PAGE ONE

PAGE ONE

Major Events 1920–1995 as Presented in

The New York Times

GALAHAD BOOKS

First Galahad Books edition published in 1995.

Galahad Books
A division of Budget Book Service, Inc.
386 Park Avenue South
New York, New York 10016

Galahad Books is a registered trademark of
Budget Book Service, Inc.

Published by arrangement with The New York Times Company.

Library of Congress Catalog Card Number: 95-79147

ISBN: 0-88365-906-9

Printed in the United States of America

The New York Times
229 WEST 43 STREET
NEW YORK, N.Y. 10036

ARTHUR O. SULZBERGER, JR.
Publisher

The Twentieth Century has been the century of the journalist. So says James B. Reston who, as one of the greatest practitioners of the craft for most of that period, ought to know.

Perhaps nothing proves his case better than a walk through the pages of this book. From the peace treaty that marked the end of the First World War through the fall of communism, the headlines and stories of the past three-quarters of a century reflect an unparalleled period of conflict and tragedy, of progress and change.

Journalism, it has been said, is the first rough draft of history. As such, it captures events which quickly pass from memory as well as those which continue to affect our lives deeply. Recorded here are some of the most significant moments of war and peace of the past century, as seen through the eyes of reporters and editors of The New York Times.

This is history at its most intimate -- for it only happened yesterday.

Contents

The New York Times

PAGE ONE

Major Events:

1920–1929

The New York Times.

THE WEATHER
Partly cloudy and warmer today; Monday, fair.
☞ For full weather report see Page 28.
Section 1

VOL. LXIX...No. 22,632. ✦✦✦   NEW YORK, SUNDAY, JANUARY 11, 1920. In Eleven Parts, Including Picture and Magazine Sections (Rotogravure) and Book Section.   FIVE CENTS In Greater New York | Elsewhere TEN CENTS

PEACE SIGNED IN PARIS AND THE TREATY IS NOW IN FORCE; WILSON TO SUMMON FIRST LEAGUE MEETING FOR FRIDAY; LODGE REBUFFS KENDRICK COMPROMISE PROPOSALS

SWEET DEFENDS ASSEMBLY'S ACTION AGAINST SOCIALISTS

Speaker Writes in Reply to Hughes and Condemns Attitude of Socialist Party.

PROMISES A SQUARE DEAL

Republican State Committee Ignores Subject—Major Mills's Protest Sidetracked.

CITY LEADERS ANGERED

Up-State Members Stand with Sweet—Text of the Speaker's Letter.

Speaker Thaddeus C. Sweet of the Assembly last night replied to the letter of Charles E. Hughes condemning the Speaker and the Assembly for suspending the five Socialist Assemblymen-elect at the opening session of the Legislature last Wednesday.

The letter was sent and made public by the Speaker after he had been in protracted conference at the Republican Club and the Murray Hill Hotel with Senator Clayton R. Lusk, who has been investigating seditious activities; Attorney General Charles D. Newton, chief counsel of the Lusk Committee; Archibald E. Stevenson, J. Henry Walters, President Pro Tem. of the Senate, and other Republican leaders.

A meeting of the Republican State Committee had brought Republican leaders from all parts of the State to this city, and that Mr. Hughes's letter had set many of them thinking and had thoroughly angered Speaker Sweet and his friends was quite evident. It was clear that a majority of the up-State leaders sided with Sweet, while with only one notable exception leaders in this city and prominent party men were vexed and disturbed as they pondered the possibility that the Assembly's action might react unfavorably in this Presidential and Gubernatorial year.

No mention was made of the Socialists at the State Committee meeting, which was attended by Sweet and many Assemblymen. Major Ogden L. Mills went to the meeting with a proxy and a prepared speech, ready to vent wrath, which he voted freely to friends.

A dozen Republican leaders, among them Senator Walters, labored with Major Mills before the meeting began and after it had been called to order. Major Mills was earnestly requested by Walters to join him in the billiard room. In the meantime Chairman Glynn rushed through with the routine committee proceedings and by the time Major Mills and Senator Walters were through talking the meeting had ended.

The proposition which contemplates the right of a majority to exclude a minority because of political beliefs, is revolutionary and as serious a threat to representative Government as can be found in our entire history," said Major Mills after the meeting. "In fact, I do not think anything like it has been attempted since the British Parliament expelled Wilkes back in the eighteenth century. I recommend to Speaker Sweet a thorough perusal of the Letters of Junius."

Speaker Sweet refused to answer questions of reporters but said he would write a letter in reply to Mr. Hughes. The Speaker's letter follows:

"New York, Jan. 10, 1920.

"Hon. Charles E. Hughes.

"My dear Judge Hughes: I notice in today's columns of the press that you communicated to me your views upon the action of the Assembly in the adoption of the resolution suspending the right of the five Socialists to seats in that body pending an investigation of the charges that they are unfit to occupy a seat in the Assembly of the State of New York. It seems from your communication that you have assumed that the action of the Assembly was in the nature of expulsion. If you read carefully and more critically the language of the resolution adopted you would see that the resolution provides as follows: 'Therefore, be it resolved, that the said (naming the five Socialist) members be denied seats in this Assembly pending the determination of their qualifications and eligibility to their respective seats.'

"You should bear clearly in mind that no attack is made upon the views of the Assemblymen-elect in question, however opposed they may be in theory to the institutions of the United States and this State. The question presented squarely is whether the different organizations of which they are members and which they seek to represent in the Legislature advocate methods and employ tactics to bring about the overturn

Continued on Page Twenty-one.

D'Annunzio May Stake Out Rome-Tokio Air Race Course

LONDON, Jan. 10.—A Caproni airplane left Rome yesterday to make a route to be covered in the Rome to Tokio flight which is being arranged and financed by the Italian Government, according to a Central News dispatch from Rome, under date of Friday. The plane was said to have reached Aviona last night and to have departed immediately for Salonlki.

Three more planes engaged in the same work are scheduled to leave Rome in ten days, and it is reported that Gabriele d'Annunzio, who made an aviation record during the war and now is in command of insurgent forces at Fiume, will be in charge of this contingent.

HOUSE AGAIN DENIES BERGER HIS SEAT

Refuses by Vote of 328 to 6 to Admit Milwaukee Socialist to Membership.

MANN OPPOSES REJECTION

Berger Reiterates Opposition to War—Promptly Renominated at Milwaukee.

Special to The New York Times.

WASHINGTON, Jan. 10.—Victor L. Berger of Milwaukee, re-elected to Congress on the Socialist ticket from that district, was today, for the second time within two months, refused a seat in the House of Representatives. The vote was 328 to 6, taken after Representative James R. Mann of Illinois, formerly Republican leader of the House, and a supporter of the McLemore resolution, had led a fight in Berger's behalf. Those voting in the negative were Representatives Mann and Voigt of Wisconsin, the latter the only member of the House who had voted for Berger, when he was first refused a seat, and Harrold of Oklahoma, Republicans, and Sisson of Mississippi, Sherwood of Ohio, and Griffin of New York, Democrats. Representative Sabath of Illinois, Democrat, voted "present."

The issue came before the House upon a resolution offered by Representative Dallinger of Massachusetts, who cited that "Victor L. Berger is hereby declared not entitled to a seat in the Sixty-sixth Congress as a Representative from the Fifth Wisconsin District and the House declines to permit him to take the oath and qualify as a Representative."

Convicted under the Espionage act and sentenced to twenty years' imprisonment, Mr. Berger presented today the credentials of his re-election last month. When the House assembled Mr. Berger walked down the aisle from the cloakroom and seated himself in the center aisle, immediately under the Speaker's rostrum, on the Republican side. He appeared to be very nervous during the one-hour debate in which he was denounced as a "traitor" and a friend of Germany. He chewed his gray mustache and moved uneasily, but when a Wisconsin member said that he had not recanted his disloyal doctrines, but continued preaching them, Mr. Berger was noticed to nod approval.

Berger Says He Will Run Again.

Following the action of the House upon its refusal to seat him, Mr. Berger gave out a statement in which he announced that he would again seek re-election, and that "he held the same position that he did during the war"—opposition to war and recruiting, which brought about his conviction under the Espionage act.

Anticipating disorder, special officers were stationed in the galleries, but while there was intense feeling against some of the utterances made in behalf of Mr. Berger, the only disapproval came from the House itself which hissed one or two points and demanded that the vote be taken after half of the one hour apportioned to debate had been consumed.

As the champion of Mr. Berger, the former Republican leader of the House, Mr. Mann, opposed the resolution, which denied a seat anywhere but in the United States, has 300,000 tons. The deficiency is due to a partial failure of the wheat crop and to a lack of facilities for threshing. Poland is at present living under a hand-to-mouth regime, which can be remedied only by a steady flow of imports from the only available surplus stocks of food, namely, those in the United States.

"The potato crop, which is the staple food of the poorer classes, has been destroyed by frosts to the extent of 30 per cent. in many districts, as it is impossible properly to care for potatoes in transit. Due to delays in transportation, Poland has been unable to procure clothing since the beginning of the war, and the result is that during the past five years practically all clothing has been worn out and has not yet been replaced.

"The food situation in Poland is so serious that the European Children's Re-

Continued on Page Nine.

GLASS URGES LOAN OF $150,000,000 TO STARVING EUROPE

Says America Alone Can Avert Anarchy in Austria, Poland and Armenia.

ASKS USE OF WHEAT FUND

Part of $1,000,000,000 Could Be Directed to Establish Credits, He Tells Committee.

AUSTRIA SEES END IN MONTH

Is Ready to Mortgage Her Forests and Customs for Food—300,000 Hungry in Armenia.

Special to The New York Times.

WASHINGTON, Jan. 10.—Secretary Glass, in a letter sent to the Ways and Means Committee today, appealed for an appropriation of $150,000,000 to aid the starving inhabitants of Poland, Armenia and Austria, giving a vivid picture of the distressing situation existing in these countries. Norman Davis, Assistant Secretary of the Treasury, presented additional details of conditions which, he said, must be remedied to prevent actual starvation and the spread of Bolshevism. He read to the committee excerpts from private reports received from American agents which bore out his statements.

Secretary Glass, appreciating the opposition to direct financial aid to the war-torn countries, recommended that the assistance be given through the grain corporation, which could use its fund of nearly $1,000,000,000 to extend aid through credits or gifts where necessary. The recommendation seemed to meet with the approval of the committee, which will probably authorize the Grain Corporation to expend $150,000,000 of its fund in aid of these countries.

The fund and food would be divided as follows: Armenia, 7,500 tons of flour and other necessities at a cost of $500,000 monthly; Austria, $100,000,000, with a probable reduction to $70,000,000 due to assistance by Great Britain; Poland, 300,000 tons of grain at a cost of $25,000,000; other parts of Europe, $25,000,000.

Norman Davis told the committee that this country must continue to supply food to these three countries until the next harvest. Austria and Poland, he said, could furnish satisfactory security for food furnished them, but in the case of Armenia the aid must be in the nature of charity as that country is without funds or means of establishing credits. Food is also needed in parts of Italy, Hungary and Czechoslovakia, he added.

"The United States has a surplus of food and is the only nation that can prevent the famine," added Mr. Davis. "Great Britain is a second food source to the United States but that her ability, which probably will be mainly in supplying ships to transport the supplies as Great Britain, France, and Italy already have lent Austria $65,000,000.

Would Mortgage Natural Resources.

"The condition in Austria is so desperate that she is willing to mortgage her forests, the tobacco monopoly, the water power facilities, and even the collection of customs, to obtain food. The Treasury does not believe that customs should be taken because it would cause great delay in economic rehabilitation. Vienna has 2,500,000 people, and it is probable that many of these will have to leave because the surrounding country, since the separation of Hungary, will not support them. Poland deserves help because she is rendering great service to the world fighting the Bolsheviki."

Secretary Glass in his letter summarizes conditions in the respective countries as follows:

"POLAND—According to the best information obtainable, the minimum grain requirement necessary to carry Poland until the next harvest, and which cannot be filled anywhere but in the United States, has 300,000 tons. ..."

Reports China and Japan Negotiating on Shantung

SAN FRANCISCO, Jan. 10.—Japan and China have started negotiations on the question of the restoration of Shantung to China, according to a cable dispatch received today from Tokio by the New World, a Japanese newspaper.

SWINDLED CLERGY, WIDOW CONFESSES

Mrs. May J. Bennett, in Tombs, Says "Divine Psychologist" Dominated Her.

WAS A MISSIONARY LEADER

Church, Social and Political Circles of Washington Heights Her Principal Field.

Blaming her downfall upon the influence of a "divine psychologist" who "dominated" her, Mrs. May Jennings Bennett, a handsome, distinguished-looking widow, confessed in the Tombs last night that she had swindled various persons out of large sums of money, and that clergymen had been her chief victims.

Mrs. Bennett, one of the Vice-Presidents of the Women's Foreign Missionary Society of the New York Presbytery, and last year its Corresponding Secretary, made her confession to newspaper men in the presence of the Tombs Warden and said that, after fleeing her bail, she had surrendered herself in the hope that the court would show her mercy and that she would be allowed her liberty that she might work to repay her victims.

The scheme she used in church, social, and political circles, particularly in Washington Heights, she said, was to pretend that she had leases on a large number of furnished room houses which she was about to convert into apartment hotels at large profit. How much she got she did not know, but it was "enough to keep me busy a long time paying it back." Of the money with which she induced sympathetic persons to part she invested $10,000 in Mexican oil wells "which aren't paying dividends."

Among those she victimized, she told, was a Pualist Father upon whom she prevailed to write a letter to Assistant District Attorney Alfred J. Talley after she had convinced him she had been badly treated. Once the priest had been won over Mrs. Bennett borrowed $200 from him.

Discussing the influence the "divine psychologist" wielded over her, Mrs. Bennett begged that his cult should not be confused with Christian Science, "which is all right."

She recalled how she was arraigned in the West Side Court last June on a charge of grand larceny, how after she had been indicted she was arraigned in General Sessions, where the case was postponed after it was learned there were three other indictments against her and, despite the urgings of several clergymen, who later proved to have been among her victims, her bail was raised to $3,500. She told of running away and of the bail furnished for her by a surety company being forfeited when she failed to appear when her case was called again last December. Then, reverting to the man upon whom she sought to cast the blame, she said:

"I met a man who exhibited a sort of 'new thought.' He told me when I went to him that he could make people wealthy. I paid him I wanted to be wealthy, and always told me to go right ahead with my scheme and he was with me, that he would pray for their success. I was under a sort of hypnotic influence; I knew what I was doing was not just right, but had not the power to resist.

"Finally, when I was indicted for grand larceny, I realized that I had been in a terrible dream and that this man, who was or called himself a 'divine psychologist,' had exercised a power for evil and not for good over me. I went to him to help me. He refused to aid me and appeared to be scared to death. I woke up then. I knew I had not been in my right mind."

While she was carrying on her swindles Mrs. Bennett lived luxuriously at Briston Hall, gave fashionable tea parties and entertained generously. She dressed well, bore herself as a woman of fashion and, in part through her church connections, gained entree to many fashionable homes.

"Under the auspices of a church she gave a 'charitable affair,' ostensibly for the Rand Crown in which she used the names of Collin H. Woodward, a Republican leader in upper Manhattan, and ex-Representative William B. Bennet. The receipts were said to have been large, but nothing remained for the Rand Crown when it was over. The charges that led her through against Mrs. Bennett, aggregate in the amount of her alleged swindles $7,000, but the sums involved in her confession would indicate that she had got more. She declared last night that her "chain" consisted of a single rooming house.

Continued on Page Nine.

REPORT OF GERMAN OVERTHROW DENIED; STRIKE SPREADING

Berlin Dispatch Declares Accounts Given by Travelers Are Untrue.

RAILROAD TIEUP IS WORSE

Communists Are Charged with Promoting It for Their Own Political Ends.

CENTRES IN RUHR DISTRICT

Not Even Food Trains Are Moved There—10,000 Berlin Clerks Walk Out of Insurance Offices.

LONDON, Jan. 10.—Reports received here early today by way of Brussels that the German Government had been overthrown, but these were later denied by an Amsterdam dispatch quoting Berlin advices received this evening. This dispatch reads:

"The report that the German Government has been overthrown is untrue, according to a dispatch received here from Berlin."

Until this dispatch was received there had been no light on the reports, storms having interrupted telegraphic and telephonic communications with Germany since Thursday.

The original Brussels dispatch said that travelers from Germany reaching there had brought unconfirmed reports that the German Government had been overthrown.

It was reported that the Socialists were masters of the situation and that all general strikes had been declared throughout the territory not under allied occupation.

Serious Strike Trouble in Germany.

BERLIN, Jan. 9.—The situation regarding the railroad strike became worse yesterday, especially in the Ruhr district, where there were additions to the ranks of the strikers.

The committee of Social Democratic railway men have charged the Communists with responsibility for the strike, alleging that while it is ostensibly an economic movement it is in reality a political measure intended to accomplish the introduction of an industrial council system on the Communist plan.

The Independent Socialists and Communists are said to be responsible for further walkouts in the Essen, Elberfeld, and Munster districts. In the Ruhr district it was impossible to move even emergency food trains. At Düsseldorf a gas and electricity shutdown is threatened owing to the lack of coal, and at Dresden the railway men have presented new demands to the Government.

At Dortmund a secret strike vote has resulted overwhelmingly in the affirmative.

Ten thousand Berlin insurance clerks struck yesterday, representing seventy-five companies. The employers claim that the walkout is not complete. The Magdeburg, Frankfort-on-Main, Potsdam, Stuttgart, and Dresden clerks are expected to join in the strike. Labor Ministry mediators are arranging for negotiations with the clerks.

WOULD SEIZE WEALTH ABROAD

Erzberger Proposes Entente Have German Fortunes in Switzerland.

BERLIN, Jan. 9.—Speaking in the Bisterich district of Württemberg last night, Mathias Erzberger, Vice Chancellor and Minister of Finance, declared that he proposed to conclude a treaty with Switzerland enabling the recovery of German capital smuggled into that country in 1919. Should the measure fail of its objective, Herr Erzberger asserted he would authorize the Entente to seize such fortunes and credit them to the indemnity to be paid by Germany.

Herr Erzberger has advertised for 3,000 additional rooms to accommodate the staff which he says will be required to administer new tax measures soon to become effective. He has announced that additional taxing measures will be submitted to the Assembly.

KING GEORGE HOPES NEW ERA HAS DAWNED

Prays People of British Empire May Forever Live at Peace with Themselves and with All Men.

LONDON, Jan. 10.—Replying to a loyal message from the citizens of London on the occasion of the ratification of the peace, the King has telegraphed the Lord Mayor of London as follows:

"With all my heart I reciprocate the good wishes of my people that please God, this day may be the beginning of a new era, in which the people of the British Empire may forever live at peace with themselves and with all men.

"It will be the duty of the League of Nations Union to formulate a policy of those matters and to weigh the nations today to lay down that noble idea.

Continued on Page Nine.

Supreme Council Prompt to Launch the League; Leon Bourgeois to Preside at the First Session

By EDWIN L. JAMES.

Copyright, 1920, by The New York Times Company. Special Cable to THE NEW YORK TIMES.

PARIS, Jan. 10.—The first meeting of the Council of the League of Nations will be opened in Paris at 10:30 o'clock on the morning of Friday, Jan. 16.

This date was set by Premiers Clemenceau, Lloyd George, and Nitti, sitting with the Supreme Council today, and was at once cabled to President Wilson in order that he might issue immediately the formal call for the historic meeting in accordance with the duty placed upon him by the Versailles Treaty. Premier Clemenceau has notified the powers concerned to have their delegates in Paris on the day set. They will gather at the French Foreign Office, where, it is understood, President Wilson's call will be read and the business of the Council started.

England, France, Italy, Japan, Spain, Belgium, and Brazil will be the nations composing the Supreme Council of the League. Leon Bourgeois, representing France, will preside at the first meeting. There will be two addresses, one by M. Bourgeois and the other by Earl Curzon, representing Great Britain. It was proposed that this gathering be made a big ceremonial event, but this suggestion was vetoed by Mr. Lloyd George and M. Clemenceau. "No, we won't need any music," declared also "the Tiger."

It has not been determined whether the Council will meet on the 16th and keep on meeting until it gets its machinery under way. That, however, will depend upon the hour before the first meeting takes place. A great deal of quiet preliminary work has been done in outlining the program for the Council prior to the first meeting of the League Assembly, and it is the desire of England to have this work started at once. France, while recognizing the need of haste, rather favors delaying important action until America shall have joined or shown that it will be a long time before she does.

In either event, if the League is to be made an issue of the next Presidential election, the League would have to go ahead before that time. If there is any chance of early ratification by the Senate, France prefers to wait for the United States.

LODGE SKEPTICAL OF DEMOCRATS' PLAN

Demands Proof of Substantial Party Support Before He Will Discuss It.

COMPROMISE SPIRIT GROWS

Neither Side Anxious to Take Up President's Challenge of Appeal to People.

Special to The New York Times.

WASHINGTON, Jan. 10.—Senator Lodge today furnished the climax to a second day of unusual activity in behalf of a treaty compromise by demanding a showdown from Democratic Senators on reservations proposed as the basis of compromise.

Mr. Lodge sent word to Senators McKellar and Kendrick, coauthors of the recently submitted Democratic reservations, that unless they could present reassurances of substantial Democratic support for their proposals further discussion of a compromise upon this basis was useless. Senators with whom Senator Lodge discussed the matter said that the Republican leader had called upon the Democrats to decide whom they would follow—whether President Wilson's warning that he would call for a "great and solemn referendum" of the American people on the treaty if the League of Nations covenant was modified other than by "interpretations" has had the effect of stimulating rather than retarding efforts at compromise between the opposing groups of Senators. Friends of the treaty, a good many of whom may find neither side, with the exception of the comparatively few irreconcilables, desire to take up the President's challenge to appeal to the people on the pending reservations are attached to the treaty.

That the majority of Senators, Republicans and Democrats, do not sympathize with the President's attitude as outlined in the letter from him read at the Jackson Day dinner in Washington on Thursday night does not mean that there is sympathy with Mr. Bryan's contrary course. That Mr. Bryan advocated the thing that most appeals to the majority of Democratic Senators and apparently to the generality of his party

Continued on Page Two.

BELLS OF LONDON PEAL FOR PEACE

But News of the Treaty Ratification Stirs Little Popular Interest.

CECIL APPEALS FOR LEAGUE

Reiterates His Declaration in Favor of the Early Admission of Former Enemy Powers.

Copyright, 1920, by The New York Times Company. Special Cable to THE NEW YORK TIMES.

LONDON, Jan. 10.—The London church bells this evening have been pealing in celebration of the conclusion of peace with Germany and the official coming into existence of the League of Nations.

The first report that the treaty had been actually ratified in Paris reached London a little after 6 P. M. But for the bell-ringing, there is no evidence of public interest, and some papers give first place in their news columns to the labor situation at home. For legal purposes in this country the war will be presumed to continue a little longer, and will be terminated by an Order in Council.

People Must Back League, Says Cecil.

LONDON, Jan. 10.—(Associated Press.)—Whether the League of Nations is to be the real thing or an imposture depends on the attitude of the peoples, and not least the British people, in the opinion of Lord Robert Cecil, who, as Chairman of the Executive Committee of the League of Nations Union, issued the following statement today:

"The Peace Treaty comes into force today, and with it the League of Nations. We, of the League of Nations Union, welcome its advent, but we must not think that we have yet achieved our aims.

"The League exists, but what is it to be? Is it to be the real thing or an imposture? Are we going to make an efficient instrument of peace, or is it to become a meaningless addition to the cumbrous forms of old-fashioned diplomacy?

"All depends upon the attitude of the peoples, and, not the least, of the British people. Are they going to throw themselves worthy of this great opportunity or not? If they are, there is no time to be lost, for there is much to be done. Scheme for the limitation of armaments must be worked out, terms of the mandates must be settled and mandatories appointed, an international court of justice must be established.

"Beyond these and other duties directly imposed upon the League by the covenant and treaty there are many circumstances at the present time which, in the words of Article XI, 'threaten to disturb international peace or the good understanding between nations upon which peace depends.'

"There is the Russian situation, economic chaos in many European countries and controversies left unsettled by the peace conference, and defects in the Peace Treaty itself and matters which are carrying German prisoners will cross the border, thus giving evidence of the good faith of France in promising to give up her prisoners at the same time as Germany allowed the Peace Treaty to go into effect.

"Although the United States did not of course sign the procès-verbal, its name figures in the document which was ..."

PEACE MADE WITHOUT POMP

Simplicity Marks Protocol Signing and Exchange of Ratifications.

LERSNER EXPRESSES JOY

Declares Germany's Determination to "Go to the Limit" in Fulfilling Terms.

GIVES WARNING TO ENTENTE

"Gravest Consequences" Foreseen if War Culprits Are Extradited.

By EDWIN L. JAMES.

Copyright, 1920, by The New York Times Company. Special Cable to THE NEW YORK TIMES.

PARIS, Jan. 10.—The Allies and Germany are at peace. The world war ended formally this afternoon, when representatives of the Allied Powers and approved the Versailles Treaty deposited their certificates of ratification and signed the procès-verbal which put the treaty into effect. The United States took no part in the proceedings.

Simplicity marked the ceremony in the Clock Hall of the French Ministry of Foreign Affairs, where the final act of the great struggle was staged. Fourteen allied and associated powers on the one hand and Germany on the other made peace and are again formally at peace.

The allied Premiers and Foreign Ministers gathered around the long green-covered tables, with Baron Kurt von Lersner and Herr von Simson, Germany's representatives, at a separate table. They arose one by one as they were designated by the master of ceremonies and affixed their signatures to the procès-verbal spread upon a stand in the middle of the long chamber. There was nothing of the dramatic in the actual proceeding; it was dramatic only in its great significance.

Before this ceremony the representatives of England, France, Italy and Japan had met the two German envoys in the office of the French Foreign Minister, and the Germans had signed the protocol binding their nation to pay for the abiding of the German fleet at Scapa Flow and to carry out the other clauses of the armistice. That done, the Premiers and the Germans were escorted to the Clock Room, where the procès-verbal setting out the existence of the League of Nations, affixed their signature to the document which ended the war. It seemed scarcely two seconds when Mr. Lloyd George was on his feet. He signed quickly and was followed by Mr. Clemenceau, and then by Signor Nitti and Baron Matsui. Then the delegates of the following Nations signed, in the order named: Belgium, Bolivia, Brazil, Guatemala, Panama, Peru, Poland, Siam, Czechoslovakia and Uruguay. China, Greece, and Rumania not having ratified the treaty with Germany, did not sign.

It was six minutes after 4 o'clock when Premier Clemenceau took his seat, closely followed by Premiers Lloyd George and Nitti, with Baron Matsui of Japan not far behind. Scarcely were they seated when Baron von Lersner arose and, walking quickly to the stand, affixed his signature to the document which ended the war. ...

Declares That Peace Is Restored.

"The protocol between the allied and associated powers and Germany has been signed. The ratifications of the treaty with Germany have been deposited. From this moment the treaty enters into effect. It will be enforced in all its terms."

That was all. The diplomats filed out, and Europe was at peace.

The absence of Ambassador Wallace, representing the United States, was a distinct disappointment on the allied statesmen. They had invited all the diplomats and hoped that Mr. Wallace would attend. A formal invitation received last night by Mr. Wallace from Premier Clemenceau, who had insisted that he attend. The American Ambassador waited until a late hour for instructions from Washington, which never arrived and returned his invitation to M. Clemenceau.

It is announced that tonight the first train carrying German prisoners will cross the border, thus giving evidence of the good faith of France in promising to give up her prisoners at the same time as Germany allowed the Peace Treaty to go into effect.

"Although the United States did not of course sign the procès-verbal, its name figures in the document which was ..."

Continued on Page Two.

Section 1

"All the News That's Fit to Print."

The New York Times.

THE WEATHER
Generally fair today and Monday, except possible local thunder showers.
☞ For full weather report see Page 31.

Section 1

VOL. LXIX...No. 22,786   ···   NEW YORK, SUNDAY, JUNE 13, 1920.—In Nine Parts, Including Rotogravure Picture Section and Book Section.   FIVE CENTS In Manhattan, Bronx, and Brooklyn; TEN CENTS elsewhere.

HARDING NOMINATED FOR PRESIDENT ON THE TENTH BALLOT AT CHICAGO; COOLIDGE CHOSEN FOR VICE PRESIDENT

The New York Times
"All the News That's Fit to Print."
PUBLISHED EVERY DAY IN THE YEAR BY THE NEW YORK TIMES COMPANY.

NEW YORK, SUNDAY, JUNE 13, 1920.

THE NOMINATION OF HARDING.

Upon a platform that has produced general dissatisfaction, the Chicago convention presents a candidate whose nomination will be received with astonishment and dismay by the party whose suffrages he invites. Warren G. Harding is a very respectable Ohio politician of the second class. He has never been a finder of men or a director of policies. For years a protégé of Foraker, he rose to a subordinate office by favor of "Boss" Cox of Cincinnati. Beaten by Judson Harmon in the contest for the Governorship in 1910, he has never shown independent strength in his own State save when he was named for Senator in 1914, having a majority of a little more than 100,000 over his Democratic competitor; and outside of Ohio he has only such strength as he now derives from his place at the head of the Republican ticket. Senator Harding's record at Washington has been faint and colorless. He was an undistinguished and indistinguishable unit in the ruck of Republican Senators who obediently followed Mr. Lodge in the twistings and turnings of that statesman's foray upon the Treaty and the Covenant.

The nomination of Harding, for whose counterpart we must go back to Franklin Pierce if we would seek a President who measures down to his political stature, is the fine and perfect flower of the cowardice and imbecility of the Senatorial cabal that charged itself with the management of the Republican Convention, against whose control Governor Beekman so vehemently protested. Rejecting Leonard Wood, probably the strongest candidate with the people the party could have chosen, because they knew he would never be dictated to by them, they favored Governor Lowden until Borah served upon them his notice of a veto of that nomination. Borah was commanding and truculent because he knew that he had to deal with a group of white-livered and incompetent politicians. If Republican leadership had not fallen into the hands of pigmies the chief men at Chicago would have told Borah to bolt and be hanged, just as upon the issue of the League they would have defied Johnson to do his worst. But they ran like a frightened flock, surrendered everything, Mr. Lodge finally throwing off all disguises and standing out as the open foe of the Covenant of the League of Nations, even with his own reservations.

What has befallen the Republican Party of the early days, the party of sixty years ago, when it was possessed of moral purposes, of forty and thirty years ago, when it could still profess to have them and find believers?

Where are its leaders that can be compared to Morrill, Seward, Hale, Platt of Connecticut, Oliver P. Morton, Sumner, Blaine, Conkling and a dozen others who rose to high places in the party councils? And, if the question be not too unfeeling, where and what are its principles, if any it have? Party control, whatever it is, is divided between a group of Senators, is divided between Lodge on the one hand and Borah and Johnson on the other. None of them, none of their accomplices in party demagogism, would have come within hailing distance of the foremost rank of party chiefs in the brilliant days of Republicanism. And for principles, they have only hatred of Mr. Wilson and a ravening hunger for the offices.

Governor Coolidge for Vice President really shines by comparison with the head of the ticket. He at least is a man of achievement. He is known to the party and to the nation. When the police force of Boston went on strike he showed himself to be a man. He met that menace to the public safety with courage and determination, and the nation rang with praise of him. It is fortunate that not a word is to be said against the character of either candidate. They are irreproachable. But that does not compensate for the lack of achievement, for the colorlessness of the candidate for first place, or for the manner in which his nomination was brought about. It will be felt and said everywhere that the Democrats at San Francisco have received from their opponents at Chicago the gift of a splendid opportunity.

HOW THE CONVENTION DID IT

Delegates Had Word Early That Leaders Were for Harding.

RECESS HASTENED CHANGE

Two Ballots Taken After Reassembling Brought Ohio Man's Nomination.

PENNSYLVANIA CLINCHED IT

Big Block of New York Votes Also Helped to Decide the Struggle.

Special to The New York Times.

CHICAGO, June 12.—The afternoon session of the Republican National Convention on its fifth day, which reached a climax in the nomination for the Presidency of Senator Warren G. Harding of Ohio, was more like a rehearsal than a star performance in the great national political drama.

Not a single time-honored device was neglected in the effort to give the performance a touch of spontaneity, a dash of surprise and setting of overwhelming approval. But the convention had "gone dead" about 3 o'clock this morning when it was first learned that conferences of Senators and other party leaders had chosen the Harding way out of the deadlock dilemma. And all the efforts of G. O. P. pulmotor-lacking as it did any modern and novel attachments—to revive it failed.

Just as the limp, wet, worn men balloting in the pit waited until they were sure the tide really was running strong, so did the throng of spectators wait to make very sure.

Harding Boom Starts Early.

The suddenly reviviling Harding boom started at the morning session. From that moment to the end it was a process of very slow and orderly rising enthusiasm to which gratitude at getting a hot and tedious job done contributed no mean element.

None of the stampede tricks of time-honored reliability worked this time. The crowd and the delegates in their separate ways seemed deliberately to prepare themselves for the finale.

As soon as it was recognized in high places that Senator Harding was to be the victor, the proper sort of stage management was set in motion. The galleries, in which were many of Mayor William Hale Thompson's supporters, who were Johnson men out of antagonism to Lowden and Wood, were glad enough to lend themselves to the task of furnishing an appropriate touch to the drama. But with all the stage management and all the willingness of the crowd to do what was expected to the best of its ability when the switching of big delegations made it a certainty, as the ninth ballot was being tallied, that Senator Harding was to be the nominee, and later, when the tenth ended the remaining speck of suspense, the performance lacked great enthusiasm.

Perhaps two-thirds of the delegates got to their feet. Maybe a hundred climbed on chairs. A few women waved damp handkerchiefs in a valiant effort to add the orthodox feminine touch to the national convention in which they had participated.

But there was no frenzy, no hat-smashing, no parading worthy of the name, and so little cheerling that three minutes after the nomination was announced those on their feet, including virtually every one in the spectators' parts of the Coliseum, were showing that listlessness.

It is a safe assertion that if Senator Lodge had elected to pound once with his cumbersome gavel, which looked to have been destined originally to be a potato masher, the hall would have been hushed in an instant.

Announced Lowden by Mistake.

There was just one touch of humor—though the careless, sopping delegates didn't see it in that way. In announcing that Senator Harding had the necessary majority the Secretary inadvertently used the name of Lowden instead of that of the successful candidate. There was a howl of protest and very manifestly even the Lowden men didn't think this mistake was funny.

Senator Lodge made the formal announcement that the Ohio Senator had become the party choice in a tired voice that reflected the weariness in his pale cheeks and dust-rimmed eyes. It didn't penetrate through the remnants of the din that the real, genuine Harding men were struggling desperately to accelerate into at least the semblance of a great occasion.

Senator McCormick of Illinois then strode to a point of strategic advantage under the mechanical amplifying apparatus.

Continued on Page Four.

REPUBLICAN NOMINEE FOR PRESIDENT
SENATOR WARREN G. HARDING
OF OHIO

WADSWORTH THREW NEW YORKERS' VOTE

Delivered 68 to Harding on Last Ballot, Acting with Senate Leaders.

20 REMAINED UNBOSSED

Organization Men Assert That They Alone Prevented Wood's Nomination.

Special to The New York Times.

CHICAGO, June 12.—The delegates from New York kept up a show of independence until the last hour of today's convention session, but then, when orders were given by the leaders of the organization, sixty-eight responded to the lash and voted for Harding. Their choice lay elsewhere, but they followed instructions. That was more votes than the organization leaders needed, yet they could have obtained several additional delegates had they been necessary. After Harding's nomination was assured these delegates were not asked to make the sacrifice.

Among the unbossed delegates who stood out on the final ballot were Robert L. Bacon of the First District, Henry L. Stimson of the Sixteenth District, George Henry Payne, alternate for George E. Medalie of the Twenty-second District, and Lansing G. Hoskins and John Taber of the Thirty-sixth District. They voted for Wood throughout and refused to yield to the wishes of Barnes, Wadsworth and the other leaders.

In the same class was Fiorello H. LaGuardia, President of the New York Board of Aldermen. His choice was Lenroot, and he voted for him to the last.

Other delegates who were not called upon to support Harding were two who favored Butler—Miss Katherine Hamman, alternate from Butler's district, and William Brice Thompson, one of the officers.

Continued on Page Three.

JOHNSON IS SILENT ON HARDING VICTORY

But Intimates He May Have Something to Say Today on Combination.

THANKS HIS SUPPORTERS

Says There Is No Rancor and That Their Hands Are Clean—Borah Also Refuses Comment.

Special to The New York Times.

CHICAGO, June 12.—Senator Hiram W. Johnson, a deeply disappointed man, refused to comment tonight upon the nomination of Senator Harding, but, according to his close friends and associates, he will not back the Republican nominee.

Mr. Johnson was approached during the noon recess of the convention by emissaries from the Harding camp with an offer to nominate him for Vice President. He is said to have turned down this offer very testily and to have said that he was after the Presidency, not the Vice Presidency. His remarks, however, are said to have indicated that he will support Senator Harding.

The news that the Vice Presidential nomination had been offered to Mr. Johnson was in line with the report, after the adoption of the foreign relations plank, that he (Johnson) could have about anything he wanted in the convention except the nomination for President. His friends and tonight that he would make a statement concerning Senator Harding's nomination tomorrow.

When Johnson stepped before his headquarters tonight to bid them good-bye he was greeted with "For He's a Jolly Good Fellow." The crowd sang lustily and with no signs of depression. When the demonstration had died down Johnson said:

"There are no tears to be shed. There is no rancor. We come out of the fight.

Continued on Page Three.

---

4 NAMED FOR SECOND PLACE

But Tired Delegates Turn To Coolidge and First Ballot Is Decisive.

LENROOT NEXT IN FAVOR

Votes Cast Also for Johnson, Allen, Anderson, Pritchard and Gronna.

DELEGATES EAGER TO LEAVE

Adjourned at 7:30 P. M., Many Leaving the Hall Before Roll Call Was Ended.

Special to The New York Times.

CHICAGO, June 12.—Governor Calvin Coolidge of Massachusetts was nominated for the Vice Presidency by the Republican Convention tonight by an overwhelming vote on the first ballot. The nomination was immediately made unanimous.

As soon as the Presidential nomination had been made, the call for Vice Presidential nominations was made by Chairman Lodge.

Medill McCormick went to the speakers' stand, and in a short address nominated Senator Lenroot of Wisconsin for the Vice Presidency. There were cheers and hisses, and the suggestion that Senator Lenroot be the running mate of Senator Harding didn't seem at first to captivate the audience.

Lenroot's nomination was seconded by A. T. Hert, National Committeeman for Kentucky; Senator Calder for New York and ex-Governor Merrick for Ohio.

The Chairman of the Oregon delegation placed in nomination Governor Calvin Coolidge of Massachusetts, and the Kansas delegation nominated Governor Henry J. Allen of Kansas. The convention presented a scene of disorder while various delegations were endeavoring to make themselves heard to second the nomination. Massachusetts seconded a demonstration for its Governor. The Virginia delegation presented the name of Colonel Henry J. Anderson of Virginia for the post, in the hope that the Republicans would turn to the South for second place on the ticket.

The most enthusiastic demonstration was for Coolidge. The delegates were worn by the hard day's work behind them, and the nomination for the Vice Presidency did not seem to give much of a thrill. Those who attempted to make seconding addresses received scant attention. It was evident that what the delegates wanted most of all was to get away. In fact, many left the hall before the roll call on the nomination was completed.

Coolidge had a runaway for the Vice Presidential nomination as soon as the balloting began. The big Eastern States, Massachusetts, New York and Pennsylvania, were lined up solidly for him, and he also got a heavy vote in the Middle West.

When Wisconsin was polled it cast two votes for Lenroot and twenty-four for Senator Gronna of North Dakota. Coolidge gained a lead so rapidly that the result was soon a foregone conclusion. When it became obvious that Coolidge would win the States down on the roll call followed the lead of the others.

The vote was:

Vote for Vice President.

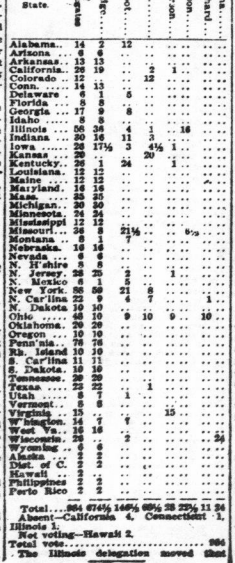

State.	No. of Delegates	Coolidge.	Lenroot.	Allen.	Anderson.	Johnson.	Gronna.	Pritchard.
Alabama.		2	12					
Arizona.	6	6						
Arkansas.	13	13						
California.	26	19		2		5		
Colorado.	12		12					
Conn.	14	13						
Delaware.	6	5	1					
Florida.	8	8						
Georgia.	17							
Idaho.	8	8						
Illinois.	58	34	4					
Indiana.	30	16						
Iowa.	26	17½	8½					
Kansas.	20			20				
Kentucky.	26		24					
Louisiana.	12	11						
Maine.	12	12						
Maryland.	16	16						
Mass.	35	35						
Michigan.	30	30						
Minnesota.	24							
Mississippi.	12							
Missouri.	36	21½						
Montana.	8	4	4					
Nebraska.	16							
Nevada.	6							
N. Hamp.	8	8						
N. Jersey.	28	28						
N. Mexico.	6	6						
New York.	88	88						
N. Car.	22		8					
N. Dakota.	10						10	
Ohio.	48	42	2					
Oklahoma.	20	9	10		1			
Oregon.	10							
Penn'nia.	76	76						
R. Island	10	10						
S. Car'lina	11	11						
S. Dakota.	10							
Tenn.	24	22	2					
Texas.	23	23						
Utah.	8	8						
Vermont.	8	8						
Virginia.	15				15			
Wash'ton.	14							
W. Virginia.	16							
Wisconsin.	26		2				24	
Wyoming.	6	6						
Alaska.	2							
Hawaii	2							
Philippines	2							
Porto Rico	2							

Total 984 674¼ 146½ 68½ 28 23¾ 11.34
Absent—California 2; Connecticut 1.
Illinois 1.
Not voting—Hawaii 2.
Total vote 984

Continued on Page Three.

ARRANGED DURING RECESS

Deal for Harding Goes Through When Lowden Frees Delegates.

BIG GAIN ON NINTH BALLOT

When the New York Delegates Swing to Him the Shouting Begins.

URGED AT NIGHT COUNCILS

But Leaders in the Race Refused to Yield at That Time—Later the Break Came.

Special to The New York Times.

CHICAGO, June 12.—Senator Warren G. Harding of Marion, Ohio, was nominated for President of the United States by the Republican Party represented by its delegates assembled in national convention at the Coliseum this evening. Calvin Coolidge, Governor of Massachusetts, was nominated for Vice President.

The nomination of the Presidential candidate came on the tenth ballot. In the ninth ballot the whole trend of the convention sentiment was toward Harding. When New York, with its heavy delegation, went to him on the tenth, everything was over except the shouting—and the shouting began immediately.

Senator Harding's nomination was the dénouement of a complex situation that did not begin to clear until last evening. After four ineffective ballots during the convention had adjourned until this morning. Four additional ballots in the forenoon and early afternoon today had developed Harding strength, but Governor Leonard Wood and Governor Frank O. Lowden had remained in the lead. A recess was taken for two hours, and during that short period combinations were formed that spade Harding's nomination certain.

The real stampede of delegates to Harding began when Governor Lowden, abandoning his intention to address the convention, issued instead a formal announcement that his delegates were released from their pledges to him.

Interesting and even thrilling, as the open proceedings in the convention were, moves behind the scenes, of which most of the convention knew nothing, had their dramatic side. The nomination of the candidate for President was arranged in conferences in hotel rooms. The prediction made in Washington weeks ago that the convention would get into a deadlock over candidates that would necessitate a combination was correct by a comparatively few of the party's dominating spirits was fulfilled to the letter.

Johnson's Strength Disintegrated.

Johnson's strength in the convention, never very potent, had begun to disintegrate this morning, under the influence of the understanding that Harding was the choice of the leaders representing the Senate group. All along it had been taken for granted that when Johnson saw that he could not be nominated he would ask his supporters to go to Knox. In conferences in which he took part last night, however, he failed to intimate that he was willing to abandon his candidacy, and no effort was made to persuade him.

In the two-hour recess this afternoon pressure seems to have been brought upon Johnson to throw his influence to Knox or some other aspirant for the Presidential honor. It is understood that he was not satisfied with Knox's views on taxation, and perhaps on other public questions. So Johnson failed to place his indorsement on the Knox boom.

Senator Knox entered the conference of the conservative group of Senators and asked them to consider Senator Johnson. Borah answered that he stood only for himself. Thereupon various objections to Mr. Knox as a Presidential candidate were raised. He was considered too old. It was said that he was not in good health. He had voted against woman suffrage and for prohibition. He was from a State that did not need a favorite son at the head of the Presidential ticket to keep it in the Republican Party, and the Knox boom died then and there.

Thought Out of the Race.

Harding entered the Presidential nomination within twenty-four hours after he was looked upon as a forlorn hope. He had made a poor showing in convention balloting yesterday and last night before midnight last night before the conferees divided into several small groups, which kept in communication with each other by members interviewing, in the Chicago clubs and at the Blackstone and the Congress Hotels.

While the convention was sitting today a dozen or so leaders met on the floor near the new responsibilities and

Continued on Page Four.

Lowden Defends Release of Delegates; Hert Says Wood Would Have Won Otherwise

CHICAGO, June 12.—Fear of a deadlock which he believed would prove detrimental to his party caused Governor Lowden to release his delegates on the convention floor at today's session, according to a statement made by him tonight. Governor Lowden said:

"After the eighth ballot, upon which I received a plurality of all votes cast, it was represented to me that the delegates were becoming restive under the delay. Fearing a protracted deadlock, which I believed would have been detrimental to the interests of the country, I decided to release all delegates and advised them to use their best judgment as to whom they should support. I have great confidence in the ability and character of the successful candidate, shall support him with all heartiness and believe the ticket will be elected. The Republican Party has not had such an opportunity for service in half a century.

"For the friendship formed during this campaign and for the loyal support of so many fine patriotic men and women I shall never cease to be grateful."

"Governor Lowden withdrew in the interest of party harmony," A. T. Hert, National Committeeman from Kentucky and one of the Lowden leaders, said tonight. Hert was a prime mover in transferring the Lowden vote to Harding and our Kentucky's 26 for the victor.

Asked if he believed Lowden had reached the height of his strength on the eighth ballot, Hert said:

"It is my judgment that Wood would have been nominated if Lowden had stayed in the fight."

THIRD SULPHUR SPRINGS, W. VA.—THE GREENBRIER—(For the information of Eastern people) AMERICAN PLAN. Opens June 15.

REPUBLICAN NOMINEE FOR VICE PRESIDENT
GOVERNOR CALVIN COOLIDGE
OF MASSACHUSETTS

HARDING DECLARES HE IS 'VERY HAPPY'

Proud to Receive "This Great Honor from the Republican Party."

COOLIDGE ACCEPTS PLACE

Taft, Hughes, Hoover and Others Congratulate Head of Ticket.

Special to The New York Times.

CHICAGO, June 12.—Senator Harding, General Wood and Governor Lowden were in rooms adjoining the Coliseum during the final balloting today. They were in different parts of the building. The result of each ballot was delivered to them by messengers.

It was a bulletin flash for a press association that gave Mr. Harding the thrill of his life. It read:

"Harding nominated."

When the news was given to the first editor ever nominated by the Republican Party for President he did not lose his equanimity. He said he was "very happy."

Later he said:

"I am very proud, as any American would be, to receive this great honor from the Republican Party. I am not unmindful of the obligations and responsibilities that come with it."

Manager Predicts Harmony.

Henry M. Daugherty, national manager for Senator Harding, issued the following statement late tonight:

"On behalf of the Republicans of Ohio, and especially on behalf of Senator Harding, his family and friends, I desire to express to Republicans of the country, men and women, our sincere gratitude for the confidence expressed in this wonderful way by nominating him as the candidate of the party for the Presidency.

"We entered this campaign with considerable reluctance because Senator Harding did not desire to make a high-powered organization campaign for the Presidency. Our plan, as is now well known, was carried out, whereby we conducted what a modest campaign and left the selection to the Republicans of the country without too much pressure.

"We have throughout the campaign had the highest respect for other candidates and for their supporters. At no time have we made any attacks upon any candidate or any candidate's supporters, and Senator Harding will receive the support no doubt of every man and woman in the country who desires to vote the Republican ticket in November."

Voicing Senator Harding's simplicity of manner Senator Harding received the newspaper correspondents tonight on the fifth floor of the Hotel La Salle, in a hall adjoining his rooms. With him were a number of old friends, including Will M. Hays, just re-elected Chairman of the Republican National Committee.

Continued on Page Four.

PROPHESIED HOW HARDING WOULD WIN

Daugherty, His Campaign Manager, Said Fifteen Tired Men Would Put Him Over.

SENATE "JUNTA" MADE DEAL

Attended All Conferences Behind Scenes and Blocked Move to Let Wood Bolster Forces.

Special to The New York Times.

CHICAGO, June 12.—"At the proper time after Republican National Convention meets some fifteen men, bleary-eyed with loss of sleep and perspiring profusely with the excessive heat, will sit down in secluded session around a big table. I will be with them and will present the name of Senator Harding to them, and before we get through they will put him over."

This statement, substantially as written here, was made by Harry K. Daugherty, campaign manager for Senator Warren G. Harding, Ohio, shortly before the Presidential primaries were held in that State. Daugherty afterward entered the primaries as a candidate for delegate at large, pledged to support Senator Harding. He was beaten but the utterance which led the Republican vote in his own State to oppose him is now full of prophetic meaning.

The sweltering crowd which sat down in the Coliseum this morning presented the usual picture of a national convention bent on getting through with the business of nominating a candidate for the President of the United States and preparing to go back home. That picture may have appeared to many of the onlookers as one fraught with unusual interest and importance, but the history of this final day of Republican Convention was really made behind the scenes and very much after the fashion suggested in Daugherty's statement.

The two days ago Senator Harding's fight was looked upon as a forlorn hope by practically every trained political observer at the convention. In fact, up to the very moment the convention took its adjournment last night his prospects were not regarded as rosy. As recently as last night Senator Harding himself could not have entertained much hope of a successful issue, for at three minutes before midnight he filed with the Secretary of State at Columbus, Ohio, the necessary papers to qualify him as a candidate for re-election to his present position in the United States Senate.

Conference Held Friday Night.

The conference at which steps were taken to break the deadlock by steering the convention toward Harding was begun soon after it finished its by mid-day's job yesterday. During the night the conferees divided into several small groups, which kept in communication with each other by members interviewing, in the Chicago clubs and at the Blackstone and the Congress Hotels.

While the convention was sitting today a dozen or so leaders met on the floor near the

Continued on Page Three.

"All the News That's Fit to Print."

The New York Times.

THE WEATHER
Thunder showers today and probably Thursday; moderate to fresh south winds.

VOL. LXIX...No. 22,810   NEW YORK, WEDNESDAY, JULY 7, 1920.   TWO CENTS

DEMOCRATIC TICKET IS COX AND ROOSEVELT; NEW YORKER UNOPPOSED AS RUNNING MATE; BRYAN IS SAD, BUT OTHER LEADERS REJOICE

LLOYD GEORGE PINS GERMANY DOWN AT SPA MEETING

In Dramatic Scene He Demands Yes or No Answer on Disarmament Question.

HERR FEHRENBACH WEEPS

Offers His Chances of Salvation as Pledge He Speaks for an Unrevengeful People.

TOLD TALK IS VALUELESS

Must Present to Conference Today a Definite Statement—Poles' Plead for Aid Is Refused.

By EDWIN L. JAMES.
Copyright, 1920, by The New York Times Company.
Special Cable to THE NEW YORK TIMES.

SPA, July 6.—The Spa conference, with all its possibilities, hangs in the balance tonight. The Allies have served an ultimatum on Germany that they must present tomorrow a definite statement of how it proposes to meet the treaty disarmament terms or the conference will at once be discontinued.

Gompers Glad Cox Was Named; Calls Him Clean and Fair

Special to The New York Times.

CHICAGO, July 6.—Samuel Gompers, President of the American Federation of Labor, who was in Chicago for a few hours today, expressed his pleasure at the action of the Democratic National Convention in nominating Governor Cox.

"He is a good, clean, fair man," said Mr. Gompers. "He was the logical candidate. Palmer's candidacy, though, was ridiculous. He never had a chance. Those delegates would have stuck if they deadlocked the convention all Summer."

Mr. Gompers had been to San Francisco with a delegation interested in the labor plank in the Democratic platform, and which will discuss the labor planks of both parties and place his views before the public.

GOV. COX ACCEPTS; MAY TOUR COUNTRY

He Intimates to Convention Chairman That He Favors a Wide Campaign.

PLEASED WITH ROOSEVELT

The Governor Calls Him a Strong Running Mate—Visits His Mother's Grave.

DAYTON, Ohio, July 6.—In a telegram to the Democratic National Convention accepting the Presidential nomination and thanking the delegates for their support Governor James M. Cox today intimated that he is ready to make an intensive speaking campaign in the country.

Following is the text of the telegram:

"Hon. Joseph T. Robinson, Chairman, Democratic Convention, San Francisco, Cal.:

"Let me thank you for your felicitous message. I shall accept the standard, even on the Democracy of America, conscious not only of the honor but the great responsibility conferred.

FEW TO WITNESS THE CLIMAX

Final Convention Thrills Staged Before Only 800 Spectators.

DETAILS OF COX LANDSLIDE

Colorado's Switch Marked the Moment When the Ohioan's Victory Became Assured.

TEXAS HEADED COX PARADE

McAdoo's Stanchest Supporters Carried Lone Star Standard to Strains of "Ohio! Ohio!"

Special to The New York Times.

SAN FRANCISCO, July 6.—There are in San Francisco today somewhat more than 9,000 angry people. Their rage is not at all lessened by the fact that they have nobody but themselves to be angry at, nor because they have no real reason to blame themselves; but still they are angry.

JAMES M. COX,
DEMOCRATIC NOMINEE FOR PRESIDENT.

BRENNAN NOW RANKS AS A PARTY LEADER

Conceded Title as Result of His Successful Fight Against McAdoo.

PUT THROUGH COMBINATION

Illinois Man Credited with Holding Anti-McAdoo Forces in Line to the End.

Special to The New York Times.

SAN FRANCISCO, July 6.—For fully half an hour after the Democratic National Convention had nominated James M. Cox for President and taken a recess early this morning, a rotund, middle-aged little man, with a beatific smile on his face, sat quietly in one of the seats assigned to the Illinois delegation.

BRYAN IN DESPAIR OVER HIS DEFEAT

"My Heart Is in the Grave with Our Cause," He Says as Convention Ends.

UNCERTAIN OF HIS FUTURE

He Will "Hesitate," He Asserts, but Democrats Fear He Will Join Prohibition Party.

Special to The New York Times.

SAN FRANCISCO, July 6.—William Jennings Bryan, eliminated as a factor and influence in Democratic politics, sat today under defeat on his dry plank, coupled with the nomination of Cox, whom he characterizes as a "wet," may go into retirement from Democratic activity or get behind the not yet ended prohibition movement.

UNANIMOUS FOR ROOSEVELT

Other Candidates for Vice President Withdrawn Without Vote.

GOV. COX WAS CONSULTED

Approved the Choice After Murphy, Brennan and Others Had Agreed.

SMITH SWAYS CONVENTION

New York Governor's Speech for Roosevelt Puts End to Other Booms.

Special to The New York Times.

SAN FRANCISCO, July 6.—Franklin D. Roosevelt of New York, Assistant Secretary of the Navy, was chosen by acclamation by the Democratic National Convention as the party's candidate for Vice President. The convention, which had been in session since June 28 and had been deadlocked on the selection of a Presidential nominee, chose Mr. Roosevelt in a few minutes.

FRANKLIN D. ROOSEVELT,
DEMOCRATIC NOMINEE FOR VICE PRESIDENT.

Enthusiasm for F. D. Roosevelt.

Franklin D. Roosevelt was next placed in nomination by Timothy L. Ansberry, a former Congressman from Ohio, who sat in the convention as a delegate from the District of Columbia.

Speech of Governor Smith.

"All the News That's Fit to Print."

The New York Times.

THE WEATHER
Fair and colder today; Thursday fair; strong southwest to west winds.
For full weather report see Page 15.

VOL. LXX....No. 22,929.　　　•••　　　NEW YORK, WEDNESDAY, NOVEMBER 3, 1920.　　　TWO CENTS

HARDING WINS; MILLION LEAD HERE;
BIG REPUBLICAN GAINS IN CONGRESS;
MILLER LEADS SMITH FOR GOVERNOR

MILLER BY 57,000

But Democrats Refuse to Concede Governor's Defeat.

SMITH'S SURPRISING RUN

In Some Up-State Strongholds He Surpassed His Former Vote.

WINS EVERY CITY BOROUGH

Strongest in Manhattan, but Could Not Overcome Miller's Up-State Lead.

75,000 VICTORY, GLYNN SAYS

Republicans Here Accuse Tammany of Holding Back City Returns.

WADSWORTH IS ELECTED

Plurality Betters Miller's, but is Far Behind That on Presidential Ticket.

NEW YORK—Voted for Presidential Electors, United States Senator, Congressmen, Governor and other State officials and an amendment to the Constitution. Vote in 1916: Democratic, 759,426; Republican, 869,671.
Polls closed at 6 P. M.

After a neck-and-neck race all evening ex-Judge Nathan L. Miller defeated Alfred E. Smith, his Democratic opponent, for the Governorship on the latest returns by about 57,000 plurality. Despite the big Harding landslide, it seemed probable for some time that Governor Smith would be able to pull through, but late returns from rural Republican districts swung a record vote for him in New York City.

The Democratic managers refused, however, to give up hope, and early this morning still claimed the election of Mr. Smith. The Governor did not put forth any claim himself, asserting that he preferred to wait until every up-State district had been heard from. The Democratic leaders based their hopes for final success upon the fact that late returns showed that the Governor had maintained his average majority in each election district in the city from 315 to 118 votes. They did not take into account, however, that Mr. Miller had also increased his average in up-State districts from 75 to 80.

If the present ratios are maintained, ex-Judge Miller's up-State plurality will be about 278,735, while Governor Smith's plurality in New York City will be 322,464, giving the Republican candidate a plurality in the entire State of 57,231. Republican leaders claimed the election of Mr. Miller by approximately 75,000. Democratic leaders and Smith's plurality would be around 40,000.

Smith Led at First.

Early reports at evening showed the Tammany Governor in the lead, but when reports from rural Republican strongholds came in Mr. Miller's slowly picked up considerably and shoved him well into the lead. At the same time Smith's vote in outlying districts in New York City did not keep pace with the huge vote he received in other parts of the city, and the indications were that ex-Judge Miller would be elected by a small plurality.

Some of the members of the Republican County Committee shortly before midnight made the charge that election returns were being held up in some Tammany districts until Mr. Miller's full strength had been reported. The First, Third and Fourth Assembly Districts, in lower Manhattan, where Tammany's strength is greatest, were among those mentioned at Republican county headquarters.

Deputy Attorney General Berger, accompanied by several members of the committee set out for the polling places in the districts to learn the true state of affairs.

Wadsworth Elected.

United States Senator James W. Wadsworth, Jr., although running behind Senator Harding did not have any difficulty in defeating his Democratic

Continued on Page Four.

State Pluralities.
FOR PRESIDENT.

REPUBLICAN.

California	500,000
Connecticut	100,000
Colorado	40,000
Delaware	5,000
Idaho	25,000
Illinois	800,000
Indiana	200,000
Iowa	200,000
Kansas	200,000
Maine	75,000
Maryland	20,000
Massachusetts	300,000
Michigan	400,000
Minnesota	100,000
Missouri	40,000
Montana	50,000
Nebraska	100,000
New Hampshire	30,000
Nevada	4,000
New Jersey	200,000
New York	1,000,000
Ohio	400,000
Oregon	5,000
Pennsylvania	750,000
Rhode Island	50,000
South Dakota	80,000
Utah	30,000
Vermont	45,000
Washington	150,000
West Virginia	50,000
Wisconsin	300,000
Wyoming	8,000

DEMOCRATIC.

Alabama	70,000
Arkansas	100,000
Florida	
Georgia	
Kentucky	20,000
Louisiana	
Mississippi	
North Carolina	60,000
Oklahoma	7,500
South Carolina	
Tennessee	40,000
Texas	50,000
Virginia	75,000

DOUBTFUL.

Arizona
North Dakota

CITY'S VOTE GOES TO HARDING AND SMITH

For Republican President by 443,000 and Democratic Governor by 325,000.

SEPARATE BALLOTS HELPED

But Some Charges Heard That Tammany Traded Votes—Socialists Make Gains.

New York City, in yesterday's election, gave its vote overwhelmingly to Senator Warren G. Harding, Republican candidate for President; to Calvin Coolidge, Republican candidate for Vice President, and to Alfred E. Smith, Democratic candidate for Governor.

Senator Harding carried every Assembly District in the Greater City with one exception—the First Assembly District, which is Governor Smith's home district. This gave him a plurality of about 400 votes.

In the minor contests the Republicans made some gains, although there was nothing like what might have been expected from the overwhelming sweep made by the Presidential ticket.

This result was greatly facilitated by the three ballots instituted by the Board of Elections, one for the Presidency, one for the State ticket (which also included the Congressional candidates), and one for the constitutional amendment and bonus proposal. The separation made ticket splitting easy, and the voters took full advantage of it.

Harding's victory in the city was overwhelming. At 3 A. M. today, on the returns then available, the plurality of the Republican candidate for the Presidency in the city was indicated at about 443,000.

Manhattan gave a Republican Presidential plurality of about 136,000; the Bronx, 62,000; Brooklyn, 177,000; Queens, 61,000, and Richmond, 7,000.

Striking Support of Smith.

But on the State ticket it was quite a different story. The same hour that found Harding victorious by 443,000 in the normally Democratic city of New York, showed Alfred E. Smith, Democrat, leading Judge Nathan Miller, his

Continued on Page Three.

OHIO FOR HARDING; 400,000 PLURALITY IS NOW ESTIMATED

Republicans Ahead in Nearly All the Large Cities of the State.

BIG LEAD IN CINCINNATI

Harding's Margin in Hamilton County Believed to be 20,000.

VICTORY IN CLEVELAND

Cuyahoga County About Two to One—Sweep in Toledo Also.

OHIO—Voted for Presidential Electors, United States Senator, Congressmen, Governor and other State officials. Vote in 1916: Democratic, 604,161; Republican, 516,755.
Polls closed at 5:30 P. M. (6:30 P. M. New York time).

COLUMBUS, Ohio, Nov. 2—Returns from 2,987 precincts out of a total of 7,145 in the State give Harding 499,355, Cox 336,352.

If this ratio is maintained, the indications are that Senator Harding carried Ohio by more than 400,000 plurality.

Under instructions from State officials county election boards counted Presidential returns first. This made returns on the State ticket and the United States Senatorship unusually slow. Many scratched ballots were voted on the State ticket.

Returns from 128 precincts out of the Governorship race show Davis (R.), 15,689; Julian (D.), 4,784.

Returns from 66 precincts for United States Senator give Willis (R.), 6,341; Julian (D.), 4,571.

Senator Harding has probably carried every large city in the State from which normally the Democrats get their majorities. In some instances his pluralities have been tremendous. He is running even in Columbus, and may have carried it.

Many of the country districts are holding up to normal for Governor Cox. In some instances he is making slight gains there.

Chairman Clark claims the election of the Republican State ticket, including Harry L. Davis for Governor, by 300,000, while Chairman Durbin claims the election of A. V. Donahey (Dem.) for Governor by at least 50,000.

The vote in Cuyahoga County, including Cleveland, is running about two to one for Harding, indicating the sentiment in Northern Ohio. Four years ago Wilson carried the county two to one. Seventy-eight percent of the 271 in the city of Cleveland gave Harding 13,840, Cox 7,037. In Cuyahoga County, outside of Cleveland, nine precincts out of 133 give Harding 2,726, Cox 830.

Hamilton County, in which Cincinnati is situated, will give 20,000 plurality for Harding. The first twenty-two precincts to re-

Continued on Page Three.

INDIANA IS SWEPT BY REPUBLICANS

Early Returns Indicate That Harding Will Carry State by Upward of 200,000.

WATSON LEADING TAGGART

He Trails Ticket, but on Basis of Returns His Election Is Expected by 185,000 Plurality.

INDIANA—Voted for Presidential Electors, United States Senator, Congressmen, Governor and other State officials. Vote in 1916: Democratic, 334,063; Republican, 341,005.
Polls closed at 6 P. M. (7 P. M. New York time).

Special to The New York Times.

INDIANAPOLIS, Ind., Nov. 2—Late returns coming in from the rural districts have piled up the Harding plurality in the State with every indication pointing that the Republican landslide will be the largest in the history of Indiana. It was estimated late tonight that Cox will be defeated by at least 200,000 votes. The former Republican record for Indiana in a Presidential race was held by Roosevelt with 85,000.

Of 1,002 precincts out of the 3,354 in the State, Harding has received 330,787 votes and Cox, 230,621.

Warren T. McCray of Kentland, Republican Gubernatorial nominee, has been swept into office by an overwhelming plurality over Dr. Carlton B. McCulloch of Indianapolis, his Democratic opponent. Although James E. Watson ran behind the ticket in several districts in his race for re-election to the Senate against Thomas Taggart, it is estimated that he will trail Harding less than 15,000 votes. Watson ran especially strong in the rural districts, with Taggart as the best showing in the laboring centres.

On the face of incomplete returns it appears that eleven of the thirteen Congressional Districts have piled up a suf-

Continued on Page Three.

ILLINOIS TREBLES REPUBLICAN VOTE

Returns Indicate Harding Has More Than 800,000 Plurality in the State.

McKINLEY CHOSEN SENATOR

Governor, State Officers and Entire Delegation to Congress Probably Republican.

ILLINOIS—Voted for Presidential Electors, United States Senator, Congressmen, Governor and other State officials and on an amendment to the Constitution. Vote in 1916: Democratic, 950,229; Republican, 1,152,549.
Polls closed at 5 P. M. (6 P. M. New York time).

CHICAGO, Nov. 2—Upon the basis of returns received up to a late hour tonight Harding and Coolidge have carried Illinois by a plurality of more than 800,000. At this hour Harding has an indicated plurality of 531,000 in Chicago. His plurality down State is estimated to be not less than 316,000.

Harding's plurality in Chicago is apparently larger than any ever given a Presidential candidate by the city. It exceeds the famous 147,477 which Mayor Thompson got in 1915.

In 966 of 5,730 Illinois precincts, including 473 in Chicago, Harding had 218,918 votes, against 78,006 for Cox.

McKinley, for Senator, had a plurality of 57,621 over Waller, and Small was leading Lewis nearly two to one for Governor.

The Republican sweep apparently is even stronger than in 1904, when Roosevelt carried Cook County by 126,000, the women not voting then. Four years ago Hughes carried the county by 56,000 over Wilson, but Harding's lead over Cox is more than five times greater.

By 1 o'clock it was estimated that 80 per cent of the 804,000 registered voters had visited the polls. During the afternoon they kept swarming in, and closing time so many still remained in line, especially in the industrial sections of Chicago. The plurality

Continued on Page Three.

United States Senators Elected.

REPUBLICANS, 20.	DEMOCRATS, 14.
S. Shortridge, Calif.	O. W. Underwood, Ala.
S. D. Nicholson, Col.	J. T. Heflin, Ala.
F. B. Brandegee, Conn.	M. A. Smith, Ariz.
F. R. Gooding, Idaho.	T. H. Caraway, Ark.
W. B. McKinley, Ill.	D. U. Fletcher, Fla.
J. E. Watson, Ind.	T. E. Watson, Ga.
A. Cummins, Iowa.	J. C. W. Beckham, Ky.
C. Curtis, Kan.	E. S. Broussard, La.
O. E. Weller, Md.	C. B. Henderson, Nev.
S. B. Spencer, Mo.	L. S. Overman, N. C.
G. H. Moses, N. H.	S. Ferris, Okla.
J. W. Wadsworth, Jr., N. Y.	G. E. Chamberlain, Ore.
E. F. Ladd, N. Dakota.	E. D. Smith, S. C.
B. B. Willis, Ohio.	C. Glass, Va.
B. Penrose, Pa.	
P. Norbeck, S. Dakota.	
R. Smoot, Utah.	
W. P. Dillingham, Vt.	
W. L. Jones, Wash.	
I. L. Lenroot, Wis.	

CONGRESS HEAVILY REPUBLICAN, GAINS IN BOTH HOUSES

Party Will Have a Majority of 12 in the Senate and 113 in the House.

54 REPUBLICAN SENATORS

House Stands: Republicans 274, Democrats 158, Independents 2, Drys 1

IRRECONCILABLES ELECTED

Brandegee in Connecticut and Moses in New Hampshire Returned.

President Harding will have a Republican Congress to support his policies in the first two years at least of his Administration. Returns received up until the time this edition of THE TIMES goes to press show that the party which was triumphant at the polls yesterday will have increased majorities in both Houses, with that in the House approaching 110.

Returns in the elections for Senators and Representatives are meager from some important States, but the trend of voting in those States in the Presidential and Gubernatorial contests indicates the probable result as far as the Senate is concerned. The returns received indicate that the two houses in the next Congress will stand as follows:

Senate—Republicans, 54; Democrats, 42.
House—Republicans, 274; Democrats, 158; Independents, 2; Prohibitionists, 1.

This gives the Republicans a majority of 12 in the Senate and a majority of 113 in the House. The present Republican majority in the Senate is 2 and in the House 29.

Senator Moses of New Hampshire and Senator Brandegee of Connecticut, both Republicans of the irreconcilable treaty group in the Senate, were strongly opposed on account of their opposition to the League of Nations, but both carried their States by substantial majorities. Senator Brandegee also had the opposition of many women on account of his effort to prevent the ratification of the Nineteenth Amendment.

Phelan Loses California.

Samuel Shortridge, Republican, who supported Senator Hiram Johnson's irreconcilable opposition to the League of Nations, appears to have been elected to the Senate, defeating Senator James D. Phelan, Democrat, a firm friend of the Wilson Administration. Senator James E. Watson, Republican, has been re-elected from Indiana, defeating ex-Senator Thomas Taggart, Democrat. Returns from Iowa are not nearly complete, but they indicate that in spite of

---

Electoral Vote.
HARDING.

California	13
Colorado	6
Connecticut	7
Delaware	3
Illinois	29
Indiana	15
Iowa	13
Kansas	10
Maine	6
Maryland	8
Massachusetts	18
Michigan	15
Minnesota	12
Missouri	18
Montana	4
Nebraska	8
Nevada	3
New Hampshire	4
New Jersey	14
New York	45
Ohio	24
Oregon	5
Pennsylvania	38
Rhode Island	5
South Dakota	5
Utah	4
Vermont	4
Washington	7
West Virginia	8
Wisconsin	13
Wyoming	3
Total	**371**

COX.

Alabama	12
Arkansas	9
Florida	6
Georgia	14
Kentucky	13
Louisiana	10
Mississippi	10
North Carolina	12
Oklahoma	10
South Carolina	9
Tennessee	12
Texas	20
Virginia	12
Total	**152**

Doubtful or Insufficiently Reported

Arizona	3
North Dakota	5
Total	**8**

Total number of votes in Electoral College, 531; necessary to a choice, 266.

GIGANTIC MAJORITIES

Pennsylvania, 750,000; Illinois, 800,000; Ohio, 400,000.

MAY BE 6,000,000 IN ALL

More Than 370 Electoral Votes Won by Harding and Coolidge.

BIG GAINS IN THE WEST

Indiana, Wisconsin, Michigan, Iowa, Kansas, Nebraska and California Won.

NEW JERSEY BY 200,000

Maine, with 75,000, Beats the Plurality She Gave in September.

SOLID SOUTH UNBROKEN

Unless Late Figures Change Tennessee—Cox May Lose All Western States.

Its majorities unprecedented in American politics, Warren G. Harding was elected President and Calvin Coolidge Vice President yesterday on Senator Harding's fifty-fifth birthday. Though the addition of women to the electorate might have been expected to make the margin of success still more somewhat larger than in past years, it could hardly account for any such unheard-of majorities as were rolled up yesterday. From coast to coast records were broken.

Harding's total pluralities in the States he carries may reach 6,000,000, and they set plurality over the vote by 4,000,000. This surpasses by 2,500,000 the previous record, which was that of Theodore Roosevelt's victory over Alton B. Parker.

The highest State plurality yet previously recorded, Roosevelt's margin of 300,000, over Parker in Pennsylvania in 1904, was surpassed by at least four States yesterday. New York State went for Harding by nearly 1,000,000; Pennsylvania gave him a plurality of 750,000; Illinois gave him 800,000; California, which went for Wilson four years ago by a majority of 2,300, gave him a plurality of perhaps 500,000 over James M. Cox. Ohio, the home State of both candidates, went for Harding by 400,000.

New York City, however, was even more surprising. Top city went for Taft in 1908 by less than 16,000; it seems to have given Harding a plurality of more than 443,000. Though the effect of the Harding sweep showed everywhere. Though the Harding sweep swept two wards in Atlanta and two Louisiana parishes. In the Middle West, Indiana and Kansas each gave him more than 200,000 plurality, Iowa about the same and Michigan nearly 600,000; Wisconsin nearly 300,000.

Maine, which surprised everyone last September by a Republican plurality of 70,000 in the Gubernatorial election, passed this figure by several thou-

Continued on Page Four.

PRESIDENT HEARD FIRST VOTES ONLY

He Retired at 9 o'Clock, His Physician Leaving the White House Earlier.

NO COMMENT ON RETURNS

Wilson at Afternoon Cabinet Meeting Expressed Confidence in Success of League.

Special to The New York Times.

WASHINGTON, Nov. 2—Although messages to the White House tonight brought the news that Harding was leading in very nearly all the doubtful localities, the attitude seemed to be sit tight and concede nothing until the actual result was ascertained. The experience of the Hughes débacle four years ago appeared to hold out a lesson in the wisdom of this course for the White House circle.

No public expressions of any kind were made. The atmosphere lacked the gloom usually associated with the news of a reversal. Visitors to the White House found the Secretaries and other members of the staff in perfect good humor.

President Wilson heard bulletins until about 9 o'clock, and this being his usual bed hour, he retired, so it was said. Admiral Cary T. Grayson, his personal physician, left the White House before his home about 8:30 o'clock. This fact seemed to set aside theories that the President would be in a nervous condition if he realized that Senator Harding was far ahead in the Presidential race. Joseph P. Tumulty, Private Secretary

Continued on Page Four.

MAP SHOWING HOW THE STATES VOTED

KEY
DEMOCRATIC
REPUBLICAN
DOUBTFUL or Insufficiently Reported

FIGURES IN CIRCLES INDICATE NUMBER OF ELECTORAL VOTES

"All the News That's Fit to Print."

The New York Times.

THE WEATHER
Generally fair today and Friday; moderate, shifting winds.
For full weather report see Page 18.

VOL. LXX....No. 23,105.   ···   NEW YORK, THURSDAY, APRIL 28, 1921.   TWO CENTS

GERMAN OFFER REJECTED, ALLIES PRESENT BILL FOR 132 BILLIONS; FORMALLY HANDED TO GERMAN AGENT IN PARIS LAST NIGHT; HUGHES AWAITS NOTICE OF ALLIED ATTITUDE ON BERLIN NOTE

BONE DRY STATE IN SIXTY DAYS, CHANDLER'S ORDER

Superintendent of State Police Tells His Troopers Two Months Is the Limit.

THEY MAKE FIRST RAIDS

Seize Liquor Worth $30,000 in Saloons in Westchester and Oneida Counties.

MILLER TO AVOID CONFLICT

Governor Opposes Enforcement by State Authorities Where They Conflict With Federal Agents.

Special to The New York Times.

ALBANY, April 27.—Major George F. Chandler, Superintendent of the State Police, began today a drive to make the entire territory in his jurisdiction bone dry within two months.

Proposes a 2½-Cent Coin To Bear Roosevelt's Likeness

WASHINGTON, April 27.—Coinage of a 2½-cent piece, bearing the likeness of Theodore Roosevelt, to provide for the date of his birth and death, is provided for in a bill introduced today by Representative Appleby, Republican, of New Jersey.

HOPE TO ESCAPE TIE-UP OF SHIPS

Both Sides Agree to Make One More Effort Tomorrow to Avert Strike.

SAYS WAGES MUST BE CUT

Benson Tells Conferees Shipping Board Holds Reduction of 15 Per Cent. Is Imperative.

Special to The New York Times.

WASHINGTON, April 27.—While no agreement as to wage reductions and working conditions was reached at the conference of marine workers and ship operators, held here today at the call of Admiral W. S. Benson, Chairman of the United States Shipping Board, hope still is held that a compromise may come which will avert a serious tie-up in New York Harbor on May 1.

BIG RING CONTROLS ALL HOUSE FIXTURES, LIKE HETTRICK PLAN

Lockwood Committee Hears of Nine Combinations Doing Hundreds of Millions Yearly.

SECRETARY $50,000 A YEAR

Members Informed Minutely of Prices by System of Colored Charts.

MORE REVELATIONS DUE

Untermyer Says 60 Combinations Grip Everything, "From Boilers to Door-Knobs."

The Lockwood committee yesterday disclosed the existence of new combinations of national manufacturers of appliances used in buildings doing an annual business of several hundred millions of dollars organized in so-called "open-price" associations, maintaining elaborate systems of price reporting by which competitors were fully informed as to each other's business.

WASHINGTON WANTS LIGHT

Not Even France's Refusal to Accept Berlin Plan Is Yet Received.

OFFICIALS KEEP SILENCE

Great Care Is Taken Not to Give Any Idea of Our Own View of Proposals.

MEANWHILE REPLY WAITS

Capital Feels That Britain Alone Can Prevent Invasion of the Ruhr Now.

Special to The New York Times.

WASHINGTON, April 27.—No formal move has been made by the United States Government in connection with the new German proposals on the reparations question, submitted to the Allies through the American Commissioner at Berlin and the State Department.

French Rejection of Offer Is Announced in Paris

PARIS, April 27 (Associated Press).—Jean Jules Jusserand, French Ambassador to the United States, has been informed by the German Government that the German reparations proposals, as transmitted to the Washington Government, are absolutely unacceptable.

German Offer Unacceptable, Belgian Official Circles Say

BRUSSELS, April 27.—The German counter-proposals with regard to reparations were declared in political circles here today to be entirely unacceptable.

ENGLAND ASKS FOR EXPLANATIONS

German Proposals Found Too Ambiguous to Permit of Definite Judgment.

CONDEMNED BY THE PRESS

Scheme Seen to Involve Allies in Further Interminable Debate—Rejection Foreshadowed.

Copyright, 1921, by The New York Times Company.
Special Cable to THE NEW YORK TIMES.

LONDON, Thursday, April 28.—The German note is too ambiguous in the view of official circles here to form a definite opinion about it.

OFFER DEAD, FRENCH HOLD

Public Opinion Strongly Supports Government's Rejection.

PLEASED WITH OUR PART

Chamber Ready for Action—Payment of Billion Marks by May 1 Might Delay Invasion.

FIND JOKERS IN PROPOSALS

Analyses of the Offer and Conditions Reject Both as Beyond Discussion.

By EDWIN L. JAMES.
Copyright, 1921, by The New York Times Company.
By Wireless to THE NEW YORK TIMES.

PARIS, April 27.—Official Paris took it for granted today that the German proposals of April 24 would not be forwarded by Washington to the Allies and that they were dead today.

German Blunder Delayed Cabling of Note to Hughes

BERLIN, April 27 (Associated Press).—Clerical blundering in the German telegraph office in Berlin caused a delay of twelve hours in transmission of the German counter-proposals on reparations to Washington.

HUGHES'S NAME IS MISUSED IN BERLIN

Suggestion for Modification Not His—Did It Come From Unofficial Intruders?

SECRETARY SENT NO WORD

It Is Also Pointed Out That British Inquiries May Have Been Erroneously Attributed to Him.

Special to The New York Times.

WASHINGTON, April 27.—The disclosure made today that the United States Government had not communicated with the German Government concerning the latest reparations proposals was intended to apply to the statement from Berlin that American suggestions for a modification of the German terms had been received by the German Government.

GERMANS GET FULL BILL

Reparation Commission Fixes Total Claims of the Allies.

LESS THAN WAS EXPECTED

Commission Finishes Its Work Three Days Ahead of Date Set in the Treaty.

EXCEEDS PARIS DEMAND

But Compares With 50,000,000,000 Marks Offered by Germany in Full Settlement.

By EDWIN L. JAMES.
Copyright, 1921, by The New York Times Company.
Special Cable to THE NEW YORK TIMES.

PARIS, April 27.—This evening at 9 o'clock the Reparation Commission summoned to the presence Dr. von Oertzen, head of the German Commission on Reparation, who replaces Herr Bergmann, and officially informed him of the sum which Germany must pay as reparation for damage done in the war. The total figure is 132,000,000,000 gold marks.

Continued on Page Four.
Continued on Page Three.
Continued on Page Seven.
Continued on Page Two.
Continued on Page Ten.
Continued on Page Ten.
Continued on Page Ten.
Continued on Page Two.

"All the News That's Fit to Print."

The New York Times.

THE WEATHER

Generally fair and warmer today; Monday, cloudy, probably thunder showers; southwesterly winds.

For full weather report see Page 19.

VOL. LXX....No. 23,171. ••• NEW YORK, SUNDAY, JULY 3, 1921. In Eight Parts, Including Rotogravure Picture Section, Book and Magazine Sections. FIVE CENTS In Manhattan, Bronx and Brooklyn. Elsewhere.

DEMPSEY KNOCKS OUT CARPENTIER IN THE FOURTH ROUND; CHALLENGER BREAKS HIS THUMB AGAINST CHAMPION'S JAW; RECORD CROWD OF 90,000 ORDERLY AND WELL HANDLED

HARDING ENDS WAR; SIGNS PEACE DECREE AT SENATOR'S HOME

Thirty Persons Witness Momentous Act in Frelinghuysen Living Room at Raritan.

DROPS BLOT ON SIGNATURE

Joint Resolution of Congress Made Effective at 4:10 P. M., Daylight Saving Time.

TEXT OF THE RESOLUTION

Steel Pen Used to Be Given to Representative Porter, Author of Historic Document.

Special to The New York Times.

RARITAN, N. J., July 2.—War with Germany ended as it began, by Congressional declaration and Executive signature on American soil.

At 4:10 P. M., local daylight saving time, in the living room of "The Hill," Senator Joseph S. Frelinghuysen's home here, President Harding placed his signature to the Porter joint Congressional resolution declaring peace with Germany and Austria, just two years and four days after the ill-fated Treaty of Versailles was signed.

By a coincidence, a year ago to the day, Warren G. Harding, United States Senator from Ohio and Republican nominee for President, left Washington for his Marion front porch to prepare his speech of acceptance containing the promise of "formal and effective peace as quickly as a Republican Congress can by its declaration for a Republican Executive to sign."

President Harding Asks, 'Was It a Good Fight?'

RARITAN, N. J., July 2.—President Harding showed little interest when informed late today that Jack Dempsey had defeated Georges Carpentier, French challenger, with a knockout in the fourth round.

"Was it a good fight?" he asked.

He made no further comment and changed the conversation into other channels.

CROWD EARLY AT GATES

Thousands Wait Through Morning Hours for Opening of Arena

POLICE IN PERFECT CONTROL

Handle Entrance and Exit of Huge Throng Without Difficulty —1,000 Firemen on Guard.

CHEER NOTABLES ON ENTRY

Spectators Eat Lunches in Streets—Bootleggers and Crooks Noticeably Absent.

More than 90,000 men and women, the biggest crowd that ever saw a sporting event in the United States, saw Jack Dempsey knock out Georges Carpentier yesterday.

Dempsey's First Thought Is Telegram to His Mother

Jack Dempsey's first thought as he came victorious from the ring was of his mother. He took a pencil and wrote her the following telegram:

Mrs. C. Dempsey, 8,572 South Ninth St., Salt Lake City, Utah.

Dear Mother: Won in the fourth round. Received your wire. Will be home soon as possible. Love and kisses.

JACK.

COBB FIGHTS IT OVER AGAIN

Calls Carpentier Soul of the Fray, Dempsey the Body.

ALL WHO'S BALLYHOO THERE

Arts, Science, Drama, Politics, Bar, Bench and Commerce Are Represented.

BOYLE'S 30 ACRES FERTILE

If There Is No New War, He Thinks Jack Will Be Best Fighter for a While.

By IRVIN S. COBB

Dempsey Says He Won Just as He Thought He Would; Carpentier Asserts He Staked His All in the Second

"Carpentier is a good, game fellow, but I think I've got it on him," Jack Dempsey remarked as he entered his dressing room after defending his title. The champion was as happy as a schoolboy and bore no marks to show the effect of the Frenchman's punches.

"I won just as I thought I would," the champion said. "It was a good fight and I think the public was satisfied. They say Carpentier staggered me with a right-hand punch in the second round. I never even remember being hit hard enough to shake me up."

DEMPSEY PROVES PROWESS

Forces Carpentier Down With Incessant Rain of Terrific Blows.

TWICE FLOORS OPPONENT

But Frenchman Is Courageous After First Knockdown and Fights Until Knocked Out.

NO "ACCIDENTAL CHAMPION"

Great Throng That Gave Louder Cheer for Georges at Start Acclaims Jack at the End.

WIFE AND MOTHER BOTH TAKE POISON

Women Go to Hotel Commodore, Swallow Mercury, and Elder One Phones Physician.

FOUND CLASPING BABY SHOE

Young Woman Was Worried Because Husband Took Child to His Mother—Both May Die.

REFORMERS DEMAND ARREST OF DEMPSEY

Police Refuse Without Warrant, and They Fail to Get Plea Before Any Judge.

NEW MOVE EXPECTED TODAY

Assault and Battery Charged in Complaint—Not So "Brutal" as They Anticipated.

Herbert Clark Gilson, attorney for the International Reform Bureau, and two other representatives of that organization were among the thousands at the ringside when Dempsey knocked out Carpentier yesterday afternoon.

CARPENTIER BROKE HIS THUMB IN FIGHT

He Also Sprained His Right Wrist on Dempsey's Jaw in Second Round.

NOT OFFERED AS EXCUSE

Carpentier Cables to Wife That He Is Uninjured and Was Beaten Fairly.

Special to The New York Times.

CARPENTIER'S TRAINING CAMP, MANHASSET, L. I., July 2.—Georges Carpentier returned to his training camp here this afternoon and informed a representative of THE NEW YORK TIMES that he knows no man in the world who is in the same class with Dempsey.

BLOW TO THE JAW ENDS THE CONTEST

Story of the Fight by Rounds Shows the Superiority of Dempsey.

ONLY ONCE IN DISTRESS

Carpentier Showed Well in Second Round, but After That Was Beaten Down.

FIRST ROUND.

The gong clanged to start the bout at 3:16 P. M. As the men advanced to the centre of the ring they were not smiling; Dempsey, a sardonic grin which was half sneer; Carpentier, a smile which reflected confidence.

Give Notice of Coming Marriage of Col. Balsan To Consuelo, Duchess of Marlborough

Copyright, 1921, by The New York Times Company.

Special Cable to THE NEW YORK TIMES.

LONDON, July 2.—Notice has been given at the Westminster Registry office in Covent Garden of the marriage of Consuelo, Duchess of Marlborough, and Colonel Jacques Balsan.

The New York Times.

THE WEATHER

Local showers today; Sunday fair; little change in temperature; moderate south and west winds.

For weather report see next to last page

VOL. LXX....No. 23,177.

NEW YORK, SATURDAY, JULY 9, 1921.

TWO CENTS In Greater New York | THREE CENTS Within 200 Miles | FOUR CENTS Elsewhere

TRUCE IN IRELAND DECLARED, TO BEGIN ON MONDAY AT NOON; DE VALERA AGREES TO MEET LLOYD GEORGE ON PEACE TERMS; DUBLIN CROWDS CHEER BRITISH COMMANDER AND UNIONISTS

FRANCE CALLS BACK MISSION IN ANGER AT LEIPSIC TRIALS

Holds That German Verdicts on Men Accused of War Crimes Are a Mockery.

THREAT OF ALLIED TRIBUNAL

Paris Is Expected to Demand the Handing Over of Offenders Under the Treaty.

BERLIN JARRED BY MOVE

Professes to Suspect a French Design to Continue the Military Occupation.

Copyright, 1921, by The New York Times Company.
Special Cable to The New York Times.

PARIS, July 8.—On the ground that the German trials of German war criminals are too plainly a farce, the French Government has withdrawn its mission to the Leipsic court, thus washing its hands of the procedure, and has notified the allied Governments of its action.

It is understood that the French Government will ask the Allies to return to the Treaty plan and demand that Germany hand over the accused men for trial by allied tribunals. It is not the purpose of the French Government to obtain the trial of some six or seven hundred accused Germans, but it believes that at least four or five prominent offenders should be punished for the sake of principle.

This move by the French Government was taken after the acquittal of General Stenger, accused by the French of having given an order to take no prisoners, and after insults to the French mission at Leipsic. Although the German Government apologized for the spat upon, the French delegates being spat upon, the procedure has reached a stage where it can no longer recognize it. Practically all the men accused by the British were freed, one test case presented by the Belgians resulted in an acquittal and the same program appears to be under way with respect to those whom the French accuse.

It is the attitude of the French Government that the Allies' treaty rights with respect to war criminals remain intact and that the German trials represented merely an opportunity given to the Germans to right the wrongs which their fighting men committed. The French say that the trials have become the trials of allied witnesses rather than of the accused Germans and that the time has come to call a halt. As the Temps says, France is going to show Germany that Germany's like Stenger are expensive luxuries.

It appears unfortunate for the tranquillity of the world at large that Franco-German relations, which were so much bettered by the progress in the reparations settlement, should become strained again. No matter how peacefully disposed he might be personally, Premier Briand is under practical compulsion to do something to meet the popular wave of indignation caused by the acquittal by the German court of Germans accused of war crimes against the French and already convicted in the court of French opinion.

The foreign tonight reviews the whole question of the war criminals. It recalls how on Dec. 31, 1919, the German Government offered to try the accused men; how on Feb. 3 Baron von Lersner, head of the German peace delegation, refused to transmit the list; how it was transmitted by the allied Ambassadors at Berlin on Feb. 8; how on Feb. 12 the Allies agreed to let the Germans show their good faith by trying forty-five of the accused men; how on May 7 it was agreed that the allied Ministers would all be the transmit, it being specified that the Allies reserved all their rights until they should have accepted the result of the German trials; and how on July 6 of last year the Allies agreed at Spa to help the German prosecutors gather evidence in allied countries. The Temps concludes that no obtention should be paid further to the procedure at Leipsic and that the Allies should at once take steps.

"The Allies' hands are free," it says, "and they must convince the Germans that crime is a bad business and that Generals à la Stenger will cost the German people dearly."

The Journal des Débats says tonight that after the acquittal of Stenger the French Government could no longer have anything to do with the Leipsic trials.

"What is serious in this business," says the paper, "is that in the farce at the whole world Germany should through the comedy of Leipsic give such an exhibition of pan-Germanism, the summer in which she started the war Germany injected into international affairs a detestable element, abolished the theory of contract. She whose who conducted the war overturned that law that all civilization had done to limit the effects of

Continued on Page Two.

President and Mrs. Harding Observe 30th Anniversary

WASHINGTON, July 8.—President and Mrs. Harding are planning a week-end cruise down the Potomac on the Presidential yacht Mayflower if public affairs will permit Mr. Harding to get away from the capital tomorrow. They do not expect to go ashore.

Today was the thirtieth anniversary of the marriage of President and Mrs. Harding, but they had no formal observance. They were married at the same house in Marion from which the front porch campaign was conducted last year.

At the White House it was stated that nothing was known there of the reported intention of the President to attend the funeral of the World War soldiers in New York Sunday.

HEAT FINDS VICTIMS FROM SEASHORE TO THE ROCKIES

High Humidity Increases Suffering and Many Deaths Are Reported.

DROWNINGS ARE NUMEROUS

One Man Seeking Relief on Roof Rolls Off When Asleep and Is Killed.

TEMPERATURE HERE 89

Thousands Sleep on Sand at the Beaches and on Park Benches—Showers Promised.

From the Atlantic Coast to the Rocky Mountains the country sweltered and sweated yesterday in the grip of a torrid wave, accompanied by high humidity that caused widespread suffering and many deaths.

Chicago reported eight heat deaths and drownings, while Syracuse five, and from Buffalo, Pittsburgh and Detroit came records of a mounting list of fatalities in which little children were most numerous among the victims.

Even Canada labored under a merciless sun. Quebec, known as a refuge for overheated New Yorkers, had an official high temperature of 96—the hottest in its recorded weather history. Remote parts of this country found things even more sizzling than they were in New York. In Arizona and the interior of Colorado, for example, the temperature went well over 100.

Late afternoon thunderstorms and local showers brought relief in areas which had suffered constantly for days. New York with its environs suffered fewer fatalities than many other parts of the country. Only one death within the city limits was due to the heat, and there was some from the direct results of the heat, though one or two were attributed to it indirectly. Several drownings were reported from nearby places, while the bodies of a number of victims of the last few days were recovered.

Highest Temperature Here 89.

The highest local temperature was 89, at 4 o'clock yesterday afternoon. At 10 o'clock last night it was 7 degrees cooler, but didn't seem so, except when a fitful breeze stirred, because the humidity had risen 10 degrees, to 67. At 8 o'clock in the morning, with the temperature only 74, the humidity was 84.

Local showers and possibly thunder storms are expected to cool things hereabouts today and Sunday, and moderate south to southwest winds were forecasted to aid in the cooling process.

Local beach reports yesterday had crowds that grew almost to holiday proportions, and last night many thousands, fleeing the stifling atmosphere of apartments and tenements, made their beds on the sands, drowsed on park benches, imperilled their lives on roofs, sheltered themselves over the grass of squares and playgrounds or sought refuge on the piers, which were thrown open as an emergency measure when Mayor Hylan issued the order:

July 8, 1921.

Otto B. Shulhof, Esq., Chairman
Mayor's Committee on Recreation and Playgrounds, 136 Madison Avenue, New York.
Dear Sir: Beginning tonight, and continuing throughout the hot weather, all piers in every part of the city are to remain open all night. Present the Gallalife of the Park Board and the Dock Commissioner have been requested to see that this is done. The Police Commissioner has also been asked to have a sufficient number of policemen in attendance at all hours on all piers.

Former Kaiser Objects To Paying Dutch Taxes

Copyright, 1921, by The New York Times Co.
Special Cable to The New York Times.

DOORN, Holland, July 8.—The Municipal Council of Doorn is discussing the vigorous protest lodged by William Hohenzollern against the tax levied by the local authorities. The ex-Kaiser maintains that they have no right whatever to tax him, as he did not come willingly to Holland, and is held practically a prisoner, and is therefore not liable to taxes as if he were a free citizen. William has also protested against the income tax.

The majority of the council, however, takes the view that the ex-Kaiser came as a free agent to Holland and himself chose Doorn as his place of residence and that therefore his protest should be disregarded and measures must be taken to secure the payment of his taxes. The ex-Crown Prince, however, is held to be exempt from taxation.

BARRICADED MANIAC TAKES LIFE IN FIGHT

Man Crazed With Drink Drove Wife From Home, Then Fought Bloomfield Police.

SHOTS KEPT ATTACKERS OFF

Firemen Failed to Subdue Pole With High-Pressure Stream Turned Into Shack.

Special to The New York Times.

BLOOMFIELD, N. J., July 8.—After turning a little one-story, tile-roofed building on the outskirts of this place into an improvised fort, and defending himself for more than an hour against the attack of policemen and firemen who tried to capture him alive, John Gruchacz, a Polish laborer, turned his pistol upon himself and committed suicide this afternoon.

During the fight the man fired twelve shots at the police and firemen, but failed to hit any of them. In the early part of the affray one of the policemen fired a shot at the barricaded man, but then ceased firing, and tried to subdue him by turning a high pressure stream of water from a fire hose through a window.

The man apparently was crazed with drink and the desire for money and more liquor. The building in which he made his stand was at 658 Broad street, where his wife, Caroline Gruchacz, had been living with her 9-months-old baby girl. It was a wooden, flat-roofed, weather-beaten structure, about eighteen feet on the street and twenty-five feet deep.

In the front is a tiny dry goods and notion shop by which the wife had been supporting herself and child since the husband deserted her several months ago. In the rear is an equally small room, which the woman and child has used as their only living quarters.

Going to Kill Somebody.

The man, who had previously threatened his wife and demanded money of her, started for her home early yesterday afternoon with the apparent intention of shooting her if she did not give him money. Persons who saw him on the way said that he was drunk and brandished a pistol.

Frank Kuttelman, the wife's landlord, met the crazed man on his way to the store, and observed the weapon.

"Let me take that gun," said Kuttelman. "You don't want to get into any more trouble."

"Keep out of this," replied the Pole, moving Kuttelman. "It's none of your business. I'm going to shoot somebody today."

Kuttelman let the man proceed, but called to the woman in the house. Forewarned in time, she fled with her daughter Louisa, who accompanied him.

DRAMATIC SCENES IN DUBLIN

General Macready, in Full Uniform, Gets Ovation From Crowds

SALUTES IRISH VOLUNTEERS

People Pray Outside the Mansion House, While De Valera Holds His Council.

WAIT HOURS FOR THE NEWS

When De Valera's Reply to the London Invitation Is Given Out, They Disperse Quietly.

Copyright, 1921, by The New York Times Company.
Special Cable to The New York Times.

DUBLIN, July 8.—Just at the stroke of 11 today the four Southern Unionists, Midleton, Woods, Jameson and Dockrell, sat down in the Mansion House at Dublin with de Valera and Griffith, President and Vice President of Sinn Fein, to discuss ways and means of an agreement on the Irish problem preparatory to the London conference. The interval since Monday gave a piece to deep anxiety, which was most manifest before the appointed hour, however, a wave of cheers swept through the crowds, heralding the arrival of the four Southern Unionist delegates. Among the first of these to enter the meeting room was Lord Midleton, immediately followed by Sir Robert Woods and Andrew Jameson, Sir Maurice Dockrell arriving later. Notwithstanding all hints that Monday, General Smuts and the Northern Premier were absent, and their absence was noted with grave disappointment.

It is again an instance of the people's hopes for success that many knelt on the gravel and prayed for the success of the deliberations. It was a striking testimony to the faith in the leaders who sat in private around a table within the building. Even the singing of patriotic songs was not as enthusiastic as on Monday, so gravely did some regard the day's proceedings.

At 1 o'clock the Lord Mayor appeared and was rushed upon for news, but he would say nothing. Then there was adjournment till 4 o'clock, and as the Unionists were passing out for lunch, Lord Midleton consoled the multitude by saying "We are coming back at 4 o'clock."

It transpired that messages of goodspeed were received from America. James J. Phelan, a Boston banker, expressed fervent hopes that the way to lasting peace would be found, as he believed the time was opportune.

When the delegates returned at 4 o'clock it was plain that there was awful seriousness in the deliberations, as each seemed determined to go through with this far-reaching attempt at a settlement of the age-long problem.

At 6 o'clock General Macready arrived as if summoned to the conference. His appearance, dramatic as it was, was a signal for a remarkable demonstration. Met by the Lord Mayor, the distinguished soldier saluted. He himself was saluted by the officer in charge of the Republican volunteers and in soldierly fashion acknowledged the salute amid enthusiastic cheers of the expectant multitude.

Macready, who was in uniform, remained fifty minutes, and on leaving was once again cheered. It was walked through a long avenue of people kept orderly by volunteers and, head erect with military bearing, entered an automobile. Macready returned at 7:45, driving through a different atmosphere only than he had experienced for a long time. He was again loudly cheered.

General Macready remained five minutes and left with the Southern unionists.

The conference closed at 5 o'clock. An hour later the letter of de Valera to Lloyd George was made public. The crowds outside the Mansion House received every word with perfect order and apparent relief.

Text of De Valera's Letter to Lloyd George; Official Announcement of Truce on Monday

LONDON, July 8.—The text of the letter sent today to Premier Lloyd George by Eamon de Valera follows:

Sir: The desire you expressed on the part of the British Government to end the centuries of conflict between the peoples of these two islands and to establish relations of neighborly harmony is the genuine desire of the people of Ireland.

I have consulted with my colleagues and received the views of the representatives of the minority of our nation in regard to the invitation you have sent me. In reply I desire to say that I am ready to meet and discuss with you on what basis such a conference as that proposed can reasonably hope to achieve the object desired.

EAMON DE VALERA.

The official wording of the statement issued from Downing Street with reference to a truce was as follows:

In accordance with the Prime Minister's offer and Mr. de Valera's reply, arrangements are being made for hostilities to cease from Monday next, July 11, at noon.

DR. BUTLER TO MEET EMPIRE PREMIERS

Is Invited by Mr. Lloyd George to Spend Week-End With Them at Chequers.

DISCUSSES BRITISH POLICY

Convinced Its Guiding Principle Is Close Accord With America —Freedom of Seas Vital.

Copyright, 1921, by The New York Times Company.
Special Cable to The New York Times.

LONDON, July 8.—Dr. Nicholas Murray Butler of Columbia University and his American friends will leave for the Continent tomorrow, but The New York Times correspondent came from an official source that Prime Minister Lloyd George today sent to Dr. Butler an invitation to pass the week-end at Chequers, the country seat donated for the use of British Premiers by Lord Lee. Among Mr. Lloyd George's other guests will be the Prime Ministers of the dominions who are attending the imperial conference.

It will be remembered that some time ago reports were circulated that Dr. Butler had been invited to address the conference here, in that form the statement was obviously incorrect, for American citizens could have no part in a purely British imperial conference. As The New York Times editorially said on June 21 last: "No spokesman for the United States is to be present at the conference. Yet it is plain from the latest official source that American interests are in the minds of all the Premiers. Unrepresented and unheard, this country will be a factor in the most important agreements reached."

The invitation extended to Dr. Butler by Premier Lloyd George to go to Chequers and spend the week-end with him and representatives of the dominions is a clear indication that in their discussions of matters which seem purely British the Premiers' eyes look outward to world relations, and particularly to relations with America.

Accord With U. S. British Policy.

Dr. Butler, who during his present visit to London has had many opportunities of exchanging views with British statesmen, is convinced that the guiding principle of British policy is close accord with the United States.

Dr. Butler's conversations have been of an unofficial kind, but they probably have been all the more intimate and penetrative on that account. Speaking to The New York Times representative today, Dr. Butler said:

"It is quite plain to me that the principle of British foreign policy following the war is the close accord with the United States and complete trust in the American Government. Great Britain does not for the faintest section of naval rivalry with us. She is an island, and sea freely open to commerce are as necessary to her food supply and her economic life as our transcontinental railways are. This is the basic fact to be reckoned with. It is agreeing to limit naval armaments she must make sure that the seas are kept free should war break out anywhere. Again, there are so many historic prejudices affecting America's settlement solution of the question, and so many unknown quantities working themselves to the front whenever a solution appears imminent.

"For my part I should like to see Ireland, in scale, of course, another America, with another declaration of independence modeled on our own. Cuba is more loyal to the United States because of the autonomy enjoyed than if our votes was constantly shouting orders at her and I am convinced that the same would be true of Ireland as regards England. The Irish would give up out of their way to please her.

"The element in Belfast and the Republicans are really very far apart; they do not understand each other, and for that reason I do not look for much from the conference. The Irish want peace, but they want self-government, with every particle of substance under it..."

IRISH HERE PLEASED OVER MONDAY TRUCE

But They Distrust Lloyd George and Expect Little of Conference.

STILL HOPE FOR REPUBLIC

Count on de Valera to Demand Full Autonomy — Some Fear Compromise.

News of the coming conference between Premier Lloyd George and Eamon de Valera wrought different reactions upon the various phases of Irish-American opinion here last night. Many preferred to await the outcome of the conference before discussing the possibilities; others viewed the news with mistrust, but all apparently were glad that a truce had been declared effective Monday.

Those who discussed the reports last night were certain that de Valera, appearing at the London conference as the President of the Irish Republic, would insist upon the recognition of the Irish Republic as a basis of peace. The Irish Republicans, or those who have held out for the Irish Republic, regarded any conference with Lloyd George as a concession to the British.

Distrusts Lloyd George.

"I haven't much confidence in Lloyd George," Mgr. Power said, "and therefore I do not look for any definite results from the proposed conference. Prejudice in Belfast against the Sinn Fein seems to be too strong to permit of the Ulster folk coming together at this time. The Irish Republicans seem to be very much in the majority in Ireland and I am sure that if the English Government approached the situation frankly—with a view to permitting the republic—neither side would be dissatisfied with the results.

"The Irish of the south are satisfied that their demands are just and legitimate—they want a republic, and will not be satisfied with anything else. They would be willing to give England every possible guarantee of protection. They would never permit Ireland to be employed as the base of a power hostile to England, for example, because they are religious people and would not violate an oath.

"On the other hand, they would be just as devoted as Australia, Canada, or any other of the Dominions of Great Britain. I do not believe the conference which de Valera has promised to attend will bring lasting peace because the Irish won't get their republic. Again, there are so many historic prejudices affecting America's settlement solution of the question, and so many unknown quantities working themselves to the front whenever a solution appears imminent."

TO MEET PREMIER FIRST

De Valera Asks to Discuss Basis of Proposed Conference

TRUCE COUNTED A BIG GAIN

Suggested by Lloyd George to Lord Midleton, It Is Agreed To by Republicans.

PEACE HOPES NOW BRIGHT

Ulster Expected to Be Called In After British Ministers Have Smoothed the Way.

Copyright, 1921, by The New York Times Company.
Special Cable to The New York Times.

LONDON, July 8.—Eamon de Valera, replying today to Premier Lloyd George's invitation to a conference of Irish and British representatives in London, agreed to meet Mr. Lloyd George to discuss "on what basis such a conference as that proposed can reasonably hope to achieve the object desired." [The text of the letter is given in an adjoining column.]

At the same time it was announced from 10 Downing Street that de Valera, Premier Lloyd George had agreed to a suspension of hostilities in Ireland beginning at noon on Monday next.

De Valera's letter to the Prime Minister intimating his readiness to meet Lloyd George and discuss the basis on which the proposed conference "can reasonably hope to achieve the object desired" was stated in authoritative quarters tonight to indicate that the Sinn Fein representatives will have a meeting with British Cabinet representatives before Ulster representatives are called into the conference. It is believed this will smooth the path of the conference and it would not imply any reluctance on the part of Sir James Craig to confer as soon as the preliminaries had been smoothed.

Before de Valera's letter was made public the Irish Bulletin issued the following:

"President de Valera informed the conference of the terms in which the Premiers' invitation was framed. In the progressive session of the conference the President expressed the view that it would be impossible to conduct negotiations with any hope of achieving results unless there was a cessation of bloodshed in Ireland. A letter to Lord Midleton from Mr. Lloyd George was read concerning this view and indicating the willingness of the British Government to come to a suspension of active operations on both sides. It is expected that an announcement of a truce to take effect from Monday next will be made early tomorrow."

Premier Suggested a Truce.

Thus it was revealed that when Lord Midleton returned to Ireland after seeing Lloyd George, he took back with him a letter from the Prime Minister in reference to a truce. It had been thought that a truce would be difficult of arrangement and that the agreement of some kind were required it would have to be in the nature of a tacit understanding.

The text of the letter which Lord Midleton took to Ireland follows:

Downing Street, July 7, 1921.

Dear Lord Midleton: In reference to the conversation I had with you this morning, the Government fully realizes that it would be impossible to conduct satisfactory results if there is bloodshed and violence in Ireland. It would disturb the atmosphere and make the attainment of peace difficult. As soon as we hear that Mr. de Valera is prepared to enter into a conference with the British Government and to give instructions to those under his control to cease from all acts of violence, we should give instructions to the forces of the crown to suspend active operations against those who are engaged in this unfortunate conflict. Yours sincerely, D. LLOYD GEORGE.

News of the truce being arrived at in Ireland came as the most auspicious fact that has grown out of the negotiations begun last Monday. It was regarded as the salient, concrete gain of the week and as lifting the general peace negotiations on to a new plane of hopefulness and reality. Hitherto hopes and fears had oscillated in the balance. Not only is it a sign that the negotiations will move constantly ahead, but it removes for much from the confusion that had obscured...

"All the News That's Fit to Print."

The New York Times.

THE WEATHER.
Rain and colder today; Sunday fair; fresh to strong northwest wind.
Temperature Yesterday—Max., 48; Min., 32.

VOL. LXXI....No. 23,303.   NEW YORK, SATURDAY, NOVEMBER 12, 1921.   TWO CENTS

OUR UNKNOWN WARRIOR BURIED, THE WORLD HONORING HIM; HARDING PLEADS FOR A BAN BY CIVILIZATION ON WAR; DELEGATES ENTER ARMS PARLEY TODAY IN HOPEFUL SPIRIT

ULSTER REJECTS PROPOSED TERMS; DRAFTS NEW ONES

Finds Fundamental Principles Involved Which Are Impossible of Attainment at Present.

WANTS THESE WITHDRAWN

Will "Indicate More Practicable Means" of Obtaining Peace Without Infringing Her Rights.

NEXT MOVE IS UNCERTAIN

British Cabinet Is Expected to Meet Today to Study Reply and to Consider Action.

Copyright, 1921, by The New York Times Company.
Special Cable to THE NEW YORK TIMES.

LONDON, Nov. 11—Ulster replied this afternoon to the British Government's draft suggestions looking to a settlement of the Irish problem with what on its face appears to be a definite rejection of the proposals. There is, however, an intimation that the Ulster Cabinet will indicate other and more practicable means for securing peace without infringing on Ulster's rights.

Boy Scouts to Gather Corn For Armenia in Iowa Fields

DES MOINES, Iowa, Nov. 11.—Thousands of Boy Scouts will scour Iowa tomorrow to gather corn for famine relief in the Near East. Farmers will co-operate, by permitting the boys to go into the fields and haul limited quantities from standing corn.

INJUNCTION STRIPS MILKMEN OF POWER TO HARASS DEALERS

Forbids 12,000 Union Members to Use Violence, Intimidation or Persuasion.

TRIED TO WRECK 4 PLANTS

Tampered With Machines, Threw Away Parts, Left Pasteurizers in Shape to Affect Milk.

SWEEPING COURT ORDER

Prohibits Crowds, Appeals to Consumers or False Reports in Five Boroughs and Westchester.

Gandhi Exhorts Hindus To Remove Lawrence Statue

LAHORE, British India, Nov. 11.—Mohandas K. Gandhi, the Indian Nationalist leader, today urged a large gathering here to remove the statue of Lord Lawrence which stands in the city. Gandhi exhorted his audience to undertake the task "even at the risk of imprisonment or death." Beneath the statue is the inscription, "Will you be governed by the pen or by the sword?"

Lord Lawrence distinguished himself in putting down the Sepoy mutiny in India. He also served as Governor-General from 1863 to 1869.

LEADERS HAIL CONFERENCE

Briand Sees No Reason to Prevent Results in a Few Weeks.

JAPANESE PREDICT SUCCESS

Millerand and Curzon Send Messages of Encouragement to Washington.

POPE TO GIVE FULL SUPPORT

Delegates Pleased With Harding's Arlington Speech—American Group Confers.

WASHINGTON, Nov. 11 (Associated Press).—With the eyes of all the world fixed hopefully upon them the accredited spokesmen of the powers will meet in Washington tomorrow to try to find a way to ease the heavy burden of armaments.

President Harding's Plea for Barring War From the Stage of Righteous Civilization

From President Harding's Speech at Arlington.

The loftiest tribute we can bestow today—the heroically earned tribute—fashioned in deliberate conviction, out of unclouded thought, neither shadowed by remorse nor made vain by fancies, is the commitment of this Republic to an advancement never made before. If American achievement is a cherished pride at home, if our unselfishness among nations is all we wish it to be, and ours is a helpful example to the world, then let us give of our influence and strength, yea, of our aspirations and convictions, to put mankind on a little higher plane, exulting and exalting, with war's distressing and depressing tragedies barred from the stage of righteous civilization.

SOLEMN JOURNEY OF DEAD

Ceremonial Procession In Which Nation's Leaders Walk Stirs Capital.

HARDING SOUNDS HIGH NOTE

His Appeal Against War Impresses Great Audience at Arlington.

NATIONS DECORATE WARRIOR

And His Body With Wreaths of War Mothers Is Lowered to Last Resting Place.

Special to The New York Times.
WASHINGTON, Nov. 11.—America buried its Unknown Warrior today—placed in the earth the body of that boy whose very namelessness symbolized 50,000 others who had given their lives for America on the field of battle in the World War.

John McCormack BUYS HALS PAINTING

Singer Pays $150,000 for "Portrait of a Man"—Now on Its Way to America.

SALE IS CONFIRMED HERE

Many Other Pictures Coming—Sir Joseph Duveen Denies "The Blue Boy" Has Been Sold.

John McCormack has paid $150,000 for the "Portrait of a Man" by Frans Hals, and the picture is now on its way to this country, after its removal from the collection of Count Maurice Zamoyski, the Polish Ambassador to France.

TROLLEY SMASHED BY WILD FIRE TRUCK

Driver Loses Control and Big Machine Hits Car Head-On —Four Men Hurt.

FIREMAN IS LIKELY TO DIE

Three-Ton Motor Truck Hits Auto on Manhattan Bridge, Injuring Two Persons.

Four men were injured when a fire truck ran wild and crashed head-on into a surface car containing twenty passengers at First Avenue and Eighty-fifth Street about 8:30 o'clock last night. The fright and excitement among the passengers as the heavy truck rammed the front vestibule of the car was intense.

HOST IN MADISON SQ. HONORS THE DEAD

Fifteen Thousand Guests of the Legion in the Garden, as Many More Outside.

FOLLOW HARDING'S VOICE

The President's Words at Arlington Clearly Heard—50,000 Parade—Thousands Pray.

President Harding's voice rang out in loud and distinct tones to a crowd of 35,000 guests of the American Legion in Madison Square Garden and in Madison Square yesterday, as he delivered his address at Arlington Cemetery in Washington over the grave of the unknown soldier.

OVATION FOR WILSON IN LINE AND AT HOME

Crowds That Watch in Silence as Parade Moves By, Cheer as ex-President Passes.

PILGRIMAGE TO HIS HOUSE

Thousands in Demonstration Lasting an Hour Move Him to Express Thanks.

Special to The New York Times.
WASHINGTON, Nov. 11.—With the last dull boom from the guns which counted off minute after minute of the hours that passed while a reverent and grateful nation paid solemn tribute to its nameless soldier dead through one of their number, and when silence had succeeded eulogy and prayer about the grave at Arlington where his remains had been added to the final rest, thousands of the throng which had taken part in those ceremonies turned their thoughts to another "soldier of the World War" who, though among the number of the living, had been grievously stricken while engaged in heroic endeavor to realize the supreme object of that great conflict.

Harvey Sees Tolerance Supplanting War, He Tells London Armistice Day Diners

LONDON, Nov. 11 (Associated Press).—"Today signalizes the joining of the past with the future," declared Colonel George Harvey, United States Ambassador to Great Britain, in an Armistice Day address here tonight.

Continued on Page Nine.

Continued on Page Seven.

Continued on Page Two.

8

The New York Times.

VOL. LXXI....No. 23,307.

NEW YORK, WEDNESDAY, NOVEMBER 16, 1921.

TWO CENTS *In Greater New York* | THREE CENTS *Within 200 Miles* | FOUR CENTS *Elsewhere*

BRITAIN AND JAPAN ACCEPT NAVAL PLAN AMID CHEERS; FAR EAST ISSUE UP TODAY; JAPAN WANTS MANCHURIA OPEN; LODGE MAY NEGOTIATE TO END ANGLO-JAPANESE ALLIANCE

TRACTION HEARINGS BEGIN OVER PROTEST; HYLAN ORDERS FIGHT

Commission Rejects City's Plea for Delay Until Legislature Can Act on Law.

PROCEDURE IS OUTLINED

Evidence Will Show Fares Have Increased and Service Decreased, Says McAneny.

WOULD RESTORE 5c FARE.

Also Keep It Indefinitely—Four Witnesses Examined—Shearn Tells Evaluation Plan.

Denying the plea of Mayor Hylan that hearings on the traction situation be delayed until after the Legislature had proved how to correct the transit law of 1921, the Transit Commission yesterday began an examination of the situation with the operation of its actual income. It was to keep the fare indefinitely at 5 cents.

Mayor Hylan were represented at the hearings by counsel to the state of the state of the city of New York.

Reparations Default Report Denied by German Officials

BERLIN, Nov. 15 (Associated Press).—The report that Germany has notified the Allies that she will be unable to meet the next reparations instalment was emphatically denied tonight in official German quarters.

A similar denial was made in Entente diplomatic circles, which are in close touch with the negotiations now proceeding with the Reparations Commission.

MRS. ENRIGHT LOSES $3,000 IN JEWELRY

Police Commissioner's Wife Misses Rings and Gems After Brooklyn Shopping Tour.

REPORT 'NOT FOR THE PRESS'

Slip to Police Stations So Noted—Chamois Bag Was Pinned to Mrs. Enright's Clothing.

BRIAND TO PICTURE DANGER

Will Set Forth to America Why France Cannot Reduce Her Army.

EXCEPT WITH GUARANTEES

He Will Quote German Documents to Prove the Fatherland Still France's Foe.

NAVAL ACCORD WITH ITALY

But Agreement of the Delegations Goes No Further, Declares French Premier.

By EDWIN L. JAMES.

Special to The New York Times.

WASHINGTON, Nov. 15.—Premier Briand of France expects to present at a plenary session of the conference, probably on Friday, the case of his country with regard to the reduction of land armament.

Cost of Army Supplies Cut $22,515,941 in Last Quarter

WASHINGTON, Nov. 15.—A difference of $22,515,941 is shown in the cost report of the Quartermaster General of the Army for supplies, clothing, food and other quartermaster properties bought for the quarter ended Sept. 30, 1921, and the same period of last year. The report was said by army officers today to reflect for the first time in official records the reduced cost of supplying the smaller army of 132,000 men as compared with 200,000 in 1920.

Another difference of $4,301,306 is shown in the net cost of operation of the quartermaster depots for the same periods. For the quarter ended September last the cost was only $3,212,199, against $7,514,496 in 1920.

LODGE MAY SOUND BALFOUR

British Treaty With Tokio Considered Inimical to Our Interests.

REGARD FOR TOKIO FEELINGS

British Want Arrangement Satisfactory to Japan—Expected to Quit Wei-hai-wei.

TODAY'S SESSION SECRET

Conference to Consider Far East in Committee of Whole—Hughes Proposal Awaited.

By RICHARD V. OULAHAN.

Special to The New York Times.

WASHINGTON, Nov. 15.—Exploding international bombshells is not to be followed by Secretary Hughes as a common practice. There is to be no bombshell exploded by him in the Washington conference in connection with Far Eastern and Pacific questions.

Takahashi Calls Conference Epoch-Making; Says Japan Welcomes Armament Relief

TOKIO, Nov. 15 (Associated Press).—"I am confident that the Washington conference will be epoch-making in the realization of peace and good-will on earth by diminishing, if not removing, causes of distrust and suspicion among nations," said Baron Korekiyo Takahashi, the new Premier, to The Associated Press today.

"The burden of armaments," the Premier continued, "tends to a waste of energy and destruction of purposes and is a curse of the times. Japan's finance feels the pain of the burden of armament as keenly as any of the other powers. Nothing would be more welcome than relief from this burden through a mutual understanding between the nations based on the principle of equality and fairness.

Here Is Japan's Far East Program; Shidehara May Present It Today

Integrity of China and Withdrawal From Shantung—Open Door Also but Recognition of Her Special Trade Needs Because Raw Material Supply Is Vital.

Special to The New York Times.

WASHINGTON, Nov. 15.—Japan has a well-defined program for consideration by the Washington conference in connection with the effort to arrive at an international agreement on Pacific and Far Eastern questions.

STIRRING CONFERENCE SCENE

British Willingness to Scrap Half Her Fleet Told by Balfour

BROAD PLAN IS ACCLAIMED

Would Go Further on Submarines Than Hughes—Favors Bringing In Other Powers.

KATO GIVES JAPAN'S ASSENT

Will Suggest Modifications Later—France and Italy Also Agree "in Principle."

By EDWIN L. JAMES.

Special to The New York Times.

WASHINGTON, Nov. 15.—Today a chapter in the history of the world was finished and a new one begun.

A white-haired man, his shoulders bowed as if weighed down by the responsibility before him, stood with folded arms within the walls which held the armament conference and declared in the name of Great Britain the abandonment of her traditional policy of supremacy on the sea.

BRITAIN WOULD END ALL SUBMARINES

Failing That, She Wants Fewer Allowed, More Small Craft, New Replacement Method.

JAPAN SEEKS BIGGER RATIO

A Permanent Tonnage of About 67 Per Cent. of Her Rivals' Total Is Her Idea.

By EDWIN L. JAMES.

Special to The New York Times.

WASHINGTON, Nov. 15.—Considerations are three in number. In the first session of the armament conference upon the modifications which will be sought to the American plan for naval limitation.

DRUG RAID IN THEATRE

Three Alleged Peddlers Arrested in Bowery Film Show.

Special Report.

Continued on Page Six.

The New York Times.

THE WEATHER
Fair today and Thursday; no change in temperature; north winds.
Temperature yesterday—Max., 40; Min., 35. For full weather report see Page 22.

VOL. LXXI....No. 23,328. ... NEW YORK, WEDNESDAY, DECEMBER 7, 1921. TWO CENTS In Greater New York | THREE CENTS Within 200 Miles | FOUR CENTS Elsewhere

IRELAND TO BE A FREE STATE WITHIN THE BRITISH EMPIRE; AGREEMENT SIGNED GIVING HER A STATUS LIKE CANADA'S; ULSTER CAN STAY OUT; PARLIAMENT CALLED TO RATIFY

HARDING PROPOSES FLEXIBLE TARIFF AND LABOR REGULATION

Asks Congress to Extend the Powers of the Present Tariff Commission.

WOULD FUND FOREIGN DEBT

Will Not Denounce Trade Treaties and Wants Merchant Marine Act Changed.

AGAINST TAX-EXEMPT BONDS

Many Arms Conference Delegates in Throng Which Listens to President's Address to Congress.

Special to The New York Times.

WASHINGTON, Dec. 6.—In an address which President Harding pointed out was not only a message to the Congress but to the people of the entire country, he made an appeal today for the unified support of his party in the accomplishment of legislation that he considers vital to the peace, prosperity and security not only of the United States but of the world. Senators and Representatives of both parties agreed that it was a very frank expression of the views and hopes of the Chief Executive. In much that he said the President won the outspoken approval of the Democrats as well as the Republicans. [The full text of the message is published on Page 8.]

Not since the war day has a more representative audience listened to an address by a President on the opening of Congress. Occupying seats of honor directly in front of the rostrum from which the President spoke were statesmen of Europe and the Orient who are representing their respective countries at the Conference for Limitation of Armament. They were an intensely interested body of men, observing the strictest decorum, who not join in the spoken applause that continually interrupted the delivery of the address.

Behind the diplomats and foreign delegates were grouped the members of the Senate and House, Secretary Hughes and the other members of the Cabinet being in the first row of seats in the House reservation. There were but two uniformed personages on the floor. One was General Pershing and the other his aid, Major Quekenmeyer.

Refers Twice to Arms Conference.

Twice in the course of his address, once at the beginning and again as he concluded, the President referred to the Conference for Limitation of Armament now in session in Washington.

Text of Agreement to Establish the Irish Free State

LONDON, Dec. 6 (Associated Press.)—The text of the agreement signed this morning by the British Government and the Irish representatives follows:

Article I.—Ireland shall have the same constitutional status in the community of nations known as the British Empire as the Dominion of Canada, the Commonwealth of Australia, the Dominion of New Zealand and the Union of South Africa, with a Parliament having powers to make laws for peace and order and good government in Ireland, and an executive responsible to that Parliament, and shall be styled and known as the Irish Free state.

Article II.—Subject to provisions hereinafter set out, the position of the Irish Free State in relation to the Imperial Parliament, the Government and otherwise shall be that of the Dominion of Canada, and the law, practice and constitutional usage governing the relationship of the Crown or representative of the Crown and the Imperial Parliament to the Dominion of Canada shall govern their relationship to the Irish Free State.

Article III.—A representative of the Crown in Ireland shall be appointed in like manner as the Governor General of Canada and in accordance with the practice observed in making such appointments.

Article IV.—The oath to be taken by the members of the Parliament of the Irish Free State shall be in the following form:

"I do solemnly swear true faith and allegiance to the Constitution of the Irish Free State as by law established, and that I will be faithful to his Majesty King George V., and his heirs and successors by law, in virtue of the common citizenship of Ireland with Great Britain and her adherence to and membership of the group of nations forming the British Commonwealth of Nations."

Article V.—The Irish Free State shall assume liability for service of the public debt of the United Kingdom as existing at the date thereof and toward the payment of war pensions as existing on that date in such proportion as may be fair and equitable, having regard for any just claims on the part of Ireland by way of set-off or counter-claim, the amount of such sums being determined, in default of agreement, by the arbitration of one or more independent persons being citizens of the British Empire.

Article VI.—Until an arrangement has been made between the British and Irish Governments whereby the Irish Free State undertakes her own coastal defense, defense by sea of Great Britain and Ireland shall be undertaken by his Majesty's imperial forces, but this shall not prevent the construction or maintenance by the Government of the Irish Free State of such vessels as are necessary for the protection of the revenue or the fisheries. The foregoing provisions of this article shall be reviewed at a conference of representatives of the British and Irish Governments to be held at the expiration of five years from the date hereof with a view to the undertaking by Ireland of a share in her own coastal defense.

Article VII.—The Government of the Irish Free State shall afford to his Majesty's imperial forces (a) in time of peace such harbor and other facilities as are indicated in the annex hereto, or such other facilities as may from time to time be agreed between the British Government and the Government of the Irish Free State, and (b) in time of war or of strained relations with a foreign power such harbor and other facilities as his Britannic Majesty may require for the purposes of such defense, as aforesaid.

Article VIII.—With a view to securing observance of the principle of international limitation of armaments, if the Government of the Irish Free State establishes and maintains a military defense force, the establishment thereof shall not exceed in size such proportion of the military establishments maintained in Great Britain as that which the population of Ireland bears to the population of Great Britain.

Article IX.—The ports of Great Britain and the Irish Free State shall be freely open to the ships of the other country on the payment of the customary port and other dues.

Article X.—The Government of the Irish Free State agrees to pay fair compensation, on terms not less favorable than those accorded by the Act of 1920, to Judges, officials, members of the police forces and other public servants who are discharged by it or who retire in consequence of the change of government effected in pursuance of the hereof paragraph.

Provided that this agreement shall not apply to members of the auxiliary police force or persons recruited in Great Britain for the Royal Irish Constabulary during the two years next preceding the date hereof. The British Government will assume responsibility for such compensation or pensions as may be payable to any of these excepted persons.

Article XI.—Until the expiration of one month from the passing of the Act of Parliament for the ratification of this instrument, the powers of the Parliament and the Government of the Irish Free State shall not be exercisable as respects Northern Ireland, and the provisions of the Government of Ireland Act of 1920 shall, so far as they relate to Northern Ireland, remain of full force and effect, and no election shall be held for the return of members to serve in the Parliament of the Irish Free State for the constituencies of Northern Ireland unless a resolution is passed by both houses of Parliament of Northern Ireland in favor of holding such elections before the end of said month.

Article XII.—If before the expiration of said month an address is presented to his Majesty by both houses of Parliament of Northern Ireland to that effect, the powers of the Parliament and Government of the Irish Free State shall no longer extend to Northern Ireland, and the provisions of the Government of Ireland Act of 1920 (including those relating to the Council of Ireland) shall, so far as they relate to Northern Ireland, continue to be of full force and effect, and this instrument shall have effect, subject to the necessary modifications.

Provided, that if such an address is so presented, a commission consisting of three persons, one to be appointed by the Government of the Irish Free State, one to be appointed by the Government of Northern Ireland, and one, who shall be Chairman, to be appointed by the British Government, shall determine in accordance with the wishes of the inhabitants, so far as may be compatible with economic and geographic conditions, the boundaries between Northern Ireland and the rest of Ireland, and for the purposes of the Government of Ireland act of 1920, and of this instrument the boundary of Northern Ireland shall be such as may be determined by such commission.

Article XIII.—For the purpose of the last foregoing article the powers of the Parliament of Southern Ireland under the Government of Ireland Act of 1920, to elect members of the Council of Ireland, shall, after the Parliament of the Irish Free State is constituted, be exercised by that Parliament.

Article XIV.—After the expiration of said month, if no such address as mentioned in Article XII. hereof is presented, the Parliament of the Government of Northern Ireland shall continue to exercise as respects Northern Ireland such powers conferred upon them by the Government of Ireland Act of 1920, but the Parliament of the Government of the Irish Free State shall in Northern Ireland have in relation to matters, in respect of which the Parliament of Northern Ireland has not the power to make laws under that act (including matters which, under said act, are within the jurisdiction of the Council of Ireland), the same powers as in the rest of Ireland, subject to such other provisions as may be agreed to in the manner hereinafter appearing.

Article XV.—At any time after the date hereof the Government of Northern Ireland and the Provisional Government of Southern Ireland hereinafter constituted, may meet for the purpose of discussing provisions, subject to which the last of the foregoing article is to operate in the event of no such address as is therein mentioned being presented, and those provisions may include; (a) Safeguards with regard to patronage in Northern Ireland; (b) safeguards with regard to the collection of revenue in Northern Ireland; (c) safeguards with regard to import and export duties affecting the trade and industry of Northern Ireland; (d) safeguards for the minorities in Northern Ireland; (e) settlement of financial relations between Northern Ireland and the Irish Free State; (f) establishment and powers of a local militia in Northern Ireland and the relation of the defense forces of the Irish Free State and of Northern Ireland, respectively, and if at any such meeting provisions are agreed to, the same shall have effect as if they were included among the provisions subject to which the powers of Parliament and of the Government

of the Irish Free State are to be exercisable in Northern Ireland under Article XIV. hereof.

Article XVI.—Neither the Parliament of the Irish Free State nor the Parliament of Northern Ireland shall make any law so as either directly or indirectly to endow any religion or prohibit or restrict the free exercise thereof or give any preference or impose any disability on the account of religious belief or religious status, or affect prejudicially the right of any child to attend school receiving public money without attending the religious instruction of the school, or make any discrimination as respects State aid between schools under the management of the different religious denominations, or divert from any religious denomination or any educational institution any of its property except for public utility purposes and on the payment of compensation.

Article XVII.—By way of provisional arrangement for the administration of Southern Ireland during the interval which must elapse between the date hereof and the constitution of a Parliament and a Government of the Irish Free State in accordance therewith, steps shall be taken forthwith for summoning a meeting of the Members of Parliament elected for the constituencies in Southern Ireland since the passing of the Government of Ireland act in 1920 and for constituting a Provisional Government, and the British Government shall take steps necessary to transfer to such Provisional Government the powers and machinery requisite for the discharge of its duties, provided that every member of such Provisional Government shall have signified in writing his or her acceptance of this instrument. But this arrangement shall not continue in force beyond the expiration of twelve months from the date hereof.

Article XVIII.—This instrument shall be submitted forthwith by his Majesty's Government for the approval of Parliament and by the Irish signatories to a meeting summoned for the purpose of members elected to sit in the House of Commons of Southern Ireland, and, if approved, it shall be ratified by the necessary legislation.

On behalf of the British delegation:

LLOYD GEORGE. WORTHINGTON-EVANS.
AUSTEN CHAMBERLAIN. GORDON HEWART.
BIRKENHEAD. HAMAR GREENWOOD.
WINSTON CHURCHILL.

On behalf of the Irish delegation:

ART O'GRIOBHTHA (ARTHUR GRIFFITH).
MICHAEL O. O. SILEAIN (MICHAEL COLLINS).
RIOBARD BARTUN (ROBERT C. BARTON).
E. S. DUGAN (EAMON J. DUGGAN).
SEOBHA GHABHAIN LI DHUBHTHAIGH (GEORGE GAVAN DUFFY).

Dated the 6th of December, 1921.

ANNEX.

An annex is attached to the treaty. Clause 1 specifies that Admiralty property and rights at the dockyard port of Berehaven are to be retained as at present date and the harbor defenses and facilities for coastal defense by air at Queenstown, Belfast, Lough and Loughswilly to remain under British care, provision also being made for oil, fuel and storage.

Clause 2 provides that a convention shall be made between the two Governments, to give effect to the following conditions: That submarine cables shall not be landed or wireless stations for communication with places outside of Ireland established, except by agreement with the British Government, that existing cable rights and wireless concessions shall not be withdrawn except by agreement with the British Government, and that the Irish Government shall be entitled to land additional submarine cables or establish additional wireless stations for communication with places outside of Ireland, that lighthouses, buoys, beacons, &c., shall be maintained by the Irish Government and not be removed or added to except by agreement with the British Government, that war signal stations shall be closed down and left in charge of care and maintenance parties, taking them over and working them for commercial purposes, subject to Admiralty inspection, and guaranteeing the upkeep of existing telegraphic communication therewith.

Clause 3 provides that a convention shall be made between the two Governments for the regulation of civil communication by air.

Continued on Page Nine.

'IRISH FREE STATE' CREATED

All of Ireland Outside of Ulster to Have Dominion Rule.

ULSTER CANNOT STOP IT

Redrawing of Her Frontiers to Follow if She Finally Refuses to Join.

NAVAL RIGHTS RESERVED

Control of Finances, Land Forces and Powers of Council of Ireland Given to New State.

Copyright, 1921, by The New York Times Company.

LONDON, Dec. 6.—Ireland shall have the same constitutional status in the community of nations known as the British Empire as the Dominion of Canada, the Commonwealth of Australia, the Dominion of New Zealand and the Union of South Africa, with a Parliament having powers to make laws for the peace and order and good government of Ireland and an Executive responsible to that Parliament, and shall be styled and known as the Irish Free State.

Such is the first article of the "treaty" between Great Britain and Ireland which was signed some minutes after 2 o'clock this morning by Lloyd George, Austen Chamberlain, Lord Birkenhead, Winston Churchill, Sir L. Worthington-Evans, Sir Hamar Greenwood and Sir Gordon Hewart, and on behalf of Ireland by Arthur Griffith, Michael Collins, Robert Barton, E. J. Duggan and Gavan Duffy.

The signatures were affixed to the document in that historic room of 10 Downing Street on whose walls hang the portraits of the greatest British Premiers of the past and of one American, George Washington, the Father of His Country.

B.R.T. DIVIDENDS PAID DAY OF RECEIVERSHIP

Checks for $236,250 Mailed by Operating Company Just Before Garrison Took Charge.

HECTIC HOLIDAY FOR HEDLEY

Got $1,000,000 on New Year's Eve to Stave Off the Failure of Interborough.

Stories of quick shifts of millions between holding companies and subsidiaries in both the Interborough and Brooklyn Rapid Transit systems on the eve of receiverships were told in the Transit Commission's housing inquiry by James R. Sheffield, trustee in bankruptcy for the Interborough Consolidated Corporation, and Howard Abel, Controller for the B. R. T.

On Dec. 31, 1918, a few hours before Lindley M. Garrison was appointed receiver for the New York Consolidated Railroad Company, which operates the subway and elevated lines of the B. R. T. system, the companys officers rushed out checks for the payment of a 1½ per cent. dividend on $15,000,000 of stock, amounting to about $236,250. The dividends had been declared in the preceding September. As holder of approximately 90 per cent. of the stock of the New York Consolidated, the Brooklyn Rapid Transit Company received the larger part of this payment.

A year later President Frank Hedley and other officers of the Interborough were spending a "hectic New Year's Eve," and finally obtained a loan of $1,000,000 from its bankrupt holding company, the Interborough Consolidated, to aid in averting a receivership for the subway and elevated lines of Manhattan and the Bronx.

A few days before this New Year's Eve loan the Interborough Rapid Transit Company had finished paying back to the Interborough Consolidated $800,000 borrowed from the treasury of the holding company the day before it went into bankruptcy in March, 1919. Mr. Sheffield, trustee in bankruptcy for the Interborough Consolidated, had demanded the return of that $800,000 on the ground that the loan was "illegal."

He also had demanded from the Interborough payment of a note for $200,000, due on April 1, 1919, but which was

Continued on Page Six.

German Explosion Kills 100, Sets Dynamite Works Afire

BERLIN, Dec. 6 (Associated Press.)—It is reported that 100 persons lost their lives today as the result of the explosion of an oil tank in the Nobel Dynamite Works at Scarbouts, Rhenish Prussia. The works are burning.

SAYS UNION ABUSES RAISE BUILDING COST

Witness Tells Lockwood Committee of Expenses Piled Up by Labor Inefficiency.

The Lockwood committee opened a new phase of its housing inquiry last yesterday afternoon by examining witnesses in an endeavor to learn to what extent housing construction was loaded with high costs due to the inefficiency of labor. C. G. Norman, Chairman of the Board of Governors of the Building Trades Employers' Association, detailed a long list of abuses in building trade unions, resulting from their severe membership and production restrictions demanded by the organizations.

Patrick J. Crowley, successor of Robert P. Brindell as Chairman of the Building Trades Council, having jurisdiction over 115,000 workers, explained the inefficiency of labor by the phrase "more pay, more pep," and declared he had heard no complaints lately regarding the inefficiency of labor.

Samuel Untermyer, senior counsel to the committee, and Henry Mayer, assistant counsel, again took up the affairs of Intensive Electrical Workers Union No. 3, which is said to have collected $250,000 a year on "permit" cards which enabled non-union journeymen to work on union jobs if they paid $2.50 a week for journeymen's cards and $1 a week for helpers' cards. Mr. Untermyer examined Joseph Lawlor, Treasurer of the union, concerning the $250,000 of the funds alleged to be missing, but Lawlor became involved in confused statements, saying he believed that William A. Hogan, the financial secretary, had turned the money over to the union, and then that he did not know whether the slogan turned the money over to him or not, finally returning to his original statement.

In introducing the examination of

Continued on Page Six.

America Will Enter No Alliance; Three More Chinese Advisers Out

No Treaty on Far East Likely, but a Less Formal Agreement—Project Shaping Slowly

By EDWIN L. JAMES.
Special to The New York Times.

WASHINGTON, Dec. 6.—Whatever plans are being worked out for an international treaty, protocol, resolution, agreement, or understanding among three, four, five, six, seven, eight or nine powers to establish a Far Eastern policy do not now form a proper subject for public consideration, according to the official view of the American delegation to the armament conference. It is stated by spokesman for the disarmament armament. But just what that "progress" means and just what it is purposed to commit the nations to the American representatives are not yet prepared to say.

While reports originating from other delegations are being published all over the world, emphasizing the idea of an alliance of the United States with other nations, the American delegates think the time is not fit to present the American views on what might be a suitable arrangement.

Efforts made today to induce the American representatives to set correspondents on the right path about the eddies of conflicting rumors as to what was being done brought only the instructive statement that what had been published about treaties and alliances was not within grasping distance of the truth. But just what the truth is—that is not forthcoming.

Observers, and many visiting diplomats, have commented frequently upon the secrecy of the conference since its first days. Not a few of the old-school diplomats who are here and are work fluxed that the Americans were going to stage the conference doings in the course taken.

China's attitude was criticised by American official, who said that China had nothing to gain by such a course. He pointed out that the conference was making great progress, and that China found herself in a very strong position. In face to face with all that representatives that this far East, with their representatives disposed to do everything possible to aid in restoring China's integrity and rehabilitating her finances.

There is divided opinion in the Chinese delegation as to the attitude that that country is facing in the conference. One Chinese adviser, deprecating the resignations, said that the action had been premature and would fail of the expected effect. Some of them resigned for the political effect at home, while others, it was said, were absolutely sincere in the course taken.

Another spokesman for China counseled caution with more determined attitude on the part of China and an insistence that the Shantung Railroad dispute be adjusted first, rather than the minor differences now under consideration in the parley. He said he was in a position to say that the leaders in the conference had decided just how far the Far Eastern matters should be settled and that China would be forced to take what was offered. In his opinion, the conference leaders have agreed not only upon a naval ratio but upon other matters. China, he said, would not be allowed to change her tariff troubles and most of the things in dispute would be left to a commission to study and report upon to another conference.

"We are not too sensitive about the

Attaches of Delegation Resign in Protest Against 'Negative Results of Conference'

Special to The New York Times.

WASHINGTON, Dec. 6.—As a protest against "negative results" of the conference concerning China's aspirations, three additional attaches of the Chinese delegation to the Washington conference, two of them superior advisers, today tendered their resignations. This action followed that of Dr. Philip K. C. Tyau, Secretary General of the delegation, yesterday.

Those who resigned today are Yuho M. T. Liang, ex-Minister of Foreign Affairs; Tzu-Chi Chow, ex-Minister of Finance, superior advisers, and Vice Admiral Ting-Kan Tsi, associate director of the naval adviser. Zo was an adviser to the office of the President of China during the incumbency of the last Yuan Shih-Kai. A report that Lieut. Gen. Fu Hwang, adviser to the delegation, also has resigned, was denied.

It was uncertain tonight whether the resignations would be accepted.

Continued on Page Four.

Carson Sees for Britain Day of 'Abject Humiliation'

Special Cable to The New York Times.

LONDON, Dec. 7.—The Morning Post says that after reading the terms of the Irish agreement the comment of Lord Carson, former Ulster leader, was:

"I never thought I should live to see a day of such abject humiliation for Great Britain."

CANADIAN ELECTION LIBERAL LANDSLIDE

Premier Meighen Loses His Seat and His Protection Policy Is Repudiated.

OTTAWA, Dec. 6.—Premier Meighen was defeated in his home constituency, Portage La Prairie, Manitoba, in the Canadian general election today. His opponent was Harry Leader, Progressive.

Returns received tonight indicated the defeat of the Meighen Government and a landslide for the Liberals, led by W. L. Mackenzie King. Seven members of the Cabinet were defeated.

Mr. King, the Liberal leader, was elected in North York, Ontario, a division normally Conservative, by 1,000 majority. T. A. Crerar, leader of the Progressive Party, was elected in Marquette, Manitoba.

Nova Scotia, with sixteen seats, gave them all to Liberals, two members of the Government going down to defeat in that province. New Brunswick returned Liberals in three out of the four Prince Edward Island divisions, and the eleven constituencies in New Brunswick.

The latest members defeated were F. McCurdy, Minister of Public Works, Defense; H. S. K. K. Spinney, Minister without portfolio, South, N. W. Rowell, President of the Privy Council, Thos. Simon, Quebec; G. G. Malantyne, Minister of Marine and Fisheries, Montreal, Quebec; A. Fauteux, Solicitor General, Terrebonne, Quebec; L. G. Belley, Postmaster General, Charlevoix, Quebec; Rodolphe Monty, Secretary of State, Beauharnois, and others.

Premier Meighen issued the following

Continued on Page Twelve.

ULSTER RESERVED; DUBLIN REJOICES

Craig Cabinet Begins Sessions to Consider the Terms of the Agreement.

NORTH DISLIKES THE OATH

But Waits to See if Sinn Fein Is Really Friendly—Dail's Acceptance Predicted.

Special Cable to The New York Times.

BELFAST, Dec. 6.—News that the settlement had been achieved between the British Government and the Sinn Fein delegates caused some surprise in Belfast, particularly in view of De Valera's declaration at Galway in regard to allegiance. The disposition of Ulster to enter upon any hasty criticism or comment, but to wait until the terms are revealed. Should the position of Ulster be safeguarded and southern Ireland accept allegiance and a recognized position within the British Empire there will be a general feeling of satisfaction in the north that the strife has been brought to an end.

A specially convened meeting of the Ulster Cabinet was held today. After considering the terms for two and a half hours the Cabinet adjourned further consideration until tomorrow.

Colonel Spender, Secretary to the Northern Cabinet, was asked for the Cabinet's first impression of the terms of settlement. He said they were somewhat puzzled and were anxious to have certain points cleared up. Colonel Spender added that if the proposed changes in area affected any great tract of territory or meant any great disturbance of population they would not be acceptable to Ulster. He understood, however, that they really meant small adjustments along the frontier.

Asked if the form of oath was acceptable, Colonel Spender said that he was surprised at it, but if it were acceptable to the British people they could not object. He regarded with suspicion the fact that the Sinn Feiners were not prepared to take the ordinary form of oath.

Likes the Option for Ulster.

In one form, Colonel Spender remarked, the latest proposals meant an advance, because the former ones provided for forcing Ulster to go in under a central Parliament while these give an option. If the good-will of the Sinn Fein was forthcoming, Ulster and the south could work in harmony.

"All the News That's Fit to Print."

The New York Times.

THE WEATHER
Unsettled today, probably light snow; Wednesday cloudy.
Temperature yesterday—Max., 40; min., 31.
For full weather report see Page 24.

VOL. LXXI....No. 23,334.   NEW YORK, TUESDAY, DECEMBER 13, 1921.   TWO CENTS In Greater New York | THREE CENTS Within 100 Miles | FOUR CENTS Elsewhere

YAP AGREEMENT MADE, JAPAN CONCEDES US LEAGUE RIGHTS; NAVY SETTLEMENT NEAR; 4-POWER TREATY TO BE SIGNED TODAY; BORAH ATTACKS IT IN THE SENATE AS AN ARMED ALLIANCE

DE VALERA DENIES HONOR REQUIRES TERMS BE RATIFIED

He Declares Plenipotentiaries Were Sent on Understanding Dail Would Act.

CROWDS FLOCK TO DUBLIN

Many Now Think That the Issue Should Be Submitted to a Plebiscite.

CRAIG REPORTS TO ULSTER

He Declares, It Is Said, That Lloyd George's Attitude Is: "This Is the Treaty, and It Stands."

Copyright, 1921, by The New York Times Company.
By Mail Cable to The New York Times.

DUBLIN, Dec. 12.—Eamon de Valera issued a further statement today on question of ratification.

Legion Head Sees Harding; Predicts Bonus Legislation

Special to The New York Times.

WASHINGTON, Dec. 12.—Hanford MacNider, National Commander of the American Legion, had a fifteen-minute conference with President Harding this morning, and as he left the White House he predicted that the present session of Congress would pass bonus legislation.

PRINCE BOYCOTTED IN ALLAHABAD VISIT

Whole Native Population Deserts the Streets at His Arrival in the City.

600 AGITATORS ARRESTED

Chairman of Allahabad Council Gets Jail Sentence—Many Imprisoned in Calcutta.

90 DRY AGENTS RAID BROADWAY RESORTS AND A VILLAGE HOTEL

Thomas Healy's, Cafe de Paris, the Little Club and the Hotel Lafayette Visited.

THIRTEEN PRISONERS TAKEN

PROTECTION BOAST A CLUE

Raiders, Posing as Western Men Seeking a Good Time, Win Confidence of Proprietors.

British Minority Laborites Ask Harding to Free Debs

LONDON, Dec. 12.—The Independent Labor Party has sent a cablegram to President Harding pleading for the immediate release of Eugene Debs and other political prisoners.

MARKETS IN A WHIRL AS EXCHANGES RISE

Continued Upswing Causes Scramble by Dealers in World's Money Centres.

STERLING TOUCHES $4.24½

Variety of Reasons Given for the Extreme Advances—Commodity Markets Unsettled.

SPIRITED SENATE DEBATE

Reed, Robinson, Stanley and Watson, of Georgia, Support Borah.

POINDEXTER BACKS TREATY

Kellogg Also Defends It—Idaho Member Wants Submarines and Poison Gas Forbidden.

PLEDGE LIKENED TO ART. X.

Long Discussion Now in Prospect, but Ratification Is Still Predicted.

Special to The New York Times.

WASHINGTON, Dec. 12.—The Conference for the Limitation of Armament had the four-power treaty were the subjects of an unexpected and spirited debate in the Senate this afternoon.

"Brilliant Success," Says Viviani in Farewell; British Delegation Plans to Sail on Dec. 31

WASHINGTON, Dec. 12 (Associated Press).—The Washington conference "is a brilliant success," M. Viviani, head of the French delegation, said tonight in a farewell conference with newspaper correspondents in anticipation of his departure tomorrow for New York, from where he will sail for Paris on Wednesday.

FOUR-POWER TREATY TO BE SIGNED TODAY

Yap Agreement, Which Was a Condition of Our Assent, May Also Be Signed.

CONFERENCE END LOOMS UP

Large Results Counted On by Our Delegates With the Further Agreements Expected.

Special to The New York Times.

WASHINGTON, Dec. 12.—The four-power treaty between the United States, France and Japan and the British Empire, relative to insular possessions and dominions in the region of the Pacific, will be formally signed at 11 A. M. tomorrow in the Diplomatic Room at the State Department.

EXTEND NAVAL RATIO TO FRANCE AND ITALY

Basis of 5-5-3-3-3 Is Studied for Inclusion in Quintuple Limitation Compact.

ORGANIZE NEW COMMITTEE

Heads of Five Delegations and Experts Are Grouped to Expedite Agreement.

Special to The New York Times.

WASHINGTON, Dec. 12.—The program of the Conference for Limitation of Naval Armament has reached the point where the major problem of ratio has been provisionally decided on—a basis of relative strength of 5-5-3-3-3 for the navies of the United States, the British Empire, Japan, France and Italy.

EQUALITY IN YAP GRANTED

We Recognize Mandate Rights of Japan in Pacific Islands.

COVENANT IS PARALLELED

Accord Reached With Tokio Insures Us Rights Equal to Any League Member.

PLAN WILL BE EXTENDED

Deals With Britain on South Pacific and With Other Mandatories Are Forecast.

By EDWIN L. JAMES.
Special to The New York Times.

WASHINGTON, Dec. 12.—The Administration reached an agreement with Japan on the covenant of the League of Nations to obtain for the United States rights and privileges of League membership in the mandated territories held by Japan in the North Pacific Ocean.

---

25 Hurt, 1 Missing, in Acid Blast And Fire at Former German Plant

Twenty-three persons were injured, six with burns, and one person was missing last night as the result of an explosion and fire yesterday afternoon at the Heyden Chemical Works, Monroe Street and River Road, Garfield, N. J.

Two Thousand Women in Leaderless Mob Storm Kansas Mine and Attack Workers

Special to The New York Times.

PITTSBURG, Kan., Dec. 12.—The Howat forces sent their women into the fight in the Kansas mining field today. Following a secret meeting at Frankfort, in the "Red" centre, yesterday, the Howat forces organized wives, daughters and other relatives of striking Howat miners into a leaderless mob.

Section 1

"All the News That's Fit to Print."

The New York Times.

THE WEATHER
Cloudy today; Monday, clear and colder; fresh west winds. Temperature Yesterday—Max. 36; min. 29.
For full weather report see Page 23.

Section 1

VOL. LXXI....No. 23,374. .... NEW YORK, SUNDAY, JANUARY 22, 1922. In Nine Parts, including Rotogravure Picture Section, Book and Magazine Section. FIVE CENTS In Manhattan, Bronx and Brooklyn; Elsewhere Ten Cents.

POPE BENEDICT XV. PASSES AWAY EARLY THIS MORNING;
LINGERS HOURS AFTER WORLD GETS REPORT OF DEATH;
TRIBUTES PAID TO THE PONTIFF BY MEN OF ALL RELIGIONS

LLOYD GEORGE ASKS NATIONS TO RESOLVE ON PEACE AT GENOA

Premier Declares International Conferences Alone Can Restore Confidence.

HITS AT POINCARE'S STAND

Those Who Fear Conferences Are Thus Unwilling to Face Realities, He Says.

FULL TEXT OF THE SPEECH

Implies Strong Hope for American Co-operation at Genoa—Warns Against Party Strife.

Copyright, 1922, by The New York Times Company.
Special Cable to THE NEW YORK TIMES.

LONDON, Jan. 21.—Prime Minister Lloyd George looks to the Genoa conference to carry the world another stage forward in the paths of peace and reconstruction after the war if the United States of America will attend and help to complete the good work done by the Washington conference.

Although he was most guarded in his expression of his views, it was obvious to the most of those who listened to the remarkable speech he made at Central Hall, Westminster, today, when he wound up the proceedings of the new Liberal Council convention held there, that he counts upon America. He did not say that without America nothing worth while would be accomplished at Genoa, but his whole speech by implication conveyed the idea that unless the United States does take a hand there progress at Genoa may be distressingly slow and limited.

He spoke as an optimist struggling hard against adversity. All his emphasis was laid on the necessity of world peace and his conviction that that could be found only through the means of international conferences. His references clear away the atmosphere of suspicion. Genoa, he believed, would remove other doubts and fears. Though he did not say it in so many words, he made it clear that his hopes lay in the English-speaking races.

He let his fancy play a little as he spoke of old hatreds, old feuds and old distrusts which complicate European problems and then he almost dramatized his experience of how conferences could solve them as with hands weighs the balance from side to side he pictured the weight of argument.

With arm slowly raised he illustrated the approach to agreement and with a blow of the right fist on the palm of the left hand he exclaimed:

"In the end reason prevails. When you are in conference some one will be there who will bring your face to face with realities, and it is those who never face realities who dislike conferences."

Although the British Premier's speech had to deal with many points of purely domestic politics, Lloyd George obviously regarded them as secondary and auxiliary to his main theme, the world reconstruction. Even his appeal for the continuance of the coalition Government in this country was based on the argument that the dominant issue of British domestic politics was need of peace in the world.

"There is one great stable country," he declared with a flash of national pride, "that is Great Britain. Do not deprive the world of the full advantages of the power and prestige of this great land by shattering them upon wretched party feeling."

Lloyd George spoke directly to his a resolution condemning the Government on the Irish settlement.

The full text of the Premier's speech is given below.

FULL TEXT OF LLOYD GEORGE'S SPEECH.

I congratulate the promoters of these meetings upon this finest gathering we have seen, representative of the Liberals who stood in the nation's need for national unity. A resolution has been moved and seconded of congratulation upon a task which if not altogether accomplished is well-nigh accomplished. Congratulations are given to myself and my colleagues on the result of our labors.

The first thing I have to say is that those congratulations have been directed to the wrong address. They ought to have been sent not to those who did it but to those who talked about it (Laughter and cheers) and never did it when they had the chance. It is a fact that we concluded long, difficult and delicate negotiations. It is true that we carried them to a successful issue. It is true we took serious decisions and faced grave responsibilities, some of us notably. (Continued on Page Nineteen.)

FLORIDA—SEABOARD FLORIDA LIM-
ited.—P. M., P. D. R. Solid Pullman with Club and Observation Car.
Sleeper Dining Car Pennsylvania. NEW-Y.—Advt.

Freighter Sinking at Sea; Rush to Save Her Crew

BOSTON, Jan. 21.—The Norwegian steamship Mod, New York for An erp, Bremen and Hamburg, is sinking in mid-ocean according to radiograms received here today. The steamer Centennial State reported that all the Mod's lifeboats and one propeller were gone, and that the steamer George Washington was going to her aid. The Mod's position was given as latitude 46:15 north, longitude 41:10 west.

The Mod left New York on Jan. 13. She is a vessel of 2,707 tons and available records indicate that she is a freighter. Her position as given in the wireless messages is about 1,200 miles east of Halifax.

STORM IN FRANCE OVER GEN. PETAIN

Poincare Sharply Criticised for Appointing Him to Post in War Ministry.

CHAMBER TO DISCUSS IT

Nationalists Not Anxious for American Participation at Genoa.

Copyright, 1922, by The New York Times Company.
Special Cable to THE NEW YORK TIMES.

PARIS, Jan. 21.—Premier Poincare's first governmental act in appointing Marshal Pétain to what is in effect not only the office of Inspector General of the Army but a position in the Ministry of War has been during the last few days one of the subjects of most controversy in all the program of the Government.

The Socialists attacked it at once as an indication of the militaristic intentions of the new Premier. Even in the general opinion it was considered as an unwise step, however fully qualified for the post the Marshal might be and however little attention there might be from his former powers.

Then in the Chamber during the debate on Thursday André Lefèvre, himself a former Minister of War, and always one of the hottest advocates of more complete disarmament of Germany, suddenly refused his support to the new arrangement on the ground of this termination. In a sharp speech he attacked the new arrangement at the Ministry of War as likely to take the army from civilian control and place it in the hands of its military leaders, and he the support he received it became at once apparent that even a great part of the enthusiasm for the Poincaré administration the Chamber was reserving its right to judge its actions in committing the country to any militarist program.

M. Maginot, the new War Minister, who formerly was, Minister of Pensions, at once replied to M. Lefèvre, but his reply was so feeble that Poincaré had to interpose and promise that the matter would be fully debated at the first convenient opportunity.

In the two days that have elapsed opinion has visibly hardened and the first symptoms have appeared of opposition to the Government within the Chamber itself. Two important groups of radicals and radical Socialists, led by M. Klotz, the former Minister, have sent a letter to the Premier informing him that they wish the debate to be fixed as early as possible and in which they characterize Pétain's appointment as "an act contrary to the principle of constitutional responsibility and to republican doctrine."

If the Premier persists in maintaining the appointment in face of the opposition which it has aroused the incident may easily become a vital issue, and though Marshal Pétain's popularity and respect for his modesty and his ability are deep and sincere in the country, there is little doubt that tremendous pressure could easily be aroused on the question.

Premier Poincaré has finished drafting his outline of the preliminary conditions for a Franco-British compact and the terms of the compact itself as he would like to see it. This draft is to be handed to the British Government through the French Ambassador in London, and presumably the reply will be sent by similar channels.

In the new project France is believed to have repeated the request which Briand made that aggression against Poland should form a ground for British intervention, and further to have asked that the treaty be operative for a longer term than ten years.

According to the formula announced in the Premier's ministerial declaration of "a treaty between equals," Poincaré is seeking to have the treaty made reciprocal so as to avoid the suggestion that France is a protected country. Just how he purposes to do this is, however, being kept secret, and even those who are most enthusiastic for "equality" profess their fear that England will not accept easily a guarantee which will appear to carry with it approval of France's military upkeep, and much less will she accept any hard and fast stipulation as to the number of army corps which she must supply in case of war.

(Continued on Page Twenty-one.)

COLLINS AND CRAIG AGREE ON BOUNDARY AT LONDON MEETING

Terms Give Hope of Peaceable Settlement of Differences of Ulster and South Ireland.

THEY CALL OFF BOYCOTTS

Decide to Devise Better System Than Council of Ireland to Handle Their Relations.

WILL TAKE UP AMNESTY

Ulster Officials Call the News "Best We Have Had, and the Most Cheering."

LONDON, Jan. 21 (Associated Press).—The Irish situation took an unexpected turn today with the announcement that Michael Collins, head of the Irish Provisional Government, and Sir James Craig, Premier of Ulster, had arrived at a mutual agreement, which holds out the promise of a peaceable settlement between the North and the South. In view of the more surprising in view of the fact that Mr. Collins had only left Dublin last night to enter into consultations with Sir James this morning.

In addition to the arrangements made to settle the boundary question, it was decided to cease forthwith mutual boycotts. What is considered of vast importance is the decision to devise a better system than the Council of Ireland as provided in the 1920 act, to deal with problems affecting the two of Ireland. The terms of the agreement are substantially as follows:

1. The boundary commission, as outlined in the Anglo-Irish treaty, will be appointed to appoint one representative each from the Irish Free State and of Northern Ireland to appoint one representative each to the Society for the Prevention of Cruelty to Children, who will mutually agree on behalf of their respective Governments regarding the future boundaries between the two.

2. Without prejudice to future consideration by his Government of the question of tariffs, Mr. Collins undertakes that the Belfast boycott will be discontinued immediately, and Sir James undertakes to facilitate in every possible way the return of Catholic workmen—without tests—to the shipyards, and whenever trade revival enables the firms concerned to absorb the present unemployed workmen. In the meantime, a system of relief on a large scale is being arranged to tide over the period of distress.

3. Representatives of both Governments are to unite in facilitating a settlement of the railway dispute.

4. The Governments are to endeavor to devise a more suitable system than the Council of Ireland for dealing with problems affecting all Ireland.

5. A further meeting will be held at a subsequent date in Ireland between the signatories to this agreement to discuss the question of amnesty for persons who have been imprisoned since the operation of the truce.

Ulster Official Is Hopeful.

BELFAST, Jan. 21 (Associated Press).—John Milne Barbour, Sir James Craig's Deputy Finance Minister, described the news of the agreement between Michael Collins and Sir James as "the best we have had yet and the most cheering." He thought it eminently desirable that the north and south combine in the interest of the common country so long as the restoration of Ulster is reserved.

The general feeling here is that the agreement is an outcome of Mr. Collins's desire to protect the Free State in the coming elections against the menace of a possible combination of Republicans and Communists, as there are many of the latter in the Transport Workers' Union. The Ulster Premier, on his part, is anxious for peace within the six-county borders.

The Ulster Unionists naturally will welcome the raising of the boycott, but are apprehensive of trouble with the shipyard workers on the question of the restoration of Catholic workmen ousted in July, 1920, after the murder of Colonel Smyth in Cork. There has been a heavy increase of unemployment in the shipyards in the last year, and it is considered definitely certain that the Protestant workmen will insist that their co-religionists be given priority in the filling of jobs.

Lord Pirrie holds the same view with regard to the situation, as does the Ulster Premier, but believes that it will be a long time before the bitterness engendered by the shootings and bombings on both sides vanishes. Matters, however, he thinks, would be facilitated if the British Government were prepared to finance a large relief scheme, as the Ulster Labor Ministry has been sorely tried by the unemployment problem.

Takes Over Dublin City Hall.

DUBLIN, Jan. 21.—The administration of the Dublin City Hall was handed over today by the British military authorities.
(Continued on Page Fourteen.)

ATLANTIC COAST LINE — Augusta, Jacksonville, Tampa, through Pullmans. Leave, New York at 1:50 P. M., 10:00 P. M., Penn. Sta. — Advt.

Senate Agrees to Take Up Foreign Debt Refunding Monday

WASHINGTON, Jan. 21.—The Senate late today cleared the way for consideration next Monday of the Allied Debt Funding bill. Before adjourning over Sunday, the Senate made the bill its privileged business. A long debate is regarded assured after final passage a Democratic amendment to require semi-annual interest payments and to require foreign bonds paying not less than 5 per cent. The Genoa Economic Conference and the armament conference are expected to be discussed in connection with the measure.

ARREST 'TEX' RICKARD ON A GIRL'S CHARGE

Boxing Promoter Is Accused of Inviting 15-Year-Old Child to 47th Street House.

HE HINTS AT AN ENEMY PLOT

Alleged Victim's 11 and 12 Year Old Companions Give Evidence to Children's Society.

"Tex" Rickard, lessee and manager of Madison Square Garden and the most conspicuous prize-fight promoter in the country, was arrested yesterday on charges involving a 15-year-old girl. 11 and 12 years respectively, have said association that began one night last association that began one night last Madison Square's swimming pool in association that began one night last Street; Elvira Renzi, 12 years old, of 221 East Twenty-fifth Street, and Lena Hess, 11 years old, of 232 East Twenty-third Street.

Rickard, who is about 50 years old, a member of the Society for the Prevention of Cruelty to Children, was arrested upon the statements, which they went to swim in the Garden pool, and invited them to visit his offices in the tower. The girls say that Rickard gave them money and offered them wine. Later, the girls say, they visited him in private houses at 20 and 24 West Forty-seventh Street.

Rickard, who is about 50 years old, was arraigned before the Magistrate George W. Simpson held him in 11,000 bail for examination Wednesday on a charge of criminal assault.

Girls' Charges Against Promoter.

Vincent D. Pisarra, Superintendent of Investigations of the Society for the Prevention of Cruelty to Children, gave reporters a detailed account of the charges against Rickard yesterday afternoon. The girls are Alice Ruck, 15 years old, of 225 East Twenty-fifth Street; Elvira Renzi, 12 years old, of 221 East Twenty-fifth Street, and Lena Hess, 11 years old, of 232 East Twenty-third Street.

"This is the story that the three girls tell," said Mr. Pisarra. "One night last August a boy friend gave the Ruck girl and the Hess girl complimentary tickets to the swimming pool at Madison Square Garden. They went that night and several times in the next few nights. One night they met Rickard, who they say was always at the pool. They just picked up an acquaintance. Those were asked if they were sure of his identity, and said that various people came up and called him 'Tex.' They say he gave them $1 each the first night he met them.

"The Renzi girl met Rickard a few nights later. All three girls then began talking to Rickard every night they went to the pool for a swim. He continued to give them money. One night, the Ruck girl said, she and several others in the sea few nights. One night they met Rickard, who they say was always at the pool. They just but they did not want it. According to the girls, Rickard attempted to attack the Hess girl and did attack the Ruck girl, in a room in the tower.

Met Him by Appointment.

"On a later occasion, the girls say, Rickard gave them a piece of paper on which was written the address, 24 West Forty-seventh Street, and made an appointment to meet them there. The Ruck and Hess girls say they met him on the evening of the shooting, and they told Mr. Dineen the refused to make a statement. Captain Fay then examined the policeman's pistol. It was fully loaded, but had been cleaned recently.

Soden was arrested and taken to the hospital in the hope that McGuiness might be able to identify him, but a few minutes before their arrival Mc-Guiness died. Soden then was taken to the West Thirtieth Street Station, where the policemen said he was scheduled to go on duty at the Glendale Station at midnight—two hours before—but had reported sick to the Lieutenant at the station over the telephone.
(Continued on Page Seventeen.)

EX-CONVICT SLAIN; POLICEMAN IS HELD FOR THE KILLING

Victim Shot Down in Dispute Said to Have Grown Out of Boyhood Enmity.

DYING, HE PROTECTS SLAYER

Refuses to Say Who Wounded Him, but Witness Names Patrolman Soden.

OFFICER ARRESTED IN HOME

Pistol Shows Recent Cleaning, but He Is Silent About Tragedy— Prompt Trial Promised.

John R. Soden, a mounted policeman attached to the Glendale Station, Queens, was held yesterday without bail for examination next Friday on suspicion of having shot and mortally wounded John McGuiness, an ex-convict, the night before in a drunken brawl in the saloon at 60 Ninth Avenue. He was arraigned before Magistrate Joseph E. Corrigan in Jefferson Market Court.

Soden, 33 years old and has been a member of the force for eleven years. He was arrested four hours after the shooting in his home, at 8 Bethune Street, a short distance from the saloon, by Captain Thomas Fay, head of the Lower West Side Detective Bureau. He refused to make any statement to Captain Fay or Assistant District Attorney William R. Dineen, an assistant District Attorney, who began an investigation shortly before McGuiness died in St. Vincent's Hospital.

The Assistant District Attorney said four or five men were in the saloon when the shooting occurred, but the police had found only one of them. This witness, Philip Comisky of 411 West Thirtieth Street, told Mr. Dineen the shooting followed an altercation growing out of ill feeling that had existed between Policemen Soden and Mc-Guiness from their boyhood.

Soden, who was in civilian clothes, is six feet one inch tall and weighs 190 pounds. He had struck McGuiness in the face when they were standing at the bar, and the men fought for five minutes, he said. McGuiness, who was two years younger than the policeman, was getting the better of the fight, Comisky said, when onlookers separated the men.

McGuiness Offers Apology.

Comisky told Mr. Dineen that McGuiness then expressed regret that they had fought over the old grudge and, walking up to Soden with his right hand extended, said:

"Well, Jack, let's forget it. We're old schoolmates together."

Soden shook hands with McGuiness, Comisky added, and said:

"Let bygone be bygones."

McGuiness then took a position beside the policeman at the bar, according to Comisky, and Soden suddenly wheeled around on him with his pistol. As Mc-Guiness backed away, the witness said, the policeman shot him in the abdomen, the chest and the right arm.

With the first shot the onlookers fled to the street, Comisky said. Policeman Soden followed.

A policeman, who had been standing a block away, ran into the barroom and found McGuiness dying on the floor. Asked who had shot him, McGuiness refused to reply. He was taken to St. Vincent's Hospital, where Captain Fay and several detectives questioned him, but he declined to answer their questions, and the only information he gave was his name and his address, 320 West Seventeenth Street.

McGuiness was in the hospital about three hours when Detective Sergeant William Quinn again pressed him to tell who shot him. McGuiness, the detective said, impatiently turned his head aside and mumbled the name of a cabaret singer who knew nothing about the shooting.

Witness Tells of Shooting.

In the meantime detectives had arrested Comisky as a material witness. Comisky told Captain Fay that Soden had fired the shots, and the Captain, accompanied by several detectives, went to the policeman's home, where they found him seated with his wife and two children. They asked him if he was in the Ninth Avenue saloon at the time of the shooting, and they told Mr. Dineen the refused to make a statement. Captain Fay then examined the policeman's pistol. It was fully loaded, but had been cleaned recently.

Soden was arrested and taken to the hospital in the hope that McGuiness might be able to identify him, but a few minutes before their arrival Mc-Guiness died. Soden then was taken to the West Thirtieth Street Station, where the policemen said he was scheduled to go on duty at the Glendale Station at midnight—two hours before—but had reported sick to the Lieutenant at the station over the telephone.

A police surgeon was summoned to learn whether Soden was drunk and told Captain Fay the policeman was "fit for duty."

Meanwhile, Mr. Dineen had endeavored to get a statement from the prisoner, but Soden, though he had conducted his cases when he was on the force, refused to answer anything. Mr. Dineen said:

"Meanwhile, Mr. Dineen had endeavored to get a statement from the prisoner, but Soden, though he had conducted his cases when he was on the force, refused to answer anything."
(Continued on Page Nineteen.)

World Is Misled by Premature Report of Death; Berlin Started Rumor, Cardinal's Aid Spread It

LONDON, Jan. 22.—All London went to bed last night in the belief that the Pope had died in the afternoon. The report appears to have been circulated throughout Europe and was accepted by church and civil authorities as true. The German Reichstag suspended proceedings, while President Ebert delivered a eulogy on the Pope.

All the London evening papers published extra editions, announcing the death of the Pontiff, and the first editions of the Sunday papers, sent to the Provinces, contained that report.

The report of the Pope's death emanated from Cardinal Bourne's residence. A member of the Cardinal's staff notified all the English press agencies before 6 P. M. that the Cardinal had received official information of the Pope's death, and confirmed this to all who made special inquiries. Bells were tolled at Westminster and the Southwark Catholic Cathedral, and an announcement of the death was made from the pulpit of the latter church, followed by a requiem mass.

Late at night the Cardinal's chief secretary informed the news agencies that the information communicated to them, that the Cardinal had received an official report of the Pope's death, was incorrect. It was impossible to obtain an explanation of the mistake.

The first report of the death of the Pope apparently came from Reuter's News Agency. An Associated Press dispatch from London (12:35 P. M.) said:

"A Berlin dispatch to Reuter's this afternoon says word has been received there that Pope Benedict is dead."

At 1:32 P. M. this Associated Press dispatch from Paris was received here:

"A Berlin dispatch to the Havas Agency quotes the Wolff Bureau as saying Pope Benedict died at 3:15 o'clock this afternoon, Rome time."

The Cardinal Bourne message to which the above London dispatch refers was timed at London (6:53 P. M. (1:53 P. M. New York time).

It read:

"Cardinal Bourne, Archbishop of Westminster, stated this evening he had been officially notified by telegraph from Rome that Pope Benedict was dead."

At 2:10 P. M. this Reuter's dispatch from Rome was issued by the Associated Press here:

"Pope Benedict died late today."

The time at which this message was filed at Rome was not given. A statement issued late last night by the Associated Press said:

"Urgent messages, asking for definite information direct from Rome, brought replies from London that the Italian telegraphic system had been in a state of chaos for more than a year and that undoubtedly the wires were overburdened with hundreds of messages regarding the Pope; that this morning messages were coming late in the afternoon, and that doubtless official Vatican messages were given precedence over press dispatches."

ADOPT PLAN TO LIST ALL CHINA TREATIES

Conferees Extensively Amend Hughes Resolution, but Principle Remains.

JAPANESE GAIN A POINT

Agreements Made by Nationals Apart From Government Need Not Be Notified.

By EDWIN L. JAMES.
Special to The New York Times.

WASHINGTON, Jan. 21.—The Far Eastern Committee of the Washington conference today adopted the Hughes resolution providing for the public listing of commitments under which rights, in China are claimed. On the motion of the Japanese, the original resolution was altered to place on China the task of publishing agreements with the nationals of the powers with relation to other than public utilities.

The Hughes plan, as adopted, is in four parts. The first lays down that the powers other than China shall file all treaties or other formal documents with relation to China, and that all future commitments shall be notified. Part two says that the powers shall file all commitments between them nationals and the Chinese governmental authorities, so far as possible, where they deal with public utilities. The third part obliges China to notify all treaties or other agreements with any outside Governments, or the nationals of any other Government. Part four provides for the notification of other powers to adhere to the arrangement.

Most of the treaties with China have been published, however, it is thought that the operation of the listing arrangement will bring some new ones to light. The provision for filing future treaties exists already in Article 18 of the Covenant of the League.

The Resolution as Adopted.

Here is the text of the Hughes resolution:

The powers represented in this conference, considering it desirable that there should hereafter be full publicity with respect to all matters affecting the political and international obligations of China and of the several powers in relation to China, are agreed as follows:

1. The several powers other than China will, at their earliest convenience, file with the Secretariat General of the conference for transmission to the participating powers a list of all treaties, conventions, exchanges of notes or other international agreements which they may have concluded with China or with any other power or powers in relation to China, which they deem to be still in force and upon which they desire to rely.

2. In any case in which the several powers concerned may deem it advisable, a copy of the text cited in the original language (or languages) in which it was concluded may be filed with the Secretariat General of the conference.

3. Every treaty or other international agreement of the character described which has not been concluded before the signing of this resolution shall be notified by the Governments concerned within sixty days after its conclusion to the powers who are signatories of or adherents to the agreement.

4. The several powers other than China will file with the Secretariat General of the conference, for transmission to the participating powers, a list of all those contracts between their nationals, of the one part, and the Chinese Government or any of its administrative subdivisions or local authorities, of the other part, which involve any concession, franchise, option or preference with respect to railway construction, mining, forestry, navigation, river conservancy, harbor works or reclamation of land.
(Continued on Page Twenty.)

WILSON SHIPPING SHOWN FOR WOMEN.

MEN OF ALL FAITHS EULOGIZE THE POPE

Protestants Unite With Catholics in Praise of His Great Service to Humanity.

HAYES PAYS HIGH TRIBUTE

"Among the Church's Greatest Pontiffs," Says Archbishop— Bishop Manning's Tribute.

Expressions of sympathy and sorrow on learning of the death of Pope Benedict XV. were given yesterday by officials and prominent citizens as well as church dignitaries throughout the city.

An early report of the Pope's death, which proved to be unfounded, stirred church circles and brought forth many eulogies. When the report of his real death was confirmed there were many more such expressions. Orders were given for the draping in purple and black of many church edifices, and announcements of masses for today were made.

Archbishop Patrick J. Hayes made the following statement before the end was announced:

"His death would be a loss not only to the church of which he is the supreme shepherd, but also to the entire world that is longing for peace and stability.

"His services during the war were of the highest order—services which he gave to all mankind, irrespective of race, nation or religion. His thought was to serve humanity, and this he did in a spirit of love and justice and conscientious neutrality.

"His ministry and influence are needed now in the restoration of order and the stabilizing of the terrified social forces and powers that are crying out for the depths of men's sorrowing and distressed souls for a better and a juster world.

"Pope Benedict's name will be placed by history among the Church's greatest Pontiffs and the world's truest benefactors."

Mayor Hylan issued this statement:

"The death of Pope Benedict is a severe loss to religion and that feeling will be universally lamented. He was an eminent ecclesiastic and a Pontiff who sought to create a real brotherhood of man. I feel a keen and deep, personal sorrow in his death, for his services have been a never-ending source of inspiration to me. His memory will ever be cherished not only at the altars of his own Church, but in the heart of every man regardless of his creed."

Tributes by Protestant Clergymen.

The Right Rev. William T. Manning, Episcopal Bishop of New York, said:

"The death of his Holiness Pope Benedict XV. is a matter of concern to the whole Christian world. All Christians will feel deep sympathy with the Bishops, clergy and people of the Roman Catholic Church in their great loss."

The Rev. Caleb R. Stetson, Rector of Trinity Episcopal Church, said:

"The whole Christian world is touched by the death of the Pope, for he is at the head of the largest body of Christian people in the world. Pope Benedict XV. has been known throughout his life as a man devoted to the service of his Church, and one whose interest in the latter years as Chief Pastor of the Roman Communion has extended to all parts of the world. His interest in this country was marked, and his expressions of sympathy were warm. My sympathy
(Continued on Page Twenty.)

END AT 6 A. M., ROME TIME

Hope Was Given Up Early Yesterday After Two Sinking Spells

BUT HIS STRENGTH REVIVED

Clear-Minded Most of the Time and Full of Affection for Those Around Him.

CROWDS AROUND VATICAN

Messages From the Great of Many Lands Are Received by Gasparri.

ROME, Sunday, Jan. 22 (Associated Press).—Pope Benedict XV. died at 6 o'clock this morning (midnight, New York time).

The end had been expected for several hours. The attending physicians, Cardinal Gasparri and other members of the Pope's household were present at the bedside.

From midnight all hope had been abandoned, and at 2 o'clock Dr. Rattisini announced that the Pope could not live longer than four hours at the maximum.

At 3 o'clock this morning Dr. Cherubini, Cardinal Giorgi and the Pope's nephew were gathered around the bedside, the end seemingly being near.

The Pope appeared then to be in considerable distress. His extremities were already becoming cold.

At one lucid period late at night the Pope was able to partake of some nourishment. He then instructed his major domo to wake him in time for mass, to be celebrated at 5:30 in the morning in his chapel adjoining the bedroom.

Great Power of Resistance.

There had been moments during Saturday when it was feared the end had come, but stimulants revived the Pontiff, and his natural powers of resistance carried him through the turning point temporarily. The Holy Father seemed to cling to life, as did Pope Pius X. in 1914, when the final outcome was in doubt for many hours.

Dr. Battistini, the chief attending physician, visited the patient several times during the night. Each time he said that any minute might see the conclusion of the long hours of suffering through which Benedict XV. had passed in his fight for life.

The last announcement of the evening to the diplomatic representatives, waiting in the antechamber, was made by Cardinal Gasparri, the Papal Secretary of State, who said:

"A catastrophe is imminent. The Holy Father is getting worse and worse. We must be prepared for the inevitable."

The Cardinal's face was downcast and sad. He spoke in quiet tones, with deep emotion, making gestures with his hands.

After the publication of the last bulletin, Cardinal Giorgi, Mgr. Migone, Father Basil and Dr. Battistini, remained by the bedside. After a time the doctor told his Holiness that the Pope would pray for the peace of the world, to which the Pope replied:

"I would willingly offer my life for the peace of the world." He then turned on his side and lay watching those near him.

Hope Revived, Only to Fade.

Yesterday was a day of great uncertainty and deep anxiety among those who watched and prayed at the Vatican. Virtually all hope of the Pope's recovery was abandoned, even in the early hours of yesterday morning, and as the hours passed the wonder grew at the recuperative powers of the Holy Father, which enabled him to pass from one sinking spell and another to periods of comparative restfulness and strength. It was this changing condition that inspired hope at one moment and gave rise to rumors of death at another.

It was thought that if the Pope passed safely through Friday night

"All the News That's Fit to Print."

The New York Times.

THE WEATHER
Rain today, rising temperature; Thursday fair; east to south winds. Temperature yesterday—Max., 48; min., 24.
For weather report see next to last page.

VOL. LXXI....No. 23,405.   NEW YORK, WEDNESDAY, FEBRUARY 22, 1922.   TWO CENTS In Greater New York | THREE CENTS FOUR CENTS Within 200 Miles | Elsewhere

GIANT ARMY DIRIGIBLE WRECKED; 34 DEAD, 11 ARE SAVED;
VICTIMS PERISH WHEN ROMA BURSTS INTO FLAMES AFTER FALL;
COLLAPSE OF RUDDER CAUSES TRAGEDY ON SHORT TRIAL FLIGHT

FOUR-POWER TREATY WILL BE REPORTED WITH RESERVATION

Brandegee's Modification of the Compact Favored by Senate Committee.

HARDING AND LODGE AGREE

Legal or Moral Obligation to Defend Rights of Other Nations in Pacific Excluded.

MAY BE REPORTED TODAY

Committee Will Choose Between Brandegee's Reservation and a Milder Substitute by Pomerene.

Special to The New York Times.
WASHINGTON, Feb. 21.—The Four-Power Treaty, with a reservation which will stipulate that the United States assumes no "legal or moral" obligation to maintain the rights of other nations signatory to the compact, and that any adjustment or agreement, arrived at under the provisions of Articles I. or II., shall not be binding, on this Government unless approved by Congress, will probably be reported out of the Committee on Foreign Relations in the next few days.

It is possible, members of the Committee said tonight, that the treaty may be in the Senate before adjournment tomorrow afternoon.

The reservation, which, it is said, Senator Lodge has accepted, and with which the President has agreed to interpose no objection to, if by so doing the situation will be, as one member of the committee expressed it, "eased up," was introduced in committee by Senator Brandegee of Connecticut, an "irreconcilable." The reservation has not been approved by the committee, although it is understood that at least one other reservation along similar lines, will command probably twelve of the sixteen votes in the committee.

The Brandegee resolution was submitted to the committee today.

The Senate advises and consents, subject to the following reservation, which is to be made a part of the Instrument of Ratification, to wit:

The United States understands that it assumes no obligation, whether legal or moral, to maintain the rights, in relation to the insular possessions or insular dominions, of any of the other high contracting parties and that the consent of the Congress of the United States shall be necessary to any adjustment or understanding under Articles I. or II. The United States is to be bound in any way and that there is no obligation either legal or moral to give such consent.

Pomerene Substitute Favored.

The Brandegee reservation would probably have been approved today had not Senator Pomerene, one of the Democratic members, offered a substitute which he intended to "soften" the language of the reservation drafted by the Senator from Connecticut. The Pomerene suggestion was favorably received by several of the members, and it is possible that it may be the reservation which the committee will report to the Senate.

The Pomerene reservation, which will be offered in committee tomorrow morning, is very short, and has nothing in it about "legal or moral" obligations, although in the opinion of some of those who favor it this is as much opposed to a bill it is just as sweeping as the Brandegee draft, in that Congress receives the right to veto any agreement or adjustment that may be reached by the representatives of the signatory nations.

The Pomerene substitute reads:

It is understood, however, that the adjustment provided for under Article I. and the understanding contemplated under Article II. shall be subject to the consent of the Congress of the United States.

According to reliable information emanating from the Committee on Foreign Relations, the following Senators will vote for a reservation along the lines indicated in the Brandegee and Pomerene drafts: Lodge, Brandegee, Johnson, Moses, McCormick and Wadsworth of the majority, and Hitchcock, Swanson, Pomerene, Pittman and Shields of the minority. Senators McCumber, New and Kellogg, Republicans, and Williams, Democrat, are understood to oppose reservations of any kind.

Senator Pomerene agrees with the President's interpretation of the Four-Power Treaty and does not think a reservation necessary; but, realizing that a reservation appears certain of adoption, is attempting to order the reservation, if possible, less objectionable.

The Brandegee reservation has been submitted to President Harding. The President is said to have informed the Senators who conferred with him on the desire that the treaty should be ratified without reservation of any kind, he will

Continued on Page Nine.

BROADWAY LIMITED.
You will find distinctive service on the Broadway. The specially select-d crews are distinguished so much for their courtesy as for their efficiency. It leaves New York 2:15 P. M. and arrives Chicago 9:15 A. M.—over the Short Line, the Pennsylvania Railroad.—Advt.

MELLON BACKS UP HARDING ON BONUS

Again Warns Ways and Means Committee That Treasury Cannot Stand the Outlay.

SALES TAX ONLY SOLUTION

Special to The New York Times.
WASHINGTON, Feb. 21.—Secretary Mellon, appearing before the Ways and Means subcommittee considering bonus legislation today, reiterated his opposition to such legislation because of the condition of the Treasury. He agreed with the President, however, that, if bonus legislation were to be passed, the only way to raise the revenue without embarrassing the Government and injuring business was through a sales tax.

Mr. Mellon was asked to appear before the committee to discuss the advantages and disadvantages of different forms of a sales tax. The conference was held in executive session. He said that he was as much opposed to a bill without any provision for the revenue as he was against a measure which found the money by the eight-point taxation scheme recently advocated by the committee or by Treasury certificates.

Experts of the Treasury who were with Mr. Mellon said that a final retail tax would be objectionable in that it would be hard to collect and would be obnoxious to the consumer. They urged that if a sales tax were adopted it be placed upon manufactured articles or on the jobber.

1 to 4 Per cent. Tax Favored.

The proposal which seemed to meet with the most favor of the committee was that placing a 2 to 4 per cent. upon specific commodities sold by manufacturers or jobbers. All iron and steel manufactured products would bear a fixed tax, and so the tax would be imposed all along the line. In some instances it would be 2 per cent., and the maximum would not exceed 4 per cent. Under such a plan, taxes would not be imposed on food products and some articles of every day household consumption. This tax, it is estimated, would raise $300,000,000 annually.

The manufacturers' tax of 1 per cent. advocated by Senator Smoot did not appear to have much support in the committee. This tax, Treasury experts estimated, would yield $250,000,000 annually.

The subcommittee is not seriously considering any form of taxation other than a sales tax. The hearings have not progressed far enough to indicate just what form the sales tax will take, but it can be said open authority that the committee intends to report a bonus bill carrying a sales tax provision.

Opposition to a sales tax is increasing among the members in doubtful whether sufficient votes can be obtained in the Rules Committee for a special rule in

Continued on Page Three.

Hughes, Mellon, Hoover, Smoot, Burton, Named on Foreign Debt Commission

Special to The New York Times.
WASHINGTON, Feb. 21.—Nominations for the Foreign Debt Funding Commission were sent by President Harding to the Senate today.

In addition to Secretary Mellon, whose appointment was expressly stipulated by the Funding bill signed by the President last week, the nominations will be made up of the following: Secretary Hughes, Secretary Hoover, Senator Reed Smoot of Utah and Representative Theodore Burton of Ohio. Upon this commission will rest the duty of working out satisfactory arrangements for the more than $11,000,000,000 loaned by this country. This total places the British negotiations first, followed by the French, Italian and Belgian.

Lloyd George Going to Paris For Conference With Poincare

Copyright, 1922, by The New York Times Co.
Special Cable to The New York Times.
LONDON, Feb. 21.—There is good authority for stating that Premier Lloyd George intends to go to Paris on Saturday to confer with Premier Poincaré on various matters affecting the relations between France and Great Britain in particular the question of the Genoa conference.

SINN FEIN BLOCKS SPLIT OF LEADERS

Senator Calder Announces in Speech Here He Will Refuse to Vote for Bonus.

Insistence of Delegates Forces de Valera and Griffith to Seek a Compromise.

NO VOTE ON THE TREATY

Parish Priests Take the Lead in Demanding Long Delay Before Elections Are Held.

Copyright, 1922, by The New York Times Company.
Special Cable to The New York Times.
DUBLIN, Feb. 21.—For the first time since their historic duel in the Dáil Arthur Griffith and Eamon de Valera met on a public platform in the Mansion House today. In a sense they were there to renew the conflict, but on this occasion the issue was as to which side should capture the organization of Sinn Fein in view of the imminent election on the treaty. Nearly 3,000 delegates from all parts of the country were present to take part in the struggle. It was a remarkable gathering of gray-bearded and young men in the green uniform of the Volunteers and others who limped in on crutches, casualties of the late war, with a sprinkling of parish priests and not a few women, some of them in mourning.

After the dispute had been stated both by de Valera and Griffith, by degrees the feeling to preserve the organization of Sinn Fein against the threatened split became apparent and a parish priest raised a storm of cheers by suggesting that both de Valera's resolution to appeal to the Republic and Griffith's amendment, which would recognize the Free State, should be deleted. Another priest urged that the pretreaty and anti-treaty parties should establish their own electoral machinery and leave the Sinn Fein organization as a weapon to enforce the strict adherence of the British Government to the spirit and letter of the treaty in the framing of the Irish constitution.

The convention was finally adjourned until tomorrow morning to give the leaders of the opposing forces an opportunity of conferring with a view to evolving a basis whereby the convention could be adjourned for a period without division.

De Valera took the chair nearly half an hour late. Wearing a heavy brown frieze overcoat, he stroke through the hall, which thousands of cigarettes and pipes were already rendering dim and

Continued on Page Two.

List of the Dead and Survivors
In the Wreck of the Big Dirigible

THE DEAD.

Major JOHN G. THORNELL, Air Service; Langley Field.
Major WALTER W. VAUTSMEIER, Coast Artillery Corps; assigned to Air Service; Rockwell Field, Cal.
Captain DALE MABRY, Air Service; Langley Field.
Captain GEORGE D. WATTS, infantry; assigned to Air Service; Ross Field, Cal.
Captain ALLEN P. McFARLAND, Air Service; McCook Field, Ohio.
Captain FREDERICK R. DURR-SCHMIDT.
Lieutenant JOHN R. HALL.
Lieutenant WALLACE C. BURNS.
Lieutenant WILLIAM B. RILEY.
Lieutenant CLIFFORD E. SMYTHE.
Lieutenant WALLACE C. CUMMINGS.
Lieutenant AMBROSE V. CLINTON.
Lieutenant HAROLD K. HINE.
Master Sergeant ROGER B. McNALLY.
Master Sergeant MURRAY.
Sergeant LEE M. HARRIS.
Sergeant LEWIS HILLIARD.
Sergeant MYRON G. FIELD.
Sergeant THOMAS YARBOROUGH.
Sergeant BILLY RYAN.
Sergeant VIRGIL C. HOFFMAN.
Sergeant SHUMAKER.
Sergeant HOLMES.
Master Sergeant HOMER GARBY.
Sergeant HEVERON.
Private KINSTON.
Private THOMAS M. BLAKELEY.
Private THOMPSON.
Private MARION HILL.
Civilian STRYKER.
Civilian HINSON.
Civilian O'LAUGHLIN.
Civilian MERRIMAN.
Civilian SCHULENBERGER.

THE SURVIVORS.

Major JOHN D. REARDON, wife, Mrs. Reardon, 230 Elm Street, Washington, D. C.
Captain WALTER J. REED; father, William J. Reed, Scarsdale, N. Y.
Lieutenant CLARENCE H. WELCH; father, W. V. Welch, Papillon, Neb.
Lieutenant BYRON T. BURT Jr.
Sergeant VIRDON T. PEEK; father, Howard Peek, 2,304 Lafayette avenue, Terre Haute, Ind.
Sergeant HARRY A. CHAPMAN.
Lowther, Mrs. J. H. Ward, 1,626 Fredericks Avenue, St. Joseph, Mo.
Sergeant JOSEPH M. BIEDEN-BACH; father, John Biedenbach, 411 East Market Street, Akron, Ohio.
Corporal ALBERT FLORES.
Civilian WALTER A. McNAIR, Bureau of Standards, Washington, D. C.
Civilian CHARLES DWORACK, McCook Field, Ohio.
Civilian RAY HURLEY, National Advisory Committee on Aeronautics.

STRIKERS SHOT DOWN IN PAWTUCKET RIOT

Police Fire on Mob Fighting to Bar Textile Workers From Mills.

ONE KILLED, SEVEN INJURED

Troops Rushed From Providence Now on Guard—Other Strike Centres Quiet.

PROVIDENCE, R. I., Feb. 21.—A fatal early-morning riot in Pawtucket, the establishment of National Guard units in three troublesome strike centres and a meeting of the State Board of Mediation and Conciliation have been the day's outstanding developments in the textile situation in Rhode Island.

The Pawtucket riot in which one strike sympathizer was killed, two critically wounded and five less seriously hurt by riot gun fire when a crowd came to grips with the police at the Jenckes Spinning Company plant, led to the immediate dispatch of four coast artillery companies to the Blackstone Valley city from Providence. The Woonsocket and East Greenwich companies were under mobilization orders tonight. Their ultimate destination is believed to be Pawtucket.

With the exception of the disturbance at Pawtucket, quiet prevailed throughout the Blackstone and Pawtuxet Valleys today. At Pontiac and Natick, where trouble was experienced yesterday, two troops of cavalry and a coast artillery company were in constant vigilance.

When the troops arrived at Pawtucket they found only guard duty awaiting them, as the strike sympathizers quieted down immediately after their encounter with the police.

Tonight soldiers guarded the Jenckes mills, the plant of the J. & P. Coats Company and the Tamarack mill as a precaution against possible disorders tomorrow. The mills expect to operate on the holiday.

The Board of Mediation and Conciliation, appointed to bring both sides of the strike controversy with a view to arriving at a settlement, declined to make public its progress today. A statement issued after the meeting said:

The convention of the occurrence today, in all sections of Rhode Island, the board of mediation feels that it should

Continued on Page Two.

BOTH HOUSES PASS PORT PROJECT BILL

Democrats Fail in Effort to Have Hylan Appoint Two Commissioners.

MILLER WILL APPROVE

Senator Straus Breaks Away From Party, Calling Plan Essential to Cheap Food Supply.

Special to The New York Times.
ALBANY, Feb. 21.—Defeating all amendments offered by the opposition, the Senate and Assembly after long debate today passed Governor Miller's Port Authority bill by very large majorities. The vote in the Senate was 37 to 9 and in the Assembly 97 to 47.

Only one Republican Senator, Smith of Richmond, voted against the bill. One Democratic Senator, Nathan Straus Jr. of New York, and four Democratic Assemblymen voted with the Republicans in support of the measure. The four Democratic Assemblymen were G. T. Cross of Sullivan, Samuel I. Roseman of New York County, Wallace H. Sidney of Schoharie and Frank J. Taylor of Kings County.

Both in the Senate and Assembly an effort was made by the leaders of the Democratic minority, Senator Walker and Assemblyman Donohue, to have the bill providing for appointment by the Board of Estimate of two members of the three on the Port Authority Commission from this State taken from the Finance Committee in the upper house and the Committee on Ways and Means in the lower house for debate and final disposition in the open. In both houses the motion was voted down, in the Senate by a vote of 36 to 14 and in the Assembly by a vote of 98 to 52.

In the upper house Senator Smith of Richmond offered several amendments substituting lines leading over State lands for the present Greenville-Bay Ridge tunnel, which under the Port Authority plan is provided for as the principal connecting link between the New Jersey terminals and the Long Island and side of the harbor. These were defeated also, by a vote of 36 to 15.

The bill now goes to Governor Miller.

Continued on Page Ten.

THE DIRIGIBLE ROMA, 410 FEET LONG, BUILT BY ITALY FOR THE UNITED STATES, BURNED AT NORFOLK YESTERDAY.

HITS HIGH TENSION WIRES

Hydrogen Ignites in Norfolk Flight and Flames Sweep Huge Structure.

FEW SAVED BY LEAPING

One Lieutenant Breaks Neck in Jump—Other Victims Buried in Wreckage.

SAFE HELIUM GAS REMOVED

Rescuers Baffled by Intense Heat—Commander Mabry Stuck to Wheel Till Death Came.

Special to The New York Times.
NORFOLK, Va., Feb. 21.—In the greatest disaster that ever befell American military aeronautics, thirty-four men died this afternoon when the army dirigible airship Roma plunged a thousand feet and crashed to earth in flames near the Hampton Roads army base. Only eleven of the forty-five men aboard with her were saved, and some of them were terribly hurt. Three were slightly injured.

The breaking of the rudder with its vertical controls, affixed in box-kite fashion to the stern, is believed to have been the original cause of the disaster. Its more horrible phase came just as the stricken craft plummeted into the earth. The metal clad nose struck high-tension electric power wires, and with a flash and a roar, the hydrogen was fired from stem to stern.

Only those whose fortunate positions in the car enabled them to take the desperate hazard of a leap before the flames ran with lightning speed through the gas bag, more than two New York City blocks long, had much chance for their lives. The thirty-three who couldn't jump died. An officer whose leg broke in a dive to earth and was dead before he could be got to a hospital.

Captain Dale Mabry, commandant of the Roma and principal pilot, died with his hands on the wheel. He stuck to his post to the last. The clothes were found burned from his body and the flesh from his fingers, but the fingers still grasped the wheel of the aircraft.

Many Officers Among Dead.

The crush'd, misshapen mass that thudded onto the field was a funeral pyre of such intense heat that the agonies of those who were not killed in the crash must have been, mercifully brief. The bodies were burned beyond recognition and the slow work of taking the victims was carried out partly by a process of elimination and partly through non-combustible objects that the aviators had carried in their pockets. That list when it was completed showed that the Majors, four Captains and seven lieutenants were among the lost.

Horrified watchers, some of them veterans of gallant affairs abroad, rushed toward the blazing wreckage. Blistering heat held them to bare the tracks. Some had associates among the crash crew, others were actuated by all the traditional daring of the service—but those walls of heat were beyond human destruction. Not until three fire departments, mobilized at breakneck speed, had exhausted their chemicals and the twisted aluminum metal work was losing its red glow could any one approach. Then there remained only the gruesome job of extricating charred bodies.

The fire burned in the wreckage nearly five hours and it was not until 7 o'clock that it was entirely extinguished and the service men could penetrate far enough to take out all the bodies. The work of examining the debris was completed shortly after 9 o'clock tonight, with the total number of dead officially placed at thirty-four.

Things might have been different had the Roma's gas bag, with its cubical capacity of 1,100,000 feet, been inflated with non-inflammable helium was the levitating gas used when the Roma, which was bought from the Italian Government, went on her first trial flight last December. But it had been planned to send the ship—the largest semi-rigid airship in the world—on a Spring cruise over the country to demonstrate her fitness to cross the Atlantic. In her bag had been the whole available supply of helium in the United States. Flying officials wanted that for the Spring journey, so they pumped it out and substituted hydrogen.

Trip to Test Liberty Motors.

The occasion for today's flight that was to prove so tremendous a blow to lighter-than-air flying was a chance for the Liberty motors which had been installed to replace the Italian motors, which functioned poorly in the cold that marked the brief trial flight last December.

In charge of Captain Dale Mabry, with full complement of officers and crew and a few civilian guests, the huge craft went aloft from Langley Field at about 12:30.

Survivor Says Roma Often Sailed With a Tilt

NORFOLK, Va., Feb. 21.—One of the survivors of today's disaster said that the Roma often sailed with a slight tilt, and that he paid little attention to the initial lift of the tail of the ship until he found a man yet that the craft refused to respond to the helm. Then came the crash.

WASHINGTON WAITS FOR A FULL REPORT

General Patrick, Flies, to Scene to Take Charge of Army Investigation.

AIR MEN NOT DISCOURAGED

Effect of the Disaster on the Future of Military Aviation Is Doubtful.

Special to The New York Times.
WASHINGTON, Feb. 21.—According to information reaching the War Department today from Langley Field, Virginia, the home station of the dirigible Roma, something went wrong with the box-kite elevating planes at the stern of the giant airship, which are used for vertical control, the pilots in charge were unable to keep the nose of the dirigible in the air and it plunged into a high-voltage electric cable, which ignited the hydrogen inside the great gas bag simultaneously with the collapse of the craft.

The capacity of the Roma is 1,100,000 cubic feet and the flames from the ignition of its great capacity of gas not only rendered it impossible for the officers and other passengers, penned within the wreckage, to escape, but made it difficult to identify the bodies of those taken later from the wreckage.

The accident occurred at 2:19 o'clock. There were forty-five passengers on board, according to information given headquarters of the Army Air Service in Washington tonight by officers making verbal report by long distance telephone from headquarters at Langley Field. This preliminary oral report stated that there were eleven survivors, that thirty-four were missing—all regarded as having lost their lives—that the injured had been taken to the hospital of the Public Health Service, near Norfolk, and that all the bodies had not been recovered. This report stated that the only body recovered that had been identified up to 8 o'clock tonight was that of First Lieut. William B. Riley, son of Mr. and Mrs. Minnie H. Riley, lives at 628 East Eighty-sixth Street, New York City. Lieutenant Riley died at the hospital to which he was taken. The hospital reported he was so badly burned that they were unrecognizable. Officials were informed that the Roma, at the time of the accident, was under command of Captain Dale Mabry of the Army Air Service, who lost his life along with most of the members of his crew.

INJURED SURVIVORS TELL OF DISASTER

Officers Coolly Remained at Their Posts of Duty Until the Roma Struck.

EXPLOSION FOLLOWED FALL

Flames, Eating Fabric, Opened a Way for Some Imprisoned Men to Escape.

Special to The New York Times.
NORFOLK, Va., Feb. 21.—Lying on cots in the United States Public Health Service Hospital, where they were taken after the Roma disaster, some of the eleven survivors tonight told of their experiences in the collapse and destruction of the giant dirigible.

Several of the survivors appeared more dead than alive. Some were swathed in bandages, some had their faces smeared with cream to relieve them of intense suffering, while others lay asleep or unconscious. Even those who were able to talk were suffering from shock.

Major J. D. Reardon, who was in the control cabin at the time of the accident, said that the work of the officers in charge was admirable.

"Lieutenant Burt and Captain Mabry were at the wheels," the Major said. "The machine gave a lurch, and I saw Lieutenant Burt pull with all his might on the elevation lever. The ship held on. 'She won't respond,' and then, 'Cut the motors.' One by one I heard the motors shut off, and then we hit. If the motors had not been shut off we would have hit the ground much harder."

When asked if he had seen any flame, Major Reardon said he had not.

Corporal Albert Flores was in the observer's pit on top of the bag.

"I felt the ship pull up from the back," he said, "and start to slide down. I tried to go down ahead, but then I decided to come out forward again. By that time we hit the ground and I was thrown out on the ground."

Flores was burned on the hands and is suffering from shock.

Engineer Was Pinned Down.

Joseph N. Biedenbach, engineer, was burned on the face and hands, in speaking of the accident, he said:

"I did not see any fire. The ship just tilted up and started to nose dive. It took about twenty seconds for us to hit the ground, and an explosion followed. I could plainly see it and I couldn't get out. The fabric was burning above me and the girders were all around where I was.

"I waited for the fabric to burn through so that I could get out. All the time I was afraid that the big gas bag behind us would explode. As it happened, the fire reached the fabric before the big explosion. If it had been the reverse, I could not have gotten out alive.

"I saw one man try to jump. I don't know who he was or even if he succeeded in making a safe landing. We hit right after that. We were too low for anybody to make a jump."

Biedenbach also spoke of the gallant way in which the officers stood at their posts. Until the instant of the crash the officers were at the wheels.

The survivors showed a peculiar curiosity to know what the wreck looked like. As it was described by others they listened with intense interest, asking questions about the debris.

"What became of the other boys? Did they get out?" one asked.

When one of them was told that the Roma was in the hospital were the only survivors, he gasped, and exclaimed, "Awful."

Everyone knew, another survivor, said that the Roma was behaving beautifully up to the moment when her rudder failed, nobody on board thought there was any danger.

From Sergeant Joseph M. Bieden-bach, who was in the motor car, received messages to the Air Service officers at Langley Field tonight that it was an "information tonight from an official at Langley Field and Mr. Ray Hurley of the National Advisory Committee on Aeronautics, who was employed by the Port Authority. All of them were in the after part of the airship and

Continued on Page Ten.

"All the News That's Fit to Print."

The New York Times.

THE WEATHER
Rain today; Sunday fair; strong northwest winds.
Temperature yesterday—Max., 45; min., 38.
[?] For weather report see next to last page

VOL. LXXI....No. 23,422.   * * *   NEW YORK, SATURDAY, MARCH 11, 1922.   TWO CENTS In Greater New York | THREE CENTS Within 200 Miles | FOUR CENTS Elsewhere

WILL DROP ELEVATED OR ACCEPT RECEIVER, INTERBORO DECIDES

New Contract Freeing Subway of $7,600,000 Annual Rent the Alternative.

OWNERS PLAN COURT FIGHT

Interborough Also Wants $30,000,000 of New Third Tracks and the New Power Houses.

TO OPPOSE BETTER SERVICE

Ready to Quit If Transit Board Compels Improvements Which Eat Up Present Savings.

The Interborough Rapid Transit Company has refused to make any further payments due on its lease of the elevated lines owned by the Manhattan Railway Company. It has asked the latter company to make a new agreement which would shift from the Interborough payments of $7,600,000 a year, save it from the responsibility of the deficits on the elevated system, and yield in return annual interest payments on betterments aggregating between $1,000,000 and $2,000,000 a year.

In this way the Interborough has answered the question, frequently asked, as to what adjustment could be made in the matter of the lease so far as it is concerned the consolidation plan of the Transit Commission.

The Interborough is prepared to consent to the appointment of a receiver for its property if it fails to obtain relief from the payments to the Manhattan Company or if the Transit Commission insists upon enforcing expected orders directing the company to increase its service to the point of absorbing the savings derived from the present restriction of service.

[remaining column text illegible]

Plan to Cut Europe's Armies in Half Submitted to League by Commission

By EDWIN L. JAMES.

Copyright, 1922, by The New York Times Company.
By Wireless to The New York Times.

PARIS, March 10.—A temporary armament commission of the League of Nations Assembly has transmitted to the Governments which are members of the League a draft plan for European armament limitation modeled on the Washington naval reduction treaty.

[remaining column text illegible]

University Course to Make Bellhops and Head Waiters

BOSTON, March 10.—Bellhops and head waiters de luxe are to be turned out by Boston University. Seventy-five men have signed for a six weeks' course for college men to work in Summer hotels during their vacation.

The course, which is to start at the university next week, will show the young men how to become any sort of hotel official. It will be given by the vocational department of the College of Business Administration.

RUM RUNNER KILLS BOOTLEGGER IN BOAT

Man Aboard the Imatra Opens Fire on Motor Craft After Dispute.

WOMAN LEADS GUN FIGHT

Wounds Detective in Fusillade Preceding Capture of $10,000 in Whisky.

An alleged bootlegger was killed in a motor boat off a Brooklyn pier last night in a controversy over several cases of liquor which men of the crew of the tramp steamer Imatra had bargained to sell to five young men who came alongside the vessel in a small power craft. A man named Fosberg was arrested and two men found in the motor boat were taken into custody. The other two are being searched for by the police.

The dead man was George Rauch, 26, of 156 South Fourth Street, Brooklyn, who was one of the five in the motor boat which was to transport the liquor.

[remaining column text illegible]

FORD'S 'FREEZE-OUT' OF RAIL PARTNERS BLOCKED BY I.C.C.

Small Stockholders of D., T. & I. Defeat Alleged Scheme to Get Rid of Them.

PREVENT LEASE OF ROAD

Commission Sustains Their Contention That It Is Against Public Interest.

WILL KEEP THEIR SHARES

Proposed Lessee Was a Company Owned Entirely by Members of the Ford Family.

Henry Ford, who urged the railroads of the country to "get rid of the unproductive stockholders," has been blocked by the Interstate Commerce Commission in an alleged attempt to "get rid of" the minority stockholders in the Detroit, Toledo & Ironton Railroad Company, Mr. Ford's interesting railroad adventure.

[remaining column text illegible]

Germans to Clear Buildings Of All Monarchical Insignia

BERLIN, March 10 (Associated Press).—All insignia of monarchical Germany must be removed from public buildings, Minister of the Interior Adolf Koester told today the Reichstag. He added that the Government had decided to fix a definite date within which this decision would be carried out.

Exceptions will be made, he said, only where these emblems have been structurally incorporated in buildings where their removal would destroy the architectural value and effect.

All paintings, busts and statues in Government offices must also be removed if their retention is incompatible with the Republican regime. This order will chiefly apply to portraits of former Emperor William, although Herr Koester said that exceptions might be made if their removal destroyed the "artistic and historical unity" of the interior decorations.

JURIES OF CITIZENS TO BAR BAD PLAYS

Conference of Actors, Dramatists, Managers and Vice Crusaders Fixes Details.

TO AVOID POLITICAL CENSOR

Theatrical Contracts to Stipulate That They Must Obey Jury's Findings.

The organization of a voluntary jury system, designed to eliminate indecent plays and thereby make unnecessary a political censorship of the stage, was launched late yesterday afternoon at a meeting of dramatists, managers and actors and vice crusaders at the American Dramatists' Society, 148 West Forty-fifth Street.

[remaining column text illegible]

SENATOR STANFIELD, THE 'WOOL KING,' ACCUSED OF FRAUD

Idaho National Bank Charges That He Formed a Company to Defraud His Creditors.

HURT BY DROP IN SHEEP

Had Just Bought 400,000—Attempt to Set Aside His Transfer of Real Estate.

THREATENS LIBEL ACTIONS

But Idaho Commissioner Defies Him and Asks Why He Doesn't Pay Farmers What He Owes.

Special to The New York Times.

PORTLAND, Ore., March 10.—Robert Nelson Stanfield, the "wool king" of and United States Senator from Oregon, elected in 1920 over former Senator Chamberlain by Gov. Olcott, is rushing home from Washington to save what he can out of property imperiled by the drop in the prices of wool and sheep.

[remaining column text illegible]

GANDHI ARRESTED ON CHARGE OF SEDITION; LONDON REPORTS INDIA QUIET THUS FAR; LORD DERBY TO TAKE MONTAGU'S PLACE

Martial Law After Day of Terror in the Rand; Strikers Kill a Manager and Ten of Police

JOHANNESBURG, Union of South Africa, March 10 (Associated Press).—Bold moves by the striking miners, accompanied by fierce fighting between strikers, commandos and police, made the day one of terror in the Rand. Martial law was eventually proclaimed.

Fighting started at Benoni early this morning. Street fighting followed, with dire suffering casualties. Many pedestrians were hit. For two hours the ground between the market square and the workers' hall was a battle area.

[remaining column text illegible]

BIG HOUSING BILL NOW SURE TO PASS

Machold Announces Support of Metropolitan $100,000,000 Building Fund Measure.

LOCKWOOD IS ACCUSED

Absence From Hearing Said to Have Endangered Other Bills—He Denies It.

Special to The New York Times.

ALBANY, March 10.—As the result of developments at the Capitol today the passage in both branches of the Legislature of the Lockwood committee's bill which would enable the Metropolitan Life Insurance Company to devote $100,000,000 of its investable funds to housing relief in New York City seems assured.

[remaining column text illegible]

OUR RHINE CLAIM IS NOT ALLOWED

Finance Ministers Continue the Division of German Payments Among Allied Powers.

BOYDEN ASKS $241,000,000

Question Will Go to Governments Upon Whom Washington Is in a Position to Use Pressure.

By EDWIN L. JAMES.

Copyright, 1922, by The New York Times Company.
Special Cable to The New York Times.

PARIS, March 10.—The Washington Government today asked the Finance Ministers of the allied nations engaged in a conference here for dividing up German payments to the Reparation Commission for a settlement of the claim of $241,000,000 of the American Government for the cost of the American Army of Occupation.

[remaining column text illegible]

ARREST IS MADE QUIETLY

Leader Taken Into Custody on Order of Government at Delhi.

NEW PLOTS WERE REVEALED

British Opinion Strongly Urged Seizure of Gandhi, First Ordered Last Month.

LORD DERBY TO TAKE OFFICE

Montagu Speaks Today at Cambridge—Resignation of Viceroy Regarded as Inevitable.

BOMBAY, March 10 (Associated Press).—India's non-co-operationist leader, Mohandas K. Gandhi, has been arrested at Ahmedabad, 310 miles north of Bombay. He is charged with sedition.

Copyright, 1922, by The New York Times Company.
Special Cable to The New York Times.

LONDON, March 10.—The announcement by the India Office late tonight that a telegram had been received stating that Gandhi had been arrested and adding there had been no trouble so far follows upon Delhi reports that the Indian Government had decided upon the arrest for today.

[remaining column text illegible]

"All the News That's Fit to Print."

The New York Times.

THE WEATHER
Fair and cold today and Sunday; northwest winds.
Temperatures yesterday—Max., 31; min., 17. For weather report see last page.

VOL. LXXII....No. 23,765. ... NEW YORK, SATURDAY, FEBRUARY 17, 1923. TWO CENTS

ESSEN IS COWED AFTER WOUNDING OF TWO SOLDIERS

Fight in Beer Hall Causes the French to Turn Out a Stronger Military Display.

CITY NOW WITHOUT POLICE

Chief Arrested, Men Disarmed and Records Seized — Frequent Clashes Elsewhere.

JAIL FOR 2 BURGOMASTERS

Electric Plant Director Is Fined 5,000,000 Marks—Berlin Supplies Funds for Strikers.

Copyright, 1923, by The New York Times Company.
Special Cable to THE NEW YORK TIMES.
DUESSELDORF, Feb. 16.—Every day in adding more and more to the casualty list of the Ruhr occupation.

---

89 M. P.'s Ask Harding's Aid; 'One Hope of Saving Europe'

Copyright, 1923, by The New York Times Company.
By Wireless to THE NEW YORK TIMES.
LONDON, Feb. 16.—Signed by eighty-nine Labor and Co-operative members of the British Parliament, the following cablegram was sent to President Harding today:

"America with Britain unwittingly made France's present destructive action possible. We appeal for American co-operation to save the one hope of saving Europe."

Among those who have signed the message are Arthur Henderson, George Lansbury, R. B. Buxton and John Hodge.

ANDERSON ENRICHED BY REALTY TRADING, IS STORY TO PECORA

Prosecutor Quotes Him as Saying $24,700 Came, in Currency, From Deals.

CONTRADICTS HIS AFFIDAVIT

Report to Anti-Saloon Directors in 1919 That Money Came From Loans Is Recalled

---

$500,000 GEM THEFT SUSPECT ARRESTED

"Marshall" Held as Leader of Gang That Robbed Mrs. Schoellkopf at Drinking Party.

CAUGHT ON MONTREAL TRAIN

Another Arrest Here Said to Have Furnished Clue—Companion Also in Custody.

Idaho Assembly Bars Japanese From Leasing Any Lands There

BOISE, Idaho, Feb. 16.—The Assembly of the Legislature, by a vote of 54 to 6, today passed a measure to prohibit the leasing of lands in the State to Japanese.

ENGINEER AMBUSHED AND SLAIN AT DOOR

Earl Remington of Los Angeles, Who Made Planes in War, Is Found Dead in Driveway.

WIFE ASLEEP IN THE HOUSE

Victim, Shot as He Stepped From Automobile, Met Death He Had Feared.

LOS ANGELES, Feb. 16.—Earl Remington, wealthy electrical engineer, found dead from gunshot wounds in the yard of his home here early today, was believed to have met death by foul play.

SENATE APPROVES BRITISH DEBT BILL; FINAL VOTE, 70-13

46 Republicans, 24 Democrats Favor It—Borah Among the Four Republicans Opposed

BITTER DEBATE TO FINISH

Many Assail "British Victory," but Glass Wins Applause by Recalling Allies' Sacrifice.

ONLY ONE AMENDMENT

Settlements With Other Allies Must Have Congress Approval—Bill Now Goes to Conference.

Special to The New York Times.
WASHINGTON, Feb. 16.—The Senate passed the British Debt Refunding bill tonight by a vote of 70 to 13, forty-six Republicans and twenty-four Democrats voting to ratify the settlement as agreed to by the Debt Funding Commission, while nine Democrats and four Republicans were recorded in favor of repudiating the settlement.

TUT-ANKH-AMEN'S INNER TOMB IS OPENED, REVEALING UNDREAMED OF SPLENDORS, STILL UNTOUCHED AFTER 3,400 YEARS

KING TUT-ANKH-AMEN,
wearing the crown and royal vestments, as he appeared to his contemporaries. From a multi-colored decoration on the walls of the tomb of Huy, his Viceroy, discovered some years ago near the tomb of the King.
Courtesy Metropolitan Museum of Art.

KING IN NEST OF SHRINES

Series of Ornate Covers Enclose Pharaoh's Sarcophagus.

WHOLE FILLS LARGE ROOM

Mortuary Chamber Opens Into Another Room, Crowded With Great Treasure.

EXPLORERS ARE DAZZLED

Wealth of Objects of Historic and Artistic Interest Exceeds All Their Wildest Visions.

The Times (London) World Copyright, by Arrangement with the Earl of Carnarvon. Copyright, 1923, by The New York Times Company.
Special Cable to THE NEW YORK TIMES.
LUXOR, Egypt, Feb. 16.—This has been, perhaps, the most extraordinary day in the whole history of Egyptian excavation. Whatever any one may have guessed or imagined of the secret of Tut-ankh-Amen's tomb, they surely cannot have dreamed the truth as now revealed.

GOV. REILY RESIGNS PORTO RICO OFFICE

Tells President Ill Health Forbids Him to Resume Executive Duties.

HAD BEEN LONG UNDER FIRE

Offended by His Inaugural Address, Unionists Made Many Charges Against Him.

WASHINGTON, Feb. 16 (Associated Press).—The resignation of E. Mont Reily as Governor of Porto Rico was received at the White House early this evening, but no announcement was made concerning it, although there was every indication that it would be accepted.

GOETHALS DEMANDS COAL FOR UP-STATE

"We Want Action, Not Conferences," He Says in Message to Federal Fuel Distributor.

SEIZURE IS THREATENED

Insists Shipments to Canada Be Diverted—People Will Get Coal, He Asserts.

General George W. Goethals, State Fuel Administrator, serving notice on the Federal Fuel Distributor that he wants action, not conferences for the relief of suffering localities in Northern New York, suggested in two telegrams yesterday immediate authorization by the Federal officials of drastic relief measures.

Harding Threatens to Cut Shipping Fleet Unless Congress Passes the Subsidy Bill

WASHINGTON, Feb. 16.—The Administration Shipping bill was restored tonight to its former place as the unfinished business of the Senate, after having been laid aside since early in the week after consideration of the British debt settlement legislation.

Doctor and Chauffeur Killed When Train Wrecks Ambulance at Jersey Grade Crossing

A fatal grade crossing accident occurred last evening at Hackensack, N. J., where a train running forty miles an hour, on the New Jersey and New York branch of the Erie Railroad, smashed into an ambulance, crushing a hospital interne and a chauffeur to death.

"All the News That's Fit to Print."

The New York Times.

EXTRA
6 A.M.
THE WEATHER: Fair Today.

VOL. LXXII....No. 23,932. ....   NEW YORK, FRIDAY, AUGUST 3, 1923.   TWO CENTS In Greater New York | THREE CENTS Within 200 Miles | FOUR CENTS Elsewhere

PRESIDENT HARDING DIES SUDDENLY; STROKE OF APOPLEXY AT 7:30 P. M.; CALVIN COOLIDGE IS PRESIDENT

COOLIDGE TAKES THE OATH OF OFFICE

His Father, Who Is a Notary Public, Administers It After Form Is Found By Him in His Library.

ANNOUNCES HE WILL FOLLOW THE HARDING POLICIES

Wants All Who Aided Harding to Remain in Office—Roused After Midnight to Be Told the News of the President's Death.

Statement by President Coolidge

Special to The New York Times.

PLYMOUTH, Vt., Aug. 3.—President Calvin Coolidge issued the following statement early this morning:

Reports have reached me, which I fear are correct, that President Harding is gone. The world has lost a great and good man. I mourn his loss. He was my chief and my friend.

It will be my purpose to carry out the policies which he has begun for the service of the American people and for meeting their responsibilities wherever they may arise.

For this purpose I shall seek the co-operation of all those who have been associated with the President during his term of office.

Those who have given their efforts to assist him I wish to remain in office that they may assist me. I have faith that God will direct the destinies of our nation.

It is my intention to remain here until I can secure the correct form for the oath of office, which will be administered to me by my father, who is a notary public, if that will meet the necessary requirement. I expect to leave for Washington during the day.

CALVIN COOLIDGE.

Takes the Oath of Office.

Special to The New York Times.

PLYMOUTH, Vt. (Friday), Aug. 3.—Calvin Coolidge took the oath of office as President of the United States at 2:47, Eastern Standard Time, this morning (3:47 New York time). The oath was administered by his father, John C. Coolidge, who found the text in a book in his library, after having expected to wait until it was received from Washington.

The taking of the oath was a simple and solemn scene. Those who gathered in the living room of the Coolidge home at Plymouth Notch, besides the President and his father, were Mrs. Coolidge, L. L. Lane, President of the Railway Mail Association of New England; Congressman Porter H. Dale, of Vermont; Joseph H. Fountain, editor of the Springfield Reporter, and Erwin C. Geisser, Mr. Coolidge's Assistant Secretary.

As the elder Mr. Coolidge read the oath Mrs. Coolidge looked on with wet eyes. As the end was reached, President Coolidge, raising his right hand, said in a low, clear voice:

"I do, so help me God."

A moment later the group dissolved, and President and Mrs. Coolidge retired.

Special to The New York Times.

PLYMOUTH, Vt., Aug. 3.—Calvin Coolidge received the news of the death of President Harding and of his own elevation to the Presidency ten minutes before 1 o'clock this morning, Daylight Saving Time.

Mr. Coolidge received the first news of President Harding's death from telegrams signed by George C. Christian, the late President's secretary, and from THE NEW YORK TIMES, whose telegram reached him at the same moment.

These telegrams were brought to the Coolidge home at Plymouth Notch by W. A. Perkins of Bridgewater, who owns the telephone line running from Bridgewater to Plymouth. About five minutes later the newspaper men arrived in Ludlow.

The following telegram was sent to Mrs. Harding:

Plymouth, Vt., Aug. 3, 1923.

Mrs. Warren G. Harding,
San Francisco, Cal.

We offer you our deepest sympathy. May God bless and keep you.

CALVIN COOLIDGE.
GRACE COOLIDGE.

The following telegram announcing the death of President Harding.

Continued on Page Five.

CALVIN COOLIDGE
Thirtieth President of the United States by the Death of President Harding.

WARREN GAMALIEL HARDING
Twenty-ninth President of the United States, Who Died Yesterday in San Francisco.

Public Men Voice Tributes To Harding's Worth and Record

Hughes Says He Was a Brave and Strong Leader—Marshall Calls Him a Great Human American—Honored as Martyr to His Duty—Sympathy Goes Out to Mrs. Harding.

Special to The New York Times.

WASHINGTON, Friday, Aug. 3.—Politics was forgotten in community public men in Washington when informed of the death of President Harding, on account of the late hour at which the news was received it was difficult to reach officials.

Secretary Hughes, who came to his office in the State Department at an early hour this morning, was shaken by the news.

"No words can express," he said, "the grief into which we are plunged by this calamity. The nation has suffered an irreparable loss. A quiet, brave, strong leader has fallen, overborne by the burden he was carrying.

"He was not only an able and faithful public servant but one of nature's noblemen. A true hearted, generous spirit, he has left with the people beloved a rare example of gentleness, high office, and of the most conscientious and unselfish devotion to public duty."

Marshall Held Him High Minded.

Thomas R. Marshall, former Vice President of the United States, expressed the deepest sorrow and paid high tribute to the integrity and worth of Mr. Harding.

"The sad intelligence of the President's death has just been communicated to me," said Mr. Marshall. "There are times when all party considerations sink into insignificance. One of them is when a man thinks of the death of his friend.

"This has been the death not only of my President but of a man who for many years in the Senate had been my friend of the personal and intimate kind. There is nothing that any man can say, on an occasion like this, that aside from political opinions he was a great human American who patriotically tried to serve his country.

"This is a tribute from a man who did not agree with him in his political principles, but it is not necessary to agree with his political principles in order to admire the integrity, patriotism and high-mindedness of a man. I think that as the years go by the people will realize that Mr. Harding tried to serve his country well."

Loss to the World, Says New.

Postmaster General New was at his home when the news of President Harding's death was flashed to him from San Francisco.

"I am simply overwhelmed," he said. "There are times when a man can not express his grief. This is one of them. The passing of President Harding is

Continued on Page Four.

editors to the world, the magnitude of which can not be overestimated."
Joseph P. Tumulty said:
"The new is a dreadful shock to me, as it must be to all who knew President Harding well. While at the White House I had many delightful associations with President Harding, who then was a member of the Senate. Like all men who came in contact with the President I knew him as a kindly gentleman and a true friend."

Says He Had People's Affection.

Senator Walsh of Massachusetts, said:

"The President's death is a terrible blow, coming as it does so soon after it was believed that he was on the way to speedy recovery. His death will be mourned in every corner of the land by every class.

"Few Presidents have had a stronger grip upon the affections of our people. His dignity, simplicity, sincerity and graciousness won the hearts of all. His personality, however, did not alone account for his popularity. He has won a place in our history among the most worthy of those who have occupied the Presidency.

"His views were statesmanlike and secure in his faith. The nation has lost a noble man, and a sound and safe leader."

Roosevelt Tells of Sacrifice.

Colonel Theodore Roosevelt, Acting Secretary of the Navy in the absence of Secretary Denby, said:

"Words cannot express my grief at the death of my chief, President Harding. It is idle to say that his death is a calamity for the United States, for every one knows it. He gave his life for the service of our country as truly as any one in our history."

Representative Stephen G. Porter of Pennsylvania, Chairman of the House Foreign Affairs Committee, a personal admirer as well as a friend of Mr. Harding said:

"I am simply overwhelmed. I hardly know what to say. He was as gentle, as kind, his every act was in the public interest. It is a terrible shock. I really can't understand it."

Mr. Porter returned recently from Europe, where he represented this country at the sessions of the commission of the League of Nations on the opium traffic.

Senator Curtis of Kansas, Republican said:

"The entire world will be shocked at the death of President Harding. In passing at this time was very unfortunate. The extent of his loss cannot be appraised in words. The entire country

DEATH STROKE CAME WITHOUT WARNING

Mrs. Harding Was Reading to Her Husband When First Sign Appeared —She Ran for Doctor

BUT NOTHING COULD BE DONE TO REVIVE PATIENT

News of Tragic End Shocks Everybody, Coming After Day Said to Have Been the Best Since His Illness Began a Week Ago.

Special to The New York Times.

SAN FRANCISCO, Aug. 2.—President Harding died at 7:30 o'clock tonight [11:30 o'clock New York time] of a stroke of apoplexy.

The end came suddenly while Mrs. Harding was reading to him from the evening newspaper, and after what had been called the best day he had had since the beginning of his illness exactly one week ago.

A shudder ran through the President's frame and he collapsed.

The first knowledge the two nurses in the sick room knew the end had come, and Mrs. Harding rushed out of the room and asked for Dr. Boone and the others to "come quick."

Dr. Boone and Brig. Gen. Sawyer reached the President before he passed away, but were not able to avert the inevitable.

This formal announcement following soon after told the story of the tragic end:

"The President died at 7:30 P. M. Mrs. Harding and the two nurses, Miss Ruth Powderly and Miss Sue Drusser, were in the room at the time. Mrs. Harding was reading to the President, when, utterly without warning, a slight shudder passed through his frame, all recognized that the end had come. A stroke of apoplexy was the cause of his death.

"Within a few moments all of the President's official party had been summoned."

Shocking in Its Suddenness.

Nothing could have been more shocking surprise. Shortly before the President's sudden collapse General Sawyer told the newspaper men that Mr. Harding had had the best day since he became seriously ill. He said that the President had definitely entered upon the stage of convalescence and that everything went to show that Mr. Harding was on the road to ultimate recovery.

The members of the official party had no warning that the President was in danger. They, like the newspaper men, had been assured that a fatal termination of the President's illness was a thing not likely and good care he would be able to recover health and strength. Most of the members of the official party were at dinner when the news came. George B. Christian Jr., secretary to the President and his devoted friend, was in Los Angeles with Mrs. Christian. He had gone there at the President's solicitation to read at a gathering of the Knights Templar tonight an address which the President had prepared in the expectation that he would deliver it in person. Mr. Christian had declined to leave San Francisco until he was positively assured of the President's physicians that there was no likelihood of any set-back in the President's condition.

The newspaper men had an engagement with General Sawyer for 8 o'clock. He was to tell them of how the President was progressing toward recovery. In view of what he had said on prior occasions during the day and statements in two official bulletins, the newspaper men had every expectation that they would be able to record that Mr. Harding was one step nearer the goal of recovery.

"There will be a bulletin," said one of the White House messengers gathered in the corridor of the Presidential suite. In a few minutes copies of the bulletin on thin white paper were handed to the waiting reporters. Instead of informing them that the President's condition continued to improve, it gave them the astounding information that was dead.

Mrs. Harding Is Brave to the End.

First reports that Mrs. Harding had collapsed were denied. The official version indicates that she was calm throughout her husband's last illness. She has been extremely courageous and by her manner and words helped him when he was suffering intensely and was apprehensive of a fatal termination. The official account says:

"Mrs. Harding, who from the beginning of the President's illness had expressed confidence in his recovery, did not break down. On the other hand, she continued, as from the beginning, the bravest member of the group.

"When it was realized that the President had actually passed away, she turned to those in the room, whose concern had turned to her and said, 'I am not going to break down.'"

Mrs. Harding was seated by the bedside when at 7:10 o'clock the President suddenly collapsed. His breathing, which had been quick ever since the illness overtook him, suddenly became spasmodic. Mrs. Harding, bidding the two nurses to take whatever steps they could in the emergency, ran to the door of the Presidential suite.

"Dr. Boone!" she called, as she ran part way into the almost deserted corridor. A Secret Service operative was seated about twenty feet down the hall. She hurriedly told the Secret Service man that the President had had a sudden and severe relapse and begged the detective to try to locate Dr. Boone or any of the other physicians.

The Secret Service men took up the search for the physicians, while

President's Death Shocks Capital, Which Had Expected Recovery

News Telephoned to Executive Clerk From San Francisco—Effort Made to Reach Coolidge in Vermont—Only Two Members of Cabinet in Washington.

Special to The New York Times.

WASHINGTON, Friday, Aug. 3.—News of the death of President Harding not only greatly shocked official and Washington but took the capital completely by surprise.

It was the sixth time in the history of the nation that the city had been brought face to face with the death of a President, but the shocking word was received under circumstances wholly different from those surrounding the death of any former President.

The only high officials of the Harding Administration in Washington are Secretary of State Hughes and Postmaster General New. All the other members of the Cabinet are out of the city, and two of them, Secretaries Mellon and Davis, are in Europe, while most of the others, with the exception of Secretaries Weeks and Denby, are in the Far West.

Calvin Coolidge, until last night Vice President, and who will immediately be sworn in as the next President of the United States, is likewise absent from Washington, but it has occurred at his home at Plymouth, Vt.

When last heard from, Mr. Coolidge was not direct from San Francisco notifying him of the death of Mr. Harding. From the Presidential party in San Francisco communications, the White House was advised late tonight, were sent direct to all other members of the Cabinet wherever they were in San Francisco and to personal friends of the President.

Rudolph Forster, Executive Clerk at the White House, was communicated with direct from San Francisco shortly before midnight by long distance telephone. He talked with Mr. Smithers, the ranking member of the White House executive forced in San Francisco in the absence of Mr. Christian who had gone to Los Angeles. Mr. Smithers confirmed the death of the President and informed Mr. Forster that messages were being sent to the Vice President and other Cabinet members.

Mr. Hughes is the ranking member of the Administration now in Washington, so that he will take such steps as are necessary in the present situation.

It will also be the duty of the Secretary of State to notify the members of the Diplomatic Corps, who will in turn officially cable their Governments that Mr. Harding is dead.

No plans have or can be made immediately for the swearing in of Mr. Coolidge as President. It is not necessary for him to take the oath of office as a member of the United States Supreme

Court. Another Judge or other officer qualified to administer an oath can act in that capacity. Even a Justice of the Peace back in Vermont, where Mr. Coolidge was last known to be located, could administer the oath.

Continued on Page Six.

The New York Times.

THE WEATHER

Fair today; unsettled tomorrow; gentle southerly winds.
Temperature yesterday—Max. 84; Min. 68.
For weather report see next to last page.

VOL. LXXII....No. 23,965.   •••   NEW YORK, WEDNESDAY, SEPTEMBER 5, 1923.   TWO CENTS In Greater New York | THREE CENTS Within 200 Miles | FOUR CENTS Elsewhere

JAPANESE DEATH TOLL MAY REACH 300,000; EARTH STILL ROCKS BUT FIRES ARE WANING; AMERICA IS RAISING MILLIONS FOR RELIEF

GREEKS OFFER PLAN FOR LEAGUE INQUIRY INTO JANINA CRIMES

Want Geneva to Direct Investigation—Will Post 50,000,000 Lire Guarantee.

ASSEMBLY SNUBS ITALIANS

Elections to Committees Result in Their Exclusion From Posts of Honor.

MUSSOLINI RENEWS THREAT

Rome Cabinet Approves Resolution to Quit League If It Intervenes.

Copyright, 1923, by The New York Times Company.
Special Cable to THE NEW YORK TIMES.

GENEVA, Sept. 4.—Nicholas Politis, delegate of the Greek Government, today proposed to the Council of the League of Nations that for the settlement of the dispute between his country and Italy the Council should appoint one or more neutral representatives.

1. To superintend in Greece the judicial inquiry already begun by the Greek authorities and the trial of those held responsible for the murder of the Italian officers of the Albanian Boundary Commission.

2. To assist in the work of a commission, the appointment of which has been proposed by the Greek Government, through the Council of Ambassadors, to investigate, both in Albania and in Greece, the circumstances which preceded and accompanied the crime.

3. That the Council should instruct a commission composed of three high judicial authorities—one Greek, one Italian and one neutral (for example, the President of the Swiss Federal Tribunal or the President of the Permanent Court of International Justice)—to meet as soon as possible in Geneva to settle the amount of indemnities which it is just that Greece should pay the families of the victims.

4. That the Council should allow the Greek Government forthwith deposit in a Swiss bank 50,000,000 lire as a guarantee for the immediate payment of whatever indemnities may be decided upon.

Discussion Put Off Till Today.

These proposals were made at a meeting of the Council held this evening at the Secretariat of the League, in the course of which Signor Salandra, head of the Italian delegation, asked for a postponement of the discussion of the Greco-Italian incident until Signor Giurati, his associate, should have returned from Rome with new instructions.

M. Politis was arguing that no sovereign nation could accept dictation as to the nature of the punishment to be inflicted upon its nationals when Signor Salandra interrupted him.

His attitude was most friendly, and it was with a smile that he declared that he could not consent to allow the Greek delegate to embark on a controversy in the course of the discussion of a simple question whether the Council should grant a postponement.

"If M. Politis is allowed to reply," he said, "I shall have to reply," he said.

The common sense of this attitude and the politeness of the Italian delegate toward his Greek colleague won general approval, and Lord Robert Cecil suggested that M. Politis should have an opportunity to submit in writing any new proposals he had to make.

M. Politis then retired from the room and at the end of half an hour brought back the suggestions already noted in this dispatch. In the circumstances they could not be immediately taken up by the Council and Lord Robert moved that the discussion of them should be withheld until tomorrow's meeting, when the Council would be in possession of full information as to the Italian attitude.

If M. Politis is allowed to reply...

[article continues]

Continued on Page Two.

DEMOTTE KILLED IN GUN ACCIDENT

International Art Dealer Shot Dead While on Hunting Expedition in France.

NEWS KEPT SECRET A DAY

Involved in Charges of Extensive Art Frauds, He Was Preparing to Push Suit Here.

Copyright, 1923, by The New York Times Company.
Special Cable to THE NEW YORK TIMES.

PARIS, Sept. 4.—George J. Demotte, art dealer of Paris and New York, was killed yesterday while hunting. His companion, Otto Wenger, dropped his gun, causing the discharge of both barrels. Demotte was struck in the shoulder and neck, the jugular vein being severed. Death was almost instantaneous.

[article continues]

Continued on Page Seven.

COAL PEACE BASIS NOW SEEMS NEAR

Indications Are That $5 Minimum for Day Men Would Satisfy Miners.

MAY DROP OTHER DEMANDS

Lewis Confers With Leaders in Preparation for Conference Today.

Special to The New York Times.

HARRISBURG, Sept. 4.—If the representatives of the anthracite operators agree to grant to day miners a minimum of $5 a day the suspension of work which began Sept. 1 will be lifted and 156,000 miners will return to work. This basis for the settlement of the strike was indicated today on good authority in advance of the meeting tomorrow between Governor Pinchot and the disputants.

[article continues]

Continued on Page Eight.

RED CROSS ASKS $5,000,000

Sets Its 3,600 American Chapters at Work at Once.

RELIEF SHIPS DUE TODAY

Six Naval Vessels Carrying Supplies Are Nearing Yokohama.

FOOD RUSHED FROM MANILA

Army Transports, Loaded to Capacity, Sail Within 24 Hours.

Prince Regent and Emperor Give $55,000,000 for Relief

SAN FRANCISCO, Sept. 4 (Associated Press).—Relief work in Japan was furthered today by several large donations. The Prince Regent gave $50,000,000 for relief; the Emperor gave $5,000,000 from the Privy Exchequer, and the Government donated $4,500,000.

Kobe $17,500 was raised for the sufferers in ten minutes.

The vessels in Yokohama harbor have given refuge to 5,000 persons.

From Shanghai it was reported that rioting had broken out in the destroyed cities and that the police were arming citizens to aid in maintaining order.

Special to The New York Times.

WASHINGTON, Sept. 4.—The Government of the United States is giving its time and attention almost exclusively to the work of extending in full measure all possible assistance to the stricken people of Japan. This was the official statement that came this afternoon from the White House, where the President is personally directing the relief activities of the Government.

The speed with which the United States is acting to bring succor to the Japanese can be appreciated when it is stated that the army transports Meigs and Merritt, each carrying a capacity cargo of relief supplies, are expected to sail from Manila within the next twelve hours, or within twenty-four hours after the order directing their dispatch is was cabled to Governor General Wood.

[article continues]

Continued on Page Four.

Islands of Bonin Group Reported Vanished, Together With Mismia Island and Its Volcano

Copyright, 1923, by The New York Times Company.
Special Cable to THE NEW YORK TIMES.

PEKING, Sept. 4.—Numerous villages along the coast of the Japanese Peninsula south of Yokohama, where many foreigners were spending the Summer, were washed away by the tidal wave that followed the earthquake.

There is no news from the Bonin Islands and it is feared they have sunk into the sea.

Nothing can be seen of Mismia Island, the volcano on which was reported on Monday to be in violent eruption, and it is believed to have disappeared.

Copyright, 1923, by The New York Times Company.

LONDON, Sept. 4.—The Bonin Islands, called by the Japanese Ogasawarajima, which are reported to have disappeared, were about twenty in number, though only ten were of appreciable size. They lay about 500 miles from the mainland of Japan on a line which would run almost due south from Yokohama or southeast from Nagasaki.

Until 1861 their few inhabitants had somewhat vaguely considered themselves as a British colony, but in that year the British Government recognized Japan's right of possession. Since then the handful of Europeans and Polynesian half-breeds had been outnumbered by Japanese colonists.

Regular steamship communication had been established and a modern system of administration introduced. Exploitation of the islands' resources—valuable timber and agricultural produce—had provided employment for the population, about 5,000.

AMBASSADOR SAFE, U. S. CONSUL DEAD

Woods and Staff Escape When Embassy Is Destroyed—Mr. and Mrs. Kirjassoff Killed.

FOREIGN CASUALTIES HEAVY

State Department Trying to Get News of Americans—All Capitals Anxious.

Special to The New York Times.

WASHINGTON, Sept. 4.—The first direct message from American representatives in Japan to the State Department today brought the news of the safety of Ambassador Cyrus E. Woods and all members of his staff in the embassy at Tokio, and the death of Max D. Kirjassoff, the United States Consul at Yokohama, and his wife.

The American Embassy at Tokio and all other embassies were destroyed, presumably by fire, which accounts for the safety of those connected with the American Embassy.

[article continues]

Continued on Page Three.

BURSTING OIL TANKS SET YOKOHAMA AFIRE

Explosions Deluged the Doomed City With Flames That Spread Death.

TOKIO BRIDGES COLLAPSE

Thousands of Victims Go Down With Them to Death—Not a House Undamaged.

Copyright, 1923, by The New York Times Company.

PEKING, Sept. 4.—The latest news received here by way of the Tomioka wireless station, 150 miles northeast of Tokio, indicates that the catastrophe in Japan equals the worst apprehensions.

In Yokohama the Government oil tanks exploded and the whole city was set on fire. The deaths alone there are still estimated at 100,000.

All bridges across the river in Tokio, which were densely crowded with refugees from the fire, collapsed during the later earthquake shocks, and many thousands were drowned or killed by the fall.

[article continues]

DEVASTATION COVERS HUNDREDS OF MILES

At Least Five Big Cities Have Been Almost Wiped Out—Millions Are Starving or Dying of Exposure.

THOUSANDS OF MADDENED PEOPLE LEAP INTO RIVER

The Sumida in Tokio Is Clogged With Bodies—Shocks and Explosions Continue—Five Billion Dollars Needed for Reconstruction.

OSAKA, Japan, Sept. 4 (Associated Press).—So vast an area of Japan has been devastated by the greatest earthquake in the history of this country that it will be long before the actual loss of life is known. The most reliable estimates of the dead up to the present are from 200,000 to 320,000.

The newspaper Osaka Asahi estimates the earthquake dead at 320,000, which includes 150,000 dead in Tokio, 100,000 in Yokohama and 60,000 in Yokosuka.

[Other dispatches estimate the casualties as high as 500,000.]

Tokio and Yokohama, with surrounding towns, which formed the centre of the disturbances, are almost completely in ruins. For two days Tokio was swept by flames, and, apart from the loss of life caused directly through the falling of buildings, thousands must have perished in their attempts to make their way through the fire zones and other thousands through exhaustion.

Yokohama, Tokio's busy port, is a city destroyed. Probably more destruction has been wrought there than in the capital itself, for its great docks were torn asunder, its shipping wrecked, its public buildings and homes levelled to the earth.

All advices received here indicate a succession of earth disturbances in that area, extending from many miles inland and to the north, and everywhere the first destructive forces were augmented by explosions, the bursting of water mains, the overflow of rivers and the terrible overpowering rush of tidal waves.

New Islands Arise From the Ocean.

Details of geographical changes are lacking, but it is reported that new islands have been forced up from the bed of the ocean, while whole sections have disappeared. Rivers are said to have changed their courses and volcanoes are erupting in various districts.

The disaster spared none who stood in its path. Many members of noble families have perished, but thus far the only notable foreign resident in the list of killed is the American Consul at Yokohama, Max D. Kirjassoff, who, with his wife, is believed to have been buried in the ruins of the consulate.

The American Ambassador, Cyrus E. Woods, and all the members of the embassy at Tokio are known to be safe, but many of the diplomatic representatives of other nations have not been accounted for, nor has any word been received of their fate.

Word is received that the fires in Tokio burned out on Monday night, but at the same time couriers carry appeals for food supplies and medical supplies and assistance for the hundreds of thousands of homeless refugees who, unless succored speedily, cannot survive.

For the moment all efforts are being directed, first, to ascertaining the extent of Japan's vast losses, both in citizens and foreign residents, and material damage to its cities, and, secondly, to rushing all assistance in every form to the stricken districts.

There has been no time yet for a summing up of the terrible consequences of the earthquake nor for the preparation of a list of the prominent dead Japanese or foreign residents.

The warships of many foreign nations are on the seas already bringing assistance, which fact serves to give encouragement to the Government and the people in their greatest calamity.

Explosion at Hakone Hot Springs.

A great explosion has occurred at Owakidini, in Hakone, one of the hot springs of Japan, located about fifty miles from Tokio.

Earthquake shocks continue at intervals around Kawaguchi, which is on the only railway open out of Tokio.

The shock of yesterday morning, followed by fire, wiped out Kawaguchi.

Reports from eyewitnesses at Hakone say the earthquake left no houses standing at Miyanoshita, the fashionable mountain resort forty-five miles south of Tokio. The Fujiya Hotel was among the buildings destroyed.

In Tokio, the Ichigaya prison was threatened by fire and about 1,500 prisoners were freed. They included Toshihiko Saki, the Communist leader, and other Communists.

Troops of the Fourteenth Division at Utsunomiya and Thirteenth Division at Takata were marching toward Tokio today.

Following the earthquake horrors many of the refugees died from extreme heat and exposure, according to eye-

[article continues]

Continued on Page Three.

Dirigible ZR-1 Makes Perfect Test Flight; 15,000 Cheer Huge Craft Made at Lakehurst

Special to The New York Times.

LAKEHURST, N. J., Sept. 4.—Exceeding the expectations of its builders, the United States Navy dirigible ZR-1 made it maiden flight this afternoon from the Lakehurst air station, where ten months ago construction was started. Cheered by 15,000 persons, the dirigible, a "made in America" product, rose gracefully, and, after circling the field, took an easterly course to Toms River. Returning to the field at dusk after a perfect landing at the station and "went to bed" in its immense hangar.

From the first preparations this morning toward releasing the ZR-1 until after the dirigible had been safely returned to its hangar, the day was replete with interesting events for naval officials. Commander Frank R. McCrary, skipper of the craft, received favorable weather reports from Washington early in the afternoon, and later went ahead with the twenty-two men in the crew who were assigned by Captain Anton Heinen, German Zeppelin authority, who has been consultant to the navy in the construction of the craft.

A force of 250 marines and enlisted men marched to their posts as guide-rope holders, and 100 civilian employees gathered at the entrance of the hangar to await the guiding the dirigible to the centre of the field.

When every man was in his place Commander Weyerbacher gave the order, "Start walking," and the small army of men began hauling the ZR-1 from the hangar.

Captain Heinen then climbed into the pilot gondola, and a moment later the order was shouted, "Let's go."

Propelled by four of its six motors, the dirigible rose to a height of about 1,000 feet, where the pilot started to circle the field. Later the big craft began its real flight, and at a height of 1,200 feet, in full view of the crowds, it soared away in perfect control.

Soon this radio message was received at Admiral Moffett: "In twenty minutes of flying all going well."

Signals is electrically illuminated signboards placed flat on the ground aided in the landing, which was made without a hitch upon an immense stretch of red and white bunting, on which a searchlight was turned.

"The flight was highly satisfactory," said Commander McCrary. "The craft steered exceedingly well, although we did not carry out any tests of several things which in our future tests we will. We only opened up the motors to half speed, and they functioned nicely on the initial trip."

Rear Admiral Moffett was enthusiastic over the results of the trip.

"One of those who made the flight was Norman O. Walker, the only American who survived the ZR-2 crash in England. He said that the dirigible seemed to him to be a much better craft.

Rear Admiral W. A. Moffett, head of the naval air forces, witnessed Commander McCrary and his crew "best voyage." McCrary, Commander Weyerbacher and

[article continues]

Dr. J. Bentley Squier Sails From Kobe To Aid Relief Measures at Yokohama

Copyright, 1923, by The New York Times Company.
Special Cable to THE NEW YORK TIMES.

KYOTO, Japan, Sept. 4.—Dr. J. Bentley Squier of New York has sailed from Kobe on the foreign relief ship West Crows, bound for Yokohama to engage in relief work there. Dr. Squier's family remain at the Miyake Hotel here.

Dr. Squier and Mrs. Squier and their son and daughter were returning via Japan from a tour in China when the Japanese earthquake occurred. They had intended to sail from Shanghai on the Empress of

[article continues]

Continued on Page Three.

"All the News That's
Fit to Print."

The New York Times.

THE WEATHER
Warmer and cloudy today; to-
morrow, fair and colder.
Temperature yesterday—Max., 4.
Ffor weather report see Page 19.

VOL. LXXIII....No. 24,105.   · · ·   NEW YORK, WEDNESDAY, JANUARY 23, 1924.   TWO CENTS | THREE CENTS

LENIN DIES OF CEREBRAL HEMORRHAGE; MOSCOW THRONGS OVERCOME WITH GRIEF; TROTSKY DEPARTS ILL, RADEK IN DISFAVOR

SOVIET CONGRESS IN TEARS

Mass Hysteria Only Averted by a Leader's Brusque Intervention.

BODY WILL LIE IN STATE

Is to Be Taken to Moscow Today From Village Where Premier Passed Away.

KREMLIN WALL HIS TOMB

Washington Expects No Immediate Change in the Policy of the Russian Government.

By WALTER DURANTY.
Copyright, 1924, by The New York Times Company.
By Wireless to THE NEW YORK TIMES.

MOSCOW, Jan. 22.—Nikolai Lenin died last night at 6:50 o'clock. The immediate cause of death was paralysis of the respiratory centres due to a cerebral hemorrhage.

NIKOLAI LENIN (VLADIMIR ILYITCH ULIANOV),
A sketch made from life for THE NEW YORK TIMES by Oscar Cesare in Moscow, November, 1922, and autographed by Lenin.

EXPERTS PROPOSE GERMAN GOLD BANK

It Would Be Absolutely Independent and Under International Control.

SCHACHT URGES MEASURE

Dawes Committee Will Go to Berlin on Monday to Discuss Proposal There.

BRITAIN ACCEPTS THE LIQUOR TREATY

Document Is Approved by All of the Dominions and Hughes Is Notified.

GEDDES MAY SIGN TODAY

Washington Makes Preliminary Proposals for Similar Compacts to Other Powers.

Captain of Tacoma and Two Radio Men Lose Their Lives in Vera Cruz Storm

Special to The New York Times.
WASHINGTON, Jan. 22.—Wireless messages from official sources tonight report that Captain Herbert G. Sparrow of the wrecked cruiser Tacoma and two radio operators have lost their lives in a severe hurricane outside Vera Cruz Harbor.

DECLARES ANDERSON FORCED HIM TO SPLIT PART OF HIS 'DRY' PAY

Chief Accuser of Anti-Saloon League Official Then Admits Trying to Sell Exposure.

DENIES HE TRIED BLACKMAIL

Defense Links Witness With Brewers and Wet Organization at Forgery Trial.

LABOR TAKES OFFICE, FULFILLING ANCIENT BRITISH CEREMONIES

Macdonald Kisses the King's Hand in Accepting Commission to Head Government.

THREE PEERS IN CABINET

New Premier Takes Foreign Office Also and Will Base His Policy on League.

By EDWIN L. JAMES.
Copyright, 1924, by The New York Times Company.
Special Cable to THE NEW YORK TIMES.

LONDON, Jan. 22.—In the historic setting of Buckingham Palace, replete with the symbolism of British monarchy of more than a thousand years, King George today entrusted to a leader of workingmen the chief post in the government of the British Empire.

COOLIDGE SENDS WATCHER TO OIL HEARING; DAUGHERTY IS ALREADY INVESTIGATING; ASK SINCLAIR TO RETURN, FALL RECALLED

Sinclair Declares Oil Inquiry Is 'Politics'; Denies Paying Fall for Teapot Dome Lease

Copyright, 1924, by The New York Times Company.
Special Cable to THE NEW YORK TIMES.

PLYMOUTH, Eng., Jan. 22.—Harry F. Sinclair was on board the liner Paris, which arrived at Plymouth this afternoon from New York. He was accompanied by Mrs. Sinclair and Mr. Day, Vice President of the Sinclair Oil Company. He did not land at Plymouth, but proceeded to Havre. His name appeared on the supplementary passenger list.

PRESIDENT READY TO ACT

Spokesman Indicates Coolidge Has His Eye on Developments.

INQUIRY TO BE PRESSED

Senate Committee Wants Fall to Explain Archie Roosevelt's Story.

SINCLAIR'S BOOKS SOUGHT

Mysterious Memorandum Appears of Fall's Ranch Purchase—No Clue to Author.

WON'T CONFER AGAIN ON ST. MARK'S RITES

Bishop-Manning Stands on His Edict Against the New Practices.

RECTOR DEMANDS A JURY

Vestry Backs Him in His Request That Services Be Judged by 50 Clergy and Laymen.

VETO THREATENED ON A HIGH SURTAX

President Stands Inflexibly for Secretary Mellon's 25 Per Cent. Rate.

COMPROMISERS UNMOVED

House Committee Decides to Act on Indirect Taxes First and Surtax Last.

"All the News That's Fit to Print."

The New York Times.

THE WEATHER
Rain today or tonight and tomorrow; no change in temperature.
Temperature yesterday—Max., 41; Min., 34.

VOL. LXXIII....No. 24,117.   •••   NEW YORK, MONDAY, FEBRUARY 4, 1924.   TWO CENTS In Greater | THREE CENTS | FOUR CENTS

WOODROW WILSON PASSES AWAY IN SLEEP; END COMES AT 11:15 A.M.; NATION SORROWS AND TRIBUTES ARE VOICED IN ALL LANDS

OIL INQUIRY PAUSES IN HONOR OF WILSON; GREGORY RETIRES

Today's Session Is Suspended and Committee May Not Resume Till After Funeral.

SENATE SANCTION AWAITED

Testimony Will Be Postponed Pending Action on Fall's Challenge of Authority.

GREGORY EXPLAINS POSITION

Writes President He Had Been Unaware of Doheny's Share in Paying Fee.

Special to The New York Times.
WASHINGTON, Feb. 3.—The death of former President Wilson may delay for several days the Congressional activities in connection with the Naval Reserve oil lease scandal.

It had been the intention of Senator Lenroot, Chairman of the Public Lands Committee, to place before the Senate tomorrow the points made by former Secretary Albert B. Fall on Saturday in refusing to answer questions and to ask for additional power to proceed with the investigation, if that were considered necessary.

But it now develops that the Senate will adjourn immediately tomorrow out of respect to the memory of Mr. Wilson, thus providing no opportunity for consideration of the oil scandals. It is possible that there may be a session of the Senate on Tuesday, at which action will be taken, but the opinion expressed tonight was that all developments might be held back until after the funeral of the former President.

Long Legal Battle in Prospect.

Mr. Fall is remaining in seclusion and his legal advisers are apparently confident that the case will uphold his right to refuse to testify on the ground that he might incriminate himself. There have been reports that the committee, after obtaining additional power from Congress, would place Fall in custody, if he persisted in defying it, but these are not confirmed. It is probable that a long legal battle will be witnessed, and in the meantime the auditing going ahead with other phases of the inquiry.

During the delay, however, the auditing experts retained by the committee will continue their examination of the books of brokerage firms which have been subpoenaed by the committee in an effort to establish whether any persons prominent in the official life of Washington who may have had advance information profited by the rise in the value of Sinclair Consolidated Securities following the announcement of the leasing of Teapot Dome Reserve to Sinclair.

Thomas Watts Gregory, Attorney General in the Wilson Administration, formally withdrew as special counsel in the oil cases today in a letter sent to President Coolidge which was given out at the White House.

Mr. Gregory made the point that while he had taken on the long distance telephone with the President on Tuesday night, he had not accepted the appointment as that time and had simply agreed to come on to Washington and discuss the proposition. He also stated that he had not recalled at that time that he ever received any money paid out by Doheny.

While the President has made no formal announcement, it was generally accepted tonight that he would appoint former Senator Atlee Pomerene as counsel representing the Democratic Party. It was indicated at the White House that the President desired to talk about it with Senator Walsh, and also would wait until the joint resolution adopted in Congress last week was placed before him.

Silas Strawn, selected as the Republican member of counsel, had a long conference today with Mr. Pomerene about the oil cases, and they said afterward that they had made a start on the preparation of the case. It is believed that the remote connection of Mr. Strawn's law firm with the Texas Oil Company will not prevent his confirmation to the White House.

"For about ten years, I think, my firm has collected bills for the Texas Company and obtained locations for their filling stations in the Chicago territory. These are matters handled by the young men of our firm and I never have had anything to do with them. My firm never has handled any of the corporate business of the Texas or any other oil

Continued on Page Ten.

Congress to Adjourn Today After Tributes to Wilson

WASHINGTON, Feb. 3.—Congress will pay its tribute tomorrow to Woodrow Wilson.

On convening at noon, both the House and Senate will adjourn out of respect for his memory.

In the House, Representative Longworth, the Republican leader, will give official notification of Mr. Wilson's death, and after a brief eulogy will yield the floor to Representative Garrett, the Democratic leader, who will deliver a eulogy.

In the Senate, Mr. Robinson, the Democratic leader, will deliver an address. Both houses will resume business Tuesday.

EUROPE IS STIRRED BY WILSON'S DEATH

Lloyd George Calls Him Glorious Failure Who Sacrificed His Life for His Ideal.

CECIL PAYS HIM TRIBUTE

France, Italy and Other Allied Capitals Recall His Services in Winning the War.

Special Cable to The New York Times.
LONDON, Feb. 3.—In common with most of the allied statesmen of Europe and other personalities whom destiny summoned to fill leading rôles in the World War, former Premier Lloyd George sees in Woodrow Wilson an idealist who stood out as perhaps the most remarkable figure of that tremendous cataclysm.

In an interview which The New York Times correspondent had with him today at his new home at Churt, Surrey, concerning the passing of Mr. Wilson, Mr. Lloyd George said:

"Woodrow Wilson was a very great man, and, like all great men, had his defects, but these will be quickly forgotten in the magnitude of his work. True he was a failure, but a glorious failure, he failed as Jesus Christ failed, and, like Christ, sacrificed his life in pursuance of his noble ideal.

"He was just as much a victim of the great war as any soldier who died in the trenches. He ruined his health in the endeavor to create a better and happier existence for the people of the whole world, and I am sure that the failure of his altruistic inspirations hastened his tragic end.

"It will perhaps be a generation before the greatness of Woodrow Wilson will be appreciated at its real value by his countrymen and the tragedy which closed his life will bring before the world the unselfishness of his ambitions as nothing else could. Like the tragedy which made for your great martyred Lincoln a permanent place in the hearts of the American people—even of those who disagreed with him, as was made very apparent to me in my recent visit to the Southern States—the sad death of this great Statesman, this great American, will indelibly stamp his name among those at the very top of your history.

Had Violent Likes and Dislikes.

"Like Theodore Roosevelt, Mr. Wilson had violent likes and dislikes, and for this, as always is the penalty of greatness, he was violently criticised. I believe I may say that never have I seen such vicious, cruel vituperation as was heaped upon him at home and in parts at the time of the Peace Conference. Such abuse never was levelled at any man in like position in history and it hurt him terribly.

"Criticism cut him like a knife. He had been a lifelong politician he could have overlooked these attacks. Thirty years or so of political life makes one invulnerable. I know. But Wilson's character was such, he received the rough stuff, that he was immensely sensitive to this public abuse and he suffered more than others would have done. I have no doubt that this helped to bring on his illness.

"Besides, he was a tireless worker. I remember when we were in Paris I would see lights in his room at all hours of the night as he worked at his League idea. The rest of us found time for golf and we took our Sundays off, but Wilson, in his zeal, worked incessantly. Only those who were there and witnessed it can realise the efforts he expended.

His Personality Grew Upon One.

"He was a man whose personality grew upon one. When I first met him here in England I did not understand him, nor did Clemenceau in Paris; but when you spend every day for five months with a man you have opportunity to become well acquainted with him, and when it was over I had learned to appreciate his great gifts and to like him very much personally, and I remember Clemenceau at the time telling me his feelings were similar.

"Yes, Woodrow Wilson was a very good fellow, and I shall mourn his passing. I had the pleasure of spending a

Continued on Page Four.

COOLIDGE ANNOUNCES DEATH

In Formal Proclamation He Calls the Nation to Mourn.

HE LAUDS WILSON'S WORK

With Mrs. Coolidge, He Drives From Church to S Street House and Leaves Cards.

FLAGS ORDERED LOWERED

Will Stay at Half-Staff 30 Days—Government Offices to Close—Receptions Canceled.

Special to The New York Times.
WASHINGTON, Feb. 3.—The death of Woodrow Wilson was formally announced to the people of the United States late this afternoon in a proclamation issued from the White House by President Coolidge, in which he paid high tribute to the war President, and directed that flags on the White House and Government buildings be half-staffed for a period of thirty days.

When the text of the proclamation was made public, the further statement was authorized at the White House that President Coolidge had directed that orders be issued closing all Government departments on the day of Mr. Wilson's funeral. Flags will fly at half-mast on war ships, at military posts and on all American diplomatic and other Government offices abroad.

President Coolidge's proclamation pays high tribute to the life and services of Mr. Wilson, saying that it brings "to many of us" a sense of profound personal bereavement.

Official Social Functions Canceled.

All official social functions—including the brilliant State reception scheduled for the White House on Thursday—have been canceled.

In ordering the flags on Government buildings half-staffed, and arranging for the issuance of orders for closing Government buildings on the day of the funeral, President Coolidge followed the customary procedure. The President feels that the Government, over which Mr. Wilson presided during eight of the most important years in American history, should in every way act in testimony of the respect in which the memory of so great and distinguished a President is held.

President and Mrs. Coolidge were in their pew in the First Congregational Church, at the corner of Tenth and G Streets, when they first heard of the death of the former President. In that church, in common with many others, announcement of the death was made during the services, at the close of which the pastor, the Rev. Jason Noble Pierce, made a special prayer in view of the occasion.

After the close of the service the Coolidges were driven directly to the Wilson home. The big White House car swept into the drive before the Wilson house at 12:25 o'clock, one hour and ten minutes after the death of the ex-President. The door of the car was opened by a Secret Service man, while another stood outside it and between the car and the spectators.

Although a few of the callers at the Wilson home had stayed in their cars and sent in cards by a footman, Mr. and Mrs. Coolidge alighted. The President got out first, assisting Mrs. Coolidge. They walked up the flight of three steps to the door. It happened to be open, because two other callers had rung the bell just as the President's car stopped.

Coolidge Hands Cards to the Butler.

Mr. Coolidge himself handed cards to the negro butler, who received them on a silver tray. They re-entered their car, but its long wheelbase was too much for the narrow arc of the Wilson driveway, and the chauffeur was obliged to back and-start twice before he could get started for the street.

The President's car started east over S Street hill and was stopped by the car to which the Secret Service men rode.

The President wore a silk hat and a black overcoat with silk lapels. Mrs. Coolidge was dressed in brown, with hat to match. Both were grave, and during their stop at the Wilson house neither was observed to speak a word.

Perhaps half an hour after the Presidential visit C. Bascom Slemp, Secretary to Mr. Coolidge, arrived alone in his car. He entered the house and was inside ten or fifteen minutes. When he emerged, Mr. Slemp said that, in addition to offering his personal condolences as a Virginian and an acquaintance of the family, he had come from the President to tell the members of the Wilson household that the Government was desirous of learning his wishes in respect to funeral arrangements, and that anything they desired would be done.

Mr. Slemp said he had talked to Joseph Wilson, the former President's brother, and John Randolph Bolling, the Secretary. They told him that funeral plans had not been discussed, but it was agreed that as soon as any decision was reached Mr. Slemp would be informed.

WOODROW WILSON

President Coolidge's Proclamation

By the President of the United States of America.

A Proclamation

To the People of the United States:

The death of Woodrow Wilson, President of the United States from March 4, 1913, to March 4, 1921, which occurred at 11:15 o'clock today at his home at Washington, District of Columbia, deprives the country of a most distinguished citizen, and is an event which causes universal and genuine sorrow. To many of us it brings the sense of a profound personal bereavement.

His early profession as a lawyer was abandoned to enter academic life. In this chosen field he attained the highest rank as an educator, and has left his impress upon the intellectual thought of the country.

From the Presidency of Princeton University he was called by his fellow citizens to be the Chief Executive of the State of New Jersey. The duties of this high office he so conducted as to win the confidence of the people of the United States, who twice elected him to the Chief Magistracy of the Republic.

As President of the United States he was moved by an earnest desire to promote the best interests of the country as he conceived them. His acts were prompted by high motives and his sincerity of purpose cannot be questioned. He led the nation through the terrific struggle of the World War with a lofty idealism which never failed him. He gave utterance to the aspiration of humanity with an eloquence which held the attention of all the earth and made America a new and enlarged influence in the destiny of mankind.

In testimony of the respect in which his memory is held by the Government and the people of the United States, I do hereby direct that the flags of the White House and of the several departmental buildings be displayed at half-staff for a period of thirty days, and that suitable military and naval honors, under orders of the Secretary of War and of the Secretary of the Navy, may be rendered on the day of the funeral.

Done at the City of Washington this Third Day of February, in the Year of Our Lord One Thousand Nine Hundred and Twenty-Four, and of the Independence of the United States of America the One Hundred and Forty-Eighth.

By the President: CALVIN COOLIDGE.

CHARLES EVANS HUGHES,
Secretary of State.

GRAYSON DESCRIBES SCENE AT DEATHBED

War President, He Says, Grew Weaker and Weaker Until He Calmly Passed Away.

ONCE CONSCIOUS AT NIGHT

Then He Relapsed Into Virtual Coma, From Which He Did Not Emerge.

Special to The New York Times.
WASHINGTON, Feb. 3.—Woodrow Wilson's death was peaceful, a gradual fading away of life after a long period of unconsciousness, according to Admiral Cary T. Grayson, who was his physician in the days of his strength and vigor at the White House and was in almost constant attendance upon him since his tragic breakdown more than four years ago.

Mr. Wilson's last spoken word was "Edith," the name of his wife, uttered in a faint whisper late yesterday afternoon, when Mrs. Wilson had left the sick room temporarily. Mrs. Wilson, sent for by Admiral Grayson, returned almost immediately. She remained in the room thereafter until the end, sitting in a chair at the bedside and holding h r husband's hand for the greater part of the time.

Mr. Wilson's last completely phrased sentence, so far as Admiral Grayson could recall, was the remark on Friday about the broken machine and the expression of his readiness to go. "I am a broken piece of machinery," he said. "When the machinery is broken—I am ready to go."

The last message to be received by Mr. Wilson from any one outside his immediate family was from Senator Glass of Virginia. Senator Glass, a close friend of Mr. Wilson and a strong supporter of his policies, asked Admiral Grayson to give "the Chief" his love. Admiral Grayson did so early Saturday

Continued on Page Two.

WAR PRESIDENT'S END CAME PEACEFULLY

His Life Ebbed Away While He Slept and His Heart Action Became Fainter Until It Finally Ceased.

WIFE AT THE DYING MAN'S BEDSIDE UNTIL THE END

Her Name Was the Last Word to Pass His Lips and His Last Sentence Was 'I Am Ready,' Spoken Friday.

Special to The New York Times.
WASHINGTON, Feb. 3.—Woodrow Wilson, twenty-eighth President of the United States, a commanding world figure and chief advocate of the League of Nations, is dead. He died at 11:15 o'clock this morning, after being unconscious for nearly twelve hours.

Mrs. Wilson, Miss Margaret Wilson, Joseph Wilson, a brother, and Admiral Grayson, his physician, were at the bedside.

Just before death the war President opened his eyes. His wife and daughter spoke to him, but he did not respond. Ten minutes later he passed quietly away. No word was uttered.

All day yesterday and last night he had been sinking rapidly, his pulse becoming fainter and fainter, until finally it ceased to beat. His "broken machinery" had collapsed.

Washington and the nation were prepared for death. The morning papers had carried the news that he had been "profoundly prostrated." The waiting groups, numbering many hundreds, outside of the Wilson home were silent when Admiral Grayson, five minutes after his patient and friend had expired, opened the door and made the announcement.

Text of the Death Bulletin.

Dr. Grayson read the following bulletin:

11:20 A. M., Feb. 3, 1924.

Mr. Wilson died at 11:15 o'clock this morning. His heart action became feebler and feebler, and the heart muscle was so fatigued that it refused to act any longer. The end came peacefully. The remote causes of death lie in his ill-health, which began more than four years ago, namely, arteriosclerosis and hemiplegia. The immediate cause of death was exhaustion following a digestive disturbance which began in the early part of last week, but did not reach an acute stage until the early morning hours of Feb. 1.

CARY T. GRAYSON.

Arteriosclerosis is a thickening and hardening of the walls of the arteries, and hemiplegia is a paralysis of one side of the body, the limbs on that side losing the power of voluntary motion. Mr. Wilson's left side was so stricken, the outward manifestation being the helpless drop of his left arm and the dragging of the left foot.

Died While Wife Held His Hand.

Mr. Wilson died in a room on the third floor of his home, where for so many months, since his retirement, he sat and looked over Washington, the scene of his greatest achievement. He expired on a large four-poster bed, a replica of the Lincoln bed in the White House.

Mr. Wilson's last word was "Edith," his wife's name. In a faint voice he called for her yesterday afternoon when she had left his bedside for a moment.

His last sentence was spoken on Friday, when he said:

"I am a broken piece of machinery. When the machinery is broken——— I am ready."

Mrs. Wilson held his right hand as his life slowly ebbed away. Admiral Grayson remained in the death room for a few minutes and then went down stairs leaving Mrs. Wilson and Margaret the only mourners at the bedside.

There had been signs during the morning that the end was a matter of minutes. The first bulletin issued by Dr. Grayson at 8:55 o'clock said:

"Mr. Wilson is unconscious and his pulse is very weak."

His 10:30 o'clock bulletin read:

"After a quiet night Mr. Wilson is very low and the end may be expected any time."

When, therefore, Dr. Grayson appeared on the steps of the house at 11:20 it was realized that he had probably come to announce the end.

Dr. Grayson Deeply Moved.

Dr. Grayson was making a strong effort to keep himself under control. In his hand he held some of the yellow slips on which the bulletins were typewritten. He came toward the newspaper men, who quickly gathered about him near the steps of the house.

"The end came at 11:15," he said in a low tone.

Immediately there was a commotion in the crowd as the newspaper men assigned to flash the news of death which would speed all over the world, broke through their comrades and rushed off.

The crowd across the street, not grown to large proportions, surged forward in an effort to hear Dr. Grayson, but the police lines held and there was nothing for them to do but to listen with painful attention.

Meanwhile Dr. Grayson had begun to read the bulletin. This was the climax of the emotional strain he has been under, and it was only with difficulty that he could force himself to go ahead.

He read slowly. His voice trembled, but did not break. But as he read, very slowly, tears kept rolling down his cheeks and he used his handkerchief.

This action, more than what they could hear, showed the spectators across the street that he was actually announcing Mr. Wilson's death. Here and there in the crowd men began to take off their hats. Soon almost all were uncovered. The women stood with lowered heads, many of them weeping.

Finally, Dr. Grayson finished reading the bulletin. The newspaper men expressed a few words of sympathy and then hurried off to send the detailed news. Dr. Grayson was left standing with only one or two before him.

The physician and friend of the former President, who has been the only link between the sick room and the outside world, was asked whether, after Mr. Wilson was dead, he would not give a detailed account of his last hours. He demurred, saying he did not believe there was anything more to be added to what had been said.

He was urged to undertake the task as a duty to the memory of his friend and patient. On this ground he assented. He said he would take an automobile ride for the purpose of resting, and that during its course

"All the News That's Fit to Print."

The New York Times.

THE WEATHER

Partly cloudy and warmer today; tomorrow probably showers. Temperature Yesterday—Max. 80; Min. 64. Full weather report see on last page.

VOL. LXXIII....No. 24,247.   • • • •   NEW YORK, FRIDAY, JUNE 13, 1924.   TWO CENTS In Greater New York | THREE CENTS Within 200 Miles | FOUR CENTS Elsewhere

EXPLOSIONS KILL 48 ON U. S. S. MISSISSIPPI; NEW BLAST FEARED

Firing Crew Wiped Out When Back-Fire Sets Off Store of Powder in Turret.

PASSENGER SHIP IN DANGER

14-Inch Gun Is Discharged in San Pedro Harbor, Shell Causing Panic on the Yale.

THIRD GUN STILL LOADED

After Landing Dead and Injured, Dreadnought Puts Back to Sea for Safety.

Special to The New York Times.

LOS ANGELES, Cal., June 12.—Three officers and forty-five enlisted men are known to have been killed, nine others probably fatally injured, and a score more hurt in various degrees in an explosion in a gun turret on the U. S. S. Mississippi, off San Pedro Harbor this afternoon.

There were two separate blasts—the first was that of 1,900 pounds of powder and a charge of a fourteen-inch rifle.

The second came as the dreadnought dropped anchor near the hospital ship Relief in the harbor proper; the charge in the second great rifle in the turret exploding, the shell was hurled out to sea, missing the outgoing liner Yale by a few hundred feet and creating a panic among its passengers.

The battleships Mississippi, Tennessee, Idaho and California, comprising a division under the command of Rear Admiral William V. Pratt, left Los Angeles Harbor today for the San Clemente drill grounds for concerted practice.

Part of this consisted in concentrated fire by the Mississippi, Idaho and Tennessee against a giant target to be towed by the California.

According to naval officers on the other ships, the three dreadnoughts were lined up. In the far distance, a tiny speck showed the California.

In gun turret No. 2, situated above and slightly abaft of gun turret No. 1, forward of the ship, were the eighty-odd men comprising the gun crews for guns Nos. 4, 5 and 6.

Part of these eighty-odd were stationed at the guns themselves; the remainder of the crews were occupied in the handling rooms and in the twin turrets leading from the ammunition stores. In command of the turret was Lieutenant Thomas Edward Zellars, a Long Beach, Cal., man. With him were Ensigns Marcus Erwin, J. J. Levasseur and James McCrea, the last two being observers from the U. S. S. New Mexico detailed to witness the target practice.

The command was given to load; the guns were elevated for the long shot.

The monster shells were brought from the ammunition stores by their mechanical carriers, lifted and shoved home in the gun barrels. Then came the great sacks of powder, 450 pounds of it in each sack, and four sacks in each charge of each gun. The three guns were loaded, and four sacks of the explosives still lay on the floor.

Gun Breech Not Closed.

The breeches in guns 5 and 6 swung slowly shut and tightly locked. In gun 4 the breech likewise swung toward closure, but something jammed. And in that moment when the breech hung slightly open, some one—no one knows who that some one was—gave the command to turn on the electrical current which detonated the explosive in gun 4. The charge exploded. The eighty-odd men, trapped in a steel cage designed to withstand the mightiest blow of an enemy fleet, were burned and crushed and mangled and gassed. Those within the turret proper were instantly killed.

The four sacks of powder still on the floor joined in the mighty blast—and the armor-plated roof of the turret dissolved into fragments.

In the handling rooms those closest to the door were instantly killed; those further away in the flat of the injured. The fireproof doors to the ammunition tunnels were blown from the hinges; the trap-doors leading to the handling rooms were totally destroyed.

Ensign Levasseur out of the corner of one eye had caught sight of that open gun-breech when the command to fire had been given. He unhesitatingly dove forty feet from the shell deck, where he was standing, down the shaft of the endless chain powder bucket. He was cut and bruised but is still alive. Ensign Erwin, by whom he was standing, was instantly killed.

The blast shook the ship from stem to stern. It seemed minutes, almost, before even the commanding officers knew what had happened. The Ensign H. D. Smith of the U. S. S. New Mexico, also detailed as an observer on the Mississippi, grabbed an air hose and, with a squad of volunteers, pushed his way into the door of the blazing turret. A fire had started which for a while menaced the safety of the entire ship. The air from the hose fanned the flames. The rescue squad was forced to retreat. Fire hose was hastily rigged and several streams poured through every point of entrance. Shortly thereafter the rescuers were able to start their work of bringing out the bodies.

Dreadnought Rushes to Port.

The Mississippi was at once put under full speed, heading for Los Angeles Harbor, and the hospital ship Relief, radio messages to the latter vessel to prepare at once for fifty victims was hurriedly sent. It was this message which gave the first news of the affair to Los Angeles.

Continued on Page Eight.

COOLIDGE AND DAWES NOMINATED; GENERAL IS NAMED FOR SECOND PLACE AFTER LOWDEN, CHOSEN, REFUSES IT

BURTON NAMES COOLIDGE

Professor Breaks Traditions and Talks Out Like a Modern Salesman.

POPULARIZES HIS VIRTUES

And Carries Audience With Him All the Way With Homely Metaphors.

JEERS AGAIN FOR WISCONSIN

But Only Laughter Greets the South Dakota Vote for Hiram Johnson.

Special to The New York Times.

CLEVELAND, Ohio, June 12.—Calvin Coolidge was nominated for the Presidency at 1:57 o'clock this afternoon on the first ballot taken in the Republican National Convention.

He received 1,065 of the 1,109 votes. Robert Marion La Follette got 34—28 of the 29 from Wisconsin and six of the 13 from North Dakota—and Hiram Johnson got 10 of the 13 votes from South Dakota.

As usual, the galleries received every mention of La Follette's name, and the report of the votes cast for him, with jeers and hisses, but they had only laughter for the name of Hiram Johnson.

When the result of the ballot had been announced, S. X. Way of South Dakota moved that the nomination be made unanimous, and Thomas Scott of Wisconsin, who cast that State's only vote for Coolidge, seconded the motion. When Chairman Frank W. Mondell put it a viva voce vote everybody shouted "Aye," but the recalcitrant handful of La Follette men in Wisconsin, and North Dakota, who at least so respects this morning's session showed a tendency to a change of long settled habits of American politics. The constitutional "demonstration" for President Coolidge, following the speech in which he was nominated, was not stretched out to the fantastic and artificial length that has been common in past conventions. It stopped after thirteen minutes, although it was two minutes later before all the delegates were in their seats.

Nominating Speech a "Sales Talk."

And the speech which had provoked it, the speech in which Dr. Marion Leroy Burton, President of the University of Michigan, placed President Coolidge in nomination, was of a type wholly new to national conventions though not unfamiliar in the commercial-cultural life of the United States. It was a sales talk, and a good sales talk at that. From some viewpoints it might be open to criticism, but it was perfectly adapted to the object for which it was designed.

The full text of Dr. Burton's speech is printed on page 6.

Dr. Burton is not a delegate. He was picked by President Coolidge himself to deliver the official advertisement for the candidate—for that is what it was, not an address to a convention already wrapped up, sealed and delivered for Coolidge, but an advertisement to the country of the personality and virtues of the head of the Republican ticket.

When the roll of States was called for nominations for the Presidency, and the head of the list, yielded to Massachusetts, President Coolidge's home State, and Governor Channing Cox of Massachusetts moved that Dr. Burton "be accorded the privilege of nominating the candidate of Massachusetts."

That was in accordance with the sacred ritual of American State religion—that the candidate must not be named until the very end of the nominating speech, when his identity is disclosed suddenly to a surprised convention. It seems to be felt that if the name is spoken during the performance of the rites the omens will be inauspicious.

But a moment later Chairman Mondell incautiously let slip the President's name, and Dr. Burton broke with tradition by telling the audience right away whom he was going to nominate.

Burton—his manner today suggested that he would feel insulted by continuing the use of his academic title—Burton looks no more like a college President than he does like a college President. Taller than Coolidge—almost as red-headed as Coolidge, smooth faced and brisk and snappy, he cast aside all formality and, through his secretary he obtained information as to what was going on behind the scenes at Cleveland. The President did not go to his executive office during the afternoon because of the desire of himself and Mrs. Coolidge to hear the convention speeches and votes. So far as known, there was no one with President and Mrs. Coolidge while they were listening in except Henry Long of Massachusetts, who was Mr. Coolidge's private secretary when he was Governor of Massachusetts.

Continued on Page Three.

REPUBLICAN NOMINEE FOR PRESIDENT.
CALVIN COOLIDGE
OF MASSACHUSETTS.

COOLIDGE IS SILENT ON HIS NOMINATION

President Feels He Can Express His Appreciation Best in His Acceptance Speech.

GETS NEWS AT LUNCHEON

Talks With Borah Before Convention Meets, and Then Listens to Its Proceedings.

Special to The New York Times.

WASHINGTON, June 12.—The White House was silent on the nomination of former Governor Lowden for Vice President, and equally uncommunicative after word was flashed to Washington that Mr. Lowden had announced his declination.

President Coolidge, it was stated by his spokesmen at the White House, was maintaining his attitude of "hands off" with respect to the selection of a running mate, and had not during the day communicated any preference to Mr. Butler or any other person in the convention city.

Nor would the President comment on his own nomination by the convention. Edward Clark, his personal secretary, in answer to inquiries by newspaper correspondents, stated that the President had requested him to say there would be no statement coming from the White House.

Mr. Coolidge intimated to friends several days ago that what he had to say in the way of appreciation could be most fittingly said when the Notification Committee arrives with the formal information of the action of the National Convention. On that occasion he will read a carefully prepared acceptance speech.

At Lunch When Nominated.

The President was at lunch at the White House when the vote of the convention was conveyed to him by Isaac Hoover, chief usher at the White House. He is reported to have nodded his acknowledgment of these tidings and resumed his meal.

President Coolidge spent practically all of the time the convention was in session "listening in" upon the convention proceedings over his radio set. Consequently he kept up-to-the-minute information as to the progress of the open proceedings, and through his secretary he obtained information as to what was going on behind the scenes at Cleveland. The President did not go to his executive office during the afternoon because of the desire of himself and Mrs. Coolidge to hear the convention speeches and votes. So far as known, there was no one with President and Mrs. Coolidge while they were listening in except Henry Long of Massachusetts, who was Mr. Coolidge's private secretary when he was Governor of Massachusetts.

Continued on Page Two.

LA FOLLETTE GROUP PREDICTS DEFEAT

Declare Blunders of Butler and Cabinet Advisers Have Beaten Coolidge.

PRAISE LEADERS' STRATEGY

Say Voters Are Alienated From Regulars and Prepare for Third Party Convention.

Special to The New York Times.

CLEVELAND, June 12.—At what one of their number referred to as "the end of a perfect day," the La Follette delegates from Wisconsin tonight are busy making hotel reservations in preparation for their attendance at what they term the "second Cleveland convention," scheduled to convene on July 4 for the purpose of nominating Senator La Follette for President of the United States on a third party ticket, which they hope, and seem to believe, will prove an insurmountable obstacle in the way of a Republican victory.

After that the leaders felt free to make against choosing President Coolidge to head the Republican national ticket in the campaign of 1924, the effort to nominate the candidate for Vice President put a fly in the Republican ointment and threatened to produce serious differences within the party management. Lack of harmony is already apparent, among those who are charged with the conduct of the Presidential campaign this year.

The futile nomination of Mr. Lowden for Vice President was in part the outcome of an abortive, inept effort to draft Senator William E. Borah of Idaho for second place on the national ticket.

At an early hour this morning William M. Butler, political manager for President Coolidge, had made known that President Coolidge desired that Senator Borah should be the Vice Presidential nominee, and that Mr. Butler had appealed to try to wreck the party and the meeting ended in great bitterness. Wadsworth, National Committeeman, Charles D. Hilles and Representative Ogden L. Mills stood together against the demand of the so-called Progressive element that a Western candidate with progressive ideas be selected for Vice President. The Progressives control of Judge Kenyon of Iowa, but Wadsworth and his followers declared he would never do, because he was not conservative enough and was not even a regular organization Republican. They declared him a follower of La Follette and not in sympathy with President Coolidge. For their candidate they brought forward Theodore E. Burton, temporary Chairman of the convention.

State Senator Frederick M. Davenport of Oneida led the Kenyon faction, and several delegates made fiery speeches sustaining his choice. One speaker declared that Kenyon had been acceptable to two Republican Presidents, Harding and Coolidge, the former having made him a Federal Judge, and therefore should be acceptable to the convention. On the vote which followed, Kenyon received 23 votes and Burton 54. There were ten absentees.

Continued on Page Seven.

REVOLT PUTS DAWES OVER

Old Timers Resent Butler's Domination of the Convention.

HE ASKED FIRST FOR KENYON

Regulars Named Lowden Instead and Then He Switched to Hoover.

DISAFFECTION SPREADING

Talk of Asking Coolidge to Select Another Man to Conduct Campaign.

By RICHARD V. OULAHAN.
Special to The New York Times.

CLEVELAND, June 12.—The Republican National Convention completed its work tonight and adjourned sine die after having chosen Calvin Coolidge of Massachusetts as its candidate for President and General Charles G. Dawes of Illinois as its candidate for Vice President.

Three sessions of the convention were held on the concluding day. The night session was made necessary by an extraordinary situation produced by the refusal of former Governor Frank O. Lowden of Illinois to be the party's candidate for Vice President after the convention had conferred that honor on him.

Mr. Lowden had been chosen on the second Vice-Presidential ballot at the afternoon, or second session. Messages from him refusing to accept the nomination, written in advance, were produced after some of Lowden's friends had sought to prevent their being presented.

This remarkable state of affairs compelled a recess to give the party leaders an opportunity to lead the party out of the maze in which it found itself. In the night session the situation was remedied by undoing the nomination of Mr. Lowden and proceeding to ballot again for a candidate for Vice President. On the first ballot at the night session, its third ballot on a candidate for Vice President, victory went to the supporters of General Dawes.

Convention Revolts on Butler.

While only a gesture of protest was made against choosing President Coolidge to head the Republican national ticket in the campaign of 1924, the effort to nominate the candidate for Vice President put a fly in the Republican ointment and threatened to produce serious differences within the party management. Lack of harmony is already apparent, among those who are charged with the conduct of the Presidential campaign this year.

Continued on Page Two.

REPUBLICAN NOMINEE FOR VICE PRESIDENT.
CHARLES G. DAWES
OF ILLINOIS.

BITTER FIGHT SPLITS NEW YORK GROUP

Wadsworth and Hayward Factions Engage in War of Words at Secret Conference.

EFFECT ON CAMPAIGN SEEN

"Old Guard" and Progressives Line Up in Opposition Through the Whole State Organization.

Special to The New York Times.

CLEVELAND, June 12.—A split that may have far-reaching consequences in the New York State fight this Fall developed in the New York delegation this afternoon just before the convention opened to nominate a Vice President. Seventy-seven of the delegates held a secret conference at their headquarters in the Cleveland hotel and the so-called Old Guard element, led by Senator Wadsworth, sought to take control. Mr. Wadsworth was denounced for trying to wreck the party and the meeting ended in great bitterness.

Wadsworth, National Committeeman, Charles D. Hilles and Representative Ogden L. Mills stood together against the demand of the so-called Progressive element that a Western candidate with progressive ideas be selected for Vice President. The Progressives counted on the part of the party who made wry faces when they were asked to support Judge Kenyon, whom they regarded as a near radical and not too loyal to the Republican cause, demanded a request direct from the White House that they put Judge Kenyon in second place on the national ticket. The whole situation split in the convention extended throughout the State and it is sure to have important results if it is not healed before the Fall campaign.

Hayward Supports Kenyon.

Colonel William Hayward, United States District Attorney for the Southern District of New York, whose candidacy for the Republican nomination for Governor is being vigorously opposed by Senator Wadsworth, sided with Davenport and advocated the selection of Kenyon. The delegates holding Federal positions in the State lined up behind Wadsworth. The vote showed a split in the organization extended throughout the State and it is sure to have important results if it is not healed before the Fall campaign.

Continued on Page Five.

DAWES WINS ON 3D BALLOT

Gets 682½ to 234½ for Hoover on Opening of Night Session.

CONVENTION THEN ADJOURNS

Lowden, Chosen First With Ovation Rivalling President's, Refuses to Accept.

KENYON AND BURTON STRONG

They Shared Lead on Early Ballots, With Watson, Dawes and Others.

By ELMER DAVIS.
Special to The New York Times.

PUBLIC HALL, CLEVELAND, Ohio, June 12.—The Republican National Convention of 1924 adjourned at 10:30 tonight, Eastern Standard Time, having renominated President Calvin Coolidge and picked Brig. Gen. Charles G. Dawes of Illinois on the third ballot with him as a candidate for Vice President.

The last day of the convention, the only one that had decently comfortable weather, the only one that saw the auditorium filled with spectators, was also the busiest and most entertaining of the three days of session.

The nomination of President Coolidge at the morning session, by 1,065 votes to 34 for Senator Robert M. La Follette and 10 for Senator Hiram Johnson, had, of course, long been foreseen; but the selection of a Vice President developed quite a struggle. Some of the struggling was done by gentlemen who wanted to be Vice President and a good many who did not want to be Vice President under any circumstances and objected to being drafted.

General Dawes was nominated on the first ballot tonight, as the last of the day's three sessions, receiving 682½ votes, as against 234½ for Herbert Hoover, Secretary of Commerce, and 75 for Judge William S. Kenyon of Iowa, and a few scattering. But at the afternoon session former Governor Frank O. Lowden of Illinois had been nominated despite his frequently expressed refusal to be a candidate, and it took two or three more refusals before the convention took him at his word.

Hoover Was Butler's Choice.

General Dawes was second choice, but Mr. Hoover, whom he defeated, was not even that. Hoover was the final candidate picked by William M. Butler, President Coolidge's campaign manager, and he was defeated by Dawes, not because the delegates had anything against Hoover, but because they had a great deal against William M. Butler.

President Coolidge and Visier Butler had been running this convention in everything, but the nomination of the Vice President, and the discontent against their domination, which has been loudly expressed in words all week, finally blossomed out into action today. The delegates couldn't be at Coolidge, nor the Coolidge platform, but they could and did beat whatever Vice-Presidential candidate was unfortunate enough to have Mr. Butler's approval. They beat one by a afternoon and they beat another tonight. And neither of those was Butler's first choice, or even his fourth or fifth honor.

All the work the delegates and workers have been trying to find somebody to take the Vice Presidential nomination. Borah refused, Kenyon was cold, Lowden refused; when the convention finally started balloting for Vice President it took the second session of the day Mr. Butler had been forced to recognize that though Judge Kenyon had been placed in nomination he stood small chance of being selected as the candidate of the party; in this situation Mr. Butler was forced reluctantly to give such support as he could to Representative Theodore E. Burton, Temporary Chairman of the convention, who is a Clevelander, and has, beside the support of Ohio, that of most of the leaders in the Eastern industrial States.

But the convention had a mind of its own and power to take action of its own—when the Presidency had been placed in nomination at the afternoon session, General Dawes, the former Lowden. He had repeatedly refused to let himself be considered for a place on the ticket; his nomination, when the ballot began to show that he wouldn't take it; but he was nominated again and on the second ballot he was put for Burton, the being necessary for a choice; but there was a rush of States to change their votes before another roll call, and J. York and Pennsylvania put Lowden over.

Lowden's Earnest Caucus a Secret.

Then it was learned that Lowden, foreseeing something of the sort, had given to friends at the convention a sealed letter, to be read in case he was nominated, absolutely refusing to be a candidate. This letter was read and William M. Butler began to chase up. Maybe he had a chance to put over a Vice President after all. By this time

DAWES PROMPTLY ACCEPTS NOMINATION

Issues Statement at Old Home in Marietta, Saying He Is "Very Grateful."

COOLIDGE CONGRATULATES

Promptly Sends Message to Running Mate—Lowden Pleased With Choice.

MARIETTA, Ohio, June 12 (Associated Press).—Brig. Gen. Charles G. Dawes, who is at the home of his sister, Mrs. A. Beach, here, said tonight:

"I accept the nomination by the Republican Party for the Vice Presidency. I deeply appreciate the honor conferred."

When the Republican Convention was taking the roll-call on the Vice Presidency, Brig. Gen. Dawes was "listening in" surrounded by two brothers with their families and friends.

When The Associated Press notified him of his nomination, General Dawes was already aware of it.

"Charley," said his brother, Henry M. Dawes, Controller of the Currency. "It's up to you again."

General Dawes came to Marietta, his native town, on Monday to attend the fortieth annual reunion of his class in Marietta College, where he was graduated in 1884.

With him tonight also was another brother, Beeman G. Dawes of Columbus. General Dawes will leave tomorrow afternoon for Chicago.

The nomination came as a surprise to General Dawes and his relatives. They knew that he had been mentioned in connection with the office but had no idea that he would be named as President Coolidge's running mate.

He will not receive the telegram of congratulation sent by President Coolidge, Governor Lowden and others tonight, as the telegraph office here closes early in the evening.

Coolidge Congratulates Dawes.

WASHINGTON, June 12.—President Coolidge sent this telegram to General Dawes late this evening:

"It will be a pleasure to be associated with you in the public service. Best wishes to you and Mrs. Dawes, in which Mrs. Coolidge joins.

"CALVIN COOLIDGE."

President wrote also in longhand and sent it by Edward B. Clark, his personal secretary, from the night part of the White House, where he had been listening in by radio, to the telegraph room of the Executive office, to be sent immediately to General Dawes.

Herbert Hoover sent the following telegram to General Dawes:

Charles G. Dawes, Chicago, Ill.

"I am more than happy at your selection and the assurance of your being again drafted to public service. The country is to be congratulated.

"HERBERT HOOVER."

Lowden Much Pleased.

OREGON, Ill., June 12 (Associated Press).—Frank O. Lowden, former Governor of Illinois, who tonight was notified by telegraph that he had been nominated for Vice President and who declined to serve, said tonight that he was much pleased with the selection of General Dawes.

Continued on Page Five.

20

"All the News That's Fit to Print."

The New York Times.

THE WEATHER
Showers today; tomorrow, fair and slightly cooler; westerly winds.
Temperature yesterday—Max. 82, min. 68.
For weather report see Page 2.

VOL. LXXIII....No. 24,274. • • • NEW YORK, THURSDAY, JULY 10, 1924. TWO CENTS

DEMOCRATS NOMINATE DAVIS AND C. W. BRYAN; FORMER, ACCLAIMED, CALLS PARTY TO BATTLE; SMITH PROMISES TO WORK HARD FOR THE TICKET

DEMOCRATS FILL THEIR TICKET

Choose Davis and Bryan After Another Day of Balloting.

CHOICE OF DAVIS UNANIMOUS

Convention Adopts Taggart Motion With a Shout While a Stampede Is On.

HE HAD MADE STEADY GAINS

Beginning the Day With 203½ Votes, He Advanced as Meredith and Others Slumped.

By RICHARD V. OULAHAN

Rising superior to the intra-party differences that have marked its session in New York, the Democratic National Convention yesterday, with impressive unanimity, ended its deadlock by choosing John W. Davis of West Virginia as its candidate for President.

At 2:30 o'clock this morning, in a session that was begun at 9:30 o'clock last night, while shouts of protest came from many delegates, the convention followed this action by choosing Governor Charles W. Bryan of Nebraska as its candidate for Vice President. With that done the convention at 2:35 o'clock adjourned sine die, thus ending one of the longest and most momentous national party gatherings ever held in America.

(remainder of column continued)

DAVIS IS PUT OVER IN WILD STAMPEDE

Weary Delegates Jump for Band Wagon and Then All Join Big Demonstration.

IT IS WEST VIRGINIA'S DAY

Convention Pays Tribute to the Men and the State That Gave It the New Leader.

By ELMER DAVIS

The Democrats have finally nominated and gone home. John W. Davis was selected as the Presidential candidate yesterday afternoon, on the 103d ballot. At 2:25 o'clock this morning Governor Charles W. Bryan of Nebraska was nominated as Vice President.

(remainder of column continued)

WIFE FIRST TO TELL DAVIS HE HAD WON

Nominee Was Having a Quiet Smoke While She Listened In on the Radio

AT HOME OF FRANK L. POLK

Reporters, Camera Men and Personal Callers Soon Brought an End to His Solitude.

John W. Davis sat alone, smoking, in the reception room of the home of his close friend and legal associate, Frank L. Polk, at 6 East Sixty-eighth Street, when he received the news of his nomination for the Presidency yesterday afternoon. It was carried to him by Mrs. Davis, who, with Mrs. Polk, had been listening in on the radio.

(remainder of column continued)

JOHN WILLIAM DAVIS
OF WEST VIRGINIA,
Democratic Candidate for President.

"There Can Be No Compromise With Reaction," Says Davis in First Statement After Nomination

John W. Davis, the Democratic Presidential nominee, gave out the following statement last night:

The history of national conventions may be searched in vain for one which has excelled this in freedom or frankness of discussion, or whose actions have been more clearly the result of the unfettered wishes of the assembled delegates. The resolution and endurance they have exhibited is but proof of their sense of the solemn responsibilities to the country under which they act and act of the supreme vitality of democracy.

I cannot but feel deeply sensible of the honor done by the convention and am even more conscious of the weighty obligations that have fallen to me by its deliberate and unanimous choice.

(remainder of statement continued)

DAVIS GETS BY WIRE CONGRATULATIONS OF SMITH AND McADOO

Governor Announces That He Will Aid in Campaign if the Nominee Desires.

McADOO IS GOING ABROAD

With Family, He Will Spend Several Weeks in Europe—Discord Among His Workers.

LEADERS ACCLAIM CHOICE OF DAVIS; SEE PARTY UNITED

"Shows Democrats Have Feet on the Ground," Says Former Governor Cox.

DANIELS PAYS TRIBUTE

Brennan of Illinois and Moore of Ohio See Breaches Healed —Bryan Pledges Support.

CHARLES W. BRYAN
OF NEBRASKA
Democratic Candidate for Vice President.

Davis and Smith Are Cheered In Speeches at the Night Session

Presidential Candidate Appeals for Party Harmony and Gives Creed as Honesty in Government—Governor Pledges Full Support to Ticket.

John W. Davis, the Democratic candidate for President, and Governor Alfred E. Smith addressed the Democratic National Committee last night.

BRYAN PICKED BY LEADERS

Daniels Suggests Him When Group Confers With John W. Davis.

ALL FACTIONS AGREEABLE

Head of Ticket Accepts Choice of Bryan's Brother as Running Mate.

SETTLED ON FIRST BALLOT

After 24 Candidates Are Voted On Host of States Swing Over to Bryan.

Governor Charles W. Bryan of Nebraska, brother of William J. Bryan, was nominated for Vice President on the first ballot, with a vote of 738, after a sweeping number of changes were recorded from the original vote of the States. The announcement of his nomination came at 2:30 A.M.

"All the News That's Fit to Print."

The New York Times.

EXTRA
5 A.M.
THE WEATHER—Fair today.

VOL. LXXIV....No. 24,392. •••• NEW YORK, WEDNESDAY, NOVEMBER 5, 1924. TWO CENTS in Greater New York | THREE CENTS Within 200 Miles | FOUR CENTS Elsewhere

COOLIDGE WINS, 357 TO DAVIS'S 136; LA FOLLETTE CARRIES WISCONSIN; SMITH BEATS ROOSEVELT BY 140,000

CITY ELECTS SMITH

Big Manhattan and Bronx Vote Wins for Governor.

UP-STATE STRONGLY G. O. P.

Roosevelt Carries Buffalo and Several Large Industrial Centres.

BROOKLYN GOES TO SMITH

Kings County Gives Him 152,000 Plurality, Although Coolidge Carries It by 80,000.

LEGISLATURE REPUBLICAN

Democrats Lose Control of Senate and Their Numbers in Assembly Are Reduced.

SOME OFFICES IN DOUBT

Whole Smith Ticket May Not Be Elected—Vote for the Socialist Nominee, Thomas, Is Small.

MRS. FERGUSON WINS 2 TO 1 IN TEXAS RACE FOR GOVERNORSHIP

Incomplete Returns Indicate That She Will Have a Majority of 225,000 Over Republican.

RUNS BEHIND IN CITIES

But the Big Majorities in the Rural Districts Carry Her to Victory.

LARGE KLAN VOTE IS CAST

COOLIDGE AND SMITH CARRY THIS CITY

The President's Plurality About 130,000 and the Governor's About 500,000.

LA FOLLETTE VOTE 250,000

Coolidge Wins in Every Borough —Democrats Elect All Local Officers.

United States Senators Elected

REPUBLICANS—18.

Colorado............*L. C. Phipps
Colorado............†Rice W. Means
Delaware............*T. C. du Pont
Idaho...............*William E. Borah
Illinois............C. S. Deneen
Kansas..............*Arthur Capper
Kentucky............F. M. Sackett
Massachusetts.......*T. H. Gillett
Michigan............‡James Couzens
Nebraska............*G. W. Norris
New Hampshire.......*H. W. Keyes
New Jersey..........*W. E. Edge
Oklahoma............*W. B. Pine
Oregon..............*C. L. McNary
Rhode Island........J. H. Metcalf
South Dakota........W. H. McMaster
West Virginia.......Guy D. Goff
Wyoming.............*F. E. Warren

DEMOCRATS—10.

Alabama.............*J. T. Heflin
Arizona.............*H. F. Ashurst
Georgia.............*W. J. Harris
Louisiana...........*J. E. Ransdell
Mississippi.........*Pat Harrison
North Carolina......*F. M. Simmons
South Carolina......C. L. Blease
Tennessee...........L. D. Tyson
Texas...............*M. Sheppard
Virginia............*Carter Glass

Result in Iowa, Minnesota, Montana and New Mexico in doubt.

*Re-elected.
†Elected for short term to fill vacancy in present term.
‡Elected for both short and long terms.

LEGISLATURE AGAIN SOLIDLY REPUBLICAN

Party Recovers Control of the Senate, With a Probable Majority of Four.

STRONGER IN THE ASSEMBLY

J. A. McGinnies of Chautauqua Is Slated for Speaker— One Woman Elected.

COOLIDGE AND EDGE WINNERS IN JERSEY

Record Vote Gives President Plurality Which Is Estimated at 350,000.

MRS. NORTON IS ELECTED

First Woman in Congress From the East—Tunnel Bond Issue Adopted.

THIRD PARTY POLLS 4,000,000 VOTES IN WHOLE COUNTRY

Showing in Electoral College Far Behind Strength in Popular Support:

CARRIED ONLY WISCONSIN

Mid-West Deserted the Senator but Industrial Districts in Cities Helped Him.

COLLAPSE IN CALIFORNIA

But the Senator Ran Second in That State, the Dakotas, Minnesota, Montana and Nevada.

Electoral Vote

COOLIDGE.

California	13
Colorado	6
Connecticut	7
Delaware	3
Idaho	4
Illinois	29
Indiana	15
Iowa	13
Kansas	10
Kentucky	13
Maine	6
Maryland	8
Massachusetts	18
Michigan	15
Missouri	18
Nebraska	8
New Hampshire	4
New Jersey	14
New York	45
North Dakota	5
Ohio	24
Oregon	5
Pennsylvania	38
Rhode Island	5
South Dakota	5
Vermont	4
Utah	4
Washington	7
West Virginia	8
Wyoming	3
Total	**357**

DAVIS.

Alabama	12
Arkansas	9
Florida	6
Georgia	14
Louisiana	10
Mississippi	10
North Carolina	12
Oklahoma	10
South Carolina	9
Tennessee	12
Texas	20
Virginia	12
Total	**136**

LA FOLLETTE.

Wisconsin	13
Total	**13**

DOUBTFUL.

Arizona	3
Minnesota	12
Montana	4
Nevada	3
New Mexico	3
Total	**25**

Total Number of Votes in Electoral College, 531; necessary to a choice, 266.

NEW YORK BY 900,000

Coolidge's Plurality in This State Little Below Harding's

DAVIS GETS THE SOUTH ONLY

La Follette Apparently Only His Own State, but Large Industrial Vote

CALIFORNIA FOR COOLIDGE

Doubtful States of the Far West Lean to the President as Returns Increase.

DAVIS LOSES WEST VIRGINIA

Refused at Late Hour to Concede Defeat and Hoped for Upset From the West.

BRYAN'S STATE TO COOLIDGE

Plurality of 50,000 in Nebraska for the President Indicated in Latest Dispatches.

REPUBLICANS MAKE GAINS IN CONGRESS

Retain Control of Senate and May Increase House Majority to 50.

BROOKHART LIKELY TO LOSE

Stanley of Kentucky and Walsh of Massachusetts, Democratic Senators, Apparently Beaten.

La Follette Wins Koenig's Home District; Coolidge Captures Davis's and Olvany's

State Pluralities Rolled Up by Coolidge.

The New York Times.

THE WEATHER
Partly cloudy, much colder today; fair tomorrow, continued cold. Temperature yesterday—Max. 41, min. 41.
☞The weather report see Section 10, Page 2.

Section 1

VOL. LXXIV....No. 24,431. •••• NEW YORK, SUNDAY, DECEMBER 14, 1924. FIVE CENTS

SAMUEL GOMPERS DIES IN SAN ANTONIO, BLESSING 'OUR GREAT INSTITUTIONS,' NATION MOURNS THE GREAT LABOR CHIEF

END COMES ON HOME SOIL

His Last Wish Granted, He Cheers Sorrowing Labor Colleagues.

STATE HONORS ARE OFFERED

Funeral Train, With Body in Bronze Casket, Starts for Washington and New York.

FUNERAL HERE THURSDAY

Body Will Lie in State in Two Cities—Burial at Sleepy Hollow.

SAN ANTONIO, Texas, Dec. 13 (Associated Press).—Samuel Gompers, for more than forty years President and active leader of the American Federation of Labor, died here this morning after a futile but gallant fight against the weaknesses that came with age and general disorders, from which he had suffered for many months. Mr. Gompers was 74 years old. He died upon American soil, realizing his last hope.

Since Saturday a week ago, when the fatal illness came upon him in Mexico City, where he had gone to attend the convocation of the Pan-American Federation of Labor, Mr. Gompers's life was all but despaired of by labor leaders and friends who had accompanied him on the last trip of his career. Fighting death valiantly, but with greatly weakened heart, due to the rigors of the Mexican trip and the higher altitudes there, he was placed aboard a special train and rushed to the United States, arriving in San Antonio last night.

THE LATE SAMUEL GOMPERS,
President of the American Federation of Labor.

DUNCAN IS LIKELY TO SUCCEED GOMPERS

Vice President of Federation Will Probably Be Named for Office Thursday.

COMMITTEE TO MEET THEM

New Executive's Term Will Hardly Extend Beyond Next October's Convention.

A successor to Samuel Gompers as President of the American Federation of Labor will be chosen at a meeting of the Executive Council, probably next Thursday in New York, following the funeral.

WOULD BAN BRINDELL 100 MILES FROM CITY

Untermyer Proposes a Geographical Limit on Labor Leader After Release.

WANTS HIM OUT OF UNIONS

Lawyer Renews Attack on Parole Board and Suggests Restrictions on Freedom.

Special to The New York Times.

OSSINING, Dec. 13.—Samuel Untermyer, who convicted wealthy Robert P. Brindell, grafting labor leader, wrote to the State Board of Parole today condemning its methods and suggesting how Brindell be curbed when he is let out of prison on Dec. 26.

Sharp Border Patrol and Bad Weather Cuts Christmas Supply of Canadian Liquor Here

OGDENSBURG, N. Y., Dec. 13 (Associated Press).—The word has gone out from points along the northern boundary of the State that down-State residents and those living in metropolitan New York will have to content with a limited amount of holiday liquor from the Northland this year.

Ralston Urges Democrats to Get Together; Asserts Party Will Live Despite Leaders

CHICAGO, Dec. 13 (Associated Press).—Senator Samuel M. Ralston of Indiana, who withdrew his name from the Democratic National Convention in New York last July when he appeared far in the lead for the Presidential nomination, in a public statement made here today, called upon Democrats to "pull themselves together, marshal their forces" and carry on.

$110,000,000 A YEAR TO KEEP NAVY RATIO URGED BY WILBUR

That Amount Is Needed for New Ships Annually for Twenty Years, He Says.

COMMITTEE DENIES ALARM

Says Our Prestige Is Not Waning—Reports Out Supply Bill of $290,485,578.

Special to The New York Times.

WASHINGTON, Dec. 13.—America should spend $110,000,000 annually for the next twenty years on new construction for the navy, if its fleets are to be maintained on an equality with Great Britain in all its branches, and superior to Japan's, thus carrying out the 5-5-3 ratio, Secretary Wilbur testified recently before the House Subcommittee on Naval Appropriations.

NATION'S DRYS SEEK TO COMPEL FEDERAL INQUIRY IN JERSEY

Attorney General Stone Has Been Asked to Detail Special Bootleg Investigator.

POLITICS ENTER SITUATION

Leaders Fear That "Rum Bottle May Replace Teapot as Emblem of Graft."

All the influence that the organized prohibition forces of the country can muster will be brought to bear on Attorney General Stone, it was learned yesterday, to induce him to send a special Assistant Attorney General to New Jersey to assume charge of the investigation and prosecution of the bootleg disclosures.

CANADIAN COURT ORDERS H.S. OSLER TO TELL INVESTIGATORS FROM THIS GOVERNMENT OF FALL'S CONNECTION WITH SINCLAIR DEAL

EX-SEC. ALBERT B. FALL.   HARRY SINCLAIR.

J. E. O'NEIL.   H. M. BLACKMER.

PRINCIPAL FIGURES IN THE GOVERNMENT'S ATTEMPT IN CANADA TO TRACE SINCLAIR PAYMENT IN LIBERTY BONDS TO ALBERT B. FALL.

DE FORD TO AID CITY IN TRANSIT INQUIRY

He Will Assist Edmund L. Mooney in Representing Transportation Board.

FIRST SESSION TOMORROW

No Indication Given as to Probable Procedure—Hylan to Start Subway Work on Heights.

MILLS URGES FUSION AT 'VICTORY' DINNER

Tells Republicans Hylanism Can Be Beaten Only by Aid of Independents.

SOUNDS PARTY RALLY CRY

Snell Says G. O. P. Here Must Mend Its Ways—Wadsworth Wants More Liberalism.

WITNESS IS NOW IN AFRICA

Formed a Trading Company for Sinclair and Paid Profits in Liberty Bonds.

$2,000,000 IN ONE DEAL

Judge Calls Company a "Fake" and Sweeps Away Objections to Testifying.

OTHER WITNESSES ABROAD

O'Neil and Blackmer in France—Teapot Dome Trial Off Awaiting Their Testimony.

Special to The New York Times.

TORONTO, Dec. 13.—Justice Riddell of the Supreme Court of Ontario handed down a sweeping decision today in connection with the Teapot Dome oil case in the United States.

"All the News That's Fit to Print."

The New York Times.

THE WEATHER

Fair and cooler today; tomorrow, fair; fresh northwest winds. Temperature yesterday—Max. 72; Min. 57. For weather report see Page 32.

VOL. LXXIV....No. 24,565.   ...   NEW YORK, MONDAY, APRIL 27, 1925.   TWO CENTS

REAL FIGHT ON HYLAN FOR RENOMINATION EXPECTED THIS WEEK

Smith Will Be in Town and Tammany Conferences May Settle Mayor's Fate.

SOME LEADERS FOR HIM

McCooey's Continued Silence Starts Reports That He May Withhold His Support.

SOMERS IS A POSSIBILITY

President of the Brooklyn Chamber of Commerce Added to List of Candidates.

The fight to prevent the renomination of Mayor Hylan by the Democratic Party of the city is expected to gain added impetus by the visit of Governor Smith here this week. The Governor will probably arrive here Tuesday night or Wednesday noon, and it was said that his visit might bring about a series of conferences in which something definite in the movement to shelve the Mayor might result.

Paris to New York Flight By French Plane Is Planned

PARIS, April 26.—There is being built secretly in Paris a large hydroplane with which it is hoped to fly without stopping 4,000 miles between Paris and New York.

This machine is being constructed on orders of the French navy according to its own plans. It will have a motor of 550 horsepower and will carry 6,000 liters of gasoline. The first trials will take place in June and the flight will be attempted during the Summer.

French aviation headquarters admit the machine is being made, but refuse to reveal any details beyond those given above.

COPPERHEAD BITES GIRL ON SNAKE HUNT

Venom Enters Veins, but First Aid and Serum Apparently Prevent Harm.

INCIDENT AMUSES VICTIM

Officer in Reptile Study Club, Miss Condon Keeps Serpents as Pets in Her Home.

1,909 MURDERS HERE IN LAST 7 YEARS, ARON REPORT SAYS

Republican Publicity Chairman Adds That Only 231 Slayers Have Been Convicted.

INCREASE OF 40 PER CENT.

There Were 333 Homicides Last Year Compared With 240 Reported in 1918.

POLICE ARE CRITICIZED

Statements of Hylan and Enright That Crimes of Violence Are Decreasing Are Denied.

VON HINDENBURG IS ELECTED PRESIDENT OF GERMANY; BEATS MARX, REPUBLICAN LEADER, BY 887,000 VOTES; TWO KILLED AND MANY INJURED IN RIOTING AT POLLS

WASHINGTON UNPERTURBED

General View Is That It Means No Sudden Shift in Berlin Policy.

OFFICIALS ARE SILENT

Question of Effect of Election on American Loans and Dawes Plan Is Discussed.

NO REACTION, SAYS LANSING

Borah Likewise Expresses Optimism—Swanson Is Not So Confident.

Hindenburg's Statement On Dawes Plan Fulfillment

Field Marshal von Hindenburg, President-elect of Germany, stated his views on the fulfillment of the Dawes program for Germany in an interview with the Associated Press correspondent at Hanover on April 9. Von Hindenburg said:

GERARD SEES DANGER FROM HINDENBURG

Ex-Envoy to Berlin Says Election Means Return to Monarchism and Militarism.

GERMANS HERE HOPEFUL

They Predict Unity and Peace —Blow to Red Influence and Treaty Protest Discerned.

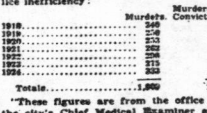

FIELD MARSHAL VON HINDENBURG
First German to Be Elected President by Popular Vote.

HINDENBURG IS IDOL OF GERMAN PEOPLE

Victory Over Russians Raised Him From Obscurity to Place of War Chief.

CALLED WOTAN AND THOR

He Insisted His Candidacy for Presidency Had No Partisan Character.

CLASHES REPORTED ALL OVER GERMANY

In Berlin Two Men Are Mortally Injured and Scores Hurt in Fighting Between Gangs.

TWO KILLED IN KARLSRUHE

Silesian Nationalists Besiege Police Headquarters After a Series of Encounters.

REPUBLICAN BLOC BEATEN

Marx Gets 13,752,000 Votes to 14,639,000 for Hindenburg.

30,000,000 BALLOTS CAST

Feverish Excitement Prevails as Early Returns Favor One, Then the Other Candidate.

WOMEN SUPPORT MARSHAL

They With Previous Stay-at-Homes Are Believed to Have Swung the Election.

Latest Official Election Totals.

BERLIN, April 27 (Associated Press).—The official provisional figures of the Presidential election follow:

Von Hindenburg	14,640,000
Marx	13,750,000
Thaelmann	1,931,001
Votes declared invalid	21,930
Total	**30,342,922**

Fleet Has "Seized" Hawaiian Flying Fields Umpires of the War Manoeuvres Decide

HONOLULU, April 26 (Associated Press).—The umpires in the naval manoeuvres here issued a communique at 2 o'clock this morning saying that the attacking "Blue" fleet had "seized" the flying field of the "Black," or defending forces, on the islands of Molokai, Lanai and Maui last night.

"All the News That's Fit to Print."

The New York Times.

THE WEATHER

Showers today and tomorrow; fresh south and southwest winds. Temperature yesterday—Max., 72; min., 62.

For weather report see page 22.

VOL. LXXIV....No. 24,651.   •••   NEW YORK, WEDNESDAY, JULY 22, 1925.   TWO CENTS

LONG STEP TO PEACE IS SEEN BY BRITAIN IN GERMANY'S REPLY

Chamberlain to Consider With Briand Chances of a Parley in August.

WANTS COMPACT PRESSED

Meanwhile the French Think There Are Traps in the Berlin Note.

GERMANS LOOKING TO US

They Want Americans Made Members of the Arbitration Tribunal.

By EDWIN L. JAMES.

Copyright, 1925, by The New York Times Company.
By Wireless to THE NEW YORK TIMES.

LONDON, July 21.—The British Government regards the German security note as a distinct step toward making the Rhine peace compact. While less favorable than London had hoped Dr. Stresemann's communication is seen as opening the way to early negotiations between the Allies and Germany.

Party Goes South on Yacht To See Dredging by Beebe

The Vanadis, the yacht of Harrison Williams, 60 Broadway, left New York early yesterday morning for Cape Hatteras, where William Beebe and the New York Zoological Society Expedition on the Arcturus are expected Friday afternoon.

ALL POLICE BELOW 14TH ST. JOIN HUNT FOR A MISSING BOY

Comb East Side Tenements Aided by Forty Detectives for Robert Peries.

ABANDON DROWNING THEORY

Marine Division Fails to Find Clue in River—Lad Seen by Man at 5 P. M. on Sunday.

LITTLE GIRL ALSO SAW HIM

Says She Played With Him but Can Tell No More—Sewers and Intakes to Be Searched Today.

Back M'Neil, Saver of 40 Lives, Gets First Honors on Tablet

"Buck" McNeil, the Battery Dock Master, who has saved more than forty persons from drowning off the sea wall at Battery Park, will be the first "Honor Man" to have his name engraved on a tablet to be placed in the office of Dock Commissioner Cosgrove, it was announced yesterday.

COAL STRIKE THREAT IS WIRED TO HOOVER

Miners' Official Warns of General Tie-Up Over West Virginia Wage Fight.

SEEKS ROCKEFELLER AID

Charges Assaults by Armed Guards—Anthracite Conferees Make Little Headway.

HYLAN REFUSES BAIT TO GO ON BENCH AND QUIT MAYOR'S RACE

Foes Realize Need for Keeping Him on Ticket to Block Third-Party Plan.

McCOOEY CALLS LEADERS

Brooklyn Chief Confers With Olvany, but Both Refuse to Tell What Was Said.

HEARST EMISSARY ACTIVE

Meeting of Borough Leaders on Mayoralty Situation Is Put Off Until Next Week.

SCOPES GUILTY, FINED $100, SCORES LAW; BENEDICTION ENDS TRIAL, APPEAL STARTS; DARROW ANSWERS NINE BRYAN QUESTIONS

Both Sides Speed Procedure for Scopes Appeal; Defense Cost $25,000, With Lawyers Serving Free

Special to The New York Times.

KNOXVILLE, Tenn., July 21.—With the conviction of John Thomas Scopes, attorneys for the defense at Dayton began at once to formulate their plans for the appeal. The case will come before the Supreme Court when that tribunal sits in Knoxville in September. Attorneys for both sides today agreed to expedite the appeal procedure in order to assure a hearing of the issues at that session.

Clarence Darrow, chief of the defense staff, is expected to argue the case before the Supreme Court here.

FINAL SCENES DRAMATIC

Defense Suddenly Decides to Make No Plea and Accept Conviction.

BRYAN IS DISAPPOINTED

Loses Chance to Examine Darrow and His Long-Prepared Speech Is Undelivered.

HIS EVIDENCE IS EXPUNGED

Differences Forgotten in the End as All Concerned Exchange Felicitations.

Special to The New York Times.

DAYTON, Tenn., July 21.—The trial of John Thomas Scopes for teaching evolution in Tennessee, which Clarence Darrow characterized today as "the first case of its kind since we stopped trying people for witchcraft," ended when Mr. Scopes was found guilty and fined $100, and his counsel will appeal to the Supreme Court of Tennessee for reversal of the verdict.

MOB CLUBS DEPUTY, FOE OF THE FASCISTI

Giovanni Amendola, Leader of Aventine Opposition, Is Attacked on Country Road.

BOOED OUT OF MONTECATINI

Assault Follows Siege of Hotel, Peace Truce and Flight From Town of Water Cures.

Copyright, 1925, by The New York Times Company.
By Wireless to THE NEW YORK TIMES.

ROME, July 21.—Deputy Giovanni Amendola, perhaps the most important leader of the Aventine opposition to the Fascist regime, was attacked and clubbed by unidentified persons presumed to have been Fascisti.

Search All London for Wisconsin Professor; He Had $3,000 and Family Suspects Foul Play

Copyright, 1925, by The New York Times Company.
Special Cable to THE NEW YORK TIMES.

LONDON, July 21.—Joseph Victor Collins, Professor of Mathematics at Wisconsin University and candidate in 1910 for the United States Senate, is missing in London and foul play is suspected by his wife and daughter.

G. G. HAVEN A SUICIDE, DUE TO ILL HEALTH

Banker and Opera Patron Shoots Himself After Vain Struggle to Recover.

FRIEND DISCOVERS BODY

Dr. E. Eliot Finds Him Dead in His Room While Wife Is Away Shopping.

George Griswold Haven, senior member of the banking firm of Strong, Sturgis & Co. of 11 Wall Street and President of the Metropolitan Opera and Real Estate Company, which controls the Metropolitan Opera House, committed suicide by shooting himself through the head with a revolver at his residence, 6 East Fifty-third Street, yesterday morning.

BONAPARTE GIVES PROPERTY TO WIFE

Great-Grandnephew of the Emperor Signs Away All but $5,000 a Year.

AGREEMENT ENDS HER SUIT

Referee Files Report and Recommends That Leon Jacobs, Lawyer, Get $5,000 Fee.

Girl, Saved by Dog, Shoots Her Assailant; Negro Again Shot by Posse Before Capture

Special to The New York Times.

NEW BRUNSWICK, N. J., July 21.—Shot twice, once by Miss Barbara Long, who lives with her brother Nicholas on a farm near the Lincoln Highway a few miles from here, and a second time by one of a posse which pursued him through the fields after he is alleged to have attacked Miss Long, Jess Williams, a negro, was arrested today on a charge of atrocious assault.

"All the News That's Fit to Print."

The New York Times.

THE WEATHER
Cloudy and warmer, probably showers, today; tomorrow showers.
Temperature yesterday—Max.; 55; min., 43.
For weather report see Page 60.

VOL. LXXV....No. 24,943. •••• NEW YORK, MONDAY, MAY 10, 1926. TWO CENTS In Greater | THREE CENTS For 8 Cents

BYRD FLIES TO NORTH POLE AND BACK; ROUND TRIP FROM KINGS BAY IN 15 HRS. 51 MIN.; CIRCLES TOP OF THE WORLD SEVERAL TIMES

BALDWIN STRATEGY IS WINNING STRIKE FOR GOVERNMENT

Aggressive Action Keeps Vital Services Going as Unions Balk at "Trump Cards."

THOMAS'S TALK SIGNIFICANT

Both Sides Spend a Quiet Sunday, While London Sees Another Food Convoy.

FOOD PRICES KEPT DOWN

Only Rise Allowed Is for Milk— Incoming Cargoes Are Unloaded and Distributed.

By T. R. YBARRA.
Copyright, 1926, by The New York Times Company.
Special Cable to The New York Times.

LONDON, May 9.—The essence of strategy is robbing the enemy of his freedom of action. If that axiom be transferred from the domain of warfare to that of strikes it must be admitted tonight that so far the British Government, led by Premier Baldwin, has robbed leaders of Britain's great general strike of their freedom of action.

At the close of the sixth day of this gigantic industrial struggle it becomes increasingly apparent that even if the British Government has not won the game yet it has manifestly forced the play.

From the very outset of the great strike, at midnight last Monday, most of the aggressiveness recorded has been contributed by those seeking to crush the strike. Each day brings increased railway service. Each day shows a more efficient organization of the Government's emergency food distributing services. Each day has shown a bigger enrollment of volunteers in every branch of strike breaking. Each day has given more hesitation on the part of the strikers to play their trump cards.

They have not tried to smash the great food distribution organization of the Government. They have not called out the "second line of defense" and the "third line of defense." Will they: That is the question, asked in a constantly growing tone of skepticism by those who have lived through these first six days of one of the greatest industrial crises in the entire history of the world.

Thomas Adds to Skepticism.

Tonight this skepticism received decided impetus from J. H. Thomas, the noted labor leader, who has consistently against extremist measures in the fight to find a panacea for British labor grievances. Speaking at Hammersmith, a London suburb, Mr. Thomas made statements which, as befits a conservative trying to please the moderates without infuriating the extremists, partook largely of the nature of those "weasel words" which so infuriated the late Theodore Roosevelt in the heyday of his acrimonious political combats.

Nevertheless, stripping the speech of all its diplomatic "I don't want to displease anybody" quality, there are in it statements which clearly imply that the general strike is not past exactly as its instigators hoped and that, therefore, Moderates like Mr. Thomas are beginning to hope that the dawn of conciliation is approaching. The most striking statement in Thomas's speech is:

"If the people who talk about a fight to a finish carried it out in that sense the country would not be worth having at the end of it."

"I have never disguised and I do not disguise now that I have never been in favor of the principle of the general strike," said Mr. Thomas. "No one will disagree, however, that the fundamental principle of trade unionism is not only the right for men and women to organize, but the essential part of that legal right is collective bargaining. The workers have no right to say to the employers, 'You must negotiate under the threat of a strike, but it is equally right and just that the workers should not be asked to carry on negotiations under the threat of a lockout.'

"From the start I deliberately went to get peace. Let there be no mistake about that, and in spite of all that has been said I repeat that it is the duty of both sides to keep the door open.

Extols Workers' Solidarity.

"The response to the appeal of the Trades Union Congress has been the most wonderful, the most marvelous demonstration of solidarity the world has ever seen and has staggered your opponents.

"All attempts to raise the constitutional issue are not only wrong, but

Continued on Page Five.

WETS NOW DEMAND SENATORS SUMMON GARY, ROCKEFELLER

In Brief Filed Today With the Committee They Call for Noted Drys' Testimony.

AIM OF GIFTS CHALLENGED

End of Anti-Trust Prosecution Is Charged When 'Big Business' Allied With Prohibition.

WAYNE WHEELER ATTACKED

Subpoenas Are Urged for Counsel of Anti-Saloon League and the Congress Members in Its Pay.

Special to The New York Times.

WASHINGTON, May 9.—A demand that the Senate Judiciary Committee reopen its prohibition hearings and subpoena Wayne B. Wheeler, John D. Rockefeller Jr., Judge Elbert H. Gary and others and ask them to disclose the sources of the great sums expended by the Anti-Saloon League, is made in a brief which will be filed tomorrow by the wets.

Denouncing Mr. Wheeler for not "keeping his word" to appear as a witness at the recent hearings, the brief declares the anti-prohibitionists wish to question him about the $35,000,000 he has asserted was used by the drys in their fight for the Eighteenth Amendment.

The wets assert that Mr. Wheeler should be forced to tell about contributions by Mr. Rockefeller, Judge Gary and other captains of industry and also "as to the significance of the strange phenomenon that after the alliance of the Anti-Saloon League and big business to keep up a continuous ferment or smoke screen over prohibition, anti-trust prosecutions suddenly ceased."

Members of the House and Senate who have admitted that they are on the League's payroll should also be summoned, as well as Dr. Ernest H. Cherrington of the World League Against Alcohol, who like Mr. Wheeler, escaped cross-examination by Senator Reed, the wets insist.

Attack Centred on Reformers.

There is a review of the testimony given at the hearings, but it is upon Mr. Wheeler that the fire is centred.

Declaring that prohibition is costing the United States $500,000,000 annually in direct enforcement and loss of revenue, the wets contend that this is too heavy a price, "even to keep the unctuous Mr. Wheeler volubly enough in the open forum but silent as a clam when it comes to testifying under oath before this committee—in a lifetime job as a parasite upon misguided religious and industrial organizations, and as a super-Government in his own divine right."

Mrs. Ella Boole, President of the Women's Christian Temperance Union is severely criticized for refusing to reply to questions as to whether it would be better to sell mild alcoholic beverages in the open or to allow them to be made at home in the presence of children.

Dr. E. C. Dinwiddie, who described as a man who has earned his living for twenty-seven years as a professional reformer, is complimented at "the highest type of professional man."

Prohibition has brought in its wake increased drunkenness, secret drinking and a widespread use of the still in the home, the wets assert in the brief. Women and children are drinking today, there is an army of rum-runners and moonshiners, demoralized alcohol can be readily secured and prohibition has been an utter failure from a temperance standpoint, the brief adds.

The example of Canada, which sells liquor under Government regulation, is contrasted with conditions in the United States where the public morals has been broken, the modificationists assert.

Reopening of Hearing Unlikely.

In spite of the strenuous nature of the plea for a reopening of the hearings, the request of the wets probably will go unheeded. The Senate subcommittee is of 1 dry, Senator Reed of Missouri, being the only modification man upon it.

So ardent is the committee that there seems to be no chance that it will favorably report any of the bills which would authorize a modification of the

Continued on Page Twelve.

Only 147 Workless in Paris, Says French Labor Minister

TOURS, France, May 9 (AP.)—There are only 147 unemployed persons in Paris, whereas London before the strike there had 800,000 and Berlin 430,000, Minister of Labor Durafour said at a banquet inaugurating the Tours exposition week.

France's birth rate, the Minister asserted, hardly varied from 1913 figures of 192 births for each 10,000 of population, whereas German statistics for the same units of population were 283 in 1913 and 200 in 1926. England, he said, shows 226 in 1913 and 186 in 1926.

"We have done this by organizing against infant mortality," the Minister affirmed, "which, although 12 per cent. before the war, had fallen to 9 per cent. in 1925. Therefore we must not despair. Our percentages will shortly equal Germany's and surpass England's."

NO TRACE OF WARD; FAMILY IS ALARMED

Brother, Fearing Foul Play, Asks Police to Broadcast Alarm for Missing Man.

SEARCH ON IN THREE STATES

Trenton Police Suspect Ruse in Abandoning His Car—Race Tracks to Be Watched.

The police began a search for Walter S. Ward yesterday at the request of his brother, Ralph D. Ward, who reported his disappearance to the Missing Persons Bureau at Police Headquarters. Mr. Ward said that his brother, who was acquitted three years ago of the murder of Clarence M. Peters, had not been seen or heard from since last Wednesday, and that his family feared foul play.

Captain John Ayres, in command of the Missing Persons Bureau, broadcast a confidential alarm for Ward, with his description, among all the police stations in the metropolitan district. Detectives working on the case said last night that they had no clue to Ward's whereabouts, and had no idea whether he had been killed or had disappeared for some reason known only to himself.

No Clue in Abandoned Car.

Ward's automobile was found in Trenton, N. J., last Friday morning, with the windshield broken and a large stone on the front seat. There was neither anything in the car nor any witness to clear up the mysterious circumstances under which the machine had been abandoned.

Ralph Ward told Captain Ayres that at the time his brother disappeared he had been on a business trip to Baltimore on behalf of the Electruck Corporation of 532 West Forty-sixth Street, of which Walter S. Ward is President. Ralph Ward did not know, he said, whether his brother had reached Baltimore and was on his way back or was driving to Baltimore when the car

To reporters who called at his home, 1,009 Fifth Avenue, at Eighty-second Street, Ralph Ward said:

"Walter went to Baltimore early in the week, but came back to New York and was seen here on Wednesday. He went away again in his car and was to have returned home again on Thursday, but we have not seen him since Wednesday."

Thinks It Was Second Trip.

"Was he going to Baltimore on the second trip?"

"I believe so," replied his brother.

"On business?"

"Presumably."

"Have you any clue to what has become of him?"

"Absolutely none," said the brother. "We have no idea what has become of him or where he is."

"Do you think that violence is indicated?"

"Yes, that is the only possible explanation."

Ralph Ward said that the family intended to investigate to see whether Walter might have had an enemy who could have had a motive for attacking him.

At Walter Ward's home, 30 West Seventieth Street, it was said that the missing man's wife was too ill to see reporters. A physician was in attendance on her yesterday morning. Ralph Ward told the police and reporters that his sister-in-law had been "prostrated" by her husband's disappearance.

George S. Ward, former head of a bakery chain company, and father of Walter and Ralph Ward, has been in the South for some time but is expected back soon, it was said at the home of Walter Ward. The Ward family is said to have engaged private detectives to search for

Continued on Page Ten.

PEARY'S OBSERVATIONS ARE CONFIRMED

Flight Is Favored by Sunlight and the Absence of Fog; Sun Compass Functions Perfectly

LEAK DEVELOPS IN PLANE'S OIL SYSTEM NEAR POLE

But Byrd Insists on Going On, Overruling Pilot Bennett—Commander's Nose and Fingers Frozen in Zero Temperature

By WILLIAM BIRD.
The New York Times Correspondent With the Byrd Expedition.
Copyright, 1926, by The New York Times Company and The St. Louis Post-Dispatch.
By Wireless to THE NEW YORK TIMES.

KINGS BAY, Spitzbergen, May 9.—America's claim to the North Pole was cinched tonight when, after a flight of fifteen hours and fifty-one minutes, Commander Richard E. Byrd and Floyd Bennett, his pilot, returned to announce that they had flown to the Pole, circling it several times and verifying Admiral Peary's observations completely.

They were favored by continued sunlight, and there was never the slightest fog, enabling Commander Byrd to use his sun compass and bubble sextant and obtain the most accurate observations possible. There were three magnetic compasses in the plane, but all of them deviated eccentrically after reaching high latitudes. Bennett declared that when he was piloting the magnetic compasses were wholly useless and would swing almost a quarter turn, returning very slowly.

Take Turns in Piloting.

Without the sunlight, navigation would have been almost impossible. Bennett and Commander Byrd alternated in the piloting, Bennett refilling the gasoline containers while the Commander piloted and navigated.

Commander Byrd found that the Bumstead sun compass worked perfectly, even when held in the hand, so when he was in the pilot's seat he held the control stick in one hand while he got his direction from the sun compass held in the other.

When they were within sixty miles of the Pole the oil system of the right-hand motor began leaking badly and it seemed necessary to choose between proceeding with two motors or attempting a landing to make repairs.

Bennett For Landing, Byrd Refuses.

In the neighborhood of the Pole numerous stretches of smooth ice were visible and a landing was favored by Bennett, but Commander Byrd, remembering his difficulties in starting at Kings Bay, vetoed this proposal.

Both agreed, however, to continue the flight to the Pole even if they went on with only two motors. To their surprise, the right-hand motor continued to work effectively, despite the ruptured oil tank, and when the Fokker returned to Kings Bay all three motors were hitting perfectly.

Chantier's Men Embrace Fliers.

The Josephine Ford, after making three circles over Kings Bay, landed at the take-off runway and taxied to her original starting position.

Commander Byrd and Bennett hurried a mile and a half to the shore, where a motor boat rushed them to the Chantier. The crew aboard her went wild with joy, waving flags and their caps. Many of the crew completely broke down with emotion, and with tears streaming from their eyes embraced the fliers.

Commander Byrd's nose and several fingers were frozen while he was taking observations in zero temperature (Fahrenheit) above the North Pole, but treatment here speedily restored circulation, and the Commander is all right now.

At 8 o'clock this morning, Greenwich Time [11 P. M. Sunday, New York Daylight Saving Time], the Norwegian radio station at Stavanger reported that heavy static was interfering with further transmission of The New York Times dispatches from Spitzbergen. These dispatches will be published tomorrow. Commander Byrd's story will be told in New York exclusively in The New York Times.

First News of Byrd's Great Feat As It Reached The New York Times

Whole Population of Kings Bay, Including the Members of the Amundsen-Ellsworth Party, Out to Welcome the Aviator.

From Staff Correspondents of The New York Times.
Copyright, 1926, by The New York Times Co. and The St. Louis Post-Dispatch.
By Wireless to THE NEW YORK TIMES.

KINGS BAY, Spitzbergen, Sunday, May 9, 6 P. M. Greenwich Time (2 P. M. New York Time). — Lieut. Commander Richard E. Byrd, U. S. N., leader of the Byrd Polar Expedition, returned from his flight

to the North Pole in the airplane Josephine Ford at 4:20 this afternoon, Greenwich Time (12:20 P. M. New York Daylight Time). The Commander reached the North Pole. He started at

PEARY'S OBSERVATIONS ARE CONFIRMED

LIEUT. COMMANDER RICHARD E. BYRD, U. S. N.
The American Naval Aviator Who Flew Yesterday to the North Pole and Back.

BLYTHE

Coolidge Sends 'Heartiest Congratulations'; Glad That Flight Was Made by an American

Special to The New York Times.

WASHINGTON, May 9.—President Coolidge received the first details of Commander Byrd's successful flight to the Pole from a radio message sent by THE NEW YORK TIMES, which is cruising tonight in the lower Potomac River.

The message, sent by the Washington Bureau soon after 5 o'clock, furnished the President with all the details known at that time. In reply he radioed:

"Thanks for your message."

Later Mr. Coolidge sent by radio the following comment:

The President sends his heartiest congratulations to Commander Byrd on the report that he has flown to the North Pole. It is a matter of great satisfaction that this record has been made by an American.

The fact that the flight seems to have been accomplished without mishap demonstrates the high development of the art in this country. That it was made by a man trained in the American Navy is a great satisfaction.

CALVIN COOLIDGE.

It is well known that the President was very anxious that the flight should be made, and, although there had been some adverse criticism of the proposal, Mr. Coolidge gave his approval to the plans.

12:50 o'clock this morning, Greenwich Time (8:50 P. M. Saturday, New York Time), which is full daylight at this time of the year in the Arctic, so that his flying time on the flight to the Pole and back was fifteen and a half hours.

Some error in the wireless transmission of these figures is possible, according to later dispatches to THE TIMES, which state that the Commander's total flying time was 15 hours 51 minutes. This is 21 minutes longer than the elapsed time here indicated. It is, however, possible that the hour 4:20, recorded as marking the commander's return, was the moment at which the returning plane was sighted.

The Josephine Ford had as its pilot on the trip Floyd G. Bennett, the American pilot of the Byrd Expedition.

The two were welcomed on their return by Captain Roald Amundsen, Lincoln Ellsworth and the entire crew of the airship Norge, now awaiting their chance to fly over the North Pole from Spitzbergen to Alaska, and the entire Summer population of Kings Bay, all of whom had been asleep when the airplane took off fifteen hours previously.

BYRD FAMILY PROUD OF FLIER'S SUCCESS

Governor of Virginia Declares His Brother Never Would Give Up—Mother Rejoices.

Special to The New York Times.

RICHMOND, Va., May 9—Richmond received the first information of the successful polar flight of Lieut. Commander Richard Evelyn Byrd about 3 o'clock this afternoon, when a message saying the flier had "returned safely" was received by Governor Harry F. Byrd by telephone. The flier's mother, Mrs. Richard Evelyn Byrd, was at the executive mansion when the message was received.

"I am tremendously gratified," Governor Byrd said, "and proud to hear of my brother's success in reaching the Pole."

"Dick has always been so lucky all his life that he believes he will come through, even though ninety-nine of a hundred chances might be against him. I am proud of him. He has always been such an adventurous fellow, we are somewhat relieved, though proud, that he has made the flight. If he had not, and believed there was a ghost of a chance to do so, he would try again as soon as possible."

This one day of the year dedicated to mothers, the message flashed across the frozen miles, brought happiness and comfort to Virginia's "Gold mother," Mrs. Richard Evelyn Byrd.

"All the News That's Fit to Print."

The New York Times.

THE WEATHER
Fair today; tomorrow fair and warmer; fresh northwest winds.
Temperature yesterday—Max. 59; min. 47.

VOL. LXXV....No. 24,945.   •••••   NEW YORK, WEDNESDAY, MAY 12, 1926.   TWO CENTS New York | THREE CENTS | FOUR CENTS

THE NORGE FLIES OVER NORTH POLE AT 1 A.M.; REPORTS HER FEAT TO TIMES BY WIRELESS; GOING ON OVER ARCTIC WASTES TO ALASKA

EFFORTS FOR PEACE ACTIVE IN LONDON; BOTH SIDES SILENT

Baldwin Waits Until a Late Hour for an Important Message From the Unions.

EXPECTED THIS FORENOON

Strike Leaders in Session Most of Day and Night, With Mac-Donald Exploring Situation.

MORE MEN ARE CALLED OUT

Meanwhile the Government Reports Still Further Progress in Maintaining Services.

By T. R. IBARRA.
Copyright, 1926, by The New York Times Company
Special Cable to THE NEW YORK TIMES.

LONDON, Wednesday, May 12.—Though the Government and the strikers continued to face each other in full battle formation throughout yesterday, the eighth day of Britain's great general strike, the dove of peace was hovering somewhere in the immediate neighborhood. Up to a late hour last night, however, nobody had quite located the bird. Many insisted, nevertheless, that they had distinctly heard the soft whirring of its wings.

They stuck to their assertion despite the declaration in last night's British Worker, the strikers' official organ, that today more workers will join the great strike—the molders and shipyard workers, members of the Amalgamated Engineering Unions and the General Engineering Unions. The strikers' organ also said that instead of "dribbling back to work," according to the Government's statement, the workers are "standing like a rock and none are coming out."

There were also two statements in the official Government communiqué last night which did not partake of the generally rosy hue pervading the bulk of the official statements. One was: "There is as yet little sign of a general collapse of the strike." The other gave the admission that the Trades Union Council "is believed to be making efforts to call out certain trades still at work."

Peace Rumors Still Persist.

But these and other similar reports current during the eighth day of the strike could not down the rumors of imminent peace.

The General Council of the Trades Union Congress met last night at strike headquarters to "explore the position with a view to leaving no door shut that could be opened." The meeting was attended by Ramsay MacDonald and J. H. Thomas, who came from Parliament for the purpose. After the meeting had been in session for some time Mr. MacDonald and Mr. Thomas hastily returned to the Commons, their arrival giving rise to the hope they might have something to announce. They found, however, that the Commons had concluded its sitting.

They went back to the meeting, which lasted until 1:35 o'clock this morning. No announcement is made at its conclusion, but it is understood that there was a spirited discussion between Mr. MacDonald, Mr. Thomas and other members of the Parliamentary Labor Party who are moderate in their views and Ernest Bevin and other leaders of more extreme opinion.

One of those stated to have been active during the day in the interests of conciliation was Ramsay M. Donald. One of the most important actions of the men, in addition to visiting the strikers' executive and the General Council of the Trades Union Congress today, MacDonald sent the following message to The British Independent, a mimeographed makeshift newspaper run by university students:

"I welcome most heartily your efforts for conciliation. This dispute ought never to have happened, and had the problem in the dispute been handled with ordinary care and common sense there would have been neither a lockout nor a strike.

"On one thing I am sure—in the confident assurance. The general strike in support of the miners was never meant as and even now is not a strike against Parliament, the Constitution. For purely war propaganda purposes the Government says it is.

"Good-will and calm heads will in the end prevail. We are working literally night and day that that may be soon. It was certainly apparent during the day that something was going on beneath the surface, that it must have concluded the surface, that it was going on beneath the surface."

Continued on Page Five.

Continued on Page Five.

'Cop Evangelist' to Retire After 25 Years on Force

Detective Alfred Smith of the Missing Persons Bureau, known as the "cop evangelist," will retire from the force on June 1, after a service of twenty-five years. He will receive an annual pension of $1,250.

In the intervals of his work of seeking missing persons for the last fifteen years Smith had devoted much time to preaching the Gospel in Chinatown, on the Bowery and in the Eighth Avenue Gospel Mission at 290 Eighth Avenue. He will continue at the head of his Bible class under Miss Sarah Gray at the Gospel Mission.

Smith is 55 years old and lives at 82 East Eighty-seventh Street. His son, Robert, is employed in a Wall Street brokerage house and his daughter, Gertrude, is at college.

RAIL LABOR BILL PASSED BY SENATE

By 69 to 13 the Upper Branch Accepts the House Measure Without Amendment.

HARD FIGHT FOR CHANGES

Curtis Fails to Get Commerce Board Power Over Wages—Coolidge's Approval Expected.

Special to The New York Times.

WASHINGTON, May 11.—The bill to abolish the Railroad Labor Board and permit railways and their employes to settle disputes over wages and working conditions by mutual agreement, passed the Senate by a vote of 69 to 13 late this afternoon. As the Senate approved the bill in identically the same form it passed the House no conference will be necessary and the bill will become law when the President affixes his signature.

Before the Senate passed the bill it was stated at the White House that it was not an Administration measure. The President, it was said, was interested in it to the extent that he believed it would work well because a majority of the railroad managers and employes favored it. But it was also understood that he did not entirely approve the bill as passed, he having suggested that it be amended so as to protect the public interest.

The detailed vote follows:

FOR THE BILL—69.
Republicans—39.

Borah,
Butler,
Cameron,
Couzens,
Cummins,
Dale,
Deneen,
Edge,
Ernst,
Fess,
Fernald,
Gillett,
Goodling,
Harreld,

Howell,
Johnson,
Jones (Wash.)
LaFollette,
Lenroot,
McMaster,
McNary,
Means,
Metcalf,
Norris,
Nye,
Oddie,
Pepper,
Pine,

Robinson (Ind.)
Sackett,
Schall,
Shortridge,
Stanfield,
Smoot,
Stanfield,
Wadsworth,
Warren,
Watson,
Weller,
Willis.

Democrats—28.

Ashurst,
Blease,
Bratton,
Broussard,
Copeland,
Dill,
Edwards,
George,
Gerry,

Glass,
Harris,
Heflin,
Jones (N. M.)
Kendrick,
McKellar,
Mayfield,
Neely,
Overman,
Pittman,

Sheppard,
Simmons,
Stack,
Stephens,
Swanson,
Trammell,
Tyson,
Walsh,
Wheeler.

Farmer-Laborite—1.

Shipstead.

AGAINST THE BILL—13.
Republicans—9.

Bingham,
Curtis,
Hale,

Keyes,
McLean,
Moses,

Norbeck,
Phipps,
Reed.

Democrats—3.

Bayard,
Ransdell.

Underwood.

Robinson (Ark.)

Provisions of the Measure.

The bill, which was agreed upon last year by most of the railway executives and heads of the four brotherhoods, and which the President endorsed in principle in his message to Congress, provides:

1. That the railroads and employes shall establish adjustment boards to arrange disputes.

2. That the President shall appoint, with the consent of the Senate, a board of mediation of five persons, none of whom has a pecuniary interest on either side, to intervene when the adjustment boards fail.

3. That boards of arbitration shall be created when both parties consent to arbitration.

4. That when the above methods fail the Board of Mediation shall notify the President, who may appoint an emergency board to investigate and report to him within thirty days. For thirty days after the report has been made there shall be no change in the status quo.

Continued on Page Twelve.

Continued on Page Twelve.

FIRST MESSAGE EVER RECEIVED FROM THE NORTH POLE

By FREDRIK RAMM.
New York Times Correspondent Aboard the Norge.
Copyright, 1926, by The New York Times Company and The St. Louis Globe Democrat.
By Wireless to The New York Times.

NORTH POLE, Wednesday, May 12, 1 A. M. (on Board the Dirigible Airship Norge)--We reached the North Pole at 1 A. M. today, and lowered flags for Amundsen, Ellsworth, and Nobile.

LATER, 3.30 A. M.--Lowering the three flags, Norwegian, American and Italian, when the Norge was over the North Pole, was the greatest of all events of this flight. Riiser-Larsen's observations showed that we were over the Pole. The Norge descended and speed was reduced, when the flags were lowered over the wastes whose edges gleamed like gold in the pale sunlight, breaking through the fog which surrounded us.

Roald Amundsen first lowered the Norwegian flag. Then Ellsworth the Stars and Stripes; finally Nobile the Italian flag.

The airship's 1 A. M. time (Norwegian time), was 8 o'clock on Tuesday night, New York daylight time.

PROGRESS OF THE NORGE AND HER PROJECTED ROUTE ONWARD TO ALASKA

Here is shown the route covered, according to the last wireless reports from the Amundsen-Ellsworth-Nobile Norge, which sailed from Kings Bay, Spitzbergen, at 10 o'clock yesterday morning, Norwegian time (5 A. M. New York daylight time) to fly over the North Pole, and her probable course onward toward her ultimate destination, Nome, Alaska.
The hours given in the hollow squares on the map show the position of the Norge at the times stated. The figures are Norwegian time, which is five hours ahead of New York daylight time. The thick black line shows the course the airship has already covered; double line shows her probable future course to Nome. Dotted lines show the routes taken to the Pole by Lieut. Commander Peary in 1909 by dogsled, and by Lieut. Commander Byrd by airplane on Sunday last.

Norge Sails Straight Into the Golden Glow of the Morning Sun, A Silver Creature of the Air, Moving With Grace and Quiet Dignity

Kings Bay Cheers and Weeps as the Giant Dirigible Starts Down the Fjord Accompanied by Commander Byrd and Bennett in Their Polar Airplane, a Striking Contrast in Arctic Exploration—Colonel Nobile Says That the Wind Is His Only Concern—Expedition May Spend Sixty Hours on the Trip to Alaska

By RUSSELL D. OWEN.
Staff Correspondent of The New York Times.
Copyright, 1926, by The New York Times Company and The St. Louis Globe-Democrat.

KINGS BAY, Spitzbergen, May 11.—At 9 o'clock this morning, Greenwich time, or 5 A. M. New York time, the Norge, of the Amundsen-Ellsworth-Nobile expedition, started for Point Barrow, Alaska.

Straight into the morning sun, a tiny speck soon lost in the golden glow of the north, the dirigible disappeared on her journey across the Pole and into the unknown wilderness of the Arctic.

The giant airship, like a silver creature of the air, rose slowly and gracefully from the hands that held her and with her motors humming sailed swiftly down the fjord, following the path Commander Byrd had taken in his spurt to the Pole. She turned over across the bay and rose over Cape Mitre. Then her black silhouette was lost in the sun.

There was rush and swift action to Commander Byrd's departure and the tense hazard of his quick take-off, but the Norge's departure was tremendously impressive because of the ponderous grace and quiet dignity of the great ship, lifting her immense burden from the ground and sailing into the unknown like a liner of the air. There were power, endurance and swiftness all embodied in her action.

Cheers and Tears at Departure.

Those below the floating fabric raised their hats in the air or flung up their arms in farewell, some cheering and a few moved to tears by the tenseness of the moment which saw their comrades departing on the greatest Arctic feat attempted. The air voyagers will spend at least sixty hours in Arctic regions never seen by man and at the end face the greatest hazard, when they may be forced to land the dirigible without assistance from the ground, something never done before.

All the day before Kings Bay was in a fever of preparation, the men of the expedition assembling equipment, packing provisions and small things for comfort, and making sure that nothing was overlooked. Mechanics swarmed over the dirigible, grooming her as though she were a race horse. Every bolt, stay, control wire and girder was gone over carefully. The full tanks were minutely examined, all pipes were overhauled and all instruments tested.

The big motors raced as they received their final turnovers, the immense green curtain near the end of the hangar billowing out in the gale created by the propellers. The new motor was put in splendid condition. Commander Gottwaldt tinkered over the wireless, making sure that the batteries and all the connections were in good condition, for on his direction-finder much depends.

Crew Spurts at Tasks.

There was uncertainty all day as to the time of departure, but late at night it was announced that the start would

Continued on Page Two.

Continued on Page Two.

NORGE SAILS OVER VAST ICE DESERT

Start Made From Kings Bay at 9 A. M. Greenwich Time and Course Is Laid Due North

VOYAGERS SEE POLAR BEARS AND SEALS BELOW

Gentle Wind, Clear Skies and Temperature A Few Degrees Above Zero Accompany Fliers on First Reach to Pole

By FREDRIK RAMM.
New York Times Correspondent Aboard the Norge.
Copyright, 1926, by The New York Times Company and The St. Louis Globe-Democrat.
By Wireless to The New York Times.

ON BOARD THE DIRIGIBLE NORGE, KINGS BAY, Spitzbergen, May 11.—The airship Norge, carrying the Amundsen-Ellsworth-Nobile expedition on its flight across the Pole to Nome, Alaska, started today at 10 A. M. Norwegian Time (9 A. M. Greenwich Time, 5 A. M. New York Time).

Make 66 Miles an Hour at Start.

ON BOARD THE DIRIGIBLE NORGE, Flying Poleward, May 11, 11:40 A. M. Norwegian Time (10:40 A. M. Greenwich time, 6:40 New York Time).—We are north of Danes Island, 80 degrees latitude, 9 east longitude. The weather is bright, with the lightest breeze from the south-southwest. The temperature is minus 7 degrees centigrade (19 degrees above zero, Fahrenheit). Our altitude is 425 meters (1,394 feet) and our speed is 107 kilometers (66 miles) an hour. The edge of the ice pack is a few kilometers north of Danes Island. We have sighted seals on the ice. Our motors are running perfectly and we are not feeling cold.

[Later] We are now in latitude 81.12. Our speed is 100 kilometers [62 miles] an hour. The weather is bright with a light easterly breeze. The temperature is minus 10 degrees centigrade (14 degrees above zero, Fahrenheit) and our altitude is 530 meters (1,732 feet).

Espy Polar Bears on Ice.

ON BOARD THE DIRIGIBLE NORGE, Flying Poleward, May 11, 2 P. M., Norwegian Time (1 P. M. Greenwich Time, 9 A. M. New York Time).—We are now in latitude 82.30, longitude 9 east. Our altitude is 560 meters (1,836 feet). The temperature is minus 9 degrees centigrade (15.8 degrees above zero, Fahrenheit). The weather stays clear, with a light southeasterly breeze. The air pressure is 730.

In the sea some lanes are covered with new ice. All the time we have used the left and back motors. Lieutenant Riiser-Larsen has been navigating, assisted by Captain Gottwaldt. Ellsworth has been measuring the atmospheric electricity. Our better speed is due to our new altitude, where the conditions are more favorable.

We have now lost all sight of land and the ice changes the whole aspect. We see several great polar bears and can discern white fish in the small openings in the ice. One meteorological report from the Stavanger radio promises that fine weather will continue far on the other side of the Pole.

All of us are naturally in the highest spirits. We are now eating our first meal and discussing how to celebrate Ellsworth's forty-sixth birthday tomorrow.

View of the Ice Desert Most Beautiful.

ON BOARD THE DIRIGIBLE NORGE, Flying Poleward, May 11, 4:15 P. M. Norwegian Time (4:15 Greenwich Time, 12:15 New York Time).—We are now in 85 degrees north latitude 10 east longitude, and heading directly north at a speed of 87 kilometers and a height of 610 meters. A gentle wind is blowing and the weather is clear. The temperature is minus 12 degrees centigrade (9.8 degrees above zero Fahrenheit) and the barometer stands at 727 millimeters.

We have now flown over the ice a long time. Despite our great height we can clearly see how the ice is cracking and screwing.

The low temperature has as yet had no effect on us. The whole view of this desert of ice is indescribable and most beautiful.

All are well.

Speed North Under Clear Sky.

ON BOARD THE DIRIGIBLE NORGE, Flying Poleward, May 11, 6:30 P. M. Norwegian Time.—We are now in 86 degrees of latitude, 10 degrees east longitude. Our course is due north and our speed is 92 kilometers (57 miles) an hour. We are 570 meters above the ice. A light south-southwest breeze is blowing and the skies are entirely clear. The temperature is minus 12 degrees centigrade [9.8 degrees above zero Fahrenheit] and the barometer stands at 727 millimeters.

Weather reports, which are constantly being received, continue to be favorable. The left engine has been stopped and the right set going. All are well.

The Pole Four Hours Ahead.

ON BOARD THE DIRIGIBLE NORGE, Flying Poleward, May 11, 8:26 P. M. Norwegian Time.—We are now at 87 d

The New York Times.

THE WEATHER
Showers today and tonight, followed by clearing and cooler tomorrow.
Temperatures yesterday—Max. 70, min. 62.
For weather report see Page 44.

VOL. LXXVI....No. 25,080.   ....   NEW YORK, FRIDAY, SEPTEMBER 24, 1926.   TWO CENTS In Greater New York | THREE CENTS Within 200 Miles | FOUR CENTS Elsewhere in the U.S.

TUNNEY WINS CHAMPIONSHIP, BEATS DEMPSEY IN 10 ROUNDS; OUTFIGHTS RIVAL ALL THE WAY, DECISION NEVER IN DOUBT; 135,000 PAY MORE THAN $2,000,000 TO SEE BOUT IN THE RAIN

FLORIDA CONSCRIPTS ALL ITS UNEMPLOYED TO CLEAR WRECKAGE

Police, Militia and Legion Round Up Men in Streets and Set Them to Work.

CALL ISSUED FOR LABORERS

Miami Wants 25,000 Men and Hollywood and Fort Lauderdale 2,000 Each.

LOSS PUT AT $165,000,000

Known Dead Now 365, With 1,100 Injured, 500 Seriously—Fight on Disease Goes On.

By WARREN IRVIN.
Staff Correspondent of The New York Times.

MIAMI, Fla., Sept. 23.—Conscription of all unemployed persons to aid in clearing away wreckage and to speed the work of rehabilitating the Florida storm-swept area was adopted every where in that area today. Militia men and police, aided by several hundred members of the American Legion who have been specially deputized, patrolled all streets and avenues, apprehending all persons who could not show that they were employed and putting them immediately to work.

At the same time the city of Miami sent out a call for 25,000 laborers, and officials of Hollywood and Fort Lauderdale announced that they would employ 2,000 laborers in each city.

Mayor E. C. Romfh of Miami predicted this afternoon that within sixty days every trace of the storm's ravages will have been removed from Miami and the city will be as prosperous as ever.

Death Lists Called Inadequate.

Many here believe that the death list lacks scores of names of persons killed. A local newspaper man declared today that he made a check-up of bodies in the city and temporary morgues last Monday, at which time there were 175, but others were given, he said, to bury the dead as quickly as possible, and many bodies were buried or shipped North for burial without any record being kept of them.

Even now it is almost impossible to get definite information as to the number of dead. [text continues...]

Continued on Page Eleven.

North Carolinians Weave Homespun Suit for Walker

North Carolina mountaineers, reputed by novelists to be a hard-drinking and generally rough lot, are now sitting peacefully in their hillside homes spinning a new suit for Mayor Walker.

The addition to the Mayor's wardrobe will be made of gray homespun and will be presented to him by citizens of Asheville, who arrive on the "Land of the Sky" special train on Oct. 6 on a boosting tour.

The color will be gray—chosen by the Mayor himself.

When the delegation reaches the city it will go directly to the City Hall, where, with appropriate ceremony, the suit will be presented.

GENEVA CONFERENCE ADOPTS COURT PLAN

Right of Powers to Withdraw Approval of American Reservations Is Recommended.

NEW PROTOCOL NEXT STEP

United States Will Be Invited to Help Draft It—President's Action in Doubt

Copyright, 1926, by The New York Times Company.
By Wireless to The New York Times.

GENEVA, Sept. 23.—With a single modification, the conference of signatories of the statute of the Permanent Court of International Justice adopted unanimously the conclusions concerning the American reservations which were presented this morning by its committee. [text continues...]

Continued on Page Sixteen.

CROWD ARRIVES SMOOTHLY

Throngs Ushered Into Philadelphia Stadium Without Confusion.

MANY NOTABLES ATTEND

Governors of Six States and Mayor Walker Among Long List of Officials.

OVER 75,000 FROM HERE

Trains Alone Carry That Number and Others Make the Trip by Automobile.

Special to The New York Times.

PHILADELPHIA, Sept. 23.—One hundred and thirty-five thousand persons, the largest crowd which ever attended a sports event in America, let out a roar when the referee placed the heavyweight crown on the head of Gene Tunney, which must have made the old Liberty Bell at Independence Hall quiver once more. [text continues...]

AIRPLANE CARRIES TUNNEY TO SCENE

Challenger Is First to Make Way to Heavyweight Title Bout Through Air.

RISK DEPLORED BY MANY

Tunney, However, Is Calm Throughout—Calls Flying Least Trying on Nerves.

Special to The New York Times.

PHILADELPHIA, Sept. 23.—Not content with the prospect of facing Dempsey and destiny, Gene Tunney had to defy death, too. For the first time in the history of heavyweight championships, the challenger flew forth to the field of battle in an airplane. [text continues...]

Continued on Page Three.

Dempsey's Share $850,000;
Tunney to Receive $200,000

Special to The New York Times.

PHILADELPHIA, Sept. 23.—The receipts of the Dempsey-Tunney fight tonight were in excess of $2,000,000. On the basis of $2,000,000, the receipts were divided as follows:

Dempsey $850,000
Tunney $200,000
Federal Tax $200,000
State $100,000
Sesquicentennial $200,000
Preliminary fights $40,000
Tex Rickard, promoter $410,000

TUNNEY ALWAYS MASTER

Challenger Bewilders His Opponent With His Speed, Accuracy.

AGGRESSIVE IN ALL ROUNDS

Sends Rain of Whiplike Lefts Which Champion Cannot Avoid.

OUTCOME IS A SURPRISE

Dempsey Lacks All Evidence of His Old Aggressiveness—Victor Is Acclaimed.

By JAMES P. DAWSON.
Special to The New York Times.

RINGSIDE, SESQUICENTENNIAL STADIUM, Philadelphia, Sept. 23.—Gene Tunney is the new world's heavyweight champion. The ex-marine fought like a marine here tonight in the Sesquicentennial Stadium, when he carried off the decision over Jack Dempsey, once known as the Manassa Mauler and the ring's man-killer, in a ten-round bout which saw the first passing of a heavyweight championship title on a decision. [text continues...]

Continued on Page Two.

GENE TUNNEY, THE NEW CHAMPION
Times Wide World Photo.

Champion Tunney Praises the Loser; "I Have No Alibis," Asserts Dempsey

Special to The New York Times.

SESQUICENTENNIAL STADIUM, PHILADELPHIA, Sept. 23.—The following statements were made after the bout tonight:

By GENE TUNNEY.

Dempsey fought like the great champion that he was. He has the kick of a mule in his fists and the heart of a lion in his breast. I never fought a harder socker nor do I hope to meet one. Dempsey fought like a gentleman and never took an unfair advantage in the ring. Once or twice he may have hit me a little low, but always it was by accident. He never meant it.

"I'm sorry," he always said following anything close to a foul blow. When the gong rang at the end of the fight he threw his arms over my shoulder and said: "Great fight, Gene, you won." I don't care what they may say about him, he is certainly a man in the ring. The hardest blows I felt were two socks on the Adam's apple. That's why I'm so hoarse. I have no plans for the future, but am content. [text continues...]

By JACK DEMPSEY.

I have no alibis to offer. I lost to a good man, an American—a man who speaks the English language. I have no alibi.

Story of the Fight by Rounds

Special to The New York Times.

RINGSIDE, SESQUICENTENNIAL STADIUM, PHILADELPHIA, Sept. 23.—The round by round detail of the Tunney-Dempsey bout fought here tonight follows:

First Round.

Dempsey was attired in blue trunks and Tunney in purple. Dempsey looked rather thin as he stepped forward for a consultation.

As the round started Dempsey, with a scowl on his face, rushed out and drove Tunney to his own corner. [text continues...]

Second Round.

Dempsey rushed over to Tunney's corner, trying to get his man. Dempsey swung his right to the body, but Tunney got out of the way. [text continues...]

Third Round.

Dempsey came out slowly for the third and they met in the middle of the ring. [text continues...]

Fourth Round.

Dempsey came out with a terrific rush and with a wild right jaw. Tunney almost over the ropes. [text continues...]

Continued on Page Three.

VICTORY IS POPULAR ONE

Ex-Marine Gets Ovation as He Enters Ring—Crowd 'Boos' Foe.

BIGGEST IN SPORT HISTORY

Rickard's Luck Turns, However, and Distinguished Gathering Is Thoroughly Drenched.

DEMPSEY'S NOSE SUFFERS

Rebuilt for Movies, It Is Target of Challenger as He Piles Up Points for Victory.

By ELMER DAVIS.
Special to The New York Times.

RINGSIDE, SESQUICENTENNIAL STADIUM, PHILADELPHIA, Sept. 23.—While the rain poured down on the greatest crowd that ever saw a sporting event, Gene Tunney beat Jack Dempsey, and captured the world's heavyweight championship in a ten-round fight here tonight.

The champion, in the phrase of one of the ringside critics, lost his title by a synthetic nose. It was by steady punching away at the built-in beak which Dempsey acquired a couple of years ago that Tunney piled up a heavy lead on points in the early rounds. [text continues...]

Crowd Is With Tunney.

It was the first time in history that the heavyweight championship of the world has changed hands on points, but there was never the slightest doubt after the start that if there were a decision Tunney would get it. [text continues...]

"All the News That's Fit to Print."

The New York Times.

THE WEATHER

Mostly cloudy today; tomorrow fair, slightly rising temperature.

Temperature Yesterday—Max. 30; Min. 25.
☞For weather report see Page 23.

VOL. LXXVI....No. 25,262. ★★★★

NEW YORK, FRIDAY, MARCH 25, 1927.

TWO CENTS In Greater New York | THREE CENTS Within 200 Miles | FOUR CENTS Elsewhere in the U.S.

AMERICANS AND BRITISH KILLED IN ATTACKS AT NANKING;
WARSHIPS THEN SHELL CITY AND RESCUE SOME FOREIGNERS;
ALLIED COMMANDERS SERVE ULTIMATUM; ALL CHINA AFLAME

DEAF TO LAST APPEAL REPUBLICANS KILL SMITH POWER BILLS

He Promises Veto in Special Message Asking That Decision Be Left to People.

BAUMES FENCE BILL DIES

Pistol Measure is Saved After Defeat—Tammany Members Less Hostile.

CHARGES ROUSE ASSEMBLY

Host of Acts Are Passed as Noon Today is Set for Final Adjournment.

Special to The New York Times.

ALBANY, March 24.—In a final drive to clear their calendars preparatory to final adjournment at noon, the Senate and Assembly labored all day, disposing of approximately 250 bills, of which less than a dozen were defeated.

Among the notable measures that were passed was the constitutional amendment providing for the creation of the Executive budget system in the State, a Smith program proposal adopted in the Senate, and the Friedsam bill providing for State contributions aggregating $16,000,000 for the common schools throughout the State, with a little more than $10,000,000 of the total going to New York City, approved in the Assembly.

The Senate amended the Assembly resolution, which in its original form called for final adjournment on March 15 so as to provide for adjournment sine die at noon tomorrow. The resolution was sent back to the Assembly for approval of the amendment, but up to the time of adjournment this evening the lower house had not concurred. There is no doubt, however, that the curtain will fall over the 1927 session some time tomorrow.

Smith Power Bill Defeated.

Defeat in the Assembly of the Governor's Power Authority bill and his measure providing for a referendum on water power in the election this year and passage of the Republican Water Power bill by a party vote in the lower house, in concurrence with the Senate, which has already approved the bill, were other outstanding features of the day.

The action on the Governor's bill was taken despite an urgent appeal made by the Chief Executive in a special message that the Legislature pass the referendum bill and let the voters determine whether the State or private interests should develop the hydroelectric resources of the State. The Governor will veto the Republican power bill.

Disposal of Baumes anti-crime bills in the Assembly provoked a bitter and prolonged debate, which ended in a second defeat for the so-called "fence" bill, which would legalize testimony by a thief against receivers of goods he had stolen. Considerable progress was made on legislation of this series, however, eight measures being passed. One, the so-called "Pistol bill," was snatched from defeat after it once had been beaten.

Measures Passed by Both Houses.

Measures upon which favorable action was taken today and in which both houses have concurred include:

The constitutional amendment.

The executive budget constitutional amendment.

The constitutional amendment providing for an increase to $25,000 in the Governor's salary and increase for Lieutenant Governor and lawmakers. The tri-State Delaware River compact.

Bills Passed by Senate.

New York City Grade Crossing Elimination bill.

Mickey bill to discourage child marriages.

Westchester Charter.

Bill to license operators at milk-gathering stations.

Lease of Ward Island in part by New York City to be used for establishment of a sewage disposal plant.

Passed by the Assembly.

Friedsam bill appropriating $16,500,000 for additional State aid to public schools.

Republic water power bill providing for a commission to investigate and recommend a State development policy.

Measures Defeated.

Governor Smith's power authority and water power referendum bills.

The Baumes series bill to legalize testimony of thiefs against receivers of stolen goods.

Democratic resolution proposing an amendment to the Constitution which would permit the State to aid or cede the Barge Canal to the Federal Government.

Continued on Page Four.

ON AIR VANDERBILT, AUGUSTA, GA. Open all year round. Ideal Southern Resort. For reservations, Vanderbilt Hotel, N.Y.—Advt.

---

14 Big Atlantic Liners Race For Spring Tourist Rush Here

Copyright, 1927, by The New York Times Co.
By Wireless to The New York Times.

LONDON, March 24.—The pick of the great Atlantic liners are racing to catch the Spring tide of American tourists headed for Europe. Fourteen of the vessels operating between New York and English ports will be on the high seas almost at the same time during the next ten days.

The Majestic and the France sailed westward yesterday. The President Roosevelt and the Antonia will sail tomorrow. The Berengaria, Washington, Ascania, Cedric, Aurania and Minnewaska will sail on Saturday. Closely following will be the Leviathan, Homeric, Lancastria, New York and Mauretania.

SAPIRO CUTS OUT 54 OF ALLEGED LIBELS

Court Tentatively Accepts New Basis of Suit, Refusing Long Recess to Study It.

LAWYERS BATTLE OVER IT

Defense Suggests a Mistrial—Court Bars Questions on Ford Ordering Attacks on Jews.

From a Staff Correspondent of The New York Times.

DETROIT, March 24.—The Sapiro-Ford libel trial produced two cardinal developments today. The first was Aaron Sapiro's elimination of 54 of the 141 libels he had alleged against Henry Ford and the Dearborn Publishing Company. The second was the vain attempt of the plaintiff to show that Mr. Ford motivated an attack on Mr. Sapiro as part of a general onslaught aimed at his race.

The alleged libels which Mr. Sapiro took out voluntarily dealt with an editorial in The Dearborn Independent, published after the series containing the alleged libels, in which the Chicago attorney was accused of unprofessional conduct and pictured as a "cheat" and "fraud" and "grafter" and "faker" and "mountebank." Mr. Gallagher said Mr. Sapiro was not mentioned in the editorial and, further, it was not part of the series which he contends were anti-Jewish. Mr. Hanley contended by saying that the defense had been ready to prove the truth of the editorial, and that the concluding paragraph of the editorial had named Mr. Sapiro.

Mr. Hanley asked that the trial be adjourned to Monday so that he and his associates could readjust their lines of defense, if necessary. Mr. Gallagher opposed that. Judge Raymond observed that there had been little "visible progress" in the case, although many issues had been clarified which would result in progress later, settled the matter by adjourning from 10 A. M. to 2 P. M. He then said that he would accept the amended declaration tentatively.

The Court explained that he provisionally accepted the document so that the taking of testimony by William J. Cameron, editor of The Dearborn Independent, could go on. He gave notice to all of the declaration except one clause. He struck that out. This paragraph sought to establish that the periodical, by earlier attacks on Mr. Sapiro's coreligionists, had made the vast "Jew" as word of contumely, hate and opprobrium in the minds of The Independent's 600,000 readers.

Amended Basis Taken Up First.

The matter of amended basis of suit was the first order of the session when court convened at 2:30 A. M. Judge Raymond had indicated that he felt the document was insufficient in some of its counts, notably where single phrases, lifted from their context, had been cited as libels. Mr. Gallagher and his associates, Judge Robert F. Marx and Walter F. Lynch, had been reviewing it since the Judge indicated his opinion. As Mr. Gallagher handed in position.

Continued on Page Twenty-four.

POISONED WHISKY IN SNYDER HOME BARES EARLY PLOT

Scheme That Failed Revealed by Gray and Chemist Finds Bichloride of Mercury.

NO TRACE IN VICTIM'S BODY

Dr. Gettler Says 20 Tablets Must Have Been Used—To Seek Other Drugs Today.

TRIAL IS SET FOR APRIL 11

Newcombe Would Try Both at Once and Will Ask Death Penalty—Woman Protests Her Innocence.

To check up a statement made by Henry Judd Gray that Mrs. Ruth Brown Snyder had tried to poison her husband some time before the murder last Sunday morning, the police took a bottle of whisky from the Snyder cellarette yesterday to Dr. Alexander O. Gettler, city toxicologist, at Bellevue Hospital.

There were several bottles in the cellarette, but the chemist was asked to analyze only the one which had been described by Gray as containing the poison, said to be bichloride of mercury.

As soon as the Snyder whisky bottle was handed to him with this explanation, Dr. Gettler heated up a shining copper wire, dipped it in hydrochloric acid and thrust it in the whisky.

This is the ordinary quick test for bichloride of mercury. If it is present, the mercury deposits on the copper in the presence of hydrochloric acid in minute globules. Usually a microscope has to be used to detect the deposit.

After leaving the copper wire in the whisky for half an hour, Dr. Gettler removed it.

Wire Thickly Coated.

"Great Scott," he exclaimed. The copper wire seemed to be silverplated. There was no need of using the microscope, so thickly was the wire coated with quicksilver (mercury).

"Enough bichloride of mercury was put into that bottle of whisky to kill any man who took one good drink of it," said Dr. Gettler.

Four other copper wires were then heated and dipped into hydrochloric acid. One was inserted into the stomach contents of the murdered man. The others were placed in contact separately with grain, kidney and liver tissue.

After half an hour they were removed. Their appearance was still that of ordinary copper wire. Each wire was examined under the microscope. No globules of quicksilver were found.

"This shows that Snyder had not touched the poisoned whisky recently," said Dr. Gettler. "It has nothing to do with his death. It is possible that he might have tasted the liquor at some time in the past. Mercury, however, remains in the system for some time. We would find traces in the organs probably for two months if he had swallowed any of the whisky with mercury in it."

Dr. Gettler did not have an opportunity yesterday to measure the quickness with which the quantity of bichloride of mercury could have made it certain that a large quantity of bichloride of mercury had been used.

"Possibly twenty tablets or more were dissolved in it," said Dr. Gettler. It is probable that the poisoner or poisoners overshot the mark by putting so many mercury tablets in the whisky as to give it a noticeable taste. Whether he was suspicious of the flavor.

Continued on Page Nine.

Calls on Gov. Smith to Give His Views On Allegiance to His Church or State

A statement from Governor Alfred E. Smith setting forth his views regarding the jurisdiction of the Roman Catholic Church, of which he is a member, is asked by Charles C. Marshall, a lawyer of this city, in an open letter to the Governor published in the April number of The Atlantic Monthly. The Governor is asked to state what would be his views in case of possible conflict regarding jurisdiction between the Church and the American Government.

Saying that letters of various Popes made it clear that the Church holds that it has divine ecclesiastical power and that, while it concedes secular power to the State, it remains the judge in its own opinion as to what constitutes secular power. Mr. Marshall contends that the Roman Catholic view is that other churches and ethical associations have no fundamental rights, and asks whether or not Governor Smith concurs in this view.

Mr. Marshall mentions divorce and annulment of marriage, education and the Mexican situation as other matters on which differences of opinion from the Church and American viewpoint are likely, in his opinion, and cites the recent annulment of the Marlborough marriage as a case in point. Mr. Marshall also cites the ratification in 1569 of John Felton, an Englishman, who was convicted of treason in 1570. Felton's offense, three centuries and a half ago, was the posting on the walls of London of the decree of Pope Pius V deposing Queen Elizabeth.

"It honors paid him were rendered 300 years after his treasonable act," Mr. Marshall says, regarding the case of Felton, in his letter to the Governor. "There lies their similar import. They are no part of the medieval mind; but of the modern milieu; they belong to the modern world and must have judgment not by medieval but by modern standards.

"Is the record of the Roman Catholic Church in England, sir, in your opinion, consistent with the peace and safety of the State? Nothing will be of greater satisfaction to those of your fellow-citizens who hesitate to trust the Roman Catholic Church in all that affects their confidence, because of religious issues involved—than a disclaimer by you of the convictions here imputed or such an exposition by others of the questions here involved as may justly turn public opinion in your favor."

Continued on Page Twenty-four.

Soviet Warned on Propaganda Hurting Stage as Church Rival

MOSCOW, March 24 (P).—Mikhail Tomsky, Chairman of the All-Russian Council of Trade Unions, has warned the Soviet authorities that the theatre in Russian villages and towns will not keep the public there from the churches unless something more than propaganda is offered to entertain audiences.

"Performances in our playhouses must be artistic, esthetic creations, designed to appeal to the taste and pocketbooks of the workers," he declares. "They must be more than propaganda vehicles."

TONGMEN KILL NINE AS WAR FLARES ANEW

Two Chinese Slain in Brooklyn Restaurant While 250 Are Dining There.

KILLINGS OCCUR IN 6 CITIES

27 Bullets Fired Into Man at Newark—Banton Warns He Will Start Deportations.

Chinese tong warfare flared anew yesterday over the eastern part of the United States after a peace had been threatened between the On Leong Tong and the Hip Sing Tong, and last night nine Chinese had been killed and two wounded in six different cities.

In Chicago one man was killed early yesterday morning and three were wounded last night. Two of these died later. In Brooklyn two were killed early yesterday morning in a crowded restaurant. In Newark a Chinese from Boston was riddled with bullets in the early morning. Cleveland and Pittsburgh each had one murder during the early hours of the day and in Pittsburgh a second Chinese was wounded.

In New York's Chinatown there was an air of fear and mystery yesterday, and a most unusual number of uniformed patrolmen and detectives. There were more police than Chinese on the three streets of Chinatown. On the "bloody angle" at Doyers and Pell Streets a single uniformed policeman remained alone most of the day.

Tongmen Out of Sight.

The ornate building of the On Leong Tong on Mott Street was deserted and the leaders of that organization congregate elsewhere. The Hip Sings gathered at 15 Pell Street in a building a darkened laundry. The one dead-line between Pell and Mott Streets was again drawn, and few if any Chinese turned from one street into the other.

Two years ago, almost to the day, the two tongs signed a peace pact. It was hailed with relief by the police and with rejoicing by the Chinese. It was to last "for all time" it was said, though the skeptical who knew the nature of the two tongs and grave doubts. The success of one tong probably said before, but I wish to reiterate it now. We has been given from time to time all the forces he has requested.

According to the reports yesterday in Chinatown, the renewal of the warfare was started by the shooting in Chicago of Chin Pock, found shot to death in a gambling house in Chicago's Chinatown. Chin, the story goes, belonged to the On Leong Tong. A few months ago he resigned and joined the Hip Sings. Recently he reversed the process, going back to the On Leongs. The Hip Sings called him a spy and a traitor. He died in Tom Jack's Chinese gambling house Wednesday night, and by morning Hip Sings had been killed in Brooklyn, Newark and elsewhere, another On Leong man was dead in Pittsburgh and a large part of the Chinese suspicious and watchful of the other.

Continued on Page Three.

WASHINGTON ACTS QUICKLY

Orders More Cruisers to China and Gives Admiral Fullest Backing.

GRAVE MESSAGES RECEIVED

Nanking Incident and Unrest Elsewhere Taken Seriously by Officials.

NO LIGHT ON CASUALTIES

Admiral Hough Simply Reports Some Americans Were Slain on Socony Hill.

Special to The New York Times.

WASHINGTON, March 24.—News of the serious incident at Nanking reached Washington early today, that 155 Americans, consisting of 90 men, 45 women and 20 children, were ashore. The rescue party made up of American and British forces, who succeeded in removing most of the stranded.

Other messages from Nanking this morning, however, told of further rescue efforts, which resulted in the rescue and evacuation of all the remaining foreigners, only after further casualties, including some Americans. These messages reported that British and American landing parties approached Socony Hill under renewed fire from the Cantonese, but ultimately rescued all the foreigners.

Nevertheless reports received from Nanking at 5 A. M. said that the fate of 155 Americans was still unknown. There were some Britishers still ashore and the Anglo-American authorities were attempting to negotiate with the Cantonese to effect the rescue of the remaining foreigners without further bloodshed, such as occurred yesterday.

The Americans ashore at Nanking are those who failed to reach the Socony compound. It is believed that they remained at mission centres which are widely separated within Nanking walls. All who reached the Socony compound were believed to have been brought out.

Reports Conflict on Americans Left in Nanking; Shanghai Hears of Negotiations for Release

By The Associated Press.

SHANGHAI, Friday, March 25.—Conflicting messages early this morning from the City of Nanking, where a number of foreigners, including Americans, were killed and wounded by Cantonese shelling yesterday, left the fate of a portion of the American community there in doubt.

Prior to yesterday's shelling of Socony Hill, which resulted in counterfire by British and American warships, it was known that 155 Americans, consisting of 90 men, 45 women and 20 children, were ashore. Some of these remained, despite the landing of a rescue party made up of American and British forces, who succeeded in removing most of the stranded.

More British Troops at Shanghai And Foreign Defenses There Hold

American Marines, Used Only in Emergency, Chafe for More Active Part—Cantonese Split—Pledges to Restore Order Unfulfilled.

By FREDERICK MOORE

Copyright, 1927, by The New York Times Company.
Special Cable to The New York Times.

SHANGHAI, March 24.—Some Americans here are complaining of the inactivities of the American marines and have started a circular letter, to which foreigners other than the British are readily affixing their signatures, thanking the British for protecting their lives and properties.

Ever since their arrival the marines have been anxious to land and participate in the preparations for the defense, but have been restrained aboard their vessels and have not placed a single sandbag or a single rifle or barbed wire in position. Finally, when a state of emergency was declared, they came ashore as soon as possible, but six hours after the British and French were in position.

They were then permitted only patrol duty, not even police service. That is, they were not permitted to search for Chinese suspects and not permitted to break up menacing gatherings. Consequently they only paraded the streets in the safer interior sections of the city.

This was commented on as not being adequate defense of American lives and property and neither did their non-civilian Americans profess that it was.

Cantonese volunteer soldiers and policemen did not serve under American command. Both of these contingents gladly accepted dangerous orders from the British police chief and commanding officer.

Marines Anxious for Action.

The marines themselves are anxious for more active duty. They themselves point out that had the British not held the lines they would have been required to shoot down many Chinese, civilians as well as soldiers, inside the settlement and that foreigners, including Americans, would have been looted and burned out. They would have been unable to keep the slaughter to a minimum.

Yesterday the marines at the request of the British twice went into machine guns, into the defenses, immediately withdrawing them in each case after the emergency terminated. In neither case, nor at any other time, have they fired a shot.

I tell this only to contradict exaggerated reports that may have gone slowly. In the meantime sniping continues in Shanghai, a British armored car being hit. The Italians today returned the fire without apparent slaughter. The warships in the harbor have been hit several times.

Denies Handicapping Marines.

Special to The New York Times.

WASHINGTON, March 24.—Positive denial that American marines at Shanghai are in any way handicapped by orders from Washington was offered tonight from officials in authority when their attention was called to the reported complaint.

Continued on Page Two.

JOINT FORCES ARE LANDED

Parties From Ships Fight Way to Socony Hill to Reach Nationals.

CHINESE FIRE ON RESCUERS

Cantonese Sympathizers Attack Foreign Consuls, Drive Them Out and Loot Offices.

ANTI-FOREIGN SPIRIT GROWS

Our Consul General Appeals Again to Americans in Interior to Go to Shanghai.

By FREDERICK MOORE

Copyright, 1927, by The New York Times Company.
Special Cable to The New York Times.

SHANGHAI, March 24.—In view of the news from Nanking, Hankow, Wuhu and other Yangtze River and neighboring coast ports, all showing that the Nationalists' success at Nanking was to assault the British, American and Japanese Consuls, as well as other foreigners. Only a partial number of these escaped through the courageous dash of a joint British-American naval landing force. There were 45 women, 20 children and 90 men, totaling 155 Americans, left to an unknown fate, besides other foreigners, whose numbers are unobtainable.

No Word of New Attempt.

A series of brief naval wireless messages to the British, American and Japanese warships stationed here told the tale, but said nothing about attempting another effort to relieve the surrounded foreigners tomorrow.

The Nanking news has been daily becoming more serious. Pieced together the story is approximately as follows:

For several days the Northerners, with little fighting, have been falling back before the Nationalists. Nanking was to assault the British, because it is the crossing place to the railway leading back to Shantung. Without the customary warning to civilians, the Southerners, following them, shelled the city.

There were not enough vessels for the Shantungese to recross the river, and they were compelled to fight or surrender to possible decapitation. Consequently the city, inside and outside the walls, became a battleground. The Northerners pillaged at will, but did not attack the foreigners. The incoming Nationalists, however, did not hesitate to attack the consulates today. They wounded the British Consul, Giles, and drove American Consul Davis with his wife and his children from the American Consulate.

A small group of foreigners accompanied by a few American sailors who were protecting the consulates made to seek safety in the Standard Oil compound immediately inside the city walls, at a point a few miles from the river, but they were unable to escape.

Warships Open Fire.

Evidently the sailors signaled the American destroyers Noa and Preston and the British cruiser Emerald, which created a barrage of shells around the Standard Oil compound, to keep off the assailants, simultaneously landing a joint American and British force, which, it is believed, crossed lowland, creek and moat, finally getting the foreigners down over the city walls and retraversing the route. Altogether it was several miles back and forth to the destroyers.

I reported erroneously yesterday that the American destroyers had left for Shanghai with their 145 American refugee women and children.

Sheet Only in Last Extremity.

The marines have been fully instructed by the British, not to fire except in the last extremity. I, myself, standing behind a Durham battalion machine gunner in a sandbagged emplacement, witnessed the self-control of the British. An unofficered group of seven Northerners, with the machine gunner aimed, but held fire till the defeated Northerners were within twenty-five feet. The Shantungese

Section 1   "All the News That's Fit to Print."

The New York Times.

THE WEATHER   Section 1
Generally fair today and tomorrow; moderate to fresh northerly winds.
Temperature yesterday—Max., 95; Min., 52.
☞ For weather report see Page 21.

VOL. LXXVI....No. 25,320.   ••••   NEW YORK, SUNDAY, MAY 22, 1927.   FIVE CENTS

LINDBERGH DOES IT! TO PARIS IN 33½ HOURS;
FLIES 1,000 MILES THROUGH SNOW AND SLEET;
CHEERING FRENCH CARRY HIM OFF FIELD

COULD HAVE GONE 500 MILES FARTHER

Gasoline for at Least That Much More— Flew at Times From 10 Feet to 10,000 Feet Above Water.

ATE ONLY ONE AND A HALF OF HIS FIVE SANDWICHES

Fell Asleep at Times but Quickly Awoke—Glimpses of His Adventure in Brief Interview at the Embassy.

LINDBERGH'S OWN STORY TOMORROW.

Captain Charles A. Lindbergh was too exhausted after his arrival in Paris late last night to do more than indicate, as told below, his experiences during his flight. After he awakes today, he will narrate the full story of his remarkable exploit for readers of Monday's New York Times.

By CARLYLE MACDONALD.
Copyright, 1927, by The New York Times Company.
Special Cable to The New York Times.

PARIS, Sunday, May 22.—Captain Lindbergh was discovered at the American Embassy at 2:30 o'clock this morning. Attired in a pair of Ambassador Herrick's pajamas, he sat on the edge of a bed and talked of his flight. At the last moment Ambassador Herrick had canceled the plans of the reception committee and, by unanimous consent, took the flier to the embassy in the Place d'Iena.

A staff of American doctors who had arrived at Le Bourget Field early to minister to an "exhausted" aviator found instead a bright-eyed, smiling youth who refused to be examined.

"Oh, don't bother; I am all right," he said.

"I'd like to have a bath and a glass of milk. I would feel better," Lindbergh replied when the Ambassador asked him what he would like to have.

A bath was drawn immediately and in less than five minutes the youth had disrobed in one of the embassy guest rooms, taken his bath and was out again drinking a bottle of milk and eating a roll.

"No Use Worrying," He Tells Envoy.

"There is no use worrying about me, Mr. Ambassador," Lindbergh insisted when Mr. Herrick and members of the embassy staff wanted him to be examined by doctors and then go to bed immediately.

It was apparent that the young man was too full of his experiences to want sleep and he sat on the bed and chatted with the Ambassador, his son and daughter-in-law.

By this time a corps of frantic newspaper men who had been madly chasing the airman, following one false scent after another, had finally tracked him to the embassy. In a body they descended upon the Ambassador, who received them in the salon and informed them that he had just left Lindbergh with strict instructions to go to sleep.

As Mr. Herrick was talking with the reporters his son-in-law came downstairs and said that Lindbergh had rung and announced that he did not care to go to sleep just yet and that he would be glad to see the newspaper men for a few minutes. A cheer went up from the group who dashed by Mr. Herrick and rushed upstairs.

Expected Trouble Over Newfoundland.

In the blue and gold room, with a soft light glowing, sat the conqueror of the Atlantic. He immediately stood up and held out his hands to greet his callers. THE NEW YORK TIMES correspondent being first to greet him.

"Sit down, please," urged every one with one voice, but Lindbergh only smiled again his famous boyish smile and said: "It's almost as easy to stand up as it is to sit down."

Questions were fired at him from all sides about his trip across the ocean, but Lindbergh seemed to dismiss them all with brief, nonchalant answers.

"I expected trouble over Newfoundland because I had been warned that the situation there was unfavorable. But I got over that hazard with no trouble whatsoever."

Sleet and Snow for 1,000 Miles.

"However, it wasn't easy going. I had sleet and snow for over 1,000 miles. Sometimes it was too high to fly over and sometimes too low to fly under, so I just had to go through it as best I could.

"I flew as low as 10 feet in some places and as high as 10,000 in others. I passed no ships in the daytime, but at night I saw the lights of several ships, the night being bright and clear."

Everyone then wanted to know if the flier had been sleepy on the voyage.

"I didn't really get what you might call downright sleepy," he said, "but I think I sort of nodded several times. In fact, I could have flown half that distance again. I had enough fuel

Continued on Page Two.

LEVINE ABANDONS BELLANCA FLIGHT

Venture Given Up as Designer Splits With Him—Plane Narrowly Escapes Burning.

BYRD'S CRAFT IS NAMED

Lindbergh Cheered at Ceremony—Commander, Now Last in Field, Waits on Weather.

Through no fault of his own, Clarence D. Chamberlin, who with Bert Acosta established a world's non-stop flying record a few weeks ago, will not fly the record-breaking monoplane in an attempt to establish a second New York-Paris non-stop flight.

G. M. Bellanca, designer of the plane, and Charles S. Levine of the Columbia Aircraft Company, owner of the ship, came to the parting of the ways last night and the designer finally severed his connection with the promoter. Then Levine issued a statement that the proposed flight, which has been talked of for weeks, was off.

"Due to the crowning blow of Mr. Bellanca's resignation, the plane will be placed in the hangar. Mr. Bellanca's resignation causes us to abandon plans for the New York-Paris flight for the present."

At the very moment that the statement was issued the plane was near the runway at Roosevelt Field with gas tanks filled and oil and equipment aboard ready for the start for Paris.

Plane Threatened by Fire.

A few minutes later, as it was being wheeled off, preparatory to being housed for the night, it narrowly escaped being destroyed by fire. When the word came to the field that the flight was definitely off the mechanics were ordered to empty one gasoline tank to lighten the machine. The gasoline spilled on the ground and while the ship was being towed away a careless spectator threw the stub of a lighted cigarette down.

In an instant there was a terrific flare and a dense burst of smoke as the gasoline blazed up.

"The Bellanca's gone," was the cry that rose from thousands of spectators who had gathered at the field.

Word was flashed to the army air station at Mitchel Field that there had been an accident and ambulances and fire-fighting apparatus were sent across the road. An ambulance from the Nassau County Hospital at Mineola was also sent to Roosevelt Field, as well as fire apparatus from Mineola.

The plane, however, was beyond the danger line and was not injured.

It had been announced that the Columbia would take off at 8 o'clock and Chamberlin was in his flying clothes ready to climb into the cockpit with the unnamed pilot who was to have accompanied him on the trip.

With the elimination of the Bellanca monoplane, only Lieut.

Over-Acidity quickly relieved by BELL-ANS for Indigestion, 25c & 75c. All druggists.—Advt.

MAP OF LINDBERGH'S TRANSATLANTIC ROUTE, SHOWING THE SPEED OF HIS TRIP.

CAPTAIN CHARLES A. LINDBERGH,
Who Flew Alone Across the Atlantic, New York to Paris, in Thirty-three and One-half Hours.
Times Wide World Photo

New York Stages Big Celebration After Hours of Anxious Waiting

Harbor Craft, Factories, Fire Sirens and Radio Carry Message of the Flier's Victory Throughout the City—Theatres Halt While Audiences Cheer.

New York bubbled all day yesterday with excitement and expectancy, first yearning for word of Captain Lindbergh, then half-doubting, gaining confidence as the afternoon progressed and finally acclaiming the victory of the young aviator with street demonstrations where the crowds were thickest, in which the ancient phrase, "I told you so," was often repeated. It was evident during the day that New York had confidence in the lad from the West.

On the streets and elsewhere Lindbergh was the one topic of conversation the whole day long. In the subway, on the elevated, in trains and cars, motion-picture houses, theatres, wherever a few had gathered, or even where one man could find another to talk to, one heard "Lindbergh — Lindbergh — Lindbergh."

And such expressions as this:
"He'll make it, all right."
"Some baby!"
"Well, if he's hit Ireland, he's safe anyway."
"He's away ahead of his time."
"What's the difference in time between here and there, anyway?"

Confused On Difference In Time.

To this latter question there were some amazing answers. One woman who had the aviator's running time mixed with the difference in time between New York and Paris solemnly informed her companion that there were thirty-six hours difference in time between the cities.

She said it with an air which signified: "I don't mean to ve." A surprising number of persons insisted that the difference in time was three hours.

Early in the day, even before there was any good reason why there should be definite news, the interest of the people was demonstrated in two ways. At every news stand there were little groups scanning the headlines and buying newspapers. In every newspaper office the switchboards were literally swamped with inquiries. It was not sufficient that the operator said there was no word, or, later, that Lindbergh's plane had been seen over Ireland. The inquirers wanted specific information:

"Well, when will you get the first news?" they asked. And later:

"If he's over Ireland how long will it be before he gets to Paris?"

"Is he all right?"

The questions that were asked, considering that no news could possibly come direct from Captain Lindbergh before he landed, were as surprising as the guesses at the difference in time.

The Times Gets 10,000 Phone Calls.

The telephone inquiries came from all sorts of people and all directions. Not a few rang up The Times office and apologetically explained that they were on golf links or elsewhere at a distance, and hence could not

Continued on Page Three.

LINDBERGH TRIUMPH THRILLS COOLIDGE

President Cables Praise to "Heroic Flier" and Concern for Nungesser and Coli.

CAPITAL THROBS WITH JOY

Kellogg, New, MacNider, Patrick and Many More Join in Paying Tribute to Daring Youth.

Special to The New York Times.

WASHINGTON, May 21.—The triumph of Captain Charles A. Lindbergh in flying from New York to Paris without a stop created a tremendous sensation in the national capital and found immediate response in a host of official messages and statements congratulating the daring aviator upon his achievement.

President Coolidge expressed his admiration in a message transmitted through Ambassador Herrick in Paris for delivery to the young flier in person.

With a single possible exception, this city has never been more thrilled since the armistice, when Woodrow Wilson mingled with the noisy thousands in celebrating the end of the war. The exception was when Walter Johnson arose from apparent defeat and won the deciding world series baseball game in 1924.

"The American people," the President said, "rejoice with me at the brilliant termination of your heroic flight. The first non-stop flight of a lone aviator across the Atlantic crowns the record of American aviation, and in bringing the greetings of the American people to France you likewise carry the assurance of our admiration of those intrepid Frenchmen, Nungesser and Coli, whose bold spirits first ventured on your exploit, and likewise a message of our continued anxiety concerning their fate."

Secretary Kellogg, in a message similarly transmitted, said:

"I heartily congratulate you on the success of your great adventure in accomplishing a non-stop flight from New York to Paris. It is a great step in the advancement of aviation. Every one in the United States is proud of your accomplishment."

Knew Lindbergh as a Boy.

In a statement issued here Mr. Kellogg referred to his personal friendship for Lindbergh, whom he has known for years through the young man's late father, a Representative in Congress from the Secretary's home State of Minnesota.

"News has just reached me," Mr. Kellogg said, "of the success of Lindbergh in completing his flight from New York to Paris. It is an achievement of which every American can justly be proud. I have known Lindbergh since he was a boy and rejoice at this culmination of his ambitions, which could only have been gained by, scientific knowledge, superb courage and physical and sterling character. Our rejoicing in Lindbergh's success, however, is tempered by our continued ignorance of the fate of Nungesser and Coli, whose courage and valor have now been equaled, but cannot be surpassed."

Hanford MacNider, Acting Secre-

Continued on Page Four.

CROWD ROARS THUNDEROUS WELCOME

Breaks Through Lines of Soldiers and Police and Surging to Plane Lifts Weary Flier from His Cockpit

AVIATORS SAVE HIM FROM FRENZIED MOB OF 100,000

Paris Boulevards Ring With Celebration After Day and Night Watch—American Flag Is Called For and Wildly Acclaimed.

By EDWIN L. JAMES.
Copyright, 1927, by The New York Times Company.
Special Cable to The New York Times.

PARIS, May 21.—Lindbergh did it. Twenty minutes after 10 o'clock tonight suddenly and softly there slipped out of the darkness a gray-white airplane as 25,000 pairs of eyes strained toward it. At 10:24 the Spirit of St. Louis landed and lines of soldiers, ranks of policemen and stout steel fences went down before a mad rush as irresistible as the tides of the ocean.

"Well, I made it," smiled Lindbergh, as the little white monoplane came to a halt in the middle of the field and the first vanguard reached the plane. Lindbergh made a move to jump out. Twenty hands reached for him and lifted him out as if he were a baby. Several thousands in a minute were around the plane. Thousands more broke the barriers of iron rails round the field, cheering wildly.

Lifted From His Cockpit.

As he was lifted to the ground Lindbergh was pale and with his hair unkempt, he looked completely worn out. He had strength enough, however, to smile, and waved his hand to the crowd. Soldiers with fixed bayonets were unable to keep back the crowd.

United States Ambassador Herrick was among the first to welcome and congratulate the hero.

A NEW YORK TIMES man was one of the first to reach the machine after its graceful descent to the field. Those first to arrive at the plane had a picture that will live in their minds for the rest of their lives. His cap off, his famous locks falling in disarray around his eyes, "Lucky Lindy" sat peering out over over the rim of the little cockpit of his machine.

Dramatic Scene at the Field.

It was high drama. Picture the scene. Almost if not quite 100,000 people were massed on the east side of Le Bourget air field. Some of them had been there six and seven hours.

Off to the left the giant phare lighthouse of Mount Valerien flashed its guiding light 300 miles into the air. Closer on the left Le Bourget Lighthouse twinkled, and off to the right another giant revolving phare sent its beams high into the heavens.

Big arc lights on all sides with enormous electric glares were flooding the landing field. From time to time rockets rose and burst in varied lights over the field.

Seven thirty, the hour announced for the arrival, had come and gone. Then 8 o'clock came, and no Lindbergh; at 9 o'clock the sun had set but then came reports that Lindbergh had been seen over Cork. Then he had been seen over Valentia in Ireland and then over Plymouth.

Suddenly a message spread like lightning, the aviator had been seen over Cherbourg. However, remembering the messages telling of Captain Nungesser's flight, the crowd was skeptical.

"One chance in a thousand!" "Oh, he cannot do it without navigating instruments!" "It's a pity, because he was a brave boy." Pessimism had spread over the great throng by 10 o'clock.

The stars came out and a chill wind blew.

Watchers Are Twice Disappointed.

Suddenly the field lights flooded their glares onto the landing ground and there came the roar of an airplane's motor. The crowd was still, then began a cheer, but two minutes later the landing glares went dark for the searchlight had identified the plane and it was not Captain Lindbergh's.

Stamping their feet in the cold, the crowd waited patiently. It seemed quite apparent that nearly every one was willing to wait all night, hoping against hope.

Suddenly—it was 10:16 exactly—another motor roared over the heads of the crowd. In the sky one caught a glimpse of a white gray plane, and for an instant heard the sound of one. Then it dimmed, and the idea spread that it was yet another disappointment.

Again landing lights glared and almost by the time they had flooded the field the gray-white plane had lighted on the far side nearly half a mile from the crowd. It seemed to stop almost as it hit the ground, so gently did it land.

And then occurred a scene which almost passed description. Two companies of soldiers with fixed bayonets and the Le Bourget field police, reinforced by Paris agents, had held the crowd in good order. But as the lights showed the plane

"All the News That's Fit to Print."

The New York Times.

THE WEATHER
Cloudy today, showers tonight or tomorrow; moderate winds.
Temperature yesterday—Max. 78, min. 64.
For weather report see Page 64.

VOL. LXXVI....NO. 25,393.   • • •   NEW YORK, WEDNESDAY, AUGUST 3, 1927.   TWO CENTS | THREE CENTS | FOUR CENTS

COOLIDGE DOES NOT CHOOSE TO RUN IN 1928; STARTLES PARTY WITH 12-WORD MESSAGE; SOME DOUBTERS, OTHERS SEE FIELD OPEN

NEW SACCO TRIAL INDICATED AS STEP FULLER WILL TAKE

Governor Is Expected to Call for Reprieve of Men and Action by the Legislature.

POLITICAL ISSUE IS RAISED

Move Would Be 'Expedient,' but Observers Say Executive Feels It Is Right.

PAIR ENTER DEATH HOUSE

Newly Found Vanzetti Alibi Is Presented as Fuller Interviews Last Witnesses.

From a Staff Correspondent of The New York Times.

BOSTON, Aug. 2.—Nicola Sacco and Bartolomeo Vanzetti will not die in the electric chair on the date set. Neither will they be pardoned. Further reprieve pending steps by the Massachusetts Legislature looking to a new trial was indicated at the State House today as the outcome of the historic case of the Italian radicals, which Governor Fuller will place before the Executive Council when it meets tomorrow. The Governor will make known the decision tomorrow night.

Commutation to life imprisonment is one alternative that has been discussed, but those who know Governor Fuller are certain that this alternative will not appeal to the State's Chief Executive.

New and overwhelming eleventh-hour evidence is the only factor likely to change the plan for a further reprieve and an appeal to the Legislature for a new trial.

Late tonight, while the Governor and his advisers worked on the report to be laid before the Council tomorrow, the defense was more cheerful than it has been since the Governor's investigation began.

This optimism is not shared by Sacco, whose mind is weakening on the eighteenth day of his hunger strike at Charlestown State Prison. Vanzetti is feeling better and partaking of a little food. His is buoyed up by the news that his sister has aided from France and is due here on Aug. 10. That is the day set for the execution under the terms of the sentence of the two men.

Every sign today pointed to the fact that Governor Fuller, despite his exhaustive and exhausting inquiry, had not made up his mind on certain phases of the case of the men convicted for the murder of a paymaster and his guard on April 15, 1920.

Interviews Last of Witnesses.

This afternoon Governor Fuller saw the last of the long line of witnesses who have filed into his office for three months, and he then closed the inquiry. He continued his work on the case after lunch from his office at 5 o'clock. When he returned he gave every indication of being in a comfortable frame of mind.

At 9:10 tonight Sacco and Vanzetti and Celestino Madeiros, facing execution for another murder, whose case is linked with that of the two radicals by his "confession" seeking to free them from the Cherry Hill section of the State Prison to the death house, about 100 yards away. The transfer was effected without incident. The removal of the men has no significance, being a routine procedure. Men condemned to die in the electric chair are, according to law, removed to the death house ten days before execution.

Until a few years ago the State House who have followed the Governor's inquiry, as well as members of the Sacco-Vanzetti Defense Committee, felt that the result would be clear cut and uncompromising. The defense hoped for an outright pardon. State House sources were of the opinion that the Governor would take no action and permit the death penalty to be imposed.

The tide apparently turned with the latest visit of Superior Court Judge Webster Thayer, who presided at the joint trial as well as at the previous trial of Vanzetti, convicted of an attempted hold-up and sentenced to from twelve to fifteen years. Judge Thayer, who refused the eight applications for a new trial, saw the Governor yesterday, and it was reported afterward that the latter indicated to him the nature of his report.

The stress placed on the meeting of the Council tomorrow is emphasized by the Defense Committee as a certain sign that the Governor could not have made up his mind to send the men to the electric chair. There are eight Councilors from widely separated parts of the State and their bearing on the case is apparent from the following provision in the State Constitution:

"The power of pardoning offenses, except such as persons may be convicted of before the Senate by an impeachment of the House, shall be in the Governor, by and with the advice of the Council.

Since yesterday the idea of a further reprieve and action by the Legis-

Continued on Page Fourteen.

Sept. 19 to Be French Holiday In Honor of American Legion

Copyright, 1927, by The New York Times Company.
Special Cable to The New York Times.

PARIS, Aug. 2.—A law proclaiming Monday, Sept. 19, as a French national holiday this year in honor of the American Legionaires returning to celebrate the tenth anniversary of their entry in the World War was promulgated in the Journal Officiel today.

In this same bill the sum of 3,700,000 francs is allocated to the Minister of Foreign Affairs for expenditures for the entertainment of the American veterans on their visit here.

The announcement declares it to be a joy and an honor for the Government and the French populace to receive the members of the American Legion, who remain an "unshakable base of friendship for France in the United States."

JAPANESE OFFER NEW NAVAL PLAN

Suggestion That May Save Conference Is Wired to Washington and London.

MAINTAINS STATUS QUO

But Gives America and Japan Chance to Catch Up With Britain on Cruisers.

By WYTHE WILLIAMS.
Copyright, 1927, by The New York Times Company.
Special Cable to The New York Times.

GENEVA, Aug. 2.—The plenary session of the tripower naval conference is still set for Thursday, and Ambassador Gibson is expected to attempt the seemingly hopeless task of obtaining a naval limitations treaty acceptable to the United States.

The delegates today were still busy suggesting new compromises, which for the most part are redressed. They gave it up after lunch and decided they might as well play golf. It is still evident, though, that all the delegations—particularly a portion of the American one—are anxious to avoid adjournment of the conference at almost any cost.

It is not generally clear just what are the newest proposals—at one time labeled Japanese and at another Japano-American—because sometimes the official spokesmen said there were no proposals and at other times there were, until interest slackened as the mystery grew. It is evident that they were sized up by Allen Dulles, the legal adviser of the American delegation, who thought they might lead to something being arranged. Thus they assumed a semi-American character.

Mr. Dulles, who recently resigned from the State Department to rejoin a New York law firm, was re-engaged this most distinguished relative is Robert Lansing, ex-Secretary of State, whom he resembles in his pacific ambition to become a treaty maker rather than a conference breaker.

Meanwhile the unconsulted American navy experts are viewing the civilian members of the delegation askance, fearful that something is being sprung that might have the same effect on the navy as the Treaty of Washington. They are anxiously counting the hours from now until the plenary session. Then if Ambassador Gibson takes the floor and brings the conference to an end they will breathe freely, but not until then.

The only delegates taking the situation placidly and unconcernedly and not indulging in gossip are the British.

The Japanese delegation gave a full dress dinner in honor of the former Crown Prince of Korea. It was followed by a dance and a midnight supper.

New Plan Submitted by Japanese.
By The Associated Press.

GENEVA, Aug. 2.—The Japanese statesman today presented to Hugh S. Gibson, chief American representative, a compromise formula on the cruiser problem which has menaced the Tripartite Naval Conference with failure. In handing their formula to the Ambassador, Viscount Ishii and his associates remarked that it was "just an idea."

Despite this new move it was said responsible quarters tonight that the spectre of failure—failure which, as a prospect, has genuinely alarmed men of many countries—should not yet be deemed definitely avoided. From the American standpoint at least, the Japanese plan to use the conference is said to appear

Continued on Page Six.

PARTY HERE IS AMAZED

State Organization in Consternation at Coolidge Statement.

IS FINAL, HILLES THINKS

Leaders Expect Effort to Force Renomination by a Popular Demand.

DR. BUTLER LAUDS ACTION

Says President Has Done Wise and Patriotic Act—Ex-Senator Butler Is Silent.

New York State Republicans, with very few exceptions, were thunder-struck yesterday by President Coolidge's announcement regarding his candidacy for another term.

Neither former Senator William M. Butler of Massachusetts, Chairman of the Republican National Committee, who happened to be in the city, nor Charles D. Hilles, the Vice Chairman, had any advance notice of the President's intention. Senator Butler was the President's personal choice for National Chairman and managed the 1924 campaign. Mr. Hilles is considered particularly close to the President and is consulted by him on all matters affecting New York State, and the fact that the President's statement came to them as a surprise indicates the degree of astonishment felt by Republicans here generally.

Mr. Hilles declared that President Coolidge had made his statement without reservation and intended his withdrawal to be final unless some emergency should confront the country in 1928. He said:

"The President's laconic statement was entirely unexpected, and I regret his action. He is a singularly self-reliant man. I believe he took his own counsel until the decision was announced. He is a man of candor and sincerity, and I think he made the statement without reservation. Except that if an emergency should confront the country in 1928, and it should clearly be a duty to run, he will be free to do so. Otherwise I think he intends this to be final.

"He has had the satisfaction of knowing that he would have been renominated by an overwhelming majority.

"I think the President was considerate in announcing his renunciation now. It gives us two months in which to prepare for the nomination of his successor. I do not agree with those who think he will lose a strategic advantage with the next Congress. He will cease to be a target for partisan attack. Members of his own party who have withheld their support as well as those of the opposition party will now have a kindlier feeling for him and an appreciation of the great service he has rendered."

By the leaders of the State party organization, President Coolidge's renunciation was regarded as virtually certain. With few exceptions, the local Republican leaders accepted the President's statement as final and at its face value, although it was said that a movement would undoubtedly develop to take advantage of the phraseology of his statement that he did "not choose to be a candidate," and seek to bring about his renomination by popular demand.

Think Field Now Wide Open.

The general feeling among those New York Republican leaders who could be found in or near the city was that the President's statement had left the field wide open for the Republican Presidential nomination in 1928, and that strong movements for former Governor Frank O. Lowden, of Illinois, and Herbert Hoover, Secretary of Commerce, were certain to develop in this State.

The one Republican of prominence who did not feel surprised at the President's announcement was Dr. Nicholas Murray Butler, president of Columbia University, who returned earlier in the day from a trip to Europe. Dr. Butler predicted last February that President Coolidge would not violate the third term tradition by becoming a candidate for renomination, and his attitude of opposition to a third term brought at that time a great deal of criticism from members of the State party organization, who had based all their plans on the probability of President Coolidge's renomination.

Dr. Butler's Statement.

Asked to comment on the President's statement, Dr. Butler said:

"As a personal friend and a political admirer of President Coolidge, although without knowledge of his purpose, I have taken it for granted, as I stated in an address to my friends and neighbors of the

Continued on Page Two.

Smith Is Silent on Coolidge, But Democrats See His Gain

President Coolidge's statement that he did "not choose to be a candidate for renomination" was met with silence by leading Democrats here yesterday.

"I have no comment to make," Governor Smith, a leading aspirant for the Democratic Presidential nomination, said at the Hotel Biltmore.

George W. Olvany, leader of Tammany, and Mayor Walker also declined to comment.

The speculation among Democrats was mostly over how the President's announcement might affect Governor Smith's chances of nomination for and election to the Presidency. The general offhand opinion was that it would have no material effect on his chances for the nomination, but probably would increase his chance for election.

COOLIDGE'S ACTION PLEASES CORN BELT

Iowa Leaders in Farm Legislation Agitation Think It Will Aid Their Cause.

BOOM IN LOWDEN'S STOCK

His Supporters Think Greatest Obstacle to His Candidacy Has Been Removed.

Special to The New York Times.

DES MOINES, Iowa, Aug. 2.—Iowa's first concern tonight over the announcement of President Coolidge that he does not choose to run for President in 1928 was manifestly as much a surprise to those who have been mentioned as probable aspirants for the nomination at the next Republican National Convention as to any one else, judging from their expressions as told in the press.

When asked to comment on Mr. Coolidge's declaration Frank O. Lowden could only say that no man could run away from the Presidency.

Leaders in the farm legislation were almost unanimous in their belief that the President's action was a victory, or at least a material aid, for the cause of agriculture. Comment also concerned itself largely with the effect of the Coolidge statement on the candidacy of Frank O. Lowden, which has been the chief concern of many of the State's political leaders.

Those who thought first of the bearing of the statement on another term for President Coolidge generally complimented the President on his "courageous act" in taking a stand against breaking the third term tradition.

Perhaps the most significant development in Iowa was the statement of Willis L. Stern, Republican State Chairman, that "this State will doubtless be united for Frank O. Lowden, as all Iowa holds him in high esteem." The statement was interpreted as placing the State party organization back of the Lowden candidacy.

Ex-Governor Lowden's most ardent supporters hailed the Coolidge withdrawal as removing the most serious obstacle to his candidacy, namely the ability of the President to obtain renomination. Organization leaders who have had nothing against Mr. Lowden but who have had to stay on the Coolidge reservation may not be disposed to advocate some other candidate against Mr. Lowden, it was pointed out.

Some observers, held that the Lowden movement made the gain by the Coolidge statement because the withdrawal of the President had left the Lowden force without an object against which to direct their attack. This attitude was reflected in the declaration of Frank J. Lund, head of the Iowa Lowden for President League, who predicted that "the East will have another candidate of the same type."

LEADERS ARE CAUTIOUS

Vice President Dawes Says Public Will Regret the Decision.

LONGWORTH KEEPS SILENT

Ex-Governor Lowden Repeats That No One Can Run Away From the Presidency.

HOOVER TO "THINK IT OVER"

Borah Accepts Announcement as Final—West Did It, Says Brookhart.

President Coolidge's sudden announcement that he did "not choose to be a candidate for renomination in 1928" was manifestly as much a surprise to those who have been mentioned as probable aspirants for the nomination at the next Republican National Convention as to any one else, judging from their expressions as told in the press.

When asked to comment on Mr. Coolidge's declaration Frank O. Lowden could only say that no man could run away from the Presidency.

Vice President Charles G. Dawes at first refused to comment on the President's statement, but later issued a statement of his own, which in effect accepted the President's statement as final on the question of his candidacy for renomination. Senator Hiram Johnson of California characterized the President's statement as "astonishing."

Speaker Nicholas Longworth of the House of Representatives, who is visiting in South Dakota, declined to comment. Secretary Hoover's views are not available.

Mr. Dawes Voices Regrets.

CHICAGO, Aug. 2 (P).—Vice President Charles G. Dawes said in a statement here tonight:

"President Coolidge enjoys the confidence and respect of the American people, and his decision will be received with regret by millions of his countrymen."

Ex-Governor Lowden's Comment.
Special to The New York Times.

ALEXANDRIA BAY, N. Y., Aug. 2.—Concerning the announcement made today by President Coolidge in 1928, former Governor Frank O. Lowden of Illinois who, with his family is visiting here, issued the following statement to which he would add nothing: "I have no statement to make beyond the one already made to different delegations calling upon me. That statement was in substance, that I know of no man in all our history who has run away from the Presidency."

Longworth Too Surprised to Talk.
Special to The New York Times.

SAN FRANCISCO, Cal., Aug. 2.—Two of the outstanding possibilities for the Republican nomination for the Presidency were in San Francisco today.

Herbert Hoover, Secretary of Commerce, was at the Bohemian Grove when the message came from the President.

Nicholas Longworth, Speaker of the House of Representatives, received the news from the President's Summer home while attending a luncheon given in his honor at the San Francisco Commercial Club. He declared that he was too surprised to say anything.

"I may have something to say later on," he remarked.

Senator Hiram Johnson admitted that when he first heard of the President's statement he was too astonished to talk. He said:

"If the statement as reported is true, the next Republican Convention will be a grand free-for-all, a regular Donnybrook Fair."

Too Soon to Discuss, Says Hoover.

PALO ALTO, Cal., Aug. 2 (P).—Herbert Hoover, Secretary of Commerce, said tonight that he had nothing to say for the present as to President Coolidge's announcement.

"I have no comment to make," the Secretary said. "It is too soon to discuss it. I must think over the President's announcement."

Finality, Borah Thinks.
By Telegraph to the Editor of The New York Times.

BOISE, Idaho, Aug. 2.—The President could have been communicated by simply remaining silent. His action seemed reasonably certain. His announcement, therefore, that he does not desire to be a candidate in 1928 must be regarded as the result of a purely conviction and finality. Naturally, other speculation will be brought out, but it will be a

Continued on Page Five.

CALVIN COOLIDGE.
"I Do Not Choose to Run for President in Nineteen Twenty-eight."

A Recent Studio Portrait. Copyright, Harris & Ewing.

Washington Sees 1928 Field Open; Some Talk of Drafting Coolidge

Hoover, Lowden, Dawes, Longworth, Borah and Norris Are Listed as the Chief of Those Whose Presidential Aspirations Will Now Take Active Form.

By RICHARD V. OULAHAN.
Special to The New York Times.

WASHINGTON, Aug. 2.—It was a real sensation for the intellectual segment of political Washington which the "hot weather has not driven away, the announcement of President Coolidge at his Summer home in South Dakota that he did not "choose" to run for President in 1928. With it was dovetailed the element of complete surprise.

While some of those concerned or interested in party politics have been expressing the opinion that Mr. Coolidge would decline to be considered as a candidate for another nomination, their number is negligible in comparison with those who were confident that he would be the Republican nominee next year. Besides, nobody expected the President to show his hand at this early date, more than ten months prior to the assembling of the Republican National Convention.

Two Features of Comment.

In the comment which followed the President's terse declaration at Rapid City there were two conspicuous features. One was the speculative slant of whether the President meant it to be understood that in no circumstances would he accept a nomination for another Presidential term. The other was the apparent evidence, cumulative over a period of many months and accentuated by what was learned today, that Mr. Coolidge did not consult close political friends or party leaders with reference to his spectacular statement. There is reason to believe that he never discussed with any member of his Cabinet the matter of becoming a candidate for President in 1928, with the possible exception of Secretary Hoover, "of whom later," as the compilers of genealogical records would say.

Very generally opinion among political observers was that Mr. Coolidge intended his announcement to mean that he had taken himself out of the running. The argument was advanced that a man occupying the high position of President of the United States could not afford, if for no other reason than that of dignity, to make a declaration of such an important character that would be open to the accusation of intentional dubiousness.

A notable exception to this view was the construction placed on the President's announcement by Senator Smoot of Utah.

"I construe the statement to mean," said Senator Smoot, "that if the Republican convention nominates him again he will accept the nomination. It does not bar him from running as an such an event."

West Coolidge, Smoot Thinks.

Senator Smoot, however, would not hazard a guess as to what the party convention would do in the face of the President's declaration. It was too early to make any guess in that respect, he explained, and then added:

"My opinion is that the American people would like to have Mr. Coolidge for President again, but that he has not yet accepted the responsibility of another nomination, I do not think that the President would refuse another nomination at the hands of the convention. At the same time I would not attempt to say whether the convention would insist on renominating him if it were convinced that Mr. Coolidge's attitude toward another term is not going to be changed."

Will Spur Lowden Boomers.

It goes without saying that the announcement from Rapid City will be followed by increased activities on the part of those who have put Frank O. Lowden forward as their choice for the Republican Presidential nomination.

Mr. Lowden is primarily the favorite of the advanced farm aid advocates and has been regarded as the candidate of the firmly leaders chiefly in the Middle West. It is expected that Senator Smoot's construction of the Coolidge statement, reading it as a declination to run, will have a stimulating effect on the movements which have been mentioned for the nomination.

His now famous announcement takes the place alongside that of his message to Congress, "I do not know." It also follows the line of his announcement on the first step in his political career which ended in his becoming President.

At the close of the legislative ses-

Continued on Page Eleven.

PRESIDENT ACTED ALONE

His Close Friends Were Unaware of His Stand on Another Term.

CALLS IN NEWSPAPER MEN

President Hands Out Typed Slip in School Room, and Declines to Comment.

DRAMATIC SURPRISE STAGED

Statement Is Issued on the Eve of Coolidge's Fourth Anniversary as President.

From a Staff Correspondent of The New York Times.

RAPID CITY, S. D., Aug. 2.—President Coolidge today dramatically and unexpectedly, and without consultation with friends, issued the following statement to the correspondents here:

"I do not choose to run for President in nineteen twenty-eight."

This brief sentence was written by him on a slip of paper at 9:23 A. M. and later transcribed by stenographers to a slip of paper four inches by two inches. The year was put in words, not figures, and so made a twelve-word statement.

The President had doubled the slip twice and held fifteen of them in his right hand, from which he gave them to the newspaper correspondents, who had been notified to return to his office at noon for a statement. This notice to the correspondents was given at the end of the regular Tuesday morning press conference, in which he had discussed the Geneva Conference and other questions before the public.

As for the odd wording of the Presidential declaration, it was pointed out by some of those who managed opinion that the President could not with propriety or with regard for his party come out with a flat declaration that in no circumstances would he accept next year's Presidential nomination. According to the generality of opinion here, must be interpreted in the light of all the circumstances. Why should there have been any announcement at all, it was asked, if the President intended to have a string tied to his disclaimer of candidacy?

Discussion of Hoover.

One of Washington's first reactions to the surprise sprung upon the country by Mr. Coolidge was the conviction that Herbert Hoover must be considered as conspicuous in the running for next year's Republican Presidential nomination. Among many political observers the belief prevails that to the country he appears as a national hero. His most recent public service in the Administration of relief measures in the flooded areas of the South has given to him a renewed prominence which has served to recall his masterful handling of Belgian and Russian relief and other work for humanity and the direction of the food administration during the World War.

No doubt exists in the minds of those who follow party political tendencies that Mr. Hoover will now be brought forward as a candidate for the Presidential nomination.

A widespread opinion exists in political quarters that his aspirations will have the moral support of President Coolidge. A knowledge of the President's mental processes which leads to the conviction that he will not make a declaration in favor of any particular candidate for the nomination, but will find means of having the word passed that Hoover is his favorite candidate.

The recent unexplained incident arising from Mr. Coolidge's voluntary assertion that if Mr. Kellogg retired from the office of Secretary of State Mr. Hoover would not be appointed to succeed him, may be cited as evidence that the President is not particularly cordial toward his candidacy, but, in the face of it, the sympathetic good wishes of the President are expected to follow Mr. Hoover's hat as it is cast into the ring.

There may be a more definite and final utterance from him, but it is regarded here as doubtful. His announcement today, it is expected here, will be the signal for the entrance of Secretary Hoover, Speaker Longworth, Vice President Dawes and the renewed activity of former Governor Lowden to gain the delegates in the coming Republican primaries.

It is believed here that the President will say nothing more and is not expected to allow his Administration to be used in the promotion of the candidacy of any others who have been mentioned for the nomination.

The New York Times.

THE WEATHER
Fair and slightly warmer today and tomorrow; moderate winds.
Temperature yesterday—Max. 71, min. 58.
For weather report see Page 42.

VOL. LXXVI....No. 25,394.   NEW YORK, THURSDAY, AUGUST 4, 1927.   TWO CENTS | THREE CENTS | FOUR CENTS

SACCO AND VANZETTI GUILTY, SAYS FULLER, AND MUST DIE; BAY STATE GOVERNOR UPHOLDS JURY, CALLS TRIAL FAIR; HIS BOARD UNANIMOUS, EXECUTION OF PAIR SET FOR AUG. 10

MESSAGES OF REGRET FLOOD COOLIDGE; STRONG DESIRE TO DRAFT HIM SHOWN AS DEBATE OVER STATEMENT GOES ON

PRESIDENT KEEPS SILENT

His Associates Declare He Issued His Statement As a Final Word.

SEEMS IN A HAPPIER MOOD

He Spends an Hour in His Office Reading Telegrams, Then Returns to Lodge.

EXPECT LATER STATEMENT

Politicians at Rapid City See Coolidge Forced by Primaries to Clarify His Stand.

From a Staff Correspondent of The New York Times.

RAPID CITY, S. D., Aug. 3.—President Coolidge, having announced that he does not choose to run for President in 1928, finds himself flooded with telegrams urging him again to lead the Republican Party.

These messages, which have poured in upon him here in the Black Hills, are most complimentary and make clear to him that he has the esteem of a great following. A large proportion of the telegrams seek to prevail upon Mr. Coolidge to accept the nomination if it should come to him after his now famous twelve-word announcement, couched in somewhat indefinite language.

Home messages told the President that he had made himself one of the greatest men in recent times by virtually refusing what they declared was certain re-election as President, and going down in history as the man who had longest held that office.

It would be a calamity to the nation, declared many of the messages, if Mr. Coolidge should eliminate himself from the race and plunge the country into an uncertain contest for the Presidency, with what was stated as the possibility of radical changes in governmental policies that have made the nation strong and prosperous.

Many Talk of Drafting Coolidge.

The nation, judged by these messages that tonight are being telegraphed by the President in his distant lodge in the hills, does not accept as final or conclusive the terse and cryptic statement that the President prepared without consultation and then personally distributed to the press yesterday in his office in the school building.

Apparently a great many people, including many of the dominant Republican leaders, do not accept the statement effectively eliminating President Coolidge from the race. They all construe the announcement as screening his state of mind and not his actual determination not to accept the nomination if in the face of it the Republican Party should cast aside President Coolidge's apparent personal desires and nominate him next year.

The trend of sentiment reflected in the messages coming here is that the admirers intend to draft Mr. Coolidge and actually show him that there is a real call from the people, a call that rises above his wishes, and disregards the so-called third term talk and the division in the Republican Party in the corn and wheat belt States.

In the opinion of some observers here who have analyzed the messages and read the interviews given in the country, it is necessary for the President to be more definite. It is stated, however, that some move, such as the entrance of a member of his Cabinet in the race, would show that he has fully made up his mind to retire at the end of his term in 1929.

The message received here indicate that only Mr. Coolidge's refusal to permit his name to be entered in the first primaries in New Hampshire and North Dakota next March will satisfy his supporters and others of the finality of the announcement.

In the last twenty-four hours the Summer White House wires have brought in reports of a great national party readjusting its entire campaign procedure, the fixed opinion of many voters altered and their views as to the strongest candidate for the Republican Party can select rendered uncertain. The wires also

Continued on Page Five.

Hoover Declares He Hopes President Will Run Again

PALO ALTO, Cal., Aug. 3 (AP).—Herbert Hoover, Secretary of Commerce, commenting today on President Coolidge's announcement that he did not choose to be a candidate for re-election in 1928, said:

"I regret the suggestion in the President's statement.

"However, I still believe as I stated in Chicago two weeks ago, that President Coolidge should be renominated and re-elected."

BULL MARKET JARRED BY COOLIDGE STAND

Fifty Representative Stocks Decline—Most of Losses Are Regained in Buying Rally.

2,767,170 SHARES SOLD

Trading Next to Heaviest of the Year—Clamor From Exchange Reaches the Street.

By RICHARD V. OULAHAN.
Special to The New York Times.

WASHINGTON, Aug. 3.—On this the day following President Coolidge's laconic announcement, "I do not choose to run for President in 1928," Washington's chief reaction is that the President owes to the country a clearer explanation of what his declaration was meant to convey.

This feeling is accentuated by editorial comment throughout the Union, showing there is widespread mystification as to the President's intention with reference to next year's Presidential nomination.

It is easily conceivable that with out clarification of the statement the President will lay himself open to the accusation of having made a deceptive utterance. Only a frank explanation from his partisans would overcome this accusatory tendency, if a cross-section of Washington opinion is well founded.

Pretty generally the Washington view is that Mr. Coolidge's purpose was to notify the electorate, and especially Republican workers, that he was out of the running. But, in another way, he took the method employed to serve notice that he was not to be considered as a candidate for his party's nomination.

Has High Regard for Dignities.

No man occupying his position, it is held, can afford to practice deception on the nation, and in this connection it may be added that so President has had a higher regard for the dignities which invest the office. Without ostentation he has adhered to the little ceremonials which carry out the idea of dignity. Despite his parading in cowboy regalia, it is the observation of those who have been brought into close contact with him that he looks upon the Presidential office with too much respect to lend his name to bring it into even the semblance of the disrepute that might attach to it through any method of deception or questionable practice by its incumbent.

But in the face of all this, the mystification continues. Those who adhere to the belief that Mr. Coolidge intended the country to understand that he would retire from the Presidency at the end of the term he is now serving concede that the element of doubt is still involved. While some of them are willing to insist that the President said all that was necessary in the circumstances, it is apparent that they cannot justify their confidence in that conviction by any positive expression in the brief words which Mr. Coolidge pronounced in yesterday's statement in Rapid City.

Enough of leading Republican regulars have commented on the President's declaration to indicate the dazed condition in which it threw them. So uniformly near unconsciousness to permit them to accept it as meaning definitely that the President is no circumstances would permit his name to be presented to the Republican National Convention next June.

A considerable number of them are resisting the interpretation that by Coolidge has withdrawn from the party contest. There is no mystery about this. The generality of party regulars, and even a large segment of those party men inclined to be spotty in their regularity, have assumed that Mr. Coolidge would be nominated for President next year.

Irregulars Wanted Coolidge.

Certain of the irregulars have been anxious to have Mr. Coolidge run again, their feeling being that of all those in the list of Presidential possibilities he was the most anti-labor. Senator Borah, although he has not hesitated to criticise Administration policies, is believed to be among these.

Another who was credited with satisfaction over the conclusion that Mr. Coolidge would be renominated

Continued on Page Four.

CAPITAL DESIRES LIGHT

Thinks President Should Remove All Doubt as to His Intent.

ACCEPTS HIS WITHDRAWAL

But Fears Accusation of Deception Might Follow Lack of Clearer Explanation.

MUCH TALK OF CANDIDATES

Lowden Held Formidable— Hoover Needs Positive Assurance of Coolidge Withdrawal.

Wall Street's "Coolidge bull market" was jarred to its foundations yesterday morning by the President's cryptic announcement that he does not choose to be a candidate for re-election in 1928. There was a pell-mell scramble to sell stocks and opening prices were from 2 to 15% points lower than the previous day's close. Then banking institutions, individual operators, pool managers and bargain hunters rushed to the market's rescue with such a volume of buying orders that the decline of stocks was turned to a rally within a brief thirty minutes.

The demonstration of the market's inherent strength and its vigorous rallying power was even more impressive than the selling which had taken place, which was mainly of the panic-stricken, save-my-profits sort characteristic of the small trader.

It was the general impression, in banking parlors and brokerage offices, after the close that most stocks had given a good account of themselves. It was a characteristic of the market, and an outstanding one, too, that the trading was most orderly. There were many wide swings, to be sure, and some hurried ones, but the market at all times—even in the hectic fifteen minutes of the first hour when the selling was heaviest—had an outward calm which inspired confidence in it and probably brought in many buying orders.

Market Caught Off Balance.

The sudden injection of an awkward and unsettling political situation into a bull market which had been built on general business prosperity, individual corporate expansion, generally good earnings, easy money conditions and the probability of an upswing in operations in basic industries this Fall was the new element which prompted many stockholders to "sell at the market." The President's announcement had not reached Wall Street until 3:15 P. M. the previous day, too late for any market reaction to it, and so nervous groups had gathered in brokerage offices after the close, trying to guess what would happen when trading was resumed in the morning.

The bolt from the Black Hills caught the market off balance. In the first place, the market had behaved in a long period of advances during July and thus far in August, so far as the leading and pivotal stocks were concerned. This strength had induced wide spread covering of short commitments, leaving many stocks without a comfortable cushion to catch the fall.

A further consideration was the fact that the market has been fairly honeycombed with stop-loss orders placed by those who desired to insure a part, at least, of their profits. Public participation has been on the increase, as was reflected yesterday in the report of a record turnover of $272,000,000, as of July 1, in Stock Exchange brokers' loans.

Selling Orders Start With Rush.

Selling orders began to come into brokerage offices before the tickers had finished tapping off the President's brief announcement on the previous day. Telephone bells in brokerage offices were jangling before 9 o'clock yesterday morning, registering the impatient calls of customers who were fearfully afraid of the uncertainty created and who wanted to save profits which might

Continued on Page Four.

Berlin Talks to Buenos Aires By 7,000-Mile Radio Telephone

Copyright, 1927, by The New York Times Co.
By Wireless to The New York Times.

BERLIN, Aug. 3.—Official tests of a radio telephone service between Berlin and Buenos Aires were carried out tonight, representatives of the various departments of the German Government sending greetings to Argentina. The voices carried over the distance of practically 7,000 miles clearly, a cable from Buenos Aires reported.

Since the South American capital was equipped with only a receiving apparatus, the greetings of the Argentine Government had to be sent via cable.

Experiments with short-wave transmitters have been conducted over a long period. Tonight's success has led to a decision to build a number of sets of this type and it is hoped that regular wireless telephone service can be opened to the public by January.

NAVAL PARLEY FAILS; FINAL MEETING SET FOR THIS AFTERNOON

Cruiser Difficulty, the Crux of Geneva Conference, Brings Break-Down.

JAPAN'S PLAN FRUITLESS

Gibson Says There Would Be No Advantage in Treaty on 'Authorized' British Program.

By The Associated Press.

GENEVA, Aug. 3.—The tripartite naval conference reached a deadlock tonight, it was stated in authoritative American circles, and the last session is planned for tomorrow. This statement was confirmed later by the Japanese spokesman.

It was stated that the delegates had mutually and sorrowfully agreed that no compact could be reached at this time to limit further the naval armaments of Great Britain, the United States and Japan.

This announcement was made after tonight's meeting of the plenipotentiaries to consider the Japanese compromise proposals. The hour of the final session was set for 3 o'clock tomorrow afternoon.

British Not Quite Clear on Plan.

When the private meeting of the delegates opened at the villa of Hugh R. Wilson, American Minister to Switzerland, with Ambassador Hugh S. Gibson, chief American delegate, presiding, the Japanese proposal was immediately brought up for discussion.

W. C. Bridgeman, First Lord of the Admiralty and chief British representative, and his colleague, Viscount Cecil of Chelwood (all accounts of the meeting agree here) were not quite clear as to whether the Japanese compromise could be acceptable to Great Britain.

This compromise virtually meant a naval holiday for Great Britain until the United States could catch up with her in naval construction. The British delegates, however, indicated that if the compromise were acceptable to both the United States and Japan, many times would be required to both take it.

In the Japanese plan the word "authorized" was employed to emphasize that Great Britain and Japan would finish only their authorized cruiser program.

Gibson-Bridgeman Exchange.

Mr. Gibson asked Mr. Bridgeman what he understood the word to signify, adding:

"Does it mean approved or authorized?"

Viscount Cecil answered that it meant "authorized."

After further dueling, Mr. Gibson asked:

"Does it mean the Birkenhead program?"

Mr. Bridgeman is understood to have answered "Yes."

"Then that means 660,000 tons for Great Britain by 1936," said Mr. Gibson.

Mr. Gibson added that this was higher than the United States could possibly go and that it would mean that American must build up to that figure in terms of naval tonnage.

Mr. Bridgeman's reply was that the British did not wish to speak in terms of total tonnage.

Mr. Gibson insisted that the United States could build only up to 400,000

When this announcement...

Continued on Page Three.

NEWS STUNS THE DEFENSE

Decision Is 'Unbelievably Brutal,' Says Statement by the Committee.

WILL CONTINUE THE FIGHT

Asks Millions Throughout the World to Join in Last Desperate Protest.

PATROLS PUT NEAR PRISON

Guard Is Thrown Around the Hotel Where Governor Fuller Spends the Night.

From a Staff Correspondent of The New York Times.

BOSTON, Thursday, Aug. 4.—Gardner Jackson, Chairman of the Sacco-Vanzetti Defense Committee, issued the following statement at 1:15 o'clock this morning:

"The decision of the Governor was delivered at such a late hour that proper answer cannot be prepared to it before morning. The decision is unbelievably brutal in its partisanship, and even more brutal in the omission of facts—not only facts brought out in the course of the case, like the frame-up of expert testimony as shown by the Proctor affidavit, but also facts of the most overwhelming significance established behind closed doors, both before the Advisory Committee and the Governor.

"Inasmuch as the committee and the Governor must justify themselves by reason, and not by partisan fiat, these facts must be disclosed in their entirety. It is a solemn truth that one cannot know the demonstrated facts of the case from the Governor's statement.

"The days separating Sacco and Vanzetti from the electric chair are few, but this defense committee will continue to fight for justice for them two men. Our faith in their innocence is unshaken. We call upon the millions of people throughout the world who have supported them to come forward and join us in this last desperate effort to stay the hand of the judicial hangman."

All through yesterday the defense headquarters were many sober-minded and conscientious men and women who were genuinely troubled about the guilt or innocence of the accused and the fairness of their trial. It seemed to me I ought to attempt to find these men guilty, but when forced to do so by the evidence.

At 10 o'clock word was telephoned that the Governor had left the State House and that the decision would be announced at 10 o'clock.

Committee in Despair.

To Miss Donovan fell the lot of going to Mrs. Sacco and breaking the news. Mrs. Sacco received the tidings stoically and would make no comment.

After the decision had reached the defense headquarters a surprise. In a closely populated Italian section, it was thought that the streets would be filled during the evening and a large squad of plainclothes men was stationed in and about the section. Not more than a handful were at the entrances all during the evening.

After the decision had reached the defense office, a throng of photographers gathered at the entrances flashing pictures of the men and women leaving, their heavy and begging stops anxiously displaying their frame of mind and spirits.

Thompson Declines Comment.

William G. Thompson, attorney for the condemned men, went to his home in Newton shortly after 6 P. M. planning to return to the office at 8 o'clock before the receipt of the news of the Governor's decision. Upon being informed that the decision would not be announced until 9:30 P. M. or later he decided

Continued on Page Three.

Crowds Awaited the Governor's Decision; Fuller's Homes and Other Buildings Guarded

BOSTON, Aug. 3 (AP).—Throngs in the streets in front of the newspaper bulletin boards tonight attested to the wide interest in the Sacco-Vanzetti case. The watchers, who included many women, waited quietly for several hours for the word to come of Governor Fuller's decision. A sprinkling of patrolmen paced the sidewalks where the crowds were the largest.

A detail of patrolmen was assigned to the vicinity of the Phillips house of the Massachusetts General Hospital, where Mrs. Fuller was at the bedside of her son, who is recovering from an operation for appendicitis. Another patrol patrolled the vicinity of the Ritz-Carlton Hotel in the early part of the evening when the Governor was there.

The Governor's city home in Beacon Street, his Summer home at Rye Beach, N. H.; the State prison, the County Courthouse and jail here and the county jail in Plymouth, Vanzetti's home, also were closely guarded.

Full Text of Gov. Fuller's Decision, Ending Long Fight of Prisoners

He Sketches the Crime of Which Sacco and Vanzetti Were Accused, Reviews the Trial in Detail and Concludes by Declaring the Verdict Right and the Men Guilty as Charged.

From a Staff Correspondent of The New York Times.

STATE HOUSE, Boston, Mass., Aug. 3.—Following is the complete text of the official decision of Governor Fuller in the case of Sacco and Vanzetti:

Decision of Governor Alvan T. Fuller in the matter of the appeal of Bartolomeo Vanzetti and Nicola Sacco from the sentence of death imposed under the laws of the Commonwealth:

On April 15, 1920, a paymaster and his guard were held up, robbed and brutally murdered at Braintree, Mass. On May 15, 1920, Nicola Sacco and Bartolomeo Vanzetti were arrested; they were later tried and found guilty of the murder. The verdict was followed by seven motions for a new trial and two appeals to the Supreme Court of the Commonwealth, all of which were heard and later denied. Prior to the trial of the two men in this case Vanzetti had been arrested, tried and convicted of an attempted hold-up on Dec. 24, 1919, at Bridgewater, Mass., and sentenced to fifteen years' imprisonment.

The appeal to the Governor was presented by counsel for the accused on May 3 of the present year. It was my first official connection with the case.

This appeal, presented to me in accordance with the provision in the Constitution of our Commonwealth, has been considered without intent on my part to violate the courts if I became convinced that the error had been committed or that the trial had been unfair to the accused.

Saw Doubt in Minds of Many.

I realised at the outset that there were many sober-minded and conscientious men and women who were genuinely troubled about the guilt or innocence of the accused and the fairness of their trial. It seemed to me I ought to attempt to find out, as well as I could, what public opinion was, and to learn whether there was substantial basis for any conclusion that I, or in fact any other one man, might reach. I believed that I could best reassure those doubters by having a committee conduct an investigation entirely independent of my own, their report to be made to me and to help in reaching correct conclusions.

I felt that if, after such a committee had conducted its investigation independently, we were not in substantial agreement, then the course of Massachusetts justice did not flow to as clear a channel as I believed it should. The final decision and responsibility was, of course, my own.

For this committee I desired men who were not only well and favorably known for their achievements in their own lines, but men whose reputation for intelligence, open-mindedness, intellectual honesty and good judgment were above reproach. I asked to serve on that committee, President Abbott Lawrence Lowell of Harvard University, former Judge Robert Grant and President Samuel W. Stratton of Massachusetts Institute of Technology.

No one of these had been asked to serve. They began work as soon as the other affairs could be arranged, labored continuously during much of June and through July, holding their sessions independently, and arrived unanimously at a conclusion which is wholly in accord with mine. The public owes these gentlemen a debt of gratitude for their high-minded, unselfish service on this disagreeable and extremely important problem.

Court Proceedings in Case.

The court proceedings in this case may be divided into two parts: First before the jury with Judge Thayer presiding; second, the hearings on the successive petitions for a new trial which were addressed to the Judge and passed upon by him. All those

Continued on Page Two.

DECISION LATE AT NIGHT

State Executive Backs the Original Verdict in Famous Case.

POSITIVE IN CONVICTION

Three Questions Involved in the Case as He Sees It, and He Answers Them Fully.

PRISONERS NOT YET TOLD

Warden Decides It Inadvisable to Inform Them of Doom Until Today.

From a Staff Correspondent of The New York Times.

BOSTON, Aug. 3.—That Nicola Sacco and Bartolomeo Vanzetti were guilty of the payroll murders and robbery at South Braintree on April 15, 1920, for which they have been condemned to die during the week of Aug. 10, was the decision of Governor Alvan T. Fuller, made public at 11:30 o'clock tonight at the State House.

Governor Fuller declared there was no sufficient reason for executive intervention; that there was no inadequate reason for granting a new trial, as the Dedham trial was conducted fairly and without prejudice by Judge Webster Thayer.

The Governor completely exonerated the Judge and jury against charges of unfairness; held that there was no valid reason for a new trial on the basis of newly discovered evidence; discarded the confession of Celestino Madeiros, who swore that, in the South Braintree murders and hold-up, Sacco and Vanzetti were not implicated; and pointed out that the advisory committee designated by him was unanimously of the same opinion.

The committee consisted of President A. Lawrence Lowell of Harvard University; President Samuel W. Stratton of the Massachusetts Institute of Technology, and former Judge of Probate Robert Grant.

Warden to Tell Men Today.

Warden Hendry of Charlestown State Prison received the news of Governor Fuller's decision almost as soon as it was given out at the State House. He said he would not convey it to the condemned men until tomorrow, after their second night in the death house.

The decision is expected to speed up world-wide protests on behalf of the two anarchists, whose sympathizers have kept up a continuous agitation for seven years.

The decision made public tonight was perhaps the most carefully guarded secret concerning an appeal in a criminal case that has ever been locked in the bosom of a Chief Executive. Yesterday, an authoritative source in the official family of Governor Fuller stated that the Governor would neither send the men to the electric chair nor would he allow them to go scot free.

The statement was made with emphasis and apparently out of full knowledge of the Governor's decision. There was no equivocation, no "ifs, buts or ands." This gave rise at the eleventh hour to the apparently well-authenticated report that a reprieve under certain conditions would be the solution.

Now that the Governor has decided to allow the law to take its course, it will not be necessary for him to consult with the State Executive Council. That body was to have held a regular meeting at noon today and was expected to hold over until tomorrow. This was irregularity by the defense as a hopeful sign, a consultation with the council meant to them anything but the death sentence.

Governor Defines His Inquiry.

The inquiry of the Governor was concerned, as he explained in his decision, with three questions:

"Was the jury trial fair?"

"Were the accused entitled to a new trial?"

"Are they guilty or not guilty?"

He declared that the eleven living members of the jury were men of the opinion that the men had a fair trial.

Discussing the subject of prejudice against Judge Webster Thayer, Governor Fuller cleared the presiding Judge and said he saw no evidence of prejudice in the conduct of the trial.

The Governor's decision had been awaited by throngs in the Boston streets, a tense situation existing as they waited for hours while copies

"All the News That's Fit to Print."

The New York Times.

THE WEATHER
Cloudy with probable showers today; tomorrow partly cloudy.
Temperature Yesterday—Max. 77; Min. 68.
☞For weather report see Page 20.

VOL. LXXVI....No. 25,413.   ....   NEW YORK, TUESDAY, AUGUST 23, 1927.   TWO CENTS *In Greater New York* | *THREE CENTS* *Within 200 Miles* | *FOUR CENTS* *Elsewhere*

SACCO AND VANZETTI PUT TO DEATH EARLY THIS MORNING; GOVERNOR FULLER REJECTS LAST-MINUTE PLEAS FOR DELAY AFTER A DAY OF LEGAL MOVES AND DEMONSTRATIONS

COOLIDGE PERCHES GOVERNMENT'S SEAT ON PEAK IN ROCKIES

He Reaches Yellowstone Park and Begins at Once His Sight-Seeing Trips.

VISITS CAMP ROOSEVELT

President Passes First Night in a Cottage Surrounded by Snow-Clad Mountains.

CROWDS EXTEND GREETINGS

Mrs. Coolidge and John Share in Ovations at Stations Where Special Train Halted.

From a Staff Correspondent of The New York Times.

MAMMOTH HOT SPRINGS, Yellowstone Park, Wyo., Aug. 22.—The seat of Government tonight is established on a high peak in the Rockies, the furthermost point west to which it has ever gone, in the majestic scenery of Yellowstone Park. With the arrival of President and Mrs. Coolidge into the national playground through the Gardiner entrance the Presidential flag was unfurled over a gray rambling cottage, the home of H. W. Child, President of the Yellowstone Transportation Company.

Here for one night the President will remain but in the next four days he will pass each night in a different place as he travels over the park.

The Presidential special train reached Gardiner in a Summer rainstorm. The mountain tops were covered with snow and through the clouds the sun was shining, presenting a rainbow that added to the first view of the President and Mrs. Coolidge had of the national playground.

Coins Word 'Avigation' For Directing of Aircraft

Special to The New York Times.

WASHINGTON, Aug. 22.—The suggestion that the word "avigation" be used in connection with aeronautics has been made by Lieutenant Lester J. Maitland, who piloted an army plane in the first successful non-stop flight from California to Hawaii. The idea has found favor with officers of the Navy Bureau of Aeronautics.

Lieutenant Maitland suggested that "we use the term 'avigation' for the directing or operating of aircraft from one place to another."

WILBUR PREDICTS STUNT FLIGHT CURB

Naval Secretary Says Federal Law Must Stop Loss of Life as in Pacific Race.

TAKES STAND WITH EBERLE

Navy Extends Search for Dole Fliers by Two Days, but Has No Clues.

By The Associated Press.

SAN FRANCISCO, Cal., Aug. 22.—While navy ships and planes searched under an extended "zero hour," Secretary of the Navy Curtis D. Wilbur, a San Francisco visitor, and officials in Washington agreed today that some Federal move must be made to prevent a recurrence of the disasters that have befallen the Dole air race entrants.

WALKER JOKES WITH BEEFEATER GUIDE IN TOWER OF LONDON

Thinks He Could Find Use for Headsman's Block in New York.

RECEIVES STATE WELCOME

Rides With Mrs. Walker From Station to Hotel in Lord Mayor's Gilded Coach.

TENEMENTS IMPRESS HIM

As Guest of Lord Mayor He Sees Greyhounds Race—Leaves for Berlin Today.

Copyright, 1927, by The New York Times Company.
Special Cable to The New York Times.

LONDON, Aug. 22.—Mayor Walker's last day in London was a busy one. He visited the Tower of London, received a delegation of advertising men, inspected model tenements and after a quiet dinner at his hotel attended the greyhound races at White City tonight as the guest of the Lord Mayor of London.

Society Gets Old Irving Home For Centre of Patriotic Work

The old home of Washington Irving at Seventeenth Street and Irving Place became the property of the National Society of Patriotic Builders of America yesterday when, in the living room, Mrs. William Cumming Story, President of the society, received the title from Algernon S. Bell, the former owner.

MRS. CHAPLIN WINS DIVORCE AND $825,000

She Gets $625,000 for Herself and $200,000 in Trust for the Two Children.

SUIT BASED ON CRUELTY

Actor Is Not in Los Angeles Court to Hear Her and Friends Tell of Alleged Neglect.

Special to The New York Times.

LOS ANGELES, Aug. 22.—Mrs. Lita Grey Chaplin received an interlocutory decree of divorce from Charles Spencer Chaplin, custody of their two small children and $825,000 in Superior Court today. The film comedian did not appear in court. A year must elapse before a final decree is granted.

FULLER HEARS PETITIONERS

Governor Is Under Steady Pressure Until the Final Hour.

WOMEN LAST TO APPEAL

Mrs. Sacco and Miss Vanzetti Leave Him and at 11:03 P. M. He Gives Decision.

DEFENSE TRIED EVERY PLEA

Stone, Taft, Holmes and Other Federal as Well as State Judges Refused to Act.

From a Staff Correspondent of The New York Times.

BOSTON, Aug. 22.—Governor Fuller, at the end of a day marked by rapid and continuous action of the defense for Nicola Sacco and Bartolomeo Vanzetti, told Michael A. Musmanno of defense counsel at 11:03 o'clock tonight that he would not interfere in the execution.

Four Final Legal Pleas Made to the Governor That Failed to Delay Execution of Death Sentence

From a Staff Correspondent of The New York Times.

BOSTON, Aug. 22.—Four final appeals to Governor Fuller for delay in the execution of the death sentences on Sacco and Vanzetti were based on the following grounds:

1. Willingness of the Department of Justice to open its files to the Commonwealth authorities.
2. The official docketing of the appeal for a writ of certiorari in the United States Supreme Court, which could not be acted on by the court until October.
3. A specific request from Arthur D. Hill, chief defense attorney, to allow alienists to examine Sacco and Vanzetti.
4. A request from Mr. Hill, dated last Friday, to delay until the matter of the Supreme Court and the Department of Justice files had been cleared up.

Governor Fuller, after a full day's consideration of these pleas, announced that he would take no further action.

CITY CROWDS SILENT ON NEWS OF DEATHS

Sacco Sympathizers Disperse After Many Protest Meetings Earlier in Night.

POLICE DOUBLY VIGILANT

Force Guards All Vital Points, While Warren and Inspectors Stay on Duty All Night.

The news that the death sentence had been carried out on Sacco and Vanzetti was received in mournful silence by their sympathizers here, who had assembled at various points in the city last night to follow the events in the case to the end.

BOSTON BESIEGED; SCORES ARRESTED

Thousands Watch Squad After Squad of Sacco Picketers March Into Police Hands.

CHEERS AND JEERS MINGLE

Advances on State House Last Till Bail Gives Out—Night Move on Bunker Hill Fails.

From a Staff Correspondent of The New York Times.

BOSTON, Aug. 22.—Boston, most of whose citizens went calmly about their business twelve days ago when the execution of Nicola Sacco and Bartolomeo Vanzetti was stayed until midnight tonight, lost its indifference today and thousands stood in the streets when the final word came.

WALK TO DEATH CALMLY

Sacco Cries 'Long Live Anarchy'; Vanzetti Insists on His Innocence.

WARDEN CAN ONLY WHISPER

Much Affected as the Long-Delayed Execution Is Carried Out.

MADEIROS FIRST TO DIE

Machine Guns Bristle, Searchlights Glare During Execution—Crowds Kept Far From Prison.

From a Staff Correspondent of The New York Times.

CHARLESTOWN STATE PRISON, Mass., Tuesday, Aug. 23.—Nicola Sacco and Bartolomeo Vanzetti died in the electric chair early this morning, carrying out the sentence imposed on them for the South Braintree murders of April 15, 1920.

Sacco marched to the death chair at 12:11 and was pronounced lifeless at 12:19.

Vanzetti entered the execution room at 12:20 and was declared dead at 12:26.

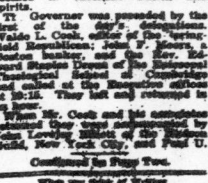

Dawes Declares He Is Not a Candidate, Declining Young America Union's Support

Special to The New York Times.

CINCINNATI, Aug. 22.—Vice President Dawes has informed Douglas T. Atkinson, Judge Advocate of the Young America Union, a secret nonsectarian political organization, that he is not a candidate for the nomination for the Presidency.

33

"All the News That's Fit to Print."

The New York Times.

THE WEATHER
Fair today and tomorrow; not much change in temperature.
Temperature yesterday—Max., 68; Min., 53.
For weather report see Page 34.

VOL. LXXVII....No. 25,444.　　　　NEW YORK, FRIDAY, SEPTEMBER 23, 1927.　　　　TWO CENTS In Greater New York | THREE CENTS | FOUR CENTS

GENE TUNNEY KEEPS TITLE BY DECISION AFTER 10 ROUNDS; DEMPSEY INSISTS FOE WAS OUT IN 7TH, AND WILL APPEAL; 150,000 SEE CHICAGO FIGHT, MILLIONS LISTEN ON RADIO

LEGIONAIRES ELECT SPAFFORD AS CHIEF, ENDING CONVENTION

New York Man Is Unanimous Choice for National Commander.

GETS OVATION AT SESSION

Veterans in Paris Approve the Stand of Administration at the Geneva Naval Parley.

PASS MITCHELL'S AIR PLAN

Project for Further Immigration Ban Is Tabled—Bissell of New York Heads '40 and 8.'

Copyright, 1927, by The New York Times Company
Special Cable to The New York Times.

PARIS, Sept. 22.—The convention in France of the American Legion, so long planned and so long heralded, is now history.

The "greatest ever," as the conventioneers term it. The convention is now known to the Legionaires, came to a close this afternoon in a typical burst of fireworks with the election of the new National Commander and other Legion officials. Edward Elwell Spafford of New York City was the man selected for the Legion's highest honor, and he was chosen unanimously, no other name being even offered to the delegates.

When the choice, which represented the wishes of Legion men from all parts of the country, as he was nominated by the North Carolina delegation and seconded by Washington, was announced the convention broke into pandemonium.

Paris had never before witnessed such a scene. The Legionaires started shouting and honking horns, while canes rapped applause like the sputter of machine guns.

Mr. Spafford was escorted to the platform amid the blare of bugles, the shrill of fifes and the thunder of the drums of the band of the Buffalo Post, while men "over the top" into the press box so as to be nearer the centre of activities, scattering the astonished newspaper men.

Nearly Mobbed in Congratulations.

Immediately a seething ocean of Legionaires was trying to shake his hands, thump his back and congratulate him in any way, form and manner as it swirled around him. He climbed into the speaker's box, which was almost the only island of safety, but it was fully ten minutes before the noise was sufficiently quieted to allow him to make a short speech of acceptance and thanks.

It was a fitting star in which to end the spectacular convention, for it was marked by the same combination of seriousness of purpose and uproarious good humor and enthusiasm which so impressed the Paris populace in the big parade of last Monday. America's unmistakable, if occasionally boisterous, sincerity is now a French byword.

It was also the right spirit in which to close the proceedings, as it wiped out any ill feeling which may have been aroused by the vehement discussions which marred the attempts to map out the Legion's policies in the earlier hours of the session.

As the nominations for the Vice Commanders were made the Legionaires reamed their good-natured gayety. The well-known cry of "Never heard of it!" rang out again and again as the various State delegations were called on. But the great opportunity for the now-renowned humorous sally of the former soldiers came when, on a point of order, a delegate from the Redwood State said, "California yields to Florida."

"What's that?" came back from every corner of the enormous room amid general laughter, while the Florida delegate cried, "Louder!" and was greeted with cheers.

Election of Vice Commanders.

The five National Vice Commanders chosen represented all sections of the country. They are Paul B. Eustis of Washington, Paul R. Younts of North Carolina, Daniel W. Spurlock of Louisiana, J. M. Henry of Minnesota and Ralph T. O'Neill of Kansas.

The Rev. Gill Robb Wilson was elected National Chaplain. He comes from Trenton, N. J., and was formerly an aviator in the Lafayette Escadrille.

The convention was called to order at 9 o'clock in the morning and lasted, without recess, until nearly 4 in the afternoon. Almost its first official act was to confer on Count Dejean, of the French Department of Foreign Affairs, the distinguished service cross of the Legion in recognition of his valuable services for Legion, to which he was assigned by Foreign Minister Briand to aid in putting out.

Continued on Page Five.

Stinson and Schilling Forced Down and Out Of New York to Spokane Non-Stop Air Derby

From a Staff Correspondent of The New York Times.

FELTS FIELD, SPOKANE, Wash., Sept. 22.—The non-stop race from New York to Spokane came to a definite end today when Eddie Stinson was forced down by engine trouble at Missoula, Mont., and C. A. (Duke) Schiller came down at Billings, Mont.

Stinson would have won the race if he had been flying over country where he could have made a landing at any time. When the intake and exhaust valves on one cylinder of his motor went out, he flew around for several hours, trying to get altitude enough to go on with sufficient gliding distance to make a safe landing.

But he could not get up high enough, and after four or five hours went down at the landing field at Missoula. The field is only 200 miles from Spokane and the time he spent flying in circles would have been sufficient for him to get here. But it was too risky and he wisely quit. Stinson came in with R. E. Duke in a Waco, the last entry in Class A to arrive. He picked Stinson up as a passenger. Stinson has become a philosopher in his attitude toward long-distance flying. "Sometimes you make it and sometimes you don't," is his motto.

"We had good weather most of the way," he said, "although there was some rain and fog over Michigan. We kept to a great circle course which took us through the centre of Lake Erie and over the other lakes. A good part of the time we were out of sight of land. It got dark while we were over Michigan and dawn found us over North Dakota. I think we kept to our course fairly well all the time until I began circling around after engine trouble developed."

There was much disappointment among the 30,000 people at the field, who had been waiting all day for the non-stop fliers to arrive. The enthusiastic crowd, which cheers every pilot who arrives as if he were a favorite son, gave a rousing reception to Stinson.

INDIANAPOLIS MAYOR QUICKLY CONVICTED

Duvall Faces 30 Days in Jail, $1,000 Fine and 4-Year Bar From Office for Corruption.

TAKES VERDICT IN SILENCE

Bitterness Marks Closing Pleas, Defense Laying Charges to a "Malicious Press."

Special to The New York Times.

INDIANAPOLIS, Sept. 22.—Mayor John L. Duvall was found guilty of violation of the Corrupt Practices act in the Marion County Criminal Court tonight. The penalty is thirty days in the Marion County Jail and a fine of $1,000.

The verdict, reported by the jury at 8 o'clock after three hours' deliberation, makes Mayor Duvall ineligible to hold public office for four years after the date of the crime.

Duvall was pale when the verdict was read and his only comment was: "I have nothing to say."

Under the Corrupt Practices act Duvall was specifically charged with promising William H. Armitage, a politician, the privilege of naming three members of the City Administration in exchange for a cash consideration and support in the 1925 mayoralty campaign. The same Grand Jury which acted upon results of a year's inquiry into alleged political corruption in Indiana also indicted Governor Ed Jackson on a charge of attempting to bribe former Governor Warren T. McCray.

Final Pleas Stir Courtroom.

Ralph Inman, defense counsel, and William H. Remy, Marion County Prosecutor, this afternoon made the packed courtroom spellbound during their pleas which at times became so bitter that the audience gasped.

The crowd got so worked up that once, when work upon a new elevator shaft in the courthouse loosened plaster and showered it through an air duct out into the courtroom, half a hundred spectators sprang to their feet in alarm.

Mr. Remy demanded that the jury send Duvall behind the bars for violating the Corrupt Practices act. Mr. Inman denounced the prosecution of Duvall as the result of acts of a malicious press and demanded that the press be "driven out of town."

With Mr. Remy's argument closing about 4:30 and Special Judge Cassius C. Shirley taking about half an hour for instructions, the case went to the jury at about 5 P. M.

Mr. Inman fired broadsides of ridicule at the State attorneys and the chief State witness, William H. Armitage, and Mr. Remy spent about half of his time in reply.

Answering Mr. Inman's charge that the prosecution of Duvall was a matter of political hatred, Mr. Remy pounded upon the railing of the jury box and declared:

"As long as I am in office this fight against political corruption is going to continue and I pledge myself to the jury and to all the people here that this case will not be the end."

Hurling invectives at the prosecution attorneys and the press, Mr. Inman, who defended D. C. Stephenson, the ex-Klan leader, at Noblesville two years ago and lost, proclaimed Duvall the victim of persecution.

Defense Denounces the Press.

Mr. Inman declared that Duvall was the victim of "a sinister influence in Indianapolis which must be satisfied and should be driven out—a malicious press."

"John Duvall isn't the first Indianapolis man made to stand and defend himself solely because he was unfortunate enough to run and be elected to office," he declared.

In his attack on William H. Freeman and William H. Armitage, the State's chief witness, Mr. Inman accused Freeman of "willful, corrupt and deliberate" perjury in part of his testimony.

"It is significant that Armitage never talked before his brother was sentenced to jail," he said. "You could tell by the look in his eyes he would tell any kind of a story to save his brother from going to prison for three months."

Continued on Page Five.

DARING FLIER, NUMB, AVOIDS CRASH IN CITY

Steve Lacey, on Western Dash, Dazed by Fumes as Gasoline Swirls About His Feet.

MOTOR SPUTTERED AN HOUR

He Fails to Dump Fuel, Fights Back to Field, Lands Safely and Falls Unconscious.

Special to The New York Times.

ROOSEVELT FIELD, L. I., Sept. 22.—A courageous pilot with a sputtering engine fought for an hour to keep his plane under control over New York City and the surrounding area yesterday afternoon, while gasoline swirled four inches deep around his feet and sent up fumes which numbed his hands and his brain. Battling these obstacles, he brought the plane down on the field here and fell over unconscious.

The pilot was Steve Lacey, who had tried so desperately to take part in the non-stop race to the Pacific against C. S. (Duke) Schiller and Eddie Stinson. With his navigator, Louis A. Yancey, he had worked most of the night repairing his blue and silver biplane Air King, which had lost its tail skid in an unsuccessful effort to take off yesterday.

Today, though the New York-Spokane air derby time limit was past and he could not hope to share in the non-stop prize money, he took off again in an endeavor to make good his promise to fly westward "just for fun." The ill luck which balked him at 12:52 P. M. again soon disappeared from sight. In a few minutes they reappeared and came down with their heavily laden plane, making a perfect landing at 300 miles an hour. Their engine was not functioning properly. It was tuned again and readjusted and up they soared once more.

Saved City From a Disaster.

Then came the mishap unique in aviation, which almost cost both men their lives and only for their heroism would have sent a plane loaded with hundreds of gallons of gasoline roaring in flames into the streets of New York.

Misfortune threatened them from the start of their last flight. It was 2:21 P. M. The Wright Whirlwind motor apparently was functioning perfectly again as Lacey gave the ship the gun and it rolled along the ground. It was running beautifully at 2,000 feet from the starting point.

Purpose of the Meeting.

Continued on Page Four.

TREND TOWARD SMITH PLAIN IN FAR WEST AS LEADERS GATHER

Indications Point to First Raising of His Banner at Ogden (Utah) Conference.

11 STATES REPRESENTED

Iowa Democrats at Own Request, Join Gathering, Which Begins Deliberations Today.

TARIFF IS ON THE AGENDA

Most Available Presidential Candidate and Two-thirds Rule Also Topics.

From a Staff Correspondent of The New York Times.

OGDEN, Utah, Sept. 22.—Democrats in the intermountain States, who went to the Democratic National Convention in 1924 for the most part as enthusiastic supporters of William Gibbs McAdoo, are swinging to Governor Alfred E. Smith of New York. There are indications that at a conference which will begin here tomorrow for the discussion of problems vital to the party they will make the Smith banner and start the first organized movement in the nation to further the Presidential aspirations of New York's Chief Executive, who, as he did in 1924, will enter next year's Democratic national conclave as the favorite son of his party in the Empire State.

At the Hotel Bigelow, where the conference will be held, fifty rooms have been reserve for prospective conferees, and it is probable that fully that many will attend. Nearly all of those who are expected to answer the roll-call when the session is called to order at 10 o'clock tomorrow morning are former adherents of Mr. McAdoo. Almost without exception, too, they are at least politically dry, as are the Democratic organizations in the several States that will be represented at the gathering.

Prominent Conferees.

At least two Democratic National Committeemen who wield considerable influence in party councils have accepted invitations to the conference. They are Isidore B. Dockweiler of California and James H. Moyle of Utah. Today, unexpectedly and to the great delight of those who have taken the initiative in calling the intermountain Democrats together, there was added to the number of prominent participants Delbert M. Draper of Salt Lake City, Chairman of the Central Committee, and, it is said here, a real power in the party organization in this State. Another spokesman for Utah will be J. W. Stringfellow, leader of the organization in Salt Lake County, which supplies approximately one-half of the votes cast in the State. He is openly for Governor Smith for President.

Fred W. Johnson of Rock Springs, Wyo., and former State Senator Joseph Chez of Utah, to whom initiative and earnest labors for many years have made the Democrats in these Far Western States own their opportunity for coming together to discuss party problems, and today that it should be clearly understood that no one will be asked at the conference to deliver the delegation from his own State to Governor Smith for President.

Purpose of the Meeting.

It is admitted, in fact, that grave doubt exists whether any of the conferees would be in a position to make such a pledge now.

Continued on Page Four.

GREATEST RING SPECTACLE

Crowd Pays $2,800,000 to Watch Contest at Soldier Field.

THRONG IN SEATS EARLY

Largest Boxing Assemblage in History Handled Smoothly by Police and Ushers.

MANY NOTABLES PRESENT

Senators, Governors and Business Leaders Rub Elbows With Obscure Sport Fans.

By JAMES R. HARRISON.
Special to The New York Times.

CHICAGO, Sept. 22.—Out of the welter and turmoil and clamor of the "fight of the ages" one clear fact stands out—that tonight Tex Rickard unveiled the most beautiful picture in the history of sports here or elsewhere.

One hundred and fifty thousand persons watched in the darkness—the greatest of all boxing crowds by about 35,000. It would fill more than two Yankee Stadiums and almost two Yale Bowls; it would pack the Polo Grounds to capacity and leave 100,000 on the outside.

The total receipts were put at $2,800,000.

Governors and Mayors and United States Senators and millionaires lent the right tone to the occasion and millions listened to the story of the fight as it went out "on the air."

Yet the facts and figures do not seem particularly important as compared to the sheer beauty of a picture that only an artist could paint. This may or may not have been "the fight of the ages," but it most certainly was the "sight of the ages."

The veil of darkness over it all, the rippling sea of humanity stretching out as far as the eye could see; the Doric columns of Soldier Field glowing a soft white along the upper battlements of the 'arena'; and finally the ring itself, where two men fought it out with their fists in a pool of white light—these were the high spots of an unforgettable spectacle.

Impressive in Its Vastness.

It was a picture that should have been seen from the air, from the cockpit of an airplane, where the lights and shadows and the blacks and whites of the panorama could have been viewed in their proper perspective.

"The ingredients of the picture were striking. A long, low oval stadium of classic lines, filled to its utmost rim. A gently sloping bank of humanity that seemed to stretch to the horizon. Set in the centre of the canvas a twenty-foot ring bathed in the fierce light that beats about a throne.

The vastness of the spectacle was its most impressive quality. It filled the eye and staggered the senses. We took the bout. "In the seventh round Tunney was down for a count of fourteen or fifteen. Every stopwatch around the ring caught the time at about fifteen seconds, and here came the same Soldier Field at the Army-Navy game, but this was the crowd of crowds and the spectacle of spectacles, lacking only the natural beauty of Poughkeepsie and New London.

Even though he did not sell all of his 163,000 seats, Tex Rickard reached a long cherished goal in his career as an impresario. The 80,000 of Boyle's Thirty Acres and the 115,000 of the Sesquicentennial were left far behind in Chicago and the influx of fight fans poured through the portals of this sports temple.

There they sat, shoulder to shoulder, packed in the top tier where American flags rippled in a brisk western wind. Not that the stadium was full. The cheaper seats, a few city blocks to the north and south, were sparsely settled, proving that you may lead a boxing fan to water but you can't make him drink.

This will probably stand as the record crowd of ring history, because people will sit only so far away from the scene of activities. And tonight Rickard reached the limit in distances. His $5 patrons were 700 or more feet from the ring, which at the Yankee Stadium would take them somewhere beyond the centre field fence.

Some Bring Radio Sets.

Time was when a fight fan could buy almost any seat and see the proceedings with the naked eye. But no more. As the citizens flocked through the gates half of them were armed with binoculars, opera glasses and telescope. Now and then one could see some shrewd lads who had brought portable radios with them. They were the $5 boys, who were going to listen even if they did not see.

The weather man was not fooling when he said fair and warmer, for the fans brought light coats with them. But they were hardly necessary, especially around the ring, where the heat of the bright lights was very noticeable.

The afternoon was gray and overcast and twilight showed a drab, threatening sky and mist which threw

Continued on Page Twenty.

GENE TUNNEY, STILL THE CHAMPION.

DEMPSEY TO APPEAL DECISION ON FIGHT

He Says Tunney Was Down for 14 or 15 Seconds in the Seventh Round.

TIMEKEEPER CITES RULE

And Boxing Commissioner Says the Point Was Explained Before Bout Started.

Special to The New York Times.

CHICAGO, Sept. 22.—Jack Dempsey and his manager, Leo Flynn, announced tonight that they intend to appeal to the Illinois Boxing Commission to reverse the decision of the referee and two judges allowing Gene Tunney to retain his world's heavyweight title.

"Intentionally or otherwise, I was robbed of the championship," Dempsey said in his dressing room after the bout. "In the seventh round Tunney was down for a count of fourteen or fifteen. Every stopwatch around the ring caught the time at about fifteen seconds, and the inefficiency of the referee or the timekeeper or both deprived me of the fight.

"Everybody knows I got out a winner. When Tunney beat me last year I admitted that he was the better man that night. I am not an alibi artist, but I know down in my soul that I knocked Tunney out tonight, and, what's more, chased him all around the ring and should have won on points at least."

Tunney Out, Says Flynn.

Flynn paced up and down the dressing room like a caged lion. "Everything Jack told you goes double for me," said Flynn. "Before the bout the Boxing Commission said they would see that we got a square deal and would step in and reverse an unfair decision. Now I'm going to take them at their word and make a formal appeal tomorrow to have tonight's verdict reversed.

"Tunney was cleanly knocked out for the count of fifteen in the seventh round. Look at that watch here. It has stopped on the figure fifteen. I have not found a watch yet that got the count under ten. I'm not saying the referee was deficient. I'm saying that he was inefficient, and it amounts to the same thing as far as we are concerned.

"He failed to take up the timekeeper's count at the start—didn't take it up until the timekeeper had got to four or five. This is the biggest injustice I have ever seen in a ring. Leaving aside the knockout in the seventh round, Jack knocked him down again in the ninth and chased him all around the ring. Why didn't Tunney come out and fight like a champ?"

Dempsey clearly won in the last three rounds.

"You can say this for me, Dempsey will fight Tunney any time and any place and knock him out."

Dempsey Wants Another Fight.

"Will I fight him again?" echoed Dempsey. "You bet your life. I beat Tunney tonight and I'll beat him again any time he wants to get into the same ring with me. I am not ready to retire, by a long shot—not before I've had another crack at Tunney."

There was plenty of high dudgeon in the Dempsey dressing room.

Continued on Page Eighteen.

STORY OF THE FIGHT TOLD BLOW BY BLOW

Detailed Description of Tunney-Dempsey Bout From the Ringside.

BOTH FIGHTERS AGGRESSIVE

Bout Is Marked by Lively Exchanges—Dempsey Hangs On at the End.

Special to The New York Times.

RINGSIDE, SOLDIER FIELD, CHICAGO, Sept. 22.—The detail of the Tunney-Dempsey bout, which was fought here tonight, follows, round by round:

First Round.

Dempsey rushed Tunney, who sidestepped, and Dempsey again swung a left and clinched and Tunney hooked a left. Tunney hit a right to face as they clinched. Referee pulled them apart. Tunney flashed left to Dempsey's face. Dempsey bobbed and weaved and jabbed to Tunney's jaw. Tunney crossed with a right to Dempsey's jaw. Tunney twice jabbed with lefts to the face and they clinched. Tunney followed with a right to Dempsey's jaw and then dodged away from Dempsey's left hook. Gene hooked to Dempsey's body. Gene again got Jack against the ropes and they clinched. Tunney then jabbed a left to the face.

Second Round.

Tunney jabbed a left to face. Dempsey sent one to chest. They clinched and Tunney held Dempsey's arm. Dempsey put a straight left to the body and Tunney a right to the jaw backing Dempsey to the ropes. Tunney missed a right to the jaw as Dempsey ducked and then Tunney drove a right to the head. Dempsey hooked a left to the head and pounded the body when Tunney held left himself open. Tunney drove two rights to the head and clinched. Tunney crossed a right to the face and Tunney then crossed away from Dempsey's left. A left to the body and Tunney a left to the body and head. Tunney drove two rights to Dempsey's head. Dempsey sent a left to Tunney's face and another to the body.

Third Round.

They danced about at start of the third and Gene led with a right as Dempsey hooked three lefts to the body. Gene started a right hook to Jack's body, but stopped the blow short as they clinched. Tunney missed Dempsey and landed with short lefts. Jack drove away at Gene's body, the blows being partly ready close to the belt line. They got in at close quarters and Dempsey shouted "Low" to the referee. Dempsey was short with a left and Tunney missed a short right and Dempsey danced away from a short right. Gene missed a left and came in at close quarters to head Dempsey.

Continued on Page Eighteen.

FIGHT FAST AND FURIOUS

On Verge of Knockout in Seventh Round Tunney Comes Back Strong.

FLOORS DEMPSEY IN EIGHTH

Referee and Judges Unanimous in Their Verdict for the Champion.

DISPUTE ON KNOCKDOWN

Challenger Went to Wrong Corner and Thus Delayed Count on Tunney for Few Seconds.

By JAMES P. DAWSON.
Special to The New York Times.

RINGSIDE, SOLDIER FIELD, CHICAGO, Sept. 22.—Observing the boxing rules of the Illinois State Athletic Commission, or his ignorance of the rules, or both, cost Jack Dempsey the chance to regain the world's heavyweight championship here tonight in the ring at Soldier Field.

By the same token this disregard of rules of ring warfare, or this surprising ignorance, saved the title for Gene Tunney, the fighting ex-marine, who has been king of the ring for just a year.

The ended with Tunney getting the decision, and the vast majority in the staggering assemblage of 150,000 people, who paid, it is estimated, $2,800,000 to see this great sport spectacle, approved the verdict.

The decision was given by Referee Dave Barry and Judges George Lytton, wealthy department store owner, and Commodore Sheldon Clark of the Sinclair Oil Company. It was announced as a unanimous decision, but this could not be verified in the excitement attending the finish of the battle. But it should have been unanimous according to all methods of reasoning and boxing scoring, for Tunney won seven of the ten rounds, losing only the third, sixth and seventh, in the last of which, Dempsey made his great mistake. It is known that Judge Lytton voted for Tunney.

Dempsey's Furious Plunge.

In that seventh round Dempsey was being peppered and buffeted about on the end of Tunney's left jabs and hooks and sharp though light right crosses, as he had been in every preceding round, with the exception of the third.

In a masterful exhibition of boxing Tunney was evading the attack of his heavier rival and was countering cleanly, superbly, skillfully, accurately the while for half of the round or so.

Then Dempsey, plunging in recklessly, charging Jack relentlessly, with an utter contempt for the blows of the champion, since he had tasted of Tunney's best previously, suddenly lashed a long, wicked left to the jaw with the power of old. This he followed with a right to the jaw, the old "iron mike" as deadly as ever, and quickly drove another left hook to the jaw, under which Tunney toppled like a falling tree, hitting the canvas with a solid thud striking Dempsey's corner, his head reaching blindly for a helping rope which somehow or other refused to be within clutching distance.

Then Dempsey made his mistake, an error which, I believe, cost him the title he values so highly.

Count Began and Halted.

The knockdown brought the knockdown timekeeper, Paul Beeler, to his feet automatically, watch in hand, eye glued to the ticking seconds and he bawled "one" before he looked upon the scene in the ring.

There he saw Dempsey in his own corner, directly above the prostrate, brain-numbed Tunney, sitting there looking foolishly anxious, while the timekeeper's count on the middle ring strand. Beeler's count stopped. Referee Barry never started one.

It is the referee's duty to see to it that a boxer scoring a knockdown goes to the corner farthest removed from his fallen foe and it is the duty of the knockdown timekeeper

Continued on Page Eighteen.

Pope Pius Sends $100,000 to Flood Sufferers; Bishops in Mississippi Area to Distribute It

Pope Pius XI has contributed $100,000 to the relief of the flood sufferers in the Mississippi Valley. The gift was made public here yesterday by the Right Rev. Dr. Edmond A. Walsh, vice president of Georgetown University and President of the Catholic Near East Welfare Association. Dr. Walsh was Director General of Papal Relief during the post-war famine in Europe.

The Pope's intention to help victims of the flood was first made known by the Pontiff during a recent visit of Dr. Walsh to the Vatican. Dr. Walsh went to Rome to report on the activities of the new association. Joseph P. Moore, General Secretary of the association, was also present when the Pope first made known his intention to make the donation.

Dr. Walsh was designated by the Pontiff to bring the gift to America and present it to the hierarchy of the United States. This he did last week in Washington, the annual meeting of the archbishops and bishops in the Catholic University of America.

Announcement of the contribution was made by Cardinal O'Connell of Boston, Chairman of the meeting. A Committee of Bishops from the flood area was formed immediately. On the committee are:

The Most Rev. John W. Shaw, Archbishop of New Orleans; the Right Rev. John B. Morris, Bishop of Little Rock, Ark.; the Right Rev. Cornelius Van de Ven, Bishop of Alexandria, Va.; the Right Rev. Jules V. Jeannard, Bishop of Lafayette, La.; the Right Rev. Richard O. Gerow, Bishop of Natchez, Miss.

The committee is now drawing up recommendations for the most economical and practical disposal of the money.

"As head of the Catholic Church, Pope Pius desired to do something proposal in addition to the help already sent to the stricken areas by the various dioceses in the United States," said Dr. Walsh yesterday at his headquarters, 480 Lexington Avenue. "The only regret of his Holiness was that he could not send more."

"All the News That's Fit to Print."

The New York Times.

THE WEATHER
Partly cloudy and continued cold today and tomorrow; west winds. Temperature yesterday—Max. 33, Min. 24.
☞For weather report see Page 42.

VOL. LXXVII....No. 25,531. ⋆ ⋆ ⋆ NEW YORK, MONDAY, DECEMBER 19, 1927. TWO CENTS ☆ ☆ ☆ THREE CENTS ☆ ☆ ☆ FOUR CENTS ☆ ☆ ☆

SIX MEN FOUND ALIVE IN TORPEDO ROOM OF SUNKEN S-4;
TAP PATHETIC PLEA 'HOW LONG WILL YOU BE?' TO DIVER;
NAVY BATTLES AGAINST TIME TO LIFT SHATTERED CRAFT

AMITY WITH MEXICO IS BROUGHT CLOSER BY LINDBERGH VISIT

Mexico City Hears President Calles Will Go to Havana to Meet Coolidge.

TOTTERING STOCKS RISE

Confidence in Efforts of Ambassador Morrow and the Flier Revives Business.

POPULAR FEELING CHANGING

Parading Workers Cheer Lindbergh and Morrow—Aviator Sees a Bullfight, but Is Silent.

By RUSSELL OWEN.
Staff Correspondent of The New York Times.
Copyright, 1927, by The New York Times Company.
By Wireless to The New York Times.

MEXICO CITY, Dec. 18.—The visit of Colonel Charles A. Lindbergh to Mexico already has brought about some remarkable results, political, economic and social. He has acted as a clarifying agent in a slowly developing situation. Not even before Ambassador Morrow, who paved the way, probably expected anything so immediately valuable to an accord between the two nations.

Out of the dramatic interest in Colonel Lindbergh, who seems destined to make men of alien race forget their differences in a common admiration of a splendid manhood, has come a definite advance toward a solution of the so-called Mexican problem.

The most significant of the movements in that direction are the reports that President Calles will go to Havana to meet President Coolidge at the Pan-American Congress.

Just what might come of such a meeting in the form of a better economic and social understanding between the two countries men grown old and discouraged in Mexican affairs do not dream of predicting.

Mexico Eager for Amity.

All they know is that with Calles apparently seated firmly in power, with a prospect of comparative internal peace in Mexico and with a wave of sentiment breaking down the barriers between the United States and Mexico, there might come from a meeting of the two Chief Executives an understanding of which the consequences could not be estimated.

Mexico is tired of fighting. Mexico wants peace and a greater degree of prosperity. There are those who believe this lie in a very distant future. But at the same time, under the stir of the emotional reaction of Mexico to Colonel Lindbergh's visit and the honest, common-sense work of Ambassador Morrow, there are many who see a new opportunity for Mexico, both financial and social.

Morrow in Leading Rôle.

As a factor in bringing about this situation Ambassador Morrow has played a leading rôle. He has placed diplomacy in Mexico on a new basis, treating those with whom he has dealt as men of their word who valued the best for their country.

If he differed with them, or failed to see their point of view, to find some point of mutual agreement. The result has been remarkable, and it is not stretching the truth to say that Ambassador Morrow is one of the most popular men in Mexico.

Slowly there has penetrated to the minds of the Mexican people a suspicion of emnity of Mexico. Ambassador Morrow's unfailing courtesy—his tact, his willingness to go personally to members of the Mexican Government instead of writing notes to them, his refusal to be anything but frank—has brought about the feeling which led today to the friendly being carried in a parade of workmen, the workmen who have been called Bolshevist, a banner with the inscription, "Morrow is an honest man."

Lindbergh Crystallizes Situation.

This tendency to change the Mexican attitude toward America and its representatives was still inchoate when Colonel Lindbergh crystallized it. When this frank, simple and courageous representative of America dropped over the famous plane, Mexico was swept by a wave of pure Americanism which is difficult to realize, even in the midst of it. There is something about this young aviator, a magnificent simple—

Continued on Page Six.

NEW YORK-FLORIDA LIMITED—6:48 P. M. Daily. Jacksonville, Tampa, Fort Myers, Sarasota, West Palm Beach, Tampa, Sarasota, Petersburg second morning. Seaboard, 143 West 42 St. Tel. Wisc. 5137.—Advt.

Lindbergh Praises Skill of Riders and Ropers Who Perform for Him

Calls Labor Parade in His Honor Expression of Friendliness for the United States—Not Certain How He Should Wear Gift Cape.

By Colonel CHARLES A. LINDBERGH.
Copyright, 1927, in the United States, Canada, Mexico, Cuba, Central and South America, Europe and the British Dominions by The New York Times Company. All rights reserved.
By Mexican War Department Wireless Direct to The New York Times.

MEXICO CITY, Dec. 18.—This has been another of these wonderful Mexican days. There seems to be no end of them. And I have seen two of the sports of Mexico under a perfect sky and brilliant sun.

The exhibition of roping and riding at the Rancho de Charros was one of the finest things of the kind I have ever seen. Then came the review of members of the Mexican Labor Unions at the National Palace, which was a gratifying expression of friendliness toward the United States.

Receives Cape From Matador.

The much debated bull fight came in the afternoon. I received a beautiful cape here, presented by José Ortiz, one of the matadors. The workmanship on it is different from anything of the kind I have ever seen and it is one of the best nationalistic gifts I have had.

I am not quite certain yet how I should wear it, but Señor Ortiz placed it over my shoulders and I suppose that is the way it should be worn.

Last night I had the first opportunity of seeing some of the country around Mexico City from an automobile in which we drove out some way toward Puebla over a wide and smooth road.

The road went up through the mountains, from which there was a splendid view of Mexico City and the valley. I should think this would be a great tourist centre.

Sees Chance for Hotels.

It is one of the most picturesque places on the continent, easy of access and with a delightful climate. If a few hotels were built on these hills, with golf courses laid out near them, so that it would be possible to stay in the country, it should be one of the most attractive places in North America.

This valley has a romantic history and contains the remains of the old Aztec and Toltec civilizations, which were the oldest north of the Isthmus. The Toltecs and Mayas people were cultured peoples whose ruins are among the most interesting in the world. I am looking forward to a visit to the famous pyramids, where I may see what is believed to be the ruins of the Toltec city.

Tourists Would Bring Air Lines.

It is hard to believe now that this whole valley was originally a huge lake, with little islands in it on which the ancient cities were built. It must have been a beautiful spot in those days, even more so than now, although Mexico City is one of the most delightful I have ever visited.

If tourists would come to Mexico in greater numbers it should be possible to build up air lines which would make it much more accessible. The United States is now two days away by railroad, but it would be only a few hours by airplane. Flying in multi-motored planes is as safe as travelling by rail and in the next few years there should be developed a series of airlines to connect all the part of the continent and extend to South America.

BEQUESTS FROM ALL SOUGHT BY COLUMBIA

Dr. Butler in Report Asserts University Merits Mention in Every Citizen's Will.

Columbia University has earned the right to be remembered by every person in every way will that is drawn in New York City because of its service to the community, according to Dr. Nicholas Murray Butler, President of the university, in his 1927 annual report to the Board of Trustees. The report, made public yesterday, again declares that Columbia University "is undercapitalized by some $60,000,000" for the successful discharge of its present obligations.

"The lack of sufficient physical equipment for the present work of the university on Morningside Heights," says President Butler's report, "is glaring and almost impossible to explain satisfactorily to students, to visiting scholars and to the public."

$3,498,380 Gifts in 1927.

The report says that Columbia's total gifts in 1927, including those to Barnard and Teachers Colleges and the College of Pharmacy were $3,498,380.20; that since 1890 gifts to Columbia University have aggregated $71,588,763.64, and that the combined resources of those institutions as of June 30, 1927, were $114,152,749.87, and their budget appropriations were $12,005,670.66. Columbia's teaching staff numbers 2,210, against 2,092 in 1926.

"It is tiresome to repeat the fact, but, as was shown in detail in the last annual report, the university is undercapitalized by some $60,000,000 for the successful and satisfactory discharge of its present public obligations," says the report. "It cannot possibly be put in funds which is to meet those obligations unless the citizens of New York and of the nation, feeling their moral responsibility for the continuance and prosperity of the great institutions that lead and serve the intellectual life and that organize and promote scientific advance, make constant and large bequests because the fortunes with which they are happily blessed.

"The time should now have come

Continued on Page Nine.

DOUBT ELIGIBILITY OF HOOVER IN 1928

Some Senators Raise Question of His Having Been Resident of Country 14 Years.

Special to The New York Times.

WASHINGTON, Dec. 18.—The question of Secretary Hoover's eligibility to the Presidency under the provision of "fourteen years a resident within the United States" is being seriously raised in Senatorial circles. It is being contended that Mr. Hoover must have been a resident within the United States for fourteen years previous to induction into the Presidency, and the question is being raised as to whether he has been a resident for that length of time.

One of the prominent Republican members of the Senate who is also a constitutional lawyer, but who did not care to be quoted tonight, said:

"The question as to whether Mr. Hoover is eligible under the fourteen-year clause has been seriously raised among some members of the Senate.

"I have no doubt myself that the Constitutional provision means that a man to be eligible for the Presidency must have been a resident within the United States for fourteen years before entering the White House. I do not think it means fourteen years inclusive of early life in the United States.

The Senator in question declined to discuss the matter, he said, because he was not aware of the facts as to the residence of Mr. Hoover here and abroad. The Constitutional provision, found in Paragraph 4, Section 1 of Article II, reads:

"No person except a natural born citizen or a citizen of the United States at the time of the adoption of this Constitution shall be eligible to the office of President; neither shall any person be eligible to that office who shall not have attained to the age of thirty-five years and been fourteen years a resident within the United States."

If Mr. Hoover was nominated and elected in 1928 he would be sworn into office March 4, 1929. Those who argue that "fourteen years a resident within the United States," as used in the Constitution, means fourteen years immediately prior to induction into office contend that Mr. Hoover must show that he has

Continued on Page Thirteen.

YOUTH ARRESTED IN CHILD SLAYING AT LOS ANGELES

Doctor's Son, a University Man, Held as Suspect in Kidnapping of Marion Parker.

ANOTHER TAKEN IN NEVADA

Clues Found in Suitcase, Abandoned Auto and Tailor's Story of Bloody Coat.

$50,000 REWARD POSTED

Volunteers Raise the Fund and Join Full Police Force in Wide Hunt for Murder Gang.

By The Associated Press.

LOS ANGELES, Dec. 18.—The police late today arrested a suspect in the Marian Parker murder case whose name they refused to divulge.

The prisoner was a man of 25 years, the son of a Los Angeles doctor, a military school and university man and known in the past to have committed offenses against young girls.

The police had earlier declared they had fingerprints of the man wanted which would convict him if captured. These prints were taken from the ransom letters and the originals of the filed telegrams.

The police further divulged that the imprisoned suspect was in a position to know intimate details of the Parker family life.

Police Describe Type of Guilty Man.

Police investigators here point out definite qualifications which the slayer and which are applied to all suspects taken into custody.

Aside from his physical appearance, which is fairly well known here, and his fingerprints taken from his letters, he is, say the officers, keen-minded, well-educated, egotistic, particularly in believing that he has a master criminal mind.

He has some knowledge of anatomy, as evidenced in the dissection of Marian Parker's body. He has a smattering of education in Greek, but only a smattering, for while he used Greek characters in spelling the word "death" in some of his messages to his little victim's father, he used two of them wrongly.

Also, say the police investigators, he had full information on residents in the neighborhood of the Parker home and was thoroughly acquainted with the district.

They point out as well that his admonition to Parker to seek "aid from God and not from man," combined with the ability to destroy innocence as he destroyed it, place him in the category of the mentally warped and the degenerate.

It may be, investigators declare, that the girl's slayer in penning his letters and telegrams to Parker patterned them after the scholarly style of Leopold and Loeb, Chicago's boy slayers.

Acting on information which they gained from a confidential source a squad of Los Angeles officers tonight descended on Tijuana, across the Mexican border from San Diego, and began combing the dives there for a clue to the killing.

Continued on Page Four.

City Watches in Vain for Newest Comet; Skjellerup Body Expected by Christmas

The latest visitor from space to make the acquaintance of the solar system, the Skjellerup Comet, which has been making progress in a northerly direction ever since it was discovered by an amateur astronomer at Melbourne, Australia, on Nov. 23, was still invisible to New Yorkers at 5:30 Saturday afternoon. It had been announced in some quarters on Friday that the new comet's appearance over the local horizon.

Dr. Clyde Fisher, curator of astronomy at the American Museum of Natural History, has been looking for it at 5:30 o'clock, just after the sun has set.

"I couldn't pick it up," he said on Saturday. Yesterday he was not at the Museum.

Dr. Harold Jacoby of Columbia University said he thought the comet was "just below the horizon."

"When an object is below the horizon," he said, "you just plain can't see it."

He said that it was barely possible that the comet would be visible tonight at 5:30, or by Christmas, anyway.

The Skjellerup is now so close to the sun that a brilliant sunset would obscure it, even if it were above the horizon. It was discovered by F. J. Skjellerup, and since Dec. 3 it has moved up by persons in Argentina, Chile, Jamaica and other places near the Equator. It is very bright, according to reports from the Southern Hemisphere.

The comet is generally thought to be a new visitor, although there is a bare possibility, according to Dr. Jacoby, that it may turn out to be one that was "discovered" many years ago. It will take close observation to be certain on this point, he said.

WHERE SIX MEN STILL LIVE IN SUNKEN SUBMARINE.
Diagram Shows the Various Compartments in a Submarine of the Type of the S-4. The Forward One, or Torpedo Room, Is Where the Only Known Survivors Have Answered Signals From the Submerged Craft. The Other Compartments in Order Are: Battery Room, Where the Crew's Quarters Are; Control Room, Directly Under the Conning Tower; Engine Room and Motor or Stern Torpedo Room.
P. & A. Photo.

SEWER CHARGES GO TO CONNOLLY TODAY

Scudder Also Expected to Fix Time and Place, Probably Jan. 3 in Queens Court House.

TWO-FOLD DEFENSE LIKELY

Friends Say Borough President Will Attack Motives of His Accusers and Uphold Costs.

Supreme Court Justice Townsend Scudder, who has been designated by Governor Smith to hear the charges of official misconduct against Borough President Maurice E. Connolly of Queens, is expected to have a copy of the charges served upon Mr. Connolly today, together with notification of the time and place of the hearings.

Justice Scudder, having spent Saturday in Utica to attend a meeting of the trustees of the Masonic Home there—he is a past Grand Master of the Grand Lodge of Masons for New York State—returned to New York yesterday. He went to his home at Glen Head, L. I., in Nassau County, which he left last night for the Hamilton Club, Brooklyn, where he stays while occupying the bench in Brooklyn or Queens. He made no announcement regarding his plans for the inquiry, and, so far as known, has not yet selected a special counsel to assist him.

Steuer Still Undecided.

Max D. Steuer, criminal lawyer, whom Connolly has asked to act as his counsel at the Scudder inquiry, said yesterday that he was still unable to say whether he could accept the retainer. He explained that he had been unable to communicate with three opposing attorneys in law suits in which he is to appear next month, in his effort to persuade them to agree to postponements so that he can accept the Connolly case. One case, he went on, was in the State courts and had been peremptorily

Continued on Page Eight.

Simon Lake Suggests Way To Rescue Men of the S-4

Special to The New York Times.

MILFORD, Conn., Dec. 18.—Simon Lake, inventor of the even keel type of submarine, told the Bridgeport Telegram tonight what he thought was the only possible manner of rescuing members of the crew of S-4 who are alive within its sunken shell.

Mr. Lake said that as long as an air line was pumping air into the submarine the only feasible plan for taking out the men would be for divers to cut a hole through the plate at the bottom of the submerged boat and enter with diving suits or helmets for the survivors.

The water would be kept out of the boat by means of air pressure pumped from above. Pressure of forty-five pounds to the square inch, making an air pressure equal to the water pressure at that depth, would allow the diver to enter with his helmets or suits. Members of the submarine's crew could put on the suits and be pulled to the surface when they came out of the submarine.

CAPITAL DUBIOUS ON MANY RESCUES

Crushing of Submarine's Hull Points to Loss of Life in Some Compartments.

SPEED NOW CHIEF FACTOR

Officials Have Full Confidence in Forces Engaged in the Rescue Operations.

Special to The New York Times.

WASHINGTON, Dec. 18.—At least six men were still alive in the sunken S-4 were being used in the Navy Department early this evening. The announcement was made tonight by Rear Admiral Frank Brumby, who is in charge of the rescue operations off the tip of Cape Cod. He stated that the information had come from the locked room by means of hammer knocks executed in the Morse code against the side of the submarine. The rescue party in this manner knocked and received responses from some of the six who survive. There was no evidence so far, he reported that any one was alive in the submarine other than in the torpedo room.

Rear Admiral Brumby's dispatch read:

"Blowing (air) from the Falcon to the tanks. Air now being hooked up to torpedo compartment.
Following messages sent and received from and to S-4:
First question: 'Is gas bad?'
Answer: 'No, but the air, how long will you be now?'
Second question: 'How many are there?'
Answer: 'There are six; please hurry. Will you be long now?'
Answer: 'We are doing everything possible.'"

These messages were by hammer knocks in the Morse code.

"No evidence so far that any one is alive anywhere but in the torpedo room.

Describes Damage to Craft.

Thomas Eadie, a diver whose rank is that of chief torpedo-man, went down at 3:15 P. M. He did not come up until 4:30, when he made a hurried report to Captain King and Rear Admiral Brumby.

Eadie said he was certain that the men alive were in the forward torpedo room. He told of his hammer signals and of receiving signals in reply.

Heartened by what he heard, he said, he began to explore. As he made his way carefully toward the stern he saw the signs of the severe damage done to the submarine in the crash. The conning tower, he declared, was ripped apart.

Closer examination revealed that a hole had been pierced in the battery compartment. Eadie said that this hole had apparently been opened by the prow of the Paulding. Further toward the stern the damage seemed worse.

The diver told of getting tangled in the wreckage of the superstructure that cluttered the muddy water and of finding it hazardous to proceed. Despite the danger he pushed his way around the craft, resuming his hammering and his listening.

Heard Sound in Rear Room.

Once, Eadie said, he thought he heard a signal from near a rear compartment. He could not be sure, though that what he heard indicated more life in the stern of the boat. Eadie went back to his examination of the damage. The battery compartment hole was on the starboard side. It was serious.

When Captain King asked the significance of Eadie's discoveries, he said:

"We are certain that men are alive aboard the submarine and we are going to do our best to get them out safely."

The damage is apparently serious

Continued on Page Two.

AIR IS BAD, VICTIMS SAY

Faint Sound Once Heard Aft in Vessel, Diver Thought.

BATTERY ROOM CRUSHED

Three to Twelve Men Met Certain Death There, Captain King Declares.

AIR PUMPED INTO TANKS

Rescue Crews Try to Up-End Ill-Fated Craft While Waiting for Pontoons.

From a Staff Correspondent of The New York Times.

PROVINCETOWN, Mass., Dec. 18.—At least six men are still alive tonight in the sunken hull of the submarine S-4, which was rammed outside the harbor here yesterday by a Coast Guard boat and went to the bottom with some forty-odd men aboard.

This announcement was made tonight by Rear Admiral Frank Brumby, directing "the efforts to bring the disabled craft to the surface and save the lives of the members of the crew." Admiral Brumby based his statement on a report received from a diver on whom the submarine rests, to converse in code with those inside in a forward compartment by hammering on the side of the steel hull.

"How long will you be?" was the pathetic message tapped out by the imprisoned men. The diver answered as best he could.

"Is the gas bad?" the diver asked. "No, but the air," was the reply from inside the hull.

"How many are you?" was slowly tapped out with the diver's hammer.

"Six," was the response. "Please hurry."

Catches Signals From Inside.

It was just about twenty-four hours after the S-4 was rammed and sunk by the Coast Guard destroyer Paulding, a mile outside the harbor that the diver, a crack navy expert, working far beneath the surface of a turbulent sea, caught the signals from inside the forward compartment.

The diver reported to Admiral Brumby that the living men who responded to his signals were in the forward part of the submerged vessel. He also brought up an account of heavy damage to the battery room and to the stern of the ship.

This report of the damage to the S-4, which went down after a collision with the Coast Guard boat while running submerged, caught Captain Ernest J. King, submarine rescue specialist, to declare that at least three or four of the crew had been killed in the battery room, which was crushed. There might have been more, he said.

But with Rear Admiral Brumby affirming that some men were surely alive in the torpedo room forward, Captain King joined him in declaring he would do everything possible with the fleet of rescue ships here to save the lives of all who might be still fighting for existence.

Admiral Hughes, chief of naval operations, who had been on duty in the Navy Department since 7 o'clock this morning, working on rescue plans, telephoned the message to Secretary Wilbur as soon as it was received.

The Secretary was informed that submarine S-4 was being used in pumping air into the S-4 and that still another submarine, the S-3, has been ordered from Portsmouth, N. H., to the scene.

Previous to this word a dispatch came from Provincetown stating that divers had heard tapping from within the submarine in response to their signals.

These sounds came from the torpedo room, which is just forward of the battery room which was shattered by the impact of the collision. Aft of the battery compartment, the long, cone shaped room that tapers toward a point and ends, so far as human life is concerned, against the bulkhead housing the torpedo tubes, this news did not greatly cheer them.

The control room is the heart of the submarine. All the main valves that control them operate from there, the engine and motor controls, the diving planes and the rising planes. About a dozen men were probably on duty at these controls, and among them several of the officers. Just forward of this compartment, which was crushed, are located the men's sleeping quarters and the ward room for the officers. Aft of that is the torpedo room, where six men are reported alive.

No one had a chance to escape either forward or aft into the engine room from the control. If men are alive, what happened is the naval men say: Some one with presence of mind closed the water-tight door between the torpedo room and the battery room and shut been the heavy steel "dogs" that fasten the door. The trapped men refused to do

Continued on Page Two.

HOPE TO SAVE MEN BY TILTING THE S-4

Experts Here Say Craft May Be Up-Ended to Surface by Air Pumped In.

With her hull smashed amidships, her control room a wreck, but with her forward compartments apparently watertight, grounded in the seaport of Diver Eadie, naval men here last night saw some hope of saving a part of the crew locked in the sunken submarine S-4 off Provincetown.

With the sweeper Falcon's powerful compressors forcing air into the forward ballast tanks and the Bushnell and the S-8 standing by with more air compressors ready to feed into the manifolds on the Falcon, it is hoped that enough buoyancy can be added to the "rigless craft to "rob" her bow first. Then the engineers say, as was the case in the rescue of the crew of the S-51, drill grinding steadily through the thick armor plate might cut the passage for the escape of the entrapped men.

When navy men heard that the control room had been crashed through by the prow of the Coast Guard destroyer Paulding they shook their heads. The diver reported the hole in her as larger than the gash in the S-51; and although later Eadie reported that men were alive in the torpedo compartment, the long, cone shaped room that tapers toward a point and ends, so far as human life is concerned, against the bulkhead housing the torpedo tubes, this news did not greatly cheer them.

Continued on Page Two.

"All the News That's Fit to Print."

The New York Times.

Copyright, 1928, by The New York Times Company.

VOL. LXXVII....No. 25,714   •••   NEW YORK, TUESDAY, JUNE 19, 1928.   TWO CENTS | THREE CENTS | FOUR CENTS

THE WEATHER
Showers today, probably tomorrow; not much change in temperature.
Temperature yesterday—Max. 84; Min. 70.
☞For weather report see Page 42.

AMELIA EARHART FLIES ATLANTIC, FIRST WOMAN TO DO IT; TELLS HER OWN STORY OF PERILOUS 21-HOUR TRIP TO WALES; RADIO QUIT AND THEY FLEW BLIND OVER INVISIBLE OCEAN

RITCHIE WITHDRAWS IN FAVOR OF SMITH, URGING PARTY UNITY

New Yorker's Nomination Will Assure Democratic Victory, He Asserts.

DIRECTS APPEAL TO SOUTH

Smith as President Would Restore Popular Government, Maryland Executive Says.

TURNS OVER HIS DELEGATES

Sees Struggle of 1924 Avoided at Houston—Reed Still in Race, Backer Declares.

Special to The New York Times.

BALTIMORE, June 18.—Governor Albert C. Ritchie tonight withdrew as candidate for the Democratic Presidential nomination, with the announcement that he would instruct the Maryland delegation to cast its sixteen votes at the National Convention at Houston next week for Governor Smith of New York.

In a formal statement, Governor Ritchie urged the Democratic Party to unite behind Governor Smith. The New York Executive, he declared, was "fitted by experience, character and ability to assume the leadership of the party and had the best chance to win in the November election.

"His record is a guarantee that with him as President, honesty in Government would take the place of corruption in Government," he said of Governor Smith.

Governor Ritchie expressed his gratitude that Maryland had advanced its own name for the Presidential nomination. "The great majority of the Democratic Party in every section of the country" was ready to back Governor Smith, however, he said, and he felt a responsibility to the party so to declare himself.

Makes Especial Plea to South.

Mr. Ritchie directed his plea in behalf of Governor Smith particularly to the South. The nomination demanded, and pointed to, the success of the Democratic Party as the champion of self-government and popular self-rule, principles which the South through the Democratic Party had saved to the nation, he asserted.

He, "as a son of the South," had fought enthusiastically for these principles. As an American and as a Democrat, he now urged a "united and unbroken front" by the party to assure its success next fall.

"Every Democrat should subordinate himself to this higher call for party unity," he said, to re-establish in national life those principles of which Governor Smith was the "exponent."

Governor Ritchie asserted that, in dropping his candidacy for the Presidential nomination, he also took himself out of the running for second place on the party ticket.

"I have not the slightest thought of the Vice Presidency, nor expectation of it being offered to me, or accepting it if it be," he said. "In taking this action, I do so without any ulterior motive whatsoever. It emanates from a profound sense of duty to the nation and to the Democratic Party, with which the country's well-being is inseparably bound up."

Governor Ritchie's Statement.

The following is Governor Ritchie's statement in full:

I am profoundly convinced that no consideration of self or of personal advancement on my own part should be allowed to stand for one moment in the way of the success of the Democratic Party, which is the natural champion of self-government and popular self-rule.

These principles are challenging the attention of the country today as they have not done for years. To them I have dedicated such political effort as I am able to exert. Faith in them saved the South during the dark days of reconstruction and made possible a reunited and happy nation; and as a son of the South I have brought to the struggle for these principles the enthusiasm and the loyalty which came to me from ancestors who were ready to die, and some of whom did die, for the cause in which they believed.

As a Democrat I have regarded this struggle as a duty, and as an American I believe that the dictates of patriotism require the re-establishment of these principles in our national life.

That my own [illegible] makes me worthy to be the standard-bearer of the Democratic Party is a distinction for which I do not [illegible] sufficiently express my gratitude, nor can I adequately express it to my friends elsewhere in the coun-

Continued on Page Ten.

SMITH SUPPORTERS SEE A QUICK VICTORY

Hope Ritchie's Withdrawal in Favor of Governor Will Be Followed by Others.

AIDES START FOR HOUSTON

Van Namee, Sure of Success, Says "Steam-Roller" Methods Will Not Be Used.

With George R. Van Namee, manager of Governor Smith's preconvention campaign for the Democratic nomination, speeding toward Houston to open headquarters in the Hotel Rice, Smith supporters here were jubilant last night at the announcement by Governor Ritchie of Maryland that he would advise the sixteen delegates from that State to cast their votes for New York's Governor on the first ballot.

Mr. Van Namee predicted, just as he boarded the train at Grand Central Station yesterday noon, that Governor Smith would be nominated on "an early ballot." The more optimistic Smith supporters contended last night that the first ballot would show a strength of 708 votes, or 29 1-3 short of the number required for nomination. The hope was expressed that Governor Ritchie's action might swing other State delegations into line before the voting starts at Houston, in which event Governor Smith might be nominated on the first ballot.

Rules Out "Steam Roller" Plan.

While declining to name the ballot on which he believed Governor Smith would be nominated, Mr. Van Namee declared that with 680 delegates already instructed and many voters known to favor the Smith candidacy, his nomination was practically assured. The Smith forces, Mr. Van Namee said, would not attempt any "steam-roller" methods at Houston and would seek in no way to prevent any candidate from presenting his claims to the nomination. The Smith forces, he added, are concerned with promoting party harmony.

With Mr. Van Namee were Mrs. Van Namee, Howard Cullman of the Port of New York Authority and George C. Norton, Norman E. Mack, Democratic National Com-

Continued on Page Nine.

Keel Laid for Biggest Ship, 1,000 Feet Long; 60,000-Ton 'Oceanic' to Cost $30,000,000

Wireless to The New York Times.

LONDON, June 18.—The biggest ship in the world was begun today at Harland & Wolff's shipyards in Belfast, when the keel was laid for a giant White Star liner to cost $30,000,000. She will be more than 1,000 feet long, with a beam of 100 feet and tonnage of about 60,000.

The ship will not be ready for sail until 1932, and experts have yet to decide what type of machinery will be installed in her.

When the new ship is added to the White Star fleet she will be called the Oceanic. She is the largest steamships in service at the present time in the Atlantic trade, are:
The Leviathan of the United States Lines, 59,957 gross tonnage, 907 feet long and 100 feet 3 inches beam.

The Majestic of the White Star Line, claimed by some to be the largest liner afloat, on the basis of its builder and designer's [illegible] measurements, which are 56,561 gross tons, 915 feet 5 inches long and 100 feet 1 inch beam.
The Cunarder Berengaria, 52,226 gross tonnage, 883 feet 5 inches long and 98 feet 3 inches beam.
The White Star Olympic, 46,439 gross tonnage, 882 feet 5 inches long, 92 feet 8 inches beam.
The Cunarder Aquitania, 45,647 gross tonnage, 868 feet 7 inches long and 97 feet beam.
The new French liner Ile de France, 43,500 gross tonnage, 791 feet 5 inches long and 91 feet 8 inches beam.

President of Porto Rican Senate Stabbed And Badly Hurt by a Maniac Anarchist

Wireless to The New York Times.

SAN JUAN, Porto Rico, June 18.—Antonio Barcelo, President of the Porto Rican Senate, was stabbed with a chisel at the close of a welcoming demonstration at City Hall today and probably owes his life to the fact that he is fat.

The chisel made a four-inch wound, then was deflected by a rib.

Justo Matos, 35 years old and believed to be demented, who attempted the assassination with the unusual instrument, was himself shot through the abdomen by an unidentified bystander after police, they say, actually had him in custody. The condition of Matos is considered critical.

In their efforts to protect Matos police were unable to detect who had shot him.

The assault on Señor Barcelo took place at the close of a noisy welcome while hundreds of persons surged about him with greetings. Señor Barcelo was just returning home from New York where Columbia University gave him an honorary degree of Doctor of Laws and President Butler had referred to him as "captain of his island people."

By The Associated Press.

SAN JUAN, Porto Rico, June 18.—Señor Barcelo tonight was in a hospital undergoing treatment for his wound. Matos was in prison, heavily guarded to protect him from an outraged populace.

A huge crowd met Señor Barcelo at the docks and escorted him to the Plaza, where on a balcony overlooking the promenade he addressed them.

It was while he was speaking that Matos edged through the crowd, pushed his way onto the low balcony and wielded the chisel. The crowd apparently did not comprehend what had happened. There was a shot from somewhere and Matos was seen to fall, writhing in pain, on the street level, where police took charge of him.

At the hospital, where Señor Barcelo was taken, doctors declined to state whether the wound was likely to prove fatal.

The motive for Matos's action is not known. Some in the crowd noticed him before his deed and he remarked he was all, and then added that he could kill ten Porto Ricans willingly.

The stabbing itself, perhaps by coincidence, followed the statement in Señor Barcelo's speech that he was not a member of any political party or faction but a Porto Rican, and was proud of the honor accorded him by Columbia University not so much for his own sake as that it went to a citizen of his country.

La Democratica, Señor Barcelo's newspaper, this afternoon and Matos had visited their office and the Barcelo home for a week asking when the legislature would return here. Other afternoon papers refer to him as a "Socialist fanatic," and one calls him a "confessed anarchist."

NOBILE VAINLY HAILS FLIERS CIRCLING OVER BUT NOT SEEING HIM

General Radios Base Ship That Rescue Planes Were Over Stranded Men an Hour.

SECOND FLIGHT ALSO FAILS

This Time Italia Castaways Sight One of Planes Piloted by Riiser-Larsen and Holm.

SAVOIA REACHES KINGS BAY

Big Italian Seaplane Ready for Dash North — French and Swedish Craft on Way.

By The Associated Press.

ROME, June 18.—The two Norwegian fliers, Captain Riiser-Larsen and Lieutenant Lutzow Holm, today made a second unsuccessful attempt to find General Umberto Nobile and the party with him north of Spitsbergen. They returned to the icebreaker Braganza without having sighted the marooned men.

Nobile, however, informed the base ship Citta di Milano by wireless that he had seen one of the planes fly within two kilometers of him.

Snow Hides Frantic Signals.

KINGS BAY, Spitsbergen, June 18.—High overhead yesterday General Umberto Nobile saw two seaplanes sent to rescue him and his five comrades from the Arctic ice-floes, but frantic efforts to signal the planes or make known their existence below failed, and, after an hour's reconnaissance above, the craft were seen to disappear in the grim Arctic horizon, flying back toward Spitsbergen.

This news came to the base-ship Citta di Milano today by wireless from the stranded Italia commander, who for days has been awaiting on the outside world who might aid in returning him and his mates on the Italia to civilization and home.

Sunday they thought their days of watching perhaps over. But they failed to count on the trickiness of the snow with visibility, and when help had passed them by their situation was if anything more difficult than before.

Good Visibility of No Avail.

The two seaplanes were those piloted by Captain Riiser-Larsen and Lieutenant Leutzow Holm, the Norwegian fliers. Both set out early Sunday and took a course over Beverly Sound, North Cape and Cape Platen, keeping at a height of from 750 to 900 feet. Both planes carried provisions and clothes for the stranded men.

Visibility was good, but when they returned to Spitsbergen they had not seen a trace of the Italia's commander and the remnant of his crew or of the silk tent he had painted red to aid them. This despite the fact that General Nobile had indicated that they had remained above him and in the vicinity for more than an hour.

Today Captain Riiser-Larsen and Lieutenant Holm set out for further reconnaissance, intending, if there were to be variations in all their course, to keep between men and the coast of Northeast Land.

No Chance to Land Amid Ice.

The fliers, on returning yesterday, said that in the area where the fliers are supposed to be they found the ice much too rough for landing. They said that the ice floes were open, considerably, but that the cracks and openings were still too narrow for landing attempts by the seaplanes. They were, however, as to foster progress by the ice breakers.

In his message to the Citta di Milano conveying the tragic irony of the situation, General Nobile, to aid further searches, gave his present position as 88 53 north and 77 12 east. This would put him about five miles to the east of Foyn Island.

Savoia's Arrival Raises Hopes.

The hydro-airplane Savoia-56, piloted by Major Maddalena, arrived here at 10:45 o'clock tonight. She was the first of the four big seaplanes en route to Spitsbergen to reach the Northern base.

Fine weather was in evidence as the big machine settled in the harbor. Her arrival and the news that at least two others of large cargo and passenger capacity were en route, raised hopes of the watchers here who for weeks have been trying to get into direct touch with General Nobile and the other survivors of the Italia.

It was a bit uncertain as to whether

Continued on Page Two.

FIRST WOMAN TO FLY THE ATLANTIC.
Amelia Earhart, Co-pilot of the Airplane Friendship, Photographed in Boston, Just Before She Started on Her Great Adventure.

Photo copyrighted by G. P. Putnam.

Eager Crowds Imperil Miss Earhart As They Welcome Fliers at Burry Port

Police Aid Weary Trio to Battle Way to Refuge in Zinc Works—Friends Fly From Southampton to Greet Them and Hear Story of Their Adventures.

By ALLEN RAYMOND.

Copyright, 1928, in the United States, Canada, Mexico, South America, Europe and the British Dominions by The New York Times Company.

Special Cable to The New York Times.

BURRY PORT, Carmarthenshire, South Wales, June 18.—The first woman to cross the Atlantic successfully by air, Miss Amelia Earhart, Boston settlement worker, alighted in the seaplane Friendship here this morning on the broad expanse of Loughor estuary, after a flight of 20 hours and 40 minutes elapsed time from Trepassey.

Few persons saw the gilt-winged Fokker monoplane descend on the Welsh coast, but this evening, when friends rushing from Southampton brought Miss Earhart ashore, she was the recipient of so enthusiastic a reception by the 2,000 inhabitants of this town that it seemed for a few minutes as if she would not outlive her triumph.

Eager Crowds Imperil Aviatrix.

The arrival of the Friendship was the greatest event this remote district has had since the end of the World War when the town's boys came home. Miss Earhart was nearly crushed by the anxiety of the crowd of men, women and children to touch the hem of her flying suit, get her autograph on a slip of paper, wring her hand and congratulate her upon her triumphant passage over the Atlantic.

The High Sheriff of Carmarthenshire, who had rowed out to greet her; the town's three policemen and a couple of friends had to form a ring with locked arms about the latest popular heroine and literally to fight their way a hundred yards from the shore to the office of the local zinc works, where they found shelter back of locked doors.

"You must remember," the local Police Chief said apologetically, "that our people never saw anything to compare with this. I advise you to remain here until we get extra police."

The Friendship's crew was marooned within the walls of the Frickers Metal Company an hour and a half before police reinforcements arrived and cleared a way to two motor cars to take them to a distant hotel where rest, food and sleep could be obtained after their arduous journey.

Poor Visibility Forced Landing.

Poor visibility forced the plane to come down on the Welsh coast after the first tentative objective—Valentia, Ireland—had been left far behind, but the possible goal of Southampton not yet reached.

Except for the first hour over the Atlantic after leaving the rugged shores of Newfoundland, the fliers never saw sea or land until they had winged their way to the Eastern Irish coast. They flew through fog, rain and snow most of the time, fighting for altitude and clearer weather, but they came fast with the wind behind of twenty to thirty miles per hour speeding them on.

They probably had plenty of gasoline left, when they descended, to reach Southampton—seventy-five gallons—but were struggling in the midst of dense fog and knew they were somewhere off the southern coast of Britain. With their object attained—that of making Miss Earhart the first woman to complete a transatlantic crossing—they decided to take no further risks.

They will go on to Southampton tomorrow.

Stultz and Gordon Elated.

The full story of the flight has yet to be told. The two airmen, Stultz and Gordon, who had the major responsibility and labor of getting the Friendship safely across the ocean, were soon fast asleep after battling their way to the hotel. Both ejaculated their joy at their success and chuckled together over the moments in mid-ocean when they seemed dubious of the outcome.

Miss Earhart, who came through her experience in fine condition and

Continued on Page Two.

12 INJURED BY BOMB 'PLANTED' IN DETROIT

County Building Shaken, Windows Shattered and Hundreds Panic-Stricken.

'PURPLE' GANG SUSPECTED

Darrow Attending Court Case Is Jarred—Jokes With Judge About Blast.

Special to The New York Times.

DETROIT, June 18.—A devastating blast which injured twelve county employes, two seriously, shattered dozens of panes of glass and rocked the Wayne County Building to its foundation this afternoon is believed by police to have been another attempt at intimidation of the county by sympathizers with the "Purple" gang, nine members of which are now on trial on charges of conspiracy to extort.

"The dynamite bomb evidently was intended for the Municipal Courts Building, where the 'Purples' are on trial," Police Inspector John T. Doyle of the First Precinct declared, "but as usual in such cases some stranger was hired to plant the bomb and probably mistook the county building for the City Court building.

"It is a miracle no one was killed. The bomb was a powerful one. If it had exploded in the confined space of the rest room instead of in the courtway I believe it would have wrecked the building and killed many persons."

The explosion occurred at about 2:50 o'clock. The bomb was left in the men's room on the first floor and was found by Frank Stolpa, a constable, who tossed it into the areaway in the centre of the building and was trying to extinguish it with water when it exploded.

One May Lose an Eye.

Stolpa and Arthur Vercrusse, another constable, who also helped in the efforts to extinguish the bomb, were struck in the face by flying glass and bits of iron from the bomb and taken to Receiving Hospital for treatment. Vercrusse, according to the physicians, may lose the sight of his right eye.

About 100 men and women clerks,

Continued on Page Nine.

FOUGHT RAIN, FOG AND SNOW ALL THE WAY

Miss Earhart Says Motors Spat and Gas Ran Low, But She Had Neither Fear Nor Doubt of Success.

PASSED OVER IRELAND WITHOUT EVEN SEEING IT

Wind Aided Plane—Girl Credits Feat to Stultz and Gordon—She Flew Because It Would Have Been 'Too Inartistic to Refuse.'

By AMELIA EARHART.

Copyright, 1928, in the United States, Canada, Mexico, South America, Europe and the British Dominions by The New York Times Company.

Special Cable to The New York Times.

BURRY PORT, Carmarthenshire, South Wales, June 18.—I have arrived and I am happy—naturally.

Why did I do it? When one is offered such a tremendous adventure it would be too inartistic to refuse it. I have been a flier for years. I had planned to spend my vacation flying. I knew the moment this chance came to me that if I turned it down I would never forgive myself.

My trip across the Atlantic aboard the airplane Friendship was all I had imagined it to be as pleasure, and much more, though pretty uncomfortable at times. This is my first trip to England, and it is rather funny dropping in by airplane. Nevertheless I hope to make the trip again some day and make it in the same way by air. What I wanted to demonstrate in this flight was that this type of travel was comparatively safe and ought to be developed.

Gives Great Credit to Companions.

I was a passenger on the journey—just a passenger. Everything that was done to bring us across was done by Wilmer Stultz and "Slim" Gordon. Any praise I can give them they ought to have. You can't pile it on too thick.

Transoceanic flying has to be done by pilots who can fly by instruments alone I am afraid that some accidents which marred past flights have been caused by pilots not too sure of instrument flying.

Despite the fact that the weather reports promised us fine visibility and fair weather, we had fog, rain and even snow practically all the way across. We only had clear weather for one hour out of the twenty-two we were on the way.

The reason we came down here was because we could not see anything. We had just about enough gasoline left, we reckoned, to make Southampton, but we did not dare attempt it because we were flying blind and we knew we had come across. We will go on there tomorrow.

Calls Waiting the Worst Part.

To go back to the beginning, the hardest strain of all this flight in a way was the waiting at Trepassey. The flight, of course, was a climax piled on top of this worry. That is what made it so tiring. But we had been trying so much to take off at Trepassey that all I can remember thinking of when we took off was that at last we were on the way. I was not really sure till we had flown for half an hour along the coast and headed against the open sea, because I knew that if everything was not all right Bill would go back.

When we started there was such a burst of spray that the outside motors started cutting out. I was afraid we had made another false start, but the motors picked up again, and although they stammered once in a while on the flight when coated with snow, I never had a moment of real trepidation about them and never doubted that we should arrive.

I did not do much. I did not handle the controls once, although I have had more than 500 hours' solo flying and once held the women's altitude record. When Bill Stultz left the controls to work the radio "Slim" would take them.

Thought of Fishing in Newfoundland.

We got two messages from ships on the way, and when I found out what ships were I did a lot of thinking and jotted down a lot of notes about my feelings, which I hope to expand some day, perhaps.

Leaving the American coast, it was beautiful weather. The jagged coastline beneath us had a grandeur one never forgets, and passing over Newfoundland one could see lots of lakes where they told me there were good trout. I hope to fish there some time.

Beneath us the water was wonderful greens and blues, and everything was serene, though, of course the first thing we did was to start looking for the fog which we knew would meet us off Newfoundland. The first hour over the open sea was the only time we saw it. We did not even see Ireland, though we passed right over it, but when we knew we were over Southern England we could not establish any landmarks and our radio had quit us. We do not know yet how it got out of order, but it was all right when Bill worked it last night and no good when he tried it this morning.

Marvelous Colors in the Clouds.

The weather was gorgeous. The billows of fog shot with pink seemed like a vast sunlit desert, and even when night came there was an interesting color effect. There was the glow of

"All the News That's Fit to Print."

The New York Times.

Copyright, 1928, by The New York Times Company.

LATE EDITION
5:30 A.M.
WEATHER—Fair today; cloudy tomorrow.

VOL. LXXVIII....No. 25,855. **★★★**

NEW YORK, WEDNESDAY, NOVEMBER 7, 1928.

TWO CENTS In Greater New York | THREE CENTS Within 200 Miles. | FOUR CENTS Elsewhere.

HOOVER WINS 407 TO 69; DOUBTFUL 55; SMITH LOSES STATE; SOUTH BROKEN; ROOSEVELT IS ELECTED GOVERNOR

HOOVER CARRIES ILLINOIS, SWEEPING IN THE STATE TICKET

Smith Wins in Chicago, but His Republican Rival Gets Big Down-State Vote.

IOWA STRONG FOR HOOVER

Nebraska Puts Republican in Lead and His Victory Seems Certain.

MICHIGAN ALSO REPUBLICAN

Hoover Sweeps Ohio by a Big Majority—Entire State Ticket Elected.

Special to The New York Times.

CHICAGO, Nov. 6.—Illinois went Republican today. Herbert Hoover and the State ticket, headed by Louis L. Emmerson, candidate for Governor, and Otis F. Glenn, nominee for United States Senator, won by such large figures in down-State territory that Emmerson would carry the State even if the eighteen electoral votes of the places in Cook County and down-State were eliminated.

Although apparently lost Chicago to Governor Smith, incomplete returns indicated that Hoover had carried Cook County, which was counted upon by the Democrats as certain for their entire ticket.

The figures received as this is written forecast a Smith victory in Chicago by about 40,000 and informal reports from the suburbs of the county promised a Republican lead of 73,000.

The vote of 3,208 precincts out of 6,942, including 1,816 from Cook County, gave Hoover 741,167; Smith 694,811. The Republican nominee for President apparently won the State by about 400,000.

Emmerson and his fellow contestants for State executive office apparently fell considerably behind Hoover both in Cook County and down-State, but all apparently were safe on the face of the incomplete figures.

Close Race for Senatorship.

The closest race of all was that for United States Senator. The first reports indicated might be a neck and neck race because of the way that Anton J. Cermak, the "wet" Democrat ran ahead of Governor Smith in Chicago. The first big batch of city precincts to be heard from promised him a Chicago lead of from 230,000 to 275,000.

It was thought that Glenn might not be able to overcome this in the down-State territory because the figures on the Governorship which had been received some time ago did not indicate that Emmerson would carry down-State by quite that big a margin. But when the outside counties began to report the returns forecast a margin for Glenn outside Chicago in excess of 250,000.

Cermak was the only Democrat who heaped abuse of all the national ticket in Chicago. Floyd E. Thompson, Democratic gubernatorial entry, was allowed by his party to trail Governor Smith and he was the only Democrat except Thomas J. Courtney, nominee for Attorney General against Oscar E. Carlstrom, the Republican who now holds that office.

The returns on these offices were far ahead of those for the rest of the offices on the State ticket, but Hoover's lead and the leads of Glenn, Emmerson and Carlstrom were taken as proof that all the Republican entries had carried the State.

On incomplete returns Judge William J. Lindsay, Democrat, was leading Judge John A. Swanson, Republican, for State's Attorney, the centre of the battle over Cook County offices.

In the battle over judges the Crowe-Thompson forces in the Board of Review, Thomas J. Nash, Democrat, is leading Edward I. Litsinger, Republican.

Much Splitting of Votes.

Scattering precinct figures from all the wards, indicate a day of prodigious vote splitting.

The Crowe-Thompson whetted their axes for the Dineen Republican candidates, and vice versa. Indications are that if Judge Lindsay maintains his early lead, the entire Democratic ticket was elected.

Continued on Page Four.

U.S. Senators Elected

REPUBLICAN—18

California............*H. W. Johnson
Connecticut..........‡F. C. Walcott
Delaware....John G. Townsend Jr.
Idaho................§John Thomas
Illinois.............§Otis F. Glenn
Indiana..............*A. R. Robinson
Maine................§Frederick Hale
Maryland............‡P. L. Goldsborough
Michigan.............*H. Vanderberg
Nebraska...........*Robert B. Howell
New Jersey...........‡Hamilton F. Kean
North Dakota........*Lynn J. Frazier
Ohio.................*Simeon D. Fess
Ohio.................†T. E. Burton
Pennsylvania........*David A. Reed
Rhode Island........*Felix Hebert
Vermont.............*Frank L. Greene
Wisconsin...........*R. M. La Follette Jr.

DEMOCRATS—9

Arizona.............*Henry F. Ashurst
Florida.............*Park Trammell
Massachusetts.......*David I. Walsh
Mississippi.........*H. D. Stephens
New York............*R. S. Copeland
Tennessee...........*Kenneth McKellar
Texas...............*Tom Connally
Utah................*William H. King
Virginia............*C. A. Swanson

FARMER-LABORITE—1

Minnesota...........*Henrik Shipstead

IN DOUBT—7

Missouri   New Mexico
Montana   Washington
Nevada   West Virginia
              Wyoming

*Elected for full term ending March 3, 1935.
‡Elected for both long and short terms.
§Elected for full term ending March 3, 1935.
†Re-elected Sept. 10, 1928, for full term ending March 3, 1935.
*Elected for short term ending March 3, 1929.

BAY STATE IS CLOSE, WITH SMITH AHEAD

Walsh, Democrat, Re-elected to Senate and Cole Is in Front for Governor.

SMITH WINS RHODE ISLAND

But State Ticket Goes Republican—Other New England States for Hoover.

Special to The New York Times.

BOSTON, Mass., Nov. 7.—At 4:30 o'clock this morning, after one of the liveliest election nights ever known in Massachusetts, and when it appeared that the Democrats had swept the State, there was a possibility that Herbert Hoover, though trailing Governor Smith, might receive the greatest electoral vote of this State.

At the same time there was a probability that the final returns would allow Frank G. Allen winner of the Gubernatorial contest over his Democratic opponent, General Charles H. Cole, despite the late returns.

Senator David D. Walsh, Democrat, running 10,000 votes ahead of Governor Smith, was clearly re-elected over Benjamin Loring Young, Republican.

Smith Carries Textile Cities.

From early in the evening, when Hoover had built up a substantial lead, the returns from Boston and some textile centres pulled him down and pushed Smith out in front.

Then followed a see-sawing back and forth, with Smith slowly forging ahead in the early morning hours, largely as a result of 10,000-vote margins which were given to him in Fall River and Lowell, 4,000 in New Bedford, 5,000 in Salem, 7,000 in Holyoke, and lesser votes in other cities.

For President, 982 precincts out of the 1,905 in the State gave Hoover 408,129, Smith 428,500.

For Governor, 843 precincts, including 300 of the 339 in Boston, gave Allen J. 346,495, Cole (D.) 351,095.

For Senator, 848 precincts gave Young (R.) 312,556, Walsh (D.) 321,002.

Unofficial Boston figures for 339 precincts out of 339 gave Hoover

Continued on Page Two.

NEW JERSEY GIVES REPUBLICAN SLATE A HEAVY MAJORITY

Incomplete Figures for State Show Hoover Leads Smith by 116,944.

LARSON AHEAD OF DILL

Victory for Republican by 166,340 Is Indicated in Gubernatorial Race.

KEAN BEATING EDWARDS

Strong Republican Showing Is a Damaging Blow to Prestige of Hague as Leader.

Herbert Hoover's indicated plurality in New Jersey was 309,420 early this morning when the tabulation of returns from 1,102 of the 2,920 districts gave Hoover 303,792 and Smith 186,848. In the metropolitan district of New Jersey the Republican and Democratic candidates ran a close race.

In Essex County, which includes Newark, tabulation of the vote in 190 of the 481 districts showed that it stood, Hoover, 39,122; Smith, 21,810.

Hamilton F. Kean was leading Senator Edward I. Edwards, Democrat, by 91,021 in 1,102 districts and his indicated plurality was 239,440.

Larson in the Lead.

In the Gubernatorial contest the returns from 1,102 districts gave Larson 269,391 and Dill 205,692, giving Larson, Republican, a lead of 63,699 and an indicated plurality of 166,340.

In 73 of 506 districts in Hudson County, the stronghold of Mayor Frank Hague, the vote was: Hoover 9,108, Smith 16,302, Kean 10,204, Edwards 18,896, Larson 10,302, Dill 18,107.

Increasing Republican pluralities reported from the counties of Southern New Jersey were not offset by expected Democratic gains in the metropolitan area.

Republican candidates for Congress were leading their opponents in all counties except Hudson, and Republican candidates for the Assembly were reported generally in the lead in all but counties which are now represented in the Assembly by Democrats.

While the Republicans of Camden County were celebrating the success of their State and national tickets there, State Senator Joseph H. Forsyth was reported to be dying from influenza at his home at Haddonfield. He was stricken several days ago. He was elected in 1926 for three years.

Reports from Trenton were to the effect that a plurality of from 150,000 to 200,000 for Hoover was indicated by the early returns. According to The Associated Press fifty-six districts out of 2,920 in strongly Republican territory gave Hoover a lead of 5,456 over Smith. The vote was Hoover 9,078 and Smith 3,622.

Forty-three districts tabulated in Jersey City gave Smith 7,761 votes, Hoover 4,024, Edwards 7,465, Kean 4,037, Dill 7,276, Larson 4,330.

Forty-three districts tabulated in the United States Senatorial and Gubernatorial races. These gave Kean, Republican, 7,090; Senator Edwards, Democrat, 2,217. The Governorship figures were William L. Dill, Democrat, 3,580; Morgan F. Larson, Republican, 5,569.

The indicated heavy pluralities for the Republican candidates for United States Senator and Governor were a damaging blow to the prestige of Mayor Hague, Vice Chairman of the Democratic National Committee, whose Democratic stronghold in Hudson has been sufficiently powerful in three Gubernatorial elections to stem the Republican tide in other sections of New Jersey and send Democratic candidates to the Governor's Mansion and to the Senate.

Fight in Hudson County.

The fight of Mayor Frank Hague of Jersey City, Democratic leader in Hudson County, was responsible for the action of election officials in striking the names of approximately 29,000 voters from the enrollment lists. It was reported that several thousand voters had been disfranchised in Hudson County because of inability of the Commissioner of Registration to deal with the situation then resulting from the County Board of Election's ruling at the eleventh hour. Election officials es-

Continued on Page Eighteen.

Gov. Smith's Message to Mr. Hoover

Governor Smith sent the following telegram just after midnight to his successful rival:

Hon. Herbert Hoover,
Palo Alto, Cal.:

I congratulate you heartily on your victory, and extend to you my sincere good wishes for your health and happiness and for the success of your Administration.

ALFRED E. SMITH.

Electoral Vote

HOOVER.			
Arizona	3	Nevada	3
California	13	New Hampshire	4
Colorado	6	New Jersey	14
Connecticut	7	New Mexico	3
Delaware	3	New York	45
Florida	6	Ohio	24
Idaho	4	Oklahoma	10
Illinois	29	Oregon	5
Indiana	15	Pennsylvania	38
Iowa	13	South Dakota	5
Kansas	10	Tennessee	12
Kentucky	13	Utah	4
Maine	6	Vermont	4
Maryland	8	Virginia	12
Michigan	15	Washington	7
Minnesota	12	West Virginia	8
Missouri	18	Wisconsin	13
Montana	4	Wyoming	3
Nebraska	8	**Total**	**407**

SMITH.			
Alabama	12	Mississippi	10
Arkansas	9	Rhode Island	5
Georgia	14	South Carolina	9
Louisiana	10	**Total**	**69**

DOUBTFUL.			
Massachusetts	18	Texas	20
North Carolina	12	**Total**	**55**
North Dakota	5		

Total number of votes in Electoral College, 531; necessary to a choice, 266.

HOOVER BREAKS THE SOLID SOUTH

He Carries Virginia and Probably Florida and North Carolina—Leads in Texas Also.

Special to The New York Times.

RICHMOND, Va., Nov. 6.—Herbert Hoover has carried the Old Dominion and broken the Solid South. State Democratic headquarters authorized the statement before midnight:

"The unofficial returns indicate that Virginia has gone for Hoover."

At a late hour he had obtained a 21,000 lead over Governor Smith with two-thirds of the State polled. His plurality had been steadily mounting from the start.

The totals in 1,429 precincts out of 1,666 were: Hoover, 145,641; Smith, 124,530.

Fifteen of forty precincts in Richmond gave Hoover 2,253 and Smith 2,381.

Danville has gone for Hoover. This is a Ku Klux Klan stronghold, but Democrats were as thoroughly organized there as anywhere in the State. Hoover, as expected, polled heavy votes in the first and second districts while Smith showed great strength in the fourth.

Only in the ninth district did the returns look normal. There were fewer Democratic defections than in other parts of the State, and Hoover and Smith were running neck and neck.

Hoover Leads in Texas.

DALLAS, Texas, Nov. 6 (P).—The possibility that a Republican Presidential candidate might carry Texas for the first time in history loomed late tonight as Herbert Hoover, for the third time during the tabulation of the vote, went into the lead.

The 11 o'clock tabulation of the Texas Election Bureau showed the Republican ahead by 2,366 votes with more than half of the ballots counted. It was the largest lead either candidate had gained in the zig and zag race. Hoover's total, as compiled by the bureau, was 208,415, Smith's 206,560, the count of 214 counties out of 253, four

Continued on Page Two.

CITY GIVES SMITH 430,000 MAJORITY

Incomplete Count Also Indicates Like Lead for Roosevelt for Governor.

Governor Smith carried New York City by about 430,000 plurality over Mr. Hoover, or about 85,000 less than the plurality he received over Theodore Roosevelt in 1924, which was the largest plurality the city gave him in any of his Gubernatorial campaigns.

With only 28 out of the 3,493 election districts of the city missing, Smith had 1,106,594 against 620,076 for Hoover, a plurality of 426,450. Thomas Norman, Socialist candidate, received less than 50,000 in the city.

Franklin D. Roosevelt, Democratic candidate for Governor, ran behind Smith in the city. With 90 districts missing, Roosevelt had 1,087,413 against 699,441 for his Republican opponent, Attorney General Albert Ottinger, a plurality of 387,977.

Herbert H. Lehman, Democratic candidate for Lieutenant Governor, and United States Senator Royal S. Copeland, Democratic candidate for re-election to the Senate, ran ahead of their ticket in the city.

Lehman Has Big Lead.

With 193 districts missing, Lehman received 1,100,088 votes, against 614,241 for Mr. Lockwood, his Republican opponent, a plurality of 491,847.

With 668 districts missing, Copeland had 808,401 to 498,599 for Alanson B. Houghton, former Ambassador to Germany and Great Britain, the Republican candidate, a plurality of 409,702 for Copeland.

Albert Conway, Democratic candidate for Attorney General, and Maurice E. Tremaine, Democratic candidate for re-election as State Controller, also ran ahead of Smith in the city. With 565 districts missing Conway had 1,026,620 votes against 585,260 for Hamilton Ward, Republican, a plurality of 495,194. With 569 districts missing Tremaine had 1,006,027, against 585,790 for

Continued on Page Seven.

ROOSEVELT IS VICTOR BY SLIM PLURALITY; COPELAND ALSO WINS

Democratic Nominee Captures Governorship by Margin Indicated to Be 40,000.

SENATOR IN BY 56,000

Re-elected Over Houghton After Running Up Lead of 523,000 in the City.

LEAVES SMITH FAR BEHIND

Polls 90,000 More Votes Than the Governor—Lehman, Conway and Tremaine Leading.

Franklin D. Roosevelt, Democrat, defeated Attorney General Albert Ottinger, Republican, for the Governorship of New York State, on the basis of returns from 7,718 election districts out of the 8,267 in the State, a plurality of about 40,000 for Mr. Roosevelt was indicated on these figures, and "it is possible that the returns from the missing districts but not enough to give Mr. Ottinger the State.

Senator Royal S. Copeland, Democrat for re-election on the Democratic ticket, apparently had won from former Ambassador Alanson B. Houghton by an indicated plurality of about 56,000. Senator Copeland ran surprisingly well in New York City, where his plurality seems likely to reach 523,000, or about 90,000 more than the plurality received by Governor Smith, heretofore regarded as the strongest candidate in the city, personally.

The victories for Mr. Roosevelt and Senator Copeland went some distance toward assuaging the 'local Democrats for Governor Smith's defeat. Governor Smith's indicated plurality in New York City was about 430,000, and his defeat in the State by about 125,000 was indicated.

Roosevelt Lead 66,568.

Mr. Roosevelt had an actual lead of 65,568, with 549 out of the 8,267 election districts in the State missing, the vote being Roosevelt 2,072,372 and Ottinger 1,864,754.

Outside New York City, 4,296 election districts out of 4,774 gave Roosevelt 929,953 and Ottinger 1,287,002, an actual plurality of 327,649 and an indicated up-State plurality for Ottinger of 367,596.

In New York City 3,400 out of 3,493 election districts gave Roosevelt 1,093,369 and Ottinger 697,752, an actual plurality of 395,617 and an indicated 1 plurality of 405,186.

Mr. Roosevelt ran ahead of Governor Smith in virtually every county up-State, while Mr. Ottinger cut into the Democratic vote somewhat in New York City, but not as much as Senator Copeland.

Senator Copeland's run in New York City was surprising. In 3,144 out of the 3,493 election districts in the city he received 1,053,045 and Houghton 561,539, an actual plurality of 491,506 and an indicated plurality of 523,000.

To offset this tremendous plurality, seemingly the largest ever received in the city by any of the candidates, Mr. Houghton in 3,640 out of 4,774 up-State election districts received 1,006,410 to 712,172 for Senator Copeland. This is an actual plurality of 294,231 and an indicated plurality of 367,500 for Houghton Up-State.

The delay in the returns from about a thousand up-State districts early this morning that there were indications which led him to suspect fraud up-State. He announced that Edward S. Dore, Chairman of the Law Committee of the Democratic State Committee, would leave for up-State early this morning for up-State "to effect the extreme delay with which about 1,000 districts are sending in election returns, the Democratic State Committee had become convinced that fraud is being committed in an attempt to elect Ottinger as Governor of the State.

On the way to Governor Smith's suite early this morning, Mr. Roosevelt said:

"Everything looks fine, all right, we are leaving New York City on the way State Supreme Court Judge (Wednesday) morning for up-State cities, together with a staff of 140 lawyers to uncover such frauds as have been

Continued on Page Seven.

HOOVER CARRIES NEW YORK BY 125,000

Republican Nominee Captures New Jersey, Takes Wisconsin; Breaks Solid South, Winning Virginia, Florida

GAINING IN NORTH CAROLINA AND BAY STATE

Most of Farm Belt in Republican Column in Record-Breaking Vote—Kentucky, Missouri and Tennessee Lost to Democrats.

Voting in unprecedented numbers, a myriad of American citizens yesterday chose Herbert Hoover of California for President of the United States and Charles Curtis of Kansas for Vice President.

How pronounced is the victory of these candidates of the Republican Party over their Democratic competitors, Governor Alfred E. Smith of New York, nominee for President, and Joseph T. Robinson of Arkansas, the Vice Presidential nominee, cannot be determined until the stupendous task of counting 40,000,000 or more votes is completed, but a Republican landslide took place at the polls, and it will be reflected in a heavy Hoover-Curtis majority of the 531 ballots in the Electoral College.

496 Electoral Votes for Hoover

Mr. Hoover is assured of more than 400 electoral votes. It is probable that his majority will increase as further returns are received. He has broken the traditionally Democratic Solid South. He has carried Virginia and returns from Florida indicate that he has won in that State. His tally in the Electoral College may go as high as 444 votes if North Carolina, North Dakota and Texas, which are very close, are added to his strength, or even to the stupendous total of 462, if the count now proceeding in Massachusetts turns in his favor.

Such an outcome would give Mr. Hoover a majority of 397 electoral votes over Governor Smith. It is already apparent that no Presidential candidate of any major party has been beaten as badly as Governor Smith, with the exception of William H. Taft, who got only 8 votes in the Electoral College in his contest for re-election against Woodrow Wilson and Theodore Roosevelt.

According to the latest returns received from Massachusetts, North Carolina, North Dakota and Texas, these States are still in the doubtful column either by reason of inadequate returns or on account of the closeness of contests as the count proceeds, and while Governor Smith may be shown to have carried some of them, his tally of electoral votes may not exceed seventy.

New York Spells Smith's Doom.

Governor Smith's hope of victory began to fade within a few hours after the polls closed in New York State when it was indicated that he had carried New York City, his great stronghold, by less than 450,000, which was much short of the estimate of his managers. As returns began to roll in from up-State it became apparent that the Hoover plurality in that strong Republican area would materially overcome the showing for Governor Smith in New York City, with the prospect that the Republican nominee would carry the State by a lead in the neighborhood of 125,000.

With New York's forty-five electoral votes placed in the Hoover column it became merely a matter of waiting until the full returns determined what the Republican candidates' majority will be in the Electoral College. The tremendous onsweep of the Hoover following was emphasized when State after State in which the Democrats had placed hope of victory went over into the Republican camp.

New Jersey was carried by the Republican national ticket by a heavy majority. Maryland followed suit. Late returns show that Hoover also took Missouri. Of other border States, he captured Kentucky and Oklahoma. Minnesota, which the Smith management was also hopeful of carrying on account of the defection among Republican voters because of Mr. Hoover's attitude on the McNary-Haugen bill, gave him a heavy plurality.

Smith States Only in South.

As for Governor Smith, there is no assurance that he has carried any State outside of the South. With the results in Florida and Texas still in doubt he must be content to be certain of having carried only Alabama, Georgia, Louisiana, Mississippi and South Carolina. In the early morning hours late returns had Hoover forging ahead even in North Carolina. Tennessee was conceded to the Republican candidate.

His victories in Alabama and North Carolina are a set back for Senator J. Thomas Heflin and Senator Furnifold M. Simmons, who deserted their party allegiance to oppose him, Simmons on the ground of Governor Smith's anti-prohibition policy and Senator Heflin for the openly stated reason that Governor Smith was a Catholic.

In the early morning hours returns from Wisconsin indicated that the portion of the State outside of Milwaukee had voted so heavily for Hoover that Smith's lead in the metropolis made famous by beer had been overcome and that the State's thirteen electoral votes would be added to the steadily mounting Hoover column.

It was after 4 o'clock this morning before virtually complete returns from Rhode Island showed that Smith had carried Rhode Island, the only State outside the Solid South that can with certainty be placed to his credit. He seems to have carried it by a small majority, probably not exceeding 2,000.

Maine, New Hampshire, Vermont and Connecticut joined the Republican procession. At an early hour this morning the prospect was that where the eighteen electoral votes of Massachusetts would be placed could not be made certain until late today.

Republican Congress Assured.

The victory for the Republican national ticket is accompanied by the assurance that, as President, Mr. Hoover will have the support of a Congress controlled by those of his own party. While returns are incomplete the indications are that the Republican majority in the House of Representatives

"All the News That's Fit to Print."

The New York Times.

THE WEATHER
Cloudy, probably rain today and tomorrow; warmer tomorrow.
Temperatures yesterday—Max. 61; Min. 51

Copyright, 1929, by The New York Times Company.

VOL. LXXIX....No. 26,212. **** NEW YORK, WEDNESDAY, OCTOBER 30, 1929. TWO CENTS

GRUNDY FOR CURBING 'BACKWARD STATES' ON THE TARIFF BILL

Veteran Republican Lobbyist Tells Senate Inquiry the West Needs "Silencing."

PENNSYLVANIA KNOWS BEST

"Unfortunate," He Holds, That the Constitution Gives Equal Voice to States in Senate.

BATTLES INVESTIGATORS

He Assails Boran—Would "Hate to Tell" His Opinion of Wisconsin.

Special to The New York Times.

WASHINGTON, Oct. 29.—Joseph R. Grundy, president of the Pennsylvania Manufacturers' Association, told the Senate Lobby Committee today that certain "backward" States of the West, through their Senators, had been altogether "too vocal" in the consideration of the current tariff bill, and that some method should be found to "silence" them at times when legislation affecting the economic welfare of the United States is under way.

Mr. Grundy declared it "unfortunate" that the framers of the Constitution had seen fit to grant to the states equal rights and representation in the Senate, some effect of the arrangement was to give sections slow in developing their resources an equal voice in legislation directly involving such great reservoirs of wealth and taxation as Pennsylvania.

Mr. Grundy was recalled today for cross-examination on testimony he gave before the lobby committee on Oct. 24. Last week Mr. Grundy and the Senate Investigating Committee got along very well, and that session was decorous and orderly in contrast with today, when the witness and his questioners appeared to be antagonistic from the outset.

Criticises Senator Walsh.

At one stage Mr. Grundy sharply described a series of questions put by Senator Walsh of Montana as "impertinent." There were frequent references to the Vare case, to the party service which Mr. Grundy had performed in the collection of Republican campaign funds, and to the relations of the witness with public men and his activities here as a part of the tariff lobby.

At times the hearing resembled a hot political debate, in which the five members of the committee were arrayed against the witness. Mr. Grundy was once reproved by Senator Blaine of Wisconsin, a member of the committee, for alleged evasion, and Mr. Blaine exclaimed heatedly:

"Look me squarely in the eye and answer my question."

The hearing was marked by frequent clashes between Mr. Grundy and senators Borah, Caraway and Blaine, and in one interchange with the witnesses Mr. Borah denied emphatically a statement that he had opposed the debenture plan at the Kansas City convention.

Chairman Caraway frankly indicated that the witness was not frank with the committee and that, while it might be "smart" for him to "sidestep," eventually the investigators would get what they were after.

Hit at "Most Vocal" States.

Mr. Grundy was impelled to enter into a discussion of his belief that "backward Western States" should be silenced on the tariff by questions asked by Senator Walsh. The Senator read from a statement submitted to the committee a week ago, in which Mr. Grundy asserted that if "volume of voice" in the Senate were proportioned to population, productive power or the total contributed toward the national upkeep, some of those States "which are now most vocal would need amplifiers to make their whispers heard."

Mr. Grundy also had declared that "such States as Arizona, South Dakota, Idaho and Mississippi, &c., do not pay enough toward the upkeep of the government to cover the costs of collection." As a result of Mr. Walsh's examination, Mr. Grundy finally included Arkansas and Montana in his list of "backward" States, thus bringing to three of them having representation on the lobby committee.

"You have not mentioned Wisconsin in your list," suggested Senator Walsh. "What do you think about that State?"

"What I think about Wisconsin I would hate to tell you," replied the witness. This evoked an outburst of laughter in the audience, in which the committee joined.

Favors a Few Concessions.

Mr. Grundy again caused laughter when he said that he would permit the "backward" States, through their Senators, to have their say on questions affecting "Junior Red Cross work and outdoor relief," but that generally speaking, they should be required to "hold their peace" on

Continued on Page Eighteen.

IT'S A SAFE TAXI IF IT'S A Kappel 1000 Yellow Taxi.—Advt.

Von Opel, Rocket Flier, Weds Woman Pilot Who Advised Him

Wireless to THE NEW YORK TIMES.

BERLIN, Oct. 29.—Fritz von Opel, the first to fly a rocket plane, and who intends to sail for New York the beginning of November to study and work at General Motors plants, was married on Saturday to Frau Selinik, née Loewenstein, the former wife of a Wiesbaden actor. For many months she has been von Opel's professional adviser on aviation and she herself is one of Germany's six women pilots, flying her Handley Page planes with the greatest skill.

Frau von Opel, who is also a daring automobilist, is handsome, slender and blonde. When the airman landed safely from his rocket flight she was the first to congratulate him, shedding tears of joy. She will accompany him to the United States.

COALITION FIGHTING MOVE TO KILL TARIFF

Will Try to Force Through Bill, While Reed Favors Ending Session Nov. 15.

WATSON QUITTING CAPITAL

Departure for Florida Tomorrow for Health Leaves Jones as Republican Senate Leader.

Special to The New York Times.

WASHINGTON, Oct. 29.—Faced with Old Guard Republican willingness to leave the Smoot-Hawley tariff bill to its fate, the Democratic-Progressive coalition was today more determined than ever to drive the bill through the Senate and force the conservatives to accept it in a completely rewritten form.

Coalition strategy was centred upon fixing on the Old Guard leaders any responsibility for abandonment of the remodeled bill with the Simmons-Norris flexible amendment to the farm debenture plan. To those coalition Republicans who are now ready to desert the measure, the coalition applied the unflattering comparison of "rats and a sinking ship."

The administration Republicans resented to be stirred by such criticism. Senator Reed of Pennsylvania reiterated his conviction that the bill would never emerge from conference. Senator Moses announced that he would vote against the bill in the Senate, before it ever went to conference. The Republicans were so dismayed that they even seriously considered a motion to adjourn the Senate about the middle of November until the regular session starts on Dec. 2.

To add to their disorganization it was revealed that Senator Watson, Republican floor leader, would leave for Florida on Thursday to rebuild his shattered health.

McNary to Act as Aide.

Old Guard lieutenants hurriedly announced that Senator Jones of Washington, assistant leader, would take charge in Mr. Watson's absence, aided by Senator McNary of Oregon, who is popular with all Senate factions, has a fine record as a conciliator and more influence than most regular Republicans on the farming public.

When it was first announced that Senator Watson was going to Florida, reports spread that his illness was so serious that he might never return to the Senate as floor leader. His friends, however, denied this. They admitted that he was an ill man and needed a complete rest for a time, but asserted that he would return to assume his duties.

There was some assumption that Mr. McNary would be made temporary leader, because Senator Jones had not sufficiently recovered from the effects of a recent operation, but Mr. Jones assured Old Guard members that he felt capable of taking over the task.

While assembled, Senator Watson, who is dropping work by his physician's orders, would not admit that the outlook for passing the tariff bill by the end of the special session was absolutely hopeless. He did not share the view that the session might as well be adjourned, which Senator Reed may propose for about Nov. 15.

Instead, Mr. Watson will work on his departure to bring about "some sort of agreement for some sort of bill," basing his plea on the idea that the coalition must concede increases on industrial as well as agricultural rates.

Says Action Would Aid Business.

"It would have a quieting effect on business to pass the tariff bill," asserted Senator Watson. "The tariff bills are always the occasion of some unrest, though this bill has caused less agitation than usual because a Republican tariff is to be superimposed on a Republican tariff and everybody knows that if this bill fails the country would continue to be prosperous.

"It is true that there might be changes in agricultural rates to meet new conditions, but it is equally true

Continued on Page Fourteen.

KAHN REFUSES POST IN SENATE CAMPAIGN; CALLS CHOICE UNWISE

He Writes to Moses to Withhold His Name for Treasurer Due to 'Divided Reception.'

WAS RELUCTANT, HE SAYS

Recalls He Told Senator of His Stand, but Yielded as a Duty to His Party.

HOLDS VIEWS CONFIRMED

Declares He Is a Wall St. Man but a Liberal in Politics—Friends See Him Put in False Light.

Otto H. Kahn in a letter to Senator George H. Moses of New Hampshire, chairman of the Republican Senatorial Campaign Committee, made public yesterday, declined the post of treasurer of that committee because of the "divided reception" which the announcement of his designation as treasurer had met.

Announcement of the selection of Mr. Kahn at the dinner given last Thursday evening at the University Club here by Jeremiah Milbank for Claudius H. Huston, the new chairman of the Republican National Committee. Publication of this announcement, together with the report that speakers at the dinner attacked the members of the Progressive Republican group in the Senate, brought protests from some of those Senators against the selection of Mr. Kahn.

Mr. Kahn in his letter to Senator Moses declared that, while a Wall Street man, he was a liberal in politics. He said some of the interpretations placed on his designation were erroneous, but added that the way it had been received justified his earlier feeling that he was not the right man for the position. No formal action for the appointment of a treasurer of the Senatorial committee has yet been taken, and Mr. Kahn requested Senator Moses not to present his name to the committee.

Mr. Kahn's Letter.

Oct. 28, 1929.

My dear Senator:

When you did me the honor to ask me to act as treasurer of the Republican Senatorial Campaign Committee I told you that I feared your kindly sentiment toward me, springing from a long friendship, was swaying your judgment, that I felt sure that I was not the right man for the position, that, moreover, I was overwhelmed with demands upon my time and energies and that I hoped very much that you would not persist in your request.

You argued to the contrary and, among other things, pointed to the fact that, while a Wall Street man, I was known to be, as classified, a liberal in politics. You repeated your invitation when I had the pleasure of seeing you at Mr. Milbank's dinner last Thursday.

I therefore stated that, though my views were unchanged, I felt that if we want effective party government, such as our political system requires, every citizen should be willing to make good his professions of party allegiance by submitting to being drafted, within the limits of reason and possibility, and that if the leaders of the party to which I belong demanded of me a service which did not conflict with my other duties and responsibilities I was not at liberty to refuse, however reluctant I was to accept.

You regarded this answer as tantamount to an acceptance in principle, as you were perfectly justified in doing, and at what was supposed and intended to be a strictly private dinner, you made informal reference to that acceptance.

Sees His Doubts Confirmed.

But the divided reception with which the report of the appointment of a separate treasurer for your committee and of my designation as such treasurer has met, however erroneous some of the interpretations placed thereon, appears to have confirmed the validity of the doubts which I ventured to express when you offered that position to me, and to justify me in concluding to abstain from occupying it.

I understand that no formal action has been taken as yet by the National Republican Senatorial committee concerning the appointment of a treasurer, and I am making free to write these lines to request that you will please refrain from bringing my name before the committee for appointment to the treasurership.

Believe me, dear Senator,
Very faithfully yours,
OTTO H. KAHN.
Hon. George H. Moses, The Senate, Washington, D. C.

Influential Republicans expressed regret that Mr. Kahn had decided not to take the post of treasurer of the Republican Senatorial committee. It was recalled that he was re-

Continued on Page Fifteen.

Newark Man, 4 Feet 10, Says He Was Smallest in A. E. F.

WASHINGTON, Oct. 29 (AP).—Nicholas Casale of Newark, N. J., wants to be known as the smallest man who went to France with the American Expeditionary Forces.

He has appealed to Representative Hartley of Kearny to establish that fact. Casale recently secured an affidavit from the Veterans' Bureau certifying that he was 4 feet 10 inches tall and weighed 106 pounds when he enlisted. The bureau has refused to declare him the "smallest man," saying it would require months for clerks to scan the record of every man who served with the A. E. F.

It was not explained how Casale secured enlistment when the minimum requirements are 5 feet and 110 pounds.

MISSING AIRLINER BROUGHT IN SAFELY

Pilot Lands Western Express Ship at Albuquerque After Being Forced Down.

WOULD NOT RISK STORM

Passengers Tell of Cold Night in Deserted Ranch House as Snow Swirled Round.

Special to The New York Times.

ALBUQUERQUE, N. M., Oct. 29.—Lost for more than twenty-four hours while marooned on a bleak New Mexico mesa, Western Air Express tri-motored liner 113 escaped today from the snow-swept stretch where it was forced down Monday and landed here with its crew of three and two passengers, chilled but safe.

Caught in a blinding swirl of snow Monday at 10:15 A. M., the plane was forced down near Mechado, seventy-five miles southeast of Gallup, N. M. The crew and passengers found refuge in an abandoned ranch house.

The passengers are Dr. A. W. Ward of San Francisco and W. E. Merz of Mount Vernon, N. Y. The crew includes James E. Doles, chief pilot, of Los Angeles; Allan C. Barrie, co-pilot, of Burbank, Cal., and R. L. Britton, steward, of Los Angeles.

Employees of the airport and pilots of two planes waiting for the weather to clear to resume the search for the 113 stood amazed as the big craft glided along the runway. They rushed out to the plane and as the group of men who had been given up for dead stepped out they danced around them, clapped them on the back and hugged them in delight.

Wild Night of Intense Cold.

Despite their fatigue, Dr. Ward and Mr. Merz were lighthearted as they stepped jauntily from the plane. They regretted only the loss of time but joined in praise of Pilot Doles for his skilful manoeuvering to save the ship in the storm when further progress could not be risked.

They told of a harrowing night which followed the forced landing, of tramping through snow to find shelter, of sleeping on an old bed spring covered with seat cushions from the plane and of shivering in intense cold while they took turns in keeping up a fire.

"A half frozen rabbit and a rabbit's foot brought us good luck," Dr. Ward said.

The half-frozen rabbit had been captured in the bushes by co-pilot Barrie. The rabbit's foot was worn by steward Britton. He had bought it the day before the flight at the T. A. T. plane City of San Francisco crashed.

Suddenly Enveloped by Storm.

"We left Holbrook, flying east," Doles said, "and were about over the edge of the plateau before a storm. I tossed her down towards St. John's. Suddenly the storm seemed to break over us all at once, and a landing became a necessity. I found a small spot, and it

Continued on Page Seventeen.

Navy Paymaster Leads Way to $47,000 Loot, Dug Up by Night in Washington Chicken Yard

Special to The New York Times.

WASHINGTON, Oct. 29.—Lieutenant Charles Muil, a navy paymaster accused of embezzling $54,600, naval authorities, in a search late at night, recently uncovered $47,000 of the loot buried in a chicken yard in Southeast Washington on the grounds of the Home of the Aged and Infirm.

When Lieutenant Muil voluntarily surrendered himself, on Oct. 14, to the naval authorities at New York, after having disappeared on Sept. 28 from his post as paymaster for Destroyer Division 40 at Charleston, S. C., he is said to have turned over $1,500 to Captain C. T. Owens, commanding the receiving ship Seattle.

This leaves $6,100 unaccounted for the navy's officers, in announcing today the discovery in the chicken yard, said they were trying to locate

the rest of the money, although they had scant hope of success.

According to the story told to the officers by Lieutenant Muil, he came here directly from Charleston and buried the money in the yard of his former home. He then left for Chicago, where he bought some stock, and went to Detroit and into Canada. From there he proceeded northward himself, on Oct. 15 to the Brooklyn Navy Yard, but when he told his story of the buried money he was brought here to direct the search for it. His now awaiting general court-martial on specifications covering embezzlement.

Lieutenant Muil was born in Illinois in 1893, enlisted in the navy twenty years ago and was commissioned in 1921. He has a wife and 9-year-old son in New York City.

STOCKS COLLAPSE IN 16,410,030-SHARE DAY, BUT RALLY AT CLOSE CHEERS BROKERS; BANKERS OPTIMISTIC, TO CONTINUE AID

LEADERS SEE FEAR WANING

Point to 'Lifting Spells' in Trading as Sign of Buying Activity.

GROUP MEETS TWICE IN DAY

But Resources Are Unable to Stem Selling Tide—Lamont Reassures Investors.

HOPE SEEN IN MARGIN CUTS

Banks Reduce Requirements to 25 Per Cent—Sentiment in Wall St. More Cheerful.

Resources of the banking group which was organized last Thursday to stabilize conditions in the stock market were utilized yesterday to break the force of the terrific flood of selling which accompanied the biggest day, from the point of view of volume, ever experienced on the New York Stock Exchange.

Despite the drastic decline, sentiment in Wall Street last night was more cheerful than it has been on any day since the torrent of selling set under way. Periodic "lifting spells" which developed between intervals of extreme weakness were cited by bankers at the close of the market, as testifying to the presence of investment buying. The public is in some measure regaining its senses and the unreasoning fear which has prompted the sacrifice of securities for any price they would bring is at length subsiding.

While even the tremendous buying power of the banking group was unable to turn the tide of selling in yesterday's market, the group did not in the least mitigate its activity. Two meetings were held during the day, one at noon and one at 4:30 P. M., the latter lasting until 6:30 P. M.

Will Continue Support.

After the evening meeting Thomas W. Lamont of J. P. Morgan & Co. spoke to reporters.

"I want to take occasion," Mr. Lamont said, "to explain again, as heretofore, that the banking group was organized to offer certain support in the market and to act as far as possible as somewhat of a stabilizing factor.

"It was not the intention of the group to attempt to maintain prices, but to maintain a free market; in other words, to correct the condition that prevailed last Thursday.

"The group has continued and will continue in a cooperative way to support the market and has not been a seller of stocks."

The statement was issued at the request of reporters to quiet rumors which had been abroad that the banking group had been selling stocks instead of supporting them.

These rumors were, of course, without foundation, for the group is known to have purchased heavily in directions where the force of its buying power would be most effective in stemming demoralization. It was reliably reported that in many instances when no bids could be obtained on the floor for large blocks of stock forced on the market the group had supplied the necessary bids and in other instances had acted as a stabilizing influence upon the list as a whole.

At the noon meeting of the group Owen D. Young, chairman of the General Electric Company, director of the Federal Reserve Bank of New York and head of the Young committee on reparations which recently developed the Young plan, joined the

Continued on Page Three.

240 Issues Lose $15,894,818,894 in Month; Slump in Full Exchange List Vastly Larger

The drastic effects of Wall Street's October bear market is shown by valuation tables prepared by THE NEW YORK TIMES, which place the decline in the market value of 240 representative issues on the New York Stock Exchange at $15,894,818,894 during the period from Oct. 1 to yesterday's closing. Since there are 1,279 issues listed on the New York Stock Exchange, the total depreciation for the month is estimated at between two and three times the loss for the 240 issues covered by THE TIMES table.

Among the losses of the various groups comprising the 240 stocks in THE TIMES valuation table were the following:

Group	Number of Issues	Decline in Value.
Railroads	25	$1,128,886,488
Public utilities	29	5,135,734,327
Motors	15	1,689,840,902
Oils	13	1,382,617,778
Coppers	7	524,403,820
Chemicals	9	1,621,897,897

The official figures of the New York Stock Exchange showed that the total market value of its listed securities on Oct. 1 was $87,073,630,423. The decline in the 240 representative issues therefore cut more than one-sixth from the total value of the listed securities. Most of this loss was inflicted by the wholesale liquidation of the last week.

U.S. STEEL TO PAY $1 EXTRA DIVIDEND

American Can Votes the Same and Raises Annual Rate From $3 to $4.

BIG GAIN IN STEEL INCOME

Earnings for Nine Months Are $15.82 a Share, Against $8.17 a Year Ago.

Two leading industrial companies yesterday declared extra dividends of $1 a share on the common stock, in each case the result of large earnings through the Summer months. The companies were the United States Steel Corporation and the American Can Company, whose interests touch every section of the country. Their action caused the Wall Street district to accept the extra dividends as final proof of the prosperity of the country, despite the breaks which have occurred in the stock market.

While the directors of neither of the companies referred to present conditions in the stock market as a reason for taking the extra dividend action at this time, the opinion was expressed in the district that the action reflecting their belief in the fundamental soundness of industry.

Directors of the American Can Company, in addition to declaring the $1 extra disbursement, also increased the regular dividend rate on the common stock from $3 a year to $4 a year, committing themselves to this payment for the future.

The United States Steel directors contented themselves with announcing that earnings for the first nine months of this year were nearly double those of the same period for 1929, namely, $15.82 a share on the common stock outstanding, compared with $8.17 for the nine months of 1928.

Steel Surplus Up $22,909,447.

Earnings of the United States Steel Corporation for the three months ended on Sept. 30 were reported as $72,009,666, equivalent to $5.57 a share on the common stock outstanding, and the extra dividend makes disbursements for the quarter less than half of the actual earnings. The operation for the three months, after the preferred and common stock dividends, including the extra dividend, increased the surplus of the company by $22,909,447.

September was the lowest for the three months which enter into the quarterly earnings. The amount reported for this month was $21,794,450, which compares with $26,290,039 in August and $24,917,157 for July. The total earnings for the quarter after deducting all expenses incident to operations, including those for ordinary repairs and maintenance of plants, taxes, including the reserve for Federal income taxes, and the interest on bonds of subsidiary companies, amounted to $70,173,717. Allowances for depreciation, depletion and obsolescence took away another $16,819,398, leaving the net income for the three months at $53,354,320. The interest for the quarter on the bonds of the company outstanding amounted to $1,178,970, and the payment of the 1¾ per cent dividends on the preferred stock amounted to $6,304,919.

Extra Due to Rise in Earnings.

The official statement issued by the company after the meeting of the directors read as follows:

The United States Steel Corporation's earnings for the first nine

Continued on Page Six.

RESERVE BOARD FINDS ACTION UNNECESSARY

Six-Hour Session Brings No Change in the New York Rediscount Rate.

OFFICIALS ARE OPTIMISTIC

Mellon Also Attends Cabinet Meeting, but Declines to Discuss Developments.

Special to The New York Times.

WASHINGTON, Oct. 29.—The further decline in stock market prices today passed without expressed apprehension on the part of Federal officials. The situation was watched intently by the Federal Reserve Board, which held a continuous session from 10 A. M. until 4 P. M. with Secretary Mellon in attendance.

Secretary Mellon, as ex-officio chairman of the board, attended the early part of the meeting before going to the White House for the Cabinet meeting. It could not be learned whether the market situation was discussed by the President and the Cabinet.

At 2:30 P. M. Mr. Mellon returned to the Reserve Board meeting, and remained until near its close. During the day he had conferred with Under-Secretary Ogden L. Mills and Roy A. Young, Governor of the Reserve Board. After the board adjourned, neither Secretary Mellon nor Mr. Young would even intimate the nature or scope of the discussions.

The board has restated to it the rediscount rate during the stock market decline, fearing that lowered rates might be employed to bolster up the market. The board's policy in not to aid in speculation, but it feels that the rediscount rate should be lowered to stimulate credits for business when it is apparent that such action would not be accepted as assistance to speculative loans. Mr. Young said there was no change in financial conditions which the board thought called for its action.

Cut in Discount Rate Expected.

It is thought the question of lowering rediscount rates may come before the Federal Reserve Board shortly. The Boston Federal Reserve Bank directors will meet tomorrow and the New York directors on Thursday. It is possible that one of these banks may suggest a lowering of the rates.

Some observers believe that a reduction in rediscount rates might have a strong psychological effect not only upon business but the market as well. There was no official indication that such a move was imminent, although some observers thought such action might come suggested by the New York bank directors, since the rate there is 6 per cent as against 5 per cent in other sections. Some thought the New York rediscount rate might be reduced to 5 per cent soon.

Continued on Page Six.

CLOSING RALLY VIGOROUS

Leading Issues Regain From 4 to 14 Points in 15 Minutes.

INVESTMENT TRUSTS BUY

Large Blocks Thrown on Market at Opening Start Third Break of Week.

BIG TRADERS HARDEST HIT

Bankers Believe Liquidation Now Has Run Its Course and Advise Purchases.

Stock prices virtually collapsed yesterday, swept downward with gigantic losses in the most disastrous trading day in the stock market's history. Billions of dollars in open market values were wiped out as prices crumbled under the pressure of liquidation of securities which had to be sold at any price.

There was an impressive rally just at the close, which brought many leading stocks back from 4 to 14 points from their lowest points of the day.

Trading on the New York Stock Exchange aggregated 16,410,030 shares; on the Curb, 7,096,300 shares were dealt in. Both totals far exceeded any previous day's dealings.

From every point of view, in the matter of losses sustained, in total turnover, in the number of speculators wiped out, the day was the most disastrous in Wall Street's history. Hysteria swept the country and stocks went overboard for just what they would bring at forced sale.

Efforts to estimate yesterday's market losses in dollars are futile because of the vast number of securities quoted over the counter and on out-of-town exchanges on which no calculations are possible. However, it was estimated that 880 issues, on the New York Stock Exchange, lost between $8,000,000,000 and $9,000,000,000 yesterday. Added to that loss is to be reckoned the depreciation on issues on the Curb Market, in the over the counter market and on other exchanges.

Two Extra Dividends Declared.

There were two cheerful notes, however, which sounded through the pall of gloom which overhung the financial centres of the country. One was the brisk rally of stocks at the close, on tremendous buying by those who believe that prices have sufficiently declined. The other was that the liquidation has been so violent, as well as widespread, that many bankers, brokers and industrial leaders expressed the belief last night that it now has run its course.

A further note of optimism in the soundness of fundamentals was expressed by the declaration by the United States Steel Corporation and the American Can Company, each of which declared an extra dividend of $1 a share at their late afternoon meetings.

Banking support, which would have been impressive and successful under ordinary circumstances, was swept violently aside, as block after block of stock, tremendous in proportions, deluged the market. Bid prices behind by bankers, industrial leaders and brokers trying to halt the decline were crashed through violently, their orders were filled, and quotations plunged downward in a day of disorganization, confusion and financial impotence.

Change Is Expected Today.

That there will be a change today seemed likely from statements made last night by financial and business leaders. Organized support will be accorded to the market from the start, it is believed, for those who are staking their all on the country's leading securities are placing a great deal of confidence, too, in the expectation that there will be an overnight change in sentiment; that the counsel of cool heads will prevail and that no deep psychology which had been so largely responsible for the market's debacle will be broken.

The fact that the leading stocks were able to rally in the final fifteen minutes of trading yesterday was considered a good omen, especially as the weakest period of the day had developed just prior to that time and the minimum prices for the day had then been established. It was a quick run-up which followed the announcement that the American Can directors had declared an extra dividend of $1. The advances in leading stocks in this last fifteen minutes represented a measurable snapback from the lows. American Can gained 10; United States Steel, common, 7½; General Electric, 12; New York Central, 14½; Anaconda Copper, 9½; Chrysler Motors, 5; and Johns Manville,

Continued on Page Three.

Section
1

"All the News That's
Fit to Print."

The New York Times.

THE WEATHER
Mostly cloudy today and tomorrow;
warmer tomorrow.
Temperatures yesterday—Max. 39, min. 29.
U. S. Weather Forecast—Page 11, Section 12.

Section
1

Copyright, 1929, by The New York Times Company.

VOL. LXXIX....No. 26,237.   * * *   NEW YORK, SUNDAY, NOVEMBER 24, 1929.   Including Rotogravure Picture Section in four parts—Magazine and Book Sections in Rotogravure   FIVE CENTS in Manhattan | Elsewhere TEN CENTS
Bronx and Brooklyn | Except in 7th and 8th Postal Zones

HOOVER ASKS THE 48 GOVERNORS TO HELP HIS PROGRAM BY SPEEDING PUBLIC WORKS, KEEPING EMPLOYMENT AT A HIGH LEVEL

WANTS STATES CANVASSED

The President Requests a Report on the Outlays Possible for Year.

LAMONT WILL COOPERATE

Commerce Secretary to Work With State, County and Municipal Officials.

5,000 MESSAGES BACK PLANS

Arizona Governor Pledges Aid—Philadelphia and St. Paul Will Expend $100,000,000.

By RICHARD V. OULAHAN.
Special to The New York Times.

WASHINGTON, Nov. 23.—The outstanding development today in President Hoover's endeavors to bring about the cooperation of all interests, governmental and private, in forestalling a recession in business because of the recent stock market decline was an appeal sent to the Governors of the forty-eight States by the President, asking them to follow the example of the Federal Government in preparing to speed up necessary construction work, thus absorbing any unemployment and contributing to the maintenance of the nation's consuming power.

Mr. Hoover said in his message that he had asked for the collective action of industry in the expansion of construction activities and in stabilization of wages, adding that he felt was one of the largest factors that could be brought to bear to supplement the efforts of private interests was the "energetic yet prudent pursuit of public works by the Federal Government and State, municipal and county authority."

Requests Official Canvass.

The Federal Government, the President said, was prepared to exert itself to the utmost "within its own province," and he desired the cooperation of the State, municipal and county authorities in a like endeavor. He suggested that it would be helpful if road, street, public building and other works could be speeded up to aid in giving additional employment.

The President asked the Governors to have an official canvass made and send to him a report as to the volume of expenditure that could prudently be arranged in their States in the next twelve months. He informed them that he had asked Secretary of Commerce Lamont to cooperate with the States.

The Federal Government, as a contribution to the program of expanded construction work, will ask Congress to grant an additional $175,000,000 for public buildings, of which $100,000,000 is to be spent outside the District of Columbia and $75,000,000 in the District. This is to extend road construction work to which the government contributes, that phase of the effort coming under the Department of Agriculture.

It is the hope of the administration that cooperation of the Federal Government and the States in large building programs and the efforts to be put forth by private industries toward business expansion will end unjustified fears of a trade depression.

The Proposed Council.

The most definite constructive step expected from the series of conferences held by President Hoover this week with men foremost in trade, finance, industry and labor, is the formation of a continuing council of business leaders which "should assume the responsibility for the mobilization of the industrial and commercial agencies," to quote the President, to bring about cooperation in keeping the country's production, trade and commerce on an even keel and prevent such as was threatened when Mr. Hoover took his initial steps to stem the tide.

The possibility of such a council has been a stream of forward-looking industrialists and others who, like the President, have made a close study of the tremendous advances made by the United States in an economic way. Such a body flows naturally from the study made by the Committee on Recent Economic Changes whose formation was the outgrowth of the President's conference on unemployment held in Washington in the Harding Administration under the chairmanship of Mr. Hoover, who was then Secretary of Commerce.

Just what will be the scope, character and particular functions of the proposed council will probably be at least partly determined at the meeting

Continued on Page Two.

Text of President's Appeal to the Governors To Aid in Stimulation of State Public Works

Special to The New York Times.

WASHINGTON, Nov. 23.—Following is the text of the telegram sent by President Hoover today to Governors of States asking their cooperation in his program of business stabilization:

With a view to giving strength to the present economic situation and providing for the absorption of any unemployment which might result from present disturbed conditions, I have asked for collective action of industry in the expansion of construction activities and in stabilization of wages. As I have publicly stated, one of the largest factors that can be brought to bear is that of the energetic, yet prudent pursuit of public works by the Federal Government and State, municipal and county authorities.

The Federal Government will exert itself to the utmost within its own province and I should like to feel that I have the cooperation of yourself and the municipal, county and other local officials in the same direction. It would be helpful if road, street, public building and other construction of this type could be speeded up and adjusted in such fashion as to further employment.

I would also appreciate it if your officials would canvass the State, municipal and county programs and give me such information as you can as to the volume of expenditure that can be prudently arranged for the next twelve months and for the next six months and inform me thereof.

I am asking Secretary Lamont of the Department of Commerce to take in hand the detailed measures of cooperation with you which may arise in this matter.

HERBERT HOOVER.

DEPARTMENT STORES FORCED TO ADD HELP

Increases in Payrolls Made to Meet Huge Holiday Trade in Spite of Stock Slump.

MACY'S SEES NEW RECORD

Altman, Arnold Constable, Wanamaker, Lord & Taylor, Bloomingdale's, Gimbels Gain.

New York City department store owners were virtually unanimous in reporting yesterday that despite the stock market crash they were enjoying a large volume of business and that they were swelling payrolls in anticipation of an increased holiday trade compared with that of last year. Their statements concerning conditions of employment and sales presumably from Wall Street, that the department stores have been laying off employes by the hundreds because of a slump in business.

Percy S. Straus, vice president of R. H. Macy & Co., said:

"The best judgment that I can bring to bear leads me to the conclusion that as the stock market panic has not thus far seriously interfered with business there is no prospect that it will. I am basing the opinion on my knowledge of conditions at Macy's, and Macy's, catering as it does to a fair cross-section of the city's population, should, I think, be an adequate basis for judgment. I therefore give you the following facts:

"Each month this year sales have been better than those of the corresponding month last year, and November is also showing good indications that it will prove to be a record one.

"As is our custom, we budget our entire business by departments at the beginning of each season. The budget set for this Fall as to numbers of employes has been maintained without interruption, and will be thus maintained. At present we have 12,622 employes, representing an increase of 2,041 over the corresponding day last year. The only discharges made were for reasons other than for business conditions. Furthermore, during the current week we employed 650 additional persons. Of course, it has been necessary to expand other facilities to meet conditions requiring the increased number of employes, such as additional motors for delivery, added selling space, improved methods of change-making, elevator replacements, and rearrangements resulting in greater ease of circulation in the building.

"Although conditions are not identical in our three affiliated stores—L. Bamberger & Co. of Newark, N. J.; the Lasalle & Koch Company of Toledo, Ohio, and the Davison-Paxon Company of Atlanta, Ga.—each of them has found it necessary to lay

Continued on Page Three.

BARNES ASSURES BUSINESS ADVANCE

Chamber Head, Disclosing Magnitude of Projects Told to Hoover, Hails Cooperation.

STRESSES 'LOGIC OF FACTS'

He Relies on 'Collective Common Sense' to Sustain Industrial Activity, Now Forging Ahead.

Special to The New York Times.

WASHINGTON, Nov. 22.—Julius H. Barnes, chairman of the board of the Chamber of Commerce of the United States, selected by President Hoover to create an executive committee from the industrial and trade association groups to cooperate with government agencies in the "expansion of construction and maintenance of employment," in a radio speech tonight revealed for the first time the actual reports on present business conditions and the outlook which were made to the President by the industrial chiefs who met at the White House on Thursday.

The speech was made over a twenty-three station network of the National Broadcasting Company's system. Mr. Barnes was introduced by Merle Thorpe, editor of The Nation's Business, a publication of the Chamber.

After reviewing the reports to the President, Mr. Barnes said:

"I again repeat that the basic element needed to maintain our high level of business activity, to preserve continuous employment, to continue wages and earnings, is the element of collective common sense, orderly conduct of every day living, guided by both prudence and courage."

Reassuring Factors Cited.

Reports of business heads to the President's conference, Mr. Barnes said, should dispel the fears that existed that the country was running into a period of great depression. Retail stores reported, he said, the usual enrollment for this period of the year, mail-order houses were going along in a normal way and the "distribution of automobiles is normal for this period of the year."

The telephone industry will expend over $700,000,000 next year, Walter Gifford, president of the American Telephone and Telegraph Company, told the conference, Mr. Barnes declared.

He quoted Walter Teagle, president of the Standard Oil Company of New Jersey, as stating that the oil industry was becoming stabilized. The steel industry, he said, announced that it expected to supply 300,000,000 tons of steel in new construction and industrial improvements. Matthew Sloan, president of the New York Edison Company, promised expansion in public utility improvements.

These reports, among others, were cited by Mr. Barnes as evidences of confidence in business progress and

Continued on Page Four.

City Gets Snow Flurry and Freezing Weather; Eight Die in South in Widespread Cold Wave

New York was visited yesterday with the coldest temperature of the season thus far, and with its second snowfall. The snow came in brief flurries during the day, too slight to register on the Weather Bureau's instruments. It was more noticeable, however, than the first snow of the season, which consisted of a few random flakes on Oct. 17.

The mercury, starting from its lowest point of 29 above zero at 5:30 A. M., hovered around the freezing point all day, rising to 39 at 6 P. M., the highest point of the day. It was a cheerless day under a dead gray sky.

The prospects for today, however, are for slightly warmer weather.

New York enjoyed a mild day in comparison with most of the rest of the country, for the northwest wind which bore the cold snap veered around the city.

New England and the Southern States, together with much of upstate New York, suffered the most. Many States in the South are blanketed with snow, ice and sleet.

Dispatches by The Associated Press gave a death list of eight persons in the South as a result of the unseasonable cold wave. Six of these were in Arkansas. Three men in that State were killed in automobile accidents resulting from the storm, one child died of exposure, a trolley car operator was killed slipping from the sleet-encrusted roof of his car, and an aged woman died of burns from an overheated stove. Two men were killed on the slippery streets of Richmond, Va. Four passengers were injured in the overturning of a bus near Greensboro, N. C.

Temperatures below zero were recorded in Western Massachusetts, New Hampshire, Vermont and Maine, dropping at some of the points to five below.

Northern New York, under a bright sun, also had zero and subzero temperatures, with light snow and frost whitening the Adirondacks.

Storm warnings against a northeast gale were set yesterday from the Virginia Capes to the tip of Cape Cod.

McMANUS TO OFFER ALIBI AS DEFENSE; TO PICK NEW JUROR

Several Witnesses to Testify He Was Not in Room When Rothstein Was Shot.

JUROR, ILL, TO BE EXCUSED

Both Sides Agree to Release Riker and to Replace Him From Special Panel of 50.

George A. McManus will set up an alibi as part of his rebuttal of the charge that he murdered Arnold Rothstein, it was learned yesterday, as a decision was reached to excuse the juror who reported illness, choose another and proceed with the trial in the Criminal Courts Building tomorrow morning.

The defendant expects to be able to account for his whereabouts during the two hours preceding and including the time, about 10:15 P. M., Nov. 4, 1928, it was said, and will call several witnesses to support his contention. They will testify that McManus was not in Room 349 of the Park Central Hotel at the time that Rothstein was wounded. The defendant will concede, it was reported, that he had hired the room under an assumed name to shield his bookmaking activities.

A vigorous fight by the defense that it has the murder weapon was indicated. Albert M. Hamilton, a small arms expert, began yesterday his tests of the pistol. He found that the barrel of the Colt .38 calibre revolver was not the one in the weapon when it left the Colt plant. The examination finish differed from the usual nickeling, and the inside of the barrel had been crudely made. Mr. Hamilton, however, admitted that his tests had not gone far enough to warrant an opinion as to how long the substitute barrel had been in place.

Agree to Excuse Ailing Juror.

The decision to excuse Eugene A. Riker of 211 West Twenty-first Street, the juror who reported illness after adjournment of the trial on Friday, was made after the prosecution, represented by Assistant District Attorney George N. Brothers, and the defense attorney, James D. C. Murray, had agreed. Riker, it was reported, is on the verge of a nervous breakdown.

Mr. Murray, the assistant District Attorney and the presiding judge,

Continued on Page Sixteen.

ROOSEVELT PLEADS FOR REAWAKENING OF CIVIC CONSCIENCE

Points to Irondequoit Inquiry Failure in Asking "What Has Become of Public Morals?"

ALSO CITES WESTCHESTER

Lauds Budget Decision in City Club Address—Sees Power Company Leaders.

Governor Roosevelt told members of the City Club and their guests yesterday at a luncheon given in his honor that he had been upheld "one hundred per cent and more" by the Court of Appeals in his opposition to a practice in vogue at the Capitol for some time, under which two legislative leaders had participated with the Governor in the segregation of items in the State budget, in conflict with the State Constitution.

He concluded his address with a strong plea for an awakening of the public conscience and a revival of public interest in the affairs of government.

As a preface to this plea, Governor Roosevelt recited the experiences of Supreme Court Justice Stephen Callaghan, whom he had sent to Rochester earlier in the year to preside at the Supreme Court's investigation of charges against public officials in the town of Irondequoit. The Governor declared that he had Justice Callaghan's word and the word of District Attorney Guy B. Moore of Erie County that the ends of justice had been defeated by the "fixing" of three successive juries.

Delayed by Power Conference.

The Governor was an hour late in arriving at the luncheon. He explained that he had been detained by an important conference on water power with "some gentlemen identified with power activities." He did not disclose the identity of the conferees, nor would he say what had occurred at the conference.

It is understood, however, that those with whom the Governor talked represented the United Corporation, a Morgan holding company.

The conference was only one of several the Governor has held recently with spokesmen for various groups interested in water power development, purely preliminary in character. He indicated that other conferences would follow after his return from Warm Springs, Ga., where he went yesterday for a ten days' stay.

Since statements emanating that this means complete victory for the Morgan firm have indicated that the door as far as they are concerned, in so far as they are concerned, to cooperation with the State in power development projects, the Governor is anxious to make the most of his opportunity, especially as he is eager to present to next year's law making body not only a plan for development under State auspices but also point a way in his message for making such a State project a going concern.

Recalls Irondequoit Trials.

In describing the Irondequoit trials, Governor Roosevelt pointed out that Irondequoit was a suburb of Rochester. A real estate man and a contractor, he said, bought a farm and on it put down sewers, streets and sidewalks, whereupon the sale of lots to people in humble circumstances was started. The purchasers were told that there would be no assessments against their properties for the improvements. However, the cost was later assessed against the property owners, he said. There was every appearance of connivance between the promoters and public officials.

"I sent Justice Callaghan up there to see if anybody ought to go to jail," the Governor said. "There were five trials. On the first the jury stood ten to two for conviction. At each of the other four the jury

Continued on Page Twenty-two.

CLEMENCEAU, 'FATHER OF VICTORY,' DIES; PASSES AWAY AT 88 AFTER HOURS IN COMA; WORLD JOINS FRANCE IN MOURNING LOSS

Associated Press Photo.
GEORGES CLEMENCEAU.

VITALITY AMAZED DOCTORS

Valiant Fight Had Stirred Friends and Old Foes to Sympathy.

MET DEATH WITHOUT PAIN

Bishop, Old Literary Friend, Visited Unconscious Man After Pleading for Admission.

STATE FUNERAL OPPOSED

Tiger's Testament Said to Ask Simple Burial Near His Father in Vendée Plot.

By P. J. PHILIP.
Special Cable to The New York Times.

PARIS, Sunday, Nov. 24.—Georges Clemenceau is dead.

The veteran statesman passed away at 1:55 this morning (8:55 P. M. Saturday, New York Time) after lingering for hours in a comatose state, with intervals of returning consciousness.

The valiant fight of the "Father of Victory" had stirred both friends and old foes to sympathy.

Earlier in the night reports had spread in Paris that the statesman had died, and these were flashed by news bureaus to all sections of the world, only to be contradicted a moment later.

Died Early in Morning.

At midnight the great heart of the fighting statesman, whose will alone kept him alive all day while his body lay inert, gave signs of collapse. Two hours later it had ceased to beat. Tired in body, but with mind and spirit breaking the spells of unconsciousness at times, he went to rest.

He did not suffer on the last day of his long life. He had no more pain. Sometimes his eyes opened, and one of the doctors was convinced that he remained fully conscious until this afternoon. But most of the day he spent in sleep. It was almost the first day of his life that he had not been fully awake and active from before dawn until night.

For those who watched it was as though they awaited something inevitable, yet feared. For since Friday, when uraemia had spread through his system, only death could be expected. It was by a miracle of strength that life clung to him. The heart alone refused to yield until it had no more functions to perform.

Oxygen Administered.

In the last few hours oxygen was administered, but it was with no hope or desire to prolong life. It was to relieve the compressed air and prevent choking.

It was at 1:55, according to official announcement, that death came in the depth of the night. As the heart grew more feeble the doctors were summoned back, and they scarcely expected to find him still alive. There was majestic deliberateness in his going.

In the last chapter of his book, "Demosthenes," which is in the nature of an autobiography, he wrote: "Call that man happy—for it is the lot of all to suffer—who has suffered for a noble cause, and grieve for him who, having sought nothing outside himself, has known nothing but the cinders of life, of egoism vainly consumed."

The words might serve for his own epitaph.

Only three persons were in the sickroom when M. Clemenceau died, his friend and executor, Francois Pietri; the nun, Sister Theonste, and his grandson, Dr. René Jacquemaire.

To M. Pietri yesterday he spoke for the last time, asking in some bewilderment, "What has happened, Pietri?" as though he had just wakened out of sleep.

"You have had an attack," his friend replied.

"This time it will be a long one," the old Tiger murmured, and he never spoke again.

Wanted Quick Burial.

M. Clemenceau's own wishes were that his chauffeur, Francois Drabant, should drive immediately on his death down to the Vendée, to prepare his grave, and that he should rest in his native province of Vendée, his former lieutenant, now Premier

Continued on Page Twenty-nine.

STRIKERS CUT OFF AIR, IMPERIL 3 IN CAISSON

As Water Rushes In on Bridge-Workers, Engineer Fights His Way to Their Rescue.

LADDER DROPPED TO THEM

Two Beaten by Strikers After Climbing 65 Feet to Safety—24 Arrested at Kearny, N. J.

Thirty compressed-air workers, members of Local 67 of New Jersey, who were discharged last Thursday when a strike was started on the State highway bridge over the Hackensack River at Kearny, attacked the new gang of workers, members of Local 2, New York City, yesterday and were subdued only after police reserves arrived.

The attackers, swarming onto a caisson where three men were working 65 feet below the river level, broke the compressed air pipe, causing water and river mud to rush in. The trapped workmen shouted for help, and John Moyer, the engineer, after having temporarily stopped the break in the pipe, fought off the invaders and managed to drop a ladder down the caisson hole.

The three clambered up, not much faster than the water was rushing upward, and felt exhausted, only to be attacked by the strikers, who beat them with 18-inch steel bolts. The engineer and his friends had been routed, but Moyer, rushing to the engine room, drew his pistol and threatened to shoot if any of the strikers advanced.

Two Rushed to Hospital.

One of the three men who climbed up from the caisson—James Withers—had 'escaped' in the general mêlée, but the two others were so badly injured that they were rushed to the City Hospital in Jersey City in an ambulance. The injured are:

LOUIS MAYS, 120 West 130th Street, Manhattan.
ROBERT HAMILTON, 25 Dellevoise Place, Brooklyn.

In the meantime the police had been informed of the fight and had reserves, under Captain Cornelius Barrett, arrived in time to stop further conflict.

Twenty-four men, including five alleged ringleaders, were arrested and later arraigned before Police Judge Anthony Cassie. The five alleged ringleaders were held in bail of $5,000 each for action by the Hudson County grand jury on charges of atrocious assault and battery. The others were convicted of the charge of malicious mischief and fined $25 each by the judge, who had got up from a sick-bed to hold court.

Engineer Fights Way to Rescue.

Moyer, the engineer, who lives at 29 Mertz Avenue, Belleville, N. J.,

Continued on Page Twenty-seven.

ALL CHINA ALARMED AS RUSSIANS INVADE

Manchurian Troops Fall Back Demoralized While Red Army Steadily Moves on Hailar.

NANKING POWERLESS TO AID

With Chiang Involved in Civil War and Treasury Bankrupt Mukden Must Fight Alone.

By HALLETT ABEND.
Special Cable to The New York Times.

SHANGHAI, Nov. 23.—With a temporary lull on the Honan-Hupeh and Canton area fronts, or a censorship so rigid that information is not obtainable, the flood of disastrous news from Manchuria, where Russians with the aid of Mongols have overrun all of Northwestern Heilungkiang well eastward toward Hailar, has shocked many Chinese circles from complacency to the realization that while the government totters on the verge of bankruptcy China's soil is actually being won by hated foreign invaders.

It has been officially announced that President Chiang Kai-shek and his staff left Honan for Nanking and from thence are likely to proceed to Canton, where the Fiftieth Division has been ordered to join the Third and Eighth, already sent there.

Government spokesmen declare that this means complete victory for Nanking in Honan and Hupeh, the government leaving the remnants of the rebels to be eliminated by General Yen Hsi-shan, who, it is asserted, has promised to dispatch troops to aid Nanking. But this claim is viewed askance here because it was often heard before last month and always proved to be groundless propaganda.

Rebel spokesmen declare that the departure of General Chiang for Nanking and thence south means the abandonment of the campaign north of the Yangtsze and an attempt to hold the country solid south of the river.

Desperate efforts are made to raise money in Hankow. Warehouses, docks and foreign firms have been repeatedly visited by illegal taxgatherers and several Chinese employes spirited away. The foreign firms have thus far refused payments of any new levies, leaving a serious situation in the hands of the various Consuls.

Official Manchurian statements charge that Russians have massacred hundreds of civilians, at the same time admitting the discouragement and breakdown in the morale of the Chinese defensive forces with the utter "disappearance" of whole brigades.

Prepare for Retreat.

TOKIO, Nov. 23.—A Harbin dispatch to the Asahi Shimbun today quoted a Tsitsihar dispatch that Chinese military headquarters on the Western Manchurian frontier were

Continued on Page Nine.

Harvard Defeats Yale, 10-6
Notre Dame and Fordham Win

Harvard triumphed over Yale at Cambridge yesterday, 10 to 6, in their forty-eighth annual football encounter before a crowd of 59,000. Albie Booth's kicks were blocked by the Crimson time and again, but his pass to Ellis brought the lone Yale touchdown.

At New York, Fordham blanked Bucknell, 14 to 0, closing its season undefeated. New York University disposed of Rutgers, 20 to 7.

In the Middle West, Notre Dame maintained its unbeaten standing by defeating Northwestern, 26 to 6, and Chicago won from University of Washington, 26 to 6. Nebraska won the Big Six title for the second consecutive year by beating the Kansas Aggies, 10 to 6.

Army defeated Ohio Wesleyan, 29 to 6, Navy halted West Virginia Wesleyan, 30 to 6, and Lehigh was victor over Lafayette, 13 to 12.

In the Far West, Stanford defeated the California Bears, 21 to 6.

The complete details of these and other games will be found in the sports section.

"All the News That's Fit to Print."

The New York Times.

THE WEATHER
Fair and continued cold today; tomorrow cloudy and warmer.
Temperatures yesterday—Max. 33, Min. 22.
[?] U. S. Weather Forecast—For details See Page 23.

Copyright, 1929, by The New York Times Company.

VOL. LXXIX....No. 26,243.   ＋＋＋＋   NEW YORK, SATURDAY, NOVEMBER 30, 1929.   TWO CENTS In Greater New York | Within 200 Miles   FOUR CENTS Elsewhere | Except 7th and 8th Postal Zones

BYRD SAFELY FLIES TO SOUTH POLE AND BACK, LOOKING OVER 'ALMOST LIMITLESS PLATEAU'; DROPS FOOD, LIGHTENS SHIP ON PERILOUS TRIP

WOMAN HEARD CRASH IN HOTEL AT THE TIME ROTHSTEIN WAS SHOT

Says She Saw Man With Angry or Agonized Look Near McManus's Room.

UNCERTAIN ON HIS IDENTITY

Mrs. M. A. Putnam, "Surprise" Witness for State, Attacked by the Defense.

RAYMOND TELLS OF BIG BET

Testifies He Won $40,000 From Rothstein on One Card—Admits That They Had a Quarrel.

A fragile woman with gray hair, but a schoolgirl complexion, took the stand yesterday in the Criminal Courts Building to aid the State in its effort to convict George A. McManus of the murder of Arnold Rothstein. In clear tones she identified herself as Mrs. Marian A. Putnam of Asheville, N. C., chief of the surprise witnesses for the prosecution.

Loosening the gray squirrel collar of a broadtail fur coat, she said that she had been a guest at the Park Central Hotel on the night of Nov. 4, 1928, when Rothstein received a bullet wound which caused his death two days later. She added that she had registered at the hotel on Oct. 30.

Assistant District Attorney George N. Brothers, urbane in manner and soothing of voice, asked her to tell what she had heard and seen that night. Mrs. Putnam turned her thin face toward the jurymen and folded her hands, asparkle with three diamond rings. Quietly she told how she had heard a "crash" and had seen a man walking down a corridor on the third floor, leading from Room 349, part of a suite hired by McManus.

Saw Agony or Anger in Face.

She had looked at the man's face. It bore the imprint of agony or anger. He had his hands clasped over his abdomen as he followed her down the carpeted passageway. Mrs. Putnam said she locked the door of her room and said nothing about the episode even the following morning when she learned of the shooting.

On through the events of the evening Mr. Brothers led the witness. She told a straightforward story under the prosecutor's questioning and now and then a faint smile curved her tight lips. Mrs. Putnam settled more comfortably in the witness chair and slipped out of the heavy fur coat. As she replied to the questions she smoothed the lace ruffles at the wristbands of her black velvet dress and adjusted the cream-colored lace fichu at her throat.

She completed her story and then the defense sought to have stricken from the record all testimony regarding the poker game. Mr. Murray told the court that the prosecution had failed to carry out its promise to show that the game gave McManus the motive for the murder. Judge Nott refused to grant the motion. Mrs. Putnam admitted that she had been registered at the Park

Continued on Page Fourteen.

Byrd Lands Radio Amateurs For Help in Message Relays

LOS ANGELES, Nov. 29 (P).—A congratulatory message sent by Commander Richard E. Byrd just before the start of his flight over the South Pole, was read before the convention of the Pacific division of the American Radio Relay League.

The message, received by B. E. Sandham, Los Angeles amateur short wave radio operator, read:

"Greetings from Little America to the radio amateurs of the Pacific division. Am glad for this opportunity to acknowledge the big debt our North and South Pole expeditions owe to the amateur radio operators.

"I wish to thank them for their helpfulness and to express my admiration of the high sense of honor they show in handling messages.

"It is radio that has made this expedition possible.

"Cordial good wishes in which all of Little America join.

"RICHARD BYRD."

WINTER GRIPS NATION; MERCURY AT 20 HERE

Icy Blast Sweeping Out of the Northwest Kills 9, Spreads Damage, Blocks Shipping.

BLIZZARDS RAGE IN WEST

One Frozen to Death in New York and No Let-Up in the Frigid Wave Is Seen.

Winter came howling out of the northwest and the Arctic wastes yesterday, bringing blizzards to the Western States and Canada, hampering shipping on the Great Lakes, and holding the West, the Middle West, the East and many Southern States in the grip of sub-freezing temperatures.

It was the frigid season's first general offensive, and it scattered death, suffering and property damage widely. White River, Ontario, which usually claims the distinction of recording low temperatures, shared with Thief River Falls, Minn., first place on the icy list yesterday, both communities recording 26 below zero. At least eight persons died in the North Central States as a result of the sudden zero snap, according to the Associated Press. New York City added one death to the list, ears were felt for the safety of hunters caught unprepared for the severe cold in the Minnesota woods. Near the cradle of Winter, where a 30-mile gale was driving a blizzard over the Saskatchewan Lakes, the fate of fifty fishermen, pushing northward on a 55-mile trip, was in doubt. The fishermen had been gone for some time.

Cold to Continue Here Today.

New York had an uncomfortable sample of Winter, and last night the local Weather Bureau gave practically no hope of a let-up today in New York's cold, with temperature of the season at 10 o'clock last night when the thermometer registered 20 degrees above zero, 12 below freezing. Even the maximum temperature at 8:30 A. M. was only 30 degrees, or 2 below freezing. The lowest temperature of the day was 20 degrees, compared with a normal Nov. 29 reading of 39. The coldest Nov. 29 on record occurred in 1873 when the thermometer registered 15 degrees.

The cold here was aggravated by a biting northwest wind, blowing at thirty-eight miles an hour. The city's firemen were put to their first severe test of the season in what was a busy "fire" day in Manhattan, the Bronx and Brooklyn. Up to 9 o'clock last night the number of fires for the day totaled thirty in Manhattan, ten in the Bronx and forty-three in Brooklyn.

Fair Weather Forecast.

Although the barometer in the New York Weather Bureau was rising last night, indicating fair weather for today, the cold snap will continue, according to the official forecaster, and the thousands of football operators who will swarm into the Yankee Stadium for the Army-Notre Dame game this afternoon will have to wear their warmest clothes and wraps.

"Fresh northeast winds and continued cold" was the prediction for today. At the Weather Bureau it was even considered possible that today might be a little colder than yesterday.

A woman on Staten Island was a victim of the cold. She was Mrs. Gladys Todd, 35 years old, who was found dead in the back yard of her home, at 4 Schrenkheisen Place, Mariner's Harbor.

Continued on Page Twelve.

FIRST MESSAGE EVER SENT FROM THE SOUTH POLE

By Commander Richard E. Byrd

WIRELESS TO THE NEW YORK TIMES.

ABOARD AIRPLANE FLOYD BENNETT, in flight, 1:55 P. M. Greenwich mean time [8:55 A. M. New York time], Friday, Nov. 29.—My calculations indicate that we have reached the vicinity of the South Pole, flying high for a survey. The airplane is in good shape, crew all well. Will soon turn north. We can see an almost limitless polar plateau. Our departure from the Pole was at 1:25 P. M.

BYRD

The difference in the times mentioned in this dispatch, that is between 1:55 P. M. in the date line and 1:25 P. M., given by the Commander as that of his departure from the South Pole, is probably accounted for by the lapse between the writing of the dispatch by the Commander and its coding and sending by the wireless operator, Harold I. June. Greenwich time is five hours ahead of New York time and twelve hours ahead of time at Little America.

The Commander's last sentence was evidently added after he began to fly away from the Pole; the first part written before he left there.

CAPITAL DISPLAYS KEENEST INTEREST

President, Waiting News, Is the First in Washington to Hear of Byrd's Success.

OFFICIALS LAUD FLIGHT

Admiral Hughes Says the Commander Is a Worthy Successor to Admiral Wilkes.

Special to The New York Times.

WASHINGTON, Nov. 29.—President Hoover, who had waited anxiously all day for word of the progress of Commander Byrd's successful flight to the South Pole, was the first person in Washington, outside of the staff of THE NEW YORK TIMES bureau, to learn of the successful flight of Commander Byrd to the South Pole and back to the base at Little America.

The word was flashed to the White House tonight from the Washington Bureau of THE NEW YORK TIMES. It was transmitted to the President before dinner by Secretary Walter H. Newton.

All day the President had asked for word of the progress of the flight and late in the afternoon had indicated his deep interest. When the news was taken to him, the President expressed his delight over the successful outcome.

Official Washington expressed the most intense relief and the greatest delight at the successful termination of the flight.

Admiral Charles F. Hughes, the Acting Secretary of the Navy, was among the first to be informed.

"We are greatly pleased at the success of Commander Byrd's flight," he said. "He is a worthy successor to Admiral Wilkes, the American naval officer who first discovered the Antarctic Continent."

Earlier in the day Admiral Hughes had said:

"The Navy Department is intensely interested and, knowing Commander Byrd, we are thoroughly confident that he will return successfully."

Davison Congratulates Expedition.

F. Trubee Davison, Assistant Secretary of War for Aeronautics, declared the success of the flight demonstrated again the value of aircraft.

"The flight of Commander Byrd and his brave companions to the South Pole," he said, "is another epic in the annals of the achievements of heavier-than-air craft and proves once again the value of the airplane in exploration of unknown areas where distances can be traversed in hours which under ordinary forms of transportation would require weeks and months. On behalf of the War Department and the Army Air Corps, I wish to congratulate the Byrd Antarctic Expedition. Their achievement will be lauded by Americans the world over."

Mr. Clarence M. Young, the Assistant Secretary of Commerce for Aeronautics, declared the Byrd flight was "simply another demonstration of the 'limitless' purposes which aviation can serve."

"The flight to the South Pole and back was surely a major accomplish-

Continued on Page Four.

President Sends His Congratulations to Byrd, Saying Spirit of Great Adventure Still Lives

Special to The New York Times.

WASHINGTON, Nov. 29.—After being informed tonight of Commander Byrd's successful flight to the South Pole and back to the base at Little America, President Hoover gave to THE NEW YORK TIMES the following message of congratulations on behalf of himself and the American people, to be transmitted by radio to Commander Byrd:

Commander Richard E. Byrd,
Little America:

I know that I speak for the American people when I express their universal pleasure at your successful flight over the South Pole. We are proud of your courage and your leadership. We are glad of proof that the spirit of great adventure still lives. Our thoughts of appreciation include also your companions in the flight and your colleagues, whose careful and devoted preparation have contributed to your success.

HERBERT HOOVER.

BYRD'S FEAT STIRS ENTHUSIASM HERE

Victorious Flight Hailed With Tributes to Commander's Daring and Foresight.

With the reception of news from Little America of the return of Commander Byrd and his companions from their flight over the South Pole, explorers, aviators, aeronautical designers and builders whose names are known throughout the world of aviation and scores of others offered their congratulations to the Commander and expressed their enthusiasm over the success of his efforts. Some of these comments follow:

Anthony H. G. Fokker, designer of the plane in which Commander Byrd made the flight: "Of course I didn't expect anything but success from Byrd and Balchen. He is an excellent organizer and Balchen is a fine pilot. With all the qualities fliers need for such an expedition, they have proved the unquestioned value and possibility of the airplane.

Mayor Walker—That's marvelous news. I can sum up the way I feel about it in a single sentence. I knew Dick Byrd would do it. He has made another great contribution to scientific advancement and world knowledge. The American flag will certainly look great down there. I know I speak for the people of this city when I say that we rejoice with him and his intrepid companions in this epoch-making exploit. We will await his return to New York City where we want back to Winchester to wait for news. The NEW YORK TIMES called me about 8 o'clock but said they would not release the news generally until later.

"Dick had sent me a Thanksgiving radio message a few hours before they hopped off. 'We are off.' We were very uneasy, but I was never so happy in my life as when we heard he had landed safely back at Little America. We really were quite uneasy because this flight seemed more hazardous than anything he ever tried. Nobody knew anything much about Antarctica.

"When Tom heard Dick had gone over safely he said he was 'tremen-

Continued on Page Four.

BYRD'S FAMILY GETS NEWS OF FLIGHT

Virginia Governor at Capitol Gets News and Mother Hears It at Winchester.

Special to The New York Times.

RICHMOND, Va., Nov. 29.—Although he knew that his brother, Commander Richard Evelyn Byrd, intended to hop to the South Pole this afternoon, Commander Richard E. Byrd Sr. and Thomas Byrd, his brother, received news of the successful flight at their home in Winchester.

Governor Byrd flew to Richmond late today from Norfolk to get news of his brother. He had been at Charles Hill for the Virginia-Carolina football game on Thanksgiving Day and stopped in the capital to be the guest of Governor O. Max Gardner of North Carolina. Accompanying Governor Byrd in another plane was Colonel Willard D. Newbill of his staff.

From The Executive Mansion the Governor relayed news of the flight to his mother at Winchester.

When Commander Byrd duplicated his top of the world feat by flying over the South Pole at the very bottom of the world he was "thrilled to death," she said tonight.

"It was in Washington when we got he saw when I phoned him and we went back to Winchester to wait for news. The NEW YORK TIMES called me about 8 o'clock but said they would not release the news generally until later.

Continued on Page Two.

BRITISH APPLAUD FLIGHT AS TRIUMPH

Thrill Over Byrd's Feat Puts Polar Land Dispute in the Background.

NEWS EAGERLY AWAITED

German Press and People Followed Commander's Course With Keen Interest.

Special Cable to THE NEW YORK TIMES.

LONDON, Saturday, Nov. 30.—Great Britain watched Commander Byrd's progress over the Antarctic wastes to the South Pole and his return as a magnificent adventure, and what claims he may make to any rich coal or mineral deposits over which he has flown or staked the American flag is an issue that is exciting no comment here.

Even the publication by New York newspapers of a summary of the State Department's answer to the British Government's year-old note concerning sovereignty over the Antarctic lands, which was read here as clearly indicating that the United States does not intend to abandon its claims based on earlier discoveries by American explorers, was not allowed to distract attention from Commander Byrd's performance or to cause a controversy almost on the eve of the five-power naval parley in London.

The Daily Chronicle outstripped its London rivals this morning by alone printing a full account of Commander Byrd's South Pole flight, as transmitted to it by THE NEW YORK TIMES and associated newspapers, with full acknowledgment of the source of their information.

The feat, therefore, was hailed here not only as a personal triumph for Commander Byrd and his three companions, Balchen, June and McKinley, but as an outstanding feat in newspaper organization.

Stupendous as is the accomplishment of a flight of 1,560 miles over the frozen wastes to the South Pole and back in 18 hours and 56 minutes in itself, it has been brought home more vividly to the public mind by the fact that within a few hours of Commander Byrd's return to his base on the Ross ice shelf, at 10:10 o'clock London time last night, the leading newspapers of the world were able to reproduce the story of the exploit.

It has not escaped notice that scientific development, from the short-wave radio to the finer details of aircraft construction, have been pressed into use on this occasion. Scientists, aviators and public men on every hand are expressing admiration for Commander Byrd's initiative and courage in carrying out successfully a flight which for scientific results may stand alone.

Commander Byrd had been flying over twelve hours before the British

Continued on Page Four.

CROSSES GLACIER PASS AT 11,500 FEET

Commander Takes Chance and Plane Roars Upward Amid Swirling Drift Out Through Gorge to Tableland

FLYING TIME FOR THE WHOLE CIRCUIT ABOUT 18 HOURS

With Two New Ranges Discovered, the Four Air Argonauts, Guided by Chief, Turn Back to Wild Welcome at Base Camp.

By RUSSELL OWEN.

WIRELESS TO THE NEW YORK TIMES.

LITTLE AMERICA, Antarctica, Nov. 29.—Conqueror of the Poles by air, Commander Richard E. Byrd flew into camp at 10:10 o'clock this morning, having been gone eighteen hours and fifty-nine minutes. An hour of this time was spent at the mountain base refueling.

The first man to fly over the North and South Poles and the only man to fly over the South Pole stepped from his plane and was swept up on the arms of the men in camp who for more than an hour had been anxiously watching the southern horizon for a sight of the plane.

Deaf from the roar of the motors, tired from the continual strain of the flight and the long period of navigation under difficulties, Commander Byrd was still smiling and happy. He had reached the South Pole after as hazardous and as difficult a flight as has ever been made in an airplane, tossed by gusts of wind, climbing desperately up the slopes of glaciers a few hundred feet above the surface.

Radiant Airmen Borne in Triumph.

His companions on the flight tumbled out stiff and weary also, but so happy that they forgot their cramped muscles. They were also tossed aloft, pounded on the back and carried to the entrance of the mess hall.

Bernt Balchen, the calm-eyed pilot who first met Commander Byrd in Spitzbergen and who was with him on the transatlantic flight, came out first. There was a little smudge of soot under the nose, but the infectious smile which has endeared him to those who know him, was radiant.

He was carried away and then came Harold June who, between intervals of helping Balchen and attending to fuel tanks and lines and taking pictures, found time to send the radio bulletins which told of the plane's progress.

And after him Captain Ashley McKinley was lifted from the doorway, beaming like the Cheshire cat because his surveying camera had done its work all the way.

Dumped Food of Forty-five Days, But Not Fuel.

Men crowded about them eager for the story of what they had been through, catching fragments of sentences. It had evidently been a terrific battle to get up through the mountains to the Plateau.

"We had to dump a month and a half of food to do it," said Commander Byrd. "I am glad it wasn't gas. It was nip and tuck all the way."

"Yes," chuckled Balchen. "Do you remember when we were sliding around those knolls picking the wind currents to help us and there wasn't more than 500 feet under us at times? We were just staggering along, with drift and clouds and all sorts of things around us."

When the plane approached the mountains on the way south, Commander Byrd picked out the Livingston Glacier, a large glacier somewhat to the west of the Axel Heiberg Glacier, as the best passageway.

Swooping Upward Through Swirling Drift.

The high mountains shut them in all around as they forced their way upward, Balchen, conserving his fuel to the utmost, coaxing his engines, picking the up-currents of air as best he could to help the plane ride upward.

Clouds swirled about them at times, puff-balls of mist driven down the glacier; drift scurried beneath them; it was a wicked place for an airplane to be, hemmed in by the wall of the towering peaks on either side.

This was the time when they had to lighten ship and Byrd, looking around for what could best be spared, decided to dump some food. There was a dump valve in the fuselage tank, but he had determined to go through and did not know what winds he might face at the top of the glacier. So food was thrown overboard, scattered over the ridged and broken surface of the Livingston Glacier.

"It is an awful looking place," Commander Byrd said.

Over the "Hump" and Vast Panorama Unfolds.

They finally reached the hump at an elevation of 11,500 feet, as indicated by the barograph, although it might have been a little more, because of the difference in pressure inland.

But there was little space under the staggering plane, buffeted by the winds that eddied through the gigantic gorge. Once at the top, Balchen could level off for a time and then gain altitude.

Then there came into view slowly the long sweep of mountains of the Queen Maud Range, stretching to the southeast, and the magnificent panorama of the entire bulwark of mountains along the edge of the Polar Plateau.

Beheld Tinted Slopes of Myriad Mountains.

"It was the most magnificent sight I have ever seen," Commander Byrd said. "I never dreamed there were so many mountains in the world. They shone under the sun, wonderfully tinted with color, and in the southeast a bank of clouds hung over the mountains, making a scene that I shall never forget."

Over the plateau the Commander set his course for the Pole. They had had a beam wind all the way into the mountains which

The New York Times

PAGE ONE

Major Events:

1930–1939

"All the News That's
Fit to Print."

The New York Times.

Copyright, 1930, by The New York Times Company.

THE WEATHER
Showers and cooler today;
tomorrow fair.
Temperature yesterday—Max. 86, min. 70.
37° S. Weather Forecast—For details see Page 41.

VOL. LXXIX....No. 26,520   ★★★★+   NEW YORK, WEDNESDAY, SEPTEMBER 3, 1930.   TWO CENTS In Greater | THREE CENTS | FOUR CENTS Elsewhere

COSTE DOES IT IN 37 HOURS, 18½ MINUTES! FIRST TO MAKE PARIS-NEW YORK FLIGHT; HOOVER, LINDBERGH AND BYRD HAIL FEAT

HEARST IS EXPELLED ON VISIT TO FRANCE FOR 'HOSTILE' ACTION

Government Says Move Was Taken Because of Use of Secret Naval Pact.

NOTE PUBLISHED IN 1928

Tardieu Reported to Have Fixed Ban Aug. 9 After American's Talk to German Press.

ORDER IS OBEYED QUICKLY

Paper Owner Asserts in London He Told French He Would "Save" Nation by Going at Once.

WIRELESS TO THE NEW YORK TIMES.
LONDON, Sept. 2.—Somewhat of a sensation was caused in London today when it was learned that William Randolph Hearst, American newspaper proprietor, who arrived here last night from France had been expelled from France because of the publication of the memorandum on the secret Anglo-French naval pact two years ago in Hearst newspapers.

Mr. Hearst arrived in Paris yesterday morning from the Italian lake district and went to the Hotel Crillon, where he received the expulsion order. He was told the French Cabinet had decided to expel him because his newspapers were "hostile" to France.

Not Molested Month Ago.

Yesterday was not the first time Mr. Hearst had returned to France since the episode of the secret document. He spent some days in Paris a month or so ago on the way to Germany and was not molested then. When Mr. Hearst reached London last night he told no one here, not even his own representatives who met him at the station, of his expulsion and sudden departure from France. It was learned only this morning when a news agency telephoned to the hotel asking for a statement, after which the American publisher was bombarded by reporters and photographers.

Later today Mr. Hearst, who is remaining in London for a while before going to his 800-year-old castle in Glamorgan, South Wales, issued a statement to the press here in which he defended publication of the secret document because it informed the American people, even though it "upset some international apple-carts."

Text of Hearst's Statement.

Mr. Hearst's statement follows:

I have no complaint to make. The officials were extremely polite. They said I was an enemy of France and a danger in their midst. They made me feel quite important.

They said I could stay a little while longer if I desired; that they would take a chance on nothing disastrous happening to the public.

But I told them I did not want to take the responsibility of endangering the great French nation; that America had saved it once during the war and I would save it again by leaving.

Furthermore, I was like the man who saw his wife was going blind and who said he did not mind as he had seen everything anyhow.

Similarly, I had seen everything interesting in France, including some very interesting governmental performances.

Then I asked Mr. Tardieu's emissary to express to Mr. Tardieu my immense admiration at his amazing alertness in protecting France from the peril of invasion, and we parted with quite elaborate politeness.

It was a little bit foolish but extremely French.

The reason for the strained relations—to use the proper diplomatic term—was really because of the secret Anglo-French treaty two years ago by the Hearst newspapers, which upset some international apple-carts and informed the American people, and of course that being the reason, the French Government was entirely right in leveling its attack at me, and quite wrong in its action toward Mr. Horan, who was only my agent.

I think, however, that the general attitude of the Hearst press in opposing the entrance of the United States into the League of Nations

Continued on Page Twenty.

Night, Virginia Rennick de Boursac, 12 hrs. from N. Y.—Advt.

Air and Rail Lines Here Open A Consolidated Ticket Office

Airlines consolidated ticket office was opened yesterday in the lobby of the Hotel Roosevelt by the Airlines Traffic Association. The office will sell tickets for air and air-rail trips on eighteen lines radiating out of the city.

The association opened a similar cooperative ticket bureau in Chicago two years ago with privilege to sell rides on thirty-two lines throughout the country. More such offices will be opened in airplane centres throughout the country soon.

Colonel L. H. Brittin, president of the association, and other officers were present at the formal opening.

HOOVER LAUDS COSTE FOR 'GLORIOUS' FLIGHT

In Cable to Doumergue, the President Calls Exploit of the French Airmen Brilliant.

LINDBERGH HAILS SUCCESS

Own Feat Surpassed, He Says —Byrd, Kimball and Aviation Leaders Add Their Praise.

Special to The New York Times.
WASHINGTON, Sept. 2.—The successful transatlantic flight of Captain Coste and M. Bellonte was a cause of general rejoicing here where interest in the daring Frenchmen had superseded all other interests.

Word that the fliers had landed was the signal for the dispatch of congratulatory messages by ranking officials of the government, while others informally expressed their gratification at the successful crossing of the Atlantic with words of high praise for the French aviators.

President Hoover, in a message to President Doumergue of France, declared that by that flight France "has established a glorious record." His message follows:

Sept. 2, 1930.
His Excellency Gaston Doumergue,
President of the French Republic,
Paris, France.

I join with the people of the American nation in rejoicing over the brilliant exploit of your distinguished aviators, Captain Dieudonné Coste and M. Maurice Bellonte, in successfully completing for the first time in history a non-stop flight from France to the United States.

France has established a glorious record. I hope that in the future many others of your citizens will come to us in this manner.

I extend to your Excellency and to the people of France my heartiest congratulations.

HERBERT HOOVER

Message to French People.

The State Department at the same time requested Ambassador Edge at Paris to extend to the Minister for Foreign Affairs, and through him to the people of France, the heartiest congratulations of the United States Government on the magnificent flight.

The department's congratulations to the fliers were contained in a message to Captain Coste from Green Hackworth, solicitor of the State Department, and in the absence of higher officials, the acting Secretary of State.

This message read as follows:
Sept. 2, 1930.
Captain Dieudonné Coste,
Curtiss-Wright Airport,
Valley Stream, Long Island.

Personally, and on behalf of the people of this country, I extend to you and Maurice Bellonte our heartiest congratulations upon your magnificent flight and safe arrival. The same splendid courage and undaunted spirit that inspired Nungesser and Coli have at last been rewarded.

GREEN HACKWORTH.

Among other officials who informally voiced their congratulations was Major Gen. J. E. Fechet, chief of the Army Air Corps, who said:

"I consider it a very marvelous flight and wish to congratulate them."

Navy Heads Add Greetings.

Secretary of the Navy Adams sent the following message to Captain Coste:

"The American Navy extends its congratulations to you and your companion, Maurice Bellonte, upon the successful completion of your first New York flight in an airplane. Your courageous feat has aroused the admiration of every officer.

COSTE'S OWN STORY TELLS OF FLYING THROUGH MIST

Like Floating Through a Hazy Dream for Hours and Hours—Felt Lucky After Conquering Three Storms Over Atlantic.

ONCE DRIVEN 100 MILES OFF THEIR COURSE

Knew That the Battle Was Over When They Sighted Land at 6 A. M., but Got Into a 'Tight Place' Between Steep Cliffs of a River.

By CAPTAIN DIEUDONNE COSTE.
Copyright, 1930, in North and South America, by The New York Times Company. All rights reserved.

When we took off from Paris the day before yesterday we knew it was the greatest moment in our lives. It was the culmination of three years of hard effort, not unmixed with many heartbreaking disappointments. If we had not left at that particular minute we might well have faced three more years of delay before accomplishing the first flight from a city of the Old World to the greatest city in the New World.

There were many exciting moments during our trip, and at times I could not be sure from one minute to the next—now that it is all over—which was the greatest thrill. I think, however, that that came after we first sighted the coast of North America. As you know, the coast of Nova Scotia is full of bends and turns, fills and rivers, promontories and little gulfs.

Followed the Winding Coast.

When we reached the coast we were determined not to lose sight of it again. In order to keep it in view we had to follow all these devious turns and that was a job. At the same time we had another problem. The sky was overcast, it was raining and we had to fly below those rain clouds. Sometimes they were extremely low, which made it necessary for us to fly as close to the water as ten meters.

We came to one bend and turned it; we flew on, skirting a precipice. Suddenly there loomed up out of the mist another precipice on our port side. We were caught between the steep banks of a river—what river, I do not know. It was a tight place.

Bellonte was at the controls at that time and he had to think fast. Fortunately, having flown thousands of miles, the ship was light. Bellonte gave her the gas and shot upward.

Decided to Fly by Instrument.

It is not pleasant to think how close we came to those cruel, jagged rocks. We went up fairly high and began to fly steadily by instrument. Some time passed before the clouds and the rain cleared somewhat and then we were over what I believe was the Atlantic off the coast of Maine. We came down a little later through a new bank of fog and headed down the coast until we were over a large city.

We were so interested in trying to determine what city it was that it never occurred to us that this was the first great city we had passed since leaving Paris. Only a few minutes later we passed another city, and now there was no doubt. We identified it as Boston. We continued the flight without further incident before landing at Valley Stream.

The tremendous load of fuel required for this flight, in which we expected to buck prevailing unfavorable winds, gave us the first real thrill of the voyage. Would the ship lift off the ground? That was our great concern. We had 5,200 litres of gasoline on board.

Storms Ahead Cause Concern.

But this great fear passed in a few moments and we found new cause for concern with each passing moment. There were storms ahead. We would have to push our over-weighted ship through them. We ran into the first of these disturbances off the Irish coast. The second gave us some trying moments, not long afterward, over the ocean. But fortunately we were able to escape the worst of it. The third—and probably the worst of all—was the storm we encountered over Nova Scotia.

That it occurred only yesterday morning seems impossible just at this moment. So many things seem to have happened since, that that storm seems remote—something that happened long, long ago.

Driven 100 Miles Off Course.

We had to find the best route to Nova Scotia, and that in short order, if we were to avoid the hazards that faced the Bremen when it ran into fog and storm of a similar nature and was forced down hundreds of miles from its goal.

In seeking to avoid this storm we were obliged to fly 100 miles out of our way to the south. We did not find land, as we had expected, so we turned northward again, flying another 100 miles. Time was swiftly passing. Each minute meant the loss of more of our precious fuel. Again we turned.

It occurred to us that three is a lucky number. We had faced three storms—were we now to be defeated? We were sure that we would not be.

Land Sighted in Early Morning.

After three hours of searching we computed that we must be very near the coast of Nova Scotia. At 3 A. M. (French time)—for we had not changed our clock—we sighted land. At the same moment it became obvious that the winds were abating. Naturally we were very happy. The only thing that could stop us now, we thought, would be failure of our motor.

It had carried us already from France to North America and we knew that it would not fail us now. We had perfect confidence in its stanch heart and that confidence was justified. The motor was wonderful. It did all that we had hoped it would.

Weather conditions, on the whole, were very favorable—at least the winds were on our side. On the other hand, almost the entire route was clouded over and we went hour after hour over that watery waste through a thick white mist. We could not see what lay ahead, below or above. It was like floating in a dream. There was something unreal about it—unreal and awesome. We were two, but we seemed so all alone.

Up and Down to Find Clear Way.

Most of the time I was at the controls and there was plenty to keep my mind busy. There was no time for dreaming. Constantly I had to shift my course to find a way out of the haze. Sometimes we dropped the plane down to less than 300 feet from the waves. At other times we were up to 2,500 feet. We seldom were above that mark, and never very much above it.

But we had our reward. Although my mind was taken up with the

Continued on Page Three.

Associated Press Photo.
FRENCH FLIER IN HIS HOUR OF TRIUMPH!
Conqueror of Atlantic Is Carried Off the Field on the Shoulders of His Admirers on His Safe Arrival From Paris.

ALL PARIS ACCLAIMS TRIUMPH BY COSTE

News of Safe Landing Here Shouted Joyfully by Great Throngs in Streets.

FELT CERTAIN OF SUCCESS

Real Demonstration Deferred Until Homecoming of the Two Fliers.

By P. J. PHILIP.
Special Cable to The New York Times.
PARIS, Sept. 2.—"Vive Coste!" "Vive Bellonte!" "Vive la France!" All over Paris these cries have sounded through the midnight hours. There is no one in the city who does not know that Coste and Bellonte have crossed safely from Paris to New York by air; crossed between breakfast time on one day and supper time on the next.

"They have done it," has been cried up every street, and every one knew who "they" were and what they had done. And so to bed, with immense, tremendous happiness, contentment and pride.

From Curtiss Field to the Place de la Concorde came the voice of Graham McNamee: "He's taxiing down the field!" The rest was interrupted by the clamor of those who did not understand. Then a French voice broke in: "Coste has landed!"

It was that way that Paris learned that the great adventure of east-to-west crossing of the Atlantic had been accomplished, that Nungesser and Coli and so many others had been avenged, that Lindbergh's great flight had been complemented and that the link between Paris and New York had been forged on both sides by air.

By tremendous handclapping Captain Coste was acclaimed, and there was an immense sigh of relief.

The great historic place, the Place de la Concorde, had been crowded. Even its immense acreage could scarcely hold those who came. It was impossible to count the multitude. Yet that was a rendezvous of all Paris. It was there that it had been arranged all news should be broadcast from the roof of the automobile club. Only that great space, it was certain, could hold the crowds of those who all day had been asking, "Where are they now; when will they arrive?"

Crowd Sure of Success.

There never was any doubt in any one's mind all day—not in that of Mme. Coste or of Mme. Bellonte; not in that of taxi drivers, who would ask their fares for the latest news; not in that of concierges who exchanged their views with passers-by. It was a day of most extraordinary camaraderie.

THE THINKING FELLOW CALLS A Yellow Taxi. Slogan 3000.—Advt.

Continued on Page Two.

10,000 STORM FIELD TO WELCOME FLIERS

Coste Cuts Whirling Propeller as Police Lines Snap and the Throngs Rush Plane.

WELCOMERS SHOVED ASIDE

Glare of Torches Lights Wild Greeting as Pilots Are Carried in Triumph From Field.

Special to The New York Times.
CURTISS FIELD, L. I., Sept. 2.—As the red biplane of Captain Dieudonné Coste and Maurice Bellonte swung out of the northeast at dusk and circled low over the Curtiss Airport here a cheer of welcome roared from the throats of 10,000 persons massed in rows behind a wire fence and strung out in a long line in front of the field's six hangars.

A large part of the crowd had waited all afternoon through a heavy rainstorm and, though most of the spectators were held behind the fence and got no more than a fleeting glimpse of the red plane, they were as vociferous in their welcome as if they had been a part of the crowd that helped to carry the two fliers off the field in triumph.

Crowd Breaks Police Lines.

As the plane glided to a graceful landing and started to taxi toward the ground stand on the west side of the field, the crowd inside the fence broke through the police lines and ran shouting and dodging policemen toward the craft. Coste, realizing the danger of the whirling propeller, cut the switch, and the metal blade swung slowly to a stop. A score of policemen and mechanics joined hands and, forming a circle about the plane, tried with scant success to hold back the crowd. At least seventy-five persons broke through the cordon and swarmed about the plane. Coste, looking hot and tired, stepped out of the plane into a seething mob, which kissed him, pummeled him, wrung his hands and all but knocked him from his feet.

"Splendid!" "Magnifique!" "Felicitations!" French as well as American voices screamed. French girls embraced the fliers, kissing them time and again, and Frenchmen followed suit. An announcer for the National Broadcasting Company, holding a microphone high above his head, was lost in the struggling throng, and gasped in the microphone:

"We seem to be having a little difficulty here at Valley Stream."

Elinor Smith, girl aviator, was in the midst of the crowd, but did not get a chance to greet the fliers until later. A delegation of French war veterans, carrying the French tricolor and the American flag, struggled inside the police cordon, but had

Continued on Page Two.

ABBOTT'S BITTERS—Delightful Flavor for Beverages.—Advt.

FLIERS LAND AT 7:12½ P. M. TO WILD CHEERS OF 10,000

Scarlet Plane Alights Smoothly at Goal With Enough Fuel for Three Hours More—Airmen, Speechless, Watch the Mad Scene of Welcome.

LINDBERGH, HIS VISIT RETURNED, HAILS COSTE

'A Great Flight,' He Says, Gripping Hand of Ace Amid Tumult at Curtiss Field—France Hears the Fliers on Radio—They Will Fly On to Texas.

By JOSEPH SHAPLEN.
Special to The New York Times.
CURTISS FIELD, L. I., Sept. 2.—Captain Dieudonné Coste and his co-pilot, Maurice Bellonte, completed tonight the first direct flight from Paris to New York when they landed at the Curtiss airport at 7:12:30 P. M., after a journey of 37 hours 18 minutes 30 seconds. They covered 6,500 kilometers, or about 4,100 miles, and when they landed had 100 gallons of gasoline left, sufficient for nearly three hours more of flight.

Their achievement marked the first non-stop crossing from Europe to the American metropolis. What others have tried to do and failed Captain Coste and M. Bellonte accomplished. In doing so they triumphed magnificently over the elements which sent Nungesser and Coli, the first two Frenchmen to try the westward crossing, to death, and took their revenge upon Neptune for the loss of other valiant aviators who sought to achieve the westward flight.

Colonel Charles A. Lindbergh's time for the eastward crossing was better. It took him only thirty-three hours and a half to fly from Roosevelt Field to Le Bourget to the credit of his visit to Coste and Bellonte repaid tonight. The Spirit of St. Louis rose from earth and started on its historic flight at 7:52 A. M., May 20, 1927. Lindbergh brought it to earth just outside of Paris at 10:24 Continental Time (5:24 P. M., New York Time), on May 21.

Ten thousand throats yelled a wild greeting to the two French masters of the air as their airplane, the scarlet, enigmatic Question Mark, bearing upon her sides the written record of a dozen odysseys of the sky, came down smoothly and gracefully on the east side of the field and taxied rapidly toward the hangars on the west side. Here among the first to greet Captain Coste and M. Bellonte was Colonel Lindbergh, whose visit to Paris had now been repaid.

"Great Flight," Colonel Lindbergh Declares.

"It's a great flight," was the enthusiastic comment of Colonel Lindbergh after he had finally managed, with the assistance of policemen, to make his way to the airmen, following their rescue from the cheering crowds, whose enthusiasm exceeded all bounds. Never before in the history of aviation in this country, according to veterans of the air, have any flying men received the reception accorded tonight to Captain Coste and his companion.

Soon after the Question Mark landed, the fliers were informed that Colonel W. E. Easterwood of Dallas, Texas, had offered $25,000 to Captain Coste and M. Bellonte if they would fly their ship to Dallas. Captain Coste said he would be glad to make the trip because it would give him an opportunity for a cross-country flight, and said he would probably take off Thursday morning, after the plane has been tuned up and tightened.

Asked if he had any plans for the future, which might include a trip around the world via the poles, as one interviewer suggested, Captain Coste replied he had no plans beyond the flight to Dallas.

It was 7:10 P. M. when the Question Mark, easily distinguished by her color and peculiar design, appeared in the sky over the airport, escorted by three Curtiss fledglings from the Naval Reserve aviation field here and flanked by a score of other airplanes which had taken off shortly before to extend a welcome to the French fliers.

After circling the field, the Question Mark came down, making a perfect landing. Veering quickly in the direction of the hangars the French victors of the Atlantic ran ahead of the crowds. But in vain. The moment Captain Coste and M. Bellonte raised their heads out of the cockpit and stepped over the fuselage they were picked up on the shoulders of several of their compatriots and carried to Hangar 2, while a small army of policemen struggled desperately to protect them against what seemed imminent injury from the ever-increasing pressure of the throng of admirers. "Vive la France," "Vive Coste et Bellonte," came the resounding, ever-mounting cries from the hundreds of Frenchmen who formed a prominent part of the surging crowds.

Police Battle Crowds in Great Rush of Welcome.

Above the unrestrained, joyous clamor of voices the boom of a hundred flashlights accompanied the triumphant procession across the field to the hangar, where the police hoped they could isolate the fliers. Here the police had to fight a veritable battle to get Coste and Bellonte to safety, but even in the hangar they found no refuge, for before the police and airport employees could close and bolt the rolling doors hundreds forced their way in, besieging the fliers, eager to shake their hands, so uncontrollable in their determination to get as close as possible to the airmen. With their faces dripping perspiration, their backs against a wall, Coste and Bellonte stood speechless for nearly ten minutes, wondering what would be the end of this mad scene which appeared beyond the powers of the police to master, until, in phalanx formation, the guards rushed the crowd back far enough to clear an exit.

With the greatest difficulty, Coste and Bellonte were finally rushed to a room upstairs, to which only a small group of their friends, members of the Nassau County and the Mayor's reception committees and representatives of the French Government made their way in the vain hope of getting a few words with the airmen.

Lindbergh Greets Fliers Returning His Visit.

Here, too, came Colonel Lindbergh, smiling with joy at the success of the flight and rushing forward to congratulate first Coste and then Bellonte.

Captain Coste's eyes flashed as he grasped the hand of the young man who more than any one else had captured the imagination of the world by his solo flight to Le Bourget, the starting point of the Question Mark.

Firmly the two heroes of the air shook hands as thousands outside, standing in the glare of scores of magnesium flares, broke into the wildest outburst of cheering that marked the arrival.

"Comment ça va?" asked Captain Coste.

"I congratulate you, I congratulate you," said Colonel Lindbergh, again pressing the Frenchman's hand and apparently so overcome by

The New York Times.

Copyright, 1930, by The New York Times Company.

VOL. LXXX....No. 26,583. ..... NEW YORK, WEDNESDAY, NOVEMBER 5, 1930. TWO CENTS

THE WEATHER
Cloudy, with probably occasional rain today; tomorrow fair, colder. Temperature Yesterday—Max. 59; Min. 44.

DEMOCRATIC LANDSLIDE SWEEPS COUNTRY; REPUBLICANS MAY LOSE CONGRESS CONTROL; ROOSEVELT WINNER BY MORE THAN 700,000

WETS GAIN IN HOUSE

Win 32 Seats and Lose None; Hold Senate Places.

AIDED BY ILLINOIS SWEEP

Also Helped by Victory of Bulkley in Ohio— Drys Win in Places.

THREE REFERENDA GO WET

Repeal Proposals Are Carried in Rhode Island, Illinois and Massachusetts.

Forces favoring repeal of the Eighteenth Amendment and liquor laws scored gains in the Congressional elections throughout the country yesterday, adding to these victories substantial majorities in favor of repeal referenda in Illinois, Rhode Island and Massachusetts.

On the basis of returns late last night, the so-called "wet bloc" in the House had picked up thirty new votes to add to the ninety-one which the most optimistic wet count in the present House.

The Senate wets had picked up several new names, of such imminence as Morrow of New Jersey, Lewis of Illinois and Bulkley of Ohio, but were battling to hold the number of eighteen in the present make-up of the Senate, because of retirements of sitting wet members from States where only dry candidates sought their seats.

Marcus Coolidge of Massachusetts was running well ahead of his dry opponent, William M. Butler, overcoming a substantial lead early in the night.

Results of Referenda.

Wet candidates were carrying with them wet referenda in every State where they were offered. In Illinois the vote went decidedly in favor of repeal of the Eighteenth Amendment. Three proposals, one for repeal of the amendment, another for modification of the Volstead act and the other proposing repeal of the State enforcement act, all carried with good majorities, with the heaviest vote and the heaviest majority recorded on the first question.

Rhode Island registered a vote of more than 2 to 1 in favor of repeal. The vote in Massachusetts was on repeal of the State enforcement act and a majority in favor of the referendum was gaining in size as Marcus Coolidge increased his lead over the dry Butler.

In his landslide in Illinois Mr. Lewis evidently had swept a number of wet Democrats into office, and in Ohio the victory of Mr. Bulkley carried with it an increase in the wet representation of that State in the lower house by at least three. At least two wet gains in the House went with the Morrow victory in New Jersey, and seven apparently had been recorded in Pennsylvania, despite the victories of dry Senatorial and Gubernatorial candidates.

Many Dry Victories Recorded.

The wets had not actually lost a seat in either house on the face of returns up until early this morning, although dry victories had been scored in a number of States, including three in the South where the prohibition figured conspicuously as an issue in the campaign.

The whole delegation in Connecticut, including Representative John Q. Tilson, Hoover spokesman and Republican leader in the House, will be listed among the wets in the next Congress. The only seat in doubt was in the First District, where C. W. Seymour, dry Republican, was pitted with A. Longergan, wet Democrat. Mr. Longergan led on the reports last night.

Four wets evidently had won in Michigan, including S. H. Person, who will occupy the seat held by Grant M. Hudson, former State Superintendent of the Anti-Saloon

Continued on Page Seven.

U. S. SENATORS ELECTED

REPUBLICANS—13.

Delaware	*D. O. Hastings
Idaho	*William E. Borah
Iowa	‡L. J. Dickinson
Kansas	*Arthur Capper
Maine	†W. H. White Jr.
Michigan	*James Couzens
Nebraska	*George W. Norris
New Hampshire	*Henry W. Keyes
New Jersey	†Dwight W. Morrow
Oregon	*Charles L. McNary
Pennsylvania	‡James J. Davis
Rhode Island	†J. H. Metcalf
Wyoming	†Robert D. Cary

DEMOCRATS—20.

Alabama	‡J. H. Bankhead
Arkansas	*J. T. Robinson
Colorado	†E. P. Costigan
Georgia	*William J. Harris
Illinois	‡J. H. Lewis
Louisiana	*Huey P. Long
Massachusetts	‡M. A. Coolidge
Minnesota	†Einar Hoidale
Mississippi	*Pat Harrison
Montana	*Thomas J. Walsh
New Mexico	*S. G. Bratton
North Carolina	‡Josiah W. Bailey
Ohio	†Robert J. Bulkley
Oklahoma	†Thomas P. Gore
South Carolina	‡James F. Byrnes
Tennessee	**William E. Brock
Tennessee	†Cordell Hull
Texas	*Morris Sheppard
Virginia	*Carter Glass
West Virginia	‡M. M. Neely

IN DOUBT—3.

Kansas   South Dakota
Kentucky

*Re-elected for full term ending March 3, 1937. †Elected for full term and short term. ‡Elected for full term ending March 3, 1937. **Elected Dec. 3, 1929 for full term ending March 3, 1937. ‡Elected for short term ending March 3, 1931. †Elected for short term ending March 3, 1931.

LEWIS, DEMOCRAT, SWEEPS ILLINOIS

Out-and-Out Wet Piles Up 2 to 1 Lead Over Mrs. McCormick, Republican, for Senate.

AHEAD 3 TO 1 IN CHICAGO

Victor Breaks Even or Better in Strong Republican Counties Down-State.

Special to The New York Times.

CHICAGO, Nov. 4.—James Hamilton Lewis, Democrat, and an out-and-out wet, won in a landslide over Representative Ruth Hanna McCormick, Republican and "provisionally wet," in today's election of a Senator from Illinois.

After a campaign in which the Democrats stressed prohibition and prosperity, something of a seismic upheaval struck the rock-ribbed Republican State—the home of Lincoln, the first Republican President—and is likely to approach 700,000. The politicians rate it the greatest blow against national prohibition thus far struck.

Incomplete returns at midnight indicated that the Democrats gained three Congressional seats from Cook County districts, two and possibly three seats down-State, and the two places as members of Congress-at-Large. Correspondingly, the complexion of the Illinois delegation to Washington had been changed by wet gains of eight or nine seats.

Figures from nearly half of the State show Mr. Lewis far in the lead both in Cook County, which includes Chicago, and down-State.

Goes Into Lead Down-State.

In Chicago he was running three to one ahead of Mrs. McCormick, the count indicating that his Chicago plurality will be around 425,000.

Mr. Lewis had 365,982 votes in 1,675 out of 3,009 city precincts; 15,400 in 50 other Cook County precincts, and 256,558 in 1,000 down-State precincts, or a total of 637,940 in 3,394 out of 7,100 precincts in the whole State. His plurality on these returns was 351,676 over Mrs. McCormick, whose vote was 126,724 in Cook County and 286,264 in the 3,394 precincts from all parts of the State. In the same number of districts, Mrs. Lottie Holman O'Neill, Independent Dry, polled 20,448 votes.

Mrs. McCormick seemed likely to

Continued on Page Five.

MORROW WINS EASILY

Majority of 100,000 In Jersey Senate Race Indicated.

PARTY LOSES IN HOUSE

Democrats Leading in Six Districts Nominally Republican.

TWO BOND ISSUES WINNING

Legislature Safely Republican —Anti-Prohibitionists Score Heavily.

Dwight W. Morrow, former Ambassador to Mexico, was leading by a wide margin his two Democratic opponents in his race for the full and short terms for United States Senator from New Jersey early this morning as the returns were coming in from the 3,321 election districts. Voters in 2,052 districts gave Mr. Morrow 322,014 and Alexander D. Simpson, former State Senator from Hudson County, 227,537.

E. Bertram Mott, chairman of the Republican State Committee, said early this morning a conservative estimate of Mr. Morrow's majority would be 100,000. Republican leaders before the election had predicted a majority of 200,000.

Tabulation of returns from 729 districts showed that Mr. Morrow was leading Miss Thelma Parkinson, Smith College Graduate, in the race for the short term or vacancy caused by the resignation of Walter E. Edge to become Ambassador to France, by a vote of 108,972 to 65,524.

Returns from 1,090 out of 3,321 election districts showed four of the $100,000,000 bond issue proposals winning and one losing as follows:

Highways, 83,653 against, 78,740 for; water supply, 78,343 against, 88,442 for, and institutional rehabilitation, 80,105 against and 84,956 for.

Democrats were leading in contests for the House of Representatives in six districts nominally Republican, and that the State Legislature was overwhelmingly Republican.

Mr. Simpson, as candidate for the full term, and Miss Parkinson, as candidate for the short term, polled a surprisingly heavy vote in the early returns although they ran ahead in only three counties, Hudson, Democratic stronghold; Mercer and Middlesex. The Democrats were greatly encouraged by the early returns giving Mr. Simpson and Miss Parkinson leads in half a dozen counties. The leads for the Democratic candidates were accounted for by the fact that they came from industrial centres.

While Mercer, a strongly Republican county, gave Mr. Simpson and Miss Parkinson substantial leads in the early returns, the Republicans expected to see those margins dwindle with the tabulation of returns outside Trenton. The strength of the Democrats in Trenton is said to have been due to the unemployment problem which has been acute there for months.

Representative Mary T. Norton, vice chairman of the Democratic State Committee, conceded the election of Mr. Morrow at 1:25 o'clock this morning.

"Senator Simpson and Miss Thelma Parkinson waged an aggressive and clean battle," said Mrs. Norton. "The opposing forces, wealth and great publicity, supporting fine personality, were hard to overcome and the inevitable resulted. I wish Mr. Morrow every success."

Mrs. Norton Re-elected.

Mrs. Norton was re-elected to the House of Representatives from the Twelfth Congressional District. Fred A. Hartley, Republican, who defeated Paul Moore, Democrat, two years

Continued on Page Five.

Roosevelt Appraises Victory As Expression of Confidence

Governor Franklin D. Roosevelt, speaking over the radio after his re-election had been conceded last night, interpreted the vote he received as one of confidence.

"I want to say a few words to the people of this State tonight," he declared over stations WEAF and WJZ. "I am overwhelmed with gratitude for the vote of confidence you have given to my administration.

"I can only say that in the next two years I will bring all my ability to serve all of the citizens, regardless of party and regardless of locality, in the interest of a program of honest government."

NEW ENGLAND HIT BY DEMOCRATIC WAVE

Massachusetts Elects M. A. Coolidge, Wet, for Senator, and Ely for Governor.

CROSS WINS IN CONNECTICUT

Former Yale Dean Surprises by Victory—Metcalf Rhode Island Winner.

New England Results.

New England Democrats were victorious in two States. Their candidates for United States Senator and Governor, Marcus A. Coolidge and Joseph B. Ely, won in Massachusetts and their nominee for United States Senator from Connecticut, former Dean Wilbur L. Cross of Yale, was elected. The Republicans carried Rhode Island, New Hampshire and Vermont.

Special to The New York Times.

BOSTON, Nov. 4.—Massachusetts saw a Democratic sweep in today's election which, while not extending throughout the entire State ticket or into the Congressional fight in the sixteen districts, carried a wet Democrat into the United States Senatorship and the Governorship, by decisive margins.

With about two-thirds of the vote counted, it is estimated that former Senator William M. Butler, dry Republican candidate for the Senate, will be defeated by about 75,000 votes by Marcus A. Coolidge, the Democratic candidate. The same returns indicated the defeat of Governor Frank G. Allen, Republican, by 25,000 votes at the hands of Joseph P. Ely, Democrat.

The vote of 1,070 precincts out of the 1,650 in the State gave:

For Governor—Allen, 245,694; Ely, 365,630.

For Senator—Butler, 319,241; Coolidge, 369,432.

State Dry Act Repeal Carried.

At the same time it was indicated that the referendum for repeal of the "baby volstead act," as the State prohibition enforcement law is known, would be carried by more than 200,000.

The vote on the question from 586 precincts, exclusive of Boston, stood: For repeal, 304,951; against repeal, 186,580.

Led by Boston, the cities of the Commonwealth were largely instrumental in piling up the winning Democratic majority. The Boston vote alone, it was estimated, would have

Continued on Page Nine.

Heflin Is Beaten in Alabama by Nearly 2 to 1; Democrats Defeat All Candidates on His Ticket

Special to The New York Times.

BIRMINGHAM, Ala., Nov. 4.—J. Thomas Heflin, senior Senator from Alabama, was defeated by the Democrats of the State today for his election from the party in the 1928 Presidential election. With three-fourths of the vote counted, John H. Bankhead, his opponent, was leading by 46,007 votes out of a total of 211,-627. The vote stood 128,817 for Bankhead and 82,810 for Heflin.

Judge B. M. Miller, for Governor, and Hugh Merrill, for Lieutenant Governor, were holding the same commanding lead over Hugh Locke and Dempsey Powell, "Jeffersonian" candidates running on the same ticket with Senator Heflin.

In a statement to The Montgomery Advertiser tonight Senator Heflin charged "fraud and corruption" in the election and said he would demand an investigation by the Senate Committee on Elections.

"While early returns indicate the vote is going against me, within two hours I will be 100,000 votes ahead."

Boxes which went overwhelmingly for Hoover in the 1928 election went just as strongly for the Democratic nominees today.

No serious political issues were at stake in the election other than whether Alabama would remain in the Democratic column or would become an active two-party State.

TUTTLE IS SWAMPED

Governor's Record Plurality Amazes His Own Party.

CARRIES TICKET WITH HIM

Lehman and Tremaine Re-elected—Bennett Also Victorious.

UP-STATE FOR ROOSEVELT

Sweep Exceeds Smith's Largest Plurality of 385,338—Lieutenant Governor Wins Easily.

Tables of the city and State votes on Pages 10 and 11.

In a Democratic landslide of unprecedented proportions, Governor Franklin D. Roosevelt was re-elected yesterday by a plurality of approximately 730,000 over Charles H. Tuttle, Republican nominee.

In his overwhelming victory, Governor Roosevelt carried with him Lieut. Gov. Herbert H. Lehman, Controller Morris S. Tremaine and John J. Bennett Jr., candidate for Attorney General, who also obtained large pluralities in New York City but ran far behind the Governor up-State.

Professor Robert P. Carroll, Independent dry, running as the candidate of the Law Enforcement party, polled a vote of nearly 170,000, all but about 8,885 of which was outside New York City. Professor Carroll carried Yates County over both Tuttle and Roosevelt and his vote cut heavily into the usual Republican vote in up-State counties.

556,868 Plurality in City.

New York City gave Governor Roosevelt 556,868 plurality. The vote in the city for Governor was: Roosevelt, 925,665; Tuttle, 369,797; Louis Waldman, Socialist, 88,329, and Carroll, 8,885.

With 168 up-State election districts missing, 4,816 districts out of 4,976 gave Roosevelt, 826,562; Tuttle, 659,-163; Carroll, 158,323, an actual plurality for Roosevelt of 167,499 and an indicated up-State plurality of 174,160 and an isolated plurality in the entire State of 730,925. The up-State vote for Roosevelt in these 4,816 districts exceeded the combined vote for Tuttle and Carroll by 10,461.

Carroll's up-State vote was 158,323. The tremendous vote for Governor Roosevelt was regarded as increasing greatly his chance for the Democratic nomination for President in 1932, for which he is known to be an aspirant. In polling up his plurality, Governor Roosevelt reached a mark never before attained by any other candidate for State office. His plurality of 556,868 in New York City would have been a record if it had not been exceeded by the city plurality of Lieut. Gov. Lehman, which was 607,087.

The largest plurality ever received in the State by Alfred E. Smith and

Continued on Page Three.

OVERWHELMINGLY RE-ELECTED.
Governor Franklin D. Roosevelt, Who, With His Entire Ticket, Is Returned to Office by a Record Plurality.

Times Wide World Photo.

REPUBLICANS RETAIN CONTROL AT ALBANY

Hold Assembly by a Reduced Margin—Advantage in the Senate Cut to One Seat.

UP-STATE WETS VICTORIOUS

Drys Who Promised to Defeat Them Fail—Bennett Elected by 227 Votes.

Despite the landslide which resulted in the re-election of Governor Roosevelt by a towering majority, the Republicans will continue its control of both branches of the Legislature.

Late returns from the legislative elections give the Republicans continued control of both the Senate and Assembly, barring upsets on revised returns in some districts where the vote was close.

Final election returns received early this morning show the Republicans failed to widen their own in the Assembly. In the present Assembly there are four Republican Assemblymen, all from Manhattan. In the 1931 Assembly there will be one from Manhattan, Abbot Lowe Moffat of the Fifteenth, and one from Brooklyn, Robert K. Story Jr. of the Seventeenth Kings District.

Wald Defeated Here.

In the Senate the day was saved to the Republicans through the re-election of Senator Samuel H. Hofstadter of the Seventeenth Senatorial District on the west side of Manhattan. Mr. Hofstadter's victory was won by a slender majority of 227 votes. He defeated Albert Wald, the Democratic nominee, for whom a terrific drive was made by the Democrats in an attempt to gain control of the upper house at Albany

Continued on Page Three.

CITY GIVES GOVERNOR GREATEST PLURALITY

Has Margin of 556,868 as Graft Issue Fails Tuttle—Lehman Leads His Ticket.

MRS. PRATT WINS BY 651

La Guardia Victorious—Miller Elected Judge, Alger Loses— Bond Issue Carries.

Governor Roosevelt carried the city yesterday by the unprecedented plurality of 556,868 votes over his Republican rival, Charles H. Tuttle. His associates on the ticket also piled up huge pluralities over Republican opponents, that of Lieut. Gov. Lehman reaching the mark of 607,087.

The city's vote for Governor was:

Roosevelt	924,665
Tuttle	360,797
Waldman	88,329
Carroll	8,885

Governor Roosevelt's tremendous plurality, although far above the pre-election estimates of John P. Curry and other Democratic leaders, did not arouse the enthusiasm which the victory of huge pluralities in the past years. The early estimate were regarded as extremely conservative, the Democratic leaders having somewhat discounted the more optimistic reports which came from the district leaders.

Mrs. Pratt Wins Close Race.

The Democratic landslide carried into office nearly all of the party's local candidates, such strong Republican candidates as Representative Ruth B. Pratt, Representative F. H. La Guardia and State Senator Samuel H. Hofstadter narrowly escaping defeat. The only upset was in Brooklyn where Robert K. Story Jr., Republican, won against his Democratic rival for an Assembly seat. This was counterbalanced by the victory of D. H. Stephens, Democrat, who was elected to the Assembly in the Nineteenth Manhattan District.

This district, incidentally, is the one in which Martin J. Healy is Democratic leader. Mr. Healy is one of the central figures in the judiciary scandals upon which Mr. Tuttle largely based his fruitless campaign. The election was one of the quietest in years, there being but few disturbances at the polling places. From the moment that the returns began to come in it was evident that the issue of judicial corruption and alleged bartering of judicial offices would have no effect upon the Roosevelt vote. Nor did the driving rain which fell throughout the day keep

Continued on Page Three.

STILL LEAD IN SENATE

But Republican Hold on House Hangs on Belated Returns.

SEE PRESAGE FOR 1932

Democrats Are Victorious in Nearly All the Chief Battles.

PINCHOT BEATS HEMPHILL

Election of Bulkley, a Wet, as Senator in Ohio Seems Indicated.

By RICHARD V. OULAHAN.

A distinct Democratic sweep, suggesting a landslide for that party, extended across the country in yesterday's elections, held in all the forty-eight States except Maine. While the outcome of a number of contests for important public offices is still in doubt, the Democrats were victorious in most of the outstanding battles from which definite returns have been received.

The general trend of these returns up to the time this edition of THE NEW YORK TIMES went to press furnished encouraging evidence to Democracy's leaders that the sentiment expressed at the polls throughout a widespread area presaged victory for their Presidential ticket in the elections of 1932.

Democratic Governors were elected in New York, Connecticut, Massachusetts, Rhode Island and Ohio, and in States normally Democratic. In such States as Kansas, Minnesota, Nebraska, Oregon and Wyoming, where the Republicans win more often than not, the result is in doubt on account of the strong trend of Democratic sentiment.

Senate Leads Slender.

Judging by the latest returns, there is a bare chance that the nominal Republican majority in the Senate will be overthrown, although the prospect is that the Republicans may still have a slight excess of members over the Democrats. It is possible, however, that the next Senate will be a tie politically.

Democratic Senators have been elected in place of Republicans in Colorado, Minnesota, Ohio, Oklahoma, West Virginia and Massachusetts, and the chance favors a victory for the Republican Senatorial candidate in South Dakota. Only one Republican Senatorial aspirant has triumphed over a sitting Democratic Senator. This happened in Iowa.

In line with the general Democratic swing, the returns showed that candidates of that party have cut heavily into the big Republican majority in the House of Representatives where a fair prospect that the Democrats will gain control, though the actual outcome remains in doubt.

The Democratic landslide carried into office nearly all of the party's local candidates, such strong Republican candidates as Representative Ruth B. Pratt, Representative F. H. La Guardia and State Senator Samuel H. Hofstadter narrowly escaping defeat. This line-up concedes the election of Klinck, Republican in South Dakota, and Schall, Republican, in Minnesota. The doubtful contests are in South Dakota, Kansas and Kentucky. Should the Democratic candidates carry all these contests the Senate would stand:

Democrats 48, Republicans 47, Farmer-Laborite 1.

Heavy gains were made by the Democrats in the contest for 435 seats in the House of Representatives, but whether these will be sufficient to wipe out the present Republican majority is uncertain, with returns incomplete from approximately threescore districts.

Results of Latest Figures.

Counting nine vacant seats which had been held by Republicans, the majority of that party in the present House is 103. The latest definite election returns give the Republicans 189 seats, the Democrats 200 and the Farmer-Labor party 1, with 44 in the doubtful column and 1 Independent Republican.

The Democrats have 185 members

"All the News That's Fit to Print."

The New York Times.

LATE CITY EDITION

THE WEATHER—Fair today and tomorrow; not much change in temperature. Temperatures yesterday—Max. 61, min. 47.

Copyright, 1931, by The New York Times Company.

VOL. LXXX....No. 26,744. ★★★★★ NEW YORK, WEDNESDAY, APRIL 15, 1931. TWO CENTS in Greater New York | THREE CENTS Within 200 Miles | FOUR CENTS Elsewhere Except 7th and 8th Postal Zones

GOVERNOR REQUESTS MINUTES ON CRAIN; QUICK DECISION SEEN

Critics of Prosecutor Predict Early Action—Albany Denies Move Is Significant.

PATHE HEARING ON MONDAY

Seabury Moves to Wind Up the Inquiry May 1—Rothstein Case Is Taken Up.

KLEIN DATA TO PROSECUTOR

Harvey Rebuffed in Plea for Bribe Evidence—Hofstadter Summons Legislative Committee.

Developments yesterday in the investigations into city affairs were:

Governor Roosevelt called upon Samuel Seabury for the minutes of the public hearings on rackets in the removal proceedings against District Attorney Crain.

State Senator Hofstadter called a meeting of the legislative inquiry committee to be held here on Monday.

Controller Berry refused to give Borough President Harvey the transcript of evidence against Irving Klein, borough highway superintendent, to be used at a public hearing on bribery charge would be sent directly to the Queens District Attorney.

GOVERNOR ACTS ON CRAIN.

Governor Roosevelt wrote to Commissioner Samuel Seabury yesterday requesting a copy of the minutes of the public hearings on rackets in the removal proceedings against District Attorney Crain. The Governor took this step twenty-four hours after the elderly prosecutor confessed helplessness against racketeers, who, he said, infest the business structure of the city.

Text of Governor's Letter.

The letter follows:

My dear Judge Seabury:

If it is not inconsistent with the progress of your work as Commissioner representing the Governor in the matter of the District Attorney in New York, I would appreciate your sending me the copy of the minutes of the public hearings held up to the present time, and also of other public hearings as they occur.

Very truly yours,
FRANKLIN D. ROOSEVELT.

Crain Had Attacked Governor.

Crowded Hours of a Busy Day In President Hoover's Life

Special to The New York Times.

WASHINGTON, April 14.—With two addresses, ten innings of an exciting American League game, a Cabinet meeting and a dinner tonight, President Hoover spent one of his busiest days since he entered the White House.

Here is the schedule of the chief events:

8:00 A. M.—Rise.
8:30 A. M.—Medicine ball.
9:00 A. M.—Breakfast.
9:30 A. M.—Brief conference with callers.
10:00 A. M.—Cabinet meeting.
11:00 A. M.—Receives delegation of tourists.
12:30 P. M.—Speech at Pan-American Day celebration.
1:30 P. M.—Luncheon.
3:00 P. M.—Attends opening American League baseball game.
5:00 P. M.—Speaks by radio from White House to Tuskegee celebration.
8:00 P. M.—Dines with Secretary of the Navy and Mrs. Adams.
11:00 P. M.—Retires.

The usual noon conference with newspaper men was omitted because of the other demands on the President's time.

BETHLEHEM BONUS GETS 72% OF PROXIES

Management Apparently Wins Approval for System That Paid Grace $1,625,753 in Year.

SCHWAB PARRIES CRITICS

Holds Practice Is an Incentive, and Says Board Voted Him $250,000 in 1930.

The Bethlehem Steel Corporation's bonus plan, under which officers received approximately $26,000,000 in fourteen years and which is being fought in the courts by a minority group, was apparently ratified overwhelmingly yesterday at the annual meeting of the stockholders in Newark.

4 AMERICANS KILLED IN SANDINO ADVANCE; WARSHIP LANDS MEN

Three Missing as Nicaraguan Rebels Near Puerto Cabezas After Jungle Skirmishes.

HEAVIER LOSSES FEARED

Fruit Company Hears Eleven Americans and Some British Employes Were Slain.

8 REBELS KILLED BY GUARD

25 Marines Board Gunboat Again When Patrols Return From Clash —300 Americans in Town.

Special to The New York Times.

WASHINGTON, April 14.—According to a report from the gunboat Asheville of the Special Service Squadron, which arrived this morning at Puerto Cabezas on the east coast of Nicaragua, preliminary skirmishes between rebel groups under Augusto Sandino, advancing toward the town, and National Guardsmen have in the past twenty-four hours resulted in four Americans being killed and three missing.

Utah Woman Is First Chosen To the Presbyterian Assembly

Special to The New York Times.

PHILADELPHIA, April 14.—Election of Mrs. E. J. Silliman of Green River, Utah, as a commissioner to the Pennsylvania General Assembly was reported today to Presbyterian headquarters here.

Mrs. Silliman, a ruling elder from the Presbytery of Southern Utah, thus becomes the first woman in the United States to be recorded as a commissioner in the highest court of the denomination. Last year's General Assembly made women eligible to the office. The General Assembly has a total membership of about 960, equally divided between ministers and ruling elders.

PAN-AMERICAN AMITY HAILED BY PRESIDENT

All Major Differences Will Be Settled by Conciliation and Arbitration, He Says.

TIES FOSTER AGREEMENT

Address Opens First Celebration of Pan-American Day Amid Banners of 21 Nations.

Special to The New York Times.

WASHINGTON, April 14.—The time is not far away when every major difference between the American republics will be settled by the orderly processes of conciliation and arbitration, President Hoover declared today at the first celebration of Pan-American Day.

KING ALFONSO QUITS, SPAIN A REPUBLIC; ALCALA ZAMORA IS FIRST PRESIDENT; NATION ORDERLY UNDER MARTIAL LAW

BRITAIN TO WELCOME EXILE

Alfonso Is Regarded as Member of English Royal Family.

HIS WIFE IS KING'S COUSIN

Much of the Huge Fortune of Deposed Monarch Said to Be Safe in London.

REPUBLICANS TO QUIT PARIS

Members of New Cabinet Pack Belongings to Rush to Madrid —They See Huge Task.

By FERDINAND KUHN Jr.
Special Cable to The New York Times.

LONDON, April 14.—The royal family and the people of Britain are prepared for the abdication of King Alfonso of Spain as the latest of royal exiles to find refuge on British soil.

KING ALFONSO XIII.

Photo by Van Dyck.

WASHINGTON ENVOY OF SPAIN TO RESIGN

Diplomatic Circles Fear Era of Chaos—State Department Awaits Official Report.

BIG CREDIT NOT WITHDRAWN

$60,000,000 Loan to Bank of Spain May Still Be Used, Say New York Financiers.

Special to The New York Times.

WASHINGTON, April 14.—The Spanish Embassy was stunned by the abdication of King Alfonso XIII today. Although, in the absence of any official information from Madrid, it declined to make any statement, there appeared to be no doubt that Señor Don Alejandro Padilla y Bell, who has been Ambassador since Oct. 11, 1926, will resign when he is officially notified of the swift turn of events in Spain.

CATALONIA TO STAY IN SPAIN AS STATE

Separatists Decide on Move After Announcing They Would Be Independent.

ROYALISTS YIELD EASILY

Colonel Macia Takes City Hall Without Resistance and Begins Emptying Jails.

By The Associated Press.

BARCELONA, Wednesday, April 15.—Francisco Macia, Provisional President of the Catalonian Republic, issued a declaration early today that he had "assumed office provisionally under Señor Zamora as head of the Federated Spanish Republic," and that the Catalonian Republic would be an integral State within the Spanish Federation.

Ousted Royalist Mayor.

MONARCH SAILS ON CRUISER

Crown Prince Is With Him —Queen and Others to Go From Madrid Today.

KING BALKED AT ABDICATION

Left to Avert Bloodshed When Revolt Threatened, but Still Claimed Throne.

MOVE REGARDED AS FINAL

New Rulers Plan New Constitution, but Won't Hold Plebiscite on Monarchy.

By FRANK L. KLUCKHOHN.
Special Cable to The New York Times.

MADRID, April 14.—King Alfonso XIII, the last of the Bourbons, yielded his throne today and Spain became a republic.

The monarchy, which had stood proudly for fifteen centuries with brief intermission, was toppled over in a few breathless hours this afternoon without a drop of bloodshed. The Republican Government, headed by Nicolo Alcala Zamora as first President, is installed peacefully in Madrid and the Republican flag is flying everywhere in the country.

Fire Wrecks the Bluecher Palace in Berlin; Just Bought for $1,800,000 for Our Embassy

Special Cable to The New York Times.

BERLIN, Wednesday, April 15.—The famous Bluecher Palace on Unter den Linden, which was recently bought by the United States for its embassy, was almost completely destroyed by fire during the night. The fire was under control early this morning.

BERLIN, April 14 (AP).—The night of the three-story Bluecher Palace was ablaze when the firemen arrived. Additional alarms emptied the firehouses and almost every piece of apparatus in the city was called out.

"All the News That's Fit to Print."

The New York Times.

LATE CITY EDITION

THE WEATHER—Generally fair and warmer today, tomorrow partly cloudy; showers. Temperatures Yesterday—Max. 74; Min. 66.

Copyright, 1931, by The New York Times Company.

VOL. LXXXI....No. 26,903.

NEW YORK, MONDAY, SEPTEMBER 21, 1931.

TWO CENTS in New York City | THREE CENTS Within 200 Miles | FOUR CENTS Except 7th and 8th Postal Zones

NANKING WILL INVOKE KELLOGG PEACE PACT; NEW FIGHTING FEARED

Foreign Minister of China Says League Also Will Be Told of Japanese Acts.

MANCHURIANS PLAN BATTLE

Kirin Troops Expected to Attack Japanese Garrison—Harbin Reported Tense.

SOVIET TROOPS AT BORDER

Foreign Observers at Mukden Hold Japanese Military Deliberately Caused Incident.

By HALLETT ABEND.
Wireless to THE NEW YORK TIMES.

NANKING, Sept. 20.—"Appropriate steps are being taken to apprise the League of Nations and the powers signatory to the Kellogg pact of the unwarranted actions of Japanese troops," C. T. Wang, Foreign Minister of the Nanking Government, declared in a statement this morning concerning the lodging of vigorous protests with the Japanese Government. Mr. Wang continued:

"The National Government is greatly exercised over the situation caused by the unprovoked attack of Japanese troops on Mukden and other cities in three eastern provinces."

Says Chinese Did Not Resist.

Mr. Wang's statement makes no reference to the charges that Chinese soldiers tried to damage the South Manchuria Railway north of Mukden, but says Japanese troops fired on Chinese soldiers encamped at Peitaying, that the Chinese withdrew without resisting and that the Japanese disarmed the Chinese and set the buildings afire.

Mr. Wang charges that simultaneously the Japanese bombarded the arsenal and the Peitaying camp, but while the arsenal was not damaged the camp's mortar depot was destroyed. The Nanking Foreign Minister also charges the Japanese fired upon and occupied all Chinese police stations inside and immediately outside Mukden and disarmed the policemen, seized the wireless station, forcibly occupied all government offices and interrupted all electrical communications.

The Japanese Consulate at Nanking announces the transmission last night to Tokyo of the formal protest of the Nanking Foreign Office in regard to the occupation of Mukden by Japanese troops and a formal request that they immediately evacuate the city.

It is officially announced that seventy-one Chinese soldiers were killed in the clash incident to the occupation of Mukden. The number of Chinese wounded is not known. No civilians were killed. The total of the Japanese casualties was one soldier killed and two wounded.

Japanese officially stress the assertion that the magnitude of the incident was due to the extreme nervousness and tension existing in the Mukden area as a result of the series of minor clashes and growing feeling on both sides of uneasiness and hostility, which resulted in the minor Japanese commanders taking the bit in their teeth and quickly extending the zone of operations without the knowledge or approval of the higher command.

More Fighting Expected.

Wireless to THE NEW YORK TIMES.

MUKDEN, Sept. 20.—More fighting was expected tonight between Japanese and Chinese between Dairen and the Mukden area at those points where Chinese soldiers are quartered along the South Manchuria Railway zone. Now everything is peaceful everywhere, with the Japanese in control.

Chinese are looting in the international section of Mukden, which area in ordinary times is under Chinese control. The Japanese are taking steps to protect the area. Foreign opinion here is that the Japanese military were angry because the Nakamura affair was about to be closed diplomatically, so, according to all foreign observers here, the outbreak on Friday night was premeditated. A Japanese statement says:

"We were always prepared for an emergency, but we were surprised on the night of Sept. 18, when Chinese tried to blow up the South Manchuria Railway tracks at two points. It was necessary to protect everybody. The incident is unfortunate."

This morning Frank Sugden, a British subject, an engineer of the Peiping-Mukden Railway workshop, attempted to go to his office, which

Continued on Page Eight.

*Imported French Natural drug.
French drug... (advertisement)*

Byrd's Old Supply Ship Sails To Load Labrador Lime Shells

By The Canadian Press.

ST. JOHN'S, N. F., Sept. 20.—Carrying out plans of a company, financed largely by Newfoundland capital, to develop the natural resources of Labrador, the steamer Eleanor Bolling sailed yesterday with fifty men and necessary machinery to take marine shell from Hamilton Inlet.

The Eleanor Bolling, which was supply ship of the Byrd Antarctic expedition, is one of several vessels chartered to convey cargoes to St. John's, where equipment for screening the product and preparing it for market has been installed.

The sun-bleached shell deposits, which have lain on the shores of Hamilton Inlet for ages, are said to be almost 100 per cent lime, valuable for poultry feeding and horticultural purposes. First shipments are expected early in October.

WALKER BACK TODAY, BUT WANTS NO 'FUSS'

Elaborate Reception Vetoed—He Will Stay Aboard Ship Until It Reaches Pier.

HE PHILOSOPHIZES ON LINER

One 'Must Laugh on the Stage of Politics No Matter What the Sadness Within,' He Remarks.

Having been widely fêted, dined and honored in Europe, Mayor Walker will return to New York today on the North German Lloyd liner Bremen, on which he sailed for a month's "rest cure" in Germany on Aug. 4.

His return, in so far as reception plans and organized welcome are concerned, will be quiet. Charles F. Kerrigan, Assistant Mayor, said yesterday. Mr. Kerrigan, Thomas F. McAndrews, the Mayor's secretary, and Police Commissioner Mulrooney will go down the harbor in a revenue cutter and board the Bremen at Quarantine.

The receiving tug Macom, the city's official craft for the reception of distinguished visitors and homecomers, will not be used. Mayor Walker will remain aboard the Bremen until she docks at Pier 4 at the foot of Fifty-eighth Street, Brooklyn, probably between 8 and 9 P. M.

May Speak Over Radio.

There he will be met by Mrs. Walker and probably by a group of friends and city officials and he will go from the pier to his home at 6 St. Luke's Place. Mr. Kerrigan said there had been some talk of having the Mayor make a short statement over the radio from the pier. While no definite plans have been made, he felt that if the microphone were installed on the pier the Mayor would make a short speech.

In the Mayor's party and returning with him are Dudley Field Malone, former Collector of the Port of New York, and Dr. William Schroeder Jr., chairman of the Department of Sanitation and the Mayor's personal physician.

It was the Mayor's own wish that his homecoming be without "fuss" or noisy reception. Plans had been made for a demonstration, with a parade, a luncheon or dinner and other details, but the Mayor, by long-distance telephone from London, was understood to have vetoed it.

It is understood that his decision was influenced by the many receptions, dinners and celebrations with which he was met in Germany, creating a spirit more festive than restful, which followed him through Europe.

Feted in Many Cities.

After a short stop in Southampton on Aug. 10 the Mayor landed in Bremen the following day and was the guest at a reception in his honor. The next day he proceeded to Berlin, where he spent several days. While there he visited the Baroness von Huenefeld, mother of the late Baron von Huenefeld, who crossed the Atlantic Ocean in the plane Bremen in 1928.

Among the German watering places he visited were Carlsbad and Marienbad. He went to Pilsen, Budapest, Vienna, Cannes, Monaco and Monte Carlo, everywhere seeking rest and finding that his leave presence prevented it. In Paris he was entertained at luncheon by President Doumer of France and was made a Commander of the Legion of Honor. In London he was the luncheon guest of Premier Ramsay MacDonald.

In Berlin he was one of the night resorts within a few hours after his arrival. The next day he was the luncheon guest of the Carl Schurz Association, and the next night, over a radio hook-up by which he was heard in Europe and the United States, he made a speech in praise of the spirit of determination to overcome...

Continued on Page Five.

PRESIDENT DEPARTS TO ADDRESS LEGION AT DETROIT ON BONUS

He Boards Special Train at Martinsburg, W. Va., After Day at Rapidan Camp.

TO WARN OF HEAVY COST

Washington Thinks He May Touch Also on Economic Situation in Europe.

LEGION COMMANDER FIRM

O'Neil Warns Against Cash-Payment Demands and Hints Danger in Prohibition Stand.

From a Staff Correspondent of The New York Times.

MARTINSBURG, W. Va., Sept. 20.—President Hoover left here on a special train at 8:30 o'clock this evening for Detroit where he will deliver an address tomorrow before the national convention of the American Legion.

The President spent the day at his Rapidan camp in Virginia working on his address, which he will deliver at noon tomorrow, but it was not completed when he left here. There were showers throughout the day, and the President remained indoors most of the time.

The President motored from his Rapidan camp to Martinsburg through Sherryville and Winchester. The last twenty-five miles of the trip were made at the slow speed of twenty-two miles an hour so that the President would arrive just before his train was scheduled to leave. As a result, a long line of automobiles which were not permitted by Secret Service men to pass the President's car trailed after it, and there was a wild blowing of horns.

At Martinsburg about 2,000 people were on hand to greet the President and he was called upon for a speech. He waved his hat, but would not make an address.

Accompanying the President are Captain Train and Colonel Hodges, his naval and military aides, and Secretaries Joslin and Richey. Governor Leslie of Indiana and Mrs. Leslie, who were his guests at the camp, will also accompany the President as far as Indianapolis.

Capital Speculates on Speech.

Special to The New York Times.

WASHINGTON, Sept. 20.—With President Hoover on his way to Detroit tonight to address the national convention of the American Legion tomorrow, speculation continues here as to whether there were several compelling motives for the President's sudden decision to attend the convention, after he had made it plain only a few days previously that he would be unable to do so.

There is unanimity of opinion that the President's chief purpose is to get the great power and authority of the influence which comes from his high office against the movements in the ranks of the Legionnaires for the adoption of a resolution calling on Congress to enact legislation permitting World War veterans to borrow from the government up to the full maturity value of their bonus certificates fourteen years before they mature.

As to Conditions Abroad.

Today's speculative comment had to do with whether the President would give attention in his address to matters of pressing public importance other than the bonus, with a rather widespread inclination to surmise that he would take occasion to sketch economic and financial conditions abroad with their effect on the United States.

Those best informed as to the Administration...

Continued on Page Four.

NEW YORK BANKERS CONFER

See No Need for Drastic Action — Investments in London Moderate.

RECENT LOANS PROTECTED

Federal Reserve Can Demand Gold—Morgan Credit Payable in Dollars.

EFFECT ON PRICES FEARED

Britain's Action Also Expected to Have Repercussions on World Credit Situation.

American security markets will not follow the lead of the London Stock Exchange, but will be open for business as usual today. No emergency had developed here to warrant any action similar to that in the foreign countries, it was stated authoritatively last night.

New York bankers held informal conferences here yesterday, at which the London crisis was discussed, but no concerted action seemed to them to be called for, it was said. The bankers were in communication with British banking authorities by transatlantic telephones.

According to a competent authority, the short-term balances of American banks in London do not exceed $50,000,000, while Great Britain's short-term obligations in this country, exclusive of the $125,000,000 credit recently granted by the Federal Reserve banks to the Bank of England and the $200,000,000 private banking credit to the British Treasury, do not exceed $500,700,000.

No further supporting measures will be taken to defend the pound sterling at this time, it was stated. The private banking credit which was opened on Aug. 28 last, while not yet actually used up, will be exhausted shortly with the taking up of forward commitments made by British banking authorities in their recent attempts to bolster the pound.

Banker Sums Up Situation.

The British financial difficulties, as they are understood here, were summed up last night by an important international banker as follows:

The emergency measures taken by the British Government to check the heavy outflow of gold from London will undoubtedly arouse widespread surprise here, although the steps to be taken are by no means unprecedented. During the early days of the Great War, it will be recalled, Great Britain suspended the Bank Act temporarily, and in 1920 sterling went as low as an exchange value of $3.20 as against parity of about $4.86½. It was not until 1925 that the country returned officially to a gold basis.

The terms of the announcement by the British authorities make it clear that the suspension of gold payments by the Bank of England is a temporary measure and in no way affects the obligation of the British Government to meet in gold such obligations as it may have outstanding in foreign currencies. Undoubtedly the government had a...

Continued on Page Two.

The British Government's Statement

Special Cable to THE NEW YORK TIMES.

LONDON, Sept. 20.—This is the statement issued by the government tonight, announcing suspension of the law requiring that the Bank of England sell gold at a fixed price:

His Majesty's Government have decided after consultation with the Bank of England that it has become necessary to suspend for the time being the operation of Subsection 2, Section 1, of the gold standard act of 1925, which requires the Bank to sell gold at a fixed price.

A bill for this purpose will be introduced immediately, and it is the intention of His Majesty's Government to ask Parliament to pass it through all stages Monday, the 21st of September. In the meantime, the Bank of England has been authorized to proceed accordingly in anticipation of the action of Parliament.

The reasons which led to this decision are as follows:

Since the middle of July, funds amounting to more than £200,000,000 (about $1,000,000,00) have been withdrawn from the London market. The withdrawals have been met partly from gold and foreign currency held by the Bank of England, partly from proceeds of a credit of £50,000,000 (about $250,000,000), which shortly matures, secured by the Bank of England from New York and Paris and partly from proceeds of French and American credits amounting to £80,000,000 (about $400,000,000) recently obtained by the government.

During the last few days withdrawals of foreign balances have accelerated so sharply that His Majesty's Government felt that they were bound to take the above decision.

This decision will, of course, not affect the obligations of His Majesty's Government or of the Bank of England which are payable in foreign currencies.

Gold holdings of the Bank of England amount to some £130,000,000 (about $650,000,000) and, having regard to contingencies which may have to be met, it is inadvisable to allow this reserve to be further reduced.

There will be no interruption of ordinary banking business. Banks will be opened as usual for the convenience of their customers, and there is no reason why sterling transactions should be affected in any way.

It has been arranged that the Stock Exchange shall not be opened on Monday, the day on which Parliament is passing the necessary legislation. This will not, however, interfere with the business of current settlement on the Stock Exchange, which will be carried through as usual.

His Majesty's Government have no reason to believe that the present difficulties are due to any substantial extent to the export of capital by British nationals. Undoubtedly the bulk of withdrawals has been for foreign accounts.

They desire, however, to repeat emphatically the warning given by the Chancellor of the Exchequer that any British citizen who increases the strain on exchanges by purchasing foreign securities himself, or is assisting others to do so, is deliberately adding to the country's difficulties.

The banks have undertaken to cooperate in restricting purchases by British citizens of foreign exchange except those required for the actual needs of trade or for meeting contracts, and should further measures prove to be advisable his Majesty's Government will not hesitate to take them.

His Majesty's Government have arrived at their decision with the greatest reluctance. But during the last few days international financial markets have become demoralized and have been liquidating their sterling assets regardless of their intrinsic worth. In the circumstances there was no alternative but to protect the financial position of this country by the only means at our disposal.

His Majesty's Government are securing a balanced budget and the internal position of the country is sound. This position must be maintained. It is one thing to go off the gold standard with an unbalanced budget and uncontrolled inflation. It is quite another thing to take this measure, not because of internal financial difficulties but because of excessive withdrawals of borrowed capital.

The ultimate resources of this country are enormous and there is no doubt that the present exchange difficulties will prove only temporary.

Gold Standard Subsection to Be Suspended.

Subsection 2 of the British Gold Standard act of 1925, which is to be suspended, reads as follows:

The Bank of England shall be bound to sell to any person who makes demand in that behalf at the head office of the Bank during office hours of the Bank, and pay the purchase price in any legal tender, gold bullion at the price of £3 17s 10½d per ounce troy of gold of the standard of fineness prescribed for gold coin by the coinage act of 1870, but only in the form of bars containing approximately 400 ounces troy of fine gold.

PARLIAMENT TO BACK MOVE

Cabinet Is Unanimous in Decision to End the Drain on Gold.

KING TO SIGN BILL TONIGHT

London Hopes Drastic Measure Will Not Be Necessary More Than Six Months.

MacDONALD EXPLAINS STEP

Government Says Withdrawals of Funds Since July Forced Its Action.

By CHARLES A. SELDEN.
Special Cable to THE NEW YORK TIMES.

LONDON, Sept. 20.—Great Britain will go off the gold standard tomorrow. Legislation accomplishing the exact time financial laws to that effect will be rushed through Parliament in the course of the day and will receive the King's royal assent tomorrow night.

To accomplish this, the new National Government, which is responsible for this drastic step, is assured of the necessary majority in the House of Commons to pass the measure through all its Parliamentary stages in one sitting. The House of Lords, which ordinarily does not sit on Mondays, has been summoned for the required concurrent action.

Bank of England Approves.

A unanimous decision to abandon the gold standard was reached at an emergency session of Premier MacDonald's Cabinet today after consultation with the Bank of England, which agreed it was the only thing to do.

The Bank of England tomorrow will raise the discount rate to 6 per cent from 4½ per cent.

The London Stock Exchange and all provincial exchanges will be closed for the day.

Although there is no suggestion in the government statement as to how long this state of affairs will continue the official announcement implies it will be only temporary by saying the suspension is "for the time being."

The expectation, or at least the hope, is that it will last only six months if within that period the country manages to balance its international trade as well as its budget.

It was hoped this week to bring to its government finance would be averted by the change in government a month ago with the subsequent achievement of balancing the budget and cutting down government expenses, but it is evident now that the change was too long delayed.

Blow Was Long Impending.

The present blow has been impending a long time. Now that it has fallen, the situation is explained as due both to international and domestic causes. The foreign factors involved, according to the British appraisal of the situation, were the hoarding of gold by the United States and France and the recent drain on sterling because of the financial difficulties of other countries.

Diminished foreign confidence in the stability of the pound was another vital factor which had gone too far to be entirely corrected by the recent change in government and by the effect of big loans from New York and Paris. The recent "pay cut mutiny" in the British navy also was one of the various causes of the cumulative effect, which is today's decision to abandon the gold standard.

Also England put a terrific strain on herself six years ago by returning to the gold standard as part of her post-war financial policy and by her whole attitude toward the payment of her war debts. Of all countries on this side of the Atlantic which participated in the war, England is the only one which has not cut the value of its currency. Great Britain alone returned to the pre-war gold parity; of its currency while France divided the franc by five.

Plus all this international strain, England has been attempting to carry on at the same time a most expensive experiment in socialism, which, with its enormous cost of unemployment insurance, caused the downfall of the Labor Government just a month ago.

Although the British public does...

Continued on Page Two.

EVENTUAL BENEFITS SEEN BY WASHINGTON

British Move Is Held Likely to Affect War Debts—Hoover Informed on Friday.

Special to The New York Times.

WASHINGTON, Sept. 20.—While government officials were unwilling to discuss formally the British financial crisis because of the delicacy of the situation, the announcement by the British government did not come as a surprise, as word had been received here as early as Friday that some drastic step was in contemplation.

While informally some experts referred to the present situation as the most serious since the world war, there was also expressed the opinion that a long-range proposition any move by Great Britain to put her financial house in order would have a salutary effect on world economic affairs.

It was reported here tonight that the White House dinner Friday evening attended by President Hoover and Secretaries Stimson, Mellon and Lamont was arranged after the President first obtained definite information of the step that Britain was contemplating.

Situation Thoroughly Discussed.

It is now understood that there was a thorough discussion at the dinner of the situation as it might affect financial interests of this country and that consideration also was given as to whether this government might be able to do anything to aid the British in facing the financial crisis. None of the officials has made known just what conclusions were reached at the dinner.

Whether the course to be followed by Great Britain would result in the ultimate revaluation of the pound sterling was a matter of considerable conjecture. In some quarters the belief was held that Great Britain would be compelled in the end to go on an "adjusted gold basis" which would in effect mean a stabilization of the pound at a lower level. One official also felt that Great Britain would find it difficult to keep her foreign obligations on a gold basis and handle her domestics financial affairs on another basis.

That any adjustments which Great Britain must make would require a...

Continued on Page Two.

Canada "Proposes to Maintain" Gold Standard, Premier Says

By The Associated Press.

OTTAWA, Ont., Sept. 20.—R. B. Bennett, Prime Minister and Acting Minister of Finance, said tonight that Canada proposed to maintain the gold standard.

"What Great Britain may do is for the government of Great Britain to determine," said Mr. Bennett. "As for Canada, we propose to maintain the gold standard."

The Prime Minister added that he had nothing further to say on the matter.

GENEVA IS SHOCKED BY CRISIS IN LONDON

High French Official There Says Paris and America Must Aid the Pound.

By CLARENCE K. STREIT.
Special Cable to THE NEW YORK TIMES.

GENEVA, Sept. 20.—The news that the Bank of England tomorrow will go off the gold standard and that the London Stock Exchange will not open came as a shock to the few in Geneva who learned of it late tonight.

"If ever there was a time when the United States and France needed to work together it is now," was the incisive comment of a high French official. "Together we can and must support the pound sterling."

Told of reports from Basle that the British development probably meant the loss in value of sterling by a third, Frenchmen here expressed surprise bordering on consternation and obviously felt every effort ought to be made to prevent it.

It was stressed in the French delegation to the League of Nations that Minister of Finance Flandin had gone last night to Paris, where he had been conversing with officers of the Bank of England. The results of the conversations were not known in the delegation, but M. Flandin was expected back here tomorrow. Whether this meant that a move through Geneva was likely none was willing to predict.

In the British delegation the gravity of the situation was indicated by the tone of voices when it was not indicated by the words used. The British stressed that their financial expert, Sir Arthur Salter, did not believe the situation would really turn out as tragically as laymen seemed to fear.

Though admitting that in such unprecedented matters incalculable factors may play a deciding role, the British seemed inclined to think that "in view of the nervousness of foreigners, who are withdrawing their money from London," the trouble had come to a head sooner than it would otherwise and that it was better that it came sooner than later. Hope was somewhat wanly expressed that everything would be all right in a few days if every one kept his head.

The reports that Sir Arthur Salter...

Continued on Page Two.

GERMANY TO CLOSE ALL BOERSES TODAY

To Keep Them Shut Indefinitely if Need Be — Reichsbank Protected by Credit Truce.

By GUIDO ENDERIS.
Special Cable to THE NEW YORK TIMES.

BERLIN, Sept. 20.—The news that the Bank of England had announced suspension of gold payments, effective tomorrow, struck Berlin banking and Boerse circles as a bolt from the blue and left leading financiers completely nonplussed as to the possible repercussions on the German financial situation.

It was uniformly asserted, however, that the Reichsbank's position was not affected as it was amply protected for the time being through the ratification of the "standstill" agreement on short-term credits.

Pending further developments in London, the German Boerses will remain closed tomorrow and, if necessary, indefinitely thereafter, in keeping with the conclusions reached late today between bank and Boerse leaders and official quarters, as it was commonly feared that the shock resulting from London's procedure would have a devastating reaction upon the German stock markets.

A preponderant number of Berlin bankers incline to the view that the Bank of England's action was an S O S to all capitalistic countries, warning them that the existing currency system was in imminent danger and that the present dislocation...

Continued on Page Two.

Most Severe Quake Since 1924 Rocks Tokyo; Slipping of Strata Alarms Indiana and Ohio

Special Cable to THE NEW YORK TIMES.

TOKYO, Monday, Sept. 21.—The worst earthquake since January, 1924, rocked Tokyo houses violently at 11:35 A. M. today, causing much alarm but apparently little damage. A second and milder shock occurred at 11:58 A. M.

Special to The New York Times.

CINCINNATI, Ohio, Sept. 20.—Earthquake shocks rocked Cincinnati and the surrounding territory shortly after 6 o'clock last night. The shocks were general, reports coming in from every part of Cincinnati—its suburbs. They were felt extensively on the Kentucky side of the river and in a number of up-State, Indiana and Kentucky cities.

No damage was reported here although large buildings were rocked on their foundations, some as much as three inches.

In Mount Adams some residents

became alarmed and rushed into their cellars.

The exact time of the tremors was variously reported from 6:05 to 6:10 o'clock. The shocks, half a dozen or more, lasted less than a minute.

CHICAGO, Sept. 20 (AP).—The earth's surface in parts of Indiana and Ohio did a little readjusting of its own today, but beyond momentarily frightening a few residents, damage was slight.

The disturbance, according to Federal geologists here, was caused by the slipping of strata under the earth's surface.

SIDNEY, Ohio, Sept. 20 (AP).—The Methodist and Lutheran churches, the high school and virtually every house in the village of Anna, Shelby County, were damaged badly by the earthquake today. Authorities said the total damage would exceed $10,000.

The New York Times.

Copyright, 1932, by The New York Times Company.

VOL. LXXXI....No. 27,066. ★★★★★ + NEW YORK, WEDNESDAY, MARCH 2, 1932. TWO CENTS In New York City | THREE CENTS Elsewhere | FOUR CENTS Except 7th and 8th Postal Zones

JAPANESE ROUTING CHINESE IN FIERCE SHANGHAI BATTLE; DEATH TOLL EXCEEDS 2,000

WHOLE CHINESE LINE FLEES

Pressure From North, of Fresh Japanese Troops Forces Quick Move.

PURSUERS LEFT BEHIND

Tachang, Miaoshin and Chapei Fall Before Advance Made Behind Smoke Screen.

TRUCE EXPECTED AT ONCE

Chinese Are Stunned by Sudden Blow—Say Retreat Meets Terms of Japanese.

By HALLETT ABEND.
Wireless to The New York Times.

SHANGHAI, Wednesday, March 2.—The Chinese were routed this morning by the Japanese in the most sanguinary battle since the World War.

The Japanese killed and wounded before 10 o'clock admittedly exceeded 200. Yesterday's advance in this region totaled two kilometres (more than a mile) and the Japanese losses up to midnight officially were admitted to be slightly in excess of 300 killed and wounded, while the bodies of 1,800 Chinese soldiers were discovered this morning on the ground won yesterday.

Brief reports from General Kenkichi Ueda's headquarters report that the Chinese retreat is degenerating into an utter, panicky rout and the rapid Japanese advance is finding difficulty in maintaining contact with the fast fleeing Chinese soldiers.

The pall of smoke from burning Chinese villages and towns was thickening over Shanghai. Immense exultation was manifested in Japanese circles and the Chinese were stunned by the suddenness and magnitude of the military disaster. The Japanese captured Tachang at 12:30 today.

Chinese in Fell Mell Retreat.

Early this afternoon the Japanese forces were rapidly approaching from beyond Tachang and the Chinese were in pellmell retreat. There was great confusion at Nantao, where Chinese soldiers were attempting to evacuate in railway trains for Hangchow.

The Nineteenth Route Army has voluntarily withdrawn from Chapei, is abandoning other fronts and concentrating at Chenju, according to official oral notification given at 13:30 by the secretary of Mayor Wu Te-chen to United States Consul General Edwin S. Cunningham in his capacity as senior consul.

This withdrawal, the official notification said, also means the evacuation of all Chinese soldiers from Nantao and Lunghua. but Mr. Cunningham was assured there was danger of disorders at Nantao because 2,000 regular police and 500 picked volunteers already have taken over the maintenance of law and order. It is understood that Chinese will not attempt to police Chapei, declaring "that is dependent upon the Japanese."

Truce Expected Soon.

Presumably the crumpling of the Nineteenth Route Army will be quickly followed by the signing of a truce and by further retirement of the Chinese forces, since Chapei is inside the twenty-kilometre zone which the Japanese insist must be evacuated.

Between 7:30 and 10 o'clock this morning the Japanese had pushed forward to within two kilometres of Tachang. A vast area was being bombed and shelled with unparalleled intensity and the region was dimmed with smoke from huge conflagrations.

The Chinese began the day's hostilities by using big batteries of big guns, firing from Chapei into the Japanese naval headquarters area in Hongkew Park, where many large fires are now burning. For an hour and a half the Chinese batteries kept the city rocking and the roar of their detonations made sleep impossible.

The Japanese had made exceedingly important gains at 10 o'clock toward Tachang, although the terrain is even more difficult than that around Kiangwan, with a multitude of vertical banked creeks and though won yesterday.

Continued on Page Twelve.

Settlement Stores Reopen And Shoppers Flock to Them

Special Cable to The New York Times.

SHANGHAI, March 1.—Acting upon the request of General Tsai Ting-chai three of the largest Chinese-owned department stores on the Nanking Road of the International Settlement reopened today and many smaller stores and shops followed suit. This action contributed largely to a return to approximate normalcy in general business conditions.

SHANGHAI, March 1 (A.P.).—Stores and offices in the International Settlement reopened today and bargain hunters turned out in droves.

The three big department stores were crowded with shoppers, but the service staff was considerably depleted. Many of the clerks used to live in Chapei and Hongkew and nobody knows where they are now.

JAPAN WILL OFFER NEW TRUCE TERMS

Accepts League Proposal for Armistice at Shanghai With Reservations.

CHINA AFFIRMS AGREEMENT

Plans for Special Assembly at Geneva Tomorrow Await Outcome of Negotiations.

By CLARENCE K. STREIT.
Special Cable to The New York Times.

GENEVA, March 1.—Naotake Sato this evening gave Joseph Paul-Boncour, President of the League Council, Tokyo's definite acceptance of the latter's so-called "President's plan" for a Shanghai truce and a round-table discussion. Mr. Sato added that the "details"—which is to say, the truce—were to be worked out in Shanghai. Later he confirmed his oral communication in a brief note.

The note merely said Japan was "happy to accept the plan the President has submitted. It mentioned none of the reservations which Mr. Sato gave M. Paul-Boncour orally regarding the details of the truce to be settled on the spot, apparently because Japan thought the terms of the "President's plan" included such reservations.

At any rate, these reservations not merely still stand, but it is understood Mr. Sato explained to M. Paul-Boncour that Japan, instead of accepting Admiral Kelly's armistice term, was taking a counter-proposal.

The United States delegation preferred to reserve comment on Tokyo's reply.

Diplomatic Move Seen.

There is a suspicion in Chinese and Soviet circles that, if Japan does really accept the truce terms, she will then try to win through diplomacy what she failed to win on the battlefield by seeking to have the boundaries of the International Settlement at Shanghai extended to include some districts largely populated by Japanese. There is hardly, certainly, in either the "President's plan" or Mr. Sato's declaration yesterday to prevent such a manœuvre, for they bar merely any concession or move which exclusively favors the Japanese.

The wording of the second point of the president's plan" and the whole of Mr. Sato's declaration, especially the third point, appear in some to be designed to facilitate such a plan by their references to strengthening the international character of the Settlement.

"The Chinese appear to regard the United States as the only one in the group on which they can count not to take advantage of the present situation to try to block China's old fight on the whole question of extraterritoriality.

New Settlement Status Hinted.

There is also something significant, although still vague, talk of the need of improving the status of the Shanghai International Settlement and possibly of putting it under League jurisdiction, like Danzig. Although the skepticism here is pointed chiefly toward Japan, some are skeptical too of the Chinese Government being able to keep its troops in the terms of the armistice.

Pending definite developments with regard to the armistice and the

Continued on Page Thirteen.

145 in House Force Vote on Dry Law Test; Texan, Last Signer, Rolls Up in Wheelchair

WASHINGTON, March 1.—An outright vote on whether the House shall consider a proposal to return liquor control to the States was assured today when the necessary 145 members had signed a petition to cite the Judiciary Committee for discharge from further study of the measure.

The vote probably will be taken on March 14, the first "discharge" day on the calendar.

The wets hailed it as the greatest day since national prohibition when the last signature necessary was obtained soon after noon. The 145th member affixing his signature was Representative Mansfield, Texas Democrat. Mr. Mansfield, who is crippled, rolled up to the desk in his wheel chair, while Representative Blanton, Democrat, of Texas, a militant dry, was on his feet chiding the wets

for their "failure" to get the required signatures.

The House was set into an uproar when at that moment it was marked that Mr. Mansfield, from Mr. Blanton's own State, had made the "wet failure" a literal "howling success." Some observers were quick to remark that March 2 is the anniversary of its Declaration of Independence from Mexico.

Representative La Guardia of New York, a wet, sprang to Mr. Blanton to task for his remarks when the news was broadcast that Mr. Mansfield had signed.

"Any time that this House has the experience of seeing the distinguished gentleman from Texas (Mr. Blanton) get unduly excited," Mr. La

Continued on Page Two.

SALES TAX ACCEPTED BY ADMINISTRATION, MILLS ANNOUNCES

Secretary Pledges Cooperation on New Bill Despite Changes in Treasury Plan.

$625,000,000 NOW IS GOAL

Basis for Manufacturers' Levy Is Widened as Subcommittee Completes Draft.

Special to The New York Times.

WASHINGTON, March 1.—Acceptance by the administration of the new tax measure, including a general sales tax applicable to practically every manufacturing industry in the country, was assured today by Secretary Mills.

Mr. Mills told a Ways and Means subcommittee that, even though the original treasury plan had been changed at nearly every major point, the administration would cooperate to the fullest extent in setting in motion and administering the new tax increases.

The subcommittee completed the new tax bill, excepting one or two minor administrative features, this afternoon.

The manufacturers' tax provisions, as agreed on, exempt only a few articles, chiefly commodities for the "poor man's breakfast table" and his daily paper, and the farmer's products, his magazines and periodicals.

The final meeting of the subcommittee resulted in a decision to recommend an even wider basis for the manufacturers' levy. Yesterday the subcommittee tentatively agreed to frame 'the tax so as to produce around $550,000,000 in additional revenue. Today it decided to extend the scope so as to produce $625,000,000.

The additions to the sales tax base were understood to have been made by adding commodities which were being held "in reserve" for special excises.

Agree on Excess Levies.

Final decision on the special excise levies was reached today. Committeemen likewise declined to discuss these, holding that to mention them would be to let loose an "avalanche" of protests on members of Congress. Other excises most prominently mentioned in discussions of the measure were a 5 to 10 per cent consumers' levy on electric energy and illuminating gas; a tax on oil, with a differential upward on oil imports, and an increase of 3 cents a share on stock transfers.

The bill probably will be presented to the full Ways and Means Committee tomorrow afternoon and may be offered to the House for action by Saturday night, according to Representative Crisp of Georgia, acting chairman.

Actual passage in the House by the end of next week was the confident hope of authors of the measure.

Representative Crisp, fatigued from his strenuous work on the bill, was confident today with the hope that it might even be introduced in the House tomorrow. He will offer "the measure as soon as the Ways and Means Committee has agreed to it. It will then be referred back to the committee, which immediately will go through the routine of making a formal report.

Being a revenue bill, it will have priority in the House and, according to Mr. Crisp, will be called up as soon as possible for action. He mentioned next Tuesday as a

Continued on Page Four.

SENATE BODY ACTS FOR BROAD INQUIRY ON SHORT SELLING

Banking Committee Will Go Beyond Hoover Idea in Stock Exchange Investigation.

EFFECTS ON TRADE SOUGHT

Subcommittee Named to Go Into Long and Short Sales and Interstate Phase.

Special to The New York Times.

WASHINGTON, March 1.—An investigation of the New York Stock Exchange was recommended today by the Senate Banking and Currency Committee. A subcommittee, headed by Senator Walcott, Republican, of Connecticut, immediately began drafting a resolution requesting authority for such an investigation from the Senate.

The subcommittee was instructed by the full committee to include in the resolution authorizations covering studies of both long and short selling, the effect of speculation on interstate commerce, the use of interstate communications systems by speculators and the value of a proposed stock transfer tax as a check on speculation.

This decision went far beyond the action believed to have been requested by President Hoover Friday when he called Senator Walcott to the White House for a conference on "bear raiding." No intimation of an investigation of trading other than short selling has come from the White House.

The subcommittee was chosen after an executive session, during which the committee members argued the constitutional right of the Senate to investigate the Stock Exchange.

The full committee finally agreed generally that such authority does exist, and the subcommittee, charged with considering this point in more detail, reached the same conclusion late this afternoon.

Regulation Not Contemplated Now.

Leading members of the full committee, including Senator Walcott, indicated that no regulatory measure affecting the New York license plates stopped a man working on highways and asked to be directed to the Lindbergh home in Hopewell."

Relayed to every outpost, this message gave the searchers their first indication of the possible description of the kidnappers' car. It was so vague, however, that they did not permit it to stop them from questioning the occupants of cars or other descriptions.

As the first alarm was being typed out the telephone connection with the Lambertville barracks had been established and Lieutenant Arthur Keaten, in command of that post, had been informed of the situation. With every available man he could be spared, he started at once for Hopewell.

Upon their arrival Corporal Joseph Wolf, at Lieutenant Keaten's direction, telephoned back confirmation of the kidnapping, but he was not at that time able to add further details to the few which had been furnished by Colonel Lindbergh.

Meanwhile injured detectives were sent on the rounds of known underworld haunts to see if they could pick up any clues as to the identity of the kidnappers.

Window Found Open.

An open window in the nursery of the "Indbergh home at Hopewell indicated how the kidnappers had gained entrance to the house. A close watch has been kept on the baby since it was born, but apparently no member of the family dreamed of the possibility of a kidnapping and no one remained in the nursery last night after the nurse had placed the child in his crib and made sure he was asleep.

The small force under Lieutenant Keaten at once began a careful search of the woody areas surrounding the Lindbergh home, on the possibility of uncovering some clue to the

Continued on Page Three.

LINDBERGH BABY KIDNAPPED FROM HOME OF PARENTS ON FARM NEAR PRINCETON; TAKEN FROM HIS CRIB; WIDE SEARCH ON

FOUR STATES JOIN HUNT

Wire Systems Flash Out Alarm on First Word of Kidnapping.

NEW YORK CAR IS SOUGHT

Roads Are Scoured for Pair Said to Have Inquired Way to the Lindbergh Home.

AUTOS STOPPED ON ROAD

Hunt Here Is Led by Mulrooney —Underworld Haunts Visited in Scores of Cities.

The Baby's Description.

HOPEWELL, N. J., March 2 (A.P.).—A chubby, golden-haired boy closely resembling his famous father—that is the description given Charles Augustus Lindbergh Jr.

He is 20 months old, has blue eyes, curly hair, fair complexion. He is about normal size for a child his age. He has just begun to toddle and is learning to talk.

At 10:40 o'clock last night Colonel Charles A. Lindbergh telephoned the New Jersey State Police headquarters at Trenton that his son had been kidnapped from the Lindbergh home to Hopewell, N. J. Within ten minutes every communication method of modern science had been utilized to broadcast the alarm and to mobilize the police systems of four States and scores of communities in the search.

Colonel Lindbergh had scarcely poured out his tale when the vast machinery of cooperating police systems began to function. While one man was calling the State police barracks at Lambertville, N. J., ten miles from Hopewell, on the telephone, another was writing out this message to be flashed over the police teletype system:

"Colonel Lindbergh's baby kidnapped from Lindbergh home at Hopewell between 7:30 and 10 P. M. Boy, 10 months, dressed in sleeping suit. Search all cars."

Pair in Stolen Car Hunted.

Shortly before 1 o'clock this morning the Princeton Police Department sent over the network of wires the same gave the searchers their first indication of the possible description of the kidnappers' car. It was so vague, however, that they did not permit it to stop them from questioning the occupants of cars or other descriptions.

The Lindbergh baby photographed a year ago. Left to right are Mrs. Dwight W. Morrow, the baby's grandmother; Mrs. Charles Cutter Long, the great-grandmother; Charles Augustus Lindbergh Jr., and Mrs. Charles A. Lindbergh, his mother.

KIDNAPPING OF BABY SPEEDS FEDERAL LAW

Demand in Capital for Statute Providing Death Penalty Expected to Increase.

OFFICIALS HINDERED NOW

Can Act in Almost Any Other Interstate Crime—Patterson Assails "Filthy Act."

Special to The New York Times.

WASHINGTON, Wednesday, March 2.—Immediate pressure for early passage of the measure making kidnapping a Federal offense is held certain to be the result of the kidnapping of Colonel Lindbergh's son.

Senator Patterson of Missouri, who recently introduced a bill to this effect, it provides a death penalty. The measure would give authority to the government when the kidnapped person is removed from one State to another. The bill was approved unanimously two weeks ago by the Senate Judiciary Committee and its supporters are confident that it will be adopted by the Senate.

A companion bill introduced by Representative Cochran of Missouri, chairman of the Committee on Expenditures, has been before the Judiciary Committee in that branch for about ten days. The hearings were scheduled for completion soon and the portraits, before this morning's news, were for a favorable report.

Patterson Denounces Crime.

"It is a shock to me to hear of this outrage," said Mr. Patterson this morning when informed by The New York Times. "I hope the child will soon be returned to its parents. This filthy act will end us in passing the needed legislation, and I am sorry it will not be retroactive, so that the Lindbergh kidnappers can be dealt with by the Federal Government."

On Jan. 23 a telephone message from Chicago to the effect that there was a plot to kidnap General Charles G. Dawes, who had just been appointed president of the Reconstruction Finance Corporation. Mr. Patterson then said that this information came from a newspaper correspondent. It created excitement in Washington official circles, although the General refused to take it seriously. However, it spurred the efforts of those behind the legislation.

Action Urged in Chicago.

As a result, when the House Judiciary Committee began hearings, Colonel Isham Randolph of Chicago, head of the "Secret Six" of that city, and former Representative Cleveland A. Newton of St. Louis came to Washington to urge early action. Mr. Newton gave a long easily list of kidnappings which he said had had

Continued on Page Three.

FATHER SEARCHES GROUNDS FOR CHILD

Lindbergh and Troopers Hunt With Flashlights for Clues on Big Estate.

NEWS ROUSES COUNTRYSIDE

Hundreds of Autos Rush to the Home in Lonely Woodland, Clogging Narrow Road.

Copyrighted, 1932, by The Associated Press.

HOPEWELL, N. J., Wednesday, March 2.—Charles Augustus Lindbergh Jr., 20-month-old son of the flying Colonel, was kidnapped last night from his country home near here. The child, clad in a blue sleeping robe, was put to bed at the usual hour, 7:30 P. M. At about 10 P. M. someone peered into the nursery. The crib was empty.

Beneath the nursery window, footprints showed in the soft earth. These indicated that the kidnappers, moving with such stealth that the Lindberghs, although in the house, heard no sound, had removed their shoes before climbing a ladder to the window. The trail of the shoeless footprints was followed by The Associated Press reporter to the rutted lane, where police believe a waiting car was parked. Feminine footprints, as well as those of a man, were worn scattered about the place.

The first news the Lindberghs had of the crime was when the frightened nurse ran downstairs, screaming that the baby had been kidnapped.

The first newspaper man to reach the home was an Associated Press reporter, who ran a mile over muddy, rut-cut roads to reach a phone to send the first direct news from the residence. This was at 12:40 A. M. Colonel Lindbergh, bare-headed as usual, was pacing the grounds, while troopers and detectives went over the place with flashlights, seeking clues. Mrs. Lindbergh, who telephoned the news to her mother, Mrs. Dwight W. Morrow, at the Morrow homes in Englewood, N. J., was inside the house. A close friend of Mrs. Lindbergh said she was expecting another child within three months.

The house, glowing with lights from top to bottom, was the only bright spot in the wooded, gloomy district. Wishing to get complete privacy, the Lindberghs picked the site from the air and it is almost inaccessible to the outside world. A winding, muddy lane—their private property—leads to the new house from a country highway, called the Stoutsberg-Woratville Road. The entrance to the Lindbergh road is more than four miles from Hopewell and there are few neighbors near enough to be of any aid in time of

Continued on Page Three.

CHILD STOLEN IN EVENING

At 10 P. M. Nurse Finds Boy, 20 Months Old, Gone, in Nightrobe.

FOOTPRINTS IN THE ROOM

Muddy Trail Leads to Ladder in Wood and Half Mile to Highway, Where Car Waited.

WOMAN BELIEVED INVOLVED

Parents, Distraught, Guarded in Home—Police Deny Report of Ransom Note.

Charles Augustus Lindbergh Jr., 20-month-old son of Colonel and Mrs. Charles A. Lindbergh, was kidnapped between 8:30 and 10 o'clock last night from his crib in the nursery on the second floor of his parents' home at Hopewell, near Princeton, N. J.

Apparently the kidnapping was carried out either while Colonel and Mrs. Lindbergh were at dinner, or soon afterward. The baby's nurse, Miss Betty Gow, visited the nursery about 8:30 o'clock and found everything in order there. When she returned at 10 o'clock, however, the crib was empty.

Muddy footprints that trailed across the floor from the crib to an open window bore mute testimony as to how the baby had disappeared. "Miss Gow dashed downstairs. 'The baby's been kidnapped!' she shouted. 'The baby's been kidnapped!' she shouted." Mrs. Lindbergh recalled that earlier in the day she had tried to fasten a screen on the window that had been opened and had been unable to do so.

Satisfied that there was no mistake and that the baby actually was gone, Colonel Lindbergh telephoned Chief of Police Charles Williamson at Hopewell. Williamson drove to the house accompanied by another officer. Outside the door they met the Colonel. He was bareheaded, as such as he frequently wears on his flights.

Footprints Under Window.

Briefly he told Williamson what had occurred. The chief telephoned first to State Police Headquarters at Trenton. Then he, his fellow officer and the Colonel began searching the grounds. Beneath the nursery window were marks where a ladder had stood and the footprints of one person. There were no shoe prints. The kidnapper, apparently, had worn socks or moccasins.

Sixty feet away in rocky ground, at the edge of a wood the Colonel and Chief Williamson found a makeshift ladder. Its rungs were caked with mud. Colonel Lindbergh could not say whether it belonged on the premises. He thought it might have been left there by the builders while the house was being constructed during his right until the spring or to the Orient last Summer with Mrs. Lindbergh.

The searchers had no difficulty in following the footprints across the muddy ground. A second set of tracks joined them near the edge of the woods. They were much smaller. The two officers thought they might be those of a woman.

The search was interrupted by the arrival of a detachment of State Troopers sent from the barracks at Lambertville and the hunt began anew. The tracks were followed to the main highway, about half a mile from the house, where they disappeared. The kidnappers evidently had entered an automobile at this point.

Lindbergh Aids Search.

Carrying a flashlight, Colonel Lindbergh stayed with the search party until long after midnight. Once or twice he returned to the house, but he declined to discuss the kidnapping with newspapermen. In stead, he referred them to Major Schoeffel of the State Police, who told the story in detail.

"I hope you boys will oblige me,"

Continued on Page Three.

"All the News That's Fit to Print."

The New York Times.

LATE CITY EDITION
WEATHER—Cloudy, probably rain today; tomorrow fair and warmer. Temperatures Yesterday—Max., 61; Min., 45.

Copyright, 1932, by The New York Times Company.

VOL. LXXXI....No. 27,138.   NEW YORK, FRIDAY, MAY 13, 1932.   TWO CENTS In New York City | THREE CENTS Within 200 Miles | FOUR CENTS Beyond 200 Miles and the Postal Zone

WALKER GOT $26,535 BONDS FROM J. A. SISTO AS 'GIFT,' TAXI FINANCIER TESTIFIES

PROFIT IN A STOCK DEAL

Control Board Advocate Bought Shares to Aid Mayor, He Swears.

McKEON WAS INTERMEDIARY

Friend of Walker Says He Took Envelope to City Hall and Handed It Over in Auto.

HASTINGS GOT CAB PROFITS

Terminal Company Hired Him at $18,000 a Year, Seabury Is Told—Unpaid Loans Bared.

J. A. Sisto, who had a hand in financing the Parmelee Transportation Company, gave Mayor Walker bonds worth $26,535.51 before the Municipal Assembly passed the Mayor's bill creating a Board of Taxicab Control, the broker testified yesterday before the Hofstadter committee.

When Mr. Sisto and John J. McKeon, who delivered the bonds to Mayor Walker in a sealed envelope in the Winter of 1929, demanded the clock that the investigating committee clerk they would say a word about that matter.

Just before Samuel Seabury, chief counsel to the committee, sprang this surprise, B. M. Seymour, vice president and general manager of the Terminal Cab Company, admitted that his company had paid $26,183 in salary to State Senator John A. Hastings, the Mayor's friend.

Colonel George W. Mixter of the firm of Day & Zimmerman testified that it was the Brooklyn Senator who got his company the job of making a traffic survey of New York in 1928. As a result of that survey, the witness said, Mayor Walker appointed a committee, with Frank P. Walsh as chairman, to study the problem of taxicab control.

That committee, of which Colonel Mixter was a member, reported in September, 1930, recommending a board of control, designed eventually to put the city's taxicab industry on a single-franchise basis, which was what the big companies wanted and the independents dreaded. Through-out the entire period of study, Colonel Mixter said, Senator Hastings was in frequent touch with Day & Zimmerman and the taxicab committee. He looked upon the Brooklyn Senator as the "Mayor's messenger or go-between."

More Hastings Loans Bared

Senator Hastings had been under fire all day at Mr. Seabury sought to show that he had borrowed heavily from companies with which the three backers of the Jamaica Central Railways, as applicant for a Queens bus franchise, were associated, while that company's application was pending in the Board of Estimate.

Park A. Rowley, president of the Manhattan Company, admitted that Hastings had borrowed $7,500 and had not repaid it. Victor A. Grave, president of New York Investors, was the victim of a $25,000 "touch," which he said he would make good himself. H. P. Williams, chairman of the executive committee of the New York Title and Mortgage Company, admitted that business exigencies had forced him to recommend that Senator Hastings be excused from making good a collateral bond on a $350,000 mortgage because it was cheaper than to resort to litigation.

Throughout the whole proceeding, members of the Democratic minority, especially Assemblyman Louis A. Cuvillier, fought to protect the "dignity of the Senate," as represented in the person of the member from Kings County, Senator Samuel Hofstadter, chairman of the committee, repeatedly overruled their objections to the testimony, and it reached the point where the spectators were laughing every time Assemblyman Cuvillier addressed the chair.

But the court room was gravely sedate and silent, and even the minority dropped their fire of objections, when Mr. Sisto, a slim, gray-haired man, dressed as carefully as the Mayor himself, took the stand and unfolded his story.

He began by refusing to waive immunity.

Continued on Page Twelve.

Seabury Has a Prior Right To Explanation, Mayor Says

When Mayor Walker was informed at City Hall of the testimony of J. A. Sisto before the Hofstadter committee he broke in and said:

"I received $26,000 in bonds as the profit from that transaction—is that it?"

Informed that his statement was substantially correct, the Mayor parried questions with:

"Well, now, don't you think that Judge Seabury has a prior right to the answer to that question? I have nothing to say about it now, but it will be answered when Judge Seabury asks about it."

METROPOLITAN LISTS NEW AMERICAN OPERA

"Emperor Jones," Gruenberg's Setting of O'Neill Play, to Be Given in Berlin Also.

TIBBETT WILL SING ROLE

14th Native Work Under Gatti Regime Will Be Produced Early in Coming Season.

The Metropolitan Opera Association will present next season a new American opera, "Emperor Jones," based on Eugene O'Neill's play, by the American composer Louis Gruenberg, it became known yesterday.

The libretto has been prepared by Mr. Gruenberg himself. When he sent Mr. O'Neill a copy of his adaptation, the playwright replied that it had been admirably prepared so that the dramatic qualities and flavor of the work were preserved.

Lawrence Tibbett will enact the part of Jones and Tullio Serafin will conduct. No decision has been made by the Metropolitan as to the date of the presentation, but it is believed it will be early in the season. Erich Kleiber, general music director of the Berlin Staatsoper, one of the largest opera companies in Europe, has already announced that he will produce the opera in Berlin this Fall. It appears, therefore, that Berlin and New York will vie for the honor to give the work its world premičre.

Tom-Tom Used in Score

Mr. Gruenberg has written the opera in two acts. He has made use, naturally, of the beat of the tom-tom which pursues Jones through the drama. This drum beat, which gradually accelerates in the opera, ceases only in certain brief scenes. These are during the visions and hallucinations which haunt Jones as he flees through the forest.

The work calls for a unique arrangement of the stage. The chorus of pursuing Negroes is grouped out of sight of the audience, below and in front of the stage flooring. At first only crossing hands and arms are seen above it. Then, as the pursuit of Jones draws nearer to its quarry, the bodies of the pursuers gradually emerge as yells of hate and triumph gather in volume.

The hallucinations of Jones—of the murdered crap player, of the sheriff whom Jones has killed, and of the auction block—are shown on small raised stages, to indicate that they are figments of the Negro's imagination.

Finally, Jones is seen, a nearly naked savage, seated on the ground with his fellows, swaying in terror as the medicine man leaps on the stage and indicates him as the tribe's victim. At the end the body of the fugitive, who shoots himself with the silver bullet, is carried by the tribesmen into the forest. Choruses of savage exultation are heard dying away in the distance.

Music Moves Swiftly

To this drama Gruenberg has written what appears to be swift and pungent music. The principal moment of lyrical expansion is his prayer for the Lord's aid in his plight, which is in the grand character, but not in slavish imitation, of a Negro spiritual. The score is also reflective of passing incident and gesture on the stage. Each one of the scenes of hallucination has its special musical counterpart. Toward the end, with an immense crescendo and acceleration, several pairs of drums are employed to intensely stirring effect. The opera takes about one hour to perform.

When Erich Kleiber, who conducted the opening weeks of the recent New

Continued on Page Nine.

Hoover Urges 3-Point Relief Plan Of $1,500,000,000 to Use as Loans

Senate Leaders Are Asked to Put the Proposal Before Colleagues—Finance Corporation Would Help States Handle Jobless and Advance Money for Spurring Business.

By ARTHUR KROCK
Special to The New York Times.

WASHINGTON, May 12.—President Hoover today asked Senators Robinson of Arkansas and Watson, the Democratic and Republican leaders of the Senate, to propose to their colleagues a three-point Federal program to stimulate private business in reproductive enterprises; to advance money for self-liquidating projects in States and municipalities, to ameliorate agricultural distress and to loan to States—but not municipalities—money for the relief of unemployed citizens.

The President's plan can be achieved simply by extending the powers and financial resources of the Reconstruction Finance Corporation. It involves no new government borrowings; it does not disturb the processes of budget balancing; it contemplates no bond issues for non-reproductive public works, as was proposed by New York financiers. If Congress will pass an amendment to the act establishing the Reconstruction Finance Corporation, the relief measures can be instituted.

The President's plan provides:

1. That the corporation be authorized to issue an additional $1,500,000,000 in debentures, of the proceeds from which $500,000,000 is to be loaned to States for general relief measures; $40,000,000 for ex- [continued] port agricultural aid, and the remaining $1,100,000,000 loaned to private business for reproductive enterprises, assured by contracts.

2. That State bonds and securities which cannot otherwise be financed be purchased by the corporation when the proceeds of these bonds and securities are to be used for unemployment relief.

3. That the corporation be authorized to loan funds for self-liquidating projects such as toll bridges, tunnels and so forth.

It provides that private business planning reproductive enterprises for which credit cannot be obtained from the banks shall but put on a loaning basis with the corporation, a plan originally proposed by Mr. Hoover but rejected by Congress.

Senator Robinson, after a morning conference with the President, called a meeting of Democrats after the Senate adjourned this afternoon and outlined the President's idea. It was favorably received.

Senator Watson talked to a number of Republicans and reported progress with the idea. Speaker Garner and Minority Leader Snell were also consulted, and tonight Republican members of the Senate Committees on Banking and Currency were called to

Continued on Page Eleven.

TAX BILL'S TARIFFS ASSAILED IN REPORT BY MINORITY GROUP

Their Elimination From Senate Measure Is Demanded and 'Log-rolling' Is Condemned.

GAIN IN REVENUE DOUBTED

Imposts on Oil, Lumber, Copper and Coal Will Mean Embargo, Opponents Assert.

Special to The New York Times.

WASHINGTON, May 12.—Five Democratic members of the Senate Finance Committee opened a fight on the tariff features of the billion-dollar tax bill today in a minority report demanding elimination of the duties on coal, oil, copper and lumber and condemning the "log-rolling" by which, they said, the items were inserted.

Consideration of the report, expected today, was delayed by further debate on the Glass banking bill. When it appeared that the Glass measure could not be disposed of, even within another day, Republican leaders asked that it be side-tracked to give right of way to the tax bill.

Senator Glass gave rather reluctant consent, explaining that he long since had found it wise "not to go up against a buzz saw."

Senator Smoot will open discussion of the tax bill tomorrow. He had finished preparation tonight of a 6,000-word speech recommending the compromise measure, as the prime step toward business recovery through the guarantee of government credit.

Senate leaders at the same time completed plans for a series of night sessions next week, by which it is hoped to complete the revenue measure well before June 10, the date tentatively set for adjournment.

Minority Questions Efficacy

The minority tax bill report was signed by Senators Harrison, George, Walsh of Massachusetts, Costigan and Hull. Democratic members of the Finance Committee whose names are not attached were Senators Barkley of Kentucky, who voted in committee for the coal tariff; Connally of Texas and Gore of Oklahoma, who favored the duty on oil, and King of Utah, who stood for the copper tariff.

The report questioned whether the duties would result in additional revenues, cited adverse decisions on some of the items by the Tariff Commission and predicted that in many cases the consumer would be a sufferer.

The "log-rolling" methods, it said, would be odious even in a general tariff measure. But to resort to "trades, exchanges of votes and on-again, off-again" practices, the minority charges, such as were used in writing the tariff items into an emergency revenue measure, was held by the Democrats to be "an exhibition that will raise serious questions in the public mind concerning the' capacity of representative government to function promptly

Continued on Page Thirteen.

NEW RELIEF GROUP WITH SMITH AT HEAD NAMED BY WALKER

Merged Bureaus on Jobs and Home Aid Have $5,000,000 to Use Until Aug. 1.

UNITY OF EFFORT IS OBJECT

Leading Lawyers, Bankers and Welfare Officials to Begin Tasks on June 1.

Members of the Emergency Work and Relief Administration, formed by a consolidation of the Home Relief Bureau and the Emergency Work Commission, who will assume their tasks on June 1, were notified of their appointments yesterday by Mayor Walker.

The new committee will consist of the following:

ALFRED E. SMITH, Empire State Building, chairman.
FRANK L. POLK, lawyer, former Under Secretary of State, 15 Broad Street.
LAWSON PURDY, executive director, Charity Organization Society, 105 East Twenty-second Street.
GEORGE V. McLAUGHLIN, president, Brooklyn Trust Company, 177 Montague Street, Brooklyn.
JOHN A. STEPHENS, Thompson Starrett Company, 101 East Twenty-third Street.
SOLOMON LOWENSTEIN, executive director, Federation for Support Jewish Philanthropic Societies, 71 West Forty-seventh Street.
FRANK J. TAYLOR, Commissioner of Public Welfare.
MARY L. GIBBONS, Catholic Charities, 10 East Thirty-fourth Street.
WILLIAM EWING, J. P. Morgan & Co., 23 Wall Street.
VICTOR F. RIDDER, president, New York State Board of Social Welfare, 25 North William Street.
WILLIAM J. HODSON, executive director, Welfare Council, 151 East Twenty-second Street.
S. SLOAN COLT, president, Bankers Trust Company, 14 Wall Street.
WILLIAM H. MATTHEWS, Association for Improving the Condition of the Poor; director, Emergency Work Commission, 105 East Twenty-third Street.
JOSEPH J. BAKER, director, Brooklyn Bureau of Jewish Charities, 285 First Street.
RALPH WOLF, president, Board of Jewish Social Service, 24 Pine Street.

Coordination of Efforts

The purpose of the joint committee will be to eliminate the duplication of investigations, obtain a closer cohesion of all public relief under moneys appropriated by the city and plan for the performance of public work other than by contract. It will also be the task of the committee to select the most beneficial method of assigning those in need to work relief or home relief.

The committee will have $5,000,000 at its disposal from June 1 to Aug. 1. Mayor Walker announced that he was pleased that so many members of the Emergency Work Commission had agreed to continue with the new organization. Cornelius N. Bliss, chairman of the Emergency Work Commission, whose term began in October, 1931, will relinquish his work on June 1.

Because of the urgent need that still persists among thousands of New York's unemployed for clothing and food the clothing relief and food relief activities of the Emergency Unemployment Relief Committee will continue indefinitely instead of being discontinued as had been planned, it

Continued on Page Eleven.

LINDBERGH BABY FOUND DEAD NEAR HOME; MURDERED SOON AFTER THE KIDNAPPING 72 DAYS AGO AND LEFT LYING IN WOODS

POLICE INTENSIFY HUNT

Curtis, Norfolk Agent, and Condon, Who Paid Ransom, at Hopewell.

TO AID PROSECUTOR TODAY

Schwarzkopf Says Restraints Designed to Safeguard Baby Now Can Be Thrown Off.

A GROUP UNDER SUSPICION

Gov. Moore Pledges Relentless Hunt—Mulrooney Also Promises Full Aid.

Dr. J. F. Condon, the Bronx lecturer who acted as intermediary in the futile payment by Colonel Lindbergh of $50,000 ransom for his son, and John H. Curtis, the Norfolk boat builder, who also has been conducting negotiations, arrived at Hopewell for questioning by the police early this morning. They were scheduled to go to the prosecutor's office in Mercer County later today.

They arrived at the Lindbergh home shortly before 2 o'clock this morning and were at once closeted with the police. A few minutes before their arrival Colonel H. Norman Schwarzkopf, commanding the New Jersey State Police, made this announcement:

"Dr. Condon and Mr. Curtis will be at these headquarters in a few minutes for questioning in connection with this case and they will be turned over by the police authorities at this point to the prosecuting authorities tomorrow morning."

May Have Secret Data

It is believed that the two intermediaries may have confidential information about the kidnappers which they are now ready to turn over to the authorities.

With this announcement the head of the New Jersey State Police indicated that the hunt for the murderers would be pursued with the aid of State, New York City and Federal authorities, throwing off the restraint that hitherto had hampered the police effort. It was disclosed further by the New Jersey authorities that immediate steps are being taken to arrest a group of persons suspected of kidnapping the Lindbergh baby.

The police started their search immediately with a close though apparently unpromising examination at the place where the baby was found.

"No footprints were found in the vicinity of where the baby's body was located," said Colonel Schwarzkopf in a statement early this morning. "This whole territory was thoroughly scoured by investigators from this office, even to the extent of scraping the surface of the ground around where the body was found and putting it all in containers and bringing it to these headquarters for the purpose of test and analysis."

Moore Pledges Every Effort

Governor A. Harry Moore of New Jersey promised that everything possible would be done to "get the murderers" and announced that he expected to confer today with Colonel Schwarzkopf, head of the New Jersey State police. Meanwhile a grand jury investigation of all the Bronx incidents in the case was predicted last night by an aide of the Bronx District Attorney, Charles B. McLaughlin.

President John Grier Hibben of Princeton University called upon the law-enforcement forces of the country to unite in their hunt for the criminals, in a statement issued after he visited the Lindbergh home with Mrs. Hibben last night.

"A national systematic effort must be made right away," he said. "The authorities have been holding off from the beginning in the fear that their actions must cause the death of the child. Now that is over. The forces of law in the country must unite to get the persons who have done this thing."

Schwarzkopf's Statement

Colonel Schwarzkopf made clear his course in regard to the hunt in an earlier statement, as follows:

"As long as there was a possibility of the baby being alive, the police have been acting with a certain amount of suppressed activity in order not to interfere with any negotiations that might result in the safe return of the baby.

"Now that the body of the baby

Continued on Page Two.

WHERE KIDNAPPERS LEFT SLAIN BABY.

SYMPATHY POURS IN FROM ALL THE WORLD

Grief and Horror Evidenced in Capital Where Hoovers Request Lindbergh News.

ORTIZ RUBIO IS SADDENED

Messages Sent From Mexico City—Inquiries Made From London to Gov. Moore.

Widespread sympathy for the bereaved parents and relatives of Charles A. Lindbergh Jr. and the American people was expressed in messages that poured into the Lindbergh home at Hopewell, N. J., last night from various parts of the world. Officials and civilians who had hastened to join the international search for the kidnappers, when the abduction became known sought to assuage the feelings they knew would follow in the wake of the announcement.

The grief and horror with which the nation received the final answer to the question regarding the safety of the child were evidenced at once in Washington, where the report reached the President and Mrs. Hoover among the first. Attachés at the White House, the Associated Press announced, immediately got in touch with the New Jersey authorities to obtain official information.

Deeply moved, Vice President Curtis said, "They have my deepest sympathy, and my most heartfelt condolences go out to the bereaved mother and Colonel Lindbergh and to their families in their sorrow." Mr. Curtis exclaimed with feeling: "It is a most shocking thing."

Unofficial like official Washington was horrified at the news and few persons were able to express their feelings about the tragedy. Captain Emory S. Land, cousin of Colonel Lindbergh, could only declare: "Anything I could say would be futile."

The shocked surprise with which Washington officials, many of them personal friends of the aviator, received the information was exemplified when the meeting of the Democratic steering committee of the Senate broke up on receipt of the barest announcement of the discovery at 6:45 o'clock.

The fifteen Senators present, including Senator Wagner of New York, dropped a momentous question under consideration to express their regrets and seek further details of the development.

"I have never heard more shocking news," Senator Wagner declared.

"It is too awful to talk about," said Senator Norris of Nebraska.

Senator Norbeck of South Dakota called the discovery "most tragic," adding "My most heartfelt sympathy goes out to Colonel and Mrs. Lindbergh."

"The world is shocked at the enormity of the crime," Senator Walcott of Connecticut said.

Mrs. Evelyn Walsh McLean, wife of Edward B. McLean, who has put forth great effort and expended upward of $100,000 in an attempt to find the baby, refused to be quoted, but was said by her attorney to be deeply shocked and grieved. He said

Continued on Page Two.

COLONEL BELIEVED ON A YACHT AT SEA

Reported Somewhere Off Block Island on Search for the Kidnappers.

INFORMED OF BABY'S DEATH

Departed May 4 With Norfolk Aides on Mission That Had Seemed Promising.

Colonel Lindbergh was believed to have been on a yacht, somewhere off Block Island, when the body of his son was discovered yesterday. He had been there searching for the kidnappers of his son. There is no question that he had heard of the finding of the body, for Colonel H. Norman Schwarzkopf said that he had been notified, and one of the men with him—telephoning to Norfolk—said that the news had been received.

Colonel Lindbergh set out from Norfolk on May 4 on board the yacht Marcon, owned by Charles H. Consolvo of Baltimore. With him were John H. Curtis, Norfolk boat builder, and one of the trio of negotiators from that city; Edwin A. Bruce of Elmira, N. Y., and Lieutenant George L. Richard, a naval flier. The Marcon cruised up and down the coast near Norfolk until last Saturday, when the men transferred to another boat, which headed out to sea.

Lieutenant Richard Telephones.

The telephone message last night was from Lieutenant Richard to Mrs. Curtis, and was merely "Mr. Curtis is well, and we have heard the news." He could not say from where he had telephoned, nor did he say definitely whether Colonel Lindbergh was still on board. But the Rev. H. Dobson Peacock, one of the other Norfolk negotiators, said that "as far as I know" he was. The second yacht carrying them was generally supposed to have headed directly for Block Island.

When the Marcon sailed from Norfolk it was reported to be going to keep a rendezvous with the kidnappers of Colonel Lindbergh's son, who, according to an unverified rumor at that time, were said to be on a foreign ship beyond the twelve-mile limit. Colonel Lindbergh boarded the yacht while in Chesapeake Bay, but bad weather kept the vessel from going out for two days.

The yacht has been running along the Atlantic Coast, it was said, searching for the other ship. Colonel Lindbergh, during the time he was on board, kept watch with the other members of the crew, sleeping in his clothes, always on the lookout for a sign of the second ship. The name of the yacht to which he transferred is not known, nor is its destination. It went straight to sea, however, as soon as he boarded it.

Quest Seemed Promising.

The Norfolk quest had been one of the most promising since the case began. Three prominent citizens of that city were involved, all of them certain that they had been in touch with the kidnappers. They were, besides Mr. Curtis, Rear Admiral Guy H. Burrage, retired, and the Rev. Mr. Peacock. Convinced that they had been in communication with the wanted men, they paid Colonel Lind- [continued on Page Three.]

BODY MILE FROM HOPEWELL

Discovered by Chance Near Centre of Wide Search for Child.

HALF-COVERED BY LEAVES

Skull Fractures Caused Death—Body and Clothing Are Identified by Nurse.

MOTHER IS BRAVE AT NEWS

Neighbors Had Complained That Hunt in Vicinity Had Not Been Thorough.

The baby son of Colonel Charles A. Lindbergh was found dead yesterday afternoon. The child had been murdered.

The body, lying face down in a depression and partly covered with dead leaves and wind-blown débris, was discovered by a Negro truck driver, in a patch of woods in the Sourland Mountains less than five miles from the Lindbergh home near Hopewell, N. J.

The discovery was made by accident at 3:15 yesterday afternoon when the driver, walking into the woods from the road, found what he thought was a child's foot sticking out of the ground and notified the police. The identification followed quickly and the official announcement of the Lindbergh baby's fate was made at the Lindbergh home at 6:45 P. M.

The child evidently had been killed soon after he was stolen from his crib in the nursery on the night of March 1. Whether he had been killed with calculating purpose by criminals who found it advantageous to them to get rid of the child, or whether he had been thrown down by kidnappers fleeing in a panic, was not determined last night.

Two Fractures of Skull.

The body showed the marks of two fractures of the skull, one on the left side and the other on the right. The latter was a hole a half-inch in diameter. It was not definitely established whether this was a bullet hole or the result of a blow with a blunt instrument, but since no bullet was found the authorities were inclined to the belief that it was the latter.

The manner in which the baby died was officially stated as follows:

"The diagnosis of the cause of death is a fractured skull due to external violence.

"Unquestionably it was a brutal murder," said Dr. Charles H. Mitchell, County Physician of Mercer County, last night, after he had completed an autopsy.

The condition of the body indicated that the child has been dead at least two months—the kidnapping occurred seventy-two days ago yesterday—and there was a strong probability that he had been killed on the very night of the kidnapping.

Mother Bearing Up Well.

Mrs. Lindbergh and her mother, Mrs. Dwight W. Morrow, were at home when the body was found, but were in complete seclusion.

Despite the shock of the discovery, Mrs. Lindbergh was bearing up courageously, as she has from the beginning, it was learned last night. Colonel Lindbergh, who has been away much of the time in recent weeks making fruitless journeys in an attempt to make contact with the kidnappers, was not at home when the discovery was made. Colonel H. Norman Schwarzkopf, commanding the New Jersey State police, said that Colonel Lindbergh had been informed of his baby's death, however, and was on his way home. He did not disclose where the Colonel had

Continued on Page Three.

"All the News That's Fit to Print."

The New York Times.

LATE CITY EDITION
POSTSCRIPT
WEATHER—Possibly showers today; tomorrow fair and warmer.
Temperatures Yesterday—Max. 81; Min. 66.

Copyright, 1932, by The New York Times Company.

VOL. LXXXI....No. 27,173. ···· ‡ NEW YORK, FRIDAY, JUNE 17, 1932. TWO CENTS In New York City | THREE CENTS Within 200 Miles | FOUR CENTS Elsewhere

HOOVER, CURTIS RENAMED ON FIRST BALLOTS; DRY-WET PLANK IS DEFENDED BY STIMSON

LAUSANNE TO OFFER REPARATIONS TRUCE TILL FINAL SOLUTION

Britain and France Agree on Plan to Be Put to Reich at Closed Session Today.

IDEA IS TO SATISFY PAPEN

Proposal Can Be Interpreted Fairly in Germany as Virtual End to War Debts.

M'DONALD ASKS BOLDNESS

In Opening Speech He Holds Out Hope That We May Cooperate in Solving Economic Problems.

By FREDERICK T. BIRCHALL.
Wireless to THE NEW YORK TIMES.

LAUSANNE, June 16.—To a private plenary meeting of the Lausanne conference tomorrow will be presented a memorandum, on which Great Britain and France have already agreed, extending the suspension of all reparations payments, including the French unconditional annuities under the Young Plan, until a final settlement can be worked out.

The idea behind this move is that it will give Chancellor von Papen of Germany something to take home that can be fairly interpreted as a practical ending of reparation payments and therefore something to talk about in the German elections. A second advantage of the step is that it removes from the Lausanne conference the curse of having to work in a hurry before payments by Germany should begin again on July 2.

Third, it is believed it will satisfy French opinion as preparing the way for a larger consideration of the entire economic situation, upon which Prime Minister MacDonald appealed in his opening speech today.

Not Moratorium Extension.

It is to be noted that this proposal is not for an "extension of the moratorium," which would bring in the matter of United States debts. It is rather for a continuation of the European status quo and therefore in full accord with the purpose of this conference. Germany, however, would not be obligated to pay indemnities to the Bank for International Settlements on the next instalments, due July 2, of non-postponable reparations she owes France, which under the present arrangement are returned to Germany in the form of railway bonds redeemable in ten years. Thereby will be removed the metaphorical sword overhanging Chancellor von Papen's head. Yet, at the same time, the end of reparations is not formally acknowledged, which satisfies Premier Herriot of France.

Should the proposal prove acceptable tomorrow it will be in fact a success for the method of temporizing as against the clean-cut method of cancellation which Germany came here to demand. On that point also von Papen is still to be heard from, but the friendliness toward him manifested by frequent visits from M. Herriot and Mr. MacDonald may not be without reward.

Pending the complete economic discussion and final settlement that Mr. MacDonald envisages, the work of exploration and liquidation, if the proposal carries, will be continued by technicians and experts. Thus the conference will in truth have fulfilled some of the expectations based on it as a preparatory movement toward a real world adjustment.

MacDonald Sounds Keynote.

By P. J. PHILIP.
Wireless to THE NEW YORK TIMES.

LAUSANNE, June 16.—Elected unanimously as president of the Lausanne conference, Prime Minister Ramsay MacDonald in a speech that strongly set forth the principles that must be established began the work of trying to get Europe to put its financial house in order.

He mentioned the United States twice, both times to emphasize her unity with the rest of the world. But there was no mention, and there was no mention, of Europe's debts to the United States. That is another problem to be settled at some other time.

Continued on Page Four.

Without Benefit of Congress—Henry Ma Elliott in July Scribner's Magazine.—Adv't.

12-Year Sentence on American In Assault Protested to Spain

Special to THE NEW YORK TIMES.

WASHINGTON, June 16.—United States Consular officers at Malaga and Seville, Spain, have intervened with the military authorities in behalf of John C. Wiley of Inglewood, Cal., who has been sentenced by a military tribunal to twelve years' imprisonment, with recommendation for commutation, on charges of assaulting a carabinero in Malaga on March 10.

The carabinero is said to have suffered a broken nose and to have been incapacitated for duty for nineteen days.

The State Department said today that the case would come up for review soon and the American officials had been promised that it would be submitted to the Premier. The consuls contend that the sentence was out of all proportion to the offense and have urged commutation or deportation.

CHILE OVERTHROWS REGIME AS TOO RED

Army Storms Palace and Captures General Grove as His Guards Quit Him.

Mobs Fight in Streets as Planes Circle Overhead, Dropping Flares.

Special Cable to THE NEW YORK TIMES.

SANTIAGO, Chile, Friday, June 17.—Colonel Marmaduke Grove was overthrown early today as provisional head of the Chilean Government, according to a manifesto by army leaders who launched a counter-revolt against him last night.

Troops opposed to communism surrounded the government palace and demanded Colonel Grove's surrender by midnight. An earlier manifesto signed by General Agustin Moreno on behalf of all sections of the army said if he did not yield by that time, planes and troops would bombard the palace if necessary to obtain control of the government.

Colonel Grove replied that he would die rather than surrender. Shortly after midnight troops began attacking the palace and soon afterward it was announced by the counter-revolutionists that their drive had been successful.

At an early hour the army leaders had not yet named the new junta to take over the government, but it was assumed that Carlos G. Dávila, who, because of his moderate views, was driven out of the junta dominated by Colonel Grove, would be a member.

Coup a Blow at Communism.

Both manifestos declared the counter-revolt was intended to prevent the establishment of communistic practices and to carry forward the socialistic principles enunciated by the junta which seized power from former President Juan Esteban Montero on June 4.

Early last evening rebellious troops began marching on the palace and surrounded it, facing a loyal guard of carabineros. Soon after the midnight attack began, it was observed that the members of the Presidential junta were quietly abandoning their arms and slipping out of the courtyard and palace. When the surrender of the men was practically complete General Moreno announced the success of the counter-revolt.

Earlier there had been considerable disorder in the city, with mobs parading and shouting for and against Colonel Grove.

The rising was made necessary, according to the counter-revolutionists, by the failure of Colonel Grove to keep promises made before the revolution of June 4 and by his encouragement of Communism. The new régime, it was declared, has the support of the entire army, will put down Communism with a firm hand and will maintain order throughout the country.

Colonel Grove Captured.

SANTIAGO, Chile, Friday, June 17 (A).—Colonel Marmaduke Grove, radical member of the new Socialist junta that deposed President Montero twelve days ago, was captured early today in a counter-revolutionary overthrow of his régime.

When the troops first approached the palace several officers got past the guards and demanded the surrender of General Grove, who re-

Continued on Page Three.

BONUS BILL REPORTED ADVERSELY, 14 TO 2; CAMP MORALE SAGS

Break-Up Starts After Senate Delays Action Till Today and Defeat Appears Likely.

CRUCIAL PERIOD AT HAND

Officials Believe Jobless Men Will Roam Nation in Bands, Hungry and Penniless.

TEMPER OF MEN ON EDGE

Former Leader Flares at the Police, Saying Veterans Are Going to Quit "Soft-Pedaling."

From a Staff Correspondent.
Special to THE NEW YORK TIMES.

WASHINGTON, June 16.—The Senate vote on the Patman bill for the payment of $2,400,000,000 to World War veterans, which was passed by the House yesterday and was scheduled for action by the upper body today, was deferred until tomorrow after the Finance Committee had reported it adversely following a swift consideration this morning.

Late this afternoon Senator Smoot, chairman of the Finance Committee, gave formal notice that the bonus bill would be taken up as soon as the Senate met tomorrow morning. Opponents of the measure say that it will be defeated in the Senate, and even should it unexpectedly succeed, its veto by President Hoover is assured. Its friends admit that it could not possibly be passed over his veto.

"Just before the Senate recessed tonight Senator Watson obtained unanimous consent to have the bonus made unfinished business. He remarked that he hoped for a final vote tomorrow, and said that if this did not materialize there would be ample time for discussion anyway.

With today's developments the morale of the bonus expeditionary force, which has remained high in the face of amazing difficulties, began almost visibly to sag. The unexpected delay, the adverse report of the committee and the growing extent of defeat began to weigh heavily on the thousands of destitute ex-service men encamped here, and the movement of the veterans homeward only a trickle thus far, was notably increased.

Officials believed that the beginning of the long-expected break-up of the camp was at hand, and would begin in earnest after the Senate vote.

Officials Plan Evacuation.

Hence they began planning for what they concede is the most dangerous period of the bonus army's existence—the period in which the men will start roving about the country as isolated bands of unemployed, without funds, without food and without the discipline to which they submitted voluntarily when they thought there was a chance of achieving their objective.

The bill was proposed in the Finance Committee by fourteen of the sixteen members present. Those voting for the adverse report were Senators Watson, Reed, Shortridge, Couzens, Keyes, Thomas of Idaho, Metcalf and Smoot, all Republicans, and King, George, Walsh of Massachusetts, Connally, Gore and Harrison, Democrats. Those voting favorably were Senators La Follette and Jones of Washington, both Republicans.

Senator La Follette later explained on the floor that he felt that a measure so important should not have had an adverse report, but should have been reported without recommendation.

A motion by Senator Connally to pay the present value of the adjusted compensation certificates, giving the veterans the option of cashing in and surrendering them now or of holding them until 1945, was defeated by vote of 11 to 4.

Senator Connally then proposed an amendment to change the interest rate on loans on the certificates from 4 per cent to 3, but this also was voted down. A similar rate cut was proposed of Senator Thomas of Oklahoma, principal proponent of the bonus payment in the Senate, that the certificates be cashed when the holders presented proof of absolute want.

When the bill was reported to the

Continued on Page Two.

DENIES IT IS A 'STRADDLE'

Secretary, Over Radio, Says Liquor Plan Is 'Definite and Logical.'

'FAITH' WITH PEOPLE KEPT

'Real Gains' Under Dry Law Must Be 'Disentangled From Evils Incurred,' He Holds.

THE ADMINISTRATION REPLY

Mr. Stimson's Address Is First Move to Justify the Party's Stand to Country.

Special to THE NEW YORK TIMES.

CHICAGO, June 16.—Defending the prohibition plank in the Republican platform, Secretary of State Stimson declared over the radio tonight that instead of being a "straddle," the proposed method of dealing with the prohibition problem was "consistent, definite, logical and well-founded in law and fact."

Secretary Stimson was speaking over a nation-wide radio hook-up of the National Broadcasting Company and his was the first move on the part of the administration to justify the party's stand before the country. Asserting that the Eighteenth Amendment represented in its adoption the hopes of millions of American wives and mothers, he added:

"To ruthlessly destroy such a faith by indiscriminately condemning an effort like the Eighteenth Amendment, instead of taking the trouble to disentangle the real gains that have been accomplished from the evils which have been incurred, would be an act of social folly and national wrong."

MR. STIMSON'S ADDRESS.

Secretary Stimson's address was as follows:

"My friends of the radio audience: "At their meeting last night the members of the Republican National Convention took a momentous step in the direction of American constitutional history. By a vote of 1,153 they have unanimously recommended to submit to the voters of this country a proposal to change the Eighteenth Amendment.

"They divided by a vote of 681 to 472 as to the form of the proposed change which should be submitted. But they were unanimous in recommending the submission of a proposal to change. Should the Democratic party in its approaching convention take similar action, the constitutional steps toward this momentous change will be well under way.

"There has been so much misunderstanding on the subject that it is well to analyze carefully the nature of what has been done. In the first place, both parties, in the convention last evening, advocated a new amendment to the Constitution. Even those who seek solely the repeal of the Eighteenth Amendment require a new amendment to accomplish such a repeal.

"The two proposals which were before the Republican National Convention last evening differed only as to the form which the new amendment should take.

Basis of the Majority Plank.

"In the second place, both propositions were clear and explicit, and the difference between them was fundamental and easily understood. The newspaper criticism that the majority plank was a straddle is quite unfounded. It is perfectly consistent, perfectly definite and perfectly logical. It is well founded in law and fact.

"Let us see what was this fundamental difference between the two proposals and the reason for that difference. One proposal was an impatient demand to abrogate the entire work of the past thirteen years under the prohibition amendment, and to confess it to be an entire failure; to go away with all direct power on the part of the Federal Government in regard to the liquor traffic, and to leave the situation in respect to liquor as it was before 1919.

"This proposal was tantamount to asserting that everything which we have done during those years was useless or evil, that we should confess it to be a great and complete failure and go back and start over again.

"Right here it is well to remind you of what is frequently forgotten, namely, that the Eighteenth Amendment did not come out of thin air

Continued on Page Seventeen.

Harris & Ewing Photo.
HERBERT HOOVER.   CHARLES CURTIS.   Harris & Ewing Photo.

HOOVER LAYS PLANS FOR COMING FIGHT

His First Move Is Selection of Everett Sanders to Be Head of Committee.

SPEAKING TOURS UNLIKELY

Friends of Executive Expect Him to Direct Much of Fight From His Camp on the Rapidan.

Special to THE NEW YORK TIMES.

WASHINGTON, June 16.—Gratified by the outcome of the Republican convention, President Hoover began preparations this afternoon for the campaign for his re-election.

His first move, after sending a message of appreciation for his nomination to Chairman Snell of the convention, was to let the national committee know that he preferred the election of Everett Sanders of Indiana as chairman of the committee.

Mr. Sanders is a former Representative, was secretary to President Coolidge and is experienced in national politics and national campaigns. Since 1929 he has been practicing law here and in Chicago.

The new chairman and the executive committee of the national committee are expected to come here shortly and map out campaign plans with the President. No definite word escaped from the White House to confirm the suggestion made today, but it was predicted by Mr. Hoover's close political advisers that he would conduct the campaign from here and make relatively few speeches. It was pointed out that this would be in accordance with past custom when Presidents standing for re-election have attended to the duties of their high office and not engaged in far-flung campaign trips or many speeches.

Trip to California Suggested.

There is some talk among friends of the President of his going to California by warship through the Panama Canal to keep an engagement tentatively set for him to open the Olympic Games at Los Angeles late in July. This would permit a campaign trip back across the country.

Close friends of the President, however, declared that practically all chance of his going to California for notification ceremonies at his Palo Alto home had disappeared, due to the pressure of public business and the efforts he is making to combat the economic depression.

The ceremonies notifying him of the nomination and his acceptance speech, it was predicted, would be held either here or at his Rapidan camp in about six weeks. The chances were said to favor Washington and there were suggestions by his advisers that his acceptance speech might be delivered from the south portico of the White House.

President Coolidge, it was recalled, delivered his acceptance speech here in 1924 at a night meeting in Memorial Continental Hall.

In any event the Rapidan camp will be the scene of important campaign activities, since the President intends to spend week-ends there during the Summer as often as possible.

Continued on Page Fourteen.

Ballot for President

Special to THE NEW YORK TIMES.

CHICAGO, June 16.—The vote of the Republican National Convention by which President Hoover was renominated here today was as follows:

State	Delegates	France	Dawes	France	Wadsworth	Hoover
Alabama	19					19
Arizona	9					9
Arkansas	11					11
California	47					47
Colorado	15					15
Connecticut	19					19
Delaware	9					9
Florida	16					16
Georgia	16					16
Idaho	11					11
Illinois	61					61½
Indiana	33					33
Iowa	29					29
Kansas	21					21
Kentucky	29					29
Louisiana	13					13
Maine	15					15
Maryland	19					19
Massachusetts	35					35
Michigan	44					44
Minnesota	25					25
Mississippi	11					11
Missouri	39					39
Montana	11					11
Nebraska	19					19
Nevada	9					9
N. Hampshire	11					11
New Jersey	35					35
New Mexico	9					9
New York	97					97
No. Carolina	28					28
No. Dakota	13					13
Ohio	55					55
Oklahoma	25					25
Oregon	13					13
Pennsylvania	75					75
Rhode Island	11					11
So. Carolina	11					11
So. Dakota	13					13
Tennessee	25					25
Texas	49					49
Utah	11					11
Vermont	11					11
Virginia	25					25
Washington	17					17
West Virginia	19					19
Wisconsin	27	4	6	13	1	1½
Wyoming	9					9
Alaska	2					2
Dist. of Col.	2					2
Hawaii	2					2
Philippines	2					2
Porto Rico	2					2
Total	**1,154**	**4**	**6**	**13**	**1**	**1,126½**

*There was nothing. †One absent.

CURTIS VICTORY WON AGAINST FIELD OF 12

Snell, Harbord, Alvin Fuller, Replogle and MacNider Were Put in Nomination.

PENNSYLVANIA TURNS TIDE

Suddenly Gives 75 to Kansan—Foes Unable to Muster Behind One Candidate.

By L. C. SPEERS.
Special to THE NEW YORK TIMES.

CHICAGO, June 16.—Charles Curtis of Kansas won renomination as the Republican Vice Presidential candidate, but it was not an easy victory, and save for the fact that Pennsylvania swung its seventy-five votes to him after the roll-call of the States was concluded, he would have been 19¼ ballots short of the majority necessary for nomination.

The anti-Curtis elements in the convention fought to the last, but were unable to concentrate on any one candidate. With General Charles G. Dawes standing as their candidate, there was apparently every justification for their boast they had Mr. Curtis stopped, but with the Illinoisan out of the picture the backbone of the opposition was broken.

Six nominations were made for Vice President, and thirteen names, all told, were on the tally sheet when the roll-call was completed. One of them was that of Senator Couzens of Michigan, who received two of the eleven "Progressive" votes in the Wisconsin delegation. The fact that Mr. Couzens was born in Canada, and therefore ineligible, did not deter the La Follettites from allotting him a share of their honorary vote.

Three ex-soldiers constituted the main opposition to the renomination of Mr. Curtis—Hanford MacNider of Iowa, former National Commander of the American Legion; Major Gen. James G. Harbord of New York, chief of staff of the A. E. F., and General Edward Martin, chairman of the Republican State Committee of Pennsylvania.

Six Placed in Nomination.

Mrs. Edward Everett Gann, sister of the Vice President, was on the firing line to the end. She was tired and smiling when "Pennsylvania withdrew the name of General Martin and cast its seventy-five votes for her brother, which assured his renomination on the first ballot.

The six nominations placed before the convention were those of Mr. Curtis, former Governor Alvin E. Fuller of Massachusetts, Mr. MacNider, J. Leonard Replogle of Florida, Representative Bertrand Snell of New York, the permanent chairman of the convention, and General Harbord.

Those who in addition to these were named in the voting that followed were Mr. Dawes, Judge William S. Kenyon of the United States Circuit Court of Appeals, Senator Couzens, Secretary Hurley of Oklahoma, David Ingalls, Republican

Continued on Page Thirteen.

REPUBLICAN PRESS SPLIT ON 'WET PLANK'

Many Papers Hold That It Is a 'Meaningless Evasion'—Others See Notable Step.

Editorial comment of Republican and independent newspapers over the nation differs on the merits of the prohibition plank in the Republican platform, telegraphed excerpts of editorials to THE NEW YORK TIMES indicated last night, with the wet papers bitter at what they called a "straddle."

In New York, The Sun declared that out of the "mountain of minds" at Chicago comes a "ridiculous mouse." The evident purpose of its authors "was to be obscure, and they have succeeded."

The Post, also Republican, headed its editorial "A moral failure at Chicago," and The World-Telegram, wet and independent, agreed with numerous other newspapers in calling the plank a "meaningless evasion."

The Herald Tribune, wet and Republican, declared that "in some paradise for politicians may yet be devised a compromise more inclusive and vague than the wet-moist-dry plank. * * * To date it has no rival."

It added that the "great compromise of Chicago can retire for a long rest, assured of the hearty disapproval of every one with an honest conviction on the subject."

The Chicago Tribune, Republican

Continued on Page Fifteen.

CHEER HOOVER 27 MINUTES

Delegates Give 1,126 1-2 Votes on First Ballot, 634 1-4 to Curtis.

NEW YORK FOR HARBORD

France Ejected From Rostrum —Coolidge's Name Fails to Stir Convention.

HOOVER VICTORY COMPLETE

Administration Had 200 Votes in Reserve—Convention Ends After Nominations.

By ARTHUR KROCK.
Special to THE NEW YORK TIMES.

CHICAGO, June 16.—Under the disclosed domination of the President, the Republican national convention at its closing session today renominated Herbert Hoover and gave a grudging but safe majority to Charles Curtis of Kansas, renominated as the party candidate for Vice President.

Mr. Hoover received 1,126½ votes on the first ballot, his nomination immediately thereafter being made unanimous. Mr. Curtis, the beneficiary of a last-minute switch of Pennsylvania's 75 votes from its Republican State Chairman, General Edward Martin, to the Vice President, had a first ballot majority of 19¼, with a total of 634¼. His nomination also was made unanimous. Until Pennsylvania responded to the Administration goad, Mr. Curtis lacked 19¼ votes of the sum required for his renomination.

It has been twenty years since the obvious will of a Republican National Committee has been so completely and publicly subordinated to a President's program. In 1912, as today, both President and Vice President were renominated, the only time in its history that the Republican party has repeated the ticket.

But then Theodore Roosevelt bolted the convention and formed the Bull Moose party, badly defeating the regular Republicans under William H. Taft in the election and assuring the victory of the Democratic ticket headed by Woodrow Wilson.

No Prospect of a Bolt.

So far as the political elements of the Republican party are concerned, there were no prospects of a bolt as the result of the defeat of the regular plank last night and the renomination of Mr. Curtis today. The only menacing element was the insurgency of the New York delegation. Today its members cast ninety-five of their ninety-seven votes for General J. G. Harbord for Vice President. Mr. Curtis stopped, but with the Illinoisan out of the picture the backbone of the opposition was broken. Had not Charles D. Hilles, the national committeeman, declined to aid the State chairman, W. Kingsland Macy, in his effort to supplant Representative Ruth B. Pratt as national committee woman, this steadfast friend of the President would have been defeated.

The church drys, and those who are dry before they are Republican or Democratic, will not be heard from until they meet in national conclave in August, after they have examined the prohibition plank which the Democrats will adopt in Chicago the week after next.

It may be that then, as they did against James W. Wadsworth Jr. and Charles H. Tuttle, they will put independent New York State and national tickets in the field. Should this happen, the effect of that action, joined to the demonstrated dissatisfaction with Mr. Hoover's program of New York's regular Republicans, may be as disastrous to the national Republican candidates as was Colonel Roosevelt's third-party movement twenty years ago.

For days before this convention opened, and for the first day of the session, administration leaders maintained the strategic fiction that the delegates were to "work their will" on all points. In every respect save

Continued on Page Thirteen.

U. S. PALE DRY—Always the Ginger Ale of the Fastidious—and, of course, the mixer that exactly meets requirements. At Regent's Hunt Club Bar. Cocktails and Cordials. (Adv.)

"All the News That's Fit to Print."

The New York Times.

LATE CITY EDITION
WEATHER—Clearing and cooler today; tomorrow fair.
Temperature Yesterday—Max. 81; Min. 70.

Copyright, 1932, by The New York Times Company.

VOL. LXXXI....No. 27,188.   ＋＋＊＊＊   NEW YORK, SATURDAY, JULY 2, 1932.   TWO CENTS In New York City | THREE CENTS Within 200 Miles | FOUR CENTS Elsewhere

ROOSEVELT NOMINATED ON FOURTH BALLOT; GARNER EXPECTED TO BE HIS RUNNING MATE; GOVERNOR WILL FLY TO CONVENTION TODAY

CONFEREES REACH RELIEF COMPROMISE UPON $2,100,000,000

Use Parts of Both Wagner and Garner Bills in Report to Reach Congress Tuesday.

BOND ISSUES ARE BARRED

$1,500,000,000 Provided for R. F. C. Loans—$300,000,000 Available for Public Works.

GRANTS TO STATES SPLIT

$300,000,000 Allowed, According to Population—$100,000,000 on a Basis of Need.

Text of Secretary Mills's review of government finances, page 2.

Special to The New York Times.
WASHINGTON, July 1.—Agreement on relief legislation, the most important subject before Congress, was reached by the conferees tonight just after the Senate and House recessed until Tuesday, when they will take up the conference report.

Compromising between the Wagner and Garner bills, each involving about $2,300,000,000, the conferees drew up a program of $2,100,000,000 divided as follows:

$1,500,000,000 for loans by the Reconstruction Finance Corporation to public and private enterprises, but only to the latter where money is unavailable elsewhere.

$300,000,000 for construction of public works, this money not to be financed by bond issues, but by the Treasury.

$200,000,000 for direct loans to the States on a basis of population.

$100,000,000 for direct loans to the States on a basis of need.

Points of Difference in Bills.

For a week the conferees have been struggling to adjust the administration's viewpoint, as well as differences between the Wagner and Garner bills, as follows:

Wagner Bill—$1,300,000,000 for loans by the Reconstruction Finance Corporation to self-liquidating enterprises a public character; $800,000,000 for public works, financed by bond issues; $600,000,000 for loans to the States on a population basis.

Garner Bill—$1,200,000,000 for loans by the Reconstruction Finance Corporation to public and private enterprises; $1,100,000,000 for public works financed by bond issues; $100,000,000 for a Presidential emergency fund.

The administration vigorously opposed bond issues, demanded that private business as well as self-liquidating public enterprises be allowed to obtain loans from the Reconstruction Finance Corporation and desired that the loans to States be granted on a need instead of a population basis.

Character and Purposes of Loans.

Announcing the agreement by the conferees, Senator Norbeck explained that the parts of the Garner bill regarding Reconstruction Finance Corporation loans had been accepted with certain restrictions and suitable safeguards.

He said the loans to private enterprises could be made only when it was impossible to obtain money from other sources, and that the loans could be granted for only four purposes—"agriculture, industry, commerce and employment."

Loans to municipalities would be permitted, he stated, only for future needs and not to settle debts already contracted. He said that this meant loans would be granted for long-day payment of school teachers as in Chicago, but might be allowed to continue employment of the teachers and other city employees.

The loans could also be made for public works and to the small cities as well as the large merchant, the Senator stated, but in all cases they would have to be adequately secured.

Continued on Page Two.

Continued on Page Two.

The Fourth and Decisive Ballot

Special to The New York Times.
CHICAGO, July 1.—The detailed vote on the fourth ballot of the Democratic National Convention nominating Franklin D. Roosevelt for President follows:

STATE	Total Vote	Roosevelt	Smith	Garner	Ritchie	Baker	Reed	Traylor	White	Byrd
Alabama	24	24								
Arizona	6	6								
Arkansas	18	18								
California	44	44								
Colorado	12	12								
Connecticut	16		16							
Delaware	6		6							
Florida	14	14								
Georgia	28	28								
Idaho	8	8								
Illinois	58	58								
Indiana	30	30								
Iowa	26	26								
Kansas	20	20								
Kentucky	26	26								
Louisiana	20	20								
Maine	12	12								
Maryland	16	16								
Massachusetts	36		36							
Michigan	38	38								
Minnesota	24	24								
Mississippi	20	20								
Missouri	36	36								
Montana	8	8								
Nebraska	16	16								
Nevada	6	6								
N. Hamp'hire	8	8								
New Jersey	32		32							
New Mexico	6	6								
New York	94	31	63							
No. Carolina	26	26								
No. Dakota	10	10								
Ohio	52	29	17		2					
Oklahoma	22	22								
Oregon	10	10								
Pennsylvania	76	49	14½			1½	5½			
Rhode Isl.	10		10							
So. Carolina	18	18								
So. Dakota	10	10								
Tennessee	24	24								
Texas	46	46								
Utah	8	8								
Vermont	8	8								
Virginia	24	24								
Washington	16	16								
West Va.	16	16								
Wisconsin	26	24		2						
Wyoming	6	6								
Alaska	6	6								
Dist. of Col.	6	6								
Hawaii	6	6								
Philippines	6	6								
Puerto Rico	6	6								
Canal Zone	6	6								
Virgin Islds.	2	2								
Totals	1,154	945	190½		3½	5½				3

Five 1½ votes not cast. Ohio cast one vote for Cox.

MADDEN MUST GO TO PRISON AGAIN

High Court Holds He and Three Others Still Under Parole, Upsetting Levy Ruling.

The police are looking for Owen Madden, former convict, and three of his associates, former Sing Sing inmates.

The search began yesterday when the Appellate Division of the Supreme Court unanimously reversed the decision of Supreme Court Justice Aaron J. Levy, who sustained a writ of habeas corpus last April freeing the four ex-convicts from the custody of the State Parole Board. Madden and his companions, Jeremiah J. Sullivan, Terence Reilly, alias Thomas Robinson, and Gustave Guillaume, alias Little Frenchy, are wanted for violation of parole.

Justice Levy, in sustaining the writ releasing Madden, had ruled that Madden was arrested on flimsy and highly technical grounds and that Madden had been discharged from parole in 1929. He also held that Madden's arrest "was an attempt to convict under color of law for wrongs which cannot be brought home to him by competent evidence." He ruled that the other three had also been discharged from parole.

Dispute Levy's Findings.

The five justices of the Appellate Division, Presiding Justice Finch and Justices Martin, Townley, McAvoy and Merrill, in their review of the proceedings before Justice Levy, commented: "No evidence, either documentary or otherwise, of the arrest..."

BINGHAM OFFERS SENATE BEER TEST

Puts 4 Per Cent Beverage Plan Into Rider for Home Loan Bank Bill—Wets Count on 49 Votes.

Special to The New York Times.
WASHINGTON, July 1.—A test in the Senate on modification of the Volstead act seemed likely when Senator Bingham today offered a proposal to legalize beer of 2.2 per cent alcoholic content by weight, or 4 per cent by volume, as an amendment to the Home Loan Bank bill.

He announced that he would not press for a vote on his amendment until the Democratic Senators returned from Chicago, where their party convention has gone on record for immediate liberalization of the Volstead act. The Senate recessed tonight until Tuesday, when the Home Loan Bank bill will come up again.

Through his rider to the bill, and my two boys, Elliott and John. That's four. Then Miss Lehand, Miss Tully, Sergeant Earl Miller and Gus Gennerich and"—

Here he paused and turned toward Justice Rosenman, who has been his constant companion for a week.

"And Sam, will he go?" interjected Mrs. Rosenman. The justice had previously indicated that he did not intend to make the trip.

"Sure he'll go," said the Governor. The justice beamed.

"We expect to have a good trip," said the Governor. Then he went on to banter with some of the correspondents whom he has known for some time, posing for a photograph.

The Democratic Nominee

FRANKLIN DELANO ROOSEVELT.

© New York Times Studio Photo.

HE IS 'READY FOR ACTION'

Plane Starts With Him at 8 A. M. for Chicago to Open Campaign.

WIFE AND BOYS GOING, TOO

On Way Governor Will Work on Speech Accepting His Party's Nomination.

EXPECTS TO MEET SMITH

Addressing 1,000 Neighbors on Lawn, He Predicts Harmony and Certain Victory.

By JAMES A. HAGERTY.
Special to The New York Times.
ALBANY, N. Y., Saturday, July 2.—Wreathed in smiles, Governor Roosevelt sat in his armchair in the Executive Mansion early this morning, jubilant at his nomination and all ready with plans for an intensive campaign to win his way to the White House.

With his wife, his sons and close friends around him, he had heard a short time before the balloting that chose him as the candidate of the Democratic party for the Presidency as it came from the radio in the corner of the room.

Then, as he received newspaper correspondents, he heard coming back over the radio from Chicago the message he had sent telling of his prospective appearance before the convention today, together with the announcement that a meeting of the national committee had been requested for tonight at the Congress Hotel to launch the campaign.

"We are ready for action," the Governor said.

Joyous Night in Mansion.

All through the evening the Executive Mansion, where four years ago Alfred E. Smith received the news of his nomination at Houston, had an atmosphere of suppressed elation. It had been intimated that Texas and California might come to the Roosevelt banner, but nothing was certain.

Just before the radio broadcast started the definite news was circulated and as members of the Governor's family and his aides hurried about the mansion they clearly showed their joy.

Throughout the broadcast the Governor sat in the workroom on the south side with his small party which included Supreme Court Justice Samuel I. Rosenman and Mrs. Rosenman, Miss Marguerite Lehand and Miss Grace Tully, his private secretaries; Detective "Gus" Gennerich, his New York City bodyguard, and several others.

When the doors were finally opened and the Governor officially became the candidate of his party, he was quick to extend the olive branch to Alfred E. Smith.

"Do you expect to see Governor Smith soon?" he was asked.

"I certainly hope so," said the Executive, smiling.

Family to Fly With Him.

"I haven't any particular statement," said the Governor. "I want to go to Chicago and there it is coming back now. The speech tomorrow will be the official notification as that we can save the expense of bringing people here from all over the country later.

"I am going to leave at 8 o'clock in the morning by airplane and expect to reach Chicago by about 2:30 our time. I am going to do some final work on the speech on the trip out."

"Mrs. Roosevelt will go along, and my two boys, Elliott and John. That's four.

GARNER WITHDRAWS, AIDING ROOSEVELT

'Politics Is Funny,' the Speaker Philosophizes as He Reveals His Decision.

PLACE ON TICKET IS SEEN

Capital Democrats Look Upon Texan as Logical Nominee for Vice Presidency.

Special to The New York Times.
WASHINGTON, July 1.—Speaker Garner, until this evening a stubborn candidate for the Democratic nomination for the Presidency, telephoned orders to Representative Rayburn and William G. McAdoo, his campaign managers, tonight to release the California and Texas delegations pledged to his support.

He ordered them to be released in favor of Governor Roosevelt, heightening, in the opinion of the capital, the chances of Mr. Roosevelt's winning the nomination.

The Speaker's action is viewed here as making himself Governor Roosevelt's logical running mate.

His announcement of withdrawal from the Presidential race was made to THE NEW YORK TIMES shortly before 9 o'clock tonight.

Long past his customary supper, Mr. Garner was on the roof garden of the hotel where he makes his home. He was pleased and apparently unrecognized by others seeking relief from the heat.

"You've gone to Roosevelt?" a reporter asked him.

"That's right, son," the Speaker replied. "And that is all I am going to say to you."

"This cigar"—he puffed slowly—"is all that"—

"Is this other than you are, son. And politics is funny"—

"You may become the first man in line," the reporter interjected.

Democratic Nominee's Name Is Pronounced "Rose-velt"

By The Associated Press.
ALBANY, N. Y., July 1.—The Democratic Presidential nominee pronounces his name "Rose-velt"; it has two syllables and the "o" instead of the way it looks as if it should be pronounced.

The name Roosevelt came over with the old Dutch patroons, and in the Dutch language double o is pronounced as a single long "o."

SMITH HEARS NEWS IN GRIM SILENCE

Refuses Comment on Rival's Victory—Friends Say He May Not Support Ticket.

By The Associated Press.
CHICAGO, July 1.—Alfred E. Smith, sitting in his hotel headquarters facing a radio and a poster spelling "Smith for President," heard, without formal comment, tonight the nomination of Governor Roosevelt.

"Do you intend to support the nominee?" he was asked.

"I have no comment to make," Mr. Smith replied, chewing vigorously at a cigar. Then he turned back to the radio and resumed his grim silence.

Mr. Smith's associates and political leaders said they did not believe he would support the Democratic ticket in November.

An expression of bitter sadness came to the face of the "Happy Warrior of 1928" as soon as William G. McAdoo began to announce the switch of California's vote. There was a change in that expression only once during the rest of the evening, when Connecticut's votes for Smith provided an outburst of cheering. He smiled slightly for the moment.

The outcome of the convention was apparently foreign to the mind of the New York Governor, for the support of the switch had changed...

Continued on Page Five.

Continued on Page Five.

15,000 IN STADIUM FOR CLIMAX SCENE

Galleries Unaware as Ballot Began That Garner Action Made Outcome Certain.

WALKER SILENT ON RESULT

He Lets Curry Acknowledge for Tammany Its Defeat in Overwhelming Vote.

From a Staff Correspondent.
CHICAGO, July 1.—Fifteen thousand persons who crowded the Stadium for the Democratic convention session tonight expecting drama were not disappointed in the spectacle they saw when Franklin D. Roosevelt was nominated, amid the cheers of delegates, and groans and boos from the galleries.

It was more time ordinary drama when William G. McAdoo, whose nomination Alfred E. Smith blocked at the Madison Square Garden convention in New York City, went to the platform to announce that California and Texas would give ninety votes for Roosevelt, making the nomination certain and preventing the balloting that convention the body longer at this convention the body.

With the local sentiment, as revealed by the gallery demonstrations, bitterly opposed to Mr. Roosevelt, the roll-call was attended with great disorder caused by interruptions from the galleries.

As State after State recorded their support for Roosevelt, the men and women in the galleries voiced their disapproval and occasionally observed wildly at the announcement of the votes which swayed with Mr. Smith.

While the Smith forces stuck by their candidate, the support of favor...

Continued on Page Four.

Continued on Page Four.

ROOSEVELT VOTE IS 945

Smith His Nearest Rival, With 190 1-2 as Four States Stick to End.

McADOO BREAKS DEADLOCK

Casts California's 44 Amid Wild Demonstration After Garner Releases Texans.

RITCHIE MEN FALL IN LINE

Tammany Holds Aloof—Cermak Forced to Appeal to the Booing Galleries.

By ARTHUR KROCK.
Special to The New York Times.
CHICAGO, July 1.—California and Texas, which came to Chicago pledged to Speaker John N. Garner, broke the deadlock on the Presidential nomination in the Democratic National Convention on the fourth ballot tonight by casting their ninety votes for Governor Franklin D. Roosevelt of New York.

This started a bandwagon rush, in which only New York—the nominee's home State—Massachusetts, Rhode Island, New Jersey and Connecticut declined to join, and Mr. Roosevelt was selected by a vote of 945, the convention's two-thirds requirement being 769 1-3. His nearest rival, Alfred E. Smith, received 190½ votes, the four States named sticking to him to the last.

Roosevelt to Fly to Chicago.

Governor Roosevelt, as soon as he heard of his success, sent a message which the permanent chairman, Senator Thomas J. Walsh of Montana read to the convention. The Governor announced that he will be here tomorrow, coming by airplane from Albany, to address the convention and to receive his formal notification, thus avoiding the expense of a more formal and distant ceremony.

The national committee will also be reorganized under the eye of the nominee tomorrow with his nomination manager, James A. Farley of New York, as chairman. A great occasion, led by Senator Walsh, and notification speeches, is to be made of the notification ceremonies.

Senator Walsh, the permanent chairman, sent the following telegram to Governor Roosevelt:

"The convention extends its greetings and assurance of fealty to our nominee and welcomes the news that he will be here with us tomorrow."

William G. McAdoo, former Secretary of the Treasury, was the voice of Mr. Roosevelt's destiny. When the name of California was called by the reading clerk he took the platform to explain the change of the vote to the Western States. The news of the impending action had spread throughout the delegates.

But the galleries had not heard about it, and, when they sensed what was happening, the boos and yells with which they expressed their anger over the defeat of Alfred E. Smith required the efforts of Mayor Anthony J. Cermak of Chicago, whose presence was demanded by Permanent Chairman Thomas J. Walsh, to restore a measure of quiet.

McAdoo Speaks for West.

Mr. McAdoo said that California had not come to Chicago to deadlock the convention, that Democracy had suffered enough, as in 1924 when he himself had almost polled a majority, by such methods. He said that the opinion of the West, in which Speaker Garner joined, was that Democrats should fight Republicans and not one another.

He did not say what has been known here for several days, that William Randolph Hearst, who has great influence in the California delegation and who "discovered" the qualification of Mr. Garner as a candidate, pressed the shift to Mr. Roosevelt because he feared that a deadlock might produce Newton D. Baker or another candidate with whose international policies he is not in agreement. Mr. Hearst also is a believer in majority rule and the Texas-California contingent was responding to his ideas on that subject. Throughout a feverish day in...

Continued on Page Four.

Continued on Page Four.

"All the News That's Fit to Print."

The New York Times.

LATE CITY EDITION
WEATHER—Thunder showers and cooler today; tomorrow fair.
Temperature Yesterday—Max., 80; Min., 69.

Copyright, 1932, by The New York Times Company.

VOL. LXXXI....No. 27,215.   Entered as Second-Class Matter, Postoffice, New York, N. Y.   NEW YORK, FRIDAY, JULY 29, 1932.   ****+ TWO CENTS In New York City | THREE CENTS Within 200 Miles | FOUR CENTS Elsewhere Except in 7th and 8th Postal Zones

---

WALKER REPLY A DENIAL OF ALL SEABURY CHARGES; CALLS 10 OF 15 OUTLAWED

GOVERNOR TO ACT QUICKLY

Turns Answer Over to His Advisers—New Move Expected in Week.

POLITICAL PLOT IS CHARGED

Mayor Says He Is the Victim of a Campaign of Calumny to Aid Hoover Regime.

DEFENDS EQUITABLE DEALS

Declares Men Who Gave Him Cash Got No Favors—Denies Sherwood Was Agent.

The text of Mayor's reply to Gov. Roosevelt, Pages 6, 7 and 8.

Terming himself the victim of political misrepresentation, and insisting that his entire official life would bear the closest scrutiny, Mayor Walker filed with Governor Roosevelt yesterday his answer to the removal charges pending against him as the result of allegations first made by Samuel Seabury, counsel to the Hofstadter committee.

The Mayor's answer, a 27,000-word document, contained specific denials of wrongdoing in connection with the Equitable Bus franchise, the receipt of securities from brokerage firms interested in taxicab legislation, the "beneficence" of Paul Block, publisher, or the huge bank accounts of Russell T. Sherwood, missing accountant. The document came from the printers yesterday forenoon, and was given at once to Thomas F. McAndrews, the Mayor's secretary, who carried it by train to the Governor at Albany.

Mr. Roosevelt, after scrutinizing it briefly, released the reply for publication. A conference between the Governor and his two legal advisers, Martin Conboy of New York and John E. Mack of Poughkeepsie, will probably be held in the near future. It was indicated, to determine the next step in the removal case that, it is held, cannot but affect the political fortunes of Mr. Roosevelt as the Democratic Presidential nominee.

Seabury Is Denounced.

In form, the Mayor's answer consisted of an attack upon Mr. Seabury before which the evidence against the Mayor was developed, followed by a point-by-point reply to the allegations made by Mr. Seabury and subsequently embodied in charges filed with the Governor by William Jay Schieffelin, head of the New York Committee of One Thousand.

Two appendices contained an answer to the separate and supplementary charges filed by James E. Finegan, Brooklyn Democrat, and legal citations and details on financial transactions covered in the main body of the answer.

Most of the legal citations were to support the Mayor's assertion that ten of the fifteen allegations advanced by Mr. Seabury related to a previous term in office, and therefore could not be made the basis of action at present by the Governor. The answer, however, also replied in detail to these allegations.

Mayor Walker did not mention Mr. Seabury's statement that he had a "metallic receptacle" in his home, where he put cash received in stock and bond deals, nor did he mention the "unnamed person" said to have received payments from both the Mayor and from Sherwood.

The payments to the unnamed person were stressed at committee hearings as tending to prove a connection between the bank accounts of Sherwood and the Mayor. Mr. Walker in his reply denied Sherwood was his financial agent.

Calls Inquiry Political Plot.

The Mayor declared that the Hofstadter committee was organized and Mr. Seabury retained as counsel "to carry out a deliberate plan of calumny" in the hope of discrediting the Democratic administration of New York City. He accused Mr. Seabury of conducting a "manhunt," and declared the counsel would have fixed upon any Democratic Mayor of New York as a victim, in order to divert attention from the shortcom-

Continued on Page Eight.

Walker Hastens to Saranac; Gets Word Brother Is Worse

Mayor Walker left on a midnight train for Saranac Lake last night, after he had received a call at City Hall informing him that the condition of his brother, George F. Walker, had taken a sudden turn for the worse.

The brother, the youngest of the three Walker brothers, has been a patient at a Saranac sanitarium for several months, and in the past few days his condition has been a source of worry to the Mayor. A report had been made at City Hall, however, that no publicity be given to the illness of the Mayor's brother, until developments forced it.

George Walker is 48 years old, is married, and has two children. He is in the insurance business, being a member of the firm of Hughes & Walker of 27 William Street.

COOLIDGE EXPECTED TO AID HOOVER DRIVE

Sanders to Spend Week-End at Former President's Vermont Home for Political Talk.

NO EASTERN MANAGER YET

Senator Hebert Is Likely to Be Named to Run Campaign in This Section.

The probability that former President Calvin Coolidge will aid President Hoover in his drive for re-election was indicated yesterday when Everett Sanders, chairman of the Republican National Committee, said that he would visit Mr. Coolidge Saturday and Sunday at the Coolidge homestead at Plymouth Notch, Vt., and expected to discuss the political situation with him.

Mr. Sanders, who was secretary to Mr. Coolidge when he was President, declined to be definite, because the invitation to visit his former chief came before he had been elected national chairman.

"I have no doubt he will take some part in the campaign," Mr. Sanders said, when asked if he expected Mr. Coolidge to make some campaign speeches for the President.

Mr. Sanders said that there had been no selection yet of an Eastern campaign manager and indicated that the choice was between Senator Felix Hebert of Rhode Island and Earl S. Kinsley, national committeeman from Vermont. From other sources it was learned that Senator Hebert probably would be named. Should Senator Hebert not be named for this post he will be the Eastern campaign manager for the Republican Senatorial Committee, Mr. Sanders said.

Mr. Sanders also indicated that General Edward Martin, who was under consideration for Eastern campaign manager, had found his duties in Pennsylvania too exacting to take on additional responsibility. General Martin, besides being active in military affairs, is the Pennsylvania State treasurer and chairman of the Republican State Committee.

Sought to Supersede Macy.

Mr. Sanders had a luncheon conference with W. Kingsland Macy, New York State Republican chairman, and earlier in the day conferred with Charles D. Hilles, national committeeman, and former Governor Henry J. Allen of Kansas, publicity director of the national committee.

Asked to make a prediction on New York State, Mr. Sanders said:

"I am very confident that the President will be re-elected, but I do not wish to discuss his chance of carrying the different States."

One point of difficulty in the Republican campaign situation in this State has been cleared up by the recent visit to Washington of Mr. Macy and conferences here with Mr. Sanders, as a result of which it has been decided that the Republican State Committee will be in complete charge of the campaign in this State and that there will be no Hoover campaign committee as there was in 1928.

Sought to Supersede Macy.

Members of the so-called Hooverite group in this State suggested the re-establishment of the Hoover campaign committee and some members of the group went so far as to make suggestions which, if adopted, virtually would have put the officers of the proposed Hoover campaign committee in charge of the campaign and

Continued on Page Thirteen.

Thousands Crowding Into Los Angeles For Opening of Olympic Games Tomorrow

By ALLISON DANZIG.

LOS ANGELES, July 28.—The biggest migration to California since the Forty-niners wrote an imperishable story of men's courage in braving the perils of the unknown has made Los Angeles the cosmopolitan capital of the world.

Not for a pot of gold at the end of the covered wagon trail has this world exodus to the jewel city of Southern California taken place, but for the tenth revival of the Olympic Games, which begin here on Saturday, with approximately 2,000 representatives of thirty-eight countries competing in an athletic plant that dwarfs the imagination, along with the colosseums and stadiums of the ancient Greeks and Romans.

Already, with the spectacular grand opening parade twenty-eight hours away, there are thousands of visitors encamped in Los Angeles and its environs.

By railroad, plane, ship and motor car they continue to pour into the city and no one knows what eager-

...of enterprise and fortitude are being written on the national highways by athletic zealots who have seized upon the most desperately dilapidated means of conveyance to bring them to the games.

Los Angeles, festooned and bedecked with flags, streamers and banners of welcome to all within its domain, is assimilating this tremendous influx of people in the same ample fashion that it has prepared, over a period of nine years, to stage this tremendous athletic carnival, the first Olympiad to be held in this country since 1904.

With its enormous hotel capacity, it is well prepared to accommodate the great burden of humanity resting within its confines and thus far there is no overcrowding or dearth of reservations.

So far as it has been possible to ascertain, there has been no mark-up in the rates for rooms, nor have prices in the restaurants or else-

Continued on Page Nineteen.

BRITAIN ASKS EMPIRE FOR MORE PURCHASES TO BALANCE HER AID

Baldwin Says United Kingdom Imports Exceeded Exports by £95,700,000 in 1930.

RHODESIA FILES DEMAND

British In Drive at Ottawa to Capture United States Sales of Machinery in Canada.

The text of Britain's trade statement is on Page 10.

By CHARLES A. SELDEN.
Special to The New York Times.

OTTAWA, July 28.—Two more cards were placed face up on the Imperial Economic Conference table today when Stanley Baldwin, leader of the British delegation, presented a statement plainly intimating to the dominions that in his opinion they were lagging behind the United Kingdom in the mutual exchange of trade benefits of the empire.

Simultaneously with this, H. W. Moffat, spokesman for Southern Rhodesia, filed a request that Britain help his country by buying more of its cattle.

The statement of the United Kingdom contained neither threat nor promise of what Great Britain would or would not do after the dominions have agreed upon what they can and cannot do for the mother country. It confined itself to what the United Kingdom already had done for the rest of the empire and showed by figures that she was buying from annually £100,000,000 worth of goods in excess of what they were buying from her.

Advantages Are Contrasted.

Mr. Baldwin called attention to the fact that practically all of the dominion products were admitted to the ports of Great Britain free of duty, whereas British exports to the dominions had only the benefit of preferences. Although the preferences are much better than nothing, Mr. Baldwin considers them far less of a boon than free entry. He spoke particularly of the fact that preferences could be based on tariffs so high that they restrict imports.

He did not refer to the fact, fully and painfully raised at Ottawa by all the dominion delegations, that after Nov. 15 the United Kingdom may deprive them of all the benefits of free entry which the empire countries now enjoy by simply applying to them the new British tariff act. That is England's trump card at this conference, which she may play to get from the trade concessions and preferences she thinks are just and fair.

Although no threats were made today nor even hinted, the British statement added nothing to the harmony of the conference and no doubt the dominions considered it as a rebuke, which they all think underserved in spite of the figures that support it.

Denies Withholding Assistance.

Perhaps Stanley M. Bruce, leader of the Australian delegation, felt personally rebuked. He told the conference the other day that Great Britain had been tardy in recognition of all the preferences the dominions had given her. No doubt Mr. Baldwin had that remark definitely in mind today when he said:

"Any suggestion that the United Kingdom has been backward in developing or assisting dominion trade or that the concessions on the side of the dominions have not been fully reciprocated, both in the letter and

Continued on Page Ten.

HERRIOT PROTESTS SCHLEICHER SPEECH; EDITORS ATTACK IT

Premier Summons Germany's Envoy to Tell Him Arms Talk Disturbs France.

CITES HIS FRIENDLY POLICY

Description of French Stand as "Hypocritical" Results in Bitter Resentment.

By P. J. PHILIP.
Wireless to The New York Times.

PARIS, July 28.—Premier Édouard Herriot summoned the German Ambassador, Dr. Leopold von Hoesch, to the Quai d'Orsay today to explain to him vigorously that the French people are considerably disturbed by the terms of Lieut. Gen. Kurt von Schleicher's radio speech Tuesday evening, in which he gave notice that Germany would arm, if necessary, contrary to the provisions of the Versailles treaty, and also attacked France.

M. Herriot's protest was the second in two days, for Ambassador André François-Poncet called at the Wilhelmstrasse in Berlin yesterday to make a formal denial of some statements made by the German Defense Minister.

In the Paris press the substance of General von Schleicher's statement is the subject of strong comment today, but all that either Premier Herriot or the French Ambassador could do was to point out that its form was distinctly impolitic, not to say impossible.

Says He Went Too Far.

Even in the midst of the German electoral period, M. Herriot is believed to have told Dr. von Hoesch that it was going too far for a Minister of the Reich to make such a speech only a few weeks after the conclusion of the Lausanne agreement, in which France showed the utmost generosity to Germany and had abandoned all claim to further reparations payments.

It was even less opportune, it was pointed out, for the German Defense Minister to speak as he did within twenty-four hours of the time when

Continued on Page Three.

Stocks Rise Again in Year's Heaviest Trading; 2,735,635 Shares Sold, Leaders Up 1 to 4 Points

Invigorated by fresh optimism, the security markets made another broad advance yesterday. The day's transactions in stocks on the New York Stock Exchange totaled 2,735,635 shares, which represented the heaviest trading since Dec. 16 of last year. The net gains in market leaders ranged from 1 to 4 points, while there were scattered advances of 6 points or more.

In the bond market the net gains were widest among domestic corporation issues, running from 2 to 10 points in the conspicuously strong favorites. The extreme gain of 22 points occurred in Schulco 6½s, due in 1946, Series B. United Biscuit 5s, due 1942, were up 9¾ points, Purity and Bakeries 5s, due 1948, were up 9 points; Alfs Chalmers 6s, due 1937, gained 6¾; Atchison, Topeka & Santa Fe bonds showed a maximum gain of 6 points; Atlantic Coast Line issues advanced as much as 7 points and Bethlehem Steel 5s of 1926 rose 4½ points. Dealings in bonds were the heaviest in a month.

Aside from a further demonstration of strength in commodities, the development which contributed most to the cheerfulness in Wall Street was a spectacular rise of the dollar in terms of foreign currencies which...

...of the gold position of the United States. Sterling fell 2½ cents, while the French franc was off 7-16 point. All the other Continental currencies except the mark, which was unchanged, lost ground.

The upswing in stock prices was most striking in the forenoon. Profit-taking at midday and in the last hour reduced the early gains to some extent, but final prices showed substantial net appreciation in the average. For instance, Allied Chemical was up 3 points on the day; American Telephone, the market leader, moved down street, clearing the path with up 4½ points after falling more than a point from its high; Santa Fe preferred was up 4¾ points and the common 2%; Bangor & Aroostock 7%, Detroit Edison 10, du Pont 2½, Norfolk & Western 3¾ and Eastman 1¾. United States Steel common touched a high of 26%, but closed at 27% with a small fractional gain. Steel preferred was up ½ point after falling 2 points from the high.

Bank stocks again advanced vigorously, the bid price of First National showing a gain of 25 points and that of the Fifth Avenue 40 points.

Continued on Page Three.

TROOPS DRIVE VETERANS FROM CAPITAL; FIRE CAMPS THERE AND AT ANACOSTIA; 1 KILLED, SCORES HURT IN DAY OF STRIFE

ANACOSTIA CAMP NO MORE

Troops Move Into Last Bonus Army Refuge as Flames Start.

AND FINISH DESTRUCTION

Marchers Stream Away, Some in Broken-Down Autos, Some Trudging Afoot.

FEW KNEW WHITHER TO GO

At Midnight the Former Home of 20,000 of Bonus Army Is Held by the Military.

Special to The New York Times.

WASHINGTON, July 28.—Flames rose high over the desolate Anacostia flats at midnight tonight and a pitiful stream of refugee veterans of the World War walked out of their home of the past two months, going they knew not where.

Cavalry stood guard at all the bridges leading across the river to the camp and thousands of onlookers gazed across the river at what had been the teeming residence of 20,000 persons.

The veterans were leaving at the behest of the military forces of the government, summoned by the President after collisions between the bonus marchers and the police. Some were departing in broken-down automobiles; some, on foot, dragging listlessly in search of new quarters.

Flames were raging in the camp. Many of the tents, numbering 2,100 and mostly belonging to the army, were ablaze and the infantry was busy trying to salvage as many as possible.

A heavy barrage of tear gas, laid down by the troops, penetrated to the houses for blocks around, and residents were forced to close their doors and windows in spite of the sweltering heat.

Had Thirty Minutes to Evacuate.

It was soon after 9 o'clock tonight that the troops, headed by General MacArthur, surrounded the main camp of the Bonus Expeditionary Force at Anacostia, wheeled their tanks into position, unlimbered their gas bombs and gave the thousands of veterans massed there thirty minutes in which to evacuate. They then sat down waiting for the order to be obeyed.

The spirit of the veterans seemed broken. Leaderless and aghast at the failure of their confident prediction that no soldier would go into action against them, they moved their women and children out of the camp and prepared to leave themselves.

General MacArthur and his staff followed the first troop of cavalry into the field at Anacostia from a road leading off from the bridge. Several veterans, as they heard the troops approach, set fire to improvised huts. The glow from the

Continued on Page Three.

Text of Hoover's Statement on Call for Troops To Put an End to Bonus Rioting in the Capital

Special to The New York Times.

WASHINGTON, July 28.—The text of President Hoover's statement explaining his action in calling out troops to combat the bonus rioters is as follows:

For some days police authorities and Treasury officials have been endeavoring to persuade the so-called bonus marchers to evacuate certain buildings which they were occupying without permission.

These buildings are on sites where government construction is in progress and their demolition was necessary in order to extend employment in the district and to carry forward the government's construction program.

This morning the occupants of these buildings were notified to evacuate and at the request of the police did evacuate the buildings concerned. Thereafter, however, several thousand men from different camps marched in and attacked the police with brickbats and otherwise injuring several policemen, one probably fatally.

I have received the attached letter from the Commissioners of the District of Columbia, stating that they can no longer preserve law and order in the district.

In order to put an end to this rioting and defiance of civil authority, I have asked the army to assist the District authorities to restore order.

Congress made provision for the return home of the so-called bonus marchers, who have for many weeks been given every opportunity of free assembly, free speech and free petition to the Congress. Some 5,000 took advantage of this arrangement and have returned to their homes. An examination of a large number of names discloses the fact that a considerable part of those remaining are not veterans; many are Communists and persons with criminal records.

There are, amongst these numbers, are no doubt many who are unaware of the character of their companions and who are being led into violence which no government can tolerate.

I have asked the Attorney General to investigate the whole incident and to cooperate with the District civil authorities in such measures against leaders and rioters as may be necessary.

[The text of the letter from the District Commissioner to the President is printed elsewhere.]

BOMBS AND SABRES WIN CAPITAL BATTLE

Cavalry, Infantry and Tanks, Advancing as Gas Spreads, Swiftly Drive Veterans

SHACKS BURN BEHIND THEM

Bayonets Clear the Section of Squatters, Who Are Ringed Finally by 1,500 Soldiers

Special to The New York Times.

WASHINGTON, July 28.—The Federal troops came out today and cleared Washington of the remnants of the Bonus Expeditionary Force. The cantonments, the "forts" in the unused Federal buildings, the huts that the men themselves had built, were evacuated by the veterans when they found themselves faced with tear-gas bombs, bayonets and tanks.

The regulars had the equipment to do the job, the equipment that the Capitol Police had lacked and they had the orders to do it. The irregulars of the bonus army had only their stubborn sullenness in most cases and bricks, rocks and epithets in other cases, and the fight did not last long.

Down Pennsylvania Avenue at 4:30 this afternoon the regulars came, cavalry leading the way, and after them the tanks, the machine-gunners and the infantry. For them the objective was the "fort" of the B. E. F. in the skeletonized building at Third Street.

There was a wait for maybe half an hour while the army officers talked it over with the police and the bonus marchers shouted defiance. They wanted action, and they got it.

Steady Sweep Down Avenue.

Twenty steel-helmeted soldiers led the way, with revolvers in their hands, and others advanced until about 300 were in position in front of the "bonus fort." Then the mounted men joined. They rode down street, clearing the path with their sabers, striking those within reach with the flat of the blades.

The action was precise, well executed from a military standpoint, but not pretty to the thoughtful in the crowd. There were those who resisted the troops, fought back, cursed and kicked at the horses; there were those who scrambled for safety and those who tried to rescue their meager belongings from the fort. Inch by inch, foot by foot, they were forced down Pennsylvania Avenue as the soldiers headed them toward Anacostia camp. They left in their path those who had been knocked over, and one passive resister, who sat down and waited unsoothed while the down blow over his head.

The success of the movement, the

Continued on Page Three.

B.E.F. TO CARRY ON, WATERS DECLARES

Men Will Organize Elsewhere if Driven From Capital, Commander Says.

WHITE HOUSE IS ASSAILED

'Political Interests' Cost a Life, He Charges, Admitting He Has Lost Control.

By The Associated Press.

WASHINGTON, July 28.—Walter W. Waters, titular head of the "Bonus Expeditionary Force," declared tonight that "no matter what may happen from now on, the B. E. F. will carry on."

"If driven from Washington, we will organize elsewhere and continue the fight for justice for the veterans and the common people of the United States" he said in a statement. "We have gone too far now to quit."

The Waters declaration, telephoned to newspaper offices, included the assertion that a life was sacrificed "to serve the political interests of the administration."

Just before arrival of the troops, Waters viewed from the sidelines while the men who formerly paid him allegiance swept completely out of his control.

Before Federal troops arrived to push former service men off their encampments in front of a cloud of tear gas, "Commander" Waters threw up his hands in a gesture of defeat. He said frankly that he be longer had any control over the men.

Accompanied by a handful of his aides, Waters viewed from the distance walks about the trouble-ridden area the swiftly breaking developments, which resulted in the death of a war veteran.

About an hour before arrival of the troops Waters wanted to a small restaurant on Pennsylvania Avenue for a cup of coffee.

Asked about the day's happenings he replied:

"The men got out completely out of control. There was nothing and is nothing I can do to control them."

"Every drop of blood shed today or that may be shed in days to come as the result of today's events can be laid directly on the threshold of the White House.

"The B. E. F. had been organized on strictly American lines of respect for law and order and is pledged to uphold American institutions.

"The men were under strictest orders to conduct themselves in orderly manner in the event of attempted

Continued on Page Two.

HOOVER ORDERS EVICTION

Blaming Reds, He Asserts Bonus Camps Included Many Criminals.

QUICK ACTION BY SOLDIERS

Eject Squatters After Police Fail and Then Burn Camps in and Near Capital.

BONUS ARMY SCATTERED

Demoralized by Soldiers' Gas Attack, Remnants Are Left Leaderless and Helpless.

Special to The New York Times.

WASHINGTON, July 28.—Amidst scenes reminiscent of the mopping-up of a town in the World War, Federal troops late today drove the army of bonus seekers from the shanty village near Pennsylvania Avenue in which the veterans had been entrenched for months. Earlier in the day the police had fought and lost a battle there which resulted in the death of one veteran, possibly fatal injuries to a policeman and a long list of other casualties, many of them serious.

Ordered to the scene by President Hoover after the District of Columbia authorities confessed defeat, detachments of infantry, cavalry, machine-gun and tank crews laid down an effective tear-gas barrage which disorganized the bonus-seekers, and then set fire to the shacks and tents left behind by the veterans on the government land near Third and Pennsylvania Avenues, scene of the earlier clash with the police.

Begin to Clear Anacostia.

After the disputed area near the Capitol had been cleared, the troops moved late in the evening on Camp Marks, on the Anacostia River, the bonus army's principal encampment. At 9 o'clock this evening a barrage of tear gas and smoke bombs was thrown into the camp, driving the crowd before them with tear gas bombs. Then they applied the torch to the shacks in which the veterans lived. Troops shortly afterward halted at the main bonus camp in response to what General Perry L. Miles, commanding the soldiers, said was a Presidential order. Theodore G. Joslin, the President's secretary, later denied positively that the President had issued any such order, and word came from the camp that the troops would resume operations within an hour.

At 11:15 P. M. the first troop of cavalry had moved into the disordered camp, now a mass of flames except for the broken-spoke veterans who were fleeing before the advancing troops. At midnight practically all the veterans had left the place.

Warning that the soldiers would use tear gas the veterans had arranged to evacuate the 600 women and children earlier.

The normal population of Camp Marks was augmented by the more than 2,000 veterans who had been evicted from other camps, bringing the total male population to 7,000.

Troops Avoid Bloodshed.

Soon after the khaki-clad regulars descended on the various camps along Pennsylvania Avenue this afternoon the bonus seekers were struggling sullenly away from the ominous blue mist of the tear gas, leaderless and apparently demoralized, seeking shelter in other open places scattered all over through the city. A few of them were sore from minor bruises, but on the whole the Federal troops had conducted their offensive without bloodshed. The veteran who was killed in the earlier clash with the police was identified tonight as William Hushka of Chicago.

The day's disturbances were blamed on the radical element among the bonus-seekers. Walter W. Waters, the young veteran from Oregon who led the unsuccessful bonus march to Washington, placed responsibility for his followers' part in resisting the first eviction effort of the police. Waters announced tonight that he

Continued on Page Two.

51

"All the News That's Fit to Print."

The New York Times.

5 A.M. EDITION
WEATHER—Rain today; tomorrow fair and colder.
Temperature Yesterday—Max. 52; Min. 41.

Copyright, 1932, by The New York Times Company.

VOL. LXXXII....No. 27,318.   Entered as Second-Class Matter, Postoffice, New York, N. Y.   NEW YORK, WEDNESDAY, NOVEMBER 9, 1932.   *****   TWO CENTS In New York City | THREE CENTS Elsewhere Except | FOUR CENTS Elsewhere in 7th and 8th Postal Zones

ROOSEVELT WINNER IN LANDSLIDE!
DEMOCRATS CONTROL WET CONGRESS;
LEHMAN GOVERNOR, O'BRIEN MAYOR

BIG VOTE FOR M'KEE

O'Brien Is 245,464 Behind Ticket as Protests Rise

BUT FINAL LEAD IS 616,736

Pounds Concedes Defeat Early, Saying 'Day of Miracles Is Past.'

McKEE TOTAL IS 137,538

Thousands of "Write-In" Votes Are Wasted as Backers Fail to Record Choice Properly.

HILLQUIT POLLS 248,425

Gets Greatest Vote in History of City for a Socialist—Runs Far Ahead of Party.

Surrogate John P. O'Brien, Tammany's candidate, was elected Mayor of New York yesterday, but overshadowing his victory, which was a foregone conclusion, was the tremendous "write-in" vote cast for Acting Mayor Joseph V. McKee.

Final returns from the city showed Judge O'Brien to have received a plurality of 616,736 over his nearest opponent, Lewis H. Pounds, Republican. Judge O'Brien's vote was 1,055,768; Mr. Pounds polled 439,032, and Morris Hillquit, Socialist, polled the highest vote ever given a candidate of his party in the city by receiving 248,425 votes.

Vote Listed by Boroughs.

By boroughs, the totals were as follows:

	O'Brien	Pounds	Hillquit
Manhattan	309,156	113,273	90,280
Bronx	181,103	43,284	67,345
Brooklyn	358,605	155,476	113,746
Queens	176,227	109,451	26,601
Richmond	30,131	16,311	3,517

City total....1,055,768 439,032 248,425

The vote for Mr. McKee, put early this morning at 137,538, actually was far more than that, if ballots in which the voters had abbreviated his name, or used initials, or spelled it wrongly, were counted.

The vote was unprecedented, particularly as the use of voting machines made it much more difficult for a name to be written in than on the old paper ballots.

Judge O'Brien had a clear majority of 215,000 over the combined vote of Pounds, Hillquit and McKee, but the McKee ballots cast aside as void would have reduced this, it was pointed out last night.

The vote for Mr. McKee by boroughs was as follows:

Manhattan, 34,336, with ten election districts missing.
Bronx, 24,443, complete.
Brooklyn, 43,227, complete.
Queens, 26,302, complete.
Richmond, 6,790, complete.
City total, 137,538.

The vote for Mr. McKee, made without any campaign on his part, and in the face of his own disavowal of the movement, kept him in the political picture as a candidate to be reckoned with for the full four-year term, to wind up on Jan. 1, 1933.

The term for which Judge O'Brien was elected starts on Jan. 1, 1933, and ends on Jan. 1, 1934.

The vote for Mr. O'Brien ran 245,263 votes behind Governor Roosevelt in the city, in actual votes cast, though his plurality was only 245,464 smaller than that given to the Presidential candidate.

Mr. Pounds conceded Mr. O'Brien's victory as early as 9:30 in the evening, and he sent the latter a telegram of congratulation.

He said later he could have been elected only by a miracle, and that the days of miracles were past. Mr. McKee, receiving election returns at the Park Lane, also sent a short

Continued on Page Seven.

FOR LOW COST HOLIDAY.
Monterey Hotel-On Beach-Asbury Park—Adv.

THE GOVERNOR-ELECT.
© New York Times Studio.
Colonel Herbert H. Lehman.

JUDGES IN 'DEAL' WIN; PROTEST VOTE HEAVY

Steuer and Hofstadter Elected With Lydon and Leary to Supreme Court Bench.

290,000 FOR INDEPENDENTS

Bar Leaders Elated by Big Count for Deutsch and Alger—Call It 'Warning to Bosses.'

City Court Justice Aron Steuer and State Senator Samuel H. Hofstadter were elected yesterday over their independent opponents, Bernard S. Deutsch and George W. Alger, by a vote of about 2 to 1.

The protest vote against the so-called deal by which Senator Hofstadter and Justice Steuer received bipartisan nominations for two of four vacancies on the Supreme Court bench in the first judicial district exceeded all expectations, but it was not enough to upset the combined strength of the Republican and Democratic organizations.

Justice Richard P. Lydon, who was nominated by both major parties for re-election, and Municipal Court Justice Timothy A. Leary, who had the Democratic nomination for the fourth vacancy on the bench, were elected with comfortable margins. Municipal Court Justice George L. Genung, who had the Republican nomination, trailed far behind the independent candidates.

Since Justice Lydon's vote was virtually uncontested, his totals were not computed in the early returns. Of the other, Justice Steuer and Judge Leary were running slightly ahead of Senator Hofstadter, whose lead was large enough, however, to preclude the possibility of his being overtaken by Mr. Deutsch, his nearest rival.

The Complete Returns.

The complete returns for the entire first judicial district, comprising the boroughs of Manhattan and the Bronx, follow:

Steuer 565,435
Hofstadter 517,112
Lydon 491,140
Leary 393,127
Genung 205,000

The totals recorded for the judiciary candidates in Manhattan follow:

Steuer 367,362
Hofstadter 331,443
Lydon 312,471
Leary 145,568
Alger 153,228
Genung 95,818

Final returns from the Bronx, where the independent candidates ran strongest, showed the following totals:

Steuer 215,479
Steuer 190,110
Hofstadter 186,902
Deutsch 143,336
Alger 141,821
Genung 66,913

The independent candidates did not

Continued on Page Twelve.

STATE VICTORY SOLID

Lehman Gets Record Party Plurality of 887,000.

WAGNER CLOSE TO HIM

National Ticket Has Margin of 615,000—Full Slate Is Elected.

RELIEF BONDS ARE VOTED

Republicans Have Narrow Edge Up-State—Hill Admits 'Protest' Defeated Them.

By JAMES A. HAGERTY.

Lieut. Gov. Herbert H. Lehman, Democratic nominee for Governor, defeated Colonel William J. Donovan, Republican, yesterday, in the Democratic whirlwind that swept New York State, by a plurality of about 887,000, a record for a Democratic candidate in this State.

Governor Franklin D. Roosevelt and Speaker John N. Garner, the Democratic candidates for President and Vice President, carried the State by a plurality of about 615,000, as against Governor Roosevelt's heretofore record Democratic plurality of 725,000, which he received as candidate for re-election to the Governorship two years ago.

With Governor Roosevelt and Colonel Lehman were swept into office the other Democratic candidates on the State-wide ticket, United States Senator Robert F. Wagner, candidate for re-election; M. William Bray, for Lieutenant Governor; State Controller Morris S. Tremaine, Attorney General John J. Bennett Jr. and the two candidates for Representatives-at-Large, Elmer E. Studley and John Fitzgibbons.

Colonel Lehman led Governor Roosevelt by 88,279 in actual votes cast in New York City and led the Governor in many cities and counties up-State. His indicated plurality exceeded that of Governor Roosevelt by more than 290,000, but exceeded the indicated plurality for Senator Wagner by only about 35,000.

Returns on the proposition and proposed constitutional amendments were slow in coming in, but a large majority for the proposal to issue $30,000,000 in bonds for unemployment relief was indicated, and scattering returns indicated that the constitutional amendment to throw open the forest preserve to the development of recreational facilities had been beaten.

The vote for President and State-wide candidates follows:

FOR PRESIDENT.
New York City, complete—Roosevelt, Democrat, 1,437,221; Hoover, Republican, 575,031; Thomas, Socialist, 120,496; actual plurality for Roosevelt, 862,200.

Up-State, 431 election districts missing—Roosevelt, 1,022,121; Hoover, 1,254,032; actual plurality for Hoover, 231,911; indicated plurality for Hoover, 247,107; indicated plurality for Roosevelt in the entire State, 615,093.

FOR GOVERNOR.
New York City, complete—Lehman, Democrat, 1,525,510; Donovan, Republican, 542,492; plurality for Lehman, 963,018.

Up-State, 561 election districts missing—Lehman, 1,056,088; Donovan, 1,141,785; actual plurality for Donovan, 85,647; indicated plurality for Donovan, 95,817.

Indicated plurality for Lehman in the entire State, 887,201.

FOR UNITED STATES SENATOR.
New York City, complete—Wagner, Dem., 1,438,343; Medalie, Rep., 517,-733; plurality for Wagner, 920,610.

Up-State, 1,301 districts missing—Lehman, 915,889; Medalie, 964,418;

Continued on Page Sixteen.

The President's Message To the President-Elect

From a Staff Correspondent.
PALO ALTO, Cal., Nov. 8.—President Hoover conceded his defeat for re-election at 9:17 o'clock tonight, Pacific Time, and dispatched this telegram of congratulations to Governor Roosevelt:

Palo Alto, Cal., Nov. 8, 1932.
The Hon. Franklin D. Roosevelt,
Biltmore Hotel,
New York, N. Y.

I congratulate you on the opportunity that has come to you to be of service to the country and I wish for you a most successful administration. In the common purpose of all of us I shall dedicate myself to every helpful effort.

HERBERT HOOVER

Governor Roosevelt had not received President Hoover's message when he left for his home shortly before 2 o'clock this morning. Pending its receipt he said he preferred not to make reply or comment on the message.

DEMOCRATS CONTROL STATE SENATE, 26-25

Republican Margin in Assembly of 6 Votes Is Reduced to 2 —Lose by 4 Up-State.

ALSO TWO SENATE SEATS

Moffatt Is Re-elected, While Hastings and Dr. Love Are Defeated in City Race.

The slender working majority of two votes by which the Republicans control the present State Senate was swept away in yesterday's Democratic landslide. The next Senate will be made up of 26 Republicans and 26 Democrats, giving the Democrats a majority of one. The present Senate has 27 Republican and 25 Democratic members. Twenty-six votes are required to pass a bill in that branch of the Legislature.

In the Assembly, where 76 votes are required to control legislation, the Republican majority of six is cut down to two in the 1933 Legislature. The Republicans won 77 seats and the Democrats 73 at yesterday's elections for the Assembly.

The Democrats won four Assembly district seats in the Republicans; one district in Monroe County, one district in Oneida and two in Sullivan and Schoharie counties. The Republicans, however, reduced the up-State Democratic gains by recapturing from them Schuyler county in the southern tier, where last year they succeeded in electing their candidate for the Lower House.

Pratt Is Defeated.

The Republicans also managed to strengthen their New York City representation by electing Herbert Brownell Jr. in the Tenth (Manhattan) District. This was the district where Langdon W. Post, Democratic incumbent was turned down by Tammany for supporting legislation to broaden the powers and continue the Hofstadter Committee and ran as an independent, polling 5,053 votes. Mr. Brownell defeated his Tammany opponent by a scant plurality of 307 votes. He received 5,807 votes. Sylva La Chappelle, the Democrat, 5,500.

The Democrats gained two Senate districts up-State, the Thirty-first, made up of Rensselaer County, and the Thirty-sixth, made up of Oneida. In the Thirty-fourth, composed of St. Lawrence and Franklin Counties, Warren T. Thayer, the present Republican incumbent, managed to win again after a hard fight.

The New York City Republicans will have three representatives in the Legislature, Senator-elect George Blumberg, who won by a plurality of approximately 500 over Senator John A. Hastings, Democratic incumbent in the Seventh Senatorial

Continued on Page Five.

OVERTURN IN SENATE

Bingham, Watson, Moses and Smoot Are Defeated.

DEMOCRATIC MAJORITY 12

Party Adds to Control in House—May Rule Both Branches This Winter.

LA GUARDIA LOSES SEAT

Mrs. Pratt Defeated, Wadsworth Wins — Texas Sends Garner Back to the House.

The Democratic wave of victory yesterday gave that party complete control of Congress and in its onrush carried down to defeat the four Republican leaders of the Senate.

Senator Smoot of Utah, Republican dean of the Senate and chairman of the powerful Finance Committee; Senator Watson of Indiana, floor leader; Senator Moses, president pro tempore and Senator Jones of Washington, chairman of the Appropriations Committee, all were relegated to the ranks of "lame ducks." No such upset has occurred in recent history.

While returns early this morning showed the new Senate will be Democratic by a majority of twelve and the House overwhelmingly Democratic, there was a possibility that, in the session of the old Congress convening Dec. 5, the Democrats with achieve a slender control of the whole body.

Changes in Coming Session.

They now have a majority of one in the House, in the old Congress that still is to hold a "lame-duck" session, and in the Senate the numbers were evened with the defeat of Senator Barbour of New Jersey for the short term beginning next month, and there was, early this morning, an even chance that Colorado would elect Walter Walker, a Democrat, provided the Senate in December would be: Democrats 49, Republicans 46, Farmer-Labor 1.

On the basis of incomplete returns, the new Senate stood at Democrats 54, Republicans 34, Farmer-Labor 1, and seven States still in doubt.

The next Congress not only will be Democratic; it will be wet.

New York Republicans fared especially ill in the election, which saw Representative La Guardia, fiery "liberal" Republican who led a bloc that controlled the House temporarily in the last session, defeated by J. J. Lanzetta, Democrat. Representative Ruth Pratt also failed of re-election.

Moses Loses in Close Race.

Of the most prominent Republicans who were unseated, Senator Watson went down first, conceding his defeat by Frederick Van Nuys, Democrat. Senator Moses ran nip and tuck with Fred H. Brown, Democrat, until after midnight in the poll of ballots, when returns from Manchester, N. H., spelled his certain defeat. Senator Smoot was defeated by Professor E. D. Thomas and Mr. Jones, who is better known as the author of the "five-and-ten" law than for his important committee chairmanship, was defeated coincident with adoption of a State referendum in Washington repealing that State's prohibition law.

An important Republican defeat in history, only nineteen outspoken drys had been returned definitely to the House, while twenty-four Senators, most of whom did not come up for re-election this year, remained among the prohibitionists. Around 200 House seats still were in doubt, and several Senators and re-elected Representatives were just undecided how to align themselves on the question.

The aggregation chosen yesterday

Continued on Page Six.

SWEEP IS NATIONAL

Democrats Carry 40 States, Electoral Votes 448.

SIX STATES FOR HOOVER

He Loses New York, New Jersey, Bay State, Indiana and Ohio.

DEMOCRATS WIN SENATE

Necessary Majority for Repeal of the Volstead Act in Prospect.

RECORD NATIONAL VOTE

Hoover Felicitates Rival and Promises 'Every Helpful Effort for Common Purpose.'

THE PRESIDENT-ELECT.
© NEW YORK TIMES STUDIO.
Franklin D. Roosevelt.

The Electoral Vote
ROOSEVELT 448.

Alabama	11	Nebraska	7
Arizona	3	Nevada	3
Arkansas	9	New Jersey	16
California	22	New Mexico	3
Colorado	6	New York	47
Florida	7	North Carolina	13
Georgia	12	North Dakota	4
Idaho	4	Ohio	26
Illinois	29	Oklahoma	11
Indiana	14	Rhode Island	4
Iowa	11	South Carolina	8
Kansas	9	South Dakota	4
Kentucky	11	Tennessee	11
Louisiana	10	Texas	23
Maryland	8	Utah	4
Massachusetts	17	Virginia	11
Minnesota	11	Washington	8
Mississippi	9	West Virginia	8
Missouri	15	Wisconsin	12
Montana	4	Wyoming	3

HOOVER—59.

Connecticut	8	New Hampshire	4
Delaware	3	Pennsylvania	36
Maine	5	Vermont	3

DOUBTFUL 24.

Michigan	19	Oregon	5

Votes in Electoral College, 531; needed to elect, 266.

Wets in Control in Both Houses, But Short of Two-Thirds in Senate

Modification of Volstead Act Appears Certain, and House Has Easy Majority for Repeal, but Upper Chamber Support Is Uncertain on Basis of Returns.

Complete control of the next Congress by forces opposed to Federal prohibition was one of the results which came with the political upheaval that took place in yesterday's election.

With full returns from the major portion of the country and definite trends established in the remainder, it appeared certain that those demanding a change in the dry laws would hold between fifty and fifty-five seats in the Senate and 300 or more in the House of Representatives.

Sixty-four Senate seats will be required for the latter, whereas only a bare majority of 49 in the Senate and 218 in the House would be needed to change the national prohibition (Volstead) law.

The House was sure of the necessary two-thirds for repeal, as early this morning the anti-prohibitionists had already captured 290 seats; the

Continued on Page Eight.

Roosevelt Statement.

President-elect Roosevelt gave the following statement to THE NEW YORK TIMES early this morning:

"While I am grateful with all my heart for this expression of the confidence of my fellow-Americans, I realize keenly the responsibility I shall assume and I mean to serve with my utmost capacity the interest of the nation.

"The people could not have arrived at this result if they had not been informed properly of my views by an independent press, and I value particularly the high service of THE NEW YORK TIMES in its reporting of my speeches and in its enlightened comment."

By ARTHUR KROCK.

A political cataclysm, unprecedented in the nation's history and produced by three years of depression, thrust President Herbert Hoover and the Republican power from control of the government yesterday, elected Governor Franklin Delano Roosevelt President of the United States, provided the Democrats with a large majority in Congress and gave them substantial control of the affairs of many States of the Union.

Fifteen minutes after midnight, Eastern Standard Time, the Associated Press flashed from Palo Alto this line: "Hoover concedes defeat."

It was then fifteen minutes after nine in California, and the President had been in his residence on the Leland Stanford campus only a few hours, arriving with expressed confidence of victory.

A few minutes after the flash from Palo Alto the text of Mr. Hoover's message of congratulation to his successful opponent was received by THE NEW YORK TIMES, though it was delayed in direct transmission to the President-elect. After offering his felicitations to Governor Roosevelt on his "opportunity to be of service to the country," and expressing wishes for success, the President "dedicated" himself to "every helpful effort in the common purpose of us all."

This language strengthened the belief of those who expect that the relations between the victor and the vanquished, in view of the exigent condition of the country, and that they may soon confer in an effort to arrive at a mutual program of stabilization during the period between now

"All the News That's Fit to Print."

The New York Times.

LATE CITY EDITION
POSTSCRIPT
WEATHER—Fair today; tomorrow cloudy, warmer, probably rain

Copyright, 1933, by The New York Times Company.

VOL. LXXXII....No. 27,417.   Entered as Second-Class Matter, Postoffice, New York, N. Y.   NEW YORK, THURSDAY, FEBRUARY 16, 1933.   TWO CENTS In New York City. | THREE CENTS Within 200 Miles | FOUR CENTS Elsewhere In 7th and 8th Postal Zones

ASSASSIN FIRES INTO ROOSEVELT PARTY AT MIAMI; PRESIDENT-ELECT UNINJURED; MAYOR CERMAK AND 4 OTHERS WOUNDED

REPEAL VOTE TODAY SET IN THE SENATE; FILIBUSTER BROKEN

Wets Win in Test Ballots as Blaine Plan is Stripped of Protective Clauses.

ROBINSON LEADS FIGHT

Borah Backs Him on Removing the Anti-Saloon Section, Voted Out 33-32.

STATE LIQUOR PLAN OUT

Commission Proposes to Bar the Saloon—Limit on Places to Sell Beer.

Report of the State Liquor Control Commission is on Page 15.

Special to The New York Times.

WASHINGTON, Feb. 15.—The Senate today stripped the Blaine prohibition repeal resolution to practically "naked" repeal and agreed to vote on the measure at 3 P. M. tomorrow.

Senator Robinson, the Democratic leader, who led the fight to simplify the resolution, predicted that the Senate would furnish the necessary two-thirds majority for adoption on the morrow.

He expressed confidence, too, that the resolution as amended tonight would be acceptable to Speaker Garner and other House leaders, who announced at the outset that the House would be allowed to vote only on the Democratic repeal plan as advocated in the last campaign.

Every prediction was that the vote tomorrow would be extremely close. Senator McNary, assistant Republican leader, described the resolution as "teetering," with the possibility of going one way or the other. He would make no forecast.

Wet leaders, scanning the votes of today, were very hopeful as to the outcome tomorrow. They had succeeded in breaking the filibuster started by the drys to prevent a vote.

Coincidental with the agreement to vote tomorrow, the Senate, by a vote of 33 to 32, struck the so-called anti-saloon provisions from the Blaine resolution and, on a ballot of 45 to 15, decreed that ratification should be by conventions in the several States instead of by Legislatures.

Passage in House Predicted.

A deciding vote on the amendment, proposed by Senator Robinson, to strike out the anti-saloon section, was cast by Senator Borah, long a dry stalwart. He held it was impossible for the government properly to exercise any supervision over saloons once the Eighteenth Amendment was repealed.

As the resolution stood tonight, its proposal was only one degree removed from outright repeal. It carried a clause directing several protection of dry States which the Garner repeal plan contained at the outset of the session, but which Senate leaders said tonight was not sufficiently controversial to bring a deadlock between the two branches.

The resolution as it emerged was believed to have a better chance of passage in the House than the proposal submitted by Speaker Garner for the first day of Congress. The Speaker's resolution failed by only six votes of obtaining the necessary two-thirds majority, and it was pointed out tonight that the six votes from Senator Robinson's own State, which were cast in the negative at that time, were sufficient to change the tide should that repeal be proposed anew to the House.

It was recalled, too, that Senator Robinson was opposed to the Garner resolution, whereas his espousal at this time of the Democratic platform plank was responsible for much of the weight given the revival of the repeal movement.

The dry filibuster against the Blaine resolution broke up in the Senate today when wets announced

Continued on Page Fourteen.

Illinois Senate Passes Bills For Repeal of Prohibition Laws

By The Associated Press.

SPRINGFIELD, Ill., Feb. 15.—The State Senate today passed two prohibition repeal measures and sent them to the House for further action.

The vote on the repeal measure, which had been delayed because of Governor Henry Horner's insistence that regulatory acts should be provided first, was preceded by promises in the debate that they would not be signed until the regulatory bills also had been adopted.

The two bills would remove from the statute books State prohibition and the search and seizure acts.

A measure designed to authorize banking holidays was introduced in the House. Under its terms, the Governor would be empowered to declare a holiday for the State and Mayors authorized to do so for municipalities.

BOY GANG CHIEF, 15, ADMITS KILLING 'FOE'

Says He Stabbed Queens Lad, 12, for "Lying" About Him and Vowed to "Get" Him.

VICTIM MISSING 2 WEEKS

Found Bound in Closet of a Vacant House to Which Killer Had Lured Him by Ruse.

Bound, gagged and stabbed through the heart, the body of 12-year-old William Bender, who disappeared Jan. 31, was found yesterday in a closet in one of a row of partly-built dwellings, less than two blocks from his home at 6 Bergen Landing Road, Richmond Hill Circle, Queens.

Nine hours after the body was found, Harry Murch, 15-year-old leader of a juvenile gang, confessed he had murdered the Bender boy. Murch and his chum, John Miller, 10, who was with him when the crime was committed, were picked up by the police yesterday afternoon. For more than five hours, despite persistent questioning by officials of the Police Department and the District Attorney's office, they calmly denied all knowledge of the crime. Then finally they broke down.

"I did it," Murch is said to have declared. "Bender lied about me. He told the whole neighborhood that I had hit Mrs. Peterson on the head with a monkey wrench. I said I'd get him and I did."

He is to be arraigned today in children's court, Jamaica, on a charge of homicide.

Tells of Meeting Victim.

Murch said that on the afternoon of Jan. 31 he and Miller had met Bender outside the latter's home.

"I told him," Murch said, "that I was going to stick up a peanut peddler and that if he'd come over to the houses in Mauretania Avenue with me I'd show him how I was going to do it. He came along all right. But he seemed a bit suspicious.

"So I tied up Miller first. Then I untied Miller and tied up Bender. As soon as I had him where I wanted him I took out my knife and stabbed him in the heart."

Miller corroborated Murch's story. Afterward, the boys said, they fled from the home and agreed to say nothing to any one. The knife which Murch used for the crime, they said, was taken from the kitchen of his home.

The clue that broke the case was a small piece of gingham cloth that had been used to gag the dead boy. The fact that Murch had threatened to "get Bender" was well known in the neighborhood and soon after the body was discovered detectives went to the home of Murch's parents, Mr. and Mrs. Charles Murch, in Philbert Avenue, just a short distance from the home of the Bender boy.

The two Murch garage the detectives found other pieces of gingham of exactly the same quality and pattern as that which had been used for the gag. Young Murch and Miller were immediately taken into custody.

Continued on Page Ten.

TAX RATE OF $2.40 SEEN AS VALUATIONS DROP $1,195,006,742

Sexton Estimates a 19-Point Reduction to the Lowest Basic Levy Since 1920.

REALTY BURDEN EASED

Assessment Totals Cut in All Boroughs—Personalty Less, Franchise Values Rise.

ALDERMEN VOTE BUDGET

Adopt $518,427,972 Document Without Change—Mayor Denies Plea on Sergeants-at-Arms.

Final adoption of the revised 1933 budget at a total of 18 per cent below that of the 1932 budget and announcement of a cut of $1,195,-006,742 in assessed valuations of city real estate, personal property and franchises provided yesterday a substantial basis for belief that the basic tax rate this year will be appreciably lower than the 1932 rate of $2.89 per $100 of assessed valuation.

For the first time in the city's history the total of assessed valuations is lower than in a preceding year. Valuations dipped upon franchises for tax purposes were increased in every borough this year. Valuations on real estate showed decreases in every borough, while in the Bronx alone valuations on personal estate showed a rise. The total valuations for all boroughs in 1932 was $19,977,077,315. For 1933 the final valuations aggregate $18,782,070,573.

The Board of Aldermen adopted a final budget of $518,427,972.16, the same total recently approved by the Board of Estimate. This figure shows a decrease of $112,932,395.51 from the total budget for 1932, which was $631,366,297.97. The budget now goes to Mayor O'Brien for his signature. It must be filed with Controller Berry by Feb. 25.

Nineteen-Point Tax Drop Seen.

James J. Sexton, president of the Department of Taxes and Assessments, said that he was certain the basic tax rate would show a decided drop. He expressed the belief that the rate would not exceed $2.40, a drop of nineteen points.

Deputy Controller Frank J. Prial, in the absence of the Controller, said that no accurate estimate of the rate could be made before the amount of the city's general fund for reduction of taxation is known. The general fund, the budget and the final total of assessed valuation, are the three factors used in computing the basic rate. Borough tax rates are added to the basic rate to pay for local improvements. Mr. Prial said that the amount of the general fund would depend

Continued on Page Nine.

SERIOUSLY WOUNDED.

Times Wide World Photo.
Mayor Anton J. Cermak of Chicago.

WOMAN DIVERTED AIM OF ASSASSIN

100-Pound Wife of Miami Doctor Tells How She Forced Up Man's Arm.

HELD ON DURING SHOOTING

Gun Had Been Pointed "Right at Mr. Roosevelt" 15 Feet Away, She Relates.

By Telephone to The New York Times.

MIAMI, Fla., Feb. 15.—Mrs. Lillian Cross, 48 years old, and weighing only 100 pounds, probably saved the life of the President-elect tonight when she forced the would-be assassin's shooting arm upward in the night when she forced the gun up so high.

"He was aiming right at the President," said Mrs. Cross.

"I saw him. That's why I caught his arm and forced the gun up. I said to myself, all in a flash, 'Oh! He's going to kill the President!'"

Mrs. Cross said that she was not frightened when she saw the weapon.

"I didn't begin to get nervous at all until it was all over," she related after she reached her home at 1,000 Northwest Second Street.

"I drove to the park tonight with my husband, Dr. W. F. Cross (he's a physician and surgeon here) and with my friend, Mrs. Willie McCrary of Atlanta, Ga. My husband got a seat somewhere in the back of the crowd, but Mrs. McCrary and I found seats right up front, by the guard rail they'd put up.

"President Roosevelt was only about fifteen feet away from us. He finished his speech and got down from the back of the automobile—an open car it was—and had settled in the back seat. I stood up on the bench on which I'd been sit-

Continued on Page Three.

Cermak in Critical Condition at Hospital; "Glad It Was I, Not You," He Tells Roosevelt

Special to The New York Times.

MIAMI, Thursday, Feb. 16.—Mayor Cermak was shot in the right side, just below the ribs, and was in a critical condition at Jackson Memorial Hospital. An X-ray showed the bullet lodged in the back of the abdomen.

An emergency operation was considered at 12:30 A. M. and plans were made to undertake it at once. A short time later physicians put off the operation.

When President-elect Roosevelt called to see Mayor Cermak at the hospital the Mayor turned his head and smiled faintly, saying:

"I'm glad it was I, instead of you. I wish you would be very careful. The country needs you badly. You should not take any more such chances as you took tonight."

The President-elect replied:

"The country needs a man like you, too. I can only express my deepest regrets. I have decided not to leave tonight and will return to see you in the morning."

The body of the missing boy was

Continued on Page Ten.

Councilman, who told of the conversation, said Mr. Roosevelt was expected to call again at the hospital about 8 A. M.

Mr. Bowler was with Mayor Cermak in the emergency room and took from the front of the Mayor's shirt a .32 calibre bullet, which was believed to be a spent shot that had hit one of the other victims.

A bulletin on Mayor Cermak's condition, issued at 2 A. M., said:

"Pulse, 88; temperature, 98.6; respiration, 16. His condition is regarded as dangerous, but not immediately critical. The bullet evidently traversed the diaphragm and margin of the liver and lodged in the body of the eleventh dorsal vertebra. Surgical intervention is deemed unwise unless his condition becomes worse."

The bulletin was signed by Dr. John W. Snyder, Dr. Thomas H. Hutson and Dr. E. B. Nichol. Dr. Snyder is in charge, and at the hospital this morning he said:

"Mrs. Gill and Mayor Cermak have more than a fifty-fifty chance to recover."

The bulletin was signed by Dr. John W. Snyder, Dr. Thomas H. Hutson and Dr. E. B. Nichol, in charge, Chicago City

WASHINGTON IS STUNNED

Hoover Wires Roosevelt; Rejoicing That He Was Not Wounded.

ASKS NEWS OF CERMAK

Senators Express Gratitude President-Elect Escaped Madman's Shots.

RISK TO PRESIDENT SEEN

Determination Is Voiced That Life of His Successor Be Safeguarded by All Means.

Special to The New York Times.

WASHINGTON, Feb. 15.—The nation's capital was deeply shocked tonight on hearing of the attempt on the life of President-elect Roosevelt.

From President Hoover to the lowliest citizen the reaction was instant that the country cast every safeguard around the President-elect.

President Hoover himself struck the keynote when he said:

"I am deeply shocked at the news. It is a dastardly act."

Hoover's Message to Roosevelt.

At the same time the President sent a telegram to Mr. Roosevelt which read:

"Together with every citizen I rejoice that you have not been injured. I shall be grateful to you for news of Mayor Cermak's condition."

Official and unofficial Washington was stunned at the first report of what appeared to be an attempt on the life of the man who within less than three weeks will become Chief Executive. Newspaper extras were on the street almost immediately, and citizens sat close to their radios, receiving the latest news flashes. General relief was expressed that Mr. Roosevelt escaped injury.

Comment of Leaders.

Speaker Garner said:

"I am thankful that our next President escaped injury and that the act of a misguided or crazy individual will not deprive the American people of their chosen leader."

"Of course, I am overjoyed that the President-elect escaped," said Senator Byrnes, one of Mr. Roosevelt's closest advisers, "but I deplore profoundly that such a thing could happen. It's awful!"

Senator Robinson of Arkansas, Senate minority leader, said:

"Assuming that the shots were fired at Mr. Roosevelt, it should be understood that this is a United States, not Russia. No fanatic, crank or revolutionist, or any number of them will be permitted to prevent the orderly transfer of power in the government of the United States."

Thinks Assailant Deranged.

"How dreadful, and how fortunate he did not hit!" said Senator Lewis of Illinois. "I do not know what to say except that it was a deplorable thing. I do hope it was not attempted out of ill will. It must have been the result of a deranged mind; certainly no one in his right mind would attempt such a thing. If, as appears possible, the shots were actually fired at Mayor Cermak, it undoubtedly was some member of the old lawless element in Chicago with a fancied grievance against the Mayor."

Chief Moran of the Secret Service, ill at his home here, received a report late this evening from Joseph E. Murphy, Assistant Chief, from the hospital in Miami where Mayor Cermak had been taken.

Commenting on the shooting, Senator Shipstead said:

"This unfortunate incident shows the risk the President and the President-elect of the United States are subject to. There are always cranks in the country. Every citi-

Continued on Page Three.

ESCAPES ASSASSIN'S BULLETS.

New York Times Studio Photo.
President-Elect Franklin D. Roosevelt.

GUNMAN LAYS ACT TO BODY 'TORMENT'

Joe Zingara, Hackensack Bricklayer, Says Pain Made Him 'Hate All Presidents.'

DESCRIBED AS ANARCHIST

Man Who Fired at Roosevelt Says He Once Tried in Italy to Kill King Victor Emmanuel.

By Telephone to The New York Times.

MIAMI, Feb. 15.—Surrounded by detectives and high police officials, the man who shot at President-elect Roosevelt tonight gave his name as Joe Zingara of New York and related, in spasms of words during questioning at Police Headquarters, how "constant torment from a stomach operation" had impelled him to attempt the life of the President-elect.

Zingara, a short, stocky man of about 35, a brick mason who came to Miami two months ago from Hackensack, N. J., betrayed by his manner even in the rational portions of his statement the warped mentality which resulted in his dead tonight.

In an almost boastful tone, he declared that he had attempted the life of King Victor Emmanuel of Italy ten years ago. That failed, he said, for the same reason as his attempt tonight—"there was too big a crowd."

He admitted he had no personal grievance against Mr. Roosevelt. Saying "No, I had none," he swept away questions of that nature.

Nor could the police discover that he had any personal grievance against the King of Italy. But he hated "rich and powerful persons," he said with a blaze, and they were figures, he indicated, for his wrath.

"I Don't Like Presidents."

"I like Roosevelt personally, but I don't like Presidents," he replied when asked if he didn't like the President-elect. He intended to kill him, he said, "and I would be glad if I had killed the President-elect." He did not like Presidents because "rich men send their children to schools."

He said this was because "when I was a young man, rich men's sons went to school while I worked in a brick factory in Italy and burned myself."

Zingara indicated a scar on his stomach which he said was the result of the burn.

He was seized with the idea of trying to kill the President-elect only two days ago, he declared.

"About two days ago I bought a paper for 2 cents and saw that the President-elect was coming to Miami," he related.

"So yesterday I went to a place

Continued on Page Two.

MRS. ROOSEVELT TAKES NEWS CALMLY

She Telephones Immediately to Husband and Is Relieved to Find Him Unhurt.

KEEPS SPEAKING PROGRAM

Assured That "He Is Not Even Excited," She Takes Train Later for Ithaca.

Mrs. Franklin D. Roosevelt returned to her home at 49 East Sixty-fifth Street about 10:30 o'clock last night and found the household upset. The Negro butler's face betrayed his agitation as he admitted her.

"What's it all about?" she demanded.

Stammering, the butler told her that her husband, the President-elect, had been fired upon in Miami. He had only the meager information gleaned from newspapers, which called the house whom the first brief reports were received.

Mrs. Roosevelt was met at her home by her daughter, Mrs. Anna Roosevelt Dall, and received the news calmly and without apparent emotion.

"These things are to be expected," she remarked.

With a calm and steady voice she placed a long distance telephone call which reached the President-elect at the bedside of Mayor Cermak. There followed a few minutes of conversation and then Mrs. Roosevelt turned to the group in the room and said:

"He's all right. He's not the least bit excited."

Leaves for Ithaca.

A few minutes later Mrs. Roosevelt, accompanied only by her maid, was on a railroad train bound for Ithaca, N. Y., to fill a speaking engagement on the program of Cornell University's Home and Farm Week. The train left at 11:25.

Mrs. Roosevelt was speaking at the Warner Club at 221 West Forty-fourth Street when the first of the dramatic incident in Miami was received in New York newspaper offices. She left there without knowledge of what had happened.

In his telephone conversation with Mrs. Roosevelt, members of the household said, the President-elect informed her that it was his belief that the would-be assassin's bullets were aimed at Mayor Cermak, and not at him.

They quoted him as saying that five persons were in the hospital as a result of the shooting, and that he wasn't even scratched. Instead of starting back for New York last night, as he had planned, however,

Continued on Page Two.

ASSASSIN SHOOTS 5 TIMES

Police and Bystanders Leap for Him and Take Him Prisoner.

ACCOMPLICE TAKEN LATER

Cermak and New York Officer Rushed to Hospital—Now in Serious Condition.

ROOSEVELT DELAYS TRIP

Had Been Warmly Welcomed and Intended to Start for North at Once.

By JAMES A. HAGERTY.
Special to The New York Times.

MIAMI, Feb. 15.—An unsuccessful attempt was made to assassinate President-elect Franklin D. Roosevelt just after he had ended a speech in Bay Front Park here at 9:35 o'clock tonight, two hours after his return from a seven-day fishing cruise on Vincent Astor's yacht Nourmahal.

Although the gunman missed the target at which he was aiming, he probably fatally wounded Mayor Anton Cermak of Chicago and four other persons were hit by five shots from his pistol before a woman destroyed his aim on the last shot by seizing his wrist and a Miami policeman felled him to the ground with a blow of his night stick.

List of the Wounded.

The wounded are:

Mayor Anton Cermak of Chicago, shot through the chest; condition critical.

Miss Margaret Kruis of the Henry Clay Hotel, Miami Beach, a visitor from Newark, N. J., shot through the hand.

Mrs. Joe H. Gill, wife of the president of the Florida Power and Light Company, shot in the abdomen; condition serious.

William Sinnott, a New York policeman, living at 612 West 178th Street, shot in the head; condition critical.

Russell Caldwell, 22, of Miami, shot in the head.

Roosevelt Was Target.

The would-be assassin, who was arrested immediately and lodged in the city prison on the nineteenth floor of Miami's skyscraper City Hall, is Giuseppe Zingara of Hackensack, N. J.

Although early reports were that he intended to kill Mayor Cermak rather than the President-elect, due to his remark, "Well, I got Cermak," it appeared later that Mr. Roosevelt was his target.

"I'd kill every President," he was reported by the police to have said after his arrest.

"I'd kill them all; I'd kill all the officers," he also is reported to have said, indicating that he may be an Anarchist.

Evidence that the attempted assassination of Roosevelt was premeditated was obtained by the police late tonight and Andrea Valenti, who lived with Zingara, was arrested on suspicion of being an accomplice.

A search of Zingara's clothing disclosed several newspaper clippings, mostly from local newspapers announcing Mr. Roosevelt's intended visit to this city.

Clipping on McKinley.

One clipping, however, contained an account of the assassination of President McKinley at Buffalo by the anarchist Czolgosz. This strengthened the police belief that Zingara might belong to some anarchist group, although no direct evidence has been obtained showing such a connection.

Detectives, deputy sheriffs and policemen were working on several clues, obtained by the questioning of Zingara and Valenti.

Zingara is charged with assault with intent to kill, pending the preferring of the more serious

"All the News That's Fit to Print."

The New York Times.

LATE CITY EDITION
WEATHER—Fair today; tomorrow cloudy, warmer, rain following. Temperatures Yesterday—Max., 40; min., 26.

Copyright, 1933, by The New York Times Company.

VOL. LXXXII....No. 27,485.   Entered as Second-Class Matter, Postoffice, New York, N. Y.   NEW YORK, MONDAY, MARCH 6, 1933.   P   TWO CENTS in New York City. | THREE CENTS Within 200 Miles | FOUR CENTS Elsewhere Except in 7th and 8th Postal Zones

ROOSEVELT ORDERS 4-DAY BANK HOLIDAY, PUTS EMBARGO ON GOLD, CALLS CONGRESS

HITLER BLOC WINS A REICH MAJORITY; RULES IN PRUSSIA

Stay-at-Homes Turn Out and Give Government 52% of 39,000,000 Record Vote.

NAZIS ROLL UP 17,300,000

Get 44% of Total Poll and Even Wrest the Control of Bavaria From Catholics.

ELECTION IS PEACEFUL

Berlin Is Closely Guarded—The Stahlhelm Holds Parade Under Sunny Skies.

By FREDERICK T. BIRCHALL
Special Cable to The New York Times.

BERLIN, Monday, March 6.—With almost mathematical precision the results in yesterday's German elections for the Reichstag and the Prussian Diet bear out the predictions based on the pre-election campaign. Just as two and two make four, so suppression and intimidation have produced a Nazi-Nationalist triumph. The rest of the world may now accept the fact of ultra-Nationalist domination of the Reich and Prussia for a prolonged period with whatever results this may entail.

At 2 o'clock this morning, when 39,000,000 out of the Reich's eligible vote of 44,000,000, counted and with every indication of a probable total vote of 90 per cent, exceeding all precedents Nazi-Nationalist control of the Reichstag was assured. The Nazis will have at least 288 seats and the Nationalists 52 more, giving them together 341 seats, or a clear 52 per cent in a total of 648.

The tabulated returns follow:

	Vote.	Seats.
National Socialists	17,300,000	288
Nationalists	3,100,000	52
Socialists	7,000,000	118
Communists	4,800,000	81
Centrists and Bavarian People's Party	5,500,000	91
People's Party and Allied Groups	1,014,000	12
State (Democratic)	333,000	5
Total	39,047,000	648

The Nazis have increased their vote to 44 per cent of the adult population, or 11 per cent over that of last November and 8⅓ per cent over their previous high-water total of last July. The Nationalist increase is barely 1 per cent over their vote of last November. This, therefore, is a Nazi rather than a Nationalist triumph.

Nazis Control Bavaria.

Apart from the size of their vote the 90 per cent of the eligible voters being as nearly unanimous as any election in any large country has ever shown—the sensation of the election is that the Nazis have wrested control of Bavaria from the Catholics. They have wiped out the deficit in the last November vote compared with that of July and have beaten the Bavarian People's party by approximately 600,000. This is likely to dispose of any dream of restoring the Wittelsbach monarchy in Bavaria, as it will of the idea of a possible secession of Bavaria from the Reich.

More than this, in the city of Cologne, the Catholic capital of Germany, under the influence of an unexpected 20 per cent increase in the total vote—three-fourths of which has gone into the Nazi column—Herr Hitler's party has come within an ace of seizing control there.

The so-called stay-at-home vote came out with a vengeance and almost the whole of it went to the Nazis; while, in addition, the Hitlerites gained a full 10 per cent from the other parties.

Gain 4,000,000 Votes.

The Nazis have increased their own vote by more than 4,000,000, or almost 30 per cent over the November total. The Centrists and Socialists throughout the country have almost held their own. The Communists lost more than 20 per cent, but their lost votes did not go to the Socialists, as had been expected. While a few may have gone

Continued on Page Eight.

[Pinchgut, N. C.—Complete change of climate, nearby; flawless service and meals, 3 days, all inclusive, $65.00 [gulf]. Carolina Hotel and T. O. Taro.; 887 at Molly Inn.—Advt.]

Mob Attacked Stalin's Home In Wide Revolt, Tokyo Hears

Wireless to The New York Times.

TOKYO, Monday, March 6.—Private information reaching Tokyo states that discontent due to famine conditions is so acute in Soviet Russia that a mob attacked Joseph Stalin's house in Moscow on Jan. 30 and was driven off by troops after 300 persons had been killed. Other reports from Siberia, partly corroborated by information reaching military circles here, indicate the farmers are in widespread revolt. Serious disturbances occurred at Irkutsk, and 80,000 men are said to have joined the revolt, including Communists and Red soldiers.

The Japanese discount a good part of these rumors, but they come from too many sources to be entirely ignored. It is believed these disturbances are much more serious than the Soviet Government has admitted.

CERMAK NEAR END; LAPSES INTO COMA

Death Is Imminent From Shot Aimed by Zangara at Roosevelt.

FAMILY AT HIS BEDSIDE

Third Transfusion Futile in 19-Day Fight to Save Chicago Mayor in Miami Hospital.

By The Associated Press.

MIAMI, Fla., Monday, March 6.—Physicians of Mayor Anton Cermak early this morning relinquished hope for his life.

In a bulletin issued at 12:30 A. M. the physicians said that Mayor Cermak was in a condition of coma and that he probably would live only a few hours. The bulletin said Mr. Cermak was "failing rapidly."

It was issued after a third blood transfusion had been administered yesterday in an attempt to save his life.

The Mayor's right lung, punctured on the night of Feb. 15 by a bullet from the pistol of the assassin, Joseph Zangara, in an attempt to kill President Franklin D. Roosevelt, was aspirated yesterday and physicians found a gangrenous condition.

Father Morrison of St. Bartholomew's Church in Chicago entered the sun parlor room at 1:15 A. M. Mayor Cermak's wife was a Roman Catholic and his children are of that faith.

Dr. Frederick Tice of Chicago told newspaper men at 1:25 A. M. that the Mayor probably would live an hour. He said Cermak's breathing was very labored. He called members of the family and said Mr. Cermak's life was "a matter of an hour."

Members of Family Weep.

Members of the family, summoned to the bedside, emerged weeping.

Joseph Cermak, a brother, his wife and Mrs. John Kallal, a sister, came from the sun porch at 12:35 A. M. Mrs. Cermak sank to the lawn before the sun porch door and wept. Vivian Graham, a granddaughter, emerged soon and joined the group. Daughters of the Mayor and his wife at his side a short time before.

At midnight newspapermen were allowed to go into the sun porch where the Mayor lies in an oxygen room and see the patient through the glass window of the oxygen apparatus.

The Mayor lay back on his pillow, hands folded over his chest, breathing heavily. Dr. Frank Jirka and Dr. E. S. Nichol were attending him.

Dr. Jirka, who is Mr. Cermak's son-in-law, said the Mayor recognized members of the family. "My wife asked him if he knew her. He told her, 'Yes, kiss me.'"

The greatest air of concern prevailed by the little sun porch, where a heavy guard of police and detectives was maintained.

"Reaction" After Transfusion.

After the blood transfusion yesterday afternoon Mr. Cermak suffered a "slight reaction," causing a weakening of the pulse and irregular respiration, the doctors said. Reports immediately upon conclusion of the transfusion were that the operation apparently was successful. One pint of blood given by Thomas Pandray Jr. of Miami was

Continued on Page Fourteen.

JAPANESE PUSH ON IN FIERCE FIGHTING; CHINA CLOSES WALL

Jehol Forces Offer Stoutest Resistance of Campaign as They Are Cornered.

BUT LOSE ANOTHER PASS

Chang's Troops at Kupei Bar Retreat Southward to the Peiping Area.

NANKING ADMITS DEFEAT

Asserts 'What Will Happen Next Depends on Military'—Tientsin Fears Clashes.

By The Associated Press.

TOKYO, March 5.—Rengo (Japanese) news agency dispatches from Chengteh (Jehol City) today said the final phase of the Japanese campaign in Jehol Province, a move to seize passes in the Great Wall north and northeast of Peiping, was producing some of the most bitter fighting of the whole drive. Cornered Chinese units were resisting desperately.

The Sixteenth Infantry Brigade of Major Gen. Tadashi Kawahara, en route to Koupei Pass through the wall, fought fiercely with remnants of the troops of Tang Yu-lin, Governor of Jehol Province, ten miles west of the provincial capital, Chengteh. Thereafter the detachment advanced to Changshanku, which is sixteen miles northeast of the pass.

Marshal Chang Hsiao-liang, military commander of North China, was reported to have sent his reserve against Governor Tang and his followers. Governor Tang himself was reported to have fled to Fengning, which is about forty miles northwest of Chengteh.

Pass in Wall Taken.

Fighting in the shadow of the Great Wall preceded the occupation by the Fourteenth Infantry Brigade of Major Gen. Heijiro Hattori of the troops of Tang Yu-lin, three important Great Wall passes south of Chengteh. General Hattori faced a large Chinese force south of the wall.

Major Gen. Kaoru Nakamura, commanding the Thirty-third Infantry Brigade, en route from Lingyu to Chiehling Pass, summoned an air squadron to aid him before he advanced to routing remnants of Marshal Chang's Sixteenth Brigade.

The Fourth Cavalry Brigade of Major Gen. Kennosuke Mogi, pushing on from Chifeng, 260 miles northeast of Chengteh, captured Weichang, fifty-five miles to the southwest, the centre of the Jehol opium-producing region, after stiff fighting.

Thousands of Chinese Dead.

Special Cable to The New York Times.

SHANGHAI, Monday, March 6.—While members of the Nanking Government are expected to discuss a unified policy at Peiping this week, Jehol reports today tell of indescribable confusion among the Chinese forces there, with thousands killed, wounded and missing among the troops in Marshal Chang Hsiao-liang's best brigades, which originally totaled 20,000.

War Minister Ho Yin-ching arrived by airplane at Peiping at noon, and Acting Premier T. V. Soong and others are expected to follow him there for a hasten stocktaking of the present situation. The Chinese troops in Jehol appear to be scrambling for the passes out through the Great Wall with the Japanese bombing Chinese concentrations near Kupei and Haifeng passes and at Dolonnor, in Northern Jehol.

The Japanese brigade led by General Hattori is expected to attack the main Chinese forces tomorrow at Palshihlatsushan Hill, twenty miles south of Pingchuan and thirty-three miles southeast of Haifeng Pass.

The Charhar Provincial Government is reported to be negotiating with the Japanese for inclusion of that province in Manchukuo, but Chinese military deny this.

The Nanking Foreign Office yesterday made this terse and incisive statement:

"Jehol is lost. What will happen

Continued on Page Eight.

Relief Wages Will Be Paid Despite Holiday, Gibson Says

Harvey D. Gibson, chairman of the Emergency Unemployment Relief Committee, declared yesterday that the bank holiday would not interfere with the payment of wages to unemployed men and women holding emergency jobs through the committee's work and relief bureau.

"Emergency wages must be paid and some way must be found to pay them," Mr. Gibson said. "I have no doubt that we will find a way to meet the situation, but it also gave the banks permission to issue scrip in the form of Clearing House certificates to take the place of regular currency.

The weekly payroll of the committee exceeds $1,000,000.

BANKS HERE ACT AT ONCE

City Scrip to Be Ready Today or Tomorrow to Replace Currency.

EMERGENCY STEP PRAISED

Financiers Look for Little Interruption in Business Under Federal Program.

'TRUST DEPOSITS' TO AID

Cash Now Can Be Placed in New Accounts and Drawn Upon Without Limitation.

Clearing House certificates will be issued in New York, if needed, just as soon as they are printed, possibly today and probably not later than tomorrow, as a result of President Roosevelt's proclamation of last night.

The President's emergency decree not only made the banking holiday national and extended it through Thursday when Congress meets in special session, but it also gave the banks permission to issue scrip in the form of Clearing House certificates to take the place of regular currency.

Thus there will be little or no interruption in the ordinary routine of New York's business affairs, which can be carried on with scrip as a substitute medium of exchange just as well as with currency. Paychecks, for instance, would be converted into scrip by the banks, which would be open for that purpose and for receiving new deposits.

Leading bankers indicated their approval of the President's proclamation last night and signified their belief that the use of scrip would be just as successful in New York as it was in the 1907 panic.

May Pay in Currency.

There is a possibility, some bankers said, that the New York banks might pay out currency when they reopen in place of, or in addition to, clearing house certificates. Such action would be possible only with the express permission of the Secretary of the Treasury under the President's order. These bankers said that the local banks have large amounts of till money on hand and that they could, if permitted, meet substantial demands from their depositors out of these cash holdings. From the standpoint of the central banking system the paying out of this till money to the public would have no effect upon the position of the national currency, since it is already a part of total money in circulation.

Subject always to the sanction of the Secretary of the Treasury, the banks will be able, under the President's proclamation, to operate along nearly normal lines. Under the provision for creation of special trust accounts, business men, merchants and wage earners will be able to find a safe depository for any cash they received without having to face the dangers of carrying large amounts of currency. Those who withdrew money from the banks just before the shutdown and who have since been worrying about the safety will be able to redeposit the funds in special trust accounts and be assured of getting it back again without limitation.

Lehman Defers State Action.

When informed of the President's proclamation late last night, Governor Lehman withheld comment for the present as to whether he would issue a new decree extending the New York State holiday. Although such an action probably would be regarded as a mere formality, it was thought likely that the Governor would take it. Before President Roosevelt's proclamation was made public, Governor A. Harry Moore of New Jersey issued a decree last night extending the banking holiday in New Jersey indefinitely.

In both New York and New Jersey the banking holiday was proclaimed first for two days—Saturday and today—and was to have ended with the close of business this afternoon. Under the original proclamations by Governors Lehman and Moore the New York and New Jersey banks were to have been reopened tomorrow morning.

All security and commodity exchanges will remain closed, barring unexpected changes in present

Continued on Page Three.

The President's Bank Proclamation

Special to The New York Times.

WASHINGTON, March 5.—The text of President Roosevelt's proclamation on the banking situation, issued at the White House at 11 o'clock tonight, was as follows:

BY THE PRESIDENT OF THE UNITED STATES OF AMERICA.

A Proclamation

WHEREAS there have been heavy and unwarranted withdrawals of gold and currency from our banking institutions for the purpose of hoarding; and

WHEREAS continuous and increasingly extensive speculative activity abroad in foreign exchange has resulted in severe drains on the nation's stocks of gold; and

WHEREAS these conditions have created a national emergency; and

WHEREAS it is in the best interests of all bank depositors that a period of respite be provided with a view to preventing further hoarding of coin, bullion or currency or speculation in foreign exchange and permitting the application of appropriate measures to protect the interests of our people; and

WHEREAS it is provided in Section 5 (b) of the act of October 6, 1917 (40 stat. L. 411) as amended, "that the President may investigate, regulate or prohibit, under such rules and regulations as he may prescribe, by means of licenses or otherwise, any transactions in foreign exchange and the export, hoarding, melting or earmarkings of gold or silver coin or bullion or currency * * *"

WHEREAS it is provided in Section 16 of the said act "that whoever shall wilfully violate any of the provisions of this act or of any license, rule or regulation issued thereunder, and whoever shall wilfully violate, neglect or refuse to comply with any order of the President issued in compliance with the provisions of this act, shall, upon conviction, be fined not more than $10,000, or, if a natural person, imprisoned for not more than ten years, or both * * *"

NOW, THEREFORE, I, FRANKLIN D. ROOSEVELT, PRESIDENT OF THE UNITED STATES OF AMERICA, IN VIEW OF SUCH NATIONAL EMERGENCY AND BY VIRTUE of the authority vested in me by said act and in order to prevent the export, hoarding or earmarking of gold or silver coin or bullion or currency, do hereby proclaim, order, direct and declare that from Monday, the sixth day of March, to Thursday, the ninth day of March, nineteen hundred and thirty-three, both dates inclusive, there shall be maintained and observed by all banking institutions and all branches thereof located in the United States, including the Territories and Insular Possessions, a bank holiday, and that during said period all banking transactions shall be suspended.

During such holiday, excepting as hereinafter provided, no such banking institution or branch shall pay out, export, earmark or permit the withdrawal or transfer in any manner or by any device whatsoever of any gold or silver coin or bullion or currency or take any other action which might facilitate the hoarding thereof; nor shall any such banking institution or branch pay out deposits, make loans or discounts, deal in foreign exchange, transfer credits from the United States to any place abroad, or transact any other banking business whatsoever.

During such holiday, with the approval of the President and under such regulations as he may prescribe, is authorized and empowered (a) to permit any or all of such banking institutions to perform any or all of the usual banking functions, (b) to direct, require or permit the issuance of clearing house certificates, or other evidence of claims of assets of banking institutions, and (c) to authorize and direct the creation in such banking institutions of special trust accounts for the receipt of new deposits which shall be subject to withdrawal on demand without any restriction or limitation and shall be kept separately in cash or on deposit in Federal Reserve Banks or invested in obligations of the United States.

As used in this order the term "banking institutions" shall include all Federal Reserve Banks, national banking associations, banks, trust companies, savings banks, building and loan associations, credit unions, or other corporations, partnerships, associations or persons, engaged in the business of receiving deposits, making loans, discounting business paper, or transacting any other form of banking business.

IN WITNESS WHEREOF I have hereunto set my hand and caused the seal of the United States to be affixed.

DONE in the City of Washington this 6th day of March, 1 A. M., in the year of Our Lord One Thousand Nine Hundred and Thirty-three, and of the Independence of the United States the one hundred and fifty-seventh.

(SEAL)   FRANKLIN D. ROOSEVELT.

By the President:
CORDELL HULL,
Secretary of State.

ROOSEVELT MEETS GOVERNORS TODAY

Conference Will Centre on Bank Problem—Confidence in President Apparent.

Special to The New York Times.

WASHINGTON, March 5.—The Governors conference which President Roosevelt called about a month ago to discuss with him interlocking governmental problems will meet with him tomorrow morning in the White House at 11 o'clock. But the discussion will be largely directed toward the more immediate issue of banking moratoriums, with the possibility that what is done may indicate the eventual Federal action to be suggested by President Roosevelt.

The present situation so far overshadows the issues which Mr. Roosevelt stressed in originally calling the conference that they have become entirely secondary. It was his first intention to confine the discussion to a limitation on overlapping Federal and State

Continued on Page Two.

ON GOLD STANDARD, WOODIN DECLARES

Other High Officials Concur in His View of Suspending Payments for Period.

Special to The New York Times.

WASHINGTON, March 5.—Secretary of the Treasury William H. Woodin declared tonight emphatically that the United States has not gone off the gold standard on account of the proclamation of the President. He was supported in this view by other high officials of the administration, both in the executive and legislative branches, among them Senator Key Pittman, chairman of the Committee on Foreign Relations.

Secretary Woodin said:
"It is ridiculous and misleading to say that we have gone off the gold standard, any more than we have gone off the currency standard.

"We are definitely on the gold standard. Gold merely cannot be obtained for several days. In other

Continued on Page Six.

USE OF SCRIP AUTHORIZED

President Takes Steps Under Sweeping Law of War Time.

PRISON FOR GOLD HOARDER

The Proclamation Provides for Withdrawals From Banks Against New Deposits.

CONGRESS SITS THURSDAY

Day of Conference With the Cabinet and Financial Men Precedes the Decree.

Special to The New York Times.

WASHINGTON, March 5.—To prevent the export, hoarding or earmarking of gold or silver, coin or bullion or currency, President Roosevelt issued a proclamation at 11 o'clock tonight, in which he ordered a bank holiday from tomorrow through Thursday, March 9. Earlier in the day he had summoned a special session of Congress to meet on Thursday.

This sweeping action was taken after a day of conference, among officials and bankers. The President taking recourse to war powers granted under the trading-with-the-enemy act.

As a result of the proclamation all banking activities will be suspended during the holiday, except as permitted by regulations of the Secretary of the Treasury, thus taking this country technically off the gold standard until the four-day period expires.

In order that there may not be a complete suspension of all banking and exchange operations, the proclamation authorizes the issuance of Clearing House certificates, which may be used as currency until the banks return to more normal functioning.

Points of the Proclamation.

The main points in the proclamation are:

1. A national banking holiday from March 6 to March 9 inclusive.

An embargo on the withdrawal of gold and silver for export or domestic use during that period, except with permission of the Secretary of the Treasury.

2. The issuance of Clearing House certificates or other evidences of claims against the assets of banking institutions to permit business to carry on.

4. Authorization to banking institutions under regulations of the Secretary of the Treasury to receive new deposits and make them subject to withdrawal on demand without any restrictions or limitations.

Friends of the President believed he had a definite three-point program for the solution of the banking problem and that tonight's action was included two of them. The first, they said, was a protection on the currency against unreasonable withdrawal. The second was to furnish a temporary currency. The third is permanent reorganization of the whole banking system, which, they predicted would be proposed to the special session of Congress meeting here Thursday.

Officials Act Quickly.

The Federal Reserve Board and Secretary Woodin, with the advice of former Secretary Ogden L. Mills, acted immediately after the issuance of the proclamation to make it effective.

The proclamation was issued at 11 o'clock, at the conclusion of a series of conferences held by Treasury officials and the new Cabinet throughout the day.

The proclamation affects all Federal Reserve Banks and national banks, trust companies, savings banks, building and loan associations, credit unions or other institutions engaged in any form of banking business.

The proclamation provides for a fine of $10,000 or imprisonment of not more than ten years as the penalty for any violation of its provisions by gold hoarding or otherwise.

The President acted under Section 5 (b) and Section 16 of the trading-with-the-enemy act to place these extraordinary restrictions on the nation's banking structure. The security being interpreted the act as giving the President authority to bring about a complete suspension of gold and silver payments as well as an embargo on their export.

Section 5 (b) of the trading-with-

BEWILDERED CITY STILL PAYS IN CASH

Faces Use of Scrip Calmly and Continues to Patronize the Theatres and Stores.

HOPEFUL MOOD PREVAILS

Merchants and Travel Lines Uncertain on Use of Tender—Many Extending Credit.

Bewildered but still cheerful, the city followed its usual routine yesterday, talked of the possibility of using scrip instead of cash, but still patronized the movie theatres, restaurants and concert halls.

Railroads reported, generally, that there had been no appreciable decrease in week-end travel, that there had been "no embarrassment" and that they were carrying on as usual, on an all-cash basis.

A spokesman for the Pennsylvania Railroad reported that the outward movement yesterday was good and an official of the New York Central reported everything going smoothly with enough cash on hand to meet all the road's needs for the present, including payrolls.

One form of nuisance cropped up at Pennsylvania Station. It started Saturday night, when persons with banknotes of large denominations demanded change. There was a tremendous number of $100 notes, quite a few $500 notes and even a few $1,000 notes were presented for change. One or two of the more timid persons tried to cover up their real purpose by buying Newark tickets.

Railroads Accept Only Cash.

None of the railroads is accepting anything but cash for transportation. This is in accord with the general practice, an official pointed out, and up to yesterday no change in that plan had been proposed. Officers of the New York Central Railroad held a special meeting yesterday apparently to arrange for eventualities that might arise from the banking situation, but no decision was reached so far as could be learned.

Airplane lines, on the other hand, were accepting checks from old clients and were following a policy of being "reasonable" about accepting checks from other customers.

"We will maintain a sensible and reasonable attitude during this crisis," said John Gammie, assistant manager of the Cunard Line. "We will try to carry on much as we did in ordinary times. We haven't taken up the matter of scrip, but it is likely that a meeting of steamship line officials may be called to decide on a policy with regard to it."

Rise in Grocery Store Sales.

Increased sales were reported in most of the chain grocery stores in the poorer districts on Saturday, owners reported yesterday. They believed it might have been caused by a desire to stock up before an inflation possibly began to be upon by the government.

The Grand Union Grocery Stores, an official said last night, are planning to issue coupon books redeemable for food at their stores. The books would be sold to industrial and commercial concerns that would use them as part payment to employees. The same official considered it likely that guaranteed Clearing House scrip might be acceptable at the Grand Union stores.

A spokesman for the Great Atlantic and Pacific Tea Company, which maintains chains of grocery stores in several States, said his concern had not yet formulated any

Continued on Page Three.

The New York Times.

NRA — "All the News That's Fit to Print."

LATE CITY EDITION
WEATHER—Fair and warmer to-day; tomorrow cloudy, showers. Temperature Yesterday—Max.; 61; Min. 50

Section 1

Copyright, 1933, by The New York Times Company.

VOL. LXXXIII....No. 27,658.   Entered as Second-Class Matter, Postoffice, New York, N. Y.   NEW YORK, SUNDAY, OCTOBER 15, 1933.   F+   Including Telegravure Pictures, Magazine and Book Sections.   TEN CENTS | TWELVE CENTS Beyond 200 Miles. Except in 7th and 8th Postal Zones.

REPUBLICANS PLAN FIGHT FOR FUSION TO END DEFECTIONS

Campaign to Begin This Week —Leaders See McKee Defeat as Blow to Roosevelt.

WEIGH NATIONAL RESULTS

Look to Party Victory Here as Step Toward State Triumph in Presidential Drive.

McKEE - LAGUARDIA CLASH

They Exchange Sharp Telegrams as Result of the Seabury Attack on Lehman.

Progress of City Campaign.

City Republicans prepared for aggressive fight for F. H. LaGuardia. National leaders of the party hold defeat of Joseph V. McKee would be a blow to prestige of President Roosevelt.

Mr. McKee demanded to know whether Mr. LaGuardia supported Samuel Seabury's attacks on Governor Lehman. Mr. LaGuardia's reply accused Mr. McKee of attack on Jews eighteen years ago. Tammany reported that "deserters" were returning to the ranks and said they would be welcomed "if they hustled."

Republican Fusion Fight.

By W. A. WARN.

The Republicans who so far have not taken a very active part in the Fusion campaign are preparing to enter the fight aggressively this week. They are determined to block attempts made by the supporters of Joseph V. McKee to bring about a Republican defection to the Recovery party.

The entry of Mr. McKee into the Mayoralty race, which inevitably will have the effect of dividing the anti-Tammany forces, it was said last night in well-informed Republican quarters, has consolidated Republican sentiment in favor of the candidates on the Fusion ticket.

Announcement is expected within a day or two of a big Republican mass meeting, to be held, probably toward the end of this week, under the auspices of the Republican Mayoralty Committee, of which Charles H. Tuttle is chairman. Plans for the meeting were discussed and perfected at a meeting held behind closed doors at the National Republican Club last week.

Financial Leaders to Meet.

Tomorrow, at a luncheon to be given at the Bankers Club under the auspices of the brokers division, F. H. LaGuardia, the Fusion standard bearer, and some of the other candidates on his ticket will make their appeal to a group of Republicans and Democrats engaged in finance who, although united in their opposition to Tammany, have not been regarded by many as friendly to the candidacy of Mr. LaGuardia.

There will be other gatherings of importance under Republican auspices to signalize the vigorous entry of the local party into the Mayoralty fight in support of the Fusion ticket.

From a purely partisan aspect, the Republicans throughout the country have come to view the Mayoralty fight now in progress in this city as of more than local significance, especially since it is understood that Mr. McKee is making his fight with the support of the Roosevelt administration at Washington.

A defeat for Mr. McKee, as the national Republican strategists look upon it, could not fail to impair the prestige of the President and correspondingly enhance that of their own party.

Republican leaders in this State have sought to impress upon the local leaders and Republicans of prominence who so far have held aloof from the contest that the election of Mr. LaGuardia would give their party a tremendous lift in its attempt to elect a Governor next year, as well as in the Congressional elections, which are of equal importance from a national Republican viewpoint.

A Republican victory in the State next year, as the national leaders view the situation, would almost certainly shift this State from the Democratic to the Republican column in 1936.

Effect on 1936 Is Weighed.

Many prominent Republicans in this city who have not been credited with any personal interest in the election of their fellow Republican, Mr. LaGuardia, are vitally interested in the Presidential campaign three years hence. Ogden L. Mills, former Secretary of the Treasury and strong supporter of Herbert Hoover, has come to be looked upon on party circles as an aspirant

Continued on Page Three.

Major Sports Results

Football—Columbia met unexpectedly strong opposition from Virginia, winning by 15 to 6. N. Y. U. beat Lafayette, 13-12, while Fordham triumphed over West Virginia, 20-0. Yale conquered Washington and Lee, 14-0, and Pittsburgh downed Navy, 34 to 6. Scores of other important games:

Army	32	Delaware	0
Colgate	25	Rutgers	2
Harvard	34	New Hamp.	0
Illinois	21	Wisconsin	0
Lebanon Val.	32	C. C. N. Y.	0
Manhattan	20	Georgetown	20
Michigan	40	Cornell	0
Notre Dame	12	Indiana	2
Princeton	45	Williams	0
Sou. Calif.	14	St. Mary's	7
Stanford	0	Northw'n	0

Racing—Mrs. T. W. Durant's Little Dan won the Long Island Hunt Cup at West Hills, L. I. Sweeping Light took the Continental Handicap at Jamaica, while Dark Secret captured the Laurel Stakes at Laurel.

Full details in Sports Section.

O'BRIEN SIGNS TAX ON UTILITY INCOMES

Levy of 1½% Monthly on Total Revenue of Companies, Effective From Sept. 1.

TO BE USED FOR RELIEF

Mayor Declines to Disclose Whether He Has Vetoed Tax on Savings Banks.

Mayor O'Brien signed yesterday the city bill placing a tax of 1½ per cent on the gross monthly income of public utility companies during the emergency for which the city must provide relief funds.

The Mayor did not disclose whether he had vetoed the city bill taxing savings banks and insurance companies. The veto of this bill was stipulated by the city's bankers as part of their agreement to finance the city and its relief needs over the next four years. The Mayor, it was understood, would defer acting on this measure until the special session of the Legislature convening this week completes its work. The session will enact into law several features of the city's four-year financing agreement.

The registration in 1932 was 2,338,604, and there were some indications that this year's total might approach that mark, although for the last few days the daily total of registrants had been gradually decreasing.

The bill, which became law yesterday with the Mayor's signature, was passed on Sept. 15 by the Board of Estimate branch of the Municipal Assembly by fifteen affirmative votes. The Board of Aldermen subsequently passed it by a vote of fifty-two to one. The bill places a tax on the gross income of every corporation, company, association, joint-stock association, co-partnership and person subject to supervision of the Public Service Commission. The levy is effective from Sept. 1, last, until Feb. 28, 1934, and the proceeds are to go for relief and redemption of relief certificates already outstanding.

Must Be Paid Every Month.

The new city tax must be paid at the end of every month, and is levied in addition to all other license fees and taxes provided by any other section of the law. At first public utilities thought they could obtain a rebate from the city on their special franchise fees, but this will be explained by the Mayor rules out this possibility.

Returns on the tax must be filed with Controller McAneny on or before the tenth day following the ending of any one month from Oct. 10 to March 10, 1934. The fee must be paid at the time the return is filed.

"In case persons or corporations liable to the payment of the tax fail to make a correct or sufficient return within twenty days after the time required, the Controller is authorized to make an estimate of the gross income of the business and to determine the amount of the tax due," the Mayor said. "The Corporation Counsel, upon request of the Controller, may bring action to enforce tax payments. A hearing is provided where exception is taken in those cases where the Controller himself makes the estimate of the gross income and fixes the tax.

"The penalty for filing a willfully false return is classed as a misdemeanor. The offense carries a punishment of a maximum fine of $1,000 and a maximum imprisonment of one year, or both.

Provision for Refunds.

"Provision is made in the bill," the Mayor said, "that refunds shall be made by the Controller where it has been legally established that a tax was erroneously or illegally collected. The bill expressly states that revenue obtained from the imposition of this tax must be looked upon as follows:

"1. To defray the cost of granting

Continued on Page Eighteen.

CITY REGISTRATION REACHES 2,322,382, 16,422 UNDER 1932

Turnout of Voters Exceeds Hopes of Leaders of the Fight on Tammany.

TOTAL ALARMS TAMMANY

Five Are Arrested on Charge of Repeating at Booth in Brooklyn.

Registration for the city election reached 2,322,382 last night as the registration period closed. The grand total for the week was only slightly under the record mark of 2,338,804 established in the registration for last year's Presidential election.

The grand total far exceeded the hopes of even the most sanguine of the anti-Tammany leaders and was taken by them as a plain demonstration that the people of the city were aroused in their determination to end the O'Brien administration at City Hall.

Both backers of F. H. LaGuardia, Fusion candidate for Mayor, and Joseph V. McKee, Recovery candidate, contended that the increase over the normal for a Mayoralty election year would go to their candidate. Tammany chieftains made no secret of their alarm at the large turn-out, which usually implies that the so-called independent voter is on the warpath.

Five-Day Record Broken.

When the booths closed Friday night the total registration for five days was 1,611,794, compared with 1,591,019 for 1932, when all previous marks were broken in the registration for the Presidential election. The registration places were only yesterday from 7 A. M. to 10:30 P. M. and far more persons than registered any other day of the week flocked to the polls.

Owing to the increased number of registrants, the final total was not immediately ascertained, but it did approximately the same number of persons registered on the final day this year as registered on the final day of the small registration year of 1929, the last regular Mayoralty election year, the total for this year would be around 2,200,000.

The registration in 1932 was 2,338,604, and there were some indications that this year's total might approach that mark, although for the last few days the daily total of registrants had been gradually decreasing.

The figures for the week showed that many persons registered earlier this year than in the past, and this too was received as evidence that voters were impatient to make themselves eligible to ballot on Nov. 7 against the political group in power in the city.

However, the final all-day listing brought the usual big rush to the registration places, but the exact total was not available some hours after the booths closed.

Five Arrested in Brooklyn.

Five men were arrested in Brooklyn charged with registering twice at a registration place at Public School 133, Fourth Avenue and Butler Street, Mrs. Caroline Maxwell, election inspector, told Lieutenant David McLunn of the Bergen

Continued on Page Two.

Two Stunt Airplanes Crash in Mid-Air; 10 Hurt as One Hits Wilmington House

Special to THE NEW YORK TIMES.

WILMINGTON, Del., Oct. 14.—Two "air circus" stunt planes crashed together 2,700 feet above the heart of Wilmington this afternoon and started dropping while several thousand horror-struck spectators looked on.

One of the planes, piloted by Roy (Speed) Hunt of Oklahoma, plunged into the roof of a two-story dwelling, while its motor, torn loose, crashed through the house and buried itself in the ground beneath the first floor. Hunt bailed out at 700 feet and floated to the middle of a street on a parachute which opened only 500 feet above the central section of the city.

The gasoline tank of his plane exploded soon after the crash, burning and injuring three policemen who had climbed to the roof to inspect the damage. Seven other persons suffered minor injuries in two dwellings badly damaged by fire after the explosion.

Lenn Povey of Boston, pilot of the second plane, managed to maneuver his ship five miles to Bellanca Airport and land it without injuring either the plane, himself or Harold Newman of Moline, Ill., his co-pilot.

Central Wilmington traffic was demoralized for almost a half hour by hundreds of automobiles and more than 5,000 pedestrians attracted by the collision.

The crashing planes were both units of the American Air Aces, Inc., which had been hired to present an air circus at Bellanca Field, Newcastle, for the Wilmington Junior League in the interest of charity.

The crash occurred just before the show was scheduled to start. Several of the stunt planes were performing high over Wilmington in an effort to arouse further interest in the circus.

Suddenly spectators saw Hunt's plane roll and drop down upon that piloted by Povey. A left wing salvo on the former craft was torn loose and Hunt appeared to go into a spin, while Povey's plane also shot downward. Povey righted his ship in a few seconds.

The plunging machine was the one in which Hunt was the transcontinental derby from Los Angeles to Cleveland at the start of the 1932 national air races.

Motorcycle Policeman Louis W. Webb was the most seriously injured. He was held under observation at the Delaware Hospital for a spinal injury. Policemen Hooper Lemmon and Emil Geiger were treated at the hospital for minor burns.

Both pilots were able to take part in the air circus.

GERMANY QUITS LEAGUE AND ARMS PARLEY; HITLER SCORES TREATY, DEMANDS EQUALITY; CALLS ELECTION NOV. 12 TO OBTAIN APPROVAL

Belgians Are Comforted By Work at Border Forts

By The Associated Press.

BRUSSELS, Belgium, Oct. 14.—Belgian political circles declared today that Germany's action in withdrawing from the disarmament conference and the League of Nations had justified last Wednesday's unanimous Cabinet decision to complete the frontier defenses.

An Anglo-French entente presenting a firm front, these circles added, would be the most satisfactory answer to the German withdrawal.

The Belgian reaction appeared to have been summed up in the expression: "Now we know where we all stand."

BERLIN JAILS NAZIS WHO HIT AMERICAN

Velz's Attackers to Be Tried at Once — Troopers Who Beat Briton and Swiss Arrested.

NEURATH GIVES US PLEDGE

Promises Dodd Germany Will Leave Nothing Undone to Render Satisfaction.

Wireless to THE NEW YORK TIMES.

BERLIN, Oct. 14.—Following the call made by Ambassador Dodd upon Foreign Minister von Neurath, at which the two discussed the state of public feeling aroused in the United States by the failure to inflict punishment upon any Nazis guilty of assault upon Americans for not giving the Hitler salute, two interesting announcements are made by a Berlin news agency tonight.

It is stated that "the persons guilty of assaulting Roland Velz (an American business man) in Duesseldorf have been tracked down" and arrested in Berlin and are "facing prompt sentence by a special court attached to the Berlin Landgericht." The trial, it is said, will probably take place Monday.

"In accord with Commander Ernst of the Berlin Brandenburg division of the storm troops," says the second announcement, "the political police arrested today four storm troopers who had taken part in the outrage on a Swiss citizen, Herr Ruegg, and Mr. Hardy, a member of the staff of the British Embassy. The storm troopers were taken to the Oranienburg concentration camp."

Briton Clerk in Embassy.

Mr. Hardy is a clerk in the British Embassy who was attacked on Unter den Linden some three weeks ago for not saluting a Nazi parade. His assailants ignored his statement that he was a British subject and are offer to produce his passport. The British Embassy has been making

Continued on Page Twenty-eight.

MOVE DISMAYS GENEVA

Bureau of Arms Parley Called to Meet Today to Study Course.

DELEGATES ARE DIVIDED

Some Favor Session Tomorrow to Prepare Treaty Without German Participation.

4-POWER PACT'S END SEEN

Conference of Leading Powers in Italy With Hitler Suggested to Save Projects.

By CLARENCE K. STREIT.
Wireless to THE NEW YORK TIMES.

GENEVA, Oct. 14.—Germany's decision to withdraw from both the League of Nations and the disarmament conference left the delegations here, including many of the Germans, incredulous at first and then dumfounded. There is apparently a unanimous agreement that it is an extremely grave and blundering move, increasing the possibility of the Austrian situation precipitating a further grave development.

The move caused greater surprise not only because of the wholly unexpected withdrawal from the League, but because it came after the Disarmament Bureau meeting this morning, in which the British, United States, French and Italian delegations, though presenting a united program, had taken pains to quit the room of the German delegation to leave the door open for negotiation.

Arthur Henderson, president of the disarmament conference, called a special meeting of the bureau for tomorrow morning to consider what to do about the meeting of the general commission scheduled for Monday.

Concessions to Germany.

The German move made a deeper impression since the united program which Sir John Simon explained to the bureau carried with it a considerable increase in Germany's arms in the next four years and promised her, at the end of the four-year period, tanks, war planes and all other weapons forbidden to her at Versailles when she others then retained. That made the break come on Germany's demand for these weapons immediately.

There are many ideas about what to do, but none of the important delegations, including the American, had apparently made up its mind tonight except to study carefully the many possibilities opened, including those of the Locarno Treaty, which is very closely related to Germany's membership in the League.

They are also agreed, as one member of the American delegation put it, that the first essential now is for "everyone to keep cool." There is no tendency here to minimize the gravity of the situation.

Five-Power Parley Urged.

One idea, which the British seem to favor, is that Premier Mussolini should invite Prime Minister MacDonald, Premier Daladier, Chancellor Hitler and Norman H. Davis to a meeting of the United States to a five-power conference in Stresa. This would not be, however, on the basis of the four-power pact which many think the German move has definitely destroyed.

The French appear opposed, the German opposed-minded. Mr. Davis taking the position that he is ready to consider anything that would help peace but that he is not sure yet whether this or any other proposal is wise or possible.

Most of the delegations, including the British and Americans and especially the French, seem favorable to continuing the Disarmament Conference, some partly to bring out more sharply Germany's isolation in the world and the issue on which the break occurred. Others favor this with the view of making a treaty without Germany, on the ground that any menace from Germany by sticking together with arms they have rather than by each nation arming more so as to meet it individually.

Some French circles also suggest that the United States delegation was seeking

Continued on Page Twenty-eight.

Germany's Note to Parley

By The Associated Press.

GENEVA, Oct. 14.—Germany's withdrawal from the general disarmament conference was announced today in a telegram from Foreign Minister von Neurath to Arthur Henderson, president of the conference, as follows:

BERLIN, Oct. 14, 1933.

On behalf of the German Government I have the honor to make to you the following communication:

In the light of the course which recent discussions of the powers concerned have taken in the matter of disarmament it is now clear that the disarmament conference will not fill what is its sole object, namely, general disarmament.

It is also clear that this failure of the conference is due solely to unwillingness on the part of the highly armed States to carry out their contractual obligations to disarm.

This renders impossible the satisfactory fulfillment of Germany's recognized claim to equality of rights, and the condition on which the German Government agreed at the beginning of this year to take part in the work of the conference thus no longer exists. The German Government accordingly will be compelled to leave the disarmament conference.

BARON VON NEURATH.

HULL HOLDS REICH BALKS ARMS CUTS

Voices Great Disappointment at Germany's Withdrawal From Geneva Parley.

FEARS THE 'ALTERNATIVE'

This Country Is Now Solidly With Former Allies, but No Sanctions Are Considered.

Special to THE NEW YORK TIMES.

WASHINGTON, Oct. 14.—The United States Government places squarely upon Germany the blame for slowing down and impeding the movement toward general disarmament, Secretary of State Hull indicated today. He said this government was greatly disappointed and very seriously regretted Germany's action at Versailles which the United States was led to believe her action, challenged the whole Wilsonian principle of international cooperation for insuring financial cooperation insuring international cooperation for insuring peace. Whatever its faults and failings, the League which Germany has rejected was consecrated to that principle.

Skeptics Will Have Their Triumph.

Certainly those who, here as elsewhere, have argued that the League was as powerless to prevent war as laws without police or punishment are to prevent crime, are now going to have their hour of triumph. Those, too, who have, especially during the past few months, been daily urging in the French press that Hitlerism must be destroyed before it gets too strong, are now assured the road has been opened to them, even if they cannot see exactly where it will lead.

For the French people today's decision by the German Government has been indeed grave. The semi-official newspaper Le Temps pleads that the situation "be examined with all calmness," in view of "the questions of paramount importance" it raises for Europe.

Whether or not the United States, Great Britain and France reached the point of agreeing on the wording of a resolution to be introduced at Monday's scheduled preliminary session of the Disarmament Conference, there was no doubt from Mr. Hull's remarks today that the three governments were in accord against any rearming by Germany. Their common meeting ground may have ended there, as the American position has been in favor of carrying on universal control of national armaments, Germany has shown by this action that she is unwilling to accept any control or any different whatever.

FRENCH ARE CALM; WEIGH NEW CRISIS

German Action Not Wholly Unexpected — Certain Relief Felt Over 'Unmasking.'

BLOW TO PEACE DEPLORED

Le Temps Sees International Efforts Doomed — Return to Versailles Urged.

By P. J. PHILIP.
Wireless to THE NEW YORK TIMES.

PARIS, Oct. 14.—France, which becomes easily excited over little matters, learned this morning with astonishing calm of Germany's decision to quit the League of Nations and the disarmament conference. There was, on the whole, a disposition to take the event calmly, now that it has happened, its extreme gravity is admitted and it is agreed its final consequences cannot be foreseen. It is felt here that Germany has, by her action, challenged the whole Wilsonian principle of international cooperation for insuring financial cooperation for insuring peace. Whatever its faults and failings, the League which Germany has rejected was consecrated to that principle.

POST-WAR ERA DENOUNCED

Hitler, Asking Solid Vote, Bars Second-Class Status for Reich.

SEES ARMS PLEDGE BROKEN

Asserting Pacific Aims, He Finds No Possibility of a Franco-German Conflict.

REICHSTAG IS DISSOLVED

State Diets Ended by Decree Wiping Out Old Federal Provinces in Unity Move.

Text of Chancellor Hitler's radio speech is on Page 28.

By FREDERICK T. BIRCHALL.

BERLIN, Oct. 14.—The National Socialist government of Germany announced today the Reich's withdrawal simultaneously from the disarmament conference and from the League of Nations.

At the same time President Paul von Hindenburg by proclamation dissolved the present Reichstag and decreed new election for Nov. 12. Thus, there will be no elections in the normal sense because there exists no organized opposition to the present government. All parties other than the National Socialist have vanished—they have been either self-dissolved or forcibly suppressed.

The new election will be rather in the nature of a plebiscite to range the people behind the present government in any course it may choose to take in foreign affairs. The people are to be enabled, as the Hindenburg proclamation says, "to give expression to their fealty to the Reich Government."

Rebels at Versailles Treaty.

The government itself has issued a statement in which, emphasizing its own and the German people's "coinciding will," it reaffirms its adherence to the completest disarmament, and goes on to say that the German Government and the German people are "determined to accept sufferings, persecution and oppression rather than submit further to a perpetuation of the conditions created by the Versailles Treaty." Therefore it asks "the German people to approve its course and thus make that course the expression of the people's will. The answer can only be unanimous approbation, because no other answer will be possible. Nor can any voice be raised within Germany to ask whether all this is leading.

This notable day has been one of many proclamations. Chancellor Adolf Hitler also has issued one individually as Chancellor and as leader of his party. Germany has suffered bitter disappointment, says the Chancellor, through the actions of former governments in putting her into the League of Nations and the disarmament conference. Repeated and studied refusals to accord Germany moral and material equality, he says, have deeply humiliated the German people and their government.

Seeks "Pacification of World."

Since discriminations against her have continued, he proceeds, Germany has no choice but to quit the conference and the League. These poses, however, that the German people shall have an opportunity to pronounce its solidarity with the government through a popular vote. He is convinced the course to a man will uphold the determination "to bring about pacification of the world" and to establish full equal rights for all.

Thus the stage is set for that unanimous vote that the election cannot fail to produce. But behind all this is something more.

Coincidentally with the calling of this plebiscite under the name of an election there is decreed today the dissolution of all State Diets. They will not be replaced by new bodies. It is even implied that before the election Chancellor Hitler may withdraw from the States his own personal delegates now the governors or Statthalters, or Federal Governors.

Thus there will be wiped out the old Federal States. There will be no more Bavaria or Saxony or Württemberg except as geographi-

Continued on Page Twenty-six.

"All the News That's Fit to Print."

The New York Times.

LATE CITY EDITION
WEATHER—Rain and warmer to-day; tomorrow fair and colder.
Temperature Yesterday—Max. 44; Min. 34.

Copyright, 1933, by The New York Times Company.

VOL. LXXXIII....No. 27,710.

NEW YORK, WEDNESDAY, DECEMBER 6, 1933.

TWO CENTS In New York City.

LINDBERGHS AT SEA ON BRAZIL FLIGHT; 'O.K.' SHE REPORTS

630 MILES FROM AFRICA

Breeze Starts Fliers After Twenty Attempts in Dead Calm.

MOON LIGHTS THEIR WAY

10,000 Natives See Take-Off as Motor's Roar Stirs Them From Slumber.

RIDE THROUGH SQUALLS

Wife Radios Every Fifteen Minutes of Progress on 1,800-Mile Flight.

Colonel and Mrs. Charles A. Lindbergh are flying across the South Atlantic from Africa to Brazil this morning, reporting their progress by radio every fifteen minutes and their location every half hour.

At 2:20 A. M., New York time, five hours and twenty minutes after taking off from Bathurst, Gambia, in bright moonlight, they were 630 miles on their way across the Southern Ocean.

The first message from the plane was picked up by the Miami, Fla., station of Pan American Airways soon after 9:02 P. M. last night, New York time. It reported that the plane had taken off from Bathurst at that time. At 10 P. M., New York time, another message picked up by the Bahia, Brazil, station of Pan American Airways advised that the plane was flying Course 224 true, and gave its position, which the American officials estimated to be about 115 miles southwest of Bathurst. At 10:40 P. M. another message, also picked up by the Bahia station, reported "everything O. K." and said that the progress O. K. was being given every half hour and a progress O. K. sent out every fifteen minutes. The first progress O. K. was received by the Pan American station at Miami at 11 P. M., New York time.

Made 240 Miles in Two Hours.

At 11 P. M., the Bahia station also picked up a message. It gave for the plane a position approximately 240 miles southwest of Bathurst and right on her course. The operators at Bahia said that in her first message, Mrs. Lindbergh reported considerable static. But her messages, they said, were coming into Bahia strong, fast and clear, as if they were being sent by an experienced wireless operator.

The next message was received by the Pan-American station at Para, Brazil, at 11:50 P. M., New York time. It reported that the plane was flying at an altitude of 2,000 feet and making about 100 knots. There was unlimited visibility, the message said, with the sky about one-tenth overcast, and a quartering ten-knot tail wind.

At 12:30 this morning, the Pan American radio station at Miami and the Chatham, Mass., station of the Radiomarine Corporation each picked up a message from the plane giving a position approximately 446 miles southeast of Bathurst. The message said the plane was flying at an altitude of 1,200 feet, the sky about nine-tenths overcast, and that there was a quartering tail wind of 10 knots.

Squalls Met at Daybreak.

A message was received at 1:27 this morning at Pará, Brazil, reporting "skies eight-tenths overcast, scattered squalls, visibility three miles, daybreak; all's well."

At 1:50 A. M. the Bahia station picked up a message, "All's well."

At 2:20 A. M. a message was received at the Pará station reporting the plane's position as 630 miles southwest of Bathurst, flying 1,000 feet, the skies nine-tenths overcast, frequent squalls, calm seas and no wind. That position indicated the Lindberghs had covered about one-third of the distance to Natal.

Natives Awaken for Start.

BATHURST, Gambia, Wednesday, Dec. 6.—With bright moonlight turning the waters around the little island of St. Mary, on which

Continued on Page Twenty-six.

Lindbergh Flight to Fame Twice as Long as New Hop

On the morning of May 20, 1927, six years and six months ago, Captain Charles A. Lindbergh, a mail pilot, left Roosevelt Field for Paris.

He flew alone, and veteran pilots shook their heads when they saw him take off. His silver plane, dripping with rain, lumbered slowly—too slowly down the muddy runway. It gathered speed, bounced back again. It barely cleared a tractor at the end of the runway and just climbed over low telephone wires at the end of the field.

Thirty-three and a half hours later the young mail pilot brought his gray plane down at Le Bourget. That famous flight covered 3,610 miles. The present flight, also in a single-engined plane, is about 1,875 miles.

PWA READY TO BAR CITY SUBWAY LOAN

Security for $25,000,000 Advance to Finish System Is Held Inadequate.

BANKERS' PACTS A FACTOR

Officials Here Say Attitude of Washington Is Based on a Misunderstanding.

WASHINGTON, Dec. 5.—Inability of New York City to furnish security satisfactory to the Public Works Administration has caused the latter to abandon the allotment of $25,000,000 for completion of the Eighth Avenue subway.

New York officials have not been notified, but it was learned from reliable sources that the application for the loan would be refused. At a press conference today Secretary Ickes said there was "nothing new" to report on the loan. He added, however, that the matter was held up by the question of security.

Application Signed by Mayor.

The application for $25,000,000, signed by Mayor O'Brien, was on a loan and grant basis, 30 per cent of the cost of materials and structure to be an outright grant and the rest a loan on security furnished by the city.

The amount of money which completion of the subway would require is indefinite. Public Works Administration officials have scaled the sum down to some $22,500,000 under one estimate.

The money would be applied to equipping, tracking and finishing some eighteen miles of subway already dug, mainly in Brooklyn and Queens, and to the building of stations. Seven thousand men would obtain work through the Winter, it was estimated, and large supplies of capital goods would be purchased.

The allotment was discussed at the recent conference between Secretary Ickes and Mayor-elect La Guardia, but it was not gone into in any detail.

The attitude of the PWA, it was learned, is that the city has tied up the revenues of the subway by its financing agreements with the banks, and would be operating on a margin too slender to enable it to guarantee any return on the investment, even if the PWA funds allowed the subway to open miles of route and thus tap new sources of revenue.

Unification Another Problem.

The PWA feels that the situation is further complicated by the competition of the other New York subway lines. If the other lines were taken over by the city under the unification plan, a campaign promise of the Mayor-elect, the PWA feels that there would be a general scaling down of the demands of creditors and a consequent loss to the government on its investment.

The question of the 5-cent fare is not worrying the administration, Secretary Ickes has said.

While Mr. Ickes has already an-

Continued on Page Twenty-seven.

TAX PLAN OFFERED TO CURB EVASIONS, RAISE $237,000,000

House Subcommittee Urges a Check on Personal Holding Concerns by 35% Levy.

WOULD INCREASE SURTAX

Normal Income Tax of 4% and Revision of Capital Gains Are Also Proposed.

WASHINGTON, Dec. 5.—Broad tax reforms designed to increase the Federal revenue $237,000,000 a year and prevent "the avoidance and evasion of the internal revenue laws" were recommended today in a report submitted to the House Ways and Means Committee by a subcommittee.

The full committee immediately began study of the suggestions, and Representative Doughton, the chairman, said a completed bill would probably be ready for presentation soon after Congress meets next month.

Changes sought are aimed principally at persons whose incomes are in the higher brackets, as well as at corporations now legally permitted to take advantage of what committee members said were "unfair but legal" provisions of the revenue laws.

Some discord was apparent within the committee, but no member would publicly express his feelings. "It isn't law yet, and it is not even past the committee," said one member. "It must go to the House and Senate."

Nine Changes Are Urged.

Nine phases of the present law were recommended for modification as follows:

1. Establishment of a normal income tax rate of 4 per cent, instead of the present 4 per cent on the first $4,000 and 8 per cent on the remainder of net income, and to increase revenue $26,000,000 annually.

2. Change for three years in the depreciation and depletion section of the 1932 Revenue Act by reducing allowances by 25 per cent; estimated to add $85,000,000 for each of the three years.

3. Revision of the capital gains and losses section by revising the method of adjustment and prescribing a scale-length of ownership; estimated to add $30,000,000.

4. Amendment of the personal holding companies' section to prevent persons with large incomes from forming companies to evade taxes; estimated to add $25,000,000.

5. Abolition of certain sections of the "exchanges and reorganization" provisions to "close the door to one of the most prevalent methods of tax avoidance"; estimated to add $18,000,000.

6. Imposition of a tax on dividends paid out of corporation earnings accumulated before March 1, 1913; estimated to add $6,000,000.

7. Amendment of the foreign tax credit sections of the 1932 act; estimated to add $10,000,000.

8. Withdrawal of permission for corporations which are affiliated through 95 per cent stock ownership to file consolidated returns; estimated to add $30,000,000.

9. Revision of the partnership losses section of the 1932 Revenue Act; estimated to add $7,000,000.

Eager to expedite the "major problems," the subcommittee passed over a group of minor matters, according to the chairman, Representative Sam B. Hill of Washington. He said the subcommittee would continue study of these problems.

Continued on Page Fourteen.

Italy to Quit League Unless It Is Reformed; Demands Altered Aims and Set-Up at Once

By ARNALDO CORTESI
Wireless to The New York Times.

ROME, Wednesday, Dec. 6.—At the end of a long sitting lasting far into the night, the Fascist Grand Council, which had been convoked to decide on Italy's relations with the League of Nations, passed a suspended sentence on Geneva.

After having discussed every aspect of the probable effect of Italy's withdrawal, the Grand Council decided "to render Italy's further participation in the League dependent on radical changes in that organization to be brought about within the shortest possible time, which changes must affect the League in its constitution, in its methods and in its objectives."

At the same time the Grand Council reached a temporizing decision also in the matter of payment to the United States of

State House Bootlegger Is Barred in Maryland

Special to The New York Times.

ANNAPOLIS, Md., Dec. 5.—Wet legislators here will patriotically support legal liquor. The State House bootlegger received formal notice today to discontinue his trade. The notice was served by a policeman on duty at the Capitol.

Throughout this session, the bootlegger has conducted a thriving business, a business which, he says, has been especially arduous because of the sudden demands made on him by legislators and their desire for prompt service.

While his services were cut off after hours before post-prohibition stuff could be bought, the bootlegger thought the legislators had obtained a sufficient reserve to carry them through until evening and legal liquor.

RATIFYING BY UTAH ENDS PROHIBITION

With Impressive Ceremony, the 36th State Follows Ohio and Pennsylvania in Day.

CONVENTIONS ALL SOLEMN

Moderation Pleas Are Made at Columbus—Hush Greets Vote at Harrisburg.

Special to The New York Times.

SALT LAKE CITY, Dec. 5.—The Eighteenth Amendment to the Constitution of the United States passed out of existence officially at 3:32½ o'clock this afternoon, Mountain time (5:32½ New York time) with the ratification of repeal by the convention of Utah, the thirty-sixth required State.

The passing of national prohibition was marked by impressive ceremony in the hall of the House of Representatives in the State Capitol here.

To Delegate S. R. Thurman, a wet leader of Salt Lake City, whose father was a member of the State's constitutional convention in 1895 before Utah was admitted to the Union, fell the honor of being the last to record his vote, the final one being called in alphabetical order.

His "Yea," placing the Twenty-first Amendment in the Constitution in effect, was greeted by enthusiastic applause from the audience of a few hundred persons.

About ninety seconds later Ray L. Olson of Ogden, president of the convention, who had been manager of the repealists' campaign, brought down his gavel and announced that the repeal amendment had been ratified. Notification was transmitted immediately to the White House by a special wire from the Capitol.

At the same time Delegate A. S. Brown, former Salt Lake Chamber of Commerce president, sent out word to President Roosevelt over the Columbia Broadcasting System. He congratulated the President on the successful culmination of the movement. The whole proceedings were in keeping with the historic aspect of the occasion. Besides high officials

Continued on Page Five.

PROHIBITION REPEAL IS RATIFIED AT 5:32 P. M.; ROOSEVELT ASKS NATION TO BAR THE SALOON; NEW YORK CELEBRATES WITH QUIET RESTRAINT

CITY TOASTS NEW ERA

Crowds Swamp Licensed Resorts, but the Legal Liquor Is Scarce.

CELEBRATION IN STREETS

Marked by Absence of Undue Hilarity and Only Normal Number of Arrests.

MANY SPEAKEASIES CLOSE

Machine Guns Guard Some Liquor Trucks—Supplies to Be Rushed Out Today.

Slowly gathering momentum from the time when the news began to spread just at nightfall that national prohibition was no more, the public rejoicing at the end of the long dry reign was carried on last night with restraint and absence of undue hilarity.

Throngs of New Yorkers ventured into Times Square and other centres of the metropolis and many of the thousand restaurants, hotels and clubs fortunate enough to have received their licenses for the sale of alcoholic beverages were swamped.

But gay as were their spirits, they were well-behaved. With the city's entire police force of 19,000 men mobilized to guard against overexuberant celebrants, arrests did not exceed the normal number for any day of the last five years. Incidentally, official word that repeal was a fact did not go out to the police until 9:30 P. M., just about four hours after Utah acted.

Stores Fail to Get Stocks.

The thronging to places of public entertainment was enhanced by the fact that only a handful of New Yorkers was able to drink a toast to the occasion with lawful liquor in their own homes. Because Utah did not make repeal effective until 5:32½ P. M., retail liquor stores with only two exceptions were unable to obtain wines and whiskies from the warehouses in the brief time left.

Indeed, the supply of lawful liquor even in the licensed places was woefully scant. Only fifty-four truckloads of bonded liquor were released from the warehouses before they closed last night, and the two largest warehouses shut their doors before the Twenty-first Amendment displaced the Eighteenth.

With 3,000 places licensed to dispense the newly legalized beverages in the metropolitan area and 2,000 more up-State, hardly one in a hundred was able to move in a stock in the few hours available. Some of the others, of course, had had the foresight to lay in supplies under medicinal permits during the dying days of prohibition.

Bootleggers and speakeasies came to the rescue, however, despite a stern warning from Police Commissioner Bolan that he men would not tolerate any such activity. They operated with a little more caution than usual, but nevertheless these took advantage of the occasion to dispose of a large part of their unlawful stocks. The raids threatened by Mr. Bolan proved few and on little known places.

Many Cordial Shops Close.

Cordial shops and other neighborhood dispensaries during the long drought showed fear of police activity last night for the first time in years. Hundreds of them closed their doors, others dealt only with long-known and trusted customers, and only a scattering number, principally in downtown Manhattan, carried on business as usual. Some of them carried signs promising to open as licensed liquor stores in a few days.

There was every indication, however, that New York's long elation on contraband cheer was near its end. The warehousemen promised deliveries on a large scale which, with 600 trucks licensed to speed legal liquors throughout the city and its suburbs.

A cargo of 6,200 cases of assorted wines and spirits worth about $170,000 arrived on the White Star liner Majestic from France and England late in the afternoon, and the ship was delayed five hours to

Continued on Page Two.

The Repeal Proclamation

Special to The New York Times.

WASHINGTON, Dec. 5.—The text of the proclamation by William Phillips, Acting Secretary of State, certifying to the adoption of the Twenty-first Amendment repealing prohibition, follows:

WILLIAM PHILLIPS,
Acting Secretary of State of the United States of America.

To all whom these presents shall come, greeting:

KNOW YE, That the Congress of the United States, at the second session, Seventy-second Congress, begun and held at the city of Washington on Monday, the fifth day of December, in the year one thousand nine hundred and thirty-two, passed a joint Resolution in the words and figures as follows:

To wit:—

JOINT RESOLUTION.

Proposing an amendment to the Constitution of the United States.

Resolved by the Senate and House of Representatives of the United States of America in Congress assembled (two-thirds of each House concurring therein), That the following article is hereby proposed as an amendment to the Constitution of the United States, which shall be valid to all intents and purposes as part of the Constitution when ratified by conventions in three-fourths of the several States:

ARTICLE.

Section 1. The Eighteenth Article of Amendment to the Constitution of the United States is hereby repealed.

Section 2. The transportation or importation into any State, Territory, or Possession of the United States for delivery or use therein of intoxicating liquors, in violation of the laws thereof, is hereby prohibited.

Section 3. This article shall be inoperative unless it shall have been ratified as an amendment to the Constitution by conventions in the several States, as provided in the Constitution, within seven years from the date of the submission hereof to the States by the Congress.

And, further, that it appears from official notices received at the Department of State that the amendment to the Constitution of the United States proposed as aforesaid has been ratified by conventions in the States of Arizona, Alabama, Arkansas, California, Colorado, Connecticut, Delaware, Florida, Idaho, Illinois, Indiana, Iowa, Kentucky, Maryland, Massachusetts, Michigan, Minnesota, Missouri, Nevada, New Hampshire, New Jersey, New Mexico, New York, Ohio, Oregon, Pennsylvania, Rhode Island, Tennessee, Texas, Utah, Vermont, Virginia, Washington, West Virginia, Wisconsin and Wyoming.

And, further, That the States wherein conventions have so ratified the said proposed amendment constitute the requisite three-fourths of the whole number of States in the United States.

NOW, therefore, be it known that I, William Phillips, Acting Secretary of State of the United States, by virtue and in pursuance of Section 160, Title 5, of the United States Code, do hereby certify that the amendment aforesaid has become valid to all intents and purposes as a part of the Constitution of the United States.

In testimony whereof, I have hereunto set my hand and caused the seal of the Department of State to be affixed.

Done at the city of Washington this fifth day of December in the year of our Lord one thousand nine hundred and thirty-three.

WILLIAM PHILLIPS.

Roosevelt Proclaims Repeal; Urges Temperance in Nation

President's Announcement Is in Accordance With the Instruction of Congress Contained in the Recovery Act—Declares Social Evils of Liquor Shall Not Be Revived.

Special to The New York Times.

WASHINGTON, Dec. 5.—President Roosevelt's proclamation of the repeal of the Eighteenth Amendment was as follows:

By the President of the United States of America.

A Proclamation.

Whereas the Congress of the United States in the second session of the Seventy-second Congress, begun at Washington on the fifth day of December in the year one thousand nine hundred and thirty-two adopted a resolution in the words and figures following: to wit—

JOINT RESOLUTION.

Proposing an amendment to the Constitution of the United States.

Resolved by the Senate and House of Representatives of the United States of America in Congress assembled (two-thirds of each House concurring therein), That the following article is hereby proposed as an amendment to the Constitution of the United States, which shall be valid to all intents and purposes as part of the Constitution when ratified by conventions in three-fourths of the several States:

ARTICLE.

Section 1. The Eighteenth Article of amendment to the Constitution of the United States is hereby repealed.

Section 2. The transportation or importation into any State, Territory or possession of the United States for delivery or use therein of intoxicating liquors, in violation of the laws thereof, is hereby prohibited.

Section 3. This article shall be inoperative unless it shall have been ratified as an amendment to the Constitution by conventions in the several States, as provided in the Constitution, within seven years from the date of the submission hereof to the States by the Congress.

Declares Amendment Repealed.

Whereas, Section 217 (a) of the Act of Congress entitled "An act to encourage national industrial recovery, to foster competition and to provide for the construction of certain useful public works, and for other purposes," approved June 16, 1933, provides as follows:

Section 217 (a) The President shall proclaim the date of (1) the close of the first fiscal year ending June 30 of any year after the year 1933, during which the total receipts of the

Continued on Page Two.

FINAL ACTION AT CAPITAL

President Proclaims the Nation's New Policy as Utah Ratifies.

PHILLIPS SIGNS DECREE

Orders 21st Amendment in Effect on Receiving Votes of Three Final States.

RECOVERY TAXES TO END

$227,000,000 a Year Automatically Dropped—Canadian Whisky Quota Is Raised.

Special to The New York Times.

WASHINGTON, Dec. 5.—Legal liquor today was returned to the United States, with President Roosevelt calling on the people to see that "this return of individual freedom shall not be accompanied by the repugnant conditions that obtained prior to the adoption of the Eighteenth Amendment and those that have existed since its adoption."

Prohibition of alcoholic beverages as a national policy ended at 5:32½ P. M., Eastern Standard Time, when Utah, the last of the thirty-six States, furnished by vote of its convention the constitutional majority for ratification of the Twenty-first Amendment. The new amendment repealed the Eighteenth, and, with the demise of the latter went the Volstead Act under which for more than a decade held legal drinks in America to less than one-half of 1 per cent of alcohol and the enforcement of which cost the nation more than 150 lives and billions in money.

Earlier in the day Pennsylvania had ratified as the thirty-fourth State and Ohio as the thirty-fifth.

Proclamation by President.

President Roosevelt at 6:55 P. M. signed an official proclamation in keeping with terms of the National Industrial Recovery Act, under which prohibition ended and four taxes levied to raise $227,000,000 annually for amortization of the $3,300,000,000 public works fund were repealed.

But the President went further. Accepting certification from Acting Secretary of State Phillips that thirty-six States had ratified the repealing amendment, he improved the occasion to address a plea to the American people to employ their regained liberty first of all for national maintenance.

Mr. Roosevelt asked personally of what he and his party had declined to make the subject of Federal mandate—that saloons be barred from the country.

"I ask especially," he said, "that no State shall, by law or otherwise, authorize the return of the saloon, either in its old form or in some modern guise."

Makes Personal Pleas.

He enjoined all citizens to co-operate with the government in its endeavor to restore a greater respect for law and order, especially by confining their purchases of liquor to duly licensed agencies. This practice, which he personally requested every individual and every family in the nation to follow, would result, he said, in a better product for consumption, in addition to the "break-up and eventual destruction of the notoriously evil illicit liquor traffic" and in tax benefits to the government.

The President then announced the policy of his administration—to see that the social and political evils of the reprohibition era shall not be revived or permitted again to exist. Failure of citizens to use their new freedom in helping to advance this policy, he said, would be "a living reproach to us all."

He expressed faith, too, in the "good sense of the American people" in preventing excessive personal use of alcoholic liquor. "The objective we seek through a national policy," he said, "is the education of every citizen toward a greater temperance throughout the nation."

As a means of enforcing his policy, the President has given the Federal Alcohol Control Administration ready to take control of the liquor traffic and regulate it at the source of supply.

In its first major step today, the

Continued on Page Two.

56

NRA · "All the News That's Fit to Print."

The New York Times.

LATE CITY EDITION
WEATHER—Showers today; tomorrow fair, somewhat cooler. Temperature Yesterday—Max., 81, Min., 70

Section 1

VOL. LXXXIII....No. 27,917.

Entered as Second-Class Matter, Postoffice, New York, N. Y.

NEW YORK, SUNDAY, JULY 1, 1934.

Including Rotogravure Picture, Magazine and Book Sections.

F

TEN CENTS | TWELVE CENTS Beyond 200 Miles. Except in 7th and 8th Postal Zones.

Copyright, 1934, by The New York Times Company.

EXCHANGE, LABOR BOARDS NAMED; FARM BILL SIGNED

KENNEDY IN 'CHANGE POST

The Others Are Mathews, Landis, Healy, Pecora for Varying Terms.

WIRE BOARD IS CHOSEN

Members Are Sykes, Brown, Case, Stuart, Payne, Gary and Walker.

RAIL PENSIONS APPROVED

Clark Howell Heads Air Study—Moffett Made Administrator of the Housing Act.

President Clears His Desk

On the eve of his departure this evening on the cruiser Houston for a month's cruise, President Roosevelt cleared his desk last night.

He named the two commissions to regulate the Stock Exchanges and the operations of telegraph, telephone and radio companies.

He signed the Frazier-Lemke bill setting up new methods for the compromising of agricultural indebtedness.

He signed the railroad employes' pension bill.

He appointed James A. Moffett of New York, prominent oil executive, Administrator of the Housing Act.

He appointed an Aviation Commission, with Clark Howell as chairman.

He created an impartial Labor Relations Board, abolishing the old one and eliminating the NRA from a rôle in settling labor disputes.

Picks Exchange Board

Special to The New York Times.

WASHINGTON, June 30.—As his last act tonight in cleaning up essential business before sailing from Annapolis for a month's holiday today, President Roosevelt named the personnel of the Securities and Exchange Commission.

He did not designate a chairman, there being some doubt as to his authority to do so, but it was understood in well-informed quarters that responsibility for the commission's work under the sweeping Stock Exchange Control Act would fall upon Joseph P. Kennedy, New York financier, who was designated to serve five years. Four other commissioners were named for periods varying from one to four years.

The personnel of the commission follows:

JOSEPH P. KENNEDY of New York, five-year term.

GEORGE C. MATHEWS of Wisconsin, four-year term.

JAMES M. LANDIS of Massachusetts, three-year term.

ROBERT E. HEALY of Vermont, two-year term.

FERDINAND PECORA of New York, one-year term.

Messrs. Mathews and Landis are members of the Federal Trade Commission. Mr. Pecora was counsel for the Senate Banking and Currency Committee during the period in which it aired publicly for the first time in twenty years the manifold operations of securities exchanges and investment banking houses. As committee counsel he played a large part in shaping the law under which the commission will operate.

The naming of the Securities and Exchange Commission came after President Roosevelt, in a day of intensive work, had also named the Communications Commission and a commission to plan coordination of aircraft development, and had issued statements announcing the signing of the Frazier-Lemke Farm Mortgage Bill and the Railroad Pensions Bill.

Kennedy Close to Farley.

The membership of the Securities and Exchange Commission had been pretty generally forecast, but even so its composition was full of surprises, particularly the order placing in line for the chairmanship of Mr. Kennedy.

This is the first emergence of the New Yorker from what seemed to be political eclipse since the campaign of 1932, when he was distinguished both as a heavy contributor and important raiser of campaign funds, and because of his

Continued on Page Twenty-one.

Major Sports Results

Track—Bill Bonthron of Princeton broke the world's record for the 1,500-meter run in the national A. A. U. championship meet at Milwaukee. Timed in 3:48.8, he beat Glenn Cunningham by two feet. It was the fifth meeting between the stars and the triumph gave Bonthron the edge with three victories.

Tennis—Four Americans advanced at Wimbledon. Frank Shields defeated Christian Boussus of France and George M. Lott Jr. halted Harry Hopman of Australia. Miss Helen Jacobs conquered Mlle. Jacqueline Goldschmidt of France and Miss J. Jedrzejowska beat Miss J. Jedrzejowska of Poland.

Baseball—Routing Carl Hubbell, the Dodgers stopped the Giants, 8—6, before 12,000 at the Polo Grounds. At Washington the Yankees were held by the Senators, 4—1, when rain caused the game to be called off in the fifth inning.

(Full details in Sports Section.)

JOHN JACOB ASTOR WEDS ELLEN FRENCH

Notables Fill Newport Church for Ceremony Climaxing Weeks of Social Activity.

ONLOOKERS PACK STREETS

Crowd Delays Both Bride and Bridegroom—Astor's Mother Sits in a Front Pew.

By RUSSELL B. PORTER.

Special to The New York Times.

NEWPORT, R. I., June 30.—Two of America's oldest families, prominent in both landed wealth and in social position, were united in marriage here today at the wedding of John Jacob Astor 3d and Miss Ellen Tuck French.

The bridegroom is the third of his name in American life. The first John Jacob Astor, fur trader, founded the family in early American days. The second lost his life in the sinking of the Titanic, and the third John Jacob Astor, today's bridegroom, was born a few months later. He is a half-brother of Vincent Astor, and inherited with the latter the great Astor fortune.

The bride is a granddaughter of Amos Tuck French and is related to the Vanderbilt family.

These young members of old families, the bridegroom only 21 years old and the bride 18, were joined together in a setting replete with symbols of early American traditions.

They were married according to the ancient simple ritual of the Protestant Episcopal Church, whose worshipers came to Old Trinity Church, a long, narrow, weatherbeaten white clapboard building with a towering white steeple and gilded spire and weather vane. It was all just as it was when the church was built more than two centuries ago, in 1726, eighty-seven years after the founding of Newport in 1639.

Shading the high steeple was a fine, old elm tree, as tall as or taller than the spire itself, with its great spreading branches almost speaking aloud the story of New England. The tree itself was as old or nearly as old as the church.

Church Recalls Colonial Days.

On the other side of the church, so that the wedding procession walked between it and the old tree to enter the building, was the old burying ground with its plain weather-beaten granite headstones bearing the names of men and women who played leading parts in shaping the history of the colonies and of the first days of the Republic.

All around the church, which is right in the centre of this fine old city, old frame buildings of Colonial architecture, with Grecian columns, steeply slanting roofs and gables, crowding close to the building line of the street, bespoke Newport's history.

The time joined with the place in celebrating the event with appropriate ceremony, for not only was it in the midst of the Summer season, when Newport's social colony is always in full swing, but it was an incident with a visit of a large part of the United States fleet. From time immemorial the navy has been associated with Newport, and

Continued on Page Eighteen.

FORD WILL ACCEPT NRA AND ITS CODE, JOHNSON IS TOLD

General Announces He Awaits Signed Certificate From Auto Maker.

SAYS HE ASKED CHANGES

Recovery Head Asserts His Suggestions Have Been Approved in Detroit.

Special to The New York Times.

WASHINGTON, June 30.—General Johnson believed tonight that he was nearing a settlement of his ten months feud with Henry Ford and would let the NRA put another feather in its cap and at the same time allow the automobile maker to re-enter the fertile field of government business.

General Johnson today read a copy of an unsigned letter purporting to be from the Ford Motor Company to a local dealer, setting forth the claims that that firm had been complying with "pertinent" provisions of the Automobile Code.

The Recovery Administrator said that if the letter, with certain revisions which he suggested, were returned to him after Henry Ford or any other authorized executive of the Ford Motor Company, he would consider it a certificate of compliance, would call off his "crack-down" campaign against the company and recommend to President Roosevelt that it be allowed to resume bidding on government contracts.

A large order of motor trucks for the army, which War Department officials prefer should be Ford products, is said to be the immediate stake in negotiations between the NRA and Mr. Ford. Harry H. Woodring, Assistant Secretary of War, has made overtures to General Johnson within the last thirty-six hours to learn what the Ford company would have to do to qualify to bid.

Representative Kvale of Minnesota, active in the House Military Affairs Committee investigating War Department purchases, accompanied the Ford dealer when he called to show the unsigned letter to General Johnson this afternoon.

Talks To Ford Adviser.

General Johnson believed the letter to be entirely authentic and to have originated at the Detroit offices of the Ford Company despite the circumstances under which it was shown to him. This belief was intensified by a telephone conversation which he had with William J. Cameron, editorial adviser to Mr. Ford, regarding the suggested revisions.

The letter, according to General Johnson, was addressed to the Northwest Motor Company of Bethesda, Md., the local dealer that had tried so consistently to keep its contractual relations with the governmental departments regardless of Mr. Ford's refusal to sign a compliance certificate for his code.

"Its original form the letter said that although the company had complied and would continue to comply with the provisions of the automobile compact, it reserved its 'constitutional rights' as guaranteed by the fundamental law.

This was the section to which General Johnson objected. He told R. P. Sabine, president of the Northwest Motor Company, and Representative Kvale that President Roosevelt would not stand for

Continued on Page Three.

POLICE FILL THE STREETS

Goering's Forces Keep Curious Throngs on Constant Move.

MACHINE GUNS MOUNTED

Public Buildings on Unter den Linden and Wilhelmstrasse Are Heavily Guarded.

NEWS IS AT A PREMIUM

Rumors Are Rampant as Only a One-Sheet Paper Provides Authentic Information.

Copyright, 1934, by The Associated Press.

BERLIN, June 30.—With the peaceful cool of a Summer evening made strangely tense by squads of armed police and the presence of machine guns, this capital city was facing tonight the possibility of a new unnamed, undefined political event.

Crowds of curious spectators, only partly informed as to events through limited press dispatches, surged up and down Wilhelmstrasse, where public buildings were massed with police ever ready to keep them on the move.

In front of the home of Captain Ernst Roehm, suicide deposed leader of the storm troops, were bristling truckloads of Prussian Premier Hermann Goering's special police. They formed a human barricade separate from the thousands who dragged their feet in slow response to demands that streets and sidewalks be kept clear.

Show of Force Excites Crowds.

The presence of police everywhere one turned was a direct stimulant to the excitement of the street and thoroughfares. Never in the history of Berlin, it was pointed out, had so many police appeared in the streets at one time with such obvious readiness for action. In addition to the regular police force, augmented by armed reserves, there was the steel-helmeted, greenclad police of Premier Goering.

The sudden appearance of a police machine gun detachment, with ammunition ready, in historic Potsdammer Platz brought a final touch to the grimness of the situation. The sight of another similar detachment idling up and down Unter den Linden left no doubt in the public mind as to the nature of the emergency.

Men and women rushed like hounds on the scent wherever carriers appeared with copies of one newspaper which had printed one page only for free distribution. This carried a brief account of Captain Roehm's discharge by Chancellor Hitler.

Reactions to the news were various and could be read at will on the faces of newspaper readers. Persons obviously of a conservative mind wreathed their faces in smiles as they read what had happened.

Continued on Page Two.

Continued on Page Two.

Dillinger Raids Bank in South Bend, Ind., Reported Shot; Officer Slain, Loot $28,000

By The Associated Press.

SOUTH BEND, Ind., June 30.—A bandit quintet with John Dillinger reported to be in command, stormed the Merchants' National Bank today, scooped up $28,430 and fled in a wild barrage of bullets, leaving a slain policeman and four wounded men in their wake.

The ruthless raiders engaged in gun battles with a detective, three officers and a jeweler as they fled from the bank and made their way to the escape car a half block away. More than fifty shots raked the street in the heart of the city.

Detective Harry Henderson, who identified the bandits' leader as Dillinger, said he believed that as Dillinger, and two henchmen, one of them believed to be "Baby Face" Nelson, rushed into the bank about noon. Covering the twenty-five customers with a machine gun, one man identified as Dillinger took up a strategic post and sent a score of slugs into the ceiling while his confederate snatched up $28,430. C. W. Coen, vice president of the institution, who took cover under a desk three feet from the gunner, declared he was positive the leader was the desperate Dillinger.

Bundling their loot, the three commandeered Stahley, Coen and several other patrons and used them as human shields as they marched out the door. Wagner ran toward them from across the crowded street. The machine gunner shot him down, three bullets entering the policeman's body.

coursed upward. His condition was described as critical. Toth was wounded in the eye as a bullet smashed the windshield of his automobile.

Leaving an outpost, believed to be John Hamilton, on guard at their automobile, and another bandit closer to the bank, the man identified by a police detective as Dillinger, with two henchmen, one of them believed to be "Baby Face" Nelson, rushed into the bank about noon.

Those wounded were P. G. Stahley, manager of the Birdsell Manufacturing Company; Jake Solomon, Delos H. Coen, a cashier, and Samuel Toth. At Epworth Hospital it was found that a bullet had struck Jeleman in the hip and

Continued on Page Eighteen.

HITLER CRUSHES REVOLT BY NAZI RADICALS; VON SCHLEICHER IS SLAIN, ROEHM A SUICIDE; LOYAL FORCES HOLD BERLIN IN AN IRON GRIP

THREE OF THE LEADERS WHO DIED IN THE REICH MUTINY.

Captain Ernst Roehm, ousted Storm Troop head, who committed suicide.
Times Wide World Photo.

Karl Ernst, Berlin Storm Troop leader, arrested and later shot.
Associated Press Photo.

General Kurt von Schleicher, slain by arresting officers.
Times Wide World Photo.

HITLER COMMANDS NAZI ABSTINENCES

Forbids the Troopers to Spend Money on Banquets and Bans Moral 'Debauches.'

WANTS 'MEN, NOT APES'

Chancellor Asserts All Must Be on Best Behavior or Be Expelled From Ranks.

Wireless to The New York Times.

BERLIN, June 30.—Chancellor Adolf Hitler issued these eleven commands today to Viktor Lutze, new Chief of Staff of the Storm Troops:

In naming you Chief of Staff of the Storm Troops I expect that you will accept the series of duties that I herewith inform you of.

1—I demand of a Storm Troop leader, just as from a Storm Trooper, blind obedience and unquestioning discipline.

2—I demand that every Storm Troop leader recognize, like every other political leader, that his behavior and reputation must be an example for his organization and for our whole body of followers.

3—I demand that Storm Troop leaders, exactly as in the case of political leaders, be expelled from the Storm Troops without hesitation as soon as their behavior disgraces them in the eyes of the public.

Demands Simplicity.

4—I demand specially from the Storm Troop leader that he be an example of simplicity. I do not desire Storm Troop leaders to give costly dinners or that they attend such dinners. There was a time when we were not invited to such affairs, and we have nothing to seek there now. Millions of our fellow citizens have not even the necessities of life. They are not oblivious of those whom fortune has favored, but it is unworthy of a National Socialist to increase the gulf between fortune and misery, which is already great enough.

5—I prohibit the use of Storm Troop or party funds for festivals and the like. It is shameless to stage debauches with the pennies of our poorest citizens. The luxurious headquarters in Berlin, in which it has now been discovered that some 30,000 marks monthly were spent for banquets, is to be done away with immediately.

State Dinners Excepted.

6—I prohibit for all party groups banquets and dinners paid for with any variety of public funds. I forbid all party and Storm Troop leaders to partake of such banquets. The only exceptions are functions necessary for reasons of State, notably those for which the Reichspresident and the Reich Foreign Minister are responsible. In that case all party leaders and Storm Troop leaders are to give so-called diplomatic dinners. A Storm Troop leader does not need to engage in representation, but simply to do his duty.

7—I do not desire Storm Troop leaders to undertake business trips in expensive limousines or cabriolets, or to employ public funds for such trips. The same

Continued on Page Eight.

Hitler Alone Had Power To Order Shooting of 7

Special Cable to The New York Times.

BERLIN, June 30.—Over the report of the deaths of seven storm troop leaders who yesterday were in power in German, the Völkischer Beobachter, Chancellor Hitler's own newspaper, carried the headline, "Seven Storm Troop Leaders Shot. End of Convicted Traitors."

The German words used for the verb and adjective taken together in this connection carry a wider meaning than the English equivalent, as is the case with so many German words. They imply that seven guilty men were proved guilty and executed.

These men were shot on the spot without trial on the mere allegation of their guilt by order of a higher authority. The only authority which could give an order for their execution unchallenged was Adolf Hitler, who, according to the same article in this newspaper, "is the supreme conscience of the German people."

GOERING POLICE NET CATCHES LEADERS

Suicides and Killings Follow Raids on Homes of Notables in Berlin and Vicinity.

By OTTO D. TOLISCHUS.

Wireless to The New York Times.

BERLIN, June 30.—General Kurt von Schleicher, former Premier, was killed with his wife while "resisting arrest with a weapon in his hand," according to an official communiqué.

The communiqué was one of a long series issued throughout the day as the criminal police of Premier Hermann Goering of Prussia rushed about Berlin and its vicinity, leaving a heavy wake of arrests, suicides and killings among prominent persons.

General von Schleicher met death at his villa in Neubabelsberg, between Berlin and Potsdam. His wife, Frau Elisabeth von Schleicher, it is stated, fell while trying to shield him with her body during an exchange of shots.

From that point tragedy spread. One squad of General Goering's police rushed to the office of Vice Chancellor Franz von Papen in Vos Strasse, next to the Chancellery, and asked the Vice Chancellor to accompany them to his home. There they kept Colonel von Papen under house arrest and questioned him regarding his relations with General von Schleicher. The amenities were preserved, and later it was stated Colonel von Papen was "at liberty."

Von Papen Visitors Barred.

Visitors to Colonel von Papen's house, however, were not allowed to see him. His secretary and a Reichswehr officer assured every one that Colonel von Papen was in good spirits, had just finished tea and was smoking his afternoon cigar.

His office meanwhile had been occupied by black uniformed special guards, men with field equipment, rifles and hand grenades. In the future he will not permit millions of decent people to be compromised by a few of such sick men. The Fuehrer instructed Premier Goering of Prussia to take similar action in Berlin and especially to arrest the reactionary accomplices of this political plot.

At noon today Der Fuehrer

Continued on Page Four.

NAZI CHIEFS TELL OF ENDING REVOLT

Hitler and Lutze Appeal to the Storm Troops to Be Faithful to Their Movement.

RAID DESCRIBED BY PARTY

Leader of War Veterans Urges Them to Be Calm and to Be Loyal to Government.

Wireless to The New York Times.

BERLIN, June 30.—A series of statements was issued today by German leaders on their success in crushing the radical Nazi revolt.

NAZI PARTY STATEMENT.

A communiqué from the National Socialist party read:

Munich, June 30.

For many months individual elements have been trying to drive a wedge and produce conflicts between the Storm Troops and the party, as well as between the Storm Troops and the State. Suspicions of this became more and more confirmed, but it was also plain that these endeavors were to be charged to a limited clique of certain leanings.

Chief of Staff Roehm, whom the leader placed an exceptional amount of confidence, not only did not oppose these endeavors but undoubtedly sponsored them. His well-known unfortunate characteristic gradually led to intolerable burdens which drove the leader of the movement and the Highest Leader of the Storm Troops [Hitler] into most serious conflicts of conscience.

Chief of Staff Roehm established contacts with General von Schleicher without the knowledge of Der Fuehrer [the leader]. His go-between was another Storm Troop leader and an obscure person well known in Berlin, to whom Der Fuehrer had always strongly objected.

Since these negotiations also of course without the knowledge of Der Fuehrer—finally to contacts with a foreign power, or rather to its representative, it was not possible to avoid intervention both from the standpoint of the party and the State.

Provocative incidents brought about according to the plan caused Der Fuehrer to fly from Bonn to Munich at 2 o'clock this morning, after visiting labor camps in Westphalia, in order to remove and arrest the most seriously compromised group of leaders. Der Fuehrer himself went with only a few companions to Wiessee in order to undo any attempts at resistance.

The execution of the arrests revealed such immorality that any trace of pity was impossible. Some of these Storm Troop leaders had taken male prostitutes along with them. One of them was even disturbed in a most ugly situation and was arrested.

Der Fuehrer gave orders for this plague to be done away with ruthlessly. In the future he will not permit millions of decent people to be compromised by a few

Continued on Page Two.

STORM TROOP CHIEFS DIE

Killed or Take Own Lives as Chancellor and Goering Strike.

REACTIONARIES ALSO HIT.

Wife Shot With Schleicher as He Resists Police—Head of Catholic Action Slain.

HITLER FLIES TO MUNICH

Tears Off Rebels' Insignia and Arrests and Ousts Roehm —Papen Held but Freed.

By FREDERICK T. BIRCHALL.

BERLIN, June 30.—On the eve of a self-proclaimed month of peace Germany has passed today through the throes of a violent purging that must profoundly affect her future. It is neither a revolution nor a coup d'état nor a counter-revolution but authoritative action intended to head off any one of the three.

Chancellor Hitler in Munich, backed by General Hermann Wilhelm Goering, Premier of Prussia, in Berlin, has struck simultaneously at the rebel elements in his own Storm Troops and at certain reactionary elements temporarily allied with them or suspected of being so allied for their own ends in an attempt to upset the present régime in Germany.

When the day was over many Storm Troop leaders had been shot to death or had committed suicide. In addition, General Kurt von Schleicher, Herr Hitler's predecessor as Chancellor, had been slain while resisting police who attempted to seize him as one of the plotters.

[Captain Ernst Roehm, committed suicide by Chancellor Hitler, according to The Associated Press, while Heinrich Klausener, chief of the Catholic Action, was shot to death by a Nazi special guard.]

The Official Version.

The official version is that the attempt was a joint effort "to bring pressure" on the government with a threat of violent action behind it. There is mention of a "foreign power" as being involved. The clearing interpret this reference as being to Russia and the ultimate aim of the rebels as a new national bolshevism.

Whatever the cause, Chancellor Hitler has acted swiftly and decisively. Flying to Munich in the early hours of this morning from Bonn, where he had been ostensibly inspecting work camps, he assembled his trusted special guards in that city and proceeded to gather in the suspected leaders, who had already proceeded to preliminary action.

Captain Roehm, the leader of the conspiracy, was arrested in his bedroom in his country house outside Munich by Herr Hitler himself and then and there deposed from all his offices. His fellow-conspirators were gathered in by the dozen in Munich and around it.

The official story told to foreign correspondents by General Goering this afternoon says that some of them, both in Munich and in Berlin, committed suicide and others were shot while resisting.

Goering Acts Swiftly.

Almost simultaneously in Berlin General Goering, by arrangement with Chancellor Hitler, was taking similar action. It came swiftly and unexpectedly just before noon. But here the members of the reactionary group believed to be acting with the rebel Storm Troop leaders were the objects of the assault.

Karl Ernst, group leader of the Berlin Storm Troops, was traced to a house near Bremen and surrounded there. He is dead and the official version is that he was shot while resisting arrest. The unofficial version is that he was caught by airplane and flown to Berlin and was executed on his arrival.

Police and special guards at the same instant sought to put General von Schleicher under arrest at his villa outside Potsdam. It is said that he attempted to draw a pistol. A volley of shots brought him down and his wife died with him.

Vice Chancellor Franz von Papen, who seems to have been under sus-

Continued on Page Two.

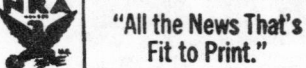
"All the News That's Fit to Print."

The New York Times.

LATE CITY EDITION
POSTSCRIPT
Fair, slightly cooler today; tomorrow fair.
Temperature Yesterday—Max. 80; min. 72.

Copyright, 1934, by The New York Times Company.

VOL. LXXXIII....No. 27,989.   Entered as Second-Class Matter, Postoffice, New York, N. Y.   NEW YORK, MONDAY, JULY 23, 1934.   TWO CENTS In New York City. | THREE CENTS Within 200 Miles | FOUR CENTS Elsewhere Except in 7th and 8th Postal Zones

15 KILLED, 18 HURT AS BUS FALLS 35 FEET AND BURNS ON AN OUTING AT OSSINING

MANY TRAPPED IN FLAMES

Machine Out of Control Plunges Off Ramp Into Lumber Yard.

GASOLINE TANK EXPLODES

Injured Struggle in Vain to Open Jammed Doors of Old-Fashioned Coach.

4, AFIRE, LEAP INTO RIVER

Members of Young Democrats' Club of Brooklyn Bound for Sing Sing Ball Game.

Fifteen persons were killed and eighteen injured, yesterday when a bus containing about forty men, women and children plunged thirty-five feet from a ramp near the Ossining railroad station and burst into flames.

The bus was one of seven that had been chartered by the Young Men's Democratic League of the Twentieth Assembly District in Brooklyn to take members of the league and their friends to a baseball game in Sing Sing.

Speeding, out of control, down the tortuous Secor Road hill, it mounted the ramp that crosses the New York Central tracks near the Ossining station, crashed through the fragile iron railing on one side of the ramp and landed on its four wheels in a lumber yard.

Gasoline Tank Explodes.

The driver, apparently, failed to turn off the ignition; and as the bus struck the ground the gasoline tank exploded with a deafening roar. Sheets of flame shot out in all directions, and while passengers inside scrambled for the exits, fire enveloped the vehicle and the adjacent lumber piles.

The bus, one of the old-fashioned type with no centre aisle, had eight seats running crosswise and doors on either side of each seat. A few of the doors were opened without difficulty, enabling those inside to escape. But many of the doors, thrown out of alignment by the crash, refused to open.

The occupants of these seats were penned inside, and with the flames mounting around them began screaming for help. Those who had escaped tugged vainly at the closed doors. With the aid of witnesses to the crash they succeeded in opening several doors and releasing some of those inside.

Four Leap Into the Hudson.

Four men, who escaped from the bus with their clothing in flames, rushed to the nearby Hudson River and threw themselves in. Two others raced down along the New York Central Railroad tracks. Those in the river were rescued by Frank McLaughlin, former Fire Chief of Ossining. What became of the two who ran along the tracks could not be definitely ascertained last night, but it is believed they were taken in charge by near-by residents and rushed to a hospital.

Thomas McGuire Jr. of 628 Halsey Street, Brooklyn, who had escaped from the bus with a broken arm and secondary burns, rushed back to rescue his father, who had been critically burned. Others who had escaped from the bus made every effort to save those still inside. So did witnesses to the accident. George Adcock, an Ossining fireman, got credit for seven rescues. But the old wooden framework of the bus and the sun-dried lumber piled near by burned like tinder and the rescue work had to be abandoned.

All ambulances were brought to the scene of the crash and the injured removed to the Ossining, Grasslands and Tarrytown Hospitals. Father John Kelly of Briarcliff, who chanced to be passing in an automobile, had arrived in time to assist in the rescue work. He also administered the last rites of the church to some of the more seriously injured. Afterward, he went to the Ossining Hospital, where he administered the last rites to others.

The regular staff at the Ossining hospital was swamped with work and was reinforced by numerous volunteers. These included Drs. Robert Bloom, James Kearney, John Schofmeister, Edward Huntington of Ossining, Edward Huntington of Croton.

Many prominent women in the vi-

Continued on Page Three.

Victims of Bus Accident

A partial list of the dead and injured in the bus accident at Ossining, as compiled last night, follows:

THE DEAD.
GALLER, ABRAHAM, 666 Hancock Street, Brooklyn.
HAYES, Mrs. WILLIAM, 27 Cornelia St., Brooklyn.
INCARNATO, FRANK, 28 years old, driver of the bus, 662 Ninety-second St., Brooklyn.
McNICHOLAS, JOHN, Jr., 36, 412 Irving Av., Brooklyn.
An unidentified person.

MISSING (BELIEVED DEAD).
GALLER, Mrs. ABRAHAM, 666 Hancock Street, Brooklyn.
LUFF, ARTHUR, 9 Woodbine St., Brooklyn.
His sister, whose name was not determined.
MEMEY, JOSEPH, 27 Cornelia St., Brooklyn. and their daughter.
McDONALD, Mr. and Mrs. JOSEPH, 109 Gates Av., Brooklyn.
McDONALD, BERNADETTE, 18 years old, their daughter.
MURRAY, Mr. and Mrs. JAMES, 19 Cornelia St., Brooklyn.
THOMPSON, Mrs. ROSE, 9 Woodbine St., Brooklyn.

THE INJURED.
(In Ossining Hospital.)
CONNORS, FRANK, 542 Bainbridge Av., Brooklyn, critical.
CORCORAN, JOSEPH, 666 Putnam Avenue, Brooklyn; not serious.

ELLERY, JAMES, 712 Knickerbocker Av., Brooklyn, left hospital after treatment.
HAYES, WILLIAM, 27 Cornelia St., Brooklyn; not serious.
HAYES, JAMES, 12, his son, critical.
HUFF, FRANK, 521 Monroe St., Brooklyn; not serious.
McCANN, DANIEL, 375 Central Av., Brooklyn; not serious.
McGUIRE, THOMAS, 636 Halsey St., Brooklyn; critical.
MERKEL, Mrs. TERESA, 280 Highland Blvd., Brooklyn, left hospital after treatment.
REITMEYER, JOHN, 1,218 Gates Av., Brooklyn, critical.
SCHWARTZ, Mrs. ARCHIBALD, 116 Liberty St. Brooklyn; not serious.

(In Grasslands Hospital.)
KNAUER, FRANK, of 73–07 Sixty-fourth St., Glendale, Queens.
LALOF, MARY, 9 Woodbine Street, Brooklyn; critical.
SCHNEIDER, EDWIN, 306–11 106th Street, Hollis, Queens; not serious.
SCHWARTZ, ARCHIBALD, 116 Liberty Street, Brooklyn; not serious.

(In Tarrytown Hospital.)
HICKEY, GEORGE, 17 Woodbine Street, Brooklyn; critical.
MURRAY, WILLIAM, 19 Cornelia Street, Brooklyn; not serious.

BUS BRAKES WEAK, SURVIVORS ASSERT

'We'll Take a Chance,' Driver Said—Stopped Twice for Makeshift Repairs.

MAN SAW WIFE PERISH

Tried to Pull Her From Wreck, but Flames Drove Him Back, He Testifies at Inquest.

Special to The New York Times.

OSSINING, N. Y., July 22.—Walter Thompson of 9 Woodbine Street, Brooklyn, a survivor of the bus accident that cost fifteen lives here today, testified tonight at the official inquest that the bus driver knew his brakes were bad.

Thompson was the first witness called by Dr. Amos O. Squire, Medical Examiner of Westchester County. His story of the bad brakes and the driver's makeshift repairs was corroborated by other witnesses and in unofficial accounts obtained by newspaper men from other survivors here and in Brooklyn.

"Several times on the way up," Thompson told Dr. Squire, "the driver had trouble with his brakes. I noticed that finally he got up and turned the foot brake around as if he were screwing it on the shaft. After each time the brake held better, and then it seemed to loosen up. At one point the emergency brake held all right, but on the hill in Ossining it was no good.

"In the neighborhood of Tarrytown, where they were fixing the brake, the cars ahead stopped for traffic and the driver had to drive off the road because the brakes wouldn't hold.

"We'll Take a Chance."

"I said to him. 'Your brakes are bad.' I told him he'd better be careful and that he ought to stop and fix them.

"The driver said: 'The hell with it. We'll take a chance. I guess we'll get through.' He was completely sober. I thought that he was a good chauffeur—that's what I told the man in the seat with me.

"When we got on the hill on Main Street here and were coming down from the top at a pretty good pace, we got to where he should have taken a turn at Hunter Street [a right-angle turn off Main Street which would have led to the prison] and there were two automobiles parked on the street which partly blocked the turn.

"The driver turned out, swung away over and cleared the automobiles and went on down the hill, swinging from curb to curb almost all the way down the hill. He couldn't get control again.

"Yelled to All to Jump.

"Just before the bus crashed through the railing the driver yelled, 'Everybody jump!' We went right through the railing, and the bus fell front first when the hind wheel hit the foundation for the railing, raising up the rear of the bus. The bus stopped on the front. The motor backed up and drove the steering wheel into the chauf-

Continued on Page Three.

TREASURY OFFERS MORTGAGE BONDS

$100,000,000 in 3% 14-Year Farm Corporation Securities to Go to Highest Bidders.

SALE USHERS NEW POLICY

Marks First Time Treasury Has Acted as Fiscal Agent—Ready Market Expected.

Special to The New York Times.

WASHINGTON, July 22.—The Treasury Department today announced an offering to the public of $100,000,000 of Federal Farm Mortgage Corporation 3 per cent bonds, thus inaugurating a new policy under which the department acted as the agent of one of the emergency recovery set-ups in floating securities which the corporation is authorized by law to sell to obtain funds.

In the past the Treasury, except in the case of short-term Treasury bills which are sold on a discount basis, has judged the market, determined upon the interest at which a security should be offered and then has sought subscriptions at par or at a small stated premium. Such offerings have been for the purpose of covering the Treasury's own requirements.

In the present offering, however, which the Treasury is making on behalf of the emergency corporations, the department did not use its discretion in fixing the interest rate the securities shall carry. It has, therefore, offered the mortgage corporation's bonds to the highest bidders, but in no case at less than par and accrued interest. The bonds will be dated May 15, 1934, mature on May 15, 1948, and may be redeemed on May 15, 1944, or on any subsequent interest payment date which comes semi-annually on May 15 and Nov. 15 of each year.

At present Treasury 3s are selling in the market at slightly over 102, and outstanding bonds of the mortgage corporation are quoted at just over 101. The latter are guaranteed as to principal and interest by law.

Substantial Premium Expected.

In connection with the present offering the Treasury Department expects to market the $100,000,000 issue readily and at a substantial premium. The bonds are exempt as to principal and interest from Federal, State, municipal and local taxation, except surtaxes. They will be issued in denominations of from $100 to $10,000.

The decision to have the Treasury market the bonds and thus further centralize the handling of government-backed security offerings in the public market was reached at conferences between Treasury officials and officials of the Farm Credit Corporation, under the supervision of which the Federal Farm Mortgage Corporation activities are brought.

To a certain extent it is in line with the policy adopted some time ago to suspend the direct sale of debentures by the RFC to banks

Continued on Page Two.

2,320 Planes for Army Asked in Baker Report

Board Declares Congress Should Provide Funds—Separate Unit Plan Rejected —Mail Flying Praised.

Special to The New York Times.

WASHINGTON, July 22.—Holding that the strengthening of the air forces was essential to adequate national defense, the War Department's special aviation committee recommended today an increase in the aviation strength of the army to 2,320 planes and a corresponding increase in the flying personnel. The present authorized strength of the army air corps is 1,800 planes, which the committee reported to be more than 300 short.

The committee, headed by Newton D. Baker, former Secretary of War, and composed of eleven civilians and generals, declared against consolidation of the army and navy aviation services into a single unit. Its report praised the spirit and manner in which the army carried the mail under difficulties during the period of the cancellation of the air mail contracts. With this was mingled criticism of the actual per-

formance, coupled as it was with fatalities, and whatever there was of failure was attributed to lack of proper equipment and to insufficient training.

While expressing the opinion that the United States was comparatively free from the threat of serious overseas air invasion because of the failure so far to develop an airplane capable of crossing the Atlantic or Pacific with an effective military load, attacking vital areas successfully and returning to its base, the committee held that the army's air corps must be ready at all times for war service.

"The next great war is likely to begin with engagements between opposing aircraft, either sea-based or land-based," the report read, "and early aerial supremacy is quite likely to be an important fac-

Continued on Page Six.

The recommendations of the Baker committee are on page 6.

FALL BUSINESS RISE PREDICTED BY NRA; SUMMER DROP CUT

Upward Trend Held Definite by Leon Henderson, Citing Homely Indicators.

LESS FAMILY DOUBLING-UP

This Despite Increase in Marriages—Small Loans Are Being Rapidly Repaid.

Copyright, 1934, by The Associated Press.

WASHINGTON, July 22.—The NRA has been informed by its experts to "gamble" on a substantial Fall rise in business and a less than usual sharp slump during the remainder of the Summer.

Leon Henderson, chief of the Blue Eagle's research and planning division, held this conclusion today on the basis of a mass of statistical and other data. His advice to NRA is based upon an expectation of an upswing.

Mr. Henderson's searchers have reported to him that the decline thus far this Summer has been less than normal, and that there are now numerous signs of an upward trend in business generally.

There is no expectation, however, of a boom development. Mr. Henderson employs most careful language in his estimate of the future. For instance, there has been a gain in the sale of living room rugs, one of the first things which housewives like to replace when funds are available.

There also has been a decline in the number of bachelors, he points out. In one city the number of bachelors before the depression was 10,000. This increased to 29,000 at the height of the depression and is now about 22,000, the expert conclusion being that men with funds are less fearful of marriage.

Families Again Spread Out.

For another thing, Mr. Henderson's "doubling up" indicator in reference to housing shows that families which have been crowded now are spreading out and filling vacant apartments and houses.

Small personal loans, his figures show, are being paid up in full at an increasing rate. The index shows the rate of repaying at a record high for the depression, and higher even than in the month when soldiers' cash bonus payments were largest. Similarly, the rate of repayment of building and loan obligations is up and the amount of unrented property held by building and loan associations is down. Repayments to the Home Owners Loan Corporation and Farm Credit Administration are also holding up well.

Mr. Henderson said he was paying increasing attention to this type of statistical indicator because, first, it shows the status of the ordinary person better than the customary type of business statistics, and second, because it tends to get at the beginning of the buying process rather than at the end.

Of particular significance, Mr. Henderson said, are the indicators showing a reduction in personal debt. He holds this to be one of

Continued on Page Two.

FRENCH FACTIONS WARNED BY LEBRUN TO RESTORE TRUCE

President Says Public Will Be Severe With Those Blocking Doumergue's Work.

PREMIER TO SEEK ACCORD

Tardieu Is Said to Be Ready to Make Peace With Herriot to Prevent Cabinet Shifts.

By The Associated Press.

AURILLAC, France, July 22.—President Lebrun took a hand in the bitter Cabinet clash today by warning that there must be no interference with the government of Premier Doumergue.

France will not tolerate anything which blocks M. Doumergue's work of restoration, M. Lebrun said as he unveiled a monument at the birthplace of the assassinated President, Paul Doumer.

M. Lebrun made no direct reference to the Cabinet dissension in which Edouard Herriot and André Tardieu, both Ministers without portfolio and both former Premiers, are the chief figures. But he said pointedly that party fights must be forgotten.

The President expressed pride in M. Doumergue's "wisdom and prudence" and asserted his work must go on.

"Public opinion will not accept a situation that stops his beneficial work," M. Lebrun said. "It will be severe toward those who do not do everything to assure for the future what the wisdom of the efforts of that already is permitting us to hope is being achieved."

Critical Week for France.

PARIS, July 22.—This coming week seems likely to be as critical for France as was that following the rioting of Feb. 6. There is only this difference in the situation, that this time there is even greater confusion.

It is believed the country as a whole at this vacation time wants a real truce to politics. It has put its trust in Premier Doumergue, and among persons of all classes of opinion one hears expressions of resentment because his Ministers could not keep the truce while his back was turned. Whatever he does will have the approval of most persons, but it also is true that whatever he does is almost certain to arouse resentment in one camp or the other.

In the two camps feeling is running high. André Tardieu's friends on newspapers are reiterating that the Radical Socialists are responsible for breaking the truce and are seeking to thrust them out of the Cabinet because they spoke the truth about Camille Chautemps.

To that the reply of the Radical Socialist press is to describe M. Tardieu as "the man who brought down French bonds."

Newspapers like the Petit Parisien, which more nearly represent average opinion, are being careful to remain outside the quarrel. They are too well aware of its dangers for France, because this quarrel strikes deeper than any political division since the days of the Dreyfus affair. There is no concealment of the fact that below the truce, which is possible only in person and authority of Premier Doumergue, there is an atmosphere

Continued on Page Four.

DILLINGER SLAIN IN CHICAGO; SHOT DEAD BY FEDERAL MEN IN FRONT OF MOVIE THEATRE

Cummings Says Slaying of Dillinger Is 'Gratifying as Well as Reassuring'

By The Associated Press.

WASHINGTON, July 22.—Smiling in elation, Attorney General Cummings tonight termed the slaying of John Dillinger by Federal agents "gratifying as well as reassuring."

The Attorney General was notified just before he boarded the train for the West, the first leg of a journey to Hawaii. At Union Station he dictated the following statement:

"The search for Dillinger has never been relaxed for a moment.

"He has escaped capture on several occasions by the narrowest of margins.

"The news of tonight is exceedingly gratifying as well as reassuring."

Mr. Cummings said the end of the Indiana bandit reflected great credit on the Chicago office of the division of investigation.

J. Edgar Hoover, chief of the Bureau of Investigation, rushed to his office at word that the desperado had been shot down. He told news men:

"This does not mark the end of the Dillinger case.

"Any one who ever gave any of the Dillinger mob any aid, comfort or assistance will be vigorously prosecuted."

He referred directly to George (Baby Face) Nelson, Homer Van Meter and another gangster. Nelson, named by the department as the killer of Special Agent W. Carter Baum in the Dillinger outbreak in the Wisconsin woods last April, was described by Mr. Hoover as a "rat."

REACHED FOR HIS GUN

Outlaw's Move Met by Four Shots, All Finding Their Mark.

HAD LIFTED HIS FACE

Desperado Had Also Treated Finger Tips With Acid to Defeat Prints.

TWO WOMEN WOUNDED

Agents, Tipped Fugitive Was Going to Theatre, Waited While He Saw Show.

Special to The New York Times.

CHICAGO, July 22.—John Dillinger, America's Public Enemy No. 1 and the most notorious criminal of recent times, was shot and killed by Federal agents a few seconds after he had left the Biograph Theatre at 2,433 Lincoln Avenue, on Chicago's North Side.

One bullet penetrated the head and another the chest of the desperate outlaw. He died as he was being taken to the Alexian Brothers Hospital. The body was later removed to the county morgue, where the identification of Dillinger was made positive.

According to Melvin H. Purvis, chief of the investigating forces of the Department of Justice in Chicago, and leader of the band of sixteen men who had waited for more than two hours while the desperado viewed his last picture show, a Dillinger attempted to put up a fight.

"He saw me give a signal to my men to close in," Chief Purvis said. "He became alarmed and reached into a belt and was drawing the .38-calibre pistol he carried concealed when two of the agents let him have it. Dillinger was lying prone before he was able to get the gun out and I took it from him."

Surgical Disguise Fails.

Dillinger had taken great precautions to prevent his being recognized. His face had been lifted his last picture was taken and he had dyed his hair a darker shade than its natural light reddish brown.

"It was a good job the surgeons did," Chief Purvis said, "but I knew him the minute I saw him. You couldn't miss it if you had studied that face as much as I have."

Two women, passers-by who had no connection with the outlaw, were wounded by stray bullets fired by Chief Purvis's men. They are Mrs. Etta Natalsky, 45 years old, of 2,428 Lincoln Avenue, and Miss Theresa Paulus. Each was struck in the left leg. Their injuries, it was said, were not serious.

Patron of Gangster Film.

Chief Purvis and twelve of his own men, accompanied by Captain Timothy O'Neill and three members of the East Chicago police force, went to the vicinity of the small theatre at about 8:30 P. M. They had received information during the afternoon that Dillinger would attend the performance of "Manhattan Melodrama," a gang and gun movie featuring Clark Gable and William Powell, in the evening.

The sixteen men were posted strategically, some at all possible exits of the theatre, with groups to the north and south, and one detail on the opposite side of busy Lincoln Avenue. Chief Purvis, seating himself in his automobile a few feet south of the show house, waited.

It was about 8:30 P. M. when Dillinger walked up to the entrance and bought a ticket, or tickets. A Chicago policeman who happened to be at the scene said he was accompanied by two women, one dressed in red, but Chief Purvis said he saw none. Passing into the theatre, Dillinger took a seat.

While he was inside, the agents completed their preparations for his emergence. There were so many of them, and their actions seemed, to the theatre manager and to observers in the neighborhood, to be suspicious that the police were notified.

Policemen Frank Slattery, Edward Meisterheimer and Michael Garrity, who investigated, were shown Federal badges by the watchers and interfered not at all, al-

Continued on Page Nine.

HOT WAVE ABATES; SEVEN DROWN HERE

Highest Temperature Is 89 at 4:30 P. M. After Cool Morning—One Heat Death.

DROUGHT SPREADS IN WEST

Total Dead in Nation From Weather 272—Cattle and Crops Loss Mounts.

After three days of oppressive heat and high humidity, the weather here moderated somewhat yesterday.

The day's maximum temperature was 89 degrees at 4:30 P. M., but the humidity remained comparatively low throughout the day, and a brisk northerly breeze tempered the heat of the sun.

The combination here of the warm sun and cool breeze made perfect weather for the seashore, and all the near-by beaches again were thronged with large Sunday crowds. For the fourth time this season the crowd at Coney Island was estimated at more than 1,000,000. At the Rockaways, it was also more than 450,000; at Long Beach, more than 300,000, and at Jones Beach, more than 150,000.

The crowd at Jones Beach was one of the largest of the year. The causeway there was lined throughout the day while automobiles, and the bathhouses did a near-capacity business.

One heat death and one prostration were reported during the day. An unidentified man about 55 years old was stricken with a heart attack induced by the heat at Sheriff and Delancey Streets and died.

Seven Persons Drowned.

Seven drownings were reported:
JOSEPH CERILLA, 18 years old, of 101 Bergen Street, Brooklyn; drowned while swimming at Coney Island.
JAMES CUNNINGHAM, 24, employed at the Overlook Hospital in Summit, N. J.; drowned off Beach 106th Street, Rockaway Beach.
ALLAN SNYDER, 23, of 632 Wrague Avenue, West Philadelphia; drowned in Mirror Lake at Browns Mills, N. J.
FRANK BELLTENRICH, 15, of 209 Seventh Street, Jersey City; drowned in New York Bay off Linden Avenue, Jersey City.
CATHERINE LeCONTE, 8, of 846 East Third Street, Brooklyn; drowned in Lake Ronkonkoma, L. I.
WILLIAM MAGUIRE, 72; drowned in Salem Creek at Salem, N. J.
MILTON WETLANDT, 15, of 363 Watchogue Road, Port Richmond, S. I.; seized with heart attack and drowned in Lake Hopatcong, N. J.

It was said last night at the Weather Bureau that today probably would be fair and slightly cooler.

272 Dead in Nation.

Deaths in the protracted heat wave covering most of the country passed 256 yesterday, The Associated Press reported.

The Southwest and Midwest were hardest hit. Only slight relief for scattered areas was in immediate prospect.

In the grain belt crops wilted and

Continued on Page Eleven.

THREE DOOMED MEN FLEE TEXAS PRISON

Another Convict Killed Climbing Wall, Two Others Shot in Death House Break.

GUARD ALSO IS WOUNDED

Trio of Killers, One of Them an Aide of Clyde Barrow, Escape in Waiting Car.

By The Associated Press.

HUNTSVILLE, Texas, July 22.—Three of the most desperate killers in the Southwest—Raymond Hamilton, Blackie Thompson and Joe Palmer—escaped from the death house of the State penitentiary here today in a daring break in which one convict was killed, two others wounded and a guard shot.

The three convicts who were shot, all bank bandits and life-termers, were moved down by the gunfire of guards as Hamilton, Thompson and Palmer scampered over the wall to two waiting automobiles.

Whitey Walker was killed by the shots of guards whom the convicts engaged in battle. Charlie Frazier, the man who engineered the break, was shot from the ladder which he was scaling the wall and was believed to be fatally wounded. Roy Johnson, the third bank robber, was shot and less seriously hurt.

H. E. George, the guard, was momentarily stunned by a bullet creased his scalp. He was not seriously hurt.

The break occurred while the prison yard was almost deserted. All officials and guards not actually on duty and practically all convicts were attending a ball game between the prison teams and a Conroe team at the athletic field beside the walls.

The escape was the first ever made from the death house, which is located in the centre of the prison. In daring and cool execution, the break has no parallel in the annals of the penitentiary.

Guard Forced to Unlock Cells.

At 4:30 P. M. inside Guard Lee Braswell approached the death house to feed the five inmates. Inside guards are not permitted to carry weapons, as they come closely into contact with the convicts, and it would be possible for the latter on occasions to overpower and disarm them.

As Braswell approached the door, Frazier, crouched against the wall, stepped forward and thrust the muzzle of a .45-calibre revolver against his ribs. In his other hand the convict held another .45.

Frazier marched Braswell into the death house and compelled him to unlock the cells in which Hamilton, Palmer and Thompson were incarcerated. These convicted murderers came out, and Frazier handed Hamilton his extra gun. Braswell was locked in Hamilton's cell.

The quartet of desperadoes sped from the death house and when they joined the other bank robbers at the door by Walker and Johnson. A few feet from the death house they encountered W. T. Mc-

Continued on Page Eleven.

The New York Times.

"All the News That's Fit to Print."

LATE CITY EDITION
WEATHER—Showers, cooler to-day; fair, cooler tomorrow.

Copyright, 1934, by The New York Times Company.

VOL. LXXXIII....No. 27,942.   Entered as Second-Class Matter, Postoffice, New York, N. Y.   NEW YORK, THURSDAY, JULY 26, 1934.   P   TWO CENTS In New York City.   THREE CENTS   FOUR CENTS Elsewhere

DEATHS FROM HEAT INCREASE TO 1,213 IN THE COUNTRY

Temperatures Continue to Stay Above 100 Degrees in Western Cities.

MISSOURI SUFFERS MOST

Records Show 312 Deaths in State—Intense Drought Suffering in Huge Area.

WALLACE IS PESSIMISTIC

He Says Situation Will Be Very Serious Unless Relief Comes in Two Weeks.

The Daily Heat Record

Following are the maximum heat records set yesterday in Western cities, with deaths for the day and the forecast:

City.	High Mark.	Deaths.	Forecast.
Chicago	98	78	Cooler.
Cincinnati ..106		27	Slightly cooler.
Des Moines..104		52	Showers, cooler.
Omaha 106		3	Possible showers.
St. Louis....106		76	Showers, cooler.
Kansas City.106		13	Showers, cooler.

By The Associated Press.

Wind and rain combined forces to afford some slight relief to people on the Atlantic, Pacific and Gulf coasts yesterday, but there was no relief for the parched fields, panting beasts and the perspiring populace of the Middle West where the toll of death and damage continued to mount.

Fatalities listed as "heat deaths" reached 1,213 persons. Thousands of head of livestock have been destroyed and the market value of many additional thousands seriously reduced during the past sixteen days, when most of the nation has suffered under temperatures around the century mark. Irreparable damage has resulted to crops in all great producing areas.

On forecasts from the Weather Bureau of continued drought, Dr. Elwood Mead, Reclamation Commissioner, said that tens of thousands of persons in the Dakotas and eastern slopes of the Rockies "must be evacuated."

The Atlantic Coast was favored with lower temperatures and showers in many places. Several baseball games were postponed. The Pacific Coast also continued to enjoy comfortable weather.

Water shortage is serious in many communities. Two down-State Illinois counties reported the situation "was becoming desperate." Some Iowa cities have been hauling water in tank cars. Hundreds of new wells have been sunk throughout the Middle West.

Grasshoppers, chinch bugs and other insect pests daily add their ravages to the farmers' worries.

Deaths Sweep States.

Missouri with 312 victims continued to lead the list of States. Illinois was second with 200 and Ohio had 127. Among the others were Indiana 54, Nebraska 61, Iowa 62, Minnesota 32, Kansas 29, Kentucky 43, Texas 22, Michigan 19, Pennsylvania 18, Wisconsin 15, Oklahoma 10, South Dakota 7, West Virginia 12, Tennessee 5, New York 4, Massachusetts 3, Maryland 3, Connecticut 4, District of Columbia 3, Arkansas 2, Alabama 1.

Chicago, where a new all-time high record of 104.9 degrees, officially 105, was recorded Tuesday, dropped to a maximum of 98 yesterday, although the humidity continued excessive. St. Louis and Kansas City, with highs of 110 for the previous day, turned in marks of 106 and 106 respectively.

Cincinnati equaled its 106-degree mark for the second successive day, but some hope of relief was held out for Thursday, after a slight drop came in the early afternoon. Cleveland, swept by a lake breeze, enjoyed a 73 at 2 P. M. (Eastern standard time).

The Pacific Coast had little change in temperature and no heat fatalities. Seattle and Los Angeles had 80, Portland 84 and San Francisco 68 degrees.

Oklahoma City dropped from 104 Tuesday to 96 at noon Wednesday. Michigan cities in the midnineties showed a 10 degree drop. Baltimore had a 98, Indianapolis 106, Lincoln 97, Huntington 104, West Virginia 104, Pittsburgh 96, Philadelphia 86, St. Paul 78, Milwaukee 84, Cumberland (Md.) 105, Ottumwa (Iowa) 104, Duluth 74, Omaha 101, Springfield (Ill.) 101, Carbondale (Ill.) 112, Louisville 100, Lawrence (Kan.) 111, Columbia (Mo.) 111, Newkirk (Okla.) 105, Topeka (Kan.) 109, Emporia 115.

Oklahoma's parched surface faced a new menace—forest fires, eighteen of which were reported licking up the valuable pasturage—and the State relief administration asked $500,000 immediately to fight conditions. "The worst on record."

Although its cattle purchase ma-

Continued on Page Eleven.

Will Not Tell of 'Hanging,' Reporters Go Back to Jail

By The Associated Press.

DANVILLE, Ky., July 25.—Jack Durham and Wesley Carty, newspaper men who have refused to tell the police court about their advance information on a hanging in effigy, went back to jail today to serve another six hours. Judge J. W. Harlan ordered them to appear in court again tomorrow.

At the close of today's hearing, after Durham and Carty repeated their refusal to disclose their information on the ground that it was given them in confidence, Judge Harlan said:

"Well, boys, if this is going to be an endurance contest, I can stand it. You understand that this is a challenge to the court."

Yesterday Durham and Carty served a jail sentence of three hours. Monday they were fined $10.

BUS CRASH WITNESS RECEIVES A THREAT

Another Tells Court 'the Boss' Ordered Him to Say Falsely He Overhauled Coach.

3 ARE HELD AS WITNESSES

De Marco, of Rialto Company, Before Grand Jury—New Jersey Pushes New Laws.

Three men were held as material witnesses and Westchester County authorities were told of a threat to one witness and an order to another to commit perjury as the grand jury opened at White Plains yesterday its investigation of the Ossining bus disaster.

Indictments for manslaughter, predicted by the District Attorney's office the day before, did not materialize, and the grand jury heard only one witness before adjourning until next Wednesday. But District Attorney Frank H. Coyne and his aides received evidence, they said.

Jersey Prepares Laws.

Before the end of the day the effects of the investigation had spread far beyond the county in which the accident that cost the lives of nineteen persons occurred.

Aroused by the tragedy and the resultant indications of faulty brakes, inadequate equipment, and lack of legislation to authorize inspection and supervision of sightseeing and chartered buses, New Jersey authorities followed the lead of New York State and prepared to provide remedial laws.

At Albany a resolution authorizing legislative investigation of the bus accident was introduced, and in New York and neighboring States local authorities of various towns and cities were taking the responsibility for inspection and supervision into their own hands.

There were suggestions that bus transportation systems be investigated with a view to more adequate control, and that the Federal Government investigate the tax returns of some companies.

Bus School Testifies.

The single witness before the White Plains grand jury yesterday was Nicola De Marco, ostensible manager of the Rialto garage at 434 East 116th Street, where the buses that took the Young Men's Democratic League of the Twentieth Assembly District, Brooklyn, on the fatal trip to Ossining were stored. De Marco, who appeared jaunty, had been described by Max E. Greenberg, attorney for the Rialto concerns, as one of those

Continued on Page Twelve.

KENNEDY PLEDGES SECURITIES ACT AID TO BUILD BUSINESS

Chairman Says Commission Will Encourage Legitimate Stock Market Operations.

PROMISES NEW STANDARDS

Speaking at Luncheon, He Assures Capital and Investors Alike of Proper Profit.

The text of Chairman Kennedy's speech is on Page 13.

Special to The New York Times.

WASHINGTON, July 25.—Joseph P. Kennedy spoke words of reassurance today to both capital and investors in connection with the new Securities Act. As chairman of the Securities and Exchange Commission he delivered his first speech since assuming office when he appeared at a luncheon of the National Press Club.

He told business generally that there would be no vindictiveness in the enforcement of the stock market law, but rather an effort to develop the financial market.

If business does the "right thing" it will be protected and have a chance to live and prosper, Mr. Kennedy said in assuring governmental protection of all interests.

The commission's job, although essentially a technical one, would be done, said Mr. Kennedy, "in a businesslike way without political publicity of any sort." Public scrutiny of the commission's activities would never be discouraged or avoided, he declared.

"In our hands has been placed the responsibility of giving all the aid of which government is capable to the better organization of the mechanism through which the savings of the people find their way into securities," Mr. Kennedy said.

Some Old Practices Past.

"Everybody says that what business needs is confidence. I agree. Confidence that if business does the right thing it will be protected and given a chance to live, make profits and grow, helping itself and helping the country. But the old things business did, the old practices it followed, are, I am sure, no longer the right ones."

The commission did not view business with suspicion, nor was there any intention by any member of it that business must be "harassed and annoyed and pushed around," he said.

"Domestic tranquillity is as essential to business as it is to our political system, and it was stated as one of the primary objects to be achieved through the Constitution," Mr. Kennedy went on. "We of the Securities and Exchange Commission do [?] regard ourselves as coroners sitting on the corpse of financial enterprise. On the contrary, we think of ourselves as the means of bringing new life into the body of the security business.

"We are not working on the theory that all the men and all the women connected with finance, either as workers or investors, are to be regarded as guilty of some undefined crime. On the contrary, we hold that business based on good-will should be encouraged so that it may be helpful."

It would be an "idle thing" to deny that business confidence was lacking in the United States, Mr. Kennedy said, and this was especially true in the case of securities. The times of change capital was notoriously timid, but there was nothing unusual in this; it was caution born of experience.

Mr. Kennedy made plain that the commission was not proceeding as a prosecutor hopeful of bringing

Continued on Page Thirteen.

French Forest Fires Menace Thousands; Whole Mediterranean Fleet Standing By

By The Associated Press.

TOULON, France, July 25.—The entire French fleet in the Mediterranean was ordered to be prepared to speed to Toulon today to evacuate thousands of persons menaced by forest fires in the region of Bormes and Lavadou.

Several thousand persons were reported to have been trapped by a serious fire, and high winds were whipping up the flames.

Orders for the fleet to stand by were radioed by Admiral DuBois after the commandant of the marines fighting the flames had reported that roads were blocked and that the fire was surrounding villages, cutting off escape.

The village of Bormes, to which inhabitants returned after having left it last night, was again evacuated.

Officials said that about 25,000 acres of pine trees have been destroyed.

ATHENS, July 25 (AP).—Six persons died of heat here today as the temperature rose as high as 115 degrees. Many forest fires were burning throughout Greece.

WARSAW, July 25 (AP).—The area around Sandomierz, where the surging Vistula River has spread itself into an enormous lake, was the outstanding danger spot today in Poland's flood-devastated scene.

Ten thousand persons already have been evacuated from the section, and as many more are expected to be ordered to move by military patrols. The evacuation everywhere was orderly.

Although it rained persistently last night, there were reassuring reports from the central section of the Vistula today.

Germany Recalls Envoy For Actions in Vienna

Special Cable to The New York Times.

BERLIN, Thursday, July 26.—The German Government at 5 o'clock this morning announced the recall of Dr. Kurt Rieth, German Minister to Austria, and Germany's intention of avenging the assassin of Chancellor Dollfuss, on behalf of whom Dr. Rieth intervened, should they reach German territory. The announcement reads:

"At the request of Austrian governmental authorities and Austrian rebels, respectively, German Minister to Vienna Rieth consented, without asking the German Government itself, to an agreement concluded between the two relative to the safe passage of the rebels to Germany. He was thereupon immediately recalled from his post."

The second official announcement said that the agreement reached between the Austrian rebels and the Austrian Government for safe passage of the rebels did not concern the German Reich and implied no legal obligations for the German Government.

BERLIN DECLARES HANDS-OFF POLICY

Asserts Austrian Revolt Is a Purely Internal Affair and No Concern of Reich.

PARIS AND LONDON GRAVE

Insist Vienna's Independence Must Be Preserved—British Fear Crisis Like 1914.

By FREDERICK T. BIRCHALL.

Wireless to The New York Times.

BERLIN, July 25.—Throughout the day there has been the keenest interest as to what was happening in Vienna. And information to the public has been correspondingly meager and inaccurate and dictated by the National Socialist interest.

Telephone communications during this afternoon were fragmentary and liable to interruption, both from the Austrian and from the German end. Tonight, when this was being written, it is cut off altogether. Since Paris, Rome and London report a similar condition, the interruption probably is from the Austrian end.

The last reliable communication between Berlin and Vienna was between two Americans at about 5 o'clock. The Vienna informant was told to assure his Berlin questioner that the Dollfuss party had regained full control and that the Chancellor "had withdrawn several promises extorted from him under duress."

Version Reaching Berlin.

At the Austrian Legation it was stated that some 300 Nazis had seized the official radio station earlier in the day, had announced that the Chancellor had resigned and had issued other falsehoods; that the police had since captured them and that the Austrian Minister of Justice had issued an explanation.

At 6 o'clock communication had ceased, and the legation professed not to know whether any Nazis had entered the Chancellery. It was stated, however, that a military cordon had been established around it and that the revolt had failed.

However, every time the press attaché at the legation tried an inquirer over the telephone that it was Austrian Nazis that had invaded the radio station, the connection with the legation was immediately broken. Eventually the abandoned all attempt at plain speech and simply said that the disturbers "belonged to the party that one would expect."

Safe Conduct Demanded.

It was understood here tonight that the assassins of Chancellor Dollfuss, wherever they came from, demanded safe conduct to Germany after their crime and further demanded and obtained intervention by the German Ambassador in this matter.

The official German reaction is that this is purely an Austrian internal situation with which Germany has nothing to do and off which she is keeping her hands. It is said that she has kept the Austrian émigrés scattered; that she has moved or called the Aus-

Continued on Page Three.

Continued on Page Eleven.

AUSTRIAN NAZIS KILL DOLLFUSS, REVOLT FAILS; 147 PLOTTERS HELD; MARTIAL LAW IN EFFECT; ITALIAN ARMY, NAVY, PLANES READY TO ACT

INTERVENTION IS HINTED

Rome Reports Appeal to Powers by Austria to Guard Independence.

75,000 TROOPS AT BORDER

Italian Forces Whip Equipment Into Order and War Fleet Is Steaming Northward.

VIENNA CONFERENCE TODAY

Representative of Italy, France, Britain and the Little Entente Expected to Act.

By The Associated Press.

ROME, July 25.—A statement emanating from official sources tonight said the Austrian Government had requested intervention by European powers to guarantee Austria's integrity.

The statement, which was given to the government-controlled press, was published soon after it was announced that Premier Mussolini had issued wartime military orders to army, navy and air forces to the north of Padua.

The inspired press reported that the diplomatic representatives of Italy, France, Britain and the Little Entente countries would hold a conference at Vienna tomorrow to determine what action should be taken. The conference also will decide which of the powers should intervene in case armed assistance is determined upon.

Italian troops are prepared to march into Austria on short notice.

Fulvio Suvich, Under-Secretary of Foreign Affairs, was remaining at the Foreign Office throughout the night to keep in touch with the Austrian situation and to confer with Premier Mussolini by telephone. The Premier at the same time was keeping a vigil at Riccione.

No effort was made to disguise the fact that the Austrian question is viewed here in a very grave light.

Responsibility of Italy.

"Italy is in the first line of defense for the peace of Europe," said an authoritative editorial in the newspaper Il Popolo di Roma. "It is difficult, if not impossible, to deny that Germany has had grave responsibility in that which has occurred in Austria.

"For months the radio at Munich has issued insult and calumny against Dollfuss and his government. All the efforts of the powers to obtain an end to this campaign, which is against all the principles of international politics, were wrecked by the ill will of German leaders."

The army and air force at Padua was commanded by the Premier to be in instant readiness to move across the Austrian frontier. Leaves were canceled, and each unit was told to keep itself in full strength with all of its mechanical war devices in order. The order applied to 75,000 men from Padua north.

At the same time, an official communiqué was issued stating that the First Naval Squadron had left Fort Adona.

The communiqué did not give the destination of the squadron, but naval circles said that it was moving into the Northern Adriatic, particularly Port Trieste, to keep in touch with Austrian developments.

Situation Is Held Grave.

By ARNALDO CORTESI.

Wireless to The New York Times.

ROME, July 25.—The Austrian Nazi outburst caused profound consternation in Italy today, but no particular surprise, as it had been felt for several days that things were rapidly approaching a crisis there as a result of the government's energetic repressive measures.

The impression tonight is that Italy probably is ready to go to any lengths, including military occupation, to prevent Nazi control of Austria. If the development of events justifies such a course, Italy will propose the occupation of Austria by international forces until such time as it is considered safe to leave her to work out her own salvation. If other powers, however, are unwilling to act, Italy is ready to go ahead on her own initiative.

There is reason to believe that preparations for such an eventuality have already been made. In-

Continued on Page Two.

KILLED IN VIENNA REVOLT.

Chancellor Engelbert Dollfuss.

Times Wide World Photo.

Eight Nazis Hold Off 1,000 Men For Hours at Vienna Radio Plant

Correspondent of The New York Times Witnesses Battle From Restaurant Table—Machine Guns and Bombs of Police and Heimwehr Force Their Surrender.

By G. E. R. GEDYE.

Wireless to The New York Times.

BRATISLAVA, Czechoslovakia, July 25.—I had to cross the Austrian frontier, because the Austrian authorities severed all telegraphic and telephonic communications and are severely censoring telegrams. I can tell the astounding story of how fewer than 200 Nazis held the Austrian Cabinet prisoners all day long in the Chancellor's office.

Chancellor Dollfuss was shot dead by the Nazi revolutionaries because he drew a revolver on being arrested by the Nazis.

Life in Vienna went on normally all day, except for the desperate battle, at which I was present.

The battle raged at the offices of Ravag, the Austrian radio broadcasting company. I left this battle in its earlier stages at 1:30 P. M. to follow an armored car which drove to the Chancellor's offices, where trucks were lining up with machine guns.

No more than any one else could I suspect that what seemed to be merely a precautionary measure was in reality an attempt to rescue members of the Austrian Government, who were being held prisoners, facing the rifles and machine guns of the desperadoes within the Chancellery.

Until late in the afternoon no one had an inkling that the Chancellor and nearly all his Cabinet, together with the huge staff of civil servants, were being held prisoners. Most of the civil servants were driven into the courtyard and kept there under guard.

Dollfuss Shot in Head.

After their release I spoke to-night with Dr. Schmitt, one of the officials of the Chancellor's Department. He seemed on the point of collapse.

"I was held prisoner all day," he said, "and, like the others, know nothing. Chancellor Dollfuss is dead. I saw wounds on his neck and on his head. He died at 6 P. M. We believe that he was shot shortly after 12 o'clock when the Nazis broke into his room. It was a terrible blow."

At 9 P. M. the Chancellor's office was finally evacuated by the rebels under a guarantee of safe conduct to the German frontier. The telephone service began to function normally again.

I learned that ten men in military uniforms confronted the Chancellor at 12:30, and when he drew a revolver they shot him down.

The first intimation I had that there was anything unusual in

Continued on Page Two.

Vienna was when I was passing through Johannesgasse shortly before 1 o'clock, when four or five revolver shots were fired. Several policemen took cover at the side of a house and occasionally fired shots at the Ravag building. They did not seem to know what was really afoot. Within a few minutes motor trucks filled with policemen with rifles, with fixed bayonets and with steel helmets began to pour into one end of Johannesgasse. In a few minutes the cracking of rifle fire was added to the popping of revolvers. The astounded passersby had no idea of what was in progress.

Woman Tells of Raid.

A woman, ashen-white and trembling, was allowed to come through the police cordon into the street where the firing was now general.

"I saw everything that happened from our house opposite Ravag," she told me. "A group of eight young men tried to enter Ravag about half an hour ago. When the policeman at the door challenged them they shot him dead.

"Inside the building they were resisted by one of the directors, a man named Holt. They shot him dead, also, and on entering the studio they placed their revolvers at the head of the announcer and forced him to broadcast a statement that the Dollfuss Cabinet had fallen. Dr. Rintelen, they stated, had become Chancellor and was forming a new Cabinet.

"Then a police alarm was given and the shooting started."

I was informed by the police that it was correct that only eight Nazi youths had carried out this coup and subsequently had repelled for nearly three hours the biggest force the Vienna police could bring to bear on them in the narrow street. With their revolvers they defended themselves against a heavy attack with machine guns.

As I watched the fighting, truck after truck loaded with police and Heimwehr men rolled up until there must have been 1,000 men taking part in the attack, which was pressed with tremendous vigor.

The police were in an ugly temper. One of them marched up to the Terrace Restaurant, where I sat, and demanded to be allowed to remain on the scene after the street had been cleared, and drove me with his clubbed rifle into the restaurant.

Machine guns were now taken

Continued on Page Two.

ALL OF REBELS PRISONERS

Passage to Germany, Arranged by German Minister, Revoked.

MOB TRIES TO LYNCH THEM

Their 'Chancellor' Is Also Held, While Kurt Schuschnigg Succeeds Dollfuss.

VIENNA IS QUIET AGAIN

But Armed Guards Patrol the Streets—Reports of Fighting in Styria, Nazi Stronghold.

Wireless to The New York Times.

VIENNA, Thursday, July 26.—Calm and quiet settled over Vienna this morning. There was no external evidence of the sensational attack on the Federal Chancellery yesterday by 147 Austrian Nazis who killed Chancellor Engelbert Dollfuss and seized members of the Austrian Cabinet as hostages.

The fate of the rebels seemed to be decided. Though they obtained a pledge of safe conduct into Germany before they released the Cabinet members the Austrian Government early this morning issued a communiqué saying this had been revoked.

The safe conduct, it was pointed out, had been granted with the consent of President Miklas, after a consultation with representatives of great powers in Vienna, on condition that nobody was killed in the building, but as Chancellor Dollfuss had died following the rebel attack the Nazis will be tried according to Austrian law.

Rebels Under Strong Guard.

The rebels are prisoners in Marokkaner Barracks in Vienna, strongly guarded. Their leader is a man named Holzweber, a former army sergeant. In addition to the barracks guard, policemen, armed with rifles, still patrolled the streets and trucks rumbled along the boulevards bringing in more troops.

[A dispatch from Vienna in a late edition of The London Mail said that Heimwehr troops and civilians had sought during the night to lynch the members of Chancellor Dollfuss. The Associated Press reported. The dispatch said police, heavily armed, had repulsed all attempts to get at the prisoners by threatening to fire into the approaching crowd.]

Dr. Anton Rintelen, the rebels' candidate for the Chancellorship, has been arrested and is now in military custody in the Building of the Ministry of War.

Reports of alleged Italian military movements along the Austrian border are believed here to be greatly exaggerated. Only those measures were taken which had been prepared automatically in the event of Austrian internal disorder. It is understood that Italian Army airplanes are held ready for flight over Austria in case of emergency.

It was believed in political circles here today that Ministers of the Great Powers will call on Acting Chancellor Kurt Schuschnigg to ask his plans and that he will accept the office of Chancellor.

Cabinet Holds Rebels.

VIENNA, July 25.—A group of Austrian Nazis today seized the federal Chancellery, killed their bitter enemy, Chancellor Engelbert Dollfuss, and held the government building until-they received a pledge of safe conduct to Germany, a guarantee which was revoked when it was discovered that Dr. Dollfuss was dead.

The Nazis were placed in Marokkaner Barracks, stripped of their uniforms and were ordered held after a Cabinet meeting under the new Chancellor, Dr. Kurt Schuschnigg, Minister of Education.

An official communiqué stated that the fact that Dr. Dollfuss was killed canceled the promise of safe conduct, in return for which the

Continued on Page Two.

The New York Times.

"All the News That's Fit to Print."

5:30 A. M. EXTRA

WEATHER—Cloudy, warmer to-day; local showers tomorrow.

Temperatures Yesterday—Max., 81; Min., 67

Copyright, 1934, by The New York Times Company.

VOL. LXXXIII....No. 27,949.

Entered as Second-Class Matter, Postoffice, New York, N. Y.

NEW YORK, THURSDAY, AUGUST 2, 1934.

P

TWO CENTS in New York City. | THREE CENTS Within 200 Miles | FOUR CENTS Elsewhere Except in 7th and 8th Postal Zones

TWO REFORM BILLS ARE SIDETRACKED; LEHMAN FIGHTS ON

Quorum Lacking for Report on County Plans as Republicans Walk Out of Committee.

BATTLE ON FLOOR IS DUE

Governor, Assailing 'Despicable' Action, Is Expected to Spur Democrats in Assembly.

SMITH TARGET IN SESSION

Republicans Deny Entering Agreement—Say He Is Trying to 'Bedevil' Situation.

By W. A. WARN.

Special to The New York Times.

ALBANY, Aug. 1.—The Assembly Judiciary Committee met this afternoon and voted to report eleven minor bills, but failed to take any action on the proposed constitutional amendments, sponsored by Senator Dunnigan and Senator Mastick, to prepare the way for county government reforms.

The Republican majority in the Assembly contrived to block these yesterday after their adoption in the Senate, sending them back to committee.

Governor Lehman pronounced as "despicable" the failure of the committee to act on the measures, the adoption of which he as ex-Governor Smith, as head of the New York City Charter Revision Commission, have so much at heart.

The Governor said he was firmly backing the publication of Mr. Smith in a telegram transmitted on behalf of the entire Charter Commission to Speaker McGinnies yesterday protesting against the action of the Republican majority in "repudiating" its agreement to pass the County Reform Bills.

Governor Is Silent on Plans.

Governor Lehman has not indicated what further steps he may be contemplating to force favorable action on the two side-tracked measures.

They have both been adopted by the Senate, together with another proposed amendment to the Constitution, in which both the Mastick and Dunnigan proposals are joined and which the Assembly yesterday concurred in by unanimous vote.

While the Judiciary Committee, like the Assembly itself, has a Republican majority, it has become apparent through developments of the last few days that the Democrats in the Legislature are no more eager to pass these constitutional amendments than are a majority of the Republicans.

While engaging on the floor of the Assembly today in an apparent effort to make political capital out of the Republican blockade established yesterday against the Dunnigan and Mastick measures, the Democrats did not bestir themselves to rescue the amendments.

Chance for Steingut to Act.

Assemblyman Steingut, minority leader, has not filed the necessary three days' notice of a motion to take the two resolutions from the Judiciary Committee, possibly on the assumption that the committee had not had an opportunity to act when the Assembly met today.

Now that the committee has met and failed to act the way is open for Mr. Steingut to proceed, but unless action is taken by the Assembly before the end of the week the adoption of the two resolutions would be to no purpose.

Under the Election Law, Monday is the deadline for the publication of notice that the amendments are to be submitted to the 1935 Legislature for concurrent action.

Governor Lehman was aroused when he learned of developments at the committee meeting.

"The action in refusing to report or act on the bills is despicable," he said. "I am back of the position taken by Governor Smith 100 per cent.

"Until I learned of the action of the Judiciary Committee in refusing to report the bills, I was convinced that in accordance with the agreement reported by former Governor Smith, the bills would be reported out and passed.

"There is still time to pass these bills, and they should be passed. I am amazed that any condition like this could exist."

Lehman Action Is Expected.

Hence, with the Governor so stirred by the situation, observers at the capital believe he will move to compel more vigorous intervention by the Assembly Democrats to save the measures.

Most of the Democrats, and Republicans also, have already quit their legislative labors for the week and returned to their homes or gone to the Saratoga races or elsewhere. In order to get anything

Continued on Page Four.

Giant Seaplane Tops All Records; Lindbergh Hails Test of Clipper

Sikorsky Machine, Under Transport Conditions With a Full Load, Averages 157.5 Miles an Hour Over a 1,242-Mile Course —Range Would Cover Ocean Trade Routes.

By REGINALD M. CLEVELAND.

Special to The New York Times.

BRIDGEPORT, Conn., Aug. 1.—All existing world's records for transport seaplane flight (previously held abroad) were toppled like ninepins here today as the giant Sikorsky S-42, the Brazilian Clipper, carrying a full transport load in charge for Pan American Airways, flew 1,242.5 miles at an average speed of 157.5 miles an hour. Eight long-standing and recent world marks were shattered by the impressive margins. The two other official ones had already been won by the plane in previous test flights.

As Edwin C. Musick, chief pilot of the airlines, sent the four-engined flying boat four times over a course of 311 miles which included Manhattan's river front, Long Island Sound and the Atlantic Ocean, it was evident that history was being written for American aviation.

Starting at the Stratford Lighthouse, the course ran through five control points, George Washington Bridge, Staten Island Lighthouse, Fire Island Lighthouse, Block Island, Point Judith Lighthouse and back to the place of beginning.

The elapsed time for the flight was 7 hours, 53 minutes, 58 seconds, for a distance equal to that from Newfoundland to the Azores. Yet Pilot Musick used only 69 per cent of the 3,000 horsepower of the four Pratt & Whitney Hornet engines streamlined into the wide silver wing. He had fuel enough for another lap when he landed. The margin of range, with a mail load, for any of the ocean trade routes, Atlantic or Pacific, by way of the islands, had been amply proved.

Cruising speed only was used and less than full horsepower because the flight was an acceptance test for the airline of this craft, which will cut two days' time from the run between Miami and Buenos Aires and put that South American capital within five and one-half days of New York.

Strictly transport conditions prevailed during the flight.

When the plane crossed the starting line against the blue of a morning sky at 9:24:38, Eastern daylight time, she had only six persons aboard. They were Colonel Lindbergh, as official representative of Pan American Airways' technical

Continued on Page Seven.

NEW ORLEANS TENSE AS POLICE AWAIT A MOVE BY TROOPS

300 More Patrolmen Sworn In as the Militia Removes Machine Guns From View.

GUARD FORCE IS REDUCED

Gov. Allen Orders Guardsmen to Investigate Alleged Gambling and Vice Graft.

Special to The New York Times.

NEW ORLEANS, Aug. 1.—New Orleans anxiously watched the growing tension tonight as armed State and city forces faced each other in a political crisis precipitated by the tactics of Senator Huey Long.

George Reyer, Superintendent of Police, completed tonight the swearing in of 500 supernumerary policemen for emergency use. The machine guns manned by National Guardsmen, which have been protruding from the windows of the registration office, were removed.

The 500 emergency policemen, called for service by order of Mayor Walmsley, were armed with automatic shotguns and pistols. They were divided into two platoons, 300 on the day shift and 200 on night duty.

Of the former, 200 will be held at police headquarters, and 100 stationed at the City Hall and the First Precinct station. All of the men on night duty are stationed at police headquarters, with police automobiles and patrol wagons held in readiness to transport them wherever they might be needed.

Policemen now ready for duty number 1,300. All regular members of the department have been instructed to be ready for duty at all times, day or night.

Explains Machine Guns.

The appearance of machine guns in the registration office was explained by Adjt. Gen. Fleming at a conference with Mayor Walmsley this afternoon.

"The members of the artillery unit guarding the registration office," Adjutant General Fleming said, "were relieved Tuesday night by members of the machine gun unit. The machine gun unit always carries its machine guns along wherever it is sent."

He denied the machine guns were intended for intimidation.

Mayor Walmsley and the Finance Commissioner, A. Miles Pratt, in statements issued today, denied there was any intention on the part of the city government to seize any records in the registration office.

The presidents of the chief organizations of business men met today and debated the situation. They adopted a resolution which censured no one and asked the world to understand that "the business of this city is being conducted along the usual, efficient lines with no interruptions whatsoever."

Three members of the police commission created by the Long-controlled Legislature to take supervision of the police force out of the hands of the Mayor and Council filed their credentials. No attempt was made to call a meeting of the board.

Prosecution of the 500 odd men charged with miscounting ballots in the last election, being regarded as impossible under a law taking effect today, District Attorney Stanley nolle prossed the cases. The charges were brought after a

Continued on Page Fourteen.

Overnight Air Service To West Coast Starts

Starting overnight service between the nation's coasts between the "Lindbergh Line," a fourteen-passenger Douglas plane of the Transcontinental & Western Air Line took off from Newark Airport yesterday afternoon at 5:25 Eastern daylight time. It is due in Los Angeles at 7 this morning.

Elliott Roosevelt, second son of the President; Lieut. Commander Frank M. Hawks, noted speed pilot; two paying passengers, newspapermen and airline officials were aboard as passengers.

The plane also carried two copies of The New York Times addressed respectively to Frank I. Shaw, Mayor of Los Angeles, and Harry Chandler, publisher of The Los Angeles Times.

20% CUT IN NAVIES URGED BY SWANSON

But Secretary, in Rejoinder to Tokyo Premier, Says 5-5-3 Ratio Should Continue.

OUR PLANE PROGRAM CUT

Navy Now Thinks Equipping of All Ships Will Require 274 Fewer Than 1st Estimate.

Special to The New York Times.

WASHINGTON, Aug. 1.—A general reduction of 20 per cent in naval armaments by all the powers signatory to the London Naval Treaty was advocated today by Secretary Claude A. Swanson, but he insisted that the 5-5-3 ratio of naval strength fixed by the Washington Treaty of 1922 should stand intact. If agreed to by the powers, the 20 per cent reduction should be a real and not a "blue print" one, he declared.

Meanwhile, Admiral William H. Standley, chief of naval operations, made known that the navy had revised its estimates, but had reached no final decision on the number of planes necessary under the Vinson Naval Building Bill to outfit old and new ships in the next five years. High navy officials now figure that only 910 new planes would be needed, or 274 fewer than previously had been estimated. The navy now has 1,000 planes.

No comprehensive reason was given by naval officials for this reduced estimate, but it was partly explained by the fact that when the earlier estimates were made no decision had been reached to abandon the building of flying-deck cruisers.

Secretary Swanson's statement came as a rejoinder to yesterday's declaration by Premier Keisuke Okada that, while Japan did not expect to attain parity with the United States and Britain at the 1935 naval conference, she could not favor continuation of the present ratio system, which "hurts the self-respect of nations."

Asked to comment on the Japanese Premier's speech, Mr. Swanson said:

"I adhere to the same position I always have. The naval powers met in London and distributed to the naval powers the naval strength they thought was just and right. Naval strength is relative. Both naval and military armaments are relative.

"I represented the navy at the Geneva conference and we offered there the proposition to have naval reductions up to 33 1-3 per cent in the different categories of ships,

Continued on Page Three.

PRESIDENT PAUL von HINDENBURG

Times Wide World Photos.

VON HINDENBURG DIES AT 86 AFTER A DAY UNCONSCIOUS; HITLER TAKES PRESIDENCY

END COMES AT 9 A. M.

Reich President Dies at His Home in East Prussia.

MADE A VALIANT FIGHT

Disappearance of House Flag at Neudeck Announces News to World.

THERE HAD BEEN NO HOPE

He Lapsed Into Coma After Hitler Reached Bedside for Last Meeting.

By The Associated Press.

NEUDECK, Germany, Thursday, Aug. 2.—President von Hindenburg died at 9 A. M. today.

The President's death was indicated to correspondents by the disappearance of the house flag from the flagstaff.

Death came to the 86-year-old leader of the German people and former war marshal after a valiant fight against a complication of ailments.

Chancellor Hitler has assumed the Presidency.

Unconscious For Hours.

By GUIDO ENDERIS.

Wireless to The New York Times.

BERLIN, Thursday, Aug. 2.—A physician's bulletin at 6 o'clock this morning stated that President Paul von Hindenburg remained in the state of unconsciousness into which he lapsed last evening. His death was believed to be a matter only of hours.

The President had consistently lost strength since early morning. All hope that his once rugged constitution would carry him along for a time was definitely dissipated by bedside bulletins that reached Berlin from Neudeck during the day.

At midnight the Propaganda Ministry announced that no further bulletin would be forthcoming during the night. This secretiveness served only to heighten the mystery surrounding Chancellor Hitler's convocation of his Cabinet. Neither foreign correspondents nor those besieging the President's estate at Neudeck had been able to break the news embargo which hedged the Field Marshal's deathbed. Only what seeped through official quarters was placed at the disposal of the German and foreign press.

Hitler Advances Time of Visit.

Chancellor Hitler advanced the time of his flight to Neudeck by more than an hour yesterday morning because of an urgent summons from Professor Ferdinand Sauerbruck, the President's chief physician. It was reported Dr. Sauerbruck notified Herr Hitler that the patient was rapidly sinking.

The last meeting between the President and the man whom he elevated to the Chancellorship after rebuffs which have now become historic, received only brief mention in the day's official bulletins. Herr Hitler found the President momentarily conscious and assured of the prayerful thoughts of the saddened nation. The President shook the Chancellor's hand and thanked him cordially for his visit; then he dropped into a fresh sleep.

Herr Hitler flew back to Berlin late in the afternoon. Among those who accompanied him to Neudeck was Ernst F. S. Hanfstaengl, chief of his Anglo-American publicity department, but only Herr Hitler was admitted to the sick chamber.

Hope that the President would linger on vanished early last evening when Dr. Sauerbruck, on the basis of the attending physicians, announced that the patient was lapsing into unconsciousness and that his heart action was fast failing. A bulletin issued at 2:30 P. M. stated that the President was then steadily losing ground, despite a restful night. He was conscious most of the forenoon and was able to converse with those around him during part of the afternoon.

Up to two months ago President von Hindenburg's rugged frame and his soldierly bearing gave no evidence of physical decline. The collapse began to assume form only a month ago when it was discovered the atrophied prostate gland precluded recourse to a major operation be-

Continued on Page 11.

[Preceding Page 4.]

SMITH ACTS TO QUIT IN CHARTER DISPUTE

Reported Ready to Resign if Board Does Not Agree to Reconsider City Rule Vote.

LETTER ALREADY DRAFTED

Seabury Said to Be Weighing Similar Action—Crucial Meeting Tonight.

Alfred E. Smith will resign from the New York City Charter Revision Commission at tonight's meeting unless the commission reverses its decision to retain the city charter in substantially its present form, according to reports last night in Albany from a source close to the former Governor.

Mr. Smith was said to have long been disgusted with the opposition to thoroughgoing reform of the city charter among members of the commission. According to reports from Albany, Mr. Smith was quoted as saying in private conversation that he was "sick and tired of the bickering and opposition in the commission" and that he "would like a vacation."

The fact that the former Governor has for some time been considering resignation or taking some other drastic action to bring sharply to public attention the failure of the commission to make real progress was confirmed by persons in the city close to Mr. Smith.

Letter Already Drafted.

It was felt that Mr. Smith might be led to resign at tonight's meeting if the commission voted to restore to the Borough Presidents their administrative and patronage powers, as some members of the commission fear will be done. According to a report by The Associated Press, Mr. Smith has already drafted his letter of resignation.

Samuel Seabury, vice chairman of the commission, declined last night to deny or to comment on a report that he also intended to resign. Earlier in the day Mr. Seabury had stated that he would make no comment until after the outcome of tonight's meeting on what he plans to do in case the opposition succeeds in restoring borough government.

These reports came as fear was expressed by members of the commission and civic organizations favoring drastic charter revision that successful drive would be made at tonight's meeting to restore to the Borough Presidents their present administrative and patronage powers. Such a result, it was said, would largely nullify all the progress made by the commission. Both Mr. Smith and Mr. Seabury have fought for stripping Borough Presidents of their powers and for a single chamber legislature.

Confusion existed yesterday among members of the commission, as well as among civic organizations, over the effect of the action taken Tuesday night by the commission to revamp the Board of Estimate and to revamp the Board of Aldermen into a smaller but much stronger Council.

Many condemned it as merely retaining the present form of city legislature, while others saw in it

Continued on Page Four.

BUSINESS TAX YIELD IS UNDER $3,000,000

$2,092,681 Total, With Mail Returns Still Due, Far Short of $8,000,000 Expected.

BUDGET NOW UNBALANCED

Mayor Denies City Plans to Restore Half of Pay Cut— Chides Levy on Figures.

The city's hope of realizing $8,000,000 from its new business tax received a severe blow last night when Controller Joseph D. McGoldrick announced that the total collected up to 6 P. M. on the final day for payment was only $2,092,681.67.

It was pointed out, however, that a last-minute rush permitting payment of taxes by mail without penalty, provided the letters containing tax checks or money orders were postmarked before midnight, would probably bring in additional payments today.

Nevertheless it was predicted that the total return, even with the last-minute checks, could not possibly come to much more than $3,000,000—only three-eighths of the sum the city had hoped to garner from the new tax.

McGoldrick Withholds Comment.

Mr. McGoldrick withheld comment on the tax payments pending the final compilation today. It was indicated, however, that he was convinced that the total returns would be materially less than the sum expected when the tax was imposed.

Failure of the revenues from the business tax to come up to expectations will have the effect of unbalancing the city budget, it was said. The budget was balanced after the passage of the City Economy Bill by salary reductions and furloughs and by imposition of new taxes, of which the business tax was one.

A total of $1,094,800.27 was received yesterday in payment of the tax in the City Collector's office in the five boroughs. During the day 16,748 returns were filed.

Several times recently administration spokesmen have expressed the fear that the business tax revenue would be materially below the original estimates. None, however, believed that the revenue would be as small as last night's figures indicated it would be.

In view of the fact that failure to pay the tax on time brings with it a 10 per cent penalty plus payment of 5 per cent interest a month on the whole tax sum due, it was left in the Finance Department that few concerns would withhold their payments. It was not disclosed how many payments were made under protest and threat of court action to test the constitutionality of the tax measure.

Cut in Reserve Is Hailed.

The revision of the bankers' agreement to provide reduction in the tax delinquency reserve fund in the budgets of 1935, 1936 and 1937 from the original $50,000,000 to $25,000,000 was praised yesterday by Peter Grimm, chairman of the Citizens Budget Commission. Mr. Grimm telegraphed Controller McGoldrick and Governor Lehman, who were mainly responsible for

Continued on Page Nine.

Wagner and Prall Hurt in Auto Plunge; Senator Drives Into Brook to Avoid Crash

Special to The New York Times.

WESTPORT, N. Y., Aug. 1.—Trapped on a curve of a narrow Adirondack highway, Senator Robert F. Wagner drove his automobile over a twenty-foot embankment into a mountain brook rather than have a collision with an oncoming car near here this morning. Senator Wagner and Representative Anning S. Prall, his only companion, were both seriously but not critically injured.

Senator Wagner suffered fractured ribs on the right side, severe lacerations of the face and knees and numerous body bruises. He may also have concussion of the brain.

Representative Prall suffered a compound fracture of both bones of his lower right leg and lacerations of the hands and forehead.

Witnesses of the crash carried the injured men three miles to the offices of Dr. Harold J. Harris here, where both remained tonight. Dr. Harris said that both were resting comfortably and in no great pain, but that because of the severe shock he did not consider it advisable to move them to a hospital.

Dr. Harris said that he thought it might be best for Senator Wagner to remain in the recovery room in his offices for several days, but that Mr. Prall might be taken to a New York hospital tomorrow. He said there was "no evidence of skull fractures or concussions, but we never are sure until after twenty-four hours."

The legislators were on their way north on a fishing expedition when the accident occurred. They were bound for the Seigneur Club at Lucerne, Que. Senator Wagner had only recently returned from Portland, Ore., where he attempted to adjust the marine workers' strike and was fired on by mistake.

The highway through the mountains between Wadhams and this village, which is on a fishing club plain, is narrow and winding. Senator Wagner attempted to pass a truck on a curve, only to find another truck approaching from the opposite direction.

Rather than hit either truck he turned his machine off the road. It tumbled down the embankment into the brook but did not overturn. Both occupants were thrown against the windshield and dashboard, but were conscious when they were extricated from the wreckage, and remained so while they were being brought to the office of Dr. Harris here.

SOCIALIST SUPPORT SOUGHT BY AUSTRIA

Neutrality of the Party in Fight With Nazis to Be Rewarded by Release of Leaders.

FOE HANGED IN INNSBRUCK

Minor Rebels to Be Held and Put at Hard Labor—Officials Linked to Putsch.

By G. E. R. GEDYE.

Wireless to The New York Times.

VIENNA, Aug. 1.—There are signs that the Austrian Government is preparing for radical changes in policy and is contemplating steps calculated to obtain from the Social Democrats assurance of at least neutrality toward the government's fight to the finish with the Nazis.

For eighteen months the Nazis have carried on terroristic activities in Austria, involving a considerable loss of life and enormous property damage. But until yesterday the death penalty had been reserved exclusively for Socialists.

Even the stern ordinance directed against Nazi terrorists, which fourteen days before he was slain, proclaiming death as the only admissible penalty for those possessing explosives, had a Socialist for its first victim. He was hanged the night before Dr. Dollfuss was assassinated.

Three Nazis Now Hanged.

Yesterday, however, two Nazis at last were hanged. Today another Nazi was hanged in Innsbruck, Friedrich Wurnig who shot and killed Police Commandant Franz Hickel of Innsbruck on the day of the Dollfuss slaying.

Still more important from the viewpoint of the government, having been committed to a final struggle, is the fact that it has arrested men like Dr. Anton Apold, director of the Alpine Mining Company, and General Karl Bardolf, former adjutant to Archduke Franz Ferdinand, who were always behind the scenes in negotiations between Germany and Austria. Governor Kernmaier of Carinthia, another prominent protector of Nazis, also has been arrested.

The first move to conciliate the Socialists would be the release of prominent leaders who have been imprisoned without trial since February. It is likely they will be free in a day or so. The leaders to be released are Burgomaster Karl Seitz, head of the party, and Herr Danneberg, Herr Helmer, Herr Proft and Frau Postranetzky, members of the central executive committee of the party, and more officers of the Republican Defense Corps, General Koerner, Major Eiffler and Captain Loew.

Whether such release will have

Continued on Page Three.

HITLER CONSULTS CABINET IN SECRET

Ministry Meets Two Hours in Emergency Session—Von Papen in Attendance.

NEW ELECTION POSSIBLE

Friend Says Chancellor Intends to Occupy the Presidency— Army an Unknown Factor.

Wireless to The New York Times.

BERLIN, Aug. 1.—Chancellor Hitler convoked the German Cabinet for an emergency session at 9:30 o'clock tonight.

The Ministers, among them Vice Chancellor Franz von Papen, had been hastily summoned. They remained with the Chancellor about two hours.

Beyond a more-than-laconic bulletin announcing that the Cabinet had been called, nothing was divulged. There was no hint as to the purpose of the session, and this quickly gave rise to rumors that President von Hindenburg had already died, but that the announcement was being withheld until tomorrow.

The reading public has received only official communiqués concerning the Reich President. The controlled press appears to have been instructed to abstain from any speculative comment on the implications involved in a vacancy in the Presidency.

Hitler Is Seen Taking Power.

Copyright, 1934, by The Associated Press.

BERLIN, Aug. 1.—Adolf Hitler intends to be both President and Chancellor of Germany, one of his close friends told The Associated Press today.

This would give to Herr Hitler a dictatorship as absolute as any in the world.

Despair gripped many Conservatives who had looked upon President von Hindenburg as an anchor against extreme Naziism.

Herr Hitler's plan, The Associated Press informant said, is to call the Cabinet together to read a brief law assigning the dual power to himself.

"The whole thing will take but a few minutes," he said, "for the Cabinet will, of course, endorse the proposal. It will simplify the Führer's [Hitler's] whole work immensely if he need not first ask somebody whether he may do this or that."

An indication of the reliability of this source is that Sunday he revealed the President's turn for the worse and was the first to tip off the fact that Herr Hitler was going to Venice to meet Premier Mussolini.

Under the German Constitution Dr. Erwin Bumke, President of the Supreme Court, would become Act-

Continued on Page Two.

NRA | "All the News That's Fit to Print."

The New York Times.

Copyright, 1934, by The New York Times Company.

LATE CITY EDITION
WEATHER—Clearing today; tomorrow generally fair.
Temperatures yesterday—Max., 75; Min., 63.
Detailed Weather Report, Page 30, Sec. 2.

Section 1

VOL. LXXXIII....No. 27,987.

Entered as Second-Class Matter,
Postoffice, New York, N. Y.

NEW YORK, SUNDAY, SEPTEMBER 9, 1934.

Magazine and Book Sections,
Including Rotogravure Picture.

F +

TEN CENTS

TWELVE CENTS Beyond 200 Miles.
Except in 7th and 8th Postal Zones.

MORRO CASTLE BURNS OFF ASBURY PARK; 200 TO 250 ARE LISTED AS DEAD OR MISSING

GORMAN PROPOSES STRIKE ARBITRATION IF ALL MILLS CLOSE

Union Leader Would 'Avoid Murders' While President's Board Settles Issue.

BUT WIDENS WALKOUT

Calls Out 50,000 More Workers as Employers Plan Mill Openings Tomorrow.

HOSIERY STRIKE ORDERED

Labor Chiefs Direct 85,000 to Quit Wednesday—Green Confers on Textile Peace Plan.

By LOUIS STARK
Special to THE NEW YORK TIMES.

WASHINGTON, Sept. 8.—Francis J. Gorman, chairman of the textile strike committee, proposed tonight that President Roosevelt's textile board arbitrate the issue in the textile strike which began Sept. 1.

In a radio broadcast over the Columbia System, Mr. Gorman suggested that arbitration begin on Monday, that both sides agree to accept the findings of the textile board and that pending arbitration the mills be closed "so that further murder of our fellow workers may be avoided."

An additional 50,000 textile workers in miscellaneous lines will be called out on Monday, said Mr. Gorman. These operatives are in the plants making upholstery and drapery, carpets and rugs, pile fabric, plush and velvets. The strike extension is made in face of the reported plan of employers to open next week mills closed by the general textile walkout.

While Mr. Gorman was still speaking over the radio, the National Executive Board of the American Federation of Hosiery Workers at an emergency session issued an order calling a strike at midnight Wednesday in all hosiery mills where no contractual relations exist between employers and employees. The order covered both seamless and full-fashioned sections of the industry and applied to about 85,000 workers in twelve States, union spokesmen said.

Strike Threat in Dye Industry.

Mr. Gorman announced that unless employers in the dye industry met demands of the union employees in that industry would be called out some time next week.

Governor J. G. Winant, chairman of the textile board, declined tonight to comment on Mr. Gorman's arbitration proposal. He would not say whether the board would take the initiative and seek the view of the employers on the arbitration request or await instead the unsolicited action of the manufacturers.

Under the President's executive order the Winant Board is authorized "upon the request of the parties to a labor dispute, [to] act as a board of voluntary arbitration or select a person or agency for voluntary arbitration."

The textile board's next appointment with George A. Sloan, president of the Cotton Textile Institute, is scheduled for Tuesday.

Green Discusses Arbitration.

Arbitration as a way out was also discussed before the board this afternoon by William Green, president of the American Federation of Labor. On leaving the board's offices Mr. Green said that he had brought up the subject of arbitration as a possible way to end the controversial issues could be settled. He declared that the employers have stated that they would open the mills on Monday, asserting that "they have hired guards, and in some places misled members of the American Legion are reported to be working with these private armies of so-called guards."

In a telegram to Edward A. Hayes, commander of the American Legion, Indianapolis, Mr. Gorman said that Mr. Sloan had announced the closed mills would resume operation on Monday. He declared that "great bands of strike-breakers have been deputized and armed and American Le-

Continued on Page Two.

Sailor Missing 12 Years 'Found' on Morro Castle

By The Associated Press.

ST. LOUIS, Sept. 8.—A St. Louisan, given up for dead by his family more than a decade ago, came back into the world for them today as a result of the Morro Castle disaster.

A crew member of the stricken vessel, carried on the roster as Roger Klinger, was identified by his brother today as Gustav Lehmann, who left his home here twelve years ago.

The brother, Edward H. Lehmann, said his missing relative had assumed "Klinger," the name of another branch of the family, to avoid rejection by navigation companies. He was turned down as Gustav Lehmann for failure to pass a physical examination the brother said.

"The last time we saw Gustav," Edward said, "was twelve years ago. He went to Detroit after that and that was the last city from which we ever received a letter from him."

5 LOST IN STORM WHEN BOATS UPSET

3 Missing, 5 Washed Ashore Off Jersey—Two on Tug Drowned in Bay.

4.8 INCHES OF RAIN HERE

Floods Disrupt Land Travel—Ships Torn From Moorings by Wind in Hudson.

A wind and rainstorm lashed the New Jersey and Long Island coasts last night, disrupting land and water transportation and capsizing two boats, causing a loss of five lives.

Two seamen were drowned and three others rescued after they had been in the water two hours when a tugboat of the Tracy Towing Company overturned in New York Bay off the foot of Sixty-fifth Street, Brooklyn. The tug, the William Tracy, was steaming from Brooklyn to New Jersey when it overturned without warning in a sudden gust of wind and plunged the five men into the water.

The drowned were Robert Whittaker, fireman, and Benjamin Elder, deckhand, both of Brooklyn. Those rescued, all of Brooklyn, were Captain William McNally, John Duffy and David Davidson. They were landed in Jersey City and taken to the Jersey City Medical Centre, where they were reported to be in serious condition.

Boat Is Washed Ashore.

The missing men are Captain Robert McCleary, 35, Harry Clayton, 45, and Edward Clayton, 30, his brother, all of Philadelphia. Coast Guard boats put out to search for them after the five survivors had been washed ashore. At 8:30 P. M. the Neshaminy, the boat in which the party of eight had been fishing, was washed up at Brigantine.

Those rescued were James Sharp, 35, of Langhorne, Pa.; George Oldham, 30, of Newportville, Pa., and Earl Widdop, 35, Claude Pieminck, 32, and Charles Wensel, 28, of Philadelphia. Wensel and Oldham were in a serious condition at Atlantic City Hospital.

They said that, although their boat was seaworthy and in good condition, it was no match for the gale that blew out of the northeast. Sharp, Harry Clayton and Oldham were in the pilot house when a big wave came along and turned the craft over. They had to break through glass windows to get free.

Craft Break Loose in Hudson.

Shipping in the Hudson River had a bad time at the height of the storm. The U. S. S. Oklahoma, anchored in midstream off Seventy-ninth Street, was forced to put her hook and manoeuvre about to escape being hit by a lighter with a derrick aboard, which had broken moorings on the Jersey side.

Continued on Page Thirty-five.

AN AIR VIEW OF THE BURNING LINER MORRO CASTLE OFF THE JERSEY COAST.

Rescue Liners Pick Up 157; Craft Near By Speed to SOS

Four Large Vessels Put Out Lifeboats to Circle Water With Coast Guard—Many of the Saved Are Injured.

From north, east and south passenger and freight ships altered their courses yesterday to go at full speed to the fire-illumined point of Shark River Inlet, above Sea Girt, N. J., where the Ward liner Morro Castle with 318 passengers and a crew of 244 was burning.

Off Ambrose Light the Monarch of Bermuda and the City of Savannah turned around and sped southward through the dark about twenty miles to the distressed ship. From the east, seven miles, came the freighter Andrea S. Luckenbach. From the south, further away than the others, the President Cleveland sped through the night.

The S O S from the Morro Castle was received by the Monarch and the Savannah line vessel at about the same time, 4:30 A. M. daylight time. The Luckenbach ship had been attracted by the sight of the flames and radio confirmation that the Morro Castle needed help came from a land station.

Rescues Began in the Dark.

The sea was turning the color of gun metal in a murky dawn when the Monarch and the Savannah arrived to find that the Luckenbach was already on the scene, as well as several Coast Guard craft.

They came upon a scene of confusion and horror. The liner was blazing from B deck upward. On the surface of the water were passengers and members of the crew who had jumped.

The water was being combed by the Coast Guard craft and two lifeboats from the Luckenbach. Four of the lifeboats from the Morro Castle had been successfully lowered, six on the port side having been made inaccessible by the flames.

The rescuing ships stood by until they could no longer be of service, and then steamed for New York, carrying in all 157 survivors including at least forty members of the Morro Castle's crew, and one woman who was dead when taken from the water.

The work of rescue began at about 5 A. M. daylight saving time, when the Morro Castle had been burning at least two hours. By 10 o'clock there were apparently no more living persons to be taken from the water.

The Monarch of Bermuda had gathered seventy-one survivors of the body. The City of Savannah, both of these ships pushed to within 100 feet of the flaming liner—had sixty-five and the Luckenbach twenty-one. The President Cleveland, from a point about half a mile away, lowered two boats, but these returned without having lifted any person from the water.

Captain A. R. Francis of the Monarch stood by for two and half hours in a choppy, wind-beaten sea while four power-driven lifeboats lowered circled the immediate water. In this way those aboard listed to safety persons, old and young, exhausted, hysterical and unconscious.

At times his ship swept within sixty feet of the burning ship and then, learning that he had nineteen persons aboard with injuries, twelve of them in a critical condition, Captain Francis headed for New York so the injured could receive adequate hospital attention as quickly as possible.

Leaves Burning Ship at Anchor.

He left the Morro Castle anchored with her prow to the wind, the flames being thus swept to stern. A few valiant seamen, 14 to 20

Continued on Page Twenty-eight.

List of Victims in Sea Disaster and Survivors

Passengers and members of the crew reported accounted for, injured or missing, together with a list of the identified dead in the burning of the Ward liner Morro Castle, on the basis of the latest available information, were as follows:

SURVIVORS.

Passengers.

ADAMS, JANE, Point Pleasant, N. J.; injured, shock and submersion.
AGUIAR, VAL, Las Vegas, Venezuela.
ARNETH, PAUL, Brooklyn.
ASCHOFF, THORP H., 150-15 Stoneford Avenue, Flushing, Queens.
ATICELLO, MARCO, Brooklyn.
ASCHOFF, Mrs. T. H., same address.
BARSTEAD, LLOYD C., 1,891 Harrison Avenue, Bronx.
BARSTEAD, Mrs., same address.
BECK, Miss EMILY C., Philadelphia.
BEACH, AGNES, 205 East Seventy-eighth Street.
BEHR, Miss V.
BEHR, Miss E.
BERGENSTEIN, Miss DOROTHY.
BIREN, ROSE, Philadelphia.
BLANCO, BOB, Havana.
BLONDEAU, Mr. JULES, Philadelphia; shock and submersion.
BLONDEAU, Mrs. JULES, Philadelphia; shock and submersion.
BODNER, S., 85 Summit Road, Elizabeth, N. J.
BODNER, Mrs. S., same address.
BORMAN, H., 362 Roosevelt Avenue, Freeport, L. I.
BRADY, Mrs. E. J., Overbrook, Pa.
BRADBERRY, Miss MARTHA, Pennsylvania.
BREGSTEIN, Dr. J.JOSEPH, 7,825 Fourth Avenue, Brooklyn.
BREGSTEIN, MERVIN G., same address.
BRENNAMAN, HARRY, Brooklyn.
BRINKMAN, Mrs.
BRODIE, Miss H.
BROWN, Miss FLORENCE.
BROWN, Miss IDA, Philadelphia.
BUDLONG, Miss MARJORIE, Hillside, N. J.
BUQUETS, OFELIA.
BUQUETS, Mrs.
BUQUETS, FRANCOIS, Brooklyn.
BURRELL, Dr. J. H., Buffalo.
BURRELL, Mrs. J. H.
BUTE, JAMES, Brooklyn.
BYRNE, W. E., 330 West Ninety-fifth Street; burns.
CALEYA, JUAN, Cuba.
CANNAVAN, Miss K., 20 Butler Place, Brooklyn.
CANNON, THOMAS.
CARPENTER, Miss MADGE, 41-08 171st Street, Flushing, Queens.
CASEY, CAROLINE, Philadelphia.
CHESLER, Miss L., Brooklyn.
CLARKE, WILLIAM F., 156-14 Channel Street, Howard Beach, L. I.; injured.
COCHRANE, Dr. CHARLES, Brooklyn.
COCHRANE, Miss C. M.
COHEN, A., Hartford, Conn.
COHEN, Mrs. A., Hartford, Conn.
COHN, Miss GERTRUDE.
COLL, Mr. J. P.
CONLAN, Miss ANNE.
CONWAY, Miss ANNE, Brooklyn.
COTTER, Miss A.
CULLEN, Miss UNA
DAVIS, Mrs. MINNIE, 200 Pine Street, Brooklyn, burns on both.
DAVIDSON, Miss LILLIAN, 23 Athens Street, Clifton, N. J.
DAVIDSON, SIDNEY.
DAVIDSON, Mrs. SIDNEY.
DESVERNINE, MADELEINE.

Continued on Page Twenty-six.

MANY BURNED IN CABINS

Flames Cut Off Escape of Tourists Returning From Cruise to Cuba.

STORM HAMPERS RESCUERS

Darkness and Pounding Seas Add to Death Toll—Captain Had Died Shortly Before.

SWEEPING INQUIRIES SET

Speed of Conflagration and Cause a Mystery—Crew Is Praised and Scored.

A page of photographs of the Morro Castle disaster, Page 24.

By RUSSELL B. PORTER.

In one of the worst marine disasters on record, the liner Morro Castle was swept by fire of unknown origin early yesterday morning off the New Jersey coast, with heavy loss of life.

The scene of the tragedy was not far from where the dirigible Akron was wrecked during a storm off Barnegat Lighthouse last year.

By a strange coincidence, Captain Robert Willmott, master of the Morro Castle, died of a heart attack following acute indigestion about 8:45 o'clock Friday night, nearly eight hours before the SOS went out at 4:23 A. M. New York daylight time. When the fire started, the liner was under the command of Chief Officer William F. Warms, who remained aboard the burning ship until taken off by a Coast Guard cutter late yesterday afternoon.

The exact number of dead and missing was not finally determined last night, but it was believed to be between 200 and 250.

Reports to the offices of the Ward Line, operators of the Morro Castle, were that 161 passengers and 147 of the crew, or a total of 308 persons, were known to have been saved. According to the line, the ship had carried a total of 562 persons, including 318 passengers and a crew of 244. This would indicate a death list of 254, but it was emphasized that other survivors may not yet have been reported.

Later information indicated that at least 325, for in addition to the 268 survivors here or bound here, there were thirty-six in the Fitkins Memorial Hospital at Asbury Park and twenty-one in the Point Pleasant (N. J.) Hospital last night. This would cut the possible dead to 237.

171 Bodies Are Recovered.

The New Jersey National Guard, which was assembling at Camp Moore, Sea Girt, all the bodies washed ashore at fifteen or more coast communities, estimated that reports from these places indicated that a total of 171 bodies had been recovered.

At midnight last night fifty-eight bodies of unidentified dead had been taken to Camp Moore from various New Jersey communities. Thirty-three were men, twenty-two women and three children. Other bodies were to be taken there during the night.

Confusion existed over the number of survivors and dead partly because of the many places to which survivors and bodies were taken at first and partly because the steamship line did not have an accurate list of the crew. The figure finally announced for the crew may be revised.

Two hundred and fifty-four survivors were brought to New York and Jersey City during the afternoon and night. These included seventy-one persons rescued by the Monarch of Bermuda, sixty-five by the City of Savannah, twenty-one by the Andrea S. Luckenbach and ninety-seven brought here by train from Jersey coast points where they had gone ashore. Fourteen more were on their way here aboard a Coast Guard vessel.

Of the 268 here or on their way here last night, 140 were members of the crew and 128 were passengers.

Nine bodies were brought to New York, and were taken to the Morgue at Bellevue Hospital. Five were men and four were women.

Continued on Page Twenty-five.

Survivors Tell of Leaping Into Sea to Escape Flames

Many Sang and Prayed on Decks—Reluctant Women Pushed Overboard or Into Boats —Ship's Plates Red Hot.

Survivors of the Morro Castle, telling of their experiences on the fire-swept liner yesterday, painted in broad strokes a story of heroism and of panic.

Some of them told of jumping from the flame-swept decks of the Morro Castle and swimming for six or seven hours before coming ashore or being picked up off the Jersey coast. Others, brought to New York on the rescue vessels, told of being picked up from the water.

Many told of being forced to jump into the sea many feet below from the crowded decks when the approaching flames left them no other course. Members of the crew described a gallant attempt to subdue the fire—a fight doomed from the start because of low water pressure.

Others told of how frightened passengers crowded aft in the vessel and were cut off from the bulk of the crew by the flames which were sweeping the midsection. They told of women weeping and praying, and of men and more courageous women banding together and singing such songs as "Hail, Hail, the Gang's All Here" in an attempt to bolster the courage of the rest.

Chief Officer Takes Charge.

The outstanding hero to the crew was W. F. Warms, the chief officer who became the acting captain of the Morro Castle. They told of his standing on the liner's bridge as it was aflame, shouting orders to his men, thinking only of saving his passengers and crew. All the passengers told of the few members of the crew who appeared among them. The crew members explained that this was due to the fact that they were cut off from the aft section of the vessel by the flames amidships.

A small group of seamen and stewards, however, aided greatly in adjusting life belts for passengers and forcing them to jump into the sea, where they stood at least some chance for their lives.

Rescued stewards laid part of the death toll to the modesty of women passengers who waited in their cabins to dress—waited too long—and found themselves cut off by the flames.

The rough weather, too, was blamed by some of the crew for the heavy loss of life. At least a third of the passengers were seasick at the time the fire began, they said. Many of these, survivors believed, were likewise trapped in their cabins.

The virtual cutting in two of the ship by the fire made it impossible to lower any number of the lifeboats. All those on the port side were inaccessible. There were ample life belts, however.

The survivors told their stories in hospitals and impromptu shelters along the Jersey coast, where they were housed after they were brought ashore. Others described their experiences when they arrived in New York on the rescue ships.

At least five couples jumped from the rails together to swim to shore and safety. The crew made frantic efforts to launch the boats. All the time the flames were creeping nearer.

"Suddenly some one gave me a violent push and I half fell and half staggered into the lifeboat. There was trouble in launching it and it seemed almost a half hour before we were in the water and pulling away from the Morro Castle. The front of the ship was a pillar of flame by this time.

"A strong gale was whipping up

Continued on Page Twenty-seven.

Doctor Awakened by Smoke.

Dr. Charles Cochrane of Brooklyn, one of the passengers, told a vivid story of his experience after he had been brought ashore at Long Branch, N. J.

Dr. Cochrane is a well-known Brooklyn surgeon. He is a fellow of the American College of Surgeons and of the American Medical Association. He is chief of the urological staff of Kings County Hospital and is a consulting surgeon at the Carson C. Peck Memorial Hospital.

"I was awakened from a sound sleep, at just what time I don't know, by clouds of suffocating smoke filling my cabin," said Dr. Cochrane. "At almost the same time some one banged and hammered at my cabin door and shouted something unintelligible.

"Confused by my sudden awakening, and choking and unable to see because of the dense smoke in the cabin, I tried vainly to find the door. Just in time my groping hands came in contact with a port hole. I crawled through it and dropped to the deck outside.

"There was no apparent panic. The crew was making frantic efforts to launch the boats. All the time the flames were creeping nearer.

NRA
"All the News That's
Fit to Print."

The New York Times.

LATE CITY EDITION
WEATHER—Cloudy, rain or snow today; tomorrow rain.

Copyright, 1935, by The New York Times Company.

VOL. LXXXIV....No. 28,145.   Entered as Second-Class Matter, Postoffice, New York, N. Y.   NEW YORK, THURSDAY, FEBRUARY 14, 1935.   P   TWO CENTS

HAUPTMANN GUILTY, SENTENCED TO DEATH FOR THE MURDER OF THE LINDBERGH BABY

MACON'S MEN LAND, SAVED FROM DEATH IN SKY AND ON SEA

Calm Heroism and Unbroken Navy Discipline Revealed as Survivors Reach Port.

ADMIRAL TELLS OF HORROR

Saw Gasoline Flames Spread Over Water to Airship's Crew as the Cruisers Came Up.

WILEY DESCRIBES PLUNGE

Naval Court Is Ordered for Today as Field Inquiry Into the Cause Is Started.

Special to The New York Times.

SAN FRANCISCO, Feb. 13.—Eighty-one officers and men of the eighty-three who set out on the dirigible Macon to join the fleet of the California Coast came home today to tell how the giant airship was destroyed yesterday evening and death which snatched at them from sky and sea was beaten back.

They stood huddled on three rescue cruisers in San Francisco Bay, laughing, asking for cigarettes, and between puffs relating this latest epic of man's defeat amid his conquests of space.

But though they could describe the first alarm and the fall, of flying minutes after the Macon struck, and dragging anxiety as the navy swept the misty seas in search of them, they were mute on the cause of the disaster.

Some fabric tore away on her fins and along her backbone; gas cells burst, the great structure shuddered and soared and descended and hit, and suddenly they were tumbled out pell mell into the water, fighting for their lives. Flaming gasoline was ignited about them by calcium flares of mercy.

This was the story in brief, different for every man, yet somehow merging into one clear picture of the whole.

Three Warships Reach Port.

The warships Richmond, Cincinnati and Concord brought in the survivors. Lieut. Commander Herbert V. Wiley, the Macon's skipper, was aboard the Concord. When he described what happened it was in terms of telephone calls, buoyancy and lack of it, jettisoned gasoline and crumbling gas cells and frames. He was in the control car, a city block from the source of trouble.

The story of men is another narrative. The Macon was humming along not far at sea south of Monterey Bay. The weather was dark gray and filled with drizzle, but the world's greatest dirigible had seen many such days. She had met the fleet plowing northward toward San Francisco; she was accompanying it, and soon she would go to her home in Sunnyvale.

The time was a little later than 5 o'clock in the afternoon, and daylight was already falling. There was a slight jar. It jerked at the wheel in the helmsman's hand. Some said they did not feel the jar, but immediately noticed the inclination of the ship, nose upward.

However, there were subsequent "jars." Lieutenant C. S. Rounds described them as a "shudder."

"But it was equally outside," he said. "I doubt if many of us in the first sixty seconds anticipated serious trouble. Even when the 'stand by' orders came, I thought it was a minor crisis of navigation."

Gas Cells Begin to Go.

But those jars were the rupturing of gas units; first No. 1, then No. 2, away aft. Lieutenant Rounds was forward and inside the ship. There was no excitement for the first four or five minutes, excepting among those aft who were whipping telephone calls into the control car. The airship was riding rapidly.

Then No. 2 cell burst. About that time it dawned on all that this was no minor crisis.

They stuck by their posts. They slipped gasoline tanks aft and devalved the forward cells to balance her out, but it was no good.

Having soared into the mist in a last living effort, the Macon lost buoyancy and began to fall. It was then that Commander Wiley sent out the message that they were falling and that first mentioned abandoning ship.

The man who sent that electric

Continued on Page Two.

CAVALIER HOTEL, Virginia Beach, Va. Opens Feb. 21. Golf and all sports—Advt.

Opera Threatened Again As Board Balks at Deficit

Metropolitan Directors Cast Doubt on Next Season Unless Production Costs Are Cut and Popular Subscription Enlarged.

There may be no opera at the Metropolitan next season. The board of directors of the Metropolitan Opera Association has decided that opera cannot be continued on the basis of the enormous losses incurred in the last five seasons.

After a meeting of the executive committee yesterday in the office of Paul D. Cravath, chairman of the board, Mr. Cravath issued the following statement:

"The directors of the Metropolitan Opera Association have decided that it is not feasible to give opera at the Metropolitan Opera House next season on the basis of continuing to incur the large deficits of the last five seasons.

"They have requested the preparation of a plan for reducing the cost of producing opera, and increasing the support of the public through subscriptions for seats, that will render the continuation of opera financially possible."

The members of the committee would not elaborate on this statement last night. One member intimated that the announcement had a twofold purpose; to quiet the rumors that have been at large in the last few weeks and to gauge the public reaction as to its willingness to participate in assuring the Metropolitan's future.

It was emphasized that neither the full board nor the executive committee had abandoned the Metropolitan, to whatever fate might befall it, and that, despite the immediate doubts, there was every intention to continue consideration of the opera's future.

Besides Mr. Cravath, the members of the executive committee who attended the meeting were Mrs. August Belmont, Cornelius N. Bliss, Frederic Potts Moore, David Sarnoff and Allen Wardwell. Robert S. Brewster, the new president of the Metropolitan Opera and Real Estate Company, and Myron C. Taylor were the only members absent.

The executive committee has been holding frequent meetings since Fall to determine ways and means of continuing opera at the Metropolitan. The first question before it was the establishment of a policy and financial program. The second, depending on the first, was the naming of a general manager to succeed Giulio Gatti-Casazza, whose resignation takes effect next April.

Many plans for the continuation of Metropolitan Opera were proposed and discussed at these meetings.

Continued on Page Twenty-five.

HOPE GAINS IN ROME FOR PEACE IN AFRICA

But Italy Is Reported Ready to Spend $850,000,000 in the Event of War.

REPLY TO DEMANDS ASKED

Plan for Solution Reported in Addis Ababa—Fascist Grand Council to Meet.

By ARNALDO CORTESI.
Wireless to The New York Times.

ROME, Feb. 13.—The optimistic forecasts made yesterday as to a peaceful solution of the Italo-Abyssinian crisis became more positive today following a meeting between Negradas Yesus, Abyssinian Chargé d'Affaires, and Fulvio Suvich, Italian Foreign Under-Secretary. Although it is stated semi-officially that no actual solution has been reached, the impression is that good progress has been made. Special emphasis is laid on the fact that Signor Suvich began by assuring the Abyssinian envoy that Italy was animated by the most peaceful intentions, to which the envoy replied that his Emperor also wished to avoid war. Signor Suvich then complained that the demands submitted to Emperor Haile Selassie by the Italian Minister at Addis Ababa remained unanswered.

Then the Italian Under-Secretary went on to discuss possible solutions of the crisis. These include the establishment of a neutral zone on the Abyssinian side of the frontier, but it is positively stated that no indication that this condition will be accepted by the Emperor has yet been received by Italy.

The Abyssinian envoy sent a long report of his conversations with Signor Suvich to Addis Ababa, and it is hoped by Italian officials that a reply will be forthcoming in the next few days.

There has been no let-up in the feverish activities to prepare a strong Italian expeditionary force for dispatch to Africa. In view, however, of today's favorable development hope is beginning to be entertained that it may never be necessary for the force to leave Italy.

Mussolini Studies Note.

By The Associated Press.

ROME, Feb. 13.—Premier Mussolini gave deep study tonight to an Abyssinian note calling Italians the aggressors in recent border conflicts. This note, Italian officials said earlier today, made the situation "very serious."

Nevertheless, there appeared this evening to be less concern in governmental circles over the prospect of hostilities in Africa, although an authoritative source said Italy was prepared to spend about $850,000,000.

Continued on Page Sixteen.

LEHMAN TAX BILLS VOTED BY SENATE

Four-Cent Gasoline Levy and Budget Are Among the 11 Measures Approved.

FEARON ATTACKS FIGURES

He Predicts a $100,000,000 Deficit at Fiscal Year End— Five Proposals Held Up.

By W. A. WARN.
Special to The New York Times.

ALBANY, Feb. 13.—Eleven of the measures included in Governor Lehman's fiscal program were passed in the Senate today. Action on five was deferred, not because the Democrats did not have the votes to pass them, but because legislative leaders doubted whether passage of them would be within the requirements of the Constitution, until after the main budget bills, already passed in the Senate, had been passed in the Assembly also.

Every Democrat in the Senate voted for the Governor's bills. The Republican vote was split in many instances. Senator Fearon, leader of the Republican minority, voted for the main budget bill, but not until he had first denounced it as a measure which did not comply with the Constitutional provision for a balanced budget and had accused Governor Lehman of financial juggling in drafting his measures.

Senator Fearon said that Mr. Lehman had constantly blundered in estimating revenues. He declared that these futile processes had been repeated by the Chief Executive in making up his new budget, with the probable result that the Governor would be confronted with a $3,000,000 deficit when the next fiscal year ends instead of the $3,000,000 surplus of the Governor's own estimate, cited in his budget message to the Legislature.

Sees 700 New Jobs.

Senator Fearon accused the Democrats of putting more than 700 new jobs into the budget bill without telling anybody anything about it. He said they had refused the taxpayers a public hearing on the budget bill at a time when the Governor himself was demanding public hearings in towns and counties on local budgets.

Senator Dunnigan, Democratic leader, came to the defense of the Governor and the debate was shot through and through with partisan charges. At times it became quite heated, with Senators Fearon and Dunnigan striding up and down the centre aisle.

Senator Fearon gave Senator Twomey, fiscal leader of the Senate, some moments of embarrassment.

Continued on Page Six.

BON AIR VANDERBILT, Augusta, Ga. 19 hrs. to machine. Round trip $33.50—Advt.

SENATE COMMITTEE ADOPTS WORK BILL; TRUCE OVER WAGES

Drive for Pay Under 'Prevailing' Rates Is Beaten and the 'Dole' Also Is Rejected.

ROOSEVELT RETAINS POWER

But His Scale Must Not Cut Private Wages—Floor Fight Due as Labor Protests.

Special to The New York Times.

WASHINGTON, Feb. 13.—After hours of struggle today, the administration leadership, supported by Senator Glass, regained control of the Senate Appropriations Committee and finished a redraft of the $4,880,000,000 relief bill deemed acceptable to President Roosevelt.

Mr. Glass expects to report the revised measure formally to the Senate tomorrow or the next day. Leaders hope it may be acted upon finally before the diminishing funds in the present relief coffers are depleted entirely.

Today's action in the Appropriations Committee was considered both by the administration and organized labor as a victory for the Roosevelt supporters. Instead of yielding to the demand of the American Federation of Labor for an irrevocable "prevailing" provision, the committee adopted an amendment giving the President control over pay rates, but with the added prescription that he must keep the "prevailing" scale if he finds the new wage program is depressing, or is likely to depress, private wage structures in any locality.

William Green, president of the A. F. of L., said tonight that the substitute was "unacceptable and unsatisfactory to labor," adding that the federation would make its appeal directly to the Senate membership.

"Dole" Amendment Is Beaten.

The committee also withstood a drive from another group and again voted down, by 12 to 11, the so-called "dole" amendment which would have provided a cut in the appropriation to $3,880,000,000 and thereby, according to its sponsors, force the President to rely more on direct relief than upon the more expensive new public works.

Thus, after three weeks of varying degrees of fight, administration leaders apparently had taken hold again. They proposed to move at once to break the log-jam of legislation which has backed up behind the relief program, and to express confidence in predicting that this measure would be well on its way through the Senate before another week had gone.

Through all of its vicissitudes in the committee, the bill emerged today without any change which leaders regarded as a serious violation of the principles laid down by the President in his annual message. He called then for a lump-sum appropriation and for adequate discretionary authority to spend it in a self-diminishing, largely self-liquidating works program, designed to return 3,500,000 able-bodied persons now on relief to employment at lower than prevailing wages.

All of the trouble on the measure

Continued on Page Eight.

ELEVATORS TIED UP IN 200 BUILDINGS IN STRIKE FLARE-UP

Union Disclaims Action After New Delay in Decision, but Admits Patience Is Gone.

UPTOWN APARTMENTS HIT

Madison Square Offices Also Are Affected—Spread of the Walkout a Possibility.

A general strike of building service employes in office and apartment house buildings loomed last night after sporadic walkouts affecting more than 200 buildings and 2,500 employes were staged in various parts of the city yesterday.

The strikes were called by a so-called "rank and file committee" of members of the Building Service Employes Union, claiming a membership of 140,000, as the arbitration committee headed by Major Henry H. Curran, appointed last December by Mayor La Guardia to settle the differences between the union and realty interests, was struggling to complete its labors and present an award.

The committee was to have made its award yesterday, but failed to do so, however, and last night Major Curran announced that the award would not be made public until today. The committee remained in session all evening at Major Curran's office, 280 Madison Avenue.

"Ill Advised," Says Mayor.

Mayor La Guardia on being informed of the walkouts, which occurred in the Harlem, Washington Heights and Madison Square sections, termed the strikes as "ill advised."

At the office of the union, 1,450 Broadway, responsibility for the strikes was disclaimed. The walkouts were characterized as "unauthorized," but the statement was added, "We cannot hold them back any longer—our men 'have lost patience waiting for the award."

Detectives of the West 123d Street Precinct, cruising in a radio car, arrested sixteen men shortly before 5 o'clock this morning, charging them with disorderly conduct for alleged intimidation of building-service employes in three Harlem apartment houses. According to the officers, the sixteen men, nine of whom were Negroes, had entered the apartment houses and compelled attendants on duty to quit their jobs.

Six of the prisoners were picked up at 50 West 112th Street, three at 86 West 112th Street, and seven at 2,180 Seventh Avenue. They will be arraigned in the Fifth District Court today.

Promised to Work for Peace.

A fortnight ago James J. Bambrick, after a meeting of the union's executive committee and the presidents of its fifteen locals in the city, had promised Major Curran that every member would be made to prevent any strikes, pending the outcome of the arbitration proceedings.

This was in response to a plea from Major Curran to keep the men from striking lest such action jeopardize the arbitration award.

Continued on Page Eight.

Girl Dies in Leap Off Empire State Tower; Impact Smashes Heavy Marquee in 33d St.

Disconsolate because of a quarrel with her fiancé, a 20-year-old girl jumped from the observation landing of the Empire State Building just before 8:30 o'clock last night, her body crashing into a glass and metal marquee nearly a quarter of a mile below.

The impact of the fall, which shattered frosted glass, light bulbs and the sheet-iron covering of the canopy, was at first mistaken for an explosion by passers-by and shop employes in the vicinity. Witnesses in the building on the opposite side of Thirty-third Street said the young woman's body had struck a sixth-floor set-back of the building before hurtling onto the marquee.

From the contents of her handbag, which was clutched tightly in her fingers, the girl was identified as Irma P. Eberhardt of the Laura Spelman Hall Branch of the Y. W. C. A., 607 Hudson Street. Except for a Y. W. C. A. membership card the black bag contained only 83 cents in change and a compact of lipstick and rouge.

At the moment Miss Eberhardt jumped from the Empire State terrace, according to the police, Raymond Rebecchi of 5,716 136th Street, Flushing, was at the Charles Street station reporting her disappearance to Detective Frank Campbell. Before he had finished, word of her death was received from the police of the West Thirtieth Street precinct.

Rebecchi is said to have told Detective Campbell that he and Miss Eberhardt had quarreled on Tuesday, but that he had called at the Y. W. C. A. last night in the hope of effecting a reconciliation. He asked her to go to dinner, he said, and while he went to a lavatory to wash his hands the young woman vanished.

Rebecchi is said to have told the police he waited about half an hour in the foyer when he received a telephone call from Miss Eberhardt. "I'm going to kill myself," she said, and hung up the receiver. Alarmed, the young man hurried to the police station.

BRUNO RICHARD HAUPTMANN
Being taken to his cell after hearing death sentence last night.
Times Wide World Photo.

HAUPTMANN IN CELL FALLS IN COLLAPSE

After Hearing Verdict Without a Sign, He Breaks Down in Fit of Weeping.

WIFE SOBS AFTER HE GOES

Both Prepared for Worst by Warning of Fisher Against Outburst in Court.

By CRAIG THOMPSON.
Special to The New York Times.

FLEMINGTON, N. J., Feb. 13.—For the first time since his arrest Bruno Richard Hauptmann was reported tonight to be in a state of collapse.

When he was marched out of the court room, manacled to Constable Hovey Low on his left and State Trooper Hugh Stockberger on his right, he was pale but erect as his step seemed firm.

He went through the back room to his cell tier, which has been occupied by him alone. The minute the door was slammed shut behind him, according to the reports, he slumped, his face striking the floor.

There was a hush in the court room when Hauptmann came in at 10:30 o'clock tonight. For the first time since the trial started he was in irons, manacled to two of his nine guards. The bell in the belfry had already announced that the jury had reached a verdict, and the shouting of the throng outside was an overtone to the inside hush.

Hauptmann walked across the room from the rear door and took his seat. He sat down stiffly, a little awkwardly, as if the manacles impeded his motions.

At almost the same moment his wife, her normally red face growing pale, edged up the outside aisle and around the seats inside the rail to a place close to her husband. She twisted her lips into a very small, but her husband, after one glance, looked away.

In the two minutes that elapsed before the jurors began to file in there was a vivid little picture. C. Lloyd Fisher, the one member of Hauptmann's counsel who has been closest to him, visiting him in the jail daily and taking his life story before the trial, leaned over and put his arm around the prisoner's shoulder.

He whispered: "This is only the beginning. Don't show a sign, because, if you do, it will count against you."

Then the attorney leaned over and placed his arm around Mrs.

Continued on Page Twelve.

ACCUSTOMED TO ENTERTAIN THE Famous—The Willard Hotel, Washington, D. C.—Advt.

JURY OUT FOR 11 HOURS

One of 2 Women Who Held Out for Mercy Near Tears at End.

DEFENDANT PALE, SILENT;

Fails to Glance at Wife as He Is Led Back to Cell— She Is Calm.

DEFENSE PLANS TO APPEAL

Execution Set for the Week of March 18—Court's Charge Attacked as Biased.

Judge's charge to the jury and exceptions argued, Pages 10, 11.

By RUSSELL B. PORTER.
Special to The New York Times.

FLEMINGTON, N. J., Feb. 13.—Bruno Richard Hauptmann was convicted of murder in the first degree at 10:45 o'clock tonight for the killing of Charles A. Lindbergh Jr. at Hopewell on the night of March 1, 1932.

He was sentenced to die in the electric chair at the State prison in Trenton some time during the week of March 18.

The jury of eight men and four women returned its verdict after having been out for eleven hours and twenty-four minutes since it retired from the court room at 11:21 o'clock this morning to deliberate in the jury room.

Handcuffed to two guards, Hauptmann stood between them silent and motionless, his face ashen white and terror in his deep-set eyes, while he heard the jury state its verdict and the judge pronounce sentence.

A few minutes later he was led away to his cell in the county jail. He did not even cast a glance of recognition toward his wife. She looked at him with red-rimmed eyes, but did not weep.

Colonel Charles A. Lindbergh, who attended every session of the thirty-two court days of the trial from its beginning on Jan. 2, six weeks ago, and who heard Supreme Court Justice Thomas W. Trenchard deliver his charge to the jury this morning, was not in court when the verdict was returned. He had returned to his home in Englewood in the afternoon.

Woman Juror Near Tears.

Mrs. Verna Snyder, juror No. 3, was biting her lips to keep from crying and her eyes were wet with tears as she left the jury box. According to well founded report, she and Mrs. Rosie Pill, juror No. 2, had held out to the last ballot for a verdict of guilty with a recommendation providing imprisonment at hard labor for life.

All the rest of the jurors were grave but appeared serene, as if they were satisfied that they had done their duty.

At 10:28 Sheriff Curtiss came out of the judge's chambers and gave an order to a deputy sheriff. The latter left the room and mounted the stairs to the cupola on the roof of the white court house. In a moment the 125-year-old bell, older than the court house itself, began to toll. By an old custom, revived a few years ago, the bell is rung to notify the town that a jury has reached a verdict and is about to return to the court room.

"There's the bell!" the whisper spread through the court room.

"Quiet! Quiet!" cried the guards as the reporters murmured among themselves, but both the murmurs and the shouts were drowned out by the noise of the crowd in the street, which at this moment rose to a roar.

Prisoner Is Brought In.

Mr. Fisher of defense counsel came in and indicated that Hauptmann was already on the way from his cell. At 10:31 the prisoner was brought in. The Sheriff and five State troopers had him.

Hauptmann's guilt was unusual as he appeared in the doorway. For the first time since the trial began, he was brought into court man-

Continued on Page Twelve.

When You Think of Writing, Think of Whiting.—Advt.

JURY COURAGEOUS, WILENTZ DECLARES

Nation Indebted to Them, He Says—Thanks Aides, Foley and New York Police.

'ENDS OF JUSTICE SERVED'

Peacock Says Verdict Is Reply to 'Mothers' Prayer'—Law Points Raised by Defense.

From a Staff Correspondent.

FLEMINGTON, N. J., Feb. 13.—Attorney General David T. Wilentz, commenting tonight upon the verdict, thanked all those associated with the prosecution, and paid special tribute to the jury.

"The tremendous responsibility imposed upon the Hunterdon County jury was shouldered without flinching," he said. "The nation is indebted to these courageous men and women.

"The proper presentation of the case was due in the main to the work of the New Jersey State police. District Attorney Samuel J. Foley of the Bronx and New York labored unceasingly and to them I extend my deep thanks, as well as to Inspectors Henry Bruckman, John J. Lyons, the members of the New York police and the agents of the Federal Government."

Mr. Wilentz added that it had been his unwelcome duty to prosecute the case and said that he hoped society would be served by his efforts and those of his associates.

Former Judge George K. Large of Flemington, special counsel to the State, said, "The verdict was fully justified by the evidence."

"Truth Will Prevail."

Assistant Attorney General Robert Peacock said:

"The verdict proves again that truth will prevail. All during the time I was preparing the case at the request of the Attorney General I felt that the simple truth presented in terms the jury could understand would adequately serve the ends of justice.

"The verdict is the answer to the prayers of the mothers of this nation that those who harm their children shall be punished and that men of the accomplishments of Colonel Lindbergh shall be able to maintain homes in the quiet assurance that their families in the hour of their absence shall be protected by the arm of the law."

Colonel H. Norman Schwarzkopf said:

"I feel that the verdict is in accordance with the evidence and that the ends of justice have been served."

Continued on Page Eleven.

"All the News That's Fit to Print."

The New York Times.

LATE CITY EDITION

WEATHER—Fair, continued warm today; tomorrow cloudy, showers.
Temperature Yesterday—Max., 80; Min., 72

Copyright, 1935, by The New York Times Company.

VOL. LXXXIV....No. 28,329.   Entered as Second-Class Matter, Postoffice, New York, N. Y.   NEW YORK, SATURDAY, AUGUST 17, 1935.   P   TWO CENTS In New York City | THREE CENTS Elsewhere | FOUR CENTS and Post Zone

ROOSEVELT CALLS CHIEFS TO ARRANGE CONGRESS WIND-UP

Conference Tomorrow Is Expected to Set Program for Adjournment Thursday.

FIVE MAJOR BILLS FAVORED

Wealth Tax, Banking, Coal, Alcohol Control and Gold Ban Measures Slated to Pass.

UTILITY DEADLOCK HOLDS

Holding Company Curb and Other Major Bills Likely to Wait Till Next Session.

By The Associated Press.

WASHINGTON, Aug. 16.—A semi-final conference of Democratic leaders to make arrangements for a prompt adjournment of Congress was called tonight by President Roosevelt for Sunday night.

The expectation of some of the party chiefs was that at that meeting the President would disclose which measures he was willing for Congress to drop and which he wanted enacted before adjournment.

Among those invited to the conference, beginning at 8:30, were: Vice President Garner, Speaker Byrns, Senator Robinson of Arkansas, the Democratic leader; Chairman O'Connor of the House Rules Committee, Chairman Harrison of the Senate Finance Committee and Chairman Doughton of the House Ways and Means Committee.

It was indicated by one of the conferees that any agreement reached Sunday night, however, would be subject to later modification if particular pressure developed for the enactment of any measure.

Conjecture on Program.

From what they already have heard directly and indirectly from the President, some of the conferees, talking privately, said the meeting made more clear the possibilities of an end to the present session by the end of next week at the latest.

Some were talking about an adjournment Tuesday, or Thursday. Most agreed that it probably would be the latter part of next week before everything could be wound up to their satisfaction or to that of the President.

The expectation of some of the conferees was that the President would renew his insistence upon enactment of:

1. The Guffey Coal Stabilization Bill, which proponents and some opponents say will pass the House Monday and be approved by the Senate early next week;
2. The Federal alcohol control plan.
3. The $250,000,000 Tax Bill.
4. The Omnibus Banking Bill, on which conferees reached an agreement late today.
5. The measure forbidding suits for gold payments on Government contracts.

Six Bills May Be Shelved.

Their belief was that unless action was hastened the following would be left behind when this session ended, with their present status remaining the same until the next session:

1. The Utilities Bill;
2. The rivers and harbors legislation;
3. The measure expanding Federal control over food and drugs;
4. Railroad reorganization;
5. General oil regulation;
6. The Ship Subsidy Bill.

Leaders said the Utilities Bill probably would be left behind, not because the President did not want the legislation, but because the conference deadlock could not be broken.

A possibility was seen by some that the Rivers and Harbors Bill might be insisted upon because it would legalize the millions already spent by the Federal Government on a number of projects, such as the Parker Dam. And they added that they had but scant doubt that before Congress had adjourned it would ratify the oil compacts entered into in Dallas last February.

House Tax Conferees Named.

Special to THE NEW YORK TIMES.

WASHINGTON, Aug. 16.—A determined drive to adjourn Congress by Tuesday night, with Thursday as the latest alternate date, was started today following formal commitment of the Wealth-Tax Bill to conference and a conference agreement on the Eccles Banking Bill.

The promise of Tuesday adjournment was held out by Senator Robinson as the Senate voted to take a recess until Monday. Early in the day he had informed the Senate of his desire to quit at that time and in so doing issued a warning.

Continued on Page Fourteen.

Davey Sets Ohio Vote for 1936, Defying Opponents of New Deal

Governor, Here, Denies Delaying Test on Advice of Roosevelt Forces, Gives Economy as Reason—He and President Are Accused of 'Conspiracy' by Republican Leader.

Governor Martin L. Davey of Ohio moved formally yesterday to defy Republican demands for a special State-wide election this year for undertaking to defeat New Deal sentiment in the State.

The Governor was visiting New York City during the day and telephoned his action to Columbus to frame an order in legal form setting the election for next year. All that remains to put the order into effect is the signature of the Governor, which he said he would affix when he reached Ohio tomorrow.

With the Republican national leaders, heartened by a victory in the Rhode Island Congressional elections, demanding that Ohio vote this November to fill the vacancy caused by the death of Representative Charles V. Truax, the Governor insisted that the election should be held next year to avoid action from $500,000 to $800,000 special election costs on hard-pressed taxpayers of the State.

He ridiculed the charge made by his political adversaries that the election was being postponed until next year, apparently under advice from the New Deal forces at Washington, to prevent an early test of the New Deal in such a key State as Ohio.

"There is no moral justification of landing that extra cost for a special election on the State," Governor Davey said at the Hotel Biltmore. "The good and ample reason for this order is that a recent referendum reducing the tax limit from 15 mills to 10 mills on the dollar has, with the aid of depression, depleted the treasuries of the counties and the cities so badly that they could not well stand the expense of a special election.

"Now I want to point out that no district in Ohio will be without representation meanwhile, since that district is that of a Representative at Large. I have an excellent precedent for this action, since the same course was followed in my own State."

Continued on Page Seven.

ROOSEVELT RESTS AT HYDE PARK HOME

Joins Family on Two-Day Visit to Celebrate 21st Birthday of Franklin Jr.

AVOIDS ISSUE ON HOOVER

President Intercedes for Man Caught at Baltimore While Stealing Ride on His Train.

From a Staff Correspondent.

HYDE PARK, N. Y., Aug. 16.—President Roosevelt returned to Hyde Park House today for a brief period of quiet contemplation of the nation's banking laws which he reached by Senate and House conferees late today and arrangements were made to hurry this highly important measure through both branches of Congress early next week.

He came here overnight aboard a special train which arrived at 8:30 o'clock this morning for the announced purpose of attending a family party tomorrow in celebration of the twenty-first birthday anniversary of Franklin D. Roosevelt Jr., his third son.

However, an impromptu "press conference" held by Mr. Roosevelt while he sat in an automobile after the ride from the train to his mother's estate overlooking the Hudson River gave ample indication of the many problems awaiting a directing hand, if not a definite solution, by the President.

The problems he plans to tackle actively on Sunday, when he will return to the White House for a long series of conferences with the individuals and groups representing the administration leadership on Capitol Hill.

A cheery confidence was radiated by Mr. Roosevelt today as he was subjected to a barrage of questions by reporters who clustered around his automobile in the bright morning sunlight.

Questioned on Utility Bill.

The questions dealt principally with the Utility Holding Company Bill, which has been deadlocked in conference between the House and Senate some time, and the Tax Bill which was sent to conference yesterday after the Senate had approved a measure considerably different than the House bill.

Asked if he expected enactment of the Utility Bill this session, Mr. Roosevelt replied smilingly that he hoped so, with an inflection in his voice which some reporters interpreted as indicating that he intended to have the done.

Would he be willing, he then was asked, to accept the House bill, which differs from the Senate bill and administration recommendations in its omission of the celebrated "death sentence" section? At this question, Mr. Roosevelt smiled and closed the topic with the assertion that he could not comment on details.

A request for comment on the action of the Senate in passing the Tax Bill in changed form brought the rejoinder from the President that the Tax Bill had not been finally passed by Congress yet; that it was still an open question.

Renewed efforts by correspondents to get specific comment from the President on the recent statement by former President Hoover requesting Mr. Roosevelt to set forth definitely his plans regarding possible changes in the Constitution, elicited from the President only the reply that he read Mr. Hoover's statement very hurriedly and therefore was in no position to comment.

Aside from the conferences at

Continued on Page Fourteen.

CONFEREES AGREE ON BANK MEASURE

Glass and His Senators Win on Nearly All Points, Ending Long Battle on Bill.

ONE VICTORY FOR HOUSE

Effort to Force State Banks Into Reserve Is Put Off—Swift Finish Planned.

Special to THE NEW YORK TIMES.

WASHINGTON, Aug. 16.—Unanimous agreement on every feature of the hotly contested bill to change the nation's banking laws was reached by Senate and House conferees late today and arrangements were made to hurry this highly important measure through both branches of Congress early next week.

Senator Glass and his conservative colleagues of the Senate conferees won a smashing victory over Representative Steagall and Goldsborough of the House conferees in almost every particular, but the two House liberals succeeded in postponing efforts to force State banks into the Federal Reserve System.

The conferees arranged to file formal reports to both branches tomorrow.

The end of the conference marks a long and bitter fight over the policies of Marriner S. Eccles, governor of the Federal Reserve Board, as expressed in the bill passed by the House, and the views of the Glass group as set forth in the Senate bill.

Opinion tonight was that Mr. Glass, veteran banking legislator, had once more come out the victor.

Reserve Board Is Interceded.

He and the other Senate conferees succeeded in carrying out their views on the open market committee, particularly in the aspect that government securities must be purchased on the open market and not direct from the Treasury.

Likewise, Senate conferees prevailed in their insistence that the Federal Reserve Board must be increased from the present six to seven members, with the Secretary of the Treasury and the Controller of the Currency eliminated as members ex officio.

The suggested permission of the Senate bill for banks of deposit to underwrite securities was stricken out at the request of President Roosevelt, Senator Glass stated.

The provision of the Senate bill that bankers may serve on not more than two bank boards simultaneously was retained but made subject to the discretion of the Reserve Board, however.

A big feature of the bill is the open market committee, which would be composed of seven Reserve Board members and five representatives of the twelve regional Reserve Banks. This committee would have power to influence the flow of credit by purchase and sale of government bonds by the Reserve Banks.

Policy Is Mandatory.

The policy laid down by the committee would be mandatory upon the Reserve Banks.

Following the view of Mr. Eccles, the House gave complete voting control of open market operations entirely to the Reserve Board.

Continued on Page Fourteen.

HOPSON ADMITS TRYING TO CONTROL PRESS WITH ADS

He Also Tells Senators He Urged Move to Kill Utility Bill in Conference.

ATTACK ON TIMES RENEWED

House Committee Told That His 1934 Income Was Between $300,000 and $500,000.

Special to THE NEW YORK TIMES.

WASHINGTON, Aug. 16.—Howard C. Hopson, who now admits that he was the guiding influence of the $800,000 lobby that the Associated Gas and Electric Company waged against the Wheeler-Rayburn bill, was forced to state before the Senate lobby inquiry committee today that the company had hesitated to use the advertising columns of newspapers as a club to minimize unfavorable publicity.

He also said he had suggested to another high utility holding company official that a campaign be waged to kill the administration's utility program in conference as matters stand tonight every indication is that the Wheeler-Rayburn bill will die in conference, where for more than a month the conferees of the Senate and House have been deadlocked. All hope had not been given up by the measure's advocates, however.

Earlier in the day, before the House investigating committee, Mr. Hopson for the first time gave figures on his income last year. He said he had received "some three or four hundred thousand dollars" from his private companies.

Admits Borrowing Millions.

He also said that the A. G. E. had borrowed several million dollars since the first of the year, and that it had it not been for the Wheeler-Rayburn bill the borrowings might have been a million dollars less.

He was directed to supply the names of the banks from which the money was borrowed, and said he would do so.

Before the Senate committee Mr. Hopson again made charges involving THE NEW YORK TIMES. He asserted that the newspaper was under "the strong influence" of the Morgan and Carlisle interests, and that because of this alleged influence the A. G. E. should expect at "more or less frequent intervals" more "unpleasant attacks from THE NEW YORK TIMES.

The charges were made in a telegram to the H. C. Hopson Company, New York, which was signed by Duncan Robertson, Mr. Hopson's private secretary.

The telegram was his own, said Mr. Hopson, explaining that it was his custom to have Mr. Robertson sign practically all of his messages to his New York office.

Messages to Hearst Admitted.

William Randolph Hearst was pictured before the committee as the writer of an editorial printed in the Hearst newspapers June 2, which Senator Black asserted was strikingly akin to a telegram sent by Mr. Hopson in a telegram to Mr. Hearst dated May 31.

Mr. Hopson admitted sending frequent messages to Mr. Hearst, who was dubbed by Senator Minton "the sage of San Simeon," but insisted that he had no reason to believe his messages inspired editorials or news articles in the Hearst papers.

Arthur Brisbane, Hearst writer, was pilloried, however, and documents placed in evidence showed

Continued on Page Twenty-six.

COAL BILL SPLITS HOUSE DEMOCRATS; PASSAGE HELD SURE

Widest Party Schism Since 'Death Sentence' Marks 'Must' Measure Debate.

VICTORY BY 30 CLAIMED

Administration Leaders Are Confident Despite Attacks as Unconstitutional.

Special to THE NEW YORK TIMES.

WASHINGTON, Aug. 16.—In the face of the most serious party schism which has yet confronted any of President Roosevelt's projects for industrial reform, the Guffey-Snyder Coal Bill was maneuvered by House leaders tonight into a position for final action on Monday.

With general debate on the measure concluded, they planned to carry it through the amending stage tomorrow and adjourn before the vote on passage.

Not since the vote on the "death sentence" for utility holding companies has the rank and file of the Democratic majority been so thoroughly split as on the merits of the Guffey-Snyder measure, and leaders were working overtime to make good their prediction that the bill would pass by about thirty votes.

Although they conceded that the final count would be close, all said enough votes had been obtained to assure passage of the administration "must" measure. Their estimate of thirty votes was verified by Republican leaders.

"Stalwarts" Oppose Measure.

Shouts of "unconstitutional," "communism," and "regimentation" from some of those who have been among the staunchest supporters of the administration on some other reform programs marked consideration of the bill on the floor today.

The opposition among Democrats was so strong that Republicans either sat back to watch them denounce the measure or left the floor entirely.

Emphasizing the broad difference of opinion on the constitutionality of the measure was the performance of such Ways and Means Committee "stalwarts" as Representative McCormack of Massachusetts, Cooper of Tennessee and Fuller of Arkansas, all of whom took the floor to oppose it, and sometimes on Republican time. The bill had been reported favorably by the committee by a vote of 12 to 11.

The special rule for consideration of the bill was adopted 241 to 64, after a perfunctory debate. Representative McCormack, one of the two Democrats on the Ways and Means Committee who abstained from voting on reporting out the measure, said that he would vote for the rule but against the bill.

He told other members that there would be no inconsistency in such a position, and that he thought the bill should have a chance for consideration on the floor.

Representative Fuller of Arkansas called Speaker Byrns's attention to the distribution by pages in the hall of copies of the bill bearing typewritten slips which said:

"Bituminous Coal Bill as amended and reprinted. Controversial proposals largely eliminated. Two-thirds of tonnage output operators favored bill and more than 80 per cent of labor."

Representative Snyder of Pennsylvania, co-author of the bill, said that he had pasted the slips on the measure and had instructed the

Continued on Page Seven.

WILL ROGERS, WILEY POST DIE IN AIRPLANE CRASH IN ALASKA; NATION SHOCKED BY TRAGEDY

Sergeant Morgan's Report of the Death Of Rogers and Post as Seen by Natives

Special to THE NEW YORK TIMES.

SEATTLE, Wash., Aug. 16.—The radio message sent by relays from Point Barrow, Alaska, to Seattle, in which Staff Sergeant Stanley R. Morgan informed the world of the tragic death of Will Rogers and Wiley Post, read as follows:

"Ten P. M. native runner reported plane crashed fifteen miles south of Barrow.

"Immediately hired fast launch, proceeded to scene.

"Found plane complete wreck, partly submerged, two feet water.

"Recovered body Rogers, then necessary tear plane apart extract body of Post from water.

"Brought bodies Barrow. Turned over Dr. Greist.

"Also salvaged personal effects, which am holding. Advise relatives and instruct this station fully as to procedure.

"Natives camping small river fifteen miles south here claim Post, Rogers landed and asked way to Barrow.

"Taking off, engine misfired on right bank while only fifty feet off water.

"Plane, out of control, crashed nose on, tearing right wing off and nosing over, forcing engine back through body of plane.

"Both apparently killed instantly.

"Both bodies bruised.

"Post's wrist watch broken, stopped 8:18 P. M."

The message was received by Colonel George E. Kumpe, in charge of the army signal corps headquarters here. It had been relayed through two radio stations and took about two hours to reach Seattle.

Sergeant Morgan won fame last Spring when he stayed at his post through a severe influenza epidemic while others, including his wife and 2-year-old son, Barrow, lay seriously ill. Sergeant Morgan and Dr. Henry W. Greist, the Presbyterian medical missionary, waged a bitter fight against the epidemic. While Dr. Greist ministered to the sick, Sergeant Morgan radioed for the aid which finally defeated the epidemic.

ETHIOPIANS OFFER ITALY GUARANTEES

Bar Military Occupation, but Propose Mine, Rail, Trade and Settlement Rights.

ASK ROME TO STATE CASE

Britain and France Hold That Frank Presentation of Demands Is Essential.

By FREDERICK T. BIRCHALL.

Wireless to THE NEW YORK TIMES.

PARIS, Aug. 16.—Throughout the day and until late this evening, with only an interval for luncheon, Premier Pierre Laval, Anthony Eden of Great Britain and Baron Pompeo Aloisi of Italy have been in conference at the Quai d'Orsay over the Italo-Ethiopian problem in an effort to avert a war, with its resultant repercussions in Europe.

The first day's deliberations closed tonight with one definite, positive step taken toward results. The British and French have made a joint formal request to Italy to state fully and frankly their complaints against Ethiopia and their consequent claims upon her.

From a British source it is learned that the Ethiopian Government, which is not represented at this conference, has shown a disposition to concede several points that may go far toward satisfying the Italian claims when these are made.

Offers Security Guarantees.

The Addis Ababa government, for instance, has expressed willingness to provide the most complete guarantees of security for Ethiopian aggression for the present Italian colonies and such economic concessions as may be agreed upon, provided the guarantees expected fall short of military occupation.

Emperor Haile Selassie is willing to grant reasonable rights for developing mineral and commercial possibilities within the Ethiopian territory, specific concessions to Italy being made in both fields.

He is further willing to consider granting some rights to Europeans to settle in Ethiopian territory and develop it while maintaining their original nationality. This last point would go a long way toward compliance with the Italian wishes.

Finally, he is willing to renew and even extend by making further concessions the old understanding with Italy, giving her permission to undertake a certain amount of commercial road and railroad construction in this country. Ethiopia anticipates an obvious Italian demand.

No answer to the Franco-British query was forthcoming from Rome tonight. Indeed, an immediate response was not expected. Baron Aloisi agreed to submit the request to Rome and to report the result as soon as possible. He received assurances from the others that if Italy would comply with this re-

Continued on Page Three.

CAPITAL SADDENED BY ROGERS DEATH

Both House and Senate Halt Business for Tribute to the Humorist and to Post.

GARNER DEEPLY AFFECTED

Robinson Hails 'Best Loved Citizen'—Deaths 'Real Loss,' Speaker Byrns Says.

Special to THE NEW YORK TIMES.

WASHINGTON, Aug. 16.—The death of Will Rogers and Wiley Post shocked and saddened the capital, which knew Rogers as a frequent visitor and liked him as an amiable "josher" of politicians.

Legislative machinery stopped briefly in tribute. The Senate dropped other business to honor the humorist, a friend of Presidents, diplomats and political leaders. The House also listened to a speech of eulogy, while from all quarters came expressions of sorrow over his death.

As soon as the Senate convened, Senator Robinson, the Democratic leader, took the floor and said:

"Probably the most widely known private citizen in the United States and certainly the best beloved met his death some hours ago in a lonely, far-away place.

"We pause for a moment in the midst of our duties to pay brief tribute to his memory and to that of his gallant companion, Wiley Post.

"I do not think of Will Rogers as dead. I shall remember him always as a sensible, courageous, loyal friend, possessed of unusual and notable talents.

"He made fun for all mankind. In nothing that he ever said was there an intentional sting. He was kind, generous, patriotic.

"His companion was a courageous representative of a gallant group who, on wings of adventure, sought remote places and conquered long distances."

News Saddens McNary.

Senator McNary, the Republican leader, said:

"Mr. Rogers has brought happiness, joy and good feeling to the hearts of millions of Americans. In common with all his fellow-citizens, I regret his tragic end and that of his doughty and valiant companion."

Vice President Garner, a friend of long standing, who shared the humorist's dislike of ceremonial attire, could only say, when informed of his death:

"Awful bad! Awful bad!"

Mr. Rogers had boomed Mr. Garner for the Presidency three years ago, and the two had a gay time together last Jan. 17 when the Vice President entertained for President Roosevelt.

Speaker Byrns, addressing the House, mentioned Mr. Rogers's in-

Continued on Page Four.

10-MINUTE HOP THEIR LAST

Engine Fails on a Take-Off for Final 15 Miles to Point Barrow.

LANDED TO GET BEARINGS

Startled Eskimos See Huge Bird Plunge to River Bank From 50 Feet Above Water.

ONE RUNS 3 HOURS TO TELL

Humorist Revealed as Financing a Trip Around the World With Famous Pilot.

(Copyright, 1935, by The Associated Press.)

POINT BARROW, Alaska, Aug. 16.—Will Rogers, beloved humorist, and Wiley Post, master aviator, were crushed to death last night when a shiny, new airplane motor faltered and became an engine of tragedy near this outpost of civilization.

Both were killed when their red Arctic sky cruiser slipped and fell fifty feet head-on into a river bank. The 550-horse-power motor, driven back into the fuselage, snuffed out the lives of the two men instantly.

A native runner raced to Point Barrow with word of a plane crash. Sergeant Stanley R. Morgan of the Army Signal Corps dashed to the scene to learn the full significance of the tragedy.

First he took the body of Rogers from the cabin. Then he was forced to tear the plane apart to recover that of the flier who twice had flown around the globe—once without settlement in America.

The bodies are taken to Barrow.

The bodies were brought here and given to the care of Dr. Henry W. Greist, a Presbyterian medical missionary.

It was a trifling ten-minute flight that ended the careers of two famous figures long accustomed to flying. Although Rogers —gentle master of the "wise crack" —never became a pilot, he was perhaps the world's foremost airplane passenger.

Resuming a happy-go-lucky aerial tour of Alaska, a prelude to a flight to Siberia and on to Moscow, the noted travelers left Fairbanks late yesterday for a 500-mile hop to Point Barrow, northernmost white settlement in America.

Fifty miles out they encountered fog. Post "sat down" on Harding Lake for a while, then resumed the journey soon.

Apparently uncertain of his bearings, he again brought his pontooned plane to the surface of a shallow river fifteen miles southwest of here to ask natives the way to Point Barrow.

The natives told the story to Sergeant Morgan. They said the motor of Post's new specially built plane misfired soon after it rose. The pilot quickly banked to the right; then the ship plummeted nose first, out of control. It dived into the edge of the stream, where the water was only two feet deep.

When Sergeant Morgan arrived at the scene by launch, he said today, he found the monoplane a complete wreck, partly submerged. The right wing was broken off.

The soldier said Post's wrist watch had stopped at 8:18 P. M., apparently the time of the accident. (The difference in time indicated by the aviator's watch and that reported by the natives probably is accounted for by the time zones through which he had flown.)

The runner arrived here at 10 P. M. with word of the tragedy. Recovering the pair's personal effects, Sergeant Morgan turned them over to Dr. Greist, awaiting instructions from Mr. Rogers and Mrs. Post and from Morgan's superior, Colonel George E. Kumpe at Seattle.

The unrelenting Arctic, grave of other such noted fliers as Carl Ben Eielson and Frank Dorbandt, played a leading part in this new tragedy.

Rogers and Post had left Fairbanks in the face of poor flying conditions. The stop at Harding Lake enabled them to await the

Continued on Page Four.

Lawyer Charges Judge Downs Beat Him; Sues for $50,000 in Contempt Case Row

County Judge Thomas Downs of Queens was sued in the New York Supreme Court yesterday by Lorenzo C. Carlino, a lawyer, for $50,000 damages. The lawyer charged that Judge Downs, after finding him guilty of contempt of court in a trial, and fining him $250, had knocked him down and kicked him at the St. Albans Golf Club in Queens.

Mr. Carlino alleges that his appeal from the contempt order was based on the ground that it was a violation of the section of the Judiciary Act which requires that a contempt order cite the specific facts upon which it is based. The lawyer further asserts that as he showed a signature of Presiding Justice Lazansky on an injunction order, "the defendant, Thom-

as Downs, struck the plaintiff, knocked him down, then kicked him—while on the ground and trampled upon the order which was served upon him. Defendant called plaintiff vile, filthy names and otherwise used vile and filthy language."

In addition to the suit against Judge Downs the lawyer asks $25,000 damages from Sheriff Peter J. McGarry of Queens for brutal treatment when he was arrested on the contempt order, which was later set aside by the Appellate Division.

Judge Downs denied last night he had assaulted Mr. Carlino.

"I was getting into my automobile parked in front of the clubhouse about 10 o'clock one night more than three months ago," the judge explained, "when a man I did not recognize in the darkness rushed out at me from some shrubbery. I was all alone and had received only a few days before an anonymous threat against me. I hit the man at once. He fell down and a paper dropped to the ground. The man picked up the paper and ran away."

The New York Times.

LATE CITY EDITION
Cloudy, slowly rising temperature today. Tomorrow cloudy, probably followed by rain or snow.
Temperature Yesterday—Max. 31; min. 25.

Copyright, 1936, by The New York Times Company.

VOL. LXXXV.....No. 28,486.   Entered as Second-Class Matter, Postoffice, New York, N.Y.   NEW YORK, TUESDAY, JANUARY 21, 1936.   P   TWO CENTS In New York City. | THREE CENTS Within 200 Miles | FOUR CENTS Elsewhere Except in 7th and 8th Postal Zones.

KING GEORGE V DIES PEACEFULLY IN SLEEP; PRINCE OF WALES BECOMES EDWARD VIII

BONUS BILL PASSES IN SENATE, 74 TO 16; HOUSE TO CONCUR

BOND PLAN IS TRIUMPHANT

All but 2 Minor Changes Are Beaten in 3-Hour Final Session.

INFLATIONISTS FIGHT HARD

But Neely Move to Pay With Currency and 'Protect' the Taxpayer Loses, 65-23.

14 'ANTIS' SWING OVER

Cost Put at $2,491,000,000 to $2,664,000,000 or More—House Acts Tomorrow.

Special to The New York Times.

WASHINGTON, Jan. 20.—By a vote of 74 to 16 the Senate today passed after about three hours' further consideration the "baby bond" Soldiers' Bonus Bill, whose total cost in outlays soon and eventually is estimated at from $2,491,000,000 to $2,664,000,000.

The measure now goes to the House, where concurrence, in a vote set for Wednesday, is regarded as certain. The vote there is being deferred, Speaker Byrns said, to allow absent members to return in time to go on record on final passage.

The overwhelming Senate support of nearly 5 to 1 for prepayment of the adjusted compensation certificates, due in 1945, was furnished by fifty-six Democrats, fifteen Republicans, two Farmer-Laborites and one Progressive.

Only nine Democrats and seven Republicans were recorded against. Thirteen names had been called without a dissenting vote before Senator Brown answered "no." Senator Bulkley voted against, as did Senators Burke and Byrd. Ten more names were called before the next opposing vote, that of Senator Couzens, the first Republican to vote "no."

The following, who voted for the baby bond bill today, had stood against the Patman currency bonus bill May 7:

Ashurst, Bailey, Barkley, Dieterich, Guffey, Harrison, Lonergan, Radcliffe, Robinson and Walsh, Democrats; Austin, Barbour, McNary and White, Republicans.

The following Senators who did not vote on passage of the Patman bill last May voted affirmatively today: Gore, O'Mahoney and Reynolds, Democrats, and Norbeck and Nye, Republicans.

Many Veterans in Gallery.

Veterans packed the galleries today and even the diplomatic section was well filled. Some of the veterans wore overcoats issued to them years ago or bought at salvage stores since. Some had apparently not shaved for several days. They had but one concern: this vote. They listened intently to the debate, to the voting—and betrayed jubilant high.

High up in one of the public galleries Ray Murphy, National Commander of the American Legion, and James E. Van Zandt, National Commander of the Veterans of Foreign Wars, took their seats soon after the session began.

On the final roll-call they kept pace with the vote on their own tally sheets.

"I am pleased, that is all, and I have nothing more to say," Mr. Murphy said afterward as he was being congratulated on all sides.

The Senate had met at noon and at 3:14 P. M. the vote was over and adjournment was quickly taken. Most observers agreed that practically every member who voted for the bill today would vote to override a veto, should President Roosevelt return the bill after the expected concurrence of the House. That would more than suffice to override.

Instead of paying the cost of the certificates in cash, as provided in

Continued on Page Fourteen.

Not a cloudbath in Atlantic City. Seek the sun at Hotel Traymore.—Adv.

House Votes Bill to Bar Foreign Mail Divorces

Special to The New York Times.

WASHINGTON, Jan. 20.—A bill designed to restrict "mail order" divorces from Mexico, by closing the mails to all correspondence about them, passed the House and went to the Senate today.

Introduced by Representative Healey, of Massachusetts, the bill provides that every sort of communication designed to give information or to solicit divorce business in a foreign country is not mailable. The bill provides a fine of $5,000 and a maximum prison sentence of five years or both.

There has been much agitation for such a bill owing to the issuance of many fraudulent Mexican divorces.

DR. ROBINSON UNFIT, ALUMNI UNIT FINDS

City College Committee Holds President Lacks Qualities Vital to Leadership.

MINORITY DEFENDS RULE

12-to-4 Report on Long Study of Campus Disorders Is Sent to Graduates.

Dr. Frederick B. Robinson, president of City College, lacks "the human qualities necessary to achieve the widespread confidence of his faculty and his student body and to provide genuinely inspired, resourceful and socially imaginative leadership," in the opinion of a special committee of the Associate Alumni of the college. The committee for more than a year has been studying the factors responsible for the frequency of undergraduate demonstrations at the institution.

Twelve members of the committee signed the report, which was mailed last night to 1,300 members of the association. Four others signed a minority draft, warmly defending the record of the Robinson administration. One committeeman did not vote because of his inability to attend meetings.

The committee was appointed on Dec. 17, 1934, by Dr. Stephen P. Duggan, director of the Institute of International Education and then president of the alumni organization. His action followed adoption of a resolution directing him to appoint a committee to "seek all significant facts concerning' present conditions in the City College and the nature of the present relations between the administration and the student body and the staff."

The group was to have reported its findings at a special meeting of the alumni a month later, but the mass of testimony gathered by it to point apparent that the committee's deliberations must be continued.

Alumni Meeting Called.

A special meeting of the Associate Alumni has been called for next Monday night at the college's Twenty-third Street building by Federal Judge Clarence G. Galston, president of the association. Both the majority and the minority reports will be discussed.

Signers of the majority draft were Dr. Henry Moskowitz, '99, chairman of the committee and executive adviser of the League of New York Theatres; Dr. Paul Abelson, impartial chairman in the arbitration of labor disputes; Dr. Louis I. Dublin, '01, third vice president of the Metropolitan Life Insurance Company; Waldemar Kaempffert, '97, science editor of THE NEW YORK TIMES; Professor Charles V. Morrill, '08, of the medical faculty of Cornell University; Dr. Henry Neumann, '00, leader of the Brooklyn Society for Ethical Culture; Louis Salant, '96, attorney; Jesse J. Shapiro, '18, attorney; Professor Herbert Wechsler, '28, of Columbia

Continued on Page Two.

QUICK AAA REFUND SHARPLY ORDERED BY SUPREME COURT

Mandate Is Swiftly Issued as Government Fights for 200 Millions Held in Escrow.

CONTRARY RULING CITED

President Calls Conference of Congress Leaders and Aides to Seek Way Out.

Special to The New York Times.

WASHINGTON, Jan. 20.—With sudden swiftness breaking a precedent of years, the Supreme Court today issued mandates making immediately effective its recent decisions declaring the Agricultural Adjustment Act unconstitutional and ordering $200,000,000 of impounded AAA taxes returned to processors.

The impact of the action was immediately felt in administration circles. President Roosevelt summoned a group of Congressional and farm leaders to meet at the White House tomorrow to discuss the situation created by the release of the $200,000,000, and the farm situation in general.

Announcement of the court's mandates came two and a half hours after the justices had left the bench and entered upon a two-week recess to catch up with their work. Court attaches said they could not remember when the justices had acted so quickly except in urgent matters such as murder cases. Usually all orders are handed down from the bench while the court is in session, and it was assumed that this would be the procedure today.

One of the orders tersely refused a government request made earlier in the day for reopening of the Louisiana rice millers' case through which the $200,000,000 was ordered turned back to the processors. It also granted the mandate sought by the rice millers and directed that their own impounded $200,000 taxes be released. The other order directed immediate issuance of a mandate releasing $90,000 in the receivership proceedings of the Hoosac Mills, victors in the AAA case decided on Jan. 6.

President Is Urged to Act.

Court action came even while government officials were studying plans to prevent the sequestered $200,000,000 from being recovered by processors without stern legal fights. In the face of the justices' swift moves, the President's advisers urged him to call tomorrow's conference as the present tentative strategy might have to be materially altered.

At the White House, it is understood, will be Senators Bankhead and Smith, and Representative Jones of Texas, Congressional farm leaders and possibly Senator Robinson, Democratic leader; Speaker Byrns, Secretary Wallace and Chester C. Davis of the AAA, M. G. White, solicitor for the Agricultural Department and representatives of the Treasury and Department of Justice are also expected to participate.

Government legal officers said it would be necessary for all processors with taxes impounded as part of the $200,000,000 to make applications in the Federal courts before their money could be released. The money, it was stated, would not be automatically given back without

Continued on Page Nine.

Lieut. Giovannoli Named for Cheney Award; Faced Death in Rescues From Burning Plane

Special to The New York Times.

WASHINGTON, Jan. 20.—Lieutenant Robert K. Giovannoli of Lexington, Ky., on duty with the Army Air Corps at Dayton, was selected today to receive the Cheney Award for 1935, in recognition of his "extreme bravery" in the rescue of two men from a burning plane at Dayton on Oct. 30.

Lieutenant Giovannoli extricated Tower through a window of the cabin. He returned, entered the compartment through the window, and began the task of releasing Major Hill. He worked with "seemingly superhuman energy" for four or five minutes and cut loose with a pocket knife the pilot's shoe which had become wedged in the wreckage. He then raised the pilot and passed him through the window to waiting hands.

"His own escape from a perilous position in which he suffered serious and painful burns was considered miraculous," the citation said.

Major Hill died several hours later and Mr. Tower several days later.

Tower, civilian test pilot, were trapped in the all-metal cockpit.

Lieutenant Giovannoli was born in 1904 in the District of Columbia, is a graduate of the University of Kentucky, and was commissioned in 1930.

"Probably not in the entire history of the Air Corps has a more heroic action been recorded," the War Department said of Lieutenant Giovannoli's act. An experimental bombing airplane crashed at Wright Field, the citation said in part, the wreckage catching fire. Three of the crew were rescued, but Major Ployer P. Hill, pilot, and Leslie

GREAT BEAR Ginger Ale, Lime Dry and Sparkling Water made with Great Bear Spring Water. Wholesale, CA, 5-8018.—Adv.

NEW KING 41 YEARS OLD

Adopts Name Edward in Signing Notice to London's Mayor.

FACES AN ARDUOUS LIFE

An Ardent Rider and Flier, He Must Settle Down to More Prosaic Tasks.

CORONATION A YEAR AWAY

Period of Court Mourning Will Precede It—Heir to Throne Flew to Sandringham.

By FREDERICK T. BIRCHALL.

Special Cable to The New York Times.

LONDON, Tuesday, Jan. 21.—Edward VIII, who at the age of 41 became King at the moment of his father's death just before midnight, will be speedily proclaimed as sovereign today.

According to ancient custom, a crier will call out from the steps of the Royal Exchange, "The King is dead, long live the King!" Ceremonial announcements of the same description will be made in every city, town and village in the country.

The new King himself, who is still at Sandringham, may be expected to remain there in such seclusion as can be permitted to him. His great loss came to him last night after a day more strenuous than most of those he has experienced in a life already inured to ceremonial hardships and quick movement.

Visited London Sunday.

King Edward, then the Prince of Wales, was in London Sunday night, having come here in the afternoon to see Prime Minister Stanley Baldwin and to arrange for a special meeting of the Privy Council at Sandringham which, in King George's presence, would appoint a Council of State, now useless and obsolete, to act should the late monarch's illness have continued over a long period.

Edward, with his brother, the Duke of York, flew back to Sandringham yesterday morning and was present when the Privy Council appointed this intended Council of Regency. Thereafter he was close by his father's death chamber until the end came.

His first task was to console his weeping mother, to whom he is deeply attached and whose favorite son he is. But his duties as King brooked no delay. Already they pressed upon him, and within less than an hour of his father's death and his own accession to the throne he had undertaken his first official act as King by sending the following telegram:

Sandringham, 12:28 A. M.
Lord Mayor, London.

I am deeply grieved to inform you that my beloved father, the King, passed away peacefully at 11:55 P. M. tonight.

EDWARD.

In the next few days, until the funeral is over, he will have a foretaste of the strenuous life of duty awaiting him. He will be consulted upon a thousand matters of procedure. He must preside over

Continued on Page Nine.

THE DEAD KING.   THE NEW KING.

MONARCH'S DEATH STIRS WASHINGTON

Roosevelt Cables Condolences —He Is Expected to Appoint Special Envoy for Funeral.

GRIEF IN WORLD CAPITALS

Bitterness Abates in Rome— New Ruler Wins Praise in Berlin—Paris Is Moved.

Special to The New York Times.

WASHINGTON, Jan. 20.—The death of King George caused deep sorrow and brought many expressions of grief here tonight. Official messages of condolence were sent to London by President Roosevelt and Secretary of State Cordell Hull.

Sir Ronald Lindsay, the British Ambassador, and the Ministers of Legations maintained here by British Dominions were deeply grieved. They refrained, however, from making any statements until they had been officially notified of the death by their governments. Official periods of mourning will be declared by those nations by authority of royal decree. In addition to the British Embassy, there are maintained here legations of Canada, the Irish Free State and the Union of South Africa.

It is likely that President Roosevelt will designate a Special Ambassador to represent him at the funeral. A decision on this question, however, is being delayed until official information on the funeral arrangements has been received from the United States Embassy in London.

Messages by the President.

The following message was sent by the President to the new King:

It is with deep sorrow that I learn of the death of His Majesty your father. I send to you my profound sympathy and that of the people of the United States, in whose respect and affection he occupied a high and unique place. I had the privilege of knowing His Majesty during the war days and his passing brings to me personally a great sorrow.

To Dowager Queen Mary the President sent this message:

Mrs. Roosevelt and I extend to Your Majesty and to the members of your family our heartfelt sympathy and join you in mourning the loss of one whose high qualities of kindness and wisdom have been so powerful an influence for universal peace and justice.

Mr. Roosevelt also sent condolences to the governmental heads of the British Dominions—Australia, Canada, the Irish Free State, New Zealand and the Union of South Africa. The message to Lord Tweedsmuir, Governor General of Canada, was typical. It follows:

Upon the sad occasion of the death of His Majesty King George, I offer to Your Excel-

Continued on Page Five.

Death Bulletin Posted At Sandringham House

By The Associated Press.

SANDRINGHAM, England, Tuesday, Jan. 21.—The last bulletin posted at "Jubilee Gate" of Sandringham House was done with rural simplicity.

Down the darkened drive a bareheaded youth rode a bicycle with a dim oil lamp flickering in front of him.

In an old brown leather case, which he carried in one hand while the other gripped a handlebar, he brought the announcement of the death of the Sovereign of the world's largest empire.

The chimes of the Sandringham church clock, striking half an hour after midnight, had just died away. Only the mourning of the wind through the elms bordering the drive broke the silence.

The youth, without dismounting, delivered the case at the lodge gate to one of the King's servants. The bulletin was taken out of the case and slowly, in the light of two great lanterns of the lodge, the gatekeeper walked across the drive and posted it.

DEATH IS MOURNED BY WHOLE EMPIRE

Aga Khan Honors the King's Memory in Bombay—Salute Is Fired in Singapore.

Special Cable to The New York Times.

LONDON, Tuesday, Jan. 21.—Within a few minutes of the King's death almost every corner of the earth had heard the news.

In Bombay, India, the Aga Khan declared that the "King Emperor was not only a great ruler but also a great man." He added:

"I am sure that the new King Emperor will, with his knowledge of the world and the whole empire, be a worthy successor."

Mahatma Gandhi announced from his Bombay sick bed that he had sent "respectful condolences" to the royal family through the Viceroy, the Earl of Willingdon.

In Cape Town most persons were asleep when the news of the King's death was received, but at the Government House high officials waited near telephones.

In Singapore a Royal Air Force airplane flying a long black streamer gave the first general indication that the King was dead. Later a battery fired a salute of seventy guns. Mohammedans, Hindus, Buddhists, Chinese and Jews, as well as Christians of all denominations, plan memorial services. The news of the death caused a suspension of Chinese New Year festivities and all markets were closed.

When Melbourne, Australia, received the news in the middle of the morning public offices were closed. All sports were canceled. The message to Lord Tweedsmuir, Governor General of Canada, was typical. It follows:

Hushed crowds in Wellington,

Continued on Page Five.

FAMILY WITH KING AT END

Queen Breaks Down as Long Vigil Closes at Sandringham.

HOPE HAD RISEN A LITTLE

Ruler, 70, Had Signed Paper Naming Council of State to Act in Illness.

PARLIAMENT MEETS TODAY

Theatres and Stock Exchange to Be Closed and Ships at Sea Will Lower Flags.

Outline of the life and reign of King George V, Pages 6 to 10.

By CHARLES A. SELDEN.

Special Cable to The New York Times.

LONDON, Tuesday, Jan. 21.—George V, King and Emperor, passed peacefully last night in his reign and the seventy-first year of his life out of a world in which he had faced manfully much tribulation. His eldest son, as Edward VIII, now reigns in his stead over Great Britain, Ireland and the great British Empire overseas.

The King died five minutes before midnight in his own house of Sandringham in Norfolkshire, where he had spent the happiest hours of his life. His Queen and his children, all except one—Henry, Duke of Gloucester, who lay himself ill in London—were at the bedside as the King's life ebbed away.

He suffered no pain, the doctors say. Throughout the last twelve hours his strength slowly failed until he fell asleep.

Canterbury Blesses Him.

Just before the end came the Archbishop of Canterbury, the King's lifelong friend, who had shared this last vigil with the royal family, bent over the dying monarch and gave him a last blessing.

A few moments later life was extinct and the news was being telephoned to Prime Minister Stanley Baldwin by Sir John Simon, Secretary of State for Home Affairs, who in virtue of his office had also remained at Sandringham near the King. And the news was being flashed also to the whole world.

The official bulletin of the death was as follows:

Death came peacefully to the King at 11:55 o'clock tonight in the presence of Her Majesty the Queen, the Prince of Wales, the Duke of York, the Princess Royal and the Duke and Duchess of Kent.

FREDERIC WILLANS,
STANLEY HEWETT,
DAWSON OF PENN.

From the death chamber there are already coming affecting stories of the last solemn scene. The Queen, who had maintained a constant watch both day and night in the room adjoining the King's bedroom, had at last been persuaded to take some food. Then she joined the others at the bedside. When the end came the iron self-control she had kept through the long, anxious days broke down at last. She turned to her son, the new King, and they exchanged an affectionate embrace. Each looked lovingly at the dead monarch, then with slow steps they turned away and went to another room, where they did their best to console each other.

Ships to Lower Flags.

Immediately on hearing the news from Sandringham the Admiralty Office in London flashed it to all British warships on the seven seas. Today all their flags will fly at half-mast.

Parliament will convene today as by law it must without summons whenever a sovereign dies. Mr. Baldwin has fixed the hour for the session at 6 o'clock in the evening.

In the House of Commons the Speaker will take the chair wearing white bands on the sleeves of his black gown and black shoe-

Continued on Page Five.

LONDON SADDENED BY NEWS OF DEATH

Hushed Crowd at Buckingham Palace Receives Word From Mourning Servant.

END SEEMED ANTICIPATED

Quietness in Piccadilly Circus Long Before Midnight Showed Stress of Nation.

By FERDINAND KUHN Jr.

Special Cable to The New York Times.

LONDON, Tuesday, Jan. 21.—The hand of death lay upon London last night. It was a stunned and silent crowd of several hundreds that stood outside Buckingham Palace just after midnight when the notice announcing that the King had died was posted on the railing.

Few in the crowd could read what it said, but all knew what it meant. Heads were bared as if by a common signal, and all conversation was hushed to whispers.

One light glowed in a window high up in a corner of the palace, but nothing else broke the gloom except the incessant popping of photographers' flashlights and the glare of headlights from automobiles that drew slowly up to the palace gates and then passed on.

Sentry Continues March.

The front of the palace loomed up dimly in the darkness across the great courtyard. A sentry in gray tramped back and forth along the sidewalk as though nothing had happened.

The crowd stayed long after midnight, apparently unwilling to believe or unable to realize the King had died. Some attraction that draws those hundreds to the palace, although the King was lying at Sandringham far away. After all, it was his home in his capital and it was to this building that thousands had come to acclaim him on Armistice Day and hundreds of thousands on the sunlit morning of his Jubilee.

Slowly the crowd melted away. By this time a newsboy was shouting through the empty streets near by and their black-bordered placards announced that a great reign had ended.

But the palace sentry still marched up and down as he had done all evening. One King had died but another was on the throne and Great Britain had not changed at all.

Even before the sad news came the King's capital seemed to anticipate it. The electric signs of Piccadilly Circus flashed their messages as brightly as ever, but all the gayety had gone out of the life of the great city.

The theatres were half empty and the streets were strangely deserted as millions sat at their radios listening for news from Sandringham. Early in the evening a vaudeville program from a broadcasting studio

Continued on Page Five.

"All the News That's Fit to Print."

The New York Times.

LATE CITY EDITION
Fair and somewhat warmer today.
Tomorrow rain and warmer.
Temperature Yesterday—Max., 20; min., 17.

Section 1

Copyright, 1936, by The New York Times Company.

VOL. LXXXV....No. 28,533.   Entered as Second-Class Matter, Postoffice, New York, N. Y.   NEW YORK, SUNDAY, MARCH 8, 1936.   P   Including Rotogravure Picture, Magazine and Book Review.   TEN CENTS | TWELVE CENTS Beyond 200 Miles Except in 7th and 8th Postal Zones.

STRIKE PEACE HOPE REVIVED AS MAYOR OFFERS A NEW PLAN

OWNERS ARE RECEPTIVE

Realty Board Acts Today on Move to Submit to Arbitration.

UNION ASSENT IS HINTED

Resumption of Negotiations Is Held Likely After La Guardia and Strikers Confer.

300 AT TUDOR CITY QUIT

More Park Av. Buildings Also Affected—Closed-Shop Issue No Longer a Factor.

Hope for settlement of the strike of elevator operators and other building service employes was revived last night after another appeal to both sides by Mayor La Guardia to submit the dispute to arbitration.

The Mayor made his proposal in identical telegrams addressed to the Building Service Employes Union, the strike organization, and the Realty Advisory Board, which has played the rôle of spokesman for large realty interests in the strike. Accompanying the Mayor's proposal was a detailed plan of settlement minus the closed shop.

The fact that the Mayor dispatched his peace plan after he had conferred at City Hall with strike leaders was taken as a clear indication that it was acceptable to the union, which had previously indicated its readiness to abandon the closed-shop demand.

William D. Rawlins, executive secretary of the Realty Advisory Board, declared after receipt of the Mayor's telegram that the peace plan might be looked upon with favor in the form in which it was submitted.

He announced that the directors of the Realty Advisory Board would consider the Mayor's proposal at a meeting this afternoon at the board's offices, 12 East Forty-first Street. The proposal will be analyzed by Walter Gordon Merritt, counsel for the board, after which a reply to the Mayor will be drafted.

New Negotiations Hoped For.

It was hoped last night that today's meeting of the Realty Advisory Board's directors would lead to a resumption of negotiations at City Hall tomorrow morning and to a settlement of the strike.

The Mayor's appeal for peace came after another day in which there were no important strike developments.

Although the union called out some 300 employes in Tudor City, preliminary to extending the walkout in the Grand Central area tomorrow, and appeared to be holding its lines in other parts of the city, there was no marked extension of the strike during the day.

Upon the intervention of the Mayor the union called off the strike in some 170 buildings controlled by the New York State Mortgage Commission after the commission had agreed to abide by any settlement ultimately reached with the realty interests of the city. The commission controls about 140 buildings in Manhattan and thirty in the Bronx.

In making known the dispatch of telegrams to the contending groups, pleading with them to bring the strike to a termination, Mayor La Guardia said:

"I am convinced that the strike can be settled if both sides are willing to do so. Resistance on one side and provocation on the other will get nowhere. The real issue now is wages and working conditions, and surely arbitration should be accepted by both sides.

"The Mayor will maintain law and order, protect life and property, and that goes for both sides. He will continue his efforts to end this controversy regardless of abuse from either side."

Closed-Shop Demand Eased.

The Mayor's plea was made public after he had conferred again with James J. Bambrick, strike leader, and other union spokesmen. His statement that "the real issue now is wages and working conditions" was taken as another indication that the union was willing

Continued on Page Thirty-seven

Butler and Shaw Swap Retorts Not 'Courteous'

By The Associated Press.

SAN PEDRO, Calif., March 7.—Nicholas Murray Butler and George Bernard Shaw let go with both barrels of caustic sarcasm today at each other through the medium of interviews.

Said Dr. Butler, president of Columbia University, with regard to the gibes of G. B. S. at the American Constitution and the President:

"Anything George Bernard Shaw may say about politics is too ludicrous to comment upon. This won't surprise Mr. Shaw because it represents an opinion I have had about him for a long time. And he knows it."

Said G. B. S.:

"I suppose if Dr. Butler had an automobile that had been running for thirty years and was still running he would insist that it shouldn't be exchanged for a new motor car. That is the way with your Constitution. Dr. Butler's antiquated automobile wouldn't bring much of a 'trade-in.'

"Anyway I'm 'G. B. S.' and Dr. Butler isn't 'N. M. B.'"

LEHMAN CRIME PLEA POLITICS, SAYS IVES

Speaker Ascribes Attack on Assembly Members to Quest for Re-election Issue.

DEFENDS ALL COLLEAGUES

He Calls on the Governor for 'Appropriate Action' on Dodge and Geoghan.

The text of Mr. Ives's address is printed on Page 38.

Special to The New York Times.

ALBANY, March 7.—Governor Lehman is making a "political football" of his crime program and picking a fight with the Legislature merely to develop an issue on which to run for re-election, Speaker Irving M. Ives of the Assembly asserted tonight in a State-wide radio broadcast.

The Speaker went on the air over WOKO and a chain of stations to reply to the radio attack of two weeks ago in which the Governor charged that "powerful groups of lawyer legislators" were banding together to hamstring his program in the Assembly.

Mr. Ives offered a detailed statement of his position on the crime bills, saying that his attitude was that of many Democrats and Republicans, and demanded that Governor Lehman "take appropriate action" in the cases of District Attorney William C. Dodge of New York and District Attorney William F. X. Geoghan of Kings. He said:

"Two glaring examples of the failure of law enforcement are to be found in New York City. The first is the case of District Attorney William F. X. Geoghan of Brooklyn, who, unable to secure convictions in the notorious Drukman case, was superseded by Special Prosecutor Hiram C. Todd, who obtained these convictions with admirable promptness.

Demands Governor Act.

"The second example is that pertaining to District Attorney William C. Dodge of New York County who, after having shown himself unable to break up racketeering gangs which for years have been preying upon the public of New York, was finally superseded by Attorney Thomas Dewey as special prosecutor. Where Mr. Dodge failed, Mr. Dewey has not failed and instead has obtained a number of convictions.

"Obviously, there must be some laxity of law enforcement somewhere in these cases, and I recommend that the Governor, in view of the facts, take appropriate action."

The Speaker enumerated "certain basic truths that have emerged from the confusion and misunderstanding which this anti-crime controversy has provoked."

He declared that "the intemperate charges directed at the Assembly by the Governor are utterly false and ridiculous."

He asserted that "the Governor has sought to claim credit for inaugurating all anti-crime programs offered in this State since the 1935 session of the Legislature, to the

Continued on Page Thirty-eight

HOOVER DECLARES FREEDOM IN PERIL, LIFE 'MORTGAGED'

He Tells Colorado Republicans We Face Enslaving Taxes, Repudiation or Inflation.

'COMMON MAN' MUST PAY

Future 'Fireside Talks' Will Be With Collector, He Says— Hits 'Planned Economy.'

The text of Mr. Hoover's speech is printed on Page 36.

Special to The New York Times.

COLORADO SPRINGS, March 7.—Crushing taxes, repudiation of debts or inflation are certain sequels to the New Deal, Herbert Hoover declared tonight before the Young Republican League of Colorado in a speech which was broadcast nationally.

The administration's spending and what he regarded as its steps toward dictatorship have failed to solve the problems of the depression and of unemployment, he said.

The former President asserted that the youth of the nation faced a choice between the old American system, with its political liberty and equality of economic opportunity, and a "planned economy" involving regimentation and bureaucracy.

The freedom and opportunities of youth "are being mortgaged," Mr. Hoover asserted, adding that "taxation enslaves as well as dictatorship."

More Taxes 'Inevitable.'

He warned that the nation's "future fireside talks" would be with the tax collector, and some believed that present taxes on wealth, designed to complete the cycle of "shirtsleeves to shirtsleeves in three generations," would take the shirt also.

"Do not mistake," he went on. "The new taxes of today are but part of them. More of them are as inevitable as the first of the month. The only alternatives are repudiation or inflation. No matter what nonsense you are told about corporations and the rich paying the bill, there will be two-thirds of it for the common man to pay after the corporations and the rich are sucked dry."

He said, further:

"And where do we get to after all this attempt to supplant the American system? At the time of the election in 1932 the American Federation of Labor estimated 11,-600,000 unemployed. Today, after three years of the New Deal, they report 11,600,000 unemployed.

"To get these people back to their jobs was the outstanding job of our government. It was the excuse given for all these doings. But the grim fact remains that it has failed in its primary purpose. And $15,000,000,000 will be added to the national debt before the New Deal is over."

The Record on Platform Pledges.

Mr. Hoover contrasted the administration's actions and party platform promises of 1932, and said that when he framed the indictment all but two of the thirty-seven Republican platform promises were carried out, despite depression difficulties. Two secondary promises, he said, "ran against the obstinacy of a Democratic Congress."

The trend of events in this country since 1932, he said, followed the pattern of European nations that succumbed to dictatorship, and he added that the New Deal had "imitated the intellectual and vocal technique of typical European revolution."

The great contributions to civili-

Continued on Page Thirty-six

Brief Attack of Cold Is Repelled by Sun; Rising Temperatures Forecast for Today

Winter tried to take possession of the city again yesterday, just two weeks before the official arrival of spring. But a bright sun in a clear sky vanquished Winter back with a jump of 7 degrees in temperature within little more than an hour in the afternoon.

A forecast for continuing rising temperatures and fair skies is expected to bring a measurably nice day of above-freezing weather today and warmer weather and rain tomorrow.

From midnight Friday until 3 o'clock yesterday afternoon the mercury remained below freezing and brought a renewed touch of Winter to the city. At 8 A. M. the temperature dropped to a low of 17—the coldest since the days of snow and ice on Fifth Avenue and Broadway.

Within the next hour the mercury rose ten degrees and then dropped back for several hours before renewing an upward course

at noon. At 3 P. M., when the mercury stood at 32, a shift in light winds from the north to the southwest sent it up quickly to a high of 39 at 4:15, after which it fell slightly.

The average temperature for the day was 28, which is seven degrees below the normal. The coldest March 7 in the records of the Weather Bureau was in 1890, when the mercury dropped to 6, and the warmest was in 1921, when it rose to 69.

Since Jan. 1, when the day was 9 hours and 17 minutes long, the length of the day has increased gradually and will be 11 hours and 52 minutes long today. On March 18 the vernal equinox will begin with the day and night each 12 hours long. Two days later, on March 20, at 1:58 P. M., Spring will begin.

Rumania's War Council Called to Special Session

BUCHAREST, March 7.—The Rumanian Defense Council tonight was called to a special session Monday, to devise means of improving and rapidly increasing the nation's armaments. The council consists of King Carol, former Premiers and the general staff of the army.

The semi-official newspaper, Dimineata, predicted that the League of Nations would apply economic sanctions against Germany as a result of reoccupation of the Rhineland.

Commenting on Chancellor Adolf Hitler's speech before the Reichstag, the newspaper said, "Germany is laughing today, but France and England will be laughing tomorrow."

PARIS APPEALS TO LEAGUE

Rejects Reich Proposal of a Substitute for Locarno Treaty.

ALLIES SUPPORT PROGRAM

Russia and Czechoslovakia to Aid to 'Limit' in Effort to Clear Rhineland.

BELGIUM ACTS AT BORDER

French Officials Say Military Moves to Drive Back Germans Await Geneva Decisions.

By P. J. PHILIP.

Wireless to The New York Times.

PARIS, March 7.—France has laid Germany's latest treaty violation before the Council of the League of Nations. That is the procedure called for in the situation.

At the same time the French Government today made it quite clear that there could be no negotiation with Germany of any substitute for the Treaty of Locarno or anything else as long as a single German soldier remained in the Rhineland in contravention of Germany's signed undertakings.

While no public mention of French troop movements is being made here, it is obvious that the necessary precautions will be taken, probably on the same scale as last March, when the Reich government denounced the military clauses of the Treaty of Versailles and reorganized her army.

[France ordered all northeastern border fortifications garrisoned at full strength, The Associated Press reports, and Belgium canceled leaves for troops garrisoning her eastern frontier.]

Withdrawal Held Essential.

What is essential, in the French view, is that the German Government must be compelled, by diplomatic pressure first and by stronger pressure if need be, to withdraw from the Rhineland. For what is found most intolerable in all today's happenings is this renewed appearance of the mailed fist in diplomacy—not, in French opinion, in the service of common peace and order, but as a menace and provocation.

Everything that can be done to avoid war will be done. But there should be no mistaking this fact in Germany or elsewhere: that rather than submit to this last crashing piece of Teutonism, France will fight.

Meanwhile, as always, the French have presented their case. The Cabinet met twice today, once in reduced numbers at the Elysée Palace with President Albert Lebrun and later at the Quai d'Orsay. Between the two meetings Foreign Minister Pierre-Étienne Flandin called in the Ambassadors of the signatory powers of the Locarno agreements for consultation and to acquaint them with his government's views.

General Marie Gustave Gamelin, chief of the General Staff, took part in the Elysée Palace meeting. The Cabinet has been summoned for tomorrow morning to be kept fully apprised of the situation and to learn the attitude of other governments whose opinions have been sought by French diplomatic representatives.

After the second Cabinet meeting, Mr. Flandin, in the famous clock room at the Quai d'Orsay, read to the biggest assembly of newspaper men there had been written off as lost. A shock to obtain a solid counter-value for a hopeless item on the balance sheet appears attractive for practical politicians in London.

The real question awaiting reply is whether Hitler offers advantages that upon closer inspection may be found ephemeral once the fact of the illegal military occupation of the Rhineland is accepted without demur.

Officials in Berlin, it is known here, were alarmed when Foreign Minister Pierre-Étienne Flandin of France put a direct question to Mr. Eden concerning British action in case of an infraction by Germany.

Continued on Page Thirty.

MUSSOLINI ACCEPTS PEACE PARLEY BID

League Invitation Satisfactory in Principle as Basis for Talks, He Tells Cabinet.

ITALY WILL NOT AID PARIS

Imposition of Sanctions Said to Have Freed Nation of Locarno Obligations.

By ARNALDO CORTESI.

Wireless to The New York Times.

ROME, March 7.—At almost the minute when Chancellor Adolf Hitler, in Berlin, was announcing the reoccupation of the Rhineland, Premier Benito Mussolini, in Rome, was informing the Italian Cabinet here that he had decided to accept "in principle" the invitation of the League of Nations to negotiate peace with Ethiopia.

These two facts, though seemingly unrelated, are likely to have some important repercussions on each other. The turmoil created in Europe by Hitler's move, which has directed attention from East Africa and pushed sanctions into the background, is expected to help Mussolini to drive a hard bargain with the Negus and to settle the Italo-Ethiopian conflict with all possible speed.

Italy, as soon as her best energies are no longer fettered in Africa, will be able to make her weight felt in the European balance of power and participate in the process of readjustment in the next few years.

The rest of Mussolini's reply to the League's peace appeal is not yet known and will not be made public until it has arrived at Geneva. Therefore, it is still uncertain whether he has agreed unreservedly to negotiate or whether he has pledged his acceptance with important reservations.

Newspapers, usually regarded as the government's mouthpieces, are at variance on this point. The Giornale d'Italia thinks, as the invitation of the League contained no limitations, there are no conditions in Mussolini's reply. The Tribuna on the contrary says that Mussolini's acceptance does not tie him down to anything and implies the widest reservations. It is also

Continued on Page Thirty-nine

HITLER SENDS GERMAN TROOPS INTO RHINELAND; OFFERS PARIS 25-YEAR NON-AGGRESSION PACT; FRANCE MANS HER FORTS, BRITAIN STUDIES MOVE

GERMAN ARMY AGAIN ON THE RHINE.
The shaded portion of the map shows the district demilitarized under the Treaty of Versailles. It included all German territory on the west of the Rhine and a zone fifty kilometers wide along the east bank. The stars show where the principal garrisons were established.

GERMANY'S ACTION ASSAILED BY EDEN

He Uses Severe Tone Toward Reich Envoy, but Attitude of Cabinet Is Deemed Milder.

By AUGUR.

Special Cable to The New York Times.

LONDON, March 7.—Foreign Secretary Anthony Eden used strong words to condemn the German Government's action when Ambassador Leopold von Hoesch of Germany presented to him this morning Chancellor Adolf Hitler's memorandum concerning the Rhineland.

Mr. Eden and the British Government must consider the entry of German regular troops into the forbidden zone to be in defiance of treaty obligations and a flagrant breach of a territorial frontier. The terms of the Treaty of Locarno impose definite duties on the British Government. The implications of the situation now created will therefore be carefully gone into. But to Charles Corbin, the French Ambassador, Mr. Eden said that the government, while determined to comply with treaty obligations, was equally desirous of avoiding any hasty action and it advised the French Government to study the points of the German offer, for they appear to be not without value.

Action Had Been Expected.

The fact is that at the bottom of their hearts Cabinet Ministers here are not so displeased with Hitler's proposals as it officially must be said they are. For sometime past the demilitarized zone has been written off as lost. A chance to obtain a solid counter-value for a hopeless item on the balance sheet appears attractive for practical politicians in London.

The real question awaiting reply is whether Hitler offers advantages that upon closer inspection may be found ephemeral once the fact of the illegal military occupation of the Rhineland is accepted without demur.

Officials in Berlin, it is known here, were alarmed when Foreign Minister Pierre-Étienne Flandin of France put a direct question to Mr. Eden concerning British action in case of an infraction by Germany.

Continued on Page Thirty-three

ARMY MARCHES IN AS HITLER SPEAKS

In Full War Equipment It Goes to Rhineland, Ending His Advance Near Frontier.

By OTTO D. TOLISCHUS.

Wireless to The New York Times.

BERLIN, March 7.—Germany today resumed her "watch on the Rhine" when, with an astonishing bravado that dared challenge Europe to war or to peace and left the world breathless for the moment, the new German Army crossed the military frontier, which hitherto had separated it from France, and occupied the demilitarized Rhineland zone created by the Versailles treaty and reaffirmed at Locarno.

The move was carried through with that German efficiency which drew from foreign military experts tribute to the German Army command and amid manifestations of both popular enthusiasm and grave apprehension. It brought back echoes of the last German westward march nearly twenty-two years ago, but also it was made to look like a dress rehearsal for more serious business.

Even while Chancellor Adolf Hitler was serving notice of the contemplated move to diplomats of the Locarno powers assembled in the chancellery at 11 A. M. field-gray masses of the troops of occupation were already on the march.

Planes Circle Cologne.

A few minutes before Hitler began to announce this move to the world in his speech before the Reichstag the first military flying squadrons already were circling Cologne's cathedral spires. As he began to talk infantry, artillery, motorized cavalry, tanks, machine-gun units, anti-aircraft artillery and all other paraphernalia of modern warfare already were closing the Rhine bridges, and two hours after he had finished, his advance guards already had reached Saarbruecken, their westernmost point for the present, only three kilometers from the French frontier.

According to an official announcement, troop movements will continue all day tomorrow, this being also the day when the zone, which comprises

Continued on Page Thirty-one

VERSAILLES CURB BROKEN

Hitler Smashes Locarno Citing Franco-Soviet Treaty as Reason.

READY TO REJOIN LEAGUE

Battle for Equality Ended, He Tells Joyous Reichstag— Sets Vote for March 29.

URGES AIR PACT IN WEST

Bilateral Neutralization of Rhine Proposed—Hand Is Extended to Lithuania.

Hitler's Reichstag speech and other texts on Pages 31, 32, 33.

By GUIDO ENDERIS.

Wireless to The New York Times.

BERLIN, March 7.—Germany today cast off the last shackles fastened upon her by the Treaty of Versailles when Adolf Hitler, as commander-in-chief of the Reich defense forces, sent his new battalions into the Rhineland demilitarized zone.

The Chancellor's marching orders were timed to synchronize with Germany's notification to the powers concerned and to a listening Reich that she no longer considered herself bound by the Locarno terms because the fundamental basis and inherent purpose of that pact had been destroyed through the conclusion of the mutual assistance treaty between France and the Soviet Union.

Hitler related to the Reichstag all he had done. After he had proposed a daring peace program he was greeted with a burst of enthusiasm when he announced that with complete sovereignty over all German territory restored, she no longer would not only to return to the League of Nations, but also to cooperate in any system of collective security that gave promise of success.

Sees Struggle Closed.

"After three years of ceaseless battle," Hitler concluded, "I look upon this day as marking the close of the struggle for German equality status and with that re-won equality the path is now also clear for Germany's return to European collective cooperation."

To give the German people an opportunity to pass judgment on his leadership, Hitler said, he decided to dissolve the Reichstag and order a plebiscite on Sunday, March 29, at which German voters will be able to record their confidence or lack of it in the government's home and foreign policies.

The announcement of Germany's denunciation of the Locarno pact, which she voluntarily negotiated with France and Belgium in 1926 and for which Great Britain and Italy stood sponsors, provoked less jubilation in the Reichstag than did the news that German troops at that very hour were again marching to their peace garrisons in the Rhineland. That news unloosed a cyclone of rejoicing as the 660 Deputies rose to greet it.

But the Chancellor's speech as a whole must be counted an outstanding political pronouncement and oratorical achievement with respect to both its contents and forceful delivery and also the intense sincerity that marked the recital of the reasons that had determined him to abrogate Locarno.

Offers Non-Aggression Pacts.

The speech was easily Hitler's biggest utterance on German foreign policy. While it was not free from recriminations and indictment of France's refusal to grasp Germany's outstretched hand, that hand was once more revealed as offering France and Belgium a twenty-five-year non-aggression pact at the very moment when the roll of German regimental drums was being heard along the Rhine for the first time since 1919.

The proposed non-aggression pact, which Hitler said was open also to the Netherlands, constituted the only part of his seven-point peace scheme that he offered as a substitute for the discarded Locarno.

Germany is also prepared, he continued, to negotiate for the creation of a demilitarized

Continued on Page Thirty.

The New York Times.

LATE CITY EDITION
Generally fair and slightly cooler
today. Tomorrow fair and warmer.
Temperatures Yesterday—Max., 77; Min., 61

Copyright, 1936, by The New York Times Company.

VOL. LXXXV.....No. 28,629. Entered as Second-Class Matter, Postoffice, New York, N. Y. NEW YORK, FRIDAY, JUNE 12, 1936. PP TWO CENTS In New York City. | THREE CENTS Within 200 Miles. | FOUR CENTS Elsewhere Except in 7th and 8th Postal Zones.

REPUBLICANS NAME LANDON UNANIMOUSLY; HE ACCEPTS PLATFORM, ADDING OWN IDEAS

SOVIET TO SET UP NEW PARLIAMENT WITH TWO HOUSES

One Chamber to Be Composed of Deputies Elected by Secret Vote of the People.

'SENATE' WILL BE PICKED

It Will Contain Delegates of the Republics—Freedom of Speech Due for All.

PRESS ALSO IS AFFECTED

Liberty of Worship and Equal Rights for Women Among Features of Charter.

By WALTER DURANTY

Wireless to THE NEW YORK TIMES.

MOSCOW, June 11.—The proposed new Soviet Constitution, which will be published tomorrow, is strikingly different from the earlier Constitution, which became law July 6, 1923.

The first difference is that in the initial section there is no reference as before to the severance of the world into the camps of socialism and capitalism—no mention of imperialist hostility or of a union of international workers or that "the bourgeoisie of the world have been unable to organize the collaboration of peoples."

Allows Private Farming

Instead, the new first section stresses the success of socialism in the Union of Soviet Socialist Republics, declares the means of production, commerce, finance, the railroads, &c., now belong to the State and outlines the position of collective farms, with the note that their property belongs to them "eternally," but the Constitution allows private farming and private sale of produce on the condition that it be direct and not involve any profit from or exploitation of a third party.

That, in short, is the basic principle of the Soviet State as expressed by the new Constitution—that no individual or group can profit by the labor of others and that everything that matters is the property of the community, worked for the community's benefit.

The first section concludes with these significant sentences: "The economic life of the U. S. S. R. is directed by the State's economic plan toward increasing the general wealth.

"In the U. S. S. R. there is established the principle of socialism, 'From each according to his capacity, to each according to his work.'"

Here you get the basic principle of Stalinism, or Soviet socialism, at its present stage as compared with the ultimate goal of Marxian communism, the motto of which is, "From each according to his capacity, to each according to his needs." In other words, the Socialist principle of greater reward for greater service still prevails over the ultimate ideal of Communist equality.

The second change is that instead of seven federated republics in the U. S. S. R. there will henceforth be eleven, the Caucasian Federation being split into three—Georgia, Azerbaijan and Armenia—and Kirghizia and Kazakstan are added. This is only a formal difference for administrative purposes, and the federated republics, as before, retain the right to secede from the union at will.

New Parliament Provided

The third change, however, is more important, affecting the whole electoral system. Instead of provincial Soviets being elected by lists on open ballot and then their chosen delegates to the All-Union Soviet Congress, there are now to be secret ballots for individual Deputies on the basis of one Deputy to each 300,000 members of the population.

These Deputies will be elected to what will be equivalent to the House of Representatives in the United States. And instead of these Deputies sitting jointly with the Congress of Nationalities, there will henceforth be two houses with equal powers of action and initiative, in which the House of Nationalities will be chosen by provincial councils in the form of ten Deputies from each federated republic, five from each autonomous

Continued on Page Five

Hoover Calls Platform 'Fighting, Progressive'

Former President Herbert Hoover last night called the Republican platform and Governor Landon's specific statements upon it, as read at the Cleveland convention, "fighting and progressive."

Through his secretary Mr. Hoover made public this statement:

"The platform admirably covers the principles and methods I have so repeatedly advocated. The platform is the fighting, definite and progressive statement the country needs.

"When put into force by the American people, these principles will regenerate the country, Governor Landon's statement amply covers any other points that may be in question."

BORAH IS 'STUNNED' BY LANDON'S PLEA

Nominee Should Have Acted 'Sooner,' He Says When Told of Gold, Wage Demands.

SILENT AS TO HIS SUPPORT

Senator Leaves for Washington After Winning Victory on His Platform Goals.

By The Associated Press.

CLEVELAND, June 11.—The Plain-Dealer says Senator Borah appeared "stunned" when informed at Akron tonight that Governor Landon had declared for a gold-backed currency and a constitutional amendment, if necessary, to permit State regulation of wages and hours.

Informed of the nominee's telegram to the Republican convention, Mr. Borah said:

"Well, that's his business. Why didn't he send it sooner?"

The Plain-Dealer says Mr. Borah ran his hands over his face four or five times. Asked if he had any more comment, he said:

"I shall wait until morning and see what they do."

Mr. Borah was on a train en route to Washington, having left Cleveland just a few minutes before the delegates adopted the platform. He had fought to have any mention of the gold standard eliminated from the platform.

Platform Pleases Him

Special to THE NEW YORK TIMES.

CLEVELAND, June 11.—Senator Borah expressed himself this afternoon as well pleased with the platform sent to the national convention by the committee on resolutions.

But the question whether he would support the man whom the convention was to select as party standard bearer remained unanswered when the Idaho Republican left for Washington.

After the final draft of the platform had been completed and become available for examination, it was reported that Senator Borah had examined it and was satisfied with the language of the planks in the

Continued on Page Thirteen

'VICTORY' LANDON PLEDGE

He Promises to Wage One of Party's Most Forceful Campaigns.

THANKS HIS TOWNSMEN

With Wife at His Side on the Front Porch He Hails Their Loyalty.

TOPEKA HAILS THE CHOICE

Citizens Decorate City and Parade to Governor's Home When Nomination Is Flashed.

By WARREN MOSCOW

Special to THE NEW YORK TIMES.

TOPEKA, Kan., June 11.—With thousands of his neighbors and other citizens of Topeka gathered around the yellow brick Executive Mansion at Eighth and Buchanan Streets, Governor Alfred M. Landon delivered to them tonight a simple message of his appreciation of their loyalty and affection as they gathered to celebrate his nomination as the Republican candidate for President.

Earlier, in a statement issued to the press, he had pledged himself to lead a harmonious party to victory next November.

It was exactly 11:14 o'clock, Central standard time, when the Governor and Mrs. Landon stepped out to meet a deafening roar of applause from the crowd.

The air rang with cheers, torches and flares blazed and band after band blared "Oh, Susanna" as the Governor and Mrs. Landon left the study in which they had spent most of the evening to appear on the front porch.

Thanks His Townsmen

The Landons' neighbors and all Topeka had been preparing to celebrate his actual nomination and had been awaiting only a radio flash from the convention hall in Cleveland apprising them of the fact. The city was decorated with flags and bunting, and paraders formed in line, with all the city's bands and bugle and fife and drum corps ready to blow their heartiest. Finally word of the nomination came and the paraders marched to the Executive Mansion.

Governor Landon, when he stepped forward into the glare of the floodlights arranged around the home, was at ease, though toward the end of his talk he was plainly affected. He wore a gray business suit, with a white shirt and attached soft collar.

Mrs. Samuel E. Cobb, Mrs. Landon's mother, and Joe Cross, a cousin of Mrs. Landon, were with the Governor and his wife. They took seats on the porch swing, while the Governor and Mrs. Landon faced the cheers of the more than 15,000 paraders.

Governor Landon in his greeting said:

"Mrs. Landon and I are deeply touched by this expression of your good will and good wishes. We are proud, too, that so many of our friends from surrounding towns

Continued on Page Thirteen

Roll-Call of the States On Landon's Nomination

Special to THE NEW YORK TIMES.

CLEVELAND, June 11.—Following is the vote by States for Governor Landon when roll was called on the nomination for President:

State or Territory	No. of Deleg.	State or Territory	No. of Deleg.
Alabama	13	New Jersey	32
Arizona	6	New Mexico	6
Arkansas	11	New York	90
California	44	North Carolina	23
Colorado	12	North Dakota	8
Connecticut	19	Ohio	52
Delaware	9	Oklahoma	21
Florida	12	Oregon	10
Georgia	14	Pennsylvania	75
Idaho	8	Rhode Island	8
Illinois	57	South Carolina	10
Indiana	28	South Dakota	8
Iowa	22	Tennessee	17
Kansas	18	Texas	25
Kentucky	22	Utah	8
Louisiana	12	Vermont	9
Maine	13	Virginia	17
Maryland	16	Washington	16
Massachusetts	33	West Virginia	15
Michigan	38	Wisconsin	6
Minnesota	22	Wyoming	6
Mississippi	11	Alaska	3
Missouri	30	Dist. of Columbia	3
Montana	7	Hawaii	3
Nebraska	14	Philippine Islands	3
Nevada	6	Porto Rico	2
New Hampshire	11	Total	984

West Virginia gave one vote for Borah. Wisconsin gave 18 votes to Borah.

VANDENBERG LOOMS AS RUNNING MATE

Senator Agrees to Reconsider Refusal and Landon Men Believe He Will Accept.

STEIWER SECOND CHOICE

Kansans May Pick Him if Other Plan Fails — Borah Backs Gannett—Knox Boomed.

By CHARLES R. MICHAEL

Special to THE NEW YORK TIMES.

CLEVELAND, June 11.—The Landon forces have not yet abandoned the hope of persuading Senator Vandenberg to accept the nomination for Vice President, despite reiteration of his announcement of last week that his decision to remain in the Senate was "final."

Although he continued his refusal earlier in the day, the Michigan Senator agreed this evening to confer again with the Landon forces after adjournment tonight. At this time he was expected to determine whether he would bow to the request of Governor Landon.

Confidence was expressed at the Kansas's headquarters that Mr. Vandenberg would be nominated tomorrow.

There is a strong movement in favor of Colonel Knox. His selection, however, is opposed by Colonel Robert R. McCormick, publisher of The Chicago Tribune.

Frank E. Gannett of Rochester, N. Y., a Borah supporter, came into the situation as a compromise candidate. Members of the New York delegation were told that Senator Borah desired his nomination and "would vigorously support

Continued on Page Twelve

THE PLATFORM IS VOTED

Containing 14 Planks, It Is Declared Largely a Liberal Victory.

WORLD COURT IS BARRED

States' Rights Are Stressed— Social Security Would Be on Pay-as-You-Go Basis.

BANS 'SCARCITY' POLICY

Farm Statement Sets Broad Aims on Crops and Credit Help —Trading Act Repeal Urged.

By FELIX BELAIR Jr.

Special to THE NEW YORK TIMES.

CLEVELAND, June 11.—After laboring for three days and nights to draft a declaration of political principles that would come near to satisfying the expected Presidential candidate and placate potential party bolters, the resolutions committee of the Republican National Convention brought forth tonight a platform on which it hopes the party can carry the national elections in November.

It was a composite of compromises in which the demands of Governor Landon, the assured nominee, were subordinated in several important instances to those of the more conservative Eastern delegations on matters of social and economic progress.

Throughout its preamble and fourteen planks the document condemned abuses it connected with the present administration.

While it urged continuance of several reforms inaugurated by the Roosevelt administration, such as regulation of security markets for the protection of investors, social security and unemployment relief—with the latter two administered by the States—these were far outnumbered by the departures from present national policy that it proposed.

Main Points of Platform

The outstanding declarations of the platform were:

1. Constitutional and local self-government must be preserved as well as the authority of the Supreme Court as final protector of citizens' rights, and maintenance of our system of free enterprise, private competition and equality of opportunity.

2. Absorption of the unemployment by private industry and agriculture holds the only answer to that problem, and to that end restriction of production should be abolished, and all policies that raise production costs and cost of living discontinued. Legitimate business should be encouraged and the government withdrawn from competition with industry.

3. Responsibility for relief of the needy should be returned to the States, which should receive Federal grants in proportion as the States contribute. This should be combined with a system of public works, such projects to be undertaken only on their merits.

4. The States should enact Old-Age Pension Laws for persons over 65 and the government make contributions to support such systems according as States contribute, but all such programs should be financed on a pay-as-you-go policy, by widely distributed taxation.

5. Labor's right to organize and bargain collectively through representatives of its own choosing without interference must be protected. State laws and interstate compacts should be undertaken to abolish sweatshops and child labor.

6. Scarcity economics should be abolished in agriculture; a national land use program should be pursued for the protection and restoration of land resources; experimental aid to farmers should be developed for production of new crops and promotions of new industrial uses of non-food crops; farmers protected from foreign importations. Farm credits at rates comparable with those in industry should be fostered together with decentralized non-partisan control of the farm credit administration. A form of subsidy should be instituted to take care of exportable surpluses with benefits based on the domes-

Continued on Page Fourteen

NOMINATED FOR PRESIDENT
Alfred Mossman Landon

© New York Times Studio Photo.

The Text of the Platform

Special to THE NEW YORK TIMES.

CLEVELAND, June 11.—Following is the text of the party platform as adopted by the Republican National Convention tonight:

America is in peril. The welfare of American men and women and the future of our youth are at stake. We dedicate ourselves to the preservation of their political liberty, their individual opportunity and their character as free citizens, which today for the first time in American history is threatened by government itself.

For three long years the New Deal administration has dishonored American traditions and flagrantly betrayed the pledges upon which the Democratic party sought and received public support.

The powers of Congress have been usurped by the President.

The integrity and authority of the Supreme Court have been flaunted.

The rights and liberties of American citizens have been violated.

Regulated monopoly has displaced free enterprise.

The New Deal administration constantly seeks to usurp the rights reserved to the State and to the people.

It has insisted on passage of laws contrary to the Constitution.

It has intimidated witnesses and interfered with the right of petition.

It has dishonored our country by repudiating its most sacred obligations.

It has been guilty of frightful waste and extravagance, using public funds for partisan political purposes.

It has promoted investigations to harass and intimidate American citizens, at the same time denying investigations into its own improper expenditures.

It has created a vast multitude of new offices, filled them with its favorites, set up a centralized bureaucracy and sent out swarms of inspectors to harass our people.

It has bred fear and hesitation in commerce and industry, thus discouraging new enterprises, preventing employment and prolonging the depression.

It secretly has made tariff agreements with our foreign competitors, flooding our markets with foreign commodities.

It has coerced and intimidated voters by withholding relief to those opposing its tyrannical policies.

It has destroyed the morale of many of our people and made them dependent upon government.

Appeals to passion and class prejudice have replaced reason and tolerance.

To a free people, these actions are insufferable. This campaign cannot be waged on the traditional differences between the Republican and Democratic parties.

The responsibility of this election transcends all previous political divisions. We invite all Americans, irrespective of party, to join us in defense of American institutions.

CONSTITUTIONAL GOVERNMENT AND FREE ENTERPRISE

We pledge ourselves:

1. To maintain the American system of constitutional and local self-government, and to resist all attempts to impair the authority of the Supreme Court of the United States, the final protector of the rights of our citizens against the arbitrary encroachments of the legislative and executive branches of government. There can be no individual liberty without an independent judiciary.

2. To preserve the American system of free enterprise, pri-

Continued on Page Fourteen

LANDON SENDS TELEGRAM

To Back Constitutional Amendment if States' Wage Laws Fail.

FOR GOLD AT PROPER TIME

In His Message to Convention He Specifies Exceptions in Accepting the Platform.

BORAH WINS HIS PLANKS

Vandenberg Is Expected to Be Vice Presidential Choice at Final Session Today.

By ARTHUR KROCK

Special to THE NEW YORK TIMES.

CLEVELAND, Ohio, June 11.—An unbossed Republican National Convention, yet working like a machine, at 11:41 o'clock tonight unanimously nominated Alfred M. Landon of Kansas for President, adopted unanimously a platform embracing certain social welfare ideas of the New Deal (which otherwise is excoriated) and seated party control in a group of young Kansas politicians and editors who entered the national political field less than two years ago.

At a final session tomorrow Arthur H. Vandenberg of Michigan is expected to accept the Vice Presidential nomination.

Eighteen Borah delegates from Wisconsin and the Senator's campaign manager (Delegate Carl G. Bachmann of West Virginia) voted for Mr. Borah on the first ballot, which prevented a nomination by acclamation under the rules. But Wisconsin then moved to make the nomination unanimous, and it was done.

Hamilton Reads Message

Two dramatic events colored the night session. Before John D. M. Hamilton, the chief of staff of the nominee, presented his name to the convention, he read at Mr. Landon's request a telegram from the Governor "interpreting" those planks of the platform and stating reservations. These planks, relating to currency, civil service and State control of wages and hours, had been revised by the resolutions committee from the text submitted by the Governor as a part of the week-long effort to placate Senator Borah and win his support in the campaign.

Governor Landon "interpreted" a "sound currency" to mean a currency eventually convertible into gold, insisted that the civil service should extend as far as the government's under-secretariat and pledged himself to support a constitutional amendment to permit State regulation of wages and hours if the statutory method were not effective. He said "in good conscience" he must make these intentions known in advance.

The other element of drama was when all the other Presidential candidates but Senator Borah, who had already left for Washington, took the platform and seconded the nomination of Mr. Landon. Mr. Borah is only fairly well-pleased with the platform, and he expects to survey Mr. Landon's speeches and the personnel of his campaign cabinet for a couple of months before deciding whether to support the candidacy. Herbert Hoover, the other eminent Republican whose opposition was feared by the Landon group, phoned here today that he was satisfied with the platform.

Senator Vandenberg was among those seconding the nomination. Colonel Knox, L. J. Dickinson, Robert A. Taft and Harry Nice, the other aspirants, followed.

Harmony the Landon Goal

Harmony among all Republicans and the support of anti-New Deal Democrats have all along been stated as the twin goals of the Landon managers, and, except for Mr. Borah, the harmony seems to have been effected.

The end of the session, amid a series of ecstatic demonstrations for Mr. Landon and Mr. Vandenberg, came after a day of anxious concern to the Kansas syndicate which, at midnight last night believed that all its worries were over, Mr. Landon's differences with the resolutions subcommittee, and with Mr. Borah, and the latter's objections to revision of planks he had seconded in the platform, caused the snarl.

But by 7 o'clock tonight, except

Continued on Page Twelve

Gov. Landon's Statement on Platform

Special to THE NEW YORK TIMES.

CLEVELAND, June 11.—Governor Landon, while approving most sections of the platform, sent the following message which was read to the convention before he was placed in nomination by John M. Hamilton:

To the delegates of the Republican National Convention:

My name is to be presented for your consideration as a candidate for the nomination for President of the United States. The platform recommended by your committee on resolutions and adopted by the convention has been communicated to me.

I note that according to the terms of the platform, the nomination tendered by this convention carries with it, as a matter of private honor and public good faith, an undertaking by each candidate to be true to the principles and program herein set forth.

If nominated, I unqualifiedly accept the word and spirit of that undertaking.

However, with that candor with which you and the country are entitled to expect of me, I feel compelled before you proceed with the consideration of my name to submit my interpretation of certain planks in the platform so that you may be advised as to my views. I could not in conscience do otherwise.

Under the title of Labor the platform commits the Republican party as follows:

"Support the adoption of State laws and interstate compacts to abolish sweatshops and child labor, and to protect women and children with respect to maximum hours, minimum wages, and working conditions. We believe that this can be done within the Constitution as it now stands."

I hope the opinion of the convention is correct that the aims which you have in mind may be attained within the Constitution as it now stands. But, if that opinion should prove to be erroneous, I want you to know that, if nominated and elected, I shall favor a constitutional amendment permitting States to adopt such legislation as may be necessary adequately to protect women and children in the matter of maximum hours, minimum wages and

working conditions. This obligation we cannot escape.

The convention advocates "a sound currency to be preserved at all hazards." I agree that "the first requisite is a sound and stable currency is a balanced budget."

The second requisite, as I view it, is a currency expressed in terms of gold and convertible into gold. I recognize, however, that the second requisite must not be made until and unless it can be done without penalizing our democratic economy and without injury to our producers of agricultural and other raw materials.

In carrying out this pledge I believe that there should be included within the merit system every position in the administrative service below the rank of assistant secretaries of major departments and agencies, and that this inclusion should cover the entire Postoffice Department.

ALF M. LANDON.

CONSTITUTIONAL GOVERNMENT AND FREE ENTERPRISE

We pledge ourselves:

1. To maintain the American system of constitutional and local self-government, and to resist all attempts to impair the authority of the Supreme Court of the United States, the final protector of rights of our citizens against the arbitrary encroachments of the legislative and executive branches of government. There can be no individual liberty without an independent judiciary.

2. To preserve the American system of free enterprise, pri-

Continued on Page Fourteen

The New York Times.

LATE CITY EDITION

Cloudy, possibly showers today, somewhat cooler. Tomorrow cloudy, possibly showers and cooler.
Temperature Yesterday—Max., 80; Min., 65

VOL. LXXXV....No. 28,644.

Entered as Second-Class Matter,
Postoffice, New York, N. Y.

NEW YORK, SATURDAY, JUNE 27, 1936.

PP

TWO CENTS In New York City. | THREE CENTS Within 200 Miles. | FOUR CENTS Elsewhere Except In 7th and 8th Postal Zones.

ROOSEVELT NOMINATED BY ACCLAMATION; DEMONSTRATIONS FOR HIM AND LEHMAN

RAIL PENSION LAW VOIDED BY COURT; WRIT HALTS TAXES

District of Columbia Court Rules 1935 Act and Its Tax Legislation Unconstitutional.

CITES FINDING ON 1934 LAW

Bailey Holds Supreme Court Decision on This Also Invalidates Substitute Measures.

CARRIERS WIN INJUNCTIONS

Federal Board Plans a Quick Appeal as 1,000,000 Workers Face Loss of the Benefits.

Text of Justice Bailey's decision on rail pensions is on Page 25.

By LOUIS STARK
Special to The New York Times.

WASHINGTON, June 26.—On grounds similar in part to those expounded by the United States Supreme Court majority on May 6, 1935, in invalidating the 1934 Railroad Retirement Act, Justice Jennings Bailey in the District of Columbia Supreme Court today declared unconstitutional the 1935 Railroad Pension Law and the companion tax measure, providing the levying and collection of taxes to finance railway men's pensions.

The Tax Act and the Pension Act itself were "inseparable," the two dovetailing "into one another so as to create a complete system," the court declared in the ruling.

The decision was the second blow delivered to the pension aspirations of a million railway workers in the last fourteen months, the Supreme Court having previously held the first Pension Law invalid as a violation of the due process clause of the Constitution.

The first decision was announced while the Social Security Act was pending, and gave rise to the question whether the taxation feature of the Social Security Act would stand up when attacked in the Supreme Court. Today's decision revived the doubts as to the constitutionality of the Social Security Act.

In today's decision, Justice Bailey stated that on Aug. 29, 1935, Congress had approved two acts, one creating a pension system for railway employees and the other levying an excise tax of 3½ per cent of the payrolls, to be paid by the carriers, and a similar tax to be deducted from the employes earning up to $300 a month.

Laws Held Interdependent

"The provisions of the two acts in question are so interrelated and interdependent that each is a necessary part of one entire scheme," the opinion stated. "This is not only apparent from the terms of the acts themselves but is shown by their legislative history. It was clearly the intention of Congress that the pension system created by the Retirement Act should be supported by the taxes levied upon the carriers and their employees."

Holding that the Taxing Act was unconstitutional, Justice Bailey said that it sought to collect revenue, not to provide for the expenses of government, "but solely for a purpose which the United States Supreme Court has held not to be within the domain of the Federal Government."

Whether the twenty-one standard railway unions would attempt to open direct negotiations with the Class I roads, which won a victory by the decision today, in an effort for an agreement on a voluntary pension arrangement, could not be ascertained in advance of early conferences among the unions.

Counsel Will Meet Judge

It was assumed that the decision would be appealed to the Supreme Court, but in the absence of Attorney General Cummings no statement was forthcoming from the Department of Justice.

Counsel for the Railroad Retirement Board and the Federal law officers will meet in Justice Bailey's chambers on Tuesday to draw up the formal court order.

The decision enjoined the Railroad Retirement Board from compelling the railroads to "assemble, compile or furnish any of the information and records required, or which may be required to be furnished under said Retirement Act."

It also enjoins Commissioner of Internal Revenue Guy T. Helvering.

Continued on Page Twenty-eight

Warships of Five Nations To Meet in Chilean Fete

Special Cable to The New York Times.

SANTIAGO, Chile, June 26.—Warships of five Latin American nations—Argentina, Brazil, Peru, Ecuador and Chile—will meet in Valparaiso Bay early in September, it was announced today.

They will be present to participate in celebrations marking the 400th anniversary of the founding of the city of Valparaiso.

The meeting is considered an excellent occasion to reawaken cordiality among Latin Americans.

A great display of Chile's air forces is contemplated.

DRUKMAN JURORS DEBATE FOR HOURS

Get Case Accusing Five of Plot in Brooklyn Murder at 2 P. M. and Sit Into the Morning.

POLICE GUARD JURY ROOM

Judge Holds Charges 'of Great Importance' and Menace to the Jury System.

By W. A. WARN
Special to The New York Times.

The Brooklyn blue ribbon jury which listened for four weeks to testimony in the Drukman conspiracy trial had not yet agreed, at 3:30 A. M. today, on verdicts for the five defendants charged with plotting to obstruct justice in the Samuel Drukman murder case.

Shortly before midnight the police cleared hundreds of persons out of the building and an army of scrub women took possession of the marble floors and corridors. The ousted crowds milled about in the street where ordinarily the sidewalks are deserted at that hour of the night. Scores of persons coming from the theatres drew up in taxicabs to get news.

At that time these had been no word from the jury room since the jurors returned from dinner. No persons were allowed above the ground floor of the building, except the uniformed court officers guarding the vicinity of the jury room. Justice Rogers had given no indication whether he would lock up the jury for the night.

Get Case at 2 P. M.

The jury had been deliberating, with time out for dinner, since 2 P. M. yesterday. Supreme Court Justice Erskine C. Rogers, presiding at the extraordinary term of the court, charged the jury for an hour and forty-five minutes in the morning. Then the jurors went out to lunch, and at 2 o'clock began their deliberations.

Shortly before 5 o'clock they sent two communications to the judge, one asking for testimony dealing with certain tapped-wire conversations and for the testimony of witnesses' whose name was kept during the week, partly contradicting each other, dealt with the State's charge that the defendant, William W. Klein, had been seen in an automo-

Continued on Page Seven

3 Guilty of Fraud, Fourth's Fate in Doubt In Failure of $81,000,000 Title Company

J. Crawford Stevens, president, and Reginald P. Ray, vice president, of the defunct Westchester Title and Trust Company, were found guilty at 12:20 A. M. today on all counts of a twenty-count mail fraud indictment by a Federal court jury which had deliberated for more than eight hours.

Philip H. Kuss, also a vice president, was found guilty on twelve of the twenty counts, and the jury failed to reach an agreement on the guilt or innocence of Frederick P. Condit, chairman of the executive committee, who is also a vice president and trustee of the Title Guarantee and Trust Company.

Judge Robert P. Patterson ordered the jury locked up for the night. It will continue its deliberation this morning on Condit.

Stevens and Ray face prison terms up to ninety-seven years and fines totaling $29,000 each, while Kuss is subject to imprisonment for up to fifty-seven years and fines totaling $12,000.

Shortly before midnight Judge Patterson called the jury into the court room and asked whether they had been able to approach a verdict Fletcher Swain, foreman, said that agreement had been reached regarding three of the defendants but that the jury was deadlocked as to the fourth. Judge Patterson then said that he would accept a

partial verdict and the jury retired to return about twenty minutes later.

Former Mayor John J. Fogarty, of Yonkers, representing Stevens and Kuss, and Monroe Cahn, attorney for Ray, objected strenuously to the court's procedure in accepting an incomplete verdict.

The Westchester Title and Trust Company failed in August, 1933, with $81,000,000 of its securities in the hands of the public. The trial has been in progress for more than seven weeks.

Of the twenty counts in the indictments, nineteen concerned the mailing of sales-promotion literature issued by the company which the government charges were misleading. The twentieth charged conspiracy. Some of the challenged statements were that mortgage certificates issued by the company were absolutely safe, completely proof and secured by Westchester County homes or improved property.

Judge Patterson pointed out that Mr. Condit was not a salaried officer of the company and was not active in its affairs. The jury's duty, he explained, was to determine only whether he participated in arranging for year-end loans in 15, and 1932 and whether, if he did so, he knew this was done to produce financial statements which might mislead the public.

LEHMAN FOR SOCIAL ISSUE

He Denounces 'Callous' Republican Fight on Security Plan.

'GHASTLY' PHILOSOPHY HIT

President's Program Is Held 'Most Humane Measure of Our Lifetime.'

'MIRACLE' UPTURN HAILED

Governor Also Predicts Fresh Business Expansion—He Will Confer With Roosevelt.

Text of Governor Lehman's seconding speech is on Page 7.

Special to The New York Times.

THE MUNICIPAL AUDITORIUM, PHILADELPHIA, June 26.—In one of the most impressive addresses of his public career, Governor Lehman of New York appeared before the Democratic National Convention tonight amid a great ovation to second the nomination of President Roosevelt on behalf of the President's and his own home State. He painted a picture of the reaction which would follow in the event of a Republican electoral victory this Autumn.

Governor Lehman said that in New York the Republicans in the Legislature had bitterly fought progressive measures, especially the social welfare legislation that had been recommended by himself and his immediate predecessor in the Governorship, now the President.

At no time did Governor Lehman mention former Governor Smith, with whom he has been on terms of warm friendship since he entered public life.

'Callous' Policies Scored

In his arraignment of Republican leaders in New York Governor Lehman described their policies as "cruel," "callous" and "reaction-ary," and declared that the social philosophy which inspired their action was undoubtedly the guiding star of Republican leaders in the nation.

Mr. Lehman declared that President Roosevelt had supplied leadership which was needed as never before when he took office and had lifted the country out of an abyss of despair and panic as by "a miracle." The Governor predicted that upon the foundation laid by the President there would be witnessed an expanding improvement in business during the present year.

"For the real progress that has been made, for the great economic reconstruction of this country, for the hope and confidence that again lie in the breasts of millions of our people—one man above all others deserves our gratitude—Franklin D. Roosevelt," Governor Lehman said. Governor Lehman met a charge

Continued on Page Seven

President Thanks Lehman, Hails Tribute to Him

Special to The New York Times.

MUNICIPAL AUDITORIUM, PHILADELPHIA, June 26.—President Roosevelt tonight sent the following telegram to Governor Lehman:

"I thank you, my old friend, from the bottom of my heart for all you said tonight.

"That wonderful tribute to you came from the hearts of every State, and you rightly deserved it. My love to you both.

"FRANKLIN D. ROOSEVELT."

The both includes Mrs. Lehman.

ROOSEVELT HINTS OF FARLEY DECISION

His Deferring of Reply Till End of Convention Is Construed as Forecasting Cabinet Change.

CLOSER TO PHILADELPHIA

President Keeps Telephone Busy—Acceptance Speech Will Dwell on Platform.

By CHARLES W. HURD
Special to The New York Times.

WASHINGTON, June 26.—President Roosevelt hinted today of early settlement of the question as to how long Postmaster General Farley would remain in the dual position of Cabinet member and chairman of the Democratic National Committee.

In response to a question at a White House press conference whether he was prepared to discuss Mr. Farley's expected resignation, President Roosevelt replied that he could not say anything until after the convention. His remark was construed as at least partial confirmation of reports that Mr. Farley would resign from the Cabinet in the near fu're.

Mr. Farley has remained in the Cabinet for more than two years since the President issued a dictum that party officials could not also hold government office, a rule which he enforced with severity except in the case of the party chairmen.

Keen Over Convention

The press conference, the President's last before he will go to Philadelphia tomorrow night to accept renomination, came in the midst of a day divided about equally between routine work on bills left by Congress and political work, including the polishing of his speech of acceptance.

The President was cheerful over the smooth running of the Philadelphia convention, but marks of fatigue on his face reflected the late and irregular hours he has kept during the week.

For the first time he admitted an active interest in the convention, saying that he had used the telephone at 1:30 this morning. Denying reports that memoranda on the final draft of the platform had been sent to him by airplane for approval, he laughingly asked newspaper correspondents if they did not agree that the telephone was a quicker means of communication.

His early morning call to Philadelphia was made to congratulate Senator Wagner, chairman of the resolutions committee, on his delivery of the platform before the convention. The radio brought it to the White House.

Mr. Roosevelt said that he also tried to reach Marvin H. McIntyre, one of his secretaries sent to Philadelphia as an observer, but was unable to do so at that hour.

Rough Draft Still "Too Rough"

As for the platform, much of which obviously was substantially written in advance of the convention with the close cooperation of, if not by, Mr. Roosevelt, he said that he had only read part of the final text.

What the President wishes to say publicly about the platform will constitute the main portion of his speech tomorrow night.

This speech, a comparatively brief document of about 2,000 words, was almost completed, having been dictated last night by the President, but he said that he probably would make several changes in it because the rough draft, in second reading this morning, appeared to be literally "too rough" in spots

In further conversation the President said that he intended to stay within the borders of the United States until after election and that there would be no cruises to Hawaii

Continued on Page Nine

DRAMA IN NIGHT SESSION

One Big Moment Is Held Back When Lehman Speech Is Delayed.

HE GETS TWO OVATIONS

Acclaim in Drafting Movement Rivals That for President as Name Is Ratified.

DOOLING LEADS PARADE

'It Was Swell,' Says Governor, but Gives No Intimation of What Answer Will Be.

By TURNER CATLEDGE
Special to The New York Times.

THE MUNICIPAL AUDITORIUM, PHILADELPHIA, Saturday, June 27.—With two prolonged demonstrations for Governor Herbert H. Lehman and another for President Roosevelt, the Democratic National Convention, at its session which ended nearly an hour after midnight this morning, attempted by a frank show of its enthusiasm to tie together the personalities of these two leaders for the campaign.

When the convention adjourned at 12:55 this morning until 10 A. M. today, it was in the midst of an ovation to President Roosevelt. It was the second given him during the day—his two sessions, the other, lasting an hour and four minutes, being when he was placed in nomination in the afternoon.

The first outburst for Governor Lehman rivaled anything seen at this convention. It came when Chairman Robinson announced at about 10 P. M. that the New York Governor would take the rostrum to second the nomination of President Roosevelt.

Culmination of "Draft" Move

It was the culmination of the "draft Lehman" movement which started even before this convention began and which last night saw every State, Territory and district represented here join in a concerted movement to add what they all considered a "dynamo of strength" to the Democratic ticket next Fall.

The demonstration was started by the New York delegation, led by James J. Dooling, leader of Tammany; Frank V. Kelly, Brooklyn leader; Senator Robert F. Wagner, and Borough President James J. Lyons of the Bronx. Just behind came George Gordon Battle. The New Yorkers were smiling and shouting as they were joined by delegates from other States.

The instant Governor Lehman's name was mentioned by Senator Robinson, permanent chairman of the convention, the delegates, alternates and spectators literally exploded with enthusiasm. They had been waiting impatiently for nearly an hour while representatives of other States paid their respects to the candidacy of Mr. Roosevelt.

Lehman Stops the Outburst

As Mr. Lehman raised his voice, however, the demonstration quickly subsided. The concerted applause eleven minutes and might have gone on for an hour had it not been halted.

The New York delegation started a new demonstration for Governor Lehman after he had completed his speech. The Buffalo women's drum and bugle corps started playing again and the "Lehman Must Run" banners began moving in all sections of the hall.

Chairman Robinson rapped for order and tried to stop it. He wanted to proceed with the seconding speeches and was ready to present Mrs. Emma Guffey Miller of Pennsylvania, but the New Yorkers kept parading. Alabama joined in, then followed Pennsylvania, Minnesota, Texas, Kansas—headed by a banner making light of Governor Landon's claims of balancing the budget—a delegate bearing the standard of the National Colored Democratic Association, North Dakota, Michigan, the Virgin Islands and others. Other delegations waved their standards.

The second Lehman demonstration continued for ten minutes be-

Continued on Page Eight

RENOMINATED FOR PRESIDENT
Franklin Delano Roosevelt,
from a photograph for which he posed at the White House last Saturday.
© Photo by New York Times Studio.

OUTBURSTS ALARM PROF. CEREBELLUM

Psychiatrist Diagnoses Campaignomania Which Affects Delegates at Times.

By F. RAYMOND DANIELL
Special to The New York Times.

THE MUNICIPAL AUDITORIUM, PHILADELPHIA, June 26.—Campaignomania, an occupational disease common to politicians at recurrent intervals, notably in Presidential years, broke out on the floor of people believe in Providence today and spread rapidly until a large proportion of the visitors in the balconies was infected.

Isolated cases of the malady have been noted among the delegates since they began assembling here early this week but the outbreak did not reach epidemic proportions until this afternoon, when the magic name of Franklin Delano Roosevelt fell from the lips of John E. Mack into the cluster of microphones before him.

The symptoms were recognized and the diagnosis provided by Professor Cerebrus Cerebellum, a noted psychiatrist from Brownsmittle, Brown County, Ind., close friend of those other Brown countians, Godfrey Gloom and Abe Martin, who once remarked that a "lot of people believe in Providence who never heard of Rhode Island."

As the professor explained it, campaignomania is a disease characterized by more or less violent manifestations of short duration. There is no immunization against it, he said, and the more dignified statesmen are especially susceptible to its ravages at convention time.

Case History Is Revealing

In the interest of science, the professor suggested that a detailed and objective study of the apparent aberrations of reflexes of the patients be made and published for the benefit of students of psychiatry and politics. Therefore the following:

At 2:22 P. M. when Mr. Mack mentioned the name of Mr. Roosevelt, the delegates and guests were slumped in their seats, listening politely and to all outward appearances behaving like perfectly normal average citizens.

A second later the entire scene had changed from a relatively dignified assemblage of patriots to one resembling what might take place in the psychopathic ward of a great

Continued on Page Nine

GARNER ON SCENE, MET WITH ACCLAIM

Vice President Passes Through Cheering Crowds From Station to His Hotel.

By CHARLES R. MICHAEL
Special to The New York Times.

PHILADELPHIA, June 26.—Jovial Jack Garner, Vice President, arrived here at 7 o'clock tonight to participate with President Roosevelt in the notification ceremonies tomorrow night. Escorted by 175 mounted policemen from the Thirtieth Street station, he was cheered by the crowds, whose attention was attracted by shrieking sirens as he and the reception committee proceeded to his hotel. He acknowledged the acclaim from the side walks by standing up in his car.

At the hotel the Texas delegates, massed in the street under the Lone Star station, gave him a rousing welcome.

Mr. Garner was met at the station by a committee composed of Attorney General Cummings, Postmaster General Farley, Senator Robinson and Connally and Governor and Mrs. Earle. As he left his car he turned to the captain commanding the police escort and said: "I have never seen a better lot of officers than you have here. You remind me of the Texas Rangers and your presence makes it home-like."

Is Guest at Reception

The Vice President attended a reception given in his honor by the Texas delegation and later participated briefly in the dinner of the Young Democrats. He did not make a speech and tarried only long enough to greet them. He told them as he left that the future of the country and the Democratic party depended upon their efforts.

Mr. Garner spent the evening in his hotel chatting with old friends. Many came to visit him. He will not make any public appearance until tomorrow night, when he is scheduled to accept renomination for the Vice Presidency before President Roosevelt makes his acceptance speech.

Since becoming Vice President, Mr. Garner has refrained from discussing public questions. He remained true to that policy tonight and declined to comment upon the platform.

He, however, did discuss the political questions with Chairman Farley and other Democratic chieftains

Continued on Page Nine

ENTHUSIASM RUNS HIGH

Eight Hours of Oratory Precede Acclamation in Early Morning.

CHEER PRESIDENT AN HOUR

Delegates in Ecstatic Climax When Name Is Presented to Convention by Mack.

LEHMAN TOPS SECONDERS

Received So Enthusiastically as to Leave No Doubt of Desire That He Run Again.

Text of former Justice Mack's nominating speech is on Page 6.

By ARTHUR KROCK
Special to The New York Times.

THE MUNICIPAL AUDITORIUM, PHILADELPHIA, Saturday, June 27.—After more than eight hours of eulogistic oratory and demonstrations, which kept the Democratic National Convention in session from 1 P. M. yesterday until 12:55 o'clock this morning, Franklin Delano Roosevelt was renominated for re-election by acclamation. Vice President Garner will share equally honored this afternoon.

Fifty-seven speeches were made by the orators in the seconding talkathon, representing every State, the District of Columbia. They included twelve Governors, eight Senators, one Senator-elect, eight women, a Cabinet officer and the Governor of the Philippine Islands, Senator McAdoo, who took the chair, also spoke in favor of the nomination but his was not strictly a seconding speech.

On motion of Governor Berry of South Dakota the rules were suspended and the roll-call was dispensed with, the nomination coming at 12:42 A. M.

Final, Noisy Celebration

Senator Robinson's announcement from the platform that the President had been chosen by acclamation—thus "beating Cleveland"—loosed another and the final demonstration of the all-day, all-night session. It was just like the rest and was still in progress when the chairman heard, put and declared passed a motion to recess until 10 o'clock this morning—an action unknown to nearly all the shouting, parading, horn-tooting demonstrators.

Rarely has the flow of harmonious oratory been equaled in a national political gathering as a few conservatives joined a long parade of New Dealers in extolling the President. Going a step beyond the Republican convention at Cleveland two weeks ago, the Philadelphia delegates cast not a single vote against Mr. Roosevelt. And West Virginia kept Governor Alf M. Landon from enjoying the same distinction.

Much more exciting than the actual nomination was a series of tumultuous uprisings to honor Governor Herbert H. Lehman of New York, who made the chief seconding speech at 10 o'clock last night. The effort was in part prearranged to convince Mr. Lehman that he must stand for re-election. At the same time a great deal of it was spontaneous and sincere. When Mr. Lehman was finally permitted to leave the platform he received a telegram of thanks from the President at Washington. Though beset with importunities, he declined to admit any change in his intention to retire.

Stresses President's Record

The Governor stressed the President's bent and record on behalf of social welfare, and by his scathing attack upon the Republican leadership at Albany, intimated what the chief campaign issue in that State will be if the Democrats can make it so.

When the President's name was formally proposed by John E. Mack of Poughkeepsie, who rendered the same service in 1932, a demonstration of more than an hour's duration interrupted the proceedings. Whatever the feelings of many Democrats who will go along this year for a number of reasons, and some of whom excused themselves from participation in the oratory of the day, there is no doubt that the tumult expressed the feeling of the overwhelming majority of the delegates.

Although a fair percentage of the

Continued on Page Eight

"All the News That's Fit to Print."

The New York Times.

FINAL EXTRA
Rain and much colder today. Tomorrow fair, with little change in temperature.
Temperature Yesterday—Max. 76; Min. 65

Copyright, 1936, by The New York Times Company.

VOL. LXXXVI....No. 28,774.   Entered as Second-Class Matter, Postoffice, New York, N. Y.   NEW YORK, WEDNESDAY, NOVEMBER 4, 1936.   TWO CENTS In New York City. | THREE CENTS Within 200 Miles. | FOUR CENTS Elsewhere Except in 7th and 8th Postal Zones.

ROOSEVELT SWEEPS THE NATION; HIS ELECTORAL VOTE EXCEEDS 500; LEHMAN WINS; CHARTER ADOPTED

FEW HOUSE SHIFTS

Democrats May Add to Vast Majorities in Both Chambers

THREE SENATORS TRAIL

Barbour, Hastings and Metcalf Appear to Have Lost Seats.

90 HOUSE RACES IN DOUBT

Democrats Elect 254, While Republicans Obtain 84, and Progressives 3.

By TURNER CATLEDGE

Republican hopes of making heavy inroads upon the huge Democratic majorities in Congress were apparently smothered under the pro-Roosevelt landslide in yesterday's election.

As the size of the New Deal avalanche continued to grow into the early morning hours the Democrats gave promise of actually increasing their lop-sided majority in the Senate and were offsetting Republican gains of new House seats by capturing places won by anti-New Dealers. If the trend of the count persists in the tardy tabulations today the Democrats may hold their own or actually add to their majorities in both branches of Congress.

In the wreckage left by the Democratic sweep also appeared the Senatorial careers of three outstanding Republican Senators—Barbour of New Jersey, Hastings of Delaware and Metcalf of Rhode Island. As the count from their respective States stood early today these three incumbents appeared defeated.

Moreover, the Democrats threatened to pick up still another Republican Senate seat, that formerly occupied by the late Senator Couzens, and they were pressing hard upon Senator Lester J. Dickinson of Iowa, whose opposition to the administration's farm relief program won for him the enmity of many farmers in his State.

Lodge Leading Curley

The only present Democratic Senate seat which appeared definitely lost to the Democrats was that held by Senator Marcus Coolidge of Massachusetts. Henry Cabot Lodge 2d, Republican, was well ahead of former Governor James M. Curley for this post, despite the State's substantial majority for the remainder of the Democratic national and State ticket.

Still another Democratic berth was threatened. Senator W. J. Bulow, Democrat, was trailing Chandler Gurney, Republican, by a slight margin in South Dakota.

The veteran Senator Norris, who left the Republican fold to stand for re-election as an Independent in Nebraska, was increasing his lead over former Representative Robert G. Simmons, Republican, and Terry Carpenter, "regular" Democrat.

Representative Ernest Lundeen, Farmer-Labor candidate, was piling up a commanding lead over former Governor Theodore Christianson, Republican, in Minnesota.

Senator Borah, Republican dean of the Senate, was doing the same to his opponent, Governor C. Ben Ross, Democrat.

As the Senate count stood early today, the Democrats appeared to have elected twenty of the thirty-five Senators who were up for election this year and the Republican six, while ten were still in doubt. On this showing the Democrats would have a membership of at least sixty-seven Democrats in the new Congress. The Republicans, seventeen, and the Progressives two. The Democrats stood a good chance to pick up still others out of the ten in

Continued on Page Three

Landon Congratulates President, Who Replies

Special to The New York Times.

TOPEKA, Wednesday, Nov. 4.—Governor Landon conceded his defeat in a message of congratulation to President Roosevelt at 1:30 o'clock this morning, Eastern standard time.

His message read as follows:

"The nation has spoken. Every American will accept the verdict and work for the common cause for the good of our country. That is the spirit of democracy. You have my sincere congratulations."

"ALF M. LANDON."

Governor Landon decided to send the message after he had retired for the night at the Executive Mansion, with the word that no statement would be issued during the night.

Special to The New York Times.

HYDE PARK, N. Y., Wednesday, Nov. 4.—Half an hour after receiving Governor Landon's message President Roosevelt sent the following reply:

"I am grateful to you for your generous telegram and I am confident that all of us Americans will now pull together for the common good. I send you every good wish."

UNION PARTY VOTE FAR BELOW BOASTS

Coughlin Group Appears to Have Exercised Little Influence on the Electorate.

SUPPORT OF LEMKE WEAK

Even in Ohio and South Dakota His Showing in the Early Returns Is Poor.

By F. RAYMOND DANIELL

Representative William Lemke, the Presidential candidate of the so-called "radical fringe," made scarcely a dent in the great total the nation piled up for President Roosevelt and Alfred M. Landon in yesterday's voting.

Showing his greatest strength in Illinois, Pennsylvania and Massachusetts, the North Dakota Representative, who had the backing of the Rev. Charles E. Coughlin, Dr. Francis E. Townsend and the Rev. Gerald L. K. Smith, still remained a negligible factor in the outcome of the election.

Despite confident predictions by the Union party's backers last August that Mr. Lemke would take enough votes from Mr. Roosevelt to deprive him of a majority in the Electoral College, thus throwing the election into the House of Representatives, nowhere did he poll a substantial enough vote to hurt either major party candidate.

In his home State of North Dakota the co-author of the Frazier-Lemke bill was trailing far behind the President and his Republican opponent. The first seventy-eight precincts reporting gave Mr. Lemke only 1,380 to Mr. Roosevelt's 11,644 and Mr. Landon's 5,333.

Here in New York, Father Coughlin's candidate for the House of Representatives in the Sixteenth Assembly District was snowed under. He was former State Senator John A. Hastings, an intimate friend of former Mayor James J. Walker. His opponent was Representative John J. O'Connor, who incurred Father Coughlin's wrath by threatening to kick the priest of Royal Oak from the Capitol to the White House. Mr. O'Connor seemed an easy winner in the Seventh.

Two reasons were advanced to explain the failure of Mr. Lemke to make a better showing. The first was that Father Coughlin, the Rev. Mr. Smith and Dr. Townsend were all inflationists when it came to estimating the size of their following, which each placed in the neighborhood of 4,000,000 voters. The second was that the men and women who cheered them so loudly at the Cleveland convention of the National Union for Social Justice and the Old Age Revolving Pensions Ltd., became Republicans and Democrats again after returning home.

The early vote for Representative William Lemke, even in States where Father Coughlin's National Union for Social Justice boasts a

Continued on Page Five

BIG CHARTER VOTE

8-Hour System for Firemen Also Wins Easily

VOTING CHANGE APPROVED

Brunner Is Victor Over Morris by Large Plurality.

ROOSEVELT SWEEP HERE

President's Vote and Margin, Which Reached 1,356,458, Set Highest City Record.

By RUSSELL B. PORTER

President Roosevelt piled up the largest vote and plurality for any office in the history of New York City at yesterday's election.

With all the city's 3,799 election districts in, the President had the extraordinary plurality of 1,356,458, which was considerably larger even than his campaign managers had estimated.

This was about 50 per cent larger than his 1932 plurality and about three times former Governor Alfred E. Smith's city plurality when he ran against Herbert Hoover in 1928.

The total Presidential vote was 2,747,240, or over 500,000 more than the total vote cast in the 1932 Presidential election and the 1933 Mayoralty election, the previous records.

Governor Lehman ran behind the President, but had a plurality of 921,938 with no election districts missing. He ran about 2 to 1 ahead of William F. Bleakley, his Republican opponent, while President Roosevelt's ratio was 3 to 1 over Governor Landon. Governor Lehman's plurality was not as large as in 1932, when it was 989,844, but was larger than two years ago, when it was 803,956.

Brunner an Easy Winner

In the day's only election for city office, William F. Brunner, Democrat, had a final plurality of 891,880 over Newbold Morris, Republican, in the contest for president of the Board of Aldermen, with no election districts missing.

The voters approved all three local questions on which referenda were taken. They accepted the new city charter by 927,396 to 583,-044, an affirmative majority of 344,354, with 689 election districts missing.

With 78 election districts missing, they voted 896,389 for and 551,914

Continued on Page Five

Smith Plans Comment On the Election Today

Alfred E. Smith, former Democratic candidate for President who espoused the cause of Alfred M. Landon in this campaign said last night that he probably would issue a statement today setting forth his views on President Roosevelt's sweeping victory.

Earlier in the evening he had called The New York Times to ask how the election was going. He was informed that President Roosevelt was leading in all but a handful of States. He made no comment but when he was asked if he were going to a party of Jeffersonian Democrats in the apartment of Raoul Desverine, Liberty League lawyer, to which he had been invited, he replied:

"No, I'm going to bed."

P. S.—The former Governor did not retire at once. He called up an hour later to get the latest returns.

DEMOCRATS RETAIN STATE SENATE LEAD

They Are Assured of 30 Seats of the 51, One More Than Their Previous Number.

FAIL TO WIN ASSEMBLY

Republicans Are Beaten for Five Places, but Still Hold a Bare Working Majority.

By W. A. WARN

The Democrats will control the State Senate by a substantial majority and the Republicans will have a bare working majority in the Assembly, according to complete returns from the legislative elections.

The latest returns give the Democrats thirty seats out of fifty-one in the Senate, a net gain of one over their present quota. The Republicans suffered a loss of five seats in the Assembly, but still retain seventy-six seats, which gives them the constitutional majority necessary to pass bills and prevail on important parliamentary motions.

The result in not a few of the districts, however, on the face of the latest returns was so close that in some instances a demand may be made by the losers for recount proceedings.

This city will lose its only Republican Senator through the defeat of Senator Joseph C. Baldwin 3d in the Seventeenth Senatorial District, situated in Manhattan. Leon A. Fischel, Democrat, carried the district by a plurality somewhat below 5,000.

The Democratic solidarity of Albany County in its legislative representation was again manifested. A Republican candidate for Assembly, John McBain, nominated in

Continued on Page Five

LEHMAN VOTE CUT

Bleakley Gets a Surprising Total in the City

SWEEP HELPS GOVERNOR

Roosevelt Strong in Industrial Cities—Gets Big Up-State Poll.

OTHER DEMOCRATS SAFE

Bray, Tremaine, Bennett and Others of State Ticket Regarded Certain of Victory.

By JAMES A. HAGERTY

Governor Herbert H. Lehman was re-elected Governor of New York yesterday for a third term. The indicated plurality for the Governor over former Supreme Court Justice William F. Bleakley, his Republican opponent, was about 600,000.

Governor Lehman, who was urged to become a candidate for re-election to help President Roosevelt, ran far behind the President in New York City. With all the election districts reported, his plurality in New York City was 921,938 as compared with the city plurality of 1,356,458, or more than the million and a quarter predicted by Postmaster General Farley, for President Roosevelt. President Roosevelt's plurality in the State was indicated at about 1,150,000.

The tremendous vote for President Roosevelt in New York City and the failure of Governor Landon to carry up-State by much more than 200,000 indicated that the defection of former Governor Alfred E. Smith and other Jeffersonian Democrats had little effect on the Presidential vote, although there apparently were influences within the Democratic party working against Governor Lehman in New York City.

With New York City complete and 480 election districts missing out of 5,151 up-State, the vote for President was:

	Roosevelt.	Landon.
Up-State	1,197,201	1,370,516
New York City	2,016,204	659,746
Totals	3,213,405	2,030,262

Actual plurality for Roosevelt, 1,183,143.

With New York City complete and 892 election districts missing up-State, the vote for Governor was:

	Lehman.	Bleakley.
Up-State	1,060,564	1,338,892
New York City	1,795,124	873,186
Totals	2,855,688	2,212,078

Actual plurality for Lehman, 643,610.

The tremendous vote for President Roosevelt swept to victory the other State-wide Democratic candidates for re-election, Lieut. Gov. M. William Bray, Controller Morris S. Tremaine, Attorney General John J. Bennett Jr., and Mrs. Caroline O'Day and Matthew J. Merritt, Representatives at Large.

Incomplete returns also indicated the election of Harlan W. Rippey, Democratic candidate for Associate Judge of the Court of Appeals over Supreme Court Justice James P. Hill, Republican candidate.

City Margin Is Unprecedented

President Roosevelt carried New York City by the unprecedented plurality of 1,356,458, the total vote being 2,016,204 for the President and 659,746 for Governor Landon. This was more than 50,000 in excess of the results forecast in the surveys made by the five Democratic county leaders, which they believed should be scaled down 10 per cent to give the probable result.

Governor Lehman's New York City plurality increased with the late returns, and he did not run as far behind the President as the early returns had indicated he would do.

With all election districts reporting, the vote for Governor in New

Continued on Page Three

©New York Times Studio Photo.

FRANKLIN D. ROOSEVELT

DEMOCRATS SWEEP ALL PENNSYLVANIA

President Wins by More Than 550,000 in First National Party Victory in 70 Years.

PHILADELPHIA IS CARRIED

Whole State Government and the Legislature Go to Democratic Control.

Special to The New York Times.

PHILADELPHIA, Wednesday, Nov. 4.—Pennsylvania, the Keystone State of Republicanism, was swept yesterday by the Democrats for the first time in a Presidential election since the Civil War era.

With unprecedented Democratic pluralities in Philadelphia and Allegheny Counties, with greatly diminished Republican pluralities in the commuting counties about Philadelphia, and with even the rural districts only half heartedly Republican, President Roosevelt carried the State by a margin which exceeded 550,000 votes.

Returns from 6,733 of the State's 8,010 divisions gave:

Roosevelt	2,010,343.
Landon	1,469,679.
Lemke	44,258.

Complete returns from the 1,391 divisions in this city gave:

Roosevelt	521,941.
Landon	222,229.

City plurality of 199,712 exceeds that for Herbert Hoover in 1932 for the whole State by 40,000.

The Democratic victory, the exact proportions of which amazed even the leaders of that party, not only gave to President Roosevelt this State's thirty-six electoral votes, but put the State government wholly in the hands of the Democrats.

Democrats Get Legislature

George H. Earle in 1934 seized the Governorship for the Democrats for the first time in forty-four years. The crowd remained for half an hour, with some enthusiastic persons shouting "How about 1940?" Governor Lehman's office he has had the past four years, but with an odds constantly with a Republican-controlled State Senate, which has succeeded in balking many of his plans for putting a "little New Deal" in effect in Pennsylvania.

As a result of yesterday's election

Continued on Page Three

JERSEY'S 16 VOTES SAFE FOR NEW DEAL

Upsets in Republican Areas Add to Huge Pluralities in Democratic Counties.

SMATHERS SEEMS WINNER

Senate Aspirant Runs Behind Roosevelt but Has Lead Over Barbour, Incumbent.

New Jersey's sixteen electoral votes seemed at 5 o'clock this morning in possession of President Roosevelt. Reports from 1,719 of the State's 3,361 election districts gave him 493,071 votes to 295,794 for Governor Landon.

Hudson County, the great Democratic stronghold run by the State leader, Mayor Frank Hague of Jersey City, was responsible for the tremendous lead in what had been a doubtful State until the count began. It seemed quite likely that, although Mr. Landon made gains in other areas, he never could overcome the Hudson County handicap, particularly since several normally powerful Republican communities deserted Landon for Roosevelt.

Keeping pace with President Roosevelt in the Democratic triumph, but dropping behind him in many Republican sections which the President dominated, State Senator William H. Smathers, Democrat, had in 1,656 districts a total of 404,546 for United States Senator.

His Republican opponent, W. Warren Barbour, the incumbent, was gathering many hundreds here and there, outside Hudson County, having a total in the same districts of 297,000. Though this seemed difficult lead to overcome, Mr. Barbour was quite confident that the great number of unreported districts would offset the absentee advantage and pull him through for another stay in Washington.

Even Mayor Hague's prediction of 125,000 plurality in Hudson County as to give him a happy surprise. In 549 districts out of 656 in that county, the President received 204,

Continued on Page Eleven

POLL SETS RECORD

Roosevelt Electoral Vote of 519 Seen as a Minimum

NO SWING TO THE BOLTERS

'Jeffersonian Democrats' Fail to Cause Rift as Expected.

NEIGHBORS HAIL PRESIDENT

Landon Concedes Defeat and Sends His Congratulations to Victorious Rival.

By ARTHUR KROCK

Accepting the President as the issue, nearly eight million more voters than ever before had gone to the polls in the United States—about 45,000,000 persons—yesterday gave to Franklin Delano Roosevelt the most overwhelming testimonial of approval ever received by a national candidate in the history of the nation.

Except for the small corner of New England occupied by Maine, Vermont and New Hampshire—which was oscillating between Republican and Democratic in the early morning hours of Wednesday—the President was the choice of a vast preponderance of the voters in all parts of the country, and with him were re-elected as Vice President John N. Garner of Texas and an almost untouched Democratic majority in the House of Representatives. The Democratic national ticket will have a minimum of 519 electoral votes and a possible popular majority of ten millions.

As the size of the President's victory grew through the morning hours it seemed that only Maine, Vermont and New Hampshire would be entered in the Republican column, giving the President 519 of the 531 electoral votes, to which the four of New Hampshire may be added:

Landon Sends Congratulations

After hours of hopeful waiting on rural States, Mr. Landon and the Republicans in the Northeast States, and their national chairman, John D. M. Hamilton, announced their intentions of letting the night pass before agreeing to the fact of the stupendous party defeat. But about 1 A. M. in Topeka, Mr. Landon sent the customary message of congratulation to the President of Hyde Park, and at 1:45 A. M., at headquarters in Chicago, Mr. Hamilton followed suit. All the important newspapers supporting the Republican ticket (about 80 per cent of the metropolitan and country

Continued on Page Three

Roosevelt, Speaking to Victory Procession At Hyde Park, Predicted Record Sweep

By CHARLES W. HURD

HYDE PARK, Nov. 3.—With wire returns indicating a landslide for President Roosevelt far in excess of the majority necessary to re-elect him, President Roosevelt said tonight that he thought the "sweep" might carry every section of the United States.

Speaking to several hundred loyal followers who staged a victory procession through rain from Hyde Park to Mr. Roosevelt's home, Hyde Park House, at 10:30 P. M., he said:

"The returns are not all in yet, so I can't say anything official or final, but it looks as though we are going to have one of the largest sweeps ever heard of in the United States."

"As a matter of fact, from the returns now, it looks as though this sweep has carried every single section of the country," he exclaimed.

The President, laughing and happy, spoke while standing on the open porch of his house, looking out over a crowd whose faces were illuminated by the calcium flares used for light for motion pictures.

He waved aside sound microphones, saying: "This is just a home party."

The crowd cheered the President, Mrs. Roosevelt, his mother, Mrs. Sara Delano Roosevelt.

The assemblage cheered loudly when Mr. Roosevelt said one of his happiest moments came with the word that he had carried the village of Hyde Park, although he lost the township.

The crowd remained for half an hour, with some enthusiastic persons shouting "How about 1940?" Mr. Roosevelt leaned on the arm of his son, Franklin Jr. Beside him were his wife and daughter. Grouped behind him were a small party including his daughter, Mrs. Anna Boettiger, and Mr. Boettiger, Mrs. James Roosevelt, her daughter-in-law, and other relatives.

Others in the party included the secretary and Mrs. Marguerite Le-Hand, and Mrs. Sam Rosenman, Frederick A. Delano and others of the White House staff and several newspaper correspondents.

Continued on Page Five

"All the News That's Fit to Print."

The New York Times.

LATE CITY EDITION
Cloudy, mild, with occasional rain today; clearing, colder tonight.
Tomorrow colder.
Temperature Yesterday—Max. 52; Min. 39

Copyright, 1936, by The New York Times Company.

VOL. LXXXVI....No. 28,811.

Entered as Second-Class Matter,
Postoffice, New York, N. Y.

NEW YORK, FRIDAY, DECEMBER 11, 1936.

P

TWO CENTS In New York City. | THREE CENTS Within 200 Miles. | FOUR CENTS Elsewhere Except in 7th and 8th Postal Zones.

EDWARD VIII RENOUNCES BRITISH CROWN; YORK WILL SUCCEED HIM AS GEORGE VI; PARLIAMENT IS SPEEDING ABDICATION ACT

CODE FOR INDUSTRY VOTED HERE TO BACK AIMS OF NEW DEAL

Association of Manufacturers Pledges Cooperation for 'Era of Good Feeling.'

ASKS FOR CENSUS OF IDLE

Moley Urges Business Join in Federal Planning—McCarl for Industrial Board.

LABOR GIVES 30-HOUR PLAN

Industrial Progress Council in Washington Hears Program for a Shorter Week.

Industry and New Deal

The National Manufacturers Association meeting here adopted a code for industry pledging cooperation with social aims of New Deal. The text of the code is on Page 30.

The Council for Industrial Progress in Washington heard labor's plan to promote employment by a thirty-hour week and Federal regulation of working conditions. Employers did not oppose new labor laws, but spokesmen insisted that they should conform to the Constitution. Page 33.

Code Is Adopted Here

A declaration of principles for American industry, calling for an era of good feeling both at home and abroad, pledging cooperation with the government in the national interest and embracing, at least in principle, some of the most important social reforms of the New Deal, was adopted yesterday afternoon at the final session of the forty-first annual convention of the National Association of Manufacturers, held in the Waldorf-Astoria Hotel.

The declaration was in harmony with the keynote speech delivered at Wednesday's session by Colby M. Chester, chairman of the General Foods Corporation and president of the association, and in striking contrast to the bitter criticism of the New Deal uttered by industrialists at previous meetings.

In closing the convention Mr. Chester asserted his belief that it had "written a new, sound and progressive note in the industrial life of this nation in its declaration of principles," and predicted that it would have the support of "a united industry" within the year.

Census of Idle Is Urged

Resolutions were adopted urging a government census of unemployed and opposing governmental ownership of the railroads or any transportation system.

Addresses were made by Raymond Moley, editor of the magazine Today; John R. McCarl, former Controller General; George H. Mead, president of the Mead Corporation and chairman of the business advisory council to the Department of Commerce, and James A. Emery, general counsel of the association.

Mr. Moley urged joint economic planning by the government and business. He warned industry that it must recognize the meaning of the election returns—that the people voted for security of wages and living standards—and offered them a rational plan to attain these ends if it does not wish to be compelled to submit to impractical and drastic legislation.

A balanced budget through the reduction of relief expenditures and other government spending was advocated by Mr. McCarl. He urged industry to accept the responsibility for reducing the need for relief by giving more jobs. He also suggested that business organize a National Industrial Board to cooperate with the government in the "collective" solution of social and economic problems.

According to Mr. Mead, business wants "constructive cooperation," contrary to a general public impression, although it is opposed to "government ownership or control." Business also believes in economic security, he said, adding that a "practical" economic security and a "sentimental" one were different.

It is pertinent to recall that Mr.

Continued on Page Thirty-one

4,336,000,000 Francs Set As French Budget Deficit

Wireless to THE NEW YORK TIMES.

PARIS, Dec. 10.—There will be a deficit of 4,336,000,000 francs in the French budget during the coming year, according to figures put before the Chamber of Deputies this morning by the finance commission.

The ordinary expenditure under the budget is estimated at slightly more than 48,000,000,000 francs and the income at 43,685,000,000 francs. With these figures before them, the Deputies began to vote in rapid succession for most of the 140 articles in the law having to do with the collection of revenue despite the protest of one Right Deputy who argued that to vote revenues before expenditures was contrary to all good sense and logic.

JAPAN WITHDRAWS DEMANDS ON CHINA

Indicates Dropping of Moves for Anti-Red Cooperation and Autonomy of North China.

ARMY IS UNDER CRITICISM

Foreign Office Wants Public to Know the Military Interfere With Major Policies.

By HUGH BYAS
Wireless to THE NEW YORK TIMES.

TOKYO, Dec. 10.—Withdrawal of all the Japanese demands regarding North China autonomy and of that for cooperation against communism was implied in a statement issued to the press today by Eiji Amau, Foreign Office spokesman.

Japan asks Nanking to fulfill the agreements already reached on lesser points, but the request is not accompanied by a threat or warning except that if Japanese lives or property are endangered or Japanese rights violated the government will take "adequate measures."

Ambassador Shigeru Kawagoe's failure to obtain satisfaction from China, even in minor matters, is explained as due to Chinese indignation over the invasion of Suiyuan Province by Mongols and Manchukuoans.

Mr. Amau said nothing to connect the Japanese Kwantung Army with these events, but the public was already aware that Manchukuo's Premier had proclaimed sympathy with the Mongolian rising and knew he would not have taken such a step without being prompted.

Mr. Amau's statement, read in conjunction with Foreign Minister Hachiro Arita's answer to the Privy Council yesterday, suggested that the Foreign Office wants the public to know how the Kwantung army interferes with major policies on which all branches of the Tokyo government have agreed.

The statement claims that a definite agreement was reached with China regarding suppression of anti-Japanese movements—including revision of the control of the press and of Kuomintang (Nationalist party) branches—engagement of Japanese advisers, control of Korean exiles and reduction of tariffs.

Concession Involved

China further agreed to reopening of the Chengtu Japanese Consulate and accepted most of Japan's demands for settlement of recent incidents.

A hitch occurred over air services. No agreement was reached regarding joint defense against communism though both sides concurred on several items.

Economic cooperation in North China was agreed on in principle. This stage having been reached, the Chinese, "taking advantage of the Suiyuan affair," broke off negotiations, threatened to repudiate all the concessions already made and evaded Ambassador Kawagoe's repeated requests for a further interview with Foreign Minister Chang Chun. Mr. Kawagoe was said to have handed Mr. Chang a note embodying the agreed points, requesting that they be put into effect.

"Japan is now watchfully waiting for China's response and is prepared to take adequate measures if China fails to control anti-Japanese movements or if Japanese life and property interests are jeopardized," said the statement.

Continued on Page Twelve

CROWDS IN LONDON CALM

News Is Received With British Reserve as Thousands Gather.

QUEEN MARY IS CHEERED

Many Break Through Police Lines When She Calls at Home of Duke of York.

TENSION OF WEEK ENDED

People Sad at Losing Edward but Relieved the Suspense Is at Last Over.

Wireless to THE NEW YORK TIMES.

LONDON, Dec. 10.—As the news of King Edward's abdication sped to the far corners of the empire this afternoon Britain received confirmation of her worst fear with mixed emotions, sadness at losing so popular and valued a sovereign and relief that the gnawing suspense of the last week at last had drawn to an end.

Massed thousands stood silently outside the towering iron gates of Parliament while the terse, restrained statement of the first monarch in England's history ever to renounce the throne voluntarily was read to the House of Commons. Presently, as the twilight shadows of Westminster Abbey lengthened over Parliament Square, word sped from mouth to mouth that the reign of Edward was coming to an end.

Although the atmosphere a few minutes before had been highly charged with tension and anxiety the news was received calmly and with typical British reserve. There was no demonstration and no show of feeling save for the serious, strained faces in the crowd and the flutter of women's handkerchiefs here and there.

Crowds Gather Throughout Day

Throughout the day, from dawn until after midnight, crowds of varying proportions gathered outside all the buildings associated with the historic happenings of the day. People clustered about No. 10 Downing Street, the Houses of Parliament and all the royal residences, standing stolidly and silently when allowed or moving along without protest if required. If any emotion was perceptible that could be described as a corporate reaction, it was one of bewilderment and incredulity that such a thing ever could actually happen.

A throng composed mostly of women, which at times reached 10,000 or more, stood on the pavement before Buckingham Palace forming

Continued on Page Twenty

Edward Plans Radio Talk To British Empire Tonight

Special Cable to THE NEW YORK TIMES.

LONDON, Dec. 10.—King Edward will broadcast to the empire tomorrow night at 10 o'clock, immediately after he has signed the Abdication Act and ceased to be King, in the character of a private person. It is expected Parliament will have disposed of its business by then.

[American networks will broadcast the message at 5 P. M., Eastern Standard Time.]

The British Broadcasting Corporation has arranged for a worldwide hook-up.

Many persons feel the King's decision to broadcast is not wise. He has already sent a message to Parliament with a penciled note to the Prime Minister, commending the Duke of York on the support of the whole empire. These will be broadcast four times tonight and printed in every British newspaper.

MRS. SIMPSON CRIES LISTENING AT RADIO

Shaken and Exhausted by the Climax in Career of King Who Forsook Throne for Her.

WILL REMAIN AT CANNES

Edward Will Not Visit Her Now—Britons in France Question Her Course.

Wireless to THE NEW YORK TIMES.

CANNES, France, Dec. 10.—With tears streaming down her face, Mrs. Wallis Warfield Simpson, for whose sake Edward VIII has abdicated as King and Emperor of the greatest empire the world has ever known, listened today as did all the rest of the world to the news over the radio from the scene in the British Parliament.

She heard the words announcing that the King Emperor of whom she had been expected had laid down his scepter and crown so as to be free to marry her some months hence and live the life of an ordinary mortal.

Says King Won't Go to Riviera

At 1 o'clock this afternoon the following statement was made by Herman L. Rogers, at whose villa Mrs. Simpson is staying:

"There is definitely no change so far as Mrs. Simpson's plans are concerned. She will stay here until after Christmas. She is now at the villa and in the best of health. There has been no change in the household.

"It cannot be stated if she has

Continued on Page Twenty

BALDWIN TELLS OF EVENTS

Relates to the Commons How He Warned King Against Marriage.

DENIES ANY BITTERNESS

Says Ruler, Far From Feeling Resentment, Had Become a Firmer Friend to Him.

LEGAL ISSUE IS REFUTED

Churchill Declares It Is Now Clear That There Was Never a Constitutional Crisis.

By CHARLES A. SELDEN
Special Cable to THE NEW YORK TIMES.

LONDON, Dec. 10.—The momentous session of Parliament that received today King Edward's message of abdication was best described by Prime Minister Stanley Baldwin himself when he said near the close of his narrative of the crisis:

"This House of Commons today is a theatre which is being watched by the whole world."

Never since the first British Parliament was called by Simon de Montfort 672 years ago had the theatre for such an impressive tragedy as that enacted today.

There have been greater political issues, perhaps, and more fateful struggles between Crown and Commons. There have been long Parliaments, short Parliaments and rump Parliaments. But there has been no precedent for today's enactment of the tragedy in which a monarch signed away his sovereignty over an empire of 500,000,000 people for his love of a woman.

And while the play was on, the wars of one hemisphere and the efforts in the other hemisphere to end wars were merely side shows.

Extra Police on Hand

Standing room only was the situation in the legislative chamber itself, while there was not even standing room left in the acres of lobbies and for many blocks outside on the streets that lead to the Houses of Parliament.

So many extra companies of police were assigned to duty around the buildings that it was feared serious disorder was anticipated by the authorities, but nothing could have been further from the fact. There was as much decorum in witnessing this self-effacement of Edward VIII as there was last January when the multitudes gathered to mourn for his father and to proclaim him.

Needless to say, the House itself was filled as it had not been since cleared in 1914. In the diplomatic gallery, every seat was taken by Ambassadors and Ministers from nearly all nations.

What little daylight sometimes seeps into the Commons chamber on a Winter afternoon was completely shut out by a leaden mass of rain clouds, but there was nothing but mellow illumination from the lights above the stained glass ceiling.

House Is Ill at Ease

The House was ill at ease during the hour's interval prior to the great moment when Prime Minister Baldwin entered with the King's message of abdication. The familiar cry, "Prayers are over," after the customary, brief devotional exercise with which every session opens, was followed by many involuntary, at least unusual, "Amens," suggestive of a devout wish that for this once they might be answered quickly.

There were no "King's men" in the House. But it was equally true there were no anti-King men.

The King's own message was received with sorrow and sympathy. When Mr. Baldwin made his long statement of the events that preceded the decision to abandon the throne, there vanished the last trace of the bitterness that had developed in the last week from fear that the Crown might try to override the Commons.

"We are not judges," said Mr. Baldwin, and it was one of his utterances that survived many shocks before this will keep its place as the keystone of the vast and loosely jointed empire.

"While there is not a soul among us who will not regret this from the bottom of his heart," the said

Continued on Page Sixteen

SUCCESSOR TO THE BRITISH THRONE
The Duke of York
Associated Press Photo.

YORK GETS OVATION AT HOME IN LONDON

Cheering and Singing Theatre Crowds Surge About His Car While Auto Horns Salute.

HE DOFFS HAT TO THRONG

New Monarch Expected to Use Name 'George' as Symbol of Strength and Steadiness.

Special Cable to THE NEW YORK TIMES.

LONDON, Dec. 10.—Thousands of Londoners shouted a welcome tonight to a shy and awkward young man who was ready to step into the dazzling light of the greatest throne on earth.

With the abdication of King Edward VIII, the 41-year-old Duke of York was about to take his place on the world wide stage as the latest in the long line of English sovereigns. And tonight, in front of his town house at 145 Piccadilly, the crowds had their first chance to show him that they were glad.

A surging throng of theatre-goers on the way home surrounded his car as he returned after having discovered that Edward was about to be returned after having dined with Edward at Fort Belvedere. Cheering and waving hats, they filled the wide roadway in front of the house and blocked traffic so completely police were powerless to keep it moving.

Before the Duke entered the house he turned to the crowd and raised his hat several times. That was the signal for a great demonstration. Hundreds of motorists set up a deafening salute with their horns, while the crowd began singing the national anthem and "For He's a Jolly Good Fellow."

Popular Reign Indicated

It was a demonstration of some importance in the story of that British throne, for it showed that the Duke may be a popular King even without any of the brilliant qualities of his elder brother.

Tomorrow night he will welcome home King, and Saturday morning his accession will be proclaimed with the stately pageantry that has come down unchanged from medieval times. For individual living may come and go, but the British monarchy that has survived many shocks before this will keep its

Continued on Page Sixteen

EDWARD CHEERFUL AFTER TAKING STEP

Reported Like Man Who Has Had Crushing Load of Worry Lifted From Shoulders.

PACKS FOR HIS DEPARTURE

Knowledge That He Will Not Be Barred From Returning to England Relieves Him.

By FERDINAND KUHN Jr.
Wireless to THE NEW YORK TIMES.

LONDON, Dec. 10.—The blue and scarlet flag of the Duchy of Cornwall fluttered slowly to the foot of its mast at 10 o'clock this morning on the high turret over Fort Belvedere.

It was a signal that made history, for at that moment King Edward VIII, the 41-year-old Duke of York was about to take his place on the earth so that he could marry the woman he loved. With his three brothers as his only witnesses, he signed the instrument of abdication as his "final and irrevocable decision" to retire into private life.

He will remain King until tomorrow afternoon, when the Abdication Bill is expected to reach him from Parliament. As soon as he signs it, however, his unhappy days as King will come to an end after the short reign of 325 years. The Duke of York will come to the throne as George VI and Edward will leave England as the first man in all the 1,000 years of the British monarchy to have left the throne of his own accord.

Edward Again Cheerful

Although he has not shown himself to the public for almost a week, it was reported on good authority tonight that he was like a man who had had a crushing load of worry lifted from his shoulders. The depression and jumpiness of the last few days had vanished and the King was said to be cheerful and purposeful, superintending the packing of his belongings, dealing with State papers, which arrived incessantly from London, and looking forward to more freedom and happiness than he has known in a long time.

Workmen and tractors were busy all day on Edward's private flying field at Smith's Lawn in Windsor Great Park, apparently preparing it for the take-off of an important airplane. Four police cars were on duty and a cordon of police and detectives surrounded the place. Even a newspaper

Continued on Page Sixteen

KING MAKES HIS DECISION

Chooses Woman Over Throne After 'Long and Anxious' Thought.

FINALE LIKELY TOMORROW

New Reign, Expected to Bring Back Calm of George V's, to Be Proclaimed Then.

CROWNING PLAN MAY HOLD

Edward Can Use Either of Two Titles, Earl of Rothesay or Baron of Renfrew.

Edward's letter, the Abdication Bill, Baldwin's speech, Page 17.

By FREDERICK T. BIRCHALL
Special Cable to THE NEW YORK TIMES.

LONDON, Dec. 10.—Some time Saturday morning, perhaps even as soon as tomorrow night, Edward VIII will cease to be a King and Emperor. He has made his choice between a woman and a throne and the woman has won.

Today at Fort Belvedere, his country home near Windsor Castle, and in the presence of his three brothers, the Dukes of York, Gloucester and Kent, the King signed a message to his Ministers announcing his determination "after long and anxious consideration" to renounce the throne to which he has succeeded on the death of his father. This, said the message, was "my final and irrevocable decision."

The message was carried by Prime Minister Stanley Baldwin this afternoon to a crowded session of the House of Commons and there read, not without emotion, by the Speaker.

Bill Introduced in House

There is no question of whether the House should accept it. Under the British Constitution there can be none, for it was an expression of the King's will, the King rule, though he does not govern, Britain and the empire. But immediately afterward, as soon as the Prime Minister in a speech that will be memorable for the restrained feeling it expressed and the leaders of the Opposition each after his fashion had voiced their regret, a bill was introduced that will implement the monarch's decision.

Tomorrow this formal bill of abdication will be rushed through all its stages in both Houses, Commons and Lords. It will then be presented to the King for the royal assent. The moment he signs it he ceases to be King and his brother, the Duke of York, who is nearest to him, will reign in his stead.

The new King will take the throne, according to the best information available tonight, as George VI and for that choice there is a reason. It is desired, now that this crisis is over and the skies are clearing, to get back to the ordered peace and quiet stability of the monarchy under the last King George, to leave behind the bitter era of conflict between will and duty and to concentrate anew on the empire and its common destiny.

Proclamation Likely Tomorrow

Another era will begin probably at noon on Saturday when the accession of the new King is proclaimed from the balcony of St. James's Palace, again at old gray Charing Cross and finally from the steps of the Royal Exchange in the City of London, each time with all the pomp and ceremony that the monarchy has upheld here throughout a thousand years and change but the old order remaineth; that is to be Britain's watchword still.

And thus, in circumstances that will arouse wonder and pity as long as history continues to be written, ends the brief reign of King Edward VIII. He has lasted ten months and twenty-two days before this strange storm that love of woman created has brought it to a close, and the empire still endures. Even a newspaper man

Continued on Page Sixteen

Soviet Orders Militia Punished for Arrests Without Warrants in Spite of New Charter

Special Cable to THE NEW YORK TIMES.

MOSCOW, Dec. 10.—The first charges of violating the new constitution were brought at Kazan today in connection with the arrests of eleven persons there by the militia on its own initiative.

According to the new Constitution, "no one may be subjected to arrest except upon the decision of a court or with the sanction of the prosecutor." Apparently no such authorization was obtained, and Moscow authorities have called the Kazan militia's action an "outrageous violation" of the Constitution and ordered that the guilty be suitably punished.

According to an investigation in Kazan, a doorman at a restaurant was arrested this week purely on suspicion. When he failed to arrive home his father made inquiries, and on finding his son in jail complained to the public prosecutor. The latter showed little interest. A correspondent of the Moscow newspaper Izvestia then took up the matter and spurred the prosecutor to visit the jail, where he found eleven persons arrested without warrants.

Today also the first Soviet & 11th sentence for the infringement of private ownership and personal property and the murder of a private individual was imposed in a Moscow court.

Two employes of a State antique

shop had been selling valuable old books to two highly paid ballet dancers. Thus the employes had learned their clients had money and valuables. They invaded the young dancers' home in Moscow, killed their mother and cook with a brass pestle and looted the apartment. The criminals were found, arrested, convicted and tonight they will be shot.

Hitherto the death penalty has been imposed in murder cases only where the safety or welfare of the State was involved, the normal penalty for an ordinary murder being not more than ten years.

Nikolai V. Krylenko has assumed his duties as head of the All-Union Commissariat for Justice, newly created under the Constitution. He today began reorganizing the whole legal profession of the country into voluntary associations, which will give legal aid to any accused persons demanding that desire. Legal aid offices are also being established by trade unions.

Because of the new legal guarantee many more lawyers than hitherto will be needed. Accordingly steps are being taken to enroll thousands more students in the law schools already established, and plans are being formed for the creation of many more schools in the various republics.

"All the News That's Fit to Print."

The New York Times.

LATE CITY EDITION
Fair today, little change in temperature. Tomorrow cloudy and warmer, followed by rain.
Temperature Yesterday—Max. 37; Min. 27

Copyright, 1937, by The New York Times Company.

VOL. LXXXVI....No. 28,868.   Entered as Second-Class Matter, Postoffice, New York, N. Y.   NEW YORK, SATURDAY, FEBRUARY 6, 1937.   P   TWO CENTS In New York City. | THREE CENTS Within 200 Miles. | FOUR CENTS Elsewhere Except in 7th and 8th Postal Zones.

PROGRESS IS MADE IN MOTORS PARLEY; EVICTION DEFERRED

WORKING ON TERMS

Subcommittee Begins Study of Specific Issues in Strike

WILL REPORT THIS MORNING

Pressure From Roosevelt Is Credited With Averting Complete Collapse

MURPHY BLOCKS OUSTERS

Halts Arrest of Union Men After Court Issues Eviction Writs at Flint

Developments in Auto Strike

DETROIT — President Roosevelt's pleas avert a new deadlock in the auto strike conferences. After all-day sessions a subcommittee is named and begins a study of specific issues pending a new joint meeting today.—Page 1.

FLINT — Judge Gadola signs writs for arrest of union leaders and sit-down strikers, but Sheriff, after asking aid of troops, delays action.—Page 2.

NEW YORK—Federal Council of Churches of Christ in America condemns sit-down strikes as a "dangerous weapon." It also assails General Motors for its speed-up program.—Page 2.

Negotiations Go On
By LOUIS STARK
Special to The New York Times.

DETROIT, Feb. 5.—John L. Lewis, chairman of the Committee for Industrial Organization, and William S. Knudsen, vice president of General Motors Corporation, comprising a subcommittee designated at today's joint conference of spokesmen for both sides in the automobile strike dispute, sat down tonight with Governor Frank Murphy to formulate a report to go before the full committee tomorrow.

The subcommittee was named today after President Roosevelt's repeated telephonic intervention had saved the deadlocked automobile conference from collapsing. When the conference closed at 8 o'clock this evening Governor Murphy announced that progress had been made.

While the Governor divulged no details of the conference session today, it was learned that Mr. Lewis had made an important concession toward meeting General Motors spokesmen part way. He agreed to drop his demand that the union be the sole bargaining agency in all the sixty-nine plants of the corporation and to limit this demand to twenty plants where union men are on strike.

Company Reported Wavering

The corporation committee, it was reported, appeared tentatively to be willing to grant sole bargaining rights to the union in six plants on certain conditions, but made no definite commitment that could be regarded by the union as unqualified acceptance of its position in these six plants. Actual and positive agreement on this point awaited further clarification at the hands of the subcommittee tonight.

In announcing progress tonight Governor Murphy, flushed and beaming, warned against over optimism. He indicated that as yet there was no absolute assurance that whatever progress had been made would broaden out until a complete settlement had been written.

Nevertheless, Mr. Murphy's announcement that a sub-committee had been appointed to meet tonight to explore the various subjects in dispute, presumably collective bargaining, wages, hours and creation of machinery for the settlement of disputes, gave rise to hope in many quarters that a settlement might be in sight.

The full joint conference of three on each side will convene again at 10 o'clock tomorrow morning to hear the reports being prepared tonight by the sub-committees.

Presses Roosevelt Plan

Governor Murphy pressed home to both sides the admonition of President Roosevelt that the nation looked to them to settle their dispute in a manner betokening public-spirited citizens in a civilized community, and without the indus-

Continued on Page Two

Great-Grandmother, 72, Joins Picket Line in Flint

By The Associated Press.

FLINT, Mich., Feb. 5.—A 72-year-old great-grandmother joined union pickets today in front of Fisher Body Plant No. 1, held by sit-down strikers.

She was Mrs. Rebecca Goddard of Clio, Mich., who said she had nine or ten relatives, including a son, inside the plant.

"I just came down from Clio to show some of my neighbors," she said. "There are a lot of sit-down grouches up there. You don't know what sit - down grouches are? Why, they're people who don't believe in the union."

She was asked if it was true she was a great-grandmother.

"Certainly," she replied. "I have six children, twenty grandchildren and about ten great-grandchildren. My youngest son, Robert, is in that plant right now."

She said she also had some grandchildren and nephews in the plant.

FRIARS FACE TRIAL AS SPANISH REBELS

'People's Court' Will Assemble Monday for Case Against 60 Escorial Guardians

1,500 OTHERS ARE INDICTED

Speedy Hearings Are Planned for Prisoners Who Fill the Jails in Madrid

By The Associated Press.

MADRID, Feb. 5.—A special "people's court" will sit in judgment on the Augustinian friars who dwelt in the Escorial monastery built by King Philip II nearly 400 years ago, the government announced today.

The monks are charged with holding "anti-government tendencies" in the civil war. So far the government has kept possession of Escorial, northwest of Madrid, despite encirclement and siege by insurgent armies.

Trials Begin Monday

The friars will be tried by a court made up of a judge and two "representatives of the people." The court's session will begin Monday, and it has been instructed to conclude the trial within twenty days.

Simultaneously, Wenceslao Carrillo, Director General of Public Safety, announced he would immediately begin to examine the cases of all prisoners in Madrid's teeming jails with a view to liberating those against whom there is insufficient evidence of Rebel activity. The others will be turned free.

State Monument Planned

Since the advent of the Spanish Republic it had been planned to remove the friars to allow conversion of the monastery into a national monument along with royal palaces and other properties. But the war gave a different aspect to their evacuation.

The mausoleum has but one vacant sepulcher, that reserved for former King Alfonso XIII, now an exile with slight chance of lying with his predecessors.

One of the friars' most-prized possessions was a rich library of Arabic, Hebrew and Spanish manuscripts. They had a school of higher education bearing the name of Alfonso's father, Alfonso XIII, and a university, similarly named, devoted to the education of the sons of the Spanish nobility.

$100,000 CAFE SHUT BY RACKET BOMBS, OWNER TESTIFIES

Stench Missiles Used for Ten Months After He Refused to Pay $3,000, He Says

FOUR OTHERS TELL ILLS

Restaurant Manager Describes Threats to His Children and $2,000 Demand

A $100,000 example was given to the Supreme Court jury hearing evidence in the restaurant racket trial yesterday by Hyman Gross, who had been one of the owners of the Gerard Cafeteria, on Broadway at Times Square, which was closed by a stench bombardment ten months after it opened.

The experience of Mr. Gross, who had refused to pay Louis Beitcher, the racket's collector, $3,000, was one of five cases, three of attempted extortion and two of extortion placed in the record before Justice Philip J. McCook during the day.

In another, John A. Miller, manager of the Anne Miller restaurant, then at 43 West Eighth Street and a place patronized by Juror No. 5, Franklin H. Middleton, told of kidnap threats against his children and a demand for $2,000. Harry A. Vogelstein, one of the defendants, Miller said, told that "only saps" picketed.

Tells of $1,750 Payment

Isidoro Coviris, one of three owners of the Broadway Cafeteria at 2,230 Broadway, testified that he paid Beitcher $1,750 to purchase protection from the "rights of the union," and Richard M. Decker, owner of a night club called the Congress Restaurant at 1,657 Broadway, told of a sudden strike called by Local 16 of the Waiters Union to force him to join the Metropolitan Restaurant and Cafeteria Association, an employers' association, which he did at a cost of $285.

Two of Mr. Decker's waiters had worked for Jules Martin, the man who organized the racket for Arthur (Dutch Schultz) Flegenheimer, when he operated a restaurant in West Forty-eighth Street.

The flow of witnesses was speeded up by the fact that attorneys for the eight defendants, including three officials of Local 16 of the Waiters Union, two of Local 302 of the Cafeteria Workers Union, and three others, two of them lawyers, connected with the Metropolitan Association, shortened their cross-examination.

Run Short of Witnesses

Toward the end of the day the prosecution, conducted by William B. Herlands and Milton C. Schilback, two of Special Prosecutor Thomas E. Dewey's chief assistants, ran short of witnesses and a half-hour wait followed while more were produced after telephone calls. Mr. Gross was examined by Mr. Schilback. He said his regular business was real estate, but in July, 1933, after he and associates "had spent $100,000 to build the place," the Gerard was opened at 1,508 Broadway. He had personally put $40,000, he said.

Before they opened, Max Pincus, then in Local 302 but now a racketeer,

Continued on Page Thirty-six

West Virginian Saved After 8 Days in Mine; Had No Food, Forced to Drink Sulphur Water

By The Associated Press.

FLEMINGTON, W. Va., Feb. 5.—Eight foodless days of utter darkness while lost in the débris-choked passageways of an abandoned mine ended today for Robert Johnson, 36-year-old rural mail carrier.

"I told myself, 'Bob, please don't lose that light.'" He didn't.

As the rescue party came closer he called to Mike Stanko Jr., Edward Whitehair and William Westfall, all his friends and neighbors:

"Take your time, I'll guide you by your light."

They cautiously approached the heap of slate, reached through a hole and gripped Johnson's hand—assurance he was safe.

Then word went to the surface, sped through this little community of about 400 population in Northeastern West Virginia. Pride and eight others gathered stretchers and blankets. They hurried into the mine, waded and swam through a deep pool of water covering nearly an acre where originally, many believed, Johnson had drowned while trying to open clogged drains.

After Johnson was taken out on the mountainside, he was carried a quarter of a mile down a snow-covered path to a waiting ambulance. There he was joined by his wife—among his first questions was "How's my wife?"—and hurried to a hospital fifteen miles away in Clarksburg, the nearest large city.

His first words were to assure himself he hadn't merely imagined a light had cut through the dark.

C. P. Pride, assistant safety director for the State Department of Mines quoted him:

"I sure thought I was a goner," he said.

Johnson told from his cot in a hospital of praying through the long hours in the damp mine, of giving up all hope, then of seeing a dim glow of lamps carried by rescue workers.

"Thank God, my prayers were answered," he sobbed fervently before a sleeping potion administered by physicians put him to sleep.

Doctors had broken his long fast—he had only sulphur water to drink in the mine—with plenty of black coffee, then with bowls of strained soup.

Rescue crews found Johnson nearly two miles from the mine entrance early today. He was huddled behind a heap of jagged chunks of slate in the mine which he operated to dig coal in his spare time for sale to neighbors.

The crews had expected difficulty in removing the slate, but had little trouble in reaching the imprisoned man.

Three of the scores of volunteers who had searched the mine day and night since Johnson disappeared on Jan. 27 heard his feeble cries for help while exploring a narrow tunnel.

ROOSEVELT ASKS POWER TO REFORM COURTS, INCREASING THE SUPREME BENCH TO 15 JUSTICES; CONGRESS STARTLED, BUT EXPECTED TO APPROVE

Supreme Court Keeps Up With Its Work, Say Aides

By The Associated Press.

WASHINGTON, Feb. 5.—Supreme Court attachés said today that the tribunal was up to date in handling its business.

They explained it had been so since soon after William Howard Taft became Chief Justice in 1921. When he went on the bench, fulfilling a lifelong ambition, the tribunal was from two to three years behind in its work. He speeded up disposition of the litigation so that soon afterward it was abreast of the docket.

SIX ON HIGH BENCH ELIGIBLE TO RETIRE

They and Six Justices of the Circuit Courts Could Come Under Roosevelt Plan

13 OTHER JURISTS LISTED

These Members of the Lower Courts Also Have Reached 70, With 10 Years of Service

Special to The New York Times.

WASHINGTON, Feb. 5.—Not only six of the nine justices of the Supreme Court but half a dozen of the judges of the Federal Circuit Courts and an undisclosed number of the judges of the District Courts would be eligible for retirement as having reached the age of 70 after ten years of service on the bench, as urged by President Roosevelt.

There are forty-three judgeships in the Circuit Courts and 163 in the District tribunals, but in some instances there are still vacancies in appointments.

As President Roosevelt stated that twenty-five out of a total judiciary of 237 could thus leave the bench, and as it is known that six Supreme Court and six Circuit justices were so classed, the thirteen others must be members of the district benches and special Federal courts.

Chief Justice Hughes is, of course, among those who will be in the 70-year-old, ten-year service class this year. In fact, he will be 75 years old April 11, and Justice Van Devanter will be 78 just six days later.

Justice McReynolds's seventy-fifth birthday fell on last Wednesday. Justice Brandeis, oldest member of the court, reached the age of 80 Nov. 13 last. Justice Sutherland will be 75 on March 25 and Justice Butler 71 on March 17. Justice Stone on last

Continued on Page Ten

BILL IS INTRODUCED

Robinson and Bankhead Act for Passage by Senate and House

MAJORITY FOR PROPOSAL

But Most Conservative Democrats Are Silent and Republicans Are Hostile

SPECULATION ON JUSTICES

Those Mentioned for New Places Include J. M. Landis, Richberg and Frankfurter

By TURNER CATLEDGE
Special to The New York Times.

WASHINGTON, Feb. 5.—President Roosevelt's proposals for a comprehensive reform of the Federal judiciary fell today like a bombshell upon a Congress which thought it already had experienced the ultimate in surprises when it heard his recent messages on reorganization of the executive branch.

Not even the closest of the President's Congressional advisers knew of the plan until this morning and told to prepare for the shock at noon.

Regardless of the far-reaching nature of the proposals, the balance of Congressional reaction was decidedly in its favor. Judging from the content of the comment, this was due to three main factors—the resentment in Congress at recent decisions of the Supreme Court holding its acts invalid, the continuing faith of the so-called "liberal" element in Mr. Roosevelt and his works, and the unquestioning loyalty of the leadership in both houses to him and his program.

Republican Protest Vehement

On the other side of the scales were the spontaneous objections of the Republicans, characterized by a vehemence akin to that of the last Presidential campaign, and the disapproving attitude of a number of conservative Democrats.

Most of the conservative Democrats declined to comment.

Although the President's plan for a non-amendment approach to the issues raised by the court's interpretations ran counter to the plans of several outstanding legislators, notably Senator Robinson and Senator Ashurst, the leadership started laying general plans for its enactment. Senator Robinson predicted that the bill would receive "favorable consideration" in the Senate, and Speaker Bankhead promised quick action in the House on what he considered a "sound principle" of judicial reform.

The details of the plan, particularly the effective proposal for appointment of six new justices to the Supreme Court, brought forth limitless speculation as to the possible appointees. High on practically every list of possibilities were Senator Robinson, James M. Landis, who will shortly resign as chairman of the Securities and Exchange Commission to become dean of the Harvard Law School; Felix Frankfurter, Professor of Law at Harvard; Donald R. Richberg, former general counsel of the National Recovery Administration; Senators Wagner and Ashurst and Chairman Summers of the House Judiciary Committee.

The reform proposals were submitted in accordance with the best approved New Deal practices. They were worked out in every essential detail by the President with his administrative advisers, then the Congressional leaders were called in and informed of the scheme. Last a message, with supporting data and the draft of a bill, was sent to Congress.

The only difference today from the practice followed with most of the other measures of major importance was that the documents—message, supporting data and bill draft—were appended together in a single sheaf of papers, and representatives of the press were called in to be informed in advance of their specifications. The latter was not exactly an innovation, as the President follows this budget matters regularly on involved budget matters and recently used it in presenting and explaining his plan on executive reorganization.

The President's attitude in explaining the proposal today was in

Continued on Page Nine

President's Message

Special to The New York Times.

WASHINGTON, Feb. 5.—Following are the text of the President's message to Congress on the judiciary, the draft of his proposed bill and the text of the letter of Attorney General Cummings to the President:

I have recently called the attention of the Congress to the clear need for a comprehensive program to reorganize the administrative machinery of the executive branch of our government. I now make a similar recommendation to the Congress in regard to the judicial branch of the government, in order that it also may function in accord with modern necessities.

The Constitution provides that the President "shall from time to time give to the Congress information of the state of the Union, and recommend to their consideration such measures as he shall judge necessary and expedient." No one else is given a similar mandate. It is therefore the duty of the President to advise the Congress in regard to the judiciary whenever he deems such information or recommendation necessary.

I address you for the further reason that the Constitution vests in the Congress direct responsibility in the creation of courts and judicial offices and in the formulation of rules of practice and procedure. It is, therefore, one of the definite duties of the Congress constantly to maintain the effective functioning of the Federal judiciary.

The judiciary has often found itself handicapped by insufficient personnel with which to meet a growing and more complex business. It is true that the physical facilities of conducting the business of the courts have been greatly improved, in recent years, through the erection of suitable quarters, the provision of adequate libraries and addition of subordinate court officers. But in many ways these are merely the trappings of judicial office. They play a minor part in the processes of justice.

Since the earliest days of the republic, the problem of the personnel of the courts has needed the attention of the Congress. For example, from the beginning, over repeated protests to President Washington, the justices of the Supreme Court were required to "ride circuit" and, as circuit justices, to hold trials throughout the length and breadth of the land—a practice which endured over a century.

In almost every decade since 1789, changes have been made by the Congress whereby the numbers of judges and the duties of judges in Federal Courts have been altered in one way or an-

Continued on Page Eight

STOCKS DROP FAST ON COURT MESSAGE

Sweeping Declines Stop a Rise, Making Market the Year's Second Largest

BRIEF RALLIES ARE FUTILE

List Closes Only Slightly Above Day's Lows—Some Bankers Say Effect Will Be Mitigated

President Roosevelt's proposals for changes in the Federal judiciary came as a stunning surprise to the financial community yesterday. They evoked uncertainty and alarm among bankers and business men which found expression in a sweeping decline of stock prices.

Prices of representative issues on the New York Stock Exchange, which had been advancing during the morning, broke swiftly as the President's message was being read. The volume of trading increased, the stock ticker fell five minutes behind the pace of trading and earlier gains were quickly turned to losses of one to three or four points.

Brief rallies in the afternoon gave way repeatedly to renewed selling and closing prices were only slightly above the lowest levels of the day.

From the standpoint of number of shares dealt in, the market was the second largest of the year, the total of transactions being 3,221,000. On the basis of number of issues to appear on the tape, 975, it was the broadest market since Nov. 12.

Course Unexpected by Bankers

A sample of the net declines among important issues showed: United States Steel down 2¾ points at 96⅜; Bethlehem Steel, off 2¾ at 81½; Allied Chemical, 5 points lower at 225; Allis Chalmers, off 2½ at 75½; Anaconda Copper, down 1½ at 54%; Chrysler, off 2 at 126¼; and Standard Oil of New Jersey, off 1¾ at 70%.

Domestic corporation bonds were irregularly weaker, while the market for government securities showed declines fairly evenly matched by advances.

The response of financiers to the news was based upon concern and uncertainty over its implications rather than upon disagreement with the President's objectives. In spite of rumors which have been heard from time to time that Mr. Roosevelt might seek to enlarge the Supreme Court, it had been felt by most bankers that such a course was unlikely.

Consequently, as the chief executive of one big bank expressed it, the financial community was "flabbergasted" at the suddenness of the announcement, the drastic character of the changes proposed and the implications of criticism of

Continued on Page Nine

SURPRISE MESSAGE

Asks Authority to Name New Justices if Old Do Not Quit at 70

SEES NEED OF 'NEW BLOOD'

Constitutional Amendment and Statutory Judiciary Curb Would Be Side-Stepped

LOWER COURTS AFFECTED

Bench Would Be Expanded, Appeals Speeded and Defense Assured in Injunctions

By ARTHUR KROCK
Special to The New York Times.

WASHINGTON, Feb. 5.—The President suddenly, at noon today, cut through the tangle of proposals made by his Congressional leaders to "bring legislative and judicial action into closer harmony" with a broad-axe message to Congress recommending the passage of statutes to effect drastic Federal court reforms.

The message—prepared in a small group and with deepest secrecy—was accompanied by a letter from the Attorney General and by a bill, drawn at the Department of Justice, which would permit an increase in the membership of the Supreme Court from nine to a maximum of fifteen if judges reaching the age of 70 declined to retire; add a total of not more than fifty judges to all classes of the Federal courts; send appeals from lower-court decisions on constitutional questions direct to the Supreme Court, and require that government attorneys be heard before any lower-court injunction issue against the enforcement of any act of Congress.

Avoiding both the devices of constitutional amendment and statutory limitation of Supreme Court powers, which were favored by his usual spokesmen in Congress, the President endorsed an ingenious plan which will on passage give him the power to name six new justices of the Supreme Court.

Power Left to the President

Under the provisions of the bill drawn by the Department of Justice for Congress, if the six now sitting justices who are more than 70 years of age do not resign, the President is empowered to name a new member for each justice in that category. These are the Chief Justice and Justices Brandeis, Van Devanter, Butler, McReynolds and Sutherland. Thus, after the passage of the bill, which is generally expected, the court will number anywhere from nine to fifteen justices.

Although the message—as unusually long one for the President—was a general criticism of the effects upon government and private litigants of overburdened and superannuated judges, and stressed a genetic plea for drastic change, its object and implication were plainly marked. The message outlined outstanding features and purposes.

Although the message outlined basic defects in the administration of justice in the United States, and contained many reforms to which no exception will be taken, Congress quickly sensed that the President had hurried the present majority of the Supreme Court on his way to the goal he outlined in his opening message of the session. This, as he stated it, is to find "means to adapt our legal forms and our judicial interpretation to the actual present needs of the largest progressive democracy in the modern world."

Variety of Emotions Aroused

That passage was the one which had brought the most cheers from the floors of Congress when the President uttered it. To achieve its aim was the object of all the proposed amendments and statutes which have heaped high in the Congressional hoppers since the opening of the session. When members of the Senate and the House became aware of the ingenious but effective manner in which the President planned to attain his objective without touching the Constitution or the powers of the court, they were torn by a variety of emotions.

Senator Robinson, the majority leader in his branch, and the men

Continued on Page Eight

AIM TO PACK COURT, DECLARES HOOVER

Roosevelt Move Transcends Any Partisanship Question, Ex-President Holds

WIDELY CRITICIZED HERE

'Shameful Day' in Our History, Colby Asserts—Justice Black Hails 'Greatest Advance'

President Roosevelt's message to Congress asking for authority to appoint Federal judges in addition to those more than 70 years old was characterized last night by Herbert Hoover, his predecessor in the White House, as a proposal for "packing" the Supreme Court to get through New Deal measures.

Mr. Hoover declared that the President's proposal went far beyond any question of partisanship, and advised that Congress delay action on it until the people had time to formulate their views. His comment, made public at his suite in the Waldorf-Astoria, was as follows:

"Stripped of subsidiary matters, some of which are admirable, the President's action amounts to this:

"The Supreme Court has proved many of the New Deal proposals as unconstitutional. Instead of the ample alternatives of the Constitution by which these proposals could be submitted to the people through constitutional amendment, it is now proposed to make changes by 'packing' the Supreme Court. It has the implication of subordination of the court to the personal power of the Executive. Because all this reaches to the very depth of our form of government, it far transcends any question of partisanship.

"The Congress should delay action until the people have had ample time to formulate their views on it. In the long sweep of the Republic a few months are not too much to consider a vital change in the repeated judgment of the American people over 150 years. The judgment has always been that their liberties have depended greatly on the independence of the court and that they themselves should determine changes in the Constitution."

Reaction to the President's proposals among New York lawyers was generally strongly unfavorable. Former Justice Clarence J. Shearn, president of the Bar Association, asserted that it was plainly an attempt to pack the Supreme Court for cases in which the Federal administration would have a political interest and called on all opposed to "moboeracy" or dictatorship to fight it.

Bainbridge Colby, Secretary of State during the Wilson administration, declared it was an attempt to

Continued on Page Eight

The New York Times.

LATE CITY EDITION
Fair today, temperature unchanged.
Tomorrow fair, little change in temperature.
Temperature Yesterday—Mon. 71; Min. 48

Copyright, 1927, by The New York Times Company.

VOL. LXXXVI.....No. 28,958.   Entered as Second-Class Matter, Postoffice, New York, N. Y.   NEW YORK, FRIDAY, MAY 7, 1927.   P   TWO CENTS In New York City. | THREE CENTS Within 200 Miles. | FOUR CENTS Elsewhere Except 7th and 8th Postal Zones

HINDENBURG BURNS IN LAKEHURST CRASH; 21 KNOWN DEAD, 12 MISSING; 64 ESCAPE

ANARCHISTS RENEW BARCELONA STRIFE; 5,000 LEAVE BILBAO

Revolters, Regaining Part of Catalan Capital, Demand Shock Troop Dissolution

SOCIALIST MINISTER SLAIN

Insurgents Reported Gaining Unresisted in Aragon as Foes Withdraw 12,000

EVACUATION IN NORTH SPED

British Warships Protect Craft Taking Women and Children From Bilbao to France

The Spanish Situation

PERPIGNAN—Anarchists were reported to have regained positions in Barcelona and to have demanded the dissolution of the government's shock troops. Withdrawal of 12,000 men from the Aragon front, to deal with the situation, was also reported, leading to an advance by the Rebel armies. Page 1.

ROME—A heavy concentration of Rebels, including Italians, to rescue the Italians cut off at Bermeo, was under way on the Bilbao front. Page 10.

BILBAO—Five thousand women and children were taken from the city, and vessels carrying them to France were guarded by British warships. More refugees were preparing to leave. (Follows the above.) Page 10.

LONDON—Foreign Secretary Eden revealed that the British Government had evidence that Guernica was destroyed by airplanes. He favored a neutral inquiry. Page 10.

Anarchists Give Ultimatum

Special Cable to THE NEW YORK TIMES.

PERPIGNAN, France, May 6.—The Anarchists are reported to have regained control in parts of Barcelona this afternoon after the Catalan Generalidad believed it had dominated the situation.

The Anarchists issued an ultimatum to the government demanding the dissolution of the shock troops patrolling the city, the government's chief support, within twenty-four hours and declaring that otherwise they would take matters into their own hands and use every means in their power to suppress the shock troops.

The Anarchists also have obtained the upper hand at Junquera in addition to Figueras, and threaten, it is alleged, to use asphyxiating gas unless their ultimatum is obeyed.

Anarchist broadcasts have been picked up here stating that the casualties in the disorders in Barcelona since the Anarchist rebellion Tuesday amounted to 400 dead and 2,000 wounded. Declaring that "enough blood has flowed," the broadcasts continue to appeal for calm every ten minutes, and it is therefore believed that trouble still persists in Barcelona.

French Consulate Menaced

The French Consulate was threatened by Anarchists, who asserted that Rightist sympathizers had taken refuge there. The consul appealed to French authorities in the harbor and 200 armed sailors reinforced the consulate guard.

Telephonic communication with Barcelona is still cut off tonight, and telegraphic and telephonic communication with the interior of Catalonia, which was re-established yesterday, was again interrupted this morning.

The Spanish Consul at Perpignan has recommended that Frenchmen and others should not go farther than Figueras, and trains do not proceed beyond Gerona.

Francisco Ascaso, leader of the Anarchists in the Aragon Government, is reported to have been murdered.

Rebels Gain on Aragon Front

By The Associated Press.

PERPIGNAN, France, May 6.—Reports of an unresisted Insurgent advance along the whole Aragon front of Northeastern Spain and of the withdrawal of 12,000 government troops from it to keep the peace in troubled Barcelona, put a new and serious face on the Catalan Anarchist insurrection tonight. The reports emanated from Insurgent

Continued on Page Ten

Judge Sentences Himself By Signing Papers Unread

Wireless to THE NEW YORK TIMES.

MOSCOW, May 6.—A judge on one of the most important benches of the Moscow District Court who has the bad habit of signing unread any document placed before him has just sentenced himself to jail!

The court clerks, deciding he needed a lesson in "Bolshevik vigilance," presented to him a sheaf of papers including one reading "To the chief of Butyrky prison. Under Magistrate Abramson is sent to you for further detention." Judge Abramson signed all the papers and picked up his newspaper again.

The clerks, of course, extracted the sentence and were passing it around laughingly when the judge found out about it. He destroyed it in a rage, declaring such jokes tended to undermine Soviet justice.

The government learned about it, however, and today Izvestia delivered to Judge Abramson a stinging rebuke for perfunctoriness, reminding him that he dealt not in inanimate goods but in human fate.

HUGHES SEES CHOICE IN LAW OR TYRANNY

Courts Must Be Maintained, He Tells Law Institute, or We Replace Reason by Force

TEST OF BAR TO ROOSEVELT

Stewardship Is Questioned by Laymen, He Writes in Warning of 'Critical Audience'

Text of Chief Justice Hughes's address is on Page 17.

Special to THE NEW YORK TIMES.

WASHINGTON, May 6.—Chief Justice Hughes made what his hearers construed as a reference to the Supreme Court when he told the American Law Institute today that if society is to choose the processes of reason as opposed to the tyranny of force, "it must maintain the institutions which embody those processes." It was the second time that the Chief Justice of the United States has broken his silence since the controversy over reorganization of the Supreme Court started three months ago.

Vigorous applause, lasting more than a minute, followed the Chief Justice's words, with which he concluded a speech in which he avoided any direct reference to the court issue.

President Roosevelt in a message to the institute likewise refrained from any positive statement about the Supreme Court, but remarked that "law interpreters," among other legal experts, are facing a sometimes critical audience.

President on Lawyers' Position

"I am happy to greet you members of the bench, the bar and the law school faculties who have assembled for the fifteenth annual meeting of the American Law Institute," the President stated.

"I have followed with interest your accomplishment within recent years in the restatement of the law and your proposals for improvement in the administration of criminal justice.

"During the World War Captain Lehmann received the German Iron Cross award. After the war, he became second in command to Eckener, and brought the dirigible Los Angeles to Lakehurst in 1924. When the Hindenburg was completed in 1936 Captain Lehmann was placed in command, a position he held until recently, when Captain Pruss was elevated as commander of the ship."

"Today our stewardship as lawyers is being questioned. The laymen of America are not, perhaps, quite so disposed to make a complete delegation of law matters to lawyers. At least the layman asserts his right to evaluate us.

"Law scholars, law practitioners, lawmakers, law administrators and law interpreters have the stage today. But more significant, they must play their rôles before an intelligent and sometimes critical audience.

"But this is well. The virtue of the common law lies in its adaptability to growth and improvement. In generations present and future the lawyer likewise will be measured by the same test.

"It is encouraging today that so many outstanding leaders of the profession assemble to give service in the important and worth-while task to which the American Law Institute is dedicated. I extend my warm and cordial greetings to your membership and best wishes for continued success."

Only at one other time since President Roosevelt made his recommendations to Congress on Feb. 5 has the Chief Justice made any

Continued on Page Seventeen

NOTABLES ABOARD

Merchants, Students and Professional Men on the Dirigible

LEHMANN IS A SURVIVOR

Veteran Zeppelin Commander, Acting as Adviser on Trip, Is Seriously Burned

CAPT. PRUSS IS ALSO SAFE

C. L. Osbun, Sales Manager, Who Survived a Plane Crash, Escapes Second Time

Notables from many walks of life were among the passengers on the ill-fated Hindenburg. They included merchants, students and business and professional men and women. Many of the survivors owed their lives to the fact that they were apparently near windows in the dirigible when the accident happened and were able to leap through them to the ground in safety.

Among the survivors, listed were Captain Ernst Lehmann, veteran Zeppelin commander; Captain Max Pruss, the new Hindenburg commander; Herbert O'Laughlin of Chicago, employed by the Consumers Company of Elgin, Ill.; Clifford L. Osbun, export sales manager of the Oliver Farm Equipment Company of Chicago, and Ferdinand Lammot Belin Jr. of Washington, D. C.

Lehmann's Condition Grave

Early this morning Dr. E. G. Herbener, staff surgeon at the Paul Kimball Hospital in Lakewood, said that Captain Lehmann was on the doubtful list. Captain Lehmann is suffering from shock and second and third degree burns of the face and body. Captain Pruss is suffering from second and third degree burns of the face, forehead and arms and will probably recover, Dr. Herbener said.

Among the passengers who were still unaccounted for were John Pannes, passenger traffic manager of the Hamburg-American Line and North German Lloyd at New York, and his wife; Ernst Rudolf Anders, partner of the firm of Seelig & Hille, tea merchants of Dresden, Germany, and his son, R. Herbert Anders, and Hermann Doehner of Mexico, D. F.

Captain Lehmann and Captain Pruss were in the control gondola when the crash occurred. Both officers, together with several other members of the crew, leaped through the gondola windows to safety.

Lehmann an Adviser

Captain Lehmann, who was serving as adviser aboard the Hindenburg, had been commander of the ship until this year. He has had long experience with the lighter-than-air craft, and has been associated with Hugo Eckener, world-famous authority on Zeppelins, since 1921.

He was born March 12, 1886, at Ludwigshafen, on the Rhine, the son of a chemist. He became a naval cadet in 1905 and later entered the Polytechnic Institute at Charlottenburg, a borough of Berlin.

Continued on Page Nineteen

DISASTER ASCRIBED TO GAS BY EXPERTS

Washington Sees Dangerous Combination of Hydrogen and Blue Gas as Cause

Special to THE NEW YORK TIMES.

WASHINGTON, May 6.—Washington airship experts and Congressional leaders received the news of the Hindenburg disaster with amazement and expressions of sorrow. But in every instance those who commented pointed out that the three disasters of the United States Navy were structural, while that of the German craft was due to the use of a combination of hydrogen and blue gas, the most dangerous of all gases for inflation of airships.

Dr. Hans Luther, the German Ambassador, said the disaster must not cause the world to lose faith in dirigibles and that it could not have been caused by technical defects.

"It is terrible," the Ambassador said. "I was horrified by the news, but it could not have been a technical matter. It must not cause us to lose faith in dirigibles because the Graf Zeppelin has operated safely and efficiently for eight years on the run from Europe to South America and elsewhere.

"It is terrible to believe," said Admiral A. B. Cook, Chief of Naval Aeronautics, when told: "From what I

Continued on Page Twenty-one

Airship Like a Giant Torch On Darkening Jersey Field

Routine Landing Converted Into Hysterical Scene in Moment's Time—Witnesses Tell of 'Blinding Flash' From Zeppelin

By CRAIG THOMPSON

Special to THE NEW YORK TIMES.

LAKEHURST, N. J., May 6.—The Hindenburg, giant silver liner of the air, suddenly became a torch plane, waiting to ferry passengers from the airship into Newark, tonight. What began as a routine landing of the transatlantic airship ended in a holocaust.

The ground crew, officials of the naval air base, spectators, reporters and press photographers were going about their customary business of aiding or watching the airship nose into the mooring mast.

Two ground lines had been dropped from the nose. These, attached to the cars running on a circular track around the mast, were holding the ship nose down at a thirty-degree angle, and helping it jockey into a position favorable for mooring.

A thunderstorm had passed over the field a short time before and a drizzly rain was still falling. Twilight was beginning, although the visibility was good.

So suddenly that it left spectators on the verge of hysteria for some time afterward, the ship burst into flame. Some one in the ground crew yelled "Run for your lives!" and the crew did. The stern of the ship settled and the photographers, squinting through the view finders of their cameras, ran toward the ship.

The occurrence sounded, witnesses said, like two explosions, one following the other about thirty seconds apart. Some said they saw one burst of flame, others two, but the noises they described as explosions gave way to the sounds of human screams.

"There was a noise that sounded like bullets coming out of the gondola," Seelig said. "I saw nobody

In the "heavier-than-air" hangar, the pilot of an American Air Lines plane, waiting to ferry passengers from the airship into Newark, watched from a window.

"It seemed to happen so fast that I didn't think anybody could escape," he said afterward.

He was wrong, for about at that moment a man ran into the hangar. "His face was black, but he seemed to be all right otherwise. He wanted to telephone his mother in Chicago."

The passenger was Herbert James O'Laughlin of Chicago. On the field was an army detachment from Philadelphia, detailed there for just such an emergency. This detail promptly went to work, trucks scurrying over the field seeking the injured, while in the hangar telephone calls were being put through to all points in New Jersey and New York City calling for ambulances, doctors, nurses, medicine.

All this occurred while the flames spread toward the uplifted nose of the ship, while the stern sank to the ground to be followed shortly by the entire length, girder and strut, the bared ribs of the ship from which the skin had disappeared.

Robert Seelig, Murray Becker and Larry Kennedy, all newspaper camera men, related what they had seen.

Continued on Page Twenty-one

SHIP FALLS ABLAZE

Great Dirigible Bursts Into Flames as It Is About to Land

VICTIMS BURN TO DEATH

Some Passengers Are Thrown From the Blazing Wreckage, Others Crawl to Safety

GROUND CREW AIDS RESCUE

Sparks From Engines or Static Believed to Have Ignited Hydrogen Gas

A page of photographs of the disaster and survivors Page 20.

By RUSSELL B. PORTER

Special to THE NEW YORK TIMES.

NAVAL AIR STATION, LAKEHURST, N. J., May 6.—The Zeppelin Hindenburg was destroyed by fire and explosions here at 7:23 o'clock tonight with a loss of thirty-three known dead and unaccounted for out of its ninety-seven passengers and crew.

Three hours after the disaster twenty-one bodies had been recovered, and twelve were still missing. The sixty-four known to be alive included twenty passengers and forty-four of the crew. Many of the survivors were burned or injured or both, and were taken to hospitals here and in near-by towns.

The accident happened just as the great German dirigible was about to tie up to its mooring mast four hours after flying over New York City on the last leg of its first transatlantic voyage of the year. Until today the Hindenburg had never lost a passenger throughout the ten round trips it made across the Atlantic in 1936.

Two Theories of Cause

F. W. von Meister, vice president of the American Zeppelin Company, gave two theories tonight to explain the crash. One was that a fire was caused by an electrical circuit "induced by static conditions" as the ship valved hydrogen gas preparatory to landing. Another was that sparks set off when the engines were throttled down while the gas was being valved caused a fire or explosion.

Captain Ernst Lehmann, who commanded the Hindenburg on most of its flights last year and was one of tonight's survivors, gasped, "I couldn't understand it," as he staggered out of the burning control car. Captain Max Pruss, commanding officer of the airship, and Captain Albert Stampf were also among the survivors.

Captain Lehmann was critically burned and injured; the other officers were also burned, but less seriously.

Experts in lighter-than-air operations who saw the accident said tonight that when the two landing lines were dropped by the dirigible at 7:20, they were immediately made fast to the mooring cars on the circular track about the mooring mast. The crew began to make the lines taut, so that the ship had gathered too much momentum, according to these observers, and drifted several hundred yards past the top. The starboard line pulled hard as the nose of the ship passed over the mooring mast at the top.

Order Not Heard

Captain Pruss, making his first trip in command of the dirigible, signaled and shouted, "Pay out!"

This order was heard by the operator on one mooring car, but not by the other, as the shout went against the wind and could not be heard. Consequently, one mooring car paid out and the other did not. The result was that the ship was thrown off its balance and lost the perfect equilibrium it had previously had.

Its nose dipped, forward ballast was dropped and the elevators were set to raise the ship. Instead the ship was held tight by one yaw line. The nose was pulled over and the elevators had an effect opposite to that which they intended to have, according to this version. The tail dropped sharply and the bottom rudder hit the

Continued on Page Nineteen

GERMANY SHOCKED BY THE TRAGEDY

At First Disbelieving, Line's Officials Tell of Receiving Message of Landing

Special Cable to THE NEW YORK TIMES.

BERLIN, Friday, May 7.—It was, a few minutes after 1 o'clock this morning when the first news of the disaster to the Hindenburg reached Berlin by telephone from The New York Times Bureau in London. The bureau forwarded the brief bulletin to the effect that the airship had been destroyed while it was landing. No details were given.

At that hour the German newspapers were without news. Several first editions, in fact, had reported the Hindenburg's supposedly safe arrival on the strength of an erroneous telegram received by the company in Frankfort on the Main. It was almost two hours later before the news of the disaster with some few details reached the newspapers through the medium of the German official news agency.

Facts Difficult to Get

In the meantime such facts about the airship and its passengers proved difficult to obtain. The Frankfort and Berlin offices of the Zeppelin company were closed and no complete list of the passengers or crew was available. A list of thirty-nine names was obtained by telephone from Frankfort, where this correspondent had retained it since the sailing day.

Dr. Hugo Eckener, veteran chief of the Zeppelin service, was in Austria, where he had lectured last night in Vienna. The Vienna bureau of THE NEW YORK TIMES traced him to Gras and obtained his address.

Continued on Page Nineteen

THE HINDENBURG IN FLAMES ON THE FIELD AT LAKEHURST
The giant airliner as she settled to the ground near her mooring mast at 7:23 o'clock last night
Associated Press Photo.

"All the News That's Fit to Print."

The New York Times.

LATE CITY EDITION
Showers and cooler today. Tomorrow generally fair and continued cool.

Temperature Yesterday—Max.; 72; Min., 56

VOL. LXXXVI....No. 28,964.

Entered as Second-Class Matter, Postoffice, New York, N. Y.

NEW YORK, THURSDAY, MAY 13, 1937.

PP

Copyright, 1937, by The New York Times Company.

TWO CENTS in New York City. | THREE CENTS Within 200 Miles. | FOUR CENTS Elsewhere Except in 7th and 8th Postal Zones.

C. I. O. STEEL STRIKE SHUTS TWO PLANTS OF JONES-LAUGHLIN

27,000 MEN ARE IDLE

Corporation Puts Blame on Murray, Says It Will Sign Pact

DRIVE AT INDEPENDENTS

Picketing Begins at Pittsburgh and Aliquippa Mills, Backing Recognition for Union

REPUBLIC BARS CONTRACT

Cleveland Letter Tells 55,000 Workers Company Will Not Agree to a Closed Shop

By The Associated Press.

PITTSBURGH, May 12.—Thousands of union steel workers picketed the giant plants of the Jones & Laughlin Steel Corporation tonight in the first major steel strike since John L. Lewis began his drive to organize the nation's millmen into one big union.

The strike began at 11 P. M. as the first move in the campaign of the Steel Workers Organizing Committee to obtain written collective bargaining contracts with the independent steel producers of the country, employing about 202,000 men.

Cheers from the picket lines greeted union members on the early night shifts who walked from the mills in Pittsburgh and Aliquippa, in answer to the strike order of Philip Murray, chairman of the S. W. O. C.

Walkout on Murray's Order

Mr. Murray ordered the walkout after a two-hour conference with H. E. Lewis, chairman of the Jones & Laughlin board, and Mr. Lewis, chairman of the Jones & Laughlin had failed to effect an agreement on the union's demand.

The corporation, in a formal announcement, stated that it had offered to sign a contract provided an identical contract could be granted to non-union workers among its 27,000 employes.

The company also announced that it had offered to grant a sole collective bargaining contract to the group obtaining a majority vote at an employes' election, supervised by the National Labor Relations Board.

A company representative said no attempt would be made to operate the plants "for the time being."

Mr. Murray declined to state what effect the Jones & Laughlin strike would have on union activities at other independent companies, and he would not comment on the company's statement.

The Steel Workers Organizing Committee, as an affiliate of the Committee for Industrial Organization, received a rebuff from Republic Steel during the day.

The Republic corporation, with 55,000 employes, made public a letter to its workers, refusing to sign a C. I. O. contract. It said: "Republic does not believe in the closed-shop principle."

Biggest Strike Since 1919

The Jones & Laughlin walkout is the biggest strike since the great steel strike in 1919. The 1919 strike cut production 40 per cent.

Mr. Murray said the Jones & Laughlin mills would be so shut "tight," except for maintenance crews, which were ordered to keep up the blast furnaces.

A further conference would be held with the company tomorrow, Mr. Murray said.

Flames from the blast furnaces shot high into the air, intermittently lighting up the faces of the crowds of men, women and children who packed the streets in front of mill gates more than an hour before the strike call went into effect.

Two score municipal police mingled with the crowd, but made no attempt to break the picket lines.

Without disorder, the union men prevented non-union workers from entering the mill gates.

They held two American flags across the main entrance at the Aliquippa works.

Night Shift Men Parade

The throng was increased by the night shift members who fell into line, clasped arms with one another, and paraded in front of the gates.

A light rain before midnight sent many of the women and children of the strikers' families to their

Continued on Page Four

Home Relief Families Get $1,200,000 WPA Clothes

Distribution to home relief families of 2,056,989 articles of clothing made by seamstresses on WPA sewing projects was reported yesterday by Miss Charlotte E. Carr, executive director of the Emergency Relief Bureau. The clothing, which had an estimated retail value of $1,200,000, was distributed between April 13, 1936, and April 23, 1937.

In addition to these WPA products, home relief families received $2,562,410 in cash for the purchase of apparel.

The cash sum to be distributed by the ERB as a clothing allowance for the quarter ending June 30 has been raised to $1,500,000, Miss Carr announced. Of this amount $750,000 was disbursed last month.

REBELS BEAT BACK ATTACK ON TOLEDO

Report Loyalists Have Lost 3,000 There—Government Claims 7-Mile Gain

BILBAO SUBURBS BOMBED

More Than 100 Missiles Were Dropped—Madrid Shelled, Toll Rising to 217

By The Associated Press.

TOLEDO, Spain, May 12.—Heavy government attacks against Insurgent-held Toledo developed today into a mass offensive in which, Insurgents said, the attackers suffered "unprecedented slaughter."

Government prisoners estimated their dead in the campaign at more than 3,000, with total casualties not calculated, Insurgent reports said.

Waves of government infantry charged Insurgent positions south of the Tagus River as a climax to four days of fighting.

Insurgents braced their lines tonight along a six-mile front south of the Tagus. Estimates of government troops in the offensive ranged from 18,000 to 22,000 men.

No-man's land was covered with dead and wounded after a terrific battle yesterday. Squads from both armies roamed the area in the night looking for wounded.

The brilliant defense of Insurgent militiamen in one sector, it is stated, won for them the collective award of the Laureada, the highest honor for bravery in the Spanish army.

Prisoners taken by the Insurgents were quoted as saying the government army in the Toledo sector included two brigades of the Lister Division and two other international outfits, the Campesina Brigade and the Dimitroff Battalion, in addition to the units already on the front. Apparently they were sent to reinforce government troops trying to recapture the city won by Insurgents last October, when they freed comrades besieged in the Alcazar.

[The government asserted its troops had advanced about seven miles on the Toledo front.]

100 Bombs Dropped Near Bilbao

BILBAO, Spain, May 12 (AP).—Insurgent airplanes dumped more than 100 bombs into the suburbs of Bilbao today but did not fulfill General Emilio Mola's threat to blast the Basque capital to bits.

Terror-stricken inhabitants, mindful of the Insurgent Northern commander's warning he would bombard the city "without mercy" if it did not surrender by today, ducked for cover three times as nine bombing planes and seven pursuit planes roared over Bilbao. Several gasoline tanks were set afire and nearby buildings were destroyed. Clouds of dark smoke billowed over the city.

Basque officials asserted they were informed General Mola had chosen today for the expiration of his ultimatum because the eyes of the world would be turned away from the Spanish civil war toward the London coronation. The indignation that would follow a violent attack on the civilians in this time would be legended, they said.

One person was killed and several wounded in the air bombing of the town of Sorrosa. Planes also bombed Lanzari and Mangula, north of Bilbao.

Bilbao's food situation was grave. Bread supplies were almost exhausted. Only enough re-

Continued on Page Thirteen

When You Think of Writing Think of Whiting.—Advt.

---

142 PLAYGROUNDS, CLOSED BY MOSES, SEIZED BY POLICE

Patrolmen Force Locks to Reopen Them as Park Head Defies Mayor on Control

STAFF FURNISHED BY WPA

Somervell, in Control Again, Provides Labor That Moses Lost in Personnel Cuts

One hundred and forty-two playgrounds in the city became the battlefield yesterday for confused conflict between Mayor La Guardia, Lieut. Col. Brehon B. Somervell, WPA Administrator, and Police Commissioner Lewis J. Valentine on the one side, and Park Commissioner Robert Moses on the other. By nightfall, however, "New York's finest" were in full control.

With the Mayor heading by train for California but keeping in touch with the situation by long-distance telephone, the police late in the afternoon picked or broke the padlocks on the playgrounds which had been closed by Mr. Moses because WPA play directors had been withdrawn, and replaced them with police padlocks.

Facilities Normal Today

Today the playgrounds will be reopened to the children, with WPA directors working for the Police Department under direct WPA jurisdiction, aided by 135 men and women from the police juvenile aid bureau. The children can play in safety, the police promised.

The police advanced on the locked gates of the playgrounds only after Mr. Moses had announced to the press there would be "no armed conflict between his park guardsmen and the police" and after he had refused the request of Commissioner Valentine for keys to the padlocks.

The Park Commissioner, asserting that no one was more interested in keeping the playgrounds open for the children than he, stood off the Police Commissioner on legal grounds. The Mayor's order to have the police take over any closed playgrounds, in effect transferring jurisdiction to the police, was a "clear violation of the charter and absolutely illegal," he declared.

Keep Up Other Play Areas

Playgrounds that had been locked "because of the outrageous way in which the WPA has done this" will stay locked, Mr. Moses said, but he added that "if the police want to take the locks off, it will be all right." The 215 playgrounds which were manned by Park Department employes will continue to be run by the department, he said.

The Mayor, anticipating a playground crisis because of the long feud between Mr. Moses and the WPA administrator, had issued his order to the police Tuesday night when he left for California. The order was made public at City Hall by his secretary, Lester Stone, after Mr. Moses had announced the closing of the playgrounds.

With the playgrounds still locked at 3 o'clock, Mr. Stone put in a telephone call for the Mayor at Toledo, and when the Mayor's train arrived informed him of the general situation. He then announced that the Mayor issued the following statement:

"I confirm my order to keep all the playgrounds open. The children of the city, for whom the playgrounds were built, cannot be made to suffer, and I expect the Police Department to reopen the play-

Continued on Page Two

GEORGE VI AND ELIZABETH CROWNED IN ABBEY; MILLIONS OF THEIR SUBJECTS ACCLAIM THEM; KING, ON AIR, PLEDGES SERVICE TO THE EMPIRE

THE ROYAL FAMILY ACKNOWLEDGES GREETINGS OF CORONATION CROWDS

King George VI, Queen Elizabeth and the Princesses Elizabeth and Margaret Rose on the balcony of Buckingham Palace after the ceremony at Westminster Abbey. Behind the Queen, on the left, is Lady Ursula Manners, daughter of the Duke of Rutland, and on the right Lady Diana Legge, daughter of the Earl of Dartmouth, both train bearers for the Queen. Behind King George are two members of the Palace staff.

Times Wide World Radiophoto.

YOUNGER PRINCESS IS BORED BY AFFAIR

Margaret Rose, 6, Even Goes to the Extent of Yawning at Archbishop of Canterbury

OLDER SISTER NUDGES HER

Elizabeth, for the First Time, Takes Precedence Over Other Ladies of Royal Family

By The Associated Press.

LONDON, May 12.—Two little Princesses saw their father crowned King today, but their reactions were very different.

Eleven-year-old Princess Elizabeth sat primly in her seat in the royal box, her attention fastened on the dramatic spectacle before her. One day she may play the leading role in such a ceremony, for she is heir presumptive to the throne.

Beside her, Princess Margaret Rose, 6½, tried her best to act as a princess should at a coronation. But she couldn't keep from squirming and lounging in her seat and she yawned right at the venerable Archbishop of Canterbury, head of the Anglican Church.

The little girls had risen at 7:30 for the great day. They peeped out of the nursery windows of Buckingham Palace to see whether

Continued on Page Sixteen

Vast Throngs Cheer Royalty In Procession and at Palace

Rain Fails to Lessen Enthusiasm of More Than 1,000,000 on London Route—Queen, Queen Mother, Baldwin Get Ovations

By CHARLES W. HURD
Wireless to THE NEW YORK TIMES.

LONDON, May 12.—The most representative military spectacle the British Empire could muster escorted King George today through six miles of London streets to signalize his coronation, while more than 1,000,000 Londoners and visitors from all countries looked on and cheered even in the last hour, when a cloudburst fell from the skies.

The procession was at once a display of most impressive pageantry and a graphic demonstration of British feeling that the monarchy is an integral part of the empire's soul.

There were plenty of cheers for the troops and the famous personages in line, but most were reserved for four persons—the King and Queen, who got the greatest ovation; Queen Mary, whose popularity is undimmed, and Prime Minister Stanley Baldwin, who steered the throne through its greatest modern crisis last December.

Following their triumphal ride the royal family had another great ovation from the crowds at Buckingham Palace when, in response to cheers, the King appeared on the balcony wearing his robe and crown. The crowd roared, "God save the King!" and then sang "For He's a Jolly Good Fellow."

More prolonged cheers were given Princess Elizabeth and Princess Margaret Rose when they joined their parents. There was an ovation for Queen Mary when she appeared to stand between the King and Queen.

The King and Queen, although tired by the day's responsibilities, made four more appearances later in the evening. Responding to the cheers of the crowds, they walked out on the balcony at 9 o'clock. Immediately after the loud-speakers were employed to announce that they would appear no more tonight. However, they made bows from the balcony three more times, the last at 11:50.

Heavy Rain in Afternoon

By seven o'clock this morning most of the stands along the parade route were filled by ticketholders who had tucked their lunches and mackintoshes under their arms and hoped they would not have to use the coats despite the lowering skies. Hope for good weather between the lips of George VI there had been a broadcast on the day of his coronation. It was evident in every sentence that he realizes the source whence his kingship comes.

With the coming of the heavy rain those who had yet to see the procession pulled on their coats, raised their umbrellas and waited. Six miles of London streets to signalize his coronation, while more than 1,000,000 Londoners and visitors from all countries looked on and cheered even in the last hour, when a cloudburst fell from the skies.

Those who left their umbrellas up after the parade appeared were pelted with balls of wet paper until they gave up the struggle to keep dry either in the open seats or among the standing crowds. It was notable that few yielded their places until they had seen the King and Queen at the close of the procession.

Britons saw their King in his full story-book rôle attired in royal raiment—the symbol of all honor and protection—riding with the Queen in a golden coach surrounded by the panoply of greatness which every Briton loves as the symbol of spiritual possessions that all share alike.

Affection for King Displayed

George, looking through the glass windows of his coach, obviously sincere but modest to the point of shyness, saw manifestations of affection and regard which promise at some future day to raise him to a statue approximating that of his father, George V, as the average Briton's ideal of a modest gentleman.

Some enthusiastic reports placed the size of the crowd greeting the King at 3,000,000 to 5,000,000, but a conservative estimate would reduce this—possibly to less than the number that turned out for George V's funeral early last year, but an extraordinary number considering the threatening weather and the bus strike which paralyzed this highly important transportation system.

Moreover, with the exception of the estimated 250,000 persons who bought reserved seats, most of the spectators had stood eight to fifteen hours by the time they saw the procession. They paid a heavy price, fainting by thousands, requiring attention by a large corps of doctors, nurses and ambulances. Durin, the wait for the Westminster Abbey ceremonies the writer saw hundreds of them in one limited area drop down to rest or sleep on the soaked ground.

Show Love of Triumphs

This picture of the sleepers on the wet ground encompassed the whole story, the love of government, King and pageantry by average Britons and their dogged determination to participate in the nation's triumphs even though many

Continued on Page Eighteen

GEORGE VI THANKS PEOPLE OF EMPIRE

His Broadcast Is Received as Promise of a Reign Like That of His Father

HE GREETS THE DOMINIONS

Recalls That Kingship Arises From 'Will of Free Peoples' Associated in Amity

By FERDINAND KUHN Jr.
Wireless to THE NEW YORK TIMES.

LONDON, May 12.—With the cheers of London crowds still ringing in his ears, King George gave his personal thanks tonight to his peoples throughout the empire and promised to serve them faithfully in the years ahead.

He chose the evening of his coronation day to speak into the microphone from his study in Buckingham Palace as his father had after his silver jubilee two years ago. He talked not only as a king who had just had a crown placed on his head but as a simple young man without great brilliants who had been called to great responsibilities and was determined to live up to them.

Voices Thanks for Loyalty

It was an unassuming little speech, and there was more than a hint of George V in the new King's voice when he said:

"I cannot find words with which to thank you for your love and loyalty to the Queen and myself. Your good will in the streets today and your countless messages from overseas and from every quarter of these islands have filled our hearts to overflowing. I will only say this: that if in the coming years I can show my gratitude in service to you that is the way above all others that I should choose."

All this, so sincerely meant and so modestly spoken, might have come from the lips of George VI there had been a broadcast on the day of his coronation. It was evident in every sentence that he realizes the source whence his kingship comes.

He called, too, of today's ceremonial as a solemn "dedication" of himself and his Queen, and in one moving passage he reminded an outnumbered millions of listeners that

Continued on Page Seventeen

RITE IS MEDIEVAL

Westminster Relives Past Age as Ruler Comes Into His Kingdom

KING A FRAIL, GRAVE FIGURE

Anointed and Robed in Regal Garb, He Receives Crown and Is Cheered by Peers

GIVES VOW WITH EMOTION

Queen, Serious and Nervous, Takes Place on Throne— Historic Service Drags

By FREDERICK T. BIRCHALL
Wireless to THE NEW YORK TIMES.

LONDON, May 12.—In a setting of medieval splendor such as seemed scarcely to belong to this day and age George VI was crowned King and Emperor in Westminster Abbey today.

He rode there with his Queen in their golden coach drawn by eight gray horses through streets lined with troops brought from all parts of the empire, and millions of his subjects acclaimed him as he passed.

In the Abbey he went through the ceremony of being accepted by his people. He took a vow to care for their welfare, to maintain and obey the laws passed by their Parliament, to be just and to temper justice with mercy.

Anointed With Holy Oil

He was disrobed of the outer garments he had worn on entering and anointed on his hands, breast and forehead with holy oil and thus dedicated to the kingship. Then he was freshly robed in cloth of gold and royal purple. The Sword of State was girt to his side and his heels were touched with the Spurs of Power.

They put the Ring on his finger. Two sceptres—emblems of power and justice, equity and mercy—were placed in his hands. Then St. Edward's ancient crown of pure gold and costly jewels was pressed upon his bowed head with a prayer to God to crown him with all princely virtues.

Trumpets sounded, drums rolled and the Abbey sprang into full illumination at his crowning, while outside the church bells rang for joy and guns thundered a royal salute. The peers of his realm surrounding him put on their own coronets and the great edifice rang with the shout, "God save the King!" Archbishops, Bishops, the King's royal brothers and the nobles of his realm knelt in turn before him and swore fealty.

Then Queen Is Crowned

Then the Queen was anointed and crowned in like manner and took her place on her lower throne beside him. They went together to the high altar, knelt in prayer and partook of the communion. Finally, in a new splendid procession, they passed down the great nave and out among the plain people, who are the mainstay of their kingdom, yet had had little part in all this ceremony. And throughout the long drive they were again acclaimed in a thunder of cheers echoing through all London—"God save the King!"

The pageant within the Abbey followed the lines that already have been so fully described in advance. The King and Queen entered the Abbey at 11:30 A. M. from the temporary annex, to which the great procession had carried them. They left it at 2:40 P. M. The historic service had dragged a little.

Most of those within the Abbey had arrived before 7 o'clock. Few were able to depart before 3:30. The last did not get away before 4:30. That was due to bad management and it made a long day for many persons no longer young.

So the sixth George and the second Elizabeth, his consort, came at last into their kingdom. Into more than a kingdom; into an empire of kindred and equal great States that overspreads the world. To keep these firmly linked and insure justice to their countless millions is no easy task in these troublous times. But that is of tomorrow.

Scene One of Splendor

The splendor of the scene in which this pageant was enacted no pen is able to convey.

Picture the great gray Abbey, shrine and temple of the English race throughout a thousand years,

Continued on Page Sixteen

Housewives Entitled to Fixed Salaries, Like Any Worker, Mrs. Roosevelt Holds

The suggestion that wives who stay at home to look after the household should receive a definite salary for their work was advanced last night by Mrs. Franklin D. Roosevelt, wife of the President.

Remarking that a housewife earns the right to a salary, "without any question," Mrs. Roosevelt said that "any girl who is needed at home has a job just as surely as the girl who operates a machine in a factory; if she is not needed at home, she loses out by not working."

Mrs. Roosevelt expressed her views in a discussion of "The Home vs. Work for Women," with Miss Rose Schneiderman, president of the Women's Trade Union League and secretary of the New York State Department of Labor. The discussion was broadcast over a radio network.

Asked for her opinion of the most vital question facing working women, Miss Schneiderman said it was "getting over their economic inferiority complex." Women often carry a feeling of inferiority into business and industry and are willing to work for much less pay, she said.

Mrs. Roosevelt remarked that "a woman who works to give her children the necessities and some of the advantages of life should have her work day limited to eight hours."

Miss Schneiderman said that when the working conditions of women were bettered "those of men automatically rise too."

"When women work long hours and for next to nothing," she continued, "they are not only competing against each other, but are pulling down the wages of their men folks."

Asked by Mrs. Roosevelt if she thought men resented women in industry, Miss Schneiderman replied that emotionally they did, "sometimes."

"But can you imagine," she continued, "what would happen if the 11,000,000 working women in the United States suddenly quit their jobs and just waited for the men to support them?"

"All the News That's Fit to Print."

The New York Times.

LATE CITY EDITION
Partly cloudy and cooler today.
Tomorrow fair with little change in temperature.
Temperatures Yesterday—Max., 70; Min., 54

Copyright, 1937, by The New York Times Company.

VOL. LXXXVII....No. 29,111.   Entered as Second-Class Matter, Postoffice, New York, N. Y.   NEW YORK, THURSDAY, OCTOBER 7, 1937.   PPP   TWO CENTS In New York | THREE CENTS | FOUR CENTS Elsewhere

61,000 SEE YANKS CRUSH GIANTS, 8-1, IN SERIES OPENER

Hubbell Routed in Sixth as Victors Stage Seven-Run Uprising at Stadium

GOMEZ PITCHES SUPERBLY

Holds Rivals to Six Hits and Yields Only Tally in Fifth—Lazzeri Gets Homer

DIMAGGIO STAR IN RALLY

Singles With Bases Full to Start the Onslaught—Gate Receipts Are $234,256

By JOHN DREBINGER

Bursting out of the misty haze like an enveloping flame such as a man might encounter on locating that leak in a gas pipe with the aid of a match, the Yankee juggernaut exploded only once at the Stadium yesterday, but that once sufficed to blow the opening clash of the 1937 world series virtually into atoms.

It came with cyclonic effect in the sixth inning, toppled Carl Hubbell like a reed in a high gale, tossed Colonel Bill Terry and his Giants into such confusion that they even nominated a relief pitcher who was sitting awed and spellbound in the dugout, and went on to hurtle seven runs across the plate.

Two rounds later the venerable Anthony Lazzeri wafted a towering home run into the stands and the sum total of all this was a smashing victory for Marse Joe McCarthy's amazing American League champions behind their own left-hander, Vernon Gomez. The final score, 8 to 1, left a crowd of 61,000 almost as stunned and bewildered as it all as were the crestfallen National Leaguers.

Clings Tenaciously to Lead

For five innings, Hubbell, ace pitcher of the circuit, strove heroically to repeat his notable triumph in the series opener of 1936. The work of these rounds, in fact, the work of the famous screwball maestro was absolutely flawless as he clung tenaciously to a one-run margin he had gained over his left-handed adversary.

But in this, perhaps, he made a mistake, for it is a matter of scientific knowledge that at times it is extremely dangerous to keep a highly volatile explosive too tightly bottled up. Something simply had to give and in the sixth it was ol' Hub himself.

Confronted by the inviting set-up of the bases full and nobody out but a few less hardy Giant rooters who doubtless already felt what was coming, Joe DiMaggio, for whom they call the wonder player of his time, crashed a single to center field to start the avalanche of Yankee runs pouring across the plate.

More Shells Are Fired

Presently the bases again filled. In fact, those Yankees seemed to keep the bases filled for an interminable period while Bill Dickey and George Selkirk fired more shells into the gaunt frame of ol' Hub, who was unmistakably going down with all his comrades on board.

Finally, with the seven big tallies tucked away, the Yankee storm subsided, leaving only Gomez to move serenely on to his fourth victory in world series warfare.

The singular Castilian, who once made the classic remark that he would rather be lucky than good, now reveled in the picture of combining both of these rare qualities so vital to success in any venture.

For not only had fortune smiled on him to the extent of having runs poured in for him in a carload lot, but he was undeniably superb as well. He pitched smoothly and easily, held the straining National League standard bearers to six blows, only two of which did any damage at all, and all in all was a far cry from the Gomez who stumbled badly to two victories last Fall behind a similar withering barrage.

Open Gaps in Stands

As had been half feared, the capacity crowd which was expected to total 70,000 did not materialize. There were a few open gaps in the lower end of the reserved sections and, what was even more surprising, the unreserved upper tier revealed vacant spaces as well.

The paid attendance totaled 60,873, more than 6,000 short of the all-time record set last year, and the receipts were $234,256.

Following a night of heavy rains which for a time threatened to postpone the whole program a day, a clear but intensely humid morning greeted the early arrivals. It assured a ball game, even if the sun remained behind a haze that hung over the arena like a smoke screen throughout the sultry afternoon.

The bulk of the crowd, in fact,

Continued on Page Thirty-two

Only Three Days Remain For Registration Here

Registration throughout the city continued yesterday to lag behind last year's figures and those of 1933, the year of the last Mayoralty campaign. The total registration in the city for the first three days of this year was 960,403, which compared with 962,072 in 1933, and 1,152,372 last year, when the all-time record was set.

Yesterday's registration did, however, show an upturn in most boroughs, and in Manhattan and the Bronx exceeded the 1933 total for the same period, although it lagged far behind the 1936 figures.

Residents of New York who desire to cast a vote in the municipal election on Nov. 2 must qualify by registering this week. There are only three days left. Registration places will be open from 5 P. M. to 10:30 P. M. today and tomorrow, and from 7 A. M. to 10:30 P. M. on Saturday.

MAYOR AND TAYLOR BREAK OVER BUDGET

La Guardia Quits Meeting in Rage, Charging Political Plot by Colleagues

WON'T CUT PAY, HE SAYS

Insists Controller Must Make Up Shortage Due to Cut in Water Rates

Enraged to the point of tears by the attempts of Democratic members of the Board of Estimate to make him responsible for finding the additional $12,000,000 that he must squeeze out of next year's budget, Mayor La Guardia slammed out of an executive session of the board yesterday after the bitterest battle he has ever had with Controller Frank J. Taylor.

Controller Taylor suggested in the course of the executive session that the Mayor order the Budget Director to reduce salaries next year to make up the $12,000,000 taken off the city's revenues when the Aldermen cut city water rates last Monday. Through the closed doors of the committee room in City Hall the Mayor's sledge-hammer blows on the table were plainly heard.

"Damn it," he shouted, "you're not going to put me on the spot. I'm a candidate too. Your Democratic Aldermen overrode my veto on the water rates, and now you want me to take the rap. I'll be damned if I will."

Tells Colleagues to Do Cutting

"Mahoney and the rest of you are going around town taking credit for getting the water rate cut through, and now you want me and my Budget Director to take the rap by trying to make us cut salaries in the budget next year.

"You cut the revenue," the Mayor stormed at his colleagues. "Now go ahead and cut the budget. I warned you that you either would have to cut relief or cut salaries, if you cut the water rate. Now, damn it, you go ahead and do it. I won't."

With a mighty tug, the door of the chamber flew open and the Mayor charged out, his face a choleric red and tears of rage starting from his eyes. He tore by everyone in the hall, clattered down the stairs and dashed into his office, and every door in his path got a resounding slam as he went.

"The Controller is the financial officer of the city—let him find the $12,000,000 to make up the water rate cut," the Mayor remarked.

"I won't take that responsibility," retorted Mr. Taylor. "It's your budget."

"Well, I can't print the money," the Mayor shot back.

Lyons in Clash

Mr. Lyons tried to introduce a motion stating that the Mayor was equally responsible with other members of the Board of Estimate to meet the budget by $22,905,033. In his budget message last Saturday the Mayor said these were items over which he had neither power nor control.

"The Borough President of the Bronx doesn't know what he's talking about and apparently can't read English," the Mayor lashed out. "He is one of those who is trying to force the tax rate up, or salaries down, through the cut in water rates."

"We're not going to tamper with

Continued on Page Eleven

LONDON AND PARIS SAID TO GIVE ITALY 24 HOURS TO REPLY

Patience is Exhausted in Issue of Withdrawal of Italians From War in Spain

SHOW OF FORCE EXPECTED

Opening of French Frontier to Arm Madrid Is Held to Be Sufficient

Twenty-four hours in which to reply to the invitation to a three-power meeting on withdrawal of "volunteers" from Spain was understood to have been given to Italy yesterday by Great Britain and France. An Anglo-French display of force was indicated if a prompt reply from Italy was not forthcoming. In Rome it was said the answer would not be ready. [Page 1.]

Rain and fog continued to hold up the Insurgent drive near Gijon on the north coast of Spain. In the southwest around Huelva the Rebels were harassed by guerrilla warfare. [Page 20.]

In London, a group of British Protestants, having issued an appeal for a united Christian front to combat anti-church activities in connection with the civil war, now resolved to help this work. [Page 20.]

Firm Stand Toward Italy

By The Associated Press.

LONDON, Oct. 6.—France and Great Britain tonight gave Premier Benito Mussolini twenty-four hours' grace to respond to their joint bid for a three-power discussion of the withdrawal of "volunteers" from Spain.

The two governments, alarmed by the new Italian aid to the Spanish Insurgents, strongly indicated their patience with Mussolini was not unlimited after Foreign Secretary Anthony Eden conferred lengthily with Prime Minister Neville Chamberlain and Ambassador Charles Corbin of France.

"The two Governments have agreed on the desirability of receiving an early reply from Italy," said a statement issued following the conferences.

Show of Force Suggested

The feeling grew in authoritative quarters that a stern show of Anglo-French force might be the only way to get Italian Black Shirt legions out of Spain, a problem that worries Britain as much as the Far Eastern crisis does.

"We may have to take quick, very decisive action to strangle at its source the prolonged Italian intervention in behalf of the Insurgents," said one informed source, though just what direct action the British Cabinet might take remained a secret.

The opinion was expressed that Italy's obvious attempts to improve Britain and France of her strength—by sending new, powerful planes and troops to Spain—actually were

Continued on Page Twenty

U. S. CONDEMNS JAPAN AS INVADER OF CHINA; DROPS NEUTRALITY POLICY TO BACK LEAGUE; GENEVA CALLS MEETING OF 9-POWER NATIONS

Rome Held Ready to Aid Any U. S. Peace Parley

By The Associated Press.

ROME, Oct. 6.—Diplomatic circles here were stirred by the potentialities of President Roosevelt's comments on world affairs.

There was considerable speculation in Fascist circles over whether the President, in announcing more active American cooperation in the cause of world peace, was planning an international conference to halt "international anarchy and instability" and if his strength was great enough to obtain a positive peace agreement.

Informed sources said Italy would be willing to take part in such a parley if sufficient preliminary work preceded the actual conference.

American condemnation of Japan as a treaty violator in China today fell sharply athwart an Italian tendency to justify Japanese activity. For example, the Popolo d'Italia of Milan said yesterday, "We fully understand and justify" Japanese efforts at expansion.

Reliable sources reported that weeks ago the Fascist press was instructed to play up the Japanese side of the Sino-Japanese conflict.

JAPANESE CONFER ON CENSURE BY U. S.

Emergency Conference Called by Foreign Office as Extras Appear With Condemnation

ROOSEVELT IS CRITICIZED

But Press Is Convinced That We Will Shun Entanglement in Other People's Quarrels

By The Associated Press.

TOKYO, Thursday, Oct. 7.—The Japanese Foreign Office called an emergency conference today following United States action condemning Japan as a treaty violator.

Simultaneously, newspaper extras began appearing with the bare text of the pronouncement issued by the State Department in Washington. No comment was published immediately. Excitement spread through the streets as crowds clustered around the newsboys.

Government officials earlier had reserved comment on the action by the United States and the League of Nations Assembly also condemning Japan for her role in the undeclared war with China.

They said they were awaiting

Continued on Page Thirteen

LEAGUE UNANIMOUS

Fifty Countries Endorse Move for a Parley to Seek Settlement

19 NATIONS ARE INVITED

Germany and Russia Also Are Expected to Be Asked—Roosevelt Speech Hailed

Wireless to THE NEW YORK TIMES.

GENEVA, Oct. 6.—With the tacit approval of fifty other countries and the remaining two, Poland and Siam, abstaining, the League of Nations Assembly adopted tonight the resolution of its Far Eastern Advisory Committee. This resolution authorizes League members who are parties to the Nine-Power treaty to invite the United States and other interested powers to initiate the consultation provided for in this treaty with a view to ending the Sino-Japanese conflict by agreement.

Then, instead of closing the session, the Assembly followed the precedents set during the Manchurian and Ethiopian crises and recessed. By this action the President, the Aga Khan, was left free to call another session whenever he considers it necessary.

Tonight's meeting was brief, lasting slightly more than a half hour. There were only two speakers, Carl J. Hambro of Norway and Stefanus F. Gie of South Africa. Both supported the resolution.

Declares Text Adopted

When they had finished and no further speakers expressed a wish to be heard the President announced that unless a vote were requested he would take it that the Assembly did not want one. There being no objection he declared the resolution adopted.

Immediately thereafter, in accordance with the Assembly's decision, he signed letters to seventeen League members who are signatories of the Nine-Power treaty, inviting them to initiate the consultation provided for under the pact's Article VII at the earliest possible moment. The seventeen League signatories are Australia, Belgium, Bolivia, Canada, China, Denmark, France, India, Italy, Mexico, the Netherlands, New Zealand, Norway, Portugal, Sweden, the United Kingdom and the Union of South Africa.

[Article VII of the Nine-Power treaty, signed at Washington Feb. 6, 1922, reads: "The Contracting Powers agree that whenever a situation arises which in the opinion of any one of them involves the application of the stipulations of the present treaty and renders desirable discussion of such application, there shall be full and frank communication between the Contracting Powers concerned.]

League circles hinted that an invitation from Washington to hold the consultation in the capital of the United States would be particularly acceptable, as under those circumstances the Japanese might be disposed to accept. The British are especially known to hold this view. Besides Japan, the United States and the seventeen other countries mentioned above, Germany and Soviet Russia are almost certain to be invited, though it is regarded as unlikely that Germany will accept. Since the Advisory Committee meets again within a month it is hoped here that consultation will be called within a fortnight. The results could then be transmitted to the Advisory Committee when it meets and, if the circumstances require it, the Assembly might be reconvened.

Other Measures Threatened

GENEVA, Oct. 6 (AP).—The League of Nations put pressure on Japan tonight to end her undeclared war on China. The League Assembly threw its "moral support" to China, called on the Nine-Power treaty group to act and told Japan there might be other measures if she did not quit her war.

The Nine-Power signatories also were expected to assemble quickly. Representatives of League members involved said the conference might be held in London within two weeks. Some suggested that the conference might meet in Washington, where the treaty was created.

Arrangements probably will be made through triangular conversation—or a passive or shameful

Continued on Page Twelve

U. S. Statement on Japan

The text of Mr. Stimson's letter is on page 12.

WASHINGTON, Oct. 6.—Following is the text of the State Department statement issued today condemning Japan's action in China:

The Department of State has been informed by the American Minister to Switzerland of the text of the report adopted by the advisory committee of the League of Nations setting forth the advisory committee's examination of the facts of the present situation in China and the treaty obligations of the Government of the United States should govern international relationships, if peace is to be maintained, as abstinence by all nations from use of force in the pursuit of policy and from interference in the internal affairs of other nations; adjustment of problems in international relations by process of peaceful negotiation and agreement; respect by all nations for the rights of others and observance by all nations of established obligations; and the upholding of the principle of the sanctity of treaties.

On Oct. 5 at Chicago the President elaborated these principles, emphasizing their importance, and in a discussion of the world situation pointed out that there can be no stability or peace either within nations or between nations except under laws and moral standards adhered to by all; that international anarchy de-

Continued on Page Twelve

STIMSON FAVORS ACTION ON JAPAN

Urges Joint Move by U. S. and Britain to Stop Supplying War Goods to Tokyo

HE PRAISES ROOSEVELT

Terms Chicago Speech 'an Act of Leadership'—Supports Our Backing of League

An appeal that the United States lend support to the League of Nations "by a statement of its concurrence" in efforts to stop Japan's war upon China was made yesterday by former Secretary of State Henry L. Stimson in a letter to THE NEW YORK TIMES discussing the Sino-Japanese situation.

Mr. Stimson, whose letter had been completed before President Roosevelt made his Chicago address, added a paragraph in which he hailed the talk, which called for "concerted action" for peace and assailed war makers. He referred to it as "an act of leadership" which, he hoped, "will result in a new birth of American courage in facing and carrying through our responsibilities in this crisis."

"In this grave crisis in the Far East we not only must not fear to face issues of right and wrong but we must not fear to cooperate with other nations who are similarly attempting to face those issues," Mr. Stimson declared.

Failure to act, he warned, will not keep this country out of war, but will endanger our own peace.

Assails Neutrality Laws

Assailing the recent neutrality legislation of the United States as "a policy of amoral drift" which, if continued, will make our entanglement in war more certain, Mr. Stimson suggested as one measure of practical action that the United States and Great Britain stop supplying Japan with commodities essential to the pursuit of her military and naval operations.

The United States and the British Empire, he pointed out, now furnish Japan with the bulk of those commodities.

"Japan's principal need is not that something should be done by outside nations to help her, but that outside nations should cease helping her enemy," Mr. Stimson declared after an exhaustive analysis of the situation, in which he branded Japan as a militarist aggressor acting in violation of international obligations under the Nine Power treaty.

While rejecting the idea of armed intervention in the Sino-Japanese conflict, Mr. Stimson emphasized that "that is very far from saying that the only alternative is inaction

Continued on Page Nineteen

OSTRACIZE JAPAN, PITTMAN DEMANDS

Senator Asserts an 'Economic Quarantine' Would End Conflict in 30 Days

HOLDS WORLD SHOULD ACT

Calls on 'Civilized' Nations, Especially Britain, to Join U. S. in Strong Move

Special to THE NEW YORK TIMES.

RENO, Nev., Oct. 6.—Senator Key Pittman, chairman of the Senate Foreign Relations Committee, recommended an economic quarantine of Japan in a statement issued here tonight.

He declared that President Roosevelt has been "very patient and has made every effort to persuade the military government of Japan to abandon its unlawful, immoral and brutal conduct in China," and that "the continued conduct of the military government of Japan" has conclusively proved to the world that Japan's "excuse" that she has been only protecting her subjects in China is false.

"The Government of the United States, while not a member of the League of Nations," said Senator Pittman, "is a signatory to the Nine-Power pact guaranteeing the territorial integrity of China and bears all of the obligations that fall upon Japan, Great Britain, France, Belgium, Russia and other great signatories. Our government can no longer refrain from asserting the facts and publicly condemning Japan."

Action Under Nine-Power Pact

"The action of our Government is taken under the Nine-Power pact and not under the covenant of the League of Nations. Japan has offered the excuse of a hold-up man that is, the hold-up man needs money and the victim has it.

"Great Britain is more directly affected by Japan's aggression than is the United States in any other country. Great Britain backed down in 1932 and left our Government out on a limb. Our government has come out of the brush and assumes their part of the responsibilities.

"The President has suggested the method of compelling Japan to desist from its barbarous warfare of destruction. He holds that Japan is disseminating war disease which may involve the world and that Japan should be quarantined as every civilized community quarantines against contagious disease.

"The Neutrality Act was never intended to meet such contagion. It was intended solely to eliminate certain causes that might lead us into foreign war. What is required now is a quarantine to prevent spread of the war disease and to stamp it out.

Continued on Page Nineteen

TWO PACTS CITED

State Department Says Tokyo Breaks 9-Power and Kellogg Treaties

EMBARKS ON NEW COURSE

Acceptance by Washington of Bid to Conference Asked by League Is Foreseen

By BERTRAM D. HULEN

WASHINGTON, Oct. 6.—Japan was condemned by the United States for her action in China and accused of having violated the Nine-Power treaty for safeguarding China and the Kellogg-Briand anti-war pact in a formal statement issued late today by the State Department.

The declaration aligned this country with the League of Nations in the condemnation of Japan as an aggressor. It is to be followed, from all indications, by American acceptance of an invitation, which has not yet been received, to participate in a conference called under the Nine-Power treaty to consider what the interested nations should do to meet the emergency.

The statement, which was issued in response to official notification of the analysis of the conclusions on the Sino-Japanese situation, marked a radical shift in American policy and represented the first step in implementing the views President Roosevelt enunciated in his Chicago speech yesterday.

New Course for U. S. Seen

Together the two moves mean, in diplomatic and political opinion, that President Roosevelt has made a dead letter of American neutrality policy and is embarked on a new course of dealing actively with aggressor nations.

The State Department statement reviewed the efforts Secretary Hull has made heretofore to encourage peace between Japan and China, recalled the pertinent points of President Roosevelt's Chicago speech, and concluded by saying:

"In the light of the unfolding developments in the Far East the action of Japan in China has been forced to the conclusion that the action of Japan in China is inconsistent with the principles which should govern the relationships between nations and is contrary to the provisions of the Nine-Power treaty of Feb. 6, 1922, regarding principles and policies to be followed in matters concerning China, and to those of the Kellogg-Briand pact of Aug. 27, 1928. Thus the conclusions of this Government with respect to the foregoing are in general accord with those of the Assembly of the League of Nations."

The condemnation of Japan marks the first time the United States has declared a nation an 'aggressor' or a violator of treaties.

First Move of the Kind

Similarly, the call for a conference under the Nine-Power treaty constitutes the first time that that pact has been invoked. Secretary of State Henry L. Stimson planned to invoke it in 1932 at the time of Japan's invasion of Manchuria, but was dissuaded when Great Britain displayed no enthusiasm for the plan. Instead, Mr. Stimson invoked American rights under the treaty and implemented the Kellogg-Briand pact by announcing that the United States would not recognize gains won contrary to its terms.

[This is the second instance within eight days in which the United States has supported action taken by the League of Nations. Secretary Hull issued a statement on Sept. 28 concerning Japanese bombings of open cities in China after the League had adopted a resolution taking a similar stand.]

Officials in issuing the statement were thoroughly aware of the significance of the step and of its implications in relation to association of the United States with the League of Nations and in the renewed force it gives the Kellogg-Briand pact.

They appreciated, although perhaps only in broad outline, that it might well lead to similar steps in future emergencies and that it might also produce adverse reactions from isolationist elements in this country. Even today peace organizations attacked President

Continued on Page Twelve

Hepburn Government Wins in Ontario; He Hails Victory as Endorsing Fight on CIO

Special to THE NEW YORK TIMES.

TORONTO, Oct. 6.—After three stormy years in office, Premier Mitchell Hepburn of Ontario was re-elected tonight by a majority almost as sweeping as that which first swept him into power in 1934.

The Conservatives lost their leader, Earl Rowe, who was defeated by Mr. Hepburn's Minister of Education, Dr. L. J. Simpson. All other Liberal Ministers were re-elected, with the exception of Duncan Marshall, who held the portfolio of agriculture.

Mr. Hepburn's Liberal party won 63 and the Conservatives 23 out of the Legislature's ninety seats.

Two Liberal Progressives, one Independent Liberal and one United Farmer were returned. Labor, Social Credit and Communist candidates were left at the post. The Cooperative Commonwealth party (Fabian Socialist) lost the one seat it held in the last Legislature.

The result was interpreted by Mr. Hepburn chiefly as an endorsement of his determined stand last Spring against the incursion of C. I. O. organizers from the United States.

"The people of Ontario," he declared, "may rest assured they will have another five years of industrial peace. Ontario has given an endorsement to the first jurisdiction in North America that enough courage openly to defy and resist the threatened C. I. O. invasion."

Ontario farmers, to whom Mr. Hepburn made his chief appeal, gave him solid support. In Oshawa,

where the General Motors strike last Spring provoked his intervention and caused the resignation of two Ministers from his Cabinet, a Liberal candidate, Gordon Conant, was returned. Northern Ontario, whose miners were recruited by the C. I. O., gave the Government almost as large a vote as in 1934.

Against this, however, was the fact that in Windsor and Toronto, David A. Croll and Arthur W. Roebuck, two former Hepburn Ministers, who lost their Cabinet portfolios as the result of an open break with the Premier over the C. I. O. issue, were re-elected with handsome majorities.

Credit for his victory is given both by the government's friends and foes to Mr. Hepburn himself. For eight weeks he waged what was virtually a one-man campaign, principally on his opposition to the C. I. O. and communism which, he contended, was following hot on its heels.

TORONTO, Oct. 6 (Canadian Press).—The Conservatives gained nine seats from the Liberals in the Ontario election: Dufferin-Simcoe, Fort William, Hastings West, Leeds, Peel, Prince Edward-Lennox, Simcoe East, Toronto Riverdale, Victoria. The Liberals gained three from the Conservatives: Peterborough, Toronto Bracondale, Toronto St. David, all from the Cooperative Commonwealth party, Hamilton East.

"All the News That's Fit to Print."

The New York Times.

LATE CITY EDITION
Partly cloudy, continued cold today. Tomorrow cloudy, probably more temperature unchanged.
Temperatures Yesterday—Max. 22; Min. 19

Copyright, 1937, by The New York Times Company.

VOL. LXXXVII....No. 29,178.   Entered as Second-Class Matter, Postoffice, New York, N. Y.   NEW YORK, MONDAY, DECEMBER 13, 1937.   PPP   TWO CENTS in New York City | THREE CENTS Elsewhere Except | FOUR CENTS in 7th and 8th Postal Zones

---

DIES CLAIMS VOTES TO BEAT WAGE BILL BY RECOMMITTAL

But Despite His Poll House Leaders Hope to Pass Measure This Week

HARD FIGHT IN PROSPECT

Some Expect Norton Change in Administration to Be Turned Down

CIO PLAN TEST IS NEAR

Senate Action This Week Seen —Harrison Predicts Tax Revision by Feb. 1

Special to The New York Times.

WASHINGTON, Dec. 12.—Congressional leaders plan to make a determined effort to send to conference this week two of the four measures for which the special session was called, the Farm Bill voted by the House last week and the Wages and Hours measure, which has long been tied up in the House Rules Committee.

The latter bill faces perhaps the bitterest fight of the session. When the House convenes tomorrow time will call up the measure, changed in many respects from the Black-Connery bill passed by the Senate at the last regular session.

By means of a discharge petition to which 218 signatures were obtained ten days ago to force it out of the Rules Committee, the bill comes before the House, where its enemies threaten the strongest kind of opposition.

Representative Dies of the Rules Committee, disclosed tonight that with other opponents he had been quietly taking a poll of the House and felt that they had enough backing to force recommittal of the bill.

Count 202 for Recommittal

"Our poll shows that 202 House members will vote for recommittal," he said. "It indicated that two-thirds of the Republicans in the House favor recommittal."

He added that at least thirty-five of the members who signed the discharge petition would vote for the motion to recommit and that Southern foes of the measure could count on enough additional votes from the Middle West and rural towns in the East to give them a majority when the time came.

"If the bill passed, taking the most optimistic figures, it would affect not more than 500,000 workers after you deduct those who are exempt and those who are engaged in intrastate employment," said Mr. Dies.

"This bill can only help a handful but at the same time its passage would increase the cost of living and thus affect the whole nation. Its real effect would be to lower wage scales and lengthen hours."

Representative Cox of Georgia, likewise a member of the Rules Committee, also expressed hostility to the bill.

"The passage of this measure is the worst thing that could take place at this time," he said. "It would throw a million out of work."

The House leadership expresses equal confidence that a wages and hours measure in some form will be passed by the end of Wednesday's session.

Boland Predicts Passage

Representative Boland, the Democratic whip, canvassed the situation over the week-end, and predicted that a bill resembling in essentials the Senate measure, which provides for a five-man administrative board with differentials as to minimum wages and maximum hours for various parts of the country, would be approved.

The leaders will fight the motion to recommit and say they regard a victory in that fight as virtually certain. Mr. Boland said a handful of those who signed the discharge petition might vote to recommit, but that there were enough votes to compensate for such a defection.

Besides having to thwart efforts of Southern members who seek recommittal, the leadership faces what may develop into a major struggle over the content of the legislation to be passed. Representative Dockweiler of California seeks to substitute for the bill a measure, strongly backed by the American Federation of Labor, which provides for a flat forty-hour maximum work week and a forty-cent minimum pay per hour and for administration by existing agencies, with Federal courts and the

Continued on Page Twelve

Convicts Kill Captive Guard As Governor Begs Mercy

South Carolina Executive Pleads 2 Hours for Hostage Held in Prison Office, Then Troops Rout 6 Men With Gas

By The Associated Press.

COLUMBIA, S. C., Dec. 12.—A machine-gun company of National Guardsmen fired tear-gas shells today to subdue six convicts who stabbed a prison guard captain to death and barricaded themselves in the captain's office in a desperate attempt to escape from the State penitentiary.

The victim, Captain Olin Sanders, was stabbed five times after the felons had defied a dramatic two-hour plea by Governor Olin Johnston to give themselves up.

The youthful Governor shouted to them through the door of their barricaded refuge, urging them to submit to avoid bloodshed and obviate the necessity of calling out the National Guard.

"Get us a car. Open the gates. Otherwise it'll be too bad for Sanders," one of the felons retorted.

In vain the Governor begged them to release their captive. Half an hour later the khaki-clad troopers arrived. Another plea was made by Adjt. Gen. James C. Dozier, commanding the guardsmen. Again the convicts bluntly refused, announcing they would stay there "until hell freezes over."

Governor Johnston made one final effort to persuade them.

"If you boys will walk out of there and let Captain Sanders walk out first, I'll see that nothing goes against your record," he promised.

A hoarse rumble of defiance replied, and Governor Johnston signaled the guardsmen.

"Go ahead, boys—let them have it."

A barrage of tear gas brought quick surrender. Gasping and choking, with tears streaming down their cheeks, the desperadoes emerged, one by one, with their hands up.

On the floor, bleeding profusely from stab wounds, lay Sanders. He died in a hospital a few minutes later.

The victim apparently was stabbed immediately after the guardsmen opened their tear-gas attack.

Prison officials said that Sanders was unarmed at the time of the attack because strict prison rules forbade carrying a gun into the prison yard.

Guards said he had "checked"

Continued on Page Four

SLOAN BACKS FUND BY $10,000,000 GIFT

General Motors Head Endows Foundation He Established for Economic Research

ASKS THAT STOCK BE HELD

Transfer of Holdings in His Own Concern Explained— Gains in Education Sought

Alfred P. Sloan Jr. announced plans yesterday for endowing the Alfred P. Sloan Foundation for economic research with securities worth about $10,000,000. A little more than one-third of the proposed endowment, his statement said, consists of common stock of General Motors Corporation, of which Mr. Sloan is chairman.

Lest the public misapprehend the situation, Mr. Sloan included in his statement announcing the gift a promise to recommend that the trustees of the fund that they retain the General Motors stock in their portfolio. Under SEC rules the transfer of ownership of the stock is a matter of public record.

The trust Mr. Sloan purposes to endow was established by him on July 6, 1936, as a non-profit corporation under the laws of Delaware. Harold S. Sloan, his brother, a former Associate Professor of Economics at State Teachers College, Montclair, N. J., was named executive director of the fund.

The organization of the trust was not announced until Feb. 27, 1937. At the time it was explained that the founder had been too busy with labor troubles to perfect the details of the fund's operation or the size of the endowment needed for its work. In the meantime, Harold Sloan established an office at 30 Rockefeller Plaza.

Sloan Explains His Gift

Mr. Sloan's statement, announcing his intention of transferring $10,000,000 of securities to the fund, follows:

"I take this means of announcing that I am in the process of making as an endowment to the Alfred P. Sloan Foundation, securities of an estimated worth of approximately $10,000,000. The specific purpose of this statement is twofold: first, to avoid any misconception as to the aims involved, and, second, to establish the objectives that I have in mind.

"I particularly wish to emphasize the fact, even if it appears self-evident, that this transaction has nothing whatsoever to do with General Motors Corporation or any official relationship with same. It is entirely a personal matter. However, among the securities involved are over 100,000 shares of the common stock of General Motors.

"Due to government regulations, any in General Motors holdings are a matter of public record on account of my official relationship with that organization; hence it is important, especially in the period of uncertainty now existing, that no prejudice should develop as to the reasons for the action that I am taking. I shall recommend to the trustees of the Foundation that they continue to hold these securities as part of its portfolio.

"As to the objectives: The Alfred P. Sloan Foundation has its general purposes, in common with all

Continued on Page Ten

PRINCETON SENIOR IS KILLED IN FIRE

Lawrence H. Clark, 21, Found Slumped in Dormitory After Flames Sweep His Room

VICTIM OF DENSE SMOKE

Fellow-Student Arouses Seven Other Sleepers, but Fails to Locate His Friend

Special to The New York Times.

PRINCETON, N. J., Dec. 12.—Lawrence H. Clark, a 21-year-old senior at the university here, was killed this morning by smoke from a fire which apparently originated in an upholstered chair in his dormitory room at 44 Mitchell Hall. He died in the room of another student across the hall from his own, his body partly draped in bedclothing which he had sought before running out into the cold.

At about 3:45 o'clock Richard B. Duane Jr., a sophomore, of Locust, N. J., and the occupant of the room in which Clark's body was found, was awakened by the noisy entrance of Clark from the hall. He saw Clark drop on one knee, seemingly having tripped over the door sill. Duane's room was instantly filled with smoke, and Clark, only in pajamas and a pair of hastily snatched shoes, he ran out of the building and to the university police office on the campus, where he turned in a fire alarm. He said he believed Clark had followed him out.

Awakens Other Students

After turning in the alarm, Duane ran back to the dormitory and awakened the other students by shouting through the building. Five students were asleep in two double rooms on the ground floor and four more in single rooms on the second floor. Only when they were all out, shivering in heavy coats over pajamas, did Duane realize that Clark was not among them.

He went back into the building, climbing the stairs to the second floor, and finding that the flames, mounting through the ceiling in Clark's room, had cut off the electric current, he struck a match. By the imperfect light he looked over his own room, but could not enter Clark's because of the smoke, and concluded that Clark had somehow got out.

Down below again, he once more became alarmed at the absence of Clark and once again went into the building. This time the smoke was so thick he could not reach the second floor.

All the fire apparatus of Princeton had arrived meanwhile. The changing had resulted in the assembly of a large number of students, police and others. The firemen, on ladders, attacked the fire through the windows of Clark's room.

In a few moments it had been subdued sufficiently to permit a more thorough search. In Duane's room Clark's body was found, wedged between a chest of drawers and the wall, at the foot of Duane's bed. Apparently he had sought to find Clark in Duane's room, became blinded by the smoke and dropped unconscious. The bedclothing from Duane's bed was draped around his body. He thought he had passed over a depression in the street and kept on toward his home.

Continued on Page Eight

RUSSIA'S MILLIONS VOTE STALIN TICKET AMID HOLIDAY AIR

Bands Play as Most of Nation's 90,000,000 Electors Join in First Secret, Direct Poll

SUPREME SOVIET CHOSEN

Heads of Air and Tank Corps, Removed From Ballot, Are Believed in Trouble

By HAROLD DENNY

Wireless to The New York Times.

MOSCOW, Dec. 12.—The Soviet Union elected its first Supreme Soviet under its new constitution today by vote today by ballot in a beautifully conducted vote that was carried out with all the precision, order and colorful decor of a May Day parade or a Bolshoi Theatre spectacle.

The authorities succeeded fully as well as they could have expected in bringing out the total electorate numbering probably 90,000,000 to vote for the only ticket in the field —the ticket headed by Joseph Stalin himself and including virtually every high government and Communist party official.

Thus the present Soviet regime can now show the world the most complete endorsement in terms of number of votes cast ever given to any government in the world's history.

As there was no semblance of opposition in today's election the only question was how many votes would be cast. It seemed tonight on the basis of this correspondent's visits to typical polling places in Moscow and several surrounding villages and of radio reports from all parts of the Soviet Union that virtually every one, male and female, above the age of 18 who was able to get to the polls afoot, on skis or in automobiles, trucks or sleighs had voted, and naturally for the one ticket.

Agitators went through searching hunting for non-voters. Where they found sick persons who were able to leave their beds cars were summoned to transport them to the polls. In one election district in Moscow a number of ill persons reported they were unable to leave their beds and requested that ballots be sent them so they could vote. It could not be determined what was done in most such cases, but in one at least an absentee vote by a bedridden elector was allowed.

This case was that of Constantin Stanislavsky, famous director of the Moscow Art Theatre, who is now 75 years old and ill of pneumonia. A ballot was sent to him and he sealed it himself and dispatched it by a member of his family, who deposited it in a box in his district at Tsinan in Shantung in 1928, when they fought with similar valor, the Chinese contested every foot of the Japanese advance.

From many vantage points on the wall at Kwanghwa gate, from Purple Mountain and from other dominant heights surrounding the city the Japanese for nearly fifty hours poured shells of all sizes and machine-gun fire into and inside Nanking's wall. There were almost hourly aerial bombings, but the Chinese continued their suicidal battle.

With the city surrounded on all land fronts the Japanese crossed the Yangtze River yesterday at Taiping, between Nanking and

Continued on Page Fifteen

Doctor Arrested in Park Ave. Hit-Run Death; Traced by Car Part Found Near the Victim

Dr. John E. Toole, 41 years old, Yale graduate and urologist, was found part of a broken automobile arrested by detectives at his home, 120 East Eighty-fifth Street, shortly after 7 o'clock yesterday morning and arrested on a technical charge of homicide. The arrest followed an all-night investigation of the death of Miss Mary McCormack, 60, of 22 East 119th Street, who was hit and dragged more than 100 feet by an automobile at 10 o'clock Saturday night as she was crossing Fifty-eighth Street at Park Avenue. The motorist failed to stop.

Detectives Charles L. McGowan and Hugh Fox took Dr. Toole to the East Fifty-first Street station, where he denied responsibility for the death of the woman, whose body was not identified at the morgue until yesterday afternoon. The identification was made by her sister, Anna McCormick, a housemaid in the home of Dr. Nicholas Murray Butler, president of Columbia University.

Although Dr. Toole insisted his automobile did not hit any pedestrian, the detectives quoted him as saying he felt a jar when the car was passing Fifty-eighth Street on Park Avenue. The doctor explained he thought he had passed over a depression in the street and kept on toward his home.

When the body of Miss McCormack was picked up, near by was radiator grill and the emblem of a Dodge car. A search of all garages in the city was started for an automobile with broken grillwork and a missing emblem. It was not until early yesterday morning that such a car, with the front blood spattered, was found in a garage at 122 East Eighty-fourth Street. The detectives said the piece of broken radiator fitted perfectly into the frame. The automobile was listed as the property of Dr. Toole. When the detectives called at his home, Dr. Toole was asleep. He was said to have admitted he drove the automobile Saturday night, but insisted that beyond the slight jar at the scene of the accident he did not notice anything out of the ordinary. Miss McCormack was crossing Park Avenue from west to east when she was struck by a northbound automobile traveling at considerable speed.

Dr. Toole was taken from the East Fifty-first Street police station to police headquarters, where he was booked and remained pending arraignment this morning in Homicide Court.

Dr. Toole, who is single, is a graduate of the Yale class of 1920. He practices here and in Hempstead, L. I., specializing in urology and radiology.

Continued on Page Sixteen

U.S. GUNBOAT SUNK BY JAPANESE BOMBS; 1 DEAD AND 15 HURT; 54 SAVED, 18 MISSING; BRITISH WARSHIP HIT, SEAMAN DEAD

NANKING INVESTED

Japanese Expect Its Fall Soon Because Troops Are Rushing In

VITAL GATE IS CAPTURED

Naval Force Is Expected to Arrive Today to Join Land and Air Assault

By HALLETT ABEND

Special Cable to The New York Times.

SHANGHAI, Monday, Dec. 13.— Japanese troops, preceded by tanks, have been pouring into Nanking since 4 A. M., when they captured Chungshan gate. The city's capitulation is imminent, according to Japanese army headquarters.

The Nanking fighting continued unabated throughout last night under clear skies and a half moon. The Japanese took yesterday the shores of Lotus Lake, which borders Nanking's north wall. Colonel and Mrs. Charles A. Lindbergh landed on this lake after their flight to China in September, 1931.

Japanese flags flew along all of the south wall before sunset yesterday. The Japanese first held Kwanghwa gate and the corner west of the gate and Chunghwa gate and another corner near it.

The Japanese Army contingent that crossed to the north bank of the Yangtze to Wukiang Sunday has captured Pukow, the southern terminus of the Tientsin-Pukow railway, directly opposite Nanking. They thus cut off the last chance of escape for the Chinese forces in the Nanking and near-by areas.

Chinese Show Bravery

Once more the rank and file of Chinese soldiery demonstrated at Nanking their extraordinary ability to take terrible punishment and hold fast under conditions which ordinarily would disharten any fighting men.

Mostly unpaid and underfed, without any provisions for their wounded, the Chinese forced the Japanese to pay a terrific price for every foot gained around the gates. As in 1900, when Chinese forces held Tientsin's walls until a mob of corpses exceeded 7,000 and conspicuously again at Tsinan in Shantung in 1928, when they fought with similar valor, the Chinese contested every foot of the Japanese advance.

Continued on Page Fifteen

Old Treaty Permits U. S. Patrol; Ships Not on Aggressive Mission

Nationals Are Protected on Yangtze Through Agreement—Silver Island Blockade by Chinese Not Responsible for Difficulties

Special to The New York Times.

WASHINGTON, Dec. 12.—The United States gunboat Panay, sunk today by bombs in the Nanking battle area, was one of six or seven such patrol boats maintained in the Yangtze River by the United States under the Sino-American treaty of 1858. Other nations also maintain patrols in the river.

This treaty was conceded to China following the joint attack on that country by Britain and France in 1857-58, when they captured Canton and reduced the Taku forts guarding Tientsin. The United States and Russia did not join in the war but they insisted on sharing the rights gained by the others.

Among these was permission for foreigners to travel in the interior of China and the entrance of Christian missionaries into this field. Four ports were opened on the Yangtze and extraterritorial rights were granted to the nations concerned so they could protect their nationals. In order to protect these

foreigners and their trade and religious activities the patrol of the river was established.

Commander I. P. Lovette, naval press relations officer, who formerly commanded such craft said tonight that these vessels comprised a sort of civil "police force" for the United States and China.

Naval orders say that these boats are on duty for the special purposes of protecting United States citizens from violence, to protect them in times of emergency, to maintain uninterrupted communications, and to protect United States diplomatic and consular establishments.

He said the ships acted as police not only for the United States but for China, offering protection to own in times of violence or emergency. Sometimes, he said, it became necessary for the United

Continued on Page Fourteen

TROTSKY CLEARED BY DEWEY BOARD

International Group Finds He and Son Were 'Not Guilty' of Plot Against Soviet

A 'FRAME-UP' IS CHARGED

New Evidence Contradicts the Moscow Verdicts on 21 Counts, Report Says

An international commission of inquiry headed by Dr. John Dewey declared last night that Leon Trotsky was "not guilty" of the charges against him in the Moscow trials of August, 1936, and January, 1937, and that the trials were a "frame-up."

The commission's verdict of "not guilty" applied also to Leon Sedov, Mr. Trotsky's son now residing in Paris and condemned in absentia with his father in the two trials.

Dr. Dewey reported the commission's findings at a mass meeting in the Hotel Center, 108 West Forty-third Street, attended by more than 2,000 persons, including many prominent liberals and representatives of various schools of political thought specially invited to hear a summary of the commission's report.

The report, a document of 80,000 words, will be published in book form, continuing the series of publications begun with the record of the preliminary hearings held by the commission last April in Mexico City and at which Mr. Trotsky testified at great length and was subjected to exhaustive interrogation.

Contradicts the Verdicts

The commission's conclusions, as reported by Dr. Dewey at last night's meeting, flatly contradicted the verdicts of the Moscow court on twenty-one separate counts, on the basis of "much new documentary evidence" assembled over a period of nine months in Mexico, the United States, Canada and European countries, and study of the official Soviet trial records, the commission reached the conclusion that Mr. Trotsky and Mr. Sedov were the victims of a conspiracy to discredit them, and that "independent of extrinsic evidence" the conduct of the Moscow trials "was such as to convince any unprejudiced person that no effort was made to ascertain the truth."

The commission found also that the confessions of the accused in the Moscow trials "contain such inherent improbabilities as to convince the commission that they do not represent the truth, irrespective of any means used to obtain them."

At the same time, the commission expressed the belief that the confessions were obtained by duress.

The Chief Findings

Supporting itself upon a "mass of new documentary evidence and affidavits," the commission affirmed

Continued on Page Sixteen

---

3 DRIVES STARTED BY SPANISH REBELS

Collapse of Loyalists Is Said to Have Resulted at Toledo, Brunete and Teruel

MADRID IS AGAIN SHELLED

Insurgents Claim 270 Planes Took Part in Friday Battle, With Victory for Them

By The Associated Press.

HENDAYE, France, at the Franco-Spanish Frontier, Dec. 12.— The Spanish Insurgent armies launched today their long-awaited general offensive, Insurgent authorities announced at Irun. This statement was made in reply to a British protest against shelling of the British gunboat Ladybird at Wuhu. A British seaman was killed and two other Britons were wounded there.

When 100 Government planes encircled the supposed raiders, 150 Insurgent warplanes suddenly swooped, putting the Government fleet to flight with a quarter of its strength lost in a few minutes.

Insurgent planes made a number of fresh incursions in Government zones Saturday, meeting renewed resistance. One Insurgent squadron invaded the Aragon front, east of Saragossa, bombing the outskirts of Castejon del Puente. A Government communiqué said the raid was checked with a minimum of damage.

270 Planes in Battle

Insurgent dispatches today gave an account of Friday's aerial battle near Saragossa. They said massed air fleets totaling 270 warplanes had clashed. Twenty-five Government planes were shot down and only one Insurgent plane was lost, it was said.

The great air battle coincided with the holiday of Notre Dame de Loretto, the patron saint of aviation. Under her auspices, twenty Insurgent planes from Saragossa flew over Government lines to lure enemy pilots.

Madrid Heavily Shelled

By HERBERT L. MATTHEWS

Wireless to The New York Times.

MADRID, Dec. 12.—Many dinners were spoiled in Madrid tonight when the Rebels chose from 7:40 to 8:00 to bombard the center of the city with considerable intensity. They may not have been good diners, for the Madrileños are not indulging id feasts this Winter.

We had a perfectly good dish of cocotail party culture in the middle of one of three shells which

Continued on Page Thirteen

JAPAN TAKES ONUS

Officers Admit Attack on Panay With Regrets— Craft Sought Safety

BRITISH VESSELS TARGETS

Two Fire at Planes as Bombs Are Aimed at Them—Two Standard Oil Ships Sunk

By The Associated Press.

SHANGHAI, Dec. 12.—Japanese bombs sank the United States gunboat Panay in the Yangtze River twenty-five miles above Nanking yesterday.

One American sailor died of his wounds. His name was not given. Eighteen other persons were unaccounted for.

There were fifty-four known survivors, some of them wounded. Among the wounded were Lieut. Comdr. James J. Hughes, commander of the Panay, and Lieutenant Arthur F. Anders, executive officer.

[Ambassador Nelson T. Johnson reported to the State Department at Washington that fifteen of the survivors had been wounded, some of them seriously, according to The Associated Press. One of the injured was an Italian subject, he said.]

The Panay's normal complement was fifty-five officers and men. In addition, the "mercy ship" carried at least nine American refugees, including four embassy officials.

Two Standard Oil Company ships were also sunk in the same melee. No word was received of the fate of those aboard these vessels.

The Japanese Navy quickly accepted responsibility for the grave incident. A Japanese communique pledged immediate steps to place the blame on the military units responsible, and it regretted the bombing "most deeply."

British Gunboat Shelled

Earlier British naval reports said that Colonel Hashimoto, senior Japanese officer, had declared he had orders to "fire on every ship on the river." His statement was made in reply to a British protest against shelling of the British gunboat Ladybird at Wuhu. A British seaman was killed and two other Britons were wounded there.

Officers of the United States flagship Augusta said they believed seventy-two persons had been aboard the Panay. Those missing apparently were killed by the Japanese bombs or were drowned when the vessel sank. However, some might have reached a place without communication facilities.

Most of the survivors were put ashore by rescue vessels at Hohsien, Anhwei Province.

Rear Admiral Harry E. Yarnell, commander of the United States Asiatic Fleet, canceled his departure for Manila, scheduled for tomorrow, in face of the serious incident.

Other Ships Rush to Aid

The U. S. gunboat Oahu and the British gunboat Bee steamed under forced draught for the scene of the sinking.

The Bee was expected to reach the scene of the sinking some time tonight, but, because of the distance, the Oahu was not expected until Tuesday.

The 450-ton Panay, especially made for river service in China, had stood by to save Americans during the Japanese siege of Nanking. Anchored in the Yangtze, the Panay was a haven for Embassy officials and other refugees until the Japanese shells crashing dangerously near caused her to seek safety up the river.

It was while steaming away from the battle zone that the vessel was sent to the bottom by Japanese bombs.

Among those aboard the Panay were George Atcheson Jr., second secretary in charge of the United States Embassy; Captain Frank Roberts, assistant military attaché, and Emile Gassie, embassy clerk.

The United States Consulate here advised that other civilians believed to have been aboard were: Norman Alley, Fox Movietone cameraman; Weldon James, United Press correspondent; Norman Soong, a newspaper correspondent of The New York Times; Roy Squires, American born in China; James Marshall, Collier's Magazine writer; J. T. Broderick, Standard Oil Company representative

Continued on Page Fourteen

"All the News That's Fit to Print."

The New York Times.

LATE CITY EDITION
Fair and moderately cold today.
Tomorrow fair, with slowly rising temperature.
Temperature Yesterday—Max., 38; Min., 29

Copyright, 1938, by The New York Times Company.

VOL. LXXXVII....No. 29,248.   Entered as Second-Class Matter, Postoffice, New York, N. Y.   NEW YORK, MONDAY, FEBRUARY 21, 1938.   PP   TWO CENTS in New York City. | THREE CENTS Within 200 Miles. | FOUR CENTS Elsewhere Except in 7th and 8th Postal Zones.

FEDERAL AGENCIES CONSIDER FORCING RAILROAD MERGERS

Groups Shaping Rehabilitation Plans Believe Plight Inclines Congress to Idea

FAVOR THREE YEARS' GRACE

Would Allow Time for Voluntary Consolidations, With Federal Action Afterward

FOR TEMPORARY POOLING

Some Officials Hold This a Need Until a Long-Range Plan Becomes Effective

By JOHN H. CRIDER
Special to The New York Times.

WASHINGTON, Feb. 20.—Legislation for forced consolidations of railroads is being considered seriously in at least three of the government offices now preparing plans to be laid before President Roosevelt at his rail conference scheduled for the coming week.

It was learned that some officials are advancing a plan which would apply the "death sentence" technique of the Holding Company Act to railroad consolidations. Under this procedure the railroads would have a certain period of years in which to submit voluntary unification plans, after which a government agency would prepare a plan for them.

Like most remedies for the nation's rail problems, the idea of forced or compulsory consolidation has been considered for years, with little favorable response from Congress, even for milder remedies than the one now gaining ground. Rail reformers are hopeful that this time Congress will relent in view of the unusually acute plight of the railroads.

"Wasteful" Competition a Factor

President Roosevelt, Senator Burton K. Wheeler, in charge of the Senate investigation of railroad finances, and the Interstate Commerce Commission in its annual report have stated that "wasteful" competition is one of the fundamental railroad ills.

The I. C. C. went so far in its annual report as to state that "no competitive industry can work out its salvation through a price-increasing policy alone." The best expert opinion in official Washington seems to be that a rate increase, such as the $517,000,000 rate rise which the I. C. C. is expected to grant to the railroads can be at most only a temporary remedy.

It is felt that compulsory consolidations cannot solve the immediate economic emergency faced by the railroads and that rate increases and perhaps some form of pooling may have to be employed until a long-range plan can be effected. Pooling is condemned by some as an incentive to inefficiency since the weak railroads are carried along by the strong.

Senator Wheeler's investigating committee, the I. C. C., the Securities and Exchange Commission and the Reconstruction Finance Corporation are among the government agencies now formulating plans to be considered at the White House conference.

Financial Position Weak

The current efforts in official circles to work out a permanent solution to the railroad problem arises from the unusually weak financial position of the country's railroads, due partly to increased operating costs, the decline in general business activity, and competition that the real work was started when the President discussed the problem at a press conference on Dec. 10. He questioned the necessity for maintaining parallel lines of railroad with inadequate traffic.

He also referred to the reports of Commissioner Joseph B. Eastman of the Interstate Commerce Commission as Federal Coordinator of Transportation in 1933 and 1934 which discussed the problems of consolidation at some length. As a consequence there has been a considerable demand for these reports, particularly for the first one, which contained in the appendix a report by Leslie Craven, counsel to the coordinator, upholding the constitutionality of compulsory consolidation and recommending a modification of the method employed in England.

Some of those now preparing plans to lay before the President feel with Mr. Craven that under "any consolidation program which is non-compulsory and not fully comprehensive, it is almost certain that uneconomic and inefficient groupings will result due to the inevitable 'inclination of the carriers which initiate consolidations to grab favorable lines in the effort

Continued on Page Eight

Swiss Make Romansh Fourth Official Tongue

By The Associated Press.

BERNE, Switzerland, Feb. 20.—Swiss voted by an overwhelming majority today to establish Romansh as the fourth official language of Switzerland.

The vote was considered by some observers as a slap at Italy, where Fascisti say Romansh, an obscure language that is spoken only in part of Grisons canton, is an Italian dialect.

German is spoken by about 71 per cent of the Swiss, French by 22 per cent, Italian by 6 per cent and Romansh by 1 per cent.

A resolution giving the Federal Council power to prevent arms shipments to warring nations and providing for partial control of armament industries also was approved.

ORTIZ INAUGURATED AMID WIDE ACCLAIM BY THE ARGENTINES

Nation Greets Six American Airplanes as a Major Part of Colorful Ceremony

PRESIDENT IS A CIVILIAN

Public Reaffirms Its Faith in Free Rule, Regarding U. S. as Example and Friend

By JOHN W. WHITE
Special Cable to The New York Times.

BUENOS AIRES, Argentina, Feb. 20.—Dr. Roberto M. Ortiz was inaugurated the twenty-first constitutional President of the Argentine Republic this afternoon in a colorful ceremony amid widespread popular acclaim. In Argentina lawyers have the title of Doctor and this puts the Presidency again under a civilian title; the last two Presidents were generals.

The presence of the giant U. S. Army monoplanes of the type known as "flying fortresses" associated the United States with Argentina on this occasion in a manner in which no foreign country has participated at any inauguration in recent years. The planes arrived on Friday after a record-smashing flight from Miami, bearing a letter from President Roosevelt to President Ortiz, expressing the best wishes of the American Government and the American people for his forthcoming government.

Nothing that the United States had done in Latin America, with the possible exception of President Roosevelt's visit a year ago, has ever aroused such an enthusiastic response on the part of the Argentine people. The newspapers have published the most laudatory editorials extending a hearty welcome to the American filers and expressing their appreciation of the goodwill of the government that sent them.

Faith in Democracy

People here have seized upon the visit of the United States filers as an opportunity to reaffirm their faith in democracy and express their disapproval of totalitarian regimes. South America, including Argentina, has been subjected to such intense propaganda from European totalitarian countries, especially Italy, during the last year that this propaganda has now reached the state expressed in the Spanish words "contra producente"—working to defeat its own aims.

The people have become resentful of this high-pressure propaganda. They have enthusiastically greeted the big American fighting planes as messengers of peace and good-will from the country to which the South Americans have always looked as their model democracy.

Public opinion in Argentina was very cold to the intimation that the Italian planes that recently visited Brazil might come to Buenos Aires for the inauguration. The Italians changed their minds and did not come. No foreign mission has ever been more enthusiastically received than the American aviators whose flight was not announced until two days before they started.

Italian newspapers both here and in Italy have not mentioned the American flight. German papers here gave it a paragraph hidden away on an inside page. Both devoted pages to two recent Italian flights.

This was an ideally beautiful Summer day with the bright blue sky and blazing sun that are featured in the Argentine flag. The Argentine Army and Navy Flying

Continued on Page Seven

TENEMENT BLAZE KILLS 3, INJURES 9

Families Routed in 165th St. Fire, Third in Building Unit in Less Than Two Years

DARING RESCUES CUT TOLL

Cripple Is Carried to Safety— Man Leaps to Death, Wife Is Killed Shielding Baby

The third fire since June, 1936, in adjoining three-story buildings at 761-63 East 165th Street, between Forest and Tinton Avenues, the Bronx, killed three persons early yesterday morning and caused injuries to nine others, including an infant orphaned by the blaze.

Hampered by the collapse of a stairway under which the flames were believed to have started, firemen of seven engine companies and two hook-and-ladder units made a series of dangerous rescues from the second and third floors of No. 763, virtually all of which was destroyed except its yellow-brick front.

One of the firemen, exhausted by the struggle in the building, which had no fire escape, was among those treated later by Dr. Harry M. Archer, honorary departmental surgeon.

Fire Not Incendiary

At first it was believed that the fire was incendiary, but after an all-day investigation Assistant District Attorney George Pilzer and Assistant Fire Marshal Martin Scott announced at 8:30 o'clock last night that the fire was not of suspicious origin. They had spent hours questioning tenants of the building and others living near by.

One of those hurt was a passer-by who aided in the rescue work. Another volunteer, boosted on the shoulders of friends before the apparatus arrived, cut his hand in smashing a second-floor window to warn tenants. The two were Thomas Smith, 38, of 1,009 Union Avenue, who suffered a sprained knee and cut thumb, and Joseph Barrett, 27, of 486 East 165th Street, who left hand was injured.

Francis Dunn, 35, of 857 Fox Street, who was later out on the head by falling glass, turned in the alarm at 3:04. He was on his way home when he noticed curling flames in the building. By the time the first fire apparatus had arrived, Smith, Dunn and others had awakened all the tenants in No. 761 and the building had been cleared.

Flames Burst Through Roof

The blaze centered, however, beneath the stairway of No. 763 and spread rapidly to the top, where it divided and ate its way into the top floor of both units of the building. One witness said it suddenly burst through the roof like a great torch. Smoke in the hallway thickened, but members of Engine Company 50 tried to get up the stairs anyway. Fireman Terence A. Nugent, who subsequently needed medical aid, was one of those nearly trapped when the stairs crumbled.

While his colleagues swung their ladders toward the building, a man appeared at the third floor window over the entrance, clambered to the sill and stared down, terrified.

A confusion of shouts rose from the street. Some cried "Jump!" and others yelled "Back! Back!" The man jumped. But while would-be rescuers extended their arms, his body struck the broad, jutting cornice between the second and ground floors. The deflection catapulted him beyond them to the street, and he was fatally injured. He was William Theofanos, 42, whose wife, Armione, 41, was burned in the bedroom while shielding their baby, 5-month-old Betsy.

With the fire-fighting crew augmented by men summoned by a second alarm, rescues by ladder were accomplished with comparatively little difficulty. But in the case of William Sculla, 65-year-old paralytic, Firemen John Mullen and Vincent Howard risked their lives to drag their way to his bed.

Continued on Page Twenty

HITLER DEMANDS RIGHT OF SELF-DETERMINATION FOR GERMANS IN AUSTRIA AND CZECHOSLOVAKIA; EDEN RESIGNS IN CRISIS OVER BRITAIN'S POLICY

Roosevelt Silent on Hitler, But May Give Views Soon

Special to The New York Times.

HYDE PARK, N. Y., Feb. 20.—The temporary White House was completely silent today on President Roosevelt's reaction to the address of Chancellor Hitler to the German Reichstag. But there were suggestions that he might soon make known in an informal way his views of his Administration toward the political situation abroad.

Marvin H. McIntyre, the President's secretary, insisted that Mr. Roosevelt passed the day resting from the cares of his office, and that he had talked only with members of his immediate family and the vestrymen of St. James Episcopal Church here.

Despite the official reticence, however, there was no doubt that the President was in close touch with the State Department.

EDEN'S RESIGNATION DISTRESSES FRANCE

Belief Prevails That British 'Capitulation' Must Reduce Leadership of Paris

SMALL ALLIES FEARED FOR

Chautemps and Delbos Confer With Ambassador Phipps, Calling Him Urgently

By P. J. PHILIP
Wireless to The New York Times.

PARIS, Feb. 20.—The resignation of British Foreign Secretary Anthony Eden has caused much more concern in France than anything that Chancellor Adolf Hitler said today. Immediately after the announcement was made, Ambassador Sir Eric Phipps hurried over to see Premier Camille Chautemps and Foreign Minister Yvon Delbos, presumably to assure them that British friendship for France and Anglo-French cooperation would remain as close as ever.

But such assurances are not likely to alter the conclusion that what is called here the Germanophile clique in Great Britain has won, and that henceforth France will be reduced to a very different role in European affairs from that which she has been accustomed to play.

It is a poor consolation to be told by Hitler that she has nothing to fear from Germany "if she minds her own business." And it will be meat for much criticism of M. Delbos and his aides that this abandonment should be the reward of their steady support of British policy during the past two years, or rather, as it will be called, their constant abasement before it.

Bitter Clash Forthcoming

It is too early to forecast what the effects will be here. What is clear, however, is that there will be a bitter fight between those who clamor for complete abandonment of the non-intervention policy in Spain and a frank espousal of the republican cause, and those who will counsel prudence and that France

Continued on Page Three

BRITAIN IS SHOCKED

Foreign Secretary Quits Over Issue of Seeking Deals With Dictators

CRANBORNE GOES OUT, TOO

Two Other Ministers Waver— Outburst Is Expected in Commons Today

By FERDINAND KUHN Jr.
Special Cable to The New York Times.

LONDON, Feb. 20.—Foreign Secretary Anthony Eden resigned from the British Cabinet tonight, no longer willing to approve or support the methods of Prime Minister Neville Chamberlain and a majority of his colleagues in seeking settlements with Italy and Germany.

He took with him into retirement Viscount Cranborne, Under-Secretary for Foreign Affairs. At least two other Ministers—Walter E. Elliot, Secretary of State for Scotland, and William S. Morrison, Minister of Agriculture—had contemplated resigning with Mr. Eden, but late tonight they had not carried their intentions to the point of action.

Viscount Halifax, Lord President of the Council, will direct the Foreign Office temporarily, with Mr. Chamberlain himself probably taking charge of foreign affairs for a time in the House of Commons.

Eden Is Adamant

The Cabinet had tried for more than three hours in the afternoon to persuade Mr. Eden to change his mind, but this time nothing could shake his determination.

As a last resort the Ministers begged Mr. Eden to accept some other office or to say he was resigning on grounds of ill health. But he refused all such suggestions. He had become on a question of policy and he saw no reason why he should conceal it.

Tonight, pale and haggard, Mr. Eden walked dejectedly across Downing Street, where a crowd was waiting to cheer him, and called at No. 10. Inside the historic Prime Minister's house Mr. Chamberlain was in anxious consultation with his Ministers.

But Mr. Eden stayed only long enough to hand in a formal letter of resignation. After four minutes he strode back to the Foreign Office in the darkness with his two years and two months of incessant responsibilities at an end.

The Foreign Secretary's later set Mr. Chamberlain's reply threw light on what had been known abroad and at home but persistently denied in official quarters and in pro-Government newspapers here. They showed that the resignation had been precipitated by the interview with the Italian Ambassador, Count Dino Grandi, on Friday, but also that disagreements between Mr. Eden and Mr. Chamberlain had been going on for months.

Refers to 'Difference'

"The events of the last few days," wrote Mr. Eden, "have made plain a difference between us on a decision of great importance in itself and far-reaching in its consequences. I cannot recommend to Parliament a policy with which I am not in agreement."

Mr. Eden went on to admit a "difference of outlook between us in respect to international problems of the day and also as to the methods whereby we should seek to resolve them." He reminded Mr. Chamberlain that it was not in the interests of the nation that Ministers should work in "uneasy partnership," especially the Foreign Secretary and the Prime Minister.

The letter ended with a note of thanks for "help and counsel" and a polite and doubtless sincere assurances that "our differences, whatever they may be, cannot efface that memory nor influence our friendship."

The stilted wording of Mr. Chamberlain's reply showed what a shock to him and his Cabinet this resignation had been. The Prime Minister wrote of his "most profound regret" and of the "distinction" with which Mr. Eden had administered the Foreign Office. His regret was all the greater, said Mr. Chamberlain, "because such differences as have arisen between us in no way concern the ultimate aims or fundamentals of our policy."

"The decision you find yourself unable to accept," wrote the Prime Minister, "is whether the present

Continued on Page Two

Eden-Chamberlain Letters

By The Associated Press.

LONDON, Feb. 20.—The texts of Foreign Secretary Anthony Eden's letter of resignation to Prime Minister Neville Chamberlain and the Prime Minister's reply follow:

My Dear Prime Minister:

The events of the last few days have made plain a difference between us on a decision of great importance in itself and far-reaching in its consequences.

I cannot recommend to Parliament a policy with which I am not in agreement.

Apart from this, I have become increasingly conscious, as I know you have also, of the difference in outlook between us in respect to the international problems of the day and also as to the methods whereby we should seek to resolve them.

It cannot be in the country's interest that those who are called upon to direct its affairs should work in uneasy partnership, fully conscious of differences in outlook yet hoping they will not recur.

This applies with special force to the relationship between the Prime Minister and the Foreign Secretary.

It is for these reasons that with very deep regret I have decided I must leave you and your colleagues with whom I have been associated during years of great difficulty and stress.

May I end on a personal note?

I can never forget the help and counsel you have always so readily given me, both before and since you became Prime Minister.

Our differences, whatever they may be, cannot efface that memory nor influence our friendship.

Yours ever,
ANTHONY EDEN.

Mr. Chamberlain's Reply

My Dear Anthony:

It is with the most profound regret, shared by all our colleagues, that I have received your intimation of your decision

Continued on Page Three

ITALY IS JUBILANT AS EDEN QUITS POST

Sees Relations With Britain Improved With Change in the Foreign Office

HITLER SPEECH IS HAILED

But Strain on Friendship Is Seen if Reich Interferes Actively in Austria

By ARNALDO CORTESI
Wireless to The New York Times.

ROME, Feb. 20.—The news of the resignation of Anthony Eden, British Foreign Secretary, reached Rome late this evening and quickly spread throughout the city, causing great satisfaction everywhere, as was to be expected. In the Foreign Office Mr. Eden's resignation is believed to remove one of the great obstacles to the conclusion of an Italian-British understanding and, as this is still one of the main objectives of the present foreign policy, it is thought that official negotiations soon will be opened with better chances of success than in the past.

Italians have, whether rightly or wrongly, been convinced that for a long time there has been a conflict of opinion in the British Cabinet between one school of thought, headed by Prime Minister Neville Chamberlain, that was in favor of an agreement with Italy, and another school, headed by Mr. Eden, that made an agreement dependent on conditions, such as the withdrawal of Italians from Spain, that Italy could not accept or was not willing to accept.

Mr. Eden's resignation is regarded as a victory for Mr. Chamberlain's faction and, therefore, likely to bring an Italian-British understanding nearer by insuring that Italy's desire to make friends with Britain is met by an equal desire on Britain's part to make friends with Italy.

Claim Personal Defeat

It is thought in Italy that Mr. Eden is more or less smarting under the failure of his scheme to upset Premier Benito Mussolini's plans in Ethiopia by means of sanctions which it is believed were actuated by personal animosity against Italy.

Mr. Eden has, therefore, always been the target of strong attacks by the Italian press which, sometimes openly and sometimes by innuendo, accused him of allowing his private grudges to play too large a part in his handling of his country's foreign affairs. Italians feel, in other words, that Mr. Eden's fall has caused a personal enemy to disappear as head of the British Foreign Office.

It cannot be doubted that Italy will take advantage of the new sit-

Continued on Page Five

NAZIS CELEBRATE IN AUSTRIAN FETES

Great Strength Is Shown in the Provinces, but Numbers Are Small in Vienna

HITLER THREAT IS FEARED

Patriots Are Bitter, Hearing No Pledge of Independence in Chancellor's Talk

By G. E. R. GEDYE
Wireless to The New York Times.

VIENNA, Feb. 20. — Throughout Chancellor Adolf Hitler's speech Vienna's streets were like those of a dead city. Patriots and Nazis alike were indoors, patiently listening, the former hoping to hear the promises made at the Berchtesgaden meeting with the Chancellor fulfilled, the latter to learn whether there would be flaming words with which to light the torch of a Nazi uprising.

Instructions had come from Munich for small but peaceful Nazi demonstrations today. A Nazi journalist told me today, however, that three or four days hence there would be large-scale demonstrations. He would not give the date. Presumably it is Thursday, when Chancellor Kurt Schuschnigg speaks.

It has become fairly common knowledge here that Hitler solemnly promised Dr. Schuschnigg that if he accepted the terms dictated under the threat of invasion Germany would today recognize Austria's independence, the political monopoly of the Fatherland Front and guarantee suspension of the support of the Austrian Nazis with money and propaganda material from Germany.

Threat to Austria Seen

When the speech ended without the least effort by Hitler to fulfill his part of the bargain, there was great indignation. But more serious than this was the bitterness caused by Hitler's silence on the question of Austrian independence, which was taken as equivalent to a threat that will soon be put into execution.

During the broadcast Vienna Nazis listened quietly in their favorite cafés. Immediately after, suppressed "cheers" began. Immediately ward street demonstrations began, but not on any serious scale. Three hundred Nazis marched past the German Legation singing the "Horst Wessel Song" and shouting "Heil Hitler." The police allowed the demonstrators to parade but then ordered them to stand outside the legation.

Soon afterward similar small

Continued on Page Three

NAZI POWER CITED

Status Quo Repudiated by Fuehrer—Restates Colonial Demands

TONE OF TALK ANTI-BRITISH

Resignation of Eden Is Hailed as Greatest Victory of German Diplomacy

Chancellor Hitler in a militant speech to the Reichstag yesterday made a strong point of the right of "self-determination" for the 10,000,000 Germans in Austria and Czechoslovakia. He indicated force must be used in the end to break the status quo. He promised to go ahead with plans to enlarge the army. He assailed British policy, making a direct attack on Mr. Eden, and demanded colonies.

Disputes in the British Cabinet over proposed negotiations for a settlement with Italy and Germany led to the resignation of Foreign Secretary Eden. Viscount Halifax took temporary control of the Foreign Office, but Prime Minister Chamberlain will direct his policies.

France was fearful of losing her position as leader on the European Continent as a result of Mr. Eden's retirement. Italians, on the other hand, were jubilant over the passing of the Secretary, long regarded as a foe of their country.

Nazis held large demonstrations in Austrian provinces, but made a poor showing in Vienna.
[All stories on Page 1.]

Main Points of Hitler's Speech to the Reichstag on Page 4.

Hitler Shows Militancy

By OTTO D. TOLISCHUS
Wireless to The New York Times.

BERLIN, Feb. 20.—In the most militant speech of his career, which is already hailed here as the final cause for the overthrow of British Foreign Secretary Anthony Eden, Chancellor Hitler outlined before the Reichstag three principles and conditions through which National Socialist Germany proposes to retain her place in the sun and which, in her view, are alone able to preserve peace.

In some respects this most anxiously awaited speech was sufficiently vague to allay some of the worst fears in certain capitals, already primed for sensational extras. In respect to the two events which have most alarmed the world recently, namely the reorganization of the government and the army command and Austria's "cold Anschluss" with the Third Reich, it was even disappointing in its paucity of new revelations.

In both of these cases Hitler has stuck entirely to the understatements of the official communiqués previously published.

Right of Self-Determination

The speech's real keynote was the proposition that by virtue of national rights and accomplishments the German people, organized in and represented by the National Socialist Third Reich, constituted a great power therefore entitled to equal rights with all other great powers, including the right of self-determination. This right of self-determination, according to Wilson's fourteen points, was specifically proclaimed by Hitler for the "10,000,000 Germans" living in the two states adjacent to German borders.

These states are Austria, with nearly 7,000,000 inhabitants, and Czechoslovakia, with a German minority of more than 3,000,000.

Despite the occasional vagueness there was no possibility of mistaking the final implications of this speech, with which the world will have to reckon henceforth. It was a frank repudiation of the status quo and many more legalistic conception of world politics and an equally frank avowal of power politics based on the vital, if egotistic, interests of nations—a dedication to the proposition that might creates new right.

League Policies Repudiated

It is in this sense that the whole speech was also an outspoken repudiation of the legalistic League of Nations policy of Mr. Eden. It was further underlined by the ironic attacks on Mr. Eden per-

Continued on Page Three

King Issues Fascist Charter for Rumania; Constitution Sets Up a Corporative State

Wireless to The New York Times.

VIENNA, Feb. 20.—A dictatorial Constitution was given to Rumania tonight by a proclamation signed by King Carol. It was not countersigned by any of his Ministers.

The democratic parliamentary system is abolished and replaced by a Fascist corporative Chamber and Senate, where various trades and occupations will be represented. The distribution of land under the land reform scheme stands, but increased compensation will be given for mineral rights taken over by the State. Special measures will be taken against corruption. Trial by jury is abolished.

In the proclamation Carol says: "I have been moved by one noble only—the love of my people and the need to rescue the fatherland."

The Constitution promises to peoples that have lived for centuries on the soil of present-day Rumania the same treatment as the "Rumanian race" will receive, but it indicates that State jobs will go mostly to ethnical Rumanians.

There are rumors that Rumania will go through the Thursday form of taking a plebiscite of the people's views on this dictated Constitution.

King Carol assumed direct control of the Rumanian Government early this month, when he forced the pro-Fascist Premier Octavian Goga out of office to make way for a national Cabinet headed by Dr. Miron Cristea, Patriarch of the Rumanian Orthodox Church.

The King suspended the Constitution, promising to replace it as soon as the situation created by M. Goga's leanings toward Germany and Italy and his anti-Semitism had calmed.

The new Constitution had been generally expected to provide for a dual administration or a Crown Council, composed of distinguished Rumanians, that would lay down general principles of policy, and a Cabinet to frame legislation that would be submitted to the King and the Crown Council.

Under a corporative State, such a dual system would resemble that of Italy, with her Fascist Grand Council and Cabinet.

"All the News That's
Fit to Print."

The New York Times.

LATE CITY EDITION
Generally fair and warmer today.
Tomorrow mostly partly cloudy, mild
temperature, colder at night.

Copyright, 1938, by The New York Times Company.

VOL. LXXXVII..No. 29,267.   Entered as Second-Class Matter,
Postoffice, New York, N. Y.   NEW YORK, SATURDAY, MARCH 12, 1938.   PP   TWO CENTS In New York
City.   THREE CENTS Elsewhere Except
within 200 Miles.   FOUR CENTS Elsewhere Except
in 7th and 8th Postal Zones.

A. E. MORGAN DEFIES PRESIDENT'S AIRING OF TVA BOARD ROW

Again and Again He Declines at Hearing in Roosevelt's Office to Give 'Facts'

SAYS IT IS UP TO CONGRESS

He Is Told He Should Resign if Not Willing to Support Accusations He Made

TWO COLLEAGUES HEARD

Lilienthal and H. A. Morgan Put Before Chief Executive Data Defending Their Course

A summary of Mr. Roosevelt's inquiry in TVA on Page 8.

By TURNER CATLEDGE
Special to The New York Times.

WASHINGTON, March 11.—President Roosevelt met open defiance today in his efforts to investigate dissension in the Tennessee Valley Authority when Arthur E. Morgan, chairman of the board, refused to submit evidence in support of his charges against his fellow-directors and reiterated, instead, his demand for a Congressional investigation.

Chairman Morgan sat with the other board members, Dr. Harcourt A. Morgan and David E. Lilienthal, for six hours in the President's office, the most unusual meeting of its kind ever held in Washington.

Time and time again the TVA chief heard the President repeat demands for him to bring forth evidence to back his charges. He heard the other directors spread before the President the grounds on which they had counter-charged that the chairman was undermining the TVA and that they could work with him no longer.

Dr. Morgan even based the suggestion from the President's lips that he should resign if he were unwilling to support with facts his accusations that "fairness" and "decency" were impossible in the TVA administration with the other two members on the board.

Says He Is an "Observer"

Except for rare intervals when he defended himself with a sentence or two against the charges of his associate directors, Chairman Morgan remained openly defiant of the proceedings. Throughout, he maintained the position he had stated shortly after 11 A. M. when he marched into the President's office behind the others:

"I am an observer and not a participant in this alleged process of fact finding."

As the conference temporarily ended early tonight, President Roosevelt told the three TVA board members that it was their duty to the country not to continue their "personal" row any longer. He told them that if they could not reach a settlement among themselves, it was the duty of those who could not see their way to do so, to resign. He gave them until 11 A. M. next Friday to submit any other statements or evidence to prove their charges, and, furthermore, to determine whether they would be able to compose their differences without a resignation.

This statement from the President was widely interpreted in Washington as an ultimatum to Chairman Morgan to drop or substantiate his statement by next Friday or quit.

Expect Morgan to Resist

Simultaneously the Presidential statements aroused wide speculation as to whether Mr. Roosevelt had the power to remove Chairman Morgan or any of the other two TVA directors. From Dr. Morgan's attitude, observers concluded that he would resist any effort at ouster until his case was heard before a Congressional committee.

Various data concerning the dissension were brought into the open at the Presidential hearing and the two groups made it plainer than ever that they are separated by a chasm of professional and personal feeling which will require little short of a political miracle if it is to be patched up.

Opening the meeting with a statement of the necessity, in the public interest, of disclosing the facts upon which Chairman Morgan had based his charges against the other directors, the President turned to Dr. Morgan for a reply, but received, instead, a refusal to answer. The President read the accusations made in recent statements by Chairman Morgan and at the end of each asked for specifications. As often as Mr. Roosevelt demanded "facts," Dr. Morgan stood on his previous statement, in which he had said in effect that he would have nothing to do with the President's personal inquiry.

The questioning revealed that Dr.

Continued on Page Nine

Flower Peddler Freed By Defiant Magistrate

In defiance of a letter from Chief Magistrate Jacob Gould Schurman urging city magistrates to impose heavier fines on flower vendors, Magistrate Sabbatino suspended sentence yesterday on a peddler in Coney Island Court, declaring that "nobody can tell me what to do except my Creator, through my conscience."

After releasing Thomas Hyden, 22-year-old peddler, of 337 Eighty-seventh Street, Brooklyn, Judge Sabbatino made public the letter from his chief. Terming the instructions "insulting," he said:

"In the letter I received, I was told that I should sentence floral peddlers to pay fines of $5 or to serve two-day jail terms, and should be even stricter with second offenders. The people of this city should heed the many robberies that are committed instead of worrying about floral peddlers."

WHITNEY ARRESTED ON SECOND CHARGE

Accused by the State of Using $109,384 Yacht Club Fund to Get a Loan

BAIL PLACED AT $25,000

Prompt Indictment Will Be Sought—Bennett-Dewey Feud Is Revealed

For the second time in two days Richard Whitney, senior partner of the brokerage firm which bears his name and former president of the New York Stock Exchange, was arrested, fingerprinted, photographed, haled into court and held in bail yesterday on a charge of grand larceny in the first degree.

This time he was accused of the theft of bonds with a face value of $153,200 and present market value of $109,384 belonging to the New York Yacht Club, of which he had custody as treasurer of the club, and their use as collateral for a personal loan of $450,000 from the Public National Bank and Trust Company of New York without the sanction or knowledge of the club. He was released in $25,000 bail on this charge after arraignment in the Felony Court before City Magistrate Thomas A. Aurelio, who held him for the grand jury.

The penalty fixed by law for conviction on the charge of grand larceny in the first degree is from five to ten years in State's prison for each offense.

Total Bail $35,000

Mr. Whitney now has his liberty on $35,000 bail, as he was freed in $10,000 on Thursday by Judge William Allen in the Court of General Sessions on the charge of stealing $105,000 in securities from the estate of his father-in-law, George R. Sheldon, of which he was an executor and trustee, and of which his wife, his sister-in-law, the widow of Judge Daniel F. Murphy of the Court of Special Sessions; Harvard University and St. Paul's School at Concord, N. H., were the beneficiaries.

Ambrose V. McCall, Assistant State Attorney General, who has been conducting daily hearings on behalf of Attorney General John J. Bennett Jr. since the Whitney firm was suspended by the Stock Exchange on Tuesday, informed Magistrate Aurelio that his investigation had already shown shortages of nearly $1,000,000 in the Whitney accounts. He said that in view of this and other circumstances Attorney General Bennett regarded the $10,000 bail asked by District Attorney Thomas E. Dewey of New York County in the Sheldon estate case as entirely insufficient.

Feud Is Revealed

Mr. McCall's statements brought into the open a feud that has been developing behind the scenes since District Attorney Dewey called a witness from the Attorney General's inquiry before the grand jury and obtained the indictment in the Sheldon case by a surprise move.

Hurrying here from Albany yesterday morning, Attorney General Bennett made no secret of his resentment at Mr. Dewey's action. He said that a district attorney had never before stepped into a case while it was under investigation by the Attorney General, and that he saw no necessity of Mr. Dewey acting as he had done. In the ordinary course of events, Mr. Bennett explained, his office would have prosecuted the Sheldon case to the grand jury and prosecuted it just as it intends to do with the yacht club case, under Article 22-A of the General Business Law. He said his office has concurrent jurisdiction with the county prosecutor.

In view of the indictment obtained by Mr. Dewey, the Attorney General said he did not intend to accept Mr. Whitney's offer to testify. If it had not been for Thursday's indictment, he added, the broker would have

Continued on Page Eighteen

Mechanic on New Army Planes Held as Spy; Trapped by Counter-Espionage in Plant

Following several days of intensified counter-espionage activities around Long Island air fields, Federal authorities yesterday arraigned Otto Hermann Voss, a naturalized German mechanic employed in the Seversky aircraft plant, for espionage. Waiving examination, Voss was held in $10,000 bail.

The government invoked the same severe World War statute under which two renegade soldiers and a German woman were held as German spies on Feb. 26. Voss was charged with delivering and inducing others to deliver "to agents of a foreign power certain documents, writings, code books, signal books, photographs, instruments and information relating to the defense of the United States." The maximum punishment for conviction is imprisonment for twenty years.

The Seversky Aircraft Corporation at Farmingdale, L. I., is now building pursuit planes for the army that have broken several world records at speeds over 300 miles an hour and are recognized as one of the best types of fighting ships.

The defendant, 39 years old, was silent at his arraignment. He is 5 feet tall with old scars on both cheeks. Mr. Dunigan said Voss worked at the plant at intervals for several years. He alleged illegal activities were dated from Jan. 2, 1936.

Dunigan said that after a conference with John F. Dailey, Acting United States Attorney, it had been decided that any statement at this time "would be out of order."

It was reported, however, that four men who were once mechanics worked near Voss for three weeks until two Department of Justice agents arrested him Wednesday. Then they disappeared. Voss worked in the "day-dreaming" or experimental, section of the plant's assembly division, where Major de Seversky tests new ideas and materials.

Voss, it was learned, visited Germany for about a month last Summer. His wife at their home at 225 Jericho Turnpike, Floral Park, was on the verge of collapse after two long sessions of questioning by Federal agents. They were at her home on Wednesday and Thursday. Mrs. Voss asserted her husband was innocent and believed he came under suspicion when his name was found in a paper on the person of a friend arrested as a spy recently.

The background of the case was not revealed beyond what appeared in the complaint and the warrants spoken by Lester C. Dunigan, Assistant United States attorney, at the arraignment before United States Commissioner Isaac Platt. Mr.

TAX BILL IS PASSED BY HOUSE, 294 TO 97; SENATE TO SPEED IT

Three Hours of Continuous Voting on Amendments Precede House Action

'THIRD BASKET' IS OUT

Liquor, Pork Import Levies Replace It—Profits, Gains Imposts Are Retained

By CHARLES W. HURD
Special to The New York Times.

WASHINGTON, March 11.—The House passed the new Tax Bill today after three hours of continuous voting, in which a roll-call confirmed its former informal action eliminating a special levy of 20 per cent on the income of large closely held corporations. Adopted in place of the "third basket" surtax were new taxes on liquor and imported pork products. Final passage was voted 294 to 97.

Although now expected to be sent to the Senate immediately, the bill is expected to yield between $5,000,000,000 and $5,300,000,000 annually as ordered sent to the Senate immediately. There the Finance Committee will begin studies of it on Monday in expectation of a quick report.

Final House action on the bill occurred in the presence of almost all members on the floor, that being in itself a rare occurrence.

These members, permitted by the leadership only to vote and not to debate, carried on loud conversations among themselves, laughed and occasionally applauded as some member shouted "Aye" or "Nay" in response to his name through the dreary succession of roll-calls, one teller count and one standing division.

New Corporation Clause Voted

The most important change in the bill, as compared with current tax laws, consists of readjusted rates and schedules for corporation taxes, reported in detail previously, which are expected to make their burden more equitable.

However, the House refused again today, by an overwhelming vote on a roll-call, to reconsider its action continuing in effect the much criticized undistributed profits tax and the capital gains tax.

The results of the roll-calls, in the order in which they were taken, follow:

The House adopted, 233 to 153, the McCormack Amendment which eliminated the "third basket" contained in Section 1B.

It adopted, 201 to 182, an amendment by Representative Thompson of Illinois placing a new excise of six cents a pound on imported pork and three cents a pound on imported meats.

It approved, 290 to 96, an additional tax of 25 cents a gallon on spirits, proposed by Representative Robertson, to be added to the $2 rate now in effect.

It defeated, 292 to 94, a motion by Representative Treadway of Massachusetts, to recommit the bill to the Ways and Means Committee with instructions to eliminate the undistributed profits tax and to modify the corporate gains.

The final roll-call was on adoption of the bill.

A teller vote resulted in approval, by 135 to 96, of an amendment by Representative Boileau to include Engleman spruce among woods ex-

Continued on Page Nine

Netherlands Likens Crisis To Invasion of Belgium

Wireless to The New York Times.

THE HAGUE, The Netherlands, March 11.—The news of the dramatic events in Austria has seriously impressed The Netherlands, where it is considered the most alarming intelligence for smaller European countries since August, 1914, when German troops invaded Belgium.

Although German relations with The Netherlands are quite different from those with Austria, it is felt that some pretext or other might serve the Reich some day to intervene in The Netherlands' internal affairs as well.

The attitude of the British Government in the face of the new situation is impatiently awaited. In any case the lesson of Austria will not be lost on The Netherlands.

ROME CHECKS PARIS ON AID FOR VIENNA

Refuses to Cooperate With France and Britain for the Support of Austria

FAILURE FOR BLUM IS SEEN

Premier Designate Is Unable to Form Union Government From All the Parties

By P. J. PHILIP
Wireless to The New York Times.

PARIS, March 11.—It was learned here tonight that yesterday the French and British Governments jointly sounded out Italy as to whether cooperation could be expected in maintaining Austrian independence and that they received a firm negative reply.

However, Nazi Germany's annexation of Austria this evening has profoundly affected the French political situation and, in the opinion of every political party, made the immediate constitution of a government essential. That being so, Premier-designate Léon Blum tonight, after a day of continuous negotiation and argument with one party and another, informed the press that toward noon tomorrow he will announce his decision and intentions.

It is believed that he hopes to be able to announce the formation of a national government including most, if not all, of the parties. Before then, however, he will meet the National Council of the Socialist party, which last January ran counter to his wishes and by a small majority opposed entry through the Chautemps Cabinet.

What course events will take depends on M. Blum's ability to persuade his own party that the time has come for them to take the lead in the formation of a government which will represent France and not

Continued on Page Two

ITALY GETS SHOCK

Visit of Hitler Probably Will Be Canceled as Result of the Coup

ROME-BERLIN AXIS SHAKEN

Parleys With Britain Likely to Be Speeded and Accord Is Now Thought Probable

By ARNALDO CORTESI
Wireless to The New York Times.

ROME, March 11.—The news from Austria struck Italy with the impact of a exploding bomb and left the official world here aghast. An official spokesman told an unusually large audience of newspaper men this evening that the Italian Government considered the situation as grave that it did not feel it could make any statement at present.

The general impression is, however, that whatever Italy may decide to do she will not make any attempt to intervene in Austria militarily and will not concentrate divisions at the Brenner Pass as in July, 1934, after the assassination of Chancellor Engelbert Dollfuss. Certainly no troop movements have been reported.

The greatest uncertainty and confusion reigned in Italian quarters, where the day's developments apparently were entirely unexpected. But it seems clear that Chancellor Kurt Schuschnigg's resignation has shaken the Rome-Berlin axis to its very foundations, Whether the axis will be able to survive depends on the turn of events in the next few days and the explanations Berlin furnishes in reply to Rome's inquiries. Worth recording in any case are the widespread rumors that Hitler's visit to Italy in May will be canceled. Such a cancellation would be an unmistakable symptom that the axis was doomed.

No Hint as to Rome

The very surprise and shock caused by Dr. Schuschnigg's resignation prove that Hitler acted without giving the Rome end of the axis the slightest inkling of his intentions. As late as last night Italian circles close to the government were still saying that the Austrian plebiscite would lead to a clarification, which Rome heartily favored. Now the latest developments have brought everything to a climax.

It is declared here that Hitler could not have chosen a better moment for a coup in Austria. The Anglo-Italian negotiations are not yet properly under way and therefore Italy cannot definitely count on British support in any action she might mediate in Central Europe. France is in the throes of a Cabinet crisis, while Russia also is going through a far from happy period internally.

The events in Austria are also likely to have deep repercussions on the Anglo-Italian negotiations. Italy obviously will now enter them in a much weaker position, since her principal strength in bargaining to Britain hitherto was that in the field of foreign politics she and Germany acted as a unit. The wabbling of the axis cannot but increase for Italy the "necessity" of reaching an understanding with Britain and thus deprive her of a considerable part of her bargaining points.

Agreement Facilitated

On the other hand, the events in Austria cannot but make both Italy and Britain more determined to reach an agreement as soon as possible.

Even if the Rome-Berlin axis survives this blow, it is doubtful whether it will ever again regain the strength it had hitherto. Public opinion is convinced Germany has betrayed Italy; therefore it is difficult to imagine that the atmosphere of perfect cordiality and mutual confidence existing hitherto can ever be restored. Perhaps an open break will be avoided so as to gloss over the fact that a pillar that has upheld the whole of Italian foreign policy in the last two years has fallen to the ground, but it seems that the process of a breaking up of the axis has begun.

No course appears open to Italy but to save what she can of her position in Central Europe by diplomacy. Germany today is very different in a military sense from the Germany of 1934, so the use of force can in all probability be ruled out.

Perhaps Germany still counts

Continued on Page Two

The Austrian Situation

Following an ultimatum from Berlin, the Schuschnigg government in Austria retired yesterday evening and was succeeded by one headed by the Nazi leader, Arthur Seyss-Inquart, as Chancellor. He immediately asked Germany to send troops to help in preserving order. Some 50,000 highly armed and mechanized forces marched to the border. Both Munich and Vienna report some crossed into Austria. Berlin denies this. Nazi mobs took possession of Vienna and raided the Jewish quarter. The swastika was flown over public buildings, and Fatherland Front forces were disarmed. There were similar demonstrations in other cities.

Europe was aghast at the coup of Hitler. His action struck Italy with the force of an exploding bomb. The impression was that Italy would not retort with force, but it was believed the Rome-Berlin axis had been shaken and that Hitler's visit to Rome might be canceled. No advance notice of Germany's intention is believed to have been given to Mussolini.

Britain delivered a sharp protest to Berlin, saying Germany's action was bound to produce "the gravest reactions, of which it is impossible to foretell the issue." Other warnings were delivered earlier, but Foreign Minister von Ribbentrop retorted that Germany saw no reasons to confer with Britain until her purposes had been achieved elsewhere.

In Paris it was understood that Italy had been asked if she would join in a united effort to save Austria, but had refused. France, however, took action similar to that of Britain in protesting the Reich's action. The parties tried to get together to form a new Cabinet to deal with the situation, but they were still too deeply divided to make that accomplishment possible. It was believed Léon Blum would not be able to gain sufficient support to head a government. [All the above dispatches on Page 1.]

Premier Negrin of Spain announced that Italy and Germany had made unofficial proposals for some agreement with the Loyalists, but they were determined not to enter on negotiations.
[Page 2.]

BRITISH APPALLED BY REICH METHODS

Government Sends to Berlin a Sharp Rebuke Assailing the Tactics Employed

LONDON NOT TO INTERVENE

German Troops Start Across Border While Ribbentrop Is Guest of Chamberlain

By FERDINAND KUHN Jr.
Special Cable to The New York Times.

LONDON, March 11.—At the very moment when German troops were crossing the Austrian frontier the British Government tonight delivered to Berlin one of the sharpest protests it has yet made in its post-war relations with Germany.

[France also protested to Germany along the same lines as the British rebuke, it was reported in Paris.]

The strength of the protest showed how strongly the British Government felt over the day's events and particularly over the methods by which Germany had finally attained her ends in Austria. Referring especially to the second German ultimatum that preceded the actual invasion, the British described it as the "coercion, backed by force, of an independent State in order to create a situation incompatible with its national independence."

Such action, it was pointed out, was bound to produce the "gravest reactions of which it is impossible to foretell the issue."

The protest was delivered at the Wilhelmstrasse by Sir Nevile Henderson, the British Ambassador.

British Warning Disregarded

In invading Austria tonight Germany flatly disregarded the warnings of the British Government earlier in the day that the threat or use of force would damage the prospects of the Anglo-German talks and threaten future chances for reconciliation in Europe.

On the other hand, the events in Austria cannot but make both Italy and Britain more determined to reach an agreement as soon as possible.

Even if the Rome-Berlin axis survives this blow, it is doubtful whether it will ever again regain the strength it had hitherto. Public opinion is convinced Germany has betrayed Italy; therefore it is difficult to imagine that the atmosphere of perfect cordiality and mutual confidence existing hitherto can ever be restored. Perhaps an open break will be avoided so as to gloss over the fact that a pillar that has upheld the whole of Italian foreign policy in the last two years has fallen to the ground, but it seems that the process of a breaking up of the axis has begun.

While these words were being spoken the German Army was rolling along the express highways leading to the Austrian border and Berlin was preparing the ultimatums that forced the Austrian Government from power.

Britain will, of course, do nothing in the way of intervention. At this late stage in the absorption of Austria there is little left for Britain

Continued on Page Three

SCHUSCHNIGG GOES

Resigns After Threat of Invasion as Powers Fail to Back Him

PLEBISCITE IS CALLED OFF

Goering and Hess Expected in Vienna Today—Nazis Rule Streets, Rout Foes

Censorship Imposed

By The Associated Press.

VIENNA, March 11.—Censorship has started.

An order posted in the correspondents' room in the Central Telegraph Office tonight said all telephone conversations from the room must be in German.

Correspondents for the International News Service, an American organization, were detained against their will, without charges, at the office.

By G. E. R. GEDYE
Wireless to The New York Times.

VIENNA, Saturday, March 12.—Under threats of force from Berlin, Chancellor Kurt Schuschnigg of Austria yielded last evening and resigned in dramatic circumstances. The Nazis, with Dr. Arthur Seyss-Inquart, Interior Minister in the Schuschnigg Cabinet, as Chancellor, are in power.

To an unexpected public listening over the radio to a typical program of pleasant Viennese melodies the voice of the man who may have been the last Chancellor of an independent Austria announced at 7:45 P. M. that, in his own words, he had "yielded only to force" to avoid bloodshed and that under the threat of a German invasion that was to start at the very moment he spoke, he had resigned his office.

Plebiscite Is Postponed

Apart from the statement in a broadcast at 4 o'clock that "the Chancellor and Fatherland Front Leader, in consultation with President Miklas, had decided to postpone the plebiscite," there was no warning for the public when the program was interrupted for the announcer to say, "An important declaration is just coming." Then, without even mention of Dr. Schuschnigg's name, his voice was heard at the microphone.

When Dr. Schuschnigg had finished, thousands of Nazis began swarming into Vienna's streets to take over control unopposed. An hour afterward German forces, some 50,000 strong, made up of infantry, cavalry, artillery, motorized divisions, air force units and engineers with bridge building materials were moving to the Austrian frontier. Their mission was to avenge what is termed in Germany "the betrayal of Berchtesgaden"—Chancellor Kurt Schuschnigg's recent proclamation of a plebiscite on Austrian independence.

Last night, following Dr. Schuschnigg's overthrow and a telegram from the new Chancellor, Dr. Arthur Seyss-Inquart, to Chancellor Hitler requesting German military aid in preventing bloodshed, German troops were reported to have marched into Austria in close formation at three points—Salzburg, Kufstein and Mittenwalde.

[According to an Associated Press dispatch from Vienna, German troops crossed also at Passau, on the way to Linz, Austria, and a contingent of Reich troops, numbering about 1,000 men in three columns, was expected to reach Vienna at 6 A. M., New York time.]

Orders No Resistance

Information given out at the Munich army headquarters said the troops had begun to cross the border shortly after 10 o'clock, although their coming had been heralded by Dr. Seyss-Inquart in semi-hourly broadcasts beginning soon after 7 o'clock. The broadcasts included instructions to the Austrian military and civil authorities and the population not to resist the troops.

Whether the statements of the Munich army headquarters are correct or whether insistent denials in Berlin of a German march into Austria are the real truth does not much matter, for, even if the German troops were not already marching in, there is still the victory. The war that march that turned the tide in Austria and, after a bloodless taking, enabled the Austrian Nazis to take over their country unopposed.

REICH ARMY MOVES; 50,000 AT FRONTIER

Force of Infantry, Artillery and Engineers Said to Have Entered Austria With Planes

BUT BERLIN MAKES DENIAL

Bavarian Roads Choked, Cars Taken Over—Border Towns Fired by Excitement

Wireless to The New York Times.

MUNICH, Germany, Saturday, March 12.—With a dramatic suddenness that stunned the world the German Army embarked yesterday on its first campaign beyond the Reich's borders and without firing a shot achieved a victory that laid Austria prostrate at its feet, transformed the European equilibrium and set the borders fixed by the peace treaties into motion for a readjustment, of which the end is not yet in sight.

All day yesterday German forces, some 50,000 strong, made up of infantry, cavalry, artillery, motorized divisions, air force units and engineers with bridge building materials were moving to the Austrian frontier.

Final Ultimatum Delivered

The final ultimatum was delivered in Vienna. It brought Dr. Schuschnigg a final and, this time, an official ultimatum. The man who delivered it was believed to have been Josef Buerckl, Nazi leader in the Saar.

At first it was rumored that Field Marshal Hermann Goering and Rudolf Hess, deputy leader of the German Nazi party, had arrived with the ultimatum and were going to speak to the crowds in the Karlsplatz at 10 P. M., but this proved untrue. It was stated later, however, that Marshal Goering and Herr Hess would arrive today.

In any event, this ultimatum was quite different from that Dr. Glaise-Horstenau had delivered. It was so

Continued on Page Three

"All the News That's Fit to Print."

The New York Times.

LATE CITY EDITION
POSTSCRIPT
Showers today, cooler tonight.
Tomorrow fair.
Temperature Yesterday—Max., 75; Min., 69

Copyright, 1938, by The New York Times Company.

VOL. LXXXVII....No. 29,454.   Entered as Second-Class Matter, Postoffice, New York, N. Y.   NEW YORK, THURSDAY, SEPTEMBER 15, 1938.   P   THREE CENTS NEW YORK CITY and Vicinity | FOUR CENTS Elsewhere Except in 7th and 8th Postal Zones

GEORGE IS WINNING IN GEORGIA POLL; CAMP RUNS THIRD

TALMADGE SECOND

Choice of President in 'Purge' Primary Admits His Defeat

TALMADGE CLAIMS VICTORY

Former Governor Lost Lead Won in the Early Returns in Rural District Counts

Senator George went into the lead on the late count from the Georgia Senatorial primary after a nip-and-tuck race in the returns with Former Governor Eugene Talmadge, an even more direct critic of the Senator than the Senator whom President Roosevelt marked for elimination in the party "purge" campaign. Lawrence Camp, the choice of the President, trailed throughout the count and conceded defeat. [Page 1.]

Democrats of Connecticut, in State convention, renominated Senator Lonergan and Governor Cross; Attorney General Cummings advocated letting "the dead past bury its dead." [Page 14.]

Former Governor Frank D. Fitzgerald of Michigan won over two opponents and will oppose Frank Murphy for the Governorship. [Page 16.]

Senator Tydings's lead in Maryland's popular vote rose to 56,000 on late returns. [Page 12.]

'Purge' Again Defeated

By TURNER CATLEDGE
Special to The New York Times.

ATLANTA, Thursday, Sept. 15.—President Roosevelt's drive to "purge" less than 100 per cent followers from the Senate was rounded out here early today in an apparently disastrous finish.

Senator Walter F. George, whom the President personally requested Georgia voters to oust from the seat which he has held in the Senate for 18 years, forged ahead in the returns from yesterday's Democratic Senatorial primary. The Senator was leading both in popular and county unit votes at midnight.

The runner-up was former Governor Eugene Talmadge, a more consistent and certainly more bitter critic of the President and the New Deal than Senator George. After running ahead in the returns, Mr. Talmadge dropped behind the Senator, but at the same time went on the radio and claimed the nomination, saying that if he lost, it would be stolen from him.

Federal District Attorney Lawrence Camp, over whom the President waved the once-magic New Deal wand in his celebrated speech at Barnesville three weeks ago today, ran a poor third and conceded defeat at 11:30 P. M.

70 of 159 Counties Complete

At midnight 70 of the State's 159 counties had reported complete returns, accounting for 170 of the total 410 county unit votes, a majority of which a candidate must receive to be nominated. Out of the number Senator George had collected a total of 110 county unit votes in forty-two counties; Mr. Talmadge had 14 votes in twenty-six counties, and Mr. Camp six in two counties.

Senator George had amassed 100,002 popular votes; Mr. Talmadge 75,931 and Mr. Camp 55,265. Senator George was leading in counties having a total of 192 unit votes; Mr. Talmadge in counties having a total of 194 and Mr. Camp in counties with a total of 7. However, a trend toward late in the evening was still running.

In a radio broadcast at 11:30 P. M. Mr. Camp said:

"I am deeply grateful to all the people who have supported me in this fight. I regret the fight was not successful at this time, but I believe that the fight for liberalism will be successful in the end and that the people will demand liberal representation. I bow to the will of the electorate and offer my congratulations to the successful candidate."

On many of the first returns Mr. Talmadge would be leading in one county after another, with only one to three boxes in each to be heard from. But in most of these, when the county tabulation was completed

Continued on Page Eighteen

Corcoran 'Dead and Dumb' When Queried on Tydings

Thomas G. Corcoran, one of President Roosevelt's closest advisers in the current "purge" campaign, visited the local WPA offices yesterday to renew an old friendship with Lieut. Col. Brehon B. Somervell, Works Progress Administrator. He smilingly denied that there was any political significance to his visit.

Asked whether he had anything to say about Senator Millard Tydings's renomination in Maryland, Mr. Corcoran replied:

"I never have anything to say. Professionally I am deaf, dumb and blind."

TRANSIT EXPANSION TO COST $827,102,344

Delaney Submits Long-Range Program to Planning Board —Many Items Must Wait

A long-range program for expansion of the city's rapid transit facilities, at an estimated total cost of $827,102,344, was submitted to the City Planning Commission yesterday by the Board of Transportation.

In submitting the program, John H. Delaney, chairman of the board, explained that it was not to be regarded as inflexible, but as subject to changes in the city's financial condition, the volume of rapid transit traffic, the fate of pending transit unification proposals and other factors.

"This board," Mr. Delaney wrote, "is aware that the present financial resources of the city are not sufficient to permit the adoption at this time of any considerable part of this future program, but is of the opinion that the City Planning Commission should have before it a comprehensive outline of what this board deems to be the most useful development of transit facilities during the coming years."

Early Unification Assumed

Explaining that the list of projects was arranged generally in the order of priority desired, Mr. Delaney declared that it was drawn on the assumption that "rapid transit unification will be effected in the near future."

The list is a comprehensive summary of the many rapid transit projects put forward by the Board of Transportation since it began to function in 1924. It includes the proposed additional system based upon a trunk line subway under Second Avenue, the proposed acquisition of parts of the Long Island Railroad right of way in Queens, the recapture of the Hudson & Manhattan Railway tubes in Manhattan and the building of a rapid transit tunnel between Brooklyn and Staten Island.

The list, which will come before the City Planning Commission for consideration this afternoon, includes the proposed demolition of the Sixth Avenue elevated line at an estimated cost of $225,000, less possible salvage. Proceedings are now pending under which the city hopes to acquire the line itself at a cost of $12,500,000.

Projects as Submitted

Following is the complete list of projects submitted by the Board of Transportation:

Transportation building......$3,000,000
Rockaway Line, Acquisition and Reconstruction, Queens—Four and two tracks; subway, embankment and elevated......$49,365,844
Fulton Street Line Extension:
Via Pitkin Avenue and Linden Boulevard, Grant Avenue to 229th Street, with provision for a connection to the Rockaway line, Brooklyn and Queens; four tracks, subway......$21,300,000
Connection from Rockaway line to Fulton Street extension, Queens—two tracks, subway cut......$3,230,000
Hillside Avenue Extension—178th Street to 212th Street, Queens; four tracks, subway......$23,730,000
Flushing Line—I. R. T. Extension, Via Roosevelt Avenue, public streets and private property parallel and adjacent to L. I. R. R.; Main Street, Flushing, to Bell Boulevard, Bayside, Queens; two tracks to 169th Street, thence two tracks to Bell Boulevard; subway, embankment and open cut......$8,200,000
Via 149th Street and 212th Avenue, from Roosevelt Avenue to 212th Street, College Point, Queens; two tracks, elevated throughout......$7,500,000

Continued on Page Fourteen

RED HOOK HOUSING TO COST $12,000,000, A $4,600,000 SAVING

Total Per Room of $1,125 is About Half That for Harlem and Williamsburg Projects

BIDS FAR BELOW BUDGET

Rheinstein Wires Mayor That Queensbridge Should Now Provide for 9,000 More

The total cost of the Red Hook low-rental housing development, including land, will be about $12,000,000, or approximately $4,600,000 less than the $16,592,766 provided in the budget allowed by the United States Housing Authority, it was announced yesterday by Alfred Rheinstein, chairman of the New York City Housing Authority.

Mr. Rheinstein, who is also Commissioner of Housing and Buildings, telegraphed Mayor La Guardia at Prescott, Ariz., that the bids for the Red Hook superstructures, which were opened Tuesday, showed that the project could be completed at a cost per room, including land, carrying charges and overhead, of $1,125.

Cost of Other Projects

The cost per room of the Williamsburg Houses, built by the housing division of the Public Works Administration, was $2,284, while Harlem River Houses cost $2,150 a room, Mr. Rheinstein said, adding that the lower cost for Red Hook was due to "an accurate definition of the problem, careful planning, unusual cooperation of the building industry and a favorable market."

Mr. Rheinstein expressed confidence that similar economies would be revealed when bids for the $16,500,000 Queensbridge development were opened some time next month. He advised Mayor La Guardia that as a result it would be possible to provide housing in the Queensbridge development for 21,000 persons, or 9,000 more than the plans approved by the Federal authorities contemplated.

"This saving undoubtedly will permit slum clearance which, in the past, was a doubtful prospect because of the high cost of land in New York City," Mr. Rheinstein said in discussing the reduction in cost.

"This is the first fruit of intensive effort by an organization which has labored with great skill and faithfulness. Credit is due Alfred Easton Poor, the chief architect, and his associates; to the engineers and to our own technical staff, which is headed by Allan S. Harrison."

Rheinstein Praises Builders

Mr. Rheinstein paid tribute to the cooperative attitude of the building industry, which he said had been a factor in the saving. He said the building industry and the Housing Authority had worked in close harmony and "on a practical basis" for many months.

The text of Mr. Rheinstein's telegram to the Mayor follows:

"Bids on the superstructures for Red Hook opened last night. Total cost, including land, carrying

Continued on Page Thirteen

Ultimatum of Henlein Disavowed in Germany

Wireless to The New York Times.

BERLIN, Sept. 14.—The ultimatum sent to the Czech Government by the Sudeten party yesterday is declared here to have been drawn up without Chancellor Adolf Hitler's approval.

It was stated here today that Konrad Henlein did not communicate with Berchtesgaden yesterday because of alleged intervention by Prague in telephonic communication with Germany. Herr Henlein is thereupon said to have dispatched his belligerent statement to the Czech Government on his own responsibility.

Apparently he was not sharply reproved for doing so, and his subsequent decision to break off negotiations with Prague had Hitler's complete approval.

The German Foreign Office stated today that it was unable to get in touch with the German Legation in Prague yesterday between 8 P. M. and midnight.

PRESIDENT SPEEDS BACK TO CAPITAL

Tells Rochester, Minn., Crowd That the European Crisis Changed His Plans

By HENRY N. DORRIS
Special to The New York Times.

ON BOARD THE PRESIDENTIAL TRAIN EN ROUTE TO WASHINGTON, Sept. 14.—President Roosevelt sped toward Washington tonight to be at the seat of government during the present crisis in Europe.

Concerned over what he described in extemporaneous remarks at Rochester, Minn., as the "extremely serious" situation in Europe, Mr. Roosevelt cut short his visit to his son, James, who was reported to be progressing well after his operation Sunday for a gastric ulcer.

Standing on the rear platform of his special train after he had paid his son a morning visit, the President said to several hundred Rochester citizens gathered to bid him farewell:

"I am going back now, not to straight through to Washington, because, as you know, having read the newspapers, the condition of affairs in other parts of the world is extremely serious. That is why, as President, I have to go back to the national capital."

Until this morning the President was undecided as to going to Hyde Park or Washington, but after a long conversation with Secretary Hull, Mr. Roosevelt ordered that the train go direct to the capital. After he reaches Washington tomorrow night he is expected to go

Continued on Page Twelve

Americans Informally Told to Return Home; Many Ship Bookings to Europe Canceled

By The Associated Press.

BERLIN, Sept. 14.—American travelers have been advised "unofficially and informally" by the United States Consulate here to return home "if they could conveniently alter their European travel plans," officials said today.

Members of the consulate staff disclosed that "numerous United States citizens had inquired what they ought to do in view of the critical situation in Central Europe." The officials said, however, that American residents here have not been advised to leave Germany. Consulates of other countries have given their nationals similar advice.

Special to The New York Times.

WASHINGTON, Sept. 14.—Asked about a press report that the American consulate in London was advising Americans to book early passages for home, Secretary of State Cordell Hull today said he had received nothing officially on that subject.

He pointed out that three years ago a survey was taken of possible eventualities in various parts of the world and general instructions were then issued to consulates for their guidance "in such matters as a threatening war situation. Those instructions, he said, had not been supplemented by special instructions in the present crisis."

Special Cable to The New York Times.

LONDON, Sept. 14.—The United States consulate advised Americans in the Thames off Gravesend today after a special trip from Hamburg. The Europa, which will dock here today after a trip from Portland, a move which can ostensibly to "let the

men see another port" but in reality, London suspected, to care for American residents in case of danger.

WASHINGTON, Sept. 14 (P).—It was announced today that a bombproof cement and steel shelter was being built under a wing of the American Legation in Prague, Czechoslovakia.

It was authorized by the State Department after the Czech Government had given its approval.

The American Embassy in Berlin is also about to undergo extensive repairs, and it is reported another bombproof shelter may be built there.

Shipping executives said last night that European developments of the last few days had "affected shipping in both passenger and freight fields.

Trans-ships of foreign registry, which are generally available for service to any part of the world depending upon the nature of the freight, were said yesterday to have been withdrawn from the market.

In the passenger field cancellations of bookings have already been reported. Nine cancellations were reported last night on a ship scheduled to sail during the next few days.

The ship lines also have notified their booking clerks to restrict their promises of accommodations on ships in overbound sailings during the next few weeks.

There have been no cancellations of sailings from Europe as yet. The Europa will dock here today and the New York of the Hamburg Line tomorrow.

FIGHTING IS BITTER

Dead Mount to 23 as Six Are Killed in a Struggle in Eger

GERMAN ARMS ARE SEIZED

Troops Victorious After Long Struggle in Schwaderbach —Martial Law Extended

By G. E. R. GEDYE
Wireless to The New York Times.

PRAGUE, Czechoslovakia, Thursday, Sept. 15.—After perfect order had apparently been restored in most of the Sudeten German areas yesterday, further serious firing on the police occurred in Eger last night that developed into a pitched battle, with six killed.

A government communiqué last night said that representations to events in various parts of the frontier areas had established that the shooting of individual police and attacks on various government stations and State buildings that set in immediately after Chancellor Adolf Hitler's speech at Nuremberg Monday night were part of an attempted revolt.

Despite the restoration of order, it asserted, danger still remained that irresponsible elements would continue their "cruel and ruthless attempts at violence against fellow citizens of a different race and of different political opinions."

"Altogether," the communiqué declared, "there have been twenty-three deaths—thirteen Czechs, whom belonged to the forces of public order. Of the German assailants ten were killed. Of the seventy-five wounded fourteen are Germans; thirty-seven of the others are police and gendarmes."

Moderate Measures Stressed

These figures clearly show with what reserve and moderation the necessary measures have been taken. Firearms have been employed only on absolutely unavoidable occasions; the attackers have had machine guns and even hand grenades among their arms.

"The government has had every right to suppress this revolt and to do it energetically in the interests of the State and for the sake of European peace."

The writer had left Eger absolutely normal in the afternoon, save for many drawn shutters concealing the wreckage of Monday night's war of violence following Hitler's speech. An occasional double police patrol with rifles and bayonets indicated that martial law was in force.

Late in the evening it was reported that a police patrol had been fired on from the headquarters of the Henlein party in the Hotel Victoria in the town.

The fighting began, according to the official account, when, acting on information that there was a secret munitions depot in the party headquarters, two police detachments in armored cars were sent to carry out a search. They found the doors of the hotel closed and were received with fire from the windows.

Armored Cars Return Fire

The armored cars returned the fire and with the help of hand grenades the doors were finally burst open. Inside a considerable armory of German revolvers and automatic pistols and a train-smitting station were found. Those who had not already escaped were arrested.

During these operations the police were constantly fired on from the cellars of the neighboring Hotel Wenzel. The shooting continued until late in the evening, when that hotel was taken by storm and every one found inside was placed under arrest.

The six persons killed included one policeman, one Czech railwayman and one Henleinist. Three bodies of persons apparently killed by stray bullets were lying in the market square. One was a woman. Their identity has not yet been established.

At 9:20 P. M. order was stated to have been fully restored in Eger. The ringleaders were arrested and will be tried summarily by a military court.

The only other place in the republic where the Sudeten revolutionaries were still causing trouble last night was the village of Schwaderbach, near Graslitz. Schwaderbach is really a suburb of the German township of Sachsenberg. There the Henleinists had been armed, allegedly by Germany, and

Continued on Page Four

CHAMBERLAIN OFF BY PLANE TO SEE HITLER; WILL MAKE A PERSONAL PLEA TO AVERT WAR; PRAGUE FIRM AS SUDETENS BATTLE THE POLICE

Chamberlain Visit Stuns Reich; Hitler Looks to British Fair Play

Czech-Sudeten Crisis Seen as Drawing Further Away From Brink of War as Result—Berlin to Delay Action

By GUIDO ENDERIS
Wireless to The New York Times.

BERLIN, Sept. 14.—The Czech-Sudeten German crisis drew further away from the brink of war tonight with the announcement that Prime Minister Neville Chamberlain and Chancellor Adolf Hitler would meet in Berchtesgaden tomorrow afternoon for a man-to-man talk.

Following a day of nervous apprehensions over the intensification of the situation in Sudetenland and the breakdown of negotiations between the Czech Government and Konrad Henlein the news that the British Prime Minister had sought an appointment with Hitler stunned the unsuspecting radio public tonight. Mr. Chamberlain's visit was announced in a communiqué containing the Prime Minister's messages and Hitler's reply, which was remarkable both for its informally personal formulation and its dramatic contents.

This statement apparently implies an immediate spread of a European conflict to the Far East and places enormous interests in jeopardy.

Mr. Chamberlain, it is expected, will reach Hitler's mountain chalet early tomorrow afternoon. He will land at Munich and will immediately motor to Berchtesgaden, which once again is to become a cynosure of world-wide curiosity. The an-

Continued on Page Two

TOKYO CZECH STAND ALARMS SHANGHAI

Pledge to Back Reich and Italy by Arms, if Necessary, Seen as Threat to Foreigners

By HALLETT ABEND
Special Cable to The New York Times.

SHANGHAI, Sept. 14.—Consternation over the European crisis spread and deepened here and in other centers of foreign residence in China upon receipt from Tokyo of a declaration by a Foreign Office spokesman to the effect that Japan is prepared to join forces with Germany and Italy in accordance with the anti-Comintern agreement.

An immediate question arises concerning the British and French concessions in Tientsin, where there are stationed only a handful of troops of each nation. There, presumably, Japan and Italy has her own Tientsin concession, a considerable Tientsin garrison and a river gunboat.

Limited Forces

At Shanghai there are only two regiments of British troops, about 4,500 French forces and Annamites and 1,200 United States Marines. Anchored in the Whangpoo River are three French warships, one British cruiser, the U. S. S. Asheville, ocean-going gunboat, and the U. S. S. Oahu, river gunboat, while far miles downstream are many Japanese warships of all sizes. Other fighting craft, however, are within striking distance. The British have a force at Hong Kong while the United States Asiatic Fleet bases at Manila and spends its Summers on the China coast.

British interests in the International Settlement and also the French Concession at Shanghai are utterly indefensible and the entire surrounding countryside is in the hands of the Japanese Army.

At Canton there are only two foreign concessions, the British and French, both on the island of Shameen. There is nothing larger than the river gunboats that could be dispatched from Hong Kong, which is well-garrisoned and stoutly defensible from land and sea.

Inexplicable to Americans

TOKYO, Sept. 14.—A statement by a Foreign Office spokesman early today that the Comintern is primarily responsible for the Sudeten troubles is considered inexplicable by Americans and other foreign circles in Tokyo.

The afternoon edition of the newspaper Miyako editorially supports this statement but all other papers at present are silent.

The Miyako repeatedly praises Chancellor Adolf Hitler's Nuremberg speech, saying that it will then

Continued on Page Seven

LONDON HAILS PLAN

Prime Minister Hopeful of a Temporary Accord at Berchtesgaden

KING HASTENS TO CAPITAL

In Case of a Rebuff Britain Will Have Stressed to World Her Efforts for Peace

Prime Minister Chamberlain, in a dramatic move to avert Europe's threatened war, is flying to Germany to meet Chancellor Hitler face to face. The step, which was approved by the full British Cabinet yesterday, was understood to have been suggested by Premier Daladier of France. [Page 1.] It electrified Germany, where Hitler conferred all day with his diplomatic advisers. [Page 1.]

This development came after a day of continued violence in the Sudeten areas of Czechoslovakia. In the border town of Schwaderbach the police station and fire house were held the Czech forces at bay. Prague charged that they were helped by arms from abroad. In Eger six were killed in a police attack on Henleinist headquarters. [Page 1.]

Meanwhile Konrad Henlein said events had left his original demands far behind and he balked at further negotiations. [Page 10.]

As a solution to the Sudeten German problem a letter published in Italy, attributed to Premier Mussolini, called on Viscount Runciman, British mediator, to sponsor a plebiscite. [Page 5.]

At Geneva preparations were made to convene the League Council immediately after any German invasion of Czechoslovakia. [Page 6.]

A Tokyo statement that Japan would support her anti-Communist allies, Germany and Italy, with arms if necessary aroused alarm in foreign circles in China because of the peril to huge foreign interests there. [Page 1.]

While Washington took hope from the Chamberlain development [Page 2], American tourists in Germany were advised as a precautionary measure to leave the country. [Page 1.]

Locally, the stock market again was hit by a wave of selling [Page 2], and underwriters suspended rates on marine insurance, with higher ones likely to be fixed today. [Page 3.]

FRENCH HOPES RISE ON BRITAIN'S MOVE

Daladier Not Only Endorses the Chamberlain Plan, but Claims Initiative in It

By P. J. PHILIP
Wireless to The New York Times.

PARIS, Sept. 14.—With special trains ready outside Paris to take the civilian population away and with the president of the American Chamber of Commerce here making notifications difficult, I took the initiative in establishing direct personal contact with the British Prime Minister with a view to examining with him the possibility of attempting exceptional procedure that would permit an examination into the differences that separate the two governments and the Prague government and, in consequence, of maintaining peace in Europe.

"I am, therefore, extremely happy at the agreement in the ideas of Sudetens and the Prague government and the two governments."

The British Prime Minister's action has, therefore, official French sanction and approval. At the same time the French, because of the fact that the British are acting alone, are relieved of certain grave embarrassments. They are bound by their treaties with Czechoslovakia to go to that country's aid if her territorial integrity is threatened.

But the French are also on record as defenders of minorities, and the behavior of the Sudeten Nazis during these last few weeks has left no doubt in any French mind that, whatever they may want, the French do not want to continue under the old regime or anything like it. From a purely French viewpoint, therefore, the whole basis on which war might

Continued on Page Three

Chamberlain Flying to Reich

By FERDINAND KUHN Jr.
Special Cable to The New York Times.

LONDON, Thursday, Sept. 15.—Prime Minister Neville Chamberlain flew today from the Heston Airdrome for Berchtesgaden, Germany, to keep an appointment with Chancellor Adolf Hitler in a last attempt to save Europe from war.

At 8:36 A. M. the wheels of the big silver Lockheed monoplane lifted from the runway into a cloudless sky. Its first stop will be Munich, 600 miles away, whence Mr. Chamberlain will go to Hitler's mountain chalet by automobile.

He made a statement for the newsreels as follows:

"I am going to meet the German Chancellor because the situation seems to me to be one in which discussions between me and him would be fruitful. My policy has always been to seek peace. The Fuehrer's ready acceptance of my invitation leads me to hope my visit will not be without result."

Only about 100 newspapermen, photographers and officials were allowed near the airplane. They cheered and shouted, "Good luck! God speed you!"

A moment later Mr. Chamberlain turned and bowed his head to the plane. But photographers called him back and then the Prime Minister found time to joke. He struck a stiff attitude, his hands on his hips, like an old-fashioned daguerreotype.

The crowd gasped and then gave three cheers, waving hats. The individual cries redoubled and Mr. Chamberlain's face broke into a superior smile and he waved his own hat. Within five minutes the engines had been warmed up

Continued on Page Three

"All the News That's Fit to Print."

The New York Times.

LATE CITY EDITION
Cloudy, little change in temperatures today; showers tonight.
Temperature Yesterday—Max. 71; Min. 55

Copyright, 1938, by The New York Times Company.

VOL. LXXXVIII...No. 29,466.   Entered as Second-Class Matter, Postoffice, New York, N. Y.   NEW YORK, TUESDAY, SEPTEMBER 27, 1938.   PPPP   THREE CENTS NEW YORK CITY | FOUR CENTS Elsewhere and Vicinity | in 7th and 8th Postal Zones

TRUCK FIRMS HALT THE MAYOR'S PLAN; DRIVERS ACCEPT IT

Operators Reject Peace Terms as 'Unfair' After All-Day Conference Fails

CITY HAS A FLEET READY

1,000 Sanitation Vehicles Are Mobilized for Emergency—15,000 Quit in Jersey

Convinced that further negotiations between union and operator representatives would produce no settlement of the truck drivers' strike that has paralyzed shipping in New York City for more than a week, Mayor La Guardia submitted a compromise proposal to the negotiators whom he locked in City Hall last night and demanded an end to the strike by noon today.

Michael J. Cashal, vice president of the International Brotherhood of Teamsters, submitted the Mayor's proposal to the strikers' committee and within a few minutes announced their acceptance.

The Mayor's proposal was unanimously rejected by the truck operators early this morning at a meeting at the Capitol Hotel, Eighth Avenue and Fifty-first Street, attended by more than 300 members of the Merchant Truckmen's Bureau and the Highway Transport Association.

The vote was taken at about 1 A. M. at the end of a two-hour meeting at which members of the operators' negotiating committee reported on the Mayor's proposal and asked for instructions.

The operators also voted to set up a committee to enlist support among shippers and to seek to persuade operators not to sign separate agreements.

Although the committee made no formal recommendations for acceptance or rejection of the Mayor's proposal, members of the committee assailed it as "unfair" and requiring the operators to concede everything while the union gave nothing in return.

Rise in Costs Seen

D. L. Sutherland, president of the Highway Transport Association, estimated that the proposal, if accepted, would raise costs between 7 and 9 per cent. He termed the proposal "not a compromise but a piece of political skulduggery." Operators at the meeting applauded declarations from the floor that it was time to make a stand and fight it out.

The operators met late in the afternoon, and recessed until evening to hear reports on the City Hall negotiations. The committee arrived from City Hall at about 11:30 P. M., and discussion of the Mayor's plan began a few minutes later. The operators will meet again at the Capitol Hotel at 3 P. M. today.

The operators' committee is to report its answer at City Hall at 9 o'clock this morning, in accordance with the Mayor's request. Arthur G. McKeever, managing director of the Merchant Truckmen's Bureau, told the Mayor at the conclusion of the City Hall conference last night that some points would require clearing up and would have to be submitted to the operators' organizations.

In the meantime, the Mayor ordered mobilization of the Department of Sanitation's emergency fleet of 1,000 trucks, which began arriving at City Hall Plaza shortly after 12 o'clock. The fleet was being mobilized to handle any essential food stuffs or other material held up by the strike.

2-Year Contract Urged

Mayor La Guardia's proposal was for an agreement to run for two years. Where the union had demanded a forty-hour week at the forty-four-hour rate of pay, the Mayor proposed a forty-four-hour week at forty-seven hours' pay, an eight-hour day, beginning at 8 A. M. with four hours on Saturday, no man to be permitted to work more than forty-four hours weekly.

The Mayor submitted his compromise plan at a joint meeting of driver and operator committees of eleven members each at City Hall. He expressed a determination to end today the strike which he pointed out had caused not only losses to the business community but hardship to citizens, particularly those in the storm-stricken areas.

The plight of the hurricane-swept communities of New England, which need building supplies and other materials, was described by Governors Robert M. Quinn of Rhode Island and Wilbur L. Cross of Connecticut in telegrams to the Mayor to start storm relief supplies moving again. Meanwhile, the strike of 15,000 drivers in New York City had spread to 12,000 drivers in North New Jersey, while a strike of bus drivers, not involved in the dispute, had halted the transportation of

Continued on Page Six

Southampton Declines WPA Storm Clean-Up Aid

Special to The New York Times.
SOUTHAMPTON, L. I., Sept. 26.—The Village Board of Southampton voted today to decline an offer of WPA aid in cleaning up after Wednesday's hurricane. Many trees were blown over and considerable damage was done to the waterfront of this exclusive Summer resort.

After the Village Board meeting Mayor Albert P. Loening said:

"The Village Board has declined WPA aid in cleaning up the highways and for other rehabilitation work in the village. In Southampton we have always been able to handle our own affairs in the 300 years of our existence. The Village Board appreciates WPA offers of help, but the members feel that the sister communities of Southampton, which sustained greater damage, should have whatever assistance they need have gone to us."

LABOR LAW CHANGE DEMANDED BY FREY

Its Administration 'Disrupting' Factor in Industry, He Tells Metal Trades Group

By The Associated Press.
HOUSTON, Texas, Sept. 26.—John P. Frey, chief of the A. F. of L. Metal Trades Department, attacked Federal regulation of wages and industrial relations today in his annual report to the metal trades conference, and called for greater cooperation between labor and industry.

Mr. Frey said that the trade union movement was founded on "self-government in industry instead of government by bureaus and administrators."

Congress, he declared, would do much to prevent recurring depressions by establishing "the proper and adequate rules under which business is to be conducted."

"Business and organized labor, through the conference room and collective bargaining, must then work out the problem of stable production and the economically sound division of the wealth being created," he said.

Mr. Frey's report criticized both the Wage-Hour Law and the National Labor Relations Act. The administration of the latter, he said, was a "disrupting" factor in American industry.

"Both the law and the personnel must be changed before the board under the Wagner act can constructively and sanely apply its authority to protect the right of wage-earners to be represented by organizations of their own choosing," he said.

The Wage-Hour Law, he continued, conferred "extraordinary authority" on the administrator amounting to "bureaucratic or commissar control."

Communist Activity Assailed

The metal trades chief also criticized the activity of Communists in the labor movement, the political ventures of the rival C. I. O. and its contributions to political campaigns.

In less specific terms, he struck at centralization of government authority, "college professors and theorists in administrative posts," and at a "super-intelligent, highly educated minority" that would be preaching that workers should trade their independence for security.

"Should the day come," he continued, "when American workmen, instead of depending upon themselves, depend upon outsiders for leadership and guidance, then American wage-earners will have lost their independence, and their capacity for self-government."

Recalling some of the political activities of the C. I. O., Frey said: "The definite entry of the C. I. O. into the political fields creates an issue which we cannot escape. The political activities of the C. I. O. have led many representatives in State Legislatures and in Congress to give more consideration to the probabilities of C. I. O. strength than the merits of the legislative measures coming to their attention.

"The nonpartisan political policy of the American Federation of Labor serves to indicate the most effective method of meeting this problem." (The federation's policy has been to reward its friends and punish its enemies regardless of party.)

The political expenditures of the C. I. O.'s United Mine Workers in the 1936 Democratic Presidential campaign and later in the 1936 Pennsylvania Democratic primary, Mr. Frey declared, "eclipsed all political records."

"These enormous campaign expenditures," he added, "are an evidence of what labor may expect if it is to indulge in partisan politics, a larger expenditure for political purposes than for all other trade union activities combined."

Reiterating some of his anti-communist testimony before the Dies House committee investigating un-American activities, Mr. Frey

Continued on Page Five

PREPARE TO FIGHT 'OLD GUARD' SLATE ON DEWEY TICKET

Republican Liberals Fear Move to Give All Other Places to Conservatives

SPRAGUE BOOM IS HINTED

Young Element in Party Hears He Is Talked for Long-Term Senate Nomination

By JAMES A. HAGERTY
Special to The New York Times.
SARATOGA SPRINGS, Sept. 26.—Reports of a possible clash between the liberal and Old Guard elements in the Republican party over the nomination of candidates other than for Governor reached here tonight as the first of the delegates arrived for the opening of the State convention Wednesday.

There was no difference of opinion over the desirability of nominating District Attorney Thomas E. Dewey of New York County for Governor, but fear was expressed by some of the liberal faction that the conservative party leaders might try to name conservatives for the rest of the ticket.

This feeling is likely to be reflected at meetings of the board of governors of the State Association of Young Republican Clubs tomorrow afternoon and of the executive committee of the association tomorrow evening. The board of governors will confine itself to making suggestions for the platform while the executive committee will make recommendations concerning candidates.

The Young Republicans favor the nomination of Edward Corsi of Manhattan for the short Senatorial term. They are not wholly satisfied with all of those suggested for nomination for the full Senatorial term of six years.

Mentioned for Long Term

The word here is that J. Russell Sprague of Nassau County and Representative Bruce Barton of Manhattan are under consideration for this nomination in addition to Edward H. Butler, publisher of The Buffalo Evening News, and Jerome D. Barnum, publisher of The Syracuse Post-Standard.

District Attorney Alfred L. Simon of Saratoga County, president of the Association of Young Republican Clubs, has the support of this section for nomination for Attorney General. State Senator Benjamin F. Feinberg of Clinton County also has strong support for this nomination.

The boom for Assemblyman Jeremiah J. Wadsworth of Livingston County arrived tonight in the custody of Mark Welch, his campaign manager. State Senator Frederic H. Bontecou of Dutchess County also is a candidate for this nomination. Delegates from Western New York brought a boom for E. E. Holmquist, Jamestown furniture manufacturer, for the nomination for Controller.

Miss Katherine Kennedy, acting secretary of the Republican State Committee, was overwhelmed with requests for tickets of admission to the convention on her arrival. There will be 1,936 delegates and the same number of alternates, in excess of 1,000, more than at any previous convention of the party, and the convention hall seats will

Continued on Page Four

BRITAIN PLEDGES AID IF CZECHS ARE ATTACKED; ALSO GUARANTEES SURRENDER OF SUDETEN AREA AS HITLER IN SPEECH KEEPS PEACE DOOR OPEN

Reich Is Accelerating Inflation of Currency

Wireless to The New York Times.
BERLIN, Sept. 26.—Inflation of German currency is being accelerated alarmingly by military preparations. Contrary to the general rule for the third week in September the Reichsbank return for Sept. 23 shows a large increase in loans and a substantial rise in banknote and total circulation.

In consequence the Sept. 30 return will show a very serious situation in the total.

On Sept. 23 the bills portfolio was 1,785,000,000 marks higher than in the same period in 1937. The note circulation was 2,078,000,000 marks higher, which means a 40 per cent rise in one year.

The total note circulation is 8,756,000,000 marks, against 6,565,000,000 marks for the same period in 1937. Reichsbank gold and exchange reserves show virtually no change.

3 NATIONS IN REPLY PRAISE ROOSEVELT

Germany Is Silent, but Czechs, British and French Send Notes—U. S. Cabinet Called

Replies by Benes, Chamberlain and Daladier are on Page 10.

Special to The New York Times.
WASHINGTON, Sept. 26.—A Presidential call for a special meeting of the Cabinet tomorrow afternoon, "because of the existing situation," coupled with feverish activity at the State Department of Americans stranded in European danger zones, combined today to make official Washington keenly aware of the fast-developing war crisis in the wake of Chancellor Adolf Hitler's Berlin address.

At the White House and at the State Department, particularly, there was an obvious effort to present an appearance of calm in the face of an admittedly serious situation in Europe. President Roosevelt remained in his home throughout the day in the White House, from which in the early hours this morning he authorized his appeal for peace to the European powers directly concerned.

Replies were received from the British, French and Czechoslovak Governments expressing gratification at President Roosevelt's eleventh-hour peace plea and they were relayed to the White House as quickly as they were received at the State Department. At the close of business for the day no reply had been received from the German Government, and officials did not know when to expect one.

[Advices from Berlin showed that no mention was made of Mr. Roosevelt's message in the German press and Herr Hitler did not mention it in his speech.] Mr. Roosevelt conferred with

Continued on Page Ten

BENES IS ASSAILED

Hitler Says Czech State Was Conceived as Lie by 'Mad' Statesmen

SUDETENLAND ONLY CLAIM

Address Seen as Facade Behind Which Anything Can Happen —Oct. 1 Still Deadline

Text of Chancellor Hitler's speech is on Page 17.

By FREDERICK T. BIRCHALL
Wireless to The New York Times.
BERLIN, Sept. 26.—For an hour tonight, facing directly an audience of 15,000 in the Sportpalast, Chancellor Hitler addressed the German people listening in by order at loudspeakers over all the land and his speech was far from being the expected defiance of British and French public opinion steadily rising against his Czechoslovak ultimatum.

Uncompromising in the matter of his demands for the evacuation of Sudeten German areas, he stressed equally his having agreed to a plebiscite in the disputed territory after German forces came into possession of them.

It was notable that Herr Hitler had really harsh words only for President Eduard Benes and the present Czechoslovak State, which he characterized as "conceived as lie and conducted as a swindle for twenty years." The Czech people escaped vituperation, and Herr Hitler addressed soothing phrases to the Poles, Ukrainians, Slovaks, French, British and even Hungarians, all of whom he reminded of his manifested desire to seek no quarrel with them.

It was almost as though, knowing himself about to take an action that would be universally reprehended, he sought in advance to create a friendlier atmosphere.

Last Territorial Demand

Twice he asserted that if the Sudeten territories were ceded this would be the last territorial demand Germany would make in Europe. There was no special emphasis on the last two words, but there might have been. Not once did Herr Hitler demand the alienation of the Czechoslovak State entirely.

While utterly uncompromising in his insistence that the Sudeten areas should be surrendered by Saturday he stressed the sweet reasonableness of this demand rather than the desire to acquire them forcibly. The Czech Government, he argued, had already consented to surrender the territories; he only wanted it to keep its word. The British and French had agreed to it and they should stand by their agreement.

The fact that his memorandum handed to Prime Minister Neville Chamberlain had extended beyond the original limits of the areas to be surrendered and that the conditions for evacuation were harsh and humiliating beyond any expectation, Herr Hitler ignored. He glossed over the demand for German military occupation of the disputed areas also pending and during the plebiscite stressing instead that he had granted Mr. Chamberlain's request to have an international commission manage the plebiscite.

Way Left Open for Hitler

The speech, in fact, while fervent and impassioned in the Hitler manner, left the impression on account of its very reticences that it was a facade behind which anything can happen without in the least controverting its contents. Herr Hitler can negotiate - through France and Britain for a peaceful surrender or he can have the prescribed period and then march in dealing as harshly as he chooses with the Czech resistance. Either way he will be consistent and he can claim and will probably receive the initial applause of his people.

It is common knowledge that Sir Horace Wilson of the British Foreign Office arrived by air from London bringing a message from Mr. Chamberlain that had the endorsement of the French authorities who had gone to London as well as the French Cabinet, and that Sir Horace was closeted with Herr Hitler for more than a half hour before his speech. The message, it is understood, was a final appeal not to close the door to negotiations

Continued on Page Twelve

Two British Declarations

By The Associated Press.
LONDON, Tuesday, Sept. 27.—Following are the texts of the authoritative statement issued yesterday on Britain's decision to join in defending Czechoslovakia in case of attack and of Prime Minister Chamberlain's statement early this morning replying to Chancellor Hitler's speech:

Statement of Policy

It is stated in official quarters that during the last week Prime Minister Chamberlain has tried with the German Chancellor to find a way of settling peacefully the Czechoslovak question.

It is still possible to do so by negotiation.

Germany's claim to transfer of the Sudeten areas has already been conceded by the French, British and Czechoslovak Governments.

But if, in spite of all efforts made by the British Prime Minister, a German attack is made upon Czechoslovakia, the immediate result must be that France will be bound to come to her assistance and Great Britain and Russia will stand by France.

It is still not too late to stop this great tragedy and for the peoples of all nations to insist on settlement by free negotiation.

Chamberlain Declaration

I have read the speech of Chancellor Hitler and I appreciate his reference to the efforts I have made to save peace.

I cannot abandon those efforts since it seems to me incredible that the peoples of Europe who do not want war with one another should be plunged into a bloody struggle over a question on which agreement has already been largely obtained.

It is evident that the Chancellor has no faith that the promises made will be carried out. These promises were made not to the German Government direct but to the British and French Governments in the first instance.

Speaking for the British Government, we regard ourselves as morally responsible for seeing that the promises are carried out fairly and fully and we are prepared to undertake that they shall be so carried out with all reasonable promptitude, provided that the German Government agree to settlement of terms and conditions to the transfer by discussions and not by force.

I trust that the Chancellor will not reject this proposal, which is made in the same spirit of friendliness as that in which I was received in Germany and which if it is accepted will satisfy the German desire for union of the Sudeten Germans with the Reich without the shedding of blood in any part of Europe.

ENTENTE REVIVING

London Warns It Will Share Defense With Paris and Moscow

APPEALS TO HITLER ANEW

Offers to Enforce the Cession Pledge of Czechs—Meeting of Parliament Tomorrow

Britain announced last night that she and Russia "will certainly stand by France" if that nation should go to the defense of Czechoslovakia. This information was not delivered to Herr Hitler before his speech but a personal note from Prime Minister Chamberlain was given to him urging further negotiations. Mr. Chamberlain announced he would see that Sudeten territory was transferred to Germany fairly if she did not go to war.

Herr Hitler refrained from defiance in his speech to the German people. He was uncompromising in his demands for annexation of Sudeten territory and threatened to take it if surrender was denied but was believed to have left the door open to negotiations.

Czechoslovakia gave no indication that she would make a reply to Herr Hitler's speech, and the people resigned themselves to the worst. It was felt in Prague that the speech made war inevitable by Saturday.

The French Premier and Foreign Minister, on their return from London, declared the issue had boiled down simply to whether Hitler wanted war. If Germany should attack, the League Council is to be convened to give Russia a chance to intervene with Rumania's consent.

President Roosevelt called a special session of the Cabinet for today "because of the existing situation" and the State Department rushed activities in getting Americans out of Europe. [All the above dispatches are on Page 1.]

Premier Mussolini appealed to Britain and France to abandon Czechoslovakia before it was too late. [Page 16.]

Germans and French strung barbed wire along their frontiers and challenging signs were erected on both sides. [Page 14.]

Britain Is Pledged to Fight

By FERDINAND KUHN Jr.
Special Cable to The New York Times.
LONDON, Tuesday, Sept. 27.—The British Government took its most momentous decision in twenty years yesterday by accepting a clear-cut military commitment in case of German aggression against the Czechoslovak Republic.

An authoritative statement came from Downing Street last night that if a German attack was made against Czechoslovakia "the immediate result must be that France would be bound to come to her assistance and Great Britain and Russia will certainly stand by France."

So at the eleventh hour and as a last resort the hesitations of the past months and years have been wiped away. Prime Minister Neville Chamberlain's carefully qualified warning to Germany on March 24 and that of Sir John Simon, Chancellor of the Exchequer, last month have been swept into the forgotten past by the rush of tremendous events.

Triple Entente Revived?

From now on France knows that she can count definitely, without quibbles and evasions, upon British help if she springs to the defense of Czechoslovakia. Britain has had to swallow her dislike of Continental commitments and by an odd twist of history Conservative Britain and Bolshevist Russia will find themselves, if war breaks out, allied once more in defense of all their mutual antipathies of the past twenty years.

In other words, if Chancellor Hitler fulfils last night's threat to "go and liberate our Germans" in Czechoslovakia he will find himself confronting a revival of the old Triple Entente.

There is one big "if" in the decision taken by the united British Cabinet early yesterday morning and approved by the heads of the British and French Governments later in the day. The very substance...

Continued on Page Fourteen

CZECHS RESIGNED AFTER HITLER TALK

No Hope Taken by the People From Speech—Officials Are Urged to Stand Fast

By G. E. R. GEDYE
Wireless to The New York Times.
PRAGUE, Czechoslovakia, Sept. 26.—Knowledge that Chancellor Adolf Hitler would speak tonight hung like a thundercloud over the political atmosphere of this capital all day. Czechoslovakia had already rejected the Godesberg memorandum as furnishing no basis whatever for discussion, and it was felt quite possible that Herr Hitler's speech would contain an announcement that German troops would be ordered to attack Czechoslovakia.

People hurried from shops and offices with unusual speed or security of their homes and far more than the usual number of gas masks were carried by civilians in the streets during the afternoon and evening.

The fact that Dr. Joseph Goebbels, German Propaganda Minister, with his well-known desire for war, introduced Herr Hitler tonight seemed at once an ominous sign. When the speech of the German Chancellor closed without a declaration of hostilities there was a slight relaxation of tension here. The relaxation, however, did not go very far because it is universally felt that the speech of Herr Hitler now makes war inevitable by Saturday.

Czechoslovakia Is Silent

It is not likely that there will be any official Czechoslovak reply to the speech, which, it is felt here, did nothing but repeat the Godesberg memorandum, with no important variations. That memorandum had already been rejected, and Czechoslovakia has nothing more to say.

There is full confidence that when the blow falls both of Czechoslovakia's allies, France and Russia, will fulfill their treaty obligations to the letter, as will her allies of the Little Entente, Rumania and Yugoslavia, should their intervention be necessary by reason of Hungary's participation in an attempt to wreck this country.

As for Britain, the news received here concerning last night's Cabinet sitting awakened a strong hope that she also would join her friends. Meanwhile, until dusk falls with its unconditionally darkened streets and pitch black windows, daily life continues almost normal in Prague. The virtually complete absence of taxicabs—perhaps six are plying in the entire city, but nobody sees them—makes it necessary to fight for a place in street cars, where Russian conditions prevail. The cars are packed from morning to night with passengers clinging to every inch of space, even on the steps.

For those who have no automobiles of their own, the street cars are now the only means of trans-

Continued on Page Fourteen

FRANCE SEES ISSUE DRAWN FOR HITLER

Ministers Say Chancellor Must Choose Now Between War and Peace

By P. J. PHILIP
Wireless to The New York Times.
PARIS, Sept. 26.—From their London conference Premier Edouard Daladier and Foreign Minister Georges Bonnet returned this afternoon by air to find there was no necessity even for calling a Cabinet meeting before tomorrow morning. Events had spoken for themselves. There was no need to explain.

M. Daladier's reply to President Roosevelt, Prime Minister Neville Chamberlain's final appeal to Chancellor Adolf Hitler, the decision of Foreign Minister Georges Bonnet to summon at once the Council of the League of Nations if Czechoslovakia should be attacked, interviews that General Marie Gustave Gamelin, Chief of Staff of the French Army, had had, London warnings, preparations against air attack that are being made in Paris and finally Chancellor Hitler's speech all contributed to make the situation clear to every one. If Herr Hitler insists on having his way, he will have war. There is no other issue.

Opens Way for Russia

By deciding to summon at once the League Council, M. Bonnet is opening the way for Russian intervention with the consent of Rumania. The only uncertain element in today's doings, as far as the French public was concerned, was exactly what was contained in Mr. Chamberlain's appeal to Herr Hitler, which had been sent with M. Daladier's full approval. Everything else that had been done and said seemed to point to war. London reports late today of a proposal to Herr Hitler to negotiate with the Czechoslovaks and a warning that if he does not reach a satisfactory settlement and tries force, Great Britain and Russia will automatically join France in protection of Czechoslovak independence, swiftly changed the outlook. Even Chancellor Hitler's speech was found, in the light of these new reports, to read somewhat differently than it had sounded. There were significant omissions. It was not until his reply, which Sir Horace Wilson is taking to London tomorrow, is made public, that any one can be quite sure, if even then.

Fears of the general public who were concerning last night's Cabinet sitting changed the outlook. It looked like war. In inner circles of those engaged in this immense diplomatic game it is still hoped, even believed, that inch by inch the German leader will be forced from his position. No one here has any quarrel with the German people. It is the Nazi system, personified in Hitler, Goering and Goebbels that is the cause of what France believes is the danger.

Continued on Page Fourteen

Geoghan, Angered by Rumors, Subpoenas Officials to Inquiry Into 'Corruption'

For the second time within two months, District Attorney William F. X. Geoghan of Brooklyn proceeded yesterday to conduct a personal investigation into rumors of "official corruption" involving a member of his office and this time centering about a fur swindle in which five policemen and four other persons have been indicted.

Making one of his rare appearances before a grand jury, Mr. Geoghan spent several hours in the afternoon interrogating three witnesses, including Police Inspector Michael F. McDermott. Afterward, he announced that he had issued grand jury subpoenas for the appearance today and tomorrow of William B. Herlands, Commissioner of Investigation, Chief City Magistrate Jacob Gould Schurman Jr., Magistrate Matthew J. Troy, S. Harvey Posner of the Citizens Committee for Crime Control, and "others reported to know something about this matter."

"Aspersions have been cast upon my office and I now propose to have a show-down," Mr. Geoghan, angered, declared. "With the aid of this grand jury, I am going to probe these charges of reported, or rumored, official corruption in connection with this case.

"I will subpoena every single person connected in any way with this matter. If anyone has anything to say, let him say it before this grand jury. I want it all on the record in black and white. I'm the prosecutor of this county and if there is anything to this I'll prosecute it to the limit."

Later in the day Mr. Geoghan announced that the investigation concerned Isidore Jaffe, 48 years old, of 332 East Fourteenth Street, Brooklyn, a suspect in the fur swindle, against whom grand larceny charges twice have been dismissed because of insufficient evidence, and who is alleged to have said that he was freed "because I paid plenty." Mr. Geoghan said that Jaffe had been an informer in the case and that he had made a statement regarding denying the payment of money and explaining that he "was only trying to throw the others off the trail."

It was just two months ago that Mr. Geoghan, acting on the basis of rumors and official charges, initiated a personal investigation into reports that one of his staff assistants had accepted a bribe of $100 to "fix" a perjury case. As a result William F. McGuinness, suspended assistant district attorney of Brooklyn, and George F. Murphy, city-employed elevator operator, recently were indicted for conspiracy to obstruct justice and are awaiting trial.

ADELPHIA HOTEL, Philadelphia, Pa. (advt.)

Continued on Page Fourteen

The New York Times.

LATE CITY EDITION

Generally fair, cooler today. Tomorrow cloudy, probably followed by rain; temperature moderate.

Temperatures Yesterday—Max., 73; Min., 54

VOL. LXXXVIII...No. 29,468.   Entered as Second-Class Matter, Postoffice, New York, N. Y.   NEW YORK, THURSDAY, SEPTEMBER 29, 1938.   PPP   THREE CENTS   NEW YORK CITY and Vicinity | FOUR CENTS Elsewhere Except in 7th and 8th Postal Zones

---

DEWEY SLATE HITS CONVENTION SNAG; KEY POSTS IN DOUBT

Barton and Heck, at Opening Session, Score New Deal on 'Vote Buying' and 'Waste'

LEHMAN UNDER PRESSURE

Farley Says He Will Be Drafted—Hoover in West Backs Roosevelt Peace Plan

The Republican State Convention opened with a snag developing over completing the Dewey slate. Bruce Barton and Oswald D. Heck condemned the New Deal on "vote buying" and as failing to solve the unemployment problem. [Page 1.]

At Rochester, on the eve of the Democratic state convention, the leaders were exerting all their pressure to induce Governor Lehman to run again and Chairman Farley expressed the opinion that the convention would draft him. [Page 21.]

Herbert Hoover in a speech in Kansas City backed President Roosevelt's peace efforts, but attacked his home policies. [Page 22.]

Senator Vandenberg told the Michigan League of Women voters that the "yes-but-man" was the essential factor in a system of "nonpartisan politics" that he asserted would be a strengthening element in the development of the two major parties. [Page 23.]

Speeches at the Republican Convention, Pages 18, 19; Hoover's Kansas City speech, Page 22.

State Republicans Meet

By JAMES A. HAGERTY
Special to The New York Times.

SARATOGA SPRINGS, Sept. 28.—With complete agreement on District Attorney Dewey as the candidate for Governor, the Republican State Convention struck a snag today when Mayor Rolland B. Marvin of Syracuse refused to be drafted for the nomination for the long Senatorial term.

Concurrently, a difference of opinion developed between Kenneth F. Simpson, New York County chairman and national committeeman, and Edwin F. Jaeckle, Erie County leader, and there was a revolt of a minority of the Brooklyn delegation, who expressed opposition to the candidate for the nomination for Controller suggested by John R. Crews, Brooklyn leader.

Agreement seemed to have been reached on the nomination of Edward Corsi of Manhattan for the short Senatorial term, to fill the vacancy caused by the death of Senator Royal S. Copeland, and on the nomination of Richard B. Scandrett Jr. of Orange County and Mrs. Helen Rogers of Buffalo for Representatives at Large. The selection of candidates for the long Senatorial term, Lieutenant Governor, Attorney General and Controller awaited the results of further conferences to be held after the night session of the convention.

The name of Jerome B. Barnum, publisher of The Syracuse Post-Standard, was the only one mentioned for the long Senatorial term nomination after it became known that Mayor Marvin had repeatedly refused efforts to draft him.

Marvin Favors Present Posts

Mr. Marvin is under commitment to serve the three remaining years of his Mayoralty term. He also is the head of the Onondaga Republican organization, and is reported to be reluctant to leave these two positions.

The nomination of Mr. Barnum, understood to be opposed to any possible alliance with the American Labor party, would not be satisfactory to sponsors of Mr. Dewey's candidacy, it was said.

Mayor Marvin this evening called members of the Onondaga County delegation together for a conference. He said at midnight that his position was unchanged and that he would not take the nomination for Senator. Reluctant to lose his candidacy will make a further effort of tomorrow to get him to run. In case of failure, the indications tonight were that the nomination would go to Mr. Barnum.

No meeting of the executive committee of the State committee was held tonight and the conferences which went on were confined to a small number of the party leaders. Resentment among the delegates and leaders of the less populous counties increased as no apparent progress was made in agreeing on a ticket, and a meeting of the county chairmen of rural counties was called for tomorrow morning in the Grand Union Hotel at which it is expected that pressure will be

Continued on Page Eighteen

Gain of 369,000 Jobs Shown in August Survey

The National Industrial Conference Board reported yesterday that 10,890,000 workers were unemployed in August, a drop of 369,000 from the July total. This estimate included as unemployed 2,475,000 workers in the WPA, Civilian Conservation Corps and other government works agencies.

The hiring of 338,000 additional workers in manufacturing helped increase total industrial employment to 41,453,000, or 422,000 above the July figure. Construction employment rose by 126,000, transportation 12,000, forestry and fishing 5,000 and agriculture 3,000, according to the report.

Declines of 41,000 in employment in the service industries and of 32,000 in trade, distribution and finance were recorded.

TRUCK PEACE NEAR; MANY OWNERS SIGN

Only the Out-of-Town Haulers Still Oppose Mayor's Plan—Shipments Move Again

An end of the two weeks' strike of 15,000 truck drivers today was expected last night when the Merchant Truckmen's Bureau, representing local operators, voted to accept the compromise terms of Mayor La Guardia. The Highway Transport Association, representing long-distance haulers, voted to reject the terms, but decided later to defer action until today.

The Highway Transport Association adopted a five-point resolution to send a committee to see Mayor La Guardia this morning, to defer action meanwhile on the Mayor's compromise, to register a vote of confidence in its wage scale committee, to draw up as soon as possible a new contract to be submitted to the Mayor and to meet again this evening at 8 o'clock. At the second meeting the long-distance haulers rescinded their rejection of the Mayor's plan.

The operators, in settling in the day had declared they would stand pat "until hell freezes over," quickly came to terms after Mayor La Guardia had appeared at a joint meeting of the two groups at the Hotel Capitol, Eighth Avenue and Fifty-first Street.

The Mayor appealed to the operators to end the dispute, told them that disaffections in their ranks had resulted in separate agreements releasing 2,500 trucks during the day and, incidentally, admitted that he had no desire to continue "in the trucking business," referring to his emergency mobilization of 800 obsolete trucks of the Department of Sanitation.

Offers to Name Committee

The Mayor's appearance before the operators apparently turned the tide in favor of a settlement. He offered to appoint a fact-finding committee to study economic and other factors in the trucking industry and to make recommendations on wages and working conditions. Furthermore, the Mayor was able to cite the widespread response of truck operators to sign separate agreements following the appeal he made to the operators when their organizations rejected his compromise offer.

As a result of these disaffections the movement of commerce had resumed to such an extent that merchants reported increasing shipments and Port Authority executives noted a rise in truck traffic through the Holland Tunnel.

The compromise plan which the Mayor submitted late Monday night provides among other things for a forty-four-hour week at the rate of forty-seven hour pay. The strikers originally demanded a forty-hour week at forty-seven hours' pay.

Decide to Vote Separately

The Merchant Truckmen's Bureau and the Highway Transport Association, which had met jointly 500 strong to consider every proposal up to last night, finally decided to vote separately on the Mayor's compromise terms. At the time of the division their number had dwindled to about 300 and of that number only half cast ballots. The ballot of the Merchant Truckmen's Bureau totaled about eighty.

The business members accepting the Mayor's terms, it was learned, after their joint wage scale committee of nineteen had been reduced to four members by disaffections. The four members of the "old guard" who stood pat were P. J. Murphy, president; Arthur G. McKeever, managing director; Ted Ficke, past president, and Hugh E. Sheridan, chairman of the joint wage scale committee.

The end of the strike was assured when the United States Trucking Corporation and other important operators announced soon after Mayor La Guardia's decision and that they would follow the lead of Daniels & Kennedy and others and signed separate agreements with the International Brotherhood

Continued on Page Twenty-six

BERLIN IS RELIEVED

Hopes Talks on Czechs May Lead to Wider European Accord

ROOSEVELT PLEA A FACTOR

Hitler Described as Desirous of Removing Parley From 'Benes Atmosphere'

By GUIDO ENDERIS
Wireless to The New York Times.

BERLIN, Sept. 28.—Announcement today of the four-power conference in Munich tomorrow followed a day of high-pressure diplomatic exchanges and long-distance telephone calls between Berlin, London, Paris and Rome. It burst in upon the stagnant political atmosphere like a freshening breeze.

The circumstances under which the four Premiers will meet is not unlike that existing when Neville Chamberlain, the British Prime Minister, undertook his dramatic flight to Berchtesgaden.

With the German ultimatum nearing its deadline it was recognized that the statesmen concerned with the Czech crisis were largely talking past each other and that only a frank, intimate exchange across a conference table gave promise of breaking the deadlock. Chancellor Adolf Hitler was reported determined not only to reset to Mr. Chamberlain's appeal but to expand the British Prime Minister's suggestion by making further conversations a four-power affair.

Roosevelt's Plea a Factor

There were other factors, too, that pressed for early inter-governmental action. One of decisive weight, it was admitted here, was President Roosevelt's second appeal to Chancellor Hitler, which reached Berlin early this morning.

In view of the atmosphere of recrimination engendered by foreign and German press controversies over the German memorandum, the proposal that four statesmen meet provoked no surprise in Berlin diplomatic quarters. It was realized that important time had been lost through the fruitless Hitler-Chamberlain negotiations at Berchtesgaden and Godesberg.

The outcome of those negotiations, it now seems, contributed to making the Czech crisis more complicated and acrimonious. Charges that Czech mobilization was undertaken at British instigation also provoked irritation here. Meanwhile Herr Hitler watched developments with a calm born of unconcern, convinced that the German case was securely grounded and that Great Britain would not abandon her peace initiative merely because of conflicting interpretations of the German memorandum.

Continued on Page Six

Chamberlain Off to Reich; Cites 'Try, Try, Try Again'

By The Associated Press.

HESTON AIRPORT, London, Thursday, Sept. 29.—Prime Minister Neville Chamberlain took off for the Munich four-power conference at 8:35 o'clock this morning (2:35 A. M. in New York).

Most of the Cabinet and a large crowd cheered him. Like admiring schoolboys, the Ministers had brought a gift of fruit for him to eat en route on this third journey to Chancellor Adolf Hitler in the cause of peace.

Standing outside his plane, the Prime Minister said:

"When I was a little boy, I used to repeat: 'If at first you don't succeed, try, try, try again.' That's what I'm doing."

BRENNER PASS, Thursday, Sept. 29 (AP)—Premier Benito Mussolini and his Foreign Minister, Count Galeazzo Ciano, arrived here today by special train at 6:06 A. M. (12:06 A. M. in New York) on their way to Munich. They were greeted by Rudolf Hess, Chancellor Hitler's deputy in party affairs. An hour later the train continued toward Munich.

PARIS, Thursday, Sept. 29 (AP).—Premier Edouard Daladier, accompanied by his staff, left Le Bourget Field by airplane today at 8:45 A. M. (2:45 A. M. in New York) for Munich.

CZECHS SUSPICIOUS OF MUNICH PARLEY

Fear Four-Power Accord at Their Expense—Hope Hitler Simply Aims to Save Face

By G. E. R. GEDYE
Wireless to The New York Times.

PRAGUE, Czechoslovakia, Sept. 28.—Prime Minister Neville Chamberlain's speech tonight and the forthcoming conference in Munich had a mixed reception here. In official circles a reserved attitude was maintained.

For years what Europe's small nations that have remained outside the German orbit have most dreaded is a four-power pact in which the so-called Western democracies would in the end find themselves led by the nose by the two Fascist powers. This four-power conference looks to Czechoslovak eyes alarmingly like such a move.

An early release of the Czechoslovak News Agency tonight labeled it the "Puehrer Conference," an innocent misprint, which was corrected subsequently to the "Vierer Conference," or Conference of Four.

There is another interpretation that seems not without foundation—that Chancellor Adolf Hitler and the Nazi party find themselves losing the war within their own

Continued on Page Seventeen

Italy Reported Forsaking General Franco; Angry at His Neutrality in Czech Quarrel

Wireless to The New York Times.

ROME, Sept. 28.—In connection with the other problems now confronting Europe, a report circulated in Rome today that, although still lacking confirmation and indeed officially denied, nevertheless is worth noticing.

It was stated that the Italian Government, incensed at Generalissimo Francisco Franco's declaration of absolute neutrality in the present European crisis, had decided to withdraw all Italian troops from Spain immediately. Some reports even went as far as to say the first contingents were already on their way back.

It is obviously useless, say many indignant Italians, to continue spending Italian money and shedding Italian blood in Spain if Italy cannot count on General Franco in an hour of need.

All such reports would be accepted with the greatest prudence, since Italy is heavily committed in the Spanish conflict and can scarcely afford to see General Franco lose. Nevertheless, Italian enthusiasm for the Spanish cause has waned noticeably of late. Recent it is not to be concluded that some compromise solution may be broached at the conference in Munich, Germany, tomorrow.

The offer of the Spanish Premier, Dr. Juan Negrin, to withdraw all foreign volunteers on the Loyalist side seems to offer a possible starting point for negotiations aiming at the institution of a constitutional monarchy in Spain with definite safeguards for the two warring parties.

Elimination of the Spanish question would have the immediate advantage for Italy of permitting application of the Anglo-Italian agreement and facilitating the resumption of Italo-French negotiations. It is deemed significant, in any case, that the Italian Foreign Minister, Count Galeazzo Ciano, before his departure for Munich, had a long conversation with the Spanish Ambassador here.

Wireless to The New York Times.

GENEVA, Sept. 28.—In the League of Nations Assembly's political committee tonight the request of the Spanish Premier, Dr. Juan Negrin, for a League Commission to verify the withdrawal of non-Spanish combatants from the Loyalist army hit a snag.

The British and French agreed to it on the condition, which Spain accepted, that this should not prevent the London Non-Intervention Committee later from sending the committee to each sides for the same purpose if Generalissimo Francisco Franco ever accepted its plan. Portugal, Albania and Poland, however, opposed even the slightest commitment and insisted that only the Non-Intervention Committee should act in this respect.

DUCE SWAYS HITLER

Persuades Him by Phone to Delay Mobilizing and Join Parley

HEEDS CHAMBERLAIN PLEA

Appeal by Roosevelt Is Also Delivered to Mussolini—Italian Hopes Soar

By ARNALDO CORTESI
Wireless to The New York Times.

ROME, Sept. 28.—The war clouds hanging over Europe were torn asunder in dramatic fashion this morning and admitted a pale ray of sunshine when Premier Benito Mussolini had a long personal telephone conversation with Chancellor Adolf Hitler of Germany and prevailed upon him to postpone German mobilization and give his adherence to a conference in Munich at noon tomorrow among Prime Minister Neville Chamberlain of Britain, Premier Edouard Daladier of France, Herr Hitler and Signor Mussolini himself.

Premier Mussolini telephoned the German Chancellor after the first of two calls by the Earl of Perth, the British Ambassador to Rome, on Count Galeazzo Ciano, the Italian Foreign Minister. On his first visit Lord Perth delivered the following message to Signor Mussolini from Mr. Chamberlain:

I have today addressed an appeal to Chancellor Hitler to abstain from the use of force to solve the Sudeten problem, which I feel sure could be solved by means of a brief discussion while giving him essential territory, population and the protection of both Sudetens and Czechs during the transference.

I offered to go myself to Berlin to discuss a compromise with the German and Czech representatives and, if the Chancellor so desires, also with the representatives of Italy and France.

I trust that Your Excellency will inform the German Chancellor that you are willing to be represented and will exhort him to adhere to my suggestions. I have guaranteed that the Czech promises will be carried out and I am confident that complete agreement could be reached within a week.

Roosevelt Appeal Received

William Phillips, the United States Ambassador, was received by Premier Mussolini at 6 o'clock this afternoon and delivered a personal message from President Roosevelt. It is understood that Signor Mussolini expressed his appreciation of the President's efforts on behalf of peace and declared himself happy to be able to announce that a solution in accordance with Mr. Roosevelt's suggestion had already been adopted with the decision to hold the Anglo-French-Italian-German conference in Munich tomorrow.

[A summary issued by Stefani, official Italian news agency said, according to The Associated Press, that the President in his message, "after having recalled efforts exerted by him to assure a peaceful solution of the German-Czechoslovak conflict and after having emphasized the tragic consequences that a European war would have for every one, asked Il Duce to lend his aid to settle the controversy by negotiation or other peaceful means and without recourse to force."]

Lord Perth first called on Count Ciano at 10 A. M. and then at noon. As Signor Mussolini's telephone conversation with Herr Hitler occurred between the two visits, Count Ciano was able to inform the British Ambassador on the second that Signor Mussolini had induced Herr Hitler to agree to a conference.

Signor Mussolini assured Herr Hitler personally, as well as through an official step through the Italian Ambassador to Berlin, that Italy was ready to stand by her pledge to Germany but begged him not to disregard the opportunity Mr. Chamberlain offered for getting what he wanted without using violence.

The Italian Premier left for Munich by special train at 8 o'clock this evening accompanied by Count Ciano.

The wave of hopefulness that swept over Italy when this news became known is heightened by reports that Signor Mussolini succeeded in inducing Herr Hitler not only to meet Mr. Chamberlain and

Continued on Page Nine

German Liners Are Called Home; Thousands of Tourists Stranded

Other Lines Take as Many as Possible—2,000 on the Washington—Freighter Slips From Puerto Rico and Eludes a Cutter

Germany withdrew the far-flung tentacles of her mercantile marine yesterday in a drastic move that threw shipping on the Atlantic into unprecedented confusion, turned liners around at sea and sent two vessels out from New York Harbor empty, before all their prospective passengers could be warned.

With other steamship companies altering schedules on a moment's notice in efforts to accommodate stranded passengers and shipping on extra ecto, lifebelts and other equipment required by international safety laws, the entire industry was in a state of disruption unknown here since the World War.

German shipping officials, long accustomed to soldierly discharge of orders from the Reich Government, said they knew only that the order had been issued and had been complied with as quickly as circumstances permitted. It was construed here as an attempt to get the fleet into safe German harbors to avoid possible repetition of the elimination of the German merchant marine in the World War.

All the way across the Atlantic, from the North Sea to America, ships were either plowing along on their usual courses devoid of passengers and carrying only such cargo as could be shipped at the last moment or are retracing their courses and omitting ports that in more peaceful times are regularly on their schedules.

The first ship affected was the 50,000-ton express liner Europa, which turned around in the English Channel before reaching Cherbourg and Southampton and hurried back toward Bremerhaven, leaving hundreds of passengers waiting on piers in the French and English ports.

Her sister ship, the Bremen, had sailed from New York at 12:25 A. M. yesterday, on schedule. At the end of the day, however, the recall order had been extended to the entire fleet of the German lines with a few exceptions in which execution of the order was impossible.

Early yesterday morning, after a few hours of hurried preparation, the Hamburg-American liner Hansa steamed out of New York, leaving

Continued on Page Twelve

WASHINGTON'S HOPE FOR PEACE MOUNTS

Roosevelt Made Final Plea to Hitler on Hearing Reich Might March Yesterday

Special to The New York Times.

WASHINGTON, Sept. 28.—Upon receiving official confirmation through diplomatic channels of the summoning of the four-power conference at Munich tomorrow, the White House, through Stephen T. Early, secretary to the President, said today that the meeting "offered hope and encouragement."

This was the one definite Administration comment on the development, but the relief here was evidenced in a relaxation of the tension that had gripped the government. For the first time in several days it was really believed that the grave danger of war could be averted.

Mr. Early revealed that President Roosevelt had decided upon his final plea to Chancellor Hitler for peace last night after having received press and radio reports that Germany might march into the Sudeten area of Czechoslovakia today. There was no official confirmation, but Mr. Roosevelt felt that he should make his last effort then or never. If the troops marched today it would be too late.

Stresses No Involvements

It was also disclosed by Mr. Early that the President's suggestion of a conference to decide the detailed questions at issue would enlarge the negotiations to include Poland, Russia and Hungary. At the same time Mr. Early stressed that the United States has no involvements in Europe.

According to Mr. Early the President decided to make his plea early last night during a two-hour conference on the day's developments with Secretary of State Cordell Hull and Sumner Welles, Undersecretary of State.

Previously, at his late afternoon press conference, the President had rather indicated that there would be no developments during the night, but the unofficial reports of possible German military movements this morning decided his course. When he reached his decision the telegram instead of writing it in longhand, as he did his earlier peace appeal that was dispatched early Monday morning.

This illustrates, Mr. Early said, how closely the President has watched the situation by reading press dispatches and listening to the radio when he was confined to the Executive Mansion by a head cold.

"It is a great advantage," Mr. Early said, "to have the President sitting in the White House Mansion in a rather detached way, and his cold, therefore, has been a blessing."

There was no attempt here to forecast what the result of the Munich conversations would be.

Continued on Page Eight

FRENCH NOW WANT SOLID PEACE BASIS

Nation Firmer Toward Hitler—Mussolini Moves Watched —Many Abandon Paris

By P. J. PHILIP
Wireless to The New York Times.

PARIS, Thursday, Sept. 29.—How will they line up, two and two or three and one? Is Premier Edouard Daladier of France strong enough to carry this immense argument? In which camp will Premier Benito Mussolini of Italy be? Will Chancellor Adolf Hitler scream, as he did at Berchtesgaden? Will it bring real peace?

All these and a thousand other questions poured out in an uneasy stream yesterday as bit by bit the news leaked out in France that this ever-towering crisis, which has seemed each day certain to crash in a great welter of blood and ruin, had shot up to a new pinnacle with hope perched higher than ever.

And now what? After these successive days crowded with events, with their alternating hopes and fears, even peace will seem an anti-climax. To satisfy France in her present grim mood it must at least be a real peace, such a peace of confidence as there is between Britain and France or between France and the United States. Is that possible with Adolf Hitler and Benito Mussolini in power in their respective countries with Nazi and Fascist systems?

Daladier Must Be Wary

M. Daladier will have to go warily. His people are not trustful by nature—and, perhaps, with cause. And yet it is realized that the French Premier cannot go to this conference with nothing to offer. There must be something for Signor Mussolini, whose ways have seemed devious, but to whom in the end for whatever cause a debt of gratitude seems due for yesterday's action.

There must be something for Herr Hitler, if only a Roman triumph in a Mercedes car through the winding streets of Karlsbad, Czechoslovakia. M. Daladier is big enough to do it, but he will need Prime Minister Neville Chamberlain's protecting shadow if he is to bring back honor with peace in a manner sufficient to satisfy even some of his immediate colleagues.

What comes first, of course, is a settlement of the Sudeten issue. There the line-up seems almost certain to be three to one, for Signor Mussolini knows that anything more than the first Anglo-French settlement proposal will mean the Czechs will fight, and the chances that such a war might be localized are small. He has other reasons, some of which go back to the assassination of Austria and others that look forward to the future on the necessity of doing a service for those who have something to give.

Can Herr Hitler, who has never gone back from what he said he would, do so now? That is the great question of tomorrow. Signor

Continued on Page Thirteen

COMMONS JUBILANT

Chamberlain's News of a Delay by Hitler on Czechs Stirs Bedlam

FINAL PLEAS SUCCESSFUL

Mussolini and Roosevelt Are Credited—Germany Warned She Would Attack Today

As Prime Minister Chamberlain was delivering a grave speech to the House of Commons yesterday two slips of paper were handed to him that bore tidings which instantly dispelled the war clouds hanging over Europe. The slips related that Chancellor Hitler had agreed to meet Mr. Chamberlain, Premier Daladier and Premier Mussolini at Munich today for a peace conference, and meanwhile had deferred his war measures.

This development resulted from a Chamberlain appeal to Herr Hitler, a second Roosevelt appeal to the Chancellor and especially from an appeal by Mr. Chamberlain to Signor Mussolini. The Italian Premier promptly got in touch with the Chancellor and begged him not to disregard the opportunity for peace.

There was talk in Rome that the Munich conference would range over the entire European situation, including Spain, and also that Signor Mussolini might forsake the cause of the Spanish insurgents.

Washington was hopeful. It was revealed in the capital that President Roosevelt had sent a personal message to Premier Mussolini asking his intervention.

Berlin was relieved by the new turn, as was Paris, but the French are insistent that a real settlement must develop out of the four-power talks. Prague was suspicious, fearing that a settlement would be at its expense.

Meanwhile, as a result of German action in recalling merchant ships, many of which sailed swiftly without passengers, the Atlantic tourist trade was thrown into confusion.

[All the above dispatches on Page 1.]

The stock market here reacted to the good news in Europe with gains of 1 to 4 points. [Page 7.]

Mr. Chamberlain's speech is printed on Page 14; British White Paper, Pages 16-17.

Hitler Agrees to Parley

By FERDINAND KUHN Jr.
Special Cable to The New York Times.

LONDON, Thursday, Sept. 29.—Prime Minister Neville Chamberlain won the greatest, and sweetest triumph of his life yesterday when he suddenly announced to a wildly cheering House of Commons that Chancellor Adolf Hitler had summoned a four-power meeting for today at Munich, Germany, to find a peaceful way out of the Czech crisis.

A "last last" appeal from Mr. Chamberlain to Herr Hitler and another to Premier Benito Mussolini, together with the second message from President Roosevelt, had produced the desired result in Berlin when all hope of averting war appeared lost. It came only twenty-four hours after Herr Hitler had sent word to London that Germany would mobilize yesterday and march across the Czech frontier today unless its demands upon Czechoslovakia were fulfilled.

Instead Mr. Chamberlain is flying to Munich this morning and hopes to meet Herr Hitler, Signor Mussolini and Premier Edouard Daladier of France about midday. Some advisers who went to Godesberg are accompanying Mr. Chamberlain, with the addition of Frank Ashton-Gwatkin, the expert who served with Viscount Runciman's mediatory mission in Prague.

Whether the meeting at Munich succeeds or not, there was a strong belief throughout Britain today that Europe might soon awaken from its nightmare. Relief and thanksgiving without parallel since the Armistice swept the country as

Continued on Page Fifteen

WALTER WINCHELL SAYS: "FRED More from an American through a 'Legation' at the John Golden Theatre."

"All the News That's Fit to Print."

The New York Times.

LATE CITY EDITION
Mostly cloudy, not quite so cool today. Tomorrow probably fair with moderate temperatures.
Temperature Yesterday—Max., 46; Min., 44

Copyright, 1939, by The New York Times Company.

VOL. LXXXVIII...No. 29,680.

Entered as Second-Class Matter,
Postoffice, New York, N. Y.

NEW YORK, SATURDAY, APRIL 29, 1939.

P

THREE CENTS NEW YORK CITY and Vicinity | FOUR CENTS Elsewhere Except in 7th and 8th Postal Zones

MOSCOW AVIATORS DOWN IN CANADA; RELIEF IS RUSHED

One Flier Hurt and Plane Is Badly Damaged in Landing on New Brunswick Marsh

ON DASH TO NEW YORK

Mishap in Northern Wilds Comes After 23 Hours and 40 Minutes in the Air

By Telephone to The New York Times.

MISCOU PLAIN, N. B., April 28.—Forced down on their Arctic Circle route from Moscow to New York, Colonel Vladimir Kokkinaki and his co-pilot, Major Mikhail Gordienko, Soviet airmen, wrecked their twin-motored monoplane in landing in a marsh five miles from this village on Miscou Island, northeasternmost point of the Province of New Brunswick.

Clearing the ice covering Chaleur Bay on the west and the Gulf of St. Lawrence on the east, the airmen found a landing spot on the snow-covered marsh to bring their flight to a halt, but in making the landing both right and left wings were smashed, the two propellers shattered and one of the two engines was torn from the fuselage.

One of the fliers was injured in landing, but it was believed that he was not badly hurt. He made light of his injury, indicating that it was only a broken rib and, with the aid of his comrade, made himself comfortable in an improvised bed beside the wrecked plane, sheltered from the frozen marshland by a single blanket. It was cold, but not severely so.

The fliers had made their presence known to the residents of this hamlet and others of the 1,200 on Miscou Island by circling before landing. Their motors sputtered as if they were having engine trouble or were running short of fuel. It was thought at first, because they were flying so low, that they might land here, but they continued on.

Inhabitants Finds Plane

When the big red plane swung down toward the marsh and it was apparent the fliers were going to land, Lawrence Vibert of this village set out to find them. He discovered them on the marsh, five miles from the village, resting beside their plane. Vibert was unable to speak to them, however, for the fliers spoke only Russian.

For several minutes Vibert tried to make himself understood in English and French and the Russians attempted to talk with him in their native tongue. Gesticulating, the uninjured airman at last hauled out a map and showed Vibert that the plane had flown from Moscow along a course set out on the paper and that it was due in New York at 8 P. M. The plane had been 23 hours 40 minutes in the air.

Vibert, by gestures, attempted to get the fliers to leave their wrecked plane in the desolate marsh and come to his house for shelter. Both pilots gestured that they would remain on guard beside their plane, and the injured man, lying on the frozen ground in his improvised bed, indicated that he was comfortable so long as he did not attempt to move.

Returning to the village, Vibert telephoned to Miss Jeannette Newton, telephone operator at Shippigan, a railroad trunk station on the mainland twenty-five miles from here, and reported his discovery. Loading up with food and fuel and blankets at his house, he started trudging back to the plane, intending to stay through the night with the airmen.

Vibert said as far as he could discover the men had a single blanket and no tent or other material to afford shelter from the cold.

Stay to Guard Plane

It was believed the men were remaining by their plane to guard it, as the injured flier did not indicate that he felt he was hurt too badly to be moved by villagers, who were ready to send out a stretcher for him. However, no medical aid could be sent to the men as Dr. A. Robichaud of Shippigan (the nearest physician) would have to cross two dangerous ice-covered strips of water and two islands to reach them.

A rescue party headed by Constable Marcel Theriault of the Royal Canadian Mounted Police, stationed at Shippigan, will escort Dr. Robichaud to the scene at dawn. Once the party takes the men off the island, they will be able to go from Shippigan to the railroad terminal at Bathurst and thence away to Moncton and St. Johns.

The end of the flight in this section of the Canadian wilds was caused by lack of knowledge of the terrain, the same cause which prevented several Moscow-New York airmen, flying the Pacific route, from reaching their destination non-stop. Colonel Kokkinaki and

Continued on Page Two

Daylight-Saving Time Starts At 2 Tomorrow Morning

Daylight-saving time will go into effect at 2 A. M. Eastern standard time, tomorrow. Before retiring many New Yorkers will turn their clocks and watches forward one hour.

More than 30,000,000 persons in the United States are affected by the time change, of whom about 10,000,000 are in New York. Daylight saving will continue in effect until the last Sunday in September, when the lost hour of sleep will be regained.

As has been the custom in past years, most railroad time-tables will continue to show Eastern standard time, while nearly all the trains will be changed an hour to conform to the new daylight time. The Long Island Railroad, however, will operate all its trains on the new time.

THRONGS ARRIVING FOR START OF FAIR

Incoming Travel Rises, Hotels Filling Up With Visitors for Opening Fete

The advance guard of World's Fair visitors began to trickle through New York's railroad terminals, bridges and tunnels yesterday, with indications that many thousands would arrive today, tonight and tomorrow morning for Sunday's official opening.

With the Weather Bureau predicting "probably fair" for tomorrow, with more than thirty vessels of the Atlantic fleet nearing port, and, with the Bronx-Whitestone Bridge to be dedicated today, Fair officials were confident that their estimate of an attendance of 1,000,000 for the opening day would be realized.

Although the Fair will not be 100 per cent ready, by any means, when the gates open, the management was satisfied that it would be as nearly ready as any other World's Fair has been, or more so. They felt that this one will be so much bigger than previous fairs that even so much more to see than any one can possibly cover in a day that no one will be disappointed at the failure of some of the exhibits to be ready.

Most of Features Ready

Bad weather in the last few weeks, labor troubles and the foreign situation were given as factors that have delayed construction and the receipt of exhibits in some cases. It was emphasized, however, that the buildings that will not open, or will open in a seriously incomplete condition, will be in a distinct minority.

Even in the amusement zone, which is the most retarded part of the Fair from a construction standpoint, it was said that fifty-five or more attractions would be ready for business when the first-day crowds arrive. The management promised that the streets in the amusement zone would be satisfactorily paved by tomorrow.

Grover A. Whalen, president, and Bayard F. Pope, treasurer of the Fair Corporation, made a tour of the grounds last night and expressed themselves afterward as satisfied with the conditions they found. They saw thousands of painters, carpenters, landscape gardeners and other artisans working through the night to get things ready both outside and inside the exposition buildings.

40,000 Work at High Speed

Despite the damp, misty rain that prevailed most of the day, about 40,000 men were working at high speed inside the Fair Grounds, putting up many-colored flags, pennants and banners, taking down scaffolding and doing other last-minute jobs. Trucks and automobiles, which will be barred from the grounds after today, continued to dash about, and the wheel-chairs and buses in which visitors will be able to go from place to place throughout the 1,216-acre tract began to appear in large numbers.

Hotels, restaurants and bars, as well as railroad stations, throughout the city also were filling up with people from out-of-town who exhibited an eager friendliness and talkativeness unusual to New Yorkers, and told stranger their personal histories and their views on the foreign situation, as well as their plans for visiting the Fair.

The police, especially the traffic policemen, began to have their hands full with visitors unaccustomed to the ways and regulations of the metropolis. Just outside Pennsylvania Station yesterday afternoon an elderly woman, evidently from out-of-town, put a traffic policeman to the test, and he came through with flying colors under

Continued on Page Three

LEGISLATURE VOTES REPUBLICAN BUDGET, SLASHING LEHMAN'S

Both Houses, on Party Lines, Pass $388,000,000 Bill, a $31,000,000 Reduction

GOVERNOR PLEADS IN VAIN

Warns of Harm to Public Service—Majority Holds Cut Vital—Court Test Ahead

By WARREN MOSCOW

ALBANY, April 28.—Both houses of the Legislature, by practically a straight party vote, adopted the Republican budget late today. The Assembly balloted 82 to 64 for the measure and the Senate approved it, 27 to 24.

The total of the budget, as revised by the Republican majority, is $388,-000,000, as contrasted with the $419,-000,000 budget submitted by Governor Lehman, a reduction on paper of $31,000,000. The Governor submitted a budget of $415,000,000, but by transferring special fund revenues and appropriations to the general fund the totals of the Governor's budget and that of the Republican majority were raised by about $4,000,000 of bookkeeping transactions.

The vote in the Assembly came late in the afternoon after an all-day debate wherein the Democrats charged the Republicans with crippling State services, and the repudiation of platform pledges, and the Republicans retorted that a check in spending was necessary.

Senate Session Is Short

The Senate, worn out by the Assembly debate, to which most of the Senators listened as visitors, cut its discussion to less than an hour. The only deviation from party affiliation in either house came in the Assembly, where Joseph Boccia, Republican of New York City, elected with the support of the American Labor Party, voted with the Democrats against the revised budget.

Both houses acted after they had received another special message from Governor Lehman, in which the Governor accused the Republicans of hampering State services, and pursuing an unconstitutional course of action.

The budget will now go to the Governor, who has the power to veto any addition to estimates and also any of the special acts necessary to carry out the Republican program. These special acts have not yet been passed. He has no power to veto cuts in the budget. Both sides have served notice that the question of the constitutionality of the "lump sum" budget prepared by the Republicans will be carried to the Court of Appeals, but it is not now known whether the Governor will attempt to veto the budget on the grounds that it is unconstitutional or sign it for the purpose of expediting a test case.

Nor is it certain how the test case will be brought. The most probable sponsor is the State Association of Civil Service Employes, which has announced that it would bring an action if the Republicans carried out their announced plans. This they did today.

On the floor of the Assembly the

Continued on Page Four

Riot in Saar Reported Over New 60-Hour Week

Special Cable to The New York Times.

PARIS, April 28.—A French news agency reports that twenty Saar workers have been jailed for rioting against the new sixty-hour week.

At Forbach on the French frontier gendarmes reported that all was quiet on the eastern front. Metz and Strasbourg also reported apparent quiet across the frontier.

VIENNA, April 28.—Twelve men, most of them former officers of the Austrian Army, were arrested today in a wine cellar in the center of Vienna. They are suspected of a monarchist conspiracy. All are known to have monarchist sympathies.

ROME-LONDON PACT MAY BE NEXT TO GO

Following of Hitler's Lead Is Rumored in Italy — Public Fears Step Toward War

By HERBERT L. MATTHEWS

ROME, April 28.—Amid a general fear of an approaching war, which Chancellor Adolf Hitler's address intensified here today, came rumors that Italy might in her turn denounce the Anglo-Italian Pact of April 16, 1938. These reports, however must be taken cautiously and they cannot be confirmed in official quarters.

These reports are, perhaps, more symptomatic of the rising tension in Italy since the announcement of British conscription than a true foreshadowing of events to come. But something is expected.

Herr Hitler's reply to President Roosevelt was very different from Premier Benito Mussolini's mild protestation of peace, and there well may be some move from this end of the Axis to bring Italy's policies into line with Germany's.

Alarm Felt by Public

Herr Hitler's speech has been interpreted by the ordinary Italian as another step toward war and from that viewpoint it has brought regret and disappointment. Such feelings, of course, are not expressed in official circles or in the first reactions that are to be found in the press.

Herr Hitler's reaffirmation of the strength of the Axis is constantly being said here and because of that the official attitude on everything that Herr Hitler states is prima as a matter of policy. The newspapers reflect the same attitude and outwardly one gets the impression of complete harmony.

Yet, when there is a controlled press, the commentator has to distinguish between spontaneous and natural feelings, as far as they are

Continued on Page Five

$325 Car Set to Go 50 Miles Per Fuel Gallon; Crosley Puts Its Speed at 50 Miles an Hour

Special to The New York Times.

INDIANAPOLIS, April 28.—A new low-cost, two-cylinder automobile, designed for a top speed of fifty miles an hour and a gasoline mileage of fifty to the gallon, was introduced to distributors and newspaper men today at the Indianapolis Motor Speedway here by Powel Crosley Jr., Cincinnati manufacturer and owner of the Cincinnati Baseball Club.

Radical in design, the car will sell f. o. b. for $325 for the two-passenger convertible coupe and $350 for the four-passenger convertible sedan, the only models in which it is to be manufactured, at Richmond, Ind. The car will be manufactured in Cincinnati as well, but Richmond will be the final shipping point.

It is said that the car will accommodate persons taller than six feet, although the automobile itself is only ten feet long from bumper to bumper, mounted on a wheelbase of eighty inches. It has three speeds forward and reverse, four-wheel mechanical brakes and is equipped with safety glass.

The two-cylinder engine is of a light variation four-cycle type. An aviation-type suction blower, an integral part of the flywheel, provides air cooling. The drive shaft runs straight to the rear axle without

going through universal joints as in the conventional car.

The Crosley automobile weighs only 925 pounds and has a gasoline tank of four-gallon capacity which is estimated to be at least a 200-mile fuel supply. The crankcase holds only two quarts of oil.

The gear shift and steering arrangements are not essentially different from those of other makes. The cars shown at the introductory display today were in the standard colors of gray, yellow and blue. They had red wheels with chrome hub caps and black tops. The car can be used as a light commercial vehicle by the removal of one of the seats in the convertible coupe for added transportation space, offering a quarter-ton carrying capacity, Mr. Crosley said.

"I always have wanted to build a practical car that would not only operate at a low cost, but also would sell at a low price," Mr. Crosley stated. "I have been dreaming about this for a good many years."

The car was christened by Lewis L'Hommedieu Crosley, grandson of the manufacturer, who broke a bottle containing a sample of its standard brands of gasoline.

Crosley officials announced that the new cars could be manufactured at the rate of about 250 a day.

HITLER SAYS NO TO ROOSEVELT, INSISTS ON DANZIG; SCRAPS POLISH, BRITISH NAVAL AND MUNICH PACTS; WARSAW DEFIANT; ITALY MAY END LONDON TREATY

POLAND PREPARED

Return of Danzig to the Reich Opposed as Well as a Corridor Road

ARMS PLAN TO BE RUSHED

Attempts to Exert Pressure Will Be Met by Poles—End of Pact Seen as Warning

By JERZY SZAPIRO
Wireless to The New York Times.

WARSAW, April 28.—The memorandum from the Reich government outlining its views in the present state of Polish-German relations was delivered to the Foreign Office here today by the German Charge d'Affaires at the very moment Chancellor Hitler began his speech.

No information is obtainable here as to the contents of the memorandum but official circles declare that it will be examined carefully and attentively. There is a tendency to regard the document as a preliminary step to the opening of new negotiations between Poland and Germany with a view to concluding a new agreement replacing the 1934 non-aggression pact that Herr Hitler denounced today.

The Poles, it is understood, are prepared to negotiate a new understanding and to discuss the Danzig problem but under normal conditions without pressure or intimidation.

[Poland intensified her military precautions at the Polish-German frontier where many of Poland's 1,300,000 men now under arms are stationed and military activity especially was noticeable near Danzig. The Associated Press reported.]

The memorandum, it is believed, repeats in more diplomatic form the views Herr Hitler expressed in his speech and declares that the non-aggression pact must be considered non-existent because it was violated by the Poles when they entered an agreement with Britain.

Official circles interpreted thus so far as Danzig is concerned the German, during the last five years, have always maintained that the fate of this provincial city was of minor importance to them but that the Danzig problem should not adversely affect Polish-German relations and undermine the non-aggression agreement.

As far as German communications through the so-called Corridor, they have always been treated favorably by the Polish Government although Germany violated certain conventions in connection with traffic such as, for instance, the prompt payment for railroad transit.

Road Held Out of Question

The extra-territorial road through the Corridor is out of the question, it was added. Such a demand, it was said, had already served the Germans as a pretext to disrupt a neighboring country; such methods could not be applied to Poland.

The Polish-German non-aggression pact, it was further said, was a bilateral arrangement and a unilateral denunciation of the agreement was sure to provoke a strong reaction. Germany never received the right to decide what was best for Poland's interests, it was added, and the 1934 pact could never be interpreted as preventing Poland's cooperation with the western powers.

The question of whether the Polish-British agreement was contrary to the non-aggression pact should be left for diplomatic exchanges, it was said. In this case such exchange were rendered impossible by the fact that since April 5—the date of Prime Minister Neville Chamberlain's pronouncement of the Polish-British guarantee—diplomatic contacts with the Reich government have been little good but because Foreign Minister Joachim von Ribbentrop would not see the Polish Ambassador, Josef Lipski, and the German Ambassador here, Hans Adolf von Moltke, never returned from his Easter vacation.

Statesmen Surprise Warsaw

Warsaw was surprised by Herr Hitler's revelation that he had offered the extension of the Polish-German non-aggression pact for twenty-five years and to conclude a Polish-Slovak-German guarantee of Slovakia's independence in return for Danzig's incorporation in the Reich and a motor road through the Corridor. It was indicated in official circles that up to

Continued on Page Seven

President Tells Norwegian Guest Hitler Leaves Door Open 'an Inch'

Remark to Crown Princess at Poughkeepsie Roosevelt's Only Comment on Speech— He Slept Through the Broadcast

By FELIX BELAIR Jr.
Special to The New York Times.

POUGHKEEPSIE, N. Y., April 28.—"It left the door about an inch open," President Roosevelt commented on Chancellor Adolf Hitler's reply to his proposal that the Rome-Berlin Axis pledge a ten to twenty year guarantee of the territorial integrity of thirty-one European States, in which the Nazi chief called for specific proposals on the basis of absolute reciprocity.

The Chief Executive's off-hand judgment, presumably directed at the opportunities for an amicably negotiated settlement of Germany's demands within the limits of Chancellor Hitler's statement of his attitude, was offered in response to a direct question from Crown Princess Martha of Norway as to what he thought of the speech.

Fewer than fifty persons were within earshot of the exchange that followed, and some of it was missed entirely amid the hub-bub that followed the handshaking and picture taking of the President and Mrs. Roosevelt with the Princess Martha and Crown Prince Olav and their entourage as they debarked at a lumber yard dock at Poughkeepsie.

"What did you think of Hitler's speech, Mr. President?" inquired the Crown Princess.

"Six o'clock in the morning is rather early, don't you think?" Mr. Roosevelt parried first, referring to the hour the broadcast of the speech started here.

Newspaper photographers and newsreel cameramen began jostling each other, and for a moment or two the President's conversation was blanked out. Then he was heard by those closest to remark:

"How can any one have a reaction to a speech that lasts more than two hours?"

The remark about the door's being left open about an inch followed a few seconds later.

Exactly to what part of the Hitler address the President directed this remark was left to the imagination of those who heard it. From as much of the context as was heard

Continued on Page Eight

FRENCH SEE PERIL IN BOND TO POLES

Fear Call to War for Danzig Which They Do Not Regard as a Good Issue

By P. J. PHILIP
Wireless to The New York Times.

PARIS, April 28.—Both in official circles and among the general public Chancellor Hitler's speech today has been judged as unlikely to increase, although it does not diminish, the present state of tension.

In manner it sounded aggressive. In matter it is described as being a very astute lawyer's presentation of the German case, carefully compiled, well argued and marked by tendency toward caution.

This tendency is shown in the disinclination to appeal to juries—the British, French and American peoples—by insinuating that their governments are hostile judges. It is shown also, it is considered here, in the manner in which, while the Chancellor denounces the Anglo-German naval agreement and the German-Polish accord he leaves the doors open for future arrangements.

Where he was least at ease was in defense of his action regarding Bohemia. He devoted twenty-five written pages, nearly a fifth of the whole speech, to that question as if it needed all that space to convince himself as well as his listeners that he had not departed form his doctrine and policy. It seemed, French experts judged, uncomfortably, as if he knew instinctively that he had acted in contradiction to himself.

Uneasiness Over Danzig

By far the greatest importance is attached to the denunciation of the pact with Poland and his account of the rejection by Warsaw of the offer he had made concerning Danzig and operation through the Polish Corridor. While the Chancellor based his denunciation of the pact with Poland on the fact that that country had joined the ranks of the western nations in an agreement that he considers hostile to Germany there seems little doubt but that his major reason was the rejection of the Danzig agreement by Warsaw, for the Franco-Polish treaty existed when the Germano-Polish pact was signed.

There is uneasiness here because Warsaw was solely responsible for rejection of the German proposal. Paris was not informed until afterward and even then not fully of all its terms. That Germany had proposed that Poland and Hungary should participate in a guarantee of the independence of the Slovak State was news to the French Foreign Office.

Regarding the Chancellor's proposals Warsaw was 'not, therefore,

Continued on Page Six

BRITAIN UNSOLACED BY HITLER'S SPEECH

Finds Situation Full of Danger —Home Fleet Concentrates —Russian Plan Speeded

By FERDINAND KUHN Jr.

LONDON, April 28.—The British Government pushed ahead today with its conscription plans and its defensive alliances in spite of the comparatively mild and almost apologetic tone of certain passages in Chancellor Adolf Hitler's speech.

Prime Minister Neville Chamberlain met his leading Cabinet colleagues to discuss the draft of the conscription bill that will be published Monday night and debated in the House of Commons Thursday. At the same time British diplomacy showed no signs of slackening in its efforts to bring Russia and Turkey into the anti-aggression front of Europe.

Soviet Ambassador Ivan M. Maisky returned here today from his consultations in Moscow and found a message saying that Viscount Halifax, Foreign Secretary, would be delighted to see him at the Foreign Office at his earliest opportunity. So the two men arranged to compare notes tomorrow morning on the progress of the Anglo-Russian talks, which aim to create a solid front against Germany in case of war.

British Fleet Assembles

By coincidence or design, warships of the British Home Fleet, led by the giant battleship, Nelson, assembled at Portland today after their Easter leave. The ships concentrated while Herr Hitler was speaking, just as last September they arrived at their battle stations in Scotland on the day of the Nuremberg speech that helped to precipitate the Czech crisis.

Such friendly references as Herr Hitler made to Britain today may, no doubt, be reciprocated publicly by Mr. Chamberlain in the House of Commons next week. Taking a leaf from Herr Hitler's book, the Prime Minister can say with equal fact sincerity that he admired Germany's past achievements and would regard war between Britain and Germany as a needless tragedy for mankind, but the British found nothing in the speech to justify even the slightest abandonment of their new policy, which has led them in six short weeks to assume military responsibilities in Eastern Europe and to impose compulsory military training in peacetime.

Continued on Page Six

BID TO POLES BARED

Chancellor Reports 25-Year Pact Offer for Free City's Return

SPEECH A BLISTERING ONE

Nazi Leader Willing to Give Non-Aggression Pledges to Nations Asking for Them

Chancellor Hitler, in a scornful speech before the Reichstag yesterday, denounced three treaties, replied in critical tones to President Roosevelt's truce proposal and defended his actions in Europe. One pact he abrogated was the non-aggression treaty with Poland [text of note to Warsaw, Page 7], and at the same time he emphasized he wished the return of Danzig and cession of a right-of-way across Pomorze. Another accord he canceled was the Anglo-German naval treaty [text of note to London, Page 6], and the third was the Munich consultative agreement with Britain. To Mr. Roosevelt, the Chancellor declared he was ready to pledge non-aggression to the thirty-one nations named by the President provided such pledges were reciprocal and the other nations took the initiative. [Page 1; text of the speech, Pages 9, 10 and 11.]

Poland's reaction was one of firm refusal to cede any territory and of renewed military precautions. [Page 1.]

Rumors circulated in Rome that Premier Mussolini might follow his partner's lead by denouncing the Anglo-Italian agreement. [Page 1.]

In the opinion of President Roosevelt the Chancellor "left the door about an inch open" [Page 1], and the State Department seemed to agree. [Page 8.]

London found the speech had done nothing to relieve the tension [Page 1]. Paris was somewhat encouraged but was apprehensive over the danger spot at Danzig [Page 1], while Moscow took solace in the thought that the Chancellor had divided Europe into two camps and thus removed the long-standing Bolshevist bogey. [Page 5.]

Chancellor Hitler Speaks

By GUIDO ENDERIS
Wireless to The New York Times.

BERLIN, April 28.—An American President's political philosophy underwent searching scrutiny by Chancellor Adolf Hitler before the National Socialist Reichstag today and he found it wanting.

But President Roosevelt's peace appeal of April 15 to Herr Hitler was not the only document to crumble in the white heat created by one of the most blistering speeches that the Chancellor has delivered before the Reichstag.

Today that body literally worked itself into a frenzy of approval as Herr Hitler announced the abrogation of the German-Polish non-aggression pact of 1934, the Anglo-German naval agreement of 1935 and the Anglo-German consultative pact concluded between Herr Hitler and Prime Minister Neville Chamberlain in Munich last September.

If the political equilibrium in Europe is already restless Europe is not placed further in jeopardy by the German Government's decisions an nounced today it will be because of calmer judgments in Chancelleries elsewhere, which probably have discounted today's speech on the ground that it was motivated by internal considerations.

Diplomats Keep at Decisions

The tension in the chamber of the Kroll Opera House mounted as Herr Hitler announced the decisions, which made neutral spectators and the occupants of the diplomatic gallery gasp at the manner in which he defied Britain and forecast the nerves of Polish statesmen.

His caustic rejection of President Roosevelt's message concluded a two-hour speech already laced with thrills. The climactic effect was attributable to the devitalizing sarcasm bestowed upon the President's proposals.

Herr Hitler dealt with them as twenty-one points, each of which gave him a succulent opportunity

Continued on Page Eight

"All the News That's Fit to Print."

The New York Times.

LATE CITY EDITION
Generally fair and continued cool today. Tomorrow fair, slowly rising temperature.
Temperature Yesterday—Max. 50; Min. 45

Copyright, 1939, by The New York Times Company.

VOL. LXXXVIII...No. 29,682.   Entered as Second-Class Matter, Postoffice, New York, N. Y.   NEW YORK, MONDAY, MAY 1, 1939.   PP   THREE CENTS NEW YORK CITY and Vicinity | FOUR CENTS Elsewhere Except in 7th and 8th Postal Zones.

POLES CONSIDERING COUNTER DEMANDS IN REPLY TO HITLER

Military Circles Say Claim on Danzig Should Be Dropped Before Further Parleys

BALTIC OUTLET STRESSED

Reich Specification of Width of Right of Way in Corridor Said to Be 15.5 Miles

In Warsaw there were indications yesterday that the Polish reply to Germany might call for a dropping of the Nazi demands regarding Danzig and the replacing of the League of Nations link to the Free City by a new Polish one. It was also reported that Chancellor Hitler in a detailed demand had asked a fifteen-and-a-half-mile motor road right-of-way across Pomerania. [Page 1.]

Both Paris and London seemed to be hopeful that a Polish-German compromise on Danzig could be reached. Reports from the two capitals indicated a disinclination to be forced to fight on this issue. [Page 12.]

The question of peace or war, however, was considered by Nazi spokesmen to have been put up to the democracies and their partners. [Page 13.]

With the arrival of the German Army commander in Rome it was believed new pressure was being put on Italy by Germany for a full-fledged military alliance. But it was significant that according to all reports the Brenner Pass between the two countries was being fortified on both sides. [Page 11.]

Poles to Use Hitler Tactics

By JERZY SZAPIRO
Wireless to THE NEW YORK TIMES.

WARSAW, Poland, April 30.—The German memorandum to the Polish Foreign Office delivered on Friday while Chancellor Adolf Hitler was attacking Poland will be answered in the same manner. A Polish memorandum, repudiating the German accusation and rejecting Danzig's incorporation into Germany and a highway across Pomorze (the Polish Corridor), but leaving the door open for further negotiations, will be delivered at the Berlin Foreign Office while Foreign Minister Josef Beck and Premier Felicien Slawoj-Skladkowski are addressing the Sejm [Parliament], probably on Friday.

[It was reported in Poland that Chancellor Hitler had demanded a German motor road right of way across Pomorze 15.5 miles wide, The Associated Press stated.]

Certain influential military circles hold that Warsaw should not enter into new negotiations with the Nazis unless the Germans withdraw their demands regarding Danzig. This view is expressed in the military journal, Polska Zbrojna, which published one of the strongest criticisms of Herr Hitler's speech and of German policy generally.

"Danzig is at the mouth of a great Polish river," it says, "and we cannot give it up. The Polonization of Danzig is notable; wherefore, why should the Germans show so much interest in what to them is but one of their provincial towns?"

Poland to Make Demands

The Gazeta Polska, official organ of the Polish Government, tomorrow will publish a noteworthy statement concerning the position of Danzig.

"Germany," it will say, "has shown her regard for international engagements by her recent occupation of Memel, by her denunciation of solemn treaties. She has demonstrated quite clearly that German policy aims at separating Poland from her outlet on the Baltic Sea, the importance of which to Poland needs no emphasis.

"The policy of Berlin thus creates a situation that forces Poland to go further in her demands concerning the status of Danzig than she did formerly when concluding with Germany the pact of 1934."

Although it is not explicitly stated, there is reason to believe that Poland's demands will include the transference of the functions of the League Commissioner to the Polish Government.

Will Close Exchanges

The Polish official answer to the German memorandum, it is believed, will close German-Polish exchanges for the time being. The Poles expect to delay the negotiations until there is a general clarification of the European situation. No chances are being taken, however. All the military precautions ordered last month are still in force and the army is strengthened every day.

Continued on Page Twelve

Rider Will Ask Pensions For Congress Members

By The Associated Press.

WASHINGTON, April 30.—A quiet campaign to give pensions to members of Congress has materialized into a legislative proposal.

Chairman Ramspeck of the House Civil Service Committee said today that he intended to add provisions for the pensions to a bill making amendments to the Civil Service Law which has just been passed by the Senate.

Under the proposal, the government and the members would bear about equal shares of the cost. Five per cent of the salary of each member would be deducted monthly and would go toward the purchase of an annuity to be added to the amount to be paid by the government.

Civil service workers receive pensions which increase with length of service. They contribute 3½ per cent of their salaries.

Mr. Ramspeck reported that almost every member he had talked to favored the pension idea.

"They're getting security-minded," he added, laughing.

PARI-MUTUEL VOTE AGAIN UP IN STATE

Republicans Plan Assembly Test on Betting System— Democratic Split Reported

Special to THE NEW YORK TIMES.

ALBANY, April 30.—The question of pari-mutuel betting on horse-racing is returning to plague the 1939 session of the Legislature.

Pressure from pari-mutuel advocates has resulted in a decision on the part of Republican leaders to put the matter to a vote on the Assembly floor. If the proposed constitutional amendment should be passed by both Houses this year, it would be submitted to the people for approval in the Fall, as the 1938 Legislature approved the system.

Despite considerable support on the Republican side, there is no guarantee that the pari-mutuel proposal will pass in either house. The Democrats, who have blown hot and cold on the measure for years, are again reported to be divided on the subject.

In one recent year the proposed amendment was passed by the Senate, and when it came up a second time as is required by the Constitution, its original sponsor voted against it. Last year John J. Dunnigan, the Democratic leader of the Senate, pushed the proposal through the Upper House, and it gained approval in the Republican controlled Assembly as well.

Senate Sponsor Now Lacking

With the intervening elections, the Republicans gained control of the Senate as well and Senator Dunnigan has made no move to introduce the proposal in the Senate. In fact, it has yet to have an official sponsor there. However, John D. Bennett and Norman F. Penny's Nassau County Republican Assemblymen, have introduced in the Assembly resolutions identical with the Dunnigan resolution of the year before, and passage this year by both Houses would constitute the required second action by the Legislature, even if the sponsors are not the same.

In the Assembly the practice of the Republican leadership, under Speaker Heck, is to refuse to throttle in committee any bill of the type of the pari-mutuel proposal, because of rumors always circulated about bookmakers' lobbies. Putting the bill out for a vote leaves it up to the individual membership. The Republicans will seek passage of the measure in the Assembly, but its final fate would appear to rest on the number of Democratic votes only two votes. The political aspects of the battle over the budget itself appear to make it unlikely that the Republican sales tax idea can gain any Democratic votes on the Senate side.

Local bills have been cleaned up to a large extent in both houses and after the enactment of the tax bills, the settling of the sales tax problem, the revision of the unemployment insurance law, and the enactment of a housing measure the Legislature will be in a position to quit and go home, to await a possible special-session call.

CONGRESS FACING SEVEN BIG ISSUES AS TIME SHORTENS

None Is on Week's Calendars, But All Except Taxes Are in Legislative Process

WAY CLEARED FOR ACTION

Routine Money Bills Passed, Reporting of Vital Measures to Floor Is Expected

By LUTHER A. HUSTON
Special to THE NEW YORK TIMES.

WASHINGTON, April 30.—Congress has been in session nearly four months and has disposed of only two of the major controversial items on its calendar. At least seven important issues remain to be settled in the two months that remain of the session if present plans are followed and a late Summer sitting is avoided by adjournment around July 1.

None of the major measures is on the calendar of either chamber for this week. The most progress that can be expected is that one or more of these measures may come from committees to the floor of the House or Senate.

The two issues that have been settled are the limited authorization for the President to reorganize executive agencies and the expansion of national defense, for which necessary appropriation bills have been passed. The decks also have been cleared of considerable of the routine, most of the important departmental appropriation bills having been disposed of.

Major Questions Outstanding

The following matters remain to be dealt with:

Amendments to the Social Security Act, the National Labor Relations Act and the Wages and Hours Law.

Revision or extension of existing neutrality laws.

The amount of the appropriation and the method of disbursement for relief during the 1940 fiscal year.

A farm program including the highly controversial question of export and domestic subsidies on farm products.

Legislation to repeal, modify or continue in effect certain tax provisions of the tax laws that are estimated to yield an annual revenue of around $2,000,000,000 even if general tax revision is not attempted.

Except for tax proposals, all of these measures are in the legislative mill. On some of them committee hearings are in progress; on others committee action has ended. There is a possibility that proposed amendments to the Wages and Hours Law may come up in the House tomorrow. Representative Mary Norton, chairman of the Labor Committee, has indicated that she will try to bring up under suspension of the rules the proposal that her committee has approved. If this is not done, the proposals must lie over at least a week.

To Hear Green on C. I. O. Question

On Capitol Hill tomorrow, however, interest probably will center in the hearing by the Senate Education and Labor Committee on proposed amendments to the National Labor Relations Act, at which William Green, president of the American Federation of Labor, will be the witness.

Mr. Green is expected to reply to

Continued on Page Twenty-four

Times Sq. May Be Closed To Autos During Fair

Times Square may be turned over as a playground for World's Fair visitors if their numbers become great enough to warrant special police arrangements in the theatrical area.

Police Commissioner Valentine said yesterday that the Fair crowds may approximate the number of American Legion members who came to New York for their national convention in September, 1937. If that should develop, Mr. Valentine said, it would be advisable to turn over Times Square to the city's guests. Automobile traffic would be routed north and south on either side of the Square, as in the American Legion convention. For the last two weeks heavy police details have handled the crowds in Times Square, directing pedestrians to the right to obtain the maximum amount of order.

RUSSIAN AVIATORS, RESCUED, ARRIVE

Two Who Crashed in Canada Here in American Plane— One Fainted During Flight

Brig. Gen. Vladimir Kokkinaki and Major Mikhail Gordienko, the two Soviet airmen who crashed Friday night in a swamp off the coast of New Brunswick were landed in a rescue plane last night at Floyd Bennett Field at 10:31 o'clock.

The two men were brought to New York in the plane of Commodore Harold Vanderbilt, which was chartered by Soviet and American officials for the rescue work, which took more than thirty hours.

They and the rescue party, which left here Friday night after word of the crash of the Moscow-New York non-stop flight came through from Miscou Point, N. B., were "ferried" to the end of the scheduled flight in an American airplane.

Their own craft, in which they sped toward New York from Moscow in 23 hours and 40 minutes, still lay in the frozen morass where Major Gordienko squashed it in an emergency landing. He landed it, because General Kokkinaki fainted at an altitude of more than 27,000 feet. It was learned yesterday when the party first brought the two men as far south as Moncton, N. B.

In recounting last night the events which led up to the forced landing at the field General Kokkinaki said the main difficulty of flying in the substratosphere was at 27,000 feet, where his compass liquids froze and his radio reception was so poor that he could not tune in the directional beams. He offered this explanation as a reason why the ship apparently lost its course, having been reported in the same area for nearly four hours and hours prior to its final landing.

In the plane were the two Russian aces; Russell Thaw, pilot, and his co-pilot, John Revely; V. P. Butosov, Dr. Louis S. Spector and Peter Baranov, all of the Am

Continued on Page Twenty-four

PRESIDENT OPENS FAIR AS A SYMBOL OF PEACE; VAST SPECTACLE OF COLOR AND WORLD PROGRESS THRILLS ENTHUSIASTIC CROWDS ON THE FIRST DAY

ROOSEVELT SPEAKS

He Sees Nations of This Hemisphere United in Desire for Peace

U. S. DEMOCRACY STRONG

Exposition Here and in West Born of Singleness of the American Ideal, He Says

By FELIX BELAIR JR.

In his first public utterance since Chancellor Hitler's virtual rejection of his plan to assure the peace of Europe for another ten years, President Roosevelt served notice on the world yesterday that the nations of the Western Hemisphere were "united in a desire to encourage peace and good-will among all nations" and voiced their hope that time would break down the barriers to tranquillity on the Continent.

In a brief address dedicating the New York's World's Fair to the cause of international amity and declaring it "open to all mankind," the President said that the American wagon was hitched to the star of peace, and asked that the months ahead "may carry us forward in the rays of that hope."

Avoids Any Direct Reference

For those who had expected a more direct reference by President Roosevelt to the state of affairs in Europe or something that might be interpreted as a reply to the German Chancellor's all but complete throwdown of his peace guarantee proposal there was disappointment, for his attitude regarding that had to be inferred from what he said of the traditional aspirations of the American republics.

Of recent years American historians would write that "sectionalism and regional jealousies diminished and that the people of every part of your land acquired a national solidarity of economic and social thought such as had never been seen before," the President said. He added that "wise tolerance" almost as much as the American form of government had made possible this unity of sentiment in a nation made up of so many different creeds and national derivations. The President recalled that democratic government had endured unchanged in this country longer than in any other country on the globe at any period of history, a circumstance he attributed to the wisdom of the framers of the Constitution.

He Sees Aim Accomplished

"That this has been accomplished," the President added a little later, "has been due first to our own form of government itself and, secondly, to a spirit of wise tolerance which, with few exceptions, has been the rule.

"We in the United States, and, indeed, in all the Americas, remember that our population stems from many races and kindreds and tongues. Often, I think, we Americans offer up the silent prayer that on the continent of Europe, from which the American hemisphere was principally colonized, the years to come will break down many barriers to intercourse between nations—barriers which may be historic, but which so greatly, through the centuries, have led to strife and hindered friendship and normal intercourse."

Of recent years American historians would write that "sectionalism and regional jealousies diminished and that the people of every

Continued on Page Four

Crowds Awed by Fair's Vastness And Medley of Sound and Color

Opening Day Has Everything, Including All Kinds of Weather—Spirit of Gayety Wanes When Pelting Rain Menaces Finery

The Fair had everything for its opening yesterday, including all kinds of weather. Early trains rolled to the Flushing Meadows under skies clear and blue, flooded with rich sunlight, carrying thousands come to look upon the miracle wrought by Grover Whalen's armies in the last three years.

Silk-hatted dignitaries, sailors on leave, men and women of all ages, dressed for fair weather and a great holiday. They came in hordes down the railroad and subway ramps, forty and fifty abreast, to the waiting stand and crossed to the outer border of the Fair. The crowds craned their necks to watch this activity in the sky, and drivers of observation cars kept sounding their musical horns to warn them to safer spots.

Wealthier fairgoers climbed into motor-driven and man-powered chairs for their first tour of the grounds. Hundreds of thousands preferred to make it on foot, all a little bewildered and puzzled by the tremendous sweep of grounds, by the dazzling color, almost blinding in the bright sun. Guides, ushers, policemen and policewomen were breathless the first hour trying to keep up with the flood of questions. Men and women, rank amateurs at reading maps, assembled in the walks or took over the benches, to puzzle out the direction of the various exhibits. Thousands were

Continued on Page Two

CITY AND THE FLEET TAKE TURN AS HOST

1,000 Officers and Men Under Admiral Johnson Help Open Fair—Ships Draw Crowds

By HANSON W. BALDWIN

The city played host to the navy yesterday and the navy played host to the city.

It was—all things considered—an even exchange. Some 1,000 officers and men of the thirty-five visiting men-of-war, led by Rear Admiral Alfred W. Johnson, commanding the Atlantic Squadron, took part in the opening ceremonies for the World's Fair, and thousands of others rolled along Broadway and throughout the five boroughs that walk peculiar to sailors home from the sea.

But the boats that brought the parties ashore took crowds of visitors out to the ships, while other thousands climbed the gangways of ships berthed at piers and stared with absorbing interest at turrets, the burnished muzzles of guns, the ranks of planes aboard the aircraft carrier Ranger, the ominous black hulls of the submarines and the torpedo tubes of the destroyers.

It was the visiting squadron's second day—and first Sunday—in port, and the public took full advantage of it. The men-of-war were a rival attraction, and a stellar one, to the World's Fair, and the crush of visitors was more than the navy could handle.

Estimates of Throng Vary

The crowd estimates varied widely. The police said 25,000 got aboard, while the navy thought 50,000 had crowded onto the battleships, cruisers, destroyers, submarines and auxiliaries in the few hours of the afternoon that the ships received the public. Perhaps 10,000 to 15,000 others were turned away—some of them after several hours in line—when ships' officers and the beach guard said the men-of-war were unable to accommodate any more visitors.

The visiting hours were supposed to have been from 1 to 5 P. M., but at the Ninety-sixth Street landing no more visitors were permitted to leave shore after 3:25 P. M. Naval officials explained that it took some time to clear the ships of visitors, especially when the vessels were lying out in the stream and all visitors had to be transported by small boats.

They explained that it was necessary at times to allow no visitors to leave the shore landing places later than 4 P. M. This was, however, despite the navy's announcement that all ships would be open daily from 1 to 5 P. M., considerable variation on individual ships.

The Ranger, aircraft carrier berthed alongside a pier at Canal

Continued on Page Ten

LIGHT AUTO TRAFFIC SURPRISE TO POLICE

Elaborate System to Cope With Expected Snarls on Roads Goes Unused

Although Police Department traffic experts were ready for the worst, streams of automobiles flowed evenly along principal Queens highways yesterday and not a single accident involving a serious injury was reported.

An elaborate system for emergency communications, worked out to cope with expected road snarls, went unused as 3,300 patrolmen, 523 of the traffic division, and 300 detectives—a total of 4,123—worked overtime to assure a safe and orderly opening to the World's Fair.

By 11 P. M. most of the motorists had either gone home or were on their way there and a report to police centers indicated there was no more congestion than there had been on the way out.

The only mishap was the record-spoiling what otherwise would have been a virtually incredible perfect mark—occurred at 1:10 P. M. just outside the Fair Grounds, at Lawrence and Sanford Avenues.

Louis Hoffman, 70 years old, of 1,366 Spofford Avenue, the Bronx, suffered lacerations of the left leg when struck by a car that the police said was driven by Louis Anselone of 37-41 106th Street, Corona. Mr. Hoffman went home after Flushing Hospital. The driver was not held.

Policeman Is Injured

A patrolman was hurt inside the grounds a little later, when a crush developed outside the French Building. There were seven children lost, a man had an epileptic fit, and fifty peddlers were arrested for operating on the ramp leading from the combined I. R. T.-B. M. T. subway terminal, but otherwise, the first day was as safe as a lawn party.

A false fire alarm was turned in at the box in the R. C. A. building shortly before the opening parade, while the walks near the theme center were cleared when Fire Chief Thomas F. Dougherty said it was "malicious."

Patrolman Bartholomew Nicastro, 35 years old, of 118-02 175th Street, St. Albans, was the man most injured. A policeman, he was trying to keep back throw him against a wooden "horse," which had been used in construction work. He was treated for a cut right leg by one of the Fair surgeons under Dr. Joseph Foster in Hoguet, and remained on duty. In addition, the Fair's six first aid stations had a dull day.

A checkup by the Fair police and at 10 P. M. indicated that the stations,

NATIONS IN PARADE

Mayor and the Governor Voice Welcome to the 'World of Tomorrow'

WEATHER REDUCES THRONG

Attendance Reported Above 600,000—Centers of Religion and Freedom Dedicated

By RUSSELL B. PORTER

The biggest international exposition in history was officially opened at 3:12 o'clock yesterday afternoon when President Roosevelt formally dedicated the New York World's Fair 1939 in an address before a gathering of 60,000 persons in the open-air Court of Peace.

Governor Lehman, Mayor La Guardia, Sir Louis Beale, British Commissioner General to the Fair and spokesman for the nearly sixty foreign nations that have exhibits, and Grover A. Whalen, president of the Fair Corporation, also made speeches at the opening ceremonies. They joined the President in emphasizing the message of peaceful progress that the Fair brings to mankind in an era when the whole world is troubled by war and threats of war.

When the President officially declared the Fair open he brought to a climax ceremonies that included a parade of 20,000 uniformed soldiers, sailors and marines, fraternal groups in picturesque native costumes from nearly all the countries of Europe, Asia and the Americas, and the workmen who built the Fair, in their overalls and white caps.

Starting at the Trylon and Perisphere, the Theme Center of the Fair, the parade passed down Constitution Mall to the Court of Peace with flags waving, bands playing and spectators applauding until it ended with a colorful pageant in the Court of Peace.

Spectacle Impresses Visitors

Although the official exercises were the important part of the day from a formal viewpoint, actually the Fair itself made the greatest impression upon the visitors, judging from their comments as they strolled through the 1,216-acre Fair Grounds and as they journeyed homeward last night.

What they saw was a spectacle of surprising beauty and magnificence, especially last night when the whole Fair and the heavens above it were bathed in soft, glowing colors with the most modern lighting effects, and when fireworks combined with flame, water and color displays on the Lagoon of Nations, the pools in Constitution Mall and the surface of Fountain Lake.

In the daytime also the Fair is a beautiful sight, with the whole scene dominated by the 700-foot Trylon and the 200-foot Perisphere, from which radiates a rainbow of many-colored buildings of modernistic, functional architecture, some bizarre in shape and hue, others strikingly handsome and impressive in their suggestion of strength and use.

Green trees, shrubbery and lawns, playing fountains, shady benches and restful spots on all sides make a garden spot of this artificial city within a city which has been constructed within the past three and one-half years on what was formerly the ash dumps of the Flushing Meadows, and will be a great city park after the Fair is over.

See "World of Tomorrow"

In the huge crystal ball of the Perisphere, visitors peered to see what "the World of Tomorrow" would be like, finding it to be a conception of more and more progress in democracy and in the advance of science, industry, communications, transportation, communication, the arts and the professions to bring to peace and happiness to mankind. They found the same ideas expressed in the streamlined, futuristic dimensions of the buildings, statues, murals, dioramas, landscapes and exhibits of the Fair.

Like the worlds of yesterday and today, and also like the City of New York, which has the reputation of never being finished but of always changing, the "World of Tomorrow" was a great deal of unfinished business before it. The heart of the Fair, the half-mile stretch between the Theme Center and the Court of Peace where the official ceremonies were held, was virtually complete yesterday, but many other sections,

Continued on Page Three

Hague Ignores Own Plea for Patriotic Rally; Skips Americanization Fete for Ball Game

Special to THE NEW YORK TIMES.

JERSEY CITY, N. J., April 30.—Mayor Frank Hague, who issued a proclamation yesterday calling on residents of Jersey City to "show your Americanism" by attending the city's tenth annual celebration today of Americanization Day, did not appear at that event this afternoon. Instead he attended the double-header baseball game between the Jersey City and Toronto teams of the International League at Roosevelt Stadium.

"As Mayor of Jersey City, I earnestly and respectfully invite all the people of our city to participate actively in the Americanization Day exercises, Sunday, April 30, 2 P. M., at Pershing Field," declared the Mayor's signed proclamation, published yesterday in newspaper advertisements.

"Show your Americanism by parading or being present Sunday afternoon. It is my request that the American flag be displayed on all homes and buildings Sunday. Every citizen should remove his hat as the colors pass by."

The proclamation listed Mayor Frank Hague among the speakers at Pershing Field, yet when Representative Jerry O'Connell, Montana Democrat and foe of the Jersey City Mayor, was whisked away by police several months ago when he attempted to speak there.

A crowd estimated at 4,000 persons assembled in the field today and 10,000 others marched there. During the parade and speechmaking, however, the Mayor was one of 29,362 baseball fans who did not take part in the Americanization celebration. He occupied a box at the baseball stadium with his nephew and private secretary, former Judge Frank Hague Eggers.

The Jersey City team won both games.

Commissioner Arthur Potterton, who spoke at Pershing Field, declared that "Jersey City takes the lead to show the world that nothing un-American will creep into our lives in this part of the State." He referred to other parts of the State as having "no idea of the dangers that beset the nation, he said that "we have given them the courage they did not possess."

Representative Edward J. Hart, Democrat, was another speaker. Governor A. Harry Moore was present, but did not speak.

The Americanization Day celebration is sponsored by Captain Clinton Fisk Post, Veterans of Foreign Wars.

Continued on Page Four

"All the News That's Fit to Print."

The New York Times.

Copyright, 1939, by The New York Times Company.

LATE CITY EDITION
Partly cloudy and warm with scattered showers today and tomorrow.
Temperature Yesterday—Max., 85; Min., 70

VOL. LXXXVIII...No. 29,797.   Entered as Second-Class Matter, Postoffice, New York, N. Y.   NEW YORK, THURSDAY, AUGUST 24, 1939.   PP   THREE CENTS NEW YORK CITY and Vicinity | FOUR CENTS Elsewhere Except in 7th and 8th Postal Zones

GERMANY AND RUSSIA SIGN 10-YEAR NON-AGGRESSION PACT; BIND EACH OTHER NOT TO AID OPPONENTS IN WAR ACTS; HITLER REBUFFS LONDON; BRITAIN AND FRANCE MOBILIZE

U.S. AND ARGENTINA PLAN TRADE PACT, WELLES DISCLOSES

Our Commerce Will Get Full Equality With That of All Foreigners, He Asserts

BEEF NOT TO BE INCLUDED

Long Preliminary Talks Ease Difficulties, With Offset Seen to Our Recent Losses

Special to The New York Times.

WASHINGTON, Aug. 23.—The United States intends to negotiate a reciprocal trade treaty with Argentina as a move to put American commerce on a footing of equality with that of European competitors, Sumner Welles, Acting Secretary of State, stated today. There have been more than four years of preliminary discussions.

The State Department, making public a list of products upon which this country would make tariff concessions, set Oct. 4 as the closing date for submission of briefs by interested Americans and Oct. 16 for the opening of public hearings.

It was emphasized that fresh, chilled or frozen Argentine meats, the entry of which into this country is banned by the Tariff Act of 1930, and fine wools would not be a subject of discussion in the negotiations. This was expected by officials to remove the most serious objections which might have been advanced to conclusion of a reciprocal agreement. Barring at the entry of Argentine fresh beef here has long been a subject of some friction between the two countries in their commercial relations.

"It may be noted that during the fifteen-year period 1924-38 our exports to Argentina have exceeded our imports from that country by $486,900,000," Mr. Welles said in a statement.

Trade Cut by Foreign Pacts

"Our trade with Argentina has suffered in recent years for lack of a trade agreement. The trade of certain European countries with Argentina has been developing at our expense under the influence of their commercial agreements with Argentina. The placing of American commerce in Argentina on a footing of full equality with that of our European competitors was a subject which has gone into fully in preliminary discussions leading up to the present announcement.

"The agreement will enable us to maintain our competitive position in a market of great present and prospective importance.

"On our side we must, of course, offer reciprocal benefits. The products of interest to Argentina with respect to which concessions will be given in the course of the negotiations, with a view to seeing what concessions could be granted, are listed in connection with the announcement of the proposed negotiations. The concessions, which will in due course be formulated, should, of course, permit an increase in Argentina's exports to this country, but will not have injurious effect upon American production.

"The types of wool included in the list are the coarser types, of which there is only a very small production in this country."

Barter Agreement With Germany

It was presumed that in referring to European competitors Mr. Welles was speaking principally of Germany, which concluded a barter agreement with Argentina after the Pan-American Conference in Lima last December. England was a large trader with Argentina, however, and is a heavy buyer of Argentine beef.

Among the products upon which the United States would consider lowering duties in favor of Argentina are:

Tallow, oleo oil and oleo stearin, extract of meat, including fluid, pickled or cured beef packed or not packed in air-tight containers, dried turkeys, dead birds, chicken eggs, corn or maize, including cracked corn; asparagus in its natural state, and some wools.

With the possible exception of that made with Brazil, a reciprocal trade treaty with the Argentine would be the most important pact to be consummated with a Latin-American country, officials indicated. Be-

Continued on Page Thirty-five

BRITAIN ACTS FAST

Air Force Is Ready for Hostilities—Warships Mass in Skagerrak

EXPORT EMBARGO IS FIXED

Parliament Meets Today in an Emergency Session—King to Convene Privy Council

By FERDINAND KUHN Jr.
Special Cable to The New York Times.

LONDON, Aug. 23.—The British Government prepared for action today with every indication that it was ready to go to war with Germany whenever a call for help from Poland should come.

Warning notices went out to reservists in all departments of the armed and civilian services; the King was returning to London to hold a meeting of the Privy Council tomorrow; Londoners were ordered to darken their windows until further notice; the air force was poised for instant action, and a concentration of an undisclosed number of British warships was reported in the Skagerrak, off the Norwegian and Danish coasts, as if to remind Germany of the blockade that she had to endure during the World War.

The emergency was underlined by a Board of Trade announcement placing an immediate embargo on unlicensed exports of essential war materials "in order to conserve the stocks in this country." The list included copper, nickel and rubber, which the Germans have been buying in large quantities in the past week or two, and also aluminum, lead, iron and steel scrap and raw cotton.

Parliament Session Today

Tomorrow both houses of Parliament will meet in emergency session to give the government sweeping powers of a sort unknown in democratic England since the World War days. The new law will be something like the old Defense of the Realm Act, enabling the government to issue Orders in Council, without prior or subsequent Parliamentary sanction, for any purpose that the national interest may require.

Trade-union leaders were invited to examine the bill today and they came away satisfied that all possible safeguards of individual liberty would be included.

The real business of the Parliamentary session, however, will be to hear a complete review of the international situation by Prime Minister Chamberlain in the House of Commons and by Viscount Halifax, the Foreign Secretary, in the House of Lords. All indications are that the Prime Minister's words and the subsequent debate will be more sombre in tone than anything heard in the Commons chamber since Aug. 3, 1914, when Sir Edward Grey made his famous speech on the eve of the World War.

Everywhere it was expected that a crisis of the utmost gravity now confronts Britain, a crisis far more serious than that of last Autumn, when this country was not committed as it is now. The British determination to carry out all the pledges to Poland was reaffirmed in the government message handed to Chancellor Hitler today by Sir

Continued on Page Five

Sidney Howard Killed by Tractor on Estate; Playwright Is Crushed in Berkshire Garage

Special to The New York Times.

TYRINGHAM, Mass., Aug. 23.—Sidney Coe Howard, playwright, was crushed to death today by a two and a half ton tractor in his garage on his 700-acre estate here.

Mr. Howard had put in a morning of hard work on a new play based on Carl Van Doren's "Benjamin Franklin" and, as was his custom, was going to seek relaxation in physical work on his estate, which included one of the most modern dairy farms in this part of the State. The chore he had set for himself was harrowing a twenty-eight-acre field which he had recently bought to extend his property.

Driving alone to the garage a quarter of a mile from his studio in the fields, Mr. Howard entered, turned on the ignition switch of the tractor and cranked it. The machine lurched forward, pinning the playwright against the wall of the structure. The tractor, put in the garage the night before by an employe, was believed to have been left in high gear.

Fred L. Fairbanks, superintendent of the estate, discovered Mr. Howard while on an inspection trip. The garage, a former Shaker schoolroom, is set off by itself on the estate and is seldom visited by any one except by those on business.

Mr. Fairbanks found his employer in an upright position, his head bent over his chest. He was pinned at the chest by the hood of the tractor, which had stalled after crushing him against the wall.

After starting the tractor and moving Mr. Howard's body, Mr. Fairbanks ran to the nearest telephone on the estate to notify Mrs. Howard and summon aid. Mr. Howard was shopping in Lee, five miles away. When she returned

Continued on Page Nineteen

The Developments in Europe

The signing of the Russo-German non-aggression pact, which many world capitals feared might be Chancellor Hitler's "go-ahead signal," took place in Moscow early this morning, half a day after German Foreign Minister von Ribbentrop had arrived in the Russian capital. The pact, which runs for ten years, in addition to prohibiting attack by either party against the other, forbids either to join any association of powers aimed at the other. Moreover, it provides that if one party is an "object of warlike acts" the other will not support such acts. [Page 1; text of the treaty, also Page 1.]

Signature of the pact followed a day that seemed to bring Europe closer to the brink. When the British Ambassador to Germany conveyed to Chancellor Hitler a warning that Britain would fight for Poland he was bluntly rebuffed. In Berlin word freely circulated that the German Army would march at 6 P. M. today (noon in New York). [Page 4.]

In the face of Herr Hitler's rebuff Britain went ahead with war preparations, including the sending of notices to reservists, poising of the air force and concentration of warships in the Skagerrak, north of Denmark. Parliament prepared to meet today to grant the government sweeping emergency powers. [Page 3.] The emergency here reported being sent to the Mediterranean, where the bases at Gibraltar and Malta were on the alert. [Page 3.] The dominions, led by Canada and Australia, were beginning to swing into line behind Britain. [Page 6.]

France, convinced that Germany intends to invade Poland within a few days, called up further reservists after a meeting of the Permanent Committee on National Defense. [Page 1.]

Poland remained outwardly calm, still doubting that Herr Hitler would risk precipitating a general war. [Page 2.]

In Turkey allegiance to the coalition powers was affirmed, although German Ambassador von Papen was flying to Angora from Germany, presumably to try to break that allegiance. [Page 1.] But in Rumania, another State guaranteed by France and Britain, informed circles said that country would strive to remain neutral. [Page 7.]

Only in Rome were signs of war lacking. Although the press continued to attack Poland, no unusual defense preparations were evident. [Page 1.]

In an attempt to head off disaster King Leopold of the Belgians, speaking for the seven Oslo powers, appealed for peace. [With the text of the appeal, Page 5.]

President Roosevelt, disturbed by the outlook, was speeding back to Washington [Page 1], where officials were clearing the decks for action if it became necessary to safeguard United States neutrality and help Americans to escape from danger zones. [Page 3.] The State Department advised citizens not to go to Europe [Page 3] and those who were trying to return home found ships still running normally from foreign ports. [Page 3.]

In the Far East the army and navy leaders in Japan were understood to have shaped a policy to be followed in view of the new situation arising from the Russo-German treaty. [Page 4.] In China some observers believed the treaty would mean increased Soviet aid in resisting Japan. [Page 4.]

FRANCE MOBILIZES; NOW EXPECTS WAR

People Confident of Strength to Meet Aggressor as Hopes of Peace Diminish

By P. J. PHILIP
Wireless to The New York Times.

PARIS, Thursday, Aug. 24.—Convinced by a report from French Ambassador Robert Coulondre at Berlin and by a reply that Chancellor Adolf Hitler gave yesterday to Prime Minister Neville Chamberlain's message through British Ambassador Sir Nevile Henderson at Berchtesgaden that an invasion of Poland is intended by the German Government within the next few days, the French Government last night decided to call up a further contingent of reservists.

This decision was communicated to the press in an official statement from Premier Edouard Daladier's office as follows:

"On account of the international situation the French Government has decided to complete military measures already taken by calling up an additional contingent of reserve soldiers."

During last night notices were

Continued on Page Two

TURKEY REAFFIRMS PLEDGES TO ALLIES

Will Honor Pact With France and Britain—German Envoy Flies to Woo Her

Special Cable to The New York Times.

ISTANBUL, Turkey, Aug. 23.—No official pronouncement has yet been made about the Russo-German non-aggression pact. In official quarters the position of Turkey is said to be unchanged; she has made agreements for mutual assistance against aggression with France and Britain and stands by them.

The Turkish people are still bewildered over yesterday's news, but see alarm about its possibilities is noticeable since last night's official British communiqué was published.

Until the Turkish Government has authentic information about the non-aggression pact the newspapers will be reticent. Cumhuriet, the only Turkish newspaper with an editorial on the subject today, assumed the Soviet Union would stipulate that if Germany was guilty of aggression against any of her Western neighbors, the pact would become null and void.

In this case, the newspaper said, it should act as a deterrent against war in Europe, for the newspaper could not believe the Soviet Government will remain indifferent to the fate of its neighbors on the Baltic and Black Seas simply because it signed a pact of non-aggression with Germany.

Cumhuriet added that although a pact of non-aggression was not an alliance, it implied friendly feelings, and it believed, therefore, that the anti-Comintern pact was political, not ideological, and that the Russo-German pact may be regarded as a truce.

Von Papen Flies to Turkey

BUDAPEST, Hungary, Aug. 23 (P).—Franz von Papen, Germany's Ambassador to Turkey, passed by plane through Budapest today, en route from Salzburg to Angora.

Diplomatic circles conjectured his mission now was to renew attempts to draw Turkey out of the British-French bloc. They recalled German and Italian claims that Turkey's alliance with Britain and France was dependent upon Russia's not joining the opposition camp.

Wireless to The New York Times.

BUDAPEST, Hungary, Aug. 23.—The international situation was dis-

Continued on Page Five

QUICK ACTION SEEN

Berlin Talks of 6 P. M. Deadline for Move Against Poland

DICTATOR WARNS BRITISH

Henderson So Wrought Up on Leaving Parley With Hitler That He Is Speechless

By OTTO D. TOLISCHUS
Wireless to The New York Times.

BERLIN, Thursday, Aug. 24.—While Foreign Minister Joachim von Ribbentrop was in Moscow discussing, in the view of some German quarters, not so much a new non-aggression pact as "Poland's fourth and final partition," Chancellor Hitler yesterday received Sir Nevile Henderson, the British Ambassador, for a fifteen-minute conference.

According to reliable information, the conference ended on a rather blunt note that is interpreted in diplomatic quarters as possibly Herr Hitler's last word. The communiqué, issued last night, reads:

"Complying with the wish of the British Government, the Fuehrer received Sir Nevile Henderson at the Berghof today. The Ambassador delivered a letter from the British Prime Minister addressed to the Fuehrer, which was drawn up in the same sense as yesterday's British communication regarding the Cabinet session.

"The Fuehrer left no doubt in the mind of the British Ambassador that the obligations assumed by the British Government could not induce Germany to renounce the defense of her vital national interest."

Hitler's Tone Reported Blunt

Actually Herr Hitler's tone to Sir Nevile was reported to have been even more blunt than the communiqué indicates. In effect, Herr Hitler told the Ambassador that Britain had no business in Eastern Europe and that her guarantee of Poland merely encouraged Polish resistance to German demands, and that Britain was up to Britain to persuade the Poles to yield or face the consequences.

Sir Nevile left the conference so wrought up he was speechless. Not trusting his memory to repeat the exact shadings of Herr Hitler's answer, he asked that it be put in writing and he returned for it a half hour later. He got it couched in the same strong terms that Herr Hitler used to him before.

At the same time there are also well-authenticated reports that, in addition to Prime Minister Chamberlain's letter, Sir Nevile also delivered to Herr Hitler an oral message that if Herr Hitler would try to induce Poland to come forth with new proposals. In that connection some circles launched—perhaps not unintentionally—the suggestion that Foreign Minister Josef Beck of Poland might after all ask to see Herr von Ribbentrop and even Herr Hitler. A preliminary meeting with the former might be arranged at Riga, Latvia, on their return from Mos-cow. But Polish circles declare the suggestion was "extremely unlikely" because it spelled surrender.

As during the last few days the word in Berlin is that the zero hour, which will set the German Army on the march, will come today, and these rumors are supplemented with the additional detail that the exact hour is 6 P. M. (noon, New York time), which might mean "contact with the enemy" some time tomorrow. Furthermore, orders to postpone action, issued after Herr von Ribbentrop's departure for Moscow, have been canceled again.

Germans Elated by News

How much all that is merely a matter of "war of nerves" and how much is bitter reality remains to be seen. In fact the tension developing in Germany, at least in an atmosphere of fantastic unreality, is made no more real by the delayed Summer heat that lures the populace to the woods and beaches, and, together with the elation over the Russian pact and renewed confidence in Herr Hitler's diplomatic superiority over the democratic powers, helps to hide the war clouds.

However, the rebuff to Britain yesterday, which in some quarters is compared with the rebuff administered to the French Ambassador by King William of Prussia just preceding the Franco-Prussian War

Continued on Page Four

Text of the Berlin-Moscow Treaty

By The Associated Press.

MOSCOW, Thursday, Aug. 24.—The text of the German-Russian non-aggression pact announced here today follows:

The German Reich Government and the Union of Soviet Socialist Republics, moved by a desire to strengthen the state of peace between Germany and the U.S.S.R., and in the spirit of the provisions of the neutrality treaty of April, 1926, between Germany and the U.S.S.R., decided the following:

Article I

The two contracting parties obligate themselves to refrain from every act of force, every aggressive action and every attack against one another, including any single action or that taken in conjunction with other powers.

Article II

In case one of the parties of this treaty should become the object of warlike acts by a third power, the other party will in no way support this third power.

Article III

The governments of the two contracting parties in the future will constantly remain in consultation with one another in order to inform each other regarding questions of common interest.

Article IV

Neither of the high contracting parties will associate itself with any other grouping of powers which directly or indirectly is aimed at the other party.

Article V

In the event of a conflict between the contracting parties concerning any question, the two parties will adjust this difference or conflict exclusively by friendly exchange of opinions or, if necessary, by an arbitration commission.

Article VI

The present treaty will extend for a period of ten years with the condition that if neither of the contracting parties announces its abrogation within one year of expiration of this period, it will continue in force automatically for another period of five years.

Article VII

The present treaty shall be ratified within the shortest possible time. The exchange of ratification documents shall take place in Berlin. The treaty becomes effective immediately upon signature.

Drawn up in two languages, German and Russian.

Moscow, 23d of August, 1939.

For the German Government:
RIBBENTROP.

In the name of the Government of the U.S.S.R.:
MOLOTOFF.

BARS HOSTILE UNION

Treaty Forbids Either to Join Any Group Aimed at Other

ESCAPE CLAUSE OMITTED

Von Ribbentrop's Car, Flying Swastika, Passes Beneath Red Flag at Kremlin

By The Associated Press.

MOSCOW, Thursday, Aug. 24.—Germany and Soviet Russia early today signed a non-aggression pact binding each of them for ten years not to "associate itself with any other grouping of powers which directly or indirectly is aimed at the other party."

By the pact they also agreed to "constantly remain in consultation with one another" on their common interests and to adjust differences by arbitration.

The non-aggression clauses bound each power to refrain from any act of force against the other and if either party is "the object of warlike acts by a third power" to refrain from supporting that third power.

The pact did not include the usual escape clause providing for its denunciation in case one of the contracting parties attacked a third power. This provision has been written into most non-aggression agreements signed in the past by Moscow.

Arrives by Plane

Special Cable to The New York Times.

MOSCOW, Thursday, Aug. 24.—With the meticulous punctuality of a perfectly staged arrival, two huge Focke-Wulf Condor planes conveying Joachim von Ribbentrop, the German Foreign Minister, and his thirty-two assistants, landed at the Moscow airdrome on the stroke of 1 P. M. yesterday.

Adequate but not excessive police precautions were taken at the airdrome. For the first time since the Soviet authorities displayed the swastika banner, five of which flew from the front of the airdrome building, but were placed so as not to be visible from the outside.

Vyacheslaff M. Molotoff was not present to welcome Herr von Ribbentrop, probably because he is not only Commissar of Foreign Affairs but also Premier, and therefore higher in rank than Herr von Ribbentrop. Instead the visitor was received by Vladimir P. Potemkin, Vice Commissar of Foreign Affairs; Mr. Barkoff, protocol chief; Mr. Merkuloff, Vice Commissar of Internal Affairs, under whom falls the NKVD, formerly the OPU; Mr. Alexandroff, chief of the Central European Department of the Foreign Office, and General Suvoroff, commander of the Moscow garrison.

Almost the entire staff of the huge German Embassy, headed by the Ambassador, Count Friedrich Werner von der Schulenburg, with the military, naval and air attachés in uniform, was present. The German civilians mostly wore top hats and cutaway coats.

The Italian Ambassador, Augusto Russo, with his military attaché in uniform, also was present. The reason of the reception most commented upon was the absence of any Japanese representative.

The German Embassy staff stood lined up like troops on parade. As each was presented to Herr von Ribbentrop he sprang to attention, clicked his heels, gave the Hitler salute and shook hands, again saluting and heel-clicking.

In Old Austrian Embassy

From the airdrome the party drove to the city through streets where police in their white Summer jackets stood every ten paces. For Herr von Ribbentrop the Soviet Government provided a large American car from the Kremlin car park, flying the swastika flag.

The party drove directly to the former Austrian Embassy, where they are being housed. Subsequently Herr von Ribbentrop and leading members of his mission had luncheon at the embassy with Count von der Schulenburg.

At about 5:30 P. M. Herr von der Schulenburg, accompanied by Count von der Schulenburg and an expert translator whom the Germans brought from Berlin, drove through the gates of the Kremlin on the

Continued on Page Six

NO MILITARY MOVES APPARENT IN ITALY

Country Remains Tranquil as Regime Fails to Whip Up Any War Fervor Among People

By HERBERT L. MATTHEWS
Wireless to The New York Times.

ROME, Aug. 23.—The Italian ship of state sailed tranquilly on the edge of the European tornado today. There have been no conferences, communiqués, evacuation orders, special mobilization or troop movements.

There have been only some diplomatic visits to Count Ciano, the Foreign Minister, including those of the British and French Ambassadors. This is the fourth time since last Thursday that Sir Percy Loraine saw Count Ciano, which shows the degree of pressure the British are bringing to bear as well as their anxiety to make the Italian leaders realize Britain's determination to support Poland. Presumably, Sir Percy delivered a copy of the same note that was presented to Chancellor Hitler, although that has not been admitted.

André François-Poncet's visit was his first since returning to Rome last Friday. He has tried steadily to see the Foreign Minister but hitherto without success. It is believed he also impressed on Count Ciano France's intention to abide by her pledges.

The Hungarian Minister, Baron Frederick Villani, also saw Count Ciano today, reviving reports about Germany's demands on Budapest.

Italian People Are Calm

The Italian people as well are not whipped up to the fervor that would be required to enter a war in the next few days. Nowhere do you see air shelters being hastily dug or gas masks being distributed.

Only in the newspapers do the commentators warn their readers that a conflict seems near, while relatively full accounts of the developments in various capitals are given. The British Cabinet's statement last night is published fully in all newspapers here, whereas the German press ignored it. If readers trusted their Italian newspapers this evening they would have a biased but reasonably correct appreciation of the dangers of the situation.

On the one hand, so far as they know their country is making no last-minute efforts to meet the

Continued on Page Three

PRESIDENT SPEEDS TO ACT ON CRISIS

Disturbed by War Threat, He Will End Cruise Today and Board Train at Red Bank

By FELIX BELAIR Jr.
Special to The New York Times.

RED BANK, N. J., Aug. 23.—Admittedly disturbed by the European war crisis, President Roosevelt is hurrying here aboard the navy cruiser Tuscaloosa after scrapping plans for a more ceremonious landing at Annapolis in order to be at the White House in the event of an outbreak of hostilities.

A small White House secretarial staff is awaiting the arrival of the President off Sandy Hook early tomorrow to give him a bundle of the latest diplomatic reports on the latest developments abroad. Mr. Roosevelt plans to study the reports aboard his special train en route to Washington.

After debarking from the Tuscaloosa about 8 A. M. tomorrow the President will motor here with Brig. Gen. Edwin M. Watson, his secretary, and Rear Admiral Ross T. McIntire, White House physician. He is expected to stop long enough before entraining for the capital to telephone Secretary of State Cordell Hull, as well as to the embassies in London and Paris about overnight developments.

To Get War Supplies Report

Back at the White House in the early afternoon the President will have before him a report of the War Industries Committee on the status of the nation's munitions and other heavy industries. The committee has been canvassing the aviation and other industries in the past few days with a view to American preparedness.

Prior to the departure of the White House staff here today it was understood the War Industries Committee had drafted a report informing the President that the aviation and several other industries were prepared for any emergency that might arise and that aircraft manufacturers were ahead of schedule on orders of military planes from France and Great Britain.

Among Presidential intimates as well as the capital's political observers interest centered during the day on the question of whether Mr. Roosevelt considered the situation abroad sufficiently grave to call a

Continued on Page Three

"All the News That's
Fit to Print."

The New York Times.

Copyright, 1939, by The New York Times Company.

EXTRA
Partly cloudy and somewhat warmer today. Tomorrow generally fair
with moderate temperatures.
Temperature Yesterday—Max. 67; Min. 61

VOL. LXXXVIII...No. 29,805.   Entered as Second-Class Matter,
Postoffice, New York, N. Y.   NEW YORK, FRIDAY, SEPTEMBER 1, 1939.   THREE CENTS NEW YORK CITY | FOUR CENTS Elsewhere Except
and Vicinity | In 7th and 8th Postal Zone

GERMAN ARMY ATTACKS POLAND;
CITIES BOMBED, PORT BLOCKADED;
DANZIG IS ACCEPTED INTO REICH

BRITISH MOBILIZING

Navy Raised to Its Full Strength, Army and Air Reserves Called Up

PARLIAMENT IS CONVOKED

Midnight Meeting Is Held by Ministers—Negotiations Admitted Failure

By The Associated Press.
LONDON, Friday, Sept. 1.—The British Parliament was summoned to meet today at 5 P. M. [12 noon in New York.]

British Call Up Forces

By FERDINAND KUHN Jr.
Special Cable to The New York Times.
LONDON, Friday, Sept. 1.—All attempt to bring about direct negotiations between Germany and Poland appeared to have broken down tonight as Great Britain mobilized her fleet to full strength, stretched her other defensive preparations close to the limit and began moving 3,000,000 school children and invalids from the crowded cities into the safety of the countryside.

Censorship was established over cables after London had been cut off for hours from communication with the Continent.

It was the peak of the crisis, but a day of rumors had not shifted the fundamental issue nor given a conclusive answer to the question of peace or war.

At midnight the British Government was not yet convinced that Germany really intended to attack Poland and provoke a world war.

Terms Called Smoke Screen

All that had happened during yesterday, including the sudden broadcasting of Chancellor Hitler's sixteen-point demands, was interpreted here as a smoke screen rather than as the flash of guns.

After hearing Herr Hitler's "terms" officials here quietly announced tonight that "the government primarily interested in the proposals is, of course, the Polish Government."

Until the Polish Government has had time to consider them, it was said in Whitehall that "it would be highly undesirable for any comment to be made."

It was fully expected that Poland would reject them later today; indeed, Polish circles here were describing them tonight as "utterly unacceptable," for they would involve dismemberment of Poland and loss of Poland's capacity to defend her independence. In any event, there was no sign of any intention here to put pressure on Warsaw to accept.

Much might have been said about the German "proposals" here tonight if the government had not been so anxious to leave the first decision to Warsaw without any prompting. That the British regarded them as artful went without saying, since they conveyed a first impression of reasonableness that was not borne out by the terms themselves.

Until the announcement on the German wireless tonight, the British Government had not been told about them officially, and the Polish Government was not informed until Josef Lipski, Polish Ambassador to Berlin, visited Foreign Minister Joachim von Ribbentrop a few minutes before the broadcast took place.

Shortly after midnight last night, Sir Nevile Henderson, the British Ambassador in Berlin, heard the "points" read to him by Herr von Ribbentrop, but the reading was so fast that the Ambassador could not even take notes of them in detail. In any event, he was told Herr Hitler's "points" were not being given to him or his government officially, on the ground that it was already too late.

Time Limit Expired

On Tuesday Herr Hitler had asked that a Polish negotiator should arrive in Berlin within twenty-four hours; and as nobody had arrived from Warsaw when the limit expired, Sir Nevile was told that the "points" could not be communicated officially as German time table with the

Continued on Page Four

Bulletins on Europe's Conflict

London Hears of Warsaw Bombing

LONDON, Friday, Sept. 1 (AP).—Reuters British news agency said it had learned from Polish sources in Paris that Warsaw was bombed today.

French Confirm Beginning of War

PARIS, Friday, Sept. 1 (AP).—The Havas news agency said today that official French dispatches from Germany indicated that "the Reich began hostilities on Poland this morning."

The agency also reported that the Polish Embassy here had announced that "Germany violated the Polish frontier at four points."

"German reports of pretended violation of German territory by Poland are pure invention, as is the fable of 'attack' by Polish insurgents on Gleiwitz," the embassy announcement said.

Attack on Entire Front Reported

LONDON, Friday, Sept. 1 (AP).—A Reuters dispatch from Paris said:

"The following is given with all reserve: According to unconfirmed reports received here, the Germans have begun an offensive with extreme violence on the whole Polish front."

First Wounded Brought Into Gleiwitz

GLEIWITZ, Germany, Friday, Sept. 1 (AP).—An army ambulance carrying wounded soldiers arrived at the emergency hospital here today at 9:10 A. M.

The men, carried in a wagon, were on stretchers. One had on a first-aid field bandage. It could not be ascertained where the ambulance came from.

At about 9:30 a half-mile long truck train manned by the engineering corps drove through the heart of the city with pontoon bridge building material. In the train were caterpillar tread, twenty-passenger motor vans.

Obviously the train had been on the road for a considerable time. All equipment was thickly covered with gray mud.

A scouting plane of the air force was patrolling an area over Gleiwitz.

Early today Gleiwitz residents reported that artillery fire

Continued on Page Four

DALADIER SUMMONS CABINET TO CONFER

News of Attack on Poland Spurs Prompt Action—Military Move Thought Likely

By The Associated Press.
PARIS, Friday, Sept. 1.—Edouard Daladier, Premier and War Minister of France, informed that German troops crossed the Polish frontier today, summoned an urgent meeting of his Cabinet for 10:30 A. M.

It was probable that Parliament would be called tomorrow.

Reports of the German invasion came from Berlin and from the Polish Embassy here. The Ministers were called to the Elysee Palace to meet with President Albert Lebrun.

Upon receipt of word of the German operations M. Daladier rushed to the War Ministry and called General Marie Gustave Gamelin, supreme commander of land, sea and air forces, into consultation.

A little later Daladier summoned Foreign Minister Georges Bonnet.

The Polish Embassy said that Germans violated the Polish frontier at four points and at the same time it characterized German charges that Poland had crossed into Germany as "pure invention."

Havas, French news agency, announced that "a German declaration of war against Poland probably will lead France and Great Britain to take new military measures."

Britain and France are committed to aid Poland in any fight to save her independence.

Continued on Page Four

BRITISH CHILDREN TAKEN FROM CITIES

3,000,000 Persons Are in First Evacuation Group, Which Is to Be Moved Today

By FREDERICK T. BIRCHALL
Special Cable to The New York Times.
LONDON, Friday, Sept. 1.—The greatest mass movement of population at short notice in the history of Great Britain is under way. It is an evacuation, under government order, of little children, invalids, women and old men from congested areas.

From London, Birmingham, Manchester, Liverpool, Edinburgh, Glasgow and twenty-three other cities the great exodus is going on as this dispatch is being written. The numbers are stupendous. More than 3,000,000 of these helpless human beings are being taken out of danger of German bombs.

Nothing like it has ever been attempted anywhere; yet it is going on without mishap—so far, indeed, without serious confusion.

Scenes everywhere were much the same whether in the aristocratic West End or the proletarian East Side, but one that this correspondent

Continued on Page Five

Soviet Ratifies Reich Non-Aggression Pact; Gibes at British and French Amuse Deputies

By G. E. R. GEDYE
Special Cable to The New York Times.
MOSCOW, Aug. 31.—With Premier and Foreign Commissar Vyacheslaff M. Molotoff, working under high pressure—so suddenly applied without any previous indication and contrasting so sharply with earlier delaying tactics this week as to prepare that German insistence that the matter be finally settled—the Supreme Soviet [Parliament] tonight constantly ratified the Russo-German non-aggression pact.

Ratification was first foreshadowed by a speech by Mr. Molotoff so precise in its definition of Soviet obligations to refrain from participating on the side of Great Britain and France in any war against Germany, so voluble in its defense against charges of inconsistency in embracing Fascist Germany, and so in-

sistent on the inevitability of friendship between "not merely the governments but also the peoples" of Germany and Russia as to extinguish the last faint hopes of the western democracies that Moscow might yet find loopholes or excuses for joining them at some subsequent date in resisting German aggression against Poland.

Mr. Molotoff's speech contained nothing to justify constantly recurring suspicions of the existence of a secret German-Soviet pact entitling the two nations to participate in a partition of Poland.

The Premier's speech contained much trenchant and seemingly irrefutable evidence of blunders by the British and French Governments in handling the question of Soviet cooperation. It was not diffi-

Continued on Page Eight

HOSTILITIES BEGUN

Warsaw Reports German Offensive Moving on Three Objectives

ROOSEVELT WARNS NAVY

Also Notifies Army Leaders of Warfare—Envoys Tell of Bombing of 4 Cities

By JERZY SZAPIRO
Wireless to The New York Times.
WARSAW, Poland, Friday, Sept. 1.—War began at 5 o'clock this morning with German planes attacking Gdynia, Cracow and Katowice.

At Gdynia three bombs exploded in the sea.

The regular German Army started an offensive in the direction of Dzialdowka—in Upper Silesia and Czestochowa. The German plan apparently is to cut off Western Poland along the line of Dzialdowka-Lodz-Czestochowa.

The offensive is developing, from East Prussia, toward Silesia and northwards from Slovakia.

At 9 o'clock an attempt was made to bombard Warsaw. The planes, however, did not reach even the suburbs.

A military attack on the garrison at Westerplatte in the Danzig area was reported.

The Foreign Office at 8:45 A. M. issued a communiqué saying that military action had begun in Westerplatte in the Danzig area as well as in Buschkowa near Gdynia, and in Dzialdowa, Chojnice and Lowa.

Hostilities have begun and Poland has been attacked, said the communiqué.

Three cities in Upper Silesia suffered artillery bombardment, particulars of which are lacking, it was said.

While this dispatch was being telephoned, the air-raid sirens sounded in Warsaw.

Danzig Fighting Reported

WARSAW, Poland, Friday, Sept. 1 (AP).—It was reported today that Tcsew and Czestochowa were bombed by German airplanes early this morning.

There was no official confirmation of the bombing.

Fighting was reported at Danzig.

It was reported officially that German troops had attacked Polish defenses near Mlawa, bordering the southern part of East Prussia.

There was no announcement of the damage resulting from the bombing.

Mist and clouds were overhanging the city. A light drizzle apparently afforded momentary protection against air raids. Warsaw went to work as usual.

Roosevelt Warns Navy

WASHINGTON, Friday, Sept. 1 (AP).—President Roosevelt directed today that all naval ships and army commands be notified at once by radio of German-Polish hostilities. The White House issued the following announcement:

"The President received word at 2:50 A. M. Eastern standard time

Continued on Page Five

FREE CITY IS SEIZED

Forster Notifies Hitler of Order Putting Danzig Into the Reich

ACCEPTED BY CHANCELLOR

Poles Ready, Made Their Preparations After Hostilities Appeared Inevitable

Special Cable to The New York Times.
DANZIG, Friday, Sept. 1.—By a decree issued early this morning Albert Forster, Nazi Chief of State, proclaimed the annexation of the Free City to the Reich, thus settling by a fell stroke the original point of contention in the international crisis.

In a telegram to Chancellor Hitler Herr Forster explained his action as necessary to remove "the pressing necessity of our people and State." Herr Forster also issued a proclamation to the people of Danzig saying the hour awaited for twenty years had arrived because "our Fuehrer, Adolf Hitler, has freed us."

[A New York Times dispatch from Berlin this morning said Herr Hitler telegraphed Herr Forster today thanking him and all Danzigers, and stating:

"The law for reannexation is in effect immediately."

The Chancellor stated, furthermore, that Herr Forster was appointed head of the civil administration of the Danzig area.]

In a four-article decree Herr Forster declared the Constitution of Danzig no longer valid. He declared himself sole administrator of the Danzig part of the German Reich, and he declared that until the Reich's legal system had been introduced by command of Herr Hitler all laws except the Constitution remained in effect. Then Herr Forster immediately wired Herr Hitler of his action, begged the Chancellor to give his approval of the move and through Reich law complete the annexation.

The German flag is now flying everywhere over Danzig, Herr Forster said, and all church bells resound to the event. "We thank God," he declared, "that He gave the Fuehrer the strength and the possibility to free also us from the evil Versailles treaty."

Hitler Accepts Danzig

BERLIN, Friday, Sept. 1.—The German official news agency, D. N. B., announced today that Albert Forster, Nazi Chief of State in Danzig, had proclaimed the reunion of the Free City with the Reich.

Herr Hitler today accepted the Free City of Danzig into the Reich.

"I acknowledge your proclamation of the return of the Free City of Danzig to the Reich," Herr Hitler's telegram said. "I thank you, Gauleiter Forster, and all Danzig men and women, for your loyalty which you have displayed for so many years.

"Greater Germany welcomes you with joy in her heart.

"The law of reunion will be enacted forthwith. I appoint you, Herr Forster, chief of the civil administration in the Danzig territory."

Forster's telegram to Herr Hitler read:

My Fuehrer,

I have just signed and then put into effect the following basic law, concerning the reunion of Danzig with the German Reich:

The basic State law of the Free State of Danzig and the reunion of Danzig with the German Reich is effective Sept. 1, 1939.

To lift the immediate distress of the people and State of the Free City of Danzig, I decree the following basic State law:

ARTICLE I

The Constitution of the Free City of Danzig has been suspended forthwith.

ARTICLE II

All legal and administrative power will be executed exclusively by the head of State.

ARTICLE III

The Free State of Danzig with its territory and its peoples forms

Continued on Page Five

Hitler Acts Against Poland

The port of Gdynia, north of Danzig (toward top of map), was blockaded this morning. At Gleiwitz (shown by cross) artillery fire was heard after a Polish-German skirmish had been reported there. Cracow, to the east, was among Polish cities said to have been bombed.

Hitler Tells the Reichstag 'Bomb Will Be Met by Bomb'

Chancellor Vows 'Fight Until Resolution' Against Poland—Gives Order of Succession As Goering, Hess, Then Senate to Choose

Chancellor Adolf Hitler of Germany, in a world broadcast this morning, opened "a fight until the resolution of the situation" against Poland, announcing that "from now on bomb will be met by bomb."

At the same time he announced, to face any eventuality, that if anything "happened" to him, Field Marshal Hermann Goering was to be in charge; if to Marshal Goering, Rudolph Hess; if to Herr Hess, the Senate, which he proposes to appoint, will select a successor.

The Chancellor, after attempting to narrow the conflict with Poland by assuring the Western powers that he had no designs on their frontiers, by assuring the neutrality of the sideline powers and by acknowledging the friendliness of Italy and the new relations with Russia, issued a defy to Poland's allies.

Says He Will Carry on

"I shall carry on this fight regardless of against whom I may come," he declared.

At the same time he held the door open for Poland to capitulate to his demands, declaring that he did not intend to make war against women and children. He said that if a solution did not come from the present Polish Government, it would come from a future Polish Government.

The Chancellor expressed confidence, toward the close of his address, that his decision, which was being broadcast over amplifiers hastily erected by electricians at the last moment in the streets of Berlin and the provincial capitals, would be accepted by the German people.

The scene enacted in the Kroll Opera House in Berlin was carried over sound waves to most of the nations of the world. From Berlin hook-up, hook-ups had been arranged with the three major networks of the United States and, according to the announcer of the German broadcasting system, over the Italian, Hungarian, Spanish, Norwegian, Swedish, Danish, Yugoslav, British and French national networks.

The summons to the Reichstag, ordered by Herr Hitler himself, had been sent out only a few hours before the meeting. Most of the mem-

bers had been awaiting the signal, and when the opera house opened at 10 o'clock [5 o'clock, New York time] this morning, they were dressed in the uniforms of their military formations.

After Herr Hitler finished speaking the deputies enacted a law incorporating Danzig into the Reich, declaring Danzig citizens were now Germans, voiding the Constitution of the Free City and extending to its territory the jurisdiction of German law.

At 5:10 A. M., Marshal Goering opened the meeting and turned the floor over to the Chancellor.

In the early part of his address, Herr Hitler electrified his audience with this declaration:

"We have all been suffering under the tortures that the Versailles treaty has been inflicting upon us."

Then, speaking with measured deliberateness of Germany's claims to the pre-war German areas, he announced, as he had on a previous occasion:

"The Treaty of Versailles is, for us Germans, and has been, for us Germans, not a law."

Anticipating what the announcement's reiteration would lead to, the Deputies roared applause. Then Herr Hitler, his indignation rising to the German case, asserting that his proposals for a peaceful solution of the problem of Danzig and the Polish Corridor had been rejected, and charging that the Poles had visited atrocities on Germans, especially women and children, were "killing many of them."

SUMMARY OF SPEECH

A summary of Herr Hitler's speech was translated as follows:

"For months we have been suffering under the burdens of the Treaty of Versailles. Danzig was and is a German city. All these regions have only Germany to thank for their cultural development.

"Minorities in the Polish Corridor have been shamefully mistreated. Here, as in other respects, I have tried to solve the problems by peaceful means. In the fifteen years of National Socialism I have

Continued on Page Three

HITLER GIVES WORD

In a Proclamation He Accuses Warsaw of Appeal to Arms

FOREIGNERS ARE WARNED

They Remain in Poland at Own Risk—Nazis to Shoot at Any Planes Flying Over Reich

By OTTO D. TOLISCHUS
Special Cable to The New York Times.
BERLIN, Friday, Sept. 1.—Charging that Germany had been attacked, Chancellor Hitler at 5:11 o'clock this morning issued a proclamation to the army declaring that from now on force will be met with force and calling on the armed forces "to fulfill their duty to the end."

The text of the proclamation reads:

To the defense forces:

The Polish nation refused my efforts for a peaceful regulation of neighborly relations; instead it has appealed to weapons.

Germans in Poland are persecuted with a bloody terror and are driven from their homes. The series of border violations, which are unbearable to a great power, prove that the Poles no longer are willing to respect the German frontier. In order to put an end to this frantic activity no other means is left to me now than to meet force with force.

"Battle for Honor"

German defense forces will carry on the battle for the honor of the living rights of the reawakened German people with firm determination.

I expect every German soldier, in view of the great tradition of eternal German soldiery, to do his duty until the end.

Remember always in all situations you are the representatives of National Socialist Greater Germany!

Long live our people and our Reich!

Berlin, Sept. 1, 1939.

ADOLF HITLER.

The commander-in-chief of the air force issued a decree effective immediately prohibiting the passage of any airplanes over German territory excepting those of the Reich air force or the government.

This morning the naval authorities ordered all German mercantile ships in the Baltic Sea not to run to Danzig or Polish ports.

Anti-air raid defenses were mobilized throughout the country early this morning.

A formal declaration of war against Poland had not yet been declared up to 8 o'clock [3 A. M. New York time] this morning and the question of whether the two countries are in a state of active belligerency is still open.

Reichstag Will Meet Today

Foreign correspondents at an official conference at the Reich Press Ministry at 2:30 A. M. [New York time] were told that they would receive every opportunity to facilitate the transmission of dispatches. Wireless companies had been instructed to speed up communications and the Ministry is installing additional batteries of telephones.

The Reichstag had been summoned to meet at 10 o'clock [5 A. M. New York time] to receive a more formal declaration from Herr Hitler.

The Hitler army order is interpreted as providing, for the time being, armed defense of the German frontiers against aggression. This action is also suspected of forcing international diplomatic action.

The Germans announced that foreigners remain in Polish territory at their own risk.

Flying over Polish territory as well as the maritime areas is forbidden by the German authorities and any violators will be shot down.

When Herr Hitler made his ad-

Continued on Page Three

CHAMBERLAIN ANNOUNCES BRITAIN IS AT WAR WITH GERMANY

"All the News That's Fit to Print."

NEWS INDEX, PAGE 21, THIS SECTION.

The New York Times.

Copyright, 1939, by The New York Times Company.

EXTRA

Generally fair, little change in temperature today. Tomorrow cloudy, showers in afternoon or night.
Temperature Yesterday—Max. 80; Min. 64

Section 1

VOL. LXXXVIII....No. 29,807

Entered as Second-Class Matter, Postoffice, New York, N. Y.

NEW YORK, SUNDAY, SEPTEMBER 3, 1939.

P

Including Rotogravure Picture, Magazine and Book Review.

TEN CENTS | TWELVE CENTS Beyond 200 Miles Except in 7th and 8th Postal Zones.

BRITAIN AND FRANCE IN WAR AT 6 A. M.; HITLER WON'T HALT ATTACK ON POLES; CHAMBERLAIN CALLS EMPIRE TO FIGHT

SOVIET IN WARNING

British-French Action to Bring Western Border Revision, Berlin Hears

NAZIS GREET MISSION

Hitler to Receive New Russian Ambassador and General Today

By OTTO D. TOLISCHUS
Wireless to THE NEW YORK TIMES.

BERLIN, Sunday, Sept. 3.—According to well-informed quarters here Moscow is already supposed to have notified Paris and London that if France and Britain join in the present Reich-Polish conflict Russia will find herself compelled to revise her Western borders.

This is tantamount to the threat that any British and French help to Poland will merely hasten the partition of Poland between Germany and Russia. There are hints that Russia might also seek other "compensation" in regions even less convenient to Britain.

As an impressive demonstration of this new cooperation there arrived today by air from Stockholm a new Russian embassy secretary, each of whom were said to be very close to Premier Vycheslaff Molotoff, and a Russian military mission headed by a commanding general.

Officials Greet the Mission

The new Ambassador is Alexander Shkhartzeff, who, it is pointed out here, collaborated with Mr. Molotoff in the Commissariat of Foreign Affairs in Moscow. The new embassy secretary is Vladimir Perloff, up to now Mr. Molotoff's secretary and interpreter.

The military mission consists of General Maxim Purjakoff, designated as the Military Plenipotentiary of the U. S. S. R.; and his staff; Brig. Gen. Michae' Beljakoff, Colonel Nikolai Skornjakoff, Major Basanoff and Captain Alexander Seditch.

To show the importance of the occasion the members were met at Tempelhof Airfield by Dr. Ernst Woermann, Under-Secretary of State in the Foreign Office; Baron Alexander von Doernberg, Chief of Protocol, and other Foreign Office officials. Lieut. Gen. Seifert, commander of Berlin, headed the list of army officers greeting the Russians. A guard of honor presented arms.

The Russians received an ovation as their automobiles, flying the hammer-and-sickle flag of the Soviet Union, passed the Reich Chancellery. Those assembled along the street gave the Nazi salute.

Hitler to Receive Envoy

Adding importance to all this is the fact that it was announced at midnight that Herr Hitler would receive the new Ambassador, together with the Military Plenipotentiary, for the submission of credentials later today, which sets a precedent for diplomatic speed.

That such a formidable military mission was sent here to work out 'close cooperation with the German Army is taken for granted now. But German quarters still hold that the consultative clauses of the German-Russian pact are sufficient to cover all the collaboration necessary and a formal military alliance may be signed only as the last trump card to impress London and Paris.

Ambassador Joseph Lipski and his whole embassy staff left Berlin this morning under safe conduct en route to Sweden, which has also taken over the representation of Polish interests. The German Embassy staff was supposed to have left Warsaw at the same time. German interests in Poland are being represented by the Netherlands. Official quarters hold, however, that this merely represents a "cessation of direct diplomatic relations," not a formal break of relations, just as there is no declared state of war.

Meanwhile, since the German-Polish conflict is now being arbitrated by the roar of cannon and the re-

Continued on Page Sixteen

Announcement of Final Ultimatum

By The Associated Press.

LONDON, Sunday, Sept. 3.—Following is the text of today's communique revealing the final ultimatum to Germany:

On Sept. 2 His Majesty's Ambassador in Berlin was instructed to inform the German Government that unless they were prepared to give His Majesty's Government in the United Kingdom satisfactory assurances that the German Government had suspended all aggressive action against Poland and were prepared promptly to withdraw their forces from Polish territory, His Majesty's Government in the United Kingdom would without hesitation fulfill their obligations to Poland.

At 9 A. M. this morning His Majesty's Ambassador in Berlin informed the German Government that unless not later than 11 A. M., British Summer time, today, Sept. 3, satisfactory assurances to the above effect had been given by the German Government and had reached His Majesty's Government in London a state of war would exist between the two countries as from that hour.

His Majesty's Government are now awaiting the receipt of any reply that may be made by the German Government.

The Prime Minister will broadcast to the nation at 11:15 A. M.

21 CIVILIANS KILLED IN RAID ON WARSAW

Women, Children Die as Bomb Hits Workers' Apartment— State of War Decreed

By The Associated Press.

WARSAW, Poland, Sept. 2.—Twenty-one dead and more than thirty wounded were counted late tonight after German bombs had struck an apartment house in a Warsaw workingmen's quarter.

The bombs tore off the side of the apartment house as if it had been made of paper. Rescue workers still were clearing away the resultant pile of debris in a search for further casualties when this correspondent inspected it.

One of the bombs had dug a crater fully twenty feet in diameter, and the open ground was piled high with furniture and belongings.

In the center of a large park in the southern section of Warsaw, this writer also saw where a bomb had struck a simple wooden dwelling, killing two persons and wounding one. In an open field near the Vistula River, where ten light bombs apparently had been released simultaneously, they had dug craters in a 100-yard circle.

With the writer on this tour of inspection of damage done by the German air bombings were C. Burke Elbrick, secretary of the American Embassy; Clifford Norton, chargé d'affaires of the British Embassy, and officials of the Polish Foreign Office.

During the tour the party twice was forced to take refuge because of air-raid alarms, five of which in all sounded through the city today. Once the party took cover in a shallow dugout filled with working men, their wives and their crying children.

The worst scene of damage was at Kolo, the workingmen's quarter, where, in addition to wrecking one apartment building, the bombs had smashed windows in several others.

An old man gulped back tears as he said his wife and two children were dead. A woman, still staring blankly into space, said:

"My husband is gone."

An official news service communique stated that yesterday German raiders dropped 120 bombs on Warsaw and its vicinity, killing ten and wounding twenty-five in Warsaw proper, with the number of casualties in the suburbs still undetermined.

President Ignaz Moscicki declared that Poland was under a "state of war" today as official reports said that Polish forces were resisting German invasion on three fronts. The "state of war" supersedes the

Continued on Page Fourteen

News dispatches from Europe are now virtually all subject to censorship

PARIS AUTHORIZED WAR DECLARATION

Chamber Voted Credits After Hearing Daladier — New Ultimatum Being Drawn

By The Associated Press.

PARIS, Sept. 2.—Premier Edouard Daladier today received implied authority from the Chamber of Deputies to declare war on Germany.

With that to support them, he and his Cabinet met at the War Ministry at 7:30 tonight to frame a demand that Chancellor Hitler reply to the British-French "last warning" of yesterday.

The power to declare war was vested in a war budget bill of 69,-000,000,000 francs, which the sober Deputies, many wearing army uniforms, adopted unanimously by a show of hands after hearing M. Daladier say the government was still willing to negotiate if Germany would cease hostilities in Poland.

Whether the Premier uses the authority vested in him by adoption of the budget depends upon the possibility—really a bare possibility—that Herr Hitler would avail himself of a last-minute loophole for peace.

The Premier told the finance committee after the Chamber session that he planned to call the Chamber to approve an actual declaration of war if that became necessary, but he may simply ask for approval after, rather than before, the action is taken.

"The government will take the same chance as Parisians," M. Daladier told a Deputy who asked whether the government planned to leave Paris immediately.

The session was held in a tense atmosphere from 3 to 3:55 P. M.

Continued on Page Fifteen

ROME ASKED PEACE

Pressed Its Proposal for a 5-Power Parley on Britain and France

WAR MEASURES CUT

Press Expressed the Hope Germany Would Win in Poland

By The Associated Press.

ROME, Sept. 2.—Premier Mussolini tonight sought to prevent Polish-German hostilities from spreading into a general European war by arranging a negotiated settlement.

Conferences that the British and French Ambassadors had with Foreign Minister Count Ciano were believed to be connected directly with an Italian proposal of a five-power conference disclosed in London by Prime Minister Neville Chamberlain and Foreign Secretary Viscount Halifax.

The possibility of halting the German-Polish conflict and arranging a peaceable settlement was believed to have been discussed at the diplomatic conferences, but no official information was forthcoming.

Some foreign observers believed, however, that Signor Mussolini had been asked to use his influence on Adolf Hitler to halt fighting in Poland, call his army back and negotiate a settlement of his demands on the Poles.

For Wide Settlement

Here it was regarded as certain that any five-power conference proposed by Premier Mussolini would not be merely for settling the German-Polish conflict but would be aimed at complete revision of the Treaty of Versailles.

Under such a revision Italy and Germany would seek the political and economic concessions that they consider necessary to end European tension once and for all. This has long been Signor Mussolini's idea and Italian newspapers recently have been stressing it as the only real solution. [Italy has been demanding from France concessions concerning Tunisia, the Suez Canal and Jibuti, French Somaliland port.]

While the Ambassadors of France and Britain conferred with Foreign Minister Ciano continued her policy of watchful waiting and avoidance of any military "initiative".

The important commentator, Virginio Gayda, in the Giornale d'Italia noted uneasily that French and British war preparations made it seem that only a miracle could prevent a "more general explosion." Italy, he said, rested on her arms, confident she would win everything possible to avoid war. He said she was following events

Continued on Page Three

NAZIS REPORT GAINS

Hitler's Aims in Corridor Already Won, They Say, Telling of Big 'Trap'

RESISTANCE IS NOTED

But Armies Drive On and Navy Is in Command of Baltic, Germans Hold

Special Cable to THE NEW YORK TIMES.

BERLIN, Sunday, Sept. 3.—Defying the British and French ultimatums, the German armies reported continued advances into Poland yesterday.

By nightfall, it was asserted, not only had they attained the German war aims in the Polish Corridor as outlined in Chancellor Hitler's "sixteen points" but they were pushing forward in a concentric drive toward Warsaw. According to one report, the German forces stood less than fifty miles north of the Polish capital, and a big battle was believed developing along the Vistula River.

According to the latest communique of the army command, which apparently have already been overtaken by developments, the German armies operating out of East Prussia and Pomerania had virtually cut the Corridor along the Netze and Vistula Rivers, so that all Polish troops remaining in the bottleneck north of it were hopelessly trapped.

Claim Capture of Teschen

In the South the Germans were reported to have taken the heavily fortified Jablunka Pass, the main strategic highway from Slovakia into Poland; to have captured Teschen and Pless [Pszczyna] and to be breaking through the Polish bunker line approaching Biala. This group apparently has the task of capturing the Upper Silesian industrial section and the Teschen coal mines, taken by Poland from Czecho-Slovakia, and then of advancing along the Vistula toward Sandomierz, the new Polish armament and industrial center.

At the same time two other German Army groups, operating from the north out of East Prussia and from the southwest out of Silesia, apparently were conducting a pincers movement on Warsaw. The southwestern group was declared to have taken Wielun and to be advancing toward Radomsk and Sierads.

The Northern army group, according to a communiqué, was advancing on Przasnysz, but, according to private reports, is already disputing a larger Polish army that is supposed to have taken a stand on the Narew, where the first real battle of the undeclared war may take place.

Reich Claims "Air" Domination

The communique asserted also that the German air force, after many bombing expeditions against air fields, railroads, military transports, retreating marching columns and other military objectives, in which many planes and the munition factory at Skarzysko-Kamienna were destroyed, now has "unchallenged air domination over the entire Polish territory and so is now free for other tasks in protection of the Reich."

In addition, the German Navy, which said it had bombed the fortifications and port of Hela and also Gdynia, reported the sinking of a Polish torpedo boat off Hela. It was said to command the Baltic so completely that the fishing embargo was lifted last night.

A communiqué issued by the high command early today, according to the official German News Bureau, declared:

"The German air force yesterday again proved its absolute superiority. The totals of six areas over the battle zone and the hinterland is completely controlled by the German air force. Attacks were confined exclusively to military objectives.

"After units of the German armored cars had reached the Vistula, approximately at noon, the German

Continued on Page Twelve

Text of Chamberlain Address

The following is the text of the address by Prime Minister Chamberlain from 10 Downing Street this morning:

I am speaking to you from the Cabinet Room at 10 Downing Street. This morning the British Ambassador in Berlin handed the German Government the final note stating unless we heard from them by 11 o'clock [6 o'clock New York time] that they were prepared at once to withdraw their troops from Poland a state of war would exist between us. I have to tell you now that no such undertaking has been received and consequently this country is at war with Germany.

You can imagine what a bitter blow it is to me that all my long struggle to win peace has failed. Up to the very last it should have been quite possible to carry on the work of the nation in these days of stress which may be ahead, but these plans need your help. You may be taking part in one of the fighting services or one of the other branches.

It is of vital importance that you carry on with your jobs. May God bless you all and may He defend the right for it is the evil things we shall be fighting against—brute force, broken promises, bad faith. But I am certain that right shall prevail.

Hitler has evidently made up his mind to attack Poland whatever may happen. Hitler claims that his proposals were shown to Poland and to us. That is not a true statement. The proposals never were shown to the Poles or to us.

The German Government prepared the proposals in German and the same night the German troops crossed the Polish frontier. Germany will never give up force and can only be stopped by force.

We are prepared to uphold our treaty with Poland and to protect them from the wicked and unprovoked attacks on the Polish people. France is joining Britain in fulfillment of her pledges. We have a clear conscience and the situation has become intolerable. Now that we have determined to finish it I know that you will all play your part.

When I have finished speaking several detailed announcements will be made in addition of the government giving you plans under which it will be possible to carry on the work of the nation in these days of stress which may be ahead, but these plans need your help. You may be taking part in one of the fighting services or one of the other branches.

Bulletins on European Conflict

Air Raid Warning in London

LONDON, Sept. 3 (Sunday).—Air raid sirens sounded an alarm in London today at 11:32 A. M. (5:32 A. M., E.S.T.).

The whole city was sent to shelters by the wail of the alarm but all clear signals were sounded seventeen minutes later.

Ribbentrop Gives Reply to British Envoy

BERLIN, Sunday, Sept. 3 (AP).—German Foreign Minister Joachim von Ribbentrop received British Ambassador Sir Nevile Henderson at 9 A. M. [4 A. M. in New York] today to hand him Germany's answer to the "final warnings" of Britain and France. Herr von Ribbentrop was expected to see the French Ambassador, Robert Coulondre, shortly before noon.

American Diplomats' Families Leave Reich

BERLIN, Sunday, Sept. 3 (AP).—About fifty women and children of the United States Embassy and consular staffs, as well as several other American families, left Berlin today at 8:50 A. M. [3:50 A. M. in New York] for Copenhagen in compartments reserved for them in a regular train.

They were due in Copenhagen at 5:35 P. M. [12:35 A. M. in New York].

War Announced in France

PARIS, Sunday, Sept. 3 (AP).—The radio announced to the French nation today that British Prime Minister Chamberlain had proclaimed Great Britain at war with Germany.

"No News" at the German Embassy

LONDON, Sunday, Sept. 3 (AP).—At the German Embassy in London at 9:30 A. M. today [5:30 A. M., New York], a half hour before the expiration of the British ultimatum, it was said, "There is no news." A spokesman said, "We are in constant communication with Berlin."

Denies Poles Got Five-Power Parley Offer

LONDON, Sunday, Sept. 3 (AP).—Exchange Telegraph Agency, British news agency, said today that Count Edward Raczynski, Polish Ambassador in London, informed it that "the Italian Government did not approach Poland" concerning a reported five-power conference to settle German-Polish issues.

"Apart from the declarations made yesterday in the British Parliament and apart from contradictory reports in the press," the agency quoted him, "the Polish Government has not knowledge of such a scheme."

Exchange Telegraph said the Ambassador declared that "any talk of such a conference" would be "ludicrous and fantastic" as long as "a single enemy soldier stands on Polish soil."

1,000 Americans Sail on French Liner

PARIS, Sunday, Sept. 3 (AP).—The French Line said today that the Ile de France had sailed from Havre with more than 1,000 Americans on board, bound for home.

Heavy Fighting Is Reported in Silesia

WARSAW, Sept. 2 (AP).—Although official information was lacking, it was reported tonight that severe fighting be-

TO END OPPRESSION

Premier Calls It 'Bitter Blow' That Efforts for Peace Have Failed

WARNING UNHEEDED

Demand on Reich to Withdraw Army From Poland Ignored

Prime Minister Neville Chamberlain announced to the world at 6:10 o'clock this morning that Great Britain and France were at war with Germany. He made the announcement over the radio, with short waves carrying the measured tones of his voice throughout all continents, from 10 Downing Street in London.

Mr. Chamberlain disclosed that Great Britain and France had taken concurrent action, announcing that "we and France are, today, in fulfillment of our obligations, going to the aid of Poland."

France, however, had not made any announcement beyond stating that the French Ambassador to Berlin would make a final call upon Foreign Minister Joachim von Ribbentrop at 6 o'clock this morning, and it was assumed the French had proclaimed the existence of the state of war.

Speaks With Solemnity

With the greatest solemnity Mr. Chamberlain began his declaration by reporting that the British Ambassador had handed in Great Britain's final ultimatum and that it had not been accepted. Without hesitation he announced Britain's decision and, after touching briefly on the background of the crisis, he expressed the highest confidence that "injustice, oppression and persecution" would be vanquished and that his cause would triumph.

Mr. Chamberlain appealed to his people, schooled during the last year as the crisis deepened in measures of defense and offense, to carry on with their jobs and begged a blessing upon them, warning that "we shall be fighting against brute force."

The declaration came after Great Britain had given Chancellor Adolf Hitler of Germany extended time in which to answer the British Government's final ultimatum of Friday. In the final ultimatum Herr Hitler had been told that German aggression in Poland ceased, Britain was prepared to fulfill her obligations to Poland.

Warning Was Sharp

Britain's last warning at 4 o'clock this morning, New York time, left no doubt of her stand, for the phrase, "fulfillment of Britain's obligations to Poland," was replaced by a flat statement that a state of war would exist between the two countries as of the hour of the deadline.

After Mr. Chamberlain had finished his statement, which had been introduced as "an announcement of national importance," the announcer warned the British people not to gather together, broadcast an order that all meeting places for entertainment be closed, and gave special precautions to prepare the people against air bombings and poison gas attacks.

Mr. Chamberlain began his

Continued on Page Fifteen

Fuller Breaks Own Bendix Race Records; Crosses Continent in 8 Hours 58 Minutes

Frank Fuller, San Francisco sportsman pilot, broke his own record in the Bendix Trophy Race from Burbank, Calif., to Cleveland yesterday and then kept on to Bendix, N. J., to break his own record for a transcontinental crossing in the event, opening feature of the National Air Races and the country's outstanding air derby.

Flying a stripped-down Seversky military plane equipped with the same twin Wasp engines he had in the 1937 race, when his earlier records were set, Fuller flew the 2,650 miles from Burbank to Bendix in an elapsed time of 8 hours 58 minutes 45 seconds. His average speed was 273.34 miles an hour. His elapsed time in 1937 was 9 hours 25 minutes.

The record for a transcontinental flight is 7 hours 28 minutes, established by Howard Hughes in a specially built plane about two years ago.

In crossing the finishing line at Bendix, Fuller, a wealthy paint manufacturer, won three prizes totaling $12,900. For being the first to reach Bendix he received a

prize of $9,000. As the first to fly over the line at Bendix he won another $1,000, and for breaking his 1937 record he won $2,500.

Fuller reached Bendix at 4:24:53 P. M., Eastern daylight time, and proceeded, without landing, to Floyd Bennett Field, where he brought his plane to earth at 4:35 P. M.

Max Constant of Burbank was the second racer to fly over Bendix, reaching there at 6:13:30 P. M. Arthur C. Bussy of Hoytsford, Pa., appeared at 7:08:15 P. M.

Although Constant arrived at Bendix ahead of Bussy, he took off from Burbank before him and Bussy was declared the second prize winner of $5,000 for the flight to Cleveland and an additional $900 for continuing to Bendix and Floyd Bennett Field.

Mrs. Arline Davis of Cleveland landed at Newark Airport at 8 P. M., believing that she had crossed the official marker at Bendix and thereby won the $2,500 prize for the first woman to finish

Continued on Page Three

The New York Times.

VOL. LXXXVIII...No. 29,808.   Entered as Second-Class Matter, Postoffice, New York, N. Y.   NEW YORK, MONDAY, SEPTEMBER 4, 1939.   P   THREE CENTS NEW YORK CITY and Vicinity | FOUR CENTS Elsewhere Except in 7th and 8th Postal Zones.

Copyright, 1939, by The New York Times Company.

BRITISH LINER ATHENIA TORPEDOED, SUNK; 1,400 PASSENGERS ABOARD, 292 AMERICANS; ALL EXCEPT A FEW ARE REPORTED SAVED

ROOSEVELT IN PLEA

President, on Air, Asks the Nation to Observe True Neutrality

CALLS ALL TO UNITY

Draws Ring Around Americas—'Even a Neutral' May Judge, He Says

By TURNER CATLEDGE
Special to THE NEW YORK TIMES.

WASHINGTON, Sept. 3.—In an extraordinary message broadcast by radio to "the whole of America," President Roosevelt tonight called for an adjournment of all partisanship and selfishness and substitution of complete national unity in the United States to the end that the newest world war may be kept from the Western Hemisphere.

He declared that, as long as it remained within his power to prevent, "there will be no blackout of peace in the United States."

Linking the present European conflagration to the "invasion of Poland by Germany," the President announced that a proclamation of American neutrality was being prepared for issuance under the present Neutrality Act.

"I trust that in the days to come our neutrality can be made a true neutrality," he said.

Would Seek a "Final Peace"

But it seemed clear to him, he said, "even at the outbreak of this great war," that the influence of America should be consistent in seeking for humanity a final peace which will eliminate, as far as it is possible to do so, the continued use of force between nations.

In his flat declaration that "this nation will remain a neutral nation," the President said he could not ask that every American remain neutral in thought as well. "Even a neutral has a right to take account of facts," he said. "Even a neutral cannot be asked to close his mind or his conscience."

The President gave no inkling of his intentions about calling Congress into special session to revise the stringent Neutrality Law which places certain mandatory obligations upon him. The universal opinion among observers at the capital was that he would issue a call soon, and that it might come upon the heels of the obligatory neutrality proclamation, placing an embargo on arms and munitions of war to Germany, Poland, France and England. White House sources said the neutrality proclamation could be expected within the next forty-eight hours.

Gives Idea of Safety

Under the law, the neutrality proclamation, which carries with it the proclamation of an arms embargo, is required as soon as the President makes a finding that a state of war exists between two or more countries. Officials were standing today on the technicality that this government had not been officially notified of Britain's and France's declarations. They conceded, however, that this was a mere technicality.

In the course of his message, the President drew a ring around the Western Hemisphere, saying in substance that this was the area which the United States must and would seek to protect and keep neutral.

This country, he said, had certain ideas and ideals of national safety "and we must act to preserve that safety today and to preserve the safety of our children in future years."

That safety, he continued, is and will be bound up with the safety of the Western Hemisphere "and the seas adjacent thereto.

"We seek to keep war from our firesides by keeping war from coming to the Americas," he said.

Recalls Efforts for Peace

He claimed historic precedent, going back to the days of George Washington, for this country's assuming the responsibility of protecting the whole of the Americas. It is serious enough and tragic enough to every American family in every State in the Union to live in a world torn by wars on other continents, he said. Therefore he considered it our national duty to use

Continued on Page Six

Poles Charge Aerial Gas Attacks on Cities As Germany Agrees to 'Humanize' the War

LONDON, Sept. 3 (AP).—The Polish Ambassador to London, Count Edward Raczynski, tonight declared that new German air attacks in all parts of Poland had disclosed that the civilian population was suffering with the Germans using gas in their raids.

WARSAW, Sept. 3 (Polish Telegraphic Agency).—German bombers threw gas bombs on the unfortified village of Grudisk in the county of Ciechanow.

Wireless to THE NEW YORK TIMES.

BERLIN, Sept. 3.—It was announced today that Germany and the Western Powers had agreed to "humanize" the war by not employing poison gas, not bombing open cities from the air, even when in the zone of war operations, and not taking military measures against civilians as long as both sides observed the agreement.

The reported dropping of gas bombs on Polish towns represents the first use of gas from planes in European warfare.

The inauguration of this form of attack recalls that in 1915 the Germans began the use of poison gas on the battlefields and the Allies followed suit.

In 1917 the German General Staff gave consideration to the use of gas from planes in attacking cities, but after a long debate it was decided not to do so. The reason was that the British and French air forces combined were superior to the air force of the Germans, and the fear of what might happen to German cities deterred the Germans from using gas in air attacks at that time.

ITALY FAILS TO ACT AS HER ALLY FIGHTS

Rome Plans to Stay Neutral Unless Attacked—Fascist Moves Kept Secret

By HERBERT L. MATTHEWS
Special Cable to THE NEW YORK TIMES.

ROME, Monday, Sept. 4.—Although Great Britain and France are at war with Germany, Italy has taken no step to join her Axis partner. She remains friendly to Germany but neutral, and she will make no move against the French and British unless attacked. This was made clear in Premier Mussolini's newspaper, the Popolo d'Italia, this morning, which confirmed the declaration of neutrality contained in the Council of Ministers' communiqué Friday.

Whether there is any possibility of Italy going beyond that attitude toward one side or the other cannot be stated yet, for the Italians continue to be completely secret. Since history always repeats itself, one may well suppose that the French and British are doing everything they can to win Italian benevolence, if not aid. That is the normal and natural thing for them to do whether they have hopes for success or not. After all, diplomatic relations between Rome and Paris and London continue on a friendly basis, and none need be surprised if André François-Poncet and Sir Percy Loraine, the French and British Ambassadors, are today exerting their greatest efforts to win Italy away from Germany. It is their business to do so.

Attitude Is Not Changing

None can say yet what success, if any, they are having. So far as today is concerned there is that Popolo d'Italia article to go upon, which indicates clearly enough that Italy is not changing her attitude because Britain and France have entered the conflict. Although it was printed before those countries acted it was written at a time when there could be no doubt of what was going to happen.

First, that notwithstanding certain foreign interpretations which are too hasty or ingenious nothing is changed on the plane of Italo-German friendship.

Second, that Signor Mussolini has worked not only for the solution of the German-Polish problem but for all other problems which like this one now being solved by arms, have their origin in the Versailles Treaty.

"It is therefore natural," the article goes on, "that whatever happens, whether the German-Polish conflict remains localized or spreads to a catastrophe, the Duce's work—that is to say the work that

Continued on Page Seven

HITLER WITH ARMY ON EASTERN FRONT

Leaves Berlin After Placing Blame for War on Britain— Allied Envoys Depart

By OTTO D. TOLISCHUS
Wireless to THE NEW YORK TIMES.

BERLIN, Sept. 3.—At 9 o'clock tonight Chancellor Hitler left Berlin, presumably for the Eastern Front. He had previously sent a message to the Eastern Army stating that he was joining them.

He left the city in a heavily guarded special train that mounted anti-aircraft artillery. He was accompanied by his Foreign Minister, Joachim von Ribbentrop, and by Field Marshal Hermann Goering. It was supposed that their destination was Stolp, Pomerania, where the headquarters of the Eastern Army is believed to be located.

The departure of the Chancellor ended a day of proclamations from the chancellery. There was an appeal to the German people, a proclamation to the Nazi party, a message to the soldiers of the East Army and another to the troops manning the Westwall. There was also given out the text of a German memorandum answering the British ultimatum.

Perhaps the most significant feature of all these proclamations and of the memorandum is that they do not mention France, sidetrack

Continued on Page Nine

POLES REPORT GAIN

Tell of Fighting on Foe's Soil After Horsemen Retake 2 Towns

SHELL GERMAN AREA

But Invaders Announce Wide Advances—They Capture Rail Center

By The Associated Press.

LONDON, Monday, Sept. 4.—An Exchange Telegraph dispatch from Warsaw reported early today that Polish troops that crossed the German frontier north of Breslau and were fighting on German soil.

Quoting a Polish short-wave radio broadcast, the news agency said the troops had crossed between Rawicz and Leszno. These towns are on the border about twenty-five miles apart and approximately forty-five miles north of Breslau. The report said Polish cavalry was in the action.

[The Polish Telegraphic Agency reported earlier that Polish cavalry had driven German forces from Rawicz and Leszno, which they had captured in furious attacks on Friday.]

The agency quoted the following communiqué issued last night by the Polish supreme command:

"During the day the German air force carried out raids on numerous unfortified towns, including Warsaw, Deblin, Radom and Cracow. Near Radom six enemy aircraft were brought down. The total number brought down today was sixty-four. The Polish losses amounted to eleven machines. German raiders did not spare the peasant population working in the fields near the villages.

"Considerable enemy forces launched a strong attack in the direction of Silesia and the district of Podhale. Under the pressure of the enemy, Polish troops were compelled to abandon Czestochowa on the Silesian frontier.

"Our lines were slightly pressed back in the Silesian sector. In the north Polish troops recaptured Puck and Orlowo,"

In an air encounter over Poznan late yesterday, Exchange Telegraph said, six German bombers were shot down near Wolbrom after they had dropped a number of gas bombs.

The agency said that the German radio had announced that a German Army had crossed the Warta (Warthe) River yesterday east of Wielun in Western Poland.

An attempt by Polish troops cut

Continued on Page Four

BRITISH NAVY ACTS

It Cuts Off Entrances to the Baltic, North and Mediterranean Seas

LONDON IS UNSHAKEN

Declaration of War Is Met With Resolve— Air Alarm Orderly

Special to THE NEW YORK TIMES.

WASHINGTON, Sept. 3.—The British Government has ordered a naval blockade of Germany, according to information reaching officials here tonight. This government has not been informed officially by the British Government of this fact, however.

It was understood here that the naval blockade went into effect immediately upon the declaration of war and that British naval vessels were blocking the entrance to the Baltic Sea near Skagerrak and were stretched across the North Sea near the Scandinavian peninsula. It was also understood here that the entrances to the Mediterranean at Gibraltar and Suez were being carefully controlled.

Both Britain and France were cloaking their naval and military moves with utmost secrecy and neither the Navy nor the War Department had specific information about them up to 8 o'clock, Eastern standard time, tonight.

Britain Is Determined

By FREDERICK T. BIRCHALL
Special Cable to THE NEW YORK TIMES.

LONDON, Monday, Sept. 4.—At last midnight Great Britain had been at war with Germany for thirteen hours. France had been at war for seven hours—since 5 o'clock.

A darkened London, in which only hooded red and green crosses at the traffic halts, invisible from above, indicate that there are streets, houses and human life below a dreary starry sky, awaits calmly the air attacks that it confidently expects despite Chancellor Hitler's professed desire to avoid bombing open cities. Even these tiny indications will be extinguished the moment that sirens hoot their warnings of approaching raiders.

There are few people in the streets because the authorities have broadcast warnings to every one to stay at home and to go out no more than is necessary. Cinemas, theatres and every other form of entertainment likely to draw a crowd have been shut down by order for the time being, at least. Only the churches have held their customary services.

People Grimly Determined

Thus war has come to Britain, to a people grimly determined to meet it and to see it through. The predominating sentiment, if any, is one of relief that the long period of suspense is over. Throughout the land the watchword now is: "Let's get on with it."

War became a reality yesterday morning just after the church bells had ceased ringing. It came in the shape of a sudden interruption of the regular radio program by an announcer:

"The Prime Minister will broadcast an important announcement to the nation."

Then came Mr. Chamberlain's well-known voice, quiet and sad but clear and firm:

"I am speaking to you from the Cabinet room at 10 Downing Street."

Then followed his terse narration of the course of events. That morning (it was actually at 9 o'clock, two hours earlier) the British Ambassador at Berlin had handed Foreign Minister Joachim von Ribbentrop a final note stating that unless the Germans had agreed by 11 o'clock to withdraw their troops from Poland, a "state of war would exist between us."

"I have to tell you now," continued Mr. Chamberlain in the same level tones, "that no such

Continued on Page Five

FIRST SHIP SUNK IN THE WAR

The Athenia, with 1,400 aboard, torpedoed off the Hebrides.

Wired Photo—Times Wide World

List of the American Passengers Aboard the Torpedoed Athenia

Special to THE NEW YORK TIMES.

WASHINGTON, Monday, Sept. 4.—The list of American citizens who embarked on the liner Athenia in Liverpool follows; no addresses were given in the cable received at the State Department from Ambassador Joseph P. Kennedy:

Ralph Ruffieau
Katheryn McGuire
Hazel Casserly
Charles Grant
Florence Malik
Edith Bridge
Harry Bridge
Robert Harris
Gustaf Petersen
Margaret Buchan
Laura Cattle
Mrs. Thomas Kerr
Kate Hinds
Herbert Spieleiberg
Mrs. Davis
Margaret McGuire
Elizabeth Wise
William Buchanan
Master Charles Grant
Bernice Jansen
Constance Bridge

Sarah Warenreich
John Hughes
Gertrude Reed
George Cattle
Thomas Kerr
Rhoda Thomas
William Hinds
J. Davis
William Peers
Lillian Peers
Charles Prince
Harold Etherington
Ellen Harrington
Jessie Forie
Francis Cooley
Charles Prince (two Charles Princes)
Geoffrey Etherington
R. Casey
George Keither
Harry Trehearne
Ella Trehearne
Annie Word
Duncan Wood
(Two Duncan Woods)

Joseph MacDonald
Elmetta MacDonald
Harriet Roney
Wendell Sherk
Nicola Lubitsch
Henry Smith
Ellen Smith
Jeannette Smith
Carolina Stuart
Frieda Windmann
Matthew Brown
Mary Brown
Alice Robinsons
Robert Townsend
Bainbridge Hay
Dirus Ekaube
Doris Elaine
Kent William Ralph Singleton
Margaret Moore
Sarah Bloom
Olive Bloom
Fred Tinney
Madeline Tinney
Charles Corterman
Susson Price
Elizabeth Alton (two listed)
Louis Burns
Mary Burns
Harriette Jones
Joan Moffett
Elsie Moffett

Ernest Ratcliffe
Faith Ratcliffe
Irene de Munn
Edward O'Connell
Aileen Philipsen
Mary Steinberg
Ralph Child
Peter Birchall
Duncan Wood
Ellin Ratcliffe
Donald Gifford
Jozef Karnowski
Dorris O'Connel
John Youngquist
Donald Edwards
John Lawrence
Tryphene Humphry
Louise Horte
Mary, Dick and Edward Belton
Elise Philipsen
Adolph Sedowski
Adolph Leocha
Florence Dary
Wikter Poujola

Ethel Russell
William Bohn
Ada Bohn
Montgomery Evans
Franklin Dexter
Cathleen Schurr
Agnes Stappel
Lillian Ellstrap
Rose Churchill
Ellen Howland
Marine Dexter
Maud Shearer
Alexander Sheshunoff
Cosby Eilstrap
Sarah Burdett
Yvette Pepin
Ena Logan
Herbert Bonn
Thomas Quine
Lulu Sweigard
Ramona Allen
Gus Anderson
Eleanor Crowley
Harriet Tolley
Janet Eleen
Annie Quine
Carol Allen
Susan Allen

Gus Anderson
Caroline Rice
William Bown
Ada Bown
Elizabeth Lewis
May Lewis
Donald Lewis
William Aitken
Anne Baker
Alma Bloom
Dorothy Feder
Martha Bonnet
William Brown
George Calder (Two listed)
Margaret Calder
Alice Chalmers
William Chalmers
Margaret Doggett
Eileen Duncombe

The names of the Americans who boarded the Athenia at Belfast could not be obtained up to 5 o'clock this morning.

HIT OFF HEBRIDES

Ship Bound for Canada Carried Some Children Among Americans

CAPITAL IS SHOCKED

President's Aide Notes Liner Had Refugees, Not Munitions

By The Associated Press.

BELFAST, Northern Ireland, Monday, Sept. 4.—All persons aboard the sunken British liner Athenia, except some killed by a German torpedo, were reported saved today.

An agent of the ship's owners here issued the report. He said all survivors had been picked up by other vessels.

By The Associated Press.

LONDON, Monday, Sept. 4.—The British Liner Athenia, with 246 United States citizens among her 1,400 passengers, was torpedoed and sunk 200 miles west of the Hebrides, the British Ministry of Information announced early today. [Washington reports said 292 Americans were aboard the Athenia.]

The United States Embassy, checking on the departures of Americans hurrying home in flight from the European war, said 101 boarded the ship at Liverpool and 145 at Glasgow. [Forty-six more Americans boarded the vessel at Belfast, Washington was informed.]

The Athenia sailed Saturday from Liverpool.

The British Ministry of Information said the 13,581-ton ship had been torpedoed 200 miles off the Hebrides, west of Northern Scotland.

The Ministry of Information said the last official information received by the Admiralty from the ship was that she was sinking "rapidly." Since there were no further advices, it was then assumed she had gone down.

[Stephen Early, secretary to President Roosevelt, said in Washington that official reports indicated the Athenia was carrying "mostly Canadians and some Americans."

["I'd like to point out," he said, according to The Associated Press, "that, according to official information, the ship had gone from Glasgow to Liverpool and was bound for Canada, bringing refugees.

["I point this out to show that there was no possibility, according to official information, that the ship was carrying any munitions or anything of that kind."]

292 Americans Were Aboard

WASHINGTON, Monday, Sept. 4 (AP).—Dispatches to the State Department indicated today that at least 246 [later news brought the figure to 292] Americans were aboard the liner Athenia, torpedoed in the North Atlantic.

White House Is Informed

Special to THE NEW YORK TIMES.

WASHINGTON, Monday, Sept. 4.—Information received here last night that the Cunard White Star liner Athenia had been torpedoed off the coast of Ireland while en route to the United States brought a prompt statement from the White House acknowledging receipt of the news and information from the State Department that it had received eighteen long-distance calls within a few minutes of a radio broadcast of the news. The calls appealed for information about relatives aboard.

The White House said the vessel was bound from Glasgow and Liverpool to Montreal with a large group of Canadian passengers and with an undetermined number of Americans among them. [At 6 A.M. in New York time] Ambassador Joseph P. Kennedy to the State Department cabled as follows:

"Admiralty unable as yet to indicate whether Athenia has sunk or rescue arrangements; 101 American citizens embarked on her at

Continued on Page Five

The Developments in Europe

Britain and France plunged into war yesterday morning and once events began to gather momentum.

The most sensational was the torpedoing and sinking of the British liner Athenia off the Hebrides this morning. She was carrying 1,400 passengers, including 292 Americans, from Liverpool to Montreal. The news shocked the White House. [Page 1.]

On top of this came charges by Poles that the Germans had dropped gas bombs on towns. [Page 1.]

Britain, following her tactics of the last war, quickly blockaded Germany and closed the entrances to the Mediterranean Sea as well. The British public was calm and grimly determined after it had heard Prime Minister Chamberlain gravely announce on the radio that "this country is at war with Germany." [Page 1.] He made the same announcement in the House of Commons, where he immediately received the support of such former opponents as Winston Churchill and David Lloyd George. In a new War Cabinet Mr. Churchill resumed the post of First Lord of the Admiralty, which he had held in the last war; Lord Hankey, the other veteran statesman of that conflict, became Minister Without Portfolio, and Anthony Eden

became Secretary for the Dominions. [Page 5; texts of Mr. Chamberlain's addresses and addresses in the Commons, Page 3.]

In France Premier Daladier, declaring that the responsibility for bloodshed was Chancellor Hitler's, said that France's cause was the cause of justice. [Page 1; text of Daladier's radio speech, Page 8.]

Herr Hitler in a series of statements during the day put the blame for the strife on the British whom he accused of seeking to encircle Germany. He left for the Polish front. [Page 1; texts of these statements, Page 2.]

On that front the Poles were reported to have carried the fighting to German soil in one sector, but were declared to be giving ground in Silesia and at their side. [Page 1.]

Italy still took no step to join her Axis partner in the conflict and it seemed obvious that the British and the French were doing what they could to win her to their side. [Page 1.]

Russia likewise kept a middle-of-the-road position. [Page 6.]

President Roosevelt, in an extraordinary message radioed to "the whole of America," called for national unity as a measure for keeping the Western Hemisphere from becoming embroiled. [Page 1; text of the message, Page 6.]

News dispatches from Europe and the Far East are now virtually all subject to censorship.

The New York Times.

LATE CITY EDITION
Generally fair and cooler today and tonight Tomorrow fair with moderate temperature.
Temperature Yesterday—Max., 84; Min., 64

Section
1

Copyright, 1939, by The New York Times Company.

VOL. LXXXVIII....No. 29,821 | Entered as Second-Class Matter, Postoffice, New York, N. Y. | NEW YORK, SUNDAY, SEPTEMBER 17, 1939. | PPP | Including Rotogravure Picture, Magazine and Book System. | TEN CENTS | TWELVE CENTS Beyond 200 Miles Except in 7th and 8th Postal Zones.

SOVIET TROOPS MARCHED INTO POLAND AT 11 P. M.; NAZIS DEMAND WARSAW GIVE UP OR BE SHELLED; FIERCE BATTLE IS RAGING ON WESTERN FRONT

2 SENATORS BLAST EMBARGO REPEAL AS LEADING TO WAR

Clark, Disavowing Filibuster, Asks Prolonging of Session to Curb Rule by Decree

DEFENDS 'INSULATIONISTS'

Vandenberg Calls Favoring Any Belligerent 'Unneutral' and Urges 'Middle Ground'

By TURNER CATLEDGE
Special to The New York Times.

WASHINGTON, Sept. 16—The fight over lifting the embargo against export of arms was intensified further today as Senators Clark of Missouri and Vandenberg of Michigan aimed new blasts at the Administration's program to alter the Neutrality Act at the special session of Congress.

Following upon the radio address last night of Colonel Lindbergh, the Senators, a Democrat and a Republican, took up Senator Borah's thesis—that the issue was more of intervention or non-intervention in the affairs of Europe than of mere methods of neutrality.

Senator Clark's remarks were contained in a statement telegraphed from his home in St. Louis for release at the capital.

Senator Vandenberg made his plea to his own constituents at a Republican rally at Grand Rapids, telling them not to allow their minds to be taken off domestic problems by the agitation over the conflict abroad.

In his address, Senator Vandenberg declared that the arms embargo should not be repealed by a revision of the present neutrality laws.

"In my view," he said, "it is not 'neutrality' for us to change that code today to make it fit some ill-favored belligerent, no matter what our sympathies. In my view, that is unneutrality. It is trying to be half in this war and yet to safely stay out. I do not believe there can be any such middle ground."

Clark for Check on Executive

"I welcome the President's call for an extraordinary session of the Congress," Senator Clark said in his statement.

"Since the President has by proclamation declared the existence of a national emergency, it is the duty of the Congress to remain in session and share fully in the responsibilities of government during the duration of the national emergency. This is and should remain a government by law and not by decree.

"So far as the Neutrality Act is concerned there has been no suggestion of a 'filibuster' on the part of any of the Senators who oppose the emasculation and perversion of the whole neutrality policy heretofore adopted by the Congress and approved by the President by the repeal of the provision for a mandatory arms embargo.

"The suggestions of a 'filibuster' have been put out in inspired articles from Washington and Hyde Park designed to promote gag rule and stifle free and fair discussion of perhaps the most important question of public policy which has confronted the Congress of the United States since that tragic day in 1917 when the decision was made to throw the United States into the World War.

Sees Decision on 'Taking Sides'

"We are now to determine whether or not we have learned anything from that awful experience by deciding whether by repealing the arms embargo we shall again deliberately set our feet on the path which inevitably leads to war.

"Those of us who oppose the abandonment of a bona fide neutrality policy stand precisely where President Roosevelt stood in his eloquent Chautauqua speech in 1936 when he was a candidate for re-election when he said in defending the law containing a mandatory arms embargo:

"'We are not isolationists except in so far as we seek to isolate ourselves completely from war.'

"My friend, Senator Elbert Thomas of Utah, one of the leading revisionists, let the cat out of the bag the other night as to the real point"

Continued on Page Thirty-seven

White House Gate Closed To Keep Out Trysting Cars

Special to The New York Times.

WASHINGTON, Sept. 16—Neither wars nor rumors of wars, but the popularity among motorists of the White House grounds on Summer nights is the reason one of the iron gates on Pennsylvania Avenue is now closed after dark and a guard stands at the other, day and night, to tell all comers that only those having appointments may park their cars inside.

People have been driving in, especially at night, and parking there, Mrs. Roosevelt revealed at a press conference today. And though it is a pleasant place to sit, under the trees, the White House driveway is really not a good trysting place, she said. Too many motorists were attracted by it.

As the number of parking parties increased, so did the problem of keeping the driveway open and free of obstruction. Now an extra all-night guard is on duty, from dark to dawn, to keep it so.

LATIN TRIP FOR FAIR PLEDGED BY MAYOR

'If They Want Me to Go, I Am Going,' He Says—Crowds Set New Record for Saturday

By SIDNEY M. SHALETT

Clarifying his position as the possible World's Fair ambassador of good-will to South America, Mayor La Guardia, in one statement yesterday, agreed that he would go "if necessary," but hinted that the trip might not take place for at least several months.

There was even a third statement issued by Stanley Howe, the Mayor's executive secretary, to settle the "incident" created Friday night when Grover A. Whalen, Fair president, announced in the Mayor's absence that Mr. La Guardia would fly "at an early date" to sell the United States' neighbors to the South on the idea of participating in the 1940 exposition.

As Mr. Howe viewed it, the Mayor would like, with permission of the State Department, to make a trip both to sell South American nations on the 1940 Fair and to "unsell" them on any totalitarian ideas that may have crept in.

These matters yesterday were exceedingly important to the administrators who run the Fair, but despite all the flurry about South American envoys and European participation the Fair itself was entertaining the biggest Saturday crowd in its history. From early morning on thousands of visitors streamed past the turnstiles, and early in the evening it became evident that a new record for a Saturday would be set.

The Mayor issued his first statement shortly after noon, after a hurried dash from the World's Fair City Hall to Hoboken to see Mr. Whalen off on the Statendam. The Fair president, who had made the announcement Friday in which the Mayor did not fully concur, was sailing for Europe as salesman for the 1940 Fair.

Boat Held Up for Mayor

Arriving at the dock only four minutes before sailing time, Mayor La Guardia induced the captain to hold up the boat until he could hurry aboard, have a word with Mr. Whalen and pose with him for a farewell picture. It was such an eleventh-hour affair that the last gangplank was partly dismantled and had to be made secure again before the Mayor and his retinue could leave the ship.

Then, on the pier, the Mayor gave out the following statement concerning his South American plans:

"There are a great many preliminaries. If it can do the Fair any good, and if these necessary preliminaries can be made, and if there is a real need, I'll go. But there is nothing definite yet."

Then he whisked off in his car. His next appearance, late in the afternoon, was at a ceremony of the United Spanish War Veterans in the Court of Peace at the Fair. There he was asked again if he would fly south, and this time he made it a little stronger.

"I'll do anything that is helpful and necessary for the World's Fair," the Mayor said. "If they want me to go, I am going. Of course, that requires a good deal of preliminary preparation and is"

Continued on Page Forty-eight

6 U. S. SHIPS KEPT IN PORT AS SEAMEN HOLD OUT FOR PAY

Stalemate Results Over War Risk Insurance Demands— No Solution Seen Near

FRIED CALLS 12 SAILORS

Plans Inquiry on Tie-Up of American Trader—Owners Say Capital Must Act

American merchant shipping was badly hampered in New York harbor yesterday when the crews of six vessels refused to sail their ships, insisting on concrete concessions to their demands for extra compensation for entering European waters affected by the war.

With Federal agencies already overburdened by the unusual duties laid on them as a result of the war, confusion reigned on the waterfront, and at a late hour there appeared to be little chance of solution or compromise.

Two of the ships, one with passengers, were to have sailed Friday afternoon but their crews staged a sit-down strike after signing the ship's articles. In other cases, the men declined to sign the articles, leaving vessels with no manning force.

Fried Sends Out Summonses

On the United States liner American Trader, which was at the Chelsea piers of the company with passengers and cargo, twelve union men received summonses from the office of Captain George Fried, supervising inspector of the Bureau of Marine Inspection and Navigation.

The summons in each case was returnable immediately at 45 Broadway, but a representative of the National Maritime Union appeared in the men's stead and received an adjournment until 10 A. M. tomorrow, allowing the union time to obtain counsel for them.

Captain Fried had boarded the American Trader on Friday night and had been at the piers yesterday, but he declined to reveal the nature of the charges to be filed against the men, saying that the public would be admitted to the hearing.

He also declined to explain why only twelve of the seventy seamen had been called, or to say how they had been selected.

Will Set Up Special Board

He planned to constitute a "C" board to preside at the inquiry, headed by himself and including Captain Karl Nielsen and Howard C. Bridges, inspectors of the district. The "C" board would sit in the same manner as a grand jury, to determine if charges should be filed against the men.

The National Maritime Union, which has disclaimed responsibility for the strike on the American Trader, issued

Continued on Page Forty-six

Blast Shakes Offices Of Reich Air Ministry

By The Associated Press.

BERLIN, Sunday, Sept. 17—An explosion occurred in the Air Ministry headquarters on the Leipzigerstrasse early today. Firemen and police closed off an extensive area around the building.

The Propaganda Ministry acknowledged that there had been an explosion, but no immediate explanation was forthcoming. It was reported that no one had been injured. There was shattered glass in the street, but the extent of the damage was not immediately apparent.

The Propaganda Ministry refused to speculate whether the blast might have been caused by a bomb. It said merely that an investigation was under way.

"The persons responsible are being sought energetically," a Propaganda Ministry spokesman declared.

The blast came during the regular nightly blackout and the streets were deserted.

TOKYO MINIMIZES SOVIET AGREEMENT

Denies Non-Aggression Pact Is to Follow Truce—Policy on Russia Is Held Unchanged

By HUGH BYAS
Wireless to The New York Times.

TOKYO, Sept. 16—Japanese officials emphatically deny and characterize as "absolute nonsense" reports that a non-aggression pact with Russia is under negotiation or is contemplated. They also deny that Germany had a hand in arranging the armistice on the Manchukuoan-Mongolian border or that German influence could induce Japan to change her policy toward the Soviet.

The Japanese Government regards the armistice as a means of terminating the border fighting. It is part of the new Cabinet's policy for a speedy settlement of the China "incident." Nor does it assure peace on the Mongolian frontier, it is asserted, but it shows Generalissimo Chiang Kai-shek that he cannot expect further diversions in the north, and it helps demonstrate that the Soviet has lost faith in the possibility of a Chinese victory.

According to Domei, the Japanese news agency, the armistice is a definite help toward a settlement in China by enabling Japan to devote her entire power to the impending peace moves. When asked what Russia receives, the Japanese answer is that she wins a cessation of potentially serious disputes with Japan and possibly certain territorial concessions during the forced adjustment.

On the broader question whether the armistice is a first step toward a revolutionary realignment of world forces, officials suggest that the move is adequately explained

Continued on Page Thirty-two

Major Sports Yesterday

BASEBALL

The Yankees clinched their fourth consecutive American League pennant under Manager Joe McCarthy and equaled the record set by John McGraw's Giants of 1921 to 1924. It was the eleventh flag victory for the New Yorkers, who beat the Tigers at the Stadium, 8–5. The second-place Red Sox lost. In Cincinnati the Reds halted the Giants, 6–1, and maintained their lead of three and a half games over the victorious Cards.

GOLF

Marvin (Bud) Ward of Spokane defeated Ray Billows of Poughkeepsie, N. Y., 7 and 5, to win the national amateur championship on the North Shore Country Club links, Glenview, Ill. Ward is the first Pacific Coast golfer to take the title.

TENNIS

Welby Van Horn upset John Bromwich, 2–6, 6–4, 6–3, 2–6, 8–6, to gain the final of the national singles championship with Robert L. Riggs, who eliminated Joe Hunt, 6–1, 6–2, 6–4, 6–1. Miss Alice Marble and Miss Helen Jacobs entered the women's final.

HORSE RACING

Hash won the Edgemere Handicap at Aqueduct, where Merry Knight annexed the Junior Champion Stakes. At Chicago, Challedon captured the Hawthorne Gold Cup. Fandale took the Foxcatcher National Cup Steeplechase at Fair Hill, Md.

POLO

The Bostwick Field four beat Westbury, 9–6, in the first match of the national open tournament.

(Complete Details of These and Other Sports Events in Section 5.)

GERMANS SET BACK

Heavy Counter-Attacks Repulsed by the French Drive

NAZIS BLAST TOWNS

Gamelin Hits at Three Points in Saar Area, Hardest on Moselle

By G. H. ARCHAMBAULT
Wireless to The New York Times.

PARIS, Sept. 16—The Germans are bringing up more and more troops on the western front, where the fighting grows fiercer daily. That is the salient point in the French headquarters communiqué today. This morning's bulletin, Communiqué 25, said:

"There was a restless night on numerous parts of the front. Enemy artillery was very active in the region east of Saarbruecken.

"Our troops made some progress east of the Moselle.

"A strong enemy counter-attack, following artillery preparation, was driven back in the region near the lower valley of the Nied River."

This evening Communiqué 26 announced:

"There was great activity on both sides on the part of artillery and of first-line troops on the entire front.

"The enemy is constantly reinforcing before us.

"At several points the enemy abandoned and destroyed several of his villages from which he had retreated."

Battle West of Saarbruecken

The heaviest fighting at present is on that portion of the front running some twenty miles west of Saarbruecken. The object is the possession of observation points dominating not only the Saar Valley but also certain parts of the Westwall.

The specific purpose of the German attack near the River Nied, which is a tributary of the Saar, is to regain a number of observation points along the plateau from which the town of Saarlautern can be brought under the fire of French guns.

After artillery preparation the German infantry left its cover for a swift attack. The duration of this preparation, however, had sufficiently indicated to the French that the French guns came into action as soon as the infantry got on the move and the attack was soon stopped. It is reported that the Germans employed a relatively large force for this attempt.

There is also heavy fighting for the establishment of the Saar bridgeheads. The possession of the banks of the river at divers points is important for the bringing up of heavy tanks.

That the Germans should be bringing up reinforcements continuously, as reported in the evening communiqué, may imply the intention of attempting stronger counter-attacks than any hitherto. It was suggested an endeavor to wrest the initiative from the French. It is manifest that important developments may be expected soon.

Three Main Sectors

As the second week of the war ends, the operations on the west front are clearly divided into three main sectors. These are, reading the map from the east to the west:

1. From the Rhine, in the vicinity of Lauterbourg to the highway from Zweibruecken to Bitche.

2. From this highway to a point on the Saar north of Forbach, taking in Saarbruecken, the industrial heart of the Saarland.

3. From this point west of Saarbruecken to the Moselle River in the vicinity of the village of Perl.

In two of these three sectors French troops are operating on German soil.

At the beginning of the hostilities the eastern sector was the most active, with the French occupation of the forest called Bienwald, in order to gain ground at the point where the Maginot Line and the Westwall describe a right angle before following the Rhine Valley southward. In that valley itself scarcely a shot has been fired as yet; the garrisons of the respective fortified lines are merely sentries.

Continued on Page Forty-six

The International Situation

A Poland already tottering under the blows of the German military machine was subjected to another invasion last night, this time by Soviet forces, according to an official announcement in Berlin.

It was declared that the Russian Government had informed the Polish Ambassador that it was marching in "to protect its own interests and to protect the White Russian and Ukrainian minorities."

Nevertheless, Moscow said, Soviet neutrality is being maintained. Berlin said the action had German sanction. [Page 1.]

The German sweep in Poland was unabated. Kutno, Bialystok and Przemysl fell. But at Warsaw the invaders were still encountering ferocious resistance. As a result they issued an ultimatum to the Poles to quit Warsaw within twelve hours or pain of bombardment of the entire city. [Page 1.] The effects of previous bombardments and air raids on the Polish countryside were described by a correspondent, who found towns in flames, inhabitants wailing over ruins of homes and chaos everywhere. [Page 28.] In general, military experts found that Poland's despair was undermining her resistance. [Page 40.]

Meanwhile, the "Battle of the Saar," snowballing daily into a major engagement, was being fiercely fought. The French reported that after a heavy artillery exchange the Germans had destroyed and abandoned several villages and had retreated. [Page 1.]

In the face of continued harrying of commerce by German submarines, which yesterday sank two more British ships, the Admiralty set up a convoy service for merchant vessels. [Page 1.] Three South American countries, Argentina, Brazil and Uruguay, fearing violations of their neutrality by belligerent warships, were negotiating to pool their naval strength for protection of the entire east coast of South America. [Page 31.]

The full significance of the Russo-Japanese truce on the Mongolian frontier was still unclear, as was Germany's role, if any, in its conclusion. Japanese officials emphatically denied reports that a non-aggression pact with Russia would follow, insisting that Japan would remain an anti-Comintern power. [Page 1.] But one result of the new truce that the Japanese, freed of fears for the Manchukuoan border, had launched a general offensive in Central China. [Page 30.] In London news of the truce was received with equanimity; statesmen there had become accustomed to surprises from Moscow. [Page 34.]

In this country Senators Clark and Vandenberg rallied to Senator Borah's fight against alteration of the Neutrality Act. [Page 1.]

MERCHANT CONVOYS SET UP BY BRITAIN

Guard Pressed After Her Loss of 21 Ships—Three More Vessels Are Victims

By The Associated Press.

LONDON, Sept. 16—The British Admiralty pressed into service tonight convoys for merchant shipping after it was disclosed authoritatively that enemy craft had sunk twenty-one British ships, involving a tonnage of 122,863, during the first two weeks of the war.

The use of convoys was not instituted by the British in the last war until 1917.

While slim cruisers and racing destroyers roved and struck on the shipping lanes, planes of the Royal Aircraft patrolled the skies around the United Kingdom in redoubled efforts to halt the persistent shipping losses to U-boats or mines.

Despite the casualties, naval quarters expressed optimism about the situation at sea.

Understatement in Reports

Increasing patrol activity and the Admiralty's cautious announcement that "a number of U-boats have been destroyed," was taken by naval authorities to tell a story of far greater successes than the guarded statement indicated.

Britain placed responsibility on Germany for the sinking last night of the 5,000-ton Belgian motorship Alex Van Opstal in the Channel off Weymouth, asserting she was sunk by mine or torpedo in violation of international law.

[In Brussels, Belgian authorities refrained from lodging a protest, pending a report from the master of the vessel as to whether she was sunk by torpedo or mine.]

A British communiqué said there were no British mines in the neighborhood, that Germany had sent no notification of German mines there and that that attack without warning was in violation of the submarine protocol to which Germany subscribed.

[The Alex Van Opstal left New York on Sept. 6 for Antwerp with eight passengers and 3,400 tons of grain.]

The latest ship to be added to the list of British losses was the tanker Cheyenne of the Anglo-American Oil Con., any, which was announced officially to have been attacked and sunk by a submarine off the southwest coast of Ireland.

[The Anglo-American Oil Company, according to Poor's Manual]

Continued on Page Forty-six

ORDER GIVES POLES 12 HOURS TO LEAVE

Nazis Say Citizens Will Have to Take 'Consequences' Today Since Army Is Defiant

Wireless to The New York Times.

BERLIN, Sept. 16—The German Army High Command has given Warsaw until 3:10 o'clock tomorrow morning to decide whether or not to surrender. In the event the Polish capital does not give in to the German troops now surrounding it on all sides, the city will "take full consequences of being regarded as a military sector."

[The German High Command reported at 4:30 o'clock this morning, an hour and twenty minutes after expiration of the ultimatum, that its army in the field had had no word from the Polish authorities. The Associated Press reported.]

Warsaw's reply to a first German ultimatum of a double ultimatum: First, a military ultimatum expiring at 3:10 o'clock tomorrow morning, and the second ultimatum to the civilian population to leave the city by 3:10 o'clock in the afternoon (10:10 A. M. New York time.)

A German officer entered Warsaw with a white flag at 8 o'clock this morning to demand the surrender of the city. According to the report of the official German News Agency the commandant of the city refused to see him or accept a written demand for the surrender of the city.

The officer, it is stated, thereupon returned to the German lines and this afternoon a squadron of the German air force distributed the pamphlets.

Nazis Cite Law Violation

Warsaw already has been subjected to a partial bombardment by the German air force and artillery but, according to German report, only objects of a military nature have been fired upon. Preparations for defense by the civilian population, however, are regarded by the German High Command as being a "violation of international law depriving the city of its character as an open city." German shells and German bombs will crash into the city tomorrow afternoon unless it is "surrendered without resistance" by that hour.

"The patience of the German Army is now exhausted," states the official news agency. "The German Army is no longer willing to observe inactively the conditions which are a slap in the face of all international law, but is determined to put an end to these activities of the Warsaw power holders which, though of no importance whatever in a military sense, constitute a

Continued on Page Forty

FRONTIER CROSSED

Reich Ministry States That Invasion Has German Sanction

ENVOY IS NOTIFIED

Soviet Pleads Need to Aid Minorities, but Claims Neutrality

By The United Press.

BERLIN, Sunday, Sept. 17—A spokesman for the Propaganda Ministry announced that Russian troops had marched into Poland today at 4 A. M. Moscow time (11 P. M. Saturday in New York).

The Soviet troops entered Poland with the full knowledge and approval of the German Government, he said.

The spokesman made his statement after D. N. B., the official German news agency, had reported from Moscow that the Soviet Government had informed the Polish Ambassador, Dr. Waclaw Grzybowski, Saturday night that Soviet troops were about to cross the frontier.

The agency said that the note handed to the Ambassador informed the Poles that the troops would cross the frontier along its entire length from Polesk in the north to Kamieniec-Podolski in the south in order to protect our own interests and to protect the White Russian and Ukrainian minorities."

The Soviet Government, the agency said, told the Poles that it maintained its neutrality despite its military action, but that treaties with the Polish State could be regarded as canceled because the Polish State could no longer be regarded as existing.

To Occupy Two Districts

MOSCOW, Sunday, Sept. 17 (UP)—Soviet Russia has decided to send her army across the Polish frontier today and to occupy the Polish Ukraine and White Russia.

The government was understood here saying that the Red Army would enter the Polish Ukraine and White Russia today from Polesk to Kamieniec-Podolski.

Copies of this note were said to have been sent simultaneously to all diplomatic representatives here saying the action was taken because Poland no longer exists. It was said to have declared there no longer is a Polish Government because its whereabouts are unknown.

The note was said to have declared that "the Soviet Union will retain strict neutrality, but feels it necessary to protect White Russian and Ukrainian minorities in Poland and will do everything to keep peace and order."

[Poland not only has a non-aggression pact with Russia, but in mutual assistance treaties by which the British and French are pledged to aid Poland in defense of her independence against any aggression. Polish invocation of this treaty brought Great Britain and France into war against Germany on Sept. 3, two days after a German army invaded Western Poland.]

Covers Entire Frontier

The scene of the Russian action would extend across the whole of Russia's Polish frontier.

It would increase considerably Russia's frontier with Rumania. Rumania holds Bessarabia, wrested from Russia after the World War, and the Soviet Government never has relinquished its claims on this territory.

Russia's decision to act came after she had sent a vast number of men to her western frontier in semi-mobilization and had followed with her "peace" pact with Japan.

It was believed here that the Polish Embassy in Moscow would leave and that, possibly, the British also would leave, since they are allies of Poland.

Man Power Is Threat

If necessary, Soviet Russia could throw nearly 3,000,000 trained soldiers against the struggling Poles.

The official Communist party newspaper Pravda this Spring estimated Russia's peacetime army at 1,500,000. This estimate did not include the millions of semi-trained

Continued on Page Thirty-six

Dispatches from Europe and the Far East are now subject to censorship.

The New York Times.

Copyright, 1939, by The New York Times Company.

VOL. LXXXIX...No. 29,895.

Entered as Second-Class Matter, Postoffice, New York, N. Y.

NEW YORK, THURSDAY, NOVEMBER 30, 1939.

P

THREE CENTS NEW YORK CITY and Vicinity | FOUR CENTS Elsewhere Except in 7th and 8th Postal Zones

RUSSIANS START THEIR INVASION OF FINLAND; PLANES DROP BOMBS ON AIRFIELD AT HELSINKI; WAR STARTS AS U. S. MOVE FOR PEACE IS MADE

KUHN FOUND GUILTY ON ALL FIVE COUNTS; HE FACES 30 YEARS

Leader of the Bund Here Will Be Sentenced Tuesday as Thief and Forger

JURY OUT FOR 8½ HOURS

Defense Counsel Rebuked by the Court as Clashes Mark Final Day of Trial

Fritz Kuhn, the leader of the German-American Bund, was convicted shortly after 10 o'clock last night of grand larceny and forgery in General Sessions Court.

He stood up, with only his forefinger on his left hand waving along the side seam of his trousers, and heard without a blink the verdict of a jury that had deliberated eight and a half hours. The maximum sentence he can receive is thirty years, and the day on which he will hear his fate was set by Judge James G. Wallace as Tuesday.

Pending the sentence Judge Wallace told Peter L. F. Sabbatino, the counsel who had defended Kuhn during his trial in General Sessions Court, that action on a promised contempt of court would be suspended until then. He gave Mr. Sabbatino leave to make any motions he desired in the intervening time.

Kuhn marched off to the Tombs with the stolical attitude of a good German soldier, which he says he once was. There was no tremor on his face, and the three courtroom bailiffs who surrounded him when Morris C. Bullock, the foreman of the jury, pronounced him guilty, had only to tug at his sleeve to lead him away to prison. There was not even an interchange of glances between him and Mr. Sabbatino or Wilbur V. Keegan, associate counsel.

What the Verdict Meant

The verdict was that he was guilty of grand larceny in the first and second degree in the theft of $717 from the bund to pay for the transportation of the furniture of Mrs. Florence Camp across the country, and of second degree larceny and two counts of forgery in the "Murray transaction."

The Murray transaction was a $500 item which Kuhn listed on the bund books of record and told the bund members that he had paid to James D. C. Murray for legal services. These two items, totaling $1,217, were all that the jury had to pass on of an indictment which originally charged thefts amounting to more than $14,000.

One pair of counts, dealing with more than $5,000 charged against Kuhn as a theft had been eliminated before the trial began and Judge Wallace knocked out another pair charging that he had stolen $4,424 of the bund funds because, the Judge ruled, the prosecution had not proved this beyond a reasonable doubt.

During a long afternoon and early evening while the jury was out, Kuhn sat in the court room talking to his counsel. He had sandwiches brought in to him and munched on them while Assistant District Attorney Herman J. McCarthy, who prosecuted him, walked the corridors of the Criminal Courts Building.

The precaution of three men surrounding the man who says his war record covered service as a machine gunner in Alpine service during the World War I was not necessary. He made no move and there was no sign of emotion on his face.

The index finger of his left hand wiggled spasmodically. But he did not even move his hand.

Then, in a voice that was not even audible a few feet away, he gave his "pedigree" to a bailiff. He said he was born in Germany forty-two years ago and revealed

Continued on Page Twelve

Must Stay Day in Mexico Or Pay San Diego Duties

Special to The New York Times.

WASHINGTON, Nov. 29 — The twenty-four hour limit goes into effect Friday on the Mexican border in the San Diego Customs District and persons wishing to avail themselves of the $100 customs exemption on goods brought into this country must stay in Mexico at least twenty-four hours. Collectors have been instructed that in their discretion they may permit tourists staying a shorter time to bring in goods with an aggregate value of not more than $5 without paying duty.

The unusual situation in the San Diego district is created by the proximity of the Free Port of Tijuana, into which European merchandise may enter duty-free. Large retail establishments there maintain billboards along the roads to Tijuana advertising bargains on selected European imports.

CITY WILL SET UP A 'BOOSTER' BUREAU

Mayor Reveals Plans for New Department to Attract More Business Here

Reviewing the accomplishments of his administration before a gathering of merchants and property owners yesterday, Mayor La Guardia disclosed plans for still another project for the betterment of the city—a Department of Commerce—to bring more business and industry here.

He told the Central Mercantile Association at its Fall luncheon in the Hotel Pennsylvania that he had often boosted New York on his frequent flights out of town and that now he would have a municipal organization for this purpose. "And I am going to out-small-town the smallest town in the country."

Will Combat Adverse Reports

"We have been confronted with a lot of small-town stuff about business in New York being more costly than elsewhere," he then went on. "I am going to out-small-town the smallest town in the country. I am going to establish a Department of Commerce which will have the function of providing information and advice to business men interested in coming to New York."

The Mayor's bureau will add no cost to the city government, he said, because he will "pick up employees from various city departments to do the work." He also will invite business and labor here to cooperate, he said, adding that "labor will have to assume its responsibility and I expect it to do its part."

The first step in the functioning of such a new program, the Mayor said, has already been taken in his invitation to the film industry to return to New York. He said there was no reason why this industry should be centered in our city "but we should have our share." He reported that, "notwithstanding ridicule and opposition, we are making progress."

Ryan Seen as Likely Head

A report that a municipal department of commerce would be established was published last Sunday but had not been publicly acknowledged by the Mayor until yesterday. The report said that Clendenin J. Ryan, Deputy Commissioner of Sanitation, would head the new department and would be sworn in as the first Commissioner this week.

In his address, lasting for more than an hour, the Mayor dwelt particularly on his new pension plan for policemen and firemen. The establishment of the plan was prompted by the fact that any pension plan in existence July 1, 1940, will, under constitutional amendment, become a contractual obligation of the city.

The Mayor noted that the Legislature had failed to put the policemen and firemen pension system on a

Continued on Page Twelve

DIES AT RALLY HERE WARNS U.S. TO STOP ITS 'APING' OF EUROPE

10,000 Cheer His Plea for National Unity and a Fight on All Alien Forces

HE PLEADS FOR TOLERANCE

Calls on Administration to Provide Funds to Continue Work of His Committee

Speaking last night in Madison Square Garden before an enthusiastic throng estimated at 10,000 to 12,000 persons, representing many patriotic and religious organizations, Representative Martin Dies of Texas denounced communism, fascism and nazism as alien forces tearing at American unity. He made a strong plea also for racial and religious tolerance.

Asserting that there was an organized campaign to discredit the work of the Congressional Committee Investigating un-American Activities which he heads, Mr. Dies made a demand for public funds with which to continue the investigation into subversive groups next year. He also called on the Administration, which he implied was opposed to the committee, to come out openly and say whether or not it favored the drive against foreign "isms."

On this question Mr. Dies got strong support from the audience and from the other speakers, who urged those present to demand from Congress an appropriation that would preserve the committee as it is.

The husky, 6-foot Representative who has achieved national prominence since he was named chairman of the committee in 1938 was escorted to the platform by a guard of American Legionnaires while the drums of the Seventh Regiment band announced him with a fanfare.

Mr. Dies had reviewed the difficulties of city finance, education costs, the new pension plan for policemen and firemen, the Sixth Avenue improvement, transit unification, plans for Ninth and Second Avenues, the North Beach Airport and the new information bureau under the Park Avenue ramp in Pershing Square, not mentioning other accomplishments.

As chairman of the meeting, Merwin K. Hart, president of the New York State Economic Council, opened the meeting at 8:30 P. M. Frederick Jagel of the Metropolitan Opera sang the "Star-Spangled Banner," although he advocates the adoption of a new anthem for the United States.

Among those who attended, it was reported but not confirmed, were

Continued on Page Seven

Intelligence Chief Quits; Dutch Blame Venloo Case

Wireless to The New York Times.

AMSTERDAM, the Netherlands, Nov. 29—Major Gen. J. W. van Oorschot, 64-year-old head of the Netherlands intelligence service, resigned today. He had headed the department since 1919.

Observers are inclined to link his resignation with the Venloo frontier incident.

THE HAGUE, the Netherlands, Nov. 29 (UP)—The Venloo incident involved the shooting of a Netherlands intelligence officer, Lieutenant Klop, and the kidnapping of two British intelligence agents and a chauffeur by German Gestapo (secret police) agents. General J. W. van Oorschot, who resigned today, was responsible for sending Lieutenant Klop to Venloo.

The British version of the incident was that two British intelligence officers, Sigismund Payne Best and Captain Richard Henry Stevens, went to Venloo to investigate presumably legitimate German peace talk on Nov. 9.

REICH OIL SITUATION VIEWED AS CRITICAL

Germany Isolated From Great Sources of Supply—Imports From U. S. Virtually Ended

Special to The New York Times.

WASHINGTON, Nov. 29—The oil situation in Germany, especially the Reich's reserve of fuel oils, is the most serious problem facing the Hitler government today, in the opinion of American naval and military experts. Export data in the Department of Commerce appear to substantiate this opinion.

Germany is one of the few great nations without oil resources and since the war started she has received virtually no crude, lubricating or gasoline supplies from the United States. One market that under normal conditions would be in a position to make up at least part of the deficit.

Official statistics, plus reports considered reliable, all indicate that Germany is completely isolated from the great oil markets of the world. So grave is the situation that Germany is making frantic efforts to develop synthetic gasoline plants, which, it is hoped, may be in partial operation by the middle of 1940. Even the Germans do not expect the plants to be operating to capacity before the end of 1941.

Any hopes the Germans might have of getting appreciable quantities of oil from the Russian fields are dispelled, according to official information, by the fact that Russia is having a hard time producing enough for her own needs. This is

Continued on Page Seven

HULL ACTS QUICKLY

Offer of Good Offices in Ending Dispute Sent to Finland and Russia

HELSINKI LIKELY TO AGREE

But Moscow's Reaction Is Held to Be Highly Problematical —Pittman Assails Soviet

U. S. Offer Received

By The United Press.

MOSCOW, Thursday, Nov. 30—The United States' offer to mediate in the Soviet-Finnish dispute was received at the American Embassy here at 10:30 A. M. (3:30 A. M. Eastern Standard Time).

The offer will be presented or delivered to the Soviet Foreign Office some time this morning by Walter Thurston, Chargé d'Affaires.

By BERTRAM D. HULEN

Special to The New York Times.

WASHINGTON, Nov. 29—The increasingly serious developments in relations between Russia and Finland led the United States today to proclaim her readiness to extend good offices for a pacific adjustment of the points at issue, if that should be agreeable to both parties.

The move was made in an effort to leave no stone unturned that would prevent a spread of European hostilities. It was in the form of a statement issued by Secretary of State Cordell Hull after several telephone conversations with President Roosevelt. In particular, it represented their views of a way in which the American Government could throw its weight into the scales for peace after consideration had been given in the State Department to possible courses of action.

The text of the statement follows:

This government is following with serious concern the intensification of the Finnish-Soviet dispute. It would view with extreme regret any extension of the present area of war and the consequent further deterioration of international relations.

Without in any way becoming involved in the merits of the dispute, and limiting its interest to the solution of the dispute by peaceful processes only, this government would, if agreeable to both parties, gladly extend its good offices.

Text Is Cabled to Envoys

The force of a diplomatic appeal was given the statement when Secretary Hull late yesterday cabled the text to the United States Legation in Finland and the United States Embassy in Russia with instructions that it be delivered to the Foreign Offices.

The statement was issued at 3:05 P. M., one hour before word was received of Russia's severance of diplomatic relations with Finland, and an hour and a half before the press carried reports of the speech of Vyacheslaff M. Molotoff, Soviet Premier and Foreign Commissar.

In comment on the statement the State Department said it did not constitute intervention, nor did it necessarily mean mediation. It simply meant, it was stated, that this government is using what efforts it can to help Russia and Finland settle the dispute themselves.

Although Secretary Hull merely expressed a readiness to extend good offices if Russia and Finland are agreeable, his action threw open the possibility of an adjustment that might be worked out along any one of several lines. An offer of good offices, mediation and arbitration are the three recognized methods for pacific adjustment of disputes under The Hague convention of 1907 and have been used on many occasions, particularly in Latin America.

In the case of an offer of good offices the country making the tender sets no limitations upon the form that will be used in seeking to facilitate an adjustment. It could be by diplomatic conversation, mediation, arbitration, reference to a commission of inquiry or any other method. The country making the tender, moreover, usually does not figure in the ad-

Continued on Page Three

The International Situation

Soviet Russia severed diplomatic relations with Finland last night and this morning the Red Army crossed the border while Soviet planes bombed the airfield at Helsinki. Explaining the break over the radio, Premier Molotoff said that Finnish hostility had become "unbearable," and virtually demanded that a different government be set up in Helsinki. He also indicated rejection of a tender of good offices by the United States. [Page 1.] This offer had been made by Secretary Hull after he had been in touch with President Roosevelt. [Page 1.]

Finland, meanwhile, revealed that the Russian action had been taken before she had delivered a note to the Kremlin offering to withdraw forces from the border and suggesting conciliation. [Page 1.]

London evinced friendliness for the Finns and welcomed the news of the American offer. [Page 5.] Likewise Italy, fearing that near-by Rumania might next claim Russia's attention, expressed through her press sympathy for the Finns. [Page 7.] Germany, on the other hand, supported Russia, although she indicated that her attitude if a conflict began would be one of "benevolent neutrality." [Page 4.]

Japan, a possible sufferer from the hostilities at sea, studied measures of reprisal against the Anglo-French blockade of German exports. It was reported that such measures might include seizure of Allied cargoes in the Orient. [Page 1.]

In the Balkans the Rumanian Foreign Minister turned down Hungary's revisionist demands, but at the same time invited her to help improve relations between the two countries. [Page 10.]

Today Premier Daladier will go before the French Parliament and ask, with every expectation of success, that his emergency powers be continued. [Page 9.]

The Reich's most serious problem of the moment, according to Washington experts, is its critical oil situation. Germany was revealed as completely isolated from the world's oil markets. [Page 1.]

There was little actual war activity during the day. The British reported having driven off two German air raid attempts. [Page 2.] The French said one of their patrols had penetrated deep into German territory in the Vosges sector and had brought back valuable information. [Page 8.] And at sea two more British ships were sunk. [Page 3.]

JAPAN MAY SEIZE CARGOES OF ALLIES

Studies Plan for Reprisals if Anglo-French Ban on Reich Exports Continues

By HUGH BYAS

Wireless to The New York Times.

TOKYO, Thursday, Nov. 30—The Japanese Government is considering retaliatory measures against Great Britain's two-way blockade of Germany. These might include seizure of Anglo-French ship cargoes in Far Eastern waters.

This threat appears in the newspaper Nichi Nichi this morning as part of its report of a conference held at the Foreign Office yesterday to discuss the British reply to Ambassador Mamoru Shigemitsu's protest against the Order in Council for seizure of German exports on neutral ships.

Reports from other sources indicate that interference with Anglo-French shipping in the Far East still is a somewhat distant possibility, depending on the British response to Japan's demand for special consideration of her German imports. Asahi says that Mr. Shigemitsu has been instructed to press the British Government to give assurances that Japanese trade will receive special consideration in enforcement of the blockade.

The Foreign Office conference in which Foreign Minister Kichisaburo Nomura, Vice Foreign Minister Masayuki Tani and several bureau chiefs participated, found the British order had been formulated in flexible terms so that its effect could not be ascertained until it has been enforced. It was decided to await the text and to continue the policy of pressing Britain to give consideration to Japan's "important" imports from Germany.

In comment on the statement the British representations to Britain are disregarded, a further measure will be considered in the terms of Japan's original protest, which threatened appropriate countermeasures.

Norway Adds Her Protest

OSLO, Norway, Nov. 29 (UP)—Foreign Minister Halvdan Koht announced today that the Norwegian Government has made representations to the Allied Governments regarding their decision to seize German exports.

The Norwegian Government, Mr. Koht said, "fails to see how such a move can be in accord with international law." He added that Norway claimed the right to demand compensation for any losses involved, and urged Great Britain to reconsider her decision. Norway is

Continued on Page Three

BORDER IS CROSSED

Soviet Artillery Opens Fire as Troops March in Karelian Sector

AIR RAID WARNING SOUNDED

People Run to Shelters as the Capital Sees Russian Planes —Five Bombs Are Dropped

Special Cable to The New York Times.

COPENHAGEN, Denmark, Thursday, Nov. 30—At 9:15 A. M. today the first Russian troops crossed the Karelian frontier into Finland. At 9:20 o'clock an air raid warning was sounded in Helsinki, causing panic in the streets.

At 9:25 o'clock Russian bombers flew over the Finnish capital.

Five Bombs Dropped

HELSINKI, Finland, Nov. 30 (UP)—Five bombs were dropped on the city's airfield today. A report from the border station at Terijoki said Russian troops had opened artillery fire against the Finns early this morning.

Terijoki is on the Karelian Isthmus, twenty-two miles from Leningrad.

The bombing of Helsinki occurred a few minutes after a Russian two-motored airplane flew over the city, driving people to shelter.

Earlier, a squadron of six Russian airplanes had been sighted over the Gulf of Finland, approaching the city.

Finnish anti-aircraft guns fired on the squadron as well as on the single plane over the capital. Finnish anti-aircraft batteries fired on the plane here and coastal batteries attacked the Russian squadron in the gulf.

Molotoff Proclaims Split

By G. E. R. GEDYE

Wireless to The New York Times.

MOSCOW, Thursday, Nov. 30—Premier Vyacheslaff M. Molotoff announced in a thirteen-minute radio speech last midnight the breaking off of diplomatic relations with Finland by the Soviet Union through the recall of all Soviet diplomatic, consular and economic representatives in Finland. At the same time he warned all units of the Red Army and Red Navy to stand ready for every emergency.

In contrast to the last Soviet note to Finland and in glaring contrast to the abusive violence of the inspired press and radio campaign, Mr. Molotoff's speech, except for one important particular, conformed entirely to international usage.

Although if accepted, of course, without any effort to substantiate their accuracy, all the Soviet charges concerning the alleged extraordinary violations of the frontier by the Finns in the last few days, the language was restrained and contained indications that the Soviet was prepared to reach a settlement—with the "Finnish people." In that, however, lay the important exception to conformity with international usage.

Appeals to 'Finnish People'

Despite the sentences asserting no desire to interfere in internal Finnish affairs and in the Finnish regime's relations with other States exclusively the affair of Finland, the speech directly appealed over the heads of the present Finnish Government "to the Finnish people." Thus it confirmed the belief expressed here more than once that the Soviet Union intended to try to force the surrender of the bases demanded from Finland through a change in the Finnish Government rather than through involving the Soviet Union in an invasion of Finnish territory.

By these passages of his speech Mr. Molotoff would seem to have confronted the Finnish Government with the alternatives of immediately recalling its diplomatic mission from Moscow at the peril of a still further increase in Soviet military pressure, if not of invasion, or of resignation. If the latter alternative were chosen, it would open the

Continued on Page Four

FINLAND IS BLOCKED IN MEDIATION PLEA

Note Delivered After Rupture Offers to Recall Troops— Soviet Move Awaited

The text of the last Finnish note appears on Page 5.

By The Associated Press.

HELSINKI, Finland, Thursday, Nov. 30—Profoundly disturbed by Moscow's action rupturing diplomatic relations, but still determined to stand fast, Finns early today awaited developments at any time. But early this morning officials said there had been no troop movements across the borders so far as they could learn.

It was all the more shocking to the Finns because the Moscow action came before they could deliver a note to the Kremlin offering to withdraw Finnish defense forces from the frontier as a gesture toward settling their quarrel.

The offer was made by Foreign Minister Eljas Erkko in his reply to Russia's denunciation of the 1932 Finnish-Soviet non-aggression treaty.

"My government is ready to settle with the Soviet Government the question of the removal of Finnish defense forces on the Karelian Isthmus, with the exception of frontier customs guard forces, to such a distance from Leningrad that it could not even be alleged that they threaten its security," Mr. Erkko's note said.

Making a Sincere Effort

He prefaced this statement with the explanation that Finland was motivated by a desire "to prove physically that there is a sincere effort to reach an accord with the Soviet Government and refute the Soviet Government's allegations that Finland has adopted a hostile attitude toward the U.S.S.R. and is desirous of threatening the security of Leningrad."

Despite the breaking off of diplomatic relations, and despite the midnight broadcast of Soviet Premier Vyacheslaff M. Molotoff, which announced the action, Finland's note answering Moscow's denunciation of their non-aggression pact was delivered to the Kremlin at 1:10 A. M., Moscow time.

This was almost three hours after the Vice Commissar of Foreign Affairs, Vladimir Potemkin, had notified the Finnish Minister that relations were broken.

The Finnish answer said the Helsinki Government thought Russia unjustified in denouncing the non-aggression pact and suggested that a conciliation commission be named to examine the controversy.

The news from Moscow spread rapidly through Helsinki. Grim Finns gathered in clusters to discuss the situation. Government of-

Continued on Page Five

Unofficial Thanks to Be Given Here Today By Irreconcilables Clinging to 'Old Style'

It will be just another day on New York's official calendar today, but half the nation, led by New England, will observe Thanksgiving with a determination to make the celebration of the traditional date outshine the "new Thanksgiving" fixed by President Roosevelt and marked by the other half of the country a week ago.

They will be joined here in unofficial joy by those New York irreconcilables who refuse to set turkey on any but the last Thursday of November, by those who have children coming home from school or college in "old-style" States, and by those who feel that any holiday is worth celebrating again even if it did occur only seven days before. These double celebrators will be following the example of Colorado, Mississippi and Texas, which are observing a second holiday in addition to the one last week.

Including these three, twenty-six States have proclaimed today as Thanksgiving Day. Americans in Sao Paulo, Brazil, denounced their fellows in Rio de Janeiro, and most other Americans abroad will observe the day—which has been termed the "Republican Thanksgiving" in contrast to the "New Deal Thanksgiving" of Nov. 23.

In New York many theatres are giving special matinees, and numerous restaurants will have turkey dinners for those who wish to partake. Private clubs are in some cases holding special events which were scheduled for today before the President changed the date. The Volunteer Rescue Army, which fed turkey to 2,018 unemployed last week, will give the same menu today for 3,000 at its chapel at 379 First Avenue.

Magistrate Henry H. Curran, sitting in Felony Court yesterday, declared he would observe the holiday today to "give thanks for the twenty-three States that didn't fall for this tyrannical novelty which came out of Washington." But he will eat chicken because "it's not fair to make the turkeys suffer on two days."

In Highland Park, N. J., a suburb of New Brunswick, school pupils will be dismissed at 1 P. M. as a "gesture toward those who believe the day is still the oldtime Thanksgiving."

Rutgers University, in New Brunswick, will observe its second Thanksgiving today to permit students to go to Providence, R. I., to see the Brown-Rutgers football game. Mayor C. D. White of Atlantic City has also proclaimed today as a second Thanksgiving.

The nation's principal observance

Continued on Page Fifteen

Dispatches from Europe and the Far East are subject to censorship.

"All the News That's Fit to Print."

The New York Times.

LATE CITY EDITION
Cloudy and colder today. Tomorrow partly cloudy with slowly rising temperatures.
Temperature Yesterday—Max. 43; Min. 31

Copyright, 1939, by The New York Times Company.

VOL. LXXXIX...No. 29,909.   Entered as Second-Class Matter, Postoffice, New York, N. Y.   NEW YORK, THURSDAY, DECEMBER 14, 1939.   PP   THREE CENTS NEW YORK CITY and Vicinity | FOUR CENTS Elsewhere Except in 7th and 8th Postal Zones

BRITISH DEFEAT NAZI RAIDER IN ALL-DAY FIGHT; SHE RUNS TO MONTEVIDEO WITH 36 DEAD, 60 HURT; U-BOAT SUNK, REICH CRUISER HIT IN NORTH SEA

A. F. L. LEADER SAYS NLRB 'PLAN' SAVED LEWIS' COAL UNION

Area Jurisdiction Ruling Led Thousands to Quit the Rival P.M.W., Ozanic Tells Inquiry

'SHOOTING' ORDER CHARGED

NLRB Report Said U. M. W. Officer Urged This Treatment for Progressive Miners

By The Associated Press.

WASHINGTON, Dec. 13—Joe Ozanic, young leader of the Progressive Mine Workers (A. F. L.), charged before a House investigating committee today that the National Labor Relations Board had followed a "plan" to give the United Mine Workers (C. I. O.) a "way out" in the desperate rivalry between the two unions.

The "plan," as he described it, was embodied in a controlling decision, which certified the C. I. O. union as the bargaining agent for all the coal mines in a specified geographic area. This was done, he said, despite probable majorities for the Progressives in individual mines affected.

As a result, he asserted, the United Mine Workers and employers in the field had forced thousands of Progressive members to switch to the C. I. O. union, and pay its dues, regardless of their own desires in the matter.

In one instance which he cited, that of the Acme Semi-Anthracite Coal Company of Williams, Okla., members of the Progressive union were unemployed, he said, because their jobs had been taken by miners imported by the United Mine Workers.

Bitterness of Feud Evidenced

All the accumulated bitterness of the fierce battle between the C. I. O. and the American Federation of Labor was epitomized for the committee in the day's testimony. Mr. Ozanic spoke repeatedly of "Dictator John L. Lewis," and of alleged "coercion" by C. I. O. members against his own followers.

At one point Edmund M. Toland, the committee's counsel, introduced a memorandum from Philip G. Phillips, the West Virginia regional director of the Labor Board, which quoted "Van Bitner" as having advised United Mine Workers' organizers to move the Progressive organizers "faster than they would shoot a rabbit."

"Who is Van Bitner?" Chairman Smith, Democrat of Virginia, inquired.

"Van Bitner," Mr. Ozanic replied, "why, he's the provisional district president for District 17 of the United Mine Workers. He was appointed by Dictator John L. Lewis and never in his life elected by the United Mine Workers. That, gentlemen, is Mr. Bitner."

Later Van A. Bitner, who spells his name with two "t's" and is president of District No. 17 and also a member of the U. M. W. International Board, denied that he had ever made the shooting statement.

Denied by U. M. W. Official

"That statement of Phillips is absolutely untrue and made out of whole cloth," he told reporters. The memorandum mentioned that "Bitner" spoke at a Labor Day meeting in Charleston, W. Va., but the U. M. W. official said that the union held no Labor Day meeting in Charleston in 1939.

When Mr. Ozanic took the stand he told the committee that he started work as a coal miner at the age of 18 and was a member of the United Mine Workers of America.

After twenty-two years in that union, he said that he and fellow-miners in the Illinois fields "seceded" because of the U. M. W.'s dictatorial policies" and formed the Progressive Mine Workers of Illinois in 1932.

The new union soon recruited 35,000 of the State's 42,000 miners, he said, and, he added, still had them. After the Progressives received an A. F. L. charter as an international union the A. F. L. in 1938, Mr. Ozanic said, it recruited an additional 50,000 workers in coal fields outside Illinois. To the latter, however, re-

Continued on Page Eighteen

When you think of Writing Think of Whiting.—Advt.

Revolutionary Landmark In Queens Being Razed

The old frame building in Elmhurst, Queens, used during the Battle of Long Island as the headquarters of the British Army, is being razed by its present owner yesterday despite efforts of Borough President George U. Harvey to have the property purchased by the city and restored as a historic landmark.

The building, which stands at what is now Fifty-seventh Avenue and Queens Boulevard, was erected in 1763. On Sept. 3, 1776, General William Howe, commanding the British forces, moved his official report to the King on what happened during the Battle of Long Island six days before, while using the house as his headquarters.

The present owner, Dr. Hevia, Cuban tobacco planter, who has a home in Richmond Hill, decided to raze the building when it became in need of repair. He has no plans for future use of the land.

RALLY HERE SCORES REICH AND SOVIET

Hoover, Landon, La Guardia and Green Are Heard by 20,000 in Garden

Before a mass meeting of more than 20,000 persons who filled every seat in Madison Square Garden last night, former President Herbert Hoover, former Governor Alf M. Landon of Kansas, Mayor La Guardia and William Green, president of the American Federation of Labor, headed prominent Christian and Jewish speakers who joined in protest against the persecution of Jews by Nazi Germany and in an appeal for the mobilization of the moral forces of the world against Hitlerism and Stalinism.

The meeting, held under the auspices of the American Jewish Congress and the Jewish Labor Committee, unanimously adopted by rising vote a resolution asking President Roosevelt to convey American condemnation of the persecution of the Jews in Nazi Poland to the German Government and to use every possible means to succor the victims of the oppression. It was decided to appoint a committee representing the two organizations to take the resolution to Washington.

Hitler and Stalin Booed

Every vague reference to President Roosevelt's neutrality program, the audience booed equally every mention of Hitler and Stalin. They laughed loudly when speakers ridiculed Mad and Communist propaganda that Hitler and Stalin are working for peace against the imperialistic war aims of England and France.

They also applauded statements that the real issue was the defense of democracy against totalitarianism, whether its label was Nazi, Fascist or Communist, and that anti-Semitism was only the first step toward the destruction of all religions, labor unions and civil liberties. Many in the audience came in delegations from New York labor unions in which Jewish membership predominates.

The speakers and the audience made it clear that their protests were aimed at the Russian invasion of Finland as well as German aggression in Poland, and that their appeals for help were directed in behalf of the Finns as well as the Jews in Poland, Austria, Czechoslovakia and Germany.

It was announced that part of a collection taken up at the meeting to defray its expenses and to help Jewish victims of Hitlerism would be turned over to former President Hoover's Finnish relief fund if the collection was large enough. The total was not announced, as the contributions were not to be counted until today.

About seventy policemen were stationed outside the Garden in case of disturbances, but there was no trouble.

Several hundred persons who turned away when the gates of the Garden were closed by Fire Department order at 8:25 P. M., half an hour after the meeting opened. Mayor La Guardia received the biggest ovation of all the speakers when he arrived on the platform after flying in from Chicago on a night plane. He expressed his "horror" at what is taking place in Europe and said he hoped that what

Continued on Page Eight

RUSSIA CONDEMNED

League Certain to Expel Her as Committee of 13 Calls Her Aggressor

PLANS AID TO FINNS

U. S. Will Be Invited to Help—Victim One of Invader's Judges

Text of League report on Russia is on Page 6.

By P. J. PHILIP
Wireless to THE NEW YORK TIMES.

GENEVA, Dec. 13—Soviet Russia, it is now considered certain, will be thrust forth from the company of the League of Nations, having, in the opinion of her fellow-members, by her own acts placed herself outside the Covenant.

A report by thirteen of them—the committee appointed by the Assembly to consider Finland's appeal—held today that Russia has been the aggressor and called on member States to lend all possible aid to the victim. It also offered the facilities of the League to coordinate such help and suggested that non-members be invited to cooperate.

The report was drafted by a subcommittee composed of the representatives of Great Britain, France, Sweden, Bolivia and Portugal.

In the public meeting of the Assembly during the morning Argentina demanded the expulsion, declaring that she would no longer remain a member of the League if the Soviet Union continued to enjoy that title.

Russia Not Represented

The Russian Government was not there to defend itself and no one cared to assume its defense. Jacob Suritz, Soviet Ambassador to France, anticipating events, had left Geneva on the morning train.

Alternative suggestions to that of expulsion proposed by Argentina were invited. It was stipulated that they should be heard in private committee so as to avoid embarrassment to those who feel that their geographic position as Russia's neighbors affects their judgment of both the legal and moral aspects of the question.

Cuba wanted to speak after Argentina in the Assembly, but was overruled as Mexico and India already had agreed to submit their proposals in private.

The Assembly then prepared one more step on the way to expulsion by electing the Union of South Africa and Finland to the council in the place of New Zealand and Sweden, re-electing Bolivia and shelving until after the council shall have taken its decision on the Russian issue the re-election of

Continued on Page Six

Liner Columbus Cleared For Transatlantic Dash

By The Associated Press.

VERACRUZ, Mexico, Dec. 13—Port authorities disclosed tonight that the 32,581-ton German liner Columbus had obtained clearance papers for a transatlantic voyage and was prepared to sail without further notice.

All crew members on shore leave have been ordered to report aboard to prepare for a "long voyage."

The ship's representatives said her destination was Oslo, Norway.

It was believed that the Columbus would slip from port shortly, but in view of persistent rumors of British warships in the Gulf of Mexico and Caribbean she was expected to sail as secretly as possible, probably at night without lights.

The same agency also arranged for the departure of the German freighter Arauca, also here since the start of the war. There was busy this afternoon painting herself black.

VALPARAISO, Chile, Dec. 13—The 4,930-ton German steamer Dusseldorf sailed from this Pacific Ocean harbor today, the fourth to sail of five German ships here at the outbreak of war. The only remaining one is the school ship Velero Priwall.

FINNS REPORT GAIN IN COUNTER-THRUST

Say Russians Are Hurled Back as Major Battle Impends— Soviet Is 'Invaded'

By The United Press.

COPENHAGEN, Denmark, Thursday, Dec. 14—Heavily reinforced Finnish troops early today were reported to be laying siege to the strategic town of Salla, just above the Arctic Circle, where the Russians were said to have lost 7,000 men.

The Finns, concentrating large forces in an effort to prevent the Red Army from reaching the Gulf of Bothnia and cutting Finland in two, hoped to recapture Salla today, frontier dispatches said.

Salla is about 125 miles northeast of the top of the Gulf of Bothnia at the Swedish-Finnish border and slightly northeast of the town of Kemijaervi, where fierce fighting was reported.

Thrust Into Russia Reported

[Finnish forces had carried the war to Russian soil in a strong drive north of Lake Ladoga, according to unofficial reports in Helsinki. This followed closely the reported bombing of the Soviet's Leningrad-Murmansk railway, which was said to have halted an attempt to transport submarines to the Arctic.]

Against the Russians' reported losses of 7,000 men in the new Finnish counter-offensive, the Finns claim to have lost only 250 men.

Continued on Page Nine

Davies Will Resign as Envoy to Belgium To Become an Adviser on Europe to Hull

By FELIX BELAIR Jr.
Special to THE NEW YORK TIMES.

WASHINGTON, Dec. 13—Joseph E. Davies is soon to give up his post as Ambassador to Belgium and take a place in the special division of the State Department dealing with war emergencies.

The Ambassador's resignation is lying on the President's desk. Whether it was offered when Mr. Davies called on the President today or was sent ahead of his return to the United States was not ascertained. The resignation was technical, in any event. Arrangements for the transfer were completed several weeks ago.

The duties to be assigned to Mr. Davies will be similar to those now being performed by Hugh R. Wilson, who recently resigned as Ambassador to Germany, and Breckinridge Long, former Ambassador to Italy. President Roosevelt is said to be desirous of getting the details of the emergency situations abroad in the hands of diplomats who have had experience in the field.

Mr. Davies entered the diplomatic service as Ambassador to Russia and later was transferred to Brussels. He has been credited at various times with an ambition to represent this country in London. He returned to this country yesterday.

...tentionsly to participate in negotiations over revision of the reciprocal trade agreement with Belgium.

As he left the Executive Office today after conferring with the President, Mr. Davies said that he wanted to be on record as having stated that he was not a candidate for the Secretaryship of the Navy, a post with which his name had been connected in recent rumors.

Mr. Davies will probably go back to Brussels to wind up the affairs of his ambassadorship and also to participate in official activities incident to the start of operation of the trade agreement.

It became known that information regarding Mr. Davies's resignation had been obtained by THE NEW YORK TIMES, a spokesman of the State Department said that Mr. Davies had been instructed to return here and that he reported today to the President, Secretary Hull and Under-Secretary Welles.

The spokesman issued the statement:

"No decision has been reached with regard to the future duties of Mr. Davies, either in Washington or in the event that he returns to Belgium."

Continued on Page Three

NORTH SEA SUCCESS

British Submarine That Spared Bremen Said to Have Scored Twice

NEW TACTICS IN AIR

Planes Patrol Nazi Base to Prevent Laying of Mines at Night

Special Cable to THE NEW YORK TIMES.

LONDON, Dec. 13—The British Admiralty announced tonight that the British submarine that sighted and spared the German liner Bremen a few days ago had sunk a German U-boat and torpedoed a German cruiser in the North Sea.

The announcement marked the first time that any British submarine had been in action against enemy aircraft. Details of the British submarine's exploit were not given and officials would not make any comment on the identity of the German cruiser involved.

When asked whether the cruiser had sunk after the torpedoing the officials pointed out that the communiqué specified sinking in the case of the U-boat but used the word "torpedoed" in the case of the cruiser. This was taken to mean the cruiser had been damaged. When the action took place was not revealed.

New Air Patrol Fixed

The Air Ministry issued today a statement hinting at new tactics in the evolving strategy of war in the air and on the sea. British planes, it was said, had maintained an all-night watch over the German seaplane bases at Sylt, Borkum and Norderney in Helgoland bight.

The official announcement indicated that a new arm of defense against air attack had been formed and that it was its duty to squelch attacks from the air on enemy territory instead of awaiting the arrival of Nazi air armadas.

Hindsight is sometimes helpful in interpreting the mysterious diplomatic manoeuvring in these uncertain times, but yesterday's announcement that a British submarine had sunk the Bremen and the latest announcement that British planes roared harmlessly over German naval bases last night do not help much in understanding the way this strange war is developing.

Presumably, the British Admiralty thinks more was gained diplomatically by the strict observance of international law than could have been gained by the sinking of the queen of Germany's merchant navy. Likewise, it may be presumed the British feel there is more to be gained by sending planes to hover over the nests of Germany's mine-laying flying boats than by bombing their bases and that it is better to hold the threat of attack above the Nazi fliers' heads than to try to drive them from British coasts with all the advantage that falls to the fighter who rises fresh to the fray.

Nazis Scoff at Statement

The Germans, of course, scoff at the British statement that they could have sunk the Bremen but did not think it sporting or legal. The truth is, the Germans say, that the British are just trying to put the best face possible on their naval impotence.

The official announcement of the new patrols over the German bases in Helgoland Bight said they were "continuously maintained." Their purpose, it was said, was "to interrupt the activities of mine-laying aircraft operating from these bases." Despite anti-aircraft opposition "the operations were successfully carried out."

Today's Air Ministry statement indicated that Britain's method of meeting the new magnetic mine menace included not only some method of sweeping up the destructive eggs laid by planes and submarines in coastal shipping channels but also contemplated measures to prevent their being laid at all. Aviation experts said there was much about the establishment of what already have been dubbed "security patrols" that is mysterious.

It was pointed out, for instance, that the official statement rather indicated that bombing planes were used, that they circled more or less

Continued on Page Three

The International Situation

Britain's far-flung sea power caught up with a raiding German pocket battleship yesterday in the Western Hemisphere.

A running battle was fought during the day and last night off the Uruguayan coast between the Nazi craft, identified as the Admiral Graf Spee, and two small British cruisers, the Ajax and the Achilles. The cruiser Exeter had also been in the battle, but was damaged and forced to drop out. The pursuit continued with hits scored on both sides until the pocket battleship raced into neutral Montevideo harbor badly damaged and with thirty dead aboard. The Ajax and the Achilles followed and lay outside the harbor. [Page 1.]

Under international law Uruguay must now determine the minimum repairs needed to make the German ship seaworthy, and when these repairs have been made the vessel must either put to sea or be interned for the duration of the war. [Page 4.]

London claimed another naval success, reporting that the British submarine that had sighted the liner Bremen on her dash to Germany had sunk a U-boat and torpedoed a German cruiser. At the same time the Air Ministry indicated a new policy of an all-night air patrol over German seaplane bases to frustrate aerial mine-laying. [Page 1.]

Following his adventurous voyage homeward, the Bremen's commander declared at a reception that he believed the liner had been held up in New York last August to help the British. [Page 2.]

While the Finns reported having thrown the Russians back in counter-offensives and were unofficially said to have carried the war to Russian soil [Page 1], a League of Nations committee condemned Russia as an aggressor, called for all possible aid to the Finns by members and non-members alike and suggested expulsion of the Soviet, a development that now seems certain. [Page 1.]

What the League was doing was still kept from the Soviet people. [Page 8.] But a hint that Moscow was not insensitive to criticism was seen in the hasty summoning home of the new Russian Ambassador to Rome, who had not yet had time to present his credentials. [Page 1.]

While the British House of Commons in its first secret session since the World War debated Opposition charges of government bungling on supplies [Page 11], peers talk in the House of Lords by a few members caused Foreign Secretary Halifax to characterize the debate as "unfortunate." [Page 1.]

PREY OF 3 CRUISERS

Pocket Battleship Puts In South America Port After 18-Hour Fight

EXETER FORCED OUT

Foe Badly Damaged; 1 Ship, but Two Others Continue Chase

By JOHN W. WHITE
Special Cable to THE NEW YORK TIMES.

BUENOS AIRES, Argentina, Thursday, Dec. 14—The German pocket battleship Admiral Graf Spee struggled into Montevideo harbor shortly before midnight with thirty-six of her crew dead, sixty wounded and the ship badly damaged as the result of an eighteen-hour running battle with the British cruisers Exeter, Ajax and Achilles.

Shortly after the Graf Spee's arrival two British cruisers, the Ajax and the Achilles, arrived at the outer roads off Montevideo, but at an early hour this morning had not reported to the authorities ashore regarding their casualties.

[Returning from a visit aboard the Admiral Graf Spee, the German Minister to Uruguay, Otto Langman, said that the dead included a lieutenant and the wounded the commander of the ship, The Associated Press reported. His statement that the ship was the Spee and not the Admiral Scheer as reported at first was the first indication that the Graf Spee had been operating in the Atlantic.

[The spokesman for the German Legation at Montevideo said that "there are thirty-six dead and sixty wounded aboard the Graf Spee, mostly because the British used mustard gas shells." The spokesman said that the damage to the battleship was insignificant.

[Captains of six British ships captured by the Graf Spee off the South American and South African coasts will be landed at Montevideo, the spokesman added.]

Open Fire on the Spee

The British squadron was under the command of Commodore H. H. Harwood.

Contact with the Graf Spee was established at his time during the morning when the pocket battleship attacked the Ajax while the latter was convoying the French passenger liner Formosa from Rio de Janeiro to Montevideo. The Ajax called for help and the Exeter and Achilles arrived at full speed and opened fire on the battleship.

The four warships fought an intense artillery duel from 6 o'clock until 12. Despite the Admiral Spee's speed and heavier armament she was repeatedly hit by shells from the British cruisers, especially the Exeter. The Spee, accordingly, directed her main efforts to putting the Exeter out of commission. By this time all four warships were running southward, the Formosa having dropped back for safety.

The Exeter, finally disabled, was forced to drop out of the battle but by this time the Spee was so badly damaged that the commander began running at full speed for the River Plate, closely followed by the Ajax and Achilles.

The battle apparently lasted on and off all day, as the firing was renewed twice after the warships were within sight of the Uruguayan shore. Under cover of night the Graf Spee changed her course and finally reached the refuge of Montevideo.

Spee Changes Her Course

This forced the Spee to change her course disadvantageously to the southeast. Then the British warships renewed their heavy firing, which continued until well after dark. Under cover of night the Graf Spee changed her course and finally reached the refuge of Montevideo.

Continued on Page Four

SOVIET CALLS HOME NEW ROME ENVOY

Italians Believe He Will Be Asked How Seriously They Mean Balkan Warning

By HERBERT L. MATTHEWS
By Telephone to THE NEW YORK TIMES.

ROME, Dec. 13—Nikolai Gorelchin, the new Russian Ambassador, who has not yet had time to present his credentials, was hastily summoned back to Moscow by telegram and left Rome on Monday, it was learned today. The Russian Embassy claims it is a mere informative visit without particular significance and that Mr. Gorelchin, who saw Count Ciano, the Foreign Minister, last week, will return to Rome shortly.

However, it is at least a coincidence that his sudden recall should come at a time when there are almost daily hostile demonstrations against Russia and when the Fascist Grand Council, to say nothing of the entire Italian press, has been issuing warnings to Moscow to keep out of the Balkans. One is entitled to suppose that Joseph Stalin wants to know just what the Italians mean and how serious they are with their threats.

Italy's Earnestness Clear

If that is what his visit is about, Mr. Gorelchin will doubtless inform his government that Italy means business, for genuinely strong measures are being taken to parry the expected Russian thrust, should it try to go beyond Bessarabia. On the other hand, the Soviet Government may become more sensitive about criticism and hostility and may not intend to send Mr. Gorelchin back here.

In connection with the press criticism, Roberto Farinacci's newspaper, the Regime Fascista, offers a novel explanation for the Russo-German alliance. After saying that Finnish resistance has proved Russian weakness, the writer concludes:

"So when England, France and the Osservatore Romano (the Vatican City newspaper) speak of the Russian peril, it is in bad faith. Russia preferred the German alliance because she thought that it had to be feared, whereas she would be bested."

Premier Georges Kiosseivanoff of Bulgaria, in an interview with the Giornale d'Italia's correspondent today, says that while Bulgaria has not renounced "the realization of

Continued on Page Seven

BRITISH PEERS URGE NEW PEACE MOVES

Mediation Call Hurts Nation, Halifax Replies—Commons Holds Secret Session

Special Cable to THE NEW YORK TIMES.

LONDON, Dec. 13—The question of making peace now and without military victory arose in the House of Lords today in a heated violence and terror in Germany, "and as long as that persisted any idea that there was a change of heart or that a freely negotiated peace was possible was illusory."

Lord Darnley maintained that Chancellor Hitler's actions were aimed partly to make Germany free and prosperous but chiefly to make her free from any danger in the future, and every threat made against him made him think aggression more necessary.

Lord Arnold said it was unfortunate the Earl's proposal could not be discussed at a secret session. He contended that laying down peace conditions in advance did not help negotiations, but hindered them. He added:

"If a satisfactory peace could be secured in other respects, this country would not wish to continue the war on account of Austria."

Lord Arnold believed that if the war continued until Herr Hitler was overthrown by revolution, Germany would become Communist and enter into an alliance with Russia. He feared that communism might spread over Eastern Europe and "not only would any peace at the end of a long war be without value but the greatest calamity in the history of the world would have occurred."

Three Peers Reply

Lord Balfour, Viscount Samuel and Lord Snell opposed the Earl amid cheers. Lord Balfour declared there was a reign of violence and terror in Germany, "and as long as that persisted any idea that there was a change of heart or that a freely negotiated peace was possible was illusory."

The debate was precipitated by a suggestion from the Earl of Darnley that Britain take up the Belgian and Netherland proposal for mediation, which, he said, still is open. Supported by Lord Arnold and the Bishop of Chichester, he said Britain had not done enough after the Versailles treaty to conciliate Germany and warned against a "revenge-producing victory."

[Meanwhile the House of Commons in its first secret session since the last war debated for seven hours and a half Opposition charges that the government was bungling the production of vital war supplies.]

Continued on Page Twelve

Dispatches from Europe and the Far East are subject to censorship.

88

The New York Times

PAGE ONE

Major Events:

1940–1949

The New York Times.

VOL. LXXXIX...No. 30,026.   Entered as Second-Class Matter, Postoffice, New York, N. Y.   NEW YORK, TUESDAY, APRIL 9, 1940.   P   THREE CENTS NEW YORK CITY and Vicinity | FOUR CENTS Elsewhere Except in 7th and 8th Postal Zones

GERMANS OCCUPY DENMARK, ATTACK OSLO; NORWAY THEN JOINS WAR AGAINST HITLER; CAPITAL IS REPORTED BOMBED FROM AIR

HOUSE TO CONSIDER WAGE ACT CHANGES EARLY NEXT WEEK

Leaders in Surprise Moves Also Slate Bill for Court Review of Agency Rulings

LABOR LAW ACTION LIKELY

Proponents of Amendments Expect Drive to Dispose of All Labor Legislation

House consideration next week was slated for the bill to amend the Wages and Hours Act and for the Logan-Walter bill to provide for a court review of decisions by governmental agencies. [Page 1.]

A refusal by the Supreme Court to review the Labor Board's order in the Republic Steel case sustained the reinstatement of 5,000 C. I. O. strikers with $5,000,000 back pay. [Page 20.]

The Socialist party convention, at Washington, stated in a resolution that "the interests of American working men and women will best be served by the making of an immediate peace between the C. I. O. and A. F. L." [Page 1.]

Colonel Harrington, WPA Administrator, will be questioned Thursday by the House Appropriations Subcommittee on evidence gathered by its investigators bearing on the 1941 relief outlay. [Page 20.]

The NLRB refused to relieve Mrs. Elinore M. Herrick of further responsibility in connection with the election of employees of the Consolidated Edison Company of New York after a charge of collusion with the company. [Page 20.]

Two Revision Bills Slated

By HENRY N. DORRIS
Special to The New York Times.

WASHINGTON, April 8—House leaders decided on consideration early next week of the Barden bill to amend the Wages and Hours Act, a decision which occasioned surprise in labor quarters since it had been assumed this measure would follow the Smith or Norton amendments to the National Labor Relations Act.

But this was not the only surprise, because the tentative calendar for next week also contained a place for the Logan-Walter bill providing court review of any decision of a governmental agency which has the force of law.

When these two measures are out of the way, proponents of amendments to the Wagner Act expect to win consideration of these measures. Just how they will manage this was not revealed, but it was said by one member that the procedure was for a "Bang! Bang! Bang!" program that would wipe the House calendar clean of labor legislation that has "plagued" it for more than a year.

The Barden bill has been pending since last August, when a rule was granted for its consideration. It was never considered, however, because of the "compromise" by which the lending-spending and United States Housing Authority bills—desired by the Administration—were taken up. Both of these failed to obtain consideration, but they served to crowd out the Barden bill, which primarily aims at a redefinition of the "area of production" provision of the Wages and Hours Act.

Would Remove "Ambiguities"

The amendment proposed by Representative Barden of North Carolina, a member of the House Labor Committee, proposes to remove the "ambiguities" of the "area of production" clause and the ruling subsequently made on it by the former Wages and Hours Administrator, Elmer F. Andrews.

Under that ruling processing plants located within ten miles of the area where agricultural products are grown or harvested are exempt from the provisions which require them to pay a minimum wage of thirty cents an hour or work their employees not to exceed forty-two hours per week without overtime pay of time and a half. The Barden amendment proposes

Continued on Page Twenty

The International Situation

War caught up two more countries in its clutches today as the Germans invaded Denmark and attacked Norway.

In the early morning Nazi troops crossed the southern border of Denmark, landed on Danish soil from warships and occupied the Danish capital, Copenhagen—all apparently without resistance. [Page 1.]

Almost at the same time a diplomatic dispatch to Washington announced that Norway was at war with Germany. [Page 1.] This development followed an attempt by German warships—more than 100 of which had been sighted last night moving northward in the Kattegat—to force an entry, with aerial support, into Oslo Fjord. At latest reports German troops were debarking on the Norwegian coast and had entered Narvik, Bergen and Trondheim, while the Norwegians were said to have moved their capital, which was reported bombed.

Berlin explained it was taking Denmark and Norway under its "protection" to prevent any hostile attack upon them. [Page 4.]

There had been at least one suggestion yesterday of German troop movements in Scandinavia. A Nazi transport had been torpedoed off Southern Norway with a loss of 150 out of some 300 uniformed men aboard. In the same neighborhood a large German tanker was sent to the bottom. [Page 1.]

The mining of Norwegian waters had taken Norway completely by surprise and eight German freighters were apparently in the same predicament, as they were trapped in those waters and unable to get home. With British warships patrolling the mine fields the ore traffic at Narvik was halted and it seemed likely that Swedish iron shipments would be halved. [Page 3.] Norway protested to both Britain and France against the mining, terming it "an open breach of international law" and demanding that the mines be removed. [Page 1.] London had expected the protest and discounted it. But the British were believed to be ready to go to Norway's aid against the Germans. [Page 2.]

With a loophole in the blockade apparently plugged in Scandinavia the British gave some of their attention to the Balkans; their envoys to the countries of that region began their conferences. [Page 9.] At the same time Southeastern Europe was startled by Rumania's detention of a fleet of British barges carrying dynamite, which, according to the Germans, was to have been used for blocking the Danube. British quarters insisted the explosives were to have been used only for destroying river craft in the event of a German invasion of Rumania. [Page 1.]

REICH SHIP IS SUNK

150 Lost Off Transport Torpedoed by British Off South Norway

ALL' MEN IN UNIFORM

Large Nazi Tanker Also Sunk by Allies, but Crew Is Rescued

Special Cable to The New York Times.

OSLO, Norway, April 8—A British submarine torpedoed and sank the German troop ship Rio de Janiero today off Lillesand, on the south coast of Norway. At least 150 German soldiers are believed to have perished.

It is reported here that the German transport, formerly a freighter on the South American run, had at least 300 men aboard and that fewer than 150 are accounted for. The ship, of 5,261 tons, was out of Hamburg and was classified here as a transport because all the men aboard were in uniform.

Another large German vessel, the tanker Posidonia, was also reported torpedoed today off the south Norwegian coast, but without loss of life.

[Lloyd's Register of Shipping does not list a German tanker Posidonia. The Associated Press, in recording the report of still a third sinking, that of the German tanker Kreta, indicated that there might be some confusion over the Posidonia's case, since the Kreta, apparently to conceal her identity, had sent out the call letters of the Posidonia. Other reports said that the Posidonia used the Kreta's signals.]

The report of the torpedoing of the Rio de Janiero received here states that the British submarine intercepted the transport off the Norwegian coast, hailed her and fired a warning shot across her bows. This was disregarded and the troopship altered her course, speeding toward land or territorial waters. The submarine then fired a torpedo.

Some Jump Overboard

With the explosion some of the Germans immediately jumped overboard. A Norwegian fishing vessel was near by and went to the rescue, taking these men out of the water.

As the transport appeared to be settling, the submarine fired a second torpedo, with terrific result. An iron bar from the ship was hurled 150 feet and struck the rescuing fishing vessel, killing three of the Germans who had been taken aboard.

The fishing vessel continued its work of rescue and was aided by other fishing craft that hurried out when an alarm was sounded along the coast. These ships took a total

Continued on Page Five

NAZIS IN NORWAY

Troops Debark at Ports —Government Leaves Oslo for Hamar

NARVIK IS OCCUPIED

Air Attacks on Capital Reported—Civilians Are to Be Evacuated

Sweden Is Mobilizing

By The United Press.

STOCKHOLM, Sweden, April 9—The Swedish radio announced today that the government had ordered general mobilization.

Wireless to The New York Times.

LONDON, Tuesday, April 9—The Paris correspondent of Reuters, British news agency, reported this morning that the Oslo radio had announced that German troops had debarked in Norwegian ports at 3 A. M.

[Mrs. J. Borden Harriman, United States Minister to Norway, notified the State Department early this morning that she had been informed by the Foreign Minister that Norway considered herself at war with Germany.

[Mrs. Harriman also reported that at 5:30 A. M. Norwegian shore batteries were still engaged in battle with four invading German warships that were trying to force entry into Oslo Fjord.]

It was also announced that the Norwegian Government had left Oslo for Hamar, in Central Norway.

Reuters further reported that the Germans had occupied the cities of Bergen and Trondheim.

[The Oslo radio announced this morning that the Norwegian Government had ordered general mobilization after an all night session of the Cabinet, The Associated Press reported.]

Reuters also reported from Paris that the Oslo radio announced this morning that the Germans had occupied Narvik.

The Norwegian legation here issued the following communiqué:

"The German Minister in Oslo saw the Norwegian Foreign Secretary at 4:30 o'clock this morning and demanded that Norway should be handed over to the German administration. If this was not done all resistance would be defeated. This demand was refused and hostilities have started."

LONDON, Tuesday, April 9 (UP)—A Reuters, British news agency,

Continued on Page Two

NEW THEATRE OF WAR IS OPENED

German troops invaded Denmark at 5 A. M. today. A few hours previously German warships attempted to force an entry into Oslo Fjord (cross). This action, which brought Norway into the war against the Reich, followed the sighting last night of a German armada steaming northward off Lesoe (3). Near Lillesand (1) a German troop transport was torpedoed by a British submarine and a U-boat was rumored to have been sunk. Off Faerder Light (2) one and perhaps two German tankers were sent down. The Allied mine fields off Norway are indicated by arrows.

NORWAY DECLARES WAR ON GERMANY

Washington Notified of Action by U. S. Minister at Oslo— Warships Sent There

Special to The New York Times.

WASHINGTON, Tuesday, April 9—Norway is at war with Germany. This was the word received soon after 1 o'clock this morning by the State Department from Mrs. J. Borden Harriman, the American Minister at Oslo.

The startling information was received less than two hours after equally disturbing intelligence had been received of the German occupation of Denmark.

[President Roosevelt, at Hyde Park, kept in close touch with the State Department and his special train was held ready for a quick return to Washington, The United Press reported.]

The State Department announced the state of war in the following communiqué:

"The American Minister at Oslo, Mrs. J. Borden Harriman, telegraphed the Department tonight that the Foreign Minister had informed her that the Norwegians had fired on four German warships coming up Oslo Fjord and that Norway was at war with Germany. In response to a request by the British Minister to Norway the American Legation at Oslo has been authorized to take over British interests in Norway in case he is forced to leave."

Envoy's Request Explained

State Department officials, in answer to queries regarding the apparently ambiguous last paragraph of Mrs. Harriman's cable, said that there could be no doubt that Norway was at war against Germany. They pointed out that the Norwegians were firing on German warships and the British envoy, was apprehensive of the possibility that he might have to evacuate, although he was not certain he would have to do so.

[The United Press said Mrs. Harriman reported that she had taken charge of the British and French Legations.]

It was reported on usually good authority that American warships in European waters had been ordered to proceed northward so they could take part in the evacuation of American citizens in Denmark.

Any or all of these topics may be profitably discussed between the

Continued on Page Four

ALLIED MINES BRING A PROTEST BY OSLO

Breach of International Law Charged by Koht—Sweden Takes Defense Measures

By The Associated Press.

OSLO, Norway, April 8—Foreign Minister Halvdan Koht told Parliament today that Norway had protested to Paris and London against the mining of her waters at dawn, a sudden move by which the Allies hope to cut off Germany's Swedish ore shipments through Norway's western coastal waters.

In a public statement Mr. Koht charged the Allies with an "open breach of international law" and demanded that the mines "be removed at once and that the guard by foreign warships cease." Britain was patrolling Norway's waters near the new mine fields, stating such action would be for forty-eight hours to warn away neutral vessels.

In all Scandinavia statesmen, in realization that the dreaded day had arrived bringing the European war to the north, gathered to discuss the cloudy future and await a feared retaliation from Germany. Leaders of the Norwegian Parliament, which was called into special session, and they were behind the government's action in the crisis. A Cabinet meeting was held in Oslo, which military and naval leaders attended.

Political Leaders Meet

Leaders of all of Denmark's political parties met in Copenhagen, and in Stockholm Swedish leaders watched gravely. The Swedish Foreign Office announced there had been no violation of Swedish waters, but officials admitted they were worried.

The Oslo newspaper Arbejderbladet, a government organ, said that "the situation is particularly grave for our country, but in such times we must keep our heads cool."

"Any tendency toward nervousness or panic would only make it worse," the paper said. "Norway naturally will protest in a most emphatic way against any closing of her waters and demand respect for international laws. But it is a ques-

Continued on Page Four

ROOSEVELT EFFIGY 'FRONT' GUN TARGET

Healy Also Swears Cassidy Wanted 12 in Congress Shot in Capital as Gesture

Denis A. Healy, star prosecution witness in the trial of seventeen men indicted for conspiring to overthrow the United States Government, testified yesterday in the Brooklyn Federal Court that some of the defendants had used a likeness of President Roosevelt's head as a target during rifle practice.

He swore that John F. Cassidy, a defendant who was prominent in the Christian Front, had favored "going to Washington and shooting twelve Congressmen to show that the Christian Front means business," and he testified that William Gerald Bishop, another defendant, wanted to place Major General Van Horn Moseley, U. S. A. retired, at the head of a dictatorship after overthrowing the present government.

"Telling of how members of the group practiced making crude bombs out of empty beer cans, Healy said that they had discussed committing acts of sabotage here if the United States entered the war. He said that Bishop had boasted to him of knowing who was responsible for an explosion he said had occurred on an oil tanker in the lower bay a few days earlier.

Cross-Examination Begun

Healy finished his direct testimony at 2:30 P. M. yesterday after having been on the witness stand for five hours, beginning Friday afternoon. He began at once a hammering cross-examination at the hands of defense counsel, which they estimated would last for at least two full court days in their effort to discredit his story of having posed as one of the plotters meanwhile keeping the Federal Bureau of Investigation informed of every development.

He was forced to admit that he had lied on numerous occasions, that he had pretended to be anti-Semitic in order to "carry out my role"; that he had once approached Bishop for aid in smuggling a relative into this country from Canada, and that he had once been convicted of street fighting, for which he received a suspended sentence.

Conceding that he had testified for the government in a previous case, Healy denied that he was a "professional witness," as was charged by former Magistrate Leo J. Healy, counsel for eleven of the defendants. He said the government had arranged a leave of absence for him from the New York Central Railroad, and was paying him the same salary while he was

Continued on Page Sixteen

BRITISH EXPLOSIVES HELD BY RUMANIANS

Fleet of Barges Detained at Danube Port—Nazis Charge Plot to Block River

By The Associated Press.

BUCHAREST, Rumania, April 8—Detention of a fleet of dynamite-laden British barges, said by Germans to be designed to blow up a narrow Danube gateway and block a German supply line, today electrified Southeastern Europe with the fear war soon might spread to this quarter of the world.

Rumanian police, acting on a tip said to have been supplied by the pro-Nazi Iron Guard, halted the fleet near Giurgiu, Danube River port whence Germany ships much-needed Rumanian oil supplies. Aboard were tons of dynamite.

Germans alleged the British planned to blockade the spot in the Danube known as the Iron Gate by sinking the barges and wrecking the narrow channel where the river cuts through the Carpathian barrier between high cliffs. The Iron Gate is 280 miles up river from Giurgiu.

Official British quarters, acknowledging the barges were loaded with explosives, insisted they were to be used only for destroying Allied river craft in case of a German invasion of Rumania.

The only official British statement on the matter was a communiqué saying merely that Rumanian authorities had seized two cases of firearms which a British barge captain had neglected to declare in passing customs.

Troops Guard Gateway

The British aim was reported in Germany to be the blocking of the Iron Gate with sunken barges and blasting of the narrow artificial channel through which all river shipping must pass.

Two hundred Rumanian and Yugoslav soldiers armed with machine guns tonight were guarding the gateway where the Danube forms the boundary between Rumania and Yugoslavia. Giurgiu was turned into a military zone by the Rumanian Army, which banned all entries without special permits.

The German version of the seizure, said to have taken place Saturday, reported more than 100 British Army, Navy and Air Force men, who were to have participated in the coup, had been arrested.

Both the Rumanian Foreign Office and British quarters, however, insisted there was no basis for the German reports that Britons had been seized aboard the barges, and official London sources declined to

Continued on Page Eight

Canadian Premier to See Roosevelt Soon, Stopping Off En Route South for a Vacation

By FREDERICK T. BIRCHALL
By Telephone to The New York Times.

OTTAWA, April 8—Prime Minister W. L. Mackenzie King will leave Ottawa in a few days for a short holiday in the South of the United States. On his way through Washington he will pay a visit to President Roosevelt at the White House.

This will be Mr. Mackenzie King's first visit to Washington since war was declared. There are several questions he would like to take up with Mr. Roosevelt. There are doubtless also matters the President will be glad to discuss with the Canadian Prime Minister.

While there is no information here as to the precise subjects that may figure in the conversation, there are those ripe for discussion which are well known. Among these are the progress of the St. Lawrence Waterway project, continuance of the trade agreements renewed last year and the extent to which the United States can aid Canada's war effort.

As to the St. Lawrence project, it is known that both administrations are anxious to have the treaty signed with as little delay as possible so that it may be submitted to Congress in time for consideration before adjournment. Since the

---

German tanker was sent to the bottom. [Page 1.]

War caught up two more countries in its clutches today as the Germans invaded Denmark and attacked Norway.

Leaders in the Christian Front means business.

Among matters even more pressing are the exemption of Americans resident in Canada from the conditions affecting the ownership of foreign currency and securities and the status of American fliers who desire to come here and enlist under the Air Training Plan and for overseas service.

It has been strongly urged that Canada modify for these the oath of allegiance now required from all who join her forces, which does not automatically give them Canadian citizenship, while causing them to lose their own.

Another point of interest is Canada's desire to obtain from the United States more airplanes for use in the initial stages of the commonwealth air training plan. The present prospect is that there will be a shortage of planes until Canadian plants, now in receipt of about $40,000,000 worth of orders, can reach the stage of advanced production.

Any or all of these topics may be profitably discussed between the

Continued on Page Five

COPENHAGEN TAKEN

Troops Cross Border as Ships Debark Others in Sudden Nazi Blow

DANES FALLING BACK

Germans Say They Act to Forestall Foe and Protect Neighbor

By SVEND CARSTENSEN
Wireless to The New York Times.

COPENHAGEN, Denmark, Tuesday, April 9 — German troops crossed the Danish frontier at 5 o'clock this morning.

Three German cruisers arrived at that same hour at Middelfart and troops immediately occupied the streets of the town.

Copenhagen was also occupied by German troops this morning.

The invasion came some hours before the crossing of the border reports had circulated here that the Germans of South Jutland were expecting German troop trains carrying 45,000 men to arrive at the town of Flensburg during the night. That German town on the border was characterized as a convenient post for shipping troops northward, and although Danish border guards had been put in the highest state of preparedness it was not thought that there would be any threat to Denmark.

This belief had been bolstered by the fact that the fleet of more than a hundred German warships that passed through the Great Belt into the Kattegat and Skagerrak yesterday and early today included troopships—and it was presumed that this fleet was on the way to Norway to retaliate against the British Navy.

More Centers Seized

Mr. Carstensen left Copenhagen after the entry of German forces and went to Kolding, where he filed the following dispatch:

Special Cable to The New York Times.

KOLDING, Denmark, Tuesday, April 9—The German occupation continues here. It is reported that two ferry points on the Great Belt — Nyborg and Korsoer—have been occupied.

Troops have landed at Middelfart on a large scale. A Little Belt bridge has been reported seized and the city of Aalborg in North Jutland has been occupied.

Although there were no reports of clashes between Danish troops and the invaders today, military resistance was expected at Haderslev, about thirty miles north of the German border. The placing of guns and erection of barricades were reported from that town.

After leaving Copenhagen I observed from my automobile swarms of fast German planes flying over towns dropping badly printed leaflets that laid responsibility for Germany's invading Denmark and Norway to what was termed a British intention to make Scandinavia a theatre of war. The leaflets termed Winston Churchill, Britain's First Lord of the Admiralty, "the century's greatest warmonger," who planned to police Norwegian and Danish waters against the wills of the two countries.

The statement said that, since Norway and Denmark were unable to resist effectively, Germany had resolved to act in advance of a British attack and, by her own forces take over "protection" of Danish and Norwegian neutrality and "guard" the countries during the war. It was asserted that Germany did not intend to obtain bases for her fight against Britain but solely aimed at preventing Scandinavia from being a battlefield for "British expansion of the war."

According to the statement, negotiations were going on between the German and Danish Governments to make Denmark "secure" and assure that her army and navy were maintained and the Danish people's freedom respected. The country's independence, it was said, is fully secured. The sol-

Continued on Page Two

"All the News That's Fit to Print."

The New York Times.

LATE CITY EDITION
POSTSCRIPT
Fair, not much change in temperature today. Tomorrow cloudy.
Temperatures Yesterday—Max. 64; Min. 47

Copyright, 1940, by The New York Times Company.

VOL. LXXXIX...No. 30,057.   Entered as Second-Class Matter, Postoffice, New York, N. Y.   NEW YORK, FRIDAY, MAY 10, 1940.   THREE CENTS NEW YORK CITY and Vicinity | FOUR CENTS Elsewhere Except in 7th and 8th Postal Zones

NAZIS INVADE HOLLAND, BELGIUM, LUXEMBOURG BY LAND AND AIR; DIKES OPENED; ALLIES RUSH AID

U.S. FREEZES CREDIT

President Acts to Guard Funds Here of Three Invaded Nations

SHIP RULING TODAY

Envoy Reports to Hull on Germany's Attacks by Air and Land

Special to THE NEW YORK TIMES.

WASHINGTON, Friday, May 10—President Roosevelt early today ordered the freezing of all credits held by Belgium, the Netherlands and Luxembourg in this country.

He called a conference for 10:30 A. M. of heads of the State, War and Navy Departments to consider pressing problems of neutrality.

The President acted swiftly after news of Germany's invasion of the three European neutral countries reached Washington and galvanized high officials into action. His order with regard to the freezing of all the invaded countries' credits and cash balances here was a counterpart of the action taken after Germany invaded Norway and Denmark.

Congress this week completed action on legislation that specifically authorizes the President by decree to freeze all such cash and credits of any belligerent. The object is to prevent these resources from falling into the hands of the invading power.

Ships to Be Considered

The President's order directed Secretary of the Treasury Henry Morgenthau Jr. to freeze all Belgian, French and Luxembourg credits before the markets open this morning.

It was announced also that the conference to be held at 10:30 will consider the question of Belgian and Netherland ships that may be in United States ports. Attorney General Robert H. Jackson will also attend this conference.

The White House, meanwhile, indicated some skepticism of the official explanation of the invasion given by German Propaganda Minister Joseph Goebbels, who was reported to have said that the Germans had ordered information from official sources that Great Britain and France intended to invade the countries involved.

"Nevertheless," said Stephen T. Early, Presidential secretary, after he had quoted the Goebbels statement, "it remains to be seen who invaded who."

It was announced that the President would remain awake throughout the night, if necessary, to receive reports and consult with officials. Sumner Welles, Under-Secretary of State, at 1:45 A. M. joined the group of State Department officials who remained on duty at the department.

Report From Ambassador

A general invasion of the three neutrals by heavy German land and air forces was reported to the State Department and the Navy Department early today by Ambassador John J. Cudahy at Brussels.

After trying vainly to re-establish telephone connection with Secretary of State Cordell Hull, over which he had relayed a "blow-by-blow" description of developments several hours earlier, the Ambassador got through the following terse message:

"German planes continue to cross the border and are bombing the airport near Brussels. It seems to be a general attack on all three countries."

A State Department press liaison officer who was relaying latest diplomatic bulletins to reporters as they came in by transatlantic telephone, dropped the cryptic remark:

"As the American Ambassador spoke from Brussels, an enemy military attaché stood at his elbow."

After relaying the information to the President that the Belgian Government had ordered all hands to stand by, Ambassador Cudahy again called Secretary Hull between 10 and 11 o'clock and said he had been informed by officials in Brussels that one German and another

Continued on Page Two

The International Situation

In the midst of Britain's Cabinet crisis Germany struck another powerful blow early this morning by invading the Netherlands, Belgium and Luxembourg.

After swarms of planes had engaged in air fights over Amsterdam, parachute troops, some of them clad in Netherland uniforms, descended at strategic points while planes bombed air fields. The Netherlands resisted the incursion and promptly opened the dikes that are part of her water defense system. [Page 1.]

Parachute troops likewise made surprise landings in Belgium and bombs from 100 planes blasted the Brussels airport. [Page 1.]

Appeals for help were dispatched to the Allies by the invaded countries and it was understood that machinery of assistance was being set in motion. Queen Wilhelmina in a proclamation issued at The Hague declared, "I and my government will do our duty." [Page 1.]

As in the case of Norway, Berlin explained that the German action had been taken to forestall the Allies; an announcement said that an attack on Germany had been planned through the territory of the Low Countries. What the Reich was doing, it was declared, was safeguarding the neutrality of those countries. [Page 1.]

President Roosevelt lost no time in acting on the new situation. After night conferences he ordered the freezing of credits of the three invaded countries. Further measures are to be taken today. [Page 1.]

London, meanwhile, announced that British troops had occupied Iceland to prevent a possible German seizure of that former Danish possession. [Page 1.]

Before all these happenings Neville Chamberlain had appeared to be on his way out as Prime Minister, but today it was expected the new developments might save him.

Following upon his relatively narrow escape in the House of Commons vote on Wednesday night, Mr. Chamberlain set about yesterday to see what could be done to satisfy his critics. He offered Cabinet posts to two leaders of the Labor Opposition, but they refused to serve under him. As to whether they would serve under another Conservative, they delayed their reply. If Mr. Chamberlain steps out of office, it is thought probable his [Page 1.]

Bombs Drop on Swiss Soil

By The United Press.

BERNE, Switzerland, Friday, May 10—The army staff announced today that foreign airplanes had dropped bombs in the Berne Jura Alpine district between Delémont, near the frontier, and Mount Terr, damaging a railroad.

Traffic continued over the road, the army staff said. It added that other foreign planes were flying over Swiss territory near Basle but that no details had been received.

Special Cable to THE NEW YORK TIMES.

LONDON, Friday, May 10—The British Government received appeals for help early today from both the Netherlands and Belgium.

The British and French reply to the Netherland-Belgian appeals was prompt. Representatives of the respective governments here were told by 8:30 A. M. (3:30 A. M. New York time) they could expect all the help Britain could give them.

The Netherland Legation here received assurances that this country and Belgium were now regarded as Allies of Britain and France.

Within a few minutes after receipt of official news of the invasion of the Low Countries, the British Cabinet was called to 10 Downing Street and was in session with Prime Minister Neville Chamberlain.

According to information here, the German invasion of the Low Countries had been expected in London, and it must be presumed the Allies were ready for it to some extent.

Allies Visible to Planes

The biggest handicap to the British and French was in the timing of the German thrust at dawn. This prevented the Allies moving troops under cover of darkness, and since hundreds of German planes already had flown over practically all of Netherland and Belgian territory for some hours, the disposition of Allied troops and their every movement must have been known to the German High Command.

While the Netherlanders and Belgians had taken every precaution

Continued on Page Four

MUSSOLINI TO LET 'ONLY FACTS' SPEAK

Press Assures Yugoslavia, but Reminds Her of Fate of Poland and Norway

By HERBERT L. MATTHEWS
By Telephone to THE NEW YORK TIMES.

ROME, May 9—The fourth anniversary of the founding of the new Italian Empire was celebrated today in an atmosphere of warlike preparation. The army was honored, Italian armed strength was glorified and the country was told by its leading commentators that the empire would soon earn that "freedom of the seas" which to Italians means domination of the Mediterranean.

Rome, like every other city in the empire, resounded today to martial music while thousands of soldiers paraded through streets from whose buildings hung innumerable flags. The great ceremony was at the Piazza Venezia this morning. Premier Mussolini awarded gold and silver medals to the kin of soldiers fallen in Fascismo's three wars in Ethiopia, Spain and Albania. Later, from his balcony, he spoke very briefly, only to say that he was resuming his cloak of silence.

"May 9, 1936, was a great day in the history of the country, a day of solar victory," he said. "After my speeches, you must accustom yourself to my silence. Only facts will break it."

Small groups in the crowd thereupon began yelling "Tunisia!" and "Malta!" but the cries were not general.

At the same time this morning

Continued on Page Seven

ICELAND OCCUPIED BY BRITISH FORCE

Secret Expedition Is Justified as Thwarting Action There by Germany

By JAMES MacDONALD
Special Cable to THE NEW YORK TIMES.

LONDON, Friday, May 10—Forestalling a possible German swoop on the strategically valuable former Danish dominion of Iceland, the British have landed an expeditionary force there, it was announced this morning by the Foreign Office here.

Neither the size of the British contingent, which was sent out in the deepest secrecy, nor its place of landing was revealed in the official communiqué.

It was believed that the Labor party, which so far has refused to serve under him in a truly national government, would now close ranks, forget political difficulties and take any Cabinet job offered to its leaders. Furthermore, the expeditionary force was still going at an early hour this morning. Observers guessed that the landing place must be Reykjavik.

TEXT OF COMMUNIQUE

The official announcement read as follows:

Since the German seizure of Denmark it has become necessary to reckon with the possibility of a sudden German descent on Iceland.

It is clear that in the face of an attack on Iceland, even on a very small scale, the Icelandic Government would be unable to prevent their country from falling completely into German hands.

His Majesty's Government have accordingly decided to preclude this possibility which would ex-

Continued on Page Three

ALLIED HELP SPED

Netherland and Belgian Appeals Answered by British and French

TACTICS ARE WATCHED

London Thinks Move an Effort to Get Bases to Attack Britain

Italians Reported Massing

By The United Press.

BUENOS AIRES, Argentina, Friday, May 10—The Madrid radio was heard broadcasting today that the British had closed the Strait of Gibraltar and that Italy was massing troops on the French frontier.

BRUSSELS IS RAIDED

400 Reported Killed— Troops Cross Border at Four Points

PARACHUTE INVASION

Mobilization Is Ordered and Allied Aid Asked— Luxembourg Attacked

Wireless to THE NEW YORK TIMES.

BRUSSELS, Belgium, Friday, May 10—The invasion Belgium had feared since the outbreak of the European war came before dawn this morning. About a hundred German planes flew over this city and bombed the airport.

The airfield at Antwerp also was bombed. Parachute troops were landed at Hasselt in Eastern Belgium. Artillery fire was reported heard along the German and Luxembourg frontiers.

Anti-aircraft guns at the airport commenced firing with the appearance of the first invaders and kept up a steady barrage. Those in the center of the city went into action at 5:30 A. M.

Above the drone of airplane engines could be heard the staccato of machine guns. Bombs wrecked many houses in the vicinity of the airport and caused some loss of life. [Exchange Telegraph (British news agency) said 400 persons had been killed in the first raid.]

Reports from Antwerp and other parts of the country said German planes had flown constantly over since 4:30 A. M., keeping anti-aircraft batteries steadily in action.

According to information here, the Belgian Cabinet was in Brussels and Premier Hubert Pierlot conferred with King Leopold.

The German invasion of the Low Countries had been expected in London, and it must be presumed the Allies were ready for it to some extent.

Above the drone of airplane engines could be heard the staccato of machine guns. Bombs wrecked many houses in the vicinity of the airport and caused some loss of life. [Exchange Telegraph (British news agency) said 400 persons had been killed in the first raid.]

German parachute troops had fluttered down at Nivelles, less than twenty miles south of Brussels, and at Saint Trond, about thirty-five miles east of the capital. The broadcast stated that German bombs had made no demarche in the Brussels before the invasion.

Wireless to THE NEW YORK TIMES.

LONDON, Friday, May 10—The Germans crossed the Belgian frontier at four points this morning, according to an announcement over the

Continued on Page Two

Chamberlain Saved by Nazi Blow In Low Countries, London Thinks

By RAYMOND DANIELL
Special Cable to THE NEW YORK TIMES.

LONDON, Friday, May 10—The first effect of the German attack on the Low Countries is expected to be that Prime Minister Chamberlain will be saved just when it looked as if he was sure to fall.

It was believed that the Labor party, which so far has refused to serve under him in a truly national government, would now close ranks, forget political difficulties and take any Cabinet job offered to its leaders. Furthermore, there was a possibility that Mr. Chamberlain may quit immediately and turn his seals of office over to First Lord of the Admiralty Winston Churchill. This was a strong but unconfirmed rumor as a Cabinet meeting held this morning came to an end.

In addition, it was said that under Mr. Churchill, Alfred Duff Cooper would receive the Admiralty post, Anthony Eden the War Office and that Viscount Halifax would remain at the Foreign Office.

Until the invasion of the Low Countries was known, the con-

Continued on Page Five

NAZIS SWOOP ON THE LOW COUNTRIES

By land and air German troops descended this morning upon the Netherlands, Belgium and Luxembourg. The principal land incursion into the Netherlands was at Roermond.

Ribbentrop Charges Allies Plotted With the Lowlands

By GEORGE AXELSSON
Wireless to THE NEW YORK TIMES.

BERLIN, Friday, May 10—Foreign Minister Joachim von Ribbentrop at 9 o'clock this morning announced that Reich forces had launched military operations against Holland, Belgium and Luxembourg to "protect their neutrality."

Earlier it was reported that German troops had occupied Maastricht, the Netherlands, and had "landed" contingents in Brussels, probably meaning parachute troops.

Herr von Ribbentrop said that Germany had received unimpeachable proof that the Allies were engineering an imminent attack through the Lowlands into the German Ruhr district wherefore the Germans felt compelled to take corresponding measures. He said the time had come for settling the final account with the "Franco-British leaders."

And thus the war to a decisive finish was at last started in the West. This was the assumption when Herr von Ribbentrop informed the world through newspaper men that the German action meant that she had decided to settle all accounts with the Allies. "France and Britain dropped their mask," said Herr von Ribbentrop. "The alarm in the Mediterranean was a feint behind which the Allies were preparing an onslaught on German territory which the Reich could not tolerate."

The notes handed to The Hague and Brussels simultaneously with a shorter note to the Grand Duchy of Luxembourg just prior to their invasion by Germany—accused the Lowlands with having been overwhelmingly partial toward the Allies, adding that the attitude of the press was objectionable to the Reich.

A memorandum similar in tone to that handed to Denmark and Norway last month explained:

"In the life-and-death struggle thrust upon the German people, the government does not intend to await an attack by Britain and France inactively allowing the war to be carried through Belgium and Holland onto German soil. The government, therefore, has issued orders to safeguard the neutrality of the two countries with all the military means of the Reich."

Ribbentrop Reads Statement

In eight points the memorandum outlines the German argument that Belgium and Holland had not observed the strictest neutrality upon which German respect for their territories was founded. This argument reads: Berlin slept peacefully unaware

Continued on Page Four

HOLLAND'S QUEEN PROTESTS INVASION

Wilhelmina Vows She and the Government Will Do Duty— Bars Negotiation With Foe

By The United Press.

THE HAGUE, the Netherlands, Friday, May 10—Queen Wilhelmina said today in a statement on the German invasion of the country that "I and my government will do our duty."

The Queen, in a proclamation addressed to "my people," said:

"Since 3 A. M. German troops have crossed the Netherland frontier and German planes have tried to attack airports. Inundations are effective according to plans. The army anti-aircraft batteries were found prepared. So far as is known six German planes have been shot down."

[French, Belgian and British planes were sighted over the Netherlands this morning, a Reuters (British news agency) dispatch said in quoting The Netherland radio station at Hilversum, near Amsterdam.]

German troops were first reported crossing the Netherland frontier near Roermond, eight miles north of the Belgian frontier. German planes landed troops by parachute at strategic points near Rotterdam, The Hague, Amsterdam and other large cities.

A large number of the German troops landed by parachute were said to be dressed in Netherland military uniforms.

Other Germans crossed the Maas River in rubber boats to Netherland territory. They were said to be reaching the Netherland side in "considerable numbers."

A fierce air battle raged over Amsterdam as Netherland fighter planes dived repeatedly on German bombers and troop transport planes with chattering machine guns.

Schiphol Airdrome outside Amsterdam, the nation's largest, was heavily bombed. Military authorities immediately threw a heavy guard around the airdrome in an effort to defend the airdrome against German planes.

Planes identified as German Heinkels bombed Schiphol Airdrome repeatedly, loosing some thirty heavy caliber bombs on the landing field while the all-clear signal was given at 5:15 and 5:30 A. M.

Reports poured in of planes in great numbers over a score of Netherland cities. Netherland authorities, hurriedly organizing defense, flashed orders to the whole country to be on the alert against parachute troops.

Fifty planes were over Nijmegen, sixty miles southeast of Amsterdam on the German border.

A number of parachute troops reportedly landed at Sliedrecht, Delft and several other points. Delft is twelve and a half miles from The Hague. About 100 parachute troops

Continued on Page Three

AIR FIELDS BOMBED

Nazi Parachute Troops Land at Key Centers as Flooding Starts

RIVER MAAS CROSSED

Defenders Battle Foe in Sky, Claim 6 Planes as War Is Proclaimed

First Bombing in France

Special Cable to THE NEW YORK TIMES.

PARIS, Friday, May 10—The Bron airdrome, a big airport near Lyon, was bombed by German planes today. One German aircraft was shot down. The alarm was first given at 4:25 A. M. The all-clear signal was given at 6:45 A. M.

WASHINGTON, Friday, May 10 (UP)—United States Ambassador William C. Bullitt telephoned the State Department from Paris at 4 A. M. today that the Germans had bombed a number of fortified towns in France, "such as Dunkerque and Calais."

By The United Press.

AMSTERDAM, The Netherlands, Friday, May 10—Germany invaded the Netherlands early today, land troops being preceded by widespread air attacks on airdromes and by the landing of parachute troops.

The Netherlands resisted and announced she was at war with Germany. Anti-aircraft batteries and fighter planes engaged swarms of German aircraft when they appeared simultaneously over a score of Netherland cities.

An official proclamation said:

"Since 3 A. M. German troops have crossed the Netherland frontier and German planes have tried to attack airports. Inundations are effective according to plans. The army anti-aircraft batteries were found prepared. So far as is known six German planes have been shot down."

[French, Belgian and British planes were sighted over the Netherlands this morning, a Reuters (British news agency) dispatch said in quoting The Netherland radio station at Hilversum, near Amsterdam.]

Dispatches from Europe and the Far East are subject to censorship at the source.

"All the News That's Fit to Print."

The New York Times.

LATE CITY EDITION
Fair, continued cool today. Tomorrow increasing cloudiness, slightly warmer.
Temperature Yesterday—Max., 64; Min., 52

Copyright, 1940, by The New York Times Company.

VOL. LXXXIX...No. 30,065.   Entered as Second-Class Matter, Postoffice, New York, N. Y.   NEW YORK, SATURDAY, MAY 18, 1940.   PPPP   THREE CENTS NEW YORK CITY and Vicinity | FOUR CENTS Elsewhere Except in 7th and 8th Postal Zones

NAZIS PIERCE FRENCH LINES ON 62-MILE FRONT; TAKE BRUSSELS, LOUVAIN, MALINES AND NAMUR; WASHINGTON SPEEDS ITS BIG DEFENSE PROGRAM

ROOSEVELT IS BUSY

Calls Parley on Great Air Force, Considers Bigger Sea Patrol

UNITY IN CONGRESS

Partisanship Shelved in Drive—Midwest May Get Arms Plants

By FELIX BELAIR Jr.
Special to The New York Times.

WASHINGTON, May 17—National defense preparations were begun by government agencies today on a scale unapproached since the World War.

In response to President Roosevelt's preparedness message calling for an impregnable America, first steps were taken toward proposed far-reaching undertakings, such as construction of airplane and munitions factories in the Middle West, out of reach of possible quick bombing raids.

The President followed his request to Congress for a goal of 50,000 first-line fighting planes by calling a conference of aviation industry officials with army, navy and Treasury officials to be held in the office of Secretary Morgenthau Monday morning. Earlier in the day he disclosed plans to recommission thirty-five more World War destroyers for emergency patrol duty at a cost of $6,000,000.

Developments of the Day

As the executive and legislative branches gave evidence of the "partnership" for which the President appealed in his $1,182,000,000 national defense message yesterday, the preparedness campaign brought the following developments:

1. The House Military Affairs Committee began hearings on the President's defense program envisaging an army nucleus of 750,000 regulars and 250,000 reserves, fully equipped for active service by June 30, 1941.

2. Military authorities shaped plans calling for a $300,000,000 outlay to bring actual aircraft production up to 50,000 planes a year as quickly as possible under a program specifying a number of factories between the Allegheny and Rocky Mountains capable of producing a hundred planes a month, and rent them on a "fixed-fee basis."

3. House leaders organized a drive for modification of the Walsh-Healey Act to permit the President to waive forty-hour week limitations governing shipbuilding to speed up the present expansion program.

4. Mr. Roosevelt made known plans to call to Washington soon several recognized industrialists to speed industrial mobilization required to carry out his unprecedented peacetime defense program.

5. The White House placed its reliance upon the plans of Colonel Frank Knox, Chicago publisher, to sponsor the creation of a chain of aviation training camps throughout the country to supplement the military and naval training facilities.

6. The Navy Department considered proclaiming all industrial navy yards, air bases and fields as restricted areas and sought ways and means of increasing the number of its skilled mechanics from 75,000 to 150,000 or 200,000 men. The President's defense plan included the placing of the navy's expansion program on a twenty-four-hour basis instead of eight hours as at present.

Leaders Discard Partisanship

Political leaders, meanwhile, declared a moratorium on partisanship to expedite early enactment of legislation carrying out the President's plan to make our defenses invulnerable. The statement of former President Hoover endorsing Mr. Roosevelt's message to Congress was received by the White House as "an indication of national unity which we welcome and that political differences are being cast aside in the emergency."

The President, apparently convinced of Republican good will for his program, invited Alfred M. Landon to a White House luncheon conference next Wednesday.

In announcing the President's endorsement of the aviation training plan suggested by Colonel Knox, Stephen T. Early, White House

Continued on Page Six

The International Situation

The War in the West

German arms struck yesterday along the whole Western Front from the Netherland border to the northern anchor of the Maginot Line at the Luxembourg corner. As night fell the situation was as follows:

The Nazis claimed that on the northern wing against the British and Belgians they had penetrated to the outlying forts of Antwerp and occupied Malines and Louvain and that advance units were in Brussels, the Belgian capital. On the southern wing, against the French, the German High Command said it had broken through the fortifications along the Belgian-French border for a distance of 100 kilometers (62 miles) from just south of Maubeuge to Carignan, south of Sedan, and had penetrated into France as far as Le Cateau, La Capelle and to a point north of Rethel. The communiqué admitted, however, that the lines were changing hourly. The Germans claimed 12,000 French prisoners, including two generals. On the central Belgian front advances were reported at Namur and Wavre. [Page 1.]

The Allies did not deny that the situation was critical. General Gamelin, supreme commander of the Allies, issued a general order to all troops stating that the "fate of our country, of our Allies, the destiny of the world depend on the battle now being fought." The order recalled Marshal Joffre's famous message to the French Armies before the 1914 First Battle of the Marne, where the "taxicab army" from Paris stopped the Kaiser's legions, and saved Paris. A communiqué said that the Germans had penetrated as far as Avesnes and Vervins, about fifteen miles into France along the Belgian border. It estimated the Germans had engaged the "greatest part" of their heavy tank divisions in the attack. Attacks south of Sedan in the vicinity of Montmedy and Sedan were said to have been repulsed. Allied bomber and fighter squadrons were reported carrying out their missions of harassing enemy troop concentrations and rear lines of communication. [Page 1.]

While London admitted a withdrawal of its forces to a new defense line behind Brussels, advices from field headquarters in Belgium indicated that the retreat had been orderly and that the British air forces were more than holding their own in harassing the enemy and protecting their own rear from German bombing and machine-gunning attacks on communication lines. [Page 1.]

The Air Ministry at London said the German advance was not being made without cost. It estimated German plane losses in the last seven days at 1,000. However, it said, large reserves (estimated at 23,000 planes) made it probable the German air effort could be sustained for some time. [Page 4.]

Tragic victims of the horror were uncounted numbers of refugees who choked all roads in Belgium not already filled with troops and guns moving up to the fighting lines. Homeless, unfed, many wounded, seeking a sanctuary which appeared not to exist. [Included in the above.]

King Leopold of the Belgians, his capital lost, moved his government to Ostend. [Page 1.]

Repercussions Elsewhere

Scenes in government departments reminiscent of World War days were seen in Washington as the Federal agencies involved moved to put into effect the needed defense measures outlined by President Roosevelt in his speech to Congress Thursday. The President called a conference of Army, Navy and Treasury officials and aviation leaders to discuss his program to build up the United States air force to 50,000 planes. [Page 1.]

War fever mounted in Rome. Premier Mussolini's newspaper, Popolo d'Italia, thundered: "The Italian people must now or never achieve their Mediterranean destiny." The Senate, in an atmosphere of war hysteria, heard a budget report with a record deficit and warning of more taxes; the stock market suffered another "Black Friday" recession. [Page 1.]

On the Balkan diplomatic front Russia was reported bringing pressure on all interested countries to retain the status quo there under threat of forming an alliance with Yugoslavia and Bulgaria and reviving the idea of a union of all the Slavs in Europe. [Page 5.]

GAMELIN IN APPEAL

Says Fate of Nation and World's Destiny Hang on Present Conflict

FIGHTING IS AT PEAK

Full Air Forces Battle—Attacks at Sedan and Montmedy Repulsed

By G. H. ARCHAMBAULT
Wireless to The New York Times.

PARIS, May 17—"The fate of our country and that of our allies and the destiny of the world now being fought."

Thus begins a general order to all troops issued this evening by General Maurice Gustave Gamelin, supreme Allied commander.

Taken in conjunction with the communiqué issued from General Headquarters tonight, it reveals the situation as tragic.

"Today the German attack developed on a massive scale," the communiqué stated, "not only in Belgium but in the region of Avesnes and Vervins. On those fronts the enemy engaged a greater part of his heavy tank divisions. The battle took the form of a veritable melee."

Avesnes and Vervins are in the North of France, the latter some fifteen miles from the Belgian border.

[Cannonading was heard today on the outskirts of Paris, according to The Associated Press. It was not learned whether this was anti-aircraft or other fire.]

All United in Battle

General Gamelin's order adds that British, Belgian and Polish soldiers are fighting by the side of the French, together with foreign volunteers. The British Air Force, he added, like the French, is fighting to the last man.

Every troop that cannot advance, must die where it stands rather than abandon the portion of national soil entrusted to it. Concluding, he said:

"As always in the critical hours of our history, the watchword is 'Conquer or die.' We must conquer."

This general order so reminiscent of that issued by Marshal Joffre in 1914 on the first day of the Battle of the Marne tells the story. There is no detail. A terrific struggle is being fought for the future of mankind. All else is of no moment.

That the Allied General Headquarters has not departed from its calm is indicated in the remainder of the communiqué, which proceeds to refer to minor incidents as follows:

"Further to the east the enemy attacked in the region of Sedan and Montmedy without success.

Aviation Continues Activity

"In close collaboration with the Royal Air Force our aviation continued its energetic and efficacious action against ground troops, crossroads and railways. While assuring the protection of our troops our fighters engaged in numerous encounters. Many enemy planes were brought down. In the present conditions of open warfare it is not possible to know the exact number."

Nor is it of moment to refer to this morning's news relating to the actions on the Meuse. They all pale into insignificance with the day's developments. Since the outline of the pocket formed by the Germans was indicated by a spokesman for the general staff that pocket has been burst.

Any appreciation of the situation, any comment would be mere guesswork utterly out of place in the circumstances.

Decisive Victory Sought

PARIS, May 17 (AP)—The French armies, under orders from General Maurice Gustave Gamelin to "die on the spot rather than give further ground," battled a massive German tank drive into Northern France tonight in a clash described by the high command as "a veritable melee."

Adolf Hitler's fighters carried their week-old offensive on the Western Front to a peak during their day of most violent blows both in Belgium and France in a desperate effort to drive home a decisive victory.

The German thrust through Bel-

Continued on Page Three

GERMANY'S SWIFT COLUMNS SWEEP TO NEW SUCCESSES

Nazi forces, breaking through the extension of the Maginot Line in Northern France across the Belgian border, have reached the vicinity of Avesnes (4) and Vervins (5) and are reported north of Rethel (6) in a thrust toward Laon. The Allies claim to have halted a further attempt to widen the gap south of Sedan (7). In Belgium the Germans occupied Louvain and Malines (1) and claim to have reached the outer fortifications of Antwerp; they also crashed through the Dyle River defenses and marched into Brussels (2) as British forces withdrew to the west, and reported the capture of Namur (3). The dotted line indicates approximate Allied fixed positions.

NAZIS REPORT ROUT

Allies 'in Full Retreat' Westward Into France, Germans Declare

AIR VICTORIES NOTED

Sedan Prisoners Said to Total 12,000, Among Them 2 Generals

By GEORGE AXELSSON
Wireless to The New York Times.

BERLIN, May 17—Brussels, Malines and Louvain have fallen to the relentlessly advancing Germans, who also claim to have broken into France across the defenses of the Maginot Line extension on a wide front, standing not more than ninety miles from Paris at the nearest point.

The German High Command today broke a three days' silence on its Western Front operations to announce two major successes. First was the driving of a sixty-two-mile wedge into the French lines from south of Maubeuge to Sedan, southeast of Sedan. Second was a break through the Belgian Dyle line positions south of Wavre, along with the capture of Namur.

The spearhead of the German advance into France—where, a General Headquarters communiqué significantly says, "Our infantry units and air force are pursuing the enemy in full retreat westward"—is tonight said to be in the vicinity of La Capelle and Le Cateau, on the railway between Maubeuge and St. Quentin.

In the sector southeast of Sedan the Germans, according to their communiqué, have taken 12,000 prisoners, including two generals, and also captured abundant war material.

British Throw in Tank Units

In Belgium, the Germans early this morning already had advanced their lines to Malines, the vicinity of Louvain and south of Brussels in the Waterloo area, making the military situation of the capital seem hopeless for the defenders.

Here, it is admitted, the British had thrown in particularly powerful tank units in a desperate attempt to stem the German advance to the coast. The lines were swaying back and forth along this entire sector, with tank meeting tank and infantry against infantry in vicious hand-to-hand encounters of a ceaseless attack and counterattack.

The Germans evidently were following the Polish campaign method of launching giant tanks in wild forward lunges fanwise, as though along the fingers of an outspread hand, and trusting to skill and chance to hold the spearheads and eventually close the gaps between.

With Paris and the English Channel coast directly threatened, the military plight of the Allies appears most grave, as seen from Berlin. The British, it is said, must now devote every ounce of their resources to saving the coast, while the French must be equally occupied with the defense of their capital, rendering mutual aid difficult but impossible.

French Attacks Said to Fail

The Germans admit violent French attacks on their south flank, presumably in the Longwy sector, saying these attempts to relieve the main fronts met with no success. Instead, it is claimed, the Germans gained further ground in their counter-attacks.

That the struggle in Belgium and France have changed their aspect in the last forty-eight hours is asserted by military observers here. Only Wednesday the two battles were separate, one that in front of Brussels and the other to the south in France, formed one connected from Antwerp by Charleville to Sedan.

The German break through between Namur and Givet and through the Maginot Line across the Meuse was thrust at the point where the south flank of the Belgian battle zone joined the northern flank of the French. Widening of the breach between Namur and Givet and the rapid German push westward in the Maubeuge sector are said to have cooperated the two battle lines and doubled over the front.

The Belgian front is now reported turned back on the Sambre River westward where, according to the Germans, the Allied forces now are threatened with a flanking movement.

Continued on Page Two

COL. KNOX TO FORM AIR 'PLATTSBURGS'

Roosevelt Authorizes Civilian Groups to Promote Training of Students as Pilots

Special to The New York Times.

CHICAGO, May 17—With the authorization of President Roosevelt, Colonel Frank Knox, publisher of The Chicago Daily News and Republican Vice Presidential nominee in 1936, stated here today that a civilian group would be formed to cooperate with the government in training 10,000 pilots at volunteer camps this Summer in the nine army corps areas. Colonel Knox discussed the project in a White House conference yesterday with the President.

The training camps will be opened about July 1, Colonel Knox said, and will be designed primarily to accommodate 10,000 college students who have been receiving preliminary training through the Civil Aeronautics Authority.

"What we are undertaking," Colonel Knox said, "is not to replace any of the present activities, but to extend and increase them. We can turn out airplanes rapidly, but not top pilots, and we need at least two pilots for each plane."

World War Comparison

Colonel Knox described the new organization as a parallel to the army training camps of the last World War, such as Plattsburg, N. Y.

The cost of promoting the volunteer enlistments in the camps will be financed privately, he continued. The army has agreed for its part to provide tents, reserve officers for training, cooks and camp sites.

"Most of all," Colonel Knox said,

Continued on Page Seven

WAR BASIS EVIDENT IN ITALIAN BUDGET

With Record Deficit Figures, Senators Cheer Belligerent Speeches of Leaders

By HERBERT L. MATTHEWS
By Telephone to The New York Times.

ROME, May 17—While nothing startling happened in Italy today, there have been a number of minor developments to drive home further the feeling that Italian intervention in the European war is not very far off.

The Senate held a session in the morning full of genuine war fervor. The Minister of Finance, Count Paolo Thaon di Revel, presented what amounts to a war budget and admitted a deficit for this year of more than 26,000,000,000 lire. Premier Mussolini's own newspaper, in a highly significant editorial, as good as told the nation that it was about to enter the conflict.

The Stock Exchanges had a singularly black day; the great successes claimed by Germany on the French front provided a temptation of the first magnitude for the Fascist leaders.

The temperature in the Senate session was feverish. Every time the name of King Victor Emmanuel or of Premier Mussolini was mentioned there was a remarkably emotional reaction. Count Suardo, the President of the Senate, spoke words like these:

"The Italian people press around you, Duce, to form an iron block of energy and will, ready for your orders wherever you wish to guide them, because they know that the road you will take at their head to preserve our vital rights has just gained the grandeur and power of Italy."

At the end of Count Suardo's

Continued on Page Five

Gamelin, 1940; Joffre, 1914

Gamelin Order
By The United Press

PARIS, May 17—Following is the text of General Maurice Gustave Gamelin's order of the day to the French armies:

"The fate of our country and that of our Allies and the destiny of the world depend on the battle now being fought.

"English, Belgian and Polish soldiers and foreign volunteers fight at our side.

"The British Air Force is engaged up to the hilt like ours.

"Every unit that is unable to advance must accept death rather than abandon that part of the national territory entrusted to it.

"As always in the critical hours of our history the watchword today is 'Conquer or die.' We must conquer."

Joffre Order

Following is the text of the order addressed by Marshal Joffre to all army headquarters and to troops on Sept. 8, 1914:

"We are about to engage a battle on which the fate of our country depends and it is important to remind all ranks that the moment has passed for looking to the rear; all our efforts must be directed to attacking and driving back the enemy.

"Troops that can advance no further must, at any price, hold on to the ground they have conquered and die on the spot rather than give way. Under the circumstances which face us, no act of weakness can be tolerated."

BRITISH FALL BACK BEHIND BRUSSELS

'Adjustment' West of City is Announced—Troops Steady Against Nazi Blows

Special Cable to The New York Times.

LONDON, May 17—The War Office announced tonight that the British Army in Belgium had retired the night before to positions west of Brussels, "certain adjustments at the front having become necessary."

This "adjustment," the communiqué said, "was carried out without interference. There is no question of any collapse or break through in this sector as suggested by the German communiqué."

By HAROLD DENNY
Wireless to The New York Times.

WITH THE BRITISH ARMY IN BELGIUM, May 17—The Germans renewed today their assaults on the British positions, hurling tanks supported by airplanes with especial severity on the right side of the British line.

The British are withstanding these terrific mechanized assaults with great steadiness and can be counted upon to continue doing so. The briefest explanation is that the Allies have paid that price for moving immediately to the aid of Belgium and the Netherlands despite the fact that both countries steadily refused to consider any joint plan of campaign in the event of invasion.

Apparently what seems most inexplicable to the layman is that of vicious necessity. The Allied troops are defending themselves step by step, but the rapidity of movement that armies have today causes events to transpire with greater rapidity than ever. After a few days of war we find ourselves now in a situation which, without being so grave, recalls in certain respects what it was after the first weeks of war in 1914. We shall soon witness, we firmly believe, the same recovery which took place then."

Second, that the value of field works is determined by the forces behind them.

Since the Allied High Command decided early in the campaign to

Continued on Page Three

BELGIANS REMOVE CAPITAL TO OSTEND

Vacating of Brussels Laid to 'Obvious Necessity'—U. S. Envoy Remains at Post

Wireless to The New York Times.

PARIS, May 17—The removal of the Belgian capital from Brussels to another point in Belgian territory was announced today in a broadcast from Brussels by M. Vanderpoorten, Minister of the Interior, speaking for Premier Hubert Pierlot.

[The Belgian Government is now established at Ostend, on Belgium's North Sea coast, The Associated Press reported in a dispatch from Ostend.]

"This painful decision," he said, "has been forced upon us by obvious necessity.

First, these defenses were not of the Maginot Line of solid permanent concrete works that extends only from Montmedy eastward to the Rhine, but field fortifications—trenches, ditches, pits and the like—reinforced since the war by pill boxes and blockhouses.

Continued on Page Four

FRANCE PAYS PRICE FOR SHIFTING UNITS

Penetration by Nazi Armored Forces Laid to Fact Aid Had to Be Rushed to Neutrals

Wireless to The New York Times.

PARIS, May 17—Outside military circles, the public mind not only here but seemingly all over the world is much exercised over the swift advance of German armored columns into French territory.

The fact that the Allies have had to pay this price for moving rapidly to the aid of the neutrals seems not to be generally understood. They are equally confident of the ability of the French High Command to meet any situation presented by the German drive. The French must have foreseen every emergency which could develop and devised effective countermeasures. The French seem to have the gift of choosing the exact moment to strike most effectively.

The British now are fighting side by side with the Belgians, who made contact with them in the vicinity of Malines.

British resistance to the German

Continued on Page Four

Dispatches from Europe and the Far East are subject to censorship at the source.

"All the News That's
Fit to Print."

The New York Times.

LATE CITY EDITION
Cloudy, little change in temperature today. Tomorrow rain, not
much change in temperature.
Temperature Yesterday—Max., 79; Min., 55

VOL. LXXXIX No. 30,069. NEW YORK, WEDNESDAY, MAY 22, 1940. THREE CENTS NEW YORK CITY | FOUR CENTS Elsewhere Except in 7th and 8th Postal Zones.

NAZIS AT CHANNEL, TRAP ALLIES IN BELGIUM; CROSS AISNE RIVER 60 MILES FROM PARIS; FRANCE CAN'T DIE, REYNAUD TELLS PEOPLE

PRESIDENT SPEEDS DEFENSE PROGRAM; APPEALS FOR UNITY

At Press Talk He Condemns Nazis as Machine-Gunning Fleeing French Civilians

MOVES ON 'FIFTH COLUMN'

New Reorganization Order Will Put Immigration Bureau in Justice Department

As President Roosevelt outlined yesterday at his press conference further details of plans for the nation's defense [Page 1] various departments of the government took action to speed up preparedness. The navy submitted to Congress a program calling for 10,000 planes and 16,000 pilots. It also ordered a forty-eight-hour work week in navy yards and the hiring of 15,000 more civilian employes. [Page 13.]

Senator Pepper offered a resolution authorizing the President to sell to any invaded country any of the army's or navy's airplanes. The Senate sped action on the War Department Appropriation Bill, now increased to almost $1,500,000,000 in cash grants and close to $325,000,- 000 in contract authorizations. [Page 10.]

The President asked the House to lift its $50,000,000 limit on WPA grants, because such a restriction would hamper projects for defense. [Page 8.] He also vetoed a $109,985,450 Rivers and Harbors bill in order to give preference to military projects. [Page 11.]

States 3-Point Plan

By FELIX BELAIR Jr.
Special to The New York Times.

WASHINGTON, May 21—President Roosevelt today coupled an appeal for national unity behind his preparedness drive with the grimmest picture of German military tactics yet painted in any official American quarter—a picture of the deliberate machine-gunning of millions of fleeing French women, children and old men by Nazi war planes. He said Americans well understood the implications of such ruthless methods and would be guided accordingly.

Then the President, employing the gravest terms he has used in referring to the war in Europe, outlined the following three-point policy which he said would govern the nation's defense preparations:

Not a single war measure will be created in this country as a result of the war disaster.

Labor will not attempt to take advantage of its collective power to foment strikes and interfere with the national defense program to squeeze higher wages from employers in the so-called war industries. Under no circumstances will the Administration sanction a weakening of the social legislative gains attained during the last seven years. Labor standards prescribed in the Walsh-Healey act and the Wage-Hour Law must not be relaxed in the name of the national defense.

Plans Attack on 'Fifth Column'

As the President gave further impetus to the preparedness drive there were the following developments in his national defense program:

1. Mr. Roosevelt sought to strengthen the country against "fifth column" activities by providing for an early transfer of the Bureau of Immigration and Naturalization from the Labor Department to the Department of Justice. He said he would send to Congress tomorrow another reorganization plan giving effect to the transfer proposal.

2. With full Administration backing, chairmen of the Senate and House Naval Affairs Committees introduced companion bills to spend an additional $124,000,000 for a naval air armada of 10,000 planes and 16,000 pilots. Introduced by Senator Walsh and Representative Vinson after a White House conference, the proposed legislation would increase the navy's authorized aerial fleet by 7,000 units.

Continued on Page Two

The International Situation

On the Battle Fronts

Eleven days after the start of their offensive on the Western Front, the Germans yesterday drove a spearhead into the English Channel, cutting off the Allied troops in Belgium and the northwest tip of France from the main body of the French army. The German command estimated that half a million to a million men had thus been trapped between a steadily pressing mass of German attackers and the North Sea. [Page 1.]

The German thrust, described by Berlin as "the greatest attack of all time," swept sixty miles along the valley of the Somme, reaching Abbeville, on the estuary of that river. Amiens and Arras fell. The Germans claimed that their air force, aided by submarines and torpedo-carrying mosquito boats, was in command of the Channel. However that may be, French and Belgian ports, from which the British must embark if all effort to hold the northern line is abandoned, were being unmercifully bombed last night. Despite all this activity in the west, the Germans did not let up in the southern part of their huge salient. The push toward Paris continued, with semi-official sources in Berlin saying the invaders had crossed the Aisne at Soissons, sixty miles from the capital. [Included in foregoing.]

Paris contended that only motorcycle troops had reached Abbeville. Despite the breakthrough, French authorities said, there still was furious fighting in the neighborhood of Cambrai, far to the German rear, where the invaders had not yet succeeded in consolidating their positions. But there was as yet no sign of large-scale counterattack. [Page 1.]

The French admitted that the Somme Valley above St. Quentin was in chaos. Parachutists were being dropped by the hundreds and fires were springing up between the Belgian border, Amiens and the Channel, not one railway station stood intact. [Page 1.]

The Germans apparently had succeeded in capturing the commander of the French Ninth Army, General Henri Honoré Giraud. A Berlin dispatch said the capture had been "half-tragic, half-comic"—that the general had walked into his headquarters and found German officers there. Paris admitted there had been no communication with the general for forty-eight hours. [Page 1.]

Early this morning waves of Allied fliers bombed Aachen (Aix-la-Chapelle), on the west border of Germany. Bombs showered on the city and on Westwall fortifications. This raid was outstanding among many aimed at the German rear. The British Air Ministry announced that during the night German planes had dropped bombs on two districts in Southeastern England; no damage or casualties were reported. [Page 1.]

Alfred Duff Cooper, British Minister of Information, warned his countrymen by radio that they might expect invasion at any time. Volunteer "parachutists" were trained to take positions guarding points vulnerable to attack by German soldiers floating down from the skies. [Page 3.]

Premier Reynaud, addressing the French Senate, said the inefficient training and handling of General André Georges Corap's army was responsible for France's plight. "Unbelievable faults" would be punished, he declared. The Premier said the classic French conception of war had been demolished by armored divisions, fighting planes and disorganization of the rear by parachutists. He emphasized his faith in France to surmount her period of trial, and asserted: "Abroad they are beginning to understand * * * that what is happening affects them and their children. Let them not come to this understanding too late." [Page 1.]

Repercussions Elsewhere

Italy, which is expected shortly to join the German side, closed the border between Italian-owned Albania and Yugoslavia, where Allied sentiment has been strong. There were reports in Yugoslavia that munitions were being rushed in below the border and that barrack and other military construction work was being pressed in twenty-four-hour shifts. [Page 5.]

President Roosevelt, at a press conference in Washington, appealed for national unity in preparedness. He set forth three points to govern policy in building up our defenses: (1) No war measures will be created; (2) labor must not take advantage of its collective power to foment strikes interfering with the defense program; (3) there must be no weakening of social legislation of the last seven years, notably laws affecting labor standards. [Page 1.]

PREMIER IS CANDID

'Unbelievable Faults' in Allied Defense to Be Punished, He Says

'DISASTER' ADMITTED

But France Is Told Hope and Savage Energy Can Still Bring Victory

The text of Premier Reynaud's address is on Page 6.

By P. J. PHILIP
Wireless to The New York Times.

PARIS, May 21—Announcing quietly, amid a chilly silence, that since 8 o'clock this morning the advancing German forces had occupied Amiens and Arras, Premier Paul Reynaud in the Senate this afternoon called on the people of France, soldiers and civilians alike, to be worthy of "the grandeur of the hour in which we are living" and to "rise to the height of the misfortunes of our country."

Succinctly, sparing no one, he told the tragic story of the mistakes that had been made in the Belgian campaign, of the lack of preparation, of the miscalculations of the terrible exactness of the German calculations and their consequences.

The Germans had broken the hinge on which the whole left wing of the Allied armies swung, the Premier explained. They had pounded through the breach and driven forward with their armored divisions and airplanes far behind the French northern defense line. The French classic conception of war had been utterly routed by this new conception which disorganized the country behind the lines while it piled hammer blow on hammer blow at strategic points.

Cites 'Unbelievable Faults'

There had been, he went on, "unbelievable faults which will be punished." Bridges over the Meuse that should have been destroyed had not been destroyed. Describing what happened to General André Corap's army, he called it a "disaster" and "total disorganization." M. Reynaud seems not to have given up hope. The mistakes that had happened, that hope should be backed by confidence and savage energy on the part of all who are fighting and working for the salvation of the country.

This new method of war must be met by new methods of defense, he held. France had in the past repeatedly overcome such initial mistakes and miscalculations; she had risen from the pit of defeat to victory under Marshal Henri Philippe Pétain and Marshal Foch's lieutenant, General Maxime Weygand, in the past and could do so again.

There was an indirect word directed toward America and all the peoples far removed from the struggle. They were beginning to understand and to see that their future also was involved, M. Reynaud declared.

Continued on Page Six

NAZIS SPRINT TO COAST AND PUSH NEARER TO PARIS

Allied forces have been put in peril by a German spearhead driven between French and Belgian troops at Valenciennes (2) and by the westward push of the German right wing in Belgium, where the Belgians were engaged east of Ghent (1). Even more serious, however, was the advance to Abbeville (4) near the shore of the English Channel. As fighting raged north of Cambrai (3) motorized units swept south of that town and then, while some of them moved northwest to Arras, the rest raced along the Somme valley, took Amiens and continued on to the coast. Now was the threat to Paris renewed. At Amiens the Nazis claimed to have a bridgehead across the Somme, while to the east the German advance beyond Laon (5) was semi-officially declared to have resulted in the capture of Soissons, within sixty miles of Paris, and threats to both Noyon and Compiègne. At Rethel (6), however, the French said they were clinging to the south bank of the Aisne. The approximate limit of the German advance is shown by the broken line, which is based on dispatches received from both Berlin and Paris.

'Chutists and Cyclists Set Fires Behind Allied Lines

By The United Press.

PARIS, May 21—Germany unleashed the full fury of "total war" on Northern France today, dropping parachutists with torches to set fire to wide areas around Arras, Amiens and other cities in the Nazi drive to the English Channel.

Hundreds of German planes rained incendiary bombs on every city, village and community in the Picardy and Flanders lowlands, military dispatches said.

The action follows an official announcement today that General Sir Clive Liddell, had received instructions from the War Cabinet that owing to the international situation the evacuation of women and children from Gibraltar would be compulsory immediately.

The British have their choice of attempting evacuation under a rain of German bombs over the entire Channel ero or facing the enemy in a last-ditch effort to hold the only avenue of escape left to them—the Channel ports of Calais, Boulogne, Ostend and Blankenberge.

In either event, the B. E. F. is fighting desperately to escape annihilation.

[In Berlin it was said that the British had received orders to embark for England and that "our planes are bombing embarkation centers."]

Le Touquet Threatened

The Germans are completing encircling tactics in their drive to the coast between Abbeville and Le Touquet, which they are due to reach at any hour.

[Le Touquet is about twenty miles north of Abbeville, with a double-trunk railroad line runs to the French resort.]

German mechanized divisions were rumbling along roads leading to the principal ports. Allied forces were rushing to oppose them, but the Nazis were flushed with victory and no obstacle seemed capable of checking them.

The roads were crowded with refugees from Northern France, Belgium and the Netherlands. They blocked the roads and made Allied military manoeuvres more difficult.

The B. E. F. at present is awaiting the order of the Commander in Chief to make a terrific last stand in which it would be hoped that it possesses of gun power, tanks, infantry divisions and aircraft.

Continued on Page Four

500,000 'ISOLATED'

Swift Thrust to Coast Cuts Off Huge Force, Berlin Claims

SOISSONS 'TAKEN,' TOO

Invaders Stab at Paris as Threat to Britain Progresses

By GEORGE AXELSSON
Wireless to The New York Times.

BERLIN, May 21—In a crowning series of staggering blows dealt to the Allies in the last few days, the Germans claim tonight to have reached Abbeville on the Picardy coast, fifteen miles from Le Tréport on the English Channel. Thus they have now virtually achieved their aim to isolate the combined Allied armies in the western corner of Belgium and the northwestern tip of France. Unless they can fight their way out, this should seal the fate of the Belgian Army and numerous divisions of the French, altogether totaling perhaps between 500,000 and 1,000,000 men, to avoid whatever British forces are left in this area.

[The German thrust toward Paris has reached the region of Reims, it was said in official German circles early today, according to an Associated Press dispatch from Berlin.]

In an apparently masterful enveloping movement rapidly closing in, the Germans claim to have definitely broken up the entire French Ninth Army, taking prisoner its commander, General Henri Giraud, with his complete staff. The mission of the Ninth Army was to insure liaison between the strong Allied units in Belgium and the Maginot Line south of Sedan.

In the advance to Abbeville, the Germans say, they occupied Amiens and Arras. The River Somme up to the estuary the Germans tried in vain to breach "at all" drive in March, 1918, should thus be in their hands after brisk fighting that apparently lasted fewer hours than it did months during the World War.

Soissons Reported Taken

At the same time they are pushing toward Paris, they it is semi-officially said here tonight that they have taken the city of Soissons, a bare sixty miles by air from the French capital. Noyon and Compiègne, in this same area, appear to be seriously endangered and likely to be occupied at one moment or another.

With perhaps 1,000,000 Allied troops hopelessly cut off and squeezed by powerful German armored divisions toward the mouths of the Rivers Scheldt and Somme, the question arises here in the minds of neutral military observers: How could the Allied Army leaders have permitted a situation threatening such a major disaster?

One explanation is that it is perhaps the outcome of a desperate French attempt at a counter-offensive aimed at the flank of the German right wing without having sufficiently insured the rear lines of communication. It is suggested that Germans may have charged the mastodon type may have charged the French laterally, cutting off their supply lines and forcing the bulk of the attackers clear through the fronts into the jaws of Nazi dive-bombers efficiently supported the deadly ground work of the tank divisions.

French Effort Criticised

In this connection, it is asked here: What has happened to the French artillery? It is a matter of record here that the French have the most efficient artillery, from light field pieces including the famous 75's up to railway and other heavy long-range guns.

None of these, any more than French superb tanks reputedly weighing in the neighborhood of fifty tons, have figured in reports of the fighting available here. The superiority of the German tank and of the German planes seems definitely established, in the eyes of observers here.

With the Channel ports strongly commanded, a powerful German bid for final victory seemingly enters a decisive stage. As seen from here, the Allied position is not altogether

Continued on Page Two

BRITISH FIGHT HARD TO AVOID DISASTER

Their Whole Force in Belgium Is Trapped in Untenable Position, Allies Admit

By The United Press.

LONDON, May 21—The lightning German thrust to the English Channel has separated the main French and British armies and trapped the entire British expeditionary force in an untenable position, the Allied High Command recognised tonight.

The writer left one of the Channel ports today when the German drive was reaching its peak. It was directly menaced by advancing German mechanized units.

Women, Children Begin Evacuation of Gibraltar

Wireless to The New York Times.

GIBRALTAR, May 21—Women and children are being evacuated from Gibraltar. The first batches left today for French Morocco. Others will follow tomorrow and subsequent days.

AACHEN IS BOMBED HEAVILY BY ALLIES

Troop Concentrations There —German Bombs Dropped in Southeast England

By The Associated Press.

AACHEN, Germany, Wednesday, May 22—Waves of Allied bombing planes early today attacked this German city along the German Westwall fortifications, bombing and battling Nazi Messerschmitt fighters.

The first air raid alarm was sounded at 12:45 A. M., when the first enemy bombers appeared over the city and began dropping bombs. The attack was met by anti-aircraft fire for fifteen minutes, and Messerschmitt fighters went into the sky to battle the raiders. From then on the Allied planes came in waves and were still sweeping upon the city at 1:05 A. M.

[Aachen, also known as Aix-la-Chapelle, lies at the point of the German, Netherlands and Belgian borders and was the "jumping off" place for the German

Continued on Page Four

HENDRICKSON LEADS IN JERSEY PRIMARY

Willkie Gets Surprise Write-In Vote Against Dewey in Presidential Contest

A write-in vote for Wendell L. Willkie in the New Jersey primaries yesterday disclosed surprising strength for the utilities executive as a candidate for President. State Senator Robert C. Hendrickson of Gloucester County was the leading candidate and former Governor Harold G. Hoffman for the Republican nomination for Governor.

A total of 2,285 election districts out of 3,651 in the State gave 195,- 680 votes to Mr. Hendrickson and 144,280 to Mr. Hoffman, a commanding lead of 21,390 for Mr. Hendrickson.

Contrary to pre-election predictions, Hendrickson carried Bergen and Union Counties on the basis of incomplete returns. He made in both counties was small, however. His plurality in Essex County was larger than had been expected.

State Senator Winant Van Winkle, a Hendrickson supporter, was defeated for renomination in Bergen County by a Hoffman candidate, Lloyd L. Schroeder. Complete returns gave Schroeder 37,380 votes to 29,251 for Van Winkle.

District Attorney Thomas E. Dewey entered the Republican primary as a preferential candidate

Continued on Page Sixteen

ALLIES FIGHT BACK AT FURIOUS DRIVES

Admit Penetration of Nazis to Abbeville, but Look for Re-forming of Lines

By The Associated Press.

PARIS, May 21—The Allies, with their backs to the English Channel, tonight fought against a new German advance that spread a path of fire across Northern France and threatened to isolate England.

The French High Command's night communiqué admitted the Germans had driven their advance point to Amiens and Arras, on the edge of the coastal plain leading to the English Channel.

A War Ministry spokesman added that German motorcycle troops had pushed on to penetrate the outskirts of the Abbeville region. The city of Abbeville is on the Somme estuary, twelve miles from the Channel's open waters, and about twenty-five miles west of Arras and Amiens. The War Ministry spokesman said he believed the French still held Abbeville itself, but that he could "give no official confirmation."

German motorcycle units thrust along roads to the west of Arras and Amiens behind advance formations of Nazi planes. Other roads radiating from the French towns, filled with refugees, were reported strafed by the Germans from the

Continued on Page Four

Nazis Report Capture of Giraud; Say General Walked Into a Trap

Wireless to The New York Times.

BERLIN, May 21—The German told an astounding story today of how General Henri Giraud, commander of the French Ninth Army, was captured. In a lightning advance in the Cambrai sector, Nazi forces occupied the château headquarters of the French Ninth Army. Here they learned that the commanding general had left, having been relieved by order of the new Commander in Chief, General Maxime Weygand by General Giraud, who had been head of the Seventh Army.

According to accounts here, the Germans did their best by merely remaining and telling General Giraud and his staff into custody as they arrived to take charge, ignorant of the situation. The story of the capture turned out to be even more fantastic, for the High Command did not want it spread, hoping that dispatch riders and others attached to the Ninth Army headquarters,

uninformed of the change, would fall into the net.

BERLIN, May 21 (UP)—General Henri Honoré Giraud, commander of the French Ninth Army, which struggled to stem the German tide for eleven days, was said to have been taken prisoner in a "half-tragic, half-comic manner" when he walked into his headquarters and found German officers there.

General Giraud, 61 years old and one of France's most famous strategists, had been placed in command of the main Allied defense along the German "bulge" front in Northern France and Southern Belgium only on Saturday, it was said by German officials.

As a captain in the World War, he was captured by the Germans two weeks after the outbreak of the conflict and finally escaped through Belgium and the Netherlands.

Continued on Page Five

Dispatches from Europe and the Far East are subject to censorship at the source.

The New York Times.

Copyright, 1940, by The New York Times Company.

VOL. LXXXIX...No. 30,077.   Entered as Second-Class Matter, Postoffice, New York, N. Y.   NEW YORK, THURSDAY, MAY 30, 1940.   THREE CENTS NEW YORK CITY and Vicinity | FOUR CENTS Elsewhere Except In 7th and 8th Postal Zones

LATE CITY EDITION
Partly cloudy today, showers tonight, little change in temperature. Tomorrow showers.
Temperature Yesterday—Max., 64; Min., 53

ALLIES ABANDONING FLANDERS, FLOOD YSER AREA; A RESCUE FLEET AT DUNKERQUE; FOE POUNDS PORT; ONE FORCE CUT OFF FROM THE SEA AS LILLE FALLS

PRESIDENT TO ASK $750,000,000 MORE FOR ARMY PROGRAM

Nazi Blitzkrieg Held to Show the $3,300,000,000 Allotted Fails to Meet Needs

FOR TANKS, GUNS, PLANES

Tax Bill to Be Offered in House Today—D. M. Nelson Named Procurement Director

By FELIX BELAIR Jr.
Special to THE NEW YORK TIMES.

WASHINGTON, May 29—On the eve of his first meeting with the reconstituted Council of National Defense, President Roosevelt was putting finishing touches today on a new request for $750,000,000 as a supplemental appropriation for further expansion and mechanization of the military establishment to take account of European war developments since he sent his preparedness message to Congress two weeks ago.

The projected increase in funds for the Army, over and above the omnibus $3,300,000,000 defense program already mapped by the President in a White House conference with Treasury and War Department officials.

It was the President's plan to send up the supplemental request in a few days. Subject to additions, the new program contemplates placing orders immediately for the following:

About 3,000 new pursuit and bombing planes.
Between 1,500 and 2,000 tanks.
About 500 heavy howitzers.
A supply of aerial bombs of various sizes, to cost between $20,000,-000 and $30,000,000.

Other modern weapons of war which have been developed in Army laboratories, but not yet put into actual production.

German Drive Appraised

There was no official announcement on the results of the meeting, and Secretary Woodring, who acted as spokesman for the group, said only that they had reviewed "the whole military situation."

From others present, however, it was learned that the nation's military establishment had been reappraised in the light of Germany's advances in Western Europe since the President's preparedness message was first submitted to Congress.

Other developments in the national defense program were:

1. The Senate Naval Affairs Committee brought out a measure increasing the air force limit of the Navy to 10,000 planes and 16,000 pilots, with a report warning that the "country at this time is facing the possibility that the Allies may be defeated and that we may have to defend ourselves in both oceans at the same time."

2. Senate leaders were planning to take up tomorrow the $1,500,-000,000 bill providing an 11 per cent increase in under-age surface tonnage, with indications that the measure would be disposed of without delay.

Procurement Officer Named

3. Secretary Morgenthau named Donald M. Nelson, executive vice president of Sears, Roebuck & Co., as director of the Treasury's Procurement Division, thereby adding another business executive to the list of those on whom the administration is relying for the success of the defense program.

4. Administration — Congressional plans for placing emergency rearmament financing on a "pay-as-you-go" basis gathered momentum, with an announcement by Representative Doughton, chairman of the House Ways and Means Committee, that he would introduce tomorrow a measure raising the statutory debt limit by $3,000,000,-000 and imposing upward of $656,-000,000 in new defense taxes.

5. Secretary Hull modified aviation restrictions under the Neutrality Act to permit the delivery of American planes by American pilots to Halifax, N. S., thereby removing the ban on through deliveries over the Maritime Provinces.

6. White House sources explained that there would be the closest possible relations between Presi-

Continued on Page Eight

When You Think of Writing Think of Whiting—Advt.

ALLIES STRIKE FOR COAST IN EVER-TIGHTENING POCKET
To keep the exit at Dunkerque (1) open French and British sea, land and air forces were waging a furious struggle yesterday to retard the German advance the Allies were understood to have opened sluice gates on the Yser to flood the region below Nieuport (2). In the sector that had been held by the Belgians the Nazis pushed to Ostend and Dixmude (3). Farther south they were reported to have taken Ypres (4). Their most important operation of the day, however, was the bisecting of the pocket by the capture of Lille and Armentieres (5), thus cutting off from the sea the Allied forces in the lower section. Along the Somme the French eliminated a German bridgehead west of Amiens (6). The broken lines show the approximate battlefronts.

HULL ORDER SPEEDS PLANES TO ALLIES

Allows Our Pilots to Fly Craft Over Three Canadian Maritime Provinces

Special to THE NEW YORK TIMES.

WASHINGTON, May 29—The way was opened today for expediting deliveries of American airplanes to the Allied fighting lines when Secretary Hull modified regulations of the Neutrality Act to permit the delivery of such aircraft by American pilots to ports in the three eastern Canadian cities.

The step was designed to facilitate deliveries to the Allies because of the urgency of their military situation. It was taken at the request of the French Government.

Mr. Hull ruled that "American nationals may travel in belligerent aircraft over the Canadian Provinces of New Brunswick, Nova Scotia and Prince Edward Island."

This means that pilots from the United States may fly new planes to Halifax, whence they will be flown across the Atlantic by pilots of the Allies or sent across by ship. American pilots have been delivering planes in Ottawa and other Canadian cities. As before, they must still conform under the new order to regulations by pushing planes over the Canadian border from the United States.

Previously, American pilots could fly planes over Canadian territory, once they were pushed over the border the fliers could not enter the three eastern maritime Provinces because American ships are barred from them and aircraft regulations conform to shipping rules. Newfoundland was excluded from the modification today because there was no actual need for including it.

The Department of Commerce announced that April shipments of aircraft and equipment to the Allies included 195 planes and 285 engines.

Of the planes, France received seventy completely powered craft and ninety-eight in a knock-down condition. The United Kingdom obtained twenty-three assembled and powered and Canada four.

With a variety of other equipment included, French purchases for the month totaled $14,448,671; those of the United Kingdom $2,905,621 and those of Canada $725,329.

The Department of Commerce announced that total exports of aero-

Continued on Page Two

Berlin Exchange Slumps As Optimism Is Decried

Wireless to THE NEW YORK TIMES.

BERLIN, May 29—In what was apparently a strong reaction to warnings against over-optimism, which have been circulated generally among the population following the German victories in the West, the Berlin Boerse today took a sudden nose dive.

Most issues dropped between 1 and 4 per cent. In shipping, Hapag dropped 5 per cent and North German Lloyd dropped 3 per cent. Fixed interest securities were quiet and generally unchanged. The close was irregular, with call money at 1¾-2¾.

Utilities, motor works and other heavy industries led the recession, while metal works in the Rhineland were among those that showed the maximum decline.

URUGUAY ON GUARD FOR FIFTH COLUMN

Check on Assembly, Increase in Army Urged—Nazis Take Bold Tone in Ecuador

Special Cable to THE NEW YORK TIMES.

MONTEVIDEO, Uruguay, May 29 —The Uruguayan Government is frankly alarmed over Nazi fifth column activities.

After several Cabinet meetings at which the problem was closely studied, President Alfredo Baldomir has sent to Congress, with a request for urgent action, two bills. One provides for general rearmament and the other modifies Article 38 of the Constitution, which guarantees the right of assembly.

It has been rumored in well-informed diplomatic circles in more than one South American capital yesterday and today that Uruguay fears an invasion of Nazi fifth columnists from Southern Brazil. Official circles tonight emphatically denied any such fear and also denied that Uruguay had requested assistance from any other government.

The President's office earlier in the day, however, had published the details of the plans for rearmament and for modifying the constitutional guarantees.

Article 38 of the Constitution says that "all persons have a right to utilize association except 5,000,-000 times this power output of coal, assemble freely in time association, whatever may be the object sought, except they do not constitute an association declared by the law to be illicit.

Since the law doesn't define what constitutes an illicit association, the bill that President Baldomir sent to Congress yesterday defines such il-

Continued on Page Six

ITALY BARS IMPORTS EXCEPT BY BARTER

Cancels Permits to Bring In Goods or to Buy Exchange for Payments Abroad

By HERBERT L. MATTHEWS
By Telephone to THE NEW YORK TIMES.

ROME, May 29—The Ministry of Foreign Exchange issued an order today to all banks and industrial firms canceling permits for importation and permission to acquire foreign currency to pay for imports. Thus Italy cuts herself off commercially from the world, except for barter agreements, and even there Italian ships coming in are not departing to bring back further imports.

This is the most serious indication yet given of the expectation of war, certainly as serious as the postponement of the sailing of Italian vessels announced last Friday.

The Conte di Savoia is due back from New York Sunday. No one expects her to depart, even on June 23, when she is scheduled to go. That will leave only the Conte Grande out of the Mediterranean among the large Italian ships. She sailed for South America a week ago.

[The steamship Roma arrived yesterday at Naples, according to The Associated Press, and is now expected to remain there instead of proceeding to Genoa, as scheduled. The Roma was to have left Genoa for New York June 29.]

Trade with the United States will suffer most heavily by the decision taken today. It has been possible for importers to acquire dollars at

Continued on Page Four

11,000 Times Speedier Way Found To Obtain Atomic Power Element

By WILLIAM L. LAURENCE

Development of a process that speeds up by 11,000 times the extraction of U-235, the element recently discovered to possess 5,000,-000 times the power output of coal, promising to make it possible to utilize atomic energy as a new source of enormous power for all purposes, and to place in the hands of the nations at war, especially Germany, the most powerful fuel ever to be discovered, is to be announced in the forthcoming issue of Nature, leading British scientific weekly, advance proofs of which have reached THE NEW YORK TIMES.

On May 5 it was announced that a tiny amount of U-235, a relative of uranium, had been isolated at the University of Minnesota and that General Electric Company, and that pioneer experiments at the physics laboratories at Columbia University, under the direction of Professor

blockade could be materially offset.

The new process for extracting U-235 that promises to revolutionize methods of power production and to usher in a new civilization based on the utilization of atomic power, was developed by Professor Wilhelm Krasny-Ergen of the Wenner-Grens Institute, Stockholm, Sweden, one of the leading scientific research institutions in Europe.

On May 8 it was announced that Germany positions on the Rhine German positions on the Ofotes railway. In a narrow part of the fjord the Germans have sunk ten ships in an attempt to block off the British naval vessels.

Other reports reaching London today said German planes had raided Bodoe, at the entrance to Vest Fjord, about ninety miles north of Narvik, last evening, dropping 200 bombs and machine-gunning the town. Of the population of 6,000, it is said at least 5,000 are now

Continued on Page Five

NAZIS TIGHTEN TRAP

They Drive a Line Across Pocket, Encircling Foes in South

SAY YPRES IS TAKEN

Zeebrugge and Ostend Fall—Large Stores Are Reported Seized

By GEORGE AXELSSON
Wireless to THE NEW YORK TIMES.

BERLIN, May 29—Remnants of the Allied Armies cut off in Flanders came a step nearer to being wiped out today when the Germans, simultaneously pressing from east and west toward the middle, managed to drive a wedge right across the pocket, thus separating the French and British divisions north of Lille from those in the south, who now are surrounded on all sides, no longer having access to the sea.

The Germans tonight claim to be in the city of Lille, in Ypres and Armentieres and to have burned Dunkerque under heavy artillery bombardment. The Belgian capitulation permitted the Germans to take Bruges, Zeebrugge, Ostend and Thourout without a struggle.

Piercing the Allied lines at Lille, where, however, fortifications still seem to hold out, permitted the Germans to make two pockets out of the big one. The smaller of these, south of Lille, is square with the sides between nine and twelve miles long, and inside this narrow space are compressed the French divisions that only a few days ago tried to break the strong German hold at Valenciennes, as well as British contingents that figured in desperate resistance in the sector between Arras and Cambrai.

Refugees Also in Trap

Hemmed in with these troops is an incalculable number of refugees and other civilians, who are exposed to bombs and shell fire on the same terms as the soldiers fighting one another in this area.

The larger northern pocket reaches from Lille to the sea, and although it is some thirty miles wide the situation of the troops enclosed in it appears to be hardly more enviable than that of their comrades surrounded to the south. They are being hard pressed on three sides by withering German fire as well as from the air.

Their only chance of retreat, should they choose this way out, seems to be the narrow strip of coast between Dunkerque and Nieuport, but the Germans are said to be continuously shelling and bombing this district, making it scant, even if protected by Allied warships, seem most difficult.

Crowded together in an area bounded by Dixmude, Ypres—which the Germans claim to have taken by storm tonight — Armentieres, Bailleul and Bergues, remnants of the British Expeditionary Force and whatever French and Belgians remain thereabout appear to have a choice only between death or surrender.

The situation up there, according to latest reports received in Berlin, indicates that the Allies have chosen to fight to the last. The Germans stand before Dixmude, where the Allies are holding them, and a similarly bitter struggle is raging at

Continued on Page Four

The International Situation

On the Battle Fronts

The Battle of Flanders became yesterday a wholly rear-guard action, with the Allies trying to evacuate as many as possible of the troops caught in the German pocket. The trapped men fought on "desperately but not despairingly," Paris reported. [Page 1.]

The port of Dunkerque was still in Allied hands (although the Germans reported its embarkation area in ruins), as was Nieuport, just above the Belgian border. Ships were said to be waiting at the coast to take off the men who could get to them, although how they stayed afloat in the torrent of German bombing seemed a mystery. The British and French fleets were furiously bombarding German forces on the Channel, hoping to cover the withdrawal. The task of evacuation was made doubly difficult by a German force that, Paris reported, had straddled the Franco-Belgian border near Cassel and Mount Kemmel. The French said that defense floodgates had been opened, inundating part of the area west of the Yser. On other fronts the French asserted that they had eliminated a German bridgehead on the Somme west of Amiens, and had repulsed a German thrust near Rethel, on the left flank of the invaders. [Included in the foregoing.]

The desperate situation of the Allied army of the north was made evident by Berlin dispatches telling of the success of the German effort to cut the opposing forces in two. The invaders drove a wedge between the two and Allied wings to the north of Lille. Thus there are now two pockets; the forces south of Lille are completely surrounded, in a square-shaped area whose sides measure only nine to twelve miles. The pocket above Lille was greatly reduced by German advances pressing down from the north and up from the south. [Page 1.]

Early this morning shattered remnants of the British Expeditionary Force began arriving at British ports. Most of them were wounded. To the survivors still in Flanders King George sent a message saying they had displayed "gallantry that has never been surpassed in the annals of the British Army." [Page 1.]

The Allies recorded a victory in Norway. They took Narvik, and the Germans admitted its loss. The British said their warships had sunk seven German troop transports in the Narvik area in the last three days. [Page 1.]

Repercussions Elsewhere

Britain took drastic measures to guard against possible fifth column activities on the part of aliens. Beginning June 3, all aliens must be in their "ordinary place of residence" from 10:30 P. M. to 6 A. M.; they are forbidden to own bicycles, boats or aircraft without special permission. [Page 2.]

Italy, by decreeing an end to import and foreign currency permits, cut herself off from the world commercially, except for barter arrangements. And even they have ceased to mean anything, as Italian vessels no longer are being sent abroad for cargoes. The new regulations gave the strongest indication yet of Italy's intention to join Germany in the field soon. [Page 1.]

Because Russia had refused to accept Sir Stafford Cripps, Left-Wing Labor member of the British Parliament, as a "special trade envoy," London conferred Ambassadorial status on him. Sir Stafford is in Athens, en route to Moscow. With offers of improved trade with Britain, he will seek to woo Russia away from Germany. [Page 4.]

The Nazi fifth-column technique stirred fears in South America. Uruguay's Congress received from President Baldomir two bills, one of which would provide for rearmament, the other modifying the Constitution to deny the right of assembly to anti-democratic organizations with foreign connections. [Page 1.]

What has happened in Flanders impelled a reappraisal in Washington of American defense plans, with the result that President Roosevelt decided to ask Congress for $750,000,000 (in addition to the $3,300,000,000 already budgeted) to be used to buy 3,000 pursuit and bombing planes, 1,500 tanks, 500 heavy howitzers and at least $20,000,-000 in aerial bombs. The Senate Naval Affairs Committee, recommending House-adopted bills to speed air and naval preparedness, said the country's defense plans must be based on the possibility of defeat for the Allies. [Page 9.]

ALLIES GET NARVIK IN LAND-SEA FIGHT

Warships Support Troops in Final Thrust From Beis and Rombaks Fjords

By JAMES MacDONALD
Special Cable to THE NEW YORK TIMES.

LONDON, May 29—Narvik, Norway's important iron ore port, the prize of an unrelenting struggle ever since Germany invaded Norway on April 9, has been captured by Allied forces, the War Office and Admiralty announced in a joint communiqué today. The communiqué also announced the capture of Pagernaes, on the shore of Narvik Harbor, and Forsnaeset, five miles east of Narvik on the railway line over which Swedish iron ore reaches Narvik for shipment to Germany.

Fierce fighting by Norwegian, French, British and Polish forces continues in the district. An unofficial report received here today said British naval forces had sunk seven German troop transports in Narvik waters since Sunday.

British warships are reported high up in Rombaks Fjord, shelling German positions on the Ofotes railway. In a narrow part of the fjord the Germans have sunk ten ships in an attempt to block off the British naval vessels.

Other reports reaching London today said German planes had raided Bodoe, at the entrance to Vest Fjord, about ninety miles north of Narvik, last evening, dropping 200 bombs and machine-gunning the town. Of the population of 6,000, it is said at least 5,000 are now

Continued on Page Five

COAST FIGHT RAGES

Communications Lines and Bases Bombarded Constantly by Nazis

DUNKERQUE SHELLED

Allies Inflicting Heavy Losses as They Battle in Rear-Guard Actions

By G. H. ARCHAMBAULT
Wireless to THE NEW YORK TIMES.

PARIS, May 29—The full import of the Belgian defection during the course of the battle in Flanders may be gathered from the indication given tonight by a spokesman for the General Staff that King Leopold's army represented about half the Allied forces engaged on that front.

French and British in that area continue to fight desperately, though not despairingly yet, with the knowledge that at present at least little help can be given them. Their valor is described as very comforting in the circumstances, and it is added that whatever happens their honor will be safe.

Breaking the anonymity rule that has prevailed hitherto, it is announced this evening that, under General Georges Maurice Jean Blanchard's direction, General René-Jacques-Adolf Prioux is striving to fight his way to the coast in the general direction of Dunkerque, where Vice Admiral Jean Marie Abrial of the French Navy is cooperating and is holding that base, where he has organized a service of supplies with vessels of all kinds of tonnage.

Prioux a Cavalry Man

General Prioux was a corps commander at the beginning of the war; he is sixty-one years of age and comes from the cavalry arm.

No one has yet come from that inferno in Flanders to describe the scene; doubtless it baffles the imagination. For the battle is being waged on land, in the air, on the sea and under the sea. Every engine of death yet devised by man is in action and the fight never ceases day or night. Nor is it confined to the actual battlefield. All bases, all lines of communication are bombed continually on both sides, with the Germans concentrating a great effort on Dunkerque.

The communiqué issued from French General Headquarters this morning said that "information from accurate sources warrants the affirmation that the losses suffered by the Germans in the engagements yesterday and last night were particularly high."

The French and British are fighting mostly rear-guard actions against very superior numbers, but whenever any unit finds itself in approximately equal strength it counter-attacks "to progress over the enemy dead."

Position Very Critical

Nevertheless despite heroic deeds it cannot be gainsaid that the position of the Allied division is very critical.

The exact position of General Blanchard's forces is not known; his front on any case must be very fluid. Doubtless he has shortened his lines in order to constitute a sort of mobile fortress moving toward the sea and fighting every inch of the way. This rescue aspect of his situation lies in the fact that the prime task of Leopold's army was to cover the coast.

It is revealed today in this connection that it was at the Belgian King's repeated insistence that the Allies took up positions on the Scheldt to protect Antwerp and also that the order to retreat was deferred until May 15, although the Allied High Command had urged withdrawal on the eleventh or twelfth.

There is confirmation today of the indication given yesterday in these dispatches that before the capitulation there were French detachments between the Belgians and the sea. It is hoped that though relatively small they may have acted effectively along the coast. It is believed, moreover, that it has been possible to flood part of the country west of the Yser River. Water lines of this sort proved of great value in the last war in this very region.

On the coast the Allies have lost Ostend. They hold Nieuport and

Continued on Page Two

HARRIED B. E. F. MEN ARRIVING IN BRITAIN

Many of Wounded Had to Wade Out to Boats Under Constant Fire of German Forces

By The United Press.

LONDON, Thursday, May 30—Shattered remnants of the British Expeditionary Force—blood-stained, muddy and walking like men asleep —began arriving in British ports early today.

Most of the first arrivals were wounded. They described a constant, pitiless German bombing and strafing bombardment of the French ports from which Viscount Gort is attempting to save his trapped divisions.

They said the shattered British lines were "sliding off a stretch of coast thirty miles long."

German bombs rained down continually, even on hospital ships, they said. Quays and harbor works of the French ports were under terrific German air attack, which went on all through last night.

Allied warships and the Royal Air Force worked and fought like beavers to aid the rescue of the battered armies of Flanders whose fate was tested on on the Channel's brink. Under a screen of intense curtain fire from long-range naval guns, the B. E. F. was backing out through the Dunkerque area.

The New York Times.

LATE CITY EDITION
Cloudy with showers and little change in temperature today and tomorrow.
Temperature Yesterday—Max. 65; Min. 57.

VOL. LXXXIX..No. 30,089.

Entered as Second-Class Matter, Postoffice, New York, N. Y.

NEW YORK, TUESDAY, JUNE 11, 1940.

THREE CENTS NEW YORK CITY and Vicinity | FOUR CENTS Elsewhere Except in 7th and 8th Postal Zones.

ITALY AT WAR, READY TO ATTACK; STAB IN BACK, SAYS ROOSEVELT; GOVERNMENT HAS LEFT PARIS

NAZIS NEAR PARIS

Units Reported to Have Broken Through Lines to West of Capital

SEINE RIVER CROSSED

3 Columns Branch Out From Soissons—Enemy Held, French State

By The Associated Press.

PARIS, June 10—Marauding German tanks were reported tonight to have reached the Paris region itself as the government left the capital. While some German armored advance guards were said to have penetrated to the environs of Paris in isolated raids through the French lines, the main front was about thirty-five miles west and northwest of the capital. Although steadily approaching, the battle's roar still could not be heard here.

[The German High Command has no knowledge that Nazi tank units have reached the Paris region, The United Press reported.]

The battle, which had been waged heretofore all along the entire World War territory for the most part, swung into virgin soil as the Germans advanced west of Paris.

In the triangle bounded by Amiens on the Somme, Rouen, seventy miles west of Paris on the Seine, and Vernon, forty miles west on the Seine, the Germans redoubled their attacks, crossing the river at several points. An armored column, which crossed the Bresle last week, led the assault.

The French took their main stand west of Paris all along the Seine in an effort to prevent the Germans from effecting further passages and taking the capital from the rear.

In the central sector of the Oise Valley, directly north of Paris and farther east, where they had crossed the Aisne. Three columns fanned out from Soissons through La Ferte Milon and Fere en Tardenois and toward Reims.

Hold Firm on East Flank

They were just north of Chateau-Thierry and the Marne, where they by Americans fighting with the French.

On the east flank, below the French have been holding firm, fresh German infantry, tanks and planes battered the French lines, but with small gains.

But France, besieged on two sides by Germans driving on Paris from the north and the Italians entering the war on the south, proclaimed her grim determination to carry on the fight.

The main combats were centered in the Seine Valley to the west of Paris, with the High Command declaring that some German elements had crossed the Seine River at certain points, and in the Ourcq River Valley to the northeast of the capital.

The communiqué, however, said the "enemy is held everywhere by vigorous counter-attacks."

The French communiqué was filed from Paris, but was issued "Somewhere in France." The regular press conference of the War Office was not held this morning, as only a few attachés were in the office.

The High Command reported that the German break-through in the Seine resulted from increased pressure applied by the Nazis between the route from Amiens to Rouen and from Amiens to Vernon as far as the lower Seine.

In the other principal area of combat, east of the Oise River, German columns coming down from the region of Soissons have resumed their attack toward the Ourcq River.

The German offensive in the

Continued on Page Two

The International Situation

On the Battle Fronts

Italian guns will speak today in Europe. Italy's declaration of war against France and Britain became effective at 12:01 A. M. Rome time. Before 100,000 men and women, packed in the Piazza Venezia and near-by streets, Premier Mussolini yesterday announced his decision. It was war against "the plutocratic and reactionary democracies of the West." For the present that does not include the United States, but Rome reports that few Italians, from Signor Mussolini down, believe they will see the end of this war without having America against them.

The Italian Premier specifically excluded Turkey, Switzerland, Yugoslavia, Greece and Egypt from his military designs. Rome hoped Turkey would fail to keep her agreement to support the Allies in a Mediterranean war. Demonstrators in Rome carried placards naming Italian objectives in the war—Tunisia, Jibuti, Corsica, Suez, Malta, Cyprus. There were reports that action against some of these places already had started. But Rome was convinced that nothing big would get under way until today. [All the foregoing, Page 1, Column 8.]

The Canadian Parliament declared war against Italy; Prime Minister Mackenzie King denounced Premier Mussolini as "a carrion bird waiting for brave men to die." [Page 4, Column 5.]

Premier Reynaud, broadcasting to the French people after Italy's announcement, said France had won out over greater difficulties in the past. He asserted France always had been willing to negotiate Italian demands peaceably. [Page 12, Column 1.]

Berlin, jubilant over the entry of the Italians, expressed the belief that Premier Mussolini's military effort would be concentrated in the Mediterranean. It was said that no immediate Italian land attack on France was expected. [Page 5, Column 1.]

Switzerland reported much military activity, but no rumble of guns, in mountain passes between France and Italy. The Swiss were concerned about rumors that there were new German troop concentrations on the country's northern frontier. [Page 5, Column 3.]

Turkey stood ready to fulfill her engagements to the Allies under the mutual-assistance pact of last October. It was said that the first step, once Italy made that pact operative by an aggressive move in the Mediterranean, would be the placing of Turkish ports and air fields at the disposal of the Allies. [Page 1, Column 7.]

Belgrade heard reports that the Italians had landed troops and much mechanized equipment at the Italian-owned port of Zara, which is on the Yugoslav coast, and on the Italian-owned island of Lagosta, near by. [Page 1, Column 6.]

velop the capital. In the center, they pushed through to the Ourcq Valley, a movement that similarly threatened to flank Reims. On the French right wing the German pressure was furiously increased; but the French said no great gains had resulted. Information from the French side was less complete than usual because the government press bureau was evacuated from Paris and had not yet established a stable headquarters. [Page 1, Column 1.]

The French Government moved, apparently to the neighborhood of Tours. An exodus of civilians from Paris got under way. [Page 1, Column 2.]

Berlin analyzed the front thus: a semicircle had been thrown around Paris, from which three wedges were being driven into the defense lines. The first, in the lower Seine Valley, succeeded in cutting off the extreme left of the French Army, which can now be pushed to the coast. The second was progressing toward the Marne from the Aisne below Soissons. The third, on the French right, had pierced the Aisne and was headed toward Reims. [Page 1, Column 1.]

London admitted the loss of the airplane carrier Glorious, two destroyers, a transport and an oil tanker—totaling 50,706 tons—in an engagement in the North Sea. King Haakon of Norway arrived in Britain with his government. Some Norwegian troops also were carried off and will continue the war on the Western Front. [Page 16, Column 3.]

Repercussions Elsewhere

President Roosevelt, in a broadcast speech, termed Italy's entry into the war a threat to the American way of life. "The hand that held the dagger has struck it into the back of its neighbor," he said. Declaring in an "obvious delusion that we of the United States can safely permit the United- States to become a lone island in a world dominated by the philosophy of force," he advocated all possible material aid to the Allies. [Page 1, Column 4.]

OUR HELP PLEDGED

President Offers Our Full Material Aid to Allies' Cause

AMERICA IN DANGER

Fate Hangs on Training and Arms, He Says at Charlottesville

The text of the President's speech will be found on Page 6.

By FELIX BELAIR Jr.
Special to THE NEW YORK TIMES.

CHARLOTTESVILLE, Va., June 10—"On this 10th day of June, 1940, the hand that held the dagger has struck it into the back of its neighbor." In these words tonight President Roosevelt condemned the decision of Premier Mussolini which took Italy into the war on the side of Germany.

The remark was interpolated by the President in an address at the graduation exercises of the University of Virginia here. There could be no missing the depth of his feeling, since he put into the words all the emphasis at his command.

Italy's intervention was denounced furthermore as a definite threat to the way of life and the trade and commerce of the American. This government, he said, would give all material aid to France and Great Britain as "opponents of force."

The Chief Executive of the United States spoke to the nation and to the world only a few hours after Premier Mussolini announced his decision to join hands with Chancellor Hitler and unleashed his fascist legions against France and Great Britain. More details were revealed by Mr. Roosevelt of his correspondence with the Italian dictator in an effort to keep Italy at peace and to prevent the spread of war to the Mediterranean basin.

"To the Regret of Humanity"

"Unfortunately—unfortunately, to the regret of all of us and to the regret of humanity—the chief of the Italian Government was unwilling to accept the procedure suggested, and he has made no counter proposal," the President said.

And a moment later:

"The Government of Italy has now chosen to preserve what it terms its freedom of action and to fulfill what it states are its promises to Germany. In so doing it has manifested disregard for the rights and security of other peoples, disregard for the lives of the peoples of those nations which are directly threatened by the spread of this war, and has evidenced its unwillingness to find the means, through pacific negotiation, for the satisfaction of what it believes are its legitimate aspirations."

The President bespoke the prayers and hopes of this nation for those peoples beyond the seas who were battling for their freedom.

"In our American unity," he

Continued on Page Six

Nazi Tide Laps at Paris as Italy Joins War

On the western end of the line the Germans pushed a wedge to the Seine southeast of Rouen (1) and struck mighty blows in the region of Beauvais (2). In the center they reached the Ourcq River below Soissons (3). To the east they crossed the Aisne at two points near Vouziers (4).

Italy's announcement of her entry into the war was accompanied by no attack anywhere. One report had Italian troops invading the French Riviera (1), but this was unsupported. Rome's troops landed at two Italian-owned points on the Yugoslav coast: Zara (2) and Lagosta (3). In Albania (4) Italian military preparations were accelerated.

NAZIS CLAIM BREAK IN SUPPLY ARTERY

Paris Cut Off From Havre by Thrust to Seine East of Rouen, Berlin Says

By C. BROOKS PETERS
Wireless to THE NEW YORK TIMES.

BERLIN, June 10—German forces in Northern France tonight are fighting tonight to shorten the radius of a semicircle they are drawing about Paris, according to reports received here. Apparently they are attempting to drive three wedges into the remaining French territory north of the capital.

The first is on the Germans' extreme right wing, which is reported to have reached the lower Seine east of Rouen and therewith cuts off Paris from Havre. Mass tank formations, assisted by light motorized units, are claimed to have made more than a sixty-mile ad-

Continued on Page Eleven

Three Italian Freighters Are Scuttled by Crews

By The Associated Press.

LA LINEA, Spain, Tuesday, June 11—Two Italian merchant ships, the 10,000-ton Chelina and the 2,000-ton Numbolla, were scuttled by their crews in Gibraltar waters late yesterday [Monday] when their crews heard the radio news that Italy had gone to war.

RIMOUSKI, Que., June 10 (UP)—The 3,921-ton Italian freighter Capo Noli was set afire by her crew tonight as she proceeded down the St. Lawrence, but the scuttling attempt failed.

The Marine Department said the Canadian pilot grounded the freighter near the Father Point pilot station. A naval control boat extinguished the flames.

The government salvage boat Lord Strathcona left Quebec tonight for the site with a large derrick in tow. The Capo Noli will be taken over by the Canadian Government and her crew probably will be interned.

TURKEY PREPARES UNDER ALLIED PACT

Partial Mobilization Expected Today—Troops Are on Move —Precautions in Balkans

By J. W. KERNICK
Special Cable to THE NEW YORK TIMES.

ISTANBUL, Turkey, June 10—Turkey, speeding her military preparations as a result of Italy's entry into the war, stood ready tonight to fulfill her obligations under her mutual-assistance agreement with Britain and France.

That accord, concluded last October, stipulates that Turkey will lend the Allies every assistance in her power in the event of hostilities in the Mediterranean as a result of aggressive action by a European power. Hence Turkish aid can be invoked as soon as the first shot is fired.

The Italian action has already resulted in the calling of several classes to the colors by the Turkish Government. It is believed that the next move will be to place ports and airfields at the disposal of the Allies.

The Turkish Cabinet met last night to consider the question of war or peace, The Associated Press reported, but it was believed that Turkey's entrance into the war would be by gradual steps, not immediately.]

DUCE GIVES SIGNAL

Announces War on the 'Plutocratic' Nations of the West

ASSURES 5 NEUTRALS

Bid Is Made to Russia, But Rome Has No Pledge of Aid

'Hostilities' Are Reported

"Hostilities were started four hours ago, Central European time," Radio Roma, the official Italian short-wave radio, said last night at 11 o'clock Eastern daylight time in a broadcast recorded by Columbia Broadcasting System's short-wave listening station.

"The first Italian war bulletin is expected to be issued within a few hours."

At 2:15 A. M. today, however, the official British wireless said that "there have been no reports as yet of any engagements growing out of Italy's entrance into the war," Columbia's listening station reported.

By HERBERT L. MATTHEWS
By Telephone to THE NEW YORK TIMES.

ROME, Tuesday, June 11—Italy declared war on Great Britain and France yesterday afternoon, to take effect at one minute past midnight. The land, air and sea forces of the Italian Empire were already in motion.

It is a war, as Premier Benito Mussolini announced in the people from his balcony at the Palazzo Venezia at 6 in the evening, against the "plutocratic and reactionary democracies of the West." For the moment that does not include the United States, but few Italians believe that they will see the war to a finish without having the Americans against them.

Signor Mussolini expressly excluded Turkey, Switzerland, Yugoslavia, Greece and Egypt as enemies unless they attacked Italy or the Italian possessions.

Turkey provides the burning question of the war. Italian are absolutely convinced that the Turks will not move against them and will not honor their agreement with the Allies. It is hoped to confine Italian activity to France, Great Britain and the Mediterranean and to keep the Balkans tranquil. If that can be done, Italians think, the Turks will remain quiet.

Soviet Action Discounted

Russia has washed her hands of the struggle. Any disturbance in the Balkans will immediately bring her in; but as long as the struggle is confined to the west and south the Soviet will do nothing either to hinder or help. This was told to your correspondent a few hours ago by a very authoritative source.

It was emphasized there were no agreements about materials or anything else, nor any threats or promises.

The Italian Ambassador, Augusto Rosso, left in the morning for Moscow and Ivan Gorelkin, Soviet Ambassador, is coming back to Rome, thus ending a long period without representation. The Italians were anxious to restore full diplomatic relations in the critical period, according to this writer's information, and the Russians agreed, but without compromising themselves.

It thus appears that Premier Mussolini has embarked on this dangerous venture without really knowing what Soviet Russia will do in the long run.

President Roosevelt spoke clearly. There was too late. There was nothing that the United States could do to halt this conflict, the Italians say. Whatever brake Mr. Roosevelt may have exercised was overcome by the momentum of the whole Fascist policy. Once it was set in motion, nothing could stop it.

The Italians do not believe that the United States can affect the issue, whatever it does. They are

Continued on Page Four

FRENCH MINISTRIES MOVED SOUTHWARD

Tours Is Believed New Capital, but Reynaud Goes to Army —No Civilian Panic

By The Associated Press.

PARIS, June 10—The French Government left Paris tonight.

"Paul Reynaud, Premier, has gone with the armies," said a communiqué, which also declared:

"The High Command asked the Ministers to effect their withdrawal to the provinces in conformity with established dispositions. This withdrawal has been effected."

The announcement of the departure of the Ministers was made only after they were safely installed "somewhere in France" in the southern provinces.

The government transfer at General Maxime Weygand's request was approved last night at a Cabinet meeting.

Under cover of darkness the Ministers drove to their new offices

Continued on Page Ten

BRITISH NAVY GUNS HAMMER AT NAZIS

Shelling From Sea, Rushing of Troops and Planes Mark London's Share in Battle

By HAROLD DENNY
Wireless to THE NEW YORK TIMES.

LONDON, June 10—Britain is rushing all available fighting today into the battle in France, which was officially called here the "Battle of Paris and London" because of the Nazi threat to England. This reinforcement across the English Channel will continue, it was stated, "despite the imminent danger of German invasion of the United Kingdom."

The guns of British warships pounded the Germans near the coast.

"Important contingents" of new troops have already gone to France, it was announced. Meantime, Morris B. Novik, director of the station, had made arrangements to rebroadcast the Mayor's talk over five commercial stations at intervals later in the day.

Even closer cooperation with

La Guardia Warns of Strict Neutrality Here; Consuls Told to 'Adhere to Consular Duties'

Mayor La Guardia went on the air over WNYC, the city broadcasting station, yesterday afternoon with a strong plea to the million persons of Italian blood in this city to preserve strict neutrality in the face of Italy's declaration of war.

Moving with characteristic rapidity, the Mayor telephoned the city broadcasting studio in the New York City Building at the World's Fair and said he would be on the air nine minutes later. He thought over the message he wanted to deliver while driving over from the World's Fair Hall, and was prepared to speak immediately upon his arrival.

The Mayor stated his policy that the European war must be fought on the battlefields of Europe and not on the sidewalks of New York.

Recalling his war service as an ally of the Italian forces in Italy, the Mayor said he fully realized that the Italian entry into the war on the opposite side must be as painful to others of Italian blood as it was to him. Nevertheless, he insisted that the national policy of neutrality must be observed in the city, while he pledged full protection to consular officers of various European governments in the city, the Mayor made clear that these officials must stay within the bounds of their consular duties.

The Mayor's speech follows:
This is F. H. La Guardia, Mayor of the City of New York, talking. On Sept. 2, 1896, when the Nazi

Continued on Page Eight

ITALIANS REPORTED ON YUGOSLAV COAST

Said to Have Landed at Two Places Controlled by Rome— Mass on Greek Border

By The United Press.

BELGRADE, Yugoslavia, Tuesday, June 11—Large numbers of Italian troops were reported early today to have been landed along the Yugoslav coast at two Italian points as the Yugoslav Government prepared to fight in defense of its territory if necessary.

[It was reported from Berlin yesterday that Italian forces had invaded France through the Riviera, but this was denied in Rome, and German military quarters said later that they had no knowledge of any such movement.]

Reports from Split on the Adriatic coast said that large columns of Italian troops had been landed at

Continued on Page Four

Dispatches from Europe and the Far East are subject to censorship at the source.

"All the News That's Fit to Print."

The New York Times.

LATE CITY EDITION
Partly cloudy, warmer today, followed by showers tonight. Tomorrow fair, temperature unchanged.
Temperature Yesterday—Max., 70; Min., 65.

Copyright, 1940, by The New York Times Company

VOL. LXXXIX...No. 30,093.   Entered as Second-Class Matter, Postoffice, New York, N. Y.   NEW YORK, SATURDAY, JUNE 15, 1940.   THREE CENTS NEW YORK CITY | FOUR CENTS Elsewhere Except in 7th and 8th Postal Zones.

GERMANS OCCUPY PARIS, PRESS ON SOUTH; CAPTURE HAVRE, ASSAULT MAGINOT LINE; FRENCH ARMY INTACT; SPAIN SEIZES TANGIER

HITLER IS DOUBTED

Roosevelt Skeptical of Pledge He Will Not Cross Atlantic

HAS RECOLLECTIONS

U. S. Doing All It Can for Allies, He Asserts of French Appeal

By FELIX BELAIR Jr.
Special to THE NEW YORK TIMES.

WASHINGTON, June 14—President Roosevelt replied today to Adolf Hitler's reported denial of territorial aspirations in the Western Hemisphere with a reference to the German Chancellor's record of broken pledges to respect the integrity of European nations over a considerable period of time.

As a part of the same answer the President said the United States was doing and would continue to do everything in its power to give aid to the Allies. He said, in effect, that Chancellor Hitler's statement in an interview that he would confine his activities to Europe was to be taken with considerable quantities of salt.

The President followed up with an announcement of plans to mobilize American scientific genius in the interest of national defense.

"That brings recollections," the President said when asked at his press conference for his reaction to statements credited to the German Chancellor in an interview published in Hearst newspapers today. Reporters were not permitted to quote directly the rest of the President's statement, in which he said his observation might be enlarged upon with dates and nations going back over quite a period of years.

Many Rumors in Washington

Mr. Roosevelt's press conference remark was the high point of a day in which Washington was thick with rumors of the formation of a new French Cabinet without Premier Reynaud, that France would soon seek a separate peace with the Germans and that the President had been asked by France or Great Britain to propose a declaration of war against the Nazi government.

Both the White House and State Department denied that any proposal had been received from the Allied governments that the United States declare war.

Secretary Hull was asked in connection with the French situation whether the question of a declaration of war by the United States had been projected or raised in any way. He replied that so far as he knew nothing was involved beyond the sale of supplies, under terms and conditions that every one knew.

The question was asked of the Secretary of State at his press conference, which was held at 1 o'clock. Mr. Hull said the appeal Premier Reynaud made to President Roosevelt was then being decoded, that he had not seen it, but he understood it was the same that the French Premier gave by radio last night. Later the French Ambassador, Count de Saint-Quentin, said he assumed it was that or its equivalent.

Day's Other Developments

These other developments in the legislative and executive branches during the day stood as:

1. The President let it be known, by inference, that no accumulation of circumstances in the European war would alter this country's determination to arm to the teeth.

2. The House passed and sent to the Senate a bill authorizing the Reconstruction Finance Corporation to organize and lend money to corporations for plant expansion and acquisition of strategic materials for national defense.

3. State Department officials expressed their belief that France would soon undertake negotiations with Germany looking to a separate peace, and the reorganization of the French Government probably would be attempted with this in mind.

4. Administration sources said legislation would be introduced next week to embargo exports of scrap iron as a measure of national defense.

5. Attorney General Jackson

Continued on Page Two

The International Situation

On the Battle Fronts

Paris was taken over yesterday by the German war machine. Led by dust-stained tanks, followed by motorised divisions and then by infantry, the German Army marched down the Champs Elysées. Tense, grim-faced Parisians—the few who had remained behind—stood silently on the curbs as a hostile force marched through the famous boulevards of the "City of Light" for the first time since 1871. Shops were closed and shuttered. [Page 1, Column 7.]

In Berlin there were scenes of wild rejoicing. On Chancellor Hitler's orders church bells were rung for a quarter of an hour and the Nazi flag was ordered displayed for three days. [Page 2, Column 3.]

Berlin said that the fall of Paris—described as "catastrophic" morally and economically for the French—had completed the second phase of the war. The first was the Battle of Flanders. The third, the High Command communiqué said, was pursuit and "final destruction" of all the French forces. The chief drive of this "final" phase appeared to be directed against the flank of the Maginot Line through Champagne and the Argonne Forest—famous World War battlefield of American troops. Montmédy, western anchor of the line, was reported conquered. Spearheads had driven as far east as Vitry-le François, between Paris and Nancy. Verdun was said to be threatened. On the coast Havre's fall was claimed. [Page 1, Column 8.]

Hitler's personal press representative in the field said that the German leader considered the fall of Paris only an incident on his road of conquest and that he was not interested

in peace now. [Page 2, Column 8.]

The French High Command said it had abandoned Paris because there was no "valuable strategical reason" why it should be defended and it did not want the city devastated. The communiqué said the French Army was retreating in good order. A slackening of the German drive was reported at several points, but the heavy push in Champagne, threatening the rear of the Maginot Line, was still in progress. The armament of the line is useless against an attack from the rear. A frontal attack on the line west of the Saar was reported repulsed. [Page 1, Column 5.]

High sources in London said that Britain had agreed to accept any military or political decision the French Government might make but would fight on whatever it was. [Page 1, Column 6.] If the war is to be waged successfully, however, informed sources said, every available piece of war material in the United States must be sent to the Allies at once. [Page 1, Column 4.]

The war appeared to be developing for Italy. First reports of action on her Alpine frontier were reported in a communiqué. It was divulged for the first time, too, that the Italian fleet was at sea in force. [Page 1, Column 3.] Attacks in Africa were reported, both by the Italian air arm and by Allied troops against Libya, Eritrea and Ethiopia. Successes were claimed by the Italians in all actions. [Page 4, Column 1.]

The French Government abandoned Tours as its provisional capital and started southward, apparently for the port of Bordeaux. It was the seat of the French Government for a short time in 1914. [Page 1, Column 6.]

Repercussions Elsewhere

Spanish troops yesterday took over control of Tangier, the small internationally-policed territory in Northern Africa fronting on the Straits of Gibraltar. Madrid said the action had been taken to "guarantee its neutrality" and had been done with the full consent of the other three guarantors—Britain, France and Italy. Berlin said the consent of the Allies was given after the act. Return of Tangier has been one of the most frequently expressed territorial demands of the Franco-Spain. That of British-held Gibraltar is the other. [Page 1, Column 4.] In Washington Secretary Hull said the United States would insist on its

extraterritorial rights in Tangier under the treaty of 1906. [Follows the foregoing.]

"That brings up recollections," President Roosevelt said at his press conference when he was asked to "guarantee its neutrality" in an apparently interview with Chancellor Hitler was shown to him quoting the German leader as saying he had no aspirations in this hemisphere. The President's reference was to similar statements made about European countries. Driving ahead with the American defense program, the President announced the appointment of a scientific research commission to work with the defense advisory commission. [Page 1, Column 1.]

MOROCCANS MOVE IN

Spanish Troops Take Over Zone in Which U. S. Has Rights

'GIBRALTAR' NOW CRY

Madrid Students Parade and Shout for Return of the Famous Rock

By T. J. HAMILTON
Special Cable to THE NEW YORK TIMES.

MADRID, June 14—The Spanish Government announced early this afternoon that in the role of guaranteeing "the neutrality of the international zone" in Morocco, Moroccan troops entered Tangier this morning.

It was stated officially that the action had been taken in agreement with Great Britain, France and Italy, who are other guarantors of the zone under a convention of 1903. The United States, which is also a signatory to the convention, received a copy of the announcement in a note delivered to the United States Embassy here at 11 A. M. The text of the communiqué follows:

"With the object of guaranteeing the neutrality of the international zone and the city of Tangier, the Spanish Government has decided to take charge provisionally of the surveillance, police and public safety services of the international zone; forces of Moroccan troops entered this morning with this object.

"All existing services are assured and they continue functioning normally."

Coveted by the Spanish

Next to Gibraltar, Tangier occupies the front rank in Spanish territorial aims. In the last few days newspapers have devoted special attention to it among African territories that the French, assertedly with the connivance of the British, took away from Spain.

Although the first extra newspapers did not appear on the streets until 4 P. M., word that Tangier had been occupied spread quickly. By noon flags were appearing on houses throughout Madrid and members of the Falange youth movement were marching in uniform through the streets.

The news helped to bring an extra welcome for General Franco when he arrived late in the afternoon to open an exposition showing accomplishments of the government in rebuilding devastated regions. The press confined itself to printing the text of the government communiqué and relating the history of the international zone.

However, there were four demonstrations during the day, in which university student Phalangists predominated, all shouting, "Tangier is ours!" Some of these demonstrations passed the French and British Embassies.

British circles emphasized tonight that the occupation of Tangier had taken place with the complete agreement of Britain and France, who along with Italy and Spain were guarantors of the interna-

Continued on Page Six

FRENCH NOTE LULL

Battle Continues Along Front—At Some Points Its Violence Abates

ATTACK IS REPULSED

Nazi Losses Are Heavy in Maginot Assault— Loire Next Barrier

By G. H. ARCHAMBAULT
Wireless to THE NEW YORK TIMES.

TOURS, France, June 14—Is there any significance in the fact that although the battle continued to be waged today all along the front from the coast to the Argonne, it was notable that at certain points its violence was abating?

That question is in every mind tonight, for it may contain confirmation of the belief that the Germans have now engaged the maximum of their available forces.

The communiqué issued tonight gives little information on the day's operations, but it implies that all the retreating French forces continue to fight rear-guard actions and that at several parts of the front they have, in addition, counter-attacked the advancing Germans.

The only reference to Paris is as follows:

"The prescribed withdrawal has been effected in conformity with our plans."

But if there has been a relative lull on the main line of battle the Germans were very active in front of the Maginot Line, especially west of the Saar River. Early in the morning they launched a violent attack with the now customary accompaniment of tanks and dive-bombing planes. The French claim to have thrown back the attacking forces, on which they inflicted heavy losses.

Present Front Uncertain

Manifestly this attack must be considered in correlation with the fighting in the Argonne, farther to the west.

It is impossible tonight to indicate the present front even approximately. It is really one long line of pockets and salients, a situation calling for great qualities of generalship in order to preserve cohesion of the French forces.

Meanwhile, with the withdrawal of the French troops charged with the defense of Paris the first phase of the Battle of France was ended in defeat. It may be called the Battle of the Seine. The next phase may be the Battle of the Loire.

The issue was clear from the moment it was decided to declare Paris an open city and the news of withdrawal cannot have surprised many. A communiqué issued this morning from French General Headquarters explained that there were insufficient strategic reasons for defending the capital to justify risking destruction of France's very heart.

From the military point of view it is clear now that a battle for Paris would merely have immobilised troops, added to the loss of life and brought about no com-

Continued on Page Three

Will Fight On, British Insist, Even if the French Capitulate

London Letting Ally Make Decision on the Immediate Course as Help Is Speeded— New Nazi Peace Offensive Expected

By The United Press.

LONDON, June 14—Britain has agreed to accept any decision France may make regarding military and political policy, but if France is lost as an ally the British will fight on alone against Chancellor Hitler's war machine, it was understood tonight.

The British Government was understood to have agreed this week to any choice the French Government might make in regard to these military and political matters, which weigh more heavily in favor of Germany's increased drive, provided the choice had the approval of Generalissime Maxime Weygand.

Foreign observers in London today regarded the German assault against the Maginot Line, particularly the strong flanking attack south of Montmedy around Vitry-le-François, as of far greater strategic importance than yesterday's German occupation of undefended Paris. The psychological importance of the fall of Paris and the effect on French morale are not underestimated.

The impression prevails in foreign embassies in London that Herr Hitler would respond affirmatively to any possible French peace overture, but would impose harsh con-

Continued on Page Five

2 FORCES TAKE CITY

Berlin Says Industrial Losses May Be Worst Feature for French

MONTMEDY CAPTURED

Anchor of Maginot Line Lost—Nazis Report Foe Is Routed

By C. BROOKS PETERS
Wireless to THE NEW YORK TIMES.

BERLIN, June 14—Today, for the third time within the last century and a quarter, victorious German troops marched into Paris. This time, however, the legions, the clatter of whose hobnailed boots resounds throughout Paris and the entire world, are more than just German soldiers. They are the bearers of a proposed new order for Europe and perhaps the world, a major tenet of which is to destroy the old one.

With the capitulation of Paris, a German claim that the destruction of the remaining French forces is but a matter of "the shortest time." Well-informed quarters in Berlin put that time at two weeks at most.

For the German High Command announced today that the second phase of the western campaign had been completed successfully, the resistance of the French northern fronts has been broken and the enemy is "in full retreat along the entire front from Paris to the Maginot Line near Sedan."

Retreat Called Rout

If the statements of German military officials in Berlin are correct, this "full retreat" is really a rout. For the French, forced from their positions, have had no time to construct new ones but are being constantly harassed by German tanks, other motorised units and planes as they move southward, it is reported.

Early this morning, the Germans declare, they unleashed a frontal attack on the Maginot Line along the entire Saar front. Farther east, the fall of Montmedy, "anchor" of the Maginot Line, was claimed as well.

The extreme right wing of the German forces was not idle either. For yesterday it captured Havre, Berlin heard, and thus added approximately another hundred miles to the stretch of French coast that already is in German hands.

Advance on Cherbourg

The lower Seine, moreover, according to the High Command, was crossed on a wide front. The extreme right wing, it is believed, now is advancing on Cherbourg further to cut France off from Great Britain and provide the Germans with still another base for a future raid on the British Isles.

The front is now about 300 miles long as the crow flies, Germans declare, from Havre to the Rhine.

Although no information has been officially released here relative to the progress of the attack on the Maginot Line, it was said in usually accurately informed quarters tonight that the force of the German drive in this sector already has borne fruit and that Reich troops have broken through in several places.

Escape Held Impossible

Forces of the German left wing are reported pushing forward in a southeastwardly direction in what now appears to be a plan to storm the triangle of the Maginot fortifications from several sides, while an advance west of the fortifications to Belfort—southern tip of the Maginot Line—would cut off the avenue of escape for the French troops manning the line.

This German left wing yesterday was said to have captured Vitry-le François and crossed the Marne-Rhine Canal, which connects that town with Strasbourg. Still farther west another tentacle of the German left wing but sweeping we reported to have stormed the famous Hill 304 (Dead Man's Hill) northwest of Verdun, in which sector in 1916, Germans say, they lost 80,000 men.

The southern tip of the Argonne Forest also has been reached, Germans declare.

The Meuse defenses and Verdun

Continued on Page Two

TOURS ABANDONED AS FRENCH CAPITAL

Government Is Expected to Make Seat at Bordeaux— U. S. Move Is Awaited

By F. J. PHILIP
Wireless to THE NEW YORK TIMES.

TOURS, France, June 14—Tours has ceased to be the substitute capital of France after a brief three-day career. Premier Paul Reynaud's speech last night and other symptoms showed clearly before we went to bed that that would be so.

There were already signs of packing up again in different administrations. Sleep seemed, however, more urgent than flight, especially as we ourselves had just obtained a bed—the first we had slept in since Sunday. In that we were luckier than most, although it does seem expensive to have had only one night's sleep in a two-room apartment rented for a month. However, it permitted a proper wash and a change of linen.

And now we and everybody else are on our way again. We don't know what is happening because the information service installed here with so much trouble on Monday has opened its wings and fled with a part of the censorship service. Press Wireless is functioning for a few hours and then good-bye to Tours.

Avalanche Advancing

The morning communiqué told the story of why this should be so—in part at least. The avalanche is advancing from all sides, closing in around Paris and pushing forward in Champagne. The problem is where to go to escape it.

During the day, while we are on the road, things are likely to happen that will change the whole situation. It is too much now to hope that they will change it in any way that can be counted as satisfactory.

Along the roads through here the stream of civilian and military cars has recommenced. The embassies and legations have already pulled out. Wherever we go is going to be so congested that the remnants of that camping outfit we started are going to be invaluable. Only 5,000 American bombers and fighters flying across the Atlantic in response to Premier Reynaud's desperate appeal could restore to the French people their belief that they are not alone in this terrible fight. Words and promises and vague expostulation of political circumstances will not suffice. They will serve only to break further the dying hope there is today in every French heart.

For the British all the French feeling is as if they were of the

Continued on Page Three

REICH TANKS CLANK IN CHAMPS-ELYSEES

Berlin Recounts Parade Into Paris—Third of Citizens Reported Remaining

By The United Press.

BERLIN, June 14—German tanks today clanked across the Seine bridges, past the Arc de Triomphe and down the tree-lined Champs Elysées into the heart of Paris at the head of the first cavalcade of invaders to enter the French capital in nearly seventy years.

Flanked by armored cars, the dust-stained tanks swung triumphantly into Paris from the northwest at the head of Nazi units occupying the "City of Light," German accounts of the event said.

It was the ninth recorded invasion since Bismarck's legions trod the broad boulevards in 1871. The jubilant German press proclaimed the fall of Paris to be the "symbol of decision" in Chancellor Adolf Hitler's Western offensive.

Entry From Northwest

The advance into Paris, through the suburbs of Argenteuil and Neuilly and into the aristocratic western part of the city began early in the morning, the Germans said. It was exactly five weeks after the massive western offensive began with the German drive into the Netherlands and Belgium.

The tanks rumbled between thin lines of tense and silent Parisians, the Germans said. Reports from the French capital estimated that probably a third of the city's normal population of 2,800,000 had remained in Paris.

Behind the tanks rolled anti-tank units, still dusty and laden with evidence of the furious fighting in the north.

As the long shadows of the early morning retreated, more and more Nazi contingents streamed into the capital, evacuated by French Armies hoping to save the fate of Warsaw.

Motorised infantry, riding in steel-shielded trucks mounting machine guns to command the broad streets, converged on the Place de l'Étoile.

In that hub from which radiate eleven streets stands the Arc de Triomphe and under it the tomb of the Unknown World War Soldier, where flickers the Eternal Flame.

German reports indicated that the parade through Paris swung around

Continued on Page Two

COLONNA PROTESTS ON ITALIAN CHARGES

Envoy Sees Hull—Inquiry Here Widened—German Agent to U. S. Warns of Reprisals

Special to THE NEW YORK TIMES.

WASHINGTON, June 14—The Italian Ambassador, Don Ascanio dei Principi Colonna, protested to Secretary of State Cordell Hull today what he considered to be an unjustified effort to foment anti-Italian feeling in the United States. The protest was directed specifically to the charges made in New York yesterday that the Italian Consulate General there, under orders of Premier Benito Mussolini, was seeking to promote fascism in this country by ideological propaganda. He also implied there were similar activities against Italy in other American cities.

His concern was especially manifested over publication of these charges by newspapers. The fact that the New York charges were issued through Police Commissioner Valentine apparently was not mentioned. No reference was made directly to President Roosevelt's Charlottesville address denouncing Italy.

In making the protest, Prince Colonna declared that Italian consuls in this country restrict their activities to their legal functions and that Italian nationals in the United States are careful to avoid

Continued on Page Nine

ITALIANS IN CLASH ON FRENCH BORDER

Report Attack Repulsed— Fleet Action Revealed— Coast Is Shelled

By HERBERT L. MATTHEWS
By Telephone to THE NEW YORK TIMES.

ROME, June 14—The war began to develop for Italy on land, sea and air, according to this morning's communiqué, with the first activity on the Italo-French frontier and an indication that the Italian fleet was on its way on some great mission.

The taking of Tangier by the Spaniards is considered a first-rate victory for the Axis, but, of course, the fall of Paris dominates everything else.

Among Fascisti here there is rejoicing over the fate of Paris. The newspaper Lavoro Fascista cheers in an eight-column box whose sentiments are typical.

"C'est Paris," it says. "Capitalists, Jews, Masons and snobs all over the world are in mourning. The spiritual capital of all the old fallen. Paris itself 'la ville lumière'—Paris tout entier.'"

As the war shapes up, even this early, the Mediterranean seems more than ever certain to become Italy's main theatre of operations. To be sure, there was some activity for the first time yesterday on the French frontier. There were clashes by patrols and "enemy, at-

Continued on Page Four

British Call on U. S. for Munitions at Once; French Order 120 Bombers Here for 1941

By RAYMOND DANIELL
Special Cable to THE NEW YORK TIMES.

LONDON, June 14—In circles close to the government it was said today that every gun, every ounce of war materials that the United States can spare was needed urgently and needed quickly if the cause for which the Allies were fighting was not to be lost on the battlefields of France. It is not a matter of months but of weeks, even days, it was said. France is in a position to know the facts, of which the ordinary people in this country only now are becoming dimly aware.

Withdrawal of the battered French armies behind their abandoned capital and contemplation of the possibility that the Government of France may be forced to withdraw from Europe to Africa, led to apprehension that increasingly apparent the extent to which

After the Anglo-French Purchasing Commission yesterday announced that French purchases of war material in the United States were being stepped up, the French signed a contract at 7 P. M. for 120 "flying fortresses" to be delivered in the second and third quarters of 1941. The planes are to be built by the Consolidated Aircraft Corporation.

In an interview earlier in the day a spokesman for the Anglo-French commission said that contracts for "many millions of dollars" had been placed during the day.

Instead of curtailing purchases following the capture of Paris by the Germans, France is sending more purchasing experts, the spokesman said. In response to a question relative to the ability to pay cash for purchases, he added:

"There is no immediate and of our

Continued on Page Four

"All the News That's Fit to Print."

The New York Times.

LATE CITY EDITION
Cloudy today with little change in temperature. Tomorrow cloudy and slightly warmer.
Temperature Yesterday—Max., 72; Min., 52

NEWS INDEX, PAGE 33, THIS SECTION

Section 1

VOL. LXXXIX. No. 30,101.

Entered as Second-Class Matter, Postoffice, New York, N. Y.

Copyright, 1940, by The New York Times Company.

NEW YORK, SUNDAY, JUNE 23, 1940.

Including Rotogravure Picture Magazine and Book Review.

TEN CENTS

TWELVE CENTS Beyond 200 Miles, Except West of Pa.—South of Md.—North of Mass.

FRENCH SIGN REICH TRUCE, ROME PACT NEXT; BRITISH BOMB KRUPP WORKS AND BREMEN; HOUSE QUICKLY PASSES 2-OCEAN NAVY BILL

REPUBLICAN FIGHT LOOMS ON WAR ISSUE AT THE CONVENTION

Dewey, Taft and Willkie Reach Philadelphia to Appeal to the Delegates

NO GROUP HAS CONTROL

Rival Candidates Make Ballot Claims—Willkie Stronger— Hoover Possibility Seen

A battle between divergent views on the war and peace issue loomed yesterday among delegates to the Republican National Convention, opening tomorrow. Messrs. Dewey, Taft and Willkie, rival candidates for the Presidential nomination, reached Philadelphia to press their campaigns. No leader or group of leaders was in a position to dominate the proceedings or the committee on resolutions. The effect of a speech by Mr. Hoover to the convention is expected to decide what, if any part, he will play as a Presidential nominee. [All the foregoing page 1, Column 1.]

In press conferences Mr. Dewey declared for aid to the Allies without violating international or domestic law or entering the war; Mr. Willkie for aid to the Allies without going to war, and for reciprocal trade treaties. [Page 2, Column 1.]

The national committee approved a change in the rules under which districts which fail to show a poll of 1,000 Republicans would be deprived of representation at future conventions. Other rules changes approved would make penalties on States which do not give a majority for the national ticket. [Page 2, Column 4.]

Drafters of the platform, split over aid to the Allies, hinted that a stand on the foreign policy plank might be left largely to the decision of the Presidential nominee. [Page 3, Column 1.]

Convention Unbossed

By JAMES A. HAGERTY
Special to THE NEW YORK TIMES.

PHILADELPHIA, June 22—The Republican National Convention, which will convene here Monday in the Municipal Auditorium, will open without a boss or even a man in control of any particular group of minor bosses.

This was the indication today, when District Attorney Thomas E. Dewey of New York, Senator Robert A. Taft of Ohio and Wendell L. Willkie, president of the Commonwealth and Southern Corporation, just now regarded as the three leading candidates for the Presidential nomination, arrived in the convention city to make direct appeals to the delegates.

With no leader or group of leaders in a position to dominate either the convention or the committee on resolutions, the delegates face the prospect of a hotly contested fight for the nomination for President, and an equally bitter floor contest on the resolution on foreign relations.

Little difficulty is expected in putting through the rest of the platform which is expected to follow the recommendations of the program committee of the National Committee, headed by Dr. Glenn Frank.

Alfred M. Landon, nominee for President in 1936, who is chairman of the subcommittee on foreign relations of the committee on resolutions, continued today his efforts to get a plank that would be satisfactory both to the isolationists and those favoring a declaration of aid to the Allies, but the formula, so far as could be learned, had not been found tonight.

Candidates Give Views

Mr. Dewey, Mr. Willkie and Senator Taft each had a press conference. Mr. Dewey declared for aid for the Allies without violating international or domestic law or getting into the war. Mr. Willkie, who was nearly mobbed by supporters in the Bellevue-Stratford Hotel, also declared for aid to the Allies without going to war and

Continued on Page Two

Major Sports Results

BASEBALL

New York's major league teams all met defeat yesterday. The Reds downed the Giants, 3–1, on Ernie Lombardi's homer with one man on base, the Pirates beat the Dodgers, 7–2, and the Tigers won from the Yankees, 3–2. Despite the setback, the Dodgers stayed in first place in the National League.

RACING

Your Chance won the $13,350 Dwyer Stakes at Aqueduct after Snow Ridge, first past the finish line, was disqualified for bumping in the stretch. Gen'l Manager was placed second and Andy K. third. The crowd of 20,520 bet $1,076,417 on the seven races, this being Aqueduct's first million-dollar day.

TRACK AND FIELD

The University of Southern California won its sixth successive National Collegiate A. A. championship in the meet at Minneapolis. The New York A. C. easily retained the metropolitan A. A. U. senior title.

(Complete Details in Section 5.)

CITY WPA TO PURGE 1,000 NAZIS, REDS

Signing of Affidavits to Be Started Tomorrow—FBI to Aid in Investigations

Without waiting for President Roosevelt to sign the new Relief Appropriations Act, Colonel F. C. Harrington, National Work Projects Commissioner, set in motion yesterday the machinery for purging the WPA rolls of Communists and Nazis by July 1.

The purge in this city will begin tomorrow, and the local administrator, Lieut. Col. Brehon B. Somervell, estimated that at least 1,000 WPA workers would lose their jobs before it was completed. Of the 101,000 persons on the rolls here, and 1,700,000 in other parts of the country, will be required to sign affidavits disavowing Communist or Nazi affiliations. The maximum penalty for false statement will be $2,000 fine and two years' imprisonment.

Colonel Somervell made clear that his office would not rely on affidavits alone in carrying out the mandate of the new law. The registration lists of the Board of Elections will be compared with the WPA payroll to turn up the names of Communists. The full facilities of the Federal Bureau of Investigation, the Police Department and the WPA's own Bureau of Investigation will be invoked as a further means of identification.

Dies Records to Be Used

Still another source of data, Colonel Somervell revealed, will be the reports and testimony gathered by the Dies committee and the record compiled in the recent trial of Fritz Kuhn, leader of the German-American Bund.

Because of "the well-known practice of Communists to deny membership in the party and to use false names in enrollment with the WPA," the administrator called upon all "responsible citizens" to make available any information they had on subversive activities among Federal relief employes. He said he expected at least 50,000 letters, and he promised that "grudge letters would be carefully sifted out from those submitting authentic information."

Although Congress did not complete action on the new Relief Act until yesterday morning, WPA officials in this city have been collecting material on Communists and Nazis on their rolls for several weeks. More than 1,000 names of persons tentatively identified as members of un-American groups are now under scrutiny, it was learned.

Under the wording of the law, Colonel Somervell said, a person does not have to be a member of the Communist party to be ineligible for WPA employment. He would be regarded as a Communist within the meaning of the law, and indicated that other "splinter groups" would be subject to a similar interpretation. The administrator said he would function as the court of last resort in determining whether a person entertained subversive views.

The WPA purge creates a problem for municipal relief authorities.

Continued on Page Thirteen

FOR 200 NEW SHIPS

70% Increase in Fleet Authorized as Congress Recesses Till July 1

TO COST 4 BILLIONS

Chambers Enact Tax, Defense and Relief Fund Measures

Special to THE NEW YORK TIMES.

WASHINGTON, June 22—Congress took a recess at 9:10 o'clock tonight, adopting a resolution to reassemble on July 1 after the Republican National Convention in Philadelphia, and to take a similar week's recess during the Democratic National Convention at Chicago.

As a night session began to clear the decks for the recess, the House gave a dramatic flourish to a day devoted to pressing legislation by passing and sending to the Senate the "two-ocean" navy bill. No dissent was heard in the voice vote.

Within less than two hours, the House thus gave its approval to the construction of the world's mightiest navy, designed for defense of the United States and the Western Hemisphere. The Senate did not have time to act.

The "two-ocean" navy bill would authorize about 200 warships, a 70 per cent increase in the nation's fleet, or an expansion of 1,325,000 tons of combatant and auxiliary vessels to be built in the next six years at an estimated cost of $4,000,-000,000.

Naval Air Force Augmented

Besides the increase in ship tonnage, the two-ocean navy measure also would increase the naval air force authorized strength from 10,-000 to 15,000 planes.

It provides for $35,000,000 for "mosquito" torpedo boats, and authorizes an appropriation of $150,-000,000 to expand shipbuilding facilities at government and private yards.

It provides also for the expenditure of $20,000,000 for expansion of facilities for armor plate manufacture and $50,000,000 for added facilities for construction of guns.

In calling for enactment of the bill, as recommended by Admiral Harold R. Stark, Chief of Naval Operations, Chairman Vinson of the House Naval Affairs Committee said that when the bill became law the Administration would ask for $175,000,000 for an immediate start on the program.

Mr. Vinson and Representative Maas of Minnesota, ranking minority member on the committee, led the brief debate by asserting that the United States should not depend upon the Navy of any other power for its defense.

"The time has come to realize that if the United States is to remain free and independent it must depend upon itself," Mr. Maas said. "It is foolish to risk our defense on the thin thread of a (the Panama) canal."

The Navy now has 307 ships in

Continued on Page Fourteen

British Torpedo and Bomb the Scharnhorst; Submarine, Planes Waylay Nazi Battleship

By HAROLD DENNY
Wireless to THE NEW YORK TIMES.

LONDON, June 22—The Germans' 26,000-ton battle cruiser Scharnhorst has been seriously damaged by a British submarine and airplane off the Norwegian coast, according to reports given out tonight by the Admiralty and the Air Ministry.

The Scharnhorst was believed to be lying at bay with German destroyers and war planes clustering about her protectively, awaiting further attack by British naval units summoned by the Royal Air Force bombers.

The battle with the Scharnhorst and her escorting forces was the most important of three attacks on German and Italian naval craft reported in London.

The other incidents were the almost unbelievable exploit of the capture of an Italian submarine by a British trawler in the Gulf of Aden opposite British Somaliland and the sinking by an airplane of a German supply ship in the North Sea.

The Scharnhorst, with her sister ship the Gneisenau, the most powerful of German war vessels, had previously taken severe punishment. She was heavily pummelled in April by the British battleship Renown off Narvik, Prime Minister Winston Churchill then reported.

On June 13 she was reported hit near by, badly bombed, with one—perhaps two—British bombs making direct hits on the center of the ship when she was in Trondheim Fjord.

"One of our submarines sighted the Scharnhorst soon after she left Trondheim Fjord," the day's reports said. "The battle cruiser was clearly on passage to a safe port where she could repair damage previously taken by her. British heavy bomb during an attack by the aircraft of the fleet arm on June 13."

This latest encounter with the Scharnhorst touched off a

Continued on Page Twenty-two

$5,377,552,058 Voted For Defense This Year

By The Associated Press.

WASHINGTON, June 22—Here are the defense appropriation totals, including contract authorizations, which Congress has approved thus far this session:

*Regular Army $3,254,624
*Regular Navy bill........ 1,492,542,750
Supplemental defense
                            1,768,913,906
Urgent deficiency   28,000,000
Emergency deficiency   252,340,776
Strategic materials
  (in Treasury appropriation)   12,500,000
  Total $5,377,552,058
*To which supplemental sums were added by the Senate.

There are also items included for defense in the Civil Aeronautics Authority, Civilian Conservation Corps, WPA and the Army Civil Functions Supply Bills.

COMMITTEE LEANS TO KNOX REJECTION

But Senate Naval Group Votes to Hear Him July 1—Stimson Will Testify Next Day

By HAROLD B. HINTON
Special to THE NEW YORK TIMES.

WASHINGTON, June 22—Confirmation of Colonel Frank Knox as Secretary of the Navy probably will be opposed by the Senate Naval Affairs Committee, according to some members questioned after a stormy executive session today. If members maintain the opposition shown today, and if there were the nominations of Colonel Knox and of Henry L. Stimson as Secretary of War have been referred, will give Colonel Knox a more searching examination, it was believed. Some members, it was reported, favored rejecting the nomination today, but counsel prevailed that no nominee should be disapproved without having a chance to be heard.

Senator Walsh, its chairman, announced after the meeting that Colonel Knox would be invited to appear on July 1. In other quarters it was said that eleven members attended today's meeting and that most of those who spoke were opposed to the nomination. Only Senators Hale and Barbour took no part in the discussions.

The most outspoken opponents, according to these reports, included Senators Walsh, Tydings, Smith of South Carolina, Byrd, Holt and Gillette, all Democrats. Senator Johnson of California, a Republican, also indicated his opposition. Others attending the meeting were

Continued on Page Fifteen

ARMS PLANT IS HIT

R.A.F. Raiders Continue Assault Upon Nazis' Bases of Supply

SCORE NEAR BERLIN

Plane Factory Is Target —Germans Retaliate Along English Coast

By JAMES MacDONALD
Special Cable to THE NEW YORK TIMES.

LONDON, June 22—Royal Air Force bombers pounded the big Krupp arms works at Essen and important aircraft factories and military stores at Bremen, Kassel, Rothenburg and Goettingen and a big naval depot at Willemsoord in German-occupied Netherlands in a heavy series of air raids last night, according to the Air Ministry's communiqué today.

As against their boast of heavy damage done to the Nazis, British officials insisted that Nazi airmen had accomplished little in their retaliatory raids in this country this morning and last night.

Three persons were killed in a Suffolk town and three wounded elsewhere, it was announced. It was declared that bombs burst sporadically in "several counties on the east coast," but that most of them fell in open country, causing small damage. The German raids, it was said, were less intense than those of Tuesday and Wednesday nights. The Ministry did not state whether or not any Nazi planes were shot down, or if any defending fighter machines were lost.

All Appears Quiet

Meanwhile all appeared quiet on the British home air front tonight. There were no unwelcome noises of purring enemy motors that were picked up by the sensitive sound-detecting devices on the ground.

[Alexandria, Egypt, fought off three Italian air raids yesterday, the first of the war. British fliers attacked Tobruk, Libya, and reported hitting a large warship. Rome said bombers had destroyed a British naval base in Egypt and raided Marseille and Bizerte, Tunisia.]

Many sections of British planes are reported to have taken part in widespread raids on German objectives last night, but only one was shot down and only two are reported missing.

Two Planes Missing

Many planes were engaged in big raids over Germany. They returned with only two missing.

British raiders out Bremen directed their attack against the large Focke-Wulf airplane factory, which previously had been severely punished. Two fires, direct hits with incendiary and explosive bombs in the middle of the factory buildings. Two violent explosions were seen by the British fliers after the bombs burst.

The airfield adjoining the factory was also bombed and one hangar was badly damaged, according to another section of the raiders reported that they had hit several buildings of the Krupp plant at Essen as well as railroad sidings near by. The exact extent of the damage done there, however, was not disclosed in London.

The objective at Kassel was the Fieseler aircraft factory and it was said that several bombs were seen exploding directly on the target.

Airplane hangars were bombed at Rothenburg, where also military buildings and air field were hit. Another attacking force dropped bombs on the aircraft storage depot

Continued on Page Twenty-two

The International Situation

In Europe and Africa

An armistice between Germany and France was signed in the Forest of Compiegne yesterday at 6:50 P. M. German time (12:50 P. M. New York time). Immediately after the signing the French representatives left by a German plane, Germanpiloted, for Rome, where they will sign a companion document with Italy. Six hours after the signatures have been appended to the Italian armistice the order to cease fire will become effective. The terms of the armistice are still withheld; in Bordeaux they were described as "hard but honorable." London reported, without confirmation, that these were the principal provisions: (1) Occupation of France by Germany and Italy for the duration of the war with Britain; (2) surrender of all war stores; (3) surrender of all foreign currency reserves; (4) delivery of coal and other raw material supplies to Germany for a fixed period. [Page 1, Column 8.]

Prime Minister Churchill said he had heard "with grief and amazement" of the French acceptance of terms that, to his mind, would mean that France and her empire would be entirely at the mercy of the dictators. He called on the French people to continue resistance. This call was reiterated by General Charles de Gaulle, former French Under-Secretary of War, who broadcast from London, calling on all French people not under Axis guns to mobilise to carry on the war. [Page 1, Column 6.]

The French negotiators arrived in Rome by plane from Compiegne. [Page 27, Column 1.]

Berlin announced that 500,000 French soldiers, encircled in Alsace-Lorraine, had surrendered, among them three army commanders. Only isolated resistance was left in that part of France. The Germans took the port of Lorient, on the southern coast of Brittany. According to Swiss reports, the French repulsed a German attack on L'Ecluse Fort, which dominates the Rhone at the Swiss border. [Page 22, Column 1.]

British bombers struck at the famous Krupp armaments works at Essen and at aircraft factories at several other points in Germany. In a raid on Willemsoord, German-held base in the Netherlands, the British said they had sunk two ships, set one afire and destroyed naval storehouses. Berlin reported that nearly 100 planes took part in Friday night's bombing of Britain. The Germans said that in recent actions they had sunk two British transports, one of 11,000 tons, the other of 32,000, the latter carrying about 5,000 men who were lost. British bombers reached the Berlin area Friday night, the Germans admitted, injuring seven persons and damaging buildings. [Page 1, Column 5.]

The British reported that the German battleship Scharnhorst, 26,000 tons, had been both torpedoed and bombed, with "considerable damage" resulting. The action took place off the Norwegian coast. A destroyer was torpedoed in the same fight, London said. The British trawler Moonstone informed the Admiralty that it had captured a large Italian submarine in the Gulf of Aden. Depth charges forced the submarine to the surface, where guns were brought into play. The Italian commander and several officers were reported killed; three officers and thirty-seven men were captured. [Page 1, Column 3.]

Three groups of Italian bombers attacked the Allied naval base at Alexandria, Egypt, early yesterday. They were driven off, the British reported, by the combined fire of both French and British naval units, and no warship were hit. Rome claimed to have sunk three enemy ships in the Mediterranean. [Page 1, Column 7.]

By the emphatic means of an official government statement, Russia denied that troops were being concentrated on the German frontier. [Page 22, Column 7.]

Developments Elsewhere

Within less than two hours, the House of Representatives adopted the "two-ocean" navy bill, which will give the United States the most powerful navy in the world—a navy 70 per cent greater than the present one. [Page 1, Column 3.]

After a stormy session of the Senate Naval Affairs Committee, it appeared in Washington that Colonel Frank Knox, Republican, would not be approved by the committee for Secretary of the Navy. Colonel Henry L. Stimson, Republican, nominated for Secretary of War, also faces hard going before the Military Affairs Committee. Confirmation of both appointments is expected when the issue gets to the floor. [Page 1, Column 4.]

In Hyde Park, where he was spending the week-end, President Roosevelt contemplated the possibility that the United States might have to shift the fleet to the Atlantic to face a superior sea power of the totalitarian nations. [Page 16, Column 1.]

GENERAL SUMMONS FRENCH TO RESIST

De Gaulle Offers to Organize Fight Abroad—Churchill Supports His Stand

By RAYMOND DANIELL
Wireless to THE NEW YORK TIMES.

LONDON, Sunday, June 23—A broadcast to the French people by one of their own military leaders calling on them to continue the fight against Germany by every means in their power was made from here last night.

General Charles de Gaulle, assistant and adviser to Paul Reynaud when the former Premier was also War Minister, told his countrymen that the proposed armistice might not only capitulation but "submission and slavery."

[The general undertook to organize armed French resistance as was possible himself and urged French fighting men and technicians everywhere to join him in the task, according to The United Press.]

General de Gaulle's arguments were reinforced early this morning by Prime Minister Winston Churchill in a statement expressing "grief and amazement" at the French decision. He indicated they would transform France into an active enemy, and he urged all loyal French-

Continued on Page Twenty-seven

NAZI TERMS SIGNED

But Hostilities Persist as French Fly to Get Italy's Demands

SEVERITY PROTESTED

Huntziger Voices View at Close of 27-Hour Compiegne Parley

By GUIDO ENDERIS
Wireless to THE NEW YORK TIMES.

BERLIN, June 22—The armistice treaty between Germany and France was signed today in the forest of Compiegne at 6:50 P. M. German Summer time (12:50 P. M. New York time). Col. Gen. Wilhelm Keitel, Chancellor Hitler's plenipotentiary, signed for Germany and General Charles Huntziger for France.

Its contents will not be made public for the present, but it is announced that the agreement does not provide for immediate cessation of hostilities. The fighting is to end six hours after the Italian Government has notified the German High Command of the signing of an armistice treaty between Italy and France.

As the latter is believed to be a mere formality, already agreed upon by the leaders of the Axis Powers in their discussion in Munich last Tuesday, its conclusion is expected within the next forty-eight hours. The French delegation that conferred at Compiegne also will negotiate with Italy. Such procedure, it is predicted, will end the war on the Continent early in the coming week.

Scene in Car Dramatic

The French delegation returned to Compiegne from Paris at 10 A. M. and continued its deliberations throughout the day, during which it was in constant communication with the Bordeaux government. To expedite contacts, German military authorities installed a direct telephone wire connecting the armistice car with Bordeaux.

The German radio broadcast announcing the signing of the treaty closed with the words "We thank our Fuehrer." There was a dramatic scene in the armistice car at Compiegne before the formalities were completed. General Huntziger, in a subdued voice, announced that his government had ordered him to sign.

"Before carrying out my government's order," he said, "the French delegation deems it necessary to declare that in a moment when France is compelled by fate of arms to give up the fight, she has a right to expect that the coming negotiating nations a chance to live and work once more. As a soldier you will understand the onerous moment that has now come for me to sign."

After the signatures were affixed, General Keitel requested all delegates to rise from their seats, and he said:

"It is honorable for the victor to do honor to the vanquished. We have risen in commemoration of those who gave their blood to their countries."

Talks With Italy Speeded

The French delegation left Compiegne for Paris tonight and is expected to meet Italy without further delay to bring the hostilities to a quick close.

With an Italian-French armistice in imminent prospect, military activities are now expected to give way to diplomatic negotiations and it is not improbable that Germany, Italy, France and possibly also Belgium will meet in conference soon in some German city to discuss steps for an approach to honorable peace.

Meanwhile there is no indication in German official quarters that Germany is anxious to suggest that Germany is still grimly determined to prosecute her war on Britain with all possible speed, and this determination has received fresh impetus through uninterrupted attacks by British bombers on German objectives.

With French Channel ports now available as German air bases, raids on English coastal points also have increased in recent days and with the final liquidation of the

Continued on Page Twenty-eight

ALEXANDRIA FIGHTS FIRST ITALIAN RAIDS

20 Bombs Fall in 3 Attacks— Warship Reported Fired by R. A. F. at Tobruk

By JOSEPH M. LEVY
Special Cable to THE NEW YORK TIMES.

CAIRO, Egypt, June 22—Alexandria experienced its first bombing this morning when twenty bombs were dropped in three Italian air raids. Two persons were killed; twenty-three were injured.

The dead were a native woman, who was killed when bombs hit among palm trees growing in a village close to the city, and a man who was killed by a bomb that demolished four Alexandria houses. Here nineteen persons were injured.

[Another air raid warning sounded in Alexandria early this morning, The Associated Press reported, and the all-clear signal was given in fifteen minutes.]

Bombs were reported dropped indiscriminately on the city, harbor and native villages, the bombers flying high and dodging in the attempt to avoid anti-aircraft fire. Two Italian planes were reported badly damaged. It is not certain whether either was shot down.

Only a few bombs fell in the city.

Continued on Page Twenty-three

"All the News That's Fit to Print."

The New York Times.

LATE CITY EDITION
Fair, with little change in temperature today and tomorrow.
Temperature Yesterday—Max. 80; Min. 65

Copyright, 1940, by The New York Times Company.

VOL. LXXXIX..No. 30,174.

Entered as Second-Class Matter, Postoffice, New York, N. Y.

NEW YORK, WEDNESDAY, SEPTEMBER 4, 1940.

THREE CENTS NEW YORK CITY | FOUR CENTS Elsewhere Except and Vicinity | In 7th, 8th and 9th Postal Zones

ROOSEVELT TRADES DESTROYERS FOR SEA BASES; TELLS CONGRESS HE ACTED ON OWN AUTHORITY; BRITAIN PLEDGES NEVER TO YIELD OR SINK FLEET

R. A. F. REPELS RAIDS

Fliers Turn Back Three Drives on London—Reich Perfecting Technique

PLANES REACH BERLIN

2¼-Hour Alarm in City —British Hit Hard at French Coast

By JAMES B. RESTON
Special Cable to The New York Times.

LONDON, Wednesday, Sept. 4—German bombers started ringing that big London doorbell early yesterday morning. They rang it again in the afternoon while Prime Minister Winston Churchill and his Ministers were commemorating the first anniversary of the war, and they kept ringing it right up till last midnight, when the final "all clear" of the day was sounded for the capital.

It was a day of fierce air battles, fought at great height in blue and silver sky all over southeast England, and at the end, though Reich Marshal Hermann Goering's night shift was still operating all over the island, the British Air Ministry announced that twenty-five Nazi planes had been shot down to fifteen of Britain's planes. Eight British pilots were said to be safe, though it is not known whether they are in condition to fly.

[British bombing planes flew high over Berlin shortly after last midnight. Berlin spokesmen were quoted as saying that most of the Royal Air Force planes were turned back by severe anti-aircraft fire between Wittenberg and Magdeburg, but several planes escaped through the anti-aircraft barrage and reached Berlin, where they were again met with anti-aircraft fire.]

These German bombers, which have already instructed five countries in the past twelve months, have now perfected a technique in attacking this vast, sprawling city, and they tried to work it again yesterday morning in the first raid.

Two Formations Meet

Just at 10 o'clock, timed to perfection, one wave of bombers approached the Thames Estuary from their bases in Belgium. Simultaneously, another formation, flying high through a light haze, came up from bases in France and met them over the Kentish coast. Altogether they were about 250 of them, and defying anti-aircraft batteries at first they started along the banks of the Thames toward London.

As they came inland, however, they met first one, then a second squadron of British fighters, who dived through Nazi fighter patrols into the bombers, broke up the formation and then attacked them singly and drove them back over the coast.

Some German bombers dropped their dynamite in Kent and Essex, but all that is said about the effect of these bombs is that they caused few casualties and little damage.

What can be said is that, if these bombers were trying to get into the heart of London to attack objectives here, they certainly failed, for while sirens were sounded everywhere in Greater London nobody in the heart of the city saw any fighting.

There was an interesting sidelight to the second mass raid of the day. At 2:45 P. M. Mr. Churchill, who somehow contrives to look more confident every day, walked into Westminster Abbey to attend the special service in commemoration of the day a year ago when Britain declared war on Germany. Alongside him walked tall, gaunt Viscount Halifax, Foreign Secretary; dapper Arthur Greenwood, Minister without portfolio; Sir Kingsley Wood, Chancellor of the Exchequer; Anthony Eden, War Secretary, and Joseph P. Kennedy, United States Ambassador to Great Britain.

They took their places in the cool church beside a great audience. At 2:50 P. M., as they were sitting there waiting for the service to start, air-raid sirens started echoing through the great cathedral.

Mr. Churchill got up, walked over to the cloisters and had a long talk with the Dean. In a few minutes he returned and took his place beside his Ministers in the chancel. It was announced that the service would proceed.

Around the city the British fight-

Continued on Page Three

The International Situation

Destroyer-War Base Deal

Completion of a deal by which the United States will transfer to Britain fifty over-age destroyers and obtain ninety-nine-year leases on eight shore and island bases stretching from Newfoundland to British Guiana was announced by President Roosevelt yesterday in a message to Congress. Coincidentally, the British Government pledged not to scuttle or surrender its fleet under any conditions. [Page 1, Column 8.]

The objective of the arrangement with Britain is to build a 4,500-mile iron fence in the Atlantic to assure this country's safety for a century, an authoritative State Department source said. To attain this, any interpretations of international law and parts of treaties in conflict must be subordinated, he said. Since this country's purpose is its defense, no well-intentioned nation can call the move a hostile act, he declared. [Page 1, Column 7.]

President Roosevelt, en route to Washington, disclosed that he looked upon the agreement as a means of keeping an enemy from the country's front door. Listing it as in some ways more important for defense than Jefferson's

Louisiana purchase, he hinted there might be other similar arrangements. [Page 1, Column 6.]

The President had acted on an opinion from Attorney General Jackson, who held that the Executive had the right to negotiate the transfer without Senate consent and the constitutional power to dispose of the vessels. [Page 1, Column 5.]

Wendell L. Willkie, Republican Presidential nominee, said the country would undoubtedly approve the arrangement, but criticized Mr. Roosevelt's failure to obtain Congress's approval. [Page 1, Column 3.]

London rejoiced. A Foreign Office spokesman described the agreement as a practical method for each nation to contribute to the other's defense requirements. [Page 1, Column 4.]

Axis spokesmen did not challenge the deal's legality under neutrality laws. In Berlin it was belittled as unlikely to affect the war's outcome. It was said to be a bargain for the United States and evidence that Britain was "cracking up." In Rome it was expected the Italians would be embittered. [Page 15, Column 1.]

Developments in Congress

The House opened debate on the Selective Service Training Bill, the discussion following the lines of the Senate's deliberations. Indications were that the bill would pass by a good margin, the principal controversy centering on the question of industrial conscription. Leaders

planned for final action Friday. [Page 17, Column 1.]

The Senate Finance Committee opened hearings on the excess profits tax and defense expansion amortization bill. The probability of changes in the measure increased as witnesses hit at its effects on business. [Page 10, Column 1.]

The War in Europe, Asia and Africa

German bombers hammered at Britain's airfields, harbors and naval bases, engaging the Royal Air Force in battles all over Southern England. Three raids on London were repelled. [Page 1, Column 1.]

Several R. A. F. bombers reached Berlin early today to provoke violent anti-aircraft fire after the British had loosed a powerful aerial counter-offensive in which their planes had smashed German industrial centers, the French coast and Italian power stations. [Page 3, Column 1.]

In the central Mediterranean, new type Italian bombers scored a victory, damaging a British battleship, an aircraft carrier, a cruiser and a destroyer, the Rome High Command announced. The R. A. F. again pounded Assab, port in Italian Eritrea. [Page 4, Column 6.]

Led by Tahiti, France's most important colony in Oceania, the French-protected Society Islands have voted to throw in their lot with Britain, repudiating Vichy, it was reported. [Page 6, Column 1.]

A virtual Japanese ultimatum demanding a military base and passage for troops was reported to have been rejected by French Indo-China and conflict there was believed inevitable. [Page 6, Column 3.]

In an attempted Iron Guard coup three gunmen broke through King Carol's palace guard and fired several shots into the air. Others equally vainly besieged a radio station, fought with troops. [Page 1, Column 2.]

A clash between Hungarian and Rumanian troops over the occupation of Transylvania was reported at Bucharest. [Page 4, Column 1.]

BUCHAREST CHECKS IRON GUARDS' COUP

Shots Fired in Front of Royal Palace — Handbills Call On Carol to Abdicate

By EUGEN KOVACS
Wireless to The New York Times.

BUCHAREST, Rumania, Sept. 3—A group of the Iron Guards, dissatisfied with the conduct and policy of other Iron Guards who are Ministers and who participated in the Crown Council, organized and carried out several attempts tonight against different public buildings in Bucharest. All these attacks failed.

A small group consisting of three persons appeared in an automobile this evening at 8:30 before the Royal Palace and one of them fired two shots in the air. A policeman on duty in front of the gates of the palace fired at the car but failed. The man who fired the shots tried to escape, however, but was arrested, while the car disappeared.

The regular news bulletin broadcast at 10 o'clock was canceled.

A second group, consisting of young men wearing military uniforms and disguised as Iron Guards, attacked the Bucharest radio station. The guard fired and succeeded in repelling the attacking group.

At the cable of transmission of this attack a man found who cut off some lines so that the telephone connection with abroad was cut off for a while. At the State Railway station these times when the struggle in the suburb of Grivitsan an-

Continued on Page Four

WILLKIE FOR PACT, BUT HITS SECRECY

Regrets President Did Not Deal With Britain Before Congress and People

By JAMES A. HAGERTY
Special to The New York Times.

RUSHVILLE, Ind., Sept. 3—Asked tonight to comment on President Roosevelt's announcement of the agreement to turn over to Great Britain fifty over-age destroyers in return for air and naval bases in British Western Hemisphere areas, Wendell L. Willkie, Republican nominee for President, declared that the country would undoubtedly approve the program, but criticized the President's failure to obtain prior approval of Congress as smacking of totalitarianism.

In a statement prepared with care and with realization that it might have important foreign repercussions, Mr. Willkie said:

"The country will undoubtedly approve of the program to add to our naval and air bases and assistance given to Great Britain. It is regrettable, however, that the President did not deem it necessary in connection with this proposal to secure the approval of Congress or permit public discussion prior to adoption.

"The people have a right to know of such important commitments prior to and not after being made. We must be extremely careful in these times when the struggle in the world is between democracy and to-

Continued on Page Fourteen

BRITISH JUBILANT

Destroyers Strengthen Their Fleet at Point of Greatest Strain

MORAL EFFECT GREAT

But Press Warns People Gesture Does Not Mean U. S. Will Enter War

By RAYMOND DANIELL
Special Cable to The New York Times.

LONDON, Sept. 3—It would be impossible to overstate the jubilation in official and unofficial circles caused today by President Roosevelt's announcement that fifty United States destroyers were coming to help Great Britain in her hour of peril. They will be manned by British crews and will fly the white ensign of the Royal Navy, it is true, but they are coming, nevertheless.

It was tangible proof that American talk of giving "all aid short of war" was more than idle chatter and that this country's friends across the Atlantic, despite German propaganda and the heavy bombardment of British cities and towns, had decided there was still lots of fight left in the British lion and that it was not too late to help turn the tide against totalitarian domination of Europe.

Destroyer Losses Offset

Under the arrangement, it was pointed out by authoritative sources, the United States gained security against future aggression, while the British fleet at one stroke acquired fifty 1,300-ton destroyers as an offset to the thirty lost since the beginning of hostilities.

These destroyers are badly needed at this stage of the war with British seapower engaged in a death grapple with the German Empire. Since the French were knocked out as an ally, the whole job of protecting convoys and maintaining the lifelines of the Empire against the new enemy in the Mediterranean has fallen upon the British fleet, while the air force has concentrated chiefly on destroying the enemy's supplies and defending the homes of the people of this island, which is under repeated bombardment from the air throughout its length and breadth.

Added to the multiplication of the navy's duties has been the necessity of blockading the whole Continent of Europe while standing by to resist the very real threat of a German invasion which, as War Secretary Anthony Eden warned today, still hangs over this country.

As great as was Britain's need this action was matched in British minds by the intangible implications of most open indication yet of Anglo-American cooperation for defense against the Nazi threats.

The Times, London, will point out editorially tomorrow that such cooperation between a belligerent and a neutral is "a new departure" but one that is dictated by the necessities of modern war. The editorial goes on to say:

"The tragic fate of some of the smaller peoples of Europe might have been averted if they had not been restrained from planning for

Continued on Page Fifteen

RULING BY JACKSON

Opinion Holds Transfer by President Needs No Senate Action

AN 'EXECUTIVE' DEAL

Opponents in Congress Seek to Find Means of Obstructing It

Attorney General Jackson's opinion is printed on Page 16.

By LEWIS WOOD
Special to The New York Times.

WASHINGTON, Sept. 3—President Roosevelt has unqualified power to exchange fifty over-age destroyers for British naval and air base sites in the Western Hemisphere without Senate consent, in the opinion of Attorney General Jackson, made public today, but, while Mr. Jackson asserted the Executive's right to dispose of naval vessels, he again refused to sanction the legality of delivery of "mosquito boats" now under construction.

Under a World War law the Attorney General ruled that it would be entirely proper to transfer the destroyers, since these were not built "with the intent that they should enter the service of a belligerent," but turning over the uncompleted mosquito boats, he argued, would be impossible, as this would legally mean that they were intended for a belligerent.

Opponents of the British-American deal sought tonight to find means of obstruction and delay, but this seemed to hinge upon the extent to which the direct interest of a taxpayer could be proved and the general opinion here was that the adversaries were blocked from court action and could depend only upon sufficient massing of public opinion. Apparently the Administration felt legally secure.

Writing his opinion to President Roosevelt last Tuesday, Mr. Jackson went into detail as to constitutional power and especially stressed the responsibility of the Executive to use every authority for national defense at a time when "present world conditions forbid him to risk" any constitutionally avoidable delay.

"No Future Commitments"

The Attorney General conceded that the wide Presidential power over foreign relations was not unlimited, but in this case, Mr. Jackson contended, there were no promises or future commitments by the United States which would require Senate consent or, indeed, any Congressional action. The agreement provided an opportunity to establish naval and air bases for coastline defense, he maintained, but needed no appropriation of money. Thus it was unnecessary for the Senate to ratify "an opportunity that entails no obligation," he declared.

Alluding to precedents, Mr. Jackson remarked that the "proposition falls far short" of the acquisition of the Louisiana Territory by President Jefferson from a belligerent during a European war. Outside of constitutional power, he went on,

Continued on Page Sixteen

UNITED STATES ACQUIRES DEFENSE BASTIONS
Bases at the places indicated by circled dots are being leased by Great Britain to this country for ninety-nine years. The bases for those in Newfoundland and Bermuda are in effect outright gifts; the leases for the others are in exchange for fifty over-age United States destroyers. The bases in the Caribbean area will supplement present American defense centers (black diamonds) in guarding approaches to the Panama Canal.

LINE OF 4,500 MILES

Two Defense Outposts Are Gifts, Congress Is Told—No Rent on Rest

FOR 50 OLD VESSELS

President Holds Move Solely Protective, 'No Threat to Any Nation'

Texts of messages on leasing of naval bases, Page 10.

By FRANK L. KLUCKHOHN
Special to The New York Times.

WASHINGTON, Sept. 3—President Roosevelt informed Congress today that he had completed an arrangement by which the United States will transfer to Great Britain fifty over-age destroyers and obtain from Britain ninety-nine-year leases for sea and air bases at eight strategic continental and island points in the Western Hemisphere.

The new American defense line thus established will stretch 4,500 miles from Newfoundland to British Guiana and include other bases on the islands of Bermuda, the Bahamas, Jamaica, St. Lucia, Trinidad and Antigua.

It is intended to make difficult, if not impossible, naval and air attacks upon the United States and much of the New World. The exact sites of the bases will be determined later by the two governments.

A solemn pledge by the British Government to the United States not to scuttle or surrender the British fleet under any conditions was revealed coincidentally with the State Department's publication of correspondence between Secretary Hull and the British Ambassador, the Marquess of Lothian.

Secretary Hull was informed that it represented the "settled policy" of His Majesty's Government not to "surrender or sink" the British fleet.

Reshaping of Naval Defense

The deal, carrying with it far-flung international as well as domestic defense implications, was hailed by President Roosevelt as the most important for the defense of this country since the Jefferson Administration completed the Louisiana Purchase in 1803.

Informed official circles contended that it assured the British Fleet as an Atlantic sea-screen for the United States and made it possible for the American Fleet to remain in the Pacific.

Some thought it might lead to an informal defensive alliance between this country and Australia similar to the arrangement recently completed administratively with Canada, although others disagreed on this point.

President Roosevelt informed Congress that the British Government had given the right to bases in Newfoundland and Bermuda as an outright gift, "generously given and gladly received," but that "the other bases mentioned have been acquired in exchange for fifty of our over-age destroyers."

Previously, the President had insisted that the destroyer and base deals were separate.

Legal Basis for Procedure

Mr. Roosevelt explained in his message that he had acted upon a legal opinion by Attorney General Jackson which held that the Chief Executive had the right to dispose of the deal without consultation with the Senate or without its approval. The President made clear that he would not seek the Senate's endorsement by remarking that he sent his statement merely "for the information of Congress."

Chairman Walsh of the Senate Naval Affairs Committee and several other Senators publicly condemned the proposed deal as illegal under domestic and international law when it was reported in the press some weeks ago that President Roosevelt had agreed to give Britain fifty destroyers at pleas from Prime Minister Winston Churchill.

In view of Senator Walsh's stand, some Senators privately expressed the opinion that there might be an attempt to have the Naval Affairs Committee open an investigation of the whole transaction.

After the President's message was

Continued on Page Twelve

ROOSEVELT HAILS GAIN OF NEW BASES

Exchange of Over-Age Ships for British Leases Offers Outer Defense Line, He Says

By CHARLES HURD
Special to The New York Times.

ON BOARD ROOSEVELT TRAIN, Sept. 3—President Roosevelt indicated that the chief value of the trade with Great Britain of fifty over-age destroyers for naval and air base sites in British crown colonies in the Western Hemisphere lay in the fact that this outer line of defense would keep any enemy away from this country's front door.

For that reason, he said, his agreement with the British Government was more important for the defense of this country than anything since the Louisiana Purchase in 1803, which assured American military control over the Mississippi River.

There may be other similar negotiations, he added, but he cautioned newspaper reporters not to try to guess where they would be, listing the odds at 10 to 1 that such guesses would be wrong.

The President did not deny a suggestion made by a reporter that perhaps Greenland might be the site for another base. He merely renewed his caution against speculation.

The President's view of the agreement, which has been known to be in progress for several weeks, was given at a special press conference on his private train at the same hour that his offices in Washington sent to Congress a message that the exchange was accomplished.

A dozen newspaper reporters heard Mr. Roosevelt read the text of the message to Congress, which he completed during a trip from Hyde Park, N. Y., to Tennessee, North Carolina and West Virginia. He read the message, after laughingly telling them that there was no story. While the document, with supporting papers, was being made public in Washington at noon, he began his press conference at 11:50 A. M. Eastern time.

Mr. Roosevelt called the press conference to meet in the tiny vestibule of his private car forty-five minutes after he departed from South Charleston, W. Va., where he engaged work being done to restore to high productivity a long abandoned Navy ordnance plant built in 1917-18 to construct armor plate and shells.

Among the statements he made, one could accurately visualize the

Continued on Page Ten

SHIP TRADE IS HELD NOT HOSTILE ACTION

State Department Stresses Defense Phase of Exchange of Vessels for Bases

Special to The New York Times.

WASHINGTON, Sept. 3—No country could consider the transfer of fifty United States destroyers to Great Britain and the obtaining by this country of naval and air bases in British New World territory as a hostile act, an informed State Department source said today.

Only a nation seeking world conquest could use this as a pretext for belligerent action, the source asserted.

The intention of this government in completing the agreement was merely to strengthen its own defenses and no other considerations were entertained, State Department officials said, in insisting that the United States had the opportunity to obtain a 4,000 or 5,000 mile ring of steel around the eastern part of the hemispheres on terms unequaled since the Louisiana Purchase. They added that the protection would last for 100 years.

It was made clear that it was no time to consider any technical provisions which might be sought in international law by opponents of the agreement but that in these dangerous days, when the world is almost literally on fire, defense considerations must come first.

This view was expressed in answer to questions of correspondents about the Second Hague Convention of 1907, of which the United States and Germany are signatories, but Great Britain is not.

Hague 1907 Convention Is Quoted

Article VI of this convention asserts:

"The supply in any manner, directly or indirectly, by a neutral power of a belligerent power, of warships, ammunition or war materials of any kind whatever, is forbidden."

Article VIII says:

"A neutral government is also bound to display the same vigilance to prevent the departure from its jurisdiction of any vessel intended to cruise, or menace in hostile operations, which had been adapted empirely to high productivity a long abandoned Navy ordnance plant built in 1917-18 to construct armor plate and shells.

Article XXVIII, however, states:

"The provisions of this present convention do not apply except to the contracting powers and then only if all the belligerents are parties to the convention."

One could accurately visualize the

Continued on Page Sixteen

Writer on British Destroyer Sees U-Boats in Raids and One Sunk

By BRYDON TAVES

ABOARD A BRITISH DESTROYER, in the North Atlantic, Sept. 3—(UP)—Somewhere it is shooting the works to make good the threat of total blockade of the British Isles, but after eight days aboard a little British flotilla leader I can say that hundreds of ships are entering and leaving British ports each week.

German submarine and air attacks marked my voyage. Not one day passed without action. The British crew was either manning gun and depth-charge stations to fight off a U-boat or manning anti-aircraft stations to fight attacking planes.

I saw one British merchantman take a long-range torpedo squarely amidships and sink within a yard hour. The next day our destroyer avenged the score.

"A 'tin fish,' meant for us, missed by a scant thirty feet as we

whipped around. Then we rocked from the concussion of our own depth charges and I saw an oil patch spread slowly over the surface, marking that U-boat's end.

The destroyer was engaged in a typical convoy job, and its duties were something between those of a conscientious sheep dog and a sister of charity leading a bunch of orphans across Times Square.

We were one destroyer and one smaller warship escorting a thirty-ship convoy over fifteen square miles at sea. Watching the lines of hulls stretching out behind us, I remembered what a naval officer in a convoy control room on a West coast port told me just before I sailed:

"Give me fifty over-age American destroyers," he said, "and I will

Continued on Page Four

"All the News That's Fit to Print."

The New York Times.

LATE CITY EDITION
Fair and cooler today. Tomorrow fair and continued cool.
Temperature Yesterday—Max., 72; Min., 64

Copyright, 1940, by The New York Times Company.

VOL. LXXXIX .. No. 30,181.   Entered as Second-Class Matter, Postoffice, New York, N. Y.   NEW YORK, WEDNESDAY, SEPTEMBER 11, 1940   THREE CENTS NEW YORK CITY and Vicinity | FOUR CENTS Elsewhere Except in 7th and 8th Postal Zones

BRITISH BOMB BERLIN, HIT REICHSTAG BUILDING AND OTHER LANDMARKS IN CENTER OF THE CITY; GERMANS POUND AT LONDON IN 8-HOUR ATTACK

ROOSEVELT TO TALK 'POLITICS' TONIGHT BEFORE TEAMSTERS

First Avowed Campaign Talk Will Be a Paid Broadcast Over Two Networks

'HISTORY' WILL BE A TOPIC

President Professes Not to Know if 8-Year Survey Would Be Political or Historical

By CHARLES HURD
Special to The New York Times.

HYDE PARK, N. Y., Sept. 10—President Roosevelt dropped tonight the nonpolitical attitude which he has heretofore adopted. He will deliver tomorrow night a major speech in Washington before the annual convention of the Brotherhood of Teamsters, Chauffeurs, Stablemen and Helpers, A. F. of L.

He will speak over two nation-wide radio networks on broadcast time to be paid for by the Democratic National Committee, instead of getting facilities free from all four networks available.

The decision was announced by Stephen T. Early, White House secretary, who told news correspondents:

"I expect that President Roosevelt in all probability will deliver his first avowed talk of the campaign.

The decision to be Mr. Roosevelt's first bid for re-election apparently was made at the last minute. The President at a press conference earlier indicated that he did not consider the speech to be political.

Mr. Early, who acted as Presidential spokesman later, said that the decision was dictated ... some extent by a desire not to burden the radio circuits by carrying the talk as an unpaid news service by all the radio companies and thereby making them liable for granting equal facilities and time to Wendell L. Willkie.

New Phase of the Campaign

The White House announcement, made only a few hours before the President left on his train for the capital, opened a new phase of his activities as they concern this election year. Heretofore he has stated that his inspection trips and his talks were made as duties of the President.

He will speak nonpolitically in Philadelphia on Sept. 20, when he receives a degree from the University of Pennsylvania, and here on Oct. 5, when he dedicates in one ceremony a new high school and two grade schools.

This attitude also will characterize other similar trips and talks in the future, but White House sources recalled that Mr. Roosevelt made for himself a loophole in the non-campaign rule in his radio address to the Democratic National Convention at Chicago on July 19.

In that speech he said:

"Since last Summer I have been compelled to abandon proposed journeys to inspect many of our great national projects from the Alleghenies to the Pacific Coast. Events move so fast in other parts of the world that it has become my duty to remain either in the White House itself or at some near-by point where I can reach Washington and even Europe and Asia by direct telephone.

"I do expect, of course, during the coming months, to make my usual periodic reports to the country through the medium of press conferences and radio talks. I shall not have the time or the inclination to engage in purely political debate, but I shall never be loath to call the attention of the nation to deliberate or willful falsifications of fact which are now being made by political candidates.

Early Recalls President's Stand

On retreating from a work session with the President at the Hyde Park home in late afternoon, Mr. Early gathered reporters in his office and recalled that statement by Mr. Roosevelt, laying emphasis on the President's earlier stipulation that he would use the press conferences and radio speeches to reply to political attacks.

The address tomorrow night will be on radio time to be paid for by the Democratic National Committee," Mr. Early said, and he added, "That's all."

This campaign served to let the prepared speech, which Mr.

Continued on Page Fifteen

La Guardia to Reveal Choice for President

Special to The New York Times.

WASHINGTON, Sept. 10—Mayor La Guardia will announce his choice for President in a nation-wide radio broadcast Thursday evening over the NBC Red Network, he announced here today.

The Mayor, here as chairman of the United States section of the United States-Canadian Joint Defense Commission, issued a type-written announcement to this effect. It had been reported that the Mayor would work for President Roosevelt's re-election, but he refused to go beyond his formal announcement.

The Democratic National Committee will pay the bill for Mayor La Guardia's broadcast tomorrow evening, Edward J. Flynn, chairman of the committee, said yesterday. The speech will be delivered from 7:15 to 7:30 P. M. and will be repeated later from 11:15 to 11:30 P. M. for the Pacific Coast listeners.

Mr. Flynn said that the Mayor had suggested the broadcast to him several days ago.

LEHMAN DEPLORES STATE TAX CURBS

Asserts Attempts at 'Economic Isolation' Are a Threat to Democratic Way of Life

Charging that several States have deliberately attempted a policy of "economic isolation" in recent years, Governor Lehman warned last night that their efforts to "stifle the flow of trade across State lines" might eventually threaten our democratic way of life.

Governor Lehman, Governor A. Harry Moore of New Jersey and Governor Raymond E. Baldwin of Connecticut spoke at the annual dinner of the National Tax Association, which is holding its thirty-third annual conference at the Hotel Pennsylvania. Their addresses followed a day of discussion of current tax problems by many governmental and university specialists in the field.

Governor Moore pointed out that at present three-quarters of the cost of government in New Jersey is borne by taxes on real property, and he contended that this is too narrow a tax base. In working out replacement taxes, however, he said, care must be taken not to impose taxes that would harm the State's industries in their competitive position with other States.

Governor Baldwin, pointing out that Connecticut has a balanced budget without a sales tax or a State income tax, said that in his State an indicated deficit of $3,500,000 when the took office in January, 1939, has been changed to a surplus of $1,000,000 by a policy of government "friendly" to business, labor and agriculture, with resultant increased production.

Sees Struggle by States for Gain

In his assault on State tax policies that are creating interstate trade barriers, Governor Lehman said that over a period of years there has arisen "a shameless struggle for gain at the expense of our States." He said that these policies were of "questionable material benefit" to the States that employ them.

"Laws have employed the power of government not for purposes of revenue but rather to stifle the flow of trade across State lines in behalf of domestic interests and enterprises," Governor Lehman said. "The net result has been to limit open competition, raise prices, lower standards of quality and, finally, to affect adversely the national income."

Turning to the "political and social implications" of this trend, Governor Lehman said that this development was "one of the most geographically hardened manifestations of that trend toward an economic and a democracy is doomed," Governor Lehman continued. "National strength and solidarity in times of crisis are strongly dependent upon singleness of purpose, pooling of resources and a willingness ...

"If the time ever arrives when boundary lines of the forty-eight States assume greater significance than as mere geographic units ...

Continued on Page Twenty-nine

WILLKIE OPPOSES DELAYING OF DRAFT DESPITE PRESSURE

Hopes the Senate and House Conferees Will Eliminate the Fish Amendment

HE REBUFFS ISOLATIONISTS

Takes Stand in Face of 140 House Republicans Who Voted to Wait

By JAMES A. HAGERTY
Special to The New York Times.

RUSHVILLE, Ind., Sept. 10—Disregarding strong pressure from members of the Republican organization, Wendell L. Willkie came out today against the House amendment to the Burke-Wadsworth selective service bill, which, if accepted by the Senate, would delay the draft until after the November election.

"I hope that, as a result of the conference between House and Senate conferees on the selective service bill, the Fish amendment is eliminated," Mr. Willkie said in a formal statement.

In opposing any delay in the draft, or selective service for national defense as Mr. Willkie prefers to phrase it, the Presidential nominee ran counter to 140 Republicans in the House who voted for the amendment, including Representative Joseph W. Martin Jr., chairman of the national committee. Only twenty-two Republicans voted against the amendment.

Resists Isolationist Pressure

Mr. Willkie's declaration confirmed the assertion he made in his speech Saturday night that never during his campaign would he take any position in which he did not believe. He is known to regard the international situation as so serious that there should be no avoidable delay in any of the preparations for national defense. He declared for "selective service" in his acceptance speech and explained afterward that he meant selective service now, not later.

Since that time he has resisted pressure from leading members of his party to modify his position and take more of an isolationist stand. He has been frank at all times regarding his views on foreign policy.

He has said frequently that he favored aid to Great Britain, short of war, adding that when he said "short of war" he meant "short of war." In criticizing President Roosevelt's exchange of over-age destroyers for defense bases in British possessions, he favored the trade but attacked the method used by the President as dictatorial.

Research Aides Arrive

Members of the research staff which will accompany Mr. Willkie on his trip to the Pacific Coast arrived here today. Among them were Russell W. Davenport, who resigned as managing editor of Fortune to join the movement to nominate Mr. Willkie; Raymond Leslie Buell, former director of The Foreign Policy Association, and Elliott

Continued on Page Seventeen

Italians Jail Prince Doria as Anti-Fascist; Prince Torlonia Also Reported Arrested

By CAMILLE CIANFARRA

ROME, Sept. 10—Prince Filippo Andrea Doria-Pamphili-Landi, 54-year-old head of an Italian princely family, has been put in a concentration camp, it is learned.

It is also reported, but without confirmation, that 28-year-old Prince Alessandro Torlonia, whose mother was Elsie Moore of New York and who married a daughter of the King of Spain, also has been arrested.

Circles close to the government emphatically denied the evening that the "alleged" arrests were part of a round-up of anti-Fascists.

"No such round-up has taken place," they stated, "and all reports to the contrary are completely unfounded."

Prince Doria's arrest is stated to have been caused by remarks unfriendly to the Fascist regime, which he made publicly less than a fortnight ago; at present, according to friends of the family, he is

doing manual labor. Since it is feared he is affected by heart trouble and rheumatism, there is considerable apprehension for his life among his friends.

Prince Doria, after the death of his first wife, married his English nurse, Gesine Mary Dykes, who is generally credited with having kept him alive with her constant care.

His anti-Fascist feelings are well known in Rome. He heartily disapproved the Ethiopian campaign.

On Dec. 1d, 1935, the "day of faith," when, following the adoption of sanctions against Italy by the League of Nations, Italian women were asked to donate their wedding rings to demonstrate their solidarity, Prince Doria refused to display the Italian flag at the balcony of his beautiful sixteenth-century palace in the Corso Umberto, Rome's main street.

This gesture did not escape

Continued on Page Six

Ford's Party Leaves $46 As Tip After Luncheon

By The Associated Press.

DETROIT, Sept. 10—Ethel Gaff, 19-year-old Fort Wayne (Ind.) hotel waitress, need not worry about the $46 left on the table after Henry Ford and his party ate a $4 luncheon. It was the change from a $50 bill which paid for the luncheon.

Miss Gaff was reported in doubt as to whether the money was a tip or whether the automobile manufacturer had forgotten it in his hurry to resume his motor trip.

"I paid the check, and I left the money purposely as a tip for the young lady," Harry Bennett, personal director of the Ford Motor Company, said today. "She did a very good job in taking care of us, and particularly in keeping curiosity seekers away from Mr. Ford."

PLANE PRODUCTION HAILED BY KNUDSEN

He Says in Buffalo Interview We Will Have 11,000 Combat Craft by April, 1942

By The Associated Press.

BUFFALO, Sept. 10—In nineteen months the Army and Navy will have about 11,000 combat airplanes, fighters and bombers, William S. Knudsen of the National Defense Commission said today as he approached the end of a nation-wide tour of aircraft plants with Major Gen. H. H. Arnold, chief of the Army Air Corps.

"We know the United States is making the best airplanes," he said, and added:

"I believe that presently we can say we are making the most airplanes."

The figure of 11,000 was based on a total production by April 1, 1942, of 33,000 planes, 14,000 destined for the armed services of the United States. General Arnold said that of these he believed 9,000 would be delivered to the Army and Navy, about 60 per cent would be so-called combat types.

Mr. Knudsen said the current American airplane production of 800 a month, including both military and large commercial types, would be doubled in twelve months. Seated in the office of Burdette S. Wright, president of the Curtiss Aeroplane Division of the Curtiss-Wright Corporation, he fixed at three a day the delivery of new Curtiss P-40 fighter planes to the Air Corps.

General Arnold added that 534 P-40's, one of the newest types of American fighters, were on order for the Air Corps, and that 140 had been delivered.

The visitors saw two of these fighter planes, the almost completed corpart of British and German pursuit craft, streak at 330 miles an hour across Buffalo's Municipal Airport in a rare public demonstration of the progress of the nation's air rearmament drive.

Delivery of P-40's to both the Air Corps and to Great Britain's Royal Air Force has been slowed down by the limited manufacture of engines by the Allison Engineering Corporation, a General Motors subsidiary at Indianapolis, but Mr.

Continued on Page Fourteen

LONDON IS HARRIED

Night Invaders Resume Bombing After 4 Raids by Day Are Repelled

BRITONS CARRYING ON

People Now Sleep in the Shelters—Water and Gas Impaired

By RAYMOND DANIELL
Special Cable to The New York Times.

LONDON, Wednesday, Sept. 11—As darkness fell last night a waning half-moon rose above the smoldering embers of the previous night's great fires, which threatened for a time to destroy the beautiful St. Paul's Cathedral and St. Mary-le-Bow Church, whose sweet-toned chimes for generations have lulled the Cockney children to sleep. The German Air Force then returned in force to London to continue the attack that has made life in this capital a nightmare since Saturday.

The all clear was sounded at 4:39 this morning, after the raid had been in progress for eight hours and twenty-four minutes.

[Nazi bombers smashed at London with increasing violence early today, The Associated Press reported. Until early this morning, it was stated, the attack was much less ferocious than the previous three. Then the pace stepped up until four separate squadrons were wheeling about the capital at the same time at opposite points of the compass.]

The screams of their bombs, the earth-shaking crashes, the blazes that lit the sky, the clangor of fire engines and ambulances, the bark of anti-aircraft guns and nerve-racking hum of engines droning like a mosquito that does not bite, brought another sleepless and nidious night to 7,000,000 harried persons who are trying to carry on in the face of an attack that spares neither humble workmen's homes nor the homes of the nobility.

Bombing Is at Random

For nine hours last night explosive-laden planes roared overhead, dropping high explosive and incendiary bombs apparently wherever the spirit moved the man in charge of the bomb racks to press the button. They released death and destruction upon helpless civilians who shuddered each time the ground shook beneath them.

Two hospitals, one filled with ailing children and the other a maternity hospital, suffered heavy damage. It is not accurately known at present, while the raid is still going on, how many homes were wrecked or persons killed, for that rescue workers are still digging among the ruins.

It was estimated, however, that last night's raid caused at least 286 deaths and sent 1,400 persons, including the lame, halt and blind, into hospitals, seriously injured.

Question of Morale

But it is not the dead or the injured, or even the extensive property damage that really counts in this battle for London, which is a mere prelude to the Battle for Britain. It is what is happening to the city's life and the nerves of its people that matters the most.

They are standing up to the punishment that is being rained on them from the skies with a courage that makes the eyes of a neutral observer smart at times. There is no doubt about their bravery, but one cannot help but wonder how long any people's nerves can stand up under this kind of bombardment, in which every one knows that each breath may be the last one, and in which the suspense is awful.

That does not mean that a defeatist attitude is growing. Far from it. These people are getting madder by the minute.

Many homes are without gas and water. Citizens are forced to undergo tremendous inconveniences in getting to and from the places where they earn their livelihood, and their ingrained politeness to one another is becoming a little strained.

There is hardly any one who has not a friend who has been bombed out of his home or has had a narrow escape from death or injury.

Monday night bombs dropped on every section of London. Slum hovels, wealthy houses, warehouses and luxury apartments, all felt the

Continued on Page Two

The International Situation

The War in Europe and Africa

Berlin last night suffered the most intense raid yet inflicted by Royal Air Force planes. Earlier British craft had ranged over Northwestern Germany, Belgium, the Netherlands, France and the Norwegian coast, raiding twenty-five places. Relays of planes blasted Hamburg wharves, a Berlin power plant, docks, factories, barges and supplies at Continental ports. Four bombers failed to return, the Air Ministry reported. [Page 1, Column 8.]

With fires from Monday's attack still smoldering, Nazi bombers swooped down upon London again last night to give the harassed city last night its fourth sleepless night. The crash of descending bombs started at dusk, when the air-raid sirens sounded the fifth warning of the day. Previous raids had been limited apparently to reconnaissance flights and the planes had been driven off by British fighters. The early alarms were so timed that they drove workers to air-raid shelters at lunch time, at tea time, and again at the height of the evening rush hour with people jammed around crippled transit facilities. Though harassed at their daily tasks after a sleepless and strained night Londoners' morale was unbroken and they were getting "madder by the minute." [Page 1, Column 5.]

Women and children, many dazed from shell shock, jammed the railroads, begged rides from motorists and pleaded with the authorities to find havens for them in an exodus from battered London. The menfolk were carrying on. The Minister of Transport asked that every one refrain from unnecessary travel; the Minister of Health broadcast a plea for aid to the homeless

and warned of increasing destitution as a result of bombing. [Page 3, Column 4.]

Announcing more raids against the British capital, German official sources said that new waves would strike London until the British people being to power a government willing to accept German terms. The present heavy on being wrought in London, German spokesmen said, is not the Battle of Britain but merely the Battle of London, and they promised that the Battle of Britain would follow when London, as the nerve-center of the British Isles and an important military objective, had been destroyed. [Page 4, Column 7.]

London and Berlin reports told of a new secret British weapon, a "self-igniting leaf" of cardboard and phosphorus, that had started fires in Germany. [Page 1, Column 6.]

In what was reported to have been the worst raid in the Middle East, Italian fliers bombed Tel Aviv, Palestine, killing 150 civilians. British claimed there were no military objectives there. Rome reported bombing of the Jaffa harbor, the Alexandria-Matruh Railroad and Port Sudan. [Page 6, Column 2.]

Prince Filippo Andrea Doria-Pamphili-Landi, 54-year-old head of an Italian princely family, has been put in a concentration camp for remarks unfriendly to the Fascist regime, it was learned in Rome. Reports that Prince Alessandro Torlonia, whose mother was Elsie Moore of New York and who married a daughter of the King of Spain, also has been arrested were unconfirmed. The government denied that there had been a round-up of anti-Fascisti. [Page 1, Column 3.]

American Developments

The American Red Cross sped plans to provide relief for victims of German air raids in London and other British cities. The Washington office of the Red Cross ordered 500,000 garments shipped from its New York warehouses, made preparations to send additional medical supplies, and cabled funds for purchase in London of twelve mobile canteen units of eight vehicles each for feeding homeless civilians. [Page 14, Column 4.]

Bombing Is at Random

versions of the measure without conclusive result. Washington opinion is that the final version will accept the House age limits of 21 to 45 and that the Fish amendment to delay the draft sixty days will be dropped. [Page 12, Column 3.]

The Senate agreed to limit debate on the Export-Import Bank Bill to ten minutes today after spending yesterday in fruitless discussion. Senator Taft has offered the only amendment, restriction of loans to help Latin-American production of strategic, critical or non-competitive products. [Page 11, Column 1.]

RAID NAZI CAPITAL

Miss U. S. Embassy, Hit Brandenburg Gate, Germans Say

AIM HELD DELIBERATE

R. A. F. Hammers 25 Vital Points to Weaken Foe's Offensive

By PERCIVAL KNAUTH
Wireless to The New York Times.

BERLIN, Wednesday, Sept. 11—The Royal Air Force this morning attacked the heart of Berlin's governmental center, dropping explosive and incendiary bombs in the immediate vicinity of the Wilhelmstrasse and the Reich's Chancellory. Appearing over the capital a few minutes after midnight with the moon nearly at full to guide them, the British fliers steered their course straight down "Via Triumphalis" bisecting Berlin from east to west and dropped a veritable hail of incendiary bombs on the famous Unter den Linden and Brandenburg Gate.

Two houses away from the American Embassy incendiary bombs set a small fire. Three hundred yards up the "East-West Axis" a bomb estimated at between 500 and 1,000 pounds in weight smashed into the broad asphalt speedway, rocking buildings in a half-mile radius. Incendiary bombs splattered on the rooftops, on the Brandenburg Gate, the Academy of German Art, the House of German Engineers and the old Reichstag building, setting small fires, which, however, were said to have been quickly extinguished.

In The New York Times office near the Wilhelmplatz detonations of half a dozen explosive bombs in the vicinity of the cellar were heard in the underground air-raid shelter. Incendiary bombs were said to have set small fires in a Jewish hospital, and the Charite Hospital.

The Catholic Saint Hedwig's Hospital, second largest in Berlin, likewise was said to have been struck by incendiary bombs which started several fires.

Two Injured by Bombs

In the Invalidenstrasse, close to the governmental center, a house was badly hit, injuring two persons and blasted the front of an apartment house as well as part of another house. In Dorotheenstrasse, which runs parallel to Unter den Linden, a dud bomb buried itself many feet deep in the street, while another ripped a wide hole in the office building.

An American news agency, with offices on the top floor of a building on this street, had a narrow escape when a bomb struck a house next door.

The British apparently attacked in four waves coming from the west. German military observers estimated the altitude of the first wave at about 18,000 feet, with each successive wave flying at a lower height, the last dropping its bombs from an altitude of about 8,000 feet. They flew straight into the city and when over the governmental district dropped numerous flares, which were followed by both explosive and incendiary bombs.

Some planes were reported to have flown low and machine-gunned anti-aircraft, artillery and searchlight batteries. The ground defenses followed the planes with a steady barrage, which was louder over the center of the capital than any heard before.

Official German quarters asserted the attack on the governmental district were obviously premeditated and designed to destroy government buildings. R. A. F. fliers, it is asserted, that the order had been given to concentrate on the governmental district, for it is claimed that "all military objectives were strictly avoided."

When from the German retaliation for this attack will take place cannot as yet be said. However, German quarters always have been very clear in stating that retaliation will follow a hundred thousandfold in the same manner as the British attack. Never before have governmental districts in Berlin

Continued on Page Four

INCENDIARY 'CARDS' A BRITISH WEAPON

Damp Discs, Dropped by R.A.F. by Thousands, Dry and Ignite—Nazis Incensed

By The Associated Press.

LONDON, Sept. 10—Britain disclosed tonight a new "secret weapon" in the form of innocent-looking bits of chemically treated cardboard dropped by the millions on Germany as delayed fire-bombs that burst into flame in unexpected quarters.

Germany, in first making public the new British tactics, acknowledged that the fire-scattering "calling cards" carried something more than a mere nuisance threat.

British authorities, in subsequently admitting use of the new weapon, described it only as a "self-igniting leaf," and declined to furnish details.

But the authentic German description, given after chemical analysis, sounded like a sequence from some fertile adventure cartoon or a passage from a detective thriller.

The cards, composed of guncotton and phosphorus, are carried in a moist state, the Germans said. Scattered over the countryside in lots of a quarter-million from a single plane, they dry out naturally and spring suddenly into flame about eight inches high when warmed by natural processes to a moderate temperature.

Implying that the cards may bear a printed message, the Germans said they were particularly dangerous because people had been picking

Continued on Page Four

NAZIS SEE BATTLE AS FIGHT TO FINISH

Air Attacks on London Will Be Pressed Till British Yield, It Is Said in Berlin

By The United Press.

BERLIN, Sept. 10—Nazis, angered by British bombing of Berlin and other cities, reported tonight that the German Air Fleet was roaring against London again in an offensive that would be pressed relentlessly until the British capitulate.

New waves of German bombers flying against London will carry out remorseless and incessant warfare, Nazis said, until "the smoking ruins of industrial and military objectives, decimation of the British Air Force and shattered morale of the British people bring into power a government that will accept German terms."

The German terms were regarded as unconditional capitulation.

Official German quarters were silent regarding any peace terms, but there were many unofficial suggestions that the collapse of Britain is "only a matter of weeks."

The Nazi press said that "now it is an eye-for-an-eye and a tooth-for-a-tooth" battle and said that "the sword of the German air force strikes pitilessly."

"What effects the heavy caliber bombs have were clearly revealed by Warsaw and Rotterdam," one newspaper said. "If London wishes to taste a similar fate to the full extent, then let Herr Churchill and his criminal clique continue to send pirates at night to Germany."

The Propaganda Ministry said

Continued on Page Four

"All the News That's Fit to Print."

The New York Times.

LATE CITY EDITION
Cloudy, much colder today. To-morrow partly cloudy and rather cold
Temperature Yesterday—Max., 66; Min., 52

VOL. XC. No. 30,237.

Entered as Second-Class Matter, Postoffice, New York, N. Y.

NEW YORK, WEDNESDAY, NOVEMBER 6, 1940.

Copyright, 1940, by The New York Times Company.

THREE CENTS NEW YORK CITY and Vicinity | FOUR CENTS Elsewhere Except in 7th and 8th Postal Zones

ROOSEVELT ELECTED PRESIDENT; CERTAIN OF 429 ELECTORAL VOTES; DEMOCRATS KEEP HOUSE CONTROL

RETAIN HOUSE GRIP

Democrats, Holding 225 Seats, Gain at Least Ten From Rivals

65 ARE NOW IN DOUBT

Latest Figures Indicate Republican Gain of 1 to 3 Senators

By TURNER CATLEDGE

Unless further complete returns today show more Republican winners in yesterday's election, the Democrats not only will have met successfully the challenge of their opponents to control the house but may actually repair some of the damage to their huge majority in the 1938 Congressional election.

The Republicans, on the other hand, may have added from one to three to their roster in the Senate, but this remains to be determined by complete reports.

Returns received up to 4 o'clock this morning indicated that the President's party had dropped only four seats to the opposition, while they had picked up at least ten now held by Republicans. This made the count 225 Democrats, 143 Republicans, one Independent Democrat and one American Labor with sixty-five seats still in doubt.

The present House is composed of 262 Democrats, 167 Republicans, one Farmer-Laborite, two Progressives and one American Labor member, with five vacancies due to deaths and resignations.

The status of the Senatorial tabulation at that hour, with thirty-six States in contest—thirty-three for full and three for unexpired terms—showed Democrats, 18; Republicans, 7, and 11 still in doubt. This made sure that the new Senate would have at least 62 Democrats, 23 Republicans, 1 Independent, leaving the 11 in doubt. The present ratio of the Senate is 69 Democrats, 24 Republicans, 1 Progressive, 1 Independent and 1 Farmer-Laborite (Senator Shipstead of Minnesota, who ran this year as a Republican).

The Senate's lone Progressive, Senator Robert M. La Follette, trailed Fred E. Clausen, his Republican opponent, in the earlier returns from Wisconsin, but late in the morning hours he forged ahead and word from the Badger State indicated that he might pull through in the toughest fight of his career.

The four seats dropped by Democrats to Republicans were in the Eighth Oklahoma, Sixteenth New York, Fourth California and the Sixth Missouri districts. More than offsetting these were the ten picked up by the Democrats, including the First, Second and Fourth Connecticut at large of that State; the First and Second Rhode Island districts, the Fifth and Twenty-second Pennsylvania districts and the Forty-first New York and the Sixteenth Ohio districts. The Democrats made a clean sweep of the delegations in Connecticut and Rhode Island, annexing six seats held in these two States. Perhaps the greatest upsets in the House were the defeats of Representative Phil Ferguson, Democrat of Oklahoma by Ross Rizley, Republican, and of the Democratic Representative James Fay of the Sixteenth New York by William E. Pheiffer, Republican.

Incumbent Democrats Sticking

Incumbent Democrats were holding tenaciously to leads in most of the other contests in which they were involved and New Deal leaders were threatening sitting Republican Congressmen in a number of districts, particularly in States where the Roosevelt victory was assuming landslide proportions in the popular vote.

The Republicans had entertained no hope from the start of capturing the leadership of the House, but they claimed chances of picking up from five to ten new seats to add to the twenty-four they now have.

Continued on Page Two

The PLACE to Want Ad just telephone The New York Times—LAckawanna 4-1000.

THE VOTE FOR PRESIDENT

State	Districts Total. Reported.	Roosevelt, Democrat.	Willkie, Republican.	Thomas, Socialist.	Electoral vote. Roos.-Will.
Alabama	2,200 1,107	140,984	21,224		11
Arizona	430 270	40,287	21,803		3
Arkansas	2,160 642	37,258	8,586		9
California	13,602 9,384	1,043,300	743,523		22
Colorado	1,610 387	43,180	54,301		
Connecticut	169 166	412,048	358,186		8
Delaware	249 200	80,880	60,812		3
Florida	1,451 686	246,182	82,521		7
Georgia	1,730 895	196,657	39,046		12
Idaho	792 300	26,113	30,155		
Illinois	8,375 6,017	1,514,763	1,375,082		29
Indiana	3,890 2,188	876,754	876,872		
Iowa	3,453 1,000	388,687	276,809		
Kansas	3,734 1,277	147,831	216,803		
Kentucky	4,341 2,240	297,123	193,622		11
Louisiana	1,712 481	187,513	22,967		10
Maine	629 624	154,733	163,762		
Maryland	1,231 1,194	351,234	241,447		8
Massachusetts	1,810 1,151	636,856	576,950		17
Michigan	3,630 1,349	287,245	287,726		
Minnesota	3,696 910	258,715	216,433		11
Mississippi	1,695 685	87,130	4,179		9
Missouri	4,479 2,914	536,687	420,110		
Montana	1,196 262	43,057	26,820		4
Nebraska	2,043 1,227	134,825	169,083		
Nevada	260 177	16,545	11,312		3
New Hampshire	297 287	115,932	103,671		4
New Jersey	3,630 2,038	829,922	564,294		
New Mexico	914 413	60,999	39,300		3
New York	9,319 9,397	3,231,083	3,021,536		47
North Carolina	1,926 -608	580,355	175,507		13
North Dakota	3,282 631	72,669	73,330		
Ohio	8,675 7,722	1,488,514	1,385,759		26
Oklahoma	3,613 2,805	355,764	349,117		11
Oregon	1,693 933	59,971	59,639		
Pennsylvania	8,113 7,152	1,913,401	1,670,023		36
Rhode Island	289 250	181,881	138,423		4
South Carolina	1,377 903	81,867	4,144		8
South Dakota	1,936 1,034	61,311	62,369		
Tennessee	2,190 1,891	207,724	119,836		11
Texas	254 244	804,453	118,198		23
Utah	831 345	63,396	30,941		4
Vermont	348 248	44,344	78,356		
Virginia	1,714 1,623	233,386	108,030		11
Washington	3,018 1,068	194,300	103,023		8
West Virginia	2,300 1,016	317,084	185,890		
Wisconsin	3,038 1,782	408,665	377,717		12
Wyoming	696 480	33,889	21,765		
					429 51

Hudson County returns incomplete.

ROOSEVELT WINNER IN MASSACHUSETTS

Indicated Margin Is Below That of 1936—Saltonstall Ahead in a Close Race

Special to THE NEW YORK TIMES.

BOSTON, Nov. 5—President Roosevelt carried Massachusetts over Wendell Willkie in today's election. Indications tonight were that his margin would be smaller than the 174,000 by which he captured the State's 17 electoral vote four years ago.

The Democratic surge was great enough to re-elect Senator Walsh over Henry Parkman Jr. by a substantial margin and to endanger Governor Leverett Saltonstall's re-election in his contest with Attorney General Paul A. Dever.

Lieut. Gov. Cahill, State Secretary Cook, State Treasurer Hurley and State Auditor Cook apparently were re-elected, while Robert T. Bushnell seemed to have won his contest for Attorney General on the basis of returns which had been counted late tonight.

President Roosevelt was strongest in the industrial city outside Boston. He carried Lynn by almost 6,000 votes and New Bedford by a ratio of nearly 2 to 1. It was estimated that Roosevelt's margin in Boston would approach 100,000. He carried Somerville by 4,100 votes.

Governor Saltonstall was running

Continued on Page Four

The War

Leading developments yesterday in the war, accounts of which appear on Page 25—the first page of the second section, —were as follows:

1. A German pocket battleship appeared in mid-Atlantic and shelled a British convoy.

2. Prime Minister Churchill emphasized before the Commons the growing U-boat threat and said bases in Ireland were needed by Britain.

3. In the Greek-Italian hostilities Rome reported an advance in the Yanina sector, the Greeks were said to be closing in on Koritza and a Yugoslav town was bombed by Italian-type planes.

The summary headed "International Situation" also appears on Page 25.

NEW JERSEY VOTE GOES TO PRESIDENT

Willkie Margin Cut in Normal Republican Areas—Edison and Barbour Win

By RUSSELL B. PORTER

On the basis of incomplete returns at 4 o'clock this morning, President Roosevelt appeared to have carried New Jersey with its sixteen electoral votes by a safe plurality—over Wendell Willkie—drastically defeated from 364,000 margin in 1936 and closer to his 31,000 edge in 1932.

The same returns indicated the election of Charles Edison, former Secretary of the Navy and son of the late Thomas A. Edison, the inventor, over his Republican opponent, State Senator Robert C. Hendrickson. Mr. Edison appeared to have polled more votes than the President.

United States Senator W. Warren Barbour, Republican candidate for re-election, ran far ahead of his ticket, and decisively defeated James H. Cromwell, former Minister to Canada and husband of Doris Duke, the tobacco heiress.

Eight hours after the polls closed at 8 P. M. there was still uncertainty over State-wide totals. Only one-half of the State's 3,631 election districts had reported their results by that time, and only a few comparatively of these were from the strong Democratic counties—Hudson, where Mayor Frank Hague of Jersey City, vice chairman of the Democratic National Committee, piled up a big Roosevelt vote, and Camden and Middlesex, where big industries with strong Roosevelt labor strength are located.

Big Vote Adds to Delay

The delay in recording the vote from these counties was caused partly by the record-breaking vote, brought out by perfect weather and unprecedentedly heavy registration, partly by the fact that voting machines are not used in these counties, and partly by the traditional withholding of the Hudson County vote until after the Republican counties have reported.

Surrogate John H. Gavin of Hudson County, spokesman for Mayor Hague, estimated early this morning, with the vote still incomplete, that Hudson would give the President and Mr. Edison a plurality of 110,000, including 60,000 in Jersey City. Mr. Cromwell was running far behind.

Four years ago Mr. Roosevelt re-

Continued on Page Twelve

CITY MARGIN WIDE

Lead Totals 727,254— Queens, Richmond Won by Willkie

P. R. SYSTEM UPHELD

Abolition Move Defeated by About 206,550— Simpson Is Elected

By LEO EGAN

Franklin D. Roosevelt piled up a plurality of 727,254 in New York City yesterday as voters in record-breaking numbers went to the polls under clear skies to record their choice for President. This was far short of the 1,375,356 plurality given to him in 1936, when he was a candidate for a second term.

The President carried the three most populous counties in the city, but lost Queens and Richmond. Queens gave Wendell Willkie a plurality of 36,673.

Senator James M. Mead, seeking re-election on the Democratic ticket, ran slightly ahead of the President. He carried the city by 945,063, carrying all five counties.

The President's pluralities of 350,-610 in Kings, 219,066 in the Bronx and 195,017 in Manhattan were much less than his supporters had counted on except in Manhattan, but they were enough to please them. The Manhattan plurality was larger than expected.

Results in Other Contests

Other features of yesterday's voting in the city were the defeat by an indicated plurality of 206,550 of the proposal to repeal the proportional representation method of selecting members of the City Council, the apparent defeat of Representative Vito Marcantonio, outstanding Congressional foe of conscription and the Roosevelt defense program, in the Twentieth Congressional District on Manhattan's upper East Side.

The President carried all but two Assembly district in Manhattan, losing the Fifteenth and Tenth, and all but three in King's—losing the Ninth, Tenth and Twentieth. He swept all eight districts in the Bronx and lost three out of six in Queens.

In all but one borough the friends of proportional representation were able to beat down the proposal to repeal it. If the proposal had been carried the voters would have elected Councilmen next year on the basis of State Senate districts within the victory.

Continued on Page Four

Willkie Retires Refusing to Give Up; He Declines Any Statement Before Today

Grimly clinging to his avowed determination not to give up the fight, Wendell L. Willkie said at 1:30 this morning that he intended to go to bed in his suite at the Hotel Commodore, and that he would have no statement to make concerning the election until some time after he wakes up this morning.

This information, relayed from his sixteenth-floor suite to the waiting crowd of reporters in the press headquarters downstairs, was the only word that came from Mr. Willkie after he had briefly appeared before a crowd of cheering campaign workers at 12:20 A. M. that he was neither afraid nor disheartened, and repudiate indignantly suggestions that he should concede his defeat.

When he appeared at that time before about 1,500 faithful supporters in the Grand Ball Room of the Commodore Hotel, Mr. Willkie pleaded with them not to quit and expressed his confidence that the fight they had jointly waged would eventually be won.

His appearance before his own campaign workers came after hours of seclusion in his private suite, where he repeatedly characterized the election as "a horse race" and predicted that the result would not be known definitely until some time today. Mr. Willkie appeared before the crowd of campaign workers at 12:19 A. M.

Holding up both hands to ask for silence while they gave him an ear-splitting ovation, Mr. Willkie said: "Fellow workers: I first want to say to you that I never felt better in my life. I congratulate you in being a part of the greatest crusade of this century. And that the principles for which we have fought will prevail as sure as that the truth will always prevail.

"And I hope that none of you are either afraid or disheartened because I am not in the slightest.

"I just wanted to come down and thank you so much for being my fellow fighters in this struggle—to

Continued on Page Five

WINNERS OF PRESIDENCY AND VICE PRESIDENCY
Franklin Delano Roosevelt   Henry Agard Wallace

DEMOCRATS CARRY STATE BY 230,000

Mead, O'Day, Merritt and Desmond Join President in New York Victory Column

By JAMES A. HAGERTY

For the third time President Franklin D. Roosevelt carried his home State of New York with its forty-seven electoral votes in yesterday's election, this time by a plurality of about 230,000, over Wendell L. Willkie, his Republican opponent.

The vote in New York State with 40 election districts missing out of 4,051 gave Willkie 1,241,501 and Roosevelt 1,937,017, an actual plurality for Roosevelt of 695,516 and an indicated plurality of 700,823.

Outside New York City in 5,004 out of 5,268 election districts, the vote was Willkie 1,685,043, Roosevelt 1,219,817, an actual plurality of 465,276 for Willkie and an indicated plurality of 480,924. This gave the President an actual plurality of 230,240 on these returns and an indicated plurality of 215,000, which may be slightly higher because of the small number of votes in the unreported districts.

Continued on Page Ten

Bonfires of All Buttons Urged to Heal Bitterness

Public bonfires of all the Democratic and Republican campaign literature and buttons were suggested yesterday by William Allen White, national chairman of the Committee to Defend America by Aiding the Allies, as a means of "healing partisan bitterness and for launching a nation-wide campaign to safeguard American democracy."

Mr. White, in a statement issued last night, urged "unity mass meetings" as soon as possible after election, in a message to the representatives of the group's 717 local chapters in the forty-eight States.

The meetings should be held, he said, "not in the spirit of exaltation on the part of the victorious party but with the idea that we destroy the symbols of partisan bitterness and unite now on a national program of safeguarding American democracy."

Bruce Barton, Republican candi-

Continued on Page Four

PRESIDENT TAKES KEYSTONE STATE

Republican Chairman Concedes Pennsylvania—Guffey Ahead in Senate Race

Special to THE NEW YORK TIMES.

PHILADELPHIA, Wednesday, Nov. 6—Aided by impressive strength in the industrial areas, President Roosevelt apparently duplicated his feat of 1936 and won the thirty-six electoral votes of traditionally Republican Pennsylvania in yesterday's election.

The trend in the senatorial contest between Senator Joseph F. Guffey, Democrat, and Jay Cooke, chairman of the Philadelphia Republican Committee, was in the direction of the re-election of Mr. Guffey, who campaigned on his record of "100 per cent Roosevelt support."

The Democrats, it seemed likely, would gain an undetermined number of seats in the State's Congressional delegation, which had been Republican by nineteen to fifteen, and they appeared to have an even chance of wresting control of the State House of Representatives from the Republicans, who took it over with the election of Governor James two years ago. The Republicans were hopeful of salvaging their majority in the State Senate.

James F. Torrance, Republican State Chairman, conceded Pennsyl-

Continued on Page Four

BIG ELECTORAL VOTE

Large Pivotal States Swing to Democrats in East and West

POPULAR VOTE CUT

First Time in History That Third Term Is Granted President

By ARTHUR KROCK

Over an apparently huge popular minority, which under the electoral college system was not able to register its proportion of the total vote in terms of electors, President Roosevelt was chosen yesterday for a third term, the first American in history to break the tradition which began with the Republic. He carried to victory with him Henry A. Wallace to be Vice President, and continued control of the House of Representatives by the Democrats was also indicated in the returns.

But in many of the States so many precincts were still missing early this morning, and the contest in these States was so close, that Wendell L. Willkie, the Republican opponent, whose name Mr. Roosevelt never mentioned throughout the campaign, refused to concede defeat. He said it was a "horse race," and that the result would not be known until today. As the returns mounted there seemed little, however, to sustain Mr. Willkie's hope. New York, Massachusetts, Connecticut, Rhode Island, Pennsylvania, Ohio and Illinois, of the greater States, all appeared to have been carried safely by the President. The Solid South had resisted all appeals to revolt against Mr. Roosevelt's quest for a third term. The Pacific and Mountain States were following the national trend.

States for Mr. Roosevelt

States sure or probable for the President are:

Alabama, Arizona, Arkansas, California, Connecticut, Delaware, Florida, Georgia, Illinois, Kentucky, Louisiana, Maryland, Massachusetts, Missouri, Minnesota, Mississippi, Montana, Nevada, New Hampshire, New Jersey, New Mexico, New York, North Carolina, Ohio, Oklahoma, Pennsylvania, Rhode Island, South Carolina, Tennessee, Texas, Utah, Virginia, West Virginia and Wisconsin—electoral votes, 429.

States sure or probable for Mr. Willkie:

Kansas, Maine, Michigan, Nebraska, North Dakota, South Dakota, Vermont—electoral votes 51.

States doubtful or insufficiently reported:

Colorado, Idaho, Indiana, Iowa, Oregon, Washington and Wyoming—electoral votes, 51.

The Electoral Vote

Listing as doubtful nine States, including several like California, Ohio and Indiana, which seem certain to join the Democratic column, there were at 3 A. M. only 51 electoral votes in possible dispute. The President had an apparently certain total of 429, while with more or less security in Mr. Willkie's column were only 51 votes.

No shift or series of shifts would affect the electoral result and the indications were that the President's total would reach from 430 to 470.

Either figure would be much less than the nearly clean sweep he had in 1932, when he carried forty-two States, and in 1936, when only Maine and Vermont went Republican. And unless the Far West and the Mountain States shall be shown to have given incredible majorities and late returns from the Eastern States pile up the President's popular majority, Mr. Roosevelt's popular majority will be far less than he had against Herbert Hoover and Alf M. Landon.

It appeared early this morning that a maximum of 5,000,000 and a minimum of 2,000,000 votes would represent the final difference between the popular votes cast for the two major Presidential candidates. The Associated Press tabulation at 1:50 A. M. was 14,879,930 for Mr.

Continued on Page Two

ROOSEVELT LOOKS TO 'DIFFICULT DAYS'

But Tells Celebrators That He Will Carry On for the Country 'Just the Same'

By CHARLES HURD

Special to THE NEW YORK TIMES.

HYDE PARK, Wednesday, Nov. 6—Standing on the portico of his mother's home here, Franklin D. Roosevelt early today acknowledged his re-election with a promise to continue to be "the same Franklin Roosevelt you have known."

He made this statement to several hundred residents of Hyde Park and vicinity who formed a torchlight procession that carried out a tradition marking Democratic political victories with rallies at the old house, a parade formed by Democrats as soon as returns indicated the victory.

"We are facing difficult days in this country," Mr. Roosevelt told the throng, "but I think you will find me in the future just the same Franklin Roosevelt you have known great many years."

The President beamed on the crowd as he leaned on the arm of his third son, Franklin Jr., in the bright light of flares set in place by motion-picture camera men.

He smiled and waved his hands through the grounds from cars parked first in the driveways and afterward on the Albany Post Road, some of them a quarter of a mile away.

President Faces His Neighbors

Behind the President were grouped about forty guests who had been entertained by Mrs. Roosevelt at supper at her cottage at Val-Kill. But the President faced a crowd in which there were no prominent politicians, no industrial leaders.

These were exclusively his neighbors, who bear to him the same relationship as the villagers bore to his father when he was a minor Democratic leader and a friend of President Cleveland.

President Roosevelt walked on to the front porch of Hyde Park house just before midnight, when he finally broke a vigil over returns behind locked doors in the dining room of his home.

The first glare of red flares was seen far off down the driveway. Ten minutes later, exactly at midnight, a town band marched into the car park in front of the house.

The President, with Franklin Jr., stood at the right side of the porch.

Continued on Page Two

"All the News That's Fit to Print."

The New York Times.

LATE CITY EDITION

Section 1

NEWS INDEX, PAGE 51, THIS SECTION

VOL. XC No. 30,388.

NEW YORK, SUNDAY, APRIL 6, 1941.

TEN CENTS

GERMANS INVADE YUGOSLAVIA AND GREECE; HITLER ORDERS WAR, BLAMING THE BRITISH; MOSCOW SIGNS AMITY PACT WITH BELGRADE

U. S. STEEL STRIKE IS CALLED BY C. I. O., EFFECTIVE TUESDAY

Murray Says Wage Talks Failed and Plans Picketing in Tie-Up Involving 261,000 Men

ROOSEVELT MAY STEP IN

President Is Reported to Have Summoned C. I. O. Chief in Move to Bar Walkout

By The Associated Press.

PITTSBURGH, April 5.—The C. I. O. Steel Workers Organizing Committee tonight ordered its members in all steel mills of the giant United States Steel Corporation, employing about 261,000 wage-earners, to stop work at midnight next Tuesday.

The union said that negotiations for a wage increase and other benefits had collapsed.

Philip Murray, C. I. O. president and chairman of the Steel Workers Organizing Committee, telegraphed instructions to local union chiefs of the corporation to establish continuous picket lines at all plant gates.

[The United Press reported from Pittsburgh last night it had learned authoritatively that President Roosevelt, concerned over the threatened stoppage, had invited Mr. Murray to a White House conference tomorrow or Tuesday.]

The company produces more than one-third of America's steel, an amount exceeding all of that made in England. It hold millions of dollars in defense contracts.

Mr. Murray termed the cessation of work a "lockout" rather than a strike, asserting that the company had rejected his suggestion to continue negotiations, which began March 20, another week, with any agreement to be retroactive to April 1. The company was said to be willing to make the agreement retroactive only to April 8.

The sudden development, threatening to spread the nation's strike area to the vital steel industry, came during an interim of wage negotiations, which still are scheduled to be resumed Monday at 10 A. M.

Mr. Murray called in 100 local union leaders today for conference. It was the third such meeting since the union made known its nine-point demands, which included a closed shop, check-off of union dues by the company, liberalized vacations and establishment of seniority rights.

The company's minimum pay, established in 1937, is 62½ cents an hour, with the average pay of wage-earners about 87 cents an hour. This contract expired April 1 and was extended to April 8.

The company's original counter-offer of a 3% cents an hour wage rise was rejected by Mr. Murray. Tonight it was learned this offer had been raised to five cents an hour but again was refused by the union. The company contended it made $60,000,000 of its $102,000,000 profit last year in its steel plants. The other profits came from coal, cement shipping and other subsidiaries. The company has insisted it cannot increase wages without increasing the price of steel. The Government has firmly refused to sanction any such price advance.

In his instructions to local unions, Mr. Murray said:

"The Carnegie-Illinois Steel Company has either rejected entirely or submitted unsatisfactory counter proposals with respect to each of the points offered by the S. W. O. C. in its program.

"The S. W. O. C. will attempt to arrive at an agreement with the companies involved to provide for the continuance at work of the necessary maintenance men during the suspension of operations. Further instructions regarding this situation will be forwarded to you by wire.

"Peaceful picket lines shall be established at all plant gates and maintained at all times during the cessation of work. There should be no violence or other unlawful acts on the part of members or representatives of the S. W. O. C."

No comment was forthcoming from the company on the development.

Continued on Page Forty-one

The International Situation

SUNDAY, APRIL 6, 1941

Germany's armies this morning launched a vast attack upon Yugoslavia and Greece. The move was announced over the Berlin radio in an order of the day from Reichsfuehrer Hitler, read by Propaganda Minister Goebbels; it denounced "the Belgrade government of intrigue" and said German troops would not lay down their arms until "this band of ruffians" and every last Briton had been eliminated from Southeastern Europe. [Page 1, Column 8.]

As Belgrade's first air raid was reported, it was believed the principal Nazi attacks had been launched from Bulgaria, one across Southern Yugoslavia and another southward toward Salonika. Bulgaria's army was said to have an active role, but Hungary's was believed inactive for the present. The Yugoslavs were expected to fight a rear-guard delaying action until they reached their strong natural defense positions. The Belgrade Government had planned to evacuate the capital, going to some southern point. The United States Minister was reported remaining in Belgrade. [Page 1, Column 5.]

With dramatic suddenness Yugoslavia and Soviet Russia signed a five-year non-aggression and friendship pact providing that if either signatory became the victim of aggression by a third State the other would maintain a policy of "strictest friendship." The pact will take effect immediately and the articles of ratification will be exchanged in Belgrade "at the earliest possible moment." [Page 1, Column 4.]

On the African front, British Headquarters in Cairo reported that an Axis advance east of Bengasi, Libya, "has been successfully held and the situation is well in hand." Empire forces in Ethiopia crossed the Awash River, to a point only eighty miles from Addis Ababa, while other units driving down on the capital from Eritrea captured Adowa and Adigrat. [Page 1, Column 6; Map, Page 7.]

The British Air Ministry augmented very brief accounts of the R. A. F. attack on Brest Friday night and early Saturday by stating that the 26,000-ton German battleships Gneisenau and Scharnhorst had been "very, very lucky" if they had escaped serious damage from new and powerful British bombs. R. A. F. aircraft, it was said, had dived to 1,000 feet to unleash their missiles on the Nazi raiders and had fired oil stores and warehouses near by, while other British planes dropped bombs on Rotterdam and the Ruhr. [Page 9, Column 1.]

The sharp British blow at the two German raiders coincided with a Berlin claim that 718,000 tons of British and Allied shipping had been sunk during March by German surface craft, U-boats, mines and airplanes. A German auxiliary cruiser operating "overseas" was said to have sunk the British auxiliary cruiser Voltaire of 13,255 tons. Moreover, Berlin said, U-boats in two days had sunk eighteen ships, totaling 106,000 tons, in a British convoy. [Page 13, Column 1.]

President Roosevelt's hint that he might soon lift combat-zone restrictions on the Red Sea to permit passage of American ships with war supplies for Britain aroused considerable interest in Washington. Senator George, chairman of the Senate Foreign Relations Committee, was said to feel that such action would necessitate Congressional amendment of the Neutrality Act; other members of Congress were believed to hold the President already had power to do this through provisions of the Lease-Lend Law. [Page 21, Column 1.]

Uruguay formally seized two Italian and two Danish ships in her harbors and placed the crews, comprising 119 men, under the direction of the Italian and Danish consuls, respectively. Many of the Danish seamen were reported to have expressed pleasure over the seizures and to have exhibited pro-British emblems. [Page 19, Column 1.]

COAL TIE-UP ENDED IN 65% OF THE MINES

Southern Operators Hold Out but Contract for Rest Will Be Signed Tomorrow

Yielding to pressure from the Federal Government, representatives of 65 per cent of the nation's soft-coal producers agreed yesterday to sign a new contract with the United Mine Workers tomorrow. At least 300,000 miners are expected to return to work Tuesday or Wednesday, ending a week's stoppage that threatened to cut off vital coal supplies for the war industries.

Dr. John R. Steelman, director of the United States Conciliation Service, who succeeded in breaking the four-week deadlock between the C. I. O. union and the operators, predicted that virtually all the mines would be open within a week. Other government officials said they believed settlement in the soft-coal fields would provide a key to peaceful adjustment of employer-union differences in steel and anthracite, thus removing two additional threats of delay in the defense program and insuring uninterrupted work for 1,000,000 men.

Thirteen associations of Southern bituminous operators were the sole holdouts against the tentative accord effected by Dr. Steelman, and there were indications that their ranks were beginning to crumble. Union officials said several companies in the Southern States had indicated their intention of signing with the John L. Lewis organization, whether or not their associations went along. The union relied on the pressure of competition to bring the others into line in a few days.

Under the terms of the proposed contract the United Mine Workers will win its full demand for a basic wage of 87 a day. This represents an increase of $1 over the rate previously in effect in the North and $1.40 over the Southern rate. The union's insistence on abolition of the

Continued on Page Forty-two

KNUDSEN ASSAILS RADICALS IN LABOR

Charges They Hamper Output for Defense—Cooperation by All Vital, He Warns

Text of Mr. Knudsen's address appears on Page 40.

Asserting that the most serious thing about the strike in the Allis-Chalmers plant in Milwaukee was not the time lost in the production of defense materials but the fact that it showed that "radical" labor leaders could tell the State and Federal Governments "where to get off," William S. Knudsen last night proposed a program for dealing with labor difficulties that he said would eliminate 90 per cent of the strikes.

The director-general of the Office of Production Management, who spoke at the Army Day dinner of the Military Order of the World War at the Hotel Waldorf-Astoria, said the labor situation during the last month had grown worse and warned that the epidemic of strikes must be stopped or the effort for defense and aid to Great Britain, Greece and Yugoslavia would fail.

Interrupted by applause when he started to discuss the labor situation, Mr. Knudsen declared that time was the all-important element in America's defense program and declared that if the nation could put on a "little steam" in production during the eighty-nine days remaining before the Fourth of July "we might save a lot of blood later on."

"I do not believe that legislation against strikes is necessary or enforceable," Mr. Knudsen said, "but I do believe that during the emergency period a definite procedure should be followed in order that strikes may be held to a minimum.

"For instance, I believe that strike votes should be taken under the supervision of the Labor Department. I believe a certain min-

Continued on Page Forty.

TREATY NOW VALID

Moscow Discloses That Pledge of Friendship Was Made Yesterday

PEACE IS TERMED AIM

Strictest Neutrality Is Provided—Accord Is Hailed in London

By The Associated Press.

MOSCOW, Sunday, April 6—Soviet Russia and Yugoslavia have signed a treaty of friendship and non-aggression after several days of negotiation, Tass, Soviet official news agency, announced early today.

The agency said the pact was signed yesterday by the Russian Premier and Foreign Commissar, Vyacheslaff M. Molotoff, and Milan Gavrilovitch, former Yugoslav Cabinet Minister and Yugoslavia's representative in Moscow.

The treaty declared that Russia and Yugoslavia were "inspired by the friendship existing between the countries and convinced that the preservation of peace forms their common interest" and hence had decided to conclude the pact.

Its first article provided neither country would attack the other and that each would respect the sovereign rights and territorial integrity of the other.

It provided that, in case of aggression against one of the countries by a third power, the other would observe a policy of friendly relations with the country attacked.

TEXT OF THE TREATY

MOSCOW, Sunday, April 6 (UP) —Tass News Agency gave out today the text of the treaty between the Soviets and Yugoslavia, as follows:

A treaty on friendship and non-aggression between the Union of Soviet Socialist Republics and the Kingdom of Yugoslavia.

The Presidium of the Supreme Soviet U. S. S. R. and His Majesty the King of Yugoslavia, inspired by the friendship existing between the two countries and convinced that preservation of peace forms their common interest, decided to conclude a treaty on friendship and non-aggression and appointed for this purpose their representatives:

Presidium of the Supreme Soviet U. S. S. R.—Vyacheslaff M. Molotoff, chairman of the Council of Peoples Commissars and Peoples Commissar of Foreign Affairs; His Majesty the King of Yugoslavia — Milan Gavrilovitch, Envoy Plenipotentiary and Minister Plenipotentiary of Yugoslavia, Bozhin Simitch and Colonel Dragutin Savitch, which representatives, after exchanging their credentials found in proper form and due order, agreed on the following:

ARTICLE I

The two contracting parties mutually undertake to desist from

Continued on Page Twenty-five

YUGOSLAVIA FIGHTS

Belgrade Has Air Raid as Armies Resist, Berne Hears

DRIVE FROM BULGARIA

Greeks Announce Nazi Attack—Stukas Clear Path, Germans Say

By RAY BROCK

Wireless to THE NEW YORK TIMES.

BELGRADE, Yugoslavia, Sunday, April 6—At 3:25 o'clock this morning the air-raid sirens in Belgrade sounded an alarm. For the Yugoslavs it was the first indication that the nation was at war.

An hour later, at 4:32, two Yugoslav fighter planes appeared over the city, flying in an easterly direction. They came from the Zemun airdrome. Two more fighter planes appeared a short time later.

[At this point wireless communications with Belgrade were cut.]

Greeks Announce Attack

The Greek High Command announced in a communiqué broadcast from Athens that since 5:15 A. M., Athens time, the German troops had been attacking Greek troops on the Bulgarian border, the Columbia Broadcasting System announced this morning. No further details were in the communiqué as it was received here.

The German Propaganda Ministry announced in a broadcast from Berlin, according to CBS, that swarms of German planes, including Stuka dive bombers, were "pouncing like hornets" on Greek and Yugoslav airdromes and railways in an effort to cripple the resistance to the invading German armies. The Nazi Propaganda Ministry also asserted that the planes were clearing a path for tanks and infantry, and that parachute troops were landing at strategic points within the Greek-Yugoslav defenses. There was no confirmation of these claims, however.

Belgrade Has Second Alarm

By Telephone to THE NEW YORK TIMES.

BERNE, Switzerland, Sunday, April 6—The Belgrade correspondent reported at 5:30 o'clock this morning that naturally he had heard of the situation, but that "you wouldn't know the difference." Aside from two air-raid alarms in the night there was nothing, no incident had yet occurred. Reports as to the exact location of the fighting were very scant.

On the Greek frontier the invasion doubtlessly came from Bulgaria through the Struma Valley and southward down the Vardar Valley. This latter attack, however, would entail driving across the southeastern border of Yugoslavia—the Third Army region based on Skoplje under General Ilija Brasitch.

Continued on Page Twenty-four

Hitler's Order of the Day

Adolf Hitler's declaration that Germany was at war with Yugoslavia was read over the Berlin radio early today by Propaganda Minister Joseph Goebbels. As heard by the National Broadcasting Company's station in New York and translated from the German, it read:

In the name of the Fuehrer, Adolf Hitler, I am reading the following order of the day to the German armies of the East:

Berlin, April 6, 1941.

Soldiers of the Southeast Front:

Since early this morning the German people are at war with the Belgrade government of intrigue. We shall only lay down our arms when this band of ruffians has been definitely and most emphatically eliminated, and the last Briton has left this part of the European Continent, and that these misled people realize that they must thank Britain for this situation, they must thank England, the greatest warmonger of all time.

The German people can enter into this new struggle with the inner satisfaction that its leaders have done everything to bring about a peaceful settlement.

We pray to God that He may lead our soldiers on the path and bless them as hitherto.

In accordance with the policy of letting others fight for her, as she did in the case of Poland, Britain again tried to involve Germany in the struggle in which Britain hoped that she would finish off the German people once and for all, to win the war, and if possible to destroy the entire German Army.

In a few weeks long ago the German soldiers on the Eastern Front, Poland, swept aside this instrument of British policy. On April 9, 1940, Britain again attempted to reach its goal by a thrust on the German north flank, the thrust at Norway.

In an unforgettable struggle the German soldiers in Norway eliminated the British within a period of a few weeks.

What the world did not deem possible the German people have achieved. Again, only a few weeks later, Churchill thought the moment right to make a renewed thrust through the British Allies, France and Belgium, into the German region of the Ruhr. The victorious hour of our soldiers on the West Front began.

It is already war history how the German Armies defeated the legions of capitalism and plutocracy. After forty-five days this campaign in the West was equally and emphatically terminated.

Then Churchill concentrated the strength of his Empire

Continued on Page Twenty-six

NAZI TROOPS MARCH

Goebbels Reads Order to Germans to Rid Europe of All Britons

QUICK BLOW PLEDGED

Greece Told She Invited It—U. S. Is Said to Share Blame

By DANIEL T. BRIGHAM

By Telephone to THE NEW YORK TIMES.

BERNE, Switzerland, Sunday, April 6—At 5 o'clock this morning German forces attacked Yugoslavia and Greece in the long-awaited culmination of the Balkan war of nerves.

The news broke on the world with startling suddenness when a German radio station announcer with a triumphant blast this morning introduced Dr. Joseph Goebbels, Minister of Propaganda, who then read Reichsfuehrer Hitler's order of the day to "my forces in Southeast Europe."

"Since dawn this morning," said Dr. Goebbels, "the German Reich has been at war with Yugoslavia and Greece."

It was indicated that the friendship pact signed between Yugoslavia and Russia yesterday was one of the factors of which Germany complained. This was the new charge of "aggressive encirclement of Germany," which have been used since Herr Hitler's advent to power.

Yugoslav Arming Held Cause

Another source of grievance, it would seem, was Belgrade's mobilization, a point that Herr Hitler mentioned in his order of the day as one of the chief reasons for the attack.

Immediately after Dr. Goebbels's broadcast, telephone communications to the eastward from this city —and south to Rome—were cut off.

[United States and British encouragement to the Yugoslavs in their resistance to German demands was also cited as grounds for Germany's attack, according to The Associated Press. Alleged American offers of material aid were also quoted.]

The German Army was told it would not lay down its arms until the "ruffians" had been deposed and the last Briton driven out of this territory.

Friendship for Greeks

German soldiers have been fighting in Greece since dawn today, the proclamation stated. It was indicated that the battle in Greece was not directed against the population but only against the "world enemy," Great Britain, who had dispatched troops there for an attack against the interests of the Reich.

Germany, Herr Hitler was quoted as saying, does not consider herself at war with Greece and will not molest any Greek who does not take up arms against the German Army, but any who lends his support to the British will be crushed.

"Soldiers of the Southeast Front," the Reichsfuehrer proclaimed, "your hour has now come."

He then told these troops that they must emulate their comrades in Poland, Scandinavia, the Lowlands and France. He added that the general mobilization in the Balkans was considered by the Reich as final proof that Britain had mixed into the internal affairs of Yugoslavia and would lead that country into hostile acts against Germany.

Yugoslav Provocation Charged

BERLIN, Sunday, April 6 (U.P.)— The German radio, in broadcasting Reichsfuehrer Hitler's order to the German Army, quoted him as saying Germany was unable longer to endure the Yugoslav attitude.

The Reich was said to be reacting to the mistreatment, "attacks and murdering" of Germans in the Yugoslav Kingdom.

The order had the greatest portions had been exercised by Germany respecting Yugoslavia and Greece, but that now the moment for action had arrived.

It was said that Herr Hitler had frequently called attention to the dangers in the Southeast.

Now, it was said, Germany was

Continued on Page Twenty-five

BRITISH HALT DRIVE IN LIBYA, GET ADOWA

Axis Checked East of Bengasi —South Africans Within 80 Miles of Addis Ababa

Wireless to THE NEW YORK TIMES.

CAIRO, Egypt, April 5—The British announced today that their forces in Libya had halted the advance of German and Italian armored units somewhere east of Bengasi. The situation here after the recapture of that port by the Axis was said to be "well in hand."

At the same time the swift progress of the British Imperial forces in East Africa resulted in the capture of Adowa (and of near-by Adigrat, according to The Associated Press) while South African troops in Ethiopia crossed the Awash River and struck to within eighty miles of Addis Ababa.

[Massawa, the Red Sea port toward which the British armies of East Africa are racing, was reported to have defied a British demand for surrender, according to an Associated Press dispatch from Khartum.]

South African Advance

After the British in the last two days took the two most easily defendable areas in East Africa, Italian resistance appeared to be crumbling fast. The South African troops, who have marched all the way from Italian Somaliland and are moving westward along the Jibuti railway, after a brisk but brief battle at the crossing of the Awash, this column is pushing through the African hill country toward the higher rolling grassland plateau around Addis Ababa.

It is said the South Africans averaged a twenty-five-mile advance every day in the last two months. North of the capital, combined British and Indian forces are pursuing the fleeing Italians toward Dessye through difficult mountainous terrain. Between Asmara and Adowa they advanced with only slight skirmishing at many points that might have been some Cheren and Italian morale had good.

The occupation of Adowa frees the battle site where in 1896 Ethiopia's Emperor Menelik routed the Italians, killing 6,000 and capturing 4,000, thus preserving his nation's independence until 1935. The town itself has a population of 6,000.

Despite the lightness of the fighting in this area, advancing British forces surprised and captured a battalion of Italian infantry. Italians are running southward, apparently almost wholly disorganized, throwing away their arms, and rendering on the slightest excuse.

Continued on Page Seven

NAZI UNITS CROWD YUGOSLAV BORDERS

Some Are Reported in Albania, Many in Southern Hungary— German Plane Downed

By C. L. SULZBERGER

BELGRADE, Yugoslavia, April 5 —The German mobilization around Yugoslavia was nearing completion of the Yugoslav situation reportedly jammed the Hungarian roads, a powerful armored unit concentrated at Bela Crkva, on the Rumanian frontier one and a half hours' drive from Belgrade, and the first Nazi troops entered Albania.

British information sources from Bucharest and Budapest that the invasion of Southeastern Yugoslavia by the German Army of the Struma was ready to begin at any moment.

An absolutely reliable source said that more than one of the more pessimistic predictions emanate from German-controlled countries, such as Hungary, Rumania and Bulgaria, or from the Croat capital of Zagreb, which is the center of the small but active German-inspired Fascist movement.

The facts of the situation are clear. Once more the normal peace-time life of Hungary has been thrown into turmoil by the huge disruption caused by the passage of German Armies, and eight separate divisions were said to have been sighted. The motorized units on three points of the Hungarian southern frontier—Mohacs, Szeged and Nagy Kanizsa—were increased, as were the concentration in the Rumanian Banat.

British information sources report from Bucharest and Budapest that the invasion of Southeastern Yugoslavia by the German Army of the Struma was ready to begin at any moment.

It is only worth noting that most of the more pessimistic predictions...

Continued on Page Twenty-five

New Army Marches in Rain Here; Nation Joins in Military Tribute

By HANSON W. BALDWIN

The new Army of the United States paraded down the Fifth Avenue in many cities yesterday as the nation opened an unprecedented week-end celebration of Army Day.

Veterans of past wars marched with youngsters who may become veterans of a future war, as the muffled beats of drumheads dampened by the rain epitomised the somber attitude with which thousands of spectators in many cities viewed their marching men. Not since 1917 and another war has the nation so taken the Army—now truly a national army—to heart with quiet, restrained pride.

For the minds of the bands was but a faint echo in people's minds of the growing thunder of Europe's guns, and the serious attitude of the onlookers was matched in New York, Washington and other Eastern cities by the weather. The skies were a sullen gray and the peaks of New York's skyscrapers were veiled in mist as the Army marched and drumbeads burst and stickers poured off torrents of the rain.

The New York parade along upper Fifth Avenue, which had been expected to be the greatest Army Day event in the city's history, lost considerably in volume but gained in solemnity because of the weather. Not many more than half of the expected 30,000 marchers participated, and the sparse, umbrellaed crowd that watched could not have numbered at its peak more than 30,000 to 40,000. The crowd dwindled as time during the two-hour parade to less than half that number. The weather, too, turned the marching men into a real test of soldiering, particularly for 4,500 men of the Forty-fourth Division from Fort Dix, N. J., who had negotiated seventy-eight miles of roads slick with rain in motor convoys to participate in the parade.

Mayor La Guardia, huddled be-

Continued on Page Forty-two

"All the News That's Fit to Print."

The New York Times.

LATE CITY EDITION
Fair and continued cool today and tomorrow.
Temperature Yesterday—Max., 62; Min., 49

Copyright, 1941, by The New York Times Company.

VOL. XC..No. 30,425.   Entered as Second-Class matter, Postoffice, New York, N. Y.   NEW YORK, TUESDAY, MAY 13, 1941.   THREE CENTS NEW YORK CITY and Vicinity

HESS, DESERTING HITLER, FLIES TO SCOTLAND; BERLIN REPORTED HIM MISSING AND INSANE; DARLAN MEETS HITLER; R. A. F. POUNDS PORTS

COAST SHIPYARDS SHUT BY PICKETS; RETURN REJECTED

Navy and Maritime Work Stops as Other Crafts Refuse to Pass Heavy Lines

POLICE STAY IN RESERVE

Union Leaders Declare Fight to Finish as Meeting Votes Against Lapsing Strike

By FOSTER HAILEY
Special to The New York Times.

SAN FRANCISCO, May 12—A request from the Office of Production Management that striking journalists in eleven shipbuilding yards in the San Francisco Bay area return to work pending an attempt to settle their wage and hour demands in conference was unanimously rejected today by a mass meeting of those of the strikers affiliated with the American Federation of Labor.

Picket lines around the eleven plants, established by the 1,200 A. F. of L. machinists and the 700 who belong to the Congress of Industrial Organizations, brought a complete halt to operations as 15,000 to 18,000 other workers who are not on strike refused to pass through the machinists' picket lines.

The strike was called Friday midnight by Local 68 of the A. F. of L. and Lodge 1304 of the C. I. O. The latter is affiliated with the Steel Workers Organizing Committee, headed by Philip Murray, president of the C. I. O. The walkout is in protest against hourly wage and overtime provisions of a master contract signed April 23 in Seattle by representatives of labor, the OPM and the shipbuilders.

Reason for Refusal to Return

The request to go back to work pending a conference came from Joseph Keenan, A. F. of L. representative of the OPM. It was presented to a mass meeting of about 3,000 members of Local 68 by its business agents, E. F. Dillon and Harry Hook, who later said:

"Our members took the position, and passed a resolution to the effect, that inasmuch as we've never been able to get an agreement out of Bethlehem in the past twenty-two years, we don't feel any good purpose would be served by sending the men back to work before an agreement is reached now.

"We feel it would only prolong the controversy and probably result in a repetition of what we are going through now."

Although Bethlehem Shipbuilding, a division of Bethlehem Steel, is only one of the eleven plants involved in the strike, it is by far the largest, employing about 900 of the 1,200 A. F. of L. machinists who are on strike, and it is considered the bellwether of the group.

Out to Compel Settlement

"We intend to tell Mr. Keenan, if he telephones us from Chicago, the attitude of the strikers," Mr. Dillon said. "When he made the request yesterday he said he would call back today. (He had not called up to late tonight.)

"We would be glad to have a representative of the OPM on the ground here to go into a thorough analysis of the situation.

"As things stand now, the strike will continue in effect until we are able to make some agreement with Bethlehem and the rest."

No formal action was taken by the C. I. O. machinists, since the request was not directed to them, but pickets handed out leaflets signed by J. P. Smith, business agent of Lodge 1304, asserting that "hard-won conditions must be preserved and employers, under a smoke screen of national defense, are not going to destroy them."

The C. I. O. was not represented in the negotiations for the master contract.

In a joint statement, Mr. Dillon and Mr. Hook said that the "friendly attitude and fine spirit of the other metal trades organizations," intend to see to it "that all such metal trades men that respected our picket lines will be returned to their jobs without discrimination" and on a basis satisfactory to them.

Appraisal of the strikers' position, Frank H. Fox, chairman of the Bay Area Shipbuilders Personnel Committee and authorized spokesmen

Continued on Page Sixteen

'Peace' Pickets Routed At White House Gates

Special to The New York Times.

WASHINGTON, May 12—One soldier and one Marine tonight broke up a line of eight pickets marching in front of the White House who represented the American Peace Mobilization. This organization has been charged with being a Communist Front group.

At the hour all Washington theatres were letting out, police emergency cars and motorcyclists roared through downtown Washington to the White House. The two assaulters were arrested and one picketeer was removed to Emergency Hospital where he was reported slightly injured. The picketing continued.

Tonight's fracas followed one at 3 A. M. when a larger group of soldiers and Marines attacked the pickets, tore up their placards and warned them they would be back if the picketing continued. In an earlier assault the policemen did not interfere. Tonight the assailants were seized and one was charged with simple assault. The police then closed and barred the White House gates for the night.

ROOSEVELT TO TALK TO NATION MAY 27

'Fireside Chat' Two Weeks From Today Is Substituted for Address Tomorrow

By FRANK L. KLUCKHOHN
Special to The New York Times.

WASHINGTON, May 12—President Roosevelt will make a "fireside chat" to the nation May 27, but will not make his scheduled speech before the Pan American Union Wednesday night, it was announced at the White House today.

This change in plans was interpreted generally to mean that the President has in mind no important announcement on American foreign policy for two weeks and that, at least for this period, he does not contemplate any new type of aid for Britain.

The Executive seldom makes fireside chats except upon important matters, however, and his talk on the 27th is generally expected to present an outline of the current position of the United States as he sees it and the future steps that should be taken.

Mr. Roosevelt cancelled his seventh day in bed because of illness today, and his widely publicized speech was cancelled to give him time to recover fully, according to official statements.

Stephen T. Early, White House Secretary, emphasized, however, that the President had never intended his talk before the Pan American Union to be of "world-shaking" importance.

Pressure on President

In informed circles it was understood that the Executive did not intend to be pushed into any important steps and that he considered the present time poor for any announcement of vital importance. Speaking of the canceled Wednesday address, Mr. Early said:

"So, despite reports from abroad, there will be no world-shaking pronouncement made Wednesday. President Roosevelt Wednesday night, as this office has stated right along."

Three Cabinet members, Secretaries Henry L. Stimson, Frank Knox and Claude Wickard, have urged use of the American Navy to protect Britain, their speeches generally being interpreted as an appeal for escort of convoys by the American Navy. Other individuals or groups publicly have urged the Executive to go so far as ask for a declaration of war. Pressure has come from all sides on these controversial questions and others.

The decision to cancel Wednesday night's speech was revealed through White House announcement of a resolution adopted by the Board of Governors of the Pan American Union.

Diplomats Ask Postponement

The Ambassadors, Ministers and chargés d'affaires of the republics of Latin America," the resolution said, "realizing that President Roosevelt has recently been indisposed and in view of the fact that the reception to be tendered him would involve strain upon him, take the liberty of suggesting that the reception be postponed until such time as President Roosevelt may

Continued on Page Eight

HAMBURG HIT HARD

Miles of Docks Fired in British Bombing a Second Night

BREMEN LIKE TARGET

U-Boat Yards and War Plants of Reich Bases Kept Under Attack

By DAVID ANDERSON
Special Cable to The New York Times.

LONDON, Tuesday, May 13—Nine miles of docks along the River Elbe at Hamburg were laced with heavy British bombs and thousands of incendiaries over Sunday night when the Royal Air Force followed up its attack of the previous night with another vigorous raid on German war ports.

The Hamburg docks were "threaded and crossed with fire, continuing the destruction and disorganization of vital parts of this great seaport," the British Air Ministry reported.

Bremen, the Reich's second port in the size of its war activities, was attacked also with what R. A. F. officials moderately termed a "heavyweight of high-explosive and incendiary bombs."

Shipbuilding yards and especially the plants of the two ports where Germany has built most of her U-boat fleet were blasted.

Previous Attack Extended

Explosives hammered down on industrial works in both cities, the Air Ministry stated, and vast fires were started to continue the havoc of previous attacks.

Last night "objectives" at the great German industrial center of Mannheim, also a frequent target for the British, were attacked by R. A. F. bombers, a brief official report early today said.

Sunday night attacks were made by the R. A. F. on a number of other targets in the Reich, including Emden again, and the docks of Rotterdam were also bombed.

Four aircraft of the Bomber Command were missing from all these operations, British officials said.

The Coastal Command carried out Sunday night attacks on docks at the Netherland port of Ijmuiden, and on the Nazi seaplane base on the island of Texel without loss.

The attacks seemed to mark a definite stepping-up of the R. A. F. offensive, as officials of the Bomber Command, in giving some detail of the operations, said the objective was to strike Hamburg again before that city could "recover from the impact of the attacks made Saturday night."

Weather Right for Bomb-Aimers

Fine weather and the brilliant moonlight enabled the British pilots to pick their spot with relative ease over "the vast expanse of docks which was the particular focus" of this raid, it was stated.

An R. A. F. flier's account of the Bremen attack said:

"It was not so cold as when we visited Bremen three nights before, but there was the same bright sky. All the way over there were patches of cloud which looked like stepping

Continued on Page Six

Russians See Advantage In R.A.F. Planes' Big Load

By The Canadian Press.

LONDON, May 12—Increased bomb loads carried by Royal Air Force bombers "partly offset" the German advantage of having air bases close to Britain, Red Star, organ of the Soviet Army, said in an article quoted today by the British Broadcasting Corporation.

The article commented on "the tremendous load of bombs that now can be carried by a single British machine."

In a review of war developments, the newspaper observed that "the hardest blows delivered by the German Air Force in recent weeks have been aimed at British ports and centers of shipbuilding" and also that "the experience of the last war proved that British and United States industry made up for sinkings by U-boats."

PAPEN SEES HITLER, RETURNS TO TURKEY

Envoy Is Expected to Reveal Nazi Plans for Near East— Soviet Move Studied

The following dispatch was received by direct voice broadcast through the Ankara wireless station last night. C. L. Sulzberger prefaced the broadcast in this way:

"The following direct broadcast from Ankara to THE NEW YORK TIMES, New York City, contains news dispatches for THE TIMES. These are exclusive property of The New York Times Company. Dispatches follow."

By C. L. SULZBERGER
Special Broadcast to The New York Times.

ANKARA, Turkey, May 12—Franz von Papen, the German Ambassador to Ankara, came back to his post today aboard a large camouflaged Junkers troop transport plane, following a series of last-minute conferences with Reichsfuehrer Hitler at the latter's Obersalzburg retreat.

The Ambassador, who was accompanied by his wife and daughter, was met at the Ankara Airport by the diplomatic representatives of the countries that have signed the tripartite accord. He appeared in excellent spirits and conferred for several minutes with the Italian Ambassador.

Herr von Papen has been expected back almost daily for the better part of the last fortnight and the fact that he continually delayed his return and then at the last minute had a long personal conversation with Herr Hitler is regarded as significant.

Events are shaping up rapidly in the Middle East, and the only hand that now remains to be disclosed fully is that of Germany. Russia has abandoned her disinterest in this area by according full diplomatic recognition to the bellicose Rashid Ali Beg Gailani government of Iraq.

Britain, already engaged in extensive military operations in Iraq, has

Continued on Page Two

ADMIRAL HAS TALK

Berlin Says Ribbentrop Was Present—Place Is Not Disclosed

VICHY PRESS TENSE

U. S. Attitude Is Cause of Worry—Leahy May Protest Attacks

By The Associated Press.

BERLIN, Tuesday, May 13—Reichsfuehrer Hitler has received the French Vice Premier, Admiral François Darlan, in the presence of German Foreign Minister Joachim von Ribbentrop, it was officially announced early today.

The communiqué announcing the meeting did not say where or when it took place.

The announcement said:

"The Fuehrer, in the presence of the Reichsminister of Foreign Affairs, received the vice president of the French Ministerial Council, Admiral Darlan."

Hitler-Stalin Talk Discussed

VICHY, France, May 12 (AP)—Separate meetings of Reichsfuehrer Hitler with Premier Joseph Stalin and Premier Benito Mussolini were considered in diplomatic circles here tonight as likely to result from the political moves over Europe.

The object of the meetings, these circles said, probably would be complete economic if not military organization of the Axis-dominated Continent.

Observers listed the current shakeup of Spain's civil and military organization and Vice Premier Admiral François Darlan's negotiations with the Germans as indications of the forthcoming conferences of Herr Hitler and Mr. Stalin and Signor Mussolini.

U. S. Gives Press Concern

By G. H. ARCHAMBAULT
Wireless to The New York Times.

VICHY, France, May 12—For the time being it is not possible to appraise the two hemispheres in any discussion here of the world situation.

That the situation is tense and is likely to remain so, at least until President Roosevelt has spoken, is admitted.

In every newspaper as well as in every conversation the United States and what it may or may not do is a recurrent topic.

There are here a few who surmise that it may have been mentioned in Paris during the visit there of Vice Premier Admiral François Darlan, who is expected back in Vichy tomorrow to report to Marshal Henri Philippe Pétain, who himself returned this morning after a few days' rest in his Riviera estate.

A semi-official commentary declared today that the Marshal has expressed his satisfaction to the Admiral with the progress of his negotiations hitherto.

It is understood that another Admiral—William D. Leahy, the United States Ambassador—may also see Marshal Pétain in the near future for one of their periodical conversations on food supplies and cognate subjects.

To Stick to Collaboration

While there is complete official silence regarding the negotiations with Germany, as also regarding the United States, the Inter-France News Service, not situated in Vichy, which circulates editorials "for free reproduction by any newspaper," advanced the following arguments:

"Should war occur between the United States and Germany and should it be prolonged, the political reasons which led France to follow the road of collaboration would be reinforced by even more decisive practical reasons. For war between the United States and the Axis would immediately create a European solidarity that would be stronger than any sentimental factor.

"An American blockade, which would necessarily be extended to all our coasts, will develop the notion of a common interest among the peoples of Europe, since from Brest to Koenigsberg and from Narvik (Norway) to Cadiz (Spain) we should be compelled to do without meat from Argentina and coffee from Brazil, to say nothing of cotton from the United States and oil from Mexico. The French

Continued on Page Five

Nazis Allege 'Hallucinations'; Silent on Glasgow Arrival

Arrest of Hess's Aides Ordered Since Hitler Forbade Him to Fly—Letter He Left Said to Show Disordered Mind

Special to The New York Times.

BERLIN, May 12—Authoritative quarters in Berlin refused to comment late tonight on a British statement that Rudolf Hess, 47-year-old deputy leader of the National Socialist party and Reichsfuehrer Hitler's personal representative, had bailed out of a Messerschmitt plane near Glasgow, Scotland, and was in the hands of the British authorities. Earlier in the evening the German had officially reported Herr Hess to be missing.

The man who, on Sept. 1, 1939, was designated by Herr Hitler as his second choice, next to Reich Marshal Hermann Goering, in the line of succession for leadership of the German State, was last heard of in Augsburg, in Bavaria, on Saturday. He was reported to have taken an airplane there for an unknown destination in violation of Herr Hitler's orders prohibiting him from flying because of physical disability.

THE GERMAN STATEMENT

The news of the mysterious disappearance of Herr Hess was released, forty-eight hours after he had been reported missing, in the following communiqué:

Party Comrade Hess met with an accident.

Party Comrade Hess, who because of a disease that for a year was progressively worsened has been categorically forbidden by the Fuehrer to continue his flying activities, recently found means in violation of this command to come into possession of an airplane.

Continued on Page Four

BRITISH ASTOUNDED

Hitler's Deputy Is in Hospital After Bailing Out of War Plane

HAS A BROKEN ANKLE

London Believes Hess's Flight May Portend a New Purge in Reich

By ROBERT P. POST
Special Cable to The New York Times.

LONDON, Tuesday, May 13—Rudolf Hess, deputy leader of the German Nazi party and the third-ranking personage in the German State, parachuted to earth in Scotland on Saturday night and is now a prisoner of war.

That may sound like something from a mystery thriller by Oppenheim. But in sober truth, 10 Downing Street issued a communiqué last night that is probably the strangest and most dramatic announcement ever to come from the official home of a British Prime Minister.

THE BRITISH STATEMENT

This statement said:

Rudolf Hess, the Deputy Fuehrer of Germany and party leader of the National Socialist party, has landed in Scotland in the following circumstances:

On the night of Saturday, the tenth, a Messerschmitt 110 was reported by our patrols to have crossed the coast of Scotland and to be flying in the direction of Glasgow. Since a Messerschmitt 110 would not have fuel to return to Germany, this report was at first disbelieved.

Later on a Messerschmitt 110 crashed near Glasgow with its guns unloaded. Shortly afterward a German officer who had bailed out was found with his parachute in the neighborhood, suffering from a broken ankle.

He was taken to a hospital in Glasgow, where he at first gave his name as Horn, but later on he declared that he was Rudolf Hess.

He brought with him various photographs of himself at different ages, apparently in order to establish his identity.

These photographs were deemed to be photographs of Hess by several people who knew him personally. Accordingly, an officer of the Foreign Office who was formerly acquainted with Hess before the war has been sent up by air-plane to see him in the hospital.

Identified by Official

Ivone A. Kirkpatrick, who used to be first secretary in the British Embassy in Berlin, was the official sent to Scotland, and the Ministry of Information announced early this morning that Herr Hess's identification had been definitely established.

Earlier the Germans had announced that Herr Hess, who was outranked only by Reichsfuehrer Hitler and Reich Marshal Hermann Goering in the Nazi hierarchy, had been suffering from hallucinations and had violated Herr Hitler's orders in taking the plane.

It was just before nightfall Saturday that Herr Hess was found by a Scottish farm worker; he was groaning in agony, with his parachute wrapped around him. He was taken first to a little two-roomed cottage and then was turned over to the military authorities. This morning he was in a military hospital somewhere near Glasgow.

That is the bare outline of the facts as they are known so far. What do they mean? The Germans have already announced that Herr Hess's "adjutants" have been arrested. The British are inclined to believe that there may be another purge in Germany—a purge similar to the one following the arrest of Captain Ernst Roehm, who was also one of Herr Hitler's closest collaborators, on June 30, 1934.

But from this distance it is almost impossible to say what this development means as far as Germany is concerned. One can record only what the British believe it means. One Briton told the writer that "this is the first 'break' we have had since the war started."

Continued on Page Four

PAPEN SEES HITLER, RETURNS TO TURKEY

The International Situation

TUESDAY, MAY 13, 1941

A laconic announcement from 10 Downing Street gave to an astounded world last night the news that Rudolf Hess, deputy leader of the Nazi party in Germany and the third most powerful figure in the Reich, had landed by parachute in Scotland and was in safe custody in a Glasgow hospital suffering from a broken ankle. The official statement gave no direct explanation for the dramatic development, but it was presumed that the man who was named at the outset of the war by Adolf Hitler as his second in succession had deliberately deserted Germany. [Page 1, Column 6.]

Herr Hess flew to Scotland in a Messerschmitt 110, a plane incapable of carrying sufficient fuel for his return to Germany. The plane crashed Saturday night on the Duke of Hamilton's estate. The flier established his identity in the hospital, and the Foreign Office dispatched an official to interview him there. [All the foregoing, Page 1, Column 3.]

Berlin issued a communiqué earlier in the day stating that Herr Hess, apparently suffering from "hallucinations" induced by a long-standing ailment, had taken off by plane from Augsburg Saturday evening against the express orders of Herr Hitler and was "missing" and presumably had "met with an accident." It was announced that Herr Hess's adjutants had been arrested. [Page 1, Column 6.]

Hundreds of German bombers flew over South England and the Midlands Sunday night, attacking airdromes and other objectives, and causing destruction over widespread areas. Nine Nazi planes were shot down. A Berlin statement that forty-five British airfields were attacked was contradicted by the British, who said the military damage was "not considerable." Few raiders were reported over Britain last night. [Page 6, Column 1.]

Over Sunday night the R. A. F. was sending wave after wave of bombers against German ports, particularly Hamburg and Bremen. Nine miles of docks and shipyards on the River Elbe were laced with fires from British incendiaries, and attacks were made on Emden, Rotterdam and Ijmuiden. Last night British planes again bombed Mannheim. [Page 1, Column 3.]

The return to Ankara of German Ambassador von Papen

from an extended visit to Berlin gave rise to a belief that Germany would propose a far-reaching economic treaty to all but isolated Turkey. Ankara also looked for an early meeting between the Ambassador and the Iraqi Defense Minister, who has been visiting Ankara. [Page 1, Column 4.]

The situation in Iraq was described by the British as now "stabilized." R. A. F. planes harried remnants of Iraqi forces, and British mechanized forces completed the occupation of Rutbah, a vital point on the oil pipe line and site of an airplane base. [Page 2, Column 6.]

The British forces in Ethiopia tightened their pincer around Alagi, the last Italian stronghold on the Asmara-Dessye road. The Italian garrison at Gondar was said to be virtually isolated. In North Africa, the Admiralty announced, British warships bombarded Bengazi Saturday night, but Rome asserted the British vessels had been routed after having suffered direct hits. [Page 3, Column 4.]

In Washington the ship-seizure bill sponsored by the Administration passed its first test in the Senate when the Commerce Committee reported it favorably by a vote of eleven to four, thus making it possible to bring the measure to the floor later this week. The committee defeated an attempt to prevent transfer to a belligerent of any of the ships that might be seized. [Page 7, Column 1.]

President Roosevelt's scheduled speech before the Pan-American Union tomorrow night has been canceled, but he will make a fireside chat to the nation on May 27, when it is expected that he will deal with the position of the nation in the international situation and the future steps that should be taken. [Page 1, Column 2.]

Bodies of Brewster and Wife Found In Plane Wreckage in Alleghenies

The bodies of Benjamin Brewster, New York investment broker, and his wife, the former Leonie de Bary Lyon, who disappeared Friday on a projected flight from Roosevelt Field to Warren, Ohio, were found last night in the charred wreckage of their plane on a rugged mountain top forty miles north of Harrisburg.

The discovery was made after several pilots reported they had seen the badly damaged wreck nestled in tree branches on Shade Mountain near Beavertown.

The report that the bodies had been found was telephoned to Private Charles Isicklin of the Pennsylvania Motor Police by Private John Zeigler, one of a party sent out from the barracks at Selinsgrove.

The bodies were taken in charge by Dr. Charles W. Strand, coroner of Snyder County, who will remove them to Middleburg as soon as permission is received from members of the Brewster family.

Late last night positive identification was made by Whitney Stone,

vice president of the Stone & Webster Company, a brother-in-law of Mr. Brewster. In a telephone conversation with his sister, Mrs. Edward C. Brewster, Mr. Stone said the plane crashed against the side of a 1,800-foot mountain and then exploded. A reward of $1,000 had been offered by Mr. Stone to the person locating the plane.

The Brewsters' plane was a radio-equipped black and green Beechcraft with a Wright motor. Mr. Brewster was a prominent sportsman pilot and had more than 1,000 flying hours to his credit.

The tangled, charred wreckage was sighted at about 5 P. M. (daylight saving time) by two private pilots from Philadelphia, who were among more than seventy who searched the mountain area by air. They reported having circled the scene and sighted a twisted wing lying near by. The wing, they said, apparently had escaped the flames, and its black and green striping could be seen clearly. These fliers,

Continued on Page Nineteen

"All the News That's Fit to Print."

The New York Times.

LATE CITY EDITION
Partly cloudy and continued warm today and tomorrow.
Temperatures Yesterday—Max., 91; Min., 72

Section 1

NEWS INDEX, PAGE 35, THIS SECTION

VOL. XC. No. 30,465.   Entered as Second-Class Matter, Postoffice, New York, N. Y.   NEW YORK, SUNDAY, JUNE 22, 1941.   Including Rotogravure Picture, Magazine and Book Sections   TEN CENTS   New York City and Vicinity

HITLER BEGINS WAR ON RUSSIA, WITH ARMIES ON MARCH FROM ARCTIC TO THE BLACK SEA; DAMASCUS FALLS; U. S. OUSTS ROME CONSULS

MUST GO BY JULY 15

Ban on Italians Like Order to German Representatives

U. S. DENIES SPYING

Envoys Told to Protest Axis Charges—Nazis Get 'Moor' Text

By BERTRAM D. HULEN
Special to The New York Times.

WASHINGTON, June 21—The Italian Embassy was directed by the State Department in a note published today to close all its consular offices and other agencies in this country having connections with the Italian Government by July 15. This was the reply to the Italian demand for the closing of all American Consulates in Italy.

At the same time Summer Welles, Under-Secretary of State, announced that he had sent to Dr. Hans Thomsen, the German Chargé d'Affaires, the text of President Roosevelt's message to Congress yesterday denouncing the sinking of the American freighter Robin Moor in the South Atlantic on May 21.

This message, which accused Germany of being an international outlaw, engaging in piracy and attempting to intimidate the United States by the sinking and to drive American commerce from the seas, contained notice that this country would not yield before such measures and stated that compensation would be sought for the sinking.

It was transmitted "for the information" of the German Government, but constituted in effect a note of protest. A further communication will be sent asking damages when a final determination has been reached of the extent of damages that should be sought.

Will Deny Improper Acts

In addition, the State Department instructed the American Embassies in Berlin and Rome to inform the respective governments that the United States objects to all allegations of improper acts by American consular officials in those countries and to complete arrangements for the withdrawal of the consular officials and their staffs by July 15, the limit set by the German and Italian Governments.

The Axis governments had charged that the American Consuls had spied for the British. No reply has been made by the State Department to the German protests against the order closing Italian consulates in this country, but the protest will be rejected. The notes to the German and Italian Embassies were sent by messenger last night. However, no direct charge of improper activities was made against the Italian Consuls in the note Mr. Welles sent to Don Ascanio dei principi Colonna, the Italian Ambassador. He merely stated that the continued functioning of Italian consular establishments within United States territory "would serve no desirable purpose."

In addition, the closing of Italian agencies having connections with the Rome government was requested. The Italian Embassy, as in the earlier case of the German Embassy, was exempted, but the closing of the office of the Italian Commercial Counselor in New York was demanded, along with the consulates.

Welles Note to Colonna

The note from Mr. Welles to Prince Colonna follows:
June 20, 1941

His Excellency
Don Ascanio dei principi Colonna
Royal Italian Ambassador

I have the honor to inform Your Excellency that the Italian Government has directed me to request that the Italian Government promptly close all Italian consular establishments within United States territory and remove therefrom all Italian consular of-

Continued on Page Two

FOR WANT AD RESULTS Use The New York Times. It's easy to order ad. Just telephone LAckawanna 4-1000.—Advt.

Hope Dims for Submarine; Diver Balked at 370 Feet

Knox Believes All 33 Are Dead on the O-9 and Expects Rites at Scene for Navy 'Heroes'—Pressure Halts Descent

By RUSSELL PORTER
Special to The New York Times.

PORTSMOUTH, N. H., June 21—As hope faded rapidly for the crew of the Submarine O-9, which failed to rise after submerging yesterday morning twenty-four miles east of this city, it became known tonight that the Navy might be unable to complete its salvage operations, and might be compelled to leave the bodies entombed where they lie—440 feet below the surface of the Atlantic.

This theory was based upon the assumption that the two officers and thirty-one men must already be given up as lost, but that assumption has become stronger with every hour's progress since the submarine was reported missing.

Last night cork insulation from the interior of the hull was picked up, showing that at least part of the submarine had collapsed, and early today, after fourteen hours of dragging, grapnels located an object believed to be the sunken craft. Since then no signals from the O-9 had been received on the sensitive sound-detection devices on the salvage ships in response to their repeated messages.

The view that the O-9's fate was sealed was strengthened this afternoon when reporters and photographers, visiting the scene in a

Navy press boat, saw one of the Navy's most experienced divers fail in an attempt to reach the O-9 after descending 370 feet, or within seventy feet of where the Navy believes it has located the submarine with grapnel lines.

The diver, George Crocker, 30 years old, of Seattle, asked to be hauled up when he became convinced that he was not getting enough air pressure from his life lines of helium-oxygen mixture to overcome the increasing sea pressure as he went lower and lower.

A message from the Falcon said: "Diver descended 370 feet. Had difficulty in breathing. Brought to surface. Will continue attempts by varying diving techniques."

On the salvage ship the dive was called "the most dangerous in submarine history." It was pointed out that no one had ever made a successful "working" dive at 440 feet and that any diver who went down so far, where he would have to grope his way in complete darkness under terrific sea pressure, 195.8 pounds to the square inch, could do so only at extreme risk to his life.

Colonel Frank Knox, Secretary of the Navy, returning tonight on

Continued on Page Thirty

ARMY ASKS GUARD BE KEPT IN SERVICE

Recommends Congress Act to Hold State Troops, Reserve Officers Indefinitely

By HALLETT ABEND
Special to The New York Times.

WASHINGTON, June 21—Members of the National Guard and Reserve Officers Corps will be kept in active service beyond the single year planned when they were called, if a recommendation made today by the War Department is approved by President Roosevelt and Congress.

Instead of a return to civilian life, starting Sept. 15, their terms of service in uniform may be extended indefinitely, or at least until the Army selectees have been sufficiently trained in ample numbers to permit the Guardsmen to be demobilized. The recommendation to the President does not specify any limit to the proposed extension of service.

At present there are 289,800 National Guardsmen, including their 21,800 officers, on active duty with the Federal Army. They were inducted into service in increments beginning Sept. 15 of last year. Some went into uniform as late as March of this year. Their terms of service, at time of induction, were limited to twelve months, which may not be extended except by act of Congress.

341,300 Would Be Affected

In addition to the National Guardsmen, who comprise eighteen divisions and one cavalry brigade now on active service, the government has called up 51,500 Reserve officers under the same terms, making collectively 341,300 officers and men who would be affected.

Today's War Department recommendation to the President that the steps be taken to retain in the service these Guardsmen and Reserve officers was taken, according to the official announcement, because "the War Department has been flooded with queries from the field" as to whether or not the specified one-year limit of service would hold good or be changed.

"These queries are to be expected," continues the announcement, "because whatever the decision, there are many adjustments which the citizen-soldier must make in his affairs."

As yet no decision has been reached in the War Department whether or not to seek authority to retain selectees in the Army beyond the one-year limit specified in the Selective Service Act, but presumably such a step

Continued on Page Nineteen

NAVY MAY REPLACE SHIPYARD STRIKERS

Weighs Putting Own Machinists to Work to End Long Tie-Up in San Francisco

By The Associated Press.

SAN FRANCISCO, June 21—Striking A. F. L. machinists in a $300,000,000 defense program have come to a showdown with the United States Navy and their own international officers.

Reliable reports, not officially denied, indicated that the Navy might install its own machinists in the huge Bethlehem shipyards Monday if the local union did not heed the order of its international president to call off the strike by that time.

The same reports indicated that the Army also might be on hand

Continued on Page Twenty-eight

R. A. F. BLASTS FOE

Bags 26 Nazi Planes in Record Day Raids on Invasion Coast

GERMANY IS BOMBED

British on 11th Straight Night Offensive Into Western Reich

Special Cable to The New York Times.

LONDON, Sunday, June 22—Twenty-six Nazi fighter planes were destroyed in daylight yesterday by Royal Air Force fliers on their fifth straight day of raiding the Germans' invasion coast and air bases in Northern France.

Twice before dark, waves of R. A. F. warcraft—reportedly numbering at least 150 planes each—swept over the Channel in offensive operations.

Bombers attacked the Nazis' airdromes on each occasion while strong forces of fighters blasted the way for the big planes through formations of German defense fighters. While the major raids were going on, other strong R. A. F. units patrolled over the French coast and battled Messerschmitts.

Attack Goes On; Big Bombs Used

Last night and early this morning the R. A. F. was still attacking the invasion coast, using some of the latest type of high-powered bombs.

Explosions rolled across the Channel like peals of thunder, shaking the ground and rocking buildings for miles along the Kentish coast, observers there reported.

A night curtain of fog hung over the Strait of Dover and little could be seen of the raids. The latest British attacks were apparently being made in the Boulogne area, where some of the heaviest daylight bombing was carried out.

Meanwhile R. A. F. bomber forces were again attacking Western Germany, officials here said briefly early today. The attacks marked the eleventh consecutive night in which the British have bombed industrial centers and war bases in the Reich.

Two Nazi bombers were shot down during the night in small scattered enemy raids on the east and southeast coasts of England. A few German bombs were reported dropped there; there were no accounts of casualties or damage.

The R. A. F. coastal patrol squadrons reported destroying at least two enemy planes and one Nazi

Continued on Page Eighteen

SYRIAN CITY TAKEN

French Withdraw After a Hard Fight—British Closer to Beirut

TADMUR PUSH IS ON

Allied Planes Harassing Vichy Troops, Whose Defense Falters

By C. L. SULZBERGER
By Telephone to The New York Times.

ANKARA, Turkey, June 21—French troops evacuated the city of Damascus today after a persistent bombardment by British artillery and withdrew to new positions outside the Syrian capital, according to official advices from Beirut. Early in the afternoon it was learned that the Allied vanguard was already beginning to enter the city. This evening the British reported complete occupation.

The Damascus airport at Mezze has been taken by Indian detachments of the Allied forces and one of the key points east of Damascus has been surrounded by Druz tribesmen fighting on the side of the British.

The Beirut radio announced tonight that a British motorized column pushing westward from Iraq was now heading toward Tadmur. The British column, it was said, has been bombed constantly by the French Air Force, which has just been reorganized and reinforced by French squadrons coming from North Africa. Some German planes also were said to have arrived in Syria.

Advance in High Gear

It is clear that the Allied advance is beginning to move into high gear. Unconfirmed reports that the British forces have reached Beirut indicate that it may also fall soon. Beirut's fate depends largely on whether the British will call in their superior naval forces to shell the city proper. So far this has been avoided in order to keep damage and casualties at a minimum.

[A dispatch from Cairo said that Australian forces had been progressing toward Beirut for two days and had passed Ras Damour.]

The Allies, convinced of the seriousness of the French resistance, evidently have begun to fight this undeclared war in earnest and intend to get it over with fast at any cost. The main center of French resistance in the east has been Damascus, and the capture of the city is of great importance.

The Allied counter-move to the French attack in the south, which developed earlier in the week, is now proceeding with dispatch in the Merdjayoun district. The fortress of Merdjayoun is in Allied hands and it is obvious that the region is being rapidly cleared, since the coastal advance is so dependent to a large degree on a corollary advance in the center.

Considerable concentrations of French artillery had been brought up around Damascus. The French dug in and placed batteries in many of the villas and gardens in the outer sections of the city. These batteries were slowly picked off by British gunners with Royal Air Force support, but the principal British effort was artillery shelling. The British sought to avoid excessive damage by aerial bombardment, which is less accurate than artillery fire.

Tadmur Believed in Peril

The French admission that a British column is pressing toward Tadmur would seem to indicate that perhaps the town is endangered. Several days ago reliable sources here reported the existence of the column, but this was steadfastly denied by Beirut.

While there have been new reports that the trouble for the British in Iraq is far from over, the fact that they are able to spare considerable forces from what would indicate that everything is well under control. It is known that British forces also are working westward along the North Syrian frontier toward Aleppo, but the exact strength of these units is not known here.

British military circles admit that the Syrian adventure can no

Continued on Page Twelve

WHERE GERMAN ARMIES MARCH ON RUSSIA
Shown on the map is the western frontier of the Soviet Union, a battle line of more than 2,000 miles. Berlin indicated an attack from Norway to Rumania.

The Hitler Proclamation

The text of Adolf Hitler's proclamation, as recorded here by Columbia Broadcasting System, follows:

It was a difficult step for me to send my Minister to Moscow in order to attend to work against the policy of encirclement of Britain.

I hoped that at last it would be possible to put away tension.

Germany never intended to occupy Lithuania. The defeat of Poland induced me to again address a peace offer to the Allies. This was declined because Britain was still hoping to bring about European coalition.

That is why Cripps [Sir Stafford Cripps, British Ambassador] was sent to Moscow. He was commissioned under all circumstances to come to an agreement with Moscow. Russia always put out the lying statement that she was protecting these countries [evidently Lithuania, Estonia and Latvia, the Baltic States].

The penetration of Russia into Rumania and the Greek liaison with England threatened to place new, large areas into the war. Rumania, however, believed she was able to accede to Russia only if she received guarantees from Germany and Italy for the remainder of the country. With a heavy heart, I did this, for if Germany gives guarantees, she will fulfill them. We are neither Englishmen nor Jews.

I asked Molotoff [Soviet Foreign Commissar V. M. Molotoff] to come to Berlin, and he asked for a clarification of the situation. He asked, "Is the guarantee for Rumania directed also against Russia?"

I replied, "Against every one."

And Russia never informed us that she had even more far-reaching intentions against Rumania.

Molotoff asked further, "Is Germany prepared not to assist Finland, who was again threatening Russia?"

My reply was that Germany has no political interests in Finland, but our attack on Finland could not be tolerated, especially as we do not believe that Finland is threatening Russia.

Molotoff's third question was, "Is Germany agreeable that Russia give guarantees to Bulgaria?"

My reply was that Bulgaria is a sovereign State and I did not know that Bulgaria needed guarantees. Molotoff said Russia needed a passage through the Dardanelles and demanded bases in the Bosporus.

A few days later she [Russia] concluded the well known friendship agreement which was to incite the Serbs against Germany. Moscow demanded the mobilization of the Serbian Army.

When I still was silent, the men in the Kremlin went one step further. Russia offered to deliver war material against Germany. This was at the same time that I advised Matsuoka [Japanese Foreign Minister Yosuke Matsuoka] to bring about a lessening of the tension with Russia.

Serbian officers flew to Russia, where they were received as allies. Victory of the Axis in the Balkans at first foiled the plan to involve Germany in a long war and then, together with England and with the hope of American supplies, to throttle Germany.

Now the moment has come when I can no longer look at this development. Waiting would have been a crime against Germany.

For weeks the Russians have been committing frontier violations. Russian planes have been crossing the frontier again and again to prove that they are the masters. On the night of June 17 and again on June 18 there was large patrol activity.

The march of the German Armies has no precedent. Together with the Finns we stand from Narvik to the Carpathians. At the Danube and on the shores of the Black Sea under Antonescu [Rumanian Dictator Ion Antonescu], German and Rumanian soldiers are united.

The task is to safeguard Europe and thus save all. I have therefore today decided to give the fate of the German people and the Reich and of Europe again into the hands of our soldiers.

BAD FAITH CHARGED

Goebbels Reads Attack on Soviet—Ribbentrop Announces War

BALTIC MADE ISSUE

Finns and Rumanians Are Called Allies in Plan of Assault

Statement by von Ribbentrop is printed on Page 6.

By C. BROOKS PETERS
By Telephone to The New York Times.

BERLIN, Sunday, June 22—As dawn broke over Europe today the legions of National Socialist Germany began their long-rumored invasion of Communist Soviet Russia. The non-aggression and amity pact between the two countries, signed in August, 1939, forgotten, the German attack began along a tremendous front, extending from the Arctic regions to the Black Sea. Marching with the forces of Germany are also the troops of Finland and Rumania.

Adolf Hitler, in a proclamation to the German people read over a national hook-up by Propaganda Minister Dr. Joseph Goebbels at 5:30 this morning, termed the military action begun this morning the largest in the history of the world. It was necessary, he added, because in spite of his unceasing efforts to preserve peace in this area it had definitely been proved that Russia was in a coalition with England to ruin Germany by prolonging the war.

Saw Stalemate in West

Herr Hitler, in his proclamation as reported here, made one vitally interesting statement, namely, that the supreme German military command did not feel itself able to force a decisive victory in the West—apparently on the British Isles—when large Russian troop concentrations were on the Reich's borders in the East.

These troop concentrations in the East began in August, 1940, Herr Hitler asserted. "Thus, there occurred the effect intended by the Soviet-British cooperation," he added, "namely, the binding of such powerful German forces in the East that a radical conclusion of the war in the West, particularly as regards aircraft, could no longer be reached for by the German High Command."

[The German radio announced early today that documentary proof would shortly be given of a secret British-Russian alliance, made behind Germany's back.]

Designed "to Save Reich"

The German action, Herr Hitler explained to his fellow-National Socialists, is designed to save the Reich and with it all Europe from the machinations of the Jewish-Anglo-Saxon warmongers.

The German Foreign Minister, Joachim von Ribbentrop, followed by Dr. Goebbels on the air with a declaration of the Reich Government read before the foreign correspondents in the Foreign Office. Herr von Ribbentrop said he received V. G. Dekanosoff, the Russian Ambassador, this morning and informed him that in spite of the Russian-German non-aggression pact of Aug. 23, 1939, and an amity pact of Sept. 28, 1939, Russia had betrayed the trust that the Reich had placed in her.

"Contrary to all engagements which they had undertaken and in absolute contradiction to their solemn declarations, the Soviet Union had turned against Germany," the Reich note asserted. "They have not only continued, but even since the outbreak of war intensified their subversive activities against Germany in Europe. They have, second, in a continually increasing measure, developed their foreign policy in a tendency hostile to Germany, and they have third massed their entire forces on the German frontier ready for action."

The Soviet Government, it was charged, had violated its treaties

Continued on Page Seven

The International Situation

SUNDAY, JUNE 22, 1941

At 5:30 o'clock this morning, Berlin time, two statements were read over the German radio that constituted a declaration of war upon the Soviet Union by Germany. A proclamation of Adolf Hitler, read by Propaganda Minister Goebbels, said that Russia, with Britain and the United States, had sought to "throttle" Germany and that he had therefore decided to put the fate of the German people in the hands of the army. A statement by Foreign Minister von Ribbentrop contained the actual declaration of war. The Finns and the Rumanians were mentioned as allies. Berlin reported subsequently that troops were on the march in East Prussia. [Page 1, Column 8; with map.]

Yesterday was a good day for British arms.

In the Syrian campaign Damascus was occupied. The British announced its capture and Vichy reported its evacuation to avoid street fighting and destruction of the city. Another British force was pushing nearer Beirut, supported by the fleet and the air arm, while a third column was moving toward Tadmur. [Page 1, Column 5; Map on Page 12.]

No less encouraging to the British was a victory much closer to home in the largest British daylight attack of the war. In a sweep two waves of 150 planes each pounded the French Channel coast, going particularly for airdromes, and engaged German air defenses. The British reported downing twenty-six Nazi planes in these attacks for a loss of five of their own. Late last night the British were continuing their attacks across the Channel. [Page 1, Column 4; Map, Page 18.]

The Libyan pressure was quiet, but British pressure in East Africa was indicated by a protest from Vichy against what was declared to be a virtual ultimatum from General Wavell to French Somaliland to join the Free French or suffer an intensified blockade. London condemned the representations of General Wavell. [Page 24, Column 1.]

Washington continued the accelerated pace of its anti-Axis diplomatic offensive. The Italian Embassy was instructed to close the forty-nine Italian consulates and seven agencies in this country before July 15. President Roosevelt's message to Congress on the Robin Moor was handed to the German Embassy while the State Department instructed the United States embassies in Berlin and Rome to inform those governments that the United States objected categorically to any allegations of improper acts by United States consuls. [Page 1, Column 1.]

Italian consular circles were silent concerning the Washington order, but Italian anti-Fascist quarters expressed jubilation. [Page 2, Column 1.]

104

"All the News That's Fit to Print."

The New York Times.

LATE CITY EDITION
Increasing cloudiness with rising temperature today. Tomorrow cloudy, somewhat colder.
Temperatures Yesterday—Max.,34; Min.,25

Copyright, 1941, by The New York Times Company

VOL. XCI No. 30,634.

Entered as Second-Class Matter, Postoffice, New York, N. Y.

NEW YORK, MONDAY, DECEMBER 8, 1941.

THREE CENTS NEW YORK CITY and Vicinity

JAPAN WARS ON U. S. AND BRITAIN; MAKES SUDDEN ATTACK ON HAWAII; HEAVY FIGHTING AT SEA REPORTED

CONGRESS DECIDED

Roosevelt Will Address It Today and Find It Ready to Vote War

CONFERENCE IS HELD

Legislative Leaders and Cabinet in Sober White House Talk

By C. P. TRUSSELL
Special to THE NEW YORK TIMES.

WASHINGTON, Dec. 7—President Roosevelt will address a joint session of Congress tomorrow and will find the membership in a mood to vote any steps he asks in connection with the developments in the Pacific.

The President will appear personally at 12:30 P. M. Whether he would call for a flat declaration of war again Japan was left unannounced tonight. But leaders of Congress, shocked and angered by the Japanese attacks, were talking of a declaration of war on not only Japan but on the entire Axis.

The plans for action tomorrow were made tonight in a White House conference at which the President, surrounded by his Cabinet and by Congressional leaders of both parties, went through reports, some official, some unconfirmed, of the continued assaults of the Japanese upon American Pacific outposts.

Meet Far Into Night

The conference lasted until after 11 o'clock and at its close an official statement was issued. This said that the President had reviewed for his conferees the latest advices from the Pacific and declared:

"It should be emphasized that the message to Congress has not yet been written and its tenor will, of course, depend on further information received between 11 o'clock tonight and noon tomorrow. Further news is coming in all the time."

Congressional leaders asserted as they left the White House that they did not know what the President would say tomorrow.

"Will the President ask for a declaration of war?" Speaker Rayburn was asked.

"He didn't say," answered the Speaker.

Asked whether Congress would support a declaration of war, Mr. Rayburn observed:

"I think that is one thing on which there would be unity."

Politics Declared Dropped

"There is no politics here," said Representative Joseph W. Martin Jr., Minority House Leader. "There is only one party when it comes to the integrity and honor of the country."

"The Republicans," said Senator Charles L. McNary of Oregon, the Senate minority leader, "will all go along, in my opinion, with whatever is done."

Unless international developments and plans changed overnight, it was indicated, the Presidential recommendations would be directed for the present, at least, at Japan only. This was asserted authoritatively in the face of widespread expectation that any

Continued on Page Six

TOKYO ACTS FIRST

Declaration Follows Air and Sea Attacks on U. S. and Britain

TOGO CALLS ENVOYS

After Fighting Is On, Grew Gets Japan's Reply to Hull Note of Nov. 26

By The Associated Press.

TOKYO, Monday, Dec. 8—Japan went to war against the United States and Britain today with air and sea attacks against Hawaii, followed by a formal declaration of hostilities.

Japanese Imperial headquarters announced at 6 A. M. [4 P. M. Sunday, Eastern standard time] that a state of war existed and these nations in the Western Pacific, as of dawn.

Soon afterward, Domei, the Japanese official news agency, announced that "naval operations are progressing off Hawaii, with at least one Japanese aircraft carrier in action against Pearl Harbor," the American naval base in the islands.

Japanese bombers were declared to have raided Honolulu at 7:35 A. M., Hawaii time [1;05 Sunday, Eastern standard time].

Premier-War Minister General Hideki Tojo held a twenty-minute Cabinet meeting at his official residence at 7 A. M.

Soon afterward it was announced that both the United States Ambassador, Joseph C. Grew, and the British Ambassador, Sir Robert Leslie Craigie, had been summoned by Foreign Minister Shigenori Togo.

The Foreign Minister, Domei said, handed to Mr. Grew the Japanese Government's formal reply to the note sent to Japan by United States Secretary of State Cordell Hull on Nov. 26.

[In the course of the diplomatic negotiations leading up to yesterday's events, the Domei agency had stated that Japan could not accept the premises of Mr. Hull's note.]

Sir Robert was summoned by

Continued on Page Five

PACIFIC OCEAN: THEATRE OF WAR INVOLVING UNITED STATES AND ITS ALLIES

Shortly after the outbreak of hostilities an American ship sent a distress call from (1) and a United States Army transport carrying lumber was torpedoed at (2). The most important action was at Hawaii (3), where Japanese planes bombed the great Pearl Harbor base. Also attacked was Guam (4). From Manila (6) United States bombers roared northward, while some parts of the Philippines were raided, as was Hong Kong, to the northwest. At Shanghai (5) a British gunboat was sunk and an American gunboat seized. To the south, in the Malaya area (7), the British bombed Japanese ships, Tokyo forces attempted landings on British territory and Singapore underwent an air raid. Distances between key Pacific points are shown on the map in statute miles.

JAPANESE FORCE LANDS IN MALAYA

First Attempt is Repulsed— Singapore is Bombed and Thailand Invaded

By The Associated Press.

SINGAPORE, Monday, Dec. 8—The Japanese landed in Northern Malaya, 300 miles north of Singapore, today and bombed this great British naval stronghold, causing small loss of life among civilians and property damage.

About 300 Japanese troops landed on the east coast of Malaya and began filtering through jungle-fringed swamps and rice fields toward Kota Bahru airdrome, which is ten miles from the northern terminus of a railroad leading to Singapore.

An official report from the

Continued on Page Two

Tokyo Bombers Strike Hard At Our Main Bases on Oahu

By The United Press.

HONOLULU, Dec. 7—War broke with lightning suddenness in the Pacific today when waves of Japanese bombers attacked Hawaii this morning and the United States Fleet struck back with a thunder of big naval rifles. Japanese bombers, including four-engined dive bombers and torpedo-carrying planes, blasted at Pearl Harbor, the great United States naval base, the city of Honolulu and several outlying American military bases on the Island of Oahu. There were casualties of unstated number.

[The United States battleship Oklahoma was set afire by the Japanese attackers, according to a National Broadcasting Company observer, who also reported in a broadcast yesterday that two other ships in Pearl Harbor were attacked.]

[The Japanese news agency, Domei, reported that the battleship Oklahoma had been sunk at Pearl Harbor, according to a United Press dispatch from Shanghai.]

[Governor Joseph B. Poindexter of Hawaii talked with President Roosevelt late yesterday afternoon, saying that a second wave of Japanese bombers was just coming over, and the Gov-

Continued on Page Thirteen

ENTIRE CITY PUT ON WAR FOOTING

Japanese Rounded Up by FBI, Sent to Ellis Island—Vital Services Are Guarded

The metropolitan district reacted swiftly yesterday to the Japanese attack in the Pacific. All large communities in the area, including New York City, Newark, Jersey City, Bayonne and Paterson, went on immediate war footing.

One of the first steps taken here last night was a round-up of Japanese nationals by special agents of the Federal Bureau of Investigation, reinforced by squads of city detectives acting under FBI supervision. More than 100 FBI men, fully armed, were assigned to the detail.

The prisoners were sent to Ellis Island, where they will be held pending action at Washington. It was indicated hundreds would be detained.

Earlier Mayor La Guardia had convened his Emergency Board and directed that Japanese nationals be confined to their homes pending decision as to their status and had their clubs and other meeting places closed and put under police guard.

A police sergeant and five policemen immediately went to the Japanese Consulate at 630 Fifth Avenue in Rockefeller Center where the Consul General, Morito Morishima, and his staff were preparing to leave, and posted a guard there. The Consul General and his staff were escorted to their homes when they left. They were not to move about the city without police in attendance.

Rear Admiral Adolphus Andrews, commander of the North Atlantic Squadron, told reporters at a conference in the Federal

Continued on Page Three

HULL DENOUNCES TOKYO 'INFAMY'

Brands Japan 'Fraudulent' in Preparing Attack While Carrying On Parleys

Texts of Secretary Hull's note and Japan's reply, Page 10.

By BERTRAM D. HULEN
Special to THE NEW YORK TIMES.

WASHINGTON, Dec. 7—Japan was accused by Secretary of State Cordell Hull today of making a "treacherous and utterly unprovoked attack" upon the United States and of having been "infamously false and fraudulent" preparing for the attack while conducting diplomatic negotiations with the professed desire of maintaining peace.

But even before he knew of the attack, Mr. Hull had vehemently brought the diplomatic negotiations to a virtual end with an outburst against Admiral Kichisaburo Nomura, the Japanese Ambassador, and Saburo Kurusu, special envoy, because of the insulting character of the reply they deliv-

Continued on Page Eleven

GUAM BOMBED; ARMY SHIP IS SUNK

U. S. Fliers Head North From Manila— Battleship Oklahoma Set Afire by Torpedo Planes at Honolulu

104 SOLDIERS KILLED AT FIELD IN HAWAII

President Fears 'Very Heavy Losses' on Oahu— Churchill Notifies Japan That a State of War Exists

By FRANK L. KLUCKHOHN
Special to THE NEW YORK TIMES.

WASHINGTON, Monday, Dec. 8—Sudden and unexpected attacks on Pearl Harbor, Honolulu, and other United States possessions in the Pacific early yesterday by the Japanese air force and navy plunged the United States and Japan into active war.

The initial attack in Hawaii, apparently launched by torpedo-carrying bombers and submarines, caused widespread damage and death. It was quickly followed by others. There were unconfirmed reports that German raiders participated in the attacks.

Guam also was assaulted from the air, as were Davao, on the island of Mindanao, and Camp John Hay, in Northern Luzon, both in the Philippines. Lieut. Gen. Douglas MacArthur, commanding the United States Army of the Far East, reported there was little damage, however.

[Japanese parachute troops had been landed in the Philippines and native Japanese had seized some communities, Royal Arch Gunnison said in a broadcast from Manila today to WOR-Mutual. He reported without detail that "in the naval war the ABCD fleets under American command appeared to be successful" against Japanese invasions.]

Japanese submarines, ranging out over the Pacific, sank an American transport carrying lumber 1,300 miles from San Francisco, and distress signals were heard from a freighter 700 miles from that city.

The War Department reported that 104 soldiers died and 300 were wounded as a result of the attack on Hickam Field, Hawaii. The National Broadcasting Company reported from Honolulu that the battleship Oklahoma was afire. [Domei, Japanese news agency, reported the Oklahoma sunk.]

Nation Placed on Full War Basis

The news of these surprise attacks fell like a bombshell on Washington. President Roosevelt immediately ordered the country and the Army and Navy onto a full war footing. He arranged at a White House conference last night to address a joint session of Congress at noon today, presumably to ask for declaration of a formal state of war.

That was disclosed after a long special Cabinet meeting, which was joined later by Congressional leaders. These leaders predicted "action" within a day.

After leaving the White House conference Attorney General Francis Biddle said that "a resolution" would be introduced in Congress tomorrow. He would not amplify or affirm that it would be for a declaration of war.

Congress probably will "act" within the day, and he will call the Senate Foreign Relations Committee for this purpose, Chairman Tom Connally announced.

[A United Press dispatch from London this morning said that Prime Minister Churchill had notified Japan that a state of war existed.]

As the reports of heavy fighting flashed into the White House, London reported semi-officially that the British Empire would carry out Prime Minister Winston Churchill's pledge to give the United States full support in case of hostilities with Japan. The President and Mr. Churchill talked by transatlantic telephone.

This was followed by a statement in London from the Netherland Government in Exile that it considered a state of war to exist between the Netherlands and Japan. Canada, Australia and Costa Rica took similar action.

Landing Made in Malaya

A Singapore communiqué disclosed that Japanese troops had landed in Northern Malaya, and that Singapore had been bombed.

The President told those at last night's White House meeting that "doubtless very heavy losses" were sustained by the Navy and also by the Army on the island of Oahu [Honolulu]. It was impossible to obtain confirmation or denial of reports that the battleships Oklahoma and West Virginia had been damaged or sunk at Pearl Harbor, together with six or seven destroyers, and that 350 United States airplanes had been caught on the ground.

The White House took over control of the bulletins and the Navy Department, therefore, said it could not discuss the matter or answer any questions how the Japanese were able to penetrate the Hawaiian defenses or appear without previous knowledge of their presence in those waters.

Administration circles forecast that the United States soon might be involved in a world-wide war, with Germany supporting Japan, an Axis partner. The German official radio tonight attacked the United States and supported Japan.

Axis diplomats here expressed complete surprise that the Japanese had attacked. But the impression gained from their attitude was that they believed it represented a victory for the Nazi attempt to divert lease-lend aid from Britain, which has been

Continued on Page Four

The International Situation

MONDAY, DEC. 8, 1941

Yesterday morning Japan attacked the United States at several points in the Pacific. President Roosevelt ordered the United States forces into action and a declaration of war is expected this morning. [Page 1, Columns 7 and 8.] Tokyo made its declaration as of this morning against both the United States and Britain. [Page 1, Column 2.] The first Japanese assault was directed at Pearl Harbor Naval base in Hawaii. Many casualties and severe damage resulted. [Page 1, Columns 4 and 5; Map, Page 12.] United States Army aircraft took off from the Philippines this morning and some points in the Archipelago were bombed. [Page 3, Column 2.] Singapore and Hong Kong were bombed and a Japanese landing in Northern Malaya and a move on Thailand were reported. [Page 1, Column 3.] In Shanghai, Japanese marines occupied the waterfront; a British gunboat was sunk, a United States gunboat seized. [Page 9, Column 1.]

Factional lines dissolved as an angered Congress rose to meet this morning. [Page 1, Column 1.] Secretary of State Hull denounced Japan of having made a "treacherous and utterly unprovoked attack" after having been repeated again "infamously false and fraudulent." [Page 1, Column 6.] He released the text of diplomatic exchanges with Japan [Page 10].

while the President gave out the text of the Japanese Emperor. [Page 12.] The White House was the hub of Washington activity and news bulletins were released there. [Page 12, Column 3.]

The Federal Bureau of Investigation was ordered to begin a round-up of some Japanese in this country. [Page 1, Column 4.]

As New York City went on a war footing and public precautions were taken, the FBI began the detention of Japanese nationals. [Page 1, Column 4.]

Prime Minister Churchill notified Tokyo that a state of war existed. [Page 4, Column 1.] Declarations were made last night or early today by Australia, Canada [Page 14 Column 2], the Netherlands Indies [Page 7, Column 2] and Costa Rica. [Page 15, Column 1.]

Libya was the scene of a renewed tank battle and the Tobruk corridor was reported again clear of Axis forces. [Page 20, Column 2, with map.] On the Moscow front the German line was broken at two places, said Soviet sources. [Page 37, Column 2.]

Lewis Wins Captive Mine Fight; Arbitrators Grant Union Shop

The three-man arbitration board appointed by President Roosevelt to arbitrate the union shop dispute in the captive coal mines last night reversed the decision of the National Defense Mediation Board and ruled that all workers in the captive mines should be required to join John L. Lewis's United Mine Workers as a condition of employment.

The decision was made by a two-to-one vote, with Benjamin F. Fairless, president of the United States Steel Corporation, dissenting. Dr. John R. Steelman, who took a leave of absence from his post as director of the United States Conciliation Service to serve as chairman of the arbitration panel, and Mr. Lewis voted in favor of extension to the captive mines of the union shop provision of the standard Appalachian agreement.

Despite his dissent, Mr. Fairless promised that the coal mining subsidiaries of United States Steel would put the ruling into effect. All eight steel companies operating captive mines had given formal as-

surances before the decision was reached that they would accept it as binding.

The arbitration award ended a dispute in which Mr. Lewis had repeatedly defied the President by calling strikes that menaced the production of steel and that had had its repercussions in the enactment by the House of the Smith anti-strike bill.

In explaining his vote for the union shop, Dr. Steelman pointed out that 95 per cent of the 53,000 captive miners had voluntarily assumed membership in Mr. Lewis's C. I. O. union and that 99.5 per cent of all the miners in the nation were now members of the union.

Since the bulk of the industry, including many owners of captive mines, was already operating under the union shop, it could not be argued that the United Mine Workers was endeavoring to take

Continued on Page Forty-three

The New York Times.

LATE CITY EDITION
Cloudy followed by clearing and
colder today. Tomorrow fair
and moderately cold.
Temperatures Yesterday—Max., 44; Min., 25

Copyright, 1941, by The New York Times Company.

VOL. XCI. No. 30,635. — Entered as Second-Class Matter, Postoffice, New York, N. Y. — NEW YORK, TUESDAY, DECEMBER 9, 1941. — THREE CENTS NEW YORK CITY and Vicinity

U. S. DECLARES WAR, PACIFIC BATTLE WIDENS; MANILA AREA BOMBED; 1,500 DEAD IN HAWAII; HOSTILE PLANES SIGHTED AT SAN FRANCISCO

TURN BACK TO SEA

Two Formations Neared City on Radio Beams, Then Went Astray

ALARM IS WIDESPREAD

Whole Coast Has a Nervous Night—Many Cities Blacked Out

By LAWRENCE E. DAVIES
Special to The New York Times.

SAN FRANCISCO, Dec. 8—Two formations of "many planes," described as undoubtedly enemy aircraft, flew over the San Francisco Bay area tonight, it was announced officially by Brig. Gen. William O. Ryan, commander of the Fourth Interceptor Command, after a progressive blackout had blotted out naval and military establishments and whole cities along the Pacific Coast.

Conflicting reports spread, contributing to the "war of nerves," as the sirens wailed and broadcasting were silenced.

After another spokesman, through an error, had declared the blackout to be an air raid test, General Ryan said the report was that it was no test but "the real thing."

The ships were detected first about 100 miles at sea, he said. In two formations they headed for the Monterey Peninsula, about eighty miles south of this city, and for San Francisco Bay itself.

Radio detectors plotted their course, bringing one formation in just north of the Golden Gate and the other to a point near Fort Barry, at the south end of the Golden Gate Bridge.

Planes Turn Back to Sea

After flying northward for some distance the planes turned south to a point thirty-five or forty miles down the peninsula section below San Francisco. Apparently trying to orient themselves, they flew about a while longer and then headed southwest to sea, General Ryan said.

The commanding officer, whose station is at Riverside and who said he just "happened" to be at the Presidio tonight, declared that the planes followed radio beams to these shores. When radio stations on the West Coast were silenced as part of the blackout, the enemy craft apparently were not sure of their position.

No American planes were sent to the attack, he said, because "you don't send planes up unless you know what the enemy is doing you know what you are going and you don't send planes up in the dark unless you know what you are doing."

Although there was no official explanation for the absence of antiaircraft fire, it was indicated that the planes were hardly close enough for effective use of the guns.

Plane Carriers Rumored

Although General Ryan had no information, he said, as to the presence of enemy aircraft carriers hovering off the Pacific Coast, rumors of their presence had been broadcast during the day and this, it was acknowledged, would be the logical explanation for the appearance of the planes.

Lieut. Gen. John L. Dewitt,
Continued on Page Twenty-eight

NEWS BULLETINS

Please do not telephone The New York Times for war news. Every hour on the hour news bulletins are broadcast over Station WMCA—570 on the dial.

WEEKDAYS
8 a. m. through 11 p. m.
SUNDAYS
9 a.m., 1 p.m., 5 p.m., 11 p.m.

Philippines Pounded All Day As Raiders Strike at Troops

Air Base Near Capital Among Targets Hit by Japanese—Landing on Lubang With Aid of Fifth Columnists Reported

By H. FORD WILKINS
Wireless to The New York Times.

MANILA, Tuesday, Dec. 9—After a day of widespread aerial attacks throughout the Philippines, Japanese bombers swept in over Manila Bay early this morning and attacked Nichols Field, the United States Army air base on the outskirts of this capital, and simultaneously reports were received of a Japanese landing on Lubang Island, off the northwestern tip of Mindoro.

This morning's attack, which began shortly after 3 o'clock, was the first in the Manila area. The damage is believed to have been slight, but some casualties were reported. [A National Broadcasting Company correspondent reported that an official statement issued in Manila after the raid said: "In the

raid on Nichols Field, which was conducted by approximately ten Japanese bombers, one hangar was damaged and one officers' quarters was burned. The casualty list consists of one soldier killed and twelve wounded—all Americans."]

The reported landing on Lubang, sixty miles southwest of Manila, was not officially confirmed, but the reports received credence here. [Other unconfirmed reports, relayed by the Columbia Broadcasting System, told of landings in the Davao region, on the southern island of Mindanao.]

The Manila area's first experience with bombs was a climax to a day and night of tension and activity. The explosions could be
Continued on Page Nine

PLANES GUARD CITY FROM AIR ATTACKS

Army Interceptors Join the Navy Patrols—Anti-Aircraft Apparatus Set Up Here

While long lines of men of fighting age waited impatiently outside of every Army, Navy and Marine Corps recruiting office in the city yesterday, representatives of the city, State and Federal Governments went ahead with the grim business of making New York City ready for war.

Beginning at dawn yesterday Army fighting planes took off at regular intervals from Mitchel Field to maintain, in conjunction with a Navy patrol, a constant fighting force in the air, so there could be no repetition here of the surprise in Hawaii. At the same time the First Interceptor Command called to active duty 40,000 volunteer civilian aircraft spotters at 1,300 posts scattered through thirteen eastern coastal states and the District of Columbia.

Anti-Aircraft Guns Set Up

The Sixty-second Coast Artillery of Fort Totten, Bayside, Queens, set up anti-aircraft apparatus at vantage points around the city. One base was in Prospect Park, Brooklyn.

Air raid wardens went on duty at midnight in every part of the city, as a result of a series of conferences among Police and Fire Department officers and representatives of the Board of Education and the Department of Housing, at which it was agreed that air raid warnings would be broadcast by the blowing of the sirens of all police radio cars and emergency trucks and all Fire Department apparatus.

Alternating long and short blasts of the sirens will be sounded from the moment the Army notifies the Police and Fire Departments of the approach of an enemy and will be continued throughout the duration of the raid. The all-clear signal will be given by a series of short blasts from the sirens, it was agreed.

Teachers to Be Warned

The Police and Fire Departments, with their network of communications reaching into every neighborhood in the city, also undertook to advise the 800 public schools of an impending raid when the alarm is sounded, so the teachers can shepherd their pupils to their homes in accordance with plans already made.

Precautions against sabotage of bridges, tunnels, railroads, reservoirs, dams, power plants and other points of key importance throughout the city also were discussed at conferences of high police officials with Commissioner
Continued on Page Twenty-six

MALAYA THWARTS PUSH BY JAPANESE

Thailand Capitulates and Is Seen Virtually in Axis—Two Raids on Singapore

By F. TILLMAN DURDIN
Wireless to The New York Times.

SINGAPORE, Dec. 8—The Japanese in the first eighteen hours of their attack on the Malaya peninsula have forced Thailand to capitulate, but do not now appear to have achieved any appreciable success in an invasion of British Malaya.

There was an air raid on Singapore this morning. Prai, on the mainland opposite Georgetown, more commonly known as Penang from the name of the island on which it is located, was also bombed, but damage was said to be slight.

[Bombs again started dropping on Singapore at 4 A. M. today, The Associated Press re-
Continued on Page Ten

The International Situation

TUESDAY, DECEMBER 9, 1941

The United States yesterday made a formal declaration of war on Japan after President Roosevelt had addressed a joint session of Congress. [Page 1, Column 8.] The Senate approved by unanimous vote [Page 6, Column 1] while one woman in the House of Representatives dissented. [Page 6, Column 4.]

In the national effort the Supply, Priorities and Allocations Board mapped expanding production [Page 36, Column 1], leaders of organized labor pledged support [Page 36, Column 4], and Mayor La Guardia issued a proclamation giving air raid defense instructions [Page 34, Column 1.]

In San Francisco two formations of enemy aircraft were sighted over the city, which was blacked out. [Page 1, Column 1.]

White House announcements indicated that the battle of the Pacific was raging with the United States still on the defensive. [Page 1 Column 1: Map, Page 4.] There were extensive air attacks in the Philippines [Page 1, Columns 2 and 3: Map, Page 9], raids on Hong Kong [Page 11, Column 1] and a Tokyo report that both Guam and Wake had been put under the Japanese flag. [Page 12, Column 1: with map.] The British were mopping up on a Japanese landing party in Malaya, but Thailand had yielded. [Page 1, Column 3; Map, Page 10.]

The small detachment of United States Marines at Tientsin and Peiping were disarmed and detained by the Japanese

and they closed the United States Consulate in Shanghai. [Page 3, Column 1.] Imperial Headquarters in Tokyo made sweeping claims of victory in the battle of the Pacific, listing great damage to the United States forces. [Page 1, Column 5.]

In London, Prime Minister Churchill announced Britain's declaration of war to Parliament and made a stirring address to the world. [Page 14, Column 1.]

The American nations began to line up behind the United States. A conference was held, but seven countries have already declared war on Japan, two have broken diplomatic relations and several others are preparing to act. [Page 22, Column 3.] China decided to declare war not merely on Japan but on Germany and Italy as well. [Page 9, Column 4.] The various European governments in exile also supported the United States. [Page 18, Column 1.] Russia's position is obscure. [Page 2, Column 2.]

The United States accused Germany of having egged Japan on; said lease-lend aid would continue. [Page 1, Column 6.] Berlin gave out word that Winter had stopped the Germans short of Moscow and that the capture of the Russian capital had been put off until Spring. [Page 1, Column 7.]

In Libya, the Axis armored forces were attacked from three directions by the British and what was expected to be a major engagement was eventually merely a rearguard action. [Page 24, Column 3.]

1 BATTLESHIP LOST

Capsized in Pearl Harbor, Destroyer Is Blown Up, Other Ships Hurt

FLEET NOW IS FIGHTING

Aid Rushed to Hawaii— Some Congressmen Sharply Critical

By CHARLES HURD
Special to The New York Times.

WASHINGTON, Dec. 8—The Battle of the Pacific spread tonight over a 3,000-mile "front" from Hawaii to the Philippines while a badly battered United States Fleet fought back at Japanese air and sea forces that launched severe attacks yesterday afternoon.

Tonight the Japanese were reported to be launching their main attack at the Philippines, particularly at Palawan, the greatest natural harbor in the archipelago. That attack was preceded today, according to reports from Manila, by an onslaught against the United States military air fields there, which put three out of commission for the time being and set fire to storage tanks containing vital gasoline for air operations.

The Japanese Sunday attack on Hawaii was reported in informed quarters to have been launched from the mandated islands, rather than from Japan proper, and aircraft carriers apparently approached undetected within 250 or 300 miles of Pearl Harbor.

3,000 Casualties on Oahu

The White House announced officially that the attack on the Island of Oahu, site of Honolulu and the Pearl Harbor naval base, probably has cost about 1,500 lives and resulted in an equal number of wounded persons.

To the toll of lives announced for this region, and undisclosed casualties in the Philippines and at other points, was added official word that one "old battleship" had capsized in Pearl Harbor, a destroyer had exploded and that several other
Continued on Page Four

The President signs the declaration of war — Associated Press Wirephoto

LARGE U. S. LOSSES CLAIMED BY JAPAN

Tokyo Lists 2 Battleships, 1 Mine-Sweeper Sunk, 4 Capital Ships, 4 Cruisers Damaged

TOKYO, Tuesday, Dec. 9 (From Official Broadcasts, Distributed by The Associated Press)—Japanese Imperial Headquarters announced last night the sinking of two United States battleships and a mine-sweeper, severe damage to four other American capital ships and four cruisers and the destruction of about 100 American planes in Japan's surprise blows at Hawaii, the Philippines and Guam.

The official news agency, Domei, quickly interpreted "these magnificent early gains" as giving Japan naval mastery over the United States in the Pacific, and said that force that the United States could muster now "would be regarded as utterly inadequate to accomplish any successful outcome in an encounter with the thus-far-intact Japanese fleet."

In addition, "many enemy merchant ships were captured" in the Pacific, it was announced, and the communiqué listed an unconfirmed report that a Japanese submarine had sunk an American aircraft carrier off Honolulu.

"No Japanese ships were lost during the fighting," it added.

Domei said today it was "understood that Japanese forces had destroyed more than 300 American planes, including 200 in dogfights and on the ground in Hawaii. The others, it said, were "believed" destroyed in the Philippines. Of the total, the news agency said, they were Fortress planes and thirty long-range bombers.

Japanese newspapers identified two American battleships declared sunk Sunday at Pearl Harbor, Hawaii, as the 31,800-ton West Virginia and the 29,000-ton Oklahoma. [An Italian broadcast, however, quoted Domei as listing the Oklahoma and the 33,100-ton Pennsylvania as lost.] In Berlin, D. N. B. said in a Tokyo dispatch that an American transport ship carrying 350 men had been sunk off Manila.

Japanese planes were reported to have again attacked the Philippines and British Hong Kong yesterday, inflicting "heavy damage" in a follow-up of the raids launched Sunday. "Twelve out of fourteen enemy planes on the ground were
Continued on Page Thirteen

The President's Message

Following is the text of President Roosevelt's war message to Congress, as recorded by The New York Times from a broadcast:

Mr. Vice President, Mr. Speaker, members of the Senate and the House of Representatives:

Yesterday, Dec. 7, 1941—a date which will live in infamy—the United States of America was suddenly and deliberately attacked by naval and air forces of the empire of Japan.

The United States was at peace with that nation, and, at the solicitation of Japan, was still in conversation with its government and its Emperor looking toward the maintenance of peace in the Pacific.

Indeed, one hour after Japanese air squadrons had commenced bombing in the American island of Oahu, the Japanese Ambassador to the United States and his colleague delivered to our Secretary of State a formal reply to a recent American message. And, while this reply stated that it seemed useless to continue the existing diplomatic negotiations, it contained no threat or hint of war or of armed attack.

Attack Deliberately Planned

It will be recorded that the distance of Hawaii from Japan makes it obvious that the attack was deliberately planned many days or even weeks ago. During the intervening time the Japanese Government has deliberately sought to deceive the United States by false statements and expressions of hope for continued peace.

The attack yesterday on the Hawaiian Islands has caused severe damage to American naval and military forces. I regret to tell you that very many American lives have been lost. In
Continued on Page Six

U. S. TO CONTINUE AID TO BRITAIN

White House Charges Nazis Sought Pacific War, but Will Fail to Gain Ends

Special to The New York Times.

WASHINGTON, Dec. 8—A statement accusing Germany of having done everything in her power "to push Japan into the war" was issued this evening at the White House.

The statement declared that Germany's objective was "to put an end to the lease-lend program," which has aided the European enemies of Germany, including Britain and Russia and their allies and Turkey. It added that this program would continue "in full operation" and that the German attempt to end lease-lend shipments was "100 per cent" mistaken.

[A surprise Russian attack on Eastern Crimea from the Caucasus was revealed in a Moscow broadcast. A counter-attack from Sevastopol also was reported. The Soviet claimed important progress around Taganrog and on Moscow's defense lines.]

It seemed likely from the spokesman's statement that until Spring there could be no further major German offensive except along the extreme southern front. This word reduced the Russian campaign to secondary interest for the Germans for the first time, and attention focused instead on Ja-
Continued on Page Seventeen

NAZIS GIVE UP IDEA OF MOSCOW IN 1941

Winter Forces Abandonment of Big Drives in North Till Spring, Berlin Says

By The Associated Press.

BERLIN, Dec. 8—Winter has stopped the Germans short of Moscow and the capture of the Soviet capital is not expected this year, a military spokesman announced tonight.

It is not expected that Spring weather will permit resumption of full-scale operations against Moscow. For the time being the Russian attacks will carry out its pledges to Japan, its Axis ally, by declaring war on the United States and that Italy would
Continued on Page Twenty-five

UNITY IN CONGRESS

Only One Negative Vote as President Calls to War and Victory

ROUNDS OF CHEERS

Miss Rankin's Is Sole 'No' as Both Houses Act in Quick Time

By FRANK L. KLUCKHOHN
Special to The New York Times.

WASHINGTON, Dec. 8—The United States today formally declared war on Japan. Congress, with only one dissenting vote, approved the resolution in the record time of 33 minutes after President Roosevelt denounced Japanese aggression in ringing tones. He personally delivered his message to a joint session of the Senate and House. At 4:10 P. M. he affixed his signature to the resolution.

There was no debate like that between April 2, 1917, when President Wilson requested war against Germany, and April 6, when a declaration of war was approved by Congress.

President Roosevelt spoke only 6 minutes and 30 seconds today compared with Woodrow Wilson's 29 minutes and 34 seconds.

The vote today against Japan was 82 to 0 in the Senate and 388 to 1 in the House. The lone vote against the resolution in the House was that of Miss Jeanette Rankin, Republican, of Montana. Her "No" was greeted with boos and hisses. In 1917 she voted against the resolution for war against Germany.

The President did not mention Germany or Italy in his request. Early this evening a statement was issued at the White House, however, accusing Germany of doing everything possible to push Japan into the war. The objective, the official statement proclaimed, was to cut off American lend-lease aid to Germany's European enemies, and a pledge was made that this aid would continue "100 per cent."

A Sudden and Deliberate Attack

President Roosevelt's brief and decisive words were addressed to the assembled representatives of the basic organizations of American democracy—the Senate, the House, the Cabinet and the Supreme Court.

"America was suddenly and deliberately attacked by naval and air forces of the empire of Japan," he said. "We will gain the inevitable triumph, so help us God."

Thunderous cheers greeted the Chief Executive and Commander in Chief throughout the address. This was particularly pronounced when he declared that America "will remember the character of the onslaught against us," a day, he remarked, which will live in infamy.

"This form of treachery shall never endanger us again," he declared amid cheers. "The American people in their righteous might will win through to absolute victory."

Then, to the accompaniment of
Continued on Page Five

President to Talk On Radio Tonight

By The Associated Press.

WASHINGTON, Dec. 8—President Roosevelt will make a radio address to the nation tomorrow night at 10 P. M., Eastern standard time, at which time the White House said he would make "a more complete documentation" of the Japanese attack than has yet been possible.

Stephen Early, Presidential secretary, announced that the Chief Executive would speak for half an hour and that the address would be carried by all networks.

Mr. Roosevelt began dictating the speech tonight in his White House study.

"All the News That's Fit to Print."

The New York Times.

LATE CITY EDITION
Fair, slowly rising temperature today. Tomorrow cloudy, moderately cold, occasional snow.
Temperatures Yesterday—Max.,34; Min.,24

VOL. XCI..No. 30,638.
Entered as Second-Class Matter,
Postoffice, New York, N. Y.
NEW YORK, FRIDAY, DECEMBER 12, 1941.
THREE CENTS NEW YORK CITY and Vicinity

Copyright, 1941, by The New York Times Company.

U.S. NOW AT WAR WITH GERMANY AND ITALY; JAPANESE CHECKED IN ALL LAND FIGHTING; 3 OF THEIR SHIPS SUNK, 2D BATTLESHIP HIT

BLOCKED IN LUZON

But Japanese Put Small Force Ashore in South of Philippine Island

SABOTEURS ARE HELD

Some in Manila Seized for Spreading Rumor About City Water

By H. FORD WILKINS
Wireless to THE NEW YORK TIMES

MANILA, Friday, Dec. 12—The United States Army Far East headquarters announced today that a small Japanese invasion force was reported to have pushed ashore at Legaspi, Southern Luzon, and "the enemy has improved his strength in Northern Luzon," where, however, the situation remains unchanged materially. The announcement added that the report of the Legaspi landing was still unconfirmed and there were no details.

[Small forces of Japanese apparently have been landed at Legaspi, about three hours after the morning communiqué had said merely that the Legaspi development had not yet been confirmed, a United Press dispatch from Manila said.]

There was no further indication of the progress of the sea war. The office of Admiral Thomas C. Hart, commander in chief of the United States Asiatic Fleet, remained silent.

One Japanese plane was shot down by an American fighter near Bancayan, in the mountain mining district.

2,000 Families Are Moved

Manila took further emergency measures to evacuate portions of the old walled city. The Red Cross supervised the removal of 2,000 families, loading them into buses and trucks and taking them to safety zones comparatively removed from the city. Identification cards were issued and checked as the evacuees lined up for removal. With Lieut. Gen. Douglas MacArthur's United States Far Eastern forces fully in control of the North Luzon invasion threat and his air force sufficiently active to disperse Japanese raiders turned yesterday to mopping up fifth columnists.

Their latest trick was to circulate rumors that the city water supply had been poisoned. Army, city and government officials quickly scotched the rumors with assurances and proof that nothing whatever was wrong with the water supply. Several persons were arrested, including air-raid wardens, on a city-wide house-to-house campaign warning the people against "impure water."

Several persons entered hospitals asserting that they had been poisoned, but examination disclosed that nothing was wrong with them but upset stomachs and fear. Elaborate analysis proved that the water they drank was not contaminated.

The official communiqué asserting that mopping-up operations were progressing heightened the morale of the nation, suddenly plunged into total war and the first taste of conflict in forty years.

The sinking of a United States Army transport in Manila Bay, as announced by Tokyo, was denied officially here yesterday.

Interned Japanese, numbering around 2,000, were revealed to be extremely uncomfortable under the threat of bombs from Japanese planes, recognizing that bombs do not distinguish nationalities.

Legaspi Move Discounted

MANILA, Friday, Dec. 12 (UP)—The small Japanese landings at Legaspi, a port of about 36,000

Continued on Page Eight

TO PLACE a Want Ad just telephone The New York Times—LAckawanna 4-1000.

Line-Up of World War II

THE ALLIES

Australia	Haiti
†Belgium	*Honduras
Canada	Netherlands
China	Indies
Costa Rica	New Zealand
Cuba	Nicaragua
†Czecho-Slovakia	†Norway
Dominican	*Panama
Republic	†Poland
*El Salvador	South Africa
Free France	†Soviet Union
Great Britain	United States
†Greece	†Yugoslavia
Guatemala	

THE AXIS

Finland	Japan
Germany	Manchukuo
Hungary	Rumania
Italy	Slovakia

*Have declared war on Japan only.

†At war only with Germany, Italy and their European allies.

CITY CALM AND GRIM AS THE WAR WIDENS

Loyalty and a Determination to Win Are Evident in Every Class and National Group

The people of New York City received the news that we are at war with Germany and Italy as well as Japan with profound calm and a quiet, stern determination to see it through, no matter how long it takes. Patriotism and loyalty were the spontaneous order of the day in every household, every business office, every factory, every school and every institution. The whole city rallied in support of the war.

All over the city the Stars and Stripes flew proudly from public and private buildings, and those in charge of Army, Navy, Coast Guard and civilian defense organizations swung promptly and forcefully into action to protect the city

Continued on Page Twenty-one

U. S. FLIERS SCORE

Bombs Send Battleship, Cruiser and Destroyer to the Bottom

MARINES KEEP WAKE

Small Force Fights Off Foe Despite Loss of Some of Planes

By CHARLES HURD
Special to THE NEW YORK TIMES

WASHINGTON, Dec. 11—A Japanese battleship, a cruiser and a destroyer have been sunk in the Pacific and a second battleship badly damaged by bomb hits, the United States forces announced in communiqués today recording their first major victories in the warfare that began last Sunday with surprise Japanese attacks.

Damage to the second battleship was revealed tonight in a Navy communiqué, which said a man-of-war of the Kongo class had been hit by Navy patrol planes off the coast of Luzon. The second battleship to be bombed effectively by United States forces, the communiqué asserted.

The battleship sunk, also of the Kongo class, was believed to have been the 29,330-ton Haruna. She went down after having been set afire by aerial bombardment north of Luzon. She had been supporting an attack in which the Japanese effected a landing at Aparri, a remote village on the northern Philippine coast, separated from Manila by mountains and forests.

The cruiser, unidentified except that it was of the light class, and the destroyer were sunk also by fliers who took off from Wake

Continued on Page Six

Left: The President set his signature to the act against Germany. Center: He checked the time with Senator Tom Connally. Right: After that he placed the United States officially at war with Italy.

Associated Press Wirephotos

AXIS TO GET LESSON, CHURCHILL WARNS

He Announces Replacement of Libyan General—Upholds Phillips's Judgment

Text of Mr. Churchill's speech will be found on Page 16.

By CRAIG THOMPSON
Special Cable to THE NEW YORK TIMES

LONDON, Dec. 11—Prime Minister Winston Churchill delivered a review of the war in the Pacific, North Africa, Russia and the Atlantic today that contained a compound of gloom and of optimism, but he ended with this ringing declaration:

"Just handfuls and cliques of wicked men and their military or party organizations have risen to bring these hideous evils upon mankind. It would indeed bring shame upon our generation if we did not teach them a lesson which will not be forgotten in the records of a thousand years."

Precedes Declarations

He spoke to the House of Commons before the Axis war declarations and the United States' reply.

Mr. Churchill gave hitherto unpublished details about the sinkings of the Prince of Wales and the Repulse, which made plain that the British lost the use of airdromes on the Malay Peninsula and that the ships had had to rely solely on their anti-aircraft guns for protection against the attacking planes. In so doing he stoutly defended the judgment whereby Vice Admiral Sir Tom S. V. Phillips, who appeared tonight to have been lost, undertook an attack on Japanese transports that resulted in the sinkings of the warships.

Mr. Churchill announced that Lieut. Gen. Sir Alan Gordon Cunningham had been replaced in Libya by Major Gen. Neil Methuen Ritchie, adding that General Cunningham "has been reported by medical authorities to be suffering from serious overstrain and was granted sick leave."

President Roosevelt called upon industrial and labor representatives, whom he will meet next week and reach a voluntary agreement to end labor disputes for the duration. [Page 29, Column 2.] It was revealed also that the Administration was considering the registration of all men between the ages of 18 and 65 for military and civilian service. [Page 34, Column 1.]

On the European fighting front the Russians reported further gains against German forces. [Page 18, Column 3.] The Berlin radio replaced that the Nazis had replaced their commander on the Moscow front. [Page 19, Column 1.] In Libya, the main Axis forces were still withdrawing westward, Cairo announced. [Page 17, Column 1.]

Our Declaration of War

Special to THE NEW YORK TIMES.

WASHINGTON, Dec. 11—Following are the texts of the documents wherein the President asked a war declaration against Germany and Italy, and Congress acted:

The President's Message

To the Congress of the United States:

On the morning of Dec. 11 the Government of Germany, pursuing its course of world conquest, declared war against the United States.

The long-known and the long-expected has thus taken place. The forces endeavoring to enslave the entire world now are moving toward this hemisphere.

Never before has there been a greater challenge to life, liberty and civilization.

Delay invites great danger. Rapid and united effort by all of the peoples of the world who are determined to remain free will insure a world victory of the forces of justice and righteousness over the forces of savagery and of barbarism.

Italy also has declared war against the United States.

I therefore request the Congress to recognize a state of war between the United States and Germany, and between the United States and Italy.

FRANKLIN D. ROOSEVELT.

The War Resolution

Declaring that a state of war exists between the Government of Germany and the government and the people of the United States and making provision to prosecute the same.

Whereas the Government of Germany has formally declared war against the government and the people of the United States:

Therefore, be it

Resolved by the Senate and House of Representatives of the United States of America in Congress assembled, that the state of war between the United States and the Government of Germany which has thus been thrust upon the United States is hereby formally declared; and the President is hereby authorized and directed to employ the entire naval and military forces of the United States and the resources of the government to carry on war against the Government of Germany; and, to bring the conflict to a successful termination, all of the resources of the country are hereby pledged by the Congress of the United States.

(An identic resolution regarding Italy was adopted)

Secretary Knox Visits Honolulu; Bases There Were Raided 5 Times

Special to THE NEW YORK TIMES.

WASHINGTON, Dec. 11—The Navy Department announced tonight that Secretary Frank Knox had arrived in Honolulu this afternoon.

There was no previous announcement that he had left for Hawaii, nor was there any intimation of the specific purpose of his visit.

WASHINGTON, Dec. 11 (UP)—Delegate Samuel W. King of Hawaii disclosed tonight after a telephone conversation with Governor Joseph B. Poindexter that twenty Japanese planes were shot down during the Sunday raid on Pearl Harbor.

Mr. King said the information was authorized for release in Hawaii by Lieut. Gen. Walter C. Short and that Mr. Poindexter was permitted to make the disclosure by transpacific radio-telephone.

Mr. Poindexter told Mr. King that "civilian morale is 100 per cent throughout the territory.

"Civilian defense measures are working without a hitch," he added.

HONOLULU, Dec. 11 (UP)—In addition to two deadly attacks on the United States naval base at Pearl Harbor last Sunday, Japanese bombers followed with a third attack later that day and with a fourth Monday morning, it is possible to disclose today for the first time.

Censorship permits a cautious description of the attack. A few seconds after the first bombers came over, with the rising sun insignia of Japan on their wings, defending anti-aircraft batteries sent up a heavy barrage.

Within a few minutes heavy clouds of black smoke began rolling up from Pearl Harbor, fourteen miles from Honolulu.

Planes roared in over the harbor, dropping bombs on navy centers and ships. Torpedo planes splashed

Continued on Page Eleven

CONGRESS KILLS BAN ON AN A. E. F.

Swift Action Without Debate— Service Terms Are Extended to Six Months After War

Special to THE NEW YORK TIMES.

WASHINGTON, Dec. 11—Congress swiftly eliminated prohibitions against American expeditionary forces today and continued terms of enlistment or induction to a date six months after hostilities end. Acting without debate, the two houses dropped the A. E. F. ban by removing restrictions in the Selective Service Act on the use of troops outside the Western Hemisphere.

The Senate Appropriations Committee, meanwhile, added an undetermined sum to the $8,246,000,000 third supplemental national defense appropriation bill as passed by the House. This change was said to have raised the bill's total above $10,500,000,000.

A ranking member of the committee was unable to say tonight what the exact amount of the bill was, but he said he was "satisfied it is above $10,500,000,000." He added that the amendments approved by the committee were mostly for new items, regarded as emergency ones by the Army and the Navy and Coast Guard. If approved, the measure would set a record for the size of a single appropriation bill.

Fund for Army Pay Specified

Among the amendments approved by the committee was one setting at $314,000,000 the supplemental item for pay of the Army, but immediately following it was a proviso that this amount should not be taken to mean the limit if the Army inducted or enlisted thousands of new personnel. If this took place, under the amendment practical authority would be granted for pay of the personnel under Congressional promise to pass deficiency bills to whatever extent was necessary.

Some $390,000,000 was added to the bill for military air construction. The Signal Corps also received a sizable increase for construction and equipment, while to the Navy were granted increases of many millions for landing fields, yards and docks. The Coast Guard received $4,750,000 for extraordinary expenses and $8,743,000 for new equipment.

The Army Chief of Staff received $125,000,000 as an emergency fund, to be accounted for to Congress every three months, and various sums were voted for additions to forts and posts within the United States.

The measure changing the Selective Service Act regarding the tenure of service and the extent of service came on the heels of action by both houses in declaring war on Germany and Italy, following

Continued on Page Thirty-four

WAR OPENED ON US

Congress Acts Quickly as President Meets Hitler Challenge

A GRIM UNANIMITY

Message Warns Nation Foes Aim to Enslave This Hemisphere

By FRANK L. KLUCKHOHN
Special to THE NEW YORK TIMES.

WASHINGTON, Dec. 11—The United States declared war today on Germany and Italy, Japan's Axis partners. This nation acted swiftly after Germany formally declared war on us and Italy followed the German lead. Thus, President Roosevelt told Congress in his message, the long-known and the long-expected has taken place.

"The forces endeavoring to enslave the entire world now are moving toward this hemisphere," he said.

"Never before has there been a greater challenge to life, liberty and civilization."

Delay, the President said, invites great danger. He added:

"Rapid and united effort by all of the peoples of the world who are determined to remain free will insure a world victory of the forces of justice and righteousness over the forces of savagery and barbarism."

For the first time in its history the United States finds itself at war against powers in both the Atlantic and the Pacific.

Quick and Unanimous Answer

Congress acted not only rapidly but without a dissenting vote to meet the Axis challenge. Within two and three-quarters hours after the reading of Mr. Roosevelt's message was started in the Senate and House at 12:26 P. M., the President had signed the declarations against Germany and Italy. Seventy-two hours previously the Japanese attack on Hawaii had brought about the declaration of war against the other Axis partner.

Congress also quickly completed legislation to allow selectees and National Guardsmen to serve outside the Western Hemisphere and set the term of service in the nation's forces until six months after the termination of the war.

In the Senate the vote was 88 to 0 for war against Germany and 90 to 0 for war against Italy. The vote in the House was 393 to 0 for war against Germany and 399 to 0 for war against Italy. The larger Congressional vote against Italy was attributable to the fact that some members reached the floor too late to vote on the declaration against Germany.

In the House, Miss Jeannette Rankin, Republican, of Montana, who cast the lone dissenting vote on Japan, today voted a non-committal "present" with regard to Germany and Italy.

Ignoring Hitler's declarations before the Reichstag today regarding American policy, and Mussolini's to a crowd before the Palazzo di Venezia in Rome, Congress adopted identical resolutions against Germany and Italy. It merely noted that their governments had thrust war upon the United States.

Grim Mood in Congress

Congress acted in a grim mood, but without excitement. Not only on the floors of the Senate and House, but in the galleries the grim mood prevailed. President Roosevelt, busy at the White House directing the battle and production effort as Commander in Chief, did not appear to read his message, as he did when war was declared upon Japan.

There was a deeply solemn undemote as the members assembled at noon. Senator Walsh, chairman of the Senate Naval Affairs Committee, had announced that the

Continued on Page Five

The International Situation

FRIDAY, DECEMBER 12, 1941

The United States declared war yesterday on Germany and Italy. Congress acted swiftly without a dissenting vote. [Page 1, Column 1; Map, Page 2.] Then, without debate, it passed a bill to permit the use of all United States land forces anywhere in the world. [Page 1, Column 7.]

This action coincided with good news from the Pacific. Washington announced the sinking of a Japanese battleship, a cruiser and a destroyer and reported severe damage to a second battleship by bomb hits. [Page 1, Column 3, Map, Column 5.]

Tokyo claimed the destruction of a American destroyer, a submarine and eighty-one planes, in addition to the capture of 350 Americans on Guam. [Page 8, Column 5.] With the announcement of Britain's Far Eastern Fleet among 15,000 casualties. [Page 11, Column 1, map.]

The American declaration came within a few hours after Germany and Italy had declared war on the United States. The Reich's declaration was in a diplomatic note and in a Reichstag address by Adolf Hitler. [Page 4, Column 5.] Benito Mussolini proclaimed Italy's declaration. [Page 4, Column 5.]

In London, where news of America's full entry into the world war brought predictions of an Allied grand strategy [Page 13, Column 5], Prime Minister Churchill declared that the Allies would win ultimately at any cost. [Page 1, Column 4.] Mexico broke off relations with Germany and Italy, while ten other Latin-American countries declared war on those countries or prepared to take that step. [Page 9, Column 1.]

The Soviet radio asserted that any Axis hopes for a separate peace with Russia were in vain. The radio declared that Russia was determined to fight alongside the United States and Britain until the Allies won. [Page 19, Column 1.]

In all of yesterday's land fighting, Japan was checked. In the Philippines, attempts to win a firm foothold on Luzon appeared smashed, except for a landing of parachutists at an airport 120 miles northeast of Manila and another small landing on the southeastern coast of the island. [Page 1, Column 1; Map, Page 2.]

The British reported a slow-down of Japanese attacks in Malaya. [Page 13, Column 1.] While British forces fought off new assaults on Hong Kong, a two-day Chinese offensive to relieve pressure there was reported to have inflicted 15,000 casualties. [Page 11, Column 1.]

Amid debate in Washington over a proposed investigation of what happened at Pearl Harbor Sunday [Page 10, Column 1], Secretary of the Navy Knox arrived in Honolulu, presumably to seek first-hand information on that attack. [Page 1, Columns 5 and 6.]

President Roosevelt called upon industrial and labor representatives, whom he will meet next week and reach a voluntary agreement to end labor disputes for the duration. [Page 29, Column 2.] It was revealed also that the Administration was considering the registration of all men between the ages of 18 and 65 for military and civilian service. [Page 34, Column 1.]

On the European fighting front the Russians reported further gains against German forces. [Page 18, Column 3.] The Berlin radio replaced that the Nazis had replaced their commander on the Moscow front. [Page 19, Column 1.] In Libya, the main Axis forces were still withdrawing westward, Cairo announced. [Page 17, Column 1.]

miles northeast of Manila and another small landing on the southeastern coast of the island. [Page 1, Column 1; Map, Page 2.]

The British reported a slow-down of Japanese attacks in Malaya. [Page 13, Column 1.] While British forces fought off new assaults on Hong Kong, a two-day Chinese offensive to relieve pressure there was reported to have inflicted 15,000 casualties. [Page 11, Column 1, map.]

Tokyo claimed the destruction of a American destroyer, a submarine and eighty-one planes, in addition to the capture of 350 Americans on Guam. [Page 8, Column 5.] With the announcement of Britain's Far Eastern Fleet among 15,000 casualties, the sinking of the Prince of Wales and the Repulse, the British named a new commander. [Page 14, Column 3.]

Mr. Churchill announced that Lieut. Gen. Sir Alan Gordon Cunningham had been replaced in Libya by Major Gen. Neil Methuen Ritchie, adding that General Cunningham "has been reported by medical authorities to be suffering from serious overstrain and was granted sick leave." [Page 1, Columns 5 and 6.]

President Ritchie, the new commander of the Eighth Army, is 44 years old. His was one of three "young-men" appointments to the General Staff that were made last June. In the last war he was commissioned a second lieutenant at the age of seventeen and was a captain when he was twenty. He fought in France, Mesopotamia and Palestine, and received the Distinguished Service Order and the Military Cross.

Mr. Churchill gave an indication of the size of British and Allied losses in merchantmen in the Battle of the Atlantic for November that would, from his statement, appear to have been no greater than 100,000 tons. This would be a

Continued on Page Seventeen

The New York Times.

Copyright, 1941, by The New York Times Company.

VOL. XCI..No. 30,642.

Entered as Second-Class Matter, Postoffice, New York, N. Y.

NEW YORK, TUESDAY, DECEMBER 16, 1941.

THREE CENTS NEW YORK CITY and Vicinity

KNOX REPORTS ONE BATTLESHIP SUNK AT HAWAII, 5 OTHER CRAFT LOST, BUT MAIN FLEET IS AT SEA; PRESIDENT LAYS PERFIDY TO JAPAN'S EMPEROR

AIR WARDEN ORDERS WILL BE BACKED UP BY $500 PENALTIES

Alternate Jail Sentences Are Provided in Bill Council Will Act Upon Today

5 NEW SIRENS DELIVERED

Devices May Be Heard One to Two Miles—Tests Tomorrow —School Rules Unchanged

Failure to obey civil defense regulations or refusal to comply with the orders of air raid wardens would be made punishable by a jail term of not more than six months or a fine of not more than $500 by a local law to be introduced at this afternoon's meeting of the City Council by majority leader Joseph T. Sharkey of Brooklyn.

The measure, which was requested yesterday by Mayor La Guardia, also provides that during an air raid all except duly authorized persons must immediately leave streets, parks and open spaces and proceed to the nearest cover, and that vehicles must be parked immediately and their passengers take to the nearest shelter.

After the air-raid alarms last Tuesday and Wednesday many air-raid wardens complained that crowds thronged into the streets to see what was going on and ignored their directions to seek shelter. The legislation sought by the Mayor is intended to correct this condition and to give the wardens legal authority to disperse crowds which might be subject to heavy casualties in an actual raid.

Warden Cards Printed

The Police Department has completed the printing of 200,000 identification cards for air-raid wardens, it was learned last night at the office of the Coordinator of Civilian Defense at Police Headquarters, and is about to begin issuing them to qualified wardens. Zone wardens will receive white cards, sector wardens yellow cards and post wardens salmon-colored cards.

Each warden must affix a photograph of himself, chauffeur size, to his card and return it to the police through his local precinct. A Police Department seal will then be placed over his picture and signature to guarantee the validity of the card, and then it will be returned to the holder. The cards will be two by three inches in size.

Five big "siro-drones," the first of seventy to be delivered this week, arrived yesterday at the office of Thomas W. Rochester, chief engineer of the Police Department. The five included two different types, one of which is supposed to be audible within a radius of two miles and the other with a range of one mile.

Can Be Heard Mile

Both sirens are about three feet high, with horns twenty inches in diameter, and are electrically operated. The type with a radius of one mile is operated by a two-horsepower motor and the louder horn by a five-horsepower motor. They are ordinarily used as factory whistles and fire alarms in small towns and are manufactured by the H-O-S Company, Inc., of Stapleton, S. I.

Mayor La Guardia, Police Commissioner Valentine, and other local officials and civilian defense leaders will attend tests of both types of the new "siro-drones" tomorrow afternoon. The Mayor's party is to arrive at Spring and Lafayette Streets, near Police Headquarters, at 4:30 P. M. to try out the sirens after they have been placed on a Police Department tower truck.

Earlier tomorrow afternoon, at 4 o'clock the Mayor and his entourage will visit the building of the New York Edison Company at Fortieth Street and the East River for a trial of the big whistle, operated by steam and electricity, that is mounted on the structure.

Continued on Page Twenty-four

'Keep Flag Flying,' MacArthur's Order

Wireless to THE NEW YORK TIMES.

MANILA, Dec. 15—Morale at headquarters of the United States Army's Far Eastern Forces is above par.

An officer on the staff of General Douglas MacArthur, Commander in Chief, suggested to him that the American flag atop the bastion that marks the headquarters might serve as a target for Japanese planes. General MacArthur laughed and said:

"Take every other normal precaution for the protection of the headquarters, but let's keep the flag flying."

18-64 AGE LISTING FOR DRAFT RUSHED

House Committee for Military Service at 21, Senate Group for Minimum of 19

By HENRY N. DORRIS
Special to THE NEW YORK TIMES.

WASHINGTON, Dec. 15—Congressional committees speeded legislation today to give full wartime powers to the President and to extend the registration requirements of the Selective Service Act to all men from 18 to 64, inclusive.

The House Military Affairs Committee gave final approval to a bill carrying the Selective Service changes. The Senate bill was pushed toward the front rank, important rail point on the Senate Military Affairs Committee gave tentative approval to a bill, withholding full approval pending testimony in executive session tomorrow by Brig. Gen. Lewis B. Hershey, Selective Service Administrator.

The bills as they stood tonight differed on the ages subject to military service. The Senate bill contains tentatively the War Department recommendation for the age brackets 19 to 44, inclusive. The House committee approved the bracket 21 to 44, inclusive.

About 41,000,000 men would be affected by the overall registration requirement, which is planned not only to provide an army of 2,800,000 to 7,500,000 but to ascertain

Continued on Page Fifteen

The International Situation

TUESDAY, DECEMBER 16, 1941

Secretary of the Navy Knox yesterday reported losses to the United States Fleet in the Pearl Harbor attack as one battleship, a target ship, a minelayer and three destroyers. Casualties, he gave them out, were heavier than had been previously reported. He said that the American flag atop forces were "not on the alert" and that the Japanese had been aided by a great "fifth column." An investigation is going forward. [Page 1, Column 8.]

The situation in the Philippines appeared to be stabilized, with an air raid on the naval station at Olongapo the only major operation. Midway, as well as Wake, was said in reports from Washington to be still holding out. [Page 1, Column 5; Map, Page 2.] British troops, resisting a Japanese attack in force on the Malay Peninsula, were declared to have dug in on a stronger defense line in southern Kedah and to have abandoned the southern tip of Burma. [Page 14, Column 3.] British and Netherland air units fought off strong Japanese forces. [Page 1, Column 5 and 6.] At Hong Kong the British had retired from the mainland and were strongly defending the island. The Chinese thrust in relief was gaining momentum. [Page 10, Column 2.]

Tokyo's Premier pictured his foes in collapse, but warned of a long war. [Page 1, Columns 6 and 7.]

President Roosevelt, in a message to Congress outlining the events leading up to the war, laid stress on the Japanese bad faith, in which, he implied, the Emperor himself was involved. [Page 1, Column 4.] In a broadcast to the nation on the anniversary of the ratification of the Bill of Rights, he made Adolf Hitler the chief object of his attack and pledged

our victory for the sake of liberty. [Page 30, Column 2.]

The President also made his quarterly report to Congress on lease-lend aid and emphasized that our entrance into the war increased its necessity. [Page 4, Column 1.] Military Affairs Committees of the Senate and House approved bills to register all males between 18 and 65 years, but differed slightly on the age for military service. [Page 1, Column 2.]

Moscow reported the recapture of the city of Klin and said the drive around Tula was successful; indeed, there was continued victories of the Russian offensive on all fronts. [Page 1, Column 3; Map, Page 15.]

The Axis also continued to give ground in Libya and the Nazis were reported to be throwing their last tank and infantry strength into a desperate delaying action. [Page 16, Column 1.] Their supply lines were said to have been further impaired with the sinking in the Mediterranean of a large supply ship and the sinking or damaging of half a dozen smaller vessels. [Page 17, Column 1.]

Vichy heard of fresh attacks on Nazis in Paris, including the bombing of a restaurant. There were reports that Marshal Pétain had refused the Germans the use of the French fleet and base in Tunisia. [Page 18, Column 3.] Secretary of State Hull expressed friendly and encouraging sentiments toward the French people at his press conference. [Page 19, Column 4.]

As the American republics took further actions in support of the United States, Argentina contemplated instituting a state of siege to curb Axis activities. [Page 9, Column 3.]

RUSSIANS TAKE KLIN

Vital Rail Point in Center Seized as Push Gains on Every Front

NAZIS FLEE IN NORTH

Lose 3 Towns in Tula Area—Soviet Claims Crimean Advance

By DANIEL T. BRIGHAM
By Telephone to THE NEW YORK TIMES.

BERNE, Switzerland, Tuesday, Dec. 16—Smashing through ever-weakening German lines of defense, Soviet troops continued their brilliant operations in the fighting yesterday, recapturing Klin, important rail point on the Moscow-Leningrad line, and three communications centers south of Moscow.

The Red Army also advanced in the Volkhov area, southeast of Leningrad, and in Crimea the Germans were pushed back to the outskirts of Balaclava by Russian troops from Sevastopol, a Russian military spokesman announced on the Moscow radio this morning.

In operations intended to disengage the entire Leningrad-Moscow rail line, the Russians carried out encircling movements north of the Valdai Heights that enabled them to smash the German Thirty-ninth Army Corps. According to the spokesman, 20,000 Germans were killed or wounded in this action.

The remainder of the German force was reported to be fleeing in a southwesterly direction in an attempt to rejoin a "fairly large German force" with its back to Lake Ilmen. However, a Russian column threatens the Germans' southern wing on that sector.

On the Leningrad end of the front Red Army troops began a wide-scale operation southwestward from Tosna. It is understood that the main objective is to straighten out a deep salient that the Germans have held for more

Continued on Page Fifteen

U. S. 'WHITE PAPER'

President in Message Reveals How Tokyo Hid Treacherous Aims

AS HITLER DID LATER

Tyrants Will Fall in End to the Free Peoples, He Says on Radio

The President's message to Congress is on Page 6.

Special to THE NEW YORK TIMES.

WASHINGTON, Dec. 15—Emperor Hirohito was accused today by President Roosevelt, in effect, of personal complicity in Japan's course of carrying on peace negotiations with the United States while putting into operation the plan for a treacherous attack upon this country.

The Emperor is regarded by most Japanese as a divinity whose personal honor must be above reproach, and diplomatic circles here expressed the opinion today that the revelation of perfidy might have serious repercussions within Japan later.

The President revealed in a message transmitted to Congress the details of the reply from the Emperor to his personal appeal for peace on Dec. 6. The message, which was looked upon as the equivalent of an American White Paper, outlined the whole course of American-Japanese relations and of step-by-step execution of the joint German-Japanese-Italian plan for world conquest.

[The issue of the war is whether a revival of barbarism is to be forced on the self-respecting peoples of the world by tyrants, President Roosevelt declared last night in his radio address on the 150th anniversary of the ratification of the Bill of Rights. Whereas Hitler's idea is that the individual has no rights whatsoever under an absolute master, the state, the President pledged that this nation will not lay down arms until "liberty is once again secure in the world we live in."]

Talked Peace After War Started

The President emphasized that Hirohito's reply to his peace appeal was delivered orally to Ambassador Joseph C. Grew in Tokyo three ,hours and forty minutes after Japanese planes and submarines had started the war by a surprise attack on Pearl Harbor.

The full text of the Emperor's reply was not made public, but he was quoted as saying, in part, after Japan had begun the war:

"Establishment of peace in the Pacific, and consequently of the world, has been the cherished desire of His Majesty, for the realization of which he has hitherto made his government to continue its earnest endeavors."

Japan's real reply, the President stressed, had been given earlier by the long-prepared attack without warning on American bases in the Pacific. "There," he said, "as the record, for all history to read in amazement, in sorrow, in horror and disgust."

After outlining the attempt by the United States to maintain friendly relations with the Japanese from the time Commodore Perry opened Japan to the outside world in 1853, and telling of continued American efforts to maintain a peace program of justice and fair-dealing in the Orient, the President stated that Japan openly entered a league of fascism against the free world under the pretext of signing the anti-Comintern Pact in 1936.

Tells of Axis Accord Against Us

He offered evidence to show that Japan, Germany and Italy arranged together to time their blows against free nations in the best manner to effect joint plans for world dominance, and mentioned how the three finally and openly concluded last year "a treaty of

Continued on Page Six

British defenders of Victoria Point (1) were reported to have withdrawn as a Japanese force pushed westward across the Kra Isthmus. An announcement of fighting in Southern Kedah (2) indicated that the Japanese had made progress in that area. "Some activities" were reported in Kelantan (3). Ipoh (4) had an air-raid alarm. Frame on inset shows the area covered by large map.

Allied Fliers Match Japan's In North Malaya Fighting

By F. TILLMAN DURDIN
Special Cable to THE NEW YORK TIMES.

SUNGEI PATANI, North Malaya, Dec. 14 (Delayed)—Against Japanese based on airdromes in Thailand that apparently had been prepared for them long before the attack on Malaya began, British, Australian and Netherland air units in this region are putting up courageous and effective opposition. One Royal Air Force source told me that the Japanese were operating from five different airfields in Southern Thailand within forty-eight hours after the war broke out.

[Japanese forces pushed into the southern part of the State of Kedah, Northern Malaya, and took Victoria Point, the tip of Southern Burma, the British announced. The Japanese, however, moved at a heavy cost in lives, it was said. The defenders were entrenched on the eastern side of the peninsula south of Kota Bharu. Penang was not raided yesterday, but Japanese bombers attacked Ipoh, tin mining center.]

The fighting lasted three days. It began last Wednesday night and at last report the Filipinos were holding the beach. The colonel in command sent word to Manila that his force would stand their ground "to the last man."

Details were brought here by a correspondent of The Philippines Herald. He quoted the colonel, whom he did not identify, as having said:

"We eagerly awaited the Japanese attempt to land. The enemy showed up Wednesday night. I counted 154 motorboats in all. We held our fire until they were near.

"Then our artillery roared into action. Most of the boats were destroyed. A few managed to escape to warships which must have been anchored far beyond the horizon. Since then the enemy has attempted to land, but each time he has been frustrated."

The correspondent reported that when the colonel promised to fight to the last man "he was merely voicing the sentiments of men of all ranks whom I interviewed."

The colonel was said to be con-

Continued on Page Six

FILIPINOS BEAT OFF 154 ENEMY BOATS

Lingayen Guns Blast Japanese for 3 Days—Invading Planes Bomb Olongapo Naval Base

By The United Press.

MANILA, Tuesday, Dec. 16—First details reached here today of an engagement at Lingayen Beach, 110 miles northwest of Manila, where a Filipino Army division, lining the shore with artillery, blasted 154 motorboat loads of invading Japanese soldiers without letting one of them reach land alive.

Tokyo Premier Claims Triumph, Then Warns of War to Be Fought

By The Associated Press.

TOKYO, Tuesday, Dec. 16 (From Japanese Broadcast) — Premier Hideki Tojo, addressing an extraordinary session of the Japanese Diet, today reiterated his assertions that Japan had declared war on the United States only after trying all means of peaceful settlement. He declared:

"Your fighting services have speedily broken through the enemy key positions within less than ten days. The bulk of the American Fleet which has been at Hawaii is destroyed; the main body of the British Far Eastern Fleet is crushed; the encircling front against Japan, the strength of which the enemy has exaggerated and given wide publicity in an attempt to intimidate Japan, is shattered at various places."

"The anti-Japanese encircling front already is on a fair way to collapse."

He nevertheless cautioned the Japanese that "a war remains waiting to be fought."

Japanese Imperial Headquarters reported that Japanese expeditionary forces had landed on British Borneo at dawn today despite a heavy gale.

The headquarters also reported that Japanese Army and Navy forces completed occupation of the island of Guam last Friday.

A joint communiqué of the army and navy sections of Imperial Headquarters warned Japanese yesterday "against the lurking danger of enemy submarines" off Japan's island coasts and urged them to

Continued on Page Seven

HEROIC ACTS CITED

2,897 Defenders Killed in Gallant Battle— Base Not 'on Alert'

FIFTH COLUMN ACTIVE

2-Man Submarine Used —Roosevelt to Name Inquiry Board

By CHARLES HURD
Special to THE NEW YORK TIMES.

WASHINGTON, Dec. 15—Japan did not administer a knockout blow or destroy the effectiveness of American naval forces in the Pacific when she attacked at Pearl Harbor, Hawaii, at dawn on Dec. 7, and thus failed to achieve her objective, Secretary of the Navy Frank Knox reported today on his return from a flight to Hawaii to investigate the attack.

High Japanese officials had asserted that the blow struck at Pearl Harbor destroyed American naval supremacy in the Pacific. Mr. Knox evidenced a different view when he said:

"The Japanese failed to knock out the United States before the war began."

Fleet Now Hunts Enemy

The Secretary said the United States Army and Navy forces in Hawaii "were not on the alert against the surprise attack" and in consequence losses had been heavy. After the action started, however, he said, our soldiers and sailors fought bravely, and he added that all remaining effective units of the Pacific Fleet "are at sea seeking contact with the enemy."

He listed the destroyed vessels as the battleship Arizona, the destroyers Cassin, Downes and Shaw, the minelayer Oglala and the target and training ship Utah. In addition, he said that the battleship Oklahoma had capsized and that an unannounced number of vessels had been damaged.

The Navy casualties in this action were given by Mr. Knox as 91 officers and 2,638 men killed and 20 officers and 636 men wounded. Late this evening the Army announced that its losses in this engagement totaled 168 officers and men, bringing the aggregate service losses to 2,897.

Attack's Objective Failed

Mr. Knox gave his report at a special press conference a few hours after his return from Honolulu. He supplemented a prepared statement with replies to questions that emphasized the fact that the Japanese, launching their attack with carrier-borne planes and submarines, eluded the naval patrols at sea, caught the Army Air Force on the ground and destroyed the great majority of planes there, and showed a detailed knowledge of objectives.

Against these adverse reports, Mr. Knox reported that the sailors and soldiers fought bravely and well after the action started, and he told reporters that the Japanese failed in their objective, which was to knock out the Pacific fleet before the war started.

Responsibility for the errors committed, he said, will be investigated immediately by a Presidential commission. He declined to anticipate the results of such an investigation. After calling on President Roosevelt this evening, Mr. Knox said the President would name the inquiry board tomorrow.

The Japanese losses for this engagement were listed by the Secretary as three submarines, including one large and one small one destroyed and a small one captured, and forty-one planes.

One reason for the success of the Japanese, he asserted, was co-operation from the Hawaiian Islands themselves.

"The most effective fifth-column work in this war was done in Hawaii, with the exception of Norway," Mr. Knox said.

He declined to elaborate on steps

Continued on Page Seven

Knox Statement on Hawaii

By The Associated Press.

WASHINGTON, Dec. 15—The text of Secretary Knox's statement detailing losses in the Japanese attack on Pearl Harbor follows:

My inspection trip to the island enables me to present the general facts covering the attack which hitherto have been unavailable.

1. The essential fact is that the Japanese purpose was to knock out the United States before the war began. This was made apparent by the preparations which had gone on for many weeks before the attack, and the attacks themselves, which were made simultaneously throughout the Pacific. In this purpose the Japanese failed.

2. The United States services were not on the alert against the surprise attack on Hawaii. This fact calls for a formal investigation, which will be initiated immediately by the President. Further action is, of course, dependent on the facts and recommendations made by this investigating board. We are all entitled to know it if (a) there was any error of judgment which contributed to the surprise, (b) if there was any dereliction of duty prior to the attack.

3. My investigation made clear that after the attack the defense by both services was conducted skillfully and bravely. The Navy lost:

(a) The battleship Arizona, which was destroyed by the explosion of, first, its boiler and then its forward magazine due to a bomb which was said to have literally passed down through the smokestack;

(b) The old target ship Utah, which has not been used as a combatant ship for many years, and which was in service as a training ship for anti-aircraft gunnery and experimental purposes;

(c) Three destroyers, the Cassin, the Downes and the Shaw;

(d) Minelayer Oglala. This was a converted merchantman, formerly a passenger ship on the Fall River Line and converted into a minelayer during the World War.

The Navy sustained damage to other vessels. This damage varies from ships which have been already repaired and are ready for sea, or which have gone to sea, to a few ships which will take from a week to several months to

Continued on Page Seven

"All the News That's Fit to Print."

The New York Times.

LATE CITY EDITION
Rain today and not much change in temperature.
Temperature Yesterday—Max., 53; Min., 35

Copyright, 1942, by The New York Times Company.

VOL. XCI..No. 30,757.   Entered as Second-Class Matter, Postoffice, New York, N. Y.   NEW YORK, FRIDAY, APRIL 10, 1942.   THREE CENTS NEW YORK CITY and Vicinity

JAPANESE CAPTURE BATAAN AND 36,000 TROOPS; SINK TWO BRITISH CRUISERS; ITALIANS LOSE ONE; INDIA REPORTED AGREEING ON NATIVE COUNCIL

SENATOR AND JONES CLASH OVER ATTACK ON WAR PLANT DEAL

Bunker Charges DPC Condones 'Unconscionable Profits' for Nevada Magnesium Plant

UNTRUE, SAYS SECRETARY

Fees Paid to 9 Contractors, He Adds, Will Be Less Than 2% of Cost of 70 Millions

Special to THE NEW YORK TIMES.

WASHINGTON, April 9—Senator Bunker, Democrat, of Nevada, today attacked the Defense Plant Corporation, an RFC subsidiary, charging that the terms of its contract with Basic Magnesium, Inc., for a plant at Las Vegas, Nev., meant "unconscionable profits."

Secretary Jones, as head of the RFC, immediately replied that the charges were misleading and untrue, and, in effect, challenged Senator Bunker to press further without benefit of Senatorial immunity.

The Secretary of Commerce replied to Senator Bunker in a statement:

"Senator Bunker's statements accusing RFC officials of wrongdoing," he said, "are unworthy of a United States Senator and cannot go unchallenged. The Senator must know these statements are untrue.

"The magnesium plant that is being built by the government near Las Vegas, Nev., will cost approximately $70,000,000 and have an estimated annual capacity of 112,000,000 pounds of metallic magnesium.

Says Fees Total Less Than 2%

"Nine separate contractors are participating in the construction. The fees to be paid the nine contracting and engineering firms, together with the fee to Basic Magnesium, Inc., for its engineering plans, supervision and 'know-how,' will aggregate less than 2 per cent of the total cost of the plant.

"The operating or management fee of the plant is to be half cent per pound of magnesium produced, which is approximately 2 per cent of the estimated cost.

"The royalty for the ores will not exceed ¼ cent per pound of magnesium metal produced.

"No irregularities have been discovered in the construction of the plant that would warrant the irresponsible statements made by Senator Bunker. The plant is wholly owned by the government and will be operated for its account. All expenditures in connection with the construction of the plant as well as its operation are carefully audited as the work progresses.

"Defense Plant Corporation contracted with Basic Magnesium, Inc., for the construction of this plant at the request of OPM and the War Department, and the government's interest is fully protected.

"Senator Bunker's speech contains many false and misleading statements, which it takes no courage to make under his cloak of immunity."

"Sinister," Bunker Contends

In his speech in the Senate the Nevada Senator said:

"Those individuals who have participated in unconscionable profits in America and who have slowed down our war production are worthy of the disgust and contempt of every American."

He contended that the data he presented was sufficient "to warrant the conclusion that the Defense Plant Corporation has entered into an agreement that is so sinister as to indicate that some officials in our government are guilty of malfeasance in the performance of their duties."

"If the agreement between the Defense Plant Corporation and Basic Magnesium, Inc., represents a cross-section of conduct on the part of the Defense Plant Corpora-

Continued on Page Eighteen

Cripps Said to Have Accord On National Regime in India

Plan Is Reported to Envisage Rule by a Council With Briton Directing Army and Native in Defense Ministry

By The United Press.

NEW DELHI, India, April 9—Great Britain and India are in general agreement on a self-government plan that will establish the first all-Indian national government in two centuries and provide for an executive council of fifteen members, all but one of them to come from the various political parties, it was learned tonight.

The plan was reported to be acceptable, with the exception of a few minor adjustments, to the two major political groups—the All-India Congress party and the Moslem League.

Under the plan a native government Minister will handle all Indian defense matters except war strategy and tactics, which a British military chief will control.

With only final details to be smoothed out, formal announcement of the settlement was predicted for late tomorrow or Saturday.

Inquiries late tonight revealed that under the agreement reached between the Congress party and Sir Stafford Cripps, British negotiator, the new national government would be directed not by a Cabinet but by the Executive Council of the Viceroy of India, the Marquess of Linlithgow.

The importance of that point in the agreement, it was said, was the fact that a Prime Minister would not be appointed and asked to form a Cabinet—the usual constitutional procedure—but that the Viceroy would appoint members to the council, after receiving the names of nominees by the various Indian parties.

Under the new government, the country will be mobilized to resist the Japanese, who are pressing closer.

It was learned that an executive

Continued on Page Six

2 Police Officials Suspended On Amen's Charges of Graft

In an unexpected move that may present a test case of far-reaching effect in the Police Department, Special Prosecutor John Harlan Amen's two extraordinary grand juries returned supplemental presentments yesterday against two high-ranking police officers who had sought retirement while under investigation in connection with alleged police protection of a $100,000,000 city-wide gambling racket.

The two, Inspector Camille C. Pierne of the Tenth Division in Brooklyn and Lieutenant Terence J. Harvey of the Brooklyn Borough headquarters squad, were named in Wednesday's presentments that bared the existence of police graft estimated at more than $1,000,000 a year, but no specific charges were lodged against them on the theory that a mere application for retirement was sufficient to preclude the prosecution of departmental charges against them.

However, Police Commissioner Valentine, after conferring behind closed doors with his aides and later in the afternoon with Mayor La Guardia, issued a statement Wednesday night asserting that he had notified Mr. Amen that inasmuch as the retirement applications of several police officers had not been acted upon by the Police Pension Fund he regarded them as members of the uniformed force and would like to be advised if the grand jury had made any charges against them so that he could be "guided accordingly."

Mr. Amen's reply yesterday was to send a letter to Commissioner Valentine asserting that it was because of his misunderstanding of Mr. Valentine's earlier advice that he had not filed charges against men

Continued on Page Thirty-eight

GASOLINE SUPPLIES CUT AGAIN BY WPB

Deliveries to East and 2 States in Northwest Will Be Reduced From 80 to 66⅔ Per Cent

Special to THE NEW YORK TIMES.

WASHINGTON, April 9—The War Production Board issued today an order further curtailing gasoline deliveries to filling stations and bulk consumers in seventeen Eastern States, the District of Columbia and Oregon and Washington.

Effective April 16, deliveries of gasoline to filling stations and bulk consumers in curtailment areas will be cut to 66 2-3 per cent of average deliveries in December, January and February, adjusted for seasonal variations. Deliveries have been reduced 20 per cent since March 19.

Secretary Ickes, Petroleum Co-ordinator, discussing the WPB order, said at his press conference:

"If this curtailment proves satisfactory, we may go to Leon Henderson and tell him we see no need for rationing."

Mr. Ickes added that the matter

Continued on Page Twenty-six

Jesse Jones Shakes Eugene Meyer; Eye-Glasses Broken in Encounter

Special to THE NEW YORK TIMES.

WASHINGTON, April 9—Jesse Jones, Secretary of Commerce, and Eugene Meyer, editor and publisher of The Washington Post, were participants in a fistic encounter at the annual dinner of the Alfalfa Club at the Hotel Willard tonight.

A sharp verbal exchange arising from resentment by the Secretary of an editorial in which his testimony before the Senate's Truman committee investigating the rubber situation was criticized preceded the encounter, club members said.

As told by eyewitnesses, Secretary Jones was approached by Mr. Meyer, a long-time critic of the banker, as Mr. Jones entered the small ballroom of the hotel. Accounts of witnesses vary as to the words which immediately preceded the encounter, but most members agreed that Secretary Jones

grasped Mr. Meyer by the coat and started to shake him. As Mr. Meyer wrenched himself free his eye-glasses fell to the floor and were smashed.

Mr. Meyer, the accounts continue, swung at the Secretary but friends, including John J. O'Connor, former New York Representative, pushed them apart. Secretary Jones left immediately after a time chatting with friends.

The men have been frequent adversaries since the Hoover Administration, when both served with the Reconstruction Finance Corporation, of which Mr. Jones was then chairman. Mr. Jones is also a publisher, owning The Houston Chronicle.

Today's editorial asserted that Mr. Jones had shielded himself behind the President, the British and the Netherlands in defending his handling of the rubber situation.

Continued on Page Six

PLANES GET SHIPS

Japanese Sink Big Naval Units in Bay of Bengal, Blast Base in Ceylon

BRITISH RAID CARRIER

Score Near-Misses, Get 4 Aircraft—2 Fleets Massing for Battle

By RAYMOND DANIELL
Wireless to THE NEW YORK TIMES.

LONDON, April 9—The Japanese have struck a heavy blow against the British Navy in the struggle for mastery of the Bay of Bengal, which is the key to the Indian Ocean, in sinking by air attack the heavy cruisers Dorsetshire and Cornwall. In return, near-misses were scored by bombers in an attack on a Japanese aircraft carrier in the Bay of Bengal.

Full enemy control of the Bay of Bengal, the eastern half of which the Japanese command already, would lay the eastern coast of India open to invasion. Renewed aerial attacks today on Trincomalee, the main British naval base on the island of Ceylon, off the south coast of India, made it more apparent than ever that the Japanese were seeking to extend their domination westward.

1,100 Are Rescued

News of the sinking of the 10,-000-ton Cornwall and 9,975-ton Dorsetshire was given in an Admiralty communiqué, which placed the encounter with the Japanese planes in the Indian Ocean. The announcement said 1,100 survivors, —including the commanders, Captain A. W. S. Agar of the Dorsetshire and Captain P. C. W. Mainwaring of the Cornwall—had been picked up. The Dorsetshire was the ship whose torpedoes administered the coup de grace to the German battleship Bismarck in the Atlantic last year.

The attack on the Japanese aircraft carrier was announced in a communiqué received tonight from Colombo, Ceylon. In the action, which followed today's attack on Trincomalee, four Japanese planes were shot down. Some of the attacking planes did not return, but their number was not disclosed. While Trincomalee was being raided a couple of Japanese planes appeared over Colombo, but dropped no bombs.

[The Colombo communiqué also revealed that in the attack on Trincomalee the Japanese damaged harbor and airdrome facilities and caused a few casualties among dockyard personnel. The Associated Press reported: Six of the Japanese planes were shot down, six others were probably destroyed and two were listed as damaged. The Japanese, who attacked with "a large force of bombers and fighters," caused no damage in the town of Trincomalee.]

Allied Cargo Ships Sunk

The loss of the Cornwall and the Dorsetshire, coupled with an official statement from New Delhi, India, that several merchantmen have been sunk in recent enemy air and naval attacks in the Bay of Bengal, represents a serious blow not only at British naval strength in the Asian area but against United Nations lines of communication.

The number of merchant vessels lost was not announced, but the total of survivors from them—between 400 and 500, who have landed on the coast of Orissa in India—indicates a considerable number. Tokyo said today that the number of ships sunk was twenty-one, with twenty-three others so severely damaged that they must be regarded as lost.

The Japanese naval force in the Bay of Bengal is operating hundreds of miles from its presumed base in the Andaman Islands. The distance from the Andamans to Ceylon is more than 1,000 miles. Before the occupation of

Continued on Page Six

IN THE FOX HOLES OF BATAAN

U. S. Troops in action on the Philippine peninsula, the fall of which was announced yesterday.
Associated Press Wirephoto (U. S. Army Signal Corps)

ITALIAN CRUISER SUNK BY BRITISH

10,000-Ton Vessel Destroyed by Subm——Foes Spar in Libyan Fighting

By ROBERT P. POST
Wireless to THE NEW YORK TIMES.

LONDON, April 9—A 10,000-ton eight-inch-gun Italian cruiser has been sunk in the Central Mediterranean by torpedoes from a British submarine, the Admiralty announced today.

The cruiser, which may have been convoying reinforcements for Marshal Erwin Rommel in Libya, was accompanied by destroyers and aircraft when Lieut. Comdr. E. P. Tomkinson, who received the Distinguished Service Order with bar in December for his work on submarine patrol, ordered the attack. Eight minutes after his torpedoes struck home, the commander risked attack by the cruiser's escort to show his periscope. The cruiser was heard to break up and sink while the destroyers picked up survivors.

Lieut. Commander Tomkinson's earlier exploits were carried out with the Urge, one of the smallest British submarines. Last April he sank a heavily laden oil tanker of more than 10,000 tons. For this he

Continued on Page Eight

Sacred Saffron of Priests Aids Foe's Burma Advance

By HARRISON FORMAN
Wireless to THE NEW YORK TIMES.

CHUNGKING, China, April 9—Clad in the sacred saffron robes of the Poongee—literally meaning "great glory"—the fifth column in Burma is taking advantage of the historic sanctuary provided by Burmese Buddhism. In the past the Poongees have included, besides the genuinely devout, many thieves, bandits and general malcontents, and they have always been a major problem for British administration.

Unlike most other priesthoods, the Poongees require no special training or following here. Any man may in practice become a Poongee for any period desired, days or years, by the simple procedure of shaving his head, donning a saffron robe, formally renouncing all things worldly before a temple and thereafter living solely by begging, which is not permitted for more than daily needs.

In practical example, a business man may welch on a contract or a debt by simply becoming a Poongee, and he thereby is cleansed of all worldly obligations and responsibilities. The Poongees are arrogant and sacrosanct in so far as the police are concerned. The Poongees are publicly regarded as holy men who can do no wrong, and the British military confess they are practically helpless in the face of such fanaticism.

An eyewitness on the Burma front reports that at a certain supposedly secret airport there ap-

Continued on Page Five

AMERICANS BAG TEN IN BURMA AIR FIGHT

A. V. G. Routs Twenty of Foe Without One Loss—Lull in Land Fighting Continues

By The United Press.

CHUNGKING, China, April 9—Reinforced American Volunteer Group fliers have roared back into the Battle of Burma, destroying ten planes and damaging two others in a mass dogfight with twenty Japanese Zero fighters in which one American plane was lost but its pilot saved, an A. V. G. communiqué announced tonight.

The battle was fought over the Burmese town of Loi-Win, the communiqué said. [An Associated Press dispatch from Chungking, based on the same official source, said the encounter took place south of China's Yunnan Province. Neither Loi-Win nor Leiyun appears on available maps.]

Continued on Page Two

War News Summarized

FRIDAY, APRIL 10, 1942

Rocky Bataan Peninsula, the finger of land that still defied the Japanese after they had conquered most of the Southwest Pacific, finally succumbed yesterday. Its 36,853 remaining American and Filipino defenders—drained by hunger, exhaustion and disease—could no longer rally to beat off an enveloping movement that broke their lines on the east flank. For three months they had fought against ever-growing odds. Although Corregidor Island and the other forts in Manila Bay stayed in American hands, it was questionable how long they could hold out. [1-8; map, P. 2.]

The naval defeat in the Indian Ocean was offset somewhat by the sinking of a 10,000-ton Italian cruiser by a British submarine in the Mediterranean. In Libya, the British were jockeying for position against strong Axis forces, whose movements no longer seemed to indicate a large-scale offensive. [1:5.]

Germany flung large units of tanks and planes into the Russian front to feel out the Red Army's strength in virtually every sector. Moscow reports said, but the reinforced Soviet forces broke up their attacks and clung to the initiative. [1:1, with map.]

In occupied Europe, the embittered Norwegian people observed the second anniversary of the German invasion with a "strike" of silence and German troops marched in the streets. [9:1.]

Allied aerial successes were reported from Burma and Australia. Reinforced American volunteer pilots in the Burma theatre shot down ten enemy fight-

ers and damaged two others without a loss of their own. [1:7.] United Nations bombers blasted planes and military targets in a surprise raid on Rabaul, New Britain. [3:1.]

With the threat to India growing daily, the drawn-out negotiations in New Delhi appeared nearing a successful compromise—the establishment of an Indian national government in which the defense minister would share responsibility with General Wavell. [1:2-3.]

DEFENSE CRUSHED

Stimson Reveals Defeat Followed Failure to Get in More Food

CORREGIDOR IS HELD

Wainwright on the Isle Free to Set Course, Roosevelt Tells Him

TOKYO, Friday, April 10 (From Japanese broadcasts recorded in New York)—The Domei news agency said today that "60,000 Filipino and American troops resisting the Japanese on Bataan Peninsula have begged for a halt in hostilities after six days of fierce Japanese assault."

"Details of the conditions of surrender are not yet disclosed," said the Domei dispatch, "nor is it known yet whether the Japanese forces have decided to accept the terms."

Corregidor was raided twice yesterday by Japanese bombers and tons of explosives were unleashed on military installations, Domei reported.

By CHARLES HURD
Special to THE NEW YORK TIMES.

WASHINGTON, April 9—An overwhelming Japanese Army, aided by the allies of hunger, fatigue and disease, today crushed the small mixed force that had held Bataan Peninsula since December.

Japanese forces, heretofore estimated at 200,000 men, including fresh assault troops, and supported by tanks, artillery, bombers and attack planes in profusion, enveloped an exhausted defending army of 36,853 men, as counted officially yesterday afternoon.

The defeat of the American and Filipino forces was officially announced as a "probability" in a War Department communiqué issued as of 5:15 A. M. today. A few hours later Secretary of War Henry L. Stimson announced the defeat at his regularly scheduled weekly press conference. He already had carried the word to President Roosevelt.

Reveals Supplies Were Sent In

When Secretary Stimson met reporters in his conference room he paid the highest praise to the spirit of the defenders in a fight recognized as hopeless from the beginning and pledged that the Philippines would be reconquered. In the same talk he described the extraordinary efforts made to provision the garrison, saying that "several shiploads of supplies" were sent into the Philippines, "but for every ship that arrived safely we lost nearly two."

As far as was known here today the rocky fortress of Corregidor Island still held its own astride the entrance to Manila Bay and other troops held adjacent fortified islands. The decision as to whether they should continue fighting was laid squarely on Lieut. Gen. Jonathan M. Wainwright, to whom President Roosevelt yesterday sent a message giving him absolute authority to continue the fight or make terms, as he might see fit.

Army Records Position

This responsibility is a heavy one for General Wainwright, for it is assumed here that he lacks transport to take more than a handful of the Bataan forces across the two miles of water that separates Bataan Peninsula from Corregidor. Even so his food is desperately short, Secretary Stimson having said this morning that every man in Bataan had been on short rations since Jan. 11. This was a primary reason for the collapse of the defense after five days of savage hand-to-hand fighting.

The long-expected defeat, which by its deferment wrote an epic in American military history, was officially indicated in a War Depart-

Continued on Page Two

The New York Times.

"All the News That's Fit to Print."

LATE CITY EDITION
Mild today.
Temperature Yesterday—Max. 74; Min., 52

Copyright, 1942, by The New York Times Company.

VOL. XCI. No. 30,783.

Entered as Second-Class Matter,
Postoffice, New York, N. Y.

NEW YORK, WEDNESDAY, MAY 6, 1942.

THREE CENTS NEW YORK CITY
and Vicinity

CORREGIDOR SURRENDERS UNDER LAND ATTACK AFTER WITHSTANDING 300 RAIDS FROM THE AIR; BRITISH HIT MADAGASCAR BASE; VICHY RESISTS

CHARGE ACCOUNTS ARE DUE IN 40 DAYS AS INFLATION CURB

Reserve Board's Regulation, in Effect Today, Is First Check on Such Retail Customers

Bringing retail charge accounts under control for the first time and ruling that installment purchases must be liquidated in twelve months the Federal Reserve Board promulgated yesterday amendment No. 4 to its consumer credit regulation W, carrying into effect the seventh point in President Roosevelt's anti-inflation program.

Under the amendment, which is effective today, charge account customers of retail stores will be required to speed up their payments to complete them within forty days after the end of the month in which purchase is made. If this is not done the account will be transferred to an installment basis requiring liquidation within six months and no further charge account purchases will be permissible until the items are in default are paid for.

The amendment also tightened substantially the earlier restrictions on installment sales and broadened the scope of the merchandise covered to forty-six listed classifications, including almost every item used in the American home, and clothing and jewelry as well. The down payment was generally raised to 33 1/3 per cent and the payment period to twelve months.

Explains Aim of Rules

Allan Sproul, president of the Federal Reserve Bank of New York, in announcing the amendment here, said:

"As amended, the regulation is extended to cover a comprehensive list of durable and semi-durable goods for civilian consumption and contemplates that the volume of outstanding consumer credit, already substantially diminished, will be further contracted in keeping with the government's purpose to prevent the rapid bidding up of prices.

"The purpose of this revision is to help make effective the last point in the seven-point program which the President set forth in his special message to Congress of April 27, 1942, as follows: 'To keep the cost of living from spiraling upward, we must discourage credit and installment buying, and encourage the paying off of debts, mortgages and other obligations; for this promotes savings, retards excessive buying and adds to the amount available to the creditors for the purchase of war bonds.'"

With respect to charge accounts, the regulation, in effect and depending upon the date of the purchase, provides for a forty to a seventy day payment period, similar to that in effect in Canada. The average period for payment of

Continued on Page Fourteen

Mrs. Rosenberg in 2 Federal Jobs While Making $22,500 on the Side

By LOUIS STARK
Special to The New York Times.

WASHINGTON, May 5 — Some members of the House Appropriations Committee asserted today that they were determined to write into all future supply bills a provision prohibiting Federal administrative employment outside the government. This came following the disclosure at a closed meeting of an appropriations subcommittee today that Mrs. Anna M. Rosenberg of New York, regional director of the Social Security Board, receives a large income from private industry and also draws pay from another agency.

Mrs. Rosenberg's Social Security Board post pays $7,500 on a full time basis. Besides this Federal position she revealed to the subcommittee that she received $20,000 a year for part time work as public and labor relations consultant to the Macy-Bamberger

Nazis' War Industry Spurs Plane Output

By Telephone to The New York Times.

BERNE, Switzerland, May 5 — German war industry has been ordered to devote all its attention henceforth to turning out airplanes, even to the detriment of tanks and other matériel. This news from Berlin tonight confirms indications reaching foreign circles here that mastery of the air is the paramount consideration for the moment.

Figures declared to be trustworthy indicate that the peak of plane production in the Reich was reached in June, 1941, when 3,300 were turned out. Now it has fallen to between 2,700 and 2,800. Italy's contribution does not exceed 700 machines a month.

It is understood the Germans' estimate of their opponents' production is: United States, 3,300 planes a month; Britain, 2,400; Russia, 2,600 to 2,900. But the Nazis can draw upon considerable reserves.

WPB CUTS GASOLINE 50 PER CENT IN EAST

Non-Essential Users May Be Down to 5 Gallons a Week After May 16 Order

By The Associated Press.

WASHINGTON, May 5 — Gasoline consumption in the East will be slashed 50 per cent below normal starting May 16, the War Production Board said tonight. This means that many of the area's 10,000,000 motorists probably will have to get along with as little as five or six gallons a week.

The reduction will become effective the day the seaboard area begins using ration coupons.

[In New York motorists will register for gasoline rationing next Tuesday, Wednesday and Thursday. Rationing will begin on May 15.]

While the actual curtailment will be one-half, informed sources explained that it would amount to about 60 per cent cut for nonessential users of automobiles, since necessary vehicles will continue to receive their full requirements of fuel.

Action Recommended by Ickes

The WPB action, taken on recommendation of Harold L. Ickes, petroleum coordinator, came shortly after Joseph B. Eastman, defense transportation director, declared "every owner of a motor vehicle in public or private service should realize that he holds this vehicle in trust for the national war effort and that it should be used only for purposes of necessity."

This statement of Mr. Eastman's applied to the whole country, not merely to the East.

Simultaneously with the gasoline order, WPB directed that the

Continued on Page Thirteen

BRONX GRAND JURY CLEARS EVERYONE IN THE FLYNN CASE

County is 'Singularly Free of Fraud and Corruption,' Presentment Says

The Bronx County grand jury that has been hearing evidence on the paving of a courtyard at the Lake Mahopac estate of Edward J. Flynn, chairman of the Democratic National Committee, handed up a seventeen-page presentment yesterday, finding that Bronx County is "singularly free of fraud and corruption," but that many irregularities are prevalent.

The grand jury declared that after hearing all the evidence submitted, it did not find that the facts warranted the indictment of any one.

Work on Flynn Estate Reviewed

In discussing the work done on the Flynn estate on Nov. 14, 15, 17 and 18 of last year, the presentment said city employes had been transported to the estate from the city by city-owned station wagons and that the work had consisted of laying 8,000 second-hand granite blocks.

The city employes, the presentment said, were paid in full for their services; 8,000 blocks were returned to the city and the gasoline and oil issued to the city station wagons for the Mahopac trip were returned in full. The cost of trucking the blocks by private concerns was paid by Mr. Flynn. The courtyard was only part of a general alteration on the estate, with the total job to cost more than $30,000.

The evidence adduced, it continued, showed that Mr. Flynn had never expressed any desire that the work be done under city auspices or by city employes and without expense to him, but that the job would be done by a private contractor and paid for by Mr. Flynn; that the work done by city employes was under the supervision of Robert J. Moran, Bronx Commissioner of Public Works.

Paul J. Kern, deposed president of the Civil Service Commission, who conducted an investigation in the paving job while still in office, was severely rebuked by the grand jury for hampering the investigation conducted by William B. Herlands, Commissioner of Investigation.

No Conspiracy Found

"In respect to the second phase of the investigation," the presentment said, "the alleged conspiracy between Mayor La Guardia, Mr. Flynn and Commissioner Herlands to suppress the Kern investigation, the charge was entirely without foundation and we feel that it never would have been made but for the fact that Mr. Kern is greatly influenced by what he terms 'his intuition.'"

Mr. Kern had charged that Mayor La Guardia was trying to suppress his investigation in Mr. Flynn's behalf, and that in return Mr. Flynn was to obtain for the Mayor the Democratic nomination for United States Senator.

The grand jurors found that the records of the Department of Highways and Sewers under Commissioner Moran were in a "deplorable condition." They said they believed Borough President James J. Lyons when he testified that he was ignorant of the Mahopac paving job, and "we strongly condemn Commissioner Moran, who said Mr. Lyons's appointee and the Borough President could not avoid responsibility for the manner in which any subordinate conducted a department."

In its presentment the grand jury said:

"The subject matter of our investigation resolved itself, naturally, into three phases; 1, the Mahopac

Continued on Page Twenty-eight

Direct Hit on Tirpitz By British Reported

By Telephone to The New York Times.

STOCKHOLM, Sweden, May 5 — British Royal Air Force bombs scored a direct hit on the battleship Tirpitz when she was in Kiel harbor prior to her transfer to her present anchorage at Trondheim, Norway, according to an eyewitness account by a Swedish seaman published in Ny Dag. The observer also reported a great change of morale among German civilians.

"Although the British attacks on Kiel were usually made from a great height, sometimes from 20,000 feet," he is quoted as saying, "the bombs hit their targets with astonishing precision. Thus in every bombing the biggest wharf in Kiel was regularly set ablaze, and on one occasion a British bomber scored a direct hit on the Tirpitz."

FOE ENTERS CHINA ACROSS BURMA LINE

Advance Units Over Border While Main Columns Wait— Planes Aid British Retreat

By DAVID ANDERSON
Wireless to The New York Times.

LONDON, May 5 — The Japanese have entered Yunnan Province in China via the Burma Road, it was announced today. Their vanguards reached the suburbs of Wangting, which is on a small river dividing Burma and China, and Chungking said the Japanese were being engaged by Chinese troops in the hills. The main enemy column was waiting within Burma at Chukok, near by.

The invading force must have made a detour around the Chinese fighting at Kutkai because the battle there was reported still going on. Other Chinese units were believed holding out north of Mandalay on the banks of the Irrawaddy River. British soldiers were continuing their slow retreat west of Mandalay.

"At times their [the Japanese]

Continued on Page Four

BRITISH ADVANCING

Landing Force Reported Within Four Miles of Madagascar Base

'CHUTISTS ARE USED

Warships and Aircraft Make Frontal Assault to Help Troops

By RAYMOND DANIELL
Wireless to The New York Times.

LONDON, May 5 — Small units of British Commandos and regular troops won a bridgehead at Courier Bay in the action against Madagascar and were reported tonight to be fighting their way across a ten-mile-wide isthmus toward the important naval base of Diego Suarez.

[A London dispatch of The Associated Press quoted Vichy reports that waves of British parachutists had been landed at the outset of a double attack in which warships and squadrons of aircraft made a frontal thrust from the sea timed to coincide with the overland assault on the rear of the base by British light armored units landed at Courier Bay.

[The Associated Press said that, according to advices released by Vichy sources, the British occupying forces had reached Andrakaka, four miles from Diego Suarez. The French estimated that the attacking forces numbered 20,000 and the French and native defenders about 7,000.]

There were only sketchy accounts of the battle for the big French island, which lies athwart vital United Nations supply routes. However, a joint Admiralty-War Office communiqué issued this afternoon clearly indicated that opposition 'had been offered by the Vichy French garrison. The capture of a defending battery was reported.

A communiqué issued late to

Continued on Page Two

Laval Protests 'Aggression' But Won't Seek U. S. Break

By LANSING WARREN
By Telephone to The New York Times.

VICHY, France, May 5 — Replying to the American note expressing approbation of the British occupation of Madagascar, Pierre Laval as Chief of the French Government and Foreign Minister, tonight protested the move as an aggression. He rejected as inadmissible the "pretension of the Government of the United States to forbid France to defend her territory when attacked," and declared that he leaves "to President Roosevelt the share of responsibility that may fall to him in consequence of this aggression."

[In Washington, Secretary Hull made it clear that there would be no deviation from the approval of the British action at Madagascar. After a White House session, Pacific War Council members praised the move.]

M. Laval, in handing his note to the American Chargé d'Affaires, S. Pinckney Tuck, recalled the long record of friendship between France and the United States and added:

"You were present at my recent interview with your Ambassador, Admiral Leahy, and I wish again to repeat to you what I said to him, that no definitive gesture leading to a break will be initiated by France."

Indicates Grave Situation

M. Laval read his reply to the assembled French and foreign press in a salon of the Hotel du Parc, and completed it with comments that indicated the full seriousness for French-American relations because the United States for the first time was directly involved in diplomatic controversy with France.

Following is the text of the note as read to the correspondents by M. Laval:

In replying to the note handed in today by the Chargé d'Affaires of the United States of America, the French Government raises the most energetic protest against the aggression of which Madagascar has just been the object on the part of British forces.

It notes the assurance given that Madagascar will be returned to France some day.

It rejects as inadmissible the pretension of the Government of the United States to forbid France to defend her territory when attacked.

The French Government is the sole judge of the obligations imposed by its honor. In that manner, the defenders of Madagascar are understood correctly their duties. They have not hesitated, despite their numerical inferiority, to carry out their duties according to the most noble tradition of the French Army.

England ever since the Armistice has manifested hostility to France and the aggression

Continued on Page Two

RED ARMY ATTACKS KEY GERMAN BASES

Timoshenko Smashes at Kursk, Kharkov and Taganrog to Forestall Nazi Drive

By The Associated Press.

MOSCOW, May 5 — Stealing the jump on Reichsfuehrer Hitler, hundreds of thousands of Russian soldiers, tanks and planes smashed head-on today at three key German bases from which it was believed the Nazi leader was planning his Spring or Summer drive.

Under command of Marshal Semyon Timoshenko, the first Russian general to turn back the German military machine with the recapture of Rostov last November, the Red Army struck at Kharkov, Kursk and Taganrog in the strongest Nazi-held section of the long battle line.

Action was also stepped-up in the northern sectors, particularly the hard-fought Kalinin area northwest of Moscow. The army newspaper Red Star said the Germans were

Continued on Page Ten

OTHER FORTS FALL

American Soldiers Had Held Out in Spite of Supply Shortage

COURAGE IS PRAISED

Roosevelt Views Their Example as Guarantee of Final Victory

By The Associated Press.

AT UNITED NATIONS HEADQUARTERS, Australia, Wednesday, May 6 — The American fortress of Corregidor and the other fortified islands in the entrance to Manila Bay surrendered today, it was officially announced here.

Besides the rock that is Corregidor, the United States forts that had held out were Fort Hughes, Fort Drum and Fort Frank.

The end came in the second day of the final Japanese assault, launched at midnight Tuesday, Manila time, with landings from Bataan Peninsula after Corregidor had been pounded again and again by Japanese big guns and aerial bombs. Corregidor alone had had 300 air raids since Dec. 29, when thirty-five Japanese bombers attacked for three hours.

A spokesman for General Douglas MacArthur, who led the brilliant defense of Bataan and the forts at the mouth of Manila Bay until ordered to Australia, made this announcement:

"General Wainwright has surrendered Corregidor and the other fortified islands in Manila Harbor."

There were believed to be about 7,000 men and women altogether on Corregidor and the other fortified islands. Besides the original garrisons, there was a naval detachment consisting originally of some 3,500 Marines and bluejackets who were removed to Corregidor when fighting ceased April 9 on Bataan Peninsula. A group of Army nurses also reached Corregidor.

Troops Half-Starved

WASHINGTON, May 5 — The fortified island of Corregidor in Manila Bay, last bastion of the American defenders of the Philippine Island, Luzon, was fighting a landing attack by Japanese troops today.

The issue of the fighting was not known in Washington at 8 P. M., when the War Department issued a communiqué, but two factors indicated grave concern over the outcome of a contest in which the defenders were outnumbered.

Continued on Page Five

War News Summarized

WEDNESDAY, MAY 6, 1942

Corregidor, the island fortress at the entrance to Manila Bay, was surrendered to the Japanese after a furious assault. The British were engaged in breaking French resistance to their landing in Madagascar. Japanese forces reached and crossed the Burma-China frontier. Other war fronts were largely unchanged.

The surrender of Corregidor and other island bases was announced by United Nations Headquarters in Australia, following an earlier Washington communiqué stating that the Japanese had started landing operations. The defenders were reported to be short of both food and ammunition. [1:8.]

British landing forces on Madagascar were reported to be within four miles of the Diego Suarez naval base at the northern extremity of the island. The French garrison was resisting, and Vichy reported that some 20,000 British had landed or were preparing to land. London said the Commandos had encountered little resistance. [1:5; map, P. 2.]

The Vichy regime ordered the garrison at Madagascar to resist. Pierre Laval in a note to the United States Government rejected Washington's warning against French belligerent action, but he insisted his government would not be the first to take measures to break relations with the United States. Admiral Darlan, chief of the Vichy military forces, expressed extreme bitterness toward Britain. [1:6-7.]

Secretary of State Hull indicated clearly at his press conference that the United States would adhere to a policy of full support of British occupation of Madagascar. [5:1.]

Meanwhile, Japanese forces

in Burma had reached the Chinese frontier in the Burma Road sector and had penetrated a slight distance into China. A battle was raging on the frontier, and the Japanese. had been halted, according to Chungking. United States bombers from India attacked successfully Mingaladon airport north of Rangoon. The Japanese said their planes had set on fire the Chinese city of Yungchang, 120 miles inside China in Yunnan Province. [1:4; map, P. 4.]

Chungking said that Chinese guerrillas in Eastern China had raided fifteen Japanese-occupied cities during the past two weeks and destroyed power plants and communications. [6:3, with map.]

The United Nations Australian Headquarters announced successful air attacks on Lae, New Guinea, and Rabaul, New Britain. A Japanese air attack on Port Moresby was repulsed. [4:4.]

On the other side of the world, London announced Royal Air Force attacks on the Skoda munitions plant in Czechoslovakia and factories at Stuttgart in Southwestern Germany. The Germans raided points on the British south coast. [10:2.]

The story was heard in London that a group of German generals had informed Adolf Hitler that if the campaign in Russia this year should fail, they would seek to abolish the National Socialist system. [8:4-5.]

Moscow reported an offensive in the south against German-held Kharkov, Kursk and Taganrog. [1:7.]

Washington disclosed the sinking of three more merchant vessels off the United States east coast. [5:1.]

G. M. Defies WLB on Double Pay; Hearing Will Take Up Issue Today

Special to The New York Times.

DETROIT, Mich., May 5 — On the eve of the start of negotiations before a panel of the National War Labor Board between the General Motors Corporation and the United Automobile Workers, C. I. O., C. E. Wilson, president of the corporation, revealed today that it had defied the board on the issue of double-time pay for Sunday and holiday work.

The disclosure came in the release by Mr. Wilson of the texts of exchanges of correspondence among the corporation, the board and the union. The correspondence dated from April 27. It included a copy of the order by the board to Mr. Wilson May 1 that double-time pay for Sunday work be continued by the company to May 15.

In reply to the order, the release by Mr. Wilson showed, H. W. Anderson, vice president of General Motors, sent the board on May

Continued on Page Fourteen

110

"All the News That's Fit to Print."

The New York Times.

LATE CITY EDITION
Little change in temperature today.
Temperature Yesterday—Max., 85; Min., 69

Copyright, 1942, by The New York Times Company.

VOL. XCI..No. 30,830.

Entered as Second-Class Matter,
Postoffice, New York, N. Y.

NEW YORK, MONDAY, JUNE 22, 1942.

THREE CENTS NEW YORK CITY
and Vicinity

TOBRUK FALLS, AXIS CLAIMS 25,000 PRISONERS; GERMANS DRIVE WEDGE INTO SEVASTOPOL LINES; JAPANESE ASHORE ON KISKA IN THE ALEUTIANS

'GAS' DROUGHT CUTS HOLIDAY PLEASURE AS CITY SWELTERS

New Yorkers Stay at Home or Drive Only to Suburbs— Many Avoid Main Roads

CROWDS AT SOME RESORTS

Others Are Hard Hit as Travel Is Spotty—Humidity Soars and Mercury Reaches 84°

New Yorkers, afflicted with the first sweltering Sunday of the season under the gasoline shortage, stayed at home yesterday, sitting on the sidewalks or in penthouse or roof gardens, or went to near-by parks and beaches. Pleasure driving was only half of normal, by and large, and the resorts, particularly the distant ones, bore the brunt of the decline. Relatives and friends in the suburbs apparently had many visitors.

The heat was not record-breaking. Temperatures rose from a low of 69 degrees at 8:45 A. M. to a high of 84 degrees at 5:30 P. M. The humidity, however, remained at 75 per cent, which the Weather Bureau said was extremely high for such high temperatures. In the morning two-tenths of an inch of rain fell and skies were overcast long after, accounting for many of the stay-at-homes in the city.

Brooklyn's first heat prostration of the season was reported last night, when John Chambers, 45 years old, of 244 West 23d Avenue, Coney Island, collapsed as he was walking in Flatbush Avenue near East Twenty-sixth Street, Brooklyn. He was removed to Coney Island Hospital, where his condition was described as fair.

Motoring Is Spotty

The drop in pleasure driving, although marked as far as resorts were concerned, and severe if parkway use was an accurate indication, did not fully reflect the gasoline supply situation. With many stations dry, traffic on the George Washington Bridge was reported normal for a Sunday, through the Holland Tunnel a third off, and over other bridge and tunnel exits the reduction was not significant.

Yet on the Westchester parkways motor traffic was 30 per cent of normal and on the Long Island parkways about 60 per cent of normal. Police traffic experts believed that this reflected the spotty character of the gasoline shortage, which was acute in Westchester and near-by Long Island and some sections of New Jersey, but not serious in others.

Those who had gasoline in their tanks apparently went pleasure driving in spite of the appeals to save gasoline, but avoided the parkways and resorts, where they would be conspicuous. Many, the traffic experts thought, must have gone to visit friends and relatives.

Continued on Page Nine

If in Doubt, Put It Out

Carelessness remains the greatest enemy of the Army's dimout regulations, it was said yesterday by civilian lighting experts who have been working with the Army on ways of cutting down the nightly illumination over the city that is used by enemy submarines in spotting shipping off our coast.

Windows and doors thoughtlessly opened for relief from the heat continue to loose light rays that help build up the sky glow over the metropolitan area, these experts said. They urged that whenever a window or door is opened for this purpose, it should be properly shaded or screened to prevent direct rays of light from emerging. These and other precautions should be placed in effect by one hour after sundown, which is at 8:31 P. M. tonight.

Meanwhile, the Army adjures all citizens: "If in doubt, put it out."

Peter of Yugoslavia Reaches Washington

Special to THE NEW YORK TIMES.

WASHINGTON, June 21—King Peter of Yugoslavia arrived here by airplane today. He was accompanied by M. Nincitch, the Yugoslav Foreign Minister.

They will discuss with President Roosevelt and other officials their country's continued opposition to the Axis. One of their objectives, it is understood, will be to obtain lease-lend aid for the guerrilla forces resisting the Nazis in Yugoslavia.

The King and his entourage will spend tonight at Blair House and will leave tomorrow to spend a few days in the country. He is traveling incognito until Wednesday, when he will return to Washington to begin the official program of his visit to the United States.

DIMOUT 'FAILURE' IS LAID TO MAYOR

Defense Council Members Say He Has Not Ordered Police to Enforce Army Rules

Charges that Mayor La Guardia has failed to give the Police Department orders to enforce the Army's dimout regulations, but has endeavored unsuccessfully to get the Army to modify its specifications, were advanced yesterday by two members of the executive board of the Lower West Side Defense Council, acting as a special committee in behalf of the council. Howard Mulligan, a lawyer, of 103 Waverly Place, and J. B. C. Woods of 38 Perry Street, made public copies of a letter they had sent to the Mayor charging that conditions in their area were "deplorable." Mr. Mulligan explained that he and Mr. Woods had been authorized to take this action at a meeting at the council's headquarters, 27 Barrow Street, last Tuesday evening.

"Nightly, men are dying and ships are being sunk by the enemy off our coast because you, sir, prefer not to carry out the Army's orders," the letter charged.

In his weekly radio broadcast on June 7 Mayor La Guardia an—

Continued on Page Thirteen

RED ARMY RETIRES

Paris Radio Says Nazi Troops Have Reached Town of Sevastopol

AXIS LOSSES SEVERE

Placed at 7 Divisions— Germans Repelled on Kharkov Front

By RALPH PARKER
Wireless to THE NEW YORK TIMES.

MOSCOW, Monday, June 22—The Russian High Command acknowledges in its communiqué this morning that the Germans have succeeded, at a high cost in lives lost, in driving a wedge into the defenses of Sevastopol. But the bulletin also reports the repulse of numerous German assaults on the Sevastopol front.

[The German-controlled Paris radio said that German troops had reached the town of Sevastopol after breaking through the Russian inner defense lines, The United Press reported from London. German sappers smashed their way through the final defense line outside the town with flame throwers, the Paris broadcast claimed.]

[The Germans reported the Red Army forces on the Kharkov front, where fighting on any considerable scale appears to be confined to one narrow sector, are said to have achieved an important success. After two enemy regiments had crossed a river barrier and advanced on the eastern bank, the Russians struck back, driving the Germans into and across the river. The Russians themselves then crossed the river and captured points on the western bank.]

Press reports yesterday indicated that the Germans were continuing to pour troops into the Sevastopol fighting and that the situation there was grave. These reports said that waves of German and Rumanian infantry, attacking Russian lines in the southern sector of the Crimean base defenses while planes dive-bombed Soviet artillery positions, had

Continued on Page Five

NEW LANDING MADE

Japanese Cruiser Is Hit in Army Air Blow at Kiska's Harbor

TRANSPORT IS SUNK

U. S. Fliers See Enemy's Temporary Buildings on Aleutian Isle

By C. BROOKS PETERS
Special to THE NEW YORK TIMES.

WASHINGTON, June 21—The Japanese forces that have been operating in the western Aleutian Islands since June 3 have succeeded in occupying Kiska, 650 miles west of Dutch Harbor, strategic American operations base, the Navy Department announced today.

Enemy occupation of Attu, westernmost island of the American chain and some 275 miles northwest of Kiska, was acknowledged in a Navy announcement on June 12.

Flying conditions in the Aleutian region—in which "foul weather and fog" are the general rule, the Navy reported recently—were sufficiently satisfactory in the last few days to permit "some restricted air operations against Kiska," today's Navy communiqué asserted.

Long-range Army aircraft attacked a small force of Japanese ships in Kiska's harbor and reported hits on a cruiser, the Navy announced. An enemy transport was sunk.

Tents of Japanese Seen

The American planes that finally were able to penetrate to the remote island of Kiska, where until the Japanese occupation the United States Navy maintained a weather station, observed that the enemy had set up tents and "minor temporary structures on land."

The communiqué added that operations in that area continued to be restricted "by considerations of weather and great distances."

Last Monday the Navy Department reported that Army and Navy planes were continuing air assaults "against the Japanese forces which recently were reported to have landed on western islands of the Aleutian group." At that time the Navy asserted that at least three Japanese cruisers, one destroyer, one gunboat and one transport had been damaged, "some of them severely," by air attacks.

Since the announcement on June 12 of the occupation of Attu naval circles in Washington have minimized the seriousness of Japanese landings in the western Aleutians, characterizing them as having been inspired primarily by a desire "to save face" after the defeat administered by American Army and Navy forces in the Coral Sea and off Midway Island.

Supply Problem Difficult

Military experts here have stated that supply would be a major problem for any enemy forces that endeavored to establish themselves in the Aleutians. The distance from bases in Japanese territory to the Aleutian Islands is so great, these circles have contended, that aerial transport is not feasible, particularly in view of the uncertain weather conditions. Therefore, supplies must be transported by surface craft, which are constantly exposed to attack by American submarines.

There is, however, a possibility that in the Rat Island group, of which Kiska is one island, the Japanese could conceal submarine mother ships and perhaps even small aircraft carriers, the experts here said. Submarines from such bases might prove effective should Japan attack Russia, they added.

But for the most part, according to the opinion conveyed to reporters in Washington by military circles, the enemy will have to be

Continued on Page Four

ROMMEL'S FORCES TAKE IMPORTANT PORT IN LIBYA

Tobruk (1) has been overwhelmed and captured with its garrison by the Axis, which also claimed the capture of Bir el-Gobi (2) and the minor port of Bardia (3). There were indications that the Germans were working their way from Bardia southward to Capuzzo for an assault across the border into Egypt. Here they will find defenses between Solum and Sidi Omar (4).

Vancouver Island Shelled; Northwest Coast Dims Out

By P. J. PHILIP
Special to THE NEW YORK TIMES.

OTTAWA, June 21—Estevan Point on Vancouver Island was shelled by an enemy submarine at 10:35 o'clock, Pacific time, last night (1:35 A. M., Sunday, Eastern war time), Colonel J. L. Ralston, the Defense Minister, announced here today. The submarine was presumed to be Japanese.

The enemy's objective was the government wireless and telegraph station there. No damage was done, said a report from Lieut. Gen. Kenneth Stuart, Canadian Chief of Staff and acting Commander in Chief of the West Corps defenses.

[Coastal dimouts in the State of Washington and Oregon were put into effect last night, following the shelling of Estevan Point, which is about 125 miles north of the United States border.]

There is an airfield near Estevan Point, but no report has come through as to whether action was taken against the attacking submarine.

The attack was the first against Canadian soil in the history of Canada as a Dominion. Last month two ships were torpedoed and sunk in the Gulf of St. Lawrence.

The Defense Minister's announcement said:

"The Commander in Chief, West Coast defenses, reported that the Dominion Government telegraph station at Estevan Point, Vancouver Island, was shelled by a submarine at 10:35 P. M. (Pacific time) on Saturday night. No damage resulted."

Estevan Point lies halfway along the western shore of Vancouver Island, about 150 miles northwest of Victoria. Its only importance seems to be the estab—

Continued on Page Four

R. A. F. PAYS EMDEN 2D VISIT IN 2 NIGHTS

Also Hammers Other Targets in Northwest Reich—Hits Ship Off Dutch Coast

By JAMES MacDONALD
Wireless to THE NEW YORK TIMES.

LONDON, June 21—A large number of British bombers hammered Emden, Germany, last night for the second night in succession and also other objectives in Northwest Germany and air bases in the Netherlands.

At the same time American-built Hudson planes of the Coastal Command, ever on the lookout for enemy shipping, searched waters off the Netherland coast, where a Canadian flying crew dropped two bombs on a medium-sized cargo vessel.

The communiqué announcing these operations did not divulge the number of planes engaged, but said the raids cost the Royal Air Force six bombers and one Coastal Command plane. The R. A. F. losses were increased today when one fighter plane failed to return home from a daylight attack on Dunkerque.

[The Berlin radio went off the air at 1:50 A. M. today, a possible sign that British bombers were again over Germany, The United Press reported from London.

[German planes dropped bombs early today in a sharp attack on the south coast of England, The Associated Press reported. Two of the raiders were shot down and two more Nazi planes destroyed over Europe.]

As in the case of the R. A. F. raids on Emden late Friday night and early yesterday morning, the Air Ministry did not go into details about the targets for the night or indicate the extent of damage.

While patrolling along the Netherland coast during the night Coastal Command fliers caught up with an enemy convoy of three ships. The rear gunner on a Canadian-manned plane said on his return to his base that he saw two bombs hit one vessel amidship, hurling debris high in the air in the resulting explosions. Whether the vessel sank was not determined. What became of her two companion ships was not learned here.

Although the sky was clear, there was less daylight activity to—

Continued on Page Five

NEWS PUTS DAMPER ON CHURCHILL VISIT

But Washington Sees Mid-East Crisis as Incidental in His Planning With Roosevelt

By JAMES B. RESTON

WASHINGTON, June 21—Washington was in a sober and realistic mood tonight. The fall of Tobruk and the situation of the Russians at Sevastopol have put a damper on the unrestrained second-front speculation that has surrounded the Roosevelt-Churchill talks. The chief immediate concern was viewed as the holding of the second front the United Nations now have in Egypt, rather than opening up new fronts on the European Continent.

The President and Mr. Churchill continued their talks during the day, and the chiefs of staff of the United States and Britain. General George C. Marshall and General Sir Alan Brooke, who came to the United States with Mr. Churchill, continued their exchange of information and their planning for the future.

The plain and simple truth about these important discussions is that only a few persons know what has gone on since Mr. Churchill arrived, and they are not telling what they know.

The purpose of the conversations is much less complicated, dramatic and urgent than one would tend to deduce from the secrecy with which they have been surrounded.

It is undoubtedly true, as Stephen Early, White House secretary, has said, that they are dealing with the future plans of the

Continued on Page Eight

'Never a Dull Moment' at Midway, Reporter Watching Battle Found

The following account of the Battle of Midway is by a correspondent of THE NEW YORK TIMES who was aboard one of the United States warships.

By FOSTER HAILEY
Special to THE NEW YORK TIMES.

WITH THE PACIFIC FLEET, at Sea, June 4 (Delayed)—Today is the day. Mark it on your calendar in red ink. Thursday, June 4. It may be the one on which the tide definitely turned in the battle of the Pacific.

This morning at dawn the Japanese launched planes from a strong striking force northwest of Midway. We are in a position to strike them on the flank. If our planes can only get to their carriers before the Japanese planes attacking Midway can return, the result may be a naval disaster for the Japanese.

White water is curling away from the clipper bows of the cruisers and the big carriers, whose escort we are, as we drive along at high speed with the destroyers ahead and on the flanks. It is a relief for the nerves when the first alarm is sounded. It turns out to be false, but the activity has eased the tension.

There is another spurt of activity as another air contact is reported, but it turns out to be a big patrol plane from Midway that joins the force to act as an antisubmarine guard.

"Midway was attacked at 8:48 A. M.," our Admiral and Chief of Staff says crisply when an inquiry on the situation is made.

"We should be in launching distance soon."

The dawn was a gloomy one, but now the clouds are breaking up.

Continued on Page Four

NAZIS NEAR EGYPT

British Are on Border as Rommel Presses On After Victory

PORT'S LOSS SERIOUS

Plan for a Second Front Seen Upset by Need to Hold New Line

By DAVID ANDERSON
Special Cable to THE NEW YORK TIMES.

LONDON, June 21—A smashing blow delivered yesterday by waves of German tanks, heavily supported from the air, crushed the defenses of Tobruk in Libya. The War Office tonight confirmed the loss of the town, already claimed by the enemy, who said 25,000 prisoners, including "several generals" had been captured.

The story of what happened, as given by both German and Italian sources, appears to cover the battle fairly fully, but the accuracy of these reports cannot be checked at present. Briefly, it can be said Field Marshal Erwin Rommel's armored units that had passed Tobruk in pursuit of the British Eighth Army did so to make certain whether the British showed any signs of preparing a counterattack.

When the German Marshal was satisfied this was not the case he reversed his forces, bringing back tanks against Tobruk from the south, driving from the vicinity of Ed Duda, and did this fiercely with every ounce of power at his command. At the same time the Luftwaffe began intensive bombing of Tobruk's defenses. Within a matter of hours the battle was over.

Tobruk Long in Battle

Tobruk must have been softer in its last moments than during the many other attacks it beat off during the last seventeen months since it was captured from the Italians on Jan 22, 1941. It has been on the fringe of the Libyan battlefield for some weeks with inevitable strain as strategy wavered between one of concentration of strength there and one of evacuation.

Despite the presence of a large garrison when Tobruk fell it is believed there was not time to lay minefields on its perimeter or otherwise strengthen its defenses to face an immediate storming.

A Cairo communiqué, released here at noon today, paved the way for the worst. It read:

"Yesterday the enemy attacked the perimeter of Tobruk in great strength. In spite of most determined resistance by our forces the enemy succeeded in penetrating the defenses and in occupying a considerable area inside them."

Twelve strong points in the defense were taken by the first wave of enemy tanks, according to Berlin. This made a wedge two and a half miles wide, and German sources state the British defenders then realized that further resistance was useless.

Bombers Blast Defenses

But they had other reasons for weighing most seriously the advantages of carrying on the fight. The Germans said today that "numerous bombers' ceaseless attack wrought great destruction in the fortifications and other military works of the port and town."

It was not long after noon yesterday when large formations of German bombers swooped down on a group of four anti-aircraft batteries, all of which were silenced, it was reported by Berlin. Still more of the Luftwaffe's heavy aircraft, laden with high explosives, cruised over a column of twenty tanks, setting many of them alight.

Finally, the German radio said, "About 2 P. M. another great attack was made on Tobruk, which lasted three hours without interruption and caused numerous fires.

Continued on Page Two

War News Summarized

MONDAY, JUNE 22, 1942

Tobruk fell yesterday, and the resultant threat to Egypt and the British position in the Eastern Mediterranean changed the war picture drastically, while the Russians acknowledged a significant German advance at Sevastopol, though at the cost of heavy enemy losses.

Tobruk fell to a smashing blow delivered by waves of German tanks according to London reports. The Germans claimed that 25,000 prisoners had been taken. In London the opinion prevailed that there had not been time to lay minefields around Tobruk before the Axis attack. [1:8.]

Military observers in London referred to the fall of Tobruk as an "incontestable disaster." The Germans were believed to have obtained a large quantity of stores. General Rommel was expected to drive on Suez. [2:2.]

British bombers attacked Emden, German submarine base, for the second successive night, airfields in the Netherlands and enemy shipping off the Netherland coast. Heavy air attacks were also made on the French and Belgian coasts. [1:5.]

Moscow granted that the defenders of Sevastopol had been forced to fall back as the enemy forced a wedge in their lines, but declared that the action had crippled four German and two Rumanian divisions. Sharp activity was reported in the Kharkov and Leningrad sectors. [1:3.]

President Kalinin of the Soviet Union, in a review of a year of war, stated that the Germans no longer were capable of a general offensive. [5:5; map, P. 5.]

Lord Beaverbrook, addressing a "Salute to Russia" meeting in Britain, again urged the United Nations to open a second front. He asserted that the British Army was now sufficiently prepared. [3:1.]

Chungking reported that the Japanese had been halted in Kiangsi and had lost 1,300 troops in Honan. The Minister of War asserted that the Japanese soon would be so bogged down in China that they would not be able to attack Russia with full strength. [4:1.]

The United States Navy announced that Japanese forces in the Aleutians had succeeded in occupying the island of Kiska, 650 miles west of Dutch Harbor. Bomb hits were made on a Japanese cruiser and a Japanese transport was sunk. [1:4; map, P. 4.]

Colonel J. L. Ralston, Canadian Defense Minister, disclosed that a government telegraph station at Estevan Point, Vancouver Island, had been shelled by a submarine Saturday night, but no damage was done. [1:5-6.]

As President Roosevelt and Prime Minister Churchill continued their conversations yesterday Washington reported that the fall of Tobruk and Russian withdrawals at Sevastopol had checked "second front speculation." Concern was being drawn over the necessity for holding the present front in Egypt. [1:7.]

"All the News That's Fit to Print."

NEWS INDEX, PAGE 56, THIS SECTION

The New York Times.

LATE CITY EDITION

Continued cool today with light winds.
Temperature Yesterday—Max., 57; Min., 45
Sunrise, 7:34 A. M.; Sunset, 5:18 P. M.

Section 1

VOL. XCII—No. 30,965.

Entered as Second-Class Matter, Postoffice, New York, N. Y.

NEW YORK, SUNDAY, NOVEMBER 8, 1942.

Copyright, 1942, by The New York Times Company.

Including Magazine and Book Sections

TEN CENTS
New York City and Vicinity

AMERICAN FORCES LAND IN FRENCH AFRICA; BRITISH NAVAL, AIR UNITS ASSISTING THEM; EFFECTIVE SECOND FRONT, ROOSEVELT SAYS

U.S. DRIVES ON BUNA

American Troops Flown to Area Closing In on Big Japanese Base

PAPUA IS OVERRUN

All Except Beachhead of Buna-Gona Seized in New Guinea Push

By The Associated Press.

AT UNITED NATIONS HEADQUARTERS, Australia, Sunday, Nov. 8 — American combat troops are in action near Buna, vital Japanese base on the north New Guinea coast, General Douglas MacArthur disclosed today.

Simultaneously, General MacArthur disclosed that the Allies have occupied Goodenough Island, off Collingwood Bay, in an obvious flanking movement.

[American Army troops on Guadalcanal advanced on Friday (Solomons time) in the area to the west of Henderson airfield, the Navy reported yesterday. They crossed the Malimbul River a few miles south of Koli Point, where the Japanese recently landed reinforcements, but met little opposition.]

It was from Buna, in midsummer, that the Japanese began a drive across tortuous trails of the Owen Stanley Mountains which carried to within thirty-two miles of Port Moresby, Allied base on the south coast, before it was stalled. Late in September the Allies began encircling and infiltration movements which rolled the Japanese back and yesterday's communiqué had mentioned bitter fighting at Oivi, which is fifty-five miles south of Buna.

Japanese Resist at Oivi

"American ground troops in force, transported by air from Australia during the last month, have penetrated Central and Southeastern Papua to the vicinity of Buna," a communiqué stated.

"The Allied forces now control all of Papua except the beach head in the Buna-Gona area."

The surprising development came as a thrust around the eastern end of New Guinea from Milne Bay where Japanese troops landed in July only to be pinned against the sea and slain or forced to their ships.

"Units from Milne Bay," the communiqué said, "have now completed clearing remnants of hostile forces from the islands to the north and have occupied strategic points."

While this disclosure was being made, Australian ground forces still were meeting fierce resistance at Oivi. Today's communiqué said the Australians maintained constant pressure and were resorting to their hitherto successful tactics of local encircling movements in efforts to dislodge the defenders.

The Allied air force continued to support the overland drive with strafing attacks on the Japanese troops.

Island Attacked Oct. 22

AT UNITED NATIONS HEADQUARTERS, Australia, Sunday, Nov. 8 (AP)—The announcement of sweeping Allied gains in New Guinea came as a surprise to observers here, although an Australian offensive through mountainous central New Guinea had been making steady progress toward the north coast for the past five weeks.

[Delayed dispatches from Harold Guard, United Press staff correspondent in New Guinea, revealed that the Americans had been

Continued on Page Forty-five

LEADS IN AFRICA

Lieut. Gen. Dwight Eisenhower
Associated Press

R.A.F. ROCKS GENOA; U.S. RAID ON BREST

Bombers From Britain Pound North Italy 2 Nights in Row —Hit Nazis on Coast

Special Cable to THE NEW YORK TIMES.

LONDON, Sunday, Nov. 8—Bombers from Britain struck a heavy blow at Northern Italy on Friday night, blasting the port of Genoa again in support of the Eighth Army's battling of the Nazis and Italians in the African desert.

Again last night the Royal Air Force sent its big bombers over Northern Italy, British officials reported briefly early today. The announcement meant that the R.A.F. from here was seeing to it that the Axis forces in Africa got no help from home.

American heavy bombers, both Flying Fortresses and Liberators, escorted by Allied fighters, carried out a smashing attack on the docks and U-boat pens at Brest in occupied France yesterday afternoon, United States Army headquarters here announced.

Bombs were seen to strike the targets at Brest. The communiqué stressed that sharp Nazi antiaircraft fire and enemy fighter opposition were encountered over the coast of Brittany.

The Brest raiders shot down four Nazi fighters. All the United States bombers returned, but one Allied fighter was lost.

The R.A.F.'s fighter squadrons

Continued on Page Four

NAZIS NEAR LIBYA

British Drive Out to Bar New Stand by Enemy or Reinforcements

FOE BOMBED ALL NIGHT

Pursuers Reported to Be Within 40 Miles of Halfaya Pass

By The United Press.

CAIRO, Egypt, Nov. 7—The British Eighth Army under Lieut. Gen. Bernard L. Montgomery hurled armored forces, motorized infantry and swarms of planes tonight at the remnants of German General Field Marshal Erwin Rommel's once-proud Afrika Korps—possibly only 25,000 out of an original 140,000—now trying to brace for a stand at Halfaya [Hellfire] Pass on the Libyan frontier, 240 miles west of the Alamein battleground.

The main body of the British was reported to be well west of Matruh, 110 miles west of El Alamein, and advance striking forces were believed to be as far as 200 miles west of El Alamein, or close to the Egyptian-Libyan frontier, 240 miles west of El Alamein.

How many men Marshal Rommel had left in the Halfaya area could not be established. Already 20,000 prisoners had been counted in British hands. Marshal Rommel's desert casualties were estimated at approximately 20,000 more. In addition, 75,000 Italian troops had been left far behind the swirling battleground, ready to surrender when the British could find time and men to round them up.

Marshal Rommel entered the battle with a maximum of 140,000 troops in the forward area. It was doubted whether he had more than one or two divisions left to attempt another stand at Halfaya unless he had been able to rush large reinforcements from the rear.

It appeared possible tonight that the Axis forces might not even attempt to stand at Halfaya, but would, instead, continue their headlong flight as deeply as possible into Libya in an effort to open a gap between themselves and the Eighth Army.

Such a manoeuvre, however, may already be doomed to failure. General Montgomery has ordered all his forces to make to cut off Marshal Rommel's retreat. It was believed that he might have sent a hard-hitting, fast-moving

Continued on Page Five

SHOCK TROOPS LEAD

Simultaneous Landings Made Before Dawn at Numerous Points

PLANES GUARD SKIES

An Armada Pours Men on the Beaches—Early Actions Satisfactory

By WES GALLAGHER
Associated Press Correspondent

ALLIED HEADQUARTERS IN NORTH AFRICA, Sunday, Nov. 8—American soldiers, marines and sailors from one of the greatest armadas ever put into a single military operation swarmed ashore today on the Vichy-controlled North Africa shore before dawn, striking to break Hitler's hold on the Mediterranean.

[Reports reaching Allied headquarters in North Africa today disclosed that successful landings had been made by American assault parties on beaches of North Africa near two main objectives outlined in operational plans as announced by an Associated Press dispatch stated.

[British forces reported attempting a landing at Algiers after a bombardment were said by the Vichy radio to have been "beaten off."]

Tall, decisive Lieut. Gen. Dwight D. (Ike) Eisenhower, supreme commander of the huge forces involved in the operation, worked throughout the night directing the first great American blow at the Axis.

Included in the forces were crack combat troops, Rangers (airborne units) and the cream of America's airmen.

British naval and air force units supported the American landing forces, who were preceded by a snowstorm of leaflets and a radio barrage promising the French that the United States had no intention of seizing French possessions and only sought to prevent Axis infiltration.

It undoubtedly was the longest over-water military operation ever attempted, with hundreds of ships in great convoys coming thousands of miles under the protection of British and American sea and air might.

I came on one of these big convoys.

Fighting-fit American soldiers

Continued on Page Fourteen

WHERE THE UNITED STATES PREPARES FOR NEW FRONT

As the survivors of Marshal Rommel's beaten German legions fled westward toward the Libyan border (1), powerful American land, sea and air forces landed behind them at various places in Vichy France's colonies along the Mediterranean (2) and on the shores of the Atlantic, apparently in Morocco (3). British naval and aerial units are assisting them. There was no indication of military action against Vichy's possessions on the western bulge of the Atlantic (4). A large and comprehensive map of the African and Mediterranean theatre of war will be found on Page 1 of Section 4 of this issue of THE TIMES. However, Section 4 had gone to press before the announcement last night of the landing of American troops.

LANDING PLAN KEPT SECRET BY WRITERS

Americans Selected for Duty, Bureaus Sworn to Silence— Eisenhower Slipt Away

By RAYMOND DANIELL
Special Cable to THE NEW YORK TIMES.

LONDON, Sunday, Nov. 8—For weeks American newspaper men have been the custodians of one of war's biggest secrets. It was not an easy secret to keep because through all that time they had to improvise excuses for the absence of a large number of the members of their London staffs to conceal the fact that they had gone with the expeditionary forces.

Most London offices of Amer-

Continued on Page Fourteen

President's Statement

Special to THE NEW YORK TIMES.

WASHINGTON, Nov. 7—President Roosevelt's statement announcing the opening of a second front in French North and West Africa follows:

In order to forestall an invasion of Africa by Germany and Italy, which, if successful, would constitute a direct threat to America across the comparatively narrow sea from Western Africa, a powerful American force equipped with adequate weapons of modern warfare and under American command is today landing on the Mediterranean and Atlantic coasts of the French colonies in Africa.

The landing of this American Army is being assisted by the British Navy and air forces, and it will, in the immediate future, be reinforced by a considerable number of divisions of the British Army.

This combined Allied force, under American command, in conjunction with the British campaign in Egypt is designed to prevent an occupation by the Axis armies of any part of Northern or Western Africa and to deny to the aggressor nations a starting point from which to launch an attack against the Atlantic coast of the Americas.

In addition, it provides an effective second-front assistance to our heroic allies in Russia.

The French Government and the French people have been informed of the purpose of this expedition and have been assured that the Allies seek no territory and have no intention of interfering with friendly French authorities in Africa.

The government of France and the people of France and the French possessions have been requested to cooperate with and assist the American expedition in its effort to repel the Germans and Italian international criminals, and by so doing to liberate France and the French Empire from the Axis yoke.

This expedition will develop into a major effort by the Allied Nations and there is every expectation that it will be successful in repelling the planned German and Italian invasion of Africa and prove the first historic step to the liberation and restoration of France.

Blow to Knock Italy Out of the War Called Goal of American Invasion

Special Cable to THE NEW YORK TIMES.

LONDON, Sunday, Nov. 8—Allied Army, Navy and air forces commanded by Lieut. Gen. Dwight D. Eisenhower, commander of all American forces in the European theatre, have struck a powerful blow to free the Mediterranean from Axis control and knock Italy out of the war. That, in the opinion of military observers here, is the meaning of the movement of United States forces that now become part of the gigantic pincers with which it is expected that the last vestiges of the German and Italian forces in North Africa will be annihilated.

The first stage of the battle just beginning will be a struggle for the control of roads, railways and airfields in Algeria and the neighboring colony of Tunisia. Once the three have been won, Allied reinforcements and supplies will be able to dispense with the long journey around the Cape of Good Hope that has been one of

Continued on Page Thirteen

U.S. MEETS 'THREAT'

Big Expeditions Invade North and West Africa to Forestall Axis

EISENHOWER AT HEAD

President Urges French to Help, Calls Move Aid to Russia

Roosevelt's appeal to French people and Eisenhower's message to North Africans, Pg. 8.

By C. P. TRUSSELL
Special to THE NEW YORK TIMES.

WASHINGTON, Nov. 7—Powerful American forces, supported by British naval and air forces, landed simultaneously tonight at numerous points on the Mediterranean and Atlantic coasts of French North Africa, forestalling an anticipated invasion of Africa by Germany and Italy and launching effective second-front assistance to Russia, President Roosevelt announced tonight.

Lieut. Gen. Dwight D. Eisenhower is in command.

The President made the announcement even as the American forces, equipped with adequate weapons of modern warfare, he emphasized, were making the landings.

President Speaks to France

Soon he was speaking direct to the French Government and the French people by short-wave radio and in their own tongue, giving assurances that the Allies seek no territory and have no intention of interfering with friendly French, official or civilian. He called upon them to cooperate in repelling "the German and Italian international criminals."

By doing so, he said, they could help liberate France and the French Empire.

[United States and British planes dropped leaflets in France and French Africa containing messages to the people from President Roosevelt and General Eisenhower, London reported.]

General Eisenhower himself, the White House let it be known, also spoke by radio to the French people, explaining the purposes of the invasions.

His proclamation, delivered while the American troops were making their landings, gave specific directions to French land, sea and air forces in North Africa as to how they could avoid misunderstanding and prevent action against them by a system of signals. This is a military operation, General Eisen-

Continued on Page Three

Petain Says Vichy Will 'Defend' Lands

By The Associated Press.

LONDON, Sunday, Nov. 8—The Vichy radio said today that Marshal Henri Philippe Pétain had sent President Roosevelt a message expressing his "astonishment and sadness" at learning of "the aggression of your troops against North Africa."

Marshal Pétain said that the reasons given by the President for the landings failed to justify them and added:

"France and its honor are involved. We are attacked and we will defend ourselves."

The Vichy government issued a communiqué opening with an "appeal to Frenchmen not to allow yourselves to be swayed by foreign broadcasts."

Major Sports Yesterday

FOOTBALL

Making both touchdowns in the second half, Notre Dame defeated Army before 75,142 spectators at the Yankee Stadium. With a scoring pass in the first period and several goal-line stands, Navy thrilled 74,000 fans at Philadelphia by upsetting Penn. Both Fordham and Columbia lost free-scoring contests and the Big Three—Princeton, Yale and Harvard—all went down to defeat. Iowa toppled hitherto unbeaten Wisconsin. Scores of leading games:

Alabama ...29	So. Carolina... 0	Miss. State... 7	Tulane ... 6
Amherst ...35	Trinity ... 6	Missouri ...26	Nebraska ... 6
Boston Coll...28	Temple ... 0	Moravian ...32	C. C. N. Y.... 0
Brown ...20	Holy Cross...14	Navy ... 7	Penn. ... 0
Colgate ...35	Columbia ...26	Notre Dame.. 6	Army ... 0
Cornell ...13	Yale ... 7	Ohio State...59	Pittsburgh ...19
Dartmouth ... 7	Princeton ... 7	Oklahoma ...76	Kan. State... 0
Duke ...42	Maryland ... 0	Oregon 10	U. C. L. A... 7
Duquesne ... 7	St. Mary's... 2	Penn State...13	Syracuse ...13
Georgia ...75	Florida ... 0	Rice 40	Arkansas ... 6
Ga. Pre-Fl...41	Maryland ... 0	So. Calif...21	California ... 7
Ga. Tech...47	Kentucky ... 7	Stanford ...20	Washington . 7
Great Lakes..42	Purdue ... 0	Texas 20	Baylor ... 0
Illinois 14	Northwestern. 7	Tex. A. & M.27	S. M. U....20
Indiana 7	Minnesota ... 0	Texas Tech...13	T. C. U. ... 6
Iowa 6	Wisconsin ... 0	Vanderbilt ...19	Mississippi ... 7
La. State...26	Fordham ...13	Wash. State...23	Mich. State...13
Michigan ...35	Harvard ...13	Williams 31	Wesleyan ... 6

HORSE RACING

Good Morning won the Florence Nightingale Purse by about a length from Too Timely on the war-relief program before 22,099 racegoers who bet $1,550,089 at Belmont Park. Aonbarr defeated Riverland by a neck in the Grayson Handicap at Pimlico.

HOCKEY

The New York Rangers downed the Montreal Canadiens, 4–3, in the overtime opening game at Madison Square Garden.

(Complete Details of These and Other Sports Events in Section 5.)

War News Summarized

SUNDAY, NOVEMBER 8, 1942

The White House announced last night that powerful American forces were landing on the Atlantic and Mediterranean coasts of French North Africa to forestall a German invasion. The announcement stated that the landing was to prevent the creation of an Axis threat to the Atlantic coast of the Americas across the narrow sea in Western Africa. France has been assured that the Allies seek no territory. [1:8.]

American correspondents with the African expeditionary force told of simultaneous landings by the United States troops at many points hundreds of miles apart. [1:4.]

Britain's Eighth Army continued its pursuit in North Africa of Marshal Rommel's shattered army. Twenty thousand prisoners had been taken, according to Cairo. British columns were said to be 200 miles west of El Alamein, close to the Libyan border. [1:3; map, P. 4.]

London announced that British heavy bombers had launched a "concentrated and effective" attack on Genoa Friday night and again raided Northern Italy last night. United States bombers attacked the U-boat base at Brest, France, and other planes from Britain pounded Nazi targets from the Netherlands to the Bay of Biscay. [1:2; map, P. 21.]

Moscow reported that the Soviet armies held on all fronts and killed some 1,800 of the enemy on the Stalingrad and Caucasus fronts. The German advances in the Nalchik region had apparently been halted. [1:5.]

General Douglas MacArthur's headquarters announced that American troops in force had been transported by air to New Guinea and had penetrated to the vicinity of Buna, Japanese base on the north coast. [1:1; map, P. 45.]

The United States Navy announced that Army forces on Guadalcanal Island in the Solomons had attacked Japanese troops to the east of the airfield Nov. 6 and had encountered little opposition. Announcement was also made that at least 5,188 Japanese had been killed in land fighting on Tulagi and Guadalcanal since the United States occupation Aug. 7. [46:1 with map.]

United States bombers attacked successfully the docks at Rangoon, Burma, and returned to their bases in India. [46:8.]

The New York Times.

LATE CITY EDITION
Continued cool with moderate winds today.
Temperature Yesterday—Max., 82; Min., 69
Sunrise, 5:31 A. M.; Sunset, 8:31 P. M.

VOL. XCII—No. 31,204.

Entered as Second-Class Matter, Postoffice, New York, N. Y.

NEW YORK, THURSDAY, JULY 1, 1943.

Copyright, 1943, by The New York Times Company.

THREE CENTS NEW YORK CITY

M'ARTHUR STARTS ALLIED OFFENSIVE IN PACIFIC; NEW GUINEA ISLES WON, LANDINGS IN SOLOMONS; CHURCHILL PROMISES BLOWS IN EUROPE BY FALL

MAYOR FACES FIGHT WITH OPA ON PLAN FOR HANDLING MEAT

Gives Approval for Sales by Slaughterers to Retailers on Consignment Basis

FEDERAL ACTION LOOMS

Price Agency Director Here Promises Move Should Violation be Found

A direct conflict between Mayor Fiorello H. La Guardia and the Office of Price Administration appeared inevitable last night, after the Mayor had announced that he had approved, on his own responsibility, a plan for independent slaughterers to sell meat to the public at consumer ceiling prices through consignments to retailers, despite the OPA's objections to the plan.

"If they go ahead with a plan that is in violation of the regulations, OPA will be forced to take action," Frank C. Russell, district OPA director, retorted when informed of the Mayor's decision. "Apparently the Mayor has given his permission for something which the OPA legal department has turned down."

Former Municipal Court Justice Nathan Sweedler of 225 Broadway, who, as counsel for the Eastern States Independent Meat Packers and Slaughterers, proposed the plan approved by the Mayor after the OPA had turned it down, announced that his organization hoped to have meat on sale in some retail shops today and expected to have a large quantity available by Saturday.

Sees Quick Meat Supply

Mr. Sweedler has estimated that his group could provide 25,000 pounds of beef within twenty-four hours after the Mayor gave his approval to the plan and eventually could gear its output to 1,000,000 pounds a week, but the Mayor was even more optimistic. He said that the plan might provide the city with 1,000,000 pounds a week "and it may be 5,000,000 pounds."

Under the plan the meat would be sold on consignment, the retailer keeping 21 per cent of the selling price. According to Mr. Sweedler, the remaining 79 per cent would pay for the cost of livestock, freight and slaughtering. He contends that under his plan meat could be sold at the consumer ceiling prices, and any butcher violating the ceiling would be deprived of meat through a voluntary policing system.

The Mayor announced his approval of the plan to reporters at City Hall and then released a letter to Commissioner of Markets Daniel P. Woolley in which he argued that the plan did not conflict with any existing regulations and that it should be accepted as a temporary measure.

Holds Plan Feasible

"I have carefully studied the report you submitted to me with plan for direct consignment of food from the original processor to the retailer direct, and selling by such retailer to consumer at ceiling prices or lower," the Mayor said in his letter. "I do not see how any such plan could conflict with any existing rules or regulations of any Federal agency, provided the producer, farmer or livestock man is paid the market price and the retailer sells at ceiling prices or lower.

"The whole purpose of food control is to make food available and fix ceiling prices. There is nothing in the rules that prevents anyone from selling below ceiling prices. Surely, in the protection of the consumer, we could not or would not prosecute a retailer for selling below ceiling prices provided his food is wholesome and complies with all health requirements and government inspection.

"In fact, if an original processor or retailer wanted to give food

Continued on Page Seventeen

OWI Closes Twelve Regional Branches

By The Associated Press

WASHINGTON, June 30—Twelve regional and thirty-six branch offices of the Office of War Information throughout the country began closing at midnight tonight as the fiscal year ended.

The OWI said an official would remain in each of the twelve regional offices for a few days to liquidate the affairs of both the regional and branch offices.

The shutdown was made necessary, the OWI said, because the Senate voted to appropriate only $3,000,000 for the domestic branch of the organization and earmarked the amount, allowing none for maintaining the regional and branch offices. The House had voted to abolish the domestic service entirely.

"It isn't likely that the Congressional conference committee, which has yet to act finally, would go above the Senate's $3,000,000, so we are closing down the offices," an agency spokesman said.

CONGRESS CRUSHES SUBSIDY PROGRAM

Ban on Payments to Cut Prices Stays in CCC Bill Passed by Overwhelming Majorities

By The Associated Press

WASHINGTON, June 30—Congress, handing the Roosevelt Administration another legislative setback, today forbade use of subsidies to push down retail food prices and ordered the meat-butter price "roll back" ended by Aug. 1.

The ban was incorporated in legislation extending the life of the Commodity Credit Corporation for two more years from midnight tonight and adding $750,000,000 to its present 2,650,000,000 lending powers. Both Senate and House approved the measure by far more than the two-thirds majority which would be necessary to override a veto. The House vote was 160 to 32, and the Senate vote, 62 to 13.

Less restrictive than the original House measure, the bill permits continued use of subsidies, up to $150,000,000 to meet increased transportation costs such as are now being paid on the movement of oil to the East Coast and on coffee imports, and to promote production of critical metals and war-essential foods. It also allows incentive payments on canning and specialty crops, price support for domestic vegetable oils and fats, and payments for sale of wheat for feeding purposes. However, no subsidies could be paid simply to reduce prices.

Before final passage, a provision prohibiting Government agencies from deducting farm benefit payments in calculating agricultural parity prices was stricken out.

Just before final Congressional action, Leo R. Maxon, deputy administrator of the Office of Price

Continued on Page Eleven

Cattle Grower Says 'Policymakers' Are to Blame in Meat Shortage

By JAY G. HAYDEN
North American Newspaper Alliance

WASHINGTON, June 30—Joseph G. Montague, general counsel for the Texas and Southwestern Cattle Raisers Association, put the blame for the meat shortage today on "the unofficial policymakers close to the President."

Mr. Davis is believed to have had substantially this same thought in mind when he gave as his first reason for resignation that "I find I have assumed a public responsibility which brings me into the open a charge which figured behind the scenes in the Congressional rejection of food subsidies and the retirement of Chester C. Davis as Food Administrator.

Speaking before the Senate Agricultural Committee, Mr. Montague said:

"Surrounding this situation are a group of people who have no responsibility, yet determine policy and cause confusion in the meat situation. They are entrenched in

When You Think of Writing Think of Whiting.—Advt.

WALLACE AND JONES RENEW THEIR ROW AFTER 2-HOUR TALK

Conference Called by Byrnes Fails 'to Resolve and Determine' Controversy

SHARP STATEMENTS ISSUED

Secretary Says Charge of Delay by RFC in War Effort is 'Dastardly' and 'Untrue'

By JOHN H. CRIDER
Special to THE NEW YORK TIMES.

WASHINGTON, June 30—An attempt by the War Mobilization Director, James F. Byrnes, to harmonize the differences between Vice President Henry A. Wallace and Secretary of Commerce Jesse H. Jones failed today after he had summoned them to his office for a two-hour discussion this afternoon.

Tonight the Vice President issued a statement which somewhat tempered his bitter accusations against Mr. Jones made yesterday but said the fundamental differences remained.

To this the Secretary replied:

"Mr. Wallace in his statement tonight repeats that delays of the RFC have retarded the war effort. This dastardly charge is as untrue as when he first made it. As for the rest of his statement, Mr. Wallace was not authorized to speak for me, and I will continue to speak for myself, and as previously stated, I shall insist upon a Congressional investigation."

The Vice President's statement made it clear that the basic differences between himself and Mr. Jones had been altered only to the extent that "Mr. Jones did not object" to Mr. Wallace's plan to ask Congress after its recess for funds for foreign procurement which would make it independent of the Reconstruction Finance Corporation, headed by the Secretary of Commerce.

There was no mention of Mr. Byrnes in the Vice President's statement, although it was the fruit of the War Mobilization Director's efforts to play the role of peacemaker for the Federal Bureaucracy cast for him by President Roosevelt's Executive Order of May 28 calling upon him to "resolve and determine controversies between such agencies or departments."

Meanwhile, the Senate, showing little indication at this point of being in a mood to grant the broad authority over foreign procurement expenditures sought by Mr. Wallace, inserted in the War Agencies Appropriation Bill an amendment by Senator Kenneth McKellar, Democrat, of Tennessee, providing that BEW could not use for foreign purchases any of the $36,000,000 appropriated without approval of a majority of the

Continued on Page Seventeen

76 BILLIONS SPENT IN U.S. FISCAL YEAR

71 of the Total Were for War—Public Debt Up to 140 Billions, Deficit to 55

Special to THE NEW YORK TIMES.

WASHINGTON, June 30—The United States ended its fiscal year tonight with a record of expenditures of more than $76,000,000, receipts of more than $21,000,000, a gross public debt of more than $140,000,000,000 and a deficit of more than $55,000,000.

The latest figures available at the Treasury were for June 26, four days before the actual end of the fiscal year. On that date total war expenditures for the year were $71,014,000,000, as against $25,515,000,000 on the same date in 1942.

Spending for civilian purposes was $5,375,000,000, as compared with $5,800,000,000 on the same day a year earlier. The War Department spent $41,690,000,000 and the Navy $20,513,000,000. War expenditures of the Agriculture Department totaled $2,005,000,000, and the Maritime Commission spent $2,733,000,000.

In one year the public debt increased from $78,580,000,000 to $140,028,000,000 and the deficit advanced from $19,152,000,000 to $55,242,000,000.

Receipts of $21,625,000,000 dur-

Continued on Page Twelve

Prime Minister Warns Axis Allied Attacks Are Imminent

By RAYMOND DANIELL

LONDON, June 30—Prime Minister Churchill warned the Axis today that the Allies were preparing heavier blows on land and sea and by air from east, south and west to bring about the unconditional surrender that he and President Roosevelt declared at Casablanca was the price of peace.

In the Mediterranean and "elsewhere," he said, heavy fighting probably would develop "before the leaves of autumn fall," but he added that large-scale amphibious operations take months to prepare.

Significantly, he dwelt at length and in considerable detail upon the growing scale and intensity of the British-American air offensive against Germany from this island, and indicated that Russian air power, long tied down to the battle lines, would soon be able to join in the attack on Nazi industry from the east.

A Major Victory at Sea

Reviewing the Battle of the Atlantic, he said a victory had been won at sea against the submarines two months ago comparable with the Allied conquest of Africa with the capture of 350,000 German and Italian prisoners and vast quantities of war material. He likened the victory in Tunisia to the Russian triumph at Stalingrad.

The Prime Minister was speaking in the ancient Guildhall, where he received freedom of the City of London, that square mile of the British capital that still bears the

Continued on Page Four

The text of Mr. Churchill's address is printed on Page 4.

BERLIN EVACUATION REPORTED PLANNED

Swedes Hear Exodus Is to Start in Fall—Wuppertal Held Beyond Rebuilding

By GEORGE AXELSSON
By Telephone to THE NEW YORK TIMES.

STOCKHOLM, Sweden, June 30—Berlin will evacuate in the Fall women and children not engaged in the war industries, according to reliable information received here today through private channels.

Fear of heavier and more frequent Allied air raids with the coming of longer nights has prompted this decision, and authorities have already begun the preliminary arrangements, it is stated.

The extent to which the Ruhr has been hit by the RAF raids is indicated by a statement by Adolf Hitler's chief city planning consultant, Armaments Minister Albert Speer, just back from a tour of inspection of the devastated area.

He said it was not worth while to try to rebuild Wuppertal.

Continued on Page Three

UNITED NATIONS FORCES MOVE FORWARD IN THE SOUTHWEST PACIFIC

July 1, 1943

American troops landed on Rendova and New Georgia Islands without opposition. In New Guinea they occupied Nassau Bay (4), (1), in the vicinity of the enemy air base at Munda, and engaged just below Salamaua; the landing craft encountered only slight the Japanese. The inset shows this area in detail. To the west the resistance. Apparently these widespread operations had as their Allies occupied Woodlark Island (2) and the Trobriand Islands (3) ultimate goal the reduction of Rabaul (5), which was bombed.

2-PRONGED DRIVE

Americans Battle Enemy on New Georgia and Rendova Islands

SALAMAUA IN PERIL

Allies Seize Trobriand and Woodlark Isles—Rabaul Pounded

By SIDNEY SHALETT
Special to THE NEW YORK TIMES.

WASHINGTON, Thursday, July 1—Combined Army and Navy forces under General Douglas MacArthur have opened the long expected offensive against the Japanese in the south and southwest Pacific.

Fighting was in progress on Rendova and New Georgia Islands, which were hit by ground, naval and air forces in "closest synchronization," a communiqué from General MacArthur's headquarters in Australia reported today. Nassau Bay, ten miles south of the big Japanese base of Salamaua in New Guinea, fell to the Allies after a slight skirmish, and the Trobriand and Woodlark island groups, 300 to 400 miles west of the New Georgia group, were occupied without opposition.

The Allied push—aimed, observers here believe, at the major Japanese base of Rabaul, on New Britain Island—got under way yesterday, Solomons time, which was Tuesday here.

Nutcracker Move Seen

It was believed here, on the basis of early reports, that the fighting and occupations reported so far were preliminary to major actions to come. If bases in the New Georgias are consolidated, a two-way push against Rabaul might be developing, with one arm advancing northwestward from the Central Solomons and the other swinging across eastward from our new bases in New Guinea.

United States heavy bombers carried out an attack on Rabaul during the night, dropping nearly twenty-three tons of high-explosive, fragmentation and incendiary bombs throughout the dispersal areas at the Vunakanau and Lakunai airdromes, the communiqué from Australian headquarters reported. "Several explosions" and "numerous fires" were observed, one of which was visible for 100 miles, the announcement said.

The big bombers, which have punished Rabaul extensively in recent weeks, ran into heavy Japanese anti-aircraft fire and interference from some enemy night fighters. One American bomber was missing after the raid.

The Trobriand and Woodlark islands will be valuable as stepping-stones in a chain of fighter-plane bases from the Allied stronghold of Milne Bay, on the tip of New Guinea. Japanese-held Gasmata and Rabaul could be raided with comparative ease with the aid of these bases.

Navy Gives First News

The first report of landing actions came early yesterday when the Navy announced here in a communiqué that combined United States forces had landed June 30 (Solomons time) on Rendova Island, in the "New Georgia group, which is only five miles from the important Japanese air base of Munda, on New Georgia Island. The dispatch said that communiqué said, "No details have been received."

A hint that the fighting has extended came later from Secretary of the Navy Frank Knox in Los Angeles, where he is inspecting Pacific Coast installations. The Secretary declared that the Rendova attack was the beginning of "an offensive against the Japanese base at Munda and surrounding bases." Navy officials in Washington yesterday declined, however, to con-

Continued on Page Three

MARTINIQUE YIELDS, ASKS TERMS OF U.S.

Robert, 'to Avoid Bloodshed,' Ready to Accept Change of French Authority

The Martinique radio broadcast a statement last night by Admiral Georges Robert, Vichy's High Commissioner on the island, asserting that he had asked the United States Government to dispatch a "plenipotentiary to fix the terms for a change of French authority."

The broadcast said that Admiral Robert had taken the action "to avoid bloodshed." It was recorded by Federal Communications Commission monitors, The United Press said.

The admiral has, since the fall of France, stood firm in his determination to hold Martinique and nearby French islands in the Caribbean under his own rule, loyal to Marshal Henri-Philippe Pétain, French Chief of State.

The reception of the broadcast was marred by technical difficulties, but those portions of the broadcast that could be heard said:

"Communiqué to the population:

"In order to avoid bloodshed between the French and * * * I have asked the Government of the United States, under the double condition of its renewing the guarantee to maintain French sovereignty in these islands and of the nonintervention of American forces, to send a plenipotentiary to fix the terms for a change of French authority.

"* * * my duty to the people and the Marshal * * *

"Admiral Robert."

Recently there have been unconfirmed reports of clashes between the admiral's troops and elements favoring the end of the islands by

Continued on Page Eight

Laundry Workers Held Essential But the WMC Restricts Services

Special to THE NEW YORK TIMES.

WASHINGTON, June 30—The War Manpower Commission intended to the country's laundries today the same preferential treatment in the allocation of manpower as is given to essential war industries.

Laundries classified as "locally needed" by regional directors of the WMC will be supplied with workers by the United States Employment Service, will be protected from labor piracy and will have their existing labor force stabilized, except that there will be no occupational deferment under the Selective Service Act. They will receive this aid only if they discontinue luxury services to their patrons.

To be classified as "locally needed" they must meet standards agreed upon by the War Labor Board's Office of Civilian Requirements and the WMC. These standards are designed to enable the

Continued on Page Ten

War News Summarized

THURSDAY, JULY 1, 1943

The Allied Southwest Pacific and South Pacific Commands have started a broad offensive against Japanese positions. The first results of the combined naval, air and land operations are:

Landings on Rendova and New Georgia Islands in the Central Solomons, where fighting is going on.

Occupation, without opposition, of the Trobriand Islands and Woodlark Island off the southeastern tip of New Guinea at the north end of the Coral Sea.

A landing at Nassau Bay, ten miles south of Salamaua in New Guinea.

Heavy aerial bombardment of the big Japanese base at Rabaul, New Britain.

Gen. Douglas MacArthur is in general command of the combined operations, with Admiral William F. Halsey Jr. directing the offensive of the South Pacific forces. The battle area extends 500 miles north of Guadalcanal to Rabaul and 750 miles northwest to Salamaua [All the foregoing, 1:8.]

In London, Prime Minister Churchill pledged that after Hit-

ler's defeat "every man, every ship and every airplane in the King's service that can be moved to the Pacific will be sent and there maintained in action * * * for as many years as are needed to make the Japanese, in their turn, submit or bite the dust."

Mr. Churchill then announced that "very probably there will be heavy fighting in the Mediterranean and elsewhere before the leaves of autumn fall." He characterized Tunisia and the campaign against the U-boat as the two greatest Allied victories of the war, and promised that every corner of Germany would be bombed as thoroughly as the Ruhr had been. [All the foregoing, 1:5-6.]

On the other war fronts, Flying Fortresses raided Le Mans in France and the RAF hit targets in western Europe [5:2-3]. Reggio Calabria and Messina were bombed in the Mediterranean [6:2], and Russian troops captured a strong position on the Velikiye Luki front. [7:1.]

Admiral Robert, Vichy's High Commissioner in Martinique, asked the United States for terms under which the West Indies islands could be transferred to other French authority. [1:7.]

The New York Times.

LATE CITY EDITION
Moderately cool with gentle winds today.

Temperature Yesterday—Max., 80; Min., 72
Sunrise, 6:25 A. M.; Sunset, 7:27 P. M.

VOL. XCII.—No. 31,268.   Entered as Second-Class Matter, Postoffice, New York, N. Y.   NEW YORK, FRIDAY, SEPTEMBER 3, 1943.   THREE CENTS NEW YORK CITY

Copyright, 1943, by The New York Times Company.

ALLIES LAND IN ITALY OPPOSITE MESSINA; 8TH ARMY LEADS, WITH AIR-NAVAL COVER; RUSSIANS DRIVE AHEAD, CAPTURING SUMY

HULL TO TAKE REINS OVER ALL AGENCIES IN ECONOMIC FIELD

Coordination of OEW, OFRRO and Lend-Lease Under State Department Is Due Soon

NOT ALL FRICTION ENDED

WFA and OEW at Odds—Capital Speculates on What Course Lehman Will Pursue

By JOHN MacCORMAC
Special to The New York Times.

WASHINGTON, Sept. 2—The coordination of the Office of Economic Warfare, the Office of Lend-Lease Administration and the Office of Foreign Relief and Rehabilitation Operations by the State Department in a way which will give the department complete control over their activities and leave them as instruments executing its policies has been planned and will shortly be put in effect, it was learned today.

Part of the plan is the formulation of a definite and coordinated policy with regard to the international economic activities of the Government. Hitherto there has been a general understanding in theory, but in practice some of the agencies which were supposed to execute economic policy have worked at cross-purposes.

The conflict between the foreign activities of some of the Reconstruction Finance Corporation subsidiaries and those of the Board of Economic Warfare exploded recently in the row between Vice President Wallace and Secretary Jones, which led to the coordination of these activities by the OEW under Leo T. Crowley as its new head.

Some Friction Still Exists

But there is still uncertainty regarding the representative spheres of OEW, Lend-Lease and OFRRO and, for that matter, friction between OEW and the War Food Administration as regards foreign food purchases. The plan, therefore, is to have the State Department effect a final coordination of their efforts, and there is a possibility that some or all of them might be absorbed in the process.

This is not only believed to be the policy of the President and Secretary Hull, but it is understood to be approved by Mr. Crowley and Edward Stettinius Jr., lend-lease administrator. There is some doubt, however, whether ex-Gov. Herbert H. Lehman is willing to subordinate OFRRO to the State Department to the extent desired.

From a spokesman for Mr. Crowley it was learned that close collaboration with the State Department has from the first been one of his objectives. Mr. Crowley has indicated that as soon as the coordination is made and the administrative facilities have been set up, the time will have arrived for a substantial simplification of the Government's foreign economic set-up.

OEW Changes Held Temporary

It was because of these views that the reorganization of OEW announced Tuesday was regarded as of a transitory rather than permanent character.

For instance, James L. McCamy, who was appointed assistant to the director, will soon leave again to join the Bureau of the Budget. Hugh B. Cox, who will act as general counsel, will work only part time with OEW, and the rest of the time as assistant attorney general of the United States. No executive director was named, and Lauchlin Currie, who will act as executive officer, is on "loan" from the President's office.

Before OEW and lend-lease are placed under the State Department, however, the details of foreign economic policy will have been worked out and men of the requisite business ability will have been added on

Continued on Page Seven

Meat Ration Points Are Cut But Butter Will Need More

Thirty-five Meat Items Are Reduced 1 to 2 Points on Report of Larger Supplies— Changes Take Effect Sunday

Special to The New York Times.

WASHINGTON, Sept. 2—Point values of most meats were lowered today by the Office of Price Administration, effective Sunday through September. An exception to the increased purchasing power of red stamps was creamery butter. It will call for twelve instead of ten points a pound. The buying power of blue stamps was reduced by an increase in the point values of many processed fruits and vegetables.

The changes in red stamp values were based on the belief that more meat would be available to civilians for the rest of this month. The ration costs of most lamb and bacon cuts were reduced one to two points a pound. Lower values were fixed for sirloin steak, roasts of beef and several variety meats.

The increase in the point value of creamery butter is not likely to be noticed in most urban areas, where dealers, because of acute shortages, have been restricting customers to a quarter pound at a time and getting three points for the quarter pound, or twelve points a pound.

Farm or country butter was listed separately for the first time in the new point value schedules. To it a point value of six points a pound was assigned. Previously country butter had the same point value as creamery butter. The reduction was intended to spur the movement of farm-churned butter to urban markets to relieve the shortage of creamery butter.

"The further increase in the point value of creamery butter is necessary because purchases near butter-producing areas have been so large at a ten-point value that shortages developed in other parts of the country," the OPA said. "In addition butter production during

Continued on Page Eight

CONGRESS TAX MOVE IRKS MORGENTHAU

Joint Committee Plans to Subpoena Data Direct From Internal Revenue Body

Special to The New York Times.

WASHINGTON, Sept. 2—A conflict has arisen between the joint committee of Congress on internal revenue taxation and the Treasury over the committee's power to obtain tax data direct from officials of any Government department or agency and this may lead to a test in the courts of the committee's authority.

The 1942 revenue act empowered the committee to obtain such data from officials of the Bureau of Internal Revenue or any other department without sending its requests through departmental heads. The committee, jointly set up by the Senate Finance and House Ways and Means Committees, has seldom agreed with the Treasury on tax matters in recent years. Of late it has been paying less and less attention to the Treasury's views and insisting on writing its own tax bills.

It was up to give Colin F. Stam, the committee's chief of tax experts, opportunity to make use of the fiscal and economic experience to be found in Government departments and particularly in the Internal Revenue Bureau that Congress was asked to authorize it to go over the head of Secretary Morgenthau to his subordinates and to deal similarly with other divisions.

Although neither the Treasury nor Mr. Stam would comment on

Continued on Page Ten

1,330 JAPANESE SAIL ON EXCHANGE LINER

Gripsholm Leaves on Second Trip—Teia Maru to Bring Americans Back Home

The exchange liner Gripsholm, painted white and carrying in huge letters on her side the word "Diplomat," sailed from her anchorage in New York Harbor early yesterday on her second mission to exchange Japanese civilians for Americans who have been interned in the Orient since December, 1941.

Gaily painted like the cruise ship she was before the United States Government chartered her in the spring of 1942 from the Swedish-American Line, the big vessel carried the gold and blue marks of Sweden, painted flags and brilliant lighting arrangements to identify her through submarine-infested waters.

In her cabins there were, according to announcements of the War and State Departments in Washington, 1,330 Japanese civilians who will be exchanged for Americans and nationals of other Western Hemisphere nations in the port of Mormugao, Portuguese India, on or about Oct. 15.

The Americans and their fellow internees—1,500 of them, including 1,250 citizens of the United States—are to travel from the Orient on the Japanese-flag liner Teia Maru. The Washington announcement said that the Teia Maru was scheduled to leave Japan on Sept. 15, touching at ports in China, the Philippines and Indo-China to take on additional passengers, and calling at Singapore for fuel and wa-

Continued on Page Five

Browder Charges 'Bad Faith' Delays Opening a Second Front

Earl Browder, general secretary of the Communist party of the United States, asserted at a party meeting last night in Manhattan Center, 311 West Thirty-fourth Street, that Anglo-American relations with Soviet Russia would "deteriorate sharply" unless a second front in Western Europe was opened before the end of summer.

The meeting was a special one called to hear Mr. Browder discuss the present situation. About 3,000 persons were in the hall.

Mr. Browder argued that we should not wait until next spring in the hope that victory can then be "bought much more cheaply," but should land in full force now in an effort to win a quick victory and take some of the burden of land fighting off the Red Army. He held that military occupation

by "fighting armies" was the only way nazism could be ended.

Mr. Browder, who is not a military expert, vigorously expressed the opinion that our troops were overwhelmingly able to open a second front whenever their leaders gave the word. But the British and American general staffs, he charged, have acted in the role of "politicians subject to reactionary influence," and have overruled themselves as military leaders, in which capacity, he said, they realize the need for a second front. Counting out "weakness" as a reason for not opening a second front, he said the only alternative was "bad faith."

Mr. Browder charged that "dark and sinister forces" in this country were accusing the Soviet Union of

Continued on Page Four

AIR BLOWS PRESSED

French Fields Pounded as Fortresses Join British in Sweeps

POWER PLANT IS HIT

Canal Locks Smashed on Key Dutch Route Serving Antwerp

New, Heavy Air Raids As Allies Land in Italy

By The United Press.

LONDON, Friday, Sept. 3—Powerful forces of Allied bombers ranged over the northern flank of the European continent early today, almost simultaneously with the invasion of Italy.

A long procession of bombers streamed out over the British coast, flying so high they could not be seen from the ground, although the roar of their motors was audible.

By The United Press.

LONDON, Friday, Sept. 3—American Flying Fortresses, culminating an evening of widespread activity that saw Royal Air Force Fighter Command planes in their biggest operation of the year, blasted enemy airfields at Mardyck and Denain in northern France late yesterday, a joint British-American communiqué reported today.

Squadrons of British Spitfires and Typhoons escorted medium B-26 Marauder bombers of the Eighth United States Air Force Spitfires. One medium and one light bomber and two fighters were lost in the heavy operation.

Fast and deadly P-49 Thunderbolts covered the Fortresses in their hard-hitting foray against the northern French airfields. "Good bombing results were observed on all targets," the joint communiqué said, adding that four enemy aircraft were destroyed—one by the Fortresses and three by Spitfires. One medium and one light bomber and two fighters were lost in the heavy operation.

The B-26 Marauder medium bombers of the Eighth United States Air Force attacked the power station at Mazingarbe, near Bethune, France, "with good results," the fighter pilots reported.

Continued on Page Six

RED ARMY ROLLING

Storms Ukraine Citadel and Seizes Towns on Kiev Rail Line

DONBAS KEYS TAKEN

Nazis Retreat Toward Dnieper—550 Places Fall in Two Days

By The Associated Press.

LONDON, Friday, Sept. 3—Moscow announced early today that five Red armies plunging westward had cut the Bryansk-Kiev railway 150 miles from Kiev, smashed German reinforcements in a six-mile gain on Smolensk and rolled up Axis lines in a forty-five-mile-wide spurt in the Donets Basin.

Premier Joseph Stalin, in an order of the day, announced late yesterday that the Ukraine citadel of Sumy, ninety miles northwest of Kharkov, had fallen to Gen. Nikolai Vatutin's army, and a communiqué announced the capture of Krolevets and Yampol, two points on the vital Bryansk-Kiev railway linking the enemy's central and southern fronts.

Lisichansk, Voroshilovsk, Slavyanoserbak and other cities were seized in the Donets Basin, while Budennovka, twenty miles from Mariupol, was taken in the push along the rim of the Sea of Azov, said the communiqué, as recorded by the Soviet monitor.

250 More Places Overrun

The swiftness of the Russian advances and the tone of the communiqué indicated that the Germans were engaged in a large-scale retreat toward the Dnieper River, particularly in the huge Donets Basin. The bulletin, however, emphasized that the Germans were fighting stubbornly all along the 600-mile front.

More than 9,000 Germans were killed yesterday as the Red Armies overran nearly 250 cities and villages, many of them strategic prizes, for a two-day bag of nearly 550 localities.

Germany's 1941 invasion lines have now been cracked by the Russians in a 1943 offensive that has carried the Red Army more than half way along the comeback trail.

Continued on Page Four

ACROSS NARROW WATERS TO EUROPE

Sept. 3, 1943
Allied forces spanned the Strait of Messina this morning to land on the toe of Italy. This map, a perspective view looking eastward, gives an idea how the mainland appeared to the invaders.

Other Invasions This Year Anticipated in Washington

By ROBERT F. WHITNEY
Special to The New York Times.

WASHINGTON, Friday, Sept. 3—While Washington slept, its somnolent thousands secure in the knowledge that plans laid at Quebec last week would be efficiently carried out, the word was flashed to the capital that the invasion of the Italian mainland had begun. It was the first penetration by the Allies of Europe's "Fortress Europe" and thus a historic event which defied the pledge of Adolf Hitler that his Reich, by its aggressions, would secure its future for a "thousand years."

Unlike the invasion of North Africa by American troops nearly a year ago and the opening of the Sicilian campaign about two months ago, the invasion was not announced in Washington. The first news to the public came in flashes from North Africa.

The announcement, as received here, told of Allied troops swarming across the Strait of Messina. Only on Tuesday Prime Minister Churchill, in his Canadian speech, had stated that the Germans had augmented their forces in Italy and intended to make a battleground of that country.

The Allied invasion was seen here as an answer both to that challenge by the Germans and to the demands that a second front be opened in Europe this year.

When the news came, it is probable that the President and Mr. Churchill, the pair who are directing the strategy of the two English-speaking nations of the United Nations, were awaiting the news of a successful landing together in the White House study, as it is known that when they meet neither one retires early.

It was hoped here in semi-official quarters that the invasion of Italy would answer the prayers of Russia that her Allies in the west would lift some of the load off her shoulders by an attack on the European Continent.

While it was confidently expected that the invasion of Italy

Continued on Page Three

PLANE OUTPUT 7,700 FOR AUGUST, A JUMP

Production This Month May Reach 8,000, WPB Says— Rise Despite New Designs

Special to The New York Times.

WASHINGTON, Sept. 2—Aircraft production last month totaled 7,700 planes, compared with 7,373, it was announced today, and the WPB reported today in tones of elation.

On the basis of the August figure, airplane production in September will top 8,000, it was said.

The rise in output last month as compared with July was at the rate called for in the production schedule. Both July and August production were below the original schedule, WPB officials said. But they maintain that the schedules are "unrealistic" in that they do not take into consideration the shifts in production occasioned by design changes and by many other factors.

Schedules have been adjusted three times so far this year, one official said, and are likely to be changed again. He added that "I'd rather make 6,500 planes of the type we needed than to meet the schedules which include many of the types we don't need and would rather not have."

He contended that "we got the planes we wanted. Those we didn't want we didn't get."

The discrepancy between the

Continued on Page Seven

DAWN IS ZERO HOUR

British and Canadians Storm Over Narrow Strait of Messina

ROME SAYS NOTHING

Allies Invade on Fourth Anniversary of Their War Declaration

By MILTON BRACKER

ALLIED HEADQUARTERS IN NORTH AFRICA, Friday, Sept. 3—The Allies have breached the "Fortress of Europe." On the fourth anniversary of the British and French declaration of war against Germany, Allied troops are striving to establish a bridgehead on the Italian side of the Strait of Messina.

Under the thunderous support of Allied sea and air power, British and Canadian units of the British Eighth Army crossed the narrow strip of water to bring the war at long last to the mainland of the Continent that Germany has enslaved.

Preceded by a pounding artillery barrage across the strait and by a number of reconnaissance landings, the main party set foot on the tip of the Calabrian Peninsula, opposite Messina, at 4:30 A. M. today (10:30 P. M. Thursday, Eastern War Time).

No details were available on either this morning's historic assault or the previous reconnaissance missions. The latter were, plainly, those referred to in German broadcasts as landing attempts beginning on Aug. 29, which the Germans said had been repulsed with heavy losses.

[A Mutual Broadcasting System commentator, speaking from Algiers, quoted an official Allied spokesman today as saying that the Allies were "apparently engaged in heavy fighting." The Associated Press reported from London.]

A special communiqué issued here at 7:20 A. M. said merely: "Allied forces under General Eisenhower continued their advance. British and Canadian troops of the Eighth Army, supported by Allied sea and air power, attacked across the Strait of Messina early today and landed on the mainland of Italy."

Field Guns Pave Way

ALLIED HEADQUARTERS IN NORTH AFRICA, Sept. 3—British, Canadian and other troops of the British Eighth Army spearheaded the invasion armies, swarming across the Strait of Messina from Sicily under cover of Allied aircraft and the big guns of British and American warships. The Eighth Army's field guns helped to pave the way for the invasion troops with a thunderous barrage that silenced several of

Continued on Page Two

Arnold in Britain To Meet Air Chiefs

By The Associated Press.

LONDON, Sept. 2—Lieut. Gen. Henry H. Arnold, chief of the United States Army Air Forces, and Maj. Gen. William E. Lee, commander of an air-borne division, who is known as the father of American parachute troops, arrived in Britain today from the United States. They plunged immediately into a study of the military set-up and recent operations by the Eighth United States Air Force.

General Arnold is here for conferences with Air Chief Marshal Sir Charles Portal, Lieut. Gen. Jacob L. Devers, commanding all United States forces in the European theatre; Maj. Gen. Ira C. Eaker, commander of the Eighth Air Force, and other British and American officers.

War News Summarized

FRIDAY, SEPTEMBER 3, 1943

Allied forces crossed the Strait of Messina from Sicily and landed in southern Italy early this morning to start the long-awaited invasion of Europe, according to a communiqué issued by the Allied Headquarters in North Africa. The landing was the culmination of a series of devastating air blows. [1:8, maps pages 1, 2 and 3.]

The Russian war machine rolled relentlessly on yesterday. The important Ukrainian town of Sumy was captured, the Bryansk-Kiev railway was severed and a wide advance was made in the Donets Basin, with every indication that a German retreat to the Dnieper River was in full swing. [1:5, map P. 4.]

Continuing the softening-up process on the Continent, Allied fighters and bombers hit airfields in Northern France shortly after RAF fighters had returned from the Netherlands. They were swept from some of the most vital water communications controlled by the Germans. The bomb racks were unloaded on the strategic Hansweert Canal, where three locks were hit. The RAF reported that 107,520 American tons of bombs had been dropped on Germany in the first eight months of 1943. [1:4, map P. 6.]

The Navy Department in Wash-

ington still withheld details of Tuesday's raid on the Marcus Islands, but some of the mystery was dispelled by the Japanese, who acknowledged damage to the strategic air and observation base and estimated the American task force at 160 fighter and bomber planes from two carriers. Military observers at Pearl Harbor believe that the Marcus raid was just a feint and that a major blow against Japan's outer defenses is near. [5:1.]

Allied bombers dropped a record of 206 tons of bombs on the Japanese bases at Madang, New Guinea, General MacArthur reported. Ground troops also were strafed at Salamaua. [5:5, with map.]

The Pacific phase of the war is believed to be one of the principal subjects being discussed by Prime Minister Churchill and President Roosevelt in Washington. They have been holding day and night sessions. Prime Minister also has conferred with high military and supply mission heads. [4:4.]

Another indication of the stepped-up pace to launch a second or a third front was the report from Washington of an August output of 7,700 planes as against 7,373 for July and indications that the figure might top 8,000 in September. [1:7.]

Portugal Weighs Idea of Fighting; Premier Tells People to Prepare

Neutral diplomatic quarters in London reported yesterday that Portugal was contemplating a declaration of war against Japan and might follow it with declarations against other Axis powers, according to The United Press.

The Portuguese action is said to arise from the fact that the Japanese established military control over Macao, as well as from Japanese-held Hong Kong, as well as from Japanese-held Timor. They have been holding day and night sessions. Prime Minister also has conferred with high military and supply mission heads.

Portuguese naval reservists have been called up during the past ten days. It was understood reliably that 10,000 reservists were being called to the Army. It was suggested that Portugal was now preparing to send expeditionary forces to free Macao and Timor.

The Government of Portugal on Wednesday night issued a formal

LISBON, Sept. 2 (UP)—Premier Antonio de Oliveira Salazar stated today that Portugal's stepped-up military preparations were defensive but "in the unfortunate times in which we are living may have to be used against foreign enemies as much as against internal elements of national disintegration."

Clamping a tight censorship on speculation regarding the military preparations, Dr. Salazar cautioned against expecting any change in the country's foreign policy.

[The London Evening Standard interpreted the "mobiliza-

Continued on Page Five

The New York Times.

LATE CITY EDITION
Continued moderately cool today; moderate winds.
Temperature Yesterday—Max., 74; Min., 67

VOL. XCII..No. 31,274.

Entered as Second-Class Matter, Postoffice, New York, N. Y.

NEW YORK, THURSDAY, SEPTEMBER 9, 1943.

Copyright, 1943, by The New York Times Company.

THREE CENTS NEW YORK CITY

ITALY SURRENDERS, WILL RESIST GERMANS; ALLIED FORCES LAND IN THE NAPLES AREA; RUSSIANS IN STALINO, CLEAR DONETS BASIN

SOVIET TIDE RISES

Swift Red Army Blows Capture Key City, Free Rich Region

DRIVE NEARS DNIEPER

More Rail Hubs Fall— Thrust Toward Kiev Also Extended

By The United Press.

LONDON, Thursday, Sept. 9— The Red Army recaptured Stalino, Russia's twelfth city, yesterday and freed the Donets Basin, which before the war produced more steel than Japan and Italy combined, in a great surge that took it to Grishino, ninety miles east of Dniepropetrovsk on the lower Dnieper River.

While the armies of Gen. Rodion Y. Malinovsky and Gen. Fedor Tolbukhin drove the enemy from the rich Donets Basin, crowded with coal mines and factories, the army of Gen. Konstantin Rokossovsky drove to a point ninety-six miles northeast of Borzna, twenty-three miles west of Bakhmach.

Bakhmach and Romni, forty-two miles to the southeast, were surrounded on three sides, a Moscow radio bulletin reported, and thus the Bakhmach-Kremenchug railroad was cut. The roads leading from Bakhmach to Kursk and Gomel had been cut previously and only the lines to Kiev and Odessa remained open.

Picked Troops Take Stalino

Red Army shock troops, picked from the sixteen infantry divisions that had driven the Germans through city after city in six days of tireless fighting, took Stalino by storm.

The Russian communiqué said the Red Army troops drove in on Stalino throughout Tuesday night and yesterday morning. They fought through the suburbs and then stormed the city from north and south, routing the enemy in a street-by-street fight and capturing a great store of spoils.

Twenty-five miles northwest of Stalino the Russians took Krasnoarmeiskoye, a big railroad junction controlling two of four rail roads leading west from the basin.

In all the Russians took, in addition to Stalino, a city of 462,000 persons, more than 150 towns in the Donbas alone, twenty of them important, in gains of up to twelve and a half miles. During their Donbas offensive the Russians took twelve towns of more than 50,000 persons each.

The Germans at Krasnoarmeiskoye so swiftly beaten that the Russians took nineteen guns and several loaded railroad trains.

March on Kiev Gains

On the Kiev front, the Russians took more than sixty towns in advances of up to twelve and a half miles. Their capture of Borzna in that area meant that the battle for the Dnieper River line had started. An advance of twenty-three miles to Nezhin would put the only remaining German supply line east of the river. The Russians had already advanced 101 miles in nine days from Rylsk, half the distance to Kiev.

More than 1,000 Germans were killed at Borzna, and 1,000 were killed in another sector.

South of Bryansk the Russians advanced up to six miles to take several villages. They were reported only twenty miles south of Bryansk. The Soviet communiqué, recorded from the Moscow radio, reported that the Russians were advancing west of the Naviya railroad junction in the area, driving the Germans through dense forest.

West and southwest of Kharkov nearly four miles were gained in some sectors and 1,200 Germans were killed.

The Russians were first to advance.

Continued on Page Twenty-two

New Fascist Regime Set Up, Nazis Report

By Cable to THE NEW YORK TIMES.

LONDON, Thursday, Sept. 9— The German radio announced early today that a "National Fascist government has been set up in Italy and functions in the name of Benito Mussolini."

The announcement, called a "proclamation by the National Fascist Government of Italy," said "this Badoglio betrayal will not be perpetrated. The National Fascist Government will punish traitors pitilessly."

The broadcast, in Italian, said nothing about the whereabouts of Mussolini, who has been reported under arrest. It was preceded by the playing of "Giovinezza," the Fascist anthem.

FOE'S MARCUS LOSS 80% NIMITZ SAYS

U. S. Carrier Planes Alone Hit at Japanese Isle—Hell Cat Fighter Excels in Test

By ROBERT TRUMBULL
By Telephone to THE NEW YORK TIMES.

PEARL HARBOR, Sept. 8—Admiral Chester W. Nimitz, Commander in Chief of the Pacific Fleet, issued today a communiqué that gave the first details of the raid on Marcus Island Sept. 1. Coincidentally three naval air officers who participated in the action gave an interview covering all phases of the raid, which they said destroyed a surprisingly well-fortified Japanese air base.

Action Consisted of Bombing

Admiral Nimitz's communiqué said that a United States Pacific Fleet task force under command of Rear Admiral Charles A. Pownall attacked the little island, 1,185 miles southeast of Tokyo, at dawn Sept. 1. The air officers revealed that the action consisted entirely of bombing and strafing by carrier-borne aircraft.

They said that the new Grumman F6F Hellcat fighter was employed in combat for the first time in the

Continued on Page Twenty-two

IN HEART OF ITALY

American 7th Army Is Reported in Van of Naples Operation

MORE POINTS NAMED

Landings Rumored at Genoa, Pizzo, Gaeta and Leghorn

By Wireless to THE NEW YORK TIMES.

ALLIED HEADQUARTERS IN NORTH AFRICA, Thursday, Sept. 9—The Allies have carried the land campaign against the Nazis in Italy to the vicinity of Naples in new operations announced within twelve hours of the disclosure by Gen. Dwight D. Eisenhower that the Italian armed forces had unconditionally surrendered.

The news was announced here a few minutes past 6:30 A. M. in the following thirteen words:

"Further operations have started on the Italian mainland in the vicinity of Naples."

In the absence of the slightest expansion of the communiqué, no details are available as to the forces participating. The single fact remained that the attack had been pressed near Italy's southern metropolis and port, second only to Genoa, in what obviously was a major amphibious thrust.

Naples is a city of more than 700,000 population—nearer 1,000,000 if the suburbs are included. The assault was launched eighty-three years and two days after Garibaldi entered the city alone in a dramatic liberation gesture, which culminated in the unification of the country ten years later.

Although there is no indication just how near the city itself the landing or landings were carried out, it is plain that Naples is the objective of the sea-borne invaders.

[This dispatch did not indicate the make-up of the landing parties. A Tunis radio broadcast

Continued on Page Four

U. S. SOLDIERS IN LONDON CHEER THE NEWS

Americans in front of the Red Cross Washington Club in the British capital when the news of Italy's surrender was announced.

Associated Press Radiophoto, passed yesterday by censor

Announcements of the Surrender

By Broadcast to THE NEW YORK TIMES.

ALLIED HEADQUARTERS IN NORTH AFRICA, Sept. 8—The texts of the proclamations by Gen. Dwight D. Eisenhower and Premier Pietro Badoglio follow:

By GENERAL EISENHOWER

This is Gen. Dwight D. Eisenhower, Commander in Chief of the Allied Forces.

The Italian Government has surrendered its armed forces unconditionally. As Allied Commander in Chief, I have granted a military armistice, the terms of which have been approved by the Governments of the United Kingdom, the United States and the Union of Soviet Socialist Republics. Thus I am acting in the interest of the United Nations.

The Italian Government has bound itself to abide by these terms without reservation. The armistice was signed by my representative and the representative of Marshal Badoglio and it becomes effective this instant.

Hostilities between the armed forces of the United Nations and those of Italy terminate at once. All Italians who now act to help eject the German aggressor from Italian soil will have the assistance and the support of the United Nations.

By PREMIER BADOGLIO

The Italian Government, recognizing the impossibility of continuing the unequal struggle against the overwhelming power of the enemy, with the object of avoiding further and more grievous harm to the nation, has requested an armistice from General Eisenhower, Commander in Chief of the Anglo-American Allied forces. This request has been granted. The Italian forces will therefore cease all acts of hostility against the Anglo-American forces wherever they may be met. They will, however, oppose attack from any other quarter.

CITY 'JUMPS GUN' IN WAR BOND DRIVE

Rallies, Sales Begin on Vast Scale—State Savings Banks Will Invest $600,000,000

As President Roosevelt and Secretary of the Treasury Henry J. Morgenthau Jr. opened the Third War Loan Drive for $15,000,000,000 last night over the radio, it was announced here that in the campaign to raise the State's quota of $4,709,000,000 the mutual savings banks in the State would buy $600,000,000 in Government bonds. The United States Steel Corporation and its subsidiaries will buy $100,000,000 in Government securities, with parts of the total allocated to districts where the corporation operates.

Restive to get its drive under way, New York City held preliminary rallies yesterday as Army convoys took into the five boroughs Navy gunners who had been rescued at sea. The largest meetings were held in Times Square and on the steps of the Sub-Treasury Building at Wall and Broad Streets.

Burgess Hails Italy's Surrender

The thousands assembled in the streets for these two gatherings cheered wildly as speakers announced the capitulation of Italy. Ticker tape, confetti and torn paper were thrown from the windows of buildings where workers in the financial community were listening to the rally.

The unconditional surrender of Italy is "bullish news" and will be a great help in the bond drive, W. Randolph Burgess, chairman of the War Finance Committee for New York State, said later in the

Continued on Page Sixteen

President Hails Victory But Warns of Real Foes

By JOHN H. CRIDER
Special to THE NEW YORK TIMES.

WASHINGTON, Sept. 8—President Roosevelt hailed the surrender of Italy tonight as "a great victory for the United Nations" and also "a great victory for the Italian people" against "their real enemies, the Nazis," but cautioned against over-optimism. Addressing the nation on the opening of the Third War Bond drive, the President said "the time for celebration is not yet" and added that "our ultimate objectives in this war continue to be Berlin and Tokyo."

"This war does not and must not stop for one single instant," he declared. "Your fighting men know that. Those of them who are moving forward through jungles against lurking Japs—those who are landing at this moment in barges moving through the dawn up the strange enemy coasts—those who are diving their bombs down on the target at roof-top level at this moment—every one of these men knows that this war is a full-time job and that it will

Toward the middle of his speech

the President interpolated three words which gave basis to reports that Allied armies already were on the move again in the Mediterranean when he spoke of troops in landing barges moving up to enemy coasts "at this moment."

Continued on Page Seventeen

Germans Charge Betrayal by Italy In Plot With Russian Government

By GEORGE AXELSSON
By Wireless to THE NEW YORK TIMES.

STOCKHOLM, Sweden, Sept. 8— Berlin's newspapers branded Italy's capitulation as cowardly treachery last night. The German press abounds in scathing denunciation of Premier Pietro Badoglio and King Victor Emmanuel, as well as the Italian people.

"Mussolini was too great a person for a nation like that," a German official said. This is the second time that Victor Emmanuel has broken his word, the newspapers say, because the King "left Germany in the lurch" in 1915 when he joined the Allies.

Forgetting its praise of the Italians during the heyday of their pact, Berlin now condemns the Italians as third-rate individuals. "The cowardly betrayal of Badoglio caps the crime," one paper said.

...by being committed in collusion with the Soviet Government, which is treason not only against Italy and Germany but also against all Europe.

Berlin added that the Germans had no intention of giving up their entrenchments in Italy, where they hoped to offer efficient resistance. Italy, since last night, is German-occupied territory to the extent that the Germans have been able to gain a firm footing there. In the Italian provinces occupied by the Germans, Berlin boasts fascism will be revived even if "we leave it to the Italians in those provinces to organize themselves along fascist lines."

Official circles are reviving accusations of broken words of honor

Continued on Page Nine

GEN. EISENHOWER ANNOUNCES ARMISTICE

Capitulation Acceptable to U. S., Britain and Russia Is Confirmed in Speech by Badoglio

TERMS SIGNED ON DAY OF INVASION

Disclosure Withheld by Both Sides Until Moment Most Favorable for the Allies—Italians Exhorted to Aid United Nations

By MILTON BRACKER
By Wireless to THE NEW YORK TIMES.

ALLIED HEADQUARTERS IN NORTH AFRICA, Sept. 8—Italy has surrendered her armed forces unconditionally and all hostilities between the soldiers of the United Nations and those of the weakest of the three Axis partners ceased as of 16:30 Greenwich Mean Time today [12:30 P. M., Eastern War Time].

At that time, Gen. Dwight D. Eisenhower announced here over the United Nations radio that a secret military armistice had been signed in Sicily on the afternoon of Friday, Sept. 3, by his representative and one sent by Premier Pietro Badoglio. That was the day when, at 4:50 A. M., British and Canadian troops crossed the Strait of Messina and landed on the Italian mainland to open a campaign in which, up to yesterday, they had occupied about sixty miles of the Calabrian coast from the Petrace River in the north to Bova Marina in the south.

The complete collapse of Italian military resistance in no way suggested that the Germans would not defend Italy with all the strength at their command. But the capitulation, in undisclosed terms that were acceptable to the United States, the United Kingdom and the Union of Soviet Socialist Republics, came exactly forty days after the downfall of Benito Mussolini, the dictator who, by playing jackal to Adolf Hitler, led his country to the catastrophic mistake of declaring war on France three years and three months ago this Friday.

Negotiations Begun Several Weeks Ago

The negotiations leading to the armistice were opened by the war-weary and bomb-battered nation a few weeks ago, it was revealed today, and a preliminary meeting was arranged and held in an unnamed neutral country.

The Italians who approached the British and American authorities were bluntly told that the terms remained what they had been: unconditional surrender. They agreed, and the document was signed five days ago. But it was agreed to hold back the announcement and its effective date until the moment most favorable to the Allies.

That moment came today, when the Allied Commander in Chief, in a historic broadcast, announced the armistice. He concluded with the reminder that all Italians who aided in the ejection of the Germans from Italy would have the support and assistance of the United Nations.

One hour and fifteen minutes after the General's voice had gone out over the air, Marshal Badoglio faced a microphone in Rome and confirmed the armistice. He concluded with the promise that the Italian forces would oppose attacks "from any other quarter," although they were laying down the arms that they had taken up against the Anglo-American armies.

Military Aspect Emphasized

Although it was emphasized that the armistice was a strictly military instrument, "signed by soldiers," it was disclosed that it contained a clause binding Italy to comply with political, economic and financial conditions to be imposed at the Allies' discretion.

[It was believed that the armistice conditions were substantially the same as those imposed on France in 1940, which allowed the Germans to use all strategic French ports and military bases to wage war against Britain, The United Press reported.]

Immediately after the announcement of the armistice, the Allies made two appeals—one to the Italian people and one to the Italian Fleet—urging them to rally to a cause that was, in effect, the liberation of their own country. The appeal to the people was disseminated by radio and air-borne leaflet, while that to the Navy was delivered by Admiral Sir Andrew Browne Cunningham, the Allies' Mediterranean naval commander.

The Italian people, particularly transport, railroad and dock workers, were asked not to give the slightest aid to the Germans. The men who ran Italian ships received specific instructions how to bring their vessels into the protection of the United Nations.

Although the fear was proved unjustified by Marshal Badoglio's broadcast, the Allies had taken no chances of a German move to forestall his giving the news to the people. As a safeguard, they had obtained from the Italians an agreement to leave one senior military representative behind when the others returned to Rome. This man is now in Sicily and presumably had broadcast the decision to the Italian public.

As a further earnest of good faith, Marshal Badoglio had arranged to send the text of the proclamation that he made this evening to Allied Headquarters here. He kept his word.

1,181 Days at War and Losses

Italy quit the war after 1,181 days, during which she steadily lost territory and prestige. Last May 7, with the fall of Tunis and Bizerte, the last Italian soldier in North Africa was doomed. Since then, Sicily, part of Metropolitan Italy, was occupied in thirty-eight days.

The Italians endured two raids on military targets in Rome

Continued on Page Three

War News Summarized

THURSDAY, SEPTEMBER 9, 1943

Italy has surrendered unconditionally, and all hostilities between that country and the United Nations ceased yesterday. An armistice was signed last Friday, the same day that Italy was invaded, but the victors reserved the right to withhold announcement until the most favorable moment for the Allies. The armistice terms had been approved by the United States, Britain and Russia.

General Eisenhower, announcing the surrender, promised support to all Italians who would help fight the Germans. Marshal Badoglio issued a proclamation ordering all fighting against the "Anglo-American forces" to cease and commanding resistance to "attacks from any other quarter."

Allied radios and planes carried messages urging the Italians to take vengeance on their "German oppressors" and to prevent trains, ships and trucks from carrying German troops or supplies. [All the foregoing. 1:8; map, P.3.]

Landings in the Naples area followed only a few hours after the surrender announcement and it was believed the Allies were attempting to cut off German troops in southern Italy. The American Seventh Army was reported among the invading forces. [1:3; map, P. 4.] Earlier, the Italian Navy and merchant marine had been urged to take their ships to designated points or to scuttle the vessels as a last resort to keep them from the Germans. [7:4.]

Wild demonstrations of joy were reported from all over Italy, but in the north they gave way to sober realization of continued danger when the Germans occupied Milan and other cities and imposed martial law. [3:1.]

No official comment came from Berlin, but the German radio, after withholding the news for hours, was furious at the "treachery." [1:5-6.]

Germany's Balkan satellites were so shaken by the Italian surrender that Bulgaria, Rumania and Hungary were reported ready to follow Italy out of the war. [10:3.]

President Roosevelt, in a radio address last night, termed the surrender a great victory for the Italian people as well as for the United Nations. But he warned: "The time for celebration is not yet. Our ultimate objectives in this war continue to be Berlin and Tokyo." [1:5-6.]

The actual fighting in Italy was of a minor nature. Land forces advanced on both coasts. [3:6.] Airfields were hit by Allied bombers and the Rome radio reported heavy raids on suburbs of the city. [4:1.]

With one Axis partner out of the war, the two others continued to be hit hard. The Red Army captured Stalino and cleared the Germans out of the Donets Basin. [1:1; map, P. 22.] Allied bombers from Britain struck enemy airfields in France and Belgium [22:2], while down in New Guinea Japanese troops were providing weak opposition as the Allies closed in on Lae. [22:1.]

The naval task force that raided Marcus Island Sept. 1 destroyed 80 per cent of the Japanese military installations. We lost three planes. [1:2.]

The New York Times.

LATE CITY EDITION
Cloudy and warmer today; fresh winds.
Temperature Yesterday—Max., 30; Min., 9
Sunrise, 6:18 A. M.; Sunset, 4:36 P. M.

VOL. XCIII. No. 31,381.
Entered as Second-Class Matter,
Postoffice, New York, N. Y.
Copyright, 1943, by The New York Times Company.
NEW YORK, SATURDAY, DECEMBER 25, 1943.
THREE CENTS NEW YORK CITY

EISENHOWER NAMED COMMANDER FOR INVASION; 3,000 PLANES SMASH FRENCH COAST; BERLIN HIT; ROOSEVELT PROMISES NATION A DURABLE PEACE

STRIKE CALLED OFF BY 230,000 IN TRAIN AND ENGINE UNIONS

But Non-Operating Men Meet Carriers and Reject Offer Made for Overtime Pay

GIVE BYRNES NO ANSWER

He Says Agreement Must Meet Requirements Set Forth in the Stabilization Program

By LOUIS STARK
Special to The New York Times.

WASHINGTON, Dec. 24—The Brotherhood of Locomotive Engineers and the Brotherhood of Railroad Trainmen today canceled notices for a strike of their 230,000 members on Dec. 30 in view of President Roosevelt's offer and their acceptance of arbitration by the Chief Executive.

The conductors, firemen and switchmen's unions, also members of the "Big Five" operating and transportation brotherhoods, representing more than 120,000 employes, have rejected arbitration by the President and have not called off the strike of their members set for Dec. 30.

The other major development today in the railroad wage situation was a three-hour conference in the office of James F. Byrnes, chief of the Office of War Mobilization, participated in by committees of the railroads and of spokesmen for the fifteen non-operating unions, whose 1,100,000 members are scheduled to strike on Dec. 30.

At this meeting it was reported that the non-operating unions asked for a wage increase of 6 cents an hour as compensation for overtime after forty hours. These employes receive overtime after forty-eight hours of service. The carriers are reported to have offered 4 cents an hour for overtime, but it is understood that this was rejected by the unions.

Insists on Negotiations

B. M. Jewell, chief negotiator for the unions, is said to have been pressed by Mr. Byrnes for a reply to the President's demand that the non-operating employes permit him to act as sole and final arbiter in their dispute with the carriers.

The union leader is said to have replied with some asperity that the President last night gave the unions until Monday to reply to the arbitration proposal, and that in the meantime they had obtained from the President authority to proceed and seek an agreement with the carriers, whose committees were headed by Jacob Aronson, vice president of the New York Central Railroad.

The offer of 4 cents an hour for overtime was understood to be above the 4 to 10 cents an hour sliding scale wage increase recommended in the non-operating unions' case by an emergency board, convened after Frank M. Vinson, the Economic Stabilization Director, had rejected the 8 cents an hour proposal of a previous emergency board.

Byrnes' Statement

The conference in Mr. Byrnes' office, which was attended for a short time by Mr. Vinson, ended at 5:30 P. M. and the following statement was issued on Mr. Byrnes' behalf:

"The representatives of the carriers and the non-operating brotherhoods met in the conference room of the Office of War Mobilization.

"The representatives of the carriers were not present at the conference the President held with representatives of the brotherhoods yesterday afternoon. Justice Byrnes advised the carriers' representatives that the President desired to know whether they would object to his arbitrating the differences between the carriers and the non-operating brotherhoods.

"The representatives of the carriers stated that they were entirely willing to agree that the President should arbitrate the differences just as they had agreed to in

Continued on Page Twenty-six

17 Perish as Fire Sweeps 42d Street Lodging House

Scores Hurt in 'Bowery-Type' Building Disaster, Worst of Its Kind Here in Years—Many Trapped Asleep

Sixteen bodies had been removed last night from a five-story brick structure at 437-439 West Forty-second Street, between Ninth and Tenth Avenues, the four upper floors of which were occupied by a "Bowery-type" lodging house, after one of the city's worst fires in years virtually had consumed the entire interior.

A seventeenth victim died at 7:15 P. M. in Roosevelt Hospital, to which most of the scores of injured were removed.

The actual loss of life probably never will be known. With most of the victims burned beyond recognition and in many cases nothing remaining but bones, the task of counting the dead and identifying them was proving almost impossible. Authorities, after checking for hours, could not even determine how many persons were in the building at the time of the fire. They were faced with the fact that the lodging house had beds in three-foot by six cubicles, separated by flimsy plywood partitions, and in hall-like dormitories "accommodating" 248 persons. It was said the beds were well filled with restaurant and other night workers.

The fire, believed to have smoldered for three hours, started at 2 P. M. as if set by a hundred torches. Trapped in their sleep many were burned to death in their "cells," rooms so tiny that a lodger had literally to crawl into bed through a special door on a central vertical hinge that folded to permit entry.

The victims groped through confusion

Continued on Page Twenty-six

WLB PEACE OFFER WIRED STEEL UNION

Davis Tells Murray Retroactivity Can Be Reconsidered Within Wage Formula

Special to The New York Times.

WASHINGTON, Dec. 24—William H. Davis, chairman of the War Labor Board, telegraphed today to Philip Murray, president of the CIO United Steel Workers, that if labor members of the board desired to reconsider their vote on the retroactive pay issue the public members will favor such reconsideration.

But, while he indicated that a retroactive basis might be approved within the framework of the present ("Little Steel") wage stabilization formula, Mr. Davis stated in his message that the public members could not now determine "any question of retroactivity that might come up in any future change in the wage stabilization policy."

Presuming that any such future change would be applied to "all wage-earners," he wrote that retroactivity in general or in particular ought to be decided when and if the change is made.

[A production stoppage was reported early this morning by The Associated Press with the expiration of contracts at midnight covering 35,000 employes at the Republic Steel Corporation and Youngstown Sheet and Tube Company. At these plants in Youngstown and in Cleveland picketing began.]

"Misunderstanding" Deplored

Mr. Davis' telegram said:

"You are quoted as saying that the proposal of the public members of the War Labor Board was framed by permission of Archbishop Francis J. Spellman. Episcopal churches celebrated communion, while many churches of other faiths held can

Continued on Page Twenty-six

CITY AN OPEN HOUSE FOR WARTIME YULE

Heart-Warming Parties for Service Men and Women Are Chief Among Festivities

New York was far from a big, cold, gray city as it ushered in its third wartime Christmas last night with heart-warming church services, gay parties, gifts for the ill and unfortunate, and messages of good-will that brought cheer to its teeming millions and to the men and women visitors in the services.

It will not be a white Christmas, according to the weather man, but it will be cold.

Tens of thousands of visitors, many of them members of the families of service men, were in the city for the week-end. Railroads, doing a peak business, were handicapped by the bitter cold in the surrounding country. Virtually every train to and from the city was loaded to capacity, with standees in the aisles. Because of the cold, many trains were late.

Grand Central Terminal and the Pennsylvania Station were packed. Policemen kept the crowds moving. Buses and bus terminals throughout the city did a land-office business, too.

Stores Experience Let-Up

Only in the stores did Christmas bring a let-up. While business was brisk, the real crush had subsided and only last-minute shoppers were on hand.

The churches of all faiths welcomed the Holy Day with midnight services, offering prayers for a victorious peace. There were many men in uniform at masses, carol services and communion.

Virtually every Roman Catholic church celebrated a midnight mass

Continued on Page Nine

Biggest of War Plants Will Make Army Bomber Engines at Chicago

By The United Press.

CHICAGO, Dec. 24—The country's largest war plant, a series of structures sprawling over 500 acres of land, was ready today to turn out an unending stream of engines for Army bombing planes.

The giant inland plant on Chicago's South Side was built by the Dodge division of the Chrysler Corporation. Willow Run could be set down in the main building with enough room left to lay out twenty baseball diamonds.

There are nineteen buildings in the plant, all ready for production. The main building, the machining-assembly unit, covers eighty-two acres.

The plant has fourteen cafeterias and kitchens, butcher shops and bakeries to feed employes.

A parking lot a mile and a quarter long will accommodate 14,000 automobiles. The interplant communication system has 500 miles of telephone lines. Utility services are sufficient for a city of 75,000 population.

Officials revealed that the machine shops had been turning out parts for 2,000-horsepower, eighteen-cylinder Wright engines.

The plant, already called "Hitler's headache," will employ more than 25,000 persons when it enters mass production.

Prior to the completion of the Chicago plant, the bomber factory owned by the Government and operated by Henry Ford at Willow Run, twenty-five miles from Detroit, was called the largest war production unit in the world. It covers two square miles.

RECORD AIR BLOW

'Forts,' Liberators and Medium Bombers Rock 'Special' Targets

ALL CRAFT RETURN

RAF Pounds the German Capital With 1,120 Tons Before Dawn

By DAVID ANDERSON
By Cable to The New York Times.

LONDON, Dec. 24—The greatest number of American heavy bombers ever to take off from Britain attacked "special military installations" of the Germans along the coast of northern France today as part of record operations of probably 3,000 Allied warplanes across the Channel.

Before dawn hundreds of the most powerful bombers of the Royal Air Force struck Berlin again with more than 1,120 tons of high explosives and fire missiles.

Several features of this two-fisted battering by the Allied air forces on the eve of Christmas made the day a memorable one for the enemy, even taking into account the Anglo-American achievements of recent weeks.

Headquarters of the United States Eighth Air Force announced that 1,300 planes handled by American crews took part in the daylight missions.

An even greater number of RAF, Dominion and Allied planes were out. Every one of the bombers and fighters of the joint forces returned to its base, according to a communiqué issued by headquarters of the United States Army here and the British Air Ministry.

Included in the American force were the largest formations of Flying Fortresses and Liberators ever sent into the air. Since an estimated 750 United States "heavies" at one time have attacked targets in western Germany within the past month, the day's operations entailed the use of close to, if not exceeding, 800 four-motored bombers.

The most concentrated attacks were carried out in the Pas-de-Ca-

Continued on Page Three

TO KEEP IT BY ARMS

President Says 4 Nations Agree on This for as Long as Necessary

'COST MAY BE HIGH'

German Might Must End, He Says on Air, Warning 'Japs' of Bad News

By JOHN H. CRIDER
Special to The New York Times.

HYDE PARK, N. Y., Dec. 24—President Roosevelt promised the country and the world this Christmas Eve that they could look for insured peace with "certainty," even though "the cost may be high and the time long," and said that the United States, Great Britain, Soviet Russia and China were agreed to use force to maintain that peace "for as long as it may be necessary."

Speaking from the study in the Franklin D. Roosevelt Library, one of his favorite rendezvous, with his family gathered informally around him, the President gave his first comprehensive report on his recent conferences in the Middle East over the most extensive broadcast facilities ever set up in this country.

For the first time the President tempered his "unconditional surrender" ultimatum of Casablanca by stating that the United Nations did not want to enslave the German people but wanted them to have "a normal chance to develop in peace as useful and respectable members of the European family."

Here appeared to be one of the great achievements of the conference at Teheran—a united view by the Allies in Europe on what kind of a post-war Germany they would look for, which closes the gulf which appeared to exist between the Anglo-American "unconditional surrender" demand, and the more hopeful outlook for the future which the Russians have been

Continued on Page Eight

The text of the President's address appears on Page 8.

NEW INVASION COMMANDER IN CHIEF

Gen. Dwight D. Eisenhower
The New York Times, 1943

Pope Prays for Just Peace Kept by Wise Use of Force

By The Associated Press.

LONDON, Dec. 24—Praying that this may be the last war Christmas and that a truly Christian peace may be celebrated in the coming year, Pope Pius XII today called for the world's responsible leaders to check the instincts of hate and vengeance and give rise to "the resplendent dawn of a new spirit of world union."

Raising his voice to a vibrant ring in outlining "the principles for a peace program," the Pontiff called for a "normal measure of power," sanctions and "the employment of force" to achieve and maintain peace, but warned that true peace "can never be a harsh imposition supported by arms' alone.

"An hour like the present—so full of possibilities for vast beneficent progress no less than for fatal defects and blunders—has perhaps never been seen in the history of mankind," said the Holy Father, who spoke on Christmas Eve from the bayonet-circled Vatican, where he has been isolated except by radio since the Germans occupied Rome in September.

The 35-minute address was delivered on the radio in Italian, but an official English language translation later was made available.

Juridical Basis for Peace

"A true peace is not the mathematical result of a proportion of forces, but in its last and deepest meaning is a moral and juridical process," said the Pope, speaking from what he called the "abysmal ruins of this terrible war."

"It (peace) is not, in fact, achieved without the employment of force, and its very existence

Continued on Page Ten

The text of the Pope's address appears on Page 10.

RED ARMY TAKES KEY TO VITEBSK

Gorodok, 17 Miles From Goal, Falls After Russian Feint Outwits Nazi Defense

By The Associated Press.

LONDON, Saturday, Dec. 25—The Russian Baltic Army cracked a model German defense-in-depth line and captured the heavily fortified lake town of Gorodok, seventeen miles north of Vitebsk yesterday, sweeping on over 2,000 German dead in a continuing offensive to take sixty more towns and hamlets, Moscow announced early today.

Resuming their drive after a two-day slow-down, the Russians swept to within fifteen miles of the Vitebsk-Polotsk rail line, an important east-west supply artery for the Germans, as they advanced southward along the Nevel-Vitebsk railroad.

In another fighting area, the Russians moved southward of Zhlobin, south-southwest of Zhlobin—the

Continued on Page Five

GENERAL IS SHIFTED

Choice of 'Big 3' Parley, He Has Montgomery as British Field Leader

WILSON IS SUCCESSOR

Mid-East Head Honored —Spaatz to Direct U. S. Air Strategy

Special to The New York Times.

HYDE PARK, N. Y., Dec. 24—President Roosevelt announced today the appointment of Gen. Dwight D. Eisenhower to lead the invasion of Europe from the north and west, and from London came word that Gen. Sir Bernard L. Montgomery of North African fame would lead the British troops under General Eisenhower to form a proved and hard-hitting team to lead the assault on Adolf Hitler's "Fortress Europe."

The President's announcement of General Eisenhower's selection at the recent Teheran conference to lead the main attack on Germany also set to rest the old rumors regarding the probable appointment of Gen. George C. Marshall, Army Chief of Staff, to that post.

The President, in his radio report today on the recent conferences at Teheran and Cairo, also named Lieut. Gen. Carl A. Spaatz as commander of "the entire American strategic bombing force operating against Germany."

This was taken to mean that while General Eisenhower will confine his command to the mass attack on Europe from the north and west, General Spaatz' command over all American strategic bombardment of Germany extends to operations against Germany from all neighboring bases.

Quashes Marshall Rumors

The President gave a vivid picture in his radio report of the complete agreement between Prime Minister Churchill, Premier Stalin and himself regarding a detailed program for the annihilation of Germany by land and air from all directions.

He also paid high tribute to General Marshall, presumably to set old rumors at rest. Some persons have argued that the position to be occupied by General Eisenhower is of greatest importance, but the official decision now revealed seems to give credence to the opinion that the most important position in the Army is that of Chief of Staff, just as Washington is the only place from which the whole global operation can be commanded.

"To the members of our armed forces, to their wives, mothers and fathers, I want to affirm the great faith and confidence that we have in General Marshall and Admiral King (Chief of Naval Operations), who direct all of our armed might throughout the world," the President declared.

Their Military Genius Stressed

"Upon them," he said, "falls the responsibility of planning the strategy; of determining where and when to fight. Both of these men have already gained high places in American history; places which will record in that history many evidences of their military genius that cannot be duplicated today."

The announcement from London told not only of General Montgomery's appointment to head the British invasion forces under General Eisenhower but also of Gen. Sir Henry Maitland Wilson's appointment to replace General Eisenhower as commander of the Mediterranean Theatre and Gen. Sir Harold R. L. G. Alexander's appointment to command all Allied forces in Italy.

The Teheran military decision announced by the President proved as much as anything else that the American handling of the invasion of North Africa and of Italy had deeply impressed the Allied leaders. Those invasions may now be regarded as the testing phase of the main European invasion, since the American officers identi-

Continued on Page Two

War News Summarized

SATURDAY, DECEMBER 25, 1943

President Roosevelt proudly announced to the world yesterday the appointment of General Dwight D. Eisenhower as supreme commander of the Anglo-American invasion forces—a selection, he said, that was made at the Teheran conference, where every point concerning the impending east-west-south attack on Germany had been decided.

It was announced from London that General Wilson would succeed General Eisenhower as commander of the Allied forces in the Mediterranean theatre; that General Montgomery would be chief of British Army units under General Eisenhower; that General Alexander would head the Allied forces in Italy, and that General Spaatz would be American Air Force commander against Germany. [All the foregoing, 1:8.]

Peace is certain, but the cost of bringing it about will be high and the realization may be delayed, President Roosevelt declared during the Christmas Eve broadcast from his Hyde Park home. He said the United Nations had no desire to enslave the German people but wanted them to develop as respectable members of the European family. As for Japan, he said that empire is being enveloped in a band of steel and there is plenty of bad news for the Japanese in the offing. [1:5.]

Speaking from the German-surrounded Vatican, Pope Pius XII made a plea for a just peace and declared that a normal measure of power and the employment of force were needed to achieve it, but he decried any harsh imposition supported by arms alone. [1:6-7.]

An estimated 3,000 American and British planes of virtually all types—the greatest concentration in air history—bombed the Pas-de-Calais area of France, where, it is believed, the Germans had no desire to complete the German people but wanted assault on these targets, the American Eighth Air Force sent 1,300 planes, a record number for any single operation. All Allied planes returned. The attack followed a Royal Air Force blow at Berlin, reportedly hitting the southeast industrial area near Tempelhof. [1:4, map P. 3.]

The fortified town of Gorodok, seventeen miles from Vitebsk and on the Vitebsk-Nevel railroad, was successfully stormed by the Russian Army, which drove ahead to capture sixty other places. Southwest of Zhlobin, in southern White Russia, large German tank and infantry attacks were beaten back. [1:7, map, P. 5.]

The British Eighth Army captured Vezzani, three miles southwest of the Adriatic port of Ortona, where fighting continued in the streets. There was little activity except for patrol thrusts on the Fifth Army front, because of deep mud. Medium Allied bombers struck at the Riviera coast, hitting bridges, railroads and viaducts. Cape Gloucester, which seems to be shaping up as another possible invasion point on New Britain Island, was hit by 300 more tons of Allied aerial bombs, bringing the total tonnage dropped since Dec. 1 to 2,500. [6:1.]

The Navy announced that the United States submarine Grayling was presumably lost with her complement of sixty-five men. [6:2]

8th Army Wins Town Near Ortona; Americans Take a Hill, Lose One

By MILTON BRACKER
By Wireless to The New York Times.

ALGIERS, Dec. 24—The Allied armies in Italy kept up pressure all along the line yesterday despite the imminence of Christmas, but were unable to complete the capture of Ortona or accomplish substantial gains on the Fifth Army front.

Although Canadian units of Gen. Sir Bernard L. Montgomery's Eighth Army had driven back the last German defenders of Ortona to the northwest corner of the shell-blasted and tank-razed town, the defenders kept returning fire and apparently intended to deprive the Allies of the full use of the most important port immediately below Pescara as long as possible.

Evidence of the toll the Germans have been paying for their desper- ate defense of the area was the discovery of a new cemetery at the crossroads just southwest of Ortona with at least 100 German graves.

The Eighth Army did manage to wrest from the enemy another village three miles southwest of Ortona and a mile beyond the Ortona-Orsogna road. It was Vezzani, which is three and a half miles from the coast and, like Ortona, just about twelve miles from Pescara. Other units of General Montgomery's veteran army have also penetrated to the outskirts of Villa Grande, a mile northeast of Vezzani, a secondary road paralleling the coast.

On the Fifth Army front the

Continued on Page Three

"All the News That's Fit to Print"

The New York Times.

LATE CITY EDITION
Partly cloudy, slightly warmer today; gentle to moderate winds.
Temperatures Yesterday—Max., 63; Min., 55

Copyright, 1944, by The New York Times Company.

VOL. XCIII.—No. 31,544.

Entered as Second-Class Matter, Postoffice, New York, N. Y.

NEW YORK, MONDAY, JUNE 5, 1944.

THREE CENTS NEW YORK CITY

ROME CAPTURED INTACT BY THE 5TH ARMY AFTER FIERCE BATTLE THROUGH SUBURBS; NAZIS MOVE NORTHWEST; AIR WAR RAGES ON

TRANSIT MEN BALK AT MAYOR'S INQUIRY INTO OUTSIDE JOBS

Demand for Sworn Statements Covering Family Earnings Evokes Union Protest

RESENTMENT WIDESPREAD

Many Department Heads Cold Toward Policy and Some Authorize Dual Work

By PAUL CROWELL

Widespread resentment among city employes against Mayor La Guardia's crusade to keep them from holding outside jobs on their own time was intensified yesterday. It became known that Investigation Commissioner Edgar Bromberger, by direction of the Mayor, had asked the 35,000 employes of the unified transit system to make sworn answers to forty questions concerning their own employment and that of all working members of their families.

The Transport Workers Union and other organizations representing city transit workers already have registered informal protests and are considering formal action. It was reported that the TWU was prepared to ask its members receiving such questionnaires from Commissioner Bromberger's office to turn them over to the union.

The questionnaire, of a type said to have been sent to employes of other city agencies, asks the transit worker to give full details about his own job, any job he may have outside, any job his wife may hold, any jobs his children may be filling. Full details concerning pay rates on all such jobs are demanded. The workers are asked also how they obtained outside jobs, whether they paid anyone to get them and whether they are making payments to anyone in connection with outside jobs.

Board Members Dislike Policy

The regulations of the Board of Transportation do not forbid the holding of outside jobs and individual members of the board were known to feel that so long as employes were punctual and punctilious in their tasks their outside activities were their own affair. Despite this feeling, however, the board is prepared to carry out the policy laid down by the Mayor. An informal survey of other city agencies conducted last week indicated that most of their heads held about the same attitude, but felt that the Mayor's policy must be carried out if he insisted upon it.

The Mayor's insistence that city employes, regardless of departmental rules forego such activities, led him recently to demand that charges be brought against an electrical engineer employed by the Board of Transportation who was teaching one night a week at City College, receiving $12 for each night's work. An exchange of views between the Mayor and the Board of Transportation resulted in a decision to let the employe continue teaching until the end of the current term, with the understanding that he would not resume teaching in the fall.

The electrical engineer, who is a graduate of one of the country's leading technical schools, was certified by the Board of Transportation, after investigation, to be efficient, painstaking and punctual, and the Mayor was told that his outside work made him a better city servant, while the small additional income was a welcome addition to his modest salary. It was also pointed out to the Mayor that there was nothing in the board's rules or the law to bar the outside work. The Mayor is reported to have replied that the man must keep one job or the other, but could not hold both.

Outside work by employes is a live issue in the Board of Transportation, where it is estimated that at least 10 per cent of the 35,000 transit workers have extra work to increase family income.

Resentment against the Mayor's

Continued on Page 11

Laval Tries to Shift Funds to Argentina

Pierre Laval, chief of the Vichy government, recently tried to transfer $50,000 from Spain to Argentina, the Brazzaville radio said yesterday in a broadcast recorded at the Columbia Broadcasting System's short-wave listening station.

"A Madrid bank revealed to the Spanish authorities that a deposit of $50,000 had been made with them for transfer to an Argentinian bank," the French radio said. "An inquiry was opened, and the person behind the depositor was discovered: He is Pierre Laval."

The same broadcast reported: "Germans in France have been buying gold at very high prices. Among the German agents arrested by French police for illegal traffic in gold was one who identified himself in order to be freed. He told the police commissioner that he was the director of a bank in a small German town. Because of his age, he had not been drafted into active military service, but his competence in financial matters made possible his being used in this work, in which he had been engaged since 1940."

JOHNSTON IN RUSSIA SCOFFS AT U. S. REDS

Business Leader Also Praises Soviet 'Capitalism'—Calls Ideologies Bridgeable

By The United Press.

MOSCOW, June 4—With straight-from-the-shoulder frankness, Eric Johnston, president of the United States Chamber of Commerce, told 100 Soviet trade leaders yesterday that a gulf separated the economies of the United States and Russia, but that bridges of practical cooperation could be thrown across the other.

Mr. Johnston advocated extensive post-war trade and visits between American business and "Soviet capitalists" as one bridge, and said that "each of our countries should be allowed to pursue its own unique economic experiment unimpeded by the other."

Bluntly, he told the Russians that Americans "were most private-minded and most individual-minded and, make no mistake, we are determined to remain so and even become more so."

Mr. Johnston, who arrived in Russia last week, was luncheon guest of A. I. Mikoyan, Soviet Foreign Trade Commissar, at Spiridonovka House. At the table sat the top experts of the Soviet Foreign Office, United States Ambassador W. Averell Harriman and Soviet military men.

At first the Russians appeared nonplused by Mr. Johnston's bluntness, but later they burst into gales of mirth at his sallies at American Communists and Marxians.

"I shall try to show you my admiration for your heroic deeds and

Continued on Page 6

Enraged Bull Kills 2 Brothers, Gores Neighbor on Long Island

Special to The New York Times.

BABYLON, L. I., June 4—Two dairy farmers, brothers, were found this morning gored and trampled to death on the Ames Farm in North Babylon, victims of their Guernsey bull, which had run wild and scattered their herd of thirty cows over near-by roads. A neighbor, trying to round up the scattered herd, was gored in the groin by the infuriated animal.

State troopers were forced to shoot and kill the belligerent bull.

The victims were George W. Ames, 41 years old, and his brother, James Hawley Ames, 35, of North Babylon. So far as is known no one saw the unequal encounter that cost them their lives. Their bodies were discovered, lying about 100 feet apart, several hundred yards from the cow barn.

The first intimation that anything was amiss came with com-

Continued on Page 29

FOE 'EXPLAINS' STEP

Hitler Ordered Troops Out to Save Rome, Germans Assert

ENEMY PLEA BARED

Kesselring Made Last-Minute Renewal of Open-City Offer

By The Associated Press.

LONDON, June 4—The Germans announced tonight in a special communiqué—broadcast after the Allies had liberated Rome—the withdrawal of German troops to the northwest of the city and said that the Allies had received a plan whereby Rome would have been regarded as an "open city."

The open-city proposals were said to have been advanced at 11 P. M. on Saturday, less than twenty-four hours before Rome changed hands. The first word from Adolf Hitler's headquarters in several days asserted that the fight in Italy would continue and that measures were being taken "to force final victory for Germany and her allies." The communiqué said:

"As the front line, in the course of the present fighting in Italy, was gradually approaching nearer and nearer to the city of Rome, there was danger that Rome, one of the oldest cultural centers of the world, would be directly involved in the present fighting. Hitler has ordered the withdrawal of German troops to the northwest of Rome to prevent the destruction of Rome.

"The struggle in Italy will be continued with unshakable determination to break the enemy attacks and to force final victory for Germany and her allies. The necessary measures for an eventual German victory are being taken in close collaboration with fascist Italy and other allied powers.

"The year of invasion will bring Germany's enemies an annihilating defeat at the most decisive moment."

Kesselring's Proposals Listed

Field Marshal Gen. Albert Kesselring, the German commander in Italy, sent the Allies proposals that Rome be regarded as an open city, a special announcement from Hitler's headquarters said. The statement was broadcast by the German radio and was received only after a dispatch filed from Rome had announced the crushing of the last German resistance units within the city. The broadcast said:

"The German High Command announced that the supreme commander of German troops in Italy, Field Marshal Kesselring, had submitted proposals to the Vatican with the request that they should be conveyed to the Anglo-American High Command. The proposals confirmed the recognition of Rome

Continued on Page 4

U. S. 'HEAVIES' BOMB IN FRANCE ALL DAY

Attack Boulogne Area Twice, Rip Rail, Air Targets Near Paris—Genoa Blasted

By JAMES MacDONALD
By Cable to The New York Times.

LONDON, Monday, June 5—Continuing to pave the way for the Allied invasion of the Continent hundreds of Allied bombers and fighters from Britain scorched a 200-mile stretch of the French coast yesterday and penetrated inland.

Three separate missions were carried out by the Flying Fortresses and Liberators of the United States Eighth Air Force with fighter escort over northwestern France. They met little Luftwaffe opposition; the enemy flak ranged from moderate to heavy.

In the morning and again in the afternoon strong formations of the

Continued on Page 5

THE FIRST OF EUROPE'S WAR CAPITALS TO FALL TO THE ALLIES

The sign tells the troops they have entered Rome.
The New York Times (U. S. Signal Corps Radiotelephoto)

Road to Rome Hard Fought, Yet Crowded With Civilians

By MILTON BRACKER
By Wireless to The New York Times.

IN THE OUTSKIRTS OF ROME, June 4—The Fifth Army's entry into the suburbs of Rome was made along Highway 6—the Via Casilina, which runs into Rome at Centocelle, a suburb best known for its airport. But the advance did not mean a simple triumphal procession into the heart of Rome. It meant going in careful infantry columns along the sides of the road. Most of the men had their bayonets fixed and they wore deadly earnest expressions because two wrecked Sherman tanks along the approaches told what had happened to other Americans earlier today.

Just before 4 P. M., a huge column of smoke billowed up from the southwest corner of the city, indicating a demolition. At the same time, a mine went off with a terrible burst beyond the farthest of the two tanks, and it tore an Italian woman to pieces. As the afternoon wore on, the sniping

Continued on Page 4

CITY'S FALL FOCUSES POLITICAL CHANGES

Victor Emmanuel's Promise to Retire Recalled—Badoglio Cabinet May Step Down

Special to The New York Times.

WASHINGTON, June 4—Pending receipt of final details of the fall of Rome, most Government leaders tonight refrained from direct comment. It was felt that the first official reaction to the Allied victory would come from President Roosevelt in the radio address that the White House announced that he would make tomorrow night.

Interest in the news of the capture of the Italian capital centered not so much in the military victory as in the possible political consequences, particularly those stemming from King Victor Emmanuel's recent statement that he planned to retire as Italy's ruler as soon as Rome fell to the Allies.

The King announced April 12 that he intended to turn Italy's affairs over to Crown Prince Humbert, and said the transfer of power would take place "on the day on which the Allied troops entered Rome."

But Rome has been reached—the goal of conquerors throughout the ages, though none was ever before able to make the almost impossible south-north campaign. What Hannibal did not dare to do, the Allies' generals accomplished, but at such a cost in blood, materiel and time that it will probably never again be attempted.

All roads from all over the world led to Rome today as a United

Continued on Page 5

CONQUERORS' GOAL REACHED BY ALLIES

Fifth and Eighth Armies Drive Up From South on Rome in a Historic Campaign

By HERBERT L. MATTHEWS

ROME, June 4—The Allied troops fought their way into Rome this morning and at nightfall they were still fighting on the outer edges, which the Germans were defending despite all their protestations about considering Rome an open city. Other large German units faced entrapment south of Highway 6 unless they could be pulled back across the Tiber or through Rome.

But Rome has been reached—the goal of conquerors throughout the ages, though none was ever before able to make the almost impossible south-north campaign. What Hannibal did not dare to do, the Allies' generals accomplished, but at such a cost in blood, materiel and time that it will probably never again be attempted.

All roads from all over the world led to Rome today as a United

Continued on Page 5

War News Summarized

MONDAY, JUNE 5, 1944

Rome was liberated from the Nazi-Fascist aggressors last night. The first European capital to be wrested from the enemy came under full Allied control when a force that had fought its way up from the Anzio beachhead knocked out a German scout car in the center of the city. There was fierce fighting with enemy rear-guard detachments at the outskirts of Rome before the city was liberated.

Fifth Army units and the vanguard of the Eighth Army later, were sent in hot pursuit of the fleeing Germans. Rome was found to be 95 per cent intact, with destruction centered in the railroad yards. [All the foregoing 1:8; maps P. 2.]

German artillery and snipers held off the Allied advance between the airport at Centocelle and the city limits. Civilians, obviously happy over the departure of the Nazis, remained calm as United Nations troops moved in. [1:5-6.]

Hitler's headquarters announced after the Fifth Army had entered the city that the Germans had withdrawn to new lines northwest of the city. Shortly before the city fell they dispatched a proposal that Rome be declared an open city. [1:2.]

Capture of Rome, according to military observers in London, made it much more likely that the main objective of the offensive—destruction of the German Tenth and Fourteenth armies—would be accomplished, with possible enemy losses reaching up to 100,000. [3:1.]

The AMG, following closely upon the victorious Allied forces, was fully prepared to undertake the gigantic task of feeding some 2,000,000 civilians. Vast stocks of food have been accumulated for distribution. [1:6-7.]

Washington withheld official comment until President Roosevelt's radio address tonight, but the capital was interested in how soon King Victor Emmanuel would fulfill his promise to retire when Rome had fallen to the Allies. [1:7.]

American heavy bombers from Britain smashed three times at enemy installations in France yesterday as the air invasion continued unabated against little or any opposition. Italian-based aircraft struck rail lines on the French-Italian border. [1:4.]

United States troops resumed the offensive against the three airfields on Biak Island, off New Guinea. Thirty Japanese planes were shot down in widespread fights from Biak to Truk. [8:2.] Continued improvement in Allied positions was reported from Burma [8:3] although in China the Japanese made some gains toward Changsha while losing ground in other sectors. [8:4-5.]

Allied authorities have stocks of wheat, canned milk and dehydrated vegetables ready to send to Rome quickly with the cooperation of the Fifth and Eighth Armies regarding transport by trucks. At Anzio landing facilities have

AMERICANS IN FIRST

U. S. Armor Spearheads Thrust Through Last Defenses of Rome

FINAL BATTLE BITTER

Fifth and Eighth Armies Rush On Beyond City in Pursuit of Foe

By The United Press.

NAPLES, June 4—The Fifth Army captured Rome tonight, liberating for the first time a German-enslaved European capital. German rear guards were fleeing in disorganized retreat to the northwest.

Except for the railway yards, smashed by the Allies' bombs, the city is 95 per cent intact United Press correspondents reported, after their arrival in the city.

Late tonight, the British Eighth Army, rushing into Rome from the southeast along the Via Casilina, was reported to be joining the Fifth Army in close pursuit of the hard-pressed enemy remnants, under orders to destroy them to a man if possible. Only enough troops to maintain order and ferret out any German snipers or suicide nests were to be left in Rome as the Allies' main armies pounded on, without pausing to celebrate their greatest triumph, coming 270 days after the start of the Italian campaign.

[The Allies battled German rear guards along the edge of the ancient Forum, The Associated Press reported. A force from the old Anzio beachhead completed the mopping up of German forces at 8:15 P. M. by knocking out an enemy scout car in front of the Bank of Italy, almost within the shadow of Trajan's Column.]

Final Stand at Rome's Gates

At the very gates of Rome, the Germans had made a final stand but Lieut. Gen. Mark W. Clark, after having waited three hours for the enemy troops to withdraw in accordance with their own declaration of Rome as an open city, ordered a violent anti-tank barrage. Then masses of Fifth Army snipers and a few tanks and mobile guns trying to cover the retreat.

More of the enemy survivors of the Allies' whirlwind offensive were streaming in congested retreat to the northwest at the mercy of the Allies' planes, which, during the day, destroyed or damaged 600 enemy trucks and other traffic columns stretched fifty-five miles to Lake Bolsena.

Direct radio contact with American correspondents in Rome was established tonight. A United Press reporter said that the main entry into the city had been made along the Via Casilina, which passes through the Porta Maggiore at the southeastern edge of the city. Other Allied troops were reported to have fought their way through the Ostiense freight yards, just south of St. Paul Gate, the main entrance to the city from due south and only one and one-quarter miles from the Venice Palace.

The entry into Rome came with dramatic suddenness after the Al-

Continued on Page 3

AMG Will Rush Food for Rome, Teeming With 750,000 Refugees

By HAROLD CALLENDER

ALGIERS, June 4—The fall of Rome will add about 2,000,000 persons to those whom the Allies have assumed responsibility of feeding, Allied authorities estimated today. But the Allied Military Government, now operating under the Allied Control Commission, has long prepared for the task and is believed to be ready.

The normal population of the Italian capital is estimated to have been swollen by 750,000 refugees from Naples and other places.

Allied authorities have stocks of wheat, canned milk and dehydrated vegetables ready to send to Rome quickly with the cooperation of the Fifth and Eighth Armies regarding transport by trucks.

Eric Johnston, president of the United States Chamber of Commerce, told 100 Soviet trade leaders at a Moscow luncheon that the way to bridge the economic gulf separating American and Russian economies lay in closer knowledge and greater mutual respect. [1:2.]

been built since the establishment of the bridgehead, and ships can be unloaded at Gaeta.

In the plans already made Rome has been divided into regions for the distribution of foodstuffs by Italian and Allied personnel under the authority of the commission. An emergency system has been prepared to provide strict control over the black market, which otherwise might absorb the local produce destined to go into the Allied pool for distribution on a ration basis to the masses who cannot afford the black market.

Capt. Matthias F. Correa, former United States Attorney for the Southern District of New York, has a staff of investigators, including 150 Guardia di Finanza, ready to combat the black market.

President to Talk On Rome Tonight

By The United Press.

WASHINGTON, June 4—A fifteen-minute radio address will be made by President Roosevelt to the nation tomorrow night on the liberation of Rome, the White House announced tonight. Mr. Roosevelt will speak from 8:30 to 8:45 P. M.

The President's message will be broadcast over all major networks.

"All the News That's Fit to Print"

The New York Times.

6 A.M. EXTRA
Partly cloudy and warmer today; moderate to fresh winds.
Temperature Yesterday—Max., 67; Min., 51

Copyright, 1944, by The New York Times Company.

VOL. XCIII..No. 31,545.

Entered as Second-Class Matter, Postoffice, New York, N. Y.

NEW YORK, TUESDAY, JUNE 6, 1944.

THREE CENTS NEW YORK CITY

ALLIED ARMIES LAND IN FRANCE IN THE HAVRE-CHERBOURG AREA; GREAT INVASION IS UNDER WAY

ROOSEVELT SPEAKS

Says Rome's Fall Marks 'One Up and Two to Go' Among Axis Capitals

WARNS WAY IS HARD

Asks World to Give the Italians a Chance for Recovery

The text of President Roosevelt's address is on Page 5.

By CHARLES HURD
Special to The New York Times.

WASHINGTON, June 5—President Roosevelt hailed tonight the capture of Rome, first of the three major Axis capitals to fall, as a great achievement on the road toward total conquest of the Axis. Rome, he said, marked "one up and two to go."

The President spoke for a quarter-hour on the radio, as had been announced yesterday, but his speech was notable for its lack of heroics. It was in no sense a speech of triumph, but rather a tribute to the United Nations forces and leadership that drove the Germans from Rome.

With this tribute he combined a solemn warning that much greater fighting lies ahead before the Axis is defeated, as well as high tributes to the Italian people, whom he again welcomed as a people into the family of nations opposed to the Axis.

"Italy should go on," Mr. Roosevelt said, "as a great mother nation, contributing to the good and the progress and the good-will of mankind, developing her special talents in the arts, crafts, and sciences, and preserving her historic and cultural heritage for the benefit of all peoples.

"We want and expect the help of the future Italy toward lasting peace. All the other nations opposed to fascism and nazism ought to help to give Italy a chance."

Shrines Should Live, He Says

President Roosevelt saw considerable significance in the fact that Rome should be the first Axis capital to fall. He remarked that the "visible symbols of the faith and determination of the early saints and martyrs that Christianity should live and become universal," and added that "it will be a source of deep satisfaction that the freedom of the Pope and of Vatican City is assured by the armies of the United Nations."

There is significance, too, he added, in the fact that Rome was liberated by a composite force of soldiers from many nations.

Reviewing the military picture, the President pointed out that "it would be unwise to-inflate in our own minds the military importance of the capture of Rome." He cautioned his auditors that while the Germans have retreated "thousands of miles" across Africa and back through Italy "they have suffered heavy losses, but not great enough yet to cause collapse."

"Therefore," he added, "the victory still lies some distance ahead. That distance will be covered in due time—have no fear of that. But it will be tough and it will be costly."

Turning to the relief problem in the newly liberated portion of Italy, Mr. Roosevelt noted that some persons thought of the financial cost, but he maintained that the work would pay dividends "by eliminating fascism" and any future desire by Italians to "start another war of aggression." Relief has been planned, he added, but transport demands are so great that "improvement must be gradual."

He warned Italy that it "cannot grow in stature by seeking to build up a great militaristic empire," but ——

Continued on Page 5

Conferees Accept Cabaret Tax Cut

By The Associated Press.

WASHINGTON, June 5—A House-Senate conference committee agreed today to cut back the cabaret tax from 30 to 20 per cent, but eliminated a provision exempting service men and women from the levy.

The group decided to put the national debt limit at $260,000,000,000 as originally requested by the Administration.

The action is subject to House and Senate votes. The conferees met informally today, but members said that the decisions probably would stand as their final recommendation.

The House, at the insistence of a group of Republicans, passed a bill raising the debt ceiling only from $210,000,000,000 to $240,000,000,000. The Senate then put the figure at $260,000,000,000 and attached a rider reducing the cabaret tax from 30 to 20 per cent and exempting men and women in uniform from paying the tax on their checks.

Some tax experts argued that this exemption would make administration of the excise on night clubs impossible.

FEDERAL LAW HELD RULING INSURANCE

Supreme Court, 4-3, Decides Business Is Interstate and Subject to Trust Act

Special to The New York Times.

WASHINGTON, June 5—The Supreme Court, by a four-to-three decision today, held that the insurance companies of the country, with assets of $37,000,000,000 and annual premium collections in excess of $6,000,000,000, are interstate commerce and thus subject to the Sherman Anti-Trust Law.

The decision upset precedents which began with a contrary decision by the court more than seventy-five years ago and have been reaffirmed repeatedly since the adoption of the anti-trust law in 1890.

The majority decision, written ——

Continued on Page 13

PURSUIT ON IN ITALY

Allies Pass Rome, Cross Tiber as Foe Quits Bank Below City

PLANES JOIN IN CHASE

1,200 Vehicles Wrecked —Eighth Army Battles Into More Towns

By The Associated Press.

ROME, June 5—The Allies' armor and motorized infantry roared through Rome today without pausing, crossed the Tiber River and proceeded with the grim task of destroying two battered German armies fleeing to the north.

Fighter-bombers spearheaded the pursuit, jamming the escape highways with burning enemy transport and littering the fields with dead and wounded Germans. The enemy was tired, disorganized and bewildered by the slashing assault, which in twenty-five days had inflicted a major catastrophe on the Germans and liberated Rome almost without damage.

Railway Yards Bombed

Five hundred American heavy bombers blasted railway yards at five points in northern Italy between Venice and Rimini along which the Germans might attempt to move reinforcements and equipment to bolster their beaten armies. Hour after hour, the Allies' planes swept down on highways leading northward and tore the fleeing enemy apart. Twelve hundred combat vehicles were destroyed from dawn to dark yesterday, and hundreds more today. Farther north, medium bombers smashed bridges and rail facilities.

[The Germans have abandoned the entire left bank of the Tiber from Ostia, at its mouth, to Rome, according to a Vichy broadcast quoted by The Associated Press.

[The Germans are already entrenched in mountain positions ——

Continued on Page 2

FIRST ALLIED LANDING MADE ON SHORES OF WESTERN EUROPE

General Eisenhower's armies invaded northern France this morning. While the landing points were not specified, the Germans said that troops had gone ashore near Havre and that fighting raged at Caen (1). The enemy also said that parachutists had descended at the northern tip of the Normandy Peninsula (2) and heavy bombing also been visited on Calais and Dunkerque (3).

POPE GIVES THANKS ROME WAS SPARED

Voices Appreciation to Both Belligerents in Message to Throng at St. Peter's

By Wireless to The New York Times.

VATICAN CITY, June 5—Pope Pius XII appeared on the balcony of St. Peter's at 6 P. M. today to thank God that Rome had been spared from the ravages of war while before him in the densely packed square of St. Peter's and the new broad Via Della Conciliazione tens of thousands of Romans cheered themselves hoarse.

It was the third time today that the Pontiff had showed himself to cheering crowds, as he had appeared twice at a window of his office this morning. But this was a solemn, sacred occasion and no one knowing anything about Pius XII could doubt the fervor of his thankfulness that Rome had been saved.

The Pontiff seemed strong and well and his voice carried far, though it was difficult to hear every word he said because of the crowd.

"We must give thanks to God for the favors we have received," said the Pope. "Rome has been spared. This day will go down in the annals of Rome."

He went on to say he hoped that Italians would be worthy of the grace shown them and put aside hatred and all personal vendetta. He then thanked both belligerents—the Allies and Germany—for having left Rome intact.

After a prayer of thankfulness to the Blessed Virgin and Saints Peter and Paul, guardians of Rome, the Pontiff gave his blessing, "urbe et orbis," as the immense crowd knelt before him.

[The Associated Press estimated the crowd was between 250,000 and 500,000.]

Continued on Page 5

Italy's Monarch Yields Rule To Son, but Retains Throne

By The Associated Press.

NAPLES, June 5—Victor Emmanuel III stepped aside as King of Italy today, as he previously had said he would do upon the liberation of Rome, and turned to his 39-year-old son, Crown Prince Humbert, all "royal prerogatives." Italian political pressure had been brought to bear against him since the occupation of Naples.

In a decree signed by himself and countersigned by Premier Pietro Badoglio, head of the Italian Liberation Government, the King named his son Lieutenant General of the Realm. The monarch, however, retained his title as head of the House of Savoy and remains as King without power.

[The first act of the Council of Ministers after the transfer of royal powers was a formal denunciation of the 1940 armistice treaty inflicted on France, The United Press said.]

Victor Emmanuel, who became King July 29, 1900, had made his "irrevocable" decision to withdraw from public life "on the day on which Allied troops enter Rome."

Little more than a figurehead since Benito Mussolini assumed the dictatorship of Italy, Victor Emmanuel had won a reputation in the first years of his reign as a sympathetic monarch, interested in his people and their problems.

Prince Humbert, tall and erect, despite heavy opposition, especially northeast of Valmontone, captured a number of strategic towns. He declared that the group at the start, but later made a truce with Mussolini. In effect, Humbert becomes the King's regent.

TEXT OF ROYAL DECREE

The King's withdrawal decree:

I, Victor Emmanuel III, by the grace of God and by the will of the nation King of Italy, in collaboration with the President of the Council of Ministers and with the agreement of the Council, have ordered and order as follows:

My beloved son, Humbert of Savoy, Prince of Piedmont, is nominated our Lieutenant General. In collaboration with responsible Ministers he will in our name superintend all matters of administration and exercise all royal prerogatives without exception, signing royal decrees which will be countersigned and authenticated in the usual way.

We order all concerned to observe this decree and see that it is observed as the law of the State.

Given at Ravello June 5, 1944.
VICTOR EMMANUEL.
(Countersigned) PIETRO BADOGLIO.

The withdrawal was presented to ——

Continued on Page 4

EISENHOWER ACTS

U.S., British, Canadian Troops Backed by Sea, Air Forces

MONTGOMERY LEADS

Nazis Say Their Shock Units Are Battling Our Parachutists

Communique No. 1 On Allied Invasion

By Broadcast to The New York Times.

LONDON, Tuesday, June 6—The Supreme Headquarters of the Allied Expeditionary Force issued this communiqué this morning:

"Under the command of General Eisenhower, Allied naval forces, supported by strong air forces, began landing Allied armies this morning on the northern coast of France."

By RAYMOND DANIELL
By Cable to The New York Times.

SUPREME HEADQUARTERS, ALLIED EXPEDITIONARY FORCES, Tuesday, June 6—The invasion of Europe from the west has begun.

In the gray light of a summer dawn Gen. Dwight D. Eisenhower threw his great Anglo-American force into action today for the liberation of the Continent. The spearhead of attack was an Army group commanded by Gen. Sir Bernard L. Montgomery and comprising troops of the United States, Britain and Canada.

General Eisenhower's first communiqué was terse and calculated to give little information to the enemy. It said merely that "Allied naval forces began landing Allied armies this morning on the northern coast of France."

After the first communiqué was released it was announced that the Allied landing was in Normandy.

Caen Battle Reported

German broadcasts, beginning at 6:30 A. M., London time, [12:30 A. M. Eastern war time] gave first word of the assault. [The Associated Press said General Eisenhower, for the sake of surprise, deliberately let the Germans have the "first word."]

The German DNB agency said the Allied invasion operations began with the landing of airborne troops in the area of the mouth of the Seine River.

[Berlin said the "center of gravity" of the fierce fighting was at Caen, thirty miles southwest of Havre and sixty-five miles southeast of Cherbourg, The Associated Press reported. Caen is ten miles inland from the sea, at the base of the seventy-five-mile-wide Normandy Peninsula, and fighting there might indicate the Allies' seizing of a beachhead.

[DNB said in a broadcast just before 10 A. M. (4 A. M. Eastern war time) that the Anglo-American troops had been reinforced at dawn in the Havre area.]

[An Allied correspondent broadcasting from Supreme Headquarters, the Columbia Broadcasting System, said this morning that "German tanks are moving up ——

Continued on Page A
Following Page 5

PARADE OF PLANES CARRIES INVADERS

Witness Says First 'Chutists Met Only Light Fire When They Landed in France

The first eyewitness account of the Allies' invasion of Europe was given in a pool broadcast from London this morning by Wright Bryan of the National Broadcasting Company, who accompanied the airborne troops in their landings.

His account said the first spearhead of Allied forces landed by parachute in northern France in the first hour of D-day.

"In the navigator's dome in the flight deck of a C-47, I rode across the English Channel with the first group of planes from the United States Ninth Air Force Troop Carrier Command to take our fighting men into Europe," Mr. Bryan said. He added that just before he left French soil for the return trip he saw seventeen American paratroopers, led by a lieutenant colonel, jump with their arms, ammunition and equipment into German-occupied France.

ALLIED WARNING FLASHED TO COAST

People Told to Clear Area 22 Miles Inland as Soon as Instructions Are Given

By Cable to The New York Times.

LONDON, Tuesday, June 6—The British Broadcasting Corporation in its 8 A. M. news bulletin this morning with quotations from a Supreme Headquarters "urgent warning" to inhabitants of the enemy-occupied countries living near the coast.

Gen. Dwight D. Eisenhower had directed that whenever possible in France a warning shall be given to towns in which certain targets will be intensively bombed.

This warning, the broadcast said ——

Continued on Page B

Eisenhower Instructs Europeans; Gives Battle Order to His Armies

Following are the texts of a statement by Gen. Dwight D. Eisenhower broadcast to the people of western Europe and his Order of the Day to the Allied Expeditionary Force as recorded by The New York Times and the Columbia Broadcasting System:

People of western Europe! A landing was made this morning on the coast of France by troops of the Allied Expeditionary Force. This landing is part of the concerted United Nations plan for the liberation of Europe made in conjunction with our great Russian Allies. I have this message for all of you. Although the initial assault may not have been made in your own country, the hour of your liberation is approaching.

Citizens of France! I am proud to have under my command the gallant forces of France. Fighting beside their Allies, they will play a worthy part in the liberation of their ——

Continued on Page 3

War News Summarized

TUESDAY, JUNE 6, 1944.

The invasion of western Europe began this morning.

General Eisenhower, in his first communiqué from Supreme Headquarters, Allied Expeditionary Force, issued at 3:30 A. M., said that "Allied naval forces supported by strong air forces began landing Allied armies this morning on the northern coast of France."

The assault was made by British, American and Canadian troops who, under command of Gen. Sir Bernard L. Montgomery, landed in Normandy. London gave no further details but earlier Berlin had broadcast that parachute troops had landed on the Normandy Peninsula near Cherbourg and that invasion forces were pouring from landing craft under cover of warships near Havre. Dunkerque and Calais were being heavily bombed, the Germans said.

Later announcements from Berlin said that there was fighting between Caen and Trouville and that shock troops had swung into action to halt the invasion. [All the foregoing, 1:8.]

General Eisenhower, in an order of the day to each member of the "great crusade," told his men the enemy would fight savagely and added: "We will accept nothing less than full victory. Good luck." In a broadcast to the "Peoples of Western Europe," he said the day would come when he would hold their full help. A special word to France added that Frenchmen would rule the country. [1:6-7.] Almost simultaneously it was announced that General de Gaulle had arrived in London. [6:2.]

The liberation of Rome in no way slowed the Allied pursuit of the tired and disorganized German armies in Italy yesterday. Armored and motorized units sped across the Tiber upon the retreating enemy's heels. Five hundred heavy bombers joined with lighter aircraft to smash rail and road routes leading to northern Italy and to add to the foe's demoralization. The Eighth Army, despite heavy opposition, especially northeast of Valmontone, captured a number of strategic towns. [1:3; map P. 2.]

General Clark said that parts of the two German armies had been smashed. He doubted the ability of the German Fourteenth to put up effective opposition and declared that the Tenth had taken a bad beating. [3:1.]

King Victor Emmanuel fulfilled his promise and turned over all authority to his son, Crown Prince Humbert. [1:5-6.]

President Roosevelt warned the people of the United States in a radio talk last night not to over-emphasize the military significance of the liberation of Rome. "Germany has not yet been driven to surrender," he said. "Victory still lies some distance ahead. * * * It will be tough and it will be costly." The President appealed to the world to give Italy a chance to contribute her share to a lasting peace. [1:1.]

In the Pacific theatre Americans were converging on the Biak airfields. Allied planes sank one and damaged two Japanese destroyers and shot down at least eighteen aircraft. [8:1.]

"All the News That's Fit to Print"

The New York Times.

LATE CITY EDITION
POSTSCRIPT
Partly cloudy and warm today
Temperature Yesterday—Max. 84; Min. 64
Sunrise, 5:28 A. M.; Sunset, 8:32 P. M.

VOL. XCIII. No. 31,566.

Entered as Second-Class Matter,
Postoffice, New York, N. Y.

NEW YORK, TUESDAY, JUNE 27, 1944.

THREE CENTS NEW YORK CITY

CHERBOURG FALLS TO AMERICAN TROOPS; ENEMY LEADERS AMONG 30,000 PRISONERS; RUSSIANS CAPTURE VITEBSK AND ZHLOBIN

REPUBLICANS MAKE QUICK END TO WAR THEIR BATTLE CRY

Warren, Keynoter, Says Party Will Bring Victorious Boys Home With All Speed

DISPUTES OVER PLATFORM

Dewey Avalanche Piles Up, With Californian Unchallenged as His Running Mate

Governor Warren's keynote address is printed on Page 10.

By TURNER CATLEDGE
Special to THE NEW YORK TIMES.

CHICAGO, Tuesday, June 27—A triple pledge to bring the boys back home quickly and "victorious," to reopen the doors of opportunity to "all Americans," and to guard the peace in the future, was sounded yesterday as the Republican battle-cry at the opening of the party's twenty-third national convention.

While it was being uttered by Gov. Earl Warren of California, temporary chairman, in his keynote address to a cheering throng in the Chicago Stadium, THE NEW YORK TIMES gained access to a plank which policy writers had evolved Saturday, pledging the party to a post-war cooperative organization "among sovereign nations," to prevent military aggression and attain permanent peace in the future.

Word had come meanwhile from Wendell L. Willkie, the nominee of 1940, that he considered the foreign policy plank, as he understood it, ambiguous, and therefore was disappointed in it.

Willkie's Backers Upset

This note of controversy came as a distinct shock to a group of former backers of Mr. Willkie who have been attempting these last few days to bring him in line with the platform, and with a ticket of Thomas E. Dewey of New York for President and Governor Warren for Vice President, which is considered certain of nomination by tomorrow night.

Meanwhile, another complication appeared in the hitherto placid convention picture when the seventeen Governors who are delegates demanded opportunity to examine and possibly suggest changes in the platform before it is submitted to the convention, probably tonight, for ratification.

The Governors did not protest any particular item in the platform as it was agreed to in principle last night. They did protest the fact, however, that, as one of them put it, an "oligarchy" of Senators, members of the House and other party leaders, had assumed the prerogative of speaking for the party.

The Governors feel, as Governor Warren reflected in his keynote address, that they have been the spearhead, more than members of Congress, in the resurgence of Republicanism during the last three years. What happened here when the Governors demanded and obtained permission to appear before the resolutions committee was another chapter in a protest which first came to light at the Mackinac Island conference in September.

Led by New Englanders

The action was led, as was the move at Mackinac, largely by a New England group, in which Gov. Raymond E. Baldwin of Connecticut and Gov. Sumner Sewall of Maine were active.

These new possibilities of trouble ahead did not divert the main line of appeal upon which the party was centering—an appeal to the soldier vote, to those Americans who are weary of the New Deal and, above all, to those wanting to avoid the tragedy of war in the future.

It was the note on which Gov. Dwight Green of Illinois opened the meeting with a welcoming address.

Continued on Page 9

Convention Events Listed for Today

Special to THE NEW YORK TIMES.

CHICAGO, June 26—The official program for tomorrow's sessions of the Republican National Convention is as follows:

Tuesday, June 27, 10:15 A. M.
(Central War Time)
Convention called to order by the temporary chairman.
National Anthem: Miss Mildred Maule of East St. Louis, Ill.
Prayer: The Rev. Joseph Simonson, pastor of Christ Lutheran Church, St. Paul.
Report of Committee on Credentials.
Report of Committee on Permanent Organization.
Election of permanent chairman and permanent officers.
Address by permanent chairman.
Report of Committee on Rules and Order of Business.
Election of National Committee.
Report of Resolutions Committee.
Recess until 8:15 P. M.

Tuesday, June 27, 8:15 P. M.
Convention called to order by the permanent chairman, Representative Joseph W. Martin Jr.
National Anthem: Miss Mona Bradford of the Chicago Civic Opera Company.
Prayer: Rabbi Abba Hillel Silver of The Temple, Cleveland.
Music.
Address: Herbert Hoover.
Address: Representative Clare Boothe Luce of Connecticut.
Adjourn until Wednesday.

WILLKIE CONDEMNS PEACE-POLICY PLAN

Republican Draft on Foreign Relations Could Be Used to Balk Cooperation, He Says

A few hours after Wendell Willkie had received the text of the proposed Republican foreign-policy plank, the 1940 Presidential candidate issued a statement denouncing the plan as ambiguous, subject to opposing interpretations and capable of being used to throttle effective collaboration by the United States with other countries to maintain peace.

Mr. Willkie's views on the platform committee's suggestions were presented to reporters who had been invited to visit his offices at 15 Broad Street. He explained that he chose this form of making them public because he was not a delegate to the convention.

Likening the language proposed for this year's platform to that employed in 1920, Mr. Willkie recalled that thirty-one leading Republicans had assured the country that the 1920 formula "was the surest road to an effective international organization," but that President Harding, immediately after the election, "announced that the League of Nations was dead."

"A Republican President elected under the proposed platform of

Continued on Page 12

ACCORD OF NATIONS FAVORED IN PLANK ON FOREIGN POLICY

'Participation in Cooperative Organization' Provided 'to Attain Permanent Peace'

TAFT PREDICTS ADOPTION

Declaration Calls for Seeking 'Economic Stability,' Pledges Constitutional Procedure

By JAMES B. RESTON
Special to THE NEW YORK TIMES.

CHICAGO, Tuesday, June 27—The Republican party platform will favor "participation by the United States in post-war cooperative organization among sovereign nations to prevent military aggression and to attain permanent peace."

The party's Foreign Affairs Committee, headed by Senator Warren Austin of Vermont, has approved unanimously a plank which calls on the future world peace organization to "develop effective cooperative means to prevent or repel military aggression."

Pending the formation of this world peace organization, the plank recommends that the United States should "pledge continuing collaboration with the United Nations."

Senator Robert A. Taft, chairman of the party's Resolutions Committee, to which the platform will be submitted later this morning, said he was certain that the foreign affairs plank as recommended by Senator Austin's committee would be adopted.

Objectives of Peace Treaties

After stating that the party favored "prosecution of the war to total victory against all our enemies in full cooperation with the United Nations and the speedy return of our armed forces," the plank emphasized that justice in the writing of the peace was the essence of realism.

"We believe that peace and security do not depend upon the sanction of force alone, but should prevail by virtue of reciprocal interests and spiritual values recognized in these security agreements," the Foreign Affairs Committee said.

"The treaties of peace should be just; the nations which are the victims of Axis aggression should be restored to sovereignty and self-government, and the organized cooperation of the nations should concern itself with basic causes of world disorder."

Elaborating on "cooperation," the committee continued:

"We shall seek, in our relations with other nations, conditions calculated to promote world-wide economic stability, not only for the sake of the world, but also the end that our own people may enjoy a high level of employment in an increasingly prosperous world. We

Continued on Page 14

ALLIED WARSHIPS SHELLING GERMAN POSITIONS IN CHERBOURG

The U. S. S. Quincy (left) and H. M. S. Glasgow bombarding the port
The New York Times (British Admiralty via U. S. Signal Corps Radiotelephoto)

U. S. TROOPS SCALE LOFTY SAIPAN PEAK

Tapotchau, Dominating Island, Is Reported Won — Carrier Planes Batter Guam and Rota

By GEORGE F. HORNE
By Telephone to THE NEW YORK TIMES.

PACIFIC FLEET HEADQUARTERS, Pearl Harbor, June 26—Mount Tapotchau on Saipan Island has been scaled by United States Marines who are now established in positions near the summit. Marines and Army troops have made substantial gains on both the eastern and western shores of the island.

[A front dispatch said that Tapotchau which dominated the island and has been the goal of our men ever since they landed on Saipan, had been captured by troops who held it against a before-dawn Japanese counter-attack Sunday.]

Admiral Chester W. Nimitz stated that the Kagman Peninsula, forming the upper arm of Magicienne Bay, was now entirely in our hands and that troops had

Continued on Page 7

Russians Begin Encircling Mogilev and Orsha Citadels

By The United Press.

LONDON, Tuesday, June 27—The Red Army, tearing out the northern and southern anchors of the German defense line in White Russia, captured the fortress cities of Vitebsk and Zhlobin yesterday and seized more than 1,700 towns and settlements, while the vanguard of their victorious forces advanced more than twenty-two miles toward Minsk for a great pincer assault on that city.

Striking with unprecedented power and speed, four Soviet armies sprinting along a 285-mile front raced to within eighty-four miles of Minsk, approached to within thirty-five miles of the Polish border, outflanked Orsha and drove to within six miles of Mogilev.

Vitebsk, the most powerful Nazi stronghold on the route to East Prussia, and Zhlobin, 157 miles to the south, fell on the fourth day of the Red Army's summer offensive—four days in which Russian troops advanced as much as fifty-six miles, seized 3,040 towns and settlements and killed more than 31,500 Germans.

More than 6,000 of the German garrison of five infantry divisions

Continued on Page 6

14 WARSHIPS SHELL CHERBOURG AT ONCE

British Newsman Describes Destruction of Batteries Defending Harbor

By DESMOND TIGHE
Reuter Correspondent

ABOARD H.M.S. GLASGOW, off Cherbourg Harbor, June 25 (Delayed)—American battleships and heavy cruisers, supported by two British cruisers and seven destroyers, are firing broadside after broadside into German shore batteries at vital key points on the fringes of Cherbourg harbor in support of the Army.

Air Resounds With Crashes

Our six-inch guns are blazing away as shells scream into a German fort. The air resounds with the crash of broadsides and destroyers. The Channel sea is whipped with wicked looking grey-black splashes as we fire broadside and time by German shore batteries.

The German gunnery is good and although we are plastering their concrete gun emplacements with tons of high explosives some of them keep on firing.

The United States bombardment task force is commanded by Rear-Admiral Morton L. Deyo, United States Navy. Admiral Deyo is flying his flag in the heavy cruiser Tuscaloosa. Among the warships in his battle squadron are the battleships Texas, Nevada, Arkansas; the American cruiser Quincy, and the two British cruisers, Glasgow and Enterprise. We are escorted by

Continued on Page 4

VIENNA WAR PLANTS GET HEAVY BOMBING

Italy-Based Planes Pound Oil, Aircraft Works — Weather Cuts Invasion Support

By The Associated Press.

SUPREME HEADQUARTERS, Allied Expeditionary Force, Tuesday, June 27—United States Flying Fortresses and Liberators 500 to 750 strong roared from Italian bases to the Vienna area yesterday through the heaviest Luftwaffe opposition in recent weeks and attacked oil refineries, rail yards and a Nazi aircraft plant.

Poor weather over western Europe halted for the day the pounding from Allied air bases in Britain and Normandy of German supply and communication lines behind the French front.

Indications of renewed Allied aerial activity came last night as the German radio interrupted programs to say an alert had been sounded in all parts of southwestern Germany. In Hungary, where British bombers of the Mediterranean Allied Air Forces attacked oil works Sunday night, the Budapest radio went off the air again at 10 P. M.

The Flying Fortresses and Liberators and their escorting Mustangs, Lightnings and Thunderbolts of the United States Fifteenth Air Force shot down large numbers of enemy planes on the route to the Vienna area, headquarters announced.

They struck refineries at Schwechat, ten miles southeast of

Continued on Page 5

VICTORY IN FRANCE

Capture of Port Seals First Phase of Allied Liberation of Europe

FIGHT SHARP TO END

British Reported Near Main Enemy Highway at Base of Peninsula

5 A. M. Communique

By The Associated Press.

SUPREME HEADQUARTERS, Allied Expeditionary Force, Tuesday, June 27—The capture of Lieut. Gen. Carl Wilhelm von Schlieben, commander of the Cherbourg garrison, and Rear Admiral Hennecke, Nazi sea defense commander of Normandy, was announced today in Allied communiqué No. 43 confirming the fall of Cherbourg.

"Cherbourg's liberation came after a final day of fierce fighting in the northwestern part of the city," the communiqué said.

"In the battle the enemy has lost the greater part of four infantry divisions, numerous naval and marine units and line of communication troops."

Of the British gains on the east side of the beachhead, it said:

"A strong attack toward the Villers-Bocage-Caen main road has secured Cheux and Fontenay, and has advanced several miles in the face of heavy German armor and infantry. Progress continues."

By DREW MIDDLETON
By Cable to THE NEW YORK TIMES.

SUPREME HEADQUARTERS, Allied Expeditionary Force, Tuesday, June 27—Cherbourg, France's third greatest port, has fallen to the American troops in the first outstanding victory of the Allied campaign to liberate France.

The fall of Cherbourg, after a siege that lasted a week from the moment the first Allied field guns began to pound its defenses, was officially announced here this morning just after 7 o'clock double British summer time [1 A. M. in New York.]

With the taking of the city the first phase of the campaign in which the Allies were forced to build up their armies without the use of a large port came to an end. It was estimated here recently that supplies for two divisions could be moved through Cherbourg within forty-eight hours after its fall.

Captives May Total 30,000

Last night American patrols mopped up the remaining German resistance in the vicinity of the naval base and arsenal and cleaned out snipers from buildings along the waterfront, where individual Germans held out until the last.

Although there has been no official estimate of the number of prisoners yet, it is probable this city's fall will bring more than 30,000 German soldiers and sailors into the Allied cages.

Cherbourg was the second French port and naval base to fall to Lieut. Gen. Omar N. Bradley.

Bizerte in Tunisia was taken by the United States Second Army Corps under his command on May 7, 1943.

The struggle for Cherbourg drew to its victorious close yesterday when in the rain and chill American doughboys mopped up the port. By nightfall more than one-third of the port had been occupied and by midnight two-thirds of the city was in Allied hands.

At dawn Monday 3,400 German prisoners had been taken and it is probable that twice that number was captured in the mopping up operations yesterday.

The Germans were driven from five remaining strongholds during the early morning by grenade, bay-

Continued on Page 3

3-Cornered Baseball Game Yields $56,500,000 in Fifth Bond Drive

A crowd of 50,000 baseball fans, all of whom paid their way into the park by buying war bonds, turned out last night at the Polo Grounds to witness a bizarre contest in which the Yankees, Giants and Dodgers participated in a nine-inning contest. The Brooklyn nine won the game, tallying five runs; the Yankees scored one and the Giants nothing.

These new possibilities of trouble ahead did not divert the main line of appeal upon which the party was centering.

The program, as arranged by the Fifth War Loan Sports Committee, helped to swell New York's quota in the current bond drive by $56,500,000. Fifty million dollars of this sum came, according to an announcement by Mayor La Guardia, from the coffers of the City of New York. The remainder was contributed by the crowd as "admission fee," plus a one-million-dollar bond purchase of an autographed score card by the Bond Clothing Stores.

During the day the drive moved into high gear with the announcement of many large subscriptions here totalling around $1,000,000,000 and the disclosure that purchases throughout the nation had reached $4,261,000,000, or 29 per cent of the quota for the campaign.

Devised and conceived by Stanley Oshan of the War Finance Committee, the baseball game was followed closely by the huge league teams tangle with each other on the same field for the first time. While Mr. Oshan was the originator of the idea it was Professor Paul J. Smith, to produce a method of scoring it.

Professor Smith's assistance proved helpful, indeed, for the

Continued on Page 20

War News Summarized

TUESDAY, JUNE 27, 1944

Cherbourg fell to the Americans this morning after General Bradley's troops had fought the desperate German defenders from dock to dock along the ruined waterfront. The enemy held out in four or five strong points, principally around the naval base, until each fortified nucleus had been overrun. Lieut. Gen. von Schlieben, Cherbourg garrison commander, and Admiral Hennecke, head of the German sea force off Normandy, were captured. The total of prisoners may reach 30,000.

At the eastern end of the Normandy line the British opened a new drive from Tilly-sur-Seulles and gained as much as four miles, threatening to cut the Caen-Avranches highway at the base of the Cotentin Peninsula. Since the initial landings three weeks ago the Allies have liberated more than 1,000 square miles of France, have taken more than 50,000 prisoners and have destroyed four German divisions. [All the foregoing 1:8; map, P. 2.]

Three United States battleships headed a force of fourteen Allied vessels that pounded Cherbourg's main fortifications into rubble shortly after noon Sunday. The massed naval rifles poured shells into the targets for more than three hours, clearing the way for the troops. [1:7.] A British naval intelligence officer said in this city that the Germans had been so skillfully outmaneuvered that they massed their air defenses to counter a feint invasion aimed at Calais and Boulogne, leaving Normandy without protection. [9:1.]

Dense fog halted air operations from Britain, but a heavy

force of American bombers from Italy smashed oil refineries, rail yards and an airplane plant in the Vienna area. The Luftwaffe offered the heaviest opposition in weeks. [1:6.]

Another vaunted German line crumbled when the Red Army captured Vitebsk and Zhlobin, anchors of the "Fatherland Line." More than 45,000 enemy troops were trapped at Vitebsk, and at one point the Russians were thirty-four miles from the old Polish frontier. A record number of 1,700 places was liberated in the general advance. Gains were also registered from the Karelian Isthmus on the Finnish front. [1:5-6; map, P. 6]

The Fifth Army in Italy entered the port of Piombino without a fight and, inland, advanced to within fifteen miles of Siena and forty-five miles of Florence. The Eighth Army crossed the Chienti River northwest of Foligno in hard fighting. [6:1.]

Marines on Saipan, in the Marianas, have scaled Mount Tapotchau and dug in at the summit. The southern part of Garapan, on the west, was in American hands, and the Japanese have been cleared from Kagman Peninsula on the east. Carrier planes did widespread damage to shipping, installations and grounded enemy aircraft at enemy bases on Guam and Rota. [1:4; maps P. 7.]

Allied forces have captured Mogaung in Burma and closed in on all fronts from the Indian border to China, where Hsiangyang was recaptured. [7:5.] The Japanese, after seizing Hengshan and Tuhsien, were unable to push closer to Hengyang in China's Hunan Province. [7:4.]

Pockets of Nazis Kept on Sniping As Americans Overran Cherbourg

By HAROLD DENNY
By Wireless to THE NEW YORK TIMES.

WITH THE AMERICAN FORCES at Cherbourg, June 26—The Germans fought a last-ditch defense in Cherbourg this evening, though the outcome was inescapable. Substantial elements of the American forces got into the city from the south only after a piece-by-piece conquest of succeeding strong points and the Germans were still firing on them in the city and from two pillboxes remaining on Fort du Roule with 88-mm. fieldpieces and machine guns. The city has been considerably damaged but less than one would have thought. As a whole it is intact, though many individual buildings have been smashed.

Dominating all was the arsenal, where the last important holdout

group was still firing rifles while large portions of the structure were burning with a red glow and towering black smoke.

Holding out about equally with the arsenal was one last desperate little group of cannoniers at Fort du Roule.

It stands like Gibraltar and should have been impregnable. Its fortifications of reinforced concrete, several stories deep and tunneled into solid rock, remind one of the Maginot Line fortresses which I visited the first winter of this war. They include an electric light plant, underground barracks, an underground hospital and abundant stores of everything conceiv-

Continued on Page 6

119

The New York Times.

LATE CITY EDITION
Fair today and tomorrow with mild afternoons and cool nights.
Temperature Yesterday—Max., 75; Min., 55

VOL. XCIII..No. 31,626.

Entered as Second-Class Matter, Postoffice, New York, N. Y.

Copyright, 1944, by The New York Times Company.

NEW YORK, SATURDAY, AUGUST 26, 1944.

THREE CENTS NEW YORK CITY

ALLIES SWEEP TO TROYES, NAZI ROUT GROWS; GERMAN COMMANDER SURRENDERS IN PARIS; RUMANIA DECLARES WAR, BULGARIA TO QUIT

NELSON UNDER FIRE OF BRADLEY DEWEY; WPB POST IN DOUBT

Former Head of Rubber Agency Defends Program, Accuses Nelson of 'Sniping'

ISSUE PUT TO PRESIDENT

Question of Production Chief's Future Is 'Iffy,' He Says —Krug Takes Firm Hold

By CHARLES E. EGAN
Special to The New York Times.

WASHINGTON, Aug. 25—The question whether Donald M. Nelson will resume his chairmanship of the War Production Board on his return from a special mission to China for President Roosevelt was raised today when the President told his press conference that he did not know whether Mr. Nelson would resume his duties at that time.

The President's statement came soon after Mr. Nelson departed on the first leg of his China journey the day after the chairman had apparently won a fight with his executive vice chairman, Charles E. Wilson, who resigned yesterday after charging that his usefulness was being impaired by attacks from Mr. Nelson's staff. It supplied another surprising development in the explosive situation which had developed in the WPB over reconversion.

While official Washington speculated whether the President had a more important job than WPB head in prospect for Mr. Nelson or whether the war agency chairman was to be "let out" along with his first assistant, Mr. Nelson came under fire from another quarter when Col. Bradley Dewey, retiring rubber director, accused him of engaging "in typical Washington sniping" at the rubber director's office.

Dewey Takes Issue on Rubber

Colonel Dewey referred to the testimony given by Mr. Nelson before a closed session of the Senate's committee investigating national defense as the type "that has made many good Americans unwilling to give services that otherwise would be of value to the country and to the conduct of the war."

Mr. Nelson had testified that the rubber program was completed, "all but getting the tires." Questioned about Colonel Dewey's then-recent resignation, Mr. Nelson said that to call the rubber program completed would be "like the Army saying they are completed except for the shooting."

Colonel Dewey told reporters that he had never said the task of providing tires was completed, but rather that the synthetic rubber plants were turning out rubber in surplus.

The problem of providing manpower and tire cords no longer required the special powers which were reposed in the Office of Defense Rubber, Colonel Dewey added.

Krug Demands End of Sniping

"These powers are of no value to the problem of manning the plants and providing the much-needed tires," he concluded. "By Presidential directive these were and are the responsibilities of the WPB and of the War Manpower Commission."

J. A. Krug, who was named yesterday by President Roosevelt as acting chairman of the WPB in the absence of Mr. Nelson, took over the reins today. He called the vice chairmen of the agency into conference this afternoon, and according to reports, told them that he received a clear grant of authority to run the WPB and to get it back on the track.

He warned that certain fights within WPB should end and that he would "fire" anyone who engaged in the future in internal disputes.

Mr. Krug told reporters later

Continued on Page 24

Must Post Ceilings For Diners Monday

The Regional Office of Price Administration reminded restaurant managements yesterday that they have until Monday to file a list of forty food items and the ceiling prices they are required to post on their premises. The list in triplicate must be filed with local war price and rationing boards.

The new OPA national restaurant regulations require the posting of the forty food items and the ceiling prices. Restaurants violating the provisions of the regulation face enforcement action, OPA attachés pointed out. Each list filed by a restaurant will be compared with menus of May, 1943, and, upon approval, a copy of the list, bearing an official stamp to show approval, will be returned to the restaurant owner.

OWN MEN AT FRONT APPEAL TO LABOR

AFL and CIO Leaders in France Link War Supply Shortages to 'Our Quarrels at Home'

By SIDNEY SHALETT
Special to The New York Times.

WASHINGTON, Aug. 25—"We cannot let the men whose lives depend on this equipment pay the price for our quarrels at home," six American labor leaders who are visiting the French battlefields under War Department sponsorship have declared in a message sent back here to their unions.

The message was transmitted through the War Department by William Green, president of the American Federation of Labor, and Philip Murray, head of the Congress of Industrial Organizations.

"Conscious of the partnership that exists between the fighting fronts and the factory," it read, "the War Department has made it possible for us to travel through the battle areas and see at first hand how our soldiers are using the weapons and equipment made by American labor.

Need of Supplies to Save Lives

"As we travel along roads lined with the wreckage of American and German equipment and pass through shattered French cities and, above all, as we pause at military cemeteries and hospitals that are all too plentiful here, we are struck more forcibly than ever before with the horrible destructiveness of modern war and the importance of superior supplies in cutting down the toll of our dead and wounded.

"We are filled with pride for our Army. Its combat efficiency and morale are high. It is well-staffed and well-manned—an Army representative in the highest sense of our great American democracy.

"Everybody knows his job—from generals to privates—and we are determined to get ourselves to the job of finishing this war with the same single-minded determination the men at the front.

"We do not know whether the war will last a short time or a long

Continued on Page 24

RED ARMY RACES ON

Russians Attack Galati Gap and Encircle 12 German Divisions

REACH DANUBE DELTA

205,000 Enemy Troops Killed or Taken in Six Days—Tartu Seized

By The Associated Press.

LONDON, Saturday, Aug. 26—Two Russian armies racing toward the heart of Rumania at a better than a mile-an-hour clip yesterday reached the Galati Gap defenses at Tecuci and also drove a spearhead down to the Danube River delta at Kiliya in a six-day whirlwind offensive that Moscow announced had cost the enemy nearly 205,000 in killed or captured.

In perhaps the greatest defeat yet inflicted on the Axis in a comparable period, the Russians also announced they had encircled twelve German divisions of upward of 60,900 men southwest of fallen Kishinev, provincial capital of Bessarabia. Thirteen thousand Germans already have surrendered in two days, and the remainder are being annihilated, said the Moscow broadcast bulletin.

Thousands of Rumanians were abandoning the struggle against the Russians and turning to fight the Germans, dispatches said, as the Second and Third Ukrainian Armies under General Rodion Y. Malinovsky and Feodor I. Tolbukhin linked up in a quick drive on Bucharest, within 113 miles of the Bariad River.

Danube Delta Reached

A total of 550 towns and villages were swept up by the two armies, and the capture of Tecuci found the Russians within ninety miles northeast of the Ploesti oil wells. General Malinovsky's troops now were at the Galati Gap, a forty-five-mile stretch of defenses prepared along the Putna, Siret and Bariad Rivers just above where those streams empty into the Danube.

To the southeast, a Soviet communiqué said, the Russians had captured Kiliya on the Danube, fifteen miles west of the Black Sea port of Vilkov at the mouth of the delta, and twenty-two miles east of the port of Ismail. General Tolbukhin's Third Army seized that point. To the northwest his troops reached the Prut River on a seventy-mile front between captured Leusheny and Kagul, the latter being thirty miles northeast of the Galati Gap. The capture of Gasanbatyr put the Russians thirty miles from the port of Ismail on the northeast.

Soviet aircraft added to the slaughter by attacking Axis military trains at Galati, the supplementary communiqué said.

In six days the Russians have captured nearly all of lower Bessa-

Continued on Page 6

ALLY FIGHTS REICH

Nazis' Bombers Attack Bucharest—City Held Cleared of Germans

FIGHTING CONTINUES

Bulgaria Called Willing to Surrender to Allies Unconditionally

By SIDNEY GRUSON
By Cable to The New York Times.

LONDON, Aug. 25—The new Rumanian Government, after having denounced German perfidy tonight, openly declared war on the Reich, thereby fulfilling a Russian prerequisite for acceptance of the Rumanian offer to change to the Allied side.

The United States and Great Britain, moreover, have received word from Bulgaria that she is ready to accept unconditional surrender terms. The western allies, it was learned tonight, are now filling in details of the terms. The Rumanian declaration of war came after the Nazis, according to a proclamation broadcast by the Bucharest radio, had bombed the capital heavily and German units had attacked Rumanian forces and machine-gunned civilians of Bucharest and of other places.

Nazis' Flight Called Hopeless

"By these acts of aggression, which occurred simultaneously in various parts of the country, Germany has placed herself in a state of war with Rumania," the proclamation declared. "The Government therefore orders the Rumanian Army to begin the struggle against all German military forces on Rumanian territory for the liberation of the country from German usurpation."

The Germans themselves have acknowledged their position in Rumania as being hopeless. The Nazi-controlled Scandinavian News Service said that encircled German units were trying to break through the Russian lines toward the Carpathians and Transylvania to fight their way to Hungary.

The German "Danube" radio station appealed to the Rumanian Army tonight to "refuse to fight against your former allies." But the appeal was falling on deaf ears, for the Bucharest radio shortly before had declared that the capital had been completely

Continued on Page 6

PARISIANS CELEBRATE ARRIVAL OF ALLIES

Patriots crowding around a jeep after its arrival in the French capital yesterday. This picture, one of the first to be taken inside the city, was sent from the new transmitting station set up in Cherbourg.

The New York Times (U. S. Signal Corps Radiotelephoto)

JAPANESE CRUISER FIRED BY U.S. FLIERS

Mast-Head Strike at Manado Also Smashes 7 Freighters —40 Barges Riddled

By FRANK L. KLUCKHOHN
By Cable to The New York Times.

ALLIED HEADQUARTERS IN AUSTRALIA, Aug. 25—A Japanese cruiser and seven Japanese freighters were sunk or severely damaged and forty barges and luggers were shot up as a force of fewer than twenty-five of Lieut. Gen. Douglas MacArthur's Liberators made a surprise low-level attack yesterday on Manado, in Netherland Celebes, which is the enemy supply point for Halmahera.

The Mitchells braved heavy ack-

Continued on Page 3

Allied Forces Help French To Rid Capital of Nazis

By The Associated Press.

SUPREME HEADQUARTERS, Allied Expeditionary Force, Aug. 25—The Paris radio announced late tonight that the French capital had been liberated and that the German commander had signed a document ordering his troops to cease fire immediately.

The announcement followed entry of American and French troops into the capital during the day. There was no immediate confirmation here.

The latest word at headquarters was that American and French troops had joined Fighting French patriots on the Ile de la Cité in the heart of the capital after bitter fighting with Germans and French collaborationist militiamen.

Gen. Charles de Gaulle, President of the French Committee of National Liberation, said in a speech broadcast from Paris:

"France will take her place among the great nations which will organize the peace. We will not rest until we march, as we must, into enemy territory as conquerors."

The commander of the Paris region for the French Forces of the Interior, Colonel Raoul, issued this proclamation to his forces, the radio said:

"FFI of the Ile de France (the Paris region), you have unleashed a rising that has liberated Paris. You have improvised your tactics, animated by the strong desire to win, and you have won."

In another broadcast the Paris radio said that the German com-

Continued on Page 5

AMERICANS SEIZE CANNES, PUSH EAST

Drive to 20 Miles From Italy, Spear Along Rhone—Lyon Is Reported in Patriots' Hands

By The Associated Press.

ROME, Aug. 25—American troops lunging suddenly eastward from their Riviera beachhead, on southern France, have captured the famous resort towns of Cannes and Antibes and tonight were fighting forward less than twenty miles from the Italian frontier.

Nice, within short artillery range of the advancing Americans, was expected to fall at any hour.

Other swift Allied columns drove methodically toward the heart of France and a junction with Gen. Dwight D. Eisenhower's armies in the north. Tonight's communiqué said forces probing into the plains of the Rhône valley were close to

Continued on Page 5

THIRD NEAR MARNE

Berlin Says Americans Have Driven to Reims, 80 Miles Above Paris

SEINE FOE CRUSHED

River Becomes a Scene of Carnage as Bombs Rain on Germans

By DREW MIDDLETON
By Cable to The New York Times.

SUPREME HEADQUARTERS, Allied Expeditionary Force, Saturday, Aug. 26—Three resounding victories were won along the 200-mile-long front in northern France yesterday.

Armored patrols of the United States Third Army rumbled into Troyes, a great road and railroad center 130 miles from the German frontier as the thrust eastward on the extreme right flank of the Allies' line broke through German offensive positions in front of Troyes, thirty-seven miles from the Marne River.

Bridgeheads across the Seine south of Paris were widened, and the enemy was driven from Montereau, ten miles east of Fontainebleau, and was retreating hurriedly from the area northeast of Montargis, taken by other American forces late Thursday.

Report Reims Reached

An unconfirmed report, published in The London Chronicle, said the Germans declared that American troops had reached Reims, eighty miles northeast of Paris.

French and American columns penetrated into the center of Paris yesterday.

Aside from its tremendous effect on French morale, the Allies' occupation of Paris, the most important communications center in France, is a military triumph of first magnitude.

Finally, far to the west, British, American and Canadian forces were driving the remnants of the German Seventh Army pell-mell into the Seine. The Elbeuf pocket replaced Falaise as a graveyard. Enemy forces are now contained in an area less than 300 miles square, with the Seine to the east and north and the Risle to the west and the steadily advancing Allied line to the south.

Planes Batter Fleeing Foe

While field guns and tanks searched the forests for fleeing Germans, hundreds of medium and light fighter bombers scourged the Germans seeking to escape across the Seine.

The battle has become a race for Seine crossings, with Allied forces confident they will have killed, wounded or captured at least 40,000 of the Germans before they reach the Seine.

As ground forces drove the Germans to the Seine, American and British light naval craft, attacking German ships leaving Le Havre, blew up an escort vessel, an armed trawler and a German E-boat, and damaged at least five other craft. Between 3 and 4 o'clock yester-

Continued on Page 4

Von Kluge Killed, Stockholm Hears

STOCKHOLM, Saturday, Aug. 26—Field Marshal Gen. Guenther von Kluge has been killed, the newspaper Dagens Nyheter said today on the basis of information received from Germany.

Circumstances of his reported death were not known here and the newspaper had no additional details.

[There was no immediate confirmation of this report in either Axis or Allied official quarters.]

Von Kluge, 61 years old, had held command of the German armies on the western front since July 6, when he succeeded Field Marshal Gen. Karl von Rundstedt.

"Will Host 'Allies in Command.'"

Army Rules Roosevelt Address Was Political, Then Denies It

Special to The New York Times.

WASHINGTON, Aug. 25—The War Department changed its mind today on whether President Roosevelt's speech at Bremerton, Wash., on Aug. 12 was "political," holding first that it was and several hours later reversing itself to hold that it was "not political."

The issue was raised by the Socialist party, which applied to the War Department for equal radio time to address fighting men overseas on the grounds that the President's Bremerton speech, in which he mainly reviewed his trip to Hawaii and the Aleutians, was "political."

"The War Department," said a memorandum, issued in reply to press inquiries, "has indicated to the Socialist party that, under the statute, it will accede to this request. The other major political parties have asked for and have been furnished copies of the correspondence between the War De-

Continued on Page 5

War News Summarized

SATURDAY, AUGUST 26, 1944

American forces in northern France entered Troyes, 130 miles from the German frontier, as Allied armies continued yesterday to move forward along a 200-mile front. Our bridgeheads across the Seine south of Paris were widened. The enemy was driven from Montereau, ten miles east of Fontainebleau and was in hurried retreat from the area northeast of Montargis. Far to the northwest, the remnants of the German Seventh Army, trapped with their backs to the Seine, were being driven into the river. [1;8; map P. 4.]

As the famous spire of the Eiffel Tower pierced the early morning fog, French and American forces smashed through to the heart of Paris amid a tumultuous welcome. The Free Paris radio reported that the German commander of the city had surrendered. [1:8-7; map P. 5.]

In southern France, Allied troops captured Cannes and Antibes and stood less than twenty miles from the Italian frontier. Other Allied columns were reported closing in on Lyon, Rhône Valley industrial center 170 miles inland from the Mediterranean, and French patriots were said to be in control of the city. [1:7; P. 2.]

General de Gaulle—who is in Paris—and his committee will have a greater place in the administration of civil affairs in France by now generally [2:1.]

More than 3,000 planes from Britain and Italy ranged over Czechoslovakia and Germany, pounding aircraft plants, airfields and experimental and research centers for Hitler's flying bombs and other new weapons of destruction. [4:6.]

The Red Army has reached the Galati Gap, a forty-five-mile path between the Danube delta and the mountains to the west, and seized Tecuci, a railway junction within that gateway to the Balkan plains. Twelve enemy divisions have been encircled southwest of Kishinev. Moscow also reported the capture of the key city of Tartu in the Riga-Tallinn railroad in Estonia in the Russian drive to wipe out two German Baltic armies. [1:3; map, P. 6.]

Chaos mounted in the Balkans. After German planes had bombed the Rumanian capital, Rumania declared war on the Reich and proceeded to fulfill a Russian condition for armistice by proceeding to proclaim that King Michael's pro-Ally Government was at war with Germany. Rumanians were battling Hungarians as well as Germans. [1:4.] The Russian sweep led Bulgaria to send word to the Allies that she was ready for unconditional surrender. [1:7.]

Allied planes sank a Japanese cruiser offsite and sank or damaged seven enemy freighters near Celebes, an important Japanese supply center for Halmahera Island. [1:5.]

Dulles Indicates Republican Idea Is to Cooperate, Yet Criticize

By JAMES B. RESTON
Special to The New York Times.

WASHINGTON, Aug. 25—Apparently the Republican party will try to lift the specific question of American participation in a world security organization out of party politics in the Presidential campaign, but there will be no moratorium on discussion of the Administration's conduct of foreign policy as a whole.

Mr. Dulles told reporters that he hoped the two major parties could reach an agreement on the American security plan now being discussed at the Dumbarton Oaks Conference.

Mr. Dulles, Gov. Thomas E. Dewey's representative on foreign affairs, who issued a joint statement which indicated that they had not reached complete agreement on the subject of international re-

... to discuss foreign policy during the campaign or complete agreement on the American security plan now before the Dumbarton Oaks Conference.

This seemed clear today at the close of the first phase of the discussion between Secretary Hull and John Foster Dulles, Governor Dewey's representative on foreign affairs, who issued a joint statement which indicated that they had not reached complete agreement as yet and emphasized that the Republicans would retain their right to criticize freely the Administration's past conduct of foreign relations.

The joint statement by Secre-

Continued on Page 24

The New York Times.

LATE CITY EDITION
Sunny, cool and windy; fair and becoming cooler tonight.
Temperatures Yesterday—Max., 60; Min., 51
Sunrise, 7:29 A. M.; Sunset, 6:41 P. M.

VOL. XCIV..No. 31,687.   Entered as Second-Class Matter, Postoffice, New York, N. Y.   NEW YORK, THURSDAY, OCTOBER 26, 1944.   Copyright, 1944, by The New York Times Company.   THREE CENTS   IN NEW YORK CITY

U. S. DEFEATS JAPANESE NAVY; ALL FOE'S SHIPS IN ONE FLEET HIT; MANY SUNK; BATTLE CONTINUES

SPECIAL PRIVILEGE SOLD BY NEW DEAL, DEWEY CHARGES

Says Roosevelt Backs Plan for 1,000 to Put '$1,000 on the Line' to Aid Campaign

PARTY LETTER IS QUOTED

Governor Declares in Chicago Administration Lacks 'Honesty' to Solve Post-War Problems

The text of Mr. Dewey's speech will be found on Page 13.

By ALEXANDER FEINBERG
Special to The New York Times.

CHICAGO, Oct. 25—Governor Dewey declared tonight that "for $1,000 laid on the line to finance the fourth-term drive, this Administration boldly offers for sale 'special privilege,'" which includes the "assisting in the formulation of Administration policies."

Attacking the "rudimentary honesty" of the New Deal, Mr. Dewey, in a major campaign address preceding the appearance of President Roosevelt here Saturday, charged that the Chief Executive himself was the sponsor of the fund raising idea.

The Chicago Stadium, which accommodates 25,000 persons, was packed to capacity, with several —and others clamoring to obtain admittance. Gov. Dwight H. Green of Illinois presented Mr. Dewey, who was received with tumultuous acclaim. He kept pointing to the microphone to still the demonstration, but it was just short of five minutes before he could begin his speech.

Governor Dewey said that the fund raising plan was disclosed in a letter signed by H. L. McAlister and Sam J. Watkins, State finance chairman, and written on the letterhead of the National Democratic Campaign Headquarters, Little Rock, Ark.

Dewey Quotes Letter

Mr. Dewey quoted the letter as follows:

"This is an invitation to you to join the One Thousand Club.

"The idea of such a club originated at a recent conference at the White House between the President, Robert E. Hannegan, chairman of the Democratic National Committee, and Edwin W. Pauley, treasurer of the committee. At this meeting the President commented:

"I think it would be a good idea to have a list of one thousand persons banded together from all over the United States to act as a liaison to see that facts relating to the public interest are presented factually to the President and members of Congress.'

"Members of this organization undoubtedly will be granted special privilege by party leaders. These members will be called into conference from time to time to discuss matters of national importance and to assist in the formulation of Administration policies.

"To be eligible for membership in the One Thousand Club will require a contribution of $1,000 to the National Democratic campaign fund."

Mr. Dewey declared that "there in crude, unblushing words is the ultimate expression of New Deal policies," adding:

"And the sponsor of this idea is frankly stated in that letter to be the President himself. The man who holds the highest office within the gift of the American people at a conference in the White House sponsors an idea to sell 'special privilege' and a voice 'in the formulation of Administration policies' for one thousand dollars on the barrelhead."

The Governor said that New

Continued on Page 13, Column 1

No Extra Gasoline For Trip to Polls

By The Associated Press.
WASHINGTON, Oct. 25—Chester Bowles, OPA head, in a letter to Senator Davis, Republican, of Pennsylvania today stated that the OPA could not allow extra gasoline rations for private automobiles to take voters to the polls if other means of transportation are available.

Pennsylvania has no absentee voting law and Senator Davis contended that many persons from his State working elsewhere would be unable to return to cast their ballots unless they received extra gas rations.

"A special ration may be granted to carry persons to and from the polls for the purpose of voting in public elections (including primary elections), provided reasonably adequate alternative means of transportation are not available," Mr. Bowles wrote.

Where no other form of transportation is available those wishing to use cars for voting may apply to their local ration boards on special forms which the boards have available.

WAGNER ACCLAIMS PARTY FARM POLICY

He Says That Dewey Is Vague on Agriculture—Calls His Platform 'Double Talk'

By CLAYTON P. KNOWLES

SYRACUSE, N. Y., Oct. 25—The farm plank in the Republican platform offers nothing but "double talk" and Governor Dewey, rather than clarifying the issue, puts forward proposals "as vague and airy as a wisp of smoke," Senator Robert F. Wagner declared tonight as he carried his campaign for re-election into this city in the heart of the farm area.

"Come quick," he cried, slapping his palms together for emphasis. Rushing to the President's oval-shaped office, the reporters found him seated at his desk, smiling broadly. Obviously he had been interrupted in his late afternoon dictation. Before him lay scattered papers, but directly in front of him was a single sheet of paper, inscribed apparently with his own handwriting.

"Mr. Dewey ridicules the socalled alphabetical agencies," he declared. "But how could low-interest loans have been provided without the Farm Mortgage Corporation? How could farm prices have been supported without the Agricultural Adjustment Administration? How could the number of farms with central electric service have been multiplied three times without the Rural Electrification Administration?

"These programs are not perfect. They need to be improved, but they are solid, they can be seen, they can be felt. When Mr. Dewey talks about the farmer, what he proposes is as vague and airy as a wisp of smoke."

His address, broadcast over a State-wide hook-up by the Columbia Broadcasting System, said that Governor Dewey's Commissioner of Agriculture last spring set minimum milk prices "far above

Continued on Page 12, Column 4

PRESIDENT ELATED

Gives News From Halsey That Foe Is 'Defeated, Damaged, Routed'

TEST IS ON, KING SAYS

Practically All Japanese Fleet in the Battle, Admiral Believes

By LEWIS WOOD
Special to The New York Times.

WASHINGTON, Oct. 25—President Roosevelt exultantly announced late today the receipt of a report from Admiral William F. Halsey saying that the Japanese Navy in the Philippine area had been "defeated, seriously damaged and routed" by our forces.

Two hours earlier Admiral Ernest J. King, Commander in Chief of the United States Fleet and Chief of Naval Operations, had disclosed that virtually all of the long elusive Japanese Fleet had been engaged at last in the furious sea battle off the Philippines.

These two startling revelations, exciting Washington as nothing has done since the European invasions, were taken here to mean that the vaunted Japanese naval power had been seriously crippled and the road to Tokyo made much easier. At last, it was presumed, the principal part of Japanese naval strength had been nettled out of hiding and then decisively beaten.

Announcement Is Dramatic

The circumstances of the President's statement were thrilling. When only a half dozen newsmen remained in the White House press room at 5:20 P. M., Press Secretary Stephen T. Early appeared at the door.

"Come quick," he cried, slapping his palms together for emphasis. Rushing to the President's oval-shaped office, the reporters found him seated at his desk, smiling broadly. Obviously he had been interrupted in his late afternoon dictation. Before him lay scattered papers, but directly in front of him was a single sheet of paper, inscribed apparently with his own handwriting.

He had, said the President beamingly, a "real flash," just telephoned to him by Admiral William D. Leahy, Chief of Staff to the President as Commander in Chief of the Army and Navy. Picking up the paper, Mr. Roosevelt slowly and distinctly read:

"The President received today a report from Admiral Halsey that the Japanese Navy in the Philippine area has been defeated, seriously damaged and routed by the United States Navy in that area."

For a moment there was a pause. No one said a word. Then

Continued on Page 3, Column 3

U. S. and Britain Recognize Italy; Action Is First With an Ex-Enemy

By BERTRAM D. HULEN
Special to The New York Times.

WASHINGTON, Oct. 25—Diplomatic relations with Italy were resumed by the Allies tonight.

Recognition is being accorded by the United States, the other American republics in the United Nations and Britain. The Soviet Union had previously accorded recognition to the Government of Premier Ivanoe Bonomi.

Our action was announced by Edward R. Stettinius Jr., acting Secretary of State, who said that Alexander C. Kirk, who has been serving as our diplomatic representative in Rome with the personal rank of Ambassador, would now be accredited to the Italian Government with the rank of Ambassador.

It is expected that Italy will now send an Ambassador here. The appointment of Count Carlos Sforza, long a friend of the United States, to the post, has been forecast since it became evident that recognition would not long be delayed.

Announcement of the recognition has been made at London and is expected at the Latin-American capitals, except for Buenos Aires. Argentina never severed relations with Italy, although she did with Germany and Japan.

The announcement by Mr. Stettinius follows:

"After consultation with the other American republics, as provided in the Resolutions of Rio de

Continued on Page 10, Column 6

SEA POWER OF LAND OF THE RISING SUN SHATTERED IN BATTLE

Oct. 26, 1944

SCALE OF MILES

Piecing together the statements of Admiral Nimitz and General MacArthur gives this picture of the battle around the Philippines: One Japanese force, including four battleships, ten cruisers and thirteen destroyers, first sighted south of Mindoro (1) steamed east, across the Sibuyan Sea, through San Bernardino Strait and down the coast of Samar (2), where Admiral Kinkaid's combined force (5) attacked it and forced it to retire northward with perhaps ten ships damaged. It was apparently in this action that the American light carrier Princeton was sunk. A second Japanese force, first sighted southwest of Negros (3), included two battleships, one or two cruisers and four destroyers. It moved east across the Sulu Sea and through Surigao Strait (4). Admiral Kinkaid attacked this group and it lost one battleship and several cruisers and destroyers; the rest of the force retreated west through the strait. This whole battle scene is at (A) on the inset. A third Japanese force was engaged southeast of Formosa (B).

ALLIES CUT UP FOE IN WEST HOLLAND

British Hammer Germans in One Area of 's Hertogenbosch —Canadians Tighten Traps

By CLIFTON DANIEL
By Wireless to The New York Times.

SUPREME HEADQUARTERS, Allied Expeditionary Force, Oct. 25—The Germans are rapidly losing their grip tonight on their stronghold between the North Sea and the British Second Army's salient in the Netherlands.

British forces converging from three sides drove them out of all

Continued on Page 7, Column 2

'17 Hours of Hell' Raised In Sea Battle Off Leyte

By RALPH TEATSORTH
United Press Correspondent

ABOARD ADMIRAL KINKAID'S FLAGSHIP, off the Philippines, Thursday, Oct. 26—The Tokyo Express rammed into the American Navy Limited today. The pride of Japan was wrecked so badly it may never make another long run. It was the day our Navy had dreamed about for considerably more than a year.

It was seventeen hours of concentrated hell and the most amazing thing about the battle was that our Pacific Fleet Carrier Force which nobody thought could deliver such a terrific punch—held off the bulk of the Japanese fleet all day and had it on the run all afternoon.

When evening came and most of

Continued on Page 4, Column 7

AIR PLANT IN JAPAN SMASHED BY B-29'S

Omura Target Is 'Perfectly Patterned,' Pilots Say—Foe Lists 100 Planes in Attack

Special to The New York Times.

ADVANCED TWENTIETH AIR FORCE HEADQUARTERS here announced that a medium-sized task force of the mammoth bombers, operating from Twen-

Continued on Page 4, Column 4

AMERICANS MAKE BIG LEYTE JUMPS

Troops Push Westward on Isle —Southern Coast of Samar to the North Now Held

By The United Press

ADVANCED HEADQUARTERS ON LEYTE, Thursday, Oct. 26.—American dismounted cavalry troops have invaded Samar, third largest of the Philippines and last island barrier on the road to Luzon and Manila, while forces fighting on Leyte have punched nine miles inland to seize the key road junction of Burauen.

Gen. Douglas MacArthur also announced in a special communiqué that Field Marshal Count Juichi Terauchi's Japanese defenders of the northern Leyte front were "disintegrating" under the American hammer blows.

The three-mile American advance that occupied Burauen, southern terminus of an inland highway, split the Japanese lines in northern Leyte and threw the enemy back toward the coast, where Filipino guerrillas were reported in action.

The new American triumphs pushed our lines nine miles inland to thirty-one miles of seized. Six airfields also have been seized. The invasion of Samar, with an

Continued on Page 4, Column 5

War News Summarized

THURSDAY, OCTOBER 26, 1944

The Japanese Navy came out to fight in the waters of the Philippines and was severely mauled. One force of four battleships, ten cruisers and thirteen destroyers moved up south of Mindoro into the Sibuyan Sea. Every battleship and at least one cruiser was hit. This flotilla rounded Samar and fled north. We lost an escort carrier.

A second force of two battleships, two cruisers and four destroyers came into the Sulu Sea from southwest of Negros Island. After all the ships had been hit it turned tail and retreated.

A third force, this one with carriers, came down from home waters and the battle was still going on. Most of the engagements were fought from the air and the enemy suffered heavily in plane losses. Our light carrier Princeton was hit and its magazine subsequently exploded. Most of the crew were saved. The Third Pacific Fleet took on the enemy carrier force and the Seventh took back the two others. [All the foregoing 2:8.]

President Roosevelt, in an impromptu press conference, said that Admiral Halsey, commanding the Third Fleet, had just reported that the Japanese Navy had been "defeated, seriously damaged and routed." Earlier Admiral King had said that almost the entire enemy naval strength was involved in the Philippines battle. Fighting covered an area 600 miles north and south and 250 east and west. Navy officials were elated and felt the whole course of the war might be speeded. [1:3.]

On Leyte American troops had pushed twenty miles north of Tacloban and nine miles inland from Dulag. Additional landings on the northern part of Leyte and the southern part of Samar won control of San Juanico Strait, which separates the two. [1:7; map P. 2.]

Superfortresses delivered a smashing assault on Japan's key aircraft plant at Omura on the island of Kyushu. One B-29 was missing. [1:6.]

German positions in the Belgium - Netherland pocket were becoming increasingly untenable as Canadian and British troops drew closer and menaced the enemy retreat line. [1:4; map P. 7.] More than 2,200 American and British bombers lashed rail and oil targets in the Reich. Six bombers and one of a great fighter escort were missing. [9:1.]

Russian forces captured the German port and U-boat base of Kirkenes in Norway and thirty other Norwegian villages. [1:6-7; map P. 11.] To the south the Red Army renewed its drive on Warsaw, gained more ground in East Prussia and liberated all of Transylvania by capturing Satu-Mare and Carei. [12:1, with map.]

Mount Belmonte, guarding the southern approaches to Bologna, was captured by Americans of the Fifth Army in Italy. The British Eighth Army gained three miles in the Adriatic sector. A German withdrawal was indicated. [10:7.]

The United Nations have resumed diplomatic relations with Italy, the first former enemy state to receive recognition. [1:2-3.]

BATTLESHIP IS SUNK

Seventh Fleet Smashes Two Japanese Forces Converging on Leyte

REMNANTS IN FLIGHT

They Are Hotly Pursued —Third Enemy Force Is Hit Off Formosa

The Imperial Japanese Fleet has been brought to battle. It is suffering a crushing defeat. Two of its divisions have been routed. One has been almost destroyed. Contact has been made with the main force southeast of Formosa by Admiral William F. Halsey's Third Fleet. That engagement is continuing, said the last communiqué.

Two strong Japanese naval forces converged on Leyte Gulf through the San Bernardino Strait in the Philippines to the north and the Surigao Strait to the south. Vice Admiral Thomas C. Kinkaid's Seventh Fleet smashed these two forces and put the remnants to flight after sinking or heavily damaging every ship in the southern enemy forces.

One big Japanese carrier has been sunk. Two more have been put out of action. One Japanese battleship of the Yamasiro class has been sunk. At least four others have been heavily damaged. Several enemy cruisers and destroyers have been sunk. Many others have been hit, both by bombs and torpedoes.

Enemy Defeated and Routed

The only announced American loss is the converted cruiser-carrier Princeton sunk. Other escort carriers or one of the enemy battleships sunk.

Gen. Douglas MacArthur reported triumphantly that the Japanese Navy has suffered its most crushing defeat of the war." Admiral Ernest J. King, in Washington, said that "practically all" of the Japanese fleet was engaged and that he was confident of the outcome. President Roosevelt called a special press conference to announce receipt of a message from Admiral William F. Halsey reporting that the enemy has been "defeated, seriously damaged and routed."

Pending official word from Pearl Harbor, it appeared the greatest surface and naval air action in the history of naval warfare was being fought and won by the Pacific Fleet, the greatest naval force that ever went down to the sea.

Fate of Leyte Decided

SEVENTH FLEET HEADQUARTERS, Philippines, Thursday, Oct. 26 (UP)—Japan lost the first, and possibly the decisive, round in an all-out battle to halt the Philippines line the American advance toward her home islands.

This occurred early yesterday morning when Admiral Kinkaid's outnumbered fleet attacked and put to rout Japanese battle forces converging on Leyte Gulf.

Complete results are lacking as the action is continuing, with planes from Admiral Kinkaid's fleet but still fighting carrier force hitting the surviving enemy warships as they are retiring. [General MacArthur said the Japanese force that came through Surigao Strait fled back through it to the west and the other was in flight in a northerly direction.]

[Gordon Walker in a Mutual broadcast from the Philippines said "a Navy spokesman here claimed that practically every

Continued on Page 5, Column 2

Russians Invade North Norway; Take Kirkenes in Wide Advance

By W. H. LAWRENCE
By Wireless to The New York Times.

MOSCOW, Oct. 25—Entering their ninth country in less than seven months, Red Army forces smashed across the "Norwegian frontier today and liberated the Barents Sea port of Kirkenes and thirty other Norwegian villages just fifty-four months and twenty-one days after the beginning of Adolf Hitler's treacherous invasion of the Scandinavian country.

This new expedition of Russian troops outside the Soviet Union was announced by Premier Joseph Stalin in a special order of the day and was saluted by Moscow's massed guns and highlighted in tonight's communiqué.

The Soviet Union's Norwegian campaign brings Allied armies

back on the soil of that restless country for the first time since June 15, 1941, when the British had to withdraw their poorly equipped forces in the face of numerically superior German forces.

On its European front the Red Army reopened the battle for Warsaw by outflanking the Polish capital on the north, drove farther into East Prussia against desperate resistance and completed the liberation of Transylvania.[2]

It would be wrong to assume from this dash across the Norwegian frontier that this is the northern-most point that the liberation of

Continued on Page 11, Column 4

"All the News
That's Fit to Print"

The New York Times.

LATE CITY EDITION
POSTSCRIPT
Considerable cloudiness and milder
today; moderate winds.
Temperatures Yesterday—Max., 51 ; Min., 37
Sunrise, 7:33 A. M.; Sunset, 3:45 P. M.

Copyright, 1944, by The New York Times Company.

VOL. XCIV No. 31,700.   Entered as Second-Class Matter,
Postoffice, New York, N. Y.   NEW YORK, WEDNESDAY, NOVEMBER 8, 1944.   THREE CENTS   NEW YORK CITY

ROOSEVELT WINS FOURTH TERM; RECORD POPULAR VOTE IS CLOSE; DEMOCRATS GAIN IN THE HOUSE

2-DAY LUZON BLOWS SMASH 440 PLANES, 30 JAPANESE SHIPS

Halsey's Fliers Destroy 249 Aircraft, Sink Four Vessels in Sunday Sweep

MANILA FIELDS RAVAGED

Ports and Installations Hit Hard—Enemy Lines to Leyte Defenders Are Strained

BY GEORGE HORNE
By Telephone to The New York Times.

PEARL HARBOR, Nov. 7—Admiral William F. Halsey's Third Fleet carriers spread death and damage over southern Luzon Island in the Philippines for the second successive day on Sunday, sinking another five ships and destroying 249 additional enemy aircraft.

It was a major air strike, apparently an all-out effort to annihilate the Japanese air force supporting enemy counter-attacks on Leyte, where American military leaders have reported the campaign nearing its final stages.

Over the two days, according to Admiral Chester W. Nimitz's communiqué today, the enemy has lost 440 aircraft, 327 of which were caught and destroyed on the ground and 113 shot down in the air. The principal plane concentrations were found on seven fields in the Manila network. They were Nichols, Clark, Nielson, Lipa, Tarlac, Bambam and Mabalacat.

[The two-day toll of enemy ships sunk or damaged was about thirty.]

Unable to Rise in Strength

As the widespread attacks continue, the enemy air opposition is becoming steadily weaker, as is evidenced by the fact that on the second day all but a few of the lost enemy aircraft were caught on the ground, unable to get into the air.

Terrific damage is being inflicted on port facilities and ground installations in and around Manila harbor. In addition to ships sunk and planes destroyed, many air and surface craft were listed as damaged. Reports on the action were still of a preliminary nature and there was no count of our own losses.

Admiral Nimitz said three oil storage areas were left blazing at the northern section of Clark Field and at the northeast of the field a tremendous explosion was observed, followed by fire. North of Malvar a railroad engine and five tank cars were blown up.

Five Ships Sunk at Manila

In the harbor of Manila the fighters, torpedo planes and dive-bombers sank three cargo ships and an oil tanker, probably sank a destroyer and damaged two destroyers, two destroyer escorts, a tanker and several cargo ships. Fourteen cargo ships were damaged during the two-day attack, in which wave after wave of American planes swept in from the sea to wipe out available enemy strength that might be used to bolster the hard-pressed Japanese forces on Leyte.

Meanwhile the steady attacks on the Bonins and Kuriles are continuing. On Sunday a squadron of the Eleventh Army Air Force, flying hundreds of miles from our Aleutian bases, hit three small transports off Onnekotan Island in the Kuriles and other Liberators flying with it concentrated on land targets of the island base.

Seven enemy fighters fought the big bombers in a running battle, and guns from three Liberators brought down one and probably destroyed another. Two Liberators were damaged.

Otomari and Tori Island, also in the Kuriles, were attacked.

Seventh Air Force Liberators

Continued on Page 19, Column 2

War News Summarized

WEDNESDAY, NOVEMBER 8, 1944

Japanese Lose 440 Planes

Japanese air power in the Philippines received a staggering blow on Saturday and Sunday when Third Fleet carrier planes destroyed 440 enemy aircraft in the Manila and southern Luzon areas. Nearly thirty ships, including a number of warcraft, were also destroyed or damaged. Our fliers reaped their greatest harvest at seven airfields where they wiped out 327 planes on the ground. Port and ground installations suffered terrific damage. Reports were still incomplete and our own losses were not known. [1:1.]

Battle Joined on Leyte

American troops on Leyte were battling elements of four Japanese divisions in the hills north of Ormoc and repulsed three heavy attacks, inflicting great loss on the enemy. The area of Valencia, north of Ormoc, was under American artillery fire. [19:1, with map.]

Tokyo Sees B-29's

The jittery Japanese reported more Superfortresses on reconnaissance flights over Tokyo and surrounding territory. They also said that the Bonins and Volcanoes had been bombed. [19:2.] In China the enemy scored by driving to within twenty miles of Liuchow, but in Burma the British captured Kennedy Peak and threatened Fort White and Paletwa. [21:1.]

Grim Fight Below Aachen

The United States First Army fought its way back into the streets of Vossenack in some of the bitterest fighting of the war.

Three German counter-attacks from Schmidt were repulsed. The Sixth Army Group made important advances in the Vosges Mountains and in the Netherlands Allied troops were mopping up the liberated areas. [19:8, with map.]

Soviet Drive Forecast

Behind the lull on Russia's fighting fronts the Red Army was reported to be preparing for a great new offensive. [19:4.] The Athens radio announced that the Greek Government had ordered dissolution of the guerrilla bands Edes and Elas. [19:5.]

Robot Blows at U. S. 'Possible'

A joint Army-Navy statement said that it was "entirely possible" for flying bombs to reach the United States from Europe, but gave no indication such an attack was expected. [19:6-7.]

GET 11 TO 20 SEATS

Victories Blast Hopes of Rivals to Control the House

SENATE UNCHANGED

Democrats Have 180 in House, Republicans 155, 98 in Doubt

By TURNER CATLEDGE

Democratic gains of from eleven to twenty seats in the House and a possible new place or two in the already one-sided Senate, appeared on returns received up to 5 A. M. today to have followed in the wake of yesterday's fourth-term landslide of President Roosevelt.

Republican hopes of controlling the House appeared to have been blasted beyond any possibility of realization and what in the earlier count seemed to portend a G. O. P. gain in the Senate began to fade with the later returns.

These same reports showed the defeat of Representative Hamilton Fish, Republican, of New York, one of the most controversial figures in the lower house; the possible defeat of Senator John A. Danaher, Republican, of Connecticut; a victory for Mrs. Clare Luce, Republican, in a close race in the Fourth Connecticut Congressional District; a trend in the early count against Senator Gerald P. Nye, Republican "isolationist" of North Dakota, and a neck-and-neck contest in which Senator James J. Davis, Republican, of Pennsylvania, was trailing his Democratic opponent, Representative Francis J. Myers, by a slight margin.

Leading Senators Re-elected

These returns also revealed the re-election of Senator Alben W. Barkley, Democratic Majority Leader, in Kentucky; of Senator Scott Lucas, Democrat, in Illinois; of Senator Robert A. Taft, Republican, in Ohio; of Senator Millard Tydings, Democrat, in Maryland, and numerous other sitting Senators, both Democratic and Republican.

With 98 House seats still in doubt, the Democrats had clinched 180 seats in the House of Representatives of the Seventy-ninth Congress; the Republicans were certain of at least 155; the American Labor party of 1 an dthe Progressives of 1.

Seventeen Senate places were still awaiting the decision of the final count, but the Democrats were certain of 48, or an actual majority. The Republicans appeared certain of thirty-one and the Progressives of one.

With the latest returns received the Democrats had gained at least

Continued on Page 2, Column 5

ELECTED TO PRESIDENCY AND VICE PRESIDENCY

Franklin D. Roosevelt   Harry S. Truman

ROOSEVELT STRONG IN WAR VOTE TALLY

Partial Count of Ballots of Armed Forces Increases President's Majority

By CHARLES GRUTZNER Jr.

The majority given to President Roosevelt by civilian voters who went to the polls throughout the nation yesterday was increased by the count of war ballots marked, some of them as long as two months ago, by members of the armed forces in camps here and in far-flung theatres of operations.

The decisiveness of the President's victory over Governor Dewey removed the possibility that the outcome of the election might hinge on the soldier vote in some of the eleven States that delayed counting their war ballots, but partial returns from States that counted their war ballots yesterday made it clear that the support of the men and women in the armed forces would be a strong factor in building up the final majority of their Commander in Chief.

A breakdown of the vote into civilian and war ballots was slow in coming in from nearly all of the thirty-seven States that counted their soldier vote yesterday, because election officials were concerned chiefly with transmitting

Continued on Page 4, Column 2

Roosevelt Leads as Davis Trails, In Mounting Pennsylvania Count

Special to The New York Times.

PHILADELPHIA, Wednesday, Nov. 8.—On the basis of partial returns from all but three of the sixty-seven counties in Pennsylvania, it appeared early that President Roosevelt for the third successive time had captured the State's electoral vote.

Swept on the Roosevelt wave, it appeared, was Representative Francis J. Myers in his race to unseat James J. Davis, 71-year-old Republican Senator who was elected first in 1932 and re-elected six years ago.

Whether the Roosevelt impetus would be sufficient to sweep into office the Democratic candidates for the five State offices remained in doubt. Reports in these instances, lagging far behind the count on the two top contests, were inconclusive.

With 6,012 of 8,202 precincts reporting, President Roosevelt was

leading Governor Dewey, 1,282,392, to 1,238,986. Among the returns were all the 1,338 precincts in this city where the President gained a lead of 117,000.

The returns showed that Philadelphia once again was leading the State's electoral vote.

The returns showed that once again the soft coal miners in western Pennsylvania and the anthracite miners in the East repudiated John L. Lewis, president of the United Mine Workers of America, by turning in thumping pluralities for Mr. Roosevelt.

On the other hand, with less than half the precincts reporting and Governor Dewey reducing the President's lead, Republican leaders were hoping that late returns and a fair share of the soldier vote, to be counted on Nov. 22, would mean victory for the party in this State.

Although the President seemed

Continued on Page 8, Column 4

DEWEY CONCEDES

His Action Comes as Roosevelt Leads in 33 States

BIG ELECTORAL VOTE

Late Returns in Seesaw Battles May Push Total Beyond 400

By ARTHUR KROCK

Franklin Delano Roosevelt, who broke more than a century-old tradition in 1940 when he was elected to a third term as President, made another political record yesterday when he was chosen for a fourth term by a heavy electoral but much narrower popular majority over Thomas E. Dewey, Governor of New York.

At 3:15 A. M. Governor Dewey conceded Mr. Roosevelt's re-election, sending his best wishes by radio, to which the President quickly responded with an appreciative telegram.

Early this morning Mr. Roosevelt was leading in mounting returns in thirty-three States with a total of 391 electoral votes and in half a dozen more a trend was developing that could increase this figure to more than 400. Governor Dewey was ahead in fifteen States with 140 electoral votes, but some see-sawing away from him and back again. Typical of these were Wisconsin, where he overtook the President to lead about 2 A. M.; Nevada, where Mr. Roosevelt passed him at about the same time, and Missouri.

In the contests for seats in Congress, the Democrats had shown gains of 11 to 20 in the House of Representatives, assuring that party's continued control of this branch. In the Senate the net of losses and gains appeared to be an addition of one Republican to the Senate, which would give that party twenty-eight members—far short of the forty-nine necessary to a majority. A surprise was the indicated defeat of the veteran Pennsylvania Republican, Senator James J. Davis.

Mrs. Luce's Opponent Concedes

The Congressional races were featured by a mass defeat, in attempt, in which the President and Vice President Henry A. Wallace personally participated, to unseat Representative Clare Boothe Luce of Connecticut. But shortly after 3 A. M., following a night in which the lead had swung back and forth, her election was conceded by her opponent, Miss Margaret Connors. Some hours before, to his neighbors at Hyde Park, the President had expressed rejoicing over Mrs. Luce's "defeat." Her success was the vitriol in the Democratic honey.

Despite the great general victories by the Democrats, the popular vote will evidently show a huge minority protest against a fourth term for the President. Tabulations by the press associations indicated that the disparity between the ballots cast for the two candidates will be so small that a change of several hundred thousand votes in the key States, distributed in a certain way, would have reversed the electoral majority. At 4:40 A. M. The Associated Press reported 16,387,999 for Mr. Roosevelt and 14,235,051 for Mr. Dewey from about one-third of the country's election districts. This ratio, if it carried through, would leave only about 3,000,000 votes between the candidates.

One of the most interesting struggles for the Presidency was that in Wisconsin, where Mr. Dewey took an early lead, lost it and regained it again. Wisconsin is the State where the late Wendell L. Willkie made his stand for renomination, posing the issue of

Continued on Page 2, Column 2

FISH IS DEFEATED; CLARE LUCE WINS

Congress Veteran Concedes Bennet's Victory—Close Finish in Connecticut

Special to The New York Times.

NEWBURGH, N. Y., Wednesday, Nov. 8.—Representative Hamilton Fish, for twelve years a Republican member of the House and a leading isolationist and critic of President Roosevelt's foreign policy, conceded his defeat by Augustus W. Bennet just before 1 o'clock this morning.

"From reports I have received to date, it looks like I have lost the district by a 5,000 vote majority," he said.

"It looks as if the Republicans have lost the House, and if that is so, as much as I regret it, I have no great desire to continue to serve as a minority member, which I have for the last fourteen years in an uphill fight."

Mr. Bennet, in a victory statement, paid tribute to those who had supported him from all parties, "including the much-abused Political Action Committee." He hailed his election as the result of the citizens' determination "to eliminate Ham Fish from Congress."

Factors in the Result

Heavy Republican defections to Mr. Bennet in Orange County and strong support for Mr. Fish's opponent in the parts of the district in Rockland, Sullivan and Delaware counties sent the Republican nominee down to defeat in the bitterest Congressional election in this part of the State in years.

Complete returns from Orange County gave Fish 35,126 votes to 27,371 for Bennet, a majority for Fish of 7,755. This indicated that Mr. Bennet's majority for the whole Twenty-ninth Congressional District would be about 5,600.

Complete returns for Bennet 19,706 votes to 12,323 for Fish, a majority of 7,383.

In Sullivan County, with twenty-four election districts missing, including those where Mr. Bennet was expected to run strongest, the vote was Fish 3,877, Bennet 3,776.

Continued on Page 2, Column 7

ROOSEVELT VICTORY CLAIMED IN JERSEY

Hague Spokesmen Also Say Wene Will Win—Constitution Revision Is Rejected

Despite greatly reduced pluralities in Hudson County, Democratic stronghold of New Jersey, lieutenants of Mayor Frank Hague of Jersey City, Democratic boss of the State, predicted shortly before 4 A. M. today that the State's sixteen electoral votes would be delivered to President Roosevelt, largely by virtue of an estimated plurality of 75,000 votes in Hudson. In 1940 Mr. Roosevelt carried the county by a plurality of 100,877.

Mayor Hague's spokesman also predicted victory for the party nominee for the United States Senate, Representative Elmer H. Wene, although by a close vote, and rejection of the proposed revised State Constitution by a substantial margin.

Mr. Hague himself left headquarters in Jersey City early today without making any statement.

The Jersey City predictions were made despite the fact that eight of the twelve wards in the city had not reported returns up to that hour, but the estimates on the fate of charter revision appeared to be borne out by State-wide returns.

At the same hour Mr. Wene was leading Roosevelt by a vote of 481,677 to 456,275, with 1,819 districts missing, and H. Alexander Smith, Mr. Wene's Republican opponent, was leading the Democratic nominee by a vote of 562,-261 to 503,763, on the basis of returns from 2,226 districts.

Five Hudson Communities Bolt

The apparent rebellion of the Hague machine could not be fully estimated in the early morning hours, but it was clear that the expected large Democratic plurality in the county had surprised some political observers to shave some substantial margin in the State in the doubtful column.

Continued on Page 9, Column 4

New York for Roosevelt; Wagner Re-elected Senator

By JAMES A. HAGERTY

For the sixth consecutive time, four times as a candidate for President and twice as a candidate for Governor, President Roosevelt carried his home State of New York in yesterday's election and won its forty-seven electoral votes.

With 3,609 of the 5,421 election districts in New York City and 4,978 of the 5,421 election districts outside New York City reporting, President Roosevelt had an actual lead over Governor Dewey, his Republican opponent, of 300,831 and a plurality of about 283,000 for the President in the State was indicated.

Returns from 3,609 election districts out of 3,700 in New York City gave Dewey 1,240,216, Roosevelt 1,966,539. This is an actual plurality of 726,273 and an indicated plurality of 743,700 for Roosevelt.

Returns from 4,978 election districts out of 5,421 outside New York City gave Dewey 1,585,771, Roosevelt 1,160,329. This is an actual plurality of 425,442 and an indicated plurality of 460,785 for Dewey.

Re-elected in the sweep for the President was United States Senator Robert F. Wagner, who defeated Secretary of State Thomas J. Curran by a plurality probably greater than that for Mr. Roosevelt. Also elected was Associate Judge of the Court of Appeals, Marvin R. Dye, who defeated John Van Voorhis, Republican. The President, Senator Harry S. Truman, candidate for Vice President, Senator Wagner and Mr. Dye, all Democrats, also were nominees of the American Labor and Liberal parties.

Returns from 3,566 election districts out of the 3,700 in New York City gave Curran 1,183,020, Wagner 1,957,026. This is an actual plurality of 774,006, and an indicated plurality of 802,900 for Wagner.

Returns from 4,797 of 5,421 election districts outside of New York City gave Curran 1,468,985, Wagner 1,086,736. This is an actual plurality of 382,249, and an indicated plurality of 433,680 for Curran.

Both Houses of the State Legislature remain Republican. Among the greatest upsets in the State was the defeat of former Mayor Rolland B. Marvin of Syracuse, Republican candidate for State Senator in the Forty-third Senatorial District, by Richard J. Byrne, Democratic and American Labor party nominee. On incomplete returns, Senator John J. Dunnigan, Democratic leader of the

DEWEY STATEMENT ADMITS HIS DEFEAT

Candidate Concedes Loss of Election at 3:12 A. M. and Congratulates Victor

Gov. Thomas E. Dewey, Republican candidate for President, conceded defeat at 3:12 o'clock this morning.

His statement was made at Republican National Headquarters in the Hotel Roosevelt, where both he and Herbert Brownell Jr., chairman of the National Committee, earlier had refused comment on the growing indication of a lopsided electrical college vote for his Democratic opponent, President Franklin D. Roosevelt.

Mr. Dewey said:

It is clear that Mr. Roosevelt has been re-elected for a fourth term, and every good American will whole-heartedly accept the will of the people.

I extend to President Roosevelt my hearty congratulations and my earnest hope that his next term will see speedy victory in the war, the establishment of lasting peace and the restoration of tranquillity among our peoples.

I am deeply grateful for the confidence expressed by so many million Americans for their labors in the campaign.

The Republican party emerges from the election revitalized and a great force for the good of the country and for the preservation of free government in America.

I am confident that all Americans will join me in a devout hope that in the years ahead Divine Providence will guide and protect the President of the United States.

President Roosevelt, from his Hyde Park home, acknowledged, at 3:28 o'clock this morning Gov-

Continued on Page 2, Column 2

Continued on Page 6, Column 4

"All the News That's Fit to Print"

The New York Times.

LATE CITY EDITION
Fair and cold today. Cloudy and slightly warmer tomorrow.

Temperatures Yesterday—Max., 23; Min., 19

Copyright, 1945, by The New York Times Company.

VOL. XCIV...No. 31,771.   Entered as Second-Class Matter, Postoffice, New York, N.Y.   NEW YORK, THURSDAY, JANUARY 18, 1945.   THREE CENTS NEW YORK CITY

RUSSIANS TAKE WARSAW, REPORTED IN CRACOW; WIN A CITY 14 MILES FROM REICH IN 24-MILE GAIN; BRITISH ADVANCE, AMERICANS CLOSE ON ST. VITH

ROOSEVELT URGES WORK-OR-FIGHT BILL TO BACK OFFENSIVES

Letter to May Calls for Prompt Action on 18-to-45 Measure—King, Marshall Tell of Needs

RECENT LOSSES ARE HEAVY

House Group Abruptly Ends Hearings—Approval of Legislation Expected by Tonight

Appeals by the President, Gen. Marshall, Adm. King, Page 13.

By C. P. TRUSSELL
Special to The New York Times.

WASHINGTON, Jan. 17.—President Roosevelt called on Congress today for prompt action on a work-or-fight bill for men between 18 and 45, since it was vital that the Allied "total offense should not slacken because of any less than total utilization of our manpower on the home front."

In support of his appeal, which was addressed to Chairman Andrew J. May of the House Military Affairs Committee, the President attached a copy of a joint letter sent to him by General Marshall and Admiral King.

Replacements Needed

As "the agents directly responsible" for the conduct of military operations, they also urged "immediate action" on the home front to meet requirements for young and vigorous replacements in battle zones and to provide the necessary manpower to multiply production of critical munitions, build new ships and repair those damaged in combat.

Mr. Roosevelt said that the need for statutory controls to channel 4-F's into essential war work was more urgent now than it was eleven days ago when he asked for it as a stop gap, pending enactment of a national service law, and urged action "without delay" on the May-Bailey bill providing for "limited national service" and covering all 18 to 45 deferred registrants.

Hearings on the May-Bailey bill were ended abruptly, and Mr. May called an executive session of the committee tomorrow. He predicted that the measure, in some form, would be approved by nightfall.

"Time to Act," May Says

"We've discussed this matter long enough," Mr. May said. "It's now time to act."

Committeemen joined their chairman in expected approval of the bill, but they predicted that changes would be made, warned that much care must be exercised in revising the measure, and looked for a "tough" fight when it reached the House floor.

Earlier, the National Association of Manufacturers joined organized labor in opposing the bill, as well as national service generally, before the committee.

Frederick C. Crawford, chairman of the NAM executive committee, testified that it legislation were to be written, it should only put teeth into the controls of existing machinery and program. He said that intensified cooperation between Government, management and labor could supply the manpower demands for the armed service and war production for replacements now and in the future, when an estimated 1,500,000 men will be required. Recent employment gains were cited.

The President in his letter to Mr. May said it was true that there had been a trend toward increased placement of manpower in the last fortnight, but he added that there was danger that this trend, accelerated by belief that Congress was about to act on work-or-fight measures, build action was likely to be delayed.

Although the May-Bailey bill is not a complete national service measure, Mr. Roosevelt said, it would "go far" to effect essential

Continued on Page 13, Column 2

Russian Super-Tank Reported by Nazis

By The Associated Press.

LONDON, Jan. 17.—A German reporter, speaking on the Berlin radio from the Kielce sector of Poland tonight, paid high tribute to the power of a new Red Army heavy tank, called the Joseph Stalin.

"The Russians are using their new Joseph Stalin super-tank on an ever-increasing scale," the Nazi reporter, Heinz Megerlein, said. "This most powerfully gunned and armored vehicle in the world is more than a match for our best tank, the Royal Tiger."

The German broadcaster said the Russian super-tank carried a 122-mm. [4.8-inch] gun.

The German Royal Tiger tank has been reported to mount a new version of the famous 88-mm. gun.

U.S. POLICY ON ROWS IS FIRM, GREW SAYS

Position, Stated Vigorously, Is Not to Allow Differences to Mar Unity, He Asserts

Joseph C. Grew, Under Secretary of State, declared last night that our State Department had vigorously stated, and would continue to state to its allies, the American position on issues in dispute, but that it was the policy of this Government not to allow these differences to interfere with the unity of action essential to winning the war, or to disrupt that unity after the war.

He made this reply to recent critics of our foreign policy at a meeting in The Town Hall, 240 West Forty-fourth Street, at which Senator Warren R. Austin of Vermont called for the earliest practicable meeting to establish the Dumbarton Oaks Organization, and Senator J. William Fulbright of Arkansas assailed our handling of foreign affairs as hesitant, timid, and lacking in forthrightness.

Nicholas Roosevelt was moderator of the meeting, which was arranged by THE NEW YORK TIMES on the topic, "America's Place in World Affairs." The prepared addresses of the three speakers were broadcast over radio stations WQXR and WQXQ. Senators Austin and Fulbright then took part in a discussion and question-and-answer period that followed, for which Mr. Grew was unable to remain.

Fulbright Assails Delay

Senator Fulbright said that our failure to take part in formulating decisions in such pressing situations as the situations in Greece, Italy and Poland was forcing Great Britain and Russia to make their own decisions. He declared that our failure to assume a share of the responsibility for the decisions in the case of Greece had had the effect of making one of our Allies, Great Britain, "the undeserved goat" and had stirred up feeling

Continued on Page 8, Column 1

FOE STIFF IN WEST

Fog and Tanks Help the Germans Slow British and U.S. at Front

OUR AIR ARM BARRED

Montgomery Push Gains Town—Americans Lift Threat to Strasbourg

By CLIFTON DANIEL
By Wireless to The New York Times.

SUPREME HEADQUARTERS, Allied Expeditionary Force, Jan. 17.—While the drive to beat back the German salient continued despite thick, freezing weather and repeated German counter-attacks, which cost the Germans at least twenty-four tanks today, British forces northeast of Aachen also made painful progress into the flank of the Maaseyck bulge.

Beating their way with a flail of tanks through mine fields, dense fog and stinging sleet, they advanced 2,000-odd yards in the first twenty-four hours. Their progress was marked on the map by two river crossings and a village captured—Dieteren. The attack seemed less ambitious than originally appeared, but it still held symbolic value as representing a resumption of the Allied initiative.

The American threat to St. Vith, the last important road junction on the Germans' retreat route from the Ardennes, grew serious today as the battle-wise Old Hickory Division pressed down on the devastated town through knee-deep snow, thick woods and treacherous hills, reaching within five miles of St. Vith's outskirts. A forest belt of two and a half miles and a maze of knobby hills still stand between the town and the attacking Americans, however.

Americans Gain in Alsace

In Alsace American forces attacking the perimeter of the German bridgehead over the Rhine north of Strasbourg not only redressed the setback inflicted by the Germans last night but pushed their way into the western stronghold of the German pocket at Herrlisheim. This advance, though local and limited, will be regarded with satisfaction, particularly by the French, who have been viewing the bridgehead and its threat to Strasbourg with apprehension for many days.

Militarily, Strasbourg does not seem more important than any other city, but politically it is a far greater prize for either the Germans or the French. As the capital of the lost and regained province of Alsace and the "second symbol for France," it is a major symbol for France, and its loss might have a painful effect on French morale, already at a low ebb because of the unduly severe winter.

However, French forces holding the city are regarded as sufficient at the moment to counter any

Continued on Page 9, Column 1

RED ARMY TEARS GERMANS' DEFENSES IN POLAND ASUNDER

Breaking from their Narew River positions, the Russians punched out a salient between Ciechanow and Pomiechowek (1). In an encircling operation they finally toppled Warsaw and some units sped westward to Lesmo (2). South of the Polish capital the Warsaw-Lodz railroad was cut with the capture of Zyrardow (3). The rail junction of Skarzysko-Kamienna was being encircled as Soviet forces moved into Szydlowiec and Konskie (4). The Red Army's closest approach to Germany was at the important Polish city of Czestochowa, fourteen miles from the Silesian border (5). Although the Lublin radio reported the fall of Cracow, Moscow merely said that Sadowie (6), eight miles away, had been taken, but the city's capture was obviously at least imminent.

U.S. MEN USE TNT TO SLIT ICY GROUND

Fight Polar Weather in Hills of Ardennes as Well as Atrocity-Bent Germans

By Wireless to The New York Times.

SUPREME HEADQUARTERS, Allied Expeditionary Force, Jan. 17—Up in the Ardennes hills, where the United States First Army is attacking toward St. Vith, the ground is so hard that the troops have to use dynamite and mortar shells to dig slit trenches.

The hills are so steep and slippery with snow that tanks sometimes slide down them like sleds. When pinned down by enemy fire or while waiting to attack Americans

Continued on Page 3, Column 2

MacArthur Protects Flank By 17-Mile Dash Along Gulf

By LINDESAY PARROTT

ALLIED HEADQUARTERS, on Leyte, Thursday, Jan. 18—The pace of the American advance on Luzon in the Philippines has been fastest in the extreme northwest where Gen. Douglas MacArthur's infantrymen have been feeling their way into Bolinao Peninsula, which forms the western shore of Lingayen Gulf. Here, in a sprint of seventeen miles from captured Alaminos, Sixth Army men reached Bolinao, a town on the extreme point of the peninsula.

Other detachments are moving southwestward toward Dasol Bay and the highway that leads west of the Zambales Mountains toward Bataan, a communiqué announced today.

[The capture of Bolinao sealed

Continued on Page 3, Column 3

War News Summarized

THURSDAY, JANUARY 18, 1945

Warsaw, the first European capital to fall to Hitler's blitzkrieg five years and four months ago, was liberated by Russian and Polish troops yesterday. The First White Russian Army captured the city after it had swept up more than 800 other places.

The Red Army steamroller, which at its closest point was 260 miles from Berlin, moved north of the Polish capital when the Second White Russian Army, from its two bridgeheads across the Narew River, advanced twenty-four miles on a sixty-two-mile front, freeing Makow, Pultusk, Ciechanow and 500 other communities.

At the southern end of the long surging line the First Ukrainian Army liberated Czestochowa, Radomsko and 700 more inhabited places, and Lublin reported that Cracow had also fallen. This Russian army was only fourteen miles from the Reich. [All the foregoing 1:8.]

Gloom hung heavy over Germany. The enemy press and radio prepared the people for retreat on the Eastern front as the "final onslaught against Germany launched at Teheran" got under way. [6:1.]

The Warsaw victory brought to a climax the diplomatic impasse over recognition of a single Polish Government by all the Allies. The Polish Government in London indicated it would seek an early return to Warsaw and the Moscow-fostered Lublin regime was expected to move into the capital immediately. [1:7.]

Reverses in the east did not prevent the Germans from stiffening against the new British Second Army drive north of Aachen. The British advanced 2,000 yards, crossed the Roode River in two places and captured two villages, one of which was Dieteren. To the south, Americans took Vielsam and were five miles from St. Vith. The Third Army trapped a German force in the woods southeast of Tettingen. Inconclusive small battles were fought in the Alsace area. [1:2; map, P.9.]

Some 700 American heavy bombers and 350 fighters carried the air war to oil and submarine plants in the Hamburg-Harburg area and rail targets in northwest Germany. [8:3-4.]

Americans on Luzon speared seventeen miles from Alaminos on the extreme right of the line to capture Bolinao, at the southwest tip of Lingayen Gulf. They also cut across the peninsula toward Dasol Bay, on the China Sea. At the other end of the line patrols entered Pozorrubio while main forces were half a mile from Rosario. Allied planes, in their best day, destroyed sixty-two enemy aircraft, all but one of which were caught on the ground. [1:5-6; map, P.3.]

Tokyo said that Pacific Fleet carrier planes had hit China for the fourth day, 200 of the Navy's aircraft striking Hong Kong, Canton and Hainan Island. A sizable force of B-29's — Tokyo said eighty — hit air installations at Shinchiku, on Formosa's northwest coast, with good effect, and General MacArthur's fliers again struck Okayama, on the southwest coast. [1:5.]

ACCORD ON POLAND AT ONCE HELD VITAL

Red Armies' Sweep to West Seen Spurring Need for 'Big 3' Agreement

By RAYMOND DANIELL
By Cable to The New York Times.

LONDON, Jan. 17.—The fall of Warsaw and the swift advance of the Red Armies across western Poland toward the old frontiers of Germany have made it imperative that President Roosevelt and Prime Minister Churchill reach a final agreement with Premier Stalin on Poland's territorial and political future at their next meeting, it is believed here.

There are signs that the exiled Polish Government under Premier Tomasz Arciszewski is approaching the problems of its relations with Russia with a new sense of urgency but without much outward evidence to support an optimistic view of the outcome.

Mr. Arciszewski, in a statement on the liberation of Warsaw, cited the words of Lieut. Gen. Tadeusz Komorowski [General Bor], just before he and his underground army defending Warsaw yielded to the Germans after a heroic sixty-three-day struggle: "We are fighting for freedom, we are fighting for the right to be free!" Mr. Arciszewski commented: "At this moment these words embody, as

Continued on Page 5, Column 6

OUR CHINA STRIKE IN 4TH DAY, FOE SAYS

Tokyo Cites 300-Plane Blow at Coast Ports—B-29's Join in Attack on Formosa Base

By The United Press.

PEARL HARBOR, Jan. 17—Tokyo reported today that more than 300 American carrier planes hit the China coast for the fourth successive day, battering Hong Kong, Canton and Hainan Island. B-29 Superfortresses joined the mounting two-way offensive with new blows against Formosa.

[A new attack on Formosa Wednesday night was reported by General Douglas MacArthur's headquarters on Luzon. The report stated that long-range patrol planes harassed the Okayama airdrome.]

There was no immediate confirmation that Admiral William F. Halsey's Third Fleet planes had

Continued on Page 5, Column 6

McGuire, Pacific Air Ace, Killed; He Downed 38 Japanese Planes

By The Associated Press.

SAN ANTONIO, Tex., Jan. 17—Major Thomas B. McGuire Jr. of San Antonio and Ridgewood, N. J., the leading American active ace with thirty-eight Japanese planes to his credit, was shot down and killed in the Philippines Jan. 7, Lieut. Gen. George C. Kenney, commanding the Allied Air Forces in the Pacific, informed Mrs. McGuire in a letter dated Jan. 8.

Mrs. McGuire received General Kenney's letter today. The letter said that the word Major McGuire had been shot down brought him the worst of a number of bad moments he had had to face since the war began.

"I felt that he would make a name for command as well as for leadership and for great personal courage," the letter stated.

The accident, which left still Major McGuire's plane in such a manner that the cause of his death was sheer chance as Major McGuire was one of the most capable fighter pilots I have ever known.

"Your husband was one of the men the Air Forces can never forget. We will find it more difficult to carry on without him," General Kenney added.

The letter indicated that Major McGuire's plane in some way disabled in the air, making him an easy prey to defending enemy fighters. Mrs. McGuire said she had received no official notification of her husband's death from the War Department.

Major McGuire became the leading ace when Maj. Richard I. Bong of Poplar, Wis., returned to the United States in December. Major

Continued on Page 5, Column 3

RIPS LINE IN POLAND

Red Army Races West After Storming Into Vistula Citadel

KONEFF NEAR SILESIA

Capture of Czestochowa Threatens Heart of Reich's Industries

By The United Press.

LONDON, Thursday, Jan. 18.—Russian and Polish troops yesterday captured devastated Warsaw to free its last survivors of five years of Nazi tyranny as the Red Army's greatest offensive surged twenty-four miles across western Poland, taking Czestochowa and reaching within fourteen miles of the German border.

At the same time the Red Army launched another offensive north of Warsaw that carried within 130 miles of Danzig and twenty-two miles south of the East Prussian border. Cracow, the fourth city of Poland, also was reported to have been liberated, and Moscow said only that Russian armored spearheads were eight miles north-east of the city at Sadowie.

Shoulder to shoulder, three crack Soviet armies were driving westward across Poland along a twisting 450-mile front. They were headed straight for Germany and were 260 to 288 miles from Berlin.

Racing Toward Lodz

With Warsaw, the first European capital to be overrun by Adolf Hitler's victory-flushed troops, behind them, the Russians were racing westward toward Lodz, second city of Poland, and Russian spearheads already were at Babsk, thirty-six miles east of Lodz on the main Warsaw-Berlin highway.

German troops were retreating hastily toward the borders of the Reich and Berlin reports indicated that the Nazis might be pulling out of Poland entirely, writing off their 1939 and France in 1940, and though Berlin protested that its troops were fighting far behind advance Soviet lines, the German Army appeared to be in full rout.

More than 2,000,000 Soviet soldiers were committed to the huge offensive and Moscow dispatches said savagery unparalleled in four winters of war raged on the East-ern Front as the Russians tore gaps in the German lines and split and resplit enemy groups falling back toward the Oder River—the Rhine of the east.

Silesian Center Outflanked

Thousands of German troops were killed yesterday as Soviet troops, advancing at a mile-an-hour clip, outflanked the coal and steel region of upper Silesia and split its defenders from the main German armies in the Lodz area. Capturing Slawnow, the Russians were only twenty-four miles north-west of Dabrowa, easternmost industrial center of Silesia.

Premier Joseph Stalin announced the capture of Warsaw, the capital of our ally, Poland," just five years, three months and twelve days after Hitler's troops marched into the bombed city, and the free Warsaw radio broadcast to the world: "The city is razed, but we live on."

Marshal Stalin announced the victory in an order of the day. In Moscow victory guns fired without interruption for three hours to mark it and two subsequent orders of the day from the Red Army's Commander in Chief.

The second total of the new offensive, the fall of Warsaw by the Second White Russian Army under the command of Marshal Konstantin K. Rokossovsky, which had ad-

Continued on Page 4, Column 2

Douds Receives Formal Charges Aimed at Removal From NLRB

Formal charges aimed at forcing his resignation as regional director of the National Labor Relations Board were received yesterday by Charles T. Douds. This document was signed by Lester A. Asher, associate administrative examiner of the board in Washington.

Filing of the charges was announced in a statement on Tuesday by Harry A. Millis, chairman of the board, who said that Mr. Douds' removal was being brought "to promote the efficiency of the service" and on grounds of a "lack of fitness and capacity to supervise and direct the work of the staff" of the New York office. In making known that removal proceedings had been instituted against Mr. Douds, Dr. Millis voiced an implied reprimand for Douds for carrying the controversy

between himself and the board into the press.

Mr. Douds, who had refused to comply with the board's previous request that he resign, demanding that formal charges be filed against him so that he might answer them in accordance with prescribed procedure, confirmed receipt of the charges yesterday but declined to discuss them. He made the following statement:

"This afternoon I received formal charges from the board. I first learned of the transmission of these charges from the papers this morning. I will answer these charges to the board and not through the newspapers.

"Dr. Millis implied in his statement this morning that the information already made public on this matter emanated directly or indirectly

Continued on Page 34, Column 6

"All the News That's Fit to Print"

The New York Times.

LATE CITY EDITION
Fair and warm today. Cloudy and warm tomorrow.

Copyright, 1945, by The New York Times Company.

VOL. XCIV..No. 31,836.

Entered as Second-Class Matter,
Post-office, New York, N. Y.

NEW YORK, SATURDAY, MARCH 24, 1945.

THREE CENTS NEW YORK CITY

PATTON CROSSES RHINE IN A DARING DRIVE WITHOUT BARRAGE, EXPANDS BRIDGEHEAD; NAZIS SAY RUSSIANS ARE MOVING ON BERLIN

SENATE, BY 52 TO 36, REJECTS WILLIAMS AS DIRECTOR OF REA

Nineteen Democrats Join With 33 Republicans to Defeat the Former Chief of NYA

HE DENOUNCES HIS FOES

And Declares With Patton of Farmers Union That Issue Is Whether People Shall Rule

By WILLIAM S. WHITE
Special to The New York Times.

WASHINGTON, March 23—The Senate rejected today, 52 to 36, President Roosevelt's nomination of Aubrey Williams to be Rural Electrification Administrator. The adverse vote came through a coalition of Republicans and Conservative Democrats. Most of the latter came from the South, and some of them had been termed "Tories" by the nominee.

Nineteen Democrats joined thirty-three Republicans in voting to deny confirmation to Mr. Williams, the first such denial of an important executive appointment since 1939. Thirty-one Democrats, four Republicans and the Senate's single member of the Progressive party, LaFollette of Wisconsin, voted for the nomination.

Immediately after the Senate vote, the National Farmers Union, of which Mr. Williams has been national director of organization, vowed political vengeance on his opponents, and said that Mrs. Franklin D. Roosevelt would address a "Victory Dinner" for Mr. Williams here Wednesday night that would begin "a total war of issues."

The Southern Democrats who opposed Mr. Williams were principally those whose views on economics are radically opposed to the New Dealism of Mr. Williams.

Barkley Upholds Nominee

A last minute speaker for Mr. Williams was Senator Barkley of Kentucky, the majority leader.

"The record shows," he said, "that Williams was not connected with communism, but that he combated communism."

Mr. Williams asserted that he had been rejected by "those who stand for control by the few, fearing an economy in which everybody would share."

Then, in a joint press conference at the headquarters of the Farmers Union, both he and James G. Patton, president of the National Farmers Union, indicated that the Senate's action would be used as the starting point of an intensive national organizing and political campaign by the union to be concentrated in the Deep South.

"We'll be seeing some of those Senators out where the people live," Mr. Patton declared. Remarking that the forthcoming "Victory Dinner" for Mr. Williams had been so named because the vote in the Senate "showed us how we stand," he added:

"This is the first battle in a total war of issues in this country to decide whether the country is to be conducted for the people or for the vested interests. The Farmers Union have become much more intense in their feelings because of Mr. Williams' rejection. We are going to take whatever steps are necessary to begin to implement our feelings more drastically."

Denies Competence an Issue

Mr. Patton and Mr. Williams have been associated, as individuals, with the CIO's Political Action Committee, although the Farmers Union as an official entity has not been so connected. What the union's precise mechanism would be in its new campaign had not been determined, Mr. Patton said, although he indicated that no consideration had been given to the question of setting up a separate political organization.

Mr. Williams declared that "such Senators" as Bushfield, Republican of South Dakota; Willis, Republican, of Indiana; McKellar, Democrat, of Tennessee; Taft, Republi-

Continued on Page 15, Column 7

Women's Jury Bill Goes to Governor

Special to The New York Times.

ALBANY, March 23—With unanimous adoption by the Senate, Governor Dewey received today Assemblyman Philip Schuyler's bill making jury service for women mandatory instead of optional. The only exceptions permitted under the bill are those where a woman has children under 16 years of age or is caring for a sick or invalid person.

Enactment of the measure after several years of experience under permissive jury service follows a considerable demand from women's groups, notable among which is the League of Women Voters.

A year ago former Assemblywoman Jane H. Todd sponsored a similar bill, which passed the Assembly, but died in committee in the upper house. There has been no indication as to what Governor Dewey's views are with regard to the proposal.

RISE OF $14,000,000 IN SCHOOL AID VOTED

Legislature Moves to Adjourn Today—Assembly Passes Merit Rating Truce

By LEO EGAN
Special to The New York Times.

ALBANY, March 23—By unanimous vote in both houses, the Legislature passed and sent to Governor Dewey today a bill revising the apportionment of State aid for education to increase the total by about $14,000,000 that provided by existing law and $18,000,000 over that required for the old formula.

The Assembly rejected, 66 to 78, the Young-Demo merit rating bill after a debate lasting almost five hours and then passed unanimously the "harmonizing" merit rating proposal, which had the endorsement of Governor Dewey, the Ives Committee on Labor and Industrial Conditions, the AFL and the CIO.

A majority of the Assembly Republicans favored the Young-Demo bill and threatened for a time to revolt against their leaders, who, along with Governor Dewey, opposed it.

Bowing to Labor Charged

In private conversation and, according to some reports, at a closed party conference, the Young-Demo backers accused the leadership of bowing to organized labor. There was a great deal of private bitterness over the action of Irving M. Ives, the majority leader, and Oswald D. Heck, the Speaker, in persuading a number of Republicans favoring the Young-Demo plan to switch to the "harmonizing" bill.

The "harmonizing" bill, which in most essentials is identical with the last of the Falk-Gugino bills, will be taken up in the Senate tomorrow, with passage, in view of the Assembly action, regarded as certain.

By disposing of the education-aid and merit rating measures, which rank among the most impor-

Continued on Page 15, Column 2

HOUSE UNANIMOUS IN VOTE TO EXTEND DRAFT ACT A YEAR

Senate Leaders Seek Rapid Action on Measure Free of Civilian Job Issue

NO BREAK IN DEADLOCK

New Compromise to 'Freeze' Workers Is Considered by Conferees—Vote Set Today

By C. P. TRUSSELL
Special to The New York Times.

WASHINGTON, March 23—The House quickly passed by unanimous vote and sent to the Senate today a bill to extend the Selective Service Act for one year beyond May 15.

On the Senate side leaders assumed that chamber also would act promptly on the bill, without the attachment of riders which would link the drafting of men for the armed services to the mobilization of manpower on the home front.

The question of a "labor draft" remained deadlocked, with Senate and House conferees seeking to find a compromise in the conflicting civilian manpower bills which the two branches have passed.

A new compromise, or trade, was proposed today and was scheduled for a vote tomorrow. It was suggested that if the House would abandon its "limited national service," or draft, provisions, the Senate would agree to impose penalties on workers as well as employers for violations of employment ceilings and other War Manpower Commission controls.

Workers Would Be "Frozen"

Under the proposed compromise there would be a "freezing" of essential war workers into their present jobs as long as they were needed.

An expected move to prohibit the sending of draftees into combat zones within five months after their induction into the Army failed to develop in the House.

The Military Affairs Committee, which reported the extension bill yesterday, was told by Maj. Gen. Idwal Edwards, Assistant Chief of Staff in charge of training, that such a restriction would be "very definitely harmful" to an orderly system of providing men for the fighting fronts.

While the House was acting with unanimity, conferees spent hours this afternoon studying the compromise offered by Senator Austin, Republican, of Vermont, and the amendments to it which have been presented by Representative May, Democrat, of Kentucky.

As a recess was taken, the conferees had before them a proposal for the newer compromise. Concededly, it was not certain that the Senate conferees would be willing to apply penalties to employers when WMC regulations were violated, even though the House conferees should agree to abandon all "labor draft" concepts.

Among Senate conferees there

Continued on Page 14, Column 5

Moses Threatens to Resign in Row Over 'Talk Out of Mayor's Office'

Park Commissioner Robert Moses, for years one of Mayor La Guardia's stanchest political and administrative supporters, told the Board of Estimate yesterday that he keenly resented "talk right out of the Mayor's office" insinuating that he favored a free-removal appropriation of $145,000 because it "had to take care of favored contractors."

Discussion of the Burke proposal provoked a heated argument between Commissioner Moses and Deputy Mayor Rufus E. McGahen, who insisted that the proposal be referred to Budget Director Thomas J. Patterson for a report in accordance with routine procedure. Before the argument ended Commissioner Moses, pale with anger, indicated his willingness to

and Brooklyn. The hurricane left 16,730 trees to be removed from the streets. Of these 7,933 have been removed by contract and 3,467 by departmental forces of the Park Department, cooperating with employes of the Department of Sanitation and the offices of the borough presidents.

Thousands of Allied bombers again struck in support of the ground forces, seeking to pulverize enemy installations east of the Rhine and soften the foe's power and will to resist. Countless fires were started in the industrial areas of the Ruhr as our flying artillery pounded marshalling yards. [1:7]

The Red Army has renewed its drive on Berlin after breaking through German defenses along the Oder River line. The Nazis also said the Russians had smashed six

Continued on Page 15, Column 5

THE RHINE IS BRIDGED AND OUR MATERIEL ROLLS ACROSS

A strong span is stretched on pontoons, over which heavy trucks are carrying supplies to our forces on the east bank.
The New York Times (U. S. Signal Corps)

ODER BRIDGEHEADS REPORTED MERGED

Foe Puts Red Army 6 Miles Past Kuestrin—Danzig and Gdynia Split—Push in South Gains

By The Associated Press.

LONDON, Saturday, March 24—Berlin said last night that the Red Army had reopened a blazing battle for the imperiled German capital, while Moscow announced that Russian forces had split the defenders of the prize Baltic ports of Danzig and Gdynia.

Waves of Russian infantry and tanks were reported by the enemy to have broken through defenses along Berlin's Oder River line and to have swept six miles beyond captured Kuestrin to within thirty-one miles east of the capital. [German reports cited by The United Press said that two Oder bridgeheads had been linked.

Continued on Page 7, Column 2

New Rhine Bridgehead Won Without Loss of Single Man

By EDWARD D. BALL
Associated Press Correspondent.

WITH THE UNITED STATES THIRD ARMY east of the Rhine, March 23—The United States Third Army stormed across the Rhine at 10:25 o'clock last night without loss of a man and without drawing a single shot from the Germans until a good twenty minutes after the crossing was made good.

By dawn today a solid bridgehead had been driven into Hitler's inner fortress against opposition that still was spotty and erratic despite some artillery and mortar fire.

Most of the enemy weapons were soon silenced.

By dawn many infantry units had gone across, and by that time the first waves of doughboys had pushed inland.

There was a minimum of noise and confusion at the bridgehead, where droves of assault boats were speeding back and forth with men and supplies.

Within eight hours Lieut. Gen.

Continued on Page 4, Column 4

War News Summarized

SATURDAY, MARCH 24, 1945

The American Third Army has stormed across the Rhine in large force and established a firm bridgehead, the second one now held by our troops. The new crossing was made at 10:25 P. M. Thursday and the bridgehead has been expanded since then. Its site was not officially disclosed, but the Germans said it was near Frankenthal, four and a half miles north of Ludwigshafen.

The mighty German armies once deployed west of the Rhine have been either destroyed or driven to the east bank almost in their entirety. American tanks crashed into Speyer, one of the last enemy strongholds west of the Rhine, while the enemy bridgehead in the Palatinate was compressed further to an area about fifteen miles deep but thirty miles along the river. Tremendous aerial blows on German communications north of the Ruhr may be part of preparations for a new offensive by Marshal Montgomery. [All the foregoing 1:8; map, P. 2.]

Thousands of Allied bombers again struck in support of the ground forces, seeking to pulverize enemy installations east of the Rhine and soften the foe's power and will to resist. Countless fires were started in the industrial areas of the Ruhr as our flying artillery pounded marshalling yards. [1:7]

The Red Army has renewed its drive on Berlin after breaking through German defenses along the Oder River line. The Nazis also said the Russians had smashed six

miles beyond Kuestrin to within thirty-one miles of the capital, reaching Golzow on the main Kuestrin-Berlin railroad. Soviet troops on the Baltic split the enemy before Danzig and Gdynia by knifing to the Bay of Danzig midway between the two ports. [1:4; map P. 7.]

An American escort carrier, the Bismarck Sea, was lost to enemy action off Iwo Feb. 21, the Navy announced. Another naval bulletin revealed that our carrier planes had caused extensive damage at seven Japanese ports and bases on Kyushu Island during the attack by Fifth Fleet forces early this week. Further details also put at 731 the number of enemy planes destroyed or damaged. [1:6; map P. 10.] The B-29 attack on Tokyo March 9 knocked out 20 per cent of the city's productive facilities for at least three months and did the punishment given the Japanese in the five recent aerial assaults against their industrial cities probably was the most severe suffered by any people in a similar period, it was emphasized by General Norstad. [9:4.]

In the Philippines American forces took Naguilian and its airfield, twelve miles northwest of Baguio, on Luzon. [10:8.]

The Japanese opened a new offensive northwest of Hankow in central China with 60,000 troops. The drive apparently had the twin aims of capturing several Allied airfields in its path and seizing the wheat crop. [9:2; with map.] The British, striking out south of Mandalay in Burma, continued to cut up the foe. [9:5.]

3D WINS FIRM HOLD

Spans the River at Night Above Ludwigshafen, Catches Foe Asleep

1ST SPEEDS UP PUSH

Palatinate Escape Gap Cut Again—Thousands More Captured

By DREW MIDDLETON
By Wireless to The New York Times.

PARIS, March 23—Troops of Lieut. Gen. George S. Patton's United States Third Army have established a bridgehead over the Rhine in a bold, skillful assault.

The river was crossed at 10:25 o'clock Thursday night. The bridgehead established at that time has been steadily expanded since. [Press services said the crossing was virtually unopposed for two hours.]

The Twelfth Army Group, whose announcement was released here tonight, did not locate the bridgehead, but the German radio said that it was east of Frankenthal, four and a half miles north of the northern outskirts of Ludwigshafen.

[Earlier German broadcasts said that Third Army had crossed the Rhine at Oppenheim, ten miles south of Mainz, and that other American troops had attempted crossings at Duesseldorf and six miles south of Cologne, The Associated Press reported. The Germans said the crossings at Duesseldorf and in the Cologne area had been repulsed.]

Crossing Is Bold Stroke

At his headquarters, Lieut. Gen. Omar N. Bradley, Twelfth Army Group Commander, said that the Allies were in a position to cross the Rhine virtually "anywhere at any time."

The Third Army's crossing of the Rhine was an operation as daring as the character of its commander. General Patton hurled his troops across the river without preparation by artillery or air force in a surprise move that evidently caught the enemy asleep.

Since that time his troops have been striking out from the bridgehead and expanding it.

A great east-west highway runs through Frankenthal. There was a bridge under construction there in May, 1944. No recent information concerning the bridge is available.

Frankenthal, where the Germans said the crossing was made, is six miles northwest of Mannheim on the east bank of the Rhine opposite Ludwigshafen. If the crossing was made in this area, as the enemy claimed, then General Patton has placed his troops in a fine position to attack Mannheim from the north or east. Frankenthal also is twenty-five miles southwest of the industrial city of Darmstadt.

Germans Nearly Wiped Out

Meanwhile Gen. Dwight D. Eisenhower's order to destroy the German Armies west of the Rhine is almost fulfilled.

Tanks of General Patton's Third Army rumbled into Speyer, one of the last German strongholds west of the Rhine, today, while a series of savage blows by armored and infantry divisions of the Third Army and Lieut. Gen. Alexander M. Patch's Seventh Army hammered down the enemy bridgehead in the Palatinate to a rough triangle fifteen miles from east to west with a base of less than twenty miles along the west bank of the Rhine.

The tremendous aerial assault on the German Army's defense posts and communications in the area north of the Ruhr and west of the Rhine opposite the front of Field Marshal Sir Bernard L. Montgomery's Twenty-first Army Group was maintained from early morning today.

Nothing more than routine ac-

Continued on Page 5, Column 5

AIR FLEETS FLATTEN NAZIS AROUND RUHR

U. S. 'Heavies' Strike at 12 Rail Yards, RAF Hits Bridges and Enemy Troops

By SYDNEY GRUSON
By Wireless to The New York Times.

LONDON, Saturday, March 24—Allied airmen poured more thousands of tons of bombs on the Germans east of the Rhine, especially in the Ruhr area, yesterday, in the third successive day of record operations to flatten everything in the path of the American and British Armies massing for a crossing of the Rhine on the northern sector of the Western Front.

Last night, as the Ruhr's industrial towns and the great plain leading to north Germany blazed from countless fires set by thousands of heavy, medium and light bombers, more blows were struck in the aerial softening-up.

[A powerful fleet of British heavy bombers battered German troops and positions on the east bank of the Rhine during the night, London officials announced early Saturday. The Associated Press said British planes also bombed Berlin for the thirty-second straight night.]

More than 1,250 Flying Fortresses and Liberators of the United States Eighth Air Force and three fleets of Lancasters and Halifaxes of the Royal Air Force, all of them escorted by fighters, flew by daylight through towering clouds of smoke rising from the ashes of dead cities.

In weather so clear the heavy bombers' targets could be picked up by naked eye from five miles up, the American and British crews pounded rail yards and

Continued on Page 5, Column 2

U. S. CARRIER LOST IN BATTLE OFF IWO

Bismarck Sea, Escort Craft, Is Victim of Air Blow — Fleet Strike in Ryukyus Reported

By The Associated Press.

GUAM, Saturday, March 24—Loss of the U. S. S. Bismarck Sea, an escort aircraft carrier, to enemy aerial attack off Iwo Island on Feb. 21 was announced by Admiral Chester W. Nimitz today. Most of the Bismarck Sea's company was rescued, he stated. The normal complement of an escort carrier is about 1,500 officers and men.

[Delayed dispatches from the fleet off Iwo said there were more than 300 casualties among the crew of the Bismarck Sea, including 100 who, struggling in the water, were strafed and killed by Japanese fliers.]

An American escort carrier, the Bismarck Sea, was lost to enemy action off Iwo Feb. 21, the Navy announced. Another naval bulletin revealed that our carrier planes had caused extensive damage at seven Japanese ports and bases on Kyushu Island during the attack by Fifth Fleet forces early this week.

Continued on Page 10, Column 2

Germans Speed Arms to Mountains As Allies Map Their Destruction

By Wireless to The New York Times.

PARIS, March 23—The Germans are speeding work on a great national redoubt, a defensive position based on the mountains of the southern Reich, where SS divisions, some regular soldiers and Nazi party officials hope to continue the war after the German field armies have been destroyed.

A reliable source who recently returned from Switzerland said the work on the redoubt has been rushed since the last Russian offensive and the Anglo-American victories west of the Rhine and that, according to neutrals who lately had been in the Reich, the Germans were also constructing another redoubt in the Kiel Canal in the north.

The Swiss, he said, are extreme-

ly worried, since the preparation of the redoubt in the south foreshadows heavy fighting near their borders by Russian as well as American and British armies.

According to this source a nobleman, who must remain unidentified, recently drove from his domain to Vienna and back. Both trips were exceedingly difficult because the Germans had closed many of the roads leading into the redoubt and he had to detour around the position. He reported that the Germans were pouring many hundreds of tons of supplies of all kinds into the redoubt.

The exact limits of the position where the Germans hope to retire

Continued on Page 5, Column 1

The New York Times.

LATE CITY EDITION
Clearing and warm today.
Fair, continued warm tomorrow.
Temperature Yesterday—Max. 74; Min. 54
Sunrise today, 5:51 A. M.; Sunset, 7:25 P. M.

Copyright, 1945, by The New York Times Company.

VOL. XCIV...No. 31,856.

Entered as Second-Class Matter,
Postoffice, New York, N. Y.

NEW YORK, FRIDAY, APRIL 13, 1945.

THREE CENTS NEW YORK CITY

PRESIDENT ROOSEVELT IS DEAD; TRUMAN TO CONTINUE POLICIES; 9TH CROSSES ELBE, NEARS BERLIN

U. S. AND RED ARMIES DRIVE TO MEET

Americans Across the Elbe in Strength Race Toward Russians Who Have Opened Offensive From Oder

WEIMAR TAKEN, RUHR POCKET SLASHED

Third Army Reported 19 Miles From Czechoslovak Border—British Drive Deeper in the North, Seizing Celle—Canadians Freeing Holland

By DREW MIDDLETON
By Wireless to The New York Times.

PARIS, April 12—Thousands of tanks and a half million doughboys of the United States First, Third and Ninth Armies are racing through the heart of the Reich on a front of 150 miles, threatening Berlin, Leipzig and the last citadels of the Nazi power.

The Second Armored Division of the Ninth Army has crossed the Elbe River in force and is striking eastward toward Berlin, whose outskirts lie less than sixty miles to the east, according to reports from the front. [A report quoted by The United Press placed the Americans less than fifty miles from the capital.] Beyond Berlin the First White Russian Army has crossed the Oder on a wide front and a junction between the western and eastern Allies is not far off.

[The Moscow radio reported that heavy battles were raging west of the Oder before Berlin, indicating that Marshal Gregory K. Zhukoff had launched his drive toward the Reich's capital. The Soviet communiqué announced further progress by the Red Army forces in and around Vienna.]

Paris is wild with excitement tonight. A special edition of the newspaper France-Soir carries a report by the radio station "Voice of America" that places American forces fifteen and five-eighths miles from Berlin after an airborne landing that had linked up with Lieut. Gen. William H. Simpson's forces advancing eastward from the Elbe. This would put American forces only seventy-five miles from the Red Army vanguard.

No Confirmation at Headquarters

There was no confirmation of this report at Allied Supreme Headquarters, whose latest admission was thirty-six hours behind developments on some sectors of the front.

Resistance was continuing only on the northern and southern flanks. The center had burst wide open. Weimar fell to Lieut. Gen. George S. Patton's infantry, and reports from the front said Erfurt also had been cleared. Schweinfurt and Heilbronn, two German bastions on the south, had fallen to United States Seventh Army forces, who were driving on Bamberg, while farther north Third Army forces were about thirty-five miles from the Czechoslovak frontier in the area east of Coburg.

[The German radio reported American Third Army forces at Lichtenberg, nineteen miles from the Czechoslovak border, The United Press said.]

The offensives to liberate the Netherlands and reduce the Ruhr

Continued on Page 12, Column 2

Army Leaders See Reich End at Hand

By The Associated Press.

WASHINGTON, April 12—High Army officials told Senators today that the end of organized fighting in Germany probably would come within a few days. In describing the pell-mell dash of American armies across Germany, General Staff officers expressed the opinion to members of the Senate Military Committee that a collapse of German arms was imminent.

Those who attended said the army chiefs declared that they were so sure of the results that orders had been drawn for a drastic reduction in shipments of durable equipment to Europe.

OUR OKINAWA GUNS DOWN 118 PLANES

Japanese Fliers Start 'Suicide' Attacks on Fleet, Sink a Destroyer, Hit Other Ships

By W. H. LAWRENCE
By Wireless to The New York Times.

GUAM, Friday, April 13—Japanese attempting to halt the American march to Tokyo, have started "desperate, suicidal" aerial attacks upon our ships and men in the Okinawa area, losing 118 planes on Thursday alone, Fleet Admiral Chester W. Nimitz announced today.

The Japanese succeeded in sinking a destroyer and damaging several other surface units, the communiqué said. All of the damaged vessels remained in action.

It was the first time that the Navy had revealed the suicidal nature of the Japanese air missions against our ships and men. The Japanese radio has been saying that this type of assault was being carried on by a "special attack corps" known in Japanese as "kamakasi," which, translated literally, means "divine wind."

Attack at Low Levels

The Japanese fliers launched their attacks upon our ships and men at a high speed and from low levels, diving directly into a ship or troop concentration to explode their bombs as they crashed. About 2:15 Eastern war time he said, there was no official estimate of the total number of enemy aircraft engaged in the Okinawa area, other than that the report of the 118 enemy planes destroyed.

Admiral Nimitz reported that the attacks began early on April 12 (Eastern Longitude time) with seven enemy planes shot down during the morning in the vicinity of the Hagushi beaches.

The tempo of the attack was stepped up in the afternoon as the Japanese bore in on our ships in wave after wave. Admiral Nimitz said that ships' guns, carrier aircraft and shore-based anti-aircraft shot down 111 of the attackers.

The revelation of the suicidal Japanese air attacks was the highlight of Admiral Nimitz' regular morning communiqué, which also disclosed the identity of two Marine and two Army divisions that have gone into action on Okinawa. These included the Twenty-seventh Army Division, formed from New York National Guard units, which are seeing action for the first time since the Saipan campaign and previously had engaged in the Gilbert Islands assault. It is com-

Franklin Delano Roosevelt
1882-1945

© Perskie

SECURITY PARLEY WON'T BE DELAYED

State Department Urges That World Be Shown We Plan No Changes in Policy

By JAMES B. RESTON
Special to The New York Times.

WASHINGTON, April 12—The United Nations Security Conference will open in San Francisco on April 25, despite the death of President Roosevelt, Secretary of State Edward R. Stettinius Jr. announced tonight.

Mr. Stettinius said that he had been authorized by President Harry Truman to make this announcement after a meeting of the Cabinet at the White House.

Most of the overseas delegations to the San Francisco conference have either arrived in this country or are now on their way, but while this was said to have been a factor in the decision to proceed with the conference, State Department officials urged that every attempt be made to give immediate evidence to the world that President Roosevelt's foreign policy would be sustained by the new Administration.

President Roosevelt had planned to address the San Francisco conference. His interest in an international organization of nations to maintain peace and security had gone back to his service in the Wilson Administration, when he sat in the gallery of the Senate and listened to the debate that resulted in the rejection of the League of Nations Covenant. He had expressed to friends his desire to participate in the San Francisco conference and to see the United States enter the new league during his term in office.

The sudden elevation of Presi-

Continued on Page 2, Column 1

War News Summarized

FRIDAY, APRIL 13, 1945

President Roosevelt died yesterday afternoon, suddenly and unexpectedly. He was stricken with a massive cerebral hemorrhage at Warm Springs, Ga., on the eve of his greatest military and diplomatic successes—the impending fall of Berlin and the opening of the San Francisco Conference to set up a World Security Organization that would make the world free from martial and economic strife [1:7-8.]

Mr. Roosevelt had been sitting in front of the fireplace of his Little White House, having gone to Warm Springs on March 30 for a three-week rest. About 2:15 Eastern war time he said, "I have a terrific headache," lost consciousness in a few moments and died at 4:35. He was 63 years old. [1:6.]

The tragic word spread quickly around the world. Expressions of sorrow poured in from all sections. [4:5.] American soldiers and sailors refused to believe the reports until there was no longer doubt that their Commander in Chief had gone. [4:2-3.]

Harry S. Truman was sworn in as President at 7:09 o'clock last night, and a few minutes later Mrs. Roosevelt left for Warm Springs. [1:7.] The new President immediately called a Cabinet meeting and declared that Mr. Roosevelt's policies would be continued, that the war would be carried on until Germany and Japan surrendered unconditionally and that the San Francisco conference would open April 25 as scheduled. [1:3.]

Some 500,000 American soldiers of the Third and Ninth Armies, and thousands of tanks, sped along a 150-mile front toward Berlin and Leipzig. The Ninth, surging across the Elbe, according to delayed reports was less than fifty miles from the

German capital and 115 from the Russians along the Oder. The Third Army captured Weimar, home of the late German Republic, and was twenty-three miles below Leipzig, with the First closing a pincers from the north. [1:1-2; map P. 2.]

The Moscow radio reported that the Red Army was waging fierce battles west of Berlin, indicating resumption of the drive on that city. Elsewhere Russian troops scored wide gains and cut the last escape railroad from Vienna. [13:1.]

Open cities were ruled out and every German town ordered by Himmler to fight to the death, although Goebbels said "the war cannot last much longer." [12:6-7.]

The Ninth Air Force destroyed at least 117 more German planes yesterday. [11:8.]

In Italy the Eighth Army advanced along a thirty-mile front toward Bologna and the Po Valley; the Fifth Army also made good gains and was eleven miles from La Spezia. [13:8, with map.] Japanese planes resumed their suicide attacks on American ships off Okinawa, sinking a destroyer and damaging several other vessels. One hundred and eighteen enemy planes were shot down. [1:2.] The Americal Division invaded Bohol, last of the enemy-held central Philippines. [18:6.] The B-29 attack on Koriyama, 110 miles north of Tokyo, set a new Superfortress distance record. [18:2.]

Secretary of State Stettinius and Secretary of War Stimson, denouncing Germany's "steadily increasing" mistreatment of American prisoners, said those responsible would be brought to justice. [13:6-7.]

Clashes between Right and Left wing elements in Iran were reported from Moscow. [13:2.]

END COMES SUDDENLY AT WARM SPRINGS

Even His Family Unaware of Condition as Cerebral Stroke Brings Death to Nation's Leader at 63

ALL CABINET MEMBERS TO KEEP POSTS

Funeral to Be at White House Tomorrow, With Burial at Hyde Park Home— Impact of News Tremendous

By ARTHUR KROCK
Special to The New York Times.

WASHINGTON, April 12—Franklin Delano Roosevelt, War President of the United States and the only Chief Executive in history who was chosen for more than two terms, died suddenly and unexpectedly at 4:35 P. M. today at Warm Springs, Ga., and the White House announced his death at 5:48 o'clock. He was 63.

The President, stricken by a cerebral hemorrhage, passed from unconsciousness to death on the eighty-third day of his fourth term and in an hour of high triumph. The armies and fleets under his direction as Commander in Chief were at the gates of Berlin and the shores of Japan's home islands as Mr. Roosevelt died, and the cause he represented and led was nearing the conclusive phase of success.

Less than two hours after the official announcement, Harry S. Truman of Missouri, the Vice President, took the oath as the thirty-second President. The oath was administered by the Chief Justice of the United States, Harlan F. Stone, in a one-minute ceremony at the White House. Mr. Truman immediately let it be known that Mr. Roosevelt's Cabinet is remaining in office at his request, and that he had authorized Secretary of State Edward R. Stettinius Jr. to proceed with plans for the United Nations Conference on international organization at San Francisco, to begin April 25. A report was circulated that he leaned somewhat to the idea of a coalition Cabinet, but this is unsubstantiated.

Funeral Tomorrow Afternoon

It was disclosed by the White House that funeral services for Mr. Roosevelt would take place at 4 P. M. (E. W. T.) Saturday in the East Room of the Executive Mansion. The Rev. Angus Dun, Episcopal Bishop of Washington; the Rev. Howard S. Wilkinson of St. Thomas's Church in Washington and the Rev. John G. McGee of St. John's in Washington will conduct the services.

The body will be interred at Hyde Park, N. Y., Sunday, with the Rev. George W. Anthony of the St. James Church officiating. The time has not yet been fixed.

Jonathan Daniels, White House secretary, said Mr. Roosevelt's body would not lie in state. He added that, in view of the limited size of the East Room, which holds only about 200 persons, the list of those attending the funeral services would be limited to high Government officials, representatives of the membership of both

Continued on Page 5, Column 3

TRUMAN IS SWORN IN THE WHITE HOUSE

Members of Cabinet on Hand as Chief Justice Stone Administers the Oath

By C. P. TRUSSELL
Special to The New York Times.

WASHINGTON, April 12—Vice President Harry S. Truman of Missouri, standing erect, with his sharp features taut and his eyes looking straight ahead through his large, round glasses, became the thirty-second President of the United States in a ceremony lasting not more than a minute in the Cabinet Room of the White House at 7:09 o'clock tonight.

The oath was administered by Chief Justice Harlan F. Stone two hours and thirty-four minutes after the sudden death of President Roosevelt at Warm Springs. Mr. Truman had picked up a Bible from the end of the big Cabinet conference table, held it with his left hand and placed his right hand upon the upper cover. After repeating the oath, he bowed his head, lifted the Bible to his lips and kissed it.

Even before he had taken the oath Mr. Truman had asked President Roosevelt's Cabinet to continue in service. He also authorized Edward R. Stettinius Jr., Secretary of State, to announce that the United Nations Conference for International Organization would go on as scheduled.

To the newsmen at the White House he sent this word, through Stephen Early, press secretary:

"For the time being I prefer not to hold a press conference. It will be my effort to carry on as I believe the President would have done, and to that end I have asked the Cabinet to stay on with me."

Soon after he became President, Mr. Truman left the White House for the five-room Connecticut Avenue apartment where he has resided with Mrs. Truman and their 20-year-old daughter, Mary Margaret, for four years. He said he was "going home, to bed."

It was shortly after he had finished presiding over the Senate debate on the United States-Mexican Water Treaty late this afternoon that Mr. Truman received word from the White House of President Roosevelt's death. This was at about 5.15 P. M., a half hour before the news was made public. Reaching for his hat, he dashed out of the office, calling back to his staff that he was going to the White House.

Arriving at the White House, the

Continued on Page 3, Column 6

LAST WORDS: 'I HAVE TERRIFIC HEADACHE'

Roosevelt Was Posing for Artist When Hemorrhage Struck —He Died in Bedroom

By The Associated Press.

WARM SPRINGS, Ga., April 12—President Franklin D. Roosevelt's last words were:

"I have a terrific headache."

He spoke them to Comdr. Howard G. Bruenn, naval physician.

Mr. Roosevelt was sitting in front of a fireplace in the Little White House here atop Pine Mountain when what was described as a massive cerebral hemorrhage struck him.

The President's Negro valet, Arthur Prettyman, and a Filipino messboy carried him to his bedroom. He was unconscious at the end. It came without pain.

Dr. Bruenn said that he saw the President this morning and he was in excellent spirits at 9:30 A. M.

"At 1 o'clock," Dr. Bruenn added, "he was sitting in a chair while sketches were being made of him by an artist. He suddenly complained of a very severe occipital headache (back of the head).

"Within a very few minutes he lost consciousness. He was seen by me at 1:30 P. M., fifteen minutes after the episode had started.

"He did not regain consciousness and he died at 3:35 P. M. (Georgia time)."

The artist sketching Mr. Roosevelt was N. Robbins of 530 West 159.3. Street, New York.

Only others present in the cottage were Comdr. George Fox, White House pharmacist and long an attendant on the President; William D. Hassett, Presidential secretary; Miss Grace Tully

Continued on Page 4, Column 2

Byrnes May Take Post With Truman

Special to The New York Times.

WASHINGTON, April 12—James F. Byrnes, recently resigned as Director of War Mobilization and Reconversion, known to be one of President Truman's warmest friends in official Washington, is expected to be called to the White House for consultation, and possibly to take an important post in the Cabinet, in the immediate future.

President Truman's admiration of former Justice Byrnes is well known here. He undoubtedly would have been Mr. Truman's choice as a successor to Cordell Hull as Secretary of State.

"All the News That's Fit to Print"

The New York Times.

LATE CITY EDITION
Clearing and warmer today. Cloudy with moderate winds tomorrow.
Temperature Yesterday—Max., 61; Min., 44
Sunrise today, 5:54 A. M.; Sunset, 7:55 P. M.

VOL. XCIV. No. 31,875.

NEW YORK, WEDNESDAY, MAY 2, 1945.

THREE CENTS NEW YORK CITY

Copyright, 1945, by The New York Times Company.

HITLER DEAD IN CHANCELLERY, NAZIS SAY; DOENITZ, SUCCESSOR, ORDERS WAR TO GO ON; BERLIN ALMOST WON; U. S. ARMIES ADVANCE

MOLOTOFF EASES PARLEY TENSION; NEW MOVES BEGUN

Russian Says Country Will Cooperate in World Plan Despite Argentine Issue

4 COMMISSIONS SET UP

They Will Deal With Council, Assembly, Court and Some General Problems

By JAMES B. RESTON
Special to The New York Times.

SAN FRANCISCO, May 1—The United Nations Conference on International Organization has survived its first basic crisis and after six days of political maneuvering on secondary issues, it began to move at rapid tempo today toward its primary task—the creation of a world organization which would stop what Field Marshal Jan Christiaan Smuts called "this pilgrimage of death."

The test came last night. Rebuffed by the conference on his attempts to keep Argentina out of the conference and bring the Warsaw Poles in, Soviet Foreign Commissar Vyacheslav M. Molotoff went late last night to Secretary Stettinius' penthouse at the Fairmont Hotel. He immediately made his position clear.

He still disapproved the conference actions on the Poles and the Argentine, but he wanted the conference to succeed; he would cooperate in its labors, and while he was under urgent pressure by the events in Europe to return to Moscow, he would remain at least for a few days until the major issues on the charter were threshed out among the four sponsor powers. Then, he said, he would have to leave, probably at the week-end or early next week.

"Friendly Meeting" Is Held

Immediately, in what the Foreign Ministers of the United States, Great Britain and China described to their colleagues as "the most friendly meeting of the conference," the big four approved the formation of the working committees and committees of the conference, and other committees began discussing, not the personalities or procedures of the conference, but the basic questions of creating an organization which would win the support, with the power, of, the great nations without violating the rights and principles of all nations.

The three main developments of the day were as follows:

First, the conference approved four commissions to deal with the security council of the proposed organization, the general assembly, the judicial agency and general problems, and established twelve committees to handle specific problems under these four commissions.

The heads of the four commissions were: Trygve Lie of Norway, Security Council; Field Marshal Smuts, General Assembly; Carraciolo Parra Perez of Venezuela, judicial organization; and Paul Henri Speak of Belgium, general provisions.

Second, Field Marshal Smuts called on the four major powers to accept the special responsibilities which flow from the special authority given them under the Dumbarton Oaks proposals and urged all the nations here to pay more attention to the spiritual and economic aspects of the new charter than they had in the past.

Third, the Russians began studying in some detail the sixteen amendments to the Dumbarton Oaks proposals which have been submitted by the United States. The other delegations started circulating amendments and exchanging views on proposals already circulated.

The facts on the crisis among the Big Three over Poland, Argentina, White Russia and the Ukraine can now be put down with assur-

Continued on Page 13, Column 4

Allies Invade North Borneo; Fighting Fierce, Tokyo Says

Australia Informed of Landing by Treasury Minister—MacArthur Reports Only Air Attacks and New Gains on Luzon

By The United Press.

MANILA, Wednesday, May 2—An official Australian announcement said yesterday that Allied troops had invaded Borneo, the world's third largest island, but Gen. Douglas MacArthur's communiqué early today reported only that heavy bombers were neutralizing enemy bases and airdromes on the oil-rich island.

Tokyo also reported the landings and said they had been made on the ten-square-mile island of Tarakan on the northeast coast, a region rich in oil wells, which the Netherlands destroyed before the Japanese captured them in 1942. The enemy broadcast said "fierce fighting" was in progress.

[A later Japanese broadcast, picked up in San Francisco, reported that Allied units had landed on Tarakan Island at 6:30 A. M., Tuesday, Tokyo time. The broadcast said "the enemy had been bombarding the island since April 27, and on Monday morning began approaching the island in their landing attempts." It reported the landing force consisted of "about 5,000 soldiers" and said Japanese forces on the island "are holding secure their positions, obstructing the enemy's advance."]

General MacArthur announced that heavy bombers in attacks on Borneo had struck Kuching, Macassar and Kendari, while medium units and fighters had attacked Japanese gun positions on Tarakan.

General MacArthur announced that on Mindanao Island the Twenty-fourth Division, in another swift drive, had advanced eleven miles

Continued on Page 18, Column 2

NEW CIGARETTES FACE PRICE INQUIRY

OPA Calls on Manufacturers of 21-Cent Brands to Prove Quality Merits Charge

By JAMES E. POWERS

Manufacturers of hitherto unheard of brands of cigarettes that have appeared on the market in recent weeks and are being retailed at four or more cents a package higher than ceiling prices for scarce popular brands will be called upon by the Office of Price Administration to show that the new products are of a quality meriting the prices charged, it became known yesterday.

Daniel P. Woolley, regional OPA administrator, said an investigation was in progress as a result of complaints by smokers who said they had paid 21 cents a package for cigarettes "they had previously never heard of."

The United Wholesale Tobacco and Cigarette Distributors Association, a sub-jobbers' group, in a telegram to Senator William Langer of North Dakota, who recently introduced a resolution to set up a committee to look into the "black market" in cigarettes, demanded an immediate investigation of the entire cigarette shortage.

Mr. Woolley declared that as a result of OPA prosecution of violators of price ceilings, the black-market condition largely had been corrected here. He said he was investigating on the pricing of the new cigarette brands.

Mr. Woolley added that studies were being made to determine

Continued on Page 40, Column 4

HARD COAL 'HOLIDAY' BRINGS WLB BAN

New Order by Board Asserts Output Is Urgent—Seizure Action Is Postponed

By JOSEPH A. LOFTUS
Special to The New York Times.

WASHINGTON, May 1—The War Labor Board issued a new order tonight to the United Mine Workers and the operators to resume the production of hard coal. To give the UMW leaders an opportunity to act on the order it decided to defer for twenty-four hours a recommendation to President Truman for Government seizure of the mines.

The miners went on a holiday today after expiration of their contract at midnight.

Dr. George W. Taylor, WLB chairman, in a telegram to both parties took cognizance of the miners' traditional "no contract, no work" policy.

"The board's order provides for a continuing contract," he said. "It is urgent that production should be immediately resumed."

As in acting on the soft coal dispute a month ago, the WLB provided in the new order that any legal wage adjustment agreed upon or finally ordered be retroactive to the expiration date of the old contract.

Union spokesmen told the WLB at a brief hearing that the Tri-District Scale Committee had voted to advise the miners to return to work when the operators accepted the settlement proposal made by Secretary of Labor Perkins.

Dr. Taylor, in questioning John Owens of the UMW, noted that

Continued on Page 40, Column 2

Eisenhower Halted Forces at Elbe; Ninth Had Hoped to Storm Berlin

By The Associated Press.

WITH THE UNITED STATES NINTH ARMY, in Germany, April 26 (Delayed by Censorship)—A direct order from Supreme Allied Headquarters halted the United States Ninth Army's drive to Berlin at the Elbe River at a time when the most pessimistic officers could push on to the capital without great difficulty. While the order disappointed some staff officers, it was not altogether unexpected. It was known that the Ninth Army had pushed past the eventual British-American occupation area when it crossed the Weser River.

While the staff officers were disappointed, the American doughboys and tankmen who had to do the fighting and dying to get to Berlin expressed no regret. Almost to a man, they felt they could do with-

Eisenhower's order was dictated by political policy agreed upon by the Great Powers or in a belief that it was a military necessity.

It was felt by high staff officers in the field, however, that the Ninth and other American forces could push on to the capital without out difficulty.

General Eisenhower's order would reduce the German capital in ten days, "even if the Germans fought hard."

General Eisenhower's order would halt the Ninth on the Elbe and await the arrival of Russian forces from the east, thereby leaving the capture of the capital to the Red Army. It also was understood that the American First and Third and British and Canadian armies received similar orders to halt at the Elbe.

It was not clear whether General

Continued on Page 4, Column 4

REDOUBTS ASSAILED

U. S. 3d, 7th and French 1st Armies Charging Into Alpine Hideout

NEAR BRENNER PASS

British in North Close About Hamburg—Poles Gain in Emden Area

Von Rundstedt Caught

By The Associated Press.
WITH UNITED STATES SEVENTH ARMY, Wednesday, May 2—Field Marshal Karl von Rundstedt has been captured by United States Seventh Army troops.

The Seventh Army caught the former German commander in the west in the Nazis' southeastern redoubt area.

By DREW MIDDLETON

PARIS, May 1—The last defenses of the Third Reich were crumbling as Allied tanks and infantry swept almost unopposed into the northern and southern redoubts.

Gen. George S. Patton's United States Third Army has resumed its offensive into Austria, crushing to within twenty miles of Linz, and is only fifty-four miles from Amstetten, where Marshal Fedor I. Tolbukhin's Third Ukrainian Army was last reported. According to reports from the front, radio contact has been established between tanks of the United States Eleventh Armored Division and the vanguard of the Soviet armies.

Other armored columns of the

Continued on Page 14, Column 1

NAZI CORE STORMED

Russians Drive Toward Chancellery Fortress, Narrowing Noose

BRANDENBURG TAKEN

Stralsund Port Swept Up in New Baltic Gains— Vah Valley Cleared

By C. L. SULZBERGER

MOSCOW, Wednesday, May 2—Street battles within smoldering Berlin today entered its twelfth day since the Russians first broke into the city, with Nazi die-hards still holding grimly to the central part of the town, whittled down by yesterday's fighting, in which Marshal Gregory K. Zhukoff's First White Russian Army group completely occupied Charlottenburg and Schoeneberg and more than 100 blocks in the capital's central region.

Some 14,000 prisoners were taken within the city on Monday, the Russians announced. At the same time, the remnants of a hold-out group south of Berlin, part of which had been annihilated at Wendisch Buchholz, was split in two and the survivors are being ground to death by Marshal Zhukoff's men.

Curiously enough, the midnight communiqué does not mention Marshal Ivan S. Koneff's First Ukrainian Army group, which has been working from the southwestern sector of the city toward the desperately defended Tiergarten.

Marshal Zhukoff's forward spearheads meanwhile struck deep into Brandenburg Province, capturing the city of Brandenburg, halfway to Magdeburg from Berlin.

While Gen. Andrei I. Yeremenko proceeded apace in his lightning

Continued on Page 3, Column 2

ADOLF HITLER
The New York Times, 1933

Clark's Troops Meet Tito's In General Advance in Italy

By VIRGINIA LEE WARREN
By Wireless to The New York Times.

AT ADVANCED ALLIED HEADQUARTERS, in Italy, May 1—After advancing fifty-five miles in less than a day along the coastal road rimming the Gulf of Venice, units of one division of the Fifteenth Army Group made contact this afternoon with Marshal Tito's forces at Monfalcone while other troops under Gen. Mark W. Clark continued to sweep German remnants from the valleys of north Italy and to seal off the few remaining escape routes through the Alps.

No details of the meeting at the small seaport northwest of Trieste between Marshal Tito's men, who had driven fourteen miles from Trieste, and leading elements of the Eighth Army's Second New Zealand Division were given in tonight's communiqué.

On the other side of Italy another historic meeting was imminent as Fifth Army troops, continuing their drive along the Aurelian Way to within sixty miles of Genoa, advanced on the Aurelian Way to within sixty miles of the French border, which has already been crossed by French troops headed this way.

General Clark announced yesterday that the military power of Germany had virtually collapsed, but there still are drives for his two armies to make and engagements still to be won. The Germans, trying to regroup for further flight across the Alps, have been deprived of two key road junctions leading to mountain passes west of Brenner when Belluno and Udine were occupied this afternoon by units of the Eighth Army.

Udine, which was taken by the British Sixth Armored Division, is twenty-eight miles southwest of Caporetto, the scene of the Italian disaster in World War I. The forces that entered Belluno went on five miles to Ponte nell' Alpi, guardian of the approach to Italy's

Continued on Page 18, Column 5

ADMIRAL IN CHARGE

Proclaims Designation to Rule This Afternoon—Appeals to People and Army

RAISES 'RED MENACE'

Britain to Insist Germans Show Hitler's Body When War Ends

By SYDNEY GRUSON
By Cable to The New York Times.

LONDON, May 1—Adolf Hitler died this afternoon, the Hamburg radio announced tonight, and Grand Admiral Karl Doenitz, proclaiming himself the new Fuehrer by Hitler's appointment, said that the war would continue.

Crowning days of rumors about Hitler's health and whereabouts, the Hamburg radio said that he had fallen in the battle of Berlin at his command post in the Chancellery just three days after Benito Mussolini, the first of the dictators, had been killed by Italian Partisans. Doenitz, a 53-year-old U-boat specialist, broadcast an address to the German people and the surviving armed forces immediately after the announcer had given them news of Hitler's death.

[The British Foreign Office said that it would demand the production of Hitler's body after the end of hostilities, The Associated Press reported.]

First addressing the German people, Doenitz said that they would continue to fight only to save themselves from the Russians but that they would oppose the western Allies as long as they helped the Russians. In an order of the day to the German forces he repeated his thinly veiled attempt to split the Allies.

Radio Prepares Germans

Early this evening the Germans were told that an important announcement would be broadcast tonight. There was no hint of what was coming. The standby announcement was repeated at 9:40 P. M., followed by the playing of excerpts from Wagner's "Goetterdaemmerung."

A few minutes later the announcer said: "Achtung! Achtung! In a few moments you will hear a

Continued on Page 5, Column 4

DOENITZ ACCESSION VIEWED AS A BLIND

Capital Lays His Designation to General Ignorance of His Allegiance to Party

By The Associated Press.
WASHINGTON, May 1—If Adolf Hitler really designated Grand Admiral Karl Doenitz his successor, military men here believe, he did so for the following reasons:

1. Doenitz is a Nazi supporter who could be counted on to keep German resistance going if possible.

2. But he is not associated in the Allies' minds with German atrocities and the extreme policies of the Nazi party. Therefore, Hitler probably figured that he might be able to get better treatment from the Allies when the hour of surrender came.

3. He is immensely popular with the German people.

There was a disposition here tonight to look for continued organized resistance whose core would now be centered in the Baltic and North Sea port areas. Those places are the homes of the German Navy, and especially of the U-boat fleet that Doenitz commanded from 1936 until he succeeded Grand Admiral Erich

Continued on Page 5, Column 1

Copenhagen Writer Again Phones Story

By Cable to The New York Times.
STOCKHOLM, May 1—For the first time in more than five years THE NEW YORK TIMES correspondent in Copenhagen, Svend Carstensen, tonight telephoned a story from the Danish capital. The Nazi-imposed censorship there has been lifted. Mr. Carstensen said:

"The Danes are overjoyed at their imminent liberation, but it is not noticeable on the Copenhagen streets.

"Anxious to avoid trouble on May Day, Copenhageners have been staying indoors. The blackout is still enforced and it is glued to radios listening to broadcasts on Hitler's death.

"We expect King Christian will resume his functions and name a new Cabinet any day now. In the meantime the strictest discipline is being observed so as not to give the Germans any excuses for starting more trouble."

On April 9, 1940, Mr. Carstensen was the first to flash to the world the news of the German invasion of Denmark in a wireless dispatch to THE NEW YORK TIMES. His dispatch was the last from Copenhagen until the Nazis seized the radio station and was the last to be sent.

War News Summarized

WEDNESDAY, MAY 2, 1945

Hitler is dead, according to the Hamburg radio and, on Monday, the day before he allegedly fell at his command post in the Chancellery in Berlin, he appointed Admiral Karl Doenitz to be the new Fuehrer. The head of the German Navy, who had made his mark directing the enemy's U-boats campaign, pledged continuance of the war. [1:8.]

Washington received the news, as did London, with some skepticism and a desire to see the body. Selection of Admiral Doenitz was considered logical in view of his strong Nazi feelings. [1:7.]

The new development was interpreted in London as a move to counteract Himmler's reported peace bids, and Prime Minister Churchill broadly intimated in the Commons that he might have "information of exceptional importance" to impart before Saturday. Peace will probably come before all enemy forces have surrendered, he said. [1:6-7.] Germany was reported to have begun evacuation of Denmark and to be ready to leave Norway. Count Bernadotte said in Sweden he had no new Himler proposals, and the Nazis' Scandinavian withdrawals were related there to a prospective general capitulation. [11:1.]

Meanwhile, general Allied progress on the battlefields against all Nazi resistance continued. The United States Third Army, on the day Hitler was declared to have died, captured Braunau, his birthplace. The drive into Austria resumed and had reached to within twenty miles of Linz and fifty-four of the last known Russian position. The Seventh Army smashed through the Tyrol on a broad front and cleared Munich. The British Second Army, by-passing Hamburg, raced to within eight-

een miles of the Baltic port of Luebeck. [1:4; map P. 14.]

General Eisenhower, it was revealed, personally ordered the halt of the Allied drive on Berlin from the west to permit the Russians to take the capital. [1:2-3.]

The Russians greatly cut down the German holding in Berlin, capturing the districts of Charlottenburg and Schoeneberg. West of the city they occupied Brandenburg and along the Baltic they seized Stralsund. [1:5; maps Pages 2 and 14.]

New Zealand troops in Italy made contact with Yugoslav Partisans at Monfalcone near Trieste and the British entered Udine. While the Eighth Army was closing a trap along the Swiss border, the Fifth neared France. [1:6-7; map P. 14.]

Mussolini and his mistress were buried in unmarked paupers' graves in Milan. [13:1.] Admiral Horthy, former Regent of Hungary, was captured. [4:3.]

Invasion of Borneo was officially disclosed in Australia, although no word of the break into the Japanese-held Netherlands East Indies had come from General MacArthur. On Mindanao in the Philippines, Americans were within six miles of the city of Davao. [1:2-3; map P. 16.]

Seventh Division troops on Okinawa resumed their southward advance, entering the village of Kuhazu. [15:1.] More than 400 starved, naked Allied prisoners of war were liberated by the British as they drove on Rangoon in Burma. [15:3.]

Good progress was made at the San Francisco Conference. Foreign Commissar Molotoff, after assuring Secretary of State Stettinius of his desire that the conference succeed, announced that pressure of events would compel his return to Moscow within a few days. [1:1.]

Churchill Hints Peace This Week; 2-Day Celebration Is Authorized

By CLIFTON DANIEL
By Wireless to The New York Times.

LONDON, May 1—The general belief that peace with Germany will be announced this week persisted in Britain today, encouraged by Prime Minister Churchill himself and by Grand Admiral Karl Doenitz's announcement of the death of Adolf Hitler.

The War Cabinet again held a session tonight but so far as was known did not have any concrete proposal to consider. The chances that Heinrich Himmler ultimately will deliver an acceptable peace are now held in some official quarters to be only "fifty-fifty."

Nevertheless, the buoyant Prime Minister told the House of Commons today that he might have "information of importance" to announce before Saturday.

The public's hopes were raised still further by a Home Office circular giving the Government's views on how Britain should observe V-E Day, which the British, it appears, will be expected to celebrate strictly according to form.

[Stockholm reported, with the return there of Count Bernadotte, the "imminent liberation" of Denmark and Norway, already taking effect locally in Denmark —as a phase of a prospective general German capitulation.]

The hurrahing will begin with the announcement of the cessation of hostilities by Mr. Churchill over a nation-wide radio network. The King will speak at 9 o'clock that evening. And throughout that day

Continued on Page 10, Column 6

The New York Times.

LATE CITY EDITION
Cloudy with showers today. Partly
cloudy and cooler tomorrow.
Temperatures Yesterday—Max., 64; Min., 47
Sunrise today, 5:55 A. M.; Sunset, 7:59 P. M.

VOL. XCIV..No. 31,881.

Entered as Second-Class Matter,
Postoffice, New York, N. Y.

Copyright, 1945, by The New York Times Company.

NEW YORK, TUESDAY, MAY 8, 1945.

THREE CENTS NEW YORK CITY

THE WAR IN EUROPE IS ENDED! SURRENDER IS UNCONDITIONAL; V-E WILL BE PROCLAIMED TODAY; OUR TROOPS ON OKINAWA GAIN

ISLAND-WIDE DRIVE

Marines Reach Village a Mile From Naha and Army Lines Advance

7 MORE SHIPS SUNK

Search Planes Again Hit Japan's Life Line— Kyushu Bombed

By WARREN MOSCOW
By Wireless to THE NEW YORK TIMES.

GUAM, Tuesday, May 8—In an island-wide American advance on Okinawa yesterday the First Marine Division drove south to the edge of Dakeshi Village, about a mile from Naha, the capital, straightening out the line on our right flank. In the center the Seventy-seventh Army Division used flame-throwing tanks for considerable advances, while the Seventh Army Division moved forward on the left flank.

[Airfields on Kyushu, southern Japan, were bombed Monday and Tuesday by Superfortresses, two of which were lost in heavy air opposition.

[Allied fliers started operating from the Tarakan airfield although fighting continued on that island off Borneo, and in the Philippines American troops made advances on Mindanao and Luzon.]

Japanese Dead at 36,535

As the United States forces on Okinawa resumed their drive, Fleet Admiral Chester W. Nimitz revealed that Japanese killed on the island had mounted to 36,535 on Monday, showing that the Americans were maintaining their rate of 1,000 a day.

The Americans have not yet taken the main Japanese artillery emplacements on Okinawa, which were the principal targets of the fleet off the island. The fleet's guns continued yesterday, along with carrier aircraft, to support the ground movements.

Meanwhile search bombers of Fleet Air Wing 1 continued to give an impressive demonstration of what the tightening air blockade of Japan will mean. Attacking at mast-head height with bombs and machine guns, these long-range aircraft, based in the Okinawa area, sank four more ships in waters off Korea and damaged five others.

The ships sunk were a large cargo ship, a medium cargo ship, a medium oiler and a large fleet tanker. Two small freighters were

Continued on Page 12, Column 2

Leopold Rescued By 7th Army Troops

By The Associated Press.

WITH THE UNITED STATES SEVENTH ARMY, Tuesday, May 8.—Leopold III, King of Belgium, and his wife, Princess Rethy, have been liberated by the Seventh Army, it was announced today.

They were found near Strobl, eight miles east of Salzburg. The Americans had been told of their whereabouts by civilians.

With the King and his wife were eighteen members of their staff and four children. All were in good health.

Elements of the American 106th Cavalry Group had to overpower German Elite Guards to make the rescue. Seventh Army troops are now closely guarding the royal party.

The Pulitzer Awards For 1944 Announced

The Pulitzer Prize awards announced yesterday by the trustees of Columbia University included: For a distinguished novel, to "A Bell for Adano," by John Hersey; for an original American play of the current season, to "Harvey," by Mary Chase.

Among the newspaper awards were those to Hal Boyle, Associated Press war reporter, for distinguished correspondence; to James B. Reston of THE NEW YORK TIMES for his reporting of the Dumbarton Oaks Security Conference; to Joe Rosenthal, Associated Press photographer, for his photograph of marines raising the American flag at Iwo and to The Detroit Free Press for "distinguished and meritorious public service" in its investigation of legislative corruption at Lansing, Mich.

Further details of the awards will be found on Page 16.

MOLOTOFF HAILS BASIC 'UNANIMITY'

He Stresses Five Points in World Charter, but His View on One Is Questioned

By JAMES B. RESTON
Special to THE NEW YORK TIMES.

SAN FRANCISCO, May 7—The major allies who forced Germany's unconditional surrender have reached "unanimity" on the kind of world security organization which should be created at the United Nations conference to protect their newly won victory, Vyacheslav M. Molotoff, Russian Foreign Commissar, said today.

While the delegates at the conference celebrated the end of the European war, and three Foreign Ministers, T. V. Soong of China, Paul Henri Spaak of Belgium and Trygve Lie of Norway left the conference to deal with urgent official business elsewhere, Mr. Molotoff told the press that the Soviet Union attached the "greatest importance" to five agreements reached by the heads of the Big Four delegations.

First, he said, these leaders agreed to support the principles of justice, international law, human rights and fundamental freedom for all.

Second, he added, the Big Four agreed not to make provision in the security charter for the revision of treaties.

His statement on this point was ambiguous and led to some speculation as to the unanimity of all four on the question.

Revision Power Called Danger

A reference in the United Nations charter to the necessity of revising treaties, Mr. Molotoff stated, "would play into the hands of enemy countries, which would certainly like to undermine and emasculate these treaties." Furthermore, he declared, to give the new League of Nations authority to consider revision of treaties would be a violation of national sovereign rights, which are guaranteed in the Dumbarton Oaks Charter.

For these reasons, he concluded, "the idea of revising treaties was rejected as untenable."

Third, Mr. Molotoff said, it was agreed among the Big Four that treaties directed against Germany, such as Russia's twenty-year alliances with Britain, France, Czechoslovakia, Yugoslavia and the Warsaw Poles, "should remain in force until such time as the Government concerned felt that the international security organization was really in a position to undertake the accomplishment of the tasks of

Continued on Page 15, Column 2

GERMANY SURRENDERS: NEW YORKERS MASSED UNDER SYMBOL OF LIBERTY

Thousands filling Times Square in spontaneous celebration yesterday
The New York Times

PRAGUE SAYS FOES ACCEPT SURRENDER

Czechoslovak Radio Reports All Fighting in Bohemia Will Be Ended Today

By The Associated Press.

LONDON, Tuesday, May 8—The Czechoslovak - controlled Prague radio announced today that the Germans in Prague and throughout Bohemia, a last major holdout pocket of German resistance, had accepted unconditional surrender.

The announcement came as the United States Third Army was reported to have advanced to the outskirts of the Czechoslovak capital, and three Russian armies hammered toward the same goal from the east and north.

"The German military plenipotentiary is negotiating with the Czechoslovak National Council on the modalities of unconditional surrender," said the broadcast, detailing what purported to be the

Continued on Page 11, Column 2

Wild Crowds Greet News In City While Others Pray

By FRANK S. ADAMS

New York City's millions reacted in two sharply contrasting ways yesterday to the news of the unconditional surrender of the German armies. A large and noisy minority greeted it with the turbulent enthusiasm of New Year's Eve and Election Night rolled into one. However, the great bulk of the city's population responded with quiet thanksgiving that the war in Europe was won, tempered by the realization that a grim and bitter struggle still was ahead in the Pacific and the fact that the nation is still in mourning for its fallen President and Commander in Chief.

Times Square, the financial section and the garment district were thronged from mid-morning on with wildly jubilant celebrators who tooted horns, staged impromptu parades and filled the canyons between the skyscrapers with fluttering scraps of paper. Elsewhere in the metropolitan area, however, war plants continued to hum, schools and offices and

factories carried on their normal activities, and residential areas were calmly joyful.

One factor that helped to dampen the celebration was the bewilderment of large segments of the population at the absence of an official proclamation to back up the news contained in flaring headlines and radio bulletins. With the premature rumor of ten days ago fresh in everyone's mind, and millions still mindful of the false armistice of 1918, there was widespread skepticism over the authenticity of the news.

By mid-afternoon loudspeakers were blaring into the ears of the exciting thousands in the amusement district the news that President Truman's proclamation was being held up by the necessity of coordinating it with the announcements from London and Moscow, and that the formal celebration of the long-awaited V-E Day would be delayed until today.

This sobering note gradually

Continued on Page 7, Column 6

SHAEF BAN ON AP LIFTED IN 6 HOURS

Action Comes After Protests From Newspapers and Public —Writer Still Barred

Suspension of filing facilities of The Associated Press in the European theatre was clamped on by Supreme Headquarters, Allied Expeditionary Forces (SHAEF), yesterday in an unprecedented action and was lifted six hours and twenty minutes later.

The ban was continued, however, on all copy submitted for clearance by Edward Kennedy, chief of the press association's staff on the Western Front, who sent the momentous story announcing Germany's final surrender in a dispatch from Reims, France, which was received in New York over the AP wires at 9:35 A. M. (EWT).

It was not until seven hours and fifty-five minutes had elapsed aft-

Continued on Page 4, Column 2

GERMANS CAPITULATE ON ALL FRONTS

American, Russian and French Generals Accept Surrender in Eisenhower Headquarters, a Reims School

REICH CHIEF OF STAFF ASKS FOR MERCY

Doenitz Orders All Military Forces of Germany To Drop Arms—Troops in Norway Give Up —Churchill and Truman on Radio Today

By EDWARD KENNEDY
Associated Press Correspondent

REIMS, France, May 7—Germany surrendered unconditionally to the Western Allies and the Soviet Union at 2:41 A. M. French time today. [This was at 8:41 P. M., Eastern Wartime Sunday.]

The surrender took place at a little red schoolhouse that is the headquarters of Gen. Dwight D. Eisenhower.

The surrender, which brought the war in Europe to a formal end after five years, eight months and six days of bloodshed and destruction, was signed for Germany by Col. Gen. Gustav Jodl. General Jodl is the new Chief of Staff of the German Army.

The surrender was signed for the Supreme Allied Command by Lieut. Gen. Walter Bedell Smith, Chief of Staff for General Eisenhower.

It was also signed by Gen. Ivan Susloparoff for the Soviet Union and by Gen. Francois Sevez for France.

[The official Allied announcement will be made at 9 o'clock Tuesday morning when President Truman will broadcast a statement and Prime Minister Churchill will issue a V-E Day proclamation. Gen. Charles de Gaulle also will address the French at the same time.]

General Eisenhower was not present at the signing, but immediately afterward General Jodl and his fellow delegate, Gen. Admiral Hans Georg Friedeburg, were received by the Supreme Commander.

Germans Say They Understand Terms

They were asked sternly if they understood the surrender terms imposed upon Germany and if they would be carried out by Germany.

They answered Yes.

Germany, which began the war with a ruthless attack upon Poland, followed by successive aggressions and brutality in internment camps, surrendered with an appeal to the victors for mercy toward the German people and armed forces.

After having signed the full surrender, General Jodl said he wanted to speak and received leave to do so.

"With this signature," he said in soft-spoken German, "the German people and armed forces are for better or worse delivered into the victors' hands.

"In this war, which has lasted more than five years, both have achieved and suffered more than perhaps any other people in the world."

LONDON, May 7 (AP)—Complete victory in

Continued on Page 3, Columns 2 and 3

Summary of News of the War and German Surrender

TUESDAY, MAY 8, 1945

The war ended in Europe yesterday after five years, eight months and six days of the bloodiest conflict in history. Grand Admiral Karl Doenitz surrendered unconditionally to the Allies in a little red schoolhouse at Reims, France. At 8:41 P. M. Sunday, New York time, Col. Gen. Gustav Jodl signed for the enemy and Lieut. Gen. Walter Bedell Smith, General Eisenhower's Chief of Staff, for the Allies. In the absence of any official announcement there was some confusion as to the compliance with the surrender. Fighting had been going on in compliance with Czechoslovakia and nothing had been heard from German pockets along the French coast. [1:7-8.]

President Truman planned a broadcast from the White House at 9 o'clock this morning. Washington, gratified that the war in Europe was over, was confused by lack of confirmation. [2:2.]

Prime Minister Churchill will also broadcast at 9 A. M. from London and Premier Stalin is

expected to make a simultaneous announcement in Moscow. King George will talk over the radio six hours later. [2:8.] London will celebrate V-E Day today, but, unable to restrain its joy, staged many impromptu celebrations yesterday. [2:7.]

Most New Yorkers took the news calmly and thankfully, sobered by realization that the war in the Pacific was far from over. There were, however, noisy outbursts in such centers as Times Square and Wall Street. Scrap paper showers fluttered from roofs and windows. [1:4-5.]

German Foreign Minister Lutz Schwerin von Krosigk broke the news to his people. The future will be difficult, he warned, and then added: "We must make right the basis of our nation. In our nation justice shall be the supreme law and the guiding principle. We must also recognize law as the basis of all relations between the nations." This sudden, complete reversal in German policy was received with

skepticism by the Allies. [3:1.]

Perhaps one reason for this was the announcement from Moscow that 4,000,000 men, women and children had been done to death by gas, shooting, famine, poisoning and torture in the German extermination camp at Oswiecim, Poland. [12:5.]

The actual situation in Czechoslovakia was obscure. Late last night a Patriot broadcast said the Germans were negotiating with the Czechoslovak National Council details of surrender in Prague and Bohemia. Fighting had continued throughout yesterday and German planes had bombed public buildings and hospitals. [1:3; map P. 11.]

The United States Third Army continued its general advance into Czechoslovakia and the Fifth and Seventh Armies joined again in the Alps. The British Second Army moved to Denmark and Poles entered the shattered port of Wilhelmshaven. [11:1.] Breslau fell to the Red Army after an eighty-four-day siege; 40,000

Germans were captured. [11:5.]

Infantry and marines on Okinawa scored another general advance after naval bombardment had pulverized Japanese strong points. Pacific Fleet planes sank or damaged thirteen more ships off Korea and Japan. [1:1; map, P. 12.] B-29's maintained their assault on Kyushu airfields. Two of the big planes were shot down. [14:3-4.] On Tarakan Allied troops were within a mile and a half of the eastern shore. Americans gained on Mindanao and Luzon in the Philippines. [12:3-4.]

Foreign Commissar Molotoff said in San Francisco that unanimity on amendments to success of the conference. He declared that the Big Four consultations had ended. [1:2.]

The New York Times.

LATE CITY EDITION
Showers, thunder showers; warm
and humid today and tomorrow.
Temperature Yesterday—Max.: 72; Min.: 67
Sunrise today: 5:49 A. M.; Sunset, 8:15 P. M.

Section
1

NEWS INDEX, PAGE 41, THIS SECTION

Copyright, 1945, by the New York Times Company.

VOL. XCIV..No. 31,963.

Entered as Second-Class Matter,
Postoffice, New York, N. Y.

NEW YORK, SUNDAY, JULY 29, 1945.

Including Magazine
and Book Review.

TEN CENTS
New York City and Suburban Areas (15c Elsewhere)

SENATE RATIFIES CHARTER OF UNITED NATIONS 89 TO 2; TRUMAN HAILS AID TO PEACE

FOES ARE CRUSHED

With Hiram Johnson Ill, Only Shipstead and Langer Vote 'No'

WORLD OBLIGATION CITED

Leaders Say Today's Ratification Is 'Master Plan,' With Military Pacts Secondary

By JAMES B. RESTON
Special to The New York Times.

WASHINGTON, July 28—The United States Senate paid a first installment on an old debt today. It ratified, 89 to 2, the United Nations Security Charter, successor to the League of Nations Covenant which it rejected twenty-six years ago, and thereby fulfilled Woodrow Wilson's prophecy that one day the upper chamber would reverse its decision.

The vote came 107 days after the death of Franklin D. Roosevelt, who helped guide the Charter past the pitfalls that defeated Wilson's Covenant, and at a moment when American statesmen were settling the fate of a defeated Germany and American warships were closing in on the heart of Japan.

The two Senators who voted against ratification were William Langer of North Dakota and Henrik Shipstead of Minnesota, both Republicans. Mr. Langer, who worked actively for Hiram Johnson and Robert M. La Follette when those two "irreconcilables" were candidates for President, said he was voting against the Charter because it would mean "perpetual war" and the "enslavement" of millions of poor people from Poland to India.

Hiram Johnson Sends Word

Senator Hiram Johnson, Republican, of California, sent word from the Naval Medical Center outside Washington that if he had been well enough to be present he would have joined Mr. Langer and Mr. Shipstead in opposition, but the four other members of the Senate who were with Mr. Johnson in the upper chamber during the League of Nations debate—Arthur Capper, Republican, of Kansas, and Peter G. Gerry of Rhode Island, Kenneth McKellar of Tennessee, and David I. Walsh of Massachusetts, Democrats, all voted for ratification.

As soon as the results were made known, President Truman and Cordell Hull, former Secretary of State, who started work on the Charter in the State Department in 1942, issued statements praising the Senate's action.

"It is deeply gratifying that the Senate has ratified the United Nations' Charter by a virtually unanimous vote," the President's message from Potsdam said. "The action of the Senate substantially advances the cause of world peace."

It was a grim-appearing Senate that rolled off the "ayes" on the final count this evening. Despite the long parliamentary debate in the chamber on the subject, and despite its overwhelming approval at the end, there was no sense of the British delegation experts had first been mentioned to members of this chamber by Woodrow Wilson in 1914, some 40,000,000 human beings, armed and unarmed, had been killed in two great wars. In the first German war total military casualties were estimated at 37,000,000 men; in the European phase of the second German war some 14,000,000 men had been killed, and our own casualties in this war, still unfinished, were over the million mark.

Chaplain Tells Senate's Hopes

Throughout the debate, the Senate seemed to realize this and to approach the problem more in hope than anything else.

"Under the old order of strife," the Senate's chaplain said in his prayer opening today's session, "we learned how to destroy ourselves. Under a new charter of mutual aid and tolerance of diversity, may we learn at last how to save ourselves."

Today's vote does not put the

Continued on Page 33, Column 4

Truman Deeply Gratified, He Says in Cable Message

President Promptly Recognizes Senate's Action as Advancing 'the Cause of World Peace'—Grew and Hull Applaud

WASHINGTON, July 28—President Truman was swift to applaud the passage of the World Security Charter. In a message from Potsdam he said:

"It is deeply gratifying that the Senate has ratified the United Nations Charter by a virtually unanimous vote.

"The action of the Senate substantially advances the cause of world peace."

Joseph C. Grew, Acting Secretary of State, and Cordell Hull, former Secretary of State, also commended the Senate for its approval of the Charter.

Mr. Grew said:

"The passage of the United Nations Charter by the Senate today is a memorable event in the history of the United States and the world. By their action, the members of the Senate have taken a most important step toward establishing security and peace throughout the world.

"Millions of men, women and children have died because nations took to the naked sword instead of the conference table to settle their differences.

"The United Nations Charter, approved by such an overwhelming majority, represents the labor of citizens of fifty nations, united in their desire for a peaceful world. The Charter itself is the foundation and cornerstone on which the international organization to keep the peace will be built. This organization can survive only through the faith and labor of the citizens of all these nations.

"I congratulate the members of the Senate for their work today."

Continued on Page 33, Column 1

Poles, at Big 3 Meeting, Ask Stettin, Oder-Neisse Border

By RAYMOND DANIELL
By Wireless to The New York Times.

BERLIN, July 28—A delegation of the Polish Government, including Vice Premier Stanislaw Mikolajczyk and, it is believed, Labor Minister Jan Stanczyk, has been here this last week to ask for a final delimitation of their country's western frontier to include Stettin and run from there southward along the east bank of the Oder-Neisse River line.

It was officially announced that Britain's new Prime Minister, Clement R. Attlee, and his Foreign Minister, Ernest Bevin, after formal calls on President Truman, Secretary of State James F. Byrnes, Premier Stalin and Foreign Commissar Vyacheslaff M. Molotoff, had participated today in a plenary session of the tripartite conference.

It has been believed, although there has been no inkling of their plans from official sources, that neither Winston Churchill nor former Foreign Secretary Anthony Eden will return. The new Prime Minister and his Foreign Secretary, who as Labor Minister in Mr. Churchill's coalition Government had access to all secrets of the War Cabinet, are the only new members of the British delegation. Inasmuch as Mr. Attlee sat in at all sessions of the Big Three before his election and saw all the official documents at the conference, it can hardly be said that he is a newcomer to the council table.

Parley Continuity Maintained

The downfall of the Churchill Government has caused little break in the continuity of the conference. Little more than forty-eight hours elapsed between Mr. Churchill's departure from Berlin and Mr. Attlee's return today.

In the absence of the head of the British delegation experts worked steadily to clear the decks

Continued on Page 5, Column 4

WOOLLEY DISMISSES ROSS IN OPA DISPUTE

Refuses to Grant the Public Hearing Demanded by Aide He Suspended June 22

Paul L. Ross, regional enforcement executive of the Office of Price Administration, who was suspended June 22 on charges of maladministration, was discharged yesterday by Daniel P. Woolley, regional OPA administrator, who refused to grant Mr. Ross the public hearing for which he had pleaded.

The discharge, effective at once, was contained in a registered letter mailed to Mr. Ross at noon, and followed by less than forty-eight hours the filing of Mr. Ross' reply to the administrator's charges.

In a brief statement, Mr. Woolley declared "utterly untrue and unfounded" serious counter-charges against him preferred by Mr. Ross in his answer. The enforcement officer had accused Mr. Woolley of hampering the enforcement of OPA regulations, interfering in behalf of certain alleged violators and obstructing the Federal enforcement policies.

Upon learning of his discharge,

Continued on Page 37, Column 5

Kweilin and Three Airfields Seized; Chinese Also Gain in Other Areas

By The Associated Press.

CHUNGKING, China, July 28—Chinese troops recaptured the airbase city of Kweilin yesterday and seized its three former American airfields from the Japanese, the Chinese High Command said tonight. The victory ended a six-week battle.

Kweilin, walled capital of Kwangsi Province, once was the biggest United States airbase in South-Central China. It had been occupied by the Japanese since last November. Its recapture was the most significant victory in the recent comeback of the Chinese armies.

Generalissimo Chiang Kai-shek's veterans smashed into the rubbled streets of Kweilin, 360 miles southeast of Chungking, at 4 P. M. yesterday after mowing down the defenders of the city's south and west gates. Most of the Japanese garrison had fled and enemy rearguard remnants swiftly were routed from machine-gun nests in cellars and on roofs, a communiqué said.

The Japanese, headquarters added, withdrew to the northwest to escape annihilation. Their escape route northeastward to Hengyang was severed several days ago. The Chinese said: "Our troops are in hot pursuit."

Kweilin, abandoned by the United States Fourteenth Air Force eight months ago, was the third former American airbase recovered in three days by the Chinese, whose current drive is rapidly strengthening American air power on the Asiatic mainland. It was

Continued on Page 3, Column 5

CRIPPLED WARSHIPS OF JAPANESE NAVY SMASHED BY FLIERS

2 Battleships and 3 Cruisers Set Afire in Saturday Strike by the Third Fleet

HYUGA IS FOUND SUNK

Returning U. S. Pilots Report Waters Off Kure Strewn With Burning Vessels

By Wireless to The New York Times.

GUAM, Sunday, July 29—Two Japanese battleships, the Haruna and Ise, and three cruisers were set afire and a third battleship, the Hyuga, which was heavily damaged on Tuesday, was found to be resting on the bottom at her anchorage as United States Third Fleet carrier planes struck heavily Saturday at crippled remnants of the Japanese Navy in the Inland Sea.

An aircraft carrier also was further damaged.

Fleet Admiral Chester W. Nimitz today announced the results of the strike, which were incomplete. No reports had yet been received from British carrier pilots, who also participated.

Enemy Air Opposition Sporadic

The enemy's air opposition was sporadic, with American fighters shooting down one Japanese plane near Task Force 38, another eighteen near the target areas and destroying seventy-five on the ground. Fifty-six other parked enemy aircraft were damaged.

[Pilots returning from the Saturday strike reported waters off the Kure naval base littered with burning ships, and fleet dispatches said every major Japanese warship was believed to have been put out of action for the duration of the war, The United Press stated.]

The Third Fleet assault was directed at Japanese shipping between the once great ports of Kobe and Kure.

Pilots reported that the Hyuga, a modernized battleship with carrier type runway aft permitting it to handle aircraft, was on the bottom, water lapping over her main deck amidships.

It was disclosed also that Saturday's aerial assault resulted in the sinking of three submarines, presumably in dry dock, and damage to four destroyers, two destroyer escorts, two medium-size freighter transports, three small cargo ships and an unidentified vessel.

Five Warships Left Burning

Whether these ships were among those damaged in the Tuesday attack, which battered twenty-three warships, was not revealed. However, it is definite that yesterday's attack further damaged six warships Haruna and Ise, the cruisers Tone, Aoba and Oyodo and the escort carrier Kaiyo. All of these ships except the carrier were left burning in the latest assault.

Thus it seems that Admiral Halsey is well along toward his objective—the neutralization of Japan's remaining naval warships in order to provide a thoroughly clear field for future amphibious

Continued on Page 3, Column 2

BOMBER HITS EMPIRE STATE BUILDING, SETTING IT AFIRE AT THE 79TH FLOOR; 13 DEAD, 26 HURT; WIDE AREA ROCKED

WHERE BOMBER CRASHED INTO EMPIRE STATE BUILDING

Hole torn between seventy-eighth and seventy-ninth floors   The New York Times (by Sisto)

B-29'S FIRE 6 CITIES IN PROMISED BLOWS

Oil Refinery Target on Honshu Added to List LeMay Gave Japanese in Advance

By Wireless to The New York Times.

GUAM, Sunday, July 29—The Twentieth Air Force early today bombed six out of eleven Japanese cities that hardly twenty-four hours previously had been told that they were on a list of enemy communities marked for aerial destruction by Superfortresses.

Seven task forces of the B-29 bombers, totaling 550 to 600 planes, dropped more than 3,500 tons of incendiaries on the six industrial centers situated from Shikoku in the south to northern Honshu and demolition bombs on an oil refinery near Osaka.

[Gen. Douglas MacArthur reported Okinawa-based Army planes had sunk enemy shipping in Japan's Inland Sea area. He disclosed that our new B-32 super-bomber has been in action since May against the foe on Formosa and along the China coast.]

One of the B-29 task forces, sent

Continued on Page 4, Column 1

Catholic War Relief Office Is Chief Victim of Tragedy

By LARRY RESNER

An agency that has been in the vanguard of supplying aid and comfort to thousands of homeless and destitute persons in the war zones became yesterday, through one of those curious quirks of fate, the victim of the worst local tragedy of the war. The point of greatest impact of the low-flying bomber that crashed into the Empire State Building was at the seventy-ninth floor, where the principal tenant was the War Relief Services of the National Catholic Welfare Conference.

Throughout the war years, this agency has sent many field representatives into the lands laid waste by war to work with other relief and welfare agencies in helping war victims.

And only yesterday, as the bomber struck and destroyed their office, the reduced Saturday staff of workers was busily engaged in arranging the final details of a trip to Europe on Tuesday of two of their principal functionaries.

Only five of an estimated working staff of thirteen to twenty persons in the office, including men and women, were known to have escaped the flames that swept the skyscraper floor as the gasoline of the crashing plane exploded.

W. Paul Dearing, correspondent here for The Buffalo Courier-Express and publicity director of the War Relief Services for the last year, either jumped or was blown from his seventy-ninth-floor office to his death on a ledge on the sev-

Continued on Page 32, Column 3

SURVIVOR LIKENS CRASH TO A QUAKE

Building Moved Twice, Then Settled, Says Occupant Who Felt Shocks in China

By ALEXANDER FEINBERG

The towering Empire State Building that is a city of 102 stories, reaching 1,250 feet high, "moved" twice yesterday when a plane hit the bomber and then it "settled." That was a dread moment for one who had felt that double movement and the settling many times before.

Recently returned from China after twenty-seven years, the man who told of his sensations when the B-25 struck said the impact was precisely that of an earthquake, to which he is no stranger. Preferring not to give his name, he said he was in an office on the sixty-eighth floor of the building when he felt the double "move-

Continued on Page 28, Column 1

B-25 CRASHES IN FOG

Hole 18 by 20 Feet Torn Through North Wall by Terrific Impact

BLAZING 'GAS' SCATTERED

Flames Put Out in 40-Minute Fight—2 Women Survive Fall in Elevator

By FRANK ADAMS

A twin-engined B-25 Army bomber, lost in a blinding fog, crashed into the Empire State Building at a point 915 feet above the street level at 9:49 A. M. yesterday. Thirteen persons, including the three occupants of the plane and ten persons at work within the building, were killed in the catastrophe, and twenty-six were injured.

Although the crash and the fire that followed wrecked most of the seventy-eighth and seventy-ninth floors of the structure, causing damage estimated at $500,000, Lieut. Gen. Hugh A. Drum, president of the Empire State, Inc., Corporation, said last night that an inspection by the city's building department and by other engineers and architects showed that the structural soundness of the building had not been impaired.

Landing Advice Disregarded

The plane, en route from Bedford, Mass., to Newark on a cross-country mission, had flown over La Guardia Field a few minutes before the crash, and its pilot, Lieut. Col. William F. Smith Jr., deputy commander of the 457th Bomber Group and recently decorated for his service overseas, was advised by the control tower to land. Instead he asked for the weather at Newark Airport and headed in that direction.

Horror-stricken occupants of the building, alarmed by the roar of engines, ran to the windows just in time to see the plane loom out of the gray mists that washed the upper floors of the world's tallest office building. The plane was banked at an angle of about fifteen degrees as Colonel Smith swung it to a course off to the northeast.

It crashed with a terrifying impact midway along the north or Thirty-fourth Street wall of the building. Its wings were sheared off by the impact, but the motors and fuselage ripped a hole eighteen feet wide and twenty feet high in the outer wall of the seventy-eighth and seventy-ninth floors of the structure.

Brilliant orange flames shot as high as the observatory on the eighty-sixth floor of the building, 1,050 feet above Fifth Avenue, as the gasoline tanks of the plane exploded. For a moment watchers in the street below saw the tower clearly illumined by the glare. Then it disappeared again in gray murk and the smoke of the burning plane.

Motor Hits Another Building

One of the plane's two motors hurtled clear across the seventy-eighth floor, tore a hole in the south wall of the building, and plummeted to the roof of the twelve-story office building at 10 West Thirty-third Street, where it started a fire that demolished the penthouse of Henry Hering, noted sculptor, with resulting damage estimated at $75,000.

A propeller was imbedded in the wall of the Empire State Building; the other motor and part of the landing gear crashed into an elevator shaft, whence they fell to the floor a thousand feet below, and other sections of the fuselage were blown as high as the eighty-sixth floor observatory. The steel girder at the seventy-ninth floor level was bent inward eighteen inches by the shock.

Cascading torrents of flaming gasoline poured through the seventy-eighth and seventy-ninth floors, setting fire to everything that was combustible. The burning fuel ran down stair wells into hallways as far as the seventy-fifth floor, while choking fumes

Continued on Page 25, Column 1

Red Cross and Hospital Groups Speed to Aid of Victims, Rescuers

The last fireman barely had leaped from his truck to the ragging four-alarm blaze caused by the bomber crash in the Empire State Building when hospital disaster units and two Red Cross Service canteen wagons were on the scene to aid the victims and rescuers of the catastrophe.

While fifteen Red Cross aides set up shop and dispensed hot coffee and doughnuts to the toiling fire fighters and others helping them, two disaster units from Bellevue Hospital, replete with the latest equipment, were making their way into the upper reaches of the building to assist in the rescue work.

Only twelve minutes elapsed between the sounding of the first alarm at 9:49 A. M. and the fourth alarm and from the moment the Telegraph Bureau at Police Headquarters received the first report

Continued on Page 32, Column 6

the city's fire-fighting equipment, a small army of police and squads of Army and Navy units, mostly military police and more patrols moved with clock-like precision through the fog-shrouded streets.

The fire sirens screeched continuously as apparatus sped to the scene. The second alarm hit at 9:57 A. M., the third at 10 A. M. and the last at 10:01 A. M. After that there were other calls but only for specialized equipment.

The four alarms brought to the scene more than sixty pieces of fire-fighting apparatus, including "walkie-talkie" radio units. All were under the immediate command of Fire Commissioner Patrick Walsh. Almost simultaneously the Police Department's ranking officers dispatched more than 400 policemen

Continued on Page 25, Column 1

War News Summarized

SUNDAY, JULY 29, 1945

The United States Senate ratified, 89 to 2, the United Nations Security Charter. The two Senators who voted against ratification were William Langer of North Dakota and Henrik Shipstead of Minnesota, both Republicans. [1:1.]

Two battleships and three cruisers, all previously damaged, were hit again in the latest Third Fleet attack on the Inland Sea area, Admiral Nimitz disclosed, and it was found another battleship had been sunk. Returning pilots reported that the Japanese Navy probably was out of action for the rest of the war. [1:4.]

Between 550 and 600 Superfortresses set fire to six of the eleven Japanese cities warned previously of their coming destruction. [1:5; map P. 2.]

General Minami, of Tokyo's would-be-totalitarian party, said Japan would be ready to discuss peace when East Asia was free from British-American "colonial exploitation." [9:1.]

Captain Zacharias, United States naval spokesman, broadcast to Japan a declaration that peace with Japan had now been made possible by the Potsdam proclamation. [4:5.]

Chinese forces took Kweilin and three former United States airfields. Other Chinese pressed toward Kukong, 120 miles north of Canton, gaining thirty miles in two days. [1:2-3; map P. 3.]

The British in Burma reported that the Japanese Twenty-eighth Army had been annihilated with more than 5,500 killed and the remnant fleeing toward Thailand. [3:1.]

Prime Minister Attlee and his new Ministers took the oath of office in London. [1:4.]

A Polish Government delegation was in Potsdam pleading for a western frontier running along the Oder and Neisse Rivers. Meanwhile, the conference was resumed with Mr. Attlee and Foreign Secretary Bevin in the places of Winston Churchill and Anthony Eden. [1:2-3; map P. 5.]

Michel Clemenceau accused Marshal Pétain at the latter's treason trial of having been indirectly responsible for handing over Georges Mandel, former Minister of Colonies, to the Germans who killed him. [12:1.]

"All the News That's Fit to Print"

The New York Times.

LATE CITY EDITION
Partly cloudy, less humid today.
Cloudy and warm tomorrow.
Temperatures Yesterday—Max., 72; Min., 66
Sunrise today, 5:57 A. M.; Sunset, 8:06 P. M.

Copyright, 1945, by The New York Times Company.

VOL. XCIV..No. 31,972.

Entered as Second-Class Matter,
Postoffice, New York, N. Y.

NEW YORK, TUESDAY, AUGUST 7, 1945.

THREE CENTS IN NEW YORK CITY

FIRST ATOMIC BOMB DROPPED ON JAPAN; MISSILE IS EQUAL TO 20,000 TONS OF TNT; TRUMAN WARNS FOE OF A 'RAIN OF RUIN'

HIRAM W. JOHNSON, REPUBLICAN DEAN IN THE SENATE, DIES

Isolationist Helped Prevent U. S. Entry Into League—Opposed World Charter

CALIFORNIA EX-GOVERNOR

Ran for Vice President With Theodore Roosevelt in '12 —In Washington Since '17

Special to THE NEW YORK TIMES.

WASHINGTON, Aug. 6.—Senator Hiram Warren Johnson of California, lifelong isolationist, who helped prevent this country's entry into the League of Nations and fought all "foreign entanglements" through a second World War, died in his sleep this morning at Bethesda Naval Hospital, nine days after, ill but consistent, he had paired his vote against ratification of the United Nations Charter. Death was caused by a thrombosis of a cerebral artery. Mrs. Johnson was with him when the end came.

When word reached the Capitol of the passing of the oldest member of the Senate in point of service, save Senator Kenneth McKellar, the President pro tempore, the mourning was deep. With great personal affection colleagues paid humble tribute to his integrity of character, his liberalism and his steadfastness to his ideals and convictions. They joined in declaring the country had lost a great statesman.

Senator Johnson, who was serving the fourth year of his fifth term in the Senate, would have been 79 years old on Sept. 2. Although his health had been failing during the last two years and though the thundering voice which had conveyed his eloquence through innumerable stirring debates had become little more than a whisper, friends believed he planned to seek a sixth term in 1947.

He went to the hospital July 18. Five days before that he had cast the lone vote in the Foreign Relations Committee, of which he was the ranking minority member, against reporting the new World Charter to the Senate without change. He did not participate in the floor debate on this document, which won Senate approval by a vote of 82—2. However, he clashed spiritedly with colleagues while the hearings were in progress.

Funeral arrangements await the arrival of the Senator's son, Lieut. Col. Hiram W. Johnson Jr., who was flying here from California.

Capper Becomes the Dean

The death of Senator Johnson made Senator Arthur Capper of Kansas, who last month made his eightieth birthday, the Republican dean of the Senate. It also elevated him to the ranking minority membership on the Foreign Relations Committee, with which Senator Johnson had been so conspicuously identified through the many years of his unshaken position on foreign policy. Mr. Capper, too, with Senators McKellar, Carter Glass of Virginia, David I. Walsh of Massachusetts and Peter G. Gerry, was in the League that of 1919 and 1920. He supported it, with reservations.

The career of Senator Johnson, from his entrance into the Senate from the Governorship of California in March of 1917, was one distinctly lacking in compromise or reservation. In 1912 he had bolted his party with Theodore Roosevelt and had become the Vice-Presidential nominee on the Bull Moose ticket. In 1932 he again bolted to support Franklin D. Roosevelt for the Presidency but broke bitterly with the President when he ran for his third term.

In 1919 Mr. Johnson joined with Senators Lodge, Borah, Reed,

Continued on Page 22, Column 4

Jet Plane Explosion Kills Major Bong, Top U. S. Ace

Flier Who Downed 40 Japanese Craft, Sent Home to Be 'Safe,' Was Flying New 'Shooting Star' as a Test Pilot

By The United Press.

BURBANK, Calif., Aug. 6.—Maj. Richard Bong, America's greatest air ace, died today in the flaming wreckage of a jet propelled fighter plane which crashed while he was testing it.

Only 24 years old, he wore twenty-six decorations including the nation's highest award, the Congressional Medal of Honor. He had survived countless air battles and shot down forty Japanese planes without a scratch.

The knowledge he gained in those battles was too valuable to risk, so he was brought home to "safe" duty. He was on that "safe" duty today when his P-80, the Shooting Star, hurtled over a clump of trees and burst like a bomb in a field.

Witnesses did not agree on the cause of the crash. One Army flier said that Major Bong overshot the Lockheed airport. Another witness, John McKinney of North Hollywood reported that he saw something fall out of the plane's tail.

"The plane started to wobble up and down, then went into a left bank and hit the ground," he stated. "It exploded and burned and scattered wreckage over half a block square."

Major Bong was trying to get out of the ship when it crashed. He had released the escape hatch and was partly clear. He had pulled the ripcord to his parachute, and the silken folds lay about the body as the flames swept over it.

With a roaring sigh, the plane, like a giant blowtorch, shot over the airport just before 3 P. M. and then lurched over the trees and nosed down into the field, a mile away.

Smoke and flame surged up and crowds rushed from the airport. By the time anyone could reach the scene the ship had been almost consumed.

The crash scene was near the intersection of Cahuenga and Oxnard Boulevards and barely outContinued on page 15, Column 2

KYUSHU CITY RAZED

Kenney's Planes Blast Tarumizu in Record Blow From Okinawa

ROCKET SITE IS SEEN

125 B-29's Hit Japan's Toyokawa Naval Arsenal in Demolition Strike

By FRANK L. KLUCKHOHN
By Wireless to THE NEW YORK TIMES.

MANILA, Tuesday, Aug. 7.—More than 400 fighters and bombers, speeding at chimney-top level for two hours Sunday over Tarumizu in southern Kyushu in the largest single attack launched by Gen. George C. Kenney's Far East Air Forces to date, leveled that city's munitions factories and aircraft and munitions storage depots and waterfront installations.

Rockets and demolition bombs were poured by waves of B-26 Invaders, B-25 Mitchells and Mustangs and Thunderbolts of the Fifth and Seventh Air Forces from Okinawa, supported by a few B-24 Liberators carrying big bombs.

[Tarumizu, about 350 miles from Okinawa, appeared to be a site at which the Japanese might be preparing a rocket campaign against the American base, said a United Press dispatch. FEAF pilots reported seeing in the area, which has extensive cave construction, what seemed to be Japanese robot planes and also a huge catapult-like machine, extending over the water, that might be a rocket launcher.

[About 125 B-29's hit the Toyokawa naval arsenal of Japan in a demolition bombing Tuesday noon, Strategic Air Force headquarters at Guam reported.]

The planes over Tarumizu met scant resistance, as our fliers took their time to assure the highest
Continued on Page 11, Column 2

REPORT BY BRITAIN

'By God's Mercy' We Beat Nazis to Bomb, Churchill Says

ROOSEVELT AID CITED

Raiders Wrecked Norse Laboratory in Race for Key to Victory

The text of Mr. Churchill's statement is on Page 8.

By CLIFTON DANIEL

LONDON, Aug. 6.—The hitherto secret details of the grisly race between Germany and the Allies to find a weapon so destructive that it would insure absolute victory—a race not only between scientists but also between under-cover agents—were recounted in London tonight after it had been disclosed that the first atomic bomb had been dropped on Japan.

"By God's mercy" British and American science outpaced all German efforts," said a statement by former Prime Minister Churchill written before he left office and issued from 10 Downing Street by his successor, Clement R. Attlee.

"The possession of these powers by the Germans at any time might have altered the result of the war," Mr. Churchill said, "and profound anxiety was felt by those who were informed."

The British Isles, which endured the terrors of flying bombs and rockets, did hear repeated rumors that Adolf Hitler's V-3 weapon was to be an atomic bomb, but they never knew until tonight how close they came to being the first victims of its destructive power. Much less did they suspect what
Continued on Page 9, Column 1

Steel Tower 'Vaporized' In Trial of Mighty Bomb

Scientists Awe-Struck as Blinding Flash Lighted New Mexico Desert and Great Cloud Bore 40,000 Feet Into Sky

By LEWIS WOOD
Special to THE NEW YORK TIMES.

WASHINGTON, Aug. 6.—A blinding flash many times as brilliant as the midday sun and a massive, multi-colored cloud boiling up 40,-000 feet into the air accompanied the first test firing of an atomic bomb on July 16, three weeks ago today. Set in the remote desert lands of New Mexico, the experiment was seen against a wild background where rain poured in torrents, and lightning pierced the sky up to the zero hour of the explosion at 5:30 A. M.

A steel tower from which the atomic weapon hung was vaporized. In its place was only a huge, sloping crater. At the moment of the explosion a mountain range three miles distant stood out sharply in brilliant light.

"Then," said the War Department in a description, "came a tremendous, sustained roar and a heavy pressure wave which knocked down two men outside the control tower (10,000 yards, or more than five miles, away.)"

The scene of the great drama was the Alamogordo Air Base, 120 miles southeast of Albuquerque. Here the scientists strove to unlock the secret upon which $2,000,000,000 had been spent.

Graphic word pictures of the
Continued on Page 5, Column 1

ATOM BOMBS MADE IN 3 HIDDEN 'CITIES'

Secrecy on Weapon So Great That Not Even Workers Knew of Their Product

By JAY WALZ
Special to THE NEW YORK TIMES.

WASHINGTON, Aug. 6.—The War Department revealed today how three "hidden cities" with a total population of 100,000 inhabitants sprang into being as a result of the $2,000,000,000 atomic bomb project, how they did their work without knowing what it was all about, and how they kept the biggest secret of the war.

One of these, Oak Ridge, situated where only oak and pine trees had dotted small farms before, is today the fifth largest city in Tennessee. Its population of 75,000 persons has thirteen supermarkets, nine drug stores and seven theatres.

A second town of 7,000 was built for reasons of isolation and security on a New Mexico mesa. The third, named Richland Village, houses 17,000 men, women and children on remote banks of the Columbia River in the State of Washington.

None of the people, who came to these developments from homes all the way from Maine to California, had the slightest idea of what they were making in the gigantic Gov-
Continued on Page 3, Column 2

NEW AGE USHERED

Day of Atomic Energy Hailed by President, Revealing Weapon

HIROSHIMA IS TARGET

'Impenetrable' Cloud of Dust Hides City After Single Bomb Strikes

Truman, Stimson statements on atomic bomb, Page 4.

By SIDNEY SHALETT
Special to THE NEW YORK TIMES.

WASHINGTON, Aug. 6.—The White House and War Department announced today that an atomic bomb, possessing more power than 20,000 tons of TNT, a destructive force equal to the load of 2,000 B-29's and more than 2,000 times the blast power of what previously was the world's most devastating bomb, had been dropped on Japan.

The announcement, first given to the world in utmost solemnity by President Truman, made it plain that one of the scientific landmarks of the century had been passed, and that the "age of atomic energy," which can be a tremendous force for the advancement of civilization as well as for destruction, was at hand.

At 10:45 o'clock this morning, a statement by the President was issued at the White House that sixteen hours earlier—about the time that citizens on the Eastern seaboard were sitting down to their Sunday supper—an American plane had dropped the single atomic bomb on the Japanese city of Hiroshima, an important army center.

Japanese Solemnly Warned

What happened at Hiroshima is not yet known. The War Department said it "as yet was unable to make an accurate report" because "an impenetrable cloud of dust and smoke" masked the target area from reconnaissance planes. The Secretary of War will release the story "as soon as accurate details of the results of the bombing become available."

But in a statement vividly describing the results of the first test of the atomic bomb in New Mexico, the War Department told how an immense steel tower had been "vaporized" by the tremendous explosion, how a 40,000-foot cloud rushed into the sky, and how observers were knocked down at a point 10,000 yards away, and President Truman solemnly warned:

"It was to spare the Japanese people from utter destruction that the ultimatum of July 26 was issued at Potsdam. Their leaders promptly rejected that ultimatum. If they do not now accept our terms, they may expect a rain of ruin from the air the like of which has never been seen on this earth."

Most Closely Guarded Secret

The President referred to the joint statement issued by the heads of the American, British and Chinese Governments, in which terms of surrender were outlined to the Japanese and warning given that rejection would mean complete destruction of Japan's power to make war.

[The atomic bomb weighs about 400 pounds and is capable of utterly destroying a town, a representative of the British Ministry of Aircraft Production said in London, the United Press reported.]

What is this terrible new weapon, which the War Department also calls the "Cosmic Bomb"? It is the harnessing of the energy of the atom, which is the basic power of the universe. As President Truman said, "The force from which the sun draws its power has been loosed against those who brought war to the Far East."

"Atomic fission"—in other
Continued on Page 2, Column 1

MORRIS IS ACCUSED OF 'TAKING A WALK'

Fusion Official 'Sad to Part Company'—McGoldrick Sees Only Tammany Aided

The No Deal ticket, headed by Council President Newbold Morris, "can only serve the interests of Tammany Hall," Controller Joseph D. McGoldrick, candidate for re-election on the Republican-Liberal-Fusion party slate, declared yesterday in a fresh attack on the third-party ticket injected over the week-end into the city Mayoralty campaign.

A short while later Gabriel A. Wechsler, general secretary of the City Fusion party, which supported Mayor La Guardia and Mr. Morris in previous city campaigns, accused Mr. Morris of "taking a walk away from the good government forces."

To both charges Mr. Morris declared he would stand on his statement of Sunday that he was not interested in "just taking votes" away from Judge Jonah J. Goldstein, Republican-Liberal-Fusion candidate for Mayor, or from William O'Dwyer, his Democratic-American Labor party opponent.

"I have no comment," he said, "since I stand on my statement of Sunday. We are waging an affirmative campaign."

Informed that Hyman Blumberg,
Continued on Page 19, Column 6

CHINESE WIN MORE OF 'INVASION COAST'

Smash Into Port 121 Miles Southwest of Canton—Big Area Open for Landing

By The Associated Press.

CHUNGKING, China, Aug. 6.—Chinese troops have broken into the South China port of Yeungkong and cleared a fifty-mile stretch of the Chinese "invasion coast" west of Hong Kong, Generalissimo Chiang Kai-shek's headquarters said today.

Swaying block-by-block street fighting is raging in the strategic coastal highway town, 121 miles southwest of Canton, a communiqué said.

By breaking into Yeungkong Chinese forces won control of a fifty-mile coastal stretch leading west to Tupak, which lies east of Luichow Peninsula on the South China Sea. The coastal area now is open to a virtually unopposed landing should American forces choose it for a staging point for supplies to the armies of South China.

West of Luichow Peninsula another 145-mile coastal improvement stretching to the Indo-China frontier is under Chinese control and observers believe the Chinese soon may launch a concerted drive from the west and east that would seal off the Japanese on the Luichow
Continued on Page 2, Column 2

TRAINS CANCELED IN STRICKEN AREA

Traffic Around Hiroshima Is Disrupted — Japanese Still Sift Havoc by Split Atoms

By The United Press.

WASHINGTON, Aug. 6.—Japan, in broadcasts without referring to the atomic bomb dropped on Hiroshima, hinted tonight at the terrific damage it must have caused by announcing that train service in the Hiroshima and other areas had been canceled.

First mention of the bomb came in a Japanese Domei agency dispatch announcing that President Truman and Prime Minister Attlee had disclosed that the new missile had been dropped on Hiroshima.

The Office of War Information began telling the Japanese today what hit them. OWI branch transmitters in San Francisco, Hawaii and Saipan beamed President Truman's announcement on the atomic bomb to Japan.

Edward Barrett, director of the OWI's overseas branch, said that the President's announcement and related information on the atomic bomb will dominate the OWI's normal Japanese transmissions for the next several days.

LONDON, Tuesday, Aug. 7 (UP)—The Japanese Domei news agency, in a dispatch recorded by the British radio, said today that
Continued on Page 7, Column 3

War News Summarized

TUESDAY, AUGUST 7, 1945

One bomb hit Japan on Sunday night, but it struck with the force of 20,000 tons of TNT. Where it landed had been the city of Hiroshima; what is there now has not yet been learned.

The attack, dramatically announced by President Truman sixteen hours after the missile had struck, was with an atomic bomb, a "harnessing of the basic power of the universe," he said. "The force from which the sun draws its power has been loosed against those who brought war to the Far East. And the end is not yet."

Details of the missile are closely guarded, but the 125,000 workers who saw materials pour into their factories never saw anything go out. The bomb is the result of pooling British-American scientific knowledge begun in 1940. "We have spent two billion dollars on the greatest scientific gamble in history —and won," Mr. Truman said, and warned:

"We are now prepared to obliterate more rapidly and completely every productive enterprise the Japanese have above ground in any city. It was to spare the Japanese people from utter destruction that the ultimatum of July 26 was issued at Potsdam. If they do not now accept our terms they may expect a rain of ruin from the air." Secretary of War Stimson detailed the story of research and production and forecast improvements to increase the effectiveness of the "atomic bomb" several times. Congress will be asked to establish a committee to control peacetime use. [13:1.]

Hiroshima was a major military target, a city of 318,000 persons thickly settled around a quartermaster's depot, an embarkation port, armament and airplane parts plants. [All the foregoing in 1:8.]

All production was in the United States at two plants at Oak Ridge, near Knoxville, Tenn., and one at Richland, Wash. A scientific laboratory was maintained in Sante Fe, N. M. [1:6.]

Former Prime Minister Churchill told of Britain's part, including costly attacks on German "heavy water" plants and the race to outstrip the Nazis. He praised American scientific achievement and gave full credit to President Roosevelt and his advisers. [1:5.]

Tokyo made no mention of what had happened to Hiroshima but rail service in that area was canceled. [1:7.]

Okinawa sent out 400 planes that left Tarumizu, on Kyushu's Kagoshima Bay, in flaming wreckage. About 125 "Superforts" bombed Toyokawa naval arsenal by daylight. [1:4; map p. 11.]

Chinese troops have broken into the port of Yeungkong and have cleared a large stretch of the south China coast west of Hong Kong and east of the Luichow Peninsula. [1:3; map P. 2.]

Moscow, moving to implement Potsdam decisions, has resumed diplomatic relations with Finland and Rumania. [11:4.]

The Germans received an opportunity to develop democratic talents when the United States and Great Britain authorized local trade unions and political parties in their zones of occupation. [12:2.]

France is expected to ratify the United Nations Charter and then the Bretton Woods monetary plan in the near future. [13:6.] Marshal Pétain was accused of having asked Hitler for help in regaining France's colonial status. [13:1.]

Argentina has lifted the state of siege in effect since Pearl Harbor. [14:6.]

Turks Talk War if Russia Presses; Prefer Vain Battle to Surrender

By SAM POPE BREWER
By Wireless to THE NEW YORK TIMES.

ANKARA, Turkey, Aug. 6.—Russo-Turkish relations weigh heavy on Turkish minds these days. All leading editors comment today on various aspects of the Russian claims against Turkey.

The Potsdam conference leaves the situation virtually unchanged so far as the Turks can see, but they seem to agree that they would go to war, however hopeless such a war might be, rather than yield before the threat of force. Suggestions from London and Washington that the Russians have been asked to moderate their demands give little reassurance here.

The Potsdam communiqué created more confusion than confidence and the Turks are still trying to decide whether the fact that the conference did not deal with certain specific questions means that it was a failure

Many point out that all the really thorny questions still are unsettled. The Turks probably do not see a relative importance among world problems of Russian demands on Turkey, but point out that the important question of principle is involved. The general and apparently official argument is that the status of the Straits cannot be modified by a bilateral agreement but must be discussed at a conference of the signatories of the Montreux Convention, with America replacing Japan. The signatories were Great Britain, France, Russia, Japan, Turkey, Greece, Rumania, Yugoslavia and Bulgaria.

The grounds for the Russian claims to Kars and Ardahan are not clear, but throughout the Near and Mideast in recent months
Continued on Page 13, Column 1

Reich Exile Emerges as Heroine In Denial to Nazis of Atom's Secret

Special to THE NEW YORK TIMES.

WASHINGTON, Aug. 6.—How Germany twice narrowly missed the secret of harnessing atomic energy by splitting atoms and releasing the most powerful destructive force on earth was recalled today in War Department reports on the atomic bomb. Development of the bomb after more than ten years of experimentation and research marks the climax of the long search for a method of releasing atomic energy is Dr. Lise Meitner, a woman physicist whom the Nazis regarded as "non-Aryan." With her associates, Dr. Otto Hahn and Dr. F. Strassmann, both chemists, she had been working in the Kaiser Wilhelm Institute in Berlin, bombarding uranium atoms with neutrons and then submitting the uranium to chemical analysis.

As the War Department tells the story:

To their amazement, they found in the debris of the smashed uranium atoms one-tenth of 1 per cent of the total energy present in the material. But even one-hundredth of 1 per cent is still the most destructive force by far on this earth."

The principal character in the dramatic story of the long search for a method of releasing atomic energy is Dr. Lise Meitner, a woman physicist whom the Nazis regarded as "non-Aryan." With her associates, Dr. Otto Hahn and Dr. F. Strassmann, both chemists, she had been working in the Kaiser Wilhelm Institute in Berlin, bombarding uranium atoms with neutrons and then submitting the uranium to chemical analysis.

"The energy we are now able to utilize in the atomic bombs, at 100 per cent efficiency, constitutes
Continued on Page 7, Column 1

The New York Times.

LATE CITY EDITION
Sunny with low humidity today.
Partly cloudy, warmer tomorrow.

Temperature Yesterday—Max. 77; Min. 66
Sunrise today, 5:59 A. M.; Sunset, 8:01 P. M.

Copyright, 1945, by The New York Times Company.

VOL. XCIV..No. 31,974. Entered as Second-Class Matter, Postoffice, New York, N. Y. NEW YORK, THURSDAY, AUGUST 9, 1945. THREE CENTS NEW YORK CITY

SOVIET DECLARES WAR ON JAPAN; ATTACKS MANCHURIA, TOKYO SAYS; ATOM BOMB LOOSED ON NAGASAKI

TRUMAN TO REPORT TO PEOPLE TONIGHT ON BIG 3 AND WAR

Half-Hour Speech by Radio to Cover a Wide Range of Problems Facing the World

HE SIGNS PEACE CHARTER

And Thus Makes This Country the First to Complete All Ratification Requirements

By The Associated Press.

WASHINGTON, Aug. 8—President Truman will report to the country on the Potsdam conference over all radio networks at 10 P. M., Eastern war time, tomorrow in a thirty-minute speech.

The Presidential secretary, Charles G. Ross, said today that the speech, which probably would also be short-waved abroad, would go into greater detail than the Big Three statement issued by the Big Three at the close of the meeting July 26.

Mr. Truman worked on the speech today as well as on a mass of other paper work which accumulated during his month-long absence, and signed into full ratification the United Nations Charter.

He held his calling list to a minimum, including brief conferences with Senators Hatch of New Mexico and Kilgore of West Virginia, and Henry L. Stimson, Secretary of War.

The Stimson conference was devoted to further discussion of the atomic bomb.

Associates of the President indicated that his report on the Potsdam conference would probably mention the new and revolutionary bomb used for the first time against Japan.

Full Appraisal May Be Given

A full appraisal of revised conditions, including Russia's declaration of war against Japan, may come in Mr. Truman's broadcast.

Originally the speech was expected to be primarily a report on the Soviet-British-American agreements announced at the end of the Potsdam conference. These dealt mainly with Europe, keeping Germany under strict surveillance, and the writing of peace treaties.

It became known today that Mr. Truman had four or five names under consideration for the vacancy on the Supreme Court, and the decision appeared imminent.

One of the names is that of Senator Austin, Republican, of Vermont, who has been endorsed by his Democratic colleague, Senator Hatch. It was to renew his suggestion that Mr. Austin be appointed to succeed Justice Owen Roberts, who retired, that brought Mr. Hatch to the White House today.

"Of course the President made no commitments," Mr. Hatch told reporters later, "but he definitely is considering both the appointment of a Republican and Senator Austin. Of course that is only a possibility."

Justice Roberts, appointed by President Hoover in 1930, was one of two Republicans in the present makeup of the high court. Chief Justice Harlan F. Stone is the remaining member of that party.

Charter Goes to Archives
Special to THE NEW YORK TIMES.

WASHINGTON, Aug. 8—When President Truman signed today the document by which he ratified the Charter of the United Nations, the United States became the first country to complete its action for bringing the Charter into force.

Several other countries have ratified or taken action with a view to ratification, but no instrument of ratification has yet been received from any of them by the State Department, which is the

Continued on Page 5, Column 3

Foreigners Asked To Stay at Home
Special to THE NEW YORK TIMES.

WASHINGTON, Aug. 8—Discouragement of unessential travel by foreigners to the United States was ordered by the Government today through the State Department.

"The Department of State has always traditionally done everything in its power to promote the travel of citizens of other countries of the Western Hemisphere to the United States," said the announcement. "However, the United States Government is now engaged in a gigantic military operation in deploying forces and supplies from the European theatre to the Pacific area. This tremendous task places an unprecedented burden on the transportation system."

The citizens of other countries should realize the situation, the statement said, and postpone trips to the United States unless they were directly connected with the war.

TAMMANY OUSTS LAST OF REBELS

County Committee Ratifies Executive Group's Action— Meeting Picketed

Without the slightest opposition, the New York County Democratic Committee, popularly known as Tammany, last night ratified the selection of an executive committee on which there remained no opposition to the leadership of Edward V. Loughlin or to the influence in the organization repeatedly exercised by Bert Stand, secretary, and Clarence H. Neal Jr., chairman of its elections committee.

In Brooklyn the Kings County Democratic Committee nominated United States Attorney Miles F. McDonald for District Attorney of Kings County to run for the vacancy by the resignation of William O'Dwyer, Democratic and American Labor party candidate for Mayor. Mr. McDonald, a graduate of Holy Cross College and Fordham Law School, in accepting the nomination, told the members of the committee that he would resign as United States Attorney.

Nearly 2,000 members, the largest number in recent years, attended the Tammany meeting in the Central Commercial High School, 214 East Forty-second Street. All resolutions presented were adopted unanimously by voice vote.

The committee ratified action taken by the executive committee in seating Robert B. Blaikie as leader of the Seventh Assembly District in place of Joseph H. Broderick and Assemblyman Patrick H. Sullivan, in spite of the claim of Mr. Broderick that he had elected a majority of county com-

Continued on Page 17, Column 2

Allies Cut Austria Into Four Zones With Vienna Under Joint Control

By LANSING WARREN
Special to THE NEW YORK TIMES.

WASHINGTON, Aug. 8—A four-power control machinery, including France with the Big Three, has been established in Austria in accordance with an agreement between the Soviet Union, the United States, the United Kingdom and France, it was announced today.

The system resembles the military control arrangement for Germany. It divides Austria into four zones of occupation and provides that Vienna, the capital city, shall be occupied by the forces of the four controlling powers. It creates an Allied Council, consisting of the four military commissioners, who will govern Austria

as a whole. The commissioners will make the decisions for all Austria and will insure a uniformity of action in the different zones.

[The text of the statement on Austria is on Page 11.]

Under the direction of this combined Allied council each military commander will have full authority in his zone. The council will act through the commanders and through an executive committee, which will advise the council on and carry out its decisions.

By this means the agreement seeks to prevent a situation that would separate too rigidly the

Continued on Page 11, Column 5

2D BIG AERIAL BLOW

Japanese Port Is Target in Devastating New Midday Assault

RESULT CALLED GOOD

Foe Asserts Hiroshima Toll Is 'Uncountable' —Assails 'Atrocity'

By W. H. LAWRENCE
By Wireless to THE NEW YORK TIMES.

GUAM, Thursday, Aug. 9—Gen. Carl A. Spaatz announced today that a second atomic bomb had been dropped, this time on the city of Nagasaki, and that crew members reported "good results."

The second use of the new and terrifying secret weapon which wiped out more than 60 per cent of the city of Hiroshima, according to the Japanese radio, killed nearly every inhabitant of that town, occurred at noon Japanese time. The target today was an important industrial and shipping area with a population of about 253,000.

The great bomb, which harnesses the power of the universe to destroy the enemy by concussion, blast and fire, was dropped on the second enemy city about seven hours after the Japanese had received a political "roundhouse punch" in the form of a declaration of war by the Soviet Union.

Vital Transshipment Point

GUAM, Thursday, Aug. 9 (UP)—Nagasaki is vitally important as a port for transshipment of military supplies and the embarkation of troops in support of Japan's operations in China, Formosa, South-east Asia and the Southwest Pacific. It was highly important as a major shipbuilding and repair center for both naval and merchantmen.

The city also included industrial suburbs of Inase and Akunoura on the western side of the harbor, and Urakami. The combined area is nearly double Hiroshima's.

Nagasaki, although only two-thirds as large as Hiroshima in population, is considered more important industrially. With a population now estimated at 253,000, its twelve square miles are jam-packed with the eave-to-eave buildings that won it the name of "sea of roofs."

General Spaatz' communiqué reporting the bombing did not say whether one or more than one "mighty atom" was dropped.

Hiroshima a 'City of Dead'

The Tokyo radio yesterday described Hiroshima as a city of "ruins and dead" "too numerous to be counted," and put forth the claim of Mr. Broderick that he had

Continued on Page 6, Column 3

RED ARMY STRIKES

Foe Reports First Blow by Soviet Forces on Asian Frontier

KEY POINTS BOMBED

Action Believed Aimed to Free Vladivostok Area of Threat

By The United Press.

SAN FRANCISCO, Aug. 8—Russia's mighty Far Eastern Army began hostilities against Japan at 12:10 A. M. Thursday [Russian time], launching a sudden attack along the eastern Soviet-Manchuria border only nine minutes after Moscow's declaration of war became effective, the enemy reported today.

A Kwantung Army headquarters communiqué issued at Changchun [Hsinking] and recorded here reported the attack and also announced that the Red Air Force already was bombing strategic points in Manchurian territory in high Japanese time.

No details of the attack were given, but presumably the Russians would drive west from the attack—part of the Soviet Union's Far Eastern Army of more than 1,000,000 well-equipped troops, who never were called into action against Germany, but remained along the border, a constant threat to Japan.

Although the communiqué did not locate the fighting, it was believed the Russians would strike out as quickly as possible from the Vladivostok region, which is highly

Continued on Page 4, Column 6

CIRCLE OF SPEARHEADS AROUND JAPAN IS COMPLETED

With the entry of the Soviet Union into the war against Japan, the enemy is confronted with armed might from new directions—the north and northeast. Japan was already being bat-tered by American power pressing in from the northeast and the south and by Chinese and British power from the west and southwest. The Russians are reported attacking Manchuria.

385 B-29'S SMASH 4 TARGETS IN JAPAN

Tokyo Arsenal and Aircraft Plant Are Seared—Fukuyama and Yawata Cities Ripped

By The United Press.

GUAM, Thursday, Aug. 9—Gen. Carl A. Spaatz, armed with the confirmed knowledge that his Strategic Air Force possesses in the atomic bomb the most powerful destructive agent devised by man since gunpowder was discovered, sent four separate forces

Continued on Page 2, Column 1

War News Summarized

THURSDAY, AUGUST 9, 1945

Russia has declared war against Japan because that country is the only great power standing in the way of peace. Foreign Commissar Molotoff so informed Ambassador Sato in Moscow yesterday. He said it was in the interests of shortening the war and bringing peace to the world that Moscow acceded to the Allied request to join the war in the Far East and subscribed to the Potsdam ultimatum of July 26. Mr. Molotoff revealed that Japan had asked the Soviet Union to mediate for peace, but that proposal "lost all foundation" when Tokyo rejected the Potsdam demands. [1:8.]

Hostilities were begun nine minutes after the war declaration went into effect at 12:01 this morning, according to Tokyo, when Soviet troops struck along Manchuria's eastern frontier with Siberia. Air attacks, it was said, quickly followed. [1:4.]

President Truman broke the news when he told a hastily called press conference: "Russia has declared war against Japan —that is all." [1:7.] Secretary of State Byrnes declared there was "still time—but little time— for the Japanese to save themselves from the destruction which threatens them" and Mr. Byrnes said the President had convinced Premier Stalin that Russia must enter the war if she was to be responsible for peace. [4:2.]

Congress, jubilant and confident that Russia's aid and the atomic bomb would shorten the war materially, expected to be called back soon. [4:1.]

Japan received another blow when the second atomic bomb to

fall struck Nagasaki on Kyushu. Crew members reported good results. "Practically all living things" in Hiroshima were destroyed beyond recognition by heat and pressure from the first atomic bomb, Tokyo reported. [1:3.] Fires leaped seven rivers. [6:3, with map.]

The Third Fleet, after nine days of silence, sent its carrier planes in a strong attack, still continuing at last reports, against northern Honshu and its score of airfields. [1:6-7.] B-29's hit four Japanese cities in twenty-four hours and mined home waters. [1:5; map P. 2.]

Wuhu Island, at the mouth of the Min River east of Foochow, was captured by the Chinese. [8:2, with map.]

Russia, Britain, France and the United States have signed an agreement for the occupation and administration of Austria similar to that in effect in Germany. Complete separation from Germany, restoration of the 1937 frontiers and return of democratic government were set as Allied goals. [1:2-3; maps P. 11.]

A new code of international law was adopted by the Big Four listing wars of aggression as a crime against peace. [1:5-7.] General de Gaulle and his Cabinet, contrary to the wishes of the Consultative Assembly, will submit the questions of a wider constitutional and governmental responsibility to a referendum on Oct. 21. [12:3.]

President Truman signed the United Nations Charter yesterday. He will discuss the Potsdam Conference and the military situation in a broadcast at 10 o'clock tonight. [1:1.]

U. S. Third Fleet Attacking Targets in Northern Honshu

By ROBERT TRUMBULL
By Wireless to THE NEW YORK TIMES.

GUAM, Thursday, Aug. 9—Admiral William F. Halsey's mighty Third Fleet, including British carriers, is now throwing strong air attacks at northern Honshu in the Japanese home islands, where the enemy has twenty to twenty-five airfields, Fleet Admiral Chester W. Nimitz announced this morning.

Although no specific targets were designated, the communiqué said shipping, air installations and "other military targets" were hit by strong air attacks beginning at dawn.

Today's communiqué broke nine days of silence by the Third Fleet after strikes in the Tokyo area July 30. It is possible that persistent fogs, caused by the warm Japanese Current at this time of year, forced Admiral Halsey to desist during that time from the sea-borne attacks carried out in conjunction with land-based air activity over the empire.

Northern Honshu, an area of 30,669 square miles, a little smaller than Maine and populated by 8,-500,000 persons, has twenty to twenty-five operational although some are small, poorly developed bases and probably are used only for the dispersal of the Japanese air force hiding out in that area.

While the northern Honshu district geographically defined is outside the main military and industrial area of the island there is

Continued on Page 2, Column 3

TRUMAN REVEALS MOVE OF MOSCOW

Announces War Declaration Soon After Russian Action —Capital Is Startled

By FELIX BELAIR Jr.
Special to THE NEW YORK TIMES.

WASHINGTON, Aug. 8—President Truman announced a few minutes after 3 P. M. today that Russia had just declared war on Japan. The dramatic statement, issued with all the casualness of a routine proclamation, came in the shortest White House press conference on record.

Flanked by Secretary of State James M. Byrnes and Admiral William D. Leahy, his Chief of Staff, the President stood before hastily summoned reporters and in steady, matter-of-fact tones declared: "I have only a simple an-

Continued on Page 5, Column 1

4 Powers Call Aggression Crime In Accord Covering War Trials

By CHARLES E. EGAN
By Wireless to THE NEW YORK TIMES.

LONDON, Aug. 8—A new code of international law, defining aggressive warfare as a crime against the world and providing punishment for those who provoke such wars, was announced here today.

By agreement among representatives of the United States, Great Britain, the Soviet Union and France, the legal framework necessary for the trial of the key German and Italian leaders held by the Allies was promulgated this afternoon. The document sets precedents in international law and, in the words of United States Supreme Court Justice Robert H. Jackson, the American representative, "ought to make clear to the

world that those who lead their nations into aggressive war face individual accountability for such acts."

"If we can cultivate in the world the idea that aggressive war-making is the way to a prisoners' dock rather than the way to honors," he said, "we will have accomplished something toward making peace more secure."

[The texts of the War Crimes Committee report and Mr. Jackson's statement are on Page 10.]

The agreement, upon which the international committee has been laboring since June 26, represents

Continued on Page 11, Column 6

RUSSIA AIDS ALLIES

Joins Pacific Struggle After Spurning Foe's Mediation Plea

SEEKS EARLY PEACE

Molotoff Reveals Move Three Months After Victory in Europe

By BROOKS ATKINSON
By Wireless to THE NEW YORK TIMES.

MOSCOW, Aug. 8—Russia declared war on Japan tonight. In a dramatic press conference at 8:30 P. M., Foreign Commissar Vyacheslaff M. Molotoff read the declaration, which was announced to the public at 10 P. M. Moscow time [3 P. M. New York time].

In view of Japan's refusal of the Allies' demand for unconditional surrender, Mr. Molotoff said, the Soviet Union "join the war against Japanese aggression, and thus shorten the duration of the war, reduce the number of victims and facilitate the speedy restoration of universal peace.

"Loyal to its Allied duty," the Foreign Commissar continued, "the Soviet Government has accepted the proposal of the Allies and has joined in the declaration of the Allied Powers of July 26. The Soviet Government considers that this policy is the only means able to bring peace nearer, free the people from further sacrifice and suffering and give the Japanese people the possibility of avoiding the dangers and destruction suffered by Germany after her refusal to capitulate unconditionally."

Closing his concluding statement, Mr. Molotoff declared:

"In view of the above, the Soviet Government declares that from tomorrow, that is Aug. 9, the Soviet Union will consider that it is at war with Japan."

The Soviet Government's declaration comes three months after the victory over Germany, supporting rumors that some months ago the Soviet Government intimated it would join in the war against Japan three months after victory in Europe.

For the first time Mr. Molotoff revealed that the Japanese Government had asked the Soviet Union to mediate for a cessation of hostilities about the middle of June. Japanese Ambassador Naotaka Sato delivered the message, and also a special message from

Continued on Page 5, Column 2

Tokyo 'Flashes' News 3 Hours After Event

By The Associated Press.

SAN FRANCISCO, Aug. 8—Japan's first recorded wireless reaction to Russia's war declaration was a brief factual announcement of that action by the Domei agency in an English-language transmission to Europe.

The Domei account, broadcast three hours and fifty-five minutes after the Moscow announcement, reported:

"Flash! Flash! Tokyo, Aug. 9 —Tass News Agency announced late last night that Foreign Commissar Vyacheslaff M. Molotoff communicated to Naotaka Sato, Japanese Ambassador to Russia, that the Soviet Union would consider itself in a state of war with Japan from Thursday, Aug. 9, according to the Moscow radio recorded here this morning."

By the time the "flash" was read, the state of war already had existed for several hours.

"All the News That's Fit to Print"

The New York Times.

LATE CITY EDITION
Thunderstorms, warm, humid; clear and cooler tonight. Fair tomorrow.
Temperature Yesterday—Max., 84; Min., 71
Sunrise today, 6:02 A. M.; Sunset, 7:52 P. M.

Copyright, 1945, by the New York Times Company.

VOL. XCIV..No. 31,980.   Entered as Second-Class Matter, Postoffice, New York, N. Y.   NEW YORK, WEDNESDAY, AUGUST 15, 1945.   THREE CENTS NEW YORK CITY

JAPAN SURRENDERS, END OF WAR!
EMPEROR ACCEPTS ALLIED RULE;
M'ARTHUR SUPREME COMMANDER;
OUR MANPOWER CURBS VOIDED

HIRING MADE LOCAL

Communities, Labor and Management Will Unite Efforts

6,000,000 AFFECTED

Draft Quotas Cut, Services to Drop 5,500,000 in 18 Months

By LEWIS WOOD
Special to The New York Times.

WASHINGTON, Aug. 14—All manpower controls over employers and workers were abolished tonight, the War Manpower Commission announced, enabling employers to hire men where and when they pleased.

The end of the war threw on the Government the difficult task of trying to readjust perhaps 3,000,000 over workers into new employment. Nevertheless, the WMC said, all its facilities would be used to help workers find new places, with preference going to veterans, displaced migratory war workers and other preferentials.

At the same time President Truman announced that monthly inductions into the Army would be immediately slashed from 80,000 to 50,000, and said 5,000,000 to 5,500,000 men probably would be released from the service within the next year or eighteen months.

The induction rate of 50,000 monthly, the President said, would be sufficient to maintain the occupation forces and allow men of long service overseas to return to their homes.

Under the WMC program, the manpower controls are to be lifted at once and voluntary community action to hurry reconversion will be substituted. In every community, the number of displaced workers and returning veterans will be ascertained in cooperation with local management-labor groups. Full facilities of the United States Employment Service offices will be made available to all employers. Service for veterans will be enlarged.

The WMC program embraced these seven points:

1. All manpower controls are to be lifted at once and in their place voluntary community action to

Continued on Page 13, Column 4

Hirohito on Radio; Minister Ends Life

The Japanese Domei agency said at 11 o'clock last night that Emperor Hirohito had been "graciously pleased to personally read an imperial rescript accepting the Potsdam declaration.

The Domei English-language wireless dispatch, directed to the United States and recorded by the Federal Communications Commission, said that the Emperor had read the rescript over a nation-wide broadcast at noon Wednesday, Tokyo time.

Previously Domei had reported that weeping people had gathered before the Imperial Palace and "bowed to the very ground" in shame.

Japanese War Minister Korechika Anami committed suicide, Domei reported this morning. The wireless dispatch, directed to the American news, said Anami had taken his life as an "official residence" to "atone for his failure in accomplishing his duties as His Majesty's Minister."

A complete story appears on Page 3.

Third Fleet Fells 5 Planes Since End

By The Associated Press.

GUAM, Wednesday, Aug. 15—Japanese aircraft are approaching the Pacific Fleet off Tokyo and are being shot down, Admiral Chester W. Nimitz announced today.

Five enemy planes have been destroyed since noon today, Japanese time, or 11 P. M. EWT. Gen. Douglas MacArthur has been requested to tell the Japanese that American defense measures require the Third Fleet to destroy any Japanese planes approaching United States warships.

GUAM, Wednesday, Aug. 15 (UP)—When Admiral Halsey received word of Japan's capitulation today, he sent this message to his fliers:

"It looks like the war is over, but if any enemy planes appear shoot them down in friendly fashion."

SECRETS OF RADAR GIVEN TO WORLD

Its Role in War and Uses for Peacetime Revealed in Washington and London

By WILLIAM S. WHITE

WASHINGTON, Aug. 14—The great drama of radar, the war's most powerful "secret weapon" until the atomic bomb was devised, was displayed before a world audience today.

The Joint Board on Scientific Information Policy permitted the Office of Scientific Research and Development, the War Department and the Navy Department to tell the story of a device of which millions had known vaguely for two years, a device which at least three times stood between survival of the United States and Great Britain.

It was radar, short for "radio detection and range," that helped the small surviving British air squadrons to beat the German blitz of 1940, thus not only saving the home islands but preserving them as the essential Anglo-American movement forward on June 6, 1944.

It was radar, which "sees through the heaviest fog and the blackest night," that more than any other factor broke in 1942 the German submarine attack in the Atlantic which was threatening to starve and strangle the British homeland.

And it was radar that permitted the remnants of the blasted United States Pacific Fleet to stay alive

Continued on Page 16, Column 2

ALL CITY 'LETS GO'

Hundreds of Thousands Roar Joy After Victory Flash Is Received

TIMES SQ. IS JAMMED

Police Estimate Crowd in Area at 2,000,000— Din Overwhelming

By ALEXANDER FEINBERG

Five days of waiting, of rumor, intimation, fact, distortion—five agonizing days following the first indication of a Japanese surrender, days of alternately rising hopes and fears—came to an end for New York, as for the nation and the world, a moment or two after seven o'clock last night. And the metropolis exploded its emotions, harnessed for the most part during the day, with atomic force.

"Official — Truman announces Japanese surrender."

These were the magic words, flashed on the moving electric sign of the Times Tower, at 7:03 P. M. that touched off an unparalleled demonstration in Times Square, packed with half a million persons.

The victory roar that greeted the announcement beat upon the eardrums until it numbed the senses. For twenty minutes wave after wave of that joyous roar surged forth.

Restraint was thrown to the winds. The'ss in the crowds in the streets tossed hats, boxes and flags into the air. From those leaning perilously out of the windows of office buildings and hotels came a shower of paper, confetti, streamers. Men and women embraced—there were no strangers in New York yesterday. Some were hilarious, others cried softly.

By 7:30 P. M. the crowd in the Square had risen to 750,000 persons; by 8:45 it had swelled to 800,000 and the number continued to rise. People were packed solidly between Forty-third Street and Forty-fifth Street. Individual movement was virtually impossible; one moved not in the crowd but with it.

At 10 P. M. Chief Inspector John J. O'Connell estimated that 2,000,000 persons were in the Times Square area from Fortieth to Fifty-second Street, between Sixth and Eighth Avenues. This conservative estimate placed police officials aghast at that hour people were still pouring into the Square from subways, buses and on foot. Those at the north end of the

Continued on Page 5, Column 1

Two-Day Holiday Is Proclaimed; Stores, Banks Close Here Today

By The Associated Press

WASHINGTON, Aug. 14—Tomorrow and Thursday are days off for Government workers and holidays for pay purposes for workers in general.

And V-J Day, when it comes, will be a premium pay day, too. President Truman announced both rulings tonight.

He directed agency heads throughout the Government to cut their forces down to a bare skeleton staff Aug. 15 and 16 and not to charge the two days against the employes' annual leave. He said it was in "inadequate" recognition of the four-year efforts and "one of the hardest working groups of war workers."

For other workers under wage control, Wednesday and Thursday count like Christmas and the few other accepted holidays for purposes of overtime pay and in figuring the number of days worked

Continued on Page 6, Column 7

PRESIDENT ANNOUNCING SURRENDER OF JAPAN

Mr. Truman reading the message in the White House. Seated are Admiral William D. Leahy, Secretary of State James F. Byrnes and former Secretary of State Cordell Hull. Standing (left to right) are Maj. Gen. Philip Fleming, head of the Federal Works Administration; William H. Davis, Economic Stabilizer; John W. Snyder, Reconversion Director; James Forrestal, Secretary of the Navy; Fred Vinson, Secretary of the Treasury; Tom Clark, Attorney General, and Lewis Schwellenbach, Secretary of Labor.
Associated Press Wirephoto

PETAIN CONVICTED, SENTENCED TO DIE

Jurors Recommend Clemency Because of His Age—Long Indictment Upheld

By G. H. ARCHAMBAULT
By Wireless to The New York Times.

PARIS, Wednesday, Aug. 15—Marshal Henri-Philippe Pétain was convicted at 4:15 A. M. today of intelligence with the enemy and sentenced to death. Because of his age—the former head of the Vichy regime is 89—the jury expressed the hope that the death sentence might not be carried out.

Guards had to arouse Pétain in

Continued on Page 15, Column 5

Terms Will Reduce Japan To Kingdom Perry Visited

By JAMES B. RESTON

WASHINGTON, Aug. 14—The Allied terms of surrender will not only demobilize and demilitarize Japan but also deprive her of 80 per cent of the territory and nearly one-third of the population she held when she attacked Pearl Harbor. Thus these terms, already approved by President Truman and our major Allies, will not only destroy the vast empire she conquered in the first eighteen months of this war but also reduce her to little more than the territory she occupied when Commodore Perry introduced her to the western world in 1853.

The main terms of surrender, as

Continued on Page 11, Column 2

TREATY WITH CHINA SIGNED IN MOSCOW

Complete Agreement Reached With Chungking on All Points at Issue, Russians Say

By Cable to The New York Times.

LONDON, Aug. 14—The Soviet Union and China have signed a treaty of friendship and alliance, the Moscow radio announced tonight, and have reached "full agreement on all other questions of common interest."

The broadcast said the treaty and "other agreements" would be published shortly after they had been ratified by the two countries.

These are the first fruits of the talks that have been proceeding in

Continued on Page 6, Column 3

Cruiser Sunk, 1,196 Casualties; Took Atom Bomb Cargo to Guam

Special to The New York Times.

WASHINGTON, Aug. 14—The American heavy cruiser Indianapolis was sunk by enemy action in the Philippine Sea with 1,196 casualties, every man aboard, the Navy announced today.

The 9,950-ton ship left San Francisco on July 16 on a special high-speed run to deliver essential atomic bomb materials to Guam. The cargo was delivered. The cruiser was lost after having left Guam.

The sinking, which took one of the Navy's heaviest tolls of lives since Pearl Harbor, was disclosed a few minutes before President Truman announced Japan's surrender.

Casualties included five Navy dead, including one officer; 946

Continued on Page 10, Column 8

World News Summarized

WEDNESDAY, AUGUST 15, 1945

World War II became a page in history last night.

President Truman announced at 7 P. M. that he had received the Japanese reply to the Allied note of last Saturday and that he deemed it full acceptance of the Potsdam declaration of July 26. The Chief Executive said that the Japanese surrender would be made to Gen. Douglas MacArthur in his capacity as Supreme Allied Commander in Chief. Allied military commanders were ordered to stop fighting, but the proclamation of V-J Day will await the signing of the peace treaties. [1:7-8.]

Simultaneously with the President's announcement, Admiral Nimitz flashed a "cease fire" order to all units under his command. [6:2-4.]

The official announcement that the Japanese sneak attack on Pearl Harbor had resulted three years and 250 days later in the inglorious end of the Japanese Empire touched off unrestrained celebrations throughout the Allied world. Here in New York the flash on the moving electric sign on The Times Tower, "Official—Truman announces Japanese surrender," signaled a wild demonstration. [1:2.]

Emperor Hirohito announced the Japanese surrender to his people in his first broadcast to the nation. Weeping Japanese gathered outside the Emperor's palace to bow to the ground in

their shame because their "efforts were not enough." [3:2.]

The fury of Allied military might continued to strike at Japanese up to the very last. Even as the Tokyo radio announced that the Japanese reply to the Allied note of surrender was on its way, our Superfortresses were winging from the Marianas to the Japanese homeland. More than 1,000 planes struck Honshu with 6,000 tons of bombs in a fourteen-hour assault ending early yesterday. [6:6; Pacific area map P. 8.]

The Red Army unleashed fierce new attacks. Russian armored forces raced ninety-three miles unchecked across western Manchuria toward Harbin and other Soviet columns scored new gains all along the 2,300-mile front. [6:6; Pacific area map P. 8.]

The Soviet Union signed "a treaty of friendship and alliance" with China after an agreement had been reached between the two nations on all questions of common interest. [1:6.]

Chinese Communists informed the Generalissimo that they refused to accept his command to remain at their posts. [6:1.]

A French jury sentenced Marshal Pétain to death. [1:4.]

YIELDING UNQUALIFIED, TRUMAN SAYS

Japan Is Told to Order End of Hostilities, Notify Allied Supreme Commander and Send Emissaries to Him

MACARTHUR TO RECEIVE SURRENDER

Formal Proclamation of V-J Day Awaits Signing of Those Articles—Cease-Fire Order Given to the Allied Forces

By ARTHUR KROCK
Special to The New York Times.

WASHINGTON, Aug. 14—Japan today unconditionally surrendered the hemispheric empire taken by force and held almost intact for more than two years against the rising power of the United States and its allies in the Pacific war.

The bloody dream of the Japanese military caste vanished in the text of a note to the Four Powers accepting the terms of the Potsdam Declaration of July 26, 1945, which amplified the Cairo Declaration of 1943.

Like the previous items in the surrender correspondence, today's Japanese document was forwarded through the Swiss Foreign Office at Berne and the Swiss Legation in Washington. The note of total capitulation was delivered to the State Department by the Legation Charge d'Affaires at 6:10 P. M., after the third and most anxious day of waiting on Tokyo, the anxiety intensified by several premature or false reports of the finale of World War II.

Orders Given to the Japanese

The Department responded with a note to Tokyo through the same channel, ordering the immediate end of hostilities by the Japanese, requiring that the Supreme Allied Commander—who, the President announced, will be Gen. Douglas MacArthur—be notified of the date and hour of the order, and instructing that emissaries of Japan be sent to him at once—at the time and place selected by him—"with full information of the disposition of the Japanese forces and commanders."

President Truman summoned a special press conference in the Executive offices at 7 P. M. He handed to the reporters three texts.

The first—the only one he read aloud—was that he had received the Japanese note and deemed it full acceptance of the Potsdam Declaration, containing no qualification whatsoever; that arrangements would be made for the formal signing of the "earliest possible moment"; that the Japanese surrender would be made to General MacArthur in his capacity as Supreme Allied Commander in Chief; that Allied military commanders had been instructed to cease hostilities, but that the formal proclamation of V-J Day must await the formal signing.

The text ended with the Japanese note, in which the Four Powers (the United States, Great Britain, China and Russia) were officially informed that the Emperor of Japan had issued an imperial rescript of surrender, was prepared to guarantee the necessary signatures to the terms as prescribed by the Allies, and had instructed all his commanders to cease active operations, to surrender all

Continued on Page 2, Column 2

MacArthur Begins Orders to Hirohito

By Wireless to The New York Times.

MANILA, Wednesday, Aug. 15—Gen. Douglas MacArthur in his first action as Allied Supreme Commander today directed Emperor Hirohito and the Japanese Government to furnish a radio station in the Tokyo area for "continuous use in handling radio communications between this headquarters and our headquarters." The message, sent in the clear, called for the "earliest practicable" arrangements to end hostilities.

"All the News That's Fit to Print"

The New York Times.

NEWS INDEX, PAGE 33, THIS SECTION

VOL. XCIV..No. 31,998.

LATE CITY EDITION

Clearing early today; cooler. Clear and cool tomorrow.
Temperature Yesterday—Max., 88; Min., 72
Sunrise today, 6:32 A. M.; Sunset, 7:29 P. M.

Section 1

NEW YORK, SUNDAY, SEPTEMBER 2, 1945.

Copyright, 1945, by The New York Times Company.

Including Magazine and Book Review

TEN CENTS

New York City and Suburban Areas (In Elsewhere)

JAPAN SURRENDERS TO ALLIES, SIGNS RIGID TERMS ON WARSHIP; TRUMAN SETS TODAY AS V-J DAY

HOLIDAY TRAFFIC NEAR 1941 LEVEL; 'GAS' IS PLENTIFUL

Exodus From City Is Greatest Since Pre-War Days but Congestion Is Avoided

GOOD WEATHER PROMISED

Near-by Resorts Do Capacity Business—3 Persons Die in Queens Accidents

America's millions, deprived since 1941 of the chance to cruise the highways of their nation, hit the road in traditional Labor Day week-end style yesterday.

There was a plentiful supply of gasoline, the sun shone warm out of blue skies, and everyone felt free from war worries. This combined to roll up traffic that continued heavy all day.

The temperature yesterday reached 88 degrees at 3:30 P. M. with the humidity at 52 per cent. The all-time high for the date was set in 1926 with 92.5 degrees and the low in 1872 with 51.

Many Cars Come Into City

Travel in the city was two-way. As cars streamed out of the city over bridges, on ferries and through tunnels, out-of-towners poured in. The main idea for Labor Day seemed to be change of scenery.

Thousands of automobiles, many of them looking as though they had just been taken off the jacks for the first time in years, formed a continuous procession along the main highways leading up-State, out on Long Island and to the South Jersey shore.

The Port of New York Authority reported that 60,400 automobiles had crossed the George Washington Bridge into New Jersey. Forty-five thousand cars passed through the Holland Tunnel during the sixteen hours preceding 6 o'clock last night. Lincoln Tunnel police said traffic was heavier than usual.

Few serious accidents were reported. "Maybe it's because the cars just don't have the pep," remarked a Westchester County policeman.

Slights along the parkways bore out his contention. Many cars became pathetically silent as their drivers resignedly hauled them over to the side of the road to patch up tires or to fume over engine repairs.

Gasoline Supplies Abundant

Assured of as much gasoline as they wanted, motorists traveled leisurely and did not cause congestion. Filling station operators perceived their heaviest workout in years. Station operators estimated that demands for gasoline ranged from 10 to 30 per cent over last week-end, but they reported there was no difficulty in obtaining supplies.

The Cities Service Oil Company said it was having difficulty in meeting orders for premium gasoline, ordinarily accounting for 25 per cent of sales, as the supply was limited, but no company reported shortages of non-premium gasoline. No motorist was forced to stay in town because of lack of fuel.

Trains, buses and airlines were crowded, as they have been all through the war. The airlines re-

Continued on Page 36, Column 2

Times Sq. Takes V-J News Quietly

Times Square throngs, which had greeted Japanese capitulation explosively last month, took the formal signing of terms in much calmer fashion last night.

Two hundred policemen, including twenty-five mounted patrolmen, who had been assigned to the area in case of another outburst of feeling, reported that the street crowds took the flashing of the bulletin from Times Tower at 10:04 P. M. with a few cheers and good-natured remarks, and did not attempt to start a celebration.

In numbers the crowd was no larger than an average Saturday night, and of the persons present perhaps half or more were out-of-town visitors here for the Labor Day week-end, the police estimated. Other parts of the city were similarly quiet.

Mayor La Guardia had said earlier that the people "have had their big time and are satisfied." He decided not to hold a celebration in Central Park today as had been planned.

PRESIDENT STRESSES LABOR DAY OF PEACE

But He Warns That After Six Holidays of Hostilities Great New Problems Lie Ahead

Special to The New York Times.

WASHINGTON, Sept. 1—President Truman hailed the first Labor Day of peace in six years today and declared a grateful world would always remember the workers and all free nations for their contribution to victory.

Secretary Forrestal and J. A. Krug, chairman of the War Production Board, also lauded the men and women of labor, and Philip Murray, chairman of the Congress of Industrial Organizations, told a radio audience that America's vast war plant must be put to work on peacetime products which would give prosperity unlimited to this country.

Mr. Truman's statement said that six years ago today the workers of the United States, and of the world, awoke to a Labor Day in a world at war, and added:

"We in the United States had two years of grace, but the issue was squarely joined at that hour, as we now know. There was to be no peace until tyranny had been outlawed.

"Today we stand on the threshold of a new world. We must do our part in making this world what it should be, a world in which the bigotries of race and class and creed shall not be permitted to warp the souls of men.

"We enter upon an era of great problems, but to live is to face problems. Our men and women did not falter in the task of saving freedom. They will not falter now in the task of making freedom

Continued on Page 24, Column 3

HAILS ERA OF PEACE

President Calls On U.S. to Stride On Toward a World of Good-Will

SALUTES HEROIC DEAD

Cautions Jubilant Nation Hard Jobs Ahead Need Same Zeal as War

Text of the President's address proclaiming V-J Day, P. 4.

By WILLIAM S. WHITE

WASHINGTON, Sept. 1—President Truman, in remembrance of all who have fallen and in an appeal to all Americans to go forward now in hope and fraternity toward "a new and better world of peace and international good-will," tonight solemnly proclaimed tomorrow as V-J Day.

The moment that he began to speak was in the official and historical sense, the first moment of peace this country had known since a December day nearly four years ago, when, at a sudden, a harsh and an incredible blow the whole of the Pacific world went into flames.

Into the human calendar of great American holidays, like the Fourth of July and the Eleventh of November, the President thus entered another date, the Second of September, although it does not technically signify the end of the "duration" and will have no basis as a legal end of the war. The termination of hostilities, for purposes of computing military service, for setting the limit to war agencies and for all other like formalities, will be set only by final decision of Congress.

Japanese Surrender Signaled

But Mr. Truman's speech was a speech to the heart of a country that had had the skill to make the atomic bomb and could now "use the same skill and energy and determination to overcome all the difficulties ahead," rather than to be the keepers of its books of law.

It was notice from the White House, so long awaited, that nearly four years of war, a struggle of sacrificial grandeur such as the United States had never known, had at last come to an end, and that the terrible ledger opened at Pearl Harbor had now been balanced and closed.

The President spoke in this mood, a mood of valedictory and of dedication, as he proclaimed "this . . . victory of more than arms alone . . . this . . . victory of liberty over tyranny." He had just received the signal from across the world that the Japanese had signed, aboard the great battleship Missouri, the last, humiliat-

Continued on Page 4, Column 1

JAPANESE FOREIGN MINISTER SIGNING SURRENDER ARTICLES

Mamoru Shigemitsu (right, seated), on behalf of Emperor Hirohito, affixes his signature to document as Gen. Douglas MacArthur (left) and Lieut. Gen. Richard K. Sutherland (center) look on during ceremony aboard the Missouri in Tokyo Bay.

Associated Press Wirephoto (via Navy Radio from U.S.S. Iowa)

BYRNES FORESEES A PEACEFUL JAPAN

Says People Are Expected to Force Development—World Amity Vital, Hull Warns

Special to The New York Times.

WASHINGTON, Sept. 1—Secretary of State James F. Byrnes declared tonight that with Japan's surrender we have entered the second phase of our war—"what might be called the spiritual disarmament of Japan, to make them want peace instead of wanting war."

The intention of this Govern-

Continued on Page 5, Column 1

Japan's Surrender Ordered Over Militarist Opposition

By FRANK L. KLUCKHORN

TOKYO, Sept. 1—In the rubble of this once-proud imperial capital the story of how the Japanese Army opposed the surrender and how the Emperor made the final decision to capitulate after having heard the opinions of all his advisers, and how War Minister Korechika Anami had committed suicide has unfolded today by one of a handful of those in a position to know without bias what occurred.

It was also learned how the Japanese reacted step by step to wartime developments and how propaganda that Japan could win had been continued to the last moment, thus leaving the industrious long-

Continued on Page 7, Column 1

World News Summarized

SUNDAY, SEPTEMBER 2, 1945

The rulers of Japan, who set the Pacific ablaze nearly four years ago with their surprise attack on Pearl Harbor and hoped to culminate that assault with a peace dictated in the White House, formally signed their unconditional surrender to the Allied powers in Tokyo Bay. Foreign Minister Shigemitsu signed the historic document for his country in the shadow of the sixteen-inch gun muzzles of the battleship Missouri. General MacArthur, who signed in behalf of the Allies, said mankind hoped a better world would result from the solemn occasion. [1:8; map P. 12.]

President Truman proclaimed today as V-J Day. He urged the nation to observe the day of victory over Japan in a spirit of dedication and as a symbol of "victory of liberty over tyranny." He also asked his countrymen to remember "our departed gallant leader, Franklin D. Roosevelt." [1:1.]

Japan's decision to surrender was dictated by Emperor Hirohito after he had overruled a strong faction within the Cabinet and the army that wanted to keep on with the war in the belief that the Japanese could defeat an invasion of the homeland, according to well-informed observers in Tokyo. [1:5-6.]

Medical "experiments" recalling medieval sadism were carried out on dying American prisoners of war by young Japanese Army doctors, two American physicians interned with their compatriots said aboard a United States hospital ship. [1:6-7.]

With the Foreign Ministers' Council scheduled to meet in London next week to begin consideration of peace terms, it was learned that a serious division of opinion over the disposition of the Italian colonies had developed in the State Department. [1:8.] Former Secretary of State Stettinius said in London that the development of the atomic bomb emphasized the need for "the speedy creation of the United Nations Organization to keep the peace of the world" and predicted that as soon as the organization began functioning it would provide a military staff to deal with the use of atomic bombs, as well as all other types of force, in preserving peace. [12:3.]

WAR COMES TO END

Articles of Capitulation Endorsed by Countries in Pacific Conflict

M'ARTHUR SEES PEACE

Emperor Orders Subjects to Obey All Commands Issued by General

The texts of the surrender documents and statements, P. 3.

By The Associated Press.

ABOARD THE U. S. S. MISSOURI in Tokyo Bay, Sunday, Sept. 2—Japan surrendered formally and unconditionally to the Allies today in a twenty-minute ceremony which ended just as the sun burst through low-hanging clouds as a shining symbol to a ravaged world now done with war.

[A United Press dispatch said the leading Japanese delegate signed the articles at 9:03 A. M. Sunday, Tokyo time, and that General MacArthur signed them at 9:07 A. M.]

Twelve signatures, requiring only a few minutes to inscribe on the articles of surrender, ended the bloody Pacific conflict.

On behalf of Emperor Hirohito, Foreign Minister Mamoru Shigemitsu signed for the Government and Gen. Yoshijiro Umezu for the Imperial General Staff.

MacArthur Voices Peace Hope

Gen. Douglas MacArthur, who accepted on behalf of the United Nations, declaring:

"It is my earnest hope and indeed the hope of all mankind that from this solemn occasion a better world shall emerge out of the blood and carnage of the past."

One by one the Allied representatives stepped forward and signed the document that blighted Japan's dream of empire built on bloodshed and tyranny.

First was Admiral Chester W. Nimitz for the United States, then the representatives of China, the United Kingdom, the Soviet, Australia, Canada, France, the Netherlands and New Zealand.

The stage of the United States, Britain, the Soviet and China fluttered from the veranda deck of the famed superdreadnaught, polished and scrubbed as never before. More than 100 high-ranking military and naval officers watched.

Pledges Justice and Tolerance

"As Supreme Commander for the Allied powers," General MacArthur told the Japanese, "I announce it my firm purpose, in the tradition of the countries I represent, to proceed in the discharge of my responsibilities with justice and tolerance, while taking all necessary dispositions to insure that the terms of surrender are fully, promptly and faithfully complied with."

All through this dramatic half hour, only those aboard the battleship knew of what was taking place, because the Missouri has no broadcasting facilities.

But recordings were rushed to the near-by communications ship Ancon, and the solemn words of General MacArthur beginning the ceremony—"We are gathered here, representatives of the major warring powers"—were flashed around the world.

The Japanese representatives were present at the command of Emperor Hirohito contained in a proclamation issued by order of the Supreme Allied Commander.

The Emperor further commanded his officials "to issue general orders to the military and naval forces in accordance with the direction of the Supreme Commander.

Continued on Page 2, Column 3

TOKYO AIDES WEEP AS GENERAL SIGNS

Imperial Staff Chief Hastily Scrawls His Signature— Shigemitsu Is Anxious

By The Associated Press.

ABOARD U. S. S. MISSOURI in Tokyo Bay, Sunday, Sept. 2—The solemn surrender ceremony on this battleship today, marking the first defeat in Japan's 2,600-year-old semi-legendary history, required only a few minutes as twelve signatures were affixed to the articles.

Surrounded by the might of the United States Navy and Army, and under the eyes of the American and British commanders they so ruthlessly defeated in the Philippines and Malaya, the Japanese representatives quietly made the marks on paper that ended the bloody Pacific conflict.

The Japanese delegation came aboard at 8:55 A. M., 7:55 P. M. Saturday, E. W. T., as scheduled. They reached the Missouri in personnel speed boats flying the American flag.

Foreign Minister Mamoru Shigemitsu led the delegation. He climbed stiffly up the ladder and limped forward on his right leg, which is artificial. He was wounded by a bomb tossed by a Korean terrorist in Shanghai many years ago.

On behalf of Emperor Hirohito, Mr. Shigemitsu signed first for

Continued on Page 9, Column 1

U. S. CHIEFS DIVIDED ON ITALY'S COLONIES

State Department Split Over Russia and Influence Zones Is Projected by Issue

By JAMES B. RESTON

Special to The New York Times.

WASHINGTON, Sept. 1—A fundamental issue has developed in the Department of State over the future of the Italian colonies, particularly Eritrea, Libya and Italian Somaliland.

The issue is whether these colonies should go back to Italy as part of her sovereign territory, be taken from her and administered by the United States, Britain, France and the Soviet Union under the United Nations Organization or be administered by a neutral international commission under the United Nations.

The major powers that defeated Germany are soon to start drafting

Continued on Page 10, Column 1

PRESIDENT STRESSES LABOR DAY OF PEACE

Public Gets Big Army Food Stocks; Whipping Cream Is Freed of Bans

Special to The New York Times.

WASHINGTON, Sept. 1—The national food situation continued its steady improvement today as the Department of Agriculture, with four orders, increased the supplies of butter, canned salmon and ice cream and signaled the return of whipping cream.

This action was a direct consequence of the sharp reduction of military requirements of these foods. With the discontinuance of butter purchases by the armed forces, the Department explained, it is now possible to revoke the limitations on the sale of heavy cream and the use of butter fat in the production of all frozen desserts. Both these rulings will make

whipping cream and ice cream of a higher butter fat content readily available.

In a simultaneous direction, the agency ordered released for civilian use all butter currently held by creameries and receivers for the armed forces and other Government buyers. Although as much as 20,000,000 pounds of butter may be returned to civilian consumers under this ruling, ration values will not be changed, it was indicated.

"At the time ration point values were established for September, the Office of Price Administration recognized the possibility that

Continued on Page 38, Column 1

Enemy Tortured Dying Americans With Sadist Medical 'Experiments'

By ROBERT TRUMBULL

By Wireless to The New York Times.

ABOARD THE HOSPITAL SHIP BENEVOLENCE, in Tokyo Bay, Sept. 1—Seriously ailing American prisoners at Shinagawa, the only hospital serving 8,000 prisoners of war held in the Tokyo area, were guinea pigs for fantastic experiments recalling the sadistic excesses of the middle ages, Drs. Mack L. Gottlieb and Harold W. Keschner, both of New York, told this correspondent today.

Both doctors are recuperating aboard this ship after their rescue from Shinagawa on Wednesday by a special Navy evacuation mission headed by Comdr. Harold A.

minnesota and now Assistant Chief of Staff and Flag Secretary to Admiral William F. Halsey, commander of the Third Fleet.

[In an interview in Tokyo the Japanese Army doctor to whom some of these practices were charged confirmed the cruel treatment of American prisoners.]

Dr. Gottlieb, who had his home and office at 207 East Forty-fourth Street, was a naval officer captured at Guam. Dr. Keschner, of 451 West End Avenue, was taken with an Army force in the Philippines. Both are in good physical

Continued on Page 14, Column 1

"All the News That's Fit to Print"

The New York Times.

LATE CITY EDITION
Cloudy with showers today. Considerable cloudiness tomorrow.
Temperature—Max., 75; Min., 62

Copyright, 1945, by The New York Times Company.

VOL. XCIV..No. 32,011.

NEW YORK, SATURDAY, SEPTEMBER 15, 1945.

THREE CENTS NEW YORK CITY

M'ARTHUR PLEDGES IRON RULE, REBUKES CRITICS ON POLICY; CURBS DOMEI NEWS AGENCY

FIRM GRIP MAPPED

General Says All Terms of Surrender Will Be Imposed on Japan

HOMMA READY TO GIVE UP

Japanese Premier Asks U. S. to 'Forget Pearl Harbor' in Interests of Peace

By GEORGE E. JONES
By Wireless to The New York Times.

YOKOHAMA, Sept. 15, Saturday.—Gen. Douglas MacArthur took cognizance yesterday of criticism of his so-called "soft policy" toward Japan. In an extraordinary statement defining his problems and policies, he emphasized that surrender terms imposed on the beaten empire would be carried out in a stern, uncompromising fashion.

At the same time the Supreme Commander for the Allied Powers admitted that it was difficult for him to "exercise that degree of patience which is unquestionably demanded if the long-time policies which have been decreed are to be successfully accomplished without repercussions which would be detrimental to the well being of the world."

This was General MacArthur's rebuttal to the criticism, particularly that of the American press, of his policy of working to the fullest possible extent through the existing Japanese Government.

Domei Curbed, Put Under Censor

General MacArthur's patience evidently had worn thin as he ordered the suspension of Domei, the Japanese news agency, which had been foremost in propagating stories of American "brutalities" toward Japanese civilians.

Today Supreme Headquarters rescinded the suspension and permitted Domei to reopen at noon after a shutdown of nearly eighteen hours.

Henceforth, however, Domei must use for its foreign news only what it receives from the United States Office of War Information broadcasts and its local news will be subjected to strict American censorship. Presumably the censorship will be applied also to local news matter gathered by the Japanese newspapers.

This backdown from General MacArthur's original order ended a news drought for Tokyo's large papers that sent them scurrying to American press associations and syndicates seeking to arrange for reception of foreign news from American sources.

The shutdown order was rescinded after conversations between representatives in which the Japanese agency was reminded sharply that Japan was a defeated nation and that Domei would take its orders from the occupation authorities without "ifs" and "buts." General MacArthur has been placing great stress on the tendency of the Japanese press, particularly Domei, to assume that Japan enjoyed equal status with other nations and as such considered prerogatives of sovereignty in dealings with the American occupation forces.

Still in First Phase of Action

In effect General MacArthur stated that we were still in the first phase, which is primarily one of military considerations—that of deploying sufficient American troops onto Japanese soil and of mobilizing Japanese forces. He promised that when this phase had been completed "no one need have any doubt about the prompt, complete, entire fulfillment of the terms of the surrender."

He added that Japan was in a state of utter collapse industrially and militarily and said that her existing structure was controlled completely by the American occupation forces. This amounts in effect to no explanation of his present policy in terms of promises for a stern policy in the future when military conditions permit.

[Lieut. Gen. Masaharu Homma, held responsible by General MacArthur for the Bataan death march, arrived in Tokyo and said he was preparing to surrender himself, The Associated Press reported.

[Earlier Premier Prince Naru-

Continued on Page 4, Column 3

Big 5 Invite Other Powers To Present Views on Italy

Evatt Is Credited With Winning Voice for Smaller Allies on Peace Treaty—Parley Picks Up Speed, Forms Secretariat

By HERBERT L. MATTHEWS
By Cable to The New York Times.

LONDON, Sept. 14—The Council of Foreign Ministers of the five great powers, pushed by internal and external pressure, suddenly came to its majority today as a full-fledged organization to settle the peace problems of the world.

The Foreign Ministers began their detailed discussions of a treaty with Italy and found surprisingly easy going. The Council called in a number of other powers for discussions, established a joint secretariat to carry on through the coming months and in general adopted methods of procedure that show that this body, which began as a council of five powers, is really a world organization.

If any one man deserves the credit for forcing this issue so quickly it is the fiery Australian Minister for External Affairs, Dr. Herbert V. Evatt, who came to London last week brimming with determination that the smaller powers would have their say, and today's development was his triumph. The essential points were set forth in two communiqués, one from the Council and the other from Dr. Evatt himself.

The first communiqué begins by saying that there were two meetings today, one presided over by Foreign Minister Wang Shih-chieh of China and the other by Secretary of State James F. Byrnes of the United States, in accordance with the rotation decided upon on the first day. Encouraged by their progress today, the Foreign Ministers decided to forget about the traditional British week-end and to work tomorrow and perhaps Sunday.

"The Council began its discussion of terms for the peace settlement with Italy," the communiqué said. "It was agreed all the United Nations at war with Italy would be invited to submit, if they wished, their views in writing on this subject. It was also decided that the president of the session,

Continued on Page 7, Column 4

POLAND DENOUNCES VATICAN CONCORDAT

Asserts Holy See Violated It —Arrests and Deportations of Clerics Reported

By Wireless to The New York Times.

LONDON, Sept. 14—The Warsaw Government has denounced the concordat that has governed relations between Poland and the Holy See since 1925, it became known here today. The decision was taken on Sept. 4, with fifteen Cabinet Ministers voting in favor against.

It also was reported in Catholic circles here that two Polish priests were arrested this week on charges that are not known. They are Dr. Albert Stajer, who was attached to Cardinal Hlond's cathedral in Poznan, and Father Kuhn, a German priest of the Danzig diocese. Dr. Stajer will be put on trial shortly. Father Kuhn already has been sentenced to death.

These arrests followed alleged deportations to Russia of the Bishop of Luck and to Central Poland of the Archbishop of Vilna and the arrest of the Bishop of Danzig, all of which were reported by Polish circles in London opposed to Warsaw.

In an article on religious conditions in Poland, the Catholic weekly Tablet will say tomorrow that these events "confirm the view already forced upon us 'that the present limited freedom enjoyed by Polish Catholics is only temporary and will end when it is decided that Japan enjoyed equal status with other nations' but that 'the occupation order was rescinded.'"

Father Piotr Kruszynski, Vicar General of the diocese of Lublin,

Continued on Page 9, Column 2

ARGENTINE REPLY FOUND MISLEADING

Many Errors Shown in Answer to U. S. Charges of Failure to Live Up to Obligations

By ARNALDO CORTESI

BUENOS AIRES, Sept. 14—On Tuesday the Foreign Ministry published a 10,000-word document to prove that the Argentine Government had complied faithfully with the commitments it assumed when it signed the final Act of Chapultepec. A careful study of this document shows that it contains so many hiatuses and makes so many erroneous or misleading statements that it can confidently be described as a very poor attempt to justify the Government's far from brilliant position.

Far from proving that Argentina carried out her commitments, it convicts the Government of the most astonishing laxness in almost all matters of fundamental importance. Since the Argentine document was provoked by former Assistant Secretary of State Nelson Rockefeller's charges that Argentina had not taken the measures necessary to eliminate Axis firms, it perhaps would be best to start from this point.

The Argentine Government substantially confirms Mr. Rockefeller's figures. To date the Government has eliminated only two small subsidiaries of the Thyssen-Lametal Company and two German banks, while six German insurance companies are in the process of liquidation. Bids also have been requested for the sale of merchandise belonging to about 10

Continued on Page 10, Column 1

Chinese Communists Claim Gains Ranging From Yangtze to Peiping

By TILLMAN DURDIN
By Wireless to The New York Times.

CHUNGKING, China, Sept. 14—Sweeping territorial gains from the Yangtze Valley to areas north and west of Peiping are claimed for the Communist armies in a communiqué issued today from Communist headquarters in Chungking. The communiqué summarized Communist army activities of the last week.

The Communists claim to have "fairly complete control of everything but points on the railways" in an area stretching from Kalgan to the mouth of the Yangtze River and from the Shantung Peninsula to east of Shansi and including northern and northwestern Shansi. The communiqué said "puppet armies" in the big cities were strong enough to resist attacks.

At a meeting with the press in Chungking today Mao Tse-tung,

Continued on Page 5, Column 6

Storm Races to Florida; 2 Subways Flooded Here

6th and 8th Ave. Lines Tied Up 3 Hours as Half Inch of Rain Falls in 10 Minutes—Boy Drowned on Newark Street

Exposed Areas Are Prepared as Hurricane With 150-Mile Winds Moves Toward Coast —Bahamas Await Big Blow

A torrential rainstorm that began at the start of the rush hour last evening halted service on the Sixth and Eighth Avenue subways through midtown Manhattan for three hours last night, flooded thousands of cellars and delayed millions on their way home. In New Jersey it was responsible for two deaths, one by electrocution, the other by drowning, in addition to uprooting trees and tearing the roof from a home in Elizabeth.

Half an inch of rain fell in Manhattan in the ten minutes between 5 and 5:10 P. M., according to Weather Bureau measurements. This was not a record fall. Last year .76 inches fell in ten minutes on Aug. 16 and .85 inches in ten minutes on Sept. 13, the eve of last year's hurricane.

There was no connection between yesterday's storm and the hurricane moving toward Miami out of the Caribbean, according to the Weather Bureau. The local storm, it was explained, was part

Continued on Page 30, Column 4

By The Associated Press.

MIAMI, Fla., Sept. 14—A tropical hurricane which is reported to have created great havoc in Turks Island with 150-mile winds swirled toward the Florida Keys tonight, and at 11 o'clock was about 210 miles southeast of Miami.

Thousands of persons began to move from exposed areas under Coast Guard, Red Cross and Weather Bureau urgings. Schools, police stations and other public buildings were thrown open to refugees throughout south Florida.

The Federal storm warning service estimated that squalls would be felt in this area tomorrow morning, building up to gales and then howling hurricane winds as the center passed, probably over the Florida Keys, tomorrow afternoon.

The red, and black flags of the hurricane warning signal were up from Fort Lauderdale to Key West and Dry Tortugas.

Army, Navy and commercial airplanes sped out of the danger

Continued on Page 30, Column 2

TROLLEY CARS HERE ON WAY TO OBLIVION BY NEXT YEAR'S END

700 New Buses to Assume Travel Burden on Lines in Manhattan and Bronx

The antiquated, clangorous and slow trolley car is to disappear from the streets of Manhattan and most of the Bronx by the end of next year, according to an announcement yesterday by the Third Avenue Transit Corporation.

As replacements for 450 trolleys that are to be scrapped, 700 new buses will travel the seventy-five miles of surface lines scheduled for abandonment in Manhattan and the Bronx, and thirty miles in Yonkers, New Rochelle and Mount Vernon. Most of the buses already have been ordered from General Motors Corporation.

Announcement of the company's program, involving $11,000,000 of financing, was made by its president, Victor McQuistion. He said, would cost an average of $15,000 each.

In Manhattan the street car lines hat will meet the passing of an era are those running up Broad-

Continued on Page 11, Column 5

VALENTINE RETIRES; LA GUARDIA DELAYS NAMING SUCCESSOR

Mayor Tells Police at Promotion Ceremonies New Head Will Come From Ranks

The Police Department is operating today without a commissioner, as the resignation of Lewis J. Valentine, its chief for almost eleven years, became effective at midnight without the appointment of a successor by Mayor La Guardia.

As the time drew near for Mr. Valentine to perform his last official act by presiding at departmental promotion ceremonies at noon yesterday, Centre Street gossip predicted confidently that the climax of the proceedings would be the naming of a new commissioner. The 500 members of the force present in the line-up room sat up expectantly as the Mayor walked to the rostrum, waited eagerly for him to broach the subject and then relaxed as he made it clear that he would take his legal time about swearing in Mr. Valentine's successor.

With Mr. Valentine out of the department after forty-two years

Continued on Page 11, Column 1

FORD ENDS ALL PRODUCTION, BLAMES CRIPPLING STRIKES; ALL AUTO INDUSTRY MENACED

Labor Rows Worry Capital; Detroit Situation 'Ominous'

Officials Fear Crisis Before Peace Parley of Unions and Management, and Want Early Meeting—Congress Ponders Steps

By LOUIS STARK
Special to The New York Times.

WASHINGTON, Sept. 14—A national labor-industry crisis, which might even precede President Truman's scheduled "industrial peace" meeting, was regarded as a possibility today by labor officials, who felt that Detroit labor developments were "ominous."

Secretary Schwellenbach called for reports from the Conciliation Service, which has had a commissioner in close touch with the Detroit labor situation.

Other officials felt that the piling up of wage demands by unions and the comparative slowness in settling problems of reconversion pay may touch off a series of strikes and disputes that will keep the Labor Department and the War Labor Board as busy as at some periods during the war.

The difficulty facing the board, however, is that neither labor nor industry fears any possible "sanctions." To labor the no-strike agreement is no longer binding. While high international union officials have in some cases sought to minimize strikes, they have not always succeeded in checking the walkouts that threatened to get out of hand.

Decision by the shop craft unions to ask the railroads for reduction of the forty-eight-hour week to thirty-six hours without loss of pay will go through the procedure provided under the Railway Labor Act, beginning with direct conferences, mediation, proposal for voluntary arbitration and then, if a crisis develops, for investigation by a Presidential fact-finding board.

This slow, step-by-step procedure, with "cooling off" periods during each step, was contrasted by officials today with strikes now under way on short notice now and all and with threats by the CIO United Automobile Workers Union to "blockade" plants of General Motors Corporation.

Members of Congress, who are

Continued on Page 2, Column 6

50,000 ARE LAID OFF

Company Head Charges Irresponsible Groups Balk Reconversion

UNION PLANS CAMPAIGN

UAW-CIO Leaders Insist on 30% Auto Pay Rise Under Sweeping Strike Plan

The Ford Motor Company halted all production at its plants throughout the country and laid off 50,000 workers, blaming "irresponsible labor groups" for strikes against its supplies [1:8.]

Meanwhile at Flint the Automobile Workers Union's executive board moved to demand a 30 per cent nation-wide pay rise under threat of strikes, and a labor-management showdown loomed. [2:5.]

Washington feared a labor crisis before the labor-management conference, and called the Detroit situation ominous. [1:6-7.]

A CIO Electrical Workers Union began an enrollment drive among 12,000 striking "white-collar" workers of Westinghouse Electric. [2:1.]

The AFL railway unions will demand a thirty-six hour week with no pay cut. [2:7.]

Benjamin Fairless, president of the United States Steel Corporation, said a union demand for $2 a day wage increase cannot be granted without a sharp rise in steel prices. [2:8.]

Company in Blunt Attack

By JAMES B. RESTON

DETROIT, Sept. 14—The Ford Motor Company halted virtually all production in its plants throughout the country today and laid off 50,000 workers, basing its action upon "crippling and unauthorized strikes" against complete with parts.

The company's action, set forth in a statement signed by Henry Ford 2d, executive vice president, applied to all plants except its Lincoln and Rouge steel factories. The statement said that "continued outbreaks by irresponsible labor groups are impeding the regular progress of reconversion."

The development came as the entire automotive industry appeared heading for a labor-management showdown after the International Executive Board of the CIO United Automobile Workers Union had demanded earlier today a 30 per cent wage increase throughout the industry under a threat of strikes to enforce the demand.

Period of Tension Starts

A period of tension in the automotive capital began this morning when the 22-man Executive Committee of the UAW, largest CIO union in the country with a membership of about 1,250,000, announced at a union meeting in Flint that the UAW would either get its 30 per cent raise or call a series of concentrated strikes, first against one of the Big Three auto companies and its suppliers and then against another, but on a basis of one at a time so that the full force of the international union could be thrown against each individual of the Big Three.

In outlining this "divide and conquer" policy, R. J. Thomas, international president; Walter Reuther, vice president, and George F. Addes, secretary-treasurer, stated that their new drive would be carried out under the law, and that the union would "crack down" on wildcat strikes.

The Ford company statement, coming soon afterward, was blunt. It read as follows:

"After several weeks operations in the face of crippling and unauthorized strikes against many of our suppliers, the Ford Motor Company is being forced to halt virtually all of its production operations late today.

"We have considered all angles of the situation. We wanted to keep men at work. We had hoped that by this time we would be hiring more men. Instead we are telling 50,000 of our employes to

Continued on Page 2, Column 3

COLLEGES CHART 2 BILLION OUTLAY

Survey Discloses a Building Program Marking Greatest Expansion in Their History

By BENJAMIN FINE

Colleges and universities in all parts of the United States face the greatest period of expansion in their history, involving a post-war building program of possibly more than $2,000,000,000, a survey conducted by THE NEW YORK TIMES has disclosed.

After four years of war-enforced delay, the colleges report that new dormitories, laboratories, classrooms, gymnasiums and other necessary buildings will be constructed just as soon as help and priorities can be obtained. Almost every one of them needs repair and reconstruction work.

A sampling of forty representative institutions of higher learning showed that blueprints have been prepared for buildings and development of campus facilities which will cost $250,000,000. This sampling, which is less than 10 per cent of the 600 recognized liberal arts institutions and State universities, did not cover the professional schools or junior colleges, where an even greater expansion is planned.

Plainly, the college heads are preparing for a substantial rise in enrollment. Many institutions predict that their building will increase by 50 to 100 per cent. As a result, building must start at once. Since Pearl Harbor little, if any, work has been done on the campuses. Almost every college and university reported that buildings

Continued on Page 16, Column 2

BRADLEY REVAMPS VETERANS' SERVICE

Sweeping Decentralization to Give 13 Districts Controls— Hospital Changes Planned

By CHARLES HURD
Special to The New York Times.

WASHINGTON, Sept. 14—The modernized Veterans Administration ordered by President Truman took shape today when Gen. Omar N. Bradley, new administrator, announced a decentralization program for the organization together with innovations in medical service designed to meet criticisms.

General Bradley made public his reorganization program less than twenty-four hours after it was reduced to tabular form, cautioning reporters that for the most part it existed as yet only on paper. But he said he hoped to be able to show accomplishment soon.

"Don't get the idea," he said at a news conference, "that we think this plan will perform a miracle or get things done right now. But we hope it will show definite improvement in the work of the Veterans Administration."

General Bradley plans to:

1. Decentralize supervision and control over veterans' facilities into thirteen branch offices that will have absolute control over its facilities and offices in their areas.

2. Raise the medical establishment to rank equal to other departments, add a planning section and break insurance away from general finance.

3. Separate vocational training from other activities and make it a specialized project equal in importance to medical care.

4. Reform veterans' hospitals to

Continued on Page 5, Column 5

World News Summarized

SATURDAY, SEPTEMBER 15, 1945

General MacArthur pledged that Japan would be made to carry out her terms of unconditional surrender in a stern, uncompromising manner. Taking note of criticism of the occupation as indicating "a soft policy," he said this was an "erroneous concept." He emphasized that the occupation was still in its first phase and that when this phase was completed "no one need have any doubt about prompt, complete, entire fulfillment of the terms of surrender." The Allied commander also curbed the Domei agency, foremost Japanese news outlet. [1:1.]

Premier Higashi-Kuni asked Americans to "forget Pearl Harbor" and declared a new Japan would emerge after reconstruction that would be shorn of militarism and would be "as peace-loving as the United States." [4:1.]

General Homma, Japanese commander in the Philippines during the Bataan "death march," arrived in Tokyo to surrender as a war criminal. [4:3.]

A Communist communiqué issued from Chungking reported large-scale territorial gains and said the Chinese Communists had "fairly complete" control between Kalgan and the mouth of the Yangtze River and from the Shantung Peninsula east of Shansi. [1:7.]

Japanese forces surrendering on Morco Island were to have reported to annihilation. [5:2.]

On the eve of Viceroy Wavell's return the All-India Congress party working committee voted to contest all elections in India and to continue its program of negotiation and cooperation in

seeking independence. [6:2.]

The Foreign Ministers' Council in London began detailed discussions of the treaty with Italy and made encouraging progress. All nations that were at war with Italy will be asked to submit their views. The council also set up a joint secretariat consisting of the secretaries of the five delegations to speed its work. [1:2-3.]

Exchange of operational information between the Red Army and the American-British forces during the war was called "wholly satisfactory" by General Deane, head of the American military mission in Moscow. [9:4.]

Poland denounced its concordat with the Vatican. [1:6.]

Study of a 10,000-word document issued by the Argentine Foreign Ministry led to the conclusion that it was a poor attempt to justify the Argentine Government's position and tended to convict that Government of laxity in carrying out its commitments under the Act of Chapultepec. [1:3.]

The tempo of reconversion suffered a serious setback as the Ford Motor Company shut down after hitting out at "unauthorized" strikes that were interfering with its supplies. [1:8.]

The British Trades Union Congress adopted a resolution urging a general forty-hour week in industry and a more vigorous housing program. [9:2.]

The Pearl Harbor disaster will be investigated by a joint Senate-House committee of six Democrats and four Republicans. Senate Majority Leader Barkley is expected to act as chairman of the inquiry. [1:4-5.]

Ten Lawyers in Congress Named To Conduct Pearl Harbor Inquiry

By WILLIAM S. WHITE
Special to The New York Times.

WASHINGTON, Sept. 14—A joint Congressional committee of ten members, all lawyers, was appointed today to investigate the Pearl Harbor disaster.

For the Senate, Senator McKellar of Tennessee, the presiding officer, chose Senators Barkley of Kentucky, the majority leader; George of Georgia and Lucas of Illinois, Democrats, and Brewster of Maine and Ferguson of Michigan, Republicans. Senator George withheld a final acceptance, pointing out that a great amount of work was pending before his own finance committee but would reach a decision by early next week.

On the part of the House, Speaker Rayburn said he had followed no precise criterion in appointing the House members of the committee. He disclosed that he had acted upon the recommendations of Representative Martin of Massachusetts, the House Republican leader, in selecting the minority members.

The Speaker, who has made it plain that he suggested Congress demand insistence on an inquiry and

Continued on Page 5, Column 7

133

"All the News
That's Fit to Print"

The New York Times.

LATE CITY EDITION
Sunny, warm today. Sunny, with
increasing cloudiness tomorrow.

Temperatures Yesterday—Max., 70; Min., 49
Sunrise today, 5:48 A.M.; Sunset, 6:13 P.M.
Full U. S. Weather Bureau Report, Page 51

Copyright, 1946, by The New York Times Company.

VOL. XCV..No. 32,205.   Entered as Second-Class Matter,
Postoffice, New York, N. Y.   NEW YORK, THURSDAY, MARCH 28, 1946.   THREE CENTS NEW YORK CITY

RUSSIAN, DEFEATED ON IRAN, WALKS OUT OF UNO; TEHERAN'S ENVOY PUTS PLEA BEFORE COUNCIL; SAYS SOVIET ASKED OCCUPATION AND OIL RIGHTS

REUTHER ELECTED PRESIDENT OF UAW BY NARROW MARGIN

8-Year Reign of Thomas Is Ended in Balloting Marked by Fist Fights, Near-Riots

VICTOR MAKES UNITY PLEA

Plans Campaign Among Farm Equipment Makers, Pledges Assistance to Murray

By WALTER W. RUCH
Special to The New York Times.

ATLANTIC CITY, N. J., March 27—The United Automobile Workers, CIO, crowned ten years of trade unionism for Walter P. Reuther today by electing the 38-year-old 'red-head to the union presidency that had been held for eight years by R. J. Thomas.

In an election in the Municipal Auditorium that was as close as it was bitter, the delegates at the tenth convention of the huge union elevated the fiery leader from his post of vice president to one of the most powerful positions in the labor movement by a majority of only 124.4 votes.

The final tabulation, under a system of fractional voting, gave Reuther 4,444.8 and Thomas 4,320.4.

Mr. Reuther's first gesture was one of friendliness toward the Left Wing element that had battled furiously to keep him from office, and his first promise was one that he would exercise every power at his command to bring unity into an organization that has, admittedly, been disintegrating at the top level.

Plans Membership Drive

As for the "common enemy," he immediately outlined plans to expand the membership through drives to organize the farm machinery workers, the white collar workers and the engineers and technicians of the automotive industry as part of the UAW.

In his first address as president, Mr. Reuther sought to scotch, once and for all, rumors of dissension between him and Philip Murray, president of the Congress of Industrial Organizations, by extending full cooperation and expressing an anxious desire to walk at Mr. Murray's side to help bear "his heavy burden."

In a word, Mr. Reuther stepped into the presidency with a plea for unity that he might bind up the factionalism that abounds in a union harboring virtually every breed of political faith in the nation.

The man he had defeated, who had lost in a seventh attempt at re-election, was on the verge of tears as he gave up the office he held since Homer Martin, the first president, was ousted in 1938. He accepted a hearty handshake from the winner, who was heard to say: "Well, Tommy, now we can work together for a better union."

Mr. Thomas was understood reliably to be slated for appointment by Mr. Murray to serve as vice president of the CIO on the newly formed World Federation of Trade Unions.

A movement was under way late tonight, however, to draft Mr. Thomas as a candidate for one of the two vice-presidential posts, which will be filled tomorrow. Among those urging such action were a number of Reuther delegates, who called at the Thomas headquarters to express their personal good-will toward the defeated candidate. Mr. Thomas promised an answer in the morning.

Fights Enliven Voting

Fist fights and near-riots enlivened the voting session, which began with nominations at noon and ended at 4:30 P. M., with the most tumultuous demonstration of the convention. So near exhaustion were the frenzied partisans as a result of the narrow margin separating the candidates throughout the day that an overnight recess was taken before proceeding with the election of a secretary-treasurer and two vice presidents.

His red locks flecked with red,

Continued on Page 51, Column 5

U. S. Tutor Sought For Hirohito's Son

By Wireless to The New York Times.

TOKYO, March 27—Emperor Hirohito has asked the members of the American education mission at present here under the chairmanship of Dr. George D. Stoddard, New York State Commissioner of Education, to recommend an American tutor for the 12-year-old Crown Prince Akihito, it was learned in palace circles today.

The report came as members of the mission were received in audience this afternoon, later attended a tea party and witnessed court dances in the presence of the Emperor and his younger brother, Prince Nobuhito Takamatsu.

Prince Akihito now is enrolled in the Peers School, of which his father also is a graduate. He also has the tutorial services of R. H. Blythe, an Englishman long resident in Japan, who is teaching him English. It is understood that an American tutor is being sought to supplement Mr. Blythe's teachings.

DRASTIC PROGRAM ON FOOD ADOPTED

UNRRA Resolution Outlines Steps, Including Rationing, to Meet Famine Crisis

UNRRA resolution outlining world food policy, Page 14.

By BESS FURMAN
Special to The New York Times.

ATLANTIC CITY, N. J., March 27—The eleven-nation special food committee, which has been hard at work here since Friday on ways of meeting the famine crisis, recommended today rigorous food-saving measures. It also called for a recess in this United Nations Relief and Rehabilitation Administration Council to permit assessing the scarce supply situation, with provision to reconvene in Washington as soon as the director general can report.

With a few slight word changes, the resolution of the food committee was adopted unanimously at a session of the committee of the whole on policy held tonight to close the two weeks debate here on world food.

The expectation here was that the Council would reconvene in Washington in two or three weeks. In the interim the UNRRA director general would be requested under the resolution of the food committee "to consult immediately and continuously with representatives of the supplying Governments and with the combined food board to consider the effectiveness of steps being taken and to report thereon to the Central Committee and the Council." This duty no doubt will devolve on Fiorello H. La Guardia, slated to succeed Director General Herbert H. Lehman, although Mr. Lehman earlier had agreed to serve through the Council, not anticipating a recess.

Dallas W. Dort, second alternate of the American delegation, who served as chairman of the eleven-

Continued on Page 14, Column 2

10c Fare Resolution Withdrawn; Defeat by Board Was Indicated

By PAUL CROWELL

Cornelius A. Hall, Borough President of Richmond, withdrew yesterday, "pending further conferences with Mayor O'Dwyer," the ten-cent subway fare resolution submitted by him to the Board of Estimate on March 14.

Mr. Hall's announcement came soon after the committee of the whole of the Board of Estimate ended a three-hour executive meeting at City Hall. Mayor O'Dwyer and the other Democratic members of the board declined to discuss Mr. Hall's announcement, but it was reliably reported that he decided to withdraw the higher-fare resolution after his colleagues had indicated that they would vote it down today and would not agree

to lay it over for consideration at some future meeting.

The resolution called for a ten-cent fare on all transit lines owned and operated by the city, with "free transfers for any single continuous trip. It also provided for a ten-cent fare on the Staten Island ferries, with free transfers to subways and certain bus lines. Another provision called for retention of a five-cent fare for school children traveling to and from school.

Mr. Hall declined to discuss details of the proceedings at this executive meeting, but did say that "it was a lengthy discussion."

"I am withdrawing my resolution pending further conferences with Mayor O'Dwyer," he declared. Mayor O'Dwyer recently indi-

Continued on Page 29, Column 5

IRAN'S STORY TOLD

Ambassador Ala Says He Does Not Know of Any Agreement in Force

DISCLOSES DEMANDS

Byrnes Asks That Case Be Confined to Purely Procedural Issue

Iranian Ambassador's statement of his country's case, P. 9.

By WILL LISSNER

In relief at becoming a participant in the deliberations of the United Nations Security Council on Iran's case, Ambassador Hussein Ala of Iran took a place at the Council table at 5:50 o'clock yesterday afternoon and disclosed demands made by the Soviet Union upon his country in secret Moscow negotiations between Feb. 19 and March 3 of this year.

The Iranian Ambassador plunged almost at once to one of the most vigorously discussed points, the question of whether or not there was a Soviet-Iranian agreement, as both Marshal Stalin and the Soviet delegate had indicated, when he stated:

"May I say once and for all that I know of no agreement or understanding, secret or otherwise, having been entered into between my Government and the Soviet Union with respect to any of the matters involved in the dispute now referred to this Council."

Mr. Ala, a short, spare man of quiet dignity, moved on the invitation of the chairman, Dr. Quo Tai-chi, from the seat in the front row reserved for Iran to the medium of Soviet officials and armed forces," he asserted.

When Prime Minister Ahmad Ghavam of Iran went to Moscow on Feb. 19 to negotiate, as directed by the Security Council in its resolution of last Jan. 30, Mr. Ala continued, the Soviet officials "would not agree to withdraw their troops from Iran or to refrain from interfering in the internal affairs of Iran."

Instead, he said, the Soviet officials made a series of proposals. Soviet troops were to continue to stay in some parts of Iran indefi-

Continued on Page 11, Column 2

SOVIET DELEGATE WALKS OUT OF UNO—IRAN'S ENVOY TAKES A SEAT

Ambassador Andrei Gromyko is flanked by newspaper men as he leaves the chamber after the delegates refused to postpone discussion of the Iranian dispute until April 10.
The New York Times

Ambassador Hussein Ala addressing the delegates. At the left is an assistant to Dr. Oskar Lange, Poland's representative, and at the right is Akbar Daftari of the Iranian Embassy.
Associated Press

IRAN AGAIN DENIES NEW SOVIET PACT

Premier Reiterates No Written or Oral Accord Was Reached in Talks in Moscow

By GENE CURRIVAN
By Wireless to The New York Times.

TEHERAN, Iran, March 27—Official sources here reiterated today that there was no new agreement with the Soviet Union despite the clamoring for details from other parts of the world. Premier Ahmad Ghavam has not altered his position one degree since he returned from his conference in Moscow.

He said then that he had failed

Continued on Page 11, Column 5

Gromyko Is Stern and Silent As He Leaves UNO Chamber

By W. H. LAWRENCE

With grim, stony-faced determination, young Andrei A. Gromyko took a fateful walk out of the United Nations Security Council at 5:19 P. M., yesterday. He went because the Kremlin had told him that under no circumstances would the Soviet Union present to the Council before April 10 a defense of its actions in Iran. The Council had just rejected, 9 to 2, his motion to postpone the case for two weeks.

He did not wait for the report to begin to speak. He did not wait until the Council had decided the issue affirmatively by inviting his opponent, Hussein Ala, Iranian Ambassador to the United States, to join the Council table.

But Mr. Gromyko will be back.

Continued on Page 3, Column 5

World News Summarized

THURSDAY, MARCH 28, 1946

The Soviet Union walked out of the UNO Security Council session late yesterday afternoon after the Russian proposal to defer consideration of the Iranian question until April 10 had been defeated, 9 to 2. Only Russia and Poland voted for it. When it became evident that Iranian Ambassador Ala would be invited to the table to present his case, Ambassador Gromyko announced he was unable to participate further in the discussions or remain present, picked up his papers and departed. [1:8.]

Mr. Gromyko's withdrawal is in conformity with strict instructions from Moscow and he is expected to attend any sessions before April 10 at which the merits of the Iranian question are not discussed. [1:5-6.] Oskar Lange, Poland's delegate, defended Mr. Gromyko's action and declared that Poland would continue in attendance. [1:1.]

Russia, at the Moscow conferences with Premier Ghavam, instead of agreeing to withdraw from Iran, made counter-proposals that were unacceptable, Mr. Ala disclosed to the Council. The Russians wanted Soviet troops to remain in some parts of Iran "for an indefinite period"; they demanded recognition of Azerbaijan's autonomy and proposed a joint Soviet-Iranian oil company in which Russia would hold 51 per cent of the stock. There have been no further discussions or agreements, he said, and he had not been authorized to agree to a delay. The session adjourned before Mr. Ala finished. [1:3.]

Official sources in Teheran confirmed the lack of any agreement. [1:4.]

The day of debate was marked by frequent sharp exchanges. The Council will meet in executive session this afternoon. [4:2.]

The Military Staff Committee began work on the international police force to maintain world security and peace through the UNO. [10:2.]

Russian Naval Lieutenant Redin was held in $25,000 bail in Portland, Ore., on espionage charges that Soviet officials called a "frame-up" to damage Russian prestige. He was accused of having induced some unnamed person to obtain data about the destroyer-tender Yellowstone, described as a "floating shipyard." [6:3.]

The British Labor party attacked Communists and dissident left-wingers in a manifesto rejecting a proposal to affiliate with the Communist party, which was accused of harboring fifth columnists. [10:3-4.]

In this country, observers saw a rebuke to leftists in the labor movement [31:2] in the defeat of R. J. Thomas by Walter P. Reuther for president of the United Auto Workers Union, CIO. [1:1.]

All nations were urged to their greatest efforts to cut food consumption and increase production to meet the world famine crisis in an UNRRA resolution. [1:2.]

Yugoslavia was warned in a sharp Allied communiqué that American and British occupation troops would oppose any sudden attempt by Marshal Tito's men to seize part of the Venezia Giulia area. [1:7; map P. 15.] Russia presented new draft peace treaties for Bulgaria and Hungary designed to meet Anglo-American objections. [15:2.]

Léon Blum told American negotiators that France would have to spend at least $17,000,000,000 in five years to re-establish her economic position and to permit her to play her full part in collective security. [3:6.]

IRAN AGAIN DENIES

ALLIES WARN TITO ON VENEZIA GIULIA

Issue Blunt Statement Against Any Yugoslav Move to Invade Disputed Zone at Trieste

By SAM POPE BREWER
By Wireless to The New York Times.

ROME, March 27—The Allied Governments issued a firm warning tonight to the Yugoslavs against any effort to stage a sudden invasion of the disputed Zone A of Venezia Giulia, now occupied by Anglo-American forces.

In the most blunt statement made on the subject in many months, Lieut. Gen. William D. Morgan, Supreme Allied Commander in the Mediterranean theatre, from his headquarters in Caserta, speaking in the names of the American and British Governments, said: "Public order will be enforced with justice, and in our zone we shall tolerate no attempt to prejudice in any way the final disposition of the territory.

"To this end, the American and British Governments have authorized me to declare that it is their firm intention to maintain their present position in Venezia Giulia until an agreed settlement of the territorial dispute has been reached and put into effect."

Allied Forces Reduced

This is the first time since the agreement was signed with Marshal Tito last June for the present division of Venezia Giulia into Zones A and B that such action has been necessary by the British and Americans.

[Zone A constitutes about a quarter of the area on the western side of the peninsula against the Italian frontier, and includes

Continued on Page 15, Column 2

BLUM PUTS NO TOP ON SIZE OF U. S. LOAN

Emissary Says France Needs $5,000,000,000 of Our Goods to Modernize Industry

By JOHN H. CRIDER
Special to The New York Times.

WASHINGTON, March 27—Léon Blum, special French emissary to the United States, opened the current financial negotiations by painting a pitiable picture of France as "a nation twice ruined in thirty years," but citing the post-war accomplishments of her people as evidence of their courage and determination to recover.

The release today by the French Embassy of excerpts from M. Blum's lengthy presentation at the opening session on Monday was the first of a series of official releases under the rule of liberal public information adopted yesterday by the negotiators.

M. Blum opened on a note of "great solemnity" to stress the unity of all French political parties in supporting the "principles of democracy" and the "unconditional and unqualified" acceptance by France and all her constituent parties of the "principles of collec-

Continued on Page 17, Column 2

Braden Bars a Break With Peron; Says Europe Needs Argentine Aid

Spruille Braden, Assistant Secretary of State and leading exponent of a firm policy in dealing with Argentina, indicated yesterday that there was nothing we could do at the moment about the Perón regime, recently victorious in the election held there.

In a frank discussion here, Mr. Braden ruled out the breaking of diplomatic relations as "silly," and any attempt to impose sanctions as futile, because neither France nor Britain would back us, nor would we, in this country, want to assume the responsibility of depriving the starving of Europe of the food Argentine could supply.

Mr. Braden told American women at a seminar for women's clubs, arranged by The New York Times in cooperation with the General Federation of Wom-

en's Clubs, held at Times Hall, 240 West Forty-fourth Street.

Other speakers on the program, the first of three scheduled, included Turner Catledge, assistant managing editor; Foster Hailey, editorial writer; James B. Reston, national correspondent; Anne O'Hare McCormick, editorial columnist, all of The Times; John J. McCloy, former Assistant Secretary of War; Mrs. William Dick Sporborg of the General Federation of Women's Clubs and Mrs. Arthur Hays Sulzberger, who welcomed the guests.

Mr. Braden was the principal speaker at a seminar for women's clubs, arranged by The New York Times in cooperation with the General Federation of Wom-

Continued on Page 19, Column 1

COUNCIL PROCEEDS

Soviet Departure Fails to Swerve Body in Hearing of Issue

SOVIET COURSE HAZY

She Will Be Present at a Meeting Today— Poland Backs Her

Transcript of UNO proceedings on Iran question, Page 8.

By JAMES B. RESTON

The Soviet Union took a walk at the United Nations Security Council meeting yesterday, but it will be represented at the Council's Committee of Experts today, and it will come back to the Council when it feels like it, which will probably be on April 10.

This action, which broke, temporarily, the rule of Big Five unanimity, was not a break with the UNO. It was opposed, as some observers have been comparing it, with the German, Italian and Japanese departures from the League of Nations; nor was it an indication that the coalition that produced victory had been dissolved.

It is a decision by the Soviet Government, carried out in the Ambassador to Washington, Andrei A. Gromyko, to leave the Council for two weeks while the question of Red Army troops in Iran is being discussed. It is a parliamentary maneuver. It is an expression of protest against the Council. It is, admittedly, a psychological blow to the new organization and an illustration of the Soviet thesis that the great powers should direct, and even dictate, procedure as well as issues of substance in the Council.

Not a Break With Council

But it is not a break with the Council. In fact, not only do the Soviet representatives say they will be in the meeting of the Committee of Experts today, but it is reported that if today's closed session of the Council deals only with the procedural aspects of the Iranian question, they may even attend that, though this is not at all certain.

At 5:04 yesterday afternoon, at the end of what began to look strangely like a filibuster by the Soviet Union, the Council defeated the Soviet Union's motion to postpone discussion of the Iranian case until April 10. Only the U.S.S.R. and Poland voted for it.

At 5:19, before the Council had voted to invite the Iranian Ambassador to sit at the Council table and tell why he thought the case of the Soviet troops in Iran was urgent, the youthful, pokerfaced Soviet delegate, Ambassador Gromyko, raised his hand and addressed the chair.

Soviet Statement on Withdrawal

As he was recognized, the spotlights in the chamber room went on slowly. The chamber was crowded. The delegates, weary of endless argument and pleas, frustrated by the lack of any rules of procedure and frankly out of sorts, turned indulgently toward what looked like another long speech. But he rose only to the point.

"For reasons which I explained clearly enough in our meeting of yesterday and in today's meeting, Mr. Chairman," he said in Russian, "I, as representative of the Soviet Union, am not able to participate further in the discussions of the Security Council because my proposal has not been accepted by the Council, nor am I able to be present at the meeting of the Council, and I therefore leave the meeting."

For a few minutes the audience did not understand the meaning of this, for when he finished speaking he waited expressionless in his chair until the translators finished. The first indication of

Continued on Page 3, Column 1

"All the News That's Fit to Print"

The New York Times.

LATE CITY EDITION
Partly cloudy and mild today. Occasional showers tomorrow.

Temperature: Max., 64; Min., 42
Sunrise, 5:53 A. M.; Sunset, 7:58 P. M.
Full U. S. Weather Bureau Report on Page 23

VOL. XCV. No. 32,239.

Entered as Second-Class Matter,
Postoffice, New York, N. Y.

NEW YORK, WEDNESDAY, MAY 1, 1946

Copyright, 1946, by The New York Times Company.

THREE CENTS NEW YORK CITY

WARSHIP BLOWS UP AT MUNITIONS PIER IN PORT, KILLING 5

60 on Escort Vessel Injured—Blasts Shake New Jersey Towns Near Big Depot

BOMBS ASHORE SET OFF

Sailor Is Only Slightly Hurt as Depth Charge Explodes as He Is Carrying It

By MEYER BERGER
Special to The New York Times

LEONARDO, N. J., April 30—One officer and four sailors of the destroyer escort Solar's complement of fourteen officers and 136 enlisted men vanished utterly before noon today in an ammunition explosion that tore away one-third of the 306-foot ship's forward structure.

About sixty of the ship's crew were injured, but only thirty-five were hospitalized, and of them only a handful remained tonight for further treatment. The Navy withheld the names of the five missing men and the names of the injured because not all their families had been officially notified.

The explosion damaged the Solar's crew was unloading her ammunition supply in preparation for an overhaul. Normally she carries about fifteen tons of assorted ammunition, including depth bombs and smaller charges, torpedoes and shells for her cannon. Only one-third of this amount was still aboard when the blast occurred.

Tons of Explosives Near by

Near by, when the detonation shook the New Jersey coast in and around the Raritan Bay district, were a number of other vessels preparing to unload ammunition. It was unofficially estimated that these vessels held, all told, about 25,000 tons of explosives. Tugs dragged these craft out of the danger zone.

Burning fragments from the Solar, hurled at tremendous force against freight cars on the pier, started other explosions. One car in a freight string, filled chiefly with depth charges, blew up and all but vanished in dust and smoke, scattering its parts in all directions. Three strings of cars were hauled backward by their locomotive crews, at great risk.

No one seemed certain tonight what had caused the explosion, but what seemed like a possible explanation came from Jack Borns, fireman second class, of Charlotte, N. C. He thought a piece of ammunition carried by Joseph Stuchinski, seaman, of Baltimore, might have done it.

"Ski," the fireman said, "was carrying a 'hedgehog' from the forward magazine. While he was holding it, it just went off. He must have bumped it against something, because those things go off when anything touches them."

Seaman Stuchinski, oddly enough, was not seriously injured. He was deafened, a few minor scratches showed on his chest when he got to the first-aid station and his dungarees were split.

"It went off. The thing just went off," he said.

The "hedgehog" Stuchinski carried was an anti-submarine depth charge. Metal-cased, weighing about sixty pounds, it is generally cylindrical, about thirty inches long and between four and five inches in diameter.

Like Like Elephant's Trunk

The Solar lay at the northern, or bay end, of the easternmost of the three great piers that jut out from the Navy's Earle Ammunition Depot, when she blew up. She was approximately one and one-half miles from the beach end of the depot. The blast curled her bow in much the same shape as an elephant's back-bent trunk.

The concussion was felt twenty to thirty miles around. The detonation rushed across Raritan Bay to shake homes in Tottenville, Richmond Valley, Pleasant Plains, Princess' Bay, Great Kills, Oakwood and New Dorp, all on Staten Island and shattered panes in some of those communities.

Ground tremors were felt to the west and to the southwest. There were some freakish effects. Residents in Middletown Township, including Rumson, Fair Haven, Red Bank and Little Silver, for example, assumed certain the explosion was local. Several frightened housewives called the police to say, "The boiler just blew up in my cellar."

Dogs raced away from the beach

Continued on Page 2, Column 2

AFTER EXPLOSIONS RIPPED DESTROYER ESCORT

The wrecked U. S. S. Solar at the Navy Ammunition Depot at Earle, N. J., yesterday.
The New York Times (U. S. Navy)

BAN BY MUSICIANS BLOW TO TELEVISION

Petrillo Plans to Prolong the Refusal of Union Men to the Industry Indefinitely

By JACK GOULD

The American Federation of Musicians, headed by James C. Petrillo, plans to forbid its members to work in television until some indefinite date in the future when the union can determine the effects of video's advent on present-day radio, it was learned yesterday.

Television broadcasters were agreed that Mr. Petrillo's stand would retard the development of video programs, since it could be a matter of months if not years before anyone could determine to what extent television would supplant or complement sound broadcasting.

Use of "live" musicians was first denied the television industry in February, 1945, by the international executive board of the federation, but yesterday was the first time that Mr. Petrillo explained the action and indicated that the ban would be of prolonged duration.

Musical Films Already Banned

Last week Mr. Petrillo's union and the Hollywood motion picture producers entered into an agreement not to permit films containing music to be used in television, a move leaving the telecasters with only records as a possible source of music. Beginning July 1, under a rule of the Federal Communications Commission, the television stations are scheduled to offer twenty-eight hours of programs a week, but under Mr. Petrillo's edicts they will be forced to rely primarily on talks, sporting events and other non-musical fare.

Coincidentally with stating the union's position on television, Mr. Petrillo also reiterated his stand against permitting standard radio programs containing music to be presented simultaneously on frequency modulation outlets. The union is insisting on double crews of musicians in the event of such duplication.

The re-statement of the union's views on FM were regarded with

Continued on Page 26, Column 3

Stalin Warns of War Plot By 'International Reaction'

By The Associated Press.

LONDON, April 30—Generalissimo Stalin promised tonight that the Soviet Union would be true to a policy of peace and security but charged that what he described as "international reaction" was "hatching plans of a new war." In an order of the day broadcast by the Moscow radio the Russian leader also declared that it was necessary to be constantly vigilant, "to protect as the apple of one's eye the armed forces and defensive power of our country."

TEXT OF STALIN ORDER

His broadcast order, issued in connection with the Soviet Union's May Day celebration, was heard in London by the Soviet monitor, who issued the following text:

Comrades, Red Army and Red Navy men, sergeants and petty officers, comrade officers, generals and admirals, working people of the Soviet Union:

Today, for the first time since the victorious termination of the Great Patriotic War, we celebrate May 1—the international holiday of working people—in conditions of peaceful life, won in a hard struggle against the enemies at the cost of heavy sacrifices and privations.

One year ago the Red Army hoisted the banner of victory over Berlin and completed the defeat of fascist Germany. Within four months after the victorious termination of the war against Germany, imperialist Japan downed her arms. The Second World War, prepared by the forces of international reaction and unleashed by the chief fascist states, ended in a full victory of the freedom-loving nations. The smashup and liquidation of the main hotbeds of fascism and world aggression resulted in changes in the political life of the nations of the world, in a wide growth of the democratic movement of the nations.

Taught by the experience of war, the popular masses realized that the destinies of states cannot be entrusted to reactionary leaders, who pursue the narrow caste and selfish anti-popular aims. It is for this reason that nations, which no longer wish to live in the old way, take destinies of their states into their own hands, establish democratic order and actively fight against the forces of reaction, against instigators of a new war. The nations of the

Continued on Page 5, Column 4

INQUIRY FINDS 'PERIL TO SECRETS OF WAR

Senators Hear Radar Makers on Russian Buying and Urge Law Tightening

By C. P. TRUSSELL
Special to The New York Times

WASHINGTON, April 30—Need for a tightening of the laws to provide protection for wartime secrets in the electronics and other fields was declared by Senate investigators today to be "very definite."

The statement came after a closed-session inquiry into negotiations for sales of radar and similar equipment to Russia.

Members of a special Senate Judiciary subcommittee, conducting the investigation, said that there was no evidence that "classified,"

Continued on Page 4, Column 2

World News Summarized

WEDNESDAY, MAY 1, 1946

Palestine should become neither a Jewish state nor an Arab state, the Anglo-American Committee of Inquiry declared in its report made public simultaneously last night in Washington and London. Admission of 100,000 Jews this year and virtual abrogation of the 1939 British White Paper with the restrictions on land holdings were recommended. Other suggestions included continuation of the present mandate until establishment of a United Nations trusteeship and readouts suppression of violence and terrorism by Jews or Arabs. [1:8.]

Although President Truman expressed pleasure over certain parts of the report, it was felt in Washington that neither the Jews nor Arabs would be satisfied. [12:1.] In fact, Arab leaders threatened to combat any additional Jewish immigration [13:3] and Zionists expressed their opposition. Bartley C. Crum, a member of the committee, predicted that a directive authorizing the entry of 100,000 Jews into Palestine would "issue forthwith." [1:6-7.]

British reaction counted heavily upon American support in whatever was done, but regretted the absence of any long-term solution. [1:6-7.]

Italy will be permitted to retain most of northern Tyrol despite Austrian claims, the Foreign Ministers tentatively agreed at their conference in Paris, but they were as wide apart as ever on what to do about Trieste and the Venezia Giulia area. It was decided to invite Yugoslavia and Italy to present their cases anew. [1:5.]

Britain tried to meet French demands by suggesting internationalisation of either the Ruhr or both the Ruhr and the left bank of the Rhine for fifty years. [3:1.] Secretary Byrnes proposed four-power treaty to keep Germany disarmed was favorably received in the Senate Foreign Affairs Committee. [3:5.] The United Nations Security

Council subcommittee opens its investigation into Franco Spain this afternoon. [1:7.] Europe's ruined industries should be restored before attempts to eradicate world unemployment, the Economic and Employment Commission heard [8:5], while the Transport and Communications Commission debated the relative merits of free enterprise and government control of shipping. [7:1.] The Commission on Human Rights may seek a new international bill of rights and ask authority to supervise its implementation. [8:2.]

Tabriz, capital of Azerbaijan, has been formally evacuated by Russian troops, the Tabriz radio reported. [3:6.] Premier Etalin declared that, while the world must remain vigilant against reaction, it had "no reason to doubt" that Russia would remain steadfast in its devotion to international peace and security. [1:3-4.]

Japan was shocked at the plot to assassinate General MacArthur and the Government offered its apologies. No arrests have been announced. [1:6-7.]

Ammunition being unloaded from the destroyer-escort Solar at Raritan Bay exploded, killing an officer and four sailors. [1:1.]

John L. Lewis served notice that anthracite miners intended to strike on May 31 unless they obtained the same demands that led to the soft-coal strike. Negotiations will start in New York on May 10. No progress was made toward settling the bituminous dispute. [29:1.]

Further restrictions were placed on the use of grain by distillers in order to make more food available for world famine relief. [1:2-3.]

General Motors was authorized by the OPA to raise prices of its cars from $16 to $60 to cover wage increases. [27:6-7.] House members returned to Washington still opposed to extending price control without heavy restrictions. [30:5.]

Sharp Restrictions in Distilling Ordered in Food Conservation

By CHARLES E. EGAN
Special to The New York Times

WASHINGTON, April 30—World famine is more than a short term problem, and plans to meet its reappearance next winter should be drafted immediately, Chester C. Davis, chairman of the President's Special Famine Emergency Committee, asserted today.

Mr. Davis, who conferred with President Truman, later said that emergency measures, taken to insure larger relief shipment of grains and other foods to famine stricken areas in the next few weeks, could not be considered as final, but were merely "the first sprint" in a continuing "race to avert death for millions who otherwise would starve."

Meanwhile, Secretary Anderson issued an order restricting distilleries who operated for five days at full mashing capacity in April to three capacity days in May.

The order also limited the use of grain by the entire distilling industry to 1,200,000 bushels of wheat in the

Continued on Page 22, Column 3

manufacture of spirits and restricted distillers to the use of corn which is unsuitable for human consumption.

In January, distillers were permitted ten capacity mashing days, but were cut to seven and one-half in February and to five days in March and April.

Brewers, operating on a 30 per cent reduction of grain, were not included in today's order.

"Every report coming before us makes it plain that the present famine is not a short run emergency that ends on July 1," Mr. Davis' statement said, adding:

"The present food shortages have been seriously aggravated by drought in many parts of the world, but even with good weather the wartime destruction of agricultural facilities will be felt for a long time.

"Farm animals and farm machinery have been destroyed, the strength of farm workers has

Continued on Page 22, Column 3

BIG FOUR RULE OUT AUSTRIA'S DEMAND FOR SOUTH TYROL

Paris Conference Rejects Any Major Frontier Revision in That Region of Italy

NO PROGRESS ON TRIESTE

Rome and Belgrade Are Asked to Send Delegates—Report of Experts Confusing

By C. L. SULZBERGER
By Cable to The New York Times

PARIS, April 30—Italy's retention of most of the Province of Bolzano [South Tyrol], which is claimed by Austria, was virtually assured tonight after the Council of Foreign Ministers had agreed that no requests for a major frontier change would be accepted in that area so valuable in hydroelectric power.

At the same time, after examining a verbose and confused report on Trieste and Venezia Giulia, submitted at long last by the special commission sent by the Foreign Ministers' deputies to investigate the Italian-Yugoslav border area, the ministers agreed to invite the Yugoslav and Italian Governments to send delegates here on Friday to present once again their views on this hotly disputed and vitally important region.

The report showed a complete divergence in opinion between the Soviet investigator and the three other participants on the value of a census taken in 1945 by a Yugoslav, Professor Rodich. The Soviet member of the commission said the census was fine and the three others said it was just the opposite. Since this census is of vital importance in deciding the ethnic basis for a decision, that leaves everything up in the air.

Suggested by Molotov

The move to widen the scope of the Foreign Ministers' meeting by inviting the Italians and Yugoslavs was suggested by Vyacheslav M. Molotov. The Soviet Foreign Minister recalled that the Potsdam declarations, the "bible" under which the peace treaties are being drafted, provided that the interested parties should be included when necessary. Thus, the doors have been opened to permit entry of those delegations—Greek, Italian, Yugoslav, Hungarian and Bulgarian—now clamoring for

Continued on Page 4, Column 2

JOINT PALESTINE BODY BARS A JEWISH STATE, BUT URGES ENTRY OF 100,000 REFUGEES

Arabs 'Outraged' by Report; Jews Are Far From Satisfied

Rival Agencies Reiterate Their Arguments—U. S., British Talks Are Forecast on Easing Burden Too Big for London

By HERBERT L. MATTHEWS
By Wireless to The New York Times

LONDON, April 30—Now that the report of the Anglo-American Committee of Inquiry on Palestine has been published, one can safely predict tonight that the next step will be for the British to consult the United States Government about it. The British have reached the point at which they consider that Palestine is far too great a burden for them to be forced to handle alone.

No Government spokesman would say anything about the report tonight because the Cabinet and other officials have not had time to study it. One must keep in mind that the members of the committee had a mandate only to make recommendations, which do not in any sense involve Governmental responsibility.

The Arab Office in London has lost no time in issuing a scorching statement condemning the report lock, stock and barrel. The Jewish Agency for Palestine gave the report a mixed reception. It was

Continued on Page 14, Column 5

TRUMAN FOR ACTION

Inquiry Upholds His Visa Proposal, Urges End of White Paper

WOULD GUARD ARAB RIGHTS

Report for Change in Holy Land Property Curbs—Demands a Firm Stand on Violence

The text of the report of the Anglo-American Committee of Inquiry on Palestine, Pages 15 to 21, inclusive.

By FELIX BELAIR JR.
Special to The New York Times

WASHINGTON, April 30—The Anglo-American Committee of Inquiry on problems of Jews in Europe and Palestine, reporting to the two Governments today on its four-month investigation, urged admission of 100,000 European Jews into the Holy Land as soon as possible, but flatly rejected the idea of a Jewish state, together with Arab claims for dominance. It asserted Christendom's own interest in the area.

Released simultaneously for publication in Washington and London, the report drew from President Truman an expression of satisfaction that his proposal for the admission of 100,000 Jews into Palestine had been recommended. He added that "the transference of these unfortunate people should now be accomplished with the greatest dispatch." The President declared it significant that the report aimed at guarantees for Arab civil and religious rights and urged measures to improve Arab cultural, educational and economic positions.

Land Changes Asked

"I am also pleased," he said, "that the committee recommends, in effect, the abrogation of the White Paper of 1939."

The report repudiated the 1939 White Paper principles, which made further Jewish immigration dependent on Arab consent and banned Jewish land purchases in a major part of Palestine.

Dependent for its final effect on adoption by both Governments, the report covered a wide range of controversial subjects on which President Truman gave no hint of his attitude except to say that he was taking them under advisement.

However, Mr. Truman seemed to have embraced the major policy alternatives rejecting "once and for all the exclusive claims of Jews and Arabs to Palestine," which the committee enunciated as follows:

"(I. That Jew shall not dominate Arab and Arab shall not dominate Jew in Palestine. (II.) That Palestine shall be neither a Jewish state nor an Arab state. (III.) That the form of government ultimately to be established shall, under international guarantees, fully protect and preserve the interests in the Holy Land of Christendom and of the Moslem and Jewish faiths."

Stress on Unique Status

With deliberate emphasis, the Committee of Inquiry declared that "Palestine is a Holy Land, sacred to Christian, to Jew and to Moslem alike; and because it is a holy land, Palestine is not, and can never become, a land which any race or religion can justly claim as its very own."

With equal emphasis, the committee said the same considerations set Palestine apart from other lands, and dedicated it to the precepts and practices of the brotherhood of man rather than to the narrow nationalism.

The 42,000-word report was signed in Lausanne, Switzerland, by Judge Joseph C. Hutcheson, United States chairman; Sir John E. Singleton, British chairman, Frank Aydelotte, Frank W. Buxton, Bartley C. Crum, James G. McDonald and William Phillips, American members, and W. F. Crick, R. H. S. Crossman, Frederick Leggett, R. E. Manningham-Buller and M. Morrison for Britain. For the immediate future the

Continued on Page 14, Column 2

Truman Said to Plan Start Of Jewish Entry 'Forthwith'

By LAWRENCE RESNER

Bartley C. Crum, one of the six United States members of the Joint Anglo-American Committee of Inquiry on Palestine, predicted here yesterday, on the basis of a discussion he had with President Truman at the White House on Monday, that the directives authorizing the admission of 100,000 European Jews into Palestine would "issue forthwith."

Mr. Crum, a San Francisco lawyer, also expressed the belief that most Jewish groups would endorse the affirmative aspects of the report, although reserving their right to continue a fight for the achievement of their ideological tenets, principally a Jewish state.

An immediate endorsement of the recommendation to obtain the admission of the 100,000 European Jews came from Joseph M. Proskauer, president of the American Jewish Committee, who said the provisions for immediate action were "obviously based on the highest considerations of statesmanship and humanity."

The World Zionist Emergency Council, which speaks for some of the largest and most active Zionist groups in the United States, said a statement outlining its position probably would be issued tomorrow, after the report had been studied.

The initial negative response by a Jewish group came from the Political Action Committee for Palestine, whose executive vice chairman, Dr. Baruch Korff, said that despite "the report's few fine points, the commission had proved

Continued on Page 13, Column 6

U. N.'S SPAIN INQUIRY COMMENCES TODAY

5-Man Subcommittee to Meet Here in Secret—No Outside Witnesses at First Session

By W. H. LAWRENCE

The United Nations subcommittee investigating the Franco regime in Spain goes on trial today on charges that it is a cause of international friction and a threat to world peace.

Meeting privately at 3 P. M., representatives of Australia, China, France, Poland and Brazil will be in motion the first formal investigation by the United Nations, authorized Monday by a 10-to-0 vote of the Security Council, in which Russia did not participate but refrained from exercising an asserted right to veto the inquiry.

How, where and when the Council subcommittee will function presumably will be decided in the early part of today's meeting, and the members then will turn to analyzing the evidence now being laid before them, listing the specific charges

Continued on Page 7, Column 2

MacArthur Plot Alarms Japanese; They See Possible Repercussions

By The Associated Press.

TOKYO, April 30—News of Japanese reporters speculated that frustrated assassination plot they discussed tighter precautions against General Douglas MacArthur tonight shocked the Japanese.

Their first reaction was two-fold: A feeling that their country had lost face; fears that repercussions might be felt in every household.

The Government officially apologized. Katsuo Okazaki, representing Foreign Minister Shigeru Yoshida, visited General MacArthur's office two hours after Allied Headquarters had announced discovery of the plot. He did not see the general personally, but delivered a verbal message to aides.

Mr. Okazaki expressed "deep regret and concern" and said his Government was "greatly embarrassed." He added that there was mention in the Government could do. Earlier, Premier Kijuro Shidehara, Mr. Yoshida and Home Minister Chuzo Mitsuchi conferred.

than previously were planned for the May Day demonstrations.

Many Japanese immediately asked, "Will this create more anti-Japanese feeling in America?" They linked this with fear that adverse American reaction might complicate efforts to obtain food and might mean a longer, harsher occupation.

They also expressed regret that the incident might mar the occupation and change the attitude of General MacArthur, whom the Japanese generally respect.

Allied headquarters had previously given some details of the plot. One conspirator was dead and a nation-wide hunt was launched for a die-hard Japanese militarist named as the arch-plotter.

The accused and hunted plot leader was Hideo Tokugawa, former member of the dread Kempeital of "thought police."

Continued on Page 12, Column 6

"All the News That's Fit to Print"

The New York Times.

LATE CITY EDITION
Mostly sunny today. Fair and warmer tomorrow.

Temperature Yesterday—Max., 54; Min., 41
Full U. S. Weather Bureau Report, Page 44

VOL. XCVI...No. 32,393.

Entered as Second-Class Matter, Postoffice, New York, N. Y.

NEW YORK, WEDNESDAY, OCTOBER 2, 1946.

Copyright, 1946, by The New York Times Company.

THREE CENTS NEW YORK CITY

12 NAZI WAR LEADERS SENTENCED TO BE HANGED; GOERING HEADS LIST OF THOSE TO DIE BY OCT. 16; HESS GETS LIFE, SIX OTHERS ORDERED TO PRISON

SHIP OFFICERS QUIT, PARALYZING PORT 2D TIME IN MONTH

Never Before Have Masters Been Called From Bridges —Engineers Also Strike

WASHINGTON PLEAS FAIL

But Efforts to Settle Dispute Over Wages and Working Conditions Are Continued

By GEORGE HORNE

The cogs of the nation's merchant marine slowed to a standstill yesterday for the second time in a month as the unprecedented strike of licensed officers got under way.

It was unprecedented because never before in the country's shipping history have shipmasters—captains earning as much as $500 and $600 a month—been called from the bridges in a union action to enforce wage and working demands. But they are leaving their ships on order, along with brother engineer officers of the Marine Engineers Beneficial Association.

Reaction among the captains was mixed, and the situation affecting them at a late hour last night was obscure, after a welter of messages to and from the negotiating headquarters in Washington, where Government authorities were still trying to effect a settlement before the walkout could settle down to a long-term affair.

Many Captains Not in Union

Many captains are not members of the National Organization of Masters, Mates and Pilots (AFL), even on such ships as have MMP contracts. Shipping operators said the captains, who are the owners' supreme representatives aboard, and as such considered beyond the call of strike action, were "being threatened."

They declared that Capt. Harry Martin, East Coast president of the MMP, had agreed in Washington yesterday to leave security watches aboard all ships, including a captain and a day and night mate for stand-by duty. But they said the pledge was not being honored.

At a special meeting of the AFL Maritime Trades Department at the office of the International Longshoremen's Association last night it was announced that the "status quo" remains. That meant that captains were being called off, whether they agreed or not. The AFL spokesman said the response among all MMP officers was excellent.

Ship operators took the position that the masters were "in the middle" and "behind the eight-ball," and they agreed that many would have to leave their ships at the union's call.

The MMP leaders have stood by their original conception of the walkout as being no strike. It was, in the case of the men not moving

Continued on Page 4, Column 2

Cards Beat Dodgers In First Game, 4-2

Despite a muscle ailment, Howie Pollet pitched the Cardinals to a 4-2 victory over the Dodgers at St. Louis yesterday in the first of a three-game play-off series for the National League pennant. The Cards meanwhile routed Ralph Branca, first of five Brooklyn pitchers, with three runs in as many innings.

Howie Schultz momentarily tied the score for the Dodgers with his homer in the third and also batted in their second run with a single in the seventh.

The play-offs, first such in the history of major league baseball, will be resumed tomorrow at Ebbets Field, and the third contest, if necessary, will be played there Friday.

(Complete details on Page 35.)

Write "SKY-RITE" for sample Give six-mail envelope, 74 Varick St., N. Y.—Advt.

12 Inches of Snow Blanket Several Up-State Areas

Flurries Are Reported as Far South as the Pennsylvania Line—Temperature Here Is Near Record Low for Date

By The Associated Press

ALBANY, Oct. 1 — Canadian-border areas of upper New York dug out tonight from more than a foot of snow as high winds churned the tail-end of the season's first storm into near-blizzard fury.

It was still snowing early tonight, but a United States weather forecaster described the pre-winter blast as a one-day storm. He predicted low temperatures for another 48 hours.

The storm, whipping across the Adirondack area from Canada, forced some schools to close, blocked secondary highways and disrupted power and communications lines in northern New York.

Although the brunt of the storm was felt in the upper Adirondacks, its effect was State-wide. Temperatures plummeted near the freezing mark and snow flurries were reported in western and southern New York, along the Pennsylvania line.

Syracuse, reporting its earliest snow in forty-four years of official records, had a half-inch.

New York City's 45-degree temperature early this morning was within three degrees of the 1916 record low for the date.

Some up-State areas without snow had steady rain. Saratoga Springs reported a twenty-four-hour fall of 1.5 inches and Schenectady had 2.08 inches in the thirty-six hours ending at 8 A. M.

The villages of Malone in Franklin County and Potsdam in St. Lawrence apparently were hardest hit, with traffic crippled and heavy damage caused by falling trees and branches. Malone had 13 inches of snow and Potsdam a foot. Both were without electric power.

Malone's gas service was cut partly when a falling tree damaged a main. The Alice Hyde Memorial Hospital was without electricity all morning and gas most of the day. Power was re-

Continued on Page 27, Column 2

LEHMAN 'STRADDLE' CHARGED BY IVES

Says Rival Evades Wallace Foreign Policy Issue With Aim to Placate Left

Special to THE NEW YORK TIMES.

ALBANY, Oct. 1—Irving M. Ives, Republican candidate for United States Senator, charged tonight that former Governor Herbert H. Lehman, his Democratic opponent, had issued a "shadow doctrine" on foreign policy designed to placate both ends the Democrats and left-wing groups.

Mr. Lehman, he declared, straddled the issue and took a "vague and insecure" stand which had something to please "each of the political organizations and splinter parties he represents in this campaign."

Challenge on "Enslavement"

"Mr. Wallace believes in drawing an iron curtain across eastern Europe," he said, adding:

"We have seen that wars arise when people are enslaved and the truth kept from them. Does my opponent favor a policy which would permit this condition to ex-

Continued on Page 5, Column 5

HULL, 75, STRICKEN AFTER PEACE PLEA

United Nations' 'Father' Calls on Powers to Renew Zeal— His Condition Serious

Text of Mr. Hull's statement appears on page 18.

By BERTRAM D. HULEN

Special to THE NEW YORK TIMES.

WASHINGTON, Oct. 1—Cordell Hull, former Secretary of State, suffered a stroke in the United States Naval Hospital at Bethesda, Md., last night, a few hours after he had completed a statement appealing to the Great Powers to compose their differences for the sake of world peace.

Mr. Lehman, he declared, straddled condition. The improvement has been noted in his condition since the last bulletin," it said. "No change" was reported at midnight.

The stroke was officially described at first as "light," but the hospital announced later that Mr. Hull's condition had become "more serious during the day." Friends meanwhile had described him as extremely weak and had expressed grave concern. They considered his condition to be critical.

A hospital bulletin issued at 10 o'clock tonight said Mr. Hull remained in serious condition. "The

Nevertheless, the former Secretary's statement for world peace was issued on his behalf tonight, carrying out his instructions.

Continued on Page 18, Column 3

City's Search for Meat Supplies Fails to Uncover Any Hoarding

A meat search by three city departments was three-quarters finished yesterday and disclosed holdings in local slaughterhouses, storage plants and railroad cars of 13,312,580 pounds—not much compared to New York's normal consumption of 3,800,000 pounds a day.

With fewer than fifty of the city's 400 major repositories of meat still to be visited by the task force of 225 policemen and inspectors of the Health and Market departments, Mayor O'Dwyer said he saw nothing in the findings so far to warrant municipal action.

Meat supplies in retail stores, meanwhile, continued to shrink, and the Office of Price Administration reported that the black market was shrinking even faster than the supply of available meat. This did not seem any great victory to housewives, since the race was in the direction of a zero supply.

OPA enforcement agents, continuing their daily check on prices and, incidentally, supply, found

only one out of ten butcher shops with meat to sell. Many were short and many others sold only poultry. There was more sausage meat than any other kind. Last week the district OPA had reported one shop out of five selling meat.

Yesterday's report by the district enforcement staff was to the effect that only 5 per cent of the meat being offered for sale was at black market prices, whereas the same office had estimated last week that 20 to 35 per cent of the local sales were at over-ceiling prices.

The City Council, in a majority resolution sent to its rules committee, called upon the Federal Government to seize all cattle and meat in the country and blamed the meat industry for "open defiance to the American people for the creation of a meat famine." The resolution, which also urged that the Government make available to the public as an emergency health measure the most ac-

Continued on Page 33, Column 3

11,236-MILE RECORD SET AS NAVY PLANE LANDS IN COLUMBUS

Truculent Turtle Smashes Old Mark by 3,300 Miles in Non-Stop Flight From Australia

UP 55 HOURS 15 MINUTES

Four-Man Crew, Fresh Despite Rough Hop, Is Disappointed at Not Finishing in Washington

By FREDERICK GRAHAM

Special to THE NEW YORK TIMES.

COLUMBUS, Ohio, Oct. 1—A non-stop flight distance record that surpassed the previous mark by more than 3,300 miles was set today when the Truculent Turtle, the Navy's new twin-engine, land-based patrol bomber, landed here to complete an 11,236-mile flight that started Sunday morning in Perth, Australia.

The plane touched down here at 12:25 P. M., Eastern standard time.

The time for the flight, which started in the warm spring weather of Australia and ended in chilly winds here, was 55 hours 15 minutes. Despite a heavy load of fuel and constant headwinds that averaged 11.5 miles an hour for the entire trip, the average speed of the plane was 203.4 miles an hour.

The old distance record, set by the four-motored Dreamboat, a Superfortress, in a flight from Guam to Washington, was 7,976 miles.

Like "Long Patrol Mission"

"You might say it was no tougher than a good, long patrol mission," Comdr. Thomas D. Davies, chief of the four-man crew that manned the flat-sided Lockheed plane, said when he dropped from the exit hatch in the belly of the fuselage and greeted Navy officers at the municipal field.

"We had turbulent air, headwinds and some instrument weather," Commander Davies con-

Continued on Page 12, Column 3

RECEIVING THEIR FREEDOM FROM NUREMBERG COURT

Col. Burton C. Andrus, who headed the prison where the defendants were confined during their trial, handing out letters certifying their liberty to Hans Fritzsche (left), Franz von Papen (second from right) and Hjalmar Schacht (right).
Associated Press Radiophoto

GERMANY NOT FREE, SCHACHT COMPLAINS

Von Papen Says He Has Given Up Politics—Austria Seeks Extradition for Trial

By DANA ADAMS SCHMIDT

Special to THE NEW YORK TIMES.

NUREMBERG, Germany, Oct. 1—Frans von Papen said that his political career was "absolutely ended," Hans Fritzsche said he would like to try again by a German court and Hjalmar Schacht asked for choice late for his two children today when the three men acquitted by the International Military Tribunal appeared before 200 representatives of the world press.

Schacht got his candy bars and all reaped a harvest of cigarettes

Continued on Page 26, Column 3

Russian and Jackson Object; Schacht Called a Swindler

By The Associated Press

NUREMBERG, Germany, Oct. 1—Soviet Justice J. I. Nikitchenko tonight assailed the acquittal of three high Nazis by the International Military Tribunal, asserting that the opinion freeing Hjalmar Schacht, banker, was in "obvious contradiction to the evidence." [Justice Nikitchenko also declared Schacht a "swindler," according to a Reuters dispatch.]

The Russian Major General also dissented from the acquittal of the German General Staff, the Reich Cabinet and the decision imprisoning Rudolf Hess for life instead of giving him the death penalty.

Justice Robert Jackson of the United States, speaking for what he called the prosecutors of all nations, declared the decisions on individuals were of secondary importance compared to the fact that the principle was established making aggressive war a crime punishable by death. However, Justice Jackson also assailed the Schacht verdict.

Justice Nikitchenko said Fritzsche, as a radio propagandist, "had a most basic relation to the preparation and conduct of aggressive warfare." The most detailed dissent was in the case of the German General Staff and High Command, of which Justice Nikitchenko said:

"Without their advice and active cooperation, Hitler could not have solved [his] problems. In the majority of cases their opinion was decisive. * * * The General Staff issued most brutal decrees and orders for relentless measures against unarmed, peaceful population and prisoners of war."

Justice Nikitchenko said bluntly

Continued on Page 24, Column 6

SLAV BLOC STALLS VOTING ON TRIESTE

Connally Disputes Vishinsky's Charge That U. S. Seeks to Violate Big Four Accord

By LANSING WARREN

PARIS, Oct. 1—Making use of procedural entanglements in an atmosphere of raw nerves, the Slav States succeeded tonight in blocking a vote on the United States proposal to implement the Italian draft treaty's general clauses on a statute for Trieste.

During a tense discussion in the peace conference's Italian Political Commission, Senator Tom Connally of the United States and Andrei Y. Vishinsky, Soviet Vice Foreign Minister, exchanged accusations and retorts. Other leading delegates made contradictory suggestions on procedure, and finally the lateness of the hour forced adjournment.

Mr. Vishinsky charged that the United States proposal was an adroit and deliberate effort to evade an agreement by the Big Four's Council of Foreign Min-

Continued on Page 17, Column 2

Baruch Rebukes Wallace Groups For Distorting U. S. Atom Plan

By A. M. ROSENTHAL

LAKE SUCCESS, N. Y., Oct. 1—In a sharp reply to followers of former Secretary of Commerce Henry A. Wallace, Bernard M. Baruch, American representative on the United Nations Atomic Energy Commission, categorically denied tonight that this country was asking the rest of the world to stop nuclear research and reveal its uranium resources while the United States retained complete freedom of action.

No progress was made toward ending the Pittsburgh power walkout that has halted production on vital materials [2:3], and a strike of CIO warehouse and office workers threatens to paralyze the dress manufacturing industry in New York. [3:4.] Thirty-seven persons were in a picketing riot at Hollywood studios. [5:1.]

Mr. Baruch's strongly-worded denial was the result of statements made in Chicago on Saturday at a conference of the National Citizens Political Action Committee, Independent Citizens Committee of the Arts, Sciences and Professions, and the Congress of Industrial Organizations' Political Action Committee. It was sent as a telegram addressed to Henry Morgenthau, Harold Ickes and Philip Murray, president of the CIO, who were speakers at the conference.

After noting that the conference had gone on record as saying that the United States was trying to have other nations accept "binding agreements" while keeping its technical knowledge to itself as long as it saw fit, Mr. Baruch declared:

"I say without reservation that this is either misinformation or complete distortion. Nowhere does such a statement occur in the American proposal."

Mr. Baruch followed his denial with a pointed request for a correction.

"I am sending this to you," he said in the telegram, "in order that you may see that this is correct and rectified immediately."

The Baruch statement was issued by the American delegation at 7 P. M., on the eve of a meeting tomorrow morning of the Atomic Energy Commission's Committee 2, which will discuss the

Continued on Page 14, Column 2

World News Summarized

WEDNESDAY, OCTOBER 2, 1946

Twelve high Nazi conspirators were sentenced by the International Military Tribunal in Nuremberg yesterday to death by hanging for the supreme crime of aggressive war; three received life sentences in prison, four received lesser terms and three were acquitted.

The men who will be executed not later than Oct. 16 are Goering, von Ribbentrop, Kaltenbrunner, Rosenberg, Frank, Frick, Streicher, Sauckel, Seyss-Inquart, Keitel and Jodl. Bormann was sentenced to death in absentia. Hess, Funk and Grand Admiral Raeder received life sentences, von Schirach and Speer twenty years, von Neurath fifteen years and Grand Admiral Doenitz ten years. Schacht, von Papen and Fritzsche were acquitted. [All the foregoing 1:8.] The verdicts on Hess, von Papen and Schacht and the exoneration of the General Staff, Cabinet and Storm Troops as organizations brought a strong dissent from the Russian Justice, Maj. Gen. Nikitchenko. The chief American prosecutor, Justice Jackson, said he was "disappointed" in the liberation of von Papen and Schacht because it would adversely affect further prosecution of industrialists and militarists. [1:6-7.]

Russia accused the United States at a commission meeting of the Conference of Paris of attempting to change agreements reached by the Foreign Ministers Council on Trieste, and the Slav bloc succeeded in delaying a vote. [1:7.]

Former Secretary of State Hull, who is 75 years old today, was stricken in Bethesda Naval Hospital shortly after completing a statement urging the Great Powers to compose their differences for the sake of peace. His condition is serious. "Incalculable disaster" would follow any

irreconcilable division in this "most perilous juncture in history," Mr. Hull said. [1:3.]

A House committee, it was disclosed, has been quietly laying the basis to ask Congressional approval for this country's first integrated, permanent world-wide espionage and counterespionage service. [13:1.]

Iran, rejecting Britain's disavowals, has asked for the recall of a British Embassy secretary accused of conspiring to bring about a revolt of southern Iranians. [11:1.]

Dmitri Shostakovich's new Ninth Symphony has been condemned in the Soviet press for ideological weakness and failing to reflect the true spirit of the Russian people. [23:3-4.]

Bernard M. Baruch characterized as "either misinformation or complete distortion" charges at a political rally by supporters of former Secretary Wallace that the United States expected other nations to give up their atomic energy secrets while this country withheld all information. [1:6-7.]

The American Merchant Marine was almost completely tied up by the strike of engineers and dock officers that began at midnight yesterday. Federal conciliation efforts continued without result. [1:1.]

No progress was made toward ending the Pittsburgh power walkout that has halted production on vital materials [2:3], and a strike of CIO warehouse and office workers threatens to paralyze the dress manufacturing industry in New York. [3:4.] Thirty-seven persons were in a picketing riot at Hollywood studios. [5:1.]

The Navy bomber Truculent Turtle landed at Columbus, Ohio, establishing a new world-distance record of 11,236 miles in its non-stop flight from Perth, Australia. [1:4; map P. 12.]

By KATHLEEN McLAUGHLIN

Special to THE NEW YORK TIMES.

NUREMBERG, Germany, Oct. 1—Death by hanging was decreed this afternoon for twelve of the original twenty-four defendants indicted in the Nuremberg war crimes trials. The others—Dr. Hjalmar Schacht, Frans von Papen and Dr. Hans Fritzsche—were acquitted by the International Military Tribunal over the dissent of the Soviet member of the court, Maj. Gen. Iola T. Nikitchenko.

Those who will die by the noose within fifteen days, unless reprieved through an appeal within four days to the Allied Control Council in Berlin, are Hermann Goering, Joachim von Ribbentrop, Field Marshal Gen. Wilhelm Keitel, Ernst Kaltenbrunner, Dr. Alfred Rosenberg, Hans Frank, Wilhelm Frick, Julius Streicher, Fritz Sauckel, Col. Gen. Alfred Jodl and Arthur Seyss-Inquart.

Martin Bormann, who succeeded Rudolf Hess as Deputy Fuehrer and who was tried in absentia, owing to the lack of conclusive evidence that he is dead, also was sentenced to death by hanging if and when he ever is apprehended.

Mitigation in von Neurath Case

Life imprisonment was meted out to Hess, Walther Funk and Grand Admiral Erich Raeder. General Nikitchenko dissented likewise from his colleagues' judgment on Hess, expressing the opinion that he had merited death by hanging.

Baldur von Schirach, formerly supreme leader of the Hitler Jugend, and Albert Speer, Reich Minister for Armament and Munitions and chief of the Todt Organization, received twenty-year terms.

Possibly in consideration of his advanced years, Baron Constantin von Neurath, former Foreign Minister, although adjudged guilty on all four counts, received the comparatively mild sentence of fifteen years' imprisonment. He is 73. The Tribunal said in mitigation that he had been dismissed by Adolf Hitler for having been too lenient in his administration as Protector for Bohemia and Moravia and that he had intervened to obtain the release of many Czechoslovaks who had been arrested.

The mildest punishment of all fell to Grand Admiral Karl Doenitz, once Commander in Chief of the German Navy and, during the last days of the war, successor to Hitler as head of the German Government. He must serve ten years in prison.

[Six of those convicted—von Ribbentrop, Frank, Seyss-Inquart, von Schirach, Speer and Doenitz—have appealed their sentences, the British Broadcasting Company said, quoting official sources. The BBC broadcast was recorded by the National Broadcasting Company.]

Pattern Is Similar

In the courtroom, which over the last ten months has echoed unceasingly to the testimony of the unprecedented horrors precipitated upon the world through the Nazi hierarchy, the profound drama of the concluding phase of the trial lasted only fifty minutes. Lord Justice Sir Geoffrey Lawrence, as presiding jurist, announced all the sentences to the eighteen convicted men as they were summoned singly throughout the grim ordeal. An atmosphere of utter solemnity prevailed throughout the proceedings.

Beginning with Goering, former

Continued on Page 31, Column 3

"All the News That's Fit to Print"

The New York Times.

LATE CITY EDITION
Fair and continued cold today and tomorrow.
Temperature Range Today—Max. 39; Min. 30
Temperature Yesterday—Max. 49; Min. 39
U. S. Weather Bureau Report, Page 32, Sect. 1

Section 1

NEWS INDEX, PAGE 78, THIS SECTION

Copyright, 1947, by The New York Times Company

VOL. XCVII..No. 32,817.   NEW YORK, SUNDAY, NOVEMBER 30, 1947.   FIFTEEN CENTS

SCHUMAN BARS DISCUSSION OF FRENCH LABOR OVERTURE; COMMUNIST PAPERS SEIZED

PREMIER ADAMANT

Strikers Must Go Back on Regime's Terms— Labor Curbs Urged

ASSEMBLY SPLIT ON CODE

324 Saboteurs Are Arrested— Paris to Expel Aliens Who Help Ruin Economy

By HAROLD CALLENDER
Special to The New York Times.

PARIS, Sunday, Nov. 30—Premier Robert Schuman refused early today to meet the leaders of the Confederation of Labor to discuss a strike settlement different from that offered by the French Government.

Meanwhile, the Premier pressed hard for immediate passage by the Assembly of a law to strengthen the Government's hand by enlarging its police force and enabling it to imprison those who sought to force men to strike or who committed or urged sabotage.

As intense activity continued throughout the night inside and outside the Assembly, it became clear that the labor leaders who had encouraged the strikes had at last taken the initiative in seeking to end them, and that the Cabinet was divided regarding the policy the Government should adopt.

Early last evening Paris police surrounded the plants of the two Communist newspapers, l'Humanité and Ce Soir, entered the buildings and seized the plates of special editions whose publication had been forbidden. No papers were allowed to leave the plants. Later the police vacated the premises.

The special edition of l'Humanité, in large headlines printed in red ink, proclaimed: "They wish to assassinate the Republic!"

Minister Begins Parley

Shortly after M. Schuman had placed his proposed law before the Assembly early yesterday, Pierre Lebrun, a Communist secretary of the labor confederation, issued a statement urging renewed negotiations and mentioning that the striking workers would have a hard time when the Dec. 1 pay day came on Monday without pay envelopes.

At the same time, Daniel Mayer, Socialist Minister of Labor, who is understood to have opposed the law that M. Schuman sought, opened negotiations with the executive committee of the labor confederation, which met most of the night in his office while the Cabinet met in the Palais Bourbon. Through M. Mayer the committee asked to see M. Schuman, but the Premier refused his request and denied that the Government was negotiating with the strike leaders.

A sharp divergence of view became

Continued on Page 45, Column 3

U. S. Troops to Stay in Italy Beyond Dec. 3 Sailing Date

Change in Plans Is Linked to Disturbances Led by Communists—Milan Is Calm Following Compromise on Prefect

By ARNALDO CORTESI
Special to The New York Times.

ROME, Nov. 29—The United States Army Department today ordered Maj. Gen. Lawrence Jaynes, commanding the Mediterranean Theatre of Operations, and his entire staff to postpone their departure from Italy. With them will remain about 2,500 officers and men who are leading specialists of the United States Army in Italy.

The order is believed to reflect the anxiety with which the Government in Washington views the Communist-fomented disturbances in Italy.

General Jaynes and his officers and men had planned to leave from Leghorn on Dec. 3 aboard the Admiral Sims. Washington ordered a postponement of departure until Dec. 14, the deadline set by the Italian peace treaty. No explanation was given for the change of plans and this strengthened the impression that it was dictated by preoccupation over Italy's political outlook.

The officers and men who will form the skeleton organization for a large army. They include highly trained specialists, familiar with conditions in Italy. They belong to the Engineer, Signal, Ordnance, Secretariat, Quartermaster, Medical and Military Police Corps and other auxiliary services.

Washington's change of plans came after General Jaynes had said farewell to Pope Pius and President Enrico de Nicola. Ambassador James C. Dunn called on Premier Alcide de Gasperi two days ago, and it is presumed that he informed the Italian Government then of the postponement of the American troops' departure.

Though the American troops should, under present plans, leave

Continued on Page 45, Column 1

No-Parking Area Is Created From City Hall to Canal St.

After a two-hour conference with Mayor O'Dwyer at Police Headquarters, Police Commissioner Arthur W. Wallander announced yesterday two further moves in the department's efforts to ease traffic congestion in the city.

Commissioner Wallander added the section of Manhattan north of City Hall as far as Canal Street and west to but not including West Street to the restricted parking areas already established in a large part of the borough below Fifty-ninth Street.

He also said that a survey was being made throughout the city in an effort to discover additional sites for municipal parking lots like the one established at the old World's Fair parking lot in Flushing, Queens. "The lot set up experimentally there 'looks promising,'" he said, reporting that 766 motorists had used it on Friday.

Mayor Explains Needs

The Commissioner announced the moves at a press conference at the end of his talk with the Mayor. Mr. O'Dwyer sat in on the press conference and added some comments of his own after his aide had made the announcement.

About forty traffic policemen will be needed to enforce the parking restrictions in the new area, the Mayor said. Commissioner Wallander asked for 2,000 additional men for the Police Department to take care of this and other needs, which would add $6,000,000 to the department's budget, he continued.

Together with $4,000,000 for the men added to the force last July, this would amount to a total of $10,000,000 that would have to be appropriated for the Police Department next year in addition to

Continued on Page 37, Column 1

Congress Action Lags on Aid Bill Despite Warnings Need Is Urgent

By JOHN D. MORRIS

WASHINGTON, Nov. 29—Congress set aside the troublesome problems of European aid and domestic inflation today and attended the Army-Navy game practically en masse, while pressures for accelerated action on the legislative problems awaited members' return to work Monday.

Despite repeated representations of urgency in both fields, the Congressional machinery faced a slowdown in production of the authorizing legislation still needed for winter relief to France, Italy and Austria.

Formulation of anti-inflation legislation still had hardly begun, and completion of the task was far out of sight.

The Senate was prepared to resume consideration Monday of the foreign relief bill, but earlier expectations of passage on that day had been diminished by failure yesterday to dispose of four amendments proposed by Senator

James P. Kem, Republican, of Missouri.

While some of them are acceptable to the bill's managers, at least one is expected to cause considerable discussion and possible delay of a vote on the bill itself until Tuesday.

This would require detailed, written acknowledgement by every recipient of relief supplies that the goods were gifts of the United States.

Senator Kem successfully opposed action on the amendments yesterday, asserting that he wanted Thanksgiving holiday absentees to be present when the votes were taken. He thus disrupted leaders' plans for cleaning the slate of all proposed amendments so that the bill itself could be disposed of Monday.

Hope for a final vote Monday

Continued on Page 26, Column 4

VAST GI HOUSING TO RISE NEAR SITE OF WORLD'S FAIR

21 14-Story Apartment Units to Form Nation's Largest Veterans' Cooperative

COST PUT AT $58,000,000

Occupancy on Tenant-Owner Basis—Work Will Start Before End of Year

By LEE E. COOPER

On a fifty-five-acre tract overlooking the site of the World's Fair of 1939, the country's largest veterans' cooperative apartment community soon will begin to take form, it became known last night.

After nearly a year of negotiations, and with the official blessing of the city and of the Veterans Administration, plans for the $58,000,000 project were revealed by Frederick Briggs, chairman of the board of the Communities Inc. development corporation, which is sponsoring the enterprise.

The new Queens housing center, which will occupy a large part of the former Arrowbrook Golf Club grounds, will be for occupancy exclusively by veterans of World War II and their families on a tenant-ownership basis.

Plans call for the erection of twenty-one fourteen-story apartment houses of the fireproof type, to accommodate 5,699 families. Each building will have its own garage facilities, to be rented separately, for tenants' automobiles.

Shopping Centers Will Rise

In furtherance of the plan to create a self-contained community, the builders will erect shopping centers at the edges of the property, which is bounded by Main Street, Jewel Avenue and Park Drive East, within the boundaries of Flushing Meadow Park. A promenade, with stores beneath it, will be constructed on the hillside overlooking Flushing Meadow Park. The residential buildings will be set amid winding tree-lined walks and landscaped park spaces.

The Board of Estimate gave its unanimous sanction to the project at a special closed session last Wednesday, after receiving a favorable report on it from Robert Moses, City Construction Coordinator who had been in consultation with the sponsors.

The city's cooperation will be limited to street changes and zoning aids permitting stores and the erection of fourteen-story buildings on the site. No municipal financial

Continued on Page 12, Column 3

World News Summarized

SUNDAY, NOVEMBER 30, 1947

The General Assembly of the United Nations yesterday approved the plan for the partition of Palestine by a vote of 33 to 13 with ten abstentions and one absence. After the vote there were repeated statements of bitterness and disillusion from the Arab representatives. One after another they asserted that the Charter had been violated and that their nations would not be bound by the action and would reserve "freedom of action." The Arabs then walked out of the Assembly. [1:8.]

The Arabs subsequently pronounced the United Nations "dead," and disavowed any intention of playing a part under the partition plan. They went on to say, however, that this did not mean their retirement from the United Nations. Zionist leaders were jubilant over the outcome. [1:6-7.]

Zionists attending the Assembly expressed their joy with tears and excited laughter. Dr. Oswaldo Aranha praised the public for its good behavior. [1:7.] The Palestine debate concluded the business of the current session of the General Assembly, and Dr. Aranha of Brazil gave his closing address. He declared that this second meeting had made a notable contribution to world peace, and after the delegates had risen to applaud him the session adjourned. [1:5.]

In London, Soviet Foreign Minister Molotov demanded the early establishment of a German government to accept the peace treaty. The other Ministers, seeing this as a move to commit themselves against any possible partition of Germany, opposed him. [1:6-7.] Secretary Marshall drew an eager crowd at the Council of Foreign Ministers next week to achieve the economic unification of Germany through the removal of all

sonal barriers in what is expected to be the most important United States proposal at the conference. [5:0.3.]

In this deputies' meeting the Soviet delegation continued to study the French proposals on Austria and refused to agree on principle at any point. Action was delayed, but it was felt the Russians might accept. [5:1.1.]

In Paris, Premier Schuman declined to discuss with leaders of the Confederation of Labor any strike settlement on terms other than the Government's. He asked for police powers to suppress Communist agitators and moved against Communist papers. They had charged that a "revolutionary coup" was planned, that midnight and that "assassination of the Republic" was its objective. The editions were suppressed. [1:1.]

In Italy, the United States commander and 2,500 American troops were ordered by Washington to postpone departure, presumably because of the troubled situation. The general strike in Milan, however, was ended. [1:2-3.]

The Ronne Expedition in the Antarctic reported the exploration and mapping of a total of about 100,000 square miles of territory in the name of the United States. [56:3.]

A scientific advance that may be of importance in insect pest control was announced by the United States Army. Ultrasonic waves have been developed that are lethal to mice and small insects. [14:4.]

Defense Secretary Forrestal has been instructed by President Truman to turn over the records of 28,000 wartime Army officers who have been retired for disability on tax-free pay, in the determination to "wipe out any possible 'racket.'" [1:2.]

U. S. REJECTS DELAY

Proposal Driven Through by U. S. and Soviet Will Set Up Two States

COMMISSION IS APPOINTED

Britain Holds Out Hand to It— Arabs Fail in Last-Minute Resort to Federal Plan

By THOMAS J. HAMILTON

The United Nations General Assembly approved yesterday a proposal to partition Palestine into two states, one Arab and the other Jewish, that was to become fully independent by Oct. 1. The vote was 33 to 13 with ten abstentions and one delegation, the Siamese, absent.

The decision was primarily a result of the fact that the delegations of the United States and the Soviet Union, which were at loggerheads on every other important issue before the Assembly, stood together on partition. Andrei A. Gromyko and Herschel V. Johnson both urged the Assembly yesterday not to agree to further delay but to vote for partition at once.

The Assembly disregarded last-minute Arab efforts to effect a compromise. Although the votes of a dozen or more delegations seesawed to the last, supporters of partition had two votes more than the required two-thirds majority, for a margin of three.

How Members Voted

The roll-call vote was as follows:

For (33)—Australia, Belgium, Bolivia, Brazil, Canada, Costa Rica, Czechoslovakia, Denmark, Dominican Republic, Ecuador, France, Guatemala, Haiti, Iceland, Liberia, Luxembourg, the Netherlands, New Zealand, Nicaragua, Norway, Panama, Paraguay, Peru, Philippines, Poland, Sweden, the Ukraine, South Africa, Uruguay, the Soviet Union, the United States, Venezuela, White Russia.

Against (13)—Afghanistan, Cuba, Egypt, Greece, India, Iran, Iraq, Lebanon, Pakistan, Saudi Arabia, Syria, Turkey, Yemen.

Abstentions (10) — Argentina, Chile, China, Colombia, El Salvador, Ethiopia, Honduras, Mexico, United Kingdom, Yugoslavia.

Absent (1)—Siam.

All other questions before the Assembly were disposed of a week ago, and it ended its second regular session at 6:37 P. M. after farewell speeches by Dr. Oswaldo Aranha, its President, and Trygve Lie, the Secretary General. The Assembly's third regular session is to open in a European capital on Sept. 21.

The vote on partition was taken at 5:35 P. M. Representatives of Iraq, Saudi Arabia, Syria and Yemen, four of the six Arab member states, announced that they would not be bound by the Assembly's decision and walked determinedly out of the Assembly Hall at Flushing Meadow. The Egyptian and Lebanese delegates were silent but walked out, too.

Briton Seeks Contact

Sir Alexander Cadogan, representative of Britain, which is to terminate the League of Nations mandate over Palestine and withdraw all British troops by Aug. 1, made a brief statement after the vote. He requested the United Nations Palestine Commission to establish contact with the British Government about the date of its arrival in Palestine and the coordination of its plans with the withdrawal of British troops.

The United Nations commission, which will be responsible to the Security Council in the event that the Arabs carry out their threats to fight rather than agree to partition, will be composed of representatives of Bolivia, Czechoslovakia, Denmark, Panama and the Philippines.

The commission, as proposed by the partition subcommittee of the

Continued on Page 60, Column 2

ASSEMBLY VOTES PALESTINE PARTITION; MARGIN IS 33 TO 13; ARABS WALK OUT; ARANHA HAILS WORK AS SESSION ENDS

PEACE GAINS NOTED

Brazilian Says Contacts Inspired No Forecast of Imminent War

CITES ROLE OF MINORITY

Lie Regrets That Economic Issues Were Sidetracked —Others Hail Aranha

By MARSHALL E. NEWTON

It is the mission of the United Nations to achieve world peace and the General Assembly made a memorable contribution in that direction, Dr. Oswaldo Aranha of Brazil, president of the Assembly, told the delegates of the fifty-seven member nations yesterday in his speech closing the second regular session in Flushing Meadow.

When he finished his address the delegates rose and applauded Dr. Aranha, whose talents and statesmanlike handling of the difficult task of presiding at the international assembly had been lauded by several preceding speakers.

Dr. Aranha pointed out that the present post-war period had not been marked by the armed conflicts that had followed the Peace of Versailles and he said that we lived today in a different era, in which our minds must turn to the future and not the past.

Calls for Foresight

"But close contact with international political life leads to no forecast of world war in the near future," he said. "The world seeks, however, new forms of political, economic and social integration in which the contest of ideas will supersede the clash of arms. The status quo is no longer possible. A new reality is rising in sour days, to which we must impart the spirit of the United Nations, the only conception capable of insuring peace, solidarity, dignity and equality for all peoples.

"Our action should not be post factum. Our task is one of foresight and of organized prevention to eliminate the elements and factors capable of disturbing world

Continued on Page 67, Column 3

Arabs See U. N. 'Murdered,' Disavow Any Partition Role

Angry Delegates Stalk From Assembly Hall Before Formal Closing—Silver Voices Gratification, Offers Friendship

By A. M. ROSENTHAL

Bitter Arab delegates walked out of the General Assembly hall at Flushing Meadow last night after the vote for the partition of Palestine and solemnly announced that in their eyes the United Nations had died.

"No, not died," said Faris el-Khouri of Syria. "Murdered."

The representatives of the Arab states swept out of the building without waiting for the formal end of the Assembly and the farewell speeches. But before they announced that they would have absolutely nothing to do with the United Nations Commission for Palestine, nothing to do with the transitional period after the end of the mandate and nothing to do with partition.

There was an open thread of Arab delegates' comments on the Assembly's action. They spoke of bloodshed to come and said the

responsibility would not be theirs, but would be on the shoulders of the countries that had pressed for partition.

On the other side of the quarter-century Arab-Zionist dispute there was jubilation and hope for the future. Dr. Abba Hillel Silver, chairman of the American section of the Jewish Agency for Palestine, expressed his gratitude to the United States and especially to the Soviet Union.

Dr. Silver's statement follows:

"We are deeply gratified with the action of the United Nations. It marks a turning point in Jewish history. It is an impressive reaffirmation of the just claim of the Jewish people to rebuild its national life in its ancestral home.

"This noble decision to re-establish the Jewish state and restore

Continued on Page 60, Column 1

Molotov Insists on Regime Before Treaty on Germany

By DREW MIDDLETON
Special to The New York Times.

LONDON, Nov. 29—Soviet Foreign Minister Molotov urged with new fervor in the Council of Foreign Ministers today the early establishment of a central German government as a precondition of the peace treaty.

Mr. Molotov's argument was based on the futility of completing a German peace treaty with no German government to sign it or assist in its preparation. But it was obvious that the Soviet delegate was moved by fears that the Western Allies, if this Council meeting failed, would make their own arrangements for a German government and treaty.

With a stridency that disrupted an otherwise decorous meeting, Mr. Molotov declared that the Soviet Union would never recognize a peace signed by Western Germany and the Western powers. No government set up in Frankfort on the Main in the United States zone and no "ersatz government for Bizonia" will be an adequate substitute for the Soviet proposal, he asserted.

Secretary of State Marshall and French Foreign Minister Bidault both flatly opposed any tendency to make the establishment of a German government a precondition of signing the German peace treaty.

A compromise proposal presented by British Foreign Secretary Bevin was as abruptly turned down by Mr. Molotov, who said it did not go far enough. Then he proceeded to add a clause that made the British proposal an echo of the Soviet suggestion.

This brisk exchange of German participation in the peace making followed an encouraging agreement by the Big Four on the ad-

Continued on Page 54, Column 3

ZIONIST AUDIENCE JOYFUL AFTER VOTE

Tears, Excited Laughter Mark Tension—Aranha Commends Public's Good Behavior

By WALTER S. SULLIVAN

The attention of the entire Arab and Jewish worlds was focused on Flushing Meadow yesterday to hear the verdict of the United Nations General Assembly on the future of Palestine.

The reaction in the packed main hall to the decision for partition typified that of listeners far and near. While members of the Arab delegations walked out, Zionists in the audience rejoiced.

It was a rejoicing that started with silence and grew as the meaning neared its end. In the public lobby there were kisses and tears and excited laughter. In the delegates' lounge a rabbi cried, "This is the day the Lord hath made! Let us rejoice in it and be glad!"

The initial silence resulted from a call to order by the Assembly's president, Dr. Oswaldo Aranha. A burst of applause had greeted the surprise vote of France in favor of partition, and it was this that had

Continued on Page 57, Column 3

Company Asks Rise in Gas Rate From $1.15 to $2 Sliding Scale

The Consolidated Edison Company of New York, Inc., announced yesterday it had applied to the State Public Service Commission for permission to increase the maximum charge for gas from $1.15 a thousand cubic feet to $2 with declining rates after the first thousand.

The petition said that neither Consolidated Edison nor any of its predecessor companies had increased its rates since Oct. 1, 1922, and that existing rates were confiscatory of the company's property. It was estimated that the company would lose $1,498,500 in 1947 from its gas operations.

According to the company, 57 per cent of the gas it supplies is sold at the maximum rate of $1.15 a thousand cubic feet. The company's service area includes 1,100,000 customers in Manhattan, the Bronx and the first and third wards of Queens—Astoria, Long

Island City, Flushing, College Point, Whitestone, Douglaston, Bayside, Little Neck and Bellerose.

The company proposed an immediate schedule of temporary rates, which it estimated would increase its annual revenues approximately $6,289,700 on the basis of estimated gas sales for 1947.

If this increase had been in effect through 1947, the company said, it would have provided its stockholders with a net return after taxes of $4,200,000 in connection with its gas operations.

If approved by the Public Service Commission, the new classifications would provide a maximum charge of $2 for the first thousand cubic feet or less of gas consumed in any bi-monthly billing period.

For the first 4,000 cubic feet consumed bi-monthly after the initial 1,000-foot block, residential customers would be charged 12 cents a hundred; 10 cents a hun-

Continued on Page 12, Column 1

WAR PAY 'RACKET' HUNTED BY TRUMAN

Gen. Vaughan Says President Wants Army, Navy, Air House-Cleaning on Disability Cases

Special to The New York Times.

WASHINGTON, Nov. 29—The armed services are preparing to turn over to President Truman at his request the records of 28,000 wartime Army officers who have been retired for disability on tax-free pay normally amounting to three-fourths of their active service remuneration.

This became known as an aftermath of the case against Maj. Gen. Bennett E. Meyers and was confirmed today by Maj. Gen. Harry H. Vaughan, the President's military aide, who said at Philadelphia that Mr. Truman was determined to "wipe out any possible 'racket'" in tax-free disability retirement pay.

The President has already spoken about the matter to James Forrestal, Secretary of Defense, and it is expected that a formal directive will be received soon.

Presumably the order will apply also to naval officers retired for disability so that once the President has the records in hand he

Continued on Page 27, Column 1

Major Sports Results

FOOTBALL

With Rip Rowan passing for the first touchdown and dashing ninety-two yards for the second, Army beat Navy yesterday for the fourth straight year. N.Y.U. rallied to defeat Fordham. Scores of leading games:

Alabama 21	Miami, Fla.... 6
Army 21	Navy 0
Florida 25	Kansas State 7
Fordham 16	N.Y.U. 18
Ga. Tech.... 7	Georgia 0
Holy Cross..26	Boston Coll.. 7
Maryland ... 0	N. C. State.. 0
Mich. State..55	Hawaii 19
Mississippi ..33	Miss. State .14
N. Carolina..40	Virginia 7
Oklahoma ...21	Okla. A.&M..13
Oregon Sta...27	Nebraska ... 6
Rice 34	Baylor 4
S. M. U. 19	T. C. U. 19
Tennessee ...12	Vanderbilt .. 7
Texas Tech..14	Hardin-Sim.. 6
West Va. ...17	Pittsburgh .. 2

CROSS COUNTRY

Curtis Stone of Philadelphia won the National A.A.U. championship at Van Cortlandt Park, but the New York A.C. took the team title for the third successive time.

HORSE RACING

Inchac outran Gallorette to capture the Bryan and O'Hara Memorial Handicap at Bowie on the last day of the major Eastern season.

(Full details in Section 5.)

"All the News That's Fit to Print"

The New York Times.

LATE CITY EDITION
Increasing cloudiness, cold today. Snow, not so cold tomorrow.
Temperature Range Today—Max.,18; Min.,6
Temperature Yesterday—Max.,24; Min.,5.5
Full U. S. Weather Bureau Report, Page 21

Copyright, 1948, by The New York Times Company

VOL. XCVII No. 32,879.

Entered as Second-Class Matter, Postoffice, New York, N. Y.

NEW YORK, SATURDAY, JANUARY 31, 1948.

THREE CENTS NEW YORK CITY

MANY HOMES WITHOUT HEAT AS ZERO COLD IS DUE HERE; U. S. CUTS OIL EXPORTS 18½%

FUEL CRISIS GROWS

Hundreds of Families Reported Suffering in City Area

BAY STATE SEIZES PLANT

Bradford Acts When Walkout Threatens Boston Gas—Oil Diversion Denied Here

By WILL LISSNER

Hundreds of families in the city were reported by their landlords to be in cold homes for lack of fuel oil last night as temperatures dropped toward zero in Manhattan and toward subzero levels in the suburbs.

At 3 A. M. today the temperature dropped to 2.2 degrees, establishing a new low record for the season. The previous record was 5 degrees, registered last Saturday.

The winter's coldest winds gripped not only New York but the whole Northwest. The Midwest and South, however, got some relief yesterday from the protracted cold spell. The fuel situation was reported acute in many cities throughout the East.

Temperatures, after falling to points between zero and 5 degrees above in Manhattan and zero and 10 degrees below in the suburbs, are expected to rise today to 20 degrees. The cold is due to continue, according to the United States Weather Bureau, but whereas yesterday was sunny, increasing cloudiness was expected today. More snow is threatened tomorrow. The lowest temperature yesterday was 5.5 degrees at 9:50 A. M.

Yesterday's hourly temperatures were:

1 A. M.	.23	2 P. M.	.15
2 A. M.	.23	3 P. M.	.15
3 A. M.	.22	4 P. M.	.14
4 A. M.	.18	5 P. M.	.12
5 A. M.	.12	6 P. M.	.12
6 A. M.	.9	7 P. M.	.11
7 A. M.	.8	8 P. M.	.9
8 A. M.	.6	9 P. M.	.9
9:50 A.M.	5.5	10 P. M.	.7
10 A. M.	.7	11 P. M.	.7
11 A. M.	.7	12 M.	.4
Noon	.9	1 A. M.	.4
1 P. M.	.10	2 A. M.	2.2

Petroleum Exports Cut

As the fuel shortage produced critical conditions for many apartment and home owners in this and other cities, officials took steps to relieve the situation.

The Commerce Department announced in Washington that it had ordered exports of petroleum products cut 18½ per cent from 11,850,000 to 9,650,000 barrels during the first quarter of the year. Oil exports to Japan and the Ryukyus were cut 1,600,000 barrels to 100,000. Exports will be allowed only from areas where fuel can be spared best, the department said.

In Massachusetts Gov. Robert F. Bradford ordered the seizure of a gas plant in Everett when a walkout of 900 workers was threatened that would have affected service to sixty-four hospitals and 1,500,000 residents of Greater Boston. After seizure and issuance of a temporary injunction, union leaders ordered their followers to remain at work.

In Tennessee, Governor James McCord proclaimed a state of emergency and announced a voluntary fuel conservation program.

In Rochester, Sheriff's deputies and city policemen were organized to make emergency deliveries of fuel oil in extreme cases.

In Endicott, Mayor E. Raymond Lee declared an emergency due to the gas shortage and urged residents to conserve fuel. Many homes there and in Binghamton and Johnson City were without heat and residents sought emergency shelter.

Philadelphians Warned

Residents of Philadelphia were warned of a gas shortage caused by the oil shortage and were urged to restrict use of gas to the absolute minimum.

Police Commissioner Arthur W. Wallander of this city, regional fuel coordinator, sent telegrams asking supply-as terminal dealers here to remain open today and tomorrow, because of the expected severe cold, to supply fuel oil to hardship cases.

Mayor O'Dwyer declared during the afternoon that it was not necessary at this time to proclaim a state of emergency and to divert

Continued on Page 12, Column 5

Petroleum Shipment Abroad Is Curbed to Ease Shortage

Department of Commerce Orders Quotas Reduced From 11,850,000 to 9,650,000 Barrels for Quarter—Slashes Japan

Special to The New York Times.

WASHINGTON, Jan. 30—The Department of Commerce announced today that "in view of the serious shortage of fuel oils," in this country it had ordered an 18½ per cent cut in exports of petroleum products during the first quarter of the year. Its action will reduce from 11,850,000 to 9,650,000 the barrels of petroleum designated for overseas.

The Department also announced that it would limit licenses for export of petroleum products to shipments for those areas of the United States where the fuel can best be spared during the emergency.

In addition, it was disclosed that a separate quota of gas oil and distillate fuel oil had been established for the first quarter for shipments to Japan and the Ryukyus, drastically cutting their supply from 1,600,000 barrels to 100,000. The Department said that the difference would be met from oil produc-

Continued on Page 11, Column 4

ing areas outside the United States.

Proposals had been made in Congress to stop all shipments abroad except those going to American military forces. Bills to accomplish this end have been introduced in the House and the Senate.

Walter S. Hallanan, chairman of the National Petroleum Council, said today that the petroleum industry had taken "prompt and forthright action to alleviate the shortage of some petroleum products which have been rendered acute in certain sections by the severe cold weather. The industry "takes pride in the fact that it was the first to develop a voluntary agreement under the recent authorization of Congress," he added.

Canada Is Not Affected

WASHINGTON, Jan. 30 (UP)—The action today of the Depart-

Hope Wanes in Sea Search For 28 Aboard Lost Airliner

By FREDERICK GRAHAM

The Atlantic area northeast of Bermuda was being searched last night for survivors of a British South American Airways plane that disappeared in the area early yesterday morning with a crew of six and at least twenty-two passengers, but hope had almost been abandoned.

The thirty-two-passenger plane, which listed among those aboard Air Marshal Sir Arthur Coningham, Royal Air Force, who commanded the Second Tactical Air Force of the Allies at the invasion of Normandy, was out of London and on the Azores-to-Bermuda leg of the flight when last heard from about 1 A. M. (EST) yesterday.

At least fifteen United States Air Force, Navy and Coast Guard planes plus three Coast Guard cutters, two commercial steamers and a British South American Airways plane worked over a large area about 400 miles northeast of Bermuda without success. More aircraft are scheduled to continue the search today.

The plane, a converted Lancaster bomber of the type used by the RAF for saturation bombing of Germany, had stopped in Santa Maria in the Azores to refuel. An Associated Press dispatch from Bermuda said the plane, believed to have been commanded by Capt. David Colby, radioed to Bermuda that it would arrive there at midnight Thursday, an hour and a half late. One hour later it reported to Bermuda again, saying it was 440 miles northeast of Bermuda and that it was bucking strong headwinds. Nothing more has been heard from the plane.

The only other report that might

Continued on Page 10, Column 2

ORVILLE WRIGHT, 76, IS DEAD IN DAYTON

Co-Inventor With His Brother, Wilbur, of the Airplane Was Pilot in First Flight

Special to The New York Times.

DAYTON, Ohio, Jan. 30—Orville Wright, who with his brother, the late Wilbur Wright, invented the airplane, died here tonight at 10:40 in Miami Valley Hospital. He was 76 years old.

Mr. Wright, who had been confined to a hospital in October, collapsed in his office on Tuesday. He was suffering from lung congestion and coronary arteriosclerosis.

At the bedside when Mr. Wright died were Horace A. Wright, a nephew; Mrs. H. S. Miller, a niece, and Delyle Myers, a nurse.

The announcement of his death was made by Dr. A. B. Brower, family physician.

Engrossing Amusement

In the early fall of 1900 fishermen and Coast Guardsmen dwelling on that lonely and desolated spot of sand dividing Albemarle Sound from the Atlantic Ocean on the coast of North Carolina called

Continued on Page 12, Column 2

Arms Get Atomic Energy Priority In Policy Set by Congress Group

By WILLIAM S. WHITE

Special to The New York Times.

WASHINGTON, Jan. 30—The Joint Committee on Atomic Energy laid down today a firm policy that the production of atomic weapons, rather than work on peacetime applications of atomic energy, must be the "vital business" of the United States for the foreseeable future.

It declared also that "uninterrupted operation" of the "critical, or military, facilities of the Atomic Energy Commission was so essential to national security that an investigation was in motion to find a formula to assure "continuity of work" under all labor eventualities.

In its first report to the committee indicated some dissatisfaction in "a number of cases" with certain aspects of the handling of internal security within the personnel of the Atomic Energy Commission.

"In certain of these cases," the report went on, "the committee has requested that the commis-

Continued on Page 7, Column 5

sion outline in detail its security policy as applied to these specific instances."

"In the majority of these cases," it was added, the men in question had been employed while atomic energy still was under Army control.

As to the essential policy to be followed in atomic development, the committee declared:

"Until such time as an effective, enforceable and reliable program for the international control of atomic energy is in successful operation, the most vital business of the Atomic Energy Commission must be the meeting of the atomic requirements of national defense.

"The joint committee has been assured that those charged with these responsibilities are keenly aware thereof. This phase of the atomic energy program is of para-

Record 799-Million Budget Is Asked by Dewey for State

He Estimates Actual Outlay at 753 Millions for Next Fiscal Year, but Says No Rise in Taxes Is Needed—Warns on Inflation

By LEO EGAN

Special to The New York Times.

ALBANY, Jan. 30—Governor Dewey submitted another record-breaking budget to the Legislature tonight, calling for appropriations of $799,600,000, including deficiencies for the current year, but estimating actual expenditures in the new budget year at a figure of $753,500,000. The Governor regards the lower figure as his "budget" total.

Appropriations recommended are $128,200,000 higher than those carried in last year's budget message but, because of supplemental grants for teacher pay, veterans' housing, college housing, central schools and rent control, only $53,400,000 higher than actual appropriations, which were $746,200,000.

The expenditures of $753,500,000 contemplated in Mr. Dewey's message compare with an actual total of $707,500,000 in the current year, according to revised estimates. The

Continued on Page 9, Column 1

revised figure reflects increased relief contributions and higher food prices for inmates of state institutions which are being provided for in deficiency appropriations.

Allowing for continuance of the reductions made in 1946, which he recommended, the Governor estimated that existing regular taxes would produce $758,600,000 in the new budget year, enough to balance expenditures and leave a $5,000,000 surplus.

The regular tax structure does not include the additional one-cent-a-package levy on cigarettes or the 20 per cent increase in existing income tax rates which were voted to finance the $400,000,000 veterans' bonus. If the present return from these special levies continued, Mr. Dewey said, the bonus bonds might be retired in eight years.

Text of Gov. Dewey's budget message will be found on pages 8 and 9.

REALTY VALUATIONS RISE $745,775,468 IN CITY FOR 1948-49

Higher Accrued Value Is Chief Factor in $17,684,240,921 Total, Biggest Since '33

By LEE E. COOPER

New York's land and buildings, regarded as the richest segment of real estate in the world, have risen in value to $17,684,240,921 on the city's tax books for the coming fiscal year.

Municipal assessors have chalked up a tentative increase of $745,775,468 over current figures on taxable properties for the year beginning July 1, 1948, to carry the aggregate valuations to the highest level since 1933.

A report submitted to Mayor O'Dwyer yesterday by Harry B. Chambers, president of the Tax Commission, showed an average rise of about 4½ per cent for the five boroughs, accounted for largely by an upswing in "accrued value" rather than by addition of new construction to the assessment rolls.

The report set the following tentative

Continued on Page 11, Column 3

GOP GROUP SHAPES SHARP ERP REVISION WITH FUND REDUCED

A Proposal to Sell U. S. Goods to Latin America for Food for Europe Wins Favor

By FELIX BELAIR Jr.

Special to The New York Times.

WASHINGTON, Jan. 30—A fighting nucleus of eighteen Senate leaders tonight to press for important changes in the Administration's European Recovery Program as the party's legislative leaders brushed aside President Truman's demand for approval of the full $6,800,000,000 of operations.

The group of eighteen Senators, in which Westerners predominated, called for a complete shift in emphasis of the Marshall Plan "from the underwriting of trade deficits to the support of specific production programs" in which financial aid would be contingent on increased output of food, coal, steel and transportation facilities.

Senator Joseph H. Ball of Minnesota said the principles agreed

Continued on Page 6, Column 2

GANDHI IS KILLED BY A HINDU; INDIA SHAKEN, WORLD MOURNS; 15 DIE IN RIOTING IN BOMBAY

MOHANDAS K. GANDHI
The New York Times

All Britain Honors Gandhi; Truman Deplores Tragedy

By HERBERT L. MATTHEWS

Special to The New York Times.

LONDON, Jan. 30—Mohandas K. Gandhi, in death, has won the unanimous tribute of Britons—something he never hoped for or expected during his life. Nowhere outside of India has the shock of his assassination contained the feelings and emotions evident here today because Britain and Mr. Gandhi have been linked for good or evil over the last forty years.

In a special broadcast to the British people tonight the Prime Minister said:

"The voice which pleaded for peace and brotherhood has been silenced, but I am certain that his spirit will continue to animate his fellow countrymen and will plead for peace and concord."

[President Truman and Secretary Marshall expressed their grief and condolences in messages to India. Members of Congress were apprehensive. Leaders of many other lands joined in paying tribute and in deploring the manner of Mr. Gandhi's death.]

The sincerity of today's expressions of regret, which came from the King and Queen, the Prime Minister, the political parties—even the Communist—and from many humble Londoners who filed silently into India House this afternoon to pay tribute, cannot be doubted.

Those many quarrels when Mr. Gandhi fought with his passive resistance against the imperial power of Britain are truly things of the past. Mr. Gandhi himself paid high tribute to Britain for his policy of freeing India and of trying to help to keep the two dominions at peace with each other. The British, on their side, have

Continued on Page 3, Column 2

THREE SHOTS FIRED

Slayer Is Seized, Beaten After Felling Victim on Way to Prayer

DOMINION IS BEWILDERED

Nehru Appeals to the Nation to Keep Peace—U. S. Consul Assisted in Capture

By ROBERT TRUMBULL

Special to The New York Times.

NEW DELHI, India, Jan. 30—Mohandas K. Gandhi was killed by an assassin's bullet today. The assassin was a Hindu who fired three shots from a pistol at a range of three feet.

The 78-year-old Gandhi, who was the one person who held discordant elements together and kept some sort of unity in this turbulent land, was shot down at 5:15 P. M. as he was proceeding through the Birla House gardens to the pergola from which he was to deliver his daily prayer meeting message.

The assassin was immediately seized.

He later identified himself as Nathuram Vinayak Godse, 36, a Hindu of the Mahratta tribes in Poona. This has been a center of resistance to Gandhi's ideology.

Mr. Gandhi died twenty-five minutes later. His death left all India stunned and bewildered as to the direction that this newly independent nation would take without its "Mahatma" (Great Teacher).

The loss of Mr. Gandhi brings this country of 300,000,000 abruptly to a crossroads. Mingled with the sadness in this capital tonight was an undercurrent of fear and uncertainty, for none knew the strongest influence for peace in India that this generation has known is gone.

[Communal riots quickly swept Bombay when news of Mr. Gandhi's death was received. The Associated Press reported that fifteen persons were killed and more than fifty injured before an uneasy peace was established.]

Appeal Made By Nehru

Prime Minister Pandit Jawaharlal Nehru, in a voice choked with emotion, appealed in a radio address tonight for a sane approach to the future. He asked that India's path be turned away from violence in memory of the great peacemaker who had departed.

Mr. Gandhi's body will be cremated in the orthodox Hindu fashion according to his often expressed wishes. His body will be carried from his New Delhi residence on a simple wooden cot covered with a sheet at 11:30 tomorrow morning. The funeral procession will wind through every principal street of the two cities of New and Old Delhi and reach the burning ghats on the bank of the sacred Jumna River at about 4 P. M. There the remains of the greatest Indian since Gautama Buddha will be wrapped in a sheet, laid on a pyre of wood and burned. His ashes will be scattered on the Jumna's waters, eventually to mingle with the Ganges where the two holy rivers meet at the temple city of Allahabad.

These simple ceremonies were announced tonight by Pandit Nehru in respect to Mr. Gandhi's wishes, although many of the leaders desired that his body be embalmed and exhibited in state. India will see the last of Mr. Gandhi as it saw him when he lived—a humble and unassuming Hindu.

News Spreads Quickly

News of the assassination of Mr. Gandhi—only a few days after he had finished a five-day fast to bring about communal friendship—spread quickly through New Delhi. Immediately there was spontaneous movement of thousands to Birla House, home of G. D. Birla, the millionaire industrialist, where Mr. Gandhi and his six secretaries had been guests since he came to New Delhi in the midst of the disturbances in India's capital.

While walking through the gardens to this evening's prayer meeting Mr. Gandhi had just reached the top of a short flight of brick steps, his slender brown arms

Continued on Page 2, Column 6

U. S. WARNS CITIZENS IN PALESTINE FIGHT

Consulate General Says They Face Loss of Passports and All Protective Rights

By SAM POPE BREWER

Special to The New York Times.

JERUSALEM, Jan. 30—United States citizens fighting in the armed services of the Jews or the Arabs who lose their passports and their right to protection, the United States Consulate General warned Americans in Palestine tonight. Furthermore, naturalized citizens, it was said, would lose their American nationality if they fought for a foreign power.

[Zionist hopes for getting United Nations aid in arming a Jewish militia in Palestine were dimmed by the statement of Sir Alexander Cadogan, chief British representative, that the British Government would not allow formation of such forces before the end of the mandate.]

The consular warning is being twisted by Arab sources into a promise that those fighting for the Jews may have their passports back when the fighting ends. The relevant passage reads: "American passports valid only for direct

Continued on Page 4, Column 4

France Votes Free Gold Market, Legalizes Hidden Assets by a Tax

By HAROLD CALLENDER

Special to The New York Times.

PARIS, Jan. 30—Parliamentary sanction was given today for the Government's devaluation of the franc and its accompanying monetary policy.

By a vote of 308 to 242, the National Assembly passed the Government's bill to create a free gold market and to legalize the hitherto illegal possession of foreign securities held by Frenchmen, if those assets were repatriated and the owners paid a special tax of 25 per cent of the assets' value.

As a comparatively free market in dollars had already been established by decree—although its opening was delayed by the freezing of bank notes of 5,000 francs—today's vote by the Assembly completed the series of measures framed by the Government to derive maximum benefit from devaluation by getting possession of privately owned foreign securities and hoarded gold.

Estimates of the total of these illegal securities have been in the

Continued on Page 5, Column 2

neighborhood of $300,000,000 in the United States alone, while official guesses have placed the value of the hidden gold in France at $2,000,000,000.

Apparently placated by the freezing of the bank notes, the Socialists once again switched their position and voted today for the gold market bill, which they had opposed bitterly Wednesday, although their Ministers had apparently accepted it in the Cabinet meeting last Saturday. They were not reluctant to switch, for they did not desire to upset the Government and wreck the "Third Force," however. The Socialists' departure from a planned economy.

The freezing measure, taken when the Socialists had precipitated a Cabinet crisis by balking at the gold market, was considered mainly a political move. But René Mayer, Finance Minister, called the move "an instrument of justice"

Continued on Page 5, Column 2

World News Summarized

SATURDAY, JANUARY 31, 1948

Mohandas K. Gandhi, 78-year-old spiritual leader of hundreds of millions of Indians, was shot in New Delhi yesterday as he walked toward a pergola to lead 1,000 of his followers in evening prayer. He died twenty-five minutes later. His assassin, a Hindu, was seized after he had fired three quick shots into the frail leader, who only recently had ended a hunger strike in protest against communal strife. [3:8.]

News of the tragedy shocked the world. In Bombay, it touched off a new outburst of rioting. [2:3.] United Nations officials at Lake Success feared this might be the beginning of a new wave of violence throughout India. [2:4-5.] President Truman said the whole world would mourn and expressed hope that the assassination would "not retard the peace of India and the world." [2:1.] Similar expressions of regret were voiced in London, where the King and the Queen and Prime Minister Attlee were among the many leaders to pay tribute to Mr. Gandhi. [1:6-7.] The French National Assembly approved, 308 to 242, the Government's program to establish a free gold market and to allow Frenchmen to repatriate foreign assets by paying a tax. The Socialists reversed their previous stand and voted for the program. [1:6-7.]

Two recent Russian notes protesting the reopening of American use of an airfield in Tripolitania and the presence of American naval craft in Italian ports will be rejected by the State Department. [6:5.] The Navy announced that another 1,000 marines would go to the Mediterranean soon to replace an equal number now serving in that area. [6:4-5.]

Orville Wright, air pioneer, died in Dayton, Ohio, at 76. [1:2.]

in Jerusalem declared American citizens participating in the fighting would lose their passports and right to protection. [1:7.] Britain announced at Lake Success before the Palestine Commission that she could not allow the formation of any armed militia in Palestine before her mandate ends. [4:3.]

In Washington a group of eighteen Senate Republicans urged a change in the European Recovery Program to support specific production goals and brushed aside the Administration's request for approval of the full initial fund of $6,800,000,000. [1:5.]

An 18½ per cent reduction in exports of petroleum products was ordered by the Commerce Department "in view of the serious shortage" of oil in this country. [1:2-3.]

Also in Washington, the Joint Committee on Atomic Energy declared this nation must concentrate for the foreseeable future on the "uninterrupted" production of atomic weapons in preference to the peaceful utilization of atomic energy. [1:2-3.]

Governor Dewey asked the Legislature to appropriate $799,600,000 as he submitted another record-breaking budget. Appropriations last year totaled $746,200,000. [1:4-5.]

Winter's coldest weather hit the metropolitan area, with the thermometer hovering near zero in the city. In the suburbs the temperature was expected to fall to sub-zero levels during the night. Some homes suffered from a shortage of fuel oil. [1:1.]

A thirty-two passenger British plane was feared lost on its way to Bermuda. [1:2-3.]

The United States consulate

"All the News That's Fit to Print"

The New York Times.

LATE CITY EDITION
Fair and warmer today and tonight.

Copyright, 1948, by The New York Times Company.

VOL. XCVII..No. 32,984.

NEW YORK, SATURDAY, MAY 15, 1948.

THREE CENTS NEW YORK CITY

ZIONISTS PROCLAIM NEW STATE OF ISRAEL; TRUMAN RECOGNIZES IT AND HOPES FOR PEACE; TEL AVIV IS BOMBED, EGYPT ORDERS INVASION

NAVY PUSHES PLAN FOR CONSTRUCTION OF MISSILE VESSELS

Sullivan Asks House Committee to Approve Halting Work on Battleship, Destroyer Types

WANTS 65,000-TON CARRIER

Floating 'Submarine Killers' Are Also Stressed in Plea for Diverting $300,000,000 Fund

By C. P. TRUSSELL
Special to The New York Times

WASHINGTON, May 14—The Navy asked Congress today for authority to shift sharply its construction of fighting craft from battleship, cruiser and destroyer types to guided missile vessels, a 65,000-ton carrier able to bear, at sea, planes with an operating radius of 1,700 miles, and submarines and floating "enemy submarine killers."

Such new ships, John L. Sullivan, Secretary of the Navy, told the House Armed Services Committee, must have a higher priority "because of the more immediate need for them in the event of an emergency." The immediate reaction of the committee appeared to favor prompt action.

For such a shift in construction, Secretary Sullivan brought out, the Navy wanted to halt the building of thirteen naval vessels, including the battleship Kentucky, the large cruiser Hawaii, seven destroyers, two destroyer escorts and two submarines. To date about $197,000,000 has been spent on them.

However, this money was not to be abandoned, Mr. Sullivan emphasized. These craft could be converted now to the new program, he explained, or be put aside for a fitting-out later as new weapons were developed.

New Aims for $300,000,000 Fund

What the Navy wanted, Secretary Sullivan asserted, was Congressional permission to divert some $300,000,000 remaining in the present ship construction account to these purposes:

Starting the 65,000-ton aircraft carrier (the biggest ones now are the two of the Midway class, at 45,000 tons), which would cost around $124,000,000.

Building, for reproduction later, of a "submarine killer" ship. (Hearings on the defense program have indicated that Russia has made great progress in the submarine field.) A "killer" machine, it is indicated, is developing in new work on the cruiser type of sea-craft.

The construction of four submarines of types advanced beyond those now building.

In addition, there was under plan a conversion in an unidentified way of a carrier and two submarines.

Secretary Sullivan told the committee that the setbacks and the Hawaii would not have to stand by for the development of new weapons. It is planned, he disclosed, that they be converted into guided missile ships. Apparently to allay fears in Congress that large aircraft carriers make easier targets for enemy bombers, Mr. Sullivan drew upon experience in the second World War and the results of atom-bomb tests at Bikini.

Speed Held Bomb Defense

"The experiments at Bikini," Mr. Sullivan said, "have proved that a fast-moving fleet is an unprofitable target for an atomic bomb."

Members of the committee interpreted this as a Navy Department conclusion that even though a potential enemy might acquire the atomic bomb, the revised construction program proposed today promised a maximum of safety. Mr. Sullivan recalled that the Navy lost three large and two light carriers in the Pacific, but none was sunk by aircraft land-based. He indicated the mobility of a fleet, equipped to latest model, would discourage the spotting of atomic bombs, even if an enemy had some.

Today, the Senate Republicans

Continued on Page 7, Column 6

Heaviest Trading in 8 Years Marks Stock Market Spurt

3,840,000 Shares Change Hands as Wave of Bullish Enthusiasm Increases Securities 1 to 7 Points

The hectic days of the Nineteen Twenties were re-enacted yesterday on the floor of the New York Stock Exchange when the most turbulent session in recent years produce d increases of 1 to 7 points in the share list. Accompanied by a burst of bullish enthusiasm not witnessed in almost a decade, the deluge of buying orders so taxed the facilities of the Exchange that the reporting ticker tape lagged behind floor transactions by five minutes.

The cracking of the 1947 high level at the approach of mid-day served as the signal for a buying rush. Public participation suddenly enlarged and buying orders pressed floor traders to the utmost. This condition existed for forty-five minutes in the final hour when 1,350,000 shares were traded. Accompanied by the broadest market on record with a total of 1,151 issues dealt in, volume on the Stock Exchange spiraled to 3,840,-000 shares, the largest since May 21, 1940, in contrast to the Thursday turnover of 2,030,000 shares.

Brokers termed it the "wildest" bull market in twenty years on the premise that at no time in the interval had the industrials and rails advanced with such a unity of force.

While the ground had been well laid for a movement of such scope earlier this week, it was the piercing of the 1947 resistance point that confirmed the presence of a bull market to those who act by the charts, or averages. Early in the day, telegrams were sent by several advisory services to their clients urging the purchase of securities. The response to this advice showed primarily in the late

Continued on Page 23, Column 4

Truman Sees His Election; Calls GOP 'Obstructionist'

By ANTHONY LEVIERO
Special to The New York Times

WASHINGTON, May 14—President Truman asserted tonight that there would be a Democrat in the White House during the next four years and that he would be the man. He made the statement to a cheering audience of 1,000 young Democrats at their meeting here.

The President's speech was a fighting one in the new Truman manner. He spoke extemporaneously, resorting to whimsy and irony and using forceful gestures of his arms to underscore his points.

Mr. Truman accused the Republican party of stealing Democratic platform planks. "You know," he said, "it has been their habit since 1936 of taking a few planks out of the old Democratic platforms and building a platform and then saying, 'Me, too.'"

[The text of President Truman's speech is on Page 7.]

"What have the Republicans done in the last fifteen and a half years?" Mr. Truman asked, then said:

"They have been obstructionists. They spent most of their time while I was in the Senate—and I was there for ten years—in obstructing progressive legislation that was for the welfare of the common man, and throwing bricks and mud at the greatest President that ever sat in the White House."

Mr. Truman was interrupted by applause at this obvious allusion to President Roosevelt.

"That has been their record," he continued, "and they haven't changed a bit. They were against Social Security. They were against TVA. They were against wages

Continued on Page 16, Column 5

MINNESOTA'S GUARD OUT IN MEAT STRIKE

Governor Acts After 200 Raid Cudahy Newport Plant, Attack 60 Workers and Abduct 25

Special to The New York Times

ST. PAUL, Minn., May 14—National Guard troops were ordered to South St. Paul and Newport, towns on opposite banks of the Mississippi River near here, by Governor Luther Youngdahl today following violent disorders at strike-bound packing plants in the area and the statement of the local sheriffs that their forces could not maintain law and order.

The Governor did not proclaim martial law but said the troops would take their orders from the civil authorities.

The Governor's action followed a serious outbreak at the Cudahy packing plant in Newport shortly before last midnight in which a group of about 200 men raided the plant with clubs, knives and hammers. In South St. Paul on Thursday strikers forced back police who tried to open a way through picket lines at the Swift & Co. plant in

Continued on Page 7, Column 2

Princess Elizabeth, in Paris Talk, Asks Common Effort of 2 Nations

By LANSING WARREN
Special to The New York Times

PARIS, May 14—Speaking 'n faultless French with just the touch of a British accent to delight French ears, Princess Elizabeth today asked France and Britain to make a common effort from the admiring attention from the throngs that lined the streets and from all the French officials who received them throughout the day.

President Vincent Auriol voiced the general feeling when in a statement issued tonight he said:

"I have been personally struck by her grace, her charm, her modesty and her nobility. I feel sure that the sentiments that she has expressed went straight to the hearts of all the French."

Elizabeth's address, broadcast to the French nation, was delivered from the top of the monumental entry to the Galliera Museum, where she came to open the British Government's exhibition of relics and souvenirs of famous British

Continued on Page 6, Column 5

From the time they stepped down from the train at the Gare du Nord early today, Princess Elizabeth and Prince Philip, Duke of Edinburgh, were the center of admiring attention from the throngs that lined the streets and from all the French officials who received them throughout the day.

President Vincent Auriol voiced the general feeling when in a statement issued tonight he said:

"I have been personally struck by her grace, her charm, her modesty and her nobility. I feel sure that the sentiments that she has expressed went straight to the hearts of all the French."

Elizabeth's address, broadcast to the French nation, was delivered from the top of the monumental entry to the Galliera Museum, where she came to open the British Government's exhibition of relics and souvenirs of famous British

AIR ATTACK OPENS

Planes Cause Fires at Port—Defense Fliers Go Into Action

BORDER IS BREACHED

Cairo Vanguard Takes Colony—Trans-Jordan Reports a Movement

By The Associated Press

TEL AVIV, Palestine, Saturday, May 15—Air raiders bombed this all-Jewish city at about dawn today.

First reports said there were "some casualties' near the power and light station.

[Cairo reported that Egyptian armed forces had been ordered to enter Palestine. Arab armies moved from Trans-Jordan at 12:01 A. M. Saturday to "liberate the Holy Land from Zionism," said a Trans-Jordan communiqué reported by The United Press from Amman.]

Tel Aviv was under complete blackout all night but no sirens were sounded during the raid. Civil guards were alerted and fifteen to twenty ships in the port area moved out to sea.

The planes swooped over Tel Aviv little more than twelve hours after Jewish leaders proclaimed the existence of a new Hebrew state of Israel.

Some bombs fell in the vicinity of the power station along the Yarkum River near Tel Aviv.

Persons at the scene said there was one hit on or near the power station, causing "some casualties."

TEL AVIV, Palestine, Saturday, May 15 (UP) — Some ten bombs were dropped on Tel Aviv by two aircraft described as bombers and accompanied by two small fighters. One Jew was killed and three were hospitalized, Jewish army aircraft took to the skies a few minutes after the enemy planes whizzed over rooftops at an estimated altitude of 300 feet.

Several fires could be seen from

Continued on Page 2, Column 3

U. S. MOVES QUICKLY

President Acknowledges de Facto Authority of Israel Immediately

TRUCE AIM STRESSED

Soviet Gesture to New Nation Anticipated— Others Due to Act

By BERTRAM D. HULEN
Special to The New York Times

WASHINGTON, May 14—President Truman announced early tonight recognition by the United States of the new Jewish State of Israel. The President acted instantly upon being informed that the new nation had been proclaimed.

"This Government," he announced, "has been informed that a Jewish state has been proclaimed in Palestine and recognition has been requested by the provisional government thereof.

"The United States recognizes the provisional government as the de facto authority of the new State of Israel."

These two paragraphs constituted the text of the President's statement.

Coupled with the announcement was an expression of hope for peace in Palestine. This was made known through a separate White House statement issued by Charles G. Ross, Presidential press secretary.

"The desire of the United States to obtain a truce in Palestine," this said, "will in no way be lessened by the proclamation of a Jewish state.

"We hope that the new Jewish state will join with the Security Council Truce Commission in redoubled efforts to bring an end to the fighting—which has been throughout the United Nations' consideration of Palestine a principal objective of this Government."

[Pending stabilization of the Palestine situation and indications that the State of Israel

Continued on Page 2, Column 2

AT HELM OF THE JEWISH STATE

David Ben-Gurion
Premier

Moshe Shertok
Foreign Minister

The New York Times

U. N. Votes for a Mediator; Special Assembly Is Ended

By THOMAS J. HAMILTON

After hearing both the Soviet Union and the Arab delegates denounce the United States for its sudden recognition of the new Jewish state in Palestine, the United Nations General Assembly decided last night to send a Mediator to the Holy Land to do what he could to arrange a truce and carry on public services.

The vote was 31 to 7, with sixteen abstentions and four changes absent, and the General Assembly, which was called into special session at Flushing Meadow on April 16 at the request of the United States, adjourned for good at 8:32 P. M.

The failure of the General Assembly either to repeal the partition resolution of last November or to provide military force to keep the peace means that the fate of Palestine will be decided by the impending war between Jews and Arabs, not by any United Nations action.

The mediation resolution conforms substantially with a United States proposal announced last Wednesday, after it had become obvious that the General Assembly would not accept the original United States plan for a temporary trusteeship.

However, the General Assembly refused to accept a United States plan for a temporary trusteeship over Jerusalem, which was rejected earlier in the evening by a vote of 20 to 15, less than the necessary two-thirds majority.

Two other proposals regarding Jerusalem were rejected, but presumably the provisions of the partition resolution of the partition resolution of November, which was to have been considered as an international enclave under the administration of the Trusteeship Council, still stand.

In addition, the Assembly decided

Continued on Page 4, Column 4

CUNNINGHAM GOES AS MANDATE ENDS

British Commissioner Boards Cruiser Off Haifa—Jews Take Down Union Jack

By The Associated Press

HAIFA, Palestine, Saturday, May 15—Britain ended her mandate over the Holy Land last midnight. Lieut. Gen. Sir Alan Cunningham, the last British High Commissioner, sailed from Haifa port, finishing British mandate guidance.

Sir Alan's departure from Palestine's richest port caused little excitement among the Jews, who control most of the city.

The British fired a few rockets and searchlights spotlighted the cruiser as it steamed from the harbor.

Wearing the uniform of a British Army general, Sir Alan walked down a few steps of dock into a launch that took him to the cruiser Euryalus.

Upon getting into the launch, he turned and looked soberly up across the docks. There stood an honor guard of the King's Company of Grenadier Guards and Royal Marine commandos. The launch pulled away amid the

Continued on Page 2, Column 7

U. N. Bars Jerusalem Trusteeship; Vote Follows Mandate Deadline

By MALLORY BROWNE

The United Nations General Assembly rejected yesterday the United States plan for a temporary trusteeship regime in Jerusalem. Solidly opposed by the Arab States and the Russian bloc, the plan to set up a United Nations Commissioner authorized to protect the Holy City and its holy places failed to obtain the necessary two-thirds majority at the closing session at Flushing Meadow.

The vote, which came just after the bombshell of the United States recognition of the new Jewish State had burst in the Assembly, was 20 in favor, 15 against and 19 abstentions. The balance was turned by the hostility of Britain and most of the Dominions.

The United States fought hard all day, first in the Political and Security Committee of the Assembly, sitting at Lake Success, and then in the evening session of the Assembly, to get the trusteeship plan adopted before the end of the mandate at 6:01 P. M., New York time.

An Arab filibuster, aided by the Soviet bloc, defeated this effort. It was well past the one hour when a roll-call vote showed that the Assembly preferred to leave Harold Evans, newly appointed Jerusalem municipal Commissioner, in sole charge of the Holy City and its treasures.

The vote came just after another Arab filed up to the tribune and took up the maximum five-minute period allowed in repeating the arguments against a trusteeship plan, 6:01 o'clock went by.

At once Awni Khalidy of Iraq, who had led the Arab fight against the trusteeship plan, rushed up to the tribune and exultantly proclaimed that the time had passed; that the mandate was at an end, and that, since, as Francis B. Sayre of the United States had said, the measure must

Continued on Page 2, Column 5

THE JEWS REJOICE

Some Weep as Quest for Statehood Ends —White Paper Dies

HELP OF U. N. ASKED

New Regime Holds Out Hand to Arabs—U. S. Gesture Acclaimed

Text of declaration setting up new Jewish state, Page 2.

By GENE CURRIVAN
Special to The New York Times

TEL AVIV, Palestine, Saturday, May 15—The Jewish state, the world's newest sovereignty, to be known as the State of Israel, came into being in Palestine at midnight upon termination of the British mandate.

Recognition of the state by the United States, which had opposed its establishment at this time, came as a complete surprise to the people, who were tense and ready for the threatened invasion by Arab forces and appealed for help by the United Nations.

In one of the most hopeful periods of their troubled history the Jewish people here gave a sigh of relief and took a new hold on life when they learned that the greatest national power had accepted them into the international fraternity.

Ceremony Simple and Solemn

The declaration of the new state by David Ben-Gurion, chairman of the National Council and the first Premier of reborn Israel, was delivered during a simple and solemn ceremony at 4 P. M., and new life was instilled into his people, but from without there was the rumbling of guns, a flashback to other declarations of independence that had not been easily achieved.

The first action of the new Government was to revoke the Palestine White Paper of 1939, which restricted Jewish immigration and land purchase.

In the proclamation of the new state the Government appealed to the United Nations "to assist the Jewish people in the building of its state and to admit Israel into the family of nations."

The proclamation added:

"We offer peace and amity to all neighboring states and their peoples, and invite them to cooperate with the independent Jewish nation for the common good of all. The State of Israel is ready to contribute its full share to the peaceful progress and reconstruction of the Middle East."

World Jews Asked to Aid

The statement appealed to Jews throughout the world to assist in the task of immigration and development and in the "struggle for the fulfillment of the dream of generations — the redemption of Israel."

Plans for the ceremony had been laid with great secrecy. None but the hundred or more invited guests and journalists was aware of the meeting until it was started, and even the guests learned of the site only ten minutes before. It was held in the Tel Aviv Museum of Art, a white, modern-design two-story building. Above it flew the Star of David, which is the state's flag, and below, on the sidewalk, was a guard of honor of the Haganah, the army of the Jewish Agency for Palestine.

As photographers' bulbs flashed and movie cameras ground out reels of the scene, great crowds gathered and cheered the Ministers and other members of the Government as they entered the building. The security arrangements were perfect. Men guns were brandished in every direction and even the roofs were briefed with them.

The setting for the reading of the proclamation was a dropped gallery whose hall held paintings by prominent Jewish artists. Many a tribute its full share to the joys of the people of the Diaspora, the dispersal of the Jews.

The thirteen Ministers of the

Continued on Page 2, Column 5

World News Summarized

SATURDAY, MAY 15, 1948

Several hours after the state of Israel, the first Hebrew nation in 2,000 years, had been proclaimed in a Zionist declaration of independence in Tel Aviv, [1:8.], President Truman announced that the United States recognized the "provisional government" of Israel as the "de facto authority of the new state." A second White House statement expressed the hope that the new regime would cooperate with United Nations efforts to bring about peace in Palestine. [1:5.] The British High Commissioner departed from Palestine aboard a cruiser at Haifa as Britain's rule over the Holy Land formally ended. [1:7.]

The special session of the United Nations General Assembly ended last night after it had agreed to send a mediator to Palestine to try to arrange a truce. [1:6-7.] The trusteeship plan for Jerusalem sponsored by the United States was rejected by the Assembly, with the Arab states and the Soviet bloc opposed to the measure. [1:6-7.]

Tel Aviv was bombed at dawn. Egypt ordered her troops into Palestine. Trans-Jordan also reported her army on the move also. [1:4.] Haganah claimed that its forces captured Acre to the north. [2:8.]

In Moscow the newspaper Pravda, in the first editorial comment on the recent exchange between Washington and Moscow, accused the United States of double-dealing. [4:8.]

Paris crowds gave an enthusiastic welcome to Princess Elizabeth and the Duke of Edinburgh when they arrived for a visit. [1:2-3.]

Congress received a request from the Navy for authority to shift the emphasis in its construction of fighting craft to guided-missile vessels. [1:1.] President Truman predicted that he would be re-elected next November. [1:2-3.]

Minnesota National Guard troops were rushed to South St. Paul and Newport after 200 persons had raided the Cudahy meat packing plant at Newport, where a strike is in progress, attacking about sixty workers and abducting twenty-five of them. [1:2.]

The New York Stock Exchange enjoyed one of its biggest days in recent years as an avalanche of buying orders sent stocks up from 1 to 7 points. Trading reached a total of 3,840,000 shares, the largest since May 21, 1940. [1:2-3.]

Winston Churchill's War Memoirs

See Page 17 for today's installment, in which Mr. Churchill describes the invasion of Norway and the clash of the British and German fleets.

The New York Times.

7 A.M. EDITION

Partly cloudy today with occasional
rain tonight and tomorrow.

Temperature Range Today—Max.54; Min.43
Temperature Yesterday—Max.54; Min.46

Full U. S. Weather Bureau Report, Page 16

Copyright, 1948, by The New York Times Company.

VOL. XCVIII No. 33,156.   Entered as Second-Class Matter. Postoffice, New York, N. Y.   NEW YORK, WEDNESDAY, NOVEMBER 3, 1948.   Times Square, New York 18, N. Y. Telephone LAckawanna 4-1000   THREE CENTS NEW YORK CITY

TRUMAN LEADS DEWEY IN LATE RETURNS; THURMOND GETS 40 VOTES; WALLACE TRAILS; DEMOCRATS GAIN IN HOUSE AND SENATE

SHIFT IN CONGRESS

Democrats Win Control of Senate by Wresting Six Seats From GOP

LEADING FOR 3 MORE

Republicans' House Rule Endangered as Rivals Surge in East, West

By C. P. TRUSSELL

Democratic control of both the Senate and House of the Eighty-first Congress was probable if not a certainty on the basis of returns at 6 A. M. today from yesterday's dramatic and surprise-laden election.

From the Senate returns it had been made certain that Democrats had wrested Republican seats from Illinois, Iowa, Oklahoma, West Virginia, Minnesota and Wyoming. It requires a net gain of only four for the Democrats to acquire a majority from the present division of 51 to 45 in favor of the Republicans.

The Democratic sweep, however, had not ended there. They were riding to indicated victory over Republicans in three other states, Kentucky, Delaware and Idaho.

This, it appeared, was a virtual promise to the Democrats that they would have a bare majority, plus four and thus remove, or at least lessen, doubts that they could reorganize the Senate.

Republican Holds Broken

The Republicans also were in desperate danger, despite a need by Democrats of thirty-one Republican-held seats to conquer, of having the House also torn from their grasp. Republicans already had lost many seats in the industrial East, and the Democratic sweep was pressing westward.

In the Senate race the Democrats, while breaking into Republican territory, appeared to be holding solidly in those areas and preserving their present seats. In addition they were causing not only surprises but shocks at many points.

There remained a situation, however, which injected concern into the jubilation that reigned in Democratic camps. How even a "safe" majority in the upper House would make for Democratic harmony was a question left for future developments to answer. The Democratic party split had carried forty Southern electoral votes for the States' Rights party headed by Gov. J. Strom Thurmond of South Carolina—possibly sufficient to throw the whole Presidential and Vice-Presidential election into the hands of the Congress itself.

It was believed by experienced observers that Democratic voting in the Senate on many occasions would distinctly not follow the party line. Whether or to what extent the proved bitterness might delay or block a reorganization of the Senate, if it should be in order in the light of indicated returns, also remained to be seen.

Meanwhile, the completed returns and trends of others appeared to be taking persistent courses.

One of the most spectacular surprises of the Senate returns was in

Continued on Page 8, Column 2

Marshall Will Quit Jan. 20, Paris Says

By The Associated Press

PARIS, Wednesday, Nov. 3.—Secretary of State Marshall will resign next Jan. 20 regardless of the outcome of the Presidential election, an informed source in the American United Nations delegation said today.

The source said that there had been many recent reports that Secretary Marshall might resign.

Secretary Marshall, the source said, planned to retire to his farm.

Senators Elected

Democrats—19

Alabama	*John J. Sparkman
Arkansas	*John L. McClellan
Colorado	*Edwin C. Johnson
Georgia	*Richard B. Russell
Illinois	*Paul H. Douglas
Iowa	*Guy M. Gillette
Louisiana	*Allen J. Ellender Sr.
Louisiana	*Russell B. Long
Minnesota	*Hubert H. Humphrey
Mississippi	*James O. Eastland
North Carolina	‡J. Melville Broughton
Oklahoma	*Robert S. Kerr
Rhode Island	*Theodore F. Green
South Carolina	*Burnet R. Maybank
Tennessee	*Estes Kefauver
Texas	*Lyndon B. Johnson
Virginia	*A. Willis Robertson
West Virginia	*Matthew M. Neely
Wyoming	*Lester C. Hunt

Republicans—8

Kansas	*Andrew F. Schoeppel
Maine	§Margaret Chase Smith
Massachusetts	*Leverett Saltonstall
Nebraska	*Kenneth S. Wherry
New Hampshire	*Styles Bridges
New Jersey	*Robert C. Hendrickson
Oregon	*Guy Cordon
South Dakota	†Karl E. Mundt

In Doubt—6

Delaware	Michigan
Idaho	Montana
Kentucky	New Mexico

*Re-elected Tuesday for full term ending Jan. 3, 1955.
†Elected Tuesday for full term ending Jan. 3, 1955.
‡Elected Tuesday for unexpired term ending Jan. 3, 1951.
†Elected Tuesday for unexpired term ending Jan. 3, 1949, and for full term ending Jan. 3, 1955.
§Elected Sept. 13, 1948.

MARCANTONIO WINS BY NARROW MARGIN

His Vote of 35,937 Beats Ellis, Morrissey—Isacson and Pressman Defeated

By WARREN MOSCOW

Representative Vito Marcantonio last night squeaked through to a narrow victory for re-election to Congress over John P. Morrissey, Tammany Democrat, and John Ellis, Republican, in his first contest as a candidate on the American Labor party line alone.

Facing a divided opposition with the loyal support of thousands who live in the slums of East Harlem to overcome a more conservative vote lower down in Yorkville, the pep,ery Representative, who has been denounced consistently for being a close adherent of the Communist party line, won by a thin margin. His victory was a minor political miracle on the surface, yet somewhat expected by those familiar with the political conditions in the area.

He was the only leftist to win in the metropolitan area, however, as middle-of-the-road Democrats had a field day as rightist Republicans, elected in the 1946 GOP landslide, also went down in a consistent pattern of Congressional defeat.

Final figures in the contest, with no election districts missing, gave Mr. Marcantonio 35,937, Mr. Morrissey 31,184, and Mr. Ellis, 31,482. Mr. Ellis polled 26,518 Republican votes, and 4,964 on the Liberal Party line.

In one of the closest contests, attracting almost as much interest as the Marcantonio race, Representative Jacob K. Javits, Liberal and Republican nominee in the Twenty-first District, Washington Heights, overcame the normal Democratic voting tendencies in the area for the second time to win re-election. He defeated Paul O'Dwyer, brother of the Mayor, and candidate of the Democratic and American Labor parties, by a vote of 66,455 to 64,297.

When the returns showed him the winner, Mr. Javits issued the following statement:

"The victory in our district is a victory for the people of the district, and I have had the honor of carrying the fight for them in beating down an unprincipled political deal. In carrying out my functions in the Congress, I will continue to be the people's Congressman."

On the debit side for the leftists was the defeat of the incumbent Leo Isacson, ALP member from the Bronx, who won a surprising victory in a by-election last spring. Yesterday, the Democratic candi-

Continued on Page 8, Column 5

DEWEY WINS STATE

Piles Up 525,042 Lead Outside City, Loses by 489,047 Here

LABOR IS BIG FACTOR

Wallace Total 503,404 —Liberals Poll 222,217 for the President

By JAMES A. HAGERTY

Governor Dewey, Republican nominee for President, carried his home state of New York in yesterday's election by a plurality of about 37,000 over President Truman, his Democratic opponent, and won New York's important forty-seven electoral votes.

With fifteen election districts missing out of 5,592 outside New York City, and with the city complete, the vote on the two major-party candidates was:

	Dewey	Truman
New York City	1,108,054	1,597,101
Rest of State	1,720,223	1,195,181
Totals	2,828,277	2,792,281

This gave Governor Dewey an actual plurality in the state of 35,996, which probably will be increased by about 1,500 by returns from the missing up-state districts, probably all Republican. Mr. Dewey carried the state outside New York City by 525,042 on the tabulated returns. Mr. Truman's New York City plurality was 489,047.

Henry A. Wallace, Progressive candidate for President, received a larger vote in the state than had been generally expected. With fifteen up-state election districts missing, he polled 503,404 votes, of which 423,424 were in New York City and 79,980 elsewhere in the state.

The Liberal party polled 222,219 of which 194,449 were cast in New York City and 27,770 in the rest of the state.

President Truman's strong showing, which held the plurality for his Republican opponent to several hundred thousand less than most pre-election estimates, was due to strong support from members of

Continued on Page 11, Column 2

THE TRUMANS AND THE DEWEYS VOTING IN YESTERDAY'S ELECTION

The President placing his ballot in the box at the polling place in his home town of Independence, Mo. Waiting their turn to vote are Mrs. Truman and their daughter, Margaret.

Associated Press Wirephoto

Governor Dewey signing the register at the polling place in public school at 121 East Fifty-first Street. Mrs. Dewey is standing beside her husband, and the registrar is Mrs. R. V. Hough.

The New York Times

JERSEY FOR DEWEY BY 70,000 MARGIN

Governor Overtakes Truman —Hendrickson Wins, Party Loses 3 House Seats

By RUSSELL PORTER

With only 101 out of 3,707 election districts unreported at 6 o'clock this morning, New Jersey's sixteen electoral votes went to Governor Dewey by an indicated plurality of about 70,000.

This was a surprisingly small margin over President Truman, in view of claims by Republican managers as late as last night that the Dewey margin would be about 234,000.

State Treasurer Robert C. Hendrickson, Republican, of Woodbury, defeated Archibald S. Alexander, Democrat, of Bernardsville by

Continued on Page 6, Column 2

Wallace Vote Is Far Short Of His Party's Expectations

By WILL LISSNER

No signs of the 10,000,000 vote that the Progressive party leaders were counting upon for their Presidential candidate, Henry A. Wallace, appeared in returns early today from roughly half the country's projected popular vote in yesterday's election.

As the returns rolled in, it became clear that Mr. Wallace would not get even half the vote his campaign managers expected, and probably not even a quarter of it. Of 25,431,641 votes counted, Mr. Wallace polled 618,705, or about 3 per cent. Undoubtedly this figure was influenced by the failure to count minority party polls in some states in the early counting.

In New York, however, Mr. Wallace's vote was decisive, and in several other states, such as California, it made serious inroads on the Democratic showing for President Truman.

In forty of the forty-five states in which the Progressive party was on the ballot, Mr. Wallace was running better than 1 per cent of the vote in seventeen and at fractions of 1 per cent, some of them infinitesimal, in twenty-three.

The states that were giving Mr. Wallace better than 1 per cent were California, Connecticut, Florida, Idaho, Iowa, Maryland, Massachusetts, Minnesota, Montana, Nevada, New Jersey, New York, North Dakota, Oregon, Pennsylvania, South Dakota and Wisconsin.

The states that were giving him

Continued on Page 15, Column 2

40 ELECTORAL VOTES TO STATES RIGHTERS

Alabama, Mississippi, South Carolina, Louisiana Won, but Popular Vote Is Short

By CLAYTON KNOWLES

The States Rights Democratic ticket, headed by Gov. J. Strom Thurmond of South Carolina, was romping off this morning with forty electoral votes in five Southern states, an electoral total that had been as good as conceded to it even before the balloting began. With about half the projected national vote recorded, the Thurmond-Wright ticket had polled 552,417 popular votes. It was on the ballot in only thirteen states.

Not beyond the realm of possibility was the prospect that neither President Truman nor Governor Dewey would win a clear majority of the electoral vote. States Righters hoped for such an eventuality in launching their party last July. In such a situation, the election is thrown into the House of Representatives, where each state delegation casts one vote.

The forty States Rights electoral votes were made up of Alabama's eleven, South Carolina's eight, Mississippi's nine, Louisiana's ten and two of Tennessee's twelve.

Two electoral candidates, pledged to the Thurmond-Wright ticket, were running on the Democratic slate which was leading in latest tabulations in Tennessee. They also were running on the States' Rights slate which was showing up a poor third in latest reports.

The forty-vote indication fell far below the predictions of Governor Thurmond and other States' Rights leaders, who forecast that the ticket would win more than 100 electoral votes.

This, the fourth party in the national election, while living up to the great popular vote in the South that it had been expected. It did not appear to be making large enough inroads in a number of key Southern states to throw these states to the Republican ticket as some persons had expected.

States that had been placed in this category were North Carolina,

Continued on Page 7, Column 3

FORECASTS UPSET

President Surprises by Taking Early Popular Vote Lead, Holds It

AHEAD ON ELECTORS

Truman Has Indicated 227, Governor 176— 88 Are Doubtful

By ARTHUR KROCK

At 6 A. M. today, after a night in which his political fortunes waxed and waned with every passing hour, President Harry S. Truman took an impressive lead over his Republican opponent, Gov. Thomas E. Dewey of New York, in both the popular and electoral vote of the nation which went to the polls yesterday in the forty-eight states of the Union to choose a President, a Vice President, the Eighty-first Congress and thirty-two Governors.

Ahead in the popular vote at all times during the counting, the President gained the electoral lead when Illinois was conceded to him at 5 A. M. and his chance of gaining Ohio steadily improved. At 6 A. M. the division of electoral votes be.ween him and Governor Dewey that appeared to be established was:

Truman, 227; Dewey, 176; doubtful, 88.

The remaining 40 of the total of 531 electoral votes apparently had been won by the Presidential candidate of the Democratic States Rights party, Gov. J. Strom Thurmond of South Carolina.

Truman Needs 39 More

Only thirty-nine electoral votes were needed by the President to win the majority of 266 that would give him a full term in the White House in his own right. And fifty-three were in sight—in the doubtful states of Iowa, Montana, Nevada, Washington, Iowa and California. However, in the last named, with a block of twenty-five, Governor Dewey was holding a lead.

If California ends with a Dewey victory, Ohio, with twenty-five electors, can overcome that loss, and Ohio went definitely into the doubtful column in the early hours of today. Therefore the possibility that election would end without a decision, and the choice of a President would devolve on the House of Representatives in the Eighty-first Congress, remained within the area of strong possibility.

In that event Governor Dewey's chances to win the election were fading fast at dawn today.

The possibility of an election by the House is the consequence of the capture of forty electors in the South by the States' Rights Democratic party, whose nominees were Govs. J. Strom Thurmond of South Carolina and Fielding Wright of Mississippi. And, if this is the eventual outcome, the President will have been defeated by the revolt of Southern Democrats against his "civil rights" program of Federal laws to enforce anti-segregation and a "fair employment practices" act in the states.

The returns at 6 A. M., however, further upset the earlier indication that the Progressive vote candidacy of Henry A. Wallace had not proved as costly to the President, or more so, than the Southern Democratic insurrection. For if Mr. Dewey's pluralities in New York and in Ohio are as narrow as was indicated early today, Mr. Truman can attribute his failure to carry them both to the Wallace vote that was subtracted from his normal Democratic following.

The Congressional returns were more definite. Democratic candidates for the Senate appeared certain to win the four crucial contests that will give the two a numerical Senate majority over the Republicans.

Continued on Page 5, Column 3

BOWLES IS ELECTED IN GOVERNOR RACE

He Wins Connecticut by 1,400 Votes, While Dewey Carries State for GOP by 15,000

Special to THE NEW YORK TIMES.

NEW HAVEN, Conn., Nov. 2.—With only one town unreported, Chester A. Bowles, Democrat, leading by 1,322 votes, is certain of election as Governor of Connecticut over the incumbent, James C. Shannon.

Governor Dewey, the first Republican to carry the state since Herbert Hoover won it in 1932, has carried the state over President Truman by about 15,000 votes.

The Democrats also disrupted the Republican domination in Congress, which included all six Representatives in the last House. Abraham A. Ribicoff, a lawyer of Hartford, and John A. McGuire, both Democrats, upset the Republican incumbents in the First and Third Districts.

Representatives John Davis Lodge and James T. Patterson of the Fourth and Fifth Districts, respectively, are the only Republicans assured of re-election. Both candidates of the party trail in close contests for the Second District seat and Congressman-at-Large.

In the large cities of New Haven, Hartford and Waterbury, Mr. Bowles piled up a majority of 40,-

Continued on Page 2, Column 4

12,000 See Start of Horse Show; Mexican and French Officers Win

By JOHN RENDEL

New York's wealth and fashion and a large number of plain citizens divided their interest between the election returns and the annual visitations of the horse as a medium for sport and the exchange of social amenities last night. The occasion was the formal opening of the Sixtieth National Horse Show, launched again on an election afternoon for a run of eight days of matinee and evening performances in Madison Square Garden.

In some ways it was the biggest national held since the war began. There were more horses, the number exceeding 500 from this country, Canada, Mexico and France. The Royal Canadian Mounted Police, in scarlet and blue, were back with their eye-catching ride to music for the first time since 1936. France was represented by a military jumping team, also for the first time since 1936. Mexico and Canada were in the same in-

international jumping competition, as they had been a year ago.

Horse and man combined for exciting hunter and jumper contests. There were slick saddle horses, flashy harness rigs to remind the metropolis that a lot of country-side still existed where the horse had a place.

The void in the refulgent panoply was in the absence of a United States Army team, disbanded soon after last summer's Olympic Games because the horse isn't what he was in war any more. America's military riders, always hitherto present as far as memory served, were missed by the 12,000 on hand in the seats around the arena floor to honor the horse and participate, vicariously or otherwise, in the spectacle of society on parade.

There was another parade, too, that was a lot more stirring. It was the traditional one of the in-

Continued on Page 38, Column 1

World News Summarized

WEDNESDAY, NOVEMBER 3, 1948

President Truman at 7 o'clock this morning, was within sight of an electoral majority that would keep him in the White House for four years more. Maintaining an early lead in the popular vote he kept himself won more and more states in a close race with Governor Dewey [1:8.] Governor Thurmond carried four Southern states on the States' Rights ticket [1:5], but the vote for Henry A. Wallace was only a fraction of what his supporters had expected. [1:5-6.]

It was Mr. Wallace's half-million voters in New York State that enabled Mr. Dewey to win by a narrow margin. [1:3.] The New York Governor also carried New Jersey by a close vote. [1:4.] Mr. Dewey won in Connecticut, but Chester Bowles, Democrat, was elected Governor. [1:7.]

When the returns showed Mr. Truman the winner, Mr. Javits issued the following statement:

Control of Congress passed from the Republicans to the Democrats, unofficial and incomplete returns indicated. The Democrats easily won enough seats to take over the Senate [1:1] and apparently gathered more than enough Republicans to control the House. [9:3.]

In this city Representative Marcantonio was re-elected, but Representative Isacson and other American Labor party candidates were defeated. [1:2.] For the first time since 1938 the Democrats made gains in the State Legislature. [18:3.]

The coveted post of Surrogate in New York County was won by George Frankenthaler, Republi-

can, who had a plurality of 644 over Judge John A. Mullen, Democrat. [7:1.]

Chairman Spaak of the United Nations General Assembly's Political Committee admonished Soviet Deputy Foreign Minister Vishinsky during debate on the Balkan question to stop "insulting other delegates." [21:3-4.] Poland asked in the Economic Committee that action be taken against the United States for alleged economic sanctions under the Marshall Plan. [21:2.]

The Benelux countries have been asked for more detailed information on their four-year recovery plans. The Belgians fear pressure to impose a planned economy. [30:4-5.]

Plans to ban collective disobedience of taxation laws and other Communist moves will be considered by the French Cabinet today. Numerous casualties resulted from clashes between miners and Government forces seizing strike-bound mines. [24:2.]

Although it was denied that peace talks between Israel and Trans-Jordan had begun, it was reported authoritatively that King Abdullah had decided that such talks should be held. [23:4.]

Chinese planes continued to bomb Mukden, occupied by the Communists. [24:3-4.]

Washington took two steps affecting national defense. The inactive National Guard was re-established [54:2] and Selective Service recommended that qualified medical and dental students receive draft deferment until graduation. [54:5.]

"All the News That's Fit to Print"

The New York Times.

LATE CITY EDITION
Partly cloudy and mild today; fair tonight and tomorrow.
Temperature Range Today—Max., 65; Min., 47
Temperatures Yesterday—Max., 66; Min., 48
Full U. S. Weather Bureau Report, Page 35

Copyright, 1949, by The New York Times Company.

VOL. XCVIII. No. 33,346.

Entered as Second-Class Matter,
Postoffice, New York, N. Y.

NEW YORK, THURSDAY, MAY 12, 1949.

Times Square, New York 18, N. Y.
Telephone Lackawanna 4-1000

THREE CENTS NEW YORK CITY

ISRAEL WINS A SEAT IN U. N. BY 37-12 VOTE

ARABS INDIGNANT

Quit the Assembly Hall After Poll—9 Nations Abstain in Ballot

59TH COUNTRY IN BODY

Israel's Foreign Chief Sharett Pledges Peace Effort—Debate Brings Polish Attack

By THOMAS J. HAMILTON

The General Assembly admitted Israel to membership in the United Nations at 7:28 last night by a vote of 37 to 12, with nine abstentions.

The delegations of the six Arab states—Egypt, Iraq, Lebanon, Saudi Arabia, Syria and Yemen—walked out of the Assembly Hall at Flushing Meadow in protest before the applause over the election of Israel as the fifty-ninth member of the United Nations had died away. They indignantly refused to make any statement to correspondents regarding their intentions, but drove away to New York.

The Arab delegates, who also walked out when the General Assembly adopted the resolution recommending the partition of Palestine on Nov. 29, 1947 gave no hint of their impending action in the speeches in the General Assembly in the afternoon.

Charge Israeli Violation

They protested bitterly, however, that Israel had refused to comply with the provisions of a General Assembly resolution adopted on Dec. 11, 1948, calling for an international regime in Jerusalem and the repatriation of Arab refugees. Also, they challenged the validity of a Security Council recommendation for the admission of Israel, since Britain, a permanent member of the Council, had abstained.

The Charter requires the concurring votes of the Big Five on all except procedural matters, and the Arab delegates insisted that the Assembly should first get a ruling from the International Court of Justice. This procedure was contained in a resolution presented by Iraq yesterday afternoon, but Dr. Evatt ruled it out of order on the ground that the General Assembly could not examine the decision of another United Nations body.

The Yemen delegation returned shortly after 10 o'clock for the night session of the Assembly, and an Egyptian delegate came back a few minutes later, but the other desks remained vacant.

Immediately after the vote Dr. Evatt summoned to the platform Moshe Sharett, Israeli Foreign Minister, who had arrived by plane from Tel Aviv early yesterday to hear the final speeches.

"We enter this Assembly, which represents the collective statesmanship of the world, in a spirit of humility, anxious for guidance and enlightenment," said Mr. Sharett, who re-stated the Israeli policy of "loyalty to the fundamental principles of the United Nations' Charter and friendship with all peace-loving states, especially with the United States of America and the Union of Soviet Socialist Republics."

Now a Working Member

Mr. Sharett took his seat at the desk that had previously been prepared for the Israeli delegation in the back of the Assembly hall, between the Iraqi and United Nations delegations. United Nations officials said no additional facilities were required, and that Israel would have the right to participate in all further proceedings of the General Assembly on the same basis as the fifty-eight other members.

The vote was too late to permit the Israeli flag to be raised in the area in front of the main delegates' entrance. A flag pole, however, had been prepared in advance, and there will be a ceremony at Lake Success at 10:30 A. M. today.

The General Assembly took up the application at its afternoon session and the debate concluded at 7:30 as a result of the fact that the protests of the Arab delegates,

Continued on Page 13, Column 1

When You Think of Writing Think of Whiting—Advt.

Protesters in Tripoli Tear U.S. Flag to Bits

By The United Press.

TRIPOLI, LIBYA, May 11—Demonstrators tore to shreds a United States flag in front of the United States Consulate in Tripoli today and set fire to a number of Italian establishments.

The demonstrators, demanding full independence for this former Italian colony, shouted "Long live Russia! Down with America and the United Nations!"

Special to The New York Times.

LAKE SUCCESS, May 11—A United Kingdom proposal that Eritrea, except for the western province, be incorporated into Ethiopia was approved in a subcommittee of the Political Committee this morning by a vote of ten to three with two abstentions.

A second United Kingdom proposal that the western province be incorporated in the adjacent Sudan also was approved by a vote of seven to two with six abstentions.

WAR PENSION BILL IS SHARPLY LIMITED

House Group Confines Benefit to Unemployable and Reports Measure as Rankin Protests

By JOHN D. MORRIS

WASHINGTON, May 11 — The new veterans pension bill was further watered down in committee today—to such an extent that its author, Representative John E. Rankin, Democrat, of Mississippi, voted, though in vain, against reporting it to the House.

The action was taken by the House Veterans Affairs Committee at a closed meeting that had been scheduled merely to formalize its action yesterday in approving pensions on a more liberal basis.

The committee voted, 14 to 8, to confine the $72-a-month payments to unemployable veterans. By a voice vote, it then cleared the measure formally to the House.

Approval of the limitation was prompted by Veterans Administration estimates, drawn up overnight, that without it the bill would add $65,000,000,000 to the cost of veterans' benefits over the next fifty years. Yesterday's action had been based on a $12,000,000,000 estimate.

As finally approved, the measure's fifty-year cost was estimated at $8,693,000,000 by Guy M. Birdsall, assistant veterans administrator.

Mr. Rankin was joined by Representative A. Leonard Allen, Democrat, of Louisiana, in voting against reporting the bill. Shortly afterward the Mississippi legislator arose in the House to protest the action of the committee, of which he is chairman.

The employability clause, he asserted, would bar pensions from taking over, Mr. Kenny said

Continued on Page 32, Column 4

Johnson Approves Air Force Plan To Distribute Negroes Among Units

Special to The New York Times.

WASHINGTON, May 11—Latest proposals by the Air Force to conform to armed service policy on racial equality were approved today by Louis Johnson, Secretary of Defense.

W. Stuart Symington, Secretary of the Air Force, wrote to Secretary Johnson on April 30 and assured the defense chief that his directive of April 6 asking equality of treatment and opportunity "without regard to race, color, religion, or national origin" would be put into effect.

One of the principal moves in this direction is an Air Force order disbanding the all-Negro 332nd Fighter Wing at Lockbourne Air Force base at Columbus, Ohio. Its 2,000 officers and men will be distributed throughout the service in non-segregated units, it was learned.

Another assurance given to Mr. Johnson, it was learned, was that "key" positions would be open to Negroes who are individually qualified to hold them.

Mr. Johnson made his April 6 directive to the armed services public on April 20, at which time he stated that he in-

Continued on Page 54, Column 1

KENNY TO ASK COURT FOR ORDER TO SEIZE JERSEY CITY BOOKS

Mayor-Elect Seeks to Prevent Any Alterations of Records to Shield Old Regime

FULL INQUIRY IS PLANNED

'It's All Right With Me,' Says Hague of Defeat—Fight for State Rule Likely

By LEO EGAN

The political coalition that dethroned Frank Hague as boss of Jersey City has decided to seek a court order barring the outgoing city administration from destroying or altering official records before it leaves office next Tuesday.

John V. Kenny, who headed the coalition and who will become Mayor in the new administration, said a formal application for an order impounding city books and records would be submitted tomorrow to Judge William Brennan in Hudson County Superior Court.

One of the first acts of the new regime, Mr. Kenny added, will be to order a full-scale audit of the records and accounts of the outgoing administration, headed by Mayor Frank Hague Eggers, nephew of the 73-year-old former Mayor, who was one of the last of the old-time bosses in the United States to yield up his political power.

Drive to End State Rule Seen

While the new regime was making its plans for sifting city records for evidence of illegal acts and misuse of public funds on behalf of the Hague machine, Democrats in other parts of New Jersey were contemplating a drive to strip Mr. Hague of his control of the Democratic party in the state.

Many Democrats fear that unless Mr. Hague's connections with the state organizations are severed the fall elections will result in an overwhelming victory for the Republican State ticket, headed by Gov. Alfred E. Driscoll.

In any reorganization of the Democratic State Committee, Mr. Kenny, who was leader of the Second Ward in Jersey City for many years, is expected to play a leading role. So are former Mayor Meyer C. Ellenstein of Newark, who topped all candidates for City Commissioner there in Tuesday's elections, and Mayor George Brunner of Camden.

David Wilentz, who prosecuted Bruno Richard Hauptmann for the Lindbergh kidnapping, and Mayor Michael De Vito of Paterson also are expected to play important parts in any reorganization movement.

In the interview yesterday afternoon in which he told of his plans for investigating the outgoing Administration, Mr. Kenny announced also that he would support State Senator Elmer Wene for Governor in the Democratic ticket this fall. Senator Wene won the Democratic nomination with the backing of Mr. Hague in a recent primary.

The interview was sandwiched in between posing for newsreels and making an appearance on a television program. Although he looked tired and his voice was hoarse, the Mayor-elect said he felt "fine."

With respect to his plans on

Continued on Page 25, Column 2

BERLIN LAND BLOCKADE IS LIFTED; FIRST TRAIN, AUTOS REACH CITY; ZONE TROOP RETIREMENT STUDIED

U. S. PLAN WEIGHED

Big 3 Would Withdraw to Ports in the North Under Proposal

FRENCH WOULD GO HOME

Presentation of Suggestion Will Depend on Soviet Stand in Paris Talks

By JAMES RESTON

Special to The New York Times.

WASHINGTON, May 11—The United States was reported today to have under consideration a plan under which all occupation troops in Germany would be withdrawn into restricted areas at the North German ports.

Under this plan, which is being discussed with Britain and France, Soviet troops would be situated on the West Bank of the Oder in Stettin, British troops would be restricted to the area of Hamburg, and United States troops would be concentrated in Bremen.

[Stettin was included in the Soviet zone in the Potsdam pact, but under a separate agreement reached Sept. 20, 1947, the Russians turned over control of the former German port to Poland. Bremen is a United States enclave in the British zone.]

These troops, it is understood, would be obliged, under this plan, to use only sea communications, and France, which has a common frontier with Germany, would withdraw her occupation troops into her own territory.

An understanding apparently already has been reached among the Western powers to reject any Soviet proposal at the forthcoming meeting of the Council of Foreign Ministers in Paris for the complete evacuation of all occupation troops from all of Germany.

It is felt here that total withdrawal of these troops would be detrimental to the economic recovery and sense of security of Western Europe.

However, if Soviet Foreign Minister Andrei Y. Vishinsky should demonstrate in Paris that his Government was now prepared to establish a central government in Germany along the lines laid down by the Western powers for the

Continued on Page 3, Column 2

IT'S A REAL HOLIDAY FOR THESE BERLIN YOUNGSTERS

BLOCKADEFREI

Joyous children hold their lunch boxes over their heads as they get news that there will be no school in celebration of the end of the blockade. The sign reads "blockade free."

Associated Press Radiophoto

ACHESON STILL BARS FRANCO AS FASCIST

Says Spanish Regime Denies Basic Rights in the Pattern of Hitler and Mussolini

Secretary Acheson's remarks on Spanish regime, Page 10.

By BERTRAM D. HULEN

Special to The New York Times.

WASHINGTON, May 11—Secretary of State Dean Acheson declared today that the question of restoring full diplomatic relations with Spain turned primarily upon the attitude of Western European countries that were still opposed to bringing her back into their international family for military and economic cooperation.

This attitude, the Secretary told his weekly news conference, was conditioned by the absence of fundamental freedoms under the Franco regime which, he said, originally and still was patterned on Nazi Germany and Fascist Italy. At an

Continued on Page 10, Column 1

Eisler Reported Stowaway; Seizure in Britain Is Asked

By WILL LISSNER

A man who has identified himself as Gerhart Eisler, native of Germany, is fleeing from the United States aboard the Gdynia-America liner Batory, it became known yesterday. The fugitive is believed to be the former Comintern agent named by the House Un-American Activities Committee as America's No. 1 Communist, jumping $23,500 bail to escape serving a year in jail and other penalties, but his identity has not yet been definitely established.

The Federal Bureau of Investigation and the Immigration and Naturalization Service of the Department of Justice moved yesterday to fix the identity of the fugitive. If the man aboard the Batory is the German-born Communist leader Eisler, he will be placed in custody for eventual return.

The fugitive is bound for Gdynia, but the ship, which sailed last Saturday, will put into Southampton Saturday. To make sure that Polish Communists aboard the ship do not balk a return, the State Department, at the request of the Department of Justice, notified Scotland Yard of the incident and asked that top investigators meet the ship on its arrival in the English port. Scotland Yard was asked to hold the suspect.

If Eisler, the convicted Communist agent, has fled the jurisdiction of the Federal District Court, his bail would be forfeited even though the English authorities return him, it was said at the Federal Building.

The forfeiture of the $23,500 bail would be a blow to the Civil Rights Congress and the American Committee for the Protection of the Foreign Born. For a good part of

Continued on Page 4, Column 3

FIRST BERLIN TRAIN FROM WEST SEALED

Officials Lock Doors and Draw Shades to Keep Russians Out and Reporters In

By The United Press.

BERLIN, Thursday, May 12—The first western passenger train since last year arrived in Berlin at 5:11 A. M. today (11:11 P. M. Wednesday, Eastern Daylight Time)—hauled by a Soviet zone locomotive.

It carried a combined British-American train of twelve cars, it carried approximately 140 Western nationals, including seventy-three British troops and at least a score of reporters.

Anglo-American officials ordered the doors locked and the shades drawn soon after the train left Helmstedt at 1:23 A. M., the first rail stop on the West-East run on the Helmstedt-Berlin road last year.

The train officials said that the "sealing" of the cars was necessary "to keep the Russians out and to keep you newsmen in." The reporters peeked anyway but saw only a moonlit empty landscape during the eventless three hours

Continued on Page 2, Column 2

U.S. Reds Liken Pact to Hitler Axis; Norman Thomas Urges Ratification

By WILLIAM S. WHITE

Special to The New York Times.

WASHINGTON, May 11 — The Communist party of the United States, through a statement filed by its general secretary, Eugene Dennis, likened the North Atlantic treaty today to "Hitler's Axis," and demanded that the Senate withhold any action toward its ratification until after the Big Four Foreign Ministers' conference.

However, Norman Thomas, Socialist leader, supported ratification before the Senate Foreign Relations Committee, but stressed that he did so with much anxiety because of the "dangers" that might be in it.

He expressed belief that the pact should not be ratified unless the Senate made it "absolutely plain" that Spain would not be included in it, and equally plain that proposed American military aid should not be used against colonial peoples.

Communists, urging at a Senate hearing in Washington that ratification of the North Atlantic treaty be deferred until after the Paris meeting, likened the pact to "Hitler's Axis." [1:6-7.]

Victorious anti-Hague forces in Jersey City will seek a court order impounding all public records until an audit can be made. [1:3.]

Index to other news appears on Page 32.

SIEGE ON 328 DAYS

Leading Car Speeds 102 Miles From the British Zone in 1½ Hours

AIRLIFT PLANES CONTINUE

West Concerned as Russians Turn Back Some Trucks— City's Lights Turned On

By DREW MIDDLETON

Special to The New York Times.

BERLIN, Thursday, May 12—Just as the morning sun rose over the jagged skyline of this broken but defiant city a Soviet zone locomotive chugged wearily into the Charlottenburg Station in the British sector hauling the first train to reach Berlin from the West in 328 days.

Arrival of the train completed the relief of the city from the iron vise of the Soviet blockade.

At one minute after midnight [6:01 P. M. Wednesday, Eastern daylight time] two jeeps and a convoy of cars, buses and trucks roared out of the city for the Western zones. An hour and three quarters later the first cars of a flotilla that simultaneously had left Helmstedt, in the British zone at the border of the Soviet zone, swept into Berlin to re-establish the land link with the West broken since the Soviet Military administration established a complete blockade of the city last June.

By morning it was evident that the Russians had observed the letter if not the spirit of the East-West agreement reached in New York. Traffic was flowing freely along the Autobahn.

Although there had been some difficulty over locomotives, the Russians had promised to send six freight trains and one passenger train into Berlin each day. Pending settlement of the dispute the trains will be pulled by Soviet zone locomotives.

Western Officials Disturbed

To Berliners who awoke in the night to find lights burning in the streets and in their homes and intersector barriers dismantled, the blockade for the moment seemed over. Americans and British in Military Government offices, however, were distinctly disturbed by the turning back at Soviet checkpoints of trucks bound for the Western zones with Western sector exports.

This refusal to permit trucks to pass stems from a Soviet order of January, 1948. Hence it is not affected by the New York agreement on ending the blockade. But the Western Powers felt that the action indicated that the Russians would not give an inch more than called for by that agreement.

The first railroad train since June of 1948 passed through the checkpoint at Helmstedt, in the British zone at the border of the Soviet zone, at 1:23 A. M., bound for Berlin.

The first car from Helmstedt, driven by Walter G. Rundle, United Press manager for Germany, arrived at the American checkpoint outside Berlin at 1:44. Mr. Rundle had driven the distance, which the British declare is 102 miles, in an hour and thirty-seven minutes. He said that the bridge across the Elbe at Magdeburg was in good condition.

Aide's Wife Enters City

The first woman to enter Berlin after lifting of the blockade was Adelaide de Neufville, wife of Lawrence de Neufville, consultant to the civil affairs division of the United States Military Government.

The first two railroad trains to start across the Soviet zone for Berlin since June 17, 1948, left the Russian control point at Marienborn early this morning. One of these was a passenger train carrying correspondents. It moved into the moonlit landscape of the Russian zone at 1:55 after an eleven-minute wait at the checkpoint.

Eight minutes later a freight train of forty-two cars carrying coal from the Ruhr for Berlin passed through the checkpoint en route to Berlin, symbolizing the end not only of the Russian block-

Continued on Page 2, Column 2

World News Summarized

THURSDAY, MAY 12, 1949

The 328-day Soviet blockade of Berlin ended on schedule at 12:01 o'clock this morning, Berlin time, and approximately an hour and one-half later the first vehicles from the Western zones of Germany entered the city followed by the first train. [1:8; maps P. 2.]

The first Western passenger train to Berlin was sealed; a jeep led the road convoy [1:7.] Russian guards at Berlin ignored automobiles going to Helmstedt; people watched on the Autobahn. [3:1.]

Secretary of State Acheson warned that the end of the blockade did not, in itself, solve the German problem. He said Russia's willingness at the forthcoming Big Four meeting in Paris to consider proposals that would not erase the progress made in Germany by the Western powers would determine the outcome. He praised the draft constitution for a West German state. [4:2.] The United States was said to be considering a plan for withdrawal of all occupation troops to North German ports, except for French forces, which would return to France. [1:4.]

Guarded optimism was expressed by Moscow's New Times in an editorial on the Big Four meeting. The editorial said the talks could be a "turning point" in East-West relations. [4:6.]

Communists, urging at a Senate hearing in Washington that ratification of the North Atlantic treaty be deferred until after the Paris meeting, likened the pact to "Hitler's Axis." [1:6-7.]

Israel became the fifty-ninth member of the United Nations when the General Assembly voted, 37 to 12, to admit her. The six Arab states left the hall in protest. [1:1.] Foreign Minister Sharett, the first Israeli delegate to the United Nations, pledged his country to work for peace with its Arab neighbors and to remain friendly with both the United States and Russia. [12:3.]

Japan is not what she was ten years ago, Premier Yoshida said in appealing for proper understanding by the world. He asked access to materials and markets to enable Japan to become self-supporting. [19:1.]

Representative Rankin disowned his veterans' pension bill when a "watered-down" version was reported by a House committee. [1:2.]

Labor leaders and President Truman were said to have agreed on pressing passage of the Administration's labor bill with some amendments. [24:2.]

A man who identified himself as Gerhart Eisler, called this country's No. 1 Communist, sailed secretly on a Polish liner now at sea. [1:6-7.]

Victorious anti-Hague forces in Jersey City will seek a court order impounding all public records until an audit can be made. [1:3.]

Index to other news appears on Page 32.

The New York Times.

VOL. XCIX..No. 33,481.

Entered as Second-Class Matter, Postoffice, New York, N. Y.

NEW YORK, SATURDAY, SEPTEMBER 24, 1949.

Three Cents, New York, N. Y.

THREE CENTS

Copyright, 1949, by The New York Times Company.

SMALL STEEL MILL SETS PENSION PLAN, A POSSIBLE PATTERN

Proposal by Employer of 1,200, With Workers Sharing Costs, Is Held Poser for Union

LIMITS CAUSE FOR STRIKE

Murray Is Firm for 'Package' Urged by Panel — Wildcat Walkout Hits Another Plant

By A. H. RASKIN
Special to The New York Times.

PITTSBURGH, Sept. 23—The first hint at the strategy the steel industry may employ to head off a threatened strike of 500,000 steel workers Oct. 1 came today from one of the smallest companies in the industry.

While the United States Steel Corporation and other big companies marked time on the first day of their renewed negotiations with the United Steel Workers of America, CIO, the Follansbee Steel Corporation made a proposal to the union that was widely regarded here as the forerunner of similar offers to be made by the rest of the industry.

The company, which has 1,200 employes at plants in Follansbee, W. Va., and Toronto, Ohio, informed the union that it was prepared to commit itself to pay 6 cents an hour for pensions, provided its workers put up an additional 3 cents an hour.

Employes Pay for Insurance

The company already has a contributory program of social insurance, to which it gives, about 4 cents an hour and the workers 2 cents.

The proposal would bring the company's outlay for pensions and welfare into line with the 10-cent "package" recommended by President Truman's fact-finding board. At the same time it would make an end run around the union's insistence that employers pay the whole cost of industrial social security.

The Truman panel endorsed the idea that employers should meet the bill for pensions and social insurance, but opened the door for supplementary payments by workers to increase the amount of protection that could be provided. The board said such arrangements could be effected through collective bargaining.

If other steel companies subscribe to the 6-cent figure for pensions and 4 cents for health, hospital and other forms of social insurance, on condition that their workers also contribute, the union would be maneuvered into the position of having to decide whether or not to strike solely for establishment of the non-contributory principle.

Philip Murray, president of the union, has stressed the union's belief that the most important element in the Truman board's report was its recommendation that care for the "human machine" should be as much a charge on industry as care of plant equipment. The union has barred any compromise on that issue.

Murray Again Threatening Strike

At a two-hour conference with representatives of United States Steel this afternoon, Mr. Murray reiterated the union's determination to strike unless the company agreed to shoulder the full cost of pensions and welfare on the 6-cent and 4-cent basis suggested by the fact-finders.

The company made no immediate reply. Subcommittees were set up by both sides to continue negotiations Monday, five days before the strike deadline.

There was nothing to indicate that "Big Steel" had abandoned the opposition it expressed in public statements last week to incorporation of workers from any direct share of financial responsibility for their own pensions and insurance.

The company has committed itself to give 4 cents an hour for welfare, provided workers made an additional payment on their own, but it has declined to set any specific figure for pensions until a joint study of retirement benefits is completed next March 31.

Negotiations between the union and other large steel companies took place today in a dozen cities, but none of the companies gave any new indication of its position. In virtually all cases the talks were recessed until Monday without any sign of a break in the deadlock that has existed since the first negotiations got under way in June.

Union negotiators warned that the patience of the men in the steel mills was wearing thin at the lack of progress toward employer-

Continued on Page 28, Column 1

Cancer Patient Slain; Daughter Detained

Special to The New York Times.

STAMFORD, Conn., Sept. 23—Carol Paight, 20 years old, was placed under police guard in Stamford Hospital tonight pending investigation of whether she shot her police-sergeant father in pity after learning that he had an inoperable cancer.

The father, Carl Paight, 52, died seven hours after he was shot with his own service pistol at 5:45 P. M. He had been in the hospital since Sept. 15, suffering from the effects of an operation that showed he had cancer.

The daughter, who had been alone with him, became hysterical. Sedatives were administered before she could be questioned by the police and a psychiatrist. Father and daughter had been deeply attached, friends said. Police who knew both because of Sergeant Paight's twenty-eight years of service here, said that she had declared upon being told of the cancer that she did not want her father to suffer.

RED DEFENSE RESTS; REBUTTAL WAIVED

Jury in 9-Month Trial Excused Till Summaries Begin Oct. 4, May Get Case Week Later

By RUSSELL PORTER

The defense rested in the nine-month Communist trial yesterday, and the Government waived its right of rebuttal. Federal Judge Harold R. Medina gave counsel until 2 o'clock Tuesday afternoon to submit requests for instructions to be included in his charge to the jury and announced that arguments on closing motions would be heard at 10:30 o'clock Wednesday morning.

Judge Medina excused the jury until Tuesday morning, Oct. 4, when, if he denies the usual defense motions to throw out the case, summaries will begin. In the absence of unexpected developments, the case should go to the jury by the week beginning Monday, Oct. 10.

Eleven members of the Communist party's American Politburo or national board have been on trial since January 17, for criminal conspiracy to teach and advocate overthrow of the Government and destruction of American democracy by force and violence. Government witnesses have testified that the defendants reorganized the party for this purpose in 1945 on orders from Moscow.

The defense took roughly six months to present its case, including a two-month preliminary challenge to the Federal jury system. The Government introduced its evidence in two months.

The defense called thirty-five witnesses and the Government fifteen. The defense offered 429 exhibits, the Government 332.

Of the 158 trial days, the defense used 109—eighty-two in the trial proper and twenty-seven in the jury challenge. The Government spent thirty-seven days in the presentation of evidence. Ten days were devoted to picking the jury and two days to opening statements by opposing counsel.

The Government called its first witness on March 23 and rested on May 19. The defense began to present evidence on May 23, four months ago yesterday.

Nearly 20,000 pages of testimony

Continued on Page 7, Column 2

Auto Crash Kills Publisher's Wife As He Reaches for Spilling Cup

Special to The New York Times.

HARRISON, N. Y., Sept. 23—Marvin Pierce, president of the McCall Corporation, magazine and fashion publishers, at 230 Park Avenue, New York, was driving to the Rye railroad station this morning when he tried to prevent a cup of coffee from spilling on his wife's clothes. In an accident that followed, his wife, Mrs. Pauline Robinson Pierce, 53 years old, was killed and Mr. Pierce was injured.

The couple left Purchase Street home, adjoining the Westchester Country Club, soon after 8 A. M. Mr. Pierce, who is 56, was at the wheel and his wife was beside him, ready to drive home from the station after her husband had boarded a commuters' train for New York.

Mrs. Pierce held in her hands a cup of coffee that she had carried from the breakfast table. After sipping the fluid, she placed the cup for a moment on the seat between her husband and herself. From a corner of his eye Mr. Pierce saw the cup tipping toward his wife.

As Mr. Pierce reached for the cup, the auto swerved to the left side of the road, hit a soft shoulder, plunged 100 feet down a moderate embankment, slid between a pole and a tree and crashed into a tree with a stone wall. Striking the windshield, Mrs. Pierce died of a fractured skull. The accident occurred on Highland Road near Purchase Street.

Taken to the United Hospital in Port Chester, Mr. Pierce told the story to the police. Detectives found the coffee cup, some China of English manufacture, unbroken in the wreckage of the car and took it to police headquarters. Physicians listed Mr. Pierce's injuries as a cerebral concussion, fractured nose, four broken ribs and several bruises. His condition tonight was improving.

Besides her husband, Mrs. Pierce leaves two sons, James R. and Scott Pierce of Rye, and two daughters, Mrs. Walter G. Rafferty of West Hartford, Conn., and Mrs. G. H. W. Bush of Bakersfield, Calif.

CIO SEES LEFTISTS QUITTING TO FORM OWN ORGANIZATION

High Officers Say Such Action Is Called for by New Line of Communist Party

FIGHT AT CONVENTION DUE

National Body Plans to Set Up Rival Right-Wing Unions if Pro-Red Groups Depart

By LOUIS STARK
Special to The New York Times.

WASHINGTON, Sept. 23—High officers of the Congress of Industrial Organizations expressed the view today that the new Communist party line was to split all pro-Communist unions from the CIO and to form a new labor federation. This belief is supported by the following developments:

1. A factional struggle within the CIO Teachers Union in New York, in which the pro-Communists are demanding that the union leave the CIO, though their opponents proclaim loyalty to the parent body.

2. The decision of pro-Communist unions to carry the fight on autonomy and wage policies to the right wing, led by Philip Murray, president of the CIO.

3. The "impossible" demands decided on several days ago by the convention of the United Electrical Radio and Machine Workers that will be served on Mr. Murray.

4. Refusal of the Farm Equipment Workers Union to obey the CIO mandate to merge with the United Automobile Workers.

The Murray forces are prepared for a possible split. If it occurs, they will charter right-wing organizations to form the nucleus of new organizations supplanting the dissidents.

Eleven Affiliates Involved

Eleven CIO affiliates may be affected by the possible schism. While they have been generally credited with a membership of 1,000,000 members, informed officials say that their total is more nearly 600,000.

The largest of the dissidents is the UE, which says it bargains for 600,000 members. This union, however, is reported by right-wing officers to be paying to the CIO on about 350,000 members. Some of the leftist-led unions have been in arrears in payments to the national organization for some months.

The largest nut that the CIO has to crack is the UE, its third largest affiliate. This union, well entrenched in General Electric, Westinghouse and other large radio and electrical manufacturing companies, is a strong, well-disciplined organization.

Despite its strength, CIO officials indicated that they would meet any challenge of the UE's re-elected officers. If the union should decide to leave the CIO, the latter's officers feel confident of winning adherence of the workers in the big General Electric and Westinghouse plants as the nucleus of a new electrical union.

If Mr. Murray's associates are impatient for the battle because daily evidences of leftist dissidence convinces them that the latter have made up their minds to split the CIO and to put the blame on the right wing.

The latest aspect of the leftist attack on the CIO leadership is

Continued on Page 22, Column 7

ADDRESSING U. N.

Andrei Y. Vishinsky
The New York Times

VISHINSKY SAYS U.S. PLOTS ATOMIC WAR

Calls for Great Power Treaty to Strengthen World Peace in Assembly Speech

Text of Vishinsky address to U. N. Assembly is on Page 4.

By THOMAS J. HAMILTON

Andrei Y. Vishinsky, the Soviet Foreign Minister, accused the United States and Britain yesterday of planning an atomic war, and introduced a resolution at Flushing Meadow proposing that the United Nations General Assembly request the five Great Powers to conclude "a pact for the strengthening of peace."

The resolution also would call on all nations to settle their disputes without resorting to the use or threat of force, and would take note "of the unbending will and determination of peoples to ward

Continued on Page 4, Column 1

ATOM BLAST IN RUSSIA DISCLOSED; TRUMAN AGAIN ASKS U.N. CONTROL; VISHINSKY PROPOSES A PEACE PACT

CAPITOL FOR ACCORD

Lucas Says 'Future of Civilization' May Rest on Atom Control

AIRING OF VIEWS URGED

McMahon Holds U. S. Should 'Demand Right' to Put Case Before Russians Via Radio

By WILLIAM S. WHITE
Special to The New York Times.

WASHINGTON, Sept. 23—In a great anxiety that passed soon into a positive response—demands for fresh tries at international control of the atomic bomb—Congress heard today the news that an atomic explosion had occurred in the Soviet Union.

The atmosphere at the Capitol almost everywhere was consciously quiet and restrained. Some of the most responsible members of Congress issued statements saying that the American people could have confidence, in any possible crisis, in the military leadership and the military power of this country.

Beyond this, Administration Congressional spokesmen said in substance that the implications of the President's disclosure of what had happened in Russia were beyond the scope of any Congressional action. They looked toward the United Nations as the forum for this matter.

Senator Scott W. Lucas of Illinois, the Democratic leader of the Senate, and Senator Brien McMahon, Democrat, of Connecticut, the principal Congressional authority on atomic energy, came out almost at once for another attempt at bringing the bomb under the world's seal.

"I believe," said Senator Lucas, "that nothing could give the world greater confidence in survival than for the delegates at the United Nations to reconsider the question of atomic energy control, and arrive at an agreement acceptable to all.

"The world knows that our rep-

Continued on Page 3, Column 5

Soviet Achievement Ahead Of Predictions by 3 Years

By WILLIAM L. LAURENCE

President Truman's announcement that we have evidence of the occurrence of an "atomic explosion" in the Soviet Union within recent weeks ranks next only to his original announcement of the explosion of the first atomic bomb over Hiroshima on Aug. 6, 1945. It marks the end of the first period of the atomic age and the beginning of the second.

The momentous event is bound to have profound repercussions the world over. Though the scientists have predicted its coming, it came at least three years sooner than was expected. This was largely the result of an erroneous assumption that Russian scientists could do nothing about developing an atomic bomb until after we informed them about it following Hiroshima. The fact of the matter is that scientists everywhere recognized the tremendous potentialities of atomic energy for war and peace as soon as the discovery of uranium fission was announced to the world in 1939.

While it is likely that Soviet scientists tested the first and only bomb they had, it would be dangerous to assume that they are four years behind us and that it would take them that long to catch up with us. It would be much more reasonable to assume that they have geared their plants to produce at the rate of one bomb a week, so that they will have a stockpile of at least fifty bombs a year from now, enough to destroy fifty of our cities with 40,000,000 of our population.

On the other hand, it is also likely that the latest event will make possible a better understanding between us and Russia, leading toward an agreement for the international control of atomic energy. Bargaining between equals is more likely to produce desirable results than bargaining between two principals, one of which holds

Continued on Page 6, Column 2

Truman Statement on Atom

By The United Press.

WASHINGTON, Sept. 23—The text of President Truman's statement today announcing a recent atomic explosion in the Soviet Union:

I believe the American people to the fullest extent consistent with the national security are entitled to be informed of all developments in the field of atomic energy. That is my reason for making public the following information.

We have evidence that within recent weeks an atomic explosion occurred in the U.S.S.R.

Ever since atomic energy was first released by man, the eventual development of this new force by other nations was to be expected. This probability has always been taken into account by us.

Nearly four years ago I pointed out that "scientific opinion appears to be practically unanimous that the essential theoretical knowledge upon which the discovery is based is already widely known. There is also substantial agreement that foreign research can come abreast of our present theoretical knowledge in time." And, in the three-nation declaration of the President of the United States and the Prime Ministers of the United Kingdom and Canada, dated Nov. 15, 1945, it was emphasized that no single nation could, in fact, have a monopoly of atomic weapons.

This recent development emphasizes once again, if indeed such emphasis were needed, the necessity for that truly effective and enforceable international control of atomic energy which this Government and the large majority of the members of the United Nations support.

World News Summarized

SATURDAY, SEPTEMBER 24, 1949

President Truman issued yesterday a terse statement containing this dramatic disclosure: "We have evidence that within recent weeks an atomic explosion occurred in the U. S. S. R."

His announcement, indicating that United States monopoly in atomic weapons had ended, added that "ever since atomic energy was first released by man, the eventual development of this new force by other nations was to be expected." He said this "probability" had always been "taken into account" by this nation, and he renewed his plea "for that truly effective and enforceable international control of atomic energy which the Government and the large majority of the members of the United Nations support." Secretary of State Acheson said he assumed that it was an atomic weapon that had been exploded in the Soviet Union. He said the news would not lead to any shift in the United States position on international atomic control. [1:7.]

New efforts to achieve an acceptable plan for international control of atomic weapons were urged in Congress, where Mr. Truman's announcement was received with restrained anxiety. [1:3.] Reassuring statements were made by General Eisenhower and Maj. Gen. Leslie R. Groves, wartime chief of the atomic bomb project. General Eisenhower said he saw no reason why "a development that was anticipated years ago should change our thinking or 'o our actions." [2:2.] One r it expected by Washington observers was a spur to the North Atlantic defense program. Closer cooperation among the United States, Britain and Canada in atomic development was also seen. [3:4.]

Scientists who had generally predicted that the Russians would eventually succeed in discovering the secret of setting off an atomic explosion saw the Russian development as having come at least three years earlier than had been expected. [1:6-7.]

Soviet Foreign Minister Vishinsky said nothing about Russian possession of an atomic bomb in his eagerly awaited address to the United Nations General Assembly. He accused the United States and Britain of planning an atomic war. Mr. Vishinsky introduced a resolution calling for "the unconditional prohibition of atomic weapons" and another asking the five major powers to make "a pact for the strengthening of peace." [1:4.]

Renewed negotiations by the Big Four Foreign Ministers deputies on an Austrian state treaty got off to a bad start. Russian refusal to reconsider the controversial issues forced an indefinite adjournment. [6:2.]

The British Labor Government will ask for a vote of confidence after Parliament convenes next week to debate the devaluation of the pound. [6:3.]

In China the battle for the important seaport of Amoy reached new intensity. [5:1; with map.]

In a move that might set the pattern for the steel companies in the steel industry to stave off a threatened strike by 500,000 steelworkers, the Follansbee Steel Corporation offered a pension plan under which the company would pay 6 cents an hour and the employes an additional 3 cents an hour. [1:1.]

High CIO officials were reported to believe that the new Communist party line was to try to split all pro-Communist unions from the CIO to organize a new labor federation. [1:3.]

Index to other news appears on Page 14.

U. S. REACTION FIRM

President Does Not Say Soviet Union Has an Atomic Bomb

PICKS WORDS CAREFULLY

But He Implies Our Absolute Dominance in New Weapons Has Virtually Ended

By ANTHONY LEVIERO
Special to The New York Times.

WASHINGTON, Sept. 23—President Truman announced this morning that an atomic explosion had occurred in Russia within recent weeks. This statement implied that the absolute dominance of the United States in atomic weapons had virtually ended.

"We have evidence that within recent weeks an atomic explosion occurred in the U.S.S.R.," President Truman said.

These words stood out in red-letter vividness in a brief undramatic statement in which the Chief Executive said that the United States always had taken into account the probability that other nations would develop "this new force."

He pleaded once again for adoption of the system of international control of atomic energy promulgated by the United States and supported by the large majority of countries now assembled in the United Nations General Assembly at Flushing Meadow.

McMahon Reveals News

Mr. Truman announced the discovery to the Cabinet, assembled in the White House at 11 A. M. for the usual Friday meeting. Simultaneously on Capitol Hill Senator Brien McMahon, Democrat, of Connecticut, stood before the members of the Joint Congressional Atomic Energy Committee and gave them the news, which Mr. Truman had passed-on to him at 3:15 P. M. yesterday.

White House correspondents had their usual conference with Charles G. Ross, the President's secretary, at 10:30 A. M. It was routine, but as they filed out his secretary, Miss Myrtle Bergheim, advised them not to go away. A moment before 11 A. M. Miss Bergheim entered the press room and said: "Press!!"

The news men filed into Mr. Ross' office. He said he wished the door closed, and a secret service man took his post there. Then Mr. Ross said that he would pass out an announcement and that nobody was to leave the room until everyone present was a copy. He began passing around the President's mimeographed statement.

Tass Correspondent Attends

One of the first reporters to scan his copy exclaimed, "Russia has the atomic bomb!" There was a wild rush through the door and to the telephones in the near-by press room. One of the news men who sprinted out was the correspondent of Tass, the official Soviet news agency.

"The President has just given it to the Cabinet," said Mr. Ross as they went.

Thus the President did not personally appear, and there was no opportunity for questions or later to put questions to him.

Secretary of Defense Louis Johnson came out of the Cabinet meeting soon afterward. He began shaking his head as the questions came. Reporters literally clutched his arms as he headed for his limousine.

"Have we made any change in the disposition of our forces since this happened?" This question was asked twice.

"No," Mr. Johnson finally said.

"Does the Cabinet know any more about this than is contained in the President's statement?"

"It," Mr. Johnson replied to this. "It was fully informed."

"Do you have reason to believe this was the first atomic explosion in Russia?" asked another reporter.

This time Mr. Johnson smilingly shook his head, negatively.

"Don't overplay it," remarked Mr. Johnson, departing. In the cir-

Continued on Page 2, Column 5

ACHESON RULES OUT SHIFT IN U. S. PLANS

Western Diplomats and Atomic Experts at U. N. Agree to Uphold Control Program

Text of Secretary Acheson's statement is printed on Page 2.

By A. M. ROSENTHAL

Secretary of State Dean Acheson said yesterday that he assumed the explosion in Russia reported by President Truman had been caused by an actual atomic weapon. He insisted, however, that the news had come as no shock and would not change the United States-sponsored plan for international control of atomic energy.

Other Western diplomats and atomic control specialists at the United Nations Assembly at Flushing Meadow took the same line. Unanimously, they said that the majority of the members of the United Nations would stick to the plan that had been fought by the Soviet Union for more than three years.

United Nations officials took it for granted that the President's announcement had pushed the world organization back into the center of the atomic picture despite the long deadlock on control negotiations. Secretary General Trygve Lie summed up the Secretariat attitude by saying that the

Continued on Page 6, Column 6

Couple Held in Quebec Air Crash; Woman Said to Have Planted Bomb

By The Associated Press.

QUEBEC, Sept. 23—Police tonight said a drug-dazed woman confessed to carrying a package, believed to have contained dynamite, which was placed aboard an ill-fated Quebec Airways plane that blew up Sept. 9, killing all twenty-three persons aboard.

Police said the woman, identified as Mrs. Arthur Pitre, admitted taking the package to the Quebec Airport where it was placed aboard the plane, but she insisted that she did not know the contents of the package.

Royal Canadian Mounted Police claimed the woman was recovering from sleeping pills she took at the suggestion of her lover, whose wife was aboard the plane.

Provincial police detained as material witness J. A. Guay, a young Quebec jeweler, whose 28-year-old wife was one of the passengers who lost their lives when the plane was ripped open by a blast in the luggage compartment. The plane smashed into a mountain near Sault au Cochon, forty miles northeast of Quebec.

Mrs. Pitre was also being held as a material witness.

Police also are reported to have questioned a third person in connection with the case.

Police described the third person as a 36-year-old "pretty waitress." They said she was a close acquaintance of Guay.

The crash took the lives of three New York executives of the Kennecott Copper Corporation. They were President E. T. Stannard, President-designate Arthur D. Storke and Vice President R. J. Parker.

Quebec Provincial police detained Mrs. Pitre at her home in Quebec. Persons living near by are police enter the woman's Gauvreau Street home, an apartment. Crowds gathered outside and were called to keep the curious on the move.

Police Inspector René Belec told newsmen:

"We have definite proof that explosives were aboard the plane to

Continued on Page 28, Column 3

The New York Times

PAGE ONE

Major Events:

1950–1959

"All the News That's Fit to Print"

The New York Times.

LATE CITY EDITION
Cloudy, mild today and tomorrow, followed by clearing and colder.
Temperature Range Today—Max. 30; Min. 24
Temperature Yesterday—Max. 40; Min. 24
Full U. S. Weather Bureau Report, Page 92

Section 1

NEWS INDEX, PAGE 78, THIS SECTION

Copyright, 1950, by The New York Times Company.

VOL. XCIX..No. 33,601.

Entered as Second-Class Matter,
Postoffice, New York, N. Y.

NEW YORK, SUNDAY, JANUARY 22, 1950.

FIFTEEN CENTS

TRUMAN, ACHESON DEMAND CONGRESS VOTE AID TO KOREA

Rayburn Says Bill Will Come to Floor Again, and It Is 'Going to Be Passed'

SPEEDY ACTION IS SOUGHT

Secretary of State Expresses 'Concern and Dismay' — Sees Threat to U. S. Policy

By JOHN D. MORRIS
Special to The New York Times.

WASHINGTON, Jan. 21.—President Truman today deplored the House of Representatives rejection of the Korean aid bill and called for "speedy rectification."

In a statement released by the White House along with a letter in which Dean Acheson, Secretary of State, expressed "concern and dismay" over the development, the President said he would take up the matter with Congressional leaders and urge immediate action.

Even before he spoke out, however, Speaker Sam Rayburn told reporters that a bill would be brought to the floor again, and "the House is going to pass it."

The measure authorizing $60,-000,000 of appropriations to continue the $120,000,000 economic aid program for the infant Korean Republic, was killed in the House Thursday by a surprise vote of 193 to 191. The Senate had passed a separate bill last year.

"Important Foreign Policy"

President Truman called for early reversal of the House action "in order that important foreign-policy interests of this country may be properly safeguarded."

He expressed his entire concurrence in the views expressed by Mr. Acheson in a letter to the President dated yesterday.

The Secretary said the House action, if not quickly repaired, would have "the most far-reaching adverse effects upon our foreign policy, not only in Korea but in many other areas of the world" where "our encouragement is a major element in the struggle for freedom."

Mr. Acheson said our conduct in Korea was regarded by the world "as a measure of the seriousness of our concern with the freedom and welfare of peoples maintaining their independence in the face of great obstacles."

He suggested that failure to provide further aid would imperil Korea's survival as a free nation and be "disastrous" for this country's foreign policy.

Dr. John Myun Chang, the Korean Ambassador, said tonight he was gratified and "very much encouraged" by the Truman and Acheson statements.

The envoy expressed "deep gratitude" for the statements and added the hope that the United States could find a way to continue aid to Korea, which, he said, is "absolutely essential to the recovery of its domestic economy."

Parley on Another Vote

Congressional leaders have already conferred with Mr. Acheson and other State Department officials on the question of obtaining another House vote on the question.

They are now seeking to determine the best way of doing so. To bring the defeated measure up for reconsideration would require a two-thirds majority vote. Consequently, it is believed that some other method must be found.

The prevailing view appeared to be that the quickest way would be to take the Senate-approved Korean aid bill to the House floor. It would have to be reported first by the Foreign Affairs Committee, after being amended there to conform with the House bill.

Speaker Rayburn, indicating that he favored this method, said an attempt could then be made to obtain Rules Committee clearance and, if this failed, the measure could be called up through the "by-passing" procedure that the House retained yesterday.

Senator Tom Connally, Democrat, of Texas, chairman of the Senate Foreign Relations Committee, voiced his readiness to help with the problem, if necessary, by putting through a bill linking Korean aid with continuation of the authority to provide economic assistance to Nationalist China.

He said this might be done by reviving a bill sponsored by Senators H. Alexander Smith of New Jersey and William F. Knowland of California, Republicans, now pending

Continued on Page 4, Column 1

The New York Times Five Cents Tomorrow

Because of continued increasing costs in all phases of the operation of this newspaper, the newsstand price of THE NEW YORK TIMES on weekdays in New York City will be five cents beginning tomorrow. The new price of THE TIMES will be the same as that of other standard-sized newspapers in New York and generally throughout the country.

FULL ASIA VICTORY IS SEEN IN MOSCOW

Lenin Memorial Orator Says Capitalism Cannot Halt the Revolutionary Movement

By HARRISON E. SALISBURY
Special to The New York Times.

MOSCOW, Jan. 21.—Top figures of the Soviet Government and the Communist party were told tonight that capitalism and imperialism were no longer capable of halting the mass revolutionary movement of millions of Asiatic peoples inspired by successes of communism in China and the Soviet Union.

This analysis of the contemporary situation in Asia was placed before leaders of the Soviet Union and Chinese Communist chiefs at the important annual memorial meeting held at the Bolshoi Theatre on the anniversary of Lenin's death twenty-six years ago.

The Lenin memorial oration is one of the year's most important Communist party declarations. Tonight as last year, it was given by P. N. Pospelov, editor of the party's newspaper Pravda.

[The Associated Press stated that among those reported present in the Bolshoi Theatre were Chinese Communist leader Mao Tse-tung and the regime's Premier and Foreign Minister, Chou En-lai. Mr. Mao received a special ovation at mention of his name by Mr. Pospelov.]

Chinese Leaders' Presence Cited

The leaders of the new Chinese Communist regime are in Moscow conferring upon the broadest kind of understandings with the Soviet leadership. Mr. Mao has been in Moscow for nearly five weeks. Last night he was joined by Mr. Chou, accompanied by a distinguished delegation including top figures in the new Northeast China Government established in Manchuria and most of the leading specialists of the new Chinese regime in trade, commerce and industry.

Mr. Pospelov's analysis of the revolutionary successes and possibilities in Asia was coupled with the sharpest denunciation of United States imperialism and a frank prediction that "capitalism will unavoidably be replaced by socialism."

The success of Communist construction in the Soviet Union, he declared, has become "an example for the people's democracies of Europe and Asia."

"The great victory of the Chinese people already has proved that imperialism is incapable of suppressing the forces of the people, that this struggle awakens and attracts into the struggle millions of toilers," he said. "The great teaching of Leninism shows the people of all countries the road of the fight against the unheard of calamities of imperialism, shows the road of liberation from the yoke of imperialism, the road to a new Socialist life."

He declared that the leaders

Continued on Page 5, Column 1

BERLIN RAIL OFFICE IS RETURNED BY U. S. TO EAST GERMANS

Commandant Says He Yielded to Avoid New Hardships in the Western Sectors

HITS SOVIET 'PROVOCATION'

Difficulties Following Seizure Outweighed the Gain of 600 Rooms, He Asserts

Special to The New York Times.

BERLIN, Jan. 21.—Maj. Gen. Maxwell D. Taylor, United States Commandant in Berlin, this afternoon ordered the State Railway Administration building in the American sector restored to East German custody. Western sector police were withdrawn at 5 o'clock.

At a press conference called simultaneously with the release of the building, General Taylor made it clear that the basis of his action was the reprisals already taken against the population of the Western sectors and the threats of further hardships through nonpayment of wages to railway employes living in those sectors.

Confiscation of the Reichsbahn structure had been ordered, General Taylor said, as part of a program to obtain the maximum use of office and housing space in the United States sector of this badly damaged city; only forty of the 600 rooms had been used recently.

"Far from sympathizing with this purpose," his prepared statement said, "the Soviet authorities have seized upon the affair as an excuse to harass the residents of West Berlin, to threaten fresh reprisals against Reichsbahn workers and generally to disturb the peace of the city. They have not attempted to conceal their intention to discharge additional railway workers, and threaten to make further reductions in their West mark salary payments.

Claim Termed Absurd

"On Jan. 20, representatives of the Berlin press were given a tour of the Reichsbahndirektion building, where they verified the absurdity of the claim that the communications of the Reichsbahn were being interfered with. They found the usual communications personnel on the job, coming and going in the same way as during the Reichsbahn occupation. Furthermore, they verified the extent of the building space standing vacant.

"It was the American intention to put this space to use for the benefit of Berlin. Unfortunately, the unreasonable and provocative attitude of the Soviets and of the Reichsbahn makes it appear probable that the hardships which they intend to impose outweigh the benefits arising from the American plan.

"Having regretfully reached this conclusion, I am suspending the notice of custody and withdrawing the West sector police from the interior of the building.

"We now know the facts about it and shall watch to see whether the Reichsbahn puts it to a remunerative use in providing transportation service to the city.

"If our action accomplishes this, it will have served its purpose."

Obviously taken by surprise, Communist propaganda agencies were unprepared with their comment tonight as General Taylor's move. The Soviet-controlled Radio Berlin said that the United States had succumbed to "thousands of protests by workers."

Continued on Page 12, Column 2

CHURCHILL WARNS OF SOCIALIST DRIFT, ASKS END TO CURBS

Defines Big Election Issue as More Regimentation or a Return to Freedom

LABOR CLAIMS FLOUTED

Conservative Leader Credits Full Employment to Loans From U. S. and Dominions

By RAYMOND DANIELL
Special to The New York Times.

LONDON, Jan. 21.—Striking the first blow for the Conservatives in the election campaign, Winston Churchill called upon the nation's voters to set Britain free of Socialist controls and restrictions.

"The main reason why we are unable to earn our own living and make our way in the world is because we are not allowed to do so," he declared in a radio speech from his home at Westerham in Kent.

The former Prime Minister's radio address was described as a "political" but not an "election" speech. The fact is that the campaign does not officially begin until Feb. 3 when Parliament is dissolved.

As the first step toward its dissolution, taken in the orderly process of British electoral machinery, King George VI issued a proclamation today postponing the next meeting of Parliament. The call, the date on which it had been called to reconvene. This means that this Parliament, elected in 1945, will not meet again.

It was a good Churchillian speech, which "pinked" the Laborites where it hurt, on spending, housing and the high cost of living. But possibly because of the high standard of oratorical leadership that the wartime leader had set, it fell a little flat on British ears.

The first five persons this correspondent talked to after its delivery found it "disappointing." But Mr. Churchill was under the handicap of sounding a keynote for his party before his party has made known its election program. That will be issued in the coming week.

It would have been a tactical blunder for him to anticipate any surprises that this Conservative manifesto will contain. So his address to the electorate tonight was necessarily primarily a critique rather than a statement of policy, but he did manage to get across the idea that between the Laborites and the Conservatives there is no dispute about the virtue of a country's whole labor force being usefully employed.

The choice before the people on

Continued on Page 30, Column 1

HISS GUILTY ON BOTH PERJURY COUNTS; BETRAYAL OF U. S. SECRETS IS AFFIRMED; SENTENCE WEDNESDAY; LIMIT 10 YEARS

PRINCIPAL FIGURES IN THE HISS PERJURY TRIAL

Alger Hiss leaving Federal Building.   Mrs. Ada Condell, foreman of the jury.   Judge Henry W. Goddard, who presided.
The New York Times

EARLY 'RIGHTS' VOTE APPEARS UNLIKELY

Items of 'Unfinished Business' May Get Precedence Despite House Action on Rules

Special to The New York Times.

WASHINGTON, Jan. 21.—Chances for consideration by the House of Representatives on Monday of the Administration's bill to establish a Federal Fair Employment Practices code were evaluated as practically nil at the Capitol today. Some proponents of the legislation had hoped a vote on it might be taken on that day.

Being the fourth Monday in the month, it will be in order for chairmen of committees that have favorably-reported bills pending before the Rules Committee for more than twenty-one days to move on the floor to proceed to their consideration. Such discharge motions

Continued on Page 57, Column 3

Senate to Sift R. F. C. Loans With View to Writing Curbs

By H. WALTON CLOKE
Special to The New York Times.

WASHINGTON, Jan. 21.—The stage has been set for a full-scale Congressional investigation of the lending policy of the billion-dollar Reconstruction Finance Corporation. As a result of the inquiry, Congress is expected to set forth, once and for all, the terms on which it wants the RFC's lending operations to function.

Irritated by recent big loans that the RFC granted to several corporations, as well as some that were made in the earlier days of the agency, members on both sides of the aisle in Congress have been demanding a clarification of policy.

Leading this group is Senator J. William Fulbright, Democrat, of Arkansas, who recently lost a battle with the Kaiser-Frazer Corporation.

The Senator, who has not forgotten the rather sharp rebuff, has started the wheels of Congressional investigation turning. On Tuesday he will ask the Senate Banking and Currency Committee, headed by Senator Burnet R. Maybank, Democrat, of South Carolina, to inquire into the RFC's action in granting the following loans:

Kaiser-Frazer Corporation...$44,000,000
Northwest Air Lines......... 12,000,000
Waltham Watch Co........... 6,000,000
Texmass Petroleum Co....... 15,100,000

Financial observers here foresee nothing that would block the Senator's request for action. As head of the Senate Banking and Currency subcommittee on the RFC, he conducted a three-day inquiry into the loan policy of the agency last summer. It was at that time that the Senator questioned the wisdom of advancing additional funds to the Lustron Corporation, Columbus, Ohio, which is now in default on $37,580,000 of RFC loans.

Once the full committee ap-

Continued on Page 46, Column 3

MAYOR RIDICULES IDEA OF RESIGNING

Telephones From Florida That He Is Getting Rid of Virus and Will Return to Job

By JAMES A. HAGERTY

In a telephone message to THE NEW YORK TIMES from Key Largo, Fla., Mayor O'Dwyer yesterday that he had no intention of resigning.

In his telephone conversation, the Mayor appeared to be hearty of voice and very cheerful. Questioned about a report that he contemplated retirement, he said:

"It is utterly ridiculous. It touches any sense of humor."

The Mayor then laughed heartily and continued:

"I am down here to get the virus out of my system. I am going to stay till I've got it licked and I think I am well on the way to doing that. I feel much better. I want to get completely well so that I can return to the city and stay at my desk in City Hall with no program."

The Mayor said that A. Edward M. Bernecker, who left Newark Airport by plane on Friday, had not arrived but was expected to reach Key Largo today. It is understood that he will have a series of talks with the Mayor and friends

Continued on Page 57, Column 4

350,000,000-Gallon Water Loss In 24 Hours Largest Since Dec. 12

By PAUL CROWELL

The city's water storage reservoirs suffered a loss of 350,000,000 gallons in the twenty-four hours ended at 8 A. M. yesterday.

It was the first storage loss since Dec. 20 and the largest since Dec. 12. Officials of the Department of Water Supply, Gas and Electricity, attributed the loss to a slightly increased consumption of water, coupled with an absence of appreciable rain or snowfall in the up-state watershed areas.

The city's reservoirs lost 108,-000,000 gallons in the twenty-four hours ended at 8 A. M. on Dec. 17. In the twenty-four hours ended at 8 A. M. on Dec. 20, the storage loss was 662,000,000 gallons.

The reversal of the upward trend of water storage gave city officials serious concern and boosted 1,121,000,000 gallons the aver-

Continued on Page 61, Column 1

The Water Situation

The following figures as of 8 A. M. yesterday give the number of gallons of water in the city's reservoirs. The difference in the two days is the net of water intake and the day's consumption:

Friday.........106,662,000,000
Yesterday......106,312,000,000
Net loss 350,000,000
Average daily storage gain needed to fill reservoirs by June 1 1,121,000,000
Watershed snowfall:
Schoharie ....02 inch
Esopus ....04 inch
Croton ....04 inch
At present conditions there remains about ninety days' supply before pressure fails.
Catskill and Croton reservoirs at capacity hold 253,136,000,000 gallons.

JURY OUT 24 HOURS

Verdict Follows a Call on Judge to Restate Rulings on Evidence

CHAMBERS STORY UPHELD

Defendant Is Impassive — His Counsel Announces That an Appeal Will Be Taken

By WILLIAM R. CONKLIN

Alger Hiss, a highly regarded State Department official for ten of his forty-five years, was found guilty on two counts of perjury by a Federal jury of eight women and four men yesterday.

Nearly twenty-four hours after receiving the case, the jury reported its verdict at 2:50 P. M. The middle-aged jurors had begun their deliberations at 3:10 P. M. on Friday after two weeks of testimony in the second perjury trial.

By convicting Hiss on both counts, the jury found that he had betrayed his trust by passing secret State Department documents to Whittaker Chambers. The former courier for a Communist spy ring was the Government's key witness against the former official. The verdict meant that the jury believed Mr. Chambers and the corroborating evidence produced by the Government.

The convicted defendant faces maximum penalties of five years' imprisonment and a $2,000 fine on each count, a combined total of ten years and $4,000. Federal Judge Henry W. Goddard continued his bail at $5,000 and set Wednesday at 10:30 A. M. for sentencing. Sentence will be passed in the same thirteenth floor courtroom of the United States District Court where Hiss was tried.

Lapsing of Espionage Charge

The case of "The United States of America versus Alger Hiss" rested on a two-count perjury indictment. Thomas F. Murphy, Government prosecutor, had taxed Mr. Hiss with treason and sentenced him against his country. However, any possible prosecution for espionage had been ruled out by a three-year statute of limitations, which conferred immunity after March, 1941.

Hiss was thus brought to trial on one count of perjury for denying that he ever gave secret documents to Mr. Chambers. The second count charged perjury for denying that he had seen the ex-Communist after Jan. 1, 1937. The Government contended that the documents were passed in February and March, 1938.

By its verdict the jury upheld the Government's contention that Priscilla Hiss, 46-year-old wife of the defendant, had typed copies of the documents for Mr. Chambers on the Hisses' Woodstock typewriter.

Mr. Chambers had told the jury that he had been a paid functionary of the Communist party in Washington and had collected secret information for Russia from 1935 to April, 1938.

Basis Laid for Appeal

Claude B. Cross and Edward C. McLean, defense attorneys, would not say at first whether they would appeal the decision. They had established a basis for an appeal by taking exception to a part of the charge of Judge Henry W. Goddard.

"There won't be any statement," Mr. McLean said. "I do not wish to discuss the possibility of an appeal now. There is just no statement." But later Mr. Cross said that "you can be sure the verdict will be appealed."

After the jury had convicted on both counts, Mr. Murphy asked that Hiss' bail of $5,000 be increased in conformity with the custom for "all convicted defendants." After Mr. Cross protested, Judge Goddard permitted Hiss to remain at liberty under the same bail. Mr. Cross said he would make some motions on Wednesday, the day set for sentencing.

Should defense attorneys file an appeal, it would act as an automatic stay of sentence. If an appeal should reach the United States

Continued on Page 30, Column 7

World News Summarized

SUNDAY, JANUARY 22, 1950

The jury of eight women and four men in the Alger Hiss trial yesterday found the former State Department official guilty of perjury on two counts. The jury reached its verdict nearly twenty-four hours after receiving the case and its decision meant that it had accepted the testimony of Whittaker Chambers, confessed former spy, over the denials by Mr. Hiss of having passed secret documents to Mr. Chambers. Federal Judge Goddard will pass sentence Wednesday. [1:8.]

Mayor O'Dwyer characterized as "utterly ridiculous" rumors that he might resign his office because of ill health. [1:7.]

Although some supporters of the Truman Administration's Federal Fair Employment Practices code had hoped that the House might vote on it tomorrow, there was little likelihood the measure would get to the House floor by that time. [1:5.]

Congress planned a sweeping inquiry into the lending policy of the Reconstruction Finance Corporation as a preliminary to fixing the terms on which the organization's lending may operate in the future. [1:6-7.]

President Truman urged "speedy rectification" in the House of its rejection by a narrow margin of the bill providing $60,000,000 for aid to Korea. Secretary of State Acheson asserted that failure to assist Korea would jeopardize her survival as a free nation. [1:1-1.]

The journey to Moscow of Communist China's Foreign Minister, Chou En-lai, was seen as an indication that the negotiations between the Chinese Communists and the Soviet Union had reached the decisive stage. Peiping vigorously denied Russia had

---

"detaching" four north China areas as charged by Mr. Acheson. [2:3.]

The annual Lenin memorial meeting in Moscow was told that the mass revolutionary movement in Asia could not be stopped by capitalism. [1:2.]

Winston Churchill set the keynote for the campaign of the Conservative party by denial that the British voters that the "main reason why we are unable to earn our own living and make our way in the world is because we are not allowed to do so." Mr. Churchill said the choice was to regain freedom or plunge the nation deeper into socialism. [1:4.]

General Taylor, the United States commander in Berlin, ordered the seized Railway Administration building in the United States sector restored to East German custody. [1:3.]

Franco-German rapprochement once more jeopardized as the result of an announcement by the West German republic that it was suspending trade talks with France. German officials cited France's attitude on the Saar as a reason for the suspension [1:2-3] and proposed an international statute similar to that in the Ruhr. [3:1.]

The Allied High Commission, in a move hailed as a public censure of the Bonn regime for "impudent" behavior, will demand that the Germans withdraw their announcement that coal rationing would end the end of this month. [3:2.]

Finland virtually rejected Moscow's demand that she extradite 200 "war criminals" who are said to be Russians to have found refuge among the Finns. [24:2.]

Bonn Halts French Trade Talks After Clash Over Policy on Saar

By HAROLD CALLENDER
Special to The New York Times.

PARIS, Jan. 21.—A diplomatic crisis between France and Western Germany developed suddenly today when the French learned that, after challenging France's policy in the Saar, the Bonn regime had suspended negotiations for the trade treaty with France that was to have been signed a week ago.

French officials were angered by these German actions, which they considered as endangering the faint beginnings of a French-German rapprochement in the field of economic relations.

In Bonn, it was reported here as a maneuver to force reconsideration of the status of the Saar. Such was considered the purpose of the statement that Dr. Konrad Adenauer, Chancellor had proposed the creation of an international statute for the Saar that would be similar to the Ruhr statute now in force.

When asked by the French For-

---

eign Office for an explanation of their suspension of the negotiations, Bonn officials replied that they did not mean to go back on the trade pact but they must postpone its signature because of internal difficulties raised by German farmers and because of "the positions taken on the Saar question."

French officials said this reply surprised them because they considered the treaty would contribute to development of intra-European trade and desired to sign it as soon as possible.

This move by Bonn was regarded here as a maneuver to force reconsideration of the status of the Saar. Such was considered the purpose of the statement that Dr. Konrad Adenauer, Chancellor

Continued on Page 2, Column 5

The New York Times.

Copyright, 1950, by The New York Times Company.

VOL. XCIX.. .No. 33,611.

NEW YORK, WEDNESDAY, FEBRUARY 1, 1950.

LATE CITY EDITION
A little rain and cold today. Cloudy,
continued cold tomorrow.
Temperature Range Today—Max.,38 ; Min.,31
Temperatures Yesterday—Max.,37 ; Min.,32
Full U. S. Weather Bureau Report, Page 25

RAG PAPER EDITION
SEVENTY-FIVE CENTS

PRESIDENT SEEKS 70-DAY COAL TRUCE, FACT-FINDING BOARD

He Ignores Taft Law in Asking 5-Day Week at Old Wages Pending Study of Dispute

AVOIDS WORD 'EMERGENCY'

Operator Acceptance Is Seen Likely, but the Plan Holds Disadvantages for Lewis

Text of announcement by White House on coal, Page 22.

By JOSEPH A. LOFTUS
Special to The New York Times.

WASHINGTON, Jan. 31—President Truman moved into the soft coal dispute today with a proposal that John L. Lewis and the operators call a seventy-day truce and submit their arguments to a fact-finding board. He asked for an answer by 5 P. M. Saturday.

Under the truce "normal" production of coal would be resumed. This was understood to mean a return to the five-day work week by the members of the United Mine Workers, headed by Mr. Lewis. The wage scale of the expired union contract would be paid. A board would make recommendations in sixty days, but the recommendations would not be binding.

President Truman thus used the approach he used in the steel dispute last summer. This avoids use of the Taft-Hartley Law and its injunctive authority, although the President said in November that if he acted in the coal case he would use that law.

"Grave Concern" Voiced

The President's message to Mr. Lewis and the operators spoke of the "grave concern" about the dispute, but avoided Taft-Hartley words, such as "emergency" and "health and safety."

The dispute in the anthracite industry was omitted from the proposal.

The President said that in the final analysis the parties themselves must write their own agreement. "Voluntary action, not compulsion, in these matters is not only my personal conviction but the national policy," he declared.

Aware that the miners and operators were to meet at 3 P. M. tomorrow to try bargaining again, the President said he did not want to interfere with that. He told them that if they could reach an agreement to resume full production they should disregard his proposal and let him know about it by noon Saturday.

Mr. Lewis' attorneys are due in court at 10 A. M. tomorrow to answer a petition for an injunction filed by Robert N. Denham, general counsel of the National Labor Relations Board. Mr. Lewis and the other officers of the union filed affidavits in the case today. They denied violating the Taft-Hartley Law in the coal negotiations which began last May and accused the operators of refusing to bargain.

Surmise on Board Make-Up

The make-up of the fact-finding board, if the President's truce proposal goes into effect, is a matter of conjecture. When the proposal was under consideration at the White House in November the three men who had been asked if they were available were David L. Cole, who was a member of the fact-finding steel panel; John Dunlop, Harvard economics professor, and Willard Wirtz of Northwestern University, former chairman of the National Wage Stabilization Board. Neither side would say tonight.

Continued on Page 22, Column 2

Melchior Threatens To Quit Opera Here

Lauritz Melchior stepped into the Metropolitan Opera dispute last night by saying that he would not return next season "unless indicated plans change materially." He would make no comment on the possible return of Kirsten Flagstad but, like Helen Traubel, he indicated resentment at not being approached sooner by Rudolf Bing, who will be the general manager for 1950-1951.

"I would have assumed," Mr. Melchior said, "that the natural courtesy of the management to their leading artist who had appeared regularly with the company for twenty-four years would dictate a call to any leading artist who had appeared regularly with the company for twenty-four years to determine his position with

Continued on Page 24, Column 2

By Winston Churchill:

The Second World War

Volume III—The Grand Alliance
Book I—Germany Drives East

INSTALLMENT 6:

THE JAPANESE ENVOY

THE New Year had brought disturbing news from the Far East. The Japanese Navy was increasingly active off the coast of Southern Indo-China. Japanese warships were reported in Saigon harbour and the Gulf of Siam. On January 31 the Japanese Government negotiated an armistice between the Vichy French and Siam. Rumours spread that this settlement of a frontier dispute in South-east Asia was to be the prelude to the entry of Japan into the war. The Germans were at the same time bringing increased pressure to bear upon Japan to attack the British at Singapore.

* * *

About this time several telegrams arrived from our Commander-in-Chief in the Far East urging the reinforcement of Hong Kong. I did not agree with his views.

Prime Minister to General Ismay   7 Jan 41

This is all wrong. If Japan goes to war with us there is not the slightest chance of holding Hong Kong or relieving it. It is most unwise to increase the loss we shall suffer there. Instead of increasing the garrison it ought to be reduced to a symbolical scale. Any trouble arising there must be dealt with at the Peace Conference after the war. We must avoid frittering away our resources on untenable positions. Japan will think long before declaring war on the British Empire, and whether there are two or six battalions at Hong Kong will make no difference to her choice. I wish we had fewer troops there, but to move any would be noticeable and dangerous.

Later on it will be seen that I allowed myself to be drawn from this position, and that two Canadian battalions were sent as reinforcements.

* * *

IN the second week of February I became conscious of a stir and flutter in the Japanese Embassy and colony in London. They were evidently in a high state of excitement, and they chattered to one another with much indiscretion. In these days we kept our eyes and ears open. Various reports were laid before me which certainly gave the impression that they had received news from home which required them to pack up without a moment's delay. This agitation among people usually so reserved made me feel that a sudden act of war upon us by Japan might be imminent, and I thought it well to impart my misgivings to the President.

Former Naval Person to President Roosevelt   15 Feb 41

Many drifting straws seem to indicate Japanese intention to make war on us or do something that would force us to make war on them in the next few weeks or months. I am not myself convinced that this is not a war of nerves designed to cover Japanese encroachments in Siam and Indo-China. However, I think I ought to let you know that the weight of the Japanese Navy, if thrown against us, would confront us with situations beyond the scope of our naval resources. I do not myself think that the Japanese would be likely to send the large military expedition necessary to lay siege to Singapore. The Japanese would no doubt occupy whatever strategic points and oilfields in the Dutch East Indies and thereabouts they covet, and thus get into a far better position for a full-scale attack on Singapore later on. They would also raid Australian and New Zealand ports and coasts, causing deep anxiety in those Dominions, which have already sent all their best-trained fighting men to the Middle East. But the attack which I fear the most would be by raiders, including possibly battle-cruisers, upon our trade routes and communications across the Pacific and Indian Oceans. We could by courting disaster elsewhere send a few strong ships into these vast waters, but all the trade would have to go into convoy and escorts would be few and far between. Not only would this be a most grievous additional restriction and derangement of our whole war economy, but it would bring altogether to an end all reinforcements of the armies we had planned to build up in the Middle East from Australasian and Indian sources. Any threat of a major invasion of Australia or New Zealand would of course force us to withdraw our Fleet from the Eastern Mediterranean, with disastrous military possibilities there, and the certainty that Turkey would have to make some accommodation, for reopening of the German trade and oil supplies from the Black Sea. You will therefore see, Mr. President, the awful enfeeblement of our war effort that would result merely from the sending out by Japan of her battle-cruisers and her twelve 8-inch-gun cruisers into the Eastern oceans, and still more from any serious invasion threat against the two Australasian democracies in the Southern Pacific.

Some believe that Japan in her present mood would not hesitate to court or attempt to wage war both against Great Britain and the United States. Personally I think the odds are definitely against that, but no one can tell. Everything that you can do to inspire the Japanese with the fear of a double war may avert the danger. If however they come in against us and we are alone, the grave character of the consequences cannot easily be overstated.

The agitation among the Japanese in London subsided as quickly as it had begun. Silence and Oriental decorum reigned once more.

Former Naval Person to President Roosevelt   20 Feb 41

I have better news about Japan. Apparently Matsuoka is visiting Berlin, Rome, and Moscow in the near future. This may well be a diplomatic tour to cover absence of action against Great Britain. If Japanese attack which seemed imminent is now postponed, this is largely due to fear of United States. The more these fears can be played upon the better, but I understand thoroughly your difficulties pending passage of [Lend-Lease] Bill on which our hopes depend. Appreciation given in my last Personal and Secret of naval consequences following Japanese aggression against Great Britain holds good in all circumstances.

* * *

Behind the complex political scene in Japan three decisions seem to emerge at this time. The first was to send the Foreign Secretary, Matsuoka, to Europe to find out for himself about the German mastery of Europe, and especially when the invasion of Britain was really going to begin. The second was that the British forces so far tied up in naval defence that Britain could not afford to reinforce her Eastern possessions if Japan attacked them? Although he had been educated in the United States, Matsuoka was bitterly anti-American. He was deeply impressed by the Nazi movement and the might of embattled Germany. He was under the Hitler

Continued on Page 34.

FRANCE PROTESTS SOVIET RECOGNITION OF HO CHI MINH RULE

Note to Russia Asserts Action Could 'Gravely Impair' Paris-Moscow Ties

U. S. AND BRITAIN INFORMED

Government of North Korea Announces Acceptance of Viet Nam Rebel Regime

By LANSING WARREN
Special to The New York Times.

PARIS, Jan. 31—France tonight delivered to the Soviet Embassy here a vigorous protest against Soviet recognition of Ho Chi Minh, the enemy of France in Indo-China. The note charged that the Soviet action was of a nature "gravely to impair" French-Soviet relations.

In diplomatic circles here the Soviet Union's action was considered as a threat not only to the French position in Indo-China but as an effort to prevent the United States from building a policy of containment in Asia such as has been successful in Europe.

The text of the French note follows:

The French Government has learned through publication of a communiqué by the Tass Agency that the Government of the U.S.S.R. has taken the decision of recognizing as the insurrectional government of the Viet Nam the insurrectional government of Ho Chi Minh. Such a decision violates the principles of international law, since the only regular government of the Viet Nam is the government constituted by His Majesty Bao Dai, to whom the French Government has transferred the rights of sovereignty which it previously held.

In encouraging, as is the obvious intention of the Soviet Government, the insurrectional movement of Ho Chi Minh, this decision can only render more difficult the restoration of peace in Viet Nam. In taking the initiative which it has just announced, the Government of the U.S.S.R. is committing with regard to France an act whose character and consequences cannot be underestimated.

For all these reasons the French Government raises a solemn protest against a decision which is of a nature gravely to impair Franco-Soviet relations.

The note was delivered by Alexander Parodi, general secretary of the French Foreign Ministry, after Soviet Ambassador Alexandre Bogomolov, who was invited to the Quai d'Orsay, had replied he could not come today but would present himself tomorrow.

Copies of the French protest to

Continued on Page 11, Column 1

World News Summarized

WEDNESDAY, FEBRUARY 1, 1950

President Truman, acting in his capacity of Commander in Chief of the Armed Forces, yesterday directed the Atomic Energy Commission "to continue its work on all forms of atomic weapons, including the so-called hydrogen or super-bomb." The work, he said, would go forward "on a basis consistent with the over-all objectives of our program for peace and security" and "until a satisfactory plan for international control of atomic energy is achieved." [1:8.]

Congressional opinion heavily supported the President, and demands for speeding the work were made. The Atomic Energy Commission reported to Congress that atomic weapons now were being made by the "industrial type" of production and stockpiles were growing rapidly. [3:5.] New atomic safeguards were thrown about the atomic plants at Oak Ridge, Tenn.; Los Alamos, N. M., and Hanford, Wash. Any plane approaching within 100 miles of the plants without prior identification and clearance will be intercepted by Air Force fighters. [1:8.]

The hydrogen bomb, it was disclosed, is really a triton bomb, the basic element of which is tritium, a hydrogen isotope. [1:7.]

William Webster has been asked to head the Research and Development Board of the Department of Defense as successor to Dr. Karl T. Compton, who resigned. [1:6-7.]

Dealing with the major domestic problem of coal, President Truman asked John L. Lewis and the operators to call a seventy-

day truce and to submit the issues to a nonstatutory fact-finding board such as he had proposed in the steel dispute. The President asked for a full five-day week in the soft-coal mines during the truce. [1:1.] Leaders of more than 100,000 striking miners were divided over urging the men to return. Operators indicated an inclination to accept the plan. [22:3.]

This state paid $387,000,000 in jobless benefits last year, nearly twice the 1948 total, Albany reported. [21:1.]

A House committee reported, 17 to 1, a bill for economic aid to Korea and Nationalist China. [13:2.] The brutality of South Korean police was seen as a major problem of the Seoul Government. [13:4.]

France, in a strong note of protest, told Moscow that Soviet recognition of Ho Chi Minh in Indo-China "gravely" impaired French-Soviet relations. Washington called Moscow's action proof that the Ho regime was a Communist tool. [1:4.]

Senator Connally said Britain's policy of extending her embargo on dollar oil to the Commonwealth was "an act of hostility to our economy." [13:2.]

Britain won a victory in the European Marshall Plan Council when Foreign Minister Stikker of the Netherlands was elected "political conciliator." [1:5.]

French Premier Bidault won five close votes of confidence on the budget. [14:3.]

This city's tentative realty value for tax purposes was set at $18,493,559,079. [1:6-7.]

Index to other news appears on Page 30.

TRUMAN ORDERS HYDROGEN BOMB BUILT FOR SECURITY PENDING AN ATOMIC PACT; CONGRESS HAILS STEP; BOARD BEGINS JOB

DISCUSSING PLANS FOR MAKING HYDROGEN BOMB

Members of the Joint Congressional Atomic Energy Committee talk with Sumner T. Pike, right, acting head of the Atomic Energy Commission, after President Truman gave his approval. Seated are Chairman Brien McMahon, Representatives Carl T. Durham, Chet Holifield and W. Sterling Cole. Standing are Senator John W. Bricker, Representatives Paul J. Kilday, Melvin Price, Carl Hinshaw and Charles H. Elston.
The New York Times (by George Tames)

STIKKER IS NAMED E. R. P. CONCILIATOR

Council in Paris Accepts Dutch Leader Supported by Britain —E. C. A. Goals Unmet

By HAROLD CALLENDER
Special to The New York Times.

PARIS, Jan. 31—Dr. Dirk U. Stikker, Foreign Minister of the Netherlands, was named today to the post of "political conciliator" of the European Marshall Plan Council instead of Paul-Henri Spaak, former Premier of Belgium, whose appointment was vetoed by the British Government. Paul G. Hoffman, Economic Cooperation Administrator, and W. Averell Harriman, ECA Ambassador in Europe, had desired that M. Spaak be chosen.

Dr. Stikker was selected by the Council. He was the candidate of the British who had first suggested Dr. Halvard M. Lange, former

Continued on Page 14, Column 4

Truman Asks Utility Leader To Head Top Research Body

By JAMES RESTON
Special to The New York Times.

WASHINGTON, Jan. 31—President Truman has offered the Government's top scientific job—chairmanship of the Research and Development Board in the Department of Defense—to William Webster of Boston, a vice president of the New England Electric System, it was learned today.

Mr. Webster, 49 years old, a graduate of the United States Naval Academy and former chairman of the Defense Department's Military Liaison Committee with the Atomic Energy Commission, would be largely responsible for preparing an integrated military research and development program so that this weapon such as the new hydrogen bomb would take their proper place in a well-balanced defense policy.

The chairmanship of the Research and Development Board was held by Dr. Vannevar Bush from 1947 to 1948 and by Dr. Karl T. Compton, former president of Massachusetts Institute of Technology, from 1948 until Nov. 3, 1949. Since then the work of the board has been supervised by Dr. Robert F. Rinehart as deputy chairman.

Coincidental with his offer of the Government's principal scientific position to Mr. Webster, President Truman was reported to be working actively on selection of a successor to David E. Lilienthal as chairman of the Atomic Energy Commission. One person said to be under consideration is Carroll Wilson, present general manager of the AEC.

Mr. Lilienthal is reliably reported to have proposed that control of

Continued on Page 5, Column 3

City Realty Values Up for 6th Year; Assessment Total $18,493,559,079

By LEE E. COOPER

New York's taxable realty wealth this year of $316,525,750 in "ordinary" real estate, to $16,120,113,875, and of $64,802,150 in the holdings of utility corporations, which were listed tentatively for the new tax year at $1,655,893,290.

Added to these sums was $717,-551,914 for special franchises, the exact amount of which will not be set by the State Tax Commission for another month. The figure used by the city officials is based on the 1949-50 records.

Although no particular area was found by the field assessors to have increased generally in value —in contrast to last year when sharp gains were listed for the land around Stuyvesant Town and the United Nations site—there were three times as many rises as there were decreases in the city as a whole.

The report showed a net rise for

Continued on Page 26, Column 4

HISTORIC DECISION

President Says He Must Defend Nation Against Possible Aggressor

SOVIET 'EXPLOSION' CITED

His Ruling Wins Bipartisan Support on Capitol Hill--No Fund Request Due Now

By ANTHONY LEVIERO
Special to The New York Times.

WASHINGTON, Jan. 31—President Truman announced today that he had ordered the Atomic Energy Commission to continue production of the hydrogen bomb.

The Chief Executive acted in his role of Commander in Chief of the Armed Forces, ordering an improved weapon for national security. Thus, from the domestic standpoint, he removed the question of producing the super-weapon as an issue that might be argued on moral grounds.

As for international statecraft, Mr. Truman, by treating the hydrogen bomb as an addition to the American armory, also removed it as an issue that might be interpreted as an advanced threat or inducement in seeking international control of atomic weapons.

Nevertheless, Mr. Truman said that his perseverance in providing for national defense would be matched by his efforts to seek international control of atomic weapons.

New Phase of Atomic Age

In his announcement, Mr. Truman regarded the hydrogen bomb as a progressive outgrowth of United States production of the uranium-plutonium atomic bomb. He put it this way: the commission was "to continue its work on all forms of atomic weapons, including the so-called hydrogen or super-bomb."

His use of the word "continue" was understood to imply that with national security the over-riding consideration, the chief factor guiding his decision was whether it was practicable to make the weapon. Scientists have said that it is.

In effect, the President's decision, which won wide acclaim in Congress, marked the advent of a new phase of the atomic age and a surge ahead of Russia in the race to retain military ascendancy.

The bombs that visited destruction on Hiroshima and Nagasaki split the atom. The new bomb would fuse atoms instead, but with a power 100 to 1,000 times greater than the improved fission bombs that have been developed since the Japanese cities were struck.

The President's Statement

The President made his decision known in the following brief statement:

"It is part of my responsibility as Commander in Chief of the armed forces to see to it that our country is able to defend itself against any possible aggressor. Accordingly, I have directed the Atomic Energy Commission to continue its work on all forms of atomic weapons, including the so-called hydrogen or super-bomb.

Continued on Page 3, Column 2

IT'S A TRITON BOMB, MIGHTIEST POSSIBLE

Would Release Energy More Than Seven Times '45 Type —No Critical-Mass Limit

By WILLIAM L. LAURENCE

What President Truman referred to yesterday as "the so-called hydrogen bomb" is not a hydrogen bomb at all in the true scientific meaning of the term.

This, the most powerful superbomb that can be built on earth, it can now be revealed, actually is the triton bomb, in which the basic element used is tritium, a hydrogen isotope (twin) of atomic mass 3. It is an element hardly known to the public but well known to nuclear physicists. A triton is the nucleus of tritium, composed of one proton and two neutrons.

The term hydrogen, as used by scientists, refers strictly to the common form of hydrogen of atomic mass 1, a mass that cannot be made into a bomb.

While the process responsible for the vast amounts of energy released by the sun every second is

Continued on Page 4, Column 4

Air Defense Mapped For Atom Projects

By AUSTIN STEVENS
Special to The New York Times.

WASHINGTON, Jan. 31—The Air Force disclosed tonight that it planned to throw a protective aerial "wall" around key atomic installations of the country.

Under a plan worked out today at the Pentagon, the Air Force will insist on the positive identification of any airplane flying within 100 miles of three atomic plants and, failing to be advised of an aircraft's identity will send fighter planes aloft to observe its character and course.

The plan in effect is a revival of a wartime measure whereby in combat zones any aircraft picked up by radar or other means of detection was consid-

Continued on Page 3, Column 6

"All the News That's Fit to Print"

The New York Times.

LATE CITY EDITION
Drizzle and fog early today, fair later. Cloudy tomorrow.
Temperature Range Today—Max. 41; Min. 34
Temperature Yesterday—Max. 41; Min. 33
U. S. Weather Bureau Report, Page 31

Copyright, 1950, by The New York Times Company.

VOL. XCIX..No. 33,617.

Entered as Second-Class Matter,
Postoffice, New York, N. Y.

NEW YORK, TUESDAY, FEBRUARY 7, 1950.

FIVE CENTS

G. O. P. POSES ISSUE FOR '50 AS LIBERTY VERSUS SOCIALISM

FAIR DEAL IS TARGET

Republicans Want Cuts in Spending and Taxes, Revised Taft Law

BACK FOREIGN POLICY AID

But Hit Conduct of Program—Party Declaration Fails to Win United Support

Text of Republican party statement is printed on Page 26.

By W. H. LAWRENCE
Special to The New York Times.

WASHINGTON, Feb. 6—The Republican party policy makers today proclaimed "Liberty Against Socialism" to be the major domestic issue of the 1950 Congressional elections.

But the party failed to achieve complete unity, either in its denunciation of the Truman Administration's program at home and abroad, or on the alternatives which it promised.

In all-day separate and closed meetings members of the Republican National Committee and the House and Senate Republican conferences finally gave their approval to a "statement of principles and objectives" designed to serve as a national platform for the months between now and the November elections.

Party chieftains had hoped that the declaration would demonstrate party unity and purpose and bring a new flow of financial contributions to defray campaign expenses, but a group led by Senator Henry Cabot Lodge Jr. of Massachusetts, Senator Margaret Chase Smith of Maine, Representative Jacob K. Javits of New York and Representative James G. Fulton of Pennsylvania promptly made known its dissatisfaction.

"Fair Deal" Vigorously Opposed

As was to be expected, the party declaration approved by the majority was vigorous in its opposition to enactment of the most of the Fair Deal program put before Congress by President Truman.

On foreign policy questions it found a middle ground, advocating continuance of a bipartisan attitude but sharply criticizing the administration of foreign policy with particular reference to "secret agreements" made at Yalta and Potsdam "which have created new injustices and new dangers throughout the world."

An effort made by Werner Schroeder, Illinois national committeeman, to put the party on record as opposed to continuance of the bipartisan foreign policy, was overwhelmingly defeated in the national committee. Members said that a voice vote showed support for Mr. Schroeder from only one or two others.

The party statement declared:

"We advocate a strong policy against the spread of communism or fascism at home and abroad, and we insist that America's efforts toward this end be directed by those who have no sympathy either with communism or fascism."

It asserted that "basic American principles are threatened by the Administration's program for a planned economy modeled on the Socialist Governments of Europe, including price and wage control, rationing, socialized medicine, regional authorities and the Brannan Plan with its controls, penalties, fines and jail sentences."

The Republican program "to rebuild a prosperous and progressive America" included these major planks:

A return to a balanced budget

Continued on Page 26, Column 2

By Winston Churchill:
The Second World War

Installment 11 of the excerpts from Mr. Churchill's memoirs of the war will be found today on Page 29

McCloy Warns the Germans Against a Revival of Nazism

At Opening of Amerika Haus in Stuttgart He Clarifies U. S. Policy, Declaring Its Chief Concern Is to Build Democracy

By DREW MIDDLETON
Special to The New York Times.

STUTTGART, Germany, Feb. 6—The United States will use all its power to fight a revival of nazism in Germany, John J. McCloy, United States High Commissioner, asserted today.

The western Germans were bluntly warned to concentrate on internal problems, avoid "agitation" on foreign issues and to build democracy toward "unification of all Germany."

Speaking before an audience of 1,600 in the Stuttgart Opera House, Mr. McCloy turned the dedication of this city's Amerika Haus, an information center, into what was at once a major declaration of United States policy in Germany and an admission that the progress of German toward democracy had been neither as fast nor as complete as some officials had believed.

Mr. McCloy flatly told the Germans they would not be allowed a political position endangering the peace of Europe and "there will be no German army or air force."

Later at a press conference he declared he was not contemplating any changes in the occupation statute that defines the Allied powers at present and did not talk about such changes on his recent trip to Washington.

Shortly after his speech the High Commissioner intervened sharply and perhaps decisively in the denazification scandal currently shaking the government of Wuerttemberg-Baden by publicly

Continued on Page 4, Column 3

The text of the McCloy address is on Page 4.

WORLD ARMS TALK URGED BY TYDINGS TO END 'NIGHTMARE'

Senator Asks Call by Truman to Ease Fears by Reducing All Weapons Down to the Rifle

By WILLIAM S. WHITE
Special to The New York Times.

WASHINGTON, Feb. 6—Senator Millard E. Tydings, Democrat, of Maryland, appealed to President Truman today to call a world conference for disarmament, in conventional as well as atomic weapons, to "end the world's nightmare of fear."

Mr. Tydings, a powerful figure as chairman of the Senate's Armed Services Committee and a member of its Foreign Relations Committee and the Joint Congressional Committee on Atomic Energy, asked the Senate to approve a resolution "authorizing and requesting" the President to summon such a meeting.

Lacking some such "fundamental" approach to peace, he asserted, "we are up against the possible annihilation of all the human beings of this earth."

It would be "difficult" for Marshal Stalin or any other ruler, he argued, to "refuse an appeal by the President openly made on an honest and fair basis."

Senator Tydings' speech reopened a Senate debate on atomic policy, and weapons policy generally, which had been set off last week by Senator Brien McMahon, Democrat, of Connecticut, with the recommendation that this country at "almost any cost" seek an international arrangement neutralizing atomic and hydrogen weapons.

It appeared to reflect a considerable Congressional dissatisfaction at the fact that President Truman's recently announced decision to go ahead with the hydrogen bomb development was accompanied by no new approach to the Soviet Union toward atomic control.

Mr. Tydings contended that strict international inspection of

Continued on Page 5, Column 4

JAPAN SAID TO BACK GIVING BASES TO U.S.

Visit by Joint Chiefs Is Held to Have Convinced Most Party Heads on Move

By LINDESAY PARROTT
Special to The New York Times.

TOKYO, Feb. 6—Leaders of Japan's major political parties with the exception of the extreme left have become convinced as a result of the visit here by the Joint Chiefs of Staff that this nation should grant air, naval and army bases to the United States in return for a protective guarantee under the peace treaty. There are indications they believe that the view would be supported by a large majority of the post-war Japanese electorate.

The conviction of the Japanese leaders, the importance of which it is difficult to overstress, comes as a result of the emphasis they placed by the Joint Chiefs on big American installations already existing here.

The three generals and one admiral who compose the Joint Chiefs left Japan today for Okinawa after visiting the naval base at Yokosuka, Army installations in the Osaka region and the large Air Force base at Itazuke in Kyushu. They were prevented from inspecting the newly built major air base at Misawa in northeast Honshu by weather conditions.

Though no information was forthcoming, either from the chiefs or local United States military authorities, the Japanese were inclined to believe the principal point of the visit was evaluation of these and other bases and the

Continued on Page 11, Column 2

Widnall, Jersey Republican, Wins Thomas Seat in Congress by 2 to 1

Special to The New York Times.

HACKENSACK, N. J., Feb. 6—William B. Widnall, a Republican lawyer from Saddle River, tonight won a two-to-one victory in the special Seventh Congressional District election to choose a successor to J. Parnell Thomas, Republican, jailed for payroll padding.

Mr. Widnall received 31,754 votes against 15,370 for his Democratic opponent, former Mayor George T. English of East Paterson, a textile manufacturer.

The 43-year-old victor, a State Assemblyman from Bergen County, took the lead as soon as returns began to come in when the polls closed at 8 P. M. and maintained a wide margin from that time on.

A little more than two hours later Mr. English, who had predicted a "resentment vote" growing out of the Thomas scandal, conceded victory to Mr. Widnall.

"The victory is yours," he said at 10:10 P. M. in a telephone call to Mr. Widnall at the Republican campaign headquarters in Ridgewood. "My congratulations to you.

"Your support in the Seventh Congressional District apparently goes beyond partisan politics at this time."

On Mr. Widnall's invitation, Mr. English, accompanied by Mrs. English, then visited the headquarters, where a victory party was in the making. A momentary silence that greeted the Democrat and his wife when they walked in gave way immediately to a heavy burst of applause and cheers.

Mr. Widnall introduced his opponent to the gathering and read the message conceding victory. There was more applause and cheers.

The Republican said he hoped to offer a constructive program toward a better United States.

"It is my hope," he continued, "that this Republican victory is a forerunner of great Republican victories in November."

Mr. Widnall entered the primary fight for the candidacy without the force to be out of

Continued on Page 26, Column 5

TRUMAN INVOKES TAFT-HARTLEY ACT IN COAL STRIKE, NAMES FACT BOARD; 370,000 MINERS OUT, VOICING DEFIANCE

BITUMINOUS TIE-UP

Only 30,000 of 400,000 Diggers Stay on Job in Soft Coal Fields

TAFT ACT 'CLUB' ASSAILED

But Owners Hold Strikers Will Obey Writ to Work—Anthracite Mines Busy

By A. H. RASKIN
Special to The New York Times.

PITTSBURGH, Feb. 6—A general strike in the country's soft coal fields was the reply given by members of the United Mine Workers today to President Truman's request for voluntary restoration of "normal" coal production.

Two hundred and seventy thousand miners who had been working a three-day week put aside their tools and joined 100,000 others who have been on a "no-day week" for the last month. Their walkout left some 30,000 UMW members at work in bituminous mines that have signed new contracts with John L. Lewis, president of the union, and in a handful of mines west of the Mississippi.

News that President Truman had put in motion the machinery for an eighty-day injunction under the national emergency provisions of the Taft-Hartley Act brought fresh expressions of defiance from the strikers. In Pennsylvania and West Virginia, where the tie-up has been in effect for a full month, local union leaders asserted that their men did not intend to go back without a contract, even if Mr. Lewis ordered them to do so.

Sabotage Is Predicted

These statements were discounted by mine owners. They voiced certainty that the miners would go back on Mr. Lewis' signal when an injunction was issued. However, some operators said they expected many locals might be slow to return and that the injunction period would be marked by "sabotage, slowdowns and sporadic stoppages" in many areas.

The first hint that the union would instruct its members to comply with a back-to-work order

Continued on Page 19, Column 4

Ching Asks a 16-Day Delay In Call for Telephone Strike

Union, Polling Leaders Across Nation, Will Reply Today—Mediator Gravely Warns the 320,000 Set to Quit Tomorrow

A sixteen-day postponement of the threatened strike affecting 320,000 telephone workers hung in the balance last night. Acting on a proposal of Cyrus S. Ching, Federal Mediation and Conciliation Service director, the executive board of the Communication Workers of America, CIO, was being polled across the country on whether to accept the delay.

The walkout, scheduled for 6 A. M. tomorrow, would affect directly 100,000 telephone employes represented by the CWA. Another 220,000 telephone workers probably would refuse to cross picket lines. The postponement sought by Mr. Ching would delay the strike call until Feb. 24.

Before the union can answer Mr. Ching, nine members of the executive board must indicate their position to Joseph A. Beirne, president of the CWA.

These include, beside Mr. Beirne, John J. Moran, John Crull and A. T. Jones, all vice presidents of the national union; C. W. Werkau, secretary-treasurer, and four regional directors, Mrs. Mary Hanscom, Eastern region, Newark; Ray Hackney, Southwestern, St. Louis; Joseph Deirdoroff, Western, Denver, and Ray Dreyer, Central, Chicago.

Mr. Ching will receive the union leaders' decision in Washington this morning. He formulated his proposal for delay while in New York, where he sought vainly for a break in the deadlocked negotiations between the CWA and the American Telephone and Telegraph Company. The negotiations resume at 10 A. M. today in the New Yorker Hotel.

Mr. Ching warned of the grave impact should the strike take place. He told both union and company spokesmen that "many of the freedoms which both sides presently enjoy, and are enjoyed by employers and unions generally, will be endangered by a demonstration of an absence of sound and stable management-labor relations in the critical communications industry."

Despite this warning, before the

Continued on Page 18, Column 5

TRANSIT INQUIRY ON; QUILL LEADS FIGHT

Mayor's Committee Hearings Open With Union Vigorously Pressing Its Demands

By ALEXANDER FEINBERG

The Transport Workers Union, CIO, got its long-sought opportunity yesterday to start presenting to Mayor O'Dwyer's fact-finding board its case for higher wages and improved working conditions.

At the first all-day session of the board, the union restated its demands for a wage increase of 21 cents an hour across the board for all of the city's 43,000 transit workers, along with forty-eight hours' pay for a five-day, forty-hour week. Other salient points among its demands called for setting up of a grievance committee with recourse to impartial arbitration, and improved pension, vacation and holiday benefits.

John F. O'Donnell, union counsel, introduced voluminous exhibits tending to show that New York's transit workers were the lowest paid of any in twelve major cities, several of them with municipally operated systems. Other exhibits sought to show that they were paid less than railroad employes and truck drivers.

Through still other exhibits he sought to make the contrasting point that New York long took good care of its policemen, firemen and

Continued on Page 17, Column 6

WATER SUPPLY DIPS 3D SUCCESSIVE DAY

Officials Call On the Public to Reduce Consumption in 'Every Possible Way'

By CHARLES G. BENNETT

As water shortage in the city's Catskill and Croton reservoirs dipped by 134,000,000 gallons yesterday, the third successive day of storage losses, water officials issued an urgent appeal to the public to reduce water use "in every possible way."

The new appeal was underscored by the weekly consumption report. This showed that last week's water consumption averaged 868,000,000 gallons daily, an increase of 8,000,000 gallons daily over use in the previous week. It was the first week since mid-November that consumption had not declined or even done no worse than in the preceding week.

Stephen J. Carney, Commissioner of Water Supply, Gas and Electricity, noted that in spite of the one-week rise, New Yorkers still had maintained an over-all average daily reduction of 324,000,000 gallons in water consumption since the "base" week, Oct. 2 to 8, 1949.

The new series of daily storage losses, coming at a time of the year when normally the reservoirs are rising, Mr. Carney said, make it imperative that the public make even further savings.

Mr. Carney said that he thought

Continued on Page 17, Column 2

Port Body Urges Helicopter Lines; Offers Field Atop Its Bus Terminal

By FREDERICK GRAHAM

The Port of New York Authority told the Civil Aeronautics Board yesterday that it strongly recommended mail, passenger and express service by helicopters in the metropolitan area. It offered to provide a landing area atop the new bus terminal it is building on Eighth Avenue between Fortieth and Forty-first Streets.

The recommendation and offer were made by Fred M. Glass, director of airport development for the bi-state agency, at the opening session of a CAB hearing to determine whether the New York area is to have a helicopter shuttle service. The hearing was held in the assembly room of the Commerce and Industry Association, 233 Broadway.

In addition to the Port Authority, representatives of five communities in New Jersey, Connecticut and New York appeared before Ferdinand M. Moran, CAB examiner, to urge authorization of helicopter shuttle service.

Representatives of helicopter manufacturing companies also testified as to the types, performance and availability of their equipment. The sum of their testimony was that dependable helicopters were now flying and had been extensively tested both by the armed services and in commercial operations. They added that larger and faster helicopters were coming along.

After explaining that the Port Authority was appearing at the hearing because of its obligation to promote the full, efficient and economical development of transportation in its area, Mr. Glass said:

"With our greater population and more intensified commercial life, the New Jersey-New York Port District, more than any other area in the country, requires the best transportation services. The helicopter, with its unique ability to take off and land on small spaces, and to move passengers and

Continued on Page 54, Column 3

RESORT TO THE LAW

President Acts Against Lewis, Chooses Inquiry Body Headed by Cole

ASKS A REPORT BY MONDAY

Injunction Move Is Due Then if the Operators and Miners Have Not Resumed Talks

By ANTHONY LEVIERO
Special to The New York Times.

WASHINGTON, Feb. 6—President Truman invoked the Taft-Hartley Act against John L. Lewis and the United Mine Workers today as the soft-coal strike became an almost complete and virtually ended bituminous production.

Simultaneously the Chief Executive appointed an emergency board of three seasoned labor arbitrators to study the dispute and report to him on or before next Monday.

This move under the law allowed the mine owners and the miners six days in which to seek again a basis for negotiation. Failing that, the real showdown should follow next week. Under the Taft-Hartley Law, the Government is compelled to apply for a court injunction that would require the miners to go back to work for eighty days pending a renewed search for a settlement.

David L. Cole, a lawyer of Paterson, N. J., and a veteran arbitrator with experience in coal disputes, was appointed chairman of the board. The other members were William Willard Wirtz, a Professor of Law at Northwestern University and former chairman of the National Wage Stabilization Board, and John Dunlop, associate professor of economics at the Harvard School of Business Administration.

Board Holds First Meeting

The board members arrived here tonight and had a session with Peter Seitz, general counsel of the United States Conciliation Service, who briefed them on the background of the dispute. Then they held an organization meeting and planned to begin their proceedings tomorrow.

Through a spokesman, Mr. Lewis blanketed the President's dramatic action with a "no comment" and then lapsed into silence. What his course might be was a riddle. There was no assurance that he would cooperate with the board or that his miners would heed the eighty-day injunction, if the proceedings went that far.

All that appeared certain tonight was that Mr. Lewis had created an imposing dilemma for his old antagonist, President Truman, who has made the repeal of the Taft-Hartley Act a major political issue for this year's Congressional election.

Unlike his unsuccessful action of last Tuesday, when he issued a conciliatory statement and sought to bring the operators and the miners before an extralegal board, Mr. Truman today said nothing. He did what the law required—issued an executive order creating the board.

Action Forecast for Days

His action was announced by Charles G. Ross, White House press secretary. It had been forecast for several days, and a large number of reporters had gathered in the lobby of the Executive offices. Mr. Ross called them in a little after noon and said:

"The President at 11:35 this morning signed an Executive order creating a board to inquire into a dispute in the bituminous coal industry. This board is to report not later than Feb. 13. Of course, it could report earlier, but that is the terminal date."

Earlier the reporters got an intimation of this action from Speaker

Continued on Page 15, Column 1

WEST GERMANS CUT SHIPMENT OF STEEL INTO RUSSIAN ZONE

Act After East Drops Far Below Pact Figure on Sending Grain to Western Areas

By JACK RAYMOND
Special to The New York Times.

FRANKFURT, Germany, Feb. 6—The West German Government has decided to curtail steel shipments from the Ruhr to the Soviet zone, it became known today.

The reason to be given the East zone regime will be that terms of the interzonal trade agreement are in danger of being broken by Soviet zone failure to provide adequate shipments of grain. It may be assumed that recent transport difficulties imposed by the Soviet zone regime had no little to do with it.

[Monday night the Russians again delayed traffic at Helmstedt without explanation, slowing down the entry of Berlin-bound trucks to the point where a waiting line was established again, The Associated Press said. By midnight, with the entry rate cut to four or five trucks an hour, there was a line of fifteen trucks, the first such

Continued on Page 6, Column 5

World News Summarized

TUESDAY, FEBRUARY 7, 1950

President Truman invoked the Taft-Hartley Act yesterday and named a three-man fact-finding board in the soft-coal dispute. The board was instructed to report not later than Monday, and if negotiations had not been resumed the President may seek an eighty-day injunction. It was the eighth time Mr. Truman had invoked the Taft-Hartley Act, which he strongly opposes, and the third time against the coal union. John L. Lewis made no comment. [1:8.] The miners, who went on a general strike, expressed defiance of an injunction. [1:8.]

Leaders of the CIO telephone union, who have called a nationwide strike for tomorrow, were voting on a Government proposal to delay action sixteen days while Federal mediators sought a peace formula. [1:8-7.]

In this city, a fact-finding committee opened hearings on demands by the transit workers for a pay increase, shorter hours and other changes in working conditions. [1:6.] The Continental Paper Company announced it was closing its $16,000,000 Ridgefield Park, N. J., plant, which has been strike-bound seven months. [17:1.]

Concern was expressed over the growing danger to peace resulting from the inability of the United States and the Soviet Union to agree on atomic control. Senator Tydings introduced a resolution calling on the President to convoke a world conference for disarmament of conventional as well as atomic weapons under constant world-wide inspection. [1:2.] A Senate group heard pleas for a "tyranny-proof" United Nations police force to be set up with or without Soviet concurrence. [3:4.] Some United Nations observers held direct Washington-Moscow talks might prove of value. [3:2-3.]

The FBI told a Congressional committee that Dr. Fuchs, British atomic scientist who had worked on bomb research in this country, had transmitted "vital secret information" to the Russians and had a long record of "sympathy with Communist ideology." Dr. Fuchs is under arrest in Britain. [1:1.] A Justice Department official told the Jury in the Coplon-Gubitchev espionage trial how a decoy message had led to the arrest of the defendants. [14:2.]

Republican policy conference, with distinct rumblings of discontent, adopted a statement proclaiming "liberty against socialism" the keynote of this year's Congressional elections. [1:1.] In New Jersey, William B. Widnall, Republican, was elected representative to succeed J. Parnell Thomas. [1:2-3.]

"We Americans are not here exclusively to feed the German people and promote economic recovery, but to help the Germans establish a political democracy, regain economic health, rejoin the democratic world and stamp out every vestige of nazism," United States High Commissioner McCloy said in Stuttgart. [1:3-5.] His blunt speech, which was welcomed by the British and French, was said to reflect accurately this country's new policy of straight talking. [5:3.] Western Germany decided to cut steel shipments to the Soviet zone. [1:4.] Premier Bidault formed a new French Cabinet without any Socialist Ministers. [7:1.]

Index to other news appears on Page 25.

"All the News That's Fit to Print"

The New York Times.

LATE CITY EDITION
Sunny with pleasant temperatures today. Fair tomorrow.
Temperature Range Today—Max.:80 ; Min.:68
Temperature Yesterday—Max.: 90.3 ; Min.:68
Full U. S. Weather Bureau Report, Page 43

Copyright, 1950, by The New York Times Company

VOL. XCIX..No. 33,758.

Entered as Second-Class Matter
Post Office, New York, N. Y.

NEW YORK, WEDNESDAY, JUNE 28, 1950.

Times Square, New York 18, N. Y.
Telephone Lackawanna 4-1000

RAG PAPER EDITION
SEVENTY-FIVE CENTS

TRUMAN ORDERS U. S. AIR, NAVY UNITS TO FIGHT IN AID OF KOREA; U. N. COUNCIL SUPPORTS HIM; OUR FLIERS IN ACTION; FLEET GUARDS FORMOSA

114 RESCUED HERE AS LINER GROUNDS AFTER COLLISION

Excalibur, With Hole 15 Feet Wide in Side, Settles on Mud Flat Off Brooklyn

FIRES START ON FREIGHTER

One Person Slightly Injured— Responsibility for the Crash Still to Be Decided

By WILLIAM R. CONKLIN

Thirty-five minutes after a gay departure for a Mediterranean cruise, the American Export Line's Excalibur was disabled in a collision yesterday with a Danish freighter in the Narrows, but all her 114 passengers were taken off safely.

The confetti-speckled white ship left Pier 4, Jersey City, at noon for a forty-three-day voyage. At 12:35 P. M. the collision with the inbound Colombia cut across off Sixty-ninth Street, Brooklyn.

The impact crushed the bow of the freighter and tore a hole fifteen feet wide in the port side of the Excalibur forward of the bridge. Fire broke out in the Colombia's forepeak in a paint storeroom.

While passengers and both crews remained calm, water quickly flooded the forward holds of the cruise ship. The Excalibur settled with her bow on a midstream mud bank, with her screw lifted in the air.

Passengers Taken Off by Tugs

Passengers on the sinking ship donned bright orange life preservers and were taken off by tugs of the Moran Towing Company. Except for one woman who bruised three fingers of her left hand, all passengers were uninjured. They were returned to Pier 4, and the ship line arranged for hotel accommodations for them.

No official on the scene would assess responsibility for the collision. The Coast Guard required both captains to file written reports on the crash today. Under usual procedure, a Coast Guard board of inquiry takes evidence and fixes blame. Unofficially, it was said that a misunderstanding of whistle signals was the probable cause of the accident.

Capt. S. N. Groves of Brooklyn, a veteran of twenty-five years at sea, commanded the Excalibur, a ship of 9,644 gross tons with a top speed of seventeen knots. The Colombia, owned by the United Steamship Lines of Denmark, was commanded by Capt. Christian Mikkelsen of Copenhagen. The freighter was operated by the Scandinavian-American Steamship Company of 25 Broadway, Carrying cotton, was en route from Philadelphia to Pier 24 at Congress Street, Brooklyn.

When the collision occurred there was good visibility despite a light haze over the lower bay. Persons in Shore Road Park saw the collision clearly, half a mile off the Brooklyn waterfront.

As the Excalibur's forward holds filled, her bow dropped into a mudbank and she swung to face upstream on the incoming tide.

2 Fireboats Help Freighter

The fireboats William J. Gaynor and Firefighter put lines on the 5,146-ton freighter to fight the fire on board. With the help of the ship's forty-two crewmen they subdued a fire in the forward hold. A collision bulkhead between that point and the forecastle prevented them from tackling another fire in the peak.

With Army, Navy, Coast Guard fireboats and lubricating was moored near the north side of the Sixty-ninth Street ferry pier. John L. Holian, Deputy Fire Chief commanding the Marine Division, summoned a hook and ladder company to pour streams into the burning boat from the pier. Within an hour, the fire was extinguished.

Joseph H. Boggs, senior assistant purser of the Excalibur, was fortunate that the collision and occurred in shoal water.

"Immediately after the crash we

Continued on Page 29, Column 2

SANCTIONS VOTED

Council Adopts Plan of U. S. for Armed Force in Korea, 7 to 1

THE SOVIET IS ABSENT

Yugoslavia Casts Lone Dissent—Egypt and India Abstain

Mr. Austin's statement to the United Nations is on Page 6.

By THOMAS J. HAMILTON
Special to The New York Times.

LAKE SUCCESS, June 27—The Security Council adopted tonight a United States resolution recommending that members of the United Nations use armed force in repelling the invasion of southern Korea and restoring international peace and security.

The vote on the resolution, which amounted to Security Council authorization for President Truman's decision to send United States naval and air units to the defense of the Republic of Korea, was 7 to 1, with Yugoslavia voting against.

The representatives of India and Egypt did not vote because they had not received instructions from their Governments. The Soviet Union was absent.

Representatives of Britain, France, Nationalist China, Cuba, Ecuador and Norway announced this afternoon that they would vote for the United States resolution without change. However, the Council recessed at 5:12 P. M. to permit Sir Benegal Rau and Mahmoud Bey Fawzi, the representatives of India and Egypt, to try to reach their Governments by telephone.

The vote was finally taken at 10:45 P. M. after both said they had been unable to establish communication with responsible authorities. With Egypt and India again not participating, the Council then rejected, seven to one, a Yugoslav resolution proposing that the Council renew its appeal for compliance with the cease-fire resolution it adopted Sunday and request the two sides to agree to United Nations mediation.

The Council then recessed again while the invading hordes crowded around their table showed their realization that a historic decision of the United Nations and the world was being taken tonight. Warren R. Austin, the United States representative, was determined to avoid postponing a decision until tomorrow, and the Indian and Egyptian representatives cooperated by not requesting a postponement because of their failure to receive instructions.

Mr. Austin said after the meeting that the immediate effect of the resolution "should be to stop

Continued on Page 7, Column 1

President Takes Chief Role In Determining U. S. Course

Truman's Leadership for Forceful Policy to Meet Threat to World Peace Draws Together Advisers on Vital Move

By ARTHUR KROCK
Special to The New York Times.

WASHINGTON, June 27—Some of those who participated in the meetings Sunday and Monday nights, at which the momentous decisions were taken to resist further Communist aggression, beginning in the Far East, with the combat air and naval power of the United States, described the President to associates today as determined from the outset to adopt the forceful policy which was announced this morning.

As soon as the first meeting assembled, they said, Mr. Truman made it plain that these were to be the bases of his decision:

1. The situation created by Communist tactics at various points of the world, culminating in the attack of North Korea on South Korea, had been allowed to drift too long.

2. The entire Far East was deteriorating in a manner to threaten the peace of the world, a line had to be drawn at once, and the United States had to draw it.

3. National security was the primary interest, but embedded in this were world peace and the prestige and future effectiveness of the United States, which was the architect of the South Korean Government.

4. It was a time for courage, even boldness, and calculated risk, which other members of the United Nations would be asked to share as they saw fit.

5. It was not a time to give the slightest consideration to previous policies or to individuals associated with those policies. If, for example, the fundamental change in the Far Eastern sit-

Continued on Page 4, Column 3

MAINLAND ATTACKS ENDED BY FORMOSA

Chinese Nationalists Halt Air, Navy Forays in Accordance With Request by Truman

By The Associated Press.

TAPEI, Formosa, Wednesday, June 28—The Chinese Nationalists today ordered their Air Force and Navy to cease attacks on the Communist mainland in accordance with a United States request.

President Truman had ordered United States warships to protect Formosa against Communist attack and at the same time asked the Nationalists to cease offensive operations.

Nationalist Foreign Minister George Yeh hailed the President's order for warship protection as "a most welcome sign of comradeship in the fight against communism."

Generalissimo Chiang Kai-shek and his Cabinet had met after the United States note was delivered to the United States Embassy. It was understood the note carried with it instructions to see that it was brought personally to Generalissimo Chiang's attention.

Mr. Yeh translated the text to the Generalissimo last night in the presence of United States Charge d'Affaires Robert Strong.

Mr. Strong was with Generalissimo Chiang for about twenty minutes. After his departure the latter consulted with Mr. Yeh, Premier Chen Cheng and other officials.

The decision was announced after Generalissimo Chiang conferred with Gen. Chou Chih-jou, Chief of the Joint General Staff and other top Nationalist commanders.

The Nationalists were believed to have agreed to Washington's re-

Continued on Page 8, Column 4

HOUSE VOTES 315-4 TO PROLONG DRAFT

Korea Crisis Breaks Deadlock— Bill Expected to Be Sent to White House Tonight

Special to The New York Times.

WASHINGTON, June 27—The House of Representatives today passed, by a vote of 315 to 4, an extension of the draft for another year.

The bill added authority for President Truman to call to active duty members of the National Guard and the reserve forces for periods not exceeding twenty-one months.

The Senate agreed to vote on the bill tomorrow afternoon. Swift passage is expected there so that the bill may reach President Truman for his signature tomorrow night.

As recently as yesterday the Senate and the House appeared to be in a hopeless deadlock over the manner in which the selective service system could be kept alive without much leeway for the President to put it to use. Today when

Continued on Page 16, Column 5

World News Summarized

WEDNESDAY, JUNE 28, 1950

United States air and sea forces were ordered by President Truman yesterday to give Korean troops "cover and support." Moving directly to meet Communist "armed invasion and war" in Asia, the President instructed the Seventh Fleet to "prevent any attack on Formosa," called on the Chinese Nationalists to halt all attacks on the mainland, ordered United States forces in the Philippines strengthened and moved to speed military assistance to those islands and to Indo-China. He instructed Ambassador Kirk in Moscow to urge the Soviet Union to help end hostilities. [1:8; map P. 2.]

Naval and air elements are "conducting combat missions south of the Thirty-eighth Parallel of Korea in support" of the Seoul Government, General MacArthur announced. An advanced echelon of the General Headquarters has been set up in Korea, he added. Conflicting reports of the fighting showed positions little changed during the day. [1:5; maps P. 17.] In Washington it was said that General MacArthur had sufficient forces to give the South Koreans air and sea preponderance. [13:3.]

This country's new Far East policy was set at conferences during which the President's positive program and leadership convinced his top aides that his decisions "were both inevitable

and right." [1:3-4.] He brought unity to an Administration that had been split on many vital policy issues. [4:6-7.]

Governor Dewey, speaking as head of the Republican party, pledged full support to the President [4:3] and Congress was almost unanimous in its endorsement. [1:7.] The House, 315 to 4, passed a one-year extension of the draft with broad new powers for the President; the Senate will vote today. [1:4.] Senate Republicans, however, blocked a vote today on the foreign arms-aid bill. [14:3.] The National Security Resources Board was ready for introduction a sweeping bill authorizing the President to freeze prices, wages, manpower and materials. [15:2.]

The United Nations Security Council, with Russia absent and Yugoslavia voting no, approved a United States motion to permit member nations to send armed forces to help repel the Korean invasion. [1:2.]

British parties united in supporting President Truman's program. The Labor Government won confidence votes on its refusal to join talks on pooling Europe's heavy industry. [19:4.]

John S. Service, a key figure in Senator McCarthy's charges of communism in the State Department, has been cleared by the department's Loyalty Security Board. [22:3.]

Index to other news appears on Page 28.

U.S. FORCE FIGHTING

MacArthur Installs an Advanced Echelon in Southern Korea

FOE LOSES 4 PLANES

American Craft in Battle to Protect Evacuation —Seoul Is Quiet

By LINDESAY PARROTT
Special to The New York Times.

TOKYO, Wednesday, June 28—The United States is now actively intervening in the Korean civil war, an announcement from Gen. Douglas MacArthur's headquarters here made clear this morning.

[Gen. Douglas MacArthur announced Wednesday that the forces of South Korea now were holding the Communist North invaders, a United Press dispatch from Tokyo said. At the same time he reported that United States fliers had begun bombing and strafing missions against North Korean forces. Seoul was reported quiet.]

General MacArthur revealed that a "small advanced echelon" from his headquarters had been established in Korea, presumably cooperating with the United States Military Advisory Group, which has been in Korea since the republic was established there under President Syngman Rhee two years ago.

The MacArthur announcement stated that Far East air forces and elements of the naval forces under the general's command were "conducting" combat missions south of the Thirty-eighth Parallel—the dividing line between Communist North Korea and the United States-recognized Korean Republic. These operations, it was officially stated, are "in support of the Korean Republic," whose Government has now been reinstated in the capital, Seoul, after isolation of the Northern armored spearheads that had penetrated to the outskirts of the city yesterday.

The announcement said that United States planes, which were providing air cover for the evacuation of women and children at United States missions, had shot down four North Korean fighters that were interfering with the operation of

Continued on Page 17, Column 3

Statement on Korea

By The Associated Press.

WASHINGTON, June 27—The text of President Truman's statement today on Korea:

In Korea the Government forces, which were armed to prevent border raids and to preserve internal security, were attacked by invading forces from North Korea. The Security Council of the United Nations called upon the invading troops to cease hostilities and to withdraw to the Thirty-eighth Parallel. This they have not done, but on the contrary have pressed the attack. The Security Council called upon all members of the United Nations to render every assistance to the United Nations in the execution of this resolution.

In these circumstances I have ordered United States air and sea forces to give the Korean Government troops cover and support.

The attack upon Korea makes it plain beyond all doubt that communism has passed beyond the use of subversion to conquer independent nations and will now use armed invasion and war.

It has defied the orders of the Security Council of the United Nations issued to preserve international peace and security. In these circumstances the occupation of Formosa by Communist forces would be a direct threat to the security of the Pacific area and to United States forces performing their lawful and necessary functions in that area.

Accordingly I have ordered the Seventh Fleet to prevent any attack on Formosa. As a corollary of this action I am calling upon the Chinese Government on Formosa to cease all air and sea operations against the mainland. The Seventh Fleet will see that this is done. The determination of the future status of Formosa must await the restoration of security in the Pacific, a peace settlement with Japan, or consideration by the United Nations.

I have also directed that United States forces in the Philippines be strengthened and that military assistance to the Philippine Government be accelerated.

I have similarly directed acceleration in the furnishing of military assistance to the forces of France and the associated states in Indo-China and the dispatch of a military mission to provide close working relations with those forces.

I know that all members of the United Nations will consider carefully the consequences of this latest aggression in Korea in defiance of the Charter of the United Nations. A return to the rule of force in international affairs would have far-reaching effects. The United States will continue to uphold the rule of law.

I have instructed Ambassador Austin, as the representative of the United States to the Security Council, to report these steps to the Council.

NORTH KOREA CALLS U. N. ORDER ILLEGAL

Declares Security Council's 'Cease Fire' Invalid Without Assent of China and Russia

Special to The New York Times.

HONG KONG, June 27—The North Korean Government issued a statement today saying that it regarded the cease fire order of the United Nations Security Council illegal for two reasons. It said these were, one, because the Democratic Peoples Republic of North Korea was not represented when its affairs were discussed and, two, because the Soviet Union and (Communist) China did not participate.

On the latter point it cited the United Nations Charter, which requires unanimity of five permanent members of the Security Council on questions of substance. China and Russia are both permanent members. [But the Communist rulers of China have not been recognized by the United Nations as representing that country.]

Drastic measures were taken in North Korea yesterday to organize

Continued on Page 18, Column 5

BID MADE TO RUSSIA

President Asks Moscow to Act to Terminate Fighting in Korea

CHIANG TOLD TO HALT

U.S. Directs Him to Stop Blows at Reds—Will Reinforce Manila

By ANTHONY LEVIERO
Special to The New York Times.

WASHINGTON, June 27—President Truman announced today that he had ordered United States air and naval forces to fight with South Korea's Army. He said this country took the action, as a member of the United Nations, to enforce the cease-fire order issued by the Security Council Sunday night.

Then acting independently of the United Nations, in a move to assure this country's security, the Chief Executive ordered Vice Admiral Arthur D. Struble to form a protective cordon around Formosa to prevent its invasion by Communist Chinese forces.

Along with these fateful decisions, Mr. Truman also ordered an increase of our forces based in the Philippine Republic, as well as more speedy military assistance to that country and to the French and Vietnam forces that are fighting Communist armies in Indo-China.

After he had started these moves that might mean a decided turn toward peace or a general war, Mr. Truman also ordered Ambassador G. Kirk in Moscow to request the Soviet Union to use its good offices to end the hostilities. This was an obvious proffer of a peace opportunity for Russia to end the crisis before her own forces might get involved.

Door Opened to Russia

In the capital this was regarded as being at once a possible face-saving device for Russia in a showdown crisis and a feeler to determine her intentions.

The decisions amounted to a showdown in the "cold war," in which this country had at last decided to begin shooting in a limited area. Yet all the decisions followed a carefully worked out formula of action within the framework of the United Nations, as well as unilateral moves that avoided any direct provocation of the Soviet Union.

Russia Is Not Mentioned

Mr. Truman carefully avoided mentioning Russia in his statement, which was today's great shift in American foreign policy on a conclusion that the "cold war" had passed from an uneasy passive stage to "armed invasion and war." He blamed "communism":

"The attack upon Korea makes it plain beyond all doubt that communism has passed beyond the use of subversion to conquer independent nations and will now use armed invasion and war," he said.

"It has defied the orders of the Security Council of the United Nations issued to preserve international peace and security. In these circumstances the occupation of Formosa by Communist forces would be a direct threat to the security of the Pacific area and to United States forces performing

Continued on Page 2, column 3

LEGISLATORS HAIL ACTION BY TRUMAN

Almost Unanimous Approval Is Voiced in Congress by Both Sides—House Cheers

By HAROLD B. HINTON
Special to The New York Times.

WASHINGTON, June 27—President Truman's announcement today that United States air and sea power would be employed to expel the Communist invaders from South Korea evoked almost unanimous support in Congress. His statement was read by the majority floor leaders in both houses.

In the House of Representatives, the members rose to their feet and cheered as the reading was completed by Representative John W. McCormack, of Massachusetts. In the Senate the reading by Senator Scott W. Lucas, of Illinois, brought immediate declarations of support from several Republican Senators.

Showing the same spirit of solidarity in the face of crisis, as the present situation was frequently described, Senate and House conferees agreed on legislation to ex-

Continued on Page 5, Column 1

Stocks Rally After Big New Losses In War Scare; Sales Near 5 Million

By ROBERT H. FETRIDGE

Securities markets the world over were subjected yesterday to wide fluctuations as the "Korean situation approached a crisis of universal concern.

Calmer thinking emerged successful on the New York exchanges, but only after prices encountered terrific battering. Losses that at one time ranged to 3 points and even more in standard issues on the New York Stock Exchange were either trimmed or eliminated. Quotations were definitely on the recovery side at the close, with the final composite rate down only 0.75 point. As pictured by THE NEW YORK TIMES index the market was midway between the highs and lows of the day at the final bell.

London was the worst sufferer among the major exchanges, while the Canadian markets followed the lead of New York.

It was a wild day on the trading floor of the Stock Exchange. Business almost reached the 3,000,000-share mark, the reporting ticker tape was constantly thrown behind actual transactions and at one time was twenty-seven minutes behind. This necessitated "flash" quotations on the ticker to keep brokerage offices at least abreast of the price changes in the key stocks.

The trend changed with such rapidity that selling orders were still being executed after the price direction changed for the better.

City, T.W.U. in 2-Year Peace Pact; Mayor Signs Fare Rise Resolution

Officials of the Transport Workers Union, C. I. O., the members of the Board of Transportation and Mayor O'Dwyer yesterday at City Hall signed a memorandum of understanding seeking to guarantee two years of peace in the city-owned rapid transit system.

The accord closely followed recommendations made on May 31 by the Mayor's Transit Fact-Finding Board, granting an 11-cent-an-hour increase to 35,929 operating employes, a third week of vacation after ten years and an additional holiday each year. The cost of the changes recommended by the fact-finders amounts to $13,188,515 a year.

The union bound itself not to engage in any strike or other interference with transit operations and not to seek any basic changes

in the accord before July 1, 1952. It agreed to resolve all disputes in accordance with the grievance machinery set up in the pact. The union obligated itself also to recognize the board's managerial authority and to "cooperate in the attainment of efficient operations."

The Board of Transportation agreed to retain competent industrial engineers to report on a program for achieving a five-day, 40-hour week of all employes now having a scheduled work-week in excess of forty hours.

Mayor O'Dwyer also signed yesterday afternoon a resolution of the Board of Transportation, effective Saturday, increasing fares on the city-owned surface lines.

Continued on Page 28, Column 6

The New York Times.

LATE CITY EDITION
Rome cloudiness early today, fair and warmer later. Mild tomorrow.
Temperature Range Today—Max. 76; Min. 60
Temperature Yesterday—Max. 68; Min. 57
Full U. S. Weather Bureau Report, Page 32

Copyright, 1950, by The New York Times Company.
VOL. XCIX..No. 33,837.
Entered as Second-Class Matter, Post Office, New York, N. Y.
NEW YORK, FRIDAY, SEPTEMBER 15, 1950.
Times Square, New York 36, N. Y. Telephone LAckawanna 4-1000
FIVE CENTS

U. N. FORCES LAND BEHIND COMMUNISTS IN KOREA; SEIZE INCHON, PORT OF SEOUL; MOVE INLAND; U. S. WILL PRESS FOR A JAPANESE PEACE TREATY

2 GARMENT UNIONS ASK 15% WAGE RISE IN POLICY REVERSAL

Nation-Wide Demand Drafted by Big A.F.L. and C.I.O. Units to Match Costs of Living

KOREAN WAR EFFECT CITED

Long Reluctance on Economic Grounds Dropped—Mills in Northeast Grant 10%

The two largest garment unions in the United States announced yesterday that they would seek an immediate, country-wide general wage increase of 15 per cent for their thousands of members.

In this city the International Ladies Garment Workers Union, A. F. L., held a special meeting of its general executive board to formulate wage policy for 425,000 members. Locally, the union has received no pay rise since 1948, and its 80,000 dressmakers have been at the same wage level since 1947.

By a coincidence a subcommittee of the general executive board of the Amalgamated Clothing Workers of America, C. I. O., meeting in Asbury Park, N. J., drafted a similar plan to be presented to the full board today for ratification. This union will try to win higher wages for 150,000 men's clothing workers and 80,000 others engaged in the making of shirts and cotton garments.

Both organizations, which are among the most powerful and responsible in the country in wage matters, based their new demands on the rise in living costs since the start of the Korean war. Amalgamated members received their last rise, 8 cents, in 1947.

Turnabout in Attitude

In recent years the two unions, facing poor conditions in their industries, have pursued a cautious pace in moving on the wage question. Now with nearly full employment, rising prices for textiles and mark-ups on finished products, they have come to the conclusion that pay rises are both necessary and justified.

The Amalgamated, which has a total membership of 400,000-50,000 of whom are in New York—had operated on the theory that wage rises would force up clothing prices in a period of slack demand and increase unemployment among the union's members. However, it won increases in pension and medical benefits, involving no rise in employer payroll contributions.

Amalgamated officials estimated yesterday that their full 15 per cent demand would raise the cost of making a suit by less than $1. Average clothing pay ranges from $1.50 to $1.62½ an hour. The new demand would add 22½ to 24⅜ cents to those rates. Cotton wages run from $1.02 to $1.10. These would be brought up by 15 to 16½ cents an hour.

Unlike the Amalgamated, which bargains on a national level with employer associations, the Ladies Garment Workers will try to win its demands on a local basis. Word has already gone out to the union's 400 locals over the country to press for increases in talks for new contracts, under wage-reopening clauses and through requests for voluntary adjustments.

Agreement for Conference

Officials of the Amalgamated said that the United States Clothing Manufacturers Association had agreed to confer with the union's bargaining committee, but that no date had been set for the first meeting. Wage talks with shirt manufacturers will begin next week in this city and other shirt centers.

The move by the Ladies Garment Workers, fifth largest affiliate of the American Federation of Labor, represented the first such attempt by a major A. F. L. union. In the C. I. O., of which the Amalgamated is the fourth largest unit, the United Automobile Workers

Continued on Page 19, Column 2

URGENT: Hurry to the 1950 NATIONAL HOMEFURNISHINGS SHOW at GRAND CENTRAL PALACE! Last 3 days! Noon to 10 P. M. today and tomorrow! 1 to 10 P. M. Sunday! Admiss. $1. children, 50c inc. tax.—Advt.

Excess Profits Tax Now Asked by House

By JOHN D. MORRIS
Special to The New York Times.

WASHINGTON, Sept. 14—The House went on record today, 331 to 2, as favoring action this session on an excess profits tax that would be retroactive to July 1, or Oct. 1.

The vote came on a motion by Representative Herman P. Eberharter, Democrat of Pennsylvania, to amend the pending general tax-increase bill in such a way as to require the House Ways and Means and Senate Finance Committees to bring out a separate excess profits measure before adjournment. The opposition votes were cast by Representative E. E. Cox, Democrat of Georgia, and D. W. Nicholson, Republican of Massachusetts.

The directive will not be binding however, unless it is contained in the final draft of the general tax bill, which now goes to a House-Senate conference committee for adjustment of differences between versions originally passed by the two chambers.

As passed by the Senate, the bill contained a provision direct-

Continued on Page 26, Column 1

TAFT AND WHERRY OPPOSE MARSHALL

Favoritism to Chinese Reds Is Charged—Senate Puts Off Action Until Today

Special to The New York Times.

WASHINGTON, Sept. 14—A small band of Republican Senators gathered today as opposition to the bill to waive existing law and permit General of the Army George C. Marshall, a professional soldier, to serve as Secretary of Defense.

The Republican leaders, however, made no attempt to declare it an all-party issue, and the Senate's passage of the measure, probably tomorrow, was thus assured.

It had been intended to open debate tonight, but unexpected difficulties intervened in other aspects of the Administration's final "must" list for this Congress.

At length, soon after 9 P. M., Senator Scott W. Lucas of Illinois, the Democratic Senate leader, not only put over "the Marshall bill" until tomorrow but abandoned hope of bringing this Congress to a close, as had been planned, by Saturday night.

Preliminary action by the House of Representatives was expected tomorrow on the bill. The House Armed Services Committee will meet at 10 A. M. to give its approval. The House Rules committee, which governs the legislative traffic in that chamber, will meet at 11 A. M. to give it a right of way for the floor.

The bill simply specifies that, the Military Unification Act notwithstanding, "General of the Army Gen. George C. Marshall" is to be permitted to serve as Secretary of Defense.

The act forbids the office to a

Continued on page 9, Column 2

SENATE UNANIMOUS FOR BIG ARMS FUND BUT VOTES AID CURB

Approval of 17 Billion Gets Economic Help if Ally Ships War Goods to Russia

MOVE IS AIMED AT BRITISH

Proposal Would Give Defense Secretary Authority Superior to That of E. C. A. Director

By WILLIAM S. WHITE

WASHINGTON, Sept. 14—The Senate passed unanimously tonight an urgent and supplemental appropriation bill of $17,192,000,000. Nine dollars of every ten in it would go to strengthening the defense of the United States and its associates of the western world.

Added to this big measure was a rider intended to halt all Marshall Plan economic aid, but not military help, to any benefiting nation that shipped to the Soviet Union or any of its satellites any commodity or article deemed to be useful in the manufacture of "arms, armament, or military matériel."

This stipulation was offered by Senator Kenneth S. Wherry of Nebraska, the Republican Senate leader. It was approved by a voice vote, in which not a dissent was heard.

It would leave it to the Secretary of Defense to determine what commodities ought to fall under the ban. Once he had defined them, the Marshall Plan administrator, Paul G. Hoffman, would have no option but to cut off from that plan any offending country.

The stipulation was aimed mainly at the British, who long have been accused by the Republicans of sending to Russia or to Soviet friends articles that might be used in a war.

The effect was to put the Secretary of Defense in the great and delicate area of determining what would be useful to the Soviet war potential, far above the Marshall Plan agency, the Economic Cooperation Administration. Admittedly, it would give him a vast veto power over the trade practices of the European nations if he wanted to use it.

The prospective Secretary of Defense is the author of the Marshall Plan itself, General of the Army George C. Marshall.

The Senate's insistence upon this limitation over Mr. Hoffman was yet to meet the approval of the House of Representatives, as does the whole of the appropriations bill. That measure, when it passed the House in August, had been for $16,771,356,077, or about $421,000,-000 less than it stood tonight as it came from the Senate.

The additions made by the Senate were largely military, to meet needs that had been indicated by the Korean war since August, but there were other new sums, too. There was, for example, $60,000,-

Continued on Page 4, Column 3

3 Robbers Shoot 2 Payroll Guards, Flee With $23,436 in Madison Ave.

Three robbers shot down two armed payroll messengers as the victims stepped into the lobby of 625 Madison Avenue yesterday and fled with $23,436.

There were no outside witnesses to the crime and no worthwhile clues. Two small blood stains near the curb outside 35 East Fifty-eighth Street, the service entrance through which the thugs escaped, were reported as of little value but an alarm describing the getaway car with the notation that it might be blood-stained was broadcast. One robber might have been accidentally wounded by a companion, according to the police.

Fifty detectives were assigned to cover the East Side and to make a search through the city for the gunmen's car, and "o check hospitals and offices of physicians for evidence of anyone treated for a gunshot wound. By last night detectives had questioned thirty per-

sons, including a number employed in the vicinity of the crime, in their search for clues.

The thugs fired five shots as they ambushed the couriers, Harold F. O'Connor, 42 years old, of 883 Columbus Avenue, and Joseph E. Gilgar, 54, of 34-50 Twenty-eighth Street, Long Island City, Queens. Although Mr. O'Connor managed to get his pistol from his holster as the last of the attackers dashed through the side door he did not return the fire.

Herman Siegal, an employe of a laundry service, entered the building soon after the shooting and sounded the alarm. An elevator operator and a porter, the only two building service workers on duty at the time, also heard the shots but first policemen were arriving when they came up from the cellar.

Mr. Gilgar, critically wounded

Continued on Page 23, Column 2

Backbone of Attack On Taegu 'Broken'

Special to The New York Times.

TAEGU, Korea, Sept. 14—Maj. Gen. Hobart Gay, commanding the United States First Cavalry Division, said today he believed "we have 'ken the backbone' of the North Korean attack on the key United Nations advance base at Taegu.

This, General Gay said, is the situation, at least, "at the moment." For four days of seesaw fighting north and west of the city. The Communists put an estimated three divisions into the attack, with a fourth behind the lines.

General Gay said he might have to change his mind but indications today were that the situation at Taegu had considerably bettered.

ATTLEE RISKS FATE ON STEEL QUESTION

Conservatives Offer Censure Motion on Labor's Decision to Implement Nationalization

Special to The New York Times.

LONDON, Sept. 14—The British Conservatives precipitated a Parliamentary crisis today by calling for a vote of censure after an announcement by the Labor Government that it intended to implement its authority to nationalize the country's steel industry.

The matter will be debated on Tuesday. If the Government, with its slim majority, is defeated it will resign and there will be a general election.

This is how the issue arose:

There is on the statute books a law enabling the Government to take over the steel industry next January and appoint a board to do it by October. The Opposition asked today what the Government proposed to do about it. George Strauss, the Minister of Supply, said the Government intended to carry out the law, which Parliament had enacted when Labor had a bigger majority than it has now. The same sources said the United States would seek the right not

Continued on Page 15, Column 5

World News Summarized

FRIDAY, SEPTEMBER 15, 1950

United Nations forces have struck in strength against the North Koreans with landings on both coasts behind the enemy's lines. A major amphibious blow was at Inchon, the port of Seoul, where United States and British warships had shelled the area Wednesday. At least two other landings were on the east coast north of Pohang. Earlier, North Koreans claims to have sunk landing craft were disputed. Along the United Nations defense perimeter in the south relatively light action was reported, except north of Taegu. The front blamed North Korea for an unprovoked aggression. [1:7.] President Truman directed the State Department to try again to obtain a Japanese peace treaty and to seek some way to end the technical state of war with Germany. [1:5.] The State Department is studying a $250,-000,000 economic aid program for South Asia and the Middle East. [4:5.]

Foreign ministers of the United States, Britain and France discussed the "serious situation" affecting Europe and Asia. The British and French ministers agreed to seek new instructions on rearming Western Germany. Britain and France feel no military aid should go to the Germans until the North At-

lantic nations are armed. [1:6-7.] The North Atlantic Council will consider this subject at meetings opening today. [16:2.] Britain's Defense Minister predicted that a unified command would result from the talks. He disclosed that France planned to have ten divisions under arms next year and ten more later. [16:3-4.]

Britain's Labor government announced it would take over the steel industry in January. The Conservatives immediately demanded a no-confidence vote and the Commons will decide the issue next week. [1:4.] The Senate unanimously passed $17,192,000,000 money bill, mostly for defense, with a rider designed to end all Marshall Plan economic aid to nations shipping "arms, armament or military matériel" to the Soviet Union or its satellites. [1:3.] The House sent the interim tax bill to conference, but voted 33∗ to 2 for Congress to stay in session until an excess profits tax was passed. [1:2.]

A Republican charge led by Senator Taft against enabling General Marshall to become Secretary of Defense delayed a Senate vote until today. [1:2.]

The A. F. L. and C. I. O. garment unions asked an immediate 15 per cent pay increase for their 655,000 members to meet higher living costs. [1:1.]

There will be no more dry days or water curbs in this city unless the situation again gets critical, but water must not be wasted, officials said. [27:8.]

NEWS BULLETINS FROM THE TIMES
Every hour on the hour
7 A. M. through Midnight
WQXR AM 1560
WQXR FM 96.3

Index to other news appears on Page 26.

ACTION BY TRUMAN

Right to Move Forces at Will in Islands Is Held U. S. Aim

MAY IGNORE SOVIET

Factors in Ending State of War With Germany Studied, He Says

By ANTHONY LEVIERO
Special to The New York Times.

WASHINGTON, Sept. 14—President Truman announced today that he had directed the State Department to begin a new effort to obtain a Japanese peace treaty. Behind the move was this country's resolve to produce a peace agreement, with or without Soviet participation.

[The Associated Press said Secretary of State Acheson had informed British Foreign Secretary Bevin and French Foreign Minister Schuman that the United States was ready to begin informal talks on development of a Japanese peace treaty.]

Our policy with respect to Japan, said the Chief Executive, was in harmony with our general aim to "end all war situations," including the deadlocks over Germany and Austria.

The President opened his news conference by reading a formal statement, announcing the new effort on the Japanese treaty, which would be made informally in discussions with members of the Far Eastern Commission. He said this would be done "in the first instance," leaving the implication that the U. S. would proceed further if the deadlock created by the Soviet Union in the commission persisted.

Informed sources said afterward that this country was determined to make some kind of peace settlement with Japan, without the Soviet Union if that country continues her obstructive tactics. The same sources said the United States would seek the right not

Continued on Page 15, Column 1

U. N. TROOPS MAKE LANDINGS IN KOREA

The New York Times Sept. 15, 1950

United States and South Korean forces landed at Inchon (1) and drove inland, while other South Korean troops landed near Pohang (4) and at another point on the east coast about twenty-five miles north of Pohang. A fourth landing was reported made at Kunsan (3) on the west coast. Earlier, United Nations naval planes had battered targets from Pyongyang (2) and southward (points are indicated by bomb devices). South Koreans already hold islands marked by stars. The diagonally shaded area is the United Nations' southern beachhead.

'This Is Our Sunday Punch,' Task Force Observer Says

By ROBERT C. MILLER
United Press Correspondent

WITH UNITED STATES MARINES, at Sea, Friday, Sept. 15—This is the one we have been waiting for. Within a few hours ships of this blacked-out task force will begin a shore bombardment to pave the way for landing craft that will carry the Marines in for what we hope to be the final battle of the Korean war.

This is our Sunday punch. We will know by tonight whether it will knock out the North Koreans.

There are no excuses for this one—everything has been planned and worked out for weeks. The supplies are adequate, the men are trained and the plans drawn down to the merest detail.

This ship is like a highly trained boxer during those dreadful last hours before the bell, when the long weeks of training camp ordeal are finished and there is nothing to do but wait.

We are crammed with men who have been attacked into every corner of this assault ship. In the holds are the deadliest weapons we possess to arm them for the attack.

Every marine aboard is a combat veteran who came to a South Korean port directly from the front lines. They were loaded at the same port at which they arrived

Continued on Page 4, Column 5

U. S. SHUNNED SIGNS ON KOREA, U. N. TOLD

Inquiry Report Says Republic Warned General an Invasion From North Was Near

By A. M. ROSENTHAL
Special to The New York Times.

LAKE SUCCESS, Sept. 14—The United Nations Commission on Korea reported today that six weeks before the start of the war United States officers denied South Korean warnings that invasion from the north was imminent.

From January, 1950, to May 12, the commission reported, defense officials of the Korean Republic had warned that the Communist army was strong and getting stronger and that it was just a

Excerpts from findings of Commission are on Page 6.

Continued on Page 7, Column 3

Bevin and Schuman Agree to Seek Instructions on Arming of Germans

By THOMAS J. HAMILTON

Foreign Minister Robert Schuman of France and Foreign Secretary Ernest Bevin of Britain agreed yesterday to ask their governments for instructions regarding the Western Big Three discussion of the rearmament of Western Germany.

This decision was hedged with many conditions, but it is believed that it may open the door—if only partly—to acceptance of Secretary of State Dean Acheson's contention that Western German soldiers are absolutely essential for the defense of Western Europe against Soviet aggression.

According to well-informed sources, M. Schuman and Mr. Bevin agreed to send cablegrams to their Governments on the German rearmament with certain blanks. If these blanks are filled

Continued on Page 14, Column 5

Text of foreign ministers' interim communiqué appears, Page 14.

3 LANDINGS MADE

Allies Strike at Western Port and Two Points North of Pohang

4TH PUSH REPORTED

Units of U. S. Marines Join Blow Behind the Front Lines of Foe

By The Associated Press

TOKYO, Friday, Sept. 15—United Nations invasion forces landed today at Inchon, the port city for Seoul on Korea's west coast—150 miles behind the 130,000-man North Korean Army at the fighting front.

Covered by planes and warships, United States troops stormed ashore on the island of Wolmi, linked to Inchon by a causeway. South Korean Marines landed at Inchon.

In a simultaneous operation other United States forces landed immediately behind the Communist blow on the east coast. They made two landings—one two miles northeast of Communist-held Pohang, the other at Yongdok, more than twenty-five miles north of Pohang.

[Sources in Washington said the United States forces involved were units of the Second Marine Division.]

The west coast invasion, preceded by cruiser and destroyer bombardment and sweeping carrier plane strikes, swung the offensive for the first time since the Reds began the war last June 25.

Close to 38th Parallel

The invasion at Inchon, putting United Nations forces close to the Thirty-eighth Parallel which the North Koreans crossed June 25, was announced by the South Korean Commander in Chief, Maj. Gen. Chung Il Kwon.

He said that heavy pressure was quickly exerted by the invasion forces on the Communists near Kimpo airfield, Seoul's big air base. Kimpo is twelve miles northwest of Seoul and ten miles north of Inchon.

A report from Pusan said that still other United Nations forces had gone ashore at Kunsan, a west coast city 100 miles south of Seoul. The report came from Chin Soo, South Korean National Assemblyman who supported the landing.

One thousand South Korean commandos went ashore on the east coast near Pohang, striking at a coastal road that would bar the way to any retreat by the North Korean forces defending the port. The commandos quickly called for air support.

A big United States battleship was reported Thursday to be off the east coast in the Pohang-Yongdok sector.

Invasion Follows Naval Blow

The North Koreans had been expecting an invasion at Inchon since Rear Adm. John M. Hoskins, commander of Task Force 77, sent British and United States cruisers and destroyers close in to bombard Inchon Wednesday. The targets included Wolmi Island.

While their shells hit the area, carrier planes for the second straight day swept 210 miles from Kunsan to Pyongyang, capital city of the North Koreans, hitting at airfields.

B-29's coordinated these blows, blowing up an underground arsenal north of Pyongyang and severing rail lines from Pyongyang for 100 miles south to Seoul and for 200 miles southeast to Kumchon.

[Gen. Douglas MacArthur's headquarters announced at noon today, Friday, that United Nations forces were again in the walled city of Kasan, ten miles north of Taegu, from which they had been forced to retreat last week. The United Press reported.]

The Pyongyang radio broadcast claimed shore guns had sunk three destroyers and four landing craft Wednesday. United States officials in Washington quickly said the three destroyers had suffered

Continued on Page 5, Column 5

The New York Times.

VOL. C..No. 33,885.   Entered as Second-Class Matter, Post Office, New York, N. Y.   NEW YORK, THURSDAY, NOVEMBER 2, 1950.   Times Square, New York 18, N. Y. Telephone LAckawanna 4-1000.   RAG PAPER EDITION SEVENTY-FIVE CENTS

Copyright, 1950, by The New York Times Company.

KOREAN REDS HIT U. S. UNIT; NOW USE JETS

REGIMENT TRAPPED

Foe Employing Rockets Against First Cavalry Division at Unsan

U. N. TROOPS FORCED BACK

Only 24th Division Makes Gain and Then It Is Told to Halt Its Advance

By LINDESAY PARROTT
Special to The New York Times

TOKYO, Thursday, Nov. 2.—North Korean Communists, reinforced by troops of the Chinese Red Army, savagely attacked today advance guards of the United States First Cavalry Division thrown into action near the west coast of Korea to reinforce the weakening South Korean troops.

The attack made north and west of Unsan, where the Communists had concentrated their strength during the last few days and had driven back South Korean spearheads as much as thirty miles in some sectors. Using tanks, artillery and heavy mortar fire, the North Koreans cut off one regiment of the United States Cavalry Division. Other units of the division were reported to be attempting to fight their way through to reach the isolated troops.

The fighting was in progress between Unsan and Taechon, but a spokesman for the United States First Corps said the situation was too vague and confused to locate the positions to which the United States troops had been forced to retreat.

Admits Chinese Are Fighting

For the first time a corps spokesman officially admitted that "Chinese" troops were launching an assault.

"We don't know whether they represent the Chinese Government," he said, and added that it also was unknown whether or not Chinese reinforcements made up the bulk of the new strength that had enabled the shattered North Korean Army to take the offensive again—at least locally—against the United Nations move toward the Manchurian border.

The Communists launched their attack in the morning. According to reports from Korea, they used heavy rocket bombardment for the first time in the war. The latest accounts said the enemy had overrun several First Cavalry positions, capturing weapons and turning them against Americans who had been hurriedly brought up to the combat line after all but one United States division—the Twenty-fourth Infantry, was forced to the west—had been out of the contact with the enemy and behind the Korean Republican spearheads driven in by the enemy counterattack.

This morning the North Koreans were reported to be within one half mile of Unsan.

Rockets Launched on Ground

The use of the rockets, fired from launchers on the ground, represented the second new weapon introduced on the North Korean side within the last two days. Yesterday for the first time the enemy flung jet-propelled fighter planes into combat.

Meanwhile, the ground advance of the Allied forces halted at Chongko, where the United States Twenty-fourth Infantry Division stood within eighteen miles of the border city of Sinuiju, reported to be the new capital of the North Korean Communist Government.

All along the rest of the front South Korean divisions were in retreat or on the defensive against enemy attacks strengthened by contingents of Chinese Communist soldiers trained in the Chinese Red Army.

Six enemy jet fighters made their appearance yesterday over Sonchon on the west coast, fought a brief dogfight with Mustangs of the United States Fifth Air Force and then flashed back toward the Manchurian border without casualties on either side. Observers said the jet-propelled planes resembled the Soviet model MIG-15, with swept back wings and a speed of 600 miles an hour. On the previous occasion jet planes were believed to have been seen over North Korea, but this was the

Continued on Page 3, Column 1

PLAYWRIGHT DIES

George Bernard Shaw
The New York Times

BERNARD SHAW, 94, DIES IN HIS HOME

Famous Irish Wit Had Been in Coma for Day—Broken Thigh Led to Final Illness

By The Associated Press.

AYOT ST. LAWRENCE, England, Thursday, Nov. 2.—George Bernard Shaw, one of the modern age's greatest dramatists and its most caustic critic, died today at the age of 94. The white-bearded Irish-born sage, whose wit was renowned throughout the world for half a century, succumbed at 4:59 A. M. (11:59 P. M. Wednesday, Eastern standard time).

His death was announced to newsmen by his housekeeper, Mrs. Alice Laden. Wearing black, she appeared at the gates of the cottage, Shaw's Corner, and told the reporters: "Mr. Shaw is dead."

A few minutes after her announcement, Dr. Thomas Probyn, Shaw's physician, hurried into the house. Twenty minutes later Shaw's longtime biographer, F. E. Loewenstein, told newsmen that the playwright died peacefully without regaining consciousness. Only two nurses were with him when death came.

The famed dramatist, who professed himself both a Communist and an atheist, was visited in his last hours by an Anglican clergyman, who said final prayers for the old sage's soul.

"It is wrong to say that he was an atheist," said the minister, the Rev. R. G. Davies. "He believed in God."

Shaw lapsed into his coma yesterday morning at 3 o'clock (10 P. M. Tuesday, Eastern standard time) and never regained consciousness. Operated on seven weeks ago for a broken thigh suffered when he slipped and fell in his garden, he grew steadily weaker. A bladder ailment aggravated his condition.

Lights burned for two nights in Shaw's Corner, the red brick

Continued on Page 23, Column 2

Pope Affirms Dogma of Assumption Of Mary to Heaven 'Body and Soul'

By CAMILLE M. CIANFARRA
Special to The New York Times.

ROME, Nov. 1—Pope Pius proclaimed today the dogma of the Assumption into heaven of the Virgin Mary.

"We pronounce, declare and define to be a dogma revealed by God that the Immaculate Mother of God, Mary, ever virgin, when the course of her life on earth was finished was taken up body and soul into heaven," the Pope declared.

The Pontiff spoke ex cathedra as supreme pastor of the church and teacher of Roman Catholic doctrine during an open air ceremony of pomp and magnificence to an audience of thirty-six Cardinals and 480 Archbishops and Bishops in the grandiose setting of St. Peter's Square.

A throng of 200,000 faithful, including Holy Year pilgrims from so many countries that they could be said truly to represent the

Continued on Page 13, Column 1

Vatican texts on dogma and speech by Pope are on Page 12.

LIE TERM EXTENDED AS U. N. SECRETARY FOR 3 YEARS, 46 TO 5

Assembly Vote Continues Him in Office Despite Bitter Attacks by Russians

ARAB BLOC, CHINA ABSTAIN

Australia Also Shuns Support —Final Move by Vishinsky to Block Step Fails

The text of Secretary Lie's address is printed on Page 3.

By THOMAS J. HAMILTON

Overriding last-ditch Soviet opposition, the General Assembly yesterday extended the term of Trygve Lie as Secretary General of the United Nations for another three years. The vote was 46 to 5, with only the five members of the Soviet bloc opposed.

However, Australia, Nationalist China and six members of the Arab bloc—Egypt, Iraq, Lebanon, Saudi Arabia, Syria and Yemen—abstained. Haiti was absent.

Mr. Lie, whose present five-year term will expire next Feb. 2, told the Assembly when it reconvened for the afternoon session that he interpreted the extension of his term as a vote of confidence and a reaffirmation of the independence and integrity of the position.

Mr. Lie did not refer to his stand in favor of United Nations action for the defense of South Korea, which had led the Soviet Union to veto his re-election. But he said that he had worked hard for the past five years to reconcile "the conflicting interests that divide the world" and that he would continue to do so.

Iraq Explains Abstention

Immediately after the vote Dr. Fadhil Jamali of Iraq explained that he had not been able to vote for the extension of Mr. Lie's term because he felt that, despite Mr. Lie's "many fine qualities," he had not been "entirely impartial" on the Palestine question. He added that "Mr. Lie did not react toward recent Jewish aggressions in Palestine with anything like the zeal which he displayed on the question of Korea."

"With due respect to Mr. Lie, we do not believe that he helped enough to make the United Nations bring about peace and justice to the Arabs of Palestine," Dr. Jamali said.

Nasrollah Entezam of Iran, President of the Assembly, who had given Dr. Jamali the floor to explain his vote, then pounded his gavel, declaring that this was not an explanation, and that Dr. Jamali could not "continue this way in attacking a person who is not present here and who has received the confidence of the General Assembly by forty-six votes in his favor."

Dr. Jamali then stepped down from the rostrum with the statement that "it would certainly have been a betrayal of Arab public opinion and sentiment if we had not abstained."

Sir Keith Officer, who then was recognized to explain Australia's abstention, said that Australia shared the view that Mr. Lie must not be punished for doing "his clear duty as regards the action of the United Nations in Korea," but that Australia had "genuine doubts" about the legality of the extension of Mr. Lie's term, which

Continued on Page 3, Column 5

World News Summarized

THURSDAY, NOVEMBER 2, 1950

Two assassins, identified as Puerto Rican Nationalists, attempted to kill President Truman yesterday while he was taking an afternoon nap in Blair House. One assailant was killed and the other badly wounded in a gun fight outside the house with guards, one of whom died. Two policemen were seriously wounded. The President went to the window to see what had happened and was shooed to safety by alert agents. [1:8.] Later he dedicated a memorial in Arlington Cemetery honoring Sir John Dill, British Field Marshal. [1:7.]

Secret Service agents listed the two Puerto Ricans as Bronx residents, and last night six women and five men were taken to 90 Church Street for questioning. [1:6-7.] An hour before the Blair House attack an unidentified man threw two bottles of ignited gasoline into the Puerto Rican labor office in this city, but they did not explode. [17:7.] In Puerto Rico, which has been torn by Nationalist uprisings, the Government spurred its hunt for revolutionary leaders. [1:5.]

Washington, electrified by the attack, the sixth attempt on a President's life [16:8], crowded to the scene. Eyewitness reports were confusing and conflicting. [1:4.] An ironic twist to the assassination attempt was the fact that President Truman was a strong advocate of Puerto Rican independence. [16:1.]

Chinese and North Korean troops, using rockets and heavy guns, attacked the United States troops in the Unsan area, trapping one regiment. Other United

States forces were ordered to halt their advance 18 miles from the border. [1:1; map Page 2.]

India expressed "keen disappointment" in answering Communist China's rejection of her concern over the invasion of Tibet. [9:2.]

The United Nations General Assembly, 46 to 5, extended the term of Secretary General Lie for three years. Only the Soviet bloc voted no, while Australia, Nationalist China and the Arab states abstained. [1:3.]

France is ready to contribute half of forty divisions planned for Western Europe by 1953. Defense Minister Moch said. Secretary Acheson declared it was agreed there should be no German general staff, national army or war industries. [8:3.]

Pope Pius proclaimed the dogma of the Assumption of the Virgin Mary into heaven. [1:2-3.]

George Bernard Shaw died at his home in England. He was 94 years old. [1:2.]

Theodore Roosevelt, Woodrow Wilson, Alexander Graham Bell, Dr. William C. Gorgas, Josiah Willard Gibbs and Susan B. Anthony were elected to the Hall of Fame. [34:3.]

The City Planning Commission approved a record $478,761,756 capital budget for 1951 and a $1,235,850,237 five-year program. [32:1.]

NEWS BULLETINS FROM THE TIMES
Every hour on the hour
7 A.M. through Midnight
WQXR AM 1560   WQXR FM 96.3

Index to other news appears on Page 32.

CAPITAL STARTLED

Police Swiftly Cordon Blair House as Shots Attract Big Crowds

PHOTOGRAPHERS NEAR BY

Leap From Their Auto, Halted by Traffic Light, Into Action —Passers-by See Fight

By PAUL P. KENNEDY
Special to The New York Times.

WASHINGTON, Nov. 1.—This city, which has heard the sound of assassins' guns before, reacted with electric suddenness today as shots exploded before the front door of President Truman's own residence.

Within a few moments after the firing had stopped in front of Blair House hundreds of spectators were straining at police cordons almost magically thrown up at the intersecting streets bounding the block in which the President's temporary residence is situated.

Street cars, which run along Pennsylvania Avenue in front of the White House and Blair House, were backed up three blocks from Jackson Place, which bounds the Blair House block on the east, and for as many blocks from Seventeenth Street, which bounds Blair House block on the west.

Automobile traffic snarls blocked the approach of a number of ambulances and police squad cars, and wailing sirens heightened the confusion.

Approaching the scene of the shooting from the outer fringe of the crowd, one picked up at least a dozen accounts of what had happened. The accounts grew less lurid toward the core of the trouble.

Rumors Fly Among Throngs

These reports were received from spectators, at least a half block from the Blair House, from newspaper men scurrying from the scene to the nearest telephones. On the outer reaches of the crowd the rumor was that two or three persons had entered Blair House with submachine guns firing and that the President had been assassinated or wounded.

Even among the reporters and photographers directly in front of the Blair House, the early accounts were confusing. It was not until fully fifteen minutes after the firing that it was clearly established that

Continued on Page 16, Column 6

ASSASSINATION OF TRUMAN FOILED IN GUN FIGHT OUTSIDE BLAIR HOUSE; PUERTO RICAN PLOTTER, GUARD DIE

WOULD-BE ASSASSIN OF PRESIDENT SHOT DOWN

Oscar Collazo lying at the bottom of the steps to the Blair-Lee House as White House guard is putting his revolver back in his holster. This picture was made by a photographer of The New York Times, who was waiting to accompany Mr. Truman to a dedication ceremony at Arlington Cemetery.

The New York Times (by Bruce Hoertel)

PUERTO RICO'S HEAD LINKS TWO ATTACKS

Governor Says Nationalist Forces Sparked by Reds Shot at Truman, Himself

By The United Press.

SAN JUAN, Puerto Rico, Nov. 1—Gov. Luis Muñoz Marin said tonight that Puerto Rican Nationalists were being used by the Communists both in the attempt to assassinate President Truman and in the abortive revolt here, in which he also was a target.

"This further crime—the Washington attempt—further confirms me in my conviction that the Nationalists are having their lunacy, fanaticism and irresponsibility manipulated for the benefit of Communist propaganda and strategy," the Governor said.

"We all feel deeply relieved that no tragic consequences resulted from this criminal action.

"The people are profoundly

Continued on Page 19, Column 2

Assassins' Kin and Friends Are Rounded Up in Bronx

By MEYER BERGER

Thirteen Puerto Ricans—six women and seven men—were taken to the offices of the United States Secret Service at 90 Church Street last night for questioning about the attempt yesterday on President Truman's life in Washington.

Policemen said they were the families and friends of the two assassins. Unofficially, Oscar Collazo of 173 Brook Avenue, the Bronx, one of the men who fired a gun at Blair House, was described as treasurer of the New York City branch of the Puerto Rican Nationalists, bitter enemies of the United States.

Collazo, wounded, is in the Emergency Hospital in Washington. The second gunman, tentatively identified by Secret Service men as Griselio Torresola of 1259 Ward Avenue in the East Bronx, was killed by police bullets.

Mrs. Rose Collazo, 42 years old, the wounded man's wife, was one of those taken into custody. She was arraigned at 2 o'clock this morning in Federal Court before United States Commissioner Edward M. McDonald on a charge of having conspired with the two assassins and two unnamed persons to harm a member of the Government. Commissioner McDonald held her in $50,000 bail for a hearing next Thursday.

At the request of Assistant United States Attorney Irving H. Saypol, Commissioner McDonald issued John Doe warrants for two unidentified persons named in the conspiracy complaint.

Earlier Mrs. Collazo had told officials and newspaper men: "I am Oscar Collazo's wife. He

Continued on Page 18, Column 3

PRESIDENT IS CALM AT DILL DEDICATION

Speaks, After Attempt to Kill Him, at Unveiling of Statue of British Field Marshal

By The Associated Press.

WASHINGTON, Nov. 1—Less than an hour after an attempt had been made to assassinate him, President Truman calmly dedicated a memorial here in 1950, to his slain Field Marshal Sir John Dill at Arlington National Cemetery today.

"It is important to the peace of the world that peoples understand each other and have full faith in each other's sincerity," he said.

He made no reference to the gunfight in front of his Blair House residence. Many of the 600 dignitaries present at the unveiling wondered why Mr. Truman was surrounded by such an unusually heavy guard of Secret Service men.

The President in his address said that he welcomed the opportunity to remind my countrymen that the maintenance of a perfect understanding between the people of Great Britain and the United States is of great impor-

Continued on Page 17, Column 2

November Heat Record of 81° Set; Zoo and Parks Draw Big Crowds

By IRA HENRY FREEMAN

November came in like a lamb yesterday, a spring lamb.

On the fourth day of an unseasonably warm wave extending over the eastern third of the country, the temperature in this city climbed to 81 degrees at 1:15 P. M. It dropped one degree for an hour, but at 2:15 again reached 81, and the latter time was officially accepted as the record.

This was not only the warmest for any Nov. 1 but also higher than ever reached in November since the Weather Bureau began keeping records here in 1871. The previous record for Nov. 1 was 70 degrees in 1948, while the previous high for any November day was 80 on Nov. 6, 1948.

The coolest it got during the day was 59 degrees from 6 to 7 o'clock in the morning. That was two degrees above the normal maximum for Nov. 1, Col. James W. Osmun, chief assistant meteor-

ologist in charge of the New York Weather Bureau, pointed out.

During the luncheon period when the mercury was rising 4 and 5 degrees an hour, throngs of office workers and shoppers on the midtown streets were uncomfortably warm. In Bryant Park the benches were jammed with men in shirt sleeves and girls in summer blouses.

Some air-cooled restaurants and offices turned the refrigeration back on temporarily. Women shoppers in Fifth Avenue and Fifty-seventh Street strolled along with their suit jackets over their arms. The retail clothing business, incidentally, was slackened temporarily by the weather, Terry, executive vice president of the Fifth Avenue Association, reported.

The brass Prometheus bringing

Continued on Page 23, Column 1

PRESIDENT RESTING

Awakened by Shots, He Sees Battle in Which Three Are Wounded

HE KEEPS APPOINTMENTS

Documents Link 2 Assassins, Who Lived Here, to Puerto Rican Extremist Leader

By ANTHONY LEVIERO
Special to The New York Times.

WASHINGTON, Nov. 1—Quick-shooting White House guards cut down two assassins this afternoon when they attempted to invade Blair House in a Puerto Rican Nationalist plot to assassinate President Truman.

Tonight one assassin and one policeman were dead, and two policemen were wounded, one critically. The other assassin, seriously wounded, told the United States Secret Service that he and his companion had come down from New York two days ago to kill Mr. Truman.

On the body of the dead assassin Secret Service agents found a letter and a "memorandum," both cryptic but indicative of conspiracy. The missives were in the same handwriting and on the same stationery. They bore in the form of a signature, the name of Pedro Albizu Campos, leader of the Puerto Rican Nationalists who carried out the uprising in Puerto Rico Monday.

U. E. Baughman, chief of the Secret Service, cautioned reporters, however, that he had no proof that Albizu Campos was the author of the documents.

All three wounded are expected to recover.

Taking his usual afternoon nap and roused by a fury of shooting, Mr. Truman looked down from an upstairs bedroom of Blair House. In the bright sun of Pennsylvania Avenue was terror and confusion. At the foot of the stoop leading to Blair House lay one of the assassins, alive, blood flowing from the middle of his chest and staining his blue shirt.

"A President has to expect those things," Mr. Truman said, later.

Truman Keeps to Schedule

Serene, a man of good conscience, for he had told the people of Puerto Rico unequivocally that they were free to work out their own political destiny, Mr. Truman punctiliously kept his remaining appointments of the day.

The outrage, however, made the Federal police agencies increasingly alert, and new safeguards were thrown around the President and his family. Meanwhile, the Secret Service began to trace back the plot through New York, to its apparent source in the island possession in the Caribbean, which is

Continued on Page 16, Column 2

Campos Captured In San Juan Home

By The United Press.

SAN JUAN, Puerto Rico, Thursday, Nov. 2—National policemen poured five heavy volleys of rifle and pistol fire into the home of Pedro Albizu Campos early today and captured the Nationalist party leader when he fled into the street.

The Puerto Rican Governor, Luis Muñoz Marin, earlier had accused the Nationalist extremist leader of responsibility for the assassination attempt made against President Truman yesterday. The would-be assassins were said to be members of the Nationalist party.

The New York Times.

Copyright, 1950, by The New York Times Company.

NEW YORK, SUNDAY, DECEMBER 17, 1950.

LATE CITY EDITION
Mostly fair and cold today. Fair and continued cold tomorrow.
Temperature Range Today—Max., 35; Min., 27
Temperature Yesterday—Max., 42; Min., 32
U. S. Weather Bureau Report, Page 1; Sect. 1.

Section 1

FIFTEEN CENTS

PRESIDENT PROCLAIMS A NATIONAL EMERGENCY; AUTO PRICES ROLLED BACK; RAIL STRIKE ENDS; ALLIES GIVE UP HAMHUNG; WU REJECTS TRUCE

U.N. 'TRAP' ALLEGED

Peiping Representative Says He Will Start Home Tuesday

BIDS U. S. QUIT KOREA

'Volunteers' to Withdraw if Formosa Also Is Yielded, He States

Text of press statement by Mr. Wu is printed on Page 12.

By A. M. ROSENTHAL
Special to The New York Times.

LAKE SUCCESS, Dec. 16—Communist China rejected today the United Nations plan for a cease-fire in Korea as a "trap," and Peiping's representatives here said they would leave for home on Tuesday.

The Chinese Communists warned that the great problems of the world could not be settled peacefully unless Peiping got a seat in the United Nations and a major voice in Asia. They made it clear that their conditions for peace in Korea remained United States withdrawal from the country and an end to American "aggression" in Formosa. On those conditions, Communist China would withdraw its "volunteer" troops from Korea.

Peiping's stand was outlined at a special press conference here called by its chief representative at the United Nations, the impassive Wu Hsiu-chuan. Before coming to the press conference Mr. Wu informed United Nations officials that he would leave for Peiping on Tuesday by air.

Wu Complains to Lie

Mr. Wu was reported to have told Secretary General Trygve Lie last night that his delegation had come to New York several weeks ago to discuss Soviet charges of United States aggression against China and had not been invited to testify before the General Assembly's Political and Security Committee. The committee only opened debate on the item but recessed the discussion to take up the problem of Chinese intervention in Korea. Mr. Wu complained to Mr. Lie that there was no purpose in his staying if the committee did not discuss the Soviet charges, which are centered on Formosa and Korea.

The Secretary General immediately got in touch with the three-man cease-fire committee set up by the Assembly to sound out the United States and Communist China on the possibility of a cease-fire and efforts were said to have been made to persuade Mr. Wu to change his mind about leaving. But the Chinese still were planning to leave Tuesday.

Delegation May Stay

Some diplomats said that developments Monday would decide whether the Chinese Communists would leave. The Political Committee is to map its remaining work on Monday and the Chinese Communists may attend in the visitors' section. If the committee votes to resume talk on Formosa immediately, as it believed, the Chinese may stay for a while.

For its part, the cease-fire committee announced that it would present an interim report to the Assembly on Monday, and stressed the word interim. The committee released a statement saying that it intended to go ahead with its efforts for a Korean cease-fire. It was reported that the three diplomats—Lester B. Pearson of Canada, Sir Benegal N. Rau of India and Nasrollah Entezam of Iran—would now try to make direct contact with Chinese Communist leaders in Peiping.

The committee met with Mr. Lie today before the Wu press conference. In another room, a little while later, Mr. Lie met with Mr. Wu and introduced him to Mr. Entezam, who is president of the Assembly. Sometimes over the weekend, there will be another — and

Continued on Page 12, Column 3

TURNING DOWN CEASE-FIRE PLAN

Wu Hsiu-chuan, right, outlining Communist China's stand at special press conference he called at Lake Success. With him are Miss Kung Pu-sheng and Chiao Kuan-hua.

The New York Times (by Ernest Sisto)

Paris and London Void Pacts In Arming Bonn, Soviet Says

By HAROLD CALLENDER
Special to The New York Times.

PARIS, Dec. 16—The Soviet Government handed to the French and British Ambassadors in Moscow yesterday a note accusing France and Britain of violating their treaties with the Soviet Union by sponsoring rearmament of the Germans.

[Text of the Soviet note to France and Britain, Page 18.]

The step was considered an effort to hamstring defense discussions due to begin in Brussels Monday among the Foreign and Defense Ministers of the North Atlantic Treaty nations.

The new note was a sequel to that of Oct. 18 to France, Britain and the United States in which Moscow said it would not "tolerate" measures of the United States aimed at reviving the German Regular Army.

These steps, taken less than twelve hours after President Truman had proclaimed a national emergency, completed an economic embargo characteristic of a state of war.

RED CHINA'S ASSETS IN U. S. ARE FROZEN

Washington Takes Unilateral Action—Tightens Ban on Shipping to Mainland

By WALTER H. WAGGONER
Special to The New York Times.

WASHINGTON, Dec. 16—The United States, in actions believed to have fallen just short of a war declaration, froze Chinese Communist funds in United States territory tonight and prohibited United States ships from calling at Chinese ports.

The new note was a sequel to that of Oct. 18 to France, Britain and the United States in which Moscow said it would not "tolerate" measures of the United States aimed at reviving the German Regular Army.

These steps, taken less than twelve hours after President Truman had proclaimed a national emergency, completed an economic embargo characteristic of a state of war.

The State, Treasury and Commerce Departments acted in concert on the moves.

That the Government had consulted other friendly powers was not denied, and the fact that the United States acted unilaterally indicated disapproval by the other nations.

The State Department said that the freezing of Communist China's assets and the barring of United States ships from her ports had been "forced upon us" by the in-

Continued on Page 16, Column 2

The treaties that Moscow now charges were violated are Britain's pact with the Soviet Union of May 26, 1942, and France's similar treaty signed Dec. 10, 1944. The principal content of both treaties was an agreement not to make a separate peace with Germany or to make any alliance against either of the signatories.

Both treaties were made when the Soviet Union was aligned with but not formally allied with the Western powers in the war against Germany, and when both France and Britain sought to insure against a revival of German power, which then seemed to constitute the greatest possible future menace.

A warning of yesterday's note was given to the French by Jacques Duclos, French Communist leader, who, in a speech at Brest last Sunday, said that in accepting rearmament of the Germans the French Government repudiates the signature of France and "deliberately violates" the French-Soviet treaty.

M. Duclos specified that the vic-

Continued on Page 19, Column 1

Nyack Area Fears the Thruway Means Razing of 250 Buildings

Special to The New York Times.

NYACK, N. Y., Dec. 16—Fear was widespread here today that the proposed Thruway crossing of the Tappan Zee would require the razing of 250 homes and other buildings and remove half the property in the village of South Nyack from local tax rolls.

Unpopular in this area from the time it was first contemplated, the Tappan Zee bridge project aroused fresh demonstrations of hostility by messenger last night a copy of the new map from Bertram D. Tallamy, State Superintendent of Public Works and chairman of the Thruway Authority.

It was known that the Rockland residents asserted that the project would obliterate South Nyack almost as if it had been the target of an atomic bomb.

The villages of Nyack, South Nyack and Grandview, which are in the path of the Thruway, are planning a joint suit to enjoin the

State Thruway Authority from proceeding with its plans. They are also arranging to send delegations to Governor Dewey and other officials to voice their demand for a change in plans.

Harold A. Williams, supervisor of the town of Orangetown, in which Grandview, South Nyack and Nyack are situated, received a relatively detailed map of the property needed for the bridge and approaches became available.

After examining the map, the officials in this area from the time it contemplated, the Tappan Zee bridge project aroused fresh demonstrations of hostility as a relatively detailed map of the property needed for the bridge and approaches became available.

Continued on Page 72, Column 3

BEACHHEAD IS CUT

U.N. Troops Forced Back to Narrowed Area as Foe Perils Lines

NAVY SHELLS REDS

MacArthur Aides Report Chinese Build-Up for Attack in West

By LINDESAY PARROTT
Special to The New York Times.

TOKYO, Sunday, Dec. 17—United Nations forces pulled back yesterday from the wrecked industrial city of Hamhung on the beleaguered northeast Korean peninsula to form a tight perimeter around the seaport of Hungnam. Off that port lay Allied warships to pour fire on advancing columns of Chinese Communists.

Hamhung was evacuated in mid-afternoon yesterday as United States troops began to pour into the city's northeastern suburbs. United States engineers blew bridges across the Tongnonchon River and smaller tributaries to delay the pursuit.

Reports this morning said the enemy occupied the city and in this area was about seven miles from the Hungnam beaches. Attacks from the northeast and northwest continued and at the deepest penetration the Reds were only three or four miles from the port.

The withdrawal came after heavy Chinese attacks on the northern and western faces of the United Nations area around the Hungnam beaches had made some penetrations south of Oro on a mountain highway down from the Changjin Reservoir and toward Chigyong where the Chinese were thrusting toward the important Yonpo airfield.

Indications were that the Communist invaders had massed ten to twelve divisions — more than 100,-000 men — north and west of Hamhung in an attempt to drive

Continued on Page 3, Column 1

STRIKERS RETURN

Workers Heed Request of President—Freight Jam Is Melting

MAILS MOVING AGAIN

Pay Dispute Settlement Is Expected Quickly in Washington

By GEORGE ECKEL
Special to The New York Times.

CHICAGO, Dec. 16—Railroad transportation services were returning rapidly to normal today, as more than 10,000 switchmen ended their mushrooming three-day wildcat strike at the behest of President Truman.

The strikers were going back to work in fourteen of fifteen cities to which the walkout had spread. They did so without a settlement of the wage-hour dispute between the carriers and their union, the Brotherhood of Railroad Trainmen. The union, however, had not authorized the walkout.

[In Washington it was believed a quick settlement of the pay dispute underlying the strike would be effected, probably on terms long available to the union.

[In New York, mountains of mail and freight began to melt as virtually normal railroad service was restored.]

The last of the strikers to return were those at the Illinois Central yards in Birmingham, Ala. Strikers returned at the yards of the Southern Railroad in Birmingham a few hours earlier.

The Postoffice Department lifted its thirty-nine-hour embargo at 11:15 A. M., E. S. T., today, resuming "normal service" at once, and workers began the attack on mountains of backlogged Christmas parcels in the nation's key transport centers and transfer points as Chicago, St. Louis, Washington and Pittsburgh began to

Continued on Page 44, Column 1

Recent Auto Rises Canceled By First Price-Freeze Edict

'Ceiling Regulation No. 1' of Economic Stabilization Agency Holds Schedules to Dec. 1 Levels—Wage Study Set

By CHARLES E. EGAN
Special to The New York Times.

WASHINGTON, Dec. 16—The first price freeze and roll-back actions to result from the present national emergency were announced today by the Economic Stabilization Agency.

Under orders effective at once prices of passenger automobiles are frozen at Dec. 1, and companies that have increased quotations for their 1951 lines are ordered to "roll them back" to that date or face Federal penalties.

Today's order, which came soon after President Truman's action declaring a national emergency, was regarded here as a forerunner of a variety of similar edicts to issue from the agency beginning Monday.

[In Detroit, a Ford executive said the company would "conform promptly." The head of the automobile workers' union opposed "pin-prick" controls.]

The order was studied closely by representatives of business because they regarded it as setting a pattern for ensuing regulations. There was a general feeling that

Continued on Page 59, Column 1

Dec. 1 would be selected as the terminal date for price increases and that ceilings declared by the Economic Stabilization Agency over the coming month would use quotations of that date as determining factors in industries affected.

The price action in the auto industry is based upon the authority granted under the President's declaration of a national emergency. It is the first order also to affect the economy since the Office of Price Administration exercised its powers in World War II.

According to officials the order was issued to enable the Economic Stabilization Agency to make a comprehensive analysis of the effect of cost increases upon the profit position of the companies affected and to ascertain whether cost increases actually incurred justified the recent price increases. If the study justifies the price advances, it was added, the agency will make whatever changes in

U. S. Urges Defense Parley By All American Republics

Special to The New York Times.

WASHINGTON, Dec. 16—The United States proposed today an emergency meeting of the foreign ministers of the twenty-one American republics for tightening the defenses of this hemisphere against the threat of international communism.

Secretary of State Dean Acheson instructed the United States representative to the Council of the Organization of American States to request such a meeting, and he said he was acting under the direction of President Truman.

In making his request known today, Mr. Acheson declared:

"The United States, having embarked on urgent mobilization for the common defense, wishes to consult its fellow members in the inter-American community with respect to the situation which we all face and on the coordination of the common effort required to meet it."

He asserted that "the aggressive policy of international communism, carried out through its satellites, has brought about a situation in which the entire free world is threatened."

The Secretary added that the United States, after consultations with leaders of Congress and the other American Governments, would propose a time and place for the meeting and set forth an agenda for consideration.

Edward G. Miller Jr., Assistant Secretary of State for Inter-American Affairs, said it was the hope

Continued on Page 55, Column 3

DISASTER SERVICES PUT ON ALERT HERE

Wallander Orders Agencies to Be in Condition of Readiness on 24-Hour-a-Day Basis

By DOUGLAS DALES

City agencies that would have functions to perform in the event of an enemy attack were ordered yesterday to be maintained in a condition of readiness on a twenty-four-hour-a-day basis.

The order was issued by Arthur W. Wallander, Civil Defense Director, with the approval of Mayor Impellitteri after the declaration of a state of emergency by President Truman.

Twenty-two municipal divisions, including the five borough presidents' offices, were directed by Mr. Wallander to maintain at least skeleton staffs throughout the day and night. Some of the departments affected already operate on a twenty-four-hour schedule be-

Continued on Page 39, Column 2

TRUMAN SETS DRIVE

Gives Wilson Sweeping Powers, Asks 'Mighty Production Effort'

U. S. RALLIES TO CALL

Congress Speeds Action —Stand of President Praised in Europe

Texts of proclamation and executive order are on Page 30.

By ANTHONY LEVIERO
Special to The New York Times.

WASHINGTON, Dec. 16—President Truman proclaimed a state of emergency this morning and delegated many of his own war powers to Charles E. Wilson, the new Mobilization Director. Thus afterward the defense program moved into higher gear.

Today was a day of action in the White House, in Congress and elsewhere in the Government as Charles E. Wilson, the new Mobilization Director, moved the defense program into higher gear.

Today was a day of action in the White House, in Congress and elsewhere in the Government as the President's declaration to the nation and the world last night that the United States would meet the challenge of communism.

The Economic Stabilization Agency canceled the price increases made by Ford, General Motors and Chrysler in the last few days, and this was merely the harbinger of many new controls that eventually will encompass the entire economy.

Industry evinced its readiness to accept any and all production goals, striking railroad men returned to work, and the general response from the public indicated an acceptance of the austerity program suggested by the President.

Proclamation Is Signed

Mr. Truman had pleaded for unity, like past Presidents coping with crises, and in 1917 and 1941 the country was rallying with vigor.

In the free countries of Western Europe Mr. Truman was applauded for his no-appeasement speech in which he pledged to create an "arsenal of freedom" to strengthen all free countries. From Russia, which he blamed directly for the postwar troubles of the world, came a typical blast that this country was warmongering.

Mr. Truman took two actions this morning to start a drastic increase of the mobilization program. He signed the proclamation of emergency, which unleashed scores of additional executive powers, and issued an executive order granting virtually blanket authority to Mr. Wilson to carry out all aspects of war production and economic control as deemed necessary. This authority would be subject in the Executive Branch of the Government only to the veto of President Truman.

Threat to Freedoms Cited

In his proclamation President Truman declared that conquest of the world was the objective of "Communist imperialism." He said the new constituted a threat to the freedoms guaranteed by the Bill of Rights, to the free enterprise system and to other rights, like collective bargaining, that free people had chosen for themselves.

These were the elements of a "full and rich life" that could be lost by the triumph of the Communist way of life, Mr. Truman said, calling for a "mighty production effort" for defense.

Mr. Truman asked for sacrifices, for cooperation by state and local officials, for loyalty to the principles on which the nation was founded, and faith in our friends

Continued on Page 26, Column 2

In order to continue the complete presentation of the news THE NEW YORK TIMES was obliged to decline 192 columns of advertising for this issue.

World News Summarized

SUNDAY, DECEMBER 17, 1950

President Truman followed his Friday night message to the people that the nation was in grave danger by proclaiming yesterday a state of emergency. He delegated most of his own wartime powers to Charles E. Wilson, Director of the Office of Defense Mobilization, whose unparalleled controls over the country's economy will be subject only to Presidential veto. [1:8.] Shortly afterward, the Economic Stabilization Agency, in its first price-fixing action, ordered auto prices frozen at Dec. 1 levels. [1:6-7.]

In this city the declaration of emergency led to orders to twenty-two municipal departments that would have duties in the event of an attack to maintain around-the-clock vigil. [1:7.]

In response to the President's appeal to end their wildcat strike, railroad switchmen returned to work. [1:5.]

Shortly before leaving for Brussels, Secretary of State Acheson, acting with Mr. Truman's approval, proposed an emergency meeting of the foreign ministers of the twenty-one American republics to consider the strengthening of hemispheric defenses. [1:6-7.]

The United Nations' plan for a cease-fire in Korea was rejected by the Chinese Communist delegation as a United Nations "trap." The Chinese accused this country of "aggression" in Korea and Formosa, but indicated that if the "aggression" were terminated Peiping would be willing to advise the Chinese "volunteers" in Korea to quit fighting. [1:1.]

Two drastic steps directed against the Peiping regime were taken by Washington: all Chinese Communist funds in United

States territory were frozen and all American ships were told to avoid Red China's ports. [1:2.]

Hamhung, in northeastern Korea, was abandoned to the enemy, as the defenders withdrew toward Hungnam. About 100,000 Chinese were reported pressing upon the shrinking beachhead. [1:4; maps, P. 2.]

Soviet Foreign Minister Vishinsky left Lake Success for home, expressing optimism and "wishes of peace, well-being and happiness" to the people of the United States. [5:1.] According to documents made public in Washington, Moscow's slave labor system has been a major factor in the economic organization of the Soviet Union. [20:1.] In new note to France and Britain, the Soviet Government charged that London and Paris, by supporting the rearmament of Western Germany, were guilty of violating their agreements with Moscow not to participate in anti-Soviet alliances. [1:2-3.]

Prime Minister Attlee said there was no basis for the fear of wanton use of the atomic bomb by the United States. He warned Britons, however, that the future held disagreeable things in store for them, including a curb on improvements in their standard of living. [10:1.]

At the suggestion of Governor Dewey, Lieut. Gov. Joe R. Hanley has been named special counsel to the State Division of Veterans Affairs. [1:6-7.]

Hanley to Get $16,000 State Job; Dewey Makes Good His Promise

By WARREN WEAVER Jr.
Special to The New York Times.

ALBANY, Dec. 16—The appointment of Lieut. Gov. Joe R. Hanley as special counsel to the State Division of Veterans Affairs at an annual salary of $16,000 was announced today by Leo V. Lanning, director of the division. Mr. Hanley will take over the new post on Jan. 1.

Mr. Lanning said he had made the appointment "at the suggestion of Governor Dewey." Thus the Governor made good on a three-month-old pledge to give Mr. Hanley a state position, the 74-year-old official should fail to win his Senatorial campaign against Senator Herbert H. Lehman.

The question of Mr. Hanley's future was one of the issues raised in the political storm that followed release Oct. 16 of the now

Continued on Page 68, Column 1

the famed Hanley letter, which was written Sept. 5. In the letter to Representative W. Kingsland Macy, the Lieutenant Governor wrote:

"I have an iron-clad, unbreakable arrangement whereby I will be given a job with the state which I would like and enjoy (I have been told what it is) at sufficient compensation to make my net income more than I now have."

Subsequently both the Governor and Mr. Hanley denied that any specific post had been discussed between them. Both men reported, however, that Mr. Dewey had expressed reluctance to lose Mr. Han-

Continued on Page 68, Column 1

100TH ANNIVERSARY
"All the News
That's Fit to Print"
1851 1951

The New York Times.

LATE CITY EDITION
Fair today, increasing cloudiness
tomorrow and mild both days.
Temperature Range Today—Max.: 60; Min.: 45
Temperatures Yesterday—Max.: 55; Min.: 45
Full U. S. Weather Bureau Report, Page 36

Copyright, 1951, by The New York Times Company.

VOL. C. No. 34,045.

Entered as Second-Class Matter,
Post Office, New York, N. Y.

NEW YORK, WEDNESDAY, APRIL 11, 1951.

Times Square, New York 18, N. Y.
Telephone LAckawanna 4-1000

RAG PAPER EDITION
SEVENTY-FIVE CENTS

TRUMAN RELIEVES M'ARTHUR OF ALL HIS POSTS; FINDS HIM UNABLE TO BACK U. S.-U. N. POLICIES; RIDGWAY NAMED TO FAR EASTERN COMMANDS

HOUSE VOTES U. M. T. ONLY AS A PROGRAM; MARSHALL WORRIED

Chamber Accepts Compromise Setting Up Commission to Draft Details of Plan

FUTURE LAW IS REQUIRED

Congress' Approval Is Needed to Start Universal Training— General Sees Risk in This

By JOHN D. MORRIS
Special to The New York Times.

WASHINGTON, April 10—Concessions offered by advocates of Universal Military Training to save the program from outright rejection were approved today by the House of Representatives, but it remained to be seen whether the aim had been achieved.

General of the Army George C. Marshall, Secretary of Defense, meanwhile voiced the fear that current maneuvering in the House might "largely emasculate" the training features of the pending draft and training bill.

It was not clear, however, whether he was concerned over the main fight, expected later this week, over a proposal to eliminate all Universal Military Training provisions from the bill.

It was to head this off that the bill's managers headed by Representative Carl Vinson, Democrat of Georgia, offered the concessions that were approved today. The House accepted them on a voice vote.

Further Action Necessary

Consequently, as the bill now stands, little more than the principle of Universal Military Training is retained. A commission to draw up a detailed U. M. T. plan would be created. A "National Security Training Corps" would also be established, at least on paper.

But before anyone could be drafted to serve in the proposed corps, there would have to be another formal act of Congress, subject to Presidential approval or veto like any other bill, authorizing details of the training program.

At the same time, however, the revised bill retains safeguards against future pigeon-holing of U. M. T. in the House Rules Committee or elsewhere. The planning commission, which also would administer the program once Congress had authorized its institution, would be required to submit a detailed training plan to Congress within six months. The House and Senate Armed Services Committees would be required to report out a bill or resolution within forty-five days of receiving the plan. The measure then could be called up at any time.

Opponents Withhold Attack

In the House, bills ordinarily must be cleared by the Rules Committee before they can be considered on the floor. The Rules Committee bottled up a Universal Military Training Bill in the Eightieth Congress.

Opponents of any form of U. M. T. legislation did not fight the concessions approved in the House today, explaining that the proposals would make the bill less obnoxious although still unacceptable to them.

They were still hoping for approval of a substitute sponsored by Representative Graham A. Barden, Democrat of North Carolina, that would retain only what they regard as the "emergency" features of the pending draft measure. These include a three-year extension of authority to draft men 19 through 26 years of age for actual military service.

The Barden bill would eliminate authority to lower the draft age to 18½ as well as all long-range training features of the pending measure.

The Senate has already passed a draft and training bill adhering closely to the Administration's recommendations. It would authorize the drafting of men at the age of 18 and permit the President to put Universal Military Training

Continued on Page 18, Column 4

Tobey Asserts He Recorded R. F. C. Talks With Truman

President Said to Withdraw Fee Accusation—Niles Held Attempting to Aid Dawson

By C. P. TRUSSELL
Special to The New York Times.

WASHINGTON, April 10—Senator Charles W. Tobey, Republican of New Hampshire, was represented tonight as having told the Senate (Fulbright) subcommittee investigating the Reconstruction Finance Corporation that President Truman had charged in a telephone conversation with him that members of Congress had accepted fees for obtaining R. F. C. loans for constituents.

Both telephonic conversations were said to have been recorded on disks in Mr. Tobey's possession. The date, or dates, were not made public. The Senator declined to discuss the matter and members of the investigating group also were silent.

In another development in the R. F. C. inquiry, former Senator Burton K. Wheeler, Democrat of

Burton K. Wheeler
Associated Press

Montana, said today that he had asked Senator Tobey to "go easy on" Donald S. Dawson, White House aide, during the Senate investigation of the agency. Mr. Wheeler asserted that he acted at

Continued on Page 25, Column 2

Sterling Hayden Was a Red; 'Stupidest Thing I Ever Did'

Special to The New York Times.

WASHINGTON, April 10—Sterling Hayden, motion picture actor and decorated former United States Marine, told the House Committee on Un-American Activities today that he had been a member of the Communist party from June to December of 1946.

"It was the stupidest and most ignorant thing I ever had done in my life," he said. "I went into it with an emotional and very unsound approach, but I don't mean to imply that I was dragged into it. I went in voluntarily."

Mr. Hayden, a native of Montclair, N. J., said there were thousands of others like him, who should come in and tell their stories.

He added that shortly after the invasion of South Korea his attorney had written to J. Edgar Hoover, director of the Federal Bureau of Investigation, giving his Communist case history and seeking a means of eliminating any prejudice against his recall to the service.

Under questioning for more than three hours, the former husband of Madeleine Carroll, screen star, told of a restless life that started with his quitting high school at the age of fifteen and going to sea, and winding up in Hollywood. A Capt. Warwick Tompkins, described by him as an "open and avowed Communist," ran through his story.

He identified Captain Tompkins as an employe of Amtorg, the of-

Continued on Page 14, Column 3

PRICE AIDE RESIGNS, CONDEMNS DI SALLE

M. E. Thompson, Ex-Governor of Georgia, Hits 'Kansas City Crowd' in Administration

Special to The New York Times.

WASHINGTON, April 10—With bitter words for Price Stabilizer Michael V. DiSalle, and representing the "Kansas City crowd" as said was in the saddle in the national Administration, M. E. Thompson, former Governor of Georgia, resigned today as a consultant to the Office of Price Stabilization.

Mr. Thompson, once a power in Georgia politics, and who asserted that he battled successfully against the States Righters there who tried to keep President Truman's name off the ballot in 1948, declared that he would not support the Democratic party in 1952 if the "Kansas City crowd" still held control.

"If this is political treason,

Continued on Page 20, Column 1

Navy Suspends Explosives Expert; State Department Then Bars Wife

Special to The New York Times.

WASHINGTON, April 10—The Navy Department suspended Dr. Stephen Brunauer today as a "security risk," giving the 47-year-old high explosives expert thirty days in which to answer the charges.

The State Department meanwhile, suspended Mrs. Esther Caukin Brunauer, wife of the Navy scientist, pending the outcome of the investigation of her husband. The State Department made it plain in a statement that the action against Mrs. Brunauer was based not on information about her, but only as a result of the Navy suspension.

Both of the Brunauers were named by Senator Joseph R. McCarthy, Republican of Wisconsin, in the course of his charges last year of Communist infiltration of the Government.

The announcement of Dr. Brunauer's suspension, effective immediately, was made while he was on a trip to New England for the Navy. Questioned by reporters at LaGuardia Field, on his way back to the capital, he said:

"I do not know for what reason I was suspended. I think some one made a mistake. I telephoned Washington and a Navy spokesman said he did not know the reason for the suspension. I do not want to comment further on anything."

Mrs. Brunauer issued a stout denial of the McCarthy charges on March 13, 1950, defending herself and her husband against the allegations they were Communists.

The Navy announcement of the suspension of Dr. Brunauer followed the disclosure by the State Department that the action had already taken place. The Navy gave no details of the charges, but said that Dr. Brunauer would have thirty days to answer the charges and request a hearing.

The decision of Francis P. Matthews, Secretary of the Navy, will be final, it was said.

Asked whether the suspension of Mrs. Brunauer in response to charges against her husband was

Continued on Page 16, Column 3

RISE IN SALES TAX EXPECTED TO PASS CITY COUNCIL TODAY

Finance Committee Studies Bill at Length—Fight Against Measure Goes On

RUML A FISCAL ADVISER

Mayor Declines Challenge to Debate With Hoving—Joseph Suggests State-Wide Levy

The finance committee of the City Council spent an inconclusive three-hour executive session at City Hall yesterday afternoon weighing the merits of the proposed increase in the retail sales tax from 2 to 3 per cent, but when the meeting ended nothing had changed the prospect that the tax rise would be approved.

It was indicated that today the committee, after further behind-closed-doors deliberations, would favor the sales impost rise by a vote of 8 to 2, or possibly 7 to 3, and that later today the full City Council would adopt the measure by something like 19 to 6.

If the tax bill clears the Council hurdles today, as is indicated, it is expected that the Board of Estimate, whose members are committed to it, will give its approval at tomorrow's regular meeting.

Ruml to Advise Controller

Meanwhile, Controller Lazarus Joseph announced the appointment of Beardsley Ruml, business consultant, financier and economist, as a special deputy controller to advise Mr. Joseph on fiscal matters. Mr. Ruml, whose appointment was for an "indefinite" tenure, will serve without pay.

Mr. Ruml was at one time connected with the Federal Reserve Board and also with the New York Stock Exchange. He is a

Continued on Page 32, Column 4

U. S. PRODS NATIONS

Suggests U. N. Members Send More Troops to Fight in Korea

3 AVENUES ARE LISTED

Contributions Sought From Nations Not Yet Committed

By A. M. ROSENTHAL
Special to The New York Times.

UNITED NATIONS, N. Y., April 10—The United States has been quietly suggesting that members of the United Nations increase, or at least maintain, their contributions of troops for the Korean war effort.

Informed sources here report that for some time the United States has been keeping in touch with members of the world organization to see if non-United States representation in the international army could be increased.

[Chinese Communist troops in Korea clung to their positions along the Hwachon reservoir in the face of daylong United Nations attacks. Eighth Army headquarters clamped a stringent security blackout on news from the front as a major battle seemed to impend in the reservoir area.]

So far there has been no general appeal to the United Nations members to contribute more troops; it has all been on a country-to-country basis. Diplomats said that there was no indication that a new general request for troops in Korea was in the making for the time being.

But on a longer-range basis, the question of more troops may be considered by the General Assembly on Feb. 1 to plan possible sanctions

Continued on Page 5, Column 3

World News Summarized

WEDNESDAY, APRIL 11, 1951

President Truman relieved General of the Army MacArthur of his command in the Pacific because the United Nations commander had been unable to give his "wholehearted support" to United States and United Nations policies. The Presidential ouster has forced the general from all his commands, including his role in the occupation of Japan. Lieut. Gen. Matthew B. Ridgway has been designated to take over all the Far Eastern commands. [1:8.]

The United States has been asking other United Nations members to increase, or at least maintain, their forces fighting in Korea and asking for troops from countries that have sent none. [1:5.]

Enemy resistance increased in the Hwachon Reservoir area of Korea. The Communists still held the dam although Hwachon itself appeared deserted. [3:1; map P. 2.] Mao Tse-tung was said to have been officially reported ill and Liu Shao-chi was said to be acting in his place at the head of the Chinese Communist regime. [9:2.]

Britain has suggested that the United States invite Communist China to the discussions on a Japanese peace treaty and to Peiping a draft of the proposed pact. The treaty, Britain holds, should include the return of Formosa to China. [1:6-7.]

The days of "easy and automatic" relations between the United States and Canada are over, Canada's External Affairs Minister declared. "There will be frictions" that can be settled easily, he said, if the United States recognizes that Canada's acceptance of Washington leadership does not mean she is "willing to be merely an echo of somebody else's voice." [1:6-7.]

A "severe, but not crippling" budget was presented to Britain by the Labor Government, which chose to increase taxes, already heavy, rather than cut social welfare funds. [1:7.]

The bill giving West German labor equal rights with management in the operation of the steel and coal industries was passed by the lower house. [14:2.]

The House passed and sent to the Senate a supplemental defense money bill 43 per cent below Administration requests [19:1] and cut from the draft bill a provision for Universal Military Training in favor of a Presidential commission to draw detailed plans. [1:1.] Defense Secretary Marshall ordered all three armed services to share equitably draftees of superior standing. [19:3.]

Mobilization Director Wilson called for an end to complacency, selfishness and partisanship if we are to beat down the "dreadful shadow" of history's most "absolute and ruthless" dictatorship. [23:1.] M. E. Thompson resigned as consultant to the Price Stabilizer in protest against "political" control and general wastefulness. [1:2.]

Organized baseball agreed not to raise players' salaries above a club's 1950 highest. [33:2-3.] The Army halted certain pay rises for nonoperating rail workers until a special panel ruled in the case. [33:1.]

Senator Tobey was said to have disclosed that he had received telephone talks with President Truman about the Senate R. F. C. inquiry. [1:2-3.]

The Navy suspended Dr. Stephen Brunauer, a scientist, as a "security risk" and the State Department dropped his wife, Esther, until the husband's case was settled. [1:2-3.]

NEWS BULLETINS FROM THE TIMES
Every hour on the hour
7 A. M. through Midnight
WQXR AM 1560
WQXR FM 96.3

Index to other news appears on last page of this section.

DISMISSED BY THE PRESIDENT

General of the Army Douglas MacArthur

Britain Asks That Red China Have Role in Japanese Pact

By WALTER H. WAGGONER
Special to The New York Times.

WASHINGTON, April 10—Britain has suggested to the United States that Communist China be brought into the negotiations for a Japanese peace treaty. The British proposal also specifically asked that the United States send a copy of its treaty draft to the Peiping regime for its consideration and, further, that the treaty provide for the ultimate if not immediate return of Formosa to "China."

By "China" the British mean the regime of Mao Tse-tung, since that is the China now recognized by London.

These suggestions have been made in the course of recent conversations between the two Governments. They represent another difference of opinion that has developed between London and Washington on both the procedure for negotiating a Japanese treaty and the form the settlement should have.

The basis for the British request that Peiping be given a look at the United States treaty draft is to enable the Chinese Communists to reject the proposal if they want to, as the Soviet Union is expected to do.

At the same time, it is vigorously denied here that Britain will refuse to sign any treaty draft that Communist China rejects. Reports that such an "or else" position has

Continued on Page 8, Column 5

BUDGET INCREASES BRITONS' TAX LOAD

Income, Profit, Purchase, Auto and Gasoline Imposts Rise— Social Services Uncut

By RAYMOND DANIELL
Special to The New York Times.

LONDON, April 10—The already heavily burdened British people were called on today to pay even higher taxes to preserve their welfare state. Hugh Gaitskell, Chancellor of the Exchequer, introducing his first budget, told the House of Commons that there were only two ways of meeting the extra cost of rearmament. One, which brought cheers from the Conservative Opposition, was by reducing expenditures for social welfare.

The alternative he offered was a sharp rise in both direct and indirect taxes. This brought cheers

Continued on Page 10, Column 2

Canada Bars a 'Yes' Role to U. S.; Pearson Sees Unity Despite Friction

By The United Press

TORONTO, April 10—Lester B. Pearson, Canadian Secretary for External Affairs, said today that "easy and automatic" relations between Canada and the United States were a thing of the past.

In a speech apparently aimed at United States consumption, Mr. Pearson said that Canada was not willing to be "merely an echo of somebody else's voice" and reserved the right to criticize "our great friend, the United States."

Later, in a second speech, Mr. Pearson made an indirect reference to General MacArthur when he said that a successful foreign policy must work toward goals accepted by the majority of the people, and it would have a better chance of "reaching these goals if we abandon what has been called 'hoop-la diplomacy' at Lake Success, or, I hasten to add, at Tokyo."

the pursuit of objectives which we share.

"Nevertheless, the days of relatively easy and automatic relations with our neighbor are, I think, over," he added.

Mr. Pearson indicated that one of the "angry waves" that could weaken relations between Canada and the United States was the controversy over General of the Army Douglas MacArthur's statement on the war in Korea.

He said that there might be "angry waves" which may weaken the foundation of our friendship but that Canada would march forward with the United States in

Continued on Page 6, Column 3

PRESIDENT MOVES

Van Fleet Is Named to Command 8th Army in Drastic Shift

VIOLATIONS ARE CITED

White House Statement Quotes Directives and Implies Breaches

Texts of statements and orders
in MacArthur dispute, Page 8.

By W. H. LAWRENCE
Special to The New York Times.

WASHINGTON, Wednesday, April 11—President Truman early today relieved General of the Army Douglas MacArthur of all his commands in the Far East and appointed Lieut. Gen. Matthew B. Ridgway as his successor.

The President said he had relieved General MacArthur "with deep regret" because he had concluded that the Far Eastern Commander "is unable to give his wholehearted support to the policies of the United States Government and of the United Nations in matters pertaining to his official duties.

General MacArthur, in a message to House Minority Leader Joseph W. Martin Jr. of Massachusetts, made public by Mr. Martin last Thursday, had publicly challenged the President's foreign policy, urging that the United States concentrate on Asia instead of Europe and use Generalissimo Chiang Kai-shek's Formosa-based troops to open a second front on the mainland of China.

The change in command is effective at once. General Ridgway, who has been in command of the Eighth Army in Korea since the death in December of Gen. Walton H. Walker, assumes all of General MacArthur's titles—Supreme Commander, United Nations Forces in Korea, Supreme Commander for Allied Powers, Japan, Commander-in-Chief, U. S. Army, Far East.

Commanded in Greece

The Eighth Army command will pass to Lieut. Gen. James A. Van Fleet whose most recent important command was as head of the American military mission in Greece, when that country was repelling a Communist-directed guerrilla attack under the Truman doctrine.

In ousting General MacArthur for his epic public disagreement with American policy designed to localize the Asiatic war, the President said:

"Full and vigorous debate on matters of national policy is a vital element in the Constitutional system of our free democracy.

"It is fundamental, however, that military commanders must be governed by the policies and directives issued to them in the manner provided by our laws and Con-

Continued on Page 8, Column 1

News Stuns Tokyo; MacArthur Is Silent

By The Associated Press

TOKYO, Wednesday, April 11—A small Japanese boy with "flash" printed on it in red carried to General MacArthur today the news that he had been discharged from his commands by President Truman.

It was delivered by a senior aide, Col. Sid Huff, who said that the General received the news without comment. Colonel Huff indicated that the General had no forewarning that he was being relieved.

The General announced that he would have no statement immediately.

The message came as a signal Corps communication about the time and Army radio announced the news.

General MacArthur got the word while at breakfast with his wife, Senator Warren G. Mag-

Continued on Page 8, Column 4

The New York Times.

Copyright, 1951, by The New York Times Company.

VOL. CI No. 34,244.   NEW YORK, SATURDAY, OCTOBER 27, 1951.   RAG PAPER EDITION   SEVENTY-FIVE CENTS

TRUMAN PLEA TO PIER MEN IS UNHEEDED

TAFT LAW IGNORED

President Rejects Move by Industry After Talk With the Cabinet

BASES CALL ON DEFENSE

Insurgents Say No National Emergency Was Declared—Attack 'Unfair Verdict'

By GEORGE HORNE

President Truman appealed to New York waterfront strikers last night to return to work in behalf of the defense effort but the defiant strike committee immediately rejected the plea and called for widening of the costly stoppage.

The President, to whom Cyrus S. Ching, director of the Federal Mediation and Conciliation Service, had referred the dispute, discussed it with the Cabinet before making his decision not to accede to the demands of industrial leaders to invoke the procedure of the Taft-Hartley Act.

Mr. Truman said he had been informed that defense activity was being hampered and that "in the national interest" the employes ought to get back to their tasks.

The twelve-day strike started in a handful of locals on Oct. 15 and snowballed under pressure of roaming wildcat squads until it paralyzed the vast Port of New York, spread to Boston, halted work on military shipments and piled up cargoes estimated in value at nearly $300,000,000.

Demanded Pact Reopening

The intransigent strikers demanded reopening of a contract that had been negotiated through weeks of discussion with employers and was finally ratified by a 2-to-1 vote of the union's membership.

The new contract of the International Longshoremen's Association, A. F. L., and the New York Shipping Association, provided a 10-cent increase to make the basic hourly wage $2.10. It stipulated improvements in vacation terms, a single shape-up or work-call a day and other benefits which the majority of the union's 125-man wage committee approved and recommended.

Announcement of the plea from the White House was followed within ten or fifteen minutes by the insurgent response. John J. (Gene) Sampson, business agent of Local 791, spearhead local in the strike, said that the strikers would not accept the President's proposal since he had not seen fit to declare a national emergency.

The President could have invoked the Taft-Hartley Act despite the fact that the walkout involved an intra-union matter and not a labor-management dispute in which no contract existed. Moreover, he could have used a Wage Stabilization Board dispute procedure on a matter affecting national defense.

He had been urged by industrial and business associations and individuals in New York and New Jersey to apply the former procedure on the grounds that the stoppage was causing the lay-off of thousands of workers other than the 30,000 affected longshoremen and immobilizing ships, cargo and investments mounting into millions of dollars.

Two-Day Intercession Failed

Mr. Ching had sent the dispute to the White House following withdrawal of the Federal mediation agency after a boisterous and futile two-day intercession in New York.

Clyde J. Mills, No. 1 Ching aide and a trouble-shooter for the agency, had headed a Commissioner's panel in New York in efforts to end the strike's "family quarrel." The mediation men called it an "intolerable situation," a phrase that heightened the bitter feeling of recalcitrant strike leaders who described the Mills withdrawal announcement as unfair and tantamount to a verdict of guilt.

The text of Mr. Truman's statement follows:

"I have been informed by Mr. Charles E. Wilson, director of the Office of Defense Mobilization, that because of the work stoppage of the longshoremen the ports of New

Continued on Page 22, Column 2

Marciano Knocks Out Louis in 8th Round

Rocky Marciano, 27-year-old Brockton, Mass., boxer, became a leading contender for the world heavyweight championship when he knocked out Joe Louis, former holder of the title, in the eighth round of their scheduled ten-round bout in Madison Square Garden last night.

The defeat marked the end of the 37-year-old Louis' hopes of becoming the first ex-titleholder to regain the crown. Marciano dropped Louis for a count of eight before he sent him through the ropes with a right to the jaw at 2:36 of the eighth. Referee Ruby Goldstein disdained a count. It was Marciano's thirty-eighth triumph in a row, thirty-three of them by knockouts.

Louis showed no signs of weakening until the seventh round. He weighed 212½ pounds to Marciano's 187.

Details on Page 12.

FLATH'S VICE SQUAD UPSET BY MONAGHAN

Entire Personnel Transferred —Step May Foreshadow Clean Sweep of Plainclothes Men

By ALEXANDER FEINBERG

The entire personnel of the Chief Inspector's plainclothes squad, the top police unit assigned to the task of suppressing vice and gambling, was transferred yesterday by Police Commissioner George P. Monaghan.

Sixteen of the seventeen members of the squad were sent back to uniform a week after the retirement of August W. Flath as Chief Inspector and Mr. Monaghan's collateral declaration that all plainclothes squads would be reconstituted. The other member, formerly attached to the detective division, was reassigned there.

A year ago—on Sept. 29, 1950—Thomas F. Murphy, then Police Commissioner, on his fourth day in office ordered all of the 336 men in the plainclothes division back into uniform. He replaced them with selected patrolmen, "neither besmirched nor tainted," from the ranks of recruits and newly appointed policemen.

New Sweep Is Seen

Yesterday's action by Mr. Monaghan was believed to be the forerunner of a second clean sweep of all plainclothes manpower. In the shift, two acting lieutenants were reduced to sergeant, and an inspector, who headed the squad, a deputy inspector, an acting captain, two lieutenants and ten patrolmen were affected. Eight of the ten plainclothes men will take a loss of $240 a year in extra compensation.

Inspector Edward W. Lent, head of the squad under Chief Flath, who last week was succeeded by Chief Inspector Conrad H. Rothengast.

Continued on Page 7, Column 3

Error in Race Placing at Jamaica Costs $15,655, Helps Cancer Fund

By JAMES ROACH

The Damon Runyon Fund for Cancer Research was the winner in the third race on the Empire City-at-Jamaica program yesterday—a horse race that the placing judges never will be able to forget.

Place payoffs on Sao Paulo were made at the rate of $5.10 for each $2. By the time the stewards had notified the Empire City Racing Association management of the error almost all of the payoffs had been made.

What to do?

James Butler, Empire City president, conferred with other officials. There was no precedent in New York racing for their problem.

The management had an "out" in that the first general rule of New York racing reads that "final decision of the racing officials upon the running and results of races shall be conclusive." The management didn't want that "out." It wanted to pay off those who had

Continued on Page 14, Column 1

KOREAN FOE DROPS DEMAND FOR TRUCE ON 38TH PARALLEL

But Enemy's Plan for 15-Mile U. N. Retreat From the Front Is Termed Unacceptable

REDS WOULD YIELD IN PART

Communists Propose to Move Out of Last Area They Hold South of Old Boundary

By LINDESAY PARROTT
Special to The New York Times.

TOKYO, Saturday, Oct. 27—Although a Communist proposal for a fifteen-mile retreat by Allied forces in Korea was unacceptable to the United Nations Command, the negotiators for a truce were closer to geographical agreement on a cease-fire line today than at any time since the conferences started last July.

The enemy's proposal, providing for a United Nations withdrawal in the east and center, and for evacuation by the Communists of the last ground they hold in South Korea, was an abandonment of the Communist demand for a cease-fire based on the political boundary of the Thirty-eighth Parallel.

The plan was announced to Allied representatives at a ninety-minute meeting yesterday of subcommitteemen of both sides at their tent village near Panmunjom. There the United Nations on the day before had advanced its own proposal for a truce line and buffer zone close to the battle positions won by the Allied forces still grinding forward slowly into North Korea.

[The Associated Press said the third subcommittee session was held from 11 A. M. to 1 P. M. Saturday (9 to 11 P. M. Friday, Eastern standard time). The United Nations negotiators, Maj. Gen. Henry I. Hodes and Rear Admiral Arleigh A. Burke, failed to make any progress with the Communist representatives on the truce line issue. An afternoon session was scheduled for 3 o'clock.]

'Unilateral' Retreat Cited

Thus far, there has been no formal Allied rejection of the enemy proposal. But an official United Nations bulletin pointed out yesterday afternoon that the Chinese and North Korean plan required a "unilateral" withdrawal by United Nations forces from militarily important positions along virtually all of the present battle line.

Among these would be hard-won ground at "Heartbreak Ridge" and the "Punchbowl" in the rugged mountains of the peninsula's eastern watershed, and the "Iron Triangle" in the center. It was estimated that the retreat would extend along a 100-mile front, ceding almost all of the territory gained by Gen. James A. Van Fleet's summer and autumn offensives, staged since the armistice talks began.

In exchange, the Communists offered to yield the Ongjin Peninsula and an area around Yonan. There, tongues of land thrust down into the Yellow Sea below the Thirty-eighth Parallel.

But this territory generally is considered indefensible, except by a force that also could hold an enclave to the north above the old boundary, and the United Nations in the present campaign never has made any serious attempt to challenge

Continued on Page 2, Column 5

CHURCHILL IS RETURNED TO POWER WITH A MARGIN OF 26 OVER LABOR; WASHINGTON EXPECTS VISIT SOON

THE NEW PRIME MINISTER CONGRATULATED BY HIS WIFE

Winston Churchill as he appeared yesterday after late returns had assured his party of victory in the British elections
Associated Press Radiophoto

MOSES SEEKS STEEL OF FOREIGN MAKERS

Would Meet Needs for Roads by Dealing Directly With Mills in Germany and Belgium

The quest of Robert Moses, City Construction Coordinator, for imported steel to fill the construction needs of traffic relief projects in the city has been frustrated thus far by soaring prices that far exceed the limitations of the public purse, he said yesterday.

Now he is seeking ways to get the essential metal directly from German and Belgian manufacturing bases without paying a middleman's profit to the importers in this country.

Mr. Moses pointed out that the Federal allocation system had seriously restricted domestic steel for city use.

The difficulties encountered in attempts to get foreign steel were

Continued on Page 34, Column 2

Gain for U. S.-British Ties Seen by Congress Members

By WILLIAM S. WHITE
Special to The New York Times.

WASHINGTON, Oct. 26—The return of the Conservatives to power in Britain will improve British-American relations as far as both parties in Congress are concerned. The success of the ticket headed by Winston Churchill likewise will tend to ease the way for any future programs in aid of Britain, be they economic or military, other things being equal.

Washington generally expected Mr. Churchill to come to this country soon for consultation with President Truman on the coordination of United States and British foreign policy. The Prime Minister and the President are old friends, their previous meetings having included the Potsdam conference of July, 1945.

There was much speculation here that Mr. Churchill would time his visit to coincide with the President's extended vacation at Key West, Fla., which starts Nov. 5.

Continued on Page 3, Column 7

World News Summarized

SATURDAY, OCTOBER 27, 1951

Winston Churchill, as the leader of the victorious Conservative party, was asked by King George VI to become the new British Prime Minister in place of Clement R. Attlee, who resigned. With four districts still unreported, the Conservatives had an over-all majority of eighteen and a majority of twenty-six over Labor in the newly elected Parliament. [1:8.]

Mr. Churchill and his aides will face many heavy tasks, including the fulfillment of their pledge to "denationalize" the iron and steel industry and to decentralize the administration of the nationalized coal industry and of the rail and road transport system. [1:7.] Mr. Churchill, reflecting the sober mood in which the Conservative victory was accepted on all sides, said, "We shall do our very best." [3:1.]

The majority of the remnants of the once mighty Liberal party backed the Conservatives and this support was the major factor in the Conservative capture of twenty-one of the twenty-four seats won from Labor. [3:8.]

Congressional members of both parties foresaw an improvement in British-United States relations, particularly in the field of foreign policies. [1:5-6.]

In Paris European observers also were optimistic of greater Allied unity as a result of the British election. [4:3.]

next week by representatives of the two countries. [1:7.]

In the Korean truce negotiations the Communists abandoned their demand that the demarcation line between the opposing armies be set along the Thirty-Eighth Parallel, but their newer proposal, calling for a fifteen-mile retreat by Allied forces, also was unacceptable to United Nations officials. [1:3.]

Allied fliers shot down two enemy jet planes and damaged three others in another air battle over Northwest Korea. [2:8; with map.]

The peace treaty signed at San Francisco was ratified by the lower house of the Japanese Diet, which also approved the part permitting the maintenance of a United States garrison in Japan. [2:1.]

President Truman, emphasizing the serious effect on the defense program of the wildcat dock walkout here, appealed to the strikers to return to work, but his plea was promptly rejected. [1:1.]

Thomas H. White, Cleveland industrialist, his wife and daughter-in-law were killed when their private plane, piloted by Mr. White, crashed as it approached a landing at the Washington airport. [1:6-7.]

NEWS BULLETINS FROM THE TIMES
Every hour on the hour
7 A. M. through Midnight
WQXR AM 1560
WQXR FM 96.3

Index to other news appears on last page of this section.

ATTLEE STEPS DOWN

King Then Calls on War Leader to Take Over at Time of Crisis

LABOR TOPS POPULAR VOTE

Party Polls 48.8% to Rival's 48.1 While Losing Out on Seats by 293 to 319

By RAYMOND DANIELL
Special to The New York Times.

LONDON, Oct. 26—For the second time in both their lifetimes, George VI called upon Winston Churchill today to form a government at a time of national crisis.

A little earlier the King, who is convalescing from a serious operation, received Clement R. Attlee and accepted his resignation as Prime Minister because the verdict of the people of Britain had gone against the Labor party in yesterday's general election. Therefore, Mr. Churchill, leader of the Conservative party, now takes his place at the helm of the ship of state while Mr. Attlee has sailed according to Socialist navigation rules for the past six years, and with a depleted crew for nineteen months.

After the 1950 election Mr. Attlee's Labor Government never had a majority of more than seven. It seems now that Mr. Churchill in the skipper's role will not be much better off.

Over-all Margin Now 18

As matters stand now the Conservatives have a majority over all others of eighteen, and twenty-six more seats than the Labor party alone. The majority may increase or decrease but not enough to make any real difference.

There are only four constituencies remaining to be heard from. In addition there is a seat to be filled in a delayed election. If the Conservatives won all the remaining seats, which is unlikely, their over-all majority would be twenty-three. However, if these seats did not change the Conservative majority would be seventeen.

The present party standings follow:

Conservatives 319
Labor 293
Liberals 5
Independents 3

All of the Independents are Irish, two of them probably will not ever vote, and one of them leans toward Labor.

This accounts for 620 of the 625 seats in the House of Commons. Of the four constituencies remaining to be heard from, two have been heard from one by Labor and one by the Liberals.

Seat Held for Labor

The 625th seat remains vacant because one of the candidates died during the campaign. It, however, is a safe seat for Labor and when the election is held it should add one more seat to Labor's strength in the House.

Mr. Attlee probably was right in ascribing his downfall to the way the Liberals voted. At party headquarters after he had taken leave of the King he said:

"I don't think there is any reason to dispute that our loss of seats has been due to the fact that when it came to the point more Liberals were Conservative than Labor."

How many more Liberals voted

Continued on Page 3, Column 2

MANY CHANGES SET BY CONSERVATIVES

'Denationalization' of Steel, Tax Revision and Broad Housing Program Listed

By CLIFTON DANIEL
Special to The New York Times.

LONDON, Oct. 26—Former Prime Minister Attlee said in his recent ill-starred election campaign that his Labor Government could not be expected to clear up in six years the mess of six centuries.

Next week the Conservatives will set about tidying up what they regard as the mess of Labor's six years. They have promised many changes, although not as many as the ideological differences between the two parties might indicate, and they have years of legislative work ahead of them.

Their program is not as ambitious as that of the 1945 Labor Government, which came to power with plans to remake the whole economic and social structure of Britain. Among the tasks that the Conservatives have set themselves are these:

1. To "denationalize" the iron and steel industry, the last enterprise taken under public ownership by the Labor Government last March.

2. To decentralize the administration of the Nationalized Coal Industry and of the state-owned railroad and road transport systems.

3. To build more houses, 300,000 a year being the stated target, and

Continued on Page 3, Column 4

U. S. WILL INCREASE ARMS TO YUGOSLAVS

Heavy Weapons Will Help Tito Resist Aggression—Pact to Be Signed Next Week

By WALTER H. WAGGONER
Special to The New York Times.

WASHINGTON, Oct. 26—The United States and Yugoslavia will sign a military aid agreement under way here late in June, with the visit of Col. Gen. Kuca Popovic, Yugoslavia's General Staff, and concluded with the inspection trip to Yugoslavia earlier this month by Gen. J. Lawton Collins, United States Army Chief of Staff.

The agreement will bring to a close negotiations between the two Governments that formally got under way here last June, with the visit of Col. Gen. Kuca Popovic.

Arms that can be expected to start flowing to the only Government holding out in Eastern Europe against Russian domina-

Continued on Page 5, Column 4

Industrialist Flying to See Marshall Killed as Plane Crashes in Potomac

Special to The New York Times.

WASHINGTON, Oct. 26—Thomas H. White, Cleveland industrialist, his wife, the former Miss Kathleen York, and his daughter-in-law, Mrs. Robert White, were killed here this morning when a plane piloted by Mr. White fell into the Potomac River while approaching National Airport. Mr. White was on the way to keep a luncheon appointment with General of the Army George C. Marshall, former Defense Secretary.

Mr. White, 57 years old, a grandson of the founder of the White Motor Company and White Sewing Machine Company, was piloting his own plane, a single-engine Beechcraft Bonanza, from Hunting Valley, a Cleveland suburb, to Washington.

The plane had made a routine stop at Youngstown, Ohio, and was scheduled to arrive here at 10:15 A. M. The crash occurred at 10:12 A. M.

There was no immediate expla-

nation as to the cause of the accident. Radio tower operators said that the plane, after landing clearance, was apparently making a normal approach when at about 200 feet altitude it suddenly nosed down and fell into the river's edge where the water was shallow.

Crash boats were at the scene within a few minutes and their crews recovered the bodies from the plane. The nose and engine of the plane were pushed into the passenger compartment.

The Civil Aeronautics Board, the Civil Aeronautics Administration and police began an investigation.

Mr. White's purpose in visiting General Marshall today was to talk with him about Nato, an Elkhound which the children of Norway recently presented to the General. General Marshall, long an acquaintance of Mr. White, said they had exchanged some correspondence about the dog. He was indi-

Continued on Page 34, Column 4

Churchill in Office: A Wartime Study

The energy, versatility and qualities of mind that Mr. Churchill brings to the Prime Ministership are vividly illustrated in today's installment of his war memoirs. His ideas on diplomacy, his attitude toward Americans, his views on how to handle the Russians are set forth in a series of wartime minutes.

See Page 21

"All the News
That's Fit to Print"

The New York Times.

LATE CITY EDITION
Light snow this morning followed by clearing. Fair tomorrow.
Temperature Range Today—Max., 43; Min., 35
Temperature Yesterday—Max., 40; Min., 33
Full U. S. Weather Bureau Report, Page 55

Copyright, 1952, by The New York Times Company.

VOL. CI..No. 34,347.   Entered as Second-Class Matter, Post Office, New York, N. Y.   NEW YORK, THURSDAY, FEBRUARY 7, 1952.   Times Square, New York 36, N. Y.   Telephone Lackawanna 4-1000   FIVE CENTS

KING GEORGE VI DIES IN SLEEP AT SANDRINGHAM; ELIZABETH, QUEEN AT 25, FLYING FROM AFRICA; PRESIDENT AMONG WORLD LEADERS IN TRIBUTE

2½% INTEREST RATE FOR SAVINGS BANKS APPROVED BY STATE

85% of Institutions Expected to Adopt 'Permissive' Rule Lifting 17-Year Ceiling

NEW U. S. TAXES A FACTOR

Board Adjusts Payments on Commercial Deposits, Acts to Clear Extra Dividends

By GEORGE A. MOONEY

New York's thrifty received a new incentive yesterday.

Terminating a policy that dates to 1935, the State Banking Board acted to raise its ceiling on interest-dividends paid on savings and thrift deposits from a 2 per cent maximum to 2½ per cent. Eighty-five per cent of the state's 130 savings banks are expected to put the increase in effect at an early date.

Last night the Dime Savings Bank of Brooklyn became the first in this area to announce it would pay 2¼ per cent for the current quarter ending March 31.

Trustees of the Roosevelt Savings Bank announced they would meet today to increase the rate from 2 to 2¼ per cent on account balances and deposits for the three-month period starting Jan. 1.

Other savings banks and competitive commercial banks, where possible, are likely to take similar action soon.

Responding to the higher level of prevailing rates, and especially to Federal taxes imposed at the beginning of this year, several savings banks asked permission some weeks ago to pay larger dividends. Under the new tax law savings institutions are made liable for income taxes at the regular corporate rate on all earnings after surplus and reserves total 12 per cent of deposits.

Regulation Is "Permissive"

William A. Lyon, Superintendent of Banks, in announcing the board's action yesterday said the new 2½ per cent rate was "permissive."

"Banks are permitted under the regulation to pay any rate up to that maximum which directors and trustees believe to be justifiable in the light of the earning power and the capital or surplus position of their institutions," he explained.

Two other important amendments also were made in General Regulation No. 3, the dividend and interest rate regulation, Mr. Lyon said. In the first of these, relating to commercial banks' special interest and thrift deposits, the board approved a limit on interest payments at the maximum rate of 2½ per cent on the first $10,000 of any account and setting a ceiling rate of 1½ per cent on that portion of any special and thrift account in excess of $10,000.

The largest individual account that may be accepted by savings banks is $10,000, the maximum

Continued on Page 55, Column 6

Truman 'Shows Off' New White House

By W. H. LAWRENCE
Special to The New York Times.

WASHINGTON, Feb. 6.—Ducking nimbly around and under scaffolding, President Truman today took a few correspondents on a conducted tour of the White House, which is being reconstructed. He said it was still his hope that the First Family would be able to move into it early in April after three and one-half years in Blair House.

Mixing history and comment about the tribulations of a tenant who decides to get a house done over, Mr. Truman led the reporters through the building for forty minutes, answering questions and volunteering observations about nearly every room.

The hum of power saws as workmen went about their jobs sometimes drowned his

Continued on Page 25, Column 1

1-Way Traffic Signs Due Soon in Times Sq.

By JOSEPH C. INGRAHAM

Conversion of Seventh and Eighth Avenues to one-way operation has been decided upon by Acting Traffic Commissioner T. T. Wiley despite objections of the New York City Omnibus Corporation.

Preparations for the new traffic pattern were well under way yesterday, with new guideposts rising in Times Square and the fittings all set to hold the one-way arrows. Work on the other sections of the one-way route, which extend from Columbus Circle to below Canal Street, also was progressing. Seventh Avenue-Varick Street will handle southbound flow and Hudson Street-Abingdon Square-Eighth

Continued on Page 17, Column 5

CHARGES OF WASTE IN DEFENSE DENIED

Pentagon Aides Tell Senators of Savings—Admiral Calls Himself 'Oyster Fork Fox'

By HAROLD B. HINTON
Special to The New York Times.

WASHINGTON, Feb. 6.—Officials of the Department of Defense underwent a period of criticism before a Senate Appropriations subcommittee today and did not seem to like it. They were appearing in support of defense budget estimates of more than $52,000,000,000.

The principal witness was Vice Admiral Charles W. Fox, Chief of Naval Supplies, who told the Senators of the progress the Navy had made in simplifying the cataloguing of its supplies. When his presentation was interrupted by questions about allegations of waste and extravagance, the Pentagon contingent moved to the counter-offensive.

"I stand before you as Oyster Fork Fox," the admiral asserted, as the Senators and spectators laughed. "I am supposed to have bought 11,000,000 oyster forks for the Navy, and I had nothing more to do with it than you did."

He said that the Navy last

Continued on Page 4, Column 2

RED TRAPS FEARED IN FOE'S PROPOSAL FOR KOREA PARLEY

Communist Demand for Airing of Status of Formosa Viewed as Bar to U. N. Accord

TRUMAN CITED AS A GUIDE

Nam Il Argues Stand Taken by President on Blockading China Widens Issues

Text of Gen. Nam II's statement is printed on Page 2.

By LINDESAY PARROTT
Special to The New York Times.

TOKYO, Thursday, Feb. 7.—The United Nations Command began today a detailed study of the Communist proposal for a top-level political conference three months after the armistice in the Korean war to deal with related issues in the Far East.

This morning no hint of Allied reaction had come from the advance camp at Munsan, where the United Nations representatives took the Communist program after it had been delivered to them at a plenary session of the truce delegations at Panmunjom, or at the headquarters of the United Nations Commander, Gen. Matthew B. Ridgway, in Tokyo.

The enemy proposal was made by North Korean Gen. Nam Il, head of the Chinese and North Korean delegation, who drove to the meeting place in a big American limousine with whitewall tires. He nodded coldly to the senior United Nations representative, Vice Admiral Charles Turner Joy, as he launched into his prepared introductory remarks — considerably more extensive, it turned out, than the brief formal proposal for a governmental conference for "peaceful settlement of the Korean question and other questions related to peace in Korea."

Before the session adjourned it was agreed that a new plenary sitting should be held by the delegates of both sides after the United Nations study had been com-

Continued on Page 2, Column 4

World News Summarized

THURSDAY, FEBRUARY 7, 1952

King George VI died in his sleep at Sandringham Palace yesterday morning; his daughter was proclaimed Queen Elizabeth II. The King, who seemingly had recovered from an operation for the removal of a growth on his lung, had felt so well he had been out shooting the day before. [1:8.] The British people were stunned by their sudden loss. [1:7.]

King George became the British ruler in 1936 when his brother, King Edward VIII and later Duke of Windsor, abdicated. He saw little peace during his reign. Threats of war, armed conflict and the "cold war" marked his tenure. [10:1.] During the bombing of London he refused to take special precautions or leave Buckingham Palace. [13:7-8.] The new Queen started for London by plane when she learned of her father's death. She had been touring East Africa with her consort, the Duke of Edinburgh. [1:6-7.] She is the first Queen to ascend Britain's throne since 115 years ago, when Queen Victoria was crowned. [1:5-6.] The Duke of Windsor sails from New York tonight, alone, to attend his brother's funeral. [14:3.]

President Truman, Secretary Acheson and others expressed the sorrow of the United States [1:5] as did former President Hoover, Mayor Impellitteri and others in this city. [14:5.] United Nations flags were flown at half-staff. [15:1.]

The Soviet Union, for the fifth time, vetoed Italy's membership in the United Nations. [1:4.] The Russians did not join forty-seven other countries in pledging funds for expanded technical assistance this year. [3:4.]

Allied officers studied the Communist proposal for a political conference three months after a Korean armistice. [1:3.]

West German leaders were unmoved by American and British pleas to cool their anger over French moves in the Saar and not to endanger plans for West Europe's defense. [1:7.]

A masked witness told a House committee he had seen Russians kill hundreds of Polish officers in Katyn Forest in 1939. [4:3.]

Defense Department heads, testifying on the military budget before a Senate group, vigorously defended their spending. [1:2.] Mobilization heads also won an attack for plans to spread defense contracts to unemployment areas. [39:4.]

The slow-down in the military aircraft production rate will have little immediate effect on consumer goods but will avoid more stringent curbs later, a survey showed. [3:1.]

Governor Byrnes of South Carolina blamed "Negro politicians of the North" for the Democratic party's shift from a State's Rights program. [21:1.]

This state authorized banks to pay up to 2½ per cent on savings and thrift accounts. [1:1.]

Columbia University will increase tuition fees up to 25 per cent next fall and adjust faculty salaries upward. [29:1.]

NEWS BULLETINS FROM THE TIMES

Every hour on the hour 7 A.M. through Midnight
Except at 4 P.M. Today
WQXR AM 1560   WQXR FM 96.3

Index to other news appears on last page of this section.

THE NEW QUEEN AND THE LATE KING

ELIZABETH II

GEORGE VI
Associated Press

SOVIET AGAIN BALKS ITALY'S U. N. ENTRY

Russia for Fifth Time Vetoes Application—Is Beaten on En Bloc Admission Bid

By THOMAS J. HAMILTON
Special to The New York Times.

PARIS, Feb. 6.—Italy's application for membership in the United Nation's was vetoed by the Soviet Union tonight for the fifth time. Ten of the eleven members of the Security Council voted for a French resolution recommending the admission of Italy.

Jacob A. Malik, the Soviet representative, based his action on the refusal of the United States and other Western powers to accept a Soviet proposal for en bloc admission of fourteen applicants, including five Communist governments.

The Soviet resolution afterward was rejected by a vote of six to two. The United States, Brazil, Nationalist China, Greece, the Netherlands and Turkey voted against the resolution, while Pakistan joined the Soviet Union in supporting it. Britain, France and Chile abstained.

Mr. Malik accused the United States of blocking Italy's admission. He declared that "the Italian people will note that it is the United States, with the help of the United Kingdom" that had "provoked" the Soviet veto. He added that if the Western powers had wanted to get Italy admitted, they would have agreed to the Soviet proposal.

Gross Protests "Horsetrade"

Ernest A. Gross, the United States delegate, retorted that on the contrary the Italian people would hardly be grateful for being made a part of the proposed "horsetrade." He asked whether Mr. Malik really believed that Italy should be "put in the same basket" with such "a shadow state" as Outer Mongolia, one of the Communist candidates included in the Soviet resolution.

Mr. Gross also expressed regret that the new state of Libya, which came into existence on Christmas Day, 1951, had been included in the Soviet en bloc proposal—which presumably meant that it likewise would encounter a Soviet veto unless the Western powers agree to the Soviet mass entry proposal. Mr. Malik replied that Outer Mongolia deserved to be admitted. He said that its participation in the war against Japan "along with that of the Soviet Union" saved 1,000,000 American lives. He based his statement on statements by the United States high command.

Reconsideration today of Italy's long-standing application was the result of a General Assembly resolution last fall requesting the Security Council to reconsider it in the light of Italy's responsibilities

Continued on Page 2, Column 5

Ruler Becomes Elizabeth II; Her Son, 3, Is Crown Prince

By CLIFTON DANIEL
Special to The New York Times.

LONDON, Feb. 6.—Britain entered a new Elizabethan era today. Upon the death of King George VI, Princess Elizabeth Alexandra Mary, his elder daughter, automatically became Queen of the United Kingdom and the Dominions Overseas at the age of 25.

Tonight at the first meeting of her Privy Council she was formally styled Queen Elizabeth II.

[Text of the Privy Council's proclamation is on Page 14.]

Thus, for the first time in 115 years, a woman ascended the world's most exalted and stable throne. At the other law courts of the land, the judges marshal closed the court with words not heard since the end of Queen Victoria's sixty-three-year reign in 1901: "God save the Queen and my lords the Queen's justices."

For the first time in British history the sovereign was abroad at the moment of accession.

Already bearing the full responsibility of the crown, the new Queen will return home by air from Kenya in Africa tomorrow accompanied by her consort, the Duke of Edinburgh.

They were to have boarded the liner Gothic at Mombasa tomorrow to sail for Ceylon, Australia and New Zealand on a five-month ceremonial tour deputizing for the late King, whose illness prevented him from going.

With the accession of the Queen, her son Prince Charles, three years and two months old, became the Crown Prince and heir to the

Envoy Calls on Acheson

Sir Oliver Franks, British Ambassador, accompanied by seven representatives of the British Commonwealth, called on Secretary Acheson shortly after noon to inform him formally of the King's death.

"A world personage who maintained the highest conception of the English constitutional monarchy passes in the death of His Majesty King George VI," President Truman said in his statement.

"From his accession to the throne through all the ills which beset the world throughout the years of his reign—including the most disastrous war in history—he played his part nobly and with full responsibility which was his. His heroic acceptance of the pain and suffering during these past few years is a true reflection of the bravery of the British people in adversity.

"The King was ever conscious of his obligations as sovereign of a nation through centuries has been the champion of personal liberty and those free institu-

Continued on Page 5, Column 5

TRUMAN EXPRESSES SORROW OF NATION

Voices Sympathy for British Over Loss of King—Acheson and Others Pay Tribute

Special to The New York Times.

WASHINGTON, Feb. 6.—President Truman and the nation paid tribute to King George VI today in extending this country's sympathy to the British people on his death.

"He played his part nobly and with full understanding of the responsibility which was his," the President said in a formal statement.

All official Washington responded in kind following the surprise and shock at the news of the monarch's passing early this morning. Highest officials in the Government and leaders of both House of Congress joined in expressions of sympathy and praise for the man who had been a steadfast friend of the United States and, indeed, had been the first British King to visit this country.

Secretary of State Dean Acheson commented on the courage with which King George had borne his physical suffering and noted: "It is a characteristic English spirit and the King possessed it in abundance."

Continued on Page 14, Column 5

15-YEAR REIGN ENDS

British Monarch's Death at 56 Follows a Lung Operation Last Fall

PARLIAMENT HALTED

Churchill Conveys News to Commons—Attlee Suspends Party Strife

By RAYMOND DANIELL
Special to The New York Times.

LONDON, Feb. 6.—In the early hours of this morning George VI died peacefully in his sleep at the royal estate at Sandringham. As night fell upon this mourning capital of a still great family of nations, his elder daughter was proclaimed Queen of this realm and its dependencies, head of the British Commonwealth and the Defender of the Faith, with the title of Elizabeth II.

She is flying home tonight from her tragically interrupted visit to East Africa with her consort, the Duke of Edinburgh, and is expected back tomorrow to assume her royal duties as the wearer of the crown that somewhat mystically binds the British Commonwealth together.

Like the Elizabeth of England's golden age, she takes the throne at the age of 25.

Operated On 4 Months Ago

The King's death occurred just a little more than four months after an operation for the removal of a growth in his right lung. This operation resulted in the loss of the lung. His recovery seemed assured and in recent days he had been seen publicly at the theatre and at London Airport when he bade good-by to his daughter, now the Queen, as she set out with Prince Philip, her husband, on a journey that was to take her to East Africa, Australia and New Zealand, his favorite sport.

It was assumed that the King had died as a result of a heart attack, probably caused by coronary thrombosis.

Tributes to the late monarch poured into London from leading world figures and from persons of humbler station.

His death came in his 57th year. It was the beginning of the sixteenth year of an unhappy reign. He never wanted or expected the throne of Britain, but he ascended to it when his brother Edward VIII abdicated to marry "the woman I love," Wallis Simpson.

Six years of his reign were war years when he and Elizabeth, his Queen, who now becomes Queen Mother, endeared themselves to their people by their bravery and devotion to their predestined role. When he was crowned King on May 12, 1937, he was King-Emperor with the title of Emperor going with the granting of independence to India. His reign marked the end of an era of British power.

Parliament Is Suspended

His death also brought to an end this session of Parliament in the midst of a bitter and acrimonious debate on how far this country should go in aligning itself with United States policy in the Far East lest it be dragged into war. That debate, which began yesterday, was left in mid-air as Parliament put aside its controversies to swear allegiance to the new Queen and deferred its partisan arguments on controversial issues until a more seemly time.

At Sandringham when the King died there were his two grandchildren, whom he adored, Prince Charles and Princess Anne; Sir Harold Campbell, his equerry, and Lady Hyde, lady-in-waiting to his Queen. Soon after his death had been discovered by a servant bringing early morning tea, Dr. James Ansell, "Surgeon Apothecary" to the royal household at Sandringham, was called. He said that the King had died in his sleep without pain.

The news of the King's death did not go over the news tickers until 10:45 A.M. At 11:15 it was broad-

Continued on Page 13, Column 2

LONDON IS STILLED AS BRITONS MOURN

All Amusements Closed, Lights Dimmed, Streets Nearly Empty After News Stuns People

By FARNSWORTH FOWLE
Special to The New York Times.

LONDON, Feb. 6.—This was a silent city tonight, with bright lights dimmed and all places of entertainment closed, as Londoners went home shocked by the death of their King.

The news reached most office workers at noon when they went out for lunch and found venders of early editions of afternoon papers shouting "The King is dead!"

"What King!" was a typical first reaction. It was hard to believe that it was indeed their own monarch, even though it had been generally realized since the King's operation last September that he might not have many years to live. Only a week ago tonight he attended a performance of "South Pacific" at the Drury Lane Theatre.

The suddenness of the news contrasted with the memory of how the public had been prepared during the final illness of the King's father, George V, with a broadcast communiqué saying, "The King's life is moving peacefully to its close."

Flags at half-staff appeared on public buildings and many private ones by noon. Theatres, cinemas and night clubs all shut down, as did the Stock Exchange and other markets.

The laughter of London's usually cheerful office girls was muted as

Continued on Page 13, Column 6

Elizabeth Weeps at News of Death, But Is Calm in African Take-Off

By The United Press.

NAIROBI, Kenya, Feb. 6.—The local populace to spare the Young Queen Elizabeth II left Queen a further ordeal.

hurriedly for home by plane tonight only a few hours after her husband had broken the news to her of her father's death.

The 25-year-old former Princess, after having broken down in tears, was composed when she departed early tonight on the long flight to London.

With Prince Philip she left the hunting lodge where the royal couple had been staying and drove in a closed automobile eight miles to a small airport near the East African town of Nanyuki. She took off in an East African Airways C-47 from Entebbe in Uganda where the British Overseas Airways craft that had flown her to Africa waited to take her back to Britain.

The royal couple landed at Entebbe airport at 9:10 P. M. (1:10 P. M., Eastern standard time), but news of her arrival was kept from

A tropical thunderstorm at Entebbe delayed the departure of the Queen's plane for more than two hours, but it finally took off at 11:47 P. M. for Libya as the weather cleared.

[The plane made a stop at the Royal Air Force base at El Adem, Libya, landing there at 1:15 A. M., Thursday, Eastern standard time, the United Press reported.]

At El Adem and Malta the Royal Air Force had planes standing by to escort the Queen's plane over the Mediterranean. It is scheduled to reach London at 4:30 P. M. Thursday, Greenwich time (11:30 A. M., E. S. T.)

Crowds of all races and sorrowful persons of all races lined the main street of Nanyuki as the Queen's party passed through. The Queen, her face showing the strain of

Continued on Page 13, Column 8

"All the News That's Fit to Print"

The New York Times.

LATE CITY EDITION
Fair today; some cloudiness tonight. Becoming fair tomorrow.
Temperature Range Today—Max., 72; Min., 60
Temperature Yesterday—Max., 81; Min., 58
Full U. S. Weather Bureau Report, Page 39

Copyright, 1952, by The New York Times Company.

VOL. CI..No. 34,464.

Entered as Second-Class Matter,
Post Office, New York, N. Y.

NEW YORK, TUESDAY, JUNE 3, 1952.

Times Square, New York 36, N. Y.
Telephone Lackawanna 4-1000

FIVE CENTS

SUPREME COURT VOIDS STEEL SEIZURE, 6 TO 3; HOLDS TRUMAN USURPED POWERS OF CONGRESS; WORKERS AGAIN STRIKE AS MILLS ARE RETURNED

SWIFT SENATE VOTE ON BONN ACCORDS IS ASKED BY TRUMAN

Message Calls Defense Moves in Europe 'Great Forward Stride' Toward Peace

ACHESON REPORTS TO U. S.

Both President and Secretary Declare Soviet Measures Will Not Deter the West

Truman message and Acheson address are on Page 8.

By WALTER H. WAGGONER
Special to The New York Times.

WASHINGTON, June 2—President Truman urged the Senate today to approve two agreements putting West Germany on a footing of equality among nations and binding an enemy of World War II to the free world's defense alliance.

Asking for "early and favorable" action on the two pacts, signed by the diplomats of the Western Governments in Europe last week, the President, said in a message to the Senate that the documents taken together "constitute a great forward stride toward strengthening peace and freedom in the world."

Accompanying his message were the so-called peace contract with West Germany, an arrangement just short of a formal treaty, and an amendment to the North Atlantic Treaty that would extend its defense guarantees to the Bonn Government in return for reciprocal pledges. Both require approval by the Senate to become effective.

European Pact Also Sent

For the Senate's information, Mr. Truman also attached a number of other documents signed in either Paris or Bonn, the major one being the treaty constituting the six-nation European Defense Community that would bring West German troops into a European army.

[In Bonn, Germany, Dr. Kurt Schumacher, Social Democratic leader, began the Opposition's campaign against ratification of the defense arrangements. He said that under the present terms the Germans would bear the brunt of the burdens involved in those accords while the Western Allies would enjoy the benefits.]

Even before the President's message arrived, Senator Tom Connally, the Texas Democrat who heads the Senate Foreign Relations Committee, predicted that the Senate would give Mr. Truman the approval he sought.

The Senator's forecast was made on the basis of two hours of discussion, at a joint session of the Senate Foreign Relations and House Foreign Affairs Committees, with Secretary of State Dean Acheson.

Mr. Connally said that Mr. Acheson had assured the committees that "no secret or undisclosed commitments or guarantees" were made while he was on his European mission that produced the agreements.

Connally to Speed Action

The Senate's foreign policy spokesman said it was important that the treaties "go into effect as soon as possible" and he made it plain that he would do his part in speeding Senate action.

"In my view it is essential that Western Germany be accorded its proper place in the family of nations without delay so that we can proceed with the task of building the joint defense of the free world as rapidly as possible," he said in a statement.

Secretary Acheson, meanwhile, went directly to the American people for understanding and support of the new agreements, addressing the nation this evening by radio and television on the nature and necessity of the new line-up of allies.

As President Truman stressed the "very great stake" held by the United States in helping support and

Continued on Page 5, Column 2

Red Leader Named Premier of Rumania

By The United Press.

BUCHAREST, Rumania, June 2—The National Assembly proclaimed Gheorghe Gheorghiu-Dej as new Premier of Rumania today to succeed Dr. Petru Groza, who was named President of the republic.

M. Gheorghiu-Dej was named Premier by a unanimous vote. Dr. Groza, who had been Premier since March 6, 1945, was elected President of the Assembly, a post tantamount to President of the republic.

The Government changes followed a request from the former President, Dr. Constantin Parhon, that he be relieved of his functions so he could dedicate himself entirely to his scientific work.

The Assembly took no action regarding Mme. Ana Pauker.

[The Bucharest radio revealed last week that Mme. Pauker, Rumanian Foreign Minister, had

Continued on Page 13, Column 2

ALLIES TERM TRUCE UP TO FOE IN KOREA

Reds Are Told World Opinion Will Judge Refusal to Agree to New Poll of Captives

By LINDESAY PARROTT
Special to The New York Times.

TOKYO, Tuesday, June 3—Maj. Gen. William K. Harrison Jr., senior United Nations truce delegate, told the Communists today that the future of the armistice negotiations is now up to your side."

He warned the Chinese and North Koreans that the "court of world opinion" would judge their refusal to entertain the United Nations proposal that prisoners of war should be questioned by an impartial body in the presence of Communist representatives after a truce to determine how many wished to return to their former command.

General Harrison spoke during a thirty-minute session in the gravest warning given so far that the world would hold the Communists responsible for a delay in the truce and the failure of prisoners to return to their homes.

Outlining the proposal for "re-screening" of the prisoners, made after the enemy had challenged the result of an Allied poll that showed fewer than half the total

Continued on Page 2, Column 5

Another Prisoner on Koje Is Killed; Clark Set to Use Force on Captives

By GEORGE BARRETT
Special to The New York Times.

KOJE ISLAND, Korea, Tuesday, June 3—The accidental firing by an Allied soldier of a heavy machine gun near a prison stockade on this island killed one North Korean captive and wounded another this morning.

This mishap followed a statement yesterday by the new Far East Commander, Gen. Mark W. Clark, that Allied camp authorities were prepared to use "maximum force" to restore uncontested control over Communist captives.

An Army spokesman said that the North Korean who was killed had been standing near the barbed wire of Compound 78 when the machine gun went off. Other prisoners dragged the body farther inside the enclosure and refused to surrender it to United Nations medical personnel. They also refused to yield the wounded man for hospitalization.

An Army spokesman said that Brig. Gen. Haydon L. Boatner, camp commander, expressed concern over the accidental shooting, the second within a week at Koje.

Meanwhile, the prisoners resumed their demonstrations inside the enclosures, to which the camp command had attempted to put an end in them.

Gen. James A. Van Fleet, Eighth Army commander, who came with General Clark, compared the atmosphere in seventeen compounds with the prisoners' mood of only a few weeks ago and happily summed up the situation that way.

In a late development last night there was a sudden flare-up of resistance from Compound 60, where a group of North Koreans—there are about 200 prisoners in this compound on war crime charges—shouted taunts at a South Korean officer walking past the enclosure.

The South Korean listened at first to the taunting, but was fi-

on a flagpole and draped an imitation coffin with paper wreaths while General Boatner looked on from outside the barbed wire.

In Compound 602, according to pooled dispatches, the prisoners again erected the flagpole knocked down yesterday in a tank-led raid by United Nations guards, after the flying of the North Korean emblem had been forbidden. General Boatner told correspondents: "It will not be there very long."

Making his first visit to the troubled prison island yesterday, General Clark made it clear that the new United Nations policy of firmness might have taken so much starch out of the "die-hard" Communists that not much real fight was left in them.

An Army spokesman said that Communist 76 captive North Koreans held a mock funeral, presumably commemorating the five prisoners who were killed there last Friday. They hung black crepe

Continued on Page 2, Column 2

EISENHOWER YIELDS PAY IN RETIREMENT; FREE TO CAMPAIGN

He Leaves Army Duties Today—Waives $19,541 a Year to Avert Any Criticism

DECORATED BY PRESIDENT

Truman Hails Him as Symbol of Nation's Aim—General to Leave for Abilene

By JAMES RESTON
Special to The New York Times.

WASHINGTON, June 2—General of the Army Dwight D. Eisenhower has asked to be placed on the Army's retired list without pay, starting tomorrow. This request, which the Army said today had been approved by Secretary of Defense Robert A. Lovett, will release the general from the Army's regulations against political campaigning.

The current military appropriations legislation does not permit officers under the age of 62 to retire with pay unless the Department of Defense finds that this would cause personal hardship or be bad for the service.

[In South Dakota and California the final primaries will be held Tuesday, with the Dakota contest between General Eisenhower and Senator Robert A. Taft of Ohio attracting major attention. On the Democratic side, Senator Estes Kefauver is seeking delegates in both primaries. The Missouri Republican convention completed the formalities of naming a twenty-six-member delegation.]

General Eisenhower wrote to Mr. Lovett on May 28, asking that no special certification be made in his case, because his name was "directly involved in the national political campaign." The general, who is 61, would have been entitled to $19,541 a year in pay and allowances if, like General of the Army Douglas MacArthur, he had remained on the active list.

From his European headquarters, General Eisenhower wrote:

"There are a number of delegates already pledged to seek my nomination as the Republican Presidential candidate and, in the normal course of events, I will be talking to some of these delegates prior to the National Convention. As an officer on the retired list I would feel free to engage in such

Continued on Page 19, Column 1

Continued on Page 19, Column 1

TWO IMPORTANT STEPS YESTERDAY IN THE STEEL DISPUTE

Secretary of Commerce Charles Sawyer signing formal order returning nation's steel plants to owners.

Philip Murray, C. I. O. and steel union president, making call that sent 600,000 workers on strike.

Associated Press Wirephotos

REALTY TAX TO RISE 12 TO 15 POINTS HERE

Final Valuations Show Record City Rate of $3.08 Probably Will Soar to $3.21

By PETER KIHSS

A rise of twelve to fifteen points in the city's basic real estate tax rate of $3.08, already the highest in history, was forecast unofficially yesterday when the final valuations of taxable real estate and special franchises were set at $19,425,499,087 for the fiscal year beginning July 1.

The revised valuations were $58,392,794 less than the tentative valuations made public Feb. 1, but $648,742,541 above the final figure of $18,776,756,546 for the current tax year. The total was the second highest in the city's history, exceeded only by 1932's $19,616,-915,429.

While no city official would go on record with a tax forecast, pending a revised estimate of general fund revenues due from Controller Lazarus Joseph on June 20, the pencils flew at City Hall to make some approximations based on Mayor Impellitteri's budget message of April 1.

Mayor's Estimate of Need

The Mayor had estimated then that the new $1,469,265,102 expense budget would need a yield of $622,804,788 from real estate taxes. The Mayor reported that this was practically the maximum that could be levied on real estate within constitutional limitations.

Dividing this proposed yield by the final realty valuations would give a basic tax rate of nearly $3.21 for each $100 of assessed valuation, or thirteen points above the rate that has prevailed this year and last. Above this come borough rates, which this year have varied from 18 to 21 cents.

Municipal fiscal experts indicated this $3.21 basic tax rate approximation might still vary slightly, depending on revisions in the general fund. But they noted that the original general fund estimate had included $12,500,000 from an overnight parking tax, which the Mayor has been unable to get.

The main hopes in fiscal quarters appeared to be for rises in other general fund sources that might at least make up the loss from the parking tax estimate. In round numbers, each point in the city's real estate levy yields not quite $2,000,000.

The final realty valuations were transmitted to the Mayor by William E. Boyland, president of the seven-member Tax Commission. They showed ordinary real estate at $16,846,784,544, up $553,300,800 from last year; real estate of utility corporations at $1,738,-555,835, up $54,068,315, and special

Continued on Page 45, Column 7

600,000 Quit Steel Mills; Industry Offers to Bargain

By A. H. RASKIN
Special to The New York Times.

PITTSBURGH, June 2—The steel industry got its mills back today, but they were producing no steel. Six hundred thousand members of the United Steelworkers of America, C. I. O., quit work as soon as they learned that the Supreme Court had ruled that Government seizure of the steel plants.

Many did not wait even for formal strike orders from their union president, Philip Murray. They simply put aside their tools and streamed out of mills that normally produce 95 per cent of the country's steel. All who stayed were supervisors and maintenance men engaged in the orderly cooling of blast furnaces to prevent permanent damage to equipment.

[The text of Mr. Murray's strike order is on Page 22.]

Mr. Murray got word of the court's decision at luncheon in a hotel across from his Pittsburgh headquarters. He rushed back and wired all union locals to stop work.

His message said: "The act of the court leaves the members of the United Steelworkers of America without the benefit of a collective bargaining agreement. In the absence of a wage agreement, our members have no alternative other than to cease work."

Mr. Murray also called upon the major steel companies to renew contract negotiations on the basis of the wage increases and other benefits recommended by the Wage Stabilization Board.

Prompt Congressional action to meet the problem of the steel walkout was in doubt, however. Demands were made that the court's verdict be clinched, either by giving the President the powers he thought he had, or by writing into the Constitution a prohibition against the use of seizure powers without specific backing in law.

Committee Meets Tomorrow

A House Judiciary subcommittee that has on its docket a dozen or so measures to impeach Mr. Truman, to censure him or to give him powers or deprive him of them was scheduled to meet Wednesday. It appeared tonight that it might not recommend a censure on top of today's court defeat.

On the Senate calendar today was a bill that would amend the Constitution to bar the President from seizing any private property except under specific law.

This measure was "passed over." Its sponsor, Senator Pat McCarran, Democrat of Nevada and chairman of the Senate Judiciary Committee, was across the Plaza hearing the Supreme Court's decisions.

Senator Homer E. Ferguson, Republican of Michigan, obtained the Senate's unanimous consent for the McCarran bill to remain on the calendar with no prejudice.

A single objection, under the rules of the calendar, could block a proposed Constitutional amendment under this procedure.

Another measure, sponsored by Senator Wayne Morse, Republican of Oregon, would provide Presiden-

Continued on Page 22, Column 2

CONGRESS HAILS END OF STEEL SEIZURE

Some Demand Constitutional Curb on President—Censure of Truman Is Hinted

By C. P. TRUSSELL
Special to The New York Times.

WASHINGTON, June 2—Congress generally hailed today the Supreme Court's 6-3 decision holding President Truman's seizure of the steel industry unconstitutional.

Many at the Capitol held to the view that Mr. Truman still had ample legal power to invoke the Taft-Hartley Act, which he has sought unsuccessfully to have repealed, and to let its injunctions against strikes settle the problem. There was much speculation as to whether the President now would invoke that law.

Continued on Page 23, Column 7

NEXT MOVE IN CRISIS IS CALLED TRUMAN'S

President Could Use Taft Act or Appeal to Congress—No Word From White House

By ANTHONY LEVIERO
Special to The New York Times.

WASHINGTON, June 2—With steel workers walking out of mills all over the country in the wake of the decision of the United States Supreme Court nullifying the President's seizure of the industry, the next move was held to be up to Mr. Truman.

There was no indication from the White House tonight, however, as to what he might do. Meanwhile, Mr. Truman and his advisers were studying the seven opinions of the high tribunal.

Two obvious steps were presumably being considered by Mr. Truman.

The first would be to invoke the Taft-Hartley Act, which would require the union men to return to work for eighty days while a fact-finding board investigated the wage dispute. The other move might be a renewal of the plea that Mr. Truman addressed to Congress soon after the seizure for specific statutory authority to deal with labor disputes in major industries in time of emergency.

In the courts and in Congress Mr. Truman has been severely criticized for not having used Taft law that labor hates before he resorted to seizure. His answer has been that the steel workers had waited ninety-nine days while the Wage Stabilization Board studied the wage dispute. Furthermore

Continued on Page 23, Column 7

BLACK GIVES RULING

President Cannot Make Law in Good or Bad Times, Majority Says

VINSON IS DISSENTER

Rejects Idea Executive Is 'Messenger Boy' in Crisis—Steel Curbed

The majority opinion, Page 22; others in part, Pages 22 and 23.

By JOSEPH A. LOFTUS
Special to The New York Times.

WASHINGTON, June 2—The Supreme Court of the United States ruled, 6 to 3, today that President Truman's seizure of the steel industry to avert a strike violated the Constitution by usurping the legislative powers reserved to Congress.

The President bowed promptly by directing Secretary of Commerce Charles Sawyer to release the properties to their private owners, and the United Steelworkers of America, C. I. O., went on strike.

As a result of the walkout the Government ordered a halt in deliveries of steel from retail warehouses to consumer goods producers in an effort to conserve steel for defense needs.

Authorities said the action was directed at preventing a drain on warehouses by buyers who usually got their steel at the mills. Manufacturers who ordinarily receive steel from warehouses will continue to do so, they added. No order was issued against steel exports.

The Supreme Court justices who voted to uphold District Judge David A. Pine's order dispossessing the Government were: Hugo L. Black, Felix Frankfurter, William O. Douglas, Robert H. Jackson, Harold H. Burton and Tom C. Clark. Dissenting were: Chief Justice Fred M. Vinson and Justices Stanley F. Reed and Sherman Minton.

Founding Fathers' Action Cited

The court ruled in effect that when the President seized the steel mills he seized the lawmaking power, because only Congress could authorize the taking of private property for public use.

"The Constitution did not subject this law-making power of Congress to presidential or military supervision or control," said the opinion of the court, written by Justice Black.

"The founders of this nation entrusted the lawmaking power to the Congress alone in both good and bad times," it added. "It would do no good to recall the historic events, the fears of power and the hopes for freedom that lay behind their choice. Such a review would but confirm our holding that this seizure order cannot stand."

Chief Justice Vinson, writing a vigorous dissent, declared that the President's action to keep steel flowing was warranted by the current emergency.

"History bears out the genius of the founding fathers, who created a Government subject to law but not left subject to inertia when vigor and initiative are required," the Chief Justice wrote.

Vinson Criticizes Majority

"As the district judge stated this is no time for 'timorous' judicial action," he declared. "But neither is this a time for timorous executive action."

Chief Justice Vinson said the majority of the court, not the minority, was seeking to amend the Constitution. He declared:

"The broad Executive power granted by Article II to an officer on duty 365 days a year cannot, it is said, be invoked to avert disaster.

"Instead, the President must confine himself to sending a message to Congress recommending action. Under this messenger-boy concept of the office, the President cannot even act to preserve legislative programs from destruction so that Congress will have something left to act upon."

The court, contrary to a widely

Continued on Page 23, Column 5

Speedy Action by a Teller Foils Hold-Up in East 42d Street Bank

A would-be bank robber who escaped although three armed guards were near by was foiled yesterday in an attempt to hold up the Irving Trust Company at 100 East Forty-second Street by an alert 27-year-old teller, described by his superiors in the bank as a "guy with real guts."

This was the story as it was pieced together from accounts by the police of the East Thirty-fifth Street station and H. G. Brownson, vice president in charge of the bank's Forty-second Street office.

At 2:50 P. M., an hour and ten minutes before the bank's closing time, a man about 45 years old, dressed in a gray suit and wearing a dark felt hat, approached a teller's cage about 100 feet from the Forty-second Street entrance to the bank.

There were 125 employes on duty, including the armed guards, and fifteen persons at the bank

floor, which is in the second story of the Continental Can Building.

The cage then was occupied by Charles Lehanka of 460 Audubon Avenue, who had worked in the bank for a little over a year.

Without a word, the man handed to Mr. Lehanka a two-page note. The writing was a combination of lettering and script and was done in pencil on unlined paper.

Mr. Lehanka read only the first couple of sentences of the 138-word message. They said: "Don't press the alarm button if you value your life. Give me all the folding money you have in that cage."

At this point, Mr. Lehanka made a swift and courageous decision. He dropped to the floor and pressed the bank alarm, which sounded at Police Headquarters and

Continued on Page 26, Column 4

"All the News That's Fit to Print"

The New York Times.

LATE CITY EDITION
Fair and warm today and tomorrow.
Temperature Range Today-Max., 85; Min., 64
Temperature Yesterday-Max., 85; Min., 65
Full U. S. Weather Bureau Report, Page 20

VOL. CI..No. 34,503.

Entered as Second-Class Matter.
Post Office, New York, N. Y.

Copyright, 1952, by The New York Times Company.

NEW YORK, SATURDAY, JULY 12, 1952.

Times Square, New York 36, N. Y.
Telephone LAckawanna 4-1000

FIVE CENTS

EISENHOWER NOMINATED ON THE FIRST BALLOT; SENATOR NIXON CHOSEN AS HIS RUNNING MATE; GENERAL PLEDGES 'TOTAL VICTORY' CRUSADE

LONG U. N. AIR RAID POUNDS PYONGYANG AND REDS' BUILD-UP

Three-Wave Daylight Attack Is Followed by Smashing B-29 Blows at Night

NORTH'S CAPITAL AFLAME

Allied Land, Navy and Marine Fighter-Bombers Strike as Korea Truce Talks Drag On

By LINDESAY PARROTT
Special to The New York Times.

TOKYO, Saturday, July 12—Allied aircraft of many nations smashed yesterday at the North Korean capital at Pyongyang and the Communists' military build-up in western Korea in one of the largest and most devastating raids of the war.

Attacking in waves from 10 A. M. until late in the afternoon, the planes flew 1,200 sorties from ground bases and from the decks of United States and British carriers at sea.

Almost 600 tons of bombs fell on the daylight targets at Pyongyang and at Hwangju and Sariwon, on the rail line south of Pyongyang, where for months the Communist armies had stockpiled supplies of arms and munitions and placed military headquarters, communications centers and repair shops.

Meanwhile, the truce talks at Panmunjom continued, the secret sessions on the vexed prisoner question producing no indicated progress. A brief sitting was held this forenoon and another meeting was set for tomorrow.

Mass Night Strike

Last night, in what headquarters of the Far East Air Forces here called the "largest night air strike of the Korean conflict," B-29 Superforts from Japanese and Okinawan bases returned to the Communist capital in a new blow. The medium bombers also fanned out over North Korea, hitting supply concentrations at Hamhung, on the east coast; Kyomipo, near Pyongyang, and Sinmak, to the north.

Fifty-four of the B-29's unloaded 510 tons of high explosives over Pyongyang, still blazing from the attack of its fighter-bombers during daylight. Industrial plants, vehicle parks and repair shops were reported hit, with "excellent" results.

Sixty-three bombers participated in the attacks throughout North Korea, with major concentration over selected targets at Pyongyang. The clouds that moved in over the Pyongyang area during the afternoon had cleared at night and the bombardiers saw their projectiles fall in direct hits.

[Later, Far East Air Forces said one F-84 Thunderjet was lost in the day and night attacks. The Associated Press reported all the Superforts returned safely to base. The F-84 was shot down by Communist ground fire. The report did not cover Navy or Marine or other Allied planes.]

Reds' Radio Makes Claim

The Reds' Pyongyang radio, on the air a few hours after the daylight strikes, claimed ten Allied aircraft shot down.

No official estimate of the damage done in the day and night attacks had been made pending the study of aerial photographs taken from reconnaissance planes that followed close on the tails of the bombers.

Returning pilots spoke of huge secondary explosions that followed hits by bombs and rockets and big islands of fire raging last evening where hundreds of gallons of napalm—jellied gasoline—fell.

Pyongyang, the biggest railroad junction in North Korea, around which the enemy had built airfields, anti-aircraft positions and supply dumps and where some of the few remaining industrial targets north of the Thirty-eighth Parallel remained, was a mass of flames, observers said.

Pilots flying in the second wave of attack said smoke was rising thousands of feet from the Red

Continued on Page 2, Column 5

O'Dwyer Considers Staying in Mexico

By SYDNEY GRUSON
Special to The New York Times.

MEXICO CITY, July 11—Ambassador William O'Dwyer is seriously considering taking up permanent residence in Mexico when his job comes to an end.

All the Ambassador will say for public quotation at this time is that he has "made no definite plans" for the future. But he has recently told persons inquiring about his plans that settling down in Mexico is high among the possibilities.

The former New York Mayor celebrated his sixty-second birthday last Monday and in discussing the future, he has expressed concern for the financial security of his wife, the former Sloan Simpson, in the event of his death.

On his retirement from the mayoralty of New York to become Ambassador to Mexico, Mr.

Continued on Page 11, Column 5

STEEL LEADERS SEE UNION, THEN CONFER

Murray Awaits New Industry Offer in Pittsburgh—Talks Expected to Go On Today

By A. H. RASKIN
Special to The New York Times.

PITTSBURGH, July 11—Negotiations to end the crippling national steel strike waited on a new industry offer today.

After a ninety-minute meeting this morning with Philip Murray, president of the United Steelworkers of America, C. I. O., a committee representing the major steel and iron ore producers went to the headquarters of the United States Steel Corporation where they spent the afternoon in private conference with other steel company officials.

No report came from the closely guarded industry session, but there was hope that the committee would emerge with a new peace proposal to put before the union tomorrow.

Mr. Murray announced at 8:30 P. M. that no further joint meetings would be held today but that it was "reasonable" to expect there would be an industry-union meeting tomorrow.

"We did meet with the industry today, and that's that," the union leader said.

Leaders on both sides refrained

Continued on Page 23, Column 6

$445,560,000 SOUGHT FOR NEW SUBWAYS BY TRANSIT BOARD

Second Avenue Network and 2 Brooklyn Extensions Put Before Estimate Body

BENEFITS DESPITE DEFICIT

Traffic Relief Seen—Costs of Operation 17 to 20% Above Revenue Conceded

By PAUL CROWELL

The Board of Transportation authorized yesterday, subject to approval of the Board of Estimate, eight subway construction projects in Manhattan, Brooklyn, Queens and the Bronx with a total estimated cost of $445,650,000.

The projects listed were six routes of the Second Avenue trunk line, with connections with existing subway lines, and the proposed extensions of the Utica Avenue and Nostrand Avenue I. R. T. subway lines in Brooklyn. The cost of the Second Avenue project was estimated at $363,500,000, including $41,000,000 for equipment. The two Brooklyn extensions were estimated to cost $82,150,000, including $13,990,000 for equipment.

The proposals would include also a subway link-up in the form of a new line from Fifty-third Street and Avenue of the Americas to East Seventy-sixth Street and Second Avenue and thence running under the East River to Woodside Avenue and Thirty-eighth Avenue in Queens.

Not in Use Before 1957-58

In a report to the Board of Estimate the transit agency expressed the belief that ground for the eight projects could not be broken before next fall. It was indicated that the operation of the Second Avenue trunk line and its connections could not begin before 1958 and that of the two Brooklyn extensions before 1957.

The transit agency's report admitted that audition of the Second Avenue line and the two Brooklyn extensions to the existing rapid transit system would create an enlarged subway network unable to earn operating expenses under a 10-cent fare.

"The most desirable benefits to be derived from the proposed routes," the report said, "are those which will be realized by the mil-

Continued on Page 29, Column 3

THE 1952 STANDARD-BEARERS OF THE REPUBLICAN PARTY

Gen. Dwight D. Eisenhower, for President

Senator Richard M. Nixon, for Vice President
Associated Press Wirephotos

TAFT GIVES WINNER HIS PLEDGE OF AID

Pair Exchange Compliments in Cordial Chat but Supporters of Ohioan Are Bitter

By LEO EGAN
Special to The New York Times.

CHICAGO, July 11—General of the Army Dwight D. Eisenhower and Senator Robert A. Taft today had their first face-to-face meeting since the Republican convention opened and exchanged mutual professions of esteem and respect in an obvious effort to allay factional bitterness within the Republican party.

Senator Taft, his brother, Charles P. Taft, Republican candidate for Governor of Ohio, and David S. Ingalls, who managed the Senator's pre-convention campaign, all pledged themselves during the day to use their full influence to persuade the Senator's friends to give full support to the convention winner.

Usually it is the loser who calls upon the winner, but General Eisenhower reversed the custom to make a personal call on Senator Taft soon after the nomination and to bespeak the Ohioan's help in the campaign ahead.

Senator Taft, with three of his four sons standing beside him, received the general in his headquarters' suite at the Conrad Hilton Hotel and offered his congratulations. Later the two fought their way, with the help of a detail of Chicago police, into the entrance hall of the Taft headquarters where television and newsreel cameras had been set up and newspaper reporters and photographers were waiting.

General Praises Taft

As soon as he could make himself heard, Senator Taft stepped before the microphones and said:

"I want to congratulate General Eisenhower. I shall do everything possible in the campaign to secure his election and to help in his administration."

General Eisenhower, flashing the grin he has made famous, then turned to the crowd, jammed shoulder-to-shoulder in the hall, and said:

"I came over to pay a call of friendship on a very great American. His willingness to cooperate is absolutely necessary to the success of the Republican party in the campaign and in the Administration."

General Eisenhower's statement brought a chorus of cheers from Taft followers, who slightly outnumbered the reporters and television crews in the hall. Earlier, when the general first arrived, he had been greeted by a mixture of cheers and boos, followed by a "We want Taft" chant.

Obviously disturbed by the boo-

Continued on Page 6, Column 1

Nominee Asks Unity at Home And Just, Sure Peace Abroad

By JAMES RESTON
Special to The New York Times.

CONVENTION BUILDING in Chicago, July 11—General of the Army Dwight D. Eisenhower accepted the Republican Presidential nomination tonight and summoned his party to a "great crusade" for "total victory" over the Democrats in November.

[Text of Eisenhower speech of acceptance is on Page 4.]

Likening his new assignment to the historic "crusade" he led against Nazi Germany, the 61-year-old retired five-star general pledged himself to "a program of progressive politics" designed to produce unity at home and peace abroad.

To the obvious delight of a convention audience, many of whose members have feared that he would not conduct a fighting campaign against the Administration, General Eisenhower defined his first aim:

"To sweep from office an Administration which has fastened on every man of us the wastefulness, the arrogance and corruption in high places; the heavy burdens and anxieties which are the bitter fruit of a party too long in power."

The initial break that started the chain of events that led to the nomination of General Eisenhower came even before the convention opened last Monday when the Taft-dominated Republican National Committee and its pro-Taft chairman, Guy George Gabrielson, refused to permit television, radio and motion picture coverage of the committee's hearing on delegate contests. The committee had even barred newspaper photographers from the hearings where previous Republican conventions.

Eisenhower Took Control

The result was that every television and radio chain in the country filled the air with protests against what they called an "Iron Curtain" on the committee's proceedings, demanded free access to the hearings and stressed that it was supporters of Senator Taft who had imposed the ban over the objection of supporters of General Eisenhower. This television and radio barrage proved very damaging to Senator Taft's candidacy.

With supporters of Senator Taft in control of the National Committee and its Committee of Arrangements for the convention, the Eisenhower campaign managers not only overcame this handicap but in test votes involving contests in Georgia, Louisiana and Texas, took control of the convention and went on to nominate General Eisenhower.

Continued on Page 5, Column 1

VICTORS' STRATEGY OUTPACED RIVALS

Action on Doubtful Delegate Issue and on TV Ban Took Lead From Taft's Men

By JAMES A. HAGERTY
Special to The New York Times.

CHICAGO, July 11—General of the Army Dwight D. Eisenhower won the Republican nomination for President because the members of his board of strategy completely outmaneuvered the supposedly adroit group of politicians who managed the campaign of Senator Robert A. Taft of Ohio.

Control of the G. O. P. was vital, he said, and especially to put in places of power such men as Senator Robert A. Taft of Ohio. General Eisenhower's defeated antagonist for the Presidential designation.

It was only with a Republican Congress, Mr. Nixon declared, that the Republicans could successfully unite us to carry out progressive

Continued on Page 6, Column 2

Democrats Respond to Eisenhower By Urging Liberal as His Opponent

Democratic party leaders in various parts of the country reacted yesterday to the Presidential nomination of General of the Army Dwight D. Eisenhower on the Republican ticket by emphasizing the need for a liberal nominee to oppose the general.

Although many prominent Democrats, including Averell Harriman, Senator Estes Kefauver of Tennessee and Senator Richard B. Russell of Georgia, were outspoken in their views, President Truman, who stayed close to his television set in Washington watching the Republican proceedings in Chicago, maintained silence.

Mr. Truman had only one scheduled engagement yesterday forenoon, setting aside most of his time for studying the Republican situation.

Senator Robert S. Kerr of Oklahoma, a candidate for the Democratic Presidential nomination, had this to say about the winning of General Eisenhower:

"General Eisenhower will find

as did [Wendell] Willkie and [Thomas E.] Dewey before him that no matter how hard he tries to escape it the Republican party's record will be a handicap greater than he can overcome. After Nov. 4 he will be a sadder but wiser general."

At Springfield, Ill., Gov. Adlai E. Stevenson said he had no comment on the nomination of General Eisenhower. He reiterated this as an assertion that he was not a candidate for the Democratic nomination.

The labor plank in the Republican platform adopted in Chicago yesterday came under attack from the International Association of Machinists, an independent union. A. J. Hayes, the president, sent telegrams, before General Eisenhower was nominated, to the two leading Republican candidates denouncing the platform as "unfriendly to labor" and adding:

"The Republican party has long had the reputation of being the

Continued on Page 10, Column 3

REVISED VOTE 845

Minnesota Leads Switch to Eisenhower and Others Join Rush

BUT SOME HOLD OUT

First Call of the States Gave General 595 to 500 for Taft

First ballot with revised vote is printed on Page 6.

By W. H. LAWRENCE
Special to The New York Times.

CONVENTION BUILDING in Chicago, July 11—General of the Army Dwight D. Eisenhower won a hard-fought first-ballot nomination today as the Republican candidate for President and Senator Richard M. Nixon of California was chosen by acclamation as his running mate for the Vice-Presidency.

The former Supreme Allied Commander in Europe went before the 1,206 Republican delegates tonight to accept the nomination and pledge that he would lead "a great crusade" for "total victory" against a Democratic Administration he described as wasteful, arrogant and corrupt and too long in power. He said he would keep "nothing in reserve" in his drive to put a Republican in the White House for the first time since March 4, 1933.

Senator Nixon, who is 39 years old, was the choice of all the leaders who supported his senior on the 1952 Republican ticket, General of the Army Dwight D. Eisenhower, and was, of course, acceptable to the general.

Accepting the nomination in a short speech to the Republican National Convention tonight, Senator Nixon put in a strong appeal for the election of a Republican Congress.

Control by the G. O. P. was vital, he said, and especially to put in places of power such men as Senator Robert A. Taft of Ohio, General Eisenhower's defeated antagonist for the Presidential designation.

It was only with a Republican Congress, Mr. Nixon declared, that the Republicans could

Bitterly Divided Convention

General Eisenhower won in a bitterly divided Republican convention. In the last week the general had taken leadership in the contest from Senator Robert A. Taft of Ohio, the chief party spokesman in Congress, who was making his third unsuccessful bid for nomination to the office once held by his father, William Howard Taft.

Victory came for General Eisenhower on the first ballot. The official results gave 845 for General Eisenhower, 280 for Senator Taft, 77 for Gov. Earl Warren of California, and 4 for General of the Army Douglas MacArthur.

But that figure did not represent truly voting sentiments of these delegates as they faced the crucial and final showdown between General Eisenhower and Senator Taft.

When the first roll-call of the states was completed, General Eisenhower had 595 votes—nine short of the required majority of 604—and Senator Taft had 500. The balance of power rested with favorite-son candidates, such as Governor Warren, who had 81 votes, and Harold E. Stassen, former Minnesota Governor, with 20. General MacArthur had received only 10 votes.

Others Then Changed

And while Governor Warren's California delegation held firm for him in the hope of a deadlock, Mr. Stassen's Minnesota delegates, no longer bound because he had received less than 10 per cent of the vote, broke away and cast nineteen votes for General Eisenhower before a first ballot result could be announced.

The nineteen, added to the General's previous total, gave him 614, or ten more than a majority. Then other states began to change their votes in order to be recorded on the side of the winner.

Thus, while General Eisenhower's nomination later was made unanimous on the motion of principal backers of Senator Taft and Governor Warren who pledged their support for their principals to the nominee, it was made clear that General Eisenhower was the choice of a divided convention, and that one of his first tasks would be to restore party unity and heal the deep wounds inflicted during the

Continued on Page 7, Column 1

NIXON, ACCEPTING, URGES G.O.P. SWEEP

Senator Was Selected Without Opposition—His Record and Youth Strong Factors

Text of acceptance speech by Senator Nixon, Page 4.

By WILLIAM S. WHITE
Special to The New York Times.

CONVENTION BUILDING in Chicago, July 11—Senator Richard Milhous Nixon of California was nominated without opposition today as the Republican candidate for Vice President of the United States.

The whole proceeding required less than half an hour.

Senator Nixon, who is 39 years old, was the choice of all the leaders who supported his senior on the 1952 Republican ticket, General of the Army Dwight D. Eisenhower, and was, of course, acceptable to the general.

Accepting the nomination in a short speech to the Republican National Convention tonight, Senator Nixon put in a strong appeal for the election of a Republican Congress.

Control by the G. O. P. was vital, he said, and especially to put in places of power such men as Senator Robert A. Taft of Ohio, General Eisenhower's defeated antagonist for the Presidential designation.

It was only with a Republican Congress, Mr. Nixon declared, that the Republicans could successfully unite us to carry out progressive

Continued on Page 6, Column 2

Freed American Tells of Drugging With 'Truth Medicine' in China

By HENRY R. LIEBERMAN
Special to The New York Times.

HONG KONG, July 11—Robert T. Bryan, China-born American lawyer who was held incommunicado for sixteen and a half months as a political prisoner in a Shanghai jail, said today that his Communist captors had drugged him with two injections of "truth medicine" to extract an acceptable "confession" and a separate statement denouncing the United States State Department.

Mr. Bryan, who served as municipal advocate for the Shanghai International Settlement from 1928 to 1941, was arrested Feb. 14, 1951.

He was subsequently accused of espionage and also charged with responsibility for extradition proceedings in which Communist political operatives had been turned over to the Nationalist Government during the days of extraterritoriality.

"They blindfolded me, put me on a table and stuck something in my arm," he said in describing the first drug injection. "After about ten or twenty minutes when they sat me down, I felt I was sitting in mid-air.

"I wrote something, but I do not remember what happened. It took my volition away. I awoke the next morning with a terrific hangover."

This was the first report by a released political prisoner that he would have been drugged by the Chinese Communists to elicit a "confes-

sion." It raised immediate speculation about the "confessions" of Lieut. John Quinn and Lieut. Kenneth E. Enoch, the captured American fliers who were represented by the Peiping Government as having admitted the dropping of "germ bombs" in Korea.

In addition to the American military prisoners captured by the Chinese Reds in Korea, thirty-seven American civilians are officially listed here as being imprisoned in China. Thirteen more are reported to be under house arrest.

Mr. Bryan, who has resided in China about forty-five of his fifty-nine years, and who was also interned during World War II, said he underwent his first drug injection last April, after two of his "confession" drafts had been pronounced unacceptable. He said the second was administered last month, when he again failed to satisfy his interrogators after having received the option of "establishing merit" either by denouncing his friends or criticizing the State Department.

"I wrote something about the Foreign Service Act of 1946, but I did not like that, so I was again blindfolded and doped again," he recalled. "Later, when they showed me my signature, I told them I would repudiate anything obtained by drugs. They said no, this could

Continued on Page 2, Column 3

157

The New York Times.

Copyright, 1952, by The New York Times Company.

VOL. CI..No. 34,517.

Entered as Second-Class Matter, Post Office, New York, N. Y.

NEW YORK, SATURDAY, JULY 26, 1952.

Times Square, New York 36, N. Y. Telephone LAckawanna 4-1000

FIVE CENTS

STEVENSON IS NOMINATED ON THE THIRD BALLOT; PLEDGES FIGHT 'WITH ALL MY HEART AND SOUL'; TRUMAN PROMISES TO 'TAKE OFF COAT' AND HELP

MOSSADEGH HINTS AT NEW ENDEAVOR TO SOLVE OIL ISSUE

Iranian Premier Tells Nation That 'Solution of Problem' Has Now Become 'Easier'

EARLY REFORMS PLEDGED

Government Leader Confers With Communists—Feeling Against U. S. Mounts

Special to The New York Times.

TEHERAN, Iran, July 25 — Premier Mohammed Mossadegh told the nation in a radio broadcast tonight that the tangled oil problem had taken a turn for the better and that therefore he was resolved to initiate and carry out reform measures and to take fundamental speedy steps he believed the country direly needed now.

[The Associated Press reported that the Premier made his statement in these words: "In view of the fact that a solution to the oil problem now is easier, I intend to institute reforms which the country needs. These reforms can take place only in a calm atmosphere. So long as there is disorder, there is no opportunity for any kind of improvements."]

Dr. Mossadegh summoned George Middleton, British Chargé d'Affaires, to his office. They conferred for more than two hours. The purpose of the visit has not been disclosed but Mr. Middleton said that a guess that it concerned oil would not be far wrong.

Dr. Mossadegh's internal authority is now unchallenged and the decision of the International Court of Justice that the Anglo-Iranian oil complaint was outside its jurisdiction improved considerably his international situation in approaching the oil issue. Speculation naturally is to the effect that Mr. Middleton may seek again some type of solution of the oil problem.

Mossadegh Sees Communists

Dr. Mossadegh sees the leaders of the Tudeh Communist organization, which now calls itself the Association to Combat Imperialism, the subject obviously was the relation between the Government and the National Front on one hand and Communist leaders on the other after their cooperation in last Monday's violent events, which drove Ahmad Ghavam from power.

In his radio address to the nation the Premier said:

"My dear compatriots, you will admit that no social reforms can be carried out without the existence of security forces. The maintenance of peace and the security is the first condition of positive acts of the Government.

"The offenses and encroachments of some members of the security forces may have induced you to look askance on the entire security forces, but with the formation of a national government there is no reason why this suspicion should continue to exist.

Continued on Page 3, Column 5

U. S. Olympian Sets Steeplechase Mark

By ALLISON DANZIG

Special to The New York Times.

HELSINKI, Finland, July 25 — Horace Ashenfelter won today the fastest 3,000-meter steeplechase race ever run for the United States' twelfth gold medal in track and field and its first Olympic victory ever in this event.

In the remarkable time of 8 minutes 45.4 seconds, 18.4 seconds under the Olympic record that has stood in the books since 1936, the 29-year-old Penn State graduate from Glen Ridge, N. J., ran away from the world's best to win by thirty yards as the first eight to finish excelled the old mark.

Vladimir Kazantsev of Russia, the favorite, who shadowed the special agent of the Federal Bureau of Investigation virtually all the way until he stumbled in

Continued on Page 16, Column 1

Snag on Iron Ore Pay Blocks Order to Reopen Steel Mills

600,000 Union Men Await Pact for Miners —Fairless and Murray Plan to Visit Plants to Promote Labor Harmony

By A. H. RASKIN

Special to The New York Times.

WASHINGTON, July 25 — The longest and most costly steel strike in the country's history was officially called off today, but an unexpected snag over wage rates for 23,000 iron ore miners blocked the sending of union back-to-work orders to 600,000 striking steel workers.

The last-minute difficulty, which both sides hoped would blow over in a few hours, cast a shadow over settlement arrangements that had indicated the steel dispute might provide a foundation for a new era of cooperative labor-management relations in the industry that represents the backbone of the American economy.

With only one dissenting vote, the 175-man Wage Policy Committee of the United Steelworkers of America, C. I. O., voted this afternoon to accept the settlement terms agreed upon at the White House yesterday by Philip Murray,

president of the union, and Benjamin F. Fairless, president and chairman of the United States Steel Corporation.

The agreement, which was personally announced by President Truman, provided a wage increase of 16 cents an hour, retroactive to last March 1; paid holidays, higher shift differentials and other "fringe" benefits that would cost 5.4 cents an hour more, and a modified union shop.

The agreement specified that iron-ore miners were to get all the same benefits, plus additional wage increases intended to bring their pay scales up to the steel level.

It was this provision that caused the difficulty today.

Under the agreement part of the difference in wage rates was to be made up at once and the rest at the end of the first year of the

Continued on Page 30, Column 5

U. N. Truce Team Walks Out Of Korea Talks for a Week

By LINDESAY PARROTT

Special to The New York Times.

TOKYO, Saturday, July 26 — The United Nations delegates walked out of the new plenary sessions at Panmunjom today and told the Communists they would return in a week for further discussion of an armistice in the Korean war.

The senior Allied delegate, Maj. Gen. William K. Harrison Jr., led the United Nations representatives out of the conference tent after the enemy delegation had devoted much of the first of a new series of meetings to a violent repetition of charges against the United Nations Command. The two sides agreed, however, that during the week's adjournment staff officers would meet to see what could be done to draft new tentative armistice terms as a basis for further discussion.

Pooled dispatches from Korea said General Harrison was shaking with anger as he left the roadside tent, where the Chinese and North Koreans, after the breakdown of the last three weeks'

Continued on Page 2, Column 3

6 AIDES OF FAROUK RESIGN AFTER COUP

5 High-Ranking Police Officials Jailed as Maher Cabinet Acts Speedily in Egypt

By The Associated Press.

CAIRO, July 25 — Gen. Mohammed Naguib Bey's Army-backed governmental house-cleaning reached to King Farouk's own palace today. Six of the monarch's top aides resigned.

At the same time Egypt's new strong man moved anew to crush opposition to the military coup by which he had installed the anti-corruption Government of Premier Aly Maher Pasha.

Maher Pasha's new Cabinet took over today, pledged to try to end the crisis that has swept this Middle East country for six months. The Cabinet hopes to end the corruption that, according to Maher Pasha, had brought the crisis about and to settle Egypt's dispute with Britain over the Suez Canal and the Sudan.

Police Officials Arrested

General Naguib Bey flew to Alexandria for a conference with Maher Pasha, leaving behind him a series of arrests. Among those held were five high-ranking political and police officials who were accused of conspiring against the public safety, an army communiqué said. Twelve generals of the Egyptian Army also were in custody.

The officials held included Maj. Gen. Mousif Mahmoud Pasha, Under Secretary of the Interior Ministry; the commandant of the Cairo police, the director of a special section of the Interior Ministry and two high officers of the political section of the police.

The communiqué said: "Although we have detained these few people * * * a much larger number of army men have been arrested." Maj. Gen. Sirry Amer Bey, commander of Egypt's frontier corps, was arrested at Salum, on the Egyptian-Libyan border, and returned to Cairo.

General Naguib Bey received an ovation when he called on the new Premier. While they conferred for an hour, a crowd outside cheered and called the general "Protector of Egypt."

After the conference he told newsmen that his aim was to assure the people of Alexandria

Continued on Page 3, Column 5

PRESIDENT IN FORM

Talks in 'Whistle Stop' Manner, Predicting Ticket's Victory

HITS AT EISENHOWER

Says 'People Will Not Choose Man Without Faith in People'

Text of the President's speech at the Convention, Page 4.

Special to The New York Times.

CONVENTION BUILDING in Chicago, Saturday, July 26—President Truman told a cheering Democratic National Convention early this morning that it had nominated a winner in Gov. Adlai E. Stevenson of Illinois.

The President promised that he would "take off my coat and go out to help him win."

In a direct attack on Gen. Dwight D. Eisenhower, the Republican Presidential nominee, Mr. Truman declared that the "people won't choose a leader who does not have faith in the people." He said he did not think the country would be turned over to men "who are more concerned with cutting the budget than with the security of the United States."

This was a reference to General Eisenhower's pre-nomination pledge to reduce the Federal budget by $40,000,000,000 under certain conditions.

How to Win Elections

Mr. Truman started to speak at 1:42 A. M., after a four minute ovation. He reminded the delegates that four years ago at about the same hour in the morning he had predicted victory for the ticket headed by himself and Senator Alben W. Barkley of Kentucky for Vice President.

"But you didn't believe me," said the President with a grin. "I'm telling you now that Adlai Stevenson will win in 1952."

The President said that the real reason Democrats won elections "is perfectly simple—it is because they give the American people the kind of Government they want."

"The Republicans," he declared, "are going to throw millions of dollars into an attempt to confuse

Continued on Page 8, Column 8

GOVERNOR ACCEPTS

Humility Marks Speech by Nominee Before Cheering Delegates

HE HAILS PLATFORM

Illinoisan in Tribute to Losing Candidates— Bids for Unity

Text of the acceptance speech by Mr. Stevenson, Page 5.

By JAMES RESTON

Special to The New York Times.

CONVENTION BUILDING in Chicago, Saturday, July 26—Gov. Adlai E. Stevenson of Illinois, in a speech marked both by humility in the face of the high honor and by a vigorous determination in the face of its challenge, early today accepted the Democratic nomination for President.

"I will fight to win that office with all my heart and soul," he told the cheering delegates. "With your help, I have no doubt that he will win."

Earlier, the "no" man from the Lincoln country, had for the first time said "yes."

"I did not seek it. I did not want it," he said a moment after he had been nominated by the Democratic National Convention.

"The call, he continued, "asked of me nothing except that I give such talents as I have to the services of my country. That I will do."

"I feel no exaltation or sense of triumph whatever, nothing but humility. I shall go on my knees and I shall ask my God to give me strength and courage and to nourish my spirit for this great undertaking in this great hour of history."

At the outset, he said, he had never been "more conscious of the appalling responsibility of office."

He went immediately to the convention hall from the home on Chicago's "Gold Coast" where he made his short statement.

The 52-year-old Governor developed this same solemn theme after he had been driven at breakneck speed through the late night traf-

Continued on Page 5, Column 3

THE DEMOCRATIC STANDARD-BEARER

Associated Press Wirephoto
ADLAI E. STEVENSON

300-VOTE SWITCH DECIDES CONTEST

Harriman's Withdrawal Swings Big State Blocs on Third Ballot to the Governor

Harriman statement, Kefauver and Russell talks, Page 4.

By FELIX BELAIR Jr.

Special to The New York Times.

CONVENTION BUILDING in Chicago, Saturday, July 26—A sudden switch of more than 300 votes gave Gov. Adlai E. Stevenson of Illinois a third-ballot victory and the Democratic Presidential nomination here early today after Averell Harriman had announced his withdrawal from the contest and New York, Pennsylvania, Massachusetts, Michigan and Arkansas had swung in behind the choice of President Truman.

The race came out just as predicted by the managers of Governor Stevenson's floor campaign. Paul E. Fitzpatrick, the New York State party chairman, took the speaker's platform after a dinner recess to announce Mr. Harriman's withdrawal. Massachusetts' favorite son, Gov. Paul A. Dever, followed with the announcement to the convention that he, too, was withdrawing in favor of Governor Stevenson.

Mr. Fitzpatrick's statement in behalf of Mr. Harriman was followed much later in the session by speeches by Senator Estes Kefauver of Tennessee and Senator Richard B. Russell of Georgia, both conceding the nomination to the Illinoisan.

With the Harriman and Dever switches there were more than 100 votes right there to be added to Governor Stevenson's second ballot total of 423½. When Michigan switched its 40 votes from Senator Estes Kefauver it remained only for Pennsylvania to bring along the stragglers by giving the Governor all its 70 votes, a net gain of 30.

Texas held out with its big 52-vote bloc, as did other delegations favoring Senator Russell but the die was already cast.

Senator Kefauver came up the center aisle of the auditorium on the arm of Senator Paul H. Douglas of Illinois in an attempt to gain the platform to announce his plan to nominate Senator Douglas, who was not in nomination but who would then have withdrawn and urged all Kefauver delegates to vote for Governor Stevenson. But Speaker Sam Rayburn, the convention's permanent chairman, ruled that the balloting must proceed.

Governor Stevenson was within a few votes of the required 615½ majority when the roll-call of the states ended and Speaker Rayburn gave to Tennessee the first oppor-

Continued on Page 5, Column 1

LEADERS IN HUDDLE ON VICE PRESIDENCY

Balloting Is Postponed Until Noon Today as Kefauver Foes Present Objections

Special to The New York Times.

CONVENTION BUILDING in Chicago, Saturday, July 26—Democratic party leaders went into a huddle early today immediately following the Presidential nomination of Gov. Adlai E. Stevenson for talks on the Vice Presidency.

The National Convention put off its choice until a noon session. The original program had called for selection of Governor Stevenson's running mate after his acceptance speech.

It was understood that the delay stemmed principally from some objections to Senator Estes Kefauver of Tennessee, who forged to the top of the "guess" list after he dramatically yielded in the Presidential race.

A late starter among the possibilities was Representative John W. McCormack of Massachusetts. Others mentioned were Vice President Alben W. Barkley, Senator John J. Sparkman of Alabama, Secretary of the Interior Oscar L. Chapman and Senator Richard B. Russell of Georgia.

Among those in the huddle at the near-by Stockyards Inn were Averell Harriman, who last night withdrew from the Presidential race, and Jake Arvey of Chicago, Governor Stevenson's principal backer in Illinois.

Regarding the possibility of taking the post, Senator Kefauver said:

"I haven't been offered the place and I really don't believe I would want to accept it. I haven't talked

Continued on Page 8, Column 7

Two Coalitions Won Stevenson's Victory

By JAMES A. HAGERTY

CHICAGO, Saturday, July 26—The strategy used by supporters of Gov. Adlai E. Stevenson to get him the Democratic nomination for President, like the horns of a dilemma, had two prongs.

First, by a coalition with supporters of Senators Richard B. Russell of Georgia and Robert S. Kerr of Oklahoma, they brought about the seating of the Virginia, Louisiana and South Carolina delegations, which declined to take the loyalty pledge imposed by the Credentials Committee as a condition of participation in the convention.

Governor Stevenson was within a few votes of the required 615½ majority of the convention.

Having formed this temporary alliance with the conservative Southern delegates and lessened

Continued on Page 6, Column 8

RIVALS DROP OU[T]

Withdrawal of Harrima[n] Starts States' Rush to the Governor

ILLINOISAN TRAILE[D]

But Picked Up Strengt[h] From Larger States— Got C. I. O. Backing

The three ballots of Convention are printed on Page 6.

By WILLIAM S. WHITE

CONVENTION BUILDING i[n] Chicago, Saturday, July 26—Go[v.] Adlai E. Stevenson of Illinois wa[s] nominated early today on the thir[d] ballot for President of the Unite[d] States by the thirty-first Democratic National Convention.

President Truman came here to salute him and to stand with him before the delegates.

Mr. Truman, cheerful and smiling, declared to the Convention:

"I'm telling you now Adlai Stevenson is going to win in 1952 * * * I am going to take my coat off and do everything I can to help him win."

Governor Stevenson told the delegates that he could never have sought such an honor, and adding:

"I have asked the merciful Father of us all to let this cup pass from me. But from such dread responsibility one does not shrink in fear, in self-interest, or in false humility."

"So," he went on, quoting from the Bible, "'if this cup may not pass away from Me, except I drink it, Thy will be done'."

Huge Demonstration

Mr. Truman walked, as an enormous demonstration beat the walls of this hall, the length of the platform to greet Mr. Stevenson and take him to face the crowd.

The convention adjourned at 2:35 A. M. (3:35 A. M., New York time), to meet again at 11 A. M.

Governor Stevenson's nomination — the first genuine draft since the Republicans demanded and got James A. Garfield in 1880 — came after the withdrawal of Averell Harriman of New York had turned the great bulk of that delegation to the Stevenson standard. Then Senator Estes Kefauver of Tennessee put over the Stevenson selection. Tennessee cast its 28 votes for the Governor, who was then a handful short of the required 615½ needed for a majority in a total of 1,230.

'Did Best We Could'

Senator Richard B. Russell of Georgia, after Mr. Stevenson's nomination, pledged to join in efforts for a party victory in November.

Senator Kefauver told the convention that it had been "quite apparent" that someone here had to yield. His intention, he said, had been to nominate Senator Paul H. Douglas of Illinois and Senator Douglas had intended in turn to give his favor to Governor Stevenson.

But this had been made impracticable by the Stevenson rush, Mr. Kefauver said, in effect, so he was amiably retiring. It had been a good fight, he observed, "and we did the best we could."

Senator Kefauver, it appeared, was heading instead for the Vice Presidential nomination. The selection for Vice President was scheduled to be made today.

Mr. Stevenson to the end had not been a candidate.

Four aggressive aspirants—Mr. Harriman, Senator Kefauver, Senator Russell and Senator Robert S. Kerr of Oklahoma—had struggled with the Stevenson draft movement until it became apparent that there was to be no stopping it. Senator Kerr had retired early—before dinner-time last night—when his own Oklahoma delegation had left him, obviously his consent, though he did not make it formal until nearly midnight.

Mr. Harriman's announcement of retirement from the race came after Mr. Truman, the Stevenson backer, had arrived here. The

Continued on Page 5, Column 1

CONVENTION-BOUND PRESIDENT VOTES BY PROXY

Associated Press Wirephoto
At the precise moment Mr. Truman was waving farewell at the Washington Airport before starting for Chicago in his plane . . . . . . Thomas J. Gavin was casting his vote as the President's alternate on the convention floor in support of Adlai E. Stevenson.

"All the News That's Fit to Print"

The New York Times.

ELECTION EXTRA

Fair, warmer today. Some cloudiness and turning cooler tomorrow.
Temperature Range Today—Max. 62; Min. 38
Temperature Yesterday—Max. 52; Min. 30
Full U. S. Weather Bureau Report, Page 14

VOL. CII No. 34,619.

Entered as Second-Class Matter,
Post Office, New York, N. Y.

Copyright, 1952, by The New York Times Company.

NEW YORK, WEDNESDAY, NOVEMBER 5, 1952.

Times Square, New York 36, N. Y.
Telephone LAckawanna 4-1000

FIVE CENTS

EISENHOWER WINS IN A LANDSLIDE; TAKES NEW YORK; IVES ELECTED; REPUBLICANS GAIN IN CONGRESS

G.O.P. HOUSE LIKELY

But the Senate Margin Hangs in the Balance of Two Close Races

LODGE TRAILING RIVAL

President Eisenhower May Lack a Working Majority in Congress

By JAMES RESTON

It appeared at 4:30 this morning that control of the United States Senate could be determined by the outcome of the Senatorial races in Michigan and Massachusetts.

At that time the Republicans appeared to have picked up five new seats and lost three others, thus enabling them to wipe out the two-seat advantage held by the Democrats at the end of the Eighty-second Congress.

To assure the power to organize the Senate and place their Republicans at the head of its important committees, however, Senator Henry Cabot Lodge Jr., Republican of Massachusetts, would have to overcome an advantage of more than 75,000 held by Representative John F. Kennedy, his opponent.

And Representative Charles E. Potter, Republican of Michigan had to retain the 47,000 lead he held over the Democratic incumbent, Senator Blair Moody of Michigan.

Morse May Be Vital

So close was the Senate race that there was a possibility that control of the upper chamber could be determined by the decision of Senator Wayne Morse of Oregon, who was elected as a Republican, but who broke with his party during the campaign, and announced that hereafter he was an "independent."

Though it appeared that the Republicans had won control of the House, one thing was certain: that President Dwight D. Eisenhower would not have a comfortable working majority in either house and would require all his gifts of persuasion to win consent for his policies on Capitol Hill.

Several factors in the Senate race were noteworthy.

Of the ten so-called isolationist or extremist Republicans who were before the voters yesterday, seven seemed fairly sure of victory. These were Senators Joseph R. McCarthy of Wisconsin; John W. Bricker of Ohio; William E. Jenner of Indiana; Edward Martin of Pennsylvania; Arthur V. Watkins of Utah, George W. Malone of Nevada and Hugh Butler of Nebraska.

Three other Republicans in this same category, however, were in serious trouble if they had not actually been defeated. They were:

Continued on Page 15, Column 1

M'Carthy Is Winner, But Is Last on Ticket

By RICHARD J. H. JOHNSTON
Special to THE NEW YORK TIMES.

MILWAUKEE, Wednesday, Nov. 5—Wisconsin went to the Republicans today for the third time in a national election since 1920.

The predicted Republican sweep of the state and capture of its twelve electoral votes became a certainty a few minutes after midnight.

Gen. Dwight D. Eisenhower, the Republican Presidential nominee ran second on the G. O. P. ticket with Gov. Walter J. Kohler Jr. leading the slate in his bid for re-election.

As the returns from the final count, Gen. Dwight D. Eisenhower's vote indicated he would emerge as leader of the G. O. P. slate in Wisconsin, with 2,036 of the state's 3,324 voting precincts reported, his vote was 554,389 to Gov. Adlai E. Stevenson's 366,218. Gov. Walter J. Kohler, seeking

Continued on Page 23, Column 6

Electoral Vote by States

	Eisenhower's son		Eisenhower's son
Ala. ..	11	Neb. ..	6
Ariz. ..	4	Nev. ..	3
Ark. ..	8	N. H. ..	4
Calif. ..	32	N. J. ..	16
Colo. ..	6	N. M. ..	4
Conn. ..	8	N. Y. ..	45
Del. ..	3	N. C. ..	14
Fla. ..	10	N. D. ..	4
Ga. ..	12	Ohio ..	25
Idaho ..	4	Okla. ..	8
Ill. ..	27	Ore. ..	6
Ind. ..	13	Pa. ..	32
Iowa ..	10	R. Isl. ..	4
Kan. ..	8	S. C. ..	8
Ky. ..	10	S. D. ..	4
La. ..	10	Tenn. ..	11
Me. ..	5	Texas ..	24
Md. ..	9	Utah ..	4
Mass. ..	16	Vt. ..	3
Mich. ..	20	Va. ..	12
Minn. ..	11	Wash. ..	9
Miss. ..	8	W. Va. ..	8
Mo. ..	13	Wisc. ..	12
Mont. ..	4	Wyo. ..	3
		Total..	442 89

*Trend.

EISENHOWER TAKES JERSEY BY 300,000

Senator Smith Is Re-elected—Bond Issues Supported in Record Balloting

By RUSSELL PORTER

With more than three-quarters of New Jersey's vote counted early this morning, Gen. Dwight D. Eisenhower appeared headed toward a plurality of close to 300,000 in the state over Gov. Adlai E. Stevenson. This far exceeded Governor Dewey's 1948 plurality of 83,669 over President Truman.

United States Senator H. Alexander Smith, Republican candidate for re-election, won a sweeping victory over his Democratic opponent, Archibald S. Alexander, though Mr. Smith ran behind the head of his ticket. His indicated plurality was about 200,000.

The returns were:

PRESIDENT
3,461 precincts out of 3,840:
Eisenhower 1,203,120
Stevenson 921,375

UNITED STATES SENATOR
3,399 precincts out of 3,840:
Smith 1,089,883
Alexander 903,533

The Republicans appeared to have retained their majority of nine to five in New Jersey's delegation in the House of Representatives.

Both bond issues on the ballot

Continued on Page 23, Column 2

STATE LEAD 850,000

General's Upstate Edge Tops Million—He Loses City by Only 362,674

PROTEST VOTE SEEN

Albany County, Other Areas in Democratic Column Switch

By JAMES A. HAGERTY

Gen. Dwight D. Eisenhower, Republican nominee for President, carried New York State with its forty-five electoral votes with a plurality of landslide proportions that will reach nearly 850,000.

With 33 election districts missing, all outside this city, General Eisenhower led Gov. Adlai E. Stevenson, his Democratic opponent, by an actual plurality of 846,020 and an indicated plurality of 840,034.

To carry his adopted state by this astounding plurality, General Eisenhower held Governor Stevenson down to an actual plurality of 362,674 in this city, far less than the supporters of the Democratic candidate expected.

With the 33 election districts missing, General Eisenhower carried the state outside the city by an actual plurality of 1,265,789 and, assuming that his vote held up in the missing districts, by an indicated plurality of about 1,270,000.

State Presidential Vote

CITY SUMMARY

	Eisenhower (Rep.)	Stevenson (Dem.-Lib.)
Manhattan ...	300,234	447,877
Bronx	241,545	393,052
Brooklyn	447,148	656,278
Queens	449,505	331,633
Richmond	55,981	28,247
Total	1,494,413	1,857,087
Upstate	2,413,299	1,147,510
Grand total .	3,907,712	3,104,597

4,384 election districts out of 4,384 in the city reporting and 5,222 out of 5,954 upstate.

Governor Stevenson carried Manhattan by 147,633, the Bronx by 151,597 and Brooklyn by 209,130, all far below Democratic expectations. General Eisenhower carried Queens by 117,872 and Richmond by 27,834, well above

Continued on Page 24, Column 3

Hill Battle Spurts in Korea; Allies Press 'Triangle' Fight

By LINDESAY PARROTT
Special to THE NEW YORK TIMES.

TOKYO, Wednesday, Nov. 5—The hard-fighting South Korean infantry, driving for the third time in three days up the slopes of the central Korean ridges, drove a penetration today into the Communist lines on the western flank of "Triangle Hill," a strategic position north of Kumhwa.

Early this afternoon, the Republic of Korea (R. O. K.) troops had captured one of the twin peaks that project from "Triangle"—named "Jane Russell Hill." The sharp, indecisive combat continued.

The attack on the twin peaks was tied in with a new drive against the central pyramid of "Triangle Hill." The South Koreans again thrust within yards of the crest.

The Chinese Reds struck again just to the east in a new attempt to capture the summit of "Sniper Ridge," flanking "Triangle" on the United Nations' right.

The crest of "Triangle" had been lost to the Chinese Communists after the United Nations limited objective offensive took it last month. The South Koreans pushed up southern slopes today after being within fifty yards of the Reds' lines.

Some reports said the fighting again today was as furious as during the attacks Sunday and Monday, when the South Koreans desperately struggled to regain the positions.

Allied warplanes were out against the enemy guns. About fifty sorties had been flown by Fifth Air Force fighter-bombers before noon against Red artillery on high Papasan Mountain, the Communists' strongpoint just to the north of the central front.

At every opportunity, Allied guns pounded the Reds on the crest of "Triangle."

The Reds' guns dropped 5,000 rounds on the front-line positions near "Heartbreak Ridge" and the "Punchbowl" in the mountainous eastern watershed, where the heaviest fighting of yesterday occurred. A North Korean battalion hit Allied defense positions on "Heartbreak" on the heels of the barrage, but the enemy failed to make a penetration.

On "Triangle Hill" and the twin peaks to the west of it, contact was light yesterday. At least temporarily, the South Koreans broke off attempts to storm two positions they had lost to the Chinese Reds' counter-attacks, after the United Nations limited objec-

Continued on Page 5, Column 2

New President and Vice President

DWIGHT D. EISENHOWER

RICHARD M. NIXON

The New York Times

IVES IS RE-ELECTED BY RECORD MARGIN

Defeats Cashmore by Biggest Plurality of Any Republican—Harding Mark Topped

Vote for Senator

CITY SUMMARY

	Ives (Rep.)	Cashmore (Dem.)	Corsi (Lib.)
Manh'n ..	303,040	322,157	88,797
Bronx ..	233,548	277,506	101,014
B'klyn ..	398,498	522,751	147,370
Queens ..	429,225	265,812	62,558
Rich'd ..	51,939	28,742	2,044
Total .	1,416,250	1,416,968	401,783

Up-state 2,399,770 1,099,842 52,259

Gr Totl 3,816,020 2,516,810 454,042

4,394 election districts out of 4,394 in the city reporting and 5,854 out of 5,954 up-state.

By LEO EGAN

Senator Irving M. Ives won re-election in a three-cornered race yesterday by the largest plurality ever obtained by a Republican candidate in New York State, topping President Warren G. Harding's record-setting margin of 1,069,929 in 1920 by more than 200,000 votes.

The former majority leader of the State Assembly and co-sponsor of New York's law against racial discrimination in employment thus became the first Republican Senator to win re-election in New York since the late Senator James W. Wadsworth performed that feat in the Harding landslide of 1920.

Not only did Senator Ives carry the normally Republican upstate area by a plurality that may reach 1,297,972, but he came within 718 votes of capturing normally Democratic New York City as well.

The complete Senate vote in the city gave Senator Ives 1,416,250 to 1,416,968 for Borough President John Cashmore of Brooklyn, the Democratic candidate. Thus Mr. Cashmore's plurality within the city was held to 718 votes.

With 5,854 of the 5,954 districts outside the city totaled, Senator Ives had an actual plurality of 1,299,928. On this basis, his final up-state margin should reach 1,350,000.

Dr. George S. Counts, the Liberal party candidate, polled 454,042 votes in the same districts tabulated for Senator Ives and Mr. Cashmore. On this basis his final vote could reach 460,000. Corliss Lamont, the American Labor can-

Continued on Page 21, Column 2

Eisenhower Cracks South, Heads for Victory in Texas

By WILLIAM S. WHITE

Gen. Dwight D. Eisenhower, the Republican Presidential candidate, has smashed the traditionally Democratic Solid South in his national victory over Gov. Adlai E. Stevenson. He has carried outright Florida and Virginia, with their twenty-two electoral votes, winning by a margin of nearly 130,000 votes over Mr. Stevenson in final returns from the 169 cities and towns in the state.

This morning unofficial observers gave him the greatest Southern prize of all—Texas and its twenty-four electoral votes, the sixth biggest slice in the United States.

Confirmation of this indicated loss would involve a Democratic disaster.

Apart from all this and from receiving the greatest popular ballot ever given a Republican in the South, General Eisenhower was narrowly trailing this morning in Tennessee, which has eleven electoral votes. In Tennessee, the position was so close that the result probably would not be known until late this afternoon.

In Louisiana and South Carolina Governor Stevenson had slight margins trailing often in the early returns.

The victory astounded Republicans as well as Democrats. Prior to the election, Republican leaders had made cautious claims of victory by about 25,000 or 30,000 votes, while Democrats privately thought they had a chance to win the state.

The tremendous Eisenhower sweep carried two Republican United States Senators into office with him, Senator William A. Purtell of West Hartford defeated William Benton, Democrat, for the full, six-year term by a margin of 90,286, and Prescott S. Bush, Greenwich banker, defeated Representative Abraham A. Ribicoff of Hartford, Democrat, by 30,373 votes. Mr. Ribicoff made a spectacular uphill run but was edged out by Mr. Bush's lead in the small towns that are traditionally Republican.

CONNECTICUT G.O.P. SEATS 2 IN SENATE

Benton and Ribicoff Concede to Purtell and Bush While Eisenhower Sweeps State

Special to THE NEW YORK TIMES.

HARTFORD, Conn., Wednesday, Nov. 5—Gen. Dwight D. Eisenhower swept to an amazing landslide victory in Connecticut yesterday, winning by a margin of

Final returns were:

PRESIDENT
169 precincts out of 169:
Eisenhower 610,989
Stevenson 481,482

UNITED STATES SENATOR
(For six-year term)
169 precincts out of 169:
Purtell (R.) 575,445
Benton (D.) 485,159

(For Four-year Term)
169 precincts out of 169:
Bush (R.) 559,586
Ribicoff (D.) 529,213

The Eisenhower sweep enabled the Republicans to win five of the six seats from Connecticut in the House of Representatives, a gain

Continued on Page 23, Column 1

GENERAL APPEALS FOR UNITED PEOPLE

He Vows Not to Give 'Short Weight' as President—Thanks Rival for Pledge

By WILLIAM R. CONKLIN

A jubilant Gen. Dwight D. Eisenhower accepted his election as President early this morning with a pledge to the American people that he would not give "short weight" in the execution of his new responsibilities in Washington.

With his wife by his side, the Republican President-elect told 2,000 campaign supporters in the grand ballroom of the Commodore Hotel at 2:05 A. M. that it would take the support of a united people to carry his Administration to success in its efforts to build a "better future for America."

His remarks were carried by radio and television to all parts of the country.

He read a message he had sent a few minutes before to his defeated rival, Gov. Adlai E. Stevenson of Illinois, thanking him for his promise of assistance. General Eisenhower expressed hope that Americans of both parties would speedily forget campaign bitter-

Continued on Page 20, Column 2

RACE IS CONCEDED

Virginia and Florida Go to the General as Do Illinois and Ohio

SWEEP IS NATION-WIDE

Victor Calls for Unity and Thanks Governor for Pledging Support

By ARTHUR KROCK

Gen. Dwight D. Eisenhower was elected President of the United States yesterday in an electoral vote landslide and with an emphatic popular majority that probably will give his party a small margin of control in the House of Representatives but may leave the Senate as it is—forty-nine Democrats, forty-seven Republicans and one independent.

Senator Richard M. Nixon of California was elected Vice President.

The Democratic Presidential candidate, Gov. Adlai E. Stevenson of Illinois, shortly after midnight conceded his defeat by a record turnout of voters.

At 4 A. M. today the Republican candidate led in forty-one states with a total of 431 electors, or 165 more than the 266 required for the selection of a President. The Democratic candidate seemed sure of 59, with 31 doubtful in Kentucky, Louisiana and Tennessee.

General Eisenhower's landslide victory, both in electoral and popular votes, was nation-wide in its pattern, extending from New England—where Massachusetts and Rhode Island broke their Democratic voting habits of many years—down the Eastern seaboard to Maryland, Virginia and Florida and westward to almost every state between the coasts, including California.

General Wins Illinois

The Republican candidate took Illinois, Governor Stevenson's home state. In South Carolina, though he lost its electors on a technicality, he won a majority of the voters. And, completing the first successful Republican invasion of the states of the former Confederacy, the General carried Texas and broke the one-party system in the South.

The personal popularity that enabled him to defeat Senator Robert A. Taft of Ohio in the Republican primaries in Texas, and present him with the issue on which he defeated the Senator for the Republican nomination, crushed the regular Democratic organization of Texas that was led by Speaker Sam Rayburn of the House of Representatives and had the blessing of former Vice President John N. Garner.

The tide that bore General Eisenhower to the White House, though it did not give him a comfortable working majority in either the national House or the Senate (the Democrats may still nominally control the machinery of that branch), probably increased the number of Republican governors beyond the present twenty-five.

"My fellow citizens have made their choice and I gladly accept it," said Governor Stevenson at 1:46 A. M., Eastern standard time, as he asked all citizens to unite behind the President-elect. The defeated candidate said he had sent a telegram of congratulation to General Eisenhower.

At 2:05 A. M., from the Grand Ballroom of the Commodore Hotel, General Eisenhower said he recognized the weight of his new responsibilities and that he would not give "short weight" in their execution. He also urged "unity" and announced he had sent a telegram of thanks to the Democratic candidate for his support.

The issues of the unusually vigorous campaign that was waged

Continued on Page 14, Column 3

Stevenson Concedes the Victory As Weeping Backers Cry 'No, No'

By WILLIAM M. BLAIR
Special to THE NEW YORK TIMES.

SPRINGFIELD, Ill., Wednesday, Nov. 5—Gov. Adlai E. Stevenson conceded defeat early today to his Republican opponent, Gen. Dwight D. Eisenhower, and pledged the support "he will carry to carry out the great tasks that lie before him."

The Governor came from the Executive Mansion to the Democratic Headquarters in the Leland Hotel to make his announcement before a jammed ballroom of supporters, many of whom broke into tears and cried, "No, no."

Governor Stevenson said:

"General Eisenhower has been a great leader in war. He has been a vigorous and valiant opponent in the campaign. These qualities will now be dedicated to leading us all through the next four years."

"It is traditionally American to fight hard before an election.

"It is equally traditional to close ranks as soon as the people have

spoken. From the depths of my heart I thank all of my party, and all of those independents and Republicans who supported Senator Sparkman and me."

The Governor said he had dispatched to General Eisenhower in New York a telegram which he read. It said:

"The people have made their choice and I congratulate you. That you may be the servant and guardian of peace and make the dale of trouble a door of hope is my earnest prayer. Best Wishes.

Adlai E. Stevenson."

Governor Stevenson, with a grin, however, for the crowd and displayed his ever-present humor to reporters. Asked how about 1956, the next presidential election year, he echoed in a low voice and with mock surprise "'56! Examine that man's head."

As for his immediate plans, he

Continued on Page 16, Column 2

The New York Times.

Copyright, 1953, by The New York Times Company.

VOL. CII...No. 34,709. — Entered as Second-Class Matter, Post Office, New York, N. Y. — NEW YORK, TUESDAY, FEBRUARY 3, 1953. — Times Square, New York 36, N. Y. Telephone LAckawanna 4-1000 — FIVE CENTS

EISENHOWER FREES CHIANG TO RAID MAINLAND; BIDS CONGRESS VOID ALL 'SECRET' PACTS ABROAD; WOULD END CONTROLS; OPPOSES TAX CUTS NOW

EUROPE STORM TOLL EXCEEDS 1,400 DEAD AS FLOODS SUBSIDE

296 Die Along British Coast —Thousands Still Missing as Help Is Speeded

DUTCH COUNT 955 KILLED

Million in Netherlands Affected —Belgian Area Battered —Dunkirk Hard Hit

By TANIA LONG

LONDON, Tuesday, Feb. 3—As the gales abated and the raging waters of the North Sea began to recede, three nations counted their dead today and assessed the damage resulting from their worst flood disaster in recent history.

Hard hit were Britain, the Netherlands and Belgium, where tidal waves swept across large sections of the coast Saturday night and early Sunday, breaking through dikes and seawalls and swallowing entire towns and villages.

[The Associated Press said the known dead in the storm area totaled more than 1,400 early Tuesday. In the Netherlands, 955 persons drowned. The toll in Britain stood at 443, including 296 killed in floods along the east coast, 132 who lost their lives in the sinking of the ferry Princess Victoria in the Irish Sea and fifteen lost on a missing trawler. Belgium had twenty-two dead.]

Several thousand persons were still missing, and it was feared that the death roll would mount heavily as rescue squads, made up of policemen, military personnel and civilian volunteers, completed their search of the devastated areas. On Canvey Island in the Thames Estuary, for example, where there were 100 dead, 500 men, women and children were still unaccounted for. Several thousand persons were evacuated from Canvey, which suffered by far the greatest damage of any British community.

Mobilize Full Resources

When the whole magnitude of the disaster that struck most heavily at Britain and the Netherlands was realized, the full resources of the two countries were quickly mobilized to give aid in the emergency. At the same time, assistance was sped to the Netherlands from France, Belgium and Denmark, and the United States forces in Europe, which also had their casualties.

The Swiss Red Cross Society announced it would begin an immediate collection of money for the British and Dutch flood victims, and there were offers of assistance, financial or material, from many other European countries and the United States.

In the meantime, the two nations worst affected put into action emergency plans to deal with the thousands rendered homeless by the floods. In Britain, civil defense plans prepared against a possible atomic attack were put into operation to shelter and feed the dispossessed.

Government Sends Help

The Government ordered its storehouses opened and sent thousands of blankets, mattresses and other items to the distressed areas, while the women's voluntary services brought out their trucks and set into motion the Flying Food Convoys, organized during World War II and kept in reserve against the possible outbreak of another conflict.

While evacuation of many thousands was being carried on, engineers in Britain and the Netherlands began their battle to restore the broken dikes and sea walls. Using sandbags, logs and other material readily available, they filled the gaps in an effort to halt a further influx from the sea.

There was still danger that the combination of winds and high tides that caused the original disaster might bring further flood

Continued on Page 4, Column 3

REGISTER TODAY, OVER 1,200 Credit Courses for Adults. Columbia University, School of General Studies, UN 5-4000.—Advt.

Ships Arrive, Depart On Own in Tug Strike

Cargo and passenger vessels berthed and departed on their own power yesterday in New York, Philadelphia and Norfolk as the three-port strike of towboat crews continued without signs of a break.

Mild winds and calm waters here made it possible for most ships to dock or leave the harbor without the aid of tugs. A few inbound vessels, however, were held up at anchorage and several scheduled to leave were unable to do so.

Longshoremen shaped up and worked as usual. It had been feared that they might abstain from work in sympathy with the 3,500 strikers, who are members of Local 333 of the Marine Division of the International Longshoremen's Association, A. F. L.

One result of the strike was an interference with garbage dis-

Continued on Page 29, Column 4

A.F.L. ACTS TO END PIER UNION ABUSES

Breaking Traditional Policy, Its Council Orders Inquiry— Hogan Subpoenas Ryan

By A. H. RASKIN

MIAMI BEACH, Feb. 2—Acting to stamp out racketeering in its ranks, the American Federation of Labor took two sharp breaks today with its tradition of noninterference in the internal affairs of its affiliated unions.

Its executive council set up a committee of three federation vice presidents to consider means of cleaning up the gang-infested International Longshoremen's Association. The committee began its work at once and it was indicated that it would submit its report to the council within forty-eight hours.

[District Attorney Frank S. Hogan announced in New York Monday night that he had issued a grand jury subpoena for the appearance at a 2 o'clock Tuesday afternoon of Joseph P. Ryan, president of the International Longshoremen's Association.]

The council also called on another affiliated union, the United Automobile Workers, to revoke the charter of a New York local headed by a convicted extortionist. If the automobile union refuses to comply, the council has the power to recommend that it be expelled from the federation at the next annual convention.

In a third action at the opening of its mid-winter meeting at the Monte Carlo Hotel here, the executive council set Feb. 24 as the date for resumption of formal peace talks between the A. F. L. and the

Continued on Page 29, Column 1

Southeast Britain's Coast Lifeless And Awash as Seen From Plane

By THOMAS F. BRADY

LONDON, Feb. 2—A vast coastal region of southeastern Britain lay submerged by salt water today, as the Romans found it 2,000 years ago. Seen from the air the land was awash and lifeless.

This report was written after a survey flight in a little Consul plane over Essex and Suffolk where the army took several hundred lives Saturday night and Sunday. The scene from the air was a tragic disorder.

Miles of glistening gray water were broken by brown roofs of houses, telephone poles still tied together by wires, the gun barrels of an anti-aircraft battery, and, along the course of the Thames, reminders of industry and commerce—black oil tanks, stretches of raised railroad track, a long factory roof with a smokeless stack.

Above the Thames Estuary, thirty-five miles from London, the plane circled low over Canvey Island, where forty-eight hours earlier 13,000 persons had had their homes. Lower still a helicopter hovered, examining upper windows of houses for signs of life. The only other movement came

Continued on Page 4, Column 6

BRITAIN IS ANXIOUS

Makes Representations to U.S. on the Effects of Formosa Policy

PARLIAMENT AROUSED

Churchill Defers Debate Till Today, When Eden Will State Policy

By JAY WALZ

WASHINGTON, Feb. 2—Britain has made representations to the United States about President Eisenhower's decision to allow the Chinese Nationalists to raid the China mainland.

Anthony Eden, British Foreign Secretary, who is to make a statement on the subject before the House of Commons tomorrow, communicated with the State Department today.

It is understood that he advised diplomatic officials here that the British Government believed the new order to the Seventh Fleet would greatly complicate the political situation both in Europe and in the Far East.

In his communication, Mr. Eden is believed to have argued that the new order would intensify the Chinese civil war, raise the fears of a general war in the Far East and thus make any general settlement in the Far East even more difficult.

Bradley Discounts Risk

General of the Army Omar Bradley, chairman of the Joint Chiefs of Staff, said tonight that President Eisenhower's new policy on Formosa did not increase greatly the chances of the United States' becoming involved in a "big war" in the Far East.

The Eisenhower Administration contends that the United States, while intending no aggressive move, cannot permit its Navy, as the President put it, "to serve as a defensive arm of Communist China" by continuing its neutralizing function between the Nationalists and the Communists.

Some diplomatic sources feel that Britain's concern over developments may reflect general uneasiness among United States Allies in Europe over the direction of United States foreign policy.

Among these were British Embassy officials, who withheld comment pending Mr. Eden's statement in Parliament tomorrow.

However, F. S. Tomlinson, an Embassy counselor, cited an Assistant Secretary of State John M. Allison last Saturday to express "concern" over reports of President Eisenhower's decision about

Continued on Page 11, Column 2

DELIVERS FIRST STATE OF UNION MESSAGE: President Eisenhower addressing a joint session of Congress yesterday. In background are Richard M. Nixon, Vice President, and Speaker of the House Joseph W. Martin Jr.

The New York Times (by Bruce Hoertel)

RED BLOW STOPPED BY SOUTH KOREANS

650-Man Attack on the Eastern Front Repulsed — Sabres Down Two Enemy Jets

By The Associated Press.

SEOUL, Korea, Tuesday, Feb. 3—North Koreans launched a 650-man attack on the eastern Korean front today, but stout South Korean defenders repulsed the assault and pursued the Communists across the craggy No Man's Land in below-zero cold.

The Korean Communists attacked at 12:45 A. M. across one mile of the mountainous front. They threw three companies into this attack and mounted two diversionary attacks of platoon size to the east.

Moving up under cover of a 650-round artillery and mortar barrage, the main force drove within forty yards of the main South Korean defenses.

The bitterly resisting South Koreans mounted a counter-attack at 2 A. M., drove off the Reds and chased them back across the snow-clad hills. An Eighth Army staff officer reported an estimated fifty-five of the enemy were killed.

Sabres Down Two MIG's

TOKYO, Tuesday, Feb. 3—Sabre jets of the United States Fifth Air Force shot down two Soviet-designed MIG jet fighters over northwest Korea yesterday, probably destroyed another and damaged two more, while fighter-bombers and high-velocity tank-mounted guns hammered at the enemy-entrenched line across the peninsula.

Twelve Sabres clashed with eight MIG's in dogfights that ranged from 50,000 feet to 500 feet altitude, and from the Yalu River to Changchon on the west coast. The two kills were credited to Col. James K. Johnson and Maj. Foster I. Smith.

Meanwhile, more than 100 fighter-bombers, continuing the pattern of saturation raids on selected targets, plastered a big enemy troop concentration and storage area south of Chinnampo, part of the North Korean Communist capital at Pyongyang and supply and communications hub on the main route to the western front. The planes leveled forty buildings, returning pilots said, and set off six large secondary explosions, indicating that ammunition storage areas had been hit.

Other fighter-bombers flying along the front lines knocked out

Continued on Page 5, Column 2

Capehart Moves to Retain Controls on Stand-By Basis

By CLAYTON KNOWLES

WASHINGTON, Feb. 2—Opposition cropped up today in an influential Republican quarter to President Eisenhower's proposal to let price and wage controls die on April 30 without maintaining stand-by machinery to reimpose them if needed.

Senator Homer E. Capehart of Indiana, chairman of the Senate Banking and Currency Committee, introduced a bill to set up such machinery within a few minutes after the President made his point known in his State of the Union Message.

He did not challenge the President's belief that price-wage controls had outlived their present usefulness but he did question the possibility of enacting a controls law quickly if one should be needed again.

"It is the height of impracticability," Mr. Capehart said, "to expect that the Congress can do a proper job of legislating a good controls law into effect in a period of less than three months, or for such a law to begin properly functioning within seven months from the incidence of the request for the legislation."

He maintained that inaction during this enforced waiting period would promote hoarding, scare buying and indiscriminate spending, all of which contribute to inflation. He said this was precisely what happened after the outbreak of hostilities in Korea. Before a

Continued on Page 15, Column 4

CIVIL RIGHTS PLANS GET WIDE SUPPORT

Challenge to McCarthy Seen on Security Issues — Duel Over Immigration Looms

By WILLIAM S. WHITE

WASHINGTON, Feb. 2—President Eisenhower appeared to please nearly all the political center in Congress today by the civil rights, loyalty and immigration policies laid down in his State of the Union Message.

The Left Wing at some points and the Right Wing at other points were made far from happy, for varying reasons.

The prospect raised was that the President could count upon at least as much Democratic support as Republican support—and perhaps more—for his approach in these fields, which encompass some

Continued on Page 17, Column 1

Convicted Communists Snub Offer To Go to Russia Instead of Prison

By EDWARD RANZAL

Thirteen secondary Communist leaders got the chance yesterday to go to Russia as an alternative to going to prison for criminal conspiracy to teach and advocate the overthrow of the United States Government by force and violence. The offer was made by Federal Judge Edward J. Dimock.

Defense counsel and several of the defendants emphatically rejected the proposal, terming it "intolerable" and "unpalatable." Elizabeth Gurley Flynn, one of the thirteen, declared:

"We feel we belong here and have a political responsibility here. We feel we would be traitors to the American people if we turned our backs on them just to escape jail."

Judge Dimock also said he would not impose the maximum sentence of five years and $10,000 fine on the thirteen. However, United States Attorney Myles J. Lane recommended that the max-

imum sentence be imposed on each.

The actual sentencing was postponed until today by Judge Dimock after oral barrages by twelve of the thirteen defendants. At 4:40 P. M., after the court had been advised that in addition to the remaining defendant four defense attorneys would add to the voluminous record of the nine-and-a-half month trial, Judge Dimock adjourned court.

The first suggestion that Judge Dimock had an alternative plan came when the jurist asked Mr. Lane what he thought of the idea of permitting the defendants to go voluntarily to Russia rather than serve a prison sentence. Mr. Lane said he had no objection if the defendants first served their prison terms, then headed for the Soviet Union.

Then, after Miss Flynn had ad-

Continued on Page 8, Column 3

STATE OF THE UNION

President Sees No 'Logic or Sense' in Sea Patrol Helping Chinese Reds

HIS 'POSITIVE POLICY'

Reciprocal Trade Pacts, Aid to Europe Backed in Congress Message

Text of the State of the Union Message, Pages 14 and 15.

By ANTHONY LEVIERO

WASHINGTON, Feb. 2—President Eisenhower today ended the United States Seventh Fleet's protective screening of Red China, thus permitting the Nationalist forces of Generalissimo Chiang Kai-shek on Formosa to attack the Communist-held mainland.

The President also called upon Congress to repudiate any secret concessions made to the Russians at the World War II conferences at Teheran, Yalta and Potsdam.

Roars of applause greeted General Eisenhower's twin enunciations of a "new, positive foreign policy," made in his first State of the Union delivered before a joint session of Congress.

The first Republican President to chart a course for the nation in two decades, General Eisenhower dwelt on domestic affairs in his address, proposing a program that would turn the country toward a freer enterprise system and "natural" economic law.

His Program Detailed

In outlining his policies for the new Administration the President made these points:

¶There no longer was any "sense or logic" in the use of the Seventh Fleet to shield Red China.

¶The Government "recognizes no kind of commitment contained in secret understandings of the past with foreign governments which permit * * * enslavement."

¶The training and arming of South Korean troops would be accelerated.

However, as the new President made his exit, arms linked with Senator Robert A. Taft of Ohio, Senate Majority Leader, whom he defeated for the Republican Presidential nomination, the speech appeared to leave in its wake a trail of issues that spelled Congressional controversy to come.

¶Aid to Europe would be continued with the Allies required to pull their own weight and United States contributions matching according to their capabilities.

¶The new foreign policy would be the true product of bipartisanship and cooperation between the President and Congress and would be coherent and global.

¶Incontrovertible evidence is at hand of Russian possession of atomic weapons and therefore civil defense preparedness is a "sheer necessity."

¶The reciprocal trade treaties should be continued. American investments abroad should be encouraged and customs procedures simplified.

¶The Secretary of Defense would take steps to obtain the maximum in national security at minimum cost.

¶The first order of domestic business should be to balance the budget, after which a reduction in taxation would be in order.

¶Wage-price controls should be

Continued on Page 15, Column 1

CONGRESS PRAISES EISENHOWER TALK

But 7th Fleet Decision Brings Fear of War Extension and Deeper U. S. Involvement

By C. P. TRUSSELL

WASHINGTON, Feb. 2—President Eisenhower's first message on the State of the Union, delivered personally today to a joint session of the packed House of Representatives chamber, got a rousing reception.

Although the President's speech brought praise from Democrats as well as Republicans, President Eisenhower's decision to end the United States Seventh Fleet's role as a barrier against raids by the Chinese Nationalists on the Communist-held mainland seemed to bring much concern to many Congressmen. It was difficult to determine whether the Republican view that the action would end the stalemate in Korea outweighed fear, expressed largely by Democrats, that it might extend the Korean conflict and involve the United States more deeply in Asia.

Resentment Expressed

Senators and Representatives were repeatedly asking whether releasing Generalissimo Chiang Kai-shek's Formosa forces to attack the Chinese mainland would imply that the United States would have to back up such actions with American men and planes. This, they contended, would mean deeper involvement and perhaps another world war.

Influential Democrats in Congress expressed resentment over the section of the President's address in which he contended, in effect, that the present assignment of the Seventh Fleet, made by former President Truman, constituted a protection for the Communist mainland while other Communists were fighting United Nations troops, mostly American, in Korea.

Representative John W. McCormack, Democrat of Massachusetts, and House Whip, called it "hitting below the belt." He charged that President Eisenhower, while asking for bipartisan foreign policy, was acting "to destroy it."

Opponents contended the Seventh Fleet decision would not

Continued on Page 17, Column 5

To Suburban Readers

The strike of newspaper deliverymen against suburban wholesalers has curtailed distribution of The New York Times within a 50-mile radius. Times may be obtained, however, at all newsstands within the New York City line. Suburbanites in New York during the evening are advised to get their copies before going home. Temporary mail subscriptions may be ordered for the duration of the emergency at no increase over the regular newsstand price by telephoning The Times. Information on how and where to get The Times is given at the end of The New York Times News Bulletins, which are broadcast every hour on the hour over WQXR, 1560 on the AM dial, and WQXR-FM, 96.3 on the FM dial.

"All the News That's Fit to Print"

The New York Times.

Copyright, 1953, by The New York Times Company.

VOL. CII..No. 34,740.   Entered as Second-Class Matter, Post Office, New York, N. Y.   NEW YORK, FRIDAY, MARCH 6, 1953.   Times Square, New York 36, N. Y. Telephone LAckawanna 4-1000   FIVE CENTS

LATE CITY EDITION
Fair, little temperature change today. Mostly fair tomorrow.
Temperature Range Today—Max., 42; Min., 29
Temperature Yesterday—Max., 44; Min., 33
Full U. S. Weather Bureau Report, Page 47

STALIN DIES AFTER 29-YEAR RULE; HIS SUCCESSOR NOT ANNOUNCED; U.S. WATCHFUL, EISENHOWER SAYS

WORST CITY CRISIS SINCE 1933 IS SEEN IN STATE TAX PLAN

Moore and McGovern Demand Payroll Levy and Transit Unit Mandated to Raise Fares

MAYOR CALLS DEMOCRATS

Estimate Board to Get Report on Views of County Leaders —Bus Reduction Directed

By PAUL CROWELL

The city Government is facing the most serious financial and political crisis to confront any Administration since 1933, when leading banking houses rescued a Democratic regime from fiscal disaster.

This was the consensus last night of top city officials to whom Lieut. Gov. Frank C. Moore and State Controller J. Raymond McGovern had indicated earlier in the day that a sound fiscal program for 1953-54 and succeeding years should include both a city payroll tax and a transit authority with a duty to increase fares to meet operating deficits of the municipal lines.

That the city Administration realized the political dangers inherent in the adoption of the suggested fiscal program was indicated later in the day when Mayor Impellitteri, without consulting the Board of Estimate, asked the five Democratic county leaders to confer with him at noon today at City Hall. Among those invited was Tammany leader Carmine G. De-Sapio, the only member of the group who is at loggerheads with the Mayor on matters of patronage.

Leaders' Views Important

After a two-hour conference with Mr. Moore and Mr. McGovern at Mr. McGovern's office, 270 Broadway, the Mayor and Board of Estimate held an even longer closed meeting at City Hall, which was resumed at 3 o'clock this afternoon. At today's session an important factor will be the attitude of the five Democratic county leaders, as reported by the Mayor, toward the proposals upon which the two state officials apparently are insisting.

In another municipal development, the Mayor's Transit Advisory Commission demanded that the eight privately owned bus companies involved in the recent bus strike and Michael J. Quill's Transport Workers Union, C. I. O. take immediate steps to wipe out excess bus lines and to reduce the number of buses on lines that were needed. City tax relief was made dependent on such action.

The conference with Mr. Moore and Mr. McGovern was a continuation of last Monday's talks at Albany on the city's $218,700,000 fiscal program, which in effect already had been rejected by the two state officials in their joint memorandum of Feb. 22.

At the outset of the meeting

Continued on Page 19, Column 1

Eisenhower Plans to Pare Policy-Level Civil Service

Directive Will Repeal 2 That Truman Issued Anchoring Some Democrats in Their Jobs —Organization of Administration Object

By PAUL P. KENNEDY
Special to The New York Times.

WASHINGTON, March 5—Several hundred persons face the possibility of losing Civil Service status and probably their Government jobs under an Executive Order to be issued by President Eisenhower next week.

In announcing the forthcoming order, James C. Hagerty, White House press secretary, said that all those affected would not necessarily lose their jobs. The announcement was generally interpreted, however, to mean that the Administration was preparing to clear out holdover Democrats in high policy-making and administrative positions in order to replace them with Republicans of the Administration's own choosing.

President Eisenhower's order, which he directed to be drafted immediately, will repeal two Executive Orders of former President Truman in 1947 and 1948 in which certain persons on Schedule A of Civil Service rules would receive Civil Service protection against separation from the Government.

The President's order will emphasize that the rights of veterans, specified in the Veterans Preference Act of 1944 would be respected.

Schedule A is a list of positions to which appointments may be made without reference to Civil Service rules or regulations. The appointees may assume their positions without Civil Service examinations and their classifications are not subject to review by Civil Service Boards.

Mr. Hagerty said the "several hundred" persons to be affected by the order were employed in all departments and agencies of the Government. The order, he said, applied to people who had been put under Civil Service in the last twenty years.

The new Administration, since coming into office Jan. 20, Mr.

Continued on Page 15, Column 2

President May Take a Hand If Inquiries Imperil Amity

By C. P. TRUSSELL
Special to The New York Times.

WASHINGTON, March 5—President Eisenhower indicated today that if the Senate investigation into the Voice of America, being conducted by Senator Joseph R. McCarthy, or other Congressional inquiries, reached a point of inviting international misunderstandings and difficulties he might intervene.

This, he emphasized at a news conference, would mean that he would have to desert his long-held conviction that the Congress had an inherent right to investigate as it pleased. He was still hoping, he said, to avoid a situation in which a spokesman for the Executive Branch of the Government would have to take issue with actions of the coordinate Legislative Branch.

The question that prompted these responses was based upon the hearings being conducted, largely before television, by the Judiciary subcommittee headed by Senator McCarthy, Republican of Wisconsin.

The group is inquiring into the management and personnel of the Voice, the Government's radio program for telling the story of America. Broadcasts are beamed to eighty-seven countries in nearly forty languages.

At yesterday's hearing Reed Harris, deputy director of the State

Continued on Page 14, Column 6

EISENHOWER PRAISES RESTRAINT IN PRICES

Asserts There Has Been Little Evidence of Gouging—More Controls Are Removed

By CHARLES E. EGAN

WASHINGTON, March 5—President Eisenhower today complimented business for what he termed the admirable restraint it had shown in pricing policies since the removal of most price controls.

General Eisenhower said at his news conference that since the program of removing major segments of the economy from price regulation got under way Feb. 6, there had been little discernible evidence of attempts to gouge consumers.

The President's observations came immediately before an announcement from the Office of Price Stabilization that it had removed price ceilings on another wide range of items, including bread and bakery products, new and used cars, major household appliances, dry cleaning and diaper services.

Hopes for a New Climate

Another development was a Senate committee hearing at which Charles R. Sligh Jr., president of the National Association of Manufacturers, attacked proposals to establish stand-by controls authority. With such authority, the President could declare a ninety-day "freeze" of all prices and wages in event of all-out war or other critical emergency.

The only major price increase that has occurred since the Office of Price Stabilization began implementing his orders for relaxation of price ceilings, the President said, has been an expected rise of 6 to 7 cents a pound in copper.

The absence of price gouging, the President added, confirms his belief that the American people are ready to be considerate and moderate. He added that he hoped a climate might be established in labor-management relations, for instance—that would minimize harmful pressures on the economy

Continued on Page 15, Column 1

VISHINSKY LEAVING

Foreign Minister Called to Moscow to Report —Will Sail Today

U. N. TO LOWER FLAG

Lie Praises Premier as Statesman — Pearson Hails Fight on Nazis

By THOMAS J. HAMILTON
Special to The New York Times.

UNITED NATIONS, N. Y., March 5—Soviet Foreign Minister Andrei Y. Vishinsky, who was reported to have been informed of the death of Premier Stalin before the public announcement by the Moscow radio, plans to leave for Moscow tomorrow.

Mr. Vishinsky and a party of Soviet officials are scheduled to sail aboard the French liner Liberté tomorrow at 4 P. M. Plans for the sailing were disclosed at Police Headquarters. The police said they had been informed that the party would travel in seven automobiles from Glen Cove, L. I., where the Soviet delegation to the United Nations has headquarters, to Pier 88, Hudson River at Forty-eighth Street. The liner will call at Plymouth and Le Havre.

Mr. Vishinsky has a heart condition and therefore avoids air travel whenever possible.

Valerian A. Zorin, Soviet representative to the United Nations, revealed this afternoon that Mr. Vishinsky's decision was taken after he had received a telephone call from Moscow earlier in the day.

Disclosure by Consulate

There was no indication whether this telephone call had given any indication of Mr. Stalin's death. The news that Mr. Vishinsky had been informed prior to the public announcement came from a telephone inquiry at the Soviet Consulate at 680 Park Avenue.

Earlier inquiries at the headquarters of the Soviet delegation to the United Nations had brought repeated denials that Mr. Vishinsky was there. The consulate revealed, however, not only that Mr. Vishinsky was actually at the delegation headquarters but that he had been informed of the news earlier.

According to United Nations protocol, the only flag that will fly at the United Nations flagpole tomorrow is the banner of the United Nations itself, and it will be at half-staff. The same procedure will be followed during the day of the funeral of Premier Stalin.

Informed of the death of Mr.

Continued on Page 15, Column 2

CONDOLENCES SENT

President Orders Terse Formal Note on Stalin Dispatched to Soviet

TRIBUTE IS OMITTED

Eisenhower Still Ready to Confer on Peace With the Kremlin

By JAMES RESTON
Special to The New York Times.

WASHINGTON, March 5—President Eisenhower authorized John Foster Dulles, Secretary of State, tonight to send the United States' "official condolences" to the Soviet Government on the death of Premier Stalin.

Earlier the President had told reporters at his press conference that he could not tell what effect the illness of the Premier would have on the "cold war." A definite watchfulness is our policy for the moment, the President added.

The President announced the statement of condolences less than an hour after he had been informed of Mr. Stalin's death by James C. Hagerty, press secretary, at 8:25 P. M. The statement was as follows:

The President authorised the Secretary of State to send the following message to the American Embassy in Moscow: The Government of the United States tenders its official condolences to the Government of the Union of Socialist Soviet Republics on the death of Generalissimo Joseph Stalin, Prime Minister of the Soviet Union.

Dulles Informed by Hagerty

Mr. Hagerty notified Mr. Dulles, who was a guest at the British Embassy, immediately after the President had been informed.

The press secretary said the President's message would be transmitted to the Soviet Government by Jacob D. Beam, Chargé d'Affaires in Moscow.

The terse wording of the message was noted here, especially the phrase "official condolences." Diplomatic circles suggested that the wording was about as brief and formal as possible under diplomatic protocol.

They recalled, however, that the President previously had expressed condolences. In the first White House statement issued after word had been received of the serious illness of Mr. Stalin, General Eisenhower directed his words to the Soviet people rather than the Premier or the Government.

Indications were that the President's official condolences would stand in so far as the Government

Continued on Page 13, Column 5

PREMIER JOSEPH STALIN
A portrait released by Sovfoto, Soviet picture agency

Soviet Fear of an Eruption Discerned in Call for Unity

By HARRY SCHWARTZ

The fact that appeals for "monolithic unity" and "vigilance" have now become the main theme of Soviet domestic propaganda appears to be a clear indication that the present Soviet rulers fear Premier Stalin's death may result in an explosive resolution of the major tensions now repressed in the Soviet Union.

The unity theme dominates the official announcement of Stalin's death. It was first voiced in the initial communiqué regarding Stalin's illness issued by the highest Government and Communist party authorities. Unity and vigilance were the central ideas in the long leading editorials that appeared yesterday morning on the front pages of both Pravda and Izvestia.

Yesterday's Pravda editorial may also have given the first hint that Georgi M. Malenkov is leading in the succession race, but this hint seemed far from conclusive. The editorial mentioned by name only Lenin, Premier Stalin, and Mr. Malenkov, quoting the latter's speech last October when he said, "The prospects and ways of our progress are based on the laws of the national economy, on the science of the Communist social structure which have been evolved by Comrade Stalin."

The fact that Moscow has announced that Nikita S. Khrushchev will head the committee preparing

Continued on Page 12, Column 2

AMMUNITION SHORT, VAN FLEET ASSERTS

He Affirms Scarcity in Korea and Byrd Writes to Wilson Demanding Explanation

By HAROLD B. HINTON
Special to The New York Times.

WASHINGTON, March 5—Gen. James A. Van Fleet, former Commander of United Nations ground forces in Korea, told the Senate Armed Services Committee today that he had been handicapped during the entire twenty-two months he had had the command by shortages of ammunition and manpower. He specified hand grenades, and mentioned "other types" of ammunition as having been seriously short all the time and critically short on occasions.

The apparent contradiction of the General's testimony today with that of yesterday, in which he indicated there were no serious shortages of anything in Korea, was unexplained, except for the interpretation that yesterday he had been speaking for the present, whereas today he had been speaking for the past.

Praised by Symington

So much the general said before a public meeting of the committee. Senator Stuart Symington, Democrat of Missouri and former Secretary of the Air Force, praised General Van Fleet for his intelligence and courage in reporting these matters to the public. If other military figures would emulate the example, he declared, "we won't send our youth out to fight with these shortages, even if we have fewer television sets."

[In the Korean war action, Air Force Thunderjet fighter-bombers made a record 1,000-mile raid on a Communist industrial center on the northeast coast sixty miles from Siberia. Navy carrier bombers made heavy attacks in North Korea. Ground action was light.]

In a later closed session with the committee, General Van Fleet apparently amplified his discussion of the shortages. The amplification prompted Senator Harry F. Byrd, Democrat of Virginia, to write a letter to Charles E. Wil-

Continued on Page 2, Column 3

PREMIER ILL 4 DAYS

Announcement of Death Made by Top Soviet and Party Chiefs

STROKE PROVES FATAL

Leaders Issue an Appeal to People for Unity and Vigilance

Text of official announcement of Stalin's death, Page 8.

By HARRISON E. SALISBURY
Special to The New York Times.

MOSCOW, Friday, March 6—Premier Joseph Stalin died at 9:50 P. M. yesterday [1:50 P. M. Thursday, Eastern standard time] in the Kremlin at the age of 73, it was announced officially this morning. He had been in power twenty-nine years.

The announcement was made in the name of the Central Committee of the Communist party, the Council of Ministers and the Presidium of the Supreme Soviet.

Calling on the Soviet people to rally firmly around the party and the Government, the announcement asked them to display unity and the highest political vigilance "in the struggle against internal and external foes." [No announcement was made of a successor to Premier Stalin.]

The Soviet leader's death came from general circulatory and respiratory deficiency occurred just short of four days after he had been stricken with a brain hemorrhage in his Kremlin apartment.

Accompanying the final announcement was a final medical certificate issued by a group of ten physicians, headed by Health Minister A. F. Tretyakov, who cared for Mr. Stalin in his last illness under the direct and closest supervision of the Central Committee and the Council of Ministers.

Pulse Rate Was High

The medical certificate revealed that in the last hours Mr. Stalin's condition grew worse rapidly, with repeated heavy and sharp circulatory and heart collapses. His breathing grew superficial and sharply irregular. His pulse rate rose to 140 to 150 a minute and at 9:50 P. M., "because of a growing circulatory and respiratory insufficiency, J. V. Stalin died."

[The news of Mr. Stalin's death was withheld by Soviet officials for more than six hours.]

Pravda appeared this morning with broad black borders around its front page, which was devoted entirely to Mr. Stalin. The layout included a large photograph of the Premier, the announcement by the Government, the medical bulletins and the announcement of the formation of a funeral commission

Continued on Page 8, Column 2

Treaties Manifesto Shelved in Congress

By WILLIAM S. WHITE
Special to The New York Times.

WASHINGTON, March 5—President Eisenhower's proposed United States declaration against "perversion" of the wartime Yalta and Potsdam agreements into instruments for enslaving peoples was put on the shelf in Congress today.

The announced Congressional reason was that the manifesto would be inopportune now in view of the President's fatal illness, though the President himself indicated at his news conference that he thought this need not delay action. The Congressional developments came before the announcement of Mr. Stalin's death.

The Republican leaders in Congress could not close the resolution to the floor of either house

Continued on Page 6, Column 6

F.B.I. Agents Depict Rebuff by Monaghan

By LUTHER A. HUSTON
Special to The New York Times.

WASHINGTON, March 5—Leland V. Boardman, special agent in charge of the New York office of the Federal Bureau of Investigation, asserted today that Police Commissioner George P. Monaghan had notified him that he would not make New York City policemen available to any Federal law enforcement agency for questioning and that they would respond only to summonses from a Federal grand jury.

This policy, Mr. Boardman said, was founded upon a purported agreement between the New York Police Department and the Criminal Division of the Department of Justice to "block out F. B. I. investigators from cases involving police brutality in civil rights cases.

Another agent quoted Commis-

Continued on Page 16, Column 2

Pole Flies to Denmark in First Intact Russian MIG-15 to Reach West

A young Polish pilot seeking political asylum flew this Soviet-made MIG-15 into a Danish airport at Bornholm yesterday, making it the first fighter plane of its type acquired undamaged by the West. Name of pilot (center figure) was withheld.

Associated Press Radiophoto

COPENHAGEN, Denmark, March 5—The first intact Russian-built MIG-15 jet fighter—the newest known type of Russian jet fighter—to land west of the Iron Curtain came down this morning at Roenne Airport on the Danish island of Bornholm. It came from a Polish Baltic base.

The 21-year-old Polish lieutenant who fled with the fighter gave himself up to Danish authorities as a political refugee and asked for asylum. Very little is known about his story. Danish authorities are keeping it secret for the time being.

The young Pole performed a fantastic maneuver in landing the jet fighter on the grass-covered airstrip at Roenne, about 1,200 meters (3,937 feet) long. Jet fighters normally require a 3,000-meter (9,843 feet) concrete runway to start and land.

At the farther end of the air-

Continued on Page 3, Column 2

161

"All the News That's Fit to Print"

The New York Times.

LATE CITY EDITION
Mostly fair and cold today. Increasingly cloudy and cold tomorrow.
Temperature Range Today—Max., 38; Min., 30
Temperatures Yesterday—Max., 41; Min., 32
Full U. S. Weather Bureau Report, Page 31

Copyright, 1953, by The New York Times Company.

VOL. CII..No. 34,741.   Entered as Second-Class Matter, Post Office, New York, N. Y.   NEW YORK, SATURDAY, MARCH 7, 1953.   Times Square, New York 36, N. Y. Telephone LAckawanna 4-1000   FIVE CENTS

MALENKOV IS NAMED NEW SOVIET PREMIER; WIDE CHANGES DISCLOSED TO AVOID 'PANIC'; THRONGS PASS STALIN BIER; RITES MONDAY

MAJORITY OF BOARD BARS STATE TERMS FOR CITY FISCAL AID

Stands on Mayor's Plan After Democratic Leaders Report Price Politically Ruinous

VOTE ON DECISION IS 5 TO 3

New York's Legislators Held Unwilling to Support Fare Rise or Payroll Impost

By PAUL CROWELL

A majority of the Board of Estimate decided yesterday to stand firm on Mayor Impellitteri's $218,-700,000 fiscal program for 1953-54, refusing to purchase substantial financial aid from Governor Dewey's Republican Administration at a price considered politically ruinous by the Democratic leaders of the city's five counties.

At an executive meeting of the board, five members holding a majority of its sixteen votes refused to modify the Mayor's program by including, at the virtual insistence of Lieut. Gov. Frank C. Moore and State Controller J. Raymond McGovern, a city payroll tax and a transit authority mandated to increase the fare on municipal subway and surface lines to meet operating deficits.

The Moore - McGovern position was outlined to the Mayor and the Board of Estimate on Thursday at a conference in Mr. McGovern's New York office. The Mayor and his colleagues were told that a number of major items in the city's program, including the Mayor's plan for a transit authority designed to preserve the 10-cent fare by subsidizing operating deficits with an income tax on business, were unacceptable to the state.

Tax Request Discounted

The city officials also were informed that their requested increase of power to tax real estate, estimated to yield an additional annual revenue of $100,000,000, had little chance of approval at Albany unless the payroll tax and the 'higher-fare' transit authority were made part of the city program.

The state spokesmen asked for the city's decision by the end of the week. It was made known to Mr. McGovern yesterday afternoon, but he declined comment, saying that he would discuss it with Mr. Moore over the week-end and possibly with Governor Dewey tonight.

Thursday's conference between city and state officials was followed by a long meeting of the Board of Estimate, at which no decision was reached. After the meeting, the Mayor invited the five Democratic county leaders and Assemblyman Eugene F. Bannigan, minority leader at Albany, to a luncheon conference yesterday at the National Democratic Club, 233 Madison Avenue. The state's virtual ultimatum was discussed at this meeting, after

Continued on Page 21, Column 4

Rowdy Pupils Cause A School Bus Strike

Special to The New York Times.

ATLANTIC CITY, March 6— Drivers of school buses serving this resort's north side went on "strike" today against high school students because they were "fed up" with the youths' rowdy, "almost savage" antics.

The drivers, who operate four special school buses for the Atlantic City Transportation Company in the morning and afternoon, reported to work but refused to make the school trips. They made regular passenger runs, however, during other parts of the day.

Roy L. Foley, president of Local 1358, Amalgamated Association of Street Electric Railway and Motor Coach Employees of America, said the union was supporting the "striking" drivers.

"We ... not permit our men

Page 22, Column 5

Ammunition Ample to Repel Reds in Korea, Says Wilson

He Will Give 'Facts' to Senators Tuesday on Issue Raised by Van Fleet's Report —Clark Also Denies Shortage

By HAROLD B. HINTON
Special to The New York Times.

WASHINGTON, March 6 — Charles E. Wilson, the Secretary of Defense, assured the public today that "there is sufficient ammunition available in the Far East Command to counter any enemy attack in Korea."

The statement was contained in a letter to Senator Leverett Saltonstall, Republican of Massachusetts and chairman of the Senate Armed Services Committee. Most members of the committee had been aroused yesterday by testimony from Gen. James A. Van Fleet, former commander of the United Nations ground forces in Korea, that he had been handicapped during his entire twenty-two months of command by shortages of men and ammunition.

[In Korea, on an inspection, Gen. Mark W. Clark, the United Nations commander, said that "certain types" of artillery

shells had been rationed but that there was "ample" ammunition to repel any all-out Communist offensive.]

The Senate committee, after hearing General Van Fleet in two closed sessions, decided to invite Mr. Wilson, Robert T. Stevens, the Secretary of the Army, and Gen. J. Lawton Collins, the Army Chief of Staff, to give their views on the matter. Some members hoped that General Van Fleet could attend the closed hearing at which the other officials would appear next Tuesday, a resolution setting forth his next law proposals.

Senator Saltonstall said he had also invited General of the Army Omar N. Bradley, Chairman of the Joint Chiefs of Staff, but that General Bradley would be in Europe on Tuesday.

The Far East Command mentioned by Secretary Wilson includes Japan as well as Korea.

The Pentagon officials, he said, will be asked "to place the rather confusing and conflicting views which have been laid before us in

Continued on Page 2, Column 6

HALLEY DEMANDS RENT LAW BE KEPT

He Proposes That Council Ask Legislature to Let City Control as Alternative

A demand that the Legislature extend the present State Rent Law or permit the city to enact its own controls was made yesterday by City Council President Rudolph Halley. At the same time he accused the State Administration of a "rent grab."

Acting jointly with Councilman Earl Brown, Manhattan Democrat, Mr. Halley placed in the City Council hopper for introduction next Tuesday a resolution setting forth his rent law proposals.

The proposed rent control now before the Legislature, as submitted by the Temporary State Commission on Rents and Rental Conditions, Mr. Halley charged, "permits a rent grab in that it authorizes blanket increases without regard to the nature or condition of the accommodations, without a showing of landlord need and without regard to the hardships of the tenants."

There is no proof that acute housing shortage in the city has been relieved, Mr. Halley asserted, and "no evidence to show that the low and middle-income families who make up the bulk of the tenants of the city can afford to pay rent increases."

Hardship Is Predicted

The Council President predicted that the proposed new state law would work a "serious hardship" on the majority of low and middle-income tenants here, "many of whom live in substandard dwellings and most of whom can ill afford to pay rent increases at this time."

"The clear evidence is," he declared, "that if a blanket increase either in rent or percentage of rent is authorized, the great majority of tenants in New York City will have no choice but to pay oppressive rents because of the unavailability of apartments by reason of the housing shortage."

He added that the proposed state bill "ignores the problems and the needs of a great majority of the people of the city."

The resolution to be put before the Council by Mr. Halley and Mr. Brown sets forth:

"That the Legislature of the State of New York either extend the existing rent control law with-out change for another two years or, in the alternative, that it authorize the City of New York to enact its own rent control laws so that those who know the facts and understand the problems of the people of the City of New

Continued on Page 21, Column 7

POLICE ALTER PLAN TO FIGHT GAMBLING

One Officer in Each Borough to Be in Charge—Brooklyn Clean-Up Discussed

The Police Department is planning to place the enforcement of gambling and vice laws in the hands of individual commanders for each of the five boroughs in a move to "concentrate responsibility."

This plan, and another to cope with assaults on the public in Brooklyn, were announced yesterday after Commissioner George P. Monaghan conferred for an hour with District Attorney Miles F. McDonald. County Judge Samuel S. Leibowitz, Raymond H. Chadeayne, foreman of the Brooklyn rackets grand jury, and Assistant District Attorney Julius Helfand.

The meeting took place in Judge Leibowitz' chambers in the Central Court Building at the request of Mr. Monaghan.

Judge Leibowitz explained that Mr. Monaghan had asked for the meeting "so that we could sit down informally and see what we can do to correct, to clean up, the conditions that need cleaning up in the Borough of Brooklyn."

Judge Leibowitz, who acted as

Continued on Page 32, Column 2

VISHINSKY DEPARTS

Pays a Tearful Tribute to Stalin and Sails— Silent on Shake-Up

GROMYKO SENT HERE

U. N. Hears Indonesian Appeal for Eisenhower and Malenkov to Talk

By THOMAS J. HAMILTON

UNITED NATIONS, N. Y., March 6—Andrei Y. Vishinsky, in what turned out to be his last official act as Foreign Minister of the Soviet Union, delivered a tearful tribute here this morning to "the great Stalin," and sailed on the Liberté this afternoon for home and possibly an uncertain future.

He said just before the Liberté sailed that he had had no advance knowledge of the election of Georgi M. Malenkov as Premier, and declined to comment.

During the day's debate, Dr. L. N. Palar, chief Indonesian delegate, urged the United Nations to call for a direct meeting between President Eisenhower and Premier Malenkov as a move to ease world tensions and prepare the way for a settlement in Korea.

Andrei A. Gromyko, now Soviet Ambassador to London, who was permanent Soviet representative at the United Nations from 1946 until 1948, will come to New York to take over temporarily as representative to the United Nations. Mr. Gromyko left London hastily by air tonight. Headwinds forced his plane, a British Overseas Airways Stratocruiser, to stop at Shannon Airport in Ireland.

[Aboard the Liberté last night — A. A. Soldatov, a member of the Political and Security Committee of the General Assembly was made five hours before the Moscow radio announced the government changes, which included the appointment of Vyacheslav M. Molotov as Foreign Minister and the demotion of Mr. Vishinsky to Deputy Foreign Minister and permanent Soviet representative to the United Nations.

Mr. Vishinsky's statement in the Political and Security Committee of the General Assembly was made five hours before the Moscow radio announced the government changes, said that Mr. Vishinsky had been informed of his new job, but that he declined to comment for publication.]

Mr. Vishinsky showed no signs of the effect of strain and grief during his United Nations appearance this morning than a delegate was marked, after Mr. Vishinsky, returned to the Soviet delegation's

Continued on Page 3, Column 6

HUGE FUNERAL SET

Body to Be Placed With Lenin's in Red Square After Ceremonies

MEMORIAL PLANNED

New Pantheon Is Due —Mourners in Moscow Offer Quiet Homage

Special to The New York Times.

MOSCOW, Saturday, March 7— Thousands of grieving Moscow citizens have filed past Stalin's bier in the Hall of Columns through the night. A Government announcement early today said that the body of the late Premier would be taken Monday to lie beside that of Lenin in the famous tomb in Red Square.

The funeral services will be held in Red Square at noon Monday. Hundreds and hundreds of thousands of Muscovites, possibly as many as 2,000,000, will have passed Stalin's bier before the funeral services.

Like that of Lenin, Stalin's body will be subjected to the embalming process developed by Soviet scientists to preserve it in unchanged condition indefinitely, the announcement added.

The Government also announced plans for the construction of what it described as "a monumental building—pantheon-memorial."

After this building has been completed, the bodies of Lenin and Stalin, and those of other famous party figures and leaders, which now lie buried in the Kremlin wall, will be transferred, the Government said. Then the building will be opened for visitation by "wide masses of workers," the announcement said.

Meanwhile, the body of Stalin lay in state in the same chamber where his co-revolutionist lay in state on his death in January, 1924.

Throngs Fill City Streets

Mourners filled the streets for block after block around the Hall of Columns yesterday and lines stretched back as far as Moscow's Garden Circle Boulevard about a mile distant.

No man knew how many mourners would pass through the chambers while the funeral rooms during the period of lying-in-state, but it was evident that the total would be numbered in the millions—two or three.

In the hour of deep tragedy over Stalin's death, government functions operated with efficiency.

The death of Stalin was announced at 4 A. M. By 3 P. M. Stalin's body had been brought

Continued on Page 5, Column 2

NEW SOVIET LEADER: Georgi M. Malenkov, 51, succeeded Joseph V. Stalin yesterday as Premier of Soviet Union.
Sovfoto

Britain Agrees to Step Up Economic War on Peiping

By JAMES RESTON
Special to The New York Times.

WASHINGTON, March 6—President Eisenhower declined to comment today on the selection of Georgi M. Malenkov as Premier of the Soviet Union. He concentrated instead on unifying British-American policies in the war against Communist aggression and apparently made some progress, particularly in the economic war against Communist China.

Secretary of State John Foster Dulles and the British Foreign Secretary, Anthony Eden, made a tour of the world political horizon this morning, while the President was discussing the Stalin crisis with his Cabinet. Mr. Eden then had a private talk with the President and stayed on at the White House for lunch.

Results of Conversations

The results of these and yesterday's political conversations with the British were understood to be as follows:

¶The British undertook to adopt new measures to reduce the flow of strategic materials to Communist China. These measures will include adding to the items on the "forbidden" list of goods and supervising more closely the acquisition of British-owned and registered ships.

¶Agreement was reached on the advisability of disengaging United States, British and French armed forces in the Korean, Malayan and Indo-China wars and replacing them as fast as possible with dependable native troops. There was acceptance of the principle that these three wars were all part of a single campaign against the Communist aggressors and that strategy should be coordinated as much as possible.

¶Mr. Eden made clear that his Government had no intention of withdrawing recognition from the Chinese Communists. The United States also maintained its position on that subject; namely, that it would not recognize Mao Tse-tung, but continue to recognize Chiang Kai-shek.

¶However, it was reported that there was agreement on both sides that the death of Stalin and the selection of Mr. Malenkov as Soviet Premier increased the chances of a split between Moscow and Peiping, since Mr. Mao, the Chinese Communist dictator, has often regarded himself as the leading theoretician of the Communist world, next to Premier Stalin.

¶Both sides reached agreement on the policies the British were following in trying to reach a new understanding with Egypt, but found themselves far apart once more in their estimates of what would happen if the current negotiations collapsed in Iran. United States position was that the British approach to the Iran-

Continued on Page 5, Column 3

EUROPE IS CAUTIOUS ON SOVIET FUTURE

London Shuns Predictions but Asks Vigilance—Paris, Rome Pay Stalin Formal Tribute

By RAYMOND DANIELL
Special to The New York Times.

LONDON, March 6—Persons here whose business it is to forecast the course of Soviet policy received little indication of its trend from the appointment of Georgi M. Malenkov as the successor to Premier Stalin.

The elevation of Mr. Malenkov was not entirely unexpected. British betting odds were about even between him and Vyacheslav M. Molotov who, at 63—twelve year's Mr. Malenkov's senior-again becomes Soviet Foreign Minister.

To that extent the death of Stalin is regarded here as something to regret, if not to mourn over, because in the course of years, this dictator with the power of final decision had followed a pattern of action that made intelligent prediction possible.

[Elsewhere in Europe the news of Stalin's death caused some apprehension regarding future developments in Soviet policy.]

Malenkov's Mind Unknown

Nobody here—not even those charged with the responsibility of knowing—knows how Mr. Malenkov's mind works, what are his ideas of foreign policy, nor, least of all, what real power lies behind his new title.

There had been some idea that Mr. Molotov might be Stalin's heir. It is believed now that his British ruled him out but that there is a question about whether he is old enough to be ruled out for the future.

Will Lavrenti P. Beria, an aspirant for national leadership, be content to remain in what amounts to third place, in charge of home affairs?

The appointment of Marshal Nikolai A. Bulganin, who is 57, to the Ministry of War and of 72-year-old Marshal Kliment Y. Voroshilov to succeed Nikolai M. Shvernik as chairman of the Supreme Council of the Presidium, also attracted attention.

In any struggle for power that

Continued on Page 6, Column 5

FOUR TO HELP RULE

Beria, Molotov, Bulganin and Kaganovich Are Deputy Premiers

TEN-MAN PRESIDIUM

Molotov Is Again Foreign Minister—Vishinsky Demoted to U. N.

Text of announcement of Soviet changes is on Page 3.

By HARRISON E. SALISBURY
Special to The New York Times.

MOSCOW, March 6 — Georgi Maximilianovich Malenkov was named head of the Soviet Government tonight in place of the late Joseph Stalin in a series of changes in the highest Soviet leadership.

Mr. Malenkov has assumed the post of Chairman of the Council of Ministers, which was held by Stalin.

At the same time he was named as first in the list of the Presidium of the Central Committee of the Communist party, which is composed of ten members and four alternates.

Standing beside him in the chief and most responsible posts of Government and party in this reorganized structure are four veteran Soviet leaders and co-workers of Stalin—Lavrenti P. Beria, Vyacheslav M. Molotov, Nikolai A. Bulganin and Lazar M. Kaganovich. Those four become the First Deputy Chairmen of the Council of Ministers and with Mr. Malenkov constitute its Presidium.

The announcement over the Moscow radio at 11:30 o'clock tonight was made in the name of the Central Committee of the Communist party, the Council of Ministers and the Presidium of the Supreme Soviet.

Changes to Avoid 'Panic'

The changes in the directing bodies of the Government were made, it was announced, with the purpose of maintaining uninterrupted and correct leadership and avoiding "any kind of disarray and panic."

The announcement said the changes would secure the nation from any kind of interruption in directing the activity of state and party organs and "unconditionally secure" the successful carrying into effect of party and Government policies both internally and abroad.

The chief impression given by the Government both in tonight's announcement and in the proclamation of Stalin's death was one of firmness and the highest political vigilance, a sense of the rallying together of party and Government forces to withstand any threats from within or from without.

The Government was acting with the greatest resolution and with marked vigor. Mr. Malenkov lost no time in demonstrating his will and determination to prove a worthy custodian of the policies of monolithic unity and steel resolu-

Continued on Page 3, Column 2

'Voice' Aide Charges Chief Parroted 'Reds'

By C. P. TRUSSELL
Special to The New York Times.

WASHINGTON, March 6—Howard Maier, a political specialist for the Voice of America, testified today that he had received a reprimand from the State Department for having written a script for a counter-propaganda radio broadcast that had been denounced by the Communist-controlled press.

It appeared from the reprimand, Mr. Maier told the Senate investigating subcommittee, headed by Senator Joseph R. McCarthy, Republican of Wisconsin, that is investigating the Voice, that a State Department group agreed with the denunciation.

Entered among the inquiry's exhibits was a column in The Daily Compass of New York, now out of

Continued on Page 10, Column 4

Half-Staff Flags Here Stir Confusion

Most of Them Flown for the Late Head of Staten Island

Many flags flew at half staff here yesterday, but most were not a mark of respect for Premier Stalin of the Soviet Union. Only a few were.

Flags on public buildings, including the City Hall, were ordered flown at half staff as a mark of respect for Cornelius A. Hall, retired Borough President of Richmond. Mr. Hall died Thursday, too.

At United Nations headquarters the United Nations flag was at half staff too, but this was out of respect for Mr. Hall.

There were other tributes to the Premier. The national ensign of Britain was at half staff on the Queen Elizabeth, and the tricolor of France was flown similarly on the Liberté.

Officers of the Queen Elizabeth said the red ensign had been lowered in respect to the Premier. French Line officials gave no explanation. However, Andrei Y.

Continued on Page 4, Column 4

The New York Times
At City Hall for Mr. Hall

The New York Times
At U. N. for Premier Stalin

162

"All the News That's Fit to Print"

The New York Times.

LATE CITY EDITION
Fair with little change in temperature today and tomorrow.
Temperature Range Today—Max., 72; Min., 52
Temperature Yesterday—Max., 70; Min., 53
Full U. S. Weather Bureau Report, Page 29.

Copyright. 1953, by The New York Times Company.

VOL. CII..No. 34,828.   Entered as Second-Class Matter, Post Office, New York, N. Y.   NEW YORK, TUESDAY, JUNE 2, 1953.   Times Square, New York 36, N. Y. Telephone: Lackawanna 4-1000   FIVE CENTS

AUTHORITY LEASES CITY TRANSIT LINES; FARE RISE IN SIGHT

Estimate Board Votes, 11-5, for 10-Year Pact Including Terms Asked by Joseph

EFFECTIVE DATE IS JUNE 15

New Agency Seeking Tokens From Mint, Indicating New Charge May Not Be 15c

Digest of lease signed by city and Transit Authority, Page 32.

By LEO EGAN

The Board of Estimate voted 11 to 5 yesterday to lease the city's $1,700,000,000 transit system to the newly created New York City Transit Authority for a period of ten years, during which the authority will be obligated to raise enough revenue from fares and incidental charges to meet operating costs.

By approving the lease, the board made it almost certain that the authority will raise transit fares by July 30 in an amount sufficient to overcome a prospective operating deficit of $47,000,000 for the fiscal year beginning July 1. A first step in this direction was taken by the authority within a few hours after the board acted when it decided to explore the possibility of obtaining from the United States Mint an emergency supply of tokens, to be used on all three divisions of the rapid transit lines in the collection of a higher fare.

Casey Tells of Token Plans

The decision to request the Federal Government's aid in obtaining enough tokens to put a fare change into effect by July 30, the statutory deadline, was announced by Maj. Gen. Hugh J. Casey, authority chairman, after a special authority meeting at the offices of the Board of Transportation, 370 Jay Street, Brooklyn.

Sidney H. Bingham of the Board of Transportation, will confer with the Director of the Mint at Philadelphia today on the possibility of obtaining 20,000,000 tokens, General Casey said. Subsequent additions to the supply would be obtained from private suppliers, he added.

To speed the negotiations with the Mint, the authority has requested Governor Dewey to intervene with the Secretary of the Treasury, General Casey said.

A design for the token was officially approved by the authority yesterday. It is a perforated coin, somewhat smaller than a dime.

By exploring the possibility of obtaining enough tokens for use on all three divisions, the authority indicated it might reject Mr. Bingham's recommendation for a 15-cent fare in favor of a smaller charge, perhaps 12 or 12½ cents a ride. The present fare is 10 cents.

A major justification for the Bingham recommendation was that it would involve use of tokens on only the I.R.T. Division, which has electrically operated turnstiles. On the B.M.T. and IND divisions, which have mechanical turnstiles, two coins—a dime and a nickel—would be used to pay the fare.

General Casey emphasized in announcing the authority action that no decisions on a fare increase had been reached. It will not be possible to arrive at a conclusion, he said, until all pertinent facts are studied.

City Fiscal Problem Eased

The Board of Estimate's decision yesterday automatically relieved the city of the necessity of meeting the prospective operating deficit out of tax revenues in the new fiscal year that starts July 1. It likewise vested the city with power to collect $50,000,000 a year in additional taxes from real estate for general municipal purposes, for the next four years, enough to liquidate an accumulated deficit of $39,000,000 in the transit pension system.

Moreover, in accordance with special laws enacted by the Legislature earlier this year on the recommendation of Governor Dewey, transfer of the deficit-ridden transit system to the authority gives the city power at any time in the future to impose a one-half of 1 per cent payroll tax, payable in equal parts by employers and employee, estimated to yield $60,000,000 a year.

The city's budget for the new fiscal year, already approved by the Board of Estimate and City Council, contemplates full use of the additional real estate taxing powers, but no use of the payroll tax.

As had been forecast, Rudolph
Continued on Page 33, Column 2

Eisenhower Moves to Limit State Department to Policy

New Reorganization Plans Would Transfer Present Operating Functions to 2 Special Agencies, Information and Foreign Aid

By ANTHONY LEVIERO
Special to The New York Times.

WASHINGTON, June 1—President Eisenhower proposed today to restore the State Department to its traditional pre-war policy-making role and to transfer virtually all its operating functions to new organizations — the United States Information Agency and the Foreign Operations Administration.

A far-reaching reorganization of the State Department was projected by the President in two plans submitted to Congress today, with a promise of further changes to be sought early next year.

Today he stressed two objectives:

1. To invest the department with the functional tasks that had involved it in political controversy during the post-war era.

2. To make the Secretary of State supreme, next to the President, in the policy supervision of all foreign information and aid programs.

The controversial Voice of America and other information programs would be swept out of the State Department, the Mutual Security Agency and other agencies and concentrated in the new Information Agency. The Mutual Security Agency itself would become the nucleus around which would be built the new Foreign Operations Administration to take over various other programs for technical, economic and military assistance.

Of operating programs, all that would be left in the State Department would be the programs for the educational exchange of persons.

The two new agencies would have administrative autonomy, just as the Mutual Security Agency has today. But a new idea in Government organization was introduced. The directors of the two agencies not only would be subject to close
Continued on Page 24, Column 4

Text of message on propaganda and aid plans, Page 24.

RHEE BOWS TO U.S.; SAYS KOREA AGREES TO EISENHOWER AIMS

Statement on Message From Washington Hints Opposition to Truce Plans Is Easing

By The Associated Press

SEOUL, June 2—President Syngman Rhee disclosed today he had received a three-point message from President Eisenhower, and added: "We must accept anything that the United States President wants."

"Common sense and wisdom require that we cooperate with the United States at any cost," Dr. Rhee said, without saying what President Eisenhower had told him.

The statement of the 78-year-old leader of the Republic of Korea indicated that South Korean opposition to the secret proposal by the United Nations Command for bringing an armistice in Korea was lessening.

Dr. Rhee also said he was looking for some one to take the place of Maj. Gen. Choi Duk Shin as the South Korean delegate on the United Nations armistice negotiation team.

Dr. Rhee declined to elaborate on his apparently conciliatory statement. He spoke to correspondents at a parade of the British Commonwealth Division honoring the Coronation of Elizabeth II.

Nor did he make it precisely clear whether he was ready now to accept the Allied truce proposal, to which he and his Government had expressed vigorous opposition.

South Korea's acting Premier, Pyun Yun Tae, threatened yesterday a break with the Allies and a go-it-alone policy for South Korea but deferred action until after next Thursday's critical truce session.

The Communists are expected to reply to the Allied proposal at Thursday's meeting.

Rhee Said to Seek Treaty

By JAY WALZ
Special to The New York Times.

WASHINGTON, June 1—The Eisenhower Administration was reported today to have had a new request from President Syngman Rhee of South Korea for the pledge of a mutual defense pact and of military and economic help as a basis for the Seoul Government's support of present Allied truce proposals.

These conditions were said on good authority to be important features of a four-point program outlined in a letter forwarded to President Eisenhower through Ellison O. Briggs, United States Ambassador at Seoul.

The principal point in the still-secret United Nations proposal to the Communists for disposition of Korean war prisoners who refuse to return home was understood to be that final determination of the captives' fate would be left to the General Assembly of the United Nations.

Officially, the White House and State Department were silent on developments on Korea, and offered "no comment" even on reports that twelve hours then with an additional twenty-four in front of them.

Had Asked Pledge in Writing

The South Korean request for a mutual defense pact with the United States is not new. Dr. You Chan Yang, the Korean Ambassador here, has made repeated representations to the State Department for such a pledge of defense help in the event of future Communist aggression.

He has made the point that while President Eisenhower has said publicly that the United States will never desert Korea, it would be more satisfying from the Korean standpoint to have "something down in black and white."

President Rhee's four points were reported to be (1) a pledge to sign a mutual defense pact with Korea; (2) a promise by the United States to provide military and financial help to Korea on a large scale; (3) withdrawal of all foreign troops on both sides as soon as a truce has started and prisoners have been exchanged, and (4) agreement that the United States would not stand in the way of South Korea in efforts to unite that country at some future time.

As far as the last point is concerned, sources felt South Korea did not have in mind the use of military force to bring together North and South Korea.

Meanwhile, some Capitol Hill leaders spoke out on recent Korean developments.

Senator William F. Knowland of California, who is chairman of the Senate Republican Policy Committee, said the United States should "risk" war with Russia to expand the fighting, if truce negotiations with the Communists collapsed at
Continued

2 OF BRITISH TEAM CONQUER EVEREST; QUEEN GETS NEWS AS CORONATION GIFT; THRONGS LINE HER PROCESSION ROUTE

CROWDS DEFY RAIN

Face a Day of Showers After All-Night Vigil to Hail Their Sovereign

By RAYMOND DANIELL
Special to The New York Times.

LONDON, Tuesday, June 2—This is the day that all London, all Britain, all the Commonwealth and half the world have been awaiting. It is the day on which the crown of her forefathers is placed upon the head of this old country's radiantly lovely young Queen Elizabeth II whose reign, it is hoped, will usher in another golden age.

The weather for the day was uncertain. By early morning the wind still blew, but rains that fell during the night had ceased, at least temporarily. The weather forecaster, however, was not optimistic about the prospects for the day, which was chosen originally because rain had not fallen on June 2 for many years. The forecast was for cool weather and showers, with sunny intervals.

Last night's gusts and rain discomfited the hundreds of thousands of persons who squatted on the whole length of the royal way but it was unnoticeable because there were others waiting to take their places.

Some of these squatters, lacking reserved seats in the stands, began staking out their claims as early as midnight Sunday.

Squatters Sit on Curbs

By noon yesterday they were sitting on the curbs at Trafalgar Square and were packed two and three deep on the sidewalks along the Mall leading from Admiralty Arch to Buckingham Palace. By dinner time last night the East Carriage Drive in Hyde Park was filled with men, women and even young children with raincoats, blankets, lunch baskets and inflatable mattresses prepared to defend their little vantage points until the Queen's ornate gilded coach, with its eight gray horses, one named Eisenhower, had passed late in the afternoon.

During the day Queen Mother Elizabeth, accompanied by Princess Margaret, visited the palace to see the Queen on the eve of her coronation. By the time they left, an hour later, the crowd outside Buckingham Palace numbered nearly 50,000. The police, who had let the crowd swarm over the roadway, had to make strenuous efforts to clear a path for their car.

Later Princess Margaret made a visit to Westminster Abbey, where she was received by the Earl Marshal. Again the police had trouble clearing a way for her to return home.

Even Oxford Street, that busy shopping center, was taken over by sidewalk squatters almost as soon as the big stores closed. Trafalgar Square, through which the Queen will pass three times on her way from Buckingham Palace to Westminster Abbey, out again and back to the palace, was filled with curbstone sitters even at midday. Some of them had been there twelve hours then with an additional twenty-four in front of them. The litter they made of the sodden
Continued on Page 8, Column 1

AT THE TOP: Solid black line shows route of British expedition, the first to reach Mount Everest's summit.

Abbey, Bedecked and Aglow, Awaits the Coronation Hour

By TANIA LONG
Special to The New York Times.

LONDON, Tuesday, June 2—As one enters Westminster Abbey, where Elizabeth II is to be crowned in a few hours, a magnificent scene greets the eye. The austere gray interior has been converted into a rich and glowing setting for the young Queen's coronation. Carpeting and hangings in warm tones of blue and gold, banners of white embroidered with the royal coats of arms, and the deep rose of the throne and the royal chairs blend into a splendid symphony of color.

In the pale light of early morning a hush lies over the Abbey. Only a few of the great assemblage of 7,000 guests have arrived, and there is little movement in the vast edifice.

From the great west door where the Queen will enter, a thick carpet of deep azure blue reaches through the nave to the choir stalls. Hangings of blue silk with royal emblems embroidered in gold are draped over the edges of the stands and balconies, giving warmth to the gray fabric of the church.

From the choir to the altar in that area known as the Coronation Theatre the floor is covered in rich gold pile, against which the deep rose-covered throne and chairs, and the opulent blue hangings on the walls stand out in sharp contrast.

Under a huge chandelier in the center of the Coronation Theatre and raised on a dais stands the throne. Five steps lead up to it. It faces the altar, and because the Queen will be facing away from the majority of the guests, its back is low so that they too may see the Queen's crowned head during the latter part of the ceremony.

The throne chair is late seventeenth
Continued on Page 6, Column 2

HIGHEST PEAK WON

New Zealander and a Guide Made the Final Climb to Top Friday

By Reuters

KATMANDU, Nepal, Tuesday, June 2—The British expedition has conquered Mount Everest, a radio message flashed from Namche Bazar to the British Embassy here said today.

The message said Edmund Hillary, a New Zealand beekeeper and mountaineer, and Tensing Norkay, the famous Sherpa guide, had reached the hitherto unscaled summit from Camp Eight last Friday.

The news of this success had to be rushed by runner from the British expedition's base camp at Khumbu Glacier to the radio post at Namche Bazar.

It is understood here that this was the expedition's third attack on the last slopes leading to the summit, a first double attempt having failed.

Experts here said the success was largely due to the fine weather, combined with properly acclimatized climbers and the excellent organization and leadership of Col. H. C. J. Hunt.

Full details of the exploit are not expected to reach here for some days.

It is believed here that the news was transmitted specially to London by diplomatic channels so that Queen Elizabeth could be told.

Queen Told at Palace

LONDON, Tuesday, June 2 (Reuters)—The Times of London reported the news of the scaling of Mount Everest in a copyrighted message today.

The news was published in a special edition of The Times on early sale among coronation crowds in London.

Queen Elizabeth, resting at Buckingham Palace, was told on the eve of her coronation that the British expedition had conquered the mountain. The news was brought to her as she spent a quiet morning "at home." The British climbers had succeeded in their plan to give her a worldshaking coronation present.

Mount Everest, the 29,002-foot giant, was the last main outpost of the world unknown to man.

The thirteen members of the expedition formed the eleventh team to try to conquer the mountain in the past thirty years. Many climbers have died in the high ice and snow on the approaches to and the summit of the Himalaya giant.

The Sherpa guide, Tensing Norkay, is a 42-year-old native veteran of more assaults on Mount Everest than any other man.

With 362 porters, twenty Sherpa guides and 10,000 pounds of baggage the expedition left the Nepalese base of Katmandu on March 10. Thus it took eighty days from start to finish.

The climbers carried three flags —the Union Jack, the United Nations flag and the Nepalese flag— to plant on the summit.

They made an approach to the "Goddess Mother of the Snows" from the south, or Nepalese, side. The route was reconnoitered by Sir Eric Shipton, who led a British
Continued on Page 14, Column 7

Tito Abolishes Rank Of Army Commissar

By JACK RAYMOND

BELGRADE, Yugoslavia, June 1—President Tito abolished today the system of political commissars in the Yugoslav armed forces, asserting that present conditions no longer required them.

Not mentioned in Marshal Tito's order was the fact that this will undoubtedly make it easier for Yugoslavia to carry on with growing plans for integrating her military establishment with Western defense projects.

"It will be much easier to deal with Yugoslav military leaders now," said a Western military liaison expert here.

The political commissar, who wore uniforms and were equal in rank with military commanders in the Yugoslav Army, were introduced in imitation of Soviet military practice in the early days of partisan warfare against Germans. Even after the break with the
Continued on Page 15, Column 3

MRS. HOBBY WARNS DOCTORS ON TASKS

Social-Economic Problems in the Field Must Be Solved by A.M.A. or Others, She Says

By JOHN D. MORRIS
Special to The New York Times.

WASHINGTON, June 1—Mrs. Oveta Culp Hobby, Secretary of Health, Education and Welfare, declared at the annual meeting of the American Medical Association, which opened yesterday, that organized medicine must find solutions to the social-economic problems facing medicine today or the solution would be taken out of its hands. She expressed confidence that the American Medical Association "will meet this challenge."

Addressing the House of Delegates, policy-making body of the association, at the Waldorf-Astoria Hotel, Mrs. Hobby said the social and economic demands on the medical profession "are only the continuing challenge in this long history of constant adaptation to a changing society, but never have these problems been more onerous and critical than today."

The association opened its 102d annual meeting yesterday. For five days progress in all branches of medicine will be reviewed in 400 reports by leaders in their fields.

The sessions are being held in seven hotels and in Town Hall while 635 scientific and technical exhibits are being displayed on four floors of Grand Central Palace. The exhibits are open only to doctors and their guests.

Mrs. Hobby in her speech to the delegates said she agreed fully
Continued on Page 26, Column 5

HUMPHREY OPPOSES REVENUE LOSS NOW

He Calls Cut Gamble With U.S. Security—Asks House Unit to Extend Excess Profit Tax

By JOHN D. MORRIS
Special to The New York Times.

WASHINGTON, June 1—George M. Humphrey, Secretary of the Treasury, told Congress today that only "full mobilization" would justify tax increases to produce any more revenue than the Administration now is seeking.

The Government's chief fiscal officer so testified in opening the Administration's case before the House Ways and Means Committee for a six-month extension of the excess profits tax and the cancellation of automatic cuts in regular corporation and excise (sales) levies slated for next April 1.

The Administration, he said, wants those three phases of its tax program carried out in a single bill this year, though the committee has limited its present deliberations to extension of the excess profits tax, which is due to expire June 30.

The Secretary asserted that losses in Federal revenue now would be an unsafe gamble with the country's security.

Mr. Humphrey also made the following points:

¶ That he was "very strongly opposed" to any change in the excess profits tax during the extension period.

¶ That he would fight any continuation of the levy beyond Dec. 31.

¶ That tax relief starting next
Continued on Page 47, Column 2

Harvard Elects Dr. N. M. Pusey, Midwest Educator, as President

Lawrence College Head, 46, Has 3 Degrees From University— Favors Humanities Study

By JOHN H. FENTON
Special to The New York Times.

CAMBRIDGE, Mass., June 1—Dr. Nathan Marsh Pusey, president of Lawrence College in Appleton, Wis., was elected the twenty-fourth president of Harvard by the Harvard Corporation today.

Dr. Pusey, who is a native of Council Bluffs, Iowa, and 46 years old, is a scholar in Greek history, and holds three degrees from Harvard: Bachelor of Arts, magna cum laude, 1928; Master of Arts, 1932, and Doctor of Philosophy, 1937. He prepared for college at Abraham Lincoln High School in Council Bluffs.

The Iowa educator will succeed Dr. James Bryant Conant, who will become president-emeritus of Harvard University on Sept. 1. Dr. Conant, now on leave, is serving as United States High Commissioner for Germany.

Dr. Pusey's election by the Harvard Corporation is subject to the confirmation of the Board of Overseers. This confirmation, customarily a formality, is scheduled to be voted on June 10, the day before the Harvard commencement. On only one occasion, in 1869, have the overseers refused the corporation permission to elect a president.

The occasion of the only refusal was in the election of Dr. Charles W. Eliot, the original choice of the corporation, as the twenty-first president. The corporation prevailed after a delay of six months, and Dr. Eliot became president in 1869.

Dr. Pusey, reached by telephone at Appleton, said that he considered the corporation's action "a tremendous honor." But he declined
Continued on Page 27, Column 5

Dr. Nathan M. Pusey

Notables File Past Empty Thrones On Way to Offer Homage to Queen

By C. L. SULZBERGER
Special to The New York Times.

LONDON, Tuesday, June 2—At 6 o'clock this morning the most distinguished men in Britain began filing past an empty throne. Within a few brief hours, seated upon it and wearing the heavy crown of St. Edward the Confessor, a young Queen will receive their homage.

For Britain and for her still vast empire, this is a significant moment. A new Elizabethan age of challenge and uncertainty has started.

Westminster Abbey, in its fullest splendor, with gold plate and resplendid spread out on the altar, contains two thrones today. The first is that of King Edward I, a gnarled oaken chair having beneath it the Stone of Scone from the Scotland he had conquered.

Upon it the Queen is crowned. From it she will hear the acclaim of her subjects, the distant booming of her cannon and the solemn prayer of her primate, the Archbishop of Canterbury, exhorting:

"God crown you with a crown of glory and righteousness, that, having a right faith and manifold fruit of good works, you may obtain the crown of an everlasting kingdom by the gift of Him whose Kingdom endureth forever. Amen."

Only then, when she is fully consecrated and acclaimed, will the Queen, assisted by her lay and clerical peers, mount her royal throne on its dais.

Since the early dawn crept over the stirring city of London, pushing its light across gray Whitehall and through the soft rose and amber windows of this Holy Church of St. Peter, which is its royal name, the Abbey has come to life for one of those great occasions when it nurtures monarchs.

Finely attired lords and ladies are sweeping into their places, bearing
Continued on Page 12, Column 3

DULLES SAYS U.S. AIM IS TO GAIN FRIENDS

Report on Near East-Asian Trip Urges 'Impartial' Approach to Arab-Israeli Dispute

Text of Secretary Dulles' talk about recent trip, Page 4.

Special to The New York Times.

WASHINGTON, June 1—John Foster Dulles, Secretary of State, said tonight that it was the policy of the Eisenhower Administration to develop goodwill among the nations of the Near East and South Asia to thwart the Kremlin's desire to exploit their many differences.

To this end, he urged an "impartial" approach to Israeli-Arab disputes so as to win the support of both sides against the "common threat"—communism. He said the United States must make clear to all nations concerned with independence that the North Atlantic Treaty alliance was in no way related to a desire to help colonial powers keep or win back their colonies.

In a country-wide radio and television report on his twenty-day tour of the Middle East and South Asia, Mr. Dulles urged the strategic importance of that rich and populous area and said its problems could not be ignored without dangerous consequences.

'Primary Purpose' Stressed

The Secretary's half-hour address was carried over the radio and television networks of the American Broadcasting System and the Du Mont television network, and the National Broadcasting Company radio network rebroadcast it. The Secretary gave a country-by-country account of the trip, on which he was accompanied by Harold E. Stassen, Director for Mutual Security. They made stops all the way from Egypt to Pakistan and India.

Mr. Dulles declared that the "primary purpose" of the trip "was to show friendliness and to develop understanding," and he added: "These people we visited are all proud peoples who have a great tradition and, I believe, a great future."

The Eisenhower Administration, he continued, plans to make any "friendship—not fault-finding—the basis of its foreign policy."

Addressing himself to problems of the troubled Holy Land, Mr. Dulles said he had come back to Washington convinced that the Arabs were "more fearful of Zionism than of communism."

On the other hand, he added,
Continued on Page 5, Column 6

"All the News That's Fit to Print"

The New York Times.

LATE CITY EDITION
Fair and quite warm today. Hot and humid tomorrow.
Temperature Range Today—Max.: 89; Min.: 66
Temperature Yesterday—Max.: 85; Min.: 63
Full U. S. Weather Bureau Report, Page 23

Copyright, 1953, by The New York Times Company.

VOL. CII . No. 34,846.   Entered as Second-Class Matter, Post Office, New York, N. Y.   NEW YORK, SATURDAY, JUNE 20, 1953   Three Square, New York 36, N. Y. Telephone LAckawanna 4-1000   RAG PAPER EDITION SEVENTY-FIVE CENTS

REDS INSIST U.N. RECAPTURE ALL RELEASED PRISONERS; TRUCE TALKS RECESS AGAIN

FOE WRITES CLARK

Questions if Allies Can Control South Korean Leaders and Army

Text of the Communist note to General Clark is on Page 3.

By LINDESAY PARROTT
Special to The New York Times.

TOKYO, Saturday, June 20—Communist armistice delegates at Panmunjom demanded today that the United Nations recapture all 25,000 anti-Communist prisoners of the Korean war released by the order of Dr. Syngman Rhee, South Korean President.

The demand was made in the course of a twenty-five-minute meeting of the full truce delegations called for this morning by the senior Communist truce representative, Lieut. Gen. Nam Il of North Korea.

The Communist high command sent a strong protest to Gen. Mark W. Clark, United Nations commander, asserting that the Allies, equally with Dr. Rhee, must bear "serious responsibility" for the incident. The message was signed by the top enemy commanders, Marshal Kim Il Sung, North Korean Premier, and Chinese Gen. Peng Teh-huai.

The Communist protest was an angry one, and it was significant that it was made directly to the Allied commander, not to the truce delegation. Yet it seemed to indicate that the enemy was not prepared to completely end the negotiations for an armistice.

The letter to General Clark repeated many of the old charges of American coercion and duplicity, but did not slam the door to further conversations.

[The Associated Press said that Pyun Yun Tae, Acting South Korean Premier, demanded Saturday in a letter to General Clark that all anti-Communist North Korean prisoners remaining in Allied stockades be turned over to the Republic for immediate release.

[Soon afterward, in Tokyo General Clark's United Nations headquarters made public a scorching letter to the South Korean President, saying General Clark could "not at this time estimate the ultimate consequences" of President Rhee's "precipitous and shocking" release of the 25,000 anti-Communist Korean war captives. General Clark accused Dr. Rhee of breaking a "persona commitment" not to take action.]

At the armistice conference, the Communists in effect demanded that the Allied command promise to control the fiery South Korean President, from acting on his own. Pointedly, the Communists asked: "Is the United Nations Command able to control the South Korean Government and Army? If not, does the armistice in Korea include the Syngman Rhee clique.

"If it is not included, what assurance is there for implementation of the armistice agreement on the part of South Korea?

"If it is included, then your side must be responsible for recovering immediately all the 25,952 prison-

Continued on Page 3, Column 4

HIS ATTEMPT TO ESCAPE FAILS: A U. S. Marine, right, escorts a wounded prisoner in the prisoner-of-war camp at Ascom City, near Inchon, where about 500 anti-Communists escaped. Marines and other troops prevented a larger break-out.

U. S. SEES POSITION IN KOREA AS GRAVE

Dulles Meets With Both Parties and Envoys of U. N. Allies in Atmosphere of Urgency

By WILLIAM S. WHITE
Special to The New York Times.

WASHINGTON, June 19—The United States Government worked in haste today to save a Korean truce that some responsible men regarded as all but lost through South Korea's angry defiance of the United Nations.

According to an authoritative source in the Prisoner-of-War Camp since June 25, 1950—the day the Communists invaded the Republic of Korea.

There was hope, however, that if the Communists genuinely wanted peace they would not make capital of the defiance shown by Dr. Syngman Rhee, President of South Korea, in freeing the non-Communist prisoners of war.

"In the United Nations Command and its allies in the United Nations force that went to the rescue of his country three years ago.

All the possibilities seemed in the end to narrow to this one, even though there was some speculation that it might be feasible to take some sort of action to replace Dr. Rhee, Senator Walter F. George, member of the Senate Foreign Re-

Continued on Page 2, Column 2

U. N. OFFICERS FELT RHEE WAS BLUFFING

Warnings Unheeded, Prisoner Command Took No Steps to Prevent Mass Escape

By ROBERT ALDEN
Special to The New York Times.

SEOUL, Korea, June 19—The United Nations Command was not prepared for the precipitate action taken by Dr. Syngman Rhee, President of South Korea.

According to an authoritative source in the Prisoner-of-War Camp, officials in Tokyo had been warned that such a measure might be taken by the Government of the Republic of Korea. However, the Prisoner-of-War Command was assured by higher headquarters that Dr. Rhee was "bluffing."

As a result, South Korean security guards were not replaced by American soldiers and other precautionary measures were insufficient.

However, the freeing of the prisoners came as no surprise to those who have been close to President Rhee these last few weeks. Nor was it a surprise to diplomatic circles in Pusan, the temporary South Korean capital.

They knew how defiant the President's attitude has been from the start, and they regard him as a rather unpredictable individual, apt to go off on a desperate tangent at almost any time.

One reason for this reluctance to accept the facts in the matter is that it is difficult for an American to understand Dr. Rhee's reasoning. The Korean leader feels that to accept a truce agreement is drawn is tantamount to inviting self-destruction.

He is not only worried about the question of complete unification of the country. He has a great fear, for example, of allowing in the country "progressive" representatives and "pro-Communist" as border guards.

President Rhee and those close

Continued on Page 3, Column 2

AID BILL APPROVED AS DEMOCRATS SAVE MEASURE IN HOUSE

G.O.P. Split on Cutting Funds, but 280-108 Vote Prevails —4.9 Billion Authorized

By FELIX BELAIR Jr.
Special to The New York Times.

WASHINGTON, June 19—The House of Representatives authorized today an appropriation of $4,993,732,500 for military, economic and technical aid to fifty-six free governments and dependencies resisting communism. The vote sending the measure to the Senate was 280 to 108, with one Representative merely voting "present."

Throughout the afternoon, a smoothly functioning bipartisan majority shouted down repeated attempts to cut the authorization items below the recommendations of the Foreign Affairs Committee. But it was the Democrats who provided the margin of victory.

Republicans by the score deserted the leadership of Speaker Joseph W. Martin Jr. to vote for economy amendments. There was no record vote on any of the attempts to slash the measure and, although the foreign policy prestige of President Eisenhower had been thrown into the debate by the Republican leadership, it was the Democrats who gave him his vote of confidence.

On the final vote, 160 Democrats joined with 119 Republicans and an Independent, Frazier Reams of Ohio, to provide the 280 majority for the bill. A total of eighty-one Republicans and twenty-seven Democrats voted against the measure. Representative Harold A. Patten, Democrat of Arizona, was the one who voted "present."

Members Rally to Vote

The high tide of opposition to the authorization—which is $476,-000,000 less than the Administration had requested—came shortly before the final vote. Representative Hamer H. Budge, Republican of Idaho, offered an amendment to cut all the items by 10 per cent, but it was rejected by a standing vote of 152 to 101.

The same amendment had lost by a narrower margin a few minutes earlier when, on a count, the vote was put at 152 to 102. But when a vote by tellers was demanded, members input from the cloakrooms on either side of the House to provide the extra votes.

An even earlier attempt to accomplish the same result and cut the authorization by $498,000,000 was made when Representative William M. Colmer, Democrat of Mississippi, sought to place a ceiling on the total authorization of $4,500,000,000. This move was rejected, 164 to 83.

The pattern of unrecorded voting on the amendments had been set shortly after the House met for business an hour before noon.

Representative Lawrence Smith, Republican of Wisconsin, proposed to cut $529,186,000 from the section providing military aid to Western Europe. The amendment would have eliminated military aid totaling $216,906,000 for Yugo-

Continued on Page 15, Column 4

ROSENBERGS EXECUTED AS ATOM SPIES AFTER SUPREME COURT VACATES STAY; LAST-MINUTE PLEA TO PRESIDENT FAILS

SIX JUSTICES AGREE

President Says Couple Increased 'Chances of Atomic War'

Texts of related documents in case are printed on Page 7.

By LUTHER A. HUSTON
Special to The New York Times.

WASHINGTON, June 19—President Eisenhower and the Supreme Court refused to save Julius and Ethel Rosenberg from death in the electric chair.

The high court vacated the stay granted to the atomic spies on Wednesday by Justice William O. Douglas. It upheld the legality of the death sentence imposed by Federal Judge Irving R. Kaufman. Less than an hour after the court had announced its verdict, President Eisenhower refused Executive clemency for the second time. He had denied a similar petition on Feb. 11.

"I can only say that, by immeasurably increasing the chances of atomic war, the Rosenbergs may have condemned to death tens of millions of innocent people all over the world," the President said. "The execution of two human beings is a grave matter. But even graver is the thought of the millions of dead whose deaths may be directly attributable to what these spies have done."

He was convinced, the President said, that the Rosenbergs had received "the fullest measure of justice and due process of law."

"When in their most solemn judgment the tribunals of the United States have adjudged them guilty and the sentence just, I will not intervene in this matter," the President declared.

Vinson Reads Court's Ruling

The prevailing opinion setting aside Justice Douglas' stay of execution was read by Chief Justice Fred M. Vinson about 12:50 today. It was concurred in by Associate Justices Stanley F. Reed, Robert H. Jackson, Harold H. Burton, Sherman Minton and Tom C. Clark.

Justices Douglas and Hugo L. Black dissented. Justice Felix Frankfurter announced neither a concurrence nor a dissent. In a brief separate opinion he said the questions raised were "complicated and novel" and that he felt the application of the Attorney General for revocation of the stay should not be disposed of until more time had been afforded for study and argument. He promised to set forth more specifically in due course the ground for this position.

Also read from the bench were a concurring opinion by Justice Clark, in which he was joined by Justices Vinson, Reed, Jackson. Burton and Minton, and a concurring opinion by Justice Jackson.

Continued on Page 8, Column 5

Their Death Penalty Carried Out

Julius Rosenberg

Ethel Rosenberg

Associated Press

Eisenhower Is Denounced To 5,000 in Union Sq. Rally

Sympathizers of Julius and Ethel Rosenberg bombarded judges with new appeals last night and staged rallies in a desperate last-minute flurry of efforts to save the condemned atom spies from the electric chair.

As time ran out for the doomed couple, lawyers and sympathizers tried every avenue of appeal and protest in a feverish evening that included:

An order by Police Commissioner George P. Monaghan to all police commanders to maintain a special city-wide vigil against any disorder or violence in connection with the execution.

Three separate appeals to Federal Judge Irving R. Kaufman to stay the executions. These also were denied.

Two separate appeals to two Federal Circuit Court judges to grant a stay. These also were denied.

A rally by an estimated 5,000 persons in Seventeenth Street, west of the north end of Union Square, where members of the New York Clemency Committee to Secure Justice in the Rosenberg Case denounced President Eisenhower as "bloodthirsty."

Final Pleas to Kaufman

Judge Kaufman, for whom the police ordered a reinforced fifteen-man guard at his Park Avenue apartment, was importuned by attorneys making frantic new legal maneuvers to save the Rosenbergs.

Daniel C. Marshall, a Los Angeles lawyer who had pleaded with Judge Kaufman for a stay, begged Judge Kaufman to telephone the prison and delay the execution for one hour so that Mr. Marshall could elaborate his argument. But Judge Kaufman refused about twenty minutes before the executions began.

Milton H. Friedman, a lawyer representing the Rosenberg defense counsel, asked Judge Kaufman to stay the scheduled executions on the ground that they would constitute "an outrageous insult to world Jewry" if they were carried out on the Jewish Sabbath. Judge Kaufman rejected the plea, saying he had been assured the executions would not be within the Sabbath period.

Frank Scheiner, another lawyer representing the defense, asked Judge Kaufman to throw out the convictions of the couple on the same grounds argued yesterday before the Supreme Court. Judge Kaufman rejected this motion without any opinion.

Another defense lawyer, Arthur Kinoy, went to New Haven, Conn., in an unsuccessful effort to induce Judges Jerome N. Frank and Thomas W. Swan of the Federal Court of Appeals to block the executions.

Prayer Meeting Denunciation

In Seventeenth Street, more than 5,000 persons assembled for "a prayer meeting" as the Rosenbergs heard President Eisenhower denounced as "bloodthirsty."

He was linked with Attorney General Herbert Brownell Jr., Senator Joseph R. McCarthy, Republican of Wisconsin, and Senator William E. Jenner, Republican of Indiana, in "a plot" to destroy the rights and liberties of the American people.

A pre-arranged announcement at P. M. that the Rosenbergs had been put to death created such a wave of hysteria that the

Continued on Page 6, Column 6

IN HAWAII GUILTY OF RED CONSPIRACY

Director of Bridges' Union and Six Others Convicted of Violating the Smith Act

Special to The New York Times.

HONOLULU, June 19—A Federal jury today found Jack W. Hall, regional director in Hawaii for the International Longshoremen's and Warehousemen's Union, and six other defendants guilty of a Communist conspiracy to teach and advocate the overthrow of the United States Government by force and violence.

Immediately after the verdict, stevedores halted work on all island docks in the possible forerunner of a general protest strike. The United Press reported. Within two hours after the verdict was announced Hall's union suspended negotiations on a new contract and longshoremen began walking off the job at Castle and Cook Pier 32. By 3:30 P. M. Hawaii time, all Honolulu docks were abandoned and stevedores had walked off the only two ships in the port of Hilo on the island of Hawaii.

The all-male, multi-racial jury returned its verdict shortly before 1 P. M. Hawaii standard time (7 P. M., Eastern daylight time) after having deliberated for sixteen hours. Six men defendants and a spouse or aloha shirts and one woman heard the verdict read without any show of emotion as they stood behind the defense counsel's table.

A defense request for a poll of the jury revealed that the verdict was unanimous in each case.

The defense attorney, Richard

Continued on Page 5, Column 3

PAIR SILENT TO END

Husband Is First to Die —Both Composed on Going to Chair

By WILLIAM R. CONKLIN
Special to The New York Times.

OSSINING, N. Y., June 19—Stoic and tight-lipped to the end, Julius and Ethel Rosenberg paid the death penalty tonight in the electric chair at Sing Sing Prison for their wartime atomic espionage for Soviet Russia.

The pair, first husband and wife to pay the supreme penalty here, and the first in the United States to die for espionage, went to their deaths with a composure that astonished the witnesses.

Julius, 35 years old, was first to enter the glaringly lighted, white-walled death chamber. He walked slowly behind Rabbi Irving Koslowe, a chaplain at Sing Sing, who was intoning the Twenty-third Psalm, "The Lord is my shepherd, I shall not want." As Rosenberg neared the brown-stained oak chair he seemed to sway from side to side.

Guards quickly placed him in the chair. He was clean-shaven, no longer wearing his mustache, and wore a white T-shirt. At 8:04 o'clock the first shock of 2,000 volts, with its ten amperes, coursed through his body. After two subsequent shocks his life ended at 8:06½ P. M.

Dr. H. W. Kipp and Dr. George McCracken applied stethoscopes to his chest, and Dr. Kipp said: "I pronounce this man dead."

Wife Kisses Matron

Ethel Rosenberg, the 37-year-old wife, entered the death chamber a few minutes after the body of her husband had been removed. She wore a dark green print dress with white polka dots, and, like her husband, was shod in loafer-type cloth slippers. Her hair was close-cropped on top to permit contact of an electrode.

Just before she reached the chair the five-foot, 100-pound woman held out her hand to Mrs. Helen Evans, a matron. As Mrs. Evans grasped her hand, Mrs. Rosenberg drew her close and kissed her lightly on the cheek. Rabbi Koslowe, standing about ten feet from the chair, was intoning the Fifteenth and Thirty-first Psalms.

Mrs. Evans choked up at the final farewell and left the room quickly. Mrs. Lucy Many, a former matron who is now a prison telephone operator, also shook hands with the doomed woman.

Mrs. Rosenberg sat in the electric chair "with the most composed look you ever saw," one witness said.

She winced a bit as the electrode came in contact with her head, but her arms remained relaxed under their binding straps. Silent, she waited while the guards dropped a leather mask over her face. To her right stood Joseph P. Francel, the state executioner, in an alcove.

The first of three successive shocks was applied at 8:11½ P. M. After the third shock the two doctors applied their stethoscopes and Mrs. Rosenberg was still alive. After two more applications of the cur-

Continued on Page 6, Column 3

West Asks Soviet to Bar Firearms In Keeping Order in East Berlin

By WALTER SULLIVAN
Special to The New York Times.

BERLIN, June 19—The three western powers in Berlin urged the Soviet Union today to forbid the use of firearms by its troops and by the East German police in the Soviet sector of the city to prevent further bloodshed.

An announcement said Brig. Gen. Pierre Manceaux-Demiau, French Commandant in Berlin and this month's chairman of the Allied Kommandatura, had made repeated vain attempts to see high Soviet authorities to discuss the problem. It added that finally he had gone to Soviet headquarters in East Berlin to deliver in person a note stating the point of view of the Western Commandants.

Meanwhile, as the eastern part of the city continued to appear quiet, United States military delivered Otto Nuschke to Soviet officers. Herr Nuschke, East German Deputy Premier, was forced

One reason for this reluctance to accept the facts in the matter is that it is difficult for an American to understand Dr. Rhee's reasoning. The West Berlin police might determine whether he could be linked with a "kidnapping." Possibly this referred to the case of Dr. Walter Linse, anti-Communist leader, who was abducted from the United States sector last year.

East Germany's leading Communist newspaper, Neues Deutschland, conceded today that the work stoppages and disorders of the last few days had reached into the remote corners of that region. It expressed

Continued on Page 4, Column 4

4-Day Seamen's Strike Ends As Wage Demands Are Met

By GEORGE HORNE

The four-day-old seamen's strike, which immobilized 125 vessels and threatened to paralyze one-half of the nation's fleet of 1,500 ships, came to an end at 12:45 A. M. today.

National Maritime Union seamen, who struck on Tuesday when the operators refused to accede to wage demands, signed with the dry-cargo shipping employers at the headquarters of the Federal Mediation and Conciliation Service, winning wage rises ranging from 2 to 6 per cent. The settlement terms constituted a complete capitulation by the operators.

A few minutes earlier, the striking American Radio Association, also an affiliate of the Congress of Industrial Organizations, signed for a 6 per cent wage increase with a group of tanker operators.

Surrender of the employers in both cases had been foretold earlier in the day when a group of leading tanker operators submitted to the demands of the N.M.U. on the basis of similar wage rises and other terms. After this agreement was reached, it was a foregone conclusion that the rest of the industry would follow.

The mediators brought the N.M.U. into contact with agents of the Committee for Companies and Agents, Atlantic and Gulf Coasts,

and it was apparent that the costly hold-out of the companies was crumbling.

In its bargaining, the radio officer association also won its demands to gain full control over all radio telephones as well, removing this equipment from the control of captains and other bridge officers. This was a major issue with the radio men.

All details of the fringe issues won by the seamen in their negotiations with the dry-cargo operators were not available, but mediators said they had matched those won earlier by the tanker men.

The new contract for the dry-cargo men will run for only a year, with a wage reopening in the fall. Union leaders called the wage terms "the best increases won by any industry this year." They were preparing to send out telegrams releasing the immobilized ships throughout the nation, including the supertanker United States, tied up in New York.

Continued on Page 22, Column 2

Professor Loses Fulbright Award After Wife Balks at Red Inquiry

By FREDERICK GRAHAM

A Fulbright award granted last April to Dr. Naphtali Lewis of Brooklyn College to study in Italy during the next academic year has been canceled by the State Department, it was learned here yesterday.

Because she planned to go abroad with her husband for the study year at the expense of the Federal Government, Mrs. Lewis, who once held a teaching post at Brooklyn College, had been asked to appear before a subcommittee headed by Senator McCarthy, who sat as a one-member subcommittee in the Federal Courthouse in Foley Square, said that the purpose of the inquiry was to learn whether Senator McCarthy, said here yesterday.

"I think it [the cancellation] is an excellent idea," the Senator asserted at the end of a thirty-seven-minute hearing of the Senate Permanent subcommittee on Investigations into the background of Dr. Lewis and his wife, Helen B. Lewis, who once held a teaching post at Brooklyn College.

The formal title of Fulbright award is the United States Educational Exchange Award. The awards are granted to professors and students for study abroad and, under the Fulbright Act, which is named for Senator J. William Fulbright, Democrat of Arkansas, pioneered the program.

Mrs. Lewis steadfastly refused to answer questions as to whether she had held Communist cell meetings, whether she was now or ever had been a member of the Communist party.

"I think it [the cancellation] is an excellent idea," the Senator asserted. He believed it was very important to know if she was or had been a Communist. Unable to elicit an answer on that score from Mrs. Lewis, Senator McCarthy asserted that her refusal to answer on the ground that it "might tend to incriminate me" was the same as saying that "I am a member of the party."

"All the News That's Fit to Print"

The New York Times.

LATE CITY EDITION

Warm, humid, showers likely late today. Fair, not so warm tomorrow.
Temperature Range Today—Max. 85; Min. 65
Temperatures Yesterday—Max. 79; Min. 62
Full U. S. Weather Bureau Report, Page 29.

VOL. CII..No. 34,883.

Entered as Second-Class Matter,
Post Office, New York, N. Y.

NEW YORK, MONDAY, JULY 27, 1953.

Copyright, 1953, by The New York Times Company.

Times Square, New York 36, N. Y.
Telephone LAckawanna 4-1000

FIVE CENTS

TRUCE IS SIGNED, ENDING THE FIGHTING IN KOREA; P.O.W. EXCHANGE NEAR; RHEE GETS U. S. PLEDGE; EISENHOWER BIDS FREE WORLD STAY VIGILANT

GEROSA AND STARK PICKED BY WAGNER TO COMPLETE SLATE

Bronx Contractor to Run for Controller, Brooklyn Clothier for Council President

DESAPIO PRAISES CHOICE

Tammany Head Sees Approval This Week by Party Leaders Opposed to Impellitteri

By PAUL CROWELL

Lawrence E. Gerosa, a Bronx contractor, and Abe Stark, a Brooklyn merchant, were selected as running mates yesterday by Manhattan Borough President Robert F. Wagner Jr., who was chosen last week by the Democratic organizations of Bronx and New York Counties as their candidate for Mayor.

Mr. Gerosa was named as a candidate for Controller and Mr. Stark for President of the City Council. The slate headed by Mr. Wagner will wage a primary contest against the ticket headed by Mayor Impellitteri, whose running mates are City Councilman Charles E. Keegan of the Bronx for Controller and Julius Helfand, assistant district attorney of Kings County, for Council President.

The Impellitteri-Keegan-Helfand ticket has the backing of the Democratic organizations of Brooklyn, Queens and Staten Island.

At the Biltmore Hotel Mr. Wagner said that Mr. Gerosa and Mr. Stark were his personal choices but that he expected the Bronx and Tammany Hall executive committees to approve them without hesitation.

Wagner Voices Confidence

"I was given a free hand in picking my running mates," Mr. Wagner said. "I chose them after consulting with representatives of civic organizations, labor and business and the Bronx and Manhattan county leadership.

"I am confident that the Bronx and New York County executive committees will approve my choices. Speaking for myself and my running mates I am sure that we will win the primary contest next September and go on to win the November election."

Carmine G. DeSapio, the leader of Tammany Hall, expressed confidence that the executive committees of the Bronx and Manhattan organizations would approve Mr. Wagner's selections at a meeting to be held early this week. He described Mr. Gerosa and Mr. Stark as "outstanding representative business men who will make a great contribution to public service."

Mr. Gerosa, who was born in Milan, Italy, Aug. 10, 1894, lives at 615 West 252d Street in the Riverdale section. He is married and has three children.

He was designated in 1945 by four of the five Democratic county leaders as a candidate for Controller on a ticket headed by former Mayor William O'Dwyer, but withdrew in favor of Lazarus Joseph.

Continued on Page 20, Column 4

Arizona Raids Polygamous Cult; Seeks to Wipe Out Its Community

By GLADWIN HILL
Special to The New York Times.

SHORT CREEK, Ariz., July 26.—Arizona authorities, under an unusual proclamation of insurrection, raided this remote farming hamlet on the state's northern border at dawn today and placed virtually the entire adult population under arrest in an effort to wipe out the nation's last remaining center of organized polygamy.

The defendants, thirty-six men and eighty-six women, constituted the principal membership of a professed Fundamentalist sect — disowned by the Church of Jesus Christ of Latter Day Saints (Mormon) in 1939—that has continued to practice the plural marriage renounced by the Mormon church in 1890.

Separated from the outside

world by the towering cliffs and arid gorges of Arizona's wild and inaccessible "Strip" between the Grand Canyon and the Utah border, members of the cult, organized on a communal economic basis, allegedly have been maintaining as many as a half-dozen wives and thirty children, and have fostered child marriages.

In addition to 122 adults and child brides named in warrants held by a raiding force of 120 officers, the colony included some 263 children.

The state's avowed objective is to wipe out the community, imprison the adult ringleaders, and find new homes and lives for the children and for the numerous

Continued on Page 36, Column 1

Clark Ready to Start Release Of Red Captives in Few Days

But Allied Commander Says It May Be Two or Three Weeks Before Americans Freed by the Communists Arrive in U. S.

By JAMES RESTON
Special to The New York Times.

SOMEWHERE IN KOREA, July 26—Gen. Mark W. Clark said tonight he was prepared to start shipping Communist prisoners of war to North Korea and Communist China within a "few days," but he thought it would be two or three weeks before American prisoners would reach the United States.

The United Nations commander told several reporters aboard his plane en route to the signing of the truce agreement at Munsan, Korea, that while the Communists had comparatively few prisoners to send back, United Nations procedures for handling captives were undoubtedly faster.

The United Nations Command now holds 68,000 North Koreans and 5,000 Chinese Communists who want to return to their native lands, and 8,000 North Koreans and about 15,000 Chinese Commu-

Accord on plans for prisoners of war is on Page 7.

nists who have refused to return home.

In contrast, the Communists hold only 12,000 United Nations prisoners, of whom 3,000 are Americans.

Nevertheless, General Clark said, he thought it would be unwise for the Americans to expect that United States prisoners would be sent back as fast as the United Nations Command would return the Communists.

He said he expected the Communists to return the American captives at the rate of about fifty daily, while the Allies were in position to return as many as 1,500 Communists every day.

In accordance with plans that are now ready, General Clark asserted, the Communist captives would be put aboard small

Continued on Page 9, Column 2

Eisenhower Accepts Aid Cut; Drive to Adjourn Advances

Special to The New York Times.

WASHINGTON, July 26—The drive for adjournment of Congress by Saturday appeared more certain of success today as the Eisenhower Administration privately indicated it could support—under the $4,562,664,000 foreign aid fund bill approved yesterday by the Senate Appropriations Committee.

The Administration decision, already conveyed to Senate leaders, was said to represent an understanding, reluctantly reached, that little improvement could be hoped for on the committee action, which restored half the $1,115,050,000 reduction made last week in the House of Representatives.

The Administration leaders in the Senate are being asked to do no more than "hold the line" when the Mutual Security money bill comes to the floor for debate, and possibly a vote, on Wednesday.

For the record, the Administration still sought passage before adjournment of the postal rate increase bill, designed to produce an additional $240,500,000 in revenue, but the pressure for the proposal did not seem very great.

Postmaster General Arthur E. Summerfield, guest on the National Broadcasting Company's "Meet the Press" television interview, said tonight he thought Congress should stay in session to pass the bill but conceded he did not know whether it would.

"I know they've had a busy six months," he said.

The House Post Office and Civil Service Committee, which has been conducting hearings for two weeks, has given no indication when a postal bill will be reported. The House leadership tentatively has scheduled the measure for midweek consideration on the floor. There have been no Senate hearings.

Continued on Page 11, Column 2

55 REPORTED KILLED IN CUBAN REBELLION

Batista Voids Constitutional Guarantees, Hits Partisans of Ex-President Prio

By R. HART PHILLIPS

HAVANA, July 26—Fifty-five persons were reported killed and many more wounded in a rebellion today in Santiago de Cuba and near-by Bayamo. Martial law was imposed in Santiago following the uprising and military authorities began to round up members of revolutionary groups.

President Fulgencio Batista and his Cabinet in a special session tonight suspended constitutional guarantees for a period of ninety days, according to an official note from the Presidential Palace. The action was taken to enable the Government to cope with revolutionary activities following the revolt earlier in the day.

"Mercenaries in the service of those who became rich during the regime of Dr. [former President Carlos Prio Socarras]," in conjunction with Communist elements" were accused of the attacks on the military posts at Santiago and Bayamo in a joint statement signed by the Ministers.

Continued on Page 13, Column 2

TALK CONDITION SET

U. S. to Boycott Political Parleys After 90 Days if It Finds Foe Stalls

By W. H. LAWRENCE
Special to The New York Times.

WASHINGTON, July 26—The United States has agreed to join the projected Korean political conference ninety days after it begins if this Government is convinced that the Communists are not negotiating in good faith and that further sessions would be futile.

But this Government has not promised to resume hostilities in Korea at that time, nor has it promised to give South Korea any moral or material support if that Government carries out its threat to attempt to unify divided Korea by military force.

The conditional pledge to quit the Korean political conference after ninety days—if this Government believes it is futile—has been given to Dr. Syngman Rhee, South Korean President, who has already announced publicly that his agreement to cooperate in the armistice extends for only ninety days after the political conference convenes. Under the [truce] terms the conference will convene within ninety days after the signing of the armistice.

The Communists have not been asked heretofore of this American intention to quit the political talks in any specified period if they seem to this Government to be fruitless. The United States contends that a walkout from the political talks would not violate the armistice.

U. S. to Make Decision

This Government is not committed to walk out of the peace talks simply if Dr. Rhee and the South Koreans walk out. The United States will make its own decisions as to whether the political negotiations are being carried on in good faith.

There is not, so far as is known, any agreement by the other principal members of the United Nations to walk out at the same time that the United States might decide to leave the conference.

Observers here did not feel that the assurances given to Dr. Rhee were necessarily in conflict with the guarantee given the Communists by Lieut. Gen. William H. Harrison Jr., chief United Nations negotiator, that there would be no time limit on the political conference.

It was pointed out that the armistice agreement included no time limitation for success or failure of the political conference—but it also imposed no requirement on either the Communists or the Allies to continue negotiations if it

Continued on Page 3, Column 2

U.N. Assembly Meets Aug. 17 To Plan Post-Truce Parley

Special to The New York Times.

UNITED NATIONS, N. Y., July 26—Promptly upon receiving formal notification of the signing of the Korean armistice, Lester B. Pearson of Canada, President of the General Assembly, issued a call tonight to member delegations for resumption on Aug. 17 of the suspended seventh session. The Assembly will decide details of the Far Eastern political conference scheduled to take place within ninety days of the signing of the truce agreement.

Official notification that the armistice agreement had been signed was given orally to Secretary General Dag Hammarskjold and to Mr. Pearson by the permanent representative of the United States, former Senator Henry Cabot Lodge Jr., in the same committee room at headquarters here in which the Political and Security Committee held its lengthy debate on the Korean question some weeks ago.

Mr. Lodge then handed to Mr. Pearson a copy of the text of the communication, addressed to the Secretary General and issued by the United States Mission after word had been flashed from the Pentagon in Washington. It read:

"I have the honor to inform you that an armistice agreement has been entered into between the

United Nations Command and the commanders of the Communist force in Korea, i. e., the Korean People's Army and the Chinese People's Volunteers. The agreement was signed for the United Nations Command at 1000 hours [10 A. M.] on July 27, 1953, Korean time, and becomes effective at 2200 hours [10 P. M.], July 27, 1953, Korean time. [The actual signing was at 10:01 A. M., Korean time, or 9:01 P. M., Sunday, Eastern daylight time.]

"A report of the Unified Command transmitting the official text of the armistice agreement will be sent to you shortly."

Telegrams to the delegates, which had been prepared earlier, were dispatched to the delegations summoning them to report for the resumed session in mid-August.

In a joint broadcast from the committee room, which followed that of President Eisenhower from Washington, all three of the United Nations principals repeated for radio and television audiences statements about the Korean armistice.

"The whole world is thankful that the negotiations at Panmunjom have brought the fighting in Korea to an end by the signature of an armistice agreement," Mr.

Continued on Page 4, Column 5

PRESIDENT IS HAPPY

But Warns in Broadcast That Global Peace Is Yet to Be Achieved

Texts of Eisenhower and Dulles talks are on Page 4.

Special to The New York Times.

WASHINGTON, July 26—President Eisenhower greeted the news of the Korean armistice tonight with prayers of thanksgiving but warned the nation that the Allies had won an armistice only on a single battleground and had not achieved peace in the world.

The President spoke over radio and television networks about an hour after the official cease-fire documents had been signed.

General Eisenhower said the United States and all the free world must not relax its guard, or fail to be vigilant against "the possibility of untoward developments."

After the President had spoken, Charles E. Wilson, Secretary of Defense, issued a statement warning against any relaxation in the country's defense program because of the truce. He advised, too, that it would be a "long time" before American troops could be withdrawn from Korea "with safety."

"We must not be misled into the same demobilization which followed World Wars I and II," he said. "Such a demobilization would inevitably again tempt an aggressor."

Dulles Sees U. N. Victory

John Foster Dulles, Secretary of State, described the armistice as a great victory for the United Nations because "for the first time in history an international organization had stood against an aggressor and has marshaled force to meet force."

President Eisenhower spoke from the White House, across Pennsylvania Avenue and about a block east from Blair House, where President Truman decided thirty-seven months ago to commit United States forces to the defense of South Korea, then being overrun by the Communist armies from the north.

The President said he hoped that the coming of peace to Korea would at last convince all nations of the wisdom of composing their differences by negotiation beforerather than after "various resorts to brutal and futile battle."

He closed his brief speech by quoting from the final paragraph of Lincoln's Second Inaugural Address, which he said expressed the resolution and dedication of all Americans, now as in 1865.

These were Lincoln's words: "With malice toward none, with

Continued on Page 4, Column 2

REPORTS ON TRUCE: President Eisenhower making nationwide television broadcast from the White House last night.

The New York Times (by Fred J. Sass)

DEFENSE CHIEFS SEE BILLION CUT IN ARMS

Wilson Tells Quantico Parley Our Gain in Might Makes Any Attack on Us 'Foolhardy'

By AUSTIN STEVENS
Special to The New York Times.

QUANTICO, Va., July 26—Defense officials attending the high-level defense conference at the Marine Corps base here predicted today that with any kind of "decent" Korean truce defense spending could be trimmed by as much as $1,000,000,000 in the next twelve months.

Secretary of Defense Charles E. Wilson told the conference that "we have attained a strength which should make any attack upon us foolhardy in the extreme, and we are increasing our strength daily."

The previously stated defense spending figure for the fiscal year that started July 1 was $43,200,-000,000. Official announcement was made two days ago that W. J. McNeil, Assistant Secretary of Defense in charge of the budget, had told the conference, which included high military leaders, that cuts were expected in that figure. He did not indicate where the cuts would be made.

In their prediction today the defense officials said that the post-truce reductions would not be greater than $1,000,000,000 in the year because so many fixed costs would continue.

The immediate economies would come in ammunition, trucks and other "consumption items" of war. Over-all military manpower gradually would be cut back from the present 3,500,000 by 200,000, perhaps more. One item mentioned today as an example was the immediate ending of combat pay, which is budgeted at $56,000,000.

However, defense officials stated, some other costs would rise. Assuming, for instance, that large numbers of United States troops would remain in Korea for some time, it was said, it would become necessary to build barracks and other semi-permanent structures.

The three-day highly secret conference called by Secretary Wilson to have the armed services present their situations and problems and also to get members of his new defense "team" to know

Continued on Page 9, Column 1

MARINES STOP REDS IN LAST-HOUR FIGHT

Chinese Foe's Dawn Attacks Hit U. S. Units on West and South Koreans in Center

By The United Press

TOKYO, Monday, July 27—Chinese Communist troops threw "last hour propaganda" attacks at Allied forces on the central and western fronts of the rain-swept Korean battle line today, only a few hours before the armistice was signed at Panmunjom.

An estimated two enemy companies smashed into United Nations lines at the bend of the Kumsong River on the central front. South Korean forces fought the Reds hand-to-hand for more than an hour.

Allied troops all along the 155-mile line across the peninsula were ordered to hold casualties to a minimum and not to pick fights with the Reds.

The Allied orders were issued as Chinese Red shock troops just before dawn attacked United States Marines on a western front outpost for the fourth consecutive day. The Reds hit the hilltop positions northeast of Panmunjom in forces up to 200 men.

First Marine Division officers said the first wave of the attack was turned off without casualty among the Americans. The marines

Continued on Page 2, Column 5

CEREMONY IS BRIEF

Halt in 3-Year Conflict for a Political Parley Due at 9 A. M. Today

Armistice text, on Pages 6, 7; Clark and Taylor statements, 9.

By LINDESAY PARROTT
Special to The New York Times.

TOKYO, Monday, July 27—Communist and United Nations delegates in Panmunjom signed an armistice at 10:01 A. M. today [9:01 P. M., Sunday, Eastern daylight time]. Under the truce terms, hostilities in the three-year-old Korean war are to cease at 10 o'clock tonight [9 A. M., Monday, Eastern daylight time].

[President Syngman Rhee of South Korea promised in a statement at Seoul Monday to observe the armistice "for a limited time" while a political conference tried to unify Korea by peaceful means, The United Press said.]

The historic document was signed in a roadside hall the Communists built specially for the occasion. The ceremony, attended by representatives of sixteen members of the United Nations, took precisely eleven minutes. Then the respective delegations walked from the meeting place without a word or handshake between them.

The matter-of-fact procedure underlined what spokesmen of both sides emphasized: That though the shooting would cease within twelve hours after the signing, only an uneasy armed truce and political difficulties, perhaps even greater than those of the armistice negotiations, were ahead.

Signers Are Expressionless

The representatives of the two sides were expressionless as they put their names to a pile of documents, providing for an exchange of prisoners, establishment of a neutral zone for the cease-fire and a later political conference that would attempt to settle the tragic Korean questions, unsolved by three years of fighting that caused hundreds of thousands of casualties.

According to the latest figures, released July 21 by the Department of Defense, the United States has suffered a total of 139,272 casualties. This included 24,965 dead, 101,368 wounded, 2,938 captured, 8,476 missing and 1,525 previously reported captured or missing, but since returned to military control.

Early this afternoon the Allied part in conclusion of the armistice agreement was completed at advance headquarters near Munsan, where Gen. Mark W. Clark, United Nations commander, put his name to the documents previously signed at Panmunjom.

General Clark signed in the presence of some of his high-ranking officers, Vice Admiral Robert P. Briscoe, commander of the naval forces in the Far East; Gen. Otto P. Weyland, head of the Far East Air Forces; Gen. Maxwell D. Taylor, Eighth Army commander; Lieut. Gen. Samuel Anderson of the Fifth Air Force, and Vice Admiral J. J. Clark, heading the Seventh Fleet.

Also present at Munsan and

Continued on Page 2, Column 1

Skeptical G. I.'s Finally Convinced; Most Take News With Little Elation

By GREG MacGREGOR
Special to The New York Times.

SEOUL, Korea, July 26 — Tonight, on the eve of the armistice, a Marine private manning the line on the central front said with a laugh when his sergeant told him he had a full night of fighting in the thirty-seven-month-old Korean war. Only a few minor clashes had taken place by early morning, and from all indications the war would be unofficially ended by dawn. No patrols were scheduled for tomorrow.

As news of the armistice filtered down to the men at the front, it left an atmosphere of mingled disbelief and temporary confusion in its wake. In many cases the soldiers flatly refused to accept the word of their own officers and noncommissioned officers. The men had so many disappointments over cease-fire reports in the past that they were slow to accept the truth.

"It will never happen," a Marine private manning the line on the central front said with a laugh when his sergeant told him tomorrow.

Not until the Armed Forces Radio broadcast was picked up at 8 P. M. tonight by portable receivers along the front were the men willing to believe the news. Then the announcer's words struck like a bolt of lightning.

Some G. I.'s stared dumbly at each other and others broke out in howls.

"Didja hear that—didja hear that" one man kept shouting over and over as he ran from his tent.

"Wait'll they sign it—who knows what's going to happen," a skeptic

Continued on Page 3, Column 1

The New York Times.

LATE CITY EDITION
Considerable cloudiness today. Partly cloudy, cold tomorrow.
Temperature Range Today—Max. 40 ; Min. 35
Temperature Yesterday—Max. 56.4 ; Min. 47.7
Full U. S. Weather Bureau Report, Page 19.

Copyright, 1954, by The New York Times Company.

VOL. CIII..No. 35,101.   Entered as Second-Class Matter, Post Office, New York, N. Y.   NEW YORK, TUESDAY, MARCH 2, 1954.   Times Square, New York 36, N. Y. Telephone Lackawanna 4-1000   FIVE CENTS

HIDDEN OWNERSHIP OF RACEWAY STOCK BARED AT HEARING

Former Legislator, Intimate of O'Dwyer, Erickson Kin and Ex-Convict Are Identified

HOLDINGS PUT AT MILLION

Moreland Inquiry Opens Public Sessions, Gets Details of Yonkers Track Purchase

By EMANUEL PERLMUTTER

Politicians and persons with underworld backgrounds or friendships were found yesterday to have been the hidden owners of close to a million dollars' worth of stock in several New York harness racing tracks.

These disclosures were made as the Moreland Act Commission opened public hearings here on the scandal-ridden raceways. The proceedings are being held in the Criminal Court Building, 100 Centre Street.

Among those who were shown to have struck it rich secretly on the trotting tracks were former Assemblyman Elmer J. Kellam of Hancock, N. Y.; Irving Sherman, political intimate of former Mayor William O'Dwyer and admitted friend of gangsters; Frank J. Erickson, son of the convicted gambler, and Samuel J. Stirrat, an ex-convict with a long police record.

Additional testimony was introduced indicating that loans from racketeers had helped the original incorporators of the Algam Corporation to purchase the Yonkers Empire City Race Track—now Yonkers Raceway—for $2,400,000 in 1949.

Named a Racing Steward

Mr. Kellam, who served in the Assembly from Delaware County between 1943 and 1950, admitted on the witness stand that he had transferred 10,000 shares in Mid-State Raceway, near Syracuse, to a "dummy" owner after he had been appointed as a state racing steward last year.

The former Republican legislator said that he became the beneficiary of the stock, which was listed in the name of Marvin Wynkoop of Downesville, N. Y., and that he intended to sell it but had been unable to do so because of the pressure of his duties as a steward at Roosevelt Raceway, Westbury, L. I. He described the duties of a steward as "protecting the public, to see if the races are on the level."

"Did you think it was proper for a steward to own stock in a track?" Bruce Bromley, the commission chairman, asked him.

Mr. Kellam, a sandy-haired, florid-faced man, shook his head apologetically. "I don't think it's good judgment," he conceded. "But I never performed any duties at a track where I was a stockholder."

Still Owns Track Stock

The witness said he now owned 9,500 shares in the upstate track. He said he assumed he still held the job as racing steward.

At this point, Harness Racing Commissioner George P. Monaghan, sitting as a member of the Moreland Commission, interrupted to point out that stewards served for one year and that they had to be reappointed each racing season.

The testimony involving Irving Sherman, who was referred to as the contact man for Frank Costello during Mayor O'Dwyer's administration, was given by Sam Sherman, a raincoat manufacturer, of 30 West Fifty-fourth Street. He is not related to Irving Sherman.

Sam Sherman testified that although he was the listed owner of 22,500 shares of stock and $50,000 worth of bonds in the Algam Corporation, holding company for the Yonkers track, Irving Sherman actually owned 80 per cent of the investment.

In October, 1953, soon after the Moreland Commission was appointed, Algam purchased 20,000 shares from him, Mr. Sherman said. He said the purchase price was $296,000, a total of $30 a share. Of this sum, he testified, he gave $145,000 to Irving Sherman, the remainder of the latter's share being tied up in litigation.

In addition, Mr. Sherman said, the 2,500 shares of voting stock that he and his secret partner owned were sold at the same time for $75,000 to M. Duke Manacher, a stockholder in Algam. He said he gave $60,000 of this sum to Irving Sherman. The $50,000 worth of bonds

Continued on Page 12, Column 2

Jarka, Big Stevedore, Quits Port Under Fire

By A. H. RASKIN

The Jarka Corporation, one of the world's largest stevedoring enterprises, decided yesterday to stop operating in the Port of New York.

The company and its president, Frank W. Nolan, are awaiting trial in Special Sessions on charges of having paid out $119,859 in bribes to shipping executives for steering contracts to Jarka. The Waterfront Commission has been conducting an investigation to determine whether the company should be barred from doing business here.

The Jarka decision to withdraw its application for a stevedoring license was the highlight of another hectic day on the strife-swept waterfront. Other developments included:

¶A request by Charles T.

Continued on Page 11, Column 1

UNITY PLEA OPENS CARACAS MEETING

Hemisphere Accord Founded on Sovereignty and Equality Is Urged on Delegates

By SAM POPE BREWER
Special to The New York Times.

CARACAS, Venezuela, March 1—President Marcos Perez Jimenez of Venezuela opened the tenth Inter-American Conference today with a plea for closer unity among the American States on the basis of sovereignty and equality.

There is explosive material on the agenda in questions such as Communist infiltration in Latin America and rules for granting political asylum. Yet all indications today were that most of the delegates were in a conciliatory mood and that means would be sought to avoid heated clashes.

The elaborate security precautions taken for the conference seemed to grow in importance when word of the shooting in the United States Congress was received.

[Guatemala lost her first test at the parley on a procedural question, while at home President Jacobo Arbenz Guzman denied any Soviet intervention in the country's internal affairs.]

Speaking at the first session in the great modernistic assembly hall of University City, President Perez emphasized that the idea of continental unity had existed from the day the American nations won their independence.

"The existence of basic factors of a type common to all the continent, and the desire to obtain and preserve independence were the fundamental reasons for which there appeared almost simultaneously in the greater part of the peoples of America the idea of unity among them," he said.

He added, however, that "the unity of our peoples should be based on comprehension, the feeling of reciprocal assistance and mutual respect."

"We shall understand each

Continued on Page 9, Column 1

31 KILLED IN SUDAN IN NATIVES' CLASH AS NAGUIB ARRIVES

117 Hurt in Battle at Khartum Palace Between Tribesmen and Pro-Egyptian Group

Dispatch of The Times, London.

KHARTUM, the Sudan, March 1—The arrival in the Sudan today of Maj. Gen. Mohammed Naguib, Egyptian President, revived factional passions of this nascent state in a clash in which at least twenty-two persons were killed. [The Associated Press placed the toll at thirty-one.]

Among the dead were eight of the police force, including the British police commandant of Khartum, H. S. McGuigan, and the superintendent, Mustapha el Mahdi. One hundred and seventeen were wounded, of whom thirty-two were seriously injured.

The factional struggle was of a primitive nature. The dead and wounded were seen to bear the marks of clubs and spears, not gunshot wounds.

[Meanwhile, a spokesman for the ruling junta in Egypt said in Cairo Monday that General Naguib owed his reinstatement as President to agitation begun by eight Communist army officers.]

The tragedy here was enacted outside the Governor General's palace, which stands on the site of the residency where Gen. Charles G. Gordon, then Governor General, died from the thrusts of tribesmen's spears during the historic Khartum siege in 1885. Inside the residency, General Naguib, Sir Robert Howe, Governor General, and Selwyn Lloyd, Minister of State of the British Foreign Office, were at lunch during today's events.

Parliament Opening Put Off

In view of the passions aroused by the rioting, the Governor General postponed a meeting of the Sudanese Parliament, scheduled for this afternoon, until March 10.

It seemed today as though the army of Mohammed Ahmed, the Mahdi, or Moslem leader who defeated General Gordon, were on the march again. The rioters massed outside the Khartum airport, turbaned and robed in shining white, with their hundreds of banners waving above the throng. They were supporters of the patron of the Sudanese independence movement, Sir Abdel Rahman el Mahdi, mainly Baggara tribesmen from the provinces who gathered to greet General Naguib with chanted slogans demanding independence for the Sudan.

"No Egypt, No Britain!" they cried as they surged up to Sudanese Defense Force troops who barred their way to the airport.

This was no unkempt rabble; their banners were of trim red, green and black stripes, superimposed with a white spear cutting a white crescent.

General Naguib left his aircraft at Khartum airport at 10 A. M. He was accompanied by Maj. Salah Salem, Egyptian Minister of National Guidance and Minister of State for Sudanese Affairs. Sir Robert, Ismail el Azhary, Prime Minister of the

Continued on Page 2, Column 2

FIVE CONGRESSMEN SHOT IN HOUSE BY 3 PUERTO RICAN NATIONALISTS; BULLETS SPRAY FROM GALLERY

SEIZED IN SHOOTING: Capitol police hold three Puerto Rican Nationalists after they fired from gallery seats into House chamber, wounding five Representatives. Prisoners, left to right, are Lolita Lebron, Rafael C. Miranda and Andres Cordero.
Associated Press Wirephoto

CAPITOL IN UPROAR

Woman, Accomplices Quickly Overpowered —High Bonds Set

By CLAYTON KNOWLES
Special to The New York Times.

WASHINGTON, March 1—Five members of the Congress of The United States were shot down on the floor of the House of Representatives today.

Their assailants, at least three Puerto Rican Nationalists, shouted for freedom of their homeland as they fired murderously although at random from a spectators' gallery just above the House floor. Possibly twenty-five shots were fired.

Bullets rained down from two German Lugers and other pistols of lesser caliber. They crashed through the table of the majority leader and chairs around it, and struck near the table of the Minority Leader beyond. The time was 2:32 P. M.

House members at first thought the sounds were those of firecrackers. But as their colleagues fell or took cover as they heard the slugs hit around them, all realized what was happening.

The wounded House members:

ALVIN M. BENTLEY, 35 years old, multimillionaire Michigan Republican, shot through lung, liver and intestine. Condition critical.

BEN F. JENSEN, 61, Republican of Iowa, shot in back. Condition serious.

CLIFFORD DAVIS, 56, Democrat of Tennessee, shot in the leg. Condition good.

GEORGE H. FALLON, 51, Democrat of Maryland, leg wound. Condition good.

KENNETH A. ROBERTS, 41, Democrat of Alabama, leg wound. Condition good.

Assailants Subdued

Within a matter of minutes, the episode, which threw the Capitol and most of official Washington into an uproar, was at an end. Gallery attendants, aided by spectators, Capitol police and even one House member, quickly overcame and disarmed the three gun wielders.

The three Puerto Ricans, all residents of New York, were booked at police headquarters on charges of assault with intent to kill. They gave their names and addresses as:

LOLITA LEBRON, 34, 315 West Ninety-fourth Street.

RAFAEL C. MIRANDA, 25, 120 South First Street, Brooklyn.

ANDRES CORDERO, 29, of 108 East 103d Street.

A fourth Puerto Rican, also resident in New York, was arrested in a downtown section and booked on the same charge.

He was booked as Irving Flores, 27, also of 108 East 103d Street, described by Police Chief Robert Murray as a fourth member of the shooting party who had fled the Capitol successfully. When arrested, Flores still had a .45 caliber pistol.

Later, United States Commissioner Cyril S. Lawrence ordered the four held under $100,000 bonds each. He put off a preliminary hearing until March 10 to give them time to get counsel. Five counts of assault with intent to

Continued on Page 16, Column 7

M'LEOD AUTHORITY IS CUT BY DULLES

Friend of McCarthy Loses Personnel Duties, Keeps His Security Office

Special to The New York Times.

WASHINGTON, March 1—The Eisenhower Administration stripped Scott McLeod today of his authority over State Department personnel. It left him in charge of security matters.

This action, which was announced on the authority of John Foster Dulles, the Secretary of State, was widely interpreted as a thrust by the Administration at the McCarthy wing of the Republican party.

Mr. McLeod is a close friend of Senator Joseph R. McCarthy, Republican of Wisconsin. He went to the State Department last January from the office of Senator Styles Bridges, Republican of New Hampshire.

He had served as administrative assistant to Senator Bridges and at one time was an agent of the Federal Bureau of Investigation.

Mr. McLeod made five speeches for the Republican party in the recent Lincoln Week series of partisan addresses, and there were Democratic protests that he was improperly using his office. A Republican member of the Civil Service Commission, George Moore, held informally that such political activity was forbidden by the Hatch Act, which limits the partisanship of certain Federal officials and employees.

However, the counsel of the State Department ruled that Mr. McLeod was not under the Hatch Act.

Policies Criticized

On Jan. 16, five former United States Ambassadors charged in an open letter that State Department personnel and security policies might be "laying the foundations for a Foreign Service incompetent to serve a totalitarian government rather than the Government of the United States as we have heretofore known it."

They did not mention Mr. McLeod by name, but both the personnel and security policies were under his direction.

In a speech on Feb. 18 in Larchmont, N. Y., Mr. McLeod took especially heated exception to the version of State Department policy in Asia as quoted from testimony by Walter S. Robertson, Assistant Secretary of State, before a

Continued on Page 15, Column 1

McCarthy, Dirksen Suggest Labor Camps for Army Reds

By W. H. LAWRENCE
Special to The New York Times.

WASHINGTON, March 1—Senators Joseph R. McCarthy and Everett M. Dirksen suggested today "disagreeable" labor camps for armed services personnel who were Communists or who invoked the Fifth Amendment when asked about Communist associations.

Their suggestion grew out of new disclosures by the Senate Permanent Subcommittee on Investigations of "contradictions" in the Army system of handling officers and enlisted men who are alleged Communists or admitted former Communists.

Senator McCarthy, Republican of Wisconsin, is chairman of the subcommittee, and Senator Dirksen, an Illinois Republican, is a member.

The subcommittee accepted an Army suggestion that it question Robert T. Stevens, Secretary of the Army, at a closed session on Thursday or next Monday. All advance indications on both sides were that it would be a "friendly" hearing and not a controversial showdown such as was threatened but called off last week.

With four Republicans and one Democrat present, the subcommittee today questioned in secret an Army private and a former private in considering a problem of fundamental importance to all the armed forces. Stated broadly, the subcommittee raised these questions:

¶Should admitted Communists

Continued on Page 14, Column 2

U. S. Dismissed 355 In Subversive Cases

Special to The New York Times.

WASHINGTON, March 1—The Civil Service Commission reported today that 355 Federal employees whose personnel files contained some allegations of subversive associations had been separated from the Government payroll between May 28 and Dec. 31, 1953.

The report was the first overall breakdown provided by the Administration to Congress since the controversy over the 2,200 persons said by President Eisenhower to have been separated as "security risks."

Philip Young, commission chairman, said that 355 Federal employees were separated, of whom 983 were dismissed and 1,241 resigned. These figures included 211 dismissals and 231 resigna-

Continued on Page 15, Column 2

WITNESS DESCRIBES SHOOTING, CAPTURE

Reporter Sees Firing in House —Struck on Cheek by Chip Torn Loose by Bullet

By C. P. TRUSSELL
Special to The New York Times.

WASHINGTON, March 1—Until the shooting in the House of Representatives today things were somewhat dull.

So dull, in fact, that a short time before members had been summoned by bells to the floor to listen to the issue at hand, whether they wanted to or not. It concerned admittance of Mexican farm laborers.

The quorum bell was answered by 243 members, most of whom were still on the floor when the shooting started in what is called the Ladies' Gallery.

As a police reporter many years ago I was irked by eyewitnesses who had heard shots only as "backfiring automobiles," "blowouts" or "firecrackers." But this time I too thought that firecrackers were going off, and I thought it was a Latin demonstration.

But only for a moment. I saw two men and a woman, in the second row of the Ladies Gallery, pumping at pistols. The two men appeared to be aiming at the desk of Representative Charles A. Halleck of Indiana, the Republican Floor Leader.

The woman had her pistol high,

Continued on Page 16, Column 7

EISENHOWER TARGET FOR FANATICS ALSO

Secret Service Men Detected Puerto Rican Plot Against President in November

Special to The New York Times.

WASHINGTON, March 1—Puerto Rican extremists have been conspiring to harm President Eisenhower if they got the opportunity, according to the Federal Secret Service.

Henry Cabot Lodge Jr., chief of the United States delegation to the United Nations, was put under twenty-four-hour guard last November for the same reason.

U. E. Baughman, chief of the Secret Service, was asked tonight about the reports of a conspiracy against the President.

"Three or four months ago," he replied, "the Secret Service obtained information indicating the Puerto Rican Nationalists were still possibly interested in harming the President in their fight for independence."

This statement from the head of the agency charged with protecting the close watch that the Secret Service had kept on the Nationalist movement ever since two of its members tried to kill President Truman on Nov. 1, 1950.

Truman Case Still 'Open'

Although one assassin was killed in the gun battle in front of Blair House and Oscar Collazo, his companion, is serving a life sentence, the Secret Service still carries the attempted assassination of Mr. Truman as an "open case." It does this because it has not given up the possibility of rounding up the conspirators who directed the assassins.

Mr. Baughman said that the Secret Service had obtained information about designs on President Eisenhower last November. That coincided with the threats on Mr. Lodge. It was indicated tonight that there was an apparent link between the threats to Mr. Lodge and the designs on the President.

A police guard was put around

Continued on Page 17, Column 2

Nehru Decries U. S. Policy On Asia and the 'Cold War'

By ROBERT TRUMBULL
Special to The New York Times.

NEW DELHI, India, March 1—In Kashmir should be removed. Prime Minister Jawaharlal Nehru scathingly condemned virtually the entire United States policy in Asia and in the "cold war" today.

His most outspoken speech delivered to the House of the People, the lower chamber of Parliament, was repeatedly interrupted by thunderous applause. He was given a prolonged ovation at its end.

Mr. Nehru was commenting on President Eisenhower's personal letter last week informing the Indian leader of Washington's intention to furnish military aid to Pakistan and simultaneously offering the same assistance to India.

Mr. Nehru scorned General Eisenhower's suggestion with the statement that "in making this suggestion, the President has done less than justice to us or to himself."

"If we object to military aid being given to Pakistan, we would be hypocrites and unprincipled opportunists to accept such aid ourselves," he added.

The Prime Minister told the cheering House that United States members of the United Nations cease-fire observer team

He said that "these American observers can no longer be treated by us as neutrals" in India's dispute with Pakistan over possession of the strategic northern state.

[At United Nations Headquarters a spokesman said no action would be taken pending an official communication from India. In Washington a State Department spokesman said India would have to complain to the United Nations if she wanted the United States members withdrawn.]

In his tersely formal reply to General Eisenhower, which he read out, Mr. Nehru coldly thanked the President for his "assurances," but dismissed them with this curt statement: "You are, however, aware of the views of my Government and our people in regard to this matter. We shall continue to pursue that policy."

The India note ignored the offer of arms.

Mr. Nehru, in his speech, took the version of United States policy in Asia as quoted from testimony by Walter S. Robertson, Assistant Secretary of State, before a

Continued on Page 5, Column 2

WITNESS DESCRIBES continued

Atom Blast Opens Test in Pacific; No Hint of Hydrogen Plans Given

Special to The New York Times.

WASHINGTON, March 1—The Atomic Energy Commission today announced the first in a new series of test explosions at its Pacific proving ground in the Marshall Islands.

No further announcement was expected until the series ended.

A forty-two word statement which was as much of the story as the commission wanted the public to know at this stage, read:

"[Rear Admiral] Lewis L. Strauss, chairman of the Atomic Energy Commission, announced today that Joint Task Force Seven has detonated an atomic device at the A. E. C.'s Pacific proving ground in the Marshall Islands. This detonation was the first in a series of tests."

The language of Admiral Strauss' statement did not make

clear whether the "atomic device" was of the fission or thermonuclear (hydrogen) type. There has been unofficial indications, however, that a variety of hydrogen weapons or devices will be tested during the next several weeks.

The most powerful of these is expected to be an actual hydrogen bomb with perhaps twice the explosive power of the experimental device that disintegrated an island at Eniwetok atoll on Nov. 1, 1952.

Representative W. Sterling Cole of upstate New York, the chairman of the Joint Congressional Committee on Atomic Energy, disclosed two weeks ago that the first device had "completely obliterated" the island

Continued on Page 6, Column 5

"All the News That's Fit to Print"

The New York Times.

LATE CITY EDITION
Increasingly cloudy today. Rain tonight and tomorrow.
Temperature Range Today—Max., 45; Min., 31
Temperatures Yesterday—Max., 46; Min., 31
Full U. S. Weather Bureau Report, Page 43

Copyright, 1954, by The New York Times Company.

VOL. CIII..No. 35,111.   Entered as Second-Class Matter, Post Office, New York, N. Y.   NEW YORK, FRIDAY, MARCH 12, 1954.   Times Square, New York 36, N. Y. Telephone LAckawanna 4-1000   FIVE CENTS

HALF OF DOCKMEN IN BROOKLYN JOIN OUTLAW WALKOUT

Huge Food Cargoes Reported in Danger of Spoiling — Trade Losses Mounting

COURT IS PICKETED AGAIN

Rally Backs a Tie-Up Until I. L. A. Is Certified—Jersey Strikers Pledge Return

By A. H. RASKIN

The outlaw dock strike got worse yesterday.

Half of the longshoremen in Brooklyn, the only section of the port that had been operating normally, joined the week-old walkout.

Importers notified the National Labor Relations Board that millions of dollars worth of fruit and vegetables were in danger of rotting on piers and in the holds of strike-stalled ships.

The tie-up turned into a blockade when Philadelphia locals of the old International Longshoremen's Association refused to unload passenger or cargo vessels diverted from New York. Rank-and-file leaders of the local stoppage sought to make the boycott coast-wide, but received no immediate assurances of help from other ports.

The Commerce and Industry Association reported that the turbulent dock labor situation was causing many large corporations to shunt their import and export schedules to other cities. The group predicted that 10 per cent of the lost trade never would be recovered.

The one bright spot in the waterfront picture was a promise by Jersey City strikers to go back to their jobs this morning. The promise was given by spokesmen for both of the I. L. A. and its American Federation of Labor rivals—at a conference with Commissioner Lawrence A. Whipple in Jersey City.

Picket Line Is Crossed

The federation union, which has been opposing the walkout, mobilized 100 longshoremen to pierce an I. L. A. picket line at a Manhattan wharf of the United Fruit Company. Ignoring the jeers of several hundred members of the old union, five gangs of A. F. L. dock workers walked onto Pier 3, just north of the Battery, to unload coffee and miscellaneous cargo from Guatemala and Honduras. The cargo was aboard the freighter Loviland.

Two hundred and fifty I. L. A. strikers renewed the picketing of the United States Court House in Foley Square. It was the second time they had marched outside the building in protest against two anti-strike court orders.

One was an injunction forbidding the I. L. A. to strike or to interfere with waterfront truck movements. The other was a $100,000 contempt action against the union and three officers of its West Side locals.

The strike has been carried on in defiance of the two orders and in disregard of back-to-work appeals by Capt. William V. Bradley, president of the I. L. A. Strike leaders say the walkout will continue until the dock union is certified as the sole bargaining agent for the port's 24,000 dock workers.

The threat to keep the port tied up for all the months that may

Continued on Page 43, Column 2

Wilson Aide Named Secretary of Navy

Associated Press Wirephoto
Charles S. Thomas, Assistant Secretary of Defense, after he was named the successor to Robert B. Anderson, right.

Special to The New York Times.
WASHINGTON, March 11—Charles Sparks Thomas, Assistant Secretary of Defense, was nominated by President Eisenhower today to be Secretary of the Navy. Mr. Thomas, if confirmed by the Senate, will succeed Robert B. Anderson, who will become Under Secretary of Defense when Roger B. Kyes vacates the post on May 1. A successor to Mr. Thomas has not yet been chosen. The

Continued on Page 8, Column 4

'Direct' Warning to Reds Urged by U. S. at Caracas

By SYDNEY GRUSON

CARACAS, Venezuela, March 11—The United States called on the Tenth Inter-American Conference today to issue a "simple, clear and direct" warning to the leaders of international communism to keep hands off the Americas.

The best way to do this, John Foster Dulles, United States Secretary of State, said, is to adopt the United States anti-Communist resolution without crippling amendments. These, he said, would "alter the heart" of the proposed denunciation of international communism as a threat to the hemisphere.

After a week of general debate the Communist issue was joined late today in the Political Committee when consideration of the resolution began. The Secretary made his third major speech on the question in an effort to block a series of crippling amendments submitted by Mexico.

Mr. Dulles sought to eliminate the fears of some delegates that the resolution could, in his own words, "be interpreted as intervention or justifying intervention in the genuinely domestic affairs of an American state."

'Natural Historical Fears'

"This concern is, we believe, due to natural historical fears rather than to any language in the United States proposal," the Secretary said.

Delegates of Argentina, Guatemala and Mexico, all of whom spoke in the wind-up of the general debate this morning, had expressed this fear. The spokesmen for Guatemala, where the Communists have won high positions in the Government, have charged that the United States was seeking to cloak interventionist ideas in the guise of collective action against Guatemala.

Mexico's delegate spoke twice today, in the general debate and in answer to Secretary Dulles' rejection of Mexico's amendments. On both occasions Roberto Cordova of Mexico emphasized that his country was not trying to defend international communism but only the right of any people to choose their own form of government and political institutions.

Mexico, he said, would willingly subscribe to the United States proposal if his delegation were convinced that it did not represent a backward step regarding intervention. But later he brushed aside Mr. Dulles' assurances on this point and in fact took no note of the Secretary's announcement that the United States was itself proposing an addition to the declarative portion of the resolution to declare:

"This declaration of foreign policy made by the American republics in relation to the dangers originating outside this hemisphere is designed to protect and not to impair the inalienable right of each American state freely to choose its own form of government and economic system and to live its own social and cultural life."

As the resolution stood before,

Continued on Page 6, Column 6

SCHWABLE TELLS OF P. O. W. ORDEAL

Tells How His Mental Torture by Reds Almost Made Him Believe Germ 'Confession'

By ELIE ABEL
Special to The New York Times.

WASHINGTON, March 11—Col. Frank H. Schwable described today how a mature man could be conditioned to accept as real the fictions he had invented to appease the Communists.

"Taking the witness chair for the first time, the lean, nervous Marine aviator talked for six hours before a court of inquiry. He tried to explain how it felt to have his brain washed, how reality became a blur in the mind, how the judgment could be fogged and the will destroyed.

He did not quite believe his own story that the United States had waged bacteriological warfare in Korea, Colonel Schwable told the court, which is investigating his false "confession."

"I was never convinced in my own mind that we in the First Marine Air Wing had used bug warfare," he testified. "I knew we hadn't. But the rest of it [the fraudulent confession] was real to me—the conferences, the planes and how they would go about their missions."

Rear Admiral Thomas J. Cooper, who was questioning the

Continued on Page 5, Column 5

264 Exposed to Atom Radiation After Nuclear Blast in Pacific

By The Associated Press.

WASHINGTON, March 11—The Atomic Energy Commission said tonight that twenty-eight Americans and 236 natives were "unexpectedly" subjected to "some radiation" during the recent atomic test in the Marshall Islands but all those exposed were "reported well."

The commission announced on March 1 that the first of a series of nuclear tests had started in the Pacific proving grounds.

The commission announcement today said:

"During the course of a routine atomic test in the Marshall Islands, twenty-eight United States personnel and 236 residents were transported from neighboring atolls to Kwajalein Island according to plans as a precautionary measure.

"The individuals were unexpectedly exposed to some radiation. There were no burns. All are reported well.

"After completion of the atomic tests, they will be returned to their homes."

The commission made no immediate amplification of this announcement. However, it seemed probably that a "fall-out" of radioactive waste and activated moisture from a cloud drifting from the explosion probably descended on the Americans and natives on the atoll to which they had been moved.

Atomic test officials try to make careful forecasts of wind directions but sometimes miscalculate.

Exposure to mild radiation is not necessarily dangerous. Reporters last spring were within two miles of an atomic explosion at the Nevada proving ground and later walked to "Ground

Continued on Page 8, Column 4

SENATE COMBINES STATEHOOD PLANS BY VOTE OF 46-43

Ignores Eisenhower's Wishes for Action on Hawaii Alone —Democrats Score Victory

By CLAYTON KNOWLES

WASHINGTON, March 11—The Senate disregarded Administration wishes in voting today to put Hawaiian and Alaskan statehood proposals in a single bill.

The decision to join the proposals carried by a vote of 46 to 43 and came a day after President Eisenhower had urged separate consideration of the statehood measures. He had asked for immediate statehood for Hawaii alone. This is the Republican party position.

The Senate's vote was mainly along party lines, with the Democrats winning. However, the plan to combine the bills prevailed by the margin of the votes of three Republicans who broke with their party on the issue. They were Senators William Langer of North Dakota, John M. Butler of Maryland and George W. Malone of Nevada.

Forty-two Democrats and the Senate's one independent, Wayne Morse of Oregon, cast the other votes for a combined bill.

Forty-one Republicans and two Democrats, Spessard L. Holland of Florida and Russell B. Long of Louisiana, opposed the merger plan.

Knowland to Back Bill

The issue in the three-day debate preceding the vote was whether statehood aspirations of Hawaii and Alaska would be hurt or helped by putting them together. Senator William F. Knowland of California, Republican Senate leader, contended it would hurt. Senator Clinton P. Anderson, Democrat of New Mexico and sponsor of the one-package proposal, asserted it would help.

The vote along party lines stemmed largely from the fact that Hawaii is normally Republican and might be expected to send a Republican delegation to Congress, while Alaska is Democratic at the polls and probably would send Democrats to the Congress.

After the Senate action, Senator Knowland, conceding a chance to pass a combined bill, said he would vote for it. So did other Republicans in opposition on the vote today. Senator Hugh Butler of Nebraska, Interior Committee chairman who fought the Anderson amendment, said the Senate "might fool some people by passing the bill now before a conference yesterday.

The Nebraska Republican alluded to the fact that a group of Southern Democrats, numbering fifteen to twenty, had supported the Anderson amendment in the hope of defeating both statehood proposals. Senator George A. Smathers, Democrat of Florida, frankly conceded during debate

Continued on Page 13, Column 3

Lasting Prevention of Polio Reported in Vaccine Tests

Dr. Salk Says Discovery Fights Off All 3 Kinds of Crippling Disease

By WILLIAM L. LAURENCE
Special to The New York Times.

NEW ORLEANS, March 11—The latest tests on children with the anti-polio vaccine have revealed that the vaccine provides the body with lasting defensive powers against the three types of viruses causing the disease, it was reported tonight.

This was described as the long-sought answer to a vital question, making it practically certain not only that the vaccine will produce effective immunity against all the three types of polio but also that the immunity will be of the lasting type, possibly for the individual's lifetime.

This could mean that within the next three to five years polio, crippler of young and old alike, will join diphtheria, smallpox, typhoid and other formerly dreaded infectious diseases as plagues finally tamed and conquered by man.

The newest findings were described here tonight before the New Orleans Graduate Medical Assembly by Dr. Jonas E. Salk, of the Virus Research Laboratory, University of Pittsburgh School of Medicine.

Continued on Page 22, Column 3

Dr. Jonas E. Salk
Associated Press

Dr. Salk developed the vaccine against the three types of polio-producing viruses, using viruses that had been rendered incapable of producing the disease while they still retained their power to produce immunity.

The whole issue will go next week, probably on Tuesday, to the full Senate Rules Committee. The universal expectation in the Senate was that the full committee would sustain the Repub-

ARMY CHARGES M'CARTHY AND COHN THREATENED IT IN TRYING TO OBTAIN PREFERRED TREATMENT FOR SCHINE

SENATOR ATTACKS

Hits Back at Stevenson, Murrow and Flanders in Radio Broadcast

Special to The New York Times.
WASHINGTON, March 11—Senator Joseph R. McCarthy struck back tonight at criticism of him by Adlai E. Stevenson, Edward R. Murrow and Ralph E. Flanders.

The Wisconsin Republican said that Mr. Stevenson's assertion that only one alleged active Communist had been found in the Government in the last year was "absolutely false."

He called Mr. Murrow, Columbia Broadcasting System commentator, one of the "extreme Left Wing bleeding-heart elements of television and radio."

He cited an article in The Pittsburgh Sun-Telegraph of Feb. 18, 1935, to charge that Mr. Murrow had been on the advisory council for a summer session at Moscow University, where overthrow of the existing social order was taught.

[Three and a half hours after Mr. McCarthy's broadcast, Mr. Murrow issued a statement in which he said that in 1935, in his capacity as assistant director of the Institute of International Education, he was a member of a committee for a summer school in Moscow. He added, however, that "in actual fact the summer school was canceled by Russian authorities before it began."]

McCarthy Quotes Lincoln

Mr. McCarthy said he would rather stand with Abraham Lincoln, who said during Civil War times the danger to the United States was from within and not from without, rather than with Senator Flanders, a Republican of Vermont, who said the danger today is from without rather than from within.

Appearing on a question and answer radio broadcast with Fulton Lewis Jr., over the Mutual Broadcasting System, Senator McCarthy struck back at Messrs. Stevenson, Murrow and Flanders but made no mention of the implied criticism voiced by President Eisenhower at his news conference yesterday.

He also made no mention of his quarrel with the National Broadcasting Company and the Columbia Broadcasting System because they refused him free time for a reply to Mr. Stevenson and gave it instead to the Republican National Committee, which designated Vice President Nixon to make the official reply Saturday night.

Mr. Murrow had devoted a third

Continued on Page 11, Column 1

Cohn Scored When Woman Denies McCarthy's Charges

Mrs. Moss Counters Accusation as Red While Senators Decry 'Innuendo'— Crowd Applauds Hearing Scene

Special to The New York Times.
WASHINGTON, March 11—Mrs. Annie Lee Moss, suspended softly but flatly denied all Communist party activities or membership today.

The crowded caucus room of the Senate Office Building, where the Senate Permanent Subcommittee on Investigation was in session, rang with repeated applause as Democratic members struck at "convicting people by rumor and hearsay and innuendo."

The target of Democratic resentment was Roy Cohn, chief counsel for the subcommittee headed by Senator Joseph R. McCarthy, Wisconsin Republican. Mr. Cohn had countered Mrs. Moss's testimony by saying the subcommittee had still secret evidence that she was a Communist.

The Democrats, led by Senator John L. McClellan of Arkansas, demanded that he produce the evidence or refrain from public mention of it.

Senator McCarthy, in the original hearing at which the charges against Mrs. Moss were produced, had suggested she would "run the risk of indictment for perjury" when she appeared before the committee.

Senator McCarthy was absent from the committee room today when the scene over Mrs. Moss' testimony took place. He had gone to his office to prepare for his radio appearance later in which he answered criticism of him and the Republican party by Adlai E. Stevenson, the 1952 Democratic Presidential nominee.

No effort was made by the presiding officer, Senator Karl E. Mundt, South Dakota Republican, to check the crowd's applause or to interfere with the Democrats in their vigorous denunciation of Mr. Cohn's tactics.

Senator Mundt ordered Mr.

Continued on Page 10, Column 3

SENATE UNIT ASKS OUSTER OF CHAVEZ

Cites Election Irregularities in '52 but Does Not Accuse New Mexico Democrat

By WILLIAM S. WHITE

WASHINGTON, March 11—A Senate showdown on a long-forecast Republican effort to unseat Senator Dennis Chavez because of alleged election irregularities in 1952 drew near today. A Republican-controlled Senate subcommittee formally filed its expected report recommending that the New Mexico Democrat's seat be held vacant.

It also urged that the Senate find that "no member was elected from New Mexico in the 1952 general election."

The Republicans asserted that there had been no free expression of the will of the people, in part because of the alleged denial of the right of secret ballot. Senator Chavez nowhere was charged with fraud.

The Republican subcommittee chairman, Senator Frank A. Barrett of Wyoming, said there had been "no intention to cast aspersion" on Mr. Chavez. It simply had been impossible to determine whether Senator Chavez or his Republican opponent, Brig. Gen. Patrick J. Hurley, retired, actually had won, Mr. Barrett said.

The whole issue will go next week, probably on Tuesday, to the full Senate Rules Committee. The universal expectation in the Senate was that the full committee would sustain the Repub-

Democrats Are Confident

The Democrats, who had insisted on clearing the issue without further delay, plainly were confident he would be sustained. Disinterested observation seemed to support their confidence.

If Senator Chavez should be ousted and the Republican Governor of New Mexico, Edwin L. Mechem, should appoint a Republican as temporary successor, the Republican party would gain actual, as distinguished from its present nominal, control of the Senate.

The improbability of such an outcome, however, was reflected by the fact that there now were more Democrats in the Senate than Republicans and in the fact that it was the Democrats who were demanding decisive action.

The Democratic member of the subcommittee, Senator Thomas C. Hennings Jr. of Missouri, gave notice that he would file a dissenting report upholding Mr. Chavez' right to his seat.

Versions of the events leading to the meeting differed sharply. Mr. White said Mr. Murchison had arranged it on his own motion. But the Texans said it had been requested by John J. McCloy, chairman of the Chase National Bank, of which Percy J. Ebbott is president.

STEVENS A TARGET

Report Quotes Counsel As Saying Secretary Would Be 'Through'

The text of the Army's report is printed on Page 9A.

By W. H. LAWRENCE
Special to The New York Times.

WASHINGTON, March 11—The Administration said it had been subjected to direct threats by Senator Joseph R. McCarthy and his chief counsel, Roy Cohn.

The threats, the Army said, had been made in an effort to obtain preferential treatment for G. David Schine, now a private in the Army but formerly an investigator for the McCarthy subcommittee.

In a thirty-four-page report sent to each member of Senator McCarthy's Permanent Subcommittee on Investigations and some members of the Armed Services Committee, the Army declared the Wisconsin Republican and Mr. Cohn first had sought a direct commission for Private Schine.

Failing in that, the report said, they had then demanded for him an assignment in the New York area so he could study alleged subversive material in West Point textbooks.

In the period between Oct. 15 and Nov. 3, before Senator McCarthy began his open fight with the Army, John G. Adams, Army Counsel, reported he had told Mr. Cohn that it would not be in the national interest to give preferential treatment to Private Schine.

"Mr. Cohn replied that if the national interest was what the Army wanted, he'd give it a little and then proceeded to outline how he would expose the Army in its worst light and show the country how shabbily it is being run," the report declared.

Threat to Stevens Cited

The report quoted Mr. Cohn as threatening on one occasion to "wreck the Army" and make certain that Robert T. Stevens was "through" as the Secretary of the Army. At another time, the report said, "Mr. Cohn stated to Mr. Adams that he would teach Mr. Adams what it meant to go over his head."

The report is expected to spur growing demands for Mr. Cohn's ouster.

Senator McCarthy made it clear in response that he would accept battle with "one or two" in the Army high command on the Cohn-Schine case. He said he had instructed his own committee staff to pull out all its files everything bearing on the case and give them to him so they could be "made available to the American public."

"I don't like to do it," he told a New York Times correspondent. "The deeper I get into it, I'm convinced the Army as a whole is damn clean. What some people in the Army do doesn't mean the entire Army."

He said he had sought at a luncheon with Charles E. Wilson, Secretary of Defense, yesterday

Continued on Page 9-B, Col 2

SHOWDOWN NEARS ON TAX EXEMPTION

Martin Admits Some Votes of Democrats Are Needed to Defeat Increase Plan

Special to The New York Times.
WASHINGTON, March 11—The Administration will need the votes of some Democrats to win a showdown battle next week against higher personal income tax exemptions.

This was conceded by the Speaker of the House of Representatives, Joseph W. Martin Jr., Republican of Massachusetts. He said he realized some members of his party would break ranks on the issue but added:

"I am of the opinion that there will be enough responsible members of the Democratic party to more than offset what losses we may have."

His analysis was in response to a prediction by Representative Sam Rayburn of Texas, House minority leader, that the Democrats would win the fight for a $100 increase in present exemptions of $600 each for taxpayers and dependents.

Mr. Rayburn said after a caucus of House Democrats that he knew of none who would vote against the proposal. In that case, defection of half a dozen or so Republicans, depending on the absentee situation when the vote was taken, could bring victory for the Democrats.

Parliamentary preliminaries for the fight were completed this afternoon when the Rules Com-

Continued on Page 8, Column 6

White Meets Backers of Young; Denies Central Compromise Bid

By ROBERT E. BEDINGFIELD

William White, president of the New York Central Railroad Company, had two important visitors in his offices at 230 Park avenue yesterday: Clint W. Murchison and Sid W. Richardson.

They are the Texas millionaires who bought 800,000 shares of Central stock—one-eighth of the outstanding shares—last month from the Chesapeake and Ohio Railway Company to help their friend Robert R. Young in his attempt to wrest control of the $2,600,000,000 New York Central System from its present management.

Mr. White said the meeting had been arranged on his own motion. But the Texans said it had been requested by John J. McCloy, chairman of the Chase National Bank, of which Percy J. Ebbott is president.

Mr. McCloy, a spokesman said last night that the request for the meeting had originated with Mr. Murchison. But a spokesman for Mr. Young insisted yesterday that the visit had been in response to an appeal from the Central forces for a Young representative to discuss settlement of their differences.

Mr. White branded as a "plain lie" intimations that the Central management might be seeking a compromise with Mr. Young.

Mr. White summoned reporters late yesterday afternoon to deny the "compromise" rumors that had spread through Wall Street and the Grand Central Terminal area after it was dis-

Continued on Page 36, Column 3

"All the News
That's Fit to Print"

The New York Times.

LATE CITY EDITION
Clearing and continued cold to-
day; fair tonight and tomorrow.
Temperature Range Today—Max., 45; Min., 32
Temperature Yesterday—Max., 44; Min., 32
Full U.S. Weather Bureau Report, Page 63

Copyright, 1954, by The New York Times Company.

VOL. CIII..No. 35,131.   Entered as Second-Class Matter,
Post Office, New York, N. Y.   NEW YORK, THURSDAY, APRIL 1, 1954.   Times Square, New York 36, N. Y.
Telephone Lackawanna 4-1000   FIVE CENTS

SOVIET IN BID TO JOIN NATO; U. S. SAYS 'NO'

OFFER BY MOLOTOV

He Urges West to Enter All-European Pact— Deplores 'Cold War'

Text of Soviet note to West on European security, Page 4.

By HARRISON E. SALISBURY
Special to The New York Times.

MOSCOW, March 31—The So-
viet Union has proposed that the
United States and West European states join in a Soviet-spon-
sored general European security
treaty. In return the Soviet Union is prepared to examine the
question of assuming membership in the North Atlantic Treaty
Organization.

The Soviet diplomatic move
was contained in a note Vyacheslav M. Molotov, Soviet Foreign
Minister, handed to Charles E.
Bohlen, United States Ambassador, and his British and French
diplomatic colleagues, Sir William
Hayter and Louis Joxe.

There were qualifications and
provisos, both written and implied, in Mr. Molotov's proposal,
which was transmitted by the
Western Ambassadors to Washington, London and Paris.

But the essence of what Mr.
Molotov suggested was plain—
that as soon as possible the "cold
war," should be called off.

[The Soviet proposals rejected
the Soviet proposals. A State
Department spokesman said the
Soviet Government simply was
continuing its effort to block the
development of West Euro-
pean security. Paris sources
called the Soviet note an attempt to spread confusion on
the European Defense Com-
munity Treaty and to undermine the Atlantic alliance.
British sources termed the
Soviet suggestion of joining
the alliance "just a Trojan
horse."]

Defense Plan Main Target

The Soviet Foreign Minister
made it plain that his immediate
target was the European Defense
Community.

But Mr. Molotov said the Atlantic alliance was another matter.

Mr. Molotov suggested that his
proposed all-European organization and the Atlantic alliance be
placed in balance. He proposed
that all European powers, plus
the United States, could join the
Soviet - sponsored organization
while the Soviet Union might
become a member of the Atlantic
alliance.

Mr. Molotov noted that the
world was facing the peril of
war in which atomic and hydrogen bombs threatened "incalculable disaster," including the annihilation of peaceful peoples, the
wiping out of whole cities, of
contemporary industry, culture
and science of "ancient centers
of civilization" as well as "the
great capitals of the states of
the world."

Mr. Molotov asserted that in
this moment all the world .wers
bore an especially great responsibility and said the Soviet Union

Continued on Page 5, Column 3

France Ousts Juin For Anti-Pact Talk

[photo]
The New York Times
Marshal Alphonse P. Juin

Special to The New York Times.

PARIS, Thursday, April 1—
Marshal Alphonse-Pierre Juin
was disciplined by the French
Cabinet at a special meeting
early this morning for his
speech against the European
army treaty and for a snub to
Premier Joseph Laniel. The

Continued on Page 7, Column 3

PRESIDENT BACKS FIRM ASIA POLICY

Supports 'United Action' Plan of Dulles—Senator Douglas Urges Facing War Risk

By WILLIAM S. WHITE
Special to The New York Times.

WASHINGTON, March 31—
President Eisenhower made it
plain today that this Government
was deeply committed to "united
action" against any Communist
effort to overrun Southeast Asia.

He underwrote every word uttered by his Secretary of State,
John Foster Dulles, in proclaiming that policy in a speech two
nights ago.

[The Soviet Foreign Min-
istry in Moscow denied Mr.
Dulles' assertion that Foreign
Minister Molotov had agreed
the Geneva conference would
not be a five-power meeting.]

The President defined "united
action" as primarily the responsibility of the free peoples directly under threat. He declared also
that, speaking generally, the
United States could put itself under no greater disadvantages
than by spreading its ground
forces and other forces about the

Continued on Page 12, Column 4

Reds in Mass Attack Against Dienbienphu

By TILLMAN DURDIN
Special to The New York Times.

SAIGON, Vietnam, March 31—
Vietminh forces last night
launched a new mass assault
against the French defenses at
Dienbienphu.

[The French High Command
in Hanoi said three Vietminh
divisions were assaulting Dienbienphu, The United Press reported.]

During a night of savage fighting the Communist-led Vietminh
troops established a foothold
within the French positions.
However, they were pushed back
this morning at some points by
desperately resisting French Union assignments.

A late bulletin from French
headquarters here said violent
combat continued today. Bad
weather yesterday facilitated the
beginning of the Vietminh assault, but as the clouds cleared

Continued on Page 7, Column 1

I. L. A. INSURGENTS REJECT PAY RISE, STALL PIER PEACE

Eisenhower, Putting Local Action First, Says U. S. Is Prepared to Cooperate

By A. H. RASKIN

Insurgent elements in the old
International Longshoremen's Association yesterday killed a union-
inspired move to end their strike,
the longest and costliest in the
port's history.

The union's sixty-two-member
wage-scale committee spurned an
employer pay offer and demanded
a contract that would make the
I. L. A. sole bargaining agent
for the 24,000 workers on New
York and New Jersey piers.

The shipping industry retorted
that it could not legally sign such
an agreement until the National
Labor Relations Board decided
whether the old union or its
American Federation of Labor
rival was entitled to speak for
the dock workers.

The only remaining hope for
a quick end to the twenty-seven-
day tie-up was the possibility
that the union might order the
strikers back to the piers after
the labor board in Washington
had ruled on a new election. A
ruling is expected before the end
of this week.

At a City Hall conference with
Deputy Mayor Henry Epstein,
I. L. A. leaders authorized a
statement that the sooner the
board handed down its ruling the
sooner the men would be back
on the job. However, they shied
away from any clear-cut promise
that the strike would be called
off as soon as the board acted.

President Watching Strike

In Washington, President Eisenhower said the Government was
alert to the strike situation and
was prepared to take whatever
action might be necessary
to cope with it, in cooperation
with state and city authorities.
The President added that the
White House would be guided by
this rule: Everything is handled
locally as long as it can be.

The collapse of the back-to-
work effort here speeded Federal
plans to obtain a blanket injunction banning pickets and "loiter-
ers" from the waterfront. Charles
T. Douds, regional director of the
National Labor Relations Board,
laid the groundwork for such an
injunction by issuing a sweeping
complaint against the I. L. A.
last night.

The complaint, described by
members of Mr. Douds' staff as
the most drastic ever issued by
the board, accused the old union
and its locals of having intimidated dock workers through mass
picketing, blocking pier entrances,
physical assaults, overturning automobiles, slashing tires and con-
gregating in large groups" to
harass non-strikers.

Labor board' attorneys are expected to go into Federal Court
today to ask for an injunction
based on the Douds complaint.
Its purpose would be to halt all
picketing and other interference

Continued on Page 47, Column 4

H-BOMB CAN WIPE OUT ANY CITY, STRAUSS REPORTS AFTER TESTS; U. S. RESTUDIES PLANT DISPERSAL

NEW PLANS NEEDED

Defense Experts to Go to Work at Once on Factory Shifts

Special to The New York Times.

WASHINGTON, March 31—
Dispersal plans for defense production plants in major cities
will have to be redrawn in the
light of today's hydrogen bomb
disclosures.

Plans for dispersing defense
production plants to date have
been based upon a ten-mile radius
of "immediate danger," which
officials conceded was outdated.

Reliable sources indicated the
Administration's defense planners
were scheduled to go to work at
once to draw a new set of criteria
for plant dispersal.

The aim of the plant dispersal
program is to get new key production plants outside probable
target areas. To make this attractive, the Government offers
builders of such plants accelerated tax amortization certificates permitting them to write
off the cost of the plants for tax
purposes in five instead of the
normal twenty or more years.

Another plan, effective tomorrow, is to insure control of
materials and production in event
of atomic or hydrogen-bomb
attack, was announced by the
Government today. Nominal account will be kept of available
materials and production facilities so that an orderly but rapid
expansion for military atomic
production and construction will
be possible in an emergency.

Eighty-nine Surveys Undertaken

The industry dispersal program is under the supervision of
the Office of Defense Mobilization but is handled by the Area
Development Division of the
Business and Defense Services
Administration within the Department of Commerce.

The Area Development group
so far has organized committees
to make dispersal plans in many
key communities. Of eighty-nine
committees that have undertaken
such surveys, thirty-five have reported and their plans have been
approved by the Office of Defense Mobilization. Among these
is the committee for the New
York City 'metropolitan area,
which completed its work last
month.

Officials predicted that the
New York City survey, as well as
the others, probably would have
to be redone in the light of the
facts learned about the destructiveness of the hydrogen bomb.

In announcing the new De-
fense Materials System, the Business and Defense Services Administration explained that it

Continued on Page 23, Column 2

[map]
NEW YORK
CONN.
Bridgeport
Pleasantville
Torrytown
Armonk
White Plains
Scarsdale
Yonkers
Mt. Vernon
New Rochelle
Great Neck
Garden City
Morristown
Summit
NEW JERSEY
Plainfield
NEWARK
NEW YORK CITY
La Guardia Airport
Freeport
Long Beach
New Brunswick
Perth Amboy
Fort Hamilton
Atlantic Ocean
Princeton
Red Bank
Long Branch
Asbury Park
Miles

A TOTAL DESTRUCTION
B SEVERE DAMAGE
C MODERATE DAMAGE
D PARTIAL DAMAGE
E LIMIT OF INCENDIARY ACTION

50 MILES DIAMETER
32 MILES DIAMETER
28 MILES DIAMETER
16 MILES DIAMETER
8 MILES DIAMETER

The New York Times   April 1, 1954
Extent to which a hydrogen bomb explosion could devastate New York and its environs

Senate Unit Votes Changes President Asked in Taft Act

By JOSEPH A. LOFTUS
Special to The New York Times.

WASHINGTON, March 31—The Senate Labor Committee
approved a Taft-Hartley revision bill today with the Democrats
crying "steamroller." The vote was 7 to 6 along party lines.
The bill deals only with Presi-
dent Eisenhower's recommendations, minus an Administration
proposal to require Federally
conducted elections among workers before a strike could be called.

Another Administration proposal, for standards to conserve
union welfare funds, will be dealt
with separately after an inquiry.

The House Labor Committee
expects to report a bill on the
same subject next week. It will
contain many more revisions than
the Senate bill.

Two provisions dealing with
state powers were added to the
Senate committee draft today
just before the final vote to report a bill. They are certain to
be fought vigorously.

One of these new sections
deals with state emergencies. As
finally approved, it reads:

"Nothing in this act shall be
construed to interfere with the
enactment and enforcement by
the states of laws to deal in
emergencies with labor disputes
which, if permitted to occur or
continue, will constitute a clear
and present danger to the health
or safety of the people of the
state; provided, that no state
shall be authorized by this subsection to take action in any
labor dispute in which the Federal Government is acting pursuant to Sections 206 to 210, inclusive, of this act."

Sections 206 to 210 are the
national emergency provisions of
the Taft-Hartley Act. When
these are invoked, state action
would be superseded, but the

Continued on Page 34, Column 4

Calm in Middle East Urged by President

By The United Press.

WASHINGTON, March 31—
President Eisenhower called on
Israel and the Arab states today
to restrain their extremists and
permit other nations to help them
settle their disputes.

He declined to answer a question at his news conference as to
whether he believed the bitter
Arab-Israeli feud, which recently
erupted into new violence, should
be referred to the United Nations
Security Council. However, he
said the United Nations had the
full support of the United States
in its plan to seek harmony in
the Middle East.

General Eisenhower said the
United States had been giving
strong support to the plan to
develop the resources of the area
including the water resources of
the Jordan River, and hoped the
plan would be successful.

He said the Israeli-Arab issue
was so charged with emotional

Continued on Page 2, Column 2

EISENHOWER SIGNS TAX CUT MEASURE

Excise Reductions Effective Today—President Voices Hope of Business Gain

By JOHN D. MORRIS
Special to The New York Times.

WASHINGTON, March 31—
President Eisenhower signed the
$999,000,000 excise tax reduction
bill into law today. He voiced
hope that the damage to Federal
revenues would be offset to some
degree by the resulting stimula-
tion of business.

Federal sales taxes on a long
list of items, from pocketbooks
to household appliances, consequently will be reduced sharply
as of 12:01 A. M. tomorrow. The
savings are expected to be passed
along to consumers, at least in
part, by most of the industries
affected. On a majority of the
items covered, the tax cut
amounts to 50 per cent.

Enactment of the bill adds an
estimated $999,000,000 to the
Federal deficit of $2,928,000,000
projected by President Eisenhower for the 1955 fiscal year,
which starts next July 1.

On the ground that the Government could not afford such
revenue losses in addition to
those involved in other recent and
pending tax cuts, the Administration had opposed any broad-scale
reduction of excises at this time.

The President told his news
conference that, nevertheless, he
was accepting the bill whole-
heartedly. From the beginning,
he explained, there was a difference of opinion on the revenue
effects. One school of thought, he
noted, believes that the reductions can stimulate business to

Continued on Page 16, Column 7

HOUSING BAN FOES CLAIM A 'VICTORY'

G.O.P. House Chiefs Foresee 33,000 Units in Fiscal '55 —Eisenhower 'Delighted'

Special to The New York Times.

WASHINGTON, March 31—
What had been intended as a
defeat for the Eisenhower Administration developed as a probable victory today as a parliamentary tangle over public housing legislation began unraveling.

President Eisenhower himself
said he was delighted at the outcome.

Republican leaders of the House
of Representatives were said to
have claimed a victory by interpreting
the mix-up, which occurred in
the House yesterday, as meaning
that the Public Housing Administration is free to go ahead with
plans for construction of 33,000
to 35,000 new low-rent housing
units.

Today, the leaders moved to
provide authority for an additional 35,000 units in the year
starting July 1, 1955, by supporting an amendment to a general
housing bill that comes before
the House tomorrow.

Their aim is to give the President a legislative green light to
carry out the first two years of
his four-year program for 35,000
new units a year.

Action by Opposition

Yesterday's confusion in the
House resulted from the attempt
of public housing opponents, led
by Representative Howard W.
Smith, Democrat of Virginia, to
kill the entire program by striking from a pending appropriation bill a "rider" allowing construction of 20,000 new units in
the year starting July 1.

The rider was eliminated by
the bill on a point of order raised
by Mr. Smith, who successfully
challenged it as legislation on an
appropriations bill in violation of
House rules.

Killing the rider, according to
Mr. Smith, would leave the Government without authority to
start any new projects after next
July 1. He based this position on
an existing law, enacted as a
rider on the same appropriations
bill last year, limiting new construction to 20,000 units in the
present fiscal year and prohibiting any further construction
without Congressional authorization.

As soon as Mr. Smith had com-

Continued on Page 34, Column 4

VAST POWER BARED

March 1 Explosion Was Equivalent to Millions of Tons of TNT

Text of Strauss statement and conference transcript, Page 20.

By WILLIAM L. LAURENCE
Special to The New York Times.

WASHINGTON, March 31—The
United States can now build a
hydrogen bomb big enough to
destroy any city.

In revealing this today, Rear
Admiral Lewis L. Strauss, chairman of the United States Atomic
Energy Commission, hinted that
such a bomb could be delivered
by plane.

The bomb tested at the Eniwetok proving grounds on March
1, Admiral Strauss announced,
provided "a stupendous blast in
the megaton range." He said it
was "double that of the calculated estimate." A megaton is
equivalent to 1,000,000 tons of
TNT.

The explosive power attained
in the test was reported by a
member of the Joint Congressional Committee on Atomic Energy as twelve to fourteen mega-
tons. This represents an explosive force 600 to 700 times that
of the bombs that destroyed
Hiroshima and Nagasaki.

No Limit to Bomb Size

Admiral Strauss made his
statement at the President's news
conference. He declared that the
hydrogen bomb could be made as
large as desired—"large enough
to take out a city, to destroy
a city."

"How big a city?", he was
asked.

"Any city!"

"New York?"

"The metropolitan area, yes,"
he replied.

Admiral Strauss explained
later that by "metropolitan area"
he meant the heart of Manhattan and not the actual metropolitan area, which covers 3,550
square miles.

[Prime Minister Churchill,
yielding to Opposition pressure,
agreed to debate the Government's policy on the hydrogen
bomb in the House of Commons
Monday.]

Despite the hydrogen bomb's
enormous power, Admiral Strauss
said the test was "at no time
out of control." Furthermore, he
gave the nation and the world
the assurance given to him by
scientists that it was "impossible
for any such test or series of
tests to get out of control."

Admiral Strauss' appearance
at the President's press conference was at President Eisenhower's request. He made available
to the American people portions
of the report he had made to
President Eisenhower yesterday
on the hydrogen bomb tests in
the Pacific.

The tests of hydrogen weapons
on March 1 and 26, he said, have
"added enormous potential to our
military posture." He later amplified this remark with a statement that "the results of these

Continued on Page 21, Column 4

Color Film of First H-Bomb Test Is Previewed by Press in Capital

Special to The New York Times.

WASHINGTON, March 31—
The world's most fearsome
weapon, the fusion bomb, was
shown in action for the first time
here in public today before an
audience of representatives of the
press and other information
media.

They saw a reproduction on
color film of the phenomena that
followed the explosion of the first
full-scale hydrogen weapon in the
Pacific proving grounds in November, 1952.

The film was released by the
Atomic Energy Commission for
public issuance by the Federal
Civil Defense Administration. It
was intended for general release
at 6 P. M. April 7, and reviews

of it were to be embargoed until then.

However, a descriptive review
by a syndicated columnist appeared in newspapers a few hours
after the showing. Because of
this The Times is publishing its
review now.

The test in November, 1952,
was known as Operation Ivy, and
the device tested was known as
Mike. At the time it was said
the explosion was the greatest in
history. Since then, however, it
has been greatly exceeded by the
test explosions on March 1 and
26.

The event marks the entry of
mankind into the Hydrogen Age,
taking the fateful step from the
kiloton (thousands of tons) to the
megaton (millions of tons) of
explosive power in terms of TNT.

The film opens with an introduction by President Eisenhower,
who recites an excerpt from his
historic address before the United Nations on Dec. 8, 1953, relating to the need of the peoples of

Continued on Page 23, Column 2

10 Pupils Burned to Death in School Near Buffalo

[photo]
Associated Press Wirephoto
Smoke and flames billow from frame annex of an elementary school in Cheektowaga, N. Y.

Special to The New York Times.

BUFFALO, March 31—Ten
sixth grade pupils in the Cleveland Hill elementary school
died today in a fire that
trapped them in a room of the
school's one-story frame annex
on Mapleview Drive in suburban Cheektowaga. Twenty-
two other persons, nineteen of
them children, were burned or
injured and taken to hospitals.
The school has an enrollment
of more than 1,200. Hundreds

of pupils of the adjoining
Cleveland Hill High School
were sent home. The fire followed a blast that was described vari-
ously as an explosion and as a

Continued on Page 34, Column 5

The New York Times.

LATE CITY EDITION
Cloudy, scattered showers today.
Partly cloudy, cool tomorrow.
Temperature Range Today—Max., 58; Min., 47
Temperature Yesterday—Max., 60; Min., 48
Full U. S. Weather Bureau Report, Page 37

Copyright, 1954, by The New York Times Company.

VOL. CIII..No. 35,168.

Entered as Second-Class Matter.
Post Office, New York, N. Y.

NEW YORK, SATURDAY, MAY 8, 1954.

Times Square, New York 36, N. Y.
Telephone LAckawanna 4-1000

FIVE CENTS

PLEAS FOR SCHINE LACED BY THREATS, STEVENS TESTIFIES

Phone Calls Mingled Them. He Tells Jenkins, Who Brings Army Case to Sharp Focus

OFFICIAL DENIES 'BANTER'

Mundt Asserts Subcommittee Hit a 'Security Roadblock' on Monitored Conversations

Excerpts from transcript of the hearing are on Page 8.

By W. H. LAWRENCE
Special to The New York Times.

WASHINGTON, May 7—The Secretary of the Army testified today that Senator Joseph R. McCarthy and his key aides had mixed, in the same conversations, repeated requests for favored treatment for Pvt. G. David Schine with "threats" of continued exposure of alleged Communists in the Army.

Ray H. Jenkins, special counsel for the Senate subcommittee, propounded the queries to Army Secretary Robert T. Stevens that brought into sharp focus the heart of the Army case.

This was that the Senator and his staff had used the investigative power of the Senate to back up their demands for special favors for Private Schine who, until he was drafted, was an unpaid subcommittee consultant.

As Mr. Stevens, on his twelfth day on the stand, neared the end of his testimony, Mr. Jenkins propounded a series of climactic questions.

"I'll ask you," he said, "whether or not * * * many telephone calls were either transmitted to you or Mr. Adams [John G. Adams, Army Counselor] with reference to Mr. Schine?"

"Yes sir," the Secretary replied.

Subjects Intertwined

"I'll ask you," Mr. Jenkins continued, "whether or not in those [unclear] these [unclear] there were discussions not only with reference to Schine but with reference to the McCarthy investigating committee's work at Fort Monmouth. Were those two subjects discussed in the same conversations, on various occasions or on a few occasions, or on no occasions?"

"Yes, they were discussed on a number of occasions," Mr. Stevens declared.

"So that the conversations," Mr. Jenkins went on, "with reference to the investigation of Monmouth and with reference to Schine were intertwined, so to speak, in one telephone conversation. Is that right, Mr. Secretary?"

"Yes sir," the answer came.

"And did you not regard that," the counsel pursued, "as being a combination of a request for preferences for Schine, on the one hand, and correlated with a discussion or a threat of continued investigation of Fort Monmouth?"

"Yes, I couldn't separate the two," was Secretary Stevens' conclusion.

Mr. Stevens then coldly rejected suggestions by Senator Everett M. Dirksen, Illinois Republican, that the remarks taken as threatening might have been good-natured "banter." The Army Secretary said he regarded the threats as a "very serious matter."

Other major developments in

Continued on Page 8, Column 3

Seaway Bill Passed, Sent to Eisenhower

Special to The New York Times.

WASHINGTON, May 7—The Senate gave final Congressional approval today to the St. Lawrence Seaway bill.

It now goes to the White House where President Eisenhower has said he will sign the measure, which every President since Warren G. Harding has sought.

The Senate action was by voice vote. The Senate concurred in two minor changes made by the House of Representatives yesterday in giving approval of the bill by a vote of 241 to 158. The Senate had passed the measure, 51 to 33, on Jan. 20.

The bill, which authorizes the United States to join with Canada in constructing the project, calls for the establishment of a St. Lawrence Seaway Development Corporation to act for the United States subject to the supervision of the President.

General Eisenhower will name

Continued on Page 18, Column 5

State to Get $113,000,000 Under New U. S. Road Law

Grants Will Be Allocated Over 2 Years— 4 Classes of Highways to Benefit— City Expected to Gain $5,000,000

Special to The New York Times.

ALBANY, May 7—The Public Works Department estimated today that New York would get $113,000,000 Nof the $1,932,000,000 in Federal highway grants authorized by President Eisenhower yesterday.

The figure in the new law represented an increase of $41,600,000 over New York's grants under the old Federal-aid highway measure. The new amounts will be spread over a period of two years, starting July 1, 1955.

The new Federal grants, as under the old law, will have to be matched by an equal amount of state funds. This represented no problem for the state since it already was planning a huge expansion in state highway construction funds.

At this year's legislative session alternative constitutional amendments to authorize state bond issues of either $500,000,000 or $750,000,000 for highway construction received initial approval. One of the two will be taken up for final legislative ap-

proval and submission to the voters next year.

The Public Works Department analysis put the state's share of the new Federal funds at roughly $56,500,000 a year for the fiscal years 1956 and 1957. The first of these starts July 1, 1955, and the second July 1, 1956.

Four classes of roads will share in this amount: primary highways, secondary highways, urban arterial highways and interstate highway routes. More than $14,-700,000 a year is provided for primary highways. This is $3,-200,000 a year more than New York has been getting.

For secondary roads the new annual allocation is $5,900,000, an increase of $1,300,000. For urban arterial highways the new allowance is more than $22,900,000, an increase of almost $5,000,000. For interstate routes the new allocation is $12,700,000, an increase of $11,600,000.

Since New York City usually

Continued on Page 36, Column 3

Steel Workers Set to Snub Union Anti-Raiding Accord

By A. H. RASKIN
Special to The New York Times.

PITTSBURGH, May 7 — The 1,250,000-member United Steelworkers of America, C. I. O., intends to boycott the no-raiding pact between the American Federation of Labor and the Congress of Industrial Organizations.

The decision of David J. McDonald, president of the giant steel union, to withhold his signature from the peace plan represents as crippling a blow to the pact's effectiveness as the refusal of Dave Beck, an A. F. L. vice president, to bring his 1,300,-000-member International Brotherhood of Teamsters under the agreement.

Word of the steel union's plans leaked out here just one week after Mr. McDonald had forged an informal alliance with Mr. Beck and John L. Lewis, president of the United Mine Workers, independent, at a luncheon conference in Washington.

Close associates of the steel union head said his decision had been formed well before the meeting. Mr. McDonald was a member of the joint A. F. L.-C. I. O. committee that drafted the no-raiding pact last summer. The agreement was unanimous approval from the 1953 conventions of both organizations.

However, Mr. McDonald was understood to feel his own union should not commit itself until specific questions relating to the union's jurisdiction had been settled to its satisfaction.

Mr. McDonald is eager to integrate into his organization dock workers employed at Great Lakes ports through which iron ore is shipped to steel mills from the Mesabi range in upper Minnesota. The steel union recently won control over the crews on most of the ore boats and it feels

Continued on Page 10, Column 4

BUSINESS TO OFFER 3% TAX SUBSTITUTE

'Top Committee' Representing 67 Groups Seeks a Meeting With Mayor Wednesday

By PAUL CROWELL

Mayor Wagner was asked yesterday to discuss with a "top committee" of outstanding business men next Wednesday a "sound nonpartisan" proposal for added city revenue. The adoption of it would make unnecessary the extension of the 3 per cent sales tax to commercial services, the civic group said.

It was expected that the Mayor, in line with his announced policy of discussing major city problems with all responsible organizations seeking conferences, would grant the request, although the meeting might take place later in the week if the Mayor's office commitments prevented a Wednesday conference.

The request for the meeting was made in a telegram sent the Mayor by Harold W. McGraw and John T. Clancy, co-chairman of the Joint Conference for Better Government in New York City. This organization, claiming to represent sixty-seven business and taxpayers groups, is one of the leading opponents of the proposal to tax commercial services.

Asked Business to Join Plea

The telegram was in reply to the Mayor's letter of last Thursday in which he declared that extension of the sales tax to commercial services was "seemingly" inevitable unless a special session of the Legislature gave the city an acceptable substitute method of raising the $30,000,000 the broadened sales tax would yield in 1954-55.

In his letter the Mayor asked for the cooperation of the sixty-seven business and taxpayer groups in "a genuine non-partisan appeal to Albany." The McGraw-Clancy telegram assured the Mayor that the proposal to be presented for his consideration would represent the "high level non-partisan business thinking" of the "top committee," which would begin on Monday a series of executive meetings from which the plan would emerge.

The telegram expressed confidence that the plan would kill the "ruinous" sales tax proposal if the Mayor would "move sincerely" in cooperation with the business group.

The Mayor was informed that four members of the "top committee" had been chosen earlier in the day at a special meeting called to consider his letter.

They were Percy L. Ebbott, president of the Chase National Bank; Warren Lee Pierson, chairman of the board of Trans World Airlines, Inc.; Clinton W. Blume, president of the Real Es-

Continued on Page 23, Column 8

Housing Unit Counsel Ordered To Answer Charges or Be Ousted

Acting Commissioner Directs Bovard, Now on Leave, to Act in 14 Days

By The United Press.

WASHINGTON, May 7—Norman P. Mason, acting Federal Housing Administrator, charged today that the agency's counsel, Burton C. Bovard, had failed to do his job "satisfactorily" and gave him fourteen days to answer the charges or be dismissed.

Mr. Mason, named to clean up alleged widespread housing scandals, said he had "no evidence of illegal activity" by Mr. Bovard. The charges involve his "failure to satisfactorily carry out the duties of general counsel of the F. H. A.," he explained.

While he gave Mr. Bovard fourteen days to show cause why he should not be removed, he said he might extend that time. If counsel fails to answer the charges, Mr. Mason added, he will be "removed from office" within thirty days.

Mr. Mason also offered to give Mr. Bovard a public hearing within twenty-one days if he wanted to testify under oath and be subject to cross-examination.

Associated Press
Burton C. Bovard.

Meanwhile, Senator Harry F. Byrd, Democrat of Virginia, said he had sent to the Justice Department information that might be "helpful" in pinning down responsibility for Government hous-

Continued on Page 18, Column 7

TAFT ACT CHANGES KILLED BY SENATE; DEMOCRATS SOLID

Party Prevails in 50-42 Vote to Return Bill — President Rebuffed on Program

Special to The New York Times.

WASHINGTON, May 7—The Senate today killed amendments to the Taft-Hartley Law for the 1954 session of Congress.

A vote of 50 to 42 sent the Administration bill to revise the labor act back to committee.

The Democrats engineered this with solidarity, something they had not achieved on a roll-call vote in the modern cycle of labor legislation going back to the Norris-LaGuardia Act of 1932. Three Republicans joined them, but their votes did not affect the result.

Forty-six of the Senate's forty-eight Democrats were for returning the bill and the two others were paired for recommittal.

Just before the tally, Senator William F. Knowland of California, the Republican leader, sternly told his colleagues what nearly everybody understood:

"A motion to recommit this bill is a motion to kill this bill as far as this session is concerned."

Nobody challenged this on or off the Senate floor.

Senator H. Alexander Smith, Republican of New Jersey, confirmed such a conclusion after the vote. As chairman of the Labor Committee, he was in charge of the bill on the floor, and though he lost he appeared happy that the fight was over.

Feels Sense of Relief

"I feel a sense of relief," he commented. "I'm just as cheerful as a dickey bird."

He said he did not think the issue of state's rights in labor matters should be opened again at this session by his committee, and he did not think the House of Representatives would produce a bill on the subject, either. The House Labor Committee had been writing a bill, but was deferring a final vote until the Senate acted.

The Republican Senators who voted to recommit were: William Langer and Milton R. Young of North Dakota and George W. Malone of Nevada. Senator Wayne Morse of Oregon, an Independent, also voted this way.

The stated reason for the Democrats' solid vote to recommit the bill was the fact that the Republican majority on the Labor Committee would not consider amendments outside the area of President Eisenhower's recommendations.

This was not considered the final reason, however, at least not the sole reason.

The Northern Democrats, mostly friendly to labor, had been persuaded that the Administration bill would make the Taft-Hartley Law more undesirable to them and that they might fare better by waiting until the next Congress was elected.

The Southern Democrats felt that some of the President's recommendations undesirably weakened some of the labor controls. Also, if the bill were not recommitted, they would face

Continued on Page 11, Column 2

U. S. Rejects Soviet Note Seeking European Pact and Role in NATO

By DANA ADAMS SCHMIDT
Special to The New York Times.

WASHINGTON, May 7—The United States rejected today the Soviet Union's proposal of March 31 that the "cold war" be ended by formation of a new European security organization and its suggestion for Soviet admission

Text of United States reply to Soviet note is on Page 6.

to the North Atlantic Treaty Organization.

A State Department spokesman had rejected the Soviet proposal the day it was made as a transparent maneuver to upset Western security arrangements.

In the note delivered by the United States Embassy in Moscow to the Soviet Foreign Ministry, John Foster Dulles, Secretary of State, spelled out the United States rejection and proposed instead that the Soviet Union demonstrate its good intentions in a

step by step elimination of the outstanding sources of international tension.

Possibly in response to criticism in Europe of the State Department's original out-of-hand rejection of the Soviet note of March 31, the new note emphasized that this reply had been worked out in consultation with the British and French Governments.

Mr. Dulles proposed that the Soviet Government join with France, Britain and the United States in a five-point program:

1. To find a speedy settlement of the Austrian question "that will restore to Austria its full sovereignty and independence." He noted that at the Berlin conference, after the Western powers had offered to accept the Soviet text of every un-

Continued on Page 6, Column 4

DIENBIENPHU IS LOST AFTER 55 DAYS; NO WORD OF DE CASTRIES AND HIS MEN; DULLES SAYS UNITY CAN CHECK REDS

ASIA PACT PUSHED

Secretary Rules Out Armed Action Without Congress' Approval

Text of the Dulles address is printed on Page 4.

By WILLIAM S. WHITE
Special to The New York Times.

WASHINGTON, May 7—John Foster Dulles, Secretary of State, predicted tonight that the current efforts toward collective defense in Southeast Asia ultimately would halt Communist aggression short of its aims.

Reporting on the Geneva conference on the Far East, Mr. Dulles made two points plain:

1. That the possibility of ultimate United States military intervention in Indo-China, in association with other free nations, was real.

2. That there was no intention, in any event, of committing United States forces without the sanction of Congress.

The French Union fortress of Dienbienphu in Indo-China fell only at the cost of "staggering losses" to the Communists, Mr. Dulles noted.

"An epic battle has ended but great causes have, before now, been won out of lost battles," he added.

Steps Proposed for U. S.

He declared that the Eisenhower Administration regarded as important the following steps for a solution of the Indo-China crisis:

¶The French should give greater reality to their intention to grant full independence to Vietnam, Laos and Cambodia, the three Associated States of the country. This would take away from the Communists their false claim to be leading the fight for independence.

¶There should be greater reliance upon the national armies that would be fighting in their own homeland. He believed this could be done if the peoples felt that they had a good cause for which to fight and if better facilities for training and equipment were provided for them.

¶There should be greater free-world assistance. France is carrying on a struggle that is overburdening her economic resources. "Much progress" has been made toward all those goals, the Secretary asserted.

As to the current negotiations for creating a free-world alliance in Asia, Mr. Dulles reported that progress had been made and that "unity of purpose persists."

¶The fall of Dienbienphu will only "harden, not weaken, our purpose to stay unified," he added.

Geneva Hopes Stand

While "present conditions" in Indo-China do not "provide a suitable basis" for armed intervention by the United States, the possibility under other circumstances of "serious commitments" by the United States nevertheless exists, Mr. Dulles said.

The Geneva conference, he went on, may yet find a settlement by which an honorable armistice can be arranged, but the United States "would be gravely concerned" if the outcome should "provide a road to a Communist takeover and further aggression."

"If this occurs, or if hostilities continue, then the need will be even more urgent to create the conditions for united action in defense of the area," he said.

"In making commitments which might involve the use of armed force, the Congress is a full partner," Mr. Dulles continued. "Only the Congress can declare war. President Eisenhower has repeatedly emphasized that he would not take military action in Indo-China without the support of Congress.

"Furthermore, he has made clear that he would not seek that unless, in his judgment, there would be an adequate collective effort based upon genuine mutuality of purpose in defending vital interests."

This declaration took on added significance in light of the fact that earlier in the day Mr. Dulles had gone over with President Eisenhower for an hour and a

Continued on Page 4, Column 6

Associated Press Radiophoto
REVEALS MILITARY DEFEAT: Premier Joseph Laniel after he told French Cabinet of the fall of Dienbienphu.

WEST STILL PLANS ARMISTICE TALKS

Negotiations on Indo-China Set to Open in Geneva, Subject to Paris Action

By THOMAS J. HAMILTON
Special to The New York Times.

GENEVA, May 7—The United States, Britain and France decided tonight to go ahead with the opening of the Indo-China negotiations here tomorrow despite the capture of Dienbienphu. Their decision, however, was made subject to the action of the French Cabinet.

The three Western powers had previously agreed to submit to the conference on Far Eastern affairs a proposal for an armistice under which the Vietminh would withdraw from southern Vietnam and the Red River delta in northern Vietnam.

As to the current negotiations for creating a free-world alliance in Asia, Mr. Dulles reported that progress had been made and that "unity of purpose persists."

This is the program that Foreign Minister Georges Bidault has been fighting for, and if the Cabinet backs him up the Indo-China phase of the Far Eastern conference will start at 3 P. M. tomorrow.

However, if the Cabinet overrules M. Bidault and orders him to propose a simple cease-fire, the new-found unity of the Western powers will be destroyed and it will be necessary to postpone the opening of the conference while a new formula is negotiated.

Gen. Walter Bedell Smith, Under Secretary of State, busied himself

Continued on Page 4, Column 7

FRANCE IS SENDING MORE MEN TO WAR

No Protest Greets Laniel's Statement—Shock of Loss Seems to Unify Deputies

By LANSING WARREN
Special to The New York Times.

PARIS, May 7—The French Assembly heard Premier Joseph Laniel's statement on the fall of Dienbienphu in utter silence and adjourned for half an hour late this afternoon as a sign of mourning and respect for the valiant dead.

The shock was evidently great and most of the Deputies, as they discussed it, seemed to have been drawn together in a renewed determination that they would not now give up the fight. Even those members of the Assembly who had most strongly urged an end to the conflict were disposed today to show that France would not capitulate.

No one protested when the Premier made the announcement that more troops were on the way to Indo-China so that the expeditionary corps would not be weakened.

The Cabinet, in unison, decided upon military steps to aid the troops in the other parts of Vietnam to hold out.

The Vietminh tactics of overwhelming Dienbienphu on the eve of the opening of the Geneva conference on Indo-China seemed in a fair way to result in bolstering French resistance and in

Continued on Page 3, Column 2

ASSAULT SUCCEEDS

Fort Falls After 20-Hour Fight — Last Strong Point Is Silent

Special to The New York Times.

PARIS, May 7—The fall of Dienbienphu was announced today by Premier Joseph Laniel.

The news of the worst military defeat that the French have suffered since the Indo-China war began in December, 1946, came suddenly.

It was received with confused emotion. The heroic defense of Dienbienphu, besieged for fifty-five days, had been followed in screaming headlines since March 13, when the Vietminh launched its first attack — as if for the first time in more than seven years the public had fully realized that the country was fighting an enormously bloody and costly war.

M. Laniel told the Assembly that the heroic stronghold had been taken after twenty hours of fighting and continuous alertness for the last two months. He could not issue any information on the fate of the commander, Brig. Gen. Christian de Castries, or of the defenders or the wounded who have wasted underground for several weeks.

Final Concentration

All that he knew, the Premier said, was that the southern resistance point called Isabelle was still defended under the command of Col. André Lalande. French artillery with some tanks were concentrated at that center.

[Contact with the Isabelle outpost has been lost, according to an Associated Press dispatch from Saigon.]

"The Vietminh now are only a few meters away," were the last words heard from General de Castries over the radio-telephone, the French Cabinet was told. The last dispatch received from the battle was that the central strong point had been surrounded.

For the defenders of Dienbienphu there was French pride in their heroism and sadness for their fate. There was also some grim anger against those who had engulfed them in defeat and, if not anger, at least unkindly feelings for those responsible for French political and military policy.

Before last March the name of Dienbienphu, now solidly entrenched in French military annals, was unknown here, but not in Indo-China, where it had some importance.

The Vietminh has taken Dienbienphu, a peaceful community of 9,000 persons, who grew rice and poppy for opium, in February, 1953, and used it to help launch operations against Laos in the following April.

French Seizure Nov. 21

Last November when a Vietminh column started heading northwest in the Thai country to the French base of Laichau, the French decided to evacuate Laichau and seize Dienbienphu, using parachutists from the Tonkin area.

A successful operation was launched Nov. 21 and after the Laichau garrison moved in the French began daily efforts to strengthen it by building underground fortifications, improving the airfield and setting up barbed wire.

The establishment of the Dienbienphu base had strategic and political reasons. Close to the Laotian border, it helped fend off Vietminh attacks southward into Laos and against the capital of Luang Prabang by threatening the Vietminh rear and blocking supply lines.

The fact that the Vietminh withdrew from Laos and did not attack Luang Prabang is attributed to French control of Dienbienphu. The French also wished to remain in the Thai tribal country to encourage and help the Thai guerrillas hostile to the Vietminh.

Finally, Dienbienphu, because of its geographical position, was expected to require a large Vietminh force to attack it, thus relieving pressure on French defenses in the much more vital Tonkin delta area.

This is precisely what happened. The French garrison num-

Continued on Page 2, Column 4

"All the News That's Fit to Print"

The New York Times.

LATE CITY EDITION
Some cloudiness with a few showers today. Fair tomorrow.
Temperature Range Today—Max., 86; Min., 70
Temperature Yesterday—Max., 88.3; Min., 66.8
Full U. S. Weather Bureau Report, Page 47

Copyright, 1954, by The New York Times Company.

VOL. CIII No. 35,242.

Entered as Second-Class Matter, Post Office, New York, N. Y.

NEW YORK, WEDNESDAY, JULY 21, 1954.

Times Square, New York 36, N. Y.
Telephone LAckawanna 4-1000

FIVE CENTS

McCARTHY ACCEPTS COHN RESIGNATION, TRANSFERS SURINE

Puts the Assistant Counsel on Own Payroll—Panel Defers Any Action on La Venia

CONFIRMS REST OF STAFF

Carr Among 22 Approved—Senator Calls Loss of Cohn 'Great Victory' for Reds

Texts of Cohn letter, McCarthy statement are on Page 10.

By ANTHONY LEVIERO
Special to The New York Times.

WASHINGTON, July 20—Senator Joseph R. McCarthy yielded today to the insistent demand for a staff housecleaning from a majority of the members of the Senate Permanent Subcommittee on Investigations.

The results, as the subcommittee met over a steak luncheon in the old Supreme Court chamber in the Capitol, were these:

¶Senator McCarthy reluctantly accepted the resignation of Roy M. Cohn, the subcommittee's chief counsel, denouncing those who had sought it and saying the result was a "great victory" for communism.

¶Mr. McCarthy transferred the controversial assistant counsel, Don Surine, from the subcommittee staff to his personal payroll, also with a vigorous defense of him.

Action on La Venia Deferred

Both these changes were personal actions of Senator McCarthy as chairman taken before the subcommittee met. In this way he headed off inevitable defeat on a staff housecleaning demanded by a majority of four of the seven members of the subcommittee led by Senator Charles E. Potter, Republican of Michigan.

The subcommittee itself then voted unanimously to withhold "without prejudice" confirmation of Thomas La Venia in his position as office manager and investigator until further consideration of his personal record.

The subcommittee then voted to confirm twenty-two other employes of the subcommittee in their present jobs. Among them were two others who had come under fire during the thirty-six days of the Army - McCarthy hearings that ended on June 17.

One was Francis P. Carr, staff director, who had been named as a principal in the controversy but was removed from that category before the hearings ended.

Juliana Approved

The other was James N. Juliana, a staff investigator, who assumed full responsibility during the hearings for cropping an Army colonel out of a photograph introduced in evidence. As produced by the McCarthy side, this photograph showed only Robert T. Stevens, Secretary of the Army, and Pvt. G. David Schine.

There was no discussion by the subcommittee on whether to oust Mr. Carr, who said he was staying "unless I am voted out." Senator McCarthy said that all votes today were unanimous.

On Capitol Hill the staff changes were regarded as the few reversals ever suffered by Mr. McCarthy in his Senatorial career which began in 1946. The action today was a direct

Continued on Page 10, Column 5

Miss Connolly Breaks Leg, Out of U.S. Play

By The Associated Press

SAN DIEGO, Calif., July 20—Maureen Connolly, the tennis queen, was so seriously injured when she was crushed against a big cement truck while riding her horse here today that she will be unable to defend her national title next month at Forest Hills, Queens.

Surgery and X-rays determined that the small bone in her lower right leg was broken and that muscles and tendons of the calf were damaged by a deep gash.

This definitely ends her hope of winning the United States championship for the fourth straight time.

She will hardly be able to get around, doctors said, by the start of the tournament on Aug. 20.

"Little Mo," who will be 20 on Sept. 17, was wheeled into surgery within an hour after reaching the hospital.

She was conscious when she

Continued on Page 21, Column 2

House Inquiry Asked Into a House Inquiry

By C. P. TRUSSELL
Special to The New York Times.

WASHINGTON, July 20—The House of Representatives was urged today to investigate one of its investigations.

At issue was the inquiry into tax-free educational and philanthropic foundations that began in May.

Early this month the investigators decided to hold no more public hearings. At that point the witnesses, including two committee researchers, had been eleven to one in criticism of foundations. The foundations were given permission to file sworn statements in rebuttal.

A resolution was introduced in the House this afternoon by Representative Jacob K. Javits, Republican of Manhattan. It called on the Rules Committee,

Continued on Page 30, Column 7

SHOWDOWN TODAY ON T. V. A. CURB SET

Democrats Decide to Permit Vote on President's Order for Power Contract

By WILLIAM M. BLAIR
Special to The New York Times.

WASHINGTON, July 20—A band of Senate Democrats agreed tonight to a showdown vote tomorrow afternoon in their fight against President Eisenhower's order to the Atomic Energy Commission to carry out a private power contract.

They intimated, however, that if defeated they would renew what Senate Republican leaders have called a filibuster against the important atomic energy bill. The President's order directed the commission to negotiate a contract with a private utilities group to supply the Tennessee Valley Authority with power.

The general belief was that the Senate would not even attempt to reinstate the President's program since today's vote was the second in which the House had rejected it. On April 2 the House, for the first time, considering the bill for the first time, turned down the 140,000-unit program, 211 to 176.

Representative Brent Spence, Democrat of Kentucky, made the motion to reinstate the President's program, on the ground that, without it, individuals of low income could only gravitate to the slums.

Representative Jesse P. Wolcott, Republican of Michigan, defending the proposition that a unit of slum housing must be razed before a unit of public housing could be built, declared: "With these limitations, we conferees believe we have done a masterful job on public housing.

Continued on Page 8, Column 2

EISENHOWER LOSES ON PUBLIC HOUSING BY VOTE OF 234-156

House Rejects Plan to Build 140,000 Units in 4 Years —35,000 in One Voted

By CLAYTON KNOWLES
Special to The New York Times.

WASHINGTON, July 20—The House of Representatives killed the last real hope today to enact President Eisenhower's public housing program at this session of Congress.

By a vote of 234 to 156, it rejected a proposal sponsored by Democrats to write the President's request for 140,000 public housing units over a four-year period into the compromise housing bill that emerged last week from Senate-House conference.

Arrayed against the proposal were 155 Republicans and 79 Democrats. Supporting the President's position in the vote were 105 Democrats, 50 Republicans and one Independent.

Soon after this test, the House approved, 358 to 30, terms of the omnibus compromise on housing. It contained provision for only 35,000 units in a one-year extension of the public housing program. Many asserted that this authorization was meaningless because of restrictions in the provision. Some said not 10,000 units could be built under it.

Action Regarded as Final

The House action, which promises to create a major political issue for the Congressional campaign, was as good as final even though the Senate still has to ratify the conference report. The original Senate bill carried the President's public housing program, but it was pared, almost beyond recognition, in conference.

The Senate recessed at 9:57 P. M. after Senator William F. Knowland, the Republican Floor Leader, had said he hoped for a vote in the power fight tomorrow and completion of the bill by the same time tomorrow night.

He announced that he had instructed the Sergeant at Arms to set up cots in the Senate wing of the Capitol in the event it was necessary to work through the night to complete the entire atomic energy bill.

The Democrats' decision at a strategy meeting ended temporarily seven days of unlimited talking in the Senate that stalled the Administration's program.

Backed up behind the atomic

Continued on Page 16, Column 4

INDOCHINA ARMISTICE IS SIGNED; VIETNAM SPLIT AT 17TH PARALLEL; U. S. FINDS IT CAN 'RESPECT' PACT

CAPITAL CAUTIOUS

Accepts in Principle— Bars Any Guarantee Except by Alliance

Special to The New York Times.

WASHINGTON, July 20—The United States Government will issue a unilateral statement tomorrow accepting in principle the terms of the Indochina cease-fire accord. It also will acknowledge its "ability to respect" such terms under the United Nations Charter, diplomatic officials disclosed tonight.

The decision to state the United States Government's position on the agreement—probably by President Eisenhower at his regular news conference tomorrow—was disclosed after diplomatic intelligence established that this authorization was meaningless because of restrictions in the clause, which they considered would avert the swallowing up of the anti-Communist and predominantly Catholic population of parts of northern Vietnam by the Red regime.

Interruption Is Temporary

Of only slightly less importance is a provision in the agreement whereby the right of the free areas of the partitioned Indochina States to receive foreign military assistance would be interrupted only temporarily, and no interference with their sovereignty would be entailed.

It was understood the temporary restriction on the receipt of military assistance from the United States and other free nations would end after a period of "disengagement" during which forces would be withdrawn from existing front-line areas.

Diplomatic officials conversant with its terms held that the cease-fire generally came within the terms of the seven principles that President Eisenhower and Prime Minister Churchill laid down three weeks ago.

Continued on Page 3, Column 3

AGREE ON TRUCE: Pierre Mendès-France, French Premier, as he appeared yesterday with Pham Van Dong, Vietminh Foreign Minister, left, at French headquarters in Geneva. Behind them are Guy de la Tournelle, wearing eyeglasses, and Georges Boris, aides to French leader.

Associated Press Radiophoto

SENATORS TO PUSH GERMAN REARMING

Leading Republicans Will Urge Action This Year in Addition to Granting Sovereignty

By WILLIAM S. WHITE
Special to The New York Times.

WASHINGTON, July 20—Powerful Senate Republicans will advise the Eisenhower Administration that West German rearmament and sovereignty should be pushed this year.

They are prepared to suggest to the Administration that the United States-British plan to give sovereignty without the right to rearm, as an alternative to the faltering European Defense Community project, would not be realistic.

They will argue that implicit in sovereignty is the right of self-defense and that the two concepts cannot be separated validly, as John Foster Dulles, Secretary of State, has proposed to do.

Senator Homer Ferguson of Michigan, chairman of the Senate Republican Policy Committee, who is one of the leaders in this movement, expects some sort of Congressional resolution backing both German sovereignty and German rearmament to be offered before Congress adjourns this month or early next month.

Others, among them Senator William F. Knowland of California, Republican Senate floor leader, are taking a more reserved line pending a study by the State Department of the legal situation.

Mr. Dulles has adopted the position that the question of rearmament must be deferred un-

Continued on Page 5, Column 3

38 Jersey Forgeries Charged to Hoffman

Special to The New York Times.

TRENTON, July 20—The preliminary report of a handwriting expert released here today said that former Gov. Harold G. Hoffman apparently concealed his $300,000 defalcations by forging thirty-eight bank certifications in six years.

Attorney General Grover C. Richman made public the findings of Albert D. Osborne of Montclair, who for a month has been studying the signatures on the certifications from the South Amboy Trust Company.

The certifications of general state treasury funds deposited at the South Amboy bank cover a period from June 30, 1947, to Dec. 31, 1953. They all had the signature of George A. Kress, a vice president of the bank. No breakdown of the amounts of

Continued on Page 46, Column 1

French Call Pact No Victory But See Gains for Europe

By HAROLD CALLENDER
Special to The New York Times.

PARIS, July 20—The terms of agreement for the truce in Indochina were regarded here as presaging a peace without victory. Some called it a peace that would confirm a defeat for the West in Asia and would mark the most notable loss in battle of French territories since Louis XV lost Canada in the eighteenth century.

But it was expected that this ill wind in Asia might blow some good for France and the Atlantic alliance in Europe.

The truce seemed likely to give great prestige to Premier Pierre Mendès-France, to enable him to stay in office to seek a decision on the European army treaty and to press for a program to stimulate the French economy.

It appeared probable tonight that the Premier would submit the treaty to the National Assembly early in August with suggested modifications that would not require further action by the parliaments of the other signatories. The West German Chancellor, Dr. Konrad Adenauer, has indicated that he would consider changes that could be made without resort to parliaments.

New Unity a By-Product

Removal of the uncertainty that has surrounded the treaty for two years would clear up the question of West Germany's sovereignty and rearmament and permit in this sphere a unity among the United States, Britain and France that has not yet existed. Such a gain in Europe might be considered as offsetting to some extent the failure of Western policy in Indochina.

A severe blow to French prestige in Asia and probably in North Africa was foreseen in the truce. In North Africa that prestige is far more important than in Asia because France's African territories are more important to her. But M. Mendès-France's argument has been that France must cut her losses in Asia in order to conserve her strength in Europe; and if she revamps her economy, as he desires, the net result may be to increase her influence and even her prestige in Europe and Africa.

M. Mendès-France has urged that the failure to reconcile Vietnam with the French Union by prompt grant of independence should not be repeated in North Africa, where nationalist movements now are menacing.

The reconciliation of general

Continued on Page 3, Column 6

HANOI PREPARING FOR TRUCE PERIOD

French Study Plans Designed to Preserve Calm in Delta and Effect Evacuation

By HENRY R. LIEBERMAN
Special to The New York Times.

HANOI, Vietnam, July 20—Two kinds of preparations are being made here to cope with problems related to the surrender of North Vietnam to the Vietminh under a cease-fire. Hanoi will eventually be taken over by the Vietminh under a truce agreement.

French authorities were preparing security measures to "maintain calm" in this city of 340,000. Plans originally drawn up to evacuate French, foreign and a number of Vietnamese civilians under battle conditions were also being restudied in terms of a more leisurely evacuation.

It was being taken for granted today in this city, which is seven hours ahead of Geneva time, that the seven-and-a-half-year-old Indochinese war was drawing to a close.

Geneva reports aroused considerable interest in Hanoi but created no public excitement. In fact, despite a demonstration against partition yesterday by several thousand Vietnamese, there has been no major agitation

Continued on Page 2, Column 2

LONG WAR ENDING

2 Accords Completed —One on Cambodia Due Later Today

By THOMAS J. HAMILTON
Special to The New York Times.

GENEVA, Wednesday, July 21—Armistice agreements bringing the fighting in Vietnam and Laos to a halt were signed this morning by representatives of the French and Communist Vietminh forces.

A French spokesman said the armistice would take effect forty-eight hours later.

The signing ceremony, witnessed by representatives of the nine delegations participating in the Far Eastern conference here, began at 3:42 A. M. (9:42 P. M. Tuesday, Eastern daylight time). It brought to a close the eight-year struggle for Indochina.

The armistice agreements will not be signed until later this morning. The Far Eastern conference will hold its final session this afternoon to complete work on the political settlement. Under it Laos and Cambodia will be neutralized and elections to create a unified government in Vietnam will be held within two years from the date of the armistice.

Pierre Mendès-France, French Premier, who had set July 20 as his deadline to obtain an armistice or resign, had missed it by a few hours. He canceled a radio speech to the French people and went to bed before the two agreements were signed at the Palais des Nations, former headquarters of the League of Nations, where conference sessions have been held since the Indochina negotiations began last May.

Rebels Get Northern Part

Under the Vietnamese agreement, Vietnam is to be divided into two parts, about equal in area and population, between the Communist-led Vietminh rebels who will hold northern Vietnam, north of a line along the Seventeenth Parallel, and the French-sponsored Government of Bao Dai.

The partition line thus is far enough north to preserve Huc, the ancient capital of Annam; Tourane, an important port and naval and air base, and the only major highway leading to Laos from the coast.

The French will not give up Hanoi and Haiphong, in the Red River delta area, in the north, for approximately a year, which will give them time to evacuate personnel of the French expeditionary force in the territory remaining to them in the delta, plus civilians fearing persecution by the Communists.

Under the armistice agreements, the Communists recognize the Governments of Laos and Cambodia. However, regrouping areas for Communist troops were authorized in Laos. The forces of the Communist "resistance government" in Laos will be concentrated in two provinces near the frontier with Vietminh territory. [Some sources identified the two provinces as Samneua and Phongsaly.]

The Cambodian delegation held out against the provision, and prolonged sessions of the "drafting committee" of the Vietminh and Cambodian representatives

Continued on Page 2, Column 5

Reds Have Margin in Indochina Despite Even Split Under Truce

By TILLMAN DURDIN
Special to The New York Times.

GENEVA, July 20—In statistical terms, a balanced settlement on Indochina seems to have been reached.

The sum of the parts of Indochina due to the non-Communist.

However, in some respects, the Communists will have advantages not reflected by comparative figures. The Vietminh rebels will have under their control the northern Vietnamese, who are more tough and vigorous than the southern Vietnamese and the easygoing Buddhists of Laos and Cambodia. North Vietnam will envelop northern and eastern Laos and will be in a commanding strategic position with relation to Vietnam's western neighbor.

The Communist Vietminh has gained the northern half of Vietnam, inhabited by about 12,000,000 persons. If the Vietminh forces evacuate other areas according to the terms, the southern half of Vietnam and the states of Laos and Cambodia will remain in non-Communist hands.

Approximately 10,000,000 Vietnamese, 4,000,000 Cambodians and 1,400,000 Laotians live in the territories to remain outside Communist control. Northern Vietnam is somewhat smaller, both in population and area, than

Continued on Page 3, Column 2

Arrests Here Bare 'Sure Thing' Racing Fraud by Radio

Pocket transmitter at left sends race results to receiver near track, whence an agent phones data to an associate posted near a betting parlor. This man, using transmitter built into suitcase at right, relays results to a bettor, who gets electronic impulses through concealed dimes on receiver shown in left hand above. Agent then bets on horse that won.

The New York Times

The police cracked down yesterday on a gambling ring that has been using Dick Tracy techniques, complete with purse-size transmitters and skin-shock radio receivers, to flash race results far in advance of official returns. Twenty-eight

persons were rounded up in fast-hitting raids in Manhattan, Brooklyn and Queens. Fifty detectives and policemen, under the command of Supervising Assistant Chief Inspector James Nidds, fanned out through the three boroughs at 8 A. M. After the half-hour round-up, when

the twenty-eight captives were paraded before Queens Assistant District Attorney Lawrence Pelrez, a crime-comics story on the use of ingenious electronic devices was unfolded. Race-track plotters were pictured tapping

Continued on Page 28, Column 3

"All the News That's Fit to Print"

The New York Times.

LATE CITY EDITION
Fair and cold today and tonight.
Fair and milder tomorrow.
Temperature Range Today—Max., 40; Min., 25
Temperature Yesterday—Max., 37.4; Min., 28.5
Full U. S. Weather Bureau Report, Page 51

Copyright, 1954, by The New York Times Company.

VOL. CIV. No. 35,377.   Entered as Second-Class Matter,
Post Office, New York, N. Y.   NEW YORK, FRIDAY, DECEMBER 3, 1954.   Times Square, New York 36, N. Y.
Telephone LAckawanna 4-1000   FIVE CENTS

POPE IN COLLAPSE, BUT REST FOLLOWS A DIFFICULT NIGHT

Morning Announcement Tells of the 78-Year-old Pontiff's Battle Against Illness

KIN CALLED TO BEDSIDE

Trouble Laid to a Perforated Ulcer and Physicians Study Possibilities of Operation

By The Associated Press.

ROME, Friday, Dec. 3—The Vatican announced this morning that Pope Pius XII, gravely stricken, had survived the night. A spokesman said a more detailed bulletin would be issued later today.

The Pope suffered a severe collapse yesterday.

The first word this morning on his condition was given by Dr. Luciano Casimiri, spokesman for the Vatican press office, at 8:05 o'clock [2:05 A. M., Eastern standard time.]

"After a difficult night, the Holy Father is now resting," the spokesman said.

There were unconfirmed reports that the Pope had suffered a heart attack in the night, accompanied by more of the intense gastritis, nausea and hiccups for which he has been under treatment. There were indications also that the Pope's condition may be aggravated by a gastric ulcer.

His personal physician, Dr. Riccardo Galeazzi-Lisi, spent the entire night at his bedside, after making emergency X-rays yesterday and calling in a surgeon for consultation.

Grave Fears Felt

By ARNALDO CORTESI
Special to The New York Times.

ROME, Friday, Dec. 3—Pope Pius XII suffered a collapse at 3:30 o'clock yesterday afternoon due, it is believed, to a perforated ulcer.

The Pope fell into a coma and the gravest fears for his life were felt. He is 78 years old and has been weakened because for the last four days his feeding has been by artificial means.

Extreme unction was administered and Pius' nearest relatives—three nephews—were called to his bedside.

Five hours later, the Pope had overcome the crisis and his archiater, or chief physician, Prof. Riccardo Galeazzi-Lisi, said there was no immediate cause for alarm.

The Pope was stated to be resting as easily as could be expected under the circumstances, although breathing heavily and reduced to exhaustion.

It was learned that the possibility of an abdominal operation sometime today or in the next few days was being considered. The exact nature of the operation under consideration was not stated but it is understood that a noticeable swelling of the Pope's abdomen developed yesterday afternoon, accompanied by cramps and excruciating pain. Radioscopic and clinical tests were made late in the evening to ascertain both the exact nature of the Pope's ailment and whether he is in condition to undergo surgery.

From the time he fell seriously ill in January of this year, Pope Pius had refused to take the barium meal necessary if full X-ray examination of his stomach

Continued on Page 4, Column 1

Rio Conference Ends With Major Accords

By SAM POPE BREWER
Special to The New York Times.

PETROPOLIS, Brazil, Dec. 2—The twenty-one American republics ended tonight their first general economic conference with agreements on many major points and plans to hold another such meeting within two years.

Antonio Carrillo Flores, Minister of Finance of Mexico, said in the principal address at the closing session that public opinion of this hemisphere would find on studying results of the conference that its work "was not sterile."

Carlos Lleras Restrepo of Colombia introduced a dissenting note into the general air of agreement. But in this final session that his country did not feel the conference had gone far enough toward increasing international banking facilities and stabilizing commodity prices. An

Continued on Page 18, Column 5

President Rejects Blockade Of China Now as Act of War

But He Pledges No Let-Up in Efforts to Free 13 Americans Jailed by Peiping— Holds Truce Obligates U. N. to Act

By JOSEPH A. LOFTUS
Special to The New York Times.

WASHINGTON, Dec. 2—President Eisenhower asserted today he was not going to be pushed emotionally into an act of war—such as a naval blockade of Communist China.

Neither, he said, is he going to let Peiping get away with the imprisonment of thirteen Americans on spy charges.

He insisted that the United Nations act for the release of at least eleven of the Americans because they were uniformed veterans of the Korean war and as such the United Nations was obligated to act in their behalf. [At the United Nations, the United States said it wanted the world body to condemn the imprisonment by Red China of eleven American airmen shot down during the Korean war.]

"We are yet far from exhausting all of our resources to liberate these men, the President

said at his news conference: "I mention only one of those that is available to us."

He asserted that Red China deliberately timed its announcement of the imprisonment to divide the people of the United States as well as the United States from its allies. He added that the United States must be forever on its guard against this divide-and-conquer technique.

His personal feelings of anger, resentment and frustration were as great as any American's, he said, but he believed that restraint in public expression was the wiser course. To respond with patience rather than with truculence does not mean appeasement, he declared.

The President was clearly reading a lesson in the behavior of public officials to Senator Will-

Continued on Page 2, Column 4

East Bloc Says Joint Army Will Counter Bonn in NATO

By CLIFTON DANIEL
Special to The New York Times.

MOSCOW, Dec. 2—In a declaration signed in the Kremlin tonight, eight European Communist regimes gave notice that if the Atlantic powers enlisted West Germany in their alliance, an East European defense organization would be created.

Representatives of eight governments concluding a four-day conference here said another meeting would be called to plan defense measures should the London and Paris agreements for West German armament and sovereignty be finally ratified.

The envisioned defense organization would include combined military forces under a joint command like that of the North Atlantic Treaty Organization. It would be in addition to the existing framework of treaties concluded long ago among the eight powers.

Communist China's complete approval of the declaration and the measures envisioned in it was signified at the final meeting of the representatives of the eight European powers today. China's endorsement was given by Chang Wen-tien, Peiping's Deputy Foreign Minister and Ambassador to Moscow.

Having in mind the combined strength of Communist China, the Soviet Union and seven other units in the East bloc conference, the delegates declared:

"Never before have the forces of peace and socialism been so mighty and so consolidated as now. Any attempts to attack, launch a war and interfere with the peaceful life of our peoples will meet with a shattering rebuff."

The declaration, bound in a red Morocco folder with ribbons

Continued on Page 5, Column 5

ATOM POWER SEEN AS COMMON IN 1976

Half of All Electric Plants Then Building Will Use It, G. E. Head Tells N.A.M.

By A. H. RASKIN

By 1976 atomic energy will be used to fuel half of all the electric generating plants then being built, it was predicted yesterday. This forecast, was put before the National Association of Manufacturers by Ralph J. Cordiner, president of General Electric.

His estimate of the speed with which nuclear power would come into widespread use as a source of electric power was considerably more optimistic than most official calculations. Mr. Cordiner made his prediction as part of a plea to industrialists to shun "creeping conservatism" in their approach to business planning.

The head of the country's biggest electrical manufacturing company advised his fellow-executives to make their plans on a twenty-year basis, instead of limiting themselves to the ups and downs of the immediate sales market.

West Called Stronger

Other highlights at the second session of the association's thirty-ninth annual Congress of American Industry in the Waldorf-Astoria Hotel included:

¶An assertion by Gen. Walter Bedell Smith that the United States and its allies had built up a sufficient superiority over the Communist countries to "deter aggression and maintain peace." The former Under Secretary of State emphasized, however, that the balance of power was still "rather tenuous."

¶A report by a Dutch industrialist that five of his employes, who spent three months working in a Pennsylvania linoleum factory, had come home convinced that "America is a working man's world."

¶An attack by Charles R. Sligh Jr., N. A. M. board chairman, on union proposals for a guaranteed annual wage. He contended that wage guarantees would destroy business, rather than stabilize employment.

¶An assertion by Prof. Leo Wolman of Columbia University that the Taft-Hartley Act represented no substantial improvement over the old Wagner Act in curbing union power and preventing encroachment on management rights.

¶Election as N. A. M. president of Henry G. Riter 3d of Montclair, N. J., president of Thomas A. Edison, Inc., and chairman of the board of Copperweld Steel. Mr. Riter, who was an investment banker before he became an industrialist, succeeds H. C. McClellan of Los Angeles.

General Smith, who quit the State Department two months

Continued on Page 16, Column 5

'Copter Saves 5 Plane Survivors Down 45 Hours on Mountainside

Two Perish in Crash of DC-3 in New Hampshire—Work of Stewardess Praised

By JOHN H. FENTON
Special to The New York Times.

BOSTON, Dec. 2—Five survivors of the crash of a Northeast Airlines plane were plucked by helicopter today from a bleak mountainside near the Maine-New Hampshire border. They had spent forty-five hours on the snow-covered spot in bitter cold. The two others aboard the DC-3 died of injuries a few hours after the plane had fallen into a stretch of pine woods.

The dead were George McCormick, 37 years old, of Kingston, N. Y., co-pilot, and John McNulty, 39, of Boston, flight supervisor.

First to be rescued was the pilot, Capt. W. Peter Carey, 37, of Swampscott, Mass. He suffered severe head injuries. He and Miss Mary McEttrick, 23, of Boston, the stewardess, were flown here for medical treatment. Miss McEttrick suffered from shock and exposure.

The survivors praised Miss McEttrick for her coolness throughout the ordeal during which they huddled in the wrecked plane for nearly two days. Her cheerful attempts to make them com-

Associated Press Wirephoto
Stewardess Mary McEttrick in Berlin (N. H.) hospital.

fortable and her care of the injured prompted them to agree that "she's quite a girl."

Seventy-five Northeast employes, who were flown to Berlin,

Continued on Page 20, Column 4

EISENHOWER WARNS G. O. P. RIGHT WING; CHIDES KNOWLAND

Insists Party Must Follow a Progressive Course or Face Loss of Influence

Transcript and summary of the news conference, Page 18.

By WILLIAM S. WHITE
Special to The New York Times.

WASHINGTON, Dec. 2—President Eisenhower, reasserting leadership for his concept of a progressive Republican party, rebuked today the Republican floor leader, William F. Knowland of California, and the party's right wing generally.

The President did not seek to disclaim the existence of a split in the party. He said instead that the party would not long be a force in American life unless it followed a course of progressivism.

As before, he defined this progressivism as a liberal attitude in the Government's relationship with the individual and a conservative attitude concerning the national economy and the individual's pocketbook.

It was the first time since he entered the White House two years ago that General Eisenhower had publicly and without apology had criticized a leading member of his party in Congress. Always before, he had avoided such criticisms, relying frequently on the fact that the Constitution made Congress an independent branch of Government.

Even this time, the President somewhat softened his language toward the end, with the comments that while some statements sometimes made statements that certainly did not conform with the Administration's approach these normally affected method rather than principle.

China Blockade Urged

He made it clear, nevertheless, that distinction in methods were important, suggesting that the methods of Senator Knowland might mean the difference between peace and war in Asia.

Senator Knowland, in the face of rejections from John Foster Dulles, Secretary of State, and the President himself, has been calling for a blockade of Communist China to force the liberation of United States citizens in Communist prisons.

Yesterday, moreover, Mr. Knowland broke with the Administration on another sensitive issue, coming out against a Senate censure of Senator Joseph R. McCarthy, Republican of Wisconsin.

The President said little about his differences with Senator Knowland over the McCarthy issue, observing only that it was up to the Senate to determine what was required for the preservation of its dignity.

On the point of the profound division within the Republican party over policy toward Red China, however, the President spoke extensively and voluntarily. He took up Senator Knowland's

Continued on Page 18, Column 5

RANCOR CONTINUES

Welker Refuses to Let Flanders Apology Go Into the Record

By JAMES RESTON
Special to The New York Times.

WASHINGTON, Dec. 2—The McCarthy debate ended as it began in a spasm of rancor and vindictiveness that will divide the Senate and the country for a long time to come.

Though there were some lighthearted semantics at the close over whether Senator Joseph R. McCarthy was "censured" or "condemned," the underlying feeling among the principals ranged from uneasiness to sullen anger. The junior Senator from Wisconsin himself produced almost the only hint of humor all day. Asked whether he thought the Senate had passed a resolution of "censure" or "condemnation," he replied:

"I wouldn't say it was a vote of confidence."

He then announced that he was "very happy to get this circus over" and would get back to "the job of digging Communists out of the Government" on Monday.

Controversy Continues

Even after the vote was over, the controversy went on.

Senator Ralph E. Flanders, Republican of Vermont, arose and said he wanted to apologize for the Senator for some remarks he had made about Senator McCarthy some months ago. He added that he had told the Wisconsin Senator that he proposed to do so and had asked him to remain in the chamber, but Senator McCarthy had declined.

Then Senator Flanders asked for unanimous consent to have the Congressional Record amended to show that he had apologized for some of his remarks. This was blocked by Senator Herman Welker, Republican of Idaho, who angrily refused to give consent.

The usual lavish courtesy of the upper chamber gave way to biting sarcasm at the close. When Senator J. William Fulbright, Democrat of Arkansas, said he would try to answer a question by Senator Welker, the latter remarked that he would be "very surprised if a distinguished Rhodes scholar could not answer any question."

The End of a Phase

The main significance of the special session was that it ended that phase of the McCarthy controversy in which the Senate of the United States was hesitant to take action against the Wisconsin Senator.

For most of the five years since Senator McCarthy launched his anti-Communist crusade, the Senate of the United States has led a double life—critical of the Senator in private, and afraid of his political power in public.

During most of this period there has been a kind of political paralysis among the anti-McCarthy faction, which was never entirely clear who was for him and who was against him. This doubt has now been removed.

The Senator from Wisconsin will remain for a month as chairman of the Government Operations Committee. He will lose none of his rights. He will have the power of subpoena and he will wield his gavel.

What has changed is not Mr. McCarthy but his opponents. They are in the open now, willing and in some cases eager to match his criticisms with their own. In short, the balance of criticism, dominated for so long by Senator McCarthy, has been reversed.

Behind this, too, is a decision by the Executive Branch of the Government to take a firmer position against his efforts to persuade Federal employes to give him documents that are not authorized to disclose.

So long as Congress hesitated to take action against Mr. McCarthy, the Executive itself was divided about how to defend itself—regardless of what it is called—has stiffened the anti-McCarthy element in the Administration.

Thus, while he can exercise all

Continued on Page 16, Column 7

FINAL VOTE CONDEMNS M'CARTHY, 67-22, FOR ABUSING SENATE AND COMMITTEE; ZWICKER COUNT ELIMINATED IN DEBATE

Associated Press Wirephoto
CONDEMNED ON TWO COUNTS: Senator McCarthy as he left the Senate floor last night after members adopted a resolution condemning his conduct. The vote was 67-22.

PRESIDENT ALERTS MAYORS ON ATTACK

Cities Are Front-Line Targets, He Warns—Asks Teamwork in Federal-Local Defense

By ELIE ABEL
Special to The New York Times.

WASHINGTON, Dec. 2—President Eisenhower warned today that United States cities were front-line targets for modern weapons "capable" of such destruction as to appall the imagination.

The President called for closer municipal-Federal cooperation in civil-defense planning as he welcomed about 240 mayors, city manager and other local officials to a two-day conference in the State Department auditorium.

Val Peterson, Federal Civil Defense Administrator, expanded on the President's warning in a guarded discussion of radioactive "fall-out," a phenomenon that adds a new dimension to the terror of thermonuclear (hydrogen) bombs.

The idea that only city dwellers need to worry about bombing is obsolete today, Mr. Peterson said. If a hydrogen bomb is detonated on or close to the ground, he explained, tremendous amounts of earth and debris are sucked up into the fireball and made radioactive.

Although the heavy particles would not travel far, he said, the lighter ones may be swept along by winds of the upper air, at alti-

Continued on Page 19, Column 1

SENATORS CLEARED ON M'CARTHY MAIL

Inquiry Indicates Request for Check Was Handled by Staff as Routine Matter

By WILLIAM M. BLAIR
Special to The New York Times.

WASHINGTON, Dec. 2—A special Senate committee apparently will report to the Senate that a check of Senator Joseph R. McCarthy's mail in 1952 was handled as a routine matter by subcommittee staff members.

Senator Walter F. George, Democrat of Georgia, indicated as much to Senator McCarthy this afternoon as the special two-member committee completed its overnight inquiry into how the mail check was authorized.

"There's nothing to be gained from pursuing the matter further," Senator McCarthy told Senator George, who replied, "I don't think so."

Senator George and Senator Homer Ferguson, Republican of Michigan, spent the one-day session to hear testimony from persons on the staff of the Senate subcommittee on Privileges and Elections, which had inquired into Senator McCarthy's finances in 1952.

Mr. Ferguson said that a written report would be filed with the Senate. The report is expected to be filed with the secretary of the Senate tomorrow.

The two Senators were named by the Senate last night to in-

Continued on Page 15, Column 3

REPUBLICANS SPLIT

Democrats Act Solidly in Support of Motion Against Senator

Excerpts from transcript of Senate debate, Pages 12, 13

By ANTHONY LEVIERO
Special to The New York Times.

WASHINGTON, Dec. 2—The Senate voted 67 to 22 tonight to condemn Joseph R. McCarthy, Republican Senator from Wisconsin.

Every one of the forty-four Democrats present voted against Mr. McCarthy. The Republicans were evenly divided—twenty-two for condemnation and twenty-two against. The one independent, Senator Wayne Morse of Oregon, also voted against Mr. McCarthy.

In the ultimate action the Senate voted to condemn Senator McCarthy for contempt of a Senate Elections subcommittee that investigated his conduct and financial affairs, for abuse of its members, and for his insults to the Senate itself during the censure proceeding.

Lost in a day of complex and often confused parliamentary maneuvering was the proposal to censure McCarthy for his denunciation of Brig. Gen. Ralph W. Zwicker as unfit to wear his uniform.

This proposal was defeated by a parliamentary device that avoided a direct vote on the merits of the issue. Inquiry among influential Senators indicated they considered the Zwicker proposal a dilemma they wished to avoid.

Amendment Substituted

They said they wished to censure because the facts warranted it. If they failed to do so, they believed large elements of the public would feel the Senate took notice of offenses only against itself and not against ordinary citizens.

But also if they did censure for this, then Senator McCarthy could exploit the decision, contending he was being punished for his effort to expose former Maj. Irving Peress, the Army dentist who was promoted and honorably discharged, and who was denounced by Mr. McCarthy as a "Fifth Amendment Communist."

Mr. McCarthy's denunciation of General Zwicker, who was commanding officer at Camp Kilmer, N. J., when Dr. Peress was discharged, occurred when the Senator interrogated General Zwicker on the question of who had promoted Dr. Peress.

The direct test on the Zwicker issue was avoided by the substitution of the amendment to condemn Senator McCarthy for having insulted the Senate during his censure trial.

McCarthy Loses Three Tests

Thus in its final form the resolution of condemnation was in two parts, covering the offenses against the Elections subcommittee and its members in the first part, and, against the Senate in the second. Three test votes were all lost by Mr. McCarthy before the final condemnation.

First was a motion to table the Zwicker proposal, made by Senator Styles Bridges, Republican of New Hampshire, the president pro tem of the Senate, who assumed the leadership of the effort to save Mr. McCarthy yesterday.

Such a motion, if it had succeeded, might have led to a situation that would have prolonged the debate.

But amid signs that the Zwicker issue would have tough sledding, Senator Wallace F. Bennett, Republican of Utah, served notice that if Mr. Bridges' move were defeated he would attempt to substitute for the Zwicker issue his amendment for abuse of the Senate. The significance of this was that an amendment to substitution would require no time out for debate.

Then the voting proceeded. The motion to table was defeated 55 to 33. Mr. Bennett's motion to substitute passed by 64 to 23 and in the next vote his amendment was adopted by the same tally.

The final vote placing Mr. Mc-

Continued on Page 14, Column 1

G.O.P. Weighs End of Rent Curb Outside of the Metropolitan Area

By LEO EGAN

Republican legislative leaders are giving serious consideration to relaxing state rent controls outside of the New York metropolitan area, which includes Nassau and Westchester counties as well as New York City.

Such a proposal could set the stage for a major clash between Governor-elect Averell Harriman, Democratic-Liberal, and Republican majorities in the Senate and Assembly.

The Democratic platform on which Mr. Harriman was elected favored tightening rather than relaxing rent control. Moreover, Mr. Harriman affirmed his support of this position on several occasions during the campaign.

One proposal favored by some Republicans calls for decontrolling all rents outside of the New York metropolitan area. This is politically impossible or unacceptable they favor decontrolling

all one and two-family houses outside of the metropolitan area, leaving controls in effect only on apartments and tenements.

Both suggestions were informally advanced at a recent closed-door meeting of the Temporary State Commission on Rents and Rental Conditions, headed by Assemblyman Joseph F. Carlino of Long Beach, L. I.

As a result, Joseph D. McGoldrick, State Rent Administrator, was instructed to prepare a report and recommendations on the probable effect of such a relaxation of controls, the number of dwelling units involved, and the ratio of vacancies to dwelling units affected at present.

Major up-state cities that would be affected by such a

Continued on Page 24, Column 5

"All the News
That's Fit to Print"

The New York Times.

LATE CITY EDITION
Partly cloudy today. Considerable
cloudiness and milder tomorrow.

Temperature Range Today—Max., 41 ; Min., 30
Temperatures Yesterday—Max., 38; Min., 27
Full U. S. Weather Bureau Report, Page 25

Copyright, 1955, by The New York Times Company.

VOL. CIV. No. 35,445.

Entered as Second-Class Matter,
Post Office, New York, N. Y.

NEW YORK, WEDNESDAY, FEBRUARY 9, 1955.

Times Square, New York 36, N. Y.
Telephone LAckawanna 4-1000

FIVE CENTS

BULGANIN IS PREMIER AS MALENKOV RESIGNS, BUT KHRUSHCHEV IS VIEWED AS REAL LEADER; MOLOTOV, WARNING U. S., CLAIMS H-BOMB LEAD

EISENHOWER ASKS 7 BILLION PROGRAM TO BUILD SCHOOLS

Message to Congress Urges Federal-State-Local Plan for Grants and Loans

DEMOCRATS DECRY SCOPE

Leaders Denounce Proposal as 'Makeshift' — Demand Far Larger Expenditures

Text of the President's message is printed on Page 20.

By W. H. LAWRENCE
Special to The New York Times

WASHINGTON, Feb. 8—President Eisenhower proposed today a three-year $7,000,000,000 Federal-state-local school construction program.

He asked Congress to make available $220,000,000 in Federal grants and about $900,000,000 in loans to meet a current deficit of more than 300,000 school classrooms.

The message went to a Democratic-controlled Congress. Leaders in the education field in both the Senate and the House called it inadequate and "makeshift."

Some critics declared the Presidential program would be ineffective in about one-fourth of the states, which have constitutional limitations on incurring or increasing debts.

Indirectly, President Eisenhower also suggested higher pay for school teachers, but his message advanced no concrete proposals on this. He said low pay was a factor in the shortage of teachers, which he declared was "less obvious but ultimately more dangerous than the classroom shortage."

"Because of the magnitude of the job, but more fundamentally because of the undeniable importance of free education to a free way of life, the means we take to provide our children with proper classrooms must be weighed most carefully," the President said, continuing:

"The phrase 'free education' is a deliberate choice. For unless education continues to be free—free in its response to local communities——

Continued on Page 20, Column 1

A. E. C. WON'T DROP DIXON-YATES PACT

2-1 Vote Disclosed by Board —Congress Plea Rejected

By WILLIAM M. BLAIR
Special to The New York Times

WASHINGTON, Feb. 8—By a 2 to 1 vote, the Atomic Energy Commission has turned down a Democratic demand that the Dixon-Yates private power contract be canceled.

The split vote, taken on Saturday, followed the lead of President Eisenhower, who asserted three days before the vote that he would not withdraw the controversial contract to feed private power into the Tennessee Valley Authority.

Lewis L. Strauss, A. E. C. chairman, and Dr. Willard Frank Libby, a new member, voted to stick by the contract. Thomas E. Murray voted for cancellation.

As Mr. Strauss disclosed the decision today, Mr. Murray went before the Joint Congressional Committee on Atomic Energy to renew his charge that the Dixon-Yates controversy had interfered with the commission's primary job of developing atomic weapons and peacetime uses of the atom.

His main concern, he testified, was "whether we will in the future maintain our present position of world leadership in the nuclear field." He concluded:

"The attention the commission today gives to making policy de-

Continued on Page 37, Column 6

President Appeals For Satellite People

Special to The New York Times

WASHINGTON, Feb. 8—President Eisenhower urged tonight a continuing effort to "intensify the will for freedom in the satellite countries behind the Iron Curtain."

He spoke from the White House on a closed-circuit television program in behalf of the Crusade for Freedom, which operates Radio Free Europe and the Free Europe Press. The crusade hopes to raise $10,000,-000 this year.

He took no cognizance of the resignation of Georgi M. Malenkov as Soviet Premier and his replacement by Marshal Nikolai A. Bulganin. His prepared text was left unchanged after the Moscow developments had become known.

The President emphasized that the masses imprisoned behind the Iron Curtain would remain potential deterrents to

Continued on Page 6, Column 5

HOUSE, 394-4, BACKS DRAFT EXTENSION

Four-Year Continuance Finds the Democrats Unanimous —New Features Added

By C. P. TRUSSELL
Special to The New York Times

WASHINGTON, Feb. 8—The House of Representatives voted 394 to 4 today to continue the draft for four years.

This extension, the fourth since 1940, was urged by President Eisenhower. The Administration concluded that the international situation generally required the maintenance of the United States armed forces of 2,850,000 officers and men. Such a force, experience had shown, could not be mobilized through voluntary enlistments.

The four who voted against draft extension were Republicans. Democrats supported the move unanimously. The four dissenters were Representatives Noah M. Mason of Illinois, Usher L. Burdick of North Dakota; Clare E. Hoffman of Michigan, and Wint Smith of Kansas.

The extension measure now goes to the Senate. There it is expected to win approval, with its opponents agreed on the Republican side. No one predicted that the extension would not be approved finally in Congress long before the present draft authorization expires June 30.

In granting the continuance of the Selective Service the House added new features to the law. They included:

¶If the selective draft continued it should include all the benefits and allowance given to present draftees to aid their dependents. Also continued for four

Continued on Page 16, Column 4

Private Atom Reactor In This Area Planned

By PETER KIHSS

A plan for the nation's first nuclear reactor entirely owned and operated by private industry was announced here yesterday by the American Machine and Foundry Company. It would use radiations for confidential experiments for cooperating companies.

Gen. Walter Bedell Smith, retired, vice chairman of the foundry concern's board, said invitations to join the scheme had gone to companies in the fields of electronics, petroleum, food, pharmaceutical and chemical products, ceramics, rubber, metals, textiles, agriculture, machinery and others.

The project would occupy 250 acres somewhere in the New York area. A so-called swimming pool reactor would use uranium fuel surrounded by water serving as a moderator, cooler and shield.

The atomic furnace would

MIGHT IS STRESSED

Foreign Minister Says Soviet Force Is on Par With West

Excerpts from Molotov speech are printed on Page 6.

Special to The New York Times

MOSCOW, Feb. 8—Claiming superiority for the Soviet Union in hydrogen weapons, Foreign Minister Vyacheslav M. Molotov delivered to the United States today a warning of the strength of the world Communist forces.

His declaration reiterating the might of the Communist camp was made at a joint session of the Supreme Soviet, the national legislature of the Soviet Union. He spoke immediately following the change in Soviet Premiership that placed Marshal Nikolai A. Bulganin at the head of the Government.

[According to The Associated Press, the Soviet Parliament resumed its joint session at 2 A. M. Wednesday, New York time, and immediately began debating Mr. Molotov's speech.]

Laughter and applause greeted Mr. Molotov's taunts at, and defiance of, the United States, which he singled out as the leader of the "aggressive" Western coalition. He also called on the United States once again to evacuate Formosa.

Balance 'Quite Established'

In one of his most outspoken passages, Mr. Molotov declared that it must be understood that the balance of forces between the Soviet Union and the United States had been "quite established."

Comparing the two and taking into account the vast human and material resources of this country, the strength of its allies, and the justness of its cause, Mr. Molotov declared, "it will become clear that the Soviet Union is no weaker than the United States."

As for atomic strength, he said in an earlier passage that "the aggressive circles of the United States miscalculated again." They thought it would take ten or fifteen years for the Soviet Union to catch up with the United States, he asserted, but "the Soviet people have achieved such success that not the Soviet Union but the United States finds itself in the position of being behind."

In thus belittling and challeng-

Continued on Page 6, Column 4

CHANGE IN HIGH SOVIET COUNCILS: The scene yesterday in Supreme Soviet at Moscow after Marshal Nikolai A. Bulganin was elected to succeed Georgi M. Malenkov. Front row, from left, are Lazar M. Kaganovich, Marshal Bulganin, Nikita S. Khrushchev, Mr. Malenkov and Marshal Kliment E. Voroshilov. At far right in rear is Anastas I. Mikoyan.
Associated Press Radiophoto

SENATE UNIT VOTES FORMOSA TREATY

Committee Ballot Is 11 to 2 —Whole Chamber May Adopt Pact by Tomorrow Night

By WILLIAM S. WHITE
Special to The New York Times

WASHINGTON, Feb. 8—The Senate Foreign Relations Committee approved today the defense treaty with Nationalist China on Formosa. The vote was 11 to 2.

The committee's chairman, Senator Walter F. George, Democrat of Georgia, will take the pact to the Senate tomorrow in the hope that it can be cleared there by Thursday night.

Failing final action by then, there can be none before the week after next.

Beginning Friday, the Senate, by old custom, will have an unofficial holiday from all important business, for ten days while Republican speakers celebrate the birthday of Abraham Lincoln.

Mr. George recognized the possibility of delay, though he spoke out against it as undesirable in the light of the changing of com-

Continued on Page 14, Column 3

Khrushchev Comes to Fore In Compromise on Bulganin

The following article is by a member of The Times staff who is a specialist on Soviet affairs.

By HARRY SCHWARTZ

Nikita S. Khrushchev appeared to have emerged yesterday as the most powerful single person in the Soviet Union, the heir to Stalin's mantle.

Stalin ruled the Soviet Union during most of his reign without holding any Government post, content to be general secretary of the Communist party.

It was as first secretary, the new name for general secretary of the party that Mr. Khrushchev nominated Nikolai A. Bulganin to be Premier. But the largest ovation went to the first secretary, not to the new Premier.

Even before yesterday, Mr. Khrushchev had given abundant testimony that he, not some amorphous "collective leadership," is the leader.

It may be that his power is subject still to the majority of his colleagues in the Presidium of the Central Committee or to the will of the army leaders. But since last December the public image has been of a Mr. Khru-

Continued on Page 6, Column 5

This article is by a reporter of The Times who returned last fall after five years in Moscow.

By HARRISON E. SALISBURY

Marshal Nikolai A. Bulganin almost certainly is a compromise choice as Soviet Premier. He apparently represents a coalition of the party forces of Nikita S. Khrushchev and the army headed by Marshal Georgi G. Zhukov.

The heralded showdown between Mr. Khrushchev and former Premier Georgi M. Malenkov has occurred more quickly than this observer had expected.

Apparently the army threw its backing to Mr. Khrushchev.

Regardless of the fire and vigor of Foreign Minister Vyacheslav M. Molotov's address yesterday, Soviet power in the international arena will remain weakened for a considerable time. The crisis that resulted in the execution of Deputy Premier Lavrenti P. Beria left little outward signs of cracks in the Kremlin wall. However, it seemed certain the Soviet Government would be a longer time in over-

Continued on Page 6, Column 7

MOSCOW SHAKE-UP

Malenkov Avows Guilt for Shortcomings in Agriculture

Texts of Malenkov statement and Khrushchev speech, Page 2.

By CLIFTON DANIEL
Special to The New York Times

MOSCOW, Feb. 8—On nomination by Nikita S. Khrushchev, first secretary of the Communist party, Marshal Nikolai A. Bulganin became head of the Soviet Government today. He replaced Georgi M. Malenkov, who had been Premier since the death of Stalin March 5, 1953.

Reproaching himself for inadequate leadership, Mr. Malenkov offered his resignation this afternoon to the Supreme Soviet, national legislature of the Soviet Union.

[News of the resignation was published in a Late City Extra of The New York Times on Tuesday.]

Mr. Malenkov said he would fulfill "with greatest scrupulousness" the duties that would now be assigned to him. Those duties were not stated at once.

In resigning Mr. Malenkov took on himself the "guilt and responsibility" for the present state of Soviet agriculture, which has been roundly criticized by Mr. Khrushchev.

To Support Party Line

Mr. Malenkov also proclaimed his understanding of the Communist party line that forced development of heavy industry must be the basis for increased agricultural production and all other branches of the Soviet economy. That line has recently been re-emphasized with new firmness by the Central Committee of the party and its propaganda organs.

The Central Committee's decision, taken in the last days of January on the initiative of Mr. Khrushchev, gave orders for still further efforts to increase Soviet agricultural output and Mr. Malenkov said today the decision had revealed to him his shortcomings as an administrator.

The change in the Premiership, accomplished in barely ten minutes of swift political action, left two major questions unanswered for the moment:

What will be Mr. Malenkov's future position and who will be Defense Minister of the Soviet

Continued on Page 2, Column 3

U. S. SEES STRUGGLE AS FAR FROM OVER

Experts on Moscow Conclude It Is Too Early to Decide About Effect of Change

By JAMES RESTON
Special to The New York Times

WASHINGTON, Feb. 8—The United States Government, concentrating on its plans for blocking Communist expansion, refused to comment today on the battle of the dictators in the Soviet Union.

The capital hummed with speculation all day. But after hours of cooperative guesswork the official experts on the Soviet Union decided to let the events interpret the Moscow changes.

Ambassador Charles E. Bohlen's first official cablegram on the news came in at 7:49 A. M. It was discussed briefly by Secretary of State Dulles at his 9:15 staff conference.

Thereafter the official advisers on the Soviet Union were instructed to analyze the published facts. Their conclusions—less dogmatic than most opinion in the capital—were as follows:

¶There is trouble in the Soviet "paradise." Premier Georgi M. Malenkov was dismissed not because everything was going well: the dramatic news was a sign, not of Communist strength, but of weakness.

¶Nikita S. Khrushchev, the Communist party boss, is probably the most powerful figure for the moment. But the fierce struggle over succession, always a problem in Russia, even in the time of the czars, is far from over.

¶It is too early to reach any

Continued on Page 7, Column 1

TUNIS LEADER AIDS PINAY ON CABINET

U.S. Bipartisan Idea Adapted by Premier-Designate

By LANSING WARREN
Special to The New York Times

PARIS, Feb. 8—Premier-designate Antoine Pinay obtained some help today from the Tunisian Premier in his efforts to form a French Cabinet.

After their conference the Tunisian Premier, Tahar ben Ammar, said he had found that he and M. Pinay had similar ideas and that "I hope we shall continue the negotiations that were started with the Government of Mendès-France." M. ben Ammar declared that he was going full of optimism to Tunis to inform the Bey, Sidi Mohamed el Amin, about the consultations.

The statement will be used by M. Pinay in trying to convince the party groups that his Cabinet can handle the crisis in Tunisia.

In dealing with those groups today M. Pinay obtained support from M. Mendès-France's Radical group, but met a rebuff from the Socialists. The Radical executive body voted, 81 to 67, to participate in the Pinay Cabinet. This assures him of about two-thirds of the seventy-six Radical Deputies, who never vote in unison.

The Socialists, through Christian Pineau, former Minister of Finance, declined the invitation to join the Cabinet. M. Pinay had

Continued on Page 11, Column 3

U. S. Plane Downed By Reds in Tachens

By The Associated Press.

WITH UNITED STATES SEVENTH FLEET, in the Tachens, Wednesday, Feb. 9— Red anti-aircraft batteries today shot down a United States AD Skyraider plane twenty miles southwest of the Tachen Islands today, the Navy said.

The pilot and two crew members of the carrier-based plane were rescued by the destroyer Isbell, the Navy said.

WASHINGTON, Feb. 8 (AP)— The Navy said tonight that one of its patrol planes received three small holes in one wing from Chinese Communist anti-aircraft fire during the Tachens evacuation today, but returned safely from its mission.

The Navy released a brief message from Vice Admiral Alfred M. Pride:

"Vice Admiral Pride learned during the night that three small holes were discovered in one wing during inspection after returning to base."

All Civilians Off Upper Tachen; First U. S. Ship Returns to Formosa

American and Chinese military personnel, in the foreground, observe the evacuation operation on Upper Tachen Island.
Associated Press Wirephoto via Radio From Taipei

Special to The New York Times

KEELUNG, Formosa, Wednesday, Feb. 9—The first United States Navy ship with Chinese Nationalist civilians evacuated from the Tachen Islands docked here this morning. She was an 8,000-ton transport with 3,816 civilians on board. Vice Admiral Alfred M. Pride, Commander of the United States Seventh Fleet, announced last night that the evacuation of civilians was completed at 5:17 P. M. yesterday. [In Washington, the Navy announced early Wednesday that the Seventh Fleet had reported that the last "organized group" of civilians had been evacuated from South Tachen Island, The

Continued on Page 14, Column 5

"All the News That's Fit to Print"

The New York Times.

LATE CITY EDITION

Chance of some showers and mild today, tonight and tomorrow.
Temperature Range Today—Max., 65; Min., 47
Temperatures Yesterday—Max., 65; Min., 43
Full C., 8. Weather Bureau Report, Page 40

Copyright, 1955, by The New York Times Company.

VOL. CIV. No. 35,501.   Entered as Second-Class Matter, Post Office. New York. N. Y.   NEW YORK, WEDNESDAY, APRIL 6, 1955.   Times Square, New York N. Y. Telephone LAckawanna 4-1000   FIVE CENTS

MANPOWER SLASH IN MARINES, NAVY BACKED WITH 'IFS'

Carney and Shepherd Call Reduced Budget Adequate if No Emergency Occurs

DEMOCRATS CONCERNED

But They Are Assured Corps' Ability to Strike Quickly in an Attack Won't Suffer

By C. P. TRUSSELL

WASHINGTON, April 5—Top uniformed officers of the Navy and Marine Corps supported the President's reduced armed services budget today. At points, they appeared to be salting loyalty to the Commander in Chief with reservations.

The $34,000,000,000 budget for the fiscal year starting July 1 it seemed, was all right as of now. It was evident, however, that if the "international situation worsened, more money would be requested in a hurry.

Those testifying before a Senate Appropriations subcommittee were Gen. Lemuel C. Shepherd Jr., Commandant of the Marine Corps, and Admiral Robert B. Carney, Chief of Naval Operations.

Meanwhile, more civilian heads of the armed services continued to support the reduced budget. They included Charles S. Thomas, Secretary of the Navy, and Harold E. Talbott, Secretary of the Air Force.

A spokesman for Robert T. Stevens, Secretary of the Army, is expected to back the other civilian leaders tomorrow. Mr. Stevens is out of the country.

Frank Answers Sought

Democrats of the subcommittee, which is headed by Senator Dennis Chavez, Democrat of New Mexico, continued to search for blunt answers from the uniformed officers as to how they felt about the military cuts.

The Democrats do not like proposed cuts in Marine Corps forces. General Shepherd was asked how he squared his support of a reduction in the armed forces with the mission of the Marine Corps to be the first to fight in case of an attack.

"It is manifest," he replied, "that reductions of the magnitude with which we are confronted [a cut from 215,000 to 193,-000] involve some sacrifice.

"However, we are determined that the sacrifice will not be made in readiness of our basic striking forces. The reduction will be absorbed primarily by disbanding certain reinforcing combat and logistic units and by reducing the manning levels of other supporting units.

"Operationally, the effect of these actions will be to diminish somewhat the staying power of

Continued on Page 14, Column 2

JERSEY SEIZES 62 IN HOT-ROD TRAP

Racers Caught on Unlighted Road Used as Speedway

Special to The New York Times.

CHATSWORTH, N. J., April 5 —It's a rare man who can lay hands on a will-o'-the-wisp, especially if it's motor-powered. Yet that's what State Trooper Leonard Miller did under a bright moon last night.

For weeks now, nocturnal travelers through the lonely pine lands of Burlington County have been frightened almost off the highway by dabs of light whooshing past them at breakneck speed.

The police, who had their suspicions about the souped-up will-o'-the-wisps, were hard put to track them down. One night the reports came from here, the next from there. Always the apparitions appeared from unlighted stretches along Route 72, which runs from the center of the state to the coast. Among other attractions for hot-rodders it has a fourteen-mile stretch that is almost ruler-straight.

Last night the state troopers set a trap along a section that was without warning lamps but bright in the moonlight.

Trooper Miller, on watch near the Pennsylvania Railroad overpass, heard, at about 10:30 P. M., a buzz and then a roar. Out of the west came four blobs of light, spanning the two-lane roadway.

Trooper Miller stepped into the

Continued on Page 22, Column 5

Harriman and Wagner Plan Own City-State Fiscal Study

Financing by a Private Foundation May Be Sought for Project Ignored by the Legislature, Mayor Announces

By CHARLES G. BENNETT

Governor Harriman and Mayor Wagner will go ahead soon with the appointment of a committee to make a long-range study of state-city fiscal relationships. It is possible that funds will be sought from a private foundation for the study.

Mayor Wagner announced this yesterday as he discussed the city's fiscal situation in an interview in his office, 63 Park Row, and later before 300 members of the Bond Club at a luncheon at 120 Broadway. He forecast that Republicans as well as Democrats would be invited to serve on the fiscal study committee.

The Mayor expressed hope that the committee would find a formula for taking the whole city-state financial problem "entirely out of politics." He predicted that the prestige of the study committee members would be so great that the state Legislature could not afford to ignore its suggestions.

At its session just ended, the Legislature failed to take any action creating a legislative commission to make the state-city financial study. Mayor Wagner, backed by the Governor, had called for such a survey in an effort to end the recurring crises that send the Mayor and his aides to Albany each year seeking state aid and authorization for new taxes.

At his interview yesterday Mayor Wagner commented that the city had had more cooperation than usual from the Legislature in approval of city bills.

At the same time he noted that the Legislature had helped to solve city fiscal woes for "this year only" and that the city financial measures did "not call

Continued on Page 21, Column 3

Canada Cuts Income Taxes In a Bid to Spur Prosperity

By RAYMOND DANIELL

Special to The New York Times.

OTTAWA, April 5—The Canadian Government decided tonight to cut taxes. The national debt will be increased in the interest of national prosperity. Indirect and direct personal and corporate income taxes were cut to increase purchasing power and investment capital, with the advance knowledge that the Government would be collecting less than it plans to spend.

This is in accord with the expressed Liberal policy of taxing for surpluses in good and prosperous times and accepting a deficit when business, agriculture and industry run into trouble. The Canadian economy is not in serious trouble, but unemployment, a slowing down of industry and a drop in farm income have raised danger signals.

Tonight, in presenting his first budget as Minister of Finance, Walter Harris, in spite of an unexpected deficit of nearly $150,-000,000 last year, proposed new tax cuts that will reduce the Government's revenues by about $207,000,000 in a full year based on normal expectations of increased prosperity.

Mr. Harris proposed a new schedule of rates to reduce the personal income tax by 12 to 13 per cent for 85 per cent of the country's taxpayers. There are 3,800,000 persons in this category in this country of 15,000,-000 inhabitants.

This, of course, will add to the country's national debt. This, Mr. Harris asserted, should be no cause for alarm. He was taking into account an expected rise in the country's gross national product of about 5 per cent, Mr. Harris said, in reducing the scale of taxes. With more wealth being produced, he said, it was possible to reduce

Continued on Page 12, Column 5

RED CROSS EASES FUND DRIVE RULES

Permits Chapters to Join in Community Campaigns Under Some Conditions

By The Associated Press.

WASHINGTON, April 5— The American National Red Cross announced today that it had relaxed its rules so that under certain conditions local chapters could participate in Community or United Fund raising drives.

Most Red Cross chapters have refused to become a part of fund-raising campaigns such as Community Chest and United Fund Drives. In these, welfare agencies are grouped. Each receives a percentage of the funds raised.

E. Roland Harriman, national Red Cross chairman, said the board of governors had adopted the policy yesterday.

With the changes, he said, "Red Cross chapters will be able to plan in a more direct and helpful manner with other agencies and community leaders in matters of united or federated fund raising."

The board said the United States Government had established the American National Red Cross as this nation's official volunteer agency under the Geneva conventions. It added that this "unique and official" status made certain conditions of fund-raising necessary.

Units Control Own Budgets

The board said each local Red Cross chapter would keep its rights:

¶To determine and control its budget and goal.

¶To conduct a roll-call for members and funds in the month designated by the board of governors.

¶To conduct emergency campaigns in disaster, war or other unforeseen needs when authorized by the board of governors.

¶To issue a membership card to each person from whose contribution the Red Cross received $1 or more.

The amended policy keeps the provision that all chapters will "participate in annual campaigns for members and funds for the purpose of enrolling members and obtaining adequate voluntary contributions to finance the chapters and the national organization."

Red Cross headquarters here said it would be possible for a local chapter to participate in a United Fund Drive and also conduct its own campaign later if needed to reach its goal.

Local chapters may work out their own program, headquarters said. They may get all their funds from the United Drive, merely retaining the "right" to their own drive.

Since most United Fund Drives

Continued on Page 24, Column 6

WEST BIG 3 BAR AUSTRIAN ACCORD WITH SOVIET ONLY

Joint Declaration Advises Both Vienna and Moscow Big 4 Approval Is Needed

Special to The New York Times.

WASHINGTON, April 5—The Western Big Three cautioned Austria and the Soviet Union today against making bilateral commitments on the terms of an Austrian state treaty.

The United States, Britain and France issued a joint declaration noting that conclusion of the long-pending pact was of concern to all of the "Big Four powers as well as Austria.

If the Soviet Union should offer "proposals which hold clear promise of the restoration of freedom and independence to Austria, these would appropriately be discussed by the four Ambassadors in Vienna with the participation of the Austrian Government", the joint declaration said. It was made public simultaneously here and in London and Paris.

While it was not specifically directed to either the Moscow or Vienna Government, the statement was interpreted here as referring to both of the Western Big Three's attitude toward the Soviet-Austrian meeting scheduled for next week in Moscow.

West Wary on Concessions

The Western Big Three were understood to be particularly concerned lest Julius Raab, the Austrian Chancellor, make concessions to the Soviet Union that would be unacceptable to them.

Chancellor Raab and a delegation of Austrian officials will fly to Moscow Monday to discuss new ways of arriving at a treaty. The mission is being undertaken at the March 24 invitation of Vyacheslav M. Molotov, Soviet Foreign Minister.

One was a guarantee of Austrian independence that would prevent another Anschluss, or union, between Austria and Germany.

The other was an expression of Austria's willingness to guarantee that she would not join any military alliance or allow her territory to be used for foreign military bases.

The West has never opposed military neutrality for Austria and never has planned to include Austria in the North Atlantic alliance. The concern is more over a possible attempt by the Soviet Union to insist on unacceptable guarantee terms with respect to either or both of Mr. Molotov's points.

In the past, one of the main barriers to a pact restoring Austria's freedom and ending the four-power occupation has been the Soviet Union's insistence on the maintenance of occupation troops until a German treaty has been completed.

The text of today's three-power declaration follows:

"For many years the Governments of the United Kingdom, the United States and France have sought to conclude an Austrian state treaty. They have made ceaseless efforts thus to bring about the restoration of

Continued on Page 12, Column 5

DULLES SAYS U. S. WON'T START WAR

Holds Any Conflict in Formosa Area Would Be Reds' Doing —Restates Quemoy Stand

By DANA ADAMS SCHMIDT

WASHINGTON, April 5—Secretary of State Dulles said today that if there was war in the Formosa Strait it would be the Communist Chinese who started it.

The United States, he asserted, has made "perfectly clear" its desire for a cease-fire and peace in the strait. But the Chinese Communists, he declared, unfortunately do not seem to be much under the influence of the peace propaganda they disseminate.

The Secretary made his observations in reply to a request for an assessment of the prospects for war or peace in the Formosa Strait at the first news conference he has held since March 15.

"To answer that question would require me to read the minds of people to whom I have no access, that is, the Communist leaders in Peiping," Mr. Dulles replied.

The Secretary was asked about continuing demands in Congress that the United States make known now whether it will defend Quemoy and Matsu Islands against Communist attack. Mr. Dulles said he knew the answer to that one by heart. There was no commitment of any kind, sort or description, expressed or implied, he declared, binding the United States to the defense of anything except Formosa and the Pescadores.

'Very Difficult Ground'

The suggestion that the United States should announce how it proposed to fulfill its treaty commitments entered onto "very difficult ground" he said. He did not see how it could be done.

The Secretary observed that the United States also had a commitment to defend the United States of America but no one had yet asked for a commitment as to how that would be done.

Asked whether that meant the United States would not fight for the defense of Quemoy and Matsu for the sake of the morale of Chinese Nationalist troops in Formosa, he replied that it would not, "unless that was vital for the defense of Formosa and the Pescadores. It all comes back to that."

President Eisenhower has told Congress that he and he alone would make the decision whether the United States should help defend Quemoy and Matsu. He said his decision would depend on whether the invasion of the offshore islands was recognizable as a preliminary to invasion of Formosa or the Pescadores.

While Mr. Dulles was speaking to the press, Secretary of the

Continued on Page 7, Column 5

CHURCHILL QUITS AS PRIME MINISTER; DECLINES DUKEDOM TO STAY AN M. P.; EDEN TAKES OVER LEADERSHIP TODAY

ON WAY TO RETIREMENT: Sir Winston Churchill moist-eyed as he arrived in auto yesterday at Buckingham Palace to tender resignation as Prime Minister to Queen Elizabeth.

Associated Press Radiophoto

President Declares Allies Still Will Heed Churchill

By W. H. LAWRENCE

Special to The New York Times.

WASHINGTON, April 5—President Eisenhower declared today that leaders of the free world were bound to ask Sir Winston Churchill's counsel and advice, even in retirement.

Democrats and Republicans joined the President in personal tributes to the retiring British Prime Minister.

There were formal statements from John Foster Dulles, Secretary of State; Vice President Richard M. Nixon, and from a host of Senate and House members.

The President went into the White House Rose Garden to record for newsreels and television cameras his personal tribute to his long-time associate in war and peace.

It is not usual for the head of the United States Government to express himself so feelingly when the head of another government resigns from office. But Sir Winston's departure changed all the rules. The President spoke into the cameras in the obvious hope that the British statesman himself would see the pictures and hear the words.

"We have just had official word that my old and very dear friend, Sir Winston Churchill, has retired from his position as head of Her Majesty's Government in the United Kingdom," the President said.

"Naturally, an event such as this recalls to my mind many stirring incidents both of war and peace. I have greatly respected and valued my associations with a man so great as Winston Churchill.

"And now, if I dare, I should like to adress a word directly to Sir Winston.

"All of us in the free world

Continued on Page 11, Column 7

Vietnam Dissidents Give Warning to U.S.

By ROBERT ALDEN

SAIGON, Vietnam, April 5 —The groups fighting Vietnam's Government warned tonight that continued United States support of Premier Ngo Dinh Diem might lead to civil war.

They said that as far as they were concerned the truce was ended and that "all responsibility for bloodshed—Vietnamese and foreign—would rest on Ngo Dinh Diem."

It was further charged that the United States had turned over four tanks to the Government. As far as can be determined, the United States does not have any tanks in Vietnam.

The Ngo Dinh Diem Cabinet voted today to stand firm in the face of the Opposition's threat. As the situation in Saigon grew more tense by the hour, officials made it known that the Government had

Continued on Page 12, Column 3

BRITISH ERA ENDS

Aged Statesman Tells Queen of Decision— Cabinet Shifts Due

By DREW MIDDLETON

Special to The New York Times.

LONDON, April 5—Sir Winston Churchill resigned as Prime Minister today. Age has done what Britain's enemies and his political rivals could not accomplish.

Tomorrow Queen Elizabeth II will summon Sir Anthony Eden to Buckingham Palace and ask him to form a new Government. Sir Anthony's accession as Prime Minister will mark the passing of the Churchill era.

While shadows lengthened on the palace lawns, Sir Winston stood talking with the Queen at his study window. Their business was his resignation. When the audience ended he passed out of the palace, through cheering ranks of his countrymen.

The most significant change in British political life since the end of World War II was announced from Buckingham Palace in a single sentence:

"The Right Honorable Sir Winston Churchill had an audience of the Queen this evening and tendered his resignation as Prime Minister and First Lord of the Treasury, which Her Majesty was graciously pleased to accept."

Transition to Eden Era

Thus Sir Winston, Knight of the Garter, Privy Councilor, Order of Merit and Companion of Honor, left the office he has held at two different times for a total of eight years, seven months and twenty-five days.

While Sir Winston, who is 80 years old, bowed beaming to crowds shouting "Good old Winnie!" in Downing Street tonight, political London bubbled with anticipation.

When Sir Anthony is asked by the Queen tomorrow to form a Government, all the Ministers will place their offices at his disposal. This will open the way to changes that, immediately after the election, will change the Churchill Government into the Eden Government.

The decision on the date of a general parliamentary election is Sir Anthony's. Polls conducted by newspaper men in the House of Commons indicate that a great majority of the Members of Parliament expect the election will take place May 26.

If this date is chosen, the new

Continued on Page 11, Column 2

CHURCHILL BARS OFFER OF PEERAGE

Prefers to Stay Commoner. He Replies to Queen's Bid —Britons Acclaim Him

By BENJAMIN WELLES

LONDON, April 5—Sir Winston Churchill declined a dukedom today to remain in the House of Commons.

In an audience with Queen Elizabeth II in her study in Buckingham Palace, he tendered his resignation to his sovereign. The Queen accepted it and then offered him the highest titular dignity in the land. But Sir Winston, a grandson of the seventh Duke of Marlborough, humbly yet firmly declined it.

He had been a "House of Commons man" for almost fifty years, he recalled, and he preferred to remain one rather than accept a peerage and enter the House of Lords.

The decision showed that Sir Winston, after laying down the cares and responsibilities of high office, would continue as an elder statesman in the Commons, which he has loved—and which has intermittently loved him—during that half century.

Had Declined Earldom

It was not the first time Sir Winston, had turned down the offer of a peerage to remain in the lower but more powerful legislative chamber. In the aftermath of victory in 1945 he was offered an earldom, but refused it.

The 28-year-old Queen and the 80-year-old statesman each knew what was in the other's mind when they met today. He knew in advance what she would reply and she knew what his reply would be. But Elizabeth and Sir Winston, both exemplars of tradition in a tradition-loving land, observed the forms and courtesies due between the sovereign and a retiring counselor and friend.

The last non-royal dukedom was given to the Marquess of Westminster in 1874, the year of Sir Winston's birth. There are now twenty-six dukes in the United Kingdom peerage, in addition to the royal dukes—Edinburgh, Cornwall, Gloucester, Kent and Windsor.

Sir Winston's refusal of the proffered peerage means only that his name will remain as it is, His knighthood, acquired in 1953

Continued on Page 11, Column 5

SOUTH AFRICA OUT OF UNESCO RANKS

Quits United Nations Agency Over Racial Issue

By LEONARD INGALLS

Special to The New York Times.

JOHANNESBURG, South Africa, April 5—South Africa has withdrawn from the United Nations Educational, Scientific and Cultural Organization.

Eric H. Louw, Minister of External Affairs, said today in Capetown that it had been decided to terminate his country's participation in the agency because of its "interference in South Africa's racial problems."

He reported that the South African Ambassador in Paris had been instructed to inform officials of the United Nations agency of the Union's action. The decision to withdraw, Mr. Louw said, was made recently.

The Minister announced also that South Africa would not participate in deliberations of the International Court of Justice on the administration of the territory of South-West Africa under the League of Nations mandate. The territory was incorporated by South Africa in 1949.

This step of incorporation was not approved by the United Nations, which sought to have South Africa accept trusteeship of South-West Africa under United Nations supervision. South Africa ignored the United

Continued on Page 2, Column 2

3 Hefty Councilmen in Small Cab Say Rule on Front Seat Must Go

Six hundred and thirty-five pounds of City Councilmen found themselves uncomfortably squeezed recently into the back seat of one of the new small taxicabs. In front, the seat next to the driver beckoned, empty and inviting. Under the law, nothing could be done about it. The Councilmen had to stay put.

The Councilmen—there were three—decided "there ought to be a law." So now there probably will be.

The legislation authorizing use of the stock-car five-passenger cabs (driver and four fares, maximum) specifies that a passenger may ride in front with either two or three passengers on the back seat. The law says nothing about the size and weights of these back-seat riders.

Yesterday, a bill—"Fat Man's Amendment"—was introduced in the City Council to distribute the small-taxi fare weight more evenly.

The amendment, referred to the Council's General Welfare Committee, would permit a passenger to ride in front with either two or three passengers on the back seat. The sponsors of the amendment were Edward A. Cunningham, Bronx Democrat, and John J. Merli, Manhattan Democrat.

Mr. Cunningham, who weighs 225 pounds, was one of the three Councilmen who took the back-seat ride in discomfort. The others were James J. Murphy, Staten Island Democrat, weighing in at 216 pounds, and James J. Boland, Manhattan Democrat, a mere 200-pounder.

There was no ready explanation as to why Mr. Merli, who tips the beam at substantially less than 200 pounds, was a co-sponsor of the amendment. Other Councilmen guessed that he was "just going along for the ride."

Councilman Cunningham noted, in explaining his bill after yesterday's Council session, that the proposed amendment would be of aid not only to overweight passengers but also to women burdened with bundles. Referring to the plight of Mr. Murphy, Mr. Boland and himself, Mr. Cunningham said:

"When three fat guys like us try to squeeze into the back seat of one of these small-sized cabs, it is a tight fit, and something has to give."

Since Mr. Boland was not at yesterday's Council session and Mr. Cunningham and Mr. Murphy left City Hall soon after the meeting, it was impossible to

Continued on Page 26, Column 6

174

The New York Times.

LATE CITY EDITION
Fair and seasonably warm today.
Fair, quite warm tomorrow.
Temperature Range Today—Max., 86; Min., 67
Temperatures Yesterday—Max., 77.5; Min., 68.5
Full U. S. Weather Bureau Report, Page 36

VOL. CIV . No. 35,616.

Entered as Second-Class Matter,
Post Office, New York, N. Y.

NEW YORK, SATURDAY, JULY 30, 1955.

Times Square New York 36, N. Y.
Telephone LAckawanna 4-1000

Copyright, 1955, by The New York Times Company.

FIVE CENTS

TALBOTT QUITTING, PERHAPS AT ONCE, G.O.P. SOURCES SAY

But the White House Asserts 'There's Nothing Before Us' —Secretary 'Sits Tight'

ANOTHER INQUIRY LOOMS

Democrats Charge He Misled Them on Chrysler Stock by Giving It to Children

By ALLEN DRURY
Special to The New York Times

WASHINGTON, July 29—Republican Senators high in Administration councils said tonight that the resignation of Harold E. Talbott as Secretary of the Air Force was "imminent."

The Senators, who declined to be quoted by name, said the resignation might be announced over the weekend. At the White House, the Presidential press secretary, James C. Hagerty, would say only, "There is nothing before us."

Mr. Talbott said he was "sitting tight" and "has no more idea than a jackrabbit" of resigning.

He said he would be at his office in the morning and that he was "going ahead and try and run the Air Force as I have tried to do through all of this."

[A possibility, at least, that the Secretary would resign was discerned by The Associated Press, which quoted him as having said later, "I will do nothing at any time to embarrass President Eisenhower, and I will do whatever the President wishes me to do."]

The embattled Cabinet officer, already under investigation for his activities in connection with business for a management consultant corporation in which he was a partner, appeared to be headed for still another inquiry.

Senators Differ With Him

This one would revolve around a promise he made at the time of his appointment in 1953 to divest himself of 2,000 shares of Chrysler stock.

The new investigation, it was indicated, might be instigated by Democratic members of the Senate Armed Services Committee, which handled the Talbott nomination two years ago. They charged today that he had "improperly misled" them at that time concerning his plans for the stock.

Mr. Talbott testified Wednesday before the Senate Permanent Subcommittee on Investigations that he had given the stock to his four children, two of them minors. The Secretary said he had made it clear to the Armed Services Committee that he might give the stock away instead of selling it outright. But members of that committee said today they had had no such understanding.

Senator Harry F. Byrd, Democrat of Virginia, with whom Mr. Talbott said he had had an informal understanding that he might give the stock to members of his family, said he had no recollection of such a conversation. The Senator said he had understood the stock would be sold.

Senator Richard B. Russell, Democrat of Georgia, chairman of the Armed Services Committee, said today it was his "distinct impression from what Mr.

Continued on Page 6, Column 7

President Sees Party In Control 'Forever'

Special to The New York Times

WASHINGTON, July 29—President Eisenhower said today that a properly united Republican party could retain control of the national Administration "forever."

Addressing a Republican preadjournment breakfast rally, the President urged Republican legislators to get behind the principles he advocates.

He gave no sign whether he intended to lead the party again next year, but Republicans who have been urging him to run for re-election appeared encouraged.

Reporters were not invited to the meeting this morning. It was attended by all but a few of the Republicans in the Senate and House of Representatives, and members of the Cabinet and several members of the White House staff. James C. Hagerty, White House press secretary, gave a summary of

Continued on Page 6, Column 6

Court Rejects Plea To Deport Bridges

Special to The New York Times

SAN FRANCISCO, July 29—Federal Judge Louis E. Goodman today refused to strip Harry Renton Bridges, Pacific Coast labor leader, of his United States citizenship.

Judge Goodman, in the Government's fourth attempt to deport Mr. Bridges to his native Australia, ruled the prosecution had not proved its charges that the longshore leader had been a member of the Communist party before he was naturalized Sept. 17, 1945.

United States Attorney Lloyd H. Burke and Lynn J. Gillard and Robert H. Schnacke, assistant Federal attorneys, prosecuted the case. They said a decision to appeal would depend on the outcome of consultation with Department of Justice officials in Washington.

Continued on Page 10, Column 6

J. E. HOOVER SHUNS CITY POLICE POST

Declines Mayor's Bid to Be Commissioner—Wagner Is Said to Seek Outsider

By PAUL CROWELL

J. Edgar Hoover, director of the Federal Bureau of Investigation, has declined an invitation by Mayor Wagner to become the city's next Police Commissioner.

The offer of appointment to the $25,000 post now held by Francis W. H. Adams was made by the Mayor early this week through an unidentified emissary described at City Hall as a close friend of the F. B. I. chief.

Mr. Adams announced his resignation last Sunday but is remaining at his post until the Mayor appoints a successor.

The first announcement of Mr. Hoover's rejection of the Mayor's offer came from Washington. It was made by Louis B. Nichols, an assistant director of the F. B. I., after he had talked on the telephone with his chief. Mr. Nichols said Mr. Hoover was traveling "somewhere on the West Coast."

"Mr. Hoover has no plans to leave the F. B. I. and has declined Mayor Wagner's kind offer," Mr. Nichols said. He then telephoned the same announcement to William R. Peer, the Mayor's executive secretary. Mr. Peer passed the word along to the Mayor, who is spending the week-end at his summer home in Islip, L. I. The Mayor had no comment.

A report that Carmine G. De Sapio, head of Tammany Hall, was a guest at the Islip home, presumably to discuss the appointment of a new Police Commissioner, was spiked by the Mayor. Mr. DeSapio, he said, was not there and was not expected.

"I'll name the new Police Commissioner myself without consultation with anybody," the Mayor declared.

The Mayor did receive visits

Continued on Page 34, Column 6

CONGRESS CHIEFS ABANDON PLANS TO ADJOURN TODAY

House to Meet on Monday —Fuel Gas Bill Sidetracked —Public Housing Set Back

Special to The New York Times

WASHINGTON, July 29—Congress was caught tonight in the traditional minor frenzy of the eleventh hour as the controlling Democrats labored urgently toward bringing this session to an end.

All hope for an adjournment by tomorrow night, as had long been planned, was abandoned.

The Senate was in position to finish its work by then but the House of Representatives had a solid docket of work still ahead. Late in the day the House Democratic floor leader, Representative John W. McCormack of Massachusetts, officially announced that there would be a House meeting on Monday.

He prepared a calendar of business that will result in carrying Congress into next week.

The House quit for the night at 6:17 P. M. and will reassemble at 10:30 tomorrow morning.

Pressing to meet the original quitting date as nearly as they could, the Senate leaders officially cast aside until next year the most controversial single measure remaining on that side.

Defeat for President

This was a bill, passed 209 to 203 last night by the House, to exempt natural gas producers from Federal price control.

The decision was in a modified sense a blow to the President who had expressed support in principle for the bill.

It was a much heavier blow, however, to the leading Democrats of Congress, including Sam Rayburn of Texas, Speaker of the House of Representatives, and the ailing Senate Democratic chieftain, Senator Lyndon B. Johnson of Texas.

While many Republicans had gone along with the bill, its essential backers were these and other Southern and Southwestern Democratic members of Congress from the gas-producing states.

Adamantly against the project was the great bulk of the Northern wing of the Democratic party in Congress, especially the members from urban consumer areas.

The President, too, was suffering setbacks, however provisional some might turn out to be. For the White House was understood to be appealing privately for some aspects of his program.

The House, with the encouragement of the Republican Administration leadership, by 217 to 188 knocked out all public housing out of an omnibus housing bill.

The President had requested authority for the construction of 35,000 public housing units a year for two years.

One hundred fifty-one House Republicans voted with sixty-six Democrats to deny even this much public housing, though for complicated reasons not necessarily

Continued on Page 6, Column 4

U.S. TO LAUNCH EARTH SATELLITE 200-300 MILES INTO OUTER SPACE; WORLD WILL GET SCIENTIFIC DATA

MAN-MADE SATELLITE: Artist's renditions of the earth-circling satellite, based on a concept of Prof. S. F. Singer of the University of Maryland. Professor Singer's specifications—diameter of about two feet, weight 100 pounds and speed 17,280 miles an hour—conform closely with those of the announcement from the White House.

Associated Press Wirephoto (from Popular Science)

R.A.F. IS RETURNING 400 U.S. SABRE JETS

Set to Replace Fighters With British-Made Aircraft, to Be Paid For in Aid Funds

Special to The New York Times

LONDON, July 29—Britain announced today she was returning 400 Sabre Jet fighters to the United States and replacing them with British-made Hawker Hunters.

The British jets will be paid for by the United States under the Mutual Defense Assistance Program. The contract for the planes totals $140,000,000. It was signed more than a year ago, but the Hunter has been haunted by production delays.

Today's announcement indicates both the United States and Royal Air Forces are confident that the Hunter's time of trial is over, and that the planes are being produced in satisfactory numbers.

"Several" Royal Air Force squadrons are already equipped with them, an Air Ministry spokesman said.

The Hunter, which is comparable in performance with the Sabre Jet, or North American F-86F, flies about 650 miles an hour in operational trim.

The 400 Sabre Jets are being replaced not because they are

Continued on Page 3, Column 3

Russians Already Striving To Set Up Space Satellite

By HARRY SCHWARTZ

The United States and the Soviet Union now appear to be in a race for the glory of making the first major step toward interplanetary flight—the launching of an earth satellite in space. Soviet determination to achieve this objective was announced last April 15 in the newspaper Vechernaya Moskva (Evening Moscow).

The newspaper revealed then that a committee of top Soviet scientists, including the renowned physicist Prof. Peter Kapitsa, had been set up to devise a satellite in space somewhat similar to that outlined in Washington.

The announced objective of the Soviet space satellite was to photograph cloud and ice formations above the earth as an aid to weather forecasting.

[In Moscow, sources said Saturday that the Soviet Union was preparing to launch an earth satellite similar to the one planned by the United States, The United Press reported.]

Intense Soviet interest in achieving priority over all other nations in regard to all aspects of interplanetary flight has been evident for some years. The most authoritative Soviet statement of the practicability of such efforts was made in January, 1954, by the President of the Soviet Academy of Sciences, Alexander N. Nesmeyanov.

He said then: "Science has

Continued on Page 7, Column 4

U. S.-Peiping Trade Of Shows Proposed

By THOMAS F. BRADY

PARIS, July 29—A Chinese Communist theatrical company and an American theatrical company have exchanged invitations to appear in each other's country.

The reciprocal invitations are subject to Government approval on both sides, but it is known that both Governments are aware of the project.

The participants, whose cultural olive branches may add another bit of greenery to the signs of post - 'cold - war' spring, are the Peiping Opera, which is now touring Europe, and the Everyman Opera, which has presented George Gershwin's "Porgy and Bess" in most major European cities west of the Iron Curtain.

On the Chinese side the project has at least semi-official approval already. The invitation was extended by

Continued on Page 18, Column 5

PACE 18,000 M.P.H.

Rocket to Start Object Size of a Basketball in 1957 or 1958

Texts of press conference and documents, Pages 8 and 9.

By RUSSELL BAKER
Special to The New York Times

WASHINGTON, July 29—This country plans to launch history's first man-made, earth-circling satellite into space during 1957 or 1958.

Tentative plans envision an unmanned globular object about the size of a basketball. The satellite will circle around the earth about once every ninety minutes at a speed of 18,000 miles an hour in a fixed path 200 to 300 miles above the ground.

These plans were announced this afternoon at an extraordinary White House news conference attended by a battery of prominent scientists.

James C. Hagerty, White House press secretary, joined the scientists in stressing the satellite's immense scientific value to all nations and minimizing its threat as a potential instrument of war.

All nations, including the Communist countries, will have complete access to all scientific data gathered beyond the earth's known frontier, Mr. Hagerty said.

American scientists also will give the world the plot of the satellite's orbit, or course through space, so that scholars of all countries may study it.

Data Available to All

If the object carries radio equipment for transmitting scientific data to the earth, other nations will receive the broadcasting frequencies so they can tune in.

The satellite will girdle the earth "entirely for scientific purposes," Mr. Hagerty said.

"Do you mean as distinct from war-making purposes?" he was asked.

"If you wish, yes," he replied.

The scientists said they were convinced that the satellite was now "feasible" with available technological methods and materials.

Once aloft, they said, it is expected to produce new information about the unexplored outer atmosphere that is necessary before human travel in space can be undertaken.

As the scientists depicted it, the satellite would be hurled into space under rocket power. The rocket, in several stages, would fall away piece by piece as each stage burnt out its fuel load.

At a point somewhere between 200 and 300 miles above earth, the satellite—or "the bird," as the scientists call it—would get one final mighty blast from the rocket's last stage.

This would send it hurtling into its orbit at a speed of 18,000 miles an hour. A man standing on earth could perhaps barely

Continued on Page 7, Column 4

NO MILITARY ROLE FOR GLOBAL BALL

Device Cannot Survey Land Nor Can It Drop Bomb— Its Goal Is Defined

By ANTHONY LEVIERO
Special to The New York Times

WASHINGTON, July 29—The earth satellite will have no practicable military application in the foreseeable future. However, it will help man come to a better understanding of the natural laws of the universe.

Research scientists in the Pentagon said the man-made satellite, whizzing around the earth with a tumbling motion, would give them valuable information. This could be applied to flight studies for the intercontinental ballistics missile, a dread atomic weapon now being developed for wars between the continents.

There are two important things that the satellite will not be able to do:

1. It will have no utility for gaining terrestrial data that might be used as part of President Eisenhower's Geneva plan for inspecting the military establishments of the United States and Russia.

2. It will not be able to drop nuclear weapons, or anything else for that matter, back on earth for use against a hostile country.

The first satellite may have a mouse aboard, but scientists said they could not foresee the time when human beings would be able to go into outer space as passengers.

The Return Expected

The greatest return the scientists expect from the first satellite will be knowledge of conditions in the outer atmosphere —for instance, the density of a field at different altitudes, a field of knowledge with large gaps in it.

The first satellite also is expected to provide new information about:

¶The nature of the sun.
¶Solar radio noise.
¶Cosmic radiation.
¶Magnetic noises and their causes.
¶The aurora, or luminous, static - producing phenomenon that radiates from the north and south magnetic poles.

Defense Department research scientists pleaded with reporters to repress any tendency to exploit speculations that have been popularized in recent years by fiction writers. They said the possibility of human passengers in a man-made satellite and its use for military purposes was so remotely in the future that speculations about it were practically useless.

In stressing that all the data they will gain will be in abstract and basic science, the military

Continued on Page 7, Column 6

A. E. C. CITES GAINS IN H-BOMB FIELD

Designs of New Arms Based on '54 Tests—Reactors for Plane Engines Advanced

Special to The New York Times

WASHINGTON, July 29—Hydrogen weapons, apparently of several types, have been produced for the United States atomic arsenal in the first six months of this year.

The atomic energy commission disclosed this today in its eighteenth semiannual report. The design of the new weapons was based on the results of the spectacular 1954 hydrogen bomb tests in the Pacific.

The weapons advance was one of several major developments reported by the commission. Others were:

¶The commission's program for developing reactors for industrial and military electric power and for naval and aircraft propulsion "made greater strides during the first six months of 1955 than in any earlier half-year."

On the aircraft problem the

Continued on Page 15, Column 4

Three Ex-G.I. Turncoats Land in San Francisco and Are Jailed by Army

Capt. Walter B. Leahy, right, reads a summary of court-martial charges against the turncoats before formally taking them into custody. The prisoners are, from left, Otho G. Bell, William C. Cowart and Lewis W. Griggs.

Associated Press Wirephoto

By LAWRENCE E. DAVIES
Special to The New York Times

SAN FRANCISCO, July 29—Three dishonorably discharged soldiers who renounced America two years ago for life in Communist China came home today to an emotional greeting from relatives and to an Army stockade. They promised to "gladly accept whatever punishment is coming to us." When the American President Lines President Cleveland docked this afternoon after a trip from the Orient military policeman promptly arrested William C. Cowart, 22 years old, of Dalton, Ga.; Lewis W. Griggs, 22, of Jacksonville, Tex., and Otho G. Bell, 24, formerly of Hillsboro, Miss. They listened intently and soberly while Capt. Walter R. Leahy of the provost marshall's office at the San Francisco Presidio read a 400-word summary of court-martial charges based on their alleged

Continued on Page 18, Column 3

Sofia Offers Israel Air Crash Damages

Special to The New York Times

TEL AVIV, Israel, July 29—The Bulgarian Government has agreed to pay at least part compensation for the shooting down of an Israeli airliner Wednesday. Fifty-eight persons, including twelve New Yorkers, died in the crash.

A Foreign Office spokesman said today the Bulgarian promise was made yesterday in a note to Baruch Nir, Israeli chargé d'affaires in Sofia.

[Bulgaria will permit three Israeli aircraft investigators, who have been waiting in Greece, to go to the scene of the crash, Athens reported Friday.]

The Bulgarian note expressed the Sofia Government's "profound regret" and notified Israel of the appointment of a special Government commission to inquire into the circumstances of what it called "the deplorable accident." The Bul-

Continued on Page 2, Column 5

"All the News
That's Fit to Print"

The New York Times.

LATE CITY EDITION
Heavy rain and high winds today;
clearing tonight. Fair tomorrow.
Temperature Range Today—Max., 79; Min., 71
Temperatures Yesterday—Max., 78.6; Min., 67
Full U. S. Weather Bureau Report, Page 61

VOL. CV . No. 35,668.   Entered as Second-Class Matter,
Post Office, New York, N. Y.   NEW YORK, TUESDAY, SEPTEMBER 20, 1955.   Times Square, New York 36, N. Y.
Telephone Lackawanna 4-1000   FIVE CENTS

Copyright, 1955, by The New York Times Company.

GALES MOVE ON THE CITY; SOUTH IS HIT

DAMAGE IS SEVERE

New York Area Due to Feel the Effects of Hurricane Today

By PETER KIHSS

Hurricane Ione tore wide destruction in coastal North Carolina when it roared in from the Atlantic Ocean yesterday morning.

Then it slowed down and became a tricky problem that kept the entire Eastern Seaboard worried.

In Washington the United States Weather Bureau said at 3 o'clock this morning that the tropical twister was centered about twenty miles southeast of Norfolk, Va., with winds of over thirty-five miles an hour swirling outward some 200 miles to the north and east.

Swirling northeastward at eight to ten miles an hour, it is expected to pick up speed and intensity as it swings out to sea. It was expected to be off the Delaware coast this morning and southeast of Long Island in the afternoon.

Ernest J. Christie, in charge of the Weather Bureau here, said at 3 o'clock this morning that New York City would feel the worst effects of the storm later today.

The center of the storm, he said, would pass southeast of the city during the day. New York City, on the northern fringe of the storm, would have heavy rain at times with wind velocities of forty to fifty miles an hour and gusts possibly up to sixty miles an hour. Clearing weather was forecast for tonight.

Forecasts Are Qualified

Hurricane force is seventy-five miles an hour or more, according to the Weather Bureau scale.

But meteorologists were qualifying all their forecasts, warning that Ione—whose name comes from the Greek word meaning "go"—was an erratic personality.

Ione, hatched last Wednesday east of Puerto Rico, did millions of dollars worth of damage as it roared overland across the coastal areas of North Carolina with winds up to 107 miles an hour.

Communications lines were down, roads and bridges washed out, crops destroyed, large areas of cities flooded and hundreds made homeless.

Reports of the damage were fragmentary, but mounting rapidly as communications were restored. Four persons were reported dead at New Bern, N. C. and three at Beaufort, N. C. The Red Cross said it was providing shelter for 1,800 persons in the state.

New Bern, a city of 15,000 persons, was jammed before the hurricane with hundreds of refugees from tidal river lowlands. Forty blocks of the city were flooded and for fifteen hours the community was without power, communications and drinking

Continued on Page 24, Column 1

Hilda Rips Tampico In 'Worst Disaster'

By The United Press.

MEXICO CITY, Sept. 19—President Adolfo Ruiz Cortines tonight ordered unlimited Government aid for storm-lashed Tampico as Hurricane Hilda sent a flood of "catastrophic proportions" over three-quarters of the port city.

The President said Tampico, cut off by winds and water from the outside world, was confronted with the "worst disaster in its history."

[The Associated Press said Monday that Gov. Horacio Teran reported the hurricane had killed twelve persons and injured 350 in Tampico. The Governor of Tamaulipas State said 90 per cent of the buildings in the city had been damaged and 15,000 were homeless. A state of emergency was ordered.]

A medical brigade of 200

Continued on Page 24, Column 7

CITY IS PREPARED FOR STORM'S FURY

Lines Kept Open From Center at Police Headquarters to Waiting Emergency Men

Residents of the metropolitan area battened down for Hurricane Ione yesterday while Government and welfare agencies made elaborate plans to mitigate the fury of wind, rain and high tides.

New York and surrounding communities, long forewarned, appeared to be prepared as never before to weather a big storm.

The focal point of relief, rescue and damage control activities was Mayor Wagner's board of planning and operations sitting at Police Headquarters.

A communications center in the line-up room, staffed by 114 policemen, maintained open lines to all city departments and welfare agencies. Representatives of each organization were posted there at nightfall ready to flash orders to emergency crews on stand-by throughout the city.

Police Commissioner Stephen P. Kennedy urged the public, in event of emergency, to telephone available information to the Police Department.

The Civil Defense Administration, on alert since Sunday night, had its 149 fire and rescue units ready for instant action. But F. M. Robert E. Condon, City Director of Civil Defense, ordered his top personnel to remain on duty until further notice.

Two thousand Red Cross workers were standing by in the city and neighboring communities. The city's Department of Welfare was similarly prepared to staff 10¢ relief centers in the boroughs.

In Albany three units of the New York National Guard, including the Forty-second Division stationed here, were alerted

Continued on Page 24, Column 4

Democratic Farm Experts Call Republicans' Program Ruinous

By RICHARD J. H. JOHNSTON
Special to The New York Times.

CHICAGO, Sept. 19—The nation's farmers face a grim future unless action is taken immediately to relieve them of economic stress, a Democratic agricultural advisory committee said today.

Under the chairmanship of Claude R. Wickard, former Secretary of Agriculture, the fourteen-man committee met here in the Conrad Hilton Hotel to "explore all aspects of our agricultural problems."

This was the first meeting of the group that was formed to guide the Democratic farm policy fight. It was created on Aug. 31 at the behest of Paul M. Butler, chairman of the Democratic National Committee.

[Meanwhile, Democrats in Washington opened a drive to goad the Administration into unveiling its farm plans before Congress reconvenes in

Continued on Page 23, Column 4

HARRIMAN READY TO COMPETE IN '56, ADVISER DECLARES

Prendergast Says Governor Would Oppose Stevenson if Party Wanted Him

By WARREN WEAVER Jr.
Special to The New York Times.

ALBANY, Sept. 19—Governor Harriman will seek the Presidential nomination next year if "convinced the convention wanted him," the Democratic State Chairman said today.

The chairman asserted the Governor would do this even in the event of a floor fight with Adlai E. Stevenson.

Michael H. Prendergast, the Governor's chief political lieutenant, declared that under such conditions Mr. Harriman would take the nomination "regardless of whether Stevenson stepped aside or not."

This was the first public indication from within his official political family that Mr. Harriman's repeated expressions of support for Mr. Stevenson might be weakening in the face of insistence that he seek the nomination.

Charles Van Devander, the Governor's press secretary, said tonight there would be no comment from his office on the Prendergast statement. He said the Governor was in New York City. The Governor's aides in New York likewise said there would be no comment.

For the last year whenever Presidential politics were discussed, Mr. Harriman has said "I'm for Stevenson," smiled broadly and declined to discuss any other possibilities.

Says Democrats Can Win

Mr. Prendergast was the Governor's personal choice to succeed Richard H. Balch as head of the Democratic State Committee last July.

The Democratic chairman characterized as "a lot of nonsense" Republican assertions that no opponent could beat President Eisenhower.

"I don't give a damn who they run," Mr. Prendergast declared. "We can win next year with the right man, and I think Harriman is the right man. Regardless of who he says he's for, I'm representing the Democratic party—the rank and file of it—when I say I'm for Harriman."

Although Mr. Prendergast said he could not speak for the Governor, he described Mr. Harriman indirectly as a man who was thinking now in terms of his own candidacy, rather than Mr. Stevenson's or anyone else's.

"I know Mr. Harriman well enough to know that he is so definitely interested in a Democratic victory in 1956 that if he felt someone else, other than himself, were stronger and had a better chance of winning, he would be for him regardless," the state chairman declared.

Mr. Prendergast's analysis of the situation was made at a press conference. He called the session to announce that former President Harry S. Truman would speak at the state-wide Democratic candidate's rally here on Oct. 7.

The state chairman was generally deprecatory of Mr. Stevenson's chances. He said that the former Illinois Governor's announcement of his plans in November "isn't going to stampede anybody." He predicted that getting the nomination would be "no walkover for Stevenson."

Sees Swing to Harriman

On the contrary, Mr. Prendergast said, prospects that the national convention might look favorably on Mr. Harriman appear to be increasing daily.

"I think we're going into the convention with a lot of sentiment in our favor," he asserted. "Unless something unforeseen happens, I don't see how we can miss."

He later amended this to say he believed that the Governor has "a better than even chance of getting the nomination."

Mr. Prendergast was asked if the Governor had requested him to "soft-pedal" his Harriman-for-President campaign, inasmuch as Mr. Harriman was on record for Mr. Stevenson.

"No, he's said nothing about that," the chairman replied.

Mr. Prendergast also announced that he would open an upstate office for the State Committee in the Sheraton Ten Eyck Hotel here on Oct. 1. It will include offices for Miss Mary Louise Nice of Tonawanda, state vice chairman, and Carmine G. DeSapio, the party's national committeeman.

The Democratic leader said he was particularly glad to have

Continued on Page 22, Column 5

PERON'S REGIME IS OVERTHROWN; JUNTA WILL MEET WITH REBELS; CROWDS HAIL FALL OF DICTATOR

U. S. TIES HINTED

Will Grant Recognition to Insurgents as They Take Over Nation

By DANA ADAMS SCHMIDT
Special to The New York Times.

WASHINGTON, Sept. 19—Administration officials said tonight that the United States would undoubtedly recognize any new Argentine Government that showed it was in control of the country.

The State Department, insisting that any comment at this time would be a form of interference, declined to discuss the attitude the United States might take toward a new Argentine Government.

However, other officials of the Administration pointed out that the United States had followed the practice of recognizing Latin-American revolutionary governments as soon as they exercised full authority. In some cases there has been preliminary discussion with other Latin-American governments.

But the fact that relations between the United States and President Juan D. Perón were frequently strained during his nine years as President made it unlikely the United States would hesitate, these officials said.

Hostile Attitude Cited

For several years after President Perón had taken power his attitude toward the United States was hostile, thus playing upon popular antipathies toward the "Yankee imperialists." However, in recent years relations between Washington and Buenos Aires have been correct, although "hardly warm," in the view of one diplomatic student of Latin-American affairs.

President Perón has sought and obtained from the United States a number of loans that helped his Government through the difficulties that followed the application of "Peronist economics." This consisted of building up industry at the expense of agriculture.

As to whether the United States has ever "supported" the Peronist regime, there are strong differences of opinion among officials. The prevailing view is that the United States Government's attitude has been carefully "objective."

But avoiding anything that would look like official interference, a Congressional committee after the unsuccessful June 16 rising in Argentina that they were seeking to use United States influence quietly to prevent persecution of the Roman Catholic Church.

Catholic groups in the United States at that time demanded the Navy and sections of the Army as the insurgent force acted for several days.

Continued on Page 2, Column 6

COMMAND VAGUE

Rebels Believed to Be in 3 Groups, With No Over-All Chief

By TAD SZULC
Special to The New York Times.

SANTIAGO, Chile, Sept. 19—Broadcasts from Argentina indicated today that the rebel forces were operating with at least three separate commands and that no over-all chief of the movement had yet emerged.

Admiral Issac Rojas was in charge of the naval operation along the Argentine coast and of the marine units ashore. There were contradictory reports as to the identity of the leaders of the insurgent army forces operating inland.

In a telephone interview from the headquarters of the rebel-directed Second Army in Mendoza, in the foothills of the Andes, a general who identified himself as the chief of staff of the revolutionary command said that Gen. Eduardo Leonardi was the top military leader of the movement.

He said that General Leonardi was in Cordoba, where attacks on the Government forces had been fought off for several days.

General About 52 Years Old

He described General Leonardi as a "respected" officer who had served at one time as an Argentine military attaché abroad. He said General Leonardi was about 52 years old. No other data about General Leonardi were available here.

A virtually independent command in Mendoza, embracing the provinces of Mendoza, San Juan and San Luis, was held by Gen. Julio Alberto Lagos.

In an earlier telephone interview General Lagos identified himself as the chief of the revolution. But his chief of staff said later that General Lagos meant he was merely in charge of the three western provinces.

The chief of staff said that the coordination among the various commands was still deficient and he refused to say what plans the rebels had to take over the Government of Argentina. He declined to say what form of revolutionary government was being contemplated.

He declared that communication among the various commanders was by radio and courier planes.

Broadcasts picked up in Santiago told the series of dramatic events that culminated today in the virtual surrender of the man who for twelve years had ruled Argentina as a dictator.

It came on the fourth day of the bloody rebellion against President Juan D. Perón by the Navy and sections of the Army

Continued on Page 2, Column 3

Governor Calls for Federal Aid To Save Nation's Ailing Schools

But Royall Tells Conference That the Education System Should be Contracted

By BENJAMIN FINE

A sweeping program of Federal aid to education, on both school and college levels, was advocated yesterday by Governor Harriman.

Speaking before 800 community, labor, business and school leaders at the New York State Conference on Education, the Governor said that nothing but Federal support could solve the critical problem in American education.

The two-day meeting at the Biltmore Hotel is a preliminary to the White House Conference on Education in Washington from Nov. 28 to Dec. 1. Major school issues are on the agenda for both the New York and the Washington sessions.

Unexpectedly, the conference opened on a controversial note. The chairman of the New York State committee, Kenneth C. Royall, who was the keynote speaker, told the delegates they should be thinking of ways to contract, not expand, the educational system. Mr. Royall, who was Secretary of War under

Continued on Page 26, Column 6

Kenneth C. Royall

President Truman said that too many young people were attending college who should not be there.

He deplored the "widespread feeling" among educators that every high school boy and girl should go to college. He urged

---

GEN. JUAN D. PERON

MOSCOW TO INSIST ON BONN-RED TALK

Soviet Will Shun Any Voice in German Domestic Rifts in Treaty Due Today

By CLIFTON DANIEL

MOSCOW, Sept. 19—Measures to force West Germany to deal directly with the East German Communist Government were being planned today in Moscow.

Walter Ulbricht, East German Deputy Premier and Communist party chief, declared that in the future there would be no other way of settling questions in dispute between the two parts of Germany.

He said that under the treaty to be concluded with the Soviet Union here tomorrow the East German Government would control the border with West Germany and communications between West Germany and West Berlin.

"The sooner the politicians of Bonn and West Berlin realize that they cannot undermine the East German regime, the better it will be for the populace of West Berlin," Herr Ulbricht said ominously.

His implication seemed to be that the East German Government would be in a position to impose a new blockade on Berlin and that on such matters the Bonn Government would have to negotiate not with mere officials or technicians but with the East German Government itself.

Sovereign Status Due

Herr Ulbricht spoke during the negotiations with Soviet leaders on a treaty that will give to the East German regime the same sovereign status the Western Allies gave West Germany.

Upon conclusion of the treaty the Soviet Government will abolish the office of High Commissioner in Germany, Marshal Nikolai A. Bulganin, Soviet Premier, disclosed in a speech.

Henceforth, the Soviet Ambassador to East Germany will deal with United States, British and French representatives in West Germany on questions concerning Germany as a whole and on questions arising from four-power agreements, the Soviet Premier declared.

In addition, Marshal Bulganin said all laws, decrees and directives promulgated by the four-power Allied Control Council for Germany would be annulled on the territory of East Germany. Those regulations were enacted between 1945 and 1948, when the Soviet representative, Marshal Vassily D. Sokolovsky, withdrew and the Allied Control Council ceased to function.

The treaty between the Soviet Union and East Germany will provide that East Germany is free in all internal and foreign affairs, including relations with West Germany, Herr Ulbricht

Continued on Page 3, Column 3

FINNS AND SOVIET RENEW ALLIANCE

Moscow Agrees to Withdraw Its Military and Naval Forces Within 3 Months

Special to The New York Times.

MOSCOW, Sept. 19—Finland and the Soviet Union renewed their mutual defense alliance today for a period of twenty years.

At the same time the Soviet Government formally agreed to withdraw its military and naval forces from their base on Finnish territory within three months.

Those were the results of the Soviet-Finnish negotiations here today and they gave "great joy" to the witty and lively old man who is President of Finland, Juho K. Paasikivi.

"I am here in Moscow for the seventh time for negotiations on affairs of state concerning Finland and the Soviet Union," the President said this evening at a party held in the Kremlin to celebrate the signing of the two agreements.

"But this is the first time that I return to our capital satisfied," he said. "Usually I have returned unsatisfied."

His audience laughed and applauded.

Exactly eight years ago today President Paasikivi was here on one of those unsatisfying visits. He signed a fifty-year lease that gave to the Soviet Union a naval and military base on the Porkkala Peninsula as provided by the truce agreement that ended the war between the two countries in 1944.

Tonight President Paasikivi observed that the Porkkala base now to be handed back to Finland was situated only twelve

Continued on Page 6, Column 3

PEACE IS SOUGHT

Government Orders Its Forces to End Fight —Port Is Shelled

Texts of the Government and Perón statements, Page 3.

By EDWARD A. MORROW
Special to The New York Times.

BUENOS AIRES, Tuesday, Sept. 20—The Government of President Juan D. Perón fell last night.

A four-man junta of army generals assumed command of the forces that had fought unsuccessfully to keep General Perón in power. He had been master of Argentina since Oct. 17, 1945, and its President for nine years.

[A loyalist military junta told the rebels that General Perón had officially resigned the Presidency, The Associated Press reported.]

The junta quickly entered into negotiations to end the four-day civil war. Army and Navy units had joined in the rebellion and forced the resignation of the President, the Cabinet and other authorities.

Among those who tendered their "irrevocable" resignations was the Minister of the Army, Gen. Franklin Lucero, who on June 16 had quelled a navy-led revolt.

There was no news about the whereabouts of President Perón tonight. Some reports had him in asylum at the Paraguayan Embassy in Buenos Aires. The embassy denied these.

Perón Statement Read

The low ceiling prevented any planes from leaving the city's army airport and seemed to cast doubt on other reports that the President had fled to Paraguay.

General Perón offered his resignation yesterday afternoon in a statement read by him over the state radio. He suggested that the Army take charge. He had made a somewhat similar offer to resign Aug. 31 but withdrew it after "protests" from his followers.

It was widely rumored that General Perón had committed suicide. There was no official announcement to this effect, and well-informed diplomats doubted the report.

[A rebel radio broadcast from Bahía Blanca said the Argentine Confederation of Labor was planning a general strike for dawn Tuesday in an effort to restore President Perón to power, The Associated Press reported.]

The Government ordered troops that still remained loyal to it to cease fighting. It asked the rebels to do likewise to prevent further bloodshed after the Navy had shelled the seaside city of Mar del Plata and the rebels had shown other signs of strength throughout the country.

Large sections of the Buenos Aires population braved a light rain this afternoon to stage joyful demonstrations in the city's streets. The Plaza de Mayo, scene of many mass Peronist demonstrations in the past, saw a small number of the Presi-

Continued on Page 3, Column 5

U.N. Opening in Harmony Today; Chilean Next Head of Assembly

By THOMAS J. HAMILTON
Special to The New York Times.

UNITED NATIONS, N. Y., Sept. 19—A noncontroversial start is assured for the 1955 session of the United Nations General Assembly, which will convene tomorrow afternoon.

The only important business scheduled for tomorrow is the election of José Maza, a veteran Chilean diplomat, as President of the Assembly.

Delegates believe that Vyacheslav M. Molotov, the Soviet Foreign Minister, will immediately put forward the standard Soviet demand for the seating of Chinese Communist representatives.

If he does so, it would not cause more than a short flurry, since the United States is ready with its equal-and-counter-proposal that the question of Chinese representation should not be taken up at the current session. The United

Continued on Page 17, Column 1

"All the News That's Fit to Print"

The New York Times.

LATE CITY EDITION
Conclusions of U. S. Weather Bureau forecast:
Mostly fair and somewhat milder today. Partly cloudy tomorrow.
Temp. range today: 43-25; yesterday: 35-23
Full U. S. Weather Bureau Report, Page 61

© 1956, by The New York Times Company.

VOL. CV..No. 35,831.

Entered as Second-Class Matter, Post Office, New York, N. Y.

NEW YORK, THURSDAY, MARCH 1, 1956.

Times Square, New York 36, N. Y.
Telephone LAckawanna 4-1000

FIVE CENTS

EISENHOWER SAYS HE WILL SEEK A 2D TERM; CONFIDENT OF HEALTH; BARS 'BARNSTORMING'; PRAISES NIXON BUT DOES NOT ENDORSE HIM

U.S. JUDGE ORDERS ALABAMA CO-ED TO BE REINSTATED

Bids School Admit Miss Lucy by Monday—Bars Contempt Action Against Trustees

CITES THEIR 'GOOD FAITH'

He Finds That Reaction Was Underestimated—Negro Says She Will Return

By WAYNE PHILLIPS
Special to The New York Times.

BIRMINGHAM, Ala., Feb. 29—The University of Alabama was ordered today to reinstate Autherine J. Lucy, its first Negro student, by Monday morning.

Miss Lucy, 26 years old, of Birmingham, was enrolled at the university Feb. 1 after a three-year court fight. She was suspended five days later after a series of campus disorders protesting her presence.

Federal Judge Hobart H. Grooms also vacated a contempt motion, sought by Miss Lucy, against the board of trustees and officials of the university. He said the trustees had acted in good faith in suspending Miss Lucy. If they had not done so, he ruled, "she might have suffered great bodily harm."

Miss Lucy sat tense and nervous today in the Federal District Court here as a succession of witnesses recounted the events leading to her suspension. Some said that if she returned to the campus she might be killed.

Feared for Life, She Says

She said on the witness stand that while she was a virtual prisoner in a classroom building held in a state of siege by a howling mob outside, she feared that she might be killed. She said she had prayed.

With deliberation and occasional flashes of dry wit she answered the questions of the university's attorney, Andrew J. Thomas. Beside her, who sat at the counsel table, was a well-worn copy of the Bible.

After she heard the decision of Judge Grooms readmitting her, she said again that she would return to the campus.

"That girl sure has guts," her attorney, Thurgood Marshall, chief counsel for the National

Continued on Page 28, Column 1

TEAMSTERS UNION FACES SUSPENSION

Meany Weighs Tie to I. L. A. —Internal Strife Rises

By A. H. RASKIN

The International Brotherhood of Teamsters, most powerful unit in the merged labor movement, is facing possible suspension over its alliance with the expelled International Longshoremen's Association.

The possibility of punitive action by the parent federation arose yesterday amid fresh outcroppings of internal strife within the 1,300,000-member truck union. The uprisings were designed to prevent domination of the union by James P. Hoffa, international vice president and chairman of the Central States Conference of Teamsters.

The Detroit unionist announced Monday that the teamsters would deposit $400,000 to the credit of the I. L. A. to enable it to pay its debts and to participate in a joint organizing drive. The pier union was expelled from the American Federation of Labor in 1953 on charges of gang domination.

In Washington, George Meany, president of the united labor movement, announced that he had begun an investigation of the teamster-longshore pact. He pledged that he would take

Continued on Page 28, Column 3

Testimony Clashes At Gas Gift Inquiry

By RUSSELL BAKER

WASHINGTON, Feb. 29—Senate investigators were told today that John M. Neff had offered a $2,500 campaign contribution in Iowa for the chance to talk with Senator Bourke B. Hickenlooper about the natural gas bill.

However, Mr. Neff, an attorney for the Superior Oil Company of California, denied the story under oath. The conflicting testimony will be sent to the Department of Justice for possible perjury action.

The witness who testified that the offer had been made was Robert K. Goodwin, a Des Moines manufacturer and banker and Republican committeeman for Iowa.

The two men, smiling wanly, confronted each other under the great glass chandeliers in the Senate caucus room, then

Continued on Page 13, Column 3

G.O.P. TAX CUT BILL VOTED AT ALBANY

Legislature Acts in Face of Veto Threat—Committees Propose Budget Slash

By LEO EGAN

ALBANY, Feb. 29—Republican majorities rammed their $50,000,000 income tax cut bill through both Senate and Assembly this afternoon. They did this despite warnings the bill would be vetoed by Governor Harriman, a Democrat.

In the Senate the vote was 35 to 23. In the Assembly it was 84 to 58. All the Democrats voted against the measure in both houses.

The Senate deliberately voted down the Governor's plan today. The vote was 36 to 22, one Democrat, Joseph Zaretski of Manhattan, voting with the Republicans in opposition. He explained he was opposed to any tax cut this year.

While the bill was under discussion, the Republican controlled Senate Finance and Assembly Ways and Means Committees proposed reductions totaling $23,528,072 in Governor Harriman's record high $1,494,700,000 state-spending program for next year.

Democrat Hits Action

Among the suggested cuts were the elimination of a $9,900,000 appropriation to give New York City a share in motor vehicle license fees and the elimination of a $2,400,000 item for state subsidies for child day care centers, most of which would have gone to New York City.

Passage of the Republican income tax cut bill today represented an abrupt termination of negotiations between the Governor and legislative leaders for a compromise on this subject.

Assemblyman Eugene F. Bannigan, the Democratic minority leader, charged on the floor that Republican were courting a veto of the tax-cut bill to justify a return to increase gasoline and Diesel fuel taxes. Such increases have been recommended by the Temporary Highway Finance Commission to support a $500,000,000 highway bond issue and an expanded highway construction program.

Lacking the two-thirds majorities needed in each House to repass a bill over the Governor's veto, the Republicans are expected to abandon their efforts for an income tax cut after today.

Mr. Harriman announced that he was still willing to resume compromise tax-reduction negotiations. But his offer is unlikely to be accepted.

The Republican bill as passed today would give all taxpayers a credit of 20 per cent on the first $100 of taxes due on April 15 and a 10 per cent credit on the next $400, with a limit of $60 to any one taxpayer. Governor Harriman had proposed a sub-

Continued on Page 25, Column 6

DULLES SUGGESTS SOVIET MAY FAVOR CUT IN ARMS COST

Tells Senate Unit, However, U. S. Will Not Be Misled Into Weakening Defenses

By ELIE ABEL

WASHINGTON, Feb. 29—Secretary of State Dulles suggested today that the Soviet Union might welcome some reduction in the present burden of armaments.

Testifying before a special Senate Foreign Relations subcommittee on disarmament, Mr. Dulles qualified this statement with assurances that the Administration would not jeopardize the nation's security by accepting at face value Soviet promises to disarm.

"We do not minimize the difficulties of dealing in these matters with a potential enemy who is untrustworthy and who in manifold ways has demonstrated that he is a past master of the art of evasion and secretiveness," the Secretary of State said.

"However, there is some reason to believe that the Soviet Union itself would welcome relief from the present burden of armament," he added.

Russians Called Dissatisfied

Mr. Dulles said this assessment was based on the "logic" of the present situation within the Soviet Union. He depicted the Russian people as being "in a state of very considerable dissatisfaction" with their low standard of living.

It would be logical for the Soviet leaders to agree to spend less on armaments so they could apply an increased share of their production to raising the living standards of their own people, Mr. Dulles said. In addition, the Soviet Union would thus have more to spend on its new program of economic aid to underdeveloped countries in South Asia and the Middle East, he added.

The Secretary of State, who leaves for Pakistan Friday afternoon to attend the council meeting of the Southeast Asian Collective Defense Treaty in Karachi March 6 to 8, appeared before a subcommittee headed by Senator Hubert H. Humphrey, Democrat of Minnesota, who is surveying the whole disarmament problem.

Senator Leverett Saltonstall, Republican of Massachusetts, asked Mr. Dulles whether "face-to-face" meetings with the Soviet leaders offered the best hope of achieving a disarmament accord.

"I don't know any other way," Mr. Dulles replied. "In spite of

Continued on Page 6, Column 3

9,000 Jam Court as Scofflaws Rush to Beat Amnesty Deadline

By JACK ROTH

The last day of the amnesty period for scofflaws found 9,000 persons in the Criminal Courts Building at 100 Centre Street yesterday. The worst jam in Manhattan Traffic Court history ensued.

About 6,000 persons waited in long lines in the lobby to pay their fines at the court clerk's windows. Three thousand of these were scofflaws. At one point the lines backed up a stairway leading to the second floor. In addition, another 3,000 repentant drivers crowded about the Traffic Summons Control Bureau on the third floor. Tables were supplied in the corridors for the scofflaws to fill out forms.

Chief Magistrate John M. Murtagh called the amnesty a "great success" and estimated that of the 20,000 persons categorized as scofflaws all but about 6,000 had appeared.

He predicted that when all the scofflaw tickets of the amnesty period had been processed, the accounting would show that the city had collected nearly $750,000 in fines on long-ignored traffic summonses.

"Because of the last-minute influx of scofflaws," Mr. Murtagh said, "there will be a delay of perhaps a week before we can turn over the warrants to the police for the arrest of the remainder. We must make certain that none of the warrants apply to people who appeared at the last minute.

"But early next month the police will swing into action. Our goal is 100 per cent compliance with every summons issued since 1950."

He reiterated an earlier statement that this amnesty for scofflaws would be the last such grace period, because "motorists must be taught to answer summonses on time." There were two previous amnesties.

Concerning the last-minute rush, which was marked by confusion and grumbling, Mr. Murtagh admitted such great numbers had not been anticipated.

The confusion was caused by the fact that five patrolmen suddenly called to keep the lines

Continued on Page 26, Column 1

Gronchi in Congress Discounts Arms Tie

By DANA ADAMS SCHMIDT
Special to The New York Times.

WASHINGTON, Feb. 29—President Giovanni Gronchi of Italy urged Congress today to lead the Western world away from military alliances and toward economic union to counter Communist expansionism.

"The reorganization of the Western world is the central problem of the day," he declared in an address before a joint session of the Senate and the House of Representatives.

As an early step he proposed that the North Atlantic Treaty Organization be "brought into line" with today's realities, in which "military imbalance has been reduced," but in which, none the less, "the world is no more secure than it was one or two years ago."

The North Atlantic alliance,

Continued on Page 5, Column 3

PARIS ARMY CHIEF QUITS ON ALGERIA

Guillaume Out After Policy Dispute—Special Powers Asked by Government

By ROBERT C. DOTY
Special to The New York Times.

PARIS, Feb. 29—The French Government reorganized its high military command today and asked for special powers to deal with the Algerian revolt.

Gen. Augustin Guillaume was replaced as Chief of the General Staff following disagreement with his civilian chiefs over military policy in North Africa. He was succeeded by Gen. Paul Ely, a member of the high council of the armed forces.

Late today, Premier Guy Mollet submitted to Parliament a request for extensive powers in the fields of administration, economic and social affairs, and security for Robert Lacoste, Minister Residing in Algeria.

Details were not revealed, but the special powers were reported to include authority to reinstate the "state of urgency" in Algeria or even, if events should warrant it, full martial law.

Debate on this measure, probably early next week, was expected to present the left-of-center Republican Front Cabinet with its first serious political test. Some observers doubted that the National Assembly would grant the Government's request.

Neither here nor in Algeria has M. Mollet's appeal to the rebels to lay down their arms and accept the arbitration of new elections aroused any enthusiasm.

Conservatives, including most

Continued on Page 3, Column 2

2D SPOT IN DOUBT

Foes of Vice President Now May Push Drive to Block Him

By W. H. LAWRENCE
Special to The New York Times.

WASHINGTON, Feb. 29—President Eisenhower passed up today two opportunities to give an automatic immediate endorsement to renomination of Vice President Richard M. Nixon.

General Eisenhower said he properly could not speak out on the choice of a running mate until after the Republican National Convention itself had picked its Presidential nominee.

He mixed repetition of previous high praise for Mr. Nixon with what sounded at least like indirect criticism of the Vice President for his recent effort to continue a Republican party label on Chief Justice Earl Warren. The President said he personally would never admit that any Supreme Court justice continued to have a political designation while on the high court.

President Eisenhower's failure to call at once for Vice President Nixon's renomination undoubtedly will put new steam behind an effort already under way by some influential Republicans to select another running mate. These anti-Nixon men argue that the 1956 campaign involving a President who has suffered a heart attack will place new emphasis with voters on the Vice Presidential nominee.

Silent on Running Mate

In his radio-television address to the nation, the President made no mention at all of Mr. Nixon or any other possible running mate.

The omission by the President may not be meaningful, however. General Eisenhower is assured of renomination by acclamation, and the convention unquestionably will nominate any man he favors for Vice President. So he could speak up for Mr. Nixon at the last minute and insure his renomination.

The Nixon question was raised in two ways immediately after the President had disclosed he "would be available for renomination and re-election if the Republican party and a majority of the people wanted him.

He was asked directly whether he would again want Mr. Nixon as his running mate.

"As a matter of fact," President Eisenhower responded, "I wouldn't mention the Vice Presidency, in spite of my tremendous admiration for Mr. Nixon, for this reason: I believe it is traditional that the Vice President is not nominated until after a * * * Presidential candidate is * * * nominated; so I think that we will have to wait and see whom the Republican convention nominates, and then it will be proper to give an expression on that point."

Respect 'Unbounded'

Asked whether, if nominated, he would have a personal preference for Mr. Nixon's renomination, the President responded:

"I will say nothing more about it. I have said that my admiration and my respect for Vice President Nixon is unbounded. He has been for me a loyal and dedicated associate, and a successful one.

"I am very fond of him, but I am going to say no more about it."

The indirect criticism came when President Eisenhower was asked his own reaction to the Vice President's characterization of Mr. Warren as a Republican Chief Justice.

The President said he would not comment, and never had, on a comment by someone else. He added:

"But I will say this: Once a man has passed into the Supreme Court he is an American citizen and nothing else in my book and until he comes out of that court, and I believe that it would be—I would never admit that he was—longer had a political designation."

There has been sharp political controversy over the Vice President's recent contention in a New York speech that the Su-

Continued on Page 12, Column 3

Two Senators Ask Inquiry on Benson

By WILLIAM M. BLAIR
Special to The New York Times.

WASHINGTON, Feb. 29—Two Senate Democrats suggested today that the special lobby investigating committee explore what they charged were efforts by the Secretary of Agriculture to influence Southern Senators to vote against rigid farm-price supports.

Senator Hubert H. Humphrey of Minnesota said that Ezra Taft Benson, the Secretary, appeared to have violated a law prohibiting lobbying with Federal appropriations. The situation is "close enough to make it appear necessary for our new committee on lobbying to look into it most carefully," he declared.

Senator Allen J. Ellender of Louisiana accused Mr. Benson of "trying to buy votes of

Continued on Page 19, Column 2

EXPLAINS DECISION: President and Mrs. Eisenhower at the White House last night, before his TV-radio speech.

Associated Press Wirephoto

Butler Questions Fitness; Republicans Hail Decision

By JOHN D. MORRIS
Special to The New York Times.

WASHINGTON, Feb. 29—The physical fitness of President Eisenhower to serve another term was challenged sharply today within minutes of his announcement that he was willing to run. "The American people will never elect a President who, at 65, has had a serious heart attack and who is unable to be a full-time Chief Executive," Paul M. Butler, the Democratic National Chairman, declared.

While Mr. Butler raised the issue of health, other leaders of both parties hailed the President's decision.

The prevailing Democratic line was one of gratification that General Eisenhower considered his recovery sufficient to permit him to stand the rigors and pressures of four more years in the White House. But warnings of a hard campaign "on the issues," requiring vigorous activity by both candidates and ending in a Democratic victory, also came from leading party spokesmen.

Republicans responded to the announcement with enthusiasm that promised the President's renomination without a dissent by the national convention at San Francisco next August.

Predictions that the delegates would look forward to carrying the "burden of what will be a very vigorous campaign."

This was a point that other Democratic candidates, announced and unannounced, stressed as well.

In Albany, Governor Harriman asserted that the President "can no longer shift responsibility to associates and subordinates." Mr. Harriman asserted that the President must now answer for "surrender to the domination of one group in our country—the big interests"—and for "policies abroad that have "undermined our prestige and makes the confidence in us of the people of the"

Continued on Page 17, Column 1

STEVENSON CALLS DECISION PROPER

Bids President 'Set Terms of Debate' on His Health —Sees 'Vigorous' Drive

By CLAYTON KNOWLES

Adlai E. Stevenson called upon President Eisenhower yesterday to "set the terms of the debate" on the issue of his health, now that he has declared his availability for a second term.

Most active of the Democratic candidates for the Presidency, the former Illinois Governor stressed that it was General Eisenhower who had "drawn the distinction between the private matter of his personal health and the public question of how the office of President shall be conducted."

In Washington, it was felt that President Eisenhower's decision would help Mr. Stevenson's chances for the Democratic nomination.

Mr. Stevenson said it was fitting that President Eisenhower, before whom he went to defeat in 1952, should be the candidate and thus defend the policies and record of his Administration.

This view, given in a brief statement, was echoed by other Democrats across the country and by leading Republicans, too, if with a noticeable change in inflection. And Mr. Stevenson noted also that the President must look forward to carrying

Continued on Page 17, Column 2

The texts of Butler and Hall statements are on Page 17.

CAN 'LAST 5 YEARS'

President Finds 'Not Slightest Doubt' of Fitness for Duty

Conference transcript, Page 14; text of speech, Page 15.

By JAMES RESTON
Special to The New York Times.

WASHINGTON, Feb. 29—He said "yes."

Dwight David Eisenhower, the thirty-third President of the United States, agreed this morning to a second-term nomination. He explained why in a television-radio report to the nation tonight.

Speaking slowly and in a slightly hoarse voice, General Eisenhower said tonight: "After the most careful and devoutly prayerful consideration * * * I have decided that if the Republican party chooses to renominate me, I shall accept."

The 65-year-old President frankly told his party tonight, however, that because of his heart attack last Sept. 24, he must restrict his activities in the conduct of his office and in the Presidential campaign.

The President had raised personally the problems created by his heart attack at a crowded news conference earlier at which he said: "I assure you of this: My answer would not be in the affirmative unless I thought I could last out the five years."

Can Perform His Duties

And he told the nation tonight:

"As of this moment, there is not the slightest doubt that I can perform as well as I ever have all the important duties of the Presidency. This I say because I am actually doing so and have been doing so for many weeks."

Speaking of the Presidential campaign, General Eisenhower warned that "neither for renomination nor re-election would I engage in extensive traveling and in whistle-stop speaking—normally referred to as 'barnstorming.'" He added:

"I had long ago made up my mind, before I ever dreamed of a personal heart attack, that I could never, as President of all the people, conduct the kind of political campaign where I was personally a candidate. The first duty of a President is to discharge to the limit of his ability the responsibilities of his office."

General Eisenhower did not mention the Vice-Presidency in his radio address. He was cautious about committing himself

Continued on Page 15, Column 3

MARKET SURGES, THEN FALLS BACK

News Sets Off Buying Wave, but Stocks End Lower

By BURTON CRANE

Wall Street had its day of anticlimax yesterday. The President's announcement that he would seek re-election brought a boiling market of 3,900,000 shares, a ticker tape that ran nineteen minutes behind the floor for a time, an uprush of prices for a single hour—and a net loss on the day.

More stocks fell than rose. Seven of the ten most heavily traded issues closed lower. The New York Times combined average of fifty stocks fell 2.62 points to 322.98, a drop of more than 4/5 of 1 per cent.

Expectations that the President would announce his decision jammed the two galleries of the New York Stock Exchange well before its opening at 10 A. M. The east gallery was largely reserved for reporters, photographers and newsreel and television cameramen. The general public thronged the west gallery.

At the opening, the market was active and strongly higher, starting with gains of 1 and 2 points on good-sized blocks. United States Steel, for example, was up 3/4 on 10,000 shares. Volume continued heavy and

Continued on Page 47, Column 5

"All the News That's Fit to Print"

The New York Times.

7:30 A. M. EXTRA
Condensation of U. S. Weather Bureau forecast:
Mostly sunny and warm today.
Mostly fair and warm tomorrow.
Temperature range today: 84—69.
Temperature range yesterday: 85.2—67.
Full U. S. Weather Bureau Report, Page 54.

© 1956, by The New York Times Company.

VOL. CV No. 35,978.   Entered as Second-Class Matter, Post Office, New York, N. Y.   NEW YORK, THURSDAY, JULY 26, 1956.   Times Square, New York 36, N. Y. Telephone LAckawanna 4-1000   FIVE CENTS

ANDREA DORIA AND STOCKHOLM COLLIDE; 1,134 PASSENGERS ABANDON ITALIAN SHIP IN FOG AT SEA; ALL SAVED, MANY INJURED

STASSEN SUGGESTS EISENHOWER STATE IF HE IS FOR NIXON

Aide to End Pro-Herter Drive If the President Gives Nod to the Vice President

GETS NO G.O.P. BACKING

Says Hall Tries to Foreclose Choice of Delegates in Advance of Convention

By JAMES RESTON
Special to The New York Times.

WASHINGTON, July 25.—Harold E. Stassen, the loneliest man in Washington, said today he would abandon his anti-Nixon campaign if President Eisenhower personally expressed a preference for Vice President Richard M. Nixon on the 1956 election ticket.

In the absence of such a statement from the President, the White House disarmament aide made it clear that he would continue to advocate the Vice-Presidential nomination of Gov. Christian A. Herter of Massachusetts.

The President has let it be known he was "delighted" that Mr. Nixon was available for the Vice-Presidential nomination. But he has not expressed a clear preference for him over other possible candidates.

Takes Aim at Hall

However, a reliable source informed The New York Times today that Governor Herter agreed to nominate Mr. Nixon for the Vice Presidency yesterday after a telephoned message from the White House saying that it was the President's wish that he do so.

Mr. Stassen was left today without the cooperation of Governor Herter or the public support of a single influential Republican politician.

Nevertheless, he took dead aim both at Mr. Nixon and the chairman of the Republican National Committee, Leonard W. Hall.

The 43-year-old Vice President, Mr. Stassen said, ran last in a private poll he (Stassen) conducted on eight potential Republican Vice-Presidential candidates. He did not say who was polled, or who did the polling, or what questions were asked—only that Mr. Nixon, Governor Herter and Mr. Stassen himself were among the eight.

He also wrote a letter in the middle of last night to Repre-

Continued on Page 8, Column 5

Eisenhower's Four Years

An Analysis of Agriculture Policy And Steps Taken to Meet Problems

This is the fifth of a series of articles analyzing the record of the Eisenhower Administration at the start of the Presidential election campaign.

By WILLIAM M. BLAIR
Special to The New York Times.

WASHINGTON, July 25.—President Eisenhower has faced a number of stubborn dilemmas in the last four years but no other problem on the home front has been comparable to the one on farms.

Like the Communist problem overseas, it has absorbed his attention. From time to time it has been mitigated by his policies. Always, however, it has returned to plague him in one form or another.

In his home town of Abilene, Kan., in mid-1952 the President began formulating his program to reconcile freedom and prosperity for the American farmer. As he put it later, "full parity in the market place" and a minimum of Government regulation were his aims.

It has been a long, perplexing struggle for the President. Despite a notable effort, success has eluded him. The farmer still is tied up in Government con-

Jordanian Group Attacks U. N. Palestine Truce Unit

Villagers' Fire Wounds One Observer —Burns Scores Incident — Amman Puts the Blame on Israelis

By HOMER BIGART
Special to The New York Times.

JERUSALEM, July 25.—Jordanian villagers attacked a team of United Nations military observers today near Jerusalem. Lieut. Col. E. H. Thalin of Sweden was seriously wounded by the Jordanian fire, United Nations sources said.

They reported that the villagers "went berserk" after an exchange of fire with Israelis in which several Jordanians were wounded. During the engagement the Israelis employed mortar fire. There were no Israeli casualties.

[Jordanian sources in Amman said Israeli fire had been responsible, The Amman reports said ten Jordanians were wounded.]

Colonel Thalin was the third United Nations casualty in two days. Yesterday two Canadian officers were seriously wounded

Continued on Page 2, Column 3

DOWNTOWN TO GET 4TH NEW BUILDING

25-Story Structure Is Slated on Broad Street Site of R. C. A. Communications

By GLENN FOWLER

Another large office building is soon to rise in the downtown Manhattan financial district.

The building, the fourth large structure to be planned in the area within the last two years, will be twenty-five stories high. It will cover the block front on Beaver Street between Broad and New Streets, near Bowling Green.

It will stand on a plot of 48,000 square feet, running back 215 feet along Broad Street and 200 feet along New Street.

To be known as 60 Broad Street, the building will have an aluminum facade and a beacon light atop the roof. It will be fully air-conditioned, will have acoustic ceilings and will be equipped with operatorless elevators. Garage space will be provided in the basement. There will be 650,000 square feet of floor space above the ground floor.

The property on which the structure will be built is owned by R. C. A. Communications.

Continued on Page 41, Column 2

CONFEREES VOTE 3.7 BILLION IN AID

Reappropriated Fund Lifts Total to $4,006,570,000— Curb on Tito Supported

Special to The New York Times.

WASHINGTON, July 25.—Conferees from the Senate and House of Representatives agreed today on a compromise foreign aid appropriation of $3,766,570,000.

This sum to carry the Mutual Security Program for another year would be increased by $240,000,000 of reappropriated money to a total of $4,006,570,000.

The bargain struck by the conferees amounted to a substantially even split between the $4,110,920,000 in new money originally allocated by the Senate and the $3,425,120,000 provided originally by the House.

President Eisenhower initially had asked for $4,900,000,000 for the fiscal year that opened July 1, although the appropriation for the fiscal year just ended was only $2,700,000,000.

Retained by the conferees was a rider in the Senate bill directing President Eisenhower not to give new military assistance funds to Communist Yugoslavia except for spare parts and replacements.

This stipulation was primarily the work of the Senate Republican leader, William F. Knowland of California. It did not affect $100,000,000 in military aid to Yugoslavia that already is "in the pipeline," nor did it

Continued on Page 12, Column 3

Ailing Millikin Plans To Leave the Senate

By WILLIAM S. WHITE
Special to The New York Times.

WASHINGTON, July 25.—Senator Eugene D. Millikin of Colorado, a powerful member of the Republican leadership, said a farewell today in the Senate.

He was compelled by long and agonizing illness to announce that he would not seek re-election in the fall.

The decision was a heavy blow to the Republican party generally, and to its conservative wing in particular.

Mr. Millikin as a well campaigner would have been a formidable favorite to keep his seat safe for the Republicans. Even as an ailing prospective campaigner he had been greatly feared by the Democrats.

His retirement centered plainly to forward Democratic prospects for retaining control

Continued on Page 10, Column 1

CRAFT RUSH TO AID

Terse Radio Messages of the Rescue Vessels Depict Operations

Help for the stricken liners Andrea Doria and Stockholm flowed almost instantly from all points of the compass to the spot at which they collided last night.

Ships large and small, Coast Guard vessels, luxury liners, Gloucester fishing boats, coastal steamers, all headed for the spot off Nantucket Lightship where the lives of some 2,500 persons were in danger.

It was 11:22 last night when the ships collided in a dense fog. The Andrea Doria, luxury liner of the Italian Line, shaken and dangerously despite a double hull and other special safety features, sent out the first SOS less than a minute later.

The Coast Guard, with stations at Cape Ann, Cape Cod, Boston and other near-by points, sent out every available craft as soon as the position of the crash had been determined. Then came reassuring promises of help from the Ile de France and other craft within quick reach of the spot.

The Search and Rescue Division of the Coast Guard in New York received its first alert at 11:25 last night. It was then that the Coast Guard radio station at East Moriches, L. I. notified New York headquarters:

"Andrea Doria and Stockholm collided 11:22 local time Lat. 40:30' N., Long. 69:53' W."

Coast Guard Cutters Aid

The East Moriches radio had picked up simultaneous SOS messages from the ships a minute or two before. The next hour was spent verifying positions and notifying all Coast Guard and merchant ships of the disaster and calling on them for help. The Coast Guard sent out ten cutters from New York, Boston and New London, Conn., and diverted three other ships cruising in that area.

The stark drama being played on the open ocean in darkness and fog was pictured in tense, taut radio messages recorded by the wireless room of The New York Times. They read:

12:21 A. M.—S. S. Stockholm says: Badly damaged. The whole bow crushed and No. 1 hold filled with water. Have to stay in our position. If you [Andrea Doria] can lower your lifeboats we can pick them up.

12:21 A. M.—S. S. Andrea Doria replied: You have to row to us.

12:38 A. M.—S. S. Cape Ann reports: Now between the two ships and her boats are ready. Has two lifeboats.

12:45 A. M. Coast Guard boat says: Ten miles away; have eighteen boats.

1:12 A. M. Andrea Doria says: Needs more lifeboats still.

1:13 A. M. Unidentified ship, when queried, says: We have twelve lifeboats.

Stricken Ship's Boats Useless

1:21 A. M. Cape Ann asks Doria: How close do you want our ship to come to you?

1:24 A. M. Cape Ann reports: We have two boats for Andrea. Now proceeding to get close to her.

1:26 A. M. Andrea Doria reports: Danger immediate, need lifeboats, as many as possible. Can't use our lifeboats.

1:30 A. M. Stockholm gives position: Lat. 40:34' N; Long. 69:45' W.

1:32 A. M. Cape Ann asks Andrea: Want Cape Ann to move in any closer than Cape Ann is now?

1:34 A. M. Ile de France says: We are nine miles from you. Will launch as many boats as possible.

1:43 A. M. Andrea Doria repeats earlier message: Here danger immediate. Need lifeboats, as many as possible. Can't use our lifeboats.

1:46 A. M. Unidentified ship radios Andrea: Two lifeboats on way over to you.

1:53 A. M. S. S. Manaqui radios both ships: Will arrive yours at 0900 G. M. T. (5 A. M., E. D. T.) Have two lifeboats.

1:54 A. M. Andrea replies: O. K. Thanks.

1:56 A. M. Unidentified Nor-

Continued on Page 15, Column 1

The 29,000-ton Italian Line vessel, the Andrea Doria, which carried 1,134 passengers
The New York Times

The 12,644-ton Swedish American liner Stockholm, largest liner ever built in Sweden

SHIPS' PIERS QUIET IN NEW YORK PORT

Crowds Expected at Andrea Doria's Docks—Relatives Begin Calling Lines

The sea disaster had not early today awakened the pier at West Forty-fourth Street where the Andrea Doria had been scheduled to dock later in the morning.

This pier, as well as the terminal at West Fifty-seventh Street, where the Stockholm had left just before noon yesterday in a gala sailing, remained dark and quiet.

However, unaccustomed night lights began blinking on at the Italian Line's office at 24 State Street before 4 o'clock when members of the company's staff began arriving.

They had been rounded up from their scattered homes around the Metropolitan area by officials of the line against Rosmino Pernigotti, assistant general manager of the company here.

The company officials were making plans to handle expected crowds at West Forty-fourth Street during the morning. Several thousand visitors were expected to begin gathering there by 8 o'clock, some not knowing about the collision.

It is an axiom in the harbor that every arriving passenger attracts five or more relatives and friends as welcomers, and the Italian Line officials were preparing to give them the tragic news and to forestall a rush by worried relatives on the line's downtown office.

Many of the relatives already knew of the crash at sea, and the office and pier of the com-

Continued on Page 14, Column 3

Many Notables Are Listed Aboard the Andrea Doria

Persons prominent in business, the theatre, politics, journalism and government were among the passengers aboard the Andrea Doria when she collided last night with the Stockholm. Two directors of the Standard Oil Company (New Jersey) were on the passenger list. They were Stewart Coleman, traveling with his family, and Marion W. Boyer, accompanied by his wife. Mr. Coleman, 57 years old, lives at 365 Barrett Road, Cedarhurst, L. I. Mr. Boyer, 54, lives in Greenwich, Conn.

Another passenger was Richardson Dilworth, Mayor of Philadelphia, and his wife. Mr. Dilworth, is 57. He served as a Marine in both World Wars, and received the Purple Heart in World War I and the Silver Star in World War II.

Ruth Roman, Hollywood motion picture star, and her son, Richard Hall, were on the Andrea Doria. Miss Roman recently divorced Mortimer Hall, owner of a Los Angeles radio station.

Two refugees from behind the Iron Curtain, the dancers Istvan Rabovsky and his wife Nora Kovach, also were passengers. They are natives of Hungary. In May, 1953, they fled to the West from East Berlin, where they had gone for a dancing engagement. In 1954, they came to this country.

Also on board was Camille M. Cianfarra, Madrid correspondent of The New York Times, and his family. A native of New York, Mr. Cianfarra joined The Times in 1935 in Rome. He became a specialist in Vatican affairs, and has written two books about the Vatican. He became Madrid correspondent in 1951.

Others on board included Ferdinand M. Thieriot, circulation manager of The San Francisco

Continued on Page 14, Column 5

SHIP BUILT TO TAKE COLLISION SAFELY

Andrea Doria Hull Divided to Give Stability—Lifeboats Could Carry 2,000

The Andrea Doria was specially built to give her more stability in case of just such a collision as she had last night with the Stockholm.

The hull was subdivided into eleven watertight compartments extending the entire length of the ship. Bulkheads parallel with her engine rooms were designed to lessen the effect of a collision.

The ship carried lifeboats with a capacity of 2,000 persons. Some of these boats were made of light metal alloy and were hung from davits operated by motor-driven winches. Two of the boats were motor-driven and fitted with radios.

Luxurious to the last detail, the ship was completely fireproofed and radar-equipped.

The ship has two groups of turbines capable of generating 50,000 horsepower to turn its three blade propellers, each weighing sixteen tons. They are nineteen feet in diameter and turn 143 revolutions a minute.

The Andrea Doria and the Stockholm were the prides of the Italian and Swedish merchant marines.

The Stockholm, when launched in 1948, was the largest passenger vessel ever to have been built in Swedish yards. The Andrea Doria, when launched in 1951, was the last word in modern design and comfort. Each was flagship of its line until supplanted by new vessels a few years later.

When she went into service as flagship of the Swedish American Line, the Stockholm had a capacity of 364 passengers and 150 officers and crew. Alterations in 1953 increased the capacity to nearly 600 passengers with a proportionate increase in the size of the crew.

The Stockholm had an over-all length of 510 feet and a beam of

Continued on Page 15, Column 6

2D VESSEL IS SAFE

Ile de France In Today With Survivors From Crash Off Nantucket

By MAX FRANKEL

The trans-Atlantic liners Andrea Doria and Stockholm collided in a heavy Atlantic fog at 11:22 o'clock last night, forty-five miles south of Nantucket Island.

The Andrea Doria ordered her 1,134 passengers aboard to abandon ship. All were reported to have been rescued at 4:58 A. M. There was no immediate word, however, on the fate of her crew of 575.

At 5:15 A. M. today, however, the Ile de France reported from the scene that no more help was needed.

The French Liner estimated at 7 A. M. that she would arrive in New York shortly after 6 o'clock this afternoon with 1,000 survivors from the Andrea Doria. It was not clear to which ports the other survivors would be taken.

The Stockholm, although it had taken water through a crushed bow, was able to keep her 550 passengers and crew of 200 aboard. She was waiting for an escort to attempt to return to New York at a slow speed.

Many survivors of the Italian ship were said to have been seriously injured. The Stockholm said she had few "critical" cases aboard. Desperate and repeated calls for medical assistance were radioed from the score of rescue vessels in the area.

Deck Dips Into Water

The Andrea Doria lay helpless in the thick fog. The black-and-white ship reported she was listing "very badly." She gave no other indication of the extent or nature of her damage nor was there word whether she could remain afloat.

The Stockholm reported at 6 A. M. that the Andrea Doria's main deck was dipping to the surface of the water.

The 29,000-ton Italian Line vessel apparently was listing so severely that she could launch no more than two of her lifeboats. Her lifeboats can carry 2,000 persons.

The French Ile de France, largest of the rescue vessels on hand, and the Stockholm apparently recovered the bulk of the Andrea Doria's passengers. At one time as many as 100 lifeboats probably were in the area. It was not clear how the passengers were loaded into the lifeboats.

At 4:58, the master of the Ile de France told the Stockholm: "All passengers rescued." Miss Roman recently "Proceeding to New York full speed."

The Ile de France left New York yesterday bound for Le Havre.

Since shortly after the collision, the Andrea Doria had run her lights and radio on emergency power and said she did not know much longer she could keep in touch with rescue craft. Her radio was so weak she was dipping

Continued on Page 14, Column 8

Cause of the Crash Puzzles Radar Men

Experts on radar said today they could not explain how the collision between the Andrea Doria and the Stockholm could have taken place because both vessels were equipped with radar equipment.

They said that even with the "visibility nil" conditions reported in the vicinity each ship should have been able to observe the other for distances up to fifty miles.

The experts declared that, even without knowing precisely what systems the vessels carried, they almost certainly were using flexible installations such as are standard on large passenger vessels. They should have been capable of two types of operation—generalized scanning all about the vessel, and a narrower type of observation of a restricted sector of the horizon.

They should also have been

Continued on Page 14, Column 6

SCENE OF THE COLLISION: The liners Andrea Doria and the Stockholm stricken off Nantucket Island (cross).
The New York Times   July 26, 1956

The New York Times.

LATE CITY EDITION

Condensation of U. S. Weather Bureau forecast:
Warm, humid, chance of afternoon or evening showers today and tomorrow.
Temperature range today: 85—72
Temperature range yesterday: 87.1—72.5
Full U. S. Weather Bureau Report, Page 63.

VOL. CV..No. 36,000.

Entered as Second-Class Matter,
Post Office, New York, N. Y.

NEW YORK, FRIDAY, AUGUST 17, 1956.

© 1956, by The New York Times Company.

Times Square, New York 36, N. Y.
Telephone LAckawanna 4-1000

FIVE CENTS

STEVENSON NOMINATED ON THE FIRST BALLOT; OVERWHELMS HARRIMAN BY 905½ VOTES TO 210; PUTS RUNNING MATE UP TO THE CONVENTION

DULLES PROPOSES A BOARD FOR SUEZ WITH LINK TO U. N.

Agency Would Include Egypt —Shepilov Conciliatory As Meeting Opens

Texts of Dulles and Shepilov statements on Page 3.

By HAROLD CALLENDER

LONDON, Aug. 16—Secretary of State Dulles presented to the Suez Canal conference today what was, in effect, a United States-British-French plan for the future of the waterway.

His proposal, made on the first day of the conference of twenty-two nations, was that the operation of the canal should be entrusted to an international board established by treaty and "associated" with the United Nations. Egypt would be represented on the board.

From the Soviet Union, represented by its Foreign Minister, Dmitri T. Shepilov, came a long comment, not on the three-power plan but on the conference. Mr. Shepilov's speech reiterated the criticisms and reservations lengthily expressed in the Soviet note of Aug. 9 questioning the composition and competence of the conference. But it ended in an ostensible offer to cooperate to make the conference a "first step" in a negotiation on the Suez problem.

Nasser Aide Is Firm

But negotiation seemed to be rejected by an apparent spokesman for President Gamal Abdel Nasser of Egypt, who arrived here tonight by plane from Cairo. He was Wing Comdr. Ali Sabry, political adviser to the President.

To reporters who met him at London Airport he said President Nasser would not acknowledge any independent authority over the canal, which must be under Egypt's sole control. He said: "There will be no compromise that interferes with the independence and sovereignty of Egypt."

It was assumed here that Wing Commander Sabry would speak for President Nasser in the informal talks that will take place outside the conference, which decided today to meet only in the afternoons.

In a short speech welcoming the conference to London, Prime Minister Eden said the occasion

Continued on Page 3, Column 3

POLAND TO WIDEN PRIVATE BUSINESS

To Encourage Limited Group of Service Industries

By SYDNEY GRUSON

WARSAW, Aug. 16—The Polish Communist party has started to encourage limited private enterprise. Thus it is reversing one of the basic tenets of its economic philosophy.

The Government has decreed a number of inducements to rebuild small service industries where a minimum of materials is required and the most value is in the labor. Included under the decree are bakers, tailors, cobblers, plumbers, blacksmiths, mechanics and producers in the traditional cottage industries such as embroidery and woodworking.

It is not likely that this will lead to an immediate increase in retail shopkeeping because manufactured goods still will have to be bought by shopkeepers from Government stores at retail prices.

All other East European Communist countries have a small number of private shops. These are the remains of the campaign against private enterprise. But no other satellite has permitted the opening of new shops or small industries as Poland is now going to.

The Polish moves to encourage

Continued on Page 5, Column 3

AP Correspondent Freed by Hungary

By JOHN MacCORMAC

VIENNA, Aug. 16—Dr. Endre Marton, Hungarian correspondent of The Associated Press imprisoned since February, 1955, on charges of spying, was released from prison today. Word of his release came from Budapest.

His wife, Ilona Nylas Marton, who was arrested on similar charges four months later, was set free last April when accusations against her were said to have been found baseless. She had worked as United Press correspondent in Budapest.

The arrest of the Martons came shortly after the return of Matyas Rakosi to complete power in Hungary as Communist leadership.

WIDE ARAB STRIKE PROTESTS PARLEY

Egypt Virtually at Standstill but Canal Is Unaffected— Violence in Libyan City

By OSGOOD CARUTHERS

CAIRO, Aug. 16—Cairo, the greatest metropolis in Africa and the Middle East, was virtually a dead city today.

A Government-sponsored twenty-four hour strike throughout Egypt brought the nation almost to a standstill. The strike was in protest against the opening today of the London conference on the status of the Suez Canal.

Reports from the rest of the Arab world said similar peaceful demonstrations in various forms had been staged in support of Egypt's opposition to the conference.

Among the few operations unaffected by the Egyptian strike was the passage of the daily convoys of ships through Suez Canal. The state authority that has taken over control of the canal since President Abdel Gamal Nasser nationalized the Suez Canal Company ordered that work go on there as usual.

Cairo Airport Is Closed

The international airport at Cairo was closed. All airlines using it had canceled their flights for the day.

Shops in Cairo, Port Said, Ismailia, Suez and Alexandria were shuttered. The streets of these usually teeming cities were virtually deserted.

No incidents were reported throughout the country. The Government had issued orders against either rallies or street demonstrations. Security measures imposed by Colonel Nasser's police force were totally effective.

Streets approaching foreign embassies were heavily guarded by policemen on foot, on horseback and in radio cruise cars. Ordinary Government offices were closed. However, top officials stayed at their posts and continued intensive diplomatic and political activities in connection with the Suez crisis. They studied reports from London on the progress of the Suez conference.

The Soviet Union's Cairo Embassy was reported to have kept open direct telephone and telegraph lines to London throughout the day. Western embassies worked at full pace, although some of their Egyptian employees stayed away for the day.

Tear Gas Used in Tripoli

CAIRO, Aug. 16 (Reuters)—Among the incidents reported today in the Moslem world were the arrest of several Libyan demonstrators in Tripoli.

Policemen there broke up a pro-Egyptian demonstration with tear gas. Also in Tripoli, a small boy threw a stone through a window of a United States cultural affairs office.

In Casablanca, Morocco, crowds thronged the streets shouting anti-British and anti-French slogans and "Vive Nas-

Continued on Page 2, Column 4

TRUCE IN CYPRUS URGED ON BRITISH BY UNDERGROUND

Leaflet by Pro-Greek Force Proposes Negotiations— London Awaits Word

By The United Press

NICOSIA, Cyprus, Aug. 16—The Greek Cypriote underground organization, blamed for much of the terrorism that has swept this Mediterranean island in the last year and a half, offered Britain a military truce today.

The appeal for the truce by the National Organization of Cypriote Fighters, known as E. O. K. A., was made in leaflets distributed on the streets of Nicosia.

The leaflets said that E. O. K. A. was asking for a cease-fire to test the British Government's good faith. If the truce call was ignored, "operations will be resumed on a fiercer and more intensive scale."

Observers said the proposed truce might indicate the first sign of a take-over of underground activities by Anargyros Karadimas, who has been reported as successor of the long-hunted Col. George Grivas.

The Underground Leadership

The truce leaflets were signed by "Dighenis," the traditional name for a Cypriote nationalist, ethnic Greek outlaw leader. Since E. O. K. A. began its anti-British terrorism April 1, 1955, Dighenis is believed to have been Colonel Grivas, a 58-year-old former Greek Army officer.

The truce offer came shortly after Field Marshal Sir John Harding, the British Governor of Cyprus, outlined his terms in an interview with the English-language Times of Cyprus:

"Let the murderers make the first move if there is to be a stopping of violence and its consequences on this island," Governor Harding said.

The "consequences" to which he referred were a British crackdown on terrorism with added military and police force, as well as the recent hanging of at least five convicted extremists.

Governor Harding said the pro-Greek terrorists had committed more than forty murders before the first hanging took place. In July, he said, the illegal underground group committed seventeen murders.

"If we have to look for responsibility for the deaths of these men [the executed extremists], we must look back to the people who started the terrorist movement and persuaded them to take up murder," the Governor added.

The E. O. K. A. leaflets said that, awaiting a reply by the British, the underground had halted its operations. "But," the leaflets added, "E. O. K. A. is

Continued on Page 4, Column 5

Russians Exporting New Bible to U. S.

By HARRISON E. SALISBURY

Godless Russia is now exporting Bibles to God-fearing America.

In the newest twist of Communist policy the Soviet state book monopoly is shipping Bibles, in the Russian language, to the United States. They are now on sale in New York at $10 a copy.

The Russian Bibles are published in excellent type on good quality paper by the Moscow Patriarchy of the Russian Orthodox Church. They are distributed abroad, however, by Mezhdunarodnaya Kniga, the Soviet state book monopoly.

An initial shipment of fifty copies of the new Bible was received by the Four Continent Book Corporation, 821 Broadway. It was said to be selling well.

The American shipment is part of a first printing of 25,000 Bibles. A second printing, numbering 75,000, is expected soon. In view of the

Continued on Page 11, Column 1

GEROSA REBUFFED IN ECONOMY PLEA

City Units Ask $408,335,704 More in New Capital Than His Report Had Advised

By PAUL CROWELL

City departments and agencies have asked the City Planning Commission to allocate in its 1957 capital budget $589,-035,704 of new funds, chargeable against the municipal debt limit. The over-all total of capital budget requests is $1,064,-452,161.

The $589,035,704 in requests for new funds is $408,335,704 more than Controller Lawrence E. Gerosa believes the city can borrow for public works projects without having to impose new nuisance taxes to help balance its expense budget for 1957-58.

On Wednesday Mr. Gerosa warned the Board of Estimate and other city agencies that borrowing for public works projects must be curtailed if new nuisance taxes were to be avoided. He estimated that it would be unsafe for the city to borrow more than $180,300,000 within the debt limit for 'such projects in 1957.

In Chicago, where he is attending the Democratic national convention, Mayor Wagner said he was confident that the city would be 'able to produce a balanced budget for 1957-58 without recourse to any new nuisance taxes.

The Mayor took issue with

Continued on Page 12, Column 1

RACE IS LEFT OPEN

Humphrey, Kefauver Leading in Contest for Vice President

Text of Stevenson talk after nomination is on Page 7.

By JAMES RESTON

CHICAGO, Aug. 16—Adlai E. Stevenson, the Democratic party's Presidential nominee, made a dramatic personal appeal to the convention tonight to make a free and solemn choice of his Vice-Presidential running-mate.

In a move designed to point up the controversy in the Republican party over the nomination in San Francisco next week of a running-mate for President Eisenhower, Mr. Stevenson told the convention that he would not try to hand-pick the Democratic Vice-Presidential nominee.

President Eisenhower has been challenged by Harold E. Stassen, his special assistant on disarmament, to give the Republican convention a similar free choice. The President has indicated that he would be "perfectly satisfied" with Vice President Richard M. Nixon on the Republican ticket this year, but has also said he wants an open convention.

"The choice will be yours," Mr. Stevenson told the delegates shortly after 11 o'clock. "The profit will be the nation's."

Great Care Urged

Mr. Stevenson emphasized that seven of the thirty-four Presidents in the history of the United States had reached the White House as a result of the death of the President.

This, he said, placed an especially heavy obligation on the convention to choose the Vice-Presidential nominee tomorrow with great care.

There was a prolonged backstage dispute this afternoon and night over whether Mr. Stevenson would make his acceptance speech tonight immediately after he was nominated or the second time by acclamation.

Mr. Stevenson wanted to accept tonight rather than tomorrow, when he was scheduled to come before the convention and share the platform with former President Harry S. Truman, who waged an open campaign to defeat him here this week.

The chairman of the convention, Speaker Sam Rayburn, and the chairman of the Democratic National Committee, Paul M. Butler, insisted, however, that the original program be followed even if it was distasteful to the nominee.

Mr. Stevenson then asked and was granted permission to make his appeal on the Vice Presidential question.

No Mention of Truman

Unlike most of the speakers before the convention, Mr. Stevenson did not address Mr. Truman as he opened his remarks before the jammed convention hall.

Mr. Truman sat in a box on his right, but Mr. Stevenson merely addressed the chairman, Mr. Rayburn, and the delegates.

"The responsibility of the Presidency has grown so great," he said, "that the nation's attention has become focused as never before on the office of the Vice Presidency. The choice for that office has become almost as important as the choice for the Presidency."

Mr. Stevenson then added that "each political party had the 'solemn obligation" to offer the country a person fully equipped first to assist in the discharge of the duties of the most exacting job in the world, and second, "to himself assume, if need be, this highest responsibility."

"I have decided," Mr. Stevenson said, "that the selection of the Vice-Presidential nominee should be made through the free processes of this convention so that the Democratic party's candidate for this office may join me before the nation not as one man's selection but as one chosen by our great party even as I have been chosen."

He said he was confident that

Continued on Page 9, Column 1

Associated Press Wirephoto
THE WINNER: Adlai E. Stevenson as he appeared last night at the convention hall, after he had been nominated.

Stevenson Pledges to Fight 'All the Way' in Campaign

By WILLIAM M. BLAIR

CHICAGO, Aug. 16—Adlai E. Stevenson, the Democratic nomination in his pocket, lost no time tonight in starting the long hard race against President Eisenhower. "This is the end of a long journey," he told his cheering campaign workers, "but it is also the beginning of a long journey. And I'm going to fight all of the way."

The Democratic candidate addressed his supporters at the Conrad Hilton Hotel less than an hour after he told the Democratic National Convention that it would have a free choice of the Vice-Presidential candidate.

This action, together with his other activities throughout the day, was a clear indication that he had been thinking ahead and planning his campaign 'against the Republican President who is considered certain of renomination at San Francisco next week.

In a number of statements earlier in the day, Mr. Stevenson had shown solicitude for the big-city voters, with their concern over civil rights, and the traditionally Democratic states of the South.

First of all, he had said that he would have preferred a "special endorsement" of the Supreme Court's decision against school segregation in the platform.

But he had balanced this with friendly words for the South. He called the Democratic party the "only North-South party."

Continued on Page 7, Column 3

HARRIMAN PLANS '58 ALBANY RACE

Governor Also Pledges Aid to Stevenson in Drive to 'Put Him Over'

By LEO EGAN

CHICAGO, Aug. 16—Governor Harriman of New York pledged his help to Adlai E. Stevenson tonight less than half an hour after the former Illinois Governor had defeated him for the Democratic nomination for President.

Earlier, in a television appearance on the Columbia Broadcasting System, Mr. Harriman made it unmistakably clear that he intended to seek in 1958 a second term as Governor.

In the broadcast Mr. Harriman said he expected to remain as Governor of New York "for many, many years" if he failed to win the Presidential nomination. He remarked that "you know there's another election in 1958." That is the year in which the next state election of a Governor takes place.

The Governor said he intended to call on Mr. Stevenson following his television concession of defeat to congratulate the winner in person. "We are old friends, you know," he observed.

The Governor said he would campaign from one end of the state to the other because he regarded the Democratic victories in the national election and in Congressional and legislative races as important.

Continued on Page 7, Column 7

High Police Press Delinquency Drive

By CLAYTON KNOWLES

An unusual meeting at Police Headquarters, called to intensify the city's war against juvenile delinquency, last night produced demands for funds fo. 5,000 more patrolmen.

The department's entire approach to the juvenile problem was reviewed in the light of a 41.3 per cent rise in crimes by youths for the first six months of the year over the comparable period of 1955.

Commissioner Stephen P. Kennedy, conceding that the police "cannot do this job alone," appealed to leaders of the Youth Councils to step up their efforts as the new school year started. The councils are citizen groups that work with the police in the precinct level. All precinct captains and police officers who work with them were present.

Notably absent were represen-

Continued on Page 44, Column 1

VICTOR IS CHEERED

Wins by Acclamation Upon Motion of the Harriman Camp

Texts of Kennedy and Gary speeches are on Page 8.

By W. H. LAWRENCE

CHICAGO, Aug. 16—Adlai E. Stevenson won renomination for President on the first ballot at the Democratic National Convention tonight.

The roll-call gave Mr. Stevenson 905½ votes, with only 686½ required for victory. Governor Harriman of New York ran a poor second with only 210 votes despite all the help that former President Harry S. Truman could give him.

Gov. Raymond Gary of Oklahoma, who had placed Governor Harriman in nomination, moved to give Mr. Stevenson the unanimous support of the convention.

Speaker Sam Rayburn, the Permanent Chairman, put the question as one of choosing the nominee by acclamation. There was an ear-splitting roar of "ayes."

"There are no 'noes,'" announced Speaker Rayburn without asking whether there was any opposition.

Mr. Stevenson announced at once that he wanted the convention to have a free-and-open choice of his Vice-Presidential running mate without his indicating in advance any preference. That vote will be taken tomorrow afternoon.

Cheered by Delegates

The Presidential nominee received a tremendous ovation when he appeared before the convention to express his thanks and to make his suggestion that the delegates themselves choose the Vice-Presidential nominee.

He did not say so, but it was obvious that the purpose of his move was to contrast the Democratic method of choosing a Vice-Presidential nominee with that of the Republican party. The top G. O. P. leadership has joined in slating renomination of Vice President Richard M. Nixon as President Eisenhower's running mate.

Upon receiving news of the nomination, Mr. Stevenson said: "I feel relieved and happy." Later he told the delegates:

"My heart is full and I am deeply grateful but I did not come here to speak of the action you have just taken. That I shall

Continued on Page 6, Column 3

DE SAPIO SUFFERS LOSS OF PRESTIGE

But Wagner Gains Stature as Backer of Stevenson

Special to The New York Times.

CHICAGO, Aug. 16—Adlai E. Stevenson's nomination for President staked tonight the possibility of major power shifts in the Democratic party in New York State.

Carmine G. De Sapio's prestige as a state and national political leader has suffered a setback because of Governor Harriman's failure to make a better showing, in the opinion of many New York delegates.

As the leader of Tammany Hall, national committeeman for New York and unofficial manager of Mr. Harriman's campaign, Mr. De Sapio came to the convention as a prospective kingmaker. He will leave as a local politician.

Mayor Wagner, on the other hand, will leave with more prestige and possibly, political power than when he entered the convention. From the start, Mr. Wagner was outspoken in his preference for Mr. Stevenson over Governor Harriman. His one concession to party "unity" was an agreement to waive this preference for one ballot to give Mr. Harriman a courtesy vote.

Should Mr. Stevenson be elected, it is the view of most

Continued on Page 9, Column 1

4 Israelis on Bus Killed, 7 Hurt In an Ambush in Southern Negev

Attackers Said to Have Come From Jordan—Land Mine Blast Injures Five

Special to The New York Times.

ELATH, Israel, Aug. 16—Gunmen who were believed to have infiltrated from Jordan killed four Israelis today in an ambush of a bus and its military escort in the Negev. Seven others were wounded in the attack on the road to this frontier town on the shore of the Red Sea.

Elsewhere in the bleak Negev today five civilians were hurt when the truck in which they were riding north of Sde Boker was blown up by a land mine.

A Government spokesman said the Foreign Ministry had apprised Maj. Gen. E. L. M. Burns of Canada, chief of the United Nations truce team in Palestine, of the particular gravity of the situation.

Today's dead were three soldiers, who had traveled in a jeep as a vanguard, and one bus passenger.

The New York Times   Aug. 17, 1956
A bus fell into an ambush in the Negev (1) as a truck was blown up by a land mine to north of Sde Boker (2).

Among the incidents reported today in the Negev were several

He said there were several

"All the News That's Fit to Print"

The New York Times.

LATE CITY EDITION

Cloudy, cool with rain today. Fair and milder tomorrow.
Temperature range today: 58-48.
Temperature range yesterday: 55.4-45.4.
Full U. S. Weather Bureau Report, Page 43.

VOL. CVI. No. 36,071.

Entered as Second-Class Matter, Post Office, New York, N. Y.

NEW YORK, SATURDAY, OCTOBER 27, 1956.

Times Square, New York 36, N. Y.
Telephone LAckawanna 4-1000

FIVE CENTS

HUNGARIAN REVOLT SPREADS; NAGY TOTTERS; THOUSANDS IN ARMY FIGHT SOVIET TROOPS; U. S. CONSULTS ALLIES ON TAKING U.N. ACTION

STEVENSON ASKS EISENHOWER POLICY ON A COBALT BOMB

Inquires in Illinois Whether President Plans a Further Step in Nuclear Arms

Text of Stevenson speech will be found on Page 14.

By HARRISON E. SALISBURY
Special to The New York Times.

ALBUQUERQUE, N. M., Oct. 26—Adlai E. Stevenson challenged President Eisenhower today to state whether he proposed to develop the cobalt bomb or some more terrible weapon that might thrust the earth off its axis.

Mr. Stevenson suddenly renewed his nuclear offensive with an unexpected peroration to an address at Rock Island, Ill. He flew to Albuquerque later.

Tonight, in a speech here, he raised the question whether President Eisenhower had abandoned a move to halt hydrogen bomb tests "because his political opponents dared propose such a course."

The Rock Island audience of 1,300 filled the Fort Theatre, largest in the industrially depressed farm equipment center. The Democratic Presidential nominee mentioned the cobalt bomb in a new indictment of General Eisenhower's policies and position on the hydrogen bomb.

Sees Fundamental Wrong

Mr. Stevenson asserted that he had evidence provided only yesterday by four scientists that already radiation "in certain areas of the world" had passed the danger point. Mr. Stevenson did not specify the areas.

Members of Mr. Stevenson's staff identified the scientists as Walter Selove, Brookhaven National Laboratories; Louis Osborn and R. M. Weinstein of the Massachusetts Institute of Technology, and Herman P. Epstein of Brandeis University.

Mr. Stevenson charged that the President was fundamentally wrong in basing national security on reliance upon the "deterrent effect of our lead in nuclear weapons." He recalled that ten years ago similar reliance had been placed upon the original atom bombs and that "to our surprise" the Russians had caught up with the United States in no time.

"And they'll do it again in the hydrogen field," he said. "Maybe they have already."

"What does Mr. Eisenhower propose then?" Mr. Stevenson

Continued on Page 14, Column 2

EISENHOWER ADDS TENNESSEE SPEECH

Expands Campaign Again— Check-Up Begins Today

By ALVIN SHUSTER
Special to The New York Times.

WASHINGTON, Oct. 26—President Eisenhower expanded his campaign plans again today. They now include a speech next week in Tennessee, one of the four Southern states he carried in 1952.

The White House announced that the President would add Memphis to a schedule that already included Texas, Florida and Virginia, the three other traditionally Democratic states that "liked Ike" four years ago.

In addition, he will speak in Oklahoma and Pennsylvania.

On Monday he will go to Miami, Jacksonville and Richmond; on Wednesday, Oklahoma City, Memphis and Dallas, and on Thursday, Philadelphia.

The decision to broaden the President's schedule came on the eve of his pre-election physical examination. The President will enter Walter Reed Army Medical Center shortly after noon. He will stay there until Sunday when the results of the "head-to-toe" examination will be known. The President announced plans

Continued on Page 12, Column 1

U. N. Delegates Sign Atomic Energy Agreement Here

For United States, James J. Wadsworth

For Soviet Union, Georgi N. Zaroubin

The New York Times (by Edward Hausner)

STEVENSON LIKELY TO WIN IN VIRGINIA

Second Survey Finds States' Rights Bloc and Powell's Activity Hurt G. O. P.

A Times Team Report

Teams of New York Times reporters have recently surveyed political trends in twenty-seven closely contested states. They are now resurveying the most doubtful of those states. This is the first such resurvey. It comes from Clarence Dean, Tillman Durdin, Max Frankel, John D. Morris and William S. White.

By WILLIAM S. WHITE
Special to The New York Times.

RICHMOND, Va., Oct. 26—If visible trends and measurable data have their accustomed meaning, Adlai E. Stevenson should win Virginia's twelve electoral votes on Nov. 6.

On nearly every traditional basis of calculation, the Democratic Presidential nominee is ahead in the state, and should remain ahead at the decisive hour when the votes are counted on election night.

It is nevertheless necessary to put in a qualification that is both a cliché and a fact of political life in Virginia. This is that racial and other social currents run so deeply and are so unreadable that President Eisenhower might, after all, repeat his 1952 victory in this state—one of four Southern States that he carried.

A tragic, and in some degree hopeless, bitterness suffuses both the white and Negro races here. The issue of segregation versus integration is aflame, and it throws into doubt all the generally reliable political indexes.

Conclusions Indicated

These indexes, as far as they go, suggest the following conclusions:

¶The Eisenhower movement of 1952 has lost a good deal of its urgency; there is little now of the spirit of "crusade" in it. The social pressures for voting Republican are far less powerful than in 1952.

¶The President will lose some of his 1952 strength in every area of Virginia. Mr. Stevenson thus should be able to surmount the 80,000-vote plurality, out of a total of about 619,000, that General Eisenhower ran up here four years ago.

¶The third-party candidacy of T. Coleman Andrews, States' Rights Presidential aspirant, almost certainly will take more votes from President Eisenhower than from Mr. Stevenson.

This is the conclusion of a New York Times team that has just made a resurvey of this state. The team reported on Oct. 8 from Richmond that Mr. Stevenson seemed to have whatever edge there was then.

At that time there was some uncertainty about the most "Southern" part of Virginia. This

Continued on Page 12, Column 3

U.S. to Give Atom Agency 11,000 Pounds of Uranium

By LINDESAY PARROTT
Special to The New York Times.

UNITED NATIONS, N. Y., Oct. 26—President Eisenhower promised today to make available 11,000 pounds of Uranium 235 to the newly established International Atomic Energy Agency. The pledge was made in a message read this morning to the closing session of an eighty-two-state conference that debated and approved the statute of the new world organization.

Representatives of seventy of these states formally signed the statute just before noon at ceremonies in the newly decorated General Assembly Hall of the United Nations.

The President's message was read from the rostrum by Lewis L. Strauss, Chairman of the United States Atomic Energy Commission.

The message said in part:
"To enable the international atomic agency—upon its establishment by appropriate govern-

Text of message is printed on Page 12.

mental actions—to start atomic research and power programs without delay, the United States will make available to the international agency, on terms to be agreed with the agency, 5,000 kilograms of a nuclear fuel, Uranium 235."

This is one-quarter of the 20,000 kilograms (about 44,800 pounds) earmarked by the United States last February for use by friendly nations in the development of peaceful atomic programs.

In addition, the President pledged that the United States later would match the contributions of all other nations to the agency's nuclear materials "bank."

These additional supplies will become available after the establishment of the agency, after the ratification of the statute by eighteen powers, and July 1, 1960. They will be furnished as

Continued on Page 12, Column 3

CITY WARNS UNION ON SUBWAY STRIKE

Mayor Scores M.B.A. Threat as 'Political Blackmail'— Transit Board to Act

By RALPH KATZ

Mayor Wagner and the Transit Authority warned the Motormen's Benevolent Association yesterday against taking strike action on the city's subways.

In a telegram to Theodore Loos, president of the independent union, the Mayor asserted that he would not "tolerate" a strike. The authority said that if a strike vote was taken in violation of a Supreme Court injunction, "we shall take steps to meet it."

Both messages resulted from a report on Thursday by a union executive committee member that job action was planned for Nov. 5. The union official, who declined to permit the use of his name, said that the strike vote would be taken next Wednesday.

The union says it represents

Continued on Page 18, Column 6

Rioting in Singapore Takes Mounting Toll

Special to The New York Times.

SINGAPORE, Oct. 26—Rioting resulting from a strike of students spread to many parts of Singapore today. The official casualty toll reached seven dead and fifty-one injured.

The seriousness of the situation caused 27,000 police reserves and policemen to be held ready in the Federation of Malaya and in Singapore if the violence in the Crown Colony got out of hand.

[More British troops were being moved into Singapore early Saturday as the number of dead rose to eleven, according to Reuters. Ninety-nine persons were officially listed as injured, and 219 have been arrested in two days of rioting.]

Malaya's Chief Minister,

Continued on Page 10, Column 3

WEST SEEKS WAY

France, Britain, Others Study How to Appeal Russian Intervention

By EDWIN L. DALE Jr.
Special to The New York Times.

WASHINGTON, Oct. 26—The State Department disclosed today that the United States was consulting with Britain, France and other friendly governments on "the feasibility and advisability of bringing the situation in Hungary before the United Nations."

This was revealed by Lincoln White, the State Department spokesman. Officials said later that the United States was making no proposals, but was exploring various possibilities.

The Governments being consulted, other than Britain and France, were not identified.

[In Paris, Foreign Minister Christian Pineau warned the West against attempts to exploit the uprisings in Poland and Hungary.]

Mr. White said that among the questions under consideration was that of the legality of the presence of Soviet troops in Hungary under the Warsaw pact. Statements by President Eisenhower and Secretary of State Dulles on this point have appeared to be in conflict.

Troop Use Questioned

The Warsaw Pact of May 14, 1955, is a Soviet version of the North Atlantic Treaty Organization. Under the pact's provisions, Soviet troops have remained in Hungary, a member nation, to "safeguard" her security.

The view in the State Department is that there is little doubt that the troops have a right to be there. But a question might be raised about the legitimacy of their use to put down an internal rebellion.

Even this raises a problem, however. The Soviet troops are being used at the request of the Hungarian Government. There is little effort in Washington to deny that the United States forces abroad could be used in the same way if there were a Communist-led revolution in, say, Italy.

In 1944 and 1945, for example, British troops, on the request of the Athens Government, fought Communist rebels in Greece. Furthermore, any possible United Nations approach is at the moment clouded by French threats to use force in Morocco and Tunisia to protect Europeans there.

The United Nations situation

Continued on Page 5, Column 3

Reporter in Budapest Tells How Protest Grew Into War

Account From the Embattled City Says Soviet's Massed Tanks Slowed Revolt, Which the Massacre Then Rekindled

By JOHN MacCORMAC

BUDAPEST, Hungary, Oct. 26—What began here Tuesday as a demonstration turned that same night into a revolt and yesterday became a war that was still raging today.

It is war by Soviet troops and Hungarian political policemen against the mass of the Hungarian people. The war is being waged on behalf of the Soviet Union and in support of the Hungarian Communist Government, which would fall in ten minutes if it were not for the presence of Soviet tanks in Budapest.

The Soviet troops were called in by the Hungarian Government while it still was dominated by Erno Gero, who had succeeded Matyas Rakosi as First Secretary of the Hungarian Workers' (Communist) party. Imre Nagy, for whose appointment as Premier

the insurgent masses had been calling, did not take office until after the invitation to the Soviet troops had been sent, although by doing so he countenanced it.

Mr. Gero's removal from power did not occur until Mikhail A. Suslov, a member of the Soviet Presidium, and Anastas I. Mikoyan, a Soviet First Deputy Premier, who had successively visited Hungary when the fall of M. Rakosi was imminent, arrived in Budapest yesterday for a brief visit.

As late as last night the insurgents still were calling for a democratic government headed by Mr. Nagy, but one that would accede to demands that no Communist regime anywhere had yet accepted. But they were saying that Mr. Nagy already had demonstrated he was no Gomulka. This was a reference to

Continued on Page 2, Column 3

Poles, Quiet, Watch Revolt in Hungary But Get Little News

By HENRY GINIGER
Special to The New York Times.

WARSAW, Oct. 26—For the first time in almost a week Poland was reported completely quiet today.

As the ferment that accompanied changes in the country's Communist leadership died down, considerable attention was turned to events in Hungary.

Warsaw newspapers announced that in response to an appeal by the Hungarian Red Cross a special plane flew to Budapest today with blood plasma and other supplies for the victims of the fighting there. Later it was understood the plane was unable to land in Budapest and returned here with its cargo.

Of the fighting itself there was virtually no news. Communications between Warsaw and Budapest, by private phones at least, had been cut. Two regularly scheduled plane flights were canceled today.

From its "fragmentary information," Trybuna Ludu, the Polish Communist official organ, said this morning it had concluded that "the peaceful demonstration of the Hungarian

Continued on Page 3, Column 4

FIGHTING EXTENDS TO AUSTRIAN LINE

Hungarian Physicians Cross Border With Medical Plea in the Rebels' Behalf

By PAUL HOFMANN
Special to The New York Times.

VIENNA, Saturday, Oct. 27—Rebellion has spread to westernmost Hungary and has sent casualties and refugees across the border into Austria.

Shortly after 8 o'clock last night a Hungarian ambulance with three physicians appeared near the Austrian frontier village of Nicklesdorf on the main Vienna-Budapest highway and asked to see the Austrian authorities. The physicians said they were acting for the rebels and urgently requested medical supplies for their injured. They said seventy persons had been killed and 200 wounded in fighting in the Hungarian town of Magyarovar, seven miles east of the border.

The atmosphere in Vienna late last night was that of a city behind battle lines. Plasma and medical supplies were hurriedly assembled and Red Cross am-

Continued on Page 3, Column 4

NEW PEACE PLEA

Shake-Up of Regime and Revision of Tie to Moscow Vowed

By ELIE ABEL
Special to The New York Times.

VIENNA, Saturday, Oct. 27—The battle of Budapest was still in doubt early today, with Soviet troops on one side and a fiercely hostile Hungarian populace on the other.

The insurrection had spread over a large part of the country. The desperate regime of Premier Imre Nagy was struggling to maintain itself in a few scarred Government buildings along the Pest embankment with the aid of Soviet tanks and artillery.

The bulk of the Hungarian Army had given up the fight, according to reports reaching Vienna, and thousands of officers and soldiers had joined the insurrection, now in its fifth day.

[The Budapest radio said at dawn Saturday that Soviet and Hungarian troops had launched new attacks throughout Hungary against the rebels, The Associated Press reported from Vienna. The broadcast said fighting must continue because rebel elements had defied an ultimatum to surrender. No further word had been received up to 4 A. M., New York time.]

A Rebel Government

Rebel forces controlling the industrial town of Gyor in West Hungary, proclaimed their own "independent Hungarian Government." Western reporters managed to establish contact with this group from the Austrian frontier.

The anti-Communist Hungarians said they were expecting an early attack on Gyor by Soviet Army forces. The rebels told newsmen they had a number of tanks some of them captured and the rest surrendered voluntarily by Hungarian Army units.

The indication during the night was that Premier Nagy could count only on the support of the Hungarian Red Security Police and the Soviet Army. The weakness of his three-day-old Government was plain.

The Central Committee of the Hungarian Working People's (Communist) party made a fresh appeal for peace and order yesterday afternoon under the new First Secretary, Janos Kadar.

Communists' Program

The committee outlined a program virtually identical with that of the Polish United Workers (Communist) party led by Wladyslaw Gomulka. A new relationship with the Soviet Union will be worked out, the Hungarian committee promised, on the principles of "national independence, complete equality and non-interference."

The party leadership pledged that it would seek a withdrawal of Soviet forces from strongpoints as soon as order was restored, and offered an unconditional amnesty for all insurrec-

Continued on Page 3, Column 1

Sultan Strengthens Moroccan Cabinet

By THOMAS F. BRADY
Special to The New York Times.

RABAT, Morocco, Saturday, Oct. 27—A new Moroccan Cabinet of fourteen ministers, headed by Premier M'barek Bekkai, was sworn in at 3 A. M. today before Sultan Mohammed V. The Cabinet change gave predominance to the strongly nationalist Istiqlal (Independence) party.

The Sultan told his new Ministers they were chosen "to confront the difficulties" in which the country finds itself.

These difficulties are the result of the breach with France over the seizure of five Algerian nationalist rebel leaders from a Moroccan plane Monday night. The Algerians were en

Continued on Page 10, Column 3

SOVIET ARMORED VEHICLES PROWL STREETS OF BUDAPEST: A tank and a smaller vehicle moving yesterday along Kossuth Street in the embattled Hungarian capital. This picture was taken by a Western traveler, just before he left the city for Vienna. It was sent here by radio. The fighting that started on Tuesday still continued.

Associated Press Radiophoto

"All the News
That's Fit to Print"

The New York Times.

LATE CITY EDITION
Condensation of U. S. Weather Bureau forecast:
Mostly fair today and tomorrow.
Temperature range today: 65-48.
Temperature yesterday: 62.2-48.1.
Full U. S. Weather Bureau Report, Page 74.

VOL. CVI—No. 36,074.   NEW YORK, TUESDAY, OCTOBER 30, 1956.   FIVE CENTS

ISRAELIS THRUST INTO EGYPT AND NEAR SUEZ; U.S. GOES TO U.N. UNDER ANTI-AGGRESSION PACT

Budapest Rebels Refuse to Yield Until Soviet Troops Leave

EISENHOWER BIDS SOUTH FIGHT BIAS ON A 'LOCAL BASIS'

In Miami He Stresses Roles of States—Hails Byrd in Speech in Virginia

Texts of Eisenhower speeches are on Pages 24 and 25.

By RUSSELL BAKER
Special to The New York Times.

RICHMOND, Va., Oct. 29—President Eisenhower, campaigning in the South today, urged that the problem of achieving racial equality be handled largely "on a local and state basis."

He told a Miami Airport audience he was convinced that progress today in equality of opportunity and equality before the law had "to be achieved finally in the hearts of men rather than in legislative halls."

The President was applauded lightly when he said that "there must be intelligent understanding of the human factors and emotions involved if we are to make steady progress in the matter rather than simply to make political promises never intended to be kept."

In the field of civil rights, he added, he had tried to bring "reason, good sense and good judgment to the performance of clear duty."

Makes 1,800-Mile Trip

Though he delivered three airport speeches in an 1,800-mile aerial campaign in Florida and Virginia, he touched on the civil rights issue only once.

That was in Miami, in the President's first speech today.

In Jacksonville, Fla., and Richmond, Va., where the southern tradition is stronger than in Miami, he did not discuss the racial theme. Nor did he refer directly in any of his speeches to the controversial school integration issue or the Supreme Court decision.

He concentrated instead on three matters: peace, prosperity and attacks on the Democratic ticket.

And at Miami General Eisenhower tried for the first time the campaigning style of casual campaigning developed to a high art by Senator Estes Kefauver.

Surrounded by several hundred rabid admirers on his way to his plane after speaking, he shook hands by the score with a zest rarely matched by even Senator Kefauver and a folksiness as impressive as the Senator's own.

"Hi ya, folks," he said, and

Continued on Page 24, Column 4

PRESIDENT GIVEN MINNESOTA LEAD

Resurvey Finds Him Moving Ahead in a Close Contest

A Times Team Report

Teams of New York Times reporters have recently surveyed political trends in twenty-seven closely contested states. They are now rechecking the most doubtful states. Following is a resurvey report from Leonard Buder, Donald Janson and W. H. Lawrence.

By DONALD JANSON
Special to The New York Times.

MINNEAPOLIS, Oct. 29—President Eisenhower appears to hold a tenuous lead in the race for Minnesota's eleven electoral votes.

A month ago New York Times reporters found the President and Adlai E. Stevenson running neck and neck in this state. The Eisenhower victory margin of four years ago—162,000 out of 1,379,000 votes cast—had buckled under the impact of defections by farmers who were caught in a cost-price vise.

The farm revolt remains strong today in some areas.

Continued on Page 28, Column 2

Stevenson Says U. S. Gets 'Less Than Truth' on Strife

Charges President Endangered the Nation by 'Good News' From the Mideast—Boston Crowds Hail Candidate

By HARRISON E. SALISBURY

BOSTON, Oct. 29—Adlai E. Stevenson charged tonight that President Eisenhower had given the nation reassurances about the Middle East that had been "tragically less than the truth."

"The Government has not been

Texts of Stevenson statement and speech, Page 28.

telling us the whole truth," Mr. Stevenson said.

"As a campaigning politician there is none better. It is as a performing politician, as a President who knows how to control his own party, who knows how to grasp the reins of Government that he fails."

Several times Mr. Stevenson's partisan audience booed references to the President. The chorus of boos every time he mentioned Vice President Richard M. Nixon started the moment the crowd sensed that Mr.

Continued on Page 29, Column 2

POLAND'S LEADERS BACK HUNGARIANS

Support Demands for Exit of Soviet Troops—Call for End of Strife

By SYDNEY GRUSON
Special to The New York Times.

WARSAW, Oct. 29—The Polish Communist party, differing sharply once again with the Soviet Union, came out formally today in support of Hungarian demands for the withdrawal of Soviet troops from Hungary.

Yesterday the new leadership of the Polish United Workers (Communist) party rejected the Soviet allegation that foreign agents and counter-revolutionaries were responsible for the Hungarian tragedy. Today the Poles stood up again on the side of the Hungarians.

An appeal to those on both sides of the barricades in Hungary to halt fratricidal strife was issued by Wladyslaw Gomulka, the Polish party's First Secretary, and by Premier Josef Cyrankiewicz.

Emphasizing the growing insistence here for independence in foreign as well as internal affairs, the party statement ignored the Soviet charges of Western interference in Hungary.

For the Poles the statement of solidarity was a means of publicly expressing their appreciation for the Hungarian help which was threatened by the Soviet leaders a week ago. Poland escaped Hungary's fate

Continued on Page 22, Column 1

Patrols in Budapest Are Trigger-Happy From Propaganda

By JOHN MacCORMAC
Special to The New York Times.

BUDAPEST, Hungary, Oct. 29—The seventh day of the Hungarian revolution has dawned with Soviet soldiers still patrolling the Budapest street's despite a promise by Hungary's new Government that they would be withdrawn. The Government had qualified its announcement yesterday with the condition "as soon as order has been completely restored."

As far as could be learned, armed resistance in Budapest has ceased, even in the Maria Theresa barracks in Ulloi Ut, which was holding out late yesterday. But that order can ever be completely restored in Budapest as long as the Russians are here seems unlikely because of the fears and propaganda with which the Soviet troops seem to be filled.

At 10 o'clock last night, for instance, a Soviet soldier guarding an area known as Szent Istvan Ut shot and seriously wounded Noel Barber, London Daily Mail correspondent. Mr. Barber had been making a tour of inspection to get the public's reaction to Premier Imre Nagy's announcement that there would be no further firing and that the insurrection had been recognized by his Government as

Continued on Page 15, Column 1

Russians Befriend One Hungarian City

By HOMER BIGART
Special to The New York Times.

GYOR, Hungary, Oct. 29—The small Soviet garrison of this industrial city has retired to a near-by wood, leaving the townspeople free rein to rally and shout against the Nagy Government and demand democratic national elections.

The Russians here must be credited with sensible behavior. They abandoned their barracks a few days ago under no pressure and took to the wood.

There the Soviet officers are living with their wives and children in tents. They have not shot anyone. The townspeople show their gratitude by taking the Russians eggs and milk.

And although Gyor has

Continued on Page 13, Column 1

FIGHTING PERSISTS

Russians Still Pulling Out, With Hungarian Units Taking Over

Text of editorial in Communist newspaper on Page 10.

By ELIE ABEL
Special to The New York Times.

VIENNA, Tuesday, Oct. 30—Soviet troops remained in control of Budapest this morning while the Government of Imre Nagy pleaded with the stubborn revolutionaries to lay down their arms.

But the rebels refused to give up the fight until Mr. Nagy had made good on his promise that the Soviet forces would evacuate the battered city, monitored reports from the Hungarian capital said.

This morning the Budapest radio broadcast the following communiqué:

"While Soviet forces are being withdrawn from Budapest, Hungarian police and armed youth units are maintaining order. Such armed groups as are still resisting will lay down their arms at 9 A. M. [3 A. M. New York time] and will then take part in maintaining order."

[Up to 5 A. M. New York time there had been no further reports on the situation in Hungary.]

Appeal Is Pressed

Earlier this morning the Budapest radio broadcast an appeal by Karoly Janda, Defense Minister, to the rebels to lay down their arms before 9 A. M.

In spite of the gradual Soviet withdrawal, fighting in Budapest flared up again last night. Soviet tank forces engaged in heavy combat in several parts of the city. Latest reports said artillery fire was heard in Budapest all night.

Rebels from eastern Hungary and from the region of Gyor in the west were understood to have joined the insurgents in the capital.

The rebel-held Miskolc radio in northeast Hungary, in a broadcast monitored here, urged anti-Communists in Budapest not to lay down their arms before the last Soviet soldier had left the country.

A general strike called by the rebel leaders appeared to be continuing in many parts of Hungary for the fifth day. Most factory workers, railroad men and miners stayed away from their jobs again this morning despite pressing appeals from Mr. Nagy's Government to resume work.

Nearly complete was an unofficial school strike. Instead of attending classes many teen-agers in Budapest did counter work for the rebels and even

Continued on Page 10, Column 4

1950 PLEDGE CITED

White House Recalls Promise to Assist Victim of Attack

By DANA ADAMS SCHMIDT
Special to The New York Times.

WASHINGTON, Oct. 29—The United States will take the movement of Israeli forces into Egypt to the United Nations Security Council tomorrow morning.

The planned appeal to the United Nations was announced by the White House tonight after President Eisenhower had held an emergency meeting with Secretary of State Dulles and six other high officials.

[An emergency meeting of the Security Council was set for 11 A. M. Tuesday.]

The White House statement follows:

"At the meeting, the President recalled that the United States under this and prior Administrations has pledged itself to assist the victim of any aggression in the Middle East. We shall honor our pledge.

"The United States is in consultation with the British and French Governments, parties with us to the tripartite declaration of 1950, and the United States plans as contemplated by that declaration that the situation shall be taken to the United Nations Security Council tomorrow morning.

Special Session in Abeyance

"The question of whether and when the President will call a special session of the Congress will be decided in the light of the unfolding situation."

The statement was read by James C. Hagerty, Presidential press secretary. He said it had the full authority of the President and the other conferees.

Others at the meeting, in addition to Mr. Dulles, were Charles E. Wilson, Secretary of Defense; Admiral Arthur W. Radford, Chairman of the Joint Chiefs of Staff; Sherman Adams, Assistant to the President; Herbert Hoover Jr., Under Secretary of State; Allen W. Dulles, director of the Central Intelligence Agency, and Wilton B. Persons, deputy assistant to the President.

The one-and-a-half-hour meeting at the White House took place immediately after the President's return by air from a campaign trip in Florida and Virginia.

The State Department said Americans "not performing essential services" would be asked to leave the Middle East. Among the first to leave was a group that flew from Israel to Athens.

Earlier, Secretary of State Dulles had initiated the joint steps with Britain and France.

The State Department an-

Continued on Page 3, Column 1

ISRAELIS OPEN DRIVE: The advance into Egypt was reported made at and below Kuntilla, with a thrust near the Suez Canal. There was a flare-up in Gaza area (cross).

Cairo Says Egyptian Units Have Engaged the Israelis

By The United Press.

CAIRO, Tuesday, Oct. 30—The Egyptian Army said today it had begun "liquidating" an Israeli force that had thrust into Egyptian territory toward the Suez Canal. Egyptian army headquarters announced that the Israeli force had suffered "heavy casualties" in the night-long fighting. It gave no precise figures.

"The enemy's plan to penetrate deep inside Egyptian territory failed," the Egyptian communiqué said. "Egyptian armed forces early this morning started liquidating the enemy forces."

[Iraq informed Egypt early Tuesday that Iraqi troops were ready to offer immediate assistance against the Israeli thrust, The Associated Press said. The offer was announced after an urgent morning meeting of Premier Nuri as-Said's Cabinet in Baghdad.]

Leaves Are Canceled

The high command of the Egyptian armed forces recalled all officers and enlisted men on leave to meet the Israeli threat. Orders broadcast by the Cairo radio said all must "report immediately to their units." Reservists were not affected.

The Egyptian communiqué identified the three frontier checkpoints where it said the Israeli raiders had been halted at Kuntilla, Nekhet and El Mimet. All are on the eastern side of the rocky Sinai Peninsula. [No additional details on the fighting were received up to 5 A. M.]

Suez Canal authorities in Cairo said the situation along the waterway was normal. They said no blackout has been imposed and no emergency alert sounded.

Continued on Page 6, Column 2

FRANCE ACCUSES FIVE OF TREASON

Files Formal Charges Against Algerians Seized in Plane —Sends Aide to Tunisia

By ROBERT C. DOTY
Special to The New York Times.

PARIS, Oct. 29—Five leaders of the Algerian rebellion, seized a week ago, were formally charged today with treason against France. The offense is punishable by death.

The five are Mohammed ben Bella, Mohammed Khider, Mustafa Lachraf, Mohammed Boudiaf and Hossein Ait Ahmed, all members of the Algerian National Liberation Front, which has directed the two-year rebellion against France from headquarters in Cairo.

Their arrest Oct. 22, while aboard a Moroccan plane flying to a conference of North African leaders in Tunis, set off a wave of anti-French protest and violence. Arab anger was based on the theory that the five men were under the protection of Sultan Mohammed V of Morocco, with tacit French consent, at the time of their arrest.

[In the United Nations Security Council, France formally charged Egypt with gun-running for the Algerian rebels.]

As Algerians, the five seized rebel leaders are French citizens, hence subject to a treason

Continued on Page 10, Column 2

Maria Callas Bows At Opening of 'Met'

By ROSS PARMENTER

Bellini's "Norma" has never been notably popular in this country. But last night, when it opened the Metropolitan Opera's seventy-second season, it established a compound record. Never have so many Americans tried to pay so much money to hear an opera.

The actual sum paid by those who managed to crowd into the opera house was $75,510.50. This was larger by more than $10,000 than the previous box-office record of $65,336, which was set with the opening night "Faust" in 1953. The larger sum, though, was not paid by a larger number of persons. After all, sell-outs have been customary on first nights, and first-night audiences are re-

Continued on Page 43, Column 4

DEEP DRIVE MADE

Tel Aviv Declares Aim Is to Smash Egyptian Commando Bases

Text of Israeli statement will be found on Page 4.

By MOSHE BRILLIANT
Special to The New York Times.

TEL AVIV, Israel, Oct. 29—An Israeli military force thrust into the Sinai Peninsula of Egypt today. It was reported to have reached within twenty miles of the Suez Canal.

Army sources said the Israelis were west of the crossroads where the road to Kuntilla branches off from the Suez-Qoseima highway.

The Israelis were said to have halted there and to have dug in.

A Foreign Ministry statement said the operation had been started "to eliminate the Egyptian fedayeen [commando squad] bases in the Sinai Peninsula."

Army sources said the Israelis had smashed the Egyptian position at Kuntilla and Ras el Naqb at the southern end of the international border. The forces then advanced more than seventy-five miles.

No fighting was reported on the northern end of the border or in the Gaza Strip, which is heavily populated.

Too Big for a Reprisal

Reports from the Sinai area described the fighting as "too big for a reprisal and too small for a war." Details of the fighting were not available tonight, but reliable sources said there had been no aerial bombardment of Egyptian positions.

It was not clear tonight whether the Israelis proposed to push on to the Suez Canal or withdraw to Israel territory, as they have done after reprisal raids. A high official said: "I do not know. It depends on developments."

Yesterday the Israeli Government attributed its decision to call up reserves to what it said was a renewal of commando activities, to the Egyptian-Jordanian-Syrian military alliance negotiated last Wednesday, and to Arab declarations that "their principal concern is a war of destruction against Israel" and to the movement of Iraqi forces to Jordan's border.

According to information here, the Egyptians have a considerable part of their Army in the Sinai Peninsula. Their land forces are reported equipped with the

Continued on Page 5, Column 5

CITY SCHOOL AIDES SPUR INTEGRATION

District Lines Are Shifted in Some Brooklyn Areas

By BENJAMIN FINE

Without any public announcement, the Board of Education has quietly begun a program to integrate white and Negro pupils in areas where a segregation pattern has existed in the past.

A score of schools in the Bedford-Stuyvesant area of Brooklyn have become interracial since the fall term opened. Children are taken from the all-Negro schools and put into the nearby all-white schools.

At the same time, fairly large groups of children—ranging from fifty to 200—have been taken from a number of all-white schools and placed in the all-Negro schools. In doing this, the board has amended or discarded the old district and school zoning regulations.

This step is part of a "positive program" on integration, Charles H. Silver, Board of Education president, said yesterday. The board has asked its forty assistant superintendents to do everything possible to place Negro and white children in the same schools.

The superintendents are doing

Continued on Page 30, Column 8

AMERICANS LEAVE ISRAEL: Wives and children of State Department personnel boarding Air Force transport plane last night at Lydda Airport near Jerusalem. They were flown to Athens. More dependents are to follow today.

"All the News That's Fit to Print"

The New York Times.

LATE CITY EDITION
Condensation of U.S. Weather Bureau forecast:
Partly cloudy, little temperature
change today and tomorrow.

Temperature range today: 66—51.
Temperature range yesterday: 68.3—53.
Full U.S. Weather Bureau Report, Page 41.

VOL. CVI—No. 36,078.

Entered as Second-Class Matter,
Post Office, New York, N. Y.

NEW YORK, SATURDAY, NOVEMBER 3, 1956.

© 1956, by The New York Times Company.

Times Square, New York 36, N. Y.
Telephone LAckawanna 4-1000.

FIVE CENTS

BRITISH AND FRENCH PUSH TOWARD LANDING; ISRAELIS CAPTURE GAZA AND CONTROL SINAI

Hungary Protests to Soviet Against New Troop Moves; West Urges Action by U.N.; Tension Is Rising in Poland

STEVENSON OFFERS A PROGRAM TO END STRIFE IN MIDEAST

Calls for a Cease-Fire and Israel's Security—Detroit Crowd Boos President

Speech at Detroit and remarks at Cleveland, Page 20.

By HARRISON E. SALISBURY
Special to The New York Times.

DETROIT, Nov. 2—Adlai E. Stevenson offered tonight a program to restore peace in the Middle East, based on the security of Israel and restoration of the Western Alliance.

Mr. Stevenson submitted his program to an enthusiastic overflow audience at the Fox Theatre.

He charged that President Eisenhower did not know what had been happening in the Middle East and that "someone had misled him."

Mr. Stevenson's program called for these steps:

¶A cease-fire in the Middle East.

¶Restoration of the Western grand alliance of the United States, France and Britain.

¶Security for Israel against Arab attack.

¶Establishment of the principle of international concern for the Suez Canal and an end of one-man or one-country control.

¶An all-out attack on resettlement of 900,000 Arab refugees in Middle Eastern lands.

¶A joint program for improvement of economic conditions in the Middle East.

Mr. Stevenson's address was carried on a state TV network. Several thousand persons were unable to gain admission to the theatre.

Earlier today, Mr. Stevenson spoke in Cleveland's Public Square. A huge throng heard him demand United Nations action in behalf of the new Hungarian regime.

Democratic officials put the crowd at 65,000. Newspaper reporters estimated it at closer to 30,000. There was agreement, however, that it was larger than General Eisenhower drew in the same place and time three weeks ago.

Tonight Mr. Stevenson asserted that the first task in the

Continued on Page 20, Column 5

COUNCIL HEARING ON QUINN SLATED

Mayor Backs Tenney Report on Official's Carting Job

By CHARLES G. BENNETT

The City Council will hold hearings soon to consider charges against Councilman Hugh Quinn, Queens Democrat.

In a report to Mayor Wagner on Thursday, Investigation Commissioner Charles H. Tenney found that Mr. Quinn had committed an "apparent" violation of the City Charter and had given grounds for his removal from office.

Yesterday Mayor Wagner said he agreed with the Investigation Commissioner's conclusions.

Council Majority Leader Joseph T. Sharkey, Brooklyn Democrat, said he would call the Councilmen together next week, probably Wednesday, to arrange for hearings on the Quinn case. A question for the Councilmen to determine, Mr. Sharkey said, is whether the hearings will be public or private.

The Council, under the Charter, is the judge of the qualifications of its members. It may expel a member by a two-thirds vote.

Mr. Sharkey said he thought

Continued on Page 48, Column 5

HUNGARIAN PREMIER Imre Nagy, Communist who took office during national anti-Soviet uprising, addressing nation by radio. Date when photograph was taken was not given.
Associated Press Radiophoto

Eisenhower Sees Victory, Leaves Campaign to Nixon

By RUSSELL BAKER
Special to The New York Times.

WASHINGTON, Nov. 2—President Eisenhower now is so confident of re-election Tuesday that he is treating Adlai E. Stevenson's driving campaign finish with a show of indifference. This was emphasized last night in Philadelphia when he indicated that, from his point of view, the campaign was over and that henceforth he would address the nation only in the nonpartisan role of President.

It was pointedly driven home today when the White House noted that Vice President Richard M. Nixon, rather than the President, had been selected to reply tonight to the Democratic nominee's attack on foreign policy.

James C. Hagerty, White House press secretary, said the President's discussion of the Middle Eastern and Central European crises Wednesday had been "nonpolitical." Mr. Stevenson's reply last night, he added, "was strictly political."

Mr. Hagerty's implication was that the President no longer intended to trouble with replies to Mr. Stevenson's "political" charges and that this chore now could be handled adequately by Mr. Nixon.

The President, he added, knew in advance the substance of the Vice President's speech. The White House staff had helped Mr. Nixon get "the facts to refute a lot of misstatements that Mr. Stevenson made last night," Mr. Hagerty said.

The White House also an-

Continued on Page 19, Column 6

PRESIDENT LEADS IN PENNSYLVANIA

Slim Edge Not Widened Yet by Crises Abroad—Clark's Margin for Senate Cut

A Times Team Report

Teams of New York Times reporters have now completed a survey of political trends in twenty-seven closely contested states. They have rechecked eight of those states—the most doubtful ones. Following is a final resurvey report by Leonard Buder, Donald Janson and Wayne Phillips.

By WAYNE PHILLIPS
Special to The New York Times.

PHILADELPHIA, Nov. 2—President Eisenhower is clinging to a lead in this state so insubstantial that it could be washed away by a heavy rain on election day.

Depending upon developments in the Middle East crisis, he may be able to increase that lead in the four days remaining before the election. But at the moment the world crisis has served only to create doubts in the minds of voters on both sides of the fence. Those doubts have not yet crystallized in favor of either candidate.

Two weeks ago a New York Times team found the Pennsylvania Democrats well organized and confident. They were fighting an uphill battle against the appeal of the President's personality, but the odds were on their side in a state that once was a bastion of Republicanism.

They appeared to have won the public—and some Republican newspapers, too—to their Senatorial candidate, Joseph S. Clark Jr. They had created a substantial indecision among the 1952 supporters of President Eisenhower, and had won over enough of them to give some hope of carrying the state for Adlai E.

Continued on Page 15, Column 2

Nixon Hails Break With Allies' Policies

By WILLIAM M. BLAIR

HERSHEY, Pa., Nov. 2—Vice President Richard M. Nixon hailed tonight this country's break with Anglo-French policies as a "declaration of independence that has had an electrifying effect throughout the world."

Speaking with the full backing of President Eisenhower, he assailed Adlai E. Stevenson for charging that the Administration's foreign policy had "averted the Middle East crisis."

He said that the United Nations General Assembly vote gave "the lie to [Mr. Stevenson's] preposterous charge" that the United States stood alone in "an unfriendly world."

The General Assembly early

Continued on Page 15, Column 1

NEW PLEA BY NAGY

Premier Asks That U.N. Defend Neutrality of Hungary

By JOHN MacCORMAC
Special to The New York Times.

BUDAPEST, Hungary, Saturday, Nov. 3—The Hungarian Government made three oral protests yesterday to the Soviet Ambassador in Budapest, complaining that Russian reinforcements were still pouring across the frontier.

[Soviet tanks sealed the main crossings of the Austrian-Hungarian border Friday. This was regarded as a preliminary to dealing sternly with the insurgents.]

Premier Imre Nagy also sent a new appeal to the Secretary General of the United Nations to guarantee Hungary's neutrality and to bring her case before the General Assembly.

Similarly Joseph Cardinal Mindszenty, primate of Hungary, appealed to the West for political support of the revolutionaries and relief for the needy.

Soviet Forces Approaching

Early today, forces at the command of the Revolutionary Council of the Hungarian Army occupied the Foreign Ministry. Other Army units cordoned off the Parliament Building and took up posts on and near all bridges spanning the Danube. These measures were prompted by information that Soviet forces were approaching the capital.

In his plea to the Secretary General of the United Nations, Premier Nagy said that Hungary's first demand for the withdrawal of Soviet troops had been received favorably by Moscow. In spite of this, he went on, fresh Soviet troops were brought in to Hungary on Tuesday and Wednesday.

The Hungarian Government then denounced the Warsaw Pact, proclaimed Hungary a neutral state and demanded the withdrawal of all Soviet troops. Budapest also proposed the creation of two joint Hungarian-Soviet committees, one political and one military, to discuss the terms and set the timetable for this withdrawal.

The Premier said that he had protested against any further influx of Soviet soldiers, pointing out to the United Nations that new Soviet units had entered

Continued on Page 16, Column 5

TROOPS REPORTED CROSSING POLAND

Soviet Movement Is Said to Be to East Germany—Panic Buying in Warsaw

By SYDNEY GRUSON
Special to The New York Times.

WARSAW, Nov. 2—Reports reached Warsaw tonight of large-scale Soviet troop movements across Poland from Russia to East Germany. No details were available.

It was pointedly driven home today when the White House noted that Vice President Richard M. Nixon, rather than the President, had been reported they had been reported the situation in Poland had reached a point of extreme tension.

All through the day the Polish radio repeated its broadcast of an appeal by the Communist party's new leadership for "calm, discipline and a sense of responsibility" within the nation.

In Warsaw panic buying began. People bought up all the foodstuffs in the stores and then after withdrawing their money from the banks began to buy jewelry and valuables.

Word came from various parts

Continued on Page 14, Column 4

U. S. Protests Refusal by Soviet To Let Americans Quit Hungary

Special to The New York Times.

WASHINGTON, Nov. 2—The United States protested tonight to the Soviet Union against the action of Soviet troops who prevented a convoy of Americans from leaving Hungary.

A report of the incident from the United States Legation in Budapest reached the State Department in early evening. Deputy Under Secretary of State Robert Murphy called on Georgi N. Zaroubin, the Soviet Ambassador, at once.

Mr. Zaroubin told Mr. Murphy he would get in touch with his Government in Moscow about the matter.

A State Department spokesman said Mr. Murphy spoke "energetically" to the Soviet Ambassador about the "interference with American official personnel."

According to the official report, the convoy consisted of dependents—wives and children of a United States legation staff in Budapest as well as French, British and American correspondents—was turned back from the Austrian border by Soviet troops at 4:30 P. M. today.

"Polemics are useless," a Soviet officer told them. "It is requested that you turn around

Continued on Page 16, Column 3

Israelis Are Mopping Up; Egypt Braces for Landing

12,000 Prisoners Taken

By HOMER BIGART
Special to The New York Times.

TEL AVIV, Israel, Saturday, Nov. 3—Israel's lightning conquest of Egypt's Sinai Peninsula and the Gaza Strip is complete except for minor mopping-up operations. The ancient Philistine capital of Gaza was the last town to fall.

In its drive, Maj. Gen. Moshe Dayan's tough Army had killed, captured or put to flight 30,000 Egyptian troops east of the Suez Canal.

With Israel's southern flank secure after only four days of operations, the Government faced with calm confidence reports that Jordan was being reinforced by Syrian troops and that the Syrian-Jordanian-Egyptian defense pact was about to become operative.

Gaza collapsed after a three-hour fight yesterday morning. A United Nations truce aide

Continued on Page 3, Column 5

Cairo Defense Held Ready

By The United Press.

CAIRO, Nov. 2—Waves of Egyptian and French bombers and fighters blasted Cairo and outlying villages today. An Egyptian communiqué said 100 persons had been killed in one town alone.

Simultaneously, President Gamal Abdel Nasser announced that Egyptian forces in the Sinai desert had "completed their withdrawal safely."

"Now we are waiting for the British and French in the delta," he said. Only "suicide commandos" had been left in Sinai to harass the advancing Israeli forces, he added.

The communiqué asserted that fourteen British and French planes had been shot down in today's raids. An earlier communiqué had claimed three kills in the last twenty-four hours in addition to six reported downed yesterday morning. This would

Continued on Page 3, Column 2

U.N. SPEAKERS ASK HELP FOR HUNGARY

Override Soviet Objections as Security Council Argues International Action

Excerpts from Security Council debate are on Page 16.

By LINDESAY PARROTT
Special to The New York Times.

UNITED NATIONS, N. Y., Nov. 2—The Western powers overrode Soviet objections today and called on the United Nations to take measures against Soviet military action in Hungary.

An emergency meeting of the Security Council heard all nations that spoke, except the Soviet Union, appeal for international action against the reinforcement of Soviet troops in Hungary, where rebel nationalists appear to have taken control. Imre Nagy, Hungarian Premier, asked the United Nations yesterday to guarantee the country's neutralism.

No decision was reached at the two-hour session of the Council tonight. The members will meet again tomorrow afternoon in an attempt to decide on a course of action.

The meeting was sparked by a new message from Mr. Nagy distributed to Council members today.

The letter, couched in terms similar to the one Mr. Nagy sent to the United Nations yesterday, charged that "large" Soviet military units had crossed the Hungarian border. Moving toward

Continued on Page 16, Column 5

Eisenhower Offers Relief to Hungary

Special to The New York Times.

WASHINGTON, Nov. 2—President Eisenhower late today offered $20,000,000 worth of food and medical supplies to relieve the suffering in Hungary resulting from the revolt against Soviet domination.

The White House announced that offer of this offer through a conference between the President, Secretary of State Dulles, and Under Secretary of State Herbert Hoover Jr.

The aid would consist of $15,000,000 in surplus foodstuffs and $5,000,000 in specially purchased meats, oils, fats, and medical supplies.

The President urged the American people to continue sending their contributions to the American Red Cross, which is pouring relief supplies into

Continued on Page 16, Column 7

PARIS ACTS TO BAR CEASE-FIRE NOW

Fears That Immediate Halt in Military Operations Would Save Nasser

By HAROLD CALLENDER
Special to The New York Times.

PARIS, Nov. 2—The French Government moved fast today to prevent a United Nations cease-fire in the Suez Canal Zone.

It feared a halt in military operation now would save Gamal Abdel Nasser, President of Egypt, whose regime the French and British seek to liquidate. In that case the French would feel deprived of a victory they regard as already within their grasp.

This was the explanation of the hurried trip to London during the day by Christian Pineau, French Foreign Minister, that was given by high political authorities here tonight.

In London, M. Pineau, Prime Minister Eden and Selwyn Lloyd, British Foreign Secretary, were reported to have agreed they would not accept a cease-fire at least until British-French troops had landed. They were expected to land tomorrow.

Action by U. N. Noted

The United Nations General Assembly voted early today for a cease-fire in the Middle East but the question was how it could be carried out.

[Prime Minister Eden rejected a Laborite demand that he order an immediate end to British attacks on Egypt. This was in response to Laborite pressure that he comply with the resolution of the United Nations General Assembly calling for a cease-fire.]

The fear that took possession of French officials was that Prime Minister Eden might agree to a premature cease-fire. If so, he would do it, according to these officials, because he is harried by the British Labor party to call off the French-British military expedition to Egypt, and because he is pressed by Secretary of State Dulles, who is credited here with desiring a cease-fire before the United States election Tuesday. It was even suggested that the United States Sixth Fleet, now in the Mediterranean, might be mandated by the General Assembly to occupy the Suez Canal zone, instead of the French-British force now preparing to occupy it.

This fear arose because Lester B. Pearson, Canadian Minister of State for External Affairs, proposed yesterday at New York that the General Assembly should authorize the immediate

Continued on Page 6, Column 4

BOMBING PRESSED

Planes Center Attacks on Army After Cairo Loses Airpower

By DREW MIDDLETON
Special to The New York Times.

LONDON, Nov. 2—The neutralization of the Egyptian Air Force, a primary condition to successful landing operations, was claimed tonight by British and French airpower.

More than a hundred Egyptian planes have been destroyed or damaged at airfields by bombers and fighters of Royal Air Force and French Air Force. A high proportion of these were Soviet-built MIG-15 jet fighter planes and Ilyushin-28 twin-jet bombers, R. A. F. sources said.

At the outset of the operations the Egyptian Air Force had ninety MIG's and fifty Ilyushins. Since not all of them were airworthy Wednesday when the attack began, the allies' claim to have neutralized Egypt's airpower appears valid.

Transit Camp Bombed

The British-French air attack is shifting away from air bases onto the Egyptian Army's central forces, now known to be moving slowly northward and northeastward away from the Cairo area.

British air reconnaissance reported the movement of tanks and infantry into the area around Port Said, one of the three sites chosen by the allies for occupation.

One target successfully attacked was a military transit camp, around which tanks and guns were concentrated, about fifteen miles northeast of Cairo in the El Khanka area.

[The British reported that the Egyptians had sunk seven ships in an effort to block the Suez Canal. It was not known in London whether the Egyptian effort had succeeded. No word of an allied landing in Egypt had been received up to 4 A. M., New York time.]

Information that the Syrian Government was placing its armed forces under the commander in chief of the Egyptian forces has not altered British or French planning for forthcoming operations.

As part of the psychological preparation for the allied landing operations the Cairo Radio, the Voice of Arabia, was silenced

Continued on Page 2, Column 3

ARABS SAID TO PUT TROOPS IN JORDAN

Syrian and Iraqi Forces Are Reported on March

By DANA ADAMS SCHMIDT
Special to The New York Times.

WASHINGTON, Nov. 2—Syrian and Iraqi troops are marching into Jordan, according to information telephoned from Cairo, the Egyptian Embassy press counselor announced tonight.

The official, Mohammed Habib, reported also that Lebanese workers had cut one of the pipelines that carry Arabian oil to the Mediterranean.

The report of the troop movements followed announcement by Syria, in a formal note to the State Department, that she had placed her armed forces under Egyptian command.

"The Syrian armed forces are now taking orders from the Egyptian Commander in Chief, Gen. Abdel Hakim Amer," Mr. Jamail said, continuing, "Syria

Continued on Page 2, Column 3

"All the News
That's Fit to Print"

The New York Times.

LATE CITY EDITION
Continuation of U. S. Weather Bureau forecast:
Considerable cloudiness, seasonably
cool today and tomorrow.
Temperature range today: 52—60.
Temperature range yesterday: 52.5—49.2.
Full U. S. Weather Bureau Report, Page 86.

NEWS SUMMARY AND INDEX, PAGE 95

VOL. CVI—No. 36,079.   Entered as Second-Class Matter,
Post Office, New York, N. Y.   © 1956, by The New York Times Company.   NEW YORK, SUNDAY, NOVEMBER 4, 1956.   TWENTY-FIVE CENTS

SECTION ONE

SOVIET ATTACKS HUNGARY, SEIZES NAGY;
U. S. LEGATION IN BUDAPEST UNDER FIRE;
MINDSZENTY IN REFUGE WITH AMERICANS

U. N. Assembly Backs Call to Set Up Mideast Truce Force

STEVENSON HOLDS PRESIDENT LACKS 'ENERGY' FOR JOB

In Last Big Address, He Asks if Nation Is Prepared to Accept Nixon as Leader

*Stevenson statement, Page 72;
text of speech, Page 73.*

By HARRISON E. SALISBURY
Special to The New York Times.

CHICAGO, Nov. 3—Adlai E. Stevenson charged tonight that President Eisenhower "now lacks the energy" to cope with world problems such as the present crisis in the Middle East.

He asked the nation whether it was prepared to accept Richard M. Nixon "as Commander in Chief to exercise power over peace and war."

"Every consideration," Mr. Stevenson said, "the President's age, his health and the fact that he cannot succeed himself make it inevitable that the dominant figure in the Republican party under a second Eisenhower term would be Richard Nixon."

This was the first time that Mr. Stevenson in direct fashion had raised the question of General Eisenhower's health, his physical strength and his ability to survive his full term if re-elected.

It placed—on the eve of the election—the question of General Eisenhower's age and his health directly in the forefront of the campaign.

Nixon Draws Boos

Mr. Stevenson's every reference to Mr. Nixon brought forth a hurricane of boos that was equaled only by several waves of boos for General Eisenhower's foreign policy and references to the asserted errors of John Foster Dulles, Secretary of State.

Mr. Stevenson's remarks, which were carried to the nation by television, were cut off the air on a chorus of boos for Mr. Nixon. The conclusion of his address ran over the allotted air time.

General Eisenhower is 66 years old. Mr. Stevenson had foreswore any discussion of the President's health, insisting that this was a matter for each individual voter.

However, in charging tonight that the crisis in world affairs had stemmed directly from the President's "part-time conduct" of his office, Mr. Stevenson took a look into the future.

The fact is, he asserted, General Eisenhower "in the next years would inevitably recede more and more from the picture."

The President, Mr. Stevenson

Continued on Page 73, Column 2

London, Paris Bar Truce; Eden Pledges Israeli Exit

U. N. Occupation Offered

By HAROLD CALLENDER
Special to The New York Times.

PARIS, Nov. 3—Britain and France rejected today the United Nations call for a cease-fire in the Suez area.

At the same time they made a counter-proposal designed to bring their independent military action under the authority of the United Nations. They thus sought to heal the breach between the two powers on the one hand and the United Nations and the United States on the other.

The United Nations General Assembly recommended the cease-fire Thursday by adopting a resolution introduced by the United States.

The two European powers de-

Continued on Page 18, Column 1

Prime Minister Speaks

By DREW MIDDLETON
Special to The New York Times.

LONDON, Nov. 3—The British Government will insure the withdrawal of Israeli forces from Egyptian territory once British and French troops have occupied key points on the Suez Canal, Sir Anthony Eden declared tonight.

The objective of his policy of intervention in the Middle East is a lasting settlement in the area and a stronger British position, able "to act as well as to talk," the Prime Minister told

Eden's text and Gaitskell excerpts are on Page 28.

Continued on Page 28, Column 6

BID TO U. N. CHIEF

Canada's Motion That He Plan Suez Unit Adopted, 59 to 0

Texts of draft resolutions and debate excerpts, Page 29.

By KATHLEEN TELTSCH
Special to The New York Times.

UNITED NATIONS, N. Y., Sunday, Nov. 4—The General Assembly voted early today to ask the Secretary General to submit a plan for creation of a United Nations police force to obtain and supervise a cease-fire in the Middle East.

The policing proposal, sponsored by Canada, was adopted 57 to 0, at 2:17 A. M. at an emergency session of the Assembly.

Nineteen states abstained, among them Israel, France and Britain. The latter two earlier had rejected an Assembly call for a cease-fire and said they would keep on with their "police action" in Egypt to safeguard the Suez Canal.

The proposal, made by Lester B. Pearson, Canada's Secretary for External Affairs, calls on Secretary General Dag Hammarskjold to submit blueprints within forty-eight hours for an "emergency international United Nations force."

New Truce Plan Adopted

No details were suggested by Mr. Pearson, but such a police force presumably would have to include several thousand men. The Canadian spokesman has said he would recommend Canada's participation. His proposal, however, left all arrangements to the Secretary General.

Within minutes, the emergency session adopted a second resolution, co-sponsored by nineteen Asian and African countries. This renewed the cease-fire appeal made to the Assembly and asked Mr. Hammarskjold to report within twelve hours on whether the states had complied.

The second resolution was approved, 59 to 5, with twelve abstentions. Among the abstainers were France, Britain, Israel, Australia and New Zealand.

[Washington indicated that the Administration, after initial anger at the British-French and Israeli moves, was taking a more moderate, hopeful and understanding attitude.]

Weary United Nations delegates approved the new proposals at an event-filled emergency session, at which the United States presented a new Middle East plan. This seeks a long-range settlement of the Palestine problem and also of the current Suez Canal dispute. In warmly supporting the Ca-

Continued on Page 29, Column 3

SOVIET ROAD BLOCK IN HUNGARY: Soviet tank obstructs road near Magyarovar
Associated Press Radiophoto

ISRAELI PATROLS REACH SUEZ BANK

Penetrate Zone at 3 Points as Delay in British-French Landings Irks Regime

By HOMER BIGART
Special to The New York Times.

TEL AVIV, Israel, Sunday, Nov. 4—Israeli patrols reached the east bank of the Suez Canal yesterday.

A Government spokesman said Israeli columns had penetrated at three places the ten-mile buffer zone east of the canal that Britain and France wanted kept clear of warring Israeli and Egyptian forces.

Meanwhile, the Cabinet of Premier David Ben-Gurion studied reports that Syrian and Iraqi troops had entered Jordan. The developments in Jordan were being followed with "concern and alertness," according to a Foreign Ministry source.

The announcement that Israelis were within ten miles of the canal at three points—opposite El Qantara in the north, Ismailia in the center and Suez at the southern terminus—may have been timed to coincide with reports here that the British-French invasion had been put off because of United States pressure.

The British-French proposals for an international police force to occupy the canal zone were regarded here as "unrealistic."

Until its announcement, the Israeli Government had indicated compliance with the British ultimatum.

But Israel has insisted that no firm deal was made with the French about how the advance would be halted.

Meanwhile, the Israelis reported, they were rapidly occupying all key points on the conquered Sinai Peninsula.

Lieut. Col. Moshe Pearlman, Government and Army spokesman, said that the whole area was "relatively quiet" and that the "entire peninsula is in very short time well in Israeli hands."

Continued on Page 24, Column 4

British Bomb Raids On Egypt Continued In Landing Prelude

Texts of the communiqués are printed on Page 26.

By LEONARD INGALLS
Special to The New York Times.

LONDON, Nov. 3—British bombers turned their heaviest attack today from airfields in Egypt to ammunition dumps, barracks and armored weapons depots of the Egyptian Army.

There were indications that the landing by British and French forces in the Suez Canal Zone would be made by paratroopers and seaborne invasion units within the next forty-eight hours.

The Beirut radio, quoting an Egyptian communiqué, reported that a British-French force attempted to land at the southern entrance to the canal, but was driven off with heavy losses.

The Egyptians said they had sunk four British naval vessels and captured three troop landing craft at Suez with fire from shore batteries and torpedo boats. One British ship was said by the Egyptians to have been sunk by gunfire, and a British destroyer, a troop carrier and another British naval unit were said to have been sunk by torpedoes.

The Egyptians also reported they had shot down seventeen British-French planes over the Suez Canal area.

[There was little additional information on the military situation in announcements or dispatches from Cairo.]

An Admiralty spokesman said "there is no information in London to support the Egyptian

Continued on Page 17, Column 1

SOVIET VETO BARS ACTION IN COUNCIL

Censure Move in U. N. Over New Attack on Hungary Carried to Assembly

Excerpts from statements in Security Council, Page 35.

By LINDESAY PARROTT
Special to The New York Times.

UNITED NATIONS, N. Y., Sunday, Nov. 4—The Soviet Union early today vetoed a United States resolution proposing Security Council censure of the Russian military attack on Hungary.

Nine nations favored the United States proposal and one abstained, Yugoslavia.

The veto was at 5:15 A. M. Henry Cabot Lodge Jr., United States representative, immediately moved for an emergency session of the General Assembly to take up the Hungarian crisis. The Assembly already was in permanent special session over the French-British intervention in the Suez Canal area.

Council's Will 'Thwarted'

Angrily, Mr. Lodge told the Council that the will of the world organization had been "thwarted" by the Soviet veto and that the eleven-nation body had been prevented from fulfilling its responsibilities. In this "grave situation," he said, Assembly action was required.

The Council adopted the United States resolution for reference to the Assembly by a vote of 10 to 1. This ballot came at 5:21 A. M.

The Assembly meeting was set for 8 o'clock tonight.

The Council adjourned at 5:34 A. M.

The Council's action, marking the Soviet Union's seventy-ninth veto, was taken after the United States had called the group together at 3 A. M. to protest against the reoccupation of Budapest by Soviet troops. According to the latest reports here early today, the Hungarian capital was in the hands of Soviet troops after Russian tanks earlier had ringed the city.

The United States legation was understood to have been under fire. Mr. Lodge also reported that Joseph Cardinal Mindszenty and his staff had taken refuge in the legation.

The Security Council had adjourned shortly after midnight.

Continued on Page 35, Column 6

CAPITAL STORMED

Freedom Radios Fade From Air as Russians Shell Key Centers

By PAUL HOFMANN
Special to The New York Times.

VIENNA, Sunday, Nov. 4—Soviet troops started attacking Budapest and other Hungarian cities, towns and key military installations at dawn today.

At 9 A. M., local time (3 A. M. Eastern standard time) four hours after Budapest had been awakened by Russian artillery fire, overpowering Soviet tanks and infantry forces had stormed the Parliament Building and made Premier Imre Nagy and most members of his government prisoners.

Fighting in Budapest and many other parts of the country was continuing, but the prospects for the free Hungarian Government forces were nearly hopeless in the face of crushing Soviet superiority.

The Budapest radio and other Hungarian freedom stations fell silent one after another.

Before going silent, they directed desperate pleas to the West, especially to the United States, and to the United Nations for help to save the Hungarian people from "annihilation."

Mindszenty in U. S. Legation

Joseph Cardinal Mindszenty, Roman Catholic primate of Hungary, who had been freed from detention last week, and his secretary had taken refuge in the building of the United States Legation.

The United States Legation, near the Parliament Building, was under fire at 9:30 A. M.

A fierce battle was raging in the immediate surroundings.

At 7 A. M. "several hundred" Soviet heavy tanks were reported attacking key Hungarian Army positions on the outskirts of Budapest and attempting to penetrate the city. The main thrust of the Soviet forces came apparently from the southeast.

Shortly before 7 A. M. the Budapest radio repeated Premier Nagy's announcement of the Soviet attack. It directed an appeal to Dag Hammarskjold, Secretary General of the United Nations. At the same time the M. T. I. Hungarian news agency re- ported:

"Russian troops have suddenly attacked Budapest and the entire country. They have opened fire on everyone in Hungary. It is a general attack.

"Janos Kadar [since Oct. 24 secretary of the Hungarian Communist party], Gyorgy Marosan and Sandor Ronai have formed a new Government and started crushing the counter-

Continued on Page 34, Column 6

EISENHOWER PLANS TALKS TOMORROW

To Make 2 Short Speeches on TV—Mitchell Reports Advances by Labor

By CHARLES E. EGAN
Special to The New York Times.

WASHINGTON, Nov. 3—Politics held an active, if subordinate, role in White House operations on this Saturday before election.

While the President was closeted with advisers in discussions of events in the Middle East and Europe, his top aides found time:

¶To issue a special report by James P. Mitchell, Secretary of Labor, detailing aid given to workers by his department under the present Administration.

¶To give a preliminary outline of the President's two Election Eve television appearances on Monday.

Mr. Hall arrived at the White House at 11:30 this morning. He spent more than an hour there first with Sherman Adams, the Assistant to the President, and later with James C. Hagerty, White House press secretary.

Continued on Page 78, Column 4

DULLES IS GAINING AFTER OPERATION

Part of His Large Intestine Is Removed—He Will Stay in Hospital 2 Weeks

By EDWIN L. DALE Jr.
Special to The New York Times.

WASHINGTON, Nov. 3—John Foster Dulles, Secretary of State, underwent successful surgery today for removal of a perforated portion of his large intestine.

It was announced after the two-and-one-half-hour operation that Mr. Dulles had "left the operating table in good condition" and that he was "resting comfortably."

The announcement was made by a State Department spokesman, Lincoln White, at Walter Reed Army Hospital. It said Mr. Dulles, 68 years old, probably would be in the hospital for two to three weeks and that he "should be able to return to his desk in approximately six weeks." Mr. Dulles' pulse was reported to be 76, his blood pressure 126/75.

The surgery was performed by Maj. Gen. Leonard D. Heaton, commanding officer of Walter Reed, who had operated on President Eisenhower in June for ileitis. He was assisted today by

Continued on Page 78, Column 3

President Expected to Win; Democratic Congress Seen

New York Times Team Reports

Following are summaries of the apparent voting trends for President and the United States Senate and House of Representatives. They are based on the reports of New York Times teams that have surveyed twenty-seven closely contested states and of correspondents in twenty-one other states.

Presidential Race

By W. H. LAWRENCE

Surveys indicate that President Eisenhower and Vice President Richard M. Nixon will be re-elected on Tuesday by comfortable majorities of both the popular and electoral votes.

Reports from New York Times correspondents who have investigated political sentiment in the forty-eight states indicate these probable results:

For President Eisenhower—A minimum of twenty-seven states with 285 electoral votes, or nineteen more than required for a majority of the 531-member Electoral College.

For Adlai E. Stevenson—A minimum of seven states with seventy-six electoral votes.

Leaning toward President Eisenhower—Eight states with ninety-nine electoral votes.

Leaning toward Mr. Steven-

Continued on Page 69, Column 5

Congressional Races

By WILLIAM S. WHITE

The Democrats appear likely to hold Congress in Tuesday's national elections in spite of the prospect that President Eisenhower will retain the White House for the Republicans.

The outlook thus is for a continuation of the divided form of government that has guided the country since 1954.

A landslide for President Eisenhower would, of course, alter every present prospect. The weight of all current evidence suggests clearly, however, these approximate results:

¶The Democrats should at least retain their present thin margin of control in the Senate —49 Democrats to 47 Republicans.

¶There should be a Democratic House of Representatives again with no less than the

Continued on Page 66, Column 1

Major Sports News

FOOTBALL

Yale, Navy, Syracuse, Columbia and Army won major Eastern contests yesterday. Scores of leading games:

Amherst ..6 Tufts 0
Army ....55 Colgate 46
Columbia ..35 Cornell ...19
Georgia Tech 7 Duke 0
Illinois .....7 Purdue 7
Michigan ..17 Iowa 0
Michigan St..33 Wisconsin ..0
Minnesota ..9 Pitt 9
Navy ....33 Notre Dame..7
Ohio State.. 6 Northwest'n 2
Oklahoma ..27 Colorado ..19
Penn ....28 Harvard ...14
Princeton ..21 Brown 7
Rutgers ....20 Lafayette ..19
Syracuse ...13 Penn State. 9
Tennessee ..0 N. Carolina.. 0
T. C. U. ....7 Baylor 0
U. C. L. A...14 Stanford ..13
W. Virginia ..14 G. Wash'gton 0
Yale ....21 Dartmouth ..0

HORSE RACING

Summer Tan took the Gallant Fox Handicap in track record time at Jamaica.

Details in Section 5.

Mideast Oil Lines Reported Blown Up

By SAM POPE BREWER
Special to The New York Times.

BEIRUT, Lebanon, Nov. 3—Pipelines carrying more than a million barrels of oil daily from Iraq to the Mediterranean coast have stopped operating as a result of the fighting in Egypt.

Reports circulating here were that the Iraq Petroleum Company's three pumping stations in Syria known as T-2, T-3 and T-4 had been blown up and burned.

[At the United Nations an Egyptian spokesman was quoted by The United Press as having said all oil pipelines in every Middle East country except Saudi Arabia had been blown up or shut down.]

No oil installations in Lebanon were attacked. Reports abroad as to this effect are incorrect, according

Continued on Page 26, Column 4

Nutting Quits Post; Churchill For Eden

The text of Churchill letter will be found on Page 24.

Special to The New York Times.

LONDON, Nov. 3—Anthony Nutting, Minister of State in the Foreign Office, resigned from the Government tonight because he strongly disagreed with its policy of armed intervention in Egypt.

The blow to the Government represented by the defection of one of its best-known and most effective young ministers at a critical juncture was balanced by a resounding declaration of support from Sir Winston Churchill.

Writing from his lair at Chartwell, the old lion of British politics blamed Egypt for provoking war with Israel, criticized the United Nations for failing to cooperate fully and

Continued on Page 24, Column 6

Pravda Denounces Nagy for 'Reaction'

By Reuters.

LONDON, Sunday, Nov. 4—The Soviet Communist party newspaper Pravda attacked Premier Imre Nagy of Hungary today "in strong terms", according to the Moscow radio.

Pravda said: "The task of barring the way to reaction in Hungary has to be carried out without the slightest delay; such is the course dictated by events."

The broadcast quoted Pravda as saying: "Imre Nagy turned out to be, objectively speaking, an accomplice of the reactionary forces. Imre Nagy cannot and does not want to fight the dark forces of reaction."

Pravda asserted that it was Mr. Nagy who had requested bringing Soviet troops into Budapest, "as it was vital for the interests of the Socialist regime."

Continued on Page 15, Column 1

This section consists of 140 pages divided into three parts. The news summary and index will be found on Page 95. Society news begins on Page 90 and obituary articles will be found on Pages 86 and 87.

"All the News That's Fit to Print"

The New York Times.

LATE CITY EDITION
Combination of U.S. Weather Bureau forecast: Some cloudiness today; cloudy tonight. Clearing, cooler tomorrow.
Temperature range today: 66—56.
Temperature range yesterday: 65.4—52.2.
Full U.S. Weather Bureau Report, Page 61.

© 1956, by The New York Times Company.

VOL. CVI.—No. 36,082.   Entered as Second-Class Matter, Post Office, New York, N. Y.   NEW YORK, WEDNESDAY, NOVEMBER 7, 1956.   Times Square, New York 36, N. Y. Telephone LAckawanna 4-1000   FIVE CENTS

EISENHOWER BY A LANDSLIDE; BATTLE FOR CONGRESS CLOSE; JAVITS VICTOR OVER WAGNER

Suez Warfare Stopped Under British-French Cease-Fire

MAYOR CONCEDES

Javits, Swept In With the Eisenhower Tide, Wins Stiff Contest

Vote for Senator

CITY SUMMARY

	Javits (Rep.)	Wagner (Dem.-Lib.)
Manhattan	270,146	393,462
Bronx	218,895	374,810
Brooklyn	398,088	605,002
Queens	400,832	372,505
Richmond	49,694	32,881
Total	1,337,655	1,778,660
Upstate	2,362,618	1,478,238
Grand total	3,700,273	3,256,898

All E.D.'s of 4,607 in city and 6,522 of 6,525 upstate.

By DOUGLAS DALES

Attorney General Jacob K. Javits was swept to victory yesterday in the Eisenhower Republican landslide in his race against Mayor Wagner for the United States Senate.

Mayor Wagner conceded defeat in a statement at 1:22 A. M. after the trend to Javits' victory became unmistakable.

Mr. Wagner carried three boroughs in the city—Manhattan, Brooklyn and the Bronx—but lost in Queens and Richmond.

The city-wide complete totals gave Mr. Javits 1,337,655 votes to 1,778,660 for Mayor Wagner. The Mayor's total included 233,560 on the Liberal party line. The Liberal line attracted 404,769 votes in the city four years ago, when the party ran its own candidate for the Senate, George S. Counts.

The Javits' margin was expected to reach 444,000 with the final results. With all city districts and 6,522 of 6,525 districts upstate reported, Mr. Javits had an edge of 443,375.

Mayor Wagner carried two of the fifty-seven upstate counties, Erie and Albany. Eisenhower carried both.

Everywhere outside the city, Mr. Javits ran substantially behind the President's vote. On the other hand, Mayor Wagner ran well ahead of Adlai E. Stevenson, the Democratic candidate for President.

In view of the size of the

Continued on Page 22, Column 2

PRESIDENT SCORES NEW HIGH IN STATE

Plurality Tops 1,500,000 As He Cuts Rival's City Edge

State Presidential Vote

CITY SUMMARY

	Eisenhower (Rep.)	Stevenson (Dem.-Lib.)
Manhattan	299,929	378,018
Bronx	256,909	343,656
Brooklyn	459,703	558,187
Queens	471,144	313,311
Richmond	64,236	190,653
Total	1,551,921	1,614,625
Upstate	2,766,183	1,127,603
Grand total	4,318,104	2,742,228

All E.D.'s of 4,607 in city and 6,522 of 6,525 upstate.

By LEO EGAN

President Eisenhower swept New York yesterday by a plurality that dwarfed all previous records.

With sixty-one of the state's 11,132 election districts still to report this morning, General Eisenhower's margin exceeded 1,500,000.

The previous record for a Presidential plurality in New York was established in 1920, when the late Warren G. Harding, Republican, defeated James M. Cox, Democrat, by 1,139,927.

All the missing districts were in Republican territory upstate.

Continued on Page 22, Column 3

An International Summary:
The Mideast and Hungary

Following are summaries of the leading developments in the Middle East and Europe. The full foreign news report begins on the first page of the second part.

Cease-Fire Is On

Britain and France put a cease-fire into effect and halted their advance in Egypt. Prime Minister Eden told Commons that conditions had been established for an international police force under the United Nations to promote settlement of Middle Eastern issues.

Invaders Hold Canal

The invasion forces claimed control of the Suez Canal Zone. They took Port Said and drove south before the cease-fire became effective.

Egyptians Halt Fight

The Egyptians decided to hold their fire at the deadline in the hope that the United Nations resolution of Nov. 2, providing for withdrawal of all forces behind armistice lines, would be carried out.

Soviet May Send 'Volunteers'

Indications in Moscow were that Soviet "volunteers" who began applying for service

with Egyptian forces might go to the Middle East despite the cease-fire. Moscow broadcast a Cairo appeal for aid.

Troop Withdrawal Asked

Asian and Arab states drafted a United Nations resolution calling on Britain, France and Israel to withdraw their troops from Egypt immediately. A special session of the General Assembly called for last night was postponed until this morning.

Hungarian Battle Persists

Stubborn Hungarian revolutionary forces are continuing to fight the Soviet army in Budapest, according to diplomatic reports received in Vienna. Women and children were said to be fighting alongside the men in a house-to-house struggle. The General Assembly scheduled a special session this afternoon to consider Soviet intervention in Hungary.

EISENHOWER SETS RECORD IN JERSEY

Margin of 700,000 Carries All 21 Counties—G. O. P. Wins 2 Hudson Seats

By GEORGE CABLE WRIGHT

President Eisenhower yesterday scored the greatest victory in New Jersey political history.

With most of the state's ballots tallied early this morning, his margin over Adlai E. Stevenson had soared above 700,000, almost double that of 1952. He became the first candidate in modern times to carry all twenty-one counties.

The President's plurality of his victory was the complete turnabout of Hudson County, for half a century a Democratic stronghold.

This county gave the President a majority of 76,554. In 1952 Mr. Stevenson had carried Hudson by 7,586 votes.

In fact, Republicans swept every county contest. When residents of Hudson awake this morning, it is certain that many will find it hard to believe that for the next two years they will be represented in Congress by not one, but two, Republicans. There was no precedent here for that.

A third Democratic incumbent, Representative Harrison A. Williams Jr., went down to defeat in Union County.

Thus, the Democratic representation of six in the House was cut in half. All eight Republican incumbents were re-elected.

President Eisenhower became the first Presidential candidate to carry the solidly Democratic bailiwick of Jersey City since Warren G. Harding did it in 1920. Long the citadel of the late Frank Hague and now of John Kenny, it gave General Eisenhower a majority of 21,527 over Mr. Stevenson. In 1952 the Democratic candidate had carried the city by 8,251.

But the trouncing of the former Illinois Governor was by no means restricted to Hudson. Camden and Mercer Counties, which also went to Mr. Stevenson in 1952, likewise turned their backs to him this year.

Continued on Page 22, Column 5

BUSH RE-ELECTED IN CONNECTICUT

Plurality for Eisenhower 303,036 Biggest in State in a Presidential Race

By RICHARD H. PARKE
Special to The New York Times.

HARTFORD, Nov. 6—President Eisenhower scored an easy victory in Connecticut today. He carried to victory with him Senator Prescott S. Bush, the Republican incumbent.

The President's plurality of 303,036 votes over Adlai E. Stevenson, Democratic candidate, was the greatest margin the State ever has given a Presidential contender. The previous high figure was 134,128 votes, achieved by President Coolidge in 1924.

The President, whose 1952 plurality of 129,363 was considered of landslide proportions, defeated Mr. Stevenson today by 708,995 votes to 405,959, according to complete but unofficial returns.

The Republican sweep was general throughout the state. It carried in Senator Bush by a plurality of 129,544 votes. He defeated his Democratic opponent, Representative Thomas J. Dodd, by 607,330 to 477,876.

The Republicans also retained

Continued on Page 22, Column 5

SENATE IN DOUBT

Democrats Lag in East on War Issue but Gain in the West

By WILLIAM S. WHITE

The Democrats and Republicans fought along a swaying electoral battle line early today for control of the oncoming Eighty-fifth Congress.

Not all the power of President Eisenhower's landslide victory had been enough to put his Republican Congressional colleagues in front.

The Senate race, in which the Republicans were attempting to overturn a present 49-to-47 Democratic margin of control, was an affair of hairbreadth drama. Small net Republican gains for the House of Representatives were indicated. But whether these would continue or would be enough remained wholly in doubt.

The Republicans needed a net gain of 15 House seats, and the capture of 2 additional and now vacant seats that had been Republican.

The pattern of the Congressional contest was this: The East, more sensitive than other sections to the last-minute issue involved in the Middle Eastern and Central European war crises, on the whole was hitting the Democrats hard. The appeal of "don't change horses in midstream" was strong in this area. In the interior, however, Democratic organizational strength, farm discontent and other factors were turning up great Democratic strength.

Cooper Wins in Kentucky

The position on the Senate in some critical states was this:

KENTUCKY—A gain of one Republican seat in former Senator John Sherman Cooper's defeat of his Democratic challenger, Lawrence Wetherby, for the seat made vacant by the death of Senator Alben W. Barkley. The possibility of another gain for the Republicans in the fact that the assistant Democratic leader of the Senate, Earle C. Clements, was running behind Thruston B. Morton, a former assistant Secretary of State in the Eisenhower Administration.

NEW YORK—A Republican gain in the victory of Jacob K. Javits over Mayor Wagner for the seat being vacated by Senator Herbert H. Lehman, Democrat-Liberal.

OHIO—A Democratic gain in the defeat by Gov. Frank J. Lausche of Senator George H. Bender.

ILLINOIS—Senator Everett M. Dirksen, Republican, ran ahead of his Democratic opponent, Richard Stengel.

PENNSYLVANIA—Joseph S.

Continued on Page 5, Column 1

PRESIDENT EISENHOWER

VICE PRESIDENT NIXON

G. O. P. MAKES BID TO CAPTURE HOUSE

Picks Up 9 Seats in East, but Drive Eases in West —Midwest to Decide

By JOHN D. MORRIS

Republicans got off to a fast start in their bid to recapture control of the House of Representatives, but appeared to lose steam early today as returns trickled in from the West.

As of 3 A. M., results from yesterday's Congressional races indicated a decided Republican trend, with some major upsets for the Democrats. However, with control of nearly two-thirds of the 435 seats still in doubt, victory for either party was far from certain.

The undecided contests were almost entirely in the Midwest, where the issue of declining farm income was a factor favoring the Democrats, and in the Far West.

Such returns as were available from those areas indicated possible Democratic gains in Iowa, California and South Dakota.

Eastward, where the only decisive tallies were available, Republicans had picked up nine seats held by Democrats in the Eighty-fourth Congress while holding their own in all other contests where returns were conclusive. One, in New York City, was subject to a recount. Democrats had failed to capture any Republican seat except one that they took in the Maine vote on Sept. 10.

Republican incumbents were easy victors in a number of contests that had promised to be close.

The most outstanding upsets were in New Jersey, where the Hudson county Democratic stronghold of the late Mayor Frank Hague of Jersey City unseated the two Democratic Representatives, T. James Tumulty and Alfred D. Sieminski in the Thirteenth and Fourteenth Congressional Districts.

Mr. Sieminski lost to Norman H. Roth, Republican. Mr. Tumulty, a 300-pound legislator, was defeated by Vincent J. Dellay, Republican.

A third Democratic incumbent in New Jersey, Harrison A. Williams, lost to Florence P. Dwyer, Republican.

Republicans also picked up one Democratic seat in Connecticut, one in Delaware, one in Pennsylvania, one in Indiana and one

Continued on Page 22, Column 6

Stevenson Concedes Defeat and Wishes President Success

Stevenson and Kefauver talks appear on Page 13.

By HARRISON E. SALISBURY
Special to The New York Times.

CHICAGO, Wednesday, Nov. 7—Adlai E. Stevenson conceded the election of President Eisenhower in a statement made public at 12:25 A. M. Central standard time today (1:25 Eastern standard time).

In a telegram to President Eisenhower the Democratic candidate expressed his understanding of "grave difficulties" that the Administration faced and wished all success to General Eisenhower in the years ahead.

Mr. Stevenson coupled his telegram of congratulations to the President with an appeal to his followers to carry forward in the "crusade for what he called a "New America."

He called on America's leaders to recognize that the nation "wants to face up squarely to the facts of today's world."

"We don't want to draw back from them," Mr. Stevenson said. "We can't. We are ready for the test that we know history has set for us."

Mr. Stevenson in his statement took note of the troubled conditions of the world.

"Beyond the seas, in much of the world, in Russia, in China, in Hungary, in all the trembling satellites, partisan controversy is forbidden and dissent suppressed," Mr. Stevenson said.

Mr. Stevenson also took note

Continued on Page 13, Column 2

EISENHOWER VOWS TO TOIL FOR PEACE

Hails Landslide Re-election as Proof Nation Wants 'Modern Republicanism'

Texts of the Eisenhower and Nixon talks on Page 12.

By RUSSELL BAKER
Special to The New York Times.

WASHINGTON, Wednesday, Nov. 7—President Eisenhower hailed his landslide re-election victory today as proof that his "modern Republicanism has proved itself and America has approved of modern Republicanism."

He pledged in a victory statement early this morning to work with "whatever talents the good God has given me for 168,000,000 Americans here at home and for peace in the world."

Addressing a jubilant crowd of party workers at Republican election headquarters here and the nation, over television, the President declared that so long as the G.O.P. pursued the "ideals, the hopes and aspirations" of the people, it would continue to flourish.

"If it is anything less," he said, "it is only a conspiracy to seize power. And the Republican party is not that."

'Looks to the Future'

Thus, in his moment of triumph, General Eisenhower claimed a sweeping triumph for what his Administration's philosophers have styled the "new Republicanism" and what he himself termed this morning "modern Republicanism."

"Modern Republicanism," he said, "looks to the future and this means it will gain constantly new recruits." So long as it continued to remain "modern," he added, it would "continue to increase in power and influence for decades to come."

So long as it clings to its "modern" ideals, the President declared, it would "point the way to peace among nations and prosperity, advancing standards here at home in which everyone will share."

The President delivered his victory statement at 1:45 A. M. about fifteen minutes after this restive crowd gathered in the mammoth ballroom of the Sheraton-Park Hotel had heard Adlai E. Stevenson concede defeat in Chicago.

General Eisenhower had been waiting upstairs in a third-floor suite for three and a half hours.

Continued on Page 12, Column 1

---

41 STATES TO G.O.P.

President Sweeps All the North and West, Scores in South

By JAMES RESTON

Dwight David Eisenhower won yesterday the most spectacular Presidential election victory since Franklin D. Roosevelt submerged Alfred M. Landon in 1936.

The smiling 66-year-old hero of the Normandy invasion, who was in a Denver hospital recuperating from a heart attack just a year ago today, thus became the first Republican in this century to win two successive Presidential elections. William McKinley did it in 1896 and 1900.

Adlai E. Stevenson of Illinois, who lost to Mr. Eisenhower four years ago, thirty-nine states to nine, conceded defeat at 1:25 this morning.

At 4:45 A. M. President Eisenhower had won forty-one states as seven for Mr. Stevenson. His electoral lead at that time was 457 to 74 for Stevenson, and his popular vote was 25,071,331 to 18,337,434—up 2 per cent over 1952. Two hundred and sixty-six electoral votes are needed for election.

Victory in All Areas

This was a national victory in every conceivable way. It started in Connecticut. It swept every state in New England. It took New York by a plurality of more than 1,500,000. It carried all the Middle Atlantic states, all the Midwest, all the Rocky Mountain states and everything beyond the Rockies.

More than that, the Republican tide swept along the border states and to the South, carried all the states won by the G.O.P. there in 1952—Virginia, Texas, Tennessee and Florida—and even took Louisiana for the first time since the Hayes-Tilden election of 1876.

For the President and his 43-year old Vice Presidential running mate, Richard M. Nixon of California, who carried much of the Republican campaign, it was a more impressive victory than for the Republican party.

So close were many races for

Continued on Page 3, Column 3

CLARK LEADS DUFF IN PENNSYLVANIA

Democrat's Edge Dropping —President Takes State

By WILLIAM G. WEART
Special to The New York Times.

PHILADELPHIA, Wednesday, Nov. 7—Joseph S. Clark Jr., former Mayor of Philadelphia, was running ahead of Senator James H. Duff early today.

But his margin was ebbing as returns from rural areas and small towns began to offset the lead he piled up in large cities.

President Eisenhower won the state's thirty-two electoral votes by a plurality that was steadily mounting.

Mr. Clark expressed disappointment at the defeat of his party's standard-bearer. He attributed General Eisenhower's victory to his 'personal popularity.' Mr. Clark's campaign manager, Mayor Richardson Dilworth of Philadelphia, said the President's re-election was due to the "emotion caused by the war situation."

In the event the final tally in the Senatorial race is close, an estimated 50,000 absentee votes cast by servicemen and hospitalized veterans may decide the outcome. Under the law, absentee ballots are mailed to county

Continued on Page 15, Column 6

Coudert Wins in Close Contest; Vote in Queens 7th Rechecked

By CLAYTON KNOWLES

The Republicans emerged early today from a hard-fought Congressional campaign with a possible net gain of one seat in the state delegation to the House of Representatives.

At 4:20 A. M. a final decision rested on the outcome of the race in the Seventh district of Queens. Here Representative James J. Delaney, Democratic incumbent, claimed victory at 4:15 A. M. by forty votes, but a final tally was unavailable.

An hour and a half earlier, Delaney supporters were conceding the election of Joseph Stockinger, a Republican, but the contest was so close that all of Queens' 1,402 districts were being rechecked.

The announced vote for 202 districts was 72,196 for Mr. Stockinger to 72,112 for Mr. De-

lancy, who ran with Liberal party backing.

The prospect that the Republicans would pick up a House seat in the state, giving them twenty-seven of a total of forty-three, arose when Representative Frederic R. Coudert Jr. staged an eleventh-hour triumph in the Manhattan Seventeenth District.

He prevailed once more over Anthony B. Akers, Democrat-Liberal who had come within 214 votes of defeating him in 1954. This time Mr. Coudert won, 68,862 votes to 66,207.

If Mr. Delaney should go to defeat, the Republicans would have seven of the twenty-five House seats filled in the city.

President Eisenhower's land-

Continued on Page 22, Column 6

Electoral Vote by States

State	Elec. vote Eisenhower	Elec. vote Stevenson	State	Elec. vote Eisenhower	Elec. vote Stevenson
Ala.	..	11	Nev.	3	..
Ariz.	4	..	N. H.	4	..
Calif.	32	..	N. J.	16	..
Colo.	6	..	N. M.	4	..
Conn.	8	..	N. Y.	45	..
Del.	3	..	N. C.	..	14
Fla.	10	..	N. D.	4	..
Ga.	..	12	Ohio	25	..
Idaho	4	..	Okla.	8	..
Ill.	27	..	Ore.	6	..
Ind.	13	..	Pa.	32	..
Iowa	10	..	R. I.	4	..
Kan.	8	..	S. C.	..	8
Ky.	10	..	S. D.	4	..
La.	10	..	Tenn.	11	..
Me.	5	..	Texas	24	..
Md.	9	..	Utah	4	..
Mass.	16	..	Vt.	3	..
Mich.	20	..	Va.	12	..
Minn.	11	..	Wash.	9	..
Miss.	..	8	W. Va.	8	..
Mo.	13	..	Wisc.	12	..
Mont.	4	..	Wyo.	3	..
Neb.	6	..	Total	457	74

Continued on Page 12, Column 1

"All the News That's Fit to Print"

The New York Times.

LATE CITY EDITION
Condensation of U.S. Weather Bureau forecast:
Rain changing to snow today; much colder tonight. Fair tomorrow.
Temperature range today: 20—25.
Temperature range yesterday: 40—30.2
Full U.S. Weather Bureau Report, Page 38.

VOL. CVI..No. 36,146.

Entered as Second-Class Matter,
Post Office, New York, N. Y.

NEW YORK, THURSDAY, JANUARY 10, 1957.

© 1957, by The New York Times Company.

Times Square, New York 36, N. Y.
Telephone Lackawanna 4-1000

FIVE CENTS

HARRIMAN URGES NEW WELFARE AID AND CUT IN TAXES

DELIVERS MESSAGE

G. O. P. Calls Program 'Moderate'—State's Revenues Increase

Text of Harriman's message is on Pages 17, 18 and 19.

Special to The New York Times.

ALBANY, Jan. 9—Governor Harriman proposed today an increase in state social welfare benefits and an expansion of state services in several fields. He also asked, to the degree warranted, cuts in personal income and unincorporated business taxes.

His program was contained in an 18,000-word annual message which he delivered in person at the opening session of the 180th Legislature. A good part of the program had been disclosed unofficially in advance.

Of the proposals revealed today for the first time, the most startling was a suggestion that up to $150 for hospital expenses be provided as an additional benefit for 4,653,000 wage-earners covered by the state's Disability Benefits Law.

The Governor's message provided no additional details. His staff is preparing legislation on the subject.

Program Jointly Financed

This law provides for disability payments up to $40 a week for those whose wages are suspended because of an illness or disability not related to their employment. The benefits are financed by joint contributions of employers and employes.

Hospital benefits under the Governor's program would be financed without any additional employe contribution. Their cost has been estimated roughly at $15,000,000 a year. The plan has strong support from organized labor.

Democratic legislators acting on Mayor Wagner's behalf introduced fourteen measures today designed to aid the city administration in one form or another. The most important measure would provide the city with $100,000 a year in new revenue by revising the system of bidding for public contracts.

One of the notable omissions in the Governor's message was any discussion of Mayor Wagner's proposals for revising financial relations between the state and city governments. At various times in the past Mr. Harriman has endorsed, partly at least, the Mayor's repeated assertion that the city is receiving less than it deserves. This

Continued on Page 16, Column 4

RIBICOFF PROGRAM AVOIDS RISE IN TAX

More Pay for Teachers and Court Reforms Are Urged

By RICHARD H. PARKE

HARTFORD, Jan. 9—Gov. Abraham A. Ribicoff outlined today a broad legislative program that he said could be achieved without new taxes or increases in current levies.

He recommended additional expenditures in fields ranging from atomic energy to mental health. The proposals were designed, he declared, to "allow the state to live within its budget."

The Governor, a Democrat, offered his program to the opening session of the Thirty-sixth Biennial General Assembly. Republicans control the Legislature by the largest majority they have held in thirty years.

Among the Governor's major recommendations were these:

¶A $60 increase in the $180-a-year cost-of-living pay rise for state workers.

¶A $21-a-pupil increase in state aid for education, to be used exclusively for "underwriting desperately needed pay raises for 15,500 school teachers."

¶A court reform plan that would replace the local court system with a system of state courts staffed by full-time judges.

¶The construction of a $1,000,-

Continued on Page 21, Column 2

Rise in Meat Prices Predicted by U. S.

By WILLIAM M. BLAIR

Special to The New York Times.

WASHINGTON, Jan. 9—The Department of Agriculture forecast today that consumers would pay higher prices for meat this year.

Total meat production will be less than in 1956 to raise prices, particularly on pork. Retail prices on choice beef will stay above 1956 levels throughout the winter, and spring and likely climb again in the fall, but at a slower rate.

There are ample supplies of beef, the department reported, but it cast a wary eye on the drought in the Great Plains states. Persistent drought could lead to still higher prices

Continued on Page 30, Column 1

STATE G. O. P. SPLIT; SPRAGUE IS TARGET

Leader's Policies Opposed—Appointment of Lefkowitz Brings Revolt Into Open

By LEO EGAN

Special to The New York Times.

ALBANY, Jan. 9—A deep split in the Republican party has been brought into the open by the controversy that preceded today's election of Louis J. Lefkowitz as state Attorney General.

Substantial forces are in revolt against what they regard as the domination of the party by J. Russel Sprague, Republican leader of Nassau County. This was behind the severe criticism heaped on L. Judson Morhouse, state chairman, at last night's caucus of the Republican members of the Assembly. Mr. Sprague was not mentioned, but it was apparent that he and not Mr. Morhouse had been the real target.

Few Republicans will dispute that Mr. Sprague is the dominant party leader in the state. Many hold that his leadership is sound and constructive and has been responsible for improving the party's position.

Even though it was later repudiated, an implied criticism of Mr. Lefkowitz' selection by Senator Jacob K. Javits appeared

Continued on Page 20, Column 2

2 SENATE LEADERS BACK COMPROMISE ON CLOSURE RULE

Johnson Supports Knowland in Resolution for Easier Curb on Filibusters

By JOHN D. MORRIS

Special to The New York Times.

WASHINGTON, Jan. 9—Leaders of both parties and thirty other Senators joined today in sponsoring a "middle-ground" proposal to strengthen the Senate's hand in dealing with filibusters.

The Republican leader, Senator William F. Knowland of California, introduced a resolution changing Senate rules to permit closure, or limitation of debate, by two-thirds of the Senators present and voting. Two-thirds of the entire membership, or sixty-four Senators, now is required.

In a surprise move, Senator Lyndon B. Johnson of Texas, the Democratic leader, signed up as a co-sponsor. Nine other Democrats and twenty-one Republicans promptly added their names.

Hope for Action Revived

Today's development revived hope that something would be done this session to curb the power of Senate minorities to block action on legislation by the filibuster—the tactic of unlimited dilatory debate to prevent a vote.

The resolution must be approved by the Committee on Rules and Administration, but leaders spread the word privately that they would use their full influence to clear that and other prospective obstacles to early Senate action.

It was said they were even prepared to break a probable filibuster against the resolution when it reached the floor. This would be attempted, according to tentative plans, by holding the Senate in round-the-clock session to wear down filibustering opponents.

Alternatives Proposed

Alternatives to the Knowland-Johnson proposals were introduced today by two Republican Senators, Irving M. Ives of New York and Prescott S. Bush of Connecticut.

In addition, Senator Hubert H. Humphrey, Democrat of Minnesota, introduced a resolution to declare "void and of no further effect" the present rule's provision that closure cannot be invoked in debate on a motion to consider rules changes.

This so-called "built-in filibuster clause" would be repealed by the Knowland resolution without testing its constitutionality as contemplated by Senator Humphrey. Vice President Richard M. Nixon held it to be unconstitutional in an advisory

Continued on Page 21, Column 1

DULLES OPPOSES MOVE TO WEAKEN PLAN ON MIDEAST

Rejects Substitute Proposal as Violating U. N. Charter—Gordon Supports Him

By JOSEPH A. LOFTUS

Special to The New York Times.

WASHINGTON, Jan. 9—The Eisenhower Administration took a firm stand today against a move to water down its proposals for meeting Communist penetration of the Middle East.

John Foster Dulles, Secretary of State, raised detailed objections to a resolution drafted by an anonymous author as a possible substitute for the Administration's proposals.

The Administration's draft resolution submitted to Congress last week would provide for economic and military aid for Middle East nations and authorize the President to use United States forces in the event of overt Communist aggression against any of these countries.

Substance of Proposal

The proposed substitute, which Speaker Sam Rayburn said had been prepared by a former high official of the Government, would simply state:

"The United States regards as vital to her interest the preservation of the independence and integrity of the states of the Middle East and, if necessary, will use her armed forces to that end."

Mr. Dulles said the substitute also would call for military action that would violate the United Nations Charter and the position the United States took in opposing British and French military efforts "to overthrow the Nasser regime."

Representative Thomas S. Gordon, Democrat of Illinois and chairman of the House Foreign Affairs Committee, agreed with Mr. Dulles.

Democrats Surprised

However, other Democrats on the committee expressed shock and surprise at what one called the "baldness" of the Secretary's comment that the British and French sought to overthrow the regime of Gamal Abdel Nasser, President of Egypt.

The official British position, as stated by Prime Minister Anthony Eden on Oct. 31 was: "In entering the Suez Canal area, we are only protecting a vital international waterway."

Despite the fact that no one has confessed parenthood of the "short form" approach to the Middle East problem, Secretary Dulles was considerably exer-

Continued on Page 5, Column 2

EDEN RESIGNS, PLEADING ILL HEALTH; BUTLER OR MACMILLAN TO GET POST; EISENHOWER AND DULLES IN TRIBUTE

REACTION IS MIXED

Both Regret and Relief Expressed in Capital—Cairo Jubilant

By DANA ADAMS SCHMIDT

Special to The New York Times.

WASHINGTON, Jan. 9—Washington heard the news of Prime Minister Eden's resignation with a mixture of regret and relief.

President Eisenhower and Secretary of State Dulles, overlooking the sharp differences they had had with Sir Anthony over the Suez Canal and the invasion of Egypt, issued friendly tributes to the British leader.

Some Administration officials observed privately that Sir Anthony's departure might hasten the repair of the British-United States alliance as a main pillar in the foreign policies of both countries.

[Sir Anthony's resignation brought jubilation in Cairo, where it was felt his departure would make negotiations on resumption of relations easier. Paris regarded Sir Anthony as a sad but inevitable casualty of military action in Suez.]

Butler's Suez View Cited

Those Washington officials who thought relations with London would be strengthened noted reports that R. A. Butler, who might succeed Sir Anthony, had opposed the invasion of Egypt.

Others, however, expressed concern that the resignation might lead to elections in Britain and a Labor Government that might agree with the United States on Middle East policy but prove more difficult in other respects.

Washington was by no means surprised at the resignation. It had been foreseen by highly placed officials as the ultimate consequence of the Suez Canal venture.

They had watched the Prime Minister's difficulties increasing since his visit to Washington just a year ago in a vain attempt to gain backing for his Middle Eastern and other policies.

Only a few weeks ago, while Sir Anthony was convalescing in Jamaica, B. W. I., the White House rejected British suggestions that he again visit President Eisenhower.

Today, however, the President expressed hope that his "old and good friend," Sir Anthony, would soon recover and enjoy "many useful years of happiness." James C. Hagerty, White House press secretary, made public the following statement from the President:

"I have just been informed of

Continued on Page 4, Column 4

STEPS DOWN: Sir Anthony Eden going to Buckingham Palace yesterday to resign as Prime Minister of Britain.

Associated Press Wirephoto via Radio from London

Europeans See U.S. As Bypassing Allies In Mideast Policy

By HAROLD CALLENDER

Special to The New York Times.

PARIS, Jan. 9 — President Eisenhower's plan to defend the Middle East against Communist aggression is regarded by some European foreign affairs experts as a policy not of isolationism but of isolation.

It is seen as a move by the United States alone, even though in conformity with the United Nations Charter.

Much discussion has taken place among diplomats and students of the area since President Eisenhower formulated his doctrine Saturday in a speech published and studied here this week. He proposed that Congress authorize him to use the armed forces of the United States, if necessary, against any Communist or Communist-dominated aggression in the Middle East.

Although this doctrine is regarded as new by some Americans, the impression in Europe is that it amounts to a reassertion and geographical extension of the policy of containment of Soviet power. This policy was formed under the Truman Administration when Dean Acheson was Secretary of State, and a Republican, the late Senator Arthur H. Vandenberg, then chairman of the Senate Foreign Relations Committee, cooperated in a bi-partisan foreign policy.

But the containment policy, as applied in Europe, took the form of the North Atlantic alliance, which was extended to Asia when Turkey joined it. So the alliance has a flank in the Middle East.

At the meeting in December of the North Atlantic Council, which directs the alliance, the

Continued on Page 6, Column 3

PRESIDENT PLANS OATH IN PRIVATE

Only His Family and Nixon's to See Jan. 20 Swearing-In

Special to The New York Times.

WASHINGTON, Jan. 9—The White House reversed itself today and ruled that President Eisenhower and Vice President Richard M. Nixon would take their second term oaths on Sunday, Jan. 20, at a private, family ceremony in the White House.

Earlier plans had called for live telecasting and other reporting of the first ceremony.

The formal public inauguration will be held in front of the Capitol Building beginning at noon on Monday, Jan. 21. This ceremony will be televised and broadcast nationally.

The decision on the private ceremony was announced as the Union Message that General Eisenhower will deliver in person before a joint session of the House of Representatives and Senate at 12:30 P. M. tomorrow.

The advance word from the White House was that the message would not contain any major legislative surprises and would include few specific legislative proposals. The president of the legislation will be reserved for the Budget Message, which also was reviewed at the Cabinet

Continued on Page 22, Column 1

Asia-Africa Bloc Will Ask U. N. To Call on Israelis to Quit Egypt

By THOMAS J. HAMILTON

Special to The New York Times.

UNITED NATIONS, N. Y., Jan. 9—The Asian-African group decided today to seek another resolution by the General Assembly calling for the withdrawal of Israeli forces "behind the armistice demarcation lines."

This move was requested by Egypt, and the group appointed a subcommittee to draft a resolution to this effect. The subcommittee is composed of Jordan, Indonesia, India, Pakistan and Liberia. Egypt will participate in its discussions.

Although some Asian sources said the Assembly might be asked to take up the resolution this week, others said that it would not be done until next week.

Israel has withdrawn from part of the Sinai Peninsula, in fact Israeli forces are now east of a line extending southward from the Mediterranean near El Arish.

However, Israel still holds the Gaza Strip, the rest of the Sinai Peninsula, including the southernmost tip, where Egyptian coastal guns commanded the channel leading into the Gulf of Aqaba, and two small islands at the mouth of the gulf that belong to Saudi Arabia but that previously were administered by Egypt.

Mrs. Golda Meir, Israeli Foreign Minister, returned to Israel yesterday. She left the impression that Israel would not evacuate the remaining territory unless the United Nations provided guarantees against the resumption of Egyptian guerrilla raids and against the revival of the blockade of the Israeli port of Elath, on the Gulf of Aqaba.

No information on the nature of the guarantees Israel wants

Continued on Page 6, Column 6

SUEZ KEY FACTOR

Queen Is Expected to Appoint New Prime Minister Today

By DREW MIDDLETON

Special to The New York Times.

LONDON, Jan. 9—Sir Anthony Eden resigned tonight as Prime Minister of Britain, pleading ill health.

His health, and his spirit both have broken under the pressures aroused in Britain and abroad by his policy of intervention in Egypt.

Queen Elizabeth II is expected to choose his successor tomorrow. The choice lies between Richard Austen Butler, Lord Privy Seal and leader of the House of Commons, and Harold Macmillan, Chancellor of the Exchequer.

Political circles late tonight seemed to be swinging to the support of Mr. Butler as Sir Anthony's successor. But there is as yet no firm indication that "Rab," as he is known, can command a majority of the Conservative members of the House of Commons.

The new Conservative Prime Minister will face a Laborite Opposition clamoring for a general election and a national situation in which Britain's economic and international position has deteriorated sharply from the bright prospects that prevailed when Sir Anthony assumed office 644 days ago on April 6, 1955.

Bids Colleagues Good-by

A career that was thirty-three years in the making ended in Sir Anthony's forty-minute interview at Buckingham Palace with the Queen. Then he returned to 10 Downing Street to announce his decision and to say good-by to his colleagues in the Cabinet and other members of his Ministry. Later, with Lady Eden, he drove to Chequers, the country residence of British Prime Ministers.

After Sir Anthony returned from the palace the following statement was issued:

"It is announced from Buckingham Palace that the Right Honorable Sir Anthony Eden, M. P. (Prime Minister and First Lord of the Treasury) had an audience of the Queen this evening and tendered his resignation as Prime Minister and First Lord of the Treasury, which Her Majesty was pleased to accept."

The Prime Minister himself amplified this announcement in a personal statement from 10 Downing Street. The statement said:

"When I returned to this

Continued on Page 2, Column 3

FRENCH AGAIN BID U. N. SHUN ALGERIA

Premier Presents France as a Plaintiff Against Arab Nations—Defines Aims

By HENRY GINIGER

Special to The New York Times.

PARIS, Jan. 9—The French Government told the United Nations today to keep hands off Algeria. The issue is expected to be discussed at this session of the General Assembly.

A 5,000-word document, reiterating the French contention that the United Nations was incompetent to deal with the Algerian problem and explaining how France proposed to handle it, was read by Premier Guy Mollet to a large group of newsmen at his office.

Approved at a special meeting of the Cabinet in the morning, the document constituted the first major reply to the anti-French offensive launched by the Arab nations. It presented France not as a defendant but as a plaintiff against Egypt and other nations, accusing them of interference in an internal French affair.

The text contained almost nothing that had not been said before. The Premier said as much, declaring he would not be showing much consideration for the United Nations if he were to announce some radical change in the French attitude. To many observers the Government's Algerian policy appeared to be at the point where it was when the Cabinet took office in February of last year. Then, as now, it could offer no specific assurances

Continued on Page 6, Column 4

GAITSKELL SEEKS BRITISH ELECTION

Laborite, at Harvard, Says Eden Did 'the Right Thing'

Special to The New York Times.

CAMBRIDGE, Mass., Jan. 9—Hugh Gaitskell, leader of the British Labor party, called today for a general election. He indicated his belief that his party might win such a test.

The 50-year-old party spokesman, who would be Britain's Prime Minister in the event of a Labor victory, said at a news conference at Harvard University he was "sorry that Sir Anthony Eden's health has not recovered despite his trip to Jamaica."

"He has done the right thing in resigning," Mr. Gaitskell added. "But as the whole Cabinet has publicly identified themselves completely with the foreign policy pursued by the late Government in the last three months I consider that there ought now to be a general election in Britain so that the country can have an opportunity to choose a new Government."

Mr. Gaitskell is at Harvard to give two lectures. He delivered the second tonight, calling for greater cooperation among the countries of the North Atlantic Treaty Organization. He is

Continued on Page 4, Column 6

Javits Takes Oath and Brings Senate to Full Strength

Jacob K. Javits and Vice President Nixon re-enacting the induction ceremony yesterday.

Associated Press Wirephoto

Special to The New York Times.

WASHINGTON, Jan. 9—Jacob K. Javits, Republican of New York, took the oath of office today and thus brought the Senate to its full complement of ninety-six members.

The new Senator had delayed taking his oath until after New York State Republican leaders named a man to succeed him as State Attorney General. They selected Louis J. Lefkowitz.

Senator Javits told reporters his resignation became effective in Albany at 12:56 P. M. today. He appeared on the Senate floor promptly at 1 P. M. but was not sworn in until 1:22 because the Senate

was engaged in one of its favorite pastimes, the eulogizing of a member.

The member in this case was Senator William F. Knowland, the Republican leader, who yesterday announced his intention to retire two years from now at the end of his present term.

Senator Javits was sworn in by Vice President Richard M. Nixon. He received a standing ovation of applause by the Senate and spectators, including Mrs. Javits, two of their children, Joy, 5 years old, and Joshua, 7, and his brother and a nephew.

Later the Senator told re-

porters that he was "certainly not happy" with his assignment to the District of Columbia and Rules Committees. But he said he was not a novice in Congress, having served eight years in the House, and had great respect for the Senate's procedures.

Freshman Senators traditionally are assigned to the less desirable committees, and such was the case with Mr. Javits. In recent years the Democrats have been handed out new Senators one good committee post, but Republicans usually have operated on the last-come last-served basis

Continued on Page 20, Column 1

"All the News That's Fit to Print"

The New York Times.

LATE CITY EDITION
U.S. Weather Bureau report (Page 49) forecasts:
Rain, drizzle early today; brightening later. Fair and warm tomorrow.
Temp. range: 64—54. Yesterday: 59.6—50.9

VOL CVI..No. 36,252. © 1957, by The New York Times Company. NEW YORK, FRIDAY, APRIL 26, 1957. Times Square, New York 36, N. Y. Telephone LAckawanna 4-1000 FIVE CENTS

EISENHOWER ASKS FULL DISCLOSURE OF LABOR FUNDS

Administration Calls for Laws to Wipe Out 'Abomination' of Union Racketeering

RANK AND FILE PRAISED

President and Mitchell Put Stress on Moves to Block 'Punitive' Legislation

Text of Eisenhower statement appears on Page 14.

By W. H. LAWRENCE
Special to The New York Times.

AUGUSTA, Ga., April 25—The Eisenhower Administration decided today to ask Congress for full public disclosure of union receipts and expenditures.

James P. Mitchell, Secretary of Labor, reported the interim legislative program for labor after a ninety-minute conference with President Eisenhower at the President's temporary office at the Augusta National Golf Club.

Mr. Mitchell said the legislative proposals had grown out of evidence of improper practices already developed by the Senate Select Committee on Improper Activities in the Labor or Management Field. The committee is headed by Senator John L. McClellan, Democrat of Arkansas.

Secretary Mitchell warned against a "headlong" rush "impelled by the hysteria of the moment to secure punitive legislation aimed at undermining or weakening the general body of organized labor."

A Request Renewed

He said the Administration proposals were designed to strengthen the rights of the union rank and file and to "help the American labor movement to clean house in those areas where they need help."

Specifically, the President and the Secretary of Labor renewed their three-year-old request to Congress that it pass laws providing for the registration, reporting and disclosure of funds deposited under welfare and pension plans.

In addition, Secretary Mitchell said the President also had approved a proposal that Congress authorize the Labor Department to make public the reports now filed with it concerning union funds in general under the Taft-Hartley Act. Those reports now are not made public.

Secretary Mitchell indicated that the Administration later might ask Congress for Federal review and audits of the union financial statements. These are

Continued on Page 14, Column 3

CITY BARS HOUSING AT CANCER CENTER

Relocation Problems Cited —Bridge Routes Filed

By CHARLES G. BENNETT

After months of hearings, the Board of Estimate yesterday rejected a proposal to build a $6,500,000 middle-income housing project in Yorkville.

The proposal had been made by the Memorial Center for Cancer and Allied Diseases, the Sloan Kettering Institute and the Rockefeller Institute for Medical Research.

The board acted on two other major items of city business.

It received and referred to city agencies the plans for Brooklyn and Staten Island approach routes to the Narrows Bridge and for the Queens and Bronx approaches to the Throgs Neck Bridge. Robert Moses, chairman of the Triborough Bridge and Tunnel Authority, submitted the plans.

The board approved $25,000 to put under way initial studies of the rehabilitation of the downtown area of Brooklyn, including the feasibility of a sports center that would serve as a home for the Brooklyn Dodgers baseball team.

In the case of the rejected Yorkville project, the sponsoring institutions had sought permission for nearly two years to construct two buildings. One would be for nurses and would contain 287 apartments. The other was for technical, research and professional personnel. It was to have 189 apartments.

The site for the proposed im-

Continued on Page 17, Column 5

CONFER IN GEORGIA: President Eisenhower with James P. Mitchell, Secretary of Labor, in Augusta yesterday. They drew plans for laws dealing with labor unions.
Associated Press Wirephoto

M'CLELLAN WARNS OF 'GANGSTERISM'

Tells Publishers Momentum of Rackets Perils U. S. —Mrs. Luce Chides Press

Text of McClellan's speech will be found on Page 16.

The chairman of the Senate committee investigating union rackets said last night that it intended to continue its exposures of wrongdoing until Congress had enough information to "clean up the mess."

Senator John L. McClellan, Democrat of Arkansas, made his statement at a dinner of the Bureau of Advertising of the American Newspaper Publishers Association. He predicted that the investigation, which he said was still in its early stages, would produce legislation to protect union members, management and the public.

The committee chairman, speaking at the Waldorf-Astoria Hotel, warned that racketeering now had enough momentum to bring about a "gangsterism economy" and threaten liberty in the United States if it were not stopped.

'Shock Troops' of Diplomacy

Mrs. Clare Boothe Luce, former Ambassador to Italy, urged the press and public to support the American Foreign Service. Mrs. Luce spoke of the "shock troops of our diplomatic front lines" and termed them a vital instrument for the preservation of world peace.

The occasion, the Bureau of Advertising's forty-fourth annual dinner, marked the end of the seventy-first annual convention of the bureau's parent organization, the American Newspaper Publishers Association. It also marked the end of New York's annual Press Week.

As Senator McClellan spoke, preparations were made for a closed hearing on labor-management abuses in the New York area at the United States Court House today. Three officials of one of the union locals under investigation were indicted by a New York County grand jury yesterday on charges of steal-

Continued on Page 16, Column 2

De Sapio Leadership Extolled by Wagner Before Party Chiefs

By CLAYTON KNOWLES

Ringing praise for Carmine G. De Sapio and predictions of a great victory for Mayor Wagner this fall marked speeches at the annual dinner of the New York County Democratic Committee last night.

The Mayor, a candidate for re-election, was lavish in acclaiming the "forceful, dynamic, political brilliance" of Mr. De Sapio, leader of the Tammany organization for the last eight years.

About 2,200 persons attended the $50-a-plate dinner, which was held at the Commodore Hotel.

In his text Mr. Wagner said also that Mr. De Sapio had set "an example of undivided allegiance to the principles of good government—of government devoted exclusively to the needs and the welfare of the people."

Called Friend of Decency

Extemporizing in delivery, he added that Mr. De Sapio had been the "stalwart friend of decency, honesty and integrity in government." He said he was "proud to call him my friend."

The extent of the accolade took on significance in view of the start next Monday of public hearings by the Republican-dominated legislative committee into the Joseph (Socks) Lanza parole case.

Lanza has Tammany connections. And there has been reference to aid sought from "the man with the glasses," Mr. De Sapio, who wears dark tinted glasses, has scoffed at the suggestion that the reference might have been to him.

In his own speech last night, Mr. De Sapio said that he still felt, as he had when he as-

Continued on Page 12, Column 4

Recording by Lanza Is Reported Missing

By LEO EGAN

A tape recording of one conversation between Joseph (Socks) Lanza and his wife and others at the Westchester County jail was reported missing yesterday.

The disclosure was made by Arthur L. Reuter, Acting State Commissioner of Investigation. The Commissioner is conducting one of two investigations into the dismissal of parole violation charges against Lanza, a convicted extortionist.

The missing recording was made a half-hour before Lanza's release on Feb. 20. He had been arrested as a parole violator on Feb. 5. His release followed the dismissal of the charges against him by Parole Commissioner James R. Stone.

Commissioner Stone subsequently resigned from the Parole Board while being questioned about his decision to

Continued on Page 15, Column 2

PRESIDENT PLANS OIL IMPORT STUDY; SEES PERIL TO U.S.

Gets O.D.M. Report Warning of Rise in Foreign Fuel —Quotas May Result

By RICHARD E. MOONEY
Special to The New York Times.

WASHINGTON, April 25—President Eisenhower announced today he would order an investigation to determine whether imports of crude oil threatened national security. He asserted "there is reason for the belief" that such a threat exists.

The President, in Augusta, Ga., acted after receiving advice from Gordon Gray, Director of the Office of Defense Mobilization. Mr. Gray said that the trend of imports and forecasts for coming months had given reason to believe there was a threat. Mr. Gray released his and the President's memoranda at a news conference here.

If the President finds a threat to national security, he is required by law to take action that will reduce imports. This presumably would be done by placing them under quota limitations or by raising the tariff.

Independents Skeptical

General Eisenhower asked Mr. Gray to explore the possibility of limiting imports by voluntary action. This would be done while the Presidential investigation was under way.

Major importers might prefer voluntary restrictions, rather than legal quota limitations or higher tariff charges. But the independent producers in this country, with no overseas operations, feel efforts for voluntary curtailment are futile.

The question of import limitation has been introduced by the appeal of a number of independent companies. They contend that national security is being threatened because increased oil imports discourage exploration for new oil resources in this country—resources on which the United States would depend in time of war.

Voluntary Pact Sought

The Office of Defense Mobilization has tried for two years to get voluntary agreement among importers. Mr. Gray's certification to the President that a threat exists is the most forceful step that has been taken so far. In fact, it is the first such action under the law—Section 7 of the Trade Agreements Extension (Reciprocal Trade) Act of 1955.

The actual Presidential order for an investigation awaits the selection of a group to make the study, and the preparation of necessary papers.

The United States produced more than 2,600,000,000 barrels (forty-two gallons a barrel) of crude oil last year, or an average of more than 7,100,000 barrels a day. Refineries consumed a little more than 2,900,000,000 barrels.

On the basis of pure physical capacity, the nation's wells

Continued on Page 5, Column 4

KING SCORES CAIRO

Installs a New Cabinet —Vows Fight to the Finish on Reds

By OSGOOD CARUTHERS
Special to The New York Times.

AMMAN, Jordan, April 25—King Hussein proclaimed today a fight to the finish against a conspiracy to overthrow him. He imposed martial law and formed a new Government.

The 21-year-old monarch charged openly for the first time that the conspiracy was getting its support from Egypt.

Moving swiftly, the King placed the principal cities of Amman, Jerusalem, Ramallah, Nablus and Irbid under a total curfew. He also placed the Jordanian police force under direct command of the Army.

[The Associated Press reported from Amman that King Hussein had abolished Jordan's ten political parties.]

The monarch appeared to have emerged as a mature and grimly determined fighter, defending his throne against efforts by Egypt and Syria to turn Jordan into their anti-Western satellite.

His imposition of an armored fist on the Palestinian part of Jordan and his warning, in a pre-dawn broadcast, that "conspiracies might take away the remaining part of Arab Palestine" made clear that he would fight to prevent cession of the west bank and would be ready against possible Israeli attack.

Plans Carefully Laid

Events moved swiftly last night, but it was evident that the King's plans had been carefully laid. During the early evening the Government of Premier Hussein Fakhri Khalidi finally carried out an earlier decision to quit.

The Khalidi Government had been formed on the basis of support of all parties, including the National Socialists, the left-wing Baath (Resurrection) party and their pro-Communist supporters. That support was withdrawn the day before yesterday and these parties, encouraged by the Cairo radio, called the people out on a general strike and ineffective riots.

King Hussein was ready for these developments. He kept the rioters tightly confined and there was no bloodshed. In addition the monarch had a new Cabinet at his palace, ready and waiting to take over as soon as the Khalidi Government resigned.

The new Government is headed by Ibrahim Hashem, 69 years

Continued on Page 3, Column 3

A. E. C. Aide Says Dr. Schweitzer Errs

By EDWARD L. DALE Jr.
Special to The New York Times.

WASHINGTON, April 25—The scientist member of the Atomic Energy Commission sharply disputed today the contention of Dr. Albert Schweitzer that nuclear weapons tests were creating "a danger for the human race."

Dr. Willard F. Libby, the commission member, wrote to Dr. Schweitzer "as a scientist, to present data bearing on a scientific fact." He made his letter public two days after Dr. Schweitzer's warning.

After paying tribute to Dr. Schweitzer, humanitarian and winner of the Nobel Peace Prize, Dr. Libby said he feared Dr. Schweitzer's appeal was not based on the latest information on radioactive fall-out. Dr. Libby added: "I know you have the intellectual strength

Continued on Page 6, Column 4

U.S. ORDERS 6TH FLEET TO MIDEAST, SAYS COMMUNISTS MENACE JORDAN; HUSSEIN PROCLAIMS MARTIAL LAW

April 26, 1957
NAVAL MOVEMENT: Ships of the United States Sixth Fleet left Cannes (1) and Naples (2) to deploy in the eastern Mediterranean, perhaps from Egypt to Turkey (3), in a measure to help Jordan (4) remain independent.
The New York Times

Nasser Sees Syria's Leader On Mounting Jordan Crisis

By HOMER BIGART
Special to The New York Times.

CAIRO, April 25—In an atmosphere of deepening crisis, President Gamal Abdel Nasser conferred again tonight with President Shukri al-Kuwatly of Syria on what to do about Jordan. The Egyptian President is reported eager to avoid any break with King Hussein of Jordan.

But the formation of an avowedly pro-Western government in Amman has sharpened Egyptian suspicions of some grand strategic design by the Western powers to bring Jordan into the Baghdad Pact.

In an apparent effort to patch up relations with King Saud of Saudi Arabia, who has been backing Hussein, President Nasser will send a three-man mission to Riyadh tomorrow. Mr. al-Kuwatly will accompany the Egyptian team and it was reported that he would later go to Amman for a talk with King Hussein.

President Nasser's decision to send a special mission to Saudi Arabia came after he had received a message from King Saud, the contents of which were not disclosed. The Egyptian mission will consist of President Nasser's political adviser, Col. Ali Sabry, Sheikh Hassan el Bakouri, Minister of Works, and Anwar el Sadat, head of the Islamic Congress and publisher of the newspaper Al Gomhouria.

Chief Aides at Talks

Mr. al-Kuwatly arrived unexpectedly this morning from Damascus for several hours of talks. He kept his arrival secret. The Cairo radio finally broke the news at 2:30 P. M. after Damascus had announced Mr. al-Kuwatly's departure for Egypt.

President Nasser and President al-Kuwatly conferred for three hours and met again tonight in another emergency session. The Egyptian Commander in Chief, Gen. Abdel Hakim Amer, and the Syrian Chief of Staff, Gen. Tewfik Nizam el-Din, attended both meetings.

Also present were Colonel Sabry, the Syrian Foreign Minister, Salah Bitar, and the Syrian Minister of Public Works, Fakhir Kayyali.

No communiqué was issued. Diplomatic sources speculated that neither President Nasser

Continued on Page 4, Column 1

MOSCOW ACCUSES U.S. OF MEDDLING

Broadcast Attacks 'Blatant Interference' in Jordan— Hussein Also Scored

By The Associated Press.

LONDON, April 25—Moscow accused the United States tonight of "blatant interference" in the internal affairs of Jordan. An anonymous commentator on the Moscow radio's home service said the Jordanian situation remained tense amid an "atmosphere of deep internal political crisis."

The Moscow radio said the United States, "by means of behind-the-scenes machinations, is trying to set up a Jordanian Government that would adopt the aggressive Eisenhower Doctrine and give up the policy of protecting the national interests and [Jordan's] unity with other free Arab countries."

Later tonight, an Arabic-language broadcast from Moscow said, "One is surprised, to say the least, at what King Hussein said about international communism seeking to destroy Jordan." King Hussein, in interviews yesterday, attributed Jordan's troubles to international Communist propaganda and subversion.

U. S. Agitation Alleged

The commentator went on: "We cannot but see in this statement an unsuccessful attempt to stir up suspicions against the Soviet Union. It is well known that the Soviet Union has never interfered in the internal affairs of Jordan. On the contrary, the Soviet Union has always firmly supported the struggle of the Jordanian people against all imperialists to build up their free and independent country.

"We must also point out that this statement is but a repetition of the false allegations that are being used by American propaganda to lay responsibility and consequences on others."

The broadcast said "the intervention of United States diplomacy in the internal affairs [of Jordan] is getting more open and brazen."

Dulles' Speech Criticized

By WILLIAM J. JORDEN
Special to The New York Times.

MOSCOW, April 25—The Soviet Union's leaders insisted tonight they were not trying to export the Communist revolution. They said they could not understand why Secretary of State Dulles was set on advocating a policy of "liberation" for the countries of Eastern Europe.

The Kremlin roundly castigated Mr. Dulles for the speech he made before a gathering of American editors three days ago. A statement criticizing his speech and attributed to "leading circles of the Soviet Union" was

Continued on Page 2, Column 3

A SHOW OF FORCE

British Also Say a Free Jordan Is Essential to Mideast Peace

By DANA ADAMS SCHMIDT
Special to The New York Times.

WASHINGTON, April 25—The United States deployed its military and political power today to assure the survival of an independent Jordan.

It sent the Sixth Fleet, with the aircraft carrier Forrestal, hurrying back from the western to the eastern Mediterranean so suddenly that 150 sailors were left stranded on leave in Paris.

[A British Foreign Office spokesman said that Jordan's independence and integrity were "essential elements" in maintaining Middle East peace.]

The United States also began to set out the political justification for any future intervention. This justification, in the Administration's view, was that Jordan is menaced by the forces of international communism.

A State Department declaration to this effect, following a similar statement by King Hussein of Jordan yesterday, seemed designed to make the Eisenhower Doctrine applicable in the struggle over Jordan.

Statement Expanded

The declaration expanded President Eisenhower's statement yesterday in Augusta, Ga., that preservation of Jordan's independence was "vital to the national interest."

Lincoln White, press officer of the State Department, read this statement:

"The statement issued in Augusta, Ga., represented a reminder to the world by the President that a finding had been made in the Joint Resolution of the Congress on the Middle East [the Eisenhower Doctrine] that the preservation of the independence and integrity of the nations of the Middle East was vital to the national interest of the United States and to world peace.

"This reminder was appropriate because of the threat to the independence and integrity of Jordan by international communism as King Hussein himself stated."

Generally, according to Administration experts, international communism works indirectly in Jordan through the left-wing and extremist nationalists.

Continued on Page 2, Column 4

U. N. CHIEF LOOKS TO COURT ON SUEZ

Hammarskjold Says It Could Settle Israeli Ship Issue

By THOMAS J. HAMILTON
Special to The New York Times.

UNITED NATIONS, N. Y., April 25—Dag Hammarskjold suggested today that the question whether Israeli ships had the right to use the Suez Canal be decided by the International Court of Justice.

The Secretary General of the United Nations asserted at a news conference that the "Governments concerned" could decide. He added, however, that preservation of Jordan's inde-he saw a possibility that the issue could be resolved under procedures set forth in the Egyptian declaration yesterday on operation of the canal.

The declaration provided that any unresolved differences among the signatories over the meaning of the Constantinople Convention of 1888, guaranteeing freedom of navigation, would be referred to the International Court.

Egypt apparently promised to accept compulsory jurisdiction. However, Israel and the United States, which were not parties to the convention, could not use the issue to the Court.

Further questions brought out the contradictory language about the convention, which provides that while the canal should be open to the shipping of all nations, both in war and peace, Egypt is entitled to take action to guard her security. Reminded that this right was qualified by

Continued on Page 4, Column 6

N. Y. U. Hospital Is Planned, With Research Chief Goal

By ROBERT K. PLUMB

Plans for a new hospital to make the New York University-Bellevue Medical Center a pioneering scientific research institution were announced yesterday. The plans call for a nineteen-story building of

white brick and glass just south of Thirty-fourth Street and east of First Avenue. But the plans tell only part of the story. For it is the intention of New York University medical men to use the new $20,-000,000 institution to find out

how to reduce the time lag between laboratory science and bedside medical practice. Other possible improvements in medicine may in part be "built into" the new hospital.

Continued on Page 15, Column 3

This is a drawing of the new nineteen-story hospital building that will rise at New York University-Bellevue Medical Center. The architects are Skidmore, Owings & Merrill.

"All the News That's Fit to Print"

The New York Times.

LATE CITY EDITION
U. S. Weather Bureau Report (Page 26) forecast:
Some cloudiness, warm today.
Partly cloudy, humid tomorrow.
Temp. range: 88—70. Yesterday: 86.4—61.4.

VOL. CVI..No. 36,321.
© 1957, by The New York Times Company.
Times Square, New York 36, N. Y.

NEW YORK, THURSDAY, JULY 4, 1957.

10c beyond 100-mile zone from New York City

FIVE CENTS

PRESIDENT BARS BALLOT ON RIGHTS; WOULD HEAR FOES

Rejects Proposal by Russell to Hold Referendum, but Plans to Study Bill

CITES COURT'S DECISIONS

'Ready to Listen' to South's Arguments — Senator Welcomes the Offer

News conference transcript and summary, Page 13.

By WILLIAM S. WHITE
Special to The New York Times.

WASHINGTON, July 3—President Eisenhower made it plain today that he was taking another and a closer look at the implications of the Administration's civil rights bill in the wake of vehement Southern attacks on it.

At the same time, he rejected a proposal from the Southern opposition that the bill be submitted directly to the people in a national referendum.

He declared at his news conference, however, that he was "ready to listen" to any presentation of their side from the embattled Southerners.

Their chief spokesman, Senator Richard B. Russell, Democrat of Georgia, denounced the bill yesterday as so "cunningly contrived" that it could be questioned whether the President himself understood its full scope.

Opponents Map Strategy

Senator Russell was holding a strategy meeting at the Capitol with fellow Senators while the President was speaking. By coincidence, they themselves about that time were discussing the possibility of going to him in a group to offer their views.

Some were at first disposed not to attempt this course, lest it be interpreted as a sign of weakness.

Told later of the President's remarks, however, Senator Russell said:

"If the President wishes to talk to us on this matter, his wish—as would be the wish of any President of the United States—will be to us a command. I should be glad to meet with him in any circumstances he might prefer—alone or with others as he might wish."

From the Senate floor, Senator Russell charged yesterday that the Attorney General, Herbert Brownell Jr., had prepared a "deceptive piece of legislation" that would amount to "an unlimited grant of powers to the Attorney General to govern by injunction and Federal troops."

Bill Passed by House

As passed by the House of Representatives, the bill would:

¶Permit the Justice Department to intervene in behalf of any individual, with or without his consent, whose civil rights had been denied or were under threat of denial. This would be done by obtaining a Federal court injunction against the violator or imminent violator. If he refused to obey this writ, he could be held in contempt by a judge, sitting without a jury, and fined or imprisoned.

¶Set up a special civil rights division within the Justice Department.

¶Create a Federal civil rights commission to investigate and attempt to rectify cases of racial discrimination.

The civil rights advocates, Mr. Russell contended, are pretending that their main concern is to protect the right to vote, but in fact are seeking means to force racial integration in the South, in the schools and elsewhere, even to the point of possible use of Federal troops.

Russell Sees Pretense

The President at his news conference today showed that he had been disturbed by the comments of Senator Russell with whom he had had many agreeable relationships.

During his military career, General Eisenhower often appeared before the Senate Armed Services Committee, of which Mr. Russell is chairman.

On Senator Russell's suggestion of a referendum, the President said he doubted that there was any constitutional basis for such a step; that Congress itself had the responsibility to enact legislation, and that in any case the issue would not be a very good subject for a referendum, even if you could have one."

On Mr. Russell's general denunciation of the bill, however, President Eisenhower did

Continued on Page 13, Column 1

Eisenhower Raises Atomic Fuel Quota

By JOHN W. FINNEY
Special to The New York Times.

WASHINGTON, July 3—The White House more than doubled today the amount of nuclear fuel the United States would make available for atomic power plants at home and abroad.

President Eisenhower announced that he was allocating an additional 59,800 kilograms—or 131,560 pounds—of uranium 235 for peaceful purposes in domestic and foreign nuclear power projects.

Including its previous allocations, the United States has now pledged to make 100,000 kilograms—or 220,000 pounds —of uranium fuel available for peaceful purposes. At current atomic energy commission prices, the value of this fuel is $1,700,000,000.

The 100,000 kilograms will be

Continued on Page 12, Column 3

CITY BUILDING UNIT STUDIED BY STATE

Heck Announces Watchdog Inquiry—Step Welcomed by Mayor and Aides

By EMANUEL PERLMUTTER

The Republican - controlled legislative watchdog committee has begun an investigation of the New York City Department of Buildings.

This was disclosed yesterday by Assemblyman Oswald D. Heck, Republican Speaker of the Assembly. He said the committee was checking reports of "graft, corruption and 'extortion" in the department.

Confirmation was given by Senator William F. Horan, Republican of Tuckahoe, chairman of the Joint Legislative Committee on Government Operations, the official name of the watchdog unit.

Mr. Horan said the committee's staff was making "preliminary investigations into those and other matters."

Mayor Gives His Views

Mayor Wagner said his Administration welcomed the watchdog committee's investigation.

"I have said time and again that we would welcome any investigation of any city department," he declared. "We have nothing to hide. If there is wrongdoing no one is more impatient than I to root it out and take swift, decisive action.

"I have already asked those with complaints against the Department of Buildings to come in and state their complaints. I have promised full protection to all who cooperate in this fashion."

Charles H. Tenney, the City Investigation Commissioner who has begun his own inquiry into rumors that building inspectors were shaking down property-owners guilty of violations and those seeking building permits,

Continued on Page 37, Column 3

DEMOCRATS BACK EASING OF CURBS ON ALIEN QUOTAS

Key Legislators in Agreement on Compromise to Bring in 140,000 More in 2 Years

By JOHN D. MORRIS
Special to The New York Times.

WASHINGTON, July 3—Key Democrats in Congress have quietly reached substantial agreement on a compromise plan for easing restrictions on immigration.

The compromise, described as acceptable in nearly all major respects to legislators most interested in the problem, is embodied in a bill introduced last Thursday by Senator John F. Kennedy, Democrat of Massachusetts.

The measure has the backing of Lyndon B. Johnson of Texas, the Senate Democratic leader, Representative Francis E. Walter, Democrat of Pennsylvania, who holds the key to action by the House of Representatives, also participated in the unpublished negotiations that preceded its introduction. Sponsors look for his cooperation.

The bill would permit the entry over a two-year period of 140,000 to 150,000 regular immigrants and refugees who otherwise would be excluded.

Eisenhower Plan Included

While it includes features of President Eisenhower's immigration program, it stops short of making some basic changes that he had proposed in the McCarran-Walter Immigration and Nationality Act.

The President's recommendations, outlined Jan. 31 in a special message to Congress, asked authority to bring in 190,000 more persons a year.

The annual quota under present law is 154,857, of which 60,-000 quota numbers expire unused each year. Total entrances, including unrestricted immigration from Western Hemisphere countries, amounted to 321,625 in 1956.

Democratic strategists hope to obtain Republican help in steering the Kennedy bill through Congress without public hearings.

The tentative plan, similar to one that failed in the last hours of the 1956 session, is to attach the measure to a minor immigration bill passed by the House and now pending on the Senate calendar.

Tactic Failed Last Year

Senate passage of the combined bill would send it to a Senate-House conference committee for agreement on the final version.

The tactic failed last year when Representative Walter, chairman of the House Judiciary Subcommittee on Immigration, invoked a parliamentary technicality to keep a similar bill from going to conference.

This time, according to Senator Kennedy, Mr. Walter "has

Continued on Page 11, Column 1

WIDE SHAKE-UP IN KREMLIN OUSTS MOLOTOV, MALENKOV, KAGANOVICH AS KHRUSHCHEV TIGHTENS REINS

U. S. IS GRATIFIED

State Department Says Ousters Show Strain in Soviet System

By JAMES RESTON
Special to The New York Times.

WASHINGTON, July 3—Official Washington tried hard to conceal its pleasure over the latest shake-up in the Soviet Union today but didn't quite succeed.

"No comment," said James C. Hagerty, White House press secretary, grinning broadly, and the grin was the most tangible and significant act in a day devoted mainly to gleeful speculation.

News of the official Soviet announcement of the dismissal of Vyacheslav M. Molotov, Lazar M. Kaganovich, Georgi M. Malenkov and Dmitri T. Shepilov was brought to President Eisenhower during a meeting of the National Security Council in the afternoon. Reports of developments were rushed to the White House from the State Department and the Central Intelligence Agency throughout the day.

Mr. Hagerty told the press in midafternoon that the Administration had advance indication of the ouster. He noted that Nikita S. Khrushchev, First Secretary of the Soviet Communist party, and Marshal Nikolai A. Bulganin, Soviet Premier, had recently postponed a visit to Czechoslovakia, and that an aerial demonstration over Moscow, to which Communist bloc leaders had been invited, had suddenly been canceled.

Beyond that, however, he would not comment.

White Reads Statement

The State Department was more explicit. In answer to reporters' questions, Lincoln White, press officer, read the following statement:

"It has long been known that the Soviet system operates under stresses and strains. Arbitrary and abrupt dismissals without public discussion of the issues are also characteristic of the system.

"The official Soviet press has at various times suggested there have been disagreements over basic policies in such fields as Government organizations, agriculture, heavy industry, consumer goods and satellite affairs.

"The serious nature of the divergence of views is clearly shown by the number and importance of the persons dismissed or shifted. We are naturally following these developments closely for the effect they may have on Soviet basic policy."

Effect on U. S. Policy Seen

The Soviet changes have come at a critical time in the development of United States foreign policy and is expected to have some influence on that policy, particularly as it affects Communist China and the Soviet Union.

Both the Executive and Legislative branches of the United States Government have been divided about how to deal with Moscow and Peiping. Some legislators and officials have favored making a major effort to reach a disarmament agreement with the Soviet Union and acquiescing in an accommodation with the Chinese Communists.

Others have been opposing this on the ground that the whole Communist world was in ferment. They have been going along reluctantly with the current United States policy in the disarmament talks in London, but insisting that the way to break up the Communist alliance between Moscow and Peiping was to maintain the economic pressure.

Secretary of State Dulles, who left for his Great Lakes retreat on Duck Island today, said only yesterday that he was opposed to making concessions to the Chinese Communists and regarded dictatorial communism in both Peiping and Moscow as "a passing phase."

Today's developments in Moscow, coming on top of a noisy ideological dispute in Peiping over ideological questions, were expected to strengthen those who have contended that the thing to do was to keep the pressure on, not to grow weary of the long struggle, not to make risky concessions

Continued on Page 3, Column 4

The New York Times
Vyacheslav M. Molotov

Associated Press
Georgi M. Malenkov

Sovfoto
Lazar M. Kaganovich

U. S. MAY SPREAD 'CLEAN' BOMB DATA

President Weighs Proposal to Give Others Knowledge on Eliminating Fall-Out

By JACK RAYMOND
Special to The New York Times.

WASHINGTON, July 3 — President Eisenhower said today he was thinking of sharing with the Soviet Union and other countries the knowledge of how to produce "clean" hydrogen bombs.

Such a step would require legislation, he said. But he disclosed that he had asked his scientific advisers about the possibility of sharing, and they had suggested such a course might be adopted as soon as they had proved they could produce a bomb totally free of dangerous radioactive fall-out.

The President said that in the meantime he intended to invite foreign countries to make their own measurements of the percentage of radioactivity at the site of the next United States hydrogen bomb detonation.

This should serve as an appropriate test by doubters of the contention that even now only 4 per cent radioactivity results from the explosion of United States hydrogen bombs, the President declared.

U-235 Given to Others

President Eisenhower opened his news conference with an announcement that the United States was making more uranium-235 available in the peaceful uses of atomic power.

In response to questions about United States policy on disarmament and the effects on that policy of reduced radioactive fall-out in bomb explosions, the President emphasized:

¶The United States stands firm on its position at the London disarmament conference, agreeing to a temporary suspension of nuclear arms tests if it will lead to an end of bomb-making.

¶The United States disarm-

Continued on Page 12, Column 2

Moscow Ousters Termed Victory for 'Liberal' Policy

By HARRISON E. SALISBURY

Nikita S. Khrushchev, First Secretary of the Soviet Communist party, appears to have won a smashing victory for his "New Look" policies of easing tensions at home and abroad. This was the initial reaction of competent specialists in Soviet affairs to the dramatic decisions of the latest meeting in Moscow of the party's Central Committee.

With the firm support of the Soviet Army, the Communist party apparatus and the Government bureaucracy, Mr. Khrushchev has ousted from the Soviet ruling group a powerful bloc of Stalinist oppositionists.

Mr. Khrushchev's ability to remove from the party's Presidium and Central Committee such veteran party chieftains as Vyacheslav M. Molotov, Lazar M. Kaganovich and Georgi M. Malenkov was testimony to the power he had now mustered behind his leadership.

Indictment Is Stressed

Of great importance in international relations was the nature of the indictment placed against them, Mr. Khrushchev and his victorious Central Committee majority charged Mr. Molotov, Mr. Kaganovich, Mr. Malenkov and their supporters with persistent and deliberate efforts to sabotage every effort to ease international tensions, improve the life of Soviet citizens at home and destroy the vestiges of Stalinist excesses.

The communiqué announcing the expulsions contained a platform of the Khrushchev faction, which promised to continue striving for better international relations.

While the main force of the Khrushchev indictment was directed against Mr. Molotov, Mr. Kaganovich and Mr. Malenkov, they were not the only targets. In effect Mr. Khrushchev made a clean sweep.

He also ousted Dmitri T. Shepilov, the former Pravda editor and Foreign Minister who was identified with the "Young Turk" faction of the party. Mr.

Continued on Page 3, Column 2

3 STALINISTS OUT

Shepilov Also Dropped for Opposing Current Policies of Soviet

Texts of communiqué, Pravda editorial, Pages 2 and 4.

By WILLIAM J. JORDEN
Special to The New York Times.

MOSCOW, Thursday, July 4—The Soviet Communist party has accused Vyacheslav M. Molotov, Georgi M. Malenkov and Lazar M. Kaganovich of anti-party activities and has ousted them from the country's leadership.

They were removed from both the Presidium of the party's Central Committee and from the Central Committee itself. However, they remained as members of the party.

Dmitri T. Shepilov, who was said to have joined them in working against the majority, was also ousted from alternate membership in the Presidium, from the Central Committee and from his job as one of the party secretaries.

Three Linked With Stalin

The three Communist leaders, all known for their connections with Stalin, were accused of having tried to restore "methods of leadership that were condemned by the Twentieth Party Congress," an allusion to the system prevailing in Stalin's time. They were said to have tried to form an anti-party faction to achieve their aims.

The action against them was taken during an eight-day meeting of the Central Committee from June 22 through 29. The text of the committee's resolution was released by Tass, Soviet news agency, last night.

Of the former eleven members of the party Presidium only six remained. They are Nikita S. Khrushchev, Nikolai A. Bulganin, Kliment Y. Voroshilov, Anastas I. Mikoyan, Mikhail A. Suslov and Alexei I. Kirichenko.

Zhukov Is Elevated

Marshal Georgi K. Zhukov, the Defense Minister, and Miss Yekaterina A. Furtseva, the only woman on the Presidium, were among five alternate members who were raised to full rank. Four other regular members were newly added to the Presidium.

In addition to the four leading figures who were singled out for severe criticism and ousted from the Presidium, Mikhail G. Pervukhin and Maxim Z. Saburov also were dropped from the group.

Mr. Pervukhin was demoted to the position of alternate member of the Presidium, but nothing was known of Mr. Saburov's present position. He was not mentioned as having been dropped from the Central Committee itself.

Messrs. Molotov, Malenkov and Kaganovich were said to have opposed all the major policy moves of recent years that have come to be associated with Mr. Khrushchev. The Central Committee's indictment

Continued on Page 2, Column 3

SOVIET EXPECTED TO EASE BLOC TIE

Shift in Leadership Viewed as Move to Consolidate the Communist Orbit

By SYDNEY GRUSON
Special to The New York Times.

PRAGUE, Czechoslovakia, July 3—The changes in the Soviet Communist party's leadership, announced in Moscow tonight, may have ushered in a significant period of readjustment in relations between the Soviet Union and other Communist countries.

The changes, and the Pravda editorial accompanying them, were considered of such basic importance that people here and in Warsaw hesitated to comment until a more thorough study became possible. But among their first impressions were these:

¶Nikita S. Khrushchev had consolidated his position as the first among equals in the new Presidium of the Soviet party.

¶Mr. Khrushchev was bent on a determined effort to narrow the steadily widening gap between the Soviet party and some of the other Communist parties, particularly that of Communist China.

To Lessen Antagonism

¶The dismissal of Vyacheslav M. Molotov would be bound to lessen the sharp antagonism between Moscow and Belgrade, Yugoslavia, and the differences between Moscow and Warsaw as well. In both Belgrade and Warsaw Mr. Molotov had been considered the prime architect of a tough policy toward parties straying from the Soviet line.

The section of the Pravda editorial concerning the failure of "sectarians and dogmatists" [Stalinists] to understand the necessity of consolidating the Socialist camp was aimed here as aimed against Mr. Molotov.

Through the Pravda editorial the Soviet Union was assuming a posture that had already been taken up elsewhere in the Communist camp. Editorial strictures against Stalinists on the one other echoed the "struggle on two fronts" adopted as the Polish party's major ideological line months ago.

One paragraph in the Pravda particularly sounded like dozens of recent editorials of Trybuna Ludu, the newspaper of the Polish party's Central Committee. Pravda described "sectarians and dogmatists" as people "divorced from life" who have "backward conceptions."

"They do not see new situations," Pravda declared. "They stubbornly cling to obsolete forms and methods of work and reject that which is born by life. They would like to turn the party back to those incorrect methods of leadership rejected by the Twentieth Party Congress."

At long last the Russians conceded that Marshal Tito had

Continued on Page 2, Column 2

G.O.P. Picks 3-War Marine To Oppose Jack in Borough

By RUSSELL PORTER

Melvin L. Krulewitch, 61-year-old lawyer and twice-wounded Marine Corps Reserve veteran of three wars, was designated yesterday as the Republican candidate for Borough President of Manhattan. He will oppose Hulan E. Jack, the Democratic incumbent in the November election.

Mr. Krulewitch, who is a major general in the Reserve, was the only Republican named for Borough President or District Attorney at meetings of the executive committees of the New York and Kings County Republican Committees.

The following three Democrats, who already had their own party designations, were endorsed by the Republicans for re-election as Borough President or District Attorney:

Borough President John Cashmore of Brooklyn.

District Attorney Frank S. Hogan of New York County (Manhattan).

District Attorney Edward S. Silver of Kings County (Brooklyn).

Both executive committees formally approved the recent designation of three Republican city-wide candidates by the five county leaders. These candidates are Robert K. Christenberry for Mayor, Mrs. Caroline K. Simon for President of the City Council and State Senator Walter

G. McGahan of Queens for Controller.

Mr. Krulewitch's designation marked a departure from the Republican practice in the 1953 municipal campaign. At that time the Republicans picked a Negro, Elmer A. Carter, who lost to Mr. Jack, who is also a Negro.

Thomas J. Curran, the Republicans' New York County leader, said after yesterday's meeting that Mr. Carter, a member of the State Committee Against Discrimination, did not want to run for Borough President this year. According to Mr. Curran, Mr. Krulewitch was the only Republican who had served with Negro troops and could make a good campaign.

Mr. Krulewitch told Negro reporters yesterday that he had served with Negro troops at Iwo in the Pacific in World War II. "They were fine troops," he said.

He is a tall, husky, clean-shaven man of military bearing. He wears dark horn-rimmed glasses and his hair is getting thin and gray. He has been a member of the Republican County Committee for eight years but has never run for public office. He has a law office on Madison Avenue and lives at 45 Gramercy Park North, in Mr. Curran's home district.

"Are you an Eisenhower Re-

Continued on Page 29, Column 2

Holiday Traffic Exodus Begins; 952 Police Cars Will Patrol City

Police Commissioner Stephen P. Kennedy yesterday declared "all-out war" on reckless drivers in a move to help law-abiding citizens survive the Fourth of July holiday week-end.

Fifty-two unmarked cars and 900 regular radio patrol cars were assigned to watch traffic from 4 P. M. yesterday until 8 A. M. Monday.

The holiday exodus began yesterday afternoon. It was estimated that 1,000,000 persons out of the city during the four-day week-end.

Most of the nation was promised generally fair and warm weather today with which to celebrate the 181st anniversary of the adoption of the Declaration of Independence by the Continental Congress.

The Weather Bureau said temperatures here — which climbed to 86.4 degrees at 6:40 P. M. yesterday — might reach 85 to 90 degrees today. Yesterday was the first day to exceed 80 degrees since last Friday. The outlook for tomorrow and Saturday is partly cloudy, warm and humid.

The National Safety Council estimated that 45,000,000 motor vehicles would be on the roads. It feared a possible record Independence Day toll of 535 highway deaths between 6 P. M. yesterday and midnight Sunday.

The council warned that eight of every ten fatal accidents occur in rural areas; speed is involved in seven out of ten, and drinking is a factor in almost half. Indiana and Iowa detailed National Guardsmen to aid road patrols. Kentucky and Georgia planned road blocks to check drivers, and New Mexico ordered jail for reckless drivers until their records could be checked.

In the city, 1200 police cars will operate in a safety-chain plan, each patrolling back and forth on a single mile of the major parkways and highways. Six cars of the accident investigation unit will be on around-the-clock duty. Two police helicopters will help unsnarl traffic tie-ups.

The major delays yesterday affected traffic leaving the city over the George Washington Bridge. Between 5 and 6:30 P. M., cars on the West Side

Continued on Page 26, Column 2

Italy Holds TV Aide In Give-Away Fraud

By PAUL HOFMANN

ROME, July 3—One of Italy's best-known television personalities was in prison today, charged with rigging give-away shows. Giuseppe Ruggiero, 42 years old, never spoke a line before television cameras and was never introduced to watchers. But his sternly benevolent face is familiar to millions because it used to appear on the screen whenever something was to be won.

In his wordless way, Signor Ruggiero was quite a performer. To the unseen audience he was fair play personified. As chief of the promotion department of the state broadcasting and television system Signor Ruggiero presided over the distribution of thousands of television sets, record players, refrigerators and automobiles.

Now he is accused of having

Continued on Page 37, Column 2

"All the News That's Fit to Print"

The New York Times.

LATE CITY EDITION
U. S. Weather Bureau Report (Page 50) forecasts:
Mostly fair and seasonable today and tomorrow.
Temp. range: 70—57. Yesterday: 67.7—55.9.

VOL. CVII..No. 36,404.   © 1957, by The New York Times Company.
Times Square, New York 36, N. Y.   NEW YORK, WEDNESDAY, SEPTEMBER 25, 1957.   10c beyond 100-mile zone from New York City   FIVE CENTS

PRESIDENT SENDS TROOPS TO LITTLE ROCK, FEDERALIZES ARKANSAS NATIONAL GUARD; TELLS NATION HE ACTED TO AVOID ANARCHY

WEST AGAIN BARS SOVIET PROPOSAL ON MIDEAST TALK

U. S. Says Latest Moscow Note 'Cynically Distorts' American Actions

Text of U. S. note to Soviet will be found on Page 5.

By DANA ADAMS SCHMIDT
Special to The New York Times.

WASHINGTON, Sept. 24—The United States, Britain and France rejected today the latest in a series of Soviet bids for recognition of the Soviet Union's role in the Middle East.

A brief United States reply delivered in Moscow today said a Soviet note of Sept. 3 was "offensive in tone and cynically distorts United States objectives and actions in the Middle East."

It accused the Soviet Union of setting in motion "a chain of events leading to the present dangerous situation" by shipping large quantities of arms into the area.

U. S. Affirms Doctrine

The note warned the Soviet Union that the United States Government intended to carry out the national policy laid down in the Eisenhower Doctrine, which "regards the preservation of the independence and integrity of the nations of that region as vital to world peace and as vital, therefore, to its own national interests."

The doctrine, proclaimed in a Joint Resolution of the House of Representatives and the Senate on March 9, 1957, also reaffirmed the President's authority to use United States forces to aid any Middle East state that asked for help against aggression by a power controlled by international communism.

The Soviet Union's note had accused the United States of seeking to overthrow the Syrian Government and of generally fomenting trouble in the Middle East.

3d Rejection of Soviet Bid

It had proposed, for the third time, a four-power declaration renouncing the use of force in the area. Earlier Soviet proposals for such a declaration, all rejected by the West, were made Feb. 11 and April 19.

As interpreted by United States experts on the Middle East, these notes were meant to convey the idea that the four powers should meet to negotiate a settlement of their rivalries in the Middle East. The first of the notes even went into detail with a proposal for an embargo on shipment of arms to the area.

Because the Soviet Union has asserted its presence in Syria, and because there seems to be little the Western powers can do to reverse developments in the area.

Continued on Page 5, Column 3

Rebel Chief Seized In Algiers Gunfight

By THOMAS F. BRADY
Special to The New York Times.

ALGIERS, Algeria, Sept. 24—The chief of the nationalist terrorist organization in Algiers was in the hands of French parachute troops today.

The rebel leader, Saadi Yacef, 29 years old, had eluded capture in the crowded Casbah for more than two years.

With him was 24-year-old Miss Zorah Drif, an Algerian revolutionary, who was condemned to death in absentia by a French military tribunal.

A parachute colonel told reporters this evening that Mr. Yacef and Miss Drif had surrendered at 5:30 A. M. after the terrorist chief had wounded a lieutenant colonel and a master sergeant of a Foreign Legion parachute regiment. The colonel then took reporters to a hideout high in the Casbah where he described how the

Continued on Page 4, Column 5

London and Bonn Rule Out Any Currency Revaluation

Britain Tells Monetary Fund Session She Will Draw $500,000,000 in Stand-By Credit From Export-Import Bank

By EDWIN L. DALE JR.
Special to The New York Times.

WASHINGTON, Sept. 24—British and West German spokesmen and the Managing Director of the International Monetary Fund said today that the question of exchange rates for the pound and the mark was "definitely settled." There will be no change.

At the same time, Britain, through Peter Thorneycroft, Chancellor of the Exchequer, announced she would draw "over the coming weeks" the $500,000,000 stand-by credit she arranged last winter with the United States Export-Import Bank.

In his speech at the annual meeting of the fund, Mr. Thor-

neycroft indicated that Britain was drawing the money to demonstrate to speculators that she had the resources to defend the pound.

Both the British and the West Germans emphasized that the recent huge flow of gold and dollars out of Britain and into West Germany had been based solely on speculation, not on basic factors in their foreign trading accounts.

Per Jacobsson, the Fund's Managing Director, said: "The growing knowledge that there will be no alteration in the value of either the Deutsche

Continued on Page 8, Column 5

SOVIET ASSAILED BY LLOYD AT U. N.

Briton Suggests Arms Sent Arabs May Be Stocks for Future Bases

Excerpts from Lloyd's speech are printed on Page 4.

By THOMAS J. HAMILTON
Special to The New York Times.

UNITED NATIONS, N. Y., Sept. 24—Britain denounced today Soviet arms shipments to Arab countries. Selwyn Lloyd, British Foreign Secretary, suggested that the purpose might be to "pre-stock forward bases for the Soviet Union itself."

Mr. Lloyd told the General Assembly that Soviet arms had been delivered "on such a scale as to give some color to this suggestion." He added that Britain viewed the Syrian situation "with grave concern."

In addition, he criticized Soviet policy throughout the area.

Mr. Lloyd devoted most of his speech to the Middle East. He did not say what action the Assembly should take on either subject.

However, he declared that Secretary of State Dulles, in

Continued on Page 4, Column 3

City Approves Plan By Wiley to Build Midtown Garages

By JOSEPH C. INGRAHAM

The Board of Estimate has approved in principle the program of Traffic Commissioner T. T. Wiley for garage construction in the heart of lower and mid-Manhattan.

The decision clears the way for a start on $24,000,000 of garages. It also settles a three-year dispute between Mr. Wiley and other city executives that has stymied off-street parking relief.

As a result, the first of the projects—a garage in the Herald Square area—will be on the board's calendar on Oct. 9. Eight other garages are to be centrally located in Manhattan and two in the busiest parts of the Bronx.

The Herald Square garage will be east of the Avenue of the Americas between West Thirty-fifth and Thirty-sixth Streets with entrances and exits on both streets. There will be space for 610 cars on eight levels accessible by ramps. Rates will be geared to "meet the heavy unsatisfied demand" for short-time parking," Mr. Wiley said.

Rates proposed by the Commissioner would be 25 cents a

Continued on Page 25, Column 1

SOLDIERS FLY IN

1,000 Go to Little Rock —9,936 in Guard Told to Report

The texts of Executive orders on troops are on Page 16.

By JACK RAYMOND
Special to The New York Times.

WASHINGTON, Sept. 24—The Army ordered all Arkansas National Guardsmen to report for Federal duty tonight and rushed 1,000 airborne troops of the Regular Army into Little Rock to preserve order.

The Regulars were members of the 101st Airborne Division, which won fame in World War II under the command of Gen. Maxwell D. Taylor, now Chief of Staff of the Army.

Maj. Gen. Edwin A. Walker, a much-decorated combat commander with a reputation for toughness, was put in command of the Regular Army contingent and the federalized Guardsmen in Arkansas. He is the commander of the Arkansas Military District.

General Walker's mission is to make sure that no one frustrates Federal Court orders that nine Negro pupils be admitted to Central High School.

Wilson Carries Out Order

Charles E. Wilson, Secretary of Defense, carrying out President Eisenhower's mandate, earlier had called the entire Arkansas Army and Air National Guard, totaling 9,936 men, into Federal service.

The Secretary of Defense and Wilber M. Brucker, Secretary of the Army, acted two hours after President Eisenhower's executive order authorizing "all appropriate steps" to make school attendance possible for the Negroes who had been admitted to the high school.

However, an Army spokesman said that it was planned to make "the absolute minimum demonstration of force necessary."

Immediately after Secretary Wilson signed the federalization call to the Arkansas Guard at 2:25 P. M., Secretary Brucker telephoned the office of Gov. Orval E. Faubus in Little Rock.

At the same time he sent a telegram to the Governor, explaining that President Eisenhower "desires" the personnel of the Arkansas Army and Air National Guard organizations

Continued on Page 14, Column 2

SOLDIERS IN LITTLE ROCK: Residents of Arkansas capital looking on last night as men of the 101st Airborne Division took positions outside the Central High School.
Associated Press Wirephoto

GOVERNORS URGE WHITE HOUSE TALK

Southerners Move to Set Up Mediation Machinery in Use of Federal Troops

By JOHN N. POPHAM
Special to The New York Times.

SEA ISLAND, Ga., Sept. 24—Southern Governors moved tonight to establish mediation machinery that would remove Federal troops from the South. The Governors acted a few hours after the President had federalized the Arkansas National Guard.

The first group of 500 airborne soldiers came to the city this afternoon from Fort Campbell, Ky., and a second group of 500 arrived by plane this evening. The bulk of the two groups bivouacked for the night in areas away from the school.

General Issues Order

Maj. Gen. Edwin A. Walker, commander of the Arkansas Military District, issued a formal order to the people of Little Rock not to collect in crowds and to let Central High School be integrated peaceably.

With the arrival of Federal troops, including some Negro soldiers who were not expected to be on duty at the school, Negro students who were ready to try again to enter the high school.

A mob of 1,000 persons yesterday forced the city and school authorities to withdraw nine Negro students who had attended integrated classes for 3 hours and 13 minutes. The students did not try to enter the school today.

Mrs. L. C. Bates, president

Continued on Page 15, Column 1

Troops on Guard at School; Negroes Ready to Return

By BENJAMIN FINE
Special to The New York Times.

LITTLE ROCK, Ark., Sept. 24—Troops from the Army's crack 101st Airborne Division, carrying carbines and billy clubs, took posts around Central High School tonight. They were here to see that court-ordered integration is carried out.

With police sirens wailing and headlights flashing, Army trucks loaded with soldiers roared into position. The soldiers represented about a quarter of the contingent of 1,000 crack troops of the division that was ordered to Little Rock by President Eisenhower to prevent mob riots and violence.

The first group of 500 airborne soldiers came to the city this afternoon from Fort Campbell, Ky., and a second group of 500 arrived by plane this evening. The bulk of the two groups bivouacked for the night in areas away from the school.

Continued on Page 15, Column 2

CONGRESS IS SPLIT ON USE OF TROOPS

Johnston Calls for Faubus to Resist President but Others Hail His Move

By JOHN W. FINNEY
Special to The New York Times.

WASHINGTON, Sept. 24—Congressional reaction to President Eisenhower's decision to use troops in the Little Rock integration crisis ranged from angry denunciation to outright praise today.

Southern Senators sharply criticized the President and suggested he had exceeded his legal authority. Northern Senators supported the President, but some of them expressed reservations that the action was rather belated.

Expects Faubus to Act

Senator Olin D. Johnston, Democrat of South Carolina, suggested that Gov. Orval E. Faubus of Arkansas "stand up for states' rights" and force a showdown with the President by calling out the Arkansas National Guard on his own.

Senator Johnston, a former Governor of South Carolina, said if he were Governor Faubus, "I'd proclaim a state of insurrection down there, and I'd call out the National Guard, and I'd then find out who's going to run things in my state."

Asked by reporters whether he believed Governor Faubus would take such steps, Senator Johnston said, "I think he will and I hope he will."

Aiken Defends Move

Senator John L. McClellan, Democrat of Arkansas, said he believed such use of military force by the Federal Government was "without authority of law."

He said he was "very apprehensive that such action may precipitate more trouble than it will prevent."

Senator Richard B. Russell, Democrat of Georgia and leader of Southern opposition to the Civil Rights Bill in the last session, said that President Eisenhower's use of troops might "put Negro children in the white schools," but that it would have a calamitous effect on race relations and on the cause of national unity."

On the other side of the issue, Senator George D. Aiken, Republican of Vermont, said the President "is undoubtedly with-

Continued on Page 17, Column 3

EISENHOWER ON AIR

Says School Defiance Has Gravely Harmed Prestige of U. S.

Text of President's address appears on Page 14.

By ANTHONY LEWIS
Special to The New York Times.

WASHINGTON, Sept. 24—President Eisenhower sent Federal troops to Little Rock, Ark., today to open the way for the admission of nine Negro pupils to Central High School.

Earlier, the President federalized the Arkansas National Guard and authorized calling the Guard and regular Federal forces to remove obstructions to justice in the Little Rock school integration.

His history-making action was based on a formal finding that his "cease and desist" proclamation, issued last night, had not been obeyed. Mobs of pro-segregationists still gathered in the vicinity of Central High School this morning.

Tonight, from the White House, President Eisenhower told the nation in a speech by radio and television that he had acted to prevent "mob rule" and "anarchy."

Historic Decision

The President's decision to send troops to Little Rock was reached at his vacation headquarters in Newport, R. I. It was one of historic importance politically, socially, constitutionally. For the first time since the Reconstruction days that followed the Civil War, the Federal Government was using its ultimate power to compel equal treatment of the Negro in the South.

He said violent defiance of Federal Court orders in Little Rock had done grave harm to "the prestige and influence, and indeed to the safety, of our nation and the world." He called on the people of Arkansas and the South to "preserve and respect the law even when they disagree with it."

Guardsmen Withdrawn

Action quickly followed the President's orders. During the day and night 1,000 members of the 101st Airborne Division were flown to Little Rock. Charles E. Wilson, Secretary of Defense, ordered into Federal service all 10,000 members of the Arkansas National Guard.

Today's events were the climax of three weeks of skirmishing between the Federal Government and Gov. Orval E. Faubus of Arkansas. It was three weeks ago this morning that the Governor first ordered National Guard troops to Central High School to preserve order. The nine Negro students were prevented from entering the school.

The Guardsmen were gone yesterday, withdrawn by Governor Faubus as the result of a

Continued on Page 14, Column 6

Textile Union Gets 30 Days to Reform

By A. H. RASKIN

A scandal-tainted textile union was ordered yesterday to oust its two chief officers within thirty days or face possible suspension from the merged labor federation.

The ultimatum was given to the 40,000-member United Textile Workers by the executive council of the American Federation of Labor and Congress of Industrial Organizations.

It foreshadowed the fixing of a similar clean-up deadline today for the 1,400,000-member International Brotherhood of Teamsters and the 140,000-member Bakery and Confectionery Workers International Union.

The federation's Ethical Practices Committee has found all three unions guilty of violating the anti-racketeering provisions of the A. F. L.-C. I. O. constitution. The findings were based

Continued on Page 18, Column 5

U. S. Cutters Conquer Northwest Passage

3 Coast Guard Craft First of the Nation to Make Transit

By JOHN H. FENTON
Special to The New York Times.

BOSTON, Sept. 24 — Two Coast Guard cutters were saluted in Boston Harbor today at the end of a successful mission to find a practical Northwest Passage—a route around the top of the North American Continent.

A third cutter, the Spar, proceeded directly to her home port at Bristol, R. I., to be welcomed there as the first United States vessel to circumnavigate the continent.

The cutters Storis, from Juneau, Alaska, and the Bramble, from Miami, Fla., put in here for their welcoming. They will continue their homeward voyages later in the week.

The three cutters were the first United States vessels to make the passage.

The shrill sirens of water-spouting fireboats and the deeper-throated whistles of other craft sounded a "well done" as the two bulky cutters made their way up the harbor.

Ranking Coast Guard officers and civil officials joined with members of families of the crews in a dockside welcome as the cutters tied up at

Continued on Page 19, Column 1

Price Index Up .2%; Sets Another High

By RICHARD E. MOONEY
Special to The New York Times.

WASHINGTON, Sept. 24—The United States Consumers' Price Index rose two-tenths of a per cent in August, setting another record. It was the twelfth consecutive monthly increase, but among the smallest of the twelve.

The Labor Department's Bureau of Labor Statistics reported today that the index rose in August to 121, using the price average in the 1947-49 period as a comparison base of 100. All the major categories of prices increased, but food and housing were the strongest factors.

The August index was 2.6 per cent higher than a year earlier. This meant that a typical city family paid $1.03 3/5 in August of 1957 for the goods and services that cost $1 in August of 1956.

The Commerce Department

Continued on Page 24, Column 5

Coast Guardsmen on the stern of the Spar view her sister cutters, Bramble, left, and Storis, during the transit of Simpson Strait. This was a difficult part of the voyage.
U. S. Coast Guard

188

"All the News
That's Fit to Print"

The New York Times.

LATE CITY EDITION

U. S. Weather Bureau Report (Page 23) forecasts:
Cloudy and cool today and tonight.
Mostly fair tomorrow.
Temp. range: 65—53. Yesterday: 62.4—49.2.

VOL. CVII..No. 36,414.

© 1957, by The New York Times Company,
Times Square, New York 36, N. Y.

NEW YORK, SATURDAY, OCTOBER 5, 1957.

10c beyond 100-mile zone
from New York City

FIVE CENTS

SOVIET FIRES EARTH SATELLITE INTO SPACE; IT IS CIRCLING THE GLOBE AT 18,000 M. P. H.; SPHERE TRACKED IN 4 CROSSINGS OVER U. S.

HOFFA IS ELECTED TEAMSTERS' HEAD; WARNS OF BATTLE

Defeats Two Foes 3 to 1 —Says Union Will Fight 'With Every Ounce'

Text of the Hoffa address is printed on Page 6.

By A. H. RASKIN
Special to The New York Times.

MIAMI BEACH, Oct. 4—The scandal-scarred International Brotherhood of Teamsters elected James R. Hoffa as its president today.

He won by a margin of nearly 3 to 1 over the combined vote of two rivals who campaigned on pledges to clean up the nation's biggest union.

Senate rackets investigators and Hoffa critics in the union rank-and-file immediately opened actions to strip the 44-year-old former warehouseman from Detroit of his election victory.

A jubilant Hoffa exhibited, however, greater concern over the possibility that his union might be ousted from the American Federation of Labor and Congress of Industrial Organizations. He appealed for time to prove that he could make the Teamsters "a model of trade unionism."

The parent organization has ordered the 1,400,000-member Teamsters Union to get rid of corrupt leadership by Oct. 24 or face suspension. Hoffa said he felt actions by the union at its week-long convention here should satisfy the federation.

Warns Union Will Fight

He made it plain to the 1,700 cheering delegates that he did not intend to go before the convention in the role of suppliant. He said expulsion would not destroy the Teamsters. He warned that the union would fight "with every ounce of strength we possess" if it found itself outside.

In such a civil war the teamsters would start with a war chest of $38,000,000 in the hands of the international union and much more at the disposal of its locals. The teamsters could also count on their strategic power over other unions through their control of trucks and warehouses.

The Hoffa victory brought warnings of repressive legislation from James P. Mitchell, Secretary of Labor, and Senator John L. McClellan, Democrat of Arkansas. The Senator heads the Select Committee on Improper Activities in the Labor or Management Field, which has accused Hoffa of gangster associations and questionable financial practices.

Winner on First Ballot

A three-hour roll-call gave Hoffa the $50,000-a-year union presidency on the first ballot. His machine, in full command of the convention since it opened Monday, registered 1,208 votes for Hoffa.

William A. Lee of Chicago, the union's seventh vice president, was second with 313 votes. Thomas J. Haggerty of Chicago, secretary-treasurer of Milk Wagon Drivers Union, Local 753, trailed with 140 votes.

The Hoffa forces then began providing the new leader with a rubber stamp board. It elected five of thirteen vice presidents and would have elected the rest today if time had permitted completion of the cumbersome balloting procedure.

Hoffa repeatedly indicated his irritation that some of the old vice presidents marked for elimination had refused to give up without the formality of a roll-call.

Even before the voting, the McClellan committee subpoenaed the full records of the convention's credentials committee. A United States marshal served the subpoena this morning on Joseph Konowe of New York, the committee secretary. He was directed to turn over all

Continued on Page 6, Column 7

FAUBUS COMPARES HIS STAND TO LEE'S

Says He Will Remain Loyal to People of Arkansas— All Is Quiet at School

By HOMER BIGART
Special to The New York Times.

LITTLE ROCK, Ark., Oct. 4—Gov. Orval E. Faubus said today that he had made a decision as painfully difficult as the one that had confronted Robert E. Lee at the outset of the Civil War.

"Lee was offered command of the Federal Army in 1861," Governor Faubus recalled. "Lee decided to remain loyal to the people of his state.

"The Democratic party of the North wants me to go along with them on the integration issue. I will remain with the people of Arkansas."

Governor Faubus said he had come under no local pressure to change his stand on integration at Little Rock Central High School. It was a stand that forced President Eisenhower to send Federal troops into this city to uphold Federal Court decisions and to safeguard the nine Negro students registered at Central High.

Winthrop Rockefeller, chairman of the Arkansas Industrial Development Commission, broke silence today on the Little Rock integration crisis, declaring it had "damaged" the state's prospects for economic progress. He called events of the past month "tragic."

It was a quiet day in Little Rock. The nine Negro boys and girls attended school without incident. But no early solution to the crisis seemed likely.

There was no break in the impasse reached Tuesday night when a compromise plan for the

Continued on Page 18, Column 2

Flu Widens in City; 10% Rate Predicted; 200,000 Pupils Out

By ROBERT ALDEN

Asian influenza continued to spread through the city yesterday.

Commissioner of Hospitals Morris A. Jacobs reported that there were ten times more respiratory infections than during the comparable period a year ago.

Attendance in the city's schools fell again. The Board of Education said that close to 200,000 of the city's 941,000 pupils were not in their classrooms yesterday. On Thursday 160,000 pupils were absent.

The attendance estimates were based on a sampling of the schools by the board. The sampling showed that in some section in the Harlem area—the section hardest hit by the epidemic—more than 50 per cent of the pupils were absent. The board estimated that the overall city absence rate was 20 per cent.

3,000 Teachers Absent

About 3,000 teachers out of about 39,000 were not in their classrooms yesterday, compared with 2,700 absent on Thursday.

The city's acting Health Commissioner, Dr. Roscoe P. Kandle, said he expected that the total number of people affected by the highly infectious disease would run closer to 800,000 rather than 1,600,000 as predicted in some quarters.

It was estimated Thursday that 200,000 persons in New York had contracted the respiratory infection, and the total yesterday was believed to be somewhat higher.

Commissioner Kandle explained that any attempt to project the ultimate number of cases would involve conjecture.

Continued on Page 8, Column 1

ARGENTINA TAKES EMERGENCY STEPS

State of Siege Proclaimed in Buenos Aires Region —Arrests Reported

By Reuters.

BUENOS AIRES, Oct. 4—A state of siege, suspending constitutional guarantees, was proclaimed tonight in Buenos Aires city and Province.

The Under Secretary of the Ministry of Interior, Garcia Puente, announced the state of siege at a news conference.

He said the emergency move suspended for thirty days the constitutional guarantees in the capital and the Province of Buenos Aires, but not in the remainder of the nation.

He said the measure was aimed exclusively "at defending the normal development of the Government's political plan, jeopardized through sabotage and social unrest."

The proclamation of the state of siege followed the arrest of scores of labor leaders during the day. The number arrested was estimated by observers at 100 to 300.

Bankers, telephone workers, oilworkers, seamstresses and other unions reported tonight that their leaders had been detained and were taken aboard

Continued on Page 4, Column 5

City Sifts Charge That Schupler, Brooklyn Councilman, Sold a Job

By PAUL CROWELL

The city is investigating a complaint that Councilman Philip J. Schupler accepted a $500 fee last year in exchange for a promise to get a job for a Brooklyn business man.

William R. Peer, executive secretary to Mayor Wagner, said yesterday that the inquiry was started several weeks ago after the complaint had been made by Sol L. Hoffman of 1934 Sixty-third Street, Brooklyn.

At the office of Investigation Commissioner Charles H. Tenney, who is making the investigation, it was said that no findings or conclusions had been reached.

The charge was denied by Mr. Schupler, a Democrat-Liberal, in a telephone interview.

He said that he had received a $500 check from Mr. Hoffman in May, 1956, but that it was given to him as a campaign contribution. Mr. Schupler was then a candidate for re-election as a Democratic district leader. He was defeated in the primary election a month later.

Disclosure of the investigation brought from Robert K. Christenberry, the Republican candidate for Mayor, the charge that "corruption and scandal in our City Council is symptomatic of the Wagner administration."

In a formal statement commenting on the Schupler case Mr. Christenberry called upon the city's voters to support his

Continued on Page 15, Column 5

IN TOKEN OF VICTORY: Dave Beck, retiring head of the Teamsters Union, raises hand of James R. Hoffa upon his election as union's president. At right is Mrs. Hoffa.

Associated Press Wirephoto

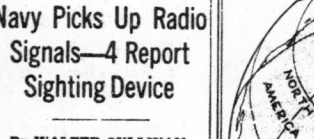

Guy Mollet
Associated Press

Ex-Premier Mollet Accepts Bid To Form a New French Cabinet

Socialist Leader Agrees With Reluctance and Without Giving Much Hope

By ROBERT C. DOTY
Special to The New York Times.

PARIS, Oct. 4—Former Premier Guy Mollet agreed reluctantly and without much hope today to try to form a new French Cabinet.

M. Mollet's pessimism, shared by many observers here, was based on the fact that both he and his party, the Socialists, still hold strongly to the policies that caused the defeat of the last two Cabinets, M. Mollet's own and that of Premier Maurice Bourgès-Maunoury, a Radical.

Thus the Socialists still support the views on economic and social questions, including the demand for extensive governmental decree powers in those domains, that brought M. Mollet's Government down last May for a record-breaking sixty-eight weeks in office. The average Cabinet's life span has been twenty-nine weeks.

At the same time the Socialists regard as a minimum of reform the program for limited Algerian home rule outlined in the framework law that was defeated in the Assembly Monday.

In both cases, opposition from the Right-wing Independents constituted the margin of defeat.

If M. Mollet should find it impossible to muster another major-

Continued on Page 5, Column 6

COURSE RECORDED

Navy Picks Up Radio Signals—4 Report Sighting Device

By WALTER SULLIVAN
Special to The New York Times.

WASHINGTON, Saturday, Oct. 5—The Naval Research Laboratory announced early today that it had recorded four crossings of the Soviet earth satellite over the United States.

It said that one had passed near Washington. Two crossings were farther to the west. The location of the fourth was not made available immediately.

It added that tracking would be continued in an attempt to pin down the orbit sufficiently to obtain scientific information of the type sought in the International Geophysical Year.

[Four visual sightings, one of which was in conjunction with a radio contact, were reported by early Saturday morning. Two sightings were reported at Columbus, Ohio, and one each from Terre Haute, Ind., and Whittier, Calif.]

Press Reports Noted

Soviet newspapers reported several weeks ago that the Soviet satellites would broadcast on frequencies in the neighborhood of twenty and forty megacycles. More exact frequencies were given by Soviet scientists at a conference on rockets and satellites that took place here this week.

Presumably the Naval Research Laboratory, which is responsible for the United States satellite program under the National Academy of Sciences, immediately set up receivers on those frequencies.

The tracking system established in this country to monitor its own satellites uses 108 megacycles, since much more accurate positions can be obtained with the higher frequencies. The Russians at first agreed to use equipment "compatible" with that of the United States, but then announced the lower frequencies.

Deception Ruled Out

American scientists believe this was because of a shortage of Soviet receivers capable of handling the higher frequency. It was not thought to be designed to hide the satellite since the Soviet signals are within easy reach of American listeners.

This was demonstrated last night as amateur and commercial radio stations, as well as the Naval Research Laboratory, reported hearing them.

Teams of visual observers at 150 stations in the United States and other Western nations were alerted during the

Continued on Page 3, Column 6

The New York Times
Oct. 5, 1957

The approximate orbit of the Russian earth satellite is shown by black line. The rotation of the earth will bring the United States under the orbit of Soviet-made moon.

Device Is 8 Times Heavier Than One Planned by U.S.

Special to The New York Times.

WASHINGTON, Oct. 4—Leaders of the United States earth satellite program were astonished tonight to learn that the Soviet Union had launched a satellite eight times heavier than that contemplated by this country.

Dr. Joseph Kaplan, chairman of the United States program for the International Geophysical Year, described the 184-pound weight as "fantastic." The heaviest American satellites are to weigh twenty-one and a half pounds.

The actual launching, nevertheless, did not take the American scientists by surprise. At the end of working sessions at the International Conference on Rockets and Satellites, which has been taking place here, some said they thought the pitching of a Soviet satellite into the sky was imminent.

The satellite must fly at a speed of about 18,000 miles an hour to counteract the force of gravity at an altitude of 560 miles. The initial announcement in Moscow did not make it clear whether or not the rocket that placed it in orbit was aimed north or south.

Its Direction in Doubt

This would determine whether or not the satellite's initial crossing of the United States was northbound or southbound. Since the earth rotates within the orbit the satellite should in one day traverse almost all nations of the world.

With an orbit inclined 65 degrees to the equator, its sweep would cover virtually the entire region between the Arctic circle and the Antarctic circle.

William A. Holaday, special assistant to the Secretary of Defense for guided missiles, said the launching was not evidence of Soviet technological superiority in missile and rocket developments.

Mr. Holaday noted that Project Vanguard, the United States satellite program, had been an "open" project as part of the International Geophysical year and there has been no

Continued on Page 3, Column 7

SATELLITE SIGNAL BROADCAST HERE

Impulse Carried on Radio and TV—First Reported by Long Island Station

By ROY SILVER

Radio signals from the first satellite launched yesterday by the Russians were broadcast to radio and television audiences here last night.

The first word that the signals had been received in this country was reported by RCA Communication, Inc. It said that its receiving station at Riverhead, L. I., had picked up impulses from the Soviet satellite.

The National Broadcasting Company and the Columbia Broadcasting System broke into their radio and television programs to enable their audiences to hear the pinging sound of the "moon's" signal. The British Broadcasting Corporation in London said it had tuned powerful receivers to the Soviet earth satellite frequencies. Reuter's radio station north of London reported hearing the signals.

RCA Communications, a subsidiary of Radio Corporation of America, said the first signal had been received at 8:07 P. M. on a frequency of 20.005 megacycles on the 15-meter wave length.

One hour and twenty-nine minutes later, at 9:36 P. M., the receiving station, situated about eighty miles from the city, reported that the satellite was making another round of the earth. Other approaches by

Continued on Page 2, Column 4

Warsaw Crushes New Protest; Clubs, Tear Gas Rout Students

By SYDNEY GRUSON
Special to The New York Times.

WARSAW, Oct. 4—Policemen and students clashed again in the streets of Warsaw tonight. Security chiefs, seemingly nervous, threw a guard of several hundred workers' militia around the downtown headquarters of the ruling United Workers (Communist) party.

For the second successive night the police broke up demonstrations by firing tear gas and beating students and others with rubber truncheons.

What began last night as a protest against the closing of one newspaper was turning tonight into a general clamor against police brutality and the suppression of free speech. By midnight the city had calmed

down and the people had left the streets.

Among those clubbed tonight was Franco Fabiani, permanent correspondent here of the Italian Communist paper L'Unita. He suffered two minor head wounds.

Signor Fabiani was caught in crowds charged by the police after about 3,000 students had met in the Polytechnic and adopted a resolution protesting both the closing of the newspaper Po Prostu and the "brutal interference" of the police at last night's meeting.

Tonight's trouble started at the Polytechnic, the huge advanced technical school near the heart of Warsaw. It was

Continued on Page 5, Column 2

560 MILES HIGH

Visible With Simple Binoculars, Moscow Statement Says

Text of Tass announcement appears on Page 3.

By WILLIAM J. JORDEN
Special to The New York Times.

MOSCOW, Saturday, Oct. 5—The Soviet Union announced this morning that it successfully launched a man-made earth satellite into space yesterday.

The Russians calculated the satellite's orbit at a maximum of 560 miles above the earth and its speed at 18,000 miles an hour.

The official Soviet news agency Tass said the artificial moon, with a diameter of twenty-two inches and a weight of 184 pounds, was circling the earth once every hour and thirty-five minutes. This means more than fifteen times a day.

Two radio transmitters, Tass said, are sending signals continuously on frequencies of 20.005 and 40.002 megacycles. These signals were said to be strong enough to be picked up by amateur radio operators. The trajectory of the satellite is being tracked by numerous scientific stations.

Due Over Moscow Today

Tass said the satellite was moving at an angle of 65 degrees to the equatorial plane and would pass over the Moscow area twice today.

"Its flight," the announcement added, "will be observed in the rays of the rising and setting sun with the aid of the simplest optical instruments, such as binoculars and spyglasses."

The Soviet Union said the world's first satellite was "successfully launched" yesterday. Thus it asserted that it had put a scientific instrument into space before the United States, Washington has disclosed plans to launch a satellite next spring, Oct. 4.

The Moscow announcement said the Soviet Union planned to send up more and bigger and heavier artificial satellites during the current International Geophysical Year, an eighteen-month period of study of the earth, its crust and the space surrounding it.

Five Miles a Second

The rocket that carried the satellite into space left the earth at a rate of five miles a second, the Tass announcement said. Nothing was revealed, however, concerning the make of which the man-made moon was constructed or the site in the Soviet Union where the sphere was launched.

The Soviet Union said its sphere circling the earth had opened the way to interplanetary travel.

It did not pass up the opportunity to use the launching for propaganda purposes. It said its announcement that people could now see how "the new socialist society" had turned the boldest dreams of mankind into reality.

Moscow said the satellite was the result of years of study and research on the part of Soviet scientists.

Several Years of Study

Tass said:

"For several years the research and experimental designing work had been under way in the Soviet Union to create artificial satellites of the earth. It has already been reported in the press that the launching of the earth satellites in the U. S. S. R. had been planned in accordance with the program of International Geophysical Year research.

"As a result of intensive work by the research institutes and design bureaus, the first artificial earth satellite in the world has now been created. This first satellite was successfully launched in the U. S. S. R. on October fourth."

The Soviet announcement said that as a result of the tremendous speed at which the satellite was moving it would

Continued on Page 3, Column 8

The New York Times.

LATE CITY EDITION
U.S. Weather Bureau Report (Page 80) forecast:
Rain early today; cloudy later;
rain late tonight and tomorrow.
Temp. range: 65—55. Yesterday: 62.0—55.2.

NEWS SUMMARY AND INDEX, PAGE 95

VOL. CVII—No. 36,443. © 1957, by The New York Times Company. Times Square, New York 36, N.Y.

NEW YORK, SUNDAY, NOVEMBER 3, 1957.

25c beyond 100-mile zone from New York City

SECTION ONE
TWENTY-FIVE CENTS

SOVIET FIRES NEW SATELLITE, CARRYING DOG; HALF-TON SPHERE IS REPORTED 900 MILES UP

Zhukov Ousted From Party Jobs; Konev Condemns Him

MEYNER'S VICTORY IS SEEN IN SURVEY OF JERSEY VOTERS

Democratic Governor Likely to Win Re-election Over Senator Forbes Tuesday

A Times Team Report

A team of New York Times reporters has just completed a survey of political trends and issues in New Jersey. Reports on the election campaign there come from George Cable Wright, Milton Honig, Alfred E. Clark, Leonard Buder, John W. Slocum and Layhmond Robinson.

By GEORGE CABLE WRIGHT

The curtain will descend tomorrow night on the New Jersey Governorship campaign. The contest—on the surface, at least—appears to have been enacted before a relatively bored audience.

Neither Gov. Robert B. Meyner, the Democratic incumbent, nor State Senator Malcolm S. Forbes, the Republican candidate, has exhibited the ability to rouse the voting public markedly from its apparent apathy.

Beyond the Hudson and the Delaware, however, far greater interest is being manifested in the contest.

The Eisenhower Administration has staked its prestige on the results of the balloting as never before in a state-wide race. Republicans and Democrats alike at the national level are eagerly awaiting the vote tally. Each party hopes to gain from it a trend in its favor.

Surprise Possible

The apparent lack of interest locally may well be misleading. It is not an uncommon trait of the state's electorate, as witness 1953, 1954 and 1956. In those years, the pre-election temper turned out to be a "sleeper." The voters, from Cape May to High Point, set their alarms for election morn, and flocked to the polls.

As the present campaign progressed, it became increasingly evident that, in all probability, it would be decided on the basis of personality rather than on issues. This was verified by a team of New York Times reporters in the field.

On the basis of findings of The Times' survey team, victory for Mr. Meyner is definitely in-

Continued on Page 60, Column 6

Major Sports News

FOOTBALL

Navy beat Notre Dame in the nation's top college contest yesterday. Scores of leading games:

Alabama .....14 Georgia 13
Amherst ....19 Tufts 6
Army ....53 Colgate 7
Auburn ......6 Florida 0
Cornell ......8 Columbia 0
Dartmouth .14 Yale 14
Delaware ..23 Rutgers 19
Georgia T. ..13 Duke 0
Harvard ....13 Penn 6
Iowa ....21 Michigan ...21
Michigan St.21 Wisconsin ...7
Minnesota ..34 Indiana 0
Missouri .....9 Colorado 0
Navy ....20 Notre Dame..6
N. C. State ..47 Northwestern .0
Ohio State ..13 Kansas St....0
Oklahoma ..27 Stanford 26
Oregon .....37 Wash. St....25
Penn St. .....7 W. Virginia..0
Princeton ...7 Brown 0
Purdue ......21 Illinois 6
Syracuse ...24 Pittsburgh ..21
T. C. U. .....19 Baylor 0
Tennessee ..35 N. Carolina..0
Texas A&M. 7 Arkansas 0
Vanderbilt ...7 L. S. U. 0

HORSE RACING

Eddie Schmidt won the $86,900 Gallant Fox Handicap at Jamaica by a length. Bold Ruler was first in the Benjamin Franklin Handicap.

HOCKEY

The Rangers routed the Boston Bruins, 5—0.

Details in Section 5.

President and Class Honor Academy

The New York Times (by Arthur Brower)

The President drinks from fountain he and other members of 1915 class gave to academy. Mrs. Eisenhower watches.

By W. H. LAWRENCE

Special to The New York Times.

WEST POINT, N. Y., Nov. 2 — President Eisenhower watched Army defeat Colgate today as the climax to a nostalgic reunion with his 1915 Military Academy classmates. Like any other old grad, the President leaped to his feet and cheered whenever Army threatened or scored—and he had many opportunities to do so. Today can be so it will be the first time since

Continued on Page 45, Column 1

DEMOCRATS COUNT ON PARTY VICTORY

Believe Wagner Can Win Without Liberal Votes in Mayoral Race

By LEO EGAN

Democratic leaders were counting confidently yesterday on obtaining enough votes on their party's line alone to insure the re-election of Mayor Wagner and his running mates next Tuesday. If they can do so it will be the first time since 1932 that a Democrat has received a majority of all the votes in a New York City Mayoral election.

Four years ago Mr. Wagner won by virtue of a split in the opposition between Harold Riegelman, Republican, and Rudolph Halley, Liberal and independent. Mr. Wagner received just over 45 per cent of the total vote cast.

This year the Liberal party is backing Mayor Wagner and his two city-wide running mates, Controller Lawrence E. Gerosa and City Council President Abe Stark. But Democratic leaders would like to be able to say they could have won without the Liberal endorsement.

Alex Rose, state vice-chairman and spokesman for the Liberal party, referred to this Democratic attitude yesterday in appealing for a large Wagner-Gerosa-Stark vote on the Liberal party line.

"A large vote on the Liberal line is a vote with a special message to the city administration to be independent and is the best guarantee for a clean and effective administration on all levels of city government," he said.

"A large vote on the Liberal line will continue the Liberal party as the political conscience

Continued on Page 53, Column 3

British and French, a Year After, Say Suez Invasion Was Justified

London Reconciled

By DREW MIDDLETON

Special to The New York Times.

LONDON, Nov. 2—In the view of some of those who planned the British-French invasion of Egypt, the situation obtaining in the Middle East a year later justifies that attempt to halt the march of Arab nationalism and its ally, Soviet communism, in the area.

A year ago the Soviet Union had one client and ally in the Middle East, Egypt. Today it has two, Egypt and Syria. The withdrawal of the British and French forces from Suez and the behest of the United Nations has been interpreted by Arab nationalists as a victory and has created a power vacuum into which Soviet imperialism has moved, it is noted.

The view that the invasion

Continued on Page 53, Column 3

Paris Still Bitter

By ROBERT C. DOTY

Special to The New York Times.

PARIS, Nov. 2 — The weekend of the first anniversary of the British-French invasion of Egypt finds most Frenchmen, including those who planned the action, convinced that it was a good idea.

There is no tendency here to push such an idea aggressively. On the contrary, French high officialdom seeks to liquidate as speedily and unobtrusively as possible the remaining economic, political and diplomatic consequences of last fall's events. This is regarded as the logical prerequisite to a restoration of complete interallied confidence and effective action to repair the Western position in the Middle East.

Furthermore, the French-

Continued on Page 53, Column 4

A.F.L.-C.I.O. TARGET RESIGNS AS CHIEF OF TEXTILE UNION

Valente Voices Hope Group Will Stay in Federation —2 More Actions Taken

Special to The New York Times.

WASHINGTON, Nov. 2—The president of the United Textile Workers, Anthony Valente, resigned today. He said he was acting to help his union retain its membership in the American Federation of Labor and Congress of Industrial Organizations.

The 44,000-member union was one of three cited for corruption last month by the executive council of the parent labor organization. Mr. Valente was declared ineligible to hold office.

Tonight, the leadership of the union accepted the resignation of Mr. Valente and announced other steps to conform with demands by the A. F. L.-C. I. O. to "clean up" the textile workers operations.

Francis Schaufenbil, secretary-treasurer of the union, told reporters at the end of an all-day meeting of the organization's executive board that "we certainly hope" the actions taken would keep the textile workers in the main body.

2 Other Measures

The board meeting was called today to answer charges brought by the A. F. L.-C. I. O. council.

In addition to accepting Mr. Valente's resignation, the board took these two actions to comply with the council's demands:

1. It agreed to call a special convention "as soon as possible" to elect new officers. The session will be in Washington, New York or Philadelphia.

2. The board "rescinded" a $104,000 severance pay deal for Lloyd Klenert, resigned secretary-treasurer, and "has not obligated" the union on any financial arrangement with any other resigned officers. This was, presumably, a reference to Mr. Valente. Senate investigators have accused Mr. Valente and Mr. Klenert of buying their homes with union funds and using devious bookkeeping to cover their tracks.

Criticizes Members of Council

Mr. Valente resigned at a meeting of the Textile Workers Executive Board, called to answer the council's charges. Talking with reporters during a recess, he loosed bitter criticism against twelve of the twenty-nine members of the A. F. L.-C. I. O. council.

He said the twelve had pledged him their support, but "they reneged on their commitments." He did not name the twelve.

This development in the labor

Continued on Page 44, Column 3

Voters Will Settle 7 State Questions; Issues Are Listed

Special to The New York Times.

ALBANY, Nov. 2—Voters who go to the polls on Tuesday will have a chance to pass on six proposed amendments to the State Constitution and whether a constitutional convention should be held.

If performance runs true, only about half those voting will bother to answer the seven questions across the top of every ballot.

The type on the ballot is small and the questions do not always express the impact of the proposition.

Following is a description of each proposal, what it would do and the arguments for and against it:

The ballot asks:

"Shall there be a convention to revise the Constitution and amend the same?"

Approval would mean the voters would elect delegates on a party basis in 1958 and those elected would hold a convention the following year, probably in the summer. The convention

Continued on Page 62, Column 1

ZHUKOV HUMBLED

He Admits 'Mistakes' —Accused of 'Cult' in Armed Forces

Text of Soviet communiqué is printed on Page 4.

By WILLIAM J. JORDEN

Special to The New York Times.

MOSCOW, Sunday, Nov. 3—Marshal Georgi K. Zhukov, dismissed a week ago as Defense Minister of the Soviet Union, has been removed from all his posts in the Soviet Communist party.

The party's Central Committee announced last night that Marshal Zhukov has lost his place on the party's central policy-making group, the Presidium, as well as on the Central Committee itself. The principal charge against the hero of World War II was that he had tried to eliminate the Communist party's direction and control of the Soviet armed forces.

The Communist party newspaper Pravda reported this morning that Marshal Zhukov had admitted his "mistakes" during the Central Committee meeting at which he was expelled from the party leadership.

Anti-Stalin Phrase Used

He tempered that acceptance somewhat by telling his party comrades that he accepted their criticism of him as being "in the main correct." He also was said to have accepted the attack on his leadership of the armed forces as being of "comradely party assistance to me personally and to other military workers."

The barrel-chested, square-jawed soldier was charged with promoting his own "cult of personality" in the army. This is the phrase used here in reference to Stalin's one-man rule, which was vigorously condemned by the Twentieth Congress of the Communist party last year.

"With the help of sycophants and flatterers," the Central Committee said, "he was praised to the sky in lectures and reports, in articles, films and pamphlets, and his person and role in the Great Patriotic War [World War II] were overglorified."

The result, the Central Committee charged, was that the whole history of the war had been "distorted." It said that by building himself up Marshal Zhukov had belittled the efforts of the Soviet people, of the

Continued on Page 3, Column 1

SOVIET 'STRESSES' SEEN BY THE U.S.

Washington Expects Strain Behind the Iron Curtain From Zhukov Disgrace

State Department statement will be found on Page 6.

By RUSSELL BAKER

Special to The New York Times.

WASHINGTON, Nov. 2—The State Department said tonight that the downgrading of Marshal Georgi K. Zhukov showed the "strains and stresses" present in the Soviet Union and countries dominated by the Soviet Communists.

In a brief formal statement, the department noted that Marshal Zhukov's "disgrace" followed only by a short time the expressed desire of Nikita S. Khrushchev, First Secretary of the Soviet Communist party, to send the military leader on a special mission to the United States.

The department said this, following so closely "similar action against" other one-time Soviet leaders, demonstrated the polit-

Continued on Page 7, Column 1

Marshal Is Linked to Stalin In Blame for '41 Reverses

Konev Charges Ex-Chief Distorted History to Create Hero's Role

Special to The New York Times.

MOSCOW, Sunday, Nov. 3—Marshal Ivan S. Konev, long companion and subordinate of Marshal Georgi K. Zhukov, condemned the former Defense Minister today for "errors in military science."

Marshal Konev's attack was the first derogatory statement leveled against Marshal Zhukov on military grounds.

Soviet commander of the Warsaw Pact forces, Marshal Konev issued his condemnation in an article in today's Pravda, the Communist party organ.

The Konev article said that Marshal Zhukov was responsible along with Stalin for lack of preparedness in the Soviet Union to meet the imminent German attack in June, 1941. It belittled Marshal Zhukov's role in the victories at Stalingrad and Berlin and accused Marshal Zhukov of undue pride and of twisting historical fact.

Associated Press

Marshal Ivan S. Konev

Marshal Konev's attack on Marshal Zhukov was bitter and extensive. Marshal Konev noted that his former comrade in

Continued on Page 3, Column 4

SATELLITE SIGNAL RECEIVED AT M.I.T.

Scientists Believe That Orbit Repeats First Sphere— Trackers Are Alerted

By The United Press

CAMBRIDGE, Mass., Sunday, Nov. 3—The first American pick-up of the new Soviet satellite's radio signal was reported early today to the Smithsonian Astrophysical Observatory.

Leon Campbell at the observatory said that the report was received from William S. Cooper of the Massachusetts Institute of Technology. Mr. Cooper said that he heard the signal at 2:02 A. M., between 20 and 20.5 megacycles.

Dr. J. Allen Hynek of the observatory staff said that the satellite apparently was in roughly the same path of 65 degrees as the first Soviet satellite.

The perigee (minimum altitude) probably is about 140 miles, the same as for the first satellite, Dr. Hynek said. "It seems like a repetition of the orbit of the first satellite," he added.

The Soviet launching of the

Continued on Page 26, Column 4

ORBIT COMPLETED

Animal Still Is Alive, Sealed in Satellite, Moscow Thinks

By The Associated Press

LONDON, Sunday, Nov. 3—The Soviet Union announced today it had launched a second space satellite, this one carrying a dog. Radio signals indicated the animal was living, the Russians said.

A satellite six times as heavy as the one sent up Oct. 4 now is circling the earth every hour and forty-two minutes at a height of 937 miles, Moscow said. This means that the speed is nearly 18,000 miles an hour for the 1,110-pound satellite.

The dog was reported hermetically sealed in a container equipped with an air-conditioning system.

Moscow Radio said data received from the second satellite indicated the "functioning of scientific instruments and control of the living activities of the animal are taking place normally."

First Trip Reported

The new satellite carries transmitting equipment and apparatus for measuring cosmic rays, temperature and pressure. It also carries equipment for reporting the condition of the dog.

It first passed over the Soviet capital at 11:20 P. M. Eastern Standard Time last night and then completed its first trip around the earth over Moscow at 1:05 A. M. today, the Soviet Union reported.

The announcement said the second satellite was "dedicated to the fortieth anniversary of the great October revolution," which the Communist world will celebrate in Moscow beginning next Thursday.

The new earth satellite is completing its orbit in about seven minutes more than the original Sputnik, still circling the earth.

Japan Receives Signals

Moscow said the second sphere was sending out two radio signals.

One, like the "beep" signal transmitted by the first satellite, is on a frequency of 20.005 megacycles. The other signal, at 40.002 megacycles, is a continuous one.

In Tokyo the Japan Broadcasting Corporation announced that radio signals from the second satellite were being heard. The corporation picked up the signals twenty-three minutes after Moscow's announcement. The "beep" was at intervals of three-tenths of a second.

A three-stage rocket shoved the original satellite into its orbit. The first Moscow announcement of the second sphere did not explain how it had been sent up.

Although the announcement of the satellite's passing over Moscow indicated an interval of one hour and forty-five min-

Continued on Page 26, Column 2

Mao Is in Moscow; He Hails Soviet Tie

By MAX FRANKEL

Special to The New York Times.

MOSCOW, Nov. 2—Mao Tse-tung, leader of Communist China, arrived in Moscow today. He is probably the most important of the gathering here to show the unity and might of international communism.

Virtually all the reigning heads of Communist nations and parties, with the notable exception of President Tito of Yugoslavia, will make the pilgrimage here to join in next week's celebrations of the fortieth anniversary of the Bolshevik Revolution.

Expected in addition to Mr. Mao, who is the Chinese Communist chief of state and party chairman, are Poland's party leader, Wladyslaw Gomulka, and Premier Josef Cyrankiewicz; Premier Janos Kadar of Hun-

Continued on Page 27, Column 2

Associated Press Radiophoto

CHINESE COMMUNIST LEADER GREETED IN MOSCOW: Mao Tse-tung, left, chief of state and Communist party chief, as he arrived yesterday at the capital airport. With him were Nikita S. Khrushchev, center, Soviet Communist chief, and Premier Nikolai A. Bulganin.

"All the News That's Fit to Print"

The New York Times.

LATE CITY EDITION
U.S. Weather Bureau Report (Page 43) forecasts
Fair, breezy, less humid today; clear and cool tonight. Fair tomorrow.
Temp. range: 78—60. Yesterday: 79.3—64.8.

VOL. CVII..No. 36,654.

© 1958, by The New York Times Company.
Times Square, New York 36, N. Y.

NEW YORK, MONDAY, JUNE 2, 1958.

15c beyond 100-mile zone from New York City.
Higher in air delivery cities.

FIVE CENTS

DE GAULLE NAMED PREMIER IN 329-224 VOTE; ASKS 6-MONTH DECREE RULE; LEFTISTS RIOT; ALGIERS IS DISPLEASED BY CABINET CHOICES

CRASHES KILL 344 ON 3-DAY HOLIDAY; RAIN CURBS TOLL

Auto Deaths Below Forecast — Temperature Climbs to 79.3 Degrees Here

By LAWRENCE O'KANE

Traffic fatalities climbed yesterday in the final, homebound hours of the Memorial Day week-end.

Bad weather over much of the nation dampened the outing spirits of many. But it also induced motorists to drive carefully.

By 2 A. M. today 344 persons had died in traffic accidents since 6 P. M. Thursday, according to The Associated Press. Altogether there were 554 accidental deaths, including 122 drownings and eight-eight from miscellaneous causes.

In New York City, three persons were killed and 556 injured in 387 road accidents, according to Police Department figures covering the period from 8 A. M. Thursday to 4 P. M. yesterday. Only property was damaged in 487 other accidents.

Cautious Optimism

Late yesterday the National Safety Council began to express cautious optimism that traffic deaths would not exceed the peak three-day Memorial Day week-end toll of 369 recorded in 1955.

Last week the council had predicted 350 deaths for the 1958 holiday week-end, but after a series of multi-death accidents Saturday it began to voice fears of a new record.

The council said rain and slippery highways had restricted short-distance travel as picnics and beach outings were canceled. Showers and thunderstorms were reported yesterday from the Gulf states to southern New England. Squalls ranged the Great Lakes and tornado alerts were issued for parts of the South and Midwest.

Rain Avoids City

In New York City, the warmest day of the year sent hundreds of thousands to beaches and parks. Afternoon rains had been predicted, but failed to materialize. The threat kept crowds from swelling to record proportions, however, and chilly offshore winds kept most beachgoers out of the water.

The year's highest temperature here—79.3 degrees—was registered at 4:20 P. M.

Today is expected to be fair, but not as warm or humid as yesterday. Afternoon temperatures are expected to be in the 70's. The prediction for Tuesday is fair with high temperatures and low humidity.

As yesterday drew to a close, city-bound traffic increased on highways and bridges and in tunnels. Most reports described the flow as heavy, but moving freely.

A 22-year-old airman was injured fatally early yesterday when his automobile struck a

Continued on Page 15, Column 2

Ernst Report on Galindez Clears Dominican Dictator

Inquiry for Trujillo Hints That Missing Columbia Scholar May Be Alive — Anti-Franco Activities Cited

By PETER KIHSS

Morris L. Ernst has filed a report in effect clearing Generalissimo Rafael L. Trujillo and his Dominican dictatorship of any role in the two-year-old disappearance here of Jesús de Galindez, a Basque scholar.

The New York lawyer's report, made after a ten-month investigation for the Dominican Republic, implied that the anti-Trujillo writer might be alive. It suggested that Dr. Galindez' disappearance March 12, 1956, might be related "to his substantial and perhaps carefully confused fiscal operations and his profound interest in Spain after Franco."

Dr. Galindez, a Spanish exile, had reported to the Department of Justice a total of $1,024,-418.24 in contributions he raised as agent for the anti-Franco Basque Government - in - exile from May, 1949, through January, 1956.

The Ernst report also rejected a theory that Gerald Lester Murphy, an American pilot who vanished in the Dominican Republic Dec. 3, 1956, might have flown Mr. Galindez to that country as a kidnap victim.

Mr. Ernst asserted that the Cuban Government had "reliable reports" that Mr. Murphy landed his plane in Cuba on March 13, 1956—before setting it down later that day in Miami.

The lawyer charged that Mr. Murphy had been "engaged in an illegal operation for hire." He recalled the pilot's reputed statements that he had flown arms and funds to Cuba for opponents of Cuban President Fulgencio Batista.

While formal comment by Government investigators in the United States was unavailable,

Continued on Page 14, Column 4

Hospital Deficits Increase With Advance in Medicine

By EMMA HARRISON

Voluntary hospitals in the New York area reported an operating loss of $23,500,000 for 1957, the United Hospital Fund disclosed yesterday. This is an increase of $3,550,000 over the 1956 figure of $19,950,000.

The operating loss for the seventy-four voluntary hospitals and convalescent homes is exclusive of the hospitals' receipts from philanthropic support and income from investment. But the figure also excludes hospital depreciation, interest on indebtedness and money spent on research and medical education, the fund noted.

The fund estimated the hospitals' net loss after all income at $6,000,000. This estimate includes an allowance of 5 per cent for plant depreciation.

However, operating income, including revenue from patients and from auxiliary activities such as nursing schools and cafeterias, went up 6.8 per cent to $176,000,000. Operating costs, meanwhile, climbed 8 per cent to $199,500,000.

Thus, with operating costs increasing partly because of better care for patients, the voluntary hospitals are faced with a paradox: The patients

Continued on Page 29, Column 2

187 MILLION URGED FOR CITY SCHOOLS

73 Projects Are Planned Over Three Budgets to House 74,740 Pupils

By GENE CURRIVAN

An extraordinary capital budget estimate of $187,600,000 for the city's school building program was announced yesterday. It would require financing in three successive budgets.

It includes seventy-three projects with an enrollment capacity of 74,740 pupils.

The proposed budget for next year is $108,200,000 for thirty-one projects.

Last year the Board of Education asked for $106,800,000 and received a little less than $96,000,000.

This year's unusual proposal was put forth by the Committee on Building and Sites headed by Charles J. Bensley. It may be predicated on the hope that a constitutional amendment giving the city the right to borrow $500,000,000 for spending on buildings will eventually be adopted. The amendment has been approved by the Legislature but must be reapproved at the next session and then submitted

Continued on Page 19, Column 4

Soviet Fishing Fleet Off Canada Causing Concern in Washington

Vessels Anchored Near Grand Banks — Each Departing Craft Always Replaced

By ALLEN DRURY

WASHINGTON, June 1—A half-dozen Soviet fishing ships riding at anchor 100 miles off the east coast of Canada have the United States Navy and Air Force puzzled.

The vessels, stationed near an area marked off with buoys flying small Soviet flags, are in international waters near the Grand Banks.

Moscow recently lodged a vigorous protest with the United States Embassy, charging that a United States military plane had flown over one of the vessels at masthead height. The accusation has been denied by a high Washington official. He told newsmen that planes in the area normally flew at several thousand feet altitude.

According to this source, the United States Government recently received from Canada a photograph of one of the buoys made from a helicopter. The photograph appeared to indicate the buoy was a conventional type, with no signs of electronic gear that might be

CANADA

The New York Times — June 2, 1958
Soviet fishing vessels are anchored 100 miles off east coast of Canada (cross).

vessel is always replaced and is causing some concern here.

Continued on Page 8, Column 4

JUNTA AIDE BITTER

'Not the Government We Hoped For,' Civil Leader Declares

By THOMAS F. BRADY
Special to The New York Times.

ALGIERS, June 1 — Léon Delbecque, vice president of the All-Algerian Committee of Public Safety, said tonight that the de Gaulle Cabinet was "not yet the Government of Public Safety we hoped for."

Looking at the list of ministers of Premier Charles de Gaulle, he said to reporters: "You call that a Government? Who is Minister of the Interior? A civil servant. Who is Minister of Foreign Affairs? A civil servant."

Emile Pelletier, the new Interior Minister, is a former Prefect. Maurice Couve de Murville, the Foreign Minister, is a career diplomat. Both are considered non-political "technicians."

Moderation Is Target

M. Delbecque was expressing the bitter disappointment that is felt among civilian insurgent leaders here at the liberal moderation shown thus far in General de Gaulle's assumption of power. No one associated with the Public Safety movement appears on the Cabinet list.

Although M. Delbecque did not appear to approve of career civil servants in the Cabinet, he expressed his confidence in Premier de Gaulle and said he regarded the Cabinet as a step toward the ultimate goal.

But outside the Government General Building, scene of regular mass demonstrations since the civil-military insurrection May 13, there was only a scattering of persons and no sign of rejoicing.

Salan Aide Sees Victory

Col. Charles Lacheroy, spokesman for Gen. Raoul Salan, military ruler of Algeria, hailed General de Gaulle's assumption of power as a victory.

"Today is Sunday. People are at home. Last Sunday, however, the peo-

Continued on Page 5, Column 1

DE GAULLE STATES HIS TERMS: The general speaking in Paris yesterday before the French National Assembly before it approved the wartime leader as the nation's Premier.
Associated Press Radiophoto

U. S. IS 'GRATIFIED' AT FRENCH ACTION

White House Gives de Gaulle Warm Welcome—Capital Hopes He Can Visit Soon

By DANA ADAMS SCHMIDT
Special to The New York Times.

WASHINGTON, June 1—The White House welcomed Gen. Charles de Gaulle as Premier of France today in a warmly worded statement issued only two hours after the news of his investiture had reached Washington.

Administration officials said unofficially that they would be glad to see General de Gaulle visit the United States soon.

They said they assumed, however, that he would be too pre-occupied with French internal affairs during his first six months to make such a trip unless he were required to prepare for a summit meeting with the Soviet Union.

The White House statement was issued from Gettysburg, where President Eisenhower is spending the week-end. It read as follows:

"We have been witnessing with sympathy and understanding the difficult days through which France has been passing, and we are gratified that the French crisis is now being resolved.

"General de Gaulle has assumed heavy responsibilities at a critical juncture in French history. Our thoughts go out to the great French nation, wish-

Continued on Page 6, Column 4

Red-Led Demonstrators Clash With Paris Police

By W. GRANGER BLAIR
Special to The New York Times.

PARIS, June 1—Communist-inspired riots erupted in Paris today a few hours before the National Assembly voted to install Gen. Charles de Gaulle as Premier. The outbreaks started at 3 P. M. in working-class quarters in northern, eastern and southern section of the city.

At almost the same time the general rose to deliver his investiture speech in a jammed and tense Parliament ringed by armed security guards.

For the next three hours thousands of policemen, crowded into heavy vans, rushed to trouble spots to clash with about 10,000 demonstrators.

Many persons were injured—"several dozen," according to the police. The injured included twenty-five members of the security forces. The police arrested 190 rioters.

Crowds Arrive From Suburbs

Besides Leftists ready for action in town, the mobs were replenished by Leftists from industrial suburbs. Even before they arrived, the police descended on key train, bus and subway exits to intercept them.

The first clash between security forces and rioters came in northern Paris near the Porte de Clignancourt. Several hundred demonstrators tried to force their way south toward the center of the city through four vanloads of policemen.

Both sides struck out with clubs. After fifteen minutes of confused fighting, the Leftists retreated northward.

These rioters, like their fellows elsewhere in the city, car-

Continued on Page 5, Column 1

DE GAULLE SHUNS ASSEMBLY DEBATE

Strides Out After He Makes Brief Statement — Anger and Fear Mark Session

By HENRY GINIGER
Special to The New York Times.

PARIS, June 1—In anger, defiance, fear and resignation, the National Assembly held today one of the last sessions of France's present parliamentary Government.

The French Republic may go on—many Deputies fear its end—but it will not be the same one that France has known since it began functioning in 1947.

This was the consensus of those who were able to fight their way into the Assembly building on the Left Bank of the Seine to witness the strangest and most memorable session the Assembly has ever had.

That France had turned a page of her history was evident in the way the session ran its course. It took the Assembly a little more than four hours to accept Gen. Charles de Gaulle by a vote of 329 to 224 and during that time the man the Deputies were debating was not present.

General Scorns System

In the past, lesser aspirants to the Premiership — those willing to work within the established system General de Gaulle has always scorned—have made their investiture speeches, then have sat down alone on the front-center benches of the semi-circular chamber to follow the debate, take notes and answer questions put to them.

When General de Gaulle, looking tired and slightly hunched in his gray, double-breasted suit, finished his seven-minute speech, he strode out and was not seen again. From about 3:45 P. M. to shortly after 7:30, the Deputies seemed to be addressing a phantom or to be arguing with each other.

It appeared to many that for General de Gaulle and the Republic representatives had ended with

Continued on Page 5, Column 6

GENERAL IS HEARD

Assembly Postpones Voting on Reforms Urged by Regime

Text of de Gaulle's speech to the Assembly, Page 4.

By ROBERT C. DOTY
Special to The New York Times.

PARIS, Monday, June 2—Gen. Charles de Gaulle has become Premier of France. The National Assembly voted last night, 329 to 224, to invest the 67-year-old leader of the wartime French liberation movement.

Approved at the same time was a fifteen-member Cabinet, including three former Premiers, representatives of seven parties on the Left, Right and Center, and five nonpolitical technicians. The most noteworthy of the latter was the choice of Maurice Couve de Murville, a career diplomat, as Foreign Minister.

General de Gaulle returns to power twelve years after renouncing the Provisional Presidency and at a moment when France faces the threat of civil war by civilians and military leaders dissatisfied with governmental efforts toward ending the rebellion in Algeria.

Terms Implicitly Accepted

By investing General de Gaulle as Premier, the Deputies implicitly accepted the terms he outlined in a seven-minute speech to the packed, breathless Assembly. He demanded:

¶Six months of full decree power, free from Parliamentary interference.

¶Immediate action to revise the Constitution in a manner to permit a popular referendum on sweeping reforms, transforming the Parliamentary regime into a Presidential one.

¶Authority to submit to a referendum reforms of the French Union, permitting a new basis of association with such overseas territories as Algeria and Central and West Africa. This was widely interpreted as opening the possibility even of full independence for some areas.

Breakdown of Vote

General de Gaulle had the almost solid support of the Center and Right wing, nearly half of the Socialist votes and more than half of the Radical votes. Voting against him were the Communists, the rest of the Socialists and Radicals, and scattered Deputies of other parties.

From Algiers came reports that the inclusion in the Cabinet of men of such liberal repute in colonial matters as former Premiers Antoine Pinay, an Independent, and Pierre Pflimlin, the Popular Republican who preceded General de Gaulle, had caused disappointment among ultra-colonialists in the dissident Committees of Public Safety.

Soon after the Assembly vote was announced General de Gaulle met with President René Coty and the new Cabinet at Elysée Palace while a violent thunderstorm lashed the capital. During the meeting, a bolt struck the palace.

At the end of the meeting,

Continued on Page 4, Column 6

Tunisian Units Fire At 3 French Planes

By Reuters.

TUNIS, June 1—Tunisian troops fired today on three French planes that "violated Tunisian air space" in the Gabès region, a Government spokesman said tonight.

No further details were given and there was no immediate comment by French sources here.

The Tunisians reported yesterday that their troops had "apparently" hit a French plane that flew over Tunisian positions in the Gabès area. The site of a French air base, is on Tunisia's east coast about 200 miles south of Tunis.

Government sources still withheld official comment on French political developments. But the

Continued on Page 4, Column 5

Mahoney Wins Upstate Support As G.O.P.'s Choice for Governor

By DOUGLAS DALES

Support for State Senator Walter J. Mahoney of Buffalo as the Republican nominee for Governor spread eastward over the week-end. Heretofore backing for the Senate leader was concentrated in western New York.

In a joint statement, county chairmen of four Hudson Valley - Catskill counties declared that no suggested candidate had Senator Mahoney's experience in state government or his capacity to present issues in a forthright and intelligent fashion.

The statement was issued by Neal Brandow of Greene, Dr. Odgen Bush of Delaware, Harold Cole of Sullivan and Kenneth L. Wilson of Ulster.

These counties, with six others whose leaders or party organizations have endorsed Mr. Mahoney, will have 181 of the 586 delegates needed for nomination at the convention Aug. 25 and 26 in Rochester.

Previously the Buffalo Senator has been assured publicly of the backing of Erie, Niagara, Chautauqua, Oneida, Madison and Herkimer Counties. In addition, he has received private assurances of support in at least ten other counties, according to close associates.

Neither of the two other potential candidates—Nelson A. Rockefeller and Leonard W. Hall — has received comparable delegate support. Mr. Hall

Continued on Page 15, Column 2

Supporters of Foreign Aid Hope For Senate Passage This Week

Special to The New York Times.

WASHINGTON, June 1—Administration supporters hope to see the $3,068,000,000 authorization for foreign aid safely through the Senate this week. They will then concentrate on getting the five-year foreign trade extension through the House of Representatives.

The prospects for the first appeared somewhat brighter today than prospects for the second. Passage of the aid bill without major change may come by Thursday.

Passage of the trade bill may not come in the House until well into the following week, and then only with drastic changes that could provoke a Presidential veto if concurred in by the Senate.

Senate debate on the aid bill started last week with major speeches by the chairman of the Senate Foreign Relations Committee, Senator Theodore Francis Green, Democrat of Rhode Island, and a top-ranking Republican, H. Alexander Smith of New Jersey. Much of the controversy, it was indicated, may center around an amendment authorizing aid to Communist-bloc nations.

This amendment would permit a broader interpretation of the Battle Act. That act now prohibits aid to Communist lands except when the President certifies to Congress that it is necessary for national de-

Continued on Page 16, Column 1

The New York Times.

LATE CITY EDITION
U. S. Weather Bureau Report (Page 63) forecasts:
Mostly fair and continued warm today, tonight and tomorrow.
Temp. range: 86—66. Yesterday: 83.2—66.5.

VOL. CVII—No. 36,683.
© 1958, by The New York Times Company.
Times Square, New York 36, N. Y.
NEW YORK, TUESDAY, JULY 1, 1958.
10¢ beyond 100-mile zone from New York City.
Higher in air delivery cities.
K
FIVE CENTS

ALASKA TO JOIN UNION AS THE 49TH STATE; FINAL APPROVAL IS VOTED BY SENATE, 64-20; BILL SENT TO EISENHOWER, WHO WILL SIGN IT

2 MORE AMERICANS ABDUCTED IN CUBA BY REBEL FORCES

44 From U. S. and Canada Now Held — Officials of Nickel Plant Latest

Special to The New York Times.

HAVANA, June 30 — Two more Americans were kidnapped today by the Cuban rebels, bringing to forty-four the number of North American servicemen and civilians seized since last Thursday.

Those kidnapped today are officers of the Nicaro nickel plant, on the north coast of Oriente Province.

Oriente is the center of operations of the rebels, led by Fidel Castro and his brother Raul, against the Government of President Fulgencio Batista. The rebels say they have carried out the kidnappings to bring pressure on the United States Government to halt military aid and assistance to the Batista regime.

Among the United States citizens seized — three of the victims are Canadians — are twenty-eight sailors and marines from the United States Naval Base at Guantanamo Bay, on the south coast of Oriente.

U. S. Denies Rebel Charge

Replying to a rebel charge that the base had been used by Cuban military planes operating against the insurgents, United States Ambassador, Earl E. T. Smith, issued a statement yesterday saying that the base was not open to planes on combat operations.

The rebels told a sailor whom they did not adduct that his kidnapped colleagues would be released tomorrow.

United States officials have been in contact with the rebels in an attempt to negotiate the release of the naval and marine personnel as well as the ten Americans and two Canadians seized last Thursday. All twelve are employes of the Moa Bay Mining Company, on the north coast of Oriente. Two civilians, an American and a Canadian, were kidnapped last night.

Mine Is Not Guarded

The Americans seized today are Sherman Avery White and J. Andrew Poll, administrator general and assistant administrator general, respectively, of the Nickel Prospecting Company, which leases the Nicaro plant from the United States Government. They were carried off at 8:30 this morning by a group of eight rebels, according to the announcement of the United States Embassy.

No details are available, but it is supposed that the two officials went to the mine, about twelve miles from the small town of Nicaro, where 6,000 workers and officials live, to check on operations. Presumably they were abducted there. The entrance of the town is guarded by an army detachment.

Continued on Page 2, Column 6

Soviet Offers Talk On Yugoslav Credit

By United Press International.

LONDON, Tuesday, July 1 — The Soviet Union proposed negotiations with Yugoslavia today on $285,000,000 in credits that the Kremlin had suspended.

The Moscow radio said the proposal was contained in a Soviet note sent to Yugoslavia June 28 and published today in Moscow newspapers.

In the note the Soviet Union said an earlier note to Yugoslavia had suggested revisions in existing economic agreements, including the postponement of one loan for several years. The Soviet Union received no reply to the suggestions, today's note said.

"The Soviet Government suggests that talks of representatives of both Governments should be held as soon as pos-

Continued on Page 2, Column 3

Russians to Attend Geneva Talk Today

By JOHN W. FINNEY
Special to The New York Times.

GENEVA, June 30 — The Soviet Union agreed today to enter into technical talks with the West on the detection of tests of nuclear weapons. As a result, talks between scientists of four Western and four Communist nations will begin here tomorrow afternoon in a conference room in the Old League of Nations headquarters.

The Soviet agreement was announced by Dr. Yevgeni K. Fedorov, head of the Soviet delegation of scientists, following a two-hour conference with Dr. James B. Fisk, chairman of the Western scientific group.

Dr. Fedorov said at a news conference later it had been agreed that the talks would begin tomorrow and that discussions would be limited to

Continued on Page 5, Column 1

BEIRUT USES JETS TO CHECK REBELS

Bombards Force Imperiling Airport — U. N. Questions Suspected Syrians

By United Press International.

BEIRUT, Lebanon, June 30 — The Government sent rocket-firing jet fighters against rebels in the hills only seven miles from Beirut International Airport today. At the same time, the Tripoli command reported it had cut the main rebel supply line into that city.

On their side, the rebels declared they had cut the main highway between Beirut and Damascus.

Druse tribesmen under the leadership of rebel chieftain Kamal Jumblatt were in the hills overlooking the airport. Jumblatt's army of 500 to 1,000 men appeared also to be poised for a night attack on Chemlain, fifteen miles southeast of the capital, which had been emptied of civilians.

[At the United Nations, Secretary General Dag Hammarskjold said United Nations observers in Lebanon had begun to question prisoners, "said to be Syrians," on their possible connection with the Lebanese uprising.]

A rebel spokesman said the Druse forces were astride the main highway to Damascus. There was no Government confirmation, but former Premier

Continued on Page 6, Column 2

N. A. ROCKEFELLER ENTERS G.O.P. RACE FOR GOVERNORSHIP

Promises Strong Fight — Mahoney and Hall Top Him in Delegate Votes

Text of Rockefeller statement is printed on Page 36.

By CLAYTON KNOWLES

Nelson A. Rockefeller announced his candidacy for Governor yesterday. He said that if nominated he would "leave no stone unturned" to win election.

The announcement, expected for some weeks, brought the declared candidacies in Republican ranks to two.

Leonard W. Hall of Oyster Bay, L. I., former Republican national chairman, announced his candidacy several weeks ago and has been campaigning vigorously. State Senator Walter J. Mahoney of Buffalo has promised to announce his position "some time in August."

In promising an "aggressive campaign," Mr. Rockefeller declared that New York's status as the Empire State had been put in jeopardy by a "complacent administration" in Albany that evaded, rather than dealt with, serious fiscal and social problems.

New Approach Held Needed

His decision to make the race, he explained, was rooted in the "deep conviction that a new approach to government must be taken in New York State." He said "new energy and efficiency, vision, courage and imagination" would be needed to enable the state "to regain its traditional pre-eminence."

Mr. Rockefeller asserted that "a lifetime spent in administration, both in government and in private and philanthropic activities," qualified him to provide the "progressive, imaginative leadership" that state conditions required.

"If nominated, I will accept the challenge and wage an aggressive campaign on the issues," he said. "If elected, I shall serve with the full awareness of the responsibility such confidence places upon me."

A member of one of America's wealthiest families, the youthful-looking board chairman of Rockefeller Center, Inc., will celebrate his fiftieth birthday next Tuesday. He is the first Rockefeller to seek elective office.

A grandson of the late John D. Rockefeller, who founded the oil dynasty, he said his family

Continued on Page 36, Column 4

DISMISSAL RULING CURBS PRESIDENT

High Court Holds He Lacks Power to Oust Wiener of War Claims Agency

By RUSSELL BAKER
Special to The New York Times.

WASHINGTON, June 30 — The Supreme Court tightened today the limitation on the President's power to remove officials of Federal quasi-judicial bodies.

Where Congress has not defined justifiable causes for dismissal, the court held, it must be assumed that Congress does not want to hang a 'Damocles' sword" over these officials by permitting the President to remove them solely to substitute "men of his own choosing."

The opinion, written for a unanimous court by Justice Felix Frankfurter, upheld Myron Wiener's contention that he was wrongfully dismissed from the War Claims Commission in 1953 so that President Eisenhower could administer the agency with personnel of his own selection.

1935 Ruling Recalled

The last significant Supreme Court ruling in the historic debate over Presidential power to dismiss was rendered in 1935. Then, in a case closely paralleling the Wiener case, the court ruled that the President could not dismiss an officer of a Federal regulatory agency for any reason except those stipulated in law.

In the 1935 case, Humphrey's Executor v. United States, President Roosevelt dismissed a member of the Federal Trade Commission on the ground that his "aims and purposes" of his Administration could be "carried out most effectively with personnel of my own selection."

The court overruled him, holding that a President could dismiss only for reasons speci-

Continued on Page 20, Column 2

Alabama Is Denied Access To Rolls of N. A. A. C. P.

Special to The New York Times.

WASHINGTON, June 30 — A $100,000 contempt fine imposed by Alabama when the National Association for the Advancement of Colored People refused to disclose its list of members in the state was struck down today by the Supreme Court.

The court held unanimously that compulsory disclosure under the circumstances in Alabama would violate constitutional guarantees of free speech and association. Justice John Marshall Harlan, writing for the court, said:

"Inviolability of privacy in group association may in many circumstances be indispensable to preservation of freedom of

Text of the opinion will be found on Page 18.

association, particularly where a group espouses dissident beliefs.

"Petitioner [the N. A. A. C. P.] has made an uncontroverted showing that on past occasions revelation of the identity of its rank-and-file members has exposed these members to economic reprisal, loss of employment, threat of physical coercion and other manifestations of public hostility."

A Major Victory

The decision was a major victory for the N. A. A. C. P. in a fight to continue operations in the South. Its activities include helping to bring suits to end school segregation.

Seven Southern states have passed legislation aimed at the association or have acted against it through state courts. Included are several statutes to require disclosure of members' names and others to restrict any financial help to Negro plaintiffs in lawsuits.

The organization has carried most of the legal burden of pushing for compliance with the Supreme Court's decision of 1954 holding school segregation unconstitutional.

In 1956 Alabama accused the N. A. A. C. P. of failing to obey a law requiring out-of-

Continued on Page 18, Column 7

HIGH COURT BARS LITTLE ROCK PLEA

Suggests Appeals Bench Set Integration Stay Review Before School Term

Text of the opinion will be found on Page 19.

By ANTHONY LEWIS
Special to The New York Times.

WASHINGTON, June 30 — The Supreme Court refused today to review on an emergency basis the order suspending school integration in Little Rock until January, 1961.

But the high court strongly suggested that the case be reviewed by the United States Court of Appeals for the Eighth Circuit before the next school term begins in September. That court has recessed for the summer.

"We have no doubt," the Supreme Court said in a short unsigned order, "that the Court of Appeals will recognize the vital importance of the time element in this litigation, and that it will act upon the application for a stay of the appeal in ample time to permit arrangements to be made for the next school year."

Summer Review Asked

Lawyers for the National Association for the Advancement of Colored People had asked the Supreme Court to by-pass the Eighth Circuit and hear the case this summer to assure early and final review.

A notice of appeal from District Judge Harry J. Lemley's suspension decision has been filed with the Eighth Circuit. So has an application for a stay of the decision pending its appeal. Judge Lemley denied a stay.

If the Eighth Circuit were to grant the stay, the need for speed would be gone, from the N. A. A. C. P.'s viewpoint. The Rock Central High School would go on with a handful of Negro children among the whites, as this last year, while the appeal was argued.

Chief Justice Earl Warren read the order to a packed courtroom at the end of a busy and dramatic day — the last in the high court's 1957-58 term. Twenty-one cases had been argued earlier in the term with forty opinions. The Chief Justice announced that the court had disposed of all its pending business before recess-

Continued on Page 19, Column 1

OPPOSITION WILTS

A Bipartisan Coalition Defeats All Efforts to Amend Plan

By C. P. TRUSSELL
Special to The New York Times.

WASHINGTON, June 30 — The Senate approved tonight the admission of Alaska as the forty-ninth state in the Union. The vote was 64 to 20.

Only President Eisenhower's signature, which is assured, and approval in a territorial referendum remain before statehood is formally achieved. Test votes indicate that the issue will carry by an overwhelming majority.

The Senate accepted the statehood bill passed by the House of Representatives word for word, beating down every effort to change it. Thus the bill goes directly to the White House.

Any change in the language would have sent the bill back to the House and invited further delays and possible death.

Final Senate action came after five days and evenings of battle, some of it bitter. The vote crossed party lines. The South fought admission, but not solidly. Senators from other sections of the country were also divided.

Stepovich in Gallery

Thirty-three Republicans and thirty-one Democrats voted in favor of admission. Opposed were seven Republicans and thirteen Democrats.

Gov. Michael A. Stepovich of Alaska sat tensely in the Senate gallery while the vote was being taken. When the result was announced he shouted:

"Thank God."

As well-wishers surrounded him he made a prediction.

"I believe that we will show the United States of America that we will be one of the greatest states in the Union within the next fifty years," he said.

It is expected that Alaska will assume full statehood by autumn or early winter. Its two Senators and one member of the House of Representatives could take their Congressional posts when the Eighty-Sixth Congress convenes next January.

Amendments Defeated

Before the final vote tonight, the Senate rejected by a vote of 62—32 a point of order entered by Senator James O. Eastland, Democrat of Mississippi.

He noted that Alaska Constitution provided that in the election of the first two Senators, one be given a six-year term and the other two or four years, to permit the staggering of Senatorial incumbencies.

Mr. Eastland said this violated the United States Constitution's provision that all Senators be elected for six years.

But the Senate decided that this was not a valid objection and overrode it.

Senator John Stennis, Democrat of Mississippi, moved that the bill be referred to the Sen-

Continued on Page 16, Column 1

ALASKANS APPEAR STUNNED BY NEWS

Civil Defense Whistles in Anchorage Signal Vote to Crowds in the Streets

By LAWRENCE E. DAVIES
Special to The New York Times.

ANCHORAGE, June 30 — Alaskans were stunned today by the realization that Congress had finally invited them to become "first class citizens."

Here in the territorial metropolis, the center of much of the agitation for statehood, it took them a while to get their bearings.

Long after the civil defense whistles had blown, signaling the Senate's action preparing the way for a forty-ninth star on the flag, unbelieving crowds almost silently walked the streets amid the tooting of automobile horns.

Texas Car Is 'Shot'

Stores did business as usual. A woman traffic policeman shook her motorcycle down Fourth Avenue putting tickets on cars that were parked overtime.

Some amateur photographers gleefully "shot" a passing car bearing a Texas license plate, emblematic of a state that would have to give up its much-loved stories of bigness as Alaska completes the transition to statehood!

Rita Martin, queen of the annual Fur Rendezvous, climbed a fire truck ladder and pinned a huge silver star — the forty-ninth — to a 60-by-40-foot flag hurriedly draped over the front wall of the Federal Building. Miss Orah Dee Clark, 83 years old, who in 1915 was the first school principal here, stood watching the star-pinning ceremony on an automobile-jammed street.

It was an emotion-packed moment for her. She had come to the territory in 1905, when the

Continued on Page 16, Column 2

Narcotics Agent Warns Inquiry Mafia Seeks to Invade Industry

By JOSEPH A. LOFTUS
Special to The New York Times.

WASHINGTON, June 30 — An expert on the Mafia told Senators today that the secret criminal organization was making a "concerted effort" to penetrate unions and management.

They are "the same people who are active in the narcotics traffic," Martin F. Pera, a Federal narcotics agent, told the Select Committee on Improper Activities in the Labor or Management Field.

Mr. Pera was the second witness as the committee laid the groundwork for extensive hearings on what the chairman, Senator John L. McClellan, "appears to be a close-knit, clandestine criminal syndicate."

The Arkansas Democrat, in his opening statement, said the committee "has become convinced that the relationship of

the national criminal syndicate with legitimate labor and business is far more critical than has heretofore been revealed."

The first witness was Sgt. Edgar D. Crosswell of the New York State police, who broke up a gangland meeting last Nov. 14 at the home of Joseph Barbara in Apalachin, N. Y. Barbara has a serious heart condition and will not testify.

Mr. Pera had barely touched on the labor-management angle when the committee recessed for the day. Photographs of him were barred because of the nature of his work.

The agent, who has worked on the narcotics problem in several foreign countries, told the committee about the origins of

Continued on Page 14, Column 6

Rayburn Bars G.O.P. Demand For Inquiry on Fox Testimony

By WILLIAM M. BLAIR
Special to The New York Times.

WASHINGTON, June 30 — Speaker Sam Rayburn rejected today a Republican attempt to have the House of Representatives investigate the conduct of the subcommittee that has been investigating the relations of Sherman Adams and Bernard Goldfine.

The Democratic Speaker ruled out of order a resolution proposed by Representative Thomas B. Curtis, Republican of Missouri. Mr. Curtis argued that the testimony of John Fox of Boston, a lawyer and business man, should have been taken in executive session, in accordance with House rules.

This move was another effort by Republicans to smother the inquiry, which they contend has developed into a "smear" of Mr. Adams and others to stem the political fears of Republican

Meanwhile, Mr. Fox announced that he had instructed his lawyers to file libel suits against Mr. Adams and four other persons for what he called "scurrilous" statements about his veracity. He said he would ask $1,000,000 damages for each.

Besides Mr. Adams, he named Roger Robb of Washington and Samuel P. Sears of Boston, lawyers for Mr. Goldfine; Robert B. Choate, publisher of The Boston Herald and Boston Traveler; William J. Dempsey, counsel for the Boston Herald-Traveler Corporation, and the corporation itself.

As the political atmosphere

Continued on Page 14, Column 4

SEEKS NOMINATION: Nelson A. Rockefeller at news conference at which he discussed his candidacy for nomination for Governor of New York on Republican slate.

ALASKA: Heavy lines define area approved for statehood. The symbols denote its present and potential resources.

The New York Times
July 1, 1958

"All the News That's Fit to Print"

The New York Times.

LATE CITY EDITION
U.S. Weather Bureau Report (Page 30) forecasts:
Fair and pleasant today;
fair tonight and tomorrow.
Temp. range: 83—67. Yesterday: 83.0—70.0.

VOL. CVII...No. 36,722.

NEW YORK, SATURDAY, AUGUST 9, 1958.

FIVE CENTS

CHIEF OF U.N. GIVES A PLAN FOR MIDEAST

ASSEMBLY MEETS

Hears Call for Step-Up of Its Economic and Political Efforts

Hammarskjold and Munro statements are on Page 2.

By THOMAS J. HAMILTON
Special to The New York Times.

UNITED NATIONS, N. Y., Aug. 8—Secretary General Dag Hammarskjold proposed today that the United Nations step up its political and economic activities in the Middle East to stabilize the area.

Mr. Hammarskjold took the floor at the opening of the General Assembly's emergency special session on the Middle East to put forward his program. He had intended to present this proposal if there was a meeting of heads of government within the framework of the United Nations Security Council.

The principal provisions of his plan are:

¶A declaration by the Arab states reaffirming their adherence to the principles of mutual respect for each other's territory, non-aggression and non-interference in each other's internal affairs.

¶The continuation and extension of present United Nations activities in Lebanon and Jordan.

¶Joint action by the Arab states, with the support of the United Nations, in economic development. This would include arrangements for cooperation between "oil-producing and oil-transiting countries" and joint utilization of water resources.

Session Is Adjourned

Mr. Hammarskjold's statement was the outstanding development of the opening session, which lasted thirty-five minutes. The Assembly adjourned until 10:30 A. M. Wednesday to give foreign ministers of some of the eighty-one member nations time to get here.

Contrary to the general expectation, Arkady A. Sobolev, Soviet delegate, did not demand the admission of Chinese Communist representatives. However, he took the floor to repeat his denunciation of the presence of United States forces in Lebanon and British forces in Jordan, and again demanded their immediate withdrawal.

Henry Cabot Lodge of the

Continued on Page 2, Column 3

U. S. MAY REDUCE FORCE IN LEBANON

Token Removal of Marine Battalion Planned

By W. H. LAWRENCE
Special to The New York Times.

BEIRUT, Lebanon, Aug. 8—The United States tentatively plans to reload a marine battalion on ships next week in a "symbolic" gesture of withdrawal from Lebanon.

A responsible source said the decision to reduce the force on shore by about 2,000 men had been communicated to the Lebanese Government and to Gen. Fouad Chehab, armed forces commander and President-elect.

Before the marine unit is pulled out, a small detachment of Army engineers and truck personnel will be moved from Lebanon to the Turkish port of Iskenderun to improve facilities at the Atlantic alliance base at Adana, which is the nerve center of air striking power and supply for the United States operation in Lebanon.

The moves will have political and military effects, it is believed. The political aims are both local and international.

Locally, leaders of the continuing insurrection against the Government of President Camille Chamoun have been insisting on speedy removal of United States troops as a condition for a cease-fire now that General Chehab has been elected. He will succeed Mr. Chamoun Sept.

Continued on Page 3, Column 2

Peronists Win Rule Of Argentine Labor

By JUAN de ONIS
Special to The New York Times.

BUENOS AIRES, Aug. 8—The Argentine Senate adopted today a controversial union organization law that virtually put the labor movement back to Peronist control.

President Arturo Frondizi's Senate majority approved the text of a bill, passed by the Chamber of Deputies, without changing a word. It did so despite fervent opposition to the measure by the Roman Catholic Church, business and professional organizations, nearly all of the press and the anti-Peronist labor unions.

The bill, which re-establishes the single General Labor Confederation, with the official right to speak for labor, awaits the President's signature only. In eighteen of the bill's fifty-

Continued on Page 5, Column 2

HOUSE VOTES BILL TO AID EDUCATION IN SCIENCE FIELD

Student Loans Raised in Place of Scholarships by 900 Million Measure

By BESS FURMAN
Special to The New York Times.

WASHINGTON, Aug. 8—The House of Representatives adopted today a four-year, $900,000,000 bill to aid science education.

No money was shorn from the bill. But the scholarship provision, on which a compromise had already been made with President Eisenhower, was deleted.

The scholarship funds were shifted to the bill's loan provisions. This was accomplished in a standing vote of 109 to 78, on a motion offered by Representative Walter H. Judd, Republican of Minnesota.

The loan provisions of the bill were increased from $40,000,000 in the first year to $60,000,000 and from $60,000,000 in each of the three succeeding years to $80,000,000.

The final adoption was by voice vote, after a motion to kill the bill by sending it back to committee had been defeated in a roll-call vote of 233 to 139. The motion was offered by Representative Ralph W. Gwinn, Republican of Westchester.

The legislation now goes to the Senate, which has already scheduled to consider on Monday its own broader science-aid bill, sponsored by Senator Lister Hill, Democrat of Alabama.

Scholarships in Senate Bill

The Senate bill includes a four-year program totaling $70,000,000 for college scholarships. If that survives on the Senate floor, some compromise will have to be worked out by House and Senate conferees.

As adopted, the House bill would cost an estimated total of $147,000,000 in the first year of operation.

It would provide:

¶Loans averaging $600 to more than 90,000 needy students, of which the Federal Government would pay a total of $60,000,000.

¶One thousand fellowships of $2,000 each to train college teachers, with reimbursement to universities for additional costs to expand graduate schools.

¶Grants to the states for scientific teaching equipment and laboratory improvement, totaling $60,000,000.

¶Grants to states to improve testing and guidance programs, $15,000,000, and $6,000,000 to set up teacher-training institutes in this field.

¶Grants to institutions to set up short-term institutes for foreign language teachers, to pay half the cost of permanent foreign language centers and stipends for those attending. This was estimated at a total of $4,500,000.

¶For research under the United States Office of Education on better educational use

Continued on Page 5, Column 3

Glennan, Ohio Educator, Named To Direct New U.S. Space Unit

Case Tech President Served on A.E.C. Under Truman—Dryden Picked as Aide

Special to The New York Times.

WASHINGTON, Aug. 8—T. Keith Glennan, a Cleveland educator and former member of the Atomic Energy Commission, is President Eisenhower's choice to head the new civilian space agency.

The President sent Mr. Glennan's nomination to the Senate today along with that of Dr. Hugh L. Dryden as Deputy Administrator of the agency.

Mr. Glennan is president of the Case Institute of Technology. Dr. Dryden is director of the National Advisory Committee for Aeronautics.

The National Aeronautics and Space Administration was created by an Act of Congress a few days ago.

Mr. Glennan's appointment is believed to be noncontroversial. There may be some objection to the choice of Dr. Dryden, however, and this could delay Senate confirmation of the nominees.

Members of the House Space Committee have criticized Dr. Dryden as presenting a program that lacked "boldness, imagina-

Continued on Page 4, Column 5

NAUTILUS SAILS UNDER THE POLE AND 1,830 MILES OF ARCTIC ICECAP IN PACIFIC-TO-ATLANTIC PASSAGE

TIME OF DECISION: Officers of the Nautilus choose a place to submerge below ice for undersea voyage across Arctic regions. Standing at the right in the conning tower of the submarine is her skipper, Comdr. W. R. Anderson.
U. S. Navy, from Associated Press

VETO THREATENED ON PENSIONS BILL

Social Security Rate Rise Backed by White House but State Plan Is Fought

By JOHN D. MORRIS
Special to The New York Times.

WASHINGTON, Aug. 8—The Eisenhower Administration raised the threat of a veto today against a bill to increase Social Security benefits.

The measure, approved by the House, calls for a 7 per cent increase in Old Age and Survivors Insurance benefits and higher Social Security taxes to finance it. Those provisions were endorsed by Arthur S. Flemming, Secretary of Health, Education and Welfare.

But the Administration is "strongly opposed," Mr. Flemming told the Senate Finance Committee, to provisions that would increase the Federal Government's share in the cost of state relief programs.

Would Recommend Veto

"Suppose we passed the House bill, would you recommend a veto?" asked Senator Paul H. Douglas, Democrat of Illinois.

"I would," Mr. Flemming replied.

Mr. Flemming was the first witness at the opening of two days of hearings on the measure, which is scheduled for Senate action before Congress adjourns. He told the Senators that his views were those of the Administration.

The bill calls for increases in monthly cash benefits under the insurance program starting

Continued on Page 5, Column 2

Hogan Is Expected To Enter the Race For Senate Monday

By DOUGLAS DALES

A statement circulated yesterday by the New York Young Democratic Club indicated that District Attorney Frank S. Hogan had made up his mind to enter the race for the Democratic Senate nomination nearly a month ago.

Mr. Hogan yesterday scheduled a news conference for Monday noon to "issue a statement."

If, as expected, he then announces his entry, he will become the fifth declared candidate in the field.

Mr. Hogan's intentions were forecast in a summary of an interview conducted by a committee of the Young Democratic Club with Mr. Hogan on July 17. The summary was submitted to Mr. Hogan for revisions before its circulation among club members.

The summary indicated that Mr. Hogan was already making plans for the future operation of his office and that he expected to have a say in the selection of a successor.

His views on this were given as follows:

"When queried as to the

Continued on Page 14, Column 5

Rackets Unit Asks Prosecution for 13

By ALLEN DRURY
Special to The New York Times.

WASHINGTON, Aug. 8—Senate rackets investigators voted unanimously today to ask the Senate to approve contempt-of-Congress citations against thirteen witnesses.

They include the president of the Carpenters Union and the reputed heir to Al Capone's gangland empire.

The action was taken by the Select Committee on Improper Activities in the Labor or Management Field. It acted in a closed meeting between morning and afternoon public sessions at which it heard witnesses give further testimony on associates of James R. Hoffa, president of the International Brotherhood of Teamsters.

Senator John L. McClellan, Democrat of Arkansas, the com-

Continued on Page 5, Column 6

POLAR TRIP OPENS DEFENSE FRONTIER

U.S. Strategic Advantage Is Seen as Temporary— Soviet Effort Expected

By HANSON W. BALDWIN

A new ocean—the frozen wastes of the Arctic—has been opened to navigation and hence to naval utilization.

This is the meaning of the transpolar, under-ice voyage from Alaska to the Greenland Sea of the nuclear-powered submarine Nautilus.

The newest achievement of the Nautilus, which had already broken all records in submarine history, has immense strategic implications.

Last year the Nautilus made a five-and-one-half-day, 1,000-mile trip under the Arctic ice pack and clearly foreshadowed the shape of things to come.

The Arctic ice pack has hitherto prevented penetration of the Arctic Ocean except, with great difficulty, by foot or by air.

Ships Skirt Land

In certain seasons of the year when the ice pack recedes from the land, or thins out, surface ships have skirted the land masses bordering the Arctic, but their cruises have been short and difficult and they have never penetrated deep into the pack.

The submerged navigation of the Nautilus under the Pole and from Pacific to Atlantic means that utilization of the Arctic Ocean for military purposes is now possible for the first time in history.

Three military capabilities for Arctic submarine operations are immediately foreseeable.

Potentially the most important—in a strategic sense—is the utilization of the Arctic for the launching of guided missiles from submarines. The fleet ballistic missile, Polaris, a two-stage, solid-fuel rocket with a range of 500 to 1,500 miles, and a powerful thermonuclear warhead, is now being developed. It has been designed for launching from a submerged submarine at considerable depths.

Nine nuclear-powered submarines, each much larger than the Nautilus and each capable

Continued on Page 6, Column 4

FOUR-DAY VOYAGE

New Route to Europe Pioneered—Skipper and Crew Cited

Text of Navy fact sheet, Page 6. The Citation, Page 7.

By FELIX BELAIR Jr.
Special to The New York Times.

WASHINGTON, Aug. 8—History's first undersea voyage across the top of the world, a distance of 1,830 miles under the polar icecap, was disclosed at the White House today.

The trip was made in four days by the Nautilus, the world's first atomic submarine. The voyage pioneered a new and shorter route from the Pacific to the Atlantic and Europe—a route that might be used by cargo submarines. It also added to man's knowledge of the subsurface of the Arctic basin.

The voyage took the Nautilus under the North Pole. The overall trip began at Pearl Harbor July 23 and ended at Iceland Aug. 7.

Dives at Point Barrow

The Nautilus went under the icecap at Point Barrow, Alaska, and surfaced four days later at a point in the Atlantic between Spitzbergen and Greenland. She is now on her way to Western Europe.

The feat of the Nautilus, with 116 crewmen and scientific observers aboard, was revealed as President Eisenhower decorated the submarine's skipper, Comdr. W. R. Anderson, with the Legion of Merit, and conferred the first-ever Presidential Unit Citation—the first ever conferred in peacetime—went to the submarine, with a ribbon and special clasp in the form of a golden "N" to all who participated in the cruise.

The Presidential citation to Commander Anderson said that the Nautilus under his leadership had pioneered a submerged sea lane between the Eastern and Western Hemispheres. It added:

"This points the way for further exploration and possible use of this route by nuclear powered cargo submarines as a new commercial seaway between the major commercial oceans of the world."

Skipper Tells Story

A few minutes after the award, Commander Anderson, admittedly "a little dazed" by the speed of events that brought him here overnight by helicopter and jet plane from Arctic waters, was telling his story of "Operation Northwest Passage."

News of the voyage reached the Capitol with electrifying effect. William F. Knowland of California, the Senate Republican leader, read a brief dispatch to the Senate and remarked:

"This should give us courage and remind us to have faith. It shows that this is no time to sell America short."

Senator Mike Mansfield of Montana, the Democratic acting

Continued on Page 6, Column 1

U.S. LEADERS SPLIT ON MIDEAST AIMS

Eisenhower Action May Be Needed to Fix Policy for Assembly Debate

By E. W. KENWORTHY
Special to The New York Times.

WASHINGTON, Aug. 8—High-level differences of opinion have developed within the Administration over the strategy and tactics to be used in the United Nations debate on the Middle East crisis, officials indicated today.

The differences are being argued out thoroughly and amicably, and a concerted position will almost certainly be arrived at during the week-end, these officials said. Nevertheless, it was considered possible that President Eisenhower might have to make the final decision on the United States approach.

Dulles Remark Recalled

The differences were said to have become apparent soon after Secretary of State Dulles' news conference a week ago Thursday. At that conference he made it clear that the United States intended to meet the Soviet charge of United States and British aggression in Lebanon and Jordan with a counter-arraignment against the Soviet Union and the United Arab Republic on "indirect aggression."

Until the problems of indirect aggression are met directly and dealt with it will not be possible to create the atmosphere of political stability in the Middle East necessary for any attack on economic problems, Mr. Dulles said.

Almost immediately some

Continued on Page 3, Column 3

NEW PASSAGE: Heavy line traces the Nautilus' route from Pacific to Atlantic Oceans.
The New York Times *Aug. 9, 1958*

Nautilus' Skipper Helps to Mitigate A Snub to Rickover

By ANTHONY LEWIS
Special to The New York Times.

WASHINGTON, Aug. 8—The man largely responsible for construction of the world's first nuclear-powered submarine was not asked to the White House today to share his moment of triumph.

Some thought was given to inviting Rear Admiral Hyman G. Rickover to the ceremony for the Nautilus, White House officials said. But only "top brass" had been asked and it was decided no exception could be made for him.

The skipper of the Nautilus, Comdr. W. R. Anderson, proved in the circumstances to be as bold a navigator in Navy politics as in the waters under polar ice.

Commander Anderson went directly from the White House to Admiral Rickover's office in the Navy Building, a few blocks away. There he paid his personal respects on the slight, frail figure whose tough-minded drive made the Nautilus a reality.

For Admiral Rickover the of-

Continued on Page 7, Column 3

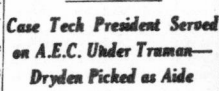

CALL TO ACTION: Dag Hammarskjold addressing the General Assembly.
The New York Times

T. Keith Glennan
Associated Press

---

479 Get Jaywalking Summonses But Public Is Hailed on Response

By BERNARD STENGREN

Pedestrians waited for traffic lights and motorists waited for pedestrians yesterday as the police began enforcing New York's new safety law.

High officials of the Traffic and Police Departments said they were gratified at the extent of compliance by drivers and walkers.

Traffic Commissioner T. T. Wiley said:

"My hat is off to New York. The reaction is wonderful."

He spoke after a tour of midtown Manhattan during which turning trucks waited for pedestrians and cab drivers not only waited but also shouted warnings to pedestrians starting to cross against lights.

John J. King, assistant Chief Inspector and head of the Safety Division, said that although some persons had argued, most

had stopped when patrolmen admonished them about jaywalking.

There were, however, exceptions. Between 8 A. M. and 4 P. M., when enforcement began, and 4 P. M., when the police day shift ended, 479 summonses returnable for $2 were issued to pedestrians.

These included 255 in Manhattan, ninety-three in Brooklyn, ninety-eight in Queens, thirty-one in the Bronx and two in Richmond—where there is only one "Don't Walk" signal.

Twenty-two motorists who failed to give the right of way to pedestrians received summonses for that infraction, which was added Thursday to violations subject to "rigid enforcement."

In Manhattan, five were is-

Continued on Page 15, Column 5

"All the News
That's Fit to Print"

The New York Times.

LATE CITY EDITION
U. S. Weather Bureau Report (Page 72) forecast
Partly cloudy and mild
today and tomorrow.
Temp. range: 72—59. Yesterday: 68.5—52.5.

VOL. CVIII..No. 36,783.   © 1958, by The New York Times Company.   NEW YORK, THURSDAY, OCTOBER 9, 1958.   10c beyond 100-mile zone from New York City.   FIVE CENTS

YANKEES WIN, 4-3, IN TENTH AND TIE BRAVES IN SERIES

McDougald's Homer Ignites 2-Run Rally and Starts Spahn to Defeat

DUREN VICTOR IN RELIEF

But Turley Collects Final Out After Losers Score and Get Two Men On

By JOHN DREBINGER
Special to The New York Times.

MILWAUKEE, Oct. 8—The Yankees kept going today in the 1958 world series. They did it by bringing down the Braves in ten innings to win the sixth game, 4 to 3.

Thus the Yankees, who only a few days ago trailed in three games to one, now are all square, with the seventh and deciding encounter coming up tomorrow.

Gil McDougald, with a home run in the tenth inning, brought to an end a heroic effort by the Milwaukee southpaw, Warren Spahn, to gain his third straight triumph of the series.

The blow broke a 2-all tie. In its wake the Bombers completed the rout of Spahn with singles by Elston Howard and Yogi Berra, a second tally coming home as Bill Skowron greeted the incoming Don McMahon with a single.

Braves Fight Back

The Yanks were ahead, 4 to 2, but the show was far from over for the crowd of 46,367. The Braves kicked up an uproar in the last of the tenth that just missed plunging the battle into another deadlock.

They routed Ryne Duren, whose blinding fast ball had baffled them in the four previous innings. They pushed across a run and got the tying run to third, with still another runner on first. But Casey Stengel, pulling out all the stops to maintain what was left of the lead, called on his other fireballing ace, Bob Turley.

Bullet Bob, who on Monday in New York had kept the Bombers in contention by winning the fifth game with a shutout, faced Frank Torre, a left-handed pinch hitter.

Torre sent a soft fly toward right and it looked every inch a single.

But McDougald, the Yankee second baseman and the hero apparent because of his homer, tore back on the grass. He leaped high in the air and pulled down the ball, which suddenly

Continued on Page 51, Column 5

MAN IN A BALLOON GIVES SPACE DATA

But Descends Prematurely After Going Up 19 Miles

By The Associated Press.

ALAMOGORDO, N. M., Oct. 8—An Air Force balloon exploring the fringe of space returned to earth early tonight after it had carried its pilot, Lieut. Clifton McClure 3d, to 99,600 feet.

The balloon, launched today, began an unexpected and unexplained descent late this afternoon. A spokesman at Holloman Air Force Base said "it must be an emergency or they wouldn't be bringing him down."

The balloon landed on the desert ranges west of here, near the San Andres Mountains about thirty miles away.

The Air Force sent a helicopter to the site of the landing to pick up the pilot and the instruments the gondola carried to the stratosphere.

[Failure of the cooling system forced the balloon down, United Press International reported, Lieutenant McClure walked out of the gondola and was taken to an Air Force hospital for a physical examination.]

At 11:05 A. M. Mountain standard time (2:05 P. M., New York time) the balloon reached an altitude of 99,600 feet—just 400 feet short of the planned goal. The balloon was launched at 5:56 A. M.

Lieutenant McClure started his descent about 4 P. M.

During his flight the 25-year-old jet pilot, who became a

Continued on Page 5, Column 2

Final Registration Is Starting Today

By LEO EGAN

The final registration period for this year's election starts today in New York City and Nassau and Westchester Counties. It will continue tomorrow and end on Saturday.

Democratic and Republican party officials are making strenuous efforts to persuade potential voters who have not registered yet to do so. Only those who have registered by Saturday night will be permitted to vote.

Those who registered for last year's municipal elections in New York City and Westchester are automatically registered this year unless they have moved outside of their election districts. All others are required by law to register to qualify as voters.

In New York City 4,613

Continued on Page 31, Column 5

FAUBUS EXPANDS SCHOOL FUND PLEA

Letters With Seal of State Going Throughout Nation in Bid for Donations

Special to The New York Times.

LITTLE ROCK, Oct. 8—Gov. Orval E. Faubus opened a nation-wide appeal today for funds to help educate Little Rock's teen-agers in a system of private high schools.

The Governor said copies of a letter appealing for contributions would be mailed to persons who had written him pledging their support in his fight against school integration.

The letters will go out on official stationery displaying the official seal of the state. They will be signed by Governor Faubus and by Dr. T. J. Raney, president of the Little Rock Private School Corporation.

For the last ten days the corporation has been accepting donations for the operations of private high schools for Little Rock's white students.

No Date Announced

The corporation has not announced an opening date for its schools, although Dr. Raney has promised it would begin operation "as soon as we can get things rolling." The classes would be held in donated buildings.

Governor Faubus revealed the contents of his appeal letter in which he said donations would benefit "all freedom-loving citizens of this nation."

He said thousands of the letters would be printed. An extra staff of thirteen stenographers was at work filling addresses gleaned from the mail received by the Governor this fall. A secretary said there were between 20,000 and 30,000 pieces of mail and telegrams.

It was the first time that the Governor had asked for money in the fight to maintain segregated schooling in the state. But Mr. Faubus had earlier pledged his support to those who had appealed for financial support.

The Governor's Letter

The appeal letter said:

"The plan set up by action of the extraordinary session of the General Assembly provided for the use of state funds, to be allocated on a per-student basis, for the student's education in whatever school he chose to attend.

"At the request of the N. A. A. C. P. [National Association for the Advancement of Colored People] and the Justice Department, the Federal courts have enjoined all public officials, including school teachers, from using the state funds, as provided by law.

"The acts have been challenged in the courts of this state, where they have already been upheld as constitutional. At the present time the schools are closed through the injunctive process of the Federal courts.

"For this reason it appears necessary that the Little Rock Private School Corporation should proceed with its plan to set up private schools in private facilities, to be operated by private funds.

"It is urgent that the students re-enter school at the earliest possible date. We would, therefore, appreciate your assistance in providing contributions to

Continued on Page 20, Column 5

PRIVATE CLASSES DIRECTED TO STOP USING VIRGINIA AID

U. S. Judge Paul Says White Units Must Drop Public Teachers or Integrate

By ANTHONY LEWIS
Special to The New York Times.

HARRISONBURG, Va., Oct. 8—Federal District Judge John Paul ruled today that "private" classes set up to replace closed Virginia schools must stop using public funds and teachers or else end segregation themselves.

"It is the opinion of the court," Judge Paul said, "that these so-called private schools are an obvious evasion of the mandate of the Supreme Court."

His order affects Charlottesville, where 1,700 children have been shut out of a high school and an elementary school, and Warren County, where 1,000 students are out of the county's only high school.

A state anti-integration law requires the closing of any public school where white and Negro children are enrolled.

Court to Rule on Norfolk

About 10,000 children are out of school in Norfolk. Judge Walter E. Hoffman will consider that case on Friday of this week.

In Charlottesville, public school teachers have been giving classes in private homes and churches and lodge halls. A similar plan for Warren County is scheduled to start tomorrow.

Attorneys of the National Association for the Advancement of Colored People had asked Judge Paul in effect to make the two school board reopen their schools. This was the burden of "motions for further relief" that they filed in the two cases.

Judge Paul said he did not think he had the right to direct the reopening of schools. He noted particularly that a suit to test the school closing law has been filed by state authorities in the Virginia Supreme Court of Appeals, and said he recognized the "propriety" of letting the issue be fought out there.

Asks State's Good Faith

But the judge said the state authorities, if they are in good faith, should not try to enforce the challenged acts until the results of the legal test are in. "The state is not pursuing that course," he said. "It has closed these schools, and it is continuing to assist education in what are called private schools but are really public. All that has happened is that they've closed the school buildings but are continuing to operate the schools in other buildings.

"If the state is going to discontinue public education in these localities," he added, "it must be a complete abandonment and not a pretext."

Judge Paul's decision was based on the doctrine—re-emphasized by the Supreme Court in its Little Rock opinion last week—that no institution that

Continued on Page 27, Column 1

U. S. ORDERS HALT IN QUEMOY ESCORT

Set to Resume Operations if Reds End Cease-Fire— Chiang Was Consulted

By E. W. KENWORTHY
Special to The New York Times.

WASHINGTON, Oct. 8—The United States announced today that its naval vessels in the Taiwan Strait had stopped escorting Chinese Nationalist convoys supplying Quemoy.

At the same time the United States made clear that it would resume the escort operations if the Chinese Communists resumed their artillery attacks on the Quemoy group.

Three days ago the Communists announced in a broadcast directed at the Nationalists that the bombardment had been ordered suspended for a week on condition that the United States stopped escorting Nationalist convoys.

Today the State Department said that the escort activity had been undertaken at the request of the Nationalist Government, and had been ordered "to the extent militarily neces-

Continued on Page 7, Column 5

President Completes His Staff, Naming Counsel as No. 2 Aide

Gerald D. Morgan   David W. Kendall

By FELIX BELAIR Jr.
Special to The New York Times.

WASHINGTON, Oct. 8 — President Eisenhower completed the reorganization of the White House staff today by designating Gerald D. Morgan as No. 2 man in the chain of command. Mr. Morgan, who is 49 years old, has been special counsel to the President since February, 1955.

The promotion of another "old hand" on the White House staff served to emphasize President Eisenhower's intention to keep reliance on the staff system rather

companied by the appointment of David W. Kendall, Washington attorney, to succeed Mr. Morgan as special counsel.

The announcement of the designation of Mr. Morgan was ac-

Continued on Page 43, Column 1

Announcement Of Pope's Death

By United Press International.

CASTEL GANDOLFO, Italy, Thursday, Oct. 9—Following is the official announcement of the death of the Pope:

The Supreme Pontiff, Pope Pius XII, is dead. Pius XII, the most esteemed and venerated man in the world, one of the greatest Pontiffs of the century, with sanctity passed away at 3:52 A. M., Oct. 9, 1958.

Eugenio Pacelli was born March 2, 1876, and elected Pope on March 2, 1939, with the name of Pius XII. He was therefore 82 years 7 months 7 days, and his pontificate was nineteen years 7 months and 7 days.

The Catholic Church and the whole world, for whose profit he spent his brilliant, intellectual energies, his heart and his actions, now gather in mourning around his body and memory, grateful for the immense and valid work he carried out to re-establish among men, children of God, the force of justice, law and peace.

Let the unanimous prayers for the repose of his lofty soul, which today passed into eternal bliss, rise from the hearts of all faithful and the entire Christianity.

COLLEGE IS CALLED

55 Princes of Church Rule Pending Vote in 15 to 18 Days

Special to The New York Times.

ROME, Thursday, Oct. 9—The death of Pope Pius XII today opened the interregnum, or régime of the Holy See vacancy. It will last until a new Pontiff is elected by the Cardinals in a secret conclave, to be convened not sooner than Oct. 24 or later than Oct. 27.

During the next few weeks the Church will be governed by the Sacred College of Cardinals. As dean of this body, Eugene Cardinal Tisserant immediately instructed the Vatican Secretariat of State to notify all his colleagues that the Apostolic See had become vacant, and to summon them to Rome.

Later today, the French-born, bearded Cardinal, who is 74 years old, is to make the formal announcement of the Pope's death to the diplomats accredited to the Holy See and, through them or through apostolic nuncios in world capitals, to heads of state.

Fastest Travel Urged

Fifteen Cardinals were present in or near Rome early this morning. Of these, thirteen are Italians. The other two are Cardinal Tisserant and Gregory Peter XV, Cardinal Agagianian, a Russian-born Armenian who has risen to prominence in the Roman Curia, or central church administration.

Italian Cardinals heading Archdioceses in various parts of the country are due to reach the capital later today. Cardinals outside Italy are expected and indeed requested to come to Rome by the fastest possible means.

With aviation just entering the jet age, it may be foreseen that members of the Sacred College will gather here much quicker than after the death of Pius XI in 1939.

Will Meet Daily

As the "Senate of the Church," the Cardinals will hold a plenary meeting later today and will reconvene every day until they enter the conclave.

One of the first items on the agenda of the Cardinals' meeting later today will be the transfer of Pius XII's body from his death bed at Castel Gandolfo to Rome.

As if he had had a premonition, the late Pontiff in his apostolic constitution of 1945 concerning the vacancy of the Holy See inserted a provision contemplating the possibility of a Pope's death outside Rome. This had not occurred since the end of the eighteenth century. The provision was that the Cardinals must see to it that the dead Pontiff is moved to St. Peter's Basilica in Rome in a "decorous and dignified manner."

Some of the powers of the Sacred College will be wielded in its name by the Cardinal Camerlengo, or chamberlain of the church. This dignitary will be elected by the cardinals in their first plenary meeting later today.

Now 55 Cardinals

The Sacred College now has fifty-five members, fifteen short of its full complement of seventy. Fifteen are in Rome. Most of the remaining forty will proceed here immediately for the exercise of the college's interim powers.

Most of these men are aged—in their seventies and eighties. Some are behind the Iron Curtain.

Jozsef Cardinal Mindszenty, Primate of Hungary, has been told that he will be allowed to go to Rome, but he has indicated that he probably will not do so, because he fears that the government might not readmit him.

The Cardinal is a refugee in the United States Legation in Budapest.

Others who may not reach Rome are Stefan Cardinal Wyszynski, Primate of Poland, and Aloysius Cardinal Stepinac, Primate of Yugoslavia. Cardinal

Continued on Page 24, Column 3

POPE PIUS XII
Associated Press

City Pays Homage On Receiving News Of Pontiff's Death

The news of the death of Pope Pius XII was received with varying manifestations in the New York area last night.

As the news became known in Times Square, many Roman Catholics paused and then continued on their way. A few inclined their heads briefly as they gave a prayer for the repose of the Pope's soul. Others made the sign of the cross unobtrusively.

Many Catholics walked to the nearest Roman Catholic church, some of which had been kept open beyond their usual 10 P. M. closing, aware that the Pope's death was imminent. There, prayers were said and impromptu services were held informally as the communicants offered prayers to the effect that Pope Pius' soul reach Heaven.

Some Churches Reopened

As some of the Catholic churches reopened their doors and their lights streamed out onto the sidewalks, patrolling policemen, many of whom had not heard of the Pope's death, stopped to investigate. Some of them stayed to pray.

Some persons, not all of a Catholic faith, felt the hard-to-describe emotion experienced when the news of the death of one of the great world figures comes to them.

The Pope's death found Cardinal Spellman, Archbishop of the Diocese of New York aboard the Greek liner, Olympia, bound for New York from Cannes, France. He had been accompanying a group of 450 Catholics visiting the Holy Places of Europe. He received an audience with the late Pope several days ago.

The Chancery, at 452 Madison Avenue, headquarters of the

Continued on Page 21, Column 4

3 Countries Named To Security Council

By KATHLEEN TELTSCH
Special to The New York Times.

UNITED NATIONS, N. Y., Oct. 8—Italy, Tunisia and Argentina were elected to Security Council membership today. They will fill the vacancies that occur when the terms of Sweden, Iraq and Colombia expire at the end of 1958.

The three new members were elected at a session of the General Assembly. The voting by secret ballot was a formality since the three nations were unanimously agreed candidates.

The six nonpermanent seats on the Council are traditionally allotted to nations of six broad geographic areas. There have been exceptions, the latest in 1957, when Japan was elected to

Continued on Page 14, Column 6

POPE, 82, DIES AFTER 2D STROKE; MILLIONS OFFER THEIR PRAYERS; CARDINALS TO NAME SUCCESSOR

PONTIFF 19 YEARS

End Comes Quietly in Papal Bedroom at Summer Palace

By ARNALDO CORTESI
Special to The New York Times.

CASTEL GANDOLFO, Italy; Thursday, Oct. 9—Pope Pius XII, the 260th successor of the Apostle Peter on the Pontifical throne of Rome, died at 3:52 A. M. today (10:52 P. M. New York time, Wednesday).

The Pontiff's death came as millions prayed for him throughout the world.

The 82-year-old Pontiff did not regain consciousness after a cerebral stroke he suffered yesterday morning.

It was the second stroke he had suffered in forty-seven hours. The first occurred at 8:30 A. M. Monday and he seemed to be recovering from it.

The second stroke struck him at 7:30 A. M. yesterday. After it the Pope sank gradually until the moment of his death.

Death occurred in a simple and unadorned bedroom on the second floor at the back of the papal palace of Castel Gandolfo.

End Comes Quietly

The Pope was passing the summer there in the cooler atmosphere of the Alban Hills as he had done every year. He had planned to return to the Vatican at the end of November in time for the spiritual exercises before Christmas.

Pius XII had been Pope for nineteen years, seven months and seven days since his elevation to the pontificate March 2, 1939. He was born in Rome March 2, 1876. He was, therefore, elevated to the pontificate on his 63rd birthday and was a week more than 82 years and seven months of age when he died.

Since the Pope had been unconscious for many hours before his death he had left no last words in the generally accepted meaning of that term. The last recorded words that he uttered were: "Pray, pray, pray that this unhappy situation for the Church may end."

At the moment of his death Pius XII was completely paralyzed and incapable of any movement. He had been un-

Continued on Page 21, Column 1

ROME HEARS TOLL OF BELLS FOR PIUS

Some Citizens in Prayer Before St. Peter's Basilica as End Is Announced

By PAUL HOFMANN
Special to The New York Times.

ROME, Thursday, Oct. 9—When Rome's many church bells started tolling before dawn today to announce the death of Pius XII, a few persons were still praying in St. Peter's Square and in the city's churches that had remained open all night.

They had remained from the throngs gathered yesterday in the Square and at the churches. Some crossed themselves at the announcement and fell to their knees to pray for the dead Pontiff's soul. Many were tearful. One elderly woman was heard to exclaim, "A saint has left us."

Attention Concentrated

At midnight thousands had still been thronging in front of St. Peter's Basilica. Among them were a group of pilgrims who had come from Germany in a dozen buses.

Although the streets and open squares of Rome had gradually emptied about 2 A. M. many Romans stayed up at their homes to follow transmissions of the Vatican radio from Castel Gandolfo.

Listeners said they were deeply impressed and moved by the post-midnight mass said at the dying Pope's bedside by one of his former closest aides, Archbishop Domenico Tardini. The homely Roman accent with which the popular prelate flavors his Latin for once sounded solemn and grave as he recited the prayers of the dying.

After the end of the mass, the Vatican radio urged listeners to keep their sets tuned in and to pray for the Pontiff while waiting that "God's will be done."

The announcement to Rome of Pius XII's death was made in a brief bulletin by the Vatican radio at 3:56 A. M. (10:56 P. M., Wednesday, New York time.) Sacred music followed.

Pilgrims at Castel Gandolfo

CASTEL GANDOLFO, Italy, Oct. 8—Thousands of Romans and pilgrims gathered in this hill town today to be near the dying Pope and to pray for him.

With few exceptions they did not object to television cameras, batteries of klieg lights and clusters of newsmen in the narrow piazza in front of the pontifical palace.

The sad accompaniment would have caused Pope Pius XII himself to smile indulgently and understandingly, a reporter told police after one of the Italian police attempted to clear part of

Continued on Page 24, Column 5

WASHINGTON SEES LEBANON SECURE

Plans to Recall All Troops —Karami Said to Quit

By DANA ADAMS SCHMIDT
Special to The New York Times.

WASHINGTON, Oct. 8 — United States troops will be "totally withdrawn from Lebanon" by the end of this month, the State Department announced today.

The department said this decision was based on improvement in "international aspects of Lebanon's security situation" and progress toward "more stable international conditions in the area."

[Reports from Beirut said Premier Rashid Karami had resigned after thirty-one of the sixty-six Deputies in Parliament said they would not support him. United States tanks were patrolling Beirut after a band disarmed three military policemen.]

State Department officials explained that Lebanon's security situation had improved mainly as a result of the election of a new President and the tapering off of the United Arab Republic's "indirect aggression" against Lebanon.

Interference in the life of Lebanon by infiltration of arms and men has apparently ceased, they said. Inflammatory broadcasts against the Government of Lebanon also have diminished, although broadcasts against the Government of Jordan have tapered off only a little, the officials reported.

In this connection the officials

Continued on Page 5, Column 1

194

"All the News That's Fit to Print"

The New York Times.

LATE CITY EDITION
U.S. Weather Bureau Report (Page 66) forecast:
Mostly cloudy today; mostly
fair tonight and tomorrow.
Temp. range: 56—44. Yesterday: 47.2—44.6.

VOL. CVIII..No. 36,803. © 1958, by The New York Times Company. Times Square, New York 36, N. Y.

NEW YORK, WEDNESDAY, OCTOBER 29, 1958.

10c beyond 100-mile zone from New York City. Higher in air delivery cities.

FIVE CENTS

PRESIDENT CALLS FOR VICTORY HERE TO AID HIS POLICY

Tells G. O. P. Workers That Democrats Lack Honest and Sane Principles

HE LAUDS ROCKEFELLER

Asks Special Aid to Keating—Meets Kean and Zeller—Talks at Sports Fete

By HARRISON E. SALISBURY

President Eisenhower yesterday attacked the "dominant wing" of the Democratic party as lacking "straightforward, honest, sound and sane principles, which make America great."

The President leveled the charge in urging Republican campaign workers here to make every effort to elect Nelson A. Rockefeller and Representative Kenneth B. Keating, the party's candidates for Governor and Senator.

The President spent the day in New York largely in political endeavors connected with the campaign. He spoke at two rallies of campaign workers and conferred with several candidates.

He traveled by bubble-topped car through midtown Manhattan streets. A persistent drizzle cut down street crowds. The police estimated that 30,000 persons saw the President.

Attends Football Dinner

The President spent just one minute less than twenty-four hours in the city. He arrived at La Guardia Airport at 11:14 P. M. Monday and departed last night at 11:13 o'clock after attending the first annual Football Hall of Fame dinner, sponsored by the National Football Foundation and the Football Hall of Fame at the Astor Hotel.

The President landed in Washington at 12:14 A. M. and went directly to the White House.

While the President's day was largely devoted to political tasks the partisan note was firmly sounded only once. This was during a brief talk he gave to workers at Republican campaign headquarters in the Roosevelt Hotel.

In making only one such call President Eisenhower generally followed the emphasis on an appeal to the independent, nonparty voter that has been stressed by Mr. Rockefeller in his gubernatorial bid.

All Deny a Split

President Eisenhower did not repeat the harsh language he employed on the Pacific Coast in characterizing Democratic "radicals" or in calling for a "fumigation" of labor unions whose leaders had been found unworthy, Mr. Rockefeller has dissociated himself from these remarks of the President.

James A. Hagerty, the President's press secretary, vigorously denied that Mr. Rockefeller had indicated a negative attitude toward campaign efforts in New York City by the President.

Mr. Hagerty did say, however, that the state Republican committee had not, to his knowledge, requested the President to come to New York.

Mr. Rockefeller went out of his way to make clear that he

Continued on Page 25, Column 1

R.C.A. Yields in Trust Suit; Will Ease Patent Licensing

Consent Action to Aid Competitors and Inventors in Radio Field—Company Fined $100,000 in Monopoly Case

By EDWARD RANZAL

The Government's antitrust suits against the Radio Corporation of America ended yesterday in Federal court with a consent judgment and a fine.

R. C. A. declined to defend itself against the charges of criminal monopoly in the licensing of electronic radio equipment patents and was fined $100,000.

At the same time, the Government's civil action was ended with the consent judgment. Competitors will now be able to obtain R. C. A. electronic radio patents under a relaxed licensing agreement.

The decree also will assure patent owners of a competitive market for their inventions and will permit them to exploit the fruits of their own research, according to Victor R. Hansen, assistant attorney general in charge of the Antitrust Division.

A statement issued by David Sarnoff, chairman of the board, and John L. Burns, president of R. C. A., declared that the terms of the decree dealt primarily with apparatus for radio purposes and did not affect the company's activities in automation, electronic computers, medical electronics and other aspects of the new industrial field.

The criminal indictment was filed Feb. 1. R. C. A. pleaded no defense to the four counts, restraint of commerce in radio

Continued on Page 35, Column 3

Survey Finds Ohio Divided Over 'Right-to-Work' Issue

A Times Team Report

This is a report from a New York Times team that surveyed political sentiment in Ohio. Team members were Wayne Phillips, Edith Evans Asbury, Stanley Levey, Joseph A. Loftus and William G. Weart. Eleven pivotal states have been surveyed previously and other reports, including some state re-checks, will continue until the elections next Tuesday.

By WAYNE PHILLIPS
Special to The New York Times.

COLUMBUS, Oct. 27—With barely a week to go before the election, Ohio is a divided and confused state.

The presence on the ballot of a proposed "right-to-work" amendment to the State Constitution has become the dominant political issue, overshadowing contests for Governor and United States Senator.

The amendment would outlaw the union shop provision contained in 82 per cent of Ohio labor-management contracts. The provision makes union membership after a stated period a requisite of employment.

Members of a New York Times team, talking to voters from the Ohio River to Lake Erie, from the Pennsylvania to the Indiana border, found people thoroughly confused on how to vote on the amendment.

"Therefore," he continued, "they had to confront a new situation. They knew that we could resupply the island, so in order to save face, they said, 'We will let you resupply the island every other day.'" [Questions 6 and 7.]

Unusual Interest in Off-Year

Republican Gov. C. William O'Neill appeared to be running behind his Democratic opponent, Michael V. DiSalle, former Mayor of Toledo and former Federal Price Administrator.

Senator John W. Bricker, a Republican, seemed to be safe in his bid for a third term unless the controversy over the "work" amendment brought out a disproportionately heavy Democratic vote.

If that happened, any of nine Republican-held Congressional seats might be in danger. Otherwise, the team saw little prospect of a change in the state's present Congressional line-up of seventeen Republicans and six Democrats.

Proponents of the amendment argue that it would help to clean up union corruption and make unions more responsive to the will of members. Opponents argue that it would destroy unions, reduce wages and undermine social benefits for which unions had fought.

The proposed amendment has created deep and bitter disputes

Continued on Page 26, Column 1

RECORD HIGH SET BY NATIONAL DEBT

Total at $280,651,429,657 Under Deficit Borrowing as Revenue Declines

By United Press International.

WASHINGTON, Oct. 28—The national debt, with larger spending and a decline in Government income as factors, has reached a record high, it was disclosed today.

The Treasury's daily financial statement showed that it was $280,651,429,657.13 on Oct. 23. Included are some non-Treasury securities the Government guarantees. The previous high was $280,821,613,238.96 on Dec. 31, 1955.

Based on the population of about 175,000,000, the new figure represents a debt of $1,604.87 for every man, woman and child in the nation. This per capita figure, however, is not a record. In the fiscal year 1946, before the post-war upsurge in the population, the per capita debt was $1,905.42. The debt then was $269,422,099,173.

The latest rise in the debt reflected recent Treasury borrowing to finance the record peacetime budget deficit of $12,000,000,000 expected for the current fiscal year. The deficit results

Continued on Page 39, Column 6

DULLES ASSAILS REDS' HALF-TRUCE AS POLITICAL STEP

Says Alternate-Day Shelling of Quemoy Results in 'Promiscuous Killing'

Transcript of the Dulles news conference is on Page 18.

By E. W. KENWORTHY
Special to The New York Times.

WASHINGTON, Oct. 28—Secretary of State Dulles said today that the intermittent shelling of Quemoy by the Chinese Communists had no military purpose and amounted to promiscuous killing for political ends.

Asked at his news conference what he thought of "the idea of having war every other day," Mr. Dulles replied:

"If you have a military purpose, you carry on your shooting for military objectives and your purpose is to destroy the capacity of your enemy to resist. When you do it only every other day and say, in between times, you can bring in supplies * * * that shows the killing is done for political purposes and promiscuously." [Question 5, Page 18.]

Red Conditions Recalled

The Chinese Communists have announced that they will not shell war military objectives on even-numbered days to enable the Nationalists to bring in supplies.

Mr. Dulles said he knew of no precedent for the alternate-day cease-fire, but he did have an explanation for what he called this "outlandish and rather uncivilized" procedure.

After seven weeks of trying to interdict resupplying of the islands, Mr. Dulles said, the Communists discovered that "the islands could not be cut off and made to wither on the vine."

No General War Seen

In view of their failure to reduce the island or cut it off, the Chinese Communists would now "engage in a level of military effort which is likely to provoke a general war." [Question 7.]

Unquestionably, Mr. Dulles said, Peiping's real objective is not the offshore islands but Taiwan itself. The Communists, he indicated, hope to achieve that objective through a long-range propaganda campaign designed "to split the inhabitants of Taiwan away from cooperation with the Americans."

To that end, he suggested, the Chinese Communists are refurbishing the pre-World War II Japanese propaganda theme of a "co-prosperity sphere of Asia for the Asians."

The Chinese Communists, he declared, are now saying, "Let us work together and get rid of these Americans; they are the

Continued on Page 18, Column 4

CARDINAL RONCALLI ELECTED POPE; VENETIAN, 76, REIGNS AS JOHN XXIII; THOUSANDS HAIL HIM AT ST. PETER'S

Associated Press Radiophoto

THE NEW PONTIFF, Pope John XXIII, raising his hand in blessing yesterday on a balcony of St. Peter's Basilica. He appeared before throng an hour after he was elected.

DULLES IS GLOOMY ON A NUCLEAR BAN

Doubts Test Suspension Can Be Negotiated as Soviet Finds It Is 'Behind'

By DANA ADAMS SCHMIDT

WASHINGTON, Oct. 28—Secretary of State Dulles said today that prospects for negotiating a ban on nuclear tests were dim because the Soviet Union had discovered it was "considerably behind" the United States in nuclear weapons development.

Soviet realization of inferiority grew out of the meetings of experts at Geneva last summer on technical means of controlling a suspension of nuclear tests, he said at his news conference.

[In Moscow, it was indicated that the three Soviet scientists would go to Stockholm to receive their prize.]

Britain Is Chemistry Winner

The 1958 chemistry prize goes to Dr. Frederick Sanger of Cambridge University's department of biochemistry. He was honored for developing a method for studying the structure of proteins and especially for isolating and identifying the components of the insulin molecule.

The prizes were announced this afternoon by the Royal Swedish Academy of Science, designated to make the annual awards under the will of Alfred Nobel, the Swedish inventor of dynamite. Each of the Nobel awards this year amounts to the equivalent of $41,420.

Like Tuesday's literature award to the poet and novelist Boris Pasternak, the physics prize constitutes a Soviet first. The only Soviet citizen to win a Nobel award before this year was Nikolai N. Semenov, who shared the 1956 chemistry prize with Sir Cyril Norman Hinshelwood of Britain.

Two Russians, Ivan P. Pavlov

Continued on Page 10, Column 2

3 Russians and Briton Win Nobel Awards for Science

By WERNER WISKARI
Special to The New York Times.

STOCKHOLM, Sweden, Oct. 28—Three Soviet physicists and a British biochemist were named today as winners of Nobel Prizes in science. The 1958 physics prize is to be shared by Dr. Pavel A. Cherenkov, Prof. Ilya M. Frank and Academician Igor Y. Tamm, all members of the Physics Institute of the Soviet Academy of Sciences.

They were cited for research beginning in the Nineteen Thirties that is credited with having opened the way to recent discoveries of atomic particles, such as the antiproton, and with spurring the study of cosmic radiation.

U.S. WON'T OPPOSE CHANGES IN NATO

However, Washington Aides Shun de Gaulle Plan for 3-Power Directorate

By JACK RAYMOND

WASHINGTON, Oct. 28—United States officials indicated today that the organizational structure of the North Atlantic alliance was as good as could be expected, but said they would not oppose some changes.

The proposal by Premier Charles de Gaulle of France for a United States-British-French political executive has found little sympathy here, regardless of whether the group is set up within NATO or outside it.

The proposal was contained in letters sent by the French leader to President Eisenhower and Prime Minister Harold Macmillan.

The chief reason for United States coolness toward the proposal is that most of the fifteen countries in the alliance have made clear that they are against it.

NATO Base Broadened

The majority, it was observed here, is composed of the small countries. They have, in recent years, forced changes that broaden rather than narrow the base of military and political responsibility in the organization.

The United States is interested in proposals for broadening the area of NATO responsibility. However, officials here are wary of any extension that would make NATO more than a "regional" organization as approved by the United Nations.

Nevertheless, peripheral problems, such as those developing in the Middle East, are recognized as having a great impact on the Western alliance. United States officials are prepared to discuss this.

At the same time it was made evident here that the United States wants to avoid participating in the formation of a Big Three political arrangement that commits Washington to consultation on its world obligations.

The United States has agreed at past NATO meetings to discuss its affairs, but only as a matter of agreement rather than formal obligation.

Premier de Gaulle's proposal, which became known last week-

Continued on Page 6, Column 5

11 BALLOTS TAKEN

New Pontiff Elevates Conclave Secretary to Cardinalate

By ARNALDO CORTESI
Special to The New York Times.

ROME, Oct. 28 — Angelo Giuseppe Cardinal Roncalli, Patriarch of Venice, was elevated to the Papacy this afternoon. He will be 77 years old Nov. 25.

He will sit on the throne of St. Peter as the 262d Supreme Pontiff of the Roman Catholic Church and will rule the Church as sovereign under the name of John XXIII. No Sovereign Pontiff has used the name John since 1334, when John XXII died.

The successor to Pope Pius XII, who died Oct. 9, was elected on the eleventh ballot by the fifty-one Cardinals assembled in conclave since Saturday. He was named as the third day of the voting in a walled enclosure in the Vatican was drawing to a close.

The conclave that elevated him was one of the fifteen shortest held since the Papacy returned to Rome from Avignon, France, in the second half of the fourteenth century. Fifty-nine conclaves have been held since then.

Coronation Likely Nov. 9

Cardinal Roncalli became Supreme Pontiff at the very moment when he replied affirmatively on being asked by the Dean of the Sacred College of Cardinals whether he accepted his election. He replied "Accepto" ("I accept") a few minutes before 5 P. M. [11 A. M. New York time]. He was invested with the full powers of the Papacy from that instant, though his reign will be counted from the day of his coronation, expected to be Nov. 9.

One hour after his election, the new Pope appeared on the outer balcony of St. Peter's Basilica and gave his first blessing as a Pope to the thousands gathered in St. Peter's Square. Before and after the blessing the crowd sang hymns. The hymns sung were "Christus Vincit" (Christ Conquers) and the Te Deum.

New Cardinal Named

As the first act of his Pontificate, Pope John XXIII conferred the Cardinal's red hat on Msgr. Alberto di Jorio, who had acted as secretary of the conclave. This return to tradition, since in the past all Popes were wont to reward the secretary of the conclave. However, Pius XII omitted to do so. The new Pope also asked all Cardinals to remain in conclave until tomorrow morning, which they did.

That the Catholic Church again had a head was proclaimed to watchers in St. Peter's Square by the white smoke emanating from a stovepipe above the roof of the Sistine Chapel, where the voting took

Continued on Page 14, Column 1

New Pontiff Faces Difficult Problems

By PAUL HOFMANN
Special to The New York Times.

ROME, Oct. 28—Pope John XXIII was a successful Vatican diplomat before he became the new Supreme Pontiff of the Roman Catholic Church.

His great experience and skill in two distant fields of work for the church should enable the former Angelo Giuseppe Cardinal Roncalli to cope with the formidable problems confronting the Papacy at present, high ecclesiastics said tonight.

In choosing the Patriarch of Venice and former Apostolic Nuncio to France the Sacred College of Cardinals overcame with great wisdom its initial uncertainty whether to place on the Throne of St. Peter a "pastoral" or a "diplomatic" Pontiff, the churchmen remarked. The personality of

Continued on Page 15, Column 4

Airliner Takes Dive To Avoid Collision

By The Associated Press.

MIAMI, Fla., Oct. 28—A Panagra airliner with forty-five persons aboard dived to safety last night under a formation of an Air Force refueling tanker and two jet fighters.

The pilot of the airliner said that he was flying at an assigned altitude on a recognized airway when the incident took place over Wilmington, N. C., at 6:47 P. M.

The Air Force said that the tanker was on a Civil Aeronautics Administration clearance within a 100-mile radius of Florence, N. C. The three Air Force craft were eighty-two miles from Florence when the incident took place.

The airliner was bound from New York to Peru, with stops at Washington and Miami. The plane was manned by a

Continued on Page 19, Column 6

Diefenbaker Sees Gain in Ties to U.S.

By RUSSELL PORTER

Prime Minister John Diefenbaker of Canada said last night that relations between Canada and the United States had improved in the last year, but that problems remained in the field of trade and economic affairs.

He urged that trade relations between the two countries be based on Canadian as well as American rights. Against the Soviet economic offensive, he declared, freedom cannot afford to allow the economic weakening of any free nation.

Mr. Diefenbaker spoke here at a dinner of the Pilgrims of the United States in his honor at the Waldorf-Astoria Hotel. Secretary of State Dulles joined in the tribute to Mr. Diefenbaker and stressed the importance of Canadian-Ameri-

Continued on Page 16, Column 3

HIGH HOPES are expressed by President Eisenhower as he leaves the Astor Hotel here. With the President yesterday were Kenneth B. Keating, left, and Nelson A. Rockefeller, the Republican candidates for Senator and Governor.

"All the News That's Fit to Print"

The New York Times.

LATE CITY EDITION
U.S. Weather Bureau Report (Page 57) forecasts:
Partly cloudy, warmer today; cloudy milder, chance of rain tomorrow.
Temp. range: 42—25. Yesterday: 35.3—27.9.

VOL. CVIII..No. 36,938.   © 1959, by The New York Times Company.   NEW YORK, FRIDAY, MARCH 13, 1959.   10 cents beyond 50-mile zone from New York City except on Long Island. Higher in air delivery cities.   FIVE CENTS

HAWAII IS VOTED INTO UNION AS 50TH STATE; HOUSE GRANTS FINAL APPROVAL, 323 TO 89; EISENHOWER'S SIGNATURE OF BILL ASSURED

ADENAUER IS FIRM AGAINST TROOP CUT IN MIDDLE EUROPE

Gets Assurance in Talks With Macmillan That the British Seek No Disengagement

By SYDNEY GRUSON
Special to The New York Times.

BONN, Germany, March 12 —Chancellor Konrad Adenauer restated to Prime Minister Harold Macmillan today West Germany's opposition to any reduction of Allied forces in Central Europe except within a general disarmament agreement.

The British leader came to Bonn today to give the Chancellor a personal report on his recent conversations in Moscow and to reassure the West Germans that Britain was not seeking the disengagement of Eastern and Western forces in Germany.

Nor, said a British Foreign Office spokesman, does London favor even a controlled thinning of forces if this would result in disequilibrium between the troops and armaments of East and West in Central Europe.

Trip Is Second of Three

Mr. Macmillan's trip here was the second of his three planned journeys to brief other Western leaders about his talks with Premier Nikita S. Khrushchev of the Soviet Union. Mr. Macmillan was in Paris earlier this week and he will cross the Atlantic for separate meetings with President Eisenhower and Prime Minister John Diefenbaker of Canada next week.

The first session between Mr. Macmillan and Dr. Adenauer, who were accompanied by their foreign ministers and two advisers each, lasted three hours. The talks were resumed tonight after a dinner in Mr. Macmillan's honor. They will continue tomorrow in the Chancellor's Palais Schaumburg offices.

The differences in outlook between the Prime Minister and the Chancellor were evident in their remarks at the airport on Mr. Macmillan's arrival.

Mr. Macmillan said the West was firm and united on the prin-

Continued on Page 3, Column 4

ROCKEFELLER ASKS A DRIVE ON CRIME

In Message to Legislature, He Urges Tighter Laws

By WARREN WEAVER Jr.
Special to The New York Times.

ALBANY, March 12—Governor Rockefeller called on the Legislature today to join him in prosecuting a war against organized crime "more vigorously than ever before."

The Governor sent a special message to the lawmakers, with a dozen recommendations for tightening the existing criminal law and making law-enforcement organizations more powerful and better trained.

In his election campaign last fall, Mr. Rockefeller was outspoken in his criticism of the increase in criminal activity during the Harriman Administration. He pledged swift action against racketeers and law violators if he should be elected.

Mr. Rockefeller urged today that the Legislature:

¶Make it a misdemeanor to defy a subpoena from the State Commission of Investigation or engage in obstructive or contemptuous conduct before the crime panel.

¶Set up a municipal police training council that would establish minimum training standards for all members of police forces.

¶Increase the statute of limitations for prosecution for tax evasion from two to six years, thus giving the state more time

Continued on Page 16, Column 2

Governor Taking Charge Of Meeting City Tax Needs

Orders Report on Costs and Resources for Conference With Mayor Tomorrow —Wants an Agreement Next Week

By DOUGLAS DALES
Special to The New York Times.

ALBANY, March 12—With his own program for higher state taxes out of the way, Governor Rockefeller has decided to take personal command of the Albany action needed to help New York City balance its budget for the fiscal year starting July 1.

The decision was made at a meeting with Republican legislative leaders today, called to discuss the conference to be held with Mayor Wagner Saturday morning on the city's budget problem.

The meeting will be held at the Executive Mansion and will be attended by Republican and Democratic legislative leaders.

In preparation for the meeting, Governor Rockefeller hastily named a task force to examine New York City's needs and the resources that might be tapped to meet them. A report has been asked by tomorrow night in time to be digested before the meeting with the Mayor.

The task force was designated at a meeting described by Mr. Rockefeller, Tax Commissioner Joseph H. Murphy, Budget Director T. Norman Hurd, Majority Leader Walter J. Mahoney of the Senate and Majority Leader Joseph F. Carlino of

Continued on Page 16, Column 4

Snowfall of 5 to 10 Inches Delays All Transit in Area

By PETER KIHSS

With spring only nine days away, the city got its heaviest snowfall of the season yesterday—5.3 inches. It was perhaps nature's way of marking the seventy-first anniversary of the famous blizzard of '88.

On March 12, 1888, that storm hurled 16 inches of snow on the city, and in two more days brought the total to 20.9 inches.

Rockland and Fairfield Counties reported ten inches of snow yesterday; Westchester, seven to nine; Bergen, six to seven; Long Island, five to six; Elizabeth, N. J., 5.4, and New Brunswick, N. J., two to three.

Rain and warming temperatures turned the snow into slush in the city. Temperatures dropped during the night, however, and turned the slush to ice on some roadways. The less heavily traveled roads in the suburbs and upstate were reported especially dangerous.

The forecast for today was for partly cloudy and warmer. The temperature may reach the low forties and cause the ice and snow to melt.

Yesterday's storm was caused by two low-pressure areas moving in from the Midwest and from the Virginia coast. Snow fell throughout the Northeast. Depths ranged up to fourteen inches in Chautauqua County on Lake Erie, the Schoharie Valley west of Albany and in western Maryland.

Seven deaths were attributed to the storm in New York, New Jersey and Ohio.

The city's public schools had only 70 per cent attendance. Radio station WOR, which gathers and broadcasts news of

Continued on Page 22, Column 1

GOVERNOR NAMES COMMERCE HEAD

Appoints McHugh, President of New York Telephone— Utility Picks Successor

Governor Rockefeller completed his Cabinet in Albany yesterday with the appointment of Keith S. McHugh to head the Department of Commerce.

Mr. McHugh, who is 64 years old, will retire as president of the New York Telephone Company on April 30 to accept the appointment.

Governor Rockefeller said he was looking to Mr. McHugh to "invigorate" the department so that its full potential to stimulate business in the state would be realized.

Mr. McHugh is leaving a $150,000-a-year job for one that pays $18,500. However, within a year, he will qualify for a company pension as a forty-year man. A company spokesman said a pension arrangement would be worked out by the board of directors.

Meanwhile, the directors of the telephone company elected Clifton W. Phalen to succeed

Continued on Page 16, Column 2

CITY VOTES DEAL ON POWER PLANTS WITH CON EDISON

But Contract Is Changed to Permit New Bids When Final Auction Is Held

By PAUL CROWELL

Contracts for the sale of the city's three rapid-transit power plants to the Consolidated Edison Company at a gross price of $125,840,000 were approved unanimously by the Board of Estimate last night.

The vote was taken after the language of the contracts had been changed slightly to make certain that bidders other than Consolidated Edison could submit offers when the power plants are disposed of at public auction, as required by the City Charter.

The changes were made after Harvey M. Spear, counsel for unidentified "substantial New York interests," had complained that his clients might not be able to submit bids technically admissible under the terms of the agreements.

Clients Not Identified

Mr. Spear declined to tell the board the names of his clients, saying that they would be disclosed when bids were received.

Mr. Spear said his clients, while preferring to submit an offer to purchase the power plants for lease back to the Transit Authority, would also be prepared to submit a bid for purchase and operation.

The contracts approved by the board paved the way for transfer of the plants to Consolidated Edison by July 1, assuming that the company was the successful bidder.

The company's bid was for at least $99,382,871 in cash in addition to concessions that would bring the total minimum purchase price up to $125,840,000. The company also offered to supply the three divisions of the city subway system with power under a ten-year contract at uniform rates.

Company Supplies IND

The company now supplies all power for the IND division. The IRT and BMT divisions obtain power from the three city plants that are on Kent Avenue, Brooklyn, and West Fifty-ninth Street and East Forty-seventh Street in Manhattan.

By its vote the Board of Estimate authorized the Mayor to execute, subject to specified conditions, a contract for selling the three plants and for purchasing power from the three divisions of the city subway system now operated by the Transit Authority.

The board also authorized the Commissioner of Marine and Aviation, Vincent A. G. O'Connor, to execute waterfront leases in connection with the transfer

Continued on Page 15, Column 2

Associated Press Wirephoto
THE BIG NEWS: Chester Kahapea, 13, offering copies of The Honolulu Star-Bulletin yesterday in the Hawaiian capital. The flag on the front page contains fifty stars.

3 OF JOINT CHIEFS WILL BE RENAMED

Twining, Burke and White Slated for New Terms— Lemnitzer to Get Post

By HANSON W. BALDWIN
Special to The New York Times.

WASHINGTON, March 12—The reappointments of three members of the Joint Chiefs of Staff will be announced soon.

Those who will be reappointed to new two-year terms starting this summer are Gen. Nathan F. Twining, chairman of the Joint Chiefs of Staff; Gen. Thomas D. White, Chief of Staff of the Air Force, and Admiral Arleigh A. Burke, Chief of Naval Operations.

Gen. Lyman L. Lemnitzer, Vice Chief of Staff of the Army, will succeed Gen. Maxwell D. Taylor, present Army Chief of Staff, whose second two-year term ends June 30. General Taylor is expected to retire.

The second two-year term of Gen. Randolph McC. Pate, as Commandant of the Marine Corps, does not expire until next Dec. 31, and as far as is known his successor has not yet been selected. General Pate also expects to retire.

The names of Lieut. Gen. Merrill B. Twining, a brother of the chairman of the Joint Chiefs, and of Lieut. Gen. Edwin A. Pollock have been men-

Continued on Page 4, Column 2

U. S. and Canada List Seaway Tolls, Effective on April 1

By RICHARD E. MOONEY
Special to The New York Times.

WASHINGTON, March 12—The United States and Canada announced the St. Lawrence Seaway tolls today, to take effect April 1.

They are identical to those proposed last June after negotiations by committees of both nations. The differences are primarily in definitions, mostly for the types of cargo that would qualify for the low rate applying to "bulk" shipments.

[Opposition to the toll set-up came from port, rail, shipping and civic interests. They called the rates unrealistically low and the estimated revenue too high. The Port of New York Authority feared a loss of 3,500 waterfront jobs because of "unfair competition" resulting from the tolls.]

Railroads Competing

The Seaway links the Great Lakes and the Atlantic for deepwater ships. Part of it was opened last summer, and the full length is scheduled to be working soon.

Interests that would benefit from the new water route and those against whom it would compete had been fighting over the toll issue.

The fight was moving into a new phase. Major railroads are considering a 20 to 25 per cent reduction of rates they charge for transporting grain for export. This would enable them better to compete with the price for shipping via the waterway.

Seaway tolls are intended to

Continued on Page 16, Column 2

HOUSE UNIT CUTS JOBLESS AID BILL

Restricts Extension of U.S. Assistance to 3 Months Instead of One Year

Special to The New York Times.

WASHINGTON, March 12—The House Ways and Means Committee approved today a bill for a three-month tapering-off of emergency Federal aid to the unemployed.

The measure falls far short of earlier plans by Democratic leaders for a year's extension of the program beyond its present expiration date of March 31.

The effect would be to prevent an abrupt cut-off of payments to about 300,000 jobless workers expected to be drawing the emergency benefits at the end of this month.

Instead, these workers would stay on the rolls until they had exhausted the benefits to which they would have been entitled in the absence of a March 31 termination date.

The committee acted in closed session by what was reported as a one-sided voice vote. The House is expected to pass the bill early next week.

Democratic sources reported that the one-year extension plan had been set aside in the interest of assuring quick enactment of a bill. President Eisenhower and House Republican leaders had voiced strong opposition to the earlier Democratic proposal.

"Apparent lack of enthusiasm with which the proposed one-year

Continued on Page 18, Column 4

MEASURE SPEEDED

A Short-Cut Sends It Direct to President, Who Is 'Delighted'

By C. P. TRUSSELL
Special to The New York Times.

WASHINGTON, March 12—The Territory of Hawaii was voted into the Union today as the fiftieth state.

The House of Representatives gave its approval by a vote of 323 to 89. Yesterday the Senate approved the Hawaii bill, 76 to 15.

President Eisenhower's approval is assured. The White House said today he was "delighted" and noted that he "has been urging it for some time."

Thus, after one of the fastest actions by Congress in years, only the mechanics of admitting a new state remain before Hawaii joins the Union.

The question arose as to whether the island territory some 2,000 miles from continental United States would seek for its fiftieth star in the flag July 4 of this year when Alaska adds its forty-ninth. There is barely enough time to do so and island leaders doubted that it would be done.

Governor Gives Word

With the galleries filled, the House started its long roll-call in midafternoon. Among the spectators was the Governor of Hawaii, William F. Quinn. When the roll-call began he quietly left the gallery and went to the office of Sam Rayburn, Speaker of the House.

At the Speaker's office Governor Quinn telephoned Acting Gov. Edward E. Johnston at Honolulu and asked him to hold the line. When he was notified that the roll-call had recorded 219 ayes—a majority of the House—Governor Quinn set off a celebration in the islands by shouting:

"Sound the sirens, close the schools and get going."

A little later he added a note of caution:

"Keep the lid on a little, Ed."

Before Hawaii can attain statehood it must hold a referendum on whether it wants to assume the burdens at this time. Besides agreeing to the ballot with provisions of the new law,

Continued on Page 13, Column 2

HAWAIIANS START 2 DAYS' FESTIVITY

Alaska Sends First 'Aloha' to Celebrating Islanders

By LAWRENCE E. DAVIES
Special to The New York Times.

HONOLULU, March 12—The kamaaina and the malihini celebrated today Congressional assurance that the nation was ready to welcome Hawaii as the fiftieth state.

That is to say, the Hawaiian version of the Alaskan sourdough—joined with the Hawaiian counterpart of the Alaskan cheechako—in opening a two-day demonstration of gratitude over the prospective ending of territorial status for the islands.

The celebration got off to a restrained start. It picked up momentum as the day wore on toward a climax here on the island of Oahu with huge bonfire, aerial and offshore military pyrotechnics and hula dancing.

At the beginning everyone seemed to be waiting for someone else to show the way. Within a half-hour after word came from Washington of the action in the House of Representatives, however, the Waikiki area was clogged with horn-tooting automobiles. Bands and colorfully clad marchers took over at midafternoon.

Colored paper streamers were flung from downtown office buildings along King and Smith Streets. Hands were thrust forward with a "happy statehood" salutation. Mayor Neal Blaisdell of Honolulu was so

Continued on Page 13, Column 1

There Are Times When Bad Weather Brings Out the Best in a Man

It was such a time yesterday at Vesey St. and Broadway

The New York Times (by Neal Boenzi)
And a man came forward to lend a gallant, helping hand

Fulton Street Widening Dropped By Jack on Protest of Merchants

The highly controversial proposal to widen Fulton Street in lower Manhattan was withdrawn from further consideration yesterday by Borough President Hulan E. Jack of Manhattan.

The action by the Board of Estimate permitting Mr. Jack to drop the project constituted a victory for a group of Fulton Street merchants.

Opponents have fought the proposal as threatening hardship to "hundreds of business men and thousands of their employees," They have also argued that the widening would not materially relieve the area's traffic situation.

Mr. Jack said he favored studies of the possibility of both an eastbound and a westbound artery in lower Manhattan.

Pending such studies, he said, it would be better to withdraw the Fulton Street proposal. In the meantime, he added, he hoped all of those who have been involved in the widening dispute would have a better understanding of the problem.

The proposal that Mr. Jack withdrew called for widening Fulton Street on its south side from Broadway to Water Street. The project was intended as the first stage of an ultimate widening of Fulton Street from South Street to West Street.

Two major slum clearance cooperative housing projects totaling $61,000,000 in cost in the Rockaways, Queens, were approved by the board. One was Hammels-Rockaway,

Continued on Page 32, Column 6

The New York Times.

LATE CITY EDITION
U. S. Weather Bureau Report (Page 61) forecasts:
Considerable cloudiness today and tonight. Chance of showers tomorrow.
Temp. range: 79—66; yesterday: 76.8—63.8.

VOL. CIX..No. 37,137.   © 1959, by The New York Times Company.   Times Square, New York 36, N. Y.   **NEW YORK, MONDAY, SEPTEMBER 28, 1959.**   10 cents beyond 50-mile zone from New York City except on Long Island. Higher in air delivery cities.   **FIVE CENTS**

PRESIDENT AND KHRUSHCHEV IN AGREEMENT ON NEW BERLIN TALKS AND MORE EXCHANGES; EISENHOWER DEFERS VISIT; PREMIER LEAVES

TYPHOON DEATHS IN JAPAN AT 1,132; 1,457 ARE MISSING

Damage Tops $100,000,000 as Storm Heads North— 927,700 Lose Homes

By The Associated Press

TOKYO, Sept. 27—Battered Japan, struck by the worst typhoon in a quarter of a century, counted more than 2,500 dead or missing today. .

As Typhoon Vera headed toward Soviet territory, the national police reported 1,132 known dead, 1,457 missing, 4,668 injured and 927,700 homeless. Damage was unofficially estimated at more than $100,-000,000.

Officials feared the toll would rise when word was received from villages isolated by floods, landslides, washed-out roads and rail lines or broken telephone lines.

Nagoya Hit Hard

The harbor of the industrial city of Nagoya, one of the hardest hit, was described as a "sea of dead." Seven ocean-going ships lay grounded like beached whales in that area. The harbor was choked with debris. In other regions, parts of villages were swept away by floods.

Typhoon Vera, the fifth to strike Japan this year, formed in the southwest Pacific, off Iwo Jima. It struck Kii Peninsula in south-central Honshu Saturday night with maximum winds of 160 miles an hour.

The storm swept across the industrial heart of central Honshu over Mie, Nara, Gifu and Aichi prefectures and into the Sea of Japan.

The typhoon then moved up the Sea of Japan off the west coast of Honshu, crossed northern Honshu and southeastern Hokkaido, the northern-most island, and was last reported

Continued on Page 3, Column 4

STRIKE-BREAKING FACES STATE CURB

Registering of Job Agencies Asked in Panel Report

By RUSSELL PORTER

A state investigating committee recommended legislation yesterday to compel registration of professional strike-breaking agencies and public disclosure of their activities.

It also urged that all employment agencies be required to inform job applicants if they are to take jobs of striking workers.

The committee was appointed in 1958 by Isidor Lubin, then State Industrial Commissioner, to investigate concerns reported to be supplying out-of-state strikebreakers to New York employers.

Mr. Lubin's action followed charges by the International Typographical Union that the Macy chain of newspapers in Westchester County had imported to break a printers' strike.

Charges Strike Is Illegal

The Macy chain has charged the strike is illegal and that the union's demands violated the Taft-Hartley law.

Two other publishers were also involved in the investigation. They were the Griscom chain of weekly papers in Nassau County and The Lockport Union-Sun and Journal, a daily newspaper in Niagara County.

The committee in its report said it had discovered only one commercial agency engaged in supplying strikebreakers to newspapers.

It is said this firm was the Schleppey-Klein Agency, owned and operated by Bloor Schleppey of Zionsville, Ind., with the help of Miss Shirley Klein, now an executive of the Macy chain.

According to the committee, this agency is exclusively engaged in recruiting and supply-

Continued on Page 12, Column 3

Red Chinese Harass Indians on Frontier

By United Press International

PAURI, India, Sept. 27—Chinese Communist troops from Tibet are taking over land previously considered India's and have reinforced their garrisons along the border, reports received here said today.

The reports said Chinese forces opposite the frontier of Uttar Pradesh were harassing Indian business men and confiscating their goods and money on the slightest pretext.

Traders and villagers said the Chinese had moved more troops into Tibetan areas facing Uttar Pradesh and had built new roads and six airstrips to supply them. Chinese planes frequently violate Indian airspace, they said.

The reports reached this

Continued on Page 3, Column 2

LAOTIANS RETAKE BORDER FORTRESS

Bastion Near North Vietnam Captured in Night Raid— Fighting Is Fierce

By GREG MacGREGOR
Special to The New York Times

VIENTIANE, Laos, Sept 27 —Muong Het, a strongly defended rebel-held fortress about eight miles from the North Vietnamese border, was reported recaptured by Government troops at dawn today in one of the sharpest encounters of the current strife.

The thrust to retake the position, which was seized by the rebels Aug. 30, began yesterday, according to informed sources. It was estimated that about 500 "Lao-Viets," the name now used in Laotian military circles to describe rebel North Vietnamese troops, had been encircled in Muong Het and forced to fight. Previous tactics adopted by both sides had been to withdraw in the face of heavy onslaught.

The size of the Government attacking force was not given. Casualties on both sides were described as heavy.

It was stated that Xieng Kho, another position in the northern part of Samneua Province near Muong Het, was still in enemy hands. Other positions along the border still held by the rebels were named

Continued on Page 2, Column 2

Dodgers and Braves End in Tie; Pennant Play-Off Starts Today

Fred Haney
The New York Times

Walter Alston
Associated Press Wirephoto

The Dodgers and the Braves finished the National League season playing tied for the pennant, the world serie. will per..ant. The two clubs will meet at Milwaukee this afternoon in the first of a three-game play-off series.

Manager Walter Alston's Dodgers defeated the Cubs, 7 - 1, and Manager Fred Haney's Braves downed the Phils, 5—2, in their final regularly scheduled games. The Giants, who had a chance for a tie in the event the Braves and Dodgers lost, bowed twice to the Cardinals.

League pennant winner, as the home team, the world serie. will start either Thursday or Friday. There will be a one day rest after the play-off, with the second game scheduled for tomorrow in Los Angeles and the third game, if necessary, in Los Angeles on Wednesday.

Sandy Koufax will pitch for Los Angeles today. Lew Burdette will hurl for the Braves.

The play-off is the third in National League history. The Dodgers lost to the Cards in two games in 1946 and to the Giants in three in 1951.

Details on Page 40

VIEWS UNCHANGED

But Both Sides Retain Reliance on Parleys to Solve Problems

By JAMES RESTON
Special to The New York Times

WASHINGTON, Sept. 27—The main result of Premier Khrushchev's visit to the United States is that it produced agreement to talk some more. This, at least, is the general view here.

It avoided the danger of personal injury. It ended without any break in the policy of settling international differences by negotiation, and it extended the negotiating period well into the middle of President Eisenhower's last year in office.

The President and his guest reached few agreements, but apparently they were impressed with each other's determination to avoid war, and to continue talking to that end.

Arms Control Urged

If there was any change in the policies of the United States and the Soviet Union, it was in the emphasis on the principle of "the strictest comprehensive control" over any disarmament agreement.

This was Mr. Khrushchev's phrase in his television address to the American people tonight. This is the principle Washington has been trying to get Moscow to accept for years. The question now is whether this principle can now be applied in specific terms to all disarmament talks coming up or only to the Soviet Union's ambitious plan of "total disarmament."

The talks on the future of Germany and Berlin did not go well. They produced more heated conversation at Camp David than anything else.

Neither Side Budges

Neither side budged from the position it held in the nine weeks of fruitless negotiation at the Big Four foreign ministers' conference at Geneva this summer. And Mr. Khrushchev went away saying that his way of settling the problem was the only way he knew of reaching a settlement.

Nevertheless, there was agreement to reopen talks on the Berlin question if the other nations concerned agreed, and a curiously worded agreement to fix President Eisenhower's return trip to the Soviet Union "next spring."

There has been some talk

Continued on Page 20, Column 1

FAREWELL: President Eisenhower wishes Premier Khrushchev a safe voyage home on steps of Blair House in Washington. At right is Andrei A. Gromyko, Soviet Foreign Minister. Oleg A. Troyanovsky, an interpreter, is in the center.
Associated Press Wirephoto

RUSSIAN EXPECTS NO QUICK CHANGE

In Talks on Last Day He Says 'Effort and Patience' Are Needed to Erase Enmity

By WILLIAM J. JORDEN
Special to The New York Times

WASHINGTON, Sept. 27—Premier Khrushchev said tonight it was "impossible to count on a sudden change" in United States-Soviet relations.

He said the main obstacle to an easing of tensions lay in certain influential forces in this country that opposed efforts to end the "cold war." He expressed confidence that common sense would prevail, but said "great effort and patience" would be required to erase the suspicions and enmity of recent years.

In his farewell appearances in this country, a news conference and a television address, the visiting Premier repeated his assertion that it was the Soviet Union that was working hardest for better relations.

U. S. Desire for Peace Seen

Mr. Khrushchev said he had no doubt that President Eisenhower shared his desire for an improvement in relations. He declared, too, that he was aware that the American people wanted peace as much as the Soviet people.

He accused those who questioned the sincerity of Soviet proposals of standing in the way of agreements. Progress is being frustrated by certain people in the United States, the Premier commented, but he did not name them or say more than that they were "still influential."

If Mr. Khrushchev was influenced in any way by his visit to the United States and his first-hand look at its wealth and variety, he gave no sign of it.

Soviet Progress Depicted

He said that what he had seen here had not shaken his "faith that the political, economic and social system in the Soviet Union is the fairest and most progressive." In fact, in most of the forty-five minutes of his television speech telling of the progress his country had made under the leadership of the Communist party.

Mr. Khrushchev's news conference held earlier in the main ballroom of the National Press Club, was a light-hearted occasion unmarred by any display of temper such as marked his previous appearance here on Sept. 16. the day after his arrival in the United States.

Five minutes before the conference was to begin at 4 P. M.

Continued on Page 19, Column 7

U.S.-Soviet Communique

Special to The New York Times

WASHINGTON, Sept. 27—Following is the text of the joint United States-Soviet communiqué issued today:

The Chairman of the Council of Ministers of the U. S. S. R. N. S. Khrushchev, and President Eisenhower have had a frank exchange of opinions at Camp David.

In some of these conversations the United States Secretary of State Herter and Soviet Foreign Minister Gromyko, as well as other officials from both countries, participated.

The Chairman of the Council of Ministers of the U. S. S. R. and the President have agreed that these discussions have been useful in clarifying each other's position on a number of subjects. The talks were not undertaken to negotiate issues.

It is hoped, however, that their exchanges of views will contribute to a better understanding of the motives and position of each, and thus to the achievement of a just and lasting peace.

The Chairman of the Council of Ministers of the U. S. S. R. and the President of the United States agreed that the question of general disarmament is the most important one facing the world today. Both Governments will make every effort to achieve a constructive solution of this problem.

A Discussion of Germany

In the course of the conversations an exchange of views took place on the question of Germany, including the question of a peace treaty with Germany, in which the positions of both sides were expounded.

With respect to the specific Berlin question, an understanding was reached, subject to the approval of the other parties directly concerned, that negotiations would be reopened with a view to achieving a solution which would be in accordance with the interests of all concerned and in the interest of the maintenance of peace.

In addition to these matters, useful conversations were held on a number of questions affecting the relations between the Union of Soviet Socialist Republics and the United States. These subjects included the question of trade between the two countries. With respect to an increase in exchanges of persons and ideas, substantial progress was made in discussions between officials and it is expected that certain agreements will be reached in the near future.

The Chairman of the Council of Ministers of the U. S. S. R. and the President of the United States should agree that all outstanding international questions should be settled not by the application of force but by peaceful means through negotiation.

Finally, it was agreed that an exact date for the return visit of the President to the Soviet Union next spring would be arranged through diplomatic channels.

Grandchildren Key To President's Trip

By ANTHONY LEWIS
Special to The New York Times

WASHINGTON, Sept. 27—Premier Khrushchev said today that it was because President Eisenhower's four grandchildren would accompany him to Russia that the President's projected Soviet visit had been postponed until next spring.

"I would like to reveal a secret," the Premier said at his news conference when he was asked the reason for the postponement. With a happy but sly smile, like a foxy grandpa, he told the story.

"Yesterday the President was kind enough to invite me to his farm, where I met his wonderful grandchildren," Mr.

Continued on Page 16, Column 2

Bonn Is Agreeable To Talks on Berlin

By SYDNEY GRUSON
Special to The New York Times

BONN, Germany, Sept. 27—Government sources said tonight that West Germany would undoubtedly be agreeable to another foreign ministers' conference on the Berlin question.

News of the communiqué issued in Washington today by President Eisenhower and Premier Khrushchev arrived too late in European capitals for high-level government comment.

Although the Eisenhower-Khrushchev communiqué did not specify at what level the Berlin negotiations should be resumed, it was assumed here that the foreign ministers were meant and that the nine weeks of dis-

Continued on Page 19, Column 6

KHRUSHCHEV OFF WITH 21-GUN POMP

Nixon Bids Him Farewell at Airport—Both Stress Need for Negotiation

Remarks by Khrushchev and Nixon at airport, Page 17.

By W. H. LAWRENCE
Special to The New York Times

ANDREWS AIR FORCE BASE, Md., Sept. 27—Premier Khrushchev took off for the Soviet Union at 10 o'clock tonight.

He flew in the giant TU-114 turbo-prop airliner that brought him here about noon Sept. 15. The flight to Moscow was scheduled to be non-stop.

Vice President Richard M. Nixon substituted for President Eisenhower in farewell ceremonies. With him were Secretary of State Christian A. Herter and Gen. Nathan F. Twining, Chairman of the Joint Chiefs of Staff.

The final ceremony at this air base about twelve miles from Washington included all the official honors usually paid a chief of state as Mr Khrushchev had been termed by the Soviet Foreign Ministry for this journey. Previously he had been considered a head of government.

Ceremonies At Airfield

Just before departure a twenty-one-gun salute from a 75-mm. howitzer boomed out after a fifty-six-piece Army band had played the anthems of the Soviet Union and the United States.

The ceremonies began shortly after 9:15 P. M., when Mr. Khrushchev arrived by car from Blair House, official guest house of the President, where he had had a quiet dinner with his family and fellow officials after a hectic day.

At the airfield he was greeted by a 128-member honor guard, including representatives of the Army, Air Force, Navy and Marines.

Mr. Nixon and Mr. Khrushchev did not, however, troop the guard, as the President and Mr. Khrushchev had done at the Premier's daylight arrival. Mr. Khrushchev and Vice

Continued on Page 17, Column 1

PEACE IS STRESSED

President Will Report His Views Today at News Conference

Khrushchev news conference and speech and U. S. news conference, Pages 18-19.

By HARRISON E. SALISBURY
Special to The New York Times

WASHINGTON, Sept. 27—Premier Khrushchev brought his historic thirteen-day visit to a conclusion today by reaching a series of understandings with President Eisenhower designed to ease "cold war" tensions.

The extent of these understandings was not immediately revealed. However, they were of a scope that suggested that the Khrushchev-Eisenhower conversations had produced at least a limited armistice in the "cold war."

High Points Delineated

The high points of the discussions held by the Soviet and United States leaders, as outlined by a communiqué, by Mr. Khrushchev at a news conference and by United States statements, were:

¶An agreement that new talks will be held on the Berlin question. These talks may be held by the foreign ministers, or at a lower level, or possibly at a summit conference.

¶Discussion of a possible summit conference. Mr. Khrushchev said the Soviet Union felt that the time was ripe for such a meeting now and that Geneva might be a suitable place. The United States position on this point was not entirely clear.

¶An agreement for President Eisenhower to postpone his trip to the Soviet Union until spring or summer. Mr. Khrushchev said he had proposed the postponement because the weather would be better at that time.

¶An understanding to broaden the present program of exchanges between the United States and the Soviet Union and to undertake explorations of questions relating to trade.

¶An agreement to reopen the long-stalemated negotiations over the World War II Lend-Lease settlement.

¶A joint declaration that "all outstanding international questions should be settled not by the application of force but by peaceful means through negotiation."

The results of the three days

Continued on Page 16, Column 1

PRESIDENT URGED TO MEET SENATORS

Mansfield Asks Consultation on Khrushchev Talks

By WILLIAM M. BLAIR
Special to The New York Times

WASHINGTON, Sept. 27—President Eisenhower was called upon today to consult with Senate Democratic and Republican leaders on his conversations with Premier Khrushchev.

Such a consultation would be a demonstration to Mr. Khrushchev and the world of the "basic unity of the American people," Senator Mike Mansfield, Democrat of Montana, declared in a statement.

The Senate's assistant Democratic leader asserted the conference also should be called because if there is to be progress toward peace beyond the President's exchange of views with Prime Minister Khrushchev any actions to that end ultimately will require the advice and consent—the sanctions—of the Senate.

The President might also discuss the "significance" of his conversations with leaders of the House as well as of the Senate, Senator Mansfield said. He suggested that the meeting might be held at Camp David, the Maryland mountain retreat where the President and the So-

Continued on Page 17, Column 3

The New York Times.

NEWS SUMMARY AND INDEX, PAGE 63

VOL. CIX....No. 37,227.   © 1959, by The New York Times Company.
Times Square, New York 36, N. Y.

NEW YORK, SUNDAY, DECEMBER 27, 1959.

5c outside New York City, its suburban area
and Long Island.   Higher in air delivery cities.

TWENTY-FIVE CENTS

LATE CITY EDITION
U. S. Weather Bureau Report (Page 63) forecasts:
Mostly cloudy, mild, some rain
today. Mostly cloudy tomorrow.
Temp. range: 50—37; yesterday: 41.6—34.5

SECTION ONE

WEST TO CONFER SPEEDILY TO SET DATE OF SUMMIT

Mid-May Is Still Favored in Washington After Reply from Khrushchev

SWIFT AGREEMENT SEEN

President Must Also Act on the Expiration of Ban on Nuclear Weapons Tests

By JACK RAYMOND
Special to The New York Times

WASHINGTON, Dec. 26—A speedy round of consultations among the Western powers was in prospect today to set a date for summit talks in Paris with the Soviet Union.

New instructions are expected to be sent to the United States, British and French Ambassadors in Moscow some time next week to discuss the subject with Andrei A. Gromyko, the Soviet Foreign Minister.

A date in mid-May was still favored in the speculation here. Much of the speculation centered on what President Eisenhower's preference might be, although no hint of his intentions was available. The President, who visited his grandchildren at his Gettysburg farm this morning, received no official visitors at the White House.

Two Urgent Issues at Hand

The summit date is one of two urgent issues awaiting President Eisenhower's action. The other is the expiration Thursday night of the fourteen-month-old ban on nuclear-weapons testing.

The prevailing belief is that the President will order an extension of the prohibition, possibly for an indefinite period. Officials said no decision had been made.

Even if an extension is ordered, the President is expected to remind the Russians, who also have unilaterally suspended nuclear-weapons tests, that further observation of the moratorium by the United States would depend upon progress in the Geneva negotiations toward a formal agreement.

Inspection Is Obstacle

The United States, Britain and the Soviet Union have failed thus far in the talks that began at Geneva fourteen months ago to get over the stumbling block of an acceptable inspection system.

This undoubtedly will be a major matter for discussion at the projected summit meeting.

President Eisenhower joined with the British and French leaders this week in inviting Premier Khrushchev to meet them in Paris April 27. The Soviet leader proposed that the proposed date was inconvenient, apparently because of his expected presence at the traditional May Day celebration in Moscow. Mr. Khrushchev suggested April 21 or May 4 instead.

The Paris summit meeting, slated to be the forerunner of

Continued on Page 2, Column 4

Sports News

FOOTBALL

The New York Giants will play the Baltimore Colts in Baltimore's Memorial Stadium today in the National Football League championship play-off. The game will be seen by a sellout crowd of 57,557 and will be telecast and broadcast nationally. The Colts are favored by 3½ points. The Colts beat the Giants, 23 to 17, in the title game last year.

In college football, the Blue defeated the Gray, 20 to 8, yesterday in their annual all-star game at Montgomery, Ala. The North beat the South, 27 to 17, in their annual all-star contest at Miami. The passing of Joe Caldwell of Army was the major factor. The National All-Stars downed the Southwest All-Stars, 21 to 6, in the Copper Bowl at Tempe, Ariz.

BASKETBALL

Cincinnati trounced St. Bonaventure, 96 to 56, in the first round of the Holiday Festival tournament at Madison Square Garden. Oscar Robertson of Cincinnati scored 47 points. In other Festival games, New York University downed Dartmouth, 78 to 68; Iowa topped St. John's of Brooklyn, 91 to 84, and St. Joseph's of Philadelphia, 84 to 70.

Details in Section 5.

Soviet Party Orders Tightened Controls Over the Collectives

By MAX FRANKEL
Special to The New York Times

MOSCOW, Dec. 26—Tighter party control was decreed today for Soviet collective farms.

The Central Committee of the Communist party ordered the organizational changes to spur agricultural production, which it said had been good in 1959, but not good enough.

The committee's decrees were made public this evening after the close of a four-day meeting of the group devoted almost exclusively to agriculture. Although the final statement contained a serious indictment of the farm leadership in Kazakhstan, no high-level personnel changes were announced.

The party said the production of 62,000,000 tons of milk this year would exceed the gross milk output of the United States. It also expect-

Continued on Page 3, Column 2

TRIBE WAR PERILS LIBERTY FOR CONGO

Barbaric Fighting Dismays Africans Who Seek Early Withdrawal by Belgians

By HOMER BIGART
Special to The New York Times

MUTOTO STATION, Belgian Congo, Dec. 26—A barbaric civil war in the heart of the Belgian Congo may wreck Congolese plans for speedy independence.

The savagery of the fighting has upset even some militant nationalists, who are beginning to dread what might happen if the restraining influence of Belgian authority were suddenly lifted.

Equally macabre has been the discovery by Belgian authorities of the mass poisoning of scores of members of the Bushongo tribe, which has been neutral in the fighting.

Old Customs Revived

The Belgians have outlawed tschipapa. But the agitation for independence apparently has encouraged the Bushongo to revert to old customs. Cynics believe that the tschipapa are rigged by witch doctors who slip poison into the cups of tribesmen of whom the chief wants to be rid.

The war, cruder and more horrible than the tschipapa, involves two closely related tribes, the Lulua and the Baluba.

They are wrestling for control of Kasai Province, which is fertile, well populated and the world's biggest producer of industrial diamonds. Here the aggressive Lulua are trying to cast out the more docile and more advanced Baluba.

King Baudouin of the Belgians, who is touring the Congo, arrived this morning in Luluabourg, the provincial capital. He received a dignified, enthusiastic

Continued on Page 8, Column 1

Deaths Exceed 350 In Holiday Driving

A rising toll of death on the highways marred celebration of the Christmas holiday during the long week-end.

By 2 o'clock this morning at least 355 persons had died in traffic accidents over the nation. In the city twelve persons were injured early today in an accident in the rain on the lower level of the Queensboro Bridge. Seven vehicles were involved.

Two tow trucks had responded after an accident between an automobile and a truck, and three other cars crashed into the tow trucks.

The injured were taken to Grand Central Hospital. Their names were not immediately available. One was reported in critical condition.

Before the three-day holiday

Continued on Page 47, Column 3

MEYNER, RIBICOFF GET STUDY HITTING TAX BY NEW YORK

Levy Tied to Services Used Is Called Fairest System— Parley Set for Tuesday

Excerpts from report on tax will be found on Page 46.

By GEORGE CABLE WRIGHT
Special to The New York Times

TRENTON, Dec. 26—A report to Gov. Robert B. Meyner and Gov. Abraham A. Ribicoff said today that New York State should aim at taxing non-residents only in proportion to the services it provided them.

It also suggested that non-residents be permitted to deduct from their New York income taxes the levies they paid on residential properties in their home states.

If New York refuses to do this at present, the report continued, it should at least earmark 30 per cent of the non-residents' taxes for aid to distressed commuter rail lines.

To Talk With Rockefeller

Governor Meyner of New Jersey and Governor Ribicoff of Connecticut will meet with Governor Rockefeller of New York on Tuesday in an attempt to solve the controversy over the taxing of out-of-state residents who work in New York.

The report was prepared by William C. Warren, interstate tax consultant to Mr. Meyner, and Roswell F. Magill, who acts in a similar capacity for Mr. Ribicoff. It comprised a detailed analysis of the effect on non-residents of New York State's income tax.

Mr. Warren, who lives in Ridgewood, N. J., is Dean of the Columbia University Law School. Mr. Magill, a tax lawyer, lives in Westport, Conn.

The report argued that unless about $15,000,000 that is cut annually from nonresident taxes there would be no equity among the states' taxpayers.

New York Plan Scored

It assailed the Rockefeller administration's plan for settling the thirty-year-old interstate tax dispute, characterizing the plan as "inherently defective and no solution to the problem." It warned that the New York proposal, if adopted, might result in still "greater injustice and disparity" than under the present law.

The Rockefeller administration's proposal would permit nonresidents who worked in New York to take exemptions proportional to the share of their incomes earned in New York.

If approved by the New York Legislature, it would become effective only when neighboring states authorized their employers to withhold taxes on employees who live in New York or to furnish Albany with data

Continued on Page 46, Column 3

Police Drop a Historic Whistle

Order Here Scraps SOS Device That Dates to 1889

By IRA HENRY FREEMAN

Another bit of old New York—the famous police whistle—is passing into history.

In an order dated Dec. 24, Police Commissioner Stephen P. Kennedy told his approximately 18,500 patrolmen and 1,500 sergeants that they would no longer be required to carry the tubular whistle.

The tubular whistle is a long, nickel-plated instrument with its own stimulating tone. It takes vigor to blow. Its sound can be heard for four or five blocks on a quiet night. For at least seventy years, it had been used by patrolmen and sometimes by civilians—to call other policemen on post to aid.

Today, Commissioner Kennedy's order said, the whistle is rarely used to call aid. The policeman uses the call-box telephone connected to his prowl car, or the radio of his prowl car, when a public telephone.

If there is no time to make telephone calls, the whistle in need can blow his traffic whistle, or bang his nightstick on the curb, or fire his revolver into the air, the Commissioner said.

The watchmen in New Amsterdam carried rattles, not whistles, after the town was

Tubular whistle is dropped

Traffic whistle will stay
The New York Times

But Traffic Variety Will Still Pierce Ears of City

incorporated in 1652. For that reason, the watchmen were called the rattle watch. The watchmen would walk their posts, swinging their rattles or cries of "evil doers," Mr. Irving said.

In 1691, under the English, the first uniformed policeman patrolled the streets of New York. Instead of a rattle, he swung a bell. The rattles, however, persisted.

Wooden whistles were used at least as early as 1854, Mr. Irving has one said to have belonged to George Washington Walling, a Police Commissioner of that period. In 1860, the pea whistle, a lead casting in which a dried pea vibrated, was used by policemen to call others from near-by posts. It is similar to the dreaded traffic whistle of today.

The practice of banging the baton, truncheon or nightstick on the curbstone or a wall or railing, and of discharging a pistol into the air, is, of course, as old as those police weapons themselves.

Although the traditional police whistle has now departed, the nasty traffic whistle will still be blown by traffic patrolmen and threatens to continue as long as traffic tickets.

Continued on Page 28, Column 3

ROCKEFELLER GIVES UP '60 RACE, CLEARING THE PATH FOR NIXON; DEMOCRATS' HOPES ARE BUOYED

LEADERSHIP WARY

But Top Democrats Appear Pleased by the Decision

By JAMES RESTON
Special to The New York Times

WASHINGTON, Dec. 26—Leading Democrats were publicly canny but privately pleased tonight by Governor Rockefeller's decision not to seek the Republican Presidential nomination.

Adlai E. Stevenson of Illinois expressed regret that the Republicans had been left "with no other choice than Mr. Nixon" as their Presidential candidate.

Representative Sam Rayburn, the Democratic Speaker of the House of Representatives, who is an old friend of the New York Governor and who recently greeted the Governor in Dallas, said he "never commented on Republican candidates" though he "sometimes commented on Republican policies."

Senator Hubert H. Humphrey of Minnesota, the most loquacious member of his party, said "no comment."

Private Opinions Given

Nevertheless, the Democrats expressed in private these reasons for being pleased with Governor Rockefeller's withdrawal:

¶They could beat Vice President Nixon more easily than Mr. Rockefeller because, they said, the New York Governor had more support among independent and Democratic voters.

¶They now knew where they stood. They had to nominate a Presidential candidate before July 11 in Los Angeles, and they could now assume in advance that Mr. Nixon would be their opponent.

¶The Rockefeller announcement revived the conservative-liberal issue between the parties, because it gave the impression that the Republican party did not want "competition" from a liberal candidate.

Mr. Nixon, who is now expected to get the Republican nomination without a contest, issued the following statement after being notified of the Governor's decision:

"Governor Rockefeller has made an excellent impression in the states he has visited in the past few months.

"People throughout the nation have recognized him as a leader of national and international stature.

"Regardless of the decision he

Continued on Page 38, Column 6

GOVERNOR ROCKEFELLER

Associated Press
VICE PRESIDENT NIXON

ROCKEFELLER SAYS IT WAS 'GREAT FUN'

Relaxed Governor Discusses a Variety of Subjects on Train to Philadelphia

By MILTON BRACKER

PHILADELPHIA, Dec. 26—Governor Rockefeller sat back with one leg over a table in a Pullman drawing room on his way here tonight, a few hours after announcing that he would not seek the Republican nomination for President.

He said "it" had been a "very invigorating business," and "great fun."

There was no particular antecedent for "it" and none was needed. The Governor had determined not to add a word of comment to his withdrawal statement, until he holds a news conference in Albany, probably next week.

He stuck to that decision but, in an informal conversation, he could not conceal some amusement at the surprise his action had caused.

He seemed to be saying, "I told them that I hadn't made up my mind—but they wouldn't believe me." Many people had insisted on making up his mind for him, he mused; well, that was their prerogative. An ironic

Continued on Page 37, Column 5

Mitchell and Halleck Gain Backing for Vice President

By W. H. LAWRENCE
Special to The New York Times

WASHINGTON, Dec. 26—Secretary of Labor James P. Mitchell and Representative Charles A. Halleck emerged tonight as the two most talked of possibilities for the Republican Vice-Presidential nomination.

Republican interest in the Vice-Presidency quickened in the wake of the surprise decision by Governor Rockefeller not to seek the Presidential nomination.

This act, virtually insuring the nomination of Vice President Richard M. Nixon, took most of the steam and interest out of the Republican convention. Delegates will meet in Chicago next July 25.

This left only a campaign for the Vice-Presidential spot to add interest to the pre-convention Republican maneuvering. But, in the final analysis, the Presidential nominee will be free—openly or by indirection—to pick whomever he wants as a running mate and the convention quickly will ratify the selection.

Many Factors in Choice

Geography, party background and, perhaps, religion may all have a bearing on the Republican Vice-Presidential choice next year. This will be true especially if the Democrats, meeting first, put a Roman Catholic like Senator John F. Kennedy of Massachusetts or Gov. Edmund G. Brown of California on the ticket.

One likely result of Governor Rockefeller's decision will be to increase the pressure on him to stand as Mr. Nixon's running mate. This will persist despite the New York Governor's firm reaffirmation of earlier statements that he would not be a candidate for Vice President under any conceivable circumstances. But many Republican leaders insist

Continued on Page 36, Column 6

GOVERNOR FACING EASIER STATE JOB

Expected to Gain a Stronger Hand in Pressing Broad Program in Legislature

Special to The New York Times

ALBANY, Dec. 26 — Governor Rockefeller's withdrawal from the Republican Presidential race will shift the national political spotlight away from the 1960 session of the State Legislature.

The result will undoubtedly be a more orderly meeting of the lawmakers. It will probably also enhance Mr. Rockefeller's prospects of winning approval of more of his first large-scale legislative program.

The Governor will have top-heavy Republican majorities in both houses of the Legislature, as have all his predecessors, Republican and Democratic, for the last twenty years.

His problem in winning support for his new programs, of which there will be plenty next year, involves the danger that conservative Republicans in the Senate and Assembly may fall off and join the Democrats in opposition.

Help for Governor Seen

Some of these upstate Republican lawmakers have made no bones about their preference for Mr. Nixon for the Presidential nomination. Mr. Rockefeller's graceful withdrawal is not likely to injure his position with this group.

Others, more sensitive to legislative prerogative than opposed to a Rockefeller candidacy, had expressed resentment over the possibility that the Governor might attempt to "use" the Legislature as a demonstration of what a strong and progressive President he would make. This is so today.

There had been talk that Mr. Rockefeller would attempt to speed the session, which normally runs from early Janary to mid-March or later, in an effort to free himself to participate in some of the Presidential primary contests in other states.

With the Governor no longer a candidate, there is no question of limiting the length of the session.

Continued on Page 37, Column 1

DECISION IS 'FINAL'

Governor Explains He Wishes to Avert a 'Massive' Fight

Text of Rockefeller statement is printed on Page 37.

By WARREN WEAVER Jr.
Special to The New York Times

ALBANY, Dec. 26—Governor Rockefeller withdrew abruptly today from competition for the Republican Presidential nomination in 1960. He said his decision was "definite and final."

He also announced an "absolutely definite" resolve not to be the party's candidate for Vice President. It was a stand he had adopted from the beginning when it appeared he might seek the Presidential nomination.

The Governor's action, unforeseen and almost inexplicable to many observers, appeared to clear the way for the unanimous nomination of Vice President Richard M. Nixon by the Republican National Convention next July.

Nixon Gets Free Hand

It also left Mr. Nixon free to select any Vice-Presidential running mate he saw fit, without reference to any Rockefeller sentiment that might have built up in recent months.

Mr. Rockefeller said he had reached the decision because an attempt to challenge Mr. Nixon would have involved "a massive struggle" and thus have forced him to slight his duties as Governor.

This was the only explanation Mr. Rockefeller offered for withdrawing at a time when virtually every political figure in the state—including many of his close associates—had become convinced he was about to become a declared candidate for President.

Obligations Are Stressed

The Governor did not say he could not defeat the Vice President in open competition in the primaries. He did not say that the Republican cause would be injured by such an intra-party contest. All he said was that the effort would "make impossible the fulfillment of my obligations as Governor of New York."

Mr. Rockefeller based his prediction that any Nixon-Rockefeller competition would be "massive" on a conclusion that "the great majority of those who will control the Republican convention stand opposed to any contest for the nomination."

This was a barely veiled method of saying that almost every leading Republican that he had met in his tours of fifteen states

Continued on Page 37, Column 1

T.W.U. Chiefs Vote Full Tie-Up Jan. 1

By STANLEY LEVEY

The leadership of the Transport Workers Union voted yesterday to recommend a New Year's Day strike on New York's private and public transit lines to support demands for a wage rise.

The vote was taken among members of the union's Local 100, representing 35,000 bus and subway workers. The recommendation, which was unanimous, will go before a mass union rally this afternoon at Manhattan Center.

Michael J. Quill, international union president, and Matthew Guinan, head of Local 100, said weeks of negotiations with the Transit Authority for a new contract had been "fruitless" and that discussions had reached a "complete deadlock."

Today's membership meeting is expected to accept the rec-

Continued on Page 46, Column 4

WANT TO PROSPER in the
Sixties? See Section 10—Advt.

The New York Times

PAGE ONE

Major Events:

1960–1969

"All the News That's Fit to Print"

The New York Times.

LATE CITY EDITION
U. S. Weather Bureau Report (Page 61) forecast:
Fair today; mostly fair tonight.
Partly cloudy and cooler tomorrow.
Temp. range: 74—54; yesterday: 69.1—52.5.

VOL. CIX . No. 37,358.
© 1960, by The New York Times Company. Times Square, New York 36, N. Y.

NEW YORK, FRIDAY, MAY 6, 1960.

10 cents beyond 50-mile zone from New York City except on Long Island. Higher in air delivery cities.

FIVE CENTS

A. M. A. DENOUNCES EISENHOWER PLAN FOR CARE OF AGED

Says Proposal Takes False Tack That Most Over 65 Are Medically Indigent

OTHERS JOIN IN ATTACK

Goldwater Sees 'Socialized Medicine'—Labor Assails Measure as Unsound

By AUSTIN C. WEHRWEIN
Special to The New York Times.

CHICAGO, May 5 — The American Medical Association assailed today the Eisenhower Administration's health-care plan for the aged.

A statement issued today in the name of the association's president, Dr. Louis M. Orr of Orlando, Fla., said the Administration plan was "based on the false premise that almost all persons over 65 need health care and can't afford it."

"This is not a fact," the statement declared.

"The truth is that a majority of our older people are capable of continuing a happy, healthy, and in many cases, productive life.

"Of the more than 15,000,000 persons in the nation over 65 years of age, only 15 per cent are on old age assistance.

Rejects 2 Proposals

"An undetermined number, although able to finance other costs, find it difficult to withstand the additional burden of the cost of illness.

"It is for these people that something should be done. Neither the Forand advocates nor the Administration proposal is tailored to meet these problems."

[In Washington, the Administration's proposal was attacked by Senator Barry Goldwater as "socialized medicine" and by the merged labor federation as unsound and politically inspired.]

The medical association's reference to "Forand" alluded to a bill sponsored by Representative Aime J. Forand, Democrat of Rhode Island. It would extend the Social Security system, and increase Social Security taxes, to provide medical care for persons over 65.

The Administration's proposal, offered yesterday, calls for Federal and state subsidies of insurance systems to be set up by the states. The estimated annual cost of $1,200,000,000

Continued on Page 32, Column 3

O'DWYER'S NIECE NAMED TO BENCH

Mayor Appoints Her Despite Bar Groups' Opposition

By LAYHMOND ROBINSON

Mayor Wagner named Joan O'Dwyer O'Neill, 33-year-old niece of former Mayor William O'Dwyer, a city magistrate yesterday, despite the objections of two of the three bar groups to whom he had submitted her name.

He reported, however, that five bar groups, including the third one asked to pass on her, had given her "unanimous approval."

The Mayor also made it clear that he regarded Mrs. O'Neill as qualified for the $16,000-a-year post on the Magistrate's Court, which basically has jurisdiction over minor crimes.

10-Year Term Slated

The appointment, which needs no further approval, is to fill out two months of a term of a magistrate who resigned. Mrs. O'Neill will then be appointed for a full ten-year term.

In commenting on the division of the bar associations over the designation, the Mayor said he had "always sought bar association approval for bench nominees," but had "never intended or pretended that such support had to be unanimous."

He emphasized that he regarded Mrs. O'Neill, "whom I know quite well," as qualified for the position.

The opposition to her appointment had stemmed largely from the feeling by some lawyers that Mrs. O'Neill had

Continued on Page 14, Column 5

FOR SUMMER COMFORT rent or buy a PURO WATER COOLER, RA 9-7000—Advt.

West Virginia Poll Finds Kennedy Gain

By W. H. LAWRENCE
Special to The New York Times.

CHARLESTON, W. Va., May 5 — Substantial voting gains for Senator John F. Kennedy were reported today in West Virginia.

Politicians and polls alike brought reports of a strong, well-financed and well-organized Kennedy drive to wrest victory from Senator Hubert H. Humphrey of Minnesota, considered the favorite in next Tuesday's Democratic Presidential preferential primary here.

One politician, who classified himself as neutral but formerly pro-Humphrey, admiringly called the Kennedy effort "a blitz." But what he and other politicians, including many in the Kennedy camp, questioned was whether the indicated gains in the southern coal fields were

Continued on Page 13, Column 1

RIBICOFF ASSAILS NEW HAVEN LINE

'This Is Not the Way to Run a Business,' He Says in Calling 4-State Parley

By RICHARD H. PARKE
Special to The New York Times.

GREENWICH, Conn., May 5 — Gov. Abraham A. Ribicoff accused the New Haven Railroad today of "shabby and shoddy" bookkeeping, of wasting "great sums" and of employing "scare words, false issues, emotional appeals and misrepresentations."

"Clearly," he said, "this is not the way to run a business and especially a business which must count so heavily on public goodwill, public support, public respect and, yes, even public affection."

Governor Ribicoff delivered his attack in announcing that he was inviting the Governors of New York, Rhode Island and Massachusetts and the Mayor of New Haven to confer with him on the New Haven's future. No date has been set for the conference.

Tax Relief Proposed

Mr. Ribicoff said he would ask them to consider taking action on the recommendations in the report issued on the New Haven yesterday by the Connecticut Public Utilities Commission.

The report, which was also critical of the railroad management, proposed several measures to aid the line. They included a joint tax-relief program by the four states and an interstate authority that would cooperate with the railroad in providing commuter service in the New York area.

Governor Ribicoff, who discussed the railroad at a meeting here of the First Selectman's Association of Fairfield County, also said he was prepared to recommend a railroad

Continued on Page 20, Column 1

DILLON CONSULTS A. F. L.-C. I. O. AIDE IN ARAB SHIP CASE

Seeks Way to End Picketing Here as Mideast Boycott of U. S. Vessels Spreads

By DANA ADAMS SCHMIDT
Special to The New York Times.

WASHINGTON, May 5—Under Secretary of State Douglas Dillon conferred today with Arthur J. Goldberg, special counsel of the American Federation of Labor and Congress of Industrial Organizations, on possible ways of ending the picketing of the United Arab Republic ship Cleopatra in New York.

Union and State Department officials spoke of the possibility of working out a statement of United States policy that would lead the Seafarers International Union to call off its pickets.

But State Department officials were emphatic in pointing out that they had no means of forcing the United Arab Republic to give up its practice of blacklisting ships that put in at Israeli ports. This boycott precipitated the picketing.

Meanwhile, concern grew at the State Department over indications that the blockade of the Cleopatra and the Arab counter-blockade were reversing the trend toward better United States relations with the Arab world.

Blockade May Spread

"From almost every post we have had laments that the diplomatic efforts of years are being upset by this affair," an official of the department said.

If the blockade continues the impact on commerce would deepen and might next spread to airlines, he added.

The reports included the following points:

¶In Khartoum, capital of the Sudan, the press for the first time in two years assumed an anti-United States tone.

¶The Bombay Port Workers Union telegraphed President Eisenhower protesting the blockade of the Cleopatra and declaring that its continuance would result in a boycott of United States ships seeking to enter the Bombay port. This was the first sign that the counter-blockade might spread beyond the Arab world.

¶A Libyan Government official suggested informally to United States diplomats that "it would be better" if United States ships avoided Libyan ports while the Cleopatra was being picketed.

¶Consulates in a number of Arab ports reported that as the result of a knifing incident in which the eye of a member of the Cleopatra crew was injured it might be unsafe for American crewmen in Arab ports.

¶The American Export liner Excalibur, due today in Alexandria, the United Arab Republic port, was diverted by its owners to a destination not yet disclosed. The United States freighter Exchequer began un-

Continued on Page 2, Column 3

London in Gala Mood for Princess' Wedding Today

Princess Margaret and Antony Armstrong-Jones as they arrived yesterday at Clarence House, the Princess' home, after rehearsing for their wedding in Westminster Abbey.
Associated Press Radiophoto

By DREW MIDDLETON

LONDON, May 5 — The Church of England stressed the spiritual aspects of tomorrow's royal wedding in a brave but unavailing attempt to modify the carnival mood that has gripped the heart of this dignified capital tonight.

Outside Westminster Abbey crowds gaped at decorations hailing the marriage of Princess Margaret to Antony Armstrong-Jones. Inside, the Very Rev. Eric Symes Abbott,

Dean of Westminster, emphasized that "here are two people—a man and a woman—for whom it is the greatest day of their lives." Westminster Abbey, the Dean observed,

Continued on Page 26, Column 3

SOVIET DOWNS AMERICAN PLANE; U.S. SAYS IT WAS WEATHER CRAFT; KHRUSHCHEV SEES SUMMIT BLOW

CAPITAL EXPLAINS

Reports Unarmed U-2 Vanished at Border After Difficulty

Text of the U. S. statement on plane is on Page 7.

By JACK RAYMOND
Special to The New York Times.

WASHINGTON, May 5—The United States said today an American weather-observation plane flown by a civilian apparently went astray near the Turkish-Soviet border Sunday when the pilot's oxygen supply failed.

This was the official explanation of the incident described by Premier Khrushchev when he had been shot down over the Soviet Union.

According to the official statement, the pilot was in a heavily instrumented U-2 single-engine plane, chartered by the Lockheed Aircraft Corporation from the National Aeronautics and Space Administration.

The pilot was identified later as Francis G. Powers, 30 years old, a Lockheed employe.

Plane Used in Research

The plane was flying at an altitude close to 55,000 feet, making weather observations over the Lake Van area of Turkey as part of a world-wide research program begun in 1956, a spokesman for the civilian space agency said.

The spokesman emphasized that the plane was unarmed and carried no military equipment of any kind. He said it was marked with the letters N. A. S. A. in black on a gold-yellow band and with an N. A. S. A. seal, a globe inside calipers. [Premier Khrushchev said the plane shot down bore no identification marks.]

Can Test Radioactivity

The U-2, in addition to its use for weather observation, was developed by Lockheed originally for the Air Force in a secret program initiated in 1954 to study radioactivity resulting from nuclear tests.

The U-2 can maintain flight at altitudes up to 55,000 feet for as long as four hours. It is powered by a single Pratt & Whitney J-57 turbojet engine.

In the high-altitude sampling program, U-2 aircraft have taken samples of radioactive fall-out by exposing filter paper to the atmosphere.

The agency spokesman denied that the U-2 missing in Turkey carried any radioactivity-detection instruments.

The incident occurred in con-

Continued on Page 7, Column 1

ANNOUNCES DOWNING OF U. S. PLANE: Premier Khrushchev speaking yesterday during opening session of the Supreme Soviet (parliament) at the Kremlin in Moscow.
Associated Press Radiophoto

U. S. ASKS DETAILS OF PLANE INCIDENT

Data Sought From Envoy in Moscow as Washington Reacts With Restraint

By WILLIAM J. JORDEN
Special to The New York Times.

WASHINGTON, May 5 — Washington reacted with restraint today to Premier Khrushchev's announcement that a United States plane had been shot down Sunday on Soviet territory.

There were some angry words on Capitol Hill—including a suggestion that President Eisenhower refuse to go to the summit meeting with Mr. Khrushchev in Paris May 16. But the Administration would say little more than that additional information was being sought from Moscow.

A message went to Ambassador Llewellyn E. Thompson Jr. in Moscow this afternoon instructing him to request more details from the Soviet authorities.

Text Made Available Late

The text of Mr. Khrushchev's long speech to the Supreme Soviet became available to officials only late this afternoon. Their first reaction was that he seemed to be preparing the way for placing the blame for a summit failure on the Western powers.

He also seemed to be giving advance warning that the Allied leaders could expect little softness from him at the Paris meeting. The consensus was that the Khrushchev address was the latest move in pre-summit maneuvering, but that it had not altered measurably the outlook for the summit meeting.

Mr. Khrushchev said that the Governments of the United States, Britain and France did not seem to be looking forward

Continued on Page 7, Column 6

Soviet Will Revalue Ruble; Income Tax to End by '65

By MAX FRANKEL
Special to The New York Times.

MOSCOW, May 5—Premier Khrushchev proclaimed a complex fiscal reform today. The changes will bring a new and more costly ruble into Soviet circulation next year and an abolition of most personal income taxes by 1965.

The Premier pledged greater take-home pay to lower-paid industrial workers and office employes and said that this would be matched by increased stocks of consumer goods in the stores.

In fact, he promised a great new drive for the production of consumer goods once his ambitious seven-year economic plan is fulfilled in 1965.

Mr. Khrushchev proposed the currency revaluation and tax revisions to the Supreme Soviet, the national Parliament. Enabling legislation as requested by the Deputies. It is expected to be some time, however, before everyone here, including experts, understands the ramifications of the program.

Unanimous Adoption Seen

There is little doubt that the changes will be unanimously adopted essentially as outlined by Mr. Khrushchev in a broadcast speech. He asked that all the arithmetic complications of the new formulas be tirelessly explained to the Soviet people, together with assurances that the country will gain by the changes and that no one will suffer.

Premier Khrushchev also promised that the currency reform would not affect the Soviet Union's foreign economic dealings or contracts. The official value of the ruble is four to $1. American tourists in the Soviet Union, however, receive a premium payment that brings them a total of ten rubles a dollar.

There was no suggestion in Moscow that the reform was a prelude to free convertibility of

Continued on Page 8, Column 3

ANKARA STUDENTS JOSTLE MENDERES

Turkish Premier Is Caught in Street Demonstration —Escapes Amid Jeers

By JAY WALZ
Special to The New York Times.

ISTANBUL, Turkey, May 5—Premier Adnan Menderes was jostled and jeered in Ankara today when he was caught by surprise in a student demonstration.

Anti-Menderes students mingled with a crowd of the Premier's supporters. They crowded around him shouting "Freedom! Freedom!" as he walked among them on his way to a political club.

One student clutched Premier Menderes' arm and asked, "How long do we suffer at your hands?" The Premier angrily called a policeman to take the young man away.

After a few minutes Mr. Menderes escaped unharmed in a small car that had been parked near by. It pushed through the throng to his own waiting automobile. President Celal Bayar and two Ministers saw the disturbance but were not involved.

Police and Cavalry Busy

About 300 policemen and a troop of cavalry dispersed the crowd, which witnesses estimated at about 3,000. A Government spokesman maintained that only 250 were demonstrators. The rest were bystanders, he said.

A few shots were fired into the air but no one was reported injured. The disturbance lasted for about an hour and a half.

Before the demonstrations in Ankara, a group of students allied with Mr. Menderes' Democratic party were waiting to greet him as he drove to the political club in Kizilay Square in the new section of Ankara. Soldiers lined his route along Ataturk Boulevard.

The anti-Menderes students had passed the word to infiltrate the throng, using the watchword "Five, Five, Five, K.," meaning "Be at Kizilay Square at 5:55 P. M."

The outbreak marked the

Continued on Page 4, Column 5

PREMIER IS BITTER

Assails 'Provocation Aimed at Wrecking' May 16 Parley

Excerpts from Khrushchev's remarks are on page 6.

By OSGOOD CARUTHERS
Special to The New York Times.

MOSCOW, May 5 — Premier Khrushchev said today that a United States plane on a mission of "aggressive provocation aimed at wrecking the summit conference" invaded Soviet territory May 1 and was shot down.

The Premier, in the most blistering speech against American policies he had made since his meetings with President Eisenhower last autumn, declared that the incursion, as well as declarations by United States policy makers, cast gloom on the prospects for the success of the summit meeting in Paris eleven days hence.

He expressed anger over the fact that President Eisenhower had supported declarations against Soviet foreign policies by Vice President Richard M. Nixon, Secretary of State Christian A. Herter, Under Secretary of State Douglas Dillon and others.

He Seems to Bar Nixon

He surmised, Mr. Khrushchev said, that General Eisenhower, while wanting peace, was a victim of tight restrictions by "imperialists and militarists" around him.

Mr. Khrushchev expressed regret that the President wanted to limit the summit meeting to one week and he virtually rejected a proposal to sit at the table with Mr. Nixon if the Vice President was delegated to take over for General Eisenhower in case the session went over the time limit.

The most sensational section of Mr. Khrushchev's three-and-a-half-hour speech, made before the opening session of the Supreme Soviet, the nation's version of a parliament, was that concerning the charges of United States violations of Soviet airspace.

Foreign Policy to Fore

Mr. Khrushchev actually had been called upon to open the Supreme Soviet session to deal exclusively with sweeping new domestic policies that will affect every Soviet worker: gradual abolition of income taxes by 1965 and a seven-hour reduction of the work day to seven hours and an upward revaluation of the ruble.

However, the Soviet leader seized the occasion to discuss foreign policy and the summit conference. He apparently had determined to tell the Soviet people that recent Western actions and statements had darkened his previous optimism.

The Premier predicted to foreign diplomats earlier this week that his talk on foreign and domestic policies would contain major surprises. Indeed, his report of the plane incident came as a shock to Westerners.

Continued on Page 6, Column 4

Harvey Firestone 3d Dies in Havana Fall

Special to The New York Times.

HAVANA, May 5—Harvey S. Firestone 3d plunged to his death from the twentieth floor of a Havana luxury hotel tonight, six hours after arriving here from Miami. The victim, who was 32 years old, was the son of Harvey S. Firestone Jr., chairman of the board of the Firestone Tire and Rubber Company.

[Cuban authorities ruled the death a suicide, The Associated Press reported.]

The Cuban police said David Morgan Firestone, 29, a cousin of the dead man, had told them that Harvey Firestone had attempted suicide on a previous occasion in the United States.

The victim had been crippled since birth by cerebral palsy.

Mr. Firestone arrived in Havana today accompanied by his

Continued on Page 32, Column 5

23 Are Killed and Scores Injured As Twisters Hit East Oklahoma

By The Associated Press.

WILBURTON, Okla., May 5—At least twenty-three persons were killed by tornadoes that slashed across eastern Oklahoma tonight. At least eleven were killed and scores injured in this college town.

A witness, Mrs. Denny Jones, said the tornado hit Wilburton about 6:45 P. M. with a "freight-train" roar.

All communications were cut and travel and rescue efforts were hampered by torrential rains.

The highway patrol and newsmen listed the Wilburton victims as:

Gordon Mote, 70 years old; Mrs. James Reeves, wife of an instructor at Eastern Oklahoma A&M Junior College; a Mrs. Porter and a Mrs. McGee; James Parks, about 70; Mr. and Mrs. Mike Brady, both about 70; Truman Clark, about 45;

Wildon Raines; Margie Bark, and one unidentified man.

Several of the older victims were killed when the twister leveled the Calvary Baptist Church where services were being held.

More than seventy-five persons were reported injured.

Ambulances raced over slick roads to hospitals at McAlester, Poteau, Hartshorne and Heavener.

A newsman on the scene said about 1,000 rescue workers rushed into the city of 2,000 in reply to a call for help.

Tornadoes killed five in the area around Moffett and Roland two small communities nestled against the Arkansas border near Fort Smith.

Sheriff Prentice Maddux of Fort Smith said four bodies

Continued on Page 62, Column 7

201

"All the News That's Fit to Print"

The New York Times.

LATE CITY EDITION
U. S. Weather Bureau Report (Page 82) forecasts:
Early showers, clearing later today; mostly fair tonight and tomorrow.
Temp. range: 78—62; yesterday: 77.0—61.5.

VOL. CIX..No. 37,370. © 1960, by The New York Times Company, Times Square, New York 36, N. Y.   NEW YORK, WEDNESDAY, MAY 18, 1960.   10 cents beyond 50-mile zone from New York City except on Long Island. Higher in air delivery cities.   FIVE CENTS

SUMMIT CONFERENCE BREAKS UP IN DISPUTE; WEST BLAMES KHRUSHCHEV'S RIGID STAND; HE INSISTS ON EISENHOWER SPYING APOLOGY

PASSENGER GAINS AND CITY SUBSIDY END TRANSIT LOSS

Board Expects $4,000,000 Surplus June 30 Instead of Deficit of $116,000

By STANLEY LEVEY

Thanks to more riders and city subsidies, the Transit Authority expects to end the present fiscal year on June 30 with a surplus of $4,000,000, instead of a deficit of $116,000.

Most of the help from the city had been anticipated in planning for 1959-60. But the sharp upturn in passenger revenues had not.

While the agency was pleased with the development, it had no explanation for it yesterday beyond the suggestion that new buses and subway cars were responsible.

"We just have more riders," Charles L. Patterson, chairman of the authority, said happily.

The prospect of a big surplus apparently made firm a previous pledge by the authority that the present 15-cent bus and subway fare would be held at least until Jan. 1, 1962. On that date contracts between the agency and the Transport Workers Union expire.

City Subsidies Counted On

The projected $4,000,000 surplus was based on the records for the first nine months of the fiscal year. From last July 1 to March 31 the authority's revenues exceeded its expenses by $2,865,021. In the same period of the preceding year the agency had a $7,822,903 deficit and it finished that fiscal year with a total deficit of $20,200,000.

Last spring, when the authority drew up its 1959-60 operating budget, it expected to end the year with a deficit of $116,-000. The officials knew then that they could count on

Continued on Page 21, Column 8

2 NETWORKS FIGHT FREE TV DEBATES

But Would Give Candidates Time Under Own Plans

By TOM WICKER
Special to The New York Times.

WASHINGTON, May 17—Adlai E. Stevenson's idea for a series of television debates between the major Presidential candidates encountered stiff opposition today from the TV industry and the opposition party.

Dr. Frank Stanton, president of the Columbia Broadcasting System, and David C. Adams, senior vice president of the National Broadcasting Company, resisted Mr. Stevenson's proposal that the networks be required by law to grant free time to the candidates.

However, both said that these networks would make free time available voluntarily, under certain circumstances.

Bill Before Senate Unit

Mr. Stevenson's "great debate" plan is embodied in S. 3171, a bill pending before the Communications Subcommittee of the Senate Interstate and Foreign Commerce Committee. The group heard and questioned the former Governor of Illinois yesterday and Dr. Stanton today.

It also received today a written statement from Mr. Adams and took written testimony against the bill from Vice President Nixon, former President Herbert Hoover and Thomas E. Dewey, twice a Republican candidate.

Mr. Adams will be questioned at an afternoon session tomorrow. His statement today described S. 3171 as "the wrong way to go about doing the right thing." The bill, he said, is "discriminatory" and "confiscatory." It is not needed, he went on, because N. B. C. already proposes to "invite the major Pres-

Continued on Page 29, Column 3

U. S. Sues to Open Biloxi Beach to All

Special to The New York Times.

WASHINGTON, May 17—The Justice Department sued Biloxi, Miss., today in a move to open the Gulf coast beach there to Negroes.

Three weeks ago, on the week-end of April 23, a group of about forty Negroes tried to swim at the beach. They were chased by white men with clubs. It has been reported that Negroes are not permitted to swim anywhere on the twenty-six-mile beach.

Gunfire and street fights in Biloxi followed the episode. Two white men and eight Negroes were wounded by bullets. Several Negroes who had tried to use the beach were arrested and fined $25 each for "disturbing the peace."

The Justice Department suit was based on the fact that

Continued on Page 22, Column 1

KENNEDY SWEEPS MARYLAND'S VOTE

Gets 70% of Total in Routing Morse for Sixth Straight Primary Triumph

By W. H. LAWRENCE
Special to The New York Times.

BALTIMORE, May 17—Senator John F. Kennedy won a landslide victory in Maryland's Democratic primary today to enlarge his claim to the Presidential nomination.

The young Massachusetts contender polled about 70 per cent of the vote and picked up twenty-four first-ballot delegate votes at the national convention opening in Los Angeles July 11.

There was no contest in the Republican preferential primary.

Senator Kennedy overwhelmed Senator Wayne Morse of Oregon and Maryland politicians who had urged a vote for an uninstructed delegation to demonstrate support for the Presidential aspirations of Senator Stuart Symington of Missouri, Senator Lyndon B. Johnson of Texas and Adlai E. Stevenson of Illinois.

Returns from 1,354 of 1,356 precincts gave:

Kennedy 199,362
Morse 49,323

Mr. Kennedy jumped far ahead in the first precinct to report, and built his lead steadily in every section.

Mr. Morse took his worst beating in Baltimore, which casts about half the Democratic vote, trailing his rival by a plurality in excess of 73,000.

The Oregonian received about 17 per cent of the vote, or 50 per cent less than the expectation he voiced Sunday, when he conceded defeat in advance.

For Senator Kennedy this was his sixth straight primary victory and an impressive show of strength before his final

Continued on Page 30, Column 4

Vatican Paper Proclaims Right Of Church to Role in Politics

Special to The New York Times.

ROME, May 17—L'Osservatore Romano, the Vatican newspaper, declared today that the Roman Catholic hierarchy had "the right and the duty to intervene" in the political field to guide its flock. It rejected what it termed "the absurd split of conscience between the believer and the citizen."

The pronouncement was in a front-page editorial described by the Vatican Press Service as "authoritative." It was presented in a special make-up that L'Osservatore Romano usually reserves for semi-official statements emanating from its Vatican superiors, as distinct from its own editorial opinion.

The article clearly referred to the 'political situation in Italy,

where some left-of-center elements in the dominant Christian Democratic party, which enjoys Vatican backing, have recently advocated collaboration with Left-Wing Socialists, against the advice of the Roman Catholic Episcopacy.

However, L'Osservatore Romano made it plain that the pronouncement was valid for Roman Catholic laymen everywhere. It explored "the great confusion of ideas that is spreading, especially in some nations, among Catholics with regard to the relations between Catholic doctrine and social and political activities, and between the ecclesiastical hierarchy and

Continued on Page 51, Column 1

SOVIET SHIFT SEEN

'Warmed-Up Cold War' Awaited—Khrushchev Will Stop in Berlin

By SYDNEY GRUSON
Special to The New York Times.

PARIS, May 17 — Western diplomats here expressed the belief today that Premier Khrushchev's break with President Eisenhower signaled a major change in Soviet policy. One Frenchman suggested that this tended toward a "warmed-up cold war."

The change will become apparent quickly, these diplomats believe, perhaps even in a session of the Supreme Soviet, the parliament in Moscow, that Mr. Khrushchev is expected to summon on his return home.

Meanwhile, the Soviet Premier plans to stop in Berlin on his way back to Moscow. His meetings in Berlin with East Germany's Communist leaders are expected by Western diplomats to open some new phase in the Soviet campaign to resolve the Berlin crisis.

Soviet-Bloc Parley Predicted

Soviet sources here said Mr. Khrushchev would also call together the Soviet Union's Eastern European allies to consider the consequences of the rupture with President Eisenhower and the failure of the Paris summit conference.

The Russians have been threatening to sign a separate peace treaty with East Germany and place access to West Berlin in East German hands unless the West negotiates a Berlin settlement.

TRANQUIL INTERLUDE: President Eisenhower and Prime Minister Macmillan stroll about the grounds of the villa in Marnes-la-Coquette, where the President lived in 1951 and 1952 as the commander of the North Atlantic Treaty Organization forces in Europe.
United Press International Radiophoto

WIELDING THE AXE: Premier Khrushchev chops wood near Sézanne, France.
Radiophoto of The New York Times (by Erich Lessing—Magnum)

DEMOCRATS HINT 'BLUNDERS' PROBE

But Mansfield and Johnson Emphasize United Front During Crisis in Paris

By RUSSELL BAKER

WASHINGTON, May 17—Democratic Congressional leaders created a temporary united front behind President Eisenhower today for the duration of the summit crisis but hinted at possible investigations to come.

Senator Mike Mansfield of Montana, the Senate's deputy Democratic leader, said that questions about Administration "blunders" preceding the Paris conference "must be asked," but only "at the proper time."

While the President is still in Paris and the Senate is threatening to create a fresh German crisis that could bring "all peoples to the edge of catastrophe" is not the right time, he told the Senate.

Lyndon B. Johnson of Texas, the Democratic leader, agreed that first priority should be given to maintaining a united national front behind the President in the present period of uncertainty.

Johnson Bars Division

"If there have been mistakes, responsibility will be assessed coolly and objectively," he said. "But one mistake that we cannot afford to make right now is to weaken the free world by division within our own ranks."

Behind these speeches by the Senate's two Democratic leaders was the conviction that to permit a great national debate at this point might strengthen Premier Khrushchev's indictment of the United States Government and further embarrass President Eisenhower.

By tacit agreement, most Congressional Democrats suspended criticism of the Administration and waited nervously for further developments in Paris.

Many Republicans were conceding today that even if the Administration got out of Paris without additional trouble, the party had been politically hurt for the election campaign ahead.

Moreover, the calm that Senators Johnson and Mansfield and Speaker Sam Rayburn have

Continued on Page 14, Column 5

The Western Communique

By The Associated Press.

PARIS, May 17—Following is a joint communiqué issued tonight by Britain, France and the United States:

The President of the United States, the President of the French Republic and the Prime Minister of the United Kingdom take note of the fact that because of the attitude adopted by the Chairman of the Council of Ministers of the Soviet Union it has not been possible to begin, at the summit conference, the examination of the problems which it had been agreed would be discussed between the four chiefs of state or government.

They regret that these discussions, so important for world peace, could not take place. For their part, they remain unshaken in their conviction that all outstanding international questions should be settled not by the use or threat of force but by peaceful means through negotiation. They themselves remain ready to take part in such negotiations at any suitable time in the future.

PRELATE IN CUBA DENOUNCES REDS

Archbishop Urges Fight— Stand Could Bring Death

By R. HART PHILLIPS

HAVANA, May 17—A pastoral letter attacking communism and urging Cuban Roman Catholics to combat this "enemy within our gates" has been issued by the Archbishop of Santiago de Cuba, Msgr. Enrique Pérez Serantes.

The letter, which was ordered read in churches of his archdiocese of Oriente Province, was published in Havana today by Información and El Crisol, Cuba's only independent newspapers. The Government press and radio ignored the pastoral.

This latest significance since anti-communism has been declared by the Government of Premier Fidel Castro to be synonymous with "counter-revolutionary activities," punishable by death before a firing squad or long imprisonment.

Castro's Ranks Split

The letter caused a sensation in the island, particularly since Archbishop Pérez Serantes has long been a close friend of Premier Castro and is credited with having saved the life of the revolutionary leader in 1953.

At that time, following an unsuccessful attack by Dr. Castro and a group of young revolutionaries on the Moncava army post of Santiago de Cuba, the Archbishop protected Dr. Castro and obtained assurances for his life from the authorities while others of the group were being hunted down and killed on sight.

Communism is a major issue in Cuba and has split the ranks of Premier Castro's own revolutionary followers. The issue has

Continued on Page 5, Column 3

LUMUMBA RISING AS A CONGO RULER

Defies Belgians as He Builds Power in Interior Region

By HOMER BIGART
Special to The New York Times.

STANLEYVILLE, Belgian Congo, May 17—Belgian authority is collapsing in part of the Congo.

Patrice Emergy Lumumba, Congolese nationalist leader, is taking over as virtual dictator of this city and much of the Stanleyville and Eastern Provinces.

Not even the arrival of Belgian troop reinforcements is likely to halt the rapid erosion of the colonial administration's authority. Forty-five days before Congolese independence the Belgian administration already seems subservient to the nationalists.

Ban on Meetings Defied

M. Lumumba saw reports of troops arrivals at the Kamina military base in Katanga Province as an "attempt to intimidate the voters and influence the election in favor of Belgian selected candidates." He said he had sent a telegram to King Baudouin of the Belgians denouncing the arrival of the troops. He did not seem unduly worried, however.

Yesterday, in a moment of painful humiliation for the Belgian settlers, M. Lumumba defied a ban on public meetings. He did it in the heart of the city that jailed him last October for inciting riots.

The incident marked the beginning of a triumphal tour by M. Lumumba of the region north of Stanleyville. There, in villages deep in the equatorial forest, he demanded and received assurances from Belgian forest watchers that watchers that he would be allowed to speak to the people. The issue has

Continued on Page 6, Column 1

CHARGES TRADED

Allies Leave the Door Open to New Talk— Soviet Scores U.S.

By DREW MIDDLETON
Special to The New York Times.

PARIS, May 17—The summit conference died tonight. The leaders of the West and Premier Khrushchev had killed it. The Russians blamed the United States.

President Eisenhower, Prime Minister Macmillan and President de Gaulle feel "complete disgust" at the attitude the Soviet delegation has taken here in the last two days, James C. Hagerty, White House press secretary, reported.

In a communique issued this evening, the three Western chiefs declared that the Soviet leader's attitude had made it impossible to begin examination of the problems that it had been agreed should be discussed.

Apology Was Demanded

Premier Khrushchev had refused to meet with the Western leaders, on the invitation of President de Gaulle, unless President Eisenhower apologized for United States espionage flights over the Soviet Union. This the President was not prepared to do.

The meeting, so long prepared and so anxiously awaited, expired in an atmosphere of gloomy foreboding. Diplomats of the three Western powers feared the world situation would deteriorate.

The Western leaders pledged their support to a settlement of all outstanding international issues by the use or threat of force. The United States, Britain and France remain ready for such negotiations "at any suitable time in the future," a communiqué said.

Soviet in Sharp Attack

A few minutes after the communiqué had been made public, a group of leading Soviet editors answered it with a sharp denunciation of the United States. The conference foundered, a Soviet statement said, because "aggressive actions" of the United States Government and the Administration's failure to accept responsibility had "torpedoed the conference which the peoples of the whole world were awaiting with such hopes."

The Western leaders will meet again tomorrow in a preliminary conference between their foreign ministers, Christian A. Herter, Selwyn Lloyd and Maurice Couve de Murville. These meetings, Western diplomats said, will review

Continued on Page 14, Column 1

KHRUSHCHEV STEP REKNITS NATO TIE

Allies Feel Premier Carried U-2 Exploitation Too Far

By ROBERT C. DOTY
Special to The New York Times.

PARIS, May 17—Soviet intransigence, applied this time to bringing the summit conference to a halt, has again served to restore the cohesion of the North Atlantic Treaty Organization.

The conclusion of NATO secretariat officials for the United States and of smaller powers today was that Premier Khrushchev had again badly overplayed his hand in exploitation of Soviet grievances arising over the downing of an American U-2 reconnaissance plane over the Soviet Union.

The same officials were unwilling to predict the long-term effects on the Atlantic alliance of the events since Sunday. New, heavy Soviet pressure on Berlin—one of the possibilities—would require severe strains on the military and political resources of NATO.

But for the present at least, resentment of Soviet tactics here has largely overshadowed Allied impatience with the

Continued on Page 14, Column 7

COLLAPSE FEARED FOR GENEVA TALK

Summit Breakdown Likely to Affect Nuclear-Test and Arms Discussion

By A. M. ROSENTHAL
Special to The New York Times.

PARIS, May 17—The East-West negotiations in Geneva on disarmament and on a nuclear test ban are collapsing today.

Premier Khrushchev's decision to boycott the summit meeting convinced Western diplomats that the chances for agreement on disarmament or the ending of nuclear tests had been blown to bits and would take considerable time to paste together again.

Russians were saying that the Khrushchev tactics at the summit did not mean that the Geneva talks would be called off. But the opinion of diplomats here was that the political foundation for agreement had been smashed.

American sources said tonight that the prospects for both conferences had been pushed back, if not destroyed. Foreign Secretary Selwyn Lloyd of Britain said the breakdown at the summit need not wreck the two Geneva meetings.

The Western delegations were expecting the Soviet Union to take the issue of the U-2 reconnaissance plane to Geneva and make it their political centerpiece at the disarmament negotiations. Moscow has repeatedly said that the West is more interested in espionage than dis-

Continued on Page 15, Column 7

Jovial Khrushchev Has Rural Holiday

By OSGOOD CARUTHERS
Special to The New York Times.

PARIS, May 17 — Premier Khrushchev spent a happy day outdoors in France today despite all the efforts of the Western leaders to get him indoors for a session of the summit conference.

With seeming abandon, the leader of the Soviet Union spent the day doing the things he wanted to do when he came to France on a state visit two months ago. Meanwhile, the tense and anxious leaders of the West waited for him to save the summit from catastrophe.

Mr. Khrushchev held sidewalk and barnyard news conferences. He dashed up to startled Frenchmen and shook their

Continued on Page 15, Column 3

"All the News That's Fit to Print"

The New York Times.

LATE CITY EDITION
U. S. Weather Bureau Report (Page 54) forecasts:
Cloudy, chance of showers today.
Fair, cooler, less humid tomorrow.
Temp. range: 84—72; yesterday: 83.2—70.
Temp.-Hum. Index: high 70's; yesterday: 78.

VOL. CIX—No. 37,427. © 1960, by The New York Times Company. Times Square, New York 36, N. Y.

NEW YORK, THURSDAY, JULY 14, 1960.

10 cents beyond 50-mile zone from New York City except on Long Island. Higher in air delivery cities.

FIVE CENTS

KENNEDY NOMINATED ON THE FIRST BALLOT; OVERWHELMS JOHNSON BY 806 VOTES TO 409

Security Council Authorizes U. N. Force to Aid Congo

PEACE UNIT VOTED

U. S. and Soviet Clash in Debate—Belgians Asked to Pull Out

Congolese texts, resolution, debate excerpts, Page 4.

By THOMAS J. HAMILTON
Special to The New York Times.

UNITED NATIONS, N. Y., Thursday, July 14 — The Security Council authorized Secretary General Dag Hammarskjold today to organize and send a United Nations force to the Congo.

The vote was eight in favor and none against, with Britain, France and Nationalist China abstaining.

The vote was taken at 3:03 A. M., nearly six and a half hours after the Security Council, at the request of Mr. Hammarskjold, began its urgent night session. The decision was delayed by bitter exchanges between the United States and Soviet representatives, Henry Cabot Lodge and Arkady A. Sobolev. The Council adjourned at 3:21 A. M.

Outcome Was Uncertain

The outcome remained uncertain until the last. It was known that Britain, France and Nationalist China would abstain. They objected to a provision in the resolution, which was introduced by Tunisia, calling for the withdrawal of Belgian troops from the Congo.

The withdrawal recommendation was included on the demand of the Soviet Union and the African states. However, word was passed during the long meeting that the Soviet Union and Poland had not received instructions on the Tunisian proposal, and would therefore abstain if the United States insisted upon a vote at this meeting.

This belief was strengthened after Walter Loridan, the Belgian representative, announced that Belgian troops would be withdrawn from the Congo when the United Nations force is able to provide "effective" maintenance of order.

Mr. Sobolev termed this statement unsatisfactory. He introduced amendments condemning Belgian "armed aggression" in the Congo, stating that the Belgian forces must be withdrawn "immediately," and limiting participation in the United Nations force to the other African states.

The first two amendments were rejected 7 to 2, with only the Soviet Union and Poland

Continued on Page 4, Column 3

Belgian Commandos Rout Congo Troops at Airport

Bunche Meets With Both Sides to Try to Halt Clashes—Congolese Open Fire on Convoy of Refugees

By HENRY TANNER
Special to The New York Times.

LEOPOLDVILLE, the Congo, July 13—Belgian commandos occupied Leopoldville's airport today and then clashed with Congolese troops. At least six Congolese and two Belgians were killed.

Belgian forces occupied the airport at midmorning. They went into action after Congolese soldiers had moved into the airport and had threatened to interfere with the evacuation of Belgian civilians by Sabena, the Belgian airline.

[Leopoldville was reported by press associations to be under the control of Belgian troops, but there was uncertainty over the extent of control. Congolese troops opened fire on Wednesday night on a convoy of 300 Belgians heading for the airport. Reuters said the Congo Government had declared that a "state of war" existed with Belgium. The Congo has asked six Congolese and two Belgians to send troops.

[In Brussels, the Belgian Government said it would keep troops at key points in the Congo.]

Dr. Ralph J. Bunche, United Nations Under Secretary, met with Congolese authorities and Ambassador Jean van an Bosch of Belgium this afternoon in an effort to halt the clashes.

Dr. Bunche was reported to have been called in by the Congolese to mediate a cease-fire between them and the Belgians. He left the United States Embassy, where he has an office, in the early afternoon with the blue United Nations flag flying

Continued on Page 3, Column 2

KISHI IS STABBED AT HOME IN TOKYO

Japan's Premier Is Reported Not Badly Hurt—Ikeda Chosen His Successor

By RICHARD J. H. JOHNSTON
Special to The New York Times.

TOKYO, Thursday, July 14—Premier Nobusuke Kishi was attacked by an assassin and stabbed in the thigh within an hour after his apparent successor had been elected by his party.

The Premier was attacked at a reception in his official residence. The attacker was identified by the authorities as Taizo Aramaki, a Rightist, about 45 years old.

Mr. Kishi was removed to a nearby hospital, where it was announced that his condition was not serious.

His assailant was arrested.

The police established the time of the attack at 2:30 P. M. This would be about forty minutes of Mr. Kishi's departure from Hibiya Hall in Downtown Tokyo, where the Liberal-Democratic party convention had been held.

The reception at the Premier's home was called to honor Hayato Ikeda, who, less than an hour before had been elected in the convention of the governing party as its new president, replacing Mr. Kishi who had resigned in the convention a short time before.

Mr. Ikeda, now Trade Minister, backs the Kishi policies.

The attack on the 63-year-old Premier was an ironic twist in the turbulent politics of recent months in Japan.

On June 23 he had announced

Continued on Page 11, Column 2

HOGAN WILL PRESS A NEW JACK TRIAL

Fall Date to Be Asked Today in Borough Chief's Case

By PETER FLINT

A date for a new trial for Borough President Hulan E. Jack of Manhattan on charges of conflict of interest and conspiracy will be requested by District Attorney Frank S. Hogan today in the Court of General Sessions.

Since the court is now in summer recess, with only three of the nine judges sitting, the prosecutor is expected to ask for a date in the fall.

Mr. Jack's first trial ended last Thursday when the jury failed to agree on a verdict after two days of deliberation and was discharged.

Mr. Jack's lawyer, Carson DeWitt Baker, said he would request an immediate trial. But he expressed the view that Mr. Hogan would "have his way as usual," and that the new trial probably would begin in October.

Mr. Baker also expressed "firm conviction" that the Borough President would continue his self-suspension from office until the case was resolved. He

Continued on Page 25, Column 5

Peru Urges O.A.S. Debate Red Threat; U. S. Favors Parley

Special to The New York Times.

WASHINGTON, July 13—Peru has suggested that the foreign ministers of the American nations meet soon to consider the Soviet threat to inter-American unity and democracy in the Western Hemisphere.

Informed sources said the Peruvian initiative was welcomed by the United States and that Washington would support the proposal. It is believed that the Peruvian suggestion will be considered at a meeting this week of the Council of the Organization of American States.

The Peruvian suggestion was circulated today among representatives of the twenty-one member of the O.A.S. It was also the subject of urgent consultation at embassies and in the State Department.

Peru's proposal was couched in careful diplomatic language, but its meaning was clear. The message stressed the necessity for the continued solidarity of the countries of this hemisphere. It called for the defense of the regional system in inter-American affairs and of democratic principles.

There was no specific reference

Continued on Page 12, Column 5

2 Planes Down Off Philippines; 86 of 88 Aboard Saved From Sea

Two Lost as U. S. Airliner Ditches—Island DC-3 Also Crashes, 30 on It Safe

By United Press International

MANILA, Thursday, July 14—An American airplane and a Philippine passenger plane went down at sea in separate accidents today with a total of eighty-eight persons aboard. But eighty-six were reported safe after swift, dramatic rescue from shark-dangerous waters.

At least thirty-four Americans were aboard one of the planes, a Northwest Orient Airlines DC7-C on the last leg of a New York-to-Manila flight with fifty-one passengers and a crew of seven.

United States air force amphibious planes from Clark Field reported the rescue of fifty-six persons from the Northwest plane. One person was reported killed and one missing.

In the southern Philippines, 500 miles from Manila between the islands of Negros and Mindanao, a Philippines Airlines plane on an inter-island flight ditched in shallow water near land and all thirty passengers and crew were safely picked up.

Passengers on the Northwest

Union Forcing Plant To Return to City

By A. H. RASKIN

An arbitrator has ordered a New York clothing manufacturer to reopen his closed factory here and to pay the Amalgamated Clothing Workers union more than $200,000 in damages for having moved its work to Mississippi.

The employer, who lost a court fight to block arbitration, made it clear yesterday that he would resist the unusual award to upset their awards will bar a successful challenge.

Jacob S. Potofsky, president of the Amalgamated, hailed the award as proof that "runaway"

Continued on Page 55, Column 2

MOSCOW BIDS U. N. CONVENE AT ONCE ON RB-47 INCIDENT

Says Flights by U. S. Planes With Reconnaissance Aim Are Threat to Peace

By OSGOOD CARUTHERS
Special to The New York Times.

MOSCOW, July 13—The Soviet Union called today for an urgent meeting of the United Nations Security Council to discuss its charges of United States "aggressive actions."

The Soviet complaint derived from the shooting down of a United States RB-47 reconnaissance plane off the Soviet coast in the Barents Sea on July 1.

[In a statement from the summer White House at Newport, R. I., the United States backed a full investigation by the United Nations of the "wanton shooting down" of the plane.]

Moscow called for the United Nations meeting in a cablegram sent by Foreign Minister Andrei A. Gromyko today to the president of the Security Council, José A. Correa of Ecuador.

Hammarskjold Gets Copy

The message, a copy of which was sent to Secretary General Dag Hammarskjold, charged that the United States flights constituted "a serious threat to the preservation of peace."

The United States has denied that the RB-47 plane had violated Soviet territorial waters as alleged by the Kremlin.

The Soviet request came on the heels of a statement yesterday by Premier Khrushchev that his Government might take the matter before the Security Council.

He said he did not expect that the Security Council, which he described as an "instrument" of the United States, would take any action satisfactory to the Soviet Union. However, he said he thought it was necessary to raise the question there anyway if only to "discredit the dishonest judges once more."

Mr. Gromyko's cablegram, which he said would be followed by an explanatory letter, noted that the Security Council had discussed the previous plane incident, in which a U-2 reconnaissance jet was shot down deep inside Soviet territory on May 1.

The message asked the Security Council to "take such measures as appear necessary to put an end to these dangerous

Continued on Page 6, Column 6

Associated Press Wirephoto
AFTER THE VICTORY: Senator John F. Kennedy of Massachusetts heads for rostrum at Los Angeles Memorial Sports Arena to address the Democratic National Convention.

JOHNSON PLEDGES HELP TO KENNEDY

He Assures Candidate of His Full Support and Issues a Call for Party Unity

By JOHN D. MORRIS
Special to The New York Times.

LOS ANGELES, July 13—Senator Lyndon B. Johnson accepted tonight "with all my heart" Senator John F. Kennedy's nomination for President.

The Texan, who had watched the convention proceedings by television in his suite at the Biltmore Hotel, issued a four-paragraph statement just as the first ballot ended. It had been prepared as Montana and some other Mountain States failed to provide expected shifts to the Johnson banner.

The statement follows:

"The delegates have made their decision and I accept it with all my heart.

"Senator Kennedy has my sincere congratulations, and my solemn assurance that in the coming months of this campaign, no one will be more dedicated than I—no one will work harder than I to make doubly sure of what all Democrats here and throughout the country know must come about for the good of the nation and the free world—that John F. Kennedy will be elected the next President of the United States.

"We have a winner—he has proved it here.

"Now, let our party unite behind our candidate—let us sweep the country this November, so that in January Demo-

Continued on Page 15, Column 6

Plan to End Strike On L.I.R.R. Offered

Governor Rockefeller's factfinding board proposed an arbitration plan last night to bring a settlement and end the Long Island Rail Road strike.

The plan was rejected almost at once by the union's negotiating committee. It charged that most arbitrators had been "so brainwashed by the propaganda of the Association of American Railroads and the National Association of Manufacturers" that labor could not trust them.

The rejection will be reviewed by the 1,350 strikers at a meeting this morning, but union leaders said they would "bet a million dollars that the men will turn the idea down unanimously."

The company said the union's reaction made further study of the plan seem academic. It

Continued on Page 20, Column 2

Symington Heavy Favorite For Second Place on Ticket

By LEO EGAN
Special to The New York Times.

LOS ANGELES, July 13—Senator Stuart Symington became a heavy favorite for the Vice-Presidential nomination tonight following Senator John F. Kennedy's first-ballot nomination for President. The Missouri delegation was the first to swing into line behind Senator Kennedy after the New Englander had clinched the nomination for first place.

At the Kennedy headquarters in the Biltmore Hotel it was announced that the Presidential nominee would meet with those under consideration for Vice President and with party leaders from all sections of the country before going to bed.

Before the convention opened, he had promised the New York delegation, which was an important factor in his victory, that he would consult with its leaders before making a choice on second place.

Senator Symington parried questions about the Vice-Presidential nomination with the comment that the matter was entirely up to Senator Kennedy.

Good Word for Jackson

Although the Missouri Senator was regarded as the front runner for the Vice-Presidential nomination, two others were receiving serious consideration.

They were Gov. Orville L. Freeman of Minnesota, who had placed the New Englander in nomination, and Senator Henry M. Jackson of Washington State.

At a meeting of the Washington delegation today, Robert F. Kennedy, the Senator's brother and floor manager, said that Senator Jackson was his (Robert's) personal choice for the place but that political considerations might force his brother to turn elsewhere.

Governor Freeman had also been informed that those around Senator Kennedy had a high regard for him and that he would be acceptable as a Vice-Presidential candidate.

Up to the hour of Senator Kennedy's nomination, both Senator Symington and Representative Charles A. Brown of Missouri, his campaign manager, were declaring that Senator Symington was not a candidate. But few delegates expected him to

Continued on Page 15, Column 6

STEVENSON GIVEN A WILD RECEPTION

His Nomination Touches Off Roaring Demonstration— It Lasts 25 Minutes

By WILLIAM M. BLAIR
Special to The New York Times.

LOS ANGELES, July 13—A wild, emotional demonstration for Adlai E. Stevenson shook the Democratic National Convention tonight.

As the name of the man who led the Democrats in 1952 and 1956 was placed before the convention, the galleries erupted in a screaming roar that dwarfed all that went before.

A rip-roaring nominating speech by Senator Eugene J. McCarthy, an "egghead" from Minnesota, set off the nearest thing to hysteria that this convention has seen.

Although the demonstrators obviously were full of enthusiasm, it was also obvious that the demonstration was at least partly contrived.

It took the convention chairman, Gov. LeRoy Collins of Florida, twenty-five minutes to slow down the stamping, shouting show to get seconding speeches.

Supporters Storm Floor

Stevenson supporters from outside the convention stormed the floor, some apparently gaining entrance by ruses, to call for the man who said he did not come West to seek the nomination.

Chanting, placard-waving demonstrators jammed the aisles while the galleries suddenly came alive with thousands of placards and hundreds of demonstrators going round and round in a deafening din.

The bobbing, weaving demonstration, in which many of them young persons, caused many delegates to cover their heads with their hands as the Stevenson rooters bounced a giant, white papier-mâché ball through the air. The ball represented a snowball intended to dramatize the "Draft Stevenson" effort.

For the most part, the delegates appeared unmoved as the

Continued on Page 15, Column 2

LONG DRIVE WINS

Wyoming's Vote Puts Bostonian Over Top Before Acclamation

Kennedy's talk on Page 14; nominating speeches, 16.

By W. H. LAWRENCE
Special to The New York Times.

LOS ANGELES, Thursday, July 14—Senator John F. Kennedy smashed his way to a first-ballot Presidential nomination at the Democratic National Convention last night and won the right to oppose Vice President Nixon in November.

The 43-year-old Massachusetts Senator overwhelmed his opposition, piling up 806 votes to 409 ballots for his nearest rival, Senator Lyndon B. Johnson of Texas, the Senate majority leader. Senator Kennedy's victory came just before 11 o'clock last night [2 A. M. Thursday, New York time].

Then the convention made it unanimous on motion of Gov. James T. Blair Jr. of Missouri, who had placed Senator Stuart Symington of Missouri in nomination.

'We Shall Win'

Senator Kennedy, appearing before the shouting convention early today, pledged he would carry the fight to the country in the fall "and we shall win." He thanked his defeated rivals for their generosity and appealed to all of their backers to keep the party strong and united in a tremendously important election. He spoke directly of Senators Johnson and Symington and the favorite sons, but made no reference to Adlai E. Stevenson.

The third session of the national convention adjourned after his speech. The next session will convene at 5 P. M. today.

Little Wyoming, well down the roll-call, provided the decisive fifteen votes that gave victory to Senator Kennedy. Two favorite-son states, Minnesota and New Jersey, waited in vain to give the on-rushing Kennedy bandwagon the final shove.

When Wyoming came in with its vote, the Kennedy total had mounted to 765 votes, or four more than the 761 votes required for nomination.

It was a tremendous victory for Senator Kennedy. Mr. Johnson, the Senate majority leader, had fought desperately to reverse a Kennedy tide that had been running for months. But Senator Johnson quickly telephoned his congratulations to

Continued on Page 14, Column 1

F.H.A. INVESTMENT OPENED TO PUBLIC

Individuals Invited to Deal in U. S.-Insured Mortgages

By RICHARD E. MOONEY
Special to The New York Times.

WASHINGTON, July 13—The Government invited individuals today to invest in mortgages insured against loss by the Federal Housing Administration.

It was, in effect, an offer of a long-term investment that could earn the investor more than 5 per cent and would be paid off by the Government if the mortgage went into default. The yields of representative stocks and bonds currently are lower than 5 per cent.

Investment in an F. H. A.-insured mortgage would not be riskless. The investor would have to hold his investment until the mortgage was paid off, if the homebuyer or F. H. A., if the house sold before that turn, he might sell at a loss.

Besides being an attractive offer, and a break with policy of twenty-five years' standing, today's action was the Government's third stimulant to sagging activity in home building in as many months.

In April, the F. H. A. reduced

Continued on Page 55, Column 4

The New York Times July 14, 1960
Sites of crash of U. S. plane (1) and Philippines plane (2)

airliner included Dr. Rodrigo L. Sarmiento, Filipino surgeon banished from the United States because of the convicted killing of a Brooklyn nurse, Margaret Kabak. Dr. Sarmiento was among the survivors.

The Northwest plane, which had come from New York via Seattle, Anchorage, Tokyo and Okinawa, crash-landed near the little island of Jimalog, of the Potillo group about 150 miles north of Manila, after a propeller "ran away" and off and a wing caught fire.

Capt. David Rall, 53 years old of Seattle, deliberately put the plane down at sea at 4:20 A. M. [4:20 P. M. ...]

Continued on Page 12, Column 4

"All the News
That's Fit to Print"

The New York Times.

LATE CITY EDITION
U.S. Weather Bureau Report (Page 54) forecast:
Mostly fair and warm today,
tonight and tomorrow.
Temp. range: 84—65; yesterday: 72.9—66.9.
Temp.-Hum. index: 76; yesterday: 71.

VOL. CIX..No. 37,441.   © 1960 by The New York Times Company.
Times Square, New York 36, N.Y.   NEW YORK, THURSDAY, JULY 28, 1960.
10 cents beyond 50-mile zone from New York City
except on Long Island. Higher in air delivery cities.   FIVE CENTS

NIXON IS GIVEN NOMINATION BY ACCLAMATION AFTER GOLDWATER GETS 10 LOUISIANA VOTES; CANDIDATE PICKS LODGE FOR SECOND PLACE

SANITATION UNION QUITS IN PROTEST; GARBAGE PILES UP

5,000 March on City Hall as Wage Talks Break Off —Walkout May Go On

By LAYHMOND ROBINSON

Thousands of tons of refuse were left lying on city streets yesterday when angry sanitation workers suddenly stopped work to protest a breakdown in wage negotiations with the city.

The Sanitation Department reported that at least 4,600 of the 5,000 garbage collectors, street cleaners and incinerator employees on the day shift had failed to report for duty at 7 A.M. They may not report today, either.

Instead, the shouting, chanting city employes, augmented by 1,000 fellow workers who were on vacation or had days off, marched to City Hall.

They besieged the building for several hours, created a traffic jam and gave a 100-man police detail some anxious moments in holding the surging crowd behind barricades. However, there was no violence, though the police took the precaution of locking the doors of City Hall.

Meeting Collapses

Later in the day, a collapse of a hastily arranged meeting between union and city negotiators brought predictions that the walkout, which the union has denied is a strike, might last for some time.

Last night, as a result of the walkout, Traffic Commissioner T. T. Wiley announced that alternate-side parking rules would be lifted here today. Motorists may ignore signs that normally prohibit parking on Thursdays between 8 A.M. and 11 A.M. and 11 A.M. and 2 P.M. The department has not decided yet what it will do about parking regulations tomorrow.

City Demands Return

At the meeting between union and city negotiators, the spokesmen for the city, acting under instruction from the Board of Estimate, demanded that the men return to work before negotiations were resumed. Union negotiators rejected the demand and vowed to stay out until the city came up with a better offer on wages and fringe benefits.

The state's Condon-Wadlin Law prohibits strikes by Civil Service employes but Mayor Wagner would not say yesterday whether he viewed the stoppage as a strike, nor would he say whether the law would be invoked for the first time here.

Union members did not report for the night shift. The Sanitation Department said only a handful had showed up for night duty, which begins at 4 P.M. Usually about 700 men work the night shift in the summer.

The Sanitation Commissioner warned the men involved that they would be docked a day's pay for each day they refused

Continued on Page 11, Column 4

Iran Cuts Cairo Tie In Dispute on Israel

By Reuters.

TEHERAN, Iran, July 27— Iran severed diplomatic relations with the United Arab Republic today and gave Cairo's Ambassador here twenty-four hours to get out of the country.

The severance was announced by Foreign Minister Abbas Aram after he had served the expulsion order on the Ambassador, Mahmoud Hammad.

Mr. Aram said the decision to oust Mr. Hammad was made after President Gamal Abdel Nasser attacked Shah Mohammed Riza Pahlevi of Iran yesterday in a speech at Alexandria. President Nasser assailed the Shah for his statement Saturday that Iran had recognized Israel.

The Iranian Foreign Minister described President Nasser as

Continued on Page 5, Column 1

Stock Margin Rate Is Cut To 70% by Reserve Board

Officials Deny Reduction From 90% Is Aimed at Shoring Up the Market— Economic Significance Minimized

By TOM WICKER
Special to The New York Times.

WASHINGTON, July 27—The margin requirement for purchases of stocks was reduced from 90 to 70 per cent today by the Federal Reserve Board.

The reduction is effective tomorrow. It reflects the belief of the board of governors of the Federal Reserve that stock market credit is relatively stable at this time.

The margin requirement governs the minimum cash payment a stock buyer must make. As an example, today's action will reduce from $900 to $700 the amount of cash that must be put up for each $1,000 of stock.

The reduction also applies to short sales, in which a trader borrows stock and sells it in the hope of buying it back later at a lower price and thus making a profit.

The margin requirement is a device by which the Federal Reserve attempts to prevent excessive use of credit in the stock market. A spokesman said today the board of governors "just thinks 70 per cent will do it" under today's conditions.

The price of common stocks has declined recently. But the spokesman denied that today's action was an attempt to shore up prices or to stimulate credit and speculative activity.

He conceded, however, that since a trader could pick up more stock with the same amount of money, beginning tomorrow, the reduction might have an initial effect on the volume of transactions.

Despite the fact that the latest change before today's in margin requirements—an advance from 70 to 90 per cent on Oct. 16, 1958—came when the

Continued on Page 37, Column 1

FRENCH 'SLIGHTS' ANGER ADENAUER

He Will Leave for Week-End Paris Talks Only Because His Hand Was Forced

By SYDNEY GRUSON
Special to The New York Times.

BONN, Germany, July 27—Chancellor Adenauer will fly to Paris for talks with President de Gaulle Friday, but in a furious mood and only because the French forced his hand.

Both Paris and Bonn announced the meeting this afternoon and said the main subject of the talks would be the political integration of Western Europe.

But the background to this laconic announcement was far more dramatic. The Chancellor had been infuriated by a number of what he considers slights to West Germany by France and had determined not to go through with the meeting this week-end.

The French, aware of his mood, let it be known last night to West German reporters in Paris and to some French newspapers that the meeting was on.

Apparently rather than permit a crack for all the world to see in the painfully restored French-German friendship, the keystone of his European policy,

Continued on Page 2, Column 5

British Earl Named Foreign Secretary In Cabinet Shuffle

By DREW MIDDLETON
Special to The New York Times.

LONDON, July 27 — Prime Minister Macmillan chose the Earl of Home as Britain's new Foreign Secretary today in a major reconstruction of the Conservative Government.

Selwyn Lloyd leaves the Foreign Office to become Chancellor of the Exchequer. A successful tenure there would improve Mr. Lloyd's prospects as the future Prime Minister.

Lord Home (whose name is pronounced Hume) is the first peer to be Foreign Secretary since Lord Halifax held the office twenty years ago. The official announcement of his appointment this evening brought to a climax the mounting criticism of the last five days.

Mr. Macmillan will be forced to defend his choice against the Labor party's censure in a House of Commons debate tomorrow night.

The objections to the appointment of Lord Home were based on two points. First, the critics said, the Foreign Secretary should be a member of the House of Commons and answerable in the House to any questions on foreign policy. Second, the objectors maintained, there was nothing in Lord Home's career to justify the appointment.

The first newspaper comment

Continued on Page 2, Column 2

CHIEFS CONSULTED

Bricker Is Expected to Place U.N. Aide in Nomination

By LEO EGAN
Special to The New York Times.

CHICAGO, Thursday, July 28—Henry Cabot Lodge, delegate to the United Nations, was picked today by Vice President Richard M. Nixon to be his running mate.

Mr. Nixon revealed his preference a few hours after he himself had been nominated for President by the Republican convention.

Mr. Nixon came out of his room and made this announcement:

"I have reached a decision that I shall recommend to the convention Henry Cabot Lodge." He said he would call Mr. Lodge at his New York home and ask if he would accept. He said he expected the decision to be affirmative.

Mr. Nixon made the announcement at 2:20 A.M. Central daylight time (3:20 A.M. New York time).

His decision all but assured Mr. Lodge's nomination for Vice President when the convention votes tonight on that post.

Mr. Nixon made the selection in consultation with leading Republicans in a meeting that began at his hotel about a half hour after the adjournment of last night's session of the convention.

Choice Not Unanimous

New York was represented at the meeting by L. Judson Morhouse, its Republican State Chairman.

The choice of Mr. Lodge was far from unanimous. However, Mr. Nixon insisted upon the Presidential nominee's right to choose his running mate.

Earlier yesterday, Mr. Nixon had listed the 58-year old former Massachusetts Senator as one of the four front runners for the vice-presidential nomination.

The three others were:

Senator Thruston B. Morton of Kentucky, the 52-year-old Republican National Chairman.

Representative Walter H. Judd of Minnesota, now 61 years old, who delivered the keynote address to the convention on Monday.

Robert B. Anderson, the 50-year-old Secretary of the Treasury, a former Texas Democrat who became an Eisenhower Republican in 1952.

To offset Midwest opposition to Mr. Lodge, an arrangement was reported to have been made to have former Senator John W. Bricker of Ohio place his name in nomination. And Representative Gerald Ford of Michigan, a

Continued on Page 12, Column 5

AFTER THE DELEGATES VOTED: Vice President and Mrs. Nixon at their hotel in Chicago last night with their daughters, Patricia, left, 14 years old, and Julie, 12.
Associated Press Wirephoto

NIXON BOLSTERS ROCKEFELLER TIE

New York Delegation Greets Him Warmly — Governor to Campaign Anywhere

By WARREN WEAVER Jr.

CHICAGO, July 27—At political sword points only a week ago, Governor Rockefeller and Vice President Nixon joined today in a powerful demonstration of concord.

Mr. Nixon made a special morning trip two miles up Michigan Avenue to visit his new-found supporters in the New York delegation. The delegation endorsed him unanimously, if belatedly, yesterday.

The Governor went to the Sheraton Towers lobby to greet Mr. Nixon, like classmates at a reunion. Beaming, he escorted him to the closed caucus. They posed for pictures with arms about each other.

Mr. Rockefeller said the Vice President's visit had given the New Yorkers "a final inspiration and emotional lift."

"We're with you all the way," he promised.

Mr. Nixon was hardly less enthusiastic about the Governor. He pleaded with the New York

Continued on Page 14, Column 5

Key Issues in Congo Awaiting U.N. Chief

By HENRY TANNER
Special to The New York Times.

LEOPOLDVILLE, the Congo, July 27 — Secretary General Dag Hammarskjold is likely to be successful in paving the way for the peaceful entry of United Nations forces into Katanga Province, diplomatic observers here predict.

Mr. Hammarskjold is scheduled to arrive here tomorrow from Brussels. Katanga, which has declared its independence of the Congo, is expected to be the dominant issue in his consultations here. He will spend four or five days talking with Congolese, Belgian and United Nations officials.

Katanga is now controlled by Belgian forces that went there at the request of the provincial Premier, Moise Tshombe. Mr.

Continued on Page 8, Column 6

13 Dead in Chicago Crash Of 'Copter on Airport Run

By The Associated Press.

CHICAGO, July 27—A helicopter carrying passengers between airports suddenly lost power and plunged in a mass of flames into a suburban cemetery tonight. All thirteen persons aboard were killed.

Wreckage was scattered over a wide area.

A swath of clipped tree tops almost 600 feet long indicated that the pilot had tried to gain altitude.

Witnesses said the craft, an S-58, carrying eleven passengers and a crew of two, stopped in air, zigzagged a moment and then plummeted, shooting flames.

The helicopter, owned by Chicago Helicopter Airways, Inc., was on an eleven-minute trip from Midway Airport on the Southwest side to O'Hare International Airport on the Northwest side.

Falls Near River

It plunged into the Forest Home Cemetery north of Roosevelt Road near the Des Plaines River. The crash site is between suburban Maywood and Forest Park.

An officer of the helicopter company landed near the crash scene and said that the pilot of the downed craft was Capt. Robert Meyer, 37 years old. The names of the other victims were not immediately available.

However, a company spokesman said "no one of national importance was known to be aboard." He apparently referred to the fact the Republican National Convention is meeting in Chicago.

The helicopter, which has a capacity of fourteen, including

Continued on Page 55, Column 2

ROBERT KENNEDY EASES SPLIT HERE

Candidate's Brother Wins Prendergast's Approval of Independent Group

By CLAYTON KNOWLES

Robert F. Kennedy came to New York yesterday and brought Michael H. Prendergast around to an agreement that an auxiliary citizens' committee could work effectively in the state for the election of Senator John F. Kennedy as President.

Mr. Prendergast, the Democratic state chairman, reversed his earlier opposition to such an auxiliary campaign unit during a two-and-a-half hour luncheon meeting with Mr. Kennedy, who is the manager of his brother's campaign for the Presidency.

Carmine G. De Sapio, Democratic national committeeman, who sat in on the session at the Hampshire House, was asked if he, too, was satisfied. "One hundred per cent!" he said with emphasis.

The conference was one of five important meetings that Mr. Kennedy held during a busy day with representatives of virtually every shade of thinking within the Democratic party.

The session with Mr. Prendergast was of particular importance because Mr. Prendergast had understood originally that the campaign would be run strictly through the Democratic state organization.

Later, when the Senator agreed to establishing a Citizens for Kennedy committee here, Mr. Prendergast viewed the enterprise as competitive with the regular organization's work. He also viewed the individual

Continued on Page 16, Column 1

UNITY IS STRESSED

Goldwater Withdraws and Asks Backing for the Nominee

*Hatfield's speech, Page 12;
Goldwater text, Page 14.*

By W. H. LAWRENCE
Special to The New York Times.

CHICAGO, Thursday, July 28 —Vice President Richard M. Nixon swept to a first-ballot Republican Presidential nomination last night and the right to face Democratic Senator John F. Kennedy in the November election.

Early today, Mr. Nixon chose Henry Cabot Lodge, chief United States delegate to the United Nations, as his Vice-Presidential running mate.

Mr. Nixon received 1,321 votes on the polling of state delegations. Senator Barry Goldwater of Arizona received ten votes, cast by members of the twenty-six-vote Louisiana delegation even after the Arizonan had asked withdrawal of his name from consideration.

At the end of the roll-call, Louisiana moved to make Mr. Nixon's choice unanimous, but balked at changing its ten votes from the Goldwater to the Nixon column without a poll. When the roll-call vote was announced as 1,321 to 10, the Arizona delegation then moved to make the nomination unanimous, and this was done by acclamation.

Goldwater Asks Unity

The convention decision pits the 47-year-old Vice President against the 43-year-old Senator from Massachusetts. Mr. Nixon is the first Vice President in the history of the modern two-party system to win a Presidential nomination in his own right.

Senator Goldwater made the dramatic appearance of the night, calling upon all conservatives to back Mr. Nixon in November and avoid any party split or stay-at-home nonvoting attitude that would help Democrats "dedicated to the destruction of this country."

Withdrawing his own name from consideration for the Presidency, the Arizona Senator, an avowed conservative, said he had been campaigning for Mr. Nixon's nomination for the last six years and would fight for his election in November.

Lecture to Conservatives

"Let us put our shoulders to the wheel of Dick Nixon and push him over across the line," Senator Goldwater said.

He lectured conservatives sternly, telling them they must "grow up" and get to work "if we want to take this party back some day—and I think we can."

He said the Democratic party no longer was the party of Jefferson, Jackson and Wilson but now was ruled by "Bowles, Galbraith and Reuther." His references were to Representative Chester Bowles of Connecticut; Kenneth Galbraith, Harvard economist, and Walter P. Reu-

Continued on Page 12, Column 1

Eisenhower Is Firm For Middle of Road

By DONALD JANSON

CHICAGO, July 27—President Eisenhower emphasized today the superiority of a middle political course over right or left extremes.

He denounced the Socialist philosophy of a "fairly friendly European country" he said he had been reading about in the last few weeks.

"The experiment of almost complete paternalism" there, he said, has resulted in a sharp rise in the suicide rate, "more than twice our drunkenness," and a "lack of moderation discernible on all sides."

It was believed that he had alluded to Sweden. Her suicide rate is 19.9 for every 100,000 persons, compared with ten in

Continued on Page 14, Column 4

PROTEST AT CITY HALL: Employes of the Department of Sanitation rally against the breakdown of wage talks
The New York Times

204

The New York Times.

LATE CITY EDITION
U. S. Weather Bureau Report (Page 96) forecast:
Fair and warm today; fair tonight.
Chance of thunder showers tomorrow.
Temp. range: 83—68; yesterday: 82.3—63.4.
Temp.-Hum. index: near 77; yesterday: 76.

SECTION ONE

VOL. CIX..No. 37,465. © 1960, by The New York Times Company. Times Square, New York 36, N. Y.   NEW YORK, SUNDAY, AUGUST 21, 1960.   5c outside New York City, its suburban area and Long Island. 10c in 17 Western states, Canada; higher in air delivery cities.   THIRTY CENTS

NIXON ENDORSES NEW JAVITS PLAN FOR CARE OF AGED

Backs Contributory Medical Insurance Based on Aid From U. S. and States

MEANS TEST RULED OUT

Senator's Proposal Faces a Showdown With Kennedy's Social Security Set-Up

By TOM WICKER
Special to The New York Times.

WASHINGTON, Aug. 20—Vice President Nixon lent his support today to a new program of contributory health insurance as the Senate opened a politically charged debate on the issue of medical care for the aged.

The new plan was introduced and strongly advocated by Senator Jacob K. Javits, the New York Republican.

It will be offered, he told reporters later, as an amendment to the relief-payments bill approved by the Senate Finance Committee. It is offered as a substitute for the Social Security plan backed by the Democratic Presidential candidate, Senator John F. Kennedy of Massachusetts.

Mr. Nixon, the Republican nominee, made no statement on the matter. Senator Javits said he had his support and a Nixon spokesman later asserted that the Vice President had helped the Senator to prepare the insurance program.

Similar Plan Recalled

Mr. Javits noted that he had introduced a similar plan in the House of Representatives in 1949. Mr. Nixon and Christian A. Herter, now Secretary of State, were among the co-sponsors.

The Javits proposal is along the lines of the Eisenhower Administration's "medicare" voluntary insurance plan but offers considerably wider benefits. It is also more liberal in its not requiring a means test for beneficiaries and in being less costly for participants.

For these reasons, Senator Javits said he could not say he had the support of President Eisenhower. The Nixon spokesman said, however, that Arthur S. Flemming, Secretary of Health, Education and Welfare had also helped prepare the Javits program.

Saltonstall Backs Plan

Among Senator Javits' co-sponsors is Senator Leverett Saltonstall of Massachusetts who introduced the Medicare scheme. Seven other Republicans also joined the New Yorker.

Their program would make about 11,000,000 persons over 65 years of age eligible for health insurance, but not those with incomes over $3,000 for individuals or $4,500 for couples. The Federal and state governments would share in the cost of the insurance.

Senator Javits put the annual

Continued on Page 44, Column 1

Sports News

BASEBALL

The Yankees beat the Washington Senators, 9—5, yesterday with four runs in the eleventh inning — two on a homer by Bill Skowron. The victory kept the Yankees a game and a half ahead of the second-place White Sox. The White Sox defeated the Athletics, 3—0, on Herb Score's two-hit pitching. The Red Sox won from the Orioles, 8—6, in the afternoon. The Orioles won their night game, 6—0. In the National League, the first-place Pirates topped the Reds, 10—7.

HARNESS RACING

Hairos II, representing the Netherlands, won the $50,000 International Trot at Roosevelt Raceway. He paid $11.90 for $2. Crevalcore of Italy was second and Silver Song of the United States third.

HORSE RACING

Tompion, the 9-to-10 choice, won the $63,100 Travers Stakes at Saratoga. One-Eyed King took the Arlington Handicap at Chicago.

TENNIS

Rod Laver of Australia and Earl (Butch) Buchholz of St. Louis gained the final of the Newport Casino tournament.

Details in Section 5.

MEETING IN INDEPENDENCE: Senator John F. Kennedy with former President Truman at the Truman Library in the Missouri city. At rear is Senator Stuart Symington.

United Press International Telephoto

Kennedy Calls on Truman; Gets a Forecast of Victory

By W. H. LAWRENCE
Special to The New York Times.

INDEPENDENCE, Mo., Aug. 20—Former President Harry S. Truman joined Senator John F. Kennedy today in what he forecast would be a winning campaign for the Democratic Presidential nominee.

The former President conferred for forty minutes with the Massachusetts Senator, whose nomination he opposed when he boycotted the Democratic National Convention at Los Angeles.

Laughing in recollection of his upset victory in 1948 over Gov. Thomas E. Dewey of New York, Mr. Truman said he had "no use" for pollsters. He added that he put no stock in a recent Gallup poll that showed Vice President Nixon leading Senator Kennedy 50 to 44 per cent.

"The Democrats are going to win," Mr. Truman said.

Talked by Telephone

The Truman-Kennedy conference was their first meeting since the Democratic convention, but they had talked earlier by telephone. At that time Mr. Truman gave assurances that he would support the ticket actively.

The groundwork for this session had been laid ten days ago when Gov. Abraham A. Ribicoff of Connecticut came as Senator Kennedy's peacemaking emissary to talk with the former President.

From all appearances, the meeting was jovial and cordial, although Mr. Truman got a little edgy when he was reminded of the harsh things he had said about Senator Kennedy before his nomination.

He was reminded that he had expressed doubts that Senator Kennedy was ready for the Presidency because he was too young and inexperienced, and that he had also asserted that the convention had been "prearranged" to produce Senator Kennedy's nomination.

To most of these, the former

Continued on Page 46, Column 1

NIXON GIVES IDEAS ON RED CHALLENGE

Says Knowledge of Ideology Is Needed to Meet It— Report First in Series

By WILLIAM J. JORDEN
Special to The New York Times.

WASHINGTON, Aug. 20—Vice President Nixon released today a thirty-page analysis of the meaning of communism. It was the first of a series of reports setting forth the thinking of the Republican Presidential candidate on major issues facing the American people.

Mr. Nixon wrote that a "major weakness" in the struggle against "the militant aggressiveness of international communism" was a prevailing lack of understanding of the character of the challenge. He said that "nothing less than a knowledge in depth of the Communist idea is necessary if we are to deal with it effectively."

The Vice President offered his study of communism as an aid to the kind of knowledge he said was necessary. It did not pretend to be an original contribution to the vast collection of studies on Communist theory. Rather it was a summation of Mr. Nixon's thoughts on some of the main features of earlier studies.

Mr. Nixon said the American people recognized that "we must retain our present military and economic advantage over the Communist bloc." He said the United States would "keep the lead that we have gained" in rocket technology and space exploration.

Sees Battle of Ideas

"What we must realize," the Vice President wrote, "is that this struggle probably will not be decided in the military, economic, or scientific areas, important as those are. The battle in which we are engaged is primarily one of ideas. The test is one not so much of arms but of faith."

The Republican candidate then explored what he considered some of the main elements of Communist thought and attacked them variously as misleading, immoral or of demonstrated ineffectuality.

He stressed that the principal appeal of Communist ideas today was not to broad masses of people but "more often to an intelligent minority in newly developing countries who are trying to decide which system offers the best and surest road to progress."

Introducing his discussion of

Continued on Page 48, Column 1

SOUTH FACES TEST IN SCHOOLS FIGHT

New Orleans Desegregation Ruling Sparks a Crisis— Election Adds Pressure

By CLAUDE SITTON
Special to The New York Times.

ATLANTA, Aug. 20—The deep South faces new steps toward desegregation of its public schools this fall under the complex pressures of a Presidential election year.

The area's response, according to the Southern Regional Council, may well affect both the election and the future pace of desegregation elsewhere.

The council, which is made up of white and Negro leaders in the South, released a study to a day of progress in the field since 1954, when the Supreme Court issued its decision on desegregation. The study also treated the outlook for this fall.

Its report noted that, after an initial surge of compliance in the border states, "desegregation has been a campaign fought by laws and lawyers over the careers of a few amazingly stanch Negro children."

As a result of a Federal court order directing New Orleans' schools to begin desegregation in September, the council said, "the deep South at last faces the demand that it comply with the law."

The outcome of that test will have far-reaching implications, the organization contended.

"Perhaps the truth has been," it said, "that desegregation cannot move more rapidly in the

Continued on Page 65, Column 3

Mali Alliance in Africa Splits; Senegal-Sudan Strife Feared

De Gaulle Invites Contending Premiers to Paris—Dakar Under Senegalese Rule

By HENRY GINIGER
Special to The New York Times.

PARIS, Aug. 20—The Mali Federation in West Africa broke up suddenly today. A civil war between its component states, Senegal and Sudan, was threatened.

The uneasy eighteen-month partnership between the former French territories, both now members of the French Community, broke down early this morning in Dakar when the Senegalese Government announced its withdrawal.

The Senegalese thus struck back at the Sudanese Premier, Modibo Keita, who also is Premier of Sudan. Late last night Mr. Keita canceled Mr. Dia's defense and external-security powers and proclaimed a state of emergency.

Shortly after the Senegalese Government had declared its withdrawal, Senegalese forces took over control of Dakar, the west-coast port that is Senegal's

Continued on Page 8, Column 1

Wagner Will Press Extra Registration

By DOUGLAS DALES

Mayor Wagner voiced regret yesterday at Governor Rockefeller's rejection of his plea for a special session of the Legislature to revise voter registration laws. He reaffirmed his intention to provide additional registration time.

The four days fixed by the Legislature for local registration, Oct. 13 through 15, conflict with Jewish religious observances. The Mayor had requested the special session to substitute Oct. 10 and 11 for Oct. 13 and 14.

Mayor Wagner said he could not understand why the Governor had turned down his request in view of its endorsement by the bipartisan Board of Elections, composed of two Democrats and two Republicans. He noted he had asked for the

DOMINICANS QUIT AMERICAS PARLEY; SANCTIONS VOTED

O. A. S. Ministers Condemn Trujillo Regime—Call for Severing of Relations

Text of O. A. S. resolution on Dominican Republic, Page 3.

By TAD SZULC
Special to The New York Times.

SAN JOSE, Costa Rica, Aug. 20—Dominican delegates abandoned the conference of the American foreign ministers today as it unanimously voted precedent - setting sanctions against the Dominican Republic.

The foreign ministers' meeting this afternoon as a general commission, approved by a roll-call vote a resolution "emphatically" condemning the Dominican Republic for "acts of aggression and intervention" against Venezuela, including an attempt to assassinate Venezuela's President, Dr. Romulo Betancourt.

The resolution also called for an immediate break in diplomatic relations with the Dominican regime by members of the Organization of American States and for "partial interruption of economic relations."

The afternoon action on the Dominican issue was final; the resolution now goes to the O. A. S. Council in Washington, which will ask member nations to carry out the terms.

New Sessions on Cuba

Next week the ministers will convene in new sessions to deal with Caribbean tensions and Soviet interests in Cuba.

The parting gesture of the Dominican delegation was to demand a fight against "American imperialism," apparently prompted by the firm position taken by the United States against the Dominican dictatorship of Generalissimo Rafael Leonidas Trujillo Molina.

As a result of a legal maneuver by Venezuela late last night, the conference members did not take any practical steps to provide for a peaceful transition to democracy in the Dominican Republic. Secretary of State Christian A. Herter had advocated the formation of a special mechanism to avert the danger of possible chaos if the Trujillo regime should crumble.

Herter States U. S. View

Speaking tonight at a formal closing session of this week's conference, Mr. Herter said that the United States, while supporting the resolution that was adopted, would have preferred to see the appointment of a special committee with power to foster true democracy in the Dominican Republic. The United States, he added adjusted its views "to maintain the solidarity and common approach of our community."

The Dominican Foreign Minister, Porfirio Herrera Baez, and several others in his delegation left San José late this afternoon for Panama en route to Ciudad Trujillo. They departed from their hotel through

Continued on Page 2, Column 1

Mrs. Powers Plans Appeal For Moscow's Clemency

Will Send a Letter Directly to Brezhnev —Wife of Pilot Is Unable to Leave 'Without Trying to Do Everything'

Special to The New York Times.

MOSCOW, Aug. 20—Mrs. Francis Gary Powers said today she would begin her fight to obtain clemency for her husband by appealing to President Leonid I. Brezhnev of the Soviet Union.

"I cannot leave Moscow without trying to do everything in the world for him," Mrs. Powers said. "But my impression on seeing Gary was that he did not think anything would help."

Mrs. Powers, who is 25 years old, was pale but composed as she answered questions. She sat on a striped blue sofa beside her widowed mother, Mrs. Monteen Beck Brown.

Mrs. Powers and the pilot's parents, Mr. and Mrs. Oliver W. Powers, expect to deliver early next week a letter to the office of Mr. Brezhnev, President of the Presidium of the Supreme Soviet (Parliament).

Mikhail I. Grinyov, state-appointed defense attorney for the 31-year-old pilot, said this afternoon that Mr. Brezhnev prob-

Continued on Page 71, Column 4

Soviet Opposes U. N. Plan; Bunche Will Leave Congo

By JAMES FERON
Special to The New York Times.

UNITED NATIONS, N. Y., Aug. 20—The Soviet Union told Secretary General Dag Hammarskjold today it opposed the week-old United Nations technical assistance program in the Congo. Vasily V. Kuznetsov, a First Deputy Foreign Minister, also demanded the immediate withdrawal of

Statements at U. N. on the Congo appear on Page 16.

"armed groups from Canada" from the African republic "because they are allies of Belgium, which is guilty of aggression in the Congo."

[In Leopoldville, Premier Patrice Lumumba abandoned his demand for the withdrawal of all white United Nations troops.]

It was also announced here that Dr. Ralph J. Bunche, who has been in charge of all United Nations operations in the Congo, would be replaced shortly by Rajeshwar Dayal, India's High Commissioner to Pakistan. United Nations officials denied the change had been prompted by any diminishing effectiveness in Dr. Bunche's relations with Congolese officials.

They also denied the shift was prompted by rising tension between Gen. Carl Carlsson von Horn, head of the United Nations force, and Maj. Gen. Henry T. Alexander, head of the Ghanaian contingent.

The discord within the United Nations forces in regard to the Ghanaian troops was brought out in documents made public by Mr. Hammarskjold. These included criticism by the Secretary General of actions of the Ghanaians and a reply by Gen-

Continued on Page 15, Column 1

Salt Inquiry Shows How Roy Cohn Lost

By CHARLES GRUTZNER

An account of how Roy M. Cohn and William Fugazy, the boxing promoters, lost a fight with Fortune Pope to control the supply of Dominican rock salt for this city is scattered through the files of the State Investigation Commission.

It depicts Joseph V. Spagna, who resigned Thursday as Purchase Commissioner, as the man who decided in favor of Mr. Pope, his friend of twenty-five years.

The state commission reported Wednesday that it had found contract-rigging, collusive bidding, bribery, shortweighting and other dishonesty in this city's annual purchase of $700,000 in rock salt for snow and ice removal. It accused Mr. Spagna of having rigged contract procedures to favor Mr. Pope, who had a financial inter-

Continued on Page 19, Column 1

TWO SOVIET DOGS IN ORBIT RETURNED TO EARTH ALIVE AS SATELLITE IS RETRIEVED

ANIMALS UNHURT

Capsule Comes Down After 17 Circuits in 24-Hour Flight

By SEYMOUR TOPPING
Special to The New York Times.

MOSCOW, Aug. 20—Living creatures have returned safely to earth from an orbit in space for the first time in history, the Soviet Union announced today.

It said its "second cosmic space ship" landed on target today after circling the earth for twenty-four hours with its cargo of two dogs, some rats and mice, flies, plants, seeds and fungi.

On its eighteenth circuit of the earth at an altitude of about 200 miles, the five-ton space ship responded to a signal from the ground and began to descend, detaching the capsule containing the animals en route.

Announced by Tass

Tass, the Soviet press agency, said:

"The space ship's control system and braking device operated with great accuracy and ensured the ship's descent to the fixed spot. The deviation from the calculated spot amounted to some ten kilometers [6¼ miles].

"The space ship, weighing 4,600 kilograms [not counting the last stage of the carrier rocket], provided as it was with a special thermal shield, safely passed through the earth's atmosphere. The space ship and the jettisoned capsule containing the experimental animals landed safely."

[In Washington, T. Keith Glennan, head of the National Aeronautics and Space Administration, saluted the Soviet Union for "a fine job." He added, however, that he did not regard the accomplishment as "a major first" in space exploration but as "just another step" toward meeting "the problems we all face."]

Television in Cabin

The space ship was launched yesterday with what was described as a cabin equipped with "everything necessary for the future flight of a man."

In the cabin, under the lenses of television cameras, were the dogs Strelka and Belka (feminine forms of the words Little Arrow and Squirrel).

Tass said scientists on the ground watched the dogs on their television screens during the flight, observed their postures "and even saw one of the dogs take food."

Meanwhile, other apparatus was recording and transmitting the animals' heart beats, blood pressure, respiration and movements, and the functioning of equipment designed to maintain

Continued on Page 53, Column 1

LOYAL LAOS UNITS MARCH ON REBELS

Five Battalions Heading for Vientiane—Opposition to New Regime Growing

By JACQUES NEVARD
Special to The New York Times.

SAVANNAKHET, Laos, Aug. 20—Five battalions of loyal Laotian troops are moving on the rebel center of Vientiane from the north and south, it was learned here today from sources close to Maj. Gen. Phoumi Nosavan.

It was not known whether their orders were to attack the capital or to lay siege to it in an effort to starve the rebels into submission.

[About 200 American women and children have been evacuated from Vientiane to neighboring Thailand to escape the threats of civil war and floods. Planes flying from Vientiane to Bangkok completed the airlift of nearly 500 foreigners Saturday.]

Deputies Joining General

The original battalion of paratroopers headed by Capt. Kong Le, which seized Vientiane Aug. 9, was reported yesterday to have been joined by two companies of pro-Communist Pathet Lao rebels.

Meanwhile, General Phoumi Nosavan, pro-Western chairman of the "Committee to Counter the Coup d'Etat in Laos," was rapidly organizing a regime here in the south of Laos. Of the twenty out of fifty-eight Deputies elected last April have arrived and others are expected.

Under Laotian law thirty Deputies are required for a quorum and if that figure is reached it is expected that the Assembly will repudiate its action in voting against the Government of Premier Tino Somsanith and setting up the present Vientiane regime of Prince Souvanna Phouma. It took the action under the guns of Captain Kong Le's troops with a mob howling outside the National Assembly.

Three of the Deputies now here escaped from Vientiane to

Continued on Page 12, Column 1

Senegal (1) broke her tie to the Sudan Republic (2).

The New York Times   Aug. 21, 1960

to be virtually a prisoner in his palace.

Communications between Dakar and the outside world were cut about 4 A. M. and news reaching Paris was sketchy. Both Dakar and Bamako, capital of Sudan, were reported to be calm.

Acting swiftly early this evening to prevent an irreparable breach in the French Community, President de Gaulle

Continued on Page 8, Column 1

The New York Times.

LATE CITY EDITION
U. S. Weather Bureau Report (Page 88) forecasts:
Cloudy, periods of rain today.
Partly cloudy, colder tomorrow.
Temp. range: 55—41; yesterday: 53.8—40.4.

VOL. CX..No. 37,546.   © 1960 by The New York Times Company. Times Square, New York 36 N. Y.   NEW YORK, THURSDAY, NOVEMBER 10, 1960.   10 cents beyond 50-mile zone from New York City except on Long Island. Higher in air delivery cities.   FIVE CENTS

KENNEDY'S VICTORY WON BY CLOSE MARGIN; HE PROMISES FIGHT FOR WORLD FREEDOM; EISENHOWER OFFERS 'ORDERLY TRANSITION'

DEMOCRATS HERE SPLIT IN VICTORY; LEHMAN ASSAILED

De Sapio Accepts Challenge for Party Control—Mayor Claims Leadership

Text of De Sapio statement appears on Page 43.

By LEO EGAN

Less than twenty-four hours after the polls closed, the political coalition that gave Senator John F. Kennedy New York's forty-five electoral votes began coming apart at the seams.

Its disintegration was signaled by a statement assailing former Gov. Herbert H. Lehman, key figure in the Democratic reform group, and Alex Rose, Liberal party master of strategy.

The statement accepted Mr. Lehman's election night challenge to a finish fight for control of the party organization in the city and state.

At the same time it appeared to rule out any chance of a Democratic-Liberal party coalition for next year's Mayoral election in New York City and for the Governorship election in the state in 1962 if Mr. De Sapio remains in control of the party machinery.

Kennedy's Delicate Problem

Mr. De Sapio, leader of Tammany and Democratic National Committeeman for New York, consulted Michael H. Prendergast, the Democratic State Chairman, and a number of party leaders in the city and upstate before issuing his statement.

The collapse of the coalition so soon after it achieved its goal gave President-elect Kennedy a delicate political problem before he takes office. At some stage soon he will have to decide whom in New York to consult about appointments for the new Administration.

Thus, in so far as New York is concerned, the election appeared to raise as many questions as it settled. Control of the Democratic party machinery is one of them. Among the others are: What is Mayor Wagner's political future? And what is Governor Rockefeller's?

When told of Mr. De Sapio's statement last night, Mayor Wagner commented that he in-

Continued on Page 43, Column 1

ATOM BILL BEATEN IN FRENCH SENATE

Debre to Push Compromise on Nuclear Force Plan

By W. GRANGER BLAIR
Special to The New York Times.

PARIS, Nov. 10.—The Senate early today rejected President de Gaulle's project for an independent French nuclear striking force.

By a vote of 186 to 83, with seventeen abstentions, this conservative Upper House approved a procedural motion to table the national nuclear deterrent bill that had been passed to it by the National Assembly Oct. 27.

Although the Senate's action was a stinging blow to President de Gaulle and a sharp indication of mounting parliamentary opposition, it did not mean that the Government's measure would not eventually become law.

It was announced after the vote that Premier Michel Debré would call for the creation of a mixed committee of Senators and Deputies to work out a compromise measure. Should this conference committee fail to find a compromise, the Government would resubmit its measure to the Assembly for a second reading, and virtually under the approval. The measure would then become law with or without the Senate's approval.

The Senate motion to table

Continued on Page 8, Column 1

Registration Set-Up Called Faulty Here

By DOUGLAS DALES

Political leaders voiced dissatisfaction yesterday over the way permanent personal registration functioned here Tuesday in its first test in a Presidential election.

Charges were made that thousands of persons had been disfranchised because they were unable to convince election inspectors that they had registered and were eligible to vote.

How many voters may have been so affected was a guess. But a check of the Supreme Courts in the five boroughs indicated that more than 1,300 persons had gone before the justices for orders directing the inspectors to permit them to vote.

"There was a minimum of 10,000 denied the right to vote," Abraham Gellinoff,

Continued on Page 43, Column 5

ASSEMBLY DELAYS U.N. CONGO DEBATE

Postpones It Indefinitely, 48-30, as Soviet Backs Step—U. S. Move Fails

By KATHLEEN TELTSCH
Special to The New York Times.

UNITED NATIONS, N. Y., Nov. 9—The General Assembly voted tonight to postpone the debate on the Congo indefinitely.

The 48-to-30 vote, with eighteen abstentions, was on a surprise move made by Ghana with the help of Guinea and Nigeria and the enthusiastic support of the Soviet bloc.

The United States tried to avoid the adjournment vote by asking for a suspension of the session until delegates could ponder the unexpected request.

Western sources said privately that Ghana's initiative appeared to have been prompted in part by the presence here of President Joseph Kasavubu of the Congo and the likelihood that the Assembly's Credentials Committee would agree to his request for the seating of a Congolese delegation of his supporters.

A Two-Hour Wrangle

Ghana, Guinea, India and five other states have joined in sponsoring a resolution that aims instead at having the Assembly seat a delegation designated by the deposed Congolese Premier, Patrice Lumumba.

The Assembly acted after a two-hour wrangle marked by two table-thumping demonstrations by the Soviet bloc and also by Ghana, both in protest against the efforts of Foreign Minister Pierre Wigny of Belgium to defend his country's position on the Congo issue.

The adjournment request was made by Alex Quaison-Sackey, Ghana's chief delegate. He appealed to the Assembly to hold off any further debate pending the efforts of a fifteen-member Asian-African commission to reconcile the clashing political factions in the Congo and restore some governmental stability.

He said that the commission probably would leave for the Congo in a week and that further acrimonious debate in the Assembly would only hamper the conciliation effort.

However, the Assembly vote did not stipulate how long the debate should be suspended. United States sources said tonight they understood this to mean that discussion could

Continued on Page 8, Column 1

WINNER'S PLEDGE

Family Is With Him as He Vows to Press Nation's Cause

Text of Kennedy's statement is printed on Page 36.

By HOMER BIGART
Special to The New York Times.

HYANNIS, Mass., Nov. 9—Senator John F. Kennedy accepted in solemn mood today his election as President.

He pledged all his energy to advancing "the long-range interests of the United States and the cause of freedom around the world."

He made this pledge inside the flag-decked Hyannis Armory at 1:45 P. M., an hour after Vice President Nixon, his Republican opponent, had conceded defeat.

His wife, Jacqueline, stood at his side as the 43-year-old President-elect faced 300 newsmen and massed batteries of TV cameras and gave his victory statement to the nation.

Behind him were arrayed the Kennedy family: his father, former Ambassador Joseph P. Kennedy; his mother, three sisters and three brothers.

No Sign of Jubilation

The Kennedys showed no evidence of jubilation. All wore expressions of solemnity. Mr. Kennedy's margin of victory was too slender to stir much elation. Some of his aides acknowledged disappointment over the startlingly narrow gap in the popular vote.

Mr. Kennedy, after responding to applause with a diffident bow and a smile, first read the telegram from Mr. Nixon conceding defeat and extending congratulations.

Replies to Nixon

Mr. Nixon wired the President-elect that all the nation would give him "united support" in the next four years.

Mr. Kennedy replied to Mr. Nixon:

"I know that the nation can continue to count on your unswerving loyalty in whatever effort you undertake, and that you and I can maintain our long-standing cordial relations in the years ahead."

Mr. Kennedy then read a congratulatory message from President Eisenhower.

In his message the President informed Mr. Kennedy that he would shortly receive suggestions from the President as to the change-over of responsibilities for national leadership.

To this Senator Kennedy had replied:

"I am grateful for your wire and good wishes. I look forward to working with you in the near future. The whole country is hopeful that your long ex-

Continued on Page 36, Column 7

10 Irish Soldiers Slain in Congo When U.N. Patrol Is Ambushed

By PAUL HOFMANN
Special to The New York Times.

LEOPOLDVILLE, the Congo, Nov. 9—A patrol of eleven Irish soldiers of the United Nations force in the Congo was ambushed in the northern part of Katanga Province yesterday. The bodies of four men were sighted.

[The United Nations Command said that ten soldiers had been slain in the ambush, Reuters reported. The Irish Army announced in Dublin that one private had survived the attack. Reports received by the United Nations in New York said the surviving soldier was "badly wounded," according to United Press International.]

The patrol belonged to the Irish Thirty-third Battalion, which has headquarters in the industrial city of Albertville. The battalion, with a strength of about 550 men, is responsible for maintaining order in a vast area of North Katanga. This region has been the scene of intertribal warfare and clashes between Baluba tribesmen and the gendarmerie controlled by Moise Tshombe, President of Katanga.

United Nations officials here were unable to say who had attacked the Irish patrol. The ambush occurred south of Niemba, a village between Albertville and Kabalo. The zone is described as "Baluba country," but it is not known whether Baluba tribesmen were responsible for the assault.

Announcing the loss, a United Nations spokesman said it brought the toll of dead in the international force to about thirty since the world organization's troops arrived

Continued on Page 2, Column 3

KHRUSHCHEV NOTE SALUTES KENNEDY

Message of Congratulations Asks for Negotiations on Tensions in World

Text of Khrushchev message will be found on Page 42.

By The Associated Press.

MOSCOW, Nov. 9—Soviet Premier Khrushchev congratulated Senator John F. Kennedy today for his Presidential victory.

He expressed hope that Soviet-United States relations would "again follow the line along which they were developing in Franklin Roosevelt's time."

He urged negotiations aimed at easing the international situation.

[In Bonn, Chancellor Konrad Adenauer said he planned to go to Washington early next year for conferences with Mr. Kennedy.]

Mr. Khrushchev's statements in a congratulatory message to Mr. Kennedy coincided with Moscow's insistence that the policies of President Eisenhower had suffered a rebuff in the election.

The Soviet press contended that the election proved "the American people have blackballed the policy on the 'cold war' and the arms race, that they want changes and expect Washington to pursue a reasonable course in international affairs, a course dictated by life and the balance of forces now prevailing in the world." Mr.

Continued on Page 42, Column 4

Electoral Vote by States

State	Rep.	Dem.	State	Rep.	Dem.	State	Rep.	Dem.
Alabama		5*	Louisiana		10	Ohio	25	
Alaska	3		Maine	5		Oklahoma	8	
Arizona	4		Maryland		9	Oregon	6	
Arkansas		8	Mass.		16	Penn.		32
California	32		Michigan		20	Rhode Island		4
Colorado	6		Minnesota		11	So. Carolina		8
Conn.		8	Mississippi	**	**	So. Dakota	4	
Delaware		3	Missouri		13	Tennessee	11	
Florida	10		Montana		4	Texas		24
Georgia		12	Nebraska	6		Utah	4	
Hawaii		3	Nevada		3	Vermont	3	
Idaho	4		New Hamp.	4		Virginia		12
Illinois		27	New Jersey		16	Washington	9	
Indiana	13		New Mexico		4	W. Virginia		8
Iowa	10		New York		45	Wisconsin	12	
Kansas	8		No. Carolina		14	Wyoming	3	
Kentucky	10		No. Dakota	4		Total	185	300

*Five electors are pledged to Kennedy and six unpledged.
**Eight electors not pledged to vote for party candidates.

LIBERALS SUFFER SETBACK IN HOUSE

G. O. P. Picks Up 22 Seats to Aid Conservative Bloc

By JOHN D. MORRIS

The House of Representatives will have a more conservative tinge in the Eighty-seventh Congress.

Inroads into the present House Democratic majority of 283 to 154 scored by the Republicans in Tuesday's elections promised to strengthen their conservative coalition with Southern Democrats.

The liberal legislative program to be submitted early next year by the new Democratic President, John F. Kennedy, may consequently face handicaps in the new Congress, which convenes Jan. 3.

In the Senate, Republicans cut the Democratic margin by two seats, to 64 to 36. That chamber remains predominantly liberal in membership, although conservatives dominate key committee posts.

Gubernatorial Shifts

The Democrats achieved a net gain of one governorship and now control thirty-four of the fifty state houses. In twenty-seven gubernatorial contests the Democrats won fifteen and the Republicans twelve, with an exchange of party control in thirteen.

In the House races, nearly complete unofficial returns showed that the Democrats had elected 257 House candidates and the Republicans 175, with five contests still in doubt.

Among the eleven states of the Old Confederacy the Republicans maintained their hold on seven seats of the Eighty-

Continued on Page 38, Column 4

NIXON WIRE GIVES HIS 'BEST WISHES'

Sends Kennedy a Message —500 in Capital Hail Him

By BILL BECKER
Special to The New York Times.

LOS ANGELES, Nov. 9—Vice President Nixon conceded today the Presidential election of his Democratic opponent, Senator John F. Kennedy.

About twelve hours after the polls had closed, the Vice President sent the following telegram to Senator Kennedy at Hyannis Port, Mass.:

"I want to repeat through this wire the congratulations and best wishes I extended to you on television last night. I know that you will have the united support of all Americans as you lead the nation in the cause of peace and freedom in the next four years."

In his telegram to Mr. Nixon

Read by Aide

The telegram was read to newsmen by Mr. Nixon's press secretary, Herbert G. Klein, at 9:45 A. M., Pacific standard time (12:45 P. M., Eastern standard time).

The Vice President did not make a personal appearance. Mr. Klein said Mr. Nixon was resting with Mrs. Nixon and their two daughters in their suite at the Ambassador Hotel. It was obvious that the Vice President had considered his remarks late on election night a virtual concession.

[A crowd of several hundred greeted Mr. Nixon as he arrived Wednesday night at Andrews Air Force Base, near Washington, after a flight of four and a half hours from Los Angeles.]

Mr. Nixon remained in seclusion most of the morning although Mr. Klein was up about 6 A. M. after little more than three hours of sleep. The secretary said Mr. Nixon

Continued on Page 42, Column 7

RESULTS DELAYED

Popular Vote Almost Even—300-185 Is Electoral Tally

By JAMES RESTON

Senator John F. Kennedy of Massachusetts finally won the 1960 Presidential election from Vice President Nixon by the astonishing margin of less than two votes per voting precinct.

Senator Kennedy's electoral vote total stood yesterday at 300, just thirty-one more than the 269 needed for election. The Vice President's total was 185. Fifty-two additional electoral votes, including California's thirty-two, were still in doubt last night.

But the popular vote was a different story. The two candidates ran virtually even. Senator Kennedy's lead last night was little more than 300,000 in a total tabulated vote of about 66,000,000 cast in 165,826 precincts.

That was a plurality for the Senator of less than one-half of 1 per cent of the total vote—the smallest percentage difference between the popular vote of two Presidential candidates since 1880, when James A. Garfield outran Gen. Winfield Scott Hancock by 7,000 votes in a total of almost 9,000,000.

End Divided Government

Nevertheless, yesterday's voting radically altered the political balance of power in America in favor of the Democrats and put them in a commanding position in the Federal and state capitals unknown since the heyday of Franklin D. Roosevelt.

They regained control of the White House for the first time since 1952 and thus ended divided government in Washington. They retained control of the Senate and the House of Representatives, although with slightly reduced margins. And they increased their hold on the state governorships by one, bringing the Democratic margin to 34—16.

The President-elect is the first Roman Catholic ever to win the nation's highest office. The only other member of his church nominated for President was Alfred E. Smith, who was defeated by Herbert Hoover in 1928.

Faces Difficult Questions

Despite his personal triumph, President-elect Kennedy is confronted by a number of hard questions:

¶In the face of such a narrow victory how can he get through the Congress the liberal program he proposed during the campaign?

¶Can so close an election produce any impetus for loosening the conservative coalition of Republicans and Southern Democrats which has blocked most liberal legislation in the House?

¶Will the new President be able successfully to claim a mandate for legislation such as the $1.25 minimum wage, Fed-

Continued on Page 35, Column 1

PRESIDENT SENDS WIRE TO KENNEDY

He Felicitates Senator and Orders Agency Chiefs to Cooperate With Him

By FELIX BELAIR Jr.
Special to The New York Times.

AUGUSTA, Ga., Nov. 9—President Eisenhower congratulated President-elect John F. Kennedy today on his election and then invited him to designate representatives to participate in all Federal policy discussions to assure an "orderly transition" to the new Administration.

The text of the President's telegram was withheld here at the request of Mr. Kennedy. But President Eisenhower is understood to have told the President-elect that he had instructed all heads of Federal departments and agencies to "cooperate fully" with Mr. Kennedy's representatives.

President Eisenhower arrived here for his customary fall holiday in midafternoon after a two-hour flight from Washington.

The President's message of congratulation to Mr. Kennedy was sent from the White House just before he took off for his favorite vacation retreat here at Augusta National Golf Course.

He also sent messages to the defeated Republican candidate, Vice President Nixon, and his running mate, Henry Cabot Lodge, as well as Vice President-elect Lyndon B. Johnson.

Continued on Page 42, Column 7

Vatican Calls Kennedy Election Proof of American Democracy

By ARNALDO CORTESI
Special to The New York Times.

ROME, Nov. 9—The election of Senator John F. Kennedy, a Roman Catholic, to the Presidency was received with keen satisfaction in the Vatican today.

During the campaign the Vatican remained neutral. Its newspaper, L'Osservatore Romano, abstained from all comment lest it be accused of siding with one candidate against the other.

Today the editor of the newspaper, former Italian Deputy Raimondo Manzini, said:

"Kennedy's victory strengthens the appreciation for the high democratic principles of freedom that guide American public life and assure access to the highest office to every citizen regardless of social class, race, or religion.

"The effective support given by large numbers of Protestant

Continued on Page 38, Column 5

THE MESSAGES WERE CONGRATULATORY: Senator John F. Kennedy displaying telegrams at Hyannis, Mass. With him are Mrs. Kennedy, his parents and Robert F. Kennedy, left, and R. Sargent Shriver, a brother-in-law.

United Press International Telephoto

206

"All the News
That's Fit to Print"

The New York Times.

LATE CITY EDITION
U.S. Weather Bureau Report (Page 46) forecast:
Cold, chance of snow flurries today;
fair and cold tonight and tomorrow.
Temp. range: 35–22; yesterday: 40.1–30.

VOL. CX..No. 37,583.
© 1960 by The New York Times Company.
Times Square, New York 36, N.Y.

NEW YORK, SATURDAY, DECEMBER 17, 1960.

10 cents beyond 50-mile zone from New York City
except on Long Island. Higher in air delivery cities.

FIVE CENTS

127 DIE AS 2 AIRLINERS COLLIDE OVER CITY; JET SETS BROOKLYN FIRE, KILLING 5 OTHERS; SECOND PLANE CRASHES ON STATEN ISLAND

STATEN ISLAND: Wreckage of Trans World Airlines Super Constellation in New Dorp.

BROOKLYN: Rescue workers gather near ruins of United Air Lines DC-8 jet in Seventh Avenue at Sterling Place, in the Park Slope section

The New York Times

ETHIOPIAN REVOLT SAID TO COLLAPSE; SELASSIE HAILED

Envoys in U. S. and Britain Report Rebels Seized —Emperor in Asmara

Special to The New York Times.

WASHINGTON, Dec. 16—The Ethiopian Embassy here reported today that the attempt by the Imperial Guard to overthrow Emperor Haile Selassie I had "ended in complete failure early this morning."

Ambassador Mikael Imru issued a statement saying that the army and air force, which had remained loyal to the Emperor, had captured Addis Ababa, the capital, and "overpowered and seized" the "disgruntled officers" of the Imperial Guard. The rebels had seized the city Wednesday.

[The Emperor arrived in Asmara, Ethiopia, Friday and received a tumultuous welcome from his loyal subjects there. He was told that the palace rebellion had failed.]

Prince Not Mentioned

The rebel group was reported at first to have been led by the Emperor's son, Crown Prince Asfa-Wossen. Later reports suggested that the Crown Prince might have acted "under duress."

The Ambassador's statement this noon made no mention of the part played by the Crown Prince and threw no light on his fate or his whereabouts.

Nor did the Ambassador say anything about his father, Ras Imru, the 68-year-old cousin of the Emperor, who was reported to have been appointed Premier of the government found by the rebels.

The Ambassador stated that the loyal forces had been led by Maj. Gen. Merod Mengsha, Chief of Staff; Maj. Gen. Kebede Guebre, army commander.

Continued on Page 2, Column 4

New Pact to Expand Cuban-Soviet Trade

By MAX FRANKEL
Special to The New York Times.

HAVANA, Dec. 16 — Cuba and the Soviet Union plan to exchange goods valued at $168,000,000 next year, the Ministry of Commerce disclosed here tonight.

The expanded trade dealings will be in addition to exchanges of sugar and other products for Soviet oil that had been agreed upon last February.

Although no details about the new arrangements were disclosed, it appeared almost certain that the Soviet Union would purchase considerably more Cuban sugar than it originally had planned.

Whatever the terms of the new trade agreement, it will

Continued on Page 6, Column 5

Dillon Appointed Secretary of Treasury; Kennedy's Brother Is Attorney General

Second Republican Gets Post in New Cabinet— President Approves

By W. H. LAWRENCE
Special to The New York Times.

WASHINGTON, Dec. 16—President-elect John F. Kennedy designated a Republican, Douglas Dillon, as his Secretary of the Treasury today and named his brother, Robert F. Kennedy, as Attorney General.

Mr. Dillon, now serving the Eisenhower Administration as Under Secretary of State, disclosed that he had sought the assent of President Eisenhower this morning and of Vice President Nixon earlier.

"Neither of them had any objection if I felt that this was something that would be in the national security interest of the country, and if we were to work toward a sound fiscal policy as is the case," Mr. Dillon said.

Both appointments long had been forecast. But the choice of Robert Kennedy, 35 years old, is expected to provoke a political storm. Senator Kennedy set a precedent by naming his brother to the Cabinet.

PRO-WEST FORCES TAKE VIENTIANE

New Premier Enters Laos Capital as Fighting Ends

Because of communications difficulties, the following dispatch was filed jointly by correspondents in Vientiane.

VIENTIANE, Laos, Dec. 16—Prince Boun Oum, the new Premier of Laos, and the rightist pro-Western leader, Phoumi Nosavan, drove into Vientiane at dusk today and announced the liberation of this shattered administrative capital.

At the same time, Capt. Peng, a cheerful Laotian tank officer, was busy cleaning from hold-out positions at the Vientiane airport the stubborn remnants of Capt. Kong Le's pro-Communist paratroops and guerrillas of the Communist-led Pathet Lao movement.

The seventy-six-hour battle for Vientiane ended at 5 P. M. local time [5 A. M., Friday, Eastern Standard Time].

Rightist Troops Hold City

By JACQUES NEVARD
Special to The New York Times.

VIENTIANE, Dec. 16—The troops of Gen. Phoumi Nosavan held the center of Vientiane this morning eighteen hours after they had captured it for a second time in a seesaw battle with tenacious pro-Communist defenders.

Mortar, machine-gun and small-arms fire could still be heard as tanks and armored cars cruised through the streets.

After a night full the battle turned hot and fierce again. The heart of this usually somnolent

Continued on Page 4, Column 2

Senator Kennedy said he would complete his Cabinet tomorrow by naming his Postmaster General from the family home at Palm Beach, Fla., where he is planning a prolonged holiday through Christmas and New Year's Day.

He left little doubt that his choice would be J. Edward Day, a California insurance executive, who flew in by jet from Los Angeles during the night and then flew South with the President-elect this afternoon.

The President-elect left Washington aboard his private twin-engine Convair, Caroline, at 4 P. M. Also aboard the airplane for the flight to Palm Beach were his brother, Robert, and two of Robert's children, Bobby and Joseph.

In two news conferences from the front stoop of his Georgetown home just after noon, Senator Kennedy announced first

the choice of Mr. Dillon and then of his brother, Robert.

At the same time, he said Byron R. White, Denver attorney and former All-America football star at the University of Colorado, would be Deputy Attorney General. Harry J. Anslinger, Commissioner of Narcotics in the Treasury Department, has agreed to stay in that position, Senator Kennedy said.

Appointments Forecast

Highly placed Democrats forecast the following other major appointments by Senator Kennedy shortly:

¶Mrs. Elizabeth Smith, California's Democratic national committeewoman, as Treasurer of the United States, replacing Mrs. Ivy Baker Priest.

¶Fred Dutton of California as secretary of the Kennedy Cabinet. He is a former executive secretary to Gov. Edmund G. Brown of California.

Mr. Dillon, 51 years old, becomes the Cabinet's second Republican. He will serve with

Continued on Page 14, Column 6

U.S. Offers NATO A Nuclear Arsenal And 5 Submarines

By DREW MIDDLETON
Special to The New York Times.

PARIS, Dec. 16—The United States offered Western Europe a mighty new nuclear armory today for defense against the Communist bloc.

Secretary of State Christian A. Herter announced what he termed a new concept for operation of medium-range ballistic missiles to the Ministerial Council of the North Atlantic Treaty Organization late this afternoon.

The offer was conditional upon agreement by the European allies on political control of the weapons, which were described by Mr. Herter as offering the best means for providing a common defense in the field of medium-range ballistic missiles.

The offer calls for commitment to the Atlantic alliance before the end of 1963 of five ballistic missile submarines armed with eighty Polaris missiles, the Secretary of State said. The step would enlarge the alliance's military capabilities and reaffirm the United States' commitment to Europe's defense, he said.

The United States would then expect other members of the

Continued on Page 13, Column 1

WIDE U. N. POWER IN CONGO IS URGED

100-Day Blanket Authority Sought for Hammarskjold

By LINDESAY PARROTT
Special to The New York Times.

UNITED NATIONS, N. Y., Dec. 16—An urgent meeting of the General Assembly heard a proposal tonight to grant blanket emergency powers to Secretary General Dag Hammarskjold for 100 days to settle the growing crisis in the Congo.

Francisco Milla Bermudez of Honduras read the text of a proposed resolution that would give effect to the plan.

Because of the series of recurring emergencies in the new African state, he said, full interim powers for the Secretary General might be the best way to bring peace and order to the country under the terms of the Charter.

The Assembly adjourned at 10:35 P. M. to meet again at 10:30 A. M. tomorrow, with the United States delegate scheduled as the first speaker.

Latin-American sources said that some Latin-American nations had been consulted on the Honduran proposal, though none joined in sponsoring the plan. Señor Milla Bermudez announced that he was prepared to consider changes in his text and would introduce it formally if others agreed.

The proposal would permit the Assembly to revoke the Secretary General's special authority if necessary or extend it beyond the 100-day period if Mr. Hammarskjold seemed to be succeeding.

The Honduran proposal was

Continued on Page 2, Column 4

A PILOT OFF ROUTE, U.S. OFFICIALS HINT

C.A.B. and F.A.A. Open Wide Inquiries—Tape Records of Flights to Be Studied

By RUSSELL PORTER

A preliminary investigation of the air disaster here yesterday suggested that the two planes collided because one was off its course.

An extensive inquiry was opened by the two Federal agencies concerned with civilian aviation, the Civil Aeronautics Board and the Federal Aviation Agency.

E. R. Quesada, Administrator of the Federal Aviation Agency, which is responsible for the operation of the airways, said last night that it was "very probable" that there had been a collision.

Alan S. Boyd, a member of the C. A. B., which investigates air accidents, was present when Mr. Quesada made his statement at New York International Airport. The two officials held a joint news conference.

They said that the investigation was just starting and little had been learned, but that the Trans World Airlines plane had fallen in three parts in Staten Island in a way indicating that it could not have been broken up by hitting the ground.

They said this made it appear likely there had been a collision, but there was as yet no positive evidence of a collision.

"All we know is that two planes crashed eleven miles apart," they said.

Shortly before the disaster, they said, the T. W. A. plane flew over the Linden, N. J., area

Continued on Page 10, Column 1

10 Brooklyn Houses Burn After Plane Hits a Church

By JOHN F. MURPHY

Ten four-story tenement buildings and an empty church were set afire when the United Air Lines DC-8 jet crashed and exploded in the populous Park Slope district of Brooklyn yesterday. More than 250 firemen and about fifty pieces of apparatus rushed to the seven-alarm blaze, which took more than two hours to bring under control.

There were several hundred persons in the buildings when the airliner plummeted through one tenement on Sterling Place and rammed into the Pillar of Fire Church across the street.

A rapid-fire series of small explosions followed, igniting roofs and spraying wreckage over a wide area.

Tenants Race From Homes

As soon as the plane crashed, women, children and elderly persons came pouring out of the buildings into the street, dressed in housecoats, sweaters and pajamas. They ran panic-stricken from the smoldering wreckage.

Aside from those on the plane who were killed, five persons on the ground died. These five presumably included three persons known to be missing. The police said even more bodies might be found beneath the fuselage.

The one victim identified was Charles J. Cooper, 34 years old, a sanitation worker, who had been shoveling snow. Those missing were Wallace E. Lewis, 90, the caretaker of the church at 123 Sterling Place; Joseph Colacano, 29, and John Oppersano, 35. Mr. Colacano Mr. Oppersano had been selling Christmas trees on the sidewalk.

The first fire alarm was sounded at 10:36 A. M. When

Continued on Page 9, Column 1

S. I. HOMES SPARED BY FALLING DEBRIS

Parts of Airliner Land in Backyards—No One on Ground Is Injured

By THOMAS BUCKLEY

Distances that can be paced off quickly—50 feet, 150 feet, 200 yards—were the measure of life and death on quiet streets on Staten Island yesterday.

Men, women and children saw the flaming wreckage of a Trans World Airlines Super-Constellation plunge toward them—and fall short. And although all forty-four persons aboard were killed, no one on the ground was even scratched by the fall of the shattered airliner.

The flaming forward section of the craft, from which twenty-nine bodies were taken, smashed to earth on the northwest corner of Miller Army Air Field, less than 150 feet from the eight-room frame home of Edward Brody, at 324 Boundary Lane, Midland Beach. Dozens of other homes on tree-lined streets stood near by.

"I saw it coming right at us," Mrs. Brody said. "I ran upstairs to get my daughters.

Continued on Page 11, Column 1

DISASTER IN FOG

DC-8 Plunges Into Park Slope Street, Missing School

By HOMER BIGART

Two airliners collided over New York harbor yesterday in fog and sleet, killing 127 passengers and crewmen. One plane crashed in Brooklyn, killing five more persons on the ground, and the other fell on Staten Island.

A United Air Lines DC-8 jet from Chicago plunged into the crowded Park Slope section of Brooklyn shortly after 10:30 A. M. All but one of its seventy-seven passengers and the crew of seven were killed. The survivor was an 11-year-old boy.

The plane demolished a church and killed a Department of Sanitation worker who was shoveling snow. Burning debris caused a seven-alarm fire, destroying two brownstone apartment buildings, several stores and a funeral home. Nine persons were injured on the ground.

Three Unaccounted For

Three persons were unaccounted for, including the 90-year-old custodian of the Pillar of Fire Church, 123 Sterling Place, a Gothic structure that was leveled by flames.

At almost the same time as the Brooklyn disaster, a Trans World Airlines Lockheed Super - Constellation crashed near Miller Army Air Field, New Dorp, S. I., eleven miles to the southwest.

This plane, out of Dayton and Columbus, Ohio, apparently exploded in the air just before the crash. All thirty-nine passengers and the crew of five were killed or fatally injured.

Parts of the plane fell in the Lower Bay and parts on the northwest corner of Miller Field.

Three victims were taken by Coast Guard helicopter to the Public Health Service Hospital

Continued on Page 8, Column 1

4 Cardinals Named; One Is an American

By ARNALDO CORTESI
Special to The New York Times.

ROME, Dec. 16—The Most Rev. Joseph Elmer Ritter, Archbishop of St. Louis, and three other prelates were named today by Pope John XXIII to become Cardinals Jan. 16.

The elevation of Archbishop Ritter will return the number of American Cardinals to six, as it was up to the death of John F. Cardinal O'Hara, Archbishop of Philadelphia, less than four months ago.

The present American Cardinals are Archbishops Francis Spellman of New York, James F. McIntyre of Los Angeles, Richard Cushing of Boston, Albert G. Meyer of Chicago and Aloysius J. Muench of Milwau-

Continued on Page 2, Column 1

Boy, 11, Only Survivor of Crash

Condition Is Critical —Parents and Sister at His Bedside

By ROBERT CONLEY

An 11-year-old boy, flying here to meet his mother and sister, was the only survivor of yesterday's airliner collision.

He was thrown from the tail section of the United Air Lines jet and found in a Brooklyn snowbank, his clothes aflame.

The youngster, Steven Baltz of Wilmette, Ill., regained consciousness last night, but was still in critical condition early today with burns and broken bones.

His mother and sister were at his bedside at the Methodist Hospital in Brooklyn. They had flown here from Chicago ahead of him. His father, William S. Baltz, flew in late in the day and reached the bedside just after dark.

"He's coming along quite well, very well," the father said after

Continued on Page 11, Column 6

Steven Baltz is comforted by passer-by at scene of crash.

© New York Journal-American

NEWS INDEX

	Page		Page
Art	47	Music	22
Books	25	Obituaries	29
Bridge	39	Real Estate	48
Business	38–39	Screen	19–22
Crossword	29	Ships and Air	44
Editorial	24	Society	32
Events Today	35	Sports	17–19
Fashions	20	Theatres	19–22
Financial	38–39	TV and Radio	46
Food	21	U. N. Proceedings	5
In the News		Wood's	

207

The New York Times.

LATE CITY EDITION
U. S. Weather Bureau Report (Page 66) forecast:
Mostly fair, seasonably cold today
and tonight. Fair, warmer tomorrow.
Temp. range 38—25; yesterday: 35—31.

VOL. CX.No. 37,601. © 1961 by The New York Times Company. Times Square, New York 36, N. Y. NEW YORK, WEDNESDAY, JANUARY 4, 1961. 10 cents beyond 50-mile zone from New York City except on Long Island. Higher in air delivery cities. FIVE CENTS

U. S. BREAKS ITS DIPLOMATIC TIES WITH CUBA AND ADVISES AMERICANS TO LEAVE ISLAND; EISENHOWER CITES 'VILIFICATION' BY CASTRO

CONGRESS OPENS WITH CONFLICTS ON PROCEDURES

Filibuster Curbs Sought in Senate—Colmer's Purge Is Believed Certain

By RUSSELL BAKER
Special to The New York Times.

WASHINGTON, Jan. 3—The Eighty-seventh Congress convened today amid clashes in both houses over rules of procedure.

In the Senate, proponents of tighter curbs on the rules of debate opened a battle to make it easier to cut off filibusters. The skirmishes ended inconclusively with a decision to postpone further action until tomorrow.

In the House of Representatives, Speaker Sam Rayburn was reported to have completed arrangements for removing Representative William M. Colmer, Democrat of Mississippi, from the Rules Committee and replacing him with a member who would reinforce the Texas Democrat's leadership.

Pledges by Leaders

The Senate session was marked by a clash between Vice President Nixon and Richard B. Russell. The Georgia Democrat, leader of the Southern bloc, normally gets deference from the chair. Twice, however, Mr. Nixon used his gavel against him with authority.

In the House's traditional opening procedures, Mr. Rayburn and Charles A. Halleck of Indiana, the Republican minority leader, made pledges to work for responsible government.

Behind the scenes, however, a liberal-conservative fight for control of the Rules Committee continued unabated. Mr. Rayburn was assured of the necessary votes in the Democratic Committee on Committees to help purge Mr. Colmer.

This presumably would create a Rules Committee majority favoring critical parts of President-elect John F. Kennedy's program. Capitol observers described the Rayburn plan as "replacing a 'no' man with a 'yes' man."

Friction in Caucus

Meanwhile, Senate Republicans joined Democrats in a standing ovation for the new and only woman member on the Democratic side, Mrs. Maurine Neuberger of Oregon.

Mr. Nixon's duty on the rostrum was to administer the oath to each Senator elected in November.

A Senate Democratic caucus this morning brought more friction. As expected, Mike Mansfield of Montana was elected to succeed Vice President-elect Lyndon B. Johnson as majority leader, and Hubert H. Humphrey of Minnesota was named assistant leader.

Mr. Mansfield, however, created a surprise when he announced that he wanted the

Continued on Page 24, Column 3

I.T.T. Voices Hopes On H-Bomb Power

By GENE SMITH

Experiments that might lead to a "low-cost nuclear fusion process" were announced here yesterday by the International Telephone and Telegraph Corporation.

No details were given, but the experiments apparently dealt with a concept that many nuclear experts have not considered promising. The company said the experiments had been conducted "for a number of years" but made no claim of success.

The problem of producing a controlled and sustained nuclear fusion, and then harnessing the reaction of the hydrogen bomb, is the goal of many experiments being conducted both here and abroad.

Temperatures of millions of degrees Centigrade are necessary

Continued on Page 16, Column 3

Legislators Choose Mahoney, Carlino

By WARREN WEAVER Jr.
Special to The New York Times.

ALBANY, Jan. 3—Senators and Assemblymen descended on the capital tonight to prepare for the opening of the 1961 legislative session here tomorrow.

The Republican majorities in the Senate and Assembly held separate caucuses to choose their leaders and housekeeping officers for the next two years.

The Democrats chose their own nominees at separate sessions, but since the Republicans control both houses their nominations were equivalent to election.

There were no surprises. Senator Walter J. Mahoney of Buffalo was chosen temporary President of the Senate, the official title of the majority leader, a post he has held for the last seven years. In the Assembly, Joseph F.

Continued on Page 14, Column 1

L.I.R.R. SEEKS AID TO AVERT 'CRISIS'

Says It Will Be Unable to Meet April Payroll—Two Rail Walkouts Cited

By CLARENCE DEAN

The Long Island Rail Road appealed yesterday for financial help to avert what it said was an impending crisis.

A statement by Thomas M. Goodfellow, president of the line, declared that unless the help was forthcoming the railroad would be unable to meet its payroll by the last week in April.

The present indications, Mr. Goodfellow said, are that the carrier's deficit by the end of this year will exceed $4,000,000.

If there is no financial help, Mr. Goodfellow said, three alternatives will arise: "a whopping fare increase," a cut in maintenance "to rock bottom" or "an arbitrary 12 per cent slash in the number of commuter trains." He declined to suggest specifically what kind of financial help the road wanted.

He attributed the railroad's predicament to unforeseen emergencies, chiefly a twenty-six-day strike on the Long Island last summer and a subsequent twelve-day shutdown of Pennsylvania as a result of a strike against the Pennsylvania Railroad.

For last October and November

Continued on Page 67, Column 2

U.S. SAYS SOVIET AND RED VIETNAM AID LAOS REBELS

Asserts 180 Air Drops Were Made in Nineteen Days— President Sees Advisers

Text of the State Department statement is on Page 8.

By WILLIAM J. JORDEN
Special to The New York Times.

WASHINGTON, Jan. 3—The United States Government charged today that the Soviet Union and North Vietnam were guilty of "extensive participation" in military operations against the Government of Laos.

To bolster its charge, the State Department released a listing of Communist supply flights over Laos, serial numbers of Soviet planes engaged in the airlift, dates and places of air drops to the anti-Government rebels and other details.

The department said the two Communist powers had carried out more than 180 air sorties into Laos in the nineteen days from Dec. 15 through Jan. 2 to drop supplies and personnel to pro-Communist forces. It said that "substantial numbers" of North Vietnamese had been parachuted into Laos to help the rebels.

Elaboration Is Declined

A department spokesman would not elaborate on the numbers. Nor would he use the term "aggression" to describe the Communists' activities.

The charges against the Communist states were attributed to "hard evidence," however. Today's list of particulars detailed earlier general charges of Communist intervention in Laos.

The catalogue of Communist involvement should be read, officials said, with the strong statement issued by the United States Government three days ago in mind. On Saturday the State Department warned that "the Government would take "the most serious view" of intervention in Laos by the Chinese Communists, North Vietnamese "or others" in support of the anti-Government rebels.

Today's Government statement on Laos was issued soon after a special briefing on the Laos situation for President Eisenhower by his top diplomatic, military and intelligence advisers. It was the third White House conference on Laos in four days.

On Capitol Hill a group of House members also received an up-to-date report on developments in Laos. John M.

Continued on Page 8, Column 5

NO ENTRY: Portion of the crowd in front of the U. S. Embassy in Havana as Cubans sought visas yesterday. When they discovered that the visa section of the embassy had been closed, there were cries of protest and dismay.
Associated Press Radiophoto

Belgian Assembly Defeats Socialists; Violence Continues

By HARRY GILROY
Special to The New York Times.

BRUSSELS, Belgium, Jan. 3—The Belgian House of Representatives rejected today a motion to withdraw the proposed new law to raise taxes and tighten up the social security administration, against which 500,000 Socialist workers are striking.

Leo Collard, president of the Socialist party, and Achille van Acker, a former Premier, presented the motion. It was defeated by a vote of 121 to 83 with 1 abstention.

The House gave the Government three votes of confidence before adjourning at 8 P. M. until 2 P. M. tomorrow. The votes followed three critical speeches by Socialists and by a Communist member on the conduct of public affairs and on the treatment of strikers.

The votes were taken in a calm parliamentary atmosphere that contrasted with an unruly session in which the measure was last discussed Dec. 23, and even more with the street demonstrations that turned up new

Continued on Page 12, Column 3

CASTRO'S CABINET DRAFTING A REPLY

Emergency Session Called After U. S. Acts—Premier Says 'Cuba Is Alert'

By R. HART PHILLIPS
Special to The New York Times.

HAVANA, Jan. 3—Premier Fidel Castro, President Osvaldo Dorticós Torrado and members of the Cuban Cabinet met at 10:30 to draft a reply to the United States' break in diplomatic relations with Cuba.

The reply will be delivered to the United States Embassy here soon, according to a statement by Dr. Carlos Olivares, Cuba's Foreign Under Secretary.

The Cabinet meeting ended without any announcement.

The Cuban people learned of the United States move tonight when the announcement was made over all radio stations.

The announcer said that "according to cables received President Eisenhower had broken off diplomatic relations with Cuba on the pretext of the order of the Revolutionary Government that he withdraw his 300 spies in the embassy from Cuba."

"Being discovered in his criminal plans of terrorism Eisenhower has responded with the habitual shamelessness of imperialism," the announcer declared.

The announcer said the radio would keep the people informed

Continued on Page 3, Column 5

U. S. Will Help Evacuate Its Citizens Living in Cuba

Special to The New York Times.

HAVANA, Wednesday, Jan. 4—The United States Embassy last night urged all Americans in Cuba to leave the island. A statement issued by the press attaché said that "all American citizens are urged to depart from Cuba immediately unless compelling reasons oblige them to remain."

The embassy has arranged for a ferry of the West Indies Fruit and Steamship Company to sail from Havana to West Palm Beach today and Friday to evacuate the Americans. Additional extra flights to Miami from the José Marti International Airport will augment the facilities for departure today and tomorrow.

Cuba Guarantees Safety

The Castro regime, in a note delivered this morning to the United States Chargé d' Affaires, Daniel M. Braddock, pledged the "most absolute guarantees" for the safety of all American citizens in Cuba, including diplomatic or consular officials "as well as residents or tourists."

Meanwhile, thousands of Cubans who for months have been seeking visas to the United States were dismayed yesterday by the Cuban-United States crisis.

A long line of Cubans appeared as usual at the United States Embassy early in the morning after Premier Fidel Castro had ordered a cut in the embassy staff. They found the

Continued on Page 3, Column 6

KENNEDY AVOIDS ROLE IN DECISION

Rusk Turns Down Herter Move to Link Democrats to Break With Cuba

By JAMES RESTON
Special to The New York Times.

WASHINGTON, Jan. 3—The Eisenhower Administration took full responsibility tonight for the diplomatic break with Cuba.

Secretary of State Christian A. Herter yesterday informed Dean Rusk, who will succeed him in less than three weeks, of the President's decision, but he did not seek the advice of the leaders of the incoming Administration on what should be done.

Mr. Herter asked Mr. Rusk whether the incoming Democratic Administration wished to associate itself with the break. Mr. Rusk replied after consultations with President-elect John F. Kennedy that the absence of complete information on all the relevant factors the new Administration did not feel that it could participate in the decision.

Both parties thus found themselves in an extremely delicate position. The Republicans were well aware of the fact that they were taking a decision that would greatly complicate the problems of the Kennedy Administration in the early days of its responsibility after the inauguration Jan. 20.

At the same time, they did not feel that they could avoid reacting quickly to Premier Castro's demand that the United States diplomatic mission in Cuba should be reduced to eleven persons.

The Democrats were equally

Continued on Page 4, Column 5

REGIME IS SCORED

People Suffer Under 'Yoke of Dictator,' President Says

Texts of President's statement and notes are on Page 3.

By E. W. KENWORTHY
Special to The New York Times.

WASHINGTON, Jan. 3—The United States formally terminated diplomatic and consular relations with Cuba tonight.

President Eisenhower announced the break with the Government of Premier Fidel Castro in a statement issued at the White House at 8:30 o'clock.

The break came a day and a half after the Cuban Government had delivered a note to the United States Embassy in Havana demanding that the staff of the embassy and the consulate there be reduced to eleven persons within forty-eight hours.

The President said in his statement:

"There is a limit to what the United States in self-respect can endure. That limit has now been reached."

Normal Situation 'Impossible'

The action of the Castro Government, the President said, "can have no other purpose than to render impossible the conduct of normal diplomatic relations with that Government."

Therefore, he said, he had instructed the Secretary of State to deliver a note to the Cuban Embassy here announcing the formal ending of relations.

The President added that "this calculated action on the part of the Castro Government is only the latest of a long series of harassments, baseless accusations and vilification."

President Eisenhower said in his statement that the friendship of the United States for the Cuban people "is not affected" by the breaking of diplomatic relations with the Castro regime.

Sympathy Expressed

"It is my hope and my conviction," the President said, "that in the not too distant future it will be possible for the historic friendship between us once again to find its reflection in normal relations of every sort."

"Meanwhile," the President said, "our sympathy goes out to the people of Cuba now suffering under the yoke of a dictator."

The United States requested the Government of Cuba, in turn, to withdraw "as soon as possible" the entire Cuban personnel in the Cuban Embassy in Washington and in all Cuban consular offices in the United States.

In a note to the Cuban Government, Secretary of State Christian A. Herter stated that it was requesting the Government of Switzerland to assume

Continued on Page 3, Column 1

Cuban U.N. Charge To Get Stern Reply

By LINDESAY PARROTT
Special to The New York Times.

UNITED NATIONS, N. Y., Jan. 3—The United States will follow up its break in relations with Cuba by sharply rejecting in the Security Council tomorrow Cuban charges of American "aggressive intentions."

Representatives of Western delegations here tonight expressed some surprise at the United States severance of relations. The American delegation, during the day, had been in contact with allied nations over the Cuban charges. It was understood, however, that the question discussed was largely whether opposition should be offered to Cuba's request to put the issue on the agenda.

The Council is to meet at 10:30 A. M. at the request of Foreign Minister Raul Roa of

Continued on Page 4, Column 4

Hammarskjold Flying to Congo To Try to End Factional Strife

By JAMES FERON
Special to The New York Times.

UNITED NATIONS, N. Y., Jan. 3—Secretary General Dag Hammarskjold left for the Congo today in an attempt to end the civil disorders threatening the work of the United Nations force there.

His departure, which had been delayed a day to study disorders in Kivu Province, remained uncertain until two hours before he left because of the changing situation in Laos.

At New York International Airport, Mr. Hammarskjold said he did not intend to visit Laos on this trip but that he might return to the United Nations earlier than he had planned if the Laotian situation required his presence.

The Secretary General was warmly applauded by a large crowd in the main lobby of the striking terminal. His plane left

for Leopoldville at 5:55 P. M.

He will spend two days in the Congo and will talk with members of the eleven-nation United Nations Conciliation Commission, the Congo Government and United Nations force leaders. Technically, this is only a side trip on the way to South Africa, where the Secretary General will spend eight days studying racial segregation.

However, United Nations sources suggested that Mr. Hammarskjold's principal concern now was the "developing civil war" in the Congo. They felt that continuing strife between opposing Congolese factions could put the United Nations force in an untenable

Continued on Page 12, Column 5

WELCOME TO WASHINGTON: Lyndon B. Johnson, right, Vice President-elect, with three others

The New York Times.

LATE CITY EDITION
U.S. Weather Bureau Report (Page 81) forecasts:
Increasing cloudiness today; chance of rain tonight and tomorrow.
Temp. range: 54—40, yesterday: 52—43.

VOL. CX..No. 37,699.

© 1961 by The New York Times Company.
Times Square, New York 36, N. Y.

NEW YORK, WEDNESDAY, APRIL 12, 1961.

10 cents beyond 50-mile zone from New York City
except on Long Island. Higher in air delivery cities.

FIVE CENTS

SOVIET ORBITS MAN AND RECOVERS HIM; SPACE PIONEER REPORTS: 'I FEEL WELL'; SENT MESSAGES WHILE CIRCLING EARTH

HEAD OF RESERVE URGES PRICE CUTS TO RELIEVE SLUMP

Martin Asserts Reductions Would Mean More Jobs and Demand for Goods

By RICHARD E. MOONEY
Special to The New York Times.

WASHINGTON, April 11—The chairman of the Federal Reserve Board made a strong appeal today for price reductions as a means of solving the nation's economic problems.

"Throughout our country, we must not only increase our productivity but also pass some of the gains on to the consumer in the form of lower prices, rather than having all of it go exclusively to labor in higher wages or to management in higher profits," he said.

The chairman, William McC. Martin Jr., said that price cuts could stimulate buying demand that would "provide more jobs for those who are now unemployed, keep the economy moving to higher levels, and [provide] still greater job opportunities in the future."

Some Gains Reported

The Labor Department reported, meanwhile, a modest increase in the factory work week and factory pay for March.

Mr. Martin spoke at the annual meeting of the Association of Reserve City Bankers at Boca Raton, Fla. Copies of his talk were made available here.

It was not the first time that a voice from Washington had been raised in favor of price cuts. It is a point that gets lost, however, in the debates most often heard here, over what the Government should or should not do. In the form presented, it is simply an exhortation. Neither Mr. Martin nor the Kennedy Administration advocates price or wage controls.

Addressing himself to the domestic economy, Mr. Martin said that "at the moment we have pressing need to reduce unemployment and to promote economic growth at the maximum sustainable speed." The way to meet the need, he said, is "a judicious blend of specific actions, monetary and fiscal policies, and wage-price policies."

Answers Critics of Policy

In such a setting, he said, interest rates need not rise so high nor fall so low as they have in past business cycles.

Mr. Martin used his speech to answer critics who have said that recent Federal Reserve strategy cannot work and has already failed. Seven weeks ago the reserve system abandoned its established policy of buying and selling only the shortest-term securities—Treasury bills—when it sought to impose its influence on credit conditions

Continued on Page 25, Column 5

Realtor Is Indicted In Expense Padding

By EDWARD RANZAL

The president of Pease & Elliman, Inc., a leading real estate concern here, was indicted yesterday on charges of income tax evasion through fraudulent claims for entertainment and travel expenses.

The indictment against the executive, Robert Neaderland, by a Federal grand jury was said to be the first of its kind in the Southern District of New York. It was expected to break ground for future prosecutions for overstatement of business expenses.

Mr. Neaderland, 53 years old, lives at 160 Central Park South. His company is one of the leading developers of apartments on the East Side. He is charged with attempting to evade $27,550 in income taxes in 1954 and 1955, according to

Continued on Page 30, Column 3

Wide College Aid Is Adopted by State

By WARREN WEAVER Jr.
Special to The New York Times.

ALBANY, April 11—A higher-education program that will make $12,300,000 in new financial assistance available to college and university students in New York State this year was approved by Governor Rockefeller today.

He said the program gave assurance that "no young man or woman with the ability and desire for a higher education need be deprived of that opportunity for lack of funds."

The seven higher education measures that were signed included a bill that gave New York City permission to establish a city university to consist of the four municipal colleges and the community colleges in the five boroughs. One of the bills provides

Continued on Page 48, Column 3

COUNCIL APPROVES OWN CHARTER BILL

Rebuffs Mayor by Spurning State Law Under Which He Named Commission

By CHARLES G. BENNETT

The City Council passed its own bill yesterday calling for the appointment of a commission to draft a new City Charter. The vote was 21 to 3.

Council officers immediately prepared to send the measure directly to Mayor Wagner for his signature or veto. This would be based on a contention that the Council's high command that since the bill merely calls for the appointment of a commission, it does not require Board of Estimate action.

The Council's stand constituted a challenge to the new state law under which Mayor Wagner already has appointed an eleven-member commission to revise the Charter.

Majority Leader Joseph T. Sharkey, who is also Democratic leader of Kings County, repeated his charge that Governor Rockefeller and Mayor Wagner had been "playing together" on Charter revision. Mayor Wagner supported the state bill.

Mr. Sharkey also said he "hoped and expected" that there

Continued on Page 26, Column 3

Population Center Moves West; Census Puts It at Centralia, Ill.

The New York Times April 12, 1961

United States center of population, which was near Portsmouth, Ohio, a hundred years ago, has continued moving west and by 1960 was just northwest of Centralia, Ill.

By The Associated Press

WASHINGTON, April 11—The population center of the United States has moved again. Secretary of Commerce Luther H. Hodges announced today that the new center, based on the 1960 census, was near Centralia, Ill., fifty-seven miles west of its 1950 location.

In general, the population

ISRAEL DEFENDS TRIBUNAL'S RIGHT TO TRY EICHMANN

Ex-Nazi Is More Confident as Jerusalem Hearing Enters Its 2d Day

By HOMER BIGART
Special to The New York Times.

JERUSALEM (Israeli Sector), Wednesday, April 12—The Attorney General of Israel, Gideon Hausner, resumed this morning his defense of the right of his country to try Adolf Eichmann for the murder of millions of Jews.

The defendant, as he entered his bulletproof glass cage on the second day of his trial seemed more confident. For the first time, he looked out at the audience. Then he sat down and engaged in an animated conversation with his German lawyer, Dr. Robert Servatius through a microphone in the glass cage. Eichmann smiled at his lawyer and seemed at ease.

On the first day of the trial, Eichmann, stonily impassive, heard his lawyer challenge the court's right to try the former Nazi leader on charges of delivering millions of Jews to Nazi annihilation camps.

The debate over Israel's right to try Eichmann was expected to continue through today's session. The court will not meet tomorrow, Holocaust Day, a day of mourning in Israel for the victims of Nazi terror.

Indictment Is Read

For seventy minutes Eichmann remained standing while the presiding judge, Justice Moshe Landau of the Israeli Supreme Court, read in Hebrew a fifteen-count indictment charging him with crimes against the Jewish people and crimes against humanity. The indictment was translated into German for Eichmann's benefit.

Rigidly erect, his head tilted back and his thin lips tightly compressed, the one-time chief of the Gestapo's Jewish Affairs Section betrayed no emotion during the opening day of trial.

His thin, hawklike visage with its large, sharply pointed nose was fixed intently on the proceedings. Not once did Eichmann turn to gaze on the throng of newsmen, foreign observers and Israeli citizens in the 750 seats in the Beit Haam (House of the People), the converted

Continued on Page 16, Column 1

Centennial of War Rocked by Dispute

By The Associated Press.

CHARLESTON, S. C., April 11—New Jersey accused the National Civil War Centennial Commission of "pathetic mismanagement" tonight and asked President Kennedy to remove Maj. Gen. Ulysses S. Grant 3d as chairman.

Joseph Dempsey, vice chairman of the Jersey Centennial Commission, made the charge at a news conference after General Grant had turned down the state's request for time to rebut a dinner speaker who had criticized its civil rights practices.

General Grant and Donald Flamm, Jersey chairman, engaged in an unscheduled standing debate at the crowded dinner at the Charleston Naval Base. General Grant, to loud applause, insisted that New

Continued on Page 36, Column 3

Former Nazi Hears Indictment Read as Trial Begins in Jerusalem

Adolf Eichmann, charged with crimes against the Jewish people and against humanity, standing in special booth in Beit Haam courtroom yesterday. Justices at bench are, from left, Benyamin Halevi, Moshe Landau, Yitzhak Raveh.

U. S. IS DISTURBED BY DELAY ON LAOS

Soviet Lag on Cease-Fire and Increase in Supplies Regarded as Ominous

By WILLIAM J. JORDEN
Special to The New York Times.

WASHINGTON, April 11—Officials said today the United States Government was disturbed by Moscow's delay in accepting a Western plan for an immediate cease-fire in Laos.

A spokesman for the State Department said that continued delay would be regarded here as "a matter of very serious concern."

Adding to the worries of Administration leaders were intelligence reports of a general increase in the flow of Soviet-bloc military supplies to the Pathet Lao movement in recent days. This was regarded as an ominous sign of Soviet intentions in Laos.

Rusk Voices Hope

High officials continued to be hopeful, however, that Moscow would soon give a favorable answer to the cease-fire plan advanced by the British several weeks ago.

That hope was voiced on Capitol Hill today by Secretary of State Dean Rusk. The Secretary told Senators that he expected a Soviet answer "within a very few days."

The presumption here is that continued fighting in Laos contains the seeds of a possibly enlarged conflict and that the Soviet bloc does not want to

Continued on Page 12, Column 4

Eichmann peers intently at tribunal during proceedings

Associated Press Radiophoto

BRITISH CONSIDER TRADE UNITY STEP

Kennedy Hopes London Will Enter Common Market

By JAMES RESTON
Special to The New York Times.

WASHINGTON, April 11—President Kennedy now has the impression that the British Government is seriously thinking about joining the European Economic Community, or Common Market.

This impression is based on the fact that during the President's conversations with Prime Minister Macmillan here last week the British leader asked what the United States Government would think if Britain decided to reverse her policy and join the Western European nations now working toward economic and political integration.

Administration to Cooperate

President Kennedy's reply was that the United States would regard this as a major advance toward the unity of the West.

The President did not in any way imply that the United States was thinking of joining the Common Market itself, but he did stress his Government's determination to cooperate fully with its allies in the Organization for Economic Cooperation and Development.

On a recent trip to London it is known that George Ball, United States Under Secretary of State for Economic Affairs, urged upon Viscount Hailsham, the British Lord President of the Council, that Britain give the most serious consideration

Continued on Page 2, Column 3

ADENAUER IN U. S. TO SEE KENNEDY

Arrives for First Talks With President—Stresses Unity

Special to The New York Times.

WASHINGTON, April 11—Chancellor Adenauer of West Germany arrived here tonight for his first meetings with President Kennedy.

He alighted at Andrews Air Force Base from the Lufthansa jet airliner that brought him without stop from Bonn.

In an arrival statement the 85-year-old Chancellor said the German people had already developed "great confidence" in the new President of the United States. He said he was looking forward to establishing personal contact with Mr. Kennedy.

Dr. Adenauer pledged that his country's considerable energy and ability would be devoted to the cause of peace and freedom. He said that his Government realized that its share of responsibility for the future of the world grew "in proportion with our efficiency and capacity."

"Our times are filled with threats and dangers," the Chancellor said, "but I feel sure that the free people of the world will overcome those dangers if they are united and resolute."

The West German leader and his party, including his daughter, Frau Libeth Werhahn, were

Continued on Page 4, Column 5

FRANCE DECLARES ANTI-U. N. 'STRIKE'

De Gaulle Bars Any Role in Armed Ventures — Warns Algerians on Partition

By HENRY GINIGER
Special to The New York Times.

PARIS, April 11—France proclaimed today a virtual strike against the United Nations.

In one of the harshest indictments he has ever made against the organization, President de Gaulle said France "did not wish to participate either by her men or her money in any present or possible enterprise of this organization—or of this disorganization."

The President, in response to a question, confirmed his country's refusal to contribute to the costs of the United Nations force in the Congo. A Foreign Ministry spokesman said that in this context the President's statement referred to present or future military enterprises, although the word "military" did not occur in the text of the news conference.

On another issue, President de Gaulle offered a mixture of incentives for Algerian rebel cooperation with France. He warned anew that a "rupture" might result in the partitioning of Algeria to protect those Algerians who wished to remain under French control.

The President called for reform of the United Nations as well as of the Atlantic Alliance. He made it clear that the future of the alliance would be a major

Continued on Page 8, Column 5

187-MILE HEIGHT

Yuri Gagarin, a Major, Makes the Flight in 5-Ton Vehicle

Text of the Tass statement is printed on Page 22.

By United Press International.

MOSCOW, Wednesday, April 12—The Soviet Union announced today it had won the race to put a man into space. Tass, the official press agency, said a man had orbited the earth in a spaceship and had been brought back alive and safe.

A brief announcement said the first reported space man had landed in what was described as the "prescribed area" of the Soviet Union after a historic flight.

A Moscow radio announcer broke into a program and said in emotional tones:

"Russia has successfully launched a man into space. His name is Yuri Gagarin. He was launched in a sputnik named Vostok, which means 'East.'"

Reports on Landing

Tass said that, on landing, Major Gagarin said: "Please report to the party and Government, and personally to Nikita Sergeyevich Khrushchev, that the landing was normal, I feel well, have no injuries or bruises."

He landed at 10:55 A. M. Moscow time [2:55 A. M. New York time].

Earlier, the major reported: "Flight is proceeding normally, I feel well."

After orbiting the earth the major applied a braking device, and the vehicle space landed in the Soviet Union, Tass said.

Major Gagarin, 27 years old, is an industrial technician, and married. He was reported to have received pre-flight training similar to that of the astronauts who will man the United States' first space ships.

Soared to 187 Miles

The announcer said the Sputnik reached a minimum altitude of 175 kilometers (109½ miles) and a maximum altitude of 302 kilometers (187¾ miles).

He said the weight of the Sputnik was 10,395 pounds, or slightly over five tons.

The announcement of the launching came at 2 A. M. New York time.

It said everything functioned normally during the flight. Constant radio contact was maintained between earth and the sputnik, the Moscow radio said.

The announcer said the duration of each revolution around the earth was 89.1 minutes.

The title of the announcement was "The First Human Flight into the Cosmos."

The radio, which was quoting a Tass press agency statement on the launching, said that Maj.

Continued on Page 22, Column 1

White House Confirms Firing; Feat Hailed by U. S. Scientists

By JOHN W. FINNEY
Special to The New York Times.

WASHINGTON, April 12—Pierre Salinger, White House press secretary, announced early today that tracking stations have confirmed the fact that the Soviet Union has launched a satellite today.

James E. Webb, head of the National Aeronautics and Space Administration, described the feat as "a significant accomplishment" that "demonstrates great technical capacity."

"I hope that they can find it possible to make the benefits of this event available to the rest of the world," he said.

Dr. Hugh L. Dryden, deputy administrator of the space agency, commented, "This is something we have been expecting for some time.

"It is only the beginning of man's continued effort in manned exploration of space," he said, "and I think we should continue as rapidly as we can with our own program."

In appraising the achieve

Continued on Page 24, Column 1

NEWS INDEX

The secret story the trial does not tell!
"OPERATION EICHMANN" Starts Today!
RKO ALBEE Fulton & DeKalb, B'klyn.
Also "Heroes Die Young."—Advt.

"All the News
That's Fit to Print"

The New York Times.

LATE CITY EDITION
U. S. Weather Bureau Report (Page 74) forecasts:
Mostly fair today.
Fair tonight and tomorrow.
Temp. range: 56—42; yesterday: 55—42.

VOL. CX . No. 37,705.   © 1961 by The New York Times Company. Times Square, New York 36, N. Y.   NEW YORK, TUESDAY, APRIL 18, 1961.   10 cents beyond 50-mile zone from New York City except on Long Island. Higher in air delivery cities.   FIVE CENTS

SUPREME COURT UPHOLDS UNIONS AGAINST N. L. R. B.

It Upsets Board's Ruling That Contracts Illegally Force Membership

MAILERS' PACTS BACKED

New York Printers' Local and California Teamsters Win on Agreements

By ANTHONY LEWIS
Special to The New York Times.

WASHINGTON, April 17—A series of decisions by the National Labor Relations Board designed to prevent the compelling of union membership was struck down today by the Supreme Court.

The court disposed of a group of major labor cases that will affect dozens of others pending in the lower courts and before the labor relations board. The court did the following things in its principal rulings:

¶It upheld, 6 to 2, contracts of the International Typographical Union with newspapers that provided that the foreman of the composing room or mail room must be an I. T. U. member and must handle all hiring in its operation.

¶By the same vote, it upheld a provision in I. T. U. contracts that made the I. T. U. "general laws" applicable unless in conflict with Federal or state laws.

¶By the same vote, it held there was nothing illegal in bargaining agreements that provided that casual workers, both union and nonunion, be hired through a union-operated hiring hall.

¶It killed, 7 to 1, an N. L. R. B. ruling making labor and management refusal to employes all union dues collected under an agreement found to constitute an illegal closed shop.

Douglas Writes Opinion

Justice William O. Douglas wrote the opinion for the court in all the cases. There was an eight-man court because Justice Felix Frankfurter took no part in the decisions.

Two cases settled long disputes over standard contracts sought by the typographical union. The first of these involved the New York Mailers' Union 6, which is affiliated with the I. T. U., and The New York Daily News and The Wall Street Journal.

The contract specified that mail room foremen must be members of the I. T. U. and must do the hiring. The N. L. R. B. had ruled that the foremen clause was a coercive device to make sure that only union members were hired and that it was thus a violation of the Taft-Hartley Law.

Justice Douglas wrote today that first, the contract said no foreman should be disciplined by the union for carrying out the publisher's instructions, and he concluded that the foreman remained the employer's agent despite his union membership.

Second, Justice Douglas said, the court would "not assume" that the foremen clause would produce discrimination in favor of union members in the absence of actual proof of discrimination. The N. L. R. B. was thus left free to bring a case to show that

Continued on Page 27, Column 3

Jersey Votes Today In Primary Election

By GEORGE CABLE WRIGHT
Special to The New York Times.

TRENTON, April 17 — New Jersey residents will nominate major party candidates for Governor tomorrow, along with candidates for ten of twenty-one State Senate seats and for all sixty seats in the Assembly.

Also at stake will be the nominations for a number of county and local posts.

The polls will open at 7 A. M. and close at 8 P. M.

Interest will center on the balloting for the Republican nomination for Governor. A bitter three-way contest for the nomination came to a close tonight with television and radio appeals by the participants.

They are James P. Mitchell, the former Secretary of Labor, and State Senators Walter H. Jones of Bergen County and

Continued on Page 38, Column 1

U. S. Finds Soviet's Reply On Laos Is Unsatisfactory

Rusk Says Note Is Unclear on Timing and Verification of Cease-Fire— Calls Issue 'Very Critical'

By E. W. KENWORTHY
Special to The New York Times.

WASHINGTON, April 17—Secretary of State Dean Rusk said today that the new Soviet note on Laos did not satisfy the United States on the timing and verification of a cease-fire. This, Mr. Rusk said at his news conference, is a "very critical matter" in any attempt to bring "the situation to a peaceful and satisfactory conclusion." [Introductory statement, Page 18.]

The Soviet note "clarifying" Moscow's first reply to the British proposals of March 23 was delivered to Sir Frank Roberts, the British Ambassador, yesterday. The British Embassy informed Mr. Rusk of the contents of the reply last night.

The British had proposed a three-step procedure—a call for a cease-fire by Britain and the Soviet Union, the co-chairmen of the 1954 Geneva Conference that brought the Indochinese

war to an end; verification of the cease-fire by the three-nation International Control Commission, which observed the carrying out of the Geneva accord in Laos, and a fourteennation conference to set up a neutral, independent Laotian Government.

It was the British intention that these steps should take place in quick order. But Britain and the United States had made clear that there could be no conference until a cease-fire was in effect.

In one respect the Soviet note represented an advance over the earlier response, according to informed sources here. Previously Moscow had indicated that the cease-fire and the conference must take place simultaneously—or very nearly so.

In yesterday's note, these

Continued on Page 2, Column 3

HIGH COURT VOIDS CAFE'S NEGRO BAN

Holds Private Restaurant on State Land in Delaware Cannot Refuse Service

Special to The New York Times.

WASHINGTON, April 17—The Supreme Court held today that a privately operated restaurant situated in a publicly owned parking garage in Wilmington, Del., could not refuse to serve Negroes.

Six justices agreed on that result. The three others thought the case should have been sent back to the Delaware Supreme Court for clarification of its views on state law.

The decision is a significant one because of the light it throws on the established doctrine that only "official action" is covered by the Fourteenth Amendment. The Constitution does not prohibit racial discrimination by private persons or enterprises.

The court concluded that the Government of Delaware was sufficiently involved in this private enterprise, the restaurant, to bring it under the Constitution. In the view of observers here, the court broke at least some new ground in reaching that conclusion.

Justice Tom C. Clark wrote the opinion of the court. He was joined by Chief Justice Earl Warren and Justices Hugo L. Black, William O. Douglas and William J. Brennan Jr.

A separate concurring opinion, resting on quite different grounds, was filed by Justice Potter Stewart. Dissents suggesting that the court should

Continued on Page 26, Column 1

HAUSNER ATTACKS EICHMANN'S PLEA

Israeli Prosecutor Details His Charges After Ex-Nazi Says He Is Not Guilty

Text of decision and Hausner excerpts are on Page 23.

By HOMER BIGART
Special to The New York Times.

JERUSALEM (Israeli Sector), April 17—Attorney General Gideon Hausner began an attack today on Adolf Eichmann's plea of innocence at his trial for responsibility in the killing of millions of Jews.

Earlier in the day Eichmann lost a challenge to the court's jurisdiction and entered his not-guilty plea when the trial was resumed after the week-end recess. Eichmann's plea for a hearing, on his kidnapping from Argentina was rejected by the court.

"In the sense of the indictment I am not guilty," Eichmann had told the three Israeli judges.

He made his statement of innocence in a precise but toneless voice in reply to charges that he had planned the annihilation of 6,000,000 European Jews for the Nazis during World War II.

From the qualified nature of his plea, it was clear that Eichmann's defense would be based on the contention that he was a mere cog in the machinery of genocide and that he was bound by higher orders when he delivered the Jews to death camps.

Standing rigidly erect and

Continued on Page 22, Column 7

GIZENGA OFFICERS ACCEPT MOBUTU AS ARMY'S CHIEF

Kasavubu Agrees to Reform Troops—Signs Accord on Congo-U.N. Cooperation

By HENRY TANNER
Special to The New York Times.

LEOPOLDVILLE, the Congo, April 17—Congolese Army headquarters announced tonight that field commanders operating under the control of the Leftist regime of Antoine Gizenga had recognized the authority of Maj. Gen. Joseph D. Mobutu as military commander in chief.

General Mobutu is the commander of the Central Government's forces.

The announcement said officers of the Gizenga regime had recognized General Mobutu during a conference at Bundoki, on the border of Eastern Province. The province is controlled by Mr. Gizenga.

The announcement also said a cease-fire had been ordered all along the border of Eastern and Equator Provinces.

Here in Leopoldville President Joseph Kasavubu and representatives of Secretary General Dag Hammarskjold signed an agreement on reorganization of the Congolese Army and the withdrawal of some foreign advisers.

Resolution 'Accepted'

The Congolese President and his Government "accepted" the Security Council resolution of Feb. 21 with the "understanding" that the United Nations, in implementing the resolution, respected the sovereignty of the Congo Republic.

The announcement on the military agreement did not say whether Gen. Victor Lundula, who has been commanding Mr. Gizenga's forces, took part in the conference.

Despite rumors of rivalry between him and Mr. Gizenga, General Lundula has consistently stressed his loyalty to his civilian superiors in Stanleyville, capital of Eastern Province.

General Mobutu left Leopoldville a week ago for the border area where the military conference took place. Talks between the two sides had continued intermittently for several weeks with and without his participation.

Kasavubu Plan Backed

In accepting the Security Council resolution the Leopoldville Government "recognized" the necessity for reorganizing the Congolese National Army. It reaffirmed President Kasavubu's earlier proposal that this reorganization take place with United Nations assistance, but under his personal authority as chief of state.

The agreement called for the United Nations to give assistance to the President so that "all foreign civil officials, military and paramilitary mercenaries and political advisers who have not been engaged under his authority" will be re-

Continued on Page 4, Column 2

ANTI-CASTRO UNITS LAND IN CUBA; REPORT FIGHTING AT BEACHHEAD; RUSK SAYS U. S. WON'T INTERVENE

The New York Times   April 18, 1961.
CARIBBEAN STRIFE: Rebel forces attacking Cuba landed in Las Villas Province in the area of Bahia de Cochinos (1, and A on the inset map). Other anti-Castro landings were said to have taken place in area of Santiago de Cuba (2) and in Pinar del Rio (3).

ROA CHARGES U.S. ARMED INVADERS

Tells U.N. That C.I.A. Aided Attacks—'Aggression' Is Denied by Stevenson

Excerpts from Stevenson and Roa statements are on Page 16.

By THOMAS J. HAMILTON
Special to The New York Times.

UNITED NATIONS, N. Y., April 17—Dr. Raul Roa, Foreign Minister of Cuba, charged today that his country had been invaded this morning "by a force of mercenaries, organized, financed and armed by the Government of the United States."

Dr. Roa told the General Assembly's Political Committee that the attack had been launched from points in Florida and Guatemala under the direction of the Central Intelligence Agency, which he called the "Gestapo." The Gestapo was the Nazi security police force.

He continued to use terms made familiar to nazism by calling Dr. José Miró Cardona, head of the anti-Castro Cuban Revolutionary Council, the "gauleiter." Gauleiters were regional party leaders under the Nazis.

Refugees Assume Control

In the last ten days, the Cuban refugees have assumed control of the operations against Premier Fidel Castro. Accordingly, official Washington could not be sure of the fate of all the small parties that went ashore.

Secretary Rusk was extremely cautious in his remarks on the situation at his news conference this morning. What happens in Cuba, he said, is for the Cuban people to decide. He added, however, that the Administration was "not indifferent" to the intrusion of the "Communist conspiracy" into this hemisphere and promised to "work together with other governments of this hemisphere to meet efforts by this conspiracy to extend its penetration." [Opening statement, Page 18.] On this point, considerable attention was being paid here

Florida Launching Denied

Adlai E. Stevenson, chief United States delegate, said in reply that "the United States has committed no aggression against Cuba and no offensive has been launched from Florida or from any other part of the United States."

[In Guatemala, the Government denied that it had participated in any attack on Cuba.]

Just before the debate ended late this evening Dr. Roa charged that two jet planes from a United States carrier had escorted a Cuban rebel plane to safety this afternoon. He also alleged that forces from the United States Naval Base at Guantanamo had entered Oriente Province, where a

Continued on Page 17, Column 1

Walker Is Relieved of Command While Army Checks Birch Ties

Special to The New York Times.

WASHINGTON, April 17—The Army said today that Maj. Gen. Edwin A. Walker had been relieved of his command in Germany while an investigation was made into reports that he had been indoctrinating his troops with the views of the John Birch Society.

The announcement said that Secretary of the Army Elvis J. Stahr Jr. had ordered General Walker transferred immediately from command of the front-line Twenty-fourth Division "pending the outcome of an official investigation."

The investigation will involve "certain published statements and actions of General Walker," the Army said.

The announcement did not mention the Birch Society. However, officials acknowledged that the transfer and investigation had been prompted by allegations that the 51-year-old general had been urging the views of the Right-Wing group upon his troops for the last six months.

The Overseas Weekly, a privately owned newspaper distributed among American troops in Europe, reported last week that General Walker had instituted a special troop-indoctrination program using materials and publications of the society.

General Walker accused the newspaper yesterday of being "immoral, unscrupulous, corrupt and destructive." The newspaper stood by its original report and said that his charges

Continued on Page 24, Column 6

Rusk Declares Sympathy Of Nation for Castro Foes

By JAMES RESTON
Special to The New York Times.

WASHINGTON, April 17—Secretary of State Dean Rusk expressed today the sympathy of the American people for those who struck against Castroism in Cuba, but emphasized "there is not and will not be any intervention there by United States forces."

The Administration did not deny that it was giving material support to the raiding parties, but this aid was undoubtedly on a much smaller

Transcript of Rusk's news conference is on Page 18.

scale than originally planned here and the landings in Cuba were much smaller than excited reports of "invasion" suggested.

No more than 200 to 300 men were involved in the week-end landings on the vast coastline of Cuba, according to reliable information reaching here.

In fact, the landings of the last forty-eight hours were not designed to get a lot of fighting men on the ground, but to provide supplies for the anti-Castro underground already operating there as a result of at least six other landings that have taken place over the last few months.

Atmosphere Is Tense

An atmosphere of tension gripped the Soviet capital after the announcement at 4 P. M. by the Moscow radio that "an armed intervention against Cuba had begun."

It was felt by most Western experts that the Soviet reaction would be confined to strong diplomatic representations, complaints in the United Nations and a propaganda onslaught against the United States.

Western experts said that Mr. Khrushchev's statement seemed to have more applicability to an invasion of Cuba by United States forces than to an attack of the type being under-

Continued on Page 17, Column 2

PREMIER DEFIANT

Says His Troops Battle Heroically to Repel Attacking Force

The texts of Castro appeals are printed on Page 14.

By TAD SZULC
Special to The New York Times.

MIAMI, Tuesday, April 18—Rebel troops opposed to Premier Fidel Castro landed before dawn yesterday on the swampy southern coast of Cuba in Las Villas Province.

The attack, which was supported from the air, was announced by the rebels and confirmed by the Cuban Government.

After fourteen hours of silence on the progress of the assault, the Government radio early today in a terse communiqué signed by Premier Castro announcing only that "our armed forces are continuing to fight the enemy heroically."

The announcement, made shortly before 1 A. M., said that within the next few hours details of "our successes" would be given.

The communiqué came amid a wave of rebel assertions of victories, new landings and internal uprisings. The rebel spokesmen were acclaiming important progress in new landings in Oriente and Pinar del Rio Provinces, but none of these reports could be confirmed.

Government Reports Battle

The Government communiqué said a battle had been fought in the southeastern part of Las Villas Province, where yesterday morning's landings occurred.

Although the communiqué was acknowledged by Premier Castro, the Cuban leader has not spoken to his nation since the attack began. An earlier communiqué, issued yesterday, reported the rebel landings.

In a communiqué issued last night, the Revolutionary Council, the top command of the rebel forces, said merely that military supplies and equipment were landed successfully on the marshy beachhead. The communiqué added that "some armed resistance" by supporters of Premier Castro had been overcome.

Premier Castro was reported to have escaped injury in an early-morning air raid yesterday near the beachhead.

The Revolutionary Council's announcement spoke of action in Matanzas Province, indicating that the rebels might have

Continued on Page 14, Column 1

MOSCOW BLAMES U. S. FOR ATTACK

Izvestia Asserts 'American Hirelings' Invade Cuba— Khrushchev Confers

By SEYMOUR TOPPING
Special to The New York Times.

MOSCOW, April 17—The Soviet Union charged tonight that the United States was responsible for the landing in Cuba by what it described as "American hirelings."

Izvestia, the Soviet Government newspaper, contended that plans for landing anti-Castro forces in Cuba had been worked out and inspired by "American imperialists."

"On all continents voices now are crying out determinedly for an end to the armed aggression against Cuba and for the defense of the freedom and independence of the Cuban people," Izvestia said.

At his vacation retreat in Sochi on the Black Sea, Premier Khrushchev conferred on the Cuban crisis with Foreign Minister Andrei A. Gromyko. A formal Government statement is expected tomorrow.

The Soviet leader also had noted that the United States was no longer out of range of Soviet missiles.

Continued on Page 17, Column 2

CHANTING CUBANS BACK CASTRO HERE

1,000 in Midtown March Dispersed by Police

Nearly 1,000 chanting, signbearing pro-Castro Cubans demonstrated last night outside the United Nations and the United States Mission to the United Nations and in the Times Square area.

Heavy police details had kept the crowds behind barriers most of the day and no violence erupted until a smaller group of pro-Castro Cubans blocked pedestrian traffic in Times Square. The police made two arrests and two policemen were injured during a brief scuffle with the demonstrators.

Many of the demonstrators carried Cuban flags and pictures of Dr. Castro as they marched along the United Nations Plaza along Forty-second Street to the corner of Eighth Avenue and Forty-third Street.

An emergency police signal brought ten radio cars and ten mounted policemen to that area. The crowd then broke up into four factions and departed in different directions.

A few minutes later, at 8 P. M., a smaller group of demonstrators formed on the sidewalk on Broadway between

Continued on Page 14, Column 5

Eisenhowers Are Welcomed Home to Pennsylvania

General and Mrs. Eisenhower in Harrisburg with Gov. David L. Lawrence of Pennsylvania
United Press International Telephoto

By The Associated Press.

HARRISBURG, Pa., April 17—Thousands of persons welcomed former President Dwight D. Eisenhower and Mrs. Eisenhower home to Pennsylvania today. The gathering was the state's official

welcome for General Eisenhower, who left the White House Jan. 20. The former President, looking tanned and rested after a six-week vacation in California, was obviously touched. Gov. David L. Lawrence, a Democrat, headed

the state and city officials on the platform. The Eisenhowers have a farm home in Gettysburg, thirty-five miles southwest of this capital city. It is the only home they have ever owned. They left for home by car after the ceremonies.

"All the News That's Fit to Print"

The New York Times.

LATE CITY EDITION
U. S. Weather Bureau Report (Page 62) forecast:
Cloudy, warm, chance of rain late today or tonight and tomorrow.
Temp. range: 61—46; yesterday: 70—47.

VOL. CX..No. 37,723.   © 1961 by The New York Times Company. Times Square, New York 36, N. Y.   NEW YORK, SATURDAY, MAY 6, 1961.   10 cents beyond 50-mile zone from New York City except on Long Island. Higher in air delivery cities.   FIVE CENTS

U. S. HURLS MAN 115 MILES INTO SPACE; SHEPARD WORKS CONTROLS IN CAPSULE, REPORTS BY RADIO IN 15-MINUTE FLIGHT

JOHNSON TO MEET LEADERS IN ASIA ON U.S. TROOP USE

President Says Decision on South Vietnam Action Will Await Report

TALKS SET IN CAPITALS

Ngo Dinh Diem Is Expected to Seek American Units to Deter Red Attack

Transcript of news conference and summary, Page 14.

By WILLIAM J. JORDEN
Special to The New York Times.

WASHINGTON, May 5—President Kennedy said today that the assignment of United States armed forces to South Vietnam would be one of several important matters Vice President Lyndon B. Johnson would discuss on his coming trip to Asia. [Opening statement and Question 4, Page 14.]

The President confirmed that the possibility of sending United States troops to Southeast Asia was under study. He indicated that the final decision would depend on the results of Mr. Johnson's talks in Saigon with President Ngo Dinh Diem and others.

Mr. Kennedy said at a news conference that a special task force in the Government was working on problems related to helping South Vietnam maintain its independence. The question has been considered by the National Security Council as well, he said.

Vital Assignment

Mr. Johnson is expected to leave next Tuesday for the Far East. He also will meet with top Government officials in Bangkok, Thailand; Manila, and other capitals.

The President today described the Johnson mission as "an extremely important assignment."

It is widely assumed here that President Ngo will ask for the assignment of at least a token force of United States troops and regard it as a guarantee of United States' involvement should his country be attacked in force by the Communist North.

Mr. Kennedy did not touch on the matter today, but it is known that the Government is also considering the possibility of sending a similar token force to Thailand. The latter is allied to the United States in the

Continued on Page 3, Column 4

NIXON ASKS DRIVE TO OFFSET SOVIET

Bids Kennedy Rally America to a Fresh Foreign Policy

Excerpts from Nixon speech are printed on Page 2.

By AUSTIN C. WEHRWEIN
Special to The New York Times.

CHICAGO, May 5—Former Vice President Richard M. Nixon urged President Kennedy today to rally the American people for a new kind of American foreign policy.

Mr. Nixon called for a "searching reappraisal of the free world's ability, particularly America's ability, to deal with the kind of aggression in which Communists are now engaging."

He further revealed that he had given President Kennedy the "assurance that I will support him to the hilt in backing positive action he may decide is necessary to resist Communist aggression."

[President Kennedy, meanwhile, sent his nuclear test-ban negotiator back to Geneva with an implied warning that the United States might not continue the talks much longer without some prospect of a safeguarded treaty.]

To meet such threats, the former Vice President said the United States should be prepared to act alone if swift action were needed when machinery for collective action was being set up.

The lesson of Cuba and Laos, he said, is this:

"We must never talk bigger than we are prepared to act. When our words are strong and our actions are timid, we

Continued on Page 2, Column 3

Talks Open in Laos On Truce Details; Meeting 'Friendly'

By JACQUES NEVARD
Special to The New York Times.

HIN HEUP, Laos, May 5—Military representatives of the pro-Western Laotian Government and the pro-Communist Pathet Lao rebels held a preliminary conference here today on machinery for continuing the cease-fire that became effective Wednesday.

The conference lasted one hour and five minutes and was described as "friendly."

According to a Laotian Army spokesman, Col. Oudom Sananikone, the meeting did not take up any political questions.

There appeared to be few tangible results of the talks, but Colonel Oudom Sananikone stressed that the meeting was a preliminary one.

He said that the first Pathet Lao request was that the next meeting take place at Namone, thirty-five miles north of here.

Continued on Page 3, Column 2

2 BILLION AID PLAN FOR BRAZIL IS NEAR

U. S. Presses World-Wide Program of New Loans and Debt Deferments

By TAD SZULC
Special to The New York Times.

WASHINGTON, May 5—An international financial rescue package worth more than $2,000,000,000 is being prepared for Brazil. Negotiations, already well advanced, involve the United States, six Western European countries, Japan and the International Monetary Fund.

The agreements, which may be announced late next week, call for new loans totaling nearly $630,000,000. About $340,000,000 of this is to be provided by the United States. The remainder will take the form of a postponement in the repayment of much of Brazil's huge foreign debt.

This international financial operation, the largest ever involving a Latin-American country and one of the largest anywhere in postwar years, is designed to provide President Janio Quadros with extra time and resources to reorganize his economy.

Broad Effort in View

The United States is playing a key role in putting together the Brazilian package. It will also supply separate smaller loans to bolster the economies of Venezuela and Bolivia. Venezuela, which is facing serious budget difficulties, expects to receive soon an initial loan of $50,000,000.

Besides these emergency measures to assist the economies of individual Latin-American republics, the United States moved today to call a special inter-American conference to blueprint long-range economic and social development programs.

President Kennedy announced at his news conference that the United States' delegation to the Council of the Organization of American States had been in-

Continued on Page 3, Column 4

Kennedy Plans Aid To Retrain Jobless And Spur Recovery

By PETER BRAESTRUP
Special to The New York Times.

WASHINGTON, May 5—The Kennedy Administration expects to ask Congress for at least $75,000,000 to provide retraining for the long-term unemployed. Other new anti-recession measures also are being considered.

The key question that President Kennedy has yet to decide is whether to break the Administration's self-imposed limit on Federal spending in an effort to stimulate the economy and spur employment.

The $75,000,000 program for retraining workers who have been laid off by technological change and by the decay of their own industries will not materially affect the budget. Nor will the President's orders to the Pentagon to channel more defense contracts to small

Continued on Page 17, Column 1

Elizabeth Visits Pope in Vatican

Pope John XXIII in private audience with Queen Elizabeth

By ARNALDO CORTESI
Special to The New York Times.

ROME, May 5—Pope John XXIII received Queen Elizabeth II and Prince Philip in a private audience today with traditional pomp and ceremony. The meeting was marked by extreme cordiality. Addressing the Queen in French, the Pope said that relations between Britain and

Continued on Page 19, Column 1

RETURN: Astronaut rides in one of helicopters carrying his Mercury capsule to the Lake Champlain

LAUNCHING: Rocket lifts the capsule   **SAFE ABOARD:** On the Lake Champlain's deck, Comdr. Alan B. Shepard Jr. views capsule he occupied
Associated Press Wirephotos

MAYOR IS UPHELD ON CHARTER LAW

But Court Reverses Ban on Action by Council, Opening Way to Rival Proposals

By RONALD MAIORANA

Mayor Wagner's right to appoint a Charter Revision Commission was upheld by Justice Irving Saypol yesterday in State Supreme Court.

However, Justice Saypol ruled invalid part of the law under which the Mayor had acted. This part excluded the City Council from Charter-revision activity.

Lawyers said the ruling appeared to make possible the enactment of the City Council's own plan for a Charter Revision Commission. Thus, it is conceivable, they said, that two competing Charters—one drawn by the Mayor's commission and the other by a commission created by the Council—could be submitted to the voters Nov. 7.

In a twenty-two-page decision that caused confusion at City Hall Justice Saypol ruled that the section of the state law that had the effect of bypassing the City Council was invalid because it was an improper delegation of legislative power. He said: "The newly enacted au-

Continued on Page 22, Column 1

Shepard Had Periscope: 'What a Beautiful View'

By JOHN W. FINNEY
Special to The New York Times.

CAPE CANAVERAL, Fla., May 5—"All systems go * * * Everything A-O.K. * * * Mission very smooth * * * What a beautiful view! * * * Coming in for a landing."

These were the reports of Comdr. Alan B. Shepard Jr. as he rode the capsule Freedom 7 115 miles up into space today in the United States' first step toward manned exploration of space. His "A-O.K.," is a rocket engineer term meaning double O.K. or perfect.

In a calm, methodical way he reported back by radio on every detail of his fifteen-minute flight, even during the moments of greatest stress as his capsule accelerated from the launching pad and then quickly decelerated upon re-entering the earth's atmosphere.

And there were moments of excitement in his voice, such as when he viewed much of the Eastern Coast of the United States through a periscope from 115 miles up in space.

"What a beautiful view!" he exclaimed into a microphone inside his visored space helmet and then, according to instructions, he returned to scientific observations to report that the cloud cover was three- to four-tenths and was obscuring much of the coast up through Cape Hatteras.

Three-to-four-tenths cloud cover is a description used by

Continued on Page 10, Column 1

14 Dead, 57 Hurt by Tornado; 2 Towns in Oklahoma Hard Hit

By The Associated Press.

POTEAU, Okla., May 5—A vicious tornado tore through two tiny eastern Oklahoma communities near here tonight, killing at least fourteen persons and injuring fifty-seven.

Ten were reported dead at Howe and four at Reichert. The death toll could go higher as rescue workers dug into the debris.

There was a report that a light plane—trying to avoid the massive storm cloud—crashed after a wing tore off. The highway patrol said that a woman who lived in the area reported she saw the plane go down west of Summerfield.

It was a grim anniversary for this rolling, wooded area some 200 miles southeast of Oklahoma City. Just one year ago twelve were killed when a twister destroyed most of the downtown area of Wilburton.

Tornadoes had plagued Oklahoma for two days, but until tonight there had been only one fatality from the scores of funnels sighted.

Two of the dead were babies. One father died with his 3-month-old son and a mother with her 14-month-old boy.

Tiny farms are scattered throughout the twister-pounded

Continued on Page 62, Column 6

NATION TO WIDEN ITS SPACE EFFORTS

Kennedy Wants More Funds —He Telephones Shepard to Offer Congratulations

Texts of Kennedy statement and call to Shepard, Page 11

By DAVID HALBERSTAM
Special to The New York Times.

WASHINGTON, May 5—An even greater effort in the exploration of space was promised today by President Kennedy.

On the day of this country's first manned space flight, he told a news conference he would make an additional request for appropriations for its space program this year.

"We are going to make a substantially larger effort in space," he declared. [Question 1, Page 14.]

Earlier in the day the President telephoned his personal congratulations to Comdr. Alan B. Shepard Jr., the nation's first space traveler, in a call from the White House to the aircraft carrier Lake Champlain.

The President also congratulated the commander's wife and his six fellow-astronauts.

Commander Shepard will visit Washington Monday. There will be a ceremony at noon on

Continued on Page 11, Column 7

PRESIDENT TO ASK INCOME TAX CUTS

Drop Next Year Is Planned, Dillon Tells House Unit

By JOHN D. MORRIS
Special to The New York Times.

WASHINGTON, May 5—The Kennedy Administration plans to lay before Congress next year a tax reform program that will include reduction of individual income taxes.

Secretary of the Treasury Douglas Dillon told the House Ways and Means Committee the plan today but gave no details. He made it clear, however, that taxpayers with high incomes would probably be among the chief beneficiaries of a proposed reduction in rates.

"I think those in high brackets deserve relief," he said.

Mr. Dillon was questioned for nearly three hours, mainly by Republican committee members, as he completed three days of testimony on tax-revision legislation being sought now by the Administration.

The pending proposals include $1,700,000,000 a year in special tax credits for business enterprise to encourage modernization and expansion of plant and equipment. Tax laws on foreign income, business expense accounts and stock dividends

Continued on Page 22, Column 3

IN FINE CONDITION

Astronaut Drops Into the Sea Four Miles From Carrier

Excerpts from radioed reports by Shepard, Page 8

By RICHARD WITKIN
Special to The New York Times.

CAPE CANAVERAL, Fla., May 5—A slim, cool Navy test pilot was rocketed 115 miles into space today.

Thirty-seven-year-old Comdr. Alan B. Shepard Jr. thus became the first American space explorer.

Commander Shepard landed safely 302 miles out at sea fifteen minutes after the launching. He was quickly lifted aboard a Marine Corps helicopter.

"Boy, what a ride!" he said, as he was flown to the aircraft carrier Lake Champlain four miles away.

Extensive physical examinations were begun immediately. Tonight doctors reported Commander Shepard in "excellent" condition, suffering no ill effects.

Major U. S. Step

The near-perfect flight represented the United States' first major step in the race to explore space with manned space craft.

True, it was only a modest leap compared with the once-around-the-earth orbital flight of Maj. Yuri A. Gagarin of the Soviet Union.

The Russian's speed of more than 17,000 miles an hour was almost four times Commander Shepard's 4,500. The distance the Russian traveled was almost 100 times as great.

But Commander Shepard maneuvered his craft in space—something the Russians have not claimed for Major Gagarin.

All in all, the Shepard flight was welcomed almost rapturous-

Continued on Page 8, Column 1

ASTRONAUT: Commander Shepard removes space suit.

Nation Exults Over Space Feat; City Plans to Honor Astronaut

By ROBERT CONLEY

The successful flight of America's first astronaut, Comdr. Alan B. Shepard Jr., roused the country yesterday to one of its highest peaks of exultation since the end of World War II.

The achievement brought relief from the strain of hearing about the Soviet Union's success in orbiting a man, feelings of new hope for the future from Maine to Hawaii and dancing in the streets at New York's Columbus Circle.

"Wonderful." "Tremendous." "The greatest thing that ever happened," thousands of persons said as the reaction took hold across the country.

"He made it," a woman gasped in Chicago, then broke into tears. "He made it."

New York City laid plans for the "most fabulous" ticker tape welcome ever given—one that a city official said would be "even bigger than the one for Charles Lindbergh."

In Washington, Congressmen moved to bestow the nation's

Continued on Page 11, Column 5

NEWS INDEX

	Page		Page
Art	63	Music	26-27
Books	23	Obituaries	29
Bridge	21	Real Estate	50
Business	36	Screen	26-27
Buying	40	Ships and Air	73
Churches	48	Society	58
Crossword	23	Sports	30-34
Editorial	20	Theatres	26-27
Events Today	32	TV and Radio	71
Fashions	24	U. N. Proceedings	3
Financial	36-47	U. S. Events	14
Food	24	Wash. Proceedings	14
Letters	20	Weather	62

News Summary and Index, Page 33

"All the News
That's Fit to Print"

The New York Times.

LATE CITY EDITION
U. S. Weather Bureau Report (Page 40) forecast:
Considerable cloudiness today;
occasional rain tonight, tomorrow.
Temp. range: 72—59; yesterday: 71—49.
Temp.-Hum. index: middle 60's; yesterday: 66.

VOL. CXI. No. 37,859.   © 1961 by The New York Times Company.
Times Square, New York 36, N. Y.   NEW YORK, TUESDAY, SEPTEMBER 19, 1961.   10 cents beyond 50-mile zone from New York City,
except on Long Island. Higher in air delivery cities.   FIVE CENTS

HAMMARSKJOLD DIES IN AFRICAN AIR CRASH; KENNEDY GOING TO U.N. IN SUCCESSION CRISIS

MAYOR APPOINTS 9 CIVIC LEADERS AS SCHOOL BOARD

Group Is Due to Be Sworn Today but Injunction Is Sought to Bar Change

By PAUL CROWELL

Mayor Wagner named a new nine-member Board of Education yesterday to replace the present board, which goes out of existence tomorrow.

The new board, which like the old one is unsalaried, is scheduled to be sworn in at City Hall today at 3:30 P. M., but there may be a last-minute hitch.

Two members of the outgoing board moved in Supreme Court late yesterday to have the Legislature's recent action dismissing the old board declared illegal and to prevent Mayor Wagner, in the meantime, from swearing in the members of the new board this afternoon.

A legal representative of the city will appear at the Brooklyn court at 10 o'clock this morning to contest both the complaint and the appeal for an injunction against the Mayor.

'Red Letter Day'

For his own part, before the legal action was instituted, Mayor Wagner expressed the hope that the swearing-in ceremony scheduled for the new board members this afternoon would mark "a red letter day for the City of New York for all the days to come."

He expressed the belief that "this can be the best board our city has ever had, possibly the best board any city ever had."

The board has seven members from Manhattan, and one each from Brooklyn and Queens.

The board was chosen from a list of twenty-six recommended by an eleven-man panel set up by the state on Aug. 21. A special session of the Legislature had passed a law to dissolve the present board and pave the way for a new one.

Appointees Listed

The Mayor's appointees are:
Brendan Byrne, public relations man, 85-19 118th Street, Kew Gardens, Queens.
James B. Donovan, lawyer, 35 Prospect Park West, Brooklyn.
Lloyd K. Garrison, lawyer, 133 East Sixty-third Street.
John F. Hennessy, engineer, 144 East Thirty-ninth Street.
Morris Iushewitz, labor leader, 386 Park Avenue South.
Samuel R. Pierce, lawyer, 2225 Fifth Avenue.
Anna M. Rosenberg, public relations consultant, 14 Fifth Avenue.
Max J. Rubin, lawyer, 101 West Fifty-fifth Street.
Clarence O. Senior, economist and sociologist, 15 Claremont Avenue.

In announcing the appointments, the Mayor said that he had chosen the board "without regard to politics."

"I do not even know the political affiliations of those I have selected," he said, "except in the cases where I have had previous personal knowledge." It was

Continued on Page 30, Column 6

Militia Seizes 176 In Cuban Outbreak

Special to The New York Times.

HAVANA, Sept. 18—Militiamen in plainclothes who had mingled with the crowd arrested 176 persons last night after a demonstration had broken out during a religious procession near here.

Eighteen demonstrators were injured, three seriously, when the militiamen swung clubs they had hidden in their clothing.

The outburst occurred one week after a larger anti-Government demonstration before a Havana church. Seven were injured, one fatally, by the militia and many were arrested in that demonstration.

The new incident took place a few hours after 136 refugees had been deported from Cuba

Continued on Page 13, Column 1

"DACRON" ® A NEW WORD FOR FALL. "Dacron" polyester fiber now improves the fall wool suit . . . adds built-in neatness to traditional wool.—Advt.

New Group Seeks Funds to Purchase And Repair Slums

By MARTIN ARNOLD

A nonprofit organization has been set up here to offer inducements to private investors to buy and improve slum tenements.

The organization, headed by former Deputy Mayor Paul T. O'Keefe, would select the buildings, find buyers and repair, operate and maintain the tenements.

Private investors would own the buildings and would collect profits agreed upon between them and the organization.

8 to 10 Per Cent Profit

The profits usually would be 8 to 10 per cent. Many unimproved slum tenements now bring profits up to 25 per cent.

Laurance S. Rockefeller, son of the late John D. Rockefeller Jr., has agreed to invest up to $750,000 in tenements to get the program started.

Mr. Rockefeller will not be part of the organization. A spokesman said last night that Mr. Rockefeller had agreed to help the program because he felt it was "a way to get responsible private money into slum housing. It was a way he could be reasonably rewarded into such housing."

The Rockefeller spokesman and other supporters of the program emphasized that the project would not be charitable or philanthropic. Rather,

Continued on Page 25, Column 1

3 STATES TO GET U. S. TRANSIT AID

New Committee Wins Pledge of Support From 2 Bodies at Orientation Meeting

By LLOYD GARRISON
Special to The New York Times.

WASHINGTON, Sept. 18—The newly created Tri-State Transportation Committee won Government support today for its plans to improve transport and commuter service in the New York metropolitan area. Committee members from New York, New Jersey and Connecticut met for more than three hours with representatives of the Housing and Home Finance Agency and the Bureau of Public Roads.

The committee did not ask for specific amounts of money, he added, but would undoubtedly seek financial support "sometime soon."

Government participants in the meeting indicated funds would be made available if requested.

Anxious to Aid

"This is the kind of program we would like to assist," said Morton J. Schussheim, assistant administrator for program policy at the Housing and Home Finance Agency. The agency is involved in transportation problems through its urban renewal service.

His enthusiasm was echoed by another Federal representative, Edward H. Holmes, assistant commissioner of the Bureau of Public Roads.

Dr. Ronan acted as regional spokesman at the meeting. The New Jersey delegation was led by Highway Commissioner Dwight R. G. Palmer and the Connecticut by Carl LaLumia, executive aide to Gov. John Dempsey.

Roger H. Gilman, on leave from the Port of New York Authority to serve as executive director of the committee, attended the meeting but departed immediately after it had ended.

The tri-state committee was established three weeks ago to study and make recommendations on improving commuter service and to attack also problems of motor traffic, air travel and freight transportation. Its

Continued on Page 18, Column 3

Rescue workers study wreckage of the Secretary General's plane in Northern Rhodesia.
Associated Press Radiophoto

Secretary General Dag Hammarskjold
The New York Times

Adenauer Begins Efforts To Form Coalition in Bonn

By SYDNEY GRUSON
Special to The New York Times.

BONN, Germany, Sept. 18—Chancellor Adenauer began fighting for his political life today as a result of his party's heavy losses in the West German elections.

With the Christian Democratic Union's parliamentary majority wiped out yesterday, the 85-year-old Chancellor lost no time in seeking a coalition with the Free Democratic party led by Dr. Erich Mende. The Free Democrats made the biggest gain in the election.

Dr. Adenauer rejected the bid of Willy Brandt, West Berlin's Mayor, for a national coalition embracing the Social Democrats as well as the two other parties. A coalition with the Socialists, the Chancellor said at a news conference, "would not correspond with our democratic feeling."

The big question was not whether Dr. Adenauer could set the terms for a coalition but whether he could survive the demands for his retirement and his replacement as Chancellor by Dr. Ludwig Erhard, the 64-year-old Minister of Economics.

There was considerable speculation that the Free Democrats would agree to Dr. Adenauer's continuing as Chancellor for a limited period—just long enough to carry the onus for accepting the hard decisions facing West Germany.

With the long, bitter campaign and the vote at last out of the way, a beginning was in sight for the long-awaited public discussion of these decisions.

The Free Democrats' news service, commenting on the election results, which left the party holding the balance of power, said:

"An epoch of German postwar history has ended. The coming months and years will destroy many illusions and place extraordinary demands on our people."

The statement reflected a continuing but decreasing reluctance to specify the demands. Two are accepted by almost all West German officials as inevitable: the acceptance of the Oder-Neisse border as Germany's frontier with Poland and some form of de facto recognition for Communist East Germany, with all that means to the loss of hope for the reunification of Germany.

No one here is yet sure whether the West Germans would

Continued on Page 3, Column 3

2D SOVIET ROCKET FIRED 7,500 MILES

Lands in Same Pacific Area as Shot Last Wednesday

By THEODORE SHABAD
Special to The New York Times.

MOSCOW, Sept. 18—The Soviet Union fired a second rocket 7,500 miles into the central Pacific yesterday.

An announcement today by Tass, the Soviet press agency, said that the dummy of the rocket's last stage had landed "in the immediate proximity" of the spot where the first rocket of the current series hit the water last Wednesday.

Today's brief Tass statement emphasized the accuracy of the Soviet shots. It referred to the "high-precision control system" of the rocket and called it "another big achievement of Soviet rocketry."

[In Washington, the Atomic Energy Commission announced that the Soviet Union on Monday exploded its thirteenth nuclear device since it resumed testing Sept. 1. The yield of the atmospheric explosion was "on the order of a megaton" and the site was "in the vicinity of Novaya Zemlya," the commission said.]

The present series of test shots was announced on Sept. 10. Ships and planes were advised to keep away from the target area, 1,000 miles southwest of Hawaii, during

Continued on Page 8, Column 1

ACTING SECRETARY IS SOUGHT AT U. N.

Delegates Favoring Proposal to Appoint Mongi Slim— Assembly Meets Today

By THOMAS J. HAMILTON
Special to The New York Times.

UNITED NATIONS, N. Y., Sept. 18—On the eve of the opening of the United Nations General Assembly session, a move was developing to have Mongi Slim of Tunisia take over the coordination of the Secretariat until the election of a successor to Dag Hammarskjold.

The death of Mr. Hammarskjold saddened delegates to the General Assembly, which will open its sixteenth session tomorrow afternoon.

Delegates and members of the Secretariat mourned the death of an able diplomat who had helped bring about compromise solutions of dangerous issues in an age of nuclear stalemates.

Long Struggle Feared

There were grave forebodings of a long struggle over the choice of a Secretary General who would be acceptable to both the Soviet Union and the Western powers.

The interim plan gained momentum after Dr. Ali Sastroamidjojo of Indonesia, Mr. Slim's only competitor for President of the sixteenth session of the Assembly withdrew this afternoon on the understanding that the African-Asian group would support him for President next year.

Frederick H. Boland of Ireland, who was President of the fifteenth session, and a number of Asian, African and European delegates are understood to favor the plan, under which Mr. Slim would, in effect, become Acting Secretary General.

Mr. Boland will call the sixteenth session to order at 3 P. M. tomorrow. Its formal business will be limited to the election of Mr. Slim and the vice presidents and committee chairmen, who will serve under Mr. Slim as the Assembly's Steering Committee.

Soviet May Force Demand

The United States and some Western delegations declined to comment on the plan, which as far as is still in the informal stage. However, other delegates expressed the belief that it would be accepted without opposition unless the Soviet Union decided to force an immediate showdown on its demand for the liquidation of the office of Secretary General and the substitution of a three-man directorate.

A Soviet spokesman said today that his delegation would press this demand, which was submitted to the General Assembly by Premier Khrushchev a year ago, at the impending session.

Although the Soviet delegate, Valerian A. Zorin, refused to join other members of the Security Council in praising Mr.

Continued on Page 16, Column 2

President to Assure U. N. U. S. Backs a Single Chief

By JAMES RESTON
Special to The New York Times.

WASHINGTON, Sept. 18—President Kennedy decided tonight to intervene personally in the constitutional crisis created at the United Nations by the death of Secretary General Dag Hammarskjold.

The White House announced that the President would address the General Assembly in New York, probably Friday. His purpose in doing so is to reassure the delegates and the Secretariat that the United States supports the coordination of the Secretariat until the election of a successor to Dag Hammarskjold and is determined to do everything possible to maintain the executive authority of the office of the Secretary General.

The President's plan to address the United Nations was made known after he had paid a tribute to Mr. Hammarskjold, in which he said:

"I am hopeful that the members of the United Nations, recognizing his untiring labors, will attempt in the coming sessions and in the years to come to try to build the United Nations into the effective instrument for peace which was Dag Hammarskjold's great ambition."

Interim Plan Sought

As for the crisis at the United Nations, the United States believes that an interim arrangement must be made quickly, with the concurrence of the Soviet Union if possible, to enable the office of the Secretary General to carry out the past instructions of the world organization.

This is an urgent matter in the Congo, where United Nations troops in secessionist Katanga Province have been under fire and must be reinforced quickly.

Officials here and in New York were in constant consultation today about how this could be done in the face of the Soviet Union's opposition to an

Continued on Page 14, Column 1

KATANGA IMPERILS MAIN U. N. AIR BASE

Loss Would Be Second Big Defeat—Tshombe Units Claim Capture of 500

Special to The New York Times.

ELISABETHVILLE, the Congo, Sept. 18—United Nations troops guarding the big air base at Kamina, in Katanga Province, were reported under heavy fire today and in danger of being overwhelmed by their Katangan attackers.

[According to The Associated Press, Katangan military radio messages reported the capture of the Kamina base and the surrender of its 500 Irish and Swedish defenders.]

The loss of the air base would be the second major defeat for the United Nations in the six days of fighting here. This morning, the surrender of a garrison of 158 Irish troops was completed at Jadotville, sixty-five miles north of Elisabethville.

With the military situation deteriorating, United Nations forces here spent an anxious morning waiting for news of Secretary General Dag Hammarskjold. Word of his death brought sorrow to the already grim band of United Nations soldiers and officials.

Outside this capital of Katanga, the secessionist forces are more numerous than they

Continued on Page 14, Column 1

French to End the Occupation Of Bizerte City, Starting Today

By THOMAS F. BRADY
Special to The New York Times.

TUNIS, Sept. 18—French and Tunisian representatives agreed today on a plan for the withdrawal of French troops from the city of Bizerte and its environs.

The withdrawal will start tomorrow morning and continue through Saturday.

Negotiations leading to the troop pullback began after a proposal by President Habib Bourguiba of Tunisia Sept. 7 to permit the French to maintain their naval-air base near Bizerte for the duration of the Berlin crisis if they would agree to a timetable for the eventual evacuation of the base.

The occupation of Bizerte and the surrounding area began July 20 when French forces moved against Tunisian troops and civilians who had barricaded roads leading to the base entrance. Fighting had broken out July 19 after France defied a Tunisian demand for a promise to evacuate the base.

In return for ending of the city's occupation, the Tunisians have guaranteed to the French the right of circulation among the scattered military installations in the Bizerte region and freedom of movement through the entrance channel from the Mediterranean Sea to the Lake of Bizerte, on which the installations are situated.

The first concrete step toward a solution of the Bizerte dispute was an exchange of prisoners Sept. 10.

The second step was the agreement just achieved on a military withdrawal for the positions held before the July

Continued on Page 2, Column 3

VIETNAM REBELS BURN CITY IN RAID

Regime Says 1,000 Reds Took Part in Attack

By The Associated Press.

SAIGON, Vietnam, Tuesday, Sept. 19—More than 1,000 Communist rebels attacked and burned the capital of Phuoc Vinh Province, sixty miles north of Saigon early yesterday, the Government said today.

It was believed to be the largest rebel assault so far in South Vietnam's civil war.

The province chief, an army major, and his deputy and a large number of Government civil guardsmen were killed.

About fifty wounded were rushed to Saigon hospitals after the rebels withdrew under attack.

The Government announced said the Viet Cong guerrillas stormed the capital at 1 A. M. yesterday in a move to liberate rebels taken prisoner. The Viet Cong held the town for several hours in pre-dawn darkness, burning and ransacking several provincial buildings.

One source estimated 1,500 Viet Cong took part in the attack, the first on a provincial capital.

It also marked a new height in violence in the areas north of Saigon where the rebels are said to be building strength.

Phuoc Thanh is a newly created province in a largely upland forest and rubber-growing

Continued on Page 3, Column 7

12 OTHERS KILLED

Lone Survivor Reports Explosions on Flight to Tshombe Talks

By DAVID HALBERSTAM
Special to The New York Times.

NDOLA, Northern Rhodesia, Sept. 18—Secretary General Dag Hammarskjold of the United Nations was killed today along with twelve other persons in the crash of a plane carrying him to a meeting with President Moise Tshombe of Katanga Province. The meeting had been called in an effort to end the fighting in Katanga.

The bodies of the Secretary General and his staff were found about four miles from the Ndola airport in Northern Rhodesia. The plane had been scheduled to land at the airport last night.

[The Associated Press said that mistaken identity and tight security led it to report erroneously Sunday night that Mr. Hammarskjold's plane had reached Ndola.]

The site of the crash is close to the border of the Congolese province of Katanga. The Congo is an area that has demanded much of Mr. Hammarskjold's time and patience in the last fifteen months.

Crash Stuns U. N. Aides

The news of the crash stunned this area. Earlier today United Nations officials at Elisabethville seemed dazed as they kept hearing reports that Mr. Hammarskjold had not arrived in Ndola.

[The Associated Press reported that the lone survivor, Harold M. Julian, a United Nations security guard, said that a series of explosions had preceded the crash. He also said that the plane had turned away from a landing, apparently on Mr. Hammarskjold's orders.]

At near-by Kitwe, in Northern Rhodesia, President Tshombe was holding a news conference and was saying that he hoped to meet in a few minutes with the Secretary General and end the war when a newsman said:

"President Tshombe, Mr. Hammarskjold is dead. His body lies not far away in the wreckage of his airplane."

Mr. Tshombe's face reflected shock and horror seemed to show in his eyes.

Tshombe Expresses Regret

"I regret it very much if what you say is true," he said. "He was a man who enjoyed the respect of many African nations and I had hoped to reach a settlement with him that would leave Katanga free."

Earlier in his news conference Mr. Tshombe had attacked United Nations policy in the Congo.

Mr. Hammarskjold's plane was a United Nations DC-6B. It left Leopoldville yesterday. Much concerning the crash remains inexplicable.

The Secretary General's plane apparently crashed after it had circled the Ndola airport twice and had been waved in. No one here could offer any explanation for the crash.

It was believed that the plane might have taken a circuitous route to avoid the Katanga area, which is patrolled by one Katanga jet fighter. This might account for the plane's late arrival here and it might account for some fatigue on the part of the pilot.

There apparently was only one survivor, a man who was found severely burned and in a delirious state near the plane. He was taken to a hospital.

Those who have been trying to end the Katanga fighting believe that Mr. Hammarskjold's death was a terrible blow to hopes for a truce.

Mr. Tshombe has refused to meet with United Nations officials in Elisabethville, the Ka-

Continued on Page 14, Column 1

NEWS INDEX

"All the News That's Fit to Print"

The New York Times.

LATE CITY EDITION
U. S. Weather Bureau Report (Page 64) forecasts
Increasing cloudiness today.
Snow, rain tonight. Rain tomorrow.
Temp. range: 39—36; yesterday: 37—30.

VOL. CXI. No. 38,014.   © 1962 by The New York Times Company.   NEW YORK, WEDNESDAY, FEBRUARY 21, 1962.   FIVE CENTS

GLENN ORBITS EARTH 3 TIMES SAFELY; PICKED UP IN CAPSULE BY DESTROYER; PRESIDENT WILL GREET HIM IN FLORIDA

CARLINO CLEARED IN SHELTER CASE BY ETHICS PANEL

Lane Scored in Unanimous Report, Which He Calls 'Cynical and Callous'

Text of concluding sections of report is on Page 50.

By WARREN WEAVER Jr.
Special to The New York Times.

ALBANY, Feb. 20—The Assembly Committee on Ethics and Guidance exonerated Speaker Joseph F. Carlino today of charges of conflict of interest made by Assemblyman Mark Lane.

In a unanimous report submitted to the Legislature, the bipartisan committee said:

¶Mr. Carlino did not "betray the public trust" by serving as a director of a company manufacturing home fall-out shelters while helping to pass school-shelter legislation last November.

¶He did not draft or support the shelter legislation "in any improper manner" for the benefit of the company, Lancer Industries, Inc.

¶The Speaker was not influenced in his official actions in behalf of the bill by the fact that he was a member of the board of directors of Lancer.

¶He did not receive any special benefit from the passage of the legislation.

Charges Unsubstantiated

"The committee concludes with respect to each and every accusation contained in the charges filed," the report said, "that Assemblyman Lane and those who testified in their support failed to substantiate their charges."

In submitting the report, the Ethics Committee requested that the full 150-member lower house vote "with respect to the conclusions reached herein" in the light of the fact that "the charges were directed against its [the Assembly's] highest ranking official."

Assemblyman Donald A. Campbell, Republican of Amsterdam, who is chairman of the committee, said he would move in the Assembly tomorrow for acceptance of the report. Mr. Carlino is expected to be absent during the debate and vote.

Assemblyman Lane, a Democrat of Manhattan, had charged that the Speaker was guilty of *Continued on Page 50, Column 1*

ROCKEFELLER BARS KOREA WAR BONUS

Voices Opposition in Face of Legislators' Backing

By LAYHMOND ROBINSON
Special to The New York Times.

ALBANY, Feb. 20—Governor Rockefeller expressed strong opposition tonight to a state bonus for veterans of the Korean war.

Mr. Rockefeller told the New York State Department of the American Legion that he could not "as a responsible leader of government" support the demand for a bonus. The veterans' group had been campaigning for a $100,000,000 bonus for the 482,000 Korean war veterans or their next-of-kin in the state.

The Governor said his stand was backed "unanimously" by the Republican leadership of the state. This was a reference to the leaders of the Republican-controlled Legislature.

He said that demands for funds for education, mental health, narcotics control and other state services were too great to permit a diversion of money for a veterans' bonus.

Mr. Rockefeller thus took a position in direct opposition to that of most of the Republican and Democratic members of the Legislature, who have been pushing for the bonus. The issue

Continued on Page 51, Column 1

READY: Lieut. Col. John H. Glenn Jr. walks to the van to take him to the launching site at Cape Canaveral, Fla.
N.A.S.A. via Associated Press Wirephoto

LIFT-OFF: The Atlas rocket booster bearing the Project Mercury spacecraft roars aloft with 360,000-pound thrust.
N.A.S.A. via United Press International Telephoto

RECOVERY: Crewmen of destroyer Noa secure capsule carrying astronaut before lifting it out of the Atlantic.
N.A.S.A. via Associated Press Wirephoto

81,000-MILE TRIP

Flight Aides Feared for the Capsule as It Began Its Re-Entry

Transcript of conversations with Glenn, Pages 25 and 26.

By RICHARD WITKIN
Special to The New York Times.

CAPE CANAVERAL, Fla., Feb. 20—John H. Glenn Jr. orbited three times around the earth today and landed safely to become the first American to make such a flight.

The 40-year-old Marine Corps lieutenant colonel traveled about 81,000 miles in 4 hours 56 minutes before splashing into the Atlantic at 2:43 P.M. Eastern Standard Time.

He had been launched from here at 9:47 A.M.

The astronaut's safe return was no less a relief than a thrill to the Project Mercury team, because there had been real concern that the Friendship 7 capsule might disintegrate as it rammed back into the atmosphere.

There had also been a serious question whether Colonel Glenn could complete three orbits as planned. But despite persistent control problems, he managed to complete the entire flight plan.

Lands in Bahamas Area

The astronaut's landing place was near Grand Turk Island in the Bahamas, about 700 miles southeast of here.

Still in his capsule, he was plucked from the water at 3:01 P.M. with a boom and block and tackle by the destroyer Noa. The capsule was deposited on deck at 3:04.

Colonel Glenn's first words as he stepped out onto the Noa's deck were: "It was hot in there."

He quickly obtained a glass of iced tea.

The 40-year-old astronaut also reported that he had felt no sickness or discomfort during his five-hour, three-orbit flight around the earth, even during the extended period of weightlessness.

Colonel Glenn landed at this small British possession at 9:11 P.M. in a Navy S-2-F submarine patrol plane. He was clad in light blue coveralls. He had co-piloted the plane from the carrier Randolph, where he spent several hours after being retrieved from the Atlantic ocean.

Around his ears were the marks of the earphones that he had worn while piloting a plane that traveled at about one-hundredth the speed of his Friendship 7 space capsule. And on his face was an excited enthusiastic smile.

Asked how he felt, the redhanded marine replied: "Fine, wonderful, I couldn't feel better."

And he was also hungry. His first comment on stepping into the small hospital arranged for him was: "First I want something to eat—I am hungry." A steak dinner was promptly arranged.

Continued on Page 22, Column 2

Jersey Bus Strike Settled; Service Is Due Tomorrow

By PETER KIHSS

An agreement to end the New Jersey bus strike was reached last night. The agreement, subject to ratification by the striking employes, was announced by Gov. Richard J. Hughes. The pact will be submitted to the union members at their garages starting at 7 A.M. today.

Union and management men expressed hope that buses could begin operating tomorrow at 4:30 A.M.

The strike against Public Service Coordinated Transport started at 12:01 A.M. Monday and halted 2,511 buses providing 1,000,000 rides a day. The company's 200 routes serve all of New Jersey's twenty-one counties except Warren and Hunterdon and go into New York City and Philadelphia. The Newark subway system was also shut.

Carlin Gets Credit

Governor Hughes credited Mayor Leo P. Carlin of Newark with having "sparkplugged" the successful negotiations. Mayor Carlin flew back from a Miami Beach vacation yesterday and arranged the talks with both sides and with Daniel F. Fitzpatrick, a Federal mediator, and the Governor and himself. The meeting started in Newark at 3:30 P.M., and the agreement was announced at 11:25 P.M.

Earlier, David L. Yunich, president of Bamberger's New Jersey, had asserted that the strike was having a "devastating • • • almost catastrophic" effect on retail business in Newark and elsewhere in the state. A Camden department store reported sales had fallen nearly 50 per cent on Monday, although not that far yesterday.

Despite the drop in shopping, most commuters managed to get to work by alternate means and with a minimum of confusion.

The agreement reached last night provides for a wage increase of 10 cents an hour retroactive to Feb. 1 and extending to next Feb. 1; 4 cents more an hour from then until Aug. 1, 1963, and another 4 cents an hour from then until

Continued on Page 29, Column 3

ROSENTHAL WINS QUEENS ELECTION

But Democrat-Liberal Has Margin of Only 193 Votes —Machines Guarded

By CLAYTON KNOWLES

Benjamin S. Rosenthal, a Democrat-Liberal backed by President Kennedy, squeaked through to victory last night in a special Congressional election in Queens's Sixth District.

The unofficial final tally, delayed as the early vote was hastily rechecked for errors, was: Rosenthal, 15,032; Galvin, 15,539, and Levin, 4,715.

Republicans immediately challenged the result, and, while Mr. Galvin did not immediately ask for a recount, he sent a telegram demanding that the voting machines be impounded. All voting machines, normally just

Continued on Page 48, Column 4

McNamara Reports Gains by Vietnamese

By JACK RAYMOND
Special to The New York Times.

WASHINGTON, Feb. 20—Secretary of Defense Robert S. McNamara returned to the capital today and reported improvement in the South Vietnamese effort against Communist insurgents.

He had presided at a meeting of United States military and civilian officials yesterday at the headquarters of Admiral Harry S. Felt, commander of United States forces in the Pacific. The meeting was the third in a series of monthly reviews on the hostilities in South Vietnam.

A spokesman for Mr. McNamara said that the forces of South Vietnam, "are hitting the United States," are

Continued on Page 2, Column 5

KENNEDY PRAISES 'WONDERFUL JOB'

Tells Glenn Nation Is 'Really Proud of You'—Welcome at White House Planned

By TOM WICKER
Special to The New York Times.

WASHINGTON, Feb. 20—President Kennedy phoned Lieut. Col. John H. Glenn Jr. today immediately after the astronaut's successful orbital flight and arranged to meet him at Cape Canaveral Friday morning.

The President also set in motion plans for bringing Colonel Glenn to Washington on Monday for receptions at the White House and the Capitol and a parade down Pennsylvania Avenue.

A television set in his office on open telephone line to Cape Canaveral had kept Mr. Kennedy informed of Colonel Glenn's progress all through the day.

The astronaut's three orbits around the earth, Mr. Kennedy said in a statement, have embarked the United States on a "new ocean"—that of space.

"I believe the United States must sail on it and be in a position second to none," the President said within minutes of Colonel Glenn's safe emergence from his Mercury capsule.

Colonel Glenn, he said, is the "kind of American of whom we are most proud." Mr. Kennedy also praised "all those who participated" in making the astronaut's flight successful.

Then, at 4:10 P.M., Mr. Kennedy *Continued on Page 22, Column 1*

The President's Statement

Special to The New York Times.

WASHINGTON, Feb. 20—Following is the text of President Kennedy's statement on Colonel Glenn's flight:

I know that I express the great happiness and thanksgiving of all of us that Colonel Glenn has completed his trip, and I know that this is particularly felt by Mrs. Glenn and his two children.

A few days ago Colonel Glenn came to the White House and visited me, and he is—as are the other astronauts—the kind of American of whom we are most proud.

Some years ago, as a Marine pilot, he raced the sun across this country—and lost. And today he won.

I also want to say a word for all those who participated with Colonel Glenn in Canaveral. They faced many disappointments and delays—the burdens upon them were great—but they kept their heads and they made a judgment, and I think their judgment has been vindicated.

We have a long way to go in this space race. We started late. But this is the new ocean, and I believe the United States must sail on it and be in a position second to none.

Some months ago I said that I hoped every American would serve his country. Today Colonel Glenn served his, and we all express our thanks to him.

ADENAUER WANTS PARLEY ON BERLIN

Suggests Foreign Ministers of Big Four Meet 'Soon'

By SYDNEY GRUSON
Special to The New York Times.

BONN, Germany, Feb. 20—Chancellor Adenauer suggested today that a Big Four foreign ministers' conference on Berlin should be "convened "soon." He was speaking to the Parliamentary group of the Christian Democratic Union.

He said that it might be "expedient" to "take a pause" in the Berlin talks now going on between André A. Gromyko, the Soviet Foreign Minister, and Llewellyn E. Thompson Jr., the United States Ambassador to Moscow.

Ambassador Thompson should not continue "negotiating" endlessly, Dr. Adenauer added. There have been four meetings in the last seven weeks between Mr. Gromyko and Mr. Thompson without any advance toward a settlement.

[A warning by Investia, the Soviet Government newspaper, that Moscow was ready to push through a separate peace treaty with East Germany if the United States did not alter its position in the talks raised the possibility of a renewal of the Soviet deadline on a peace pact.]

Dr. Adenauer's advocacy of a new conference of the United States, British, French and Soviet foreign ministers reflected his unhappiness with the course of the Gromyko-Thompson talks.

He is known to believe that *Continued on Page 2, Column 4*

URBAN PLAN VOTE PUT OFF IN SENATE

Administration Rebuffed on Forcing Issue to Floor

By RUSSELL BAKER
Special to The New York Times.

WASHINGTON, Feb. 20—President Kennedy affronted the Senate's dignity today and got a political rebuff for it.

In a surprising repudiation of the Administration's voting form sheets, the elders turned on the White House and rejected a leadership move to get a quick floor test of the President's urban affairs proposal. The vote was 58 to 43.

Thus, the White House lost the chance to get a favorable Senate vote on the plan before the House could vote to kill it. The Democrats also lost their chance to get the Senate's Republicans clearly on record for or against the plan to create a Cabinet-level Department of Urban Affairs and Housing.

Today's test came on the dusty parliamentary question whether the Senate should take the plan away from the Government Operations Committee and bring it to an immediate floor vote. This is known as "discharging" the committee. It is an extraordinary procedure that is rarely used because it is repugnant to Senate traditions.

Today it became the instrument of the President's defeat.

The move to discharge the Government Operations Committee was undertaken with misgivings yesterday by Mike Mansfield of Montana, Senate Democratic leader. The reason was a sudden threat by the

Continued on Page 16, Column 4

COL. GLENN FLOWN TO ISLE FOR CHECK

He Feels Tired but Elated —Goes to Grand Turk for Report and Examination

By JOHN W. FINNEY
Special to The New York Times.

GRAND TURK ISLAND, Feb. 20—An elated but tired John H. Glenn Jr. returned to earth tonight and reported that he "couldn't feel better."

The 40-year-old astronaut also reported that he had felt no sickness or discomfort during his three-orbit flight around the earth, and he was brought to this small British possession at 9:11 P.M. in a Navy S-2-F submarine patrol plane. He was clad in light blue coveralls. He had co-piloted the plane from the carrier Randolph, where he spent several hours after being retrieved from the Atlantic ocean.

The colonel was transferred by helicopter to the carrier Randolph, whose recovery helicopters had raced the Noa for the honor of making the pickup. After a meal and extensive "de-briefing" aboard the carrier, he was flown to Grand Turk by submarine patrol plane for two days of rest and interviews on technical, medical and other aspects of his flight.

The Noa, the ship that picked

Continued on Page 26, Column 1

NEW YORK PAUSES TO 'WATCH' GLENN

Millions Rivet Attention on Astronaut in Flight

By NAN ROBERTSON

The thoughts of millions of New Yorkers were riveted for hours yesterday on one man alone in space.

Minute by minute, they followed the orbital flight of Lieut. Col. John H. Glenn Jr. three times around the earth, waiting in agonizing suspense for his safe return. The life of New York almost stood still during the dramatic countdown.

From an orbit of Colonel Glenn scrambled "hale and hearty" out of his capsule on the destroyer Noa, people carried on absent-mindedly and in spurts. Millions of working hours were lost during the day, but no one could have begrudged them to radio and television sets.

The most spectacular display of interest occurred in the Grand Central Terminal, where throngs of up to 9,000 persons massed before a huge television screen. The police described it as the largest static crowd in the station's history. The terminal manager said those who

Continued on Page 22, Column 6

Moscow, Unmoved, Gives News of Orbit

By THEODORE SHABAD
Special to The New York Times.

MOSCOW, Feb. 20—The Russians voiced congratulations today on hearing of Lieut. Col. John H. Glenn Jr.'s orbital space flight.

But they showed no enthusiasm on the successful launching and landing of the spacecraft Friendship 7.

These reactions were reported from Moscow University by United States exchange students who had been listening with Russians to radio reports of Colonel Glenn's progress.

"They congratulated us in friendly fashion but were diffident," an American said.

Soviet radio and television were unusually prompt in reporting the flight. The first bulletin

Continued on Page 22, Column 6

Leaders of Algeria Back Peace Terms

By THOMAS F. BRADY
Special to The New York Times.

TUNIS, Feb. 20—The Algerian nationalist Provisional Government met today and gave full approval to peace accords negotiated with the French by four members of the rebel regime.

One Algerian said afterward: "All twelve members of the Government are in unanimous agreement." This was a reference to five ministers who are prisoners in France, the four negotiators and three ministers who remained in Tunis during the secret talks last week on the French-Swiss border.

The negotiators were Bel kacem Krim, M'Hammed Yazid, Saad Dahlab and Lakhdar Ben Tobbal. They met here today

Continued on Page 11, Column 1

NEWS INDEX

"All the News That's Fit to Print"

The New York Times.

LATE CITY EDITION
U.S. Weather Bureau Report (Page 95) forecast:
Sunny today; fair and cool tonight.
Mostly fair and pleasant tomorrow.
Temp. range: 70—50; yesterday: 68—54.
Temp.-Hum. index: 64; yesterday: 65.

NEWS SUMMARY AND INDEX, PAGE 95

VOL. CXII.. No. 38,235.   © 1962 by The New York Times Company. Times Square, New York 36, N. Y.   NEW YORK, SUNDAY, SEPTEMBER 30, 1962.   10c beyond 50-mile zone from New York City, except on Long Island 20c beyond 200-mile zone from New York City, higher in air delivery cities.   SECTION ONE   THIRTY CENTS

KENNEDY FEDERALIZES MISSISSIPPI'S GUARD; MOBILIZES TROOPS, ORDERS STATE TO YIELD; ADDRESSES NATION TODAY ON RACIAL CRISIS

PRESIDENT CALLS RUSK AND BRITON TO DISCUSS BERLIN

Lord Home and Envoys Will Fly to Capital Today as German Crisis Grows

By E. W. KENWORTHY
Special to The New York Times

WASHINGTON, Sept. 29—President Kennedy will meet here tomorrow with high United States and British officials to discuss the Berlin situation and other foreign policy questions.

The luncheon at the White House will be attended by Secretary of State Dean Rusk; the Earl of Home, the British Foreign Secretary; David K. E. Bruce, the United States Ambassador in London, and Sir David Ormsby Gore, the British Ambassador in Washington.

[Mr. Rusk said in New York that assertions by the Communists that they had no troops in Laos were "nonsense and the world knows it."]

Newport Trip Called Off

President Kennedy had planned to fly to Newport this afternoon and have luncheon there with the British and American officials, however, at 3 P.M. the White House said he had called off the trip.

Andrew T. Hatcher, associate press secretary, was reticent at the time about saying that the trip cancellation was related to the integration crisis in Mississippi.

The ministers and ambassadors will fly here tomorrow from New York, where they are attending sessions of the United Nations General Assembly.

The White House did not say what would be discussed. But officials here said it was obvious that Berlin and increasing tensions there would demand much of the meeting's attention.

High Administration officials have not disguised their deep concern over the lack of interest on the part of the Soviet Union in various proposals by the United States and Britain to reduce tension over Berlin. For example, Soviet officials

Continued on Page 26, Column 1

GIANTS AND COLTS SPLIT TWO GAMES

Dodgers Clinch at Least a Tie for First Place

The league-leading Los Angeles Dodgers lost to the St. Louis Cardinals yesterday but remained a game ahead of the San Francisco Giants who split a double-header with the Houston Colts. The results assured the Dodgers of at least a tie for first place.

FOOTBALL

Army and Columbia won major college football contests in New York. Scores of leading games:

Army .... 9 Syracuse 2
Auburn .. 22 Tennessee .. 21
Boston Coll. 28 Villanova ..13
California .. 22 San Jose St. 8
Colgate .. 23 Cornell 12
Columbia .. 22 Brown 20
Dartmouth .27 Mass. 3
Duke ...... 21 S. Carolina. 8
Ga. Tech ..17 Florida 6
Harvard .. 27 Lehigh 0
Holy Cross.16 Buffalo 6
Iowa ...... 28 Oregon St. .8
Michigan St. 0 Stanford ... 0
Mississippi .0 Kentucky .. 0
Navy ...... 20 W. & M. ...10
Nebraska .. 25 Michigan ...13
Notre Dame.13 Oklahoma .. 7
Ohio State .41 N. Carolina. 7
Oregon ... 35 Utah 8
Penn. ..... 13 Lafayette ..11
Penn State. 20 Air Force .. 7
Princeton .23 Rutgers 6
Stanford .. 41 Mich. St. ..13
Washington 28 Illinois ... 7
Yale ...... 13 Conn. 14

HORSE RACING

Kelso won the $115,200 Woodward Stakes at the Aqueduct meeting ended. Jaipur was a distant second to the favorite.

Details in Section 5

Brandt, Rockefeller and Wagner Lead Steuben March

Mayor Willy Brandt of West Berlin joins Mayor Wagner and Governor Rockefeller at the head of about 25,000 marchers during annual Steuben Day parade up Fifth Avenue.
The New York Times

By DAVID BINDER

The Bavarians yodeled, the Cologners danced a two-step, the Rhinelanders sang, the Hamburgers cried "Hummel Hummel" and the bands played Berliner melodies as 25,000 German-Americans marched up Fifth Avenue yesterday. The occasion was the fifth annual Steuben Parade, honoring Baron Friedrich Wilhelm von Steuben, the general from Magdeburg who helped George Washington drill the Continental Army during the American Revolution. Mayor Willy Brandt of West Berlin was the honored guest. German touches were everywhere —in black corduroy carpenter costumes, gymnastic stunts

Continued on Page 52, Column 3

KENNEDY WISHES BEN BELLA WELL

'Warmest Congratulations' Sent as U. S. Recognizes New Algerian Regime

By PETER BRAESTRUP
Special to The New York Times

WASHINGTON, Sept. 29—President Kennedy today sent "warmest congratulations" to Ahmed Ben Bella, Premier of independent Algeria's newly formed Government.

Mr. Kennedy, who as a Senator endorsed Algerian self-rule in 1957, wished Mr. Ben Bella "every success" and said that "my Government and my people share my earnest desire to foster and extend the cordial relations that exist between our two countries."

[The President's message coincided with the State Department's announcement of formal diplomatic recognition of the newly established Government of Algeria.]

New Premier to Visit Here

Yesterday Mr. Ben Bella announced his Cabinet and pledged a "neutralist and non-engaged" foreign policy in a speech before the week-old National Assembly. The Assembly subsequently approved the Cabinet list, 159 to 1 with 19 abstentions.

Secretary of State Dean Rusk sent congratulations to the Algerian Foreign Minister, Mohammed Khemisti, saying that he looked forward to a meeting "in the near future."

Informed sources said today that President Kennedy and Secretary Rusk would meet with Mr. Ben Bella sometime after the Algerian Premier's arrival in the United States, possibly late next week, to head

Continued on Page 4, Column 1

Norway Criticizes Paris Plan to Build National A-Forces

By HENRY GINIGER
Special to The New York Times

PARIS, Sept. 29—The four-day state visit by King Olav V of Norway ended today with a strong attack by the Norwegian Foreign Minister, Dr. Halvard M. Lange, on national atomic striking forces in Europe such as that planned by France.

King Olav took leave of President de Gaulle this morning. He had been warmly received and responded with the same warmth that was broadcast over the French radio and television.

It was left to Dr. Lange, who had accompanied the King, to underline the serious divergences between the Norwegian and French Governments on Western defense. He did so in a statement to the French News Agency.

Reliance Placed on the U. S.

Dr. Lange said the Western alliance must rest on confidence among its members, for "otherwise it has no sense." He said that Norway, placing her confidence in the United States' assumption of the burden and responsibility for the West's nuclear armament, was hostile to national atomic forces in Europe.

President de Gaulle has often said that France must assume responsibility for her defense, and he and his aides have left the widespread impression that they are not wholly confident of the United States' ability or willingness to defend Western Europe.

Dr. Lange said Western Europe should assume greater shares of the burden of conventional armaments and of "help to underdeveloped nations, a

Continued on Page 23, Column 2

JOHNSON IS FINED

Barnett's Lieutenant Is Liable to a Penalty of $5,000 a Day

Text of court order finding Johnson guilty, Page 66.

By HEDRICK SMITH
Special to The New York Times

NEW ORLEANS, Sept. 29—Lieut. Gov. Paul B. Johnson Jr. of Mississippi was held in civil contempt of Federal court orders today in his state's integration crisis.

A three-judge panel of the United States Court of Appeals for the Fifth Circuit tried Mr. Johnson in absentia. He was found guilty of defying court orders forbidding any official interference with the desegregation of the University of Mississippi.

The court gave Mr. Johnson until 11 A.M. Tuesday to purge himself of contempt or face a fine of $5,000 a day. The fine is to start building up immediately, but no money is to be collected until Tuesday.

Fine Might Increase

However, the court ruled that if Mr. Johnson became Acting Governor and refused to comply with its orders, he would face the same penalties as Mr. Barnett.

This means that, in such a situation, Mr. Johnson could face arrest and a fine of $10,000 a day unless he retreated and ordered Mississippi officials to comply with the court's desegregation orders.

Like Governor Barnett, Mr. Johnson did not appear at the court hearing.

There were no attorneys in court to represent him. However, the two attorneys for the state of Mississippi were in the courtroom—Charles Clarke of Jackson and John C. Satterfield of Yazoo City.

They entered no pleadings or arguments in Mr. Johnson's behalf. However, they submitted

Continued on Page 66, Column 1

U.S. TELLS SOVIET TO OUST 2 AS SPIES

Says Aides at U. N. Bought Secrets From Sailor, Held Here in $100,000 Bail

By EMANUEL PERLMUTTER

The United States yesterday demanded the expulsion of two members of the Soviet delegation to the United Nations who were involved with an American sailor in an espionage plot.

In a sharply worded note to the Soviet delegation, the United States said: "As host to the United Nations, the Government of the United States strongly protests the espionage activities directed against the internal security of the United States."

The Russians countered a few hours later with a note charging that Federal agents had illegally arrested, manhandled and questioned the two

Continued on Page 29, Column 1

Principals in Naval Secrets Case

Nelson Cornelius Drummond, a Navy petty officer, sitting between Federal officers after his arrest early yesterday.

Ivan Y. Vyrodov, member of Soviet mission to the U. N.

Yevgeny M. Prokhorov, second secretary of mission.
Associated Press

Federal Troops Massing At a Base Near Memphis

Soldiers Landed by Army Helicopters for Possible Duty in Mississippi Crisis —Engineers Ordered Into State

Special to The New York Times

MEMPHIS, Tenn., Sept. 29—Hundreds of Army troops and about 500 United States marshals were in the huge Memphis Naval Air Station near here tonight.

The Government kept flying men in during the day for a showdown next week with Gov. Ross R. Barnett of Mississippi over the court-ordered desegregation of the University of Mississippi.

[President Kennedy ordered an Army Engineer battalion to move into Mississippi to set up a tent city for 700 United States marshals, according to United Press International.]

Large Army helicopters landed 200 to 250 soldiers during the day. Newsmen were barred from the air station, 18 miles north of Memphis, but they counted 16 helicopters as they landed and discharged troops. The Pentagon in Washington admitted that the helicopters were here.

Earlier, about 400 men had been flown in by Navy transport planes. The armed soldiers were confined to the base.

Sailors leaving the base on weekend liberty told newsmen about the soldiers' being here.

The Department of Defense denied that any paratroop units had been sent to Memphis. So did Gen. C. W. G. Rich, commander of Fort Campbell, Army base in Kentucky. It was from here that 110 men of the 70th Battalion of Engineers were sent to the air station yesterday.

Gen. H. H. Howze, commander of Fort Bragg, Army base in North Carolina, would not confirm that paratroopers had been

Continued on Page 68, Column 5

Longshore Walkout Scheduled Tonight; Ships Rush to Sea

By EDWARD A. MORROW

A steady stream of ships sailed out of New York and other Atlantic and Gulf ports yesterday to avoid being caught in a longshoremen's strike that appeared certain to begin at 12:01 A.M. tomorrow.

Work on the piers continued at a record level as shipowners filed unusual weekend calls for labor with the Waterfront Commission.

The bistate agency said that 17,459 men had been hired to work 101 ships at 80 piers at time-and-a-half pay. On a normal Saturday the waterfront force is 2,000 to 3,000 men.

Sixty-two ships passed the quarantine station outbound yesterday. This number would have been even higher had not some operators decided to postpone the sailing of 12 ships until today to accept all the tonnage that could be moved off the piers before the deadline.

Cruise Liner Held Up

The 591 passengers aboard the Queen of Bermuda, which was scheduled to sail at 3 P.M. for Hamilton, Bermuda, found their voyage departure delayed until 8 A.M. this morning so the vessel could load cargo.

While the peak of the effort to get ships out was passed, a Sunday hiring record is expected to be broken today, a Waterfront Commission spokesman said.

The agency has received calls for 8,500 men to work 35 piers at double their regular pay of $3.02 an hour. The normal Sunday work force averages 1,000.

Federal mediators failed yes-

Continued on Page 44, Column 5

ACTS AT MIDNIGHT

President Holds Talks With Gov. Barnett but to No Avail

Text of Kennedy proclamation is printed on Page 68.

By ANTHONY LEWIS
Special to The New York Times

WASHINGTON, Sunday, Sept. 30.—President Kennedy committed the full weight of the Federal Government at midnight last night to end Mississippi's defiance of the Union.

He called the state's National Guard into Federal service.

He sent troops of the United States Army to Memphis, Tenn., to stand in reserve if more force were needed.

And he issued a proclamation calling on the Government and people of Mississippi to abandon what has become the most serious challenge to Federal authority since the Civil War.

Addresses Nation Tonight

Tonight, the President goes on the air to explain the situation to the American people. He will speak over all national television and radio networks at 7:30 New York time.

The President took what one official called his "irrevocable steps" after three telephone conversations yesterday with Governor Ross R. Barnett of Mississippi.

In a statement issued at five minutes before midnight, the acting White House press secretary, Andrew T. Hatcher, said that in the conversations the President was unable to receive from Governor Barnett satisfactory assurances that law and order could, or would, be maintained in Oxford, Miss., during the coming week.

Crisis Over Negro Student

Oxford is the seat of the University of Mississippi. Mississippi's defiance of Federal court orders to admit a Negro, James H. Meredith, to the university, has provoked the Federal-state crisis.

Mr. Hatcher said the action was being taken at that late hour—and telegrams dispatched to the guard commanders—so that the units "will be available for service Monday." Most Guardsmen are one-day-a-week soldiers, and it will take some time to mobilize them.

The regular Army troops sent to Memphis comprised 900 military policemen, especially

Continued on Page 68, Column 1

SUPREME COURT OPENS TOMORROW

Legislative Districting Still Among Major Problems— Goldberg to Be Sworn

Special to The New York Times

WASHINGTON, Sept. 29—The Supreme Court convenes Monday for a new term that promises to be one of high drama and significance.

Two issues that dominated the last term—legislative districting and prayers in the schools—will be back in new and difficult guises.

The court will consider such other controversial problems as restaurant segregation, contempt of Congress and censorship of books and movies.

Goldberg to Take Oath

Arthur J. Goldberg, appointed to replace Felix Frankfurter on his retirement, is scheduled to take the oath of office Monday. Byron R. White succeeded Charles E. Whittaker last April, too late to permit any real appraisal of his views last term.

Seldom, if ever, have new members of the Supreme Court faced questions so intellectually challenging or with so great a potential impact on

Continued on Page 74, Column 3

Today's Sections

Index to Subjects

U.N. Says Katanga Still Recruits Troops in Violation of Promise

BY SAM POPE BREWER
Special to The New York Times

UNITED NATIONS, N. Y., Sept. 29 — The United Nations has accused the Government of Katanga of continuing to recruit mercenaries in spite of repeated promises not to do so.

The charges were made in a letter from the chief United Nations officer in the Congo, Robert K. A. Gardiner, to President Moise Tshombe of Katanga Province, dated last Tuesday and made public here last night.

[In Elisabethville President Tshombe likened the United Nations charges to "the stories of sea serpents or the abominable snowman." He said such charges always precede an attack on Katanga.]

Mr. Gardiner charged that the Katangese gendarmerie "has been receiving reinforcements for some time both in the form of troops and material."

He said: "I am worried to see that in spite of your affirmations that there would be no more mercenaries serving the Katangese gendarmerie, bodies of Europeans killed in combat between the National Congolese Army and the Gendarmerie have been found."

In further support of the charges, Mr. Gardiner said that the United Nations organization in the Congo had a complete file of the names, addresses and photographs of mercenaries who had arrived in Katanga in recent months. It also had copies of payrolls signed by the men, he said.

Mr. Gardiner charged that recruiting was still being carried on through newspaper advertisements, especially in

Continued on Page 8, Column 1

Traffic Overhaul at Lincoln Sq. Called Basic to Orderly Growth

By JOSEPH C. INGRAHAM

The city was urged yesterday to overhaul traffic patterns around Lincoln Center before approving any future construction.

The proposal for traffic relief was submitted in a report by Day & Zimmermann, Philadelphia consulting engineers. The firm was hired by the city on April 23 to conduct a $30,000 study of the effects of future developments on traffic and mass transit, with "particular emphasis on the impact that the proposed Litho City housing development would impose."

Among the principal recommendations were the following:

¶Widening and rebuilding parts of the West Side Highway.

¶Changing the traffic pattern in local streets.

¶Adding crosstown express streets and rebuilding existing ones.

¶Changing the traffic pattern within the Lincoln Center for the Performing Arts.

The Litho City project, sponsored by Local 1, Amalgamated Lithographers of America, is planned along the Hudson River between 60th and 70th Streets.

Consisting of 17 buildings of 23 and 33 stories over the New York Central's freight yards, the project would tower above the western side of Lincoln Center.

The consultants stressed that their broad traffic study was predicated largely on the Litho City project. They noted that the original plans had called for 6,000 apartments for 15,000 to 20,000 persons, but said

Continued on Page 85, Column 3

The New York Times.

LATE CITY EDITION
U. S. Weather Bureau Report (Page 77) forecasts:
Mostly sunny today. Fair tonight and tomorrow.
Temp. range: 75—54; yesterday: 74—52.

VOL. CXII. No. 38,237.

© 1962 by The New York Times Company.
Times Square, New York 36, N. Y.

NEW YORK, TUESDAY, OCTOBER 2, 1962.

10 cents beyond 50-mile zone from New York City
except on Long Island. Higher in air delivery cities.

FIVE CENTS

3,000 TROOPS PUT DOWN MISSISSIPPI RIOTING AND SEIZE 200 AS NEGRO ATTENDS CLASSES; EX-GEN. WALKER IS HELD FOR INSURRECTION

SENATE REJECTS AID CUTS AND BAN ON HELP FOR REDS

Upholds Kennedy's Authority to Assist Nations That Do Business With Cuba

By FELIX BELAIR Jr.
Special to The New York Times.

WASHINGTON, Oct. 1—The Senate decided for the Administration today in preliminary votes on the foreign aid appropriation bill, due for passage tomorrow.

It voted, 47 to 28, against cutting $785,000,000 from the $792,400,000 of military and economic aid funds that its Appropriations Committee restored to the bill the House had cut heavily.

The effect of the vote was to hold the appropriation at $4,422,800,000, as recommended by its Appropriations Committee. The Administration had requested the full amount of the authorized ceiling of $1,-754,800,000 but the House cut this back to $3,630,400,000.

On a later vote, the Senate confirmed this action by rejecting a proposal by Senator Allen J. Ellender, Democrat of Louisiana, to adopt the House cut of $150,000,000 for military aid.

Votes Become Narrow

By increasingly narrow margins, however, it supported other Administration goals. For instance, it voted, 39-36 to continue the President's discretion to aid countries doing business with Cuba. Then it decided, 39-37, to give the President similar discretion to waive the ban on aiding Communist nations such as Yugoslavia and Poland.

All three proposals were sponsored by Senator William Proxmire, Democrat of Wisconsin.

They were intended, first, to cut back the separate money items in the bill to the low levels voted by the House. Second, they would have approved the House's ban on aiding any Communist countries or free nations that help the Castro regime or allow their ships to carry cargo to Cuba.

Only with the help of Republican members was the Democratic leadership able to turn back the Proxmire attack on the President's discretionary powers. On the proposal to ban aid to nations shipping to Cuba, 12 Republicans voted with 22 Democrats to defeat the move, while 22 Democrats and 14 Re-

Continued on Page 16, Column 4

MOSCOW FOCUSING ON BLOC IN EUROPE

Rift With Chinese Believed Behind New Emphasis

By SEYMOUR TOPPING
Special to The New York Times.

MOSCOW, Oct. 1—The Soviet Union has decided to pursue its program of rapprochement with Yugoslavia even at the risk of a further deterioration in relations with Communist China.

Diplomatic officials here have found evidence in a comparative study of Soviet and Chinese Communist documents.

These officials believe that the ideological quarrel with Peking has caused Moscow to resolve to concentrate its resources on the consolidation of the European Communist economic bloc.

Pravda, the Communist party newspaper, published today an edited version of the communiqué issued by the Central Committee of the Chinese Communist party at the conclusion of its plenary session Friday. The Soviet summary, which covered half a page in Pravda, omitted the strong attacks on President Tito of Yugoslavia for his so-called "modern revision-

Continued on Page 5, Column 1

Home Urges West to Help East's Coexistence Moves

By ARNOLD H. LUBASCH

The Earl of Home, Britain's Foreign Secretary, urged last night that the West pursue policies designed to help the Soviet bloc move toward genuine coexistence. He suggested that nuclear war was no longer a useful instrument of policy, that Communist doctrine was changing because of this and that Soviet society was changing even faster.

Lord Home's remarks were made at a dinner in the Waldorf - Astoria Hotel. The dinner was given by the Pilgrims of the United States, a friendship society devoted to cultivating understanding between this country and the nations of the British Commonwealth.

The organization, composed of 1,000 prominent persons, was founded in 1903. A sister organization across the Atlantic is known as the Pilgrims of Great Britain. The groups give dinners in honor of leading statesmen to promote understanding and brotherhood among nations.

Cites Soviet Ingenuity

Lord Home observed that the Russians exercise great ingenuity to reconcile their propaganda about peaceful coexistence with a program that permits limited force in certain regions to further the cause of Communist domination.

The West must be on guard against this technique, he said, and against the force that backs it up. He mentioned Berlin and South Vietnam as two areas of particular concern.

"I pray," he added, "that Cuba may never become a third."

Communist doctrine has begun to change, Lord Home

Continued on Page 2, Column 3

SPAAK REASSURES AFRICA ON TRADE

Tells Newer U.N. Members That Common Market Will Aid Their Development

By THOMAS J. HAMILTON
Special to The New York Times.

UNITED NATIONS, N. Y., Oct. 1—Paul-Henri Spaak, the Foreign Minister of Belgium, assured underdeveloped countries today that they could count on the cooperation of the members of the European Economic Community in the fight for economic advancement.

In addition, Mr. Spaak appealed to the entire world to understand the "new Europe" and its goal of "world cooperation."

Mr. Spaak's policy statement in the General Assembly was addressed in the first instance to 18 newly independent African states, all former possessions of France, Belgium or Italy.

Some of the states have asked the European Economic Community, or Common Market, for status as associates.

The six members of the market—Belgium, France, West Germany, Italy, the Netherlands and Luxembourg—are negotiating with the African states in Brussels.

Success Is Predicted

Mr. Spaak predicted that these talks would be concluded successfully by the end of 1962.

He also predicted that the negotiations with Britain for her admission to the market would be successful. He said the market would then have about the same productive capacity as the United States, more than the Soviet Union.

The Belgian Foreign Minister, who was one of the leaders in the formation of the Common Market, defended it against two charges: that it is a manifestation of "neo-colonialism," and that it is merely intended to provide economic support for the North Atlantic Treaty Organization.

Mr. Spaak devoted almost his entire speech to his explanation of the market's program. He received an ovation at the end, with African and Asian members joining.

The Belgian Foreign Minister emphasized that the exports of African associate members would be admitted duty-free to the Common Market countries, while the Africans would retain

Continued on Page 5, Column 2

Congo Flies Troops To End Kasai Revolt

By Reuters

LEOPOLDVILLE, the Congo, Oct. 1—Reliable sources said today that the central Congolese Government was flying troops to Luluabourg to put down a new revolt by supporters of Albert Kalonji in South Kasai. No immediate action was planned by the United Nations.

Mr. Kalonji, self - styled "king," virtually seceded from the central Government shortly after the Congo became independent two years ago. He escaped recently from a prison near Leopoldville and returned to his capital of Bakwanga.

The troop movement followed the declaration by the Government of a state of emergency in South Kasai, the Government army base nearest to the diamond-rich province.

A United Nations spokesman

Continued on Page 9, Column 2

PRISONERS ARE MARCHED TO ARMORY IN OXFORD: Army men escort a group of prisoners to National Guard Armory. The group had participated in a disturbance and was apprehended after the soldiers were ordered to fire at the feet of the rioters.

Associated Press Wirephoto

KENNEDY MOVING TO END PIER TIE-UP

He Names Board of Inquiry as First Step in Obtaining Taft-Hartley Injunction

By JOHN D. POMFRET
Special to The New York Times.

WASHINGTON, Oct. 1.—President Kennedy took the first step today toward getting an injunction to end the Atlantic and Gulf Coast longshoremen's strike for 80 days.

Declaring that continuation of the strike would imperil the national health and safety, the President issued an Executive order naming a three-man board of inquiry to investigate the dispute and to report to him by Thursday.

[Meanwhile in New York, leaders of the nation's seven major maritime unions abandoned inter-union battling to plan support for the striking longshoremen. American seamen and officers started leaving their ships, while other unions made plans to avoid servicing foreign-flag ships entering Atlantic and Gulf ports.]

The strike, which began at 12:01 A.M. today, has tied up all ports from Searsport, Me., to Brownsville, Tex. About 75,000 members of the Internation-

Continued on Page 78, Column 5

Columbia Study Scores Doctors; Says Quality of Care Lags Here

Financial Sanctions Under Blue Shield Suggested in Trussell Report

By FARNSWORTH FOWLE

The medical profession is "doing little" about the quality of medical care in the metropolitan area, the state was told yesterday in an experts' report.

The report warned that many laymen to poor medical care "is to demand firm and drastic government action—and indeed this may occur." It said that "strong medical, hospital, community and government leadership must be asserted in the public interest."

The conclusions were contained in the final volume of the Trussell-van Dyke Report, an independent study for the state by the Columbia University School of Public Health and Administrative Medicine. It was directed by Dr. Ray E. Trussell, dean of the school, now on leave from his post while serving as New York City's Commissioner of Hospitals, and Frank van Dyke, an associate professor at the school.

The report called on the medical profession to welcome cur-

WALKER IS STOPPED BY TROOPS: Former Maj. Gen. Edwin A. Walker is detained by soldiers near the courthouse in Oxford. He was turned over to U.S. marshals and is being held in $100,000 bail on charges stemming from his role in Sunday's campus riots.

United Press International Telephoto

WALKER IS FACING 4 FEDERAL COUNTS

Flown to Medical Center in Missouri to Await Trial— Bail Put at $100,000

Special to The New York Times.

OXFORD, Miss., Oct. 1—Former Maj. Gen. Edwin A. Walker was arrested today on four charges, including insurrection, for his role in last night's rioting at the University of Mississippi.

The man who commanded Federal forces during the school integration crisis at Little Rock in 1957 was held in $100,000 bail.

Unable to put up the bail, he was flown to the United States Medical Center for Federal Prisoners in Springfield, Mo., to await his trial.

[Mr. Walker, accompanied by marshals, arrived at the medical center Monday night, The Associated Press said.]

"They don't have a thing on me," Mr. Walker said after his arrest. He dictated a message to Gov. Ross R. Barnett, which said:

"Mr. Walker hopes his efforts were in your behalf and in behalf of the stand for freedom everywhere. Do nothing based on my status that is not in support of your own objectives.

Continued on Page 27, Column 3

Bidwell's Tax Trial Ends in Hung Jury

By DAVID ANDERSON

The tax-evasion trial of J. Truman Bidwell, former chairman of the New York Stock Exchange, ended early today in a hung jury.

The jury, which had been deliberating since 1 P.M., filed into the courtroom shortly after midnight and told Federal Judge Thomas F. Murphy that it was "hopelessly deadlocked."

Judge Murphy, who two hours earlier had rejected a similar report and had instructed the jurors to try once more, now said:

"I declare a mistrial. Unhappy as I am, I guess there is nothing else we can do."

The prosecutor, Assistant United States Attorney Stephen E. Kaufman, said the Government would now consider

Continued on Page 19, Column 2

SHOTS QUELL MOB

Enrolling of Meredith Ends Segregation in State Schools

By CLAUDE SITTON
Special to The New York Times.

OXFORD, Miss., Oct. 1—James H. Meredith, a Negro, enrolled in the University of Mississippi today and began classes as Federal troops and federalized units of the Mississippi National Guard quelled a 15-hour riot.

A force of more than 3,000 soldiers and guardsmen and 400 deputy United States marshals fired rifles and hurled tear-gas grenades to stop the violent demonstrations.

Throughout the day, more troops streamed into Oxford. Tonight a force approaching 5,000 soldiers and guardsmen, along with the Federal marshals, maintained an uneasy peace in this town of 6,500 in the northern Mississippi hills.

[There were two flareups tonight in which tear gas had to be used, United Press International reported. A small crowd of students began throwing bottles at marshals outside Baxter Hall where Mr. Meredith was housed. They were quickly dispersed by tear gas. Soldiers also broke up a minor demonstration at a downtown intersection.]

200 Are Seized

The troops seized approximately 200 persons.

They were seized in the mobs of students and adults that besieged the university administration building last night and attacked troops on the town square this morning.

Among those arrested was former Maj. Gen. Edwin A. Walker, who resigned his commission after having been reprimanded for his ultra-rightwing political activity. He was charged with insurrection.

The university's acceptance of Mr. Meredith, a 29-year-old Air Force veteran, followed Gov. Ross R. Barnett's retreat from his defiance of Federal court orders that the Negro be enrolled.

The 64-year-old official, a member of the militantly segregationist Citizens Councils, had vowed he would go to jail if necessary to prevent university desegregation.

Mr. Meredith's admission marked the first desegregation of a public educational institution in Mississippi. It reduced the Deep South bloc of massive-resistance states to two —

Continued on Page 24, Column 6

CAMPUS A BIVOUAC AS NEGRO ENTERS

2,000 Troops Stand Guard —Meredith Eats Alone

By McCANDLISH PHILLIPS
Special to The New York Times.

OXFORD, Miss., Oct. 1—The University of Mississippi campus was under military occupation today as James H. Meredith, its first Negro student, registered and attended two classes.

Two thousand of the more than 3,000 Army and National Guard troops have made the tree-studded, rolling campus look like a cross between a bivouac and a prisoner-of-war camp. More olive drab uniforms were evident on campus than student casual dress.

Mr. Meredith, who did not get his first meal on campus until supper was served here today, was housed in an end room in Baxter Hall. The room next door was occupied by Federal marshals.

The 29-year-old Negro was taken from his dormitory under guard at 7:45 A. M. and marched to the Lyceum, the administration building, where he was registered in 45 minutes—

Continued on Page 26, Column 1

Mississippi Aides Blamed By U.S. Officials for Riot

By ANTHONY LEWIS
Special to The New York Times.

WASHINGTON, Oct. 1—The Federal Government asserted today that the failure of Mississippi officials to keep their word led to the bloody rioting in Oxford, Miss., last night. Attorney General Robert F. Kennedy and other spokesmen said that Gov. Ross R. Barnett and his aides had repeatedly given as-

Statements by Robert Kennedy and Eastland, Page 25.

surances that they could and would maintain order when James H. Meredith, a Negro, entered the University of Mississippi last night.

Instead, the Federal spokesmen said, the state police were withdrawn at the crucial moment of the developing mob scene. Federal troops were then called in, but two men were dead and many were injured by the time they arrived.

Senator James O. Eastland, Democrat of Mississippi, read on the Senate floor this morning a report on the rioting. He said the report had been prepared by officials of the University of Mississippi.

Eastland Orders Inquiry

Tonight, Senator Eastland directed the Senate Judiciary Committee, which he heads, to make an investigation of "all events at the University of Mississippi since U.S. marshals and Army troops moved in."

The report read by Mr. Eastland this morning sought to put the blame for the rioting on "amateurism by untrained marshals." It said that the 300 marshals at the university last night had "provoked" the crowd of 2,500 persons gathered on the campus.

The university officials also

Continued on Page 25, Column 1

BARNETT CHARGES MARSHALS ERRED

Says 'Trigger-Happy' U. S. Officers Are Responsible for Campus Bloodshed

Text of Barnett statement appears on Page 25.

By HEDRICK SMITH
Special to The New York Times.

JACKSON, Miss., Oct. 1—Gov. Ross R. Barnett tonight attributed the fatal rioting at the University of Mississippi last night to "inexperienced, nervous and trigger-happy Federal marshals."

The Governor made the statement in a recorded broadcast carried by the National Broadcasting Company. In a later recorded broadcast, carried by the Columbia Broadcasting System, Mr. Barnett directly assailed President Kennedy.

"The responsibility for this unwarranted breach of the peace and violence in Mississippi rests directly with the President of the United States," he said. "He ordered armed forces to invade Mississippi and their actions were directly responsible for violence, bloodshed and death."

People Are 'Enraged'

In his earlier statement, the Governor said that the people of Mississippi are enraged, incensed—and rightly so."

"Free men do not submit meekly to the kind of treatment Mississippians received," he said.

The Governor also said that the only solution to the Mississippi integration crisis was for the Federal Government to remove James H. Meredith, a 29-year-old Negro student, from the university.

"The Federal authorities alone have the power to stop bloodshed in Mississippi," he said.

Continued on Page 25, Column 5

Dr. Ray E. Trussell
The New York Times

rent efforts of management and labor toward improving medical care.

"The organized purchasers of medical and hospital care can be the strongest arm of the community in upgrading standards, and it is to the best interest of organized medicine and hospitals to work with them,"

Continued on Page 42, Column 1

Continued on Page 26, Column 1

The New York Times.

LATE CITY EDITION
U. S. Weather Bureau Report (Page 94) forecast:
Partly cloudy, breezy, cool today.
Fair and cool tonight and tomorrow.
Temp. range: 54—45; yesterday: 66—44.

VOL. CXII..No. 38,258.

© 1962 by The New York Times Company.
Times Square, New York 36, N. Y.

NEW YORK, TUESDAY, OCTOBER 23, 1962.

10 cents beyond 50-mile zone from New York City
except on Long Island. Higher in air delivery cities.

FIVE CENTS

U.S. IMPOSES ARMS BLOCKADE ON CUBA ON FINDING OFFENSIVE-MISSILE SITES; KENNEDY READY FOR SOVIET SHOWDOWN

U.S. JUDGES GIVEN POWER TO REQUIRE VOTE FOR NEGROES

High Court Upholds Order Forcing the Registration of 54 in Alabama County

Special to The New York Times

WASHINGTON, Oct. 22—The Supreme Court held today that Federal judges have the power to make state registrars put specific Negroes on the voting rolls.

Alabama had challenged an order by Federal District Judge Frank M. Johnson Jr. requiring the registration of 54 specific Negroes in Macon County, Ala. The order was upheld by the United States Court of Appeals for the Fifth Circuit.

Today the Supreme Court unanimously affirmed the disputed order. And it did so in a way that indicated once again its mood of impatience with Southern efforts to maintain denials of Negro rights.

One-Sentence Ruling

All that was before the court was an application for review of the Fifth Circuit decision. The usual alternatives would have been to deny the petition or to grant it and hear oral argument later.

Instead, the court granted review and then, summarily, affirmed the lower court. It did so in a single sentence, with just one citation in the way of explanation.

The citation was to a decision in 1960 upholding a Federal Court order in a Louisiana voting case. There, a district judge had told Louisiana registrars to put back on their books 1,377 Negroes whose names had been removed in a purge by the segregationist Citizens Council.

Action by Congress

The Macon County case was one of the first brought by the Department of Justice under the Civil Rights Act of 1957. It is especially significant because the county is in the so-called Black Belt, with a predominantly Negro population.

In 1958, when the suit was started, virtually all of the 3,000 white persons of voting age in the county were registered. But only about 1,000 of the 12,000 eligible Negro voters were actually eligible.

In a further move, the registrars resigned, and this was held to leave no defendants to be sued. Congress in 1960 handled this problem by providing

Continued on Page 24, Column 4

102 SAVED AT SEA AS PLANE DITCHES

Rescue Is Made off Alaska Minutes After Accident

By The Associated Press

SITKA, Alaska, Oct. 22—A military-charter airliner ditched in the ocean near here today, but all 102 persons aboard were saved in a quick rescue operation.

The plane, a DC-7C of Northwest Airlines, was going from McChord Air Force Base in Washington to Anchorage, Alaska. It carried 95 passengers and a crew of seven.

The rescue was reported by Northwest and the Alaska Coastal-Ellis Airline at Sitka, which also reported that there apparently were no serious injuries.

The plane went down shortly after the Federal Aviation Agency at Anchorage got word that it was being ditched because of propeller trouble.

A Coast Guard plane alighted on the water nearby; the Air Force sent two rescue planes, and small boats from Sitka, about seven miles north of the

Continued on Page 5, Column 3

Chinese Open New Front; Use Tanks Against Indians

Nehru Warns of Peril to Independence —Reds Attack Near Burmese Border and Press Two Other Drives

Special to The New York Times

NEW DELHI, Oct. 22—Prime Minister Jawaharlal Nehru told the people of India tonight that the Chinese Communist attack was a threat to their liberty.

His grave warning followed word that the advancing Chinese had opened a third front in the Himalayas, near the Burmese border, and had used tanks for the first time. Five more Indian posts fell to the Chinese on the third day of savage fighting.

[A bid for negotiations for a peace accord was broadcast by the Chinese Communist radio early Tuesday, The Associated Press reported from Tokyo.]

In a broadcast, Mr. Nehru denounced the Peking regime as "a powerful and unscrupulous

Excerpts from Nehru's speech will be found on Page 2.

opponent, not caring for peace or peaceful methods."

"The time has come," he said, "for us to realize fully this menace that threatens the freedom of our people and the independence of our country."

Prime Minister Nehru said India would not abandon her economic development program and policy of nonalignment with international blocs, but called on the nation to switch "from the slow-moving methods of peacetime to those which produce results quickly."

"We must build up our military strength by all means at our disposal," he said.

The third front in the Himalayan fighting was opened early today when the Chinese attacked an Indian post at Kibitoo, on the border between

Continued on Page 3, Column 1

U.S. Bids U.N. Bar China; Denounces Attack on India

By SAM POPE BREWER

Special to The New York Times

UNITED NATIONS, N. Y., Oct. 22—Adlai E. Stevenson told the General Assembly today that Communist China's "naked aggression" against India was new proof that it was unfit for membership in the United Nations.

The chief United States representative at the United Nations spoke as the Assembly took up the perennial question of admitting Peking.

Mr. Stevenson told the members that by their actions on the Indian frontier the Chinese Communists "again show their scorn for the Charter of this organization."

The Vice President of the Philippines, Emmanuel Pelaez, told the Assembly that there were more than 40,000,000 Chinese living outside China who would become "a Trojan horse" if the United Nations accepted the Communist Government.

Mr. Pelaez said that the Chinese abroad, 1,000,000 of them in the Philippines, would be used for subversion by the Peking Government. He said they could not be controlled because the Communist Government did not have the means to get at them.

On the fighting in India, Mr. Stevenson declared: "Should there be some among us who think that perhaps the whole thing is a mistake that will right itself before long, let me point out that when a nation moves its troops with tanks and armor, it is no mistake. It is a premeditated act. It is naked aggression. And it has been going on with gathering momentum for some three years."

He quoted Prime Minister

Continued on Page 5, Column 3

U.S. SAID TO EASE KATANGA POLICY

Reported Willing to Put Off Any Economic Sanctions —Congolese Disturbed

By LLOYD GARRISON

Special to The New York Times

LEOPOLDVILLE, the Congo, Oct. 22—Authoritative sources said today that the United States was no longer insisting that Katanga Province strictly meet the deadlines of the United Nations plan to end its secession from the Congo.

This has alarmed Congolese officials. They say that the United States shift is reflected in United Nations policy.

The United Nations plan, introduced Aug. 2 by U Thant, Acting Secretary General, was said to have been conceived largely by the United States.

As outlined by Mr. Thant, the plan's first stage called for the following timetable:

Within thirty days a program was to be decided on for the reintegration of Katanga's army into the Congolese National Army. Sixty days were to be allowed for the program to be carried out.

Not one of these reserves has been met.

Last week Cyrille Adoula, Premier of the central Government, declared that the "deadline for the first stage has passed." He said that it was now time for the United Nations to consider the second stage — economic "sanctions."

A shift in United States policy became apparent over the weekend after the departure of George C. McGhee, Under Secretary of State for Political Af-

Continued on Page 6, Column 6

Stocks Plunge Early On Crisis, but Rally

By RICHARD RUTTER

An already badly battered stock market was hit by massive selling yesterday as talk of a new international crisis spread in Wall Street.

The selling was of dimensions reminiscent of late May when the market experienced the worst break in a generation. Yesterday, the tape ran as late as 19 minutes before a half-hearted recovery met it. That cut losses by about one-third.

On bad tape lateness and volume were the greatest since July 10. Two million shares were traded in the first two hours. Stock markets in London, Frankfurt and Brussels, following Wall Street's lead, also took large losses.

The selling was directly ascribed to news in the morning expressed the general feeling

Continued on Page 49, Column 6

SHIPS MUST STOP

Other Action Planned If Big Rockets Are Not Dismantled

By JAMES RESTON

Special to The New York Times

WASHINGTON, Oct. 22—President Kennedy drew the line tonight, not with Cuba, but with the Soviet Union. After almost a generation of trying to keep the "cold war" from reaching a direct confrontation between United States and Soviet power, a decision has been made to force Soviet missile bases from this hemisphere at the risk of war.

This is the official interpretation of President Kennedy's speech tonight, and the orders to American forces bear it out. On the highest authority, it can be said that these orders include the following:

¶Ships carrying to Cuba weapons capable of striking the continental United States must either turn back or submit to search and seizure, or fight. If they try to run the blockade, a warning shot will be fired across their bows; if they still do not submit, they will be attacked.

¶This applies not only to ships but to any planes suspected of carrying additional offensive weapons to Cuba. There is no evidence that there are nuclear warheads in Cuba, but long-range aircraft suspected of carrying these or any other offensive weapons, will be intercepted, and instructions have been issued to do everything possible to check all Communist-bloc planes en route to Cuba via Newfoundland or Africa.

Prepared to Risk War

Even this will not satisfy the new policy announced by President Kennedy. Not only must new offensive weapons be stopped, under the President's orders, but those already in Cuba must be dismantled, or the United States will take whatever additional action is necessary, beginning with a much more rigorous blockade of such things as Cuba's essential oil supplies, to force compliance.

If this leads to Soviet retaliation, such as a counter-blockade of Berlin, the United States is prepared to risk a major war to defend its present position in the former German capital. Accordingly, American forces, not only in Berlin and West Germany but all over the world, have been placed on emergency alert. The new policy has been defined in a private communi-

Continued on Page 19, Column 1

TRAFFIC DELAYED AT BERLIN BORDER

Reds Start Intensive Check of Civilian Trucks an Hour Before Kennedy Speech

By SYDNEY GRUSON

Special to The New York Times

BONN, Oct. 22—The East German police began to slow down civilian traffic between West Berlin and West Germany late tonight.

About an hour before President Kennedy announced the United States countermeasures against the Soviet build-up in Cuba, the police started intensive examination of the papers of trucks moving into East German territory.

The connection, if any, between the two actions was not immediately clear. Similar harassment of civilian traffic has occurred periodically over the years. The immediate reaction in West Berlin was to consider tonight's harassment as part of the regular order of things, rather than as an advance countermeasure to the American moves against Cuba.

Nevertheless, there was deep anxiety that the Soviet Union would retaliate by causing trouble on the West's access lines to the city.

The outcome of tomorrow's meetings between Andrei A. Gromyko, the Soviet Foreign Minister, and East German Communist leaders was awaited with concern. Mr. Gromyko

Continued on Page 17, Column 3

ANNOUNCES HIS ACTION: President Kennedy speaking to the nation last night on radio and television. He told of moves to keep offensive equipment away from Cuba.

Associated Press Wirephoto

Moscow Says U.S. Holds 'Armed Fist' Over Cuba

By SEYMOUR TOPPING

Special to The New York Times

MOSCOW, Tuesday, Oct. 23—In a broadcast before President Kennedy's speech on the missile build-up in Cuba, the Moscow radio said that the unusual activity in Washington indicated that the United States "once again was raising its armed fist over Cuba." The broadcast said there was "real hysteria" in Washington.

A Soviet reply to the United States note on Cuba that was given last night to Anatoly F. Dobrynin, the Soviet Ambassador to Washington, was expected to be delivered in 24 hours. It was expected that the reply would take the form either of a diplomatic communication or a message to President Kennedy from Premier Khrushchev.

Western observers said the reply would be a denial of any offensive Soviet intent and charge of United States aggression against Cuba.

Veracity Questioned

The veracity of the Soviet Government was directly questioned in President Kennedy's speech, which was given after delivery of the note. The President said evidence had been obtained that Moscow was constructing offensive missile bases on Cuban territory.

The Soviet Government statement of Sept. 11, which warned the United States that an attack on Cuba would mean war, contended that the Soviet weapons supplied to Cuba were of a defensive nature.

Western observers said the crisis over Cuba would enter a critical phase when and if United States war vessels sought to halt and search a Soviet ship bound for Cuba. A number of Soviet vessels carrying civilian goods and pas-

Continued on Page 18, Column 2

All Military Forces Mobilized by Castro

By The Associated Press

KEY WEST, Tuesday, Oct. 23—All of Cuba's military forces have been mobilized as a result of the news from the United States, the Havana radio said today.

The broadcast said the order was issued by Premier Fidel Castro, who will address the nation later today.

"Our combat units rapidly placed themselves on a fighting basis," said the Havana broadcast.

"Hundreds of thousands of men were mobilized in the course of a few hours," added the broadcast, which followed by some hours President Kennedy's announcement of a naval blockade against Cuba.

During the evening, Havana appeared slow to react to President Kennedy's broadcast and

Continued on Page 20, Column 1

PRESIDENT GRAVE

Asserts Russians Lied and Put Hemisphere in Great Danger

Text of the President's address is printed on Page 18.

By ANTHONY LEWIS

WASHINGTON, Oct. 22—President Kennedy imposed a naval and air "quarantine" tonight on the shipment of offensive military equipment to Cuba.

In a speech of extraordinary gravity, he told the American people that the Soviet Union, contrary to promises, was building offensive missile and bomber bases in Cuba. He said the bases could handle missiles carrying nuclear warheads up to 2,000 miles.

Thus, a critical moment in the cold war was at hand tonight. The President had decided on a direct confrontation with — and challenge to — the power of the Soviet Union.

Direct Thrust at Soviet

Two aspects of the speech were notable. One was its direct thrust at the Soviet Union as the party responsible for the crisis. Mr. Kennedy treated Cuba and the Government of Premier Fidel Castro as a mere pawn in Moscow's hands and drew the issue as one with the Soviet Government.

The President, in language of unusual bluntness, accused the Soviet leaders of deliberately "false statements" about their intentions in Cuba.

The other aspect of the speech particularly noted by observers here was its flat commitment by the United States to act alone against the missile threat in Cuba.

Nation Ready to Act

The President made it clear that this country would not stop short of military action to end what he called a "clandestine, reckless and provocative threat to world peace."

Mr. Kennedy said the United States was asking for an emergency meeting of the United Nations Security Council to consider a resolution for "dismantling and withdrawal of all offensive weapons in Cuba."

He said the launching of a nuclear missile from Cuba against any nation in the Western Hemisphere would be regarded as an attack by the Soviet Union against the United States. It would be met, he said, by retaliation against the Soviet Union.

He called on Premier Khrushchev to withdraw the missiles from Cuba and so "move the

Continued on Page 18, Column 1

BIG FORCE MASSES TO BLOCKADE CUBA

Armada Is Under Orders to Open Fire if Necessary— All Troops Are Alerted

By JACK RAYMOND

Special to The New York Times

WASHINGTON, Oct. 22—American ships and planes have begun preparing tonight to impose a blockade of Cuba. United States forces are under orders to thwart any attempt to deliver offensive weapons to Havana.

A Defense Department spokesman said that a large force of ships and planes was concentrating in the Caribbean area had instructions to use force if necessary, including sinking of ships, to carry out President Kennedy's orders for a "quarantine" of Cuba.

The Pentagon said also that United States military units throughout the world, including the garrison in Berlin and the nuclear-armed Strategic Air Command, had been placed "on alert."

Dependents of servicemen at the Guantanamo Bay Naval Base in Cuba have been evacuated, the department said.

Forces at Base Doubled

It added that the military forces there, which were previously put at 3,300 sailors and officers and men and several hundred Marines, have been doubled.

Air defense units in the United States, particularly radar warning stations, interceptor aircraft and ground-to-air missiles, "have been redeployed," the department spokesman said.

The orders for additional defense precautions were taken on the basis of aerial photographic evidence of long-range ballistic missile bases and the arrival of Soviet Ilyushin-28 bombers in Cuba.

The spokesman displayed some of the aerial photographs and pointed to some missiles sites that, he said, had been established only in the last 10 or 15 days.

He said some of the missile

Continued on Page 20, Column 1

KENNEDY CANCELS CAMPAIGN TALKS

He and Johnson Take Step to Concentrate on Crisis

By CABELL PHILLIPS

Special to The New York Times

WASHINGTON, Oct. 22—The White House announced tonight that President Kennedy and Vice President Johnson would make no further political appearances in the Congressional campaign because of the Cuban crisis.

The move by the Administration was considered evidence not only of the seriousness of the situation but also of the desire of the President to unify the country behind his blockade order and keep the issue out of partisan politics.

In this connection, the White House said the President personally informed former Republican Presidents Dwight D. Eisenhower and Herbert Hoover, as well as former Democratic President Harry S. Truman, of his decision.

And the White House announced that John J. McCloy, former disarmament adviser to the Kennedy Administration and a Republican, had been as-

Continued on Page 18, Column 7

Canada Asks Inspection of Cuba; Britain Supporting Quarantine

Diefenbaker Comments

By RAYMOND DANIELL

Special to The New York Times

OTTAWA, Oct. 22—Prime Minister John Diefenbaker of Canada declared tonight the time had come for an impartial inspection of what is happening in Cuba by eight of the "nonaligned nations."

Interrupting debate on the Canadian economic crisis in the House of Commons, Mr. Diefenbaker described President Kennedy's speech on Cuba as "somber and challenging."

"Naturally," he said, "there has been little time to give consideration to positive action that might be taken. But I suggest that if there is a desire—and I am sure there is on the part of the U.S.S.R.—to have the facts, if a group comprising the eight nations making up the 18-nation disarmament committee, were given the opportunity of making an on-site inspection of Cuba to ascertain what the facts are, a major step forward would be taken."

Meanwhile, it was disclosed that Canada has barred the use of her airfields, including that

Continued on Page 21, Column 2

British Note Peril

By DREW MIDDLETON

Special to The New York Times

LONDON, Oct. 22—Qualified sources said today that approval for President Kennedy's military quarantine of Cuba could be expected from the British government.

A Foreign Office spokesman declared, "Revelation of the Soviet build-up in Cuba will come as a shock to the whole civilized world."

Official comment cannot be given until after Prime Minister Macmillan and his Cabinet have discussed the President's speech.

Initial reaction among diplomats was that the President had taken the most reasonable course to frustrate what military circles regard as evident danger to the United States - a buildup of Soviet nuclear capacity in Cuba.

The danger that war might result from a Soviet attempt to break what amounts to a military blockade of Cuba is accepted. But one experienced airman expressed the general feeling this way: "War can come from any one of a number of causes.

Continued on Page 21, Column 1

The New York Times.

LATE CITY EDITION

U.S. Weather Bureau Report (Page 76) forecasts:
Cloudy with chance of showers today;
clear tonight. Fair, warm tomorrow.
Temp. range: 80—63; yesterday: 69°-58.
Temp.-Hum. index: high 60's; yesterday: 67.

VOL. CXII..No. 38,482.   © 1963 by The New York Times Company.
Times Square, New York 36, N.Y.   NEW YORK, TUESDAY, JUNE 4, 1963.   TEN CENTS

ARIZONA UPHELD OVER CALIFORNIA ON WATER RIGHTS

Supreme Court's 7-1 Ruling Caps 40-Year Fight on Use of the Colorado River

WIDE EFFECT FORESEEN

3 Justices Strongly Oppose Provision Allowing U.S. to Apportion Supplies

By WILLIAM M. BLAIR
Special to The New York Times

WASHINGTON, June 3 — Arizona won in the Supreme Court today in its 40-year struggle with California over how much water each state can take from the Colorado River.

The Court, voting 7 to 1, upheld a special master's recommendations on division of the water. The decision is of great economic significance to the Southwest, for the Colorado and its tributaries are the major water sources in that rapidly growing area.

The Court split, 5 to 3, however, on the majority ruling that the Secretary of the Interior had the power to apportion mainstream water among users in the lower basin states, particularly in periods of shortage.

Oppose Federal Role

The dissenters on this issue were Justices John Marshall Harlan, William O. Douglas and Potter Stewart. They sharply challenged the majority view that Congress intended a "single appointed Federal official" to have the authority to apportion mainstream waters, whether in shortage or surplus.

They found this delegation of power "extraordinary." And they argued that state law was intended to control apportionment among users within a single state and that this principle had been established by the Court in earlier water rights cases.

The majority opinion said California was entitled to 4,-400,000 acre feet of water annually from the mainstream of the Colorado, Arizona 2,800,000 acre feet and Nevada 300,000 acre feet. An acre foot is the amount of water that will cover one acre to a depth of one foot —about 325,850 gallons.

The division was confined to the area's mainstream. The Court rejected California's effort to include the Colorado's tributaries, principally the Gila in Arizona, in any water allo-

Continued on Page 23, Column 1

AGENCY SHOP WINS COURT'S APPROVAL

Ruled Permissible by U.S. Law, Optional in States

By JOSEPH A. LOFTUS
Special to The New York Times

WASHINGTON, June 3—A labor contract requiring non-members to pay service fees to a union is permissible under Federal law, but may be prohibited by state law, the Supreme Court ruled today.

The agency shop, as this type of contract is called, was reviewed in two decisions. There was no dissent. Associate Justice Arthur J. Goldberg did not participate.

Where the state's prohibition is enforceable—in state courts or before the National Labor Relations Board—was a question reserved for later decision. That point was not set for argument in the next term.

In two other labor decisions, the Court reversed damage verdicts won by individuals against unions in the state courts of Texas and Ohio. The vote in each was 6 to 2. Justices William O. Douglas and Tom C. Clark dissented. Justice Goldberg did not participate.

The central point in all four cases was the extent of state jurisdiction in the field of labor-management relations. Under the Court's doctrine of Federal pre-emption, the states have no jurisdiction except where Congress has specifically conceded it, or where the N.L.R.B. can afford no remedy, or where there is an overriding state in-

Continued on Page 24, Column 5

Douglas Upbraids Black From Bench

Special to The New York Times

WASHINGTON, June 3 — Justice William O. Douglas made an unusually sharp attack today on a major opinion by his colleague on the Supreme Court, Hugo L. Black.

The tenor of Justice Douglas's extemporaneous remarks from the bench startled those in the courtroom. His strong language was the more surprising because the two men have served together for 24 years and have been regarded as extremely close in judicial philosophy.

Justice Douglas's dissent was in the Colorado River water case. Justice Black wrote the opinion of the court deciding generally against California's claims and in favor of Arizona's.

From the bench Justice

Continued on Page 22, Column 3

PRESIDENT DELAYS RIGHTS MESSAGE

Plans Conferences in Fight on Public Discrimination —G.O.P. Offers a Bill

By E. W. KENWORTHY
Special to The New York Times

WASHINGTON, June 3 — President Kennedy decided tonight to delay for a week his civil rights message to Congress proposing legislation to outlaw discrimination in public accommodations.

He had hoped to get new legislative proposals to Congress tomorrow. He leaves on Wednesday for a Western trip and will stay out of Washington the rest of the week.

One factor in tonight's decision was that last-minute tinkering with the draft bills and the accompanying Presidential message was still going on. It was deemed wise not to rush so important a matter.

The President believed also that it would help the legislation to go ahead first with scheduled conferences. He will meet tomorrow, for example, with business executives while large holdings in the South. His brother, Attorney General Robert F. Kennedy, will meet other groups.

Democrats Briefed

The week will also be used to try to create a favorable climate at the Capitol. Democratic Congressional leaders, who were briefed on civil rights by the President today, will discuss the legislation with others in both parties.

The decision to delay the message was especially difficult for the President because 24 House Republicans introduced today their own legislation to bar racial discrimination in public accommodations. They were plainly intent on beating the Administration in offering a measure.

One of two main proposals in the Administration's legislation would deal with racial discrim-

Continued on Page 27, Column 1

PUPIL TRANSFERS TO DIVIDE RACES VOIDED BY COURT

Supreme Bench Says Plan in Two Tennessee Areas Slows Desegregation

By ANTHONY LEWIS
Special to The New York Times

WASHINGTON, June 3 — The Supreme Court held unconstitutional today a school desegregation plan that allows pupils to transfer out of schools where their race is in the minority.

Justice Tom C. Clark said that the plan was invalid because it based transfers "solely on racial factors" and led to "perpetuation of segregation." He spoke for a unanimous Court.

The transfer plan was at issue in cases from Knoxville, Tenn., and from Davidson County, adjoining Nashville. Similar provisions are in use in Memphis and in some Virginia communities.

Five other Southern states have statutes saying that no child may be compelled to attend a school where he would be in a racial minority. They are Alabama, Arkansas, Florida, Louisiana and North Carolina.

Broad Impact Likely

Thus today's decision can be expected to have a major impact on the South. It will remove the legal basis for a device widely used to cushion the effect of school desegregation.

In practice, the Tennessee provisions — and those in other areas — worked as follows:

School boards, in response to the Supreme Court's desegregation decision, abolished the former separate school maps for whites and Negroes. New school districts were drawn for a single, nonracial system.

But any white student who thereupon found himself in the district of "a school previously serving colored students" could automatically transfer to another school. So could a Negro zoned into a school formerly serving whites.

Transfers Made Easy

The plan also, significantly, permitted automatic transfers "when a student would otherwise be required to attend a school where the majority of students of that school or in his or her grade are of a different race."

A student in such a minority situation had only to ask and he would be transferred. Others who wanted to switch schools had to persuade the school board there was "good cause."

The provision was generally regarded as a way of assuring white families that their children would not be placed in a mostly Negro school. It was defended as necessary to reduce opposition to desegregation.

Negroes, on the other hand, said the transfer provision had made true integration of the schools impossible. They especially criticized the fact that there was no automatic right of a pupil to transfer from a school entirely or mostly of his

Continued on Page 25, Column 3

Army May Release Ft. Tilden for Park

By CHARLES G. BENNETT

There is a "very, very good possibility" that the Army might make Fort Tilden available to the city for the Breezy Point park development, Mayor Wagner said yesterday.

"We learned last week," the Mayor said at an impromptu press conference, "that there is a good possibility that the Army might move its installations and Nike bases from there in the near future, and then we can start negotiations."

An Army spokesman said in Washington last night that the Army had been reviewing the situation but had not made any decision.

Fort Tilden is on 317 acres next to the 236-acre Jacob Riis Park. The city proposes ultimately to have in all 1,362

Continued on Page 48, Column 5

HAITIAN CONTACTS RESUMED BY U.S.

Duvalier Regime Regarded as Firmly in Power Even if Not Constitutional

By TAD SZULC
Special to The New York Times

WASHINGTON, June 3 — The United States resumed "normal diplomatic business" with Haiti today after nearly three weeks of a suspension of contacts intended to underline Washington's disapproval of President François Duvalier.

The decision to return to normal relations and to remove a Navy task force from the vicinity of Haiti appeared to reverse last month's undisguised policy efforts aimed at Dr. Duvalier's removal.

At the peak of the Haiti crisis, the Kennedy Administration is known to have convinced itself that President Duvalier's regime was on the brink of collapse because of mounting United States pressures.

It was then expected that Dr. Duvalier would voluntarily give up office and leave Haiti on May 15. The United States regarded that date as the end of his legal term.

Marine Landing Envisaged

Accordingly, the Administration secretly prepared with at least three Latin-American governments a plan that might have involved a landing in Haiti of United States marines, it has been disclosed. An inter-American "police action" in support of a new regime in Haiti was also envisaged.

The details of this planned operation were disclosed by diplomats who participated in its preparation last month.

The operation was abandoned on May 15, however, after an all-night vigil here by officials of the Organization of American States. It then became clear that Dr. Duvalier did not intend to leave Haiti.

The State Department later that day instructed Ambassador Raymond L. Thurston in Port-au-Prince to suspend immediately his contacts with the Haitian Government. The move was made secretly and the Administration confirmed it indirectly only after it was published in press dispatches from Haiti.

Regime Still Held Illegal

Today, Lincoln White, the State Department spokesman, announced that the United States charge d'affaires in Port-au-Prince, Glion Curtis Jr., was being instructed "to resume normal diplomatic business with the Government of Haiti."

Administration officials insisted that the lifting of the short-lived diploma ic sanctions did not imply any change in the United States view that the Duvalier regime was unconstitutional. It was made clear, however, that the United States had concluded that the Haitian Government was firmly in power.

Therefore, officials said, a re-

Continued on Page 6, Column 3

POST AWAITS VOTE

Archbishop of Milan a Possible Choice as New Pontiff

By PAUL HOFMANN
Special to The New York Times

ROME, June 3—Amid the drama of Pope John XXIII's final hours, Romans speculated whether his successor would be an Italian or a "foreigner."

At the same time, ecclesiastics and laymen debated whether the next Pontiff would show the conciliatory, progressive attitude of Pope John or lead the Roman Catholic Church back to a more conservative position.

An Italian prince of the church, Giovanni Battista Cardinal Montini, 65-year-old Archbishop of Milan, was widely mentioned as the leading candidate.

Cardinal Montini is regarded as a prominent representative of the "progressive" wing of the world episcopacy, which revealed its strength with the manifest encouragement of Pope John during the first session of the Ecumenical Council in the Vatican last autumn.

A Close Aide to Pius XII

As monsignor, the present Cardinal Montini was for many years a close aide to the late Pope Pius XII, Pope John's predecessor, in the Vatican Secretariat of State. The slim, ascetic-looking churchman, who is credited with a prodigious capacity for hard work, became Archbishop of Milan, one of the largest Catholic dioceses in the world, in 1954, but still was not a Cardinal when Pope Pius XII died in 1958.

The Archbishop of Milan then already had such a reputation that some commentators suggested that the Cardinals would depart from a 600-year-old tradition and elect a prelate who was not one of their number.

Instead the Cardinals elevated one of their number, Angelo Giuseppe Cardinal Roncalli, Patriarch of Venice. As Pope John XXIII he conferred on Archbishop Montini the red hat of Cardinal in his first consistory in December, 1958. Cardinal Montini was close to Pope John throughout his pontificate and if he is elected as his successor he is expected to continue his policies.

Cardinals Take Over Rule

Soon after Pope John died tonight, the Cardinals present in the Vatican started taking over the interim government of the church on behalf of the 82 members of the Sacred College of Cardinals. The Cardinals will rule jointly until their vote in conclave results in the election of the new Pope.

Prominent among conservative Italian Cardinals thought to be of papal timber is Giuseppe Cardinal Siri, Archbishop of Genoa. He is 57 years old.

The leader of the conservative wing of the Ecumenical Council, Alfredo Cardinal Ottaviani, a 72-year-old Vatican theologian and guardian of

Continued on Page 18, Column 6

Africans Complain Of Bias in Moscow

By SEYMOUR TOPPING
Special to The New York Times

MOSCOW, June 3 — A sharp controversy has arisen between Soviet authorities and African students here who have complained of discrimination fostered by a Moscow newspaper article.

The article, published by Komsomolskaya Pravda, the newspaper of the Communist Youth League, purported to tell the experiences of a Russian girl who was sold into a harem by a Moslem student she had married.

African students here interpreted the article as a warning to Russian girls against association with them. It was published on Oct. 27 after a number of Africans had complained of being attacked by Russians because they had appeared publicly in the company

Continued on Page 5, Column 1

POPE JOHN XXIII

Associated Press

Washington Mourns Loss Of Great Force for Peace

By M. S. HANDLER
Special to The New York Times

WASHINGTON, June 3—President Kennedy paid high tribute today to the statesmanship and moral leadership of Pope John XXIII. The President said of the Pontiff: "His compassion and kindly strength have bequeathed humanity a new legacy of purpose and courage for the future."

Mr. Kennedy led official Washington in mourning the passing of Pope John as a great loss to mankind. Members of both houses of Congress and churchmen of various faiths joined in expressing the belief that the Pontiff had made an immense contribution to the reconciliation of all Christian faiths, to the reconciliation of his church with Judaism, and to the preservation of peace.

President Kennedy said the Pope had "brought compassion and understanding drawn from wide experience to the most divisive problems of a tumultuous age."

Statement by President

The President's statement said:

"The highest work of any man is to protect and carry on the deepest spiritual heritage of the race. To Pope John was given the almost unique gift of enriching and enlarging that tradition. Armed with the humility and calm which surrounded his earliest days, he brought compassion and an understanding drawn from wide experience to the most divisive problems of a tumultuous age. He was the chosen leader of world Catholicism, but his concern for the human spirit transcended all boundaries of belief or geography.

"The enabling precepts of his encyclicals and his actions drew on the accumulated wisdom of an ancient faith for guidance in the most complex and troublesome problems of the modern age. To him the divine spark which unites men would ultimately prove more enduring than the forces which divide. His wisdom, compassion and kindly strength have bequeathed humanity a new legacy of purpose and courage for the future."

The reference to Pope John's encyclicals marked the second time Mr. Kennedy had expressed such praise. At Boston College

Continued on Page 21, Column 1

WAGNER ORDERS FLAGS LOWERED

Leads City in Mourning and Picks 2 Representatives to Attend Pope's Funeral

Mayor Wagner yesterday ordered flags on all city buildings flown at half-staff until the burial of Pope John. The Mayor led the city in mourning the Pope.

"Pope John XXIII symbolized faith, goodness, courage and compassion," Mayor Wagner said, adding, "He appealed always to the best in the human heart and all humanity is uplifted by the noble example which he set."

Mayor Wagner also designated Commissioner of Public Events Richard C. Patterson Jr. and Thomas J. Deegan, chairman of the World's Fair executive committee, as official city representatives at the Pope's funeral.

Both are in Rome on other business.

Washington will not accord the Pope the flag tribute he will receive in New York. The State Department explained that flags in Washington are

Continued on Page 18, Column 4

St. Peter's Throng Silenced by Grief

ROME, June 3—A vast throng in the piazza in front of St. Peter's Basilica heard the news of the death of Pope John this evening in sad and resigned silence.

Many knelt in quiet prayer and crossed themselves as other hundreds surged toward the bronze doors leading into St. Peter's Basilica.

Many knelt in quiet prayer and crossed themselves as other hundreds surged toward the bronze doors leading into the Vatican City to watch as one of the two portals was swung shut as a traditional sign that the Pope was dead.

The Pope's death came only minutes after a choral offering brought to an end a mass celebrated for the Pontiff on the steps of the Basilica by Luigi Cardinal Traglia, pro-vicar of the Diocese of Rome.

More than 35,000 Romans, visitors, pilgrims, nuns and clergymen gathered to hear the mass, which started at 7 P.M. By the time the last sacred

Continued on Page 21, Column 2

POPE JOHN XXIII IS DEAD AT 81, ENDING 4½-YEAR REIGN DEVOTED TO PEACE AND CHRISTIAN UNITY

A LIBERAL PONTIFF

Church Council and Encyclical on Amity Marked Tenure

By ARNALDO CORTESI
Special to The New York Times

ROME, June 3 — Pope John XXIII, champion of world peace and a tireless fighter for the union of all Christian churches, died in the Vatican tonight while Cardinals and other prelates and several of his relatives prayed around his sickbed. He was 81 years old.

John XXIII was the 261st Pope to sit on the throne that was first occupied by the Apostle Peter.

In the four years, seven months and six days of his reign he conquered the hearts of people throughout the world. Few other Popes before him were so universally admired.

The Pope's death came at 7:49 P.M. (2:49 P.M. Eastern daylight time.)

After a long struggle the Pope developed peritonitis, brought on by a stomach tumor. The tumor was discovered last November.

Doctors Gave Up Hope

His doctors had given up hope at the onset of the peritonitis, an inflammation of the lining of the abdominal cavity. This was given as the cause of his death.

Much of the intervening period was passed in a state of coma or semicoma. The Pope was lucid most of yesterday, however, but in great pain, which he bore with remarkable fortitude. Early yesterday afternoon he suffered a "new crisis."

Before entering his last state of coma, he repeatedly said in Latin: "Into Thy hands, O Lord, I commit my soul."

The Pope had dedicated much of his pontificate to promoting Christian unity and the unity of all men as brothers with a common goal.

Pope's Last Words

In his last words, addressed to the assembled Cardinals and prelates around his sickbed, the Pope said:

"Ut unum sint." They are Latin words meaning "That they may be one."

The words were originally spoken by Jesus when the Last Supper.

The night of May 25 the Pope suffered a hemorrhage that brought him close to death. A series of blood transfusions saved his life. He had been improving when peritonitis developed.

John XXIII was elected Pope Oct. 28, 1958. He was born in the village of Sotto il Monte in northern Italy Nov. 25, 1881. He was 81 years, six months and nine days at his death.

Pope John passed his last days in his bedroom on the top floor of the Vatican Palace. A small crowd of ecclesiastics and laymen had congregated there when they were told that the Pope was near death.

Those at Bedside

Those around the bedside included Eugene Cardinal Tisserant, the bearded French dean of the Sacred College; Benedetto Cardinal Aloisi Masella, or Chamberlain, heads the interim administration of the Roman Catholic Church; the Pope's three brothers—Giuseppe, Alfredo and Zaverio Roncalli—and his widowed sister, Assunta; three nephews, several members of the Papal household, such as his sacristan, his confessor and his Master of the Chamber.

A larger crowd, including ambassadors and ministers, waited in an adjacent room.

Swiss guards kept all others out of the Papal apartment. About 30 minutes before the Pope died it became clear from his labored breathing and his falling pulse rate that he was near death. The Pope's personal physician, Prof. Antonio Gasbarrini, warned Cardinal Aloisi Masella that the Pope had only hours to live.

Mass for the Pope was said at an altar in an adjoining room

Continued on Page 18, Column 1

DC-7 With 101 Lost in Alaska; 95 Military Men and Kin Aboard

Vast Air-Sea Hunt Pressed for Chartered Craft After Radio Contact Breaks Off

By The Associated Press

JUNEAU, Alaska, June 3—A military-chartered airliner carrying 101 persons—men, women and children — vanished off southeastern Alaska today under circumstances suggesting sudden disaster.

The Northwest Airlines DC-7, a piston-engined aircraft, last radioed 30 to 40 miles at sea off Prince of Wales Island, requesting a change of altitude from 14,000 to 18,000 feet. Air traffic men trying to reply minutes later got no answer.

The last confirmed message from the plane was at 10:06 A.M., about two and a half hours after it had left McChord Air Force Base, Wash., with 95 military passengers, including dependents, and a crew of six.

An intensive search by planes and vessels was made in deteriorating weather.

The Coast Guard said later tonight that a Canadian plane had reported a sighting what appeared to be wreckage near

The New York Times   June 4, 1963
Cross shows where plane last reported its position.

Graham Island, in northern British Columbia.

The only detailed information concerning the sighting came

Continued on Page 13, Column 1

NEED MORTGAGE MONEY FAST? Phone
Mr. Hanson at The Dime Savings Bank
of Brooklyn—TRiangle 5-9762. Loans up to
80%.—Terms up to 30 years. Rates
low.—Answers usually within
24 hours.—Advt.

The New York Times.

LATE CITY EDITION
U. S. Weather Bureau Report (Page 50) forecast:
Sunny and cool today; clear tonight.
Sunny and warmer tomorrow.
Temp. range: 74—55; yesterday: 70—55.
Temp.-Hum. Index: 70; yesterday: 69.

VOL. CXII.,. No. 38,500.   © 1963 by The New York Times Company. Times Square, New York 36, N. Y.   NEW YORK, SATURDAY, JUNE 22, 1963.   TEN CENTS

18 UNION CHIEFS ACT TO END BIAS IN CONSTRUCTION

Bid Locals Admit Qualified Negroes as Apprentices and as Members

PROGRAM NOT BINDING

N.A.A.C.P. Aide Says Plan Sounds Good, but Notes It Must Be Implemented

Special to The New York Times

WASHINGTON, June 21—The presidents of the 18 building trades unions adopted today a program to eliminate racial discrimination in apprenticeship, union membership and assignment to job openings.

At the same time, they warned that they would fight any effort by the Government to determine qualifications necessary for admission into the industry and into union membership.

The building trades unions have been the most criticized segment of the labor movement on discrimination. The National Association for the Advancement of Colored People has long contended that most building trades locals practice systematic exclusion of Negroes. Recently, the association picketed construction projects in New York and Philadelphia.

Government Pressure

This activity and increased pressure on them by the Government to eliminate discriminatory practices prompted the building trades presidents to discuss the situation. Today's statement, adopted unanimously, was the result.

The union leaders said they recognized the Government's interest and its duty to correct economic injustice and pledged their "good faith to work toward the goal."

The program consists of the following points:

¶Local unions are urged to accept any applicant for membership who meets the required qualifications regardless of his race, creed, color or national origin.

¶If a local operates an exclusive hiring hall or a work referral system, applicants for employment are to be referred to work without discrimination as to race, creed, color or national origin.

¶Locals shall also accept and refer applicants for apprenticeship without discrimination.

Adoption of the statement does not automatically bind the local unions to abide by it.

A spokesman for the Building

Continued on Page 8, Column 1

STATE DEMOCRATS MAY SHIFT POWER

Change in Rules Proposed to Move Control Upstate

By RICHARD P. HUNT

State Democratic leaders are considering a reorganization plan that would for the first time give upstate Democrats a major, if not dominant, role in party affairs.

The plan, which is contained in a proposed set of rules of the state committee, implies that the traditional control of the party machinery by New York City Democrats will be limited or ended.

The rules have been proposed after a year of study by a nine-member committee appointed by William H. McKeon, the Democratic state chairman. They will be submitted for ratification at a state committee meeting in Albany on Tuesday.

The most important change proposed is the creation of a 38-member executive committee, which would be empowered to carry on the party's business in behalf of the full 300-member state committee.

Democrats from the 57 coun-

Continued on Page 24, Column 5

Lawyers Promise Kennedy Aid in Easing Race Unrest

Leaders of Bar Agree to Form Working Group Across Nation — President to See Negro Officials Today

By MARJORIE HUNTER
Special to The New York Times

WASHINGTON, June 21—Many of the nation's leading lawyers promised President Kennedy at a conference today that they would help open the lines of communication between the races. But they were told by a participant at the conference that they faced "a long hot summer."

At a meeting in the White House, the lawyers acceded to a Presidential request that they set up a committee that would try to ease racial tensions and provide national and local leadership.

Today's meeting was one in a series that the President has held in recent weeks with religious leaders, businessmen, Governors and labor leaders. So far, the President has conferred with several thousand persons on civil-rights matters.

Heading the lawyers' racial communications committee will be Harrison Tweed of New York and Bernard G. Segal of Philadelphia. All of the 244 lawyers attending today's meeting were invited to serve on the committee.

Another committee, also dealing with racial communications, will be established by the American Bar Association. This was announced during the White House meeting by Sylvester C. Smith Jr. of Newark, N. J., the association's president.

Joining the President in meeting the lawyers in the East Room were Vice President Johnson and Attorney General Robert F. Kennedy. Of the lawyers present, 66 were from Southern states. There were 23

Continued on Page 8, Column 3

Wagner to Help Negroes Get More Building Jobs

By CHARLES G. BENNETT

Mayor Wagner said yesterday that he would appoint "in a day or two" a panel of three qualified persons to induce construction unions to take in more Negroes. The panel will be given a week to examine employment records, talk with all groups concerned and make recommendations.

At the same time the Mayor said he had been assured by Peter Brennan, president of the Building Trades and Construction Council, that "technically qualified" members of minority groups would be put to work "right away" if job opportunities existed.

The Mayor spoke at a news conference in City Hall a few hours after his return from two weeks in Hawaii and Tokyo. Beforehand he had conferred at Gracie Mansion with Mr. Brennan and with Harry Van Arsdale Jr., president of the Central Labor Council.

Asks Special Session

Mr. Wagner dashed from the City Hall news interview back to Idlewild Airport, where he had landed early in the morning, to fly to Lake Placid, N.Y., to attend the New York State Conference of Mayors.

At the Lake Placid conference last night, Mayor Wagner called on Mayors throughout the state to join him in a request to Governor Rockefeller and the legislative leaders to summon a special session to deal with racial discrimination.

New state laws, Mr. Wagner proposed, should include financial aid to municipalities to speed desegregation in jobs, housing, education and other fields.

At City Hall the Mayor said of Mr. Brennan's promise to bring more Negroes into construction jobs as fast as possible:

"During the week the panel is preparing its recommendations, my office staff will be

Continued on Page 9, Column 2

MAYOR TO OPPOSE RACE BY DE SAPIO

Indicates He May Campaign in 'Village' in an Effort to Block Comeback Drive

Mayor Wagner made it clear yesterday that he would actively oppose Carmine G. De Sapio's attempted political comeback.

The Mayor was asked at a wide-ranging news conference about Mr. De Sapio's announcement Wednesday that he would be a candidate for the Democratic leadership of the First Assembly District South. This Greenwich Village area was the base of his former statewide political power.

"This is a free country," the Mayor replied. Then he added grimly, "My position on Mr. De Sapio has not changed."

Pressed as to whether he would actually go into Greenwich Village to oppose a De Sapio comeback, Mr. Wagner said a Mayor did not generally have time to go into the districts in district campaigns. But he conceded that he had done so, and indicated he might do so again.

He was asked, "No one should expect any encouragement from you for Mr. De Sapio?"

"That is the understatement of the year," the Mayor shot back.

Then the Mayor said: "I'll wait until the campaign begins

Continued on Page 24, Column 3

JUDICIAL INQUIRY ON PROFUMO SET; LABOR ASSAILS IT

Macmillan Announces Study of Security Aspects, but Foes Call It 'Cover-Up'

By SYDNEY GRUSON
Special to The New York Times

LONDON, June 21 — Prime Minister Macmillan announced today that a judicial inquiry would be held into the security aspects of the Profumo scandal. The form of the inquiry was immediately criticized by the Opposition Labor party as a "cover-up."

Mr. Macmillan told the House of Commons that Lord Denning, as Master of the Rolls, the third-highest judicial official in Britain, would conduct the inquiry. The Prime Minister also gravely took note of continuing rumors about the involvement of "all sorts of people" in the affair.

Asked by Harold Wilson, Labor's leader, whether he was satisfied that nothing more remained to be disclosed, Mr. Macmillan replied:

"I know of no things which I have not told the House, but I have heard these terrible things being said now of all sorts of people which, if allowed to go on, will destroy not only one side of the House of Commons but the other side of the House of Commons."

Chamber Is Crowded

To a chamber unusually crowded for a Friday session, Mr. Macmillan said that the rumors "affect the honor and integrity of public life" in Britain "and if they were true such a situation might point to a security risk."

Pressing for the appointment of a select committee of Members of Parliament to conduct the inquiry, Mr. Wilson said that Lord Denning would have no power to compel the attendance of witnesses or compel proof.

"Is the Prime Minister aware that some of the evidence required will be collected from some of the most unmitigated liars in this country?" Mr. Wilson asked.

He also referred to the rumors. In a judicial inquiry, he said, they "cannot be dissipated and the men concerned enabled to clear their names, as they have every right to do."

Blackmail Linked to Case

The rumors are boundless on Fleet Street, the home of the British press, and in Westminster, the home of Parliament. Not even the royal family has escaped.

One of the rumors has linked blackmail to the case of Dr. Stephen Ward, 50-year-old society osteopath. Dr. Ward is in custody on charges of living off the earnings of prostitution.

He introduced Christine Keeler, 21-year-old self-styled model, to John Profumo when Mr. Profumo was Secretary of State for War and to Capt. Yevgeny E. Ivanov, a Soviet deputy naval attaché until his recall last December. Miss Keeler had simultaneous affairs with the two men.

Another rumor involves the identity of a man said to be

Continued on Page 7, Column 1

FRENCH NAVY ENDS NATO ATLANTIC TIE

Paris Announces Resuming of Unrestrained Control of Virtually Whole Fleet

By DREW MIDDLETON
Special to The New York Times

PARIS, June 21—France announced today that she would resume unrestrained control of virtually the whole of the nation's naval fighting force.

A curt bulletin issued by the semiofficial French Press Agency said that "the French Government has decided to withdraw from the NATO Fleet in the North Atlantic." The bulletin cited official sources.

The Government's decision was described here as a logical consequence of France's action in 1959. In that year she withdrew her Mediterranean fleet from the alliance's control.

Effect of New Move

Earlier this year two squadrons of that fleet were transferred from the Mediterranean base of Toulon to the North Atlantic base of Brest in Brittany.

As a consequence of today's announcement, the bulk of the powerful French forces hitherto earmarked for training and planning under the ultimate command of the Supreme Allied Commander Atlantic have now been withdrawn.

[In Washington officials were distressed by the French action. The Administration was embarrassed by its timing on the eve of President Kennedy's departure for Europe.]

Allied diplomats almost universally deplored the psychological shock that the action

Continued on Page 20, Column 5

World Labor Parley Bars South African

Special to The New York Times

GENEVA, June 21 — United States Government and American worker delegates voted today for the expulsion of a South African from the International Labor Organization conference.

The credentials of the South African, a worker delegate, were rejected by a vote of 135 to 3, with 57 abstentions. His credentials had been issued by his Government.

The member states of the 108-nation organization, a United Nations specialized agency, are represented by two government delegates, a representative of employer groups and a trade unionist. Each has separate voting rights. The worker repre-

Continued on Page 4, Column 5

CARDINAL MONTINI ELECTED POPE; LIBERAL, 65, WILL REIGN AS PAUL VI; LIKELY TO CONTINUE JOHN'S WORK

POPE PAUL VI in his first public appearance gives his blessing to the crowd that had gathered outside St. Peter's Basilica. Holding missal is Msgr. Salvatore Capoferri.

United Press International Radiophoto

Rome Believes New Pope Will Press for Reforms

Clear-cut Decision Seen

By PAUL HOFMANN
Special to The New York Times

ROME, June 21 — Pope Paul VI began his pontificate today amid general forecasts that it would bring an energetic continuation of the progressive course charted by Pope John XXIII.

The consensus in Rome was that the conclave, by elevating the 65-year-old Archbishop of Milan to the papacy, had made a clear decision for a liberal pontificate—and one hopefully expected to last a long time.

First responses from world centers showed international agreement with this evaluation. The general belief here was that Pope Paul had been elected with the understanding that he would soon reopen the church's Ecumenical Council, suspended by the death of his predecessor.

Ecclesiastics who served in the past with the new Pontiff predicted that he would press for enactment

Continued on Page 3, Column 5

Choice Widely Hailed

By GEORGE DUGAN

The election of Giovanni Battista Cardinal Montini to succeed Pope John XXIII was met with worldwide acclaim.

Both Protestant and Jewish leaders said yesterday that the election of Pope Paul VI showed that the reform and renewal so close to the heart of Pope John would be emphasized in the days to come.

The new Pope, who was given the red hat of a cardinal by his predecessor, was deeply involved in the Ecumenical Council, which had been scheduled to reconvene on Sept. 8.

The election of Pope Paul aroused great interest in Washington, which is curious about the political effects the choice of a liberal will have on the European left. President Kennedy, who will visit the new Pope July 2, sent the Pontiff his "heartiest congratulations."

J. Irwin Miller, president of

Continued on Page 3, Column 3

HOUSE UNIT VOTES DEFENSE FUND CUT

Reduction of 1.9 Billion Is Protested by McNamara

By JACK RAYMOND
Special to The New York Times

WASHINGTON, June 21—The House Appropriations Committee approved a $47,092,209,-000 defense fund measure today, with only relatively small changes in the Administration's original request.

But even these changes drew an immediate protest from Secretary of Defense Robert S. McNamara. He said the cuts in airplane procurement money "would deny us necessary tactical support for our combat-ready Army divisions."

He charged also that other cuts would force a reduction in military personnel by some 60,000 men.

President Kennedy last January requested $49,014,237,000 in defense appropriations for the fiscal year 1964, beginning July 1. The committee cut the total by $1,922,028,000.

The committee noted that more than $500,000,000 of the cut represented bookkeeping shifts.

"The accompanying bill," the committee said in its report, based on four months of closed hearings, "will support programs which will promote the security of the United States and assure the continuation of the policy of military supremacy."

According to the report, the bill would provide armed forces totaling 2,695,000 officers and

Continued on Page 20, Column 3

CARDINAL MONTINI ELECTED POPE (right column)

5TH VOTE DECISIVE

New Pontiff Gives His Blessing to Crowd— Coronation June 30

By ARNALDO CORTESI
Special to The New York Times

ROME, June 21 — Giovanni Battista Cardinal Montini, 65-year-old Archbishop of Milan, was elected Supreme Pontiff of the Roman Catholic Church today. He will reign as Pope Paul VI.

The man who had been described as the most likely prince of the church to succeed Pope John XXIII manifested his intention of continuing his predecessor's policies by confirming Amleto Giuseppi Cardinal Cicognani as Apostolic Secretary of State. Cardinal Cicognani held the post under John XXIII.

Pope Paul was elected on the fifth ballot conducted in the Sacred College of Cardinals. He and 79 other Cardinals from 29 nations — both figures were records — went into conclave Wednesday evening.

The news that the more than 500,000,000 Roman Catholics in the world had a new spiritual leader was given at 11:22 A.M. by a white puff of smoke from a stovepipe on the roof of the Sistine Chapel in Vatican City.

262d on Papal Throne

The new Pope, a native of the Lombardy region, who was 65 last Sept. 26, will be, according to Catholic tradition, the 262d occupant of the throne of St. Peter.

The coronation of Paul VI will take place in St. Peter's Basilica early in the morning of June 30, the day President Kennedy is to arrive in Rome during his 10-day tour of Europe. In the Western church the day is the Feast of St. Paul, the apostle who was the first in the church to bear the name. The last Pope to use it, Paul V, a Borghese, died in 1621.

An hour after his election, Pope Paul appeared on a balcony of St. Peter's Basilica to impart an apostolic benediction to a huge crowd. There were emotional scenes as most people dropped to their knees to receive the blessing. Some women wept and others held infants toward the Pope.

Acceptance at 11:15 A.M.

The conclave that elected Pope Paul lasted 41 hours. It ranks as the sixth shortest in the last four centuries. In the last century there have been only two that were shorter, the one that elected Pius XII in 1939, which lasted 30 hours, and the one that elected Leo XIII in 1878, which lasted 36 hours. Pope John was elected in 1958 on the 11th ballot on the third day.

Paul VI assumed all papal prerogatives and rights at 11:15 A.M. (6:15 A.M., Eastern daylight time) when, after protesting that he felt unworthy, he gave his acceptance to the dean of the Sacred College, Eugène Cardinal Tisserant. The coronation is a formality and the reign

Continued on Page 2, Column 1

TAX DISCLOSURE AROUSES OTTAWA

Minister Admits Plan Was Known to 3 Businessmen

By HOMER BIGART
Special to The New York Times

OTTAWA, June 21—Walter L. Gordon, the harassed Minister of Finance in the minority Liberal Government, gave fresh ammunition to his critics in Parliament today.

He admitted that the three Toronto businessmen who helped write his budget knew in advance of the details of a controversial tax proposal. The tax had been aimed at halting the take-over of Canadian companies by foreigners.

The admission drew astonished gasps from Opposition benches in the House of Commons. Mr. Gordon had told the House yesterday that only Prime Minister Lester B. Pearson and the Cabinet knew of his decision to withdraw the tax.

The proposal would have placed a 30 per cent tax on the seller of a large block of shares in a Canadian company to a foreigner. Its withdrawal was announced while the stock markets of Canada were still open and caused frenzied speculation. Members of the Opposition have demanded an investigation to determine whether the leakage of budget secrets permitted "insiders" to make windfall profits on the markets.

Mr. Gordon had been under fire all week for enlisting three financial experts from Toronto, two of whom had re-

Continued on Page 14, Column 7

Brezhnev Advances As Khrushchev Heir

By SEYMOUR TOPPING
Special to The New York Times

MOSCOW, June 21—Leonid I. Brezhnev, a member of the ruling Presidium of the Soviet Communist party, emerged tonight after plenary meetings of the Central Committee as a likely political heir of Premier Khrushchev.

Mr. Brezhnev, who is 57 years old and a protégé of Mr. Khrushchev, has been appointed to the Secretariat of the Central Committee. The Secretariat is the chief executive body of the party.

Western analysts note that Mr. Brezhnev now holds an array of party and Government positions that make it appear that he is being groomed to assume the roles of Mr. Khru-

Continued on Page 5, Column 3

PROMISES ACTION: Mayor Wagner at City Hall news conference where he announced plans to eliminate racial discrimination in the city's construction-industry unions.

The New York Times

"All the News That's Fit to Print"

The New York Times.

LATE CITY EDITION
U. S. Weather Bureau Report (Page 58) forecasts:
Cloudy with scattered showers today; partly cloudy tonight and tomorrow.
Temp. range: 77—62; yesterday: 81—61.
Temp.-Hum. Index: 70 to 75; yesterday: 72.

VOL. CXII. No. 38,568.   © 1963 by The New York Times Company. Times Square, New York 36, N. Y.   NEW YORK, THURSDAY, AUGUST 29, 1963.   TEN CENTS

KENNEDY SIGNS BILL AVERTING A RAIL STRIKE

PRECEDENT IS SET

Arbitration Imposed by Congress—Vote in House 286-66

Text of Kennedy's statement will be found on Page 13.

By JOHN D. POMFRET
Special to The New York Times

WASHINGTON, Aug. 28 — Congress passed today a bill that prevented a national railroad strike scheduled for midnight. President Kennedy signed it immediately.

The House completed the Congressional action. It adopted by a standing vote of 286 to 66 the same joint resolution passed yesterday by the Senate. The measure provides for arbitration of the two principal issues in the railroad work rules dispute and bars a strike for 180 days.

The action was without Federal precedent. Never before in the history of peacetime labor relations has Congress imposed arbitration in a labor-management dispute.

The failure of the railroads and the five train operating unions to resolve their dispute, and the Congressional action this made necessary, is considered by many to represent a major failure for the collective bargaining system.

Many Are Reluctant

Even many Congressmen who voted for the measure, convinced that the economic consequences of a national railroad strike made action to head it off essential, did so with great reluctance. They said they feared that their action might set a precedent detrimental to collective bargaining.

An arbitration board was created by Congress to consider the two key issues. These are whether diesel locomotive firemen are necessary in freight and yard service and the size of train-service crews.

Congress ordered negotiations on the remaining issues on the theory that with the two main issues disposed of, the presumably less important matters could be settled by traditional collective bargaining.

But some well-informed Government sources do not believe the remaining issues will be

Continued on Page 13, Column 1

LODI KILLER SLAIN; 2D MAN GIVES UP

Ex-Convict Is Shot 7 Times in a Midtown Hotel

One of the killers of two New Jersey policemen was shot to death early yesterday by New York detectives during a violent struggle in his midtown hotel room. Sixteen hours later, the second man wanted in the slayings quietly surrendered.

The slain killer, 25-year-old Frank Falco, was asleep in his underwear when the police, using a passkey, entered his room at the Manhattan Hotel, at 44th Avenue and 44th Street. Although awakened with a revolver pressed to his throat, he fought desperately before being killed by seven bullets. He died snarling at the police and cursing them.

Thomas (Rabbi Tom) Trantino, 27, the second man, walked into the East 22d Street police station at 9:10 P.M., accompanied by a lawyer. He was neatly dressed and clean-shaven.

The men, both ex-convicts, had been the object of a grim police hunt since Detective Sgt. Peter Voto and Gary Tedesco, a police appointee, were gunned down early Monday morning in the Angel Lounge on Route 46 in Lodi, N. J. Mr. Tedesco was to have officially joined the Lodi force today.

A tip led the New York detectives to the hotel. They learned that Falco had checked in at 8 P.M. Tuesday under the name of J. Rello of Newport, R. I.

Lieut. Thomas Quinn, a 53-year-old veteran with 16 citations for bravery, entered Falco's 23d-floor room first, his

Continued on Page 35, Column 2

---

8 Dead in Utah Mine; Fate of 15 Unknown

Special to The New York Times

MOAB, Utah, Aug. 28 — Eight men were known dead today and 15 were trapped a half-mile underground in a potash mine rocked yesterday by a severe explosion.

Two survivors hoisted to the surface today reported that three men were dead, at least five were alive, and the fate of 15 was unknown. Later, however, rescue workers deep in the mine spotted five more bodies that officials said might be the men whom the survivors first believed alive.

Rescuers were being hampered by deadly gas, extreme heat, water and mechanical failures. A communications breakdown added to their frustrations.

Donald Hanna, 27 years old, of Price and Paul McKinney,

Continued on Page 14, Column 3

U.S. SPURNS DENIAL BY DIEM ON CRISIS

Absolves the Army Again in Vietnam Pagoda Raids and Points Toward Nhu

By TAD SZULC
Special to The New York Times

WASHINGTON, Aug. 28.— The United States reaffirmed today its belief that the South Vietnamese Government had violated pledges on the Buddhist crisis and that Vietnamese military chiefs were innocent of responsibility for assaults on pagodas.

This was the reaction of the Administration to communiqués issued in Saigon in the last 24 hours by the Government of President Ngo Dinh Diem in the name of the Vietnamese Joint General Staff.

The communiqués charged that Washington's public statements on the crisis reflected "totally erroneous information."

[In Saigon, youths loyal to the secret police were reported to be warning the population against anti-Government demonstrations.]

Change Is Held Vital

With the Vietnam crisis already regarded by the United States as extremely grave, this public dispute seemed to push it toward an unpredictable showdown.

The quarrel over who smashed pagodas and who arrested leaders of the Buddhist protest movement is understood to affect deeply the Kennedy Administration's evolving policy of encouraging Vietnamese military chiefs to reach for power.

This policy, still tentative, is that a fundamental change is required in the structure of the Saigon Government, Washington sources explain. They say the goal is national harmony that would let Vietnam concentrate again on the war against the Communist guerrillas of the Vietcong.

Specifically, Washington is said to deem internal peace out of the question as long as Ngo Dinh Nhu, chief of secret police and brother of the President, retains his vast power.

Mr. Nhu is considered also a symbol of the friction between Vietnam's Buddhists and the Roman Catholic Ngo family, which dominates the Government.

It is reported that in searching for an alternative to the regime—a course that was unthinkable here before the Buddhist crisis—the United States has almost openly been ad-

Continued on Page 5, Column 4

2 Girls Murdered In E. 88th St. Flat

Two young women, one the daughter of a writer and the other of a prominent surgeon, were bound and stabbed to death yesterday in their apartment at 57 East 88th Street.

The victims, Janice Wylie, 21 years old, and Emily Hoffert, 23, had been slashed repeatedly. Three bloodstained kitchen knives were found in the five-room apartment, which the girls shared with another young woman. The suite had been ransacked.

The bodies were found on a bedroom floor by Janice's father, the writer Max Wylie, and by Patricia Tolles, 23, the third roommate.

Mr. Wylie, who lives nearby, at 55 East 86th Street, is a

Continued on Page 35, Column 5

U. S. PRESSES U. N. TO CONDEMN SYRIA ON ISRAELI DEATHS

Stevenson Deplores Killing of Youths—Thant Assures Council on Cease-Fire

Text of Stevenson statement appears on Page 2.

By KATHLEEN TELTSCH
Special to The New York Times

UNITED NATIONS, N. Y., Aug. 28 — Adlai E. Stevenson declared today that the recent slaying of two Israeli farmers by Syrians was "wanton murder" deserving the strongest condemnation by the Security Council.

The United States delegate, followed by the British representative, gave forceful support to Israel's charges arising from the Aug. 20 ambush killing of two 19-year-old Israelis at the Almagor farm settlement.

Mr. Stevenson rejected Syria's countercharges against Israel as "not corroborated" by United Nations investigations.

The United States policy statement drew a favorable reaction from Michael S. Comay of Israel, who said it encouraged him to expect the Council to take "firm and vigorous action."

Syrian Disapproves

However, there was disapproval from Dr. Salah el-Tarazi of Syria, who criticized Mr. Stevenson as "not particularly objective." He added that Mr. Stevenson in past years had not deplored Syrian losses with equal feeling.

The Council, resuming its airing of the new crisis, was told by the Secretary General, U Thant, that United Nations inspection showed "no evidence of a military build-up on either side" of the armistice line.

Mr. Thant reported that both parties were heeding the United Nations cease-fire achieved last Friday after the ambush and subsequent exchanges of shooting greatly increased tension in the area. Bullets collected at one shooting site were on exhibit in the Council chamber.

Both Mr. Stevenson and Roger W. Jackling of Britain urged Syria and Israel to accept the suggestion by the United Nations truce chief, Lieut. Gen. Odd Bull, for avoiding new eruptions along their border, including an exchange of prisoners. Mr. Comay indicated a favorable Israeli reaction.

Evidence Questioned

Dr. Tarazi, in his turn, insisted that Israel's allegations remained unproved and that some evidence could have been faked. He noted photographs of footgear found at the ambush scene and said Syrian soldiers did not wear such shoes.

He was supported by Sidi Baba of Morocco, who accused Israel of making a "great superficial fuss" over the Almagor incident to create a climate for pressuring the Arabs into signing a peace treaty.

The United States and Britain are understood to be drafting a resolution that would condemn the killings and rebuke Syria by implication, rather than by outright condemnation, as Israel has been asking. Similar formulas have been used in the past.

Such an indirect condemnation might be blocked by a veto from the Soviet Union, however, which in the past has rejected resolutions opposed by the Arabs.

Mr. Stevenson told the 11-nation Council that General Bull's information was admit-

Continued on Page 2, Column 3

CONGRESS CORDIAL BUT NOT SWAYED

Leaders of March Pay Calls of Courtesy at Capitol

By WARREN WEAVER Jr.
Special to The New York Times

WASHINGTON, Aug. 28— The civil rights demonstration that swept more than 200,000 people through the capital today appeared to have left much of Congress untouched — physically, emotionally and politically.

In the morning, 13 demonstration leaders drove quietly up Capitol Hill and paid courtesy calls on Congressional leaders of both parties. The atmosphere was cordial, but there were no conversions.

In the afternoon, about 75 Senators and Representatives went from Capitol Hill to the Lincoln Memorial to be introduced, sit on the steps and listen to Gospel singing and speeches on civil rights.

A few demonstrators violated marching orders and went up to the Capitol to visit legislators in their offices. A few Senators welcomed trainloads and busfuls of constituents in person.

Otherwise, there was really very little contact between the marchers and the group they were working hardest to impress. And there was very little evidence that the demonstration, however large and fervent, would play a material role in advancing civil rights legislation.

Senator Hubert H. Humphrey, one of the most enthusiastic

Continued on Page 35, Column 5

200,000 MARCH FOR CIVIL RIGHTS IN ORDERLY WASHINGTON RALLY; PRESIDENT SEES GAIN FOR NEGRO

VIEW FROM THE LINCOLN MEMORIAL: The scene during the march looking toward the Washington Monument

Associated Press

VIEW FROM THE WASHINGTON MONUMENT: Marchers assembling around Reflecting Pool at the Lincoln Memorial

United Press International Telephoto

'I Have a Dream . . .'

Peroration by Dr. King Sums Up A Day the Capital Will Remember

By JAMES RESTON
Special to The New York Times

WASHINGTON, Aug. 28—Abraham Lincoln, who presided in his stone temple today over the children of the slaves he emancipated, may have used just the right words to sum up the general reaction to the Negro's massive march on Washington. "I think," he wrote to Gov. Andrew G. Curtin of Pennsylvania in 1861, "the necessity of being ready increases. Look to it." Washington was not ready for a vote today, but it is a little more conscious tonight of the necessity of being ready for freedom. It may not "look to it" at once, since it is looking to so many things, but it will be a long time before it forgets the melodious and melancholy voice of the Rev. Dr. Martin Luther King Jr. crying out his dreams to the multitude.

As Dr. King who, near the end of the day, touched the vast audience. Until then the pilgrimage was merely a great spectacle. Only those marchers from the embattled towns of the Old Confederacy had anything like the force of numbers. For many the day seemed an adventure, a long outing in the late summer sun—part liberation from home, part Sunday School picnic, part political convention, and part fish-fry.

But Dr. King brought them alive in the late afternoon with a peroration that was an anguished echo from all the old

Continued on Page 17, Column 6

PRESIDENT MEETS MARCH LEADERS

Says Bipartisan Support Is Needed for Rights Bill

Rights statement and Labor Day proclamation, Page 16.

By TOM WICKER
Special to The New York Times

WASHINGTON, Aug. 28 —President Kennedy served tea and sympathy and blunt political advice late today to the tired but proud leaders of the march on Washington.

In an hour-long conference, the President told the 10 leaders that "very strong bipartisan support" would be needed to get civil rights legislation enacted this year.

In a statement issued immediately after the conference, Mr. Kennedy said that "the cause of 20,000,000 Negroes has been advanced" by the orderly demonstration, "conducted so appropriately before the nation's shrine to the Great Emancipator."

Earlier, in a Labor Day statement released in advance of the holiday, the President called on the nation to speed up its efforts to achieve equal rights for all in jobs, education and voting.

The main discussion between the march leaders and the President concerned prospects for civil rights legislation, the leaders said after the White House meeting. They talked with Mr. Kennedy around the long table in the Cabinet Room, where the leaders were served tea, coffee

Continued on Page 16, Column 7

ACTION ASKED NOW

10 Leaders of Protest Urge Laws to End Racial Inequity

Excerpts from talks at rally are printed on Page 21.

By E. W. KENWORTHY
Special to The New York Times

WASHINGTON, Aug. 28— More than 200,000 Americans, most of them black but many of them white, demonstrated here today for a full and speedy program of civil rights and equal job opportunities.

It was the greatest assembly for a redress of grievances that this capital has ever seen.

One hundred years and 240 days after Abraham Lincoln enjoined the emancipated slaves to "abstain from all violence" and "labor faithfully for reasonable wages," this vast throng proclaimed in march and song and through the speeches of their leaders that they were still waiting for the freedom and the jobs.

Children Clap and Sing

There was no violence to mar the demonstration. In fact, at times there was an air of hootenanny about it as groups of schoolchildren clapped hands and swung into the familiar freedom songs.

But if the crowd was good-natured, the underlying tone was one of dead seriousness. The emphasis was on "freedom" and "now." At the same time the leaders emphasized, paradoxically but realistically, that the struggle was just beginning.

On Capitol Hill, opinion was divided about the impact of the demonstration in stimulating Congressional action on civil rights legislation. But at the White House, President Kennedy declared that the cause of 20,000,000 Negroes had been advanced by the march.

The march leaders went from the shadows of the Lincoln Memorial to the White House to meet with the President for 75 minutes. Afterward, Mr. Kennedy issued a 400-word statement praising the marchers for the "deep fervor and the quiet dignity" that had characterized the demonstration.

Says Nation Can Be Proud

The nation, the President said, "can properly be proud of the demonstration that has occurred here today."

The main target of the demonstration was Congress, where committees are now considering the Administration's civil rights bill.

At the Lincoln Memorial this afternoon, some speakers, knowing little of the ways of Congress, assumed that the passage of a strengthened civil rights bill had been assured by the moving events of the day.

But from statements by Congressional leaders, after they had met with the march committee this morning, this did not seem certain at all. These statements came before the demonstration.

Senator Mike Mansfield of Montana, the Senate Democratic leader, said he could not say whether the mass protest

Continued on Page 16, Column 1

Capital Is Occupied By a Gentle Army

By RUSSELL BAKER
Special to The New York Times

WASHINGTON, Aug. 28— No one could remember an invading army quite as gentle as the 200,000 civil rights marchers who occupied Washington today.

For the most part, they came silently during the night and early morning, occupied the great shaded boulevards along the Mall, and spread through the parklands between the Washington Monument and the Potomac.

But instead of the emotional horde of angry militants that many had feared, what Washington saw was a vast array of quiet, middle-class Americans

Continued on Page 17, Column 7

219

The New York Times.

LATE CITY EDITION
U. S. Weather Bureau Report (Page 58) forecast:
Cloudy, windy, chance of showers today and tonight. Cold tomorrow.
Temp. Range: 62–54; yesterday: 64–51.

VOL. CXIII...No. 38,654. © 1963 by The New York Times Company. Times Square, New York 36, N. Y.

NEW YORK, SATURDAY, NOVEMBER 23, 1963.

TEN CENTS

KENNEDY IS KILLED BY SNIPER AS HE RIDES IN CAR IN DALLAS; JOHNSON SWORN IN ON PLANE

TEXAN ASKS UNITY

Congressional Chiefs of Both Parties Promise Aid

By FELIX BELAIR Jr.
Special to The New York Times

WASHINGTON, Nov. 22—Lyndon B. Johnson returned to a stunned capital shortly after 6 P.M. today to assume the duties of the Presidency.

The new President asked for and received from Congressional leaders of both parties their "united support in the face of the tragedy which has befallen our country." He said it was "more essential that ever before that this country be united."

Partisan differences disappeared in the chorus of assurances with which the Congressional leaders responded.

Mr. Johnson was described by those who talked with him as "stunned and shaken" by the assassination of President Kennedy.

Discusses U.S. Security

But he moved quickly from problems of national security and foreign policy to funeral arrangements for Mr. Kennedy.

Across the street from the West Wing of the White House, the President conferred with officials in his old Vice-Presidential offices in the Executive Office Building.

Senator George A. Smathers, Democrat of Florida, a personal friend of the dead President, was one of those who described Mr. Johnson as shaken.

"Everyone is," he added. "But the President is the more so because he was right there when the tragedy occurred."

While flying to Washington aboard the Presidential plane, Mr. Johnson arranged for a meeting with Cabinet members to ask that they remain at their posts. He made the same request of staff members in the executive office.

Meets With Harriman

"Calm and contained" was the way Senator J. W. Fulbright described the President's manner during a discussion of foreign-policy matters with Under Secretary of State W. Averell Harriman. The Arkansas Senator said the President had been working on "what looked like a statement"—presumably an assurance of continuity of the nation's foreign policy.

The new President's first conference was aboard the helicopter that flew him the 15 miles from Andrews Air Force Base.

Continued on Page 11, Column 3

"This is a sad time for all people. We have suffered a loss that cannot be weighed. For me it is a deep personal tragedy. I know the world shares the sorrow that Mrs. Kennedy and her family bear. I will do my best. That is all I can do. I ask for your help—and God's."—President Lyndon Baines Johnson.

Henry Grossman

PRESIDENT'S BODY WILL LIE IN STATE

Funeral Mass to Be Monday in Capital After Homage Is Paid by Public

By JACK RAYMOND
Special to The New York Times

WASHINGTON, Nov. 22—The body of John F. Kennedy will lie in state in the rotunda of the Capitol Sunday and then will be borne to St. Matthew's Roman Catholic Cathedral for a pontifical requiem mass at noon Monday.

The President's body was returned to Washington today in the same Air Force jet that carried him to Texas. The airliner, with Mrs. Kennedy, the new President, Lyndon B. Johnson, and Mrs. Johnson aboard, arrived at Andrews Air Force Base at 5:58 P.M.

It was announced later that Mr. Kennedy's body would lie in the White House tomorrow from 10 A.M. to 6 P.M., during which time Government and diplomatic officials will pay their respects.

The coffin will be taken from the White House to the Capitol rotunda Sunday morning, where

Continued on Page 9, Column 2

PARTIES' OUTLOOK FOR '64 CONFUSED

Republican Prospects Rise —Johnson Faces Possible Fight Against Liberals

By WARREN WEAVER Jr.
Special to The New York Times

WASHINGTON, Nov. 22 — President Kennedy's assassination threw the American political scene into turmoil today.

It removed at a single blow the man who would have been renominated for a second term in the White House by acclamation nine months from now.

It elevated into the Presidency and the leadership of the Democratic party an older, more conservative man still emerging from his Southern heritage.

It increased immeasurably for the leaders of the Republican party prospects of electing a President next November.

The shock of the President's death stilled the official voices of politics in the capital. But so profound was the potential effect on the government and leadership that private consideration could not be silenced.

Before, there had been facts and strong probabilities on the

Continued on Page 6, Column 3

LEFTIST ACCUSED

Figure in a Pro-Castro Group Is Charged— Policeman Slain

By GLADWIN HILL
Special to The New York Times

DALLAS, Tex., Nov. 22—The Dallas police and Federal officers issued a charge of murder late tonight in the assassination of President Kennedy.

The accused is Lee Harvey Oswald, a 24-year-old former marine, who went to live in the Soviet Union in 1959 and returned to Texas last year.

Capt. Will Fritz, head of the Dallas police homicide bureau, identified Oswald as an adherent of the left-wing Fair Play for Cuba Committee.

Oswald was arrested about two hours after the shooting, in a movie theater three miles away, shortly after he allegedly shot and killed a policeman on a street nearby.

He was arraigned tonight on a charge of murdering the police officer. The charge related to the Kennedy killing was made later.

Appears in Line-Up

After the arraignment, the suspect, a slight, dark-haired man, was taken downstairs to appear in a line-up, presumably before witnesses of the Kennedy assassination.

While being escorted, handcuffed, through a police building corridor, he shouted: "I haven't shot anybody."

Captain Fritz said Oswald was employed—the exact job was unknown—at the Texas School Book Depository, a warehouse from which the assassin's bullets came. The captain said some witnesses had placed Oswald in the building at the time of the assassination.

The sequence of events leading to his arrest was as follows:

As a citywide manhunt began during the hour following the assassination, an unidentified man notified police headquarters, over a police-car radio, that the car's officer had been

Continued on Page 4, Column 1

NEWS INDEX

	Page		Page
Art	24–25	Obituaries	29
Books	27	Screen	22–23
Bridge	26	Ships and Air	52
Business	36, 44	Society	32
Churches	21	Sports	31–35
Crossword	27	Theaters	22–23
Editorial	28	TV and Radio	50
Financial	36–44	U. N. Proceedings	10
Food	20	Wash. Proceedings	10
Music	22–23	Weather	58

News Summary and Index, Page 31

John Fitzgerald Kennedy
1917–1963

Henry Grossman

Why America Weeps

Kennedy Victim of Violent Streak He Sought to Curb in the Nation

By JAMES RESTON
Special to The New York Times

WASHINGTON, Nov. 22—America wept tonight, not alone for its dead young President, but for itself. The grief was general, for somehow the worst in the nation had prevailed over the best. The indictment extended beyond the assassin, for something in the nation itself, some strain of madness and violence, had destroyed the highest symbol of law and order.

Speaker John McCormack, now 71 and, by the peculiarities of our politics, next in line of succession after the Vice President, expressed this sense of national dismay and self-criticism:

"My God! My God! What are we coming to?"

The irony of the President's death is that his short Administration was devoted almost entirely to various attempts to curb this very streak of violence in the American character.

When the historians get around to assessing his three years in office, it is very likely that they will be impressed with just this: his efforts to restrain those who wanted to be more violent in the cold war overseas and those who wanted to be

Continued on Page 7, Column 6

The City Goes Dark

By ROBERT C. DOTY

The center of New York, the restless night city, wore darkness and went in near silence after the murder of President Kennedy last night.

In and around Times Square, the normal, frenetic Friday night pulse slowed as near to a halt as it ever comes. Most legitimate and movie theaters, night clubs and dance halls closed their doors and darkened their marquees.

As dusk came, automatic devices turned on the huge, gaudy display signs that normally blot out the night. Then, one by one, the lights blinked out, turning what was almost a mourning band.

There were exceptions, of course. Restaurants, by decision of their trade associations, remained lighted and open as a

Continued on Page 5, Column 2

Gov. Connally Shot; Mrs. Kennedy Safe

President Is Struck Down by a Rifle Shot From Building on Motorcade Route— Johnson, Riding Behind, Is Unhurt

By TOM WICKER
Special to The New York Times

DALLAS, Nov. 22—President John Fitzgerald Kennedy was shot and killed by an assassin today.

He died of a wound in the brain caused by a rifle bullet that was fired at him as he was riding through downtown Dallas in a motorcade.

Vice President Lyndon Baines Johnson, who was riding in the third car behind Mr. Kennedy's, was sworn in as the 36th President of the United States 99 minutes after Mr. Kennedy's death.

Mr. Johnson is 55 years old; Mr. Kennedy was 46.

Shortly after the assassination, Lee H. Oswald, described as a one-time defector to the Soviet Union, active in the Fair Play for Cuba Committee, was arrested by the Dallas police. Tonight he was accused of the killing.

Suspect Captured After Scuffle

Oswald, 24 years old, was also accused of slaying a policeman who had approached him in the street. Oswald was subdued after a scuffle with a second policeman in a nearby theater.

The shooting took place at 12:30 P.M., Central standard time (1:30 P.M., New York time). Mr. Kennedy was pronounced dead at 1 P.M. and Mr. Johnson was sworn in at 2:39 P.M.

Mr. Johnson, who was uninjured in the shooting, took his oath in the Presidential jet plane as it stood on the runway at Love Field. The body of the President was aboard. Immediately after the oath-taking, the plane took off for Washington.

Standing beside the new President as Mr. Johnson took the oath of office was Mrs. John F. Kennedy. Her stocking was saturated with her husband's blood.

Gov. John B. Connally Jr. of Texas, who was riding in the same car with Mr. Kennedy, was severely wounded in the chest, ribs and arm. His condition was serious, but not critical.

The killer fired the rifle from a building just off the motorcade route. Mr. Kennedy,

Continued on Page 2,

THE NEW PRESIDENT: Lyndon B. Johnson takes oath before Judge Sarah T. Hughes in plane at Dallas. Mrs. Kennedy and Representative Jack Brooks are at right. To left are Mrs. Johnson and Representative Albert Thomas.

Capt. Cecil Stoughton via United Press International

WHEN THE BULLETS STRUCK: Mrs. Kennedy moving to the aid of the President after he was hit by a sniper yesterday in Dallas. A guard mounts rear bumper. Gov. John B. Connally Jr. of Texas, also in the car, was wounded.

Associated Press

The New York Times.

LATE CITY EDITION
U. S. Weather Bureau Report (Page 38) forecasts:
Sunny and cool today; fair, milder tonight. Cloudy, milder tomorrow.
Temp. Range: 46—32; yesterday: 53—37.

VOL. CXIII..No. 38,656. © 1963 by The New York Times Company. Times Square, New York 36, N. Y.   NEW YORK, MONDAY, NOVEMBER 25, 1963.   +   TEN CENTS

PRESIDENT'S ASSASSIN SHOT TO DEATH IN JAIL CORRIDOR BY A DALLAS CITIZEN; GRIEVING THRONGS VIEW KENNEDY BIER

FAREWELL: Kneeling with her mother at John Fitzgerald Kennedy's coffin in the Capitol, Caroline touches the flag
Associated Press Wirephoto

Mrs. Kennedy Leads Public Mourning

By MARJORIE HUNTER
Special to The New York Times

WASHINGTON, Nov. 24 — Mrs. John F. Kennedy, firmly holding the hands of her two children, followed the coffin bearing the body of her husband as it left the White House today for the last time.

Her eyes swollen, she moved quietly to the edge of the steps of the North Portico and paused to watch the coffin placed in the caisson by military bearers.

Her son, John Jr., tugged at her hand and pointed to a black, riderless horse, part of the ceremonial procession. She leaned down and spoke to him.

Mrs. Kennedy wore a simple black suit and black lace mantilla. John Jr., who will be 3 years old tomorrow, and Caroline, who will be 6 on Wednesday, wore similar pale blue coats, white anklets and red shoes.

As the three stood there, framed against the black-draped doorway, there was an eerie silence. It was broken only by the occasional sound of hoofs of the restless gray horses that were to pull the caisson up Pennsylvania Avenue to the Capitol.

Mrs. Kennedy was composed, but appeared to be on the verge of tears as she and the children stepped into a black limousine for the slow ride to the Capitol. In the car, too, were President and Mrs. Johnson and Attorney General Robert F. Kennedy.

Still holding the hands of her children, Mrs. Kennedy followed the flag-draped coffin into the Capitol Rotunda. She stared straight ahead as the coffin was placed on the catafalque, a simple funeral bier draped in black broadcloth.

John Jr., wide-eyed and bewildered, was restless. Clutching a tiny flag, he was led away by a military aide.

Later, after the tributes had been spoken, Mrs. Kennedy walked slowly to the coffin, touched it with her fingertips, knelt and kissed it. Caroline was by her side. They were rejoined by John Jr. at the door.

Shortly after 9 o'clock tonight Mrs. Kennedy returned to the Capitol and again knelt before the coffin and kissed it.

Mrs. Kennedy walked into the Rotunda on the arm of her husband's brother, Robert, who stopped at the rope holding

Continued on Page 2, Column 2

BUSINESS OF CITY WILL HALT TODAY

Mayor Says Only Essential Services Will Be Provided

Changes in events here are listed on Page 9.

By LEONARD INGALLS

Normal public, business and social activity in the city will be almost completely suspended today out of respect for President Kennedy.

Mayor Wagner announced yesterday that the city would continue in full mourning throughout the day. Only essential city services would be maintained, he said.

"Those city employes not engaged in activities imperative to the health, safety and welfare of our citizens are to be released from duty and their offices closed through today," Mr. Wagner said at City Hall.

Proclamation of the day as a legal holiday by Governor Rockefeller in observance of Mr. Kennedy's funeral permits banks and other institutions to close.

Classes at schools and colleges will be suspended. Department stores and specialty shops will be shut. Securities exchanges and commodity markets will not operate. Most places of entertainment will be closed. There will be no deliveries of mail and post offices will be shut.

Special memorial services for the murdered President have been scheduled at churches and synagogues.

At St. Patrick's Cathedral

Continued on Page 9, Column 1

Pope Paul Warns That Hate and Evil Imperil Civil Order

Special to The New York Times

ROME, Nov. 24 — Pope Paul VI, alluding to the assassination of President Kennedy, said today that it showed how much "capacity for hatred and evil still remains in the world."

Without mentioning Mr. Kennedy by name, the Pontiff spoke of "the crime that has aroused in these days the deploration of the whole world." He said it illustrated "how great the threat to civil order and peace still is."

The Pope was addressing thousands of people gathered in St. Peter's Square for his usual Sunday-noon benediction.

"We cannot, at this moment of prayer together, tear our thoughts from the crime that has aroused in these days the deploration of the whole world," he said.

"After dwelling upon the man who is no longer with us and after comforting those who still live in mourning and grief, our thoughts show us how much the capacity for hatred and evil yet remains in the world, how great the threat to civil order and peace still is, and how great is the need for the grace

Continued on Page 4, Column 7

JOHNSON SCORED BY CHINESE REDS

Views Called 'Reactionary' —Taiwan Aid Attacked

By United Press International

TOKYO, Nov. 24 — Communist China bitterly criticized President Johnson today and termed him a supporter of the late President Kennedy's "trickery policy."

"Since the emergence of the Kennedy regime," the Chinese Communist press agency Hsinhua said, "Johnson has positively supported various reactionary policies of the Kennedy Administration and participated in formulating and promoting such policies.

"Johnson has supported Kennedy's trickery policy and has called for the maintenance of such a policy in a series of his speeches."

The Chinese Communists reported the assassination of President Kennedy in a four-paragraph dispatch eight hours after it occurred. But they made no comment.

Hsinhua said Mr. Johnson "was one of the central figures in the Kennedy Administration and has made frequent trips abroad."

The Chinese statement added that Mr. Johnson believed "the United States, in making two-faced antirevolutionary plots, must maintain a strong position on the basis of strong force."

"He also looks toward Cuba with animosity and has called for the elimination of the Cuban revolutionary Government," it

Continued on Page 7, Column 6

NEWS INDEX

	Page		Page
Books	31	Letters	30
Bridge	31	Music	22-23
Business	27, 29	Obituaries	19-20
Buyers	39	Real Estate	39
Chess	31	Screen	22-23
Crossword	17	Ships and Air	40
Editorial	18	Society	24
Fashions	14	Sports	24-26
Financial	27-29, 30-40	Theatres	22-23
Food	14	Wea'er	38

News Summary and Index, Page 21

CROWD IS HUSHED

Mourners at Capitol File Past the Coffin Far Into the Night

Texts of eulogies spoken in Washington, Page 4.

By TOM WICKER
Special to The New York Times

WASHINGTON, Monday, Nov. 25—Thousands of sorrowing Americans passed past John Fitzgerald Kennedy's bier in the Great Rotunda of the United States Capitol yesterday and early today.

Mr. Kennedy's body lay in state in the center of the vast, stone-floored chamber. Long after midnight the silent procession of mourners continued.

Some wept. All were hushed. As the two lines moved in a large circle around either side of the flag-covered coffin, almost the only sounds were the shuffle of feet and the quiet voices of policemen urging the people to "keep moving, keep moving right along."

By 2:45 A. M. today 115,000 persons had passed the bier.

Yesterday afternoon a crowd estimated at 300,000 lined Pennsylvania and Constitution Avenues to watch the passage of the caisson bearing the body of the 35th President of the United States, slain in the 47th year of his life by an assassin's bullet.

A Riderless Horse

Behind the caisson, following military tradition, came a riderless bay gelding, with a pair of military boots reversed in the silver stirrups.

The horse was Sardar, the thoroughbred that belongs to Mrs. John F. Kennedy.

Mrs. Kennedy, her two children, President and Mrs. Johnson and Mr. Kennedy's brother, Attorney General Robert F. Kennedy, rode in the first car of a 10-car procession that followed the caisson.

The procession moved at a funeral pace, to the sound of muffled drums, from the White House to Pennsylvania Avenue. It was a journey Mr. Kennedy had made formally four times.

At the Capitol, brief ceremonies of eulogy were held in the Rotunda before the admission of the waiting thousands who swarmed over the plaza and stretched in a long line up East Capitol Street.

At the conclusion of the cere-

Continued on Page 2, Column 1

World's Leaders to Attend Requiem Today in Capital

Mrs. Kennedy Will Walk Behind the Caisson to Mass at Cathedral

By JACK RAYMOND
Special to The New York Times

WASHINGTON, Nov. 24 — Mrs. John F. Kennedy, joined by world. and national leaders, will walk behind the horse-drawn caisson that bears her husband's body from the White House to St. Matthew's Roman Catholic Cathedral tomorrow.

Following a requiem mass, John Fitzgerald Kennedy, the 35th President of the United States, will be escorted in a solemn state procession to Arlington National Cemetery to be buried with military honors. The gravesite, on a beautiful grassy knoll, provides a sweeping view of the capital city and it is itself easily in view from the Memorial Bridge approach to the national burial ground.

The state funeral procession will begin at 10:30 A.M. at the Capitol, where the closed, flag-draped coffin of the President

Continued on Page 6, Column 8

Officials of Nearly 100 Lands in U.S.—They Will Meet Johnson

By MAX FRANKEL
Special to The New York Times

WASHINGTON, Nov. 24 — An emperor, a king, a queen, princes, presidents, premiers and ministers from every continent converged on Washington this evening to pay final tribute to

List of leaders expected at the funeral, Page 6.

President Kennedy and to make the acquaintance of President Johnson.

Representing nearly 100 nations, the foreign dignitaries will include the largest assembly of ruling statesmen ever gathered in the United States for any event.

Their arrival here, through the night, virtually overwhelmed an already tense and overburdened capital. Nonetheless, each visitor received the protocol deference and police protection of more normal

Continued on Page 6, Column 1

Millions of Viewers See Oswald Killing On 2 TV Networks

By JACK GOULD

The fatal shooting of Lee H. Oswald, who was held as the assassin of President Kennedy, was seen as it occurred yesterday by millions of television viewers.

The National Broadcasting Company telecast the dramatic happening live. Less than a minute later the Columbia Broadcasting System telecast it by means of tape, made as the shooting occurred.

C. B. S. headquarters recorded the pictures from Dallas as they were received here over a closed circuit. Officials, upon seeing the moment of the Dallas relay, put the tape out over the network instantly.

The incident marked the first time in 15 years of television around the globe that a real-life homicide had occurred in front of live cameras. The closest parallel occurred in October, 1960, when Inejiro Asanuma, Japanese political leader, was knifed on a public stage in

Continued on Page 10, Column 8

ONE BULLET FIRED

Night-Club Man Who Admired Kennedy Is Oswald's Slayer

By GLADWIN HILL

DALLAS, Nov. 24 — President Kennedy's assassin, Lee Harvey Oswald, was fatally shot by a Dallas night-club operator today as the police started to move him from the city jail to the county jail.

The shooting occurred in the basement of the municipal building at about 11:20 A.M. central standard time (12:20 P.M. New York time).

The assailant, Jack Rubenstein, known as Jack Ruby, lunged from a cluster of newsmen observing the transfer of Oswald from the jail to an armored truck.

Millions of viewers saw the shooting on television.

As the shot rang out, a police detective suddenly recognized Ruby and exclaimed: "Jack, you son of a bitch!"

A murder charge was filed against Ruby by Assistant District Attorney William F. Alexander. Justice of the Peace Pierce McBride ordered him held without bail.

Detectives Flank Him

Oswald was arrested Friday after Mr. Kennedy was shot dead while riding through Dallas in an open car. He was charged with murdering the President and a policeman who was shot a short time later while trying to question Oswald.

As the 24-year-old prisoner, flanked by two detectives, stepped onto a basement garage ramp, Ruby thrust a .38-caliber, snub-nose revolver into Oswald's left side and fired a single shot.

The 52-year-old night-club operator, an ardent admirer of President Kennedy and his family, was described as having been distraught.

[District Attorney Henry Wade said he understood that the police were looking into the possibility that Oswald had been slain to prevent him from talking. The Associated Press reported. Mr. Wade said that so far no connection between Oswald and Ruby had been established.]

Oswald slumped to the concrete paving, wordlessly clutching his side and writhing with pain.

Oswald apparently lost con-

Continued on Page 10, Column 1

JOHNSON SPURS OSWALD INQUIRY

President Orders F. B. I. to Check Death — Handling of Case Worries Capital

By ANTHONY LEWIS
Special to The New York Times

WASHINGTON, Nov. 24 — President Johnson directed the Federal Bureau of Investigation tonight to look into "every aspect" of the murder of Lee H. Oswald.

He spoke with the director of the F.B.I., J. Edgar Hoover, and ordered the redoubled investigation.

The action came as official Washington was showing increasing concern about the entire handling of the aftermath of President Kennedy's assassination.

Officials were convinced that Oswald was the assassin. But their concern was over the public impression of the criminal proceedings.

Tonight they were consider-

Continued on Page 11, Column 3

JOHNSON AFFIRMS AIMS IN VIETNAM

Retains Kennedy's Policy of Aiding War on Reds— Lodge Briefs President

By E. W. KENWORTHY
Special to The New York Times

WASHINGTON, Nov. 24 — President Johnson reaffirmed today the policy objectives of his predecessor regarding South Vietnam. He called upon all Government agencies to support that policy with full unity of purpose.

This was disclosed by White House sources after a meeting between President Johnson and Henry Cabot Lodge, United States Ambassador to South Vietnam.

The meeting lasted nearly an hour. It was described as being devoted to a full review of the conclusions reached by participants in a strategy conference on South Vietnam held in Honolulu last Wednesday.

In another move today that emphasized the President's desire to convey at home and abroad the impression of continuity, Mr. Johnson asked all members of the White House staff to remain at their jobs. This was announced by Pierre Salinger, White House press secretary.

Some Expected to Leave

Mr. Salinger said the President would leave up to the officials involved how long they wished to serve him.

Inevitably some of these officials — especially those from the universities and foundations — will decide to leave their posts after an interval.

But the President's request today would seem to insure that during the difficult days of adjustment and transition he would continue to have the benefit of the experience of key policy figures.

Attending the meeting between the President and Ambassador Lodge today were Secretary of State Dean Rusk, Secretary of Defense Robert S. McNamara, Under Secretary of State George W. Ball, John A. McCone, director of the Central Intelligence Agency, and McGeorge Bundy, special assistant to the President for national security affairs.

Secretaries Rusk and McNamara, Ambassador Lodge and Mr. Bundy all took part in the Honolulu conference.

As a result of the meeting, White House informants said, President Johnson laid down a

Continued on Page 5, Column 1

OSWALD IS SHOT: Lee Harvey Oswald cringes as Jack Ruby attacks him at Dallas jail. Policeman is J. R. Leavelle.
Copyright 1963—Dallas Times-Herald and Photographer Bob Jackson, from United Press International Telephoto

The New York Times.

LATE CITY EDITION
U. S. Weather Bureau Report (Page 46) forecast:
Sunny and pleasant today; clear, cool tonight. Sunny tomorrow.
Temp. Range: 82—62; yesterday: 81—62.
Temp.-Hum. Index: high 60's; yesterday: 71.

VOL. CXIII..No. 38,906.   © 1964 by The New York Times Company. Times Square, New York, N. Y. 10036   NEW YORK, SATURDAY, AUGUST 1, 1964.   TEN CENTS

RANGER TAKES CLOSE-UP MOON PHOTOS REVEALING CRATERS ONLY 3 FEET WIDE; DATA GAINED ON LANDING SITE FOR MAN

THREE MILES FROM THE MOON: This view of lunar surface was transmitted by the Ranger 7 spacecraft 3.2 seconds before it crashed. The lens gridmarks are scale references to calibrate amount of distortion. Smallest craters shown are about 30 feet in diameter and about 10 feet in depth.

1,000 FEET FROM THE MOON: Upper photo was the last. At right it merges into blur caused by static after the Ranger 7 crashed. Below, photo taken from 3,000 feet.

Associated Press Wirephotos

U.S. STEEL WEIGHS MIDTOWN PROJECT

$100 Million Industrial and Housing Complex May Be Built Above Rail Yard

By ROBERT E. BEDINGFIELD

The United States Steel Corporation has acquired the air rights over a 40-acre railroad yard in mid-Manhattan and is considering erecting a $100 million housing and industrial complex over the site.

U.S. Steel's board of directors has approved the purchase of Webb & Knapp's lease of the air rights over the New York Central Railroad's freight yard that lies between West 30th and West 33d Streets and extends from 10th to 12th Avenue.

Webb & Knapp realized about $7 million on the deal.

It is understood that the plan being considered calls for the construction of nine apartment buildings of about 30 stories each that would provide middle-income housing for 12,000 families. The project also envisages numerous adjoining industrial buildings of several stories each.

Plan Still Studied

Last night a spokesman for U.S. Steel confirmed that the directors had authorized the acquisition of the air rights from Webb & Knapp.

He said, however, that no definite plan had yet been decided for utilization of the area. If the corporation decides to go ahead with the proposed housing development, he added, it would be for the purpose of demonstrating the company's contention that steel is useful as a prime material in middle-income housing.

Webb & Knapp since Dec. 15, 1961, has held a leasehold on the air rights to the part of the Central yard that lies between West 30th and West 37th Streets and extends from 11th to 12th Avenue and from West 30th to West 33d Street between 10th and 11th Avenues.

Webb & Knapp will net $3 million on the deal since $4 million of the proceeds will be applied to the repayment of a note of that amount owed the steel company.

The proposed U.S. Steel plans

Continued on Page 34, Column 3

Wagner Rejects Demands For Civilian Police Board

By R. W. APPLE Jr.

Mayor Wagner refused yesterday to appoint an independent civilian police review board sought by civil rights leaders.

In a long statement released at City Hall, the Mayor omitted any mention of another key demand of Negro leaders—the suspension of Police Lieut. Thomas R. Gilligan, who shot and killed a 15-year-old Negro on the East Side on July 16.

Instead, Mr. Wagner proposed a seven-point program whose main thrust was economic.

Text of Wagner's statement is printed on Page 11.

calling for the creation of about 1,500 temporary and permanent city jobs for unemployed young people.

The Mayor also set up a committee to review the findings of Deputy Mayor Edward F. Cavanagh Jr., who had been directed earlier to review the actions of the Police Department's review board.

King Voices Regret

Mr. Wagner's statement was his first since he began last Monday a series of conversations with the Rev. Dr. Martin Luther King Jr., president of the Southern Christian Leadership Conference, following racial riots here two weeks ago.

Dr. King said in a telephone interview from Atlanta that he was "very sorry" the Mayor had not ordered the creation of an independent board to evaluate allegations of police brutality. He said he had pressed the issue again and again during his talks with Mr. Wagner.

L. Joseph Overton, president of the Unity Council of Harlem Organizations, condemned the Mayor's actions and demanded again the creation of a review board composed of persons associated with neither the city government nor the police.

"I believe the Mayor has made my position untenable," Mr. Overton said. "He has made it virtually impossible for me to guarantee continued peace on the streets of Harlem."

Mr. Overton's organization was set up in an attempt to restore order in Harlem after the riots touched off by the Gilligan incident. The council was demanding that only the creation of a review board would solve the city's racial crisis.

Police Commissioner Michael

Continued on Page 36, Column 6

PAKISTAN ACCEPTS LOAN FROM CHINA

$60 Million, Interest Free, to Be Used for Imports of Industrial Goods

Special to The New York Times

KARACHI, Pakistan, July 31—Pakistan announced today that she would accept a "generous offer" by Communist China of a $60 million long-term, interest-free loan.

It is the first loan offered by Peking to Pakistan, which is allied with the West in the Central Treaty Organization and the Southeast Asia Treaty Organization, both aimed at preventing Communist aggression.

Commerce Minister Wahid-uz-Zaman, who recently returned from a tour of Communist China, said at a news conference in Rawalpindi that the loan would be used to pay for imports of machinery, cement and sugar mills.

Mr. Zaman said the Chinese Government would not even place a service charge on the loan.

United States loans offered to Pakistan are repayable in United States dollars in 40 years, including a 10-year grace period during which no payment is

Continued on Page 3, Column 2

Attitude on Soviet Is Upheld by Rusk In Policy Warning

By MAX FRANKEL
Special to The New York Times

WASHINGTON, July 31—Secretary of State Dean Rusk, in an oblique jab at Senator Barry Goldwater, said today that it was "unrealistic" to think the Soviet Union would "roll over and play dead" if its vital interests were threatened by the United States.

In answering several political questions at a news conference, Mr. Rusk said the Administration had "eminently demonstrated" that it was "just as tough and just as stubborn as is necessary" to protect its vital interests and those of the Western allies.

But he cautioned that the Soviet Union, too, would be stubborn in defending its interests. Therefore, he said, conflicts of interest must be approached with care and persistence to find ways in which the Communist and Western parts of the world can live together.

Mr. Rusk did not refer directly to Mr. Goldwater, the Republican candidate for President, or his views, but the Secretary's questioners did, leaving no doubt about the meaning of their inquiries.

Secretary Rusk said he

Continued on Page 2, Column 3

Johnson Is Said to Have Asked Kennedy to Manage Campaign

Offer Being Considered

By The Associated Press

WASHINGTON, Saturday, Aug. 1—President Johnson has asked Attorney General Robert F. Kennedy to manage his Presidential campaign, informed sources said today.

They said the offer was made Wednesday at the same time Mr. Johnson told Mr. Kennedy he was eliminating him from consideration as a Vice-Presidential candidate.

The offer reportedly is under consideration.

"I don't want to get into that," Mr. Kennedy said yesterday when asked about reports of the offer before he left for Hyannis Port, Mass., for the weekend. And Kennedy

Continued on Page 6, Column 2

Rusk Post Desired

By CABELL PHILLIPS
Special to The New York Times

WASHINGTON, July 31—Attorney General Robert F. Kennedy would like to be Secretary of State now that the Vice-Presidency has been foreclosed to him.

This is the consensus of several close friends and associates of Mr. Kennedy after President Johnson's statement yesterday that the Attorney General and others of Cabinet rank had been eliminated from consideration for the second spot on the Democratic ticket.

Mr. Kennedy, his friends say, is exerting no pressure to obtain the State Department post. But they say he has let it be

Continued on Page 6, Column 5

PRESIDENT HAILS NEW LUNAR FEAT

Calls Ranger Flight 'Basic Step' to Manned Landing —Praises Scientists

By JOHN D. POMFRET
Special to The New York Times

WASHINGTON, July 31—President Johnson congratulated today the scientists and technicians responsible for the successful flight of Ranger 7 to the moon.

The President was in the White House living quarters when Dr. William H. Pickering, director of the Jet Propulsion Laboratory at Pasadena, Calif., telephoned to inform him that the shot was a success.

The President felicitated Dr. Pickering and Dr. Homer E. Newell, assistant administrator for space science and application of the space agency, then had the White House issue a statement praising those who participated in the flight.

Mr. Johnson called the flight "a basic step forward in our orderly program to assemble the scientific knowledge necessary for man's trip to the moon."

Guide in Planning Trip

"The pictures obtained of the lunar surface should prove extremely useful," the President said, continuing:

"They will be a guide in constructing the lunar excursion module and in planning the trip.

"We shall now be able to better map out our descent to our lunar landing with greater certainty and knowledge of the conditions which our astronauts will encounter on the moon.

"I recognize that this great success has come only after a number of failures and partial successes in our efforts to send probes to the moon. This success should spur us on to added effort in the future.

"The fact that our Soviet competitors have had many unpublicized failures to the moon and the planets also confirms the complexity of today's success.

"On behalf of a grateful nation, let me again congratu-

Continued on Page 8, Column 3

Craft Hits Target Area; 4,000 Pictures Sent Back

Details of Lunar Region Seen Thousand Times Clearer Than Before—Feat Hailed as Leap in Knowledge

By RICHARD WITKIN

PASADENA, Calif., July 31—Ranger 7 radioed to earth today the first close-up pictures of the moon—a historic collection of 4,000 pictures one thousand times as clear as anything ever seen through earth-bound telescopes.

Scientists here were hailing the achievement, which exceeded all expectations, as by far the greatest advance in lunar astronomy since Galileo.

They said the pictures not only represented a great leap in man's knowledge of the moon, but also, on a more practical level, lent encouragement that the lunar surface was suitable for Project Apollo's manned lunar landings.

Taken in 17 Minutes

The still pictures were snapped and transmitted in the last 17 minutes before the spacecraft crashed into an area northwest of the Sea of Clouds.

They meant in effect that the 240,000 mile distance to the moon had been shrunk by man's ingenuity to a mere half-mile in terms of what he could see of its topography. They showed craters three feet in diameter and a foot to a foot and a half deep.

The best earthbound telescopes, handicapped by the shimmering mantle of the atmosphere, can shrink the lunar distance only to 500 miles and reveal features no smaller than about one-mile across.

The startling disclosures of what Ranger 7 had wrought were made at a packed news conference here by a team of scientists headed by Dr. Gerard P. Kuiper of the University of Arizona.

The conference, televised nationally on a closed-circuit system, was held in the auditorium of the Jet Propulsion Laboratory of the National Aeronautics Space Administration.

"This is a great day for science," the eminent astronomer

said at the start, "and a great day for the United States.

"What has been achieved is truly remarkable. We have made progress in resolution [clarity of pictures] not by a factor of 10 . . . not by a factor of 100, which would have been remarkable, but by a factor of 1,000."

As a series of ten samples of the Ranger 7 photographs were flashed on a screen, Dr. Kuiper pointed out some of the more interesting features. Among the highlights of his recital and of answers both he and another member of the scientific panel made were these:

¶A few hours' quick study of Ranger 7's massive output had not revealed that there were any totally unforeseen problems on the moon. But the numberless new details opened a region of knowledge that would keep scientists in deep study for three or four years or more.

¶There was evidence that the white rays around some major craters were caused not by light fluffy material tossed up from the moon but by sizable rocks thrown off in the formation of these large craters. The rocks made numerous secondary craters deep enough to represent an extreme hazard to a manned lunar landing craft. Such areas were to be avoided like poison, Dr. Kuiper said.

¶The tentative impression of the scientific team was that the lunar surface dust or other substance was not thick enough to swallow an astronaut landing craft. Dr. Eugene Shoemaker

Continued on Page 8, Column 1

U.S. STEEL WEIGHS MIDTOWN PROJECT

M'KESSON TO CUT ANTIBIOTIC PRICE

Plans to Sell Tetracycline at Third of Present Cost— Pfizer Says It Will Sue

By MARTIN ARNOLD

The nation's largest wholesale drug distributor announced yesterday that it would manufacture and sell tetracycline at about one-third the price at which it is sold by other manufacturers in the United States.

Tetracycline is a broad-spectrum antibiotic that is effective against a variety of bacterial infections. Yearly sales in the country total about $100 million, or about a third of the total sale of antibiotics.

The announcement was made by McKesson & Robbins, which said that it would offer pills for about 6 cents each wholesale, or $6 for 100 250-milligram tablets. A spokesman for the company said that other drug concerns that manufacture tetracycline in the United States sell it for "slightly more than" $17 a hundred tablets wholesale."

Chas. Pfizer & Co., one of the discoverers of tetracycline, immediately announced that it would file suit against McKesson & Robbins for patent infringement.

There are a number of small distributing concerns that buy tetracycline abroad, notably in Italy, and sell it for a low price here.

The importance of the McKesson & Robbins move, observers point out, is that the company's product is made American and therefore, justifiably or not, druggists and doctors will be less hesitant

Continued on Page 34, Column 3

The New York Times.

LATE CITY EDITION

U.S. Weather Bureau Report (Page 46) forecast:
Variable cloudiness today; clear tonight. Fair and cool tomorrow.
Temp. Range: 86—65; yesterday: 81—57.
Temp.-Hum. Index: low 70's; yesterday: 73.

VOL. CXIII—No. 38,910. © 1964 by The New York Times Company. Times Square, New York, N.Y. 10036.

NEW YORK, WEDNESDAY, AUGUST 5, 1964.

TEN CENTS

U.S. PLANES ATTACK NORTH VIETNAM BASES; PRESIDENT ORDERS 'LIMITED' RETALIATION AFTER COMMUNISTS' PT BOATS RENEW RAIDS

F.B.I. Finds 3 Bodies Believed to Be Rights Workers'

GRAVES AT A DAM

Discovery Is Made in New Earth Mound in Mississippi

By CLAUDE SITTON
Special to The New York Times

JACKSON, Miss., Aug. 4—Bodies believed to be those of three civil rights workers missing since June 21 were found early tonight near Philadelphia, Miss.

Federal Bureau of Investigation agents recovered the bodies from a newly erected earthen dam in a thickly wooded area about six miles southwest of Philadelphia, in east-central Mississippi.

The dam is several hundred yards off State Highway 21, near the Neshoba County fairgrounds.

Fulton Jackson, the county coroner, made a preliminary examination at the scene. The bodies were then sealed in plastic bags and brought by ambulance to the University of Mississippi Medical Center in Jackson, 70 miles to the southwest.

Pledge by Governor

Roy K. Moore, special agent in charge of the Jackson F.B.I. office, said physicians and fingerprint experts would seek to make positive identification and establish the cause of death.

[In Washington, authoritative sources said that President Johnson had telephoned Gov. Paul B. Johnson Jr. of Mississippi after having learned of the discovery of the bodies. However, this could not be confirmed immediately.]

Governor Johnson said in a statement:

"If these are the bodies of the three civil rights workers who have been missing several weeks, the investigative forces of the State of Mississippi will exert every effort to apprehend those who may have been responsible."

Area Searched Earlier

Mr. Johnson said he understood F.B.I. agents had searched the area once before and had noticed the new dam. Later, when they saw that the dam had collected no water despite heavy showers, they returned for a further investigation.

Excavation uncovered the bodies in the fill of the dam, the Governor said.

Sheriff L. A. Rainey, who had just returned from a vacation, visited the scene a short while after the discovery.

The missing men were Michael H. Schwerner, 24 years old, and Andrew Goodman, 20, both white and both from New York City, and James E. Chaney, 21, a Negro of Meridian, Miss.

All three had been taking part in the Mississippi Summer Project, a state-wide civil rights drive, which began on the week-

Continued on Page 37, Column 2

Scattered Violence Keeps Jersey City Tense 3d Night

400 Policemen Confine Most of Rioters to 2 Sections—Crowds Watch in Streets Despite Danger

By FRED POWLEDGE
Special to The New York Times

JERSEY CITY, Aug. 4—Scattered violence broke out again here tonight as roving groups of Negroes hurled crude Molotov cocktails in the streets. There was some gunfire but no injuries were reported.

About 400 city policemen contained most of the young rioters to two predominantly Negro neighborhoods. There were at least two arrests.

Although it was dangerous to be on the streets on this third night of violence, many people watched from sidewalks and front porches as police cars, their red lights flashing, sped from one pocket of violence to another.

On Ocean Avenue the police trained spotlights on the roof of a three-story block of apartments. A man had been seen on the roof, and it was feared that he was armed with a rifle, tire bombs, or both. Yet on the sidewalk below, a woman walked her dog, apparently without concern, through throngs of helmeted policemen. From a front porch across the street, a baby cried.

Since the rioting started Sunday night, more than 30 persons have been injured, two of them with gunshot wounds. None of the wounds was critical. More than three dozen persons have been arrested.

Five hundred more Jersey City policemen stood ready to

Text of Whelan's statement will be found on Page 36.

Continued on Page 36, Column 1

JOHNSON SEEKING EXTREMISM PLANK

Favors a Stand Against Far Left and Right Without Naming Any Groups

Special to The New York Times

WASHINGTON, Aug. 4—President Johnson wants the Democratic platform to take a stand against extremism of the right and the left, without naming any particular organization.

Mr. Johnson, at the moment, plans to attend the party's national convention in Atlantic City on Thursday night, Aug. 27, when he is scheduled to make his acceptance speech. But his wish on the platform is likely to be enough to make his views effective.

As yet, however, he has had no detailed discussions with the platform drafters.

The President is also planning to follow a somewhat unusual procedure in having himself placed in nomination. This is to be done by "co-nominators" — Governors Edmund G. Brown of California and John B. Connally Jr. of Texas.

These and other fairly well-advanced plans of the President have been learned from high Democratic sources.

However, on the question of most current interest, Mr. Johnson's choice for a Vice-Presidential candidate, no decision has yet been made.

Senator Hubert H. Humphrey

Continued on Page 14, Column 6

Rockefeller to Join Goldwater's Parley On Campaign Unity

Special to The New York Times

ALBANY, Aug. 4—Governor Rockefeller has accepted the invitation of Senator Goldwater to attend a meeting of Republican Governors at Hershey, Pa., on Aug. 12.

The invitation was extended by the Republican Presidential nominee in telegrams last Saturday to the 16 Republican Governors.

Mr. Rockefeller, who was a candidate for the Presidential nomination until after his defeat in the California primary June 2, was one of Senator Goldwater's severest critics through the Republican National Convention last month in San Francisco.

Mr. Goldwater has called the Hershey gathering in an effort to promote unity within the Republican party behind his candidacy.

The prospects for success of

Continued on Page 16, Column 1

REDS DRIVEN OFF

Two Torpedo Vessels Believed Sunk in Gulf of Tonkin

By ARNOLD H. LUBASCH

WASHINGTON, Aug. 4—The Defense Department announced tonight that North Vietnamese PT boats made a "deliberate attack" today on two United States destroyers patrolling international waters in the Gulf of Tonkin off North Vietnam.

The attack came two days after North Vietnamese torpedo boats attacked the Maddox, one of the destroyers in today's incident.

The destroyers and covering carrier-based aircraft fired on the vessels in today's attack, drove them off and apparently sank at least two of them, according to the announcement. The Pentagon said there were no United States casualties or damage.

The attack was made by an "undetermined number of North Vietnamese PT boats" during darkness about 65 miles from the nearest land, the Pentagon reported. It said the attack came at 10:30 P. M., North Vietnamese time, or 10:30 A. M., Washington time.

'Fabrication,' Reds Say

[The North Vietnamese regime said Wednesday that the report of another attack on United States ships was a "fabrication."]

The second attack was described in Washington as much fiercer than the first one, which was said to have lasted half an hour. The second battle was understood to have lasted about three hours in rough sea, with bad weather and low visibility.

"We are in a very serious situation," a Government official said.

The attack came shortly before the State Department made public a stern protest about the North Vietnamese attack Sunday on the Maddox, which was then patrolling about 30 miles off North Vietnam, also in international waters in the Gulf of Tonkin.

The protest over the first incident was announced shortly after noon here, when the

Continued on Page 3, Column 1

2 CARRIERS USED

McNamara Reports on Aerial Strikes and Reinforcements

By JACK RAYMOND

WASHINGTON, Wednesday, Aug. 5—Secretary of Defense Robert S. McNamara said at a postmidnight news conference that the United States planes that attacked North Vietnam yesterday and today had come from the carriers Constellation and Ticonderoga in the Gulf of Tonkin.

He said that the attacks had been directed against the bases used by the North Vietnamese PT boats that attacked two United States destroyers in international waters yesterday.

The Secretary added that the naval planes, believed to have included propeller-driven as well as jet-powered craft, had also conducted strikes against "certain other targets directly supporting the operation of the PT boats."

The United States planes used conventional weapons.

Separate Targets

Mr. McNamara, who held his news conference shortly after President Johnson had addressed the nation on television, emphasized in his report that the PT boat bases and the supporting facilities in North Vietnam had been separate targets.

He offered a guess, based on incomplete reports, that in the exchange of fire between the attacking PT boats and the United States destroyers and aircraft in international waters, at least two and possibly four of the North Vietnamese Soviet-made PT boats had been sunk. The Defense Secretary disclosed that at one point in the Vietnamese PT boat attack, the Maddox observed an unidentified aircraft on radar, but that there was no air attack and the radar image was soon lost.

Hanoi Not Attacked

The first United States reaction was a note of protest and warning. But, as announced by the President, and the Secretary of Defense, the second PT boat attack on the destroyers Maddox and C. Turner Joy yesterday precipitated the counteraction.

The Secretary of Defense said at the news conference that the retaliatory strikes were still under way at that time.

He made clear, in response to questions, that no targets outside North Vietnam had been attacked by the United States war planes. He specifically ex-

Continued on Page 4, Column 3

DECISION: President Johnson, in a nationwide broadcast, tells of action he ordered taken against North Vietnam.
Associated Press Wirephoto

FORCES ENLARGED

Stevenson to Appeal for Action by U.N. on 'Open Aggression'

By TOM WICKER
Special to The New York Times

WASHINGTON, Aug. 4—President Johnson has ordered retaliatory action against gunboats and "certain supporting facilities in North Vietnam" after renewed attacks against American destroyers in the Gulf of Tonkin.

In a television address tonight, Mr. Johnson said air attacks on the North Vietnamese ships and facilities were taking place as he spoke, shortly after 11:30 P.M.

State Department sources said the attacks were being carried out with conventional weapons on a number of shore bases in North Vietnam, with the objective of destroying them and the 30 to 40 gunboats they served.

The aim, they explained, was to destroy North Vietnam's gunboat capability. They said more air strikes might come later, if needed. Carrier-based aircraft were used in tonight's strike.

2 Boats Believed Sunk

Administration officials also announced that substantial additional units, primarily air and sea forces, were being sent to Southeast Asia.

This "positive reply," as the President called it, followed a naval battle in which a number of North Vietnamese PT boats attacked two United States destroyers with torpedoes. Two of the boats were believed to have been sunk. The United States forces suffered no damage and no loss of lives.

Mr. Johnson termed the North Vietnamese attacks "open aggression on the high seas."

Washington's response is "limited and fitting," the President said, and his Administration seeks no general extension of the guerrilla war in South Vietnam.

Goldwater Approves

"We Americans know," he said, "although others appear to forget, the risks of spreading conflict."

Mr. Johnson said Secretary of State Dean Rusk had been instructed to make this American attitude clear to all nations. He added that Adlai E. Stevenson, chief United States delegate, would raise the matter immediately in the United Nations Security Council. [The Council was expected to meet at 10:30 A.M. Wednesday.]

The President said he had informed his Republican Presidential rival, Senator Barry Goldwater, of his action and

Continued on Page 2, Column 3

The President's Address

Following is the text of the President's address on Vietnam last night, as recorded by The New York Times:

My fellow Americans:

As President and Commander in Chief, it is my duty to the American people to report that renewed hostile actions against United States ships on the high seas in the Gulf of Tonkin have today required me to order the military forces of the United States to take action in reply.

The initial attack on the destroyer Maddox on Aug. 2 was repeated today by a number of hostile vessels attacking two U.S. destroyers with torpedoes.

The destroyers and supporting aircraft acted at once on the orders I gave after the initial act of aggression.

We believe at least two of the attacking boats were sunk. There were no U.S. losses.

The performance of commanders and crews in this engagement is in the highest tradition of the United States Navy.

But repeated acts of violence against the armed forces of the United States must be met not only with alert defense but with positive reply.

Action 'Now in Execution'

That reply is being given, as I speak to you tonight. Air action is now in execution against gunboats and certain supporting facilities in North Vietnam which have been used in these hostile operations.

In the larger sense, this new act of aggression aimed directly at our own forces again brings home to all of us in the United States the importance of the struggle for peace and security in Southeast Asia.

Aggression by terror against the peaceful villages of South Vietnam has now been joined by open aggression on the high seas against the United States of America.

The determination of all Americans to carry out our full commitment to the people and to the Government of South Vietnam will be redoubled by this outrage. Yet our response for the present will be limited and fitting.

We Americans know—although others appear to forget—the risk of spreading conflict. We still seek no wider war.

I have instructed the Secretary of State to make this position totally clear to friends and to adversaries and, indeed, to all.

I have instructed Ambassador Stevenson to raise this matter immediately and urgently before the Security Council of the United Nations.

Congressional Resolution Asked

Finally, I have today met with the leaders of both parties in the Congress of the United States and I have informed them that I shall immediately request the Congress to pass a resolution making it clear that our Government is united in its determination to take all necessary measures in support of freedom and in defense of peace in Southeast Asia.

I have been given encouraging assurance by these leaders of both parties that such a resolution will be promptly introduced, freely and expeditiously debated, and passed with overwhelming support.

And just a few minutes ago I was able to reach Senator Goldwater and I am glad to say that he has expressed his support of the statement that I am making to you tonight.

It is a solemn responsibility to have to order even limited military action by forces whose over-all strength is as vast and as awesome as those of the United States of America.

But it is my considered conviction, shared throughout your Government, that firmness in the right is indispensable today for peace.

That firmness will always be measured. Its mission is peace.

Salinger Appointed to the Senate

Pierre Salinger, left, with Gov. Edmund G. Brown of California after the announcement yesterday in Sacramento.
United Press International Telephoto

By WALLACE TURNER

SAN FRANCISCO, Aug. 4—Pierre Salinger was appointed to the Senate today by Gov. Edmund G. Brown of California to fill the remaining five months of the term of the late Senator Clair Engle. Mr. Salinger is scheduled to be sworn in tomorrow about noon. He will be escorted to the rostrum by Senator Thomas H.

Kuchel of California, the assistant Republican minority leader. Governor Brown is to head a party of about 160 Democratic leaders who will be present in the Senate galleries when the new Senator takes his oath. Mr. Salinger, who was White House press

Continued on Page 16, Column 2

Auto Collision Insurance Rates In State Increased 4.3 to 25%

By JOSEPH C. INGRAHAM

Higher auto damage in-own car, is optional. The rate su. ance rates — with increases from 4.3 to 25 per cent—will go into effect today for private passenger car owners in the state.

The increases were disclosed yesterday by the National Automobile Underwriters Association, which said that sharp rises in auto thefts and in the cost of repairs had made them necessary.

The association said that although the statewide rise would be the lesser amount, the rates in most of the metropolitan area had been increased as much as 25 per cent.

Physical damage insurance, which reimburses a car owner for loss of or damage to his

revisions apply to collision insurance and to comprehensive coverage, which protects motorists against loss due to theft, fire, windstorm, glass breakage and other hazards.

While each of these coverages can be bought separately, the National Automobile Underwriters Association, rating organization for more than 400 companies here, lumps the vari-

Continued on Page 67, Column 2

Congolese Battling Inside Stanleyville

By J. ANTHONY LUKAS
Special to The New York Times

LEOPOLDVILLE, the Congo, Aug. 4—Rebels of the "Popular Army" and Government troops battled tonight in the streets of Stanleyville, the chief city in the northern Congo.

Messages from the United States consul there said heavy fighting was going on early this evening in front of the consulate, about half a mile from the center of the city.

At 6:15 P. M. Stanleyville time, the consul, Michael P. E. Hoyt, telegraphed that fighting was "advancing across front laws of consulate" and seemed to be "pushing rebels back."

Eight minutes later he wired that the army troops were "advancing rapidly and in numbers beyond consulate on road to Wanie Rukula." He said that

Continued on Page 8, Column 4

Khanh Is Fighting Threat of a Coup

By SEYMOUR TOPPING
Special to The New York Times

SAIGON, South Vietnam, Aug. 4—Premier Nguyen Khanh struggled today to strengthen the political stability of his Government as his aides privately warned of plots to drive him from office. United States officials were concerned about the political deterioration in Saigon.

The malaise in the capital was attributed more to a clash of rival political and military personalities than to pressure from the Vietcong insurgents.

United States sources said reports from provinces indicated that conditions there were generally better than in Saigon.

Once again, rumors of a coup d'état were circulating in Sai-

Continued on Page 4, Column 7

"All the News That's Fit to Print"

The New York Times.

LATE CITY EDITION
U. S. Weather Bureau Report (Page 45) forecasts.
Cloudy, then fair today; fair and cooler tonight. Fair tomorrow.
Temp. Range: 70—55; yesterday: 73—59.

VOL. CXIV.No. 38,964.
© 1964 by The New York Times Company. Times Square, New York, N. Y. 10036

NEW YORK, MONDAY, SEPTEMBER 28, 1964.

Today's Issue Contains 96 Pages in Two Sections

TEN CENTS

WARREN COMMISSION FINDS OSWALD GUILTY AND SAYS ASSASSIN AND RUBY ACTED ALONE; REBUKES SECRET SERVICE, ASKS REVAMPING

F.B.I. IS CRITICIZED

Security Steps Taken by Secret Service Held Inadequate

By FELIX BELAIR Jr.
Special to The New York Times

WASHINGTON, Sept. 27 —A sweeping revision of the organization and basic operating practices of the United States Secret Service was recommended today by the Warren Commission.

The commission sharply rebuked the Secret Service for failure to make adequate preparation for the visit of President Kennedy to Dallas last November. It reprimanded the Federal Bureau of Investigation for failure to supply the Secret Service with information concerning the presence of Lee Harvey Oswald in Dallas.

The commission deplored the fact that "there was no fully adequate liaison" between the F.B.I. and the Secret Service before the Dallas trip. It noted that some improvements had occurred since then but it insisted that, ultimately, Presidential protection required improvement in working arrangements of all Federal agencies concerned, including the Central Intelligence Agency, the State Department and the military intelligence branches.

Scrutiny Is Urged

The State Department was admonished to scrutinize more carefully requests for return to the United States of defectors

The report's appendix on Presidential protection will be printed in tomorrow's Times.

like Oswald "who have evidenced disloyalty or hostility to this country or who have expressed a desire to renounce their citizenship."

The brunt of the commission's indictment was directed at the century-old agency responsible for the safety of the President and his family. Its chief charge was that the Secret Service had not checked buildings along the route of the Presidential motorcade in Dallas nor asked the local police to do so.

The commission called for the appointment of a new special assistant to the Secretary of the Treasury with general supervisory authority over the Secret Service.

The commission found, however, that the conduct of the Secret Service agents in the Presidential motorcade "demonstrates that the President and the nation can expect courage and devotion to duty from agents of the Secret Service."

It acknowledged that whatever the human and material resources at the command of the Secret Service, a President can only be made as safe as he wants to be.

The report declared that its recommendations were "compelled by the facts disclosed in this investigation." It noted that

Continued on Page 15, Column 1

JOHNSON NAMES 4 TO ACT ON REPORT

Commission Calls for Action to Increase the Security of the Presidency

By The Associated Press
JOHNSON CITY, Tex., Sept. 27—President Johnson appointed a four-man committee today to advise him "on the execution of the recommendations of the Warren Commission.

The commission, which investigated the assassination of President Kennedy, recommended action to tighten the protection of Presidents and to make the killing of a President or a Vice President a Federal crime.

[Mike Mansfield of Montana, the Senate majority leader, said in Washington that Congress, which has been aiming at adjournment at the end of this week, "should stay here and act, if the President sends us any recommendations."]

Members of the committee are Secretary of the Treasury Douglas Dillon, Acting Attorney General Nicholas deB. Katzenbach, John A. McCone, director of the Central Intelligence Agency, and McGeorge Bundy, Special Assistant to the President for National Security Affairs.

The President named no chairman for the committee, but it was understood that Secretary Dillon, as ranking member, would have general supervision over the group.

The group will presumably

Continued on Page 17, Column 3

A New Chapter Unfolds in the Kennedy Legend

By JAMES RESTON
Special to The New York Times

WASHINGTON, Sept. 27—The Warren Commission has fulfilled its primary assignment. It has tried, as a servant of history, to discover truth. But the assassination of President Kennedy was so symbolic of human irony and tragedy, and so involved in the complicated and elemental conflicts of the age, that many vital questions remain, and the philosophers, novelists and dramatists will have to take it from here.

News Analysis

The commission has not concluded the Kennedy mystery so much as it has opened up a whole new chapter in the Kennedy legend.

It has provided the greatest repository of Presidential political history, drama and fiction since the murder of Mr. Lincoln and since legend is often more powerful than history, this may be the commission's most significant achievement.

Now the central mystery of who killed the President has been answered by the commission only in the process of raising a new catalogue of mysteries. Now the main characters in the play have been surrounded by a host of new characters, each of whom appears briefly at a critical moment with some vital testimony, only to disappear without our really knowing much about who they are.

The whole story is full of the mystery of life. Lee Harvey Oswald's motive for murdering the President remains obscure. The distinguished members of the commission and their staff obviously gave up on it.

The "might-have-beens" are maddening. If only he had been given that visa to go to Cuba and thence to the Soviet Union just before the assassination! If he had not been allowed to come back from there in the first place! Who was "the neighbor" who got him the job in the Texas Book Depository, from where he shot the President? And what were the details of Oswald's attempted suicide in Moscow?

The wild accidents are equally intriguing. There is, for example, the case of Mrs. Bledsoe, who rented Oswald a room in Dallas and then, on a 10,000-to-1 chance, just happened to be on the bus he boarded when he was running away from the crime.

Then there are the consoling yearnings and kindnesses in the midst of tragedy: Ruth Paine, who was also "alienated" and "isolated," and frustrated like Oswald, but who nevertheless "befriended" Marina Oswald in her time of

Continued on Page 15, Column 6

THE WARREN COMMISSION: President's Commission on the Assassination of President Kennedy at commission offices at Veterans of Foreign Wars Building, Washington. From left: Representative Gerald R. Ford, Representative Hale Boggs, Senator Richard B. Russell, Chief Justice Earl Warren, Senator John Sherman Cooper, John J. McCloy, Allen W. Dulles, and J. Lee Rankin, commission counsel. Portraits are of President Johnson, President Kennedy and Joseph J. Lombardo, head of Veterans of Foreign Wars.

Harris & Ewing

PANEL UNANIMOUS

Theory of Conspiracy by Left or Right Is Rejected

The text of the report begins on the first page of the second section.

By ANTHONY LEWIS
Special to The New York Times

WASHINGTON, Sept. 27 —The assassination of President Kennedy was the work of one man, Lee Harvey Oswald. There was no conspiracy, foreign or domestic.

That was the central finding in the Warren Commission report, made public this evening. Chief Justice Earl Warren and the six other members of the President's Commission on the Assassination of President John F. Kennedy were unanimous on this and all questions.

The commission found that Jack Ruby was on his own in killing Oswald. It rejected all theories that the two men were in some way connected. It said that neither rightists nor Communists bore responsibility for the murder of the President in Dallas last Nov. 22.

Why did Oswald do it? To this most important and most mysterious question the commission had no certain answer. It suggested that Oswald had no rational purpose, no motive adequate if "judged by the standards of reasonable men."

A Product of His Life

Rather, the commission saw Oswald's terrible act as the product of his entire life—a life "characterized by isolation, frustration and failure." He was just 24 years old at the time of the assassination.

"Oswald was profoundly alienated from the world in which he lived," the report said. "He had very few, if any, close relationships with other people and he appeared to have had great difficulty in finding a meaningful place in the world."

"He was never satisfied with anything.

"When he was in the United States, he resented the capitalist system. When he was in the Soviet Union, he apparently resented the Communist party members, who were accorded special privileges and who he thought were betraying Communism, and he spoke well of the United States."

The commission found that Oswald shot and wounded Maj. Gen. Edwin A. Walker in Dallas on April 10, 1963, narrowly missing him. It cited this as evidence of his capacity for violence.

It listed as factors that might have led Oswald to the assassination "his deep-rooted resentment of all authority, which was expressed in a hostility toward every society in which he lived," his "urge to try to find a place in history" and his "avowed commitment to Marx-

Continued on Page 14, Column 1

'MYTHS' OF CASE DENIED IN DETAIL

Panel Says Misinformation on the Assassination Led to 'Distorted' Views

By PETER KIHSS

The Warren Commission rejected in detail yesterday a number of charges suggesting that Lee Harvey Oswald had not acted alone in the assassination of President Kennedy.

The commission said that "publicizing of unchecked information" had led to "myths" and "distorted" interpretations. While each inaccuracy could be explained, it went on, "the number and variety of misstatements issued by the police" in Dallas would have "greatly assisted a skillful defense attorney."

On the other hand, Mark Lane, chairman of a Citizens Committee of Inquiry here, contended that if the report contained all the available evidence, "Oswald would have been acquitted" of both the President's assassination and the murder of the Dallas patrolman, J. D. Tippit.

In a news conference, Mr. Lane, a former Assemblyman, said his group would continue its efforts to "answer the unanswered questions." He said it had more than 100 workers here, with other committees in England, France and Denmark, and interested groups on 20 college campuses. His group estimated that it had raised and

Continued on Page 16, Column 4

High Clerics to Ask Stronger Statement By Council on Jews

Special to The New York Times

ROME, Sept. 27—A powerful array of Roman Catholic prelates, including at least three American Cardinals, are preparing to speak out for a strong statement by the Ecumenical Council on the Jews, clerical sources said today.

The sources said that Richard James Cardinal Cushing, Archbishop of Boston, is known to have prepared an address to be given at the Council when the issue is debated.

The draft of the declaration was introduced last Friday by Augustin Cardinal Bea, the German Jesuit, who heads the Council's Secretariat for the Promotion of Christian Unity. It is considered by many Council Fathers—the voting prelates — and observers to be a "watered down" version of an earlier draft.

Other Cardinals Named

The earlier statement, among other things, made plain that the Jews of Christ's time and of today bore no responsibility for the Crucifixion. The weakened declaration declares only that Jews of today cannot be blamed.

Among those expected to attack the newer version are two other American Cardinals—Joseph Elmer Ritter, Archbishop of St. Louis, and Albert Gregory Meyer, Archbishop of Chicago.

Cardinal Spellman of New York has also said that he favors the more forceful state-

Continued on Page 7, Column 1

2 CITIES DENY REIN ON POLICE IN RIOTS

Civilian Review Units Hold F.B.I. Criticism Unfounded

By FRED POWLEDGE

Officials of civilian police advisory boards in Rochester and Philadelphia disagreed yesterday with a statement by the Federal Bureau of Investigation that boards such as theirs had "virtually paralyzed" the police during the summer riots.

The Rev. William H. Gray Jr., executive secretary of Philadelphia's eight-member review board, said: "It's over-simplifying the situation to say that the board has an effect on the rioting or the police behavior."

Ross J. Guglielmino, the executive director and legal counsel of the Rochester board, said he did not feel the F.B.I. criticism applied to Rochester.

What the F.B.I. Found

The two men commented in telephone interviews on a report released Saturday by President Johnson. The President asked the F.B.I. to collect its investigations of summer riots in New York City, Rochester, Dixmoor, Ill.; Philadelphia, Seaside, Ore., Hampton Beach, N. H., and Jersey City, Paterson, and Elizabeth, N. J., and advise him if there were any pattern in the outbreaks.

The report, submitted to F.B.I. Director J. Edgar Hoover, concluded that the riots were not basically racial, although large numbers of Negroes did take part; that they were not organized on a national basis, and that none of them was planned by any one group or individual.

Among the several points

Continued on Page 48, Column 1

Congress Will Act On Appalachia Aid And Medical Care

Special to The New York Times

WASHINGTON, Sept. 27—The fate of two key Administration programs—health insurance for the aged and aid to Appalachia—may be decided this week as Congress pushes toward adjournment.

"We could finish up Saturday; that's my most optimistic guess," Senator Mike Mansfield of Montana, the majority leader, said today. "But I have my fingers crossed."

The health insurance issue, currently in House-Senate conference, could delay adjournment until the following week, some legislative leaders believe.

Prospects for conference approval of some form of health insurance for the aged under Social Security have ranged from bright to gloomy in recent days.

The House passed a bill this summer to increase Social Security taxes as well as cash

Continued on Page 18, Column 4

CAMPAIGN IMPACT BELIEVED LIKELY

'Kennedy Legacy' Could Aid Democrats at the Polls

By TOM WICKER
Special to The New York Times

WASHINGTON, Sept. 27—The effects of the Warren Commission's report are sure to extend far beyond its conclusion that Lee Harvey Oswald, acting alone, killed President Kennedy last Nov. 22.

The massive document could have repercussions in the 1964 elections, on the present conduct of President Johnson, and ultimately on the availability to the public of Mr. Johnson and future Presidents.

It may produce major changes for the Secret Service, the agency now assigned to protect the President.

Other Agencies Affected

The assignments and powers of other agencies such as the Federal Bureau of Investigation and even the Central Intelligence Agency might be revamped and independent review of their activities and efficiency might be increased.

In the field of legislation, the report might produce—as is recommended by the commission—a law making it a Federal crime to kill or attempt to kill a President, a Vice President or any officer next in line to the Presidency and the President-elect and Vice President-elect. Other legislation, particularly relating to security and investigative agencies and to the protection of Presidents, could also grow from the report.

Although the State Department was generally cleared of

Continued on Page 15, Column 5

G.I.'s Rescue Vietnam Captives; Uprising Stirs Mistrust of U.S.

By PETER GROSE
Special to The New York Times

SAIGON, South Vietnam, Sept. 27 — United States Army helicopters rescued 60 Vietnamese hostages today from a camp of rebel tribesmen in the central highlands.

The release of the prisoners met a Government condition for negotiations with the armed mountain tribesmen. It appeared to reduce the danger of a violent clash.

Nevertheless, the revolt is having serious political consequences, increasing growing suspicion between the United States mission and the Premier, Maj. Gen. Nguyen Khanh.

rebellion has intensified Saigon's feeling that the United States, which has supported General Khanh, is undergoing a change of policy.

[About five persons were reported shot dead when security forces fired on a crowd in Quinhon, 270 miles northeast of Saigon. Later a mob stormed a radio station and troops were called in to evict the demonstrators, Reuters reported.]

Officials around General Khanh say he no longer believes he can count on American help to stay in power and he feels he must seek firmer support from

Continued on Page 2, Column 1

NEWS INDEX

Scientific Police Work Traced Bullets to Rifle Oswald Owned

By JOHN W. FINNEY
Special to The New York Times

WASHINGTON, Sept. 27—The Warren Commission's conclusion that Lee Harvey Oswald killed President Kennedy rests in large part on scientific evidence painstakingly established through modern technology.

On the basis of the scientific evidence alone it was possible to establish that the shots were fired by a rifle owned and possessed by Oswald, that the shots were fired from the sixth-floor window of a building in which Oswald worked, and that the fatal wound could have been caused by the bullets from the high-powered rifle.

These crucial points were established through scientific detective work that combined the techniques of handwriting, ballistics, and fiber and wounds analysis. Among the devices used were microscopes, spectroscopes, X-rays, surveying instruments and skulls filled with gelatin.

Even nuclear science was employed. Paraffin casts from Oswald's hands and face were put into a nuclear reactor at the Oak Ridge (Tenn.) National Laboratory in an unsuccessful attempt to see if radiation would show up traces of gun powder. One major question left

Continued on Page 16, Column 5

"All the News That's Fit to Print"

The New York Times.

LATE CITY EDITION
U.S. Weather Bureau Report (Page 76) forecast:
Cloudy and cooler today; chance of rain tonight and tomorrow.
Temp. Range: 68—53; yesterday: 64—44.

VOL. CXIV. No. 38,982.

© 1964 by The New York Times Company
Times Square, New York, N. Y. 10036

NEW YORK, FRIDAY, OCTOBER 16, 1964.

TEN CENTS

KHRUSHCHEV OUSTED FROM TOP POSTS; BREZHNEV GETS CHIEF PARTY POSITION AND KOSYGIN IS NAMED NEW PREMIER

Labor Party Is the Apparent Victor in British Election

JOHNSON DENIES JENKINS COVER-UP; SETS F.B.I. INQUIRY

Praises His Aide's Service, but Says He Requested Resignation From Post

By TOM WICKER
Special to The New York Times

WASHINGTON, Oct. 15—President Johnson said tonight that until late yesterday he had had no information of any kind that "had ever raised a question" about the personal conduct of Walter W. Jenkins, his friend and special assistant.

The President made the statement, his first public comment on the Jenkins case, as he flew back here from a day of campaigning in New York.

In effect, he was denying Republican allegations that he had covered up knowledge of Mr. Jenkins's two arrests on morals charges. The disclosure of these arrests yesterday has shaken the Johnson Administration and the Democratic Presidential campaign.

Mr. Jenkins's resignation as special assistant to the President was announced in New York last night after the disclosure of his police record.

Mr. Johnson also disclosed in his statement tonight that he had requested the resignation of Mr. Jenkins.

'Dedication' Is Cited

The text of Mr. Johnson's statement follows:

"Walter Jenkins has worked with me faithfully for 25 years. No man I know has given more personal dedication, devotion and tireless labor.

"Until late yesterday no information or report of any kind to me had ever raised a question with respect to his personal conduct. Mr. Jenkins is now in the care of his physicians and his many friends will join in praying for his early recovery. For myself and Mrs. Johnson I want to say that our hearts go out with the deepest compassion for him and for his wife and six children—and they have our love and prayers.

"On this case as on any such case, the public interest comes before all personal feelings. I have requested and received Mr. Jenkins's resignation.

"Within moments after being notified last night, I ordered Director J. Edgar Hoover of the F.B.I. to make an immediate and comprehensive inquiry and report promptly to me and the American people."

The incident apparently is regarded by the Republicans as a major development in their

Continued on Page 20, Column 1

Cole Porter Is Dead; Songwriter Was 72

By The Associated Press

SANTA MONICA, Calif., Oct. 15—Cole Porter, the world-famed composer and lyricist, died at 11:05 P.M. today at a Santa Monica hospital, where he underwent kidney surgery last Tuesday. He was 72 years old.

Mr. Porter wrote the lyrics and music for his songs, and to both he brought such an individuality of style that a genre known as "the Cole Porter song" became recognized.

The hallmarks of a typical Porter song were lyrics that were urbane or witty and a melody with a sinuous, brooding quality. Some of his best-known songs in this vein were "What

Continued on Page 29, Column 1

"OH WHAT A LOVELY WAR"
Broadhurst Theatre W. 44th St.—Advt.

G.O.P. Hopes Rise, But Jenkins Effect On Race Is Cloudy

By EARL MAZO

The Walter W. Jenkins case inspired high hopes in the camp of Senator Barry Goldwater yesterday and dismay among supporters of President Johnson.

But by nightfall, reports from Moscow that Premier Khrushchev has been replaced led many political observers to speculate that the possible anti-Johnson impact of the Jenkins disclosure might be nullified by the effect of an international crisis upon the voters.

A leading Republican put it this way:

"That Lyndon Johnson is lucky. The arrest of his man Jenkins accented the whole Bobby Baker corruption mess, which is Barry Goldwater's strongest issue. But then comes this Khrushchev thing, taking the headlines and accenting Barry's greatest weakness."

Continued on Page 21, Column 1

JOHNSON HAILED AT LIBERAL RALLY

Asserts 'Great Society' Is a Practical Goal—He Is Acclaimed Upstate

By HOMER BIGART

President Johnson received a frenzied ovation last night from 20,000 persons who packed Madison Square Garden for a Liberal party rally.

The President expounded to the Garden audience his vision of the "Great Society" and insisted it was a practical goal —"not some vague, dreamlike utopia."

He said he would present a series of proposals dealing with the total needs of a metropolitan area.

These proposals, he said, would be built on the cooperation of government with industry—"the same sort of cooperation that has built our national defense and allowed us to explore the stars."

Campaigns With Kennedy

The President went to the Garden after stumping the state with Robert F. Kennedy, the Democratic-Liberal candidate for the Senate, and receiving tumultuous welcomes from huge crowds on a 22-mile tour of Brooklyn.

Despite the Walter Jenkins scandal, no lessening of enthusiasm was apparent in the throngs that greeted the President in Brooklyn or jammed the Garden for the Liberal party's climactic demonstration.

Roaring applause greeted the President and Mrs. Johnson when they entered the Garden at 8:20 P.M.

The President read his speech in a matter-of-fact voice and the subject matter—the "Great Society"—inspired no cheers.

Interest Stimulated

But when he turned to the day's dramatic developments in the Soviet Union, the crowd's interest was stimulated. A crescendo of applause followed his remark: "We do not intend to bury anyone anywhere and we do not intend to be buried ourselves."

The President warned that this was no time for impulsive leadership. He said "an impulsive thumb can move up toward a button," resulting in the destruction of millions of lives in a matter of moments.

Recalling the Cuban missile crisis, he declared that President Kennedy had the steadiest thumb, the greatest heart and

Continued on Page 22, Column 1

SLIM EDGE LIKELY

Wilson Aide Defeated in Campaign Marred by a Racial Issue

By SYDNEY GRUSON
Special to The New York Times

LONDON, Friday, Oct. 16—Britain apparently elected a Labor Government in yesterday's general election and sent the Conservatives, who have governed for 13 years, into opposition.

However, all indications pointed to the closest result since the Conservatives won with a majority of 17 in 1951. There is still a chance that Labor will not get a working majority.

With counting finished for the night, the standing of the parties from the results in 430 of the 630 constituencies was:

Labor—247
Conservative—181
Liberal—2

But this Labor lead of 66 House of Commons seats was misleading. Most of the results were from urban areas and the Conservatives are expected to cut deeply into the lead when counting in the rural Conservative strongholds resumes later this morning.

Labor Gains 52 Seats

The computers of the British Broadcasting Corporation and of Press Association, the cooperative newsgathering agency, both forecast an ultimate Labor majority over the Conservatives of 17.

Labor gained 52 seats, 34 from the Liberals and the rest from the Conservatives. The Conservatives lost 50 seats and took four from Labor.

Sir Alec Douglas-Home, the Conservative leader and Prime Minister, would not concede. He did not emerge from 10 Downing Street, his London office and residence, where he watched the election results on television.

So long as he did not concede, Harold Wilson, Labor's leader, refused to claim victory. Mr. Wilson would be Prime Minister in a Labor Government.

Patrick Gordon Walker, slated to be Foreign Secretary in a Labor Cabinet, lost the Smethwick constituency of industrial Birmingham to Peter Griffiths, a Conservative.

It was at Smethwick that a bitter campaign had been waged

Continued on Page 18, Column 1

Nikita S. Khrushchev
Relieved of political posts

Leonid I. Brezhnev
Named as the leader of the party

Aleksei N. Kosygin
Appointed as the Soviet Premier

Associated Press

Cholesterol Studies Bring Nobel Award To Two Biochemists

By The Associated Press

STOCKHOLM, Oct. 15—The 1964 Nobel Prize in Physiology or Medicine was awarded jointly today to Prof. Konrad E. Bloch of Harvard University and Prof. Feodor Lynen of the University of Munich.

The two were honored for their discoveries concerning the mechanism and regulation of cholesterol and fatty acid metabolism. They will share prize money equivalent to about $54,000.

In its citation, the prize-awarding body, the Royal Caroline Institute, said the therapy against circulatory diseases and related disturbances in steroid hormone metabolism would in the future rest upon the work of today's Nobel Prize winners.

Dr. Bloch, a 52-year-old naturalized American born in Germany, is Higgins Professor of Biochemistry at Harvard. He was credited with "brilliant investigations" showing how cholesterol is built up from acetic acid.

Cholesterol, a fatty substance

Continued on Page 3, Column 1

Cards Win World Series, Defeating Yankees, 7 to 5

By JOSEPH DURSO
Special to The New York Times

ST. LOUIS, Oct. 15—The St. Louis Cardinals completed their melodramatic climb from the depths of the National League to baseball's pinnacle today when they defeated the New York Yankees, 7—5, and captured the World Series.

They won it in the seventh and final game before a roaring crowd of 30,346 persons and struck, two by the Cardinals and three by the Yankees. Two were hit by the Boyer brothers—Ken of the Cards and Clete of the Yanks—while Lou Brock hit one for St. Louis and Bob Gibson, who struck out nine Yankees and survived three late home runs that knocked in all the Yankees' runs.

Five pitchers struggled against Gibson to withstand the Cardinals. But the Redbirds scored three runs in the fourth inning, three in the fifth and one in the seventh to bring St. Louis its first championship in 18 years and send the Yankees to their second straight loss of the World Series.

The Yankees have not lost two years in a row since 1921 and

Continued on Page 44, Column 2

THREATENED SUIT HALTS STATE LOAN

Deals to Borrow $17 Million Delayed by Challenge to Rockefeller Financing

By PETER KIHSS

Two state agencies have had to postpone the closing of deals to borrow $17.3 million because of a threatened court suit by the Teamsters Joint Council 16 against financing methods of the Rockefeller administration.

The Governor's office declined yesterday to say why the closing had been held up. But a high state official said the purchasers of bond-anticipation notes required standard certificates assuring that they would not become involved in litigation, and he said that such statements could not be given because of the threatened teamsters suit.

Governor Rockefeller was reported to have sought through intermediaries to get the union council president, John J. O'Rourke, to drop the threatened suit. The Governor's view was said to have been that "thousands" of jobs of currently employed construction workers would be endangered if the financing were held up.

But when Nicholas M. Kisburg, legislative and research director of the teamsters' council, said last night that the state could lose $806 million to carry on construction through bond issues already approved by the voters but not yet invoked by the Governor.

Governor Rockefeller's office said that $13.8 million in bond-anticipation notes of the State Housing Finance Agency had first been sold to five buyers Oct. 8, with delivery scheduled for yesterday. Yesterday, the agency "postponed delivery of the notes," the Governor's office said.

Similarly, it said, $3.5 million in bond-anticipation notes of the State Dormitory Authority had been sold Oct. 8, but delivery had to be "postponed" on Wednesday.

The purchasers of the Housing Finance Agency notes were

Continued on Page 31, Column 1

NEWS INDEX

SOMETHING NEW IN APARTMENT ADS.
Exclusive new feature! See actual floor plans when you check Apartment Directory ads in today's New York World-Telegram.—Advt.

U.S. Surprised but Expects No Radical Shift in Policy

By MAX FRANKEL
Special to The New York Times

WASHINGTON, Oct. 15—The Administration was surprised but not alarmed by the change of leadership in Moscow today. Analysts of Soviet affairs were almost unanimous in the view that Premier Khrushchev had suddenly been forced to step down for reasons of personality and policy, not merely age and health.

But the survival and promotion of prominent Khrushchev lieutenants, officials said, seemed to preclude any radical policy changes in the near future, at least in East-West relations.

In New York, President Johnson said that the shift in the Kremlin "may or may not be a sign of deep turmoil or a sign of changes to come." He commented at the end of his prepared remarks at a Liberal party rally.

Peace Is the Mission

"For ourselves, the need is clear—we should keep steady on our goals," he said. "Peace is the mission of the American people and we are not about to be deterred. We will be firm and restrained. We can meet any test but our quest is always for peace."

In Milwaukee, Senator Hubert H. Humphrey expressed doubt that the Soviet change would bring about a "quick" meeting of Soviet and United States leaders. Talking to newsmen

Continued on Page 15, Column 1

American Motors Struck by U.A.W.

By DAVID R. JONES

DETROIT, Friday, Oct. 16—The United Automobile Workers struck the American Motors Corporation this morning after failure to reach a new labor agreement.

Edward L. Cushman, American Motors vice president and top labor negotiator, announced at 1:05 A.M. today that the parties had agreed to retain a profit-sharing plan in a new contract. But he said the strike deadline arrived before other differences could be resolved.

The strike affects about 23,000 workers at four plants in two Wisconsin cities. The company makes Rambler automobiles.

The walkout widened labor strife in the industry, where nearly 300,000 workers already have been made idle by an auto

Continued on Page 40, Column 1

MOSCOW IS QUIET

Pravda Says Change Won't Bring Return of Harsh Policies

By HENRY TANNER
Special to The New York Times

MOSCOW, Friday, Oct. 16—Premier Khrushchev has been deprived of political power in the Soviet Union.

He was replaced by Leonid I. Brezhnev, 57 years old, as First Secretary of the Communist party and by Aleksei N. Kosygin, 60, as Premier.

Mr. Khrushchev, who is 70, even lost his seat in the Presidium of the Central Committee of the party, the third most important position he held in the leadership.

This indicated that he had fallen into disgrace.

[Dispatches did not mention if Mr. Khrushchev had been removed from the Central Committee itself. Under normal procedure such action would come at a meeting of the Soviet Communist party Congress.]

Adzhubei Reported Ousted

The changes were announced by Tass, the Soviet press agency, a few minutes after midnight. The Tass statement did not contain a single word of praise for the ousted leader.

Unofficial but reliable sources later reported that Aleksei I. Adzhubei, Mr. Khrushchev's son-in-law, had been deposed as chief editor of the Government newspaper Izvestia.

Mr. Khrushchev's whereabouts was not known. Nor was it known whether he was at liberty or under surveillance. Western diplomats assumed, however, that the changeover had been made peacefully.

Diplomats Voice Assurance

Moscow's streets were quiet. There were no signs of movements by either the army or police. Some of the smaller Western embassies, which had been without a police guard for the last several months, reported yesterday that the policemen were back in front of the gates.

Western diplomats said they did not expect the new leaders to change basic Soviet policy toward the West.

Mr. Brezhnev and Mr. Kosygin can be expected to continue Mr. Khrushchev's policy of "peaceful coexistence" with the United States, the diplomats said.

The Soviet Communist party newspaper Pravda indicated today that the party would continue to carry out policies of de-Stalinization and economic improvements under its new leadership.

The paper printed the same bare announcement that had been carried in the English-

Continued on Page 14, Column 1

STOCKS PLUMMET IN HECTIC TRADING

Changes in Kremlin Set Off Sharpest Drop in Prices Since Kennedy's Death

By RICHARD PHALON

Rumors of impending changes in the Kremlin swept Wall Street yesterday. By 1:30 P.M. a rolling tide of uneasiness had driven prices on the New York Stock Exchange to their deepest loss since the assassination of President Kennedy last Nov. 22.

Trading volume ran to 6.5 million shares, well below the record of 14.7 million shares churned up in the big market break of May 29, 1962, but much of it came in a concentrated burst after the noon hour. By 2:30 P.M. the tape lagged 27 minutes behind activity on the floor of the stock exchange.

Many brokers felt yesterday's market break followed a classic pattern. As one diagnosed it, the small investors were throwing much of the selling. "They can't see anything, they can't touch anything and they're nervous. They're selling and the professionals are bargain-hunting," he observed.

Losses Cut in Half

The first tangible sign that bargain-hunters were on the move came at 2:30 P.M. when market losses were cut in half. By 3 P.M. reports that Premier Khrushchev was retiring were confirmed and the news spread rapidly across the floor of the stock exchange.

At the close of trading, the stock market was down 6.74 points as measured by the Dow-Jones industrial average. The New York Times combined average of 50 stocks closed with a loss of 5.79 points.

Despite the late rally, it was the biggest loss since Aug. 4 when the stock prices plummeted after the Gulf of Tonkin naval action.

Boardroom habitues at midtown brokerage houses glared at the dancing symbols on the big Trans-Lux tapes with a frown

Continued on Page 53, Column 7

The TFX Unveiled; McNamara Hails It

By RICHARD WITKIN
Special to The New York Times

FORT WORTH, Tex., Oct. 15—The TFX, the plane that launched 3,000 pages of Congressional inquiry, was rolled out the factory door into public view today.

The twin-jet plane, which has revolutionary movable wings and now is called the F-111, is scheduled to make its first flight by the end of the year.

The rollout ceremony was attended by a dais full of civilian and military dignitaries, headed by Secretary of Defense Robert S. McNamara.

Mr. McNamara has been at the center of the political storm that has swirled around the F-111 program since his office overruled the unanimous judgment

Continued on Page 11, Column 1

"OH WHAT A LOVELY WAR"
Broadhurst Theatre W. 44th St.—Advt.

The New York Times.

LATE CITY EDITION

U.S. Weather Bureau Report (Page 78) forecast:
Sunny today; clear tonight.
Fair and milder tomorrow.
Temp. Range: 63—48; yesterday: 60—49.

VOL. CXIV.... No. 39,001. © 1964 by The New York Times Company. Times Square, New York, N.Y. 10036

NEW YORK, WEDNESDAY, NOVEMBER 4, 1964.

TEN CENTS

JOHNSON SWAMPS GOLDWATER AND KENNEDY BEATS KEATING; DEMOCRATS WIN LEGISLATURE

KENNEDY EDGE 6-5

Keating's Defeat Is Termed a 'Tragedy' by Rockefeller

New York Vote

PRESIDENT
Johnson, Dem.... 4,509,514
Goldwater, Rep....2,089,113
11,330 of 12,439 E.D.'s rptg.

SENATOR
Kennedy, Dem.....3,479,976
Keating, Rep......2,857,023
11,318 of 12,439 E.D.'s rptg.

By R. W. APPLE Jr.

Robert F. Kennedy was elected to the United States Senate from New York yesterday in his first bid for elective office, overwhelming Republican Senator Kenneth B. Keating.

With more than 80 per cent of the vote counted, Mr. Kennedy held a 6-to-5 lead. Because most of the untallied vote was in heavily Democratic New York City, it appeared that the former Attorney General's plurality might reach 650,000.

Mr. Keating conceded defeat at 11:39 P.M. with the announcement at the Roosevelt Hotel that he had sent a congratulatory telegram to Mr. Kennedy.

Governor Rockefeller, standing beside the white-haired Rochester legislator, said Mr. Keating's defeat was "a tragedy for the state and nation."

Runs Behind Johnson

"Senator Keating, one of the great Senators in the history of New York, has been rolled under by a national landslide," the Governor added. "He waged a magnificent campaign."

Mr. Kennedy ran well behind President Johnson. He seemed to be headed for a record margin of 2.5 million votes or more in the state. The President won all of the state's 62 counties.

It thus appeared that about a million New York voters had split their ticket to vote both for Mr. Johnson and Mr. Keating — but even this wasn't enough to make the Senate contest close.

A major surprise was the showing of the Liberal party, which had expected to deliver

Continued on Page 27, Column 1

STATE DEMOCRATS GAIN SIX IN HOUSE

Lindsay and Other Liberal Republicans Keep Seats

By WARREN WEAVER Jr.

Democrats swept through the New York Congressional delegation in yesterday's election, unseating six Republican Representatives and threatening the House seat of a seventh.

In the wake of the Johnson victory, the Democrats increased their strength in the delegation from 20 to 26 while the number of Republicans dropped from 21 to 14, with one district in doubt.

Although they failed to dislodge any of the three New York City Republican Congressmen, Democratic candidates scored victories elsewhere across the state. They took two seats in Nassau County, one in Westchester, one in the Hudson Valley and two in Western New York.

Among the chief Republican survivors was Representative John V. Lindsay of Manhattan, who won by a 65,000-vote margin in his East Side district.

Other Republicans to retain their seats were Representative Seymour Halpern of Queens, who like Mr. Lindsay had opposed Senator Barry Goldwater; and, Representative Ogden R.

Continued on Page 24, Column 3

"OH WHAT A LOVELY WAR" IS A HILARIOUS MUSICAL." — New Yorker. Broadhurst Theatre, W. 44 St.—Advt.

The Election at a Glance

President

	Number of States*	Electoral Votes
Johnson	45	486
Goldwater	6	52

*Includes Dist. of Columbia

President—New York		Senator—New York	
Johnson	4,509,514	Kennedy	3,479,976
Goldwater	2,089,113	Keating	2,857,023
(Incomplete)		(Incomplete)	

The Senate

Newly Elected Senators		Make-up of New Senate	
Democrats	25	Democrats	65
Republicans	5	Republicans	30
In doubt	5	In doubt	5

The House

Democrats elected	261
Republicans elected	127
In doubt	47

JOHNSON CRUSHES RIVAL IN JERSEY

Lead Near 900,000, Topping Eisenhower's Record— Williams Re-elected

New Jersey Vote

PRESIDENT
Johnson, Dem.......1,645,844
Goldwater, Rep...... 853,708
4,001 of 4,603 E.D.'s rptg.

SENATOR
Williams, Dem....1,474,523
Shanley, Rep...... 891,425
4,001 of 4,603 E.D.'s rptg.

By GEORGE CABLE WRIGHT

President Johnson won New Jersey's 17 electoral votes yesterday in the biggest political victory ever scored in the state.

With 91 per cent of the vote tallied, the President held a record lead of nearly 900,000 votes over his Republican opponent, Senator Barry Goldwater.

Until yesterday, the record plurality for a Presidential candidate in New Jersey was the 756,605-vote margin rolled up by President Eisenhower, a Republican, in 1956.

In sweeping at least 19, and possibly all of the state's 21 counties, Mr. Johnson carried to victory with him incumbent Democratic Senator Harrison A. Williams Jr. Democrats also captured a majority of the state's 15 seats in the House of Representatives for the first time since 1912.

In the present Congress, Republicans hold eight of the seats. On the basis of incomplete returns from yesterday's balloting, Democrats won at least 10 seats.

The Democratic candidate James J. Howard also held a narrow lead over his Republican opponent, Marcus Daly, in an

Continued on Page 32, Column 4

G.O.P. Grip Broken In Suburban Voting

By JOHN SIBLEY

Traditional Republican bastions in the suburbs crumbled before the Johnson onslaught yesterday, and the President carried with him many local Democratic candidates in nearby New York and New Jersey communities.

Widespread ticket-splitting showed, however, that Republican suburbanites were not forsaking their party so much as they were renouncing its Presidential nominee, Senator Barry Goldwater.

Westchester County, for the first time since 1912, gave a plurality to a Democratic Presidential candidate. Rockland County was Democratic for the first time since Franklin D. Roosevelt carried the county in 1936 and for only the fourth time in 100 years.

Long Island's suburbs, too, went to the President. Mr. Johnson became the first Democratic Presidential candidate in modern

Continued on Page 33, Column 2

Connecticut Votes 2-1 for President; All Democrats Win

Connecticut Vote

PRESIDENT (Complete)
Johnson, D...... 825,416
Goldwater, R...... 392,556

SENATOR
Dodd, D...... 779,252
Lodge, R...... 425,376

By RICHARD H. PARKE

President Johnson led a sweeping Democratic victory in Connecticut yesterday.

His better than 2-to-1 margin over Senator Barry Goldwater eclipsed the previous record plurality in a Presidential race in the state. Mr. Johnson's plurality was 432,860. The earlier record had been set by President Dwight D. Eisenhower in 1956 when he defeated Adlai E. Stevenson by 306,758 votes.

Senator Thomas J. Dodd, the Democratic incumbent, also triumphed easily over his Republican opponent, former Gov. John Davis Lodge. But the 57-year-old Senator ran about '5,-000 votes behind the President.

One result of President Johnson's landslide was the defeat of the state's only Republican Congressman, Representative Abner W. Sibal of the Fourth (Fairfield County) District. Mr. Sibal lost the normally Republican district to former Representative Donald J. Irwin, a

Continued on Page 32, Column 1

ROMNEY IS VICTOR; PERCY'S BID FAILS

Democrats Likely to Achieve Gain in Governorships

By JOSEPH A. LOFTUS

Democrats gave a good account of themselves in 25 contests for Governor yesterday, but it was a Republican who produced the spectacular.

Gov. George Romney, running aloof from Senator Barry Goldwater, set off a Michigan ticket-splitting spree to win re-election and thereby planted himself firmly in the thin front line of 1968 Presidential possibilities.

While Senator Goldwater gathered barely a third of Michigan's votes, the Governor defeated Neil Staebler with more than 55 per cent of the tally.

Strong Goldwater supporters "cut" Governor Romney, but the latter improved on his own 1962 vote totals in the labor Democratic areas of Detroit and Flint-Saginaw.

The Republicans failed to capture a major prize, the Illinois Governorship. The defeated candidate, Charles H. Percy, figured in Presidential talk for the future.

Gov. Otto J. Kerner won a second term in Illinois despite the failure of Mayor Richard Daley's organization to deliver Chicago majorities as big as those Mr. Kerner won there four years ago.

Nationally the Democrats seemed likely to score a net

Continued on Page 24, Column 6

Summary of International News: Wilson Acts to Nationalize Steel

Following is a summary of foreign news. A full report begins on the first page of the second part.

Labor Offers Program

Britain's new Labor Government offered a program of controversial legislation to Parliament. Headed by a demand for renationalization of the steel industry, the proposals indicate one of the bitterest sessions in parliamentary history.

French Explain Aim

Foreign Minister Maurice Couve de Murville told the French Parliament that the United States and Europe should develop separate, but not necessarily hostile, policies. In Washington, officials predicted that a major crisis for Atlantic unity would arise at a NATO meeting in December.

Bolivian Troops Revolt

A military revolt broke out in Bolivia and appeared to be spreading across the country. A truce designed to open the

UPSET AT ALBANY

Carlino and Mahoney Defeated—Special Session Expected

By LAYHMOND ROBINSON

A surge of Democratic votes swept the Republicans from control of the State Legislature yesterday for the first time in more than a quarter of a century.

The massive victory gave the Democrats a probable working majority of a dozen seats in the Assembly and a half dozen in the Senate.

Not since 1935, in the sweep of Franklin D. Roosevelt's New Deal, had the Democrats had control of both the houses. Not since 1938 had they held control of the Senate.

Toppled from their powerful posts in stunning upsets were Assembly Speaker Joseph F. Carlino of Long Beach, L. I., and Senate Majority Leader Walter J. Mahoney of Buffalo.

Beaten by Outsiders

Both suffered defeat at the hands of virtually unknown newcomers.

Mr. Carlino, the top Republican figure in the lower house for six years and an Assemblyman representing Nassau's Second Assembly District for 20 years, was beaten by Jerome R. McDougal Jr., a car salesman making his first race for public office.

Senator Mahoney, often called the most powerful man in the Legislature, was unseated by John H. Doerr of Buffalo in Erie County's 55th Senate District.

Another high-ranking Republican who lost was Senator Mac-Neil Mitchell of Manhattan, the most influential New York City member of the two houses.

In some districts in the suburbs and in upstate counties, Democrats captured Assembly and Senate seats for the first time in this century.

Districting Fight Due

At the last session, the G.O.P. had a 10-vote edge over the Democrats in the Assembly, holding 85 seats to 65 for the Democrats. In the Senate they had a 33-25 edge.

Although the Democrats ended this G.O.P. domination, the battle for control could be resumed again in December.

The Governor is expected to call a special session of the Legislature then to adopt a new plan for reapportioning seats in the two houses.

This reapportionment session will be controlled by the present members, while the Republicans in control.

Members elected yesterday do not take their seats until the

Continued on Page 33, Column 3

LYNDON BAINES JOHNSON

HUBERT HORATIO HUMPHREY

The New York Times

SOUTH REVERSES VOTING PATTERNS

Goldwater Makes Inroads, but More Electoral Votes Go to the President

By JOHN HERBERS

Special to The New York Times

ATLANTA, Nov. 3 — President Johnson carried a majority of Southern states tonight by turning the normal voting patterns inside out.

The rural Deep South, solidly Democratic in the past, voted for Senator Barry Goldwater of Arizona on the Republican ticket. The states on the border of the region, which had gone Republican in recent Presidential elections, returned to the Democrats.

But so strong was the Goldwater tide in the Deep South that seven Republican Congressional candidates rode to victory on the Senator's coattails from districts that had been Democratic since Reconstruction.

The Republicans made their biggest gains in Alabama, where five candidates for Congress defeated Democratic opponents.

President Johnson carried Virginia, North Carolina, Florida, Tennessee, Arkansas and Texas with a total of 81 electoral votes. Senator Goldwater carried Louisiana, Mississippi, Alabama, Georgia and South Carolina with a total of 47 electoral votes.

South Carolina and Mississippi had not voted for Repub-

Continued on Page 24, Column 2

WHITE BACKLASH DOESN'T DEVELOP

Vote in Suburbs in North Is Strong for President

By ANTHONY LEWIS

Rich and poor, Protestant and Roman Catholic and Jew, farmer and city-dweller and suburbanite all showed marked shifts toward President Johnson in yesterday's extraordinary election.

Only in the Deep South did Senator Barry Goldwater score any significant gains over the Republican ticket of four years ago. Riding the crest of the racial issue there, he swung Mississippi, Alabama, South Carolina and Louisiana to his party.

The white backlash, on which Mr. Goldwater had counted so strongly, failed to materialize in most parts of the North. Only among voters of Polish and other East European origins were there signs of this resentment toward Negroes, and this phenomenon was scattered

Continued on Page 26, Column 1

Democrats Are Assured Of Majorities in Congress

House Gain for Democrats

By JOHN D. MORRIS

Democrats strengthened their control of the House of Representatives in yesterday's elections, scoring substantial gains in all regions except the South.

With returns from Congressional races still incomplete early this morning, the trend indicated a Democratic pickup of at least 20 seats and possibly 30 or more.

The Republicans nevertheless scored spectacular breakthroughs in the South, winning five of Alabama's eight seats, one of Mississippi's five and at least one of Georgia's 10.

Those gains were more than offset, however, by the loss of both of their Texas seats and by heavy Democratic gains in other parts of the country.

The House division in the expiring 88th Congress is 257 Democrats and 178 Republicans. This credits five vacancies to the parties last holding the seats. Three were occupied by Democrats and two by Republicans.

With 218 needed for a major-

Continued on Page 21, Column 1

3 G.O.P. Senators Lose

By E. W. KENWORTHY

The Democrats appeared virtually certain today of maintaining a nearly 2-to-1 majority in the United States Senate.

At 3 A.M. the Democrats had won 25 of the 35 contests in yesterday's elections. These, added to their 40 holdovers, assured them of 65 seats when the Eighty-ninth Congress convenes in January.

The Republicans, at the same hour, had won only five seats—in Vermont, Nebraska, Delaware, Arizona and Hawaii—all of which were won by incumbent Senators. These, added to 25 holdovers, assured the Republicans of at least 30 seats.

The party line-up when Congress adjourned last month was 66 Democrats and 34 Republicans.

By 3 A.M. the Democrats had captured three seats from the Republicans.

In New York, Robert F. Kennedy, former Attorney General, a brother of President Kennedy,

Continued on Page 20, Column 1

PRESIDENT SEES A UNITY MANDATE

In Victory Talk, He Pays Tribute to Predecessor

The text of Johnson's talk will be found on Page 22.

By CHARLES MOHR

Special to The New York Times

AUSTIN, Tex., Wednesday, Nov. 4—President Johnson said early this morning that his election was a "mandate for unity" and for a "government that provides equal opportunity for all and special privilege for none."

Mr. Johnson, obviously deeply moved by his landslide victory, told a crowd at the Municipal Auditorium here that it was a tribute to "the program begun by our beloved President John F. Kennedy."

Of the returns, Mr. Johnson said, "I doubt there have ever been so many people seeing so many things alike" on an Election Day.

Earlier, Mr. Johnson had said of Senator Barry Goldwater's refusal to concede that it was "purely a matter for the individual involved—whatever reasons he may have, I don't know."

He also said that the election was going "about as we expected."

Mr. Johnson appeared on the Municipal Auditorium stage with his wife and two daughters to a long ovation.

He said that "no words are

Continued on Page 22, Column 6

TURNOUT IS HEAVY

President Expected to Get 60% of Vote, With 44 States

By TOM WICKER

Lyndon Baines Johnson of Texas compiled one of the greatest landslide victories in American history yesterday to win a four-year term of his own as the 36th President of the United States.

Senator Hubert H. Humphrey of Minnesota, Mr. Johnson's running mate on the Democratic ticket, was carried into office as Vice President.

Mr. Johnson's triumph, giving him the "loud and clear" national mandate he had said he wanted, brought 44 states and the district of Columbia, with 486 electoral votes, into the Democratic column.

Senator Barry Goldwater, the Republican candidate, who sought to offer the people "a choice, not an echo" with a strongly conservative campaign, won only five states in the Deep South and gained a narrow victory in his home state of Arizona. Carrying that gave him a total of 52 electoral votes.

Senator Plans Statement

A heavy voter turnout favored the more numerous Democrats.

In Austin, Tex., Mr. Johnson appeared in the Municipal Auditorium to say that his victory was "a tribute to the men and women of all parties."

"It is a mandate for unity, for a Government that serves no special interest," he said.

The election meant, he said, that "our nation should forget our petty differences and stand united before all the world."

Mr. Goldwater did not concede. A spokesman announced that the Senator would make no statement until 10 A.M. today in Phoenix.

Johnson Carries Texas

But the totals were not the only marks of the massive Democratic victory. Traditionally Republican states were bowled over like tenpins—Vermont, Indiana, Kansas, Nebraska, Wyoming, among others.

In New York, both houses of the Legislature were headed for Democratic control for the first time in years. Heralded Republicans like Charles H. Percy, the gubernatorial candidate in Illinois, went down to defeat.

Former Attorney General Robert F. Kennedy, riding Mr. Johnson's long coattails, overwhelmed Senator Kenneth B. Keating in New York.

But ticket splitting was widespread. And in the South, Georgia went Republican; never

Continued on Page 22, Column 1

Salinger Is Losing; Johnson Wins State

By LAWRENCE E. DAVIES

Special to The New York Times

SAN FRANCISCO, Wednesday, Nov. 4—President Johnson captured California's 40 electoral votes in his triumph over Senator Barry Goldwater.

On the basis of the incomplete count of ballots, however, the President's former press secretary, Senator Pierre Salinger, apparently lost his Senatorial battle to George Murphy, the Republican nominee.

Mr. Salinger late last night refused to concede defeat but said he "would be less than candid if I don't say the vote doesn't look good." Some of his campaign strategists agreed that the results "looked bad" but declared they would await developments for a few hours before having anything definite to say.

Mr. Salinger, who has been

Continued on Page 34, Column 4

NEWS INDEX

	Page		Page
Books	36-37	Music	40
Bridge	41	Obituaries	39
Business	52-61	Real Estate	63
Buyers	63	Screen	40-42
Crossword	37	Ships and Air	77
Editorial	38	Society	30-31
Events Today	41	Sports	42-50
Fashions	51	Theaters	40-42
Financial	52-61	TV and Radio	79
Food	44	U. N. Proceedings	10
Man in the News	42	Weather	78

News Summary and Index, Page 41

WORLD'S LEADING PRODUCER of Pub. Record. Write for free catalog. Overseas, 390 W. 42 St., N.Y.C.—Adv.

KAY, DRINK, and be merry about buying foods in season, reasonable in cost. Read food news features in The New York Times every day. Today!—Advt.

"All the News That's Fit to Print"

The New York Times.

LATE CITY EDITION
U.S. Weather Bureau Report (page 70).
Mostly sunny, cool today; increasing cloudiness tonight and tomorrow.
Temp. Range: 45—30; yesterday: 57—45.

VOL. CXV....No. 39,372.   © 1965 by The New York Times Company. Times Square, New York, N.Y. 10036   NEW YORK, WEDNESDAY, NOVEMBER 10, 1965.   TEN CENTS

POWER FAILURE SNARLS NORTHEAST; 800,000 ARE CAUGHT IN SUBWAYS HERE; AUTOS TIED UP, CITY GROPES IN DARK

To Our Readers

Because of the power blackout, the mechanical facilities of The New York Times were put out of operation last night and early today. Through the courtesy of The Newark Evening News this issue of The Times was set into type and printed in The Evening News's plant from The Times's own news reports. The financial tables are those of The Evening News.

Johnson Restates Goals in Vietnam

By The Associated Press

JOHNSON CITY, Tex., Nov. 9—President Johnson has restated broad American goals in Viet Nam and proclaimed Nov. 28 as "a day of dedication and prayer" for all members of the anti-Communist forces there.

The United States Government, he said, "remains ready without condition for the international discussions that can lead to lasting peace."

Mr. Johnson's proclamation, which followed a cue from Congress, was made public today though he actually signed it three days ago.

The Presidential document sidestepped one potential source of direct friction between Americans who support and oppose the Vietnam war.

Nov. 27 Suggested

Congress had suggested Nov. 27 as the day of prayer. However, a series of antiwar demonstrations, including a march on Washington, had been planned for that day.

Mr. Johnson, who had authority to fix the timing of the tribute to fighting forces in Vietnam, decided on the following day, a Sunday. In so doing, he is reported to have wanted to avoid a direct confrontation between backers and critics of American policy in Vietnam.

As the President has said on many occasions, he believes the great majority of Americans support his policy on Vietnam.

'Honored Tradition' Cited

The President proclaimed Nov. 28 as a day of dedication and prayer, honoring the men and women of South Vietnam, "of the United States, and of all other countries, who are risking their lives to bring about a just peace in South Vietnam."

He had this to say about American war aims:

"In assisting the people of South Vietnam to resist unprovoked aggression, the United States and other nations are carrying on the honored tradition of defending a people's right to freedom . . . the purpose of the United States in Vietnam is to help open the way for social justice in place of unprovoked aggression and peace instead of war."

Mr. Johnson noted that both the Senate and the House had passed resolutions saying "it would be fitting for the President to set aside a national day of remembrance dedicated to those Americans who are committing their lives, blood and energies in the defense of world peace."

G.I.'s Score Big Victory

Vietcong Force Almost Wiped Out by U.S. Airborne Unit

By R. W. APPLE JR.
Special to The New York Times

BIENHOA, South Vietnam, Nov. 9—The toll of almost 400 Vietcong killed in a battle 30 miles northeast of Saigon yesterday marked a decisive victory for troops of the US 173d Airborne Brigade.

The American paratroopers, members of one battalion, fired into waves of enemy troops at almost point-blank range in the eight-hour battle.

The United States troops suffered substantial casualties in the battle in a dense tropical thicket, but only at the battle of Chulay had an American unit inflicted heavier losses on the Vietcong.

Most of the fighting tok place at such close range that American M-79 grenades, which explode only after they have traveled 12 yards, bounced harmlessly off the guerrillas.

Assaults Thrown Back

The Americans were surrounded several times, but each time they threw back enemy assaults and held their positions. The Vietcong, using flame throwers and molten-metal thermite grenades for the first time in the war, attacked until they were almost wiped out.

This afternoon, with the battle over, the United States troops were returned by helicopter to their base camp at the sprawling installation here.

Sunday night, two platoons from the 173d, moving through the underbrush on patrol in the jungle area where they had been operating since Nov. 5, found fresh footprints and heard the frightened cackling of chickens.

At 7:30 A.M. yesterday the two platoons moved out again, clawing their way through the brush in the jungle gloom, and began climbing a pair of rocky hills. Both platoons were from C Company of the First Battalion, 503d Infantry.

'Right on Their Path'

Suddenly the platoon on the right, about 50 men, found itself in a circle of mud and thatch huts. The huts were invisible from the air because of the palmetto trees arching overhead and almost invisible from the ground because of the underbrush.

The company's commanding officer, Capt. Henry B. Tucker of Columbus, Miss., said later:

(Continued Page 5, Column 3)

CITY IN DARKNESS: Except for scattered independent lighting this is how the city looked from the Jersey side.

ON A TRAIN GOING NOWHERE: Commuters waiting on subway in Times Square area. Picture was made in
The New York Times

U.S. Orders An Inquiry

President Calls for a Study of Power Failure in East

By JOHN D. POMFRET
Special to The New York Times

AUSTIN, Tex., Nov. 9—President Johnson ordered today an immediate and complete investigation of the power failure that blacked out a large section of the East.

The President issued the order in a memorandum to Joseph C. Swidler, chairman of the Federal Power Commission.

Within minutes after the investigation was ordered, Mr. Swidler sent telegrams to all power companies in the affected areas, requesting their assistance. He also telephoned Defense Secretary Robert S. McNamara and Attorney General Nicholas de B. Katzenbach, telling them to coordinate the inquiry with them.

Time to Admire Skyline

During the evening Mr. Johnson talked by telephone with Governor Rockefeller and Mayor

(Continued on Page 3, Column 3)

Miss Liberty Shines Through Blackout

The Statue of Liberty maintained its illumination throughout last night's long blackout. Residents of lower Manhattan saw clearly the floodlit base of the statue on Liberty Island and the lighted torch. Except for an occasional passing river craft, the statue appeared to be the only beacon of light in the harbor.

Power for the statue's lights was supplied by the New Jersey Public Service Company.

City's Glitter Goes But Not Its Poise

By FRED POWLEDGE

Broadway, Manhattan and the rest of the city lost their glitter last night. Yet New Yorkers, who are used to living in crises, seemed to take the blackout in stride.

By the thousands they calmly filed out of office buildings and stores soon after the blackout started.

They grabbed every taxicab in sight. Some cab drivers turned on their "off duty" signs and headed for home themselves. Then the New Yorkers grabbed every bus in sight.

Although many merchants feared looting and violence, the police reported little such trouble. Many New Yorkers even seemed merry. There was the same air of revelry that often accompanies a heavy snowstorm.

Time to Admire Skyline

Commuters stuck in Manhattan with the prospect of a long wait, before getting to their homes found time to admire the unexpected sight of a moonlit Manhattan skyline, with stars, clouds and no neon.

Below ground, subway riders who waited in stalled trains sat quietly, resigned and good-humored.

At the Piccadilly Hotel on 45th Street in the heart of the theater district, a guest sat behind the desk helping the management dispense candles. No one seemed panicky, although a woman at the cigarette counter refused to sell anything to anyone who didn't have the correct change. Her cash register would not open.

Huckster Sells Flashlights

A huckster on Broadway sold flashlights, complete with batteries, for $1 apiece. A few doors away, in one of the shops that specializes in imported transistor radios and tape recorders, the price of dozens of flashlights at $3 each.

"It's a good quality flashlight," he said to someone who objected to the price. "It'll be working long after the current emergency is over."

Brief Thought of Disaster

A young actress who lives in Greenwich Village was taking a bath when the lights went out. She said that her first thoughts were that "we were under attack," but that she quickly dismissed such an idea and poured herself a drink.

In Times Square, pedestrians

(Continued on Page 3, Column 6)

ers gathered to listen to portable radios and wait for some form of transportation home.

Some did not wait. Thousands walked across the Queensboro and Brooklyn bridges, where the stunning night views of the city were strangely missing. The Brooklyn Bridge has a pedestrian walkway, above the automobile roadway, but the Queensboro does not. The Queens bound pedestrians walked across the south lane of the auto roadway four and five abreast. Cars crawled along behind them.

Cross Streets Jammed

Although many offices and stores closed immediately after the blackout began, some essential services stayed open.

Hospitals, using emergency generator power supplies, stayed lighted. Newspapers did too, but the light came from candles.

Manhattan's crosstown streets became unbroken ribbons of white light as automobiles, the brightest sources of light, jammed the narrow roadways.

Police cars turned on their red blinking lights. Buses crawled down the streets, their interior lamps lighting the faces of crowded passengers.

A Woolworth's store on Lexington Avenue reported a "landoffice business" in candles. People stood in lines that stretched into the street, waiting for a chance to buy a candle.

A street repair crew worked men were summoned to a halt in a pavement as their supervisor held a flashlight.

Bars filled quickly. The Astor Bar in Times Square, always a popular place, was more than usual. The candles planted in ashtrays seemed to produce more than enough light for drinkers.

Another bar in Times Square locked its doors, leaving contented drinkers within a good excuse to remain inside, but angered those who wanted to get in.

Food Is Sent To Subways

10,000 Are Stranded Long After Most Are Led Out

By SAMUEL KAPLAN

Subway trains sputtered to a halt in tunnels, on elevated tracks and in stations yesterday, stranding about 800,900 rush hour riders—10,000 of whom were still stuck at midnight.

The Transit Authority and the Police Department worked into the early hours of the morning attempting to remove passengers from crowded, stalled cars.

At midnight, food was sent to the passengers who were still waiting to be escorted out along the narrow catwalks in dark tunnels and high above rivers and streets.

Despite the anxious condition, no panic was reported, although there was confusion and fear in some of the 600 trains when they first stalled on the city's tracks.

The most difficult evacuation took place on the Williamsburg

(Continued on Page 2, Column 8)

Snarl at Rush Hour Spreads Into 9 States

10,000 in the National Guard and 5,000 Off-Duty Policemen Are Called to Service in New York

By PETER KIHSS

The largest power failure in history blacked out nearly all of New York City, parts of nine Northeastern states and two provinces of southeastern Canada last night. Some 80,000 square miles, in which perhaps 25 million people live and work, were affected.

It was more than three hours before the first lights came back on in any part of the New York City area. When they came on in Nassau and Suffolk Counties at 9 P.M., overloads plunged the area into darkness again in 10 minutes.

Striking at the evening rush hour, the power failure trapped 800,000 riders on New York City's subways. Railroads halted. Traffic was jammed. Airplanes found themselves circling, unable to land. But the Defense Department reported that the Strategic Air Command and other defense installations functioned without a halt.

National Guard Called Out

Five thousand off-duty policemen were summoned to duty here. Ten thousand National Guardsmen were called up in New York City alone. Other militiamen were alerted in Rhode Island and Massachusetts, as well as upstate New York.

The lights and the power went out first at 5:17 P.M. somewhere along the Niagara frontier of New York state. Nobody could tell why for hours afterward.

The tripping of automatic switches hurtled the blackout eastward across the state—to Buffalo, Rochester, Syracuse, Utica, Schnectady, Troy and Albany.

Within four minutes the line of darkness had plunged across Massachusetts all the way to Boston. It was like a pattern of falling dominoes—darkness sped southward through Connecticut, northward into Vermont, New Hampshire, Maine and Canada.

Sputtering at 5:27

At 5:27 P.M. the lights began sputtering in New York City, and within seconds the giant Consolidated Edison system blacked out in Manhattan, the Bronx, Queens and most of Brooklyn—but not in Staten Island and parts of Brooklyn that were interconnected with the Public Service Electric and Gas Company of New Jersey.

The darkness probed outward into northern New Jersey, up into Westchester and Rockland Counties, eastward into Long Island.

As far south as Washington, a Potomac Electric Power Company spokesman reported a power "dip" at 5:30 P.M., lasting less than a minute and virtually unnoticed in the nation's capital.

In Pennsylvania, the blackout spread through Pittsburgh and Reading into parts of Philadelphia and then into New Jersey along the coast above Atlantic City.

President Johnson, in Austin, Tex., ordered the full resources of the Federal Government thrown into an investigation by the Federal Power Commission. The Federal Bureau of Investigation, the Defense Department and other agencies were ordered to report "at the earliest possible moment."

Some Fear Sabotage

Asked whether there was any belief that sabotage might have been involved, Bill D. Moyers, the President's Press Secretary, would say only that "all of the resources of the Government" were being invoked in the investigation.

Later Mr. Johnson was advised that utility officials were "pretty well agreed upon the belief that there is substantially no chance of sabotage." Mr. Moyers said one theory was that the failure had been in automatic frequency control equipment.

Power companies, stripped of the protection of interconnected grids that usually guard against minor failures, moved to isolate their areas to restore energy on their own. This was how the Ontario Hydro Electric Commission, a Government-owned utility, cut away after loss of power for six million persons. It began bringing power back at 6:15 P.M.

In New York City, the Ravenswood plant in Queens, which provides 1.8 million kilowatts out of the 7.6 million produced by the city's Consolidated Edison plants, began sending smoke up from its stacks, as auxiliary steam power began to build up for its generators.

At 7:15 P.M. smoke began curling up also from the Hudson Avenue station in Brooklyn. It was from Hudson Avenue that the first power was restored here: Five feeder cables of 27,000 volts each sent light back into Coney Island at 8:42 P.M.

An hour later Consolidated Edison reported 17 of the

(Continued on Page 2, Column 1 and 2)

Man, 22, Immolates Himself In Antiwar Protest at U.N.

By THOMAS BUCKLEY

A 21-year-old former seminarian soaked himself with gasoline and then set himself aflame in front of the United Nations at dawn yesterday, a protest against "war, all war."

Guards from the world organization and city patrolmen beat out the flames that enveloped him as he sat cross-legged on First Avenue and then rushed him to Bellevue Hospital.

He was drifting near death in the emergency ward last night, with second and third-degree burns covering 95 per cent of his body. The hospital staff said he had almost no chance of surviving.

The youth, Roger Allen LaPorte, was a member of the Catholic Worker movement, a charitable and pacifist organization with headquarters at 175 Chrystie Street on the Lower East Side. He lived in a tenement apartment leased by the

organization at 58 Kenmare Street, a few blocks away.

Mr. LaPorte's self-immolation was the second in seven days attributable, at least in part, to continued United States' involvement in the war in Vietnam. Last Monday, Norman R. Morrison, a 32-year-old Quaker from Baltimore, burned himself to death in front of the Pentagon in Washington.

A spokesman said that Mr. Thant was "deeply grieved over this human tragedy, whatever the motivation might be. U Thant regards human life as very sacred."

Attended Union Sq. Protest

Friends of Mr. LaPorte said that he had seemed melancholy but not obviously emotionally disturbed since Saturday, when he attended the demonstration at Union Square at which five other youths burned their draft cards.

Questioned at a city reception, Mr. Goldberg said that while the youth had undoubtedly been impelled by "the highest principles and motives," his action was "terribly unfortunate and terribly unnecessary."

"Perhaps there has been a

failure on our part." he went on. "Perhaps we are not sufficiently communicating to the people of the world our dedication, our attachment and our complete commitment to the idea that peace is the only way for mankind in the nuclear age."

A spokesman said that Mr. Thant was "deeply grieved over this human tragedy, whatever the motivation might be. U Thant regards human life as very sacred."

Robert Steed, a fellow member of the Catholic Workers, said that Mr. LaPorte had been unable to make up his mind to

(Continued on Page 5, Column 1)

On street corners, New York-

How City Met the Emergency: Off-Duty Men Are Mobilized

The city's emergency services systems that they have for such emergencies. Operations were performed in some of them by lights provided by these auxiliary systems.

Five thousand off-duty policemen were summoned by a message broadcast over WNYC, the city's radio station. Some 7,000 who were on duty when the lights went out and 4,000 were held on for the emergency.

The Fire Department, too, brought in off-duty firemen because their overloaded telephone and telegraphic communications made it difficult to keep contact with scattered fire apparatus in the field.

The Fire Department radio was out of service from 5:30 p.m. to 8:30 p.m. and the dispatchers had to keep in touch with the firehouses and vehicles by telephone. They had the radio system back in operation at 8:30 and were able to communicate with men in the field until that hour.

Hospitals were generally able to carry on with the generating

small to service the massive enclave of buildings and was not used. However, in the operating and emergency rooms, the Fire Department set up emergency lights powered by small generators. One operation was finished just before the blackout occurred.

The major problems at Bellevue involved reassuring mentally disturbed patients and mixing medicine in dimly lighted pharmacies. Quantities of dry ice was obtained to keep blood plasma from spoiling.

Louis Lobo, who has been in and out of Bellevue since 1962, was transferred to a Fink Respirator, which is operated by compressed air. No ill effects were reported.

Car Battery Used

One Bellevue employee brought in his car battery, at a wheelchair and powered emer-

(Continued on Page 2, Column 7)

227

"All the News That's Fit to Print"

The New York Times.

LATE CITY EDITION
U. S. Weather Bureau Report (Page 94; forecast)
Light rain and snow, then clearing today; becoming cloudy tomorrow.
Temp. range: 46-37; yesterday: 48-42.

VOL. CXV..No. 39,408.

© 1965 by The New York Times Company.
Times Square, New York, N.Y. 10036

NEW YORK, THURSDAY, DECEMBER 16, 1965.

TEN CENTS

TWO GEMINIS FLY 6 TO 10 FEET APART IN MAN'S FIRST SPACE RENDEZVOUS; CREWS, FACE TO FACE, TALK BY RADIO

U.S. JETS SMASH BIG POWER PLANT OUTSIDE HAIPHONG

Cut Nation's Current 15% —Generators Supported Industries in Hanoi

By NEIL SHEEHAN

SAIGON, South Vietnam, Dec. 15—United States jet fighter-bombers destroyed a large power plant today 14 miles from Haiphong, North Vietnam's chief port, in the first American air strike against a North Vietnamese target of major industrial importance.

A military spokesman said the planes, flown by Air Force pilots, had struck the Uongbi thermal power plant, northeast of Haiphong. The plant has a capacity of 24,000 kilowatts, about 15 per cent of North Vietnam's total electric-power output. It supplies some of the power needs of both Hanoi and Haiphong.

The center of the plant, housing steam turbines, generators and other sensitive equipment, was smashed at 11 A.M. with 12 tons of 3,000-pound bombs. A single flight of F-105 Thunderchief fighter-bombers—apparently four to six craft—made the raid.

Secondary Blasts Sighted

A spokesman said that the pilots had encountered bad weather and heavy antiaircraft fire but reported having destroyed the plant. Several secondary explosions—detonations of explosives on the ground—were observed during the raid.

This was the first time United States aircraft had struck so close to North Vietnam's two major cities—Hanoi and Haiphong. The closest previous strike was a recent raid against a firing site for Soviet-made surface-to-air missiles, 22 miles from Hanoi.

Secretary of Defense McNamara, who arrived back in Washington shortly after midnight from the North Atlantic Alliance meeting in Paris, said the bombing of the power plant near Haiphong "is representative of the type of attack we have carried out and will continue to carry out." [The Associated Press reported Thursday, Page 3.]

Many Homes Darkened

According to military spokesmen here, the destruction of the power plant was certain to affect North Vietnamese civilians much more directly than have previous strikes, almost all of which have been aimed at road, rail and river networks and military installations.

The power-station raid will probably cut off electricity in large numbers of civilian homes as well as significantly reduce the amount of power available for industries in the Hai
Continued on Page 3, Column 1

U.S. Said to Caution Latins on Moscow

By HENRY RAYMONT

MONTEVIDEO, Uruguay, Dec. 15—The United States is warning Uruguay and other Latin-American countries against underestimating the continued aggressiveness and subversive potential of Soviet Communism, qualified sources said today.

The diplomatic initiative is directed against what United States authorities consider to be undue complacency among Latin-American leaders.

These authorities believe that the split between Moscow and Peking as well as the new attention among Latins that pro-Soviet Communists no longer threaten republican institutions in the Western Hemisphere.

According to United States officials, this assumption ignores the deterioration in East-West
Continued on Page 17, Column 1

Gemini 7 Crew

Lieut. Col. Frank Borman

Comdr. James A. Lovell Jr.

Major Steps From Launching to Rendezvous

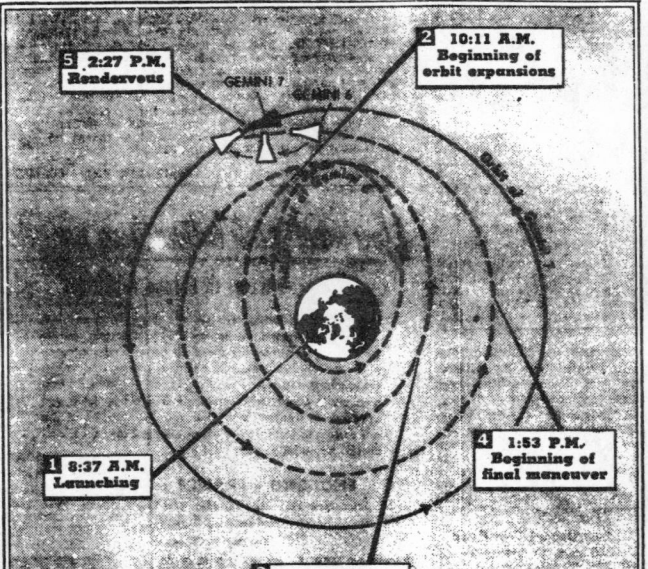

5 2:27 P.M. Rendezvous
2 10:11 A.M. Beginning of orbit expansions
GEMINI 7   GEMINI 6
1 8:37 A.M. Launching
4 1:53 P.M. Beginning of final maneuver
3 11:19 A.M. Plane adjustment

The New York Times   Dec. 16, 1965
Major steps of yesterday's rendezvous of the Gemini 6 and Gemini 7 spacecraft are shown, from the launching of Gemini 6 to its meeting with Gemini 7, orbiting about 185 miles above the earth. At rendezvous two craft were nose to nose within 10 feet of each other.

Gemini 6 Crew

Capt. Walter M. Schirra Jr.

Maj. Thomas P. Stafford

Craft in Formation Orbit 185 Miles Up

Officials of Space Agency Are Jubilant at Success—Maneuver Is Vital to a Manned Landing on Moon

By JOHN NOBLE WILFORD
Special to The New York Times

HOUSTON, Dec. 15—Four American astronauts steered Gemini 6 and Gemini 7 today to man's first rendezvous in the vastness of outer space.

In a spectacular performance of space navigation, the astronauts brought their craft within six to ten feet of each other about 185 miles above the earth. The two capsules then circled the earth nearly two times on a four-hour formation flight before Gemini 6 broke away to a lower orbit.

The pilots of the pursuing Gemini 6 were Capt. Walter M. Schirra Jr. of the Navy and Maj. Thomas P. Stafford of the Air Force. Pilots of the Gemini 7 target ship were Lieut. Col. Frank Borman of the Air Force and Comdr. James A. Lovell Jr. of the Navy.

The crews came close enough to see into each other's cabins, trade gibes and inspect details on the exteriors of their funnel-shaped spacecraft. The Gemini 6 astronauts could see Commander Lovell's beard and could tell that Colonel Borman was chewing gum.

"We have company tonight!" radioed Colonel Borman from Gemini 7, which has been in orbit 11 days of its record 14-day mission. Gemini 6, launched from Cape Kennedy at 8:37 A.M., Eastern standard time, today, is expected to splash down near the Bahamas at 10:29 A.M. tomorrow.

Officials Jubilant

The success of the mission brought jubilation at the space center here.

"It's the biggest milestone since the flight of John Glenn," Christopher C. Kraft Jr., the flight director, said. Colonel Glenn's Mercury flight on Feb. 20, 1962, was the first orbital mission by an American.

The two Gemini flights proved that two spacecraft can find each other, rendezvous and presumably link up.

Such a maneuver is necessary if astronauts are to land on the moon and then return to their mother ship, which would be circling in a lunar orbit. Space officials are aiming for such a manned landing in 1969.

Today's rendezvous also opens the way to operations in which men and supplies can be ferried out to orbiting stations, such as the Air Force's planned Manned Orbiting Laboratory.

'Made It Look Easy'

"These crews made it look easy," said Dr. Robert Gilruth, director of the Manned Spacecraft Center here, praising all those who had made the mission a success.

Just before final rendezvous, there was an anxious moment of silence. Radio contact between the craft and the ground was lost. Then a relay tracking station off Hawaii reported the two Gemini had drawn within 120 feet of each other.

"There just seems to be a lot of traffic up here," Captain Schirra commented.

"Call a policeman," Colonel
Continued on Page 28, Column 1

AT LAST, GEMINI 6 HAS A PERFECT DAY

Even Sun Comes Out in Time to Dispel Last Doubt of Jubilant Ground Staff

By EVERT CLARK
Special to The New York Times

CAPE KENNEDY, Fla., Dec. 15—After twice having had its wings clipped by failure, the Gemini satellite finally climbed to its space rendezvous today in a most spectacular way.

For 15 years, missiles have flown from this sandy point of land. But no one today could recall a flight of greater beauty.

It left behind a sense of exhilaration missing since the Mercury capsules took the first American astronauts into space four years ago.

On top of the triumph, plans were quickly made to have Gemini 6 splash down about 800 miles east of here at 10:29 o'clock tomorrow morning. The pilots will return here on Friday for the first of many days of debriefings.

A splendid sunrise had created the perfect backdrop and set the mood for the day. It dispelled a worrisome ground fog that had clung to the scrubby palmetto like the doubts that had hung over Gemini 6 in recent days.

Attitude Was Cautious

Through last night the memory of two recent false starts was so fresh that the attitude was one of caution and crossed fingers.

Yet today, from the beginning, a cockiness and almost a jubilance seemed to run through the pilots, the overworked ground crews and official observers.

It was typified by the reaction of James S. McDonnell, the 67-year-old engineer whose factory in Missouri makes the Gemini capsules.

He overslept. Awakened at 6:30 A.M. as the sun began to turn the high, scattered clouds the color of a tea rose, he looked at the sky and cried out:

"You see! I told them I'd bring them good weather from St. Louis!"

It became a day for enthusiasm.

"She looks like a dream," Navy Capt. Walter M. Schirra
Continued on Page 28, Column 8

McNamara Warns NATO Of Chinese Atom Threat

By PETER BRAESTRUP

PARIS, Dec. 15—Defense Secretary Robert S. McNamara urged the United States' Western European allies today to start worrying now about the threat posed by Communist China's growing nuclear strength.

At the same time, he pledged that the mounting United States effort in Vietnam would not require the withdrawal of "major combat units" from American forces in Western Europe.

Mr. McNamara addressed ministers of the 15-nation North Atlantic Treaty Organization in their year-end meeting, which began yesterday.

Behind Closed Doors

The Defense Secretary spoke behind closed doors. His remarks, like those of other speakers, were summarized by a delegation spokesman.

Mr. McNamara said that the Chinese Communists, having already detonated two test nuclear devices, would produce enough fissionable material in the next two years to start a small stockpile of atomic weapons.

Moreover, he continued, the Chinese, despite a "near-famine" economy, are spending 10 per cent of their gross national product on defense.

He said Peking's new mili-
Continued on Page 8, Column 3

JOHNSON AND AYUB CALL PEACE VITAL

Say Dispute With India Must Cease So Efforts Can Be Turned to Key Problems

By JOHN D. POMFRET
Special to The New York Times

WASHINGTON, Dec. 15—President Johnson and President Mohammad Ayub Khan of Pakistan said today that they agreed on the need for a peaceful resolution of all outstanding differences between India and Pakistan.

This is necessary, they said, "so that the energies and resources of the peoples of the subcontinent would not be wastefully diverted from their efforts to meet their vitally important social and economic problems."

The two leaders issued a joint communiqué at the conclusion of two days of meetings at the White House. It described the discussions as "frank, wide-ranging and productive."

Kashmir Main Issue

The main dispute between India and Pakistan is over Kashmir. This dispute led to a short war last summer.

There was no expressed agreement between the two Presidents on the specific lines along which the dispute over Kashmir should be settled.

They both were said to believe that the working out of such specific arrangements must await the outcome of further conferences that already have been scheduled.

President Ayub and India's Prime Minister, Lal Bahadur Shastri, are to meet Jan. 4 at the invitation of the Soviet Union to discuss their differences. They will confer at the Soviet Central Asian city of Tashkent.

Prime Minister Shastri and President Johnson will meet in Washington Feb. 1 and 2.
Continued on Page 6, Column 3

47-CENT FARE SEEN IN QUILL DEMANDS

Transit Authority Warns It Would Be Needed to Meet Union Pay Proposals

By EMANUEL PERLMUTTER

The Transit Authority said yesterday that if it granted the contract demands of its unions it would have to raise the 15-cent fare to 47 cents.

It asserted that a fare increase that great would lead to such a loss of riders that "the reduced use of the system would be financially catastrophic."

The authority has estimated that demands of the Transport Workers Union would cost it $680 million in a two-year contract.

"Adding an annual labor cost of $340 million annually to the T.A. budget would, in the absence of other sources of revenue, increase the present deficit incurred for each passenger carried by 19 cents, creating a 22-cent operating deficit per ride," the authority asserted. "The fare would have to be increased to not less than 47 cents."

The authority said that granting the demands would also result in increasing the "basic wage rate per hour alone
Continued on Page 58, Column 3

Staggered Working Hours Urged to Cut Transit Jam

By JOSEPH C. INGRAHAM

The chronic morning and evening subway crushes can be eliminated by staggering working hours, according to a plan made public by Mayor Wagner yesterday. The success of the proposal hinges on whether employers and employes can be persuaded to alter their traditional 9-to-5 work pattern, the Mayor said.

Only the conclusions of the voluminous, 200,000-word "report," based on a six-year study that cost $200,000, were released by the Mayor. The study was directed by Prof. Lawrence B. Cohen of the department of industrial engineering of Columbia University.

Principal Finding

The principal finding was that "work staggering is a feasible way of relieving subway congestion into and out of Manhattan's central business district during the rush hours so that standing passengers might be reasonably comfortable."

Professor Cohen held that the idea was technically and economically feasible and, within limits, which he defined very generally, was sociologically acceptable to management and labor.

In Professor Cohen's view, rush-hour crowding would be markedly alleviated if a 25 per cent spread of the peak loads
Continued on Page 58, Column 4

NASA CUTS BACK SCIENCE PROGRAM

Orbiting Solar Observatory Canceled in Move to Hold Down Expanding Budget

Special to The New York Times

WASHINGTON, Dec. 15—The National Aeronautics and Space Administration, caught in a tight budgetary squeeze, canceled today one of its most ambitious scientific projects.

"Budgetary considerations" were cited by the agency in explaining a halt in further work on the Advanced Orbiting Solar Observatory. The observatory, capable of making detailed observations of the sun, had been planned for launching in 1969.

Behind the cryptic explanation was the deliberately unpublicized fact that the agency was faced with a budgetary dilemma. It has been attempting to finance its expanding program and still heed White House directives to hold down nonmilitary spending.

Some Delays Foreseen

The present expectation is that the civilian space budget for the fiscal year 1967, beginning next July 1, will be held by the White House to about $5.17 billion, equal to the appropriation for this year, and perhaps even less. This would be about $500 million less than the space agency considered necessary to maintain the momentum of its expanding program and sought from the White House.

Enough money will be provided in the budget next year to keep Project Apollo on its schedule of landing a manned expedition on the moon before 1970. But to keep within the budgetary confines imposed by the White House, there will have to be some curtailment in the
Continued on Page 30, Column 4

Johnson Calls Feat Step Toward Moon

By JACK RAYMOND
Special to The New York Times

WASHINGTON, Dec. 15—President Johnson hailed the Gemini satellite rendezvous today as a step toward the moon. The President congratulated the astronauts and all those who had anything to do with the space feat.

"You have all moved us one step higher on the stairway to the moon," he said exuberantly. The President conveyed his feelings in a message to James E. Webb, administrator of the National Aeronautics and Space Administration. He had watched the progress of the launching and had slept anxiously throughout the day.

Bill D. Moyers, the President's press secretary, said Mr. Johnson watched the Gemini launching over his bedroom television set. Then, throughout the
Continued on Page 28, Column 4

Somerset Maugham Is Dead at 91

Novelist, Short Story Writer, Playwright Succumbs in Nice

By The Associated Press

NICE, France, Thursday, Dec. 16—W. Somerset Maugham died early today at his Riviera villa. The world-famous novelist, playwright and short-story writer was 91 years old.

Maugham fell last Friday and then suffered a stroke. He was taken to the British-American Hospital Saturday. After a medical consultation on Sunday, physicians gave him only hours to live.

He rallied slightly but weakened yesterday. When all hope was gone, he was taken from the hospital to die in his Moorish-style villa at nearby Cap Ferrat, his secretary and companion of many years, Alan

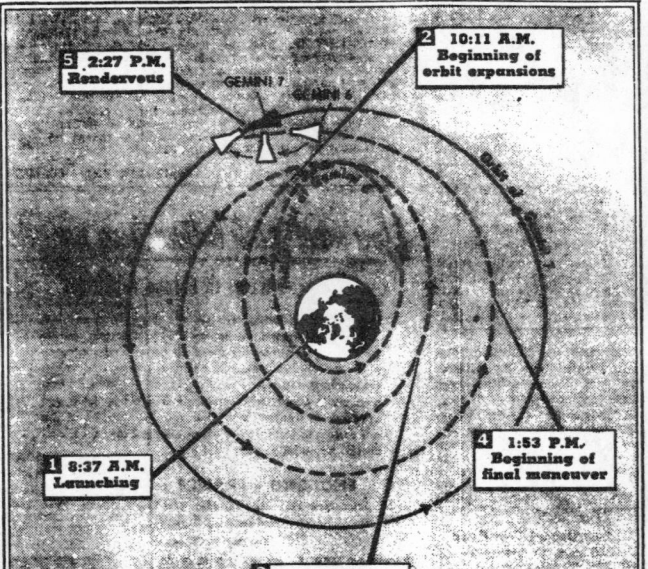

W. Somerset Maugham
Pictorial Parade

Searle, said in announcing Maugham's death.

A prolific author, Maugham turned out 30 plays, 21 novels and 120 short stories. His masterpiece was "Of Human Bondage," published in 1915 when he was 41 years old. It centered
Continued on Page 59, Column 1

228

The New York Times

VOL. CXVI..No. 39,947   © 1967 The New York Times Company.   NEW YORK, THURSDAY, JUNE 8, 1967   10 CENTS

LATE CITY EDITION
Weather: Fair and warm today and
tonight. Partly cloudy tomorrow.
Temp. range: today 85-63; Wed.
81-62. Temp.-Hum. Index: mid-70's;
Wed. 72. Full report on Page 93.

ISRAELIS ROUT THE ARABS, APPROACH SUEZ, BREAK BLOCKADE, OCCUPY OLD JERUSALEM; AGREE TO U.N. CEASE-FIRE; U.A.R. REJECTS IT

JOHNSON WILL USE CABINET TO COURT STATES' OFFICIALS

Aides Will Seek to Tighten Ties Between Governors and the White House

By WARREN WEAVER Jr.
Special to The New York Times

WASHINGTON, June 7—President Johnson has decided to use the members of his Cabinet as diplomatic agents in his campaign to improve relations between the Administration and state governments.

The President has approved a plan under which each member of the Cabinet would be assigned four or five states as his personal responsibility, with instructions to maintain personal contact between the Governors and the White House.

As part of the same effort, each of the 50 states will be given a "day" in Washington next fall and winter, when a planeload of its key officials will fly here to hold conferences all over the capital, capped by a meeting of the Governors with the President.

Bryant's Work Continued

Both projects reflect Mr. Johnson's continuing determination to build domestic as well as foreign bridges by working to sort out the tangled Federal-state relations that have been increasingly complicated by the administration of the Great Society programs.

Both are attempts to give some permanency to the contacts established during the last four months by Farris Bryant, the President's envoy to the states, on visits to 40 capitals with a squad of Federal experts.

Mr. Bryant, a former Governor of Florida who is now the director of the Office of Emergency Planning, plans to leave his White House post this summer, possibly to return to politics in his home state, and he is eager to help establish more permanent lines of communication before his departure.

As now envisioned, each Cabinet officer would visit all of

Continued on Page 29, Column 2

CONFEREES BLOCK A DRAFT LOTTERY

Compromise Bill Continues Deferment of Students

By United Press International

WASHINGTON, June 7—Senate and House negotiators reached agreement today on a new military draft bill that rules out, for the present, any lottery-like random selection system to determine the order of induction.

The bill was a compromise of differing bills that the Senate and House had passed. It would guarantee the continuation of educational deferments for college undergraduates and students enrolled in apprentice and job training programs.

Senator Richard B. Russell, Democrat of Georgia, who is chairman of the Senate conferees, said the Senate might act on the four-year draft extension bill tomorrow. House action must await approval by the Senate.

Congressional action will clear the way for President Johnson, under current discretionary powers, to reverse the order of induction and take 19-year-olds first from the Selec-

Continued on Page 3, Column 1

Rise in Debt Ceiling Rejected in House; Johnson Rebuffed

Special to The New York Times

WASHINGTON, June 7—The House of Representatives dealt the Johnson Administration a sharp setback today by rejecting a bill to increase the ceiling on the national debt $29-billion, to $365-billion.

The vote against passage was 210 to 197, with Republicans voting solidly to kill the bill. Enough Democrats, mostly Southerners, voted with them to turn the tide.

About six Northern Democratic "doves"—opponents of the war in Vietnam—also joined the opposition.

In all, 34 Democrats joined with 176 Republicans to defeat the measure.

Today's action raised the possibility—though a slim one—of financial chaos after June 30. At that time the debt limit reverts to its "permanent" ceiling of $285-billion, though the debt, at $330-billion, is already far above that level. The legal authority of the Treasury to pay its bills would be in doubt.

However, the Ways and

Continued on Page 39, Column 4

U.S. VOWS TO SEEK A DURABLE PEACE

Johnson Recalls Bundy for New Mideast Planning Unit —'Real Chance' Is Seen

By MAX FRANKEL
Special to The New York Times

WASHINGTON, June 7 — President Johnson pledged today to do his best to help translate the new Middle Eastern situation into a more lasting settlement between Israel and her Arab neighbors.

Apparently hoping to exploit Israel's lightning military success—which has surprised but not displeased the White House—Mr. Johnson ordered the drafting of special policies for a "new peace" and set up new machinery to deal with the situation.

The President said that the United States, which had worked hard to avoid the war, felt that "there is now a real chance" to turn from "the frustrations of the past to the hopes of a peaceful future."

But Mr. Johnson said the handling of the crisis and the preparations for a lasting settlement would require the most careful consideration in the United States Government. To organize that effort he recalled McGeorge Bundy to temporary duty at the White House as executive secretary to a special subcommittee of the National Security Council.

Mr. Bundy will seek a temporary leave from the presidency of the Ford Foundation, which he assumed last year after serving as special assistant for

Continued on Page 19, Column 1

EBAN SEES THANT

Says Acceptance Is Based on Enemy's Reciprocal Action

Excerpts from debate at U.N. are printed on Page 18.

By DREW MIDDLETON
Special to The New York Times

UNITED NATIONS, N. Y., June 7—The Security Council unanimously adopted a Soviet resolution today calling on the combatants in the Middle East to "cease fire and all military activities" at 4 P.M., New York time today.

The Government of Israel shortly thereafter announced that she had accepted the call of the Council for a cease-fire, provided her Arab foes agreed.

In the evening, reports from the Middle East indicated rejection of the call by the United Arab Republic, Syria, Iraq, Saudi Arabia, Algeria and Kuwait. Jordan told Secretary General Thant that she would abide by the cease-fire, except in self-defense.

Says It's in Effect

Abba Eban, the Foreign Minister of Israel, told the Secretary General that a cease-fire was already in effect between Jordan and Israel.

In presenting the resolution, the Soviet delegate, Nikolai T. Fedorenko, made it clear that if Israel failed to heed the Security Council's demands, Moscow would consider severing diplomatic relations. The original Security Council resolution, adopted yesterday, simply called for a cease-fire.

But the reports from the Arab capitals indicate, diplomatic sources here said, that military operations will continue.

According to diplomats, the best hope lies in a draft resolution presented by George Ignatieff, the Canadian delegate. This proposes that the President of the Security Council and the Secretary General take measures to insure compliance with the resolutions.

Today's resolution demanded that the combatants "cease fire and all military activities on 7 June 1967 by 2000 hours Greenwich mean time." The resolution was adopted less than an hour before this time, which is 4 P.M. New York time, 10 P.M. in Jordan and Israel and 11 P.M. in the United Arab Republic and Syria.

The Council adjourned without voting on the Canadian draft largely because Milko Ta-

Continued on Page 18, Column 2

Dorothy Parker, 73, Literary Wit, Dies

By ALDEN WHITMAN

Dorothy Parker, the sardonic humorist who purveyed her wit in conversation, short stories, verse and criticism, died of a heart attack yesterday afternoon in her suite at the Volney Hotel, 23 East 74th Street. She was 73 years old and had been in frail health in recent years.

In print and in person, Miss Parker sparkled with a word or a phrase, for she honed her humor to its most economical size. Her rapier wit, much of it spontaneous, gained its early renown from her membership in the Algonquin Round Table, an informal luncheon club at the Algonquin Hotel in the nineteen-twenties, where some of

Continued on Page 38, Column 1

OLD JERUSALEM IS NOW IN ISRAELI HANDS: Israeli soldiers in prayer at the Wailing Wall yesterday
United Press International Radiophoto

Major Mideast Developments

On the Battlefronts

Israel claimed victory in the Sinai Desert after three days of fighting. Sharm el Sheik, guarding the entrance to the Gulf of Aqaba, fell after a paratroop attack, and the Israelis said the blockade of the gulf was broken. Other Israeli units were within 20 miles of the Suez Canal, and one Israeli report placed them in the eastern section of Ismailia, on the canal itself.

In Jerusalem, for the first time in 19 years, Israeli Jews prayed at the Wailing Wall as their troops occupied the Old City. Israeli troops captured Jericho, in Jordan, and sped northward to take Nablus, giving them control of the west bank of the Jordan.

The Egyptian High Command reported that its forces had fallen back from first-line positions in the Sinai Peninsula and were fighting fiercely from unspecified secondary positions. It announced that Egyptian troops had pulled back from Sharm el Sheik to join main defense units.

In the Capitals

In the United Nations, Israel accepted the call for a cease-fire, provided the Arabs complied. Jordan announced that she would accept and ordered her troops to fire only in self-defense. But Baghdad declared that Iraq had refused. There were indications that Syria, Algeria and Kuwait were also opposed.

In Cairo, an Egyptian official said the United Arab Republic would fight on.

In Moscow, the Soviet Union threatened to break diplomatic relations with Israel if she did not observe the cease-fire.

In Paris, the French proposed an international agreement for free passage in the Gulf of Aqaba similar to the one governing the Dardanelles in Turkey.

In Washington, President Johnson promised to seek a settlement that would assure lasting peace in the Mideast.

In London, the British urged the Israelis to halt before they aroused more turmoil in the Arab world and diminished the chances for a settlement.

Israelis Weep and Pray Beside the Wailing Wall

By TERENCE SMITH

JERUSALEM, June 7—Israeli troops wept and prayed today at the foot of the Wailing Wall—the last remnant of Solomon's Second Temple and the object of pilgrimage by Jews through the centuries.

In battle dress and still carrying their weapons, they gathered at the base of the sand-colored wall and sang Halfel, a series of prayers reserved for occasions of great joy.

They were repeating a tradition that goes back 2,000 years but has been denied Israeli Jews since 1948, when the first of three wars with the Arabs ended in this area.

The wall is all that remains of the Second Temple, built in the 10th century before Christ and destroyed by the Romans in A.D. 70.

The Israelis, trembling with emotion, bowed vigorously from the waist as they chanted psalms in a lusty chorus. Most had submachine guns slung over their shoulders and several held bazookas as they prayed.

Among the leaders to pray at the wall was Maj. Gen. Moshe Dayan, the new Defense Minister. He told the troops:

"We have returned to the holiest of our holy places, never to depart from it again."

General Dayan, who was at

Continued on Page 17, Column 1

AQABA GULF OPEN

Dayan Asserts Israel Does Not Intend to Capture the Canal

By The Associated Press

TEL AVIV, June 7 — Israel proclaimed victory tonight in the Sinai Peninsula campaign against the United Arab Republic. On the eastern front, both the Old City of Jerusalem and Bethlehem were captured from the Jordanians.

"The Egyptians are defeated," said Maj. Gen. Itzhak Rabin, the Israeli Chief of Staff. "All their efforts are aimed at withdrawing behind the Suez Canal, and we are taking care of that. The whole area is in our hands. The main effort of the Egyptians is to save themselves."

Israel Losses 'Not Great'

Describing the developments through the third day of this third Arab-Israeli war in 19 years, General Rabin made these claims:

¶Sinai, the Egyptian territory between Israel's Negev Desert and the Suez Canal, is taken.

¶Most of the Jordanian territory on the west bank of the Jordan River, including Jericho, is in Israeli hands, and most of Jordan's army has been captured.

¶Relative to what was done, the number of Israeli casualties was "not great."

The Israelis were reported to have swept to the Suez Canal.

[An Israeli delegation source at the United Nations said Israeli troops had seized that part of the canal city of Ismailia that is on the eastern side of the waterway. But this was denied by an army source in Tel Aviv, who said, according to Reuters, that the Israelis had not taken any point along the canal.

[Maj. Gen. Moshe Dayan, the Israeli Defense Minister, declared that there was "no intention" of taking the canal, United Press International reported.]

'Never to Depart'

After the fall of the Old City of Jerusalem, Defense Minister Moshe Dayan said there that the Israelis had reunited their capital and would never "depart from it again."

Israel reported that paratroops aided by naval units had captured Sharm el Sheik, commanding the entrance to the Gulf of Aqaba, and said the blockade that the Egyptians had mounted from that position had been broken.

"The Strait of Tiran is now open," General Rabin said.

Israel's chief of staff said his men had taken on the United Arab Republic, Jordan, Syria and Iraq, knocked out their air forces and overrun their armor and infantry.

"All this the armed forces of Israel did alone," he declared.

The general then turned over the briefing to Brig. Mordechai Hod, commander of the air force, who announced 441 Arab

Continued on Page 16, Column 1

CAIRO ANNOUNCES A SINAI PULLBACK

Blames Foreign Aid to Foe, but Says Troops Fight On in Secondary Positions

By ERIC PACE
Special to The New York Times

CAIRO, June 7—An Egyptian military communiqué reported today that forces of the United Arab Republic had fallen back from some first-line positions on the Sinai Peninsula and were engaged in fierce fighting against Israeli troops from secondary positions.

Another statement of the High Command, broadcast four hours later by the Cairo radio, said Egyptian troops at Sharm el Sheik, guarding the entrance to the Gulf of Aqaba, had joined other Egyptian forces "now concentrated in the Sinai Peninsula."

There was no elaboration, but the communiqué, broadcast about 5:30 P.M., appeared to confirm Israeli reports that the Egyptians had been forced to retreat from Sharm el Sheik.

At night, the High Command reported that Israeli paratroops had dropped over the "second-line Egyptian front" but had been "completely wiped out."

The communiqué also said the Israelis had tried another drop at Sharm el Sheik after the

Continued on Page 17, Column 6

Pentagon Believes Israeli Jets Struck From Sea, Eluded Radar

By WILLIAM BEECHER
Special to The New York Times

WASHINGTON, June 7—At least a part of the Israeli Air Force that caught large numbers of Egyptian aircraft on the ground in the early hours of the war may have slipped through gaps in the United Arab Republic's radar net by flying in over the Mediterranean.

This possibility was raised today by Pentagon analysts. If correct, it would help to explain how Israeli pilots were able to surprise so many Egyptian jets before they could get into the air.

It might also serve to provide part of the explanation behind insistent Arab assertions that carrier-based United States and British jets participated in the raids.

Shortly after the raids, he went on, the Jordanian radio charged that Jordanian radar

Continued on Page 18, Column 8

CONQUEST IN THE MIDEAST: Israeli troops took Sharm el Sheik (1), drove on to the Suez Canal (2) and seized control of the Old City in Jerusalem (3). Photo was taken in September, 1966, during the flight of Gemini II.
The New York Times
June 8, 1967

The New York Times

LATE CITY EDITION

Weather: Fair and warm today, tonight and tomorrow. Temp. range: today 85-63; Thurs. 85-64. Temp.-Hum. Index: today 70 to 75; Thurs. 77. Full U.S. report on Page 89.

VOL. CXVI..No. 39,948   © 1967 The New York Times Company.   NEW YORK, FRIDAY, JUNE 9, 1967   10 CENTS

EGYPT AND SYRIA AGREE TO U.N. CEASE-FIRE; ISRAEL REPORTS TROOPS REACH SUEZ CANAL; JOHNSON, KOSYGIN USED HOT LINE IN CRISIS

SENATE APPROVES A TIGHTENED RULE ON REDISTRICTING

33 States Ordered to Bring Population Variant Down to 10% by 1968 Election

By JAMES F. CLARITY
Special to The New York Times

WASHINGTON, June 8—The Senate approved today a bill requiring that by the 1968 election no state have a population variance of more than 10 per cent between its largest and smallest Congressional districts.

The approval, which came in a surprise vote of 57 to 25, was a result of a fight by Senator Edward M. Kennedy, Democrat of Massachusetts, to amend a measure that would have permitted a variance of 35 per cent until the 1972 election.

The Kennedy amendment, which was soundly defeated in committee two weeks ago, is intended, according to the Senator, to make Congressional redistricting conform with the Supreme Court's one-man, one-vote ruling of 1964. The amendment also deleted language giving the states power to determine when the compactness of a district was "practicable."

An Altered Version

The measure, before it was amended today, was an altered version of a bill already passed by the House. The House bill provided for a population variance of 30 per cent, and was amended by the Senate Judiciary Committee to cover four additional states.

The version passed today, which now goes to a Senate-House conference, would apply to 33 states having variances of more than 10 per cent. Nine of these states are under Federal court orders to redistrict. The 17 states not covered by today's Senate action either elect Representatives at large or have variances lower than 10 per cent.

Mr. Kennedy's proposal was approved, first in a crucial 44-to-39 vote as an amendment, then in the final vote on the bill as amended, 57 to 25.

"We knew it would be close.

Continued on Page 26, Column 1

Arms Cost Stress Scored by Rickover

By EVERT CLARK
Special to The New York Times

WASHINGTON, June 8—Vice Adm. Hyman G. Rickover has denounced the cost-effectiveness approach to weapons development as an "ism," a "new religion" and a "fog bomb" that is keeping the nation from gaining technology that would save lives.

In Congressional testimony released today, the head of the nuclear-powered ship program attacked present management techniques in the Pentagon.

By Presidential order, many of these techniques—including the mathematical analysis of cost vs. effectiveness—are now being spread throughout the executive branch of

Continued on Page 2, Column 4

JURY FINDS LAXITY IN BUILDINGS UNIT

Graft, Shirking and Lack of Personnel Training Are Cited—Moerdler Agrees

By JACK ROTH

A New York County grand jury criticized yesterday long-standing conditions in the Buildings Department that it said had resulted in corruption among housing inspectors and landlords.

The jury also said the situation permitted some inspectors and their supervisors to quit work as early as 10:30 A.M. and go to bars and racetracks for the rest of the day.

The jury, in a presentment handed up to Supreme Court Justice Mitchell D. Schweitzer, charged that the department suffered from lack of financial and manpower resources.

It asserted that inspectors were not properly trained for their jobs, that they were unaware of their department's rules and regulations, that there was duplication in inspections, that electronic processing equipment was failing to do its job and that unauthorized persons had access to file rooms and private departmental offices.

The Buildings Commissioner,

Continued on Page 31, Column 1

ALL SINAI IS HELD

U.A.R. Loses 50 Tanks in Actions Termed Fiercest of War

By Reuters

TEL AVIV, Friday, June 9—Israeli troops have reached the bank of the Suez Canal and have taken control of the entire Sinai Peninsula, the Israeli radio reported this morning.

The radio broadcast the text of a message from the commander in the southern front, to the Chief of Staff, Gen. Yitzhak Rabin. The message said:

"Happy to inform you that our forces are stationed on the bank of the Suez Canal and the Red Sea. The Sinai Peninsula is in our hands. Greetings to you and to the whole defense forces of Israel."

Battle reports yesterday indicated that the remnants of two Egyptian armored divisions and four infantry divisions were trapped in the western part of that Sinai Desert.

50 Tanks Reported Wrecked

The news of Cairo's acceptance of the United Nations cease-fire coincided with an announcement by an Israeli spokesman that three battles in the desert yesterday had been "the fiercest in this war."

The Israelis said they had shot down eight Egyptian planes and destroyed at least 50 Egyptian tanks during the fighting.

Other tanks were wrecked and left on the road to Qantara, about 30 miles north of Ismailia, about midway along the 100-mile Suez Canal.

Among the Egyptian planes downed were a Soviet-made Ilyushin bomber and several Soviet-built Sukhoi-7's. Israeli planes also struck Soviet-made missile sites in the Suez Canal zone during daylight raids, the spokesman added.

He added that Israeli forces had captured oilfields at Ras Sudar, south of the port of Taufiq on the western coast of the Sinai Peninsula. Israeli soldiers said the wells were afire

Continued on Page 17, Column 6

AFTER THE BATTLE: Egyptian prisoners, prone on the sand, their hands behind their heads, are guarded in a compound by Israeli troops at El Arish in the northern Sinai Peninsula. El Arish was taken by Israel Tuesday.

United Press International Cablephoto

EGYPTIANS TOLD OF TRUCE DECISION

Cairo Broadcast Is Terse —Syrians Also Announce Approval of Cease-Fire

By ERIC PACE
Special to The New York Times

CAIRO, Friday, June 9—The Government told the Egyptian people this morning that it had conditionally accepted a cease-fire in the war with Israel.

There was no immediate popular reaction because the Cairo radio waited until early morning before announcing, more than three hours after the fact, that the United Arab Republic had told Secretary General Thant of the United Nations that it would agree to a truce if Israel did so.

[The Damascus radio announced that Syria, too, had accepted the cease-fire, Reuters reported. Page 17.]

Cairo was blacked out as protection against possible Israeli air raids when the news came, but nocturnal strollers reported that policemen were already taking down at least some of the anti-Israeli banners that have festooned the city for the last few weeks.

An early edition of a popular Cairo newspaper, Al Akhbar, put the news on the front page but made no comment. There was also no elaboration from the radio, which broadcast a military communiqué saying that the battle against Israel was continuing at all points along the Egyptian front.

The terse announcement of the cease-fire contrasted with

Continued on Page 17, Column 2

U.S. Planes Batter MIG Base in North

Special to The New York Times

SAIGON, South Vietnam, June 8—American fighter-bombers knocked out a MIG base near Hanoi yesterday and wrecked a surface-to-air missile storage area 50 miles southwest of the capital, the United States Command reported today.

At the same time, new fighting broke out just south of the demilitarized zone between North Vietnam and South Vietnam, where a fierce battle raged for control of three hills last month.

Navy carrier pilots attacked the Kep Airfield, 37 miles northeast of Hanoi, for the seventh time since April 24. A headquarters spokesman said the airfield was "closed temporarily.

Continued on Page 3, Column 4

Major Mideast Developments

In the Capitals

The United Arab Republic accepted a United Nations cease-fire. Israel had previously agreed to stop hostilities if her enemies were willing to go along.

In Damascus, after a series of militant vows to fight on, the Syrians announced that they would also accept the cease-fire.

President Johnson welcomed the cease-fire agreement and urged prompt action to solve the "many more fundamental" questions in the Middle East.

An emergency declaration on oil was being considered by the Johnson Administration after major oil companies reported that a worldwide transportation problem had resulted from the war.

The hot line between Washington and Moscow was used this week for the first time during a crisis.

On the Battlefronts

Before the cease-fire went into effect, Israeli planes and torpedo boats mistakenly attacked a United States communications ship about 15 miles off Sinai. The Pentagon reported that 10 Americans had been killed and 100 wounded. Israel sent an apology.

Israel reported that her troops had reached the bank of the Suez Canal and that the entire Sinai Peninsula was under her control. Earlier Israel reported three fierce desert battles in which at least 50 Egyptian tanks had been destroyed.

The United Arab Republic announced that its air force had inflicted heavy damage on Israeli armored columns trying to advance westward from El Arish in the Sinai Peninsula.

At the Strait of Tiran, a Soviet freighter bound for the Jordanian port of Aqaba was the first ship to pass since Israel declared the waterway open to shipping on Wednesday. Two Israeli ships prepared to follow.

DONATIONS POUR IN FOR ISRAELI FUND

Many Give All They Have— Some Gifts in Millions

By M. S. HANDLER

"You have got it all now," said a brief letter containing a check for $25,000.

The message was from a professor at the Jewish Theological Seminary who said he had gladly stripped himself of his worldly goods and sent the proceeds to the United Jewish Appeal for the Israel Emergency Fund.

The owner of two gas stations arrived at the appeal's offices and turned over the deeds to the stations as his contribution to the multimillion fund drive.

Other Jews cashed in with the cash-surrender values of their life insurance policies. Still others, deeply moved by the Arab-Israeli war, sold real estate and securities and sent the money to the fund's headquarters, on the Avenue of the Americas at 51st street.

These were some examples of the dramas being played out in the Jewish communities across the United States, U.J.A. officials said yesterday.

The contributions, appeal of-

Continued on Page 11, Column 1

ISRAEL, IN ERROR, ATTACKS U.S. SHIP

10 Navy Men Die, 100 Hurt in Raids North of Sinai

By WILLIAM BEECHER
Special to The New York Times

WASHINGTON, June 8—An American naval vessel was mistakenly attacked by Israeli planes and torpedo boats today in international waters about 15 miles north of the Sinai Peninsula. Reports tonight listed the toll as 10 dead and 100 wounded. Twenty of the wounded were hurt critically.

The vessel, the Liberty, was on a peaceful, though war-related mission. Pentagon sources said she had been dispatched from Spain to the war zone to provide additional communications to facilitate the evacuation of American citizens from the Middle East and North Africa.

Pentagon officials said it was too early to tell whether demnification would be asked from Israel for the loss of life and the damage to the Navy ship.

President Johnson, in a letter to the Senate majority leader, Mike Mansfield, noted that the

Continued on Page 19, Column 1

JOHNSON PLEASED BY GAINS ON TRUCE

Looks to a Stable Peace— White House Discloses Use of the Hot Line

Texts of the Mansfield letter and Johnson reply, Page 18.

By MAX FRANKEL
Special to The New York Times

WASHINGTON, June 8—President Johnson welcomed spreading acceptance of a cease-fire agreement in the Middle East today, but urged all parties to move promptly toward the "many more fundamental questions" bearing on a stable peace.

While thus pressing for more than merely another frail armistice, the White House also disclosed that its hot-line connection with Moscow had been used for the first time this week in an international crisis.

The United States used the teletype link this morning when it heard of an attack on an American communications ship off the Sinai Peninsula. At the time, the source of the attack was not known.

The Soviet Government, whose warships have been observing the movements of the United States Sixth Fleet in the eastern Mediterranean, was advised that the carrier-based American planes were scrambling into action for the sole purpose of assisting the distressed vessel.

It was later learned that Israeli forces had attacked the American ship in error.

The announcement of quick exchanges to prevent misunder-

Continued on Page 18, Column 1

Russians Continue To Harass 6th Fleet

By NEIL SHEEHAN
Special to The New York Times

ABOARD U.S.S. AMERICA, in the Eastern Mediterranean, June 8—Two Soviet warships, a destroyer and a small, highly maneuverable patrol craft, moved into the formation of this Sixth Fleet carrier task force group this morning and began systematically harassing the American ships.

The harassment was undertaken despite a warning to another Soviet destroyer yesterday from Vice Adm. William I. Martin, the Sixth Fleet commander. Admiral Martin warned the Soviet ship to withdraw from the area of the American formation. He said the Soviet ship, while following the carrier

Continued on Page 15, Column 1

A SHIFT BY CAIRO

Thant Notifies Council in Middle of Debate on Resolutions

Excerpts from the U.N. debate are printed on Page 16.

By DREW MIDDLETON
Special to The New York Times

UNITED NATIONS, N. Y., June 8—The United Arab Republic, the leader of the anti-Israel coalition, today accepted the Security Council's demand for a cease-fire in the Middle East provided Israel did the same.

Yesterday, the delegate of Israel said his country accepted the cease-fire provided Israel's foes agreed to it. Reports here yesterday indicated rejection by Cairo.

Syria gave notice tonight that she would also comply, informing the Secretary General after the Security Council recessed.

This afternoon, in his dry, precise voice Secretary General Thant read to the Council a brief letter from Mohamed Awad el-Kony, the Egyptian delegate, disclosing that President Gamal Abdel Nasser's Government had "decided to accept the cease-fire" called for in the two Council resolutions "on the condition that the other party ceases fire."

He Scraps Long Speech

Mr. el-Kony wrote the letter after a long telephone conversation with Cairo shortly before the Council meeting began. After the call, he scrapped a 20-page speech he had prepared and wrote the note to Mr. Thant.

The Israeli Foreign Minister, Abba Eban, hailed "the immediate prospect" of a cease-fire as "a notable step" and called on other Arab governments to follow the Egyptian lead.

Cairo's acceptance of the Council resolutions adopted unanimously on Tuesday and Wednesday raised rather than lowered the heat of the debate between the United States and the Soviet Union over the resolutions each has submitted to the Council.

Arthur J. Goldberg, the United States delegate, saying he hoped for a peace "stable and just to all concerned," submitted a draft of a resolution calling for the "withdrawal and disengagement of armed personnel," the renunciation of force, "the maintenance of vital international rights" and the establishment of a durable peace in the area. The Administration was said

Continued on Page 17, Column 1

SOVIET SHIP SAILS INTO AQABA GULF

Passage Is First Since Israel Lifted Arab Blockade

By Reuters

ELATH, Israel, June 8—A Soviet freighter bound for the Jordanian port of Aqaba passed through the Strait of Tiran today, the first ship to do so since Israel declared the passage an international waterway yesterday.

Two outgoing Israeli freighters were preparing to pass through the strait since the Egyptians blockaded the Gulf of Aqaba on May 23.

A report from Sharm el Sheik, which dominates the strait, dis-

Continued on Page 17, Column 7

[map of Middle East region showing LEBANON, SYRIA, JORDAN, ISRAEL, NEGEV, UNITED ARAB REPUBLIC, SINAI PENINSULA, SAUDI ARABIA]

CONVERGING OFFENSIVES: Israelis thrust westward across northern Sinai (1) to the Suez Canal after sharp fighting at Bir Gifgafa and Mitla Pass, and routed Egyptians at Nakhl and trapped in drive farther south (2). Soviet ship passed through Strait of Tiran (3), now under Israeli control. Mistaken Israeli attack on U.S. ship in Mediterranean (4) killed 10 men. Israelis held west bank of the River Jordan as far north as Jenin (5).

The New York Times

LATE CITY EDITION
Weather: Snow likely today, tonight. Partly cloudy tomorrow.
Temp. range: Today 35-31; Tuesday 41-32. Full U.S. report on Page 90.

VOL. CXVII..No. 40,177   © 1968 The New York Times Company.   NEW YORK, WEDNESDAY, JANUARY 24, 1968   10 CENTS

MILLS TURNS DOWN AIDES OF JOHNSON ON TAX SURCHARGE

Says They Did Not Convince Him They Had Done Their Best to Cut Spending

'ANOTHER LOOK' URGED

House Leader's Stand Hints at Delay Until March in Acting on New Levy

By EILEEN SHANAHAN
Special to The New York Times

WASHINGTON, Jan. 23 — Representative Wilbur D. Mills told the Administration "no" again today on the tax increase.

At the end of two days of hearings before the House Ways and Means Committee, of which he is chairman, the Arkansas Democrat told Administration officials that they had "not yet established" to his satisfaction that "you've done the best you can" to hold down Government spending.

Mr. Mills asked the officials to "take another look" at next year's planned Government spending of $147.4-billion, on the basis of the traditional administrative budget, while the committee turns its attention to another issue. That is the Administration's proposals to reduce the deficit in the United States' balance of international payments.

Date Left Undecided

Just how long the committee might take with the balance-of-payments program and when it might get back to the tax bill, Mr. Mills did not say. It seemed unlikely that the committee could resume consideration of the proposed 10 per cent tax surcharge before early March, at the soonest.

Meanwhile, the Gallup Poll reported that President Johnson faces a difficult task in trying to sell American voters on a tax increase at this time, and that the opposition comes as much from the rank and file of his own party as from others.

In addition to dealing with the balance-of-payments problem, Mr. Mills indicated that the committee might also consider, ahead of any new look at the tax surcharge, both the extension of excise taxes on automobiles and telephone service and a further step up in corporate tax collections.

Excise Action Favored

He said that an extension of the excise taxes "has to be done." Under present law they would go down on April 1 from 7 to 2 per cent on automobiles and from 10 to 1 per cent on telephone service.

In addition, he said it "might be possible, without a great deal of argument, to do some part" of what the Administration has asked to bring corporations closer to a pay-as-you-go tax basis.

Mr. Mills's reference to approval of only "part" of the corporate tax collection speed-up reflected his belief that the smallest corporations — those with tax liabilities of $25,000 or less — should probably not be put on a full pay-as-you-
Continued on Page 25, Column 1

Jersey Sues State On Price for PATH

By FRED P. GRAHAM
Special to The New York Times

WASHINGTON, Jan. 23 — New Jersey sued New York in the Supreme Court today in an unusual legal move designed to bar New York courts from approving an excessive land condemnation judgment against the Port of New York Authority.

In a suit filed directly in the Court, Attorney General Arthur J. Sills of New Jersey, contended that the New York Court of Appeals violated an agreement between the two states when it ruled that the Port Authority should pay $30 million for the assets of the Hudson Rapid Tubes Corporation.

The assets, consisting of the Hudson & Manhattan Railroad
Continued on Page 30, Column 3

City Council Votes A One-Year Trial Of Group Cab Rides

By SETH S. KING

A year-long experiment in group taxi riding was approved yesterday by the City Council.

As soon as Mayor Lindsay signs the bill his task force on taxis will be allowed to organize and supervise such rides from the Eastern Airlines Shuttle Terminal at La Guardia Airport to four zones in Manhattan.

The Council also passed a bill eliminating a requirement that cab drivers be residents of the city.

It also adopted a resolution calling upon the Police Department's Hack Bureau to require each taxi to be equipped with an exterior switch, or similar device, instead of an interior switch, to operate its off-duty sign.

This was aimed at preventing a driver from suddenly turning on his off-duty sign with an interior switch when he saw a fare he did not want to pick up. The
Continued on Page 35, Column 1

JOHNSON PROGRAM INDICTED BY G.O.P.

In TV Reply, Party Charges His Policies Led to Riots, Crime Rise and Inflation

Excerpts from the statements will be found on Page 28.

By JOHN HERBERS

WASHINGTON, Jan. 23 — Republicans in Congress told the American people tonight that President Johnson's policies had led to riots, crime and inflation at home and loss of influence and prestige abroad.

In a one-hour telecast over the Columbia Broadcasting System from the auditorium of the new Senate Office Building, eight Senators and nine Representatives delivered a harsh indictment of the Administration's record and said that President Johnson had vastly underestimated the extent of discontent in the country.

America, they said, needs a new leader who would seek a military victory in Vietnam, take a strong stand against worldwide Communism, move decisively to stamp out crime and violence at home and hold down Government spending.

The broadcast, entitled "The State of the Union — the Republican Appraisal," was a reply to President Johnson's State of
Continued on Page 28, Column 3

3,600 Drugs Facing Relabeling To List Ailments They Combat

By United Press International

WASHINGTON, Jan. 23 — Virtually every drug originally manufactured in America between 1938 and 1962 will have to be relabeled to tell exactly what ailments it is effective against, the Government told the drug industry today.

Some of the 3,600 drugs — sold in as many as 18,000 different combinations — are going to be ordered off the market, and the advertising of nearly all the drugs will have to be changed, William W. Goodrich, assistant general counsel for the Food and Drug Administration, said.

He spoke at a two-hour conference of drug manufacturers called to explain the agency's study of the effectiveness of all prescription and nonprescription drugs marketed in that 24-year period.

The review was ordered under the Kefauver-Harris Act of 1962, which requires that all drugs sold domestically be proved effective as well as safe for their intended uses. Prior to the new rules, the drugs had only to be found safe.

The first step toward removal from the market of a group of drugs was taken today with publication by the drug
Continued on Page 32, Column 1

PRESIDENT OFFERS PROJECT TO SPUR HIRING OF JOBLESS

$2-Billion Manpower Plea Stresses Industrial Effort to Assist 'Hard Core'

Text of President's message is printed on Page 24.

By MAX FRANKEL
Special to The New York Times

WASHINGTON, Jan. 23 — President Johnson asked Congress today for quick action to help him mount the first large-scale effort to induce private industry to train and hire the hard-core cases among the urban unemployed.

In the first of more than a dozen special messages covering his major legislative proposals for the year, the President urged the expansion of all Government manpower efforts by 25 per cent, from a budget of $1.65-billion in the current fiscal year, ending June 30, to $2.09-billion in the year starting July 1.

Total Is Expanding

He suggested spending the bulk of the $442-million increase on programs to find, train and employ the most disadvantaged citizens, most of whom have given up the search for work because of inadequate training, discrimination, discouragement and a general despair.

There are more than a million such persons, the Administration believes, including a still expanding total of 500,000 in 50 major cities. The President would try to place 100,000 of these in jobs in the next 18 months and aim for a target of 500,000 by mid-1971.

"It is a waste that an enlightened nation should not tolerate," Mr. Johnson said in his message. "It is a waste that a nation concerned by disorders in its city streets cannot tolerate."

National Organization

Existing manpower programs have not reached the hardcore jobless effectively, Mr. Johnson reported. Therefore he proposed the expansion of promising experiments with direct subsidies to private employers who incur the extra costs of training and making jobs available to hitherto unqualified persons.

He said he was creating a national organization of leading businessmen, headed by Henry Ford 2d, chairman of the Ford Motor Company, to enlist the cooperation of industry and to work with Government officials in the regions and cities.

At the same time, the President proposed a significant expansion of the year-old Government program to train the
Continued on Page 24, Column 1

Danish Socialists Beaten in Election; Krag Will Resign

By ALVIN SHUSTER
Special to The New York Times

COPENHAGEN, Denmark, Jan. 23 — The Social Democratic party, in power for the last 15 years, was defeated tonight in a huge protest vote.

The Danes, upset over rising prices and taxes, turned to the right in their national elections. Three non-Socialist parties won enough seats in Parliament to enable them to form a new government.

Premier Jens Otto Krag, the Social Democratic Premier, said he would resign tomorrow.

Emerging as victors today were the Radical Liberals, the Conservatives and the Agrarian Liberals. The three parties had indicated strongly before the election that if they won a parliamentary majority they would form a government.

Social Democrats Largest

Between them, with about 95 per cent of the votes counted, they had 101 seats, the Radical Liberals going from 13 to 28, the Conservatives from 34 to 38 and the Agrarian Liberals remaining unchanged at 35.

The Social Democrats will remain the largest single party in Parliament with 63 seats, a loss of six. The extreme leftist Socialist People's party, which had won 20 seats in the last elections in 1966, dropped to 11.

The voting was heavy. The final count may show that 90 per cent of the 3.3 million eligible voters cast ballots.
Continued on Page 7, Column 1

U.S. Resumes Normal Relations With Greece's Military Regime

By PETER GROSE

WASHINGTON, Jan. 23 — The United States resumed "normal" diplomatic relations with Greece today, six weeks after King Constantine failed in his attempt to oust the military regime.

The State Department said that Ambassador Phillips Talbot had been instructed to make an official call on the Greek Foreign Minister, Panayotis Pipinelis, and thus signal the resumption of formal contacts between the two governments.

Shipments of large-scale military supplies from the United States remain embargoed, the department added, as they have been since last April when the junta seized power.

on a pragmatic basis, for they fear that the Greek forces in the North Atlantic Treaty Organization are being weakened by lack of heavy matériel.

Small arms, ammunition, spare parts and other maintenance stocks continue to be supplied to the Greek forces by the United States. This kind of military aid was not suspended after the April coup.

The department spokesman, Robert J. McCloskey, swept aside a maze of protocol and political considerations by stating, "The United States Government continues to regard King Constantine as the Greek chief of state—relations between the King and the Government in Athens are an in-
Continued on Page 8, Column 1

NORTH KOREA SEIZES NAVY SHIP, HOLDS 83 ON BOARD AS U.S. SPIES; ENTERPRISE IS ORDERED TO AREA

Pueblo, seized off North Korea and taken to Wonsan, is an intelligence collection vessel of the United States Navy

Associated Press

RADIATION FOUND WHERE B-52 FELL

It Suggests Hydrogen Bombs Did Not Go Through Ice Off Greenland Base

By JOHN W. FINNEY
Special to The New York Times

WASHINGTON, Jan. 23 — Air Force search teams were reported today to have detected small amounts of radiation from some or all of the four hydrogen bombs missing after a B-52 bomber crashed on the ice off northwest Greenland.

After two days of hunting with dog sleds and helicopters, teams from the Thule Air Force Base in Greenland still had not found the unarmed thermonuclear weapons. But the detection of the radiation was taken as an encouraging sign that the bombs were scattered across the surface and had not plunged through the ice with parts of the bomber into about 800 feet of water.

If the bombs are still on the surface, recovery operations will be easier. It was first thought that the bombs had sunk to the bottom of North Star Bay, about seven miles southwest of the Thule base, raising the problem of underwater recovery operations through the sea ice.

The radiation suggested that some of the bombs might have broken apart in the impact of the crash and during the subsequent explosion in the bomber as it careened several hundred feet across the ice. If the bombs have split and
Continued on Page 6, Column 4

The American vessel was seized off Wonsan (cross)

The New York Times
Jan. 24, 1968

5,000 MEN MASSED AT KHESANH BY U.S.

Marines Rushed In as Foe Builds Up Force in Area— Supply Planes Fired On

By CHARLES MOHR
Special to The New York Times

KHESANH, South Vietnam, Jan. 23 — More than 5,000 United States marines have been concentrated at Khesanh amid indications that one of the major battles of the Vietnam war may be in the offing.

The marines were rushed in because of an increasingly obvious concentration of North Vietnamese troops in the area.

[Sixty-one enemy soldiers were reported killed by air strikes and artillery fire on Tuesday near Khesanh. In a battle on the Bongson plain, 128 Vietcong troops were reported killed by United States infantrymen.]

The nearness of the enemy forces made itself evident when the unmistakable sound of a bullet striking a fuselage rang out as a transport plane glided in to land at the Marine base here. The fat-bellied C-123 Loadmaster landed, safe despite the bullet hole.

The crew pushed pallets of 155-mm. artillery ammunition off the plane and then turned to four large wooden crates addressed to "Fifth Graves
Continued on Page 3, Column 1

RETURN OF PUEBLO ASKED BY U.S. AIDE

Immediate Action Sought at Meeting in Panmunjom of Armistice Group

By Reuters

PANMUNJOM, Korea, Wednesday, Jan. 24 — The American commander of the United Nations Command demanded at a meeting of the Mixed Armistice Commission today that the Pueblo and her crew of 83 be returned immediately by North Korea.

Rear Adm. John V. Smith also told the chief North Korean delegate, Maj. Gen. Chung Kook Pak, that the United States reserved the right to demand compensation for the capture of the vessel by the North Korean Navy yesterday.

[The North Koreans said the ship "will remain in our hands," United Press International reported.]

General Pak said North Korean naval vessels fired at the Pueblo yesterday and "several of her crew members were killed or wounded." The Defense Department in Washington had said no one was killed. Admiral Smith also protested what he said was an intrusion by a band of 31 North Korean agents into Seoul, the South Korean capital, Sunday night. The intrusion resulted in the death of 11 persons.

The meeting today in the demilitarized zone between North and South Korea was called by the United Nations Command Monday, before the Pueblo was taken, because of the infiltration incident.

The United Nations had asked that the meeting take place yesterday, but the North Koreans wanted it held today
Continued on Page 14, C

---

4 CREWMEN HURT

Rusk Says Efforts Are Under Way to Obtain Vessel's Release

U.S. statement and Pyongyang broadcast are on Page 15.

By NEIL SHEEHAN
Special to The New York Times

WASHINGTON, Jan. 23 — North Korean patrol boats seized a United States Navy intelligence ship off Wonsan today and took the vessel and her 83 crew members into the North Korean port.

The Defense Department, reporting the incident, said the ship had been in international waters about 25 miles off the eastern coast of North Korea when she was boarded by armed North Korean sailors at 1:45 P.M. (11:45 P.M. Monday, Eastern Standard time).

But North Korea, in a Pyongyang radio broadcast, asserted that the Pueblo had "intruded into the territorial waters of the republic and was carrying out hostile activities." The broadcast called the Pueblo "an armed spy boat of the United States imperialist aggressor force."

Matter of 'Utmost Gravity'

Secretary of State Dean Rusk called the seizure of the Pueblo "a matter of the utmost gravity." He said the United States was negotiating with North Korea "through the channels that are available to us to obtain the immediate release of the vessel and her crew."

The incident forced a sudden confrontation between the United States and an Asian Communist government that has long been calling for diversionary assaults against "United States imperialism" to distract American energies from the war in Vietnam.

The Defense Department said four crewmen of the Pueblo had been wounded, one critically. One report said a crew member had lost a leg. The Pentagon declined to say how the men had been wounded.

North Korean Report

Later, on Wednesday morning, Korean time—the North Vietnamese said at an armistice meeting in Panmunjom that several of the Pueblo's crew were "killed or wounded" in the incident, and a North Vietnamese broadcast monitored in Tokyo said the vessel resisted seizure. The Pentagon declined to comment.

The Pueblo carried 6 officers, 75 enlisted men and 2 civilians, whom the Defense Department identified as Navy civilian hydrographers performing oceanographic work.

Military sources said that the nuclear-powered aircraft carrier Enterprise and two destroyers
Continued on Page 14, Column 3

Seizure of Vessel Scored in Capital

By United Press International

WASHINGTON, Jan. 23 — North Korea's seizure of the United States intelligence-gathering ship Pueblo was condemned in Congress today as an act of war. Some lawmakers demanded a quick military response.

Senator Richard B. Russell, chairman of the Senate Armed Services Committee, said that the action was "a breach of international law amounting to an act of war."

The Georgia Democrat added that "it certainly behooves our Government to take a very strong position in demanding release of the ship and of the men."

Representative Bob
Continued on Page 14, Column 6

"All the News That's Fit to Print"

The New York Times

LATE CITY EDITION
Weather: Clearing today, turning cold tonight. Fair, cool tomorrow. Temp. range: today 62-44; Thurs. 73-52. Full U.S. report on Page 92.

VOL. CXVII..No. 40,249   © 1968 The New York Times Company.   NEW YORK, FRIDAY, APRIL 5, 1968   10 CENTS

MARTIN LUTHER KING IS SLAIN IN MEMPHIS; A WHITE IS SUSPECTED; JOHNSON URGES CALM

JOHNSON DELAYS TRIP TO HAWAII; MAY LEAVE TODAY

President Spends a Hectic Day Here and in Capital —Sees Thant at the U.N.

By MAX FRANKEL
Special to The New York Times

WASHINGTON, April 4 — President Johnson postponed his trip to Hawaii at least until tomorrow after he heard of the death of the Rev. Dr. Martin Luther King Jr. tonight.

The news, which visibly shocked the President, came at the end of one of the most extraordinary days in perhaps the most extraordinary week of his Administration.

Mr. Johnson was to have flown from Washington at about midnight for a weekend of strategy conferences with his military and diplomatic leaders stationed in South Vietnam. On the way, he had planned a breakfast meeting in California with former President Dwight D. Eisenhower.

Instead, the President telephoned Mrs. King in Atlanta, made a brief appeal for calm on television and went to his office to follow the reports of unrest and disturbance given him periodically by Attorney General Ramsey Clark.

Cancels Dinner Appearance

Mr. Johnson also canceled an appearance before a Democratic party fund-raising dinner here—the final event of a hectic schedule that became ever more hectic as the day unfolded.

The President began the day by making final arrangements for the Hawaii trip. It had been tentatively planned before his order Sunday to curtail the bombing of North Vietnam and the news yesterday that Hanoi was interested in establishing direct contact.

[The new United States peace moves are producing a quiet but bitter reaction in the South Vietnamese Government that is causing increasing concern among United States officials in Saigon. Page 14.]

But the diplomatic development, though not the principal subject of the Honolulu meetings, added special weight to his conversations with Gen. William C. Westmoreland, the American commander in South Vietnam, and other officials.

Mr. Johnson was careful not to arouse false hopes of peace, but he appeared encouraged and in buoyant spirit as he decided before noon to fly first to New York to attend the investiture of the Most Rev. Terence J. Cooke as Archbishop of New York.

Then, while in New York,

Continued on Page 12, Column 1

Hanoi Charges U.S. Raid Far North of 20th Parallel

By EVERT CLARK
Special to The New York Times

WASHINGTON, April 4 — North Vietnam charged in a broadcast today that United States planes had bombed a "populated area" in northwestern Vietnam far north of the 20th parallel. The Defense Department said it knew of no such raid but was investigating.

President Johnson has ordered that there be no attacks on North Vietnam north of the 20th Parallel as a step toward de-escalating the war.

[In South Vietnam, United States marines beat off an attack by about 400 North Vietnamese soldiers charging up a hill near Khesanh, killing 93, The Associated Press reported. Meanwhile, an American relief column was nearing the besieged base. Page 15.]

The Hanoi radio, in a broadcast monitored and translated here, said three waves of United States planes dropped more than 50 bombs on a "popu-

The New York Times   April 5, 1968
Hanoi said that area near Laichau (cross) was target.

lated area" about 30 miles west of Laichau, capital of Laichau Province, this morning.

The nearest village to that

Continued on Page 15, Column 1

HUMPHREY HINTS HE'LL ENTER RACE

Tells Unionists in Pittsburgh He Will Act Soon—Abel and Wirtz Back Him

By ROY REED
Special to The New York Times

PITTSBURGH, April 4—Two thousand labor representatives, including the head of the United Steel Workers union, clamorously urged Vice President Humphrey today to run for President.

The Vice President left little doubt that he would oblige them, but he indicated that he would wait until President Johnson returned from his Hawaii conference before making an announcement.

"I know what your request is, and I know what your thoughts are," he told the delegates to the Pennsylvania A.F.L.-C.I.O. convention. "I am most grateful. I am not one to walk away from a decision, and a decision will come in due time."

But nothing he does should interfere with President Johnson's peace mission, he said.

Several other political leaders urged Mr. Humphrey today to enter the race for the Democratic Presidential nomination. The most prominent among them was Secretary of Labor W. Willard Wirtz, who was addressing a union convention at Miami Beach.

I. W. Abel, president of the steelworkers Union, rose as Mr.

Continued on Page 32, Column 1

Johnson Shuns Role Of '68 'Lame Duck,' Kennedy Was Told

By JOHN HERBERS
Special to The New York Times

WASHINGTON, April 4—In his meeting with Senator Robert F. Kennedy yesterday President Johnson said he would remain out of the political fight this year because he did not believe it was appropriate for a "lame duck" President to try to pick his successor.

This and other details of the Johnson-Kennedy meeting were learned today from knowledgeable sources.

The meeting, which Senator Kennedy had requested in the interest of "national unity," was described as an extraordinarily friendly one, with both the Senator and the President speaking in a conciliatory manner.

President Johnson was pictured as the "elder statesman" of the party who had decided to remain aloof from this year's scramble for the Presidency in an effort to keep the party as strong as possible and retain his own dignity and effectiveness as President.

At one point, it was reported, the President said he did not want to make a spectacle of himself as a lame duck President attempting to dictate to the party who should be nominated at the national convention.

In this regard, he pointed out that in 1956 former President Harry S. Truman went to the

Continued on Page 31, Column 4

DISMAY IN NATION

Negroes Urge Others to Carry on Spirit of Nonviolence

By LAWRENCE VAN GELDER

Dismay, shame, anger and foreboding marked the nation's reaction last night to the Rev. Dr. Martin Luther King Jr.'s murder.

From the high offices of state to the man in the street, news of the moderate civil rights leader's violent death in Memphis yesterday drew, for the most part, stunned and sober statements.

Most major Negro organizations and Negro leaders, lamenting Dr. King's death, expressed hope that it serve as a spur to others to carry on in his spirit of nonviolence. But some Negro militants responded with bitterness and anger.

Roy Wilkins, executive director of the National Association for the Advancement of Colored People, said his organization was "shocked and deeply grieved by the dastardly murder of Dr. Martin Luther King."

"His murderer or murderers must be promptly apprehended and brought to justice," Mr. Wilkins said.

'A Man of Peace'

"Dr. King was a symbol of the nonviolent civil rights protest movement. He was a man of peace, of dedication, of great courage. His senseless assassination solves nothing. It will not stay the civil rights movement; it will instead spur it to greater activity."

Whitney M. Young Jr., executive director of the National Urban League, said:

"We are unspeakably shocked by the murder of Martin Luther King, one of the greatest leaders of our time. This is a sad reflection on America. We fear for our country.

"The only possible answer now is for the nation to act immediately on what Dr. King has been fighting for—passage of the civil rights and anti-poverty bills and a true and just equality for all men. Those of us who have remained loyal to his concept of nonviolence have been dealt a mortal blow."

Mayor Richard G. Hatcher of Gary, Ind., a Negro, termed the death of Dr. King "every man's loss."

"Men who care for humankind and struggle for its salvation through reason and faith have lost a leader of monumental stature," he said. "A man of his magnitude will not soon pass this way again."

At his home in Stamford, Conn., the former baseball star Jackie Robinson called the

Continued on Page 26, Column 1

PRESIDENT'S PLEA

On TV, He Deplores 'Brutal' Murder of Negro Leader

Statements by Johnson and Humphrey are on Page 24.

Special to The New York Times

WASHINGTON, April 4— President Johnson deplored tonight in a brief television address to the nation the "brutal slaying" of the Rev. Dr. Martin Luther King Jr.

He asked "every citizen to reject the blind violence that has struck Dr. King, who lived by nonviolence."

Mr. Johnson said he was postponing his scheduled departure tonight for a Honolulu conference on Vietnam and that instead he would leave tomorrow.

The President spoke from the White House. At the Washington Hilton Hotel, where Democratic members of Congress had gathered to honor the President and the Vice President, Mr. Humphrey, his voice strained with emotion, said:

"Martin Luther King stands with our other American martyrs in the cause of freedom and justice. His death is a terrible tragedy."

The dinner was canceled 10 to 15 minutes after the Vice President spoke. Mr. Johnson, who was scheduled to appear at the dinner, canceled his plans to attend.

F.B.I. Inquiry Ordered

Attorney General Ramsey Clark ordered an immediate inquiry by the Federal Bureau of Investigation into the shooting of Dr. King in Memphis.

He said the purpose of the investigation would be to determine whether any Federal law had been violated.

One provision of the law that could be invoked makes it a crime to engage in a conspiracy to deprive a person of his civil rights.

In addition to F.B.I. agents, Department of Justice civil rights representatives were on the scene in Memphis and were in touch with the Attorney General.

Military sources said that no National Guard units had been Federalized and no Regular Army troops had been alerted yet for possible movement to cities where violence had broken out.

National Guard troops, such as the 4,000 men who had been called into Memphis, remain under state control until the responsible Governor requests help and the President

Continued on Page 24, Column 7

Associated Press
THE REV. DR. MARTIN LUTHER KING Jr.

Scattered Violence Occurs In Harlem and Brooklyn

12 Are Arrested Here

By THOMAS A. JOHNSON

Sporadic violence erupted in Harlem and Brooklyn's Bedford-Stuyvesant section last night after news of Dr. Martin Luther King's assassination spread in the two predominantly Negro communities.

Mayor Lindsay, who went to Harlem in an effort to quiet the outbreaks, was caught in the midst of an unruly crowd and had to be hustled into a limousine by bodyguards.

Police reinforcements, including elements of the riot-trained Tactical Patrol Force, were rushed into both communities.

Two arrests were reported in Brooklyn and 10 in Harlem. A television crewman was said to have been injured by flying glass.

There were numerous instances of rock-throwing, looting and arson reported both in Brooklyn and in Harlem, starting around 11 P.M. and continuing early today.

Gangs of youth in both areas were reported roaming through the streets, now and then taunting policemen and firemen on duty.

The police fired several volleys of shots in the air to disperse crowds along Brooklyn's Fulton Street and Harlem's

Continued on Page 26, Column 2

Widespread Disorders

Disorders broke out in scattered parts of the nation last night after the slaying of the Rev. Dr. Martin Luther King Jr. The National Guard was called out or alerted in several cities.

In Washington, scattered but persistent looting and vandalism erupted, led for a time by Stokely Carmichael, former head of the Student Nonviolent Coordinating Commitee. All available policemen were being called to duty.

About 4,000 Tennessee National Guardsmen were ordered to duty in Nashville because of disorders.

In North Carolina, Gov. Dan K. Moore alerted the Guard in Greensboro at the request of Mayor Carson Bain. State Highway patrolmen were dispatched to Raleigh.

There were riotous outbursts

Continued on Page 26, Column 5

NEWS INDEX

	Page		Page
Books	44-45	Obituaries	47
Bridge	45	Real Estate	77
Business	67, 69, 75	Screen	50-58
Buyers	78	Ships and Air	92
Crossword	45	Society	40
Editorials	46	Sports	59-61, 67
Fashions	42	Theaters	50-58
Financial	68-76	TV and Radio	93, 95
Food	42	U. N. Proceedings	3
Man in the News	12	Wash. Proceedings	17
Music	50-58	Weather	92

News Summary and Index, Page 49

GUARD CALLED OUT

Curfew Is Ordered in Memphis, but Fires and Looting Erupt

By EARL CALDWELL
Special to The New York Times

MEMPHIS, Friday, April 5—The Rev. Dr. Martin Luther King Jr., who preached nonviolence and racial brotherhood, was fatally shot here last night by a distant gunman who then raced away and escaped.

Four thousand National Guard troops were ordered into Memphis by Gov. Buford Ellington after the 39-year-old Nobel Prize-winning civil rights leader died.

A curfew was imposed on the shocked city of 550,000 inhabitants, 40 per cent of whom are Negro.

But the police said the tragedy had been followed by incidents that included sporadic shooting, fires, bricks and bottles thrown at policemen, and looting that started in Negro districts and then spread over the city.

White Car Sought

Police Director Frank Holloman said the assassin might have been a white man who was "50 to 100 yards away in a flophouse."

Chief of Detectives W. P. Huston said a late model white Mustang was believed to have been the killer's getaway car. Its occupant was described as a bareheaded white man in his 30's, wearing a black suit and black tie.

The detective chief said the police had chased two cars near the motel where Dr. King was shot and had halted one that had two out-of-town men as occupants. The men were questioned but seemed to have nothing to do with the killing, he said.

Rifle Found Nearby

A high-powered 30.06-caliber rifle was found about a block from the scene of the shooting, on South Main Street. "We think it's the gun," Chief Huston said, reporting it would be turned over to the Federal Bureau of Investigation.

Dr. King was shot while he leaned over a second-floor railing outside his room at the Lorraine Motel. He was chatting with two friends just before starting for dinner.

One of the friends was a musician, and Dr. King had just asked him to play a Negro spiritual, "Precious Lord, Take My Hand," at a rally that was to have been held two hours later in support of striking Memphis sanitationmen.

Paul Hess, assistant adminis-

Continued on Page 24, Column 1

Archbishop Cooke Installed; President Looks On

By EDWARD B. FISKE

The Most Rev. Terence J. Cooke was installed as the seventh Roman Catholic Archbishop of New York yesterday in a historic pageant attended by the President of the United States and highlighted by prayers for the success of his peace efforts in Vietnam.

"Let us pray with all our hearts that God will inspire our President," the 47-year-old Archbishop said in his homily at St. Patrick's Cathedral.

"In the last few days, we have all admired his heroic efforts in the search for peace in Vietnam. We ask God to bless his efforts with success. May God inspire not only our President, but also other leaders and the leaders of all nations to find a way to peace."

Then the Archbishop, speaking from a white marble pulpit and surrounded by a blaze of purple, gold and scarlet robes, addressed himself directly to Mr. Johnson, who sat below him in a front pew.

The President, sitting with his hands clasped and his legs crossed, listened with

Continued on Page 38, Column 1

obvious intensity to the Archbishop's words.

"Mr. President," he said, "our hopes, our hearts, our continued prayers go with you."

Mr. Johnson, accompanied by his daughter, Mrs. Patrick J. Nugent, led a festive congregation of about 5,000 cardinals, bishops, priests, laymen, nuns, civic leaders

The New York Times (by Neal Boenzi)
President Johnson and his daughter, Mrs. Patrick J. Nugent, right, listening during yesterday's ceremonies. At left are Mrs. John F. Kennedy and Lieut. Gov. Malcolm Wilson. Security personnel are in the row between them.

Archbishop Luigi Raimondi, Apostolic Delegate to the U.S., speaking after Archbishop Terence J. Cooke was enthroned

"All the News
That's Fit to Print"

The New York Times

LATE CITY EDITION

Weather: Sunny and mild today;
fair tonight. Sunny, mild tomorrow.
Temp. range: today 50-35. Friday
62-46. Full U.S. report on Page 78.

VOL. CXVII..No. 40,250   © 1968 The New York Times Company.   NEW YORK, SATURDAY, APRIL 6, 1968   10 CENTS

ARMY TROOPS IN CAPITAL AS NEGROES RIOT; GUARD SENT INTO CHICAGO, DETROIT, BOSTON; JOHNSON ASKS A JOINT SESSION OF CONGRESS

SIEGE OF KHESANH DECLARED LIFTED; TROOPS HUNT FOE

Relief Column, Within Mile of Base, Presses Search —Helicopters Kill 50

By The Associated Press

KHESANH, South Vietnam, Saturday, April 6—The 76-day North Vietnamese siege of the Marine base at Khesanh was officially declared lifted yesterday.

United States marines and helicopter-borne Army troops today pushed toward what was described as North Vietnamese regimental headquarters south of the base.

The 20,000-man relief column reached the base and then fanned out on three sides in search of the vanishing enemy soldiers. Army helicopter units entered the base.

The sweep could take the Americans all the way to the Laotian border, less than 10 miles away, in the effort to root out the 7,000 men said to remain in an enemy force once estimated at 20,000. North Vietnam uses Laos as a staging area for attacks along South Vietnam's borders.

Gunships Attack Near Town

The United States command said that helicopter gunships of the First Cavalry Division (Airmobile), crisscrossing the skies ahead of the ground troops, killed 50 North Vietnamese late yesterday near the town of Khesanh, which is two miles south of the base.

Earlier, United States troops fought about 150 enemy soldiers four miles east of the town. Nine enemy soldiers and one American were reported killed.

The town was made an enemy command post after South Vietnamese troops and a small unit of United States marines abandoned it in January under a heavy siege.

Ten thousand civilians, mostly montagnard tribesmen, fled the town when fighting broke out. Many are in refugee camps in the coastal lowlands.

The relief column made no immediate attempt to enter the Khesanh base. Enemy gunners zeroed in on the outpost with 110 rounds of artillery and mortar fire.

Before the pressure on the

Continued on Page 2, Column 4

Hanoi Voices Doubt Over U.S. Sincerity

By Agence France-Presse

HANOI, North Vietnam, April 5—Hanoi protested today against what it called "savage bombings" of North Vietnam and "intensification of the war in South Vietnam" since President Johnson's announcement Sunday of restriction on attacks on the North.

Under the signature "Commentator," a pseudonym customarily indicating official authorship, an editorial in the party newspaper, Nhan Dan, questioned the sincerity of Mr. Johnson's avowed desire for peace.

[Despite the tone of the Hanoi editorial, Administration officials saw no indication that North Vietnam was backing away from talks with the United States. Page 5.]

The Nhan Dan editorial said: "The decision of the United

Continued on Page 3, Column 1

SOVIET ENDORSES ASSENT BY HANOI

Moscow Mentioned as Site of Talks With U.S.—China Urges Continued War

By RAYMOND H. ANDERSON
Special to The New York Times

MOSCOW, April 5 — The Soviet Government today endorsed the agreement by North Vietnam to start discussions with the United States toward a complete halt of bombing and to open the door to full-scale negotiations.

The statement came amid speculation that Moscow might be the site for a meeting between United States and North Vietnamese representatives.

Premier Aleksei N. Kosygin is cutting short his trip to Iran and will return to Moscow Sunday, one day early.

[Communist China, however, termed President Johnson's peace overture a smokescreen and urged the North Vietnamese and the Vietcong to continue fighting.]

The United States Embassy denied that it had any knowledge of arrangements for a meeting here. The United States, it was understood,

Continued on Page 4, Column 3

PRESIDENT GRAVE

Sets Day of Mourning for Dr. King—Meets Rights Leaders

President's statement and his proclamation, Page 23.

By MAX FRANKEL
Special to The New York Times

WASHINGTON, April 5 — President Johnson asked today to address a joint session of Congress no later than Monday evening so that he could propose "constructive action instead of destructive action in this hour of national need."

Gravely imploring Americans to "stand their ground to deny violence its victory" in the reaction to the slaying of the Rev. Dr. Martin Luther King Jr., the President set out to arouse the nation's conscience and to win quick action on the long-stalled major items in his domestic program.

He proclaimed Sunday a national day of mourning for Dr. King, who was shot yesterday in Memphis and died later in a hospital.

Meanwhile, Congressional leaders said that Dr. King's murder could assure passage next week of a landmark civil rights bill.

Conference Canceled

To deal with the divisiveness that he said was "tearing this nation apart," Mr. Johnson canceled the already delayed conference he had planned for this weekend in Hawaii with American military and diplomatic officials stationed in South Vietnam.

Gen. William C. Westmoreland, the American commander in the war zone, was flying to Washington instead and will probably see Mr. Johnson tomorrow morning.

The President spent almost the entire day working "to avoid catastrophe." He met with moderate Negro leaders and members of Congress and of his Administration to find ways of containing the violence, arson and looting that threatened many big cities and that spread here to within a few blocks of the White House.

He also conferred all day with officials of the District of Columbia and gave them Federal troops this evening to help restore order.

Mr. Johnson's demeanor all

Continued on Page 23, Column 1

ON DUTY IN WASHINGTON: A soldier with a machine gun and another with a rifle, left, stand guard on the steps outside the Senate chamber. Flag was lowered to half-staff in tribute to the Rev. Dr. Martin Luther King Jr.

Associated Press

MANY FIRES SET

White House Guarded by G.I.'s—14 Dead in U.S. Outbreaks

Text of proclamation and Executive order, Page 22.

By BEN A. FRANKLIN

WASHINGTON, April 5—President Johnson ordered 4,000 regular Army and National Guard troops into the nation's capital tonight to try to end riotous looting, burglarizing and burning by roving bands of Negro youths. The arson and looting began yesterday after the murder of the Rev. Dr. Martin Luther King Jr. in Memphis.

The White House announced at 5 P.M. that because the President had determined that "a condition of domestic violence and disorder" existed, he had issued a proclamation and an Executive order mobilizing combat-equipped troops in Washington. Some of the troops were sent to guard the Capitol and the White House.

Reinforcements numbering 2,500 riot-trained soldiers — a brigade of the 82d Airborne Division from Ft. Bragg, N. C.— were airlifted to nearby Andrews Air Force Base, to be held in reserve this weekend.

Guard Called In Other Cities

The National Guard also was called out in a half-dozen other cities in an effort to stem disorders or guard against them—Chicago, Detroit, Boston, Jackson, Miss., Raleigh, N. C., and Tallahassee, Fla.

The death toll from the violence stemming from Dr. King's assassination stood at a total of 14 tonight. Besides five deaths in Washington, they included seven in Chicago, one in Detroit and one in Tallahassee.

Mayor Walter E. Washington, who is a Negro, declared a 13-hour curfew, from 5:30 P.M. to 6:30 A.M. The Mayor's emergency order halted the sale of liquor and forbade the sale, transportation or possession of firearms, explosives or flammable liquids.

At midnight, the police reported five dead, all but one of them Negroes, in 28 hours of disorders in this city of about 800,000, 63 per cent of them Negroes. Four Negroes were killed today, including two suspected looters, one of them 14 years old, who were shot to death by policemen in separate isolated encounters across the Anacostia River, far from the areas of general disorders. The two other Negro deaths today were described as apparently the result of accidents.

The white man, George Fletcher, 28, of suburban Wood-

Continued on Page 22, Column 1

New York Volatile As Anger and Fear Set a Tense Mood

By MICHAEL STERN

A volatile mood of deep sorrow, fist-shaking anger and undefined fear settled on the city yesterday as it absorbed the impact of the death of the Rev. Dr. Martin Luther King Jr.

Many schools, colleges, offices and shops closed early partly out of respect for the memory of the slain civil rights leader, and partly because of reports that new outbreaks of violence would erupt.

The city's bustling waterfront grew still at noon as seamen and longshoremen stopped work as a tribute to Dr. King. The stoppage was announced by the International Longshoremen's Association and the National Maritime Union.

Seven thousand to eight thousand high school and college students released from classes assembled at a memorial rally for Dr. King at the

Continued on Page 26, Column 5

OUTBREAKS HERE RELATIVELY MILD

Negro Areas Are Quiet, but Bands of Young Vandals Roam Midtown Streets

By SYLVAN FOX

The streets of Harlem and Bedford-Stuyvesant were generally calm last night after a burst of violence and looting early yesterday in the wake of the assassination of the Rev. Dr. Martin Luther King Jr. in Memphis.

Half of the armed guardsmen, in fatigues and riot helmets, began patrolling glass-littered West Side streets about 10 P.M. The rest stood by in armories.

About 100 city buses were damaged by bricks and rocks. Drivers, passengers, policemen, firemen, motorists and pedestrians were among at least 75 persons injured.

Mother Beaten

Mrs. Bernadine Laskow, mother of three children, was pulled from her car by Negro youths and beaten. Some white pedestrians who were in the Negro slum suffered the same treatment.

Dozens of automobiles that entered the 12-square-mile riot zone emerged with smashed windows and dented hoods. In some blocks all store windows were boarded or broken.

Cab drivers refused to enter

Continued on Page 23, Column 8

7 Die as Fires and Looting Spread in Chicago Rioting

By DONALD JANSON
Special to The New York Times

CHICAGO, Saturday, April 6—Six thousand National Guard troops were called up yesterday as rioters pillaged stores along a two-mile stretch of Madison Street in the Negro West Side. Seven Negroes were killed and about 550 arrested, the police reported, as the violence and ransacking tapered off late last night.

Continued on Page 26, Column 6

EUROPE DISMAYED, FEARFUL FOR U.S.

Murder of Dr. King Evokes Doubts Over Stability of the American Society

By ANTHONY LEWIS
Special to The New York Times

LONDON, April 5—The murder of the Rev. Dr. Martin Luther King Jr. evoked in Europe today a reaction of intense horror at the deed and of fear for the stability of American society.

In governments, in the press and among the public, there were expressions of sympathy that went beyond formalities. Dr. King was deeply admired in Europe and held up as a symbol of hope for America.

All the concerns about the United States and its leadership that have grown here in recent years—concerns especially about the war in Vietnam and the violence in America—were fed by the killing of the civil rights leader in Memphis last night.

Everywhere in Europe, people linked Dr. King's death with the assassination of President Kennedy in 1963. That two men so admired here could so similarly be killed intensified doubts about the character of America today.

"From John Fitzgerald Kennedy to Martin Luther King,"

Continued on Page 28, Column 3

Clark Is Sure Killer Will Soon Be Seized

By MARTIN WALDRON
Special to The New York Times

MEMPHIS, Tenn., April 5—Attorney General Ramsey Clark said today that he was "confident" of a quick solution to the assassination here yesterday of the Rev. Dr. Martin Luther King Jr.

A source close to the intensive manhunt said that agents of the Federal Bureau of Investigation were close to making an arrest.

The Attorney General, who flew here this morning at the order of President Johnson with other top officials of the Justice Department, told a news conference that the F.B.I. was searching for the killer in several states.

He said that the killer, who was believed to have escaped in a white Mustang automobile,

Continued on Page 24, Column 1

Negroes Strive to Ease Tensions; False Rumors Raise City's Fears

Militants Join Effort

By THOMAS A. JOHNSON

At the height of the violence in Harlem early yesterday morning, about 30 young Negro militants fanned out from Jay's Bar and Grill on 125th Street near Eighth Avenue and tried to persuade other Negroes to stop breaking windows, looting and setting fires.

This particular group was made up of members of Harlem CORE, and they were only a part of the many hundreds of Negroes living in the violence-torn areas of Harlem and Brooklyn who worked actively to stop the disorders.

The volunteer peace-keepers tried to end the violence by a variety of methods and for a variety of reasons.

Some are church groups,

Continued on Page 26, Column 1

Racial Unrest Exaggerated

By MURRAY SCHUMACH

The city was flooded yesterday with wild and unfounded rumors that exceeded the amount of violence and heightened widespread fears of racial riots.

In some instances, the reports became so persistent that corporations allowed employes, particularly women, to leave for home early in the afternoon.

The untrue reports included subway disruptions, bombings, mass assaults and imposition of a citywide curfew. Almost any kind of holdup, apparently, was associated in the minds of some rumor-mongers with racial disturbances and was then exaggerated.

Barry H. Gottehrer, the head

Continued on Page 28, Column 1

MARCHING DOWN BROADWAY: Demonstrators protesting the slaying of the Rev. Dr. Martin Luther King Jr. crossing 23d Street on the way to City Hall yesterday. The march began after a memorial ceremony in Central Park.

The New York Times (by Barton Silverman)

If you live South of 14th St. You'll like "LOST" even Baltimore Ham.

The New York Times

LATE CITY EDITION

Weather: Sunny, warm today; fair,
continued warm tonight, tomorrow.
Temp. range 88–62; Wed.
83–59. Temp.-Hum. Index 75; Wed.
74. Full U.S. report on Page 94.

VOL. CXVII..No. 40,311   © 1968 The New York Times Company.   NEW YORK, THURSDAY, JUNE 6, 1968   10 CENTS

KENNEDY IS DEAD, VICTIM OF ASSASSIN; SUSPECT, ARAB IMMIGRANT, ARRAIGNED; JOHNSON APPOINTS PANEL ON VIOLENCE

MARCUS TESTIFIES DE SAPIO HAD ROLE IN A CON ED DEAL

Says Itkin Sought Delay of Permit to Aid Own Scheme With Ex-Tammany Head

By BARNARD L. COLLIER

Former Water Commissioner James L. Marcus testified yesterday that he had been asked to delay approval of a permit to Consolidated Edison while the former Tammany Hall leader, Carmine G. De Sapio, was trying to make a deal with the utility company.

Marcus testified that the request came last September from his business partner, Herbert Itkin, who was in turn trying to negotiate a deal with Mr. De Sapio.

The testimony was elicited from Marcus under cross-examination on the third day of a Federal bribery conspiracy trial that has been marked by the mention in Marcus's testimony of several prominent members of both the Republican and Democratic parties.

Marcus was asked if there was a time when he, as Commissioner of Water Supply, Gas and Electricity, had "done business" with Con Edison. His answer was yes.

Says Itkin Asked Delay

"Itkin came to me," he said, "and said that Con Ed wanted a permit to increase the voltage on one of their power lines for 20 miles." He added that his approval as Commissioner was needed.

"Itkin said I should hold up for a while because he was negotiating with Carmine De Sapio, who was negotiating with Con Ed."

Marcus said that Mr. Itkin asked him to delay the approval for "a few weeks."

At that point in the trial, which came at about 4:40 P.M., Herman Zoloto, a lawyer representing Henry Fried, a contractor, and Mr. Fried's company, S. T. Grand, Inc., shouted:

"You're way ahead of your story, Mr. Marcus!"

Judge Edward Weinfeld broke in and scolded Mr. Zoloto for "a highly improper re-

Continued on Page 41, Column 1

TRANSIT PACKAGE SUBMITTED TO CITY

M.T.A. Seeks Approval of 8 New Subway Routes

By EMANUEL PERLMUTTER

A $1.27-billion package of subway and commuter railroad additions and improvements was submitted to the Board of Estimate and Mayor Lindsay yesterday.

The program was presented by the Metropolitan Transportation Authority and the New York City Transit Authority with a request for speedy city agreement on the new routes and engineering designs.

The over-all plan, which would take 10 years to complete, consists of eight new subway routes, including a Second Avenue subway, and Long Island Rail Road connections to the East Side of Manhattan and to Kennedy International Airport.

City approval of the routes and designs is a first step before application can be made for $60-million set aside by the Legislature for the engineering design of the mass transportation program presented by the Metropolitan Transportation

Continued on Page 55, Column 1

France Will Meet Tariff Deadline; Strikes Dwindling

By HENRY TANNER
Special to The New York Times

PARIS, June 5 — Maurice Couve de Murville told France's partners in the Common Market today that despite the nationwide strike now ,coming to a close, the Government would honor the July 1 deadline for the abolition of remaining tariffs in the European trade bloc.

Today workers in the nationalized railroad company, the Paris transit system, the post and telegraph offices and other public administration voted to go back to work. Trains are expected to start running tomorrow on several major national lines and the Paris subways.

By the end of the week, it is expected, the nationwide strike, now in its 18th day, will be all but ended. Mr. Couve de Murville, who is the new Minister of Economy and Finance, also reassured his countrymen

Continued on Page 15, Column 1

JERUSALEM POLICE CLASH WITH ARABS

Israelis Halt Procession on Anniversary of War—U.N. Council Meets on Fighting

Special to The New York Times

JERUSALEM, June 5—A silent Arab procession commemorating the first anniversary of the Arab-Israeli war erupted into a violent clash today when Isareli policemen intercepted the marchers at the edge of the walled Old City of Jerusalem.

The clash was the most violent aspect of a widespread protest in which Arabs shuttered shops and other businesses here and elsewhere on the west bank of the Jordan and in the occupied Gaza Strip. It came after a day-long battle yesterday across the Jordan between the Israelis and Jordanians, in which aircraft and artillery were used.

[The United Nations Security Council met Wednesday at the urgent request of Israel and Jordan to consider recurrent hostilities along their cease-fire line. It postponed debate, probably until Thursday. Page 3.]

In the west-bank towns of Nablus, Jenin and Tulkarm, all centers of Arab nationalism, the general strike was 100 per cent effective. All stores, cafes and offices were closed, public transportation ceased and the streets were virtually devoid of traffic and pedestrians. Schools throughout the west bank and Gaza Strip had no

Continued on Page 2, Column 4

Italy's Cabinet Quits As Parliament Opens

By ROBERT C. DOTY
Special to The New York Times

ROME, June 5—Premier Aldo Moro and his center-left coalition Government, which has ruled Italy for four and a half years, resigned tonight with the convening of the new parliament, the fifth since World War II.

President Giuseppe Saragat asked Mr. Moro and his ministers to remain in office as a caretaker government while the search for a new government, which may be arduous, goes on.

Resignation of the government with the convening of a new parliament is automatic. But any hope that the Moro

Continued on Page 14, Column 3

6 IN RACE GUARDED

Secret Service Given Campaign Security Task by President

Text of the Johnson speech is printed on Page 23.

By MAX FRANKEL

WASHINGTON, June 5—For the second time in five years, Lyndon B. Johnson undertook today, amid national shock and outrage, to offer protection, prayer, comfort and assistance to his political rivals in the Kennedy family and then to try to heal the country's political and psychological wounds.

The President's first reaction to the shooting of Senator Robert F. Kennedy this morning was that "there are no words equal to the horror of this tragedy."

But tonight, in an emotional and at times even angry statement on television, he pleaded with all Americans to end the violence in their midst once and for all, to tolerate neither hatred nor the preaching of violence and to resolve to live under the law.

A Guard for Candidates

Mr. Johnson said he was appointing a commission of distinguished citizens to investigate both the circumstances and the causes of physical violence of all kinds in the United States, in the hope that the nation can learn "how we can stop it".

Earlier he had moved swiftly to provide protective Secret Service details to the six announced Presidential candidates of major parties, other than Vice President Humphrey, who already has such protection because of his office.

Meanwhile, in the House of Representatives, a vote of 317 to 60 cleared the way for the House to accept the Senate version of an anticrime bill, including controls over the interstate sale of hand guns. The vote rejected a move to send the legislation to a Senate-House conference.

Members of Commission

To the commission Mr. Johnson named Milton Eisenhower, former president of Johns Hopkins University; Archbishop Terence J. Cooke of New York; Albert Jenner, Chicago lawyer who worked for the commission that investigated the assassination of President Kennedy; former Ambassador Patricia Harris; Eric Hoffer, the longshoreman-turned-philosopher; Senators Philip Hart, Democrat of Michigan, and Roman L. Hruska, Republican of Nebraska; Representative Hale Boggs, Democrat of Louisiana, majority whip in the House; Representative William M. McCulloch, Republican of Ohio, and Federal Judge Leon Higginbotham of Philadelphia.

The President described himself as shocked, dismayed and deeply disturbed, as he knew all Americans were, by the shooting, which he described as the "latest spectacular example" of lawlessness and violence.

"So let us, for God's sake, re-

Continued on Page 23, Column 1

AFTER THE SHOOTING: Senator Kennedy's wife, Ethel, bends over him as a man checks pulse to determine condition

HANOI INSISTS U.S. HALT ITS BOMBING

Aides Call Talks Response to Johnson—Suspicion Voiced of a Plot Against Kennedy

By HEDRICK SMITH
Special to The New York Times

PARIS, June 5—North Vietnamese negotiators contended today that Hanoi had responded to President Johnson's restriction of American air attacks on the north by entering official talks here. They asserted that the next move, a total halt in bombing, was up to the United States.

The North Vietnamese argument, put forward in the seventh negotiating session between the two sides since May 13, produced one of the sharpest exchanges since the Vietnam talks began here.

The North Vietnamese made no direct comment on the shooting of Senator Robert F. Kennedy, but circles close to the delegation voiced suspicions in private, asking if the attack was not part of a conspiracy by the Johnson Administration. [Page 33.]

Near the end of today's session at the former Majestic Hotel, Hanoi's chief representative, Xuan Thuy, leaned across the negotiating table and asked the American delegates bluntly:

"When will the United States unconditionally cease the bombing and all other acts of war against the Democratic Republic of Vietnam so that other questions can be discussed?"

In response, W. Averell Har-

Continued on Page 8, Column 4

Big Board Weighs 4 Special Closings

By VARTANIG G. VARTAN

A securities industry panel recommended yesterday that the New York Stock Exchange, the American Stock Exchange and the over-the-counter market close down for four days over the next month to cope with the deluge of paperwork buried in brokerage offices.

The panel proposed closing the securities markets for three Wednesdays—June 12, 19 and 26—as well as Friday, July 5.

The board of governors of the New York Stock Exchange will meet this afternoon to consider the proposal. Wall Street sources said that in view of the critical situation city governors are expected to accept the pro-

Continued on Page 73, Column 4

ROBERT F. KENNEDY
The New York Times (by George Tames)

A Pall Over Politics

Murder Raises Grave Questions for Presidency Races Now and in Future

By TOM WICKER
Special to The New York Times

WASHINGTON, Thursday, June 6—The murder of Robert F. Kennedy shattered the 1968 Presidential campaign and lowered a pall of uncertainty over the years to come. For the immediate future, it may well mean emphasis to one of Robert Kennedy's major political themes—Democrats and Republicans of the present front-running candidates — Vice President Humphrey and Richard Nixon. Kennedy's death—the first assassination of an American Presidential candidate—might lead to changes in campaigning practices, even to the fundamental manner in which the nation chooses its President.

The most immediate effect, however, was that for the third —and most harrowing—time a shock wave of unexpected events had completely altered the shape of the 1968 campaign.

The first came on March 12 when Senator Eugene J. McCarthy of Minnesota won 42 per cent of the Democratic vote in the New Hampshire primary, and Mr. Kennedy immediately thereafter became an active candidate.

The second transformation

Continued on Page 25, Column 6

SURGERY IN VAIN

President Calls Death Tragedy, Proclaims a Day of Mourning

Texts of the medical reports appear on Page 22.

By GLADWIN HILL
Special to The New York Times

LOS ANGELES, Thursday, June 6—Senator Robert F. Kennedy, the brother of a murdered President, died at 1:44 A.M. today of an assassin's shots.

The New York Senator was wounded more than 20 hours earlier, moments after he had made his victory statement in the California primary.

At his side when he died today in Good Samaritan Hospital were his wife, Ethel; his sisters, Mrs. Stephen Smith and Mrs. Patricia Lawford; his brother-in-law, Stephen Smith; and his sister-in-law, Mrs. John F. Kennedy, whose husband was assassinated 4½ years ago in Dallas.

In Washington, President Johnson issued a statement calling the death a tragedy. He proclaimed next Sunday a national day of mourning.

The Final Report

Hopes had risen slightly when more than eight hours went by without a new medical bulletin on the stricken Senator, but the grimness of the final announcement was signaled when Frank Mankiewicz, Mr. Kennedy's press secretary, walked slowly down the street in front of the hospital toward the littered gymnasium that served as press headquarters.

Mr. Mankiewicz bit his lip. His shoulders slumped.

He stepped to a lectern in front of a green-tinted chalkboard and bowed his head for a moment while the television lights snapped on.

Then, at one minute before 2 A.M., he told of the death of Mr. Kennedy.

Following is the text of the statement from Mr. Mankiewicz:

"I have a short announcement to read which I will read at this time. Senator Robert Francis Kennedy died at 1:44 A.M. today, June 6, 1968. With

Continued on Page 20, Column 1

NOTES ON KENNEDY IN SUSPECT'S HOME

Cite 'Necessity' to Murder Senator Before June 5, Anniversary of War

By PETER KIHSS

A notebook found in the Pasadena home of Sirhan Bishara Sirhan had "a direct reference to the necessity to assassinate Senator Kennedy before June 5, 1968," Mayor Samuel W. Yorty of Los Angeles said last night.

The date was the first anniversary of the six-day war, in which Israeli forces smashed those of the United Arab Republic, Syria and Jordan.

Sirhan, a 24-year-old Christian Arab, who has described himself as a Jerusalem-born Jordanian, is being held in the shooting of the New York Senator.

Justice Department records indicated that Sirhan came to the United States with his family in January of 1957 as immigrants, less than three months after the Suez war in 1956. Sirhan was 12 at the time.

The family quickly broke up in discord, the father staying in New York to work as a plumber and then going back to their former Palestine home, the mother taking five children to California, where a sixth child immigrated later.

Sirhan was described yesterday by Police Chief Thomas Reddin of Los Angeles as "very cool, very calm, very stable and quite lucid."

He was quoted as having said,

Continued on Page 21, Column 6

KUCHEL UNSEATED AS RAFFERTY WINS

Conservative Beats Senator in California's Primary

By LAWRENCE E. DAVIES
Special to The New York Times

LOS ANGELES, June 5—Dr. Max Rafferty, State Superintendent of Public Instruction, defeated Senator Thomas H. Kuchel in the Republican senatorial primary in California yesterday, cutting short Mr. Kuchel's 15-year career in the Senate.

Returns from 20,714 of 21,-301 precincts gave:

Rafferty 1,056,038 50%
Kuchel 985,097 47%

As the vote count continued today, it became apparent that the conservative Republicanism of Southern California had carried Dr. Rafferty to victory over the heretofore unbeatable Republican whip in the Senate.

Mr. Kuchel, an outspoken liberal-moderate who had made many political extremists such as the John Birch Society members

Continued on Page 23, Column 3

Father of Suspect 'Sickened' by News

By TERENCE SMITH
Special to The New York Times

ET TAIYIBA, Israeli-Occupied Jordan, Thursday, June 6—Bishara Sirhan's hands trembled as he talked about his son Sirhan Bishara Sirhan, the accused assailant of Senator Robert F. Kennedy.

Mr. Sirhan dwelled on the tragedy of the shooting. He finally said: "This news made me sick when I heard it. If my son has done this dirty thing, then let them hang him."

Mr. Sirhan's memories of his five sons are those of 10 years ago, when he last saw them and their mother. After years of fierce family quarrels, Bishara

Continued on Page 21, Column 3

The New York Times

LATE CITY EDITION

Weather: Sunny, warm today; fair, seasonable tonight and tomorrow. Temp. range: today 89-73; Tuesday 91-72. Temp.-Hum. Index yesterday 81. Complete U.S. report on Page 90.

VOL. CXVII..No. 40,387 © 1968 The New York Times Company. NEW YORK, WEDNESDAY, AUGUST 21, 1968 10 CENTS

CZECHOSLOVAKIA INVADED BY RUSSIANS AND FOUR OTHER WARSAW PACT FORCES; THEY OPEN FIRE ON CROWDS IN PRAGUE

13 INDICTED HERE IN RIGGING OF BIDS ON UTILITY WORK

Contracts Worth 49-Million Involved—14 Construction Companies Also Named

By MARTIN TOLCHIN

Fourteen major construction companies, 12 top corporate executives and one employe were indicted here yesterday on charges of rigging bids on utilities contracts totaling $49.8-million.

The defendants were accused of deciding among themselves who would be low bidder in the contracts with Consolidated Edison, the Brooklyn Union Gas Company, and the Empire City Subway Company —the latter a subsidiary of the New York Telephone Company.

The indictments charge that the defendants then accommodated the selected low bidder by submitting higher bids.

The companies included such important contractors as Lipsett, Inc., a leading demolition company that razed Pennsylvania Station, the Savoy Plaza Hotel and the Third Avenue El; the Slattery Contracting Company, which held the general contract for excavating the site of United Nations Headquarters and built subway spurs and the Lincoln Center reflecting pool, and the Thomas Crimmins Contracting Company, which did the excavation for numerous skyscrapers.

1959 Activities Covered

The companies received contracts to dig trenches for electrical conduits and gas mains and for paving work. The contracts totaled $49,788,165.

The four indictments, with a total of 28 counts, were an outgrowth of the investigation of James L. Marcus, former City Water Commissioner, who pleaded guilty in Federal court to receiving a $40,000 kickback on a city reservoir cleaning contract.

"Our interest in Marcus and [Herbert] Itkin led us to the inquiry that led to these indictments," Frank S. Hogan, New York County District Attorney, said.

He noted that the indictments alleged activities in 1959, "before the community at large was aware of Marcus and Itkin."

Continued on Page 35, Column 3

OUTLOOK GUARDED FOR EISENHOWER

His Condition Still Critical Despite 'Favorable Trend'

By FELIX BELAIR Jr.
Special to The New York Times

WASHINGTON, Aug. 20 — Former President Dwight D. Eisenhower clung resolutely to life today, but with a fragile grip that his doctors acknowledged could loosen at any time.

The condition of the 77-year-old General of the Army still was listed as "critical" and the outlook for his survival as "guarded." His doctors have used this term to mean uncertain or unpredictable.

A bulletin issued at Walter Reed Army Medical Center about 11 A.M. mentioned the development of a "favorable trend" in the pattern of abnormal heart rhythm.

The episodes of rapid irregularity in the heartbeat persisted, the doctors reported, but they were isolated and did not involve the sustained fibrillating, or fluttering, reported prior to last night.

At the time of the morning

Continued on Page 13, Column 1

Democrats Debate Position on the War in Vietnam

Secretary of State Rusk defended the Administration's policies at the hearing.
The New York Times

Senator George S. McGovern of South Dakota was critical of the Administration.
Associated Press

Kenneth P. O'Donnell, left, who was an aide to President Kennedy, talks with Senator J. W. Fulbright, standing right, at the platform hearing. The Senator spoke against the war.
The New York Times (by George Tames)

NIXON INCREASES GALLUP POLL LEAD

Tops Humphrey, 45% to 29, and Maintains His Margin Over McCarthy, 42 to 37

Special to The New York Times

PRINCETON, N. J., Aug. 20 —Richard M. Nixon stretched a slim mid-July edge over Vice President Humphrey to a 45-to-29 per cent lead in voter preference immediately following the Republican National Convention, according to the latest Gallup Poll.

Against Senator Eugene J. McCarthy—Mr. Humphrey's chief rival for the Democratic Presidential nomination—Mr. Nixon held a 42-to-37 per cent lead, almost the same margin he had in the previous test in mid-July.

Mr. Nixon's improved advantage over the Vice President was caused more by Mr. Humphrey's losses than by gains by Mr. Nixon. The Republican nominee was 5 percentage points higher than the preconvention survey, while Mr. Humphrey was 9 points lower.

Support for the independent candidacy of George C. Wallace of Alabama held up. He polled 18 per cent in the Nixon-Humphrey-Wallace test and 16 per cent in the Nixon-McCarthy-Wallace post-convention survey.

Continued on Page 32, Column 2

Democrats to Seat Mississippi Rebels

By MAX FRANKEL

CHICAGO, Aug. 20—Mississippi's regular delegation to the Democratic National Convention was barred from its seats tonight by an overwhelming vote of the Credentials Committee on the ground that it had failed to meet national standards to assure the full participation of Negroes in the political process.

A biracial delegation including many members who have fought many years for this moment will be seated in place of the regulars.

At the same time, the Credentials Committee rejected by various formulas the delegate

Continued on Page 32, Column 6

Guard Is Called Up To Protect Chicago During Convention

By DONALD JANSON
Special to The New York Times

CHICAGO, Aug. 20—Gov. Samuel H. Shapiro called up the National Guard today to keep order in the city during the Democratic National Convention.

At the request of Mayor Richard J. Daley, the Governor ordered 5,649 Illinois National Guardsmen to round-the-clock duty in Chicago beginning Friday to head off threats of "tumult, riot or mob disorder."

Meanwhile, an Army spokesman in Washington confirmed in a telephone interview that about 6,000 regular Army troops received rigorous riot-control training at Fort Hood, Tex., last week as a precautionary measure.

That exercise, he said, was not Operation Jackson Park, after the park in Chicago

Continued on Page 32, Column 2

KENNEDY BACKERS OFFER WAR PLANK

But McCarthy Group Balks at Compromise—Rusk Is for General Statement

Text of plank and excerpts from statement, Page 33.

By JOHN W. FINNEY

WASHINGTON, Aug. 20—Supporters of the late Senator Robert F. Kennedy circulated in the Democratic platform committee today a compromise dovish plan on Vietnam calling for a halt in the bombing of North Vietnam, a cease-fire and negotiations between the Saigon Government and the National Liberation Front, the political arm of the Vietcong.

In the bitter fight developing within the platform committee, the proposed plank is designed to provide a common front for supporters of Senator Eugene J. McCarthy, Senator George S. McGovern and Senator Kennedy.

For the moment, however, some difficulty was being encountered in winning the approval of some McCarthy partisans, who were holding out for a plank that would be more critical of the Administration.

As the doves began to mount a concerted attack on the Administration's Vietnam policy, Secretary of State Dean Rusk was called in to defend the Administration position. Mr. Rusk,

Continued on Page 33, Column 2

SOVIET EXPLAINS

Says Its Troops Moved at the Request of Czechoslovaks

By RAYMOND H. ANDERSON
Special to The New York Times

MOSCOW, Wednesday, Aug. 21 — Moscow announced this morning that troops from the Soviet Union and four other Communist countries had invaded Czechoslovakia at the request of the "party and Government leaders of the Czechoslovak Socialist Republic."

The announcement followed unofficial information here that Alexander Dubcek, the reform leader of the Czechoslovak party Presidium, had been overthrown.

In a statement authorized by the Soviet Government, the official press agency, Tass, declared at 7:30 A.M. Moscow time (12:30 A.M., New York time) that Czechoslovakia had come under a threat from "counterrevolutionary forces" involved in a collusion with foreign forces hostile to socialism.

Friendship Stressed

Tass said that troops from Bulgaria, East Germany, Hungary, Poland and the Soviet Union, acting from motivations of "inseparable friendship and cooperation," entered Czechoslovakia early this morning.

The troops will be withdrawn as soon as the threat to Czechoslovakia and neighboring Communist countries has been eliminated, according to Tass.

"The actions that are being taken are not directed against any state and in no measure infringe state interests of anybody," the statement said. "They serve the purpose of peace and have been prompted by concern for its consolidation."

"The fraternal countries firmly and resolutely counterpose their unbreakable solidarity to any threat from outside," the Soviet explanation continued. "Nobody will ever be allowed to wrest a single link from the community of Socialist states."

Polemics Resumed

The handwriting was on the wall for the Czechoslovak reform regime last Friday when the Soviet press abruptly resumed its bitter polemics against the country.

Czechoslovakia's seven-month-old experiment with democracy under Communist rule was explicitly doomed yesterday when the Soviet Communist party warned in an editorial that imperial intrigues must be "nipped in the bud."

Rumors swept Moscow yesterday that the Soviet party's Central Committee had met in secret session, presumably to endorse intervention. Official sources insisted, however, that

Continued on Page 14, Column 6

13 Points in Delta Are Shelled by Foe

By JOSEPH B. TREASTER
Special to The New York Times

SAIGON, South Vietnam, Wednesday, Aug. 21 — The Vietcong shelled 13 cities and military installations in the Mekong Delta this morning, extending their latest wave of attacks on South Vietnam's southern-most region.

Seven of the shellings were followed by ground attacks.

Initial reports were sketchy, but a United States military spokesman said that allied casualties and damage in all of the attacks appeared to be light.

To the north, allied troops are making an increasing number of forays into the southern

Continued on Page 4, Column 3

The New York Times Aug. 21, 1968
FIVE-POWER INVASION: Soviet planes carried troops into Prague (cross). Ground forces of bloc crossed Czechoslovak borders that are indicated by heavy line.

Versions of the Two Sides

Following are the texts of the Prague radio announcement of the Soviet-bloc invasion of Czechoslovakia, as monitored in Washington, and of a Soviet statement distributed in New York by Tass, the Soviet press agency.

Czechoslovak Radio Broadcast

To the entire people of the Czechoslovak Socialist Republic:

Yesterday, on 20 August, around 2300 [11 P.M.], troops of the Soviet Union, Polish People's Republic, the G.D.R. [East Germany], the Hungarian People's Republic and the Bulgarian People's Republic crossed the frontiers of the Czechoslovak Socialist Republic.

This happened without the knowledge of the President of the Republic, the Chairman of the National Assembly, the Premier, or the First Secretary of the Czechoslovak Communist party Central Committee.

In the evening hours the Presidium of the Czechoslovak Communist party Central Committee [had] held a session and discussed preparations for the 14th Czechoslovak Communist party congress.

The Czechoslovak Communist party Central Committee Presidium appeals to all citizens of our republic to maintain calm and not to offer resistance to the troops on the march. Our army, security corps and people's militia have not received the command to defend the country.

The Czechoslovak Communist party Central Committee Presidium regard this act as contrary not only to the fundamental principles of relations between Socialist states but also as contrary to the principles of international law.

All leading functionaries of the state, the Communist party and the National Front: Remain in your functions as representatives of the people, elected to the laws of the Czechoslovak Socialist Republic.

Constitutional functionaries are immediately convening a session of the National Assembly of our republic, and the Presidium is at the same time convening a plenum of the Central Committee to discuss the situation that has arisen.

PRESIDIUM OF THE CZECHOSLOVAK
COMMUNIST PARTY CENTRAL COMMITTEE.

Announcement by Moscow

Tass is authorized to state that party and Government leaders of the Czechoslovak Socialist Republic have asked the Soviet Union and other allied states to render the fraternal Czechoslovak people urgent assistance, including assistance with armed forces. This request was brought about by the threat which has arisen to the Socialist system existing in Czechoslovakia and to the statehood established by the Con-

Continued on Page 14, Column 2

Soviet Turns Back Clock

By JAMES RESTON

The Soviet invasion of Czechoslovakia has transformed world and American politics.

It occurred in the middle of the American Presidential election of 1968, as the Soviet invasion of Hungary took place during the Eisenhower-Stevenson Presidential election of 1956. The Soviet Union moved on Prague while the United States was preoccupied in Vietnam, as they moved on Budapest in 1956 while the British and French were preoccupied with the invasion of Suez. The latest move by Moscow startled Washington just as officials were convening on new moves to reach an understanding with the Soviet Union on Vietnam.

Washington was prepared for a dramatic move by the Soviet Union against the new liberal regime in Prague, but not for anything quite so bold as an invasion by the Red Army.

The first impression of the crisis was that this Soviet intervention in Czechoslovakia, like the first one at the end of World War II, would increase

It had been observing closely the increasingly violent attacks on the Czechoslovak Government in the Soviet press, and Under Secretary of State Charles E. Bohlen, former United States Ambassador to the Soviet Union and France, had warned of the possibility of a coup d'état, followed by Soviet military intervention in Czechoslovakia. But a direct invasion at this time was discounted.

In fact, the Johnson Administration, under attack on its Vietnam policy just before the Democratic Presidential nominating convention next week in Chicago, was discussing new moves to enlist the help of the Soviet Union for a compromise in Vietnam when the Red Army moved.

News Analysis

There was no indication either of the meetings of what course the United States would take in this crisis, which clearly came as a stunning surprise here.

During the recent weeks of tension around Czechoslovakia, the Administration has insistently maintained a hands-off attitude, arguing that any gestures of support from Washington would only complicate the Prague regime's status in the Communist camp. Any move to exploit the Soviet di-

Continued on Page 15, Column 1

TANKS ENTER CITY

Deaths Are Reported —Troops Surround Offices of Party

By TAD SZULC
Special to The New York Times

PRAGUE, Wednesday, Aug. 21—Czechoslovakia was occupied early today by troops of the Soviet Union and four of its Warsaw Pact allies in a series of swift land and air movements.

Airborne Soviet troops and paratroopers surrounded the building of the Communist party Central Committee, along with five tanks. At least 25 tanks were seen in the city.

Several persons were reported killed early this morning. Unconfirmed reports said that two Czechoslovak soldiers and a woman were killed by Bulgarian tank fire in front of the Prague radio building shortly before the station was captured and went off the air.

[Soviet troops began shooting at Czechoslovak demonstrators outside the Prague radio building at 7:25 A.M., Reuters reported. C.T.K., the Czechoslovak press agency, was quoted by United Press International as having said that citizens were throwing themselves in front of the tanks in an attempt to block the seizure of the city.]

Move a Surprise

The Soviet move caught Czechoslovaks by surprise, although all day yesterday there were indications of new tensions.

Confusion was caused in the capital by leaflets dropped from unidentified aircraft asserting that Antonin Novotny, the President deposed in March by the Communist liberals, had been pushed out by a "clique." The leaflets said that Mr. Novotny remained the country's legal President.

At 5 A.M. the Prague radio, still in the hands of adherents of the Communist liberals, broadcast a dramatic appeal to the population in the name of Alexander Dubcek, the party

Continued on Page 14, Column 1

JOHNSON SUMMONS SECURITY COUNCIL

Calls Emergency Session After Seeing Soviet Envoy

By B. DRUMMOND AYRES JR.
Special to The New York Times

WASHINGTON, Aug. 20—President Johnson met with the National Security Council in an emergency session tonight to discuss the invasion of Czechoslovakia after he received a visit from the Soviet Ambassador.

The Council meeting, which was held in the Cabinet Room in the West Wing of the White House, began at 10:15 P.M. and lasted for 55 minutes.

It was followed by a 15-minute meeting at the State Department between the Soviet Ambassador, Anatoly F. Dobrynin, and Secretary of State Dean Rusk.

There was no indication after either of the meetings of what course the United States

Continued on Page 15, Column 1

NEWS INDEX

	Page		Page
Books	43	Obituaries	43
Bridge	42	Real Estate	42, 48
Business	60-70	Ships and Air	84
Buyers	44	Society	40
Editorials	50	Sports	52-59
Fashions	50	Theaters	36-41
Financial	61-69	TV and Radio	90
Food	50	Weather	90
Letters	44		

News Summary and Index, Page 47

Continued on Page 34, Column 2

"All the News That's Fit to Print"

The New York Times

LATE CITY EDITION

Weather: Rain today and tonight. Cloudy, showers likely tomorrow. Temp. range: today 52-48; Wed. 54-45. Full U.S. report on Page 93.

VOL. CXVIII..No. 40,465

© 1968 The New York Times Company.

NEW YORK, THURSDAY, NOVEMBER 7, 1968

10 CENTS

NIXON WINS BY A THIN MARGIN, PLEADS FOR REUNITED NATION

NIXON'S ELECTION EXPECTED TO SLOW PARIS NEGOTIATION

Allied Diplomats Suggest All Sides May Adopt a Wait-and-See Stance

By HEDRICK SMITH
Special to The New York Times

PARIS, Nov. 6 — Allied diplomats suggested tonight that Richard M. Nixon's election victory would add, at least temporarily, to the delays and complications of getting meaningful Vietnam peace negotiations under way.

The American, the North Vietnamese and the National Liberation Front delegations here had no comment on the election results.

But allied diplomats close to the talks suggested that the Republican victory would probably bring eventual changes in the American negotiating team, encourage delays by the South Vietnamese Government, and induce a wait-and-see attitude by all sides until Mr. Nixon's own approach to the talks became clearer.

The uncertainty about the future relationship between the outgoing Johnson Administration and Mr. Nixon is considered the primary complicating factor.

Eyes on Saigon

"Everybody has to see how Nixon and Johnson are going to handle this period," said one Western diplomat.

The Saigon Government is reported to feel that the Johnson Administration pressed it too rapidly toward expanded talks embracing the Vietcong. It now is expected to use the change-over period in the United States to play for time.

South Vietnamese officials here make no secret that they consider Mr. Nixon more sympathetic than Mr. Johnson to their position.

They have recently dropped hints that they expect no active negotiating on issues of substance until early next year.

Western diplomats now speculate that President Nguyen Van Thieu may delay sending a delegation to the talks here until he has learned Mr. Nixon's views.

But a more common opinion is that Saigon will send a delegation soon and then try to stall until the Republicans take office in January.

The Republican victory,

Continued on Page 13, Column 1

POLICE SEIZE 125 ON C.C.N.Y. CAMPUS

AWOL Soldier Taken From Student Center 'Sanctuary'

About 250 members of the Tactical Patrol Force moved early today at the request of the administration onto the City College campus and arrested more than 100 students and the AWOL soldier they had been guarding in a student center.

Under the direction of Police Commissioner Howard R. Leary, Chief Inspector Sanford Garelik and a number of other high police officials, the arrests were carried out without violence following a warning from the administration to vacate the building.

In all, about 125 persons were arrested, including supporters of the peace movement and Pvt. William Brakefield, who had been in the Finley Student Center, at 133d Street and Convent Avenue, since last

Continued on Page 4, Column 4

SHE KNEW IT ALL ALONG: President-elect Richard M. Nixon holding crewelwork, a facsimile of Presidential seal embroidered by his daughter Julie, who stands beside her fiancé, David Eisenhower. Mrs. Nixon and daughter Patricia completed the family group at the Waldorf-Astoria yesterday.

The New York Times (by Neal Boenzi)

Soviet Bids U.S. Confer; Calls for 'Normalization'

By HENRY KAMM
Special to The New York Times

MOSCOW, Nov. 6—The Soviet Union greeted the election of a new President of the United States today with a call for the "normalization" of relations between Moscow and Washington for the sake of world peace.

The demand was put forward in a speech on behalf of the ruling Politburo of the Communist party by First Deputy Premier Kirill T. Mazurov as election returns in the United States showed that Richard M. Nixon had won the Presidency. The occasion was the traditional speech in the Kremlin on the eve of the anniversary of the Bolshevik Revolution.

To underline the importance Moscow attaches to relations with the United States, Mr. Mazurov raised the issue twice. Noting Soviet proposals for mutual limitations on nuclear weapons and delivery systems, the official said:

"It is relevant to recall in this connection that we have expressed readiness to conduct negotiations with the United States on the entire range of these problems. But their positive solution does not depend on the Soviet Union alone."

Review of Soviet Actions

After a review of Soviet actions on the international scene, Mr. Mazurov returned to Soviet-American relations. He said:

"We have always attached great importance to the normalization of relations between the Soviet Union and the United States, which would be important not only to both of our countries but also to world peace."

A public offer to enter into negotiations with the United States for an accommodation on vital issues was regarded as a Soviet reaction to the

Continued on Page 14, Column 1

POSITION ON SINAI DEFINED BY ISRAEL

Note to Jarring Links Issue of Boundaries to Security Needs and Tiran Rights

By DREW MIDDLETON
Special to The New York Times

UNITED NATIONS, N. Y., Nov. 6—Israel has told the United Arab Republic that her attitude toward the boundary problem will be governed by her security needs and the maintenance of full protection of Israeli navigation in the Strait of Tiran.

This is the first time that Israel has defined with any precision her interest in the Sinai Peninsula.

The demand that Israel not reject an arrangement that returned a demilitarized Sinai to Egypt. The peninsula has been occupied by Israel since the Israeli-Arab war of June, 1967.

This information was in a memorandum that Foreign Minister Abba Eban gave yesterday to Dr. Gunnar V. Jarring, the United Nations intermediary. Mr. Eban went over the text of the memorandum with Dr. Jarring at meetings yesterday afternoon and last night.

Ambassador Jarring was asked to transmit the memorandum to Mahmoud Riad, the Egyptian Foreign Minister. The clarification of Israel's approach to the boundary question apparently was intended to rebut Mr.

Continued on Page 2, Column 3

REPUBLICANS GAIN SAFE ALBANY EDGE

Lead in Assembly Put at 77-73 and in Senate at 33-24 Unofficially

By JAMES F. CLARITY

Republican officials said yesterday that they expected to have clear majorities in both houses of the 1969 Legislature.

The Republicans, on the basis of unofficial but reliable vote-counts in the elections for the 150 Assembly and 57 Senate seats, will probably control the Assembly by 77 to 73, and the Senate by 33 to 24.

Official Count Delayed

The official count of the close races was expected to be completed early next week. The G.O.P. Senate majority was assured, regardless of the final count in a few close races.

But the Republicans' control of the Assembly, which they had lost in 1964, did not appear to give G.O.P. leaders assurance that their programs and legislation or those proposed by Governor Rockefeller would necessarily sail through the Legislature because of the majorities in both houses.

Among the Republicans who captured Democratic seats in the Assembly were several conservatives who, by combining with conservative Democrats, could obstruct, if not defeat, legislation they considered liberally oriented or objectionable for other reasons.

Three of the newly elected Republican Assembly members

Continued on Page 40, Column 5

Senate's Liberal Coalition Survives Gains by G.O.P.

By DAVID E. ROSENBAUM

Republicans made a net gain of at least four Senate seats in Tuesday's election, but the balance between liberals and conservatives did not appear to have changed substantially from the present Senate.

One Senate race remained in doubt last night. In Oregon, Wayne Morse, a Democrat, who served four terms, was running a close race with State Representative Robert W. Packwood, a Republican. Observers said it might be days before the outcome was certain.

Depending on the Oregon race, the Democrats will hold 58 or 59 seats in the new Senate to 41 or 42 for the Republicans. In the present Senate there are 63 Democrats and 37 Republicans.

Four conservative Republicans and one conservative Democrat were elected to seats that had been held by liberals or moderates. On the other hand, there was a shift in favor of liberals in at least two states.

Thus it appeared that a majority could still be formed from liberal Northern Democrats and moderate Republicans to pass legislation on such issues as

Continued on Page 29, Column 2

Election Tables

Tables reporting the vote in national, state and local contests in Tuesday's election are now scheduled for publication in The New York Times tomorrow.

The Times had expected to print them today, but breakdowns in the News Election Service's national and regional computers made a total recheck of the election results necessary. This recheck is expected to be concluded today.

civil rights and aid to education.

The Republicans' net gain of only four seats in the House of Representatives dashed the party's hopes of capturing control of that body.

In the Senate the Republicans picked up seats that had been held by Democrats in Arizona, Florida, Maryland, Ohio, Oklahoma and Pennsylvania. Democrats took Republican-held seats in California and Iowa.

Among the new conservatives was Barry Goldwater, the Republican Presidential nominee in 1964. He defeated Roy L. Elson for the Arizona

Continued on Page 21, Column 1

GOAL IS HARMONY

President-Elect Vows His Administration Will Be 'Open'

By ROBERT B. SEMPLE Jr.

President-elect Richard M. Nixon turned yesterday from the business of winning elections to the business of assembling an Administration.

Weary but thankful, he appeared before an elated band of supporters gathered in the ballroom of the Waldorf-Astoria at 11:35 A.M. He expressed his gratitude for their efforts and his admiration for the "gallant and courageous fight" of his opponent.

He also extended the hand of friendship to the disappointed partisans of Mr. Humphrey's cause—particularly the young.

Near the end of his eight-minute talk, Mr. Nixon took note of the division in the nation and pledged, in these words, to bend every effort to restore racial peace and social harmony:

"I saw many signs in this campaign. Some of them were not friendly and some were very friendly. But the one that touched me the most was one that I saw in Deshler, Ohio, at the end of a long day of whistle-stopping, a little town, almost impossible to see — but a teen-ager held up a sign, 'Bring Us Together.'

"And that will be the great objective of this Administration at the outset, to bring the American people together. This will be an open Administration, open to new ideas, open to men and women of both parties, open to the critics as well as those who support us.

"We want to bridge the generation gap. We want to bridge the gap between the races. We want to bring America together. And I am confident that this task is one that we can undertake and one in which we will be successful."

Several hours later the campaign entourage began to disassemble, its members heading home for a brief but long-overdue rest. The candidate himself flew southward for a three-day vacation in Key Biscayne, a peninsula just south of Miami where he rested occasionally during the campaign.

Although he has been urged

Continued on Page 21, Column 1

ELECTOR VOTE 287

Lead in Popular Tally May Be Smaller Than Kennedy's in '60

By MAX FRANKEL

Richard Milhous Nixon emerged the victor yesterday in one of the closest and most tumultuous Presidential campaigns in history and set himself the task of reuniting the nation.

Elected over Hubert H. Humphrey by the barest of margins —only four one-hundredths of a percentage point in the popular vote—and confronted by a Congress in control of the Democrats, the President-elect said it "will be the great objective of this Administration at the outset to bring the American people together."

He pledged, as the 37th President, to form "an open Administration, open to new ideas, open to men and women of both parties, open to critics as well as those who support us" so as to bridge the gap between the generations and the races.

Details Left for Later

But after an exhausting and tense night of awaiting the verdict at the Waldorf-Astoria Hotel here, Mr. Nixon and his closest aides were not yet prepared to suggest how they intended to organize themselves and to approach these objectives. The Republican victor expressed admiration for his opponent's challenge and reiterated his desire to help President Johnson achieve peace in Vietnam between now and his inauguration on Jan. 20.

The verdict of an electorate that appeared to number 73 million could not be declared until mid-morning because Mr. Nixon and Mr. Humphrey finished in a virtual tie in the popular vote, just as Mr. Nixon and John F. Kennedy did in 1960.

With 94 per cent of the nation's election precincts reporting, Mr. Nixon's total stood last evening at 29,726,409 votes to Mr. Humphrey's 29,677,152. The margin of 49,257 was even smaller than Mr. Kennedy's margin of 112,803.

Meaning Hard to Find

When translated into the determining electoral votes of the states, these returns proved even more difficult to read, and the result in two states—Alaska and Missouri—was still not final last night. The unofficial returns from elsewhere gave Mr. Nixon a minimum of 287 electoral votes, 17 more than the 270 required for election. Mr. Humphrey won 191.

Because of the tightness of the race, the third-party challenger, George C. Wallace, came close to realizing his minimum objective of denying victory to the major-party candidates and thereby forcing a bargain for his sup-

Continued on Page 20, Column 1

A Loser Concedes and Tries to Smile

By R. W. APPLE Jr.
Special to The New York Times

MINNEAPOLIS, Nov. 6—It was Hubert Horatio Humphrey's last hurrah in Presidential politics.

He had tried once before, in 1960, and then been crushed by the superb organization of John F. Kennedy in the West

Transcript of the Humphrey statement is on Page 22.

Virginia primary. Now he had lost again, this time to the same man whom John Kennedy had defeated, in an agonizingly close finish.

The Vice President—a hearty, sentimental man, given to laughter and to tears—tried to smile as he stood on the stage in the Leamington Hotel's ballroom this morning and listened to his faithful followers shout, "We Want Humphrey!" But what he brought forth was more a grimace than a grin.

"Thank you very much," he said in a quavering voice. "It's nice to know."

Mr. Humphrey went through

Continued on Page 22, Column 1

Vice President Humphrey with his wife after conceding

Johnson Vows Aid In Power Transfer

By NEIL SHEEHAN
Special to The New York Times

SAN ANTONIO, Tex., Nov. 6—In a telegram of congratulations this morning, President Johnson informed President-elect Richard M. Nixon that he would do "everything in my power to make your burdens lighter on that day when you assume the responsibilities of the President."

Even as Mr. Johnson's telegram was being transmitted to Mr. Nixon from the President's ranch 65 miles north of here, the machinery had been set in motion for an orderly transition from the old Administration to the new.

Lawson Knott, the administrator of the General Services

Continued on Page 20, Column 3

The Election at a Glance

President

Needed for Election—270 Electoral Votes

	Number of States*	Electoral Votes
Humphrey	14	191
Nixon	30	287
Wallace	5	45
In Doubt: Alaska, Missouri	2	15

*Includes District of Columbia.

The Senate

Newly Elected Senators		Make-up of New Senate	
Democrats	18	Democrats	58
Republicans	15	Republicans	41
In Doubt	1	In Doubt	1

The House

Democrats Elected	243
Republicans Elected	192

NEWS INDEX

	Page		Page
Books	44-45	Movies	51-54
Bridge	44	Music	51-54
Business	65, 76-77	Obituaries	47, 50
Buyers	77	Real Estate	79
Chess	44	Ships and Air	93
Crossword	45	Society	45
Editorials	46	Sports	58-63
Fashions	56	Theaters	51-54
Financial	65-78	TV and Radio	95
Food	56	U. N. Proceedings	15
Man in the News	21	Weather	93

News Summary and Index, Page 49

The New York Times

LATE CITY EDITION

Weather: Mostly sunny, cold today; fair, warmer tonight and tomorrow. Temp. range: today 30-20; Tuesday 34-24. Full U.S. report on Page 62.

VOL. CXVIII—No. 40,513   © 1968 The New York Times Company.   NEW YORK, WEDNESDAY, DECEMBER 25, 1968   10 CENTS

3 MEN FLY AROUND THE MOON ONLY 70 MILES FROM SURFACE; FIRE ROCKET, HEAD FOR EARTH

PUEBLO CREWMEN GREETED ON COAST; CAPTORS ASSAILED

Relatives Weep and Scream —Captain Asserts North Koreans Are Inhuman

By BERNARD GWERTZMAN
Special to The New York Times

SAN DIEGO, Dec. 24 — The crew of the intelligence ship Pueblo returned to the United States today in time for Christmas with many of their families.

Led by Comdr. Lloyd M. Bucher, the 82 survivors arrived at the Miramar Naval Air Station outside this city and were met immediately by emotional, sometimes hysterical, greetings and embraces of wives, mothers, fathers and children.

The one man who did not return alive, Duane D. Hodges, was carried from one of the C-141 transports in a flag-draped coffin while the air station band played the Navy hymn.

Commander Bucher, apparently overwrought with emotion, spoke in a low voice as he told the more than 250 relatives, the 300 newsmen and the national television audience about the 11 months his crew spent in North Korean captivity.

Calls Captors Inhuman

He described North Korea as a land "completely devoid of humanity, completely devoted to enslavement of men's minds."

[In Washington, the Navy named Vice Adm. Harold S. Bowen to head a court of inquiry into the Pueblo incident.]

Commander Bucher said that, during the months in North Korea, "the thought that preyed on my mind was the embarrassment to my country because of the loss of one of its fine ships."

At a news conference held in the base theater at Navy Hospital here, Rear Adm. Edwin Rosenberg, the representative of the Commander in Chief, Pacific Fleet, in charge of the Pueblo's repatriation, repeated his past praise.

Continued on Page 2, Column 1

At Least 22 Survive Pennsylvania Crash Of Plane With 45

Special to The New York Times

BRADFORD, Pa., Wednesday, Dec. 25—An Allegheny Airlines jetprop plane with 45 persons aboard crashed last night in rugged terrain during a heavy snowstorm while attempting to land at Bradford Regional Airport 15 miles south of here.

There were at least 22 survivors.

The twin-engine plane was Allegheny Flight 736, bound from Detroit to Washington. It had stopped in Erie, Pa., and had been scheduled to stop in Bradford and Harrisburg, Pa.

The wreck, about three miles southeast of the airport, was reported shortly before 9 P.M. by Allegheny Flight 734 out of Cleveland, which said it saw a fire.

It took rescue teams an hour to reach the scene on snowmobiles in freezing temperatures. Several inches of snow had fallen during the day in the heavily wooded area and

Continued on Page 62, Column 1

Pope Paul Says Mass In a Huge Steel Mill

By ROBERT C. DOTY
Special to The New York Times

TARANTO, Italy, Wednesday, Dec. 25—Pope Paul VI celebrated Christmas midnight mass here for 15,000 workers and members of their families in a huge, echoing rolling mill.

The Pontiff chose the vast Italsider steel plant at this developing industrial center in the heel of the Italian boot as the place to express "the fraternal and radiant presence of Christ among workers throughout the world."

Even while the Pope said mass at an altar consisting of a four-ton slab of steel supported on two broad sections of steel pipe, work continued elsewhere throughout the 2,000-acre plant, the largest in Europe.

Blast furnaces poured plumes of flame into a rainy

Continued on Page 34, Column 1

VIOLATIONS MAR TRUCE IN VIETNAM

80 Incidents Are Reported —22 Enemy Soldiers and an American Killed

By B. DRUMMOND AYRES Jr.
Special to The New York Times

SAIGON, South Vietnam, Wednesday, Dec. 25—The allies and the Vietcong put separate cease-fires into effect yesterday to mark Christmas, but not all the guns fell silent.

At 9 o'clock this morning, the American military command said there had been at least 80 "incidents" involving military contact since the allied cease-fire, scheduled to run 24 hours, went into effect at 6 P.M. yesterday.

The enemy cease-fire began at 1 A.M. yesterday and was scheduled to run for 72 hours. Allied military spokesmen said there were at least eight incidents involving military contact during the first hours of that stand-down.

In about 30 of the incidents, casualties were suffered by one or both sides. The allied spokesmen said that over-all South Vietnamese losses had been light. United States losses were broken down as one soldier killed and 38 wounded.

At least 22 enemy soldiers died.

It was not known whether North Vietnamese troops in South Vietnam were complying with the Vietcong cease-fire order. During previous holiday

Continued on Page 5, Column 3

Col. Frank Borman   Maj. William A. Anders   Capt. James A. Lovell Jr.

Associated Press

Moon pictures taken through the window of the Apollo 8 spacecraft that were telecast to earth last night. In picture at left of Sea of Crises area, the larger crater is 30 to 40 miles wide. The picture at right was last transmitted.

ASSOCIATED PRESS

FUEL DELIVERIES FALL SHORT HERE

City's Health Chief Warns of Danger to Sick—Flu Vaccine and Blood Low

By ARNOLD H. LUBASCH

A shortage of heat, vaccine and blood plagued the city yesterday as the Hong Kong flu epidemic continued, and the Health Commissioner warned that many sick people might die unless emergency fuel deliveries were made.

Mayor Lindsay, who said most drivers had stopped fuel deliveries for the holiday, joined Health Commissioner Edward O'Rourke in appealing for fuel deliveries today even though it was Christmas.

With the temperature dropping into the low twenties last night, hundreds of homes, apartment houses and commercial buildings remained without fuel, although oil companies sought to catch up on deliveries delayed by last week's strike.

The city's supply of flu vaccine ran out yesterday as efforts were made to arrange for further shipments for Jan. 2, when 40,000 more doses are scheduled to arrive.

A critical shortage of blood was reported by the Greater

Continued on Page 21, Column 1

Orbit Shows Lunar Interior Is 'Lumpy'

By WALTER SULLIVAN
Special to The New York Times

HOUSTON, Dec. 24—For the first time human beings took a close look today at the earth's nearest celestial neighbor, viewing it from many angles to seek out clues to the events that formed its awesomely rugged terrain.

Until now man has always been forced to look at the moon from a single direction at a great distance, although in the last few years spacecraft have provided glimpses of the far side and close-up views of the earth-facing side.

Today the three Apollo astronauts sailed serenely over the giant craters, looking down their throats, marveling at their crumbling walls and countless strange features that have long puzzled astronomers.

They reported seeing many freshly formed craters, indicating that the cataclysmic events that have pocked the moon and sprinkled it with rubble are continuing. Some of the craters, the astronauts said, looked as

Slight Wobbles Observed in Spacecraft's Course

though a giant pick had been hacking at a concrete surface, producing fine dust as well as other debris.

They became the first men to witness a lunar sunrise and found it a strange and unexpected experience. According to Capt. James A. Lovell Jr., about two minutes before sunrise a fine white haze appeared over the horizon where the sun was about to appear.

"It takes the fan shape," he said, "unlike the sunrise on earth, where the atmosphere affects it."

Meanwhile, analysis of the orbital flight by radio antennas on earth showed that, from time to time, the spacecraft wobbled slightly in its path. This confirmed earlier indications that the interior of the moon is "lumpy."

Some scientists, notably Dr. Harold C. Urey of the University of California, San Diego, a Nobel laureate, have suggested that the moon is like a giant raisin cake with lumps of dense iron embedded in material that is far less dense. Such a body could have been formed from a cloud of dust and smaller objects, including chunks of iron, during the formation of the solar system.

If the moon were uniformly dense and perfectly spherical, the gravitational field surrounding it would be perfectly symmetrical. It was this field that held the Apollo spacecraft in orbit. The fact that the spacecraft's road was slightly bumpy, so to speak, revealed an uneven distribution of mass within the moon. In particular, this was noted as the astronauts sailed over Copernicus, one of the largest and most spectacular craters on the moon. It was in darkness but was dimly illuminated by ghostly earthshine—sunlight reflected by the earth.

The lumpiness of the moon

Continued on Page 38, Column 1

Astronauts Examine 'Vast, Lonely' Place; Read From Genesis

By JOHN NOBLE WILFORD
Special to The New York Times

HOUSTON, Wednesday, Dec. 25—The three astronauts of Apollo 8 yesterday became the first men to orbit the moon. Early today, after flying 10 times around that desolate realm of dream and scientific mystery, they started their return to earth.

They fired the spacecraft's main rocket engine at 1:10 A.M. to kick them out of lunar orbit.

Excerpts from messages to and from Apollo, Page 36.

and to carry them toward a splashdown in the Pacific Ocean on Friday.

Through the static of 231,000 miles, as Apollo 8 swung around from behind the moon and started for earth, one of the astronauts dispelled any doubts, saying, "Please be informed there is a Santa Claus."

57-Hour Return Trip

It would be a 57-hour return trip from the most far-reaching voyage of the space age thus far—or of any other previous age. The astronauts had seen, as no other men had, the ancient lunar craters, plains and rugged mountains from as close as 70 miles.

At 4:59 A.M. yesterday, about 20 hours before the return trip, Col. Frank Borman of the Air Force, Capt. James A. Lovell Jr. of the Navy and Maj. William A. Anders of the Air Force, swept into an orbit of the moon by firing the spacecraft's main rocket. This occurred after they flew around the leading edge of the moon and were directly behind the earth's only natural satellite.

"We got it! We've got it!" exclaimed a mission commentator of the National Aeronautics and Space Administration as the spacecraft emerged from behind the moon 24 minutes later, and was clearly flying a safe and smooth orbit.

Businesslike Report

The calm and laconic Apollo explorers, however, were all business. Captain Lovell's first message to earth was simply: "Go ahead, Houston. Our orbit 8. Burn complete. Our orbit is 169.1 by 60.5—169.1 by 60.5."

The astronauts flew twice around the moon in the egg-shaped orbit, then dropped to a circular orbit nearly 70 miles above the ancient craters, plains and rugged mountains of the lunar surface.

As they beamed their first live television from orbit on Christmas Eve morning, they described the surface of the moon as a colorless gray, "like

Continued on Page 36, Column 1

dirty beach sand with lots of footprints on it" and said it "looks like plaster of Paris."

At about 9:30 P.M. the astronauts began their second and last television show from lunar orbit. It ran some 30 minutes and showed the bright moon, in a pitch black sky, outside the spacecraft window.

Earth Like an 'Oasis'

Colonel Borman described the moon as a "vast, lonely and forbidding sight," adding that it was "not a very inviting place to live or work."

Captain Lovell saw the earth as a "grand oasis in the big vastness of space."

Major Anders was most impressed by "the lunar sunrise and sunsets."

As the telecast neared its end, Colonel Borman said "Apollo 8 has a message for you." With that, Major Anders began reading the opening verses from the Book of Genesis about creation of the earth.

"In the beginning," Major Anders read, "God created the heaven and the earth.

"And the earth was without form and voice; and darkness was upon the face of the deep . . ."

Captain Lovell then took up with the verse beginning, "And God said let there be light, and the darkness He called night."

Colonel Borman closed the reading with the verse that read:

"And God called the dry land Earth; and the gathering together of the water called He Seas: and God saw that it was good."

Sends Holiday Greetings

After that Colonel Borman signed off, saying:

"Good-by, good night. Merry Christmas. God bless all of you, all of you on the good earth."

Glynn S. Lunney, one of the flight directors here, told reporters earlier, "we have a completely 'go' spacecraft."

George M. Low, the spacecraft manager at the Manned Spacecraft Center, said he was "altogether happy" with the mission — the most ambitious and daring thus far in the nation's $24-billion Apollo project to land men on the moon next year.

Although the mission's object was not primarily scientific, Dr. John Dietrich of the space center's geology and geochemistry branch, said that the television pictures and astro-

Continued on Page 36, Column 1

Christmas Day

Today is Christmas Day. Following is a list of services that are affected:

Public and Parochial Schools —Closed.

Post Office—Closed except for special delivery.

Stores—Most retail and department stores closed.

Banks—Closed.

Stock Exchanges—Closed.

Sanitation—No regular refuse collection.

Parking—Sunday parking regulations in force, permitting parking in alternate-side parking zones and at most parking meters.

Libraries—Closed except for the Main Reading Room of the Library at Fifth Avenue and 42d Street, which will be open from 1 to 5 P.M.

Merry Christmas, Mlle. Richmond Love, Jenn.—Advt.

A Reflection: Riders on Earth Together, Brothers in Eternal Cold

By ARCHIBALD MacLEISH

MEN'S conception of themselves and of each other has always depended on their notion of the earth. When the earth was the World—all the world there was—and the stars were lights in Dante's heaven, and the ground beneath men's feet roofed Hell, men saw themselves as creatures at the center of the universe, the sole, particular concern of God—and from that high place they ruled and killed and conquered as they pleased.

And when, centuries later, the earth was no longer the World but a small, wet, spinning planet in the solar system of a minor star off at the edge of an inconsiderable galaxy in the immeasurable distances of space — when Dante's heaven had disappeared and there was no Hell (at least no Hell beneath the feet)—men began to see themselves, not as God-directed actors at the center of a noble drama, but as helpless victims of a senseless force where all the rest were helpless atoms in a world-wide wars or in blasted cities or in concentration camps without a thought or reason for it all—or if we call it one—but force.

Now, in the last few hours, the notion may have changed again. For the first time men have seen it: seen it not as continents or oceans from the little distance of a hundred miles or two or three, but seen it from the depths of space; seen it whole and round and beautiful and small as even Dante—that "first imagination of Christendom"—had never dreamed of seeing it; as the Twentieth Century philosophers of absurdity and despair were incapable of guessing that it might be. And seeing it so, one question came to the minds of those who looked at it.

"Is it inhabited?" they said to each other and laughed—and then they did not laugh. What came to their minds a hundred thousand miles and more into space—"half way to the moon" they put it—what came to their minds was the life on that little, lonely, floating planet; that tiny raft in the enormous, empty night. "Is it inhabited?"

THE medieval notion of the earth put man at the center of everything. The nuclear notion of the earth put him nowhere—beyond the range of reason even—lost in absurdity and war. This

latest notion may have other consequences. Formed as it was in the minds of heroic voyagers who were also men, it may remake our image of mankind. No longer that preposterous figure at the center, no longer that degraded and degrading victim off at the margins of reality and blind with blood, man may at last become himself.

To see the earth as it truly is, small and blue and beautiful in that eternal silence where it floats, is to see ourselves as riders on the earth together, brothers on that bright loveliness in the eternal cold—brothers who know now they are truly brothers.

"All the News
That's Fit to Print"

The New York Times

LATE CITY EDITION

Weather: Rain, warm today; clear
tonight. Sunny, pleasant tomorrow.
Temp. range: today 80-66; Sunday
71-66. Temp.-Hum. Index yesterday
69. Complete U.S. report on P. 50.

VOL. CXVIII . No. 40,721   © 1969 The New York Times Company.   NEW YORK, MONDAY, JULY 21, 1969   10 CENTS

MEN WALK ON MOON

ASTRONAUTS LAND ON PLAIN; COLLECT ROCKS, PLANT FLAG

Voice From Moon: 'Eagle Has Landed'

EAGLE (the lunar module): Houston, Tranquility Base here. The Eagle has landed.

HOUSTON: Roger, Tranquility, we copy you on the ground. You've got a bunch of guys about to turn blue. We're breathing again. Thanks a lot.

TRANQUILITY BASE: Thank you.

HOUSTON: You're looking good here.

TRANQUILITY BASE: A very smooth touchdown.

HOUSTON: Eagle, you are stay for T1. [The first step in the lunar operation.] Over.

TRANQUILITY BASE: Roger. Stay for T1.

HOUSTON: Roger and we see you venting the ox.

TRANQUILITY BASE: Roger.

COLUMBIA (the command and service module): How do you read me?

HOUSTON: Columbia, he has landed Tranquility Base. Eagle is at Tranquility. I read you five by. Over.

COLUMBIA: Yes, I heard the whole thing.

HOUSTON: Well, it's a good show.

COLUMBIA: Fantastic.

TRANQUILITY BASE: I'll second that.

APOLLO CONTROL: The next major stay-no stay will be for the T2 event. That is at 21 minutes 26 seconds after initiation of power descent.

COLUMBIA: Up telemetry command reset to reacquire on high gain.

HOUSTON: Copy. Out.

APOLLO CONTROL: We have an unofficial time for that touchdown of 102 hours, 45 minutes, 42 seconds and we will update that.

HOUSTON: Eagle, you loaded R2 wrong. We want 10254.

TRANQUILITY BASE: Roger. Do you want the horizontal 55 15.2?

HOUSTON: That's affirmative.

APOLLO CONTROL: We're now less than four minutes from our next stay-no stay. It will be for one complete revolution of the command module.

One of the first things that Armstrong and Aldrin will do after getting their next stay-no stay will be to remove their helmets and gloves.

HOUSTON: Eagle, you are stay for T2. Over.

Continued on Page 4, Col. 1

VOYAGE TO THE MOON

By ARCHIBALD MacLEISH

Presence among us,

      wanderer in our skies,

dazzle of silver in our leaves and on our
waters silver,

O

silver evasion in our farthest thought—
"the visiting moon" . . . "the glimpses of the moon" . . .

and we have touched you!

      From the first of time,
before the first of time, before the
first men tasted time, we thought of you.
You were a wonder to us, unattainable,
a longing past the reach of longing,
a light beyond our light, our lives—perhaps
a meaning to us . . .

     Now
our hands have touched you in your depth of night.

Three days and three nights we journeyed,
steered by farthest stars, climbed outward,
crossed the invisible tide-rip where the floating dust
falls one way or the other in the void between,
followed that other down, encountered
cold, faced death—unfathomable emptiness . . .

Then, the fourth day evening, we descended,
made fast, set foot at dawn upon your beaches,
sifted between our fingers your cold sand.

We stand here in the dusk, the cold, the silence . . .

and here, as at the first of time, we lift our heads.
Over us, more beautiful than the moon, a
moon, a wonder to us, unattainable,
a longing past the reach of longing,
a light beyond our light, our lives—perhaps
a meaning to us . . .

     O, a meaning!

over us on these silent beaches the bright
earth,
     presence among us

Neil A. Armstrong moves away from the leg of the landing craft after taking the first step on the surface of the moon

The New York Times from C.B.S. News

Col. Edwin E. Aldrin Jr. climbing down the ladder. The television camera was attached to a side of the lunar module.

Associated Press

Mr. Armstrong, right, and Colonel Aldrin raise the U.S. flag. A metal rod at right angles to the mast keeps flag unfurled.

A Powdery Surface Is Closely Explored

By JOHN NOBLE WILFORD
Special to The New York Times

HOUSTON, Monday, July 21—Men have landed and walked on the moon.

Two Americans, astronauts of Apollo 11, steered their fragile four-legged lunar module safely and smoothly to the historic landing yesterday at 4:17:40 P.M., Eastern daylight time.

Neil A. Armstrong, the 38-year-old civilian commander, radioed to earth and the mission control room here:

"Houston, Tranquility Base here. The Eagle has landed."

The first men to reach the moon—Mr. Armstrong and his co-pilot, Col. Edwin E. Aldrin Jr. of the Air Force—brought their ship to rest on a level, rock-strewn plain near the southwestern shore of the arid Sea of Tranquility.

About six and a half hours later, Mr. Armstrong opened the landing craft's hatch, stepped slowly down the ladder and declared as he planted the first human footprint on the lunar crust:

"That's one small step for man, one giant leap for mankind."

His first step on the moon came at 10:56:20 P.M., as a television camera outside the craft transmitted his every move to an awed and excited audience of hundreds of millions of people on earth.

Tentative Steps Test Soil

Mr. Armstrong's initial steps were tentative tests of the lunar soil's firmness and of his ability to move about easily in his bulky white spacesuit and backpacks and under the influence of lunar gravity, which is one-sixth that of the earth.

"The surface is fine and powdery," the astronaut reported. "I can pick it up loosely with my toe. It does adhere in fine layers like powdered charcoal to the sole and sides of my boots. I only go in a small fraction of an inch, maybe an eighth of an inch. But I can see the footprints of my boots in the treads in the fine sandy particles."

After 19 minutes of Mr. Armstrong's testing, Colonel Aldrin joined him outside the craft.

The two men got busy setting up another television camera out from the lunar module, planting an American flag into the ground, scooping up soil and rock samples, deploying scientific experiments and hopping and loping about in a demonstration of their lunar agility.

They found walking and working on the moon less taxing than had been forecast. Mr. Armstrong once reported he was "very comfortable."

And people back on earth found the black-and-white television pictures of the bug-shaped lunar module and the men tramping about it so sharp and clear as to seem unreal, more like a toy and toy-like figures than human beings on the most daring and far-reaching expedition thus far undertaken.

Nixon Telephones Congratulations

During one break in the astronauts' work, President Nixon congratulated them from the White House in what, he said, "certainly has to be the most historic telephone call ever made."

"Because of what you have done," the President told the astronauts, "the heavens have become a part of man's world. And as you talk to us from the Sea of Tranquility it requires us to redouble our efforts to bring peace and tranquility to earth.

"For one priceless moment in the whole history of man all the people on this earth are truly one—one in their pride in what you have done and one in our prayers that you will return safely to earth."

Mr. Armstrong replied:

"Thank you Mr. President. It's a great honor and privilege for us to be here representing not only the United States but men of peace of all nations, men with interests and a curiosity and men with a vision for the future."

Mr. Armstrong and Colonel Aldrin returned to their landing craft and closed the hatch at 1:12 A.M., 2 hours 21 minutes after opening the hatch on the moon. While the third member of the crew, Lieut. Col. Michael Collins of the Air Force, kept his orbital vigil overhead in the command ship, the two moon explorers settled down to sleep.

Outside their vehicle the astronauts had found a bleak

Continued on Pages 2, Col. 1

Today's 4-Part Issue of The Times

This morning's issue of The New York Times is divided into four parts. The first part is devoted to news of Apollo 11 and includes Editorials and letters to the Editor (Page 16). Poems on the landing on the moon appear on Page 17.

General news begins on the first page of the second part. The News Summary and Index is on the first page of the third part, which includes sports news, obituaries (Page 51) and transportation news and weather reports (Pages 50 and 52).

Financial and business news begins on the first page of the fourth part.

Following is the News Index for today's issue:

The New York Times

PAGE ONE

Major Events:

1970–1979

"All the News That's Fit to Print"

The New York Times

LATE CITY EDITION

Weather: Cloudy but clearing today. Fair tonight. Cloudy, mild tomorrow. Temp. range: today 51-43; Tuesday 48-42. Full U.S. report on Page 85.

VOL. CXIX..No. 40,989

© 1970 The New York Times Company.

NEW YORK, WEDNESDAY, APRIL 15, 1970

10 CENTS

CREW OF CRIPPLED APOLLO 13 STARTS BACK AFTER ROUNDING MOON AND FIRING ROCKET; MEN APPEAR CALM DESPITE LOW RESERVES

Judge Blackmun of Minnesota Is Named To Supreme Court Seat by the President

Nominee, 61, Is Regarded as a Scholarly Jurist

By ROBERT B. SEMPLE Jr.
Special to The New York Times

WASHINGTON, April 14—President Nixon today nominated Harry Andrew Blackmun of Minnesota to the Supreme Court.

Judge Blackmun, a member of the United States Court of Appeals for the Eighth Circuit, is regarded in the legal profession as a scholarly and mildly conservative judge.

Mr. Nixon's third choice for the vacancy created by the resignation of Abe Fortas was announced by Ronald L. Ziegler, the White House press secretary, late this afternoon. The President did not appear and did not issue a statement.

Mr. Ziegler made the announcement while standing on the same small platform in the new White House press head-

United Press International
Judge Harry A. Blackmun in St. Louis yesterday.

quarters where Mr. Nixon last Thursday accused the Senate of hypocrisy and regional bias for refusing to approve his first two nominees for the vacancy.

A Prolonged Examination by Senate Panel Seen

ers, were Clement F. Haynsworth Jr. and G. Harrold Carswell. The Senate rejected Judge Haynsworth last November and Judge Carswell last Wednesday.

Judge Blackmun will also require Senate confirmation, but early reaction to his nomination on Capitol Hill was inconclusive. On the basis of the Senate's recent performance, however, it seemed likely that Judge Blackmun would be subjected to prolonged and searching examination by the Senate Judiciary Committee. Until that time, there may be a reluctance on the part of many Senators to commit themselves.

Senator Sam J. Ervin Jr., Democrat of North Carolina and a senior member of the Judiciary Committee, refused to

Continued on Page 34, Column 3

The two men, both Southern-

VOYAGE OF A STRICKEN SPACESHIP: Apollo 13, its hopes for America's third lunar landing dashed by a ruptured oxygen tank, arced around the moon last night on a course that would bring it back to earth on Friday.

TARGET IS PACIFIC

Chance of Safe Return Deemed 'Excellent' Despite the Risks

Excerpts from conversations with spacecraft, Page 28.

By JOHN NOBLE WILFORD
Special to The New York Times

HOUSTON, Wednesday, April 15—With the lives of its three astronauts hanging in the balance, the crippled spaceship Apollo 13 swung around the moon last night and rocketed toward an emergency splashdown in the Pacific Ocean Friday.

After the craft looped the moon, a crucial four-minute and 24-second rocket firing sent the astronauts on a fast and more accurate course — a drastic change of plans caused by Monday night's massive power failure aboard the moon-bound spacecraft.

The rocket blast started at 9:41 P.M. Eastern standard time as the astronauts, depending on their attached lunar landing craft as a back-up rocket craft, pulled away about 6,000 miles from the right side of the moon.

"That was a good burn," Mission Control radioed after the lunar module's descent rocket shut down as on schedule.

Though its success sent the first ripple of relief through Mission Control in 24 hours, Capt. James A. Lovell Jr. of the Navy and Fred W. Haise Jr. and John L. Swigert Jr., both civilians, were still a long way from home and not yet out of trouble.

A Race With Time

The three astronauts were calm, despite the fact that they were racing time, trying to reach the earth before their severely limited reserves of oxygen, electricity and water ran out.

Grim-faced flight directors here called it "the most critical situation" in the history of the American space program. But, barring any further trouble, they said the chances of the astronauts' safe return were "excellent."

A rising carbon-dioxide level in the spacecraft stirred new concern late last night for the astronauts' safety. The amount rose to the point where it triggered an alarm light, but Mission Control said it was prepared to have it go to twice that level to conserve the lithium hydroxide chemical used to cleanse the cabin atmosphere.

Laboratory tests have shown that triple the present level can be tolerated without signs of organic damage, space agency doctors said.

NASA scientists were de-

Continued on Page 28, Column 3

RISE OF 30% URGED IN CITY REALTY TAX

G.O.P. Leaders in Albany Call On Mayor to Accept $440-Million Package

By RICHARD PHALON
Special to The New York Times

ALBANY, April 14 — Mayor Lindsay arrived here tonight for talks with Republican legislators on the city's financial problems facing the possibility that he might have to adopt a $440-million package of real estate tax increases.

The package, which some Republican leaders are urging as a part-answer to the $630-million that the Mayor says he needs to balance the budget next fiscal year, would raise the real estate tax rate from $5.52 per $100 to around $7 per $100 of assessed valuation—an increase of almost 30 per cent.

City budget officials said about $200-million of the package would go in to reflect next year arrives through normal growth of assessed valuations and an expected increase in the equalization rate designed to iron out variations in assessment practices throughout the city.

The Mayor's mission here tonight is to persuade the Republican leaders that the city is entitled to more state aid on the basis of the tax effort it is already making and on the basis of the additional "do it yourself" revenue measures he has had introduced here in the closing days of the session.

Continued on Page 36, Column 4

Adm. Moorer Named To Head Joint Chiefs

Special to The New York Times

WASHINGTON, April 14 — President Nixon today named Adm. Thomas H. Moorer, Chief of Naval Operations, to succeed Gen. Earle G. Wheeler as chairman of the Joint Chiefs of Staff, the nation's highest ranking military officer.

If confirmed by the Senate—and no obstacles to confirmation are foreseen here—Admiral Moorer will be the second Navy man to hold the post. Adm. Arthur W. Radford was chairman from 1953 to 1957, in the Eisenhower Administration.

Mr. Nixon also disclosed his intention to nominate Vice Adm. Elmo R. Zumwalt Jr., commander of naval forces in Vietnam and chief of the Naval Advisory Group, United States Military Assistance Command

Continued on Page 14, Column 4

Brezhnev Says Soviet Aim Is 'Reasonable' Arms Pact

By BERNARD GWERTZMAN
Special to The New York Times

MOSCOW, April 14—Leonid I. Brezhnev, the Soviet Communist party leader, said today that the Soviet Union would welcome "a reasonable agreement" with the United States on limiting strategic arms when the second round of Soviet-American talks begins in Vienna on Thursday.

But Mr. Brezhnev, making his second televised speech in two days from the Ukrainian city

Excerpts from Brezhnev talk are printed on Page 17.

of Kharkov, indicated doubt that the United States Government was sincere in wanting an accord.

Apparently alluding to Washington's decision to go ahead with new offensive and defensive missile systems, Mr. Brezhnev shook his fist and said that if anyone tried to gain

military superiority over the Soviet Union "we will reply with the necessary increase in military might that guarantees our defense."

After loud and prolonged applause, Mr. Brezhnev added: "We cannot act otherwise."

His wide-ranging foreign policy speech covered the Middle East, Vietnam and Europe, in which he broke no new ground, and relations with China, which he said were being harmed by what he called continuing anti-Soviet war hysteria in Peking.

Last night's speech was devoted entirely to economic problems and reflected his view that the Soviet Union must adopt technological advances and rally the people to overcome its mediocre economic showing of recent years.

His critical words on how the

Continued on Page 17, Column 1

U.S. Arrests Russian Skipper In Alaska Gulf for Spilling Oil

By ROBERT M. SMITH
Special to The New York Times

WASHINGTON, April 14—A Island—about 300 miles southwest of Anchorage—and provided this account:

"We were commencing patrol, and Coast Guard aviation units were also carrying out patrol, and they located a Soviet tanker refueling Soviet fishing vessels in U.S. territory

Coast Guard cutter sent a boarding party aboard a Soviet tanker in the Gulf of Alaska last night and arrested the ship's master on charges of spilling a mile-long oil slick near Kodiak Island.

The master of the Soviet vessel, V. C. Sherstobitov, has been flown to Anchorage where he is awaiting arraignment on charges of violating the Refuse Act of 1899. His ship, the 345-foot motor vessel Mozyr, is still standing by near Kodiak Island.

In response to questions about an unconfirmed report that became available here, the State Department said the Soviet captain had been arrested.

According to information obtained by telephone from the scene, the American boarding party—consisting of a young operations officer, a representative of the Bureau of Fisheries and a seaman-photographer—encountered no resistance.

The Americans spent several hours on board the Soviet vessel while Captain Sherstobitov waited for his fleet commander in Vladivostok to tell him whether he should go with the Americans.

Comdr. John H. Byrd Jr. of New London, Conn., was the captain of the Coast Guard cutter involved, the Storis. Commander Byrd was reached by telephone at Kodiak

Continued on Page 74, Column 4

Cambodia Appeals To World for Arms

By HENRY KAMM
Special to The New York Times

PNOMPENH, Cambodia, April 14—Premier Lon Nol issued an urgent appeal tonight for arms from any country that wanted to provide them.

[The State Department said the United States had received no request. Other sources expected one and predicted that it would be granted.]

In a broadcast statement in French and Cambodian, the Premier declared:

"The Salvation Government has the duty to inform the nation that in view of the gravity of the present situation, it is necessary to accept all unconditional foreign aid, wherever it may come from, for the salvation of the nation."

The Premier underlined the

Continued on Page 3, Column 1

SENATE APPROVES TV CAMPAIGN CURB

Limit in Spending on Races for Federal Offices Voted Over G.O.P. Opposition

By JOHN W. FINNEY
Special to The New York Times

WASHINGTON, April 14—Over Republican opposition, the Senate approved today campaign reform legislation designed to limit and perhaps reduce the mounting spending on political broadcasts over television and radio.

The legislation would place a ceiling on how much a candidate for Federal office could spend on television and radio broadcasts. In addition, it would reduce the rates at which broadcasting stations sell air time to political candidates.

The spending limitations were incorporated in legislation repealing the so-called "equal time" provision in the communications act, thus permitting the television and radio networks to provide free broadcast time for the Presidential and Vice-Presidential candidates in the 1972 elections without giving comparable time to every minor candidate. Whether or not this free time is to be used for debates, as it was in the 1960 Presidential elections, or for some other format is to be worked out by the candidates and the networks.

The campaign reform legislation, first proposed two years ago, passed the Senate with unexpected ease after only one day of debate. It now goes to the House, where, as in the Senate, the Democratic majority is expected to prevail over Republican opposition.

The legislation is designed to

Continued on Page 36, Column 3

Plight of 3 Crewmen Stirs World Interest and Prayer

By MARTIN ARNOLD

Suddenly, in the moment it takes an oxygen tank to spring a leak, the flight of Apollo 13 was no longer something everybody took for granted and was even slightly bored with.

For all around the world yesterday, during the Apollo 13 emergency, there was a surge of interest in the flight and there were prayers, and anguish also, for the three men who were fighting to get their crippled spaceship home.

The world-wide shift in interest in Apollo 13 was best summed up in two printed lines—one in an Italian newspaper, the other in a French paper.

Before the bad news broke, Milan's Il Giorno commented in a headline: "Too Perfect; the Public Is Getting Bored."

Yesterday morning, in Paris, Le Monde said: "The whole human race is participating with them in the agony of their return."

In the United States there was an outpouring of prayer, and here and there, some expression of bitterness, too, that man was reaching toward space without

having first solved the problems on earth.

Both the Senate and House passed resolutions yesterday asking all Americans to pray, at 9 o'clock Eastern standard time last night, for the safe return of their countrymen. And they urged businesses and communications media to pause briefly, if they could, for the prayers at that hour.

Special services and masses were called for in thousands of churches and synagogues around the country — at St. Patrick's Cathedral and St. Thomas Episcopal Church and Temple Emanu-El in New York City, for example.

Rabbi Abraham Gross, president of the Rabbinical Alliance of America, called on all clergymen to pray for the safe return of Apollo 13, and, in Baltimore, Frank Gunter Jr., Maryland chairman of the National Conference of Christians and Jews, asked all residents of the state to observe a minute of silent prayer at 4 P.M. yesterday.

In Montgomery, Ala., T.R. Hennessey, a retired Air Force

Continued on Page 29, Column 4

BEFORE FLIGHT: Capt. James A. Lovell Jr., Fred W. Haise Jr. and John L. Swigert Jr.

Associated Press

NIXON IS BRIEFED ON APOLLO CRISIS

Meets With Space Experts During Unannounced Visit to Center in Maryland

By RICHARD D. LYONS
Special to The New York Times

GREENBELT, Md., April 14—President Nixon, looking taut and tired, met with technical experts of the space agency here for 45 minutes this afternoon and was briefed about the past and future problems of the Apollo 13 mission.

Dr. John F. Clark, director of the National Aeronautics and Space Administration's Goddard Space Flight Center here, said that the President was deeply concerned and that he asked "many knowledgeable questions" about the mission's problems and "the contingencies that have been planned."

This center is the eyes, ears and touch of Apollo 13. It is here that all the information transmitted by the spaceship is collected from 17 tracking stations around the world and sent on to the Manned Spacecraft Center in Houston for analysis.

Unannounced Visit

Hatless and dressed in a tan raincoat, dark blue suit and blue striped tie, Mr. Nixon made an unannounced visit to the center, driving from the White House, 13 miles away, through a heavy rainstorm.

The President had been briefed by his aides three times during the night and early this morning about the sudden power loss in the Apollo 13 spaceship as it was heading toward the moon. According to Ronald L. Ziegler, the White House press secretary, Mr. Nixon was informed about 4 A.M. today that the corrective firing of the lunar module's engine would bring the spacecraft on a free return to earth.

"The President will be receiving reports throughout the day

Continued on Page 29, Column 7

The New York Times (by Edward Hausner)
PRAY FOR ASTRONAUTS: Worshipers at a special mass at St. Patrick's Cathedral for the crew of Apollo 13

The New York Times

LATE CITY EDITION

Weather: Sunny, cool today; clear, cool tonight. Fair, mild tomorrow.
Temp. range: today 60-48; Monday 66-52. Full U.S. report on Page 85.

VOL.CXX..No.41,156 © 1970 The New York Times Company. NEW YORK, TUESDAY, SEPTEMBER 29, 1970 15 CENTS

VATICAN CITY: President Nixon with Pope Paul VI during special audience yesterday. Later, he flew by helicopter to U.S.S. Saratoga, with Sixth Fleet in the Mediterranean.

NASSER DIES OF HEART ATTACK; BLOW TO PEACE EFFORTS SEEN; NIXON CANCELS FLEET EXERCISE

A GESTURE BY U.S.

President Terms Loss Tragic—He Joins Fleet Off Italy

By Reuters

ABOARD U.S.S. SARATOGA, in the Mediterranean, Tuesday, Sept. 29—President Nixon last night ordered cancellation of today's exercises of the United States Sixth Fleet in the Mediterranean because of the death of President Gamal Abdel Nasser of Egypt.

The President, who arrived aboard this aircraft carrier last night, had planned to watch a demonstration of Sixth Fleet firepower, including the launching and recovery of aircraft.

Officials said: "Upon hearing of the death of President Nasser, the President ordered the cancellation of the firepower demonstrations, which were to be held in conjunction with his visit to the Sixth Fleet."

They said that Mr. Nixon's conferences with Sixth Fleet commanders aboard the flagship Springfield would go on as scheduled.

The President flew to this carrier off the coast of Italy by helicopter after a day in which he had conferred in Rome with the President and the Premier of Italy and with Pope Paul VI.

'Tragic Loss'

The President in a statement said that the death of President Nasser was a tragic loss of an outstanding Arab leader.

"I was shocked to hear of the sudden death of President Nasser," Mr. Nixon said. "The world has lost an outstanding leader who tirelessly and devotedly served the causes of his countrymen and the Arab world.

"This tragic loss requires that all nations, and particularly those in the Middle East, redouble their efforts to calm passions, reach for mutual understanding and build lasting peace.

"On behalf of the American people I extended deep sympathy to his family and to his people."

Stresses Role of Fleet

Earlier Mr. Nixon had told the men of the Saratoga that never had American military and diplomatic power been used more effectively than in the latest Middle East crisis.

Chatting with sailors who greeted his helicopter on the flight deck, Mr. Nixon spoke of "a hard two or three weeks," which he said had been capped by success. He referred to the Jordanian truce and recovery of the hostages from the hijacked airliners.

"The fact that we were successful is the fact that you were there," he told the sailors. He mentioned their
Continued on Page 19, Column 1

President Gamal Abdel Nasser bidding good-by to King Hussein of Jordan after meeting in Cairo yesterday. From ceremony, he returned home where he died of heart attack.

U.S. Officials See Period Of Instability in Mideast

By TERENCE SMITH

WASHINGTON, Sept. 28 — United States officials, startled by the death of Gamal Abdel Nasser, tended to view it today as a blow to peace-making efforts in the Middle East.

A ranking State Department official described the Egyptian President's death as a "critical loss at a decisive moment in history."

The immediate reaction of officials here was that it would bring a period of instability in the Arab world and would therefore reduce the already-thin prospects for negotiating an early resolution of the Arab-Israeli dispute.

[In Moscow, Western diplomats expected the Soviet leaders to assure the United Arab Republic that President Nasser's death would not affect Soviet support for the Arab cause. Page 17.]

An hour before the Cairo radio announcement, a cable from Donald C. Bergus, the senior United States representative in Cairo, reported a rumor that the Egyptian leader was critically ill or perhaps dead. The message was being decoded as the public announcement came.

Six hours earlier Rodger P. Davies, the Acting Assistant Secretary of State for Near Eastern and South Asian Affairs, had told a closed session of the House Foreign Affairs Committee that the Nixon Administration was "leaning to-ward optimism" about the prospects of getting the United States-sponsored peace initiative in the Middle East back on the track.

The Senate was informed of the news by Senator John C. Stennis, Democrat of Mississippi, who interrupted a debate on election reform. He described Mr. Nasser, the leader in Cairo since 1952, as "superior to most anyone who might have been in power."

"I hope his death does not mean upheaval and turmoil in
Continued on Page 19, Column 1

THE ARAB WORLD IS GRIEF-STRICKEN

Moslems Fire Rifles Into Air as Sign of Mourning —Koran Read on Radio

By JOHN L. HESS

BEIRUT, Lebanon, Sept. 28—The Arab world went into mourning tonight over the loss of its major international figure. Arab distress was heightened by the fear that instability would increase in the area and diminish the already slender prospect of peace.

Television stations went off the air and radio programs were replaced by chants and readings from the Koran. In Beirut, Moslems fired thousands of shots into the air as a sign of emotion for the loss of Gamal Abdel Nasser. Men walked in the streets in impromptu procession declaiming "Allah Akbar!"—"God is great."

Security forces raced to thwart rioting of the kind that followed President Nasser's offer of resignation after the six-day war of June, 1967.

Youths started bonfires of automobile tires and a crowd began collecting outside the United States Embassy.

[A senior Cabinet minister in Israel said that the Israelis now appeared to face an indefinite stalemate on peace negotiations. Page 18.]

Observers here said that President Nasser was the only Arab
Continued on Page 17, Column 7

ARAB-WORLD HERO

Vice President Sadat Takes Over as the Interim Leader

Obituary article will be found on Page 16.

By RAYMOND H. ANDERSON
Special to The New York Times

CAIRO, Tuesday, Sept. 29—President Gamal Abdel Nasser, leader of Egypt for 18 years and hero of much of the Arab world, died here yesterday.

The Government radio said the 52-year-old President was the victim of a heart attack.

The death was announced on Cairo's television and radio stations shortly before 11 P.M. by Vice President Anwar Sadat. An hour earlier, regular programs on television and radio were abruptly suspended and replaced with chanting of verses from the Koran. Official mourning was proclaimed for 40 days.

The President suffered the heart attack at 3 P.M. and died three hours later.

No obvious successor to Mr. Nasser was in sight, and no Egyptian seemed in a mood to-night to speculate about the matter.

Funeral Will Be Thursday

Vice President Sadat took over as interim ruler. He reported that emergency meetings had been held by the higher executive committee of the Arab Socialist Union, the political organization created by Mr. Nasser, and the Council of Ministers.

President Nasser's funeral will be held Thursday.

The impact of Mr. Nasser's death will be felt throughout the Arab world. Despite controversies and rivalries during his long years of power, he was the strongest figure of leadership among the Arabs.

Since the battlefield defeat of three Arab armies by Israel in June, 1967, Mr. Nasser was the leader who rallied his forces to rebuild their forces for a war of liberation if other means to recover the lands failed.

Favored Political Solution

But he repeatedly emphasized that he favored a political solution of the conflict with Israel if one could be achieved.

Although Mr. Nasser gained a reputation in his early years in power as a fire-breathing radical, in recent years he had become a force for moderation and pragmatism.

Even on the emotional issue of Israel, he was able to swing much of the Arab world behind his acceptance in July of a United States initiative for a cease-fire and he revived efforts for a negotiated settlement. The outlook for pursuing
Continued on Page 17, Column 1

50,000 FLEE BLAZE IN SAN DIEGO AREA

Brush Fire, 30 Miles Long, Is California's Biggest Yet —5 Die in Copter Crash

By United Press International

LOS ANGELES, Sept. 28—The largest brush fire in California history raged today through mountain canyons near the Mexican border, driving thousands of persons from their homes as the flames advanced.

In the San Gabriel Mountains to the north, a helicopter being used by the United States Forest Service to fight another fire crashed late today, killing the five persons aboard.

More than 50,000 persons were evacuated from small communities in San Diego County The 200-acre fire there erupted in the Cleveland National Forest on Saturday when a falling tree severed a power line. At least 250 structures have been destroyed.

Decreasing winds tonight and a forecast of scattered showers in mountain areas raised hopes that the blaze could be contained tomorrow.

Arson Arrests Made

The enormous blaze, 30 miles from tip to tip, eclipsed in size the Matalaja fire of 1930, which burned 125,000 acres in Kern and Los Angeles Counties.

"We've barely kept up with the situation," said Arlen B. Cartwright of the State Division of Forestry. "The problem seems to come from the fact that fire nuts run around and see flames and smoke and this makes them want to set more fires—which they do."

Arson was suspected in two other major blazes in San Diego County, and five arrests were made in Los Angeles County.

More than 5,000 men worked 36-hour shifts on the fire lines and the neighboring county of San Bernardino lost all but five of its fire engines.
Continued on Page 10, Column 2

Malpractice Suits Reported Soaring

By LAWRENCE K. ALTMAN

Witnesses at a State Senate public hearing testified here yesterday that a steep rise in medical malpractice suits is forcing physicians to practice "defensive medicine" shirk hazardous modes of treatment that could be of benefit to patients, and pass along the costs of sky-rocketing insurance premiums to patients.

"One physician in every six has been sued for malpractice," State Senator Norman F. Lent told the hearing. And more than 10,000 Americans will initiate medical malpractice suits this year, Senator Lent, who is chairman of the Senate Committee on Health, added.

Because some insurance companies find medical malpractice insurance unprofitable, wit-
Continued on Page 32, Column 1

Intrepid Wins Series, 4-1, And Keeps America's Cup

By STEVE CADY
Special to The New York Times

NEWPORT, R.I., Sept. 28—The longest series in 100 years of America's Cup challenges came to a desperately dramatic close today when Intrepid completing a 4-1 conquest of Gretel II.

Once again, the defender of yachting's most famous prize had to fight off almost constant pressure by the chunky Australian challenger.

Until a wind shift put Intrepid in clover starting the final leg of the 24.3-mile race, the action had been as close as a boat race can produce. The cynics say watching two yachts is like watching grass grow, but the grass was on fire again today, as it was so often during this controversial series.

Stage Set for Upset

When Gretel II closed to within two boat lengths at the fifth mark, the stage was set for another upset of the kind the Australian sloop brought off last Thursday. Then the wind shifted from north to east, Intrepid hit it on the right tack and the suspense evaporated.

With the final windward leg turned into a race, the redesigned 1967 defender opened up
Continued on Page 53, Column 1

John Dos Passos Is Dead at 74; Acclaimed for 'U.S.A.' Trilogy

Special to The New York Times

BALTIMORE, Sept. 28—John Dos Passos, the novelist of the post-World War I generation who wrote more than 30 books, including the trilogy "U.S.A.," died today in his apartment.

Mr. Dos Passos, who was 74 years old, had been troubled by a heart ailment in recent years and was released only Saturday from Good Samaritan Hospital. When not away on his extensive travels, he divided his time between his apartment here and a home in Westmoreland, Va.

Mr. Dos Passos is survived by his widow, the former Elizabeth Hamlin Holdridge; their daughter, Lucy, and a stepson, Christopher Holdridge.

A funeral service will be held Thursday at 10 A.M. at the William Cook-Brooks Funeral Home in the nearby town of Towson, Md.

Fame From Early Books
By ALDEN WHITMAN

The life and writings of John Dos Passos were marked by a progression from left to right. "Every day I become more Red," he said in his youth. "My one ambition is to be able to sing 'The International.'" But in middle and old age, he turned against his former ideas, berating liberals, Socialists and Communists with zeal. The one-time writer for The New Masses became a contributor to the National Review; the friend of Ernest Hemingway became that of William F. Buckley Jr.; and the supporter of

Gil Friedberg-Pix
John Dos Passos

William Z. Foster turned into the backer of Barry Goldwater.

His novels, too, marched rightward. The trilogy "U.S.A.," completed in 1936 and generally recognized as one of the hinges of modern fiction, was a painstakingly detailed and angry portrait of industrial America between 1898 and 1929. It concluded with the heroine's joining the Communist party in revulsion over what she believed were the injustices of the Sacco-Vanzetti case.

His subsequent trilogy, "District of Columbia," completed in 1949, acerbically chronicled what the author clearly viewed as the failure of the New Deal.
Continued on Page 47, Column 1

Anti-Arab Jet Plot Laid to Seized Pair

By MORRIS KAPLAN

An Israeli Army veteran and his wife, accused of trying to board a London-bound plane here with a live hand grenade and four loaded guns hidden in their clothing, were reported yesterday to have planned to hijack an Arab airliner and take it to Israel.

Law enforcement sources said the couple reportedly had planned to board a United Arab Airlines plane bound for Cairo at the London airport and divert the flight to Israel "in retaliation" for a recent attempted hijacking of an El Al airliner in London.

The sources said that the veteran, Avraham Hershkovitz, had worked as a "manager" here for the Jewish Defense
Continued on Page 12, Column 1

Arab Truce Observers Arrive In Generally Peaceful Amman

By ERIC PACE
Special to The New York Times

AMMAN, Jordan, Sept. 28—One hundred foreign Arab officers arrived here today to serve on the peace-keeping observer teams that will be deployed in Amman under the agreement reached yesterday in Cairo to end hostilities between the Jordanian Government and the Palestinian commandos.

The cease-fire instituted last Friday after nine days of civil war seemed generally effective this morning. There were no fires along the capital's skyline, although a few bursts of firing resounded in the center of Amman and on Jebel Luweibida and Jebel Amman, two of the city's seven hills.

Western diplomats also reported that shelling or shooting was continuing in part of the Palestinians' Ashrafiyeh quarter, where many of the airline hostages had been held.

There was no sign that either the army or the commandos had abandoned their positions in Amman, as the Cairo agreement called for. The guerrillas are entrenched in a populous area around the Hussein Mosque at the heart of the city, where gunfire was occasionally heard during the day.

Despite a further provision of the Cairo agreement for a release of detainees, scores were still visible this morning at the army prison camp on the way to the airport. As their women peered in through the barbed-wire fence, they were seated in orderly rows, apparently being indoctrinated by their Jordanian Army captors.

The army appeared intent to be trying to finish its clean-up of Ashrafiyeh, once a commando stronghold. Aside from that, no wide-scale military operations were known to be under way. The general calm this morning followed radio broadcasts of the 14-point agreement signed by King Hus-
Continued on Page 18, Column 5

Text of Cairo agreement is printed on Page 18.

Fourth Group of Hostages Here After Seeing President in Rome

By ROBERT D. McFADDEN

Thirty-three travel-weary Americans, whose ordinary lives became the focus of international concern during three harrowing weeks in Jordan, were hostages in Jordan, arrived at Kennedy International Airport last night and were met by loved ones, friends and a clamoring throng of newsmen.

The passengers—26 men, 6 women and an infant—were the fourth group of Americans brought home safely from an ordeal that began with multiple hijackings Sept. 6. All but two of the 33 were men over the weekend and were flown home through Nicosia, Cyprus, and Rome.

Their faces were haggard but smiling and their clothes rumpled after a 12-hour flight from Rome, where they met briefly with President Nixon in the morning. They stepped off a chartered flight at the Trans World Airlines terminal shortly after 6 P.M. They were ushered quickly through Customs and led into a private room for a reunion with 175 relatives.

Nearly 1,000 friends greeted them in the corridors and public waiting rooms as they emerged.

Six Americans are still being held of the original group on three hijacked planes. They are somewhere in Jordan.

Contrary to the confused receptions at three previous returning flights, passengers arriving last night were not besieged by newsmen thrusting cameras and microphones into
Continued on Page 18, Column 2

NEWS INDEX
	Page
Art	36
Books	41
Bridge	40
Business	63
Crossword	41
Editorials	46
Financial	59-68
Man in the News	16
Movies	34-39
Music	34-39
Obituaries	44
Society	52
Theaters	34-39
Transportation	85
TV and Radio	86-87
U. N. Proceedings	13
U.S. Proceedings	6
Washington Record	6
Weather	85
Women's	45

News Summary and Index, Page 45

242

"All the News That's Fit to Print"

The New York Times

LATE CITY EDITION

Weather: Partly sunny, mild today; fair tonight. Cloudy, mild tomorrow. Temp. range: today 49-35; Friday 40-26. Full U.S. report on Page 58.

VOL. CXX..No. 41,286   © 1971 The New York Times Company.   NEW YORK, SATURDAY, FEBRUARY 6, 1971   15 CENTS

2 ASTRONAUTS WALK AND WORK FOR HOURS ON MOON'S SURFACE

U.S. OFFICIALS FEEL NIXON HAS DECIDED ON STRIKE IN LAOS

Timing of South Vietnamese Drive Is Said to Depend on Pace of Build-up

By TERENCE SMITH
Special to The New York Times

WASHINGTON, Feb. 5 — Strong indications emerged here today that the Nixon Administration had decided to go ahead with a strike by South Vietnamese troops against enemy supply lines in southern Laos.

The Administration's official spokesmen continued, for the seventh consecutive day, to refuse any public comment on the possibility of such a strike, but officials not directly concerned with the planning said they believed the White House had decided within the last 48 hours to go ahead.

Roads and Bridges Rebuilt

The timing of the strike, the officials said, would depend upon how quickly the nearly 30,000 allied soldiers massed along the Laotian border could complete "stage one" of the new operation, called Dewey Canyon II.

In the initial stage, which began early last Saturday, the troops have swept westward across the northernmost tip of South Vietnam, scouring the countryside for enemy troops, rebuilding roads and bridges and reoccupying long-deserted allied outposts such as Khesanh and Langvei.

According to reports from the field, this work was still under way today. [Page 4.]

Army engineers were working around the clock to rehabilitate the airstrip at Khesanh and strengthen the bunkers that 6,000 American Marines occupied during a 77-day siege at the outpost three years ago.

Secure Base Sought

Little enemy resistance has been encountered in the first stage of the operation, despite intelligence reports that up to nine regiments of North Vietnamese regulars were in the rugged mountains along the border.

According to a White House source, the operation was conceived as a two-stage project, with the final decision to go into Laos hinging, among other considerations, on the amount of fighting encountered in the first stage.

The military planners reportedly considered it necessary to establish a secure base in the northwestern corner of South Vietnam before deciding whether to begin the second stage of the operation.

At least one intelligence report indicated that American

Continued on Page 5, Column 1

A Laotian General Cool to Bigger War

By HENRY KAMM
Special to The New York Times

DONG HENE, Laos, Feb. 5 —The commander of Laotian combat forces in the center of the panhandle of Laos said at his beleaguered forward command post today that the situation was critical and he did not expect to be able to hold out under mounting North Vietnamese pressure.

But the officer, Brig. Gen. Nouphet Deoheung, said nobody had told him that less than 100 miles eastward in the northwest corner of South Vietnam, a large force of American and South Vietnamese troops was driving the enemy in his direction. His meagerly equipped, ragtag forces have received no reinforcements from the Laotian Government.

Continued on Page 6, Column 4

MAN ON MOON: Capt. Alan B. Shepard Jr. steps off module ladder onto lunar surface.

FOR THE RECORD: Captain Shepard, right, stands by the U.S. flag as Comdr. Edgar D. Mitchell snaps his picture. A TV camera transmitted the scene. At left, behind Commander Mitchell, are an umbrella-like communications antenna and, rear, the module.   C.B.S. News

JURY CALLS POLICE IN GAMING INQUIRY

Looks Into Charges That 30 Were Involved With Major Gambler in Brooklyn

By DAVID BURNHAM

A Brooklyn grand jury is investigating reports of corrupt links among more than 30 policemen and former policemen, a judge and a gambling empire allegedly operated by a Brooklyn figure with a long criminal record.

The investigation is based on evidence collected during the last year by the office of District Attorney Eugene Gold and the internal affairs division of the Police Department.

More than 50 known gamblers, policemen and former policemen already have been subpoenaed. One of the first subpoenas was handed on Thursday to Thomas Marino, 72 years old, reportedly the operator of the gambling ring.

In another development involving possible corruption, the State Supreme Court yesterday upheld the legality of the subpoenas for 14 policemen, in

Continued on Page 14, Column 4

Court Upholds Patrolmen On Retroactive Pay Claim

By DAMON STETSON

State Supreme Court Justice Irving H. Saypol ruled yesterday that the Patrolmen's Benevolent Association had a valid contract with the city requiring a $100-a-month retroactive pay increase for 27,000 patrolmen.

The contract that the judge ruled "enforceable" ran from Oct. 1, 1968, to Dec. 31, 1970, so that the total of retroactive pay that the patrolmen claim is $2,700 each for the 27-month period.

The increase is based on a pay-parity provision in the contract saying the patrolmen should be paid at a rate of $3 for every $3.50 paid to sergeants.

Issue Not Settled

The issue, which has been in the courts for nearly a year and spurred a strike by the policemen last month, is still not settled, however.

A spokesman for Mayor Lindsay said that on advice of the Corporation Counsel, J. Lee Rankin, the city was going to appeal Judge Saypol's decision. The Mayor, the spokesman said, has asked the Corporation Counsel to expedite the appeal on the decision, which could cost the city hundreds of millions of dollars.

The appeal to the Appellate Division and then, perhaps, to the State Court of Appeals could take weeks or even months, lawyers said.

Edward J. Kiernan, president of the P.B.A., said the decision of Justice Saypol "reaffirmed my confidence in the court system."

Dissidents Noted

In an oblique reference to dissident members of the association who led last month's strike of policemen without P.B.A. sanction, Mr. Kiernan said the ruling should restore the faith of all policemen in the court structure. He recalled that the P.B.A. leadership had urged the strikers to get back on the job and trust the courts to deal fairly with the patrolmen's suit.

The policemen struck after the Court of Appeals ruled last month that a trial must be held to determine the validity of the contract.

John J. Loflin Jr., who represented the city in the trial be-

Continued on Page 14, Column 4

DEFECTIVE SWITCH POSED A PROBLEM

A Short Circuit That Could Have Aborted the Landing Required New Program

By RICHARD WITKIN

It took some ingenious rewriting of a computer program and about 60 rapid-fire punches on a cockpit keyboard to clear the way for the Apollo lunar landing yesterday.

The difficulty, described by officials as a "very serious" problem, was apparently in a cockpit switch that was producing intermittent short circuits.

The two astronauts aboard the lunar module were never endangered by the trouble. But it threatened to delay the landing attempt for one, two, or even three more lunar orbits. And there was an outside chance it could have canceled the landing attempt altogether.

Other Problems Cited

There were other technical aberrations that cropped up during the descent from lunar orbit to the Fra Mauro landing site, notably the distressing delay in proper functioning of the landing radar. However, it was the misbehaving switch that caused the day's biggest commotion.

The difficulty turned up at 1:30 a.m., less than three hours before the landing ship Antares was to start its final descent to the moon.

At the space agency's control center in Houston, engineers monitoring the operations of every spacecraft system saw a "spurious" number turn up on a console. The num-

Continued on Page 12, Column 2

Unemployment Rate Down For First Time in 7 Months

By EILEEN SHANAHAN
Special to The New York Times

WASHINGTON, Feb. 5—The statistics for last year changed the basis for comparison.

The unemployment rate dropped somewhat in January, its first decline in seven months, the Labor Department reported today.

The actual number of people out of work rose, however, as it generally does in January, to 5.4 million, the largest number in 10 years.

The unemployment rate is adjusted to eliminate the effects of normal seasonal changes, a procedure designed to make the underlying trend clearer.

Secretary of Labor James D. Hodgson attributed "great significance" to the downturn in the unemployment rate in January, coupled with other developments in the labor market.

On the other hand, Harold Goldstein, the Assistant Commissioner of Labor Statistics, described the change as "marginally significant." Mr. Goldstein is a career civil servant, and the Bureau of Labor Statistics, where he works, is traditionally nonpartisan division of the Labor Department.

The January statistics did present a somewhat confusing picture, partly because a routine revision in some of the

The unemployment rate for December, originally reported as 6 per cent, was revised upward to 6.2 per cent.

On the revised basis, the January rate was 6 per cent, a drop of two-tenths of a percentage point from the December level.

As it turned out, a drop of two-tenths of a percentage point would have been recorded if the revisions had not taken place. On the unrevised basis, the January rate would have been 5.8 per cent.

These revisions, which are made annually, incorporate the most up-to-date information on the adjustments in the raw figures that are needed to eliminate purely seasonal influences. The idea of revising the figures and the process by which they are revised are accepted as valid by all economists and statisticians in the field.

The differing adjustments of the figures made by Secretary Hodgson and Mr. Goldstein were unrelated to the revision in the seasonal adjustments, although some seasonal developments figured in the

Continued on Page 22, Column 1

City Seeks New Unit To Finance Housing

By STEVEN R. WEISMAN

Mayor Lindsay yesterday announced a bipartisan drive to seek the creation of a city housing finance agency that would float $700 million in bonds to provide mortgages for 25,000 new and rehabilitated apartments here in two years.

The push to gain approval of the measure by the Legislature, Mr. Lindsay said, will be "the city's No. 1 state legislative priority."

Under the bill, bonds of the proposed New York City Housing Development Corporation would be backed up by the "moral obligation," rather than the full faith and credit, of New York City. In this manner, the corporation could be created without changing the city's debt limit, which is imposed by the

Continued on Page 16, Column 5

Direct From Moon

Following are conversations between flight controllers in Houston and Capt. Alan B. Shepard Jr. and Comdr. Edgar D. Mitchell of the Navy, as recorded by The New York Times. The conversations occurred during the first moon walk yesterday, when the astronauts left the lunar lander, Antares.

ANTARES (9:49 A.M.)— Forward hatch the rest of the way open. O.K., forward hatch is open.

MITCHELL—I'll get your antenna as you go out.

SHEPARD — All right, starting out the door.

HOUSTON—Shortly Shepard will be throwing the equipment conveyor belt.

MITCHELL — While he's working on the LEC [lunar equipment conveyor] let me comment that it certainly is a stark place here. I think it's made all the more stark by the fact that the sky is completely black.

SHEPARD—Starting down the ladder.

HOUSTON—Roger . . . O.K., Al, beautiful. We see you coming down the ladder now. It looks like you're about on the bottom step—and on the surface. How's that for an old man?

SHEPARD — O.K., you're right. Al is on the surface. It's been a long way, but we're here. Now I can see

the reason we have a tilt is we landed on a slope. The landing gear struts appear to be about evenly depressed. Moving around, getting familiar with the surface. The surface in which the forward footpad landed is extremely soft. As a matter of fact, it's in a small depression. The soil is so soft that it comes up all the way to the top of the footpads.

HOUSTON—Roger.

SHEPARD—O. K., we'll move on over and take a look at Fra Mauro. Take a look at Cone Crater, which is right where it should be and is a very impressive sight.

HOUSTON—Antares, this is Houston. You are go for two-man EVA [extravehicular activity]. Over.

MITCHELL—Roger, Houston. Thank you.

SHEPARD—Continuing, we can see the boulders on the rim. It looks as though we have a good traverse route

Continued on Page 12, Column 6

2D WALK IS BEGUN

Hike to Crater Planned —Men Are to Rejoin Mother Ship Today

By JOHN NOBLE WILFORD
Special to The New York Times

HOUSTON, Saturday, Feb. 6 —Two American astronauts walked the gentle slopes of Fra Mauro yesterday, setting up instruments, collecting rocks and probing subsurface reaches in search of clues to the moon's earliest history.

While earthbound scientists eagerly watched their every televised step, Capt. Alan B. Shepard Jr. and Comdr. Edgar D. Mitchell of the Navy, the Apollo 14 explorers, spent more than four and one-half hours outside their landing craft, Antares.

Shortly before 3:30 A.M., the men began their second moon exploration.

The 47-year-old Captain Shepard opened the hatch at 9:49 A.M. Eastern standard time yesterday and stepped out on the "porch" at the top of the ladder.

The hatch remained open for four hours and 40 minutes, until 2:29 P.M.

"It certainly is a stark place here at Fra Mauro," he remarked, looking out at the undulating hills and ridges, the gray and brown soil, the distant craters and the black sky above.

Nuclear-Powered Station

During the moon walk, Captain Shepard and Commander Mitchell established a nuclear-powered scientific station to record moonquakes, measure electrically charged particles and detect the composition and energies of solar wind. The first signals from the seismometers were of the astronauts' own footsteps.

The two men also "thumped" the ancient surface with small explosive charges that sent vibrations to depths of 50 feet for indications of the rubble-like structure below the surface. In addition, the astronauts gathered soil and rocks, two of which were as big as footballs.

It was the first of the two scheduled moon excursions by the two astronauts, who landed early yesterday in the Fra Mauro highlands for a planned 33½-hour visit.

Their explorations are considered the most intensive and ambitious made thus far on the moon. Scientists are especially interested in Fra Mauro because it may have rocks as old as the solar system itself.

Men Awaken Early

The second moon walk had originally been scheduled for 5:30 this morning, but the two astronauts awoke from a nap sooner than expected and received permission to begin their walk of up to five hours.

"We're up and running this morning," Commander Shepard reported at 12:23. "The shape of the crew is excellent."

A hike out to a boulder-rimmed crater about 2,000 feet from Antares was planned.

After the second walk, the astronauts are to fire the ascent engine of Antares at 1:47 P.M. to leave the moon and rejoin the command ship Kitty Hawk.

Maj. Stuart A. Roosa of the Air Force, the third crew member, is piloting Kitty Hawk in a 70-mile-high lunar orbit.

Fra Mauro lies near the lunar equator at the eastern edge of the Ocean of Storms.

Continued on Page 12, Column 1

NEWS INDEX

WARNING! NO U.S. PERSONNEL BEYOND THIS POINT

Associated Press

NEAR THE LAOTIAN BORDER: G.I.'s posting a warning near Langvei in South Vietnam. U.S. ground forces are forbidden to cross into Laos, about 200 yards beyond the sign.

The New York Times

LATE CITY EDITION
Weather: Chance of showers today, tonight. Partly sunny tomorrow. Temp. range: today 74-94; Wed. 72-91. Temp. Hum. Index yesterday 82. Full U.S. report on Page 94.

VOL. CXX...No. 41,431   © 1971 The New York Times Company   NEW YORK, THURSDAY, JULY 1, 1971   15 CENTS

SUPREME COURT, 6-3, UPHOLDS NEWSPAPERS ON PUBLICATION OF THE PENTAGON REPORT; TIMES RESUMES ITS SERIES, HALTED 15 DAYS

Nixon Says Turks Agree To Ban the Opium Poppy

By JOHN HERBERS
Special to The New York Times

WASHINGTON, June 30—President Nixon announced today that Turkey had agreed to eliminate within a year her production of opium poppies, which account for about two-thirds of the illegal heroin reaching the United States.

Mr. Nixon, in a brief announcement delivered in the White House press room, said that as a result of negotiations between the United States and Turkish Governments, Premier Nihat Erim had agreed to ban altogether the cultivation of opium poppies by June, 1972.

He said the joint announcement, made simultaneously in Washington and Ankara, "represents by far the most significant breakthrough that has been achieved in stopping the source of supply of heroin in our worldwide offensive against dangerous drugs."

Continued on Page 22, Column 1

Soviet Starts an Inquiry Into 3 Astronauts' Deaths

By BERNARD GWERTZMAN
Special to The New York Times

MOSCOW, June 30—The Soviet authorities appointed a special commission tonight to investigate the deaths of three astronauts who perished this morning when their Soyuz 11 craft was returning to earth after the longest manned space flight in history.

News of the astronauts' deaths shocked many Soviet people. And Western specialists predicted that their deaths would retard development of the Salyut space station program. The three astronauts had spent more than three weeks working and exercising aboard the Salyut craft, described as the world's first space laboratory.

[In the United States, Amer-]

ican officials said the Soviet space disaster had probably been caused by a failure in the oxygen supply. They also said the accident should not delay United States space flights. Articles on Page 30.]

Tonight, the Soviet people seemed caught up in the human aspects of the disaster and the mystery of what caused the deaths of Lieut. Col. Georgi T. Dobrovolsky, the flight commander; Vladislav N. Volkov, the flight engineer, and Viktor I. Patsayev, the test engineer. Were their deaths caused by the weakened state of their bodies after nearly 24 days of weightlessness? Were they

Continued on Page 30, Column 3

PRESIDENT CALLS STEEL AND LABOR TO WHITE HOUSE

He Asks Both Sides to Meet With Him Tuesday Before Contract Talks Start

By PHILIP SHABECOFF
Special to The New York Times

WASHINGTON, June 30—President Nixon has called negotiators of the steel companies and steelworkers union to meet with him next Tuesday before they sit down to begin contract negotiations, a White House spokesman announced today.

It will be the first time that the President will have met with labor and management in any industry prior to nationwide contract negotiations, according to Ronald L. Ziegler, the White House press secretary.

Discussion Issues Listed

Mr. Ziegler said that the President had called the meeting to discuss general economic developments and trends in the world steel markets.

Earlier today, the chairman of the Federal Reserve Board, Arthur F. Burns, told a Congressional committee that the "first priority" should be given to a new Government move to try to moderate price and wage increases and expressed his concern over the spread of "inflationary psychology" in this country.

The Administration has repeatedly warned that excessive increases in steel wages and prices would severely retard efforts to control inflation. Hints have been dropped that import quotas that protect domestic steel from foreign competition will be eased or lifted if prices go too high.

President Nixon has been in-

Continued on Page 38, Column 1

Pentagon Papers: Study Reports Kennedy Made 'Gamble' Into a 'Broad Commitment'

By HEDRICK SMITH

The Pentagon's study of the Vietnam war concludes that President John F. Kennedy transformed the "limited-risk gamble" of the Eisenhower Administration into a "broad commitment" to prevent Communist domination of South Vietnam.

Although Mr. Kennedy resisted pressures for putting American ground-combat units into South Vietnam, the Pentagon analysts say, he took a series of actions that significantly expanded the American military and political involvement in Vietnam but nonetheless left President Lyndon B. Johnson with as bad a situation as Mr. Kennedy inherited.

"The dilemma of the U.S. involvement dating from the Kennedy era," the Pentagon study observes, was to use "only limited means to achieve excessive ends."

Moreover, according to the study, prepared in 1967-68 by Government analysts, the Kennedy tactics deepened the American involvement in Vietnam piecemeal, with each step minimizing public recognition that the American role was growing.

The expansion of that role, over three decades, is traced in the 3,000 pages of the Pentagon's study, which is ac-

companied by 4,000 pages of documents on the Vietnam era. Previous articles in The Times's presentation of this material have recounted President Johnson's movement to war in 1964 and 1965.

President Kennedy made his first fresh commitments to Vietnam secretly. The Pentagon study discloses that in the spring of 1961 the President ordered 400

The Times today resumes its series of articles on the Pentagon's secret study of the Vietnam war. The study was obtained through the investigative reporting of Neil Sheehan, and the articles were researched and written over three months by Mr. Sheehan and other staff members. The fourth and fifth articles, both by Hedrick Smith, are published today and form an account of decisions in the Kennedy Administration.

Three pages of documentary material covering the Kennedy policy begin on Page 3, and documents on the 1963 coup begin on Page 9. A summary of the three earlier articles, covering the Johnson Administration, appears on Page 15.

Special Forces troops and 100 other American military advisers sent to South Vietnam. No publicity was given to either move.

Small as the numbers seem in retrospect, the Pentagon study comments that even the first such expansion "signaled a willingness to go beyond the 685-man limit on the size of the U.S. [military] mission in Saigon, which, if it were done openly, would be the first formal breach of the Geneva agreement." Under the interpretation of that agreement in effect since 1956, the United States was limited to 685 military advisers in Vietnam. Washington, while it did not sign the accord, pledged not to undermine it.

On May 11, 1961, the day on which President Kennedy ordered to send the Special Forces, he also ordered the start of a campaign of clandestine warfare against North Vietnam to be conducted by South Vietnamese agents directed and trained by the Central Intelligence Agency and some American Special Forces troops. [See text, action memorandum, May 11, 1961, Page 3.]

The President's instructions, as quoted in the documents, were, "In North Vietnam . . . [to] form networks of resistance, covert bases and teams for

Continued on Page 6, Column 1

U.S. and Diem's Overthrow: Step by Step

The Pentagon's secret study of the Vietnam war discloses that President Kennedy knew and approved of plans for the military coup d'état that overthrew President Ngo Dinh Diem in 1963.

"Our complicity in his overthrow heightened our responsibilities and our commitment" in Vietnam, the study finds.

In August and October of 1963, the narrative recounts, the United States gave its support to a cabal of army generals bent on removing the controversial leader, whose rise to power Mr. Kennedy had backed in speeches in the middle nineteen-fifties and who had been the anchor of American policy in Vietnam for nine years.

The coup, one of the most dramatic episodes in the history of the American involvement in Vietnam, was a watershed. As the Pentagon study observes, it was a time when Washington—with the Diem regime gone—could have reconsidered its entire commitment to South Vietnam and decided to disengage.

At least two Administration officials advocated disengagement but, according to the Pentagon study, it "was never

seriously considered a policy alternative because of the assumption that an independent, non-Communist SVN was too important a strategic interest to abandon."

The effect, according to this account, was that the United States, discovering after the coup that the war against the Vietcong had been going much worse than officials previously thought, felt compelled to do more—rather than less—for Saigon. By supporting the anti-Diem coup, the analyst asserts, "the U.S. inadvertently deepened its involvement. The inadvertence is the key factor."

According to the Pentagon account of the 1963 events in Saigon, Washington did not originate the anti-Diem coup, nor did American forces intervene in any way, even to try to prevent the assassinations of Mr. Diem and his brother Ngo Dinh Nhu, who, as the chief Diem political adviser, had accumulated immense power. Popular discontent with the Diem regime focused on Mr. Nhu and his wife.

But for weeks—and with the White House informed every step of the way—

the American mission in Saigon maintained secret contacts with the plotting generals through one of the Central Intelligence Agency's most experienced and versatile operatives, an Indochina veteran, Lieut. Col. Lucien Conein. The colonel, who is now in retirement, first landed in Vietnam in 1944 by parachute for the Office of Strategic Services, the wartime forerunner of the C.I.A.

So trusted by the Vietnamese generals was Colonel Conein that he was in their midst at Vietnamese General Staff headquarters as they launched the coup. Indeed, on Oct. 25, a week earlier, in a cable to McGeorge Bundy, the President's special assistant for national security, Ambassador Lodge had occasion to describe Colonel Conein of the C.I.A. —referring to the agency, in code terminology, as C.A.S.—as the indispensable man:

"C.A.S. has been punctilious in carrying out my instructions. I have personally approved each meeting between General Don [one of three main plotters] and Conein who has carried out my

Continued on Page 12, Column 1

BURGER DISSENTS

First Amendment Rule Held to Block Most Prior Restraints

Decision, concurring opinions, dissents start on Page 17.

By FRED P. GRAHAM
Special to The New York Times

WASHINGTON, June 30 — The Supreme Court freed The New York Times and The Washington Post today to resume immediate publication of articles based on the secret Pentagon papers on the origins of the Vietnam war.

By a vote of 6 to 3 the Court held that any attempt by the Government to block news articles prior to publication bears "a heavy burden of presumption against its constitutionality."

In a historic test of that principle — the first effort by the Government to enjoin publication on the ground of national security — the Court declared that "the Government has not met that burden."

The brief judgment was read to a hushed courtroom by Chief Justice Warren E. Burger at 2:30 P.M. at a special session called three hours before.

Old Tradition Observed

The Chief Justice was one of the dissenters, along with Associate Justices Harry A. Blackmun and John M. Harlan, but because the decision was rendered in an unsigned opinion, the Chief Justice read it in court in accordance with long-standing custom.

In New York Arthur Ochs Sulzberger, president and publisher of The Times, said at a news conference that he had "never really doubted that this day would come and that we'd win." His reaction, he said, was "complete joy and delight."

The case had been expected to produce a landmark ruling on the circumstances under which prior restraint could be imposed upon the press, but because no opinion by a single Justice commanded the support of a majority, the unsigned decision will serve as precedent.

Uncertainty Over Outcome

Because it came on the 15th day after The Times had been restrained from publishing further articles in its series mined from the 7,000 pages of material—the first such restraint in the name of "national security" in the history of the United States—there was some uncertainty whether the press had scored a strong victory or whether a precedent for some degree of restraint had been set.

Alexander M. Bickel, the Yale law professor who had argued for The Times in the case, said in a telephone interview that the ruling placed the press in a "stronger position." He maintained that no Federal District Judge would henceforth temporarily restrain a newspaper on the Justice Department's complaint that "this is what they have printed and we don't like it" and that a direct threat of irreparable harm would have to be alleged.

However, the United States Solicitor General, Erwin N. Griswold, turned to another lawyer shortly after the Justices filed from the courtroom and remarked: "Maybe the newspapers will show a little

Continued on Page 15, Column 1

CHOU TIES U.N. SEAT TO TAIPEI'S OUSTER

Also Says Peking Must Have Permanent Council Post if It Is to Be Member

By TAKASHI OKA
Special to The New York Times

TOKYO, June 30 — Premier Chou En-lai of China in an interview published here today that for his country to join the United Nations it was necessary not only that all membership rights be "restored," including a permanent seat on the Security Council, but that the Nationalists be ousted from the United Nations.

Mr. Chou made the comment in a meeting with Yoshikatsu Takeiri, chairman of Komeito, the Clean Government party, who is visiting Peking with eight of his followers. The Premier's comments were published today in the party newspaper Komei Shimbun as well as in other major Japanese newspapers.

'What Steps Are Necessary'

Mr. Chou's comments, which are consistent with the line Peking has taken on prospective United Nations membership, apparently weakened attempts by the United States, Japan and other interested members of the United Nations to safeguard at least a General Assembly seat for the Nationalists while admitting the Chinese Communists to the Security Council at least as the Assembly.

"What steps do you think are necessary in order to get China into the United Nations?" Mr. Chou was asked.

Continued on Page 32, Column 4

Jim Garrison Is Arrested; U.S. Says He Took Bribes

By ROY REED
Special to The New York Times

NEW ORLEANS, June 30 — District Attorney Jim Garrison was taken into custody at his home. He was fingerprinted and placed under $5,000 bond by a Federal magistrate.

was arrested by Federal agents today and charged with taking bribes to protect illegal pinball gambling in New Orleans.

The Justice Department said that the last payment, $1,000, was delivered to Mr. Garrison at his home last night in marked $50 bills. The payment, the department said, was handed to him by a once-trusted confidant who had secretly gone to work for the Government's agents.

Mr. Garrison, 50 years old, who attempted to prove a conspiracy in the 1963 assassination of President Kennedy,

The Justice Department said that Mr. Garrison had taken up to $1,500 a month in bribes.

According to the Government, Mr. Garrison received the bribes from pinball operators since 1962.

"I've never accepted a dollar in my life," the District Attorney told reporters as he walked into the French Quarter Courthouse to face the magistrate.

Mr. Garrison was one of 10 men arrested. The others in-

Continued on Page 55, Column 3

Cousin Asserts Jerome Johnson Told of Job With Italian League

By BARBARA CAMPBELL

A cousin of Jerome A. Johnson, who was shot to death at the site of a rally in Columbus Circle after allegedly firing three bullets into Joseph A. Colombo Sr., said yesterday that Johnson told him "several months ago" he was working for the Italian-American Civil Rights League as a photographer.

This was corroborated by a close friend of Johnson's, who said the 24-year-old slain man had also told him on a May 15 visit to California that he was working for the league.

About three months before the shooting, Johnson gave his cousin a telephone number where he could be reached and

a check by The New York Times disclosed yesterday that the number had been changed. The operator said the number had been switched to a new number, that of the Italian-American League.

This latest development raised a series of questions for investigators. If Johnson was working for the league, was he known there? Was he an employee or a hanger-on, perhaps a temporary called in on occasions?

Chief of Detectives Albert A. Seedman said last night only that the telephone-number switch, if true, "certainly puts

Continued on Page 53, Column 1

THE STATES RATIFY FULL VOTE AT 18

Ohio Becomes 38th to Back the 26th Amendment

By R. W. APPLE Jr.
Special to The New York Times

WASHINGTON, June 30—The 26th Amendment to the Constitution, lowering to 18 years the minimum voting age in local and state as well as Federal elections, was ratified tonight.

Ohio became the 38th state to approve the Amendment when the state's House of Representatives, meeting in extraordinary evening session, gave its assent, 81 to 9. The Ohio Senate had approved the measure yesterday, 30 to 2.

The ratification of at least 38 states, or three-quarters of the total, is required for constitutional amendments.

An atmosphere of near-panic attended Ohio's climactic vote. The Republican Speaker of the House, Charles F. Kurfess, had planned to let a number of members, both Republicans and Democrats, speak on the issue before calling for a vote.

But after only three short speeches, the Republican floor leader, Robert E. Leavitt, interrupted to warn:

"I've just been informed that the Legislature of Oklahoma

Continued on Page 43, Column 1

Conferees Cut Military Pay Rise As Authority to Draft Runs Out

By DAVID E. ROSENBAUM
Special to The New York Times

WASHINGTON, June 30 — The Nixon Administration won a major budgetary victory today in the House-Senate conference on the draft extension bill.

The conference agreement also appeared to represent a setback for supporters of an all-volunteer Army, who had sought larger pay increases than those cleared by the conferees.

The conferees accepted a figure for military pay and allowances that was more than $900-million below what the Senate had approved. The raises voted by the conferees would cost about $1.8-billion in the fiscal year starting tomorrow and would go into effect Oct. 1.

The figure approved by the conference was still $800-million above what President Nixon sought in his budget, but the House and Senate had passed increases of about $1.7-billion over the budget.

The Nixon Administration argued than so large an increase would force severe and possibly dangerous reductions in other parts of the defense budget.

The Government's basic authority to draft men into the

military expires at midnight tonight.

The conferees completed action on all provisions of the draft bill today except the Senate-passed amendment that calls for the withdrawal of United States troops from Indochina within nine months if prisoners of war are first

Continued on Page 29, Column 1

False Advertising Laid to H&R Block

By JOHN D. MORRIS
Special to The New York Times

WASHINGTON, June 30 — H & R Block, Inc., which says it prepares income tax returns for eight million American annually, was accused by the Federal Trade Commission today of false advertising and illegally using confidential information supplied by customers.

The commission published similar but separate citations against H & R Block and the Beneficial Corporation, which offers income tax services on a smaller scale through a subsidiary, the Beneficial Management Corporation. In radio and television advertisements, the name

Continued on Page 16, Column 2

ACTION BY GRAVEL VEXES SENATORS

But No Disciplinary Action Against Him Is Expected

By JOHN W. FINNEY
Special to The New York Times

WASHINGTON, June 30—Many Senators privately expressed dismay, shock and chagrin today at Senator Mike Gravel's release of parts of the Pentagon's secret study of the Vietnam war. But it appeared that no disciplinary action would be taken against the Alaska Democrat.

Last night Senator Gravel tried to read the documents to the Senate in an all-night speech and, when he was blocked for lack of a quorum, proceeded to call an impromptu meeting of his Senate Public Works subcommittee. He read from the study for three and one-half hours, with his voice sometimes breaking into sobs and tears occasionally rolling down his face.

His action incurred the displeasure of many of his colleagues, who felt that it reflected on the dignity and composure of the Senate. But in the clublike atmosphere of the Senate there was a widespread reluctance, extending down from the leadership, to take any formal disciplinary

Continued on Page 15, Column 1

"All the News That's Fit to Print"

The New York Times

LATE CITY EDITION

Weather: Variable cloudiness, mild today; fair tonight and tomorrow. Temp. range: today 70-76; Monday 71-75. Full U.S. report on Page 81.

VOL.CXX...No.41,506   © 1971 The New York Times Company   NEW YORK, TUESDAY, SEPTEMBER 14, 1971   15 CENTS

BUSINESS FAVORS U.S. PANEL TO RULE PAY-PRICE POLICY

Leaders Urge President to Give the Private Sector Only an Advisory Role

MEET AT WHITE HOUSE

Oppose Curb on Profits in Phase Two of Program—Nixon Offers No Plan

By ROBERT B. SEMPLE Jr.
Special to The New York Times

WASHINGTON, Sept. 13—Spokesmen from the business community told President Nixon today that the next phase of the new economic strategy should be managed by the Federal Government, with the private sector playing essentially an advisory role.

Last Friday, union leaders who met with the President recommended the creation of a tripartite board representing labor, management and the general public to control wages and prices, without governmental interference, after the current 90-day freeze.

Confer Two Hours

This morning Mr. Nixon met for nearly two hours with 11 corporate executives and leaders of business associations in the second of a series of meetings designed to solicit ideas from various interest groups on what ought to be done to manage the economy after the current wage-price-rent freeze expires at midnight, Nov. 13.

Meanwhile, Secretary of the Treasury John B. Connally indicated that price controls in some form would be continued after the expiration of the freeze.

At today's meeting, according to the public statements of some participants and the private comments of others, most of the businessmen present told Mr. Nixon that the basic decisions on wage and price policy should remain with some kind of Government board.

They felt, however, that business, labor, agriculture and other groups should be consulted extensively before such decisions were made.

Typical Comment

It was not totally clear whether the business group thought that the private sector should have veto power over the decisions made by the Government board. But sources said that the consensus of the group was that business, labor and other groups should restrict themselves to offering suggestions and making recommendations, leaving ultimate wage-price decisions in the Government's hands.

A typical comment came from James M. Roche, chairman of General Motors, who was asked to address himself to labor's suggestion that a tripartite board draw up its own rules on what specific wages and prices should be controlled, rather

Continued on Page 26, Column 4

Common Market Agrees To Resist U.S. on Dollar

6 Finance Ministers Ask America to Devalue

By CLYDE H. FARNSWORTH
Special to The New York Times

BRUSSELS, Sept. 13—The European Common Market, in an assertive mood, temporarily buried its internal quarrels today to confront the United States with a uniform set of demands, including devaluation of the dollar, to resolve the monetary crisis.

Finance ministers of the six member countries of the trade bloc took the position that the United States would not get the multilateral upward revaluation of major foreign currencies that it is seeking until it agreed to eliminate its import surcharge and raise the official price of gold.

Stand Is Prepared

The six nations, which will probably be joined by other European powers (including Britain) and by Japan as well, were preparing the stand they will take at key monetary meetings later this month in London and Washington.

Observers said the effect of today's decision was to throw the ball back at President Nixon, who imposed the surcharge on Aug. 15 as a "weapon to force currency valuations upward, a greater sharing of de-

Continued on Page 25, Column 5

Basic Payments Deficit Hits $9-Billion Rate

By PHILIP SHABECOFF
Special to The New York Times

WASHINGTON, Sept. 13—Paul A. Volcker, Under Secretary of the Treasury, disclosed publicly today that the United States' basic balance-of-payments deficit reached an annual rate of $9-billion in the first half of 1971.

It had been reported earlier that the basic deficit was so large that Mr. Volcker had shocked representatives of the group of 10 major trading nations at a meeting in Paris last week when he described its dimensions.

A $9-billion deficit for the year would be almost three times higher than the highest previous such deficit in recent American history.

Panel Hears Testimony

The basic balance of payments refers to all trade and monetary transactions with foreign countries except for erratic short-term capital flows. It is often regarded as the best measure of a country's true international payments position.

Mr. Volcker told the International Trade Subcommittee of the Senate Finance Committee today, "At the heart of this deterioration in our basic accounts was a severe decline in our merchandise trade balance."

In the years 1960-1969 the

Continued on Page 25, Column 1

9 HOSTAGES AND 28 PRISONERS DIE AS 1,000 STORM PRISON IN ATTICA; 28 RESCUED, SCORES ARE INJURED

Elmer Huehn, released hostage, being greeted by his wife — The New York Times
Guard, who had been held, still dazed after being released — Associated Press

Relatives of hostages in Attica prison after being told that at least 15 of the men being held had been set free — The New York Times/Michael Evans

'LIKE A WAR ZONE'

Air and Ground Attack Follows Refusal of Convicts to Yield

By FRED FERRETTI
Special to The New York Times

ATTICA, N. Y., Sept. 13—The rebellion at the Attica Correctional Facility ended this morning in a bloody clash and mass deaths that four days of taut negotiations had sought to avert.

Thirty-seven men — 9 hostages and 28 prisoners — were killed as 1,000 state troopers, sheriff's deputies and prison guards stormed the prison under a low-flying pall of tear

Text of Oswald's statement is printed on Page 28.

gas dropped by helicopters. They retook from inmates the cellblocks they had captured last Thursday.

In this worst of recent American prison revolts, several of the hostages — prison guards and civilian workers—died when convicts slashed their throats with knives. Others were stabbed and beaten with clubs and lengths of pipe.

Most of the prisoners killed in the assault fell under the thick hail of rifle and shotgun fire laid down by the invading troopers.

Doctor Fears More Deaths

A volunteer doctor who worked among the wounded after the assault said the prison's interior was "like a war zone." Standing in front of the prison in a blood-stained white coat, he said that many more of the wounded "are likely to die."

Late today a deputy director of correction, Walter Dunbar, said that two of the hostages had been killed "before today" and that one had been stabbed and emasculated.

Of the remaining seven, five were killed instantly by the inmates and two died in the prison hospital.

Mr. Dunbar said that in addition to the 28 dead inmates, eight other convicts of the total of 2,237 were missing. Two of the dead prisoners, he said, were killed "by their own colleagues and lay in a large pool of blood in a fourth-tier cellblock."

Oswald Orders Attack

He said he considered the state's recapture of the prison an "efficient, affirmative police action."

The action was ordered with "extreme reluctance" by State Correction Commissioner Russell G. Oswald after consultation with Governor Rockefeller. It followed an ultimatum to the more than 1,000 rebellious prisoners that they release the hostages they held and return to their cells.

Most of the 28 hostages rescued by the invaders and scores of prisoners were treated for wounds and the effects

Continued on Page 28, Column 2

NIXON PANEL ASKS FREE TRADE MOVES

Urges Negotiations to End All Barriers in 25 Years—Labor Members Dissent

By EDWIN L. DALE Jr.
Special to The New York Times

WASHINGTON, Sept. 13—A Presidential commission, calling for a "new realism" in the nation's foreign economic and trade policy, said today that "the time has come to begin immediately a major series of international negotiations" with the long-term aim of "elimination of all barriers to international trade and capital movements within 25 years."

The basic thrust of the report of the 27-member Commission

A summary of the panel's recommendations, Page 24.

on International Trade and Investment Policy was in the direction of freer trade here and abroad. The two members who dissented from the entire report, calling for controls on the inflow of goods and the outflow of capital and technology.

The report, consisting of 307 pages and 147 recommendations, was presented to President Nixon today by the commission chairman, Albert L.

Continued on Page 24, Column 1

Knowles Will Head Rockefeller Fund; Lost Out on U.S. Job

By M. A. FARBER

Dr. John H. Knowles, the 45-year-old Massachusetts hospital administrator who was a controversial candidate for the nation's top health post in 1969, was named president of the Rockefeller Foundation yesterday.

He will succeed Dr. J. George Harrar next July as head of the second wealthiest foundation in the country, a multipurpose philanthropic enterprise with assets of more than $800-million and activities throughout the world. The Ford Foundation has assets of more than $2.5-billion.

Dr. Harrar, an early leader in the "green revolution" in food production in developing nations, will reach the Rockefeller Foundation's mandatory retirement age of 65 next December.

Dr. Knowles, an outspoken liberal on social as well as specifically medical issues, has been general director of the Massachusetts General Hospital in Boston since 1962.

In 1969 Dr. Knowles was proposed by Robert H. Finch as Assistant Secretary for Health and Scientific Affairs, in the Department of Health, Education and Welfare. Mr. Finch, who is now on the White House staff, was then Secretary of

Continued on Page 37, Column 3

4 Days of Attica Talks End in Failure

By TOM WICKER
Special to The New York Times

ATTICA, N. Y., Sept. 13—At 9:43:28 this morning the power went off in the small littered steward's room on the second floor of the Attica Correctional Facility's administration building.

The hands of an electric clock on the wall pointed to that second for almost two hours, while state policemen and other officers put a bloody end to a massive uprising by about 1,500 inmates—mostly black and Puerto Rican.

To the 17 men in the room, the hands marked the moment of truth—the second when the end came for four days of emotional and exhausting effort to avoid the bloodshed that every one of them feared from the beginning. For 28 of the prisoners with whom they had vainly "negotiated" and for nine of the hostages the prisoners had been holding, death had been signaled.

At 9:48 A.M., five minutes after the lights went out, armed troopers moved behind fire hoses down the littered, gasoline-smelling corridor of the 17 men and their colleagues had used in a series of harrowing visits to the prisoners' stronghold in Cellblock D and its exercise yard.

Other assaulting forces came over the walls that surrounded the exercise yard. By about 11 A.M., the prison authorities said that the institution was virtually "secure," although some cell block areas remained to be finally cleared. Active resistance had ceased.

Some members of the unusual group of 17 citizen "observers," summoned by the prisoners and authorized by the state authorities to try to find a peaceful solution, had believed all along that none could be devised. Others had hoped to the last. All had drained themselves emotionally and physically, when failure put an end to their efforts and to the lives of 37 men.

Gazing out the window of the steward's room at the helmeted troopers and the drifts of gas floating across the prison grounds, two of the 17-member group, Representative Herman Badillo of New York City and this correspondent, assured each

Continued on Page 29, Column 1

ROCKEFELLER SEES A PLOT AT PRISON

'Revolutionary Tactics' Led to Uprising, He Says—Investigation Planned

By WILLIAM E. FARRELL

Governor Rockefeller said yesterday that the uprising at Attica Prison was brought on by the "revolutionary tactics of militants" and that he had ordered "a full investigation of all the factors leading to this uprising, including the role that outside forces would appear to have played."

The Governor's comments were contained in a statement issued by his office here following one of the most critical moves of his 13 years in office—his sanctioning of the decision of State Commissioner of Correction Russell G. Oswald to storm the prison.

The action taken by the state was the subject of a telephone conversation yesterday afternoon between the Governor and President Nixon in which the President expressed support for the Governor's response to the prisoner rebellion, and in particular for his refusal to grant the amnesty demand.

Spokesmen for the Governor and the President agreed on the substance of the conversa-

Continued on Page 30, Column 1

A Hostage Says Threats Left Him 'Scared Silly'

By JOSEPH LELYVELD
Special to The New York Times

ATTICA, N. Y., Sept. 13—"I laid there on the floor and knew I was going to bleed to death right there."

As he said this, the only signs that Ron Kozlowski had been one of the hostages whose throats had been slit in the first fierce instants of the assault on the rebellious prisoners here were a small two-inch bandage at the base of his neck and a visible shakiness in his knees.

"They told us, 'As soon as the first shot is fired, you white blankety-blanks have had it.' I was scared silly up there. I really was. I didn't want them to shoot."

Mr. Kozlowski, a 23-year-old accounts clerk at the prison, said he was one of a small group of hostages who were led this morning, bound and blindfolded, out of the jerrybuilt pen in the center of the prison yard where all the hostages had been held for four days. The 30 others left in the pen were also bound and blindfolded soon after State Correctional Commissioner Russell G. Oswald delivered the ultimatum to the more than 1,000 rebellious prisoners.

First, Mr. Kozlowski said, his group was taken to a pit that was doused with gasoline and told they would be burned alive

Continued on Page 29, Column 3

BID FAREWELL TO HUSBAND AND FATHER: Nina Khrushchev paying her last respects as rain fell yesterday in Novodevichye Monastery's Cemetery in Moscow.

Daughters, Yelena, right, and Rada, behind mother, stand with friends and relatives at flower-covered bier. Cemetery is three miles from Kremlin. Dispatch is on Page 10.

GAVE ORDER: Russell G. Oswald, State Correction Commissioner, after action.
— Associated Press

"All the News That's Fit to Print"

The New York Times

LATE CITY EDITION

Weather: Cloudy today and tonight. Partly sunny and milder tomorrow. Temp. range: today 60-67; Monday 58-62. Full U.S. report on Page 82.

VOL. CXXI..No. 41,548   © 1971 The New York Times Company   NEW YORK, TUESDAY, OCTOBER 26, 1971   15 CENTS

U.N. SEATS PEKING AND EXPELS TAIPEI; NATIONALISTS WALK OUT BEFORE VOTE; U.S. DEFEATED ON TWO KEY QUESTIONS

Tanzanian and Albanian delegations applaud defeat of "important question" resolution
United Press International

WASHINGTON CALM

Officials Uncertain of Effect of Defeat on Future Relations

Special to The New York Times

WASHINGTON, Oct. 25—Official Washington reacted with outward calm tonight to the crushing American defeat in the United Nations on the China issue. But there was uncertainty as to the effect the historic vote would have on future United States relations with Taiwan, the United Nations and the Peking Government.

Although the defeat was a distinct public setback for the Administration, most knowledgeable officials here had concluded in the last 48 hours that the weeks of arm twisting and private pressure in foreign capitals would fail to save Taiwan's seat and were therefore not surprised by the outcome.

At the time the vote was being held on the "important question," many prominent Administration and Congressional figures were unaware that it was taking place. On this Veterans Day holiday, most people here had assumed that the crucial voting would not take place until tomorrow. And with a heavy rain falling all day in Washington, many officials had retired early.

U.S. Withholds Comment

Even James C. H. Shen, the Ambassador of Nationalist China, was caught by surprise by the vote tonight. He was in New Haven for a speaking engagement at Yale and had gone to sleep without knowing of the events at the United Nations. When awakened by a reporter's call, he said he would have no comment.

Both the State Department and the White House said there would be no immediate official comment, but privately some officials wondered aloud about the significance of what they called the most important defeat ever suffered by the United States in the world organization.

Senator James L. Buckley, Conservative-Republican of New York, reacted sharply. He said he had asked his staff to prepare legislation for "a major reduction" in the American financial contribution to the United Nations, which runs about one-third of the annual $200-million budget.

"The action taken by the General Assembly tonight," he said, "may well be recorded as the beginning of the end of the United Nations, as marking

Continued on Page 16, Column 6

Liu Chieh, right, Nationalists' chief U.N. delegate, and delegation walk out of the hall
United Press International

CHOW SAYS PEKING WILL SUBVERT U.N.

Nationalist Minister Sees Change to 'Maoist Front' As Result of Defeat

By SAM POPE BREWER

Special to The New York Times

UNITED NATIONS, N.Y., Oct. 25—Nationalist China's Foreign Minister, Chow Shu-kai, walked with his delegation out of the United Nations tonight and declared bitterly that Communist China, in his nation's place, would subvert the world organization.

"Once it has been seated both in the General Assembly and in the Security Council," Mr. Chow said of Peking, "it will surely transform the United Nations into a Maoist front and a battlefield for international subversion."

Mr. Chow, grave but unflinching in the glare of batteries of television lights, stood with Taiwan's delegate, Liu Chieh, at his side in a hallway outside the General Assembly Hall where the overwhelming defeat for his Government had been voted. He declared:

"There are those who think that participation of the Communist regime will enhance the prospect of peace. The idea is to subject the aggressive regime to the discipline of international public opinion. This is dangerous nonsense—it is like tying a tiger with a straw rope."

Asked if he had had a foreboding of defeat when he wrote the document, Mr. Chow said, quietly: "When you are fighting a war, you prepare for

Continued on Page 11, Column 1

U.N. Roll-Calls on China

Special to The New York Times

UNITED NATIONS, N. Y., Oct. 25—Following are two roll-call votes taken in the General Assembly tonight on seating Communist China and expelling Nationalist China.

On Two-Thirds Requirement

Resolution declaring the expulsion of Nationalist China an "important matter" and thus requiring a two-thirds vote rather than a simple majority for passage.

IN FAVOR—55

Argentina, Ghana, New Zealand, Australia, Greece, Guatemala, Nicaragua, Bahrain, Haiti, Niger, Belgium, Honduras, Panama, Bolivia, Indonesia, Paraguay, Brazil, Israel, Philippines, Burundi, Italy, Portugal, Cent. Afr. Rep., Ivory Coast, Rwanda, Chad, Jamaica, Saudi Arabia, Colombia, Japan, So. Africa, Congo (Kinsh.), Jordan, Spain, Costa Rica, Lebanon, Swaziland, Dahomey, Lesotho, Thailand, Dominican Rep., Liberia, United States, El Salvador, Madagascar, Uruguay, Fiji, Malawi, Venezuela, Gabon, Mauritius, Gambia, Mexico

OPPOSED—59

Afghanistan, Ethiopia, Norway, Albania, Finland, Pakistan, Algeria, France, Peru, Austria, Guinea, Poland, Bhutan, Guyana, Portugal, Botswana, Hungary, Romania, Britain, Iceland, Sierra Leone, Bulgaria, India, Somalia, Burma, Iran, So. Yemen, Byelorussia, Iraq, Soviet Union, Canada, Ireland, Sudan, Ceylon, Kenya, Sweden, Chile, Kuwait, Syria, China, Laos, Tanzania, Cuba, Libya, Togo, Czechoslovakia, Mali, Trinidad-Tobago, Denmark, Mauritania, Uganda, Ecuador, Mongolia, Ukraine, Egypt, Morocco, Yemen, Equat. Guinea, Nepal, Yugoslavia, Eq. Guinea, Netherlands, Zambia, Estonia, Nigeria

ABSTENTIONS—15

Austria, Italy, Qatar, Bahrain, Luxembourg, Senegal, Barbados, Malta, Togo, Cyprus, Morocco, Tunisia, Iran, Netherlands

Absent—Maldives, Oman.

On Seating Peking

Resolution to seat Communist China and expel Nationalist China.

IN FAVOR—76

Afghanistan, Guyana, Portugal, Albania, Hungary, Romania, Algeria, Iceland, Rwanda, Australia, India, Senegal, Austria, Iran, Singapore, Belgium, Ireland, Somalia, Bhutan, Israel, Soviet Union, Bolivia, Italy, Sweden, Botswana, Kenya, Syria, Bulgaria, Kuwait, Tanzania, Burma, Laos, Togo, Burundi, Libya, Trinidad-Tobago, Cameroon, Malaysia, Tunisia, Canada, Mali, Turkey, Ceylon, Mauritania, Uganda, Chile, Mexico, Ukraine, Cuba, Nepal, Soviet, Czechoslovakia, Netherlands, Yemen, Denmark, Nigeria, Yugoslavia, Ecuador, Norway, Zambia, Eq. Guinea, Pakistan, Ethiopia, Peru, Finland, Poland, France, Guinea

OPPOSED—35

Australia, Gambia, Nicaragua, Bolivia, Guatemala, Niger, Brazil, Haiti, Paraguay, Cent. Afr. Rep., Honduras, Philippines, Chad, Ivory Coast, Saudi Arabia, Congo (Kinsh.), Japan, So. Africa, Costa Rica, Lesotho, Swaziland, Dahomey, Liberia, United States, Dominican Rep., Malawi, Upper Volta, El Salvador, Malta, Uruguay, Gabon, Nicaragua, New Zealand

ABSTENTIONS—17

Argentina, Greece, Mauritius, Bahrain, Indonesia, Panama, Barbados, Jamaica, Qatar, Colombia, Jordan, Spain, Cyprus, Lebanon, Thailand, Fiji, Luxembourg

Absent—China, Maldives, Oman.

End of China's Isolation

Peking Victory Held Likely to Speed Series of International Realignments

By MAX FRANKEL

Special to The New York Times

WASHINGTON, Oct. 25—With the vote at the United Nations tonight, China burst fully and finally from the isolation first imposed on her by the United States a generation ago and periodically preferred by her own Communist Government.

Though Washington was calm or simply asleep at the symbolic moment, its rear-guard effort to save Taiwan only heightened the drama of Peking's entry onto the world stage and deepened some of the resentments in conservative circles here.

President Nixon will undoubtedly show some sympathy for those resentments. He considers his projected journey to China as far more significant than most actions of the United Nations, and he sincerely hoped that his gesture would win a more gentle handling of the Chinese Nationalists.

But there was obviously a

News Analysis

pent-up desire among many nations to make whole and unambiguous this final reversal of American policy. This will complicate the President's task in defending his new China policy and the irritations are bound to be reflected in Washington's relations with the United Nations.

There is universal agreement here, however, that whatever the consequences inside the world organization, its voting and walkout by the Nationalists will further accelerate a whole series of realignments and shifts on the international scene.

Several important trends had already combined to determine

Continued on Page 16, Column 7

SESSION IS TENSE

Washington Loses Its Battle for Taipei by 76 to 35

By HENRY TANNER

Special to The New York Times

UNITED NATIONS, N. Y., Tuesday, Oct. 26—In a tense and emotion-filled meeting of more than eight hours, the General Assembly voted overwhelmingly last night to admit Communist China and to expel the Chinese Nationalist Government.

Moments before the vote, Liu Chieh, the Chinese Nationalist representative, announced from the rostrum that his Govern-

Texts of U.N. resolutions will be found on Page 10.

ment would take no further part in the proceedings of the Assembly. He received friendly applause from most delegations, and then led his delegation out of the hall.

The vote, which brought delegates to their feet in wild applause, was 76 in favor, 35 opposed, and 17 abstentions. The vote was on a resolution sponsored by Albania and 20 other nations, calling for the seating of Peking as the only legitimate representative of Chin, and the expulsion of "the representatives of Chiang Kai-shek."

Voting Is Sudden

Thus, the United States lost —in the 22d year—its battle to keep Nationalist China in the United Nations. This development, which came with dramatic suddenness, was denounced by the chief American delegate as a "moment of infamy."

The key decision that signaled the United States defeat came an hour and a half earlier, when the Assembly voted, 59 to 55 with 15 absentees, to reject the American draft resolution that would have declared the expulsion of the Nationalists an "important question" requiring a two-thirds majority for approval.

The United States had successfully used such a resolution since 1961 to keep the Chinese Communists out and the Chinese Nationalists in. Before that time, a simple majority would have admitted Peking, but no majority could be mustered.

Pandemonium Breaks Out

Last night as the electrical tally boards flashed the news that the "important question" proposal had failed, pandemonium broke out on the Assembly floor. Delegates jumped up and applauded.

The American delegation, also in the front row, sat in total dejection. George Bush, the United States delegate, who had

Continued on Page 10, Column 2

Peking's Backers Jubilant Over Vote

By TAD SZULC

Special to The New York Times

UNITED NATIONS, N. Y., Oct. 25—Salim Ahmed Salim, the young chief delegate from Tanzania, jumped to his feet tonight and led his colleagues in a victory jig in front of the Tanzanian seats in the front row of the General Assembly hall.

At the opposite end of the hall, where the United States delegation occupies a front-row seat, George Bush, the American chief delegate, slumped dejectedly in his chair.

It was exactly 9:47 P.M. and the United Nations General Assembly had just finished its roll-

Continued on Page 10, Column 2

LINDSAY DEFENDS KNAPP HEARINGS

Tells P.B.A. Head the Inquiry is in 'The Best Interest' of Everyone' on Force

By DAVID BURNHAM

Mayor Lindsay said yesterday that while the Knapp Commission hearings meant "discomfort and shock" for many policemen and citizens, dealing decisively with police corruption was in "the best interest of every member of the police force."

Mr. Lindsay made the statement in a letter to Edward J. Kiernan, president of the Patrolmen's Benevolent Association.

The Mayor also said he intended to use the recommendations of the Knapp Commission, expected in a written report by the end of the year, "as the basis for a major campaign to build public confidence in the Police Department and the integrity of our law enforcement processes."

The Mayor's letter was in response to charges made last week by Mr. Kiernan that the Knapp Commission's hearings

Continued on Page 31, Column 5

Powell Is Seeking To Avoid Clashes Over Court Seat

By JAMES M. NAUGHTON

Special to The New York Times

WASHINGTON, Oct. 25 — Lewis F. Powell Jr., the third Southern conservative nominated to the Supreme Court by President Nixon, is attempting to avoid the collisions over ethics and racial attitudes that contributed to the Senate's rejection of his two predecessors.

Mr. Powell, aware that his life, professional record and judicial philosophy are about to undergo rigorous examination, discussed his background with unusual candor in an interview at his Richmond law office this weekend.

He pledged to use "whatever is necessary and proper" to separate himself from corporate directorships and financial holdings that might constitute potential conflicts of interest.

Mr. Powell sought to place in what he regards as the proper context the comparatively minor chinks that have appeared in his image as a racial moderate — membership in two segregated clubs in Richmond and authorship of a brief filed by

Continued on Page 22, Column 4

Pakistanis Report 501 of Foe Killed In Eastern Area

By MALCOLM W. BROWNE

Special to The New York Times

KARACHI, Pakistan, Oct. 25 —The Government reported tonight that its forces had killed 501 "enemy troops"—defined as "Indians and Indian agents" —in heavy fighting in East Pakistan.

The Government, here in Pakistan's western wing, uses the term "Indian agents" to refer to all of its adversaries in East Pakistan, including the Pakistanis there who have been battling for Bengali independence since March with Indian support.

U.N. Observers Suggested

Today the Government said some of the bodies bore identification tags of the Indian Army. If the casualties are indeed Indians and if the toll even approaches the figures given, that would indicate that the fighting has reached its greatest intensity since the brief Indian-Pakistani conflict in 1965.

[In New Delhi, Defense Minister Jagjivan Ram reiterated that India would not pull her troops back from her borders "as long as the Pakistani threat continues." Page 17.]

Meanwhile, the Government announced that President Agha Mohammad Yahya Khan had asked for the intercession of Secretary General Thant of the United Nations in the dispute.

According to the Pakistani radio, President Yahya Khan proposed that United Nations observers be posted on both sides of the border between East Pakistan and India to supervise a mutual withdrawal

Continued on Page 17, Column 1

BREZHNEV IN PARIS, BACKED ON TALKS

Pompidou Agrees to a Quick Start on Preparations for Europe Security Parley

By HENRY GINIGER

Special to The New York Times

PARIS, Oct. 25 — President Pompidou and Leonid I. Brezhnev, leader of the Soviet Communist party, agreed quickly today to begin active preparation for a European security conference.

The agreement was made known at a state dinner in Versailles that marked the end of the first day of a six-day visit by Mr. Brezhnev. The Soviet leader was received this afternoon with the honors of a chief of state, and only a few discordant notes marred the friendly atmosphere of Mr. Brezhnev's first visit to a Western country since he became party leader in 1964.

[In Washington it was reported that Mr. Brezhnev had signaled Western leaders that he had officially assumed over-all responsibility for Moscow's relations with the United States and Western Europe. Page 5.]

In toasts this evening, Mr. Pompidou and Mr. Brezhnev spoke in similar terms of the need to end hostility between blocs.

Mr. Brezhnev said that France and the Soviet Union were close "on a fundamental problem—that of ending the division of the world into political-military blocs." Mr. Pompidou declared such blocs carried within them "the certainty of

Continued on Page 6, Column 4

By Lyndon B. Johnson: First Steps Toward Peace

INSTALLMENT X

Following is the 10th of 11 installments of excerpts from Lyndon Baines Johnson's memoirs of his Presidential years, which will be published by Holt, Rinehart & Winston on Nov. 1 under the title "The Vantage Point: Perspectives of the Presidency, 1963-1969":

Wednesday, April 3, 1968, began like most days in the White House. I was up early and read through the morning papers over breakfast. I listened to the radio news and glanced again at the front pages. One item, which I had heard broadcast the previous afternoon, was receiving considerable attention. In a speech on Tuesday Senator J. William Fulbright had told the Senate that the partial bombing halt I had ordered three nights before added up to only "a very limited change in existing policy." He forecast that the halt would not move

Hanoi in the direction of peace talks. I was surprised by Fulbright's reasoning and by his timing. We had stopped bombing over more than three-quarters of North Vietnam, an area where 9 out of every 10 North Vietnamese lived. That was much more than a "limited change" in our actions. Moreover, I believed Hanoi was perfectly able to judge the significance of our move without advice from Americans.

In the Senate discussion following Senator Fulbright's speech, Majority Leader Mike Mansfield and other Senators spoke up strongly in defense of our action and disputed Fulbright's charges. Senator Mansfield recalled the long talk he and I had had on the evening of March 27 and he disclosed that I had informed him on that occasion that we were going to stop bombing north of the 20th parallel.

These reflections put me in a bad mood as I prepared to leave for the

To my mind, the principal issue was not where the precise line marking the no-bombing area was drawn but rather how Hanoi would react to our self-imposed restriction. The key question in the Senate discussion, I believed, was raised by Senator Frank Lausche of Ohio: "How can Ho Chi Minh give any affirmative action when the Senator from Arkansas and others attack the Government before Ho can respond?"

While Fulbright's allegations dominated the news stories and headlines, Lausche's pertinent question received scant attention. I saw it mentioned only once, in The New York Times on April 3, and then only in the 30th and last paragraph on Page 14.

Continued on Page 34, Column 1

NEWS INDEX

(news index listing)

"All the News That's Fit to Print"

The New York Times

LATE CITY EDITION

Weather: Cloudy and ... day colder tonight. Sun... Temp...: today 4... ... 52-62. Full U.S. report ... ... 82.

VOL. CXXI...No. 41,600

© 1971 The New York Times Company

NEW YORK, FRIDAY, DECEMBER 17, 1971

15 CENTS

INDIA ORDERS CEASE-FIRE ON BOTH FRONTS AFTER PAKISTANIS' SURRENDER IN THE EAST

CONGRESS BREAKS FOREIGN AID JAM; SEEKS TO ADJOURN

House Rejection of Vietnam Amendment Sets Stage for Conferees' Accord

By JOHN W. FINNEY
Special to The New York Times

WASHINGTON, Dec. 16 — Congress apparently broke today the impasse on foreign aid legislation that has been holding up adjournment as the House unexpectedly met Senate demands for a vote on an amendment on Vietnam troop withdrawal.

The House rejected, by a vote of 130 to 101, the withdrawal amendment offered by the Senate majority leader, Mike Mansfield, and incorporated by the Senate in the foreign aid authorization legislation. But the net effect of the House action was to reopen Senate-House negotiations on the foreign aid legislation that had been deadlocked for weeks in a conference committee.

With the foreign aid issue apparently on the way to resolution, Senate and House leaders were optimistic that the first session of the 92d Congress could adjourn by tomorrow.

Ryan Breaks Impasse

With Senate and House leaders caught up in a power struggle over foreign aid, the impasse was broken in a surprise move by Representative William Fitts Ryan, Democrat of Manhattan.

Independently of the Congressional leaders who were meeting in the Senate Appropriations Committee room seeking a way to continue the foreign aid program, Mr. Ryan unexpectedly stood up on the House floor to offer a motion instructing the House conferees to accept the Mansfield amendment.

He had found a provision in the House rules permitting such a motion to be made if a Senate-House conference committee had been deadlocked for 20 days.

Motion to Table

A surprised Representative Thomas E. Morgan of Pennsylvania, chairman of the House Foreign Affairs Committee, promptly moved to table, or lay aside, the Ryan motion, a move that carried by the 29-vote margin.

Technically, the House did not have the specific vote on the Mansfield amendment that Senate conferees had been demanding in the conference on the foreign aid legislation. It was the refusal of the House conferees to yield to this demand by Senator Mansfield

Continued on Page 45, Column 4

City Speeds Repair On Garbage Trucks

By PAUL L. MONTGOMERY

Sanitation Department officials here believe they are on the way to solving one of their most persistent problems—the inordinate number of collection trucks awaiting repairs in the department's shops.

The solution, something of a revolution in city administration, is embodied in a single sheet of statistics distributed to department mechanics this week. It lists the times the mechanics will be expected to spend to complete 18 routine tasks.

The revolution is that the times listed are an average of 46 per cent less than those that had prevailed.

The new productivity standards, reached after consultation with the mechanics' union, are frequently mentioned by city officials as an example of

Continued on Page 72, Column 1

Monthly Record Set For Housing Starts

By JACK ROSENTHAL
Special to The New York Times

WASHINGTON, Dec. 16 — Home building reached a monthly high in November, practically insuring that 1971 will be a record year, George Romney, Secretary of Housing and Urban Development, announced today at an odd, hastily called news conference.

The seasonally adjusted annual rate of housing starts in November was 2,316,000 units, Mr. Romney said, the highest figure ever. The actual 1971 figure is now likely to approach 2.1 million units, probably the highest ever.

The November figure compares with a downward revised October figure of 2,-008,000 units and with 1,-693,000 units for November, 1970.

The gain in housing starts,

Continued on Page 69, Column 5

REVAMPING URGED FOR BANK SYSTEM

Hunt Commission Proposes Change in U.S. Regulation of Money Institutions

By H. ERICH HEINEMANN
Special to The New York Times

WASHINGTON, Dec. 16 — The nation's financial structure and the Federal agencies that regulate it require a complete overhaul, a Presidential commission has concluded.

If adopted, the commission's recommendations should result in sharper competition, possibly lower prices for consumers and — over time — the gradual disappearance of the present sharp legal distinctions between different types of financial institutions.

The group is formally called the Presidential Commission on Financial Structure and Regulation and informally known as the Hunt Commission (for its chairman, Reed O. Hunt, retired chairman of the Crown Zellerbach Corporation). The commission is due to present its report to the White House in a few days. A copy of its recommendations, but not the report itself, was obtained today.

The key problem that led

Continued on Page 65, Column 1

Nixon Pledges to Seek Release Of Skipper of Ship Cuba Seized

Mr. Nixon consoles wife of José Villa, ship's captain

By JAMES M. NAUGHTON
Special to The New York Times

KEY BISCAYNE, Fla., Dec. 16 — President Nixon pledged today that he would do what he could to seek the release of José Villa, the captain of a Miami-based freighter attacked by a Cuban gunboat and seized yesterday in the Bahamas.

The President met with Captain Villa's wife, Isabel, and three children for 10 minutes at the Florida White House. The family of the captain, a Cuban exile who is now a naturalized United States citizen, had gone there to deliver a letter plead-

WEST TO FIGHT ON

Yahya Calls for Help, but Vows to Battle 'Alone if We Must'

By MALCOLM W. BROWNE
Special to The New York Times

RAWALPINDI, Pakistan, Dec. 16 — President Agha Mohammad Yahya Khan acknowledged tonight that his forces in East Pakistan had been overwhelmed but pledged to continue the war against India until final victory.

In a radio speech to the nation, he also urgently called for

Text of Yahya's speech will be found on Page 17.

help from the community of nations in Pakistan's struggle, but added: "We shall fight alone if we must."

Later, Pakistan formally acknowledged that India now controls what had been East Pakistan.

A communiqué issued here in West Pakistan said:

"Latest reports indicate that following an arrangement between the local commanders of India and Pakistan in the Eastern theater, fighting has ceased in East Pakistan, and India's troops have entered Dacca."

No Details Are Given

The communiqué said nothing more about East Pakistan and gave no details of the "arrangement."

But it indicated that fighting in West Pakistan was continuing.

For the first time since the war began, military and diplomatic spokesmen failed to hold their daily evening briefing and correspondents here had no access to Pakistani officials.

The air war in the west was apparently still in progress. Indian air raids were reported on Karachi, Sialkot and other cities with significant numbers of civilian casualties.

The President implied that he had by no means accepted the separation of East Pakistan from the West, despite Pakistan's military defeat there.

"No sacrifice will be too great to preserve this Islamic homeland of the 120 million people of Pakistan," he said.

He also said: "To all our friends we say: stand by us and rest assured that the people of Pakistan and their armed forces will not cease their struggle

Continued on Page 17, Column 4

BHUTTO SUGGESTS ACCORD ON BENGAL

Pakistani Urges Cease-fire and Negotiations With Both Indians and Insurgents

By HENRY TANNER
Special to The New York Times

UNITED NATIONS, N. Y., Dec. 16 — Pakistan's Deputy Prime Minister and Foreign Minister, Zulfikar Ali Bhutto, declared today that Pakistan should accept a cease-fire with India and should prepare to negotiate a permanent settlement with the insurgents in East Bengal as well as with the Government of India.

Mr. Bhutto, in an interview, also said that Pakistan, which is now ruled by a military government, should return to civilian democratic government "very soon." His remarks appeared to put him at odds with President Agha Mohammad Yahya Khan of Pakistan, who pledged today in a speech to continue the war against India.

Mr. Bhutto announced that he would return to Pakistan in a few days to start laying the groundwork for sweeping internal and external reform as well as for negotiation with the insurgents.

Mr. Bhutto, who is the leading civilian figure in West Pakistan, stressed that he did not concede the final loss of East Pakistan.

The Security Council, meanwhile, was close to agreement when it adjourned tonight on a resolution calling for an im-

Continued on Page 17, Column 1

Walsh at Hearing: Forgot Graft Report

By DAVID BURNHAM

Former First Deputy Police Commissioner John F. Walsh admitted in sworn testimony yesterday that he had received a report of widespread police corruption in the Bronx at least six months before an investigation was begun.

Mr. Walsh, the second-ranking New York police official for almost 10 years, told the Knapp Commission that the detailed report he had received on corruption among plainclothes men enforcing the gambling laws "left my mind."

Months later, without any orders to initiate it from Mr. Walsh, an investigation was begun by police officials in the Bronx that eventually led to criminal indictments against 10 policemen and charges against 11 others, in-

Continued on Page 44, Column 1

SIGNING THE SURRENDER AGREEMENT: Lieut. Gen. Jagjit Singh Aurora, left, commander of India's eastern forces, and Lieut. Gen. A. A. K. Niazi, Pakistani commander in East Pakistan, during surrender ceremony in Dacca yesterday.

United Press International

The Surrender Document

By Reuters

NEW DELHI, Dec. 16—Following is the text of the instrument of surrender signed today by the Pakistani and Indian commanders in East Pakistan:

The Pakistani Eastern Command agree to surrender all Pakistani armed forces in Bangladesh to Lieut. Gen. Jagjit Singh Aurora, general officer commanding in chief of the Indian and Bangladesh forces in the eastern theater.

This surrender includes all Pakistani land, air and naval forces as also all paramilitary forces and civil armed forces.

These forces will lay down their arms and surrender at the place where they are currently located to the nearest regular troops in the command of Lieut. Gen. Jagjit Singh Aurora.

Pakistani Eastern Command shall come under the orders of Lieut. Gen. Jagjit Singh Aurora as soon as this instrument has been signed. Disobedience of orders will be regarded as a breach of the surrender terms and will be dealt with in accordance with accepted laws and usages of war.

The decision of Lieut. Gen. Jagjit Singh Aurora shall be final should any doubt arise as to the meaning or interpretation of surrender terms.

"Lieut. Gen. Jagjit Singh Aurora gives his solemn assurance that personnel who surrender shall be treated with dignity and respect that soldiers are entitled to in accordance with the provisions of the Geneva convention and guarantees safety and well-being of all Pakistan military and paramilitary forces who surrender.

Protection will be provided to foreign nationals, ethnic minorities and personnel of the West Pakistan region by the forces in the command of Lieut. Gen. Jagjit Singh Aurora.

The March Into Dacca: Last Clash and Victory

2 Men at a Table

By SYDNEY H. SCHANBERG
Special to The New York Times

DACCA, Pakistan, Dec. 16—On a broad grassy field in central Dacca known as the Race Course, the Pakistani forces formally surrendered today, 13 days after the Indian Army began its drive into East Pakistan.

It was at the Race Course on March 7 that Sheik Mujibur Rahman, in a speech to thousands of Bengalis, called for the end of martial law and the transfer of power to his autonomy-minded Awami League, which had won a majority in national elections.

Today there were no speeches —just two men sitting at a single table on the green—Lieut. Gen. Jagjit Singh Aurora, chief of India's Eastern Command, and Lieut. Gen. A. A. K. Niazi, commander of the 70,000 Pakistani troops in East Pakistan—who signed the formal papers of Pakistani surrender in the East.

The final hours of the Indian drive, which ended with the ceremony at the Race Course, were punctuated by artillery and machine-gun fire as the troops pushed across the Lakhya River, just outside Dacca proper.

Seven Western journalists,

Continued on Page 16, Column 3

Joy and Marigolds

By JAMES P. STERBA
Special to The New York Times

DACCA, Pakistan, Dec. 16—Shouting "Joi Bangla!" and waving the Bangladesh flag, Indian troops poured into the Pakistani military camp north of town today just after the Pakistanis had accepted an ultimatum to surrender.

Indian soldiers with marigolds in their gun barrels passed armed Pakistani soldiers in great traffic jams within the camp. Pakistani officers saluted Indian officers. Officers of both armies, many of whom attended the same schools under the British, shook hands and asked about mutual friends. In Dacca itself, there were spontaneous eruptions of joy and celebration in the streets. Bengalis kissed Indian Punjabi soldiers, tossing flowers at them and at the rebels who accom-

Continued on Page 16, Column 7

DACCA CAPTURED

Guns Quiet in Bengali Area but War Goes On at Western Front

By CHARLES MOHR
Special to The New York Times

NEW DELHI, Dec. 16—India today ordered a complete cease-fire in the war with Pakistan after seizing Dacca, the East Pakistani capital, and accepting the surrender of Pakistan's forces there.

With guns stilled by the surrender in the East, the cease-

Statements by Mrs. Gandhi appear on Page 16.

fire on the western front, more than a thousand miles away, was set—without any agreement from Pakistan—to begin at 8 P.M. tomorrow, Indian time (9:30 A.M. Friday, New York time).

After 14 days of bitter warfare over the status of the Bengalis in East Pakistan, Prime Minister Indira Gandhi of India said, "It is pointless in our view to continue the present conflict."

Pakistani Shortages Seen

But President Agha Mohammad Yahya Khan of Pakistan asserted in a nationwide radio broadcast that the war was still on "and we will continue to fight."

Pakistan is believed by independent observers, however, to have grave supply-line problems, so that her stockpiles of fuel and ammunition may not permit a prolonged war.

A major tank battle—the largest of the war—has erupted on the western front near the little Pakistani town of Shakargarh, in the Punjab. Indian officials said India had lost 15 tanks and claimed the destruction of 45 Pakistani tanks.

Even as India celebrated her quick victory in the East, China accused her of violating the border between the Indian protectorate of Sikkim and Tibet, terming the action "a grave encroachment" on Chinese territory.

Chinese Charge Denied

Indian officials said there had been no fighting on the Chinese border, and a Foreign Ministry spokesman described the accusation by Peking—a supporter of Pakistan—as "totally without foundation." Nonetheless, the protest raised apprehensions here that the conflict might be widened.

India's offensive in East Pakistan, which began in the early hours of Dec. 4, ended at 4:31 P.M. today in the total surrender of the four divisions of West Pakistani troops there.

The surrender agreement was signed in Dacca by Lieut. Gen. Jagjit Singh Aurora, who commands India's eastern forces, and Lieut. Gen. A. A. K. Niazi,

Continued on Page 16, Column 1

CHINESE CHARGE INDIAN INCURSION

Protest May Foreshadow Use of Military Pressure in Support of Pakistan

By TILLMAN DURDIN
Special to The New York Times

HONG KONG, Dec. 16—China, in a formal Government statement today on the Indian-Pakistani war, predicted a turbulent future for India. At the same time, the Chinese pointed toward a possible trouble zone by filing a strong protest in New Delhi over alleged Indian incursions from Sikkim into Tibet.

The statement and the protest were reported here in quick succession tonight from Peking by Hsinhua, the Chinese press agency.

The protest could foreshadow military pressure from China, a strong supporter of Pakistan, along sections of the eastern Himalayan border between India and China.

The 1,600-word statement warned India that "he who plays with fire will be consumed by fire" and asserted that "henceforth there will be no tranquillity" for the Indian people.

Calling attention to India's own problems with minority nationalities, which it likened to the Bengali situation in East Pakistan, the statement said: "It may be asked how

Continued on Page 18, Column 2

Mrs. Gandhi Writes President: U.S. Could Have Averted War

By FOX BUTTERFIELD
Special to The New York Times

NEW DELHI, Dec. 16—Prime Minister Indira Gandhi has written to President Nixon, in a letter released today, that the war between India and Pakistan could have been averted if the United States had used its

Text of Mrs. Gandhi's letter is printed on Page 17.

"power, influence and authority" to achieve a political solution to the crisis in East Pakistan.

Mrs. Gandhi wrote that despite advice that she gave in August to Henry A. Kissinger, the President's adviser on national security affairs, only "lip service was paid to the need for a political settlement," and not a single worthwhile step was taken to bring it about.

"India was deeply hurt," Mrs. Gandhi wrote, "by the innuendoes and insinuations that it was she who had precipitated

Continued on Page 17, Column 1

writing at a time of deep anguish over the "unhappy turn" which relations between India and the United States have taken." The letter was sent to Mr. Nixon yesterday.

Relations between the two countries, which have been strained because the United States did not denounce Pakistan for her repression of the Bengali movement for autonomy last spring, deteriorated sharply this week with the news that the nuclear-powered aircraft carrier Enterprise and seven other American Navy ships were heading for the Bay of Bengal.

"All the News That's Fit to Print"

The New York Times

LATE CITY EDITION

Weather: Rain today; mostly cloudy tonight. Fair and milder tomorrow. Temp. range: today 51-55; Monday 53-66. Full U.S. report on Page 82.

VOL. CXXI..No. 41,744   © 1972 The New York Times Company   NEW YORK, TUESDAY, MAY 9, 1972   15 CENTS

NIXON ORDERS ENEMY'S PORTS MINED; SAYS MATERIEL WILL BE DENIED HANOI UNTIL IT FREES P.O.W.'S AND HALTS WAR

Governor Reported Irked By Nixon's Abortion Views

Rockefeller Indicates Plan to Veto Bill Stands Despite President's Support for Repeal of Present State Law

By JAMES F. CLARITY
Special to The New York Times

ALBANY, May 8 — Governor Rockefeller was reliably reported today to be angered by President Nixon's intervention in the issue of elective abortions, now pending in the Legislature.

One of the highest elected Republican officials in the state described Mr. Rockefeller as "very upset" about the President's action.

The Governor's office said that despite the President's announced support for repeal of the state's liberal abortion law, Mr. Rockefeller would veto the repeal if it was approved by the Legislature. Relations between the Governor and the President, which had improved greatly in the last several months, with Mr. Rockefeller agreeing to serve as the President's campaign manager in the state, now seem strained, at least on this one issue.

The Assembly was expected to debate the repeal legislation tomorrow.

Evidence of the Governor's pique was clear in the statement his office issued in response to requests for comments on the President's action: "We are referring all calls to the White House on this."

Mr. Nixon intervened in the state issue in a letter to Cardinal Cooke. The letter, made public Saturday, made clear the President's support for repeal of the New York law, which permits elective abortions through the 24th week of pregnancy.

The day before the letter was made public, Mr. Nixon had rejected recommendations for lib-

Continued on Page 26, Column 2

HIGH MEAT PRICES LAID TO RACKETS

City Consumers Squeezed by 15% Inflation of Costs, Law Officials Report

By LACEY FOSBURGH

The infiltration of organized crime into key positions in the New York City meat industry has artificially inflated the retail prices for fresh meat in supermarkets by 15 per cent, according to investigations developed by the Manhattan District Attorney's Office and other law-enforcement agencies here and in Washington.

Consumers buying meat in the New York-New Jersey area, they say, are putting at least a million dollars a week directly into the coffers of organized crime.

Years of Collusion Alleged

Racketeers — both in the industry and in the unions that service it — have reportedly been in collusion for at least two years "systematically" extorting "week by week, month by month," as one source put it, "vast sums of money" from the supermarket chains and the wholesale suppliers.

"This is the price they pay to stay in business," another source said, "the price of labor peace."

This picture of extortion, bribery and the ultimate victimization of the consumer

Continued on Page 66, Column 1

Local School Units Defended by Mayor

By LEONARD BUDER

Mayor Lindsay declared yesterday that the city's decentralized school boards had brought "a new vigor to the whole process of achieving quality public education."

Mr. Lindsay said that while it is "much too soon to make a final judgment on decentralization" he felt that "the community school boards have made important advances since the inception of decentralization a little less than two years ago."

The Mayor made the statement in commenting on the assertion Sunday by Dr. Kenneth B. Clark, a member of the State Board of Regents, that school

Continued on Page 53, Column 5

PAY BOARD TRIMS EAST COAST RAISE OF LONGSHOREMEN

Votes, 6-1, to Permit Rises of 9.8 to 12% Instead of 15 — Fitzsimmons Dissents

By EDWARD COWAN
Special to The New York Times

WASHINGTON, May 8 — The Pay Board directed East and Gulf Coast shippers and longshoremen tonight to roll back their agreed wage increase of 70 cents an hour to 55 cents.

About 49,000 longshoremen will be allowed increases ranging from 9.8 per cent to 12 per cent under the decision, which scaled back an agreement that had contemplated an increase calculated by the board at 15 per cent.

George H. Boldt, chairman of the seven-member board, said that he expected the International Longshoremen's Association "to look it over, be disappointed and go along with what's now the law of the land."

Boldt Declines to Predict

However, Judge Boldt, in a brief corridor meeting with newsmen, declined to prognosticate when asked if he thought the dock workers would strike.

Judge Boldt issued a brief summary of the decision after a difficult four-hour board meeting that ended with a vote of 6 to 1. The dissenter was Frank E. Fitzsimmons, president of the International Brotherhood of Teamsters, who is the only labor leader still on the board.

Four other union leaders quit the board in March after it scaled back the longshore settlement on the West Coast to 14.9 per cent from a proposed 20.9 per cent. Only Mr. Fitzsimmons remained.

President Nixon then reconstituted what had been a 15-member tripartite group as a panel of seven public members.

In New York, Thomas G. Gleason, president of the Inter-

Continued on Page 17, Column 1

State Senate Votes To Liberalize Curbs In Rape Testimony

By ALFONSO A. NARVAEZ
Special to The New York Times

ALBANY, May 8 — The Senate gave overwhelming approval today to a bill modifying the extent to which a rape victim's testimony must be corroborated to convict an alleged attacker.

The measure, which passed by a vote of 56 to 1, removes the need for testimony corroborating the identity of the alleged assailant and the fact that penetration actually took place. The bill, passed with no debate, now goes to the Governor, who is expected to sign it.

In other action today as the Legislature continued its push for adjournment:

¶Three city officials—Controller Abraham D. Beame, City Council Majority Leader Thomas J. Cuite and the Council's finance committee chairman, Mario Merola—met here with state budget officials on legislation affecting the city's proposed $9.9-billion budget. The meet-

Continued on Page 27, Column 1

New Vega Recall

The General Motors Corporation yesterday recalled 350,000 of its 1971 and 1972 Vegas to correct a safety defect. It was the second major recall of Vegas in a month. Details on Page 16.

VIETNAM ADDRESS: President Nixon speaking last night
Associated Press

Ruling Party Leads In Italian Election; Neo-Fascists Gain

By PAUL HOFMANN
Special to The New York Times

ROME, Tuesday, May 9 — The governing Christian Democrats achieved a remarkable comeback in Italy's general elections Sunday and yesterday, receiving a clear mandate to continue leading the Government as they have been doing since 1945.

At the same time, however, the neo-Fascists advanced and the Communists won gains in the Chamber of Deputies and suffered losses in the Senate. With most of the votes counted early today, increasing polarization between left and right in Italian politics became apparent.

The Christian Democrats apparently raised their share of the total popular vote close to 40 per cent again and were confirmed once more as the nation's strongest political force.

But no party was anywhere near winning a majority in the 630-seat Chamber or among the 315 elected members of the Senate. The prospects, therefore, appeared to be for another period of coalition governments and, possibly, protracted instability.

Italian commentators attributed the rightist gains and

Continued on Page 3, Column 1

CONGRESS IS SPLIT ON NIXON'S ACTION

Republicans Acclaim His Leadership—Democrats Call Him Reckless

By JOHN W. FINNEY
Special to The New York Times

WASHINGTON, May 8 — President Nixon was alternately praised tonight by members of Congress for his firm leadership and accused of setting the nation on a dangerous confrontaion with the Soviet Union that could lead to world war.

Republicans praised him on both political and military grounds for his decision to mine North Vietnam's harbors. Representative Gerald R. Ford, the House Republican leader, described Mr. Nixon as "generous in his bid for peace but firm in his determination that we will not surrender."

"The only way left to end the Vietnam war is to deprive the enemy of the supplies he needs to continue the invasion," Mr. Ford said.

Senator Robert P. Griffin of Michigan, the assistant Republican leader in the Senate, said "it was strong medicine but necessary."

Democrats, however, used

Continued on Page 19, Column 1

NEW TARGETS: Ports (underlined), rail lines from China
The New York Times/May 9, 1972

President Urges Soviet To Avoid Confrontation

By BERNARD GWERTZMAN
Special to The New York Times

WASHINGTON, May 8 — President Nixon's speech tonight appealed to the Soviet Union not to let its support of Hanoi lead it to a confrontation with the United States over his decision to try to cut off supplies to North Vietnam.

In carefully chosen language, Mr. Nixon appeared anxious to avoid turning the Vietnam war into a direct Soviet-American clash.

But some diplomats feel the mining of North Vietnam's ports has raised the possibility of cancellation of Mr. Nixon's scheduled trip to Moscow two weeks from today and even of a military confrontation if Soviet naval forces try to thwart Mr. Nixon's actions.

Dobrynin Informed

Officially, the Nixon Administration said tonight that plans for Mr. Nixon's visit to the Soviet Union were still going ahead. But a high official added that the chances that it would take place had sharply lessened because of the tensions sure to be raised as the result of the effort to prevent supplies from arriving in North Vietnam.

Anatoly F. Dobrynin, the Soviet Ambassador to the United States, was informed of Mr. Nixon's speech about an hour beforehand at a White House meeting with Henry A. Kissinger, President Nixon's adviser on national security.

Mr. Dobrynin was also the Soviet envoy in October, 1962, when President John F. Kennedy ordered a quarantine of offensive Soviet weapons being shipped to Cuba. This led to the so-called Cuban missile crisis.

Continued on Page 19, Column 5

SPEAKS TO NATION

He Gives the Ships of Other Countries 3 Days to Leave

By ROBERT B. SEMPLE Jr.
Special to The New York Times

WASHINGTON, May 8 — President Nixon announced tonight that he had ordered the mining of all North Vietnamese ports and other measures to prevent the flow of arms and other military supplies to the enemy.

Mr. Nixon told a nationwide television and radio audience.

The text of Nixon's speech is printed on Page 18.

that his orders were being executed as he spoke.

From the President's somber and stern speech and from explanations by other Administration officials, the following picture of the American action emerged:

¶All major North Vietnamese ports would be mined, ships of other countries in the harbors, most of which are Russian, would have three "daylight periods" in which to leave. After that the mines will become active and ships coming or going will move at their own peril.

¶United States naval vessels will not search or seize ships of other countries entering or leaving North Vietnamese ports, thus avoiding a direct confrontation with the Russians.

¶American and South Vietnamese ships and planes would take "appropriate measures" to stop North Vietnam from unloading matériel on beaches from unmined waters.

¶United States and South Vietnamese forces would interdict, presumably by bombing, the movement of matériel in North Vietnam over rail lines originating in China.

There was much confusion tonight about whether the United States and South Vietnam had proclaimed a blockade. The President did not use the word and Pentagon spokesmen denied that a blockade existed in the technical sense. But some observers felt that the practical effect on North Vietnam of the President's actions would be the same as a blockade.

[In Saigon, the United States command announced Tuesday that Navy planes had completed the initial phases of the mining operations in North Vietnamese harbors ordered by President Nixon.]

Two Basic Conditions

Mr. Nixon said the mining, the attacks on the rail lines within North Vietnam, and the efforts to interdict the movement of supplies by water would cease the moment the enemy agreed to two basic conditions: the return of American prisoners of war, and an internationally supervised cease-fire.

"Then," he said, "we will stop all acts of force throughout Indochina and proceed with the complete withdrawal of all forces within four months."

The White House would not say tonight whether, in these words, Mr. Nixon was in effect making the North Vietnamese a new peace proposal.

But observers here noted that he mentioned no political requirements for American withdrawal. Until now he has always insisted on some form of

Continued on Page 18, Column 3

HANOI SAYS RAIDS STRUCK AT DIKES

But U.S. Asserts Military Installations Were Hit in Attacks on North

By CRAIG R. WHITNEY
Special to The New York Times

SAIGON, South Vietnam, Tuesday, May 9 — United States Navy fighter-bombers struck at North Vietnamese storage facilities, barracks and training facilities in an area about 15 miles west of Hanoi yesterday in the closest strikes to the North Vietnamese capital since April 16, the American command announced.

The command's announcement said the planes attacked "military heartland targets" that "are helping to support the Communist invasion of South Vietnam.

The Hanoi radio, in a broadcast at noon, said American planes "deliberately struck at the dike system in Namha Province" southeast of Hanoi.

[The United States command denied that American jets had bombed the dikes, United Press International reported.]

The dikes support an elaborate system of irrigation and

Continued on Page 19, Column 7

4 Armed Arab Hijackers Hold Jet and 101 Hostages in Israel

By The Associated Press

TEL AVIV, May 8 — Despite a tip-off and a security search, four armed Arabs hijacked an Israel-bound Belgian Sabena jetliner carrying 101 persons today.

After landing in Tel Aviv, they threatened to blow up the plane and its passengers unless Israel freed 300 Palestinian guerrilla prisoners and flew them to Cairo. A senior Israeli Army officer told the hijackers that freeing hundreds of prisoners within a few hours was impossible.

The Israelis, speaking to the hijackers by radio, were reported to have offered to take 15 or 20 military prisoners of war "as a gesture of goodwill."

The gunmen, who seized the plane after it left Vienna, set a deadline of 10 P.M. Tel Aviv time to make a deal, but the

deadline passed with no explosion or other evident action.

As negotiations were being carried on by radio, the pilot, Captain Reginald Levy, said that the plane was unfit to take off. The hijackers said that it must be made ready to leave at 5:30 A.M. or that it would be blown up. They later extended the deadline again but stipulated no time.

The Arabs also demanded to talk with a representative of the International Committee of the Red Cross.

"If the plane is not refueled, I think they will blow it up," Captain Levy said by radio. "They are serious."

The police in Brussels said that they had been told by tele-

Continued on Page 7, Column 1

CITY OFFICIALS IN ALBANY: Foreground, from left: Controller Abraham D. Beame and Councilman Thomas J. Cuite, majority leader, and Mario Merola, finance com-

mittee chairman. City budget was topic. Rear, from right: State Senator John J. Marchi, Assemblyman Alexander Chananau, almost hidden; Senator Warren M. Anderson.

The New York Times/William E. Sauro

248

"All the News
That's Fit to Print"

The New York Times

LATE CITY EDITION

Weather: Cloudy, mild with chance
of showers today, tonight, tomorrow.
Temp. range: today 59-73; Monday
57-74. Full U.S. report on Page 86.

VOL. CXXI. No. 41,751   © 1972 The New York Times Company   NEW YORK, TUESDAY, MAY 16, 1972   15 CENTS

WALLACE IS SHOT; CONDITION SERIOUS; A SUSPECT SEIZED AT MARYLAND RALLY

AFTER SPEECH: Gov. George C. Wallace takes off jacket and goes to shake hands. At front is Secret Service agent.
Associated Press

DURING SHOOTING: Man at right with light hair and sun glasses holds gun as person in crowd tries to shake his arm
C.B.S. News via United Press International

Saigon's Forces Reoccupy Bastogne Base Near Hue

By MALCOLM W. BROWNE
Special to The New York Times

SAIGON, South Vietnam, Tuesday, May 16 — South Vietnamese troops, led by a platoon of 30 soldiers flown in by helicopters, reoccupied Fire Base Bastogne yesterday on the southwesterly approaches to Hue.

The five helicopters carrying the soldiers reportedly encountered no enemy fire as they landed at the base, which the South Vietnamese abandoned April 28 under heavy attack. The base had fallen after the North Vietnamese who had besieged it for more than three weeks sent commandos storming in to penetrate the barbed-wire defenses.

But after routing the defenders at the end of April, the North Vietnamese did not move their long-range 130-mm. artillery into Bastogne to shell Hue, the former imperial capital of Vietnam on the coast 15 miles away.

[The United States com-

mand announced the arrival of the carrier Saratoga off the Vietnamese coast Monday, bringing to six the number of attack carriers there. United Press International reported. The United States Seventh Fleet was now said to have 60 ships in the area.]

[In Washington, Secretary of State William P. Rogers angrily defended the mining of North Vietnam's harbors and said that if the Johnson Administration had taken the step earlier, the war might have ended long ago. Page 14.]

Allied officers in the Hue area said that if the re-entry into Fire Base Bastogne appeared to have been easy, this was only because it had capped more than a week of slow, hard fighting and several more days of heavy air and artillery bombardment.

South Vietnamese spokes-

Continued on Page 14, Column 3

Court Exempts the Amish From Going to High School

By FRED P. GRAHAM
Special to The New York Times

WASHINGTON, May 15—The Supreme Court held 7 to 0 today that the Amish religious sect is exempt from state compulsory education laws that require children to attend school beyond the eighth grade.

The Amish—the rural "plain people" who cling to a horse-and-buggy way of life—believe that education beyond the eighth grade teaches worldly values at odds with the simple life required by their creed.

With this in mind, the Court held that state laws requiring children to attend school until they are 16 years of age violate the constitutional rights of the Amish to free exercise of religion.

The decision specifically applied to Wisconsin, but it was written in terms broad enough to apply to all states that require attendance in public or private schools beyond the eighth grade. Mississippi and South Carolina are the only states that do not have compulsory school attendance laws.

The opinion, written by Chief Justice Warren E. Burger, was the first by the Court holding a religious group immune from

compulsory attendance requirements.

The Court stressed the 300-year resistance of the Amish to modern influences and served notice that faddish new sects or communes that reject formal education would probably not be granted similar exemptions.

"It cannot be overemphasized," Justice Burger wrote, "that we are not dealing with a way of life and mode of education by a group claiming to have recently discovered some 'progressive' or more enlightened.

Hogan Drops Jay Kriegel Case; Reports He Can't Prove Perjury

By DAVID BURNHAM

The question of whether one of Mayor Lindsay's closest aides, Jay L. Kriegel, committed perjury during his testimony before the Knapp Commission will not be presented to a grand jury, District Attorney Frank S. Hogan announced yesterday.

Mr. Hogan said his office was dropping the case because "the people would not be able to establish beyond a reasonable doubt that there was a willful, irreconcilable inconsistency" between Mr. Kriegel's testimony before the Knapp Commission on June 17, 1971, and Dec. 20, 1971.

The commission was created by Mayor Lindsay on the

recommendation of a special committee that included Mr. Hogan—to investigate allegations of widespread police corruption and of failure by officials in the Lindsay administration to follow up on information about cases of corruption brought to their attention.

Mr. Hogan said in a two-and-a-half-page statement, said another reason for not proceeding with the case was that "there is substantial doubt concerning the authority of the Knapp commission to administer the oath at the December hearings."

Whitman Knapp, the chairman of the commission, said in

PRESSURE GROUPS ANGER ROCKEFELLER

He Asserts Judges Blocked Court Reform and Lawyers Stymied 'No-Fault' Bill

By JAMES F. CLARITY
Special to The New York Times

ALBANY, May 15—Governor Rockefeller charged today that "inordinate pressures" placed on legislators by judges and lawyers had blocked two of his "vital programs"—court reform and no-fault insurance—in the 1972 Legislature.

Mr. Rockefeller, commenting on the action of the Legislature three days after it had adjourned for the year, said the

The no-fault insurance bill was defeated through the lobbying efforts of one small group of men—the New York State Trial Lawyers Association. Article on Page 31.

judges had stymied most of his court-reform program. The lawyers, Mr. Rockefeller said, had blocked the no-fault automobile accident insurance bill he had supported.

The Governor pledged to continue to fight for passage of the two programs next year. He said undue pressure had also been exerted on the legislators to repeal the state's liberalized abortion law. The Governor vetoed the repeal measure Saturday.

"My pledge is to make an all-out fight for no-fault automobile insurance and court reform in 1973," Mr. Rockefeller said at a news conference in the Red Room of the Capitol.

"Some headlines have interpreted the failure of the Legislature to enact these two vital programs as a setback for me. The truth is that they marked a setback for the people of New York State.

"At no time," the Governor

Continued on Page 38, Column 3

GUNMAN'S ATTACK CLOUDS CAMPAIGN

Uncertainty Created Both by Wallace's Status and Impact of Shooting

By MAX FRANKEL
Special to The New York Times

WASHINGTON, May 15—The bullets that felled George C. Wallace on the eve of his greatest achievements in national politics will cloud the conduct and the calculations of the 1972 Presidential campaign.

If he could recover in time to resume some form of campaigning, and his press secretary says he will, the Alabama Governor may find an even more aroused constituency to rally his cause. And some degree of sympathy vote may further swell his expected victories tomorrow in the Democratic primaries of Michigan and Maryland.

The Governor had 210 delegate votes of the 1,509 needed for nomination when he was struck down.

If he is forced out of the campaign, there is no one now in sight to pick up the banner of populism, tinged with an overtone of segregation, that brought the Governor 9.9 million votes, or 13.5 per cent of the total cast for President, in 1968 and seemed to promise him an equally strong following this year.

No one has ever quite

Continued on Page 34, Column 7

Shooting Suspect Shouted: 'Hey, George! Over Here!'

By WARREN WEAVER Jr.
Special to The New York Times

LAUREL, Md., May 15—George C. Wallace was shot while standing at the new crossroads of middle America today, between the drive-in bank and variety store of a suburban shopping center.

The suspected assailant, a young white man, called the Alabama Governor over to him after Mr. Wallace had stepped from behind his bullet-proof speaking stand and came down to shake hands with the crowd of about 1,000.

"Hey, George! Hey, George! Come over here! Come over here!" the man shouted insistently, according to several witnesses. The man had been standing against the ropes that cleared a space for security guards and reporters between the crowd and the small parking lot speaking stand.

Mr. Wallace heard the shouts and veered to his left, working his way down the line of admirers. He came first to Mrs. Brigitte Howkins of Hyattsville, a plump matron, who reached over a man, took Mr. Wallace's hand and said: "Good luck, Governor Wallace."

"He smiled at me," Mrs. Howkins recalled later. "I dropped my hand and reached out for another when the man who had been standing on my right lifted his right arm and suddenly there were shots."

Mr. Wallace fell to the as-phalt parking surface and lay

Continued on Page 35, Column 1

Kennedy Guarded By Secret Service

By BEN A. FRANKLIN
Special to The New York Times

WASHINGTON, May 15—Shortly after Gov. George C. Wallace of Alabama was shot today, President Nixon ordered Secret Service protection for Senator Edward M. Kennedy of Massachusetts, Representative Shirley Chisholm of Brooklyn and Representative Wilbur D. Mills of Arkansas.

Senator Kennedy, who has declared repeatedly that he is not a candidate for President, accepted the offer, and an unspecified number of agents were guarding his home tonight in nearby McLean, Va. Agents joined Mrs. Chisholm in Detroit, where she was stay-

Continued on Page 34, Column 2

3 MORE WOUNDED

Legs of Governor Are Paralyzed but Hope Is Voiced by Doctor

By R. W. APPLE Jr.
Special to The New York Times

LAUREL, Md., Tuesday, May 16—Gov. George C. Wallace of Alabama, seemingly on the verge of his greatest electoral triumphs, was shot and gravely wounded yesterday afternoon as he campaigned for President at a shopping center in this suburb of Washington.

Late last night, after the 52-year-old Governor emerged from almost five hours of emergency surgery at the Holy Cross Hospital in nearby Silver Spring, Md., one of his surgeons said that he expected Mr. Wallace "to make a full recovery."

The surgeon, Dr. Joseph Schanno, said that Mr. Wallace had suffered at least four wounds and the doctors had removed one bullet. He said that another bullet was lodged near the spine and that the Governor's legs were paralyzed as a result.

Will Continue Campaign

The Governor's wife, Cornelia, said she was "very happy that he's alive and has a sound heart and a sound brain." Billy Joe Camp, his press secretary, reported this morning, after Mrs. Wallace had talked with the Governor, that he would continue his Presidential campaign and "will be at the Democratic convention as a strong, viable candidate."

The state and local police arrested a suspect, who was identified by the Justice Department as Arthur Herman Bremer, a 21-year-old white man from Milwaukee. The department said that the Secret Service had taken custody of a .38-caliber, snub-nosed, five-shot revolver allegedly used by Mr. Bremer in the shooting. Later, Federal and state charges were filed against him.

Held in $200,000 Bond

Mr. Bremer was taken before United States Magistrate Clarence Goetz in Baltimore last night and was ordered held under $200,000 bond.

Three persons who were with Governor Wallace as he plunged into the crowd at the Laurel Shopping Center were also hit by the four or five bullets fired by the attacker.

The shooting occurred after the Governor, having finished a speech here, shed his coat and stepped from behind the protection of his bullet-proof speaking stand.

A young man wearing sunglasses and a red, white and blue shirt bedecked with Wallace buttons thrust his right hand between two other people

Continued on Page 34, Column 1

MILWAUKEE MAN HELD AS SUSPECT

Seized on Weapons Charge Last October in Wisconsin —Many Paradoxes Seen

By JAMES T. WOOTEN
Special to The New York Times

WASHINGTON, May 15—The young white man arrested as a suspect today in the shooting of Gov. George C. Wallace is a 21-year-old resident of Milwaukee who pasted Wallace bumper stickers on his car and his apartment door and was exuberantly cheering the Democratic Presidential candidate only moments before the shots rang out.

Those apparent contradictions are but a small part of the paradoxical picture now being sketched of Arthur Herman Bremer, the man accused by Federal authorities today of having tried to kill the Alabama Governor at a shopping center in Laurel, Md.

It was reported that he was arrested on a charge of carrying a concealed weapon last Oct. 18 and was subsequently convicted of disorderly conduct.

A Justice Department spokesman said that the .38-caliber snub-nosed revolver allegedly used at Laurel had been purchased in Milwaukee Jan. 13 and fired five times today.

From descriptions supplied

Continued on Page 34, Column 3

NEWS INDEX

	Page		Page
Art	48	Movies	48-51
Books	41	Music	48-51
Bridge	49		
Business	57, 60	Op-Ed	43
Chess	49	Sports	52-55
Crossword	49	Theaters	48-51
Editorials	42	Transportation	80
Family/Style	38	TV and Radio	83
Financial	57-71	U. N. Proceedings	12
Going Out Guide	48	Washington Record	18
Letters	42	Weather	86

News Summary and Index, Page 45

The New York Times

LATE CITY EDITION

Weather: Mostly sunny, mild today. Fair and mild tonight, tomorrow. Temp. range: today 54-71; Friday 46-67. Full U.S. report on Page 58.

VOL. CXXI...No. 41,762   © 1972 The New York Times Company   NEW YORK, SATURDAY, MAY 27, 1972   15 CENTS

U.S. AND SOVIET SIGN TWO ARMS ACCORDS TO LIMIT GROWTH OF ATOMIC ARSENALS; TRADE PACT DELAYED, TALKS TO GO ON

Joint Commission Set Up To Resolve Trade Issues

By ROBERT B. SEMPLE Jr.
Special to The New York Times

MOSCOW, May 26—The United States and the Soviet Union announced the formation of a joint commission today to devise a comprehensive trade agreement that has proved impossible to reach during President Nixon's visit to Moscow.

U.S. TRADE DEFICIT BIG AGAIN IN APRIL

Imports Exceeded Exports by $699-Million, Second Largest Gap on Record

By EDWIN L. DALE Jr.
Special to The New York Times

WASHINGTON, May 26—The United States recorded another huge deficit in its foreign trade in April, the Commerce Department reported today. Imports exceeded exports by $699-million, the second largest deficit for a month on record. The high was set last October, at $821-million.

In the first four months of the year the total trade deficit was $2.2-billion, almost guaranteeing that the year as a whole will see a larger deficit than last year's $2-billion, which was the first trade deficit in this century.

However, officials continue to expect some improvement as 1972 proceeds and the delayed effects of devaluation of the dollar begin to be felt.

Exports in April, seasonally adjusted, were $3.760-billion, down from $3.891-billion in March and the lowest export total of the year so far. A drop in exports of large jet aircraft was partly responsible.

Imports in April were $4.46-billion, down slightly from the figure of $4.475-billion in March. Both figures were above April a year ago—indicating a continued expansion of trade—but the rise in imports was much bigger than that for exports.

For the first four months of the year, exports were running

Continued on Page 35, Column 1

Lindsay Aide Says Council Must Raise Taxes on Property

By FRANCIS X. CLINES

Mayor Lindsay's office insisted yesterday that the City Council had no choice but to approve up to $89-million in higher property taxes to close an expected budget gap, regardless of the continuing opposition of Council members.

Councilman Matthew J. Troy Jr., the leader of the tax revolt, joined with Deputy Mayor Edward K. Hamilton that there was such an obligation in the City Charter's mandate to approve real-estate taxes by June 25. But he said he would violate it rather than vote aye.

"I'm prepared to go to jail," Mr. Troy declared.

The Mayor's press spokesman, Thomas Morgan, immediately commented: "We've alerted the Corrections Department to prepare a padded cell with a view."

Thus, a farcical tone was added to the considerable confusion as the Mayor's office tried to decide what to do next in completing a balanced budg-

Continued on Page 12, Column 5

The announcement, not altogether unexpected, represented an admission by both sides that the two countries had been unable to reconcile differences on the trade issue, and it constituted the first disappointment of the Moscow summit meeting.

Under the terms of the agreement, announced to reporters here by Peter M. Flanigan, Assistant to President Nixon, the joint commission will have these assignments:

¶To negotiate an over-all trade agreement including reciprocal "most favored nation" treatment—meaning, essentially, that imports from the Soviet Union will receive the same tariff advantages given most other United States trading partners.

¶To devise arrangements under which credits will be provided to finance sales by each nation to the other.

¶To negotiate provisions for the establishment of business offices in each country by concerns in the other.

¶To set up an arbitration mechanism for settling commercial disputes arising from trade.

President Appears Tired

The President himself appeared tired yet exhilarated after his first five days in the Soviet Union. At a dinner he gave this evening for Leonid I. Brezhnev, general secretary of the Soviet Communist party, Mr. Nixon raised his glass, and said:

"We look forward to the time when we shall be able to welcome you in our country and in some way respond in an effective manner to the way in which you have received us so generously in your country."

In effect, today was Mr. Nixon's last day of official meetings with Soviet leaders. He will pay a ceremonial visit to Leningrad tomorrow, rest for most of Sunday before delivering a televised address to the Soviet people that evening, and will participate in a reception Monday before flying to Kiev.

Yet the final day ended on what was seen by both sides as an immensely positive note, reflected not only in the arms agreement but in the words of the dignitaries here.

Mr. Nixon, in his toast tonight, called the arms accord not only an "enormously important agreement" but also an "indication of what can happen in the future as we work toward peace in the

Continued on Page 9, Column 6

AFTER SIGNING: President Nixon and Leonid I. Brezhnev exchange treaty copies at Kremlin. In center, Soviet President Nikolai V. Podgorny.

United Press International

FOE PUSHES FIGHT IN TWO KEY AREAS

Losses Heavy, but Enemy Clings to Small Gains at Kontum and Hue

Special to The New York Times

SAIGON, South Vietnam, Saturday, May 27—North Vietnamese soldiers hurled themselves against Government defenses in the Central Highlands city of Kontum and near the northern city of Hue through the day yesterday.

They suffered many casualties and lost 16 tanks, 13 at Kontum and three near Hue, according to American and South Vietnamese military spokesmen. But at nightfall they reportedly continued to hold small pockets of ground within Kontum and near the freeze from the South Vietnamese.

In Kontum, North Vietnamese infiltrators still occupied pockets in the southeastern and northeastern parts of town and continued to keep the airport closed to traffic, according to American sources.

In the northernmost part of South Vietnam, Communist forces were said to hold small bulges of territory about 20 miles northwest of Hue, having penetrated Government defenses along the Mychanh River.

Informed sources said that at one point four North Vietnamese tanks rolled into a de-

Continued on Page 6, Column 2

A First Step, but a Major Stride

By MAX FRANKEL
Special to The New York Times

MOSCOW, Saturday, May 27—The nuclear age gained its first strategic arms limitation treaty in the Kremlin last night. Its awkward name—commonly shortened to SALT — is needed because the accord involves no disarmament. Its purpose is to freeze the balance of terrifying weapons and to make sure the terror works by preventing any effective defense against them.

It is a major step forward in the already long history of nuclear arms negotiation. But it is also only a beginning.

Both President Nixon and the Soviet Party chief, Leonid I. Brezhnev, vowed to press ahead toward further limitations and perhaps eventually

News Analysis

even some reductions in arms. So this treaty is likely to be known as SALT I.

It is a beginning, achieved after seven years of effort and 30 months of negotiation in one of those fleeting moments when the two superpowers felt themselves strategic equals, despite inequality in the quality and number of their arms, and when their two leaders felt themselves strong enough politically to make the agreements stick.

The arms race will go on, not only in the regular army, navy and air force weaponry that is unaffected by the accord but also in the quality of nuclear warheads—that is, their size and accuracy and evasive skills—and in the arts of antisubmarine warfare and even in the technology of the missile defense systems that the treaty

is to limit severely at inadequate levels.

Indeed, under certain conditions or political pressures, the treaty itself may stimulate further competition in these uncovered areas. And because the accord renounces those weapons that both sides think they now possess in sufficient number, it may not even save much money in future budgets.

The United States had no plans to augment the land and submarine missiles and antimissile installations covered by the treaty. The energetic Soviet build-up of recent years was presumably intended primarily to reach a comfortable level before the freeze.

The significance of the treaty lies in that it makes the freeze legally binding. It becomes an important weapon for political

Continued on Page 9, Column 7

CEILINGS ARE SET

Nixon and Brezhnev Pledge to Abide by Treaty at Once

By HEDRICK SMITH
Special to The New York Times

MOSCOW, Saturday, May 27—President Nixon and the Soviet Communist party leader, Leonid I. Brezhnev, signed two historic agreements last night that for the first time put limits on the growth of American and Soviet strategic nuclear arsenals.

In a brief televised ceremony in the Great Hall of the Kremlin, the two leaders put their

Arms accord texts, Page 8, and toasts on Page 9

signatures to a treaty that establishes a ceiling of 200 launchers for each side's defensive missile systems and commits them not to try to build nationwide antimissile defenses. The treaty, which is to run indefinitely, requires ratification by the Senate in Washington, but both sides pledged to abide by it at once.

Applause After Signing

They also signed an interim accord on offensive systems that freezes land-based and submarine-based intercontinental missiles at the level now in operation or under construction.

After signing the two accords, Mr. Brezhnev and Mr. Nixon walked toward each other, smiling broadly, and shook hands vigorously amidst applause from a gathering of senior officials, including negotiators who had worked through the day to put the final touches on the agreement.

Mr. Nixon then said:

"We want to be remembered by our deeds, not by the fact that we brought war to the world, but by the fact that we made the world a more peaceful one for all peoples of the world."

Can Improve Quality

Mr. Kosygin said in reply:

"This is a great victory for the Soviet and American peoples in the matter of easing international tension. This is a victory for all peaceloving people, because security and peace is the common goal."

Later, American officials reported that the two leaders had resolved several deadlocks in their talks here this week.

In a toast at a dinner he gave for the Soviet leaders at Spaso House, the American Ambassador's residence, the President hailed the agreements as "enormously important."

Gerard C. Smith, the chief American negotiator, told reporters that today's two agreements were "not the end of the road by any means, but they

Continued on Page 8, Column 1

LAIRD DISCOUNTS BIG ARMS SAVINGS

Reaction to Pact in Capital Mostly Favorable but Some Conservatives Are Critical

By JUAN M. VASQUEZ
Special to The New York Times

WASHINGTON, May 26—Defense Secretary Melvin R. Laird today hailed the United States arms agreements with the Soviet Union but warned against the expectation of major cost savings.

Returning to the capital after several days of discussions with Atlantic alliance defense ministers in Brussels, Mr. Laird declared that the agreements to limit strategic arms "will enhance the national security of the United States."

He asserted, however, that "we still need to keep up our guard" and that the United States must "maintain a technological superior position."

He added, "There will be no savings as far as the request for offensive strategic weapons which have been presented to the Congress in the 1973 budget."

Specifically, he cited the Air Force B-1 bomber program and submarine construction as areas in which Congress might seek reductions, according to reports he had heard. "That just cannot be," he said.

Mr. Laird, a former Congressman from Wisconsin, told

Continued on Page 10, Column 3

Court Throws Out Jersey Law Barring Primary Cross-Voting

Special to The New York Times

NEWARK, May 26—New Jersey's primary election law prohibiting enrolled voters from casting ballots in other party contests was declared unconstitutional today by a three-judge Federal panel.

The decision specifically threw out the provisions that require enrolled voters to sit out two consecutive primary elections before switching parties. The court declared this waiting period "unreasonable and excessive."

The court directed Attorney General George F. Kugler Jr. to notify local election boards that they must permit voters to choose in which primary they want to vote on June 6 without reference to their party enrollment.

A spokesman for the At-

torney General said he would not comment on whether the decision would be appealed until he had had time to study it.

If the decision stands for the coming primary, it could affect the outcome of the contests for 109 Democratic convention delegates between Senators Hubert H. Humphrey and George McGovern. Republican voters could tip the scales in favor of the man they consider the weaker candidate against President Nixon, who is unopposed on the Republican primary ballot.

The Democratic state chairman, Salvatore A. Bontempo, said he did not know how the decision would affect the primary balloting but said he was

Continued on Page 23, Column 2

U.S. AND SOVIET NUCLEAR ARSENALS

THE ARMS RACE

LAND-LAUNCHED ICBM's

Soviet 1,510
U.S. 1,054
Soviet 1,054
934
226
'65 '67 '69 '71

SUB-LAUNCHED MISSILES

U.S. 710
Soviet 656
464
197
'65 '67 '69 '71

WHAT ACCORDS ALLOW (Basically present levels)

ICBM's
Soviet 1,618
U.S. 1,054

SUB-LAUNCHED MISSILES
U.S. 656
Soviet 710

ANTIMISSILE MISSILES
U.S. (200)
Soviet (200)

WARHEADS (Not covered by accords)

U.S. 5,700
Soviet 2,500
164

Von Braun Will Leave NASA For Job in Aerospace Industry

By HAROLD M. SCHMECK Jr.
Special to The New York Times

WASHINGTON, May 26—Dr. Wernher von Braun, one of the chief architects of man's first landing on the moon, is retiring from the National Aeronautics and Space Administration.

The German-born rocket expert, who has worked for the United States Government since the end of World War II, will leave the space agency July 1 to become corporate vice president for engineering and development of Fairchild Industries, a major aerospace company.

"Dr. von Braun's decision to retire from NASA is a source of great regret to all of us at the agency," said Dr. James C. Fletcher, NASA's administrator.

"For more than a quarter of a century, he has served the United States as the leader in space rocket development," Dr. Fletcher said in the announcement. "His efforts first put the United States in space with Explorer 1. As director of the Marshall Space Flight Center for over 10 years, he directed the development of the world's most powerful rocket, the Saturn 5—which has taken 10 American astronauts to the surface of the moon."

Two of those astronauts, Neil A. Armstrong, the first man to set foot on the moon, and Edwin E. Aldrin Jr., his companion on the historic Apollo 11 moon landing, have al-

Continued on Page 59, Column 1

MISSILE IN SILO: Above photograph, from a Czech source, is said to show a Soviet emplacement. Soviet arms totals on chart include weapons that are under construction.

Photograph from Gamma/Photoreporters   The New York Times/May 27, 1972

"All the News That's Fit to Print"

The New York Times

LATE CITY EDITION

Weather: Rain today; showers likely tonight. Fair and milder tomorrow. Temp. today 68-74; Thursday 66-76. Temp.-Hum. Index yesterday 71. Full U.S. report on Page 70.

VOL. CXXI . No. 41,796   © 1972 The New York Times Company   NEW YORK, FRIDAY, JUNE 30, 1972   15 CENTS

SUPREME COURT, 5-4, BARS DEATH PENALTY AS IT IS IMPOSED UNDER PRESENT STATUTES

Party Panel Strips McGovern of 151 California Delegates

SENATOR SET BACK

He Deplores Move by Coalition of Rivals— State Law Ignored

By WARREN WEAVER Jr.
Special to The New York Times

WASHINGTON, June 29—The Democratic National Convention's Credentials Committee stripped Senator George McGovern today of 151 delegates he thought he had won in the California primary, disregarding state law in a display of political power.

Accomplished by a coalition of his rivals for the Presidential nomination, the move abruptly slowed the momentum of the South Dakotan's campaign and heavily clouded his prospects for tying up the nomination before the convention meets July 10.

The committee ended nearly four hours of debate by voting, 72 to 66, to divide the 271-member California delegation among all the Presidential candidates who competed in the June 6 primary, instead of following the California statute, which allots all the delegates to whoever gets the most votes.

Move Called 'Outrageous'

In an unusually bitter news conference at the Capitol, Senator McGovern called the committee decision "an incredible, cynical, rotten political steal" and "an outrageous way to treat the American people."

Informed at a National Press Club luncheon about the committee action, Senator Hubert H. Humphrey said his chances for the nomination had been "markedly improved."

"I'm not going to say any more—I've got the votes," the Minnesotan said.

Authoritative sources said, meanwhile, that Senator McGovern, if he ultimately wins the nomination, viewed Senator Edward M. Kennedy of Massachusetts as his first choice for a running mate. [Details on Page 20.]

Appealed Is Planned

The Credentials Committee decision will be appealed to the convention when it opens in Miami Beach, but it may prove difficult for the McGovern forces to reverse because the 151 delegates at issue—or perhaps the entire 271 from California—will not be able to vote on their own case.

This dramatic reversal for Senator McGovern was achieved by a tight, well-disciplined coalition of committee members who were either uncommitted or favored Senator Humphrey, Senator Edmund S. Muskie of Maine, Senator Henry M. Jackson of Washington or Gov. George C. Wallace of Alabama.

The development provoked angry protests from Mr. McGovern's supporters, who maintain

Continued on Page 20, Column 2

Press Loses Plea to Keep Data From Grand Juries

Special to The New York Times

WASHINGTON, June 29—The Supreme Court held 5 to 4 today that journalists have no First Amendment right to refuse to tell grand juries the names of confidential sources and information given to them in confidence.

The decision overturned a lower Federal court ruling on behalf of Earl Caldwell, a reporter for The New York Times in San Francisco, who had refused to enter a Federal grand jury room to be questioned on information given him by the Black Panther party.

In two related cases, the Court held that Paul M. Branzburg, an investigative reporter for The Louisville Courier-Journal at the time his case arose, and Paul Pappas, a television newsman in New Bedford, Mass., must tell state grand juries names and other information given them in confidence or face imprisonment for contempt.

The sweeping decision by Justice Byron R. White, supported by President Nixon's four appointees, contained a firm rejection of the theory that the First Amendment shields newsmen under certain circumstances from having to testify when the result would be to cut off news sources and deprive the public of news.

This theory has never been considered before today by the Supreme Court. But in recent years, as a wave of subpoenas issued from grand juries for newsmen's notes, radio stations' tapes and television companies' films, some lower courts began to construe the First Amendment as giving journalists some protection against being compelled to disclose confidences.

The courts usually reasoned that if forcing a newsman to testify would cut off future information, he should be excused unless the Government could show a compelling need for his testimony.

"We cannot accept the argu-

Continued on Page 15, Column 4

Excerpts from Supreme Court action are on Page 15.

Gravel Is Denied Immunity In Case of Pentagon Papers

By ROBERT M. SMITH
Special to The New York Times

WASHINGTON, June 29—The Supreme Court ruled today, by a 5-to-4 vote, that Congressional immunity did not prevent a grand jury from asking Senator Mike Gravel or his aides certain questions about his version of the Pentagon papers—including the question where he had obtained the papers.

In a second case that turned on the same constitutional issue, the Court held, 6 to 3, that legislative privilege did not shield Daniel B. Brewster, a former Democratic Senator from Maryland, from prosecution on bribery charges.

Both decisions were handed down, with several others, on the last day of the Court's current term. The Gravel decision was written by Justice Byron R. White, who was joined by the four men President Nixon named to the Court—Chief Justice Warren E. Burger and Associate Justices Harry A. Blackmun, Lewis F. Powell Jr. and William H. Rehnquist.

Senator Gravel, Democrat of Alaska, reacted by issuing a

Continued on Page 16, Column 4

FUND MISUSE LAID TO 4 L.I. UNIONISTS

U.S. Says They Used Money in Labor-Industry Pool to Pay Ball Team's Debt

By DAVID K. SHIPLER

Four officials of a Long Island construction union were charged yesterday with using employer funds to pay off a union debt of $11,245.

The charges, filed by the Federal Organized Crime Strike Force in Brooklyn, came just hours after city officials discharged a veteran inspector in the Buildings Department who was accused of taking a $100 bribe from the owner of a Park Avenue cooperative apartment.

The two cases, while unrelated, continued to focus attention on the widespread corruption in the construction industry described early in the week by a New York Times report. According to the articles in The Times, based on a six-week investigation, builders pay at least $25-million a year here in bribes to inspectors, policemen, union

Continued on Page 28, Column 1

NIXON DISCLOSES VIETNAM PARLEY RESUMES JULY 13

He Says U.S. Is Returning on Assumption Hanoi Will Negotiate Constructively

By ROBERT B. SEMPLE Jr.
Special to The New York Times

WASHINGTON, June 29 — President Nixon disclosed tonight that the United States and North Vietnam would resume the Paris peace talks on the Vietnam war on July 13.

In a nationally televised news conference—his first in more than a year—Mr. Nixon said the United States was returning to the negotiating table "on the assumption that the North Vietnamese are prepared to negotiate in a constructive and serious way."

He said that if both sides were prepared to engage in serious talks the war could be ended by next year. He also left open the opposite possibility—that the North Vietnamese might not proceed "on that basis," in which case he vowed to continue American bombing and other forms of military pressure. [Question 1, Page 2.]

Talks 'Without Conditions'

Though Mr. Nixon seemed pleased to anounce the resumption of the talks, which were suspended by the United States on May 4, he gave no hint in his remarks that his intense diplomacy in Moscow and Peking in recent weeks had produced assurances that Hanoi was now prepared to move closer to the American position. The most he could or would say was that both sides had agreed to resume negotiating "without conditions."

The President also used the news conference to offer an unusually strong defense of his bombing policy and to give that policy an expanded rationale. In previous statements he has described the bombing as an essentially tactical act designed to protect the shrinking American ground forces in Vietnam and to compensate for the North Vietnamese attacks launched at the end of March.

Tonight he emphasized that

Continued on Page 3, Column 5

Transcript of Nixon news conference is on Page 2.

SPARED: Elmer Branch, 19, sentenced to die for nonfatal assault, in Huntsville, Tex., jail. He was one of condemned men whose sentences were upset by Supreme Court.

Associated Press

PRESIDENT WIDENS FOOD PRICE CURBS

Applies Controls to Produce After It Leaves the Farm —Seafood Also Covered

Special to The New York Times

WASHINGTON, June 29—President Nixon extended controls today to the retail and wholesale prices of such unprocessed food products as eggs, fresh vegetables, fresh fruits and all raw seafood products.

But he stopped short of the far more drastic step of placing direct controls on the prices farmers receive for these products.

The action was the President's second effort this week to impose some restraint on rising food prices, which could be a crucial issue next fall in the Presidential campaign. His reluctance to act directly on farm prices, however, appeared to reflect his concern about antagonizing the farm vote in an election year, as well as fears among some officials that direct controls might be difficult to enforce and might result in shortages.

Officials conceded at a White House briefing that the action might have little immediate effect on prices. But they expressed hope that it would exert pressure on mark-ups and profit margins at each stage of the food distribution chain that, in time, could stem the

Continued on Page 10, Column 2

$502,000 Hijacking Laid to Jobless Man

By JERRY M. FLINT
Special to The New York Times

DETROIT, June 29—Martin Joseph McNally, 28 years old, was arrested last night in front of his home in Wyandotte, Mich., outside Detroit, by agents of the Federal Bureau of Investigation and charged with air piracy in connection with an airline hijacking in the Midwest last week in which $502,000 ransom was paid. He was held today in $100,000 bond.

The hijacker bailed out over Peru, Ind., but dropped the money, which was later recovered.

Government attorneys said Mr. McNally, an unemployed

Continued on Page 9, Column 2

Nixon Backs Death Penalty For Kidnapping, Hijacking

By WILLIAM ROBBINS

WASHINGTON, June 29—President Nixon said tonight he hoped that the Supreme Court's decision restricting the death penalty "does not go so far as to rule out capital punishment for kidnapping and hijacking."

Asked about the Court's 5-to-4 decision, issued today, Mr. Nixon said that "any punishment is cruel and inhuman which takes the life of man or woman." He added that the death penalty had actually saved lives by deterring such major crimes as kidnapping. [Question 15, Page 2.]

The President acknowledged, however, that he had not had time to study all nine opinions. He said that he had read only the opinion of Chief Justice Warren E. Burger, which was a dissent from the majority ruling.

The words of the Chief Justice as well as those of another dissenter, Justice Powell, clearly bar capital punishment under both Federal and state laws as presently written.

"Not only does it [the ruling] invalidate hundreds of state and Federal laws," Justice Powell wrote in his dissenting opinion, "it deprives those jurisdictions of the power to legislate with respect to capital punishment in the future, except in a manner consistent with the cloudily outlined views of those Justices who do not support to undertake total abolition."

And Chief Justice Burger himself said: "It is clear that if state legislatures and the Congress wish to retain the availability of capital punishment, significant statutory changes will have to be made." On other domestic questions, the President did the following:

¶He declined to say whether Vice President Agnew would be his choice as a running-mate in the next election.

¶He voiced support for legislation specifically restricting the possession of handguns.

¶He said former Secretary of

Continued on Page 14, Column 5

Parole in Capital Offenses Less Likely, Officials Say

By MARTIN ARNOLD

Governors and high state officials said yesterday that the Supreme Court's ruling that capital punishment was unconstitutional could profoundly change the structure of criminal penalties in the country.

Officials in many areas said it might become much more difficult, if not impossible, to get parole in cases that were until yesterday capital offenses. Thus, when a person is sentenced to life in prison, it may mean just that, they said.

Gov. Preston Smith of Texas said that the state legislature would be called upon to pass mandatory life prison sentences for certain crimes, barring any parole.

Gov. Jimmy Carter of Georgia said:

"This decision clears the way for us to re-examine all our laws in Georgia. I still don't think seven years is long enough for a man to serve in prison who has committed premeditated murder and is given a life sentence."

Gov. Ronald Reagan of California said he believed that the ruling would allow his state to

Continued on Page 9, Column 2

COURT SPARES 600

4 Justices Named by Nixon All Dissent in Historic Decision

By FRED P. GRAHAM
Special to The New York Times

WASHINGTON, June 29—The Supreme Court ruled today that capital punishment, as now administered in the United States, is unconstitutional "cruel and unusual" punishment.

The historic decision, came on a vote of 5 to 4.

Although the five Justices in the majority issued separate opinions and did not agree on

Excerpts from Court decision on death penalty, Page 14.

a single reason for their action, the effect of the decision appeared to be to rule out executions under any capital punishment laws now in effect in this country.

The decision will also save from execution 600 condemned men and women now on death rows in the United States, although it did not overturn their convictions. Most will be held in prison for the rest of their lives, but under some states' procedures some of the prisoners may eventually gain their freedom.

Eighth Amendment Cited

The decision pitted the five holdovers of the more liberal Warren Court against the four appointees of President Nixon, who dissented. The ruling came as the Supreme Court handed down its final decisions of the year and recessed until Oct. 2.

Three Justices in the majority, William O. Douglas, William J. Brennan Jr. and Thurgood Marshall, concluded that executions in modern-day America necessarily violate the Eighth Amendment's prohibition against "cruel and unusual punishments."

The other two in the majority, the two "swing men" of the Court, Justices Potter Stewart and Byron R. White, reasoned that the present legal system operates in a cruel and unusual way, because it gives judges and juries the discretion to decree life or death and they impose it erratically.

As Justice Stewart put it, the death penalty is "so wantonly and so freakishly imposed" that those who are sentenced to death receive excessively harsh treatment.

View of Chief Justice

"These death sentences are cruel and unusual in the same way that being struck by lightning is cruel and unusual," he said.

As the dissenters pointed out, this alignment means that no death sentence can pass muster before the present Supreme Court unless it satisfies the objections voiced by Justices Stewart and White.

Chief Justice Warren E. Burger suggested that legislatures could attempt to do this in two ways. One is to state in statute books in detail the conditions under which a judge or jury can impose the death penalty—such as rape accompanied by a vicious assault, or a convict's murder of a prison guard.

The second would be to revert to the practice of more than a century ago, and impose mandatory death sentences for

Continued on Page 14, Column 4

Senate Votes Antipoverty Bill, Including Plan for Legal Aid

By The Associated Press

WASHINGTON, June 29—The Senate passed a $9.6-billion antipoverty bill today that included a provision to put the Legal Services program for the poor under an independent corporation.

The bill, passed by a vote of 74 to 16 after a week of debate, authorizes funds for two additional years for programs designed to help 26 million Americans officially defined as poor.

The Senate vote sent the legislation back to the House, which passed a version of the different version last February.

The conference to try to settle the differences between the two measures will be held after Congress returns July 17 from

its recess for the Democratic National Convention.

The bill authorizes sums well beyond President Nixon's recommendations for many programs of the Office of Economic Opportunity, the antipoverty agency. And the bill does not give the President the completely free hand he sought in handling or transferring programs.

In addition, Administration officials indicated that they still found unacceptable the form of the Legal Services Corporation set out in the bill. For these reasons, there is reason to believe that Mr. Nixon

Continued on Page 10, Column 4

U.S. Copters Ferry 1,000 To Quangtri Battleground

By MALCOLM W. BROWNE
Special to The New York Times

SAIGON, South Vietnam, Friday, June 30—About 1,000 South Vietnamese marines were flown by United States helicopters yesterday into an area between the city of Quangtri and the South China Sea in the drive to retake the Communist-held province.

With the South Vietnamese offensive in the northernmost part of the country broadened, heavy fighting was reported from the area today. The thrust was begun Wednesday by a task force of more than 10,000 South Vietnamese marines and paratroopers.

During the night, South Vietnamese troops reported that they killed 225 enemy soldiers in various enemy sectors. Two enemy tanks were reported destroyed by artillery fire near Hailang, in the southern part of Quangtri province, where the bulk of the South Vietnamese tank force was fighting.

The helicopter-borne assault yesterday brought two battalions of South Vietnamese marines into two landing zones in a region east of the city of Quangtri. That city was abandoned to Communist forces on May 1 and the present drive is intended to oust the North Vietnamese from the whole province within three months.

The main South Vietnamese force, which began a northward drive Wednesday from positions along the Mychanh river line, northwest of the city of Hue, consists of elements of South Vietnamese marine and airborne divisions.

A United States Navy spokesman said that American marine helicopters took four hours to complete the landings. While a South Vietnamese spokesman said there had been no enemy opposition, another American spokesman said enemy ground fire had been encountered in both of the landing zones east of the city.

After heavy naval bombard-

Continued on Page 3, Column 4

VISIT the historic Hudson Valley Wine Village, Highland, N.Y. for winery tour. Wine tasting. Open 10-4 daily except Sun. special champagne tour Sat. 3-5. Call (914) 691-7296.—Advt.

The 2nd Lithuanian World Youth Congress convening in Chicago today. Greetings to dependence from LITHUANIA NOW.—Advt.

News Summary and Index, Page 37

"All the News That's Fit to Print"

The New York Times

LATE CITY EDITION

Weather: Sunny and milder today; fair and mild tonight, tomorrow. Temp. range: today 58-77; Tuesday 57-74. Temp.-Hum. Index yesterday 67. Full U.S. report on Page 90.

VOL. CXXI...No. 41,864   © 1972 The New York Times Company   NEW YORK, WEDNESDAY, SEPTEMBER 6, 1972   15 CENTS

9 ISRAELIS ON OLYMPIC TEAM KILLED WITH 4 ARAB CAPTORS AS POLICE FIGHT BAND THAT DISRUPTED MUNICH GAMES

A copter making a test run before picking up Arabs involved in the attack on Israelis. At rear is the Olympic Tower. Sign in German says, "Olympic Village, Gate 6."

MRS. MEIR SPEAKS

A Hushed Parliament Hears Her Assail 'Lunatic Acts'

By TERENCE SMITH
Special to The New York Times

JERUSALEM, Sept. 5 — Her voice heavy and trembling with emotion, Premier Golda Meir today denounced "these lunatic acts of terrorism, abduction and blackmail, which tear asunder the web of international life."

Speaking to a hushed and somber parliament before the fate of the Israeli hostages held captive in Munich was known, she said, "It is inconceivable that the Olympic events should continue as long as our citizens are under the threat of being murdered in the Olympic Village."

She called on all the nations participating in the Olympics to do "whatever is necessary" to rescue the nine Israelis taken hostage by Arab guerrillas in an early-morning attack in which two other Israelis were killed.

[Official sources in Jerusalem said early Wednesday that the Cabinet would meet later in the morning and that there would be no statement on the deaths of the hostages until then.]

Cabinet Still Firm

Although she was not explicit, Mrs. Meir left the impression that Israel would continue to refuse the guerrillas' demands for the release of 200 Palestinian commandos held in this country. Cabinet sources said the Government remained committed to its hard-line policy of neither dealing with nor making concessions to the guerrillas.

Most Israelis seemed stunned by the news of the bizarre attack on the Israeli athletes, which was first reported here on a radio broadcast at 9 A.M. (3 A.M. Tuesday, New York time). Although Israeli citizens traveling abroad have been attacked by Palestinian guerrillas before, the Olympics seemed to many an unlikely setting.

"The games were going so well," one Jerusalem news dealer said, "and now this."

In parliament, where the members had gathered in an extraordinary session to confirm the Justice Minister, the attack was the sole topic of conversation.

Cabinet Ministers and members of parliament sat in the building's modern, sun-washed dining room waiting for additional news from Munich. Each hour on the hour, the large room grew silent and the ministers gathered four deep around a radio as the Israeli radio summarized the developments.

The tension was greatest at

Continued on Page 20, Column 2

West German policemen talking with a spokesman, right, for Arabs who invaded Israeli quarters at Olympic Village

A West German Army ambulance passing through the heavily guarded gate at the military airfield in Fürstenfeldbruck, near Munich, after the commandos and the hostages landed in three helicopters.

A 23-HOUR DRAMA

2 Others Are Slain in Their Quarters in Guerrilla Raid

By DAVID BINDER
Special to The New York Times

MUNICH, West Germany, Wednesday, Sept. 6—Eleven members of Israel's Olympic team and four Arab terrorists were killed yesterday in a 23-hour drama that began with an invasion of the Olympic Village by the Arabs. It ended in a shootout at a military airport some 15 miles away as the Arabs were preparing to fly to Cairo with their Israeli hostages.

The first two Israelis were killed early yesterday morning when Arab commandos, armed with automatic rifles, broke into the quarters of the Israeli team and seized nine others as hostages. The hostages were killed in the airport shootout between the Arabs and German policemen and soldiers.

The bloodshed brought the suspension of the Olympic Games and there was doubt if they would be resumed. Willi Daume, president of the West German Organizing Committee, announced early today that he would ask the International Olympic Committee to meet tomorrow to decide whether they should continue.

Policeman Killed

In addition to the slain Israelis and Arabs, a German policeman was killed and a helicopter pilot was critically wounded. Three Arabs were wounded.

There were some reports that two of the hostages said to have been killed might still be alive. "It is a dim hope," said Dr. Bruno Merk, the Interior Minister of Bavaria, "but I am skeptical on this point."

The bloodbath at the airport that ended at 1 A.M. today, came after long hours of negotiation between German and Arabs at the Israeli quarters in the Olympic Village where the Arabs demanded the release of 200 Arab commandos imprisoned in Israel.

Finally the West German armed forces supplied three helicopters to transport the Arabs and their Israeli hostages to the airport at Fürstenfeldbruck. From there all were to be flown to Cairo.

A Boeing-707 provided by the Lufthansa German Airlines was waiting.

Two of the terrorists, carrying their automatic rifles, walked about 170 yards from the helicopters to the plane. And then they started back to pick up the other Arabs and the hostages.

Positions Cited

As the Arabs were returning, German sharpshooters reportedly opened fire from the darkness beyond the pools of light at the airport. The Arabs returned fire.

The torment of the entire event was heightened by confusion created in the public mind by contradictory reports from German and Olympic officials after the gunfire erupted at the airport.

Dr. Merk, in a press conference at 3 o'clock this morning said:

"In this situation our task and goal to free the hostages was made more difficult by the lack of agreement from Israel to free prisoners or to get guarantees from the Arabs not to take action against the hos-

Continued on Page 18, Column 1

752 Air-Conditioned Cars Ordered for City Subways

By EDWARD RANZAL

Mayor Lindsay announced yesterday that 752 new air-conditioned subway cars had been ordered for $210.5-million. He said the contract was the largest ever signed in the country for the purchase of passenger railroad cars.

The first group of cars, which will be manufactured by the Pullman - Standard Company, are to be delivered by 1973.

The cars will provide a quieter ride than present equipment, according to Dr. William J. Ronan, chairman of the Metropolitan Transportation Authority.

The new equipment, which will be used on the IND and BMT lines, will enable the authority to phase out more than 1,200 pre-World War II cars which are smaller than the new ones. A study is being made, Dr. Ronan said, to produce an air-conditioned unit that can be used in cars in the smaller tunnels of the IRT system.

20% of Fleet by '75

Each car will cost more than $273,000. The city will provide one-third of the total funds—the money has been provided in the city's 1972-73 capital budget—and the Federal Urban Mass Transportation Administration will supply the rest.

By 1975 more than 20 per cent of the city's fleet of nearly 7,000 subway cars will consist of new air-conditioned cars.

The first order under the contract will be for 454 cars at a cost of $127.4-million. Some of them will be delivered in

Continued on Page 91, Column 2

Berrigan and a Nun Get Prison Terms In Letter Smuggling

By JOHN KIFNER
Special to The New York Times

HARRISBURG, Pa., Sept. 5—The Rev. Philip F. Berrigan—cleared of charges that he led a plot to kidnap President Nixon's adviser on national security affairs, Henry A. Kissinger—was sentenced in Federal District Court here today to four concurrent two-year terms for smuggling letters out of the Lewisburg Penitentiary.

Sister Elizabeth McAlister, also cleared of the plot charges, was sentenced to one year in jail and three years' probation for smuggling letters.

Moments after the sentences were announced, Government attorneys moved to dismiss the first three substantive counts of their indictment, confirming that the Justice Department would not seek a retrial of the controversial "Harrisburg Seven" case.

The Government charged Father Berrigan, Sister Elizabeth, two other Roman Catholic priests, a former priest, a former nun and a Pakistani scholar with conspiracy to kidnap Mr. Kissinger as ransom to force a halt to the bombing in Viet-

Continued on Page 16, Column 1

PARLEY REJECTS HIJACKING TREATY

U.S.-Canadian Project for Penalizing Nations Aiding Air Pirates Rebuffed

By ROBERT LINDSEY
Special to The New York Times

WASHINGTON, Sept. 5—Delegates to a 17-nation conference here rejected today United States-Canadian efforts to negotiate an international anti-hijacking treaty based on a draft proposed by the two nations.

The move for nonacceptance was led by France and Britain and supported by the Soviet Union and Egypt.

Faced with what appeared to be certain defeat of the proposed treaty if it came to a vote, the two North American nations acquiesced in a French proposal to start writing a new treaty from scratch, after debates on what "principles" should be included.

The delegates have eight working days left before the conference is scheduled to end.

Today's rejection was a significant setback for the United

Continued on Page 91, Column 2

Nixon Tightens Security In U.S. Against 'Outlaws'

By TAD SZULC
Special to The New York Times

WASHINGTON, Sept. 5 — Secretary of State William P. Rogers issued this statement on behalf of the Administration:

"There are no words which can fully express our reaction to today's tragedy at the Olympic Games. I know I speak for all Americans in extending the deepest sympathies of the

Continued on Page 18, Column 4

WASHINGTON, Sept. 5—President Nixon said today that "extra security measures" would be taken in the United States to protect American citizens as well as visiting Israelis from possible attacks by Palestinian guerrillas.

Mr. Nixon, speaking to newsmen in San Francisco, left it unclear, however, whether he meant that this new protection would cover prominent American Jews or only those whom he described as "Americans of Israeli background, American citizens."

Speaking before the gunfight at a military airport in Munich, in which the Israeli hostages were killed, Mr. Nixon discussed the capture of Israeli Olympic team members by Palestinian guerrillas and the slaying of two Israelis. He said:

"Since we are dealing with international outlaws who are unpredictable, we have to take extra security measures to protect those who might be the targets of this kind of activity in the future. That might include Americans of Israeli background, American citizens."

GAMES SUSPENDED; RITES IN ARENA SET

Halt Is the First Since 1896, When the Classic Resumed —Egypt Team in Forfeit

By NEIL AMDUR
Special to The New York Times

MUNICH, West Germany, Wednesday, Sept. 6 — The Olympic Games were suspended yesterday for the first time since competition in the modern era began in 1896.

Late-afternoon and evening events were called off in the wake of an attack staged by Arab guerrillas before dawn on the Olympic Village in which two Israelis were killed and nine others taken hostage. The hostages were later killed.

After the attack, Mark Spitz, the American swimmer who won seven gold medals at the Munich Olympics and who is Jewish, flew hurriedly to London on his way back to the United States. There were fears before his departure that he too might become a victim. [Page 20.]

The announcement of the suspension, made by the International Olympic Committee, also said that a memorial service would be held for the victims

Continued on Page 18, Column 7

Reports First Said Israelis Were Safe

Contradictory reports last night about the fate of the Israeli hostages seized by Arab terrorists in the Olympic Village threw the public into confusion all over the world.

Throughout the day, as the tragedy in Munich unfolded, millions of viewers throughout the world watched on live television. The events that had been intended for the Games. But in the evening, when the events reached their climax, viewers could get no definitive word for hours on how the hostages fared.

At first the West German Government's official spokesman, Conrad Ahlers, announced

Continued on Page 20, Column 1

Elizabeth City Hall Under Investigation

By RONALD SULLIVAN
Special to The New York Times

TRENTON, Sept. 5—Law enforcement authorities reported here today that the administration of Mayor Thomas J. Dunn of Elizabeth was the target of a Union County grand jury investigation of alleged municipal corruption.

Mayor Dunn, a Democrat running for a third term, said in an interview that he had "no knowledge of any investigation involving me or my administration." He said he volunteered last spring to go before a Union County grand jury.

According to official sources, the grand jury is investigating charges of payoffs and kickbacks involving city officials, contracts and businessmen. City license officials have already been subpoenaed, as have a number of city records and contracts.

Karl Asch, the county prosecutor, refused to comment on the nature of the reported investigation. He did say his staff had been instructed to seek indictments before the Nov. 7 elections.

Last week two of Mr. Dunn's three mayoral opponents were indicted in separate matters by a Union County grand jury. Matthew J. Nilsen, a Republican freeholder in the county, was indicted on charges of atrocious assault in August in a case involving an alleged extortion.

In the other indictment, Michael J. DeMartino, a Demo-ocratic City Councilman in Elizabeth, was charged with misconduct in office in a case involving a $3,000 bribe in 1968.

Mayor Dunn recently endorsed President Nixon for re-election. Political observers in Union County noted that the indictments of two of his opponents were sought by a Republican prosecutor, and were seen as aiding the Mayor's re-election chances.

However, Mr. Asch, who has obtained indictments against prominent Union County political figures in recent months, contended today that his anti-corruption drive was "absolutely nonpolitical" and that the investigation of the Dunn

Continued on Page 46, Column 6

IF YOU'RE NOT DRINKING WILLIAM LAWSON'S SCOTCH, DRINK DEWAR'S William Lawson is a Fine Blended Scotch Whiskies. Imported by Palmer & Lord, Ltd. Brewer, N.Y.—Advt.

"All the News
That's Fit to Print"

The New York Times

LATE CITY EDITION
Weather: Cloudy, rain likely today and tonight. Cloudy, cool tomorrow.
Temp. range: today 48-60; Tuesday 45-61. Full U.S. report on Page 93.

VOL. CXXII..No. 41,927   © 1972 The New York Times Company   NEW YORK, WEDNESDAY, NOVEMBER 8, 1972   15 CENTS

NIXON ELECTED IN LANDSLIDE; M'GOVERN IS BEATEN IN STATE; DEMOCRATS RETAIN CONGRESS

President Loses in City By 81,920-Vote Margin

By FRANK LYNN

President Nixon swept New York State yesterday, but lost to Senator McGovern in New York City by a total of 81,920 votes.

Mr. Nixon's statewide plurality was expected to be about a million votes.

With 11,521 of the 12,948 districts in the state reporting, the tally was:

Nixon 3,712,113
McGovern 2,539,326

With all of the 4,219 districts in the city reporting, the tally was:

Nixon 1,259,244
McGovern 1,341,164

The President's strong showing in the state rivaled the 1956 victory of President Dwight D. Eisenhower, who first brought Mr. Nixon to the national ticket 20 years ago.

The Nixon victory did not appear to carry too far down the Republican line. The Legislature remained Republican, but with no indication of sub-

stantially increased Republican majorities.

Three Republican candidates for the Court of Appeals held slight leads but returns were still inconclusive.

The President's capture of the state was only the third time a Republican Presidential candidate had won New York since 1928.

Dozens of sample districts showed last night that the President substantially improved his 1968 showing in virtually all ethnic groups and geographic areas in the state and city. In many cases, particularly in the cities, Mr. Nixon surpassed Governor Rockefeller's victory margins of two years ago.

In New York City, Senator McGovern carried districts that were predominantly black, Puerto Rican and Jewish. But in the Jewish areas, Mr. Nixon doubled his showing of four years before. In a middle class

Continued on Page 36, Column 2

Nixon Has a Big Plurality In Jersey and Connecticut

Case an Easy Winner
By RONALD SULLIVAN

President Nixon won the overwhelming victory predicted for him in New Jersey in yesterday's Presidential election, defeating Senator George McGovern by a 2-to-1 margin.

At the same time, Senator Clifford P. Case, the liberal Republican, won a fourth term and one of the biggest Senate election victories in New Jersey's history, defeating Paul J. Krebs, the Democratic candidate.

However, incumbent Democratic Representatives survived the G.O.P. onslaught at the top of the ballot in what political leaders described as a remarkable display of ticket-splitting.

The Presidential tally with 4,142 districts of 5,212 reporting, was:

Nixon 1,440,420
McGovern 862,582

The tally in the race for the Senate, with 3,657 of 5,212 districts reporting, was:

Case 1,112,754
Krebs 627,352

With both Mr. Nixon and Senator Case piling up 2-to-1 margins throughout the state, Republican leaders predicted that the President's margin would rival the 800,000-vote plurality achieved by Dwight D.

Continued on Page 37, Column 3

Hartford Assembly G.O.P.
By LAWRENCE FELLOWS
Special to The New York Times

HARTFORD, Nov. 7—President Nixon carried Connecticut today in a landslide victory.

The President swept the state's eight electoral votes with a plurality of 252,289, approaching the 306,758-vote margin by which the late President Dwight D. Eisenhower carried the state in 1956.

The Republicans also took control of the General Assembly, winning the State Senate by 23 to 13 and the House of Representatives by 93 to 58.

But widespread ticket-splitting enabled three of the four incumbent Democratic Representatives to keep their seats in Washington.

With all of the 169 towns in the state reporting, the Presidential tally was:

Nixon 799,249
McGovern 546,960

Continued on Page 37, Column 7

Reid Wins as Democrat; Bella Abzug Easy Victor

By RICHARD L. MADDEN

Representative Ogden R. Reid, a former Republican, was reelected yesterday as a Democrat in Westchester County, and Representative Bella S. Abzug, a one-term Democrat, won a decisive re-election in Manhattan.

In another key Westchester race, Representative Peter A. Peyser, a freshman Republican, claimed victory over his predecessor in the House, Richard L. Ottinger, a Democrat-Liberal, who was seeking to recapture his former seat.

Mrs. Abzug defeated by about 2-to-1 margin Mrs. Priscilla M. Ryan, a Liberal and widow of the late Representative William F. Ryan, who had defeated Mrs. Abzug in the Democratic primary in the 20th Congressional District last June.

With about 85 per cent of the vote reported in Westchester, but with large numbers of absentee ballots still to be counted, Mr. Reid led Carl A. Vergari, a Republican-Conservative and the county's District Attorney, by more than 8,000 votes.

Despite the strong vote for

President Nixon in the state, incumbent Democratic Representatives generally appeared to be withstanding the Republican tide. One exception was Representative John D. Dow, of Newburgh, a liberal Democrat who had strenuously opposed the war in Vietnam.

Mr. Dow, who lost his House seat in the generally conservative Rockland-Orange county area in 1968 and won it back two years ago, was substantially trailing Assemblyman Benjamin A. Gilman, a Middletown Republican.

Representative Otis G. Pike, a six-term Democrat from Suffolk County, won a three-way fight for re-election and another prime target of the Republicans, Representative James M. Hanley of Syracuse, defeated his Republican-Conservative opponent, Leonard J. Koldin.

Representative Lester L. Wolff, a four-term Democrat whose new Nassau County district now takes in part of Queens, led Assemblyman John

Continued on Page 36, Column 6

Mrs. Smith Defeated For Senate in Maine

By BILL KOVACH
Special to The New York Times

PROVIDENCE, R. I., Wednesday, Nov. 8—The 34-year Congressional career of Senator Margaret Chase Smith, the Senate's only woman member, ended last night in a major upset as Democrats showed unexpected strength in New England Senate and Gubernatorial races.

William D. Hathaway, the Democrat who gave up his Second District Congressional office to challenge the 74-year-old Mrs. Smith despite her near-legendary standing in Maine, won the seat in a hard-fought contest.

Mr. Hathaway's stunning victory was part of a Democratic surge that overcame the general New England sweep by President Nixon, and reflected stubborn ticket-splitting by

Continued on Page 21, Column 1

MANY VOTES SPLIT

G.O.P. Loses Senate Seats in 6 States and Picks Up 4 Others

By R. W. APPLE Jr.

The Democratic party withstood President Nixon's landslide yesterday to retain control of both houses of Congress.

With voters in all parts of the nation splitting their tickets in huge numbers, the Democrats brought off a series of startling upsets in Senate contests to gain at least two seats, similar to their feat in the face of Dwight D. Eisenhower's sweep of 1956.

The Democrats captured previously Republican Senate seats in six states—Delaware, Iowa, Kentucky, Maine, Colorado and South Dakota. Those pickups more than offset Republican gains in the two Southwestern states of Oklahoma and New Mexico and the two Southern states of Virginia and North Carolina.

Two Races Open

Two Senate races remained in doubt this morning—in Alaska and Nebraska. Both seats were held by the Republicans in the last Congress.

The figures for the House were far less complete, but the Republicans were not making the gains they needed to take control. It appeared that they would pick up somewhere in the neighborhood of a dozen seats; they had already gained seven.

At present, the Senate line-up is 54 Democrats, 44 Republicans, one Conservative-Republican and one independent who votes with the Democrats. In the House it is 255 Democrats, 177 Republicans and three vacancies.

Mr. Nixon's coattails proved relatively short this year, as they had in 1968. In state after state, he swept to massive vic-

Continued on Page 34, Column 7

Olympic Fund Barred

Voters in Colorado cut off public funds for the 1976 Winter Olympics yesterday. Without the tax money, the International Olympic Committee was all but forced to move the games to another site. Page 31.

M'GOVERN TO BACK MOVES FOR PEACE

But Says He Will Continue to Oppose Policies He Had Deplored in Campaign

By JAMES M. NAUGHTON
Special to The New York Times

SIOUX FALLS, S.D., Nov. 7 — Senator George McGovern conceded defeat of his Presidential candidacy here tonight but said that he would "shed no tears" because of the effort his campaign had made to draw the nation close to peace.

The Democratic nominee told 1,200 cheering enthusiasts at 10:40 P.M., Central standard time, that he had sent a telegram to President Nixon pledg-

ing support for "peace abroad and justice at home."

He said the President had his "full support" in efforts toward such goals.

But he added in his speech, which was televised, that he would, as the leader of the "loyal opposition," continue to oppose any policies that he had deplored during his long campaign.

"Now, the question is to what standards does the loyal

Continued on Page 3, Column 3

Text of McGovern's comments appears on Page 3.

The Election at a Glance

President
Needed for Election—270 Electoral Votes

	Number of States	Electoral Votes
Nixon	49	521
McGovern	2	17

The Senate

Newly Elected Senators		Make-up of New Senate	
Democrats	16	Democrats	57
Republicans	15	Republicans	41
In Doubt	2	In Doubt	2

The House

Democrats Elected	218
Republicans Elected	154
In Doubt	63

Includes District of Columbia.

Victory, 10 Years Later

Spectacular Nixon Vote Considered Vindication in Light of Past Defeats

By JAMES RESTON

It was a spectacular personal victory for Richard Nixon, 10 years to the day, and almost to the hour, after his most humiliating defeat by Pat Brown in the 1962 election for the governorship of California.

Beaten by John Kennedy by the narrowest of margins in the Presidential election of 1960, beaten again for the control of his own state in 1962, finished with

News Analysis

American politics by his own angry proclamation exactly a decade ago, here he is now, not only vindicated but triumphant in one of the most decisive victories in the history of American Presidential politics.

In a few days before he will take the oath of office for a second term as President of the United States (Jan. 9), he will be 60 years old. His thirties were a political surprise, even to himself, his forties were an agony of controversy and self-doubt, his fifties a struggle and at the end a triumph. What now will he do with his sixties? This is the question that even his most intimate associates in Washington cannot answer.

In the world, he has to achieve not only the cease-fire, but the peace he has promised in Vietnam, the "reconciliation and cooperation" with Peking and Moscow that were so central to his victory, the truce in the savage struggle between Israel and the Arab states, and some kind of new economic and political relationship with

Japan and the Common Market countries of Europe, who are now challenging the American economic leadership of the modern world.

At home, Mr. Nixon has to deal also now with the minorities who failed to support him in the election: the poor and the blacks who have been left behind in the general prosperity of the nation, the young in the universities who have been over-run but not persuaded by

Continued on Page 34, Column 3

Summary of Other News

Following is a summary of major nonelection news. A full report begins on the first page, second part.

Canarsie School Boycott

Leaders of Canarsie parents who have kept their children out of school for two weeks declared yesterday that "the boycott is over" and called on parents to return their children to school. But the prospect of full classes today remained in doubt since more than 1,000 parents shouted down the same call Monday night.

Bid by Vietcong

Agents of the National Liberation Front have made several recent contacts with Saigon's anti-Government, non-Communist opposition, according to opposition sources.

Britons Protest Price Rises

British Government offices were swamped with complaints of price increases on the first full day of Prime Minister Heath's anti-inflation freeze. But a check of London shops found no wide pattern of violations. Most of the increases involved uncontrolled items.

Soviet Parades Its Arms

The Soviet Union, marking the 55th anniversary of the Bolshevik Revolution, paraded its military might in low-key fashion. The unusually deliberate movements of Leonid I. Brezhnev, the party leader, reinforced speculation that he had been ill.

President and Mrs. Nixon and Vice President Agnew at the Republican celebration in Washington early today

MARGIN ABOUT 60%

Massachusetts Is Only State to Give Vote to the Dakotan

By MAX FRANKEL

Richard Milhous Nixon won re-election by a huge majority yesterday, perhaps the largest ever given a President.

Mr. Nixon scored a stunning personal triumph in all sections of the country, sweeping New York and most other bastions of Democratic strength.

He was gathering more than 60 per cent of the nation's ballots and more than 500 electoral votes. He lost only Massachusetts and the District of Columbia.

The victory was reminiscent of the landslide triumphs of Franklin D. Roosevelt in 1936 and Lyndon B. Johnson in 1964, although it could fall just short of their record proportions.

Tickets Are Split

Despite this drubbing of George Stanley McGovern, the Democratic challenger, the voters split their tickets in record numbers to leave the Democrats in control of both houses of Congress and a majority of the nation's governorships. Mr. Nixon thus became the first two-term President to face an opposition Congress at both inaugurals.

The turnout of voters appeared to be unusually low, despite jams at many polling places. Projections indicated a total vote of 76 million out of a voting-age population of 139.6 million, or only about 54 per cent. If accurate, that would be the lowest proportion since 51.4 per cent in 1948. The percentage has been over 60 per cent in every election since then.

May Claim Mandate

The President seemed certain, however, to claim a clear mandate for his policies of gradual disengagement from Vietnam, continued strong spending on defense, opposition to busing to integrate the schools and a slowdown in Federal spending for social programs. These are the issues he stressed through the campaign.

The 59-year-old Mr. Nixon, who will be 60 before inauguration on Jan. 20, could also claim a resounding personal vindication against the strong charges of corruption brought against him personally by the opposition.

By coincidence, the greatest triumph of his 26 years in national politics came on the 10th anniversary of his defeat for Governor of California—the time he told newsmen they would not have Nixon to kick around anymore.

McGovern Concedes

Mr. McGovern, 50, conceded defeat before midnight in the East with a telegram of support for the President if he leads the nation to peace abroad and justice at home.

The South Dakotan took credit for helping to push the Administration nearer to peace in Indochina and assured his cheering supporters at the Sioux Falls Coliseum that their defeat would bear fruit for years to come.

The President responded in a brief address from the White

Continued on Page 34, Column 1

NIXON ISSUES CALL TO 'GREAT TASKS'

At Victory Celebration, He Vows to Make Himself 'Worthy' of Victory

By ROBERT B. SEMPLE Jr.
Special to The New York Times

WASHINGTON, Wednesday, Nov. 8 — President Nixon summoned the nation last night "to get on with the great tasks that lie before us" and, in a later statement to a crowd of cheering supporters, pledged to make himself "worthy of this victory."

Mr. Nixon made two statements, both televised.

The first of these was a brief statement from his desk

Text of Nixon's remarks is printed on Page 34.

in the Oval Office of the White House in which he pledged himself to secure not only "a peace with honor in Vietnam" but also "a new era of peace" throughout the world; to "prosperity without war and without inflation" at home, and to an America in which all citizens will have "an equal chance."

"I would only hope," he said, "that in these next four years we can so conduct ourselves in

Continued on Page 34, Column 3

A Rockefeller Loses West Virginia Race

By BEN A. FRANKLIN

CHARLESTON, W. Va., Wednesday, Nov. 8—Secretary of State John D. Rockefeller 4th suffered a sharp defeat yesterday in a bid for the West Virginia governorship. The loss appeared, at least, to have postponed a possible role for him in national Democratic politics in 1976.

Mr. Rockefeller's well-financed candidacy had depended heavily on proposals on the environment in the second-ranked coal-mining state. These also suffered a setback through his defeat in a race that eclipsed all others here.

Gov. Arch A. Moore Jr., a Republican former Congressman who is the first Governor here who has been constitutionally able to succeed to a second

Continued on Page 23, Column 1

The New York Times

LATE CITY EDITION
Weather: Mostly cloudy, seasonably cold today, tonight and tomorrow. Temp. range: today 34-42; Tuesday 37-42. Full U.S. report on Page 78.

VOL. CXXII...No. 41,976
© 1972 The New York Times Company

— NEW YORK, WEDNESDAY, DECEMBER 27, 1972 —

15 CENTS

U.S. SAYS BOMBING IS BACK AT LEVEL PRECEDING PAUSE

Warplanes From Thailand, Guam and Carriers Take Off for North Vietnam

HALT LASTED 36 HOURS

Hanoi Reports 8 B-52's Shot Down in Day—Pentagon Calls Loss Rate Normal

By JOSEPH B. TREASTER
Special to The New York Times

SAIGON, South Vietnam, Wednesday, Dec. 27—With its 36-hour pause in the bombing of North Vietnam ended, the United States command said yesterday that the planes were once again operating as they had last week, when the raids were the heaviest of the war.

Maj. Jere K. Forbus, a spokesman for the command, announced yesterday afternoon that the Christmas pause in bombing had ended three hours earlier, at 1 P.M. (midnight Monday, New York time). At that time, warplanes started taking off from aircraft carriers in the South China Sea and from bases in Thailand and Guam.

Informed officers had said before the pause that about 100 B-52's and several hundred smaller fighter-bombers had been participating in the attacks.

57 Listed as Missing

Many officers in Saigon said yesterday that despite denials from the Pentagon, B-52 losses since the raids began Dec. 18 have been much higher than had been expected.

As of last evening the command had acknowledged having lost 11 of the heavy eight-engine bombers, which each carry more than 24 tons of bombs and which usually fly in formations of three. The command has also reported six fighter-bombers down.

Altogether, the command says, 57 American airmen are missing in action. Hanoi says it has captured more than 100.

The Hanoi radio said today that eight more B-52's and an F-4 Phantom fighter-bomber were shot down yesterday. The North Vietnamese now maintain that they have destroyed a total of 62 American aircraft, including 26 of the heavy bombers, which are valued at $8-million each, since the raids began Dec. 18.

[The Pentagon had no comment on the Hanoi radio report, but it said earlier that the loss rate of B-52's was not materially greater than in raids last spring though now "there are more B-52's involved."]

'Brutal and Barbaric Act'

In a statement condemning the resumption of the bombing, the North Vietnamese Foreign Ministry said over the Hanoi radio this morning that many B-52's and "scores of other aircraft" struck urban and suburban areas in Hanoi, Haiphong, Thai Nguyen — the site of the nation's principal steel mill—and other cities last night.

"This is a brutal and barbaric act aimed at killing civilians, an act that surpasses Hitler's war crimes in scope and intensity," the statement said.

Continued on Page 10, Column 1

Jury Begins Investigation Into Drug Losses by Police

Judge Threatens Murphy With Contempt for Refusal to Cooperate in Inquiry as Two Officers Fail to Appear

By EMANUEL PERLMUTTER

A grand jury began taking testimony yesterday in the recently disclosed theft of 300 pounds of heroin and cocaine from the Police Department, and a judge threatened Police Commissioner Patrick V. Murphy and two of his aides with contempt for refusing to cooperate with the jury.

Gene L. Gruposso, the police property clerk, testified before the jurors in the morning in the Manhattan Criminal Court Building. However, Assistant Chief Inspector John Guido, who is in charge of the inspection division, and Inspector Howard A. Metzdorff of the internal affairs division, were not present to testify when their names were called.

The subpoenaing of the policemen by the grand jury was a rebuff to Maurice H. Nadjari, the special state prosecutor, and to Governor Rockefeller. Last October, the Governor had directed Commissioner Murphy to send information about possible criminal-justice corruption only to Mr. Nadjari. The city's District Attorneys and Mr. Nadjari are fighting over who should investigate the narcotics thefts.

A subpoena had been served on Commissioner Murphy last Friday, calling for the three witnesses to appear before the grand jury yesterday. Mr. Murphy was also directed to turn over to the jurors department records on the stolen narcotics that had been held as evidence by the police.

Frank Rogers, a special assistant district attorney who is in charge of prosecution in the 12 narcotics courts in the city, is supervising the citywide grand jury that is investigating the drug thefts as well as other narcotics cases.

At the request of Mr. Rogers, Supreme Court Justice Sidney A. Fine issued the subpoenas last week.

In a hearing yesterday before Justice Fine, Mr. Rogers contended that the grand jury

Continued on Page 25, Column 6

School Board Plans Offer To Buy Scribner Contract

By GENE I. MAEROFF

The Board of Education was drafting a letter yesterday that it intends to send to School Chancellor Harvey B. Scribner, outlining a proposal to buy up his contract. A board member, who declined to be identified, said that there "had been no dissent" at a meeting Friday at which the five members decided to offer to pay Dr. Scribner for the remaining six months of his three-year contract and relieve him of his $53,000-a-year post.

Dr. Scribner, who was reported to be out of town and unavailable for comment, announced at a news conference Thursday that he intended to leave his post June 30. He blamed his decision on a "confidence gap" that he said had developed between him and the Board of Education.

The names of possible successors have not been mentioned by the board, but speculation centered on Irving Anker, the deputy chancellor.

Once Headed System

Mr. Anker headed the 1.1-million-pupil New York City school system on an interim basis in 1970, before Dr. Scribner assumed the job. Mr. Anker is seen as someone who could again serve on an acting basis until a permanent chancellor is chosen.

Should Dr. Scribner refuse to accept a settlement, the board—if it continues to seek his removal—would have to bring departmental charges against him, which is regarded as an unlikely possibility.

"We would rather not have to think about this aspect," one board member said yesterday.

Prior to his announcement last week, Dr. Scribner's reappointment was by no means assured, but he was regarded as still being in contention.

However, he apparently

Continued on Page 27, Column 3

GRAND JURY GETS POLICE SHOOTING

Defendant Is Central Figure in $500 Bail Dispute Involving Two Judges

By RALPH BLUMENTHAL

A grand jury here began an investigation yesterday of the holdup shooting of a patrolman—a case that has stirred controversy because of the release of the suspect in $500 cash bail.

Among the first to testify was another man shot in the holdup. He said he had told the grand jury he could identify the holdup man.

The witness, Edward M. Blagden, then returned to his hospital bed, from where he made public an open letter berating Criminal Court Judge Bruce McMarion Wright for having released the suspect in $500 cash bail.

Judge Wright said yesterday that the case was under review by the Appellate Division and a spokesman said the judge was under the division's orders not to discuss the matter publicly.

Other judicial authorities, meanwhile, said they had no jurisdiction and indicated they were not now preparing any

Continued on Page 25, Column 1

Appraisal of the Arts

The second half of an assessment of the year in art and culture by nine critics for The New York Times appears on Page 29.

CITY AIDES TO LOSE APPROVAL POWER ON NEW BUILDING

Owners to Be Responsible Under Antigraft Plan— Delays Seen Curbed

By ROBERT E. TOMASSON

In a major move aimed at reducing "graft-inducing situations" in the construction industry, the city will shift authority for initial building approval next month from its 75 plan examiners to individual owners, architects and engineers.

The "sharp departure from tradition" was announced by Joseph Stein, Commissioner of the Department of Buildings, who said the move was taken in response to the industry's complaint of excessive delays in obtaining building permits that "created graft-inducing situations to obtain expeditious approval."

Instead of the months that were often required to obtain the necessary building permits, they will be issued within days under the new system, Commissioner Stein said.

Builder Cites 'Ways'

Owners will still be held accountable for meeting requirements of the building code, Mr. Stein said, but will no longer have to suffer delays because of objections raised by individual examiners.

Building plans have often had to be submitted several times before their approval, and there has been widespread talk in the industry that there "were ways," as one major builder phrased it yesterday, to expedite approval.

One alleged widespread abuse was the consideration of plans out of sequence in which they were submitted.

In a series of articles in The New York Times last summer, it was estimated that the construction industry paid out at least $25-million in bribes annually to officials and others in connection with virtually every phase of building.

Rise of the 'Expediter'

The complexity of the city's 371-page building code has given rise to creation of the position of men known in the trade as "expediters" whose essential function is to cultivate plan examiners.

One chief executive of a large construction firm here said yesterday that plan approval was often obtained "on what amounts to a scale system, with so much graft for each apartment" in a proposed project.

John Tudda, an architect whose firm has functioned as a consultant to expedite city approval on projects including the Ruppert Brewery Urban Renewal project in the Yorkville area of Manhattan and Lincoln

Continued on Page 18, Column 4

TRUMAN, 33D PRESIDENT, IS DEAD; SERVED IN TIME OF FIRST A-BOMB, MARSHALL PLAN, NATO AND KOREA

HARRY S. TRUMAN, 1884-1972

United Press International
The Truman home in Independence, Mo., yesterday

Funeral to Be Tomorrow In Independence Library

By B. DRUMMOND AYRES Jr.
Special to The New York Times

KANSAS CITY, Mo., Dec. 26—Harry S. Truman, the 33d President of the United States, died this morning. He was 88 years old.

Mr. Truman, an outspoken and decisive Missouri Democrat who served in the White House from 1945 to 1953, succumbed at 7:50 A.M., central standard time, in Kansas City's Research Hospital and Medical Center.

He had been a patient there for the last 22 days, struggling against lung congestion, heart irregularity, kidney blockages, failure of the digestive system and the afflictions of old age.

In the more than seven years he was President, from the time Franklin Delano Roosevelt's death suddenly elevated him from the Vice-Presidency until he himself was succeeded by Dwight David Eisenhower, Mr. Truman left a major mark as a world leader.

He brought mankind face to face with the age of holocaust by ordering atomic bombs dropped on Japan, sent American troops into Korea to halt Communist aggression in Asia, helped contain Communism in Europe by forming the North Atlantic Treaty Organization and speeded the postwar recovery of Europe through the Marshall Plan.

His domestic record was

An obituary article appears on Pages 46-49. An appraisal by the late Dean Acheson, written in 1964, will be found on Page 45.

somewhat less dramatic, for his proposals and ideas were often premature on the losing side of fights other Presidents later won — Federal health care, equal rights legislation, low income housing.

His other legacies were perhaps less tangible but no less remembered — the morning walk, the "give 'em hell" campaign that nipped Thomas E. Dewey at the wire, the desk plaque that proclaimed "The buck stops here!" and the word to the timid and indecisive: "If you can't stand the heat, you better get out of the kitchen."

Toward the end of his struggle for life, the former President weakened steadily. Early yesterday, his doctors warned that death might come "within hours."

When it came, the doctors announced that the cause was "a complexity of organic failures causing a collapse of the cardiovascular system."

A state funeral will be held Thursday in nearby Independence, Mr. Truman's home

Continued on Page 44, Column 1

National Day of Mourning Proclaimed by President

By JACK ROSENTHAL
Special to The New York Times

WASHINGTON, Dec. 26—President Nixon today declared Thursday a national day of mourning for former President Harry S. Truman and made plans to pay his personal respects tomorrow in Independence, Mo.

In a proclamation issued before leaving the vacation White House in Key Biscayne, Mr. Nixon ordered all Federal of-

Text of Nixon's proclamation will be found on Page 44.

fices to close Thursday and urged that the nation pay homage to the late President in worship services.

As he returned to Washington, Mr. Nixon announced that he and Mrs. Nixon would fly to Independence tomorrow to lay a wreath at the Truman Presidential Library, where Mr. Truman's body will lie in state. Officials said that the Nixons hoped to have the opportunity to offer their condolences in person to Mrs. Truman.

The Nixons plan to return to Washington after the wreath-laying, indicating that they will not attend the funeral in Independence on Thursday.

The reason, it appeared, was the desire of the Truman family to have a private funeral.

It was announced in Austin,

Tex., that former President and Mrs. Lyndon B. Johnson and members of their family would also go to Independence tomorrow to pay their final respects. They planned to return to Texas in the late afternoon.

All stock exchanges will be closed Thursday. Most banks, with the exception of those in Connecticut, will be open. Post offices will be closed, and there will be no regular delivery of mail. [Details on Page 59.]

A memorial service for Mr. Truman here will be held in the Washington Cathedral, for Federal and foreign dignitaries. No date has been set, but the State Department said it would be within two weeks.

As a Senator and as Vice-Presidential candidate in 1952, Mr. Nixon had been bitterly critical of Mr. Truman, but today, the President voiced warm and unstinting praise.

In a statement issued an hour after word of Mr. Truman's death reached the vacation White House in Florida, Mr. Nixon said:

"Harry S. Truman will be remembered as one of the most courageous Presidents in our history, who led the nation and the world through a critical period with exceptional vision

Continued on Page 44, Column 2

Study Finds Incomes More Unequal

By PHILIP SHABECOFF
Special to The New York Times

WASHINGTON, Dec. 26—A changing population and a changing industrial structure are producing a persistent trend toward inequality in the distribution of income among wage and salary earners in the United States, a study published by the Labor Department has found.

The trend is toward a concentration of an increasingly large share of average wage and salary income among people in jobs and professions that already being higher pay, and it is likely to continue for some time, Peter Henle, author of the study, says.

The study, in the department's current Monthly Labor Review, departs from the widely accepted view that there has been little change in the distribution of income in America since World War II.

Most studies of income distribution examine family incomes, which include such nonearned incomes as welfare and Social Security payments. Family incomes also reflect the growing trend toward more than one wage earner per family.

senior specialist on labor for the Library of Congress, examines only the money earnings, wages and salaries of male workers, so as to obtain a view of shifts in the distribution of payments for work performed.

Male Workers Studied

In the period examined, 1958-1972, average earned income was steadily rising throughout the economy as a whole. But in the distribution of that income Mr. Henle found "a slight persistent trend toward inequality." This trend toward inequality was found between various occupations and industries and was also found with several occupations and industries.

Denies 'Scheme Against Poor'

In a telephone interview, he stressed that the inequality in income distribution was not caused by any "nefarious scheme against poor people." Rather, the trend reflects a tendency in the economy to produce more higher-paying jobs without reducing the number of lower-paid workers, he said.

One reason has been a heavy flow of young people into the labor force as a result of the

lowest fifth of male workers declined to 4.60 per cent from 5.10. At the same time, the share of the highest fifth of male wage and salary earners rose to 40.55 per cent from 38.15.

This trend did not necessarily affect the very highest-paid and lowest-paid workers on the earned income scale, Mr. Henle said. For example, he noted that, while there had been a marked increase in the number of professionals earning $40,000 to $50,000 a year, there had been little change in the number of executives earning $200,-000 or more.

For example, using unpublished data from the Bureau of the Census, Mr. Henle found that from 1958 to 1970 the share of aggregate wage and salary income earned by the

Continued on Page 22, Column 4

Tug of War Strains West Side Housing

By DEIRDRE CARMODY

An empty brick-strewn lot on the Upper West Side, first scheduled for middle-income housing and now slated for low-income housing, has become the symbol of controversy between groups in the neighborhood that are dedicated to preserving the ethnic and economic mix in the area but that cannot agree on how to do it.

The site, on Columbus Avenue between 90th and 91st Streets, is also a symbol of the pitfalls of the ambitious West Side Urban Renewal Project, which celebrates its 10th anniversary next month.

It is caught in a tug-of-war between those who believe there is an urgent need for middle-income housing to keep the area from becoming a slum

and those who say that the urgent need is for low-income housing to relocate the hundreds of residents who have been uprooted by the urban-renewal project.

One of the major complaints about the housing change from middle-income to low-income is Trinity School, which is directly across 91st Street from the lot. The private coeducational school, which has been on its present site since 1893, has filed suit against the city in Federal Court for allegedly having reneged on an agreement with the school that provided for a middle-income apartment house on the site across the street.

According to school officials, Trinity has long considered moving the entire institution to

Pawling, N.Y., where it owned land. As the area around the school became shabbier and increasingly less attractive to prospective parents (who today pay from $1,600 for a first-grader to $2,500 for a 12th-grader), the decision to move became more imminent.

By the mid-nineteen sixties the area, in the words of the lawsuit, was "deteriorated, substandard unsanitary" with "delapidated and crumbling structures" and a high incidence of crime.

At this time, however, the city was completing its fourth revision of the West Side Urban Renewal Project, which envisioned the refurbishing of the area from 87th Street to

Continued on Page 16, Column 4

Navy Buys $1.7-Million in Stock Of Ailing Defense Plant on L.I.

By DAVID A. ANDELMAN
Special to The New York Times

HAUPPAUGE, L.I., Dec. 26—The Navy has purchased 17,414 shares of preferred stock in the Gap Instrument Corporation here as a means of helping the company, which has been experiencing heavy cost overruns. This has made the Department of Defense the largest single stockholder in the company.

The arrangement, believed to mark the first time that the Department of Defense has purchased stock in a private corporation, provides that no dividends be paid on the $1.7-million in nonvoting, nonconvertible shares and that the stock be redeemed beginning in 1976 but only out of the company's aft-

er-tax profits.

The company has not shown a profit in the last four years, and in 1968 showed a profit of only $10,700.

Last week, Senator William Proxmire criticized the Navy for acting as "Grumman's banker" because the Navy delivered a $26-million loan at 6⅞ per cent interest to that aerospace company for the F-14, a plane that has also experienced cost overruns.

Gap first ran into trouble nearly three years ago on a contract to manufacture 31 fire-control consoles for Navy destroyers. The company had

Continued on Page 20, Column 4

The New York Times

LATE CITY EDITION
Weather: Rain late today, tonight becoming light snow early tomorrow. Temp. today 40-45; Saturday 40-44. Full U.S. report on Page 59

SECTION ONE

VOL. CXXII.. No. 42,008 © 1973 The New York Times Company   NEW YORK, SUNDAY, JANUARY 28, 1973   75c beyond 50-mile from New York City, except Long Island. Higher in air delivery cities.   50 CENTS

VIETNAM PEACE PACTS SIGNED; AMERICA'S LONGEST WAR HALTS

Nation Ends Draft, Turns to Volunteers

Change Is Ordered Six Months Early— Youths Must Still Register

By DAVID E. ROSENBAUM
Special to The New York Times

WASHINGTON, Jan. 27—Defense Secretary Melvin R. Laird announced today that the military draft had ended.

As a result of the announcement, men born in 1953 and afterward will not be subject to conscription, and men born before 1953 but not yet drafted will have no further liability to the draft.

These men will be the first in two generations to have no prospect of being drafted. Except for a brief hiatus in 1947 and 1948, men have been conscripted regularly since 1940.

President Nixon's authority to conscript troops into the military expires June 30. Since no one has been drafted since December, the President achieved his goal of turning the military into an all-volunteer force six months ahead of the deadline.

The President and Mr. Laird had promised repeatedly that the June 30 deadline would be met. But Mr. Laird had held out the possibility that as many as 5,000 men would be drafted this year from March through June.

Message From Laird

But, in a message to senior defense officials that was made public today, Mr. Laird said:

"With the signing of the peace agreement in Paris today and, after receiving a report from the Secretary of the Army that he foresees no need for further inductions, I wish to inform you that the armed forces henceforth will depend exclusively on volunteer soldiers, sailors, airmen and marines.

"The use of the draft has ended."

Although no one will be drafted, the Selective Service machinery will most likely remain on the books for standby use in an emergency. Men will continue to have to register for the draft when they turn 18, and young men will still be assigned lottery numbers based on their birthdays.

Congress has mandated, however, that the Government call up Reserves and National Guardsmen before it turns to a reinstatement of the draft to meet future emergencies.

A spokesman for the Selective Service System said that men who had refused to report for induction would still be subject to criminal prosecution. But, he said, men with induction postponements that were due to expire before June 30 will not be drafted.

"We will draft nobody," the spokesman said.

Hopes Senate Will Act

Mr. Laird's single qualification about ending the draft applied to doctors and dentists. The Nixon Administration has asked Congress to approve sizable bonuses for doctors and dentists in an effort to attract enough volunteers in those professions.

The House of Representatives passed legislation last year, and Mr. Laird said in his message today:

"I am particularly hopeful that the Senate will promptly follow the lead of the House and enact legislation giving added incentives for service from members of the health professions, so that the requirements for health services personnel can also be put on a volunteer basis."

The House is almost certainly willing to pass the bill again this year, but Representative F. Edward Hébert, chairman of the House Armed Services Committee, has said that his committee will not act until the Senate passes the legislation.

Mr. Laird also urged Congress to approve bonuses to attract men to the National Guard and

Continued on Page 28, Column 1

In the morning ceremony at the Hotel Majestic in Paris were, from the left, the Vietcong, North Vietnamese, South Vietnamese and U.S. delegations

Associated Press, United Press International and C.B.S. News
Signing, from left, William P. Rogers for U.S., Nguyen Duy Trinh for Hanoi, Mrs. Nguyen Thi Binh for the Vietcong, Tran Van Lam for Saigon

Hanoi Lists of P.O.W.'s Are Made Public by U.S.

By BERNARD GWERTZMAN

WASHINGTON, Jan. 27—The State Department tonight released the list of American civilians believed captured by North Vietnam as having been captured in South Vietnam during the Vietnam war. The list left about half the 51 American civilians believed missing or captured unaccounted for.

The list that the North Vietnamese turned over to American officials in Paris today named 27 American civilians as prisoners of the Vietcong, and listed seven other Americans as having died in captivity.

At the same time, the Defense Department began releasing, in batches, the names of the military prisoners in Communist hands who were on the list turned over in Paris along with the civilians.

2 Diplomats Listed

The United States, in Paris, provided a list of 26,000 Communist prisoners held by South Vietnam in exchange. The lists were turned over following the formal signing of the Vietnam cease-fire agreement.

Frank A. Sieverts, the State Department official charged with prisoner affairs, said that Hanoi apparently did not in-

Continued on Page 24, Column 2

The Toll: 12 Years of War

Military

United States—45,933 killed, 303,616 wounded, 587 captured, 1,335 missing (up to Jan. 13, 1973).
South Vietnam—183,528 killed and 499,026 wounded.
North Vietnam and Vietcong—924,048 (an estimate by Saigon; figures on wounded not available.)

Civilian

415,000 South Vietnamese killed and 935,000 wounded in combat (1965 through 1972).
31,463 South Vietnamese killed and 49,000 abducted as result of Vietcong actions against civilians.
20,587 killed by Saigon actions against civilian Vietcong.
North Vietnamese—Casualties not known.

CEREMONIES COOL

Two Sessions in Paris Formally Conclude the Agreement

By FLORA LEWIS
Special to The New York Times

PARIS, Jan. 27—The Vietnam cease-fire agreement was signed here today in eerie silence, without a word or a gesture to express the world's relief that the years of war were officially ending.

The accord was effective at 7 P.M. Eastern standard time.

Secretary of State William P. Rogers wrote his name 62 times on the documents providing—after 12 years—a settlement of the longest, most divisive foreign war in America's history.

The official title of the text was "Agreement on Ending the War and Restoring Peace in Vietnam." But the cold, almost gloomy atmosphere at two separate signing ceremonies reflected the uncertainties of whether peace is now assured.

The conflict, which has raged in one way or another for over a quarter of a century, had been inconclusive, without clear victory or defeat for either side.

Involvement Gradually Grew

After a gradually increasing involvement that began even before France left Indochina in 1954, the United States entered into a full-scale combat role in 1965. The United States considers Jan. 1, 1961, as the war's starting date and casualties are counted from then.

By 1968, when the build-up was stopped and then reversed, there were 529,000 Americans fighting in Vietnam. United States dead passed 45,000 by the end of the war.

The peace agreements were as ambiguous as the conflict, which many of America's friends first saw as generous aid to a weak and threatened ally, but which many came to consider an exercise of brute power against a tiny nation.

Built on Compromises

The peace agreements signed today were built of compromises that permit the two Vietnamese sides to give them contradictory meanings and, they clearly hope, to continue their unfinished struggle in the political arena without resuming the slaughter.

The signing took place in two ceremonies. In the morning, the participants were the United States, North Vietnam, South Vietnam and the Vietcong. Because the Saigon Government does not wish to imply recognition of the Vietcong's Provisional Revolutionary Government, all references to that government were confined to a second set of documents. That set was signed in the afternoon.

Continued on Page 24, Column 7

BATTLES CONTINUE AFTER CEASE-FIRE

U.S. Copter Sent to Pick Up Vietcong Officers Said to Have Been Shot Down

By FOX BUTTERFIELD
Special to The New York Times

SAIGON, South Vietnam, Sunday, Jan. 28—A cease-fire officially went into effect throughout Vietnam at 8 A.M. today, but widespread fighting continued and there were reports that an unarmed American helicopter sent to pick up a Vietcong delegation and bring it to Saigon had been shot down over Tay Ninh Province.

The helicopter, which was painted white and which is normally used for medical evacuation flights, was to bring the Vietcong's delegation to the four-power Joint Military Commission that will oversee the cease-fire. There was no immediate word on the fate of the crew.

[North Vietnam issued a statement Sunday informing its people of the cease-fire, saying, "Today, the 28th of January, war completely ends in both zones of our country," Reuters reported from Hong Kong.]

334 Incidents Reported

The South Vietnamese command reported this morning that in the 24 hours ending at dawn, North Vietnamese and Vietcong troops initiated 334 incidents throughout the country. According to Government officers, that is the highest number since they began keeping a record. However, more Communist troops were probably involved during the 1968 Tet offensive, they said.

Only an hour and a half before the cease-fire began, Communist gunners struck Tan Son Nhut airport on the outskirts

Continued on Page 18, Column 1

A Reluctant G.I.'s Life and Death

By JON NORDHEIMER
Special to The New York Times

ST. JOSEPH, Mo.—The house on Penn Street where Charley Stockbauer used to live sits near a historic crossroads of America.

It was from St. Joseph that the pioneers who won the West

a century ago set out across the prairie in rough wagons drawn by mules and oxen and gritty conviction.

They came here by railroad and steamboat in the waning days of winter and huddled in muddy encampments on the gray bluffs above the Missouri River, waiting with mounting excitement for the floodwaters to recede from the Kansas plain.

As with most American school children, the seeds of patriotism were planted deep in Charley Stockbauer, and he grew to manhood in St. Joseph surrounded by the ghosts of 19th-century heroes and the legends of the days when men strode boldly toward an uncertain horizon, enduring hardship and fear on the impulse of duty or national destiny.

Values Questioned

These values are still enshrined, but they have been questioned as never before by Charley Stockbauer's generation during the turbulent years when the vagaries of the war in Vietnam challenged traditional American attitudes about sacred abstractions such as patriotism.

Charley Stockbauer was a confused and reluctant warrior in a conflict that almost nobody fully understands, and that confusion and reluctance are mirrored here in the town that was his home before he died in Vietnam. Patriotism has not died in St. Joseph, but, here, as else-

where across the country in these days when the war has at last come to an end, there is a reticence about it all, a nervous hesitance about parading the flag.

The myths and the legends persist. Buffalo Bill and Wild Bill Hickok were raw-boned riders from the Overland Pony Express, and the mail they carried westward started out from a brick building that still stands on Penn Street. Indian fighters purchased, with leather pouches

Continued on Page 24, Column 2

Today's Sections

Nation Celebrates Peace In Prayer and Muted Joy

By MICHAEL KNIGHT

President Nixon, like millions of other Americans, watched the signing of the Vietnam cease-fire agreement on television yesterday and then, like many others, took part in a modest and somber celebration of the end of a tragic war.

Throughout the country, in cities and in hamlets, church bells tolled, fire companies sounded their horns, and small, quiet gatherings were held in homes and in public places.

Some Voice Caution

Some of those who celebrated the end of the American war did so cautiously. The executive secretary of the Washington, D. C., Council of Churches said, "The reason many of us are not throwing our hats in the air is that we are just so stunned and ashamed because the war went on so long, so needlessly."

In Elmira, N. Y., Mrs. Lucielle Cesari did not turn on the lights of a Christmas tree in her yard, lights she had lit every night for five years in a "vigil" remembering the war.

In Longmeadow, Mass., a bell forged by Paul Revere, the silversmith and patriot, was sounded in its steeple at the First Church of Christ. The bell was first sounded to signal the end of the War of 1812.

In Key Biscayne, the President attended a special service at the Key Biscayne Presbyterian Church about a mile from his home.

The minister, the Rev. John A. Huffman, Jr., borrowed from a song by two antiwar activists,

Continued on Page 20, Column 3

hour period thereafter as a day of prayer.

The President, relaxing in his home at Key Biscayne, Fla. had proclaimed 7 P.M. yesterday as "a national moment of prayer and thanksgiving" and the 24-

Continued on Page 26, Column 1

Other News About Accords

CAMBODIA — The exiled Cambodian head of state said in Peking that his guerrilla forces would fight on despite the cease-fire in Vietnam. Cambodia announced a suspension of offensive activities tomorrow. [Page 26.]

TRUCE OBSERVERS — Teams of officers from Poland and Canada left for Vietnam to join with others expected from Hungary and Indonesia. [Page 24.]

INTERNATIONAL CONFERENCE—The United States proposed Feb. 26 as the date for 12-nation meeting on guaranteeing peace. [Page 16.]

LAOS — The head of the pro-Communist negotiating team returned from Hanoi and gave no indication that a cease-fire could be arranged quickly in Laos. [Page 21.]

United Press International
President and Mrs. Nixon and their daughter, Mrs. David Eisenhower, attending a memorial service in Key Biscayne Presbyterian Church, near the Florida White House.

"All the News That's Fit to Print"

The New York Times

LATE CITY EDITION

Weather: Partly sunny today; fair tonight. Chance of rain tomorrow. Temp. range: today 50-64; Monday 45-68. Full U.S. report on Page 86.

VOL. CXXII... No. 42,101   © 1973 The New York Times Company   NEW YORK, TUESDAY, MAY 1, 1973   15 CENTS

NIXON ACCEPTS ONUS FOR WATERGATE, BUT SAYS HE DIDN'T KNOW ABOUT PLOT; HALDEMAN, EHRLICHMAN, DEAN RESIGN; RICHARDSON PUT IN KLEINDIENST POST

Biaggi Testimony to Jury Ordered Released in Full

U.S. Judge Criticizes Candidate's Petition —Delays Disclosure Pending Appeal —Troy Out as Campaign Chief

By JOHN CORRY

A Federal judge yesterday ordered the release of Mario Biaggi's testimony before a grand jury but held up the order when the mayoral candidate's lawyer said he would appeal to block disclosure.

In issuing the order, Judge Edmund L. Palmieri denied a motion by the Bronx Congressman for a panel of three judges to look over his testimony and state whether he had taken the Fifth Amendment "solely" on questions about his personal finances.

In the past, Mr. Biaggi had told leaders of the Conserva-

Excerpts from court testimony appear on Page 35.

tive party that he had answered all the questions put to him by the grand jury.

"Upon reflection," said Judge Palmieri in explaining why he ordered the minutes disclosed, "this court can only conclude that this blatantly unsanctioned petition [by Mr. Biaggi] was made with an expectation of its denial by the court, and for the purpose of publicly exploiting the court's denial of the motion."

Judge Palmieri said that he agreed with United States Attorney Whitney North Seymour Jr., who had asked for full disclosure of the testimony, that Mr. Biaggi's motion constituted an abuse of the court.

"What we have here is tantamount to a manipulation of legal procedures so that the truth can either be successfully concealed or at the very least made to appear different from the underlying facts," the judge said.

Appeal Set for Today

Mr. Biaggi's lawyer, Arthur H. Christy, said he would appeal the decision today to the United States Circuit Court of Appeals. Court sources reported that an appeal would probably be heard later this week or early next week.

Asked outside the court if Mr. Biaggi had told him to appeal, Mr. Christy said, "I follow the instructions of my client."

The political impact to the decision came quickly. Mr. Biaggi dismissed City Councilman Matthew J. Troy Jr. as his mayoral campaign manager. Mr. Troy said he had been preparing to quit anyway.

Simultaneously, leaders of the Conservative party, which has endorsed Mr. Biaggi for Mayor, were thrown into an argument.

Some of the leaders said they *Continued on Page 34, Column 5*

ROGERS DEFENDS CAMBODIA RAIDS

Facing Fulbright Committee, He Says the Constitution Justifies the Bombing

By BERNARD GWERTZMAN
Special to The New York Times

WASHINGTON, April 30 — Secretary of State William P. Rogers said today that the continued American bombing in Cambodia was legally justified by the Constitution and was "a meaningful interim action" to force the Communist-backed insurgents there to agree to a cease-fire.

Mr. Rogers, testifying before the Senate Foreign Relations

Text of Rogers memorandum will be found on Page 10.

Committee, presented the Administration's long-awaited legal justification for the Cambodian bombing, an issue that has aroused considerable criticism from members of the committee, including its chairman, Senator J. W. Fulbright.

They have argued that President Nixon has no legal basis for the bombing, now that all American troops have been withdrawn from South Vietnam.

Though the committee members generally accorded Mr. Rogers friendly treatment, his arguments, both in his comments to the committee and in a 13-page legal memorandum, failed to sway the most vocal critics such as Senators Ful- *Continued on Page 11, Column 1*

Egyptian Air Bases Reported Equipped For Libyan Planes

Special to The New York Times

BEIRUT, Lebanon, April 30 — Diplomatic sources report that ground equipment has been installed at some Egyptian air bases for French-built fighter-bombers from Libya and British-built planes from other Arab countries, and that it has been tested by the aircraft during brief visits.

Israel has been charging that French-built Mirage jets from Libya and British-built Hunter interceptors from Iraq have been transferred to Egyptian bases, but there has been no comment in Cairo. A French Government spokesman said last week that French inquiries about the charges had brought denials from Libya and Egypt.

According to informed diplomats here, however, several embassies are known to have reported to their governments that ground equipment for Mirages was installed several weeks ago. These embassies are said to believe that *Continued on Page 6, Column 1*

Kissinger Is Going to Moscow For Talks on Brezhnev's Visit

Special to The New York Times

WASHINGTON, April 30 — Henry A. Kissinger will fly to Moscow this week for talks with Leonid I. Brezhnev, the Soviet Communist party leader, on plans for Mr. Brezhnev's expected visit to the United States late in June.

While in Moscow with his top staff aides, Mr. Kissinger will also discuss Vietnam, arms control negotiations, trade questions and other matters with Mr. Brezhnev and other top officials, a senior Administration said.

The White House, in making the announcement, limited itself to saying that Mr. Kissinger would leave Thursday for four to five days in Moscow "for an exchange of views on a wide *Continued on Page 4, Column 4*

range of bilateral problems and matters of mutual interest."

But a senior Administration official said that the primary purpose of the President's adviser for national security would be to discuss the details and likely agenda for Mr. Brezhnev's visit to the United States, which will return Mr. Nixon's visit to the Soviet Union last spring.

No date for Mr. Brezhnev's trip has been announced, but an Administration official said that both sides were planning it for the middle of June.

It will be Mr. Brezhnev's first visit to the United States and the first by a top Soviet

Elliot L. Richardson, named Attorney General, yesterday

President Nixon in White House press room after address

United Press International

CONTROLS VOTED FOR ANOTHER YEAR

President Reluctantly Signs Compromise Bill Extending Wage and Price Curbs

By EDWARD COWAN

WASHINGTON, April 30— With the reluctant support of the Administration, both houses of Congress approved today, and President Nixon signed, a compromise bill extending for another year the President's authority to regulate wages and prices.

Mr. Nixon signed the bill tonight, just after making a nationwide television and radio speech. The existing law, called the Economic Stabilization Act, was scheduled to expire at midnight.

The vote in the House was 267 to 115, a larger margin than appeared likely before the Easter recess. The voice vote in the Senate was unrecorded.

Voting for the bill were 153 Democrats and 114 Republicans; opposed were 58 Democrats and 57 Republicans.

Meanwhile, the Department of Agriculture reported that prices received by farmers fell by 1.5 per cent in April, the first decline in a year. [Page 55.]

Mr. Nixon had sought a simple one-year extension of the act. But with the public frustration *Continued on Page 17, Column 1*

Ellsberg Judge Demands Affidavits on Bugging Tie

By MARTIN ARNOLD
Special to The New York Times

LOS ANGELES, April 30 — The judge in the Pentagon papers trial today ordered four figures connected to the Watergate affair to produce affidavits concerning any link between that break-in and the trial here.

Federal District Judge William Matthew Byrne Jr. said that he was not foreclosing the possibility of summoning the four men here to testify, although he denied, for now, a defense request for an immediate hearing.

The affidavit order was directed to John W. Dean 3d, former special counsel to President Nixon; L. Patrick Gray 3d, former acting director of the F.B.I., and G. Gordon Liddy and E. Howard Hunt Jr., conspirators in the Watergate bugging.

Judge Byrne indicated that he also would probably require affidavits and perhaps testimony from former Attorney General John N. Mitchell, Richard G. Kleindienst, the present Attorney General; John

D. Ehrlichman, until today the President's chief for domestic affairs; H. R. Haldeman, Mr. Nixon's chief of staff who also resigned today; Charles W. Colson, former Presidential special counsel, and Robert C. Mardian, former Assistant Attorney General.

Today's court session began with the judge announcing from the bench that about a month ago he met with Mr. Ehrlichman and President Nixon, "for approximately one minute or less," at Mr. Ehrlichman's suggestion.

At that time, he said, he was offered a new Government position, but he said he told Mr. Ehrlichman that he could not consider it "until this case is concluded." He did not say what the position was, but his name has been mentioned as a possible director of the Federal Bureau of Investigation.

Then, in response to demands from two defense lawyers, *Continued on Page 33, Column 6*

Nixon Asks Tax Law Shift To Ease Filing on Income

By EILEEN SHANAHAN
Special to The New York Times

WASHINGTON, April 30 — The Nixon Administration proposed today changes in the tax laws and tax forms that would make it easier for millions of individuals to figure out their Federal income taxes.

The Administration's proposals contained little, however,

Summary of proposed changes is printed on Page 34.

that appeared likely to satisfy the demands of those who have been calling for reform of the tax laws.

All the basic provisions of the laws that reduce taxes for those who invest in business or property — the provisions relat-

ing to capital gains, depreciation, the depletion allowance and so on — would remain untouched under the Administration's plan.

The Administration did, however, recommend enactment of two new provisions that would limit the ability of wealthy individuals to combine different preferential sections of the tax laws in ways that permit them to escape all, or most, Federal income tax.

The proposals were submitted to the House Ways and Means Committee by the Secretary of the Treasury, George P. Shultz, in the form of a 175-page booklet called "Proposals for Tax Change."

The committee chairman, Wilbur D. Mills, Democrat of Arkansas, said he thought the proposals did not go far enough and criticized particularly the lack of any proposed changes in the taxation of capital gains and in the estate and gift taxes.

The plan for simplifying *Continued on Page 35, Column 7*

2 AIDES PRAISED

Counsel Forced Out —Leonard Garment Takes Over Job

By R. W. APPLE Jr.
Special to The New York Times

WASHINGTON, April 30— Four top Nixon Administration officials resigned today as a consequence of the Watergate case, one of the most widespread scandals in American Presidential history.

H. R. Haldeman, the austere and secretive White House

Texts of Nixon announcement and resignations, Page 30.

chief of staff, and John D. Ehrlichman, the President's chief adviser on domestic affairs, maintained their innocence in letters submitting their resignations. Both said their ability to carry out their daily duties had been undermined.

The President chose Elliot L. Richardson, the Secretary of Defense, to succeed Richard G. Kleindienst as Attorney General and placed Mr. Richardson in charge of the Watergate investigation.

Mr. Kleindienst said he had quit because close friends had become Watergate suspects and "impartial enforcement of the law" ruled out such 'intimate relationships."

Dean's Departure Asked

Mr. Nixon also announced that he had "requested and accepted" the resignation of John W. Dean 3d, the White House counsel, who had threatened to implicate superiors. Leonard Garment, a special Presidential consultant, was named to replace Mr. Dean temporarily.

No replacements for the two key aides were named, and the President gave no hint as to whom he might choose.

In a related development, the United States Information Agency announced tonight that Gordon Strachan had resigned as general counsel "after learning that persons with whom he had worked closely in the White House had submitted their resignations." The statement said Mr. Strachan "stressed that he had no complicity in the Democratic National Committee break-in or in any alleged attempt to cover it up."

Mr. Haldeman's and Mr. Ehrlichman's departures strip the White House of its central operating mechanism at a time when far-reaching decisions must be made on inflation, Indochina policy and American relations with Europe.

The actions were announced *Continued on Page 30, Column 1*

NEW DATA CITED

President Tells How He Changed Mind About Charges

By JOHN HERBERS
Special to The New York Times

WASHINGTON, April 30 — President Nixon told the nation tonight that he accepted the responsibility for what happened in the Watergate case even though he had had no knowledge of political espionage or attempts to cover it up. The President went on to na-

The text of Nixon's speech is printed on Page 31.

tionwide television and radio to discuss the case after he received the resignations of three top staff members who had been implicated—H. R. Haldeman, John D. Ehrlichman and John W. Dean 3d. He also accepted the resignation of Attorney General Richard G. Kleindienst.

Wrongdoing Alleged

While the President accepted the responsibility and pledged every effort to achieve justice in the case, he alleged wrongdoing or cover-up attempts on the part of those he had delegated to run his 1972 Presidential campaign and those he appointed to investigate the matter during the campaign.

And he implied that his own election officials, in the Watergate espionage, were attempting to stop wrongdoing by the Democrats.

Mr. Nixon also said that hereafter the investigation of the Watergate matters would be delegated to his new Attorney General, Elliot L. Richardson, while he, the President, turned his attention to grave foreign and domestic matters. He added that he would leave it up to Mr. Richardson whether to appoint a special prosecutor.

Weeks of Tension

The speech, which came after weeks of growing tension at the White House as developments in the Watergate scandal implicated Administration figures, was an emotional appeal to save the integrity of his Presidency for the 1,361 days, by Mr. Nixon's count, that remain in his term. This was the 100th day of his second term.

"Tonight I ask for your prayers to help me in everything that I do," Mr. Nixon said at the end. "God bless America. And God bless each and every one of you."

He accepted responsibility for Watergate with these words: "In any organization the man *Continued on Page 31, Column 5*

SHAKE-UP LAUDED BY CONGRESSMEN

But Many Warn That Step Is Not Enough to Restore Faith in White House

By JAMES M. NAUGHTON
Special to The New York Times

WASHINGTON, April 30 — Members of Congress joined in widespread, bipartisan praise today for President Nixon's shake-up of his Administration's high command.

But many Senators and Representatives, coupled their commendations with warnings that a housecleaning of the White House staff would not be sufficient to restore faith in the Nixon Administration or the Government as a whole.

Furthermore, Representative John E. Moss of California urged House Democratic leaders to open a formal inquiry into the possible impeachment of President Nixon.

The suggestion by the long-time Democratic Congressman—which key leaders of both parties in the House described as "premature"—was the most severe reaction on Capitol Hill to the latest developments in the Watergate conspiracy case.

At Huron, Ohio, the nation's Democratic Governors joined in the call for appointment of a special prosecutor in the Watergate case.

Mark O. Hatfield, Republican *Continued on Page 33, Column 6*

End of Era in Nixon Presidency

By ROBERT B. SEMPLE Jr.
Special to The New York Times

WASHINGTON, April 30 — The resignations of H. R. Haldeman and John D. Ehrlichman from President Nixon's senior staff clearly mark the end of one era of the Nixon Presidency and the beginning of another. Things simply will not be the same. The question is how much different they will be.

The few men who remain in the President's suddenly shrunken entourage do not believe that the scandals of the moment will have much impact on Mr. Nixon's own personality. His habits are well entrenched, and 'any future White House operation will reflect the style of its master.

But there are some here

News Analysis

now, in the White House and on Capitol Hill, who hope that Mr. Nixon will seize what they sense to be a rare opening to redesign his relationships with Congress, the bureaucracy, and even the press.

They hope to increase his access to others and theirs to him, to replace the closed corporation that the White House had become with the "open Presidency" to which he once aspired, and to return to his own first principles by decentralizing some of the power that has steadily flowed from the Government agencies to a few decision-makers in the White House.

Mr. Haldeman and Mr. Ehrlichman helped design that system, ran the system and, in time, came to symbolize the style of its operation. Their Teutonic names

and mutual zeal for efficient execution gave rise to many jokes. Their enemies called them Hans and Fritz; their friends simply teased them.

In Mr. Ehrlichman's office on the second floor of the White House is a copy of Daniel P. Moynihan's "Understanding Poverty," which carries this inscription: "For John Ehrlichman. Achtung! D.P.M."

But their power was no joke. They were men with long ties and easy access to the President, men of loyalty, men who transmitted Mr. Nixon's orders to the bureaucracy and to whom, with few exceptions, Mr. Nixon's Cabinet members were forced to report before winning humble access to the Oval Office.

In all areas other than for- *Continued on Page 33, Column 4*

NEWS INDEX

The New York Times

LATE CITY EDITION
Weather: Partly cloudy today; cool tonight. Partly sunny tomorrow.
Temp. range: Today 57-69; Friday 55-75. Full U.S. report on Page 66.

VOL. CXXII...No. 42,112   © 1973 The New York Times Company   NEW YORK, SATURDAY, MAY 12, 1973   15 CENTS

PENTAGON PAPERS CHARGES ARE DISMISSED; JUDGE BYRNE FREES ELLSBERG AND RUSSO, ASSAILS 'IMPROPER GOVERNMENT CONDUCT'

White House Says Attacks Will Continue in Cambodia

By BERNARD GWERTZMAN
Special to The New York Times

WASHINGTON, May 11 — The White House said today that the United States would continue with "the right policy" of bombing in Cambodia in support of President Lon Nol's government, despite the vote yesterday in the House of Representatives blocking the transfer of military funds for such raids.

Ronald L. Ziegler, the White House press secretary, made the statement and also announced — jointly with North Vietnam — that Henry A. Kissinger and Le Duc Tho, Hanoi's chief negotiator, would resume talks on Thursday in Paris to seek ways of achieving "strict implementation" of the three-and-a-half-month-old cease-fire agreement.

In its insistence on the bombing program, the Nixon Administration is apparently heading for a possible constitutional conflict with Congress, if the Senate, as expected, supports the House action next week.

The Senate majority leader, Mike Mansfield, told reporters today: "If the will of the Congress and the intention of the Congress — the representatives

of the people—are not adhered to, then we will face a true constitutional crisis. One thing this country cannot afford at this time is a constitutional crisis."

To those who urged that any action be postponed until after Mr. Kissinger completed his talks with Mr. Tho, Mr. Mansfield said: "My sympathies are with Mr. Kissinger. But I don't think we should delay exercising our responsibilities."

Yesterday the House voted, 219 to 188, to block the transfer of funds for continued bombing in Cambodia. This was the first time that the House had supported an end-the-war amendment.

"We, of course, observed the vote in the Congress yesterday," Mr. Ziegler said. "We will continue with the policy which we feel is the right policy, and that is to provide support to the Government of Cambodia at their request. If at some time in the future the funds are not available, then the Congress will have to assume the responsibility in that matter."

Mr. Ziegler repeated that
Continued on Page 4, Column 3

Sudan Puts Off Trying 8 Who Killed U.S. Envoys

By HENRY TANNER
Special to The New York Times

CAIRO, May 11 — President Gaafar al-Nimeiry of the Sudan has decided to postpone indefinitely the trial of the eight Palestinian guerrillas who killed three diplomats, two Americans and a Belgian, while holding the Saudi Embassy in Khartoum last March 2, informed Sudanese sources said here today.

After the slayings General Nimeiry and other leading officials publicly pledged an early trial. They said that the guerrillas would be charged with murder, a capital offense in the Sudan.

Now the same officials say that the Israeli force that thrust into the heart of Beirut, the Lebanese capital, last month and killed three leading mem-

bers of the Palestinian resistance made it impossible for General Nimeiry—or any other Arab statesman—to convict Palestinian guerrillas of a crime that in Arab eyes was as much a patriotic deed as the raid into Beirut was in Israeli eyes.

The recent fighting between Lebanese troops and Palestinians is another reason why no public trial of the eight guerrillas should be held, Sudanese officials say. The trial, they maintain, would be interpreted throughout the Arab world as another instance of "fratricide."

The outlook now is for a lengthy confinement of the eight without trial, informed sources say.

General Nimeiry's decision is likely to renew friction between the Sudan and the United States, which resumed diplomatic relations less than a year ago.

The State Department is known to have served notice that no new ambassador will be sent to Khartoum unless the slayers of Ambassador Cleo A.
Continued on Page 11, Column 3

2-GERMANY PACT IS VOTED IN BONN

Parliament Also Approves Joining United Nations

By DAVID BINDER
Special to The New York Times

BONN, May 11—The treaty that will establish formal relations between the two Germanys after more than two decades of hostile nonrecognition was ratified by the lower house of the West German Parliament today by a vote of 268 to 217.

By a second vote, 365 to 121, the lower house also gave its approval to the prospective entry of West Germany into the United Nations along with East Germany.

The treaty, regarded as the crowning achievement of Chancellor Willy Brandt's policy of normalizing relations with Eastern Europe, was concluded last November. It is expected to go into effect later this month after the ratification process is completed here and in East Germany.

The upper house of the West German Parliament is expected to approve the treaty next week and send it to President Gustav Heinemann for signature. Ratification by the East German Parliament is also expected next week, with ceremonial approval by the State Council to follow.

The treaty will greatly enlarge the opportunities for the Germans of the two states to
Continued on Page 10, Column 1

GRAY CALL TO NIXON

Said to Inform Inquiry It Came 3 Weeks After Watergate

By ANTHONY RIPLEY
Special to The New York Times

WASHINGTON, May 11 — L. Patrick Gray 3d has told Senate investigators that he talked by telephone with President Nixon about three weeks after the Watergate burglary last June 17 to express concern over White House obstacles in his path and confusion that was hampering his investigation, committee sources said today.

Mr. Gray, at the time acting director of the Federal Bureau of Investigation, was concerned over the action of White House aides, these sources said.

The sources would not comment on how Mr. Gray said the President reacted to the telephone complaint. The sources did not specify the nature of the obstacles that Mr. Gray said he had faced.

Talks To Prosecution

Mr. Gray, who resigned as acting director in the wake of the Watergate scandals, was questioned by the Senate investigators last night. He spent most of today talking to the prosecution team from the Justice Department but apparently did not appear before the grand jury, which gathered at 4:30 P.M. in the Federal courthouse.

There were a flurry of news reports tonight that Mr. Gray had told the President of an attempt to impede the Watergate investigation. Mr. Gray received "no reaction" from the President, according to The Baltimore Sun.

Committee sources here said such reports were "out of focus" and did not fully reflect Mr. Gray's position.

Sought to End Confusion

"There was confusion," one source said. "Gray felt things should be straightened out so that he could carry out this investigation."

In past statements to friends and testimony before Congress, Mr. Gray has repeatedly described his troubles with the White House staff.

Mr. Gray said that the President's counsel, John W. Dean 3d, had sat in while F.B.I. agents were interviewing persons at the White House and that Mr. Dean had "probably" lied to agents. Mr. Gray also said that he had turned over raw F.B.I. investigation files to Mr. Dean. At the time the President's counsel was conducting a separate investigation of the
Continued on Page 15, Column 1

United Press International

Judge William Matthew Byrne Jr., above, threw out the Pentagon papers case and, left, defendants were freed. They are Anthony J. Russo Jr., left, and Dr. Daniel Ellsberg.

Air of Expectancy, Then Tears, Shouts, Embraces

By JUDITH KINNARD
Special to The New York Times

LOS ANGELES, May 11 — Her tears of joy had dried, but cheers still filled the courtroom when Patricia Ellsberg embraced one of many friends and said:

"I could never believe the scene of waiting for the jury to come in. I just knew it would never happen."

Federal District Court Judge William Matthew Byrne Jr. had just closed the Pentagon

papers trial with a broad decision that harshly admonished the Government for misconduct.

Dr. Ellsberg, looking gaunt as much from loss of weight as from the pressure of the last two years, spoke to a cheering crowd on the steps of the courthouse after the verdict.

Almost crushed by newsmen as he stood with his arm around his wife, he said: "This trial is not over until

that bombing is over in Cambodia." And he added that he intended to sue for damages specific individuals in the Government, perhaps the President himself.

Like every other major decision in the case since it went to trial in January, the final dramatic ruling came amid an air of expectancy that had pervaded the proceedings all week.

By 7 A.M., when the smog had already descended on

Los Angeles, spectators had begun lining up in the corridor outside the dark brown door to the courtroom for the limited passes for access to the trial, which ended almost two years after Dr. Daniel Ellsberg and Anthony J. Russo Jr. were indicted.

Photographers waited for the judge, whose latest pictures, showing shorter and fuller hair, were taken three
Continued on Page 14, Column 2

A New Grand Jury Reported Planning To Summon Biaggi

By NICHOLAS GAGE

Representative Mario Biaggi, who appeared twice before a Federal grand jury in 1971, will be called before another jury for further questioning, authoritative sources said yesterday.

On Thursday night Mr. Biaggi admitted that he had refused to answer questions before the 1971 jury after repeatedly denying it for several months.

The Bronx Representative had been scheduled to be called before a Federal grand jury on April 27, but the appearance was postponed pending resolution of the court battle—that was just then beginning—over release of his 1971 testimony. That testimony is to be released today.

The United States Attorney's office has received new infor-
Continued on Page 16, Column 3

CONNALLY TO TAKE LEAVE FROM FIRM

New Adviser to President Will Also Resign From All Corporate Boards

By JOHN HERBERS
Special to The New York Times

WASHINGTON, May 11—John B. Connally announced today that he would take a leave of absence from his law firm and resign from all corporate boards during the time he will serve as special adviser to President Nixon.

Mr. Connally's announcement, issued by his office in Houston, came after disclosure that the firm in which he is a senior partner is representing the Gulf Resources and Chemical Corporation, now under investigation by a Federal grand jury in connection with campaign contributions sent to the Committee for the Re-election of the President. The disclosure was made today in Newsday and other newspapers.

"I am today taking a leave from my law firm for the period during which I will serve as a special adviser to the President," said the former Secretary of the Treasury and former Governor of Texas.

"I am also resigning from all corporate boards on which I serve," he continued. "Notwithstanding that my service will be on an intermittent and voluntary basis and without any operational role, I will not engage in any law practice nor participate in any dividends or revenues or as a partner of the firm during this advisory pe-
Continued on Page 15, Column 5

Congress Ascending

Watergate Seen as Altering Balance Between Executive and Capitol Hill

By JAMES M. NAUGHTON

WASHINGTON, May 11—The White House is slipping and Congress is rising as the balance of power in Washington is being altered perceptibly by the Watergate conspiracy case. For the first time in six years the House of Representatives
News Analysis
went on record yesterday, by a vote of 219 to 188, in opposition to White House policies in Indochina. For the second time in five weeks, the Senate declared yesterday, 66 to 24, that the White House was obligated to adhere to the directions of Congress on government spending.

"Both houses are beginning to see eye to eye on Congres-

sional responsibility," the Senate Democratic leader, Mike Mansfield, said today in an interview.

A senior associate of President Nixon predicted privately today that the White House and the Nixon Cabinet would abandon their attitude of disregard for those on Capitol Hill and become, in the official's words, "more receptive" to Congressional viewpoints.

The change is only beginning to be visible. Much of it is atmospheric. It remains for Congress, long a slumbering giant, to take steps to "even the balance," as Mr. Mansfield put it, but he and others are becoming
Continued on Page 13, Column 1

NEW TRIAL BARRED

But Decision Does Not Solve Constitutional Issues in Case

By MARTIN ARNOLD
Special to The New York Times

LOS ANGELES, May 11—Citing what he called "improper Government conduct shielded so long from public view," the judge in the Pentagon papers trial dismissed today all charges against Dr. Daniel Ellsberg and Anthony J. Russo Jr.

And he made it clear in his ruling that the two men would not be tried again on charges

The text of Judge Byrne's decision is on Page 14.

of stealing and copying the Pentagon papers.

"The conduct of the Government has placed the case in such a posture that it precludes the fair, dispassionate resolution of these issues by a jury," he said.

David R. Nissen, the chief prosecutor, said, "It appears that the posture is such that no appeal will be possible."

Defendants Not Vindicated

But the decision by United States District Court Judge William Matthew Byrne Jr. did not vindicate the defendants; it chastised the Government. Nor did it resolve the important constitutional issues that the case had raised.

The end of the trial, on its 89th day, was dramatic. The courtroom was jammed; the jury box was filled with news reporters; defense workers in the Ellsberg-Russo cause, mostly young people, sat in chairs lining the courtroom wall.

Dr. Ellsberg and Mr. Russo, surrounded by their lawyers, stared intently as Judge Byrne quickly made his ruling.

The Government's action in this case, he said, "offended a sense of justice," and so "I have decided to declare a mistrial and grant the motion for dismissal." The time was 2:07 P.M.

The courtroom erupted in loud cheering and clapping. The judge, barely hiding a smile, quickly strode out the door behind his bench.

Tension had been building
Continued on Page 14, Column 5

NIXON AGAIN ASKS LEGAL AID TO POOR

Independent Agency Would Replace O.E.O. Unit

By LINDA CHARLTON
Special to The New York Times

WASHINGTON, May 11—President Nixon resubmitted to Congress today, in slightly revised form, his proposals for providing free legal assistance to the poor through the creation of an independent Legal Services Corporation.

A program to make available legal aid in civil matters to those unable to afford it otherwise is now a part of the Office of Economic Opportunity, which is scheduled to go out of existence July 1. Efforts to establish the program as an independent entity date back more than two years through a history of disagreement, compromise and veto. Today's bill is apparently a compromise reached after much internal Administration battling.

The new proposal would create an independent, federally funded Legal Services Corporation with an 11-member board of directors appointed by the President—a focal point of controversy in previous versions—but subject to confirmation by the Senate. Not more than six of the same political party, and a majority would be lawyers.

It also includes very specific
Continued on Page 31, Columns 3

Norton Simon Bought Smuggled Idol

By DAVID L. SHIREY

Norton Simon, the West Coast industrialist and art collector, said yesterday that he had paid $1-million for a bronze sculpture of a Hindu deity that Indian Government officials say was stolen from a South Indian temple and smuggled out of India.

"Hell, yes, it was smuggled," said Mr. Simon in a telephone interview. "I spent between $15-million and $16-million over the last two years on Asian art, and most of it was smuggled. I don't know whether it was stolen."

Indian Government officials, who have for two years been seeking the return of the 44-inch sculpture representing the deity Siva, known in this region as Nataraja, say that it was one of several stolen from a temple in Sivapuram, in southern India and smuggled out of the country. They also say that the original works were replaced in the temple by modern fakes.

The New York Times/Meyer Liebowitz
The bronze statue of the Hindu deity Siva, dancing

86th St. Toonerville Tale: 3 Flee From a Police Van

By LESLEY OELSNER

Three prisoners, two of them handcuffed together, leaped from the back of a police van yesterday and ran off along West 86th Street to freedom.

The van continued on its precinct-to-precinct morning rounds and then, 40 minutes later, at 79th Street and Lexington, two more prisoners jumped out. This time bystanders shouted and policemen jumped from the vehicle, quickly capturing the fugitives—and learning for the first time of the disappearance of the three others.

Capt. Alexander Davis of Manhattan North, said, "How's that for a Toonerville tale?"

Captain Davis, who is in charge of investigating how the escapes occurred, reported late yesterday afternoon that the fugitives—all alleged robbers—were still at large. "Four or five detec-

tives," he said, as well as the police officer who had arrested them the night before, Daniel Traynor of the 28th Precinct, were looking for the men.

The route to freedom, the captain said, appeared to have been facilitated by a defective lock on the van door.

The van began its trip early yesterday at the 28th Precinct station at 229 West 123d Street. It was to go from precinct to precinct picking up men who had been arrested the night before and then take them to the Criminal Courts Building at 100 Centre Street.

Among the men it picked up at the 28th were the three escapees—Edward McBride, 24 years old, of 215 West 101st Street, and Vincent Perry, 19, and Tony Grant,
Continued on Page 21, Column 1

"All the News That's Fit to Print"

The New York Times

LATE CITY EDITION
Weather: Very hot again today; very warm tonight. Hot tomorrow. Temp. range: today 78-96; Wed. 76-95. Temp.-Hum. Index yesterday 83. Full U.S. report on Page 66.

VOL.CXXII..No.42,222   © 1973 The New York Times Company   NEW YORK, THURSDAY, AUGUST 30, 1973   15 CENTS

JUDGE SIRICA ORDERS NIXON TO YIELD TAPES TO HIM FOR A DECISION ON GRAND JURY USE; PRESIDENT DECLARES HE 'WILL NOT COMPLY'

PEKING DISCLOSES 5-DAY CONGRESS OF CHINESE PARTY

Meeting Ousted Lin, Named Central Committee and Adopted a Constitution

By TILLMAN DURDIN
Special to The New York Times

HONG KONG, Aug. 29 — China disclosed today that the 10th Congress of her Communist party was held in Peking last Friday through yesterday.

The announcement was made in a dispatch of Hsinhua, the

Text of the communiqué is printed on Page 14.

official press agency. It said the Congress formally expelled Defense Minister Lin Piao and Chen Po-ta from the party. Mr. Lin was designated Chairman Mao Tse-tung's successor during the last Congress in 1969, and is reported to have been killed in 1971 after attempting to assassinate Chairman Mao. Both he and Mr. Chen, a former Politboro member, were denounced as renegades and traitors.

Political Report by Chou

The Congress also adopted a revised party constitution, selected a new Central Committee and approved a political report delivered by Premier Chou En-lai.

It is assumed that the new Central Committee will hold its first meeting in a day or two and name members of the all-important Politburo and the standing committee of the Politburo. These bodies run China on a day-to-day basis.

The Central Committee members were reported to include the old, middle-aged and young, which the communiqué said showed that the party "has no lack of successors."

Mao Presided

The Congress, at which Chairman Mao presided, was the briefest in the history of the Chinese party.

Attended by 1,249 delegates, the Congress was held in the greatest secrecy and confounded foreign newsmen and diplomats in Peking.

Obviously, hard decisions on sharing of power and position between factions had to be made before the Congress was held and this probably delayed its convening. The result is an apportioning of positions between the civilian moderates, represented by Premier Chou, and important career party members, military leaders and the so-called leftists generally associated with Chiang Ching, Mr. Mao's wife.

The 10th Congress appeared to have been even more of a

Continued on Page 14, Column 1

Sadat and Qaddafi Act on Unification

By HENRY TANNER
Special to The New York Times

CAIRO, Aug. 29 — President Anwar el-Sadat of Egypt and the Libyan leader, Col. Muammar el-Qaddafi, tonight proclaimed the "birth of a new unified Arab state" but made it emphatically clear that actual unification of their two countries was still a long way off.

A declaration issued in the name of the two leaders satisfied every point of the Egyptian Government's wish for a slow, gradual approach that could be broken off at any stage. It fell far short of the immediate full union that Colonel Qaddafi had urgently demanded.

Mr. Sadat and Colonel Qaddafi agreed in August, 1972, to work toward "complete unity." The process, to take a year,

Continued on Page 5, Column 1

180,000 Hit by Blackout In Four Areas of Queens

By FRANK J. PRIAL

About 180,000 Queens residents were left without electrical power last night when a group of Consolidated Edison Company cables burned out at 6:15 P.M. The blackout, the first major power failure of the summer, also darkened passenger terminals and hangars at La Guardia Airport.

The cables, and the entire Con Edison network, had been running at full capacity because of the unrelenting, record-breaking heat. Yesterday New Yorkers plodded through their second day of above 90-degree temperatures and high humidity, and there was no relief in sight.

High for the day was 95 degrees at 2:35 P.M., three degrees below Tuesday's high of 98, the record for the summer so far.

The burned-out cables, 27,-000-volt feeder lines supplying all of Jackson Heights and parts of Corona, Woodside and

Official Temperatures

	Wed.	Tues.				2 P.M.	94	95
3 A.M.	79					3 P.M.	94	92
4 A.M.	80	79				4 P.M.	94	98
5 A.M.	78	78				5 P.M.	93	98
6 A.M.	77	79				6 P.M.	92	96
7 A.M.	77	77				7 P.M.	89	93
8 A.M.	78	78				8 P.M.	86	92
9 A.M.	78	78				9 P.M.	86	87
10 A.M.	81	81				10 P.M.	86	87
11 A.M.	87	87				11 P.M.	85	86
Noon	90	89				Midnight	84	87
1 P.M.	92	92				1 A.M.	82	87

Elmhurst, as well as the airport, had been strained by a day of fires and breakdowns.

At about 11:30 P.M., at least 5,000 Con Edison customers were left without power on Staten Island, when seven feeder cables were knocked out in the Great Kills and Richmondtown sections. Full power was restored to 795 customers in Richmondtown after 65 minutes. Scattered areas of Great Kills were still blacked out at 2:30 A.M.

The power failure in Queens came just as Con Edison was about to end its second day of a 5 per cent system-wide power reduction. The cutback, which also affected the rest of the state's power companies, which are members of the New York State Power Pool, lasted from 10 A.M. to 6:25 P.M.

Throughout the day, the situation had been more serious in Jackson Heights than anywhere else in the Con Edison area, and the company had asked its Jackson Heights customers to be particularly careful about using power when they came home from work last night.

Four of eight feeder cables serving the area had burned out at about 3 A.M. yesterday. One

Continued on Page 27, Column 1

The Soviet Dissidents

Moscow Showing It Will Maintain Ideological War and Internal Curbs

By THEODORE SHABAD
Special to The New York Times

MOSCOW, Aug. 29 — The sudden upsurge in news of dissidence from Moscow has brought into sharp focus the Soviet leaders' determination to pursue their policy of improved relations with the West without giving an inch to domestic pressures for liberal reforms.

There appear to be some elements of coincidence in the timing of the current trial of two dissidents and the rash of moves and countermoves in the Soviet system—Andrei D. Sakharov, the physicist, and Aleksandr I. Solzhenitsyn, the novelist.

But the pattern of events of the last two weeks also fits in neatly with the intensification of ideological warfare that has become increasingly evident in

the Soviet Union since the meeting between President Nixon and Leonid I. Brezhnev, the Soviet Communist chief.

It seems a far cry from the smiles - and - sweetness atmosphere that was being conveyed by the Soviet mass media in those June days to the rapid-fire sequence of recent denunciations of supposedly subversive threats, foreign and domestic.

First, after a moratorium of several months coinciding with the summit period, the United States again became fair game in the Soviet media. Radio listeners were warned against writing to the Voice of America, which was presented as an intelligence-gathering organization, and "Sesame Street" was described as the kind of program that should be kept off Soviet living room screens if

Continued on Page 9, Column 1

APPEAL UNCERTAIN

White House Hints at Possible Defiance of Court Ruling

By JOHN HERBERS
Special to The New York Times

SAN CLEMENTE, Calif., Aug. 29 — The White House said today that President Nixon would not comply with Judge John J. Sirica's order to turn over his Watergate tape recordings to the court.

In a terse statement issued by its press office, the White House said the President was considering the possibility of appeal or "how otherwise to sustain the President's position."

This left open the clear possibility that the President might simply refuse to obey the order without first resorting to appeal.

Compromise Ruled Out

White House spokesmen would not elaborate on the statement, but it was plain that it was another assertion by President Nixon that he would not compromise on the issue.

In his news conference last Wednesday, Mr. Nixon said his right to withhold the tapes as a point of executive privilege was absolute.

"Let me explain the principle of confidentiality exists or it does not exist," he said. "Once it is compromised or it is known that a conversation that is held with the President can be subject to a subpoena by a Senate committee, by a grand jury, by a prosecutor, and be listened to by anyone, the principle of confidentiality is thereby irreparably damaged."

Confidentiality Needed

To conduct the affairs of the Presidency, in both foreign and domestic matters, Mr. Nixon said, "he must be able to do so with the principle of confidentiality intact."

The President seems more determined now to resist compromise on the tapes than he was a few weeks ago. Last month, Gerald L. Warren, the deputy White House press secretary, said Mr. Nixon would

Continued on Page 21, Column 6

Union Aides Indicted

Peter Ottley, president of the 20,000-member Local 144 of the Hotel, Hospital, Nursing Home and Allied Service Employees Union, and Peter Byrne, its secretary-treasurer, were indicted here yesterday by a Federal grand jury on charges of embezzling union funds. Page 44.

Judge John J. Sirica, who ruled on the Presidential tapes, in his chambers
The New York Times/George Tames

NIXON'S LAWYERS ASSAIL COMMITTEE

In Paper Filed in Court, His Counsel Rejects Demand of Senators for Tapes

Special to The New York Times

WASHINGTON, Aug. 29 — President Nixon's lawyers charged today that the Senate Watergate committee had conducted a "criminal investigation and trial" that exceeded the authority granted to Congress by the Constitution.

In papers filed in Federal District Court, the White House attorneys rejected the committee's demand for tape recordings of Nixon conversations on the ground that the Senators were illegally attempting to determine "whether or not criminal acts have been committed and the guilt or innocence of individuals."

The President's lawyers also contended that the court had no jurisdiction over their client, either as an individual or as President, and that Mr. Nixon "owes no duty," in either capacity, to the Senate committee to provide it with recordings of his confidential meetings or other material documents.

In a legal countermove, the Senate committee filed with Chief Judge John J. Sirica a motion for summary judgment in the same case, a request that the judge enforce two subpoenas already served on the President with a minimum of further court proceedings.

The motion by the committee

Continued on Page 21, Column 3

Judge Sirica's Order

This matter having come before the court on motion of the Watergate special prosecutor made on behalf of the June, 1972, grand jury of this district for an order to show cause, and the court being advised in the premises, it is by the court this 29th day of August, 1973, for the reasons stated in the attached opinion,

Ordered that respondent, President Richard M. Nixon, or any subordinate officer, official or employe with custody or control of the documents or objects listed in the grand jury subpoena duces tecum of July 23, 1973, served on respondent in this district, is hereby commanded to produce forthwith for the court's examination in camera, the subpoenaed documents or objects which have not heretofore been produced to the grand jury; and it is

Further ordered that the ruling herein be stayed for a period of five days in which time respondent may perfect an appeal from the ruling; and it is

Further ordered that should respondent appeal from the ruling herein, the above stay will be extended indefinitely pending the completion of such appeal or appeals.

JOHN J. SIRICA
CHIEF JUDGE

White House Reply

As Mr. Wright pointed out in his oral argument before the court, in camera inspection of these tapes is inconsistent with the President's position relating to the question of separation of powers as provided by the Constitution and the necessity of maintaining the precedent of confidentiality of private Presidential conversations for this President and for Presidents in the future.

The President consequently will not comply with this order.

White House counsel are now considering the possibility of obtaining appellate review or how otherwise to sustain the President's position.

Nadjari Studying Charge Of Plan to Bribe a Justice

By C. GERALD FRASER

Special Prosecutor Maurice H. Nadjari's office disclosed yesterday that it was investigating an alleged conspiracy to pay a $50,000 bribe to a State Supreme Court justice.

Although details of the conspiracy were not disclosed, sources close to the investigation said that it grew out of a case involving the Citizens Casualty Company of New York, which was declared insolvent in 1970 after fighting a long court battle to stay in business.

In that battle, the company, whose lawyer was Representative Mario Biaggi, won a brief victory before Acting Supreme Court Justice Adolph C. Orlando, an interim designate, who is now sitting in the Court of Claims. But Judge Orlando was reversed and the company was ordered dissolved.

Biaggi Received $240,000

Mr. Biaggi was paid $240,-000, but was later ordered to return $100,000 of the fee. The court order said that the $100,-000 was contingent on Mr. Biaggi's winning complete victory for the company while Mr. Biaggi maintained that he was obligated only to win the aspect of the case that came before Judge Orlando.

And he said to Justice Murtagh: "Where did the money as a result of the bribe go? ... all of the leads we have produced point to Century National Bank."

poena issued by Mr. Nadjari to the Century National Bank and Trust Company. Joseph A. Phillips, the chief assistant special prosecutor, said that bank records would be able to shed light on "the sources of moneys used to pay the bribe and to account for moneys obtained as a result of the case."

Mr. Phillips told Justice Murtagh yesterday that "in the course of that investigation, the evidence developed by the grand jury indicates that the principal officers of the Century Bank have information and evidence" relating to the alleged bribery.

Inquiry Leads to Bank

In this way, the special prosecutor got into transactions involving the Century National Bank and Trust Company of 1372 Broadway.

In an affidavit filed yesterday, Mr. Phillips said: "As a result of the alleged bribe, the conspirators obtained substantial sums of moneys due to the determination of the case."

The executive officers of the bank are Vincent F. Albano, Republican county chairman.

Continued on Page 53, Column 3

A HISTORIC RULING

President First Since Jefferson Directed to Give Up Records

By WARREN WEAVER Jr.
Special to The New York Times

WASHINGTON, Aug. 29 — President Nixon was ordered today by Judge John J. Sirica to make tape recordings of White House conversations involving the Watergate case available to him for a decision on their use by a grand jury.

Presidential aides announced, however, that Mr. Nixon "will

Text of Judge Sirica's opinion will be found on Page 20.

not comply with the order."

A White House statement said that the President's lawyers, led by Prof. Charles Alan Wright, who is chief judge of the United States District Court here, and also hinted that they might find some other method of sustaining the President's legal position.

If faced with a refusal by Mr. Nixon to accept the court's ruling or to challenge it by an appeal, Archibald Cox, the special prosecutor, might initiate contempt proceedings or begin an appeal of his own, based on the court's refusal to give him the tapes directly.

Serious Consequences

It was only the second time in the nation's history that a court had required a President, against his will, to produce his personal records as evidence, and the decision was certain to have serious political, governmental and legal consequences, both immediate and long-range. The first case involved President Jefferson.

At San Clemente, where President Nixon is vacationing, officials announced that he would not comply with the court order on the ground that inspection of the tapes by a judge "is inconsistent with the President's position relating to the question of separation of powers as provided by the Constitution and the necessity of maintaining precedents of confidentiality of private Presidential conversations . . ."

The White House statement said that the President's lawyers were considering an appeal "or how otherwise to sustain" Mr. Nixon's legal position.

The last phrase raised the possibility that the President might ignore the order rather than appeal it, thus precipitating another constitutional clash between the executive and judicial branches.

Authority Upheld

Judge Sirica said that he was "simply unable" to decide whether the President's refusal to release the tapes and related documents was valid without inspecting the recordings himself. He upheld the authority of the court to take such action.

If he finds evidence relating to criminal activity in the tapes, and it can be successfully separated from the privileged statements dealing with the President's official duties, the judge said, he will excise the privileged portions and pass the unprivileged portions along to the Watergate grand jury. Archibald Cox, the special prosecutor, is presiding over the panel.

"If privileged and unprivi-

Continued on Page 21, Column 1

BEREAVED BY EARTHQUAKE: A woman and the only one of her four children who survived sit in ruins of home in Orizaba, Mexico. Incomplete reports put the toll of Tuesday's quake at more than 600. Details, Page 12.
United Press International

The New York Times

LATE CITY EDITION
Weather: Partly sunny today; fair tonight. Partly sunny tomorrow. Temp. range: today 53-75; Saturday 53-73. Additional details on Page 91.

SECTION ONE

VOL.CXXIII..No.42,260   © 1973 The New York Times Company   NEW YORK, SUNDAY, OCTOBER 7, 1973   75¢ beyond 50-mile zone from New York City, except Long Island. Higher in air delivery cities.   50 CENTS

ARABS AND ISRAELIS BATTLE ON TWO FRONTS; EGYPTIANS BRIDGE SUEZ; AIR DUELS INTENSE

Associated Press

REDS, ORIOLES WIN PLAYOFF OPENERS: Johnny Bench after his homer won National League game for Cincinnati from New York, 2-1. Sparky Anderson, manager, is at lower left. Baltimore beat Oakland, 6-0, in the American League. Details in Section 5.

U.S. ASKS A HALT

Pleas by Kissinger to Prevent the Fighting Prove Fruitless

By BERNARD GWERTZMAN
Special to The New York Times

WASHINGTON, Oct. 6—The United States appealed to Israel and Egypt today to halt the fighting.

Secretary of State Kissinger, who was in New York, was caught by surprise when the crisis developed. He made a last-minute effort by telephone with Foreign Minister Abba Eban of Israel and Foreign Minister Mohammed H. el-Zayyat of Egypt to prevent the fighting from breaking out, but it proved fruitless.

Both men had had routine talks with Mr. Kissinger in the last two days without giving any indication that fighting was about to erupt, Administration officials said.

Kissinger Urges 'Restraint'

On instructions from President Nixon, who was in Key Biscayne, Fla., for the weekend, Mr. Kissinger "urged restraint to avoid the undermining and violation of the cease-fire" in effect since August, 1970, "and to avoid any escalation and continuation of the fighting," Robert J. McCloskey, a State Department spokesman, said in New York before Mr. Kissinger returned to Washington this afternoon.

In addition, Mr. Kissinger sent cables to King Faisal of Saudi Arabia and King Hussein of Jordan, both friendly to the United States, expressing the hope that they would "use their good office to urge restraint where they have the influence to do so," Mr. McCloskey said.

Call to Waldheim

Mr. Kissinger telephoned Secretary General Waldheim of the United Nations and Sir Laurence McIntyre of Australia, this month's President of the Security Council, to discuss possible Council action. He also called the Soviet Ambassador, Anatoly F. Dobrynin, in Washington, Mr. McCloskey said, presumably to urge Soviet restraint as well.

The crisis struck Washington without much warning. American intelligence had routinely reported signs of military build-ups in Egypt and Syria in recent weeks, but the analysts believed these were either

Continued on Page 14, Column 1

CAB DRIVER SLAIN IN TENSE BOSTON

Found Stabbed to Death in Roxbury Area Following Two Previous Killings

By JOHN KIFNER
Special to The New York Times

BOSTON, Oct. 6—The body of a young white taxi driver who had been stabbed to death was found today in the predominantly black Roxbury neighborhood as this uneasy city tried to come to grips with its racial fears.

The police identified the driver as Kirk Miller, a student at Clarkson College, who was working for the Boston Cab Company. His body was found hidden in some bushes in a vacant lot in Roxbury.

Detectives said that he had multiple stab wounds in his back and head. They said that they "had to assume" that robbery was a possible motive although they could not discount other factors. They said that no money was found on the body.

Mr. Miller was discovered by his sister Sally and a friend, Jeffrey Carter.

Tuesday night, a young white woman was burned to death by six youths in Roxbury, and less than 48 hours later an elderly white man was slain near a housing project. There

Continued on Page 77, Column 3

Tax Agents Compile Data On Net Worth of Agnew

By MARTIN WALDRON
Special to The New York Times

BALTIMORE, Oct. 6—Agents of the Internal Revenue Service are apparently compiling a statement on Vice President Agnew's net worth as part of the continuing investigation into his financial affairs.

Although the purpose of the revenue service's investigation is not known, the service often uses the technique of the net worth audit in an attempt to show that a defendant accused of evading taxes is worth more than the amounts on which he paid taxes.

Earlier this week, the Federal grand jury investigating Mr. Agnew indicted N. Dale Anderson, who succeeded Mr. Agnew as Baltimore County Executive, on income tax charges after revenue agents compiled a net worth statement on Mr. Anderson.

By law, the revenue service is prohibited from commenting on individual income tax reports or on investigations it may have under way.

But in the last few weeks its agents have been collecting data dealing with Mr. Agnew's affairs, even minor transactions, according to sources knowledgeable about the investigations.

On Oct. 3, agents from the Charlotte, N. C., intelligence office of the service subpoenaed records in Asheville, N. C., showing a gift of four yards of homespun cloth worth $16 to the United States, a consortium of United and Canadian concerns is pushing plans to tap the region's rich natural gas reserves via a different but equally controversial 2,000-mile route.

Current exploratory activities of the gas consortium, pointing toward a possible major incursion into the Arctic landscape Mr. Agnew in 1967 at the time of the Southern Governors Conference, the sources said.

Such gifts are sometimes considered as income for tax purposes.

In making a case charging income tax evasion against an individual, the revenue service sometimes alleges failure to pay tax on specific income items, which it then seeks to prove were received by the individual.

The revenue agents and agents of the Federal Bureau of Investigation are apparently checking every financial transaction that the Vice President

Continued on Page 33, Column 1

Queens Sports Center Proposed

By EMANUEL PERLMUTTER

Creation of a $275-million sports complex on air rights over the Sunnyside, Queens, railroad yards of the Penn Central was proposed yesterday by the State Racing and Wagering Board.

The project, which would be competitive with the proposed athletic complex in the New Jersey Meadows, would include two race tracks, an 80,000-seat stadium for football and other entertainments, a 1,000-room resort and convention hotel and parking for 20,000 cars.

No housing or other buildings would have to be demolished for the project since it would be built on a platform over the 300-acre yard site, which is less than a mile east of the Queensboro Bridge at the junction of Queens and Northern Boulevards and just a few minutes from Times Square by subway.

Under the proposal, the project would be financed by a bond issue and proceeds from the sale of Aqueduct Race Track. The air rights would be purchased by the Metropolitan Transportation Authority from the Penn Central and leased to the State Urban Development Corporation, which would build the necessary facilities.

Emil Mosbacher Jr., chairman of the Racing and Wager-

Continued on Page 49, Column 1

Gas Pipeline Contest Develops in Alaska

By GLADWIN HILL
Special to The New York Times

PRUDHOE BAY, Alaska, Sept. 29 — Another Alaskan pipeline dispute is brewing.

While the oil companies with the big petroleum deposits here on the North Slope await a final Congressional go-ahead to build a controversial 789-mile pipeline to Alaska's south coast, a consortium of United States and Canadian concerns is pushing plans to tap the region's rich natural gas reserves via a different but equally controversial 2,000-mile route.

Current exploratory activities of the gas consortium, pointing toward a possible major incursion into the Arctic

Continued on Page 74, Column 3

Today's Sections

Index to Subjects

U.N. COUNCIL AIDES CONFER ON CRISIS

President of Body Seeks Views on Calling Meeting to Deal With Fighting

By ROBERT ALDEN
Special to The New York Times

UNITED NATIONS, N. Y., Oct. 6—The President of the Security Council, Sir Laurence McIntyre of Australia, opened formal consultations tonight with other members of the Council to seek their views on calling a Council meeting to deal with the fighting in the Middle East.

The Western powers generally favored calling such a meeting, but not prematurely. They said that a premature meeting would result in little more than invective, claim and counterclaim.

Another proposal the Council members were discussing was for the President of the Council to appeal to both sides in the Middle East to halt the fighting. While Western powers generally supported such an appeal, the Chinese and the Russians held back endorsement; the French said they would have to study the idea.

Neither the Israelis nor the Arab states called for an urgent meeting of the Council today, though the Egyptian Foreign Minister, Dr. Mohammed H. el-Zayyat, said he wanted to

Continued on Page 8, Column 1

Israelis and Egyptians Tell Of Beginnings of Conflict

Jerusalem's Report

By TERENCE SMITH
Special to The New York Times

JERUSALEM, Sunday, Oct. 7—Heavy fighting erupted yesterday between Israeli and Arab forces along the Suez Canal and Golan heights cease-fire lines, a military spokesman announced.

The forces were still fighting early this morning in what De-

Mrs. Meir's address, Page 5; Dayan excerpts, Page 6.

fense Minister Moshe Dayan described as "all-out war."

The fighting began at 2 P.M. yesterday, Israeli time (8 A.M. New York time). Egyptian forces managed to cross the Suez Canal during the afternoon and establish bridgeheads at several points on the Israeli-held eastern bank, but Israeli military spokesmen said last night that Israeli forces had moved into position to block them.

On the occupied Golan heights, a large-scale Syrian force including armor and artil-

Continued on Page 4, Column 1

Cairo Communiques

By HENRY TANNER
Special to The New York Times

CAIRO, Oct. 6 — The Egyptian Government announced today that Israeli ground, sea and air forces attacked Egypt and Syria early this afternoon along the entire length of their front lines with Israel.

In a succession of communiques read on the Government-controlled Cairo radio, Egypt said that her forces had crossed the Suez Canal in several places and had placed Egyptian flags on the Israeli-held eastern bank.

The radio said that the Egyptians had crossed the canal—the cease-fire line since the 1967 war—after repelling Israeli landing attempts on the Egyptian-held western bank.

The radio interrupted its regular program just after 2 P.M. Cairo time (8 A.M. New York time) saying that the Israeli action had started at 1:30 local time with air attacks on Ain Sukhna, 30 miles south of the town of Suez on the Egyptian shore of the Red Sea, and

Continued on Page 7, Column 1

SYRIANS IN CLASH

Fighting Along Canal and Golan Heights Goes On All Night

By ROBERT D. McFADDEN

The heaviest fighting in the Middle East since the 1967 war erupted yesterday on Israel's front lines with Egypt along the Suez Canal and Syria in the Golan heights.

Official announcements by Israel and Egypt agreed that Egyptian forces had crossed the Suez Canal and established footholds in the Israeli-occupied Sinai Peninsula.

A military communiqué issued in Cairo asserted that Egyptian forces had captured most of the eastern bank of the 100-mile canal. An Israeli military communiqué said the Egyptians had attempted to cross the canal at several points by helicopters and small boats and had succeeded in laying down pontoon bridges at two points. Armored forces were pouring across them into Sinai, it said.

Fighting All Night

A communiqué issued early today in Tel Aviv said fighting had raged all night along the canal's eastern bank and along the entire cease-fire line with Syria.

Each side accused the other of having started the fighting. But military observers posted by the United Nations reported crossings by Egyptian forces at five points along the Suez, and said Syrians had attacked in the Golan heights at two points.

Israeli and Syrian artillery dueled in the Golan heights, and on both battlefronts there were air clashes. The Cairo radio said Egyptian forces had shot down 11 Israeli planes and lost 10 of their own in battles over the Sinai and the Gulf of Suez. The Israeli spokesman did not comment on losses but said Israeli planes had shot down 10 Egyptian helicopters carrying troops into the southern Sinai.

Shelling by Syrians

In Damascus, the military command said that Syrian pilots and ground fire had shot down 10 Israeli aircraft in renewed action over the Golan heights this morning.

Syrian artillery was reported by the Israelis to have shelled a number of settlements in the occupied Golan heights and the Hula Valley area.

The Damascus radio said that Syrian forces had reoccupied Mount Hermon in the Golan heights for the first time since 1967, and said Syrian troops were fighting on the ground with Israeli forces along the entire cease-fire line.

An Israeli spokesman said today that Israeli planes had sunk an Egyptian vessel and that the navy had sunk three troop-carrying Egyptian craft during the night.

Gunboats Reported Sunk

As fighting continued into the night, Syrian and Israeli gunboats clashed in the Syrian harbor of Latakia, 110 miles north of Beirut. An Israeli communiqué said that five Soviet-built Syrian vessels were sunk by Israeli sea-to-sea missiles being used for the first time. In Damascus, however, a military spokesman said that Syrian forces had sunk four Israeli naval vessels and shot down two Israeli helicopters in the sea battle.

No military action involving Jordan or Lebanon was reported, but King Hussein of Jordan placed his armed forces on full alert and conferred by telephone with President Anwar el-Sadat of Egypt and President Hafez al-Assad of Syria. Jordan was a belligerent in the 1967 war won by Israel.

The Government radio stations in Cairo and in Damascus

Continued on Page 2, Column 3

Heavy arrows (upper right) indicate drive by Syrians and (lower left) crossing of Suez Canal by Egyptians.

The New York Times/Oct. 7, 1973

"All the News That's Fit to Print"

The New York Times

LATE CITY EDITION

Weather: Partly sunny today; cool tonight. Fair and milder tomorrow. Temp. range: today 54-68; Wed. 52-75. Additional details on Page 90.

VOL.CXXIII...No. 42,264   © 1973 The New York Times Company   NEW YORK, THURSDAY, OCTOBER 11, 1973   15 CENTS

AGNEW QUITS VICE PRESIDENCY AND ADMITS TAX EVASION IN '67; NIXON CONSULTS ON SUCCESSOR

U.S. Believes Moscow Is Resupplying Arabs by Airlift

Soviet Could Spur Move to Aid Israel

By JOHN W. FINNEY
Special to The New York Times

WASHINGTON, Oct. 10—Administration officials said today that they believed the Soviet Union was airlifting military equipment to resupply the forces of Egypt and Syria.

The State Department said that if the Russians were in fact engaged in a huge resupply effort, this would put a "new face" on the Middle East conflict. Speaking for the department, Robert J. McCloskey said, however, that he was "not in a position to confirm that any of this is taking place at this time."

But other officials, apparently acting upon instructions laid down by the State Department, readily volunteered information. They did so, however, on a basis that precluded their identification.

The fact that officials who until today had been extremely reluctant to discuss any detail of the Middle East war were now willing to talk openly about indications of a Soviet resupply effort prompted immedi-

ate speculation that the Nixon Administration might be laying the groundwork for resupplying the forces of Israel.

There were reports that Israel was flying military supplies from the United States and from American bases in Britain and West Germany, but it was not clear whether the supplies referred to had previously been ordered. Asked about the reports, the Defense Department refused to confirm or deny them.

The exact nature of the reported Soviet airlift remains unclear, United States officials said. All that is known, according to officials, is that in the last day or so, an unusually large number of Soviet transports have been observed landing at Egyptian and Syrian airports. The presumption is that the planes are carrying military equipment.

The airlift, officials reported, was being staged primarily from Hungary, with the planes

Continued on Page 18, Column 1

A 10-Mile Egyptian Gain

By HENRY TANNER
Special to The New York Times

IN THE SINAI PENINSULA, Oct. 10 — Egyptian soldiers, tanks and equipment are continuing to pour across the Suez Canal, a group of Western correspondents confirmed from the battle area today.

On a three-and-half-mile tour into the Sinai Peninsula, this correspondent also saw evidence that Egyptian forces had reached positions 10 miles or more east of the canal in some parts of the sector.

[In the air war the Egyptians said they had shot down six more Israeli planes. Egyptian aircraft were said to have attacked Israeli command headquarters, units and administrative installations on the northern Sinai coast.]

The Egyptian soldiers in the area toured by the correspondents were in high spirits, often jubilant, and seemed oblivious to Israeli artillery shells bursting near them.

"Don't worry, God is with us!" one of three young soldiers shouted laughingly to the correspondents, who ducked for

cover when a shell burst too close for comfort. The Egyptians remained where they were, standing atop a ridge.

Shells fell every few moments but caused no casualties during a half-hour visit to the particular sector. An Egyptian officer said they were from an Israeli battery 15 miles away that was trying to hit a military bridge.

More than 50 trucks interspersed with antiaircraft guns were lined up in open country on the west bank, waiting for their turn to cross the canal. Waved onto the bridge by a young soldier with a yellow flag, they moved quickly, often with three or four vehicles on the bridge simultaneously.

On one truck two young soldiers were dancing. Others clapped their hands rhythmically.

The elation and excitement of returning to Egyptian territory occupied for more than six years by Israel was everywhere.

The loose boards and pontoons that made up the bridge

Continued on Page 18, Column 5

Israel Claiming Heights

By CHARLES MOHR
Special to The New York Times

TEL AVIV, Thursday, Oct. 11 —Israel said last night that the Syrian Army on the Golan heights had been driven back to the 1967 cease-fire line, but Israeli forces fighting the Egyptians clearly seemed to have suspended a counterat-

Text of Mrs. Meir's address is printed on Page 19.

tack aimed at pushing them from the eastern bank of the Suez Canal.

A highly informed source said that Israel estimated the Egyptian invasion force at five divisions, which could be close to 75,000 men. The force, he said, crossed with about 600 tanks, and 300 to 400 of these

may still be operational.

The Israeli Air Force bombed two air fields in the Nile delta as well as a naval headquarters, fuel installation and power plant in Syria in a day of slackening air action.

The Israeli command announced this morning that for the first time in the war Israeli forces had struck against the opposite bank of the Suez Canal. The command spokesman said that an Israeli force of unannounced size had raided convoys and rear echelon installations of the Egyptian Army.

The wording of the communiqué indicated that the operation was not an attempt to gain a foothold on the other side and that the raiding force

Continued on Page 19, Column 3

CONGRESS TO VOTE

Opposition Is Hinted if Choice Is Possible 1976 Candidate

Special to The New York Times

WASHINGTON, Oct. 10—President Nixon began his search today for a successor to Vice President Agnew amid indications that he will face stiff resistance from Congress if he chooses anyone who might qualify as a strong Republican candidate in 1976.

The Senate majority leader, Mike Mansfield, Democrat of Montana, said the choice of either John B. Connally, the former Treasury Secretary and Texas Governor, or Gov. Ronald Reagan of California—both presumed contenders for the Republican Presidential nomination in 1976—would provoke a fight from Senate Democrats.

Similar warnings had come from Democratic leaders in the House.

Quick Action Indicated

Mr. Nixon's first moves today indicated that he wished to move quickly but with some show of bipartisan consultation. Senator Mansfield said after meeting the President that Mr. Nixon had indicated he would submit the name of his nominee to Congress "at the end of this week or the first of next week."

"President Nixon intends to move expeditiously in selecting a nominee and he trusts the Congress will then act promptly to consider the nomination," Ronald L. Ziegler, the President's press secretary, announced shortly after word that the President had accepted Mr. Agnew's resignation spread through the White House.

Mr. Nixon then began meeting with Congressional leaders of both parties and with George Bush, chairman of the Republican National Committee, to reach an understanding on the procedures he will follow in selecting a Vice President ac-

Continued on Page 34, Column 2

Spiro T. Agnew speaking to reporters after appearing at court in Baltimore yesterday

Associated Press

Agnew Plea Ends 65 Days Of Insisting on Innocence

By BEN A. FRANKLIN
Special to The New York Times

BALTIMORE, Oct. 10—Vice President Agnew ended today 65 days of defiant insistence that he was innocent of any wrongdoing by pleading no contest to a charge of cheating the Government of $13,551.47 on his Federal income tax pay-

Richardson, Agnew, Hoffman statements on Page 35.

ment for 1967, his first year as Governor of Maryland. Then he resigned his Federal office.

At a dramatic, surprise appearance here before United States District Court Judge Walter E. Hoffman after two days of secret negotiations, Mr. Agnew was confronted in open court by Attorney General Elliot L. Richardson.

The Attorney General said

in a prepared statement that the Government's evidence against the former Vice President went far beyond the six-year-old tax violation. But he said that "critical national interests"—the avoidance of the "serious and permanent scars" upon the nation that would have been inflicted by months or years of a criminal prosecution of a sitting Vice President, together with the new and allied dispute over newsmen's sources—justified the agreement with Mr. Agnew. Judge Hoffman then approved the agreement.

Under it, Mr. Agnew in a 40-minute court appearance waived all his rights as a defendant—the right to be indicted and to an arraignment—and was sentenced on the spot to pay a $10,000 fine and to three years of probation. He was admonished by Judge Hoffman to violate no state or Federal laws on pain of having his avoidance of a prison term reconsidered.

A long list of other charges, involving perhaps $100,000 in payoffs by Maryland contrac-

Continued on Page 35, Column 1

Mets in World Series; Defeat Reds for Flag

By JOSEPH DURSO

The New York Mets completed their six-week odyssey from last place to the National League pennant yesterday when they overpowered the favored Cincinnati Reds, 7-2, in a tumultuous game that rocked and almost ruined Shea Stadium.

In a riotous scene that brought back memories of their "miracle" of 1969, they decided the issue with four runs in the fifth inning of a 2-2 game.

But then, in a swirling scene, thousands of persons in the crowd of 50,323 stormed the field after delaying the game in the ninth inning and caused huge chunks of fence, sod and fixtures from the arena.

Professional sports may have had more dramatic moments. But New York baseball has had none since the Mets won the World Series four years ago after eight seasons as the comic relief of the leagues.

Their rise this summer car-

ried them from medical history to baseball history, and their public responded yesterday by mobbing Willie Mays, Pete Rose and the 340 police officers struggling to prevent panic.

Repairs on the stadium were started immediately after the crowd had dispersed shortly after 5 o'clock, while the Mets celebrated their victory in champagne and prepared for the next milestone.

They will open the World Series on Saturday in the home park of the Oakland A's or Baltimore Orioles, who will decide the American League pennant this after-

Continued on Page 61, Column 4

EVIDENCE SHOWS GIFTS TO AGNEW

Cites Requests and Receipt of Over $100,000—Denial Also Entered in Record

By ANTHONY RIPLEY
Special to The New York Times

BALTIMORE, Oct. 10—Spiro T. Agnew, in three elective offices including the Vice-Presidency, asked for and accepted cash payments totaling more than $100,000, according to the evidence gathered against him by the United States Attorneys in Baltimore.

That evidence, denied by Mr. Agnew, was entered by Attor-

Charge and jury evidence are on Pages 36, 37 and 38.

ney General Elliott L. Richardson in Federal District Court today as part of the agreement between the Justice Department and Mr. Agnew's lawyers.

It became a permanent part of the record in the case, along with Mr. Agnew's denial and other terms of the agreement that included his resignation and a plea of no contest to a tax charge.

The 40-page document told of

Continued on Page 38, Column 3

I.R.S. Sees Nothing to Prevent New Tax Cases Against Agnew

By EILEEN SHANAHAN
Special to The New York Times

WASHINGTON, Oct. 10—Former Vice President Agnew's plea of "no contest" today in the income-tax evasion case against him could mark only the beginning of difficulties for him with the Internal Revenue Service.

An official spokesman for Internal Revenue said that as far as the agency is aware, there was nothing in the agreement leading to Mr. Agnew's resignation that would prohibit Internal Revenue from attempting to collect taxes on any payment to Mr. Agnew that could be documented as having been made but not reported on his tax returns.

The charge of tax evasion to

which Mr. Agnew pleaded "nolo contendere" involved $29,500. But a document released by the Justice Department detailing the evidence against the former Vice President alleges payments from contractors and others totaling as much as $100,000. The precise figure is not clear, because some of the allegations of illegal payments are stated in terms of percentages of the value of construction contracts awarded, and the figures for the contracts themselves are not given.

The Internal Revenue spokesman said, however, that it was common in tax-evasion cases for a charge of criminal tax evasion to be made involving

Continued on Page 33, Column 3

Judge Orders Fine, 3 Years' Probation

By JAMES M. NAUGHTON
Special to The New York Times

WASHINGTON, Oct. 10—Spiro T. Agnew resigned as Vice President of the United States today under an agreement with the Department of Justice to admit evasion of Federal income taxes and avoid imprisonment.

The stunning development, ending a Federal grand jury investigation of Mr. Agnew in Baltimore and probably terminating his political career, shocked his closest associates and precipitated an immediate search by President Nixon for a successor.

"I hereby resign the office of Vice President of the United States, effective immediately," Mr. Agnew declared in a formal statement delivered at 2:05 P.M. to Secretary of State Kissinger, as provided in the Succession Act of 1792.

Minutes later, Mr. Agnew stood before United States District Judge Walter E. Hoffman in a Baltimore courtroom, hands barely trembling, and read from a statement in which he pleaded nolo contendere, or no contest, to a Government charge that he had failed to report $29,500 of income received in 1967, when he was Governor of Maryland. Such a plea, while not an admission of guilt, subjects a defendant to a judgment of conviction on the charge.

Tells Court Income Was Taxable

"I admit that I did receive payments during the year 1967 which were not expended for political purposes and that, therefore, these payments were income taxable to me in that year and that I so knew," the nation's 39th Vice President told the stilled courtroom.

Judge Hoffman sentenced Mr. Agnew to three years' probation and fined him $10,000. The judge declared from the bench that he would have sent Mr. Agnew to prison had not Attorney General Elliot L. Richardson personally interceded, arguing that "leniency is justified."

In his dramatic courtroom statement, Mr. Agnew declared that he was innocent of any other wrongdoing but that it would "seriously prejudice the national interest" to involve himself in a protracted struggle before the courts or Congress.

Mr. Agnew also cited the national interest in a letter to President Nixon saying that he was resigning.

"I respect your decision," the President wrote to Mr. Agnew in a "Dear Ted" letter made public by the White House. The letter hailed Mr. Agnew for "courage and candor," praised his patriotism and dedication, and expressed Mr. Nixon's "great sense of personal loss." But it agreed

Continued on Page 33, Column 1

Agnew-Nixon Exchange

October 10, 1973

Dear Mr. President:

As you are aware, the accusations against me cannot be resolved without a long, divisive and debilitating struggle in the Congress and in the courts. I have concluded that, painful as it is to me and to my family, it is in the best interests of the nation that I relinquish the Vice Presidency.

Accordingly, I have today resigned the office of Vice President of the United States. A copy of the instrument of resignation is enclosed.

It has been a privilege to serve with you. May I express to the American people, through you, my deep gratitude for their confidence in twice electing me to be Vice President.

Sincerely,
SPIRO T. AGNEW

October 10, 1973.

Dear Ted:

The most difficult decisions are often those that are the most personal, and I know your decision to resign as Vice President has been as difficult as any facing a man in public life could be. Your departure from the Administration leaves me with a great sense of personal loss. You have been a valued associate throughout these nearly five years that we have served together. However, I respect your decision, and I also respect the concern for the national interest that led you to conclude that a resolution of the matter in this way, rather than through an extended battle in the courts and the Congress, was advisable in order to prevent a protracted period of national division and uncertainty.

As Vice President, you have addressed the great issues of our times with courage and candor. Your strong patriotism, and your profound dedication to the welfare of the nation, have been an inspiration to all who have served with you as well as to millions of others throughout the country.

I have been deeply saddened by this whole course of events, and I hope that you and your family will be sustained in the days ahead by a well-justified pride in all that you have contributed to the nation by your years of service as Vice President.

Sincerely,
RICHARD NIXON

"All the News That's Fit to Print"

The New York Times

LATE CITY EDITION

Weather: Mostly sunny, mild today; cloudy, chance of rain tonight. Temp. range: today 56-73. Friday 51-71. Additional details on Page 70.

VOL.CXXIII....No. 42,266   © 1973 The New York Times Company   NEW YORK, SATURDAY, OCTOBER 13, 1973   15 CENTS

GERALD FORD NAMED BY NIXON AS THE SUCCESSOR TO AGNEW

Appeals Court Agrees President Should Give Up Tapes

Israelis Drive Syrians Back Within 18 Miles of Damascus

Capture of Capital Thought Unlikely

By CHARLES MOHR
Special to The New York Times

EL QUNEITRA, on the Golan Heights, Oct. 12—Parts of the Syrian Army appeared to be in full retreat today as the Israeli Army advanced to within 18 miles of the Syrian capital of Damascus.

But an Israeli officer said: "We won't be having dinner together tomorrow in Damascus."

[In Tel Aviv, a well-informed Israeli source said that "the latest thinking is that we will not capture Damascus, which would be a terrible headache." An Israeli military spokesman said that Israeli forces had encountered Iraqi troops in the Golan heights for the first time.]

In at least one area of the Syrian front, northeast of the town of El Quneitra, it was apparent that Syrian forces were in retreat, although still fighting delaying actions.

Reporters following the Israeli Army—and clocking distances on the odometers of their rented sedans—could see that the Israeli forward elements were at least 30 kilometers, or 18 miles, past the old 1967 cease-fire line—and thus about 30 kilometers from Damascus.

It was apparent to neutral foreign observers that, in this

3 Freighters Sunk

By JUAN de ONIS
Special to The New York Times

DAMASCUS, Syria, Oct. 12 — Syrian air defenses today shot down 35 Israeli planes that attacked military air bases around this capital and other targets, according to a military spokesman.

Three freighters, one Soviet, one Japanese and one Greek, were sunk during attacks by Israeli missile boats on the ports of Latakia and Tartus, an official announcement said today. The Syrian spokesman said eight of the attacking Israeli craft were sunk by Syrian missile boats.

[In Cairo, military communiqués said that Egyptian forces were continuing to pour across the Suez Canal. Page 15.]

On the ground, "fierce fighting" continued all along the Syrian front, said the spokesman. He said more than 40 Israeli tanks and 20 armored vehicles had been destroyed. There was no figure on Syrian losses.

The front, along the occupied Golan Heights, was 24 miles southeast of this city of 840,000 people, which was calm tonight under a nearly full moon.

Traffic in the blacked-out streets consisted mainly of

Continued on Page 15, Column 1

To Our Readers

Distribution of this issue of The New York Times was delayed by work stoppages by the printers' union in defiance of a court order. The stoppages also made it necessary to reduce coverage of the news. Details, Page 24.

Continued on Page 14, Column 5

JUDGES RULE 5-2

Historic Decision Finds President Not Above Law's Commands

By LESLEY OELSNER
Special to The New York Times

WASHINGTON, Oct. 12—In what it called an "unavoidable" and "extraordinary" ruling, the United States Court of Appeals held tonight that President Nixon must turn over to the Federal District Court here the disputed White House tape recordings possibly bearing on Watergate crimes.

By a 5-to-2 vote, the appeals court said that the District

Excerpts from court opinions will be found on Page 21.

Court could then give the Watergate grand jury any relevant material, unless it felt that there was some public interest to be served by withholding "particular" statements or information.

"Though the President is elected by nationwide ballot, and is often said to represent all the people, he does not embody the nation's sovereignty," the court said. "He is not above the law's commands."

Order Is Upheld

Participants in today's decision were David L. Bazelon, chief judge, and J. Skelly Wright, Carl McGowan, Harold Leventhal, Spottswood W. Robinson, 3d, George E. MacKinnon and Malcolm R. Wilkey.

The court's ruling, issued at 6 P.M. through the clerk's office on the fifth floor of the Federal Courthouse here, thus substantially upheld the order last August of Federal District Judge John J. Sirica, although it appeared to take an even tougher stance against the President than Judge Sirica had.

The appellate court made its ruling in response to requests by both Mr. Nixon and Archibald Cox, the special Watergate prosecutor, to reverse Judge Sirica. Mr. Cox, who had initiated the proceedings when he had a subpoena issued for the tapes, asked the appeals court to order that the tapes be turned over directly to the grand jury.

Mr. Nixon, for his part, asked

Continued on Page 20, Column 4

Gerald R. Ford with President, after Mr. Nixon nominated him for Vice President

United Press International

Amtrak Will Double Fleet Of 'Corridor' Metroliners

By EDWARD C. BURKS

Amtrak, the nationwide rail passenger system, announced yesterday that it would virtually double its fleet of Metroliner cars and extend high-speed Metroliner service from New York to Boston.

It signed contracts in Washington for new equipment valued at $63.5-million including the following:

¶Fifty-seven new Metroliner-type coaches, capable of operation in trains pulled by either electric or diesel locomotives, for service in the Washington-New York-Boston "Northeast Corridor."

¶Eleven new 6,000-horsepower electric locomotives (added to 15 ordered earlier this year) to replace the famed but ancient Penn Central GG-1 electrics that have operated in the corridor since the nineteen-thirties.

¶Seventy new diesel passenger locomotives for other Amtrak routes around the nation.

In Philadelphia, Judge John P. Fullam, who is in charge of the Penn Central Railroad's bankruptcy case in Federal District Court, said he believed

there was no immediate need for the carrier to cease its operations. [Details Page 47.]

With the award of yesterday's contracts, Amtrak has now committed more than $110-million this year to new locomotives and passenger cars.

Started in 1969, the high-speed Metroliner service between New York and Washington has been expanded to a train every hour in each direction from early morning until evening on weekdays.

There are somewhat fewer services on the weekends. In addition, some Metroliners go on through New York as far as New Haven.

Although very-high speed service on the New York-Boston line must await the day of extensive track realignment on the curving route, new equipment ordered yesterday can substantially reduce present running times, according to Amtrak.

Bryan Duff, Amtrak's news director, said that the first of the new Metroliner-type coaches with airliner interiors should be delivered in 15 months. They are to be built by the Budd Company at Red Lion, Pa.

The 61 Metroliner cars now in operation are self-propelled and equipped with pantographs on the roof. Their use is thus limited to the relatively short stretches in this country with overhead catenary installations.

The new cars will have the

Continued on Page 70, Column 5

MOVE IS SURPRISE

House G.O.P. Leader Would Be the 40th Vice President

By JOHN HERBERS
Special to The New York Times

WASHINGTON, Oct. 12 — Gerald Rudolph Ford of Michigan, the 60-year-old minority leader of the House of Representatives, was nominated by President Nixon tonight to be the 40th Vice President of the United States.

Mr. Nixon, making the surprise announcement on national television and radio shortly after 9 P.M., said that he would

Texts of Nixon and Ford remarks are on Page 19.

send the nomination to Congress tomorrow. Because of Mr. Ford's long service in that body, 25 years, he was expected to be easily confirmed.

Under the 25th Amendment, ratified in 1967 and never used before tonight, the nomination must be approved by simple majorities of both the House and the Senate before he can take office.

Mr. Ford's selection came two days after Spiro T. Agnew, who had served in the office almost five years, resigned, pleaded no contest to income tax evasion, was fined $10,000 and was placed on probation for three years.

Move Toward Unity

In a brief announcement speech in the East Room of the White House, Mr. Nixon made it clear that he had chosen a respected memb of Congress for the post because he considered it essential for national unity to select a person who would not be the subject of a protracted and bitter fight in Congress.

It was learned that Mr. Nixon had given strong consideration to former Treasury Secretary John B. Connally but that leaders in the Democratic-controlled Congress had served notice they would oppose him. They opposed Mr. Connally because he recently switched to the Republican party and because it would have appeared that Mr. Nixon was setting him up for the Presidency in the 1976 elections.

Mr. Ford, the President said, "has earned the respect of both Democrats and Republicans."

'Unwavering' on Vietnam

"He is a man also who has been unwavering in his support of the policies that brought peace with honor for America in Vietnam and in support of the policies for a strong national defense," Mr. Nixon said.

Several score Congressional leaders, Cabinet members and other high Government officials burst into cheers and surrounded the baldish, tanned Republican and offered congratulations even before Mr. Nixon uttered his name. They knew he was the nominee when Mr. Nixon said his choice "is a man who has served for 25 years in the House of Representatives with great distinction."

Mr. Ford, the President said, met the three criteria he had set for the nominee—that "the

Continued on Page 19, Column 1

CHOICE IS PRAISED BY BOTH PARTIES

Widespread Enthusiasm Is Expressed in Congress—Fast Confirmation Seen

By RICHARD L. MADDEN
Special to The New York Times

WASHINGTON, Oct. 12—Congressional Democrats and Republicans received President Nixon's choice of Gerald R. Ford to be Vice President with widespread enthusiasm tonight.

The reaction indicated that the nomination of Mr. Ford of Michigan, who has been the House Republican leader since 1965, would be confirmed relatively quickly by both houses, barring some unforeseen development.

However, it was expected that the Senate would take more time than the House in considering the nomination.

"My own feeling is Gerry will probably be confirmed," said Speaker Carl Albert of Oklahoma, he added:

"I think I was the first in Congress to tell the President that Gerry would be the easiest candidate to sell to the House. He's a very fine man to work with. I think he earned this."

Senator Robert C. Byrd of West Virginia, the Democratic majority whip and member of the Senate Rules Committee, which will probably handle Mr. Ford's nomination, said he did not think it would be proper

Continued on Page 19, Column 3

Fumes and smoke rise as Israeli artillerymen, on the Syrian border, fire 155-mm. guns
United Press International

Israel Is Accused in U.N. Of Sinking a Soviet Ship

By ROBERT ALDEN
Special to The New York Times

UNITED NATIONS, N. Y., Oct. 12—The Soviet Union accused Israel today of "barbarous" attacks on nonmilitary targets and demanded that they be stopped at once.

Yakov A. Malik, the Soviet delegate, read to the Security Council a dispatch from Tass, the Soviet press agency, that said the Soviet merchant ship Ilya Mechnikov had been sunk in Tartus, a Syrian port, by an Israeli attack.

Tass demanded an immediate stop to the bombings of peaceful towns in Syria and Egypt, and the strict observance by Israel of the norms of international law.

"The continuation of criminal acts by Israel will lead to grave

consequences for Israel itself," the Tass article added.

Yosef Tekoah, the Israeli representative, said his information on the basis of a news dispatch was that the merchant ship had been damaged as a result of a naval battle that took place between Syrian and Israeli naval vessels outside the port. He termed the damage "unfortunate."

Reports from Damascus said that the ship had subsequently been sunk, as had a Greek and a Japanese merchant ship during attacks made by Israeli missile boats on the ports of Tartus and Latakia.

"We regret the sinking of

Continued on Page 14, Column 2

Rival Stadium Plans Stir a Bistate Furor

By FRANK LYNN

A bitter behind-the-scenes struggle has developed between New York and New Jersey over a proposed Sunnyside, Queens, sport complex that has the strong backing of Governor Rockefeller and that could effectively rival a similar New Jersey race track and football stadium.

High New York State sources said the Governor had approved the announcement of the Queens sports complex last Saturday that forced postponement of the sale of a $280-million bond issue to finance the New Jersey race track and stadium for the New York Football Giants in the Hackensack Meadows.

"We were signaling investors of New York's interest in its

Continued on Page 24, Column 5

P.S.C. Certifies Shortage Of Fuel Oil on Long Island

First in the State

By DAVID A. ANDELMAN

The State Public Service Commission certified yesterday that a sharp shortage in home and industrial fuel oils existed for Long Island—the first region in the state to be declared an "oil insufficient area."

According to the certification, between now and Jan. 15 Long Island will face a shortage of at least 150.1 million gallons of No. 2 home heating oil and 39.5 million gallons of Nos. 4 and 6 industrial fuel oils.

The certification was made to Henry L. Diamond, the State Environmental Conservation Commissioner, who must now decide whether to lift the regulations prohibiting use of high-sulphur fuel oil to ease the anticipated shortage.

Yesterday's certification applies only to fuels distributed through Northville Industries, the largest distributor on Long Island, but reportedly not the

Federal Controls Ordered

By The Associated Press

WASHINGTON, Oct. 12 — The Nixon Administration reluctantly adopted today a mandatory allocation program governing the wholesale distribution of home heating oil.

At the same time, Congress moved steadily closer to forcing a mandatory program for all petroleum products.

The Administration's limited program, which will take effect Nov. 1, requires suppliers to distribute home heating oil, jet fuel, kerosene, diesel fuel, range oil, stove oil and gas oil to their customers in proportion to purchases made in the calendar year 1972.

On Oct. 2, the Administration imposed a similar allocation program on propane gas, but so far there is no Government control over the distribution of crude oil or of gasoline and other petroleum products.

Legislation now before Congress would require mandatory allocation of all petroleum products and crude oil.

The House Rules Committee

Continued on Page 36, Column 3

Continued on Page 36, Column 5

Agnew Prosecution Took Pains To Prepare a 'Locked-Up Case'

By AGIS SALPUKAS
Special to The New York Times

BALTIMORE, Oct. 12—It started modestly.

When George Beall, the United States Attorney for Maryland, asked that a grand jury be impaneled last Dec. 1, he recalled in an interview today, the thought was: "If we ended up bringing criminal charges against a couple of building inspectors in Baltimore it would have been justified."

And the inquiry remained focused on lesser political figures, with no hint that it would lead higher, until the beginning of June when several key witnesses began to seek favored treatment from the prosecutors by telling them what they knew about making payments to the then Vice President Agnew.

By the beginning of July, Mr. Beall was convinced that the case against the Vice President was serious and on July 3 he called Attorney General Elliot L. Richardson to inform him of the explosive turn of events.

Mr. Beall comes from a long line of prominent Republicans in Maryland. He is the son of J. Glenn Beall, the former Republican United States Senator, and the brother of J. Glenn Beall Jr., who won election to the Senate in 1970. Today he recalled his feelings at that point last summer when he realized the implication of the inquiry.

"I was turning somersaults," he said as he sat at his next

Continued on Page 18, Column 2

The New York Times

LATE CITY EDITION

Weather: Chance of showers later today, tonight. Milder tomorrow. Temp. range: today 36-46; Friday 43-49. Additional details on Page 62.

VOL. CXXIII...No. 42,406   © 1974 The New York Times Company   NEW YORK, SATURDAY, MARCH 2, 1974   20c beyond 50-mile radius of New York City, except Long Island. Higher in air delivery cities.   15 CENTS

FEDERAL GRAND JURY INDICTS 7 NIXON AIDES ON CHARGES OF CONSPIRACY ON WATERGATE; HALDEMAN, EHRLICHMAN, MITCHELL ON LIST

John N. Mitchell
Former Attorney General

H. R. Haldeman
Headed White House staff

John D. Ehrlichman
Was Presidential adviser

Charles W. Colson
Former White House lawyer

Robert C. Mardian
1972 campaign coordinator

Kenneth W. Parkinson
Lawyer for campaign unit

Gordon C. Strachan
Assisted Mr. Haldeman

COLSON IS NAMED

A Question of Veracity of the President Is Indirectly Raised

By ANTHONY RIPLEY
Special to The New York Times

WASHINGTON, March 1—A Federal grand jury today indicted seven men, all former officials of President Nixon's Administration or of his 1972 re-election campaign, on charges of covering up the Watergate scandal.

Never before have so many close and trusted advisers of an American President faced criminal accusations in a single indictment.

All were charged with conspiracy — a conspiracy, the grand jury said, that continued

Five pages of Watergate material with indictment text begin on Page 14.

"up to and including" today; six were charged additionally with obstruction of justice; two with perjury and three with false statements to the Federal Bureau of Investigation, the grand jury, or both.

The indictment accused one defendant, H. R. Haldeman, the former White House chief of staff, of lying when he quoted the President as saying "it would be wrong" to raise hush money for the perpetrators of the original Watergate burglary—a break-in June 17, 1972, at the Democratic National Committee headquarters.

Endorsed Statement

This indirectly raised a question about Mr. Nixon's veracity because he endorsed Mr. Haldeman's statement at a news conference last Aug. 22. The President recalled a meeting at the White House at which clemency for the Watergate defendants and financial support for their families was discussed. Mr. Nixon said he had told his White House counsel, John W. Dean 3d, "John it is, it is wrong, it won't work."

With the indictment, the grand jury handed to Chief Judge John J. Sirica of the Federal District Court here a sealed report, accompanied by a bulky briefcase reportedly containing information about Mr. Nixon's role in the Watergate scandal.

This information was presumably intended for the House Judiciary Committee, which is considering a motion to impeach the President and put him on trial before the Senate.

The defendants and the charges against them are as follows:

John N. Mitchell, former Attorney General and director of Mr. Nixon's 1968 and 1972 Presidential campaigns—conspiracy, obstruction of justice, false statements to the F.B.I., false statements to the grand jury and perjury.

Mr. Haldeman—conspiracy, obstruction of justice and perjury.

John D. Ehrlichman, former assistant to the President for domestic affairs—conspiracy, obstruction of justice, false statements to the F.B.I. and false statements to the grand jury.

Charles W. Colson, former special counsel to the President—conspiracy and obstruction of justice.

Robert C. Mardian, former aide to Mr. Mitchell in the 1972 campaign—conspiracy.

Kenneth W. Parkinson, former attorney for the Committee for the Re-election of the President—conspiracy and obstruction of justice.

Gordon C. Strachan, former aide to Mr. Haldeman—conspiracy, obstruction of justice and false statements to the grand jury.

The key conspiracy count

Continued on Page 16, Column 1

Heath, Trailing Labor Party In Britain, Declines to Resign

Special to The New York Times

LONDON, March 1—Prime Minister Heath, deprived of his majority in Parliament by Britain's voters, declined to resign tonight. His action raised the prospect that Mr. Heath's Conservatives, outnumbered by the Labor party in the House of Commons, would try to remain in power.

Thus Britain faced one of the gravest crises in her modern political history. The last time when neither main party won an over-all majority was in 1929.

There was no official word. But sources close to Mr. Heath said that he had told Queen Elizabeth he wanted to remain in office despite his party's failure to win an over-all majority in the general election yesterday.

Wilson Prepared to Govern

A few hours earlier, Harold Wilson, the leader of the Labor party, said that he was prepared to form a new Cabinet. Labor also failed to win a majority, but it holds five more seats than the Conservatives.

With the virtual stalemate between the two big parties, the balance of power in the new House would be held by smaller ones, including the Liberals, Scottish and Welsh

Nationalists and the Members from Northern Ireland.

If Mr. Heath carries on with a minority government, despite his campaign bid for a "fresh mandate" and a "strong" majority, the question is for how long. He could go down to defeat quickly in the new House of Commons if a majority voted "no confidence" on some issue that arose for debate.

If that occurred, it is expected that he would ask the Queen to call for Mr. Wilson to form a new Government. Any call for a new election is regarded as unlikely until sometime later after the party leaders have a chance to try to win support in the House.

It was Mr. Heath, on Feb. 7, who used his power as Prime Minister to order Parliament dissolved and to call yesterday's election.

His goal was a mandate to settle a strike in the Government-owned coal mines that

British Pound Plunges

The value of the British pound fell 1.85 cents and prices of stocks went down 24 points in hectic trading in London yesterday in reaction to the setback for Britain's Conservative Government. Details on Page 41.

had crippled the country's production and forced it onto a three-day work week. Yesterday that mandate from the voters eluded him.

Tonight this was the standing of the parties in the new House of Commons, compared with their standings in the old one:

	New	Old
Labor	301	287
Conservative	296	322
Liberal	14	11
Others	23	10
Undecided	1	

Mr. Heath, after a day of meetings with his advisers at 10 Downing Street, emerged shortly after 7:30 P.M. local time (3:30 P.M., New York time) for his meeting with the Queen, who had interrupted a visit to Australia to return here.

Statement Is Issued

A statement from 10 Downing Street said:

"The Queen has granted the Prime Minister's request to her to grant him an audience at 7:45 P.M. so that he can report on the current political situation."

If Mr. Heath had submitted his resignation, the announcement would have come quickly. But it was clear that he had

Continued on Page 10, Column 1

MITCHELL JUDGE HALTS TRIAL HERE

Weighs Motion for Mistrial Over 'Apparent Excesses' in Prosecutor's Speech

By RALPH BLUMENTHAL

Federal Judge Lee P. Gagliardi abruptly suspended yesterday the conspiracy-perjury trial of John N. Mitchell and Maurice H. Stans for what he called "apparent excesses" by the chief Government prosecutor in his opening statement.

Judge Gagliardi said that he would rule Monday on demands by defense attorneys for a mistrial. He ordered the prosecutor, Assistant United States Attorney James W. Rayhill, to submit a "documented response" with his "excuses."

While neither side would comment on the surprising development, some observers in the court believed it unlikely that the judge would decide to discharge the newly picked jury, which had been carefully isolated from news of yesterday's Watergate indictments naming Mr. Mitchell along with six others.

Conspiracy Charged

The historic trial was interrupted just after the Government had told the jury that it would prove that the defendants had conspired to quash a Federal investigation of Robert L. Vesco, the fugitive financier, in exchange for his secret $200,000 cash contribution to President Nixon's re-election campaign, that the defendants covered up the scheme and lied about it when questioned under oath.

At the close of his hour and 50 minutes presentation in the fifth-floor courtroom in the

Continued on Page 18, Column 6

Nixon Urges Quick Trials, Cautions on Prejudgment

By JOHN HERBERS
Special to The New York Times

WASHINGTON, March 1 — President Nixon expressed the hope today that trials arising out of the new Watergate indictments "will move quickly to a just conclusion." He also cautioned the nation to remember that the accused are presumed innocent unless proved guilty.

"The indictments indicate the judicial process is finally moving toward resolution of the matter," Gerald L. Warren, the White House deputy press secretary, said in a statement approved by Mr. Nixon. The statement, read to newsmen, added:

"It is the President's hope that the trials will move quickly to a just conclusion. The President is confident that all Americans will join him in recognizing that those indicted are presumed innocent unless proof of guilt is established in the courts."

The statement also declared that the President had "always maintained that the judicial system is the proper forum for the resolution of the questions concerning Watergate."

Two of the seven men accused in today's indictment, Charles W. Colson and Kenneth W. Parkinson, issued personal statements of innocence and predicted their eventual exoneration on the charges. The other five relied on their attorneys to issue brief statements of innocence. [Details, Page 16.]

Word of the Watergate indictments reached the Oval Office today via the news tickers, and the President—busy with policy meetings, ceremony and entertaining of Congressmen—reacted with his brief formal statement a short time later.

Gen. Alexander M. Haig Jr. and Ronald L. Ziegler, the President's chief assistants, informed Mr. Nixon of the charges against his former high associates just as the President was ending a meeting with his economic and energy advisers and was preparing to welcome the Mayor of Meridian, Miss., Tom Stuart, who had gotten 20,000 names on a petition to

Continued on Page 17, Column 3

SIRICA SAID TO GET FINDINGS ON NIXON

Grand Jury Reported to Ask Him to Give Evidence on Watergate to House

By JAMES M. NAUGHTON
Special to The New York Times

WASHINGTON, March 1—The Watergate grand jury reportedly asked Chief Judge John J. Sirica of the United States District Court today to give the House impeachment inquiry evidence relating to President Nixon's role in the Watergate case.

The grand jury issued a sealed "report" to the judge, and investigative sources said that they understood the document contained a description of the grand jury's findings about Mr. Nixon's possible involvement in the Watergate cover-up.

Moments later, the special Watergate prosecutor's office gave Judge Sirica a large briefcase said to contain a mass of documents and other evidence sought by the House Judiciary Committee for its investigation of the President's conduct in

Continued on Page 17, Column 1

RED CROSS VISITS 65 ISRAELI P.O.W.'S

Sees Prisoners in Syria— Kissinger Confers With Assad in Damascus

By BERNARD GWERTZMAN
Special to The New York Times

DAMASCUS, Syria, March 1—Israeli prisoners held by Syria, long the focus of a dispute that prevented troop-pullback negotiations, received their first visit from Red Cross inspectors today.

The visit was arranged as part of the latest round of Middle East diplomacy, which carried Secretary of State Kissinger today from Egypt to Israel and then to Syria. He immediately began talks here with President Hafez al-Assad to convey ideas on troop disengagements that he had just received from Premier Golda Meir and other top Israeli officials.

At the end of the session between President Assad and the Secretary of State, both American and Syrian spokesmen indicated that talks on the separation of forces would continue after Mr. Kissinger left here tomorrow on his way to return to the United States. There was no announcement that any firm agreement had been reached on how negotiations would take place.

The Syrian spokesman said that Mr. Assad had not accepted the Israeli ideas presented to him by Mr. Kissinger and had offered one in return, which Mr. Kissinger "will study

Continued on Page 4, Column 3

Two-Way Radios in Taxis To Help City Fight Crime

By WILL LISSNER

The city officially began a program yesterday to put on the streets thousands of cruising taxicab drivers trained in the observation and reporting of crime and who are in radio communication with the police.

The new auxiliary arm of the police is the Civilian Radio Motor Patrol, which, Mayor Beame said, already has 500 crime watchers at work — 350 in the Bedford Park section of the Bronx and 150 in communities in Brooklyn operating from a Sheepshead Bay base.

Many taxicabs are dispatched by radio, the dispatcher having the transmitter and the cab the receiver. These one-way systems cannot be used in this program. The patrol system in use links the dispatcher and the driver by a two-way radio.

Under the system, telephone lines link the dispatcher to the switchboard operator in the police station. When necessary, the desk sergeant can then talk directly to the taxicab driver.

Two similar networks are to be opened soon in Queens, one in Long Island City and one in Richmond Hill, according to Stanley Bakalar, president of the Associated Radio Metered

Taxi Owners Council.

"Eventually Manhattan and Staten Island will be covered, too," he added.

"This is another example of how we can use the city's greatest asset—its citizens—in attacking its number one problem, crime," Mayor Beame said. He and Police Commissioner Michael J. Codd and a group of Bronx officials joined in inaugurating the system at a ceremony at the Bedford Park station in the Bronx.

The program costs the city only the services of the coordinator, Lieut. John Higgins, and the training officers. In the Bronx the cost of installing the tie-lines between the taxi dispatchers and the police was paid for by the First National City Bank and the $12 monthly service charge for the tie-line phones is paid by the taxi cooperatives—the All City Radio Taxi Association and the Bronx Two-Way Radio Metered Taxi Company. Each taxi will display a yellow and black decal announcing its participation in "Civilian Radio Patrol, Community Service."

The city's police have a number of programs in operation using civilians to supplement the department's professional manpower. A primary one is the Auxiliary Police, whose members patrol the streets and perform other police functions under the supervision of police officers.

Another is the Blockwatcher Program, in which civilians act as the eyes of the police on their own block.

NEWS INDEX

The Scene in Sirica's Court: A Historic 13 Minutes

By LINDA CHARLTON
Special to The New York Times

WASHINGTON, March 1—At 10 A.M. today, Judge John J. Sirica was sitting in his chambers, reminiscing about his 16 years on the bench, whiling away the time until he could put a black robe over his gray suit and walk into Courtroom 2 to preside over history.

He arrived to be greeted with the shuffle of a crowd rising to its feet as a court functionary intoned ceremonial phrases, ending with the prayer for the country and for "this honorable court." Some 13 minutes and surprisingly few words later, it was over.

The small, wood-paneled courtroom, with a checkerboard cork floor, an American flag and seal and two maroon ceramic water pitchers as the only decorations, was filled—with lawyers, Watergate task force staff members and reporters. The long line of would-be specta-

tors that had started forming two hours before the 11 A.M. hearing was exiled to the corridor.

The prosecution's table was crowded with lawyers and papers. At the defense table, on the right side of the courtroom, sat a lone figure, Paul Murphy of the law firm of Hundley & Gacheris, representing John N. Mitchell.

The focus of attention was a group of 21 distributed

Continued on Page 18, Column 3

Assistant U.S. Attorney James W. Rayhill, standing, making his opening statement to the jury in the trial of John N. Mitchell, seated foreground, and Maurice H. Stans. Judge Lee P. Gagliardi is at upper left.

The New York Times/Martine Church

The New York Times

LATE CITY EDITION

Weather: Fair today; rain likely tonight. Chance of rain tomorrow. Temp. range: today 61-77; Wed. 62-84. Additional details on Page 82.

VOL.CXXIII...No.42,481   © 1974 The New York Times Company   NEW YORK, THURSDAY, MAY 16, 1974   20c beyond 50-mile radius of New York City, except Long Island. Higher in air delivery cities.   15 CENTS

Busing of Pupils Upheld In a Senate Vote of 47-46

Ban Urged by Gurney Fails After 6 Hours of Debate—Revision in Aid Formula May Cost Schools Here $23-Million

By RICHARD D. LYONS
Special to The New York Times

WASHINGTON, May 15 — The Senate in effect upheld today the busing of children to end school segregation by a vote of 47 to 46.

The victory for the Senate liberals came only seven weeks after the House of Representatives by a vote of 293 to 117 approved a provision to prohibit Federal courts from ordering long-distance busing of children.

Today's vote followed six hours of emotional debate. The critical Senate vote tabled an antibusing amendment offered by Senator Edward J. Gurney, Republican of Florida, to the Federal aid to education bill that has been on the Senate floor all week.

The motion to table was made by Senator Jacob K. Javits, Republican of New York.

In a radio address in March, President Nixon supported the

antibusing language of the House version of the Gurney amendment, which was introduced in the House by Representative Marvin L. Esch, Republican of Michigan.

After defeating the Gurney amendment, the Senate approved, by a vote of 56 to 36, a more limited provision prohibiting the busing of pupils from one school district into another unless it has been found that discrimination is practiced in both districts or that district lines in both districts were drawn for the purpose of maintaining segregation.

The amendment is aimed at situations such as that in Detroit, where a Federal court has ordered busing between city schools and those in affluent white suburbs. The Detroit case

Continued on Page 9, Column 1

Beame Asks $11.1-Billion For an 'Austerity' Budget

By GLENN FOWLER

Mayor Beame formally presented his first operating budget as the city's chief executive yesterday, labeling it an "austerity" blueprint that calls for spending $11.1-billion to run the municipal government in the fiscal year beginning July 1.

Declaring that he intended to provide "little in the way

Excerpts from Mayor Beame's budget are on Page 34.

of new money for new programs," Mr. Beame detailed in a 67-page message accompanying the basic document his financial acrobatics in overcoming a threatened $1.5-billion gap between income and outgo, enabling him finally to bring the budget into balance, as required by law.

The projected 1974-75 spending level, which is almost 8 per cent higher than the current fiscal year's actual outlay, spreads most of the available money among the areas of concern that have come to absorb much of the municipal treasury: public schools ($2.7-billion), welfare and related programs ($2.6-billion), public safety ($1.3-billion for police and fire) and health services ($1.2-billion).

One unusually large item is $1.5-billion for debt service — money to pay interest and amortization on the city's mounting debt — representing in the new budget a 63 per cent increase over the cost in the current fiscal year.

Mr. Beame placed the blame for the city's fiscal condition on his predecessor, Mayor John V. Lindsay, and he had harsh words for the

Continued on Page 34, Column 1

OIL DEPLETION AID FACES HOUSE VOTE

Democrats Mandate Action on Proposal to Repeal 22% Allowance Now

By EILEEN SHANAHAN
Special to The New York Times

WASHINGTON, May 15 — Democratic members of the House of Representatives voted overwhelmingly today to force a straight yes-or-no vote in the House on immediate termination of the 22 per cent depletion allowance for the oil industry.

The action by the House Democratic Caucus, though technically only on a procedural matter, brought repeal of the depletion allowance closer than it has ever been in its 50-year history.

The vote in the caucus came about after weeks of intensive strategy planning, lobbying and nose-counting masterminded by three organizations: the American Federation of Labor and Congress of Industrial Organizations, Ralph Nader's tax reform research group and Common Cause, the citizens' lobby.

Rep. Green Is Key

The action of the caucus also brought into prominence a new leader on tax issues among the liberal Democrats in the House, Representative William J. Green of Pennsylvania.

In addition, the vote marked the first time that the new rules of the Democratic Caucus had been used to make sure that the House got to vote on a specific issue. The rules were adopted in February, 1973.

The action was deplored by Frank N. Ikard, president of the American Petroleum Institute. He said that the caucus had displayed a "lynch mob attitude" and predicted that the nation would "suffer a devastating setback in its efforts to attain a reasonable degree of energy self-sufficiency" if the ultimate victory in Congress went to those who, as he put it, "are demanding punitive tax action aimed at petroleum producers."

The caucus voted to permit

Continued on Page 17, Column 1

HOUSE UNIT ISSUES 2 NEW SUBPOENAS TO NIXON FOR DATA

Some on the Judiciary Panel Charge Transcripts Omit Significant Material

By JAMES M. NAUGHTON
Special to The New York Times

WASHINGTON, May 15—The House Judiciary Committee issued today two new subpoenas for White House tape recordings and other documents amid charges by some committee members that significant portions of President Nixon's Watergate conversations had been omitted from edited White House transcripts.

In a series of votes on the two subpoenas, the committee

Text of two memorandums on tape subpoenas, Page 26.

demanded this morning that the President turn over to its impeachment inquiry the tape recordings of 11 Watergate-related conversations as well as diaries of Mr. Nixon's White House meetings over more than eight months in 1972 and 1973.

The committee has not received any of this material, either in tape or other documentary form.

Two White House recordings previously obtained by the Judiciary Committee were played for the panel members this afternoon, prompting several Democrats to increase their resolve to obtain tapes, and not transcripts, of the relevant Watergate conversations.

Significance Disputed

Two Democratic members of the panel, Representatives Robert F. Drinan of Massachusetts and Jerome R. Waldie of California, told reporters after hearing the tape of a Sept. 15, 1972, White House conversation that material had been omitted from the White House transcripts not because it was inaudible but, as Mr. Waldie stated it, "because of the content."

Both Democrats declined to specify the nature of the missing material, however, and some Republicans on the committee said that they did not regard the omissions as serious or deliberate.

"The only thing that was deleted was the expletives, nothing of substance." Representative Delbert L. Latta, Republican of Ohio, said after the four-hour closed hearing at which recordings were played for about 40 minutes.

Renewed Effort by Panel

The new subpoenas, which "commanded" Mr. Nixon to supply the recordings and diaries by next Wednesday, were the first step in a renewed and bipartisan effort by the Judiciary Committee to obtain tapes and documents that Mr. Nixon has so far refused to yield.

Continued on Page 26, Column 1

16 YOUNG ISRAELI HOSTAGES DIE AS TROOPS KILL 3 ARAB CAPTORS; KISSINGER TALKS DELAYED A DAY

Young victims being carried from school in Maalot after the clash between Arab guerrillas and Israeli troops
United Press International

A student, wounded in chest and arm, is carried from the Natia Meir school building
Associated Press

TERROR AT SCHOOL

Soldiers Rush Building as Attempt to Trade Prisoners Fails

By TERENCE SMITH
Special to The New York Times

MAALOT, Israel, May 15—A day of terror ended in this northern town this evening with a savage, 10-minute burst of gunfire and grenade explosions that killed three Arab terrorists and 16 of the highschool students they were holding hostage.

Early this morning, terrorists took command of the school, where about 90 students out on an excursion were sleeping. The three Arabs demanded the release of 20 prisoners held by Israel in return for the lives of the students.

An Israeli attempt to meet the demand failed and, as the deadline set by the guerrillas approached, soldiers rushed the school.

On 26th Independence Day

In the fighting that ensued, besides those killed 70 students were wounded, at least nine seriously. In the morning, as the day's terror began, a family of three was cut down by the Arab guerrillas as they entered the town. One soldier was also killed.

It was one of the bloodiest terrorist incidents in Israel's troubled history and it came on the 26th anniversary of the nation's independence.

After the decision to rush the school had been made, soldiers in bullet-proof vests surrounded the three-story building while snipers trained their sights on its shallow horizontal windows.

The firing broke out suddenly, while an officer with an electric megaphone was still pleading with the guerrillas in Arabic to postpone their 6 P.M. deadline.

Two of the three Arabs were hit by the opening burst of fire. One was apparently killed instantly, but the second had the strength to turn his automatic weapon on the students, spraying the second-story classroom indiscriminately.

Sought to Explode School

The third man tossed two grenades out the windows in an attempt to scatter the attacking soldiers. Then, according to one of the officers, the terrorist raced downstairs toward the entrance of the school where explosive charges had been placed. Before he could detonate them, soldiers shot him.

The screams of the terrified teen-agers could be heard a hundred yards away as the shooting erupted. One girl shrieked over and again, "Up here, he's up here," referring to the wounded terrorist who was still firing.

Even before the shooting

Continued on Page 18, Column 3

SETBACK IS SEEN IN PEACE EFFORTS

Moves for a Compromise on Israeli-Syrian Troops Are Called Impaired

Special to The New York Times

JERUSALEM, May 15—The terrorist attack at Maalot today forced Secretary of State Kissinger to suspend his Middle East peace efforts for one day. The attack, which occupied the Israeli Cabinet through the day, was denounced by Mr. Kissinger as "this mindless and irrational action." The Secretary made it clear to his aides that he was determined not to let it undermine the progress made so far in this current Middle East negotiating trip.

But the tragic events at Maalot were viewed by both Israeli and American officials as probably having the effect of impairing his efforts to extract any last-minute compromises from either Israel or Syria on disengagement on the Syrian front before his scheduled return to Washington over the weekend.

Mr. Kissinger had been slated to meet with Israeli officials, led by Premier Golda Meir, this morning after an Israeli Cabinet meeting scheduled to discuss Israel's final ideas on disengagement to be conveyed by Mr. Kissinger to Syrian officials.

But this morning, when the dimensions of the terrorist attack became known, Mr. Kissinger put off his plans to leave Israel for Syria, preferring to wait until Mrs. Meir and other Israeli officials could deal with the disengagement problems.

Israeli officials, who spoke from time to time with Mr.

Continued on Page 19, Column 4

SCHEEL IS ELECTED PRESIDENT IN BONN

Coalition Proves Strength in First-Ballot Victory— Bitterness Dissipates

By CRAIG R. WHITNEY
Special to The New York Times

BONN, May 15 — Walter Scheel was elected to the ceremonial office of the West German presidency today in a demonstration of solidarity between the two governing coalition parties, Mr. Scheel's Free Democrats and the Social Democrats.

The 54-year-old Mr. Scheel, who has been Vice Chancellor and Foreign Minister in the coalition Government since 1969, won a comfortable majority—530 of the 1,036 votes in the presidential electoral college on the first ballot. The fourth President since the formation of the West German Federal Republic in 1949, he is the first to be chosen so easily.

It was clear that despite bickering and fears of a revolt by some Social Democrats because of the resignation of their leader, Willy Brandt, from the chancellorship last week in the wake of a divisive spy scandal, the coalition was holding firmly together. There were only five abstentions and three absences. Mr. Scheel's opponent, Richard von Weizsäcker, received 498 votes, three fewer

Continued on Page 5, Column 5

CHAPIN SENTENCED TO 10-30 MONTHS

Former Nixon Aide Appeals Prison Term for Lying to Watergate Grand Jury

By ANTHONY RIPLEY

WASHINGTON, May 15 — Dwight L. Chapin, President Nixon's former appointments secretary, was sentenced today to a minimum of 10 months in prison for lying to a Watergate grand jury about political sabotage in the 1972 campaign.

Judge Gerhard A. Gesell imposed two concurrent sentences of 10 to 30 months each, calling it "a punishment sentence for a man who is not likely to repeat and needs no rehabilitation."

When Judge Gesell read the sentence, Mr. Chapin was apparently unmoved as he stood before the bench in United States District Court here. On April 5, he was convicted by a jury on two counts of lying about his dealings with Donald H. Segretti, an old college friend. Mr. Chapin was acquitted on a third count, and a fourth count was dismissed during the trial.

"It appears to the court that your resort to the convenience of swearing falsely when called before a grand jury cannot be condoned," Judge Gesell told the 33-year-old defendant. "I have therefore decided you

Continued on Page 26, Column 4

Threats by Nixon Reported on Tape Heard by Inquiry

By DAVID E. ROSENBAUM
Special to The New York Times

WASHINGTON, May 15—The tape recording of President Nixon's Sept. 15, 1972, conversation with H. R. Haldeman and John W. Dean 3d, which was heard today by members of the House Judiciary Committee, contains at least one long passage that does not appear in the edited White House transcript of that tape, according to a committee source.

In the passage told by the source, President Nixon threatens to punish The Washington Post and its attorney, Edward Bennett Williams, and notes specifically that The Post owns television stations.

There is the clear implication, according to the source, that the President hoped to take Government action to deprive The Post of its television licenses.

The Post won a Pulitzer Prize last year for its many disclosures about the Watergate case and other scandals in the Nixon Administration.

Reading from a copy of the transcript prepared by the impeachment inquiry staff, the

Continued on Page 26, Column 1

Haig Said to Testify Simon Warned of Hughes Inquiry

By JOHN M. CREWDSON
Special to The New York Times

WASHINGTON, May 15 — Gen. Alexander M. Haig Jr., reportedly told a closed-door session of the Senate Watergate committee today that he was warned a year ago by William E. Simon, then Deputy Secretary of the Treasury, that a Federal investigation of a $100,000 political contribution from Howard R. Hughes had reached the point where it could eventually prove an embarrassment to President Nixon.

Sources familiar with his testimony said General Haig, the White House chief of staff, who was confirmed last week as Secretary of the Treasury, was the individual who told him in the spring of 1973 that an Internal Revenue Service inquiry into the trail of the Hughes

money had led to Charles G. Rebozo, Mr. Nixon's close friend.

General Haig's testimony about his knowledge of the Hughes-Rebozo matter was given under oath during an hour-and-a-half session with the Watergate committee members and lawyers, after the President had agreed to waive a claim of executive privilege invoked earlier this month before the committee by the general.

The committee voted unanimously today to ask the full Senate to extend its Watergate case through the end of June. Senate Resolution 60, which authorizes the select committee's investiga-

Continued on Page 28, Column 4

Mrs. Meir Pledges Steps To Protect Israeli People

By BERNARD GWERTZMAN
Special to The New York Times

JERUSALEM, May 15—Premier Golda Meir promised a numbed nation tonight that Israel would do everything possible to protect her people against terrorist attacks.

Speaking on television, Mrs. Meir went into detail about the

Text of Mrs. Meir's television remarks appears on Page 18.

reverse her long-standing policy of not negotiating with terrorists. The Government was prepared to release 23 prisoners in return for the safety of the approximately 90 teen-aged hostages held by three Arab terrorists, the Premier said.

But the deal fell apart, she said, partly out of confusion, when the three terrorists insisted on a code word to begin negotiations. The code word never arrived from abroad for use by the French or Rumanian Ambassadors, who were prepared to begin discussions, she said.

Talking in a firm voice that occasionally faltered, and look-

Israel, she said, will "do everything in its power to cut off the hands that want to harm a child, an adult, a settlement, a town or a village."

Mrs. Meir affirmed that Israel had decided during the day to

Continued on Page 18, Column 5

Installation in Lisbon

Gen. António de Spínola took office as President of Portugal and named a left-leaning Government promising democracy at home and in Portuguese Africa. Details on Page 3.

Police-Killing Mistrial

A mistrial was declared here yesterday in the trial of five reputed members of the Black Liberation Army who were charged with murdering two policemen. Page 45.

Ald Sternberg is President of the Jack Keller Div.of WILLCOX & GIBBS WG-AMEX.—Advt.

SANDRA Lee Church graduated from Columbia University (A.B.) yesterday.—Advt.

"All the News That's Fit to Print"

The New York Times

LATE CITY EDITION

Weather: Sunny, mild today; cool tonight. Sunny, pleasant tomorrow. Temp. range: today 66-83; Friday 73-93. Highest Temp.-Hum. Index yesterday: 81. Details on Page 62.

VOL. CXXIII..No. 42,546

© 1974 The New York Times Company

NEW YORK, SATURDAY, JULY 20, 1974

20c beyond 50-mile radius of New York City, except Long Island. Higher in air delivery cities.

15 CENTS

TURKEY LANDS AN ARMED FORCE IN CYPRUS; DROPS PARATROOPERS INTO NICOSIA SECTOR

Doar Urges Committee to Vote for Nixon's Impeachment

5 MAJOR CHARGES

G.O.P. Counsel Backs Appeal to Committee for Senate Trial

By JAMES M. NAUGHTON
Special to The New York Times

WASHINGTON, July 19—The House Judiciary Committee's senior counsels to both the Democrats and Republicans urged the committee today to recommend a Senate trial of President Nixon on one or more of five central impeachment charges.

John M. Doar, the special counsel to the Democrats, told the committee as it began im-

Text of proposed articles of impeachment, Pages 17, 18.

peachment deliberations that he could not remain "indifferent" if President Nixon or any other President committed the "terrible deed of subverting the Constitution."

The special Republican counsel, Albert E. Jenner Jr., endorsed Mr. Doar's conclusions by admonishing the committee to live up to the standards set by the nation's founders.

29 Potential Articles

Mr Doar submitted to the panel 29 potential articles of impeachment—some drafted by the committee staff and others proposed by committee members—that represented various approaches to the following five fundamental allegations against Mr. Nixon:

¶Obstruction of justice in the Watergate and related scandals.

¶Abuse of Presidential power in dealings with Government agencies.

¶Contempt of Congress and the courts through the defiance of subpoenas for evidence.

¶Failure to adhere to an explicit constitutional duty to "take care that the laws be faithfully executed."

¶Denigration of the Presidency through underpayment of Federal income taxes and use of Federal funds to improve personal property.

Harsh Judgments Suggested

Along with the 29 potential charges against Mr. Nixon, Mr. Doar submitted a thick volume outlining a summary of the inquiry's key findings and suggesting harsh judgments about the President's conduct both before and after the 1972 Watergate burglary. [Page 19.]

The proposed impeachment articles drafted at Mr. Doar's direction contained language accusing the President of "having made it his policy to cover up and conceal responsibility" for the Watergate break-in at Democratic headquarters in June, 1972. Mr. Nixon was said to have furthered the alleged conspiracy through such means

Continued on Page 18, Column 4

Ziegler Condemns A 'Kangaroo Court'

By PHILIP SHABECOFF
Special to The New York Times

SAN CLEMENTE, Calif., July 19—In its harshest attack yet on the House Judiciary Committee, the White House accused the committee's counsel today of conducting a "kangaroo court" and challenged the right of its chief counsel to present articles of impeachment against President Nixon.

Ronald L. Ziegler, the White House press secretary, charged that the committee had made "a total shambles out of what should have been a fair proceeding."

Talking to reporters outside the President's office here, Mr. Ziegler accused the counsel of the committee, Peter W. Rodino Jr. of New Jersey, of "falsely presenting a picture of fairness."

Later, at a news briefing,

Continued on Page 19, Column 1

United Press International
Prince Juan Carlos de Borbón signing Spanish-American declaration in first official act as chief of state. At ceremony was Adm. Horacio Rivero, right, U.S. Ambassador.

House Unit Releases Data On I.T.T. and Milk Affair

Antitrust Suit Inquiry

By E. W. KENWORTHY
Special to The New York Times

WASHINGTON, July 19—The House Judiciary Committee published today voluminous documentation on the tangled web known as "the I.T.T. affair."

But no document substantiated conclusively an allegation that the Nixon Administra-

tion's settlement of an antitrust suit against the International Telephone and Telegraph Corporation was in return for the conglomerate's pledge of up to $400,000 for the Republican National Convention in 1972.

The settlement permitted the corporation to retain the Hartford Fire Insurance Company.

The allegation was at the core of the committee's inquiry as it pursued evidence of impeachable offenses, as it was at the core of the Senate Judiciary Committee's resumed hearings in March-April, 1972, on the nomination of Richard G. Kleindienst to be Attorney General.

In the 980 pages of the House committee's volume No. 5 of

Continued on Page 19, Column 1

Price Supports Studied

By WILLIAM ROBBINS
Special to The New York Times

WASHINGTON, July 19—President Nixon disclosed his decision to raise milk-price supports in 1971 after listening to an exposition by John B. Connally on political and economic considerations and on dairy cooperatives' potential for campaign funding, a new transcript released by the House Judiciary Committee showed today.

The President's decision became clear, according to the document, early in a White House discussion on the afternoon of March 23, 1971, after Mr. Connally, then Secretary of the Treasury, had said that Congress would probably raise milk-price supports if the Administration did not and told Mr. Nixon:

"If you do [veto the increase], you've cost yourself the money—you've lost your political advantage."

A short while later, the transcript shows, Mr. Nixon said: "Under the circumstances, I think the best thing to do is to just uh, relax and enjoy it."

Mr. Nixon, Mr. Connally and other aides then discussed a delay in making a public an-

Continued on Page 19, Column 2

Justices' Ruling on Tapes May Follow Vote by Panel

By WARREN WEAVER Jr.
Special to The New York Times

WASHINGTON, July 19—The Supreme Court may be unable or unwilling to hand down a decision in the White House tapes case until after the House Judiciary Committee has voted late next week whether to recommend the impeachment of President Nixon.

Whichever way the Justices decide, their ruling is expected to have a substantial impact on the impeachment proceedings, either upholding the President's unlimited concept of his authority or requiring him to surrender evidence that might further incriminate him and his former colleagues.

The case was argued on July 8, and Court officials said today that a decision could not be expected until next Tuesday at the earliest. One source predicted that the decision might not be handed down next week, which would postpone it until after the Judiciary Committee voting is over.

"I can't exclude that possibility, although I'm not signalling it," Barrett McGurn, the Court information officer, said.

Congressional leaders believe that a Supreme Court ruling

against the President could influence several undecided Republican members of the committee to vote for impeachment. In turn, the number of Republicans who support impeachment at the committee level is expected to have considerable influence on the size of the Republican vote in the House.

Conversely, if the Justices support President Nixon's refusal to surrender 64 more White House tapes to Federal District Judge John J. Sirica and order Mr. Nixon's name stricken from the Watergate cover-up indictment, the decision could stiffen committee re-

Continued on Page 19, Column 3

Brasco Convicted of Conspiracy To Take Truck-Contract Bribes

By ARNOLD H. LUBASCH

Representative Frank J. Brasco was convicted last night of conspiracy to take bribes to get a Post Office contract for a Mafia-controlled truck company.

The 41-year-old Brooklyn Democrat, whose first trial on the conspiracy charge resulted in a hung jury, bowed his head but maintained his composure when the guilty verdict was announced at the end of the month-long second trial in Federal District Court here.

His wife, Linda, who sat in the front row of the courtroom throughout the trial, moved quickly to Mr. Brasco's side and put her arms around his shoulders after the jury of five men and seven women reached the verdict following almost eight hours of deliberations.

Oct. 2 for sentencing Mr. Brasco, who faces up to five years in prison and a maximum fine of $10,000.

The short, solidly built Congressman, who served as an assistant district attorney in Brooklyn before he was elected to Congress in 1966, will appeal the verdict, according to his lawyer.

Mr. Brasco declined to comment on whether he would withdraw from his current race for re-election in the 11th Con-

Continued on Page 11, Column 1

CONSUMER PRICES UP 1% FOR MONTH

Yearly Increase 11.1%— Rise in Food Slows— Real Earnings Down

By EILEEN SHANAHAN
Special to The New York Times

WASHINGTON, July 19—Consumer prices rose by 1 per cent in June, despite a slowdown in the pace of the rise of food prices, the Labor Department reported today.

The June rise brought the index to a level that was 11.1 per cent higher than in June a year ago.

In the New York-Northeastern New Jersey-Long Island area, prices rose nine-tenths of 1 per cent from the prior month and 10.6 per cent from a year ago, according to the Bureau of Labor Statistics.

The yearly increase was the largest in 27 years, said Herbert Bienstock, regional head of the bureau.

Meat Prices Down

Nationally, although there was a decline in the prices of some food items, particularly meats, the drop was less than is normally expected in June. Thus, the Labor Department's seasonally adjusted statistics, which eliminate the effects of normal seasonal changes in an attempt to focus on basic trends, showed a rise of three-tenths of 1 per cent in food prices.

The food price trend was the best for this year except for April, when seasonally adjusted food prices declined.

The prices of all commodities other than food in the index,

Continued on Page 36, Column 2

FRANCO DELEGATES POWERS AS RULER TO JUAN CARLOS

Gravely Ill Spanish Leader, 81, Issues Decree That Delegates Authority

By HENRY GINIGER
Special to The New York Times

MADRID, July 19—The ailing Generalissimo Francisco Franco, his condition suddenly worsened, delegated his powers as ruler of Spain today to his designated successor, Prince Juan Carlos de Borbón.

From the clinic where he has been under treatment for phlebitis for 10 days, the 81-year-old chief of state issued a decree that interrupted for the first time his 35 years of dominion over his people, in favor of the 36-year-old heir to a throne that has been vacant since 1931.

The six doctors treating General Franco, after talking at noon of a "setback" caused by "gastric complications," acknowledged tonight that he had vomited blood early this morning. The bulletin at 8:30 P.M. said the bleeding had been checked and that all body functions continued within normal limits. It was believed that anticoagulants, administered to inhibit blood clots in the leg, had caused internal hemorrhaging.

Pio Cabanillas, Minister of Information, said tonight that the news from the general's bedside was satisfactory. He praised the calm of the Spanish people but throughout the day and evening members of the Franco family and dignitaries of the Government indicated their alarm by streaming in general's wife, Carmen, has been staying in a room adjoining his.

General Franco acted under Article 11 of Spain's Organic Laws, which states that in case of absence or illness of the chief of state, the royal heir will assume his duties. But there was a strong feeling in the excited Spanish political world that the end of a long and often bitter era was at hand and that a new chapter in Spanish history was about to open.

Speculation about a possible momentous change, eagerly awaited by some Spaniards, feared by others, had begun the moment General Franco entered the modern hospital named for him in northern Madrid on July 9. There had been frequent meetings between the general, the prince and other officials concerning a temporary delegation of power. But optimistic medical bulletins, backed by photographs published for the first time yes-

Continued on Page 3, Column 1

Soyuz Returns Safely

Two Soviet astronauts returned to earth safely after rehearsing docking techniques for next year's Soviet-American space mission. Page 62.

United Press International
Premier Bulent Ecevit announcing invasion in Ankara

U.S. Says Soviet Alerted Seven Airborne Divisions

By JOHN W. FINNEY
Special to The New York Times

WASHINGTON, July 19—Defense Department officials said today that the Soviet Union had put seven airborne divisions on alert.

American officials said that the eventual Soviet military intentions remained unclear and the Administration chose to make no announcement of the Soviet action and ordered no reciprocal alert for American forces.

[In Moscow qualified analysts said that there were indications that the Soviet Union might have placed one division on alert, and probably not more than that.]

Diplomatically, the United States applied pressure today on both the Greek and Turkish Governments in an effort to avoid a military clash between the two Atlantic alliance allies.

Undersecretary of State Joseph Sisco flew into Athens for meetings with Greek civilian and military leaders, and then rushed to Ankara for more talks there.

And in Washington, the State Department announced that Secretary of State Kissinger would meet on Monday with Archbishop Makarios. At the same time, American officials said that the United States Embassy in Athens recently sent a cablegram to Mr. Kissinger

that detailed the direct involvement of the Greek junta in the Cyprus coup. [Page 8.]

Discussing the Soviet alert, some officials speculated that Moscow was trying to demonstrate its support if Turkey made any move to intervene militarily on Cyprus. According to well-placed officials, there were indications that the Soviet Union had suggested to the Ankara Government that it could count on Soviet support.

As analyzed by Defense Department officials, the Turkish Government was following a deliberate, step-by-step strategy of seeming to indicate a willingness to take military action if no political solution could be reached.

The prevailing Pentagon view, however, was that the Turkish Government was not intent on rushing troops to Cyprus and had little military capability to carry out such action.

Turkey has a small number of amphibious craft, most of those small, open boat not suitable for carrying troops across long stretches of open water. As a result, officials believed Turkish forces would have considerable difficulty mounting an invasion against any resistance from pro-Greek forces on

Continued on Page 8, Column 7

3d City Audit Is Believed To Be Most Devastating

By MAURICE CARROLL

Mayor Beame called back yesterday the top team that served him when he was City Controller to try to blunt the impact of still a third audit report from his successor. At City Hall the latest report was said to be "even more devastating" than the first two, which have caused the Mayor profound embarrassment.

The third report deals with the management of $6.7-billion in pension funds. It is due to be made public next week by Controller Harrison J. Goldin, whose aides carefully guarded preliminary draft copies yesterday.

From what the Beame aides have been able to ferret out, the report "comes down hard on bad management," according to one Beame sympathizer in City Hall.

Some sources said the report would cite failure to reconcile city records with bank records by several hundreds of thousands of dollars, would criticize the use of handwritten ledgers—instead of computers—to keep track of investments and would urge that a more seasoned team be put in charge of pension investments.

It would say, these sources suggested, that the investment pattern under Mr. Beame had been unimaginative and unproductive and that opportunities to earn money for the retirement funds had been missed.

If so, that will be an ironic comment, because one of Mr. Beame's boasts as Controller was that he had begun exchanging low-yield city bonds held by the pension funds for high-interest stocks, taking a short-term loss on the exchange to increase the long-run yield.

Mr. Beame, whose mayoral campaign featured the slogan "If you don't know the buck, you don't know the job," was jolted personally as well as politically by the earlier reports.

Proud of his record and well aware of the source of his political reputation, Mr. Beame was upset by the two previous reports, which charged:

¶There was $5.4-million less in vault holding security deposits from people doing work for the city than the dog-eared, handwritten ledgers said should be there. Mr. Goldin

Continued on Page 32, Column 2

CLASHES REPORTED

Capital's Airport and Northern Port Are Bombed

By NAN ROBERTSON
Special to The New York Times

ANKARA, Turkey, Saturday, July 20—Premier Bulent Ecevit announced today that Turkey had invaded Cyprus by sea and air.

The attack came after intensive diplomatic activity involving officials of Turkey, Britain and the United States had broken down. The crisis grew out of the overthrow Monday of the elected Cypriot Government of Archbishop Makarios by the Greek-officered Cypriote National Guard.

The Turkish Premier, his voice trembling with emotion, announced the invasion after meeting with Under Secretary of State Joseph Sisco of the United States at 2 A.M. today Ankara time (7 P.M., Friday, New York time). Mr. Sisco had flown here from Athens last night to try to avert war.

Bombing Reported

[Turkish forces strafed and bombed the northern port of Kyrenia and dropped paratroopers into Turkish-Cypriote areas near Nicosia, the capital, Reuters reported.

[Turkish planes bombed Nicosia airport and a Cypriote National Guard camp south of the capital. Other Turkish jets dropped bombs and rockets on a camp of the small Greek army contingent in Cyprus on the western side of Nicosia.

[Machine-gun fire and explosions were heard from many directions around the capital, and Turkish Air Force planes flew overhead.

[The Cyprus radio broadcast an appeal to all Greek Cypriot with weapons to resist the Turkish invaders, and the Turkish Cypriote radio said that a Greek Cypriote gunboat had been sunk off Kyrenia.

[In San Clemente, Calif., President Nixon conferred late last night with Secretary of State Kissinger as soon as he received news that Turkish troops had landed in Cyprus, Reuters reported. The Presidential press secretary, Ronald L. Ziegler, said that "we are following the situation" but made no other comment.]

[The Pentagon ordered the United States carrier Forrestal and other naval vessels toward Cyprus in case American citizens in the area needed to be evacuated, The Associated Press reported.]

Premier Ecevit said that the decision to intervene in Cyprus

Continued on Page 8, Column 1

U.N. Calls Session Today About Cyprus

By Reuters

UNITED NATIONS, N.Y., Saturday, July 20—The Turkish troop landing in Cyprus will top the agenda at a Security Council meeting scheduled for 11 A.M. today.

One Western diplomat predicted a cease-fire should be the logical first order of business.

The Security Council had been scheduled to meet today to consider a resolution calling for the withdrawal of the Greek Army officers serving with the Cyprus National Guard that toppled the Makarios Government last Monday.

By KATHLEEN TELTSCH

UNITED NATIONS, N.Y., July 19—Archbishop Makarios, the deposed President of Cyprus appealed to the United Nations

Continued on Page 8, Column 4

"All the News That's Fit to Print"

The New York Times

LATE CITY EDITION

Weather: Partly cloudy today; cool tonight. Fair, pleasant tomorrow. Temp. range: today 65-78; Thursday 64-85. Highest Temp.-Hum. Index yesterday: 75. Details on Page 66.

VOL. CXXIII..No. 42,566   © 1974 The New York Times Company   NEW YORK, FRIDAY, AUGUST 9, 1974   20c beyond 50-mile radius of New York City, except Long Island. Higher in air delivery cities   15 CENTS

NIXON RESIGNS

HE URGES A TIME OF 'HEALING'; FORD WILL TAKE OFFICE TODAY

'Sacrifice' Is Praised; Kissinger to Remain

By ANTHONY RIPLEY
Special to The New York Times

WASHINGTON, Aug. 8—Vice President Ford praised President Nixon tonight for "one of the greatest personal sacrifices for the country and one of the finest personal decisions on behalf of all of us as Americans."

Mr. Ford, who will take office as the 38th President at noon tomorrow, vowed to continue Mr. Nixon's foreign policy and announced that Secretary of State Kissinger had agreed to stay on in the new Administration.

"I pledge to you tonight, as

SPECULATION RIFE ON VICE PRESIDENT

Some Ford Associates Say Selecting a Successor Could Take Weeks

By CHRISTOPHER LYDON
Special to The New York Times

WASHINGTON, Aug. 8—Potentially the most revealing and most important decision of Gerald R. Ford's Presidential debut — his choice of a successor in the Vice Presidency — was a much-discussed mystery here today.

Close friends of Mr. Ford continued to feed speculation about more than a dozen possible candidates. But none of the friends claimed to have discussed the Vice-Presidential question with Mr. Ford or to be speaking for him on it. A number of Ford associates thought he might hold off the decision for days or even weeks.

"Everybody's on tenterhooks up here," a Senator remarked this afternoon in a telephone interview from the Republican cloakroom, "but I think they're wasting their time. It's going to be a week or two. So far I'd say he's a loner on this issue."

Former Defense Secretary Melvin R. Laird, a Ford counselor in the House for more than a decade, was being quoted again today as saying he believes that Nelson A. Rocke-

Continued on Page 4, Column 1

I will pledge to you tomorrow and in the future, my best efforts in cooperation, leadership and dedication to what's good for America and good for the world," he said.

The Vice President, who never sought the nation's highest office and disclaimed any intention of seeking it after Mr. Nixon's term, will take the oath of office in a private ceremony at the White House.

Thus will he become the first man to serve as President without being chosen by the American people in an election. Tomorrow night he will address the nation on radio and television. It is expected that he will speak at 6 P.M.

All day today the signs of the historic change were in the air, sensed by the crowds that gathered along Pennsylvania

Text of Mr. Ford's remarks appears on Page 2.

Avenue near the White House. Applause rang out from the crowds when Mr. Ford appeared briefly.

After watching Mr. Nixon on television tonight with his family, the Vice President stepped outside into a slight drizzle at his suburban split-level home in nearby Alexandria, Va., to face television cameras and photographers assembled in the street and about 100 cheering neighbors.

Speaks Outside Home

Speaking without notes or a prepared text, Mr. Ford pledged to continue the Nixon foreign policy and called the Secretary of State "a very great man" whom he has known for many years.

On domestic policy, he said that he had been "very fortunate in my lifetime" to have adversaries in Congress but said that he did not think he had "a single enemy" there.

President Nixon had cited in his resignation address his lack of support in Congress as one of the major reasons for his resignation.

Mr. Ford said, "The net result is that I think tomorrow I can start out working with Democrats and with Republi-

Continued on Page 4, Column 3

The New York Times/William E. Sauro
Vice President Ford meeting with newsmen last night

United Press International
President Nixon on TV as he announced his resignation

The 37th President Is First to Quit Post

By JOHN HERBERS
Special to The New York Times

WASHINGTON, Aug. 8—Richard Milhous Nixon, the 37th President of the United States, announced tonight that he had given up his long and arduous fight to remain in office and would resign, effective at noon tomorrow.

At that hour, Gerald Rudolph Ford, whom Mr. Nixon nominated for Vice President last Oct. 12, will be sworn in as the 38th President, to serve out the 895 days remaining in Mr. Nixon's second term.

Less that two years after his landslide re-election victory, Mr. Nixon, in a conciliatory address on national

Text of the address will be found on Page 2.

television, said that he was leaving not with a sense of bitterness but with a hope that his departure would start a "process of healing that is so desperately needed in America."

He spoke of regret for any "injuries" done "in the course of the events that led to this decision." He acknowledged that some of his judgments had been wrong.

The 61-year-old Mr. Nixon, appearing calm and resigned to his fate as a victim of the Watergate scandal, became the first President in the history of the Republic to resign from office. Only 10 months earlier Spiro Agnew resigned the Vice-Presidency.

Speaks of Pain at Yielding Post

Mr. Nixon, speaking from the Oval Office, where his successor will be sworn in tomorrow, may well have delivered his most effective speech since the Watergate scandals began to swamp his Administration in early 1973.

In tone and content, the 15-minute address was in sharp contrast to his frequently combative language of the past, especially his first "farewell" appearance—that of 1962, when he announced he was retiring from politics after losing the California governorship race and declared that the news media would not have "Nixon to kick around" anymore.

Yet he spoke tonight of how painful it was for him to give up the office.

"I would have preferred to carry through to the finish whatever the personal agony it would have involved, and my family unanimously urged me to do so," he said.

Puts 'Interests of America First'

"I have never been a quitter," he said. "To leave office before my term is completed is opposed to every instinct in my body." But he said that he had decided to put "the interests of America first."

Conceding that he did not have the votes in Congress to escape impeachment in the House and conviction in the Senate, Mr. Nixon said, "To continue to fight through the months ahead for my personal vindication would almost totally absorb the time and attention of the President and the Congress in a period when our entire focus should be on the great issues of peace abroad and prosperity without inflation at home."

"Therefore," he continued, "I shall resign the Presidency effective at noon tomorrow. Vice President Ford will be

Continued on Page 3, Column 1

POLITICAL SCENE SHARPLY ALTERED

G.O.P. Prospects Improved, Ford in Good Spot for '76 and Watergate Fades

By R. W. APPLE Jr.
Special to The New York Times

WASHINGTON, Aug. 8—President Nixon's resignation drastically altered the American political landscape.

It improved Republican prospects for the Congressional elections in November, thrust Vice President Ford into the favorite's role for the 1976 Presidential election, ended the Watergate agony that has served to bind together the heterogeneous Democratic party and removed from the political stage the man who was the dominant Republican for the last 15 years.

In a larger sense, it seemed to presage an era of more open government, of more cooperation and less antagonism between Capitol Hill and the White House and of decline of the White House staff as an independent power center.

Lives Are Altered

A kind of "honeymoon" between the executive and legislative branches was widely predicted by Congressional leaders today. Congressmen who knew Mr. Ford for years as a Capitol Hill colleague said that they expected to work closely with him.

At least in the beginning, pragmatic conservatism is expected to remain the dominant ideological tone in the executive branch.

How that will be translated into policies, and how those policies will shape the political future, will not be clear for weeks. But experts in the two fields forecast an essentially unchanged foreign policy and a similar, but more carefully and consistently applied, economic policy.

By his decision, Mr. Nixon

Continued on Page 6, Column 4

Rise and Fall
Appraisal of Nixon Career

By ROBERT B. SEMPLE Jr.

The central question is how a man who won so much could have lost so much. How could a public figure who so well perceived the instincts of the majority of his countrymen have misused the powers and duties those same countrymen so eagerly ceded to him?

That image has only been reinforced and deepened by the transcripts of three conversations with H. R. Haldeman on June 23, 1972, six days after the Watergate break-in, which were released on Aug. 5, and the edited transcripts of White House conversations published April 30. Whatever history's judgment of those tapes, this much was clear: Faced with mounting evidence of deception and wrongdoing in his own official family, he sought not to confront the issue but to manipulate it until he himself became part of the deception.

Mr. Nixon used the words "I am a political man" proudly, as if to challenge the moralists, but in the end they became his epitaph—a possible explanation for both his success and failure.

For if the words implied the presence of a talent for finding opportunities for political prof-

Continued on Page 11, Column 1

The historians will be kept busy on these questions, but for those who spent their time observing Mr. Nixon for the last six years the answer may well be found in a phrase he often applied to himself. "At bottom," he used to say, "I am a political man."

By his own description, he was a man of action rather than contemplation, a tactician rather than a theologian, a student of technique who seemed always impatient with substance, a figure whose exceptional antennae seemed to dwarf and even hide what lay at the core.

To his enemies, he has been both manipulative and synthetic; to his friends, a pragmatist unencumbered by inflexible principles; to those who watched him, a man who learned to run before he had learned to walk

JAWORSKI ASSERTS NO DEAL WAS MADE

Says Nixon Did Not Ask for and Was Not Given a Way to Avoid Prosecution

By RICHARD D. LYONS
Special to The New York Times

WASHINGTON, Aug. 8—Leon Jaworski, the special Watergate prosecutor, said tonight after President Nixon's resignation speech that no deals had been either made or offered and that Mr. Nixon immunity from prosecution on any charges that might stem from the Watergate scandal.

"There has been no agreement or understanding of any sort between the President or his representatives and the special prosecutor relating in any way to the President's resignation," Mr. Jaworski said in a statement issued by his office.

Mr. Jaworski's words, plus the fact that the President made no mention of the immunity issue in his address to the nation, left open the possibility, at least for the moment, that Mr. Nixon might be charged and stand trial.

No Immunity Sought

Mr. Nixon did not ask for any immunity assurances from Mr. Jaworski before the resignation speech, the prosecutor said, adding that none had been offered.

As Mr. Jaworski put it, "The special prosecutor's office was not asked for any such agreement or understanding and offered none."

"Although I was informed of the President's decision this afternoon, my office did not participate in any way in the President's decision to resign," the statement concluded.

Mr. Jaworski met earlier today with Gen. Alexander M. Haig Jr., the White House chief of staff, but that meeting was said to have been only for the purpose of informing the special prosecutor of what the President would say later in the evening.

The meeting did not take place in the White House, presumably because Mr. Jaworski would have been recognized there, and his visit would have excited speculation.

Earlier today, there were moves in both houses of Congress to grant Mr. Nixon immunity from prosecution, but

Continued on Page 2, Column 4

The Other Major News

Wholesale Prices Up

A new upward surge of farm prices joined a big jump in industrial prices to produce the year's largest monthly increase in the wholesale price index. The rise for July was 3.7 per cent, seasonally adjusted, and 3.9 per cent before adjustment. Page 45.

Election Bill Voted

The House approved by a vote of 355 to 48 a broad campaign-finance reform bill. The measure would set limits on political contributions, restrict candidate spending and provide subsidies for Presidential primaries, conventions and elections. The bill now goes to a House-Senate conference committee. Page 36.

Cyprus Talks Open

The foreign ministers of Greece, Turkey and Britain met in Geneva to try to work out an effective cease-fire on Cyprus and to tackle the political problems behind the fighting there. Page 16.

On Cyprus, acting President

Glafkos Clerides named a moderate Cabinet stripped of any militant proponents of union with Greece.

Mr. Clerides, who will occupy the key posts of Foreign Affairs and Interior, left for Athens on his way to Geneva for the talks on a political settlement. Page 16.

10 Police Accused

Ten New York City police sergeants were arrested for allegedly participating in a "club" that collected more than $250,000 over a decade from legitimate businesses and illegal rackets operations in Queens. Page 68.

Meskill Named Judge

Gov. Thomas J. Meskill of Connecticut was nominated by President Nixon to a seat on the Federal bench. Mr. Meskill, a moderate, stunned the state Republican party earlier this year by declining to run for a second term amid reports that he had been offered a judgeship. Page 38.

A Tiny G.O.P. Bastion Feels Loss and Relief

By PRANAY GUPTE
Special to The New York Times

SHELTER ISLAND, L.I., Aug. 8—Six years after he put it on his car, Evans K. Griffing sadly stripped off his bold, red-lettered bumper sticker today — the one that said "NIXON."

Mr. Griffing felt a sense of loss. So did hundreds of people in this conservative community 100 miles east of New York City.

In 1968 and 1972, Suffolk County gave Richard M. Nixon the largest single election plurality of any county in the United States. Today all that had changed on Shelter Island.

As the hour of the President's resignation announcement approached, many islanders expressed both a feeling of hurt at having been "betrayed" by Mr. Nixon and relief that he was leaving office.

"We tried to stay by him till the very end," said Thomas L. Jernick, the Town Supervisor. "But when he disclosed on Monday that he had covered

Continued on Page 7, Column 6

up his role in Watergate, we couldn't support him any more. He lied to us, and for a President of the United States to lie is inexcusable."

"We really believed in Mr. Nixon" was a phrase used again and again by dozens of islanders today.

At the same time they spoke hopefully of the Ford Administration and of moving urgently to tasks long neglected—ending the nation's political turmoil and easing its economic distress.

Shelter Island has 1,800 year-round residents, most of whom are registered Republicans.

Only last June interviews with islanders indicated that whatever else Watergate had done, it apparently had not diluted Shelter Island's faith in Mr. Nixon or relief that he was leaving office.

Only Nixon Is Serene At Sad White House

By PHILIP SHABECOFF
Special to The New York Times

WASHINGTON, Aug. 8—On his 2,027th and penultimate day as President of the United States, with his staff and family unable to conceal their anguish, Richard M. Nixon went composedly through the schedule of a busy President.

He met with his Vice President and the bipartisan leadership of Congress. He appointed Federal judges, accepted resignations from executive agencies and signed several laws.

He vetoed as inflationary an appropriation bill for the Department of Agriculture and the Environmental Protection Agency.

He also announced, over national television, that tomorrow he would resign his high office.

Mr. Nixon did not loosen his self control even when he talked of his "regret" and his "sadness" at leaving the Presidency. His delivery, with its familiar half-smiles, did not re-

Continued on Page 3, Column 6

flect the momentous message he had for his audience: that at noon tomorrow he would become the first healthy, living American President to leave office before his term expired.

At 12:30 this afternoon, the White House press secretary, Ronald L. Ziegler, announced that the President would address the nation at 9 P.M.

Mr. Ziegler did not say what the speech would be about. He did not have to. He choked on his words several times and was struggling visibly to keep himself under control as he left the rostrum of the packed but hushed briefing room of the White House.

The young women who work in the press office went through the motions of doing their jobs while tears streamed down their faces.

But the President himself, according to his appointments

Continued on Page 3, Column 6

NEWS INDEX		
		Page
About New York 37	Man in the News 7	
Art 23	Movies 19-26	
Books 31	Music 19-26	
Bridge 31	Obituaries 42	
Business 45-53	Op-Ed 35	
Crossword 31	Sports 27-30	
Editorials 34	Theaters 19-26	
Family/Style 43	Transportation 66	
Financial 43-53	TV and Radio 67	
Going Out Guide 23	Weather 66	
News Summary and Index, Page 39		

JOIN the faculty on the phone. Call Metropolitan Opera subscription.—ADVT.

"All the News That's Fit to Print"

The New York Times

LATE CITY EDITION
Weather: Partly sunny today; cool tonight. Partly sunny tomorrow. Temp. range: today 65-78; Friday 68-84. Highest Temp.-Hum. Index yesterday: 78. Details on Page 58.

VOL. CXXIII...No. 42,567   © 1974 The New York Times Company   NEW YORK, SATURDAY, AUGUST 10, 1974   20¢ beyond 50-mile radius of New York City, except Long Island. Higher in air delivery cities.   15 CENTS

FORD SWORN IN AS PRESIDENT; ASSERTS 'NIGHTMARE IS OVER'

Nixon Bids an Emotional Farewell to Washington

TEARS AT PARTING

Ex-President Warns Against Bitterness and Revenge

By JAMES T. WOOTEN
Special to The New York Times

WASHINGTON, Aug. 9 — Richard M. Nixon, his face wet with tears, bade an emotional farewell to the remnants of his broken Administration today, urging its members to be proud of their record in government and warning them against bitterness, self-pity and revenge.

"Always remember, others may hate you," he told mem-

The text of Nixon's speech is printed on Page 4.

bers of his Cabinet and staff in a final gathering at the White House, "but those who hate you don't win unless you hate them—and then you destroy yourself."

Shortly thereafter, for the last time as President of the United States, he strode up the ramp of the plane that had taken him to the capitals of the world and was flown home to California, where his career in American politics began nearly thirty years ago.

It was 11:35 A.M. here when President Nixon's letter of resignation was delivered to the office of Secretary of State Kissinger. This is what it said:

"Dear Mr. Secretary: I hereby resign the office of President of the United States. Sincerely, Richard Nixon."

Greeted by 5,000

Soon after his departure, while the giant jet was soaring high above the heartland of the country, Gerald R. Ford was sworn in here as the nation's President.

Despite that new status, 5,000 people greeted his arrival in his native state at El Toro Marine Base. They cheered and applauded when, with his wife, Pat, standing nearby, Mr. Nixon stepped to a waiting microphone, squinted into the brilliant midday heat and said: "We're home."

After a few more remarks, a helicopter whisked the former President, Mrs. Nixon, their daughter Tricia and her husband Edward F. Cox, to La Casa Pacifica, the sprawling seaside villa near San Clemente.

Mr. Nixon's day began in the mist and rain of a humid Washington morning, when Manolo Sanchez, his long-time valet, laid out the clothes he would wear during the final hours of

Continued on Page 4, Column 1

Gerald R. Ford takes the Presidential oath, administered by Chief Justice Warren E. Burger. Mrs. Ford attends the White House ceremony.
Associated Press

G.M. to Raise Prices 9.5% On 1975 Cars and Trucks

Special to The New York Times

DETROIT, Aug. 9 — The General Motors Corporation announced today that it would raise prices of 1975 model cars and trucks by an average of $480 or 9.5 per cent.

The price increase will include about $130, or 2.5 per cent for government - required pollution control equipment-catalytic converters, while $350, or 7 per cent, will be to cover added labor and material costs, the corporation said.

Mack W. Worden, G.M. vice president, said the announcement in a letter sent to dealers Thursday and released publicly today. G.M. is traditionally the price pace-setter for the auto industry. The increases it sets are expected to be matched by its competitors.

Ford Sending Notices

The Ford Motor Company has already told its dealers it is sending them advanced billing notices of an average 8 per cent increase above the 1974 prices, which is calculated to mean an increase ranging from about $225 to $800, depending on the model.

Chrysler Corporation officials have indicated their price increases will be in the same area.

A Chrysler spokesman said today that next week "we are going to be mailing tentative price bulletins on 1975 trucks.

They will be in the same ball park as the G.M. and Ford increases. But that is as much as we are going to say at the present time."

Mr. Worden, in charge of the G.M. marketing staff, said that "based on past practice we would expect the Bureau of Labor Statistics will recognize "the catalytic converter's added value and not consider it a price increase in their published data."

Mr. Worden told the dealers G.M recognized the increases were "substantial" but said the corporation had "no alternative in light of rapidly rising labor and material costs over which we have only limited control and the necessity of complying with 1975 emission standards, which have been mandated by the Government."

As for the other auto com-

Continued on Page 36, Column 4

Friedmann Case Ends

The third and last person charged with the 1972 murder of Wolfgang Friedmann, Columbia University law professor, pleaded guilty to robbery last night. The others had earlier pleaded guilty to robbery. As a result, none of those who have admitted robbing the professor will be convicted of murdering him. Page 33.

PAPERS AND TAPES ISSUES IN CAPITAL

Impoundment of Nixon Data in White House Is Urged by Some in Congress

By RICHARD D. LYONS

WASHINGTON, Aug. 9 — On the heels of Richard M. Nixon's resignation, some members of Congress were urging impoundment of Presidential documents still in the White House. A few even demanded that the Watergate investigations be continued.

But Representative Peter W. Rodino Jr. said after a morning discussion of whether his House Judiciary Committee should make another attempt to obtain the 147 subpoenaed Presidential tape recordings that "we're not an investigative body."

"I do not think the public would stand for it," Mr. Ford said then.

"Our inquiry is at an end," the New Jersey Democrat said in expressing what seemed to be the feeling of the majority of the membership of both houses of Congress.

Yet the disposition and even ownership of the vast amount of Presidential records, some of which could be used as evidence in forthcoming trials, was a recurring question that remained unresolved.

As Representative Jonathan

Continued on Page 7, Column 6

Aide Doubtful That Ford Would Give Nixon Pardon

By LESLEY OELSNER
Special to The New York Times

WASHINGTON, Aug. 9 — The new White House press secretary, J. F. terHorst, suggested today that President Ford was not likely to grant a pardon to former President Nixon. The press secretary was asked at a briefing this afternoon about the prospects of a pardon.

He replied that he had not spoken to Mr. Ford about the question directly, but that the President had apparently stated his position on the matter last fall, during the Senate confirmation hearings into his nomination as Vice President.

Mr. Nixon's prospects for avoiding criminal prosecution thus remained in doubt, with the office of the special Watergate prosecutor saying only that a decision on whether to prosecute had not been made.

Mr. Nixon lost whatever immunity from prosecution he may have had when he resigned office. According to Mr. terHorst, Mr. Nixon did not try to pardon himself before leaving office, nor did he grant pardons to anyone else.

Some Republican members of Congress urged today that Mr. Nixon not be prosecuted, saying that he had already suffered enough. But even among Republicans, the sentiment was not unanimous.

Senator Edward W. Brooke, Republican of Massachusetts, submitted a resolution to the Senate yesterday expressing the "sense" of the Congress

Continued on Page 5, Column 2

A Plea to Bind Up Watergate Wounds

By MARJORIE HUNTER
Special to The New York Times

WASHINGTON, Aug. 9 — Gerald Rudolph Ford became the 38th President of the United States today, declaring that "our long national nightmare is over."

Calling upon the nation to "bind up the internal wounds of Watergate," he said, "Our Constitution works. Our great Republic is a government of laws and not of men. Here the people rule."

And then, his voice filled with emotion, he urged the nation to pray for his predecessor

The text of Ford's address will be found on Page 3.

and friend of a quarter century, Richard Milhous Nixon.

"May our former President, who brought peace to millions, find it for himself," he said.

Mr. Ford assumed the powers of the Presidency at 11:35 A.M. the moment that Mr. Nixon's letter of resignation was handed to Secretary of State Kissinger.

Then, at 12:03 P.M., he was administered the oath of office in the historic East Room of the White House by Chief Justice Warren E. Burger before an overflow crowd of friends, Cabinet and former Congressional colleagues from both parties.

Wife Holds Bible

It was in that same room, scarcely two hours earlier, that Mr. Nixon said an emotional good-by to his Cabinet and top aides.

Raising his right hand, Mr. Ford rested his left hand on a Bible held by his wife and opened to one of his favorite passages, the fifth and sixth verses of the third chapter of Proverbs: "Trust in the Lord with all thine heart; and lean not unto thine own understanding. In all thy ways acknowledge Him, and He shall direct thy paths."

Then, in a firm voice, he took the oath of office: "I, Gerald R. Ford, do solemnly swear that I will faithfully execute the office of President of the United States and will to the best of my ability preserve, protect and defend the

Constitution of the United States."

As the heavy applause ended, the 61-year-old President began perhaps the most moving speech of his career. Speaking in his flat, Middle Western tone, but with what appeared to be a new sense of self-assurance, he said that he was assuming the Presidency under circumstances never before experienced by Americans.

Minds Are Troubled

"This is an hour of history that troubles our minds and hurts our hearts," he said.

"Therefore," he continued, "I feel it is my first duty to make an unprecedented compact with my countrymen. Not an inaugural address, not a fireside chat, not a campaign speech. Just a little straight talk among friends. I intend it to be the first of many."

As the first American to assume the office after the resignation of a President, Mr. Ford said that he was "acutely aware that you have not elected me as your President by your ballots."

"So I ask you to confirm me as your President with your prayers," he added.

He declared that he had not gained office by secret promises, that he had not campaigned either for the Presidency or the Vice-Presidency.

"I have not subscribed to any partisan platform," he said. "I am indebted to no man and only to one woman, my dear wife."

This was reminiscent of his earlier "I am my own man," a declaration that he repeated frequently in recent months as he sought to remain loyal to Mr. Nixon and at the same time hold himself above the spreading taint of the Watergate affair.

He said that while he had not sought the responsibility, he would not shirk it. He said that those who nominated him and confirmed him just eight months ago as Vice President were his friends from both parties.

"It is only fitting then that I

Continued on Page 3, Column 1

4 NAMED TO HELP FORD'S TRANSITION

All on New Panel Served in House—President Vows Open Administration

By JOHN HERBERS
Special to The New York Times

WASHINGTON, Aug. 9 — Immediately after he was sworn in today as the nation's 38th President, Gerald R. Ford took control of the Presidency and moved to give it a character and shape different from that of his predecessor, Richard M. Nixon.

After declaring in his inaugural speech that "here the people rule," President Ford named a four-member committee composed of former elected officials to oversee the transition and make recommendations for staff changes.

The four are William W. Scranton, former Governor of Pennsylvania; Donald M. Rumsfeld, Ambassador to the North Atlantic Treaty Organization and a former Republican member of Congress from Illinois; Rogers C. B. Morton, Secretary of the Interior and a former

Continued on Page 5, Column 2

President and Kissinger Confer With the Envoys of 60 Nations

By BERNARD GWERTZMAN
Special to The New York Times

WASHINGTON, Aug. 9 — President Ford undertook to convince foreign governments today that he would pursue the same foreign policy objectives that brought wide respect to Richard M. Nixon.

Two hours after taking the oath as President, Mr. Ford, assisted by Secretary of State Kissinger, who will retain his office, began meeting with about 60 envoys—some in groups and some individually—in brief sessions that lasted into the early evening.

The substance of what was said was, in general, a reaffirmation of well-known American policy positions. But Mr.

Ford and Mr. Kissinger believed the exercise to be necessary to emphasize that there would be no significant change during the transition period in which Mr. Ford, who is less experienced in foreign affairs than his predecessor, makes his leadership felt.

Priority was given to a group meeting in the Roosevelt Room of the White House with members of the North Atlantic Treaty Organization. In a pattern followed in other sessions, Mr. Kissinger and members of his staff met with 13 envoys for about 20 minutes

Continued on Page 6, Column 6

Gains of Watergate

Positive and Hopeful Results Found As the Transition Is Made Smoothly

By CLIFTON DANIEL
Special to The New York Times

WASHINGTON, Aug. 9 — Watergate has now joined Teapot Dome, Credit Mobilier and the Whisky Ring in the lexicon of political infamy. Yet, in millions of minds it also symbolizes the finest hour of American democracy. A President has been deposed, but the Republic endures. Its institutions have survived, and some are saying they have been strengthened as well. Even the Presidency, which Richard M. Nixon professed to be so anxious to protect, shows no signs of debility. The man in the White House is as powerful today as he was yesterday, although his name has changed from Nixon to Ford.

He is just as powerful, although, as the new President said today, he is "acutely aware" that he was not elected by the votes of the people, whereas his predecessor won the largest popular majority in history.

Under the United States

Constitution, removal of the President requires drastic surgery, not just a shift in the political balance, as it does in the parliamentary democracies. However, the surgery performed on the American Government this week, while agonizing and painful, has done a minimum of visible damage to the body politic.

Mr. Nixon himself has said that one way to judge a country is to see how it effects a transfer of power. Today's transfer was effected without missing a heartbeat.

"Our Constitution works," President Ford proclaimed after taking the oath of office. "Here the people rule."

"All in all," William P.

Continued on Page 7, Column 3

President Nixon at ceremony where he bade his Cabinet and staff good-by. At left is his daughter Julie Eisenhower.
The New York Times/Mike Lien

"All the News That's Fit to Print"

The New York Times

LATE CITY EDITION

Weather: Warm, partly sunny today; partly cloudy tonight, tomorrow. Temp. range: today 62-78; Sunday 58-77. Highest Temp.-Hum. Index yesterday: 72. Details on Page 66.

VOL. CXXIII .. No. 42,597   © 1974 The New York Times Company   NEW YORK, MONDAY, SEPTEMBER 9, 1974   Higher in air delivery cities.   20 CENTS

FORD GIVES PARDON TO NIXON, WHO REGRETS 'MY MISTAKES'

U.S.-Bound Plane With 88 Crashes in Sea Off Greece

All on T.W.A. Flight From Tel Aviv Are Believed Dead—Wreckage Is Sighted

By The Associated Press

ATHENS, Sept. 8 — A Trans World Airlines jet bound for the United States with 88 persons aboard crashed today in the stormy Ionian Sea off Greece. The Greek Civil Aviation Authority said there appeared to be no survivors.

T.W.A. said that the Boeing 707 fell from an overcast sky after the pilot reported that an engine had failed.

Flight 841 originated in Tel Aviv, stopped in Athens and was scheduled to make stops in Rome and New York.

The airline's Tel Aviv office said 49 passengers boarded

© The New York Times/Sept. 9, 1974

the plane there for Rome and the United States. They included 17 Americans, including a baby, 13 Japanese, four Italians, four French, three Indians, two Iranians, two Israelis, two Sri Lankans, an Australian and a Canadian.

The nationalities of 30 other passengers and the nine crew members were not immediately known. [Reuters reported a total of 37 Americans aboard.]

[In Beirut, it was reported that a Palestinian youth organization said it had placed a guerrilla aboard the plane with a bomb. In New York, however, a spokesman for T.W.A. said sabotage was "highly unlikely."]

"All that can be seen by our overflying planes are remnants of the wreckage and bodies floating on the surface," said a Greek aviation official. "The stormy sea in the area is making it difficult for our ships to approach.

"Only when our ships can get nearer will we be able to

Continued on Page 6, Column 1

State Panel Charges City Fails to Pursue Fugitives

By SELWYN RAAB

The State Commission of Investigation disclosed yesterday that the backlog of missing bail jumpers and probation violators in the city had risen during the last three years from 82,000 to 130,000.

After sifting through voluminous police and court records, the commission largely blamed the Police Department's warrant division for the 60 per cent increase since 1971 in unexecuted warrants for criminal defendants who fail to appear in court. The police division is primarily responsible for capturing such fugitives.

Sharply criticizing the performance of the division over the last three years, the investigation commission said in a report that it had found that warrant officers rarely worked at night or on weekends and that a typical attempt to track down a fugitive consisted of no

more than one or two visits to an often fictitious home address given by the suspect.

The commission described the problem of fugitives here as "critical to the public safety" and called for a major reorganization of the warrant division.

"At the present time the people of New York City are unnecessarily subjected to the risk of grave harm from known criminals because of ineffective warrant enforcement," the commission declared in its report.

In response to the findings, Police Commissioner Michael J. Codd said he was "concerned" by the growing backlog, and he hinted there might be a reorganization of the warrant division.

He also announced the assignment of First Deputy Com-

Continued on Page 21, Column 1

'PAIN' EXPRESSED

Ex-President Cites His Sorrow at the Way He Handled Watergate

By EVERETT R. HOLLES
Special to The New York Times

SAN CLEMENTE, Calif., Sept. 8—President Ford's pardon for Richard M. Nixon evoked today from the former President an expression of "regret and pain at the anguish my mistakes over Watergate have caused the nation and the Presidency."

Within 10 minutes after the Presidential pardon was announced in Washington, Mr. Nixon's statement was released at his Casa Pacifica estate, citing his sorrow in allowing Watergate to become "a national tragedy."

"That the way I tried to deal with Watergate was the wrong way is the burden I shall bear for every day of the life that is left in me," he said.

Hopes Burden Is Lifted

In a subsequent statement, given in response to reporters' questions, an aide quoted Mr. Nixon as saying that, in gratefully accepting the Presidential pardon, he hoped Mr. Ford's "compassionate act would contribute to lifting the burdens of Watergate from our country."

When the Nixon statement was released by his adviser and former White House press secretary, Ronald L. Ziegler, Mr. and Mrs. Nixon were already on the way to a new haven of seclusion away from the heavily guarded Casa Pacifica.

They left at 7 A.M., Pacific Coast time, in a large black limousine accompanied by Secret Service agents and Mr. Nixon's military aide, Lieut. Col. Jack Brennan, reportedly for the Palm Desert estate of Walter H. Annenberg, Ambassador to Britain.

A close friend of the Nixons said the former President planned to play golf on the Annenberg private 18-hole course.

[In New York, Mr. Nixon's daughter, Julie Nixon Eisenhower, said that her father had gone to the Annenberg estate "for a rest," The Associated Press reported.]

Mr. Ziegler and Mr. Nixon's appointments secretary, Stephen

Continued on Page 24, Column 1

Richard M. Nixon in a photo made earlier this year

The Statement by Nixon

I have been informed that President Ford has granted me a full and absolute pardon for any charges which may be brought against me for actions taken during the time I was the President of the United States. In accepting this pardon, I hope that his compassionate act will contribute to lifting the burden of Watergate from our country.

Here in California, my perspective on Watergate is quite different than it was while I was embattled in the midst of the controversy while I was still subject to the unrelenting daily demands of the Presidency itself.

Looking back on what is still in my mind a complex and confusing maze of events, decisions, pressures, and personalities, one thing I can see clearly now is that I was wrong in not acting more decisively and more forthrightly in dealing with Watergate, particularly when it reached the stage of judicial proceedings and grew from a political scandal into a national tragedy.

No words can describe the depths of my regret and pain at the anguish my mistakes over Watergate have caused the nation and the Presidency, a nation I so deeply love and an institution I so greatly respect.

I know that many fair-minded people believe that my motivation and actions in the Watergate affair were intentionally self-serving and illegal. I now understand how my own mistakes and misjudgments have contributed to that belief and seemed to support it. This burden is the heaviest one of all to bear.

That the way I tried to deal with Watergate was the wrong way is a burden I shall bear for every day of the life that is left to me.

Jaworski Won't Challenge Pardon, Spokesman Says

By JOHN M. CREWDSON
Special to The New York Times

WASHINGTON, Sept. 8— Leon Jaworski, the Watergate special prosecutor, apparently has no plans to challenge the validity of the unconditional pardon that President Ford bestowed today on Richard M. Nixon, according to a spokesman for Mr. Jaworski.

The special prosecutor "accepts the decision," said John Barker, the spokesman. "He thinks it's within the President's power to do it. His feeling is that the President is exercising his lawful power, and he accepts it."

Mr. Barker added that Mr. Jaworski had not been consulted in advance on the decision by either Mr. Ford or White House lawyers, and learned of the President's position less than an hour before it was announced.

Some lawyers, including Sen-

ator Edmund S. Muskie, Democrat of Maine, questioned the legal and constitutional validity of a Presidential pardon conferred before an indictment had been brought or a conviction obtained.

"It could be challenged," declared Mr. Muskie, adding "there are those who say that it ought to be challenged, lest the precedent be established in an undesirable way."

But the remarks by Mr. Barker and by other lawyers familiar with the Watergate prosecutions indicated strongly that Mr. Jaworski was little inclined to test the pardon by seeking to indict Mr. Nixon, which one authority described as "the way to do it."

The principal Watergate grand jury voted earlier this

Continued on Page 25, Column 6

Associated Press
President Ford speaking at the White House yesterday

Proclamation of Pardon

Richard Nixon became the thirty-seventh President of the United States on January 20, 1969, and was re-elected in 1972 for a second term by the electors of forty-nine of the fifty states. His term in office continued until his resignation on August 9, 1974.

Pursuant to resolutions of the House of Representatives, its Committee on the Judiciary conducted an inquiry and investigation on the impeachment of the President extending over more than eight months. The hearings of the committee and its deliberations, which received wide national publicity over television, radio, and in printed media, resulted in votes adverse to Richard Nixon on recommended Articles of Impeachment.

As a result of certain acts or omissions occurring before his resignation from the office of President, Richard Nixon has become liable to possible indictment and trial for offenses against the United States. Whether or not he shall be so prosecuted depends on findings of the appropriate grand jury and on the discretion of the authorized prosecutor. Should an indictment ensue, the accused shall then be entitled to a fair trial by an impartial jury, as guaranteed to every individual by the Constitution.

It is believed that a trial of Richard Nixon, if it became necessary, could not fairly begin until a year or more has elapsed. In the meantime, the tranquility to which this nation has been restored by the events of recent weeks could be irreparably lost by the prospects of bringing to trial a former President of the United States. The prospects of such trial will cause prolonged and divisive debate over the propriety of exposing to further punishment and degradation a man who has already paid the unprecedented penalty of relinquishing the highest elective office in the United States.

NOW, THEREFORE, I, Gerald R. Ford, President of the United States, pursuant to the pardon power conferred upon me by Article II, Section 2, of the Constitution, have granted and by these presents do grant a full, free, and absolute pardon unto Richard Nixon for all offenses against the United States which he, Richard Nixon, has committed or may have committed or taken part in during the period from January 20, 1969, through August 9, 1974.

IN WITNESS WHEREOF, I have hereunto set my hand this 8th day of September in the year of our Lord nineteen hundred seventy-four, and of the independence of the United States of America the 199th.

Nixon Tapes Must Be Kept 3 Years for Use in Court

By R. W. APPLE Jr.
Special to The New York Times

WASHINGTON, Sept. 8— Richard M. Nixon and the Ford Administration have reached an agreement under which the former President will ultimately be permitted to destroy the White House tape recordings that led to his downfall.

The agreement, announced

today by the White House, also provides that all of Mr. Nixon's Presidential papers and tapes will be preserved for three years for possible use in court cases arising out of the Watergate scandals.

Mr. Nixon signed the agreement in San Clemente, Calif., on Friday; it was countersigned yesterday by Arthur F. Sampson, head of the General Services Administration.

Philip W. Buchen, counsel for President Ford, said at a White House briefing this afternoon

Continued on Page 24, Column 4

NO CONDITIONS SET

Action Taken to Spare Nation and Ex-Chief, President Asserts

By JOHN HERBERS
Special to The New York Times

WASHINGTON, Sept. 8— President Ford granted former President Richard M. Nixon an unconditional pardon today for all Federal crimes that he "committed or may have committed or taken part in" while in office, an act Mr. Ford said was intended to spare Mr. Nixon and the nation further punishment in the Watergate scandals.

Mr. Nixon, in San Clemente, Calif., accepted the pardon, which exempts him from indictment and trial for, among

Text of the Ford statement is printed on Page 24.

other things, his role in the cover-up of the Watergate burglary. He issued a statement saying that he could now see he was "wrong in not acting more decisively and more forthrightly in dealing with Watergate."

'Act of Mercy'

Philip W. Buchen, the White House counsel, who advised Mr. Ford on the legal aspects of the pardon, said the "act of mercy" on the President's part was done without making any demands on Mr. Nixon and without asking the advice of the Watergate special prosecutor, Leon Jaworski, who had the legal responsibility to prosecute the case.

Reaction to the pardon was sharply divided, but not entirely along party lines. Most Democrats who commented voiced varying degrees of disapproval and dismay, while most Republican comment backed President Ford.

However, Senators Edward W. Brooke of Massachusetts and Jacob K. Javits of New York disagreed with the action. [Page 25.]

Dangers Seen in Delay

Mr. Buchen said that, at the President's request, he had asked Mr. Jaworski how long it would be, in the event Mr. Nixon was indicted, before he could be brought to trial and that Mr. Jaworski had replied it would be at least nine months or more, because of the enormous amount of publicity the charges against Mr. Nixon had received when the House Judiciary Committee recommended impeachment.

This was one reason Mr. Ford cited for granting the pardon, saying he had concluded that "many months and perhaps more years will have to pass before Richard Nixon could obtain a fair trial by jury in any jurisdiction of the United States under governing decisions of the Supreme Court."

"During this long period of delay and potential litigation, ugly passions would again be aroused, our people would

Continued on Page 24, Column 1

terHorst Quits Post To Protest Pardon

Special to The New York Times

WASHINGTON, Sept. 8—J. F. terHorst, whose appointment as White House press secretary was the first in President Ford's new Administration, resigned tonight in what he said was a protest over the granting of an unconditional pardon to former President Nixon.

In a statement released by the White House tonight, Mr. Ford said that he deeply regretted Mr. terHorst's decision.

"I understand his position," Mr. Ford said. "I appreciate the fact that good people will differ with me on this very difficult decision. However, it is my judgment that it is in

Continued on Page 24, Column 1

CANDIDATES SKIRT LAW ON FINANCING

Evidence Shows Big Money Played a Major Role— Voting Is Tomorrow

By FRANK LYNN

Big money—from family fortunes and large contributors—played a major role in the Democratic primary campaigns despite new state and Federal

Ballot and candidate list appear on Page 28.

campaign-finance laws that were supposed to have reduced its influence.

The question of how much money was spent and where it came from was being discussed as the primary campaigns drew to a close. The polls will be open tomorrow in the city from 6 A.M. to 9 P.M. and in the rest of the state from noon to 9 P.M.

Interviews with campaign aides and campaign financial reports show that there was considerable evidence of circumventing of the new laws in fact and in spirit, possible unrecorded cash contributions and spending and even "laundering" of campaign contribu-

Continued on Page 28, Column 1

Knievel Safe as Rocket Falls Into Snake Canyon

By JON NORDHEIMER
Special to The New York Times

TWIN FALLS, Idaho, Sept. 8—Evel Knievel failed today in an attempt to rocket 1,600 feet across the Snake River Canyon when a tail parachute deployed prematurely on the take-off of his vehicle.

The vehicle, which Mr. Knievel calls the Sky-Cycle X-2, went streaking to about 1,000 feet above the river before floating into the canyon to make a nose-down crash landing on a rocky bank at the river's edge.

But the vehicle dropped onto a boulder-strewn ledge, bounced twice on its bottom and came to rest about 20 feet from the water's edge.

The vehicle was obscured by smoke from the release 540 feet above, and some cries of anguish were heard in the crowd when several minutes went by and there was no sign of the stuntman.

A helicopter picked him

A large crowd along the canyon's south rim gasped as a 15-mile-an-hour wind blew the vehicle back toward them, rocking gently in the air nose-down like a red, white and blue Christmas ornament.

For several seconds, it appeared that Mr. Knievel, who could be seen struggling inside the open cockpit, might crash into the crowd on the rim of the canyon.

But the vehicle dropped onto a boulder-strewn ledge, bounced twice on its bottom and came to rest about 20 feet from the water's edge.

The vehicle was pulled from the craft several minutes later by a rescue team. He had superficial cuts and scrapes of the face and legs.

The flight aborted almost as soon as steam exploded from a rear nozzle of the 12-foot-long craft and propelled it along a 168-foot launching track aimed at the cloudless sky.

A drogue parachute designed to slow the vehicle's ascent at an altitude of 2,800 feet deployed while the vehicle was still on the ramp, whipping in a blast of steam.

Once the vehicle lifted off the ramp, it turned belly up and the main chute, attached to the drogue, was automatically deployed at about 1,000 feet.

Continued on Page 50, Column 5

Chris Evert Beaten

Evonne Goolagong of Australia defeated Chris Evert in the semifinals of the United States Open tennis at Forest Hills, Queens, yesterday, 6-0, 6-7, 6-3, and will meet Billie Jean King in the final today. Details, Page 45.

Some Mixed Reactions in Foley Square

By PAUL L. MONTGOMERY

A few hours after President Ford's pardon of his predecessor was announced yesterday, Mr. and Mrs. Wilson Wainwright of Olean, N.Y., were strolling in Foley Square in lower Manhattan, looking at the public buildings.

"It's going to make a lot of people mad, but I can see why he did it," Mr. Wainwright said. "It wouldn't look right to the rest of the world to have a President of the United States in jail."

Mr. Wainwright, here on a late-summer vacation, was asked if he had any doubts about former President Richard M. Nixon's guilt.

"None that I can see," his wife, Judy, replied. "I guess

some people would say it would have been better to pardon him after the courts decided."

Nearby, at 100 Centre Street, the afternoon session of the arraignment part of Criminal Court was about to begin. In the dingy, crowded room, lawyers and policemen and defendants and their families lounged on the oak benches, waiting for the judge to return from lunch.

Hal Mayerson and Peter Davis of the Legal Aid Society, which represents indigent defendants, had been discussing the pardon during the break.

"It's a bit unseemly to pardon someone before they're prosecuted," Mr. Davis said. "It doesn't do much for the

concept of equal justice under law."

"How about all the young men who refused to serve in an illegal, immoral and vicious war?" Mr. Mayerson asked. "Is he going to pardon them, too? It's like Peter was saying, maybe they should give Nixon a pardon if he does 10 months of alternate service."

Mr. Mayerson looked around the room.

"Seriously, though, it's outrageous," he continued. "You get a lady here who's going to jail for stealing a blouse, or some guy in on assault because he got tired of living with the rats and hit somebody. And here's one of the biggest plun-

Continued on Page 28, Column 6

"All the News That's Fit to Print"

The New York Times

LATE CITY EDITION

Weather: Sunny, warmer today; cold tonight. Chance of rain tomorrow. Temperature range: today 31-47; Thursday 29-38. Details on Page 74.

VOL. CXXIV..No. 42,699

© 1974 The New York Times Company

NEW YORK, FRIDAY, DECEMBER 20, 1974

Price higher in air delivery cities.

20 CENTS

ROCKEFELLER SWORN IN AS VICE PRESIDENT AFTER CONFIRMATION BY HOUSE, 287 TO 128

Congress Votes $1-Billion For Jobs for Unemployed

By DAVID E. ROSENBAUM
Special to The New York Times

WASHINGTON, Dec. 19 — The House and Senate gave final approval tonight to legislation appropriating $1-billion for jobs for the unemployed next year.

The money was part of a $5-billion appropriations bill that also allocates money for increased unemployment compensation.

President Ford supports the measure and is considered certain to sign it.

It was estimated that the measure would provide 100,000 jobs nationwide at an average salary of $7,500.

More than $2-billion would become available for unemployment compensation, with the exact amount depending on the number of persons out of work next year.

Under the bill, $875-million would be distributed to states and communities to provide public service jobs for the unemployed in such areas as health, education, recreation and sanitation.

The measure specified that $125-million would be distributed through the Economic Development Administration to stimulate public works projects in depressed areas.

Based on the September unemployment statistics and an appropriation of $1-billion, the Labor Department calculated that New York State would get $107-million, of which New York City would get $61-million; New Jersey would get $48-million, and Connecticut $18-million. [Page 4.]

The Senate had authorized $4-billion and the House $2-billion for the public service jobs program. But the authorization figures merely set ceilings on the amount of money that might be made available. The appropriation determines the amount available to be spent.

Meanwhile, today, the Democrats on the House Ways and Means Committee, which has jurisdiction over many of the important economic measures to be considered next year, created six subcommittees and appointed chairmen.

It was the first time the panel formed subcommittees since 1957.

The committee Democrats developed

Continued on Page 10, Column 2

Cuomo Selected by Carey As His Secretary of State

By FRANCIS X. CLINES

Governor-elect Hugh L. Carey announced yesterday that Mario M. Cuomo, a longtime friend, would be appointed Secretary of State, and that Raymond T. Schuler, the incumbent Secretary of Transportation, would be retained in the new administration, which takes office Jan. 1.

Mr. Cuomo, who ran unsuccessfully this year for the Democratic nomination for Lieutenant Governor, will have the responsibilities of his post expanded to include special advisory and trouble-shooting duties, Mr. Carey announced. These include the inquiry into nursing home abuses Mr. Carey charged him with earlier this week, plus executive responsibilities in programs for judicial selection, income disclosure for public officials and the current review of the New York City Charter.

Commissioner Schuler, like Mr. Cuomo, is a Democrat. H has 18 years of career service in the state bureaucracy and was appointed Commissioner two years ago by former Gov. Nelson A. Rockefeller. Under his control, the transportation agency has started to shed its traditional highway-oriented direction and to stress the need for mass transit.

Mr. Cuomo, who is 42 years old, practices law in Brooklyn and lives in Queens with his wife, Matilda, and five children. He is also a law professor at St. John's University Law School. He had been reported concerned about moving to Albany and yesterday he said that in the light of the expanded role being created for Secretary

Mario M. Cuomo

of State, he was not sure whether he would be living upstate. The Department of State, which has headquarters in Albany, oversees the licensing and registration procedures for professions and technical jobs.

Mr. Cuomo said the Governor-elect had emphasized that the post—which politicians in recent years had come to consider a Governor's symbolic Italian-American chamberlain—would not be "an ethnic position."

Mr. Cuomo first came to public

Continued on Page 25, Column 2

City's Fire Alarm Boxes Are Called Undependable

By JOHN DARNTON

The city's fire-alarm boxes, connected to a deteriorating network of cables laid more than half a century ago, are becoming dangerously unreliable, according to Fire Department dispatchers, maintenance men and fire fighters.

While some of the old mechanical "pull" boxes have failed in recent months, the new voice-alarm boxes that are replacing them at the rate of 60 a month have developed technological problems of their own. All of these Emergency Response System boxes installed in the city so far—over 1,000—will be replaced by their manufacturer because they have been found to "transmit themselves" during electrical storms.

The scope of the old fire-box problem, as the city enters its heavy fire-fatality season, is indicated by the aftereffects of one severe ice storm a year ago. The storm knocked out 2,500 of the department's 15,840 street and building boxes. Most

Continued on Page 74, Column 4

Man, 98, Strangled In Brooklyn Robbery

By JOSEPH B. TREASTER

A 98-year-old former yeshiva principal was choked to death with his yarmulke early yesterday morning by thieves who climbed into his ground-floor apartment in the Crown Heights section of Brooklyn as he slept, the police said.

The victim, Nathan Friedier, who was described by neighbors as "a nice, quiet old man," was found tied on his bed, spread-eagled with neckties to the four corner posts. He was brought by his daughter, Mrs. Sigmund Schwartz, as she brought him breakfast at about 8 A.M. from her own apartment in the same building at 899 Montgomery Street. The skull cap had been

Continued on Page 74, Column 4

CITY AND UNIONS SEEK RETIREMENT ON ELECTIVE BASIS

510 Workers Who Were to Be Let Go Today Get a Month's Reprieve

By FRED FERRETTI

The city and a group of leaders representing the municipal unions agreed yesterday to seek voluntary retirements of city employes aged 63 to 70 to save the jobs of 860 younger employes. The latter are scheduled to be dismissed in the budget-cutting layoffs recently announced by Mayor Beame.

The agreement is an alternative to an earlier plan, which would have forced the retirement of 860 older Civil Service employes to save the jobs of the younger employes — a plan that on Wednesday was declared illegal by the United States Secretary of Labor, Peter J. Brennan.

First Deputy Mayor James Cavanagh, in announcing the alternative, said that to give union actuaries time to find prospective volunteers, 510 employes scheduled to be dismissed today would get a month's reprieve.

The 510 represented part of the first wave of 1,510 municipal layoffs announced by Mr. Beame on Nov. 22 in an effort to decrease the deficit in the city's $11.1-billion budget.

The Second Wave

On Dec. 11 the Mayor called for the discharge of 6,425 more city employes, consisting of 2,200 permanent Civil Service workers, 1,525 appointed provisionals and 2,700 workers aged 65 or older who the Mayor said would not receive renewals of their work extensions and would have to retire by next June 30. In the group of 2,200 were teachers, policemen, firemen and sanitation workers and 350 other permanent Civil Service employes.

The 350, like the first group of 510, are in the New York City Employes Retirement System, one of the city's five pension programs. It was these 860 employes, mostly young members of minority groups and women, who were scheduled to be dismissed and on whom a week's effort was expected in attempts to save their jobs.

After Victor Gotbaum, executive director of the 110,000-member District 37, American Federation of State, County and Municipal Employes, and other union leaders denounced the dismissals, the Mayor met with them and announced a plan to

Continued on Page 25, Column 1

The New York Times/George Tames

Nelson A. Rockefeller being sworn in as Vice President last night by Chief Justice Warren E. Burger. In background from left are Senators Hugh Scott, Jacob K. Javits, Robert C. Byrd, James L. Buckley and Howard W. Cannon.

Nominee Takes His Oath On the Old Family Bible

By RICHARD L. MADDEN
Special to The New York Times

WASHINGTON, Dec. 19—In a simple but well-organized ceremony in the Senate chamber, Nelson A. Rockefeller held a black family Bible in his left hand tonight and took the oath of office as Vice President.

The oath was administered by Chief Justice Warren E. Burger amid a blaze of lights to accommodate television cameras, the first time they had been allowed in the room. It brought the 66-year-old Mr. Rockefeller within a heartbeat of the Presidency, a job he had been denied three times by the Republican party.

The Bible was the same one that Mr. Rockefeller had used four times when he was sworn in at Albany as Governor of New York, and in it was a note from his father, John D. Rockefeller, Jr., which said:

"This was my mother's Bible, which always lay on the table in the library at 4 West 54th Street, New York, April 1, 1946."

The 25-minute ceremony was a combination of a solemn oath, a brief speech of gratitude, formal expressions of good wishes from Senate leaders and finally hearty applause and handshakes from Representatives who had confirmed Mr. Rockefeller's nomination two hours earlier and from Senators who had done the same last week, as well as some who had pretend he was the March of Dimes poster child's father just to get into the President's office.

But the fact is that Mr. Rockefeller has the best chance of anyone who has held the Vice-Presidency in recent times to make a real impact on government and politics, despite all the continuing constraints of the No. 2 job.

This is so for two basic reasons.

First, Mr. Rockefeller himself brings to the job a depth of executive experience—years and years of running things, not just talking about them—that is unmatched in this century. He is by disposition and

Continued on Page 17, Column 1

6 SUGAR REFINERS INDICTED BY JURY

Price - Fixing Conspiracies Alleged in Three Markets in West and Midwest

By HENRY WEINSTEIN
Special to The New York Times

SAN FRANCISCO, Dec. 19—Six major sugar refining companies were indicted today by a Federal Grand Jury on charges of illegal price fixing after an 18-month investigation.

The companies indicted were the Great Western Sugar Company of Denver, the American Crystal Sugar Company, formerly of Denver; the Holly Sugar Corporation of Colorado Springs, Colo.; California and Hawaiian Sugar Company of Ogden, Utah; and the Union Sugar Division of the Consolidated Foods Corporation of Chicago. Also named as civil defendants were the National Sugar Beet Growers Federation of Greeley, Colo.; and Utah-Idaho Sugar Company of Salt Lake City, Utah.

The indictments and three companion civil antitrust suits covered acts allegedly committed through the end of 1972. Since then sugar prices have soared, and Robert J. Staal, assistant United States Attorney, stated here today that "the current pricing practices of the sugar industry are still under investigation."

Last month the staff of the Council on Wage and Price Stability said the United States sugar industry had "reaped very large windfall gains" this year from rapidly increasing sugar prices. Mr. Staal declined to state whether a grand jury

Continued on Page 62, Column 4

Export Bank Credit Curbs Are Said to Anger Moscow

By BERNARD GWERTZMAN
Special to The New York Times

WASHINGTON, Dec. 19—The Soviet Union has followed up yesterday's disavowal of a deal on emigration for trade benefits with a private denunciation of Congressional adoption of a ceiling on Export-Import Bank credits to Moscow.

According to State Department officials, Ambassador Anatoly F. Dobrynin told Secretary of State Kissinger yesterday that Moscow was angry at what it regarded as the failure of the United States to live up to its side of détente.

Without stating whether the Soviet Union would step up emigration in return for the modest trade benefits approved by Congress, Mr. Dobrynin reportedly was caustic in his complaints, particularly about the credit limitation.

Some officials said that because the additional credits—a ceiling of $300-million over four years, limited to $75-million a year—were lower than Moscow had expected, there was some question whether the Kremlin would go ahead with the informal arrangement to ease emigration restrictions in return for trade concessions. Despite the Soviet denial, the officials insist that such an arrangement exists.

The consensus was that it

Continued on Page 13, Column 1

Continued on Page 10, Column 2
Continued on Page 25, Column 2
Continued on Page 25, Column 1
Continued on Page 74, Column 4
Continued on Page 38, Column 1
Continued on Page 17, Column 1
Continued on Page 62, Column 4
Continued on Page 13, Column 1

SENATE CEREMONY

He Tells of 'Gratitude for the Privilege of Serving Country'

By LINDA CHARLTON
Special to The New York Times

WASHINGTON, Dec. 19 — Nelson Aldrich Rockefeller was sworn in tonight as the 41st Vice President of the United States.

He was sworn in by Chief Justice Warren E. Burger in a televised ceremony in the Senate chamber.

Mr. Rockefeller became Vice President one day short of four months after his nomination by President Ford. He was escorted to the Senate by Mr. Ford.

Transcript of the ceremony appears on Page 16.

Members of Mr. Rockefeller's family, Congress, the Cabinet and New York State dignitaries were among those who witnessed the ceremony.

He took the oath of office with his hand on a family Bible at 10:12 P.M.

The former New York Governor, only the second man to become Vice President without a public vote, took office after the House completed Congressional approval of his nomination by a vote of 287 to 128. The Senate approved him by a vote of 90 to 7 last week.

Ford Is Pleased

Immediately after the confirmation vote, the White House issued the following statement by President Ford:

"I am delighted that Nelson Rockefeller has been duly confirmed today to be the 41st Vice President of the United States. I congratulate him and look forward to his participation and assistance in the Administration. I commend the House of Representatives for its confirmation vote today, and the Senate for its vote earlier. Members of the 93d Congress have rendered a service to the nation by filling the constitutional office of the Vice President before adjournment. All Americans will benefit from the distinguished and devoted public service of the new Vice President."

Oath and Speech

At just past 10:11 P.M., Mr. Rockefeller raised his right hand to take the oath: "I, Nelson Aldrich Rockefeller, do solemnly swear that I will support and defend the Constitution of the United States...."

When the applause had subsided, Mr. Rockefeller read a short speech to the crowded chamber illuminated by five banks of television lights.

"I feel," he said, "a great sense of gratitude for the privilege of serving the country I love."

He went on to thank all those involved in his nomination—the President, Congress, Betty Ford for "her warmth and her courage."

"And if you'll forgive me for a personal note, my love and

Continued on Page 16, Column 1

Outlook for Rockefeller

Long Experience in Running Things Is Expected to Reinforce President

By R. W. APPLE Jr.
Special to The New York Times

WASHINGTON, Dec. 19—Even before Nelson A. Rockefeller was sworn into office, the Washington sharpshooters were reminding him that the principal assignment of most Vice Presidents has been to stay reasonably healthy. In his whimsy for today, for example, Art Buchwald wrote of the Vice President who had to

News Analysis

by training an operator, and as one Senator said, "he will find some way to operate."

Second, Mr. Rockefeller joins a President who came to office with no electoral mandate in a time of national crisis, a President who needs reinforcement in a way unique in American political history. That was one of the reasons that Mr. Ford chose him.

Not that it is going to be easy.

Continued on Page 17, Column 3

TEN ECONOMISTS FAVOR STIMULUS

Group Meets With Ford's Top Advisers — Details of Some Views Differ

By EDWIN L. DALE Jr.
Special to The New York Times

WASHINGTON, Dec. 19—Government stimulus for the sliding economy was supported favored by a group of 10 leading private economists at an unpublicized meeting at the White House today.

Participants at the meeting declined to discuss individual views in detail. However, some of the views are well known. But one participant did say, "I can't think of anyone who didn't favor stimulus in some form." The group's members, however, were reported to have differed on numerous important details, including the type of stimulus and how large it should be.

President Ford was not present, but nearly all his chief economic advisers were. Alan Greenspan, chairman of the Council of Economic Advisers, presided.

According to reports, the Government members mainly listened and asked questions and made no attempt to achieve a consensus. Mr. Greenspan has previously pledged to solicit

Continued on Page 54, Column 1

Watergate Argument

The chief prosecutor at the Watergate cover-up trial began his final argument to the jury yesterday after 46 days of testimony. The prosecutor, James F. Neal, mocked and scorned the five defendants. Page 18.

Publisher Suspends Luciano Paperback

By NICHOLAS GAGE

New American Library is suspending its plans to publish a paperback edition of "The Last Testament of Lucky Luciano," for which it was going to pay $800,000, according to a company spokesman.

The spokesman, Harold Rosenthal, said the decision was reached following a meeting Wednesday in Boston with executives of Little, Brown & Co., the book's primary publisher.

The New York Times disclosed last Tuesday that an examination of the book, including research into papers and documents concerning Mr. Luciano and more than 20 interviews, produced information that questioned the publisher's

Continued on Page 29, Column 7

The New York Times

LATE CITY EDITION

Weather: Continued mostly cloudy, cool today, tonight and tomorrow. Temperature range: today 46-58; Tuesday 45-53. Details on Page 81.

VOL. CXXIV...No. 42,830   © 1975 The New York Times Company   NEW YORK, WEDNESDAY, APRIL 30, 1975   Price higher in air delivery cities.   20 CENTS

MINH SURRENDERS, VIETCONG IN SAIGON; 1,000 AMERICANS AND 5,500 VIETNAMESE EVACUATED BY COPTER TO U.S. CARRIERS

U.S., GREECE AGREE TO END HOME PORT FOR THE 6TH FLEET

Air Base of Americans at Athens Is Also Closed, but Some Facilities Remain

By United Press International

ATHENS, April 29 — United States and Greek officials announced today the termination of the home-port arrangement for Sixth Fleet ships at the port of Eleusis near Athens and the closing of the American air base at Athens airport.

The announcement came in a joint statement at the end of a second round of talks on the status of United States military facilities in Greece.

The Greek Government threatened to close all United States bases and it withdrew from the North Atlantic Treaty Organization's military command after the invasion of Cyprus by Turkey last July.

"Certain United States facilities which contribute to Greek defense needs will continue to operate on the Greek Air Force base at Hellenikon," today's statement said.

The statement said that the second phase of the talks, held April 7 to 29 by the two delegations under the United States Embassy Minister, Monteagle Stearns, and Ambassador Petros Kalogeras of Greece also discussed the status of other facilities.

"Agreement is also expected on the elimination, reduction and conservation of other United States facilities in Greece," it said.

The two delegations said that they made progress in the review of the privileges, immunities and exemptions of American personnel in Greece.

The two Governments will

Continued on Page 4, Column 4

G.M.'s Profits Fall

First-quarter profits of General Motors declined 50.8 per cent from the depressed 1974 quarter. Page 53.

HEAVY USERS FACE CON ED INCREASE

P.S.C. Also Orders Cuts for Smaller Consumers

By WILL LISSNER

The state's Public Service Commission ordered the Consolidated Edison Company yesterday to raise its rates for those customers who accounted for the heaviest summer power demands and to cut the rates for customers whose usage did not create excess power demand.

The change — technically a revision of the rate structure approved last November to give the utility $338.7-million more a year — will not mean any extra revenue for the company. Nor will it affect the rates for the great majority of customers, the 2.5 million small residential and commercial users.

Instead, yesterday's order makes revisions in bills that will take less than $20-million from some customers and give it to others, a relatively small amount compared with its total annual billings for electricity of $2.10-billion. It affected less than 500,000 of its 2.9 million customers in New York City, Westchester County and part of Nassau County.

But the order was significant because it introduced into energy ratemaking the philosophy that the customers who are responsible for excess costs should be required to bear more

Continued on Page 34, Column 5

A crewman from an American helicopter helping evacuees to the top of a building in Saigon for flight to a U.S. carrier

United Press International

Abram Offers Bills To Curtail Abuses Of Nursing Homes

By ALFONSO A. NARVAEZ

ALBANY, April 29 — Morris B. Abram proposed today a series of changes in the laws governing nursing homes to "deal with the most serious immediate problems" uncovered during his month-long investigation.

The proposals were contained in a package of 11 bills submitted to Governor Carey and legislative leaders by Mr. Abram, head of the Moreland Act Commission investigating the nursing-home industry.

Among other things, they would authorize nursing-home residents to file class-action suits for deprivation of their rights and would entitle them to receive a minimum of 25 per cent of the daily reimbursement rate paid by government regulations for each day of a violation.

Among them were measures to make long-term care more readily available to all older Americans, improve inspection and enforcement procedures and provide training for nursing-home physicians, nurses,

Continued on Page 81, Column 3

CAMBODIA ORDERS FOREIGNERS OUT

Planned 250-Mile Road Trip to Border Is Protested by Paris as Debilitating

By FLORA LEWIS

Special to The New York Times

PARIS, April 29 — The French Government said today that the people who have been isolated in its Phnom Penh embassy since the Cambodian Communists took over two weeks ago had been ordered expelled "in the worst possible conditions."

There are 610 refugees in the embassy. They are to be sent out by truck to the town of Poipet on the Thailand border, beginning tomorrow.

Foreign Minister Jean Sauvagnargues told newsmen after having conferred with President Valéry Giscard d'Estaing:

"We fear these extremely precarious evacuation conditions will be beyond the strength of some whose health is poor."

"We continue to insist that the plane that we have held in Vientiane for evacuation of the ill be allowed to land in Phnom Penh."

However, a Foreign Ministry spokesman said that so far there has been no response to

Continued on Page 17, Column 6

2d Key Met Museum Aide Quits In Dispute Over Hoving Methods

By GRACE GLUECK

With an attack on Thomas P. F. Hoving's administration of the Metropolitan Museum of Art alleging its inability to operate "in any way that creates or preserves trust, confidence and decency," Anthony M. Clark, chairman of the museum's department of European paintings, has resigned.

Mr. Clark's resignation, one of several that have occurred among senior curatorial personnel at the museum in recent years, represents the first open

challenge to Mr. Hoving's administration.

The resignation, effective June 30, follows that of John Walsh, the vice chairman and curator of this key department a month ago. Mr. Clark would not speak for Mr. Walsh, who is abroad, but it is understood that their basic grievances are similar.

"I can't work with or for the present administration at the Met," said Mr. Clark, who had been director of the Minneapolis Institute of Arts for 10 years before his appointment to the Metropolitan in 1973. "I believe that its relation to art has become incidental, wrong and even risky. It's also hell on professionals."

In a statement last night, Mr. Hoving said that he was

Continued on Page 24, Column 1

74 Saigon Planes Fly 2,000 to Thailand

By DAVID A. ANDELMAN

Special to The New York Times

BANGKOK, Thailand, April 29 — At least 74 South Vietnamese Air Force planes fleeing the country streamed into U Taphao air base in southern Thailand without warning this afternoon.

The pilots and passengers — 2,000 people — requested asylum, American and Thai Foreign Ministry officials said.

About 30 of the planes were F-5 jet fighters and there were reports that at least one had crashed on a highway near the base as it was making its approach.

The planes began arriving at the huge naval and air base on the Gulf of Siam at about the time that the American evacuation of South Vietnam

was ending and the planes were still landing as night fell.

The aircraft were said to include C-47 transports and the C-130 cargo planes that the American military has been using to ferry refugees from South Vietnam to Guam and the Philippines. However, all the aircraft were understood to be Vietnam Air Force planes, originally supplied by the United States.

A Thai Foreign Ministry spokesman said that American authorities at U Taphao had been asked to turn over the aircraft to the Thai Government, which would return them to "the new South Vietnamese government." The pilots and passengers, the Thai spokesman said, "must leave Thailand."

"They just landed first and

asked permission afterwards," said an astounded Thai Foreign Ministry official. Other Government sources said that apparently no efforts were made to prevent the planes from landing and no aircraft went up to intercept the fighters as they roared in.

American Embassy officials in Bangkok declined to comment on the Thai request that the planes be returned since their status was unclear. An unresolved question here appeared to be whether the planes were still American property or belonged to whatever government continued in Saigon. The planes could be worth $200-million, one official said.

No details were available on the status of the refugees or

Continued on Page 16, Column 6

President Ford and Secretary of State Kissinger returning to White House to resume talks on Vietnam. They had just said good-by to King Hussein of Jordan after visit.

United Press International

FORD UNITY PLEA

President Says That Departure 'Closes a Chapter' for U.S.

By JOHN W. FINNEY

Special to The New York Times

WASHINGTON, April 29 — The United States ended two decades of military involvement in Vietnam today with the evacuation of about 1,000 Americans from Saigon as well as more than 5,500 South Vietnamese.

The emergency helicopter evacuation was ordered last night by President Ford after the Saigon airport was closed

Ford statement and excerpts from Kissinger's, Page 17.

because of Communist rocket and artillery fire. The 1,000 Americans were the last contingent of a force that once numbered more than 500,000.

They were carried by a fleet of 81 American helicopters to carriers in the South China Sea. The helicopters removed the 5,500 South Vietnamese citizens because their lives were presumed to be in danger with a Communist take-over of South Vietnam. Over the last two weeks, a total of about 55,000 South Vietnamese have been removed. Most of them will come to the United States. The helicopter flights ended the United States evacuation of South Vietnamese.

Last Marines Evacuated

The final withdrawal of Americans was completed at 7:52 P.M., about two hours after the White House had announced the evacuation was completed, when 11 marines were taken by helicopter from the roof of the American Embassy in Saigon. Officials said that the marines, the last of a security guard sent to protect the evacuation, were safely removed although small-arms fire had broken out around the deserted embassy.

President Ford, in a statement issued by the White House, said the evacuation "closes a chapter in the American experience." In a plea for national unity in the post-Vietnam period, the President said:

"I ask all Americans to close ranks, to avoid recrimination about the past, to look ahead to the many goals we share and to work together on the great tasks that remain to be accomplished."

Appeal by Kissinger

At a news conference, Secretary of State Kissinger appealed to North Vietnam not to storm Saigon by force because the United States believed the new South Vietnamese Govern-

Continued on Page 17, Column 1

DEFENSE ENDS

General Tells His Troops to Turn in Their Weapons

By The Associated Press

SAIGON, South Vietnam, Wednesday, April 30 — President Duong Van Minh announced today the unconditional surrender of the Saigon Government and its military forces to the Vietcong.

Columns of South Vietnamese troops pulled out of their defensive positions in the capital and marched to central points to turn in their weapons.

Within two hours, Communist forces began moving into Saigon. A jeep flying the Vietcong flag and carrying eight cheering men in civilian clothes armed with an assortment of weapons drove along the street a block from the United States Embassy compound.

This action followed by hours the ending of the American involvement in Vietnam through the evacuation of most of the approximately 1,000 Americans still here.

[In Washington, the White House said that President Ford had "no comment" on the surrender of Saigon, but a White House spokesman said the surrender was considered 'inevitable.' Page 16]

3 Decades of Fighting

The surrender announcement, made in a broadcast to the nation, signaled the end of three decades of fighting. It came 21 years after the 1954 Geneva accords divided Viet-

The text of President Minh's statement is on Page 16.

nam into North and South and a little more than two years after the American cease-fire agreement was signed in Paris on Jan. 27, 1973. The last American troops left the country in March of that year.

President Minh, who took office on Monday to lead South Vietnam into peace negotiations, said in his brief radio address:

"I believe firmly in reconciliation among Vietnamese to avoid unnecessary shedding of the blood of Vietnamese. For this reason, I ask the soldiers of the Republic of Vietnam to cease hostilities in calm and to stay where they are."

The President also asked the "brother soldiers" of the Vietcong to cease hostilities and added:

"We wait here to meet the Provisional Revolutionary Government of South Vietnam to discuss together a ceremony of orderly transfer of power so as to avoid any unnecessary

Continued on Page 16, Column 1

Saigon Copter Lands on Another In Stampede to U.S. Ship's Deck

By The Associated Press

ABOARD U.S.S. BLUE RIDGE, in South China Sea, April 29 — Scores of South Vietnamese helicopters filled with military men and civilians fled Saigon today and headed out to sea to search for the carriers of the United States Seventh Fleet.

Seven of the helicopters arrived unexpectedly above this vessel carrying Americans and Vietnamese evacuated from South Vietnam. The seven copters made a dash for the helipad at the rear of the ship.

One pilot dropped his helicopter on the blades of another that had just landed and chunks of metal ripped through the air. The top helicopter, with its load of women and children, nearly toppled into the sea, but they were rescued and there were no injuries.

United States sailors heaved the two damaged choppers overboard to clear the landing pad. For the Vietnamese it was a last-ditch chance to survive.

As other Vietnamese helicopters landed their passengers were pulled free. American sailors ripped the doors off the craft to make them sink and the pilots who jettisoned them in the sea to make room for other arrivals circling overhead. Two small craft rescued the swimming pilots.

The American evacuation was reported orderly, although it was delayed several times because of weather and pilot fatigue.

The Blue Ridge is the command and communications vessel of the 40-ship Seventh Fleet armada waiting off the coast of South Vietnam to evacuate Americans and other foreigners

Continued on Page 17, Colum

"All the News That's Fit to Print"

The New York Times

LATE CITY EDITION

Weather: Partly cloudy and less humid today through tomorrow. Temperature range: today 64-80; Sunday 63-82. Details on page 30.

VOL. CXXV ... No. 43,262   © 1976 The New York Times Company   NEW YORK, MONDAY, JULY 5, 1976   25 cents beyond 50-mile zone from New York City. except Long Island. Higher in air delivery cities.   20 CENTS

Nation and Millions in City Joyously Hail Bicentennial

ISRAELIS RETURN WITH 103 RESCUED IN UGANDA RAID

Toll Is Put at 3 Hostages, 7 Hijackers, Army Officer and 20 of Amin's Men

FORD LAUDS OPERATION

Freed Captives Are Received Joyously at Airport After Their 7-Day Ordeal

By TERENCE SMITH
Special to The New York Times

JERUSALEM, July 4—An Israeli commando unit that last night conducted a daring raid on the Entebbe airport in Uganda flew home today with the hostages it released.

Military officials said that 103 hostages had been flown to Israel. They said that four Is-

Text of the Rabin address will be found on page 2.

raelis, seven of the 10 hijackers and about 20 Uganda soldiers had been killed.

Some of the hostages arrived exhausted, some exuberant, to a noisy, joyous reunion here with family and friends. A majority of those freed last night were Israelis.

[President Ford sent a message of congratulation to Prime Minister Yitzhak Rabin, voicing "great satisfaction" that the passengers of the hijacked plane had been saved and "a senseless act of terrorism thwarted." Page 2. President Idi Amin of Uganda condemned the Israeli action.]

Back at Same Airport

A week to the day after they set off on an Air France airbus, the Israeli passengers and French crew members were back at the same airport where they had originally started their trip. They were weeping, laughing and literally falling into each other's arms with relief.

Their return here brought to an end seven days of terror that culminated in the spectacular rescue operation, in which Israeli airborne troops traveled 2,500 miles to pluck the hostages from the gunpoints of their captors at the Entebbe airport.

Rabin Addresses Parliament

The success of the operation, which surprised most Israelis, electrified the country. Flags were brought out, people rejoiced openly in the streets, and in the sky over Jerusalem, a skywriter wrote in Hebrew: "Kol hakavod zahal," or "All honor to the army."

Addressing a specially convened session of the Israeli Parliament, Prime Minister Yitzhak Rabin declared: "This operation will become a legend. It is Israel's contribution to

Continued on Page 3, Column 4

Preceded by a fireboat, the Coast Guard training ship Eagle leads the armada of ships past the Battery up the Hudson for the naval review
The New York Times/Edward Hausner

French Officials See Signs Amin, Hijackers Colluded

Special to The New York Times

PARIS, July 4 — Officials and released hostages said here today that they had substantial evidence that President Idi Amin had been in collusion with the hijackers of an Air France airbus in the seizure of the plane as well as after it landed in Uganda.

Although the officials refused to be quoted publicly, one said that negotiations got "much tougher" last night after President Amin returned to Uganda from a meeting of the Organization of African Unity in Mauritius.

A highly placed French source said that President Amin had refused to allow Pierre Renard, the French Ambassador to Uganda, or a special French envoy to deal with the hijackers directly.

While President Amin was out of the country, messages from Israel had to be passed by French Government representatives through the Somalian Ambassador, Hashi Abdullah Farah, to the hijackers. Messages back to the Israelis followed the same route.

Uganda Guards

When Gen. Amin returned from Mauritius yesterday, he resumed the role of mediator. He told the French Ambassador that demands for the release of 53 pro-Palestinian prisoners in Israel, Kenya and Europe must be met by early today or all the hostages would be killed.

Officials here pointed out that on the list of prisoners were five Ugandans held in

Continued on Page 4, Column 2

Kenya on charges of attempting to assassinate President Jomo Kenyatta.

They also noted that during the first 24 hours after the aircraft reached Entebbe, the hijackers withdrew to rest and Ugandans guarded the hostages.

Other evidence pointing to the Uganda President's involvement with the terrorists was included in comments by French diplomats and the reports of hostages freed earlier by the terrorists. At the time of the Israeli rescue operation nearly all of the hijackers' captives were Israelis or dual nationals.

Among the passengers released last week were Michel Cojot and his 12-year-old son, Olivier. Mr. Cojot, a French management consultant, served as interpreter for the hijackers, and negotiated on their behalf for small conveniences during the ordeal.

'Not Shadow of Doubt'

Mr. Cojot said that he had "not a shadow of a doubt" that the Uganda President knew of the hijack plan in advance and had prepared for the action.

He said that the airbus, a new European-built plane with a normal four-hour flying capacity, flew non-stop to Entebbe after a refueling stop in Benghazi, Libya — a six-hour flight. "We couldn't possibly have made any other airport by then," he said. The hijackers were obviously certain they

Continued on Page 16, Column 4

CARTER TO BEGIN TALKS ON TICKET

Will See Muskie Today and Other Possible Running Mates Soon After

By CHARLES MOHR
Special to The New York Times

PLAINS, Ga., July 4—Jimmy Carter has asked Senator Edmund S. Muskie to visit him here tomorrow and discuss the Maine Senator's qualification to serve as Mr. Carter's running mate on the 1976 Democratic ticket.

Mr. Carter told reporters gathered at the driveway of his home in this small Georgia town this morning that he expected to talk to at least four other persons about the Vice-Presidential nomination between now and the Democratic National Convention, which convenes July 12.

The former Georgia Governor, who is assured of the Presidential nomination, said that it would be wrong to assume that there was any special significance in the fact that Senator Muskie was the first to be invited to meet with him. And, indeed, few political observers seem to feel that Mr. Muskie is a front-runner for the job. He was the Vice-Presidential nominee in 1968 and an unsuccessful candidate for the Democratic Presidential nomination in 1972.

A highly knowledgeable source said that the three men

Continued on Page 16, Column 4

A Day of Picnics, Pomp, Pageantry and Protest

By JOHN L. HESS

The nation celebrated its 200th birthday yesterday with pageantry and prayer, with games and parades, with picnics and fireworks, with the peal of bells and the chant of protests.

It began with a flag-raising atop Mars Hill Mountain in Maine, where dawn reached the continent, and moved on to Fort McHenry, in Baltimore Harbor, where it was greeted by the rocket's red glare of the national anthem. The activities were to end nearly a day later with an indigenous festival in American Samoa.

At 2 P.M., Eastern daylight time, descendants of the Revolutionaries laid hands symbolically on the Liberty Bell in

Philadelphia, and bells rang in the 50 states and in American communities overseas. At Independence Hall, President Ford read the day's keynote address.

This being an American festival, many new records were claimed: the largest cherry pie (60 square feet), at George, Wash.; the largest cake (69,000 pounds), at Baltimore; the largest fireworks display, in Washington, D.C.; the largest gathering of sailing ships, in New York Harbor.

Yet many sponsors of celebrations were disappointed at the turnouts. The Philadelphia parade, planned for 70,000 marchers, drew about half that

Continued on Page 18, Column 1

PRESIDENT TALKS

Philadelphia Throngs Told U.S. Is Leader— Liberty Bell Rings

By JAMES T. WOOTEN
Special to The New York Times

PHILADELPHIA, July 4—With its famous bells ringing, bands blaring, choirs singing and fireworks exploding, this city today staged a joyous, cacophonous commemoration of that day two centuries ago when the representatives of the 13 English colonies met here to renounce their allegiance to the British Crown.

At least one million people were in Philadelphia for the centerpiece of the Bicentennial observances.

President Ford came here from Valley Forge to recall that first Fourth of July as "the beginning of a continuing adventure," unfinished, unfulfilled, but still unchallenged as a model of social and political achievement.

"The world is ever conscious of what Americans are doing, for better or for worse," he said at Independence Hall, "because the United States remains today the most successful realization of humanity's universal hope.

Says Nation Leads

"The world may or may not follow, but we lead because our whole history says we must."

Then, after he left for New York City, the Liberty Bell, that faulted but venerated symbol, was softly sounded with a rubber mallet as millions across the nation watched on television. In clamorous response, hundreds of other bells rang out in Philadelphia's steeples and towers.

Meanwhile, several miles from the official observances, more than 30,000 other Americans, most of them members of two radical coalitions, staged their own peaceful Bicentennial celebration. Mayor Frank L. Rizzo had warned of potential disorders, but there were none.

At the main celebration, blue-shirted policemen cordially gave

Continued on Page 18, Column 5

PANOPLY OF SAILS

Harbor Armada Led by Tall Ships in Salute to Fourth

By RICHARD F. SHEPARD

Buoyed by panoramic spectacles that included a unique armada of tall-masted ships, a massive fireworks display and a series of festivals that took over downtown Manhattan, millions of New Yorkers and visitors in a happy mood observed the nation's Bicentennial yesterday.

It was a day of mammoth presentations.

Uncounted crowds lining the waterfront of the magnificent but underused harbor saw a virtually unbroken bridge of small craft that reached from the shores of Brooklyn to the coast of New Jersey.

More than 225 sailing ships under 31 flags paraded up the Hudson, a river that foretold their doom in 1807 when Robert Fulton's smoky little Clermont started steamboat service on it.

International Review

A 22-nation fleet of 53 naval units gray and grim—even ships festooned with pennants—lined the upper Bay and the Hudson for the International Naval Review, which had Vice President Rockefeller as the chief United States official present.

President Ford flew onto the hulking 79,000-ton aircraft carrier Forrestal, the host ship of the review, and later went by helicopter to the U.S.S. Nashville, anchored in mid-Hudson. He watched the sailing ships and was stranded for 40 minutes by a sudden squall before taking off again, headed for Washington, without having set foot ashore in the city.

As night fell, hundreds of thousands jammed onto the shore of lower Manhattan—some dangling from trees like so many Christmas decorations—to watch the dazzling fireworks explode over the harbor and the Statue of Liberty. When it was over, the tide of the departing throngs sometimes swept people out of con-

Continued on Page 20, Column 3

President Ford waves to the crowd at Valley Forge, Pa., where he signed a bill making it a national historical site. He stands on a covered wagon that represented Michigan, his home state, in the Bicentennial wagon train.
The New York Times/Teresa Zabala

Ethnic Diversity Adds Spice to the Holiday

By FRED FERRETTI

New Yorkers and their friends poured into lower Manhattan yesterday and compressed 200 years of their history and varied ethnic heritages into a day-long birthday party crammed with prayer, martial music, high spirits and good fellowship.

It was the tall ships and the warships that drew them here, but it was Dr. Quackenbush's Traveling Medicine Show, Delancy's Loyalist Red Coat Brigade, Fraunces Tavern, Oscar Brand, falafel and pizza and egg rolls, and John Philip Sousa that kept them there.

Not even a succession of torrential downpours late in the afternoon could drive them away. They watched George III beheaded at Federal Hall National Memorial, listened to Terence Cardinal Cooke pray at Castle Clinton, watched the Turks take over Wall Street for

Continued on Page 22, Column 4

City Hall is the scene of street dancing and music in July 4th in Old New York Festival
The New York Times/Roger W. Sirone

O, Say, It Was a Glorious Patchwork-Quilt of a Fourth

By McCANDLISH PHILLIPS

The Fourth of July celebration in New York City yesterday was as American as a patchwork quilt—full of a joyous order-in-disarray and a series of brilliantly improbable juxtapositions.

It was an exercise in percussion, procession, demonstration, declamation, detonation, commemoration, vociferation, trivialization, solemnization, and, for some, indigestion.

The free and independent citizens of New York City got themselves into a good many unusual postures as they scrambled for perspec-

tive on events, sometimes at the price of mild peril.

In parks and on piers, on fences, balconies, ramps, rooftops, chimneys, ledges, abutments and the ladders of water storage tanks, they sat, stooped, stood and clung, chiefly to watch great ships come sailing out of the distant past and go up the hazy Hudson like a vision.

It was a great day for family portraits to be taken with the most senior member of the American family. The process began early in the day in front of the Federal Hall National Memorial, on Wall Street, on the site

where George Washington took the oath as President on April 30, 1789.

Washington's statue dominates the steps leading up to the eight columns of the hall, and the base of the pedestal is a stage large enough for at least half a dozen persons to stand on.

As soon as one group posed and left, the next moved up to be photographed with the unblinkingly obliging founding father.

Seven small children in bright summer colors nearly ringed the great figure, standing under his outstretched right hand their

heads reaching to half the height of the pedestal. They looked very serious for the moment or so they stood there.

Though few noticed it, Christopher Columbus was in town. Not the old boy him-

Continued on Page 20, Column 5

LATE CITY EDITION

Weather: Partly sunny today; warm tonight. Chance of rain tomorrow. Temperature range: today 65-85; range 60-88. Details on page 70.

"All the News That's Fit to Print"

The New York Times

VOL. CXXV ..No. 43,272   © 1976 The New York Times Company   NEW YORK, THURSDAY, JULY 15, 1976   25 cents beyond 50-mile zone from New York City, except Long Island. Higher in air delivery cities.   **20 CENTS**

CARTER WINS THE DEMOCRATIC NOMINATION; REVEALS VICE-PRESIDENTIAL CHOICE TODAY

AFRICANS ABANDON ANTI-ISRAEL MOVE IN U.N.'S COUNCIL

Withdraw Censure Bid When Defeat Looms—Resolution by U.S. and Britain Fails

By KATHLEEN TELTSCH
Special to The New York Times

UNITED NATIONS, N. Y., July 14—The Security Council tonight ended four days of inconclusive debate on Israel's rescue of hijacked hostages in Uganda without condemning the Israeli raid or approving a rival resolution against hijacking and terrorism.

African members of the Security Council, faced with certain defeat, withdrew a resolution that would have condemned as a "flagrant violation" of Uganda's sovereignty the July 3 raid by Israeli forces to rescue the hostages held by pro-Palestinian hijackers at the Entebbe airport.

The proposed resolution—jointly submitted by Libya, Tanzania and Benin—could have mustered only eight votes, one short of the number needed for approval, and even if it had received the nine needed votes was certain to be vetoed by the United States.

Rival Resolution Fails

In withdrawing their resolution, the supporters of Uganda announced that they would not participate in the vote on the rival resolution submitted by Britain and the United States, thus assuring that that resolution would fail.

The British-American resolution—which would have condemned the hijacking of airliners and called on all governments to "prevent and punish all such terrorist acts"—received only six votes, three short of the number necessary for approval.

Besides Britain and the United States, France, Italy, Sweden and Japan supported the resolution. Rumania and Panama abstained. Those not taking part in the vote were China, Guyana, Libya, Pakistan, Tanzania, Benin (formerly known as Dahomey) and the Soviet Union.

Israel Sees Vindication

After the vote, the Council adjourned.

Israel promptly said that it regarded the outcome of the Security Council debate as vindication of its commando raid on Entebbe because the Council, which had been called into session by the African nations to condemn Israel, had not approved a resolution to that effect.

The Council session, which began last Friday, was requested jointly by 47 members of the Organization of African Unity. In the four days of often stormy debate, Israel contended

Continued on Page 5, Column 1

City University Dropping Tenured Staff Members

By EDWARD B. FISKE

After a frenzied year of attempting to retrench without affecting long-standing traditions of job security for senior professors, the nine senior colleges of the City University system have begun to send dismissal notices to tenured faculty members.

Officials of City, Brooklyn and Queens Colleges confirmed yesterday that, in order to meet mandated budget cuts for the coming year, they were planning to dismiss a total of 921 full-time faculty members, including between 49 and 58 with tenure.

The presidents of Lehman, York and Richmond-Staten Island Colleges said that they had not yet completed their reduction plans, but that cuts among tenured professors were "possible" or "likely." Only Baruch, Hunter and John Jay College indicated that they would meet their retrenchment quotas without affecting tenured personnel.

The invasion for the first time of the academically sacred area of tenured classroom positions is expected to cause major new problems for the financially troubled university, which has been called upon to reduce its overall operating budget from last year's level of $539 million to $470 million for the coming year.

Irwin H. Polishook, president of the Professional Staff Congress, said that he was "outraged" by the news and that the faculty union would file a class-action suit to block the announced dismissals.

"To cut tenured lines is a flagrant violation of the law," he said. "They have not demonstrated that this is necessary for financial reasons, and they have violated their own procedures for due process."

The modern concept of tenure for college professors developed early in the 20th century as a means of protecting

Continued on Page 61, Column 1

Alcoa Asserts a U.S. Envoy Solicited Payment Abroad

By ROBERT D. HERSHEY Jr.
Special to The New York Times

WASHINGTON, July 14—An unidentified United States ambassador solicited at least $25,000 from the Aluminum Company of America that apparently was paid to officials and political parties of a foreign country, according to papers filed by the company recently with the Securities and Exchange Commission.

This was believed to represent the first publicly documented instance in which an American Administration official has been implicated in the continuing wave of disclosures of questionable and illegal payments by American corporations.

The incident occurred during 1971 and 1972 in a country that was not named in Alcoa's S.E.C. filing. Neither the commission nor the company would disclose today any hint of which country it was or the ambassador's identity.

A State Department spokesman denied any knowledge of the episode, commenting only that, "in principle, I would reject out of hand the notion of an American ambassador doing that."

Alcoa's disclosure came at a time of growing suspicion about the role of the United States Government in foreign pay-

Continued on Page 51, Column 1

New Taiwan Plan For Olympic Role Gets U.S. Support

By STEVE CADY

MONTREAL, July 14—Taiwan will try to take part in the Olympic Games, at least on a token basis, under a plan drawn up today with strong support from both the United States and the International Olympic Committee. Unless the new proposal is accepted by the Canadian Government, the United States is prepared to pull its 425-member team out of the Games.

The key point of the Taiwanese strategy is the use of accredited team members already inside Canada. All but a handful of the 42 Taiwanese athletes in 10 sports have been blocked from entering Canada and will not be allowed in the country.

A five-member yachting contingent consisting of three competitors and two coaches would march in the opening ceremony on Saturday. The Taiwanese are insisting that the five take part as the representatives of the Republic

Continued on Page 43, Column 1

Schools of South Africa Are Separate and Unequal

By JOHN F. BURNS
Special to The New York Times

JOHANNESBURG, July 14—Moses Pere always wanted to be one of the small band of South African blacks who graduate from high school. But when his father died last year, his mother, a kitchen hand, could no longer afford the $50 a year it cost to keep him in primary school.

The 17-year-old youth took a street-corner job selling flowers that paid $17.25 a week, enough to cover his keep and the education of the family's other hope for a graduation certificate, his 12-year-old sister.

"If I got through school, maybe I could be a doctor or a teacher," he said one evening this week, eyeing a sleek black-and-gold motorcycle with a $1,750 price tag in a showroom window. "Maybe I could buy a motorcycle."

The youth's problem is not exceptional in South Africa, where financial hardship often forces blacks to drop out of a schooling system that is vastly inferior, by every measure, to the separate system provided for whites.

Since last month's riots, which saw black students attacking and burning their own schools, the Government has stepped up efforts to publicize the improvements in black education in recent years. However, official publications offer stark contrasts.

In the school year beginning next January, the outlay for each white student will be 17 times more than for each black. Despite a growing budget for black education, the disparity

Continued on Page 10, Column 4

CANDIDATE SILENT

Mondale Named Most in Rumors—Muskie Not Ruled Out

By CHARLES MOHR

Jimmy Carter indicated yesterday that he had chosen a running mate, but he took elaborate precautions to shield the name from disclosure before he formally announces his choice today.

By last night Senator Walter F. Mondale of Minnesota, who had retreated into seclusion, appeared to be the man most frequently discussed, and often recommended, for the Vice Presidency by those with access to and influence with Mr. Carter.

But since such persons said that Mr. Carter had not told even his inner circle the name of the man he called "preeminent in my mind," there was also informed betting on Senator Edmund S. Muskie of Maine.

Mr. Carter is a person capable of springing a surprise, and thus could choose among four other Senators — John Glenn of Ohio, Frank Church of Idaho, Adlai E. Stevenson 3d of Illinois and Henry M. Jackson of Washington.

Earlier Plan Arranged

Mr. Carter had once planned, as he told reporters earlier this month, to give as much as 24 hours' notice of his selection to the winner and the losers. However, aware that his choice would almost inevitably be disclosed in such circumstances and distract attention from his own nomination, the 51-year-old Georgian decided to delay his phone calls to the contenders until just before a news conference at 10 A.M. today.

He had thus written a successful political mystery story that left even the most cynical and battlewise Democratic politicians in doubt.

One incident demonstrated the truth of that. Mayor Richard J. Daley of Chicago, a party baron of awesome influence and a man whose endorsement of Mr. Carter on June 9 helped start a landslide of other endorsements, telephoned Mr. Carter at 3:30 P.M., hoping to learn the choice, a highly placed Illinois delegate said. Mr. Carter did not tell Mr. Daley the name, the source said.

There was, however, some evidence about the thinking in the Carter campaign headquarters and among prominent

Continued on Page 25, Column 1

The New York Times/D. Gorton
Jimmy Carter in his hotel suite shortly before last night's convention session began

NEW LABOR GROUP TAKES PARTY ROLE

Coalition of 8 Unions, Not A.F.L.-C.I.O., Is Dominant Among the Democrats

By WARREN WEAVER Jr.

Organized labor, which lost much of its political effectiveness in the unorthodox Democratic National Convention of 1972, is staging a comeback in Madison Square Garden this week, but the dominant voices are not those of George Meany and the old-line unions in the American Federation of Labor and Congress of Industrial Organizations.

From 550 to 600 of the 1976 Democratic delegates are union members, a substantial increase from the drought of four years earlier. However, two-thirds of these are the product of an independent political drive by a coalition of eight unions that decided to end their risky reliance on a single labor-backed Presidential candidate.

The Labor Coalition Clearinghouse, set up in 1975 to insure a strong labor voice at the Democratic convention irrespective of the primary results, managed to elect 418 of its members this year, many under the banner of Jimmy Carter but

Continued on Page 27, Column 1

Carter Gives Insight On Decision-Making

The following article, based on an interview with Jimmy Carter, was written by R. W. Apple Jr., the national political correspondent of The New York Times.

It was the most important day in Jimmy Carter's life. As he sat and talked in his suite on the 21st floor of the Americana Hotel, the prize for which he had toiled 19 long months—the Democratic nomination for President of the United States — lay only 12 hours ahead.

He seemed as calm as if he were spending the day inspecting his orderly and almost detached manner, his choice for Vice President, his acceptance speech and his plans for the campaign.

No, Mr. Carter said. He would not name the man he had tentatively selected as his running-mate, not until a news conference this morning. He would tell the winner and the five losers in the Vice-Presidential sweepstakes by telephone only a few minutes in advance.

"I thought about it last night," he said very softly, "and by this morning there was one man pre-eminent in my mind. It's conceivable that I'll change my mind—I'm not positive yet—but I don't think so."

Why, his visitor wanted to know, had he spent so long in making up his mind? Was he really in doubt, or was the delay simply a charade to seduce the public?

"If I had had to cut the process off at some point in the past," he replied, with no trace of the famous toothy grin, "I might have chosen three different men—one right after the Ohio primary [on June 8], another late last month, and another a week or so ago.

"Now, I have in mind a fourth candidate."

He had tried to make it a habit, Mr. Carter explained, to spend as much time as he had on major decisions, "to give myself the best chance of making the right decision, so I can be at ease, even if I make a mistake—so I'll know I did my best, and not worry."

Although he had weighed dozens of factors, the 51-year-old Georgian said, he had "felt a responsibility, in contrast to my staff and to a lot of the people who have made recommendations, to

Continued on Page 24, Column 6

A QUICK VICTORY

Georgian Is Selected at the Convention by Wide Margin

By R. W. APPLE Jr.

Jimmy Carter of Georgia won the Democratic Presidential nomination last night.

By an overwhelming margin, the Democratic National Convention ratified Mr. Carter's startling electoral ascendancy of the last six months, made him the first major-party nominee from the Deep South since Zachary Taylor in 1848 and installed him as the early favorite to capture the White House in November.

It seemed appropriate when Ohio put Mr. Carter over 1,505 votes — a majority — for it was the Georgian's sweep of that state's June 8 primary that started the stampede of party leaders toward him.

Shouts and Cheers

When Christine Gitlin, the Ohio delegation chairman, announced the vote, the hall burst into shouts and cheers, and Robert S. Strauss, the national chairman, signaled the band to strike up "Happy Days Are Here Again."

An unofficial tabulation by The New York Times gave Mr. Carter a total of 2,238½ votes when the somewhat muddled roll-call ended.

The other candidates who were officially nominated—Gov. Edmund G. Brown Jr. of California, Representative Morris K. Udall of Arizona and Ellen McCormack, the antiabortion candidate—trailed far behind, as did a handful of other contenders.

Standing in the midst of his delegation, Mr. Brown switched California's votes to the former Georgia Governor, remarking, "This is the beginning of a Democratic sweep across this country that comes none too soon."

Nominee Is Declared

Gov. George Busbee of Georgia then moved that Mr. Carter, his predecessor, be declared nominated by acclamation. After a brief contretemps that prevented Massachusetts from voting, the chairman of this 37th Democratic convention, Corinne C. Boggs, declared Mr. Carter the nominee at 11:43 P.M.

In the tumult on the floor, Hamilton Jordan, Mr. Carter's campaign manager, told an interviewer: "We waited four long, hard, wonderful years for this experience and this moment."

Mr. Carter's name was placed before the convention in Madison Square Garden by Representative Peter W. Rodino Jr. of New Jersey, who two years ago this month presided over the impeachment hearings that led to the resignation of President Nixon.

"With honest talk and plain truth," he said, "Jimmy Carter has appealed to the American people. His heart is honest, and the people will believe him. His purpose is right, and the people will follow him."

Alluding several times to Watergate, Mr. Rodino said of Mr. Carter:

"As he has brought a united South back into the Democratic Party, he will bring a united Democratic Party back into the leadership of America and a united America back to a position of respect and esteem in the eyes of the world."

Then the diminutive, gray-

Continued on Page 24, Column 1

The New York Times/Gary Settle
Members of Ohio delegation cheering as their votes confirmed nomination of Jimmy Carter on first ballot at Democratic convention last night

CALL THIS TOLL-FREE NUMBER TO ORDER HOME DELIVERY OF THE NEW YORK TIMES-800-325-6400.—Advt.

The New York Times

LATE CITY EDITION

Weather: Chance of rain late today, tonight. Partly sunny tomorrow. Temperature range: today 72-86; Tuesday 66-90. Details on page 65.

VOL. CXXV .. No. 43,278

© 1976 The New York Times Company

NEW YORK, WEDNESDAY, JULY 21, 1976

25 cents beyond 50-mile zone from New York City, except Long Island. Higher in air delivery cities.

20 CENTS

VIKING ROBOT SETS DOWN SAFELY ON MARS AND SENDS BACK PICTURES OF ROCKY PLAIN

Associated Press

A composite photo showing a 300-degree panorama of the surface of Mars, made by a camera on the Viking 1 landing craft just after touchdown on the planet yesterday morning. Parts of the craft are visible in foreground.

Ford Gains 10 Delegates And Needs Only 18 More

By JAMES M. NAUGHTON
Special to The New York Times

WASHINGTON, July 20—President Ford gained substantial delegate strength today to pull within 18 votes of the total needed to gain a first-ballot nomination at the Republican National Convention.

Amid conflicting claims from the rival Republican camps, The New York Times determined from the best available information and a canvass of the delegates involved that Mr. Ford had a net gain of 10 delegates while Ronald Reagan had a net increase of one.

The new tally by The Times listed 1,112 delegates for Mr. Ford—18 short of the 1,130 needed for nomination — and 1,064 for Mr. Reagan, with 83 still uncommitted. Thirteen of the 83 said they were leaning to Mr. Ford and three to Mr. Reagan.

James A. Baker, a deputy chairman of the President Ford Committee, claimed the conversion of several delegates and proposed to certify the President's strength by making public the identities of all Ford delegates once they constitute a convention majority.

The proposal to list the delegates by name and address was the latest move in a war of nerves between supporters of the President and of Mr. Reagan.

Mr. Baker dismissed as "blowing smoke" the largely unsubstantiated claim yesterday by John P. Sears, the Reagan campaign manager, to 1,140 delegates for the former California Governor—10 more than needed for nomination.

Mr. Sears retaliated later to-

Continued on Page 8, Column 1

U.S. AGENCY FINDS DRUG TESTING LAX

Says F.D.A., Makers and Others Expose the Public to Needless Risks

By RICHARD HALLORAN
Special to The New York Times

WASHINGTON, July 20—Congressional investigators have issued a blistering indictment of the Food and Drug Administration, pharmaceutical makers, doctors and research scientists, charging them with exposing humans to unnecessary risks in testing new drugs.

The General Accounting Office also reported that the testing procedures could result in F.D.A. approval of a new drug for public use based on "inaccurate and unreliable data."

The Congressional investigating unit disclosed instances of "alarming adverse reactions" to new drugs that went unreported and the death of eight soldiers in an Army test of a drug intended to prevent malaria.

Despite continued controversy over many aspects of the regulation of prescription drugs in recent years, the general ac-

Continued on Page 42, Column 4

Rao Indictments Obtained By Nadjari Are Reinstated

By MAX H. SEIGEL

The Appellate Division in Brooklyn yesterday reinstated perjury indictments obtained by Maurice H. Nadjari against Judge Paul P. Rao Sr. of United States Customs Court; his son, Paul Jr., and another lawyer, Salvatore Nigrone.

The indictments had been dismissed last Dec. 2 by the late Justice John M. Murtagh of State Supreme Court on the ground that undercover agents had made statements to the grand jury that "were highly prejudicial to the defendants."

Justice Murtagh also had questioned whether the evidence before the grand jury was legally sufficient to establish the offense charged.

The majority found that Justice Murtagh had said improperly that he was dismissing the indictments "in the interests of justice" while he had actually ordered the dismissal

Continued on Page 67, Column 1

Long Offers 2d Vote In Tax-Aid Dispute

By EILEEN SHANAHAN
Special to The New York Times

WASHINGTON, July 20—Russell B. Long, chairman of the Senate Finance Committee, promised today to give the panel a new opportunity to vote for or against each of 73 provisions of the pending tax bill, most of which benefit just one company or industry.

Senator Long made the commitment after an unusually heated session of the committee during which Senator Edward M. Kennedy was, in effect, called a demagogue by one Republican member and accused of not knowing what he was talking about by another.

Mr. Kennedy, Democrat of Massachusetts, has emerged as a leading foe of the kind of narrow-interest tax legislation

Continued on Page 42, Column 4

Associated Press

Foot pad of the Viking 1 resting on Mars. Center of this picture is five feet from camera and the rock at center is approximately four inches across.

South African Black Is Reported Killed In Renewed Rioting

By JOHN F. BURNS
Special to The New York Times

JOHANNESBURG, July 20—At least one black man was reported killed tonight when police reinforcements were rushed to the coal-mining center of Witbank, 75 miles east of here, which was in the grip of the most serious rioting since the widespread anti-Government upheavals last month.

Reports from the scene said that about 3,000 black youths had poured out of black townships and attacked people and buildings in areas occupied by Indians and people of mixed descent, who are called colored here.

Few details were available, and it was unclear how the reported death had occurred. However, the riot policemen, armed with automatic rifles, were acting under standing Government orders to suppress fresh outbreaks of violence with all necessary force.

The possibility of a chain reaction was raised by a police report of at least one outbreak elsewhere. At midnight, rioters were said to have set fire to several buildings in Khutsong, a black township southwest of Johannesburg.

The death would be the first since the end of the rioting

Continued on Page 4, Column 7

GOLD PLUNGES 12% IN WEEK TO $107.75

Slump Hurts South Africa —Heavy Soviet Selling Is Seen as Part of Cause

By PETER T. KILBORN

LONDON, July 20 — The turmoil that has been swirling through many nations' currencies has now swept into gold, long a major component, along with the dollar, of the world's monetary reserves.

In only five business days, the price of gold has tumbled nearly 12 percent, from $122 an ounce last Wednesday to $107.75 at its close today in London. Today alone it fell nearly $6.

The drop has been so abrupt, gold experts here said, that South Africa, the world's leading producer of gold, now faces political as well as economical consequences unless the price recovers quickly.

"If you take the gold out of South Africa," said Richard Lockwood, a mining expert for a brokerage firm in London, "you've got one of the worst economies in the world."

Experts also expected difficulties for the Soviet Union, another major producer. Ironically, they said, the Russians helped bring on the decline in

Continued on Page 47, Column 5

Nitrogen, Key to Life, Is Found

By WALTER SULLIVAN

PASADENA, Calif., July 20—The first definitive analysis of the Martian atmosphere has disclosed the presence of a small component of nitrogen. Until now the absence of any evidence of that gas stood as a major obstacle to speculation that life might exist on the planet.

The analysis has also provided long-sought clues to the history of Mars, including the possibility that enough water is hidden beneath its surface to cover the planet one mile deep.

The chief surprise has been Viking's discovery that argon, an inert gas, constitutes far less of the Martian atmosphere than scientists previously believed. Whereas estimates of the argon level on Mars had been as high as 30 percent, data from Viking indicate that it is only about 3 percent, compared with about 1 percent in the Earth's atmosphere.

The analysis also put the level of nitrogen at about 3 percent.

This and other detailed determinations should bear on such questions as the history of the Earth's known atmosphere, including the proposal that the atmosphere of both Earth and Mars were formed in eruptions very early in each planet's history.

Such an early formation of the atmosphere would mean, as well, the early appearance of oceans or smaller water bodies suitable for the evolution of life.

Higher Ratio Suggested

When the Soviet Union's Mars 6 plunged into the Mars atmosphere in its unsuccessful landing attempt in 1974 it was thought that perplexing features of its data transmissions could be explained if 30 percent of the Martian air consisted of argon. The possibility of so large a percentage also offered an explanation for observations made near one of the Martian poles a few days ago by the Viking mother ship that cast loose the lander today.

Today's measurement, which is considered definitive, put the argon level at about 3 percent.

The lower abundance of argon is good news for those experimenters hoping to learn the composition of Mars's surface materials. Their instrument aboard the lander will determine such compositions with a gas chromatograph mass spectrometer that could have been rendered useless by an atmosphere rich in argon.

The project's scientists believe that today's measurements will help clarify whether, as some of them believe, there is still enough water hidden beneath the surface of Mars to cover that planet to a depth of one mile.

The abundance of argon in the air of Mars today is a critical index of the atmosphere's history. If volcanic eruptions and other processes generated the same atmospheric constituents as those produced by such activity on Earth, the present abundance of argon could, it was argued, have been as high as reported by the Russians.

The reasoning is that since

Continued on Page 12, Column 4

3¼-HOUR DESCENT

Scientists Are Jubilant as News Is Flashed, Taking 19 Minutes

By JOHN NOBLE WILFORD
Special to The New York Times

PASADENA, Calif., July 20—An explorer from Earth, the robot craft Viking 1, made the first successful landing on Mars today and transmitted spectacular photographs of a rocky, wind-scoured desert plain, the site for the first direct search for life on another world.

The squat, three-legged Viking landing craft came to rest, upright and intact, on the Chryse Plain of Mars at 7:53 A.M. Eastern daylight time after a voyage of 11 months and nearly half a billion miles. The final and most suspenseful step, the craft's descent to the surface from its mother ship in Mars orbit, took 3 hours 13 minutes.

Then, Touchdown

Responding to automatic computer commands, the lander's rockets fired, its parachute unfurled, protective shielding broke away, more rockets were fired—and then, touchdown. It was 19 minutes, because of the great distance between Mars and Earth, now more than 212 million miles, before confirmation of the safe landing reached the control rooms here at the Jet Propulsion Laboratory.

"Touchdown!" announced Richard Bender, one of the flight controllers. "We have touchdown. We have several indications of touchdown."

It was an emotional moment for the scientists and engineers of the $1 billion Viking project, many of whom had spent eight years preparing for this day.

Applause and Amazement

There was applause in the control room and throughout the laboratory. There were broad smiles and moist eyes. There were soft expressions of numbed amazement at what they had wrought.

With the Viking landing begins the first surface exploration of Mars (two Soviet landings failed to produce usable data). The planet has fascinated man for centuries and been the object of legend and endless scientific speculation.

In eight days, if all continues to go according to plan, a mechanical arm on the lander is to reach out and scoop up soil samples for chemical and biological analysis by onboard instruments. This will mark the beginning of the mission's search for signs of possible life on Mars.

Though Mars is no longer seriously thought of as an

Continued on Page 12, Column 1

Attica Is Termed as Bad As Before 1971 Rebellion

By FRED FERRETTI
Special to The New York Times

ATTICA, N.Y., July 20—The chief of a State Commission of Correction team sent into the Attica prison last week following the most recent outbreak of violence there described conditions within the facility today as "just as bad, perhaps worse" than in September 1971, just before an inmate rebellion that resulted in the deaths of 43 persons.

"What we have is a combat situation," said Scott Christianson, director of the Correction Commission's State Prison Unit, following five days of investigation and interrogation of inmates and guards. "The environment is so physical, so potentially dangerous, the power of both the inmates and the guards is so awesome, that it

Continued on Page 65, Column 1

can go off at any time. Both sides have the power of death in their hands."

The superintendent of the prison, Harold J. Smith, conceded in an interview that an inmate rebellion could happen again. "Yes, it could," he said, "I'd be a damn fool to say otherwise."

The Correction Commission has reported formally to Governor Carey that a set of parallels exists between the situation here today and what it was in Attica just before Sept. 9, 1971, when the prisoners stormed it. The prison was subsequently recaptured by state troopers who stormed it.

The new report urged the

Continued on Page 65, Column 1

United Press International

Dr. James Fletcher, left, and James S. Martin, on phones, being congratulated by President Ford as other officials watched a television set for first Mars photographs.

"All the News That's Fit to Print"

LATE CITY EDITION
Weather: Sunny today; clear, mild tonight. Sunny, warmer tomorrow. Temperature range: today 63-83; Wednesday 64-80. Details, page 70.

The New York Times

VOL. CXXV . No. 43,307   © 1976 The New York Times Company   NEW YORK, THURSDAY, AUGUST 19, 1976   25 cents beyond 50-mile zone from New York City, except Long Island. Higher in air delivery cities.   20 CENTS

FORD TAKES NOMINATION ON FIRST BALLOT; REVEALS VICE-PRESIDENTIAL CHOICE TODAY

2 AMERICANS SLAIN BY NORTH KOREANS IN CLASH AT DMZ

4 U.S. Soldiers and 5 South Koreans Hurt in Assault by Communists With Axes

Special to The New York Times

SEOUL, South Korea, Thursday, Aug. 19—North Korean soldiers, wielding axes and metal pikes, attacked a group of American and South Korean soldiers in the demilitarized zone yesterday, killing two American officers and wounding four American enlisted men and five South Korean soldiers.

The attack took place as the American and South Korean soldiers were trimming branches from a tree at the Panmunjom truce site near an allied checkpoint at the south end of the "Bridge of No Return," over which prisoners were exchanged after the Korean War.

According to the United Nations Command, the American and South Korean work group was performing a routine task when two North Korean officers and some soldiers approached and, after some discussion, demanded that the Americans and South Koreans stop trimming the tree.

Order to 'Kill' Overheard

Shortly afterward a truck carrying North Korean soldiers drove up and one of the officers was heard to tell the soldiers to "kill" the Americans and South Koreans. Then, according to the United Nations Command's account, the North Koreans rushed the Americans and South Koreans with axes, metal pikes and ax handles.

[In Kansas City, President Ford, in a statement Wednesday condemned the attack as "brutal and cowardly" and warned that the North Korean Government would be responsible for "the consequences." Page 14.]

The North Koreans charged in a radio broadcast last night that "U.S. imperialist troops" armed with "lethal weapons" had pounced on North Korean soldiers who had protested the trimming of the tree, which the broadcast said was in an area under North Korean control.

The broadcast made no mention of any casualties on either side in the clash. A Japanese news agency quoted military sources as saying said that three North Koreans had been killed in the clash, but the report could not be confirmed and

Continued on Page 14, Column 5

FILIPINOS DESCRIBE HOW DISASTER HIT

Amid Debris on Mindanao, They Tell How Quake and Tidal Wave Swept Area

By ALICE VILLADOLID
Special to The New York Times

DINAIG, the Philippines, Aug. 18—The coastal strip near this town, an hour's drive from Cotabato City, was once a scenic spot. Today it is littered with twisted coconut trees, uprooted coconut trees, battered furniture and other debris left by the earthquake and tidal wave that struck at dawn yesterday on the island of Mindanao.

The area was one of the worst hit in the quake, which the National Disaster Coordinating Center said left 3,131 dead and 3,117 missing. The head of the center said the death toll might reach 5,000. More than 28,000 were left homeless by the quake and 18-foot-high waves, and 688 were listed as injured.

One described the start of the disaster this way:

"When the earth began shak-

Burmah Oil's U.S. Aid Bid Studied for Possible Fraud

By TERRY ROBARDS

The Securities and Exchange Commission, the Federal Maritime Administration and at least one Congressional committee are investigating whether the Burmah Oil Company, a major British concern, illegally received commitments for Federal guarantees or subsidies to build at least one huge tanker ships in this country.

Hundreds of millions of dollars in shipbuilding projects and thousands of American shipyard jobs may be in jeopardy because of the possibility of fraud in applying for the Government backing, which is illegal for foreign companies under Federal law.

The ships are under construction at the Quincy, Mass., yards of the General Dynamics Corporation, which received the shipbuilding contracts from Burmah affiliates or subsidiaries. A major portion of the $1.06 billion in these contracts is understood to be in question.

At issue is whether the ships have any right to American subsidies or loan guarantees, since Burmah is not an American company. Federal law specifies that only domestic con-

cerns can receive such Government backing.

Commitments for this backing have been made to a group of companies related to Burmah and set up for the express purpose of trying to fulfill the requirements for American citizenship.

Robert J. Blackwell, Assistant Secretary of Commerce for Maritime Affairs and head of the Maritime Administration, said in a telephone interview from Washington last night that the agency "has no information to indicate that there was fraud of any type or wrongdoing" in the Burmah applications.

However, Mr. Blackwell also said that some of the original applications filed by the Burmah affiliates had been "more or less aborted" because the companies could not fulfill some of the conditions specified by his agency.

He added that the structure of the corporate entities involved in the shipbuilding contracts was being changed in an effort to assure compliance

Continued on Page 60, Column 1

Deportation Faced By Danish Widow Of Stabbing Victim

By JOYCE MAYNARD

The Danish widow of an actor fatally stabbed in Greenwich Village last June is threatened with deportation on the ground that she does not meet United States residency requirements because, in the words of immigration officials, "the marriage no longer exists."

The woman, Sus McCready, had been married 11 months and was awaiting approval of her petition for a green card signifying permanent residency when her husband, Tom, was killed.

"I try to be a hopeful person but they get me over and over and over," said Mrs. McCready in a steady voice, sitting on a single bed in the studio apartment where she moved shortly after the murder, with a few plants and some recordings and a man's rumpled brown hat on a table.

Four days after the murder, Mrs. McCready received a bill for $982 from the hospital emergency room where her husband was treated.

"There are so many papers

Continued on Page 49, Column 4

PLAN IS OUTLINED FOR 1978 FREEDOM IN AFRICAN AREA

South-West Africa Proposal for a Multiracial Regime Ignores the Guerrillas

By JOHN F. BURNS
Special to The New York Times

JOHANNESBURG, Aug. 18—Faced with a United Nations ultimatum that expires at the end of the month, a constitutional committee in South-West Africa today announced plans to lead the territory to independence from South Africa by Dec. 31, 1978.

The announcement, made with the tacit approval of the

Text of committee statement is printed on page 4.

South African Government, represented the second major move within a week to relieve international pressure on South Africa. On Friday, South Africa announced its support for the United States effort to promote a negotiated settlement of the Rhodesian crisis.

South Africa once vigorously opposed a surrender of power by the white minorities on its borders. However, its current view is that supporting moves toward majority rule outside its own borders will gain it time in which to persuade the world that white rule in South Africa, adjusted to relieve black grievances, is indispensable.

No Mention of Rebels

The statement on South-West Africa, issued in Windhoek, the territorial capital, made no mention of the South-West Africa People's Organization, recognized by the United Nations as the representative of the territory's 800,000 inhabitants. The group, which has been carrying on a guerrilla war, has been not participating in the discussions.

Nor did the statement make any reference to elections. The ultimatum issued by the Security Council called for United Nations-supervised elections in the territory, which South Africa has continued to govern in defiance of a decision by the International Court of Justice holding its occupation to be illegal.

However, the committee, representing 11 ethnic groups, appealed to all nations to counter any attempt at solving the territory's problems violently. This was seen as a reference to the South-West Africa People's Or-

Continued on Page 4, Column 4

President Ford before his nomination yesterday

— The New York Times/Teresa Zabala

PRESIDENT URGED TO NETTLE CARTER

Advisers Feel Sharp Attacks on Integrity Will Rattle Democratic Opponent

By JAMES RESTON
Special to The New York Times

KANSAS CITY, Mo., Aug. 18—President Ford is being urged by some of his closest advisers to follow a strategy of provocation against Jimmy Carter in the Presidential campaign.

"You just watch us," one of them said today. "We're going to wipe that smile off his face."

This proposed strategy rests on the assumption that the Democratic nominee is vague, self-righteous and short-tempered, and that he can be rattled by sharp attacks on his integrity and credibility.

With this in mind, the President's advisers are proposing that he put former Gov. John B. Connally of Texas in charge of the Republican campaign. Mr. Connally has a reputation as a master of political ridicule and sarcasm.

It is not clear that President Ford has agreed to this line of attack on Mr. Carter. His staff has been looking at some of the speeches made to the delegates, but there is no evidence that the President himself has been directing the

Continued on Page 30, Column 7

Reagan's Backers Stage Noisy Last-Ditch Parade

By JAMES T. WOOTEN
Special to The New York Times

KANSAS CITY, Mo., Thursday, Aug. 19—Jubilantly parading as enthusiastically as winners, Ronald Reagan's supporters celebrated his proposed candidacy at the Republican National Convention here last night with a rowdy, raucous, unscheduled demonstration that lasted 43 minutes and defied several attempts to stop it.

Moments later, equally ardent backers of President Ford responded when his name was formally placed in nomination with a shorter but similarly well-organized show of support that filled the air of Kemper Arena with hundreds of beach balls.

The Reaganites' histrionics, however, seemed finally to go beyond the control of the Californian's floor leaders

and the candidate himself eventually conceded that they were "running too long."

Armed with plastic horns and the lingering frustrations of a long campaign, the Reaganites raised the roof of the Kemper Arena, dancing in the aisles of the Convention floor and around the edges of the jammed balconies.

With the Californian's name officially entered as a candidate by his campaign chairman, Senator Paul Laxalt of Nevada, his supporters were unwilling to halt the demonstration despite the gaveling of the convention chairman, Representative John J. Rhodes.

"This is the longest demonstration of my seven convention

Continued on Page 26, Column 3

Sears Says Twists of Fate Hurt Reagan's Chances

By JON NORDHEIMER
Special to The New York Times

KANSAS CITY, Mo., Aug. 18—It was the little things—the unpredictable turns of fortune that make American politics at once so fascinating and so frustrating — that gravely wounded Ronald Reagan's chances for the Republican nomination, the open California Governor's campaign manager, John P. Sears, said today.

"It's been true at many points in this campaign that very small items have had very large significance," Mr. Sears told a news conference before the Republican National Convention met to confer its nomination for President.

The vote of the Mississippi delegation yesterday afternoon not to support Mr. Reagan's crucial floor fight last night for a rules change was the final unexpected twist that helps change history, Mr. Sears said philosophically.

Mistakes. Misunderstandings. Misinterpretation. A lost vote here and there. They all added up, he said, to bring the Reagan campaign to a point where victory after nine hotly contested months of campaigning seemed beyond reach.

In a 30-minute news conference marked by Mr. Sears's candor and crackling wit, and

Continued on Page 29, Column 3

2 RIVALS MEET

Reagan Not Running for No. 2 Spot but Doesn't Bar Draft

By R. W. APPLE Jr.
Special to The New York Times

KANSAS CITY, Mo., Thursday, Aug. 19—Gerald Rudolph Ford, who struggled for seven grueling months to avoid rejection by his party, was nominated in his own right early this morning at the 31st Republican National Convention on the first and only ballot.

The party sent Mr. Ford, a political insider who has held elective office for 28 years, into combat against Jimmy Carter, the political outsider chosen by the Democrats, after Gov. William G. Milliken of Michigan hailed him as the nation's "present and future President."

Unlike most Presidents, Mr. Ford, who inherited the White House after Richard M. Nixon resigned, will enter the general election campaign as the underdog.

West Virginia Clinches

West Virginia, the scene of intensive combat for the loyalties of delegates, gave the President 20 votes—as promised by Gov. Arch A. Moore Jr. for months—and put him over the top at 12:29 A.M. Central daylight time.

In the gallery at the south end of the hall, Betty Ford rose to her feet and waved her hands above her head in evangelistic style. Then she and her three children hugged and kissed each other.

The final count gave Mr. Ford 1,187 votes and Ronald Reagan 1,070. John J. Walsh Jr., an Illinois alternate from River Forest, abstained, and Ralph DeBlasio, a Greenwich Village district leader, voted for Commerce Secretary Elliot L. Richardson.

Despite a scattering of "noes," mainly from the pro-Reagan Texas delegation, Representative John J. Rhodes of Arizona, the convention's permanent chairman, declared Mr. Ford nominated by acclamation.

27-Minute Meeting

Mr. Ford then drove to Mr. Reagan's hotel for a 27-minute meeting with his vanquished adversary. They discussed the Vice Presidency. Mr. Reagan said at a subsequent news conference that he stood by earlier statements that he would not run with the President, but it was unclear whether he had been asked.

The Californian said he would not permit his name to be put in nomination for the Vice Presidency, but he left open the door for a draft by the delegates, many of whom appeared to want a Ford-Reagan ticket. The President, who was to announce his choice later today, smiled as Mr. Reagan responded to questions about a draft.

Describing the former Governor as "the most effective campaigner in America" and

Continued on Page 26, Column 1

Calls Swamp Police 911 Emergency Line

By PRANAY GUPTE

The 911 emergency telephone number system is being flooded by a record number of calls, and the police, citing dwindling manpower, say they cannot handle the calls as fast as they would like. This includes, they say, incidents involving what officials acknowledge are increasing activities by youth gangs.

"We need more people to handle 911 calls," Inspector Charles F. Peterson, commanding officer of the Police Department's communications bureau, said yesterday. "And we need an army to deal with these roving bands of youths."

He was responding to charges by some civic groups that the police were inefficient and tardy

in responding to three recent incidents in Manhattan, Brooklyn and Staten Island in which rampaging youths terrorized residents, shopkeepers, pedestrians and even passengers in taxis.

Such charges are currently being investigated by Police Commissioner Michael J. Codd.

Commissioner Codd and Inspector Peterson had met yesterday afternoon with John E. Zuccotti, the First Deputy Mayor, to discuss the recent incidents involving youth gangs. At that meeting the police officials were reported to have renewed their request for more manpower.

They told Mr. Zuccotti the number of personnel direct-

Continued on Page 60, Column 7

CALL THIS TOLL-FREE NUMBER TO ORDER HOME DELIVERY OF THE NEW YORK TIMES-800-325-5450.-Advt.

North Korean troops attacking a United Nations work party in the demilitarized zone, killing two U.S. officers. Photo was made by a U.S. soldier.

United Press International

CLASSIFIED advertising accepted nationally, Monday through Friday, starting September 13. Call (212) OX 5-3311 to arrange it.-Advt.

"All the News That's Fit to Print"

The New York Times

LATE CITY EDITION

Weather: Showers likely today and tonight. Partly cloudy tomorrow. Temperature range: today 63-73; Thursday 60-79. Details, page D17.

VOL. CXXV.... No. 43,329 © 1976 The New York Times Company NEW YORK, FRIDAY, SEPTEMBER 10, 1976 25 cents beyond 50-mile zone from New York City, except Long Island. Higher in air delivery cities. 20 CENTS

The Pattern of Partisan Support for Ford and Carter

People surveyed were asked if they think of themselves as Republican, Democratic or Independent. Those who answered Independent were asked toward which party they leaned.

(The height of the bars shows the percentage of registered voters in each category in The New York Times/CBS News poll.)

FORD SUPPORTERS / CARTER

Republicans | Independents (Leaning Republican) | Independents | Independents (Leaning Democratic) | Democrats

The New York Times/Sept. 10, 1976

This chart shows that President Ford's support is predominant among Republicans and that Jimmy Carter's support rises steadily along the Democratic end of the spectrum. For example, 22 percent called themselves Republicans. Among these Ford had roughly a seven-to-one advantage.

Poll Shows Ford Trailing in Bid For 2 Voter Groups G.O.P. Needs

By R. W. APPLE Jr.

President Ford is trailing Jimmy Carter among self-described independents and moderates, the two elements of the electorate without whose strong support Republican nominees have been unable to win Presidential elections in the post-World War II era.

With less than two months remaining until Election Day, the President's strength is concentrated in groups that lack the voting power to elect a President—the well-to-do, the Republicans, the white Protestants, the conservatives. In almost every other segment of the electorate, Mr. Ford is running well behind his Democratic opponent, Mr. Carter.

Those are two of the central conclusions that emerge from the first national poll taken by The New York Times and CBS News since the two party conventions—a survey of 1,703 registered voters, selected at random, who were interviewed

by telephone during the week that ended Sept. 5, immediately before the formal start of the general election campaign on Labor Day.

The New York Times/CBS News poll was not designed to predict the outcome of the election but to analyze the thinking of the electorate as it stood early this month. Nonetheless it reflected the same over-all standing of the candidates as recent surveys by the Gallup and Harris organizations, with Mr. Carter leading the President by a margin of roughly 4 to 3.

Insofar as issues determine how people cast their votes for President, the poll indicated, President Ford is suffering from the continuing deep divisions in the country over two issues he inherited from his discredited predecessor.

Continued on Page A19, Col. 3

AGREEMENT REACHED ON TAX REVISION BILL

Conferees Adopt First Reform of Estate Levies in 35 Years

By EDWIN L. DALE Jr.
Special to The New York Times

WASHINGTON, Sept. 9 — House and Senate conferees agreed tonight on all provisions of the sweeping tax revision bill after adopting the first major reform of the nation's system of estate taxes in 35 years.

The final version of the bill, it was estimated, would give the Treasury $1.6 billion more in revenues in the fiscal year 1977, thus meeting the demands of the new Congressional budget control process and greatly augmenting the bill's chances for passage.

The revenue increase would rise to $2.4 billion five years from now, offset in part by revenue losses from the new estate tax reform.

The bill has hundreds of provisions, among them a significant increase in taxes on wealthy taxpayers who avail themselves of various tax "shelters."

It also would impose tax penalties on United States companies complying with the Arab boycott of Israel.

The estate tax reform would provide

Continued on Page D17, Col. 5

Ford Asserts Rival Would Create Peril To Defense of U.S.

By JAMES M. NAUGHTON
Special to The New York Times

WASHINGTON, Sept. 9—President Ford said today that Jimmy Carter's plans to reduce Pentagon spending and troop levels overseas would make it "impossible to have a defense adequate to maintain our freedom and the freedom of our friends."

Addressing the national convention of B'nai B'rith one day after Mr. Carter did, the President departed from a prepared text to read notes sharply critical of the national security positions of his Democratic challenger.

Says Carter Invites Crisis

Mr. Ford contended that the former Georgia Governor's proposals would, among other things, require the United States to rely on "a nuclear strategy of massive retaliation" and thus "invite a major crisis with our allies, including Israel."

Mr. Carter, meanwhile, took issue with Mr. Ford's remarks yesterday, in which the President embraced proposals for a constitutional amendment to limit abortions. The Democratic nominee said that he thought the sensitive abortion issue could backfire on any Presidential candidate who attempted to exploit it.

Even Mr. Ford's running mate, Senator

Continued on Page A21, Col. 1

Radar Images From Venus Depict Vast Area of Possible Lava Flow

By JOHN NOBLE WILFORD

American astronomers who have obtained the first detailed radar images of a large portion of the surface of Venus say they reveal a possible lava flow the size of Oklahoma, an impact basin much like those on the moon and evidence of mountain-building processes similar to those that have shaped the Earth.

Since Venus is completely enveloped by thick clouds, the radar images represent the first relatively clear picture of what the planet's surface looks like. The images covered an area of about four million square miles in the northern latitudes of Venus.

The most distinctive feature in the

north of Venus, as shown by the radar, is a very bright Oklahoma size area that the scientists said looked like a broad lava field. It appears to be a sharply defined feature overlaying an older surface.

The scientists said that the area did not have a shape that might have been created by the impact of a meteorite, but instead seemed to be a result of processes internal to Venus, such as a volcanic eruption of lava. The feature has been tentatively named Maxwell, for James Clerk Maxwell, the 19th-century Scottish physicist.

Maxwell's surface appears extremely rough and apparently contains long paral-

Continued on Page A18, Col. 5

MAO TSE-TUNG DIES IN PEKING AT 82; LEADER OF RED CHINA REVOLUTION; CHOICE OF SUCCESSOR IS UNCERTAIN

KISSINGER IS CAUTIOUS

Discerns No Setback for U.S. Relations With China, but Sees Hazards in a Change

By BERNARD GWERTZMAN
Special to The New York Times

WASHINGTON, Sept. 9—Secretary of State Henry A. Kissinger said today that he did not think Mao Tse-tung's death would set back Chinese-American relations, but he cautioned that "when any historical figure disappears it is extremely difficult to predict everything his successor will do."

At a brief news conference Mr. Kissinger reflected Washington's uncertainty about the future in light of Mao's death. Officially, Secretary Kissinger and President Ford expressed confidence that the trend toward improved relations started by the Chinese leader and President Richard M. Nixon in 1972 would continue.

[In Moscow, diplomatic observers said the death of Chairman Mao raised the possibility of a relaxation of tensions between the Soviet Union and China. Page A17.]

Kissinger Met Mao Five Times

The Secretary of State, who has met Mao five times since 1971, tempered the official optimism with the caution that because China was probably on the verge of major changes, the eventual trend of its policy could not be predicted with assurance.

"We have to remember that when a towering figure disappears from the scene, not even his successors can know exactly what the shape of events will be and it is premature to speculate as to what the future evolution should be," he said in answer to a question.

Mr. Kissinger, in a signal to Chinese leaders, said that since the opening to China, it and the United States had "created a durable relationship based on mutual confidence and perception of common interests."

Pledge to Adhere to Communiqué

"For our part we will continue to cement our ties with the People's Republic of China in accordance with the Shanghai Communiqué issued at the end of Mr. Nixon's visit and calling for normalization of relations.

Earlier in the day the Secretary told newsmen that "we consider our opening to the People's Republic of China one of the most important foreign policy actions of the recent period and we don't really expect any change on the Chinese side, but the methods and the nuances

Continued on Page A17, Col. 6

Panel on Paperwork Assembling A Litany of Constant Redundancy

By MOLLY IVINS

The Commission on Federal Paperwork convened in New York City yesterday to communicate on the feasibility of implementing a restriction on the ongoing paperflow.

The commission, which reports to both the Congress and the President, has been assigned the almost insuperable task of doing something about the sea of forms, applications and reports that threatens to engulf everyone.

The members of the commission seem almost awed by the dimensions of the paperwork problem: They estimate that paperwork and red tape cost the nation's economy $40 billion a year, not counting paper clips. But they are making inroads on the problem.

They have a form that will continue to be, as was shown by Philip Toia, Commissioner of New York State's Department of Social Services, who arrived trailing a 45-foot-long string of forms—the result of one year's paperwork on a single child in the program of aid to dependent children.

The commission has been holding a series of hearings around the country, and this one focused on the paperwork in income maintenance programs.

James Reid, director of the Monroe County Department of Social Services, explained his department's procedure for Supplemental Security Income recipients. It was a five-minute litany of recipients getting ping-ponged between agencies by requirements to fill out 22-page forms.

Tales of the labyrinthine inner workings of assorted New York welfare de-

Continued on Page A18, Col. 1

Mao Tse-tung is shown in 1969 at the Ninth Party Congress, proclaiming the triumph of his Cultural Revolution over disgraced President Liu Shao-chi.

United Press International

Political Uncertainty in China

Natural Disasters and Reports of Indiscipline Leave Analysts Fearful of Forecasting Events

By FOX BUTTERFIELD
Special to The New York Times

HONG KONG, Sept. 9—The death today of Chairman Mao Tse-tung comes at a time when China's political situation seems more uncertain than at any point since the end of the Cultural Revolution.

Over the last 18 months four other members of the nine-man standing Committee of the party's Politburo, China's highest decision-making body, have died, including Prime Minister Chou En-lai. Since last winter Peking has been preoccupied with a divisive political campaign, there have been growing reports of a breakdown in public discipline, and there have even been some isolated incidents of violent conflict.

News Analysis

There have also been other misfortunes for China. Last July parts of Northern China were devastated by the world's worst earthquake in a decade, and both

northeast and southwest China have recently been hit by strong tremors.

No analysts here believe that the Communist regime is likely to be seriously jeopardized by these troubles. But few of them would dare to forecast the shape of events.

The most likely course of events in China after the funeral, some analysts believe, is that a transitional collective leadership, following current party ranking, will emerge centered on the new Prime Minister, Hua Kuo-feng.

The tall, burly, crewcut Mr. Hua, a career party administrator, seems to have swiftly strengthened his grip on the levers of leadership in Peking. He headed relief efforts after July's earthquake and last week, in a major speech, he called for the strict restoration of law and order against "class enemies."

Background and Philosophy Cloudy

Little is known about Mr. Hua's personal background or political philosophy. But judging from his few public statements, he seems to share the pragmatism of his late predecessor, Chou, and yet to be keenly aware of the need to use some of the language of Chairman Mao's more radical followers, lest the party be further split.

Whoever emerges as the dominant figure, if anyone, it is possible Peking may not actually fill Mao's place as party chairman in the immediate future. For one thing, it would be a symbolic recognition that no one was capable of succeeding Mao. North Vietnam has never filled Ho Chi Minh's post as party chairman.

Moreover, Peking's leaders may find it

Continued on Page A16, Col. 3

INSIDE

Spending Limit Voted
Congress has voted to limit spending to about $413 billion, $13 billion more than President Ford has projected, in the fiscal year 1977. Page A18.

British Strike Threat
The British Government and its allies in the labor movement held meetings in an effort to prevent a strike that could damage the economy. Page D1.

Medicaid Law
A new state law intended to prohibit kickbacks by clinical laboratories may actually have legalized the practice, city health officials said. Page B2.

PARTY IN UNITY PLEA

Appeal to People Is Coupled With Delayed Disclosure of Chairman's Death

By Reuters

PEKING, Sept. 9—Mao Tse-tung, the pre-eminent figure of the Chinese Communist revolution and the leader of his country since 1949, died today at the age of 82.

His death, at 12:10 A.M. after a long illness, left uncertain the question of who

Obituary article appears on pages A13-15; text of announcement, page A16.

was to succeed him. There is no designated heir, nor is there anyone among his subordinates who commands the awe and reverence with which he was regarded among the 800 million Chinese.

The party leadership delayed the announcement of Chairman Mao's death for about 16 hours until 4 P.M. [4 A.M. Thursday New York Time]. The announcement included an appeal to the people to uphold the unity of the party that he had headed.

Plea to Follow Mao's Policies

It said China must "continue to carry out Chairman Mao's revolutionary line and policies in foreign affairs resolutely."

It urged the people to "deepen the criticism" of former Deputy Prime Minister Teng Hsiao-ping, who was toppled in the power struggle that followed the death in January of Mao's closest comrade in arms, Prime Minister Chou En-lai.

After the disgrace of Mr. Teng, Hua Kuo-feng, regarded as a centrist, was made Prime Minister and First Deputy Chairman of the party.

Funeral music followed today's announcement broadcast over the Peking radio, and 2,000 people gathered in the vast Tien An Men Square, many wearing black armbands, some weeping. Flags fluttered at half staff.

'Internationale' Heard Across City

"The Internationale," the world Socialist anthem, echoed over the city from loudspeakers at dusk as bicyclists made their way home from work.

Eight days of memorial ceremonies were scheduled to begin Saturday and end Sept. 18 with the entire nation standing in silent tribute for three minutes but with trains, ships and factories sounding sirens.

The announcement said that no foreign leaders would be invited to Peking during the period of mourning.

Chinese embassies abroad, it said, would express gratitude to foreigners wishing to come, but would "inform them of the decision of the Central Committee of our party and the Government of our country not to invite foreign governments, fraternal parties or friendly personages."

It was believed the actual cremation or burial would be attended only by the

Continued on Page A16, Col. 1

Borman Son Denies Bribe at West Point

By CHARLES KAISER
Special to The New York Times

WEST POINT, N. Y., Sept. 9—Lieut. Frederick P. Borman, a 1974 West Point graduate, categorically denied tonight that he had received $1,200 to change his vote on an honor-code board.

"It's completely false," Lieutenant Borman said of the allegation, part of an affidavit sworn to by two cadets who had been accused of cheating at the United States Military Academy here.

[Lieutenant Borman's father, Frank Borman, the former astronaut who is president of Eastern Airlines, said in an interview with The Associated Press that he had no intention of stepping down as chairman of a five-member special West Point review panel appointed by the Secretary of the Army.]

[Robert K. Koster, another cadet accused of cheating in affidavits signed by other cadets, said he had resigned from the Academy. He is the son of Maj. Gen. Samuel W. Koster, a former West Point superintendent who stepped down from his position after charges that, when he commanded the American Division in Vietnam, he had helped to cover up the alleged massacre by American soldiers at My Lai.]

Lieutenant Borman said that he had

Continued on Page A11, Col. 1

The Commission on Federal Paperwork at the World Trade Center yesterday with a 45-foot string of forms that represents one year's paperwork on a single child on Aid to Dependent Children.

The New York Times/Neal Boenzi

HAPPY BIRTHDAY DADDY Love, Donna & Lynne—Advt.

HAPPY BIRTHDAY, J.T.—from all your staff and friends—cheers!—Advt.

"All the News That's Fit to Print"

The New York Times

LATE CITY EDITION
Weather: Partly sunny today; cool tonight. Fair and cooler tomorrow.
Temperature range: today 42-58; Tuesday 33-50. Details on page 82.

VOL. CXXVI .. No. 43,383   © 1976 The New York Times Company   NEW YORK, WEDNESDAY, NOVEMBER 3, 1976   25 cents beyond 50-mile zone from New York City, except Long Island. Higher in air delivery cities.   20 CENTS

CARTER VICTOR IN TIGHT RACE; FORD LOSES NEW YORK STATE; DEMOCRATS RETAIN CONGRESS

Moynihan Defeats Buckley For New York Senate Seat

BY MAURICE CARROLL

Daniel P. Moynihan won election to the United States Senate yesterday and shouted jubilantly to a jostling crowd in his headquarters, "It's time we made some claims on the national Government."

Mr. Moynihan topped a cautious campaign that counted on the normal Democratic sympathies of New York voters by easily defeating James L. Buckley, the Conservative-Republican incumbent.

With 12,407 of 13,844 districts reporting, the vote for Senator was:

Moynihan 2,973,200
Buckley 2,517,292

His long gray hair toppling over his forehead and perspiration gleaming on his roundish face, Mr. Moynihan told several hundred supporters in his jammed storefront office on the Avenue of the Americas: "New York was on the ballot —and New York won."

It took almost 10 minutes for Mr. Moy-nihan to squeeze through the cheering crowd and step to the platform to claim victory.

Six years ago, the cheers had been for Mr. Buckley, who won an unexpected victory as a third-party candidate. But last night, Mr. Moynihan reconstituted much of the traditional Democratic vote—with the exception of some parts of the black community and some liberals disgruntled over his narrow primary-election victory —and it was his turn to congratulate Mr. Buckley for "gracious" concession.

Then Mr. Moynihan headed for a series of celebrations, but today, his wife, Liz, said, he will go to Harvard to teach his customary class there. He did not interrupt his academic chores during the campaign and will not today, she said.

Mr Moynihan led by 2-to-1 margins in the traditional Democratic territory in

Continued on Page 19, Column 3

Atlantic City Casinos Approved

By MARTIN WALDRON

New Jersey voters yesterday approved Las Vegas-style casinos for Atlantic City, the first on the East Coast, and residents of the shore resort began celebrating as many bars handed out free drinks.

With 4,991 districts of 5,569 reporting, the vote was:

Yes 1,305,800
No 1,015,126

In the state's Congressional contests, Senator Harrison A. Williams Jr., a Democrat, easily won re-election to a fourth term, while Representative Henry Helstoski, a six-term Democrat from the Ninth District who is under indictment on Federal extortion charges, was defeated. Thirteen other incumbents—10 Democrats and three Republicans—won, as did Joseph A. LeFante, also a Democrat, who succeeded the retiring Dominick V. Daniels in Hudson County.

Two years ago, New Jersey voters defeated by more than 400,000 votes an amendment to the State Constitution that would have allowed casinos anywhere in the state.

Promoters of casinos, including Atlantic City's legislative delegation, scheduled a meeting for 9 A.M. today to begin drafting a law to implement the constitutional amendment voted on yesterday.

The Council of Churches and United States Attorney Jonathan L. Goldstein, who was the most vocal opponent of casinos, had predicted that if Atlantic City got casinos, other areas of the state would demand them also.

Mr. Goldstein also warned that gambling casinos were a magnet for organized crime, and said that loan sharks and prostitutes would flock to Atlantic City if casinos were opened there.

In the midst of the noisy crowd in the headquarters of the Committee to Rebuild Atlantic City, an organization of businessmen and public officials who led the drive for the casinos, Mayor Joseph

Continued on Page 28, Column 1

Weicker Wins a 2d Term Easily

BY MICHAEL KNIGHT
Special to The New York Times

HARTFORD, Nov. 2—United States Senator Lowell P. Weicker Jr. scored an impressive re-election victory today over Gloria Schaffer, the state's top Democratic vote-getter and the only woman running for the Senate this year.

With all of the state's 169 towns and cities reporting, the unofficial tally was:

Weicker 787,568
Schaffer 559,109

Despite an intensive effort, Mrs. Schaffer, who is Connecticut's Secretary of State, was unable to generate much excitement during the campaign or close the gap between herself and Senator Weicker, the maverick first-term Republican who earned a nationwide reputation in 1973 as a member of the Senate Watergate committee.

The clear-cut result in the senatorial race was in marked contrast to the voting in the Presidential contest in this state, where President Ford defeated Jimmy Carter by a narrow margin.

Mrs. Schaffer won handily and, sometimes even overwhelmingly, in many of the state's ethnic neighborhoods. She carried the black districts of normally Republican Stamford, for example, the Italian and Polish areas of industrial New Britain and the Italian, Irish and black districts of Hartford.

In the Congressional races, all of the state's four Democratic and two Republican United States Representatives won re-election by wide margins. The Representatives from the three western districts—Stewart B. McKinney and Ronald A. Sarasin, Republicans, and Anthony Toby Moffett, a Democrat—had faced the possibility of an upset.

The Republicans gained seven seats in

Continued on Page 29, Column 1

Jimmy Carter leaves voting booth in Plains, Ga.   *United Press International*

Walter F. Mondale waiting to vote in Afton, Minn.   *Associated Press*

Election At a Glance

PRESIDENT
Needed to Win—270 Electoral Votes

	Number of States*	Electoral Votes
Carter	23	272
Ford	23	160

THE SENATE
33 of 100 Members to Be Elected

Newly Elected Senators
Democrats	20
Republicans	8
Independent	1
In Doubt	4

Makeup of the New Senate
Democrats	61
Republicans	37
Independent	1
In Doubt	1

THE HOUSE
All 435 Seats to Be Filled
Democrats Elected	255
Republicans Elected	120
In Doubt	60

*Includes District of Columbia

A guide to election news, page 17.

METZENBAUM BEATS TAFT IN SENATE RACE

Democrat Wins Ohio Contest That Was Clear Test of Philosophies

By WILLIAM K. STEVENS
Special to The New York Times

CLEVELAND, Wednesday, Nov. 3—Robert Taft Jr., bearer of one of the most famous names in national Republican politics, lost his seat in the United States Senate yesterday to former Senator Howard M. Metzenbaum, a Democrat.

The contest between the two was a clear-cut test of orthodox Republican conservatism against classical Democratic liberalism.

With 11,138 of 13,104 polling places reporting, the tally was:

Metzenbaum 1,637,778
Taft 1,537,830

Mr. Metzenbaum rolled up a sufficient margin of votes in Cuyahoga County (Cleveland) to offset Mr. Taft's strength downstate. With 1,700 of 1,727 polling places in the county reporting, the Democrat held a 122,000-vote lead there.

The campaign was a rematch of a 1970 race in which Mr. Taft narrowly defeated Mr. Metzenbaum to win his first Senate term. In losing that race six years ago, Mr. Metzenbaum won 49 percent of the vote.

He also won statewide recognition and sufficient stature within the party to be appointed to the Senate by former Democratic Gov. John J. Gilligan in 1974. Mr. Metzenbaum subsequently ran that year

Continued on Page 24, Column 5

8 Senators Lose Seats, but Lineup Of Parties Stays About the Same

By DAVID E. ROSENBAUM

At least eight incumbent Senators were defeated yesterday, and a ninth was in a close struggle for re-election.

Nonetheless, the Democrats did no worse than retain their current 61-to-38 majority in the Senate, with one seat held by an independent, and they may have picked up one seat.

In the House, the Democrats' 2-to-1 majority was not substantially changed.

The Democratic Senators who lost were Vance Hartke of Indiana, Joseph M. Montoya of New Mexico, Frank E. Moss of Utah and Gale W. McGee of Wyoming.

The other losers were James L. Buckley, Conservative-Republican of New York, and Bill Brock of Tennessee, J. Glenn Beall Jr. of Maryland and Robert Taft Jr. of Ohio, all Republicans.

Senator John V. Tunney, Democrat of California, was in a close race with S. I. Hayakawa, a Republican, who had been president of San Francisco State College.

Fourth-Term Bids Lost

Senator Moss and Senator McGee, both committee chairmen, were defeated in their attempts at fourth terms in the Senate. Mr. Moss lost to Orrin G. Hatch, a lawyer who has never held public office. Mr. McGee lost to a State Senator, Malcolm Wallop. Mr. Hatch and Mr. Wallop are much more conservative than the incumbents.

But, in Ohio, Mr. Taft was beaten by a liberal, Howard W. Metzenbaum, a former Senator whom Mr. Taft beat in 1970.

Senator Robert T. Stafford, Republican of Vermont, won a narrow victory over Gov. Thomas P. Salmon, his Democratic challenger.

Eight senators, four Republicans and four Democrats, are retiring, but neither party was able to take advantage of the situation to gain in total strength.

Republicans John C. Danforth and John H. Chaffee took Senate seats in Missouri and Rhode Island that are held by retiring Democrats Stuart Symington and John O. Pastore.

Democrats Apparent Winners

But Democrats apparently captured seats in Arizona and Nebraska that are held by Republicans. Dennis DeConcini, a Democratic county prosecutor, was leading in the race for the Arizona seat of Paul J. Fannin, and Mayor Edward Zorinsky was ahead in the race for Roman L. Hruska's race in Nebraska.

In Pennsylvania, Representative H. John Heinz 3d held the seat for the Republicans by narrowly beating Representative William J. Green. Hugh Scott, the Republican leader, is the incumbent.

Senator Philip A. Hart's seat in Michigan was retained for the Democrats by Representative Donald W. Riegle Jr., who defeated Representative Marvin L. Esch, a Republican.

In Montana, Representative John Melcher, a Democrat, easily won the seat now held by Mike Mansfield, the Democratic leader.

The eighth Senate vacancy was that created by the retirement of Hiram L. Fong, Republican of Hawaii. Returns from Hawaii were reported late, but it was widely believed that Representative Spark M. Matsunaga, a Democrat, would win.

In the House, nearly all of the 79 freshmen Democrats, who were the principal targets of the Republicans during the campaign, managed to win re-election. With half of the House races already

Continued on Page 17, Column 3

GEORGIAN WINS SOUTH

Northern Industrial States Provide Rest of Margin in the Electoral Vote

By R. W. APPLE Jr.

Jimmy Carter won the nation's Bicentennial Presidential election yesterday, narrowly defeating President Ford by sweeping his native South and adding enough Northern industrial states to give him a bare electoral vote majority.

Three of the closely contested battleground states slipped into Mr. Carter's column shortly after midnight—New York, Pennsylvania and Texas. The President-designate lost New Jersey and Michigan, Mr. Ford's home state, while Ohio, Illinois and California were still up for grabs.

New York teetered between the rivals for hours, contrary to all expectations, before delivering a small majority to Mr. Carter—a majority that gave the Democrat a bonanza of 41 electoral votes.

When Mr. Carter finally carried Hawaii, by a far narrower margin than customary for Democratic candidates in that Democratic stronghold, he had the Georgian 272 electoral votes in 23 states. two more than a majority. Mr. Ford had 160 electoral votes in 23 states, and five states were still in doubt.

A Southern Victory

Mr. Carter was the first man from the Deep South to be elected President in a century and a quarter, and Mr. Ford, the nation's first appointive President, was the first since Herbert Hoover.

Although the President dominated the Plains and Mountain regions, he lost several middle-sized states that he had counted upon. Among them were Louisiana and Mississippi on the Gulf Coast, and Wisconsin, which went to the Democrats for only the second time in a quarter-century as the result of an outpouring of votes from industrial Milwaukee and liberal Madison.

Mr. Carter owed large debts to Mayor Frank L. Rizzo of Philadelphia, who produced the 250,000-vote margin Mr. Carter needed to carry Pennsylvania; to Robert S. Strauss, the Democratic national chairman, who worked tirelessly to put together the Texas operation, and to the South and the Border states as a whole. The Georgian won every Border state and every Southern state except Virginia, which seemed headed for the Ford column.

Division of Popular Vote

The popular vote, which was swelled by a relatively heavy turnout to roughly the same level as four years ago, appeared likely to split 51 percent for Mr. Carter, 48 for Mr. Ford and 1 for others.

With 81 percent of the nation's precincts reporting, the vote was:

Carter ..... 33,684,344—51 percent
Ford .... 31,665,958—48 percent

In the metropolitan area, Mr. Carter lost both New Jersey and Connecticut, as his backers had feared he would.

All 25,000 voting machines in New York were ordered impounded by State Supreme Court Justice Edward S. Conway. Acting at the request of state Re-

Continued on Page 17, Column 1

Summary of Other Major News

Articles on the first page of the second part of this issue are:

Indian Amendments Pass

The lower house of India's Parliament passed a sweeping set of constitutional amendments that will shift the balance of power in the Government.

No Accord on Rhodesia

Prime Minister Ian D. Smith of Rhodesia and African nationalist leaders failed to agree on a date for independence of the territory.

Burundi Chief Ousted

Burundi's armed forces deposed the President of the small central African country without violence, according to an official broadcast.

Park Tong Sun Disputed

The Gulf Oil Corporation has disputed a statement by Park Tong Sun that he received $1 million a month from his relationships with the oil company.

State U. Social Clubs

National sororities and fraternities will be allowed on the campuses of the State University of New York after a 23-year ban.

Ouster Held Illegal

The Supreme Court in effect affirmed that a company acted illegally in dismissing an employee for refusing on religious ground to work Saturday.

Pro-Statehood Candidate Stages Puerto Rican Upset

By DAVID VIDAL
Special to The New York Times

SAN JUAN, P.R., Wednesday, Nov. 3—In a staggering upset, San Juan Mayor Carlos Romero Barcelo of the pro-statehood New Progressive Party snatched the governorship of Puerto Rico from the incumbent, Rafael Hernández Colón, sending the Popular Democratic Party to only its second defeat since 1940.

The Governor, speaking to weeping campaign workers, conceded defeat and asked the party faithful "to heed this decision, if confirmed by the final official results, as the will of the people of Puerto Rico."

"That is how I accept it," he said, in a brief statement. He also called for unity but added: "The campaign for 1980 begins tomorrow."

The election was all the more surprising because the New Progressives were also on their way to assuming control of both houses of the Puerto Rican legislature as well as retaining the powerful post of mayor of San Juan.

The results reflected less a mandate for statehood than they did voter discontent with the administrative and economic problems under Mr. Hernández Colón's leadership.

In another surprise, the two parties favoring independence were running behind their 1972 pace.

With 66 of 113 precincts reporting, the tally was:

New Progressive Party 312,055
Popular Democratic Party ..297,632
Puerto Rican Independence
Party 33,170
Puerto Rican Socialist Party 4,604

A measure of the trend was seen in Barranquitas, considered a stronghold of the Popular Democrats because it was the birthplace of the father of Luis Muñoz Marin, founder of the Popular Democratic Party and of the Commonwealth. The 78-year-old leader came out of political seclusion this year to campaign personally over the weekend. The party was losing there, however, as it was in Mayaguez, called the capital of the Popular Democrats.

In 1972, when 84.14 percent of the electorate voted, the Popular Democratic Party won by 85,631 votes, taking 51.2 percent as against 44.01 percent for the New Progressives. Other parties divided the rest.

Although each major party had predictions indicating it would win this year, other polls had shown a high number of undecided voters.

That there was any doubt at all of a Popular Democratic victory was significant and indicated the changing nature of the electorate, of the perception of the party and of the party itself.

For years, islanders had grown accustomed to more and more prosperity under the "bread, land, and liberty" slogan of

Continued on Page 22, Column 5

The New York Times

LATE CITY EDITION

Weather: Sunny, hot today; warm tonight. Fair, hot, humid tomorrow. Temperature range: today 70-90; yesterday 72-93. Details, page 50.

VOL.CXXVI...No.43,636   © 1977 The New York Times Company   NEW YORK, THURSDAY, JULY 14, 1977   15 cents beyond 50-mile zone from New York City, Higher in air delivery cities.   A   20 CENTS

POWER FAILURE BLACKS OUT NEW YORK; THOUSANDS TRAPPED IN THE SUBWAYS; LOOTERS AND VANDALS HIT SOME AREAS

State Troopers Sent Into City As Crime Rises

Some Civilians Assist Police – '65 Blackout Peaceful in Contrast

By LAWRENCE VAN GELDER

Thousands of looters, emboldened by darkness and confusion, ranged through the city last night and early today in a wave of lawlessness.

Amid shattering glass, wailing sirens, and the clang of trashcans used to demolish metal storefront barricades, thieves and vandals ravaged store after store.

Governor Carey ordered the state police into the city to assist the local police.

At the same time, other people left their homes to help direct traffic in the suddenly darkened streets. Often armed with flashlights, they took up their impromptu stations at intersections and guided drivers and pedestrians.

Hundreds of Arrests

By 2 o'clock this morning, the police reported a total of 880 arrests, almost all for looting in Manhattan, the Bronx, Brooklyn, and Queens. In downtown Brooklyn and in East Harlem, where looting and rock and bottle-throwing were reported, several policemen were listed as casualties.

"It's a lot different from 10 years ago," said Daisy Voight, referring to the blackout of 1965 as she emerged from a meeting in Harlem. "Last time people were helpful. This time people are scared. They are running for buses or bars. Everybody's afraid to go out."

In Brooklyn, standing guard at an ice cream store in the downtown area at Fulton Street near Adams, the owner watched youths racing by.

"They're crazy," he shouted. "They're taking their shoes and breaking windows. They're animals. They should be put in jail and throw the key away. The cops are doing the best they can. There are about 500 kids in the street."

So accelerated was the police effort against the onslaught of looters in Brooklyn that officers bringing prisoners into the central booking facility in the 84th precinct stationhouse, at 301 Gold Street, did not wait as usual to fill out papers.

As quickly as they could, the hard pressed police—regular patrols augmented by colleagues who had responded to appeals to report to work—deposited their prisoners and · returned to the battle ground.

Mayor and Officers Meet

At 1:40 A.M. after meeting at Police Headquarters with his major commissioners to review the blackout situation, Mayor Beame characterized the looting as "sporadic." The Mayor said the police were "addressing all problems."

Vandalism and looting were reported in

Continued on Page B

A view of the darkened New York City skyline taken from New Jersey during blackout last night.   The New York Times/D. Gorton

Some Led Others by Flashlight, Some Knocked on Doors to Help

By DEIRDRE CARMODY

It is the New Yorker's real badge of pride — not the little red-apple lapel pins — that whatever else can be said about them, one truth is undeniable: New Yorkers know how to cope when trouble strikes their city.

And cope they did last night.

Some rushed undaunted into chaotic intersections and began to direct traffic. Those who had flashlights led others, Pied Piper-like, up darkened stairwells in buildings where elevators were dormant.

In the Excelsior apartment building, at 57th Street and Seventh Avenue, Roy Svendson, the manager, and members of his staff knocked on every apartment door and asked if anyone needed oxygen. They found only one lady who did, but their very helpfulness bolstered spirits and subdued a bit of the terror those who lived alone were beginning to feel.

In the cavernous waiting room of Grand Central Terminal, hundreds of people coped by simply waiting until the trains would be ready to run again. They were somber and bored and tired and hot, but they sat there and waited.

At one point, a bagpiper came through and played for about five minutes near the big clock that remained stubbornly at 9:35. Some people held flashlights up to the telephone booth so that others could dial home and reassure the people there that they were safe, albeit bored.

"Where are all those kids now with the transistor radios," muttered one passerby.

On the corner of Madison Avenue and 65th Street, a woman in a bare-backed dress and a slouched straw hat, looking the personification of East Side dinnertime chic, raced into the intersection and began to direct traffic. Dramatically but efficiently, she spread her arms. Suddenly she

Continued on Page B

Lightning Bolt: How It Struck

By JOHN NOBLE WILFORD

The blackout had its beginning in the thunderclouds that gathered last night over Westchester County. Lightning struck in the vicinity of Consolidated Edison's Indian Point Nuclear Power Plant 3, and major power transmission lines were short-circuited.

This tripped relays, shutting down transformers and other power plants throughout the New York metropolitan area, according to Con Ed officials.

Norman Terrevi, assistant vice president for transmission operations for Con Edison, said that several "massive lighting bolts" struck the 345,000-volt power lines several times. Those hit were major feeder lines running from Pleasant Valley in Dutchess County to New York City.

Reports from Indian Point indicated that there was no damage to the nuclear power plant and no threat of radiation leakage. However, state troopers had the area blocked off. People in the area reported seeing the sky light up around Buchan, near Indian Point, at 10:45 P.M. The strange light and a "whirling sound" lasted 10 seconds, witnesses reported.

Joyce Tucker, Con Edison's acting vice

Continued on Page B

Westchester Dark; Long Island's Power Interrupted Briefly

By TOM GOLDSTEIN

Although all of Westchester County was without power last night, no serious traffic or crime problems were reported.

"All's quiet," said Charles G. McLaughlin, chief of Rye Police Department. "We have a nice quiet community under any circumstances."

Hammering rainstorms hit certain parts of the county, temporarily clogging traffic. Most of the nearly 900,000 county residents who were out headed home.

On Long Island, which is served by the Long Island Lighting Company, a spokes-

Continued on Page B

Westchester Is Also Darkened After Lightning Hits Line

By ROBERT D. McFADDEN

A power failure plunged New York City and Westchester County into darkness last night, disrupting the lives of nearly nine million people.

Spokesmen for the Consolidated Edison Company said that power for all of its 2.8 million customers would not be restored until late this morning.

By 2 A.M. the utility had restored power to 150,000 customers in the Jamaica, Flushing, Queens Village and Kew Gardens sections of Queens, and to 50,000 customers in the Pleasantville area in Westchester County.

Though not as big as the nine-state blackout that hit the Northeast in November 1965, last night's power failure was in some respects an uglier experience. There was widespread looting in Manhattan, the Bronx and Brooklyn, and four hours after the blackout began, the police had arrested nearly 900 people.

Several thousand subway riders were trapped in trains between stations—but nowhere near the masses stranded 12 years ago during the rush hour.

Uprising in Bronx Jail

Thousands more were trapped last night in elevators. Homes and apartments went black. People stumbled and streamed from theaters, restaurants and late-closing shops and office buildings. In some sections, crowds milled in the streets into the early morning hours.

Prisoners in the House of Detention in the Bronx briefly took over a guard house after setting fires on four floors. The backup power in two major hospitals failed. Fires erupted in various sections of the city.

Kennedy International and LaGuardia Airports both closed, and flights were diverted to Newark, Boston and other cities.

As the ordeal continued through the night and into the morning, there were no reports of deaths or serious injuries.

The blackout struck the city shortly after 9:30 P.M. in stages, after lightning hit a major Consolidated Edison electrical transmission line in northern Westchester County. Like dominoes toppling through Westchester and the city, circuit breakers

on successively overloaded transmission lines went off automatically.

Early this morning Charles F. Luce, the chairman of Con Edison, noted that the utility's entire system of circuit breakers would have to be reset and all power lines and generators inspected, a task that he said would take until at least 8 A.M.

"When we are sure everything is set to go, we can bring the power back slowly," he said. Another utility spokesman said that the restoration would have to proceed cautiously to avoid another systemwide shutdown.

The blackout came only three days after Mr. Luce said on television that there was no immediate danger of a major blackout

Continued on Page B

To Our Readers

This is a special blackout edition of The New York Times. Regular pages of the paper's City Edition, prepared before the electrical power failed, appear inside the paper, starting on the first right-hand page. News and pictures of the blackout appear on the first two pages.

When the power failed, only a handful of copies of The Times had come off the presses in New York. Pages were taken to the plant of The Record in Hackensack, N.J., where they were photographed. Offset printing took place at The Times's satellite plant in Carlstadt, N.J.

For mechanical reasons, the size of the newspaper was limited to 40 pages, and the most important news pages were selected. Therefore, the "continued" guidelines for some articles give incorrect page numbers, as do some references in the News Summary and Index.

This page and the one following were prepared using copy and photographs provided by The Times, at The Record's plant. The Times expresses its appreciation to The Record.

Riders Safely Flee the Subway Though Some Swelter Hours

By RALPH BLUMENTHAL

Thousands of home-bound travelers were trapped in subway tunnels and along suburban railroad lines by last night's blackout.

There were no initial reports of panic, however, and although many trains remained stranded in sweltering tunnels at least two hours after the blackout began, many others were able to coast into sta-

tions and discharge passengers with ease.

In a subway tunnel at Broadway at 19th Street, for example, Officer Thomas Duffey of the Transit Authority Police guided 1,500 passengers out of a train without incident.

But George Thune, a Long Island Rail Road aide, said passengers on 12 to 14 commuter trains backed up and stranded by the power loss in Jamaica, Queens, were still awaiting buses at 11 P.M.

Trains drawing power from the Long Island Lighting Company, which was unaffected by the blackout, were able to get through, as were diesel trains on the nonelectrified portion of the line in Eastern Long Island.

Outside Grand Central Terminal, cabdrivers called out "Yonkers and Westchester," attracting a steady stream of commuters. Inside the station at 11 P.M., passengers waited in the subway aboard a Lexington Avenue downtown express.

The Times Square subway concourse was crowded with people waiting for news and snacking on donuts and fried chicken from subway stands.

The Transit Authority said that the impact on the system was lightened by quick action by transit officials and workers.

"At 9:30 sharp we began getting power surges and A.C. power failures, which took the form of signal blackouts," Jacques Nevard, an authority official, said. "Motormen started calling the train masters. The train masters have dispatchers in a ring around them, and some time between 9:30 and 9:34 they put out the word by radio to the motormen to move immediately to the closest station.

"They anticipated we may be in for a failure, so they took the precaution of ordering all trains moving to stations. As a result of approximately 150 trains normally operating at that time, only seven, as of 11:30 P.M., were caught between stations."

The seven stuck trains listed by Mr. Nevard were an IRT train north of 125th Street and Lexington Avenue, an AA local on Cen-

Continued on Page B

Bellevue Patients Resuscitated With Hand-Squeezed Air Bags

By LAWRENCE K. ALTMAN

Doctors and nurses at Bellevue Hospital had to squeeze bags of air with their hands to resuscitate patients in respiratory failure after the municipal hospital's emergency backup power supply failed at 10:10 P.M. last night.

Bellevue was one of a number of hospitals in the blacked-out area whose emergency generators — ordered after the power failure of 1965 — were unable to supply power.

About 15 Bellevue patients were on mechanical respirators in six intensive care units when the power failed. But as of midnight, officials said there had been no deaths in the hospital as a result of the power failure.

Doctors resorted to squeezing the airbags by hand to breathe for the patients. Airbags were the only form of resuscitation available before mechanical respirators became the standard form of treatment in recent years.

At 11:50 P.M., Bellevue officials closed the emergency room and referred all prospective patients to other hospitals. Bellevue was described as dark with islands of lights.

A visitor to Bellevue found the scene confused but without panic as doctors and

nurses, working with flashlights, occasionally bumped into beds and intravenous feeding equipment.

"There's no real cause for concern because we can bag-breathe [for the patients] for hours," one physician said.

At Bellevue, there were no women in labor, and no patients undergoing surgery at the time the backup power supply failed.

Bellevue's diesel auxiliary generator responded immediately to the Con Edison power failure, but the backup supply went out a few minutes later, according to Felix Calabrese, associate executive director of the hospital.

Emergency backup generators to supply hospitals with power were made mandatory by legislation after the 1965 blackout. Such units were intended to supply enough power to keep life-supporting mechanical equipment running during a power failure.

After the Bellevue emergency system failed, police and fire officials took auxiliary power units to Bellevue and Metropolitan Hospitals to help keep such equipment running.

At the New York Hospital-Cornell Medical Center, New York University Hospital, the Veterans Administration Hospital at 24th Street, and other hospitals, officials reported that the backup generators were meeting critical needs.

Continued on Page B

A doctor and a nurse aiding an injured motorist in the darkened emergency room of Bellevue Hospital last night.   The New York Times

"All the News That's Fit to Print"

The New York Times

CITY EDITION

Weather: Cold, snow late today into tonight. Partial clearing tomorrow. Temperature range: today 27-36; yesterday 44-49. Details, page D14.

VOL.CXXVII....No.43,881 Copyright © 1978 The New York Times

— NEW YORK, THURSDAY, MARCH 16, 1978 —

25 cents beyond 50-mile zone from New York City. Higher in air delivery cities.

20 CENTS

ISRAELIS SEIZE A 63-MILE 'SECURITY BELT' IN LEBANON AND SAY TROOPS WILL REMAIN; WASHINGTON SEES 'IMPEDIMENTS TO PEACE'

Senate Backers Of Canal Treaty Sure of Victory

Say They Have Votes to Win Roll-Call Today

By ADAM CLYMER

WASHINGTON, March 15—Senate supporters of the Panama Canal treaties said today that they had enough votes to win tomorrow's crucial roll-call on the first of the pacts.

On the eve of one of the most important foreign policy votes in many years, Senator Howard H. Baker Jr., the minority leader, told reporters he now believed that the treaty guaranteeing the neutrality of the canal after American control ends in the year 2000 would be approved. And the effective leader of the opposition, Senator Paul Laxalt, Republican of Nevada, characterized the situation as "not so good."

In a day of intense lobbying, beginning when Vice President Mondale appeared unannounced at the office of Senator Wendell H. Ford, Democrat of Kentucky, at 7:15 A.M., none of the uncommitted senators, including Mr. Ford, announced that they would vote against the treaty.

Two New Votes in Favor

Two uncommitted senators, Edward W. Brooke, Republican of Massachusetts, and Dennis DeConcini, Democrat of Arkansas, said they would vote for the neutrality treaty. Mr. Brooke, however, said he might vote later against the treaty turning over the canal and the canal zone to Panama.

The backing of Mr. Brooke and Mr. DeConcini, plus the expected support of Senator Bob Packwood, Republican of Oregon, gave the treaty supporters 65 votes they could count on. They would not say where they expected to get the two more votes they needed to make up the 67 required for approval.

There were still four uncommitted senators available and at least the chance of shaking one or two antitreaty senators loose. One of the the uncommitted, Senator Henry Bellmon, Republican of Oklahoma, was to announce his stand tomorrow at 9 A.M., and Senator Edward Zorinsky,

Continued on Page A3, Column 1

CAPITAL SYMPATHETIC

U.S. Officials Relieved That Heavy Combat Activity Is Apparently Over

By BERNARD GWERTZMAN
Special to The New York Times

WASHINGTON, March 15—Israel's invasion of southern Lebanon evoked a sympathetic response from the United States today, but Secretary of State Cyrus R. Vance conceded that the Israeli attack and the Palestinian raid that inspired it had raised "impediments to the peace process."

The general mood at the highest levels of the Administration was relief this afternoon that the main fighting seemed at an end.

The evidence that the Israelis were confining their ground operations to a six-mile-deep belt along the border reduced the likelihood that the Syrians would enter the conflict and spread the warfare; one high official said.

Begin Statement Causes Worry

In Beirut, however, Syrian and Lebanese officials appealed for international help in obtaining Israeli withdrawal. [Page A17.] In Cairo, Foreign Minister Mohammed Ibrahim Kamel denounced the Israeli action as "organized genocide" and said that it harmed Egyptian peace efforts. [Page A17.]

American officials said that with Prime Minister Menachem Begin due in Washington next Monday for talks with President Carter on Tuesday and Wednesday, the chances for diplomatic progress, already dim, were now more remote.

A new problem has now arisen, officials said, over a statement by Mr. Begin today that Israeli forces would remain in the belt of Lebanese territory until an agreement was reached to prevent the Palestinians from returning to the area.

The United States, a strong backer of Lebanon's sovereignty and integrity, wants the Israelis to withdraw as soon as possible and the withdrawal issue undoubtedly will now become a major topic during Mr. Begin's talks with Mr. Carter, officials said.

Late this afternoon, Ambassador Simcha Dinitz of Israel conferred for 90 minutes with Alfred L. Atherton Jr., the Administration's top Middle East negotiator, to discuss the Israeli presence in

Continued on Page A17, Column 6

Israel's Prime Minister, Menachem Begin, left, arriving at the border with Lebanon yesterday for a close look at the action. Defense Minister Ezer Weizman is at center, wearing flight jacket and sunglasses.

Guerrillas Join Civilian Retreat From Attackers

By MARVINE HOWE
Special to The New York Times

TYRE, Lebanon, March 15 — Many Palestinian and Lebanese families fled in panic today from population centers in southern Lebanon that had been bombarded by Israeli fighter-bombers, gunboats and artillery.

"We're going north, anywhere, to get away from the shelling," said Mohammed Ahmed al-Mohammed, a Lebanese farmer, as he and his family of 12 set out on foot along the Tyre-Nabatiye road carrying only small bundles of blankets and clothing.

While young Lebanese and Palestinian guerrillas in the towns and villages spoke of their "fierce resistance," it was clear they were retreating in face of the heavy Israeli odds.

"We are not going to let ourselves be annihilated," said a member of the Palestine Liberation Organization's southern military command at Saida. "We cannot destroy the Israeli forces, but we can inflict as many casualties as possible and then make a tactical withdrawal."

The Palestinian military spokesman confirmed reports that the joint Palestinian-Lebanese leftist forces had lost their principal positions in the border area: Khiam, Ibl es Saqi and Taibe in the east, Bint Jbail and Marun al-Ras in the center and Naqura and Alma 'al-Chaab in the southwest.

The city of Tyre was a prime target as the main port of entry for arms sup-

Continued on Page A16, Column 3

MAJOR FIGHTING ENDS

Forces Rout the Palestinians in Border Strongholds —Planes Bomb Bases

By WILLIAM E. FARRELL

JERUSALEM, March 15—Israeli forces routed Palestinian guerrillas today from at least seven strongholds in southern Lebanon, and Prime Minister Menachem Begin said the troops would remain until an agreement was reached to insure that the area could never again be used for raids against Israel.

With land, sea and air operations continuing from the Mediterranean to the foothills of Mount Hermon, Israelis occupied what Lieut. Gen. Mordechai Gur, the Chief of Staff, called a "security belt" along the 63 miles of its northern border, with a depth of four and a half to six miles. Late tonight, General Gur said the major fighting was over.

Mr. Begin's remarks about how long Israelis would remain in Lebanon were echoed by Defense Minister Ezer Weizman, who told reporters:

Israeli Withdrawal Demanded

"We shall continue to clear the area—prevent the area from being attack positions against us as long as we find it necessary."

The suggestion of a prolonged Israeli presence in southern Lebanon seemed likely to provoke international controversy. Even as the military drive continued, calls were being raised for Israel to withdraw.

The ground offensive, the largest that Israel has ever carried out against Palestinians, was accompanied by air strikes against Palestinian enclaves and camps far north of the Israeli border, including at least two in the vicinity of Beirut.

The Israeli Army spokesman announced that Israeli planes had bombed a Palestinian base near Damur, about 20 miles south of Beirut, which he said had been the staging area for the Arab raiders who infiltrated into Israel on Saturday and seized a bus.

Syrians Said to Fire on Planes

The seizure touched off a wild ride on the Haifa-Tel Aviv highway, with shooting and an explosion that led to the death of 35 Israelis and an American and the injury of more than 70 persons.

The army spokesman said that Israeli planes had struck targets at the Mediterranean port of Tyre and at a site near Beirut that the spokesman described as a Palestine Liberation Organization training and supply base "for terrorist naval units and for their equipment."

In the raid at Damur, the spokesman said the Israeli planes had been fired on by a Syrian guerrilla unit. The Israeli planes did not fire back at the Syrians, he said, and returned safely to base.

The Syrians have a large military

Continued on Page A16, Column 4

INSIDE

Parking Rules Reinstated
Alternate-side-of-the-street parking regulations are reinstated to let sweepers get at a 62-day accumulation of slushy litter. Page B1.

Soviet Curbs Rostropovich
The Soviet Union revoked the citizenship of the expatriate cellist Mstislav Rostropovich and his wife, Galina Vishnevskaya. Page A10.

Death-Penalty Debate
The emotional debate over capital punishment has shaken legislators in Albany, splitting some from their families and constituents. Page B12.

Rise in Fuel Prices Urged
Presidential action to raise fuel prices if Congress fails to enact the energy program was urged by G. William Miller, the Federal Reserve chief. Page D1.

Soviet Reportedly Cool to Linking Cuban, Somali Pullout in Ethiopia

By RICHARD BURT
Special to The New York Times

WASHINGTON, March 15—Contrary to what reporters were told at the State Department last week, the Soviet Union has given little sign that it is prepared to link the end of Somali-Ethiopian fighting with cuts in Cuban forces in Ethiopia, government officials said today.

They said Ambassador Anatoly F. Dobrynin, at a meeting with Secretary of State Cyrus R. Vance on Saturday,

declined to commit Moscow on the future of either its own advisers or the Cuban forces.

The previous evening, reporters were told that Moscow said the Cuban forces, estimated at 12,000, would be reduced once Somalia ended its occupation of Ogaden, an ethnic Somali region of Ethiopia. The reporters were also told that the Soviet Union had agreed to have neutral observers monitor a cease-fire. The information was supplied as "deep background," meaning that it could not be attributed.

Pullout Up to Cuba and Ethiopia

Today, a high-ranking State Department official said the information had been based on a previous "direct conversation" between Mr. Vance and Mr. Dobrynin. However, at their Saturday meeting, the Soviet envoy said the withdrawal of Cuba's forces from Ethiopia had to be taken up with those two governments, the official said.

The State Department spokesman, Hodding Carter 3d, announced that the Somali pullout, begun last week, was now complete, and he called on Moscow to facilitate the withdrawal of the Cuban troops and of the 1,000 Soviet advisers in Ethiopia.

Privately, State Department and White House officials said the Russians had been unwilling to discuss concrete plans for withdrawing the Cubans or establishing a truce-observation group.

"We have no evidence from Moscow or anywhere else that the Soviets are inclined to be cooperative on the Horn," said one White House official.

Officials expressed doubts over the likelihood of an early reduction in the

Continued on Page A6, Column 1

6 Guilty in Attack At Washington Sq.

By GREGORY JAYNES

Six of nine young men charged with taking part in a 1976 rampage in Washington Square Park that left one man dead and 13 persons injured were found guilty yesterday—three of manslaughter and three of lesser charges.

The verdict was delivered, after a nine-week trial and six days of deliberation, while a number of the defendants' parents wept in a closed courtroom in State Supreme Court in Manhattan. Parents of the three men found not guilty also cried.

Sentencing was scheduled for April 19 before Justice Robert Haft, in whose court the trial was held. Those convicted of manslaughter could be sentenced to as much as 25 years.

Calling the crime "one of great social severity," Assistant District Attorney John Moscow, the prosecutor, said that "the people will ask for imprisonment for all" those convicted.

During the trial, Mr. Moscow argued that the nine defendants had planned the attack on Washington Square to clear the park of blacks and Hispanic persons. Of the nine defendants, one, Robert

Continued on Page B6, Column 1

Israelis established "security belt" in southern Lebanon after capturing Palestinian strongholds [marked by panels]. Israeli gunboats attacked Tyre, and jets ranged from there up the coast to Beirut area.

The New York Times/John Leinung/March 16, 1978

Palestinian refugees fleeing from Damur, Lebanon, following Israeli air strikes yesterday

United Press International

The New York Times

LATE CITY EDITION

Weather:Rain, windy today, tonight;
partly sunny and milder tomorrow.
Temperature range: today 47-55;
yesterday 40-62. Details, page B6.

VOL.CXXVII....No.43,915   Copyright © 1978 The New York Times   NEW YORK, WEDNESDAY, APRIL 19, 1978   25 cents beyond 50-mile zone from New York City.
Higher in air delivery cities.   20 CENTS

SENATE VOTES TO GIVE UP PANAMA CANAL; CARTER FORESEES 'BEGINNING OF A NEW ERA'

ITALIANS FAIL TO FIND MORO'S BODY IN AREA CITED BY ABDUCTORS

Searchers Sent to Mountain Lake Report Unbroken Ice Cover and No Tracks in the Snow

By HENRY TANNER
Special to The New York Times

ROME, April 18—Italian security forces on skis and in helicopters today staged a vain search for the body of Aldo Moro, the political leader, after his kidnappers had said in a statement that he was dead and that his body had been thrown into a mountain lake about 75 miles northeast of here.

The searchers at Lake Duchessa, 5,000 feet high in the Abruzzi Mountains, found the lake covered with a blanket of ice and no human tracks on the steep snow-covered slopes around it.

Toward evening, officials of Mr. Moro's Christian Democratic party said they had reached the tentative conclusion that the terrorists' statement was a diversionary maneuver, perhaps to make it easier to move Mr. Moro from one hiding place to another.

Statement Found in Garbage Can

There was little doubt about the authenticity of the statement in which the Red Brigades, the terrorist group, announced Mr. Moro's execution by means of suicide. The statement was found in a garbage can in the center of Rome by a staff member of the newspaper Il Messaggero after it had received an anonymous phone call. Contrary to earlier messages from the Red Brigades, this one was not simultaneously distributed in Milan, Turin and Genoa.

Today marked the 30th anniversary of Christian Democratic government in Italy. The party's first Cabinet was formed on April 18, 1948, by Alcide de Gasperi. A spectacular move by the publicity-conscious kidnappers had therefore been expected.

The terrorists' statement, titled "The Trial of Aldo Moro," took note of the

Continued on Page A10, Column 4

High Court Bars Networks' Right To Nixon Tapes

Indicates U.S. Agency Could Allow Release

By WARREN WEAVER Jr.
Special to The New York Times

WASHINGTON, April 18—The Supreme Court today refused to give broadcasters and recording companies the right to copy, broadcast and sell excerpts from the White House tapes that led to the resignation of President Nixon and the criminal conviction of four of his aides.

Dividing 7 to 2, the Justices concluded that the networks had no constitutional right that was enforceable in the courts to reproduce and circulate the taped material because Congress had established a system for access to the tapes.

Texts of the taped material were printed in full at the time of the Watergate trial. The Court majority indicated today that anyone seeking sound reproductions of the tapes could apply to the General Services Administrator for permission under the Presidential Recordings Act of 1974.

No Guidelines for Access

The decision involved only the 30 tapes, covering about 22 hours of White House conversations, that were played at the Watergate trial. Eventually, as a result of the procedures that could be adopted under the recordings act, the tapes may become available for copying and broadcast. But uncertainty as to the procedure to be used, which will require further lower court consideration, makes any action in the near future unlikely.

The Court declined to give the administrator any guidelines for regulating public access to the tapes in the interests of privacy or executive privilege, saying the case before it did not require such a ruling.

In separate dissenting opinions, Associate Justices Thurgood Marshall and John Paul Stevens said that they believed Congress had intended that the tapes be made fully available to the public, includ-

Continued on Page A20, Column 3

Associated Press
President Carter shaking hands with Gabriel Lewis, Panama's Ambassador to the U.S., after Senate vote

New Chancellor Would Reward Schools That Improved Reading

By MARCIA CHAMBERS

Frank J. Macchiarola, the New York City public-school system's next Chancellor, said yesterday that he hoped to find a way to give extra money to schools that improved pupils' reading scores.

At the same time, he was critical of the state and Federal systems that first funnel compensatory funds to poverty areas where pupils often read below grade level and then may cut off the school districts if the areas improve economically or scholastically. A school may improve, Mr. Macchiarola said, but there is often a dangerous regression once the funds are removed.

At his first news conference and in an interview following his designation Monday as Chancellor, Mr. Macchiarola drew the broad outlines of his educational and fiscal philosophy and the direction he hopes the nation's largest school system will take during his tenure.

Dr. Macchiarola, the 37-year-old vice president for institutional advancement at the Graduate School of the City University, and the man who won Mayor Koch's endorsement for Chancellor, said his first priority would be to get everyone in the schools to understand that "we can do the job."

In an interview, he said excellence had to be rewarded not only to stress achievement but, also to demonstrate that many public schools were working well. Then, he said, middle-class parents will want to send their children to the city's schools.

"I think when somebody does a job you've got to pat that person on the back, and say well done," Mr. Macchiarola said. "The scale of excellence and the scale of failure is a very minuscule portion of our focus. I want to broaden that scale so that the category of excellence is one that we focus on. If you try to hit that level, inevitably others aspire to it."

Cites Success in Brooklyn

He said that an incentive system that gives financial rewards to schools that improve their reading scores had been success in District 22, in Brooklyn, where, until his taking office as Chancellor, he serves as president of the school board.

The reward was based on the ranking a school achieved on the annual citywide reading examination. Mr. Macchiarola agreed with some parents' criticism that the citywide test was given too much importance in pupil evaluation, but he said it was one measure "and not the only measure" for helping him "determine who is doing the job and who is not doing the job."

In the interview, Mr. Macchiarola said

Continued on Page B5, Column 3

Yanks Deny Abuses On Stadium's Lease

Al Rosen, president of the New York Yankees, said yesterday that a "thorough review" by the club's legal experts had shown "no evidence of impropriety" in its financial dealings with New York City, which rebuilt and owns Yankee Stadium.

He said that officers of the club remained "willing to meet with any responsible official who claims to have tangible evidence that there has been a violation of our lease."

The comments, in a statement and interview at the Stadium, came a month after Comptroller Harrison J. Goldin opened an investigation into "maintenance costs" at the Stadium. Under the terms of the lease, the Yankees were able to reduce the rent due to the city by more than $1.5 million the team said it paid in maintenance costs.

Yankee front-office executives conceded that the allegation by Comptroller Goldin that $65 of the cost of a commercial by Catfish Hunter, Yankee pitcher, in 1976, had been mistakenly charged to the city as a maintenance cost. But they added that this had been corrected when

Continued on Page D16, Column 1

PANAMANIAN LEADER ACCEPTS CANAL PACTS

Torrijos Says Approval by Senate Is Great Triumph for Nation

By ALAN RIDING
Special to The New York Times

PANAMA, April 18—Panama's leader, Brig. Gen. Omar Torrijos Herrera, accepted the new canal treaties as amended by the United States Senate tonight and declared their approval to be "one of the greatest and most awaited triumphs" in this country's history.

As firecrackers exploded and sirens wailed across Panama City, General Torrijos told a nationwide radio and television audience moments after the Senate vote, "I feel proud that I have fulfilled my mission."

Clearly seeking to stir up enthusiasm after weeks of mounting opposition to the treaties, the Government urged the people to celebrate the victory in the streets, and excited crowds gathered in the May 5 Plaza close to the United States-controlled Canal Zone.

The 48-year-old general, who has ruled Panama since 1968, declared tomorrow a national holiday and announced that some 100 political exiles could immediately return to Panama and that banned political parties might soon be legalized.

The new treaties, the result of 13 years of negotiations, recognize Panama's jurisdiction over the 553-square-mile Canal Zone and provide for the handing over of the canal itself on Dec. 31, 1999. Pana-

Continued on Page A16, Column 4

NARROW 68-32 VICTORY

Two-Thirds Majority Gained With One Vote to Spare, as in Earlier Success

By ADAM CLYMER
Special to The New York Times

WASHINGTON, April 18—The Senate voted today to turn over the Panama Canal to Panama on Dec. 31, 1999, moving to establish a new spirit of relations with Latin America and saving President Carter from a grave political defeat.

With one vote to spare, the Senate voted to approve a treaty giving up a

Text of Senate reservation, page A16.

symbol of American power and engineering that gripped the minds of so many of their constituents.

The vote of 68 to 32, one more than the two-thirds majority required by the Constitution, was identical to one by which the Senate approved a treaty on March 16 that guarantees the neutrality of the canal. The outcome was in doubt until just before the historic roll-call at 6 P.M.

New Battle Looms

Today's vote settles an issue that has existed since Panama seceded from Colombia in 1903 and entered into a treaty with the United States. It also effectively ended a 13-year negotiating process, although some financial details remain to be resolved by both Houses of Congress, probably next year.

That is expected to be the next battleground. Under an amendment agreed to last night formal ratification will be delayed until the implementing legislation is approved or until March 31, 1979, whichever comes earlier. Six months after the formal ratification, the United States will surrender large parts of the Canal Zone and a gradual Panamanian takeover will begin.

In television remarks after the vote, President Carter said, "This is a day of which Americans can always feel proud; for now we have reminded the world and ourselves of the things that we stand for as a nation."

'Mutual Respect and Partnership'

"These treaties can mark the beginning of a new era in our relations not only with Panama but with all the rest of the world," he said. "They symbolize our determination to deal with the developing nations of the world, the small nations of the world, on the basis of mutual respect and partnership."

Mr. Carter said Panama's Ambassador, Gabriel Lewis Galindo, had informed him that the country's leader, Brig. Gen. Omar Torrijos Herrera, would accept the treaties with the Senate's changes. He added that he had been invited to visit Panama and "I would like very much to accept."

The victory was critical for President Carter, who had repeatedly told wavering senators that his ability to conduct foreign affairs hung in the balance. But the

Continued on Page A16, Column 1

Basic Provisions of Treaties

WASHINGTON, April 18—Following are the basic provisions of the two treaties that provide for turning over control of the Panama Canal to Panama by the year 2000 and for the permanent neutrality of the canal thereafter.

Panama Canal Treaty

THE CANAL: Panama will assume "full responsibility for the management, operation and maintenance of the canal" on the termination of the treaty at noon Dec. 31, 1999. Until then the canal will be operated by a new United States agency, Canal Commission, whose board will include five Americans and four Panamanians.

THE CANAL ZONE: Panama will assume jurisdiction of the 553-square-mile zone when the treaty comes into force, but the zone will be integrated into Panama over 30 months.

DEFENSE: The United States will continue to have primary responsibility for the defense of the canal until expiration of the treaty in 1999, but will establish with Panama a combined

board of officers for consultation and cooperation on defense matters.

SEA LEVEL CANAL: Under the treaty, the United States will agree to negotiate only with Panama for construction of a sea-level canal across Central America, and Panama will agree not to undertake such a project except with the United States.

RESERVATIONS: The Senate adopted a measure yesterday allowing the United States to use its forces unilaterally if necessary. But another reservation specifies that any intervention would be only to keep the canal open, not to interfere in Panama's internal affairs. Another measure adopted by the Senate would nullify the mutually exclusive commitment on a new canal.

Neutrality Treaty

DEFENSE: After the treaty comes into effect on Dec. 31, 1999, the United States and Panama will each have the right to defend the canal against threats to its neutrality or to the peaceful transit of ships.

TRANSIT: Panama pledges to keep the canal open to "peaceful transit" by all nations, including warships.

RESERVATIONS: A measure adopted by the Senate last month in effect gives the United States the right to take "such steps as it deems neces-

sary," including the use of force to reopen the canal or restore its operations, should this become necessary. Another measure adopted by the Senate keeps the possibility of maintaining United States troops or bases in Panama after 1999 if Panama and the United States decided it was necessary.

AMENDMENT: Interprets the treaty to mean that Panamanian and American vessels, in an emergency, could "go the head of the line."

Ex-Diplomat to Head Met Museum

By GRACE GLUECK

After more than a year's search, the trustees of the Metropolitan Museum of Art have elected the museum's first full-time salaried president. He is William B. Macomber Jr., a 57-year-old retired diplomat whose last post was Ambassador to Turkey from 1973 to 1977.

The choice of Mr. Macomber, by unanimous vote of the board, surprised the museum world, because he is not known in the art field nor had his name been among the many reported to be in contention.

Under a reorganization of the museum's administrative structure voted by the board last March, Mr. Macomber as president will be in charge of management and finances while a subordinate director will be in charge of curatorial and artistic matters. The director, who will succeed Thomas Hoving, has not yet been chosen.

Mr. Macomber, whose salary was not disclosed, succeeds Douglas Dillon, who had served as unsalaried president since 1969 and now becomes board chairman.

Yesterday Mr. Dillon said that Mr. Macomber's extensive Washington background, which includes a stint as chief administrative officer of the State Department from 1969-1973 and as Assistant Secretary of State for Congressional Relations from 1957 to 1962 and from 1967 to 1969, would be "very useful in dealing with political figures in the city, in Albany and in Washington."

And he termed Mr. Macomber's lack of experience in the art world "a plus factor rather than a minus," adding, "We didn't want someone who'd second-guess or dominate the director and

Continued on Page C22, Column 3

INSIDE

Stocks Drop; Dow Off 6.85
The stock market declined moderately after three sessions of soaring prices and hectic trading as traders cashed in gains. The Dow was off 6.85. Pages D1.

Setbacks for Carter Tax Plan
President Carter's income tax plan suffered setbacks when a House panel rebuffed proposals on medical expenses and charitable deductions. Page D1.

We love you EDDIE KRAMER. HAPPY BIRTHDAY &
Congratulations on 10 years of Remarkable Productions
—ADVT.

The New York Times

LATE CITY EDITION
Weather: Mostly sunny, milder today;
fair tonight. Sunny, mild tomorrow.
Temperature range: today 50-70;
yesterday 53-65. Details, page B10.

VOL. CXXVII...No. 43,936   Copyright © 1978 The New York Times   NEW YORK, WEDNESDAY, MAY 10, 1978   25 cents beyond 50-mile zone from New York City. Higher in air delivery cities.   20 CENTS

Vance Offering To Sell Israel 20 More F-15's

He Informs Congress of Possible Solution to Jet Controversy

By BERNARD WEINRAUB
Special to The New York Times

WASHINGTON. May 9—Secretary of State Cyrus R. Vance offered Congress an informal compromise today in an effort to ease opposition to the Administration plan to sell advanced military jets in a package to Saudi Arabia, Egypt and Israel. Mr. Vance proposed that Israel be offered the opportunity to purchase additional planes beyond the package and that assurances be obtained from Saudi Arabia that its planes would be used solely for defense.

Mr. Vance made his offer at a private meeting with members of the Senate Foreign Relations Committee.

Administration sources said that Mr. Vance had tentatively offered to sell 20 additional F-15 fighters to Israel, to be delivered in 1983 and 1984. The extra F-15's in addition to the 15 in the current package and 25 sold earlier, would give Israel a total of 60 of the high-performance planes, the same number that the United States proposes to sell to Saudi Arabia by 1984.

Way Is Open to a Compromise

Although Administration and Congressional sources were reluctant to discuss details of the Vance offer, which was not totally fixed yet, it was evident that the Administration's plans had opened the way for a potential compromise.

"I believe we're on a road which could lead to a settlement," said Senator Jacob K. Javits, Republican of New York, one of the Foreign Relations Committee's key opponents of the package sale. "But it's a long road and we're far from home. The Administration has made proposals. We asked a lot of questions. We're thinking about it."

Two major themes dominate the Administration's compromise. One is the number of additional planes to be sold to the Israelis beyond the current package offer. The second is the Administration's willingness to give written assurances that Saudi F-15's will not be equipped with air-to-surface weapons and will not be based at sites close to Israel.

By late today, several opponents of the Administration's arms package made it clear that the number of additional planes for Israel remained an issue of discussion.

Moreover, Administration assurances involving the use of Saudi F-15's solely

Continued on Page A7, Column 1

LAW ALLOWING CITIES TO EXCEED TAX LIMIT UPSET IN NEW YORK

Appeals Court Action Also Affects School Districts—Puts Buffalo and Rochester Into Deficit

BY STEVEN R. WEISMAN
Special to The New York Times

ALBANY, May 9—The State Court of Appeals today struck down a two-year-old law that allowed localities to collect property taxes above state constitutional ceilings to pay for pensions, Social Security and other costs.

The unanimous decision by the state's highest court effectively throws into deficit the budgets of the cities of Buffalo, Rochester and the school districts of those two cities as well as the budgets of 48 other school districts across the state. It raises the possibility that residents and businesses in the areas involved may file claims for illegally collected back taxes.

According to the office of State Comptroller Arthur Levitt, the affected localities collected an aggregate of $110 million this year in excess of the property tax ceiling.

Legislative experts said that unless alternative sources of revenue were devised, the localities might have to cut spending deeply as early as July 1, when their new fiscal years begin, to bring their budgets into balance.

Legislative Leaders Meet

Aides to the legislative leaders began meeting this afternoon to review the possibility of authorizing new state aid, or new types of local levies, for the localities. Faced with the complexity of the issue, plus the unpleasant possibility of imposing new taxes in an election year, the Legislature is likely to put off moving until next month, perhaps in a special session after its regular session adjourns in two weeks.

In its unsigned opinion, the Court of Appeals noted that it had in 1974 thrown out a law permitting localities except New York City to tax above their constitutional limits for pension and other costs.

The new law, enacted in 1976, permitted the localities to go ahead anyway because they were facing a fiscal "emergency." It also sought to redefine the local property tax as a state property tax, but the court today said it viewed these tactics as creating a statute whose flaws were "indistinguishable" from the old one.

In its decision, the Court of Appeals rejected the localities' contention that they had been facing a "fiscal crisis"

Continued on Page D15, Column 5

MORO SLAIN, BODY FOUND IN ROME; WEST'S LEADERS ASSAIL TERROR

The body of Aldo Moro lies in the back of a car parked on Via Caetani in the center of Rome
United Press International

HE IS SHOT 10 TIMES

Ex-Premier Is Discovered in Car on Downtown Street 54 Days After Abduction

By HENRY TANNER
Special to The New York Times

ROME, May 9—The bullet-riddled body of former Prime Minister Aldo Moro was abandoned by his kidnappers today in a parked car in the historic center of Rome, a short distance from the headquarters of both the Communist and Christian Democratic parties, whose alliance the terrorist Red Brigades are fighting to destroy.

The discovery of the body behind the back seat of a burgundy red French Renault R-4 came 54 days after Mr. Moro, who was expected to be the next president of Italy, was abducted in a hail of gunfire in a street near his suburban home by urban guerrillas belonging to the Red Brigades.

Policemen raced to Via Caetani shortly after 1 P.M. today after intercepting an anonymous phone call to one of Mr. Moro's secretaries. The caller said, "In Via Caetani there is a red car with the body of Moro," and hung up, officials at Rome police headquarters said.

The kidnapping of Mr. Moro led to a nationwide manhunt by thousands of policemen and soldiers. Roadblocks were set up throughout the Rome area and a number of suspected terrorists were arrested in extensive house-to-house searches.

Body in Luggage Compartment

Mr. Moro was killed sometime early yesterday, according to first estimates by the police. He had at least 10 bullet holes in his chest. The cuffs of his trousers were full of sand as if he had been walking on a beach or been dragged across rough soil shortly before his death, the police said.

He was dressed in the clothes he had worn on the day of his abduction: a navy blue suit, a heavy overcoat, striped shirt and dark tie. He was found lying in the luggage compartment of the small car, his head leaning against the back of the rear seat. His face had been covered by a blanket. Next to his body was a plastic bag containing his watch, razor and other personal effects.

Mr. Moro was killed before being placed in the car, according to police sources, who said that there were no bullet holes in his overcoat. He was lying in a pool of blood.

The news of the discovery of Mr. Moro's body spread rapidly through Rome after radio stations broke into their programs with bulletins at about 1:30. There were no crowds in front of the Communist headquarters, but in front of the offices of the Christian Democrats throngs of grieving men and women shouted their anger. "Moro is alive!" some cried. Others shouted, "Death to

Continued on Page A16, Column 1

LIMIT ON ABORTIONS ADVANCES IN ALBANY

Bill Requiring Parental Notification for Minors Is Passed by Senate

By SHEILA RULE
Special to The New York Times

ALBANY, May 9—The Republican-controlled State Senate tonight passed a measure that generally requires notification of the parents of a teen-age girl before the girl can have an abortion.

Democrats denounced the measure as an attempt to legislate family relationships.

The measure requires that, if a physician does not have the parents' consent, he have proof that he had sent the parents notification by registered mail five days before the scheduled operation.

The bill, according to its sponsor, would not give objecting parents the power to veto the abortions.

After a lengthy and at times emotional debate, the Senate passed the measure 36 to 19. But the bill's fate in the Democratic-controlled Assembly is uncertain. A close vote is expected in that house's Health Committee when it considers the bill next week.

The Senate sponsor, Frank Padavan, Republican-Conservative of Queens Village, two years ago sponsored tougher parental-consent legislation that passed both houses but was later vetoed by Governor Carey.

With the Senate having recently been through a protracted battle over the

Continued on Page B20, Column 1

Europeans Pay Homage to Moro, Call for Defense of Democracy

By FLORA LEWIS
Special to The New York Times

PARIS, May 9—Throughout Western Europe today leaders paid homage to Aldo Moro, expressing horror at his death, which several considered an attack on the institutions of democracy itself. Several leaders called for a common front to fight terrorism and defend democratic regimes.

Some governments, including the Dutch and Norwegian, explicitly supported the stand of the Italian Government in having refused to accept terrorist conditions or make compromises to obtain the release of the Christian Democratic leader. Despite the sorrow and shock at the murder of a man, there was a general feeling that the very base of democratic government had been at stake.

Legislatures and international organizations, including the European Parliament and conferences of Common Market agricultural ministers and the World Health Organization, interrupted or even suspended their sessions to honor and to mourn Mr. Moro.

major developments in the kidnapping case.

Spanish and French Communists denounced the killing, in shaded terms reflecting the different positions of their parties.

The Spanish Communist Party said it was a "crime against Italian democracy and democracy in all of Europe," suggesting that the assassination was a reprisal against Mr. Moro's role in bringing the Italian Communist Party closer to a role in the Government. "It only serves the darkest forces of reaction and imperialism," the Spanish Communists said, using a phrase that they sometimes rely on in reference to the East as well as the West.

The French Communist leader, Georges Marchais, expressed his view in a telegram to the Italian Communist Party leader, Enrico Berlinguer, deploring the

Continued on Page A16, Column 1

Killing Denounced by Carter

In Washington, President Carter called the murder of Mr. Moro "a contemptible and cowardly act."

The only word from Eastern Europe so far was a brief dispatch by Tass, the official Soviet press agency, reporting the death without comment. Previously the Soviet agency had suggested that the kidnapping was a plot by both left-wing and right-wing extremists to provoke chaos in Italy, and Italian press reports that the terrorists had been armed by Communist countries were indignantly denied.

The official Chinese press agency, Hsinhua, reported the death of Mr. Moro without comment, citing reports from Western news agencies and summarizing

Lettuce: Wet Winter, High Prices

By ROBERT LINDSEY
Special to The New York Times

LOS ANGELES, May 9—As two women stood frowning before a mound of 99-cent lettuce in a suburban supermarket here the other day, one turned to the other and said, "Unbelievable, isn't it?"

The other replied, "It sure is. Three months ago I said I'd make salad for 100 people for a church party tonight."

Such reports probably will not relieve the frustration of Easterners who recently have had to pay as much as $1.49 a head for iceberg lettuce, much of it tarnished and wilted. But the supermarket encounter demonstrated that even in California, the nation's salad bowl, people are shocked by the price of produce this spring.

Lettuce prices in many parts of the country are beginning to edge down from a peak of two weeks ago. But, according to crop experts, the weeks ahead will still bring prices higher than

the 30 to 40 cents typical of the spring season in recent years.

The problem began in California, which grows more than 40 percent of the nation's fresh produce and more than 40 percent of the spring crop. This year the state's vegetable farms are operating at much less than full capacity.

North from the Imperial Valley on the Mexican border to the Salinas and Santa Clara Valleys, and up through the great San Joaquin Valley, a 500-mile spine of agriculture that is one of the richest sources of food in the world, farmers are still trying to recover from one of the state's wettest winters ever.

After a two-year drought that was one of the worst in a century, rains began to fall in December, and with

Continued on Page D15, Column 5

An Embittered Family Excludes Leaders of Italy From Funeral

By INA LEE SELDEN
Special to The New York Times

ROME, May 9—The family of Aldo Moro told Italian political leaders and members of the slain leader's Christian Democratic Party today that they would not be welcome at his funeral.

A statement issued by the family asked that there be no public expressions of mourning. It repeated a wish expressed by Mr. Moro in one of his letters toward the end of his 54-day captivity in what his abductors, the Red Brigades, termed a "people's prison."

"The family desires that the state authorities and the political leaders respect the will of Aldo Moro," the statement said. "This means no public demonstrations or speeches, no national mourning, no state funeral or medals to his memory."

'Those Who Loved Me'

Mr. Moro had asked in one of his many letters that neither state authorities nor politicians attend his funeral, and added:

"I ask to be followed only by those who loved me and are thus worthy of coming with me with their prayers and with their love." The letter was addressed to the party secretary, Benigno Zaccagnini, but intended for all the members of the Christian Democratic Party and others who had opposed an exchange of prisoners as requested by the Red Brigades for Mr. Moro's release.

Today, Eleonora Chiavaretti Moro, the widow, left her house to visit the morgue. With her were two of her daughters, her

Eleonora Moro leaving church in Rome after prayers, on Sunday.
Associated Press

son, her sister and brother-in-law and her son's fiancee.

When the family reached the room containing Mr. Moro's body, Mrs. Moro went in alone, touched the sheet covering the body, and dropped to her knees to pray.

"The family is not just embittered," said a confidant of Mr. Moro, adding that they wanted to make the political forces feel the brunt of their bitterness.

"They feel," he said "you didn't want

Continued on Page A16, Column 1

AWASH IN ESCAMBIA BAY: Water pours through the National Airlines jet that crashed while approaching Pensacola, Fla., Monday night. Three were killed but 55 survived, some saved by a passing tug. Page A18.
Associated Press

INSIDE

Massive A.M.C. Car Recall
The E.P.A. is ordering American Motors to recall nearly all its 1976 model cars to remedy a possible pollution-control defect. Page A18.

Joan Little Loses Appeal
New York State's Court of Appeals ordered the return of Joan Little to North Carolina from where she escaped last October. Page A23.

News Summary and Index, Page B1

FIRST CHOICE FOR MOTHER'S DAY DINNER
LUCHOW'S, 86-year-old restaurant landmark.
110 E. 14 at Irving Place. Res. 477-4860.—ADVT.

"All the News That's Fit to Print"

The New York Times

LATE CITY EDITION

Weather: Sunny, warm today; fair tonight. Sunny, warm tomorrow. Temperature range: today 69-84; yesterday 75-90. Details, page B17.

VOL. CXXVII....No. 43,986

Copyright © 1978 The New York Times

NEW YORK, THURSDAY, JUNE 29, 1978

25 cents beyond 50-mile zone from New York City. Higher in air delivery cities.

20 CENTS

HIGH COURT BACKS SOME AFFIRMATIVE ACTION BY COLLEGES, BUT ORDERS BAKKE ADMITTED

PRESIDENT TO ISSUE ORDER TO LIBERALIZE RULE ON SECRET DATA

Change in Procedure on Classified Documents Designed to Exhibit Interest in Open Government

By MARTIN TOLCHIN
Special to The New York Times

WASHINGTON, June 28 — President Carter plans a sweeping liberalization of the procedures governing the classification of Government documents.

He intends shortly to issue an executive order that will sharply limit the extent and duration of classifications, such as "confidential," "secret" and "top secret," and reduce the number of agencies that have classification authority.

The executive order will also provide that declassification procedures consider "whether the public interest in disclosure outweighs the damage to national security that might be reasonably expected from disclosure," according to the document, a copy of which was obtained by The New York Times.

The White House intends to present the executive order as a demonstration of the President's commitment to open government. Although civil liberty groups praised the new procedure, they said they did not believe the new policy would offset what they regarded as the Administration's commitment to secrecy in other areas.

Three Cases Cited

They cited the cases against Frank Snepp, a former agent of the Central Intelligence Agency, who wrote a book critical of the agency, and the prosecutions of David Truong and Ronald Humphrey for theft.

"Nothing that they could do in the executive order could outweigh the harm to free debate on national security issues brought about by the Snepp and Truong cases," said Morton Halperin, director of the Center for National Security Studies, who helped to formulate the new procedures.

Mark Lynch, a staff attorney for the American Civil Liberties Union who specializes in government secrecy, said that the new procedures "could be very useful" because "they'll have to think harder about what they're doing."

He agreed with Mr. Halperin, however,

Continued on Page A16, Column 3

2 U.S. NEWSMEN GET SOVIET LIBEL CHARGE

TV Agency Files Suit Stemming From Dispatches About Dissident

By DAVID K. SHIPLER
Special to The New York Times

MOSCOW, June 28 — Two American reporters were formally accused in a Moscow court today of having libeled Soviet state television by writing articles about an imprisoned dissident's televised "confession" that his friends and relatives believed had been fabricated.

It was the first time that Western diplomats and correspondents could remember the Soviet Government's taking legal action against foreign journalists for their dispatches.

The two reporters, Craig R. Whitney of The New York Times and Harold D. Piper of The Baltimore Sun, appeared in court in answer to a summons and were presented with copies of the claim against them by Lev Y. Almazov, chairman of the Moscow City Court.

Written Response Is Due Tomorrow

Judge Almazov set noon Friday as a deadline for a written response to the charge, and July 5 as a trial date. A guilty finding, according to Article 7 of the Civil Code, may result in a court order to publish a retraction and, failing that, a fine.

The claim, brought by the Soviet Government's broadcasting agency, asked that the two reporters "be held answerable for publishing in the foreign press slanderous information denigrating the honor and dignity of the members of the staff of the State Committee for Television and Radio of the U.S.S.R. and that they be caused to publish a retraction in the press."

It was not explained how a Soviet court could claim jurisdiction over newspapers

Continued on Page A13, Column 1

Associated Press
Gerard C. Smith

South Africans Reported Ready For Nuclear Ban

JOHN F. BURNS
Special to The New York Times

JOHANNESBURG, June 28 — American efforts to persuade South Africa to sign the treaty banning the spread of nuclear weapons reportedly reached an advanced stage today as high-level officials of the two Governments ended talks in Pretoria on the nuclear issue.

Sources close to the talks disclosed tonight that Gerard C. Smith, President Carter's ambassador at large in charge of efforts to prevent the spread of nuclear weapons, had been in the South African capital of Pretoria since Sunday for discussions with Foreign Minister Roelof F. Botha and other senior officials, including Abraham J. Roux, chairman of the South African Atomic Energy Board.

[Reports from Washington indicated, meanwhile, that South Africa was considering signing the treaty and was prepared to accept stricter international controls to prevent its atomic energy program from being used to develop weapons.]

Details Not Disclosed

Neither side in the Pretoria talks would divulge any details of what went on or say whether an agreement was in prospect. However, it is known that Mr. Smith, a 68-year-old veteran of arms-limitation talks, arrived here with the aim of gaining South African accession to the nuclear treaty in return for a pledge of continued cooperation between the two Governments in the peaceful applications of nuclear energy.

The talks in the South African capital are the culmination of secret negotiations that began last year, after a diplomatic flurry over fears that South Africa was preparing to test a nuclear explosive. The

Continued on Page A6, Column 3

BELL HAILS DECISION

Calls Ruling a 'Great Gain'— Plaintiff Is 'Pleased' and Others Express Relief

By LINDA GREENHOUSE
Special to The New York Times

WASHINGTON, June 28 — Among the entire spectrum of people and groups with a stake in the Bakke decision, there were degrees of satisfaction and relief today.

From Allan P. Bakke himself, who will enter medical school next September at the age of 38, to the civil rights organizations that opposed his challenge to the special minority-admissions program, people drew from the 154 pages of Supreme Court language the conclusions they most wanted to find. Mr. Bakke said he was "pleased" with the decision.

Attorney General Griffin B. Bell told reporters at the White House that he and President Carter regarded the decision as "a great gain for affirmative action." "This is what we thought the law was," the Attorney General said.

Benjamin L. Hooks, executive director of the National Association for the Advancement of Colored People, called the decision a "clear-cut victory for voluntary affirmative action," not only in education but also in other areas.

'Quotas Are Flatly Illegal'

Arnold Forster, general counsel of the Anti-Defamation League of B'nai B'rith, said his organization was "comforted that, once and for all, the United States Supreme Court has held that racial quotas are flatly illegal."

Among educators, the reaction was almost one of relief that their worst fears had not come to pass and that most existing college admissions policies could continue unchanged. [Page A23.]

Whether the decisions in Regents of the University of California v. Bakke will go down in history as "an act of judicial statesmanship," in the words of Prof. Alan Dershowitz of Harvard Law School, the nine Justices in their six opinions did seem to be offering something for everyone in a case that has been scrutinized as closely and argued as bitterly as any to reach the Court in recent decades.

The Court both ordered Mr. Bakke's admission to medical school and upheld the use of race as a factor in university admissions programs.

Black Leader Sees Threat

At a news conference of black leaders in New York City, Jesse Jackson, chairman of Operation PUSH, warned that the part of the decision striking down the minority-admissions program at the medical school of the University of California at Davis might be received by other universities as a signal to cut back programs that quite clearly have the approval of a majority of the Supreme Court.

But other civil rights leaders chose to focus on the part of the opinion establish-

Continued on Page A23, Column 6

Associated Press
Allan P. Bakke returning to home in Los Altos, Calif., after work yesterday

A Plateau for Minorities

Most College Programs Expected to Continue, But Ruling Is Seen as Brake on Rights Efforts

By JOHN HERBERS
Special to The New York Times

WASHINGTON, June 28 — The United States Supreme Court's split decision in the Allan P. Bakke case means, according to the consensus on both sides, that the great majority of affirmative action programs, public and private, will continue, as will the debate and lawsuits over what constitutes a proper racial balance.

News Analysis

For that, the leaders of the nation's minorities expressed pleasure and relief today at the 5-to-4 decision, which said that race may be considered in deciding who is admitted to colleges.

The rigid affirmative action program of the medical school of the University of California at Davis, which the Court struck down, was considered extreme in that it set aside 16 of 100 places for members of minority groups. Many other programs for enrolling minorities are more flexible and seem to fall within the boundaries set in today's decision.

A Retreat Is Seen

However, as Julian Bond, the Georgia civil rights leader and state legislator, said, affirmative action efforts reached a plateau today, and there was some fear that the decision would cause a decline in attempts to broaden educational and employment opportunities for blacks and other minorities.

Associate Justice Thurgood Marshall expressed the opinion, widely held among minority leaders, that the nation has been retreating from a commitment to racial justice made in the 1960's, in a parallel to what happened in the 19th century after the Reconstruction period.

"I fear that we have come full circle," he wrote, pointing out that "several affirmative action programs" were voided in that period by the Supreme Court. He cited the decision in Plessy v. Ferguson, which upheld segregation in public education, and said, "Now we have this Court again stepping in, this time to stop affirmative action programs of the type used by the University of California."

Although the majority decision appeared to please a broad spectrum of

people on both sides of the issue. Justice Marshall put his finger on a deep division remaining in this country between blacks and whites.

The division concerns whether the nation should give special preference to a people who in a unique way were subjected to a basic denial of human rights, beginning with slavery.

"It must be remembered," he wrote, "that during most of the past 200 years, the Constitution as interpreted by this Court did not prohibit the most ingenious and pervasive forms of discrimination against the Negro. No, when a state acts to remedy the effects of the legacy of discrimination, I cannot believe that this same Constitution stands as a barrier."

Associate Justice Lewis F. Powell Jr., who wrote the main opinion, made it clear that special preference for blacks was not what the majority had in mind when it said race could be considered in an admissions policy. He spoke of the need for diversity, for Asians, Mexican-Americans, people from rural as well as urban areas.

"The file of a particular black applicant may be examined for his potential contribution to diversity without the factor of race being decisive when compared, for example, with that of an applicant identified as an Italian-American if the latter

Continued on Page A22, Column 3

GUIDANCE IS PROVIDED

Medical School Racial Quota Voided, but Advantage for Minorities Is Allowed

By WARREN WEAVER Jr.
Special to The New York Times

WASHINGTON, June 28 — The Supreme Court by 5-to-4 vote affirmed today the constitutionality of college admission programs that give special advantage to blacks and other minorities to help remedy past discrimination against them.

But the Justices also ruled that Allan P. Bakke must be admitted to the University of California Medical College at

Excerpts from opinions, Pages A20, A21.

Davis, determining that the college's affirmative action program was invalid because it was inflexibly and unjustifiably biased against white applicants like him.

In today's opinion, the Court provided some guidance for educators trying to insure that their programs will pass judicial muster, and future cases will almost certainly shed some more light on what constitutes permissible affirmative action.

Most Significant Since '54

Both decisions involved 5-to-4 votes, with Associate Justice Lewis F. Powell Jr. joining four other Justices to force the admission of Mr. Bakke, then shifting to join the four remaining Justices in support of the constitutionality of carefully tailored flexible affirmative action plans.

Although the two-sided ruling aroused some confusion and controversy, it was generally regarded as the most significant civil rights pronouncement the high court had made since it outlawed public school segregation in 1954.

It was not initially clear whether the Bakke decision would affect future Supreme Court rulings on affirmative action in employment. Such hiring plans tend to incorporate fixed arbitrary formulas for blacks, women and others, somewhat akin to the Davis admissions program that was invalidated today, but the high court has generally approved them in the past.

Two Groups in Voting

Generally, however, civil rights advocates felt they had won a major victory by preserving the constitutionality of admissions plans to professional schools that favor minority group members, who had been all but barred from such education until recent years.

One group of Justices — William J. Brennan Jr., Byron R. White, Thurgood Marshall and Harry A. Blackmun — maintained that the special Davis admissions program was permissible because the Government could use racial classifications as long as it has the benign purpose of remedying past discrimination. They voted, as a result, to deny Mr. Bakke entrance.

A second group of four — Chief Justice Warren E. Burger and Associate Justices Potter Stewart, William H. Rehnquist and

Continued on Page A22, Column 1

Boy, 15, Who Killed 2 and Tried To Kill a Third Is Given 5 Years

By CHARLES KAISER

A 15-year-old Harlem youth who admitted killing two subway passengers and attempting to kill a subway motorman in one eight-day period last March has been sentenced to a maximum of five years in prison.

Under the terms of the sentence, imposed by Judge Edith Miller in Family Court—it was the maximum she could impose under state law—the youth will be required to spend at least 18 months in a "secure facility." After that he could be moved to a "residential facility" or kept in the secure facility, at the option of the state's Division for Youth.

Robert H. Silberling, head of the District Attorney's juvenile defense bureau, said that the state could, at its discretion, choose to keep the youth confined beyond the court-imposed five-year sentence. But when he reached the age of 21, Mr. Silberling said, he would have to be released.

Morgenthau Comments

"We've urged longer sentences," said District Attorney Robert M. Morgenthau of Manhattan, who cited the case yesterday in renewing a call for revision of the state's juvenile-offender laws. "I don't think the present law provides for adequate sentences for violent offenders. There has to be a provision for longer sentences for unusual cases like this one."

According to police and court officials,

what makes the case unusual is the violent nature of the slightly built youth, who they say has threatened to kill the detectives who arrested him, the prosecutors assigned to the case and Judge Miller herself. The police said he had also stabbed a fellow inmate in the Spofford Juvenile Center in the neck with a fork, saying: "I'll kill you if you sit down next to me."

"He's a kid who showed no remorse whatsoever," said Detective Sgt. Thomas Brady, who helped supervise the investigation that led to the youth's arrest.

Special Units Formed

Crimes by youthful repeat offenders, especially against the elderly, have generated controversy over what have been called lenient sentences sometimes handed out by judges. A highly publicized series of such crimes two years ago led to the formation in November 1976 by the Police Department of senior-citizen robbery units in all five boroughs.

Last year Mayor Koch's advocacy of the death penalty for heinous crimes was a major issue in the mayoralty campaign. Some people believe that Mr. Koch's support for the death penalty provided his margin of victory over Mario M. Cuomo

Continued on Page B7, Column 1

INSIDE

Blackout Cost Tallied

New York City's blackout last July cost at least $310 million, a study by the Library of Congress research service found. Page B9.

Levitt Disputes Vouchers

Arthur Levitt charged that the Port Authority let directors accused of falsifying expense vouchers alter them retroactively. Page B6.

United Press International
WED IN MONACO: Princess Caroline and Philippe Junot during civil marriage ceremony at palace in Monaco. They exchanged vows in same room where Prince Rainier and Grace Kelly were wed in 1956. Page C10.

"All the News
That's Fit to Print"

The New York Times

LATE CITY EDITION

Weather: Foggy, a chance of showers today and tonight. Fair tomorrow. Temperature range: today 80-71; yesterday 80-70. Details on page D8.

VOL.CXXVII...No.44,025

Copyright © 1978 The New York Times

NEW YORK, MONDAY, AUGUST 7, 1978

25 cents beyond 50-mile zone from New York City. Higher in air delivery cities.

20 CENTS

POPE PAUL VI IS DEAD OF A HEART ATTACK AT 80; GUIDED THE CHURCH THROUGH ERA OF CHANGE

Begin and Vance Consult in Israel On Reviving Stalled Mideast Talks

But Decision to Reschedule Foreign Ministers' Session Awaits Secretary's Meeting in Egypt With Sadat

By BERNARD GWERTZMAN
Special to The New York Times

JERUSALEM, Aug. 6 — Secretary of State Cyrus R. Vance and Prime Minister Menachem Begin of Israel met for more than four hours today in what they agreed were "serious, good and useful" talks.

But a decision on reviving the newly stalled Middle East peace negotiations awaited Mr. Vance's meeting with President Anwar el-Sadat in Egypt tomorrow and Tuesday.

Mr. Begin was evidently pleased that, for the moment at least, not he but Mr. Sadat was being perceived in the West as responsible for the breakdown in negotia-tions. He said that if the atmosphere was as good in Alexandria, at Mr. Vance's talks with Mr. Sadat, as it had been here today, "there will be a success" and the negotiations could resume.

Talking to reporters at the end of the day, however, the Prime Minister seemed to stand firm on previous Israeli proposals that led Mr. Sadat to break off direct talks and cancel a planned meeting of foreign ministers. And he said that Mr. Vance had not asked him to change his position.

"We were not approached to change," Mr. Begin said. "The whole problem is President Sadat's agreement to the tripartite meeting." He said he had told Mr. Vance that Israel remained ready to participate in the Egyptian-Israeli-American meeting of Foreign Ministers that had originally been planned this week as a follow-up to one held last month at Leeds Castle, near London.

"Everything hinges on President Sadat's reply" to Mr. Vance, the Israeli leader said. He added that no Israeli government could agree to what he called Mr. Sadat's precondition that direct talks take place only if Israel agrees ahead of time to withdrawal from all the territories occupied in the 1967 war.

Mr. Vance said he shared Mr. Begin's hope that the talks could be resumed, because "it's important to all of us; it's important to the world." But the Secretary of State and American officials — though Mr. Vance's prime goal on this trip is to persuade Mr. Sadat to remain involved in negotiating a Middle East peace settlement — refused to join in Mr. Begin's evaluation that all depended on President Sadat.

Israeli Flexibility Seen Necessary

American officials said again privately that for a breakthrough to take place, Israel would have to be more forthcoming on the key question of whether it is willing to withdraw from substantial parts of the West Bank of the Jordan River and the Gaza Strip. These two areas, which were occupied by Israel in 1967, are inhabited by more than a million Palestinians.

Mr. Begin, who has been ill, seemed relaxed and ebullient in his morning and late afternoon sessions with reporters. He appeared pleased that the latest turn of events had deflected American pressure for compromise away from him and to-

Continued on Page A4, Column 3

Carter Striving To Ease Strains With Congress

By TERENCE SMITH
Special to The New York Times

WASHINGTON, Aug. 6 — Like the suitor of a reluctant maiden, Jimmy Carter has been pursuing Congress in recent weeks with everything from flattery to invitations to the White House.

He has had Congressmen over in droves for working breakfasts, private luncheons, buffet dinners, tennis games and private film showings in the White House theater. In all, more than 350 of the 535 senators and representatives have trooped through the Executive Mansion in the last month.

More than mere sociability lies behind the Presidential invitations. Mr. Carter and his top aides are engaged in their most concentrated effort to date to improve the Administration's tattered relations with Capitol Hill.

House Recess Is Near

The courtship takes on a special urgency as the House approaches its Aug. 16 recess with several major Carter legislative programs still to be acted upon, including those concerning energy, Civil Service reform and taxes.

The courtship is also meant to reverse the deterioration of the President's relations with the House Democratic leadership before it is too late. That crucial relationship reached a new low last week

Continued on Page D10, Column 1

MANY VOICE SADNESS

World Remembers Leader for His Firm Guidance and Peace Efforts

Across the nation and the world, the powerful and the average parishioner yesterday mourned the man who for 15 years had been the spiritual leader of the Roman Catholic Church.

As Pope Paul VI was remembered by political and church leaders as a man who worked for world peace and guided the church during a time of social and religious unrest, the solemn hymns usually reserved for the mournful season of Lent were heard in some churches in New York. Plans were being made for special memorial masses, and some of the world's 550 million Catholics gathered to pray for the Pope, who died yesterday at his summer retreat at Castel Gondolfo.

President Carter said in a statement issued by the White House, "I was deeply saddened to learn of the death of Pope Paul VI, a man whose life and works have served personally as a great source of moral inspiration."

Remembered for Vatican II

Archbishop John Quinn of San Francisco, president of the National Conference of Catholic Bishops and the United States Catholic Conference, said: "One of the century's greatest popes has closed the long day of his earthly life. With superb skill, Paul VI brought the Second Vatican Council through three major sessions to its fruitful conclusion."

The Rev. Dario Pedroza, executive secretary of the Bishop's Commission for Evangelism and Catechism in Mexico, hailed the Pontiff's "valiant and faithful attitude toward the principles of the church and evangelism."

He added, as did many Catholic clerics, "The church is an institution that runs without dependence on any single person."

Cooke Offers Prayer

Terence Cardinal Cooke, who was named Bishop of the Archdiocese of New York by Pope Paul a decade ago, knelt at one side of the altar in St. Patrick's Cathedral and said in prayer at an evening mass, "May he now share in the joy of the Risen Lord, in the company of the Apostles, and of all those holy shepherds in whose footsteps he walked so valiantly and so selflessly."

And a statement by Governor Carey said, "His holiness Pope Paul devoted his life and his ministry to seeking world peace, to stabilizing the unity of the

Continued on Page A15, Column 1

POPE PAUL VI

©Karsh, Ottawa

Compassionate Conservative

Paul VI Was a Firm Guardian of Church Doctrine And a Champion of the Hungry and the Oppressed

By KENNETH A. BRIGGS

In contrast to Pope John XXIII, his predecessor, Paul VI was not naturally gregarious and innovative. He was the consummate bureaucrat in his Vatican career and not given to striking out in new directions.

An Appraisal If there had been no Second Vatican Council, begun under John XXIII and completed during his own reign, it is unlikely that Paul VI would have proposed such an updating of the church. But the modernizing was already well under way when he began his reign.

Paul's contribution was a product of his superior intellect, applied in the delicate application of so many Vatican II reforms. It was felt also in his unassuming presence, in which many world leaders found a poignant, peaceful respite.

Enormous Spiritual Quality

To those who met him across ideological and religious boundaries, Paul VI was first and foremost a man of surpassing spiritual quality.

He was a progressive exponent of human rights, a position that contrasted with his conservatism on church doctrine. He appealed for commitment to conventional Catholic principles as ardently as he championed the cause of the poor, the hungry and the oppressed.

To those who follow the proceedings of the church, he was much more. He performed the arduous and often thankless role as caretaker over a church that was in the midst of a tumultuous change.

In terms of particular actions, Pope Paul may be best remembered for his 1967 encyclical that underscored the church's opposition to artificial means of birth control. It caused a storm of protest, particularly in the United States, and is often cited as a major reason for the large-scale decline in mass attendance that followed in America.

For the Pope it was a matter of unshakable faith in historical Catholic reasoning rather than a question that should be rethought according to modern psychological, demographic or theological factors. He listened to the case for loosening the ban, brought forcefully by those appointed to study the problem, then made his decision.

Question of Women as Priests

The same pattern accompanied his decision in 1977 to approve a statement by the Congregation for the Doctrine of the Faith, which upheld the church's policy of refusing to ordain women to the priesthood. Since a priest must bear the image of a man because Christ was a man, he said, female priests were unthinkable.

Though these decisions often left progressives in the church disgruntled, his pleas for the downtrodden and his capacity for self-sacrifice won him a spiritual following that included all elements of the church.

His humility was epitomized when he offered himself in exchange for hostages held captive in Mogadishu, Somalia. In a political world rife with cynicism, his offer bore the stamp of sincerity.

He faithfully put in effect many of the changes that Vatican II called for. He

Continued on Page A14, Column 1

ELECTION TO BE HELD

Cardinals Are to Convene in About Two Weeks to Choose Successor

By HENRY TANNER
Special to The New York Times

ROME, Aug. 6 — Pope Paul VI, the 262d occupant of the Throne of St. Peter, died peacefully tonight at the age of 80 after a heart attack at his summer residence at Castel Gandolfo.

The death of Giovanni Battista Montini — who had served as Pope Paul VI since June 21, 1963, and had presided over major changes in the liturgy and organization of the Roman Catholic Church and had broken new ground in relations with

Pontiff's obituary begins on page A12.

Protestant and Eastern Orthodox Christians — was announced at the Vatican by the Rev. Pierfranco Pastore, acting head of the press service.

"With profound anxiety and emotion I must inform you that Pope Paul VI passed away at 2140 this evening, Aug. 6, 1978, at the papal summer residence of Castel Gandolfo," Father Pastore told reporters in the briefing hall of the Vatican press center. That time is 9:40 P.M., or 3:40 P.M. New York time.

Cardinal Assumes Role

Jean Cardinal Villot, the Vatican's Secretary of State, assumed the temporal and juridical but not the spiritual powers of the pontificate upon Pope Paul's death.

Cardinal Villot will summon the conclave of cardinals that will elect a new pope. Under a rule instituted by Pope Paul that limits voting rights to prelates under 80 years of age, 116 cardinals will be entitled to vote. Fourteen cardinals are over 80, church sources said.

The conclave will begin 15 to 18 days from now. Cardinal Villot's interregnum will last until the coronation of the new pope. The election may take several weeks.

During his reign, Pope Paul sought to mediate between the progressive and conservative forces within the church. This was true especially in his first years, when the progressive impetus given by Vatican II was at its strongest and provoked conservative counterpressures.

The Pope staked out new positions on ecumenism and carried out the sharpest liturgical changes in centuries, including abandonment of the Latin mass in favor of use of local languages. But fearing severe damage to the church, he resisted pressures to change traditional teachings on birth control, priestly celibacy and exclusion of women from the priesthood.

Bells Ring Death Knell

At Castel Gandolfo, a small town 15 miles southeast of Rome, the bells of St. Thomas Aquinas, Pope Paul's church, rang the death knell.

Outside the Pope's residence a crowd of tourists and local citizens had been waiting through the early evening. When the bells rang, many of them fell to their knees in prayer.

The lights in the square were turned off for a few minutes.

The first indication of a serious deterio-

Continued on Page A14, Column 3

Edward Durell Stone Dead at 76; Designed Major Works Worldwide

By The Associated Press

Edward Durell Stone, one of the nation's premier architects, whose designs include such public buildings as the United States Embassy in New Delhi and the Kennedy Center in Washington, died yesterday in New York City. He was 76 years old.

Mr. Stone died at Roosevelt Hospital after a brief illness, a family friend said.

Edward Durell Stone was born in Fayetteville, Ark., on March 9, 1902. He attended the University of Arkansas, and worked as an architectural apprentice at the office of Henry R. Shepley, a distinguished Beaux-Arts architect in Boston.

Started With Coveted Prize

From 1925 to 1927 Mr. Stone — who never received a college degree until his later years, when an honorary doctorate was conferred upon him by Arkansas — attended the architecture schools of Harvard and the Massachusetts Institute of Technology. In 1927 he was awarded the Rotch traveling scholarship, a coveted architectural prize that permitted him to spend two years of expense-paid travel abroad.

He went to Europe, where he had his first glimpse of modern architecture, and shortly after his return in 1929 took a job with the consortium of architects designing Rockefeller Center. There he worked on what was to be considered his first major early achievement — the design of the interiors of Radio City Music Hall.

First House in Mt. Kisco

Mr. Stone became deeply involved in the growing modern movement in New York, and in 1933 designed his first house, a starkly modern concrete and glass-blocked estate for Richard H. Mandel in Mount Kisco, N.Y. The boxy white house with strip windows and a semicircular glass-block dining area attracted wide attention, and Mr. Stone was soon called to design a compound for Mr. and Mrs. Henry R. Luce at Mepkin Plantation in South Carolina.

His next major commission was the Museum of Modern Art, and at the same time Mr. Stone designed a house in Old Westbury, L.I., for A. Conger Goodyear, the museum's president. The house's strong horizontal lines and large roof overhangs displayed a certain Frank Lloyd Wright influence that was to become even more marked in Mr. Stone's later buildings.

United Press International
Secretary of State Cyrus R. Vance listens as Prime Minister Menachem Begin of Israel discusses talks in Jerusalem

New York Hospitals Learning Economics Lessons

By RONALD SULLIVAN

The hospital's physicians were assembled for grand rounds, a hallowed monthly teaching forum at large medical centers. But Dr. Thomas C. Chalmers, the president of Mount Sinai Medical Center and the dean of its School of Medicine, did not have a fascinating disease to discuss, nor an unusual medical case history to present to the white-coated physicians gathered quietly in the hospital's auditorium.

Instead, he talked about a 60-year-old patient who had stayed at Mount Sinai for 17 days and who had run up a bill of $6,668, a considerable share of which rep-resented what he said were questionable or downright unnecessary hospital tests.

"If we don't stop runaway costs ourselves," Dr. Chalmers told his fellow physicians, "then government will come in with a meat ax and destroy the quality of medical care we have achieved."

A decade ago, when there seemed no end to the financial largesse pouring out of government-financed programs such as Medicaid and Medicare, virtually every kind of hospital procedure or grandiose expansion was approved without much thought given to the high costs involved.

Now, however, both state and Federal governments are cutting back on inflationary hospital costs. In New York City, respected medical centers in the world, the state is intent on shrinking a redundant hospital system with too many beds that will spend nearly $4 billion this year, more than two-thirds of it public funds.

In the last three and a half years, 24 hospitals have closed in New York City, many of them small, privately run facilities that health officials regarded as expendable. Increasingly, however, the city's continuing fiscal crisis, combined with the state's determination to eliminate 5,000 more hospital beds in the city,

Continued on Page B2, Column 1

FOOTBALL WINNERS VS. THE POINTSPREAD
FREE DETAILS—CALL 914-235-5100—Advt.

Glazer & BLITZ, lawyers practicing in medical malpractice, products & accident cases. First consult free. (212) 421-4624—ADVT.

"All the News
That's Fit to Print"

The New York Times

LATE CITY EDITION

Weather: Mostly cloudy, chilly today; cloudy, damp tonight and tomorrow. Temperature range: today 27-38; yesterday 39-49. Details on page B10.

VOL.CXXVIII .. No.44,043

Copyright © 1978 The New York Times

NEW YORK, TUESDAY, NOVEMBER 21, 1978

25 cents beyond 50-mile zone from New York City. Higher in air delivery cities.

20 CENTS

400 ARE FOUND DEAD IN MASS SUICIDE BY CULT; HUNDREDS MORE MISSING FROM GUYANA CAMP

Chairman Hua Kuo-feng
United Press International

2 Peking Wall Posters Raise New Questions On the Status of Hua

By FOX BUTTERFIELD
Special to The New York Times

HONG KONG, Nov. 20 — Two wall posters calling for a full public investigation into the suppression and cover-up of the major anti-Government demonstration in Peking in 1976 appeared in the Chinese capital today, raising questions about the status of Hua Kuo-feng, Chairman of the Chinese Communist Party.

The posters said an inquiry was necessary so that "those responsible for the suppression and cover-up could be brought to justice." According to diplomats in Peking, the posters demanded that the committee of investigation be made up of all major organs of the party and state.

Mr. Hua's present standing is closely linked to the incident, which took place in Tien An Men Square in central Peking on April 5, 1976 and was ostensibly in memory of the recently deceased Prime Minister Chou En-lai. At the time, Teng Hsiao-ping was blamed.

Two days later, "on the proposal" of Mao Tse-tung, Mr. Teng was purged and Mr. Hua was named party Chairman and Prime Minister. Mr. Teng, now again a Deputy Prime Minister, was reinstated in 1977 after the death of Mao and the arrest of his radical followers.

Yesterday, another poster put up in

Continued on Page A5, Column 1

SHORTAGES GROWING IN NO-LEAD GASOLINE OF HIGHER OCTANES

Although Overall Supply Appears Adequate, Some Companies Lag on Premium Grades

By ANTHONY J. PARISI

Shortages of premium unleaded gasoline are cropping up around the country, arousing fears among motorists of a general shortage of fuel for their automobiles.

Although supplies of gasoline appear adequate over all, some companies have been unable to keep up with the keen demand for high-octane unleaded gasoline, which provides superior performance for some automobiles. Some service stations have begun to turn away customers, who then find themselves waiting on longer and longer lines at stations that still have sufficient supplies on hand.

The Shell Oil Company, which has had to shut down two of its key refineries, was the first to report such shortages. Now Mobil stations are having problems, too, and other companies say their supplies are getting tighter by the day.

Some Rationing at Stations

To spread limited supplies among as many customers as possible, some stations have even begun to ration premium unleaded fuel — the first widespread example of gasoline rationing since the Arab oil embargo of 1973-74. The Bronxville Service Station in suburban Westchester County, for example, has been limiting purchases of Mobil Super unleaded to 10 gallons at a time — when it can get supplies. Yesterday it had no premium gasoline of any kind.

The shortages have appeared just as the Department of Energy is preparing to remove controls from gasoline prices. Yesterday, the department's Economic Regulatory Administration published an environmental impact statement on gasoline decontrol, recommending that the Government proceed with the plan despite concerns that the price of unleaded gasoline may skyrocket as a result.

One reason for the shortage is that motorists whose cars require unleaded gas have grown impatient with how their cars perform using regular grades of lead-free fuel. Almost a third of all the

Continued on Page D5, Column 4

Bodies lie strewn about vat containing drink laced with cyanide at the Jonestown headquarters of the People's Temple
Associated Press

LEADER OF SECT DIES

Parents Reported to Give Children Poison Before Dying Beside Them

By JON NORDHEIMER
Special to The New York Times

GEORGETOWN, Guyana, Nov. 20 — In a scene that dashed the senses, Guyanese forces today picked their way through an open-air pavilion choked with the bodies of 405 men, women and children in an American cult group who apparently committed suicide on the orders of their leader.

Wearing gaily colored clothes, the bodies were clustered in family groups, side-by-side in deathly embrace, all but three dead from drinking a concoction made of Kool-Aid and cyanide.

The setting was the jungle church of the People's Temple, the group that has been blamed for the slaying of Congressman Leo J. Ryan and four other Americans on Saturday.

Survivor Describes Scene

A surviving cult member gave the first newsmen to reach the scene today an account that was as incredible as it was filled with horror, a story of death plots and madness, of parents spooning a poisonous punch into the mouths of their babies before drinking it themselves.

And on the altar of the pavilion, surrounded in death by his followers as he had been surrounded by them in life, was the body of James Warren Jones, also known as the Rev. Jim Jones, the charismatic leader of the People's Temple, who had promised his racially integrated flock a utopia in the South American wilds. Instead, he gave them death.

"The time has come to meet in another place," he was said to have told the cultists he had assembled around him shortly after learning of the failure of a plan to kill the entire group of newsmen and parents of cultists who had flown deep into a lonely jungle airport with Congressman Ryan, according to the survivor, Odell Rhodes, 36 years old, from Detroit.

400 Are Still Missing

And then, according to the survivor's account, cyanide was dumped into a huge soup kettle, and the liquid was fed first to the babies, then to the children old enough to drink it themselves, and finally swallowed by the adults, many of whom were older people who had turned their Social Security checks and their lives over to the custody of Mr. Jones.

The leader, who at different times had described himself as the reincarnation of Christ and Lenin, died of a bullet wound in the head, according to the Guyanese police.

Nothing is known about the whereabouts of the remaining 400 or more cultists, who either fled into the jungle to escape death, or have elected to die deeper inside the canopied rain forest, where flesh-eating piranha and electric eels move in the murky jungle streams and insects swarm in the midday heat.

Cult Was Drilled in Suicide

It was learned that the cult was routinely drilled in suicide by Mr. Jones, who had a vision of a need to destroy the community if it was ever attacked.

Apparently, Mr. Ryan, who had been asked to investigate claims by his California constituents that members of the cult were being held in virtual bondage at the commune, and the party that accompanied him last Saturday, were seen as a grave danger.

Mr. Jones had decided to kill Mr. Ryan and the two dozen or so people who ac-

Continued on Page A17, Column 1

Bally Corp. Plan to Build Casino On Historic Site Backed by Jersey

By DONALD JANSON
Special to The New York Times

ATLANTIC CITY, Nov. 20 — New Jersey officials indicated today that they would permit the Bally Manufacturing Corporation, the world's leading manufacturer of slot machines, to demolish the historic Blenheim Hotel rotunda on the Boardwalk to make way for a casino.

The "preliminary" finding by the State Department of Environmental Protection is the latest step in changing the face of Atlantic City, with the classic resort hotels of the city's heyday yielding to a new line of modern casino hotels. Keeping the Moorish rotunda of the Blenheim intact — the main wing has been demolished — is the focal point of a determined drive by preservationists.

Last May 26 Resorts International opened the city's first casino in the old Haddon Hall Hotel after radically altering the structure and renaming it the Resorts International Hotel.

Since then 32 companies, including most of the major concerns operating casinos in Nevada, have either acquired potential casino sites in Atlantic City or announced plans to do so.

One company, Caesars World, operator of Caesars Palace in Las Vegas, has acquired two Boardwalk sites and has a casino under construction on one of them. Steel girders are up on the site of the Howard Johnson Regency Hotel, which will be incorporated into the new casino hotel.

Caesars hopes to open the city's second casino by next Memorial Day. It has also acquired, for possible construction of another casino, the site of the Traymore Hotel, a Boardwalk landmark that was demolished six years ago.

Bally hopes to be third to open an At-

lantic City casino. Its target date is July. It acquired three adjacent, historic hotels and wants to demolish all three eventually.

Last month Bally did demolish the Marlborough, a Queen Anne 1902 wooden structure that was one of first in the city to provide a private bath with every room.

In addition Bally is ripping out the interior of the Dennis, built in 1900 in the French Chateau style, and renovating it. The Dennis is the oldest hotel name on the beachfront today.

Last week 326 pounds of dynamite toppled

Continued on Page B7, Column 2

INSIDE

Carter Aides Named in Inquiry
A grand jury is studying charges that White House aides considered dropping the Vesco extradition case in return for $10 million in stock. Page B11.

Trucking Restriction Dropped
The Interstate Commerce Commission dropped a 40-year-old rule that barred companies that truck their own goods from hauling goods of others. Page D1.

Defectors From Sect Depict Its Rehearsals for Suicide

By ROBERT LINDSEY
Special to The New York Times

LOS ANGELES, Nov. 20 — "He has mass suicide drills, where he tells all the people, hundreds of people, to drink a certain drink, and he says, 'That's fatal, you're all going to die in 45 minutes,' I want to see how you feel about dying for socialism.'"

"He had something they called the 'blue-eyed monster,' a thing they did to children," another former member said. "They took children into a dark room and attached electrodes to them and then shocked them and told them never not to smile at Jim Jones.'"

And, said Timothy Stoen, a San Francisco lawyer and former aide to the Rev. Jim Jones, the founder of the People's Temple, when Mr. Jones ordered his followers in his Guyana commune to drink the liquid, "everybody drank."

"It was like he wanted to believe he was God," said Anna Mobley, a member

for four years. "He would get you so tired it would make you lose your mind."

"He sent spies to our home and said that if we didn't sell all our property, we would die," said Wade Medlock, the owner of a Los Angeles maintenance company, who turned over two of his homes to the cult under threats.

The remarks were made at a meeting of a group called the Human Freedom Foundation, which was set up here last summer by two psychics, Maria Papapetros and Jenita Cargile, after former cult members had sought them out for counseling on how to "deprogram" themselves. A recording of the meeting was made available to The New York Times.

According to former members, the cult was run as a police state by Mr. Jones, who was said to have enforced discipline by beatings and death threats; pursued bizarre sexual activities, and indoctrinated members in his personal brand of agrarian socialism.

According to Mr. Stoen, Mr. Jones first

enticed members with a doctrine of selflessness and a simple Christian faith of social equality that found support among blacks and upper middle-class whites who had become alienated in the 1960's.

Once he got "control of their minds," he would accept no dissent and told members that a defector had no right to live," Mr. Stoen said. He is a former deputy district attorney in Mendocino County who had been attracted to Mr. Jones's views in the late 1960's and became one of his lieutenants as the cult spread to San Francisco and Los Angeles and ultimately to the settlement in Guyana.

He said that as a sect official he had transferred more than $5 million to foreign bank accounts and said he believed the church's assets probably totaled much more.

Mr. Stoen said "people who disagreed would get phone calls at 3 A.M. with heavy breathing," or cult officials would find a drunk and pay him to read a script containing threats over the telephone. The children of parents who decided to leave the sect were often seized and kept in Guyana under guard.

Mr. Jones, he continued, had a "relationships committee" that had to approve

Continued on Page A16, Column 4

CULT LEADER: Jim Jones in Jonestown before shootings. Guyana revealed references from prominent Americans. Page A16.

Bodies of five Americans lie at ambush site in Port Kaituma, Guyana. From left, in foreground: Representative Leo J. Ryan; Don Harris, reporter for NBC; Gregory

Robinson, photographer for The San Francisco Examiner, and Patricia Parks, believed to be a member of the commune. At rear is Robert Brown, an NBC cameraman.
© 1978, The San Francisco Examiner

"All the News That's Fit to Print"

The New York Times

CITY EDITION

Metropolitan area weather: Mild today; colder tonight, tomorrow. Temperature range: today 51-30; yesterday 45-30. Details on page 39.

VOL.CXXVIII....No.44,068   Copyright © 1978 The New York Times   — NEW YORK, SATURDAY, DECEMBER 16, 1978 —   25 cents beyond 50-mile zone from New York City. Higher in air delivery cities.   20 CENTS

U.S. AND CHINA OPENING FULL RELATIONS; TENG WILL VISIT WASHINGTON ON JAN. 29

Israel Rejects New Peace Proposal; U.S., Irritated, Charges Distortion

Cabinet Backs Begin Stand

By PAUL HOFMANN
Special to The New York Times

JERUSALEM, Dec. 15 — The Israeli Cabinet decided today to reject the latest proposals by Egypt for a peace treaty as well as the "attitude and interpretation" of the United States regarding the proposals.

At the end of a special four-hour meeting, Prime Minister Menachem Begin,

Text of Israeli decision, page 3.

looking grim, said to reporters:
"The consultations, the negotiations will resume — we cannot say when."

[An official in the Egyptian Foreign Ministry denied Israeli charges that Cairo had made new demands during Secretary of State Vance's trip. Page 4.]

No Hope for Treaty by Deadline

The endorsement by the Cabinet of Prime Minister Begin's stand in talks with Secretary of State Cyrus R. Vance here Wednesday and yesterday quashed any remaining hope that the proposed Egyptian-Israeli peace treaty might be signed by this Sunday, the original deadline.

Foreign Minister Moshe Dayan warned in an interview broadcast tonight that there was a possibility the draft peace treaty might not be signed at all, and that negotiations between Israel and Egypt would have to start all over again.

The Cabinet's refusal to go along with the United States Government's view

Continued on Page 5, Column 1

Vance Reports to President

By BERNARD GWERTZMAN
Special to The New York Times

WASHINGTON, Dec. 15 — The Carter Administration accused Israel today of deliberately distorting the nature of new peace proposals taken to Jerusalem this week by Secretary of State Cyrus R. Vance in his effort to complete an Egyptian-Israeli treaty.

Obviously irritated by the Israeli Cabinet's decision to reject the proposals, announced today by Prime Minister Menachem Begin, officials accompanying Mr. Vance on his Air Force plane from Cairo to Washington, gave reporters a highly detailed briefing intended to rebut Mr. Begin's statements.

Vance Goes to White House

Mr. Vance, who arrived at Andrews Air Force Base late this afternoon, went by helicopter directly to the White House to report to President Carter on the trip to Cairo and Jerusalem.

There was no official statement by the White House after the Vance-Carter meeting. But the State Department was instructed to draft a "white paper" to put on record the complaints against the Israelis.

Relations between Washington and Jerusalem were again under severe strain, and Mr. Vance was described as "saddened" and annoyed by the Israeli Cabinet's decision, which left little room for any early progress.

The immediate reaction of American officials in the Vance party was that a

Continued on Page 3, Column 1

President Carter making announcement last night
Associated Press

Deputy Prime Minister Teng Hsiao-ping
United Press International

LINK TO TAIWAN ENDS

Carter, in TV Speech, Says 'We Recognize Reality' After 30-Year Rift

By TERENCE SMITH
Special to The New York Times

WASHINGTON, Dec. 15 — President Carter announced tonight that the United States and China would establish diplomatic relations on Jan. 1.

The President also said that Teng Hsiao-ping, the powerful Deputy Prime

Text of Carter statement, page 8.

Minister, would visit this country later in January. In a press briefing, reporters were told that Mr. Teng will visit the United States Jan. 29. It will be the first such visit by a high-level Chinese official since the Communists took power on the mainland in 1949.

In a dramatic, nationally televised speech, Mr. Carter also announced that the United States would terminate diplomatic relations with Taiwan as well as the mutual defense treaty with the Chinese Nationalists. In four months, the United States will also withdraw its remaining military personnel from Taiwan, the President said, but in remarks addressed especially to the people of the island, he pledged that the United States would remain interested in the peaceful resolution of the issue.

'Recognizing Simple Reality'

"We do not undertake this important step for transient, tactical reasons," Mr. Carter said. "In recognizing that the Government of the People's Republic of China is the single Government of China, we are recognizing simple reality."

"Normalization — and the expanded commercial and cultural relations it will bring with it — will contribute to the well-being of our own nation and will enhance stability in Asia," the President said.

In reassuring the people of Taiwan, Mr. Carter said he had taken care in reaching the agreement to make sure that the normalization of relations with the mainland "will not jeopardize the well-being of the people of Taiwan."

Certain Ties to Be Maintained

"We will continue to have an interest in the peaceful resolution of the Taiwan issue," Mr. Carter said. He added that the United States would maintain "our current commercial, cultural and other relations with Taiwan through nongovernmental means."

Mr. Teng's visit, Mr. Carter said, "will give our Governments the opportunity to consult with each other on global issues and to begin working together to enhance the cause of world peace."

The two countries will exchange ambassadors and establish embassies on March 1.

The President made special mention of the "long, serious negotiations" with China carried on before him by Presidents Richard M. Nixon and Gerald R. Ford. The results, he said, "bear witness to the steady, determined, bipartisan effort of our own country to build a world in which peace will be the goal and the responsibility of all countries."

Earlier in the evening, Administration officials confirmed that Treasury Secre-

Continued on Page 8, Column 1

CLEVELAND RACING DEFAULT DEADLINE

Bankers Grant Brief Extension — City Bond Credit Rating Cut

By REGINALD STUART
Special to The New York Times

CLEVELAND, Dec. 15 — City officials scheduled a meeting for 11 o'clock tonight to decide whether to accept Mayor Dennis J. Kucinich's sweeping fiscal rehabilitation plan for the city or find some other means of avoiding default on $15.5 million in loans that were due today.

At the same time, banker-creditors, whom the city had contracted with to repay the short-term loans, extended their hours until midnight to see if the city would either pay the debts or come up with a plan that would persuade them to renew the loans.

Mayor Assails Bank and Council

Meanwhile, Moody's Investors Service, the municipal bond credit-rating company, lowered the city's bond rating today to Caa. That was the lowest rating reached three years ago by New York City during its financial crisis. A Caa classification defines such bonds as being in default or having "present elements of danger with respect to principal or interest."

The chances for success of the Mayor's plan, which has drawn strong opposition from City Council leaders and at least two of the six lenders, were further diminished tonight when the Mayor ac-

Continued on Page 11, Column 1

China Tie Reflects Carter's Feeling That Country Was Ready for Move

By HEDRICK SMITH
Special to The New York Times

WASHINGTON, Dec. 15 — President Carter's dramatic announcement that he was taking this country into a new era of diplomatic relations with China reflects the confident political calculation that the country-at-large is now ready for this step and the hopeful diplomatic calculation that it will not jeopardize the imminent new strategic-arms agreement with the Soviet Union.

High Administration officials revealed that the breakthrough had come quicker than expected and had been pushed by the Chinese. Although the White House found the timing awkward, because of the delicate stage of negotiations with Moscow on an arms accord, Washington felt that the Chinese initiative could not be turned down.

In another way, however, the break-

through could not have come at a more opportune moment for an Administration frustrated by the latest impasse in the Middle East talks and beset by the political upheaval in Iran and the potential tremors elsewhere in the Near East.

The move appeals to the historic American fascination with the Orient since the days when clipper ships carried missionaries and merchants to distant China from the salty harbors of Massachusetts. In the modern calculus of global power politics, the tie with China offers new leverage in the triangular relationship with the Soviet Union, as well as a counter to recent Soviet gains in Afghanistan and the Horn of Africa.

As rumors swept the city tonight before

Continued on Page 8, Column 5

China: The Long Wait

By FOX BUTTERFIELD
Special to The New York Times

HONG KONG, Saturday, Dec. 16 — President Carter's announcement last night that the United States and China are finally normalizing diplomatic relations comes nearly seven years after

News Analysis

Richard M. Nixon pledged in the Shanghai Communiqué of February 1972 to work toward that goal.

The major obstacle to progress on restoring relations has been America's long-time military and diplomatic commitment to the Chinese Nationalist regime on Taiwan, a problem compounded by the continued strong support for Taiwan among many in the United States.

After the initial euphoria that accompanied Mr. Nixon's epochal trip to China, relations between the two nations seemed to languish for several years as events gave Taiwan a series of reprieves. First, Mr. Nixon's plans to improve ties were hampered by the Watergate scandal. Then President Gerald R. Ford was caught up in the debacle of Vietnam's collapse. And more recently Mr. Carter himself was sidetracked by the Panama Canal negotiations, the Middle East prob-

lems and talks to limit the spread of nuclear weapons. Fears were raised that Washington was frittering away a critical opportunity to strengthen America's interests in Asia.

But in recent months, largely at China's initiative, relations began to improve rapidly. Since the summer, in fact, the two countries have been drawing together in a process that looked like normalizing without the final actual step.

Two factors impelled this change: China's increased fears of being encircled by the new alliance between the Soviet Union and Vietnam, and its desire for expanded trade and technology to

Continued on Page 8, Column 5

Koch Gets 3 Billion School Budget; Smaller Classes Among Objectives

By MARCIA CHAMBERS

The New York City School Chancellor, Frank J. Macchiarola, submitted a $3 billion expense budget to Mayor Koch yesterday that calls for smaller classes, intensified remedial instruction and additional personnel to combat truancy, vandalism and internal mismanagement.

To finance these additional programs, the Chancellor said he had to find $130 million in the budget from sources not yet committed to the public school system's anticipated revenues. The system's costs are roughly a third of the city's overall expense budget. He said that following the Mayor's lead he intended to try to get the necessary funds from the state and Federal Governments.

The Chancellor plans to have an all-day meeting on Monday with Federal officials in an attempt to obtain changes in Federal law that would give the school system more say in how and where remedial funds can be spent. Then, Mr. Macchiarola said, he intends to talk to Albany lawmakers, who are under a court ruling to revise the state-aid allocation

formula for the financing of public schools.

If the city school district — the biggest in the country, with nearly a million students — "gets its fair share of state funding," he said, "we would get triple the

The Mayor's consultant on the City University has endorsed $160 million in priority construction projects. Page 25.

amount we get now." He said that would be more than enough for the new programs.

In an obvious criticism of his predecessor, Irving Anker, Mr. Macchiarola said in his budget message to the Board of Education that "additional funds will be required in order to begin the programing that has been neglected — not without severe effect — in recent years." Mr. Macchiarola's proposed 1979-80 budget is virtually the same as the Anker budget proposal last year. The Board of Education will hold a public hearing on the

Continued on Page 28, Column 1

Taiwan Leaders Confer Hurriedly After Learning of U.S.-China Step

Special to The New York Times

TAIPEI, Taiwan, Saturday, Dec. 16 — Leaders of the Chinese Nationalist Government were abruptly summoned into emergency meetings here early today, a few hours before the announcement in Washington that the United States was establishing diplomatic relations with Peking.

The United States, it appeared, gave only a few hours' notice to Taiwan that it was withdrawing its recognition of the Government of President Chiang Ching-kuo.

U.S. Decision a Heavy Blow

President Chiang first called several Cabinet ministers to his office to brief them on the developments. Then, official sources said, an emergency meeting of the central committee of the Kuomintang, the governing party, was scheduled to consider the most serious blow it has suffered in the three decades since Chiang Kai-shek led his defeated followers here from the mainland.

More than 50 countries have broken relations with Taiwan since the Chinese

Nationalists were replaced at the United Nations in 1971 by the Communist regime. But the American decision comes as a particularly heavy blow since the United States, the last world power to recognize the Nationalists, has supported them since 1954 with a mutual-defense treaty.

Since President Richard M. Nixon's visit to China in 1972, the Nationalists have expected that the United States would eventually break relations. The timing, however, was apparently a surprise.

It comes during a heated parliamentary election campaign on Taiwan, when some rightist candidates have been warning that it faces a possible "betrayal" by the United States. Others, however, have campaigned on the slogan that the fate of Taiwan should be decided by the island's 16 million people.

One candidate said: "We should not repeat the history in Vietnam. Taiwan's fu-

Continued on Page 8, Column 1

INSIDE

Saudis Moderate on Oil Prices
On the eve of a meeting of oil-exporting countries, Saudi Arabia's delegate called for moderation in determining an increased price of oil. Page 29.

Cults' Funds Reported Gone
A U.S. official said a Zurich bank had told the Justice Department that as much as $8 million in People's Temple funds had been removed. Page 12.

Mayor Dennis J. Kucinich of Cleveland, foreground, was accused at City Council debate of not acting to prevent default
United Press International

"THE TREE" IS LIT AT LUCHOW'S FOR THE 96th YEAR. Bring Kids (1 to 80) to ooh in awe. 110 E. 14th St. 477-4860—ADVT.

N.Y., DELTA and S.S. WELCOME BACK PETE MARK, their favorite supervisor and best friend. Love Staz. ADVT.

"All the News That's Fit to Print"

The New York Times

LATE CITY EDITION

Weather: Snow likely and cold today; snow changing to sleet or rain tonight. Temperature range: today 28-35; yesterday 25-41. Details on page B9.

VOL.CXXVIII....No.44,100   Copyright © 1979 The New York Times   NEW YORK, WEDNESDAY, JANUARY 17, 1979   25 cents beyond 50-mile zone from New York City. Higher in air delivery cities.   20 CENTS

SHAH LEAVES IRAN FOR INDEFINITE STAY; CROWDS EXULT, MANY EXPECT LONG EXILE

New York City Gets Passing Grade On $100 Million Notes It Will Sell

By ANNA QUINDLEN

The city prepared to go ahead this month with its proposed $100 million note sale after the notes received a passing, but not superior, grade yesterday. The note sale will be the city's first foray into the public borrowing market in nearly four years.

The fiscal rating is expected to be one piece of evidence of economic recovery Mayor Koch takes with him when he testifies before the Senate Banking Committee. The committee's chairman, William Proxmire, announced yesterday that he would hold hearings Feb. 7 on the city's financial condition.

The MIG-3 rating given to the notes by Moody's Investor Service yesterday was lower than city officials had hoped for, but it was still an improvement over its last investment grade, the lowest ranked MIG-4. That rating quashed a scheduled note sale in November 1977. Moody's noted in a statement that while repayment of the short-term notes seemed secure, the "chronic financial weakness" of the city made a higher rating impossible at this time.

Moody's defines MIG-3 as an investment of "favorable quality, but lacking the undeniable strength" of the two higher classifications. The letters MIG stand for Moody's Investment Grade.

'A Climate of Uncertainty'

"Reliability of pledged revenues in the quality of the mechanism to assure payment of notes provides basic security," Moody's said in issuing its grade.

"The chronic financial weakness of the issuer (continual budget balancing efforts, persistent revenue shortages, magnitude of fixed costs) still creates an overall climate of uncertainty. The balancing of this year's budget indicates financial progress."

"I'm obviously pleased that our credit rating is better," said Mayor Koch when the rating was announced, a day after the unveiling of his own plan to close the city's budget gap. "If your credit rating is better it means more people have faith in you."

Mr. Koch and Deputy Mayor Philip L. Toia said they expected the city to go ahead with the sale, although neither would speculate on how high a rate of interest the city might have to pay in the current market on such notes. The notes will be offered by a consortium of underwriters to the public in $10,000 and $25,000 denominations.

Deficit Dispute Blamed

However, Jackson Phillips of Moody's said he did not think the city would proceed with a sale if the interest rate on the notes went above the 9.5 per cent it currently pays on loans from banks. "I hear

Continued on Page B5, Column 1   Continued on Page B4, Column 5

New York State to Try New Negotiation Plan

By RICHARD J. MEISLIN
Special to The New York Times

ALBANY, Jan. 16 — Governor Carey's administration and New York's largest public-employees union agreed today to adopt an experimental bargaining method in which each side would negotiate to its "last, best offer" and an impartial arbitration panel would be forced to choose one proposal or the other.

The union, the Civil Service Employees Association, guaranteed as part of the agreement that its members would not strike and agreed to require the arbitration panel to give "substantial weight" to the "ability of the state to pay the cost of any economic benefit without requiring an increase in present taxes." The agreement covers 107,000 state workers, whose contracts expire March 31.

It will be the first use of binding arbitration to resolve impasses in negotiations between the state and its workers, which in the past have been subject to the state's Taylor Law requirements for state mediation and fact-finding and for legislative resolution.

If the new method, known as "last-offer

Continued on Page B5, Column 1

Battle Intensifies Over Authority Of President to Control Agencies

By MARTIN TOLCHIN
Special to The New York Times

WASHINGTON, Jan. 16 — President Carter's fight to control inflation is intensifying a constitutional conflict between his authority to develop national policies and Congress's power to mandate the independence of Government regulators.

In a direct challenge to the President's authority several environmentalist groups have brought a Federal court action asking that White House economic advisers be prohibited from interfering with the Interior Department's formulation of strip-mining regulations. The enforcement of the regulations was delayed for six months last week after the economic advisers expressed fears that they might be inflationary.

In recent years, Congress, suspicious of past Presidential abuses, has given no fewer than 60 agencies in the executive branch the authority to issue regulations on specific and distinct areas without reference to broader concerns. The mandates include authority to clean up the air and water, protect consumers and improve workplace health and safety, all of which affect Presidential concerns such as inflation, the energy gap and economic growth.

The White House View

The powers of such long-time regulatory agencies as the Interstate Commerce Commission and the Federal Communications Commission, whose independence from Presidential intervention is well established, are not in dispute.

But the White House does challenge the theory that executive branch agencies should perform their new regulatory functions without Presidential direction. It contends that the President's power to appoint and dismiss Cabinet officers carries an implicit authority to direct the agencies' actions.

Critics, mainly single-interest groups that have fought to get regulations through Congress, maintain that Congress intended that these Cabinet officers

Continued on Page D17, Column 1

West German Retailer Seeks 42% of A. & P. In a $75 Million Deal

By BARBARA ETTORRE

A major West German food retailer announced plans yesterday to acquire 42 percent of the Great Atlantic and Pacific Tea Company, the supermarket giant whose initials have long been a household term in American retailing.

The Tengelmann Group, a privately owned company, said that it planned to buy some A. & P. shares from the John A. Hartford Foundation, which has held a major interest in the chain for many years, and from several other major shareholders.

The 42 percent interest would mean effective control of A. & P. for the German company and would represent an investment of more than $75 million. Trading of A. & P. stock on the New York Stock Exchange was halted yesterday afternoon at 6⅝, up ⅛. The plan would involve a purchase of approximately 10 million of the 25 million A. & P. shares outstanding.

Jonathan L. Scott, chairman and chief executive officer of A.& P., said in a statement that the company "welcomes this expression of investment confidence." He continued, "We at A. & P. look

Continued on Page D4, Column 1

INSIDE

Vietnam Troops Lose Port
In their first reverse in Cambodia, Vietnamese troops were driven out of Kompong Som, a key port, according to Western analysts. Page A3.

52 Convicts Get Clemency
Freedom or parole eligibility was granted by Tennessee's governor as hearings on the alleged sale of clemency continued. Page A14.

Shah Mohammed Riza Pahlevi and his wife, Empress Farah, as they prepared to leave Teheran yesterday
United Press International

On Streets: Cheers, Roses and a Mink Coat

Statue of the Shah's father, Riza Shah, being toppled shortly after Shah left
United Press International

One Man in Crowd Hailing Shah's Departure Asks, 'Am I Dreaming?'

By ERIC PACE
Special to The New York Times

TEHERAN, Iran, Jan. 16 — "Shah raft! Shah raft!" The joyful shout announced: "The Shah is gone!"

As soon as the news broke on the Teheran radio, the cry began sounding along Vesel-e-Shirazi Street. Cheering crowds formed and happy women tossed candy and rosewater at them. Farokh Marvasti, an electrical engineer, had a dazed smile. "Am I dreaming?" he said. "What I have always hoped for has come true: The whole system of monarchy is collapsing here after 2,500 years."

"Salute to the mother of martyrs!" the throng of black-veiled women chanted at a rally in the Dehkade Vanek section of this sprouting, traffic-clogged city of five million. They waved their fists toward Zahra Rezai, who is revered by Islamic militants as the mother of four Islamic anti-Government "guerrillas" who died at the hands of the Shah's Government, one in prison and three in shootouts. "I never thought the Shah would leave so soon," Mrs. Rezai said, weeping. "I am glad the lives of my children were not wasted and now our country will have peace."

For the throng of hundreds of thousands that surged through the boulevard it was a day of reveling and roses, roses that marchers tossed in the air as they chanted: "O the anti-Islamic Shah!" "His return is impossible!" "The Shah has become a fugitive!"

Some demonstrators tried and eventually succeeded in pulling the equestrian statue of Riza Shah, the present Shah's father, from its pedestal on Sepah Square; it took a lot of pulling. On Pahlavi Avenue others toppled a statue of his son from its pedestal.

"May God help you," the militant Islamic clergyman known as Mullah Doost Mohammed said as he tried to comfort a strong-jawed woman, Nemati Roshan, who was weeping uncontrollably after the rally in Dehkade Vanek.

"Damn the Shah!" Mrs. Roshan had yelled when the rally was at its peak. Now she was sobbing as she told the

Continued on Page A8, Column 5

Iran, a Country Adrift

By R.W. APPLE Jr.
Special to The New York Times

News Analysis

TEHERAN, Iran, Jan. 16 — The din of triumph that echoed through Teheran today expressed the spirit of the moment. But the spirit of the future may have been more truly expressed by a phrase uttered at the same time near Paris by a resolute 78-year-old man who has made a revolution. The departure of Shah Mohammed Riza Pahlevi, said Ayatollah Ruhollah Khomeini, was "only a first step" toward his goals.

In the sense that little could be accomplished while the Shah remained here, his flight to Egypt and, later, to the United States removed a great obstacle to the resolution of Iran's yearlong political crisis. It also removed the man by whom and around whom the country's life has been organized since the start of World War II.

No one is really in charge here now — a situation symbolized by banknotes, held aloft by celebrants, from which the Shah's portrait has been excised. With what is probably the permanent departure of the Shah, the heir to Iran's proud 2,500-year imperial history, Ayatollah Khomeini has become the cardinal political figure. He has not yet established full control, but he more than anyone else commands the affection of the masses.

The central question tonight was this: Having brought down the Shah, with

whom he has feuded for 15 years, will he demand that the struggle continue until an Islamic republic can be established with him as the strongman, or will he mute his militancy and compromise with the struggling social democratic Government of Prime Minister Shaphur Bakhtiar?

From the answer to that question will flow the answers to many others, both do-

Continued on Page A8, Column 3

RULER GOES TO EGYPT

He Voices Hope Bakhtiar's Government Can Make Amends for Past

By NICHOLAS GAGE
Special to The New York Times

TEHERAN, Iran, Jan. 16 — Shah Mohammed Riza Pahlevi left Iran today, driven from the country he has ruled for 37 years by a popular upheaval that gathered force until it undermined his throne.

A year of demonstrations and crippling strikes culminated in a brief farewell ceremony near the imperial pavilion at Mahrabad Airport, before the Shah's departure for Aswan, Egypt, where he was to be a guest of President Anwar el-Sadat. Tears appeared to be welling in the ruler's eyes.

"I hope the Government will be able to make amends for the past and also succeed in laying the foundation for the future," he said.

Changes Aroused Resentment

The Shah had laid ambitious plans to carry his country from feudalism to the front ranks of the industrial states within a generation. But his ambitions aroused resentment at various levels of the society.

The demonstrators who took to the streets to bring down the Shah complained most loudly about the arbitrary manner in which he pressed his programs, the corruption in ruling circles and the harsh measures used to suppress opposition from the religious community and liberal political groups.

In the end, the 59-year-old Shah had accumulated so much hostility from so many quarters that his throne could be saved neither by his lavishly equipped armed forces nor by the United States, which had regarded him as a key ally.

Long Exile Thought Likely

He described his departure today as an extended vacation, but it was believed by his opponents in Iran and by government officials here and in other countries that the trip marked the beginning of a long and perhaps permanent exile.

It was at 1:24 P.M. that the royal jet, a silver-and-blue Boeing 707 named Shahin (Falcon), took off from the airport for Egypt.

[The Shah took the controls himself, The Associated Press reported, and flew the plan over Teheran and on to Egypt.]

As the jet flew over the capital, its citizens were unaware that the year of riots, which are believed to have caused the loss of more than 2,000 lives, had finally succeeded in driving out the Shah.

But within 15 minutes the news had spread throughout Teheran and hundreds of thousands of people poured out of their homes shouting "Shah raft!" — "The Shah is gone!"

The streets, nearly empty during recent days of strikes and gasoline shortages, were quickly clogged with automobiles that added the sound of their horns to the din, as people embraced, wept and

Continued on Page A8, Column 1

Other Iran News

Arriving in Aswan, Egypt, Shah Mohammed Riza Pahlevi was escorted by President Anwar el-Sadat to a secluded hotel on an island in the Nile. Page A8.

In Paris, Ayatollah Ruhollah Khomeini, the exiled leader of the Shah's religious opposition, congratulated the Iranian people for forcing the Shah's departure through their increasingly violent demonstrations over the last year. Page A8.

In Washington, the Carter Administration made no formal comment on the Shah's departure, which it had encouraged, but officials said privately that the Government of Prime Minister Shapbur Bakhtiar probably had no better than a 50-50 chance of survival. Page A10.

Also in Washington, the Iranian envoy and friend of the Shah, Ardeshir Zahedi, declared himself the "Ambassador of the Shah" and said he would continue as Ambassador despite an attempt by six employees to bar him from his embassy failed for lack of support. Page A10.

At the United Nations, Iranian diplomats closed their mission all day in what they described as solidarity with the Iranian people on the occasion of the Shah's departure. Page A10.

In Lubbock, Tex., Crown Prince Riza Pahlevi welcomed his brother and two sisters, who arrived a few hours before their father left Teheran. Page A10.

On Beekman Place in New York, neighbors of Princess Ashraf Pahlevi, the Shah's twin sister, said they thought a visit by the Shah was likely. Page B3.

In Aswan, Egypt, President Sadat took Shah on canopied ferry to hotel on Nile
Associated Press

"All the News That's Fit to Print"

The New York Times

LATE CITY EDITION

Weather: Mostly sunny, cool today; clear, cold tonight. Sunny tomorrow. Temperature range: today 32-48; yesterday 37-49. Details on page C12.

VOL.CXXVIII....No.44,169   Copyright © 1979 The New York Times   NEW YORK, TUESDAY, MARCH 27, 1979   25 cents beyond 50-mile zone from New York City. Higher in air delivery cities.   20 CENTS

EGYPT AND ISRAEL SIGN FORMAL TREATY, ENDING A STATE OF WAR AFTER 30 YEARS; SADAT AND BEGIN PRAISE CARTER'S ROLE

OPEC PARLEY WEIGHS NEW OIL PRICE RISES AND CUTS IN OUTPUT

Saudis Say They Will Try to Resist Big Increases — Carter Puts Off Decisions on Energy

By PAUL LEWIS
Special to The New York Times

GENEVA, March 26 — Pressure for another large increase in world oil prices built up today at the opening of a meeting of oil ministers of the 13 member nations of the Organization of Petroleum Exporting Countries.

The advocates of a sharp new oil price rise, of anywhere from 20 to 35 percent from current levels on April 1, also urged other oil producers to reduce output. The aim would be to keep world markets tight as Iran resumes exports to insure that the new price levels stick.

But Saudi Arabia, the world's largest oil exporter, resisted pressure for price jumps, pointing out that they could do severe damage to the economies of both the developing and the industrialized world. "There is worry particularly about the effects of price changes on developing countries," OPEC's secretary general, René Ortise, said.

Effort to Reduce Increases

Sheik Ahmed Zaki Yamani, Saudi Arabia's oil minister, interviewed after tonight's session, said the ministers faced a "deadlock," with the Saudis feeling that the increases demanded by Iran and Libya were "too steep." Observers here interpreted his stance as an effort to cut probable increases to more moderate levels.

The ministers have not yet voted themselves the power to take any pricing action at the current two-day session but are expected to do so tomorrow. A simple majority vote would grant the meeting such authority.

On the question of possible punitive cutbacks in supplies, reflecting displeasure with some consuming nations' positions on the Palestinian question, Iraqi representatives said such moves were possible, particularly against Egypt. But they carefully noted that no such moves were planned by OPEC, although the "oil weapon" could re-emerge if conditions returned to the situation of 1973.

Carter Decisions Deferred

In Washington, meanwhile, Administration officials said that President Carter's decisions on various energy proposals, expected Thursday, would be deferred, apparently because key White House officials have not been able to devote enough time to the controversial plans. [Page D12.]

When Sheik Yamani entered the OPEC

Continued on Page D12, Column 3

Leaders join hands after signing pact. President Anwar el-Sadat signed first, followed by Prime Minister Menachem Begin. President Carter was witness.
United Press International

Mood of Peace Seems Somber And Uncertain

By BERNARD WEINRAUB
Special to The New York Times

WASHINGTON, March 26 — Shortly after 6 A.M. today, President Anwar el-Sadat arose in the residence of the Egyptian Ambassador and began wandering around the five-bedroom house.

He scanned the morning newspapers, pedaled a stationary exercise bicycle, nibbled a slice of unbuttered toast, sipped a glass of orange juice and, by 7 A.M. turned on the television to watch the morning news.

Less than one mile away, in a guarded ninth-floor suite at the Washington Hilton Hotel, Prime Minister Menachem Begin of Israel peered out the windows at the traffic moving along Connecticut Avenue.

He turned away and, carrying a cup of tea, walked to a writing desk and began working on the emotional speech that he would deliver in mid-afternoon at the White House ceremony ending 30 years of war between Israel and Egypt.

It was the start of a day marked by paradox — a triumphal day of peace that seemed curiously somber, a day of celebration blurred by protest in the heart of Washington, a bright day shadowed by uncertainty.

"There is, you know, a sense of trepi-

Continued on Page A9, Column 1

Treaty Impact Still Unknown

'Hopes and Dreams' but 'No Illusions' for Carter

By HEDRICK SMITH
Special to The New York Times

WASHINGTON, March 26 — The elusive, unprecedented peace treaty that Egypt and Israel signed today has enormous symbolic importance and the potential for fundamentally transforming the map and history of News Analysis an entire region, but the agreement faces an uncertain future.

Israel has now won what it has sought since 1948 — formal recognition and acceptance from the most powerful Arab state and the ultimate prospect of exchanging ambassadors and entering into a full range of normal relations.

For all the violent denunciations that this historic breakthrough aroused in the Arab world, the best diplomatic estimate here is that the treaty has markedly reduced the risk of a major war in the Middle East for a considerable time by removing Egyptian strength from the active Arab arsenal.

And it has demonstrated American capacity to influence events in the Middle East despite the setbacks Washington has suffered since the overthrow of the

Continued on Page A10, Column 5

CEREMONY IS FESTIVE

Accord on Sinai Oil Opens Way to the First Peace in Mideast Dispute

By BERNARD GWERTZMAN
Special to The New York Times

WASHINGTON, March 26 — After confronting each other for nearly 31 years as hostile neighbors, Egypt and Israel signed a formal treaty at the White House today to establish peace and "normal and friendly relations."

On this chilly early spring day, about 1,500 invited guests and millions more watching television saw President Anwar el-Sadat of Egypt and Prime Minister

Transcripts of statements at signing are on page A11. Texts of treaty and Camp David accords are on pages A12, A13 and A14.

Menachem Begin of Israel put their signatures on the Arabic, Hebrew and English versions of the first peace treaty between Israel and an Arab country.

President Carter, who was credited by both leaders for having made the agreement possible, signed, as a witness, for the United States. In a somber speech he said, "Peace has come."

'The First Step of Peace'

"We have won, at last, the first step of peace — a first step on a long and difficult road," he added.

All three leaders offered prayers that the treaty would bring true peace to the Middle East and end the enmity that has erupted into war four times since Israel declared its independence on May 14, 1948.

By coincidence, they all referred to the words of the Prophet Isaiah.

"Let us work together until the day comes when they beat their swords into plowshares and their spears into pruning hooks," Mr. Sadat said in his paraphrase of the biblical text.

Mr. Begin, who gave the longest and most emotional of the addresses, exclaimed: "No more war, no more bloodshed, no more bereavement, peace unto you, shalom, saalam, forever."

"Shalom" and "salaam" are the Hebrew and Arabic words for "peace."

A Touch of Humor by Begin

The Israeli leader, noted for oratorical skill, provided a dash of humor when in the course of his speech he seconded Mr. Sadat's remark that Mr. Carter was "the unknown soldier of the peacemaking effort." Mr. Begin said, pausing, "I agree; but as usual with an amendment" — that Mr. Carter was not completely unknown and that his peace effort would "be remembered and recorded by generations to come."

Since Mr. Begin was known through the

Continued on Page A10, Column 1

Judge Bars Hydrogen Bomb Article After Magazine Rejects Mediation

By DOUGLAS E. KNEELAND
Special to The New York Times

MILWAUKEE, March 26 — A Federal District Court judge here, acting only after his suggestion for an attempt at out-of-court settlement was turned down, granted the Government's motion for a preliminary injunction today to keep The Progressive magazine from publishing an article about the hydrogen bomb.

In so doing, Judge Robert W. Warren became the first Federal judge ever to issue an injunction imposing prior restraint on the press in a national security case.

The magazine's attorneys said they would file an appeal shortly with the United States Court of Appeals for the Seventh Circuit in Chicago.

Court's 'Awesome Responsibility'

Before announcing his decision this afternoon, Judge Warren, a former Wisconsin Attorney General, acknowledged that he considered it an "awesome responsibility."

"Stripped to its essence, then," he said, "the question before the court is a basic confrontation between the First Amendment right to freedom of the press and national security."

The judge said "a mistake in ruling against The Progressive will seriously infringe cherished First Amendment rights." However, he added, "a mistake

Continued on Page B12, Column 3

INSIDE

Michigan State Wins
Michigan State became the National Collegiate basketball champion by defeating Indiana State, 75-64, at Salt Lake City. Page C13.

H.R.A. Administrator Quits
Blanche Bernstein, the Human Resources Administrator, resigned rather than accept Mayor Koch's offer to stay in the job without power. Page B1.

Photographs for The New York Times by TERESA ZABALA

Palestinians, Reacting to the Pact, Go on Strike and Denounce Egypt

Special to The New York Times

BEIRUT, Lebanon, March 26 — Vowing revenge, staging strikes and protest marches and calling for punitive measures against Egypt, Palestinians and other Arabs reacted angrily today against the signing of the Egyptian-Israeli peace treaty in Washington.

Yasir Arafat, chairman of the Palestine Liberation Organization, vowed to chase Americans out of the Middle East and to "chop off the hands" of President Carter, President Anwar el-Sadat of Egypt and Prime Minister Menachem Begin of Israel. He spoke to a group of guerrilla recruits at the Sabra Palestinian camp here as effigies of the three signers were burned.

The inhabitants of Lebanon's 15 Palestinian camps protested the signing today by refusing to work, as did many Lebanese Moslems. Similar protests were staged in the occupied West Bank of the Jordan River and the Gaza Strip, and in the Arab Old City of Jerusalem a grenade exploded tonight, wounding five tourists.

Iran Government Condemns Pact

In Teheran, the Iranian Government condemned the treaty, and 30 Arab students took over the Egyptian Embassy there. Protesters also stormed the Egyptian Embassy in Kuwait, where 250,000 Palestinians live, forming the largest foreign community in that small country. In Damascus, Syria, demonstrators occu-

pied the offices of the Egyptian airline, Egyptair.

Meanwhile, foreign and finance ministers of Arab League countries gathered today in Baghdad, Iraq, for a meeting tomorrow on possible economic and political measures against Egypt. The countries had vowed last November to hold such a meeting if the Egyptian-Israeli peace treaty was signed, but Saudi Arabia, Egypt's principal foreign backer, has been trying to exercise a moderating influence.

King Hussein of Jordan flew to Damascus and Baghdad during the day in what was believed to be an effort to coordinate the positions of hard-liners and moderates at tomorrow's Arab meeting.

Gromyko Comments on Treaty

In Damascus, Foreign Minister Andrei A. Gromyko of the Soviet Union ended a three-day visit to Syria today by joining with President Hafez al-Assad in denouncing the peace treaty, saying it appeared bound to increase tension in the Middle East. A joint Soviet-Syrian communiqué said the treaty was aimed at perpetuating the Israeli occupation of Arab lands, the annexation of Arab East-

Continued on Page A10, Column 5

"All the News
That's Fit to Print"

The New York Times

LATE CITY EDITION

Weather: Cloudy and hazy today;
showers likely today, tomorrow.
Temperature range: today 53-73;
yesterday 52-75. Details on page 10.

VOL.CXXVIII . No.44,173   Copyright © 1979 The New York Times   NEW YORK, SATURDAY, MARCH 31, 1979   25 cents beyond 50 mile zone from New York City.
Higher in air delivery cities.   20 CENTS

Teamster Talks Recess, and Gap Is Called Sizable

Mediator, Differing With Optimistic Report, Sees 'Tense, Difficult Spot'

By PHILIP SHABECOFF
Special to The New York Times

ARLINGTON, Va., Saturday, March 31 — Negotiations between the Teamsters and the trucking industry recessed early this morning with "substantial differences still separating the parties," according to Wayne L. Horvitz, the director of the Federal Mediation and Conciliation Service.

"We are at a tense and difficult spot right now," Mr. Horvitz said in announcing that talks would resume tomorrow morning. He added that "reports we are awfully close to a settlement are not true."

Earlier, sources close to the negotiations reported that the two sides had tentatively agreed to a wage increase of $1.50 an hour over three years plus increases in benefits totaling $30 a week over the same period.

Problems Still Unsolved

Mr. Horvitz said that there were problems still to be resolved in both economic and noneconomic areas.

Government officials said earlier in the day that they were optimistic about the prospects for a peaceful conclusion to the negotiations with a settlement that would within President Carter's wage guidelines.

In theory, the guideline would limit annual wage increases to 7 percent. However, to remove what it called inequities and to pave the way for a settlement, the Administration adjusted the guideline so that increases well over 7 percent would be technically in compliance.

26 to 30 Percent Increase

In fact, sources close to the negotiations said that they expected a total wage and benefit package providing an increase of from 26 to 30 percent over the three-year contract. A 7 percent wage guideline, when compounded, would permit a wage and benefit increase of 22.5 percent over three years.

The average wage paid to the 300,000 truckdrivers and other workers covered by the master freight agreement is estimated at about $9.50 an hour. Adminis-

Continued on Page 45, Column 1

BRITISH TORY IS SLAIN IN PARLIAMENT YARD, APPARENTLY BY I.R.A.

Bomb in Car Kills a Close Adviser to Mrs. Thatcher — 2 Groups Claiming Responsibility

By WILLIAM BORDERS
Special to The New York Times

LONDON, March 30 — A leading Member of Parliament was killed this afternoon when a bomb apparently set by Irish terrorists exploded in his car as he was driving out of the Parliament grounds.

The blast, which brought other members rushing from the House of Commons, occurred on an underground ramp in the main courtyard of the building, less than 50 yards from the clock tower. Its victim, Airey M.S. Neave, who was one of the closest advisers to Margaret Thatcher, the Conservative Party leader, died at a nearby hospital 40 minutes later without regaining consciousness.

His murder, for which two separate factions of the Irish Republican Army claimed responsibility tonight, cast a pall over the election campaign that has just begun in Britain, and it deeply shocked a nation unaccustomed to violence against its elected leaders.

'This Terrible Outrage'

Prime Minister James Callaghan, saying he was "appalled at this abhorrent act," promised that "no effort will be spared to rid the United Kingdom of the scourge of terrorism." All over London this evening, homebound workers stopped to read newspaper headlines about Mr. Neave's murder, shaking their heads and murmuring about what one of them called "this terrible outrage."

The bombing came just eight days after Britain's Ambassador to the Netherlands, Sir Richard Sykes, was shot to death in The Hague. Anonymous callers said later that the Provisional wing of the I.R.A. was responsible for his murder.

Mr. Neave, a much-decorated hero of World War II who had been in Parliament for 25 years, was the member of Mrs. Thatcher's shadow Cabinet responsible for the affairs of Northern Ireland. He knew, according to his friends, that the job made him a natural target for the terrorists who are trying to drive the British out of that province.

He was, nevertheless, outspoken on the

Continued on Page 4, Column 3

U.S. AIDES SEE A RISK OF MELTDOWN AT PENNSYLVANIA NUCLEAR PLANT; MORE RADIOACTIVE GAS IS RELEASED

The New York Times / Teresa Zabala

Elementary-school children arriving at the West Shore School in Dillsburg, Pa., after they were evacuated from Middletown, site of nuclear plant

CHILDREN EVACUATED

But Governor Says Later Further Pullouts Are Not Thought Likely

By RICHARD D. LYONS
Special to The New York Times

MIDDLETOWN, Pa., March 30 — Gov. Dick Thornburgh advised pregnant women and small children today to stay at least five miles away from the crippled Three Mile Island nuclear power plant as radioactivity continued to leak and another burst of contaminated steam had to be released for safety reasons.

Tonight, at a Harrisburg news conference, Government nuclear experts said there was no immediate threat to public health, but Governor Thornburgh said his suggestion for the women and children "remains in force until tomorrow."

Earlier in the day several thousand schoolchildren were evacuated from the plant area, 10 miles southeast of Harrisburg, and other people began leaving on the Governor's advice. More than 150 pregnant women and young children were at a shelter in Hershey, for example.

No Evacuation Order

As for others in the area, the Governor said tonight: "No evacuation order is necessary. My earlier advice that people try to remain indoors expires at midnight."

The highest levels of radioactive material yet vented were let go from the facility today, and one official of the Nuclear Regulatory Commission, Dennis Crutchfield, said that up to one-fourth of the fuel rods, or 9,000 of the 36,000 fuel elements, may have been damaged since Wednesday.

Further, Government and nuclear

Continued on Page 8, Column 3

Gov. Dick Thornburgh of Pennsylvania urged young children and pregnant women to avoid the area within five miles of the Three Mile Island plant until sometime today. His request to those within 10 miles to stay indoors expired at midnight. Earlier, residents of Lancaster, Adams, Cumberland and Dauphin counties were alerted to possible evacuation, an alert that was canceled.

The New York Times / March 31, 1979

CONGRESS IS BRIEFED

Carter Aide at Scene Says Danger to the Public Is Believed Remote

By DAVID BURNHAM
Special to The New York Times

WASHINGTON, March 30 — The Nuclear Regulatory Commission told Congress today that the risk of a reactor core meltdown had arisen at the crippled Three Mile Island atomic power plant at Middletown, Pa., an event that could necessitate a general evacuation of the surrounding area.

A core meltdown — a melting of the reactor's stainless steel fuel rods or the enriched uranium pellets within them — is second only to an explosion in terms of seriousness of a nuclear accident.

At a televised news conference in Middletown tonight, Gov. Dick Thornburgh said that no general evacuation was deemed necessary, and Harold Benton, an N.R.C. official sent to the scene as President Carter's representative, said, "There is no imminent danger to the public." He called the possibility of a core meltdown "very remote."

Bubble of Hydrogen Forms

Earlier, officials said that a large pressurized hydrogen bubble had formed in the top of the reactor's sealed core vessel, which is supposed to be full of water for cooling the fuel rods. They said that unless the bubble was removed carefully, it could expand and leave the top of the fuel rods out of the cooling water, allowing them to overheat, melt and release large amounts of radioactivity.

While calling the situation stable for the moment, they noted that both methods under discussion for removing the bubble — letting it sink to the bottom of the vessel by drawing off water, or trying to break it up with steam — involved risks of further exposure of the fuel rods and a possible meltdown.

At the request of Gov. Thornburgh, young children and pregnant women began evacuating an area within five miles of the plant today. In addition, 23 schools were closed, and 15 mass-care centers were established as a precaution in counties surrounding the Middletown area.

Evacuation Plan Developed

In Washington and elsewhere, concern mounted over what has become the nation's most serious commercial nuclear reactor accident.

At the White House, President Carter was briefed by the National Security Council, and Jody Powell, the President's Press Secretary, said that a contingency

Continued on Page 8, Column 1

Delay on U.S. Debt Ceiling Hurts Treasury and Financial Markets

By JOHN H. ALLAN

The delay by Congress in raising the legal ceiling on the national debt is disrupting financial markets across the country.

Although most observers are confident that the fiscal drama will be settled by Congressional action on Monday, the Treasury had to scramble yesterday to make sure it had enough money to last until then.

To keep its debt under the ceiling and to gather in all its tax payments being held by banks, the Treasury announced a comprehensive program.

It postponed plans to borrow $6 billion on Monday, and it also suspended sales of Government savings bonds. Banks were called on for any tax receipts they are holding, and the Treasury arranged to borrow $3 billion from the Federal Reserve. It also asked the Federal Reserve to make its monthly Government payment from earnings — about $700 million — on Monday instead of Tuesday.

In addition, the Treasury said that, starting Monday, it would not make interest payments on its trust funds for Social Security and Civil Service. If Congress

raises the debt ceiling on Monday, however, the payments would be resumed quickly.

The temporary ceiling on the debt, now $798 billion, will revert at 12:01 A.M. tomorrow to its "permanent" level of $400 billion. The reversion does not invalidate the $398 billion difference, but it prevents the Treasury from borrowing more and it means the Government must pay off its debt as it matures.

The debt ceiling limits the amount of money the Government can borrow at

Continued on Page 30, Column 4

Within Sight of Stricken Plant, A Town's Main Street Is Empty

By B. DRUMMOND AYRES Jr.
Special to The New York Times

GOLDSBORO, Pa., March 30 — At 5:15 P.M. today on Main Street here, the only living thing in sight was a brown-and-white dog, wandering aimlessly, oblivious to the radiation that was leaking from the crippled nuclear power plant just across the muddy Susquehanna.

"Almost everybody's gone," Annette Baker said, emerging from Reeser's grocery and casting a wary eye toward the plant's huge cooling towers, looming ominously above Goldsboro less than half a mile away. "Normally at this time of day, the people are around, coming home. I don't mean this place is a traffic jam or anything like that. We've only got 600 or so people. But this ..."

She gestured toward the empty town square and the surrounding houses and stores, every window and door tightly shut despite an unseasonable afternoon temperature in the 70's.

"You live with that plant over there for years and years and don't think much about it," Terry Heidler, a print shop operator, said during a quick visit to Reeser's. "But it's like living with a rattlesnake. Sooner or later it's going to bite you. You just don't know when."

'You Just Don't Know When'

The people of Goldsboro, like the 20,000 or so other Pennsylvanians living within a five-mile radius of the Three Mile Island power plant, began pulling out Wednesday within an hour or so of the malfunction that caused what appears to be America's worst nuclear accident.

Most went to the homes of relatives or friends in other counties. At first, there was only a trickle. But this morning, when the authorities advised that pre-school children and pregnant women definitely should abandon the area, the trickle became a stream, then a river.

Switchboards Tied Up

There were jammed gasoline stations. There were panicky phone calls that so cluttered up switchboards that hours went by when nothing could be heard but the buzz, buzz, buzz of a busy signal.

"This is really like '1984,'" a local radio announcer commented, searching frantically for a metaphor that would somehow put the unthinkable into perspective. He got it wrong — Big Brother wasn't really involved — but somehow the message came through.

"People have really been shaken by this," Goldsboro's Mayor, Kenneth Myers, said. "We're prepared to

Continued on Page 7, Column 4

Conflicting Reports Add to Tension

By BEN A. FRANKLIN
Special to The New York Times

HARRISBURG, Pa., March 30 — When an air raid siren shrieked what turned out to be an unauthorized alert near the state Capitol here before noon today, setting off an unscheduled midday traffic jam of jittery state employees, it was only the most dramatic result of three days of conflicting and sometimes flatly contradictory statements about the nuclear emergency at the Three Mile Island atomic plant near Middletown in south-central Pennsylvania.

The alert was variously said to have been a malfunction or to have been sounded by a Civil Defense official who misinterpreted Gov. Dick Thornburgh's widely misreported early-morning deci-

sion to prepare for, but not to carry out, a mass evacuation.

Mr. Thornburgh acted after receiving reports of what he called an "uncontrolled" release of radioactivity from the nuclear plant. And again, as has happened so often since details of the accident were announced Wednesday, the public was receiving information that was at loggerheads with other reports.

While the Governor, after four hours' sleep, said he was preparing to act "in the interest of taking every precaution" against radiation injuries, the power plant's top nuclear engineer, citing radiation readings far lower than those re-

Continued on Page 8, Column 1

United Grounds Jets As Union Walks Out

By RICHARD WITKIN

United Airlines, the nation's largest carrier, was grounded today by a strike of 18,600 mechanics and other ground workers after they voted down a new contract tentatively agreed to by their union officers.

The union, the International Association of Machinists and Aerospace Workers, notified the company at midday yesterday that the strike would get under way today at 12:01 A.M. And early last evening, United announced that it had canceled all of its 1,600 daily flights from today through April 8.

The airline said that flights that were under way at 12:01 this morning would continue to their first stop; then the crew on each flight with more than one stop was to decide whether to continue to the final destination.

There was no indication when negotiations might be resumed. The airline's switchboards were ablaze yesterday as customers with reservations sought help

Continued on Page 26, Column 1

The New York Times / Keith Meyers

Duane and Marian Shuttlesworth leave Middletown with daughter, Rebecca

INSIDE

Arabs Deadlocked on Egypt
Despite Saudi offers of concessions, an Arab conference stayed deadlocked over what to do about Egypt's signing of the treaty with Israel. Page 2.

New Sea Creatures Found
Ten-foot-long, wormlike animals that may constitute a new phylum have been discovered on the floor of the sea in the Galapagos Islands. Page 26.

"All the News
That's Fit to Print"

The New York Times

LATE CITY EDITION

Weather: Mostly cloudy, mild today; showers tonight. Showers, tomorrow. Temperature: today 52-68; yesterday 54-70. Details on page A27.

VOL.CXXVIII....No.44,207

Copyright © 1979 The New York Times

NEW YORK, FRIDAY, MAY 4, 1979

25 cents beyond 50-mile zone from New York City. Higher in air delivery cities.

20 CENTS

The New York Times/George Tames
Senator Abraham A. Ribicoff

Ribicoff Decides He Won't Seek A Fourth Term

By STEVEN R. WEISMAN
Special to The New York Times

WASHINGTON, May 3 — Senator Abraham A. Ribicoff of Connecticut announced today that he would retire from the Senate after his current term of office — his third — expires next year.

His decision startled his political colleagues, as well as his staff aides, and immediately set off a scramble to succeed him. At least three Democrats and three Republicans in Connecticut indicated their interest in running for his seat. [Page B4.]

Mr. Ribicoff, a 69-year-old Democrat, has become Connecticut's most influential elected official in modern times, and his departure from Washington would bring to a conclusion an extraordinary public career that has included service as a United States Representative, Governor, Cabinet member under President John F. Kennedy and, since 1963, United States Senator.

Today he dismissed any suggestion that he would accept either a Cabinet post or an ambassadorship after he retired.

"As Mike Mansfield said, 'There is a time to stay and a time to go,'" Mr. Ribicoff told reporters this morning, referring to the former Senate majority leader, who is now Ambassador to Japan.

"I've watched them come and go," Mr.

Continued on Page B4, Column 1

PRODUCER PRICES UP BY 0.9% FOR APRIL; FOOD DOWN A LITTLE

Rises Expected to Keep Consumer Costs High and Further Harm Carter Fight on Inflation

By STEVEN RATTNER
Special to The New York Times

WASHINGTON, May 3 — Producer prices rose by nine-tenths of 1 percent in April, and, despite a slight slowing from March, signs pointed to at least another month of substantial increases, according to Labor Department figures released today.

The increase would have been greater if food prices had not fallen slightly last month. The overall increase in prices at the producer level was the smallest for any month since last November. Food prices have been rising rapidly, and Carter Administration officials were particularly relieved by last month's abatement.

The Government now computes producer prices for finished goods ready for shipment to retailers to compile a more accurate economic indicator than the former Wholesale Price Index, which has been abandoned. But producer prices are roughly equivalent to wholesale prices.

Period of Weeks or Months

Producer price increases do not directly affect consumers but gradually work their way over a period of weeks or months to the retail level. Accordingly, last month's rise in the Producer Price Index suggests that high rates of consumer price increases will continue.

The increases would, in turn, further jeopardize President Carter's anti-inflation program, which seeks to hold wage increases to 7 percent annually. Meanwhile, consumer prices rose at a 13 percent rate in the first three months of the year. The April rise in producer prices translated into a compound annual inflation rate of 11.5 percent.

The rises last month in wholesale prices were paced by sharply higher prices for fuel, plastics, cars and leather. Home-heating oil, for example, rose by 6.7 percent in the month alone. Gasoline prices increased by 4.4 percent. The increases in energy prices reflects the worldwide shortage of oil as a result of the shutdown earlier this year of Iranian oil production and the price increases by the Organization of Petroleum Exporting Countries.

Perhaps more worrisome was the news that the increases in energy prices appeared to have begun to filter

Continued on Page D14, Column 5

CONSERVATIVES WIN BRITISH VOTE; MARGARET THATCHER FIRST WOMAN TO HEAD A EUROPEAN GOVERNMENT

United Press International
Margaret Thatcher leaving polling station after casting her vote in London yesterday

BIG SWING INDICATED

Tory Leader Given a Clear Mandate to Change the Country's Course

By R. W. APPLE Jr.
Special to The New York Times

LONDON, Friday, May 4 — Margaret Thatcher and the Conservative Party won a decisive victory in Britain's general election yesterday.

Mrs. Thatcher, an Oxford-educated chemist and lawyer who entered Parliament in 1959, won a substantial majority and a clear mandate to reverse the nation's course. She promised during her campaign to restrain the trade unions, to cut personal income taxes and to bolster the armed forces.

She will become the first woman Prime Minister of a major European nation.

Voting Pattern Shifts

Projections by the television networks and by the Press Association suggested that the Tories would hold a majority over all other parties of approximately 35 to 40 seats. But the voting pattern was not as uniform as in past elections, and the ultimate majority might therefore be somewhat smaller.

With results declared in 200 of 635 constituencies, the totals were as follows:

Conservatives	82
Labor	116
Liberals	1
Scottish Nationalists	1
Others	0

The totals reflected a gain of eight seats for the Conservatives, a loss of two for Labor and no change for the Liberals. The Scottish Nationalists lost four seats and there was a loss of two for other parties.

Jeremy Thorpe, who had represented North Devon for 20 years, was beaten by 8,000 votes. His highly publicized legal difficulties — his trial on charges of conspiracy and incitement to murder opens Tuesday — apparently proved too large an obstacle to overcome.

For Prime Minister James Callaghan and the Labor Party, the brightest spots were Scotland and Northern England, where the Conservative tide was running much less strongly. Denis Healey, the Chancellor of the Exchequer, suggested that Labor could still be saved by regional voting inconsistencies.

In the London area, the swing approached 7 percent, but in Manchester it was running at only about 2 percent.

Constituencies whose results were reported in the first few minutes after midnight suggested that the Liberal Party was doing reasonably well. However, the Scottish National vote seemed to be collapsing, and the party appeared to be in danger of losing all but one of the 11 seats it held before the voting.

Counting was slow in two of the most closely watched contests, those involving the Foreign Secretary, Dr. David Owen, at Plymouth Devonport, and Mr. Thorpe, at Devon North.

The first three Labor seats to fall to the Conservatives were two in the vital belt

Continued on Page A10, Column 1

Terrorists Bomb the Rome Offices Of the Christian Democratic Party

By HENRY TANNER
Special to The New York Times

ROME, May 3 — A group of urban guerrillas raided the Rome area headquarters of Italy's dominant Christian Democratic Party today, wrecked two floors with bombs, killed one policeman, wounded two others and escaped.

The attack, the largest terrorist operation since Red Brigade terrorists kidnapped former Prime Minister Aldo Moro last year, killing five bodyguards and subsequently Mr. Moro, came on the eve of a general election campaign.

The raiders spray-painted the walls of the party headquarters with the initials of the Red Brigades and with its emblem, a five-pointed star. They also left behind this inscription: "We shall transform the fraudulent elections into a class war."

Fears were expressed that there would be a wave of terrorist attacks during the campaign for the elections that are scheduled for June 3 and 4.

Shaken by the magnitude of today's attack, former President Giuseppe Saragat and other political figures called for stronger antiterrorist measures. Some suggested that martial law was needed, as they had done when Mr. Moro was abducted on March 16, 1978. His body was found nearly two months later.

"Political terrorism," Mr. Saragat said, "is turning into full-scale civil war and must be confronted not only by the police but also by the armed forces of the republic."

The Red Brigades, the most feared of Italy's terrorist groups, have as their aim the destruction of the Italian state and society as a step toward a revolutionary takeover. They accuse the Communist Party of having sold out to the bourgeoi-

Continued on Page A4, Column 3

'Genuine' Tory Taking Charge

Margaret Roberts Thatcher

By WILLIAM BORDERS
Special to The New York Times

LONDON, May 3 — To Margaret Thatcher, "free choice is ultimately what life is about," and she likes to illustrate what she means in political terms with this example: "If somebody comes to me and asks, What are you going to do for us small businessmen? I say, the only thing I'm going to do for you is make you freer to do things for yourselves. If you can't do it then, I'm sorry. I'll have nothing to offer you."

Woman in the News

Judging by what she has been saying over the years, in public and in private, that is the center of Mrs. Thatcher's political philosophy, — what she calls "a positive creed, to promote, not destroy, the uniqueness of the individual."

In the election campaign Mrs. Thatcher sketched a vision of a Britain that would be rebuilt, on the strong base of that kind of individualism, to the economic strength it used to know, "so that once again the products stream from our factories and workshops while the customers of the world scramble over each other to buy them." She also promised a government that "would stop trying to step in and take decisions for you that you should be free to take on your own."

Now, the British people, having chosen as their leader the first woman to head a modern European government, will have a chance to put to a practical test what she terms the genu-

Continued on Page A11, Column 1

CALIFANO REASSESSES RADIATION HAZARDS

He Now Says Some Cancer Deaths From Accident Are Possible

By CHARLES MOHR
Special to The New York Times

WASHINGTON, May 3 — Joseph A Califano Jr., Secretary of Health, Education and Welfare, said today that radiation exposure from the Three Mile Island reactor accident was higher than earlier measurements had indicated. As a result, he said, statistical probability indicates that at least one to 10 cancer deaths caused by radiation could be expected among the two million people living within 50 miles of the Pennsylvania power plant.

H.. also said that the radiation could be expected to cause as many as 10 additional nonfatal cancers.

Mr. Califano, who testified a month ago that no deaths would result from the exposure, said today that subsequent measurements showed radiation levels had been nearly twice as high as earlier estimates. He also said that the estimates were expected to rise further.

His testimony, before the Subcommittee on Energy, Nuclear Proliferation and Federal Services of the Senate Government Affairs Committee, took note of the contention of some scientists that assumptions about low-level radiation as a cause of cancer might be 10 times too low.

Under normal conditions, the number of cancer deaths in a population of two million would be 325,000.

Meanwhile, the Nuclear Regulatory Commission reported that the Oyster Creek Plant at Forked River, N.J., was shut down automatically yesterday during a test of the reactor's pressure-reading instruments. [Page B3.]

And the Nuclear Regulatory Commission, considering the status of a Maine reactor that was among five closed in

Continued on Page A19, Column 4

For Central Park Bird Watchers, Thrills Take Flight Every Spring

By ROBIN HERMAN

Why don't bird watchers get "warblers' neck" in Central Park? Why does the Police Department assign a patrolman to watch the bird watchers? And have you ever seen a rock dove?

Bird watchers don't get warblers' neck from craning to see warblers in the treetops because the hills in Central Park put bird watchers at eye level with the tops of the trees. The Police Department assigns an officer to watch bird watchers because many of them carry expensive field glasses that make them likely targets for muggers. And if you think you have never seen a

rock dove you probably have because they are otherwise known as pigeons and Central Park is full of them.

Fifty New Yorkers who went "birding" yesterday at 7 A.M. along the Central Park Ramble spotted nearly 40 species of birds in an hour and a half, including multitudes of rock doves bobbing and cooing on the paths and outcroppings. The real prizes, however, were the visiting warblers who stop in Manhattan this month for a drink and a

Continued on Page B3, Column 2

The New York Times/John Sotomayor
Bird watchers stalking their "prey" early yesterday morning in Central Park

INSIDE

Giants Pick Quarterback
The Giants' first pick in the National Football League draft was Phil Simms, a quarterback from Morehead State in Ke..tucky. Page A21.

Islanders Tie Series
Bob Nystrom's goal in overtime gave the Islanders a 3-2 victory over the Rangers, tying their playoff series at two games apiece. Page A21.

In Her Own Words

Comments by Margaret Thatcher since taking the party leadership in 1975:

Limitation of government doesn't make for a weak government — don't make that mistake. If you've got the role of government clearly set out, then it means very strong government in that role. Very strong indeed. You weaken government if you try to spread it over so wide a range that you're not powerful where you should be because you've got into areas where you shouldn't be.

•

Overtaxation is transparently foolish. Most of us are willing to work for our families and neighbors but not for the Chancellor of the Exchequer. In a free country people will work hard if it pays them to do so. At present, taxes are so high that for many it is not worthwhile working hard, and for some it is not worthwhile working at all. The first step to recovery, therefore, is to lower taxes on earnings.

•

There are two ways of making a cabinet. One way is to have in it people who represent all the different viewpoints within the party, within the broad philosophy. The other way is to have in it only the people who want to go in the direction in which every instinct tells me we have to go.

As Prime Minister I couldn't waste time having any internal arguments.

•

The power of trade unions over individual members is far too great. We shall have to stand up against those elements who are prepared to use their present freedom in society to destroy society. ... A strong trade-union movement is an integral part of modern industrial society, but it must not ride roughshod over the rest of that society.

•

On immigration from the Commonwealth: Small minorities can be absorbed — they can be assets to the majority community — but once a minority in a neighborhood gets very large, people do feel swamped. They feel their whole way of life has been changed.

•

On male colleagues: I'm not conscious of them as men at all. Don't mistake me: I see A as taller than B; I see X as more handsome than Y. What woman wouldn't? What man wouldn't have such perceptions about women? But I don't see me and my colleagues in an "I'm a woman, you are men" relationship.

"All the News That's Fit to Print"

The New York Times

LATE CITY EDITION

Weather: Cloudy, chance of showers today and tonight. Sunny tomorrow. Temperature range: today 54-66; yesterday 62-67. Details on page 8.

VOL.CXXVIII...No.44,229   Copyright © 1979 The New York Times   NEW YORK, SATURDAY, MAY 26, 1979   25 cents beyond 50-mile zone from New York City. Higher in air delivery cities.   20 CENTS

272 DIE AS JET CRASHES ON TAKEOFF IN CHICAGO AFTER LOSING ENGINE; WORST U.S. AIR DISASTER

ISRAEL LOWERS FLAG, GIVES TOWN IN SINAI BACK TO EGYPTIANS

Inhabitants of El Arish, Conquered in 1967, Cheer, Weep and Jeer at Withdrawal Ceremony

By CHRISTOPHER S. WREN
Special to The New York Times

EL ARISH, Egypt, May 25 — Egyptians cheered, prayed and wept as this town, capital of the Sinai Peninsula, was handed back to Egypt today, after 12 years under Israeli occupation.

The dusty coastal town, separated from the Mediterranean by groves of stately palms amid dunes, became the first still-inhabited Arab town conquered in the 1967 war to be relinquished.

The pullout marked the beginning of Israel's promised withdrawal from Sinai under the peace treaty signed with Egypt March 26 in Washington.

The return of El Arish and a coastal strip westward is the first step of a process that will return to Egypt nearly three-fourths of Sinai within nine months. Israel has agreed to withdraw within three years from the remainder of Sinai, to the border that prevailed before the 1967 war.

Two Sides Meet at Beersheba

As the transfer took place, Egyptian and Israeli negotiators met at Beersheba to begin negotiations on a solution to the question of autonomy for Palestinians of the West Bank and Gaza. Secretary of State Cyrus R. Vance, who attended, urged both sides, whose positions were far apart, to show "maximum restraint and farsightedness." [Page 3.]

The turnover ceremony was held in the asphalt parking lot of a former Israeli Army canteen and rest stop a mile and a half east of town. More elaborate festivities are planned tomorrow when President Anwar el-Sadat comes to El Arish.

Egyptians Whistle and Chant

As the blue and white Israeli flag was lowered to bugle accompaniment today, more than a thousand residents watching from across a road began to clap, whistle and chant.

Hundreds of young men ran toward the barbed wire of the compound where the half-hour ceremony was taking place. Armed Israeli troops in combat gear chased them back in jeeps. Four armored half-tracks were sent to assist the soldiers sent up plumes of dust.

When the red, white and black Egyptian flag was run up the pole, the nearly hysterical spectators cheered wildly and surged forth again amid cries in Arabic: "God is great!" and "Long live Egypt!"

There was scuffling between some Egyptians and Israeli soldiers, who seemed unprepared for the outburst. Although the scene briefly turned ugly, violence was averted as Egyptian military policemen rushed in to calm the people.

When the Israelis got into their trucks and jeeps and began driving to their new lines a few miles east of town, some

Continued on Page 4, Column 1

Firemen searching through the smoldering wreckage of an American Airlines jet that crashed on takeoff yesterday at Chicago's O'Hare International Airport

Associated Press

FLORIDA EXECUTES KILLER AS PLEA FAILS

Spenkelink, Electrocuted, Is First to Die Since Gilmore in 1977

By WAYNE KING
Special to The New York Times

STARKE, Fla., May 25 — The state of Florida trussed John Arthur Spenkelink immobile in the electric chair this morning, dropped a black leather mask over his face and electrocuted him.

"He simply looked at us and he looked terrified," said Kris Rebillot, a reporter who was one of 32 persons who watched through a window from an adjoining room. "It was just a wide, wide, wide stare."

The execution was carried out a few hours after the last plea in an extended legal battle. It was the third execution in the United States since Gary Mark Gilmore faced a Utah firing squad voluntarily on Jan. 19, 1977, and the first since 1967 in which the condemned person was put to death against his will.

No Final Statement — His Wish

Mr. Spenkelink made no final statement. The prison authorities said that had been his wish.

The prisoner was given three surges of electricity. The first, 2,500 volts, was administered at 10:12 A.M. Mr. Spenkelink jerked in the chair and one hand clenched into a fist.

Then came the second, and the third, by two executioners in black hoods. A doctor stepped forward after the third surge, pulled up the prisoner's T-shirt

Continued on Page 6, Column 2

Flattened Debris and 'Bodies All Over'

By WILLIAM ROBBINS
Special to The New York Times

CHICAGO, May 25 — "The plane just lost power and slowly rolled over on its side," George Owens, a witness to the worst domestic air crash in history, said today shortly after the fiery disaster at O'Hare International Airport here.

Then, he said, he "saw a huge fireball."

Hours after the crash of American Airlines Flight 191, which had just taken off for Los Angeles, smoke was still pouring from the wreckage, which was too hot for removal of many of the bodies of the victims. Red and yellow stakes marked the few charred bodies that firemen could reach. It was nearly

6 P.M. before the first bodies were moved to a nearby hangar.

One of the first physicians to arrive at the scene was Dr. Robert Loguerssio. "There were bodies all over," he said. "There were a lot of corpses on the scene. Obviously there was nothing I could do. Obviously there were no live injuries."

Helplessly, the police and firemen could only mill around the scene, keeping onlookers back and out of possible danger.

Wreckage Carried Off

But immediately after the crash, and before the police could cordon off the site, some small boys arrived and began to carry off bits of wreckage.

One was seen walking off with what looked like a fan belt in his hand.

The wreckage of the plane was spread over part of a small abandoned airport, one of the few open areas in the populated region surrounding O'Hare. It ignited three mobile homes situated in a neatly landscaped park at the edge of the field.

A resident of one of the mobile homes, Marie Nikopoulos, had been stretched out on a couch, watching television, when she heard a "big bang."

"It threw me off the couch," she said, "and the force knocked dishes off the shelves and my chandelier fell. I ran and opened the front door and saw part of the plane burning in the street. Thick black smoke filled the neighborhood and turned it pitch black. You couldn't see a foot in front of you."

Residents Ordered Out

Soon officials arrived and ordered the residents out for fear the fires might spread.

One witness, Winnann Johnson, saw what was later determined to have been an engine fall from the wing.

"I saw this silver cylinder thing fall from the plane onto the runway," she said. "It burst into flames and then smothered real quickly."

Larry Roderick saw the flight from about the same vantage point. "The left engine was smoking badly on takeoff," he said. "Then there seemed to be an explosion. There was a burst of flame and the engine fell. The plane appeared to make a steep climb. Then it swung over to the left and plunged to the ground."

NO SURVIVORS FOUND

Los Angeles-Bound DC-10 Narrowly Misses Tract of Mobile Homes

By DOUGLAS E. KNEELAND
Special to The New York Times

CHICAGO, May 25 — An American Airlines jetliner lost an engine and crashed shortly after takeoff from O'Hare International Airport this afternoon, killing all 272 persons aboard. It was the worst disaster in United States aviation history.

Flight 191, a DC-10 bound for Los Angeles at the beginning of the Memorial Day weekend, rose to the northwest from Runway 14 just after 3 P.M., central daylight time. Then, witnesses said, the plane appeared to suffer difficulties with an engine on the left wing, rolled to the left, stalled and plunged into the small abandoned Ravenswood Airport, narrowly missing a mobile home court.

Several witnesses said the engine exploded, and others reported seeing a "huge cylinder" fall from the plane to the runway and burst into flames.

No Survivors Reported

American Airlines officials said there were apparently no survivors of the crash, which scattered debris over an area about 100 by 200 yards. The crash sent up flames and black smoke that could be seen 15 miles away in Chicago's downtown Loop area, and fiery remnants struck some of the mobile homes nearby, severely damaging three of them. Two persons who were apparently working on the ground near the crash site were injured.

The plane narrowly missed a Standard Oil Company gasoline storage facility a block away.

Fire trucks, ambulances and police vehicles rushed to the area and poured water on the flames from the nearly unrecognizable wreckage of the shattered DC-10.

Late this afternoon, ambulances began removing bodies of the victims to a temporary morgue set up in an aircraft hangar. By 11 P.M., 250 bodies had been removed from the wreckage, and Douglas Dreifus, a Federal investigator, said the rest would not be removed before daylight.

Worst Previous U.S. Crash

The worst previous air disaster in the United States occurred last September, when 144 persons died in the collision of a jetliner and a small private plane over San Diego.

William Nickerson, 52 years old, of Elk Grove Village, where the plane crashed, said he saw the DC-10 take off with the left engine smoking. Almost immediately, he said, the engine fell from the plane and the massive jet lost altitude and crashed, sending flames shooting 125 feet into the air.

Danny Niemann, 25, an employee of a

Continued on Page 7, Column 1

President, Angered Over Setbacks, Urges Leadership From Democrats

By TERENCE SMITH
Special to The New York Times

WASHINGTON, May 25 — President Carter, stung by a series of defeats on Capitol Hill, lashed out today at the "demagoguery and political timidity" that he said had made the American people doubt the courage and effectiveness of their political leaders.

Displaying more passion and anger than he normally allows himself on a public forum, the President lectured about 200 members of the Democratic National Committee at their spring meeting here on the need for Congress and the party to confront the difficult choices that face the nation on energy and the economy.

"The American people are looking to us for honest answers and clear leader-

ship," Mr. Carter said. "What they see is a Government which seems incapable of action at all."

In a long answer to a question from the floor, the President also all but declared his candidacy for re-election.

"I haven't made any announcement of

Excerpts from Carter remarks, page 8.

what I'm going to do in 1980," he said, "but I have never backed down from a fight, and I have never been afraid of public opinion polls. And if and when I decide to run, it will be in every precinct in this country, no matter who else ran, and I have no doubt it will be successful."

Mr. Carter also had some thinly veiled criticism for Senator Edward M. Kennedy and the five Democratic Representatives who announced their opposition to the President's re-election earlier this week. "Press conferences will not solve the serious problems we face in energy, in inflation, in maintaining peace in a troubled world," Mr. Carter said.

At a news conference on Monday, Representatives Edward P. Beard of Rhode Island, John Conyers Jr. of Michigan, Richard M. Nolan of Minnesota, Richard L. Ottinger of Westchester and Fortney H. Stark of California announced that they were organizing a campaign to dump Mr. Carter from the Democratic ticket and replace him with Senator Kennedy, who has criticized the President's domestic policies at several meetings with the press in the last fortnight.

Mr. Carter's tone ranged from anger to

Continued on Page 8, Column 5

Gas Lines Touch Off Arguments; Price Hits a Record in Manhattan

By ALAN RICHMAN

Gasoline shortages caused arguments at service stations on Long Island yesterday and forced the posting of police officers to direct a line of waiting motorists in Manhattan. Meanwhile, prices rose to record levels — 56.5 cents a half-gallon at a Getty station in lower Manhattan.

The frantic activity was expected to end soon, because many stations indicated they would run out of gas before Monday night, the end of the Memorial Day weekend.

"My particular situation is that the company is running a day behind in deliveries," said Tim. Sullivan, owner of a Sunoco Station at the corner of 220th Street and Horace Harding Boulevard in Bayside, Queens. Mr. Sullivan, who usually sells 1,800 gallons a day, received a

3,000-gallon delivery yesterday morning and sold out by 3:30 yesterday afternoon.

At a Hess station in Manhattan offering regular gasoline for 82.9 cents a gallon, automobiles were lined up from the entrance on 10th Avenue down 44th Street to the corner of 11th Avenue.

Arguments started not only between drivers waiting in line and those pulling in front of the line, but also between drivers waiting in line and those attempting to leave the station. Finally, the Midtown North police precinct dispatched two officers, who spent the rest of the day asking "Leaded or unleaded?" and directing cars to appropriate pumps.

Mostly a Battle of Words

"There's been nothing worse than verbal altercations with some bumping into one another," explained Officer Tony Graffeo, who ordinarily drives a patrol car. "We call that a 'West Side conversation.' Anything short of shooting on the West Side is a friendly discussion."

On Long Island, fist fights started at several stations and Matthew Troy, executive director of the Long Island Gasoline Retailers Association, warned that association members might close for the weekend if drivers did not "behave themselves."

Mr. Troy reported, as of midafternoon yesterday, 50 incidents of verbal abuse by motorists against gas station owners and

Continued on Page 22, Column 5

The Israeli flag being lowered and the Egyptian flag being raised yesterday in the Sinai town of El Arish

Associated Press

INSIDE

Inflation in Double Digits Again
The Consumer Price Index rose 1.1 percent in April, making for an annual rate of 13.9 percent. April prices were up 10.4 percent from 1978. Page 38.

E.P.A. Rules on Coal Burning
The Environmental Protection Agency introduced rules on coal emissions by power plants that will please neither industry nor environmentalists. Page 6.

An Ayatollah Shot in Teheran
An Iranian religious figure believed to be a member of the secret, ruling Revolutionary Council was shot and wounded near his home. Page 2.

Spanish Army Officers Killed
A lieutenant general in the Spanish Army, two colonels and their driver were killed by Basque terrorists who ambushed their car in Madrid. Page 5.

Amy: Congratulations on your graduation. We are very proud of you. Love, Mom & Dad—ADVT

NOW! LUCHOW'S 93th ANNUAL MAY WINE & GOOSE FEST...

The New York Times

PAGE ONE

Major Events:

1980–1995

"All the News
That's Fit to Print"

The New York Times

LATE CITY EDITION

Weather: Cloudy, sporadic rain today;
rain ending tonight. Sunny tomorrow.
Temperature range: today 55-65;
yesterday 63-74. Details on page B6.

VOL.CXXIX....No. 44,590   Copyright © 1980 The New York Times   NEW YORK, WEDNESDAY, MAY 21, 1980   30 cents beyond 50-mile zone from New York City. Higher in air delivery cities.   25 CENTS

BUSH WINS MICHIGAN, SLOWING REAGAN BID TO LOCK UP VICTORY

CALIFORNIAN LOSES A KEY AIDE

Ex-Governor Sought Delegates in
2 Primary Fights to Top 998
Needed for Nomination

By ADAM CLYMER

George Bush checked Ronald Reagan's march to a delegate majority yesterday, defeating the former California Governor in the Michigan Republican primary and apparently postponing for a week Mr. Reagan's amassing the 998 convention votes needed for nomination.

The two also competed in the Oregon primary. But the solid Bush margin in Michigan, with 82 delegates, made it all but certain that Oregon, with 29, could not give Mr. Reagan the needed total last night, though it seemed sure that he would clear that numerical hurdle next week.

Even as Mr. Reagan faltered in Michigan, his campaign also suffered the resignation of Anderson Carter, his field director, the politician on the staff with the most experience in recent campaigns. In announcing that he would leave in a few days, Mr. Carter gave no reason, but some campaign sources said that he was unhappy with the dominance of other aides whom he considered inexperienced.

Leads Throughout Michigan

In a very light turnout, Mr. Bush ran well ahead of Mr. Reagan in all parts of Michigan, taking about 57 percent of the popular vote.

With more than half the returns in, Mr. Bush was winning 53 Michigan delegates to Mr. Reagan's 29.

Campaigning last night in Cleveland, the former Congressman, diplomat and Director of Central Intelligence exulted over his victory, saying: "It means I shouldn't be written off. I've been trying to make that point over and over again, and the Michigan vote states very clearly that people want a look at my candidacy."

The Democrats held a meaningful primary only in Michigan, where 39 delegates were at stake between President Carter and Senator Edward M. Kennedy of Massachusetts. The Michigan party picked

Continued on Page A24, Column 2

50,000 Warned of Volcano Flood Threat

Scientists See Danger In Overflow of Lake Dammed by Debris

By WALLACE TURNER
Special to The New York Times

VANCOUVER, Wash., May 20 — Officials said today that about 50,000 people living in Washington cities along the lower Columbia River were threatened by a flash flood that might develop in the aftermath of the eruption of Mount St. Helens.

"I think an overflow is imminent," said Dwight Crandell, one of the United States Geological Survey scientists monitoring the eruption. The threat of flooding was created when the outlet of Spirit Lake, on the mountain's shattered north flank, was plugged by dirt, rock, trees and volcanic ash from the explosion on Sunday morning. The outlet is the source of the Toutle River, the valley of which was the scene of mudflows, flooding, and flows of superheated volcanic ash.

"The best we would hope for," Mr. Crandell said, "is for the water to spill over the top and go quietly down the river. The worst would be for the whole thing to come crashing down."

Much of Valley in Path

A total, rapid deterioration of the earth plug, which scientists say is 200 feet high and 1.5 miles wide, would mean a disastrous flood that would careen down the Toutle River Valley to the Cowlitz River at Castle Rock, Wash., and then inundate much of Kelso and Longview, Wash., before pouring into the Columbia River.

The cloud of gas and particles of volcanic debris that resulted from the eruption moved east today, widening into an arc from Maine to Georgia. The cloud was not visible in New York, and environmental officials said it did not present any health hazard.

96 Reported Missing

Whether there will be any long-term health effects from the fallout is not known without more detailed analysis of the content of the cloud, but scientists say that the eruption is not likely to bring any significant changes in weather patterns, and they expect only negligible effects to be felt at ground level. [Page A20.]

The names of six persons killed in Washington were released today by the authorities, who also said that two unidentified bodies had been discovered and that they were trying to locate 96 other persons who had been reported missing.

Continued on Page A20, Column 2

© (Everett (Wash.) Herald/Vern Hodgson via Associated Press)

In what he called "a stroke of luck," Vern Hodgson, an amateur photographer of Lynnwood, Wash., was setting up his 35mm camera on a tripod when Mount St. Helens began to erupt Sunday morning. He took these pictures from a distance of 15 miles, using 400 ASA color print film. In all, he made 16 pictures in about four minutes, shifting from a 75-150mm zoom lens with an extender, making it the equivalent of a 300mm lens, to a 50mm lens and finally a 25mm wide-angle lens as the cloud from the eruption widened to about 20 miles.

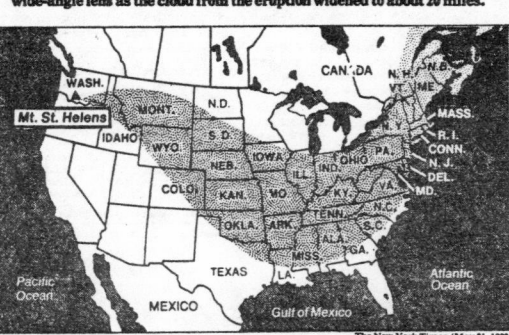

The New York Times/May 21, 1980

Dissipating cloud of fallout from eruption reached Eastern States last night

Accord Is Reported on Evacuation Of Last 710 Love Canal Families

By ROBIN HERMAN
Special to The New York Times

ALBANY, May 20 — New York State and Federal officials were reported tonight to have reached agreement on evacuating the 710 remaining families in the Love Canal area of Niagara Falls, N.Y., but were snagged on whether the relocation should be permanent or temporary.

Governor Carey told Federal officials this afternoon — including Vice President

Mondale and members of the New York delegation to Congress — that short-term assistance was unacceptable and that the

Love Canal residents were calmer yesterday after the release of two Federal officials held in a protest the night before. Page B1.

Federal Government should offer the residents of the chemically polluted area the option of permanent relocation.

A deputy assistant to the President for intergovernmental affairs, Eugene Eidenberg, said in Washington early tonight that he had been in consultation with Governor Carey but that no final decision had been reached.

Sources close to the negotiations reported, however, that the decision to relocate had been made, and that an announcement awaited only a resolution of details. It was not immediately clear when the evacuation would begin.

State and Federal officials had not

Continued on Page B4, Column 1

CONFEREES' ACCORD ON BUDGET SNAGGED

5 Liberal House Democrats Balk at $6.1 Billion Rise for Military

By MARTIN TOLCHIN
Special to The New York Times

WASHINGTON, May 20 — House and Senate budget conferees reached a tentative agreement to break an impasse in a dispute involving guns versus butter this evening but it quickly collapsed when five liberal House Democrats balked at accepting $15.5 billion in military spending for the fiscal year 1981.

"They made a firm offer and we accepted it," Senator Ernest F. Hollings, chairman of the Senate Budget Committee, said the House conferees' proposal to increase military spending by $6.1 billion from the $147.9 billion proposed by the House.

"They reneged on it," the South Carolina Democrat told reporters.

The Senate has passed a budget resolution calling for military spending of $155.7 billion. Although the Senate conferees had indicated earlier in the day that they would not accept any figure below $155.4 billion, they relented and agreed to the House conferees' proposal for spending of $154 billion, which would represent an increase of about 5 percent over 1980 after accounting for inflation.

The compromise proposal resulted from an hour-long meeting between Mr. Hollings and Representative Robert N.

Continued on Page A33, Column 2

INSIDE

Decision on Cubans' Status
The White House said arriving Cubans would be treated as applicants for asylum, so Congress need not be consulted on the number admitted. Page A24.

New York to Get U.S. Funds
New York State will get the Federal money it needs to make $40 million in Medicaid payments to New York City hospitals and nursing homes. Page B3.

Miami Police Inquiry Is Set
The Attorney General announced that a team of Federal prosecutors and agents would study alleged abuses by the Miami police. Page A22.

QUEBECERS DEFEAT SOVEREIGNTY MOVE BY A RATIO OF 3 TO 2

U.S. Scolds Paris For Secretiveness On Soviet Parley

Also Criticizes the British
for Reneging Over Iran

By BERNARD GWERTZMAN
Special to The New York Times

WASHINGTON, May 20 — The United States criticized France today for failing to consult before the French-Soviet meeting in Warsaw and criticized Britain for reneging on a Common Market commitment to block exports to Iran under contracts made since the takeover of the American Embassy.

After holding back on criticism of the French move for two days and expressing satisfaction with the Common Market steps to impose sanctions as of Nov. 4 — a move that nevertheless fell short of an earlier European pledge to cancel all trade except food and medicine — the Carter Administration found itself today in public dispute with two of its major allies.

Britain's abrupt decision against imposing the retroactive sanctions that presented on the united front that Western Europe had presented on the Iranian crisis collapse. In Paris, French officials acknowledged that the talks yesterday in Warsaw between President Valéry Giscard d'Estaing and Leonid I. Brezhnev, the Soviet leader, had achieved no major breakthrough, but they insisted that the meeting had at least kept lines of communication open. [Pages A16 and A14.]

Muskie Criticizes France

Secretary of State Edmund S. Muskie said at a news conference that France, by failing to consult with its allies about the Warsaw talks, was reasserting its independence at the cost of allied solidarity and unity.

The criticism of Prime Minister Margaret Thatcher's Government was the first by the Carter Administration. It was issued by the State Department late in the day after Britain announced that it would not carry out the Common Market decision it had participated in making on Sunday.

That decision, a compromise between those who wanted sanctions to include

Continued on Page A16, Column 1

A TRUDEAU VICTORY

Many French Canadians
Join English-Speakers
to Back Federalism

By HENRY GINIGER
Special to The New York Times

MONTREAL, May 20 — In a historic referendum, Quebec voted overwhelmingly today to reject a move to put this predominantly French-speaking province on the road out of the Canadian federation.

Federalist forces, led by Prime Minister Pierre Elliott Trudeau of Canada and Claude Ryan, leader of the Quebec Liberal party, who had cautioned against breaking up Canada and had promised constitutional changes, took 59 percent of the vote compared with 41 percent for the "yes" side led by the provincial Premier, René Lévesque.

Mr. Lévesque did not even obtain a majority of French speakers, who make up 80 percent of the province's 6.2 million people. About 54 percent of the Quebec French refused to heed his appeal for solidarity and joined with more than 80 percent of the non-French minority, mainly English-speakers, to produce the decisive federalist victory.

Lévesque Close to Tears

Close to tears, Mr. Lévesque appeared before his supporters tonight and promised "a next time." He said the vote, "an upsurge of old Quebec," had to be accepted, but he warned Mr. Trudeau that "the ball was in his court now" and that he had to make good his promises of constitutional change.

One of the heaviest turnouts in Quebec's electoral history, about 80 percent of the 4.3 million registered voters, indicated the public interest in the province's first occasion to exercise the right of self-determination for its political future.

With the count almost complete, the vote for the "no" side was 2,140,814, or 59.4 percent, while the "yes" vote was 1,475,509, or 40.6 percent.

Voters appeared unwilling to take the risk of separating their province from Canada, thus heeding the warnings of Mr. Trudeau and Mr. Ryan. At the same

Continued on Page A3, Column 1

South Korean Government Resigns As a TV Station Is Burned in Riots

By HENRY SCOTT STOKES
Special to The New York Times

SEOUL, May 20 — The South Korean Cabinet of Prime Minister Shin Hyon Hwack resigned today "to take responsibility for failure to maintain domestic calm" as riots continued in the provincial city of Kwangju.

Reports from Kwangju, a stronghold of Kim Dae Jung, the arrested opposition leader, said that a television and radio station was burned as 30,000 demonstrators, mainly students and workers, marched in groups and that some battled a division-strength army unit that was rushed to the city when troubles began there. At least five people were killed and 70 injured in clashes in Kwangju yesterday.

Seoul, situated only 25 miles from the strategic border with North Korea, was calm. But the full martial law imposed Saturday night, which gave Lieut. Gen. Chon Too Hwan, the head of the country's intelligence apparatus, virtual control of the country, appeared shaky in other provincial cities such as Mokpo, Chongju and Yosu.

Political Liberalization Asked

The imposition of full martial law followed several days of protests by university students in Seoul demanding an end of the limited form of martial law previously in force and a more rapid rate of progress toward a democratic governmental structure.

After the student leaders called off the demonstrations on Friday in response to pleas by the Government, troops raided a gathering of student leaders on Saturday. Hundreds of people have been arrested, including Kim Dae Jung, a persistent critic of the regime of the late President Park Chung Hee, and former Prime Minister Kim Jong Pil, the head of the majority Democratic Republican Party.

The leader of the opposition New Democratic Party, Kim Young Sam, another longtime opponent of President Park's regime, is under virtual house arrest here with about 100 soldiers surrounding his home.

Many South Koreans regard the weekend's events as, in effect, a coup by General Chon, who has shielded his actions with an argument that they were called for by President Choi Kyu Hah. This explanation was given credence by some South Korean officials but rejected by others, as confusion and concern spread in Seoul today after the Cabinet's resignation.

In another development in Seoul, the Supreme Court today rejected an appeal

Continued on Page A8, Column 2

157 ELDERLY WOMEN DIE IN JAMAICA FIRE

14 Missing at Kingston Institution —Question of Arson Raised

By United Press International

KINGSTON, Jamaica, May 20 — Fire swept through a two-story wooden home for poor and elderly women here early today, and officials said at least 157 were killed and 14 others were missing.

Of the 204 women asleep in their beds when the fire broke out about 1 A.M., only 33 were reported safe and accounted for hours after the blaze had been brought under control.

Prime Minister Michael N. Manley told Jamaicans in a radio broadcast that security officials thought arsonists could have started the blaze, but the city's fire chief said there was no proof of that. He suggested that an electrical short could have started the fire.

The fire chief, Allan Ridgeway, said the fire consumed the building so quickly that his men had to stand helplessly by, watching a few women jump through windows and listening to the screams of those trapped inside. Those who jumped were seriously injured.

The building collapsed four minutes

Continued on Page A3, Column 1

"All the News
That's Fit to Print"

The New York Times

LATE CITY EDITION
Weather: Partly sunny today; mostly cloudy and cold tonight and tomorrow. Temperature range: today 28-38; yesterday 36-43. Details on page D21.

VOL.CXXX... No. 44,835   Copyright © 1981 The New York Times   NEW YORK, WEDNESDAY, JANUARY 21, 1981   30 cents beyond 50-mile zone from New York City. Higher in air delivery cities.   25 CENTS

REAGAN TAKES OATH AS 40TH PRESIDENT; PROMISES AN 'ERA OF NATIONAL RENEWAL'

MINUTES LATER, 52 U.S. HOSTAGES IN IRAN FLY TO FREEDOM AFTER 444-DAY ORDEAL

'ALIVE, WELL AND FREE'

Captives Taken to Algiers and Then Germany — Final Pact Complex

By BERNARD GWERTZMAN
Special to The New York Times

WASHINGTON, Wednesday, Jan. 21 — The 52 Americans who were held hostage by Iran for 444 days were flown to freedom yesterday. Jimmy Carter, a few hours after giving up the Presidency, said that everyone "was alive, was well and free."

The flight ended the national ordeal that had frustrated Mr. Carter for most of his last 14 months in office, and it allowed Ronald Reagan to begin his term free of the burdens of the Iran crisis.

The Americans were escorted out of Iran by Algerian diplomats, aboard an Algerian airliner, underscoring Algeria's role in achieving the accord that allowed the hostages to return home.

Transferred to U.S. Custody

The Algerian plane, carrying the former hostages, stopped first in Athens to refuel. It then landed in Algiers, where custody of the 52 Americans was formally transferred by the Algerians to the representative of the United States, former Deputy Secretary of State Warren M. Christopher. He had negotiated much of the agreement freeing them.

They then boarded two United States Air Force hospital planes and flew to Frankfurt, West Germany early this morning. They will stay at an American military hospital in nearby Weisbaden, where they will be visited by Mr. Carter, as President Reagan's representative, later today. They will stay in Wiesbaden for a week or less to "decompress," as one official described it.

The 52 Americans were freed as part of a complex agreement that was not completed until early yesterday morning, when the last snags holding up their release were removed by Mr. Carter and

Continued on Page A3, Column 5

Teheran Captors Call Out Insults As the 52 Leave

By JOHN KIFNER
Special to The New York Times

TEHERAN, Iran, Jan. 20 — The 52 American hostages began to roll down the runway to freedom today minutes as President Reagan was finishing his inaugural address.

As the Algerian 727 lifted off from Mehrabad Airport, ending 444 days of captivity for the Americans, they could see, most of them probably for the last time, a full moon picking out the sharp white peaks of the Elburz Mountains to the north. The time was 8:55 P.M., 12:25 P.M., New York time.

"God is great! Death to America!" cried the young Islamic militants who kept custody of the hostages to the last minute, hustling them to the stairs of the airplane.

They Soon Are 'Former Hostages'

The American diplomats, Marine guards and the other hostages stepped one at a time from a bus, whose windows were covered with checked curtains, into a clear cold night. As they touched the tarmac, two young militants, the hoods of their parkas up against the chill, took them just above the elbows and propelled them through the shouting crowd toward the Algerian plane with its red stylized bird emblazoned on the tail.

Looking dazed, some with long hair and beards that contrasted with the neat trims of their official days before the embassy takeover Nov. 4, 1979, they stumbled into the first-class section of the plane. Now they were what a bulletin on Pars, the state press agency, would describe later as "former hostages."

"They seem stunned, as if they cannot believe they are going free," Ahmad Azizi, the Government's director of hostage affairs, remarked to an Iranian state television crew covering the departure.

At 8:20, the doors were sealed, Pars reported, and the engines began to whine. A

Continued on Page A8, Column 1

11:57 A.M.: Ronald Reagan being sworn in as 40th President by Chief Justice Warren E. Burger. Nancy Reagan held the Bible and Senator Mark O. Hatfield witnessed the ceremony.

United Press International

12:25 P.M.: Sgt. Joseph Subic Jr. propelled by militants to waiting plane at airport in Teheran

Pars via Associated Press

FREEZE SET ON HIRING

Californian Stresses Need to Restrict Government and Buoy Economy

By STEVEN R. WEISMAN
Special to The New York Times

WASHINGTON, Jan. 20 — Ronald Wilson Reagan of California, promising "an era of national renewal," became the 40th President of the United States today as 52 Americans held hostage in Iran were heading toward freedom.

The hostages, whose 14 months of captivity had been a central focus of the Presidential contest last year, took off from Teheran in two Boeing 727 airplanes at 12:25 P.M., Eastern standard time, the very moment that Mr. Reagan was concluding his solemn Inaugural Address at the United States Capitol.

The new President's speech, however, made no reference at all to the long-awaited release of the hostages, emphasizing instead the need to limit the powers of the Federal Government, and to bring an end to unemployment and inflation.

'Government Is the Problem'

Promising to begin immediately to deal with "an economic affliction of great proportions," Mr. Reagan declared: "In this present crisis, government is not the solution to our problem; government is the problem." And in keeping with this statement, the President issued orders for a hiring "freeze" as his first official act. [Page B6.]

Wearing a charcoal gray club coat, striped trousers and dove gray vest and tie, Mr. Reagan took his oath of office at 11:57 A.M. in the first inaugural ceremony ever enacted on the western front of the United States Capitol. The site was chosen to stress the symbolism of Mr. Reagan's addressing his words to the West, the region that served as his base in his three Presidential campaigns in 1968, 1976 and 1980.

Oldest to Assume Presidency

The ceremony today, filled with patriotic music, the firing of cannons and the pealing of bells, marked the transfer of the Presidency back to the Republicans after the four-year term of Jimmy Carter, a Democrat, as well as the culmination of the remarkable career of a conservative former two-term Governor of California who had started out as a baseball announcer and motion picture star.

At the age of 69, Mr. Reagan also became the oldest man to assume the Presidency, and in five months he will become the oldest man to serve in the office.

Mr. Carter, looking haggard and worn after spending two largely sleepless nights trying to resolve the hostage crisis

Continued on Page B8, Column 2

Anxious Families and Towns Erupt Into Long-Postponed Celebrations

By JOSEPH B. TREASTER

Saying his final farewells at Andrews Air Force Base yesterday, Jimmy Carter spotted Anita Schaefer, the wife of one of the hostages, and exuberantly embraced her.

"Tom is in the air," Mr. Carter said, speaking of her husband, Col. Thomas E. Schaefer of the Air Force, who was the senior military officer at the United States Embassy in Teheran.

"Really, truly, Mr. President," she whispered.

"Really, truly — at long last," he said, "Tom is safe. I'll be with him tomorrow morning in Germany."

"Oh, thank God, Mr. President."

Then they both cried. And they embraced again.

The First Glimpse

As the hostages arrived in Algiers, relatives strained close to television screens for the first glimpse of their loved ones out of captivity in more than 14 months.

"There's Billy," cried Letezia Gallegos, as her brother, Sgt. William Gallegos of the Marines, stepped down the ramp. His mother, Theresa, broke into deep sobs.

News that the plane carrying the hostages had taken off from Teheran came to Penelope Laingen, the wife of L. Bruce Laingen, the embassy's chargé d'affaires, as she sat in a reserved seat at the inauguration of President Reagan. A military policeman shouted the word for everyone to hear.

Some had gotten the word from radio and television broadcasts, and still others, like Marjorie Moore, the wife of Bert C. Moore, the administrative consul, received phone calls from the State Department.

Most of the homes of the hostages' families, torn by doubt, fear and anger for so long, exploded with joy. They cried

Continued on Page A5, Column 1

Black Star/John Troha for The New York Times

Anita Schaefer, wife of a hostage, embraced Mr. Carter at airport.

A Hopeful Prologue, a Pledge of Action

By HEDRICK SMITH
Special to The New York Times

WASHINGTON, Jan. 20 — For a President who has promised Americans a new beginning, an era of national renewal at home and restored strength and stature abroad, the release of the American hostages in Iran was exquisitely timed.

The extraordinary deadline diplomacy that put the 52 captured Americans into the air over Iran minutes after the hostages thundered a new leader into office provided a graceful exit for Jimmy Carter, a hopeful prologue for Ronald Reagan and relief for a nation weary from 14 months of humiliation and seeming impotence.

Almost unavoidably the human drama

in Iran overshadowed an Inaugural Address that was less an inspirational call to national greatness than a plain-spoken charter of Mr. Reagan's conservative creed, less a sermon than a stump speech, less a rallying cry than a ringing denunciation of overgrown government and a practical pledge to get down to the business of trimming it at once.

Although Mr. Reagan made no direct mention of the hostages, their release was on everyone's lips. Moments before Mr. Reagan took his oath of office, word that the hostages were about to be flown out of Iran swept through the crowd stretched out before the Capitol, and though that news was premature, it provided the perfect symbolic backdrop for

For all the new President's vaunted reputation as one of the nation's most polished political orators, his Inaugural Address offered surprisingly few rhetorical flourishes beyond the populist tribute to ordinary Americans that "those who say that we are in a time when there are no heroes, they just don't know where to look."

Continued on Page B7, Column 1

News Analysis

The New York Times

LATE CITY EDITION

Weather: Mostly sunny, mild today; fair tonight. Chance of showers tomorrow. Temperature range: today 48-72; yesterday 56-65. Details on page C9.

VOL.CXXX . No. 44,904

Copyright © 1981 The New York Times

NEW YORK, TUESDAY, MARCH 31, 1981

30 cents beyond 50-mile zone from New York City. Higher in air delivery cities.

25 CENTS

REAGAN WOUNDED IN CHEST BY GUNMAN; OUTLOOK 'GOOD' AFTER 2-HOUR SURGERY; AIDE AND 2 GUARDS SHOT; SUSPECT HELD

Bush Flies Back From Texas Set to Take Charge in Crisis

By STEVEN R. WEISMAN
Special to The New York Times

WASHINGTON, March 30 — Vice President Bush, cutting short a trip to Texas, returned to the White House this evening to take charge of the crisis in the Government and to assume the responsibilities of the Presidency if President Reagan's injuries prevented him from serving in the office.

It was unclear tonight how long Mr. Bush would remain in charge of Government functions, however. At George Washington Univerity Hospital, the dean of clinical affairs said that President Reagan was "alert" and that he "should be able to make decisions by tomorrow." But he said Mr. Reagan might have to remain in the hospital for two weeks.

"I can reassure this nation and a watching world that the American Government is functioning fully and effectively," Mr. Bush said this evening after presiding over a half-hour Cabinet meeting in the White House situation room, where participants also heard the televised news conference reporting on Mr. Reagan's condition.

'Officers Fulfilling Obligations'

"We've had full and complete communications throughout the day, and the officers of the Federal Government have been fulfilling their obligations with skill and with care," Mr. Bush continued. He added that "all our prayers" and "all our hope" were extended for the recovery of the two wounded law enforcement men and for James S. Brady, the White House press secretary.

White House spokesmen said this evening that no steps had been taken to install Mr. Bush as Acting President under the terms of the 25th Amendment to the Constitution, which provides for succession in case of Presidential disability.

Mr. Bush was scheduled to fill in for the President tomorrow, however, at a series of previously scheduled functions, including a Cabinet meeting, a session with Congressional leaders, and a lunch with the Prime Minister of the Netherlands, Andreas A. M. van Agt. He prepared to spend the night at his own official residence in northwest Washington, a few miles from the White House.

Contradictory Statements

There were contradictory statements in the afternoon and evening about who was in charge of the Government.

Shortly after 4 P.M., Secretary of State Alexander M. Haig Jr., who rushed to the White House minutes after the attack, announced he was in control pending the return of the Vice President to Washington. Mr. Haig also said he was in charge because the newly created system of "crisis management" was in effect, and he suggested that it was his role to serve as crisis-management coordinator until the

Continued on Page A5, Column 2

Suspect Was Arrested Last Year In Nashville on Weapons Charge

By PHILIP TAUBMAN
Special to The New York Times

WASHINGTON, Tuesday, March 31 — The 25-year-old son of a Denver oil executive was overpowered by police officers and Secret Service agents yesterday at the scene of an attack on President Reagan. He was charged with the attempted assassination of the President and the shooting of three other persons.

The suspect was identified as John W. Hinckley Jr., who was said to have been in psychiatric care recently. He was arrested in Nashville last Oct. 9 for possession of concealed weapons, according to Nashville police records, and was released after paying a fine of $62.50. President Carter had arrived in Nashville a few hours earlier that night to speak at Opry Land.

Yesterday, in the tumult that followed the firing of a series of shots at Mr. Reagan's party, Mr. Hinckley was grabbed and pushed against a wall outside the Washington Hilton Hotel. Secret Service agents said that a Harrington Richards .22-caliber pistol was recovered from him, and he was quickly taken away in a District of Columbia police car.

Mr. Hinckley, described as a blue-eyed, sandy-haired man about 5 feet 10 inches tall, was turned over by the police to the Federal Bureau of Investigation and was arraigned early this morning in Federal District Court here.

He was ordered held without bail by Federal Magistrate Arthur L. Burnett on a charge that he "knowingly and intentionally" attempted to kill President Reagan and assaulted a Secret Service

Continued on Page A2, Column 4

John W. Hinckley Jr. in photo made Jan. 21 for his driver's license. *Associated Press*

Witnesses to Shooting Recall Suspect Acting 'Fidgety' and 'Hostile'

By RICHARD D. LYONS

WASHINGTON, March 30 — "I spotted him walking rapidly up and down outside the back door of the hotel," John M. Dodson said. "He looked fidgety — agitated — a little strange, and I said to myself 'What if he takes a shot at the President?'"

Mr. Dodson, a computer specialist, was not the only person to take note of the behavior of the blond young man outside the Washington Hilton where President Reagan was making a speech. Walter C. Rogers, a reporter for Associated Press Radio, said the young man had been hostile to the group of reporters who had penetrated. And another witness, Samuel Lafta, an iron worker from Warren, Mich., said that a police lieutenant had stared at the man several times.

But, nothing was done until the shots that wounded the President, his press secretary and two guards rang out. Then, the young man was overwhelmed by police officers and Secret Service agents.

Mr. Dodson, who works for the Pinkerton Detective Agency was standing on the seventh floor of the Universal North

Continued on Page A4, Column 3

FOR HOME DELIVERY OF THE NEW YORK TIMES, call toll-free: 800-631-2500. In New Jersey, 800-932-0300. In Boston, call (617) 787-3010. In Washington, D.C. (301) 654-2771.—ADVT.

Other News

Polish Strike Suspended
A nationwide strike threatened for today was averted after leaders of Solidarity reached a tentative settlement with the Polish Government. Page A9.

Indonesians Storm Hijacked Jet
Four of five hijackers were slain and 55 hostages freed when commandos in Bangkok retook an Indonesian airliner held since Saturday. Page A8.

President Reagan leaving the Washington Hilton. At right is James S. Brady. As Mr. Reagan waved to the crowd . . . *ABC News*

Americans were saddened and outraged by news of the shooting of the President. In the business community, activity came to a standstill; stock trading was halted. Pages A5 and D1.

. . . the gunman fired, hitting the President below his left arm. In photo made over roof of Presidential car . . . *Associated Press*

. . . Secret Service agents are seen pushing Mr. Reagan into the vehicle, which immediately sped to a hospital. *Associated Press*

Circle at right shows gun held by suspect. Legs of Timothy J. McCarthy, the wounded agent, are visible at center. *NBC News*

James S. Brady lies on sidewalk. The pistol is believed to belong to a security agent, who put it down while helping. *ABC News*

LEFT LUNG IS PIERCED

Coloradan, 25, Arrested — Brady, Press Chief, Is Critically Injured

By HOWELL RAINES
Special to The New York Times

WASHINGTON, Tuesday, March 31 — President Reagan was shot in the chest yesterday by a gunman, apparently acting alone, as Mr. Reagan walked to his limousine after addressing a labor meeting at the Washington Hilton Hotel. The White House press secretary and two law-enforcement officers were also wounded by a burst of shots.

The President was reported in "good" and "stable" condition last night at George Washington University Hospital

Statements in capital, pages A5 and A7.

after undergoing two hours of surgery. "The prognosis is excellent," said Dr. Dennis S. O'Leary, dean of clinical affairs at the university. "He is alert and should be able to make decisions by tomorrow."

The hospital spokesman said surgeons removed a .22-caliber bullet that struck Mr. Reagan's seventh rib, penetrating the left lung three inches and collapsing it.

A rapid series of five or six shots rang out about 2:30 P.M. as Mr. Reagan left the hotel. A look of stunned disbelief swept across the President's face when the shots were fired just after he raised his left arm to wave to the crowd. Nearby, his press secretary, James S. Brady, fell to the sidewalk, critically wounded.

Eyewitnesses said six shots were fired at the Presidential entourage from a distance of about 10 feet. The assailant had positioned himself among the television camera crews and reporters assembled outside a hotel exit.

The authorities arrested a 25-year-old Colorado man, John W. Hinckley Jr., at the scene of the attack. He was booked on Federal charges of attempting to assassinate the President and assault on a Federal officer, and early this morning he was ordered held without bail by Federal Magistrate Arthur L. Burnett.

According to police records, Mr. Hinckley was arrested in Nashville last fall on weapons charges on a night when President Carter was speaking there.

Scene of Turmoil

Within minutes after the attack yesterday afternoon, Americans were witnessing for the second time in a generation television pictures of a chief executive being struck by gunfire during what appeared to be a routine public appearance. For the second time in less than 20 years, too, they watched as the nation's leaders scrambled to meet one of the sternest tests of the democratic system.

Mr. Reagan, apparently at first unaware that he had been wounded, was shoved forcefully by a Secret Service agent into the Presidential limousine,

Continued on Page A3, Column 3

A Bullet Is Removed From Reagan's Lung In Emergency Surgery

By ROBERT REINHOLD
Special to The New York Times

WASHINGTON, March 30 — President Reagan was treated for a partly collapsed lung today, but the bullet that entered his left side and lodged in the tissue of his left lung did not do much further damage, according to doctors who operated on him. Surgeons removed a .22-caliber bullet from the President's lower left lung.

Neither Mr. Reagan's heart nor such vital blood vessels as the aorta were affected, Dr. Dennis S. O'Leary, dean for clinical affairs at George Washington University, said at a briefing this evening. "The bullet was never close to any vital structure," he said. He called Mr. Reagan's prognosis "excellent."

Emergency surgical procedures, which took about two hours, found no bleeding or damage in the abdominal area. Mr. Reagan received five units, or two and a half quarts, of blood in a transfusion before surgery. His vital signs were stable throughout his ordeal.

The adult body contains five to six quarts of blood. The hazard of blood loss relates to how rapidly the blood is lost and whether the volume of the blood sup-

Continued on Page A7, Column 1

ALBERT G. SIMS
We miss you already. Elva and Patsy.—Advt.

The New York Times

LATE CITY EDITION
Weather: Mostly sunny, windy today;
mostly clear tonight. Sunny tomorrow.
Temperature range: today 35-50; yesterday 43-58. Details are on page B8.

VOL.CXXX.. No. 44,919   Copyright © 1981 The New York Times   NEW YORK, WEDNESDAY, APRIL 15, 1981   30 cents beyond 50-mile zone from New York City.   25 CENTS
Higher in air delivery cities.

COLUMBIA RETURNS: SHUTTLE ERA OPENS

First Re-usable Spaceship Glides to Landing in Desert; Commander Calls Flight 'Tremendous, Start to Finish'

Goal: 2d Trip in 6 Months And 100 in Ship's Lifetime

By WALTER SULLIVAN
Special to The New York Times

EDWARDS AIR FORCE BASE, Calif., April 14 — With the nearly flawless completion of the voyage of the shuttle Columbia, space agency officials began today to draw up firmer plans for the future of man in space, a future that they had always envisioned with a clarity that left their critics scoffing.

The triumph of the Columbia is expected to lead to flights with far-reaching commercial, scientific and military applications.

An agency official said at a briefing this afternoon that the Columbia would probably begin its return flight to Cape Canaveral, Fla., riding piggyback on a Boeing 747 jet in about a week.

He said that the "optimistic" estimate was that the shuttle would fly again under its own power in "less than six months" on a four-day flight from which it might be able to turn around and return to space in four months. Ultimately officials envision the shuttle being able to turn around in a matter of weeks. Each shuttle would have a life of 100 missions.

Apparently responding to the space program's critics, Christopher C. Kraft Jr., director of the Johnson Space Center in Houston, in a message relayed to the astronauts just before they left the shuttle, said: "We just became infinitely smarter."

What uncertainty remaining today centered on questions about just how quickly the spaceship could be readied for another flight. Specialists still have to determine the extent of the damage to the tiles that protect the ship from the sear-ing heat of re-entry into the atmosphere. There was also some question about the suitability for quick re-use of the launching pad at Cape Canaveral, which was significantly damaged at liftoff on Sunday. [Page A23.]

Donald K. Slayton, orbital flight test manager and a former astronaut, said that a preliminary inspection revealed no more tiles missing than had been seen earlier on television from space. He said,

The shuttle's success is sweet vindication of American know-how, but social scientists say the psychological uplift will pass. News analysis, page A22.

"minimum work" would be required to replace them. But he added that a more detailed inspection would follow.

If close inspection of the tiles here and later when the Columbia is airlifted back to Florida reveals no fundamental problems, the "optimistic" estimate of a launching in the fall would prove true, with the third test mission in the spring and the fourth and final one later in 1982. One of the last two test missions, both of which are to last for seven days, would orbit while opened to the sky, rather than the flying upside down to scan the earth.

The first operational, or nonexperimental, flight would take place by the end of that year.

The payload for that flight, as now planned, will be a TDRS or Tracking and Data Relay Satellite to be gently released into earth orbit. Among other roles, this

Continued on Page A22, Column 1

A Speck Pierces Horizon

By ROBERT LINDSEY
Special to The New York Times

EDWARDS AIR FORCE BASE, Calif., April 14 — First came the sonic boom announcing that it was near: two loud shocks that reverberated like cannon blasts across the desert floor.

Over the public address system, the voice of Mission Control read out the orbiter's speed and altitude, now rapidly declining: "Columbia, you're right on the money, right on the money,"

"Where is it, where is it?" perhaps 10,000 voices asked at once from the edge of Rogers Dry Lake.

Dropping to the Desert

Then, the sharpest eyes on the ground, squinting upward, saw it: a tiny, moving speck high over the horizon, dropping fast through a dusty, luminescent haze that rose from the surface of the parched dry lake like a cloudy mist. Suddenly, the tension broke.

"There it is!" the first voice said, and then others. The spectators, in clusters and large crowds, some who had been up all night waiting, broke into cheers as the space shuttle orbiter Columbia glided gracefully toward the hard-packed, cream-colored desert runway.

"Incredible!" shouted Joseph Lyon, who sells plywood for a living. "Can you believe it?" he asked, as he recorded the Columbia's descent with his portable home video recorder.

The Columbia, perhaps only 60 seconds after it had first been seen from the desert gallery, touched down, and the spectators continued to cheer.

The craft then rolled to a stop and seemed, from a distance, to become mired in a shimmering lake, a desert mirage that gave the illusion that the prehistoric dry lake was no longer dry.

Even before the Columbia had stopped its landing roll, a convoy of 21 service vehicles whose operators had been been training for that moment for almost three months, was moving in a phalanx toward the craft, stirring up a cloud of dust like a battalion of tanks moving over the Sahara before battle.

"It's a great day for the country," Albert Wheelon, an aerospace executive in the crowd said when he spotted a friend. "America's confidence ought to be up 100 percent."

It was a thought expressed repeatedly in the crowd of spectators, estimated by the National Aeronautics and Space Administration at more than 250,000, who had come here to watch a spaceship for

Continued on Page A23, Column 1

'Welcome Home, Columbia'
— Joseph Allen, Mission Control Communicator, 1:21 P.M.

HOUSTON: Columbia, we show you crossing the coast now.

CAPT. ROBERT L. CRIPPEN: What a way to come to California!

HOUSTON: Columbia, you're out of 130K [130,000 feet] on the tracking, 6.4 Mach, looking good.

Mach 6, 124,000 feet, range 177 miles.

JOHN W. YOUNG: John Young rolling, using manual control now.

HOUSTON: Mach 4.4, 107,000 feet, range 112.

Roll reversal complete. Control looks good.

Ejection seats can be used now, below 100,000.

You're coming right down the chute.

Rudder active now, looking good. Range 73 miles.

We now have a live television picture from the long-range optics at Dryden Flight Research Center.

Columbia, you're coming right down the track. The tracking data, map data and preplan trajectory are all one line on our plot boards here.

YOUNG: Roger, we concur.

HOUSTON: Columbia, we show you very slightly high in altitude, coming down nicely.

Mach 1 at 51,000 feet, range 28 miles.

Columbia, you're going subsonic now out at 50K, looking good.

YOUNG: Roger that.

HOUSTON: Columbia getting ready to start the big sweeping turn into the runway.

Columbia, you're really looking good, right on the money, right on the money.

25,000 feet, 1.6, range 13 miles; 22,000 feet. Control looking very smooth, speed brake at——. We have a television picture now.

You're right on the glide slope, Columbia. Right on glide slope, approaching center line, looking great.

That's TV from the chase plane. 16,000 feet.

Air speed 271 knots.

5,290.

2,500 feet.

50 feet, 40, 30, 20, 10, 5, 4, 3, 2, 1. Touchdown.

Welcome home, Columbia! Beautiful, beautiful.

More from the dialogue, page A23.

The Columbia, accompanied by two escort planes, descending toward a landing at Edwards Air Force Base
The New York Times/Jim Wilson

The shuttle's rear wheels touch the runway on Rogers Dry Lake. Craft was traveling about 215 miles an hour.
NBC News

John W. Young, left, and Capt. Robert L. Crippen walking away from their craft after landing safely in the desert
CBS News via Associated Press

FLIERS EMERGE ELATED

Crippen Says That Nation Is 'Back in the Space Business to Stay'

By JOHN NOBLE WILFORD
Special to The New York Times

EDWARDS AIR FORCE BASE, Calif., April 14 — The space shuttle Columbia rocketed out of orbit and glided to a safe landing on the desert here today to conclude the successful first demonstration of a bold new approach to extraterrestrial travel, the re-usable winged spaceship.

Heralding its triumphant return with a sharp double sonic boom, one of technology's fanfares, the 122-foot-long Columbia appeared in the clear blue sky, soared over the base, looped back and touched its wheels down in the wash of a mirage on the hard-packed clay of a dry lake bed. Touchdown came at 1:21 P.M., Eastern standard time.

"Welcome home, Columbia!" was the simple message from Joseph Allen in Mission Control.

215 Miles an Hour

Capt. Robert L. Crippen of the Navy and John W. Young brought the 80-ton gliding vehicle with its stubby delta wings to a smooth landing at a speed of 215 miles an hour, about twice the velocity of a jetliner landing.

Never before had a space vehicle returned to the earth in such a way so that it could be flown again. The Columbia and its three sister ships now under construction are each designed for as many as 100 flights to and from the space frontier.

"It was really a tremendous mission from start to finish," said Mr. Young, the commander, in a brief post-landing appearance before officials of the National Aeronautics and Space Administration.

Right on Course in Approach

Moments earlier, the Columbia had come over the California coast, and Mission Control reassured the astronauts that "we've got good data, looking good."

At 1:09, the astronauts were advised, "You've got perfect energy, perfect ground track," meaning that they were on target and slowing for the kind of landing they had practiced so many times.

"What a way to come to California!" Captain Crippen exclaimed.

The Columbia was launched Sunday morning at the Kennedy Space Center in Florida and orbited the earth 36 times over a period of 54 hours and 22 minutes. It was the first orbital test of the shuttle and the first time American astronauts had ventured into space in nearly six years.

"I think we're back in the space business to stay," Captain Crippen said.

The development of the shuttle, a hybrid spacecraft-airplane, has cost almost $10 billion since the project was initiated

Continued on Page A21, Column 1

Other News

Bloc Maneuvers Said to End
Reagan Administration officials say that unusual military activity by Warsaw Pact forces in and around Poland has virtually ended. Page A8.

Fighting Traps Beirut Premier
Artillery and mortar fire between Syrian and Lebanese Christian forces exploded around Parliament, trapping the Prime Minister inside. Page A3.

Aid Planned for Banks
Federal regulators plan to draft legislation soon to help financially troubled savings and loan associations and other institutions. Page D1.

Bradley Wins Third Term
Mayor Tom Bradley of Los Angeles was re-elected, becoming the first Mayor in the city's history to win a third term without a runoff. Page A13.

YOU ASKED FOR IT! YOU'VE GOT IT! Happy 21st Amie Beth - All the D's & Nana — ADV.

"All the News That's Fit to Print"

The New York Times

LATE CITY EDITION

Weather: Increasing cloudiness today; chance of showers tonight and tomorrow. Temperature range: today 54-71; yesterday 42-72. Details on page C18.

VOL.CXXX . No. 44,948

Copyright © 1981 The New York Times

NEW YORK, THURSDAY, MAY 14, 1981

30 cents beyond 50-mile zone from New York City. Higher in air delivery cities

25 CENTS

POPE IS SHOT IN CAR IN VATICAN SQUARE; SURGEONS TERM CONDITION 'GUARDED'; TURK, AN ESCAPED MURDERER, IS SEIZED

MADE THREAT IN '79

Alleged Assailant Wrote a Letter Saying He'd Kill John Paul on Trip

By R. W. APPLE Jr.
Special to The New York Times

ROME, Thursday, May 14 — The first reports said only that he spoke no Italian, that he was young and that he had dark hair.

But within a matter of minutes, a picture of the man accused of shooting Pope John Paul II in St. Peter's Square yesterday afternoon began to emerge, a picture of a militant Turkish terrorist, already convicted of one murder, who escaped from a maximum security prison in 1979 and then threatened in a letter to assassinate the Pope.

The Turkish Ambassador in Washington, Sukru Elekdag, said after the news of the shooting had flashed around the world, "The Turkish police have been under instruction to shoot him on sight."

Said He Was a Student

Moments after he was wrestled to the ground by pilgrims who had been standing near him, the alleged assailant told the Italian police that his name was Mehmet Ali Agca. He gave his age as 23 and said he was Turkish. He said also that he was a student at the University for Foreigners in Perugia in central Italy, but the records of the university showed that he had attended Italian-language classes there for only one day last month.

Mr. Agca was described by the police and by bystanders as a dark-haired young man, clean-shaven, with an angular face. He was wearing an open-neck white shirt under a lightweight jacket.

Mr. Agca was convicted in February 1979 of having murdered Abdi Ipekci, the editor of the independent Turkish daily newspaper Milliyet. He was jailed. But in late November, he escaped from the military prison where he was being held, and he had apparently been in hiding ever since.

When he fled from the prison, Turkish authorities say, he left behind a letter, addressed to Milliyet, threatening the life of the Pope. If the Pontiff did not cancel his visit to Turkey, which was then imminent, Mr. Agca wrote, he would shoot him in revenge for the attack by Moslem extremists on the Grand Mosque in Mecca earlier that year.

Blame Put on U.S. and Israel

The attack was considered a desecration of the Islamic holy place by Moslems, and Mr. Agca charged that the incident was of American or Israeli origin. His letter denounced the Pontiff as "the masked leader of the Crusades."

A partial text of the letter, made available by the Turkish police, reads as follows:

"Western imperialists who are afraid of Turkey's unity of political, military and economic power with the brotherly Islamic countries are sending Crusader

Continued on Page A3, Column 5

Other News

Reagan Tax Compromise Seen
President Reagan is prepared to compromise on the size of his tax cuts, an aide said, because of the financial markets' unsettled conditions. Page D1.

Social Security Plan Assailed
The Reagan Administration's plan to trim Social Security benefits aroused wide protest and the first hint of serious Congressional opposition. Page B15.

U.S. Envoy Returns to Beirut
Philip C. Habib, President Reagan's special envoy, arrived from Jerusalem with a plan for easing the crisis over Syrian missiles in Lebanon. Page A17.

U.S. Holds Soviet Cargo
Federal agents, suspecting violations, boarded a Soviet jetliner in Washington and seized gear, some of which was properly licensed for export. Page A9.

Reagan's Son Cited Ties
Michael Reagan, elder son of the President, referred to his father in letters seeking military contracts, an official of his company said. Page A24.

Plans for Battery Park Shown
Plans for the long-delayed Battery Park City commercial complex call for office buildings, plazas, parks, gardens and a skating rink. Page B1.

Pope John Paul II, with blood on his left hand, being comforted by aides moments after being shot yesterday as he rode through St. Peter's Square at the Vatican

United Press International / The Vatican

Amid Prayers, World Voices Its Indignation

Prayers, shock and indignation resounded around the world yesterday after the shooting of Pope John Paul II.

President Reagan, recovering from wounds inflicted six weeks ago by a gunman, said he would pray for the Pope. In a message Mr. Reagan said, "All Americans join me in hopes and prayers for your speedy recovery."

Queen Elizabeth II said she was horrified. President-elect François Mitterrand of France spoke indignantly of "this new manifestation of detestable violence."

In Poland, the Pope's native land, television broadcasts were interrupted with news bulletins. Stanislaw Kania, head of the Communist Party, and other leaders offered "the best wishes for a speedy recovery necessary for the mission in service of humanist ideals of peace for the benefit of mankind." In Warsaw, people gathered somberly on street corners and around television sets in hotel lobbies, and wept during church services.

Americans shared in the grief at services in cathedrals, parochial schools and neighborhood churches.

In New York, more than 2,500 people, including Mayor Koch, jammed St. Patrick's for a mass led by Terence Cardinal Cooke. Protestant and Jewish leaders joined in appeals for prayers.

The Connecticut Senate reversed itself and approved a bill calling for mandatory one-year jail sentences for illegal possession of a handgun.

"Regardless of what religion you are, he is a man of God," said Maria Lougee, a waitress on Ninth Avenue, who cried when she learned of the shooting. "Who could do something like that?"

For many, the shooting of President Reagan remained fresh in their minds. "When you shoot a President, you shoot a country," said the Rev. Miles Riley of the Archdiocese of San Francisco. "When you shoot a Pope, you shoot the church. We all felt shook, we all felt wounded."

The world, nation and region respond with shock. Pages A4-A6.

Man identified as Mehmet Ali Agca, a 23-year-old Turkish citizen, is led away

United Press International

For New York, Tearful Memories

By LESLIE BENNETTS

In the rectory basement at St. Charles Borromeo Church in Harlem, the women in the Senior Citizens Group wept quietly over the crepe paper banner they were making for a dance and recalled how the Pope leapt from his car to kiss the ground in front of their church.

Her incredulity was shared by those much older than she, many of whom had found the Pope's visit one of the great thrills of their lives. "It could not have been more wonderful," said Juanita Taylor, a retired nurse who overheard yesterday's bad news on the street and hurried to the church. "I don't think it would have been much different if Jesus Christ himself had come here. All I can do now is pray."

At the school next door, students were wide-eyed and solemn as they chanted Hail Marys and prayed for the Pope's recovery.

And in the Bronx, where the Pope had stopped on Morris Avenue on his trip to New York in 1979, worried neighborhood residents gathered on the sidewalk to exchange rumors about his condition.

Many Remember His Visit

But for those New Yorkers with personal memories of the Pope's visit to their own school or street, the news came as a particular shock. "How could somebody shoot the Pope?" wondered Lynda Anderson, a 10-year-old student at St. Charles Borromeo, who had presented the Pope with a bouquet of roses.

Many people commented on the helplessness of world leaders to defend themselves against deranged individuals. "So many people are walking around who are sick and need help," said Gwendolyn Burwell, a church volunteer. "I imagine this was a person who wanted to be seen or heard, and this was the only way he thought he could be heard."

Memories of the Pope's presence and

Continued on Page A6, Column 1

Around Nation / Music section index

A Firm Papacy For the People

Pope Strives to Deliver His Message Worldwide

News Analysis

By KENNETH A. BRIGGS

From the day that Karol Cardinal Wojtyla stepped confidently onto the balcony of St. Peter's Basilica as the newly elected Pope John Paul II, he has boldly challenged the church and the world.

Striving to make Christianity a renewed force, he has taken his message from St. Peter's Square around the globe, traveling widely with little apparent regard for his personal safety.

The "Popemobile," an open vehicle such as the one he was riding in when he was shot yesterday, has become a symbol of his mobility. Before his weekly audiences in the square, he stands in the vehicle as it winds through the crowds. The act is a byproduct of his instinctive showmanship and his irrepressible desire to bring the church to the people.

Whether his efforts have been applauded or criticized, John Paul has made the world pay attention to the church. He is a subject of great contentiousness as a leader, but he has remained personally popular to all sides in disputes and has gained a reputation for bending decorum and playing to crowds.

The Pope has undertaken nine major trips in his mission of evangelization, a concept that includes not only the preach-

John Paul II, a laborer in Poland in his youth, has won the world's affection and respect as Pope. Page A7.

ing of the Gospel as an alternative to ideologies such as Marxism but also the advocacy of the rights of the poor and oppressed. Repeatedly he has warned Roman Catholics against using violence to erase injustice. "Violence," he said during his trip to Brazil, "kills what it intends to create."

Elected to the papacy on Oct. 16, 1978, he promised "a ministry of love," and he has plunged into the world scene with a sense of fearless resolve and tireless devotion.

On his trips, he has thrived on schedules that most of his aides find exhausting. Though an intensely private man, he has a knack for stirring crowds — wandering into their midst, donning the hats worn by local people, often speaking in the local language and reaching out to touch hands.

Some of his aides have been nervous

Continued on Page A5, Column 4

2 BULLETS HIT PONTIFF

Part of Intestine Removed in 5-Hour Operation— Hand Also Injured

By HENRY TANNER
Special to The New York Times

ROME, Thursday, May 14 — Pope John Paul II was shot and seriously wounded yesterday as he was standing in an open car moving slowly among more than 10,000 worshipers in St. Peter's Square.

The police arrested a gunman who was later identified as an escaped Turkish murderer who had previously threatened the Pope's life in the name of Islam.

The Pontiff, who was struck by two pistol bullets and wounded in the abdomen, right arm and left hand, underwent 5 hours and 25 minutes of surgery in which parts of his intestine were removed. A hospital bulletin at midnight said he was in "guarded" condition, but the director of surgery expressed confidence that "the Pontiff will recover soon."

By morning the Pope was reported conscious and still in guarded but stable condition.

Pope Falls Into Aides' Arms

The attack occurred as the Pope, dressed in white, was shaking hands and lifting small children in his arms while being driven around the square. Suddenly, just outside the Vatican's bronze gate, there was a burst of gunfire.

One hand rising to his face and blood staining his garments, the Pope faltered and fell into the arms of his Polish secretary, the Rev. Stanislaw Dziwisz, and his personal servant, Angelo Gugel.

The 60-year-old Pope, the spiritual leader of nearly 600 million Roman Catholics around the world, was rushed by ambulance to Gemelli Hospital, two miles north of the Vatican, for surgery.

'How Could They Do It?'

The Pope was conscious as he was taken to the operating room and seemed to speak of the attack on him as the work of more than one person.

"How could they do it?" a nurse quoted the Pope as asking.

The gunman fired four times in the attack, the police said. Two tourists, an American and a Jamaican, were wounded by two of the bullets. Ann Odre, 60, of Buffalo, was struck in the chest; she underwent surgery and was listed in critical condition. Rose Hill, 21, of Jamaica, was slightly wounded in an arm.

The gunman, who the police said was armed with a 9-millimeter Browning automatic, was set upon in the square by bystanders, who knocked the pistol out of his hand. He was then arrested, taken away and later identified as Mehmet Ali Agca, 23. Despite reports that another man had been seen fleeing from the square, the police said they were convinced that the gunman had acted alone.

The police quoted Mr. Agca as having told them, "My life is not important."

He was said to have arrived in Italy

Continued on Page A3, Column 3

Infection Is Main Risk In Pontiff's Recovery; New Surgery Required

By LAWRENCE K. ALTMAN

The medical information on the shooting of Pope John Paul II, although incomplete, showed that the most serious damage was done to the intestines.

Three sections of the bowel, or intestines, were removed in surgery, which was termed successful, at the Gemelli Hospital in Rome.

A second operation will be needed to reconnect portions of the bowel that were surgically severed in a procedure called a temporary exclusion colostomy, which allows removal of bodily wastes through an opening of the colon part of the bowel outside the body.

The Pope received about six pints of blood, the equivalent of about 60 percent of his total blood volume.

Surgical repair of the bowel is common in gunshot wounds to the abdomen, and a temporary colostomy is often necessary in such injuries. Recovery is often complete, provided complications do not develop.

"The main risk now is infection," a hospital spokesman said.

In addition to the bullet that "went through the abdominal cavity," the Pope suffered two minor gunshot wounds in his right arm and one in his left hand, ac-

Continued on Page A2, Column 5

The New York Times

LATE CITY EDITION

Weather: Mostly sunny today; clear
tonight. Mostly sunny tomorrow.
Temperature range: today 76-99;
yesterday 74-94. Details on page B8.

VOL.CXXX... No. 45,003   Copyright © 1981 The New York Times   NEW YORK, WEDNESDAY, JULY 8, 1981   30 cents beyond 50-mile zone from New York City. Higher in air delivery cities.   25 CENTS

Rupturing of Reservoir Pipelines Imperils Newark's Water Supply

Chain Reaction Set Off as Valve Is Opened — Vandalism Suspected

By ROBERT HANLEY
Special to The New York Times

PEQUANNOCK TOWNSHIP, N.J., July 7 — A valve at an aqueduct was opened here today, apparently by vandals, starting a chain reaction that burst two huge pipelines and cut off Newark from its main water supply.

"It's an imminent catastrophe," said James F. Conley, the chief engineer of Newark's Division of Water Supply.

Mr. Conley said that unless the city could activate two existing pipeline interconnections with three other water supply systems and could build two new ones, parts of Newark "will be out of water" in five days.

Other Communities Affected

The pipelines that ruptured, he said, normally carry about 75 million of the 120 million gallons a day used by 600,000 people in Newark and parts of Elizabeth, Bloomfield, Belleville and Wayne.

Those four other communities, all of which purchase some of their water from Newark, began planning for alternative supplies.

Mayor Kenneth A. Gibson of Newark declared a water emergency in the early afternoon, prohibiting all "nonessential uses of water, including lawn watering, car washing and opening of hydrants for any purposes other than firefighting.

Douglas Eldridge, a spokesman for the Mayor, said officials did not expect any declines in water pressure or other serious difficulties in the next day or two. He said some discolored water could come from taps because of adjust-

The New York Times / July 8, 1981

ments being made on the distribution system following the huge loss of water.

But officials said that if the city could not restore a steady water source within five days, parts of Newark would run out of water. A heat wave that pushed temperatures today into the mid-90's and may see higher readings tomorrow is expected to increase water use and has heightened the officials' concern.

A 1,200-foot section of the two pipelines was torn away after they ruptured, sending tens of millions of gallons of water down a hillside here from about 4 A.M. today until the aqueduct's main supply valves at the Charlotteburg Reservoir were shut off sometime after 5 A.M., Mr. Conley said.

The cascading water, estimated at 40

Continued on Page B2, Column 4

U.S. FRAMES POLICY ON HALTING SPREAD OF NUCLEAR ARMS

American Reliability as Seller of Technology Stressed — Use Must Be Peaceful

By TERENCE SMITH
Special to The New York Times

WASHINGTON, July 7 — The Reagan Administration plans to announce shortly that while it is committed to halting the spread of nuclear weapons abroad the United States will be a "clearly reliable and credible" supplier of nuclear technology for peaceful purposes.

This policy is contained in an eight-point set of guidelines that has been prepared by the State Department and submitted to the White House. The White House is expected to issue the list before a meeting in Ottawa July 20-21 of the leaders of seven industrial nations. The spread of nuclear weapons will be one of the items on the agenda.

Although the guidelines are couched in the most general of terms, Administration officials say, they reflect a stronger commitment to halting the spread of nuclear weapons than was contained in Mr. Reagan's campaign statements last year and in a transition paper prepared by his advisers in December.

A Bigger Nuclear Umbrella

As described by Administration officials who have seen the guidelines, there are several principal points:

¶The goals of stopping the spread of nuclear weapons must be strongly reaffirmed.

¶A determined effort should be made to reduce the motivation of other countries to obtain nuclear weapons and an acknowledgement should be given that security considerations are often a basic factor in that decision. To this end, officials said, the United States should be prepared to sell conventional arms and consider extending its own nuclear umbrella.

¶The 1968 Nonproliferation Treaty, by which the nuclear powers undertook not to help others make or acquire nuclear weapons, and the 1967 Treaty of Tlatelolco, Mexico, which established a nuclear-free zone in Latin America, must be emphatically supported.

¶The International Atomic Energy Agency and its system of safeguards against the conversion of nuclear power and research facilities to weapons purposes should be strongly supported.

¶The United States should cooperate with other supplier countries to prevent the transfer of sensitive technology and material to nonnuclear countries where such transfers carry a risk of weapons production.

¶A high level of intelligence activities, including the possible upgrading of

Continued on Page A8, Column 1

REAGAN NOMINATING WOMAN, AN ARIZONA APPEALS JUDGE, TO SERVE ON SUPREME COURT

Associated Press
Judge Sandra Day O'Connor at news conference yesterday in Phoenix

'A Reputation for Excelling'

Sandra Day O'Connor

By B. DRUMMOND AYRES Jr.
Special to The New York Times

WASHINGTON, July 7 — Judge Sandra Day O'Connor's place in history is already secure, based on today's announcement that she will be President Reagan's nominee on the United States Supreme Court.

Woman in the News

But if her past is prologue, after her Senate confirmation Judge O'Connor might well go on to leave even larger "footprints on the sands of time," as Mr. Reagan, quoting Longfellow, described the mark of United States Justices. Thus far in her 51 years, Judge O'Connor has compiled an impressive list of academic, civic, political and legal achievements.

"She's finished at the top in a lot of things," said Mary Ellen Simonson of Phoenix, who was a legislative aide when Mrs. O'Connor was majority leader of the Arizona State Senate, the first woman in the nation to hold such a leadership position.

"She has a reputation for excelling," Mrs. Simonson continued. "As a result she's been one of the state's leading role models for women. Now she's a national role model."

Judge O'Connor, who currently sits on an Arizona Court of Appeals, the state's second highest court, refused this afternoon to discuss "substantive issues" when she met with reporters in Phoenix. And, because of her short, 18-month tenure on the appeals court and its somewhat limited docket, she has faced few of the nettlesome issues routinely taken up by the United States Supreme Court. Nevertheless, her past and her acquaintances provide some insights into her mind and personality.

She is said, by friend and foe alike, to be notably bright, extremely hardworking, meticulous, deliberate, cautious and, above all, a Republican conservative.

"But she has an open mind when it comes to her conservatism," said a longtime friend, Sharon Rockefeller, wife of Gov. John D. Rockefeller IV of West Virginia. "I can't conceive of her closing off her mind to anything."

A leading Democratic politician in

Continued on Page A13, Column 5

REACTION IS MIXED

Senate Seems Favorable but Opposition Arises on Abortion Stands

By STEVEN R. WEISMAN
Special to The New York Times

WASHINGTON, July 7 — President Reagan announced today that he would nominate Sandra Day O'Connor, a 51-year-old judge on the Arizona Court of Appeals, to the United States Supreme Court. If confirmed, she would become the first woman to serve on the Court.

"She is truly a 'person for all seasons,' " Mr. Reagan said this morning, "possessing those unique qualities of temperament, fairness, intellectual

Remarks on Court post, page A12.

capacity and devotion to the public good which have characterized the 101 'brethren' who have preceded her."

White House and Justice Department officials expressed confidence that Judge O'Connor's views were compatible with those espoused over the years by Mr. Reagan, who has been highly critical of some past Supreme Court decisions on the rights of defendants, busing, abortion and other matters.

Some Quick Opposition

From the initial reaction in the Senate, it appeared her nomination would be approved. However, her record of favoring the proposed Federal equal rights amendment and having sided once against anti-abortion interests while she was a legislator provoked immediate opposition to her confirmation by the National Right to Life Committee, Moral Majority and other groups opposed to abortion.

At a brief news conference in Phoenix, Judge O'Connor declined to explain her views, saying that she intended to leave such matters to her confirmation hearings before the Senate Judiciary Committee. [Page A12.]

Mr. Reagan, himself an opponent of abortions, said in response to a question that he was "completely satisfied" with her position on that issue.

No Radical Shift Expected

White House officials were hopeful that Judge O'Connor's appointment could be historic not only because she is a woman but also because her presence on the Court, as a replacement for Associate Justice Potter Stewart, who was often a swing vote between ideological camps on the Court, could shift the Court's balance to the right.

However, an examination of the Court's voting patterns suggests no radical shift is likely even if she does vote with the more conservative Justices. [News analysis, page A13.]

It is the additional hope of Mr. Reagan's aides to make the Court even more conservative in the years ahead, when more vacancies are possible.

Judge O'Connor was appointed to

Continued on Page A13, Column 2

New Pact Ends 7-Day Strike Of Garbage Haulers in Jersey

By ALFONSO A. NARVAEZ
Special to The New York Times

WEST PATERSON, N.J., July 7 — A seven-day strike against private garbage haulers in 108 northern and central New Jersey communities ended today when 1,400 drivers and loaders accepted a three-year contract that gives them a 50 percent pay increase.

Garbage trucks in the 12 affected counties will begin rolling early tomorrow, and Picket signs that had blocked municipal sanitation employees will come down from entrances to landfills.

The new contract was accepted after a long and confusing day in which the union members first rejected an agreement hammered out by negotiators in an 18-hour session at the Sheraton Heights Hotel in Hasbrouck Heights.

$155-a-Week Raise

When that proposal was rejected, the negotiators immediately went into new talks.

The union then approved a proposal that gives the drivers the $155-a-week raise over three years that was contained in the proposal they rejected, but adds three days of sick leave a year and guarantees that double time for work on the sixth day will go to workers with seniority. The drivers currently earn $310 a week for an average six-day, 48-hour week, and the loaders get about $50 less.

The union also won an additional paid holiday, four weeks of vacation after 15

years and $56 in increased health and welfare benefits.

The agreement provides for an immediate increase of $55 a week, then $35 a week on Jan. 1, 1982, $20 a week on July 1, 1982, and $45 more on July 1, 1983.

The cost of the package to residents and communities in the affected areas has not yet been calculated. However, during the negotiations, the State Attorney General, James J. Zazzali, assured the owners — members of the New Jersey State Municipal Contractors Association and the Solid Waste Industry Association — that their requests for rate increases would be handled expeditiously.

The membership did not vote on the final package. The leaders of the union,

Continued on Page B4, Column 1

Sun-Powered Airplane Crosses Channel

Special to The New York Times

MANSTON, England, July 7 — After several earlier unsuccessful attempts, the first solar-powered airplane succeeded today in crossing the English Channel.

It took an atypically sunny English summer afternoon and a five-and-a-half-hour flight, but late this afternoon, the Solar Challenger dropped slowly onto the concrete landing strip of Manston Royal Air Force Base, on the southeastern coast of England.

Designed by Paul MacCready, who also designed the first human-powered plane to cross the Channel, the 210-pound Solar Challenger is powered by 16,000 photovoltaic cells on the wings that convert solar energy to electricity, which drives the motor.

No Battery Power

Other airplanes have flown on solar power, but only the Solar Challenger has been able to do so without the help of storage batteries. The project was paid for largely by DuPont and employed many high-strength, low-weight materials made by that company.

Starting from an airport at Cormeilles-en-Vexin, 25 miles northwest of Paris, the spidery plane, which has a wingspan of 47 feet, made the 165-mile journey at an average speed of about 30 miles per hour and a cruising altitude of 11,000 feet.

Standing in the deep grass along the main east-west runway at Cormeilles, a small crowd of about 30 persons had gathered to cheer on the tiny, transparent aircraft and its pilot. They watched the delicate plane corkscrew slowly and almost silently into the sky above the airport. The 2.7 horsepower electric motor produced only a slight hum.

At an altitude of about 2,000 feet, Stephen Ptacek, the 28-year-old pilot from Golden, Colo., headed northwest in the direction of the Channel. In two or three minutes, he disappeared from sight.

Mr. Ptacek was greeted at the Man-

Continued on Page B4, Column 1

Associated Press
French policemen watch as Solar Challenger begins flight to England

Prelate, 52, Chosen By the Pope to Lead The Polish Church

By JOHN DARNTON
Special to The New York Times

WARSAW, July 7 — Bishop Jozef Glemp of Warmia was named today by Pope John Paul II as Archbishop of Gniezno and Warsaw and the Primate of Poland, succeeding Stefan Cardinal Wyszynski, who died on May 28.

The new head of the Church in this overwhelmingly Roman Catholic nation said he would continue the policies begun by his predecessor of dialogue and cooperation with both the Government and the Solidarity labor movement.

"I am convinced I must follow the road laid out by Cardinal Wyszynski," he said in an interview. "The work of the Primate is not political. It is pastoral. But if we in the church are to do our duty, we must not remain above social issues. If the Solidarity and other social movements want to follow the truth and the light, we will give them our protection. It is in line with the proper role of the church."

Archbishop Glemp, 52 years old and a specialist in both canon and civil law, said he believed in working closely with the Conference of Bishops and would strive for collegial rule. Cardinal Wy-

Continued on Page A6, Column 1

Baker Vows Support for Nominee

By FRANCIS X. CLINES
Special to The New York Times

WASHINGTON, July 7 — Anti-abortion groups today denounced President Reagan's decision to nominate Judge Sandra Day O'Connor to the Supreme Court, but initial reaction in the Senate, which will vote on confirmation, was favorable.

"I commend the President for the courage of his decision," said Howard H. Baker Jr., the Senate Republican majority leader. "I am delighted with his choice, and I pledge my full support for her confirmation by the full Senate."

The National Right to Life Committee, an amalgam of anti-abortion lobbying groups in the 50 states, said that it would mobilize its members to "prevail upon senators to oppose this nomination." The committee said that Judge O'Connor was "pro-abortion" as a member of the Arizona State Legislature.

Dr. Carolyn Gerster, a vice president of the National Right to Life Committee, said that the nominee, as a legislator, voted in 1974 not to allow an anti-abortion resolution out of caucus, thus killing it. The resolution asked Congress to pass a Constitutional amendment protecting the fetus except when the mother's life was in danger, and allowed abortions in the case of rape.

Dr. Gerster based her statement of

Continued on Page A12, Column 1

INSIDE

9 More Executed in Iran
Iran executed nine opponents in its drive against "counterrevolutionary" elements. It also ordered Reuters to close its Teheran bureau. Page A3.

Upset in Mississippi Vote
Wayne Dowdy, a Democrat, apparently won a Congressional election in Mississippi, beating a strong supporter of President Reagan. Page A18.

"All the News
That's Fit to Print"

The New York Times

LATE CITY EDITION

Weather: Chance of drizzle today and tonight. Partly cloudy tomorrow. Temperature range: today 51-63; yesterday 59-68. Details, page D24.

VOL.CXXXI.. No. 45,094

Copyright © 1981 The New York Times

NEW YORK, WEDNESDAY, OCTOBER 7, 1981

30 cents beyond 50-mile zone from New York City. Higher in air delivery cities.

25 CENTS

SADAT ASSASSINATED AT ARMY PARADE AS MEN AMID RANKS FIRE INTO STANDS; VICE PRESIDENT AFFIRMS 'ALL TREATIES'

Israel Stunned and Anxious; Few Arab Nations Mourning

Worry in Jerusalem

By DAVID K. SHIPLER
Special to The New York Times

JERUSALEM, Oct. 6 — Israel, which had such a high stake in the survival of President Anwar el-Sadat, reacted with stunned anxiety today to news of his assassination in Cairo.

A fear for the peace treaty between Egypt and Israel dominated all emotions. So thoroughly had the Egyptian leader come to personify that peace, and so deeply had Israelis distrusted the motives of other Egyptians, that his death today swept away confidence as swiftly as his historic visit to Jerusalem in 1977 had brought hope.

"The very fact that one bullet can cancel an agreement," said Geula Cohen, who heads the Tehiya Party in Parliament, "is a sign that not only the withdrawal, but all these procedures, must be stopped. There is no doubt that this incident confirms all that we have been saying; there is no stability in this region and one cannot make an agreement which is dependent on a nondemocratic regime and one man."

Question About Treaty

Even in the likelihood that Mr. Sadat's successor will adhere to the treaty's precepts, serious questions are bound to linger for some time, and the Government of Prime Minister Menachem Begin is certain to face rising political difficulties domestically in completing the return of Sinai to Egypt, scheduled for April 1982.

This afternoon, voices on the right were raised in demands that all prepa-

Continued on Page A9, Column 5

Jubilation in Beirut

By JOHN KIFNER
Special to The New York Times

BEIRUT, Lebanon, Oct. 6 — There was no mourning in most of the Arab world today for President Anwar el-Sadat of Egypt, whose separate peace with Israel had led to his isolation.

Public jubilation was reported in Syria, Iraq and Libya, and the streets of mostly Moslem, leftist-dominated West Beirut echoed with gunfire in celebration of the assassination. Most public statements attributed Mr. Sadat's death to discontent with the Egyptian-Israeli peace accord.

However, the Sudan, Egypt's closest friend in the Arab world, condemned the assassination and said it stood with the Egyptian Government against all forms of conspiracy and aggression.

Hope for Arab Unity Expressed

There was little public comment in Saudi Arabia. At the United Nations, Gaafar M. Allagany, the acting head of the Saudi mission, expressed sorrow "that this had to happen at a crucial stage." Noting Saudi opposition to Mr. Sadat's policies, he said, "We hope that our sister country will rejoin the Arab states."

An aide to Yasir Arafat, the leader of the Palestine Liberation Organization, said here on hearing of the shooting of Mr. Sadat, "We shake the hand that fired the bullets."

The aide, Saleh Khalef, better known by the code name Abu Iyad, said that "all attempts at dialogue" with Mr. Sadat had failed and that "it was inevi-

Continued on Page A9, Column 1

As President Sadat watched parade with Vice President Hosni Mubarak, left, and Defense Minister Abu Ghazala ...

Associated Press

... uniformed men, apparently part of the assassination team, approached the reviewing stand. Moments later, ...

CBS News

... after the attack, victims lay sprawled on the floor of the stand.

CBS News

Egypt After Sadat

Washington's Policies Facing New Problems

By BERNARD GWERTZMAN
Special to The New York Times

WASHINGTON, Oct. 6 — The assassination of President Anwar el-Sadat of Egypt created a new series of problems for future American policy in the Middle East at a time when the Reagan Administration was already worried about the spread of disorder in the region.

Administration officials, concerned about the chaos in Lebanon, the increased subversive activity of Libya and the Soviet inroads in Afghanistan, Southern Yemen and Ethiopia, had viewed Mr. Sadat as a solid, pro-American anchor of stability in the Middle East. With his death, there is now apprehension about the situation in Egypt as well.

At the White House, President Reagan said the United States had lost "a close friend" and "a champion of peace." But the Administration refrained from any public assessment of the possible repercussions of the assassination. [Page A12.]

The mood in Washington was one of shock and sadness at the loss of a leader who had done what would have seemed impossible a decade ago. He replaced the Prime Minister of Israel as the favorite Middle East statesman in Washington.

On virtually every Middle East, African and world issue, the Reagan Administration and Mr. Sadat saw eye to eye. With the expectation that Mr. Sadat would be in control of Egypt's policies

News Analysis

Continued on Page A9, Column 2

Cairo Regime's Plans Now Question Marks

The following article is by William E. Farrell, who has reported on Anwar el-Sadat's diplomacy from Jerusalem as well as Cairo.

Special to The New York Times

CAIRO, Oct. 6 — Anwar el-Sadat's rule in Egypt was that of one man who skillfully engineered, in his 11 years in power, the means of controlling every important facet of Egyptian life.

Although he was dismissed by many as a somewhat feckless interim leader when he became President after the death of Gamal Abdel Nasser, Mr. Sadat gradually showed that he had staying power, political skill and an ability that transformed him into a world statesman when he paid his historic visit to Jerusalem in the search for peace.

Now, with his sudden, violent death, many questions about the future of Egypt and its role in the world are beginning to be raised in this saddened capital and in many other countries.

Over the years, Mr. Sadat controlled his political party, the National Democratic Party; he supervised the Egyptian press, which lauded him; he was commander of the military, a key factor in his rule, and he had a facility for taking the pulse of Egypt's masses — about 43 million people. Some 67 percent of them are illiterate, but he was able to reach them by television and radio. He often did, in long speeches that had a pedagogical tone.

Some Egyptians opposed Mr. Sadat,

Continued on Page A8, Column 3

AT LEAST 8 KILLED

Speaker of Parliament Is Interim President — Election in 60 Days

By WILLIAM E. FARRELL
Special to The New York Times

CAIRO, Oct. 6 — President Anwar el-Sadat of Egypt was shot and killed today by a group of men in military uniforms who hurled grenades and fired rifles at him as he watched a military parade commemorating the 1973 war against Israel.

Vice President Hosni Mubarak, in announcing Mr. Sadat's death, said

Mubarak speech excerpted, page A9.

Egypt's treaties and international commitments would be respected. He said the Speaker of Parliament, Sufi Abu Taleb, would serve as interim President pending an election in 60 days.

The assassins' bullets ended the life of a man who earned a reputation for making bold decisions in foreign affairs, a reputation based in large part on his decision in 1977 to journey to the camp of Egypt's foe, Israel, to make peace.

Sadat Forged His Own Regime

Regarded as an interim ruler when he came to power in 1970 on the death of Gamal Abdel Nasser, Mr. Sadat forged his own regime and ran Egypt single-handedly. He was bent on moving this impoverished country into the late 20th century, a drive that led him to abandon an alliance with the Soviet Union and embrace the West.

That rule ended abruptly and violently today. As jet fighters roared overhead, the killers sprayed the reviewing

Of humble origin, Anwar el-Sadat became a statesman known for daring actions. Obituary, pages A8 and A9.

stand with bullets while thousands of horrified people — officials, diplomats and journalists, including this correspondent — looked on.

Killers' Identity Not Disclosed

Information gathered from a number of sources indicated that eight persons had been killed and 27 wounded in the attack. Later reports, all unconfirmed, put the toll at 11 dead and 38 wounded.

The authorities did not disclose the identity of the assassins. They were being interrogated, and there were no clear indications whether the attack was to have been part of a coup attempt.

[In Washington, American officials said an army major, a lieutenant and four enlisted men had been involved in the attack. The major and two of the soldiers were killed and the others captured, the officials said.]

The assassination followed a recent crackdown by Mr. Sadat against religious extremists and other political op-

Continued on Page A8, Column 1

Who Murdered President Sadat?

In the confusion swirling around the assassination of Egypt's President, Anwar el-Sadat, little information was made public in Cairo about the killers. Egyptian authorities were known to have several uniformed men in custody last night, but the Egyptians gave no details about the number or identity of the attackers or the reasons for the attack.

"Islamic fundamentalists" within the Egyptian Army was the characterization offered by Secretary of State Alexander M. Haig Jr. to a group of senators late yesterday afternoon. He also mentioned discontent among some Egyptian officers with the peace treaty that Mr. Sadat signed with Israel.

Reagan Administration officials said their information was that six uniformed men had taken part in the shooting, that three were killed and that the others were captured. They said that at least one was linked to the Takfir Wahigra Society, a radical right-wing Islamic group whose name translates as Repentance and Atonement. Its past actions include the slaying of the Egyptian Minister of Religious Affairs in 1977.

In Beirut, a handful of organizations stepped forward to claim responsibility for the killing, with representatives calling news agencies with their statements. But Reagan Administration officials said they doubted that any of them had been involved in the killing. Details are on page A12.

Other News

'Safety Net' Bill Passes

The House of Representatives approved spending $87.3 billion for social programs, despite President Reagan's threat to veto the bill. Page B10.

Ulster Prison Rule Is Eased

Britain gave inmates in Northern Ireland the right to wear their own clothing but stopped short of meeting the hunger strikers' demands. Page A3.

Runoff Due in Atlanta

Andrew Young, the former diplomat, and a State Representative, Sidney Marcus, won places in a mayoral runoff in Atlanta. Page A20.

Lindbergh Papers Unsealed

Evidence in the kidnapping-murder of the infant son of Charles A. Lindbergh 49 years ago will be opened to review by scholars and others. Page B1.

The New York Times/Oct. 7, 1981

The Scene Of the Assassination In Cairo

Men in military uniforms stepped from a truck and fired on President Sadat, who was in the center of the reviewing stand. The wounded president was carried to the back of the stand and flown south by helicopter to Maadi Military Hospital.

Residence

Mile

0   1

"All the News That's Fit to Print"

The New York Times

LATE CITY EDITION

Weather: Increasing cloudiness today; rain likely tonight, tomorrow. Temperature range: today 29-40; yesterday 28-38. Details, page C21.

VOL. CXXXI... No. 45,162

Copyright © 1981 The New York Times

NEW YORK, MONDAY, DECEMBER 14, 1981

30 cents beyond 50-mile zone from New York City. Higher in air delivery cities.

25 CENTS

POLAND RESTRICTS CIVIL AND UNION RIGHTS; SOLIDARITY ACTIVISTS URGE GENERAL STRIKE

Judge Reduces Westway Suits To Single Issue

Landfill's Effect on Fish Still to Be Considered

By ROBIN HERMAN

A Federal judge has whittled down the longstanding legal attacks on the Westway highway project to a single issue — the fate of fish in the Hudson River — and he will set a hearing date today for arguments on that obstacle.

The judge, Thomas F. Griesa of Federal District Court in Manhattan, has dismissed all objections to the highway contained in two remaining lawsuits except for questions on the effect the landfill for the project would have on aquatic life.

John Marino, the state's Assistant Transportation Commissioner for New York City, said that the judge's action was "a very positive development" and that it reflected the Carey administration's interest in seeing the highway built.

As for environmentalists' concern about aquatic life — especially striped bass — Mr. Marino said yesterday: "When was the last time you had striped bass from the Hudson? That's our comment on it. I don't expect that in the end this will be a serious issue. The way is clear for Westway. It's a go-ahead."

Most Objections Dismissed

The judge, meeting in private on Friday with both the plaintiffs and the state and Federal defendants, dismissed altogether a suit brought in 1974 by Action for Rational Transit, an anti-Westway group, which was attempting to block the project. The suit contended chiefly that the highway would violate Federal clean-air standards.

Also, according to both sides, Judge Griesa dismissed most objections made in a 1977 suit brought by the Sierra Club and other environmental and civic groups. That suit challenged the dredge-and-fill permit for the project granted by the Army Corps of Engineers.

The suit charged that the Government had not adequately examined alternative routes, the trade-in of the Federal Westway funds for mass-transit funds or the possibility that the landfill on which the highway would be built could threaten New Jersey with flooding. It also questioned whether the river's aquatic life had been considered in the environmental impact statement. The highway's official cost is $1.7 billion, but it is expected to exceed that figure by millions of dollars.

After a hearing, possibly next month, on the aquatic-life question, Judge Griesa has said he will issue a written decision on all claims. At that time, the two groups of plaintiffs can appeal the earlier dismissals, which the judge made orally.

Albert Butzel, the lawyer representing the Sierra Club, said yesterday that,

Continued on Page B16, Column 3

Budget Cuts, Weak Market Hurt Gasohol

By DOUGLAS MARTIN
Special to The New York Times

DES MOINES — Interest in gasohol, which has attracted more Government encouragement in recent years than any other energy source, has been fading — the result of an oversupply of crude oil and the Administration's efforts to curb Federal spending.

Enthusiasm for gasohol, a mixture of gasoline and alcohol, was born amid farmers' anger over the restrictions on grain sales to the Soviet Union and consumers' concern about the shutdown of Iran's oil fields. The fuel seemed a way for America to cultivate its way out of the energy crisis, drawing on this nation's unrivaled agricultural base. Most commercial gasohol is a 90-10 mixture of refined gasoline and ethanol derived from corn.

Pledge of Subsidies

The Carter Administration and Congress responded to the apparent groundswell by pledging subsidies for gasohol exceeding $30 billion by 1992, making it, gallon for gallon, by far the most heavily subsidized fuel.

But over the past few months, the White House has moved vigorously to slash funding for gasohol plants, large

Continued on Page D5, Column 5

HAIG WARNS SOVIET

He Says U.S. Is 'Seriously Concerned' and Backs New Warsaw Talks

By BERNARD GWERTZMAN
Special to The New York Times

BRUSSELS, Dec. 13 — Secretary of State Alexander M. Haig Jr. said today that the United States was "seriously concerned" about the imposition of martial law in Poland, and he renewed the West's warning to the Soviet Union not to interfere in the crisis.

After talking by phone with President Reagan, who was then at Camp David, Md., Mr. Haig said at a news conference here that the United States was urging

News conference excerpts, page A19.

the Polish Government to resume negotiations and to pursue a policy of compromise with the Solidarity trade union to prevent an outbreak of civil strife that could worsen the situation.

Mr. Haig said Polish authorities had assured the United States Embassy this morning that "there will be no return" to the situation that existed in Poland prior to establishment of the independent union in 1980. In addition, he said Western intelligence agencies had not detected any Soviet military moves "which would be a source of alarm."

"But we continue to watch the situation very carefully," he said.

'Very Serious' Consequences

If the Soviet Union intervened in Poland, Mr. Haig said, "the consequences would be very serious and long lasting." Western officials have previously said that, in that event, all trade with the Soviet Union would be suspended and political relations would be sharply curtailed.

President Reagan, arriving back at the White House, was asked about the danger of Soviet intervention and said that the United States had several times "made it plain how seriously we would view interference" by the Soviet Union. The Polish Ambassador and the Soviet Deputy Chief of Mission were summoned to the State Department for discussions on the situation. [Page A15.]

Mr. Haig was scheduled to leave Brussels this morning for a seven-day trip to Israel, Turkey, Pakistan, India, Egypt and Morocco. But after talking by phone with Vice President Bush and with various foreign ministers, Mr. Haig decided at the last minute to scrap his travel plans. Reporters traveling with him

Continued on Page A19, Column 4

Police in Wroclaw surround the Solidarity offices and keep crowds away. Photo was made from inside the building. Wroclaw, formerly Breslau, is an industrial city 190 miles southwest of Warsaw, near the Czechoslovak border.

Sign Press/Black Star

Communism and Better Life: Poles Found Wait Too Long

John Darnton, who has been chief of The New York Times bureau in Warsaw since September 1979, reports in the following article on the problems underlying the crisis in Poland.

Special to The New York Times

WARSAW — Behind the workers' revolt that began with strikes in the summer of 1980 and grew to a revolution on the shoulders of the Solidarity union, the operation of which was suspended when martial law was declared, lies a story of failure. It is the failure of Communism, in the eyes of the workers, to deliver on its promise of a better life.

The revolt sprang from an unspoken consensus among Poles that despite more than three decades of sacrifice and toil, conditions of everyday life were scarcely improving and that the Communist system had failed most dramatically in precisely those areas, in the realm of social welfare, where its ideology called for greater exertion and improvement.

Appalling dirt and safety conditions in factories, cramped and unavailable apartments, substandard and sloppy health care, lines in front of meat shops — food shortages in general despite a stringent rationing system — these were the distinguishing traits of what the Government referred to as "people's Po-

land." They were glossed over, ignored or denied by successive governments that pressed instead for higher production statistics in heavy industry.

They certainly did not keep pace with expectations and, compared with the West, which more and more Poles were visiting when restrictions were loosened as the cold war period came to a close, Poland was falling behind.

'My Life Doesn't Count'

"All my adult life I've been told that my life doesn't count, that I'm sacrificing myself for my children," said one well-known Polish journalist, speaking privately. "Well, now I'm 48. My son is 19. His life is no better than mine and he's being told he must sacrifice himself for his children. What's life all about, anyway?"

Satisfying the basic needs of the population was given low priority when it came to allocating investment in the national budget, but it was given lip service in public propaganda and high-

Continued on Page A18, Column 1

Army's Rule: Two Targets

General Hits at Foes In Party and Solidarity

By DAVID BINDER
Special to The New York Times

WASHINGTON, Dec. 13 — Poland's soldier-leader, Wojciech Jaruzelski, has struck at what he perceives as the two main roots of his country's current troubles: the radical "confrontationists" of the Solidarity labor movement and the still influential members of the Communist Party's old guard.

His martial law decree, accompanied by the detention of Solidarity leaders and former party leaders and an internal communications blackout, has eliminated the cadres and the instruments that might have been used to rally supporters against his rule.

A 56,000-Member Force

The state of emergency was long in the making, in the estimate of Administration specialists on Polish affairs, and was foreshadowed not only by large-scale maneuvers of Soviet troops on Poland's borders earlier in the year, but also by the brief mobilization of the Polish Internal Defense Forces last September.

The Internal Defense Forces are heavily equipped paramilitary security troops with 56,000 members. They are trained for riot control and are deployed in three contingents, one in War-

Continued on Page A18, Column 1

WALESA NEGOTIATES

New Army Council Bans Rallies and Sets Wide Grounds for Arrests

By JOHN DARNTON

WARSAW, Dec. 13 — Poland's new military leaders issued a decree of martial law today, drastically restricting civil rights and suspending the operations of the Solidarity union. The union's activists reacted with an appeal for an immediate general strike to protest.

A proclamation broadcast by the newly formed Martial Council for National Redemption, now the top authority in the country, also banned all kinds

Premier's address, page A16.

of public gatherings and demonstrations and ordered the internment of citizens whose loyalty to the state was under "justified suspicion."

The military rule was announced in a dramatic broadcast at dawn by Gen. Wojciech Jaruzelski, the Prime Minister and Communist Party leader, who said a strict regime was necessary to save Poland from catastrophe and civil war. Hours before, Solidarity leaders meeting in Gdansk had proposed holding a national referendum on forming a non-Communist government.

No Reports of Violence

Following a provision in the constitution, General Jaruzelski declared a "state of war," equivalent to a state of emergency in other countries.

There were no immediate reports of violence, but opposition to the military move seemed in the offing. Union activists, in dozens of leaflets being circulated in the streets, called for an immediate general strike.

Many Solidarity activists were in detention following coordinated police raids across the country after midnight last night. So were several former leaders of Poland's Communist Party.

Among the detained were some of the top leaders and advisers of the Solidarity union who had assembled in Gdansk to work out strategy in the latest confrontation with the Government.

Walesa Flown to Warsaw

Lech Walesa, Solidarity's chairman, who became an international figure by his role in the workers' uprising of last summer, was meeting with Government officials at a site outside Warsaw today, Jerzy Urban, a Government spokesman, said at a news conference.

Mr. Walesa was flown to Warsaw in a Government plane at 4 A.M. to begin talks with Stanislaw Ciosek, the Minister of Trade Union Affairs, according to the Interpress information agency. Mr. Urban said that Mr. Walesa had not been detained at any point.

Mr. Urban also stressed that Soli-

Continued on Page A16, Column 1

Demonstrators marching past the Polish Consulate on 37th Street near Madison Avenue. Similar protests against the military takeover in Poland were held in Paris, Vienna, London, Rome, Brussels and other European cities.

The New York Times/Dith Pran

Other Developments

Warsaw mood — Every hour on the hour beginning at 6 A.M., Poles listening to their radios heard Prime Minister Wojciech Jaruzelski speak in solemn tones about having placed the country under martial law. The interludes were filled with music. More cars were on the streets than is usual for a Sunday, particularly in a period of acute gasoline shortage. All telephones had stopped functioning, presumably to keep those who might wish to resist from coordinating actions. Page A17.

Washington concern — The Reagan Administration called in the Polish Ambassador and the Soviet Deputy Chief of Mission for discussions. Several allied diplomats were also called to the State Department. President Reagan returned ahead of schedule from a weekend at Camp David to be briefed on Poland by Administration officials. Page A15.

Soviet silence — The Soviet Union made no official comment on the declaration of martial law in Poland. The Polish developments were reported in a series of brief and largely factual dispatches by the official news agency Tass. Page A19.

Papal appeal — Pope John Paul II asked his fellow Poles to pray for peace and to do everything in their power "to peacefully build a peaceful future." Page A14.

German reaction — Chancellor Helmut Schmidt of West Germany, visiting a small East German town, seemed intent on demonstrating through his presence that there was no reason for the West to dramatize the situation in Poland. Page A20.

Polish-American reaction — Tens of

thousands of Polish-Americans across the nation voiced outrage and despair. In the New York metropolitan area and in Chicago, Philadelphia and other centers of Polish-American life, the outpouring was emotional but nonviolent as workers, scholars, writers, clergymen and diplomats spoke of their homeland. With a communications blackout severing their contacts with friends and relatives in Poland, there was also widespread concern over loved ones and acquaintances. Page A17.

INSIDE

U.S. Wins Davis Cup

John McEnroe defeated José-Luis Clerc in five sets to give the United States a victory over Argentina in the final of the Davis Cup. Page C1.

Sakharov: Weak but Elated

The Soviet dissident Andrei D. Sakharov and his wife were said to be emaciated but in high spirits at the success of their hunger strike. Page A3.

Biotechnology: Better Breeds and Crops

By HAROLD M. SCHMECK Jr.

The first major products from the young industry are expected to go on world markets next year, a development that some experts believe will usher in a new era in the prevention and treatment of disease.

Agriculture will probably be the first to benefit from such products, including vaccines against foot-and-mouth disease and scours, two economically serious diseases that afflict cattle.

Two important medical products now undergoing extensive clinical tests are expected to follow, probably in 1983 in the United States: human insulin and human growth hormone produced in bacteria by gene-splicing techniques. Animal growth hormone produced by the same techniques is also being developed for agricultural use.

The predicted uses of gene-splicing

techniques include such diverse products as industrial enzymes, food additives, medical and veterinary test chemicals and drugs, as well as improved plant species.

The long-range potential uses for the chemical, mining, energy and forest products industries, and for agriculture, dwarf all the prospective uses for medicine. Except for products related to health and food, however, the emergence of competitive major industrial

Continued on Page D13, Column 1

The New Genetics

Biology at a Turning Point

Second of three articles.

"All the News
That's Fit to Print"

The New York Times

Late Edition
Weather: Rain ending today, mostly
cloudy and cool; cloudy and cooler tonight. Partly cloudy and mild tomorrow.
Temperatures: today 61-66, tonight 54-
56; yesterday 55-60. Details, page B10.

VOL.CXXXI..No. 45,337   Copyright © 1982 The New York Times   NEW YORK, MONDAY, JUNE 7, 1982   30 CENTS

BIG ISRAELI FORCE INVADES SOUTH LEBANON; SHARP FIGHTING WITH GUERRILLAS REPORTED

Limited Summit Agreement Set on Trade and Currency

By RICHARD EDER
Special to The New York Times

VERSAILLES, France, June 6 — The eighth summit conference of the industrialized nations reached limited agreement today on two contentious subjects — East-West trade and the handling of currency fluctuations — and produced something of a breakthrough on North-South relations.

The agreements themselves were the subject of some disagreement: whether they bridged or merely papered over fundamental differences. Prime Minister Margaret Thatcher of Britain described the atmosphere as one of unanimity. Prime Minister Pierre Elliott Trudeau of Canada called it "difficult."

The conference was, in any case,

The accord fell short of American hopes and was seen as having little world impact. News analysis and economic analysis, with text of the communiqué, page D6.

shaded and sometimes interrupted by the fighting in the Falklands and Israel's invasion of Lebanon. Today's final hard bargaining on East-West trade was interrupted by the announcement by President François Mitterrand of France of the Israeli move, and the

assembled leaders approved a statement expressing shock.

The Falkland crisis, apart from producing an embarrassing flip-flop over the United States vote in the Security Council, caused Mrs. Thatcher to fly back to London tonight after the state dinner in the Versailles chateau's Hall of Mirrors.

She thus missed the musical masque and ballet and other festivities organized by France to make this the most glittering summit conference, whether or not it will have turned out to be the most productive.

The seven nations — the United States, Japan, Britain, France, West Germany, Italy and Canada — agreed to a compromise on the East-West trade issue. It fell short of American hopes for abolition of government-subsidized financing for such trade. Instead, it calls for "caution" in financial dealings with the Soviet bloc, and it says there is a need for "commercial prudence in limiting export credits."

The Reagan Administration had

Associated Press
President Reagan at economic meeting yesterday in Versailles.

Continued on Page D7, Column 1

Britain Confirms the Landing Of 3,000 Soldiers From QE2

By R.W. APPLE Jr.
Special to The New York Times

LONDON, June 6 — British troops besieging the Argentine garrison at Stanley in the Falkland Islands have been reinforced by 3,000 fresh infantrymen from the liner Queen Elizabeth 2, the Defense Ministry announced tonight.

The arrival of the Fifth Infantry Brigade, including a battalion each of Scots and Welsh Guards and Gurkha Rifles, raises British strength on East Falkland Island to about 8,000. About 5,000 paratroops and Royal Marine commandos went ashore last month, and most are drawn up opposite the 7,000 Argentine defenders of Stanley, the Falklands capital.

In Buenos Aires today, Argentina said its planes and artillery had bombarded the British positions surrounding Stanley. Senior military officers said they expected the British to launch a major assault on the Argentine garrison at any moment. [Page A6.]

There were hints in London that the long-awaited assault on Stanley had al-

ready begun in a report from Michael Nicholson of Britain's Independent Television News.

"The British push is really on," he said in a broadcast this evening. "There are under way at this moment operations which I can only describe as extraordinarily daring which cannot be revealed until they are completed, but which, almost certainly if they are successful, will surely bring the end of this war that much closer."

Mr. Nicholson reported that the Gurkhas, composed entirely of Nepalese volunteers, were operating on their own, "crisscrossing East Falkland" in a search for Argentine units lurking in the interior, between the British base at San Carlos Bay and their forward headquarters near Mount Kent.

According to unofficial sources, the Fifth Brigade transferred from the Queen Elizabeth to the assault ships In-

Continued on Page A8, Column 3

United Press International
An armored personnel carrier, part of the Israeli invasion force, breaks through the border with southern Lebanon.

U.N. COUNCIL ASKS ISRAELI PULLBACK

But Delegate, Hinting Refusal, Notes 'Limit of Endurance'

By BERNARD D. NOSSITER
Special to The New York Times

UNITED NATIONS, N.Y., June 6 — The Security Council unanimously demanded tonight that Israel pull its invading forces out of Lebanon. There was, however, no indication that Israel would pay any more attention to this order than to the unanimous Council demand Saturday night for a cease-fire.

Instead, Yehuda Z. Blum, the Israeli delegate, taunted the Council's 15 mem-

Leaders of the major industrial democracies expressed shock at Versailles over Israel's move. Page A14.

bers for "evincing not the slightest interest" in scores of terrorist acts he attributed to the Palestine Liberation Organization. "How many Israelis have to be killed by terrorists that this body can be persuaded that the limits of our endurance have been reached?" he asked rhetorically. "Israel cannot expect this body even to deplore P.L.O. barbarism against Israel's civilian population, let alone take any steps with a view towards curbing that barbarism."

Tonight's text, a compromise drafted by Ireland after a day of discussion behind closed doors, directed Israel to withdraw its forces "forthwith and unconditionally." The Soviet Union insisted on that last phrase.

At the demand of the United States, the resolution calls on Israel and the Palestinians to halt all military action "within Lebanon and across the Lebanese-Israeli border." That language was designed to cover P.L.O. shelling into Israel as well as Israeli strikes. The document directs both sides to report

Continued on Page A14, Column 5

The New York Times/June 7, 1982
Israeli tanks and troops moved into Lebanon in three columns (arrows). The land assaults, together with air and sea attacks, were aimed at the main Palestinian strongholds — Tyre, Beaufort Castle, Nabatiye and Kawkaba. Warships destroyed the Qasmiye Bridge spanning the Litani River north of Tyre, cutting the main Palestinian supply line. Towns shown in northern Israel were among those shelled last week by Palestinian forces.

THOUSANDS ATTACK

Some Syrian Units in Area Said to Have Clashed With Raiding Force

By THOMAS L. FRIEDMAN
Special to The New York Times

BEIRUT, Lebanon, Monday, June 7 — The Israeli Army invaded southern Lebanon by land, sea and air Sunday in an attack aimed at destroying the main military bases of the Palestine Liberation Organization.

More than 250 Israeli tanks and armored personnel carriers, as well as thousands of infantrymen, rolled past the observation posts of the United Nations peacekeeping troops in southern Lebanon at 11 A.M. (5 A.M., New York time) and fanned out across the frontier, according to a United Nations spokesman in Beirut.

By late Sunday evening the Israelis had taken several P.L.O. outposts in the craggy hills of southern Lebanon and were engaged in fierce firefights with the Palestinians for control of scores of other strongholds along the 33-mile front, stretching from the port city of Tyre to the foothills of Mount Hermon, the United Nations spokesman said.

Main Targets Besieged

In the first day of the invasion the Israelis besieged all their main targets — Tyre, Beaufort Castle, Nabatiye and Kawkaba — but the Palestinians stood their ground and did not flee north. The number of casualties was not known.

Israel said this morning that Beaufort Castle, a Crusader stronghold overlooking the border that the Palestinians have used as a communications and artillery base, was captured during the night by an Israeli infantry battalion. But the Palestinians denied that the castle had fallen.

It appeared that at least a few elements of Syria's force of about 25,000 men in Lebanon had become involved in confrontations with the Israelis.

The state-run Beirut radio reported Sunday night that Syrian artillery north of Hasbeya was exchanging fire with the Israelis on the eastern route of their advance. This could not be confirmed. In Damascus, a Syrian military spokesman said Israeli forces had come into contact with Syrian troops in three places, but it was not clear whether fighting had occurred. [Page A12.]

The Israel radio broadcast a state-

Continued on Page A12, Column 1

Why Israelis Invaded Now

Heavy P.L.O. Shelling Said to Tip the Scale

The following dispatch has been subjected to military censorship.

By DAVID K. SHIPLER
Special to The New York Times

JERUSALEM, June 6 — Israel's invasion of Lebanon came today as the culmination of months of military and political calculation in which Prime Minister Menachem Begin repeatedly

News Analysis

allowed the troops to be massed and the saber to be rattled, only to pull back at what seemed like the last moment.

Until today the crucial factors favoring a major assault never quite lined up, and the risks seemed greater than the potential benefits.

This time, however, Mr. Begin decided to make the military gamble and to pay the political costs that he and his advisers now exist. The crucial reason was the intensive shelling of northern Israel by forces of the Palestine Liberation Organization, which began Friday afternoon after Israeli air strikes on Palestinian bases near Beirut.

P.L.O. Has Become an Army

The Israeli command described the air raids as retaliation for the shooting Thursday of Israel's Ambassador to Britain, Shlomo Argov, who was critically wounded in London. Five suspects, all traveling on passports from Arab countries, were captured. The P.L.O. denied any responsibility for the attack.

The Palestinian shelling, with artillery and rocket launchers, was the most severe ever directed against Israeli towns and kibbutzim by the P.L.O.,

Continued on Page A13, Column 1

Begin Orders Israelis to Push Palestinians 25 Miles to North

The following dispatch has been subjected to military censorship.

Special to The New York Times

JERUSALEM, Monday, June 7 — Prime Minister Menachem Begin said Sunday that the Israeli Army had been ordered to push the Palestinian forces northward to a distance of 25 miles from the Israeli border, to place their artillery beyond the range of Israeli territory.

Mr. Begin made his statement in a letter to President Reagan, excerpts of which were reported on the Israeli radio. The Cabinet, after an emergency session, issued a statement saying Israel would not attack any Syrian forces in Lebanon or Syria unless the Syrians engaged the Israelis.

The Damascus radio said the Syrian Army was battling the Israelis near Hasbeya, 10 miles north of the border. The Israeli military spokesman said there had been no verification that any such clashes with the Syrians had occurred.

Reagan Urged Restraint

Mr. Begin's letter to President Reagan, disclosing the orders to the army to push the Palestine Liberation Organization 25 miles north of the border, came after the President sent a letter to the Israeli leader. That letter, delivered Sunday morning, requested Israeli restraint.

In his reply, as reported by the Israeli radio, Mr. Begin said that "the terrorists aim their weapons only at the civilian population." He went on: "The aim of the enemy is to kill Jews, men, women and children. Is there any people in the world that would accept such a situation?"

The invasion operation, called "Peace for Galilee," would not be aimed at acquiring any Lebanese territory and was not being undertaken

against Lebanon, according to Mr. Begin's letter. It was begun after months of sporadic terrorist attacks on Israelis here and abroad, attacks that Israel regarded as violations of the cease-fire that had been negotiated across the Lebanese-Israeli border last July.

As Israeli armored columns swept through the lines of the United Nations peacekeeping forces, a United Nations spokesman in Jerusalem reported, several United Nations units were caught in crossfire. By Sunday evening, one

Continued on Page A12, Column 3

INSIDE

Defeat for Schmidt's Party
The Social Democrats were defeated in state elections in Hamburg in what was considered a direct blow to Chancellor Helmut Schmidt. Page A9.

'Nine,' 'Nickleby' Win Tonys
"Nine," based on "8½," won the Tony award for musicals. The Royal Shakespeare Company's "Nicholas Nickleby" won for plays. Page C11.

Floods Rampage in Connecticut; 8 Believed Dead

By ROBERT D. McFADDEN

Torrential weekend rains and overflowing rivers swamped wide areas of Connecticut yesterday with the state's worst floods in decades.

The state police said that eight persons were dead or missing in the storm. More than 1,300 others were removed from their homes as floodwaters invaded residential areas, washed out roads and earthen dams and disrupted electric and telephone service and public transportation for tens of thousands of residents.

The floods, accompanied by 5 to 8 inches of pounding rain, struck a wide swath of the state, from Westport and other Fairfield County communities on the west to Waterford and New London on the east. At least 38,000 homes were hit by power blackouts, and 6,000 telephones were knocked out.

Nearly all trains in the state, including those operated by Amtrak between New York and Boston, were halted as Conrail and Amtrak used buses to carry passengers. Commuters and long-distance travelers were expected to face further delays today. Many communities in flooded areas canceled school for today.

The rest of the New York metropolitan area was relatively unscathed. But on eastern Long Island, up to 9.79 inches of rain also triggered heavy weekend flooding. Many traffic accidents were reported, and a stretch of Long Island

Continued on Page B4, Column 1

The New York Times/Alan Decker
Matthew Giurintano clearing a storm drain yesterday in Higganum, Conn.

"All the News That's Fit to Print"

The New York Times

Late Edition
Weather: Sunny today with light southeasterly winds; clear and mild tonight. Cloudy with a chance of rain tomorrow. Temperatures: today 81-83; tonight 63-67; yesterday 54-72. Details, page D24.

VOL.CXXXI . No. 45,345   Copyright © 1982 The New York Times   NEW YORK, TUESDAY, JUNE 15, 1982   30 CENTS

BRITAIN ANNOUNCES ARGENTINE SURRENDER TO END THE 10-WEEK WAR IN THE FALKLANDS

Israelis Cut Off West Beirut, Trapping P.L.O. Leaders

ACTION IN LEBANON

Tank Units Push Through the Christian Suburbs Around the Capital

By THOMAS L. FRIEDMAN
Special to The New York Times

BEIRUT, Lebanon, June 14 — Israeli tank columns completely cut off Moslem western Beirut today, trapping the military and political leadership of the Palestine Liberation Organization.

At the same time, other Israeli armored units, greeted by rice and flowers from sympathetic Lebanese Christians, began driving still deeper into Lebanon, apparently in an effort to push Syrian troops northeast of the capital into the Bekaa Valley.

There is a concentration of Syrian troops in the Khalde junction area on the coastal highway south of Beirut near the airport, and fighting was reportedly continuing there today between Israeli forces and Palestinians and Syrians.

The Israeli radio quoted Israel's Chief of Staff, Lieut. Gen. Rafael Eytan, as saying that Israeli troops had trapped guerrilla forces in Beirut and that the troops' mission was to smash the P.L.O.'s political and military nerve center there. [Page A18.]

Lebanese Leader Forms Council

The Israeli siege of guerrilla forces in Beirut came as the Lebanese Government announced the formation of a six-member Council of National Salvation to deal with the political repercussions of the Israeli invasion.

The committee, which was to consider the leading Christian and Moslem militia commanders, was formed by President Elias Sarkis and Prime Minister Shafik al-Wazzan to determine the Government's response to Israeli conditions for withdrawal.

Israel's withdrawal terms were delivered this evening to Mr. Sarkis at the presidential palace in Baabda by the special United States envoy, Philip C. Habib. Mr. Habib arrived by car from Damascus, to which he had flown earlier today from Jerusalem.

Mr. Habib declined to make any statements to the press, but Israel's conditions are reportedly the creation of a demilitarized zone stretching 25 miles north of its border to prevent attacks by Palestinian guerrillas and the withdrawal of the 30,000 Syrian peacekeeping troops from Lebanon.

Leftist Rejects Council

A meeting of the national council to consider the conditions, scheduled for this afternoon, was canceled after one proposed member, Walid Jumblat, leader of the leftist Moslem National Movement, said he would not have anything to do with the group as presently constituted.

Mr. Jumblat, who is under virtual house arrest by Israeli invasion forces occupying his mountain village of Mukhtara south of Beirut, said through a spokesman that the board should be "more comprehensive."

The other proposed council members are Bashir Gemayel, a Christian Phalangist militia commander; Nabim Berri, head of Lebanon's Shiite Moslem Party; Nasri Maalouf, another leading Christian political leader; Foreign

Continued on Page A18, Column 1

Associated Press
Israeli soldier atop armored vehicle in position overlooking western Beirut.

In Lebanon, White Flags Fly Amid the Misery and Rubble

By DAVID K. SHIPLER
Special to The New York Times

SIDON, Lebanon, June 14 — Along the battered Lebanese coast, in the wake of the invasion, white flags still fly.

They flutter from the antennas of cars without windows or windshields. They hang from bamboo poles stuck into the shell-pocked roofs and verandas of concrete houses. Even some pedestrians carried torn strips of white cloth to signify their neutrality, their surrender to the storm of war.

The Israeli Army warned residents of Lebanon's picturesque coast to leave their homes before the bombing and shelling began, and many followed the instructions on leaflets dropped from planes.

Battles Silently Traced

But when the fighting was over and they returned home from the beaches and the orange groves and the banana plantations where they had camped for days without food or water, what they saw took the strength out of them.

In Tyre, a stronghold and command center of the Palestine Liberation Organization, not a single building was untouched by the flying shrapnel.

Some high-rise apartments had collapsed like houses of cards, some villas were chewed into piles of dust and rubble.

Many other buildings revealed the course of battle: pits and chips around the doors and windows as Israeli

troops fired at guerrillas, then a single gaping hole in a wall where a heavier weapon finished off the resistance.

The Israeli military governor of the town, Maj. Joseph Dana, who in civilian life is a lecturer in Arabic at Haifa University, estimates that 30 percent of all buildings in the town were destroyed.

In Sidon, farther up the coast toward Beirut, the damage was less ex-

Continued on Page A18, Column 4

A MIDEAST WARNING

Soviet Conveys Concern Over Military Activity Near South Border

By JOHN F. BURNS
Special to The New York Times

MOSCOW, June 14 — The Soviet Government warned Israel today not to forget that the Middle East was close to the Soviet Union's southern borders and that developments in that area "cannot help affecting the interests of the U.S.S.R."

The warning was coupled with a demand, apparently directed at the United States, for "urgent effective measures" to halt Israel's "criminal

Text of Soviet statement, page A20.

act of genocide" against Palestinians and to bring about a withdrawal of Israeli troops from Lebanon.

The statement, issued through the official press agency Tass, said in part:

"The Soviet Union takes the Arabs' side not in words but in deed and presses to get the aggressor out of Lebanon.

"The present-day Israeli policy makers should not forget that the Middle East is an area lying in close proximity to the southern borders of the Soviet Union and that developments there cannot help affecting the interests of the U.S.S.R. We warn Israel about this."

Implications of Soviet Action

The statement was evidently intended to arouse concern that American inability to arrange an early cease-fire between Israeli forces and Palestinian guerrillas could provoke direct Soviet intervention.

Theoretically, Soviet options would include an emergency airlift of arms to Palestinian guerrillas by way of Syria, which has signed a Treaty of Friendship and Cooperation with Moscow, or a new supply of weapons to the Syrian forces.

As if to underscore the Soviet warning, a Soviet general was reported to have begun talks in the Syrian capital.

Sources in Damascus identified the officer as Col. Gen. Yevgeny S. Yurasov, a first deputy commander of the air defense system. The sending of the general to Syria suggested that the

Continued on Page A29, Column 1

United Press International
Prime Minister Margaret Thatcher after addressing Parliament.

Bus-Only Lanes To Be Increased To Speed Travel

By ARI L. GOLDMAN

Mayor Koch announced yesterday the creation of a system of 10 "red zone" lanes for buses in Manhattan to help relieve traffic congestion, increase bus speeds and reduce what has long been the bane of bus travelers — bus bunching.

Along the pavement at each of the 10 thoroughfares in the program, a bright red eight-inch thermoplastic strip will remind motorists of heavy fines if they park, stand or travel in the bus lane.

"Don't Even Think of Parking Here," a sign along the routes will read. Other signs will warn that fines of at least $100 will be imposed on violators. Only cars preparing to make right turns in the lanes, will be in effect at various times on major thoroughfares in both midtown and lower Manhattan. Fourteen miles of city streets will be affected.

Next Tuesday, the first of the red zone lanes will go into effect, on Third Avenue from 36th to 58th Streets from 7 A.M. to 7 P.M. The others, which will be added over the course of the summer, will be in effect at various times on major thoroughfares in both midtown and lower Manhattan. Fourteen miles of city streets will be affected.

The other streets to get red zone lanes will be: Eighth Avenue from 42d to 57th Streets between 4 P.M. and 7 P.M.; Avenue of the Americas from 40th

Continued on Page B6, Column 1

TRIUMPH BY LONDON

Commander Says Enemy Troops Are Assembled 'for Repatriation'

By R. W. APPLE Jr.
Special to The New York Times

LONDON, Tuesday, June 15 — Argentine forces in the Falkland Islands have surrendered, halting the war in the South Atlantic, Prime Minister Margaret Thatcher's office announced early this morning.

A spokesman quoted Maj. Gen. Jeremy Moore, the commander of British land forces in the archipelago, as saying that enemy troops were being rounded up for eventual repatriation to Argentina. The surrender came at 1 A.M. British time, (8 P.M. Monday New York time), the official announcement said.

There was no confirmation of the surrender from Buenos Aires by early this morning, but the Argentine high command announced Monday afternoon that an unofficial cease-fire had gone into effect on the Falklands. [Page A14.]

'God Save the Queen'

General Moore radioed from his command post on Mount Kent: "Falkland Islands once more under Government desired by their inhabitants. God Save the Queen." It had taken the British three weeks and four days of fighting on the ground to retake the islands following their landings at San Carlos Bay.

The Prime Minister signaled that the end of the conflict, or at least this phase of it, was at hand in a statement to Parliament Monday night in which she said that Argentine forces in Stanley, the last major enemy stronghold in the Falklands, had begun throwing down their arms and hoisting white flags.

As the House of Commons erupted in prolonged cheers, the Prime Minister disclosed that the deputy commander of British land forces, Brig. John Waters, was negotiating surrender terms with the commander of the 6,500 Argentine defenders of the town, Brig. Gen. Mario Menéndez. The surrender terms, she added, would cover both East Falkland, the island on which Stanley is situated, and West Falkland, where two small Argentine forces are based.

Crowds Hail Victory

Within minutes of her statement to the House, crowds gathered outside Mrs. Thatcher's residence at 10 Downing Street, singing "Rule Britannia." When she returned from the House, they cheered her and she said, "What matters is that it was everyone together — we all knew what we had to do and we went out there and did it."

Although it remained possible that fighting would continue on or around

Continued on Page A15, Column 1

1,600 Are Arrested In Nuclear Protests At 5 U.N. Missions

By PAUL L. MONTGOMERY

Offering daisies to policemen or chanting prayers for peace, more than 1,600 nonviolent demonstrators for disarmament were arrested in midtown Manhattan yesterday as they tried to block the entrances of the United Nations missions of five countries that have atomic weapons.

In an assembly-line operation that began at 7:30 A.M., the police carried the unresisting demonstrators to rented city buses to be booked for disorderly conduct. Some who had been arrested in the morning were back later in the day, encouraging their friends or sitting down again for another arrest.

The Police Department, which had 3,000 extra officers at the demonstration sites, said the total booked was a record for a civil disobedience campaign in the city. Patrick J. Murphy, the department's chief of operations, said, "almost everybody was very well-behaved — it was a textbook exercise."

The demonstrations, for which the participants were rehearsed and the police were briefed in advance, were a continuation of the protest that brought

Continued on Page A23, Column 1

INSIDE

Sports Pages

The New York Times today introduces Sports Pages, an expanded and redesigned sports section appearing Tuesday through Saturday. It will include added news as well as new columns and features. Today's section begins on page D25.

U.S. Enters Dollar Market
As the dollar reached new highs against the devalued French franc, the Administration intervened in trading to try to restore order. Page D1.

Ruling Due on Copying TV
The Supreme Court agreed to decide whether use of home video recorders to tape television broadcasts violates Federal copyright law. Page D1.

U.S. Challenged in Space
A lack of planning and foreign competition were reported to threaten United States leadership in nonmilitary space technology. Page C1.

17 Fakes at Met Museum
The Metropolitan Museum has discovered that 17 gold vessels it had believed to be ancient Egyptian are modern fakes. Page C9.

United Press International
Yasir Arafat, left, leader of the Palestine Liberation Organization, and an aide yesterday in Beirut.

U.S. Is Easing '68 Antitrust Guidelines on Mergers

By ROBERT D. HERSHEY Jr.
Special to The New York Times

WASHINGTON, June 14 — The Government, seeking to reduce uncertainty about the types of corporate mergers that it will allow, today published a new set of enforcement guidelines "more lenient" than previous antitrust policy.

Nevertheless, the Justice Department and the Federal Trade Commis-

sion, which share antitrust responsibility, said they did not believe that their long-awaited statements would lead to any significant increase in mergers, which have diminished recently.

Attorney General William French Smith described the new guidelines as an "evolutionary change — not a revolutionary change" from actual practices in recent years. William F. Bax-

ter, the Assistant Attorney General in charge of the antitrust division, said that, "in general, the new guidelines would have to be regarded as more lenient." But he added that he did not expect them to encourage more corporate combinations than guidelines that have existed since 1968. Antitrust experts said the new guidelines were more than

Continued on Page D6, Column 4

"All the News That's Fit to Print"

The New York Times

Late Edition

Weather: Overcast and mild today with scattered rainshowers likely through tonight. Cloudy, chance of rain tomorrow. Temperatures: today 73-77, tonight 61-63; yesterday 65-81. Details on page B10.

VOL.CXXXI. No. 45,437   Copyright © 1982 The New York Times   NEW YORK, WEDNESDAY, SEPTEMBER 15, 1982   30 CENTS

The New York Times / Don Hibner

Grace Kelly, the actress: In "The Country Girl," 1954, for which she won an Oscar. Princess Grace of Monaco: At a tribute in Philadelphia this year.

Princess Grace Is Dead After Riviera Car Crash

By CLYDE HABERMAN

Princess Grace of Monaco, whose stately beauty and reserve gave her enduring Hollywood stardom even long after she ended her film career, died yesterday in Monte Carlo of injuries suffered when her car plunged off a mountain road Monday. She was 52 years old.

The Princess, the former Grace Kelly, died of a cerebral hemorrhage, a palace spokesman said in Monaco.

Princess Grace was driving her British Rover 3500 on a snaking road at Cap-d'Ail in the Côte d'Azur region when she lost control and plunged down a 45-foot embankment. The car burst into flames, and the Princess suffered multiple fractures, including a broken thighbone, collarbone and ribs.

Initial reports gave no sense that her life was in jeopardy. But a Monaco Government announcement yesterday said

that her health had "deteriorated during the night."

"At the end of the day all therapeutic possibilities had been exceeded," the announcement said.

With her in the car was Stephanie, 17, her youngest child by Prince Rainier III of Monaco. Stephanie was under observation at a hospital where she had been treated for shock and bruises.

Reagan Praises 'Gentle Lady'

Princess Grace's death brought expressions of grief from former Hollywood colleagues and from residents of her hometown, Philadelphia. President Reagan called her "a compassionate and gentle lady." In Philadelphia, a spokesman for John Cardinal Krol said the Cardinal, who was a close friend, would offer a memorial mass for her at noon Friday.

Alfred Hitchcock, who directed Grace Kelly in three films and was certainly in a position to judge, once said she had "sexual elegance." And it was that very elegance that probably made its most lasting impression on movie audiences of the 1950's.

Whether playing the heiress in "To Catch a Thief" or the Quaker pacifist in "High Noon" or the amusedly detached career girl — a term still in vogue when "Rear Window" was made — Grace Kelly carried herself with straight back and clipped-voice self-assurance. Yet just beneath the frosty exterior lay a sensuality and warmth that cracked the formidable reserve.

It was this delicate balance of contrasts that helped give her legendary status — a remarkable achievement for an actress whose career encompassed only 11 films. She made more of that

Continued on Page C24, Column 1

Primaries Won By Ex-Governor, Two Incumbents

By ADAM CLYMER

A former Massachusetts Governor trying a comeback and two important members of Congress won key tests yesterday as 12 states and the District of Columbia held primary elections.

But another incumbent, Senator Howard W. Cannon of Nevada, was locked in a tight race with Representative James D. Santini as he sought the Democratic nomination for a fifth term.

In Massachusetts, former Gov. Michael S. Dukakis, attacking his successor's administration as corrupt and too supportive of President Reagan, defeated the incumbent, Gov. Edward J. King, for the Democratic nomination for Governor, just as Mr. King did four years ago when Mr. Dukakis was the incumbent. In the heavily Democratic Bay State, Mr. Dukakis will be favored over the Republican nominee in November, John W. Sears, a former Boston City Councilor.

In Vermont, Senator Robert T. Stafford, the Republican chairman of the Committee on the Environment and Public Works, defeated two conservative foes trying to end his 11-year Senate career. The two, Stewart M. Ledbetter and John McClaughry, argued that Mr. Stafford had become more interested in Washington than in Vermont.

With 93 percent of the precincts reporting, Mr. Stafford was safely ahead with 23,815 votes, or 46 percent of those

Continued on Page B11, Column 4

GEMAYEL OF LEBANON IS KILLED IN BOMB BLAST AT PARTY OFFICES

Hussein Praises Reagan's Mideast Plan

KING OFFERS HELP

But Jordanian Asserts He Lacks the Authority to Enter Peace Talks

By BERNARD GWERTZMAN
Special to The New York Times

WASHINGTON, Sept. 14 — King Hussein of Jordan, in his first public comment on President Reagan's Middle East peace plan, said in an interview that it was "a very constructive and a very positive move." He added that he would play "a very active part" in trying to bring about a federation between Jordanians and the Palestinians.

But in the interview, aired by the British Broadcasting Corporation on Monday night, the King said he did not

Transcript of interview, page A10.

have an Arab mandate to join talks with Israel, Egypt and the United States on Palestinian self-rule.

He said the Arab leaders who met in Fez, Morocco, last week did not alter the 1974 Arab League decision to give the Palestine Liberation Organization, not Jordan, responsibility for negotiations dealing with the Palestinians living in territories occupied by Israel.

'A Very Active Part'

Although the 1974 decision still holds, he said, "I am going to play a very active part in helping, pushing forth every possible attempt for the establishment of a just and durable peace."

King Hussein, in describing his ideas for an eventual settlement of the Palestinian issue, put forth a plan that was very similar to the one proposed by President Reagan in his address on the Middle East on Sept. 1.

In that speech, Mr. Reagan said the United States favored some kind of "association" between Jordan and the Palestinians. He said the United States rejected the idea of Israeli sovereignty over the West Bank and the Gaza Strip, but would not support an independent Palestinian state in the occupied territories.

Israel captured the West Bank from Jordan and Gaza from Egypt in the 1967 war.

The Fez communiqué repeated the traditional Arab demand for the establishment of an independent Palestinian

Continued on Page A10, Column 1

The New York Times / George Tames

Bashir Gemayel during a visit to Washington a year ago.

Slaying Is Denounced by Reagan; U.S. Fears New Burst of Fighting

Special to The New York Times

WASHINGTON, Sept. 14 — President Reagan said tonight that the "cowardly assassination" of President-elect Bashir Gemayel of Lebanon was a "shock to the American people and to civilized men and women everywhere."

In an unusually sharp statement, Mr. Reagan added, "We condemn the perpetrators of this heinous crime against Lebanon and against their cause of peace in the Middle East."

The White House statement, issued late tonight, expressed deepest sympathy to the Gemayel family, and said, "The tragedy will be all the greater if men in countries friendly to Lebanon permit disorder to continue in this war-torn country."

'U.S. Stands By Lebanon'

Mr. Reagan added that the "U.S. Government stands by Lebanon with its full support in its hour of need."

American officials said earlier that the assassination raised the possibility of new fighting in that country between Mr. Gemayel's Christian Phalangist forces and Moslem leftists.

New internal strife would also raise the possibility that Syrian and Israeli forces, confronting each other in Leba-

non, might enter the conflict, destroying hopes for restoring stability.

The Israelis had strongly supported Mr. Gemayel, who was an avowed enemy of Syria. Just today, the Israeli Ambassador, Moshe Arens, called on Secretary of State George P. Shultz to say Israel wanted American assistance in obtaining a peace treaty with Lebanon.

It is the American hope that Elias Sarkis, the Lebanese President, whose term of office officially ends in nine days, will remain in office pending a new consensus choice as President.

The special American Middle East envoy, Morris Draper, arrived in Israel today on his way to Lebanon to help negotiate the withdrawal of Syrian and Israeli forces and the strengthening of the Lebanese Government. His mission is even more precarious now, officials said, given the uncertain future in Lebanon.

There was no fundamental difference between Mr. Sarkis and Mr. Gemayel on the withdrawal of foreign troops from Lebanon, American officials said. They expressed hope that Mr. Sarkis

Continued on Page A9, Column 1

8 REPORTED SLAIN

President-Elect Was 34 — No Group Reports Making the Attack

By COLIN CAMPBELL
Special to The New York Times

BEIRUT, Lebanon, Wednesday, Sept. 15 — President-elect Bashir Gemayel was killed Tuesday when a bomb shattered the headquarters of his Lebanese Christian Phalangist Party in east Beirut. The Government said he would be buried today.

Mr. Gemayel, 34 years old, who was to have been inaugurated Sept. 23, was said to have died as he was about to address 400 of his followers at a weekly meeting. The state radio said the blast left at least 8 dead, among them other Phalangist leaders, and more than 50 wounded.

Prime Minister Shafik al-Wazzan deplored the killing in a statement, describing it as "a link in a chain of criminal conspiracies against Lebanon at a time when it started to restore its strength."

New Fighting Is Feared

No one took responsibility immediately for the bombing. It raised widespread fears that it would be followed by new fighting between Lebanon's Christian and Moslem militias.

Mr. Gemayel, who had been the commander of the Christian militias, was elected President Aug. 23 at a special session of Parliament that was boycotted by many Moslem legislators. To them, many other Moslems and some Christian groups, he was an enemy and an agent of Israel, whose invading troops made his election possible. [In Israel, there was no immediate official comment on the assassination.]

Until Sept. 23, the current President, Elias Sarkis, will continue as chief of state. Government sources said he could call new elections before then or appoint a presidential council to exercise presidential power until new elections could be called. Since the President in Lebanon is by tradition a Maronite Catholic, the council would also be headed by one.

400 Pounds of Explosives

The sources said another possibility was an extension of the Sarkis term, but this would require a change in the Constitution. The Lebanese President is not allowed under current law to succeed himself.

The blast, involving the detonation of what Phalangist and Government sources estimated to be more than 400 pounds of high explosives, occurred at 4:10 P.M. Tuesday. There was no immediate explanation for how so large an amount of explosive could have been introduced into the building.

For several hours reports circulated that Mr. Gemayel had survived.

There were reports that he had said "God be praised" as he left the scene for treatment of leg bruises at the nearby French-run Hôtel Dieu hospital. Those accounts were broadcast by the Phalangist radio, which quoted wit-

Continued on Page A8, Column 4

I.B.M. Accuses 3 Executives Of Stealing Computer Secrets

By ANDREW POLLACK

The International Business Machines Corporation, following its second undercover investigation in recent months, said yesterday that it had dismissed three of its executives and had sued them on charges of stealing corporate secrets.

The key figure in the month-long I.B.M. investigation, conducted by the company's own security officers, was the president of a small Cleveland computer company who pretended to negotiate a business deal with the I.B.M. executives. While he negotiated, he secretly taped the conversations on

recording equipment supplied by I.B.M.

One of the executives had approached the Cleveland company, Tecmar Inc., and had offered to sell designs for products that would enhance I.B.M.'s new and fast-selling personal computer, according to court papers. In some cases, they would compete with still-secret products I.B.M. itself is planning to introduce, the affidavits filed in connection with the lawsuit stated.

The president of the Cleveland company, Martin A. Alpert, reported the approach to I.B.M. and agreed to cooperate when I.B.M. suggested the tape-recording plan.

In one excerpt from the transcript quoted in the court papers, William W. Erdman, an I.B.M. product manager and one of the defendants, said to Mr. Alpert: "I guarantee you that we know more about the way I.B.M.'s going to put it [personal computer products] together than I.B.M. knows, because when the guys that we're talking about leave, a good deal of knowledge leaves with them."

The three men sued in the civil action included two high-level engineers who were heavily involved in the design of I.B.M.'s personal computer and follow-up products. Also sued was Bridge Technology Inc., a White Plains company that I.B.M. asserts was established by the three executives to market their products. The three executives were dismissed by I.B.M. on Monday.

Mr. Erdman, reached yesterday at his home in Stamford, Conn., said he

Continued on Page D7, Column 1

Haig, at U.J.A., Criticizes Reagan's Mideast Plan

By BERNARD D. NOSSITER

Former Secretary of State Alexander M. Haig Jr. attacked President Reagan's Middle East plan yesterday, describing the proposal for a freeze on Israeli settlements in the occupied West Bank as "a very serious mistake."

Mr. Haig also said the Administration's plans for autonomy for the Palestinians in association with Jordan threatened a "gutting session" between Israel and the United States.

"The peace process will only move forward if there is a spirit of cooperation between Israel and the United States," Mr. Haig said. "That has been shaken in recent days."

It was the first time Mr. Haig is known to have criticized the Administration in which he served until June. He spoke without a text to 300 officials of the United Jewish Appeal at the Hilton Hotel in Manhattan.

Mr. Haig made no direct reference to the speech Sept. 1 in which Mr. Reagan announced the Middle East plan, or to his successor, George P. Shultz, who is regarded as the architect of that

Don Hogan Charles

Alexander M. Haig Jr. yesterday.

funds for needy Jews around the world. It has not taken a formal position on Mr. Reagan's peace plan, but the frequent applause yesterday indicated strong agreement with Mr. Haig's criticism. Mr. Haig, who reportedly received $25,000 for his 45-minute appearance, serves as a consultant for United Technologies, a leading military contractor, and is a senior fellow at the Hudson Institute, a research center.

Mr. Haig received a standing ovation by concluding, "When we are true to Israel, we are true to ourselves."

He had earlier said, "When by our policies we can't deal effectively with our friends in Israel, we are undercutting our effectiveness throughout the Arab world."

Mr. Haig also asserted that "had the credibility" of Israel's invasion of Lebanon "been left undisturbed, the Palestine Liberation Organization would have left weeks earlier, and there would have been less bloodshed."

That was apparently an allusion to

Continued on Page A12, Column 4

speech. When Mr. Haig was asked to comment on the Reagan plan, he smiled and said it would be inappropriate to "parse the pros and cons." But he added that his own remarks contained "some pertinent observations."

The United Jewish Appeal raises

INSIDE

Doctor Shot to Death
A physician was fatally shot as he sat in his car near his Gramercy Park office. The victim, Dr. Philip Wald, 53, was shot once in the head. Page B6.

Tuition Credit Compromise
President Reagan, returning to the theme of social issues, backed legislative compromises aimed to advance a tuition tax credit bill. Page A20.

JOHN GARDNER IS DEAD: The novelist, killed in a motorcycle accident, was 49. Page D27.

"All the News
That's Fit to Print"

The New York Times

Late Edition

Weather: Increasing cloudiness, southerly winds today, cloudy, not as cool tonight. Partly cloudy, milder temperatures tomorrow. Temperatures today 53-57, tonight 43-47, yesterday 39-52. Details, page D23.

VOL.CXXXII.. No. 45,494

Copyright © 1982 The New York Times

NEW YORK, THURSDAY, NOVEMBER 11, 1982

30 CENTS

BREZHNEV IS DEAD IN SOVIET AT AGE 75; NO IMMEDIATE WORD ON A SUCCESSOR; U.S. FORESEES NO EARLY POLICY SHIFTS

Mexico Agrees to Austerity Terms For $3.84 Billion in I.M.F. Credit

By ALAN RIDING
Special to The New York Times

MEXICO CITY, Nov. 10 — The Government announced today that it had reached a long-awaited agreement with the International Monetary Fund on an austerity program aimed at easing the crisis caused by the nation's huge foreign debt.

Under the agreement, Mexico would receive $3.84 billion worth of credit from the I.M.F. over the next three years, but the Government must slash public spending, raise taxes and curb imports to qualify for the funds.

The austerity program could stabilize the Mexican peso, which has lost 70 percent of its value since February. But Government officials said today that it would also bring an economic slowdown

and thus higher unemployment and a sharp drop in living standards.

"This agreement enables us to avoid defaulting on our foreign debt of $78 billion," Finance Minister Jesús Silva Herzog said at a news conference today. He added that the Government now hoped to obtain fresh credits from private financial institutions abroad. Many of them have already lent millions of dollars to Mexico, whose foreign debt is the highest in the world.

Deep Concerns Abroad

Mexico's crisis had sent shudders through the world banking system, raising the specter of major defaults by developing countries whose economies have been undermined by the fall in commodity prices and the recession in the industrial world.

The crisis has made major banks in the industrial world reluctant to extend new loans to developing countries — loans they seek to help meet payments on their existing debt. The I.M.F. agreement eases that problem in Mexico's case by requiring an austerity program that makes this country more creditworthy in the eyes of financial institutions in the industrial world.

Argentina and Brazil, which face debt repayment problems similar to Mexico's, also received help today. The I.M.F. gave approval to a $2.1 billion credit for Argentina as the first step in a program to help that nation catch up with payments on its nearly $40 billion in foreign debt. The Argentine Government had agreed earlier to an austerity program required by the I.M.F.

Separately, six leading American banks made $600 million in emergency loans to Brazil to help that country meet debt payments abroad until it can obtain longer-term credits, banking sources said. Brazil's foreign debt is nearly as large as Mexico's.

The agreement with Mexico, the sub-

Continued on Page D3, Column 1

JOBS LEGISLATION IS GAINING SUPPORT

Reagan May Back One Plan — Two Houses Prepare Bills

By MARTIN TOLCHIN
Special to The New York Times

WASHINGTON, Nov. 10 — Bipartisan support for a public works program that would provide jobs for the unemployed solidified in Congress today. There were indications that President Reagan might support a limited jobs program.

Responding to what they regarded as a mandate from last week's Congressional elections, Democrats and Republicans vied to claim authorship of jobs legislation, and they began a bidding contest to determine who could come up with a program that would put the most people to work at the least expense.

Reagan Studies Lewis Plan

Both House Democrats and Senate Republicans were drafting public works legislation that would provide more Federal funds for construction and repair of highways and bridges, sewers, dams and public buildings. Both sides expressed hope of bipartisan agreement on such legislation in the lame-duck Congressional session that starts Nov. 29.

The President studied a more limited proposal submitted by Drew Lewis, Secretary of Transportation, which included only the rehabilitation of highways, bridges and mass transit, to be financed by an increase in the gasoline tax. Mr. Lewis initially submitted his

Continued on Page A19, Column 6

Richmond Sentenced To a Year and a Day And Fined $20,000

By JOSEPH P. FRIED

Former Representative Frederick W. Richmond of Brooklyn was sentenced yesterday to a year and a day in prison and fined $20,000 for income-tax evasion, marijuana possession and making an illegal payment to a government employee.

He had pleaded guilty to these charges and agreed to resign from Congress and not seek re-election in a plea bargaining with Federal prosecutors on Aug. 25. They agreed not to prosecute him for other matters that they had also been investigating.

Judge Is Typically Informal

No date was set for him to begin serving his term, although he will probably have to begin doing so in a few weeks, officials said.

As Chief Judge Jack B. Weinstein of Federal District Court in Brooklyn pronounced the sentence, Mr. Richmond, who will be 59 years old Monday, gazed somberly at the judge from across a polished wood conference table, at which the participants in the case were seated.

Judge Weinstein normally conducts

Continued on Page B9, Column 1

WASHINGTON REACTS

Clark Informs Reagan — Official Says President May Go to Funeral

By HEDRICK SMITH
Special to The New York Times

WASHINGTON, Thursday, Nov. 11 — The Reagan Administration expects no dramatic change in Soviet policies and no firm, quick resolution of the Soviet leadership succession in the period just after Leonid I. Brezhnev's death. The United States has already taken steps to inform Moscow that American policy will remain steady.

A high White House official said President Reagan was awakened and informed of the news at 3:25 A.M. by his national security adviser, William P. Clark. The official said the President and his top advisers would meet at 8 A.M. to assess the situation.

Military Buildup Under Brezhnev

The official said there was "some possibility" that President Reagan himself might attend Mr. Brezhnev's funeral. The Administration, having anticipated Mr. Brezhnev's death because of the Soviet leader's long illnesses, had made contingency plans for Vice President Bush to attend, but Mr. Bush left for Africa late Wednesday.

Mr. Brezhnev's 18-year rule was a period of great Soviet military buildup, and just two weeks ago the 76-year-old Soviet leader re-emphasized that policy in a major speech to top military commanders in which he pledged further increases in arms spending.

The fact that he was flanked by other top leaders, including his two ranking potential successors, was taken as a sign that these policies would be continued under new leadership.

In other areas as well, including arms negotiations with the United States and

Continued on Page D21, Column 1

Leonid Ilyich Brezhnev
Photosreporters

Polish Strike Call Goes Unheeded In Face of Government Warnings

By JOHN KIFNER
Special to The New York Times

WARSAW, Nov. 10 — A national strike called for today by the underground leaders of the Solidarity movement appeared to have been generally unsuccessful in the face of a carefully orchestrated Government campaign backed up by a display of police power.

As darkness fell, caravans of armored vehicles of the riot police fired tear gas and water cannons at any groups on the streets near the Old Town section of the capital, then took up positions at traffic circles and intersections to prevent crowds from forming.

A march through the center of Warsaw did not materialize and it appeared that there had been only spotty response to the strike call intended to protest the recent banning of Solidarity. However, in Nowa Huta, the steel center, there were clashes between demonstrators and the police. [Page A13.]

"There was not a single major strike," Jerzy Urban, a Government spokesman, said. "The day has been a full defeat for the underground and its foreign supporters."

The apparent failure of the strike call — the first stage in a planned series of demonstrations — seemed a blow to the

Continued on Page A12, Column 3

Spy in Britain Given 35 Years for Selling Secrets to the Soviet

By JON NORDHEIMER
Special to The New York Times

LONDON, Nov. 10 — A British linguistics expert pleaded guilty today to charges of passing secrets to the Soviet Union on the activities of a classified electronics listening post.

The expert, Geoffrey Arthur Prime, 44 years old, was sentenced to 35 years in prison by Lord Lane, the Lord Chief Justice, who said that Mr. Prime's treason had caused "incalculable harm" to the security interests of Britain and its allies.

According to United States sources, British intelligence officials have determined that the case represented one of the most potentially damaging penetrations of Western intelligence since World War II.

"The legal phase of the case is over, but the assessment of the intelligence implications has really only just begun," said one American intelligence official.

Details on the information supplied by Mr. Prime to the Russians in the 14 years he was in their pay were not included in the brief outline of the case presented by the prosecution today. The Attorney General, Sir Michael Havers, said the defendant's activities were "prejudicial to the national

Continued on Page A8, Column 1

DEATH IS 'SUDDEN'

Cause Is Not Revealed, but Leader Had Long Been in Poor Health

By JOHN F. BURNS
Special to The New York Times

MOSCOW, Thursday, Nov. 11 — Leonid I. Brezhnev, the Soviet leader for 18 years, died yesterday, the state television announced this morning.

The announcement, carried simultaneously on radio and television and on the official press agency Tass, said: "The Central Committee of the Communist Party of the Soviet Union, the Presidium of the U.S.S.R. Supreme Soviet and the Council of Ministers of the U.S.S.R. inform with deep sorrow

Leonid Brezhnev was a canny leader who tried to make his country the military equal of the United States. An obituary, Page D22.

that the party and the entire Soviet people that Leonid Ilyich Brezhnev, general secretary of the C.P.S.U. Central Committee and president of the Presidium of the U.S.S.R. Supreme Soviet, died a sudden death at 8:30 A.M. on Nov. 10, 1982.

"The name of Leonid Ilyich Brezhnev, a true continuer of Lenin's great cause and an ardent champion of peace and Communism, will live forever in the hearts of the Soviet people and the entire progressive mankind."

Cause of Death Not Given

The two-minute announcement was read twice on television by a dark-suited announcer. As he spoke the screen displayed a recent photograph of Mr. Brezhnev bordered by orange bands.

Mr. Brezhnev was 75 years old. The announcer gave no indication of the cause of Mr. Brezhnev's death. Nor did he give any suggestion of Mr. Brezhnev's successor as general secretary of the party or president of the Presidium of the Supreme Soviet.

Mr. Brezhnev had been in poor health for several years, apparently because of heart and respiratory problems. His last public appearance was on Sunday, when he stood for two hours atop the Lenin mausoleum in Red Square reviewing the annual military parade marking the 65th anniversary of the Bolshevik Revolution.

No Obvious Successor

Later he spoke at a Kremlin reception attended by Soviet dignitaries and the diplomatic corps.

Westerners at the parade were surprised that Mr. Brezhnev stayed so long in the subzero weather. Clad in a heavy overcoat and fur hat and with tinted sunglasses to shield the sun's glare, he stayed atop the mausoleum with other Politburo members more than twice as long as he did in 1981, when the weather was milder.

However, Soviet television offered

Continued on Page D21, Column 1

At the Vietnam War Memorial, veterans were reunited as they found the names of comrades killed on the same day.
The New York Times/D. Gorton

Tribute to Vietnam Dead: Words, a Wall

By FRANCIS X. CLINES
Special to The New York Times

WASHINGTON, Nov. 10 — President Reagan stopped by the National Cathedral to listen for a while to the reading of the names of the Vietnam war dead this evening.

His motorcade sounded fast and far-off heading northwest to the cathedral in the dusk as Tom Toohey, unheeding in another part of town, stepped up to the glossy dark wall of the war's freshly completed memorial with its long listing of its dead, touching it for the name, he emphasized, of "one good lieutenant."

"There," said Mr. Toohey, his fingers brushing the name of Richard H. Housh. "A real good lieutenant. I saw him jump up with his pump shotgun

one time and blow away four guys coming at us. He was somebody else, one good lieutenant."

Ceremony by Candlelight

While the President journeyed to one part of the capital's weeklong commemoration of the Vietnam dead, the continuous reading of their names in a candlelighted chapel at National Cathedral, Mr. Toohey and hundreds of other Americans continued to arrive at the wall even after darkness fell tonight, the eve of Veterans Day. They bore the deep grief of the Vietnam time and indulged the simplest sort of human memorial, the act of touching stone, feeling the cold, stony texture of the engraved names of the dead that showed up by flashlight and

in the wavering glow of matches struck in the dark.

Official Washington has built a week of ceremony around the opening of the simple memorial that hugs a part of the Washington earth. The first senators have already come to pose for photographs, according to attendants.

But it is already clear that the wall has touched a much more basic and human strain of response, the simple act of touching the wall as much as reading the names. Bearded veterans wearing old fatigue jackets and battle medals can be seen reaching toward the names of remembered dead war-

Continued on Page B15, Column 1

HAPPY BIRTHDAY LANCE - WITH ALL OUR LOVE - MOM & GRANDMA - ADVT.

302

The New York Times

Late Edition

Weather: Mostly cloudy, humid, chance of showers today; cloudy, chance of showers tonight. Clearing tomorrow. Temperatures: today 78-83, tonight 67-73; yesterday 67-83. Details on page 33.

VOL.CXXXII.. No. 45,714   Copyright © 1983 The New York Times   NEW YORK, SUNDAY, JUNE 19, 1983 $1.50 beyond 75 miles from New York City, except on Long Island.   ONE DOLLAR

Associated Press

Pope John Paul II at the Jasna Gora monastery in Czestochowa, Poland.

Pope Hails the 'Solidarity' of Poles And Gets a Tumultuous Ovation

By JOHN KIFNER
Special to The New York Times

CZESTOCHOWA, Poland, June 18 — Pope John Paul II, addressing a crowd estimated at more than a million people here, hailed the Polish people today for their acts of "solidarity" with those who were interned or dismissed from work under martial law. His remark drew a tumultuous ovation.

Although the Pope did not use the word solidarity to refer to the outlawed union of that name, his reference was unmistakable. The crowd rose in applause, with many people raising their arms in a V-for-victory sign signifying resistance, and they shook their red and white Solidarity banners.

Earlier in this increasingly politically charged visit, the Pope said on arriving here that the 1980 workers' uprising that led to the creation of Solidarity had "touched hearts and consciences" all over the world.

It was the Pope's strongest direct reference to the events surrounding the creation of the union since he arrived in

his homeland Thursday on an eight-day trip.

The Pope flew to the Jasna Gora monastery here by helicopter this afternoon after visiting the monastery in Niepokalanow that was founded by the Rev. Maksymilian Kolbe, who gave his life for a fellow Pole at Auschwitz and who was elevated to sainthood last fall. [Page 12.]

Speaking soon after his arrival in Czestochowa, the Pontiff said the events of 1980 marked a time "when the Polish worker stood up for himself with the Gospel in his hand and a prayer on his lips."

The commitment of Poles to that struggle, he said, was "a testimony that amazed the whole world."

—Gdansk Strikes Are Recalled

"The pictures that went around the world in 1980 touched hearts and consciences," the Pope said, referring to the August 1980 strikes that began at the Gdansk shipyard. The walkouts were settled under an agreement with the Government that permitted the creation of the first independent union in the Soviet bloc.

John Paul's first address here today was directed to members of the Baltic diocese of Szczecin. In other remarks, in which he used the word solidarity, were at a mass for Polish youths.

At that service, the Pope spoke of solidarity twice, first in reference to "historical experiences" that "tell us how much the immorality of certain periods cost the whole nation." In such circumstances, he suggested, there is a need for "love of neighbor," which he de-

Continued on Page 13, Column 1

CUBAN COMMANDER IN NICARAGUA POST

U.S. Says Intelligence Report Places Him on Duty There

By LESLIE H. GELB
Special to The New York Times

WASHINGTON, June 18 — Cuba's top military combat commander has been working in Nicaragua for about a month and has been "secretly assigned to duty" there, according to an intelligence report disclosed by a Reagan Administration official.

The commander was identified as Gen. Arnaldo Ochoa Sánchez, who as a brigade commander was said to have been instrumental in negotiating, organizing and leading the Cuban military buildup in Angola in 1976 and in Ethiopia in 1977. He is now deputy to Raúl Castro, Minister of the Armed Forces.

No Independent Confirmation

The report is based primarily on Central American military sources who, two officials said, have been reliable in their accounts of Cuban activities in Nicaragua.

These sources, according to the report, believe General Ochoa is organizing a "large-scale Cuban move into Nicaragua." One of the sources even said he would be chief of all Nicaraguan and Cuban armed forces.

Over the last few days, calm has returned to two Nicaraguan border towns where heavy fighting was reported last week between Nicaraguan forces and Honduran-based rebels. But a visit to the area turned up evidence that the insurgents caused extensive damage to farms and warehouses. [Page 10.]

Administration officials acknowledged that apart from the Central American sources, they had no independent confirmation that General

Continued on Page 10, Column 3

Today's Sections

Index to Subjects

Shuttle Rockets to Orbit With 5 Aboard

Physicist Is First U.S. Woman in Space — Satellite Launched

By JOHN NOBLE WILFORD
Special to The New York Times

CAPE CANAVERAL, Fla., June 18 — Four men and a woman, the first American woman to go into space, rocketed into orbit today aboard the space shuttle Challenger and then launched the first of two satellites in the successful beginning of a busy six-day mission.

The winged spaceship lifted off on schedule at 7:33 A.M. after one of the smoothest countdowns of the shuttle program. It carried two communications satellites, an assortment of scientific experiments and a West German satellite that is to be released and then retrieved in a critical test of the shuttle's 50-foot mechanical arm.

Deployment of Missiles

On future missions astronauts expect to release small satellites with the mechanical arm and to rendezvous with ailing satellites to retrieve them for repairs in orbit or back on the earth.

One of the communications satellites, Canada's Anik C, was launched from Challenger's cargo bay late this afternoon and, with a boost from its own small rocket, sent spinning into the darkness of space on a course toward a 22,300-mile-high orbit. The other satellite, Indonesia's Palapa B, is set to be similarly launched Sunday morning to complete the mission's primary objectives.

But what set this flight apart from the 36 other manned American space missions over the last 22 years was not the cargo but the occupant just behind the two pilots. She was Dr. Sally K. Ride, a 32-year-old physicist who has been in astronaut training since 1978. She is the third woman to fly in space, but the first on an American mission.

2d Flight for Crippen

A crowd estimated at 250,000 stood in the bright morning sun to watch the seventh shuttle launching, and many of them wore "Ride, Sally Ride" T-shirts.

In his weekly radio address, President Reagan said that Dr. Ride's flight was "another example of the great

Continued on Page 20, Column 1

NASA via Associated Press

The space shuttle Challenger lifting off the launching pad at Cape Canaveral, Fla. Inset: Dr. Sally K. Ride, the first American woman to fly in space, at work as the crew prepared to deploy a communications satellite.

Cool, Versatile Astronaut
Sally Kristen Ride

By WILLIAM J. BROAD

Woman in the News

The celebration over sending the first American woman into orbit has tended to overshadow the fact that Dr. Sally K. Ride is to be the first person to perform one of the most significant tasks of the space age.

Reaching into the void with a 50-foot robotic arm, she plans to capture a satellite as it hurtles about the earth and, using mechanical might conferred by gears and motors, bring it

safely to rest in the cargo bay of the space shuttle.

Her aerial exercise points to the not-so-distant future when it could be routine to grasp satellites, mine asteroids, build space stations — in short, to clutch and shape instead of just to pass through space as an awestruck visitor. It marks a new stage in the taming of the high frontier.

Even before liftoff, Dr. Ride had achieved world renown as the woman designated to break the all-male barrier in the American space program. There are now eight women in the astronaut corps.

Important Future Role

Dr. Ride will also play an important role in preparation for future missions. She will act as a liaison agent between the Government and private companies when clients from aerospace and military industries contract for space aboard the shuttle.

In the course of 32 years, Dr. Ride has devoted herself to the conquest of tennis, Shakespeare, physics and now the intricacies of space flight. Her diverse background, at odds with the narrow path of the speed-loving test pilots who pioneered the space program, has prepared her in an unusual way for the historic mission.

Sally Kristen Ride was born May 26, 1951, to Dale B. and Joyce Ride. Growing up in the Los Angeles neighborhood of Encino, she used to stretch

Continued on Page 20, Column 1

CHINA NAMES PRESIDENT: Li Xiannian, left, a veteran of the revolution, accepting the post in Peking. At right is Peng Zhen, new chairman of Parliament. The presidency had been vacant for years. Page 9.

New China/United Press International

Kean Orders 3d Dioxin Site Shut

By DOUGLAS C. McGILL

CLIFTON, N.J., June 18 — Governor Kean said today that preliminary tests had discovered dangerous levels of dioxin in the soil at a chemical plant near an elementary school in a mostly residential area here.

He ordered the closing of a section of the plant, which is operated by the Givaudan Corporation, pending the results of further tests and an examination of employees who may have been exposed to the toxic chemical. The area to be closed is 160 feet long and 30 feet wide and contains 14 small buildings.

The Givaudan plant, at 125 Delawanna Avenue, is the third industrial area in New Jersey where dioxin contamination has been found. However, it is the first operating plant found to be contaminated, and the first whose daily business will be affected by a gubernatorial order.

Earlier this year, the New Jersey Department of Environmental Protection checked industrial records and identified 11 areas in the state where dioxin contamination might be found. The owners of the eight remaining areas are cooperating with the state to test for dioxin.

The two other areas, both of which were abandoned industrial plants, were in Edison and in the Ironbound section of Newark.

The Governor, at a news conference at Clifton's City Hall, emphasized that there was "absolutely no evidence of off-site contamination" in Clifton. He added that "a number of precautionary steps have been taken to assure protection of public health."

The steps included covering contami-

Continued on Page 28, Column 1

VOLCKER RENAMED BY REAGAN TO RUN FEDERAL RESERVE

WIDE SPECULATION ENDED

President's Declaration Cites Chairman's Record in Fight to Bring Down Inflation

By STEVEN R. WEISMAN
Special to The New York Times

WASHINGTON, June 18 — Ending months of speculation that has roiled the financial markets, President Reagan announced today that he would reappoint Paul A. Volcker to another four-year term as chairman of the Federal Reserve Board.

Taking time from his regular Saturday radio address for what he said was "a news flash," Mr. Reagan told listeners that he telephoned Mr. Volcker this morning and asked him to accept the reappointment.

"He's agreed to do so," the President said. "And I couldn't be more pleased. He is as dedicated as I am to continuing the fight against inflation. And with him as chairman of the Fed, I know we'll win that fight."

Credited for Cutting Inflation

Mr. Volcker's tight money policies in 1981 and 1982 were credited by most economists with helping to bring down the nation's inflation rate, and by critics with causing the recession.

The chairman issued a statement saying he was "gratified and honored by the expression of confidence by the President."

"As I have said on a number of occasions, I do believe we now have a rare opportunity to achieve sustained growth on a firm foundation of stabil-

The reappointment of Mr. Volcker appears to mean a stronger recovery this year and continuing into 1984. Economic analysis, Page 26.

ity," Mr. Volcker added. "I am sure I can speak for the entire Federal Reserve System as to our commitment to work toward that objective."

Mr. Volcker was appointed chairman by President Carter in 1979. His appointment to a new term beginning Aug. 6 is subject to approval by the Senate, but he was not expected to have much difficulty winning confirmation.

Support From Eagleton

In the regular Democratic response to Mr. Reagan's address, Senator Thomas F. Eagleton of Missouri, said, "I vigorously support President Reagan's reappointment of Paul Volcker."

Another Democratic Senator, Gary Hart of Colorado, who is seeking his party's Presidential nomination, issued a statement saying that "to the degree this represents a continuation of the policies of the past two years," the selection "could be a disaster for our economy and for the unemployed."

"But it actually matters little whom President Reagan appoints to head the Federal Reserve Board if the Reagan Administration's economic policies don't change," Mr. Hart added.

Senator John Glenn of Ohio, another

Continued on Page 26, Column 1

Debate Grows Over Adoption Of National Industrial Policy

By KAREN W. ARENSON

The ills of the American economy are obvious — high interest rates, high unemployment, low productivity, uncompetitive plants.

The cures are not so evident. In recent decades, Americans have successively taken, and then discarded, a variety of economic medicines, from Keynesianism to monetarism to supply-side economics.

Now, a new prescription — industrial policy — is sweeping intellectual and political circles. It is an idea that has been spurred by the success of the Japanese economy, and by the crucial role played by Japanese industrial policy and its centerpiece, the Ministry of International Trade and Industry.

The issue is prompting much debate. To supporters, a national industrial policy, aimed at helping particular industries, holds the key to reshaping America's economy and setting the course for future growth. To others, it is simply the latest brand of snake oil or voodoo economics.

The issue is attracting high-powered attention. In the past year, the Council on Foreign Relations, the Aspen Institute, Harvard University, Columbia Law School and the Federal Reserve Bank of Kansas City have all scheduled symposiums on the topic, with participants from politics and the academic world, unions and business.

In addition, industrial policy is expected to be an important issue in the 1984 Presidential race, provided the

economy continues to have visible problems as the recovery progresses. Several Democrats have endorsed the concept, and industrial policy bills are beginning to appear in Congress.

The Republicans, on the other hand, are hoping that recovery will make the discussion moot, that the worst of the economy's troubles will disappear with the recession.

Industrial policy remains an elusive concept. It encompasses ideas, some of them contradictory, ranging from the establishment of an industrial development bank to support winning industries, to an industrial conversion agency to rehabilitate losing industries and their workers. Many proposals prescribe some type of three-way bargain-

Continued on Page 28, Column 1

INSIDE

Affirmative Action Gauged
A Labor Department study says affirmative action has raised minority employment in companies dealing with the Government. Page 16.

P.L.O. Guerrillas Clash
New fighting was reported between Palestine Liberation Organization units in Lebanon, scene of a month-old mutiny against Yasir Arafat. Page 6.

"All the News That's Fit to Print"

The New York Times

Late Edition

Weather: Mostly cloudy, warm today, light southwesterly winds; clear tonight. Sunny, more humid tomorrow. Temperatures: today 83-85, tonight 67-73; yesterday 69-84. Details, page B17.

VOL.CXXXII.. No. 45,789   Copyright © 1983 The New York Times   NEW YORK, FRIDAY, SEPTEMBER 2, 1983   80 cents beyond 75 miles from New York City, except on Long Island   30 CENTS

U.S. SAYS SOVIET DOWNED KOREAN AIRLINER; 269 LOST; REAGAN DENOUNCES 'WANTON' ACT

Begin's Party Chooses Shamir as New Leader

By DAVID K. SHIPLER
Special to The New York Times

Associated Press
Yitzhak Shamir

JERUSALEM, Friday, Sept. 2 — Yitzhak Shamir, the 68-year-old Foreign Minister of Israel, was elected early this morning to succeed Prime Minister Menachem Begin as leader of the governing Herut Party. This placed him in a favorable position to become the next Prime Minister if he can hold together Mr. Begin's coalition of right-wing and religious factions.

A former guerrilla who led the underground Stern Gang against the British in Palestine, Mr. Shamir could be expected to continue Mr. Begin's major hard-line policies, including the active program of Jewish settlement on the West Bank. In 1979 he opposed the peace treaty with Egypt.

The Foreign Minister was elected at a late-night caucus of Herut's central committee, where 745 of about 900 members voted in secret ballots. The counting at the meeting in Tel Aviv went on until nearly 2 A.M. Seven votes were invalidated.

Mr. Shamir received 436 votes to 302 for the only other contender, Deputy Prime Minister David Levy, a 45-year-old Moroccan-born Jew who rose from poverty in a Jordan Valley development town.

Had Support of Old Guard

Mr. Levy is considered somewhat more moderate and more interested in domestic social issues than Mr. Shamir, but is inexperienced in foreign affairs and military matters. Because he is young, he is still likely to be regarded as a potential leader of the party.

Former Defense Minister Ariel Sharon had withdrawn from the contest in favor of Mr. Shamir and was reported to have said that he would not serve in any government led by Mr. Levy.

Mr. Shamir had the support of the party's old guard, most of whom had fought in the underground against the British and were said to feel that Mr. Levy was not as ideological as they would have liked.

In Search of a Majority

Prime Minister Begin has said that he plans to submit his formal resignation as Prime Minister and as leader of the party within the next few days. He delayed it to give his party time to choose a new leadership.

Now Mr. Shamir's task will be to get the agreement of enough coalition partners to make up a majority in the Parliament. This should be completed by early next week.

In an acceptance speech, the new party head said he would keep the Prime Minister's job in trust for Mr.

Continued on Page A3, Column 1

U.S. Positioning 2,000 Marines Off Beirut Coast

By WILLIAM E. FARRELL
Special to The New York Times

WASHINGTON, Sept. 1 — President Reagan today ordered a 2,000-member Marine force into the Mediterranean to position itself off Beirut so "that all necessary measures" could be taken to "assure the safety" of the 1,370 marines already on shore.

Pentagon officials said the additional marine contingent would sail Friday from Mombasa, Kenya, and anchor off Lebanon in about a week. The officials said there were no plans now to send the additional marines ashore.

The announcement of the President's decision was made in California, where Mr. Reagan is vacationing, by Larry Speakes, the White House spokesman. It came during a week when two marines were killed and 14 wounded in Beirut as leftist Moslem militiamen battled the Lebanese Army.

While the army succeeded on Wednesday in taking control of major points of West Beirut from the militiamen, reports from Lebanon said fighting continued today as soldiers hunted snipers still in place on roofs and in buildings.

There was scattered shelling of Christian East Beirut areas by militiamen in the hills, and shells reportedly

Continued on Page A2, Column 3

Flight of the Korean 747

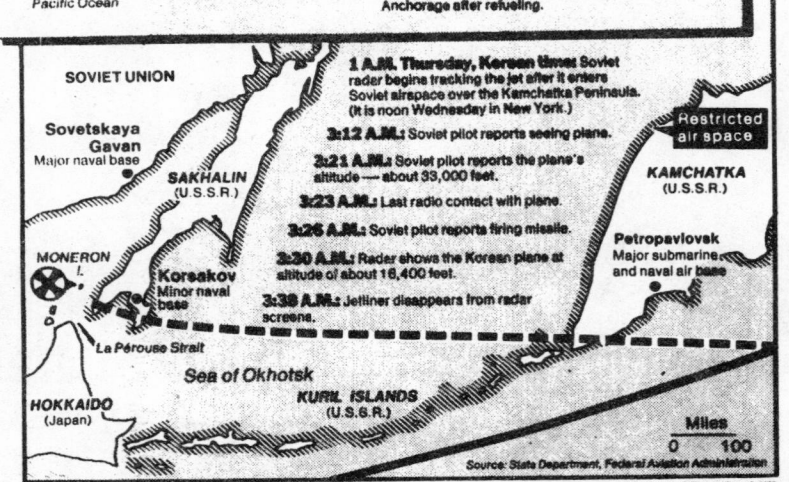

11:30 P.M. Eastern Daylight Time Tuesday: Korean Air Lines Flight 7 leaves JFK Airport with 269 people bound for Seoul.

10 A.M. Wednesday: Airliner leaves Anchorage after refueling.

1 A.M. Thursday, Korean time: Soviet radar begins tracking the jet after it enters Soviet airspace over the Kamchatka Peninsula. (It is noon Wednesday in New York.)

3:12 A.M.: Soviet pilot reports seeing plane.

3:21 A.M.: Soviet pilot reports the plane's altitude — about 33,000 feet.

3:23 A.M.: Last radio contact with plane.

3:26 A.M.: Soviet pilot reports firing missile.

3:30 A.M.: Radar shows the Korean plane at altitude of about 16,400 feet.

3:38 A.M.: Jetliner disappears from radar screens.

Source: State Department, Federal Aviation Administration
The New York Times / Sept. 2, 1983

MOSCOW CONFIRMS TRACKING OF PLANE

But Tass Statement Is Silent About an Attack on Airliner

By JOHN F. BURNS

MOSCOW, Sept. 1 — After nearly 24 hours of silence, the Soviet Union confirmed tonight only that its jet fighters in the Far East had intercepted and warned "an unidentified plane" intruding into Soviet airspace. But it made no mention of any attack on the plane.

The statement, by the Government press agency Tass, was the first acknowledgment that Moscow knew about the South Korean airliner that the United States said was shot down off southern Sakhalin.

The statement said Foreign Minister Andrei A. Gromyko had sent a message along the lines of the Tass statement, saying that the plane had violated Soviet airspace, but seeming to disclaim responsibility for the downing of the craft. Mr. Gromyko added that search planes had found "signs of a possible crash" near Moneron Island, off southwest Sakhalin.

[John Hughes, the department spokesman, said the United States "finds this reply totally inadequate and reiterates its demand for a satisfactory explanation."]

Earlier in the day the Soviet Foreign

Continued on Page A4, Column 4

President Demands Explanation For 'Horrifying Act of Violence'

By STEVEN WEISMAN
Special to The New York Times

SANTA BARBARA, Calif., Sept. 1 — President Reagan expressed revulsion today at the reported downing of a South Korean passenger airplane off the Soviet coast. He declared angrily that the Russians had "totally failed to explain how or why this tragedy has occurred."

He also decided to cut short his vacation here by three days to return to the White House Friday for a National Security Council meeting to discuss responses to the incident. In addition, Mr. Reagan asked Republican and Democratic Congressional leaders to meet with him at the White House, possibly Saturday, to discuss the situation.

Shultz Also Denunciatory

"I speak for all Americans and for the people everywhere who cherish civilized values in protesting the Soviet attack on an unarmed civilian passenger plane," Mr. Reagan said. "Words can scarcely express our revulsion at this horrifying act of violence.

"The United States joins with other members of the international community in demanding a full explanation for this appalling and wanton misdeed," Mr. Reagan said. "The Soviet statements to this moment have totally failed to explain how or why this tragedy has occurred. Indeed, the whole incident appears to be inexplicable to civilized people everywhere."

In Washington this morning, Secretary of State George P. Shultz also issued a strong statement, expressing revulsion at the reported downing of

the plane. Mr. Shultz, speaking at a news conference at the State Department, also said that he had not yet talked by telephone to Mr. Reagan.

Larry Speakes, the chief White House spokesman, said the National Security Council meeting was expected to concern "ways in which the United States may join with Korea and Japan to express effectively the disgust that the entire world feels at the utter barbarity of the action of the Soviet Government in shooting down an unarmed, nonmilitary passenger plane and their refusal thus far to acknowledge either the responsibility or their sorrow for this action."

Mr. Reagan's strong reaction to the incident was the culmination of a day in which he had been briefed by telephone by William P. Clark, the director of the National Security Council, and Edwin Meese 3d, the White House counselor. Both have been working at a resort

Continued on Page A5, Column 6

Heart Attack Kills Sen. Jackson

By LES LEDBETTER

Senator Henry M. Jackson, Washington State's senior Senator and a 44-year veteran of Congress and national politics, died in Everett, Wash., Thursday night after a massive heart attack. He was 71 years old.

Senator Jackson was taken to Providence Hospital in Everett shortly before 11 P.M., Eastern daylight time, after suffering a heart attack in his home, according to a broadcast account by Mayor Bill Moore of Everett, a family friend. He died a short time later.

The heart attack came 12 hours after the Senator held a news conference in Seattle on the destruction of a Korean Air Lines jet, apparently by the Russians.

Senator Jackson, who was a Presidential contender twice, was a power in the Democratic party and in the Senate who was known for consistency over the decades despite the prevailing political winds.

His power and prestige were so established in Washington circles that Presidents of both parties and all ideologies sought his counsel and his support for their military and international policies.

The ranking Democratic member of the Senate Armed Services Committee, he was conservative on dealing with the Soviet Union and hawkish on arms buildup.

He was a lifetime liberal in matters dealing with civil rights and organized labor. He was also a strong supporter of Israel, tying Soviet immigration policies toward Jews to any deals with

that nation. And he was an outspoken advocate for Boeing, his state's largest employer.

Some observers even complained

Continued on Page B9, Column 5

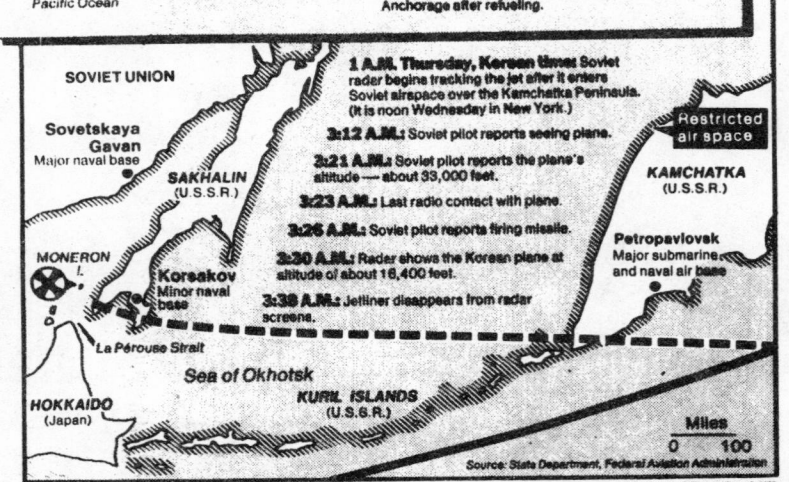

Associated Press
Sisters of a passenger weeping as South Korean official announced in Seoul that plane was probably shot down.

A FRUITLESS SEARCH

President Calls Meeting of National Security Council for Today

By ROBERT D. McFADDEN

A South Korean airliner missing with 269 people on a flight from New York to Seoul was shot down in the Sea of Japan by a Soviet jet fighter near a Soviet island off Siberia, the United States said yesterday.

There were no known survivors of the attack, in which a heat-seeking missile was said to have been fired

Statements by U.S., page A5.

without warning at the airliner by an interceptor that had tracked it over Soviet territory for two and a half hours.

President Reagan expressed "revulsion" over what he called "a horrifying act of violence." He cut short his California vacation and called a National Security Council meeting in Washington today to discuss possible reprisals.

U.N. Meeting Requested

Members of Congress and other American officials erupted in a fury of outrage, and the United States and South Korea requested a United Nations Security Council meeting on the incident. The Council was expected to begin debate today.

There was no clear explanation for the reported attack, which occurred amid several puzzling circumstances. There was an unconfirmed report that the airliner had experienced radio trouble. Soviet officials said it was flying without lights. And United States authorities acknowledged it was far off course, despite carrying what South Korean officials called sophisticated navigational equipment.

As American, Soviet and Japanese ships and planes searched frigid seas north of Japan and reportedly found traces of fuel where the jet apparently went down, Secretary of State George P. Shultz demanded an explanation from the Soviet Union and told reporters, "The Soviet pilot reported that he fired a missile and the target was destroyed." [Page A5.]

Soviet Explanation Rejected

A Soviet explanation late yesterday was rebuffed by the State Department as "totally inadequate." The Soviet statement did not acknowledge that a Soviet plane had shot down the airliner and did not accept responsibility for the incident, the State Department said.

The State Department spokesman, John Hughes, said a message from the Soviet Foreign Minister, Andrei A. Gromyko, asserted only that a plane

Continued on Page A4, Column 1

Strategic Soviet Region

Area Where Russians Say Plane Intruded Is Critical Part of Their Far East Defenses

By DREW MIDDLETON

Military Analysis

Soviet sensitivity over foreign radar penetration of defenses guarding La Pérouse Strait south of Sakhalin may have been the motivation for the reported destruction of a South Korean airliner by a jet fighter, according to American officers. In war the strait would be the direct route for the deployment of the Soviet Pacific Fleet into the northwest Pacific, the officers said.

Over the last 27 months United States and Japanese intelligence services have reported the expansion of Soviet military power on Sakhalin, on the Siberian mainland and on the island of Etorofu of the Kuril island chain. Etorofu lies 150 miles northeast of Hokkaido, the northern Japanese island. The entire area, one officer said, is of major importance to Soviet strategic planning.

A squadron of MIG-23's was deployed on Etorofu about a month ago, according to intelligence sources.

American and NATO intelligence analysts rejected the idea that the shooting down of the Boeing airliner could have been the impulsive act of a Soviet pilot. They cited the rigid, centralized command system of Soviet forces and said an attack on a civilian airliner, even when it was in Soviet airspace, could not have been carried out without the approval of a higher headquarters.

They noted that the elapsed time between the first Soviet radar sighting of the airliner and the attack was suffi-

cient for an exchange of messages between the local commander and headquarters either in Vladivostok, headquarters of the Pacific Fleet, or in Moscow.

Air Force sources were puzzled by the fact that the stricken South Korean

Continued on Page A7, Column 1

The New York Times

Late Edition

Weather: Rain ending in the afternoon, cool, southeasterly winds today; remaining cloudy tonight and tomorrow. Temperatures: today 53-57, tonight 40-45; yesterday 48-59. Details, page D12.

VOL.CXXXIII.. No. 45,841   Copyright © 1983 The New York Times   NEW YORK, MONDAY, OCTOBER 24, 1983   30 cents beyond 78 miles from New York City, except on Long Island.   30 CENTS

BEIRUT DEATH TOLL AT 161 AMERICANS; FRENCH CASUALTIES RISE IN BOMBINGS; REAGAN INSISTS MARINES WILL REMAIN

ATTACK IS ASSAILED

U.S. Says Terrorists Tied to Iran May Have Set Off the Lethal Blast

By FRANCIS X. CLINES
Special to The New York Times

WASHINGTON, Oct. 23 — President Reagan, voicing outrage over the "despicable" destruction of the Marine Corps headquarters in Lebanon, called on the nation today to be more determined than ever to keep a force in that country and resist "the bestial nature of those who would assume power."

The President, plunging into a day of emergency strategy meetings on the bombing, denounced the unidentified forces behind the attack and said the

Reagan statement, page A8.

nation "must be more determined than ever that they cannot take over that vital and strategic area of the earth."

Administration officials, emphasizing that there would be no change in the United States' military role in Lebanon, said there was "circumstantial evidence" that fanatic terrorists aligned with Iran may have been responsible for the truck bomb that razed the four-story Marine Corps headquarters in Beirut, leaving 161 dead and 75 wounded.

The White House spokesman, Larry Speakes, said this evening that the Administration was also "looking into" Syria's possible role in the incident, but he did not cite any evidence.

No Dramatic Moves Anticipated

Official spokesmen stressed that no dramatic countermoves by the military were anticipated.

In the aftermath of the attack, legislators from both parties said the Administration must redefine and clarify the role of its troops and their long-range mission in the Middle East. [Page A8.]

The troops, who were fired on by snipers even as they rescued the wounded at the Marine headquarters, have been drawing sniper fire from areas near their base at the Beirut airport for weeks. There have been reports that Palestinian guerrillas who have returned to the Beirut area were responsible.

Prime Minister Pierre Mauroy of France condemned the Beirut attacks and said French forces would stay in Lebanon. Page A7.

The bombing put the Administration at crisis alert, with Secretary of State George P. Shultz postponing a trip Monday to Brazil and El Salvador.

"There is much that points to the direction of Iran," Secretary of Defense Caspar W. Weinberger declared after the first of two emergency briefings of the President by his national security advisers. The White House said, however, that the Administration had no conclusive findings and that the President had ordered additional intelligence investigations.

The President directed the Marine Corps commandant, Gen. P. X. Kelley, to go to Beirut to inspect the scene and

Continued on Page A8, Column 2

MARINES' SECURITY RAISES QUESTIONS

Reagan Sends Commandant to Lebanon to Investigate

By CHARLES MOHR
Special to The New York Times

WASHINGTON, Oct. 23 — After a car bomb blew up the United States Embassy in Beirut on April 18, killing 63 people, the Marine force at the Beirut airport took steps to strengthen security measures against a similar incident, Marine Corps officers said today.

The embassy bombing, and at least seven other serious car bombings this year in Beirut, gave warning of a common tactic. But a determined terrorist overwhelmed the new airport defenses, raising questions about why the security measures were inadequate.

Larry Speakes, the chief White House spokesman, said tonight that President Reagan had ordered the Marine Commandant, Gen. P. X. Kelly, to go to Beirut to determine what security measures could be taken to improve protection for the marines in Lebanon.

'Unbelievable,' Kennedy Says

Senator Edward M. Kennedy, Democrat of Massachusetts, a member of the Armed Services Commitee, asked for an investitation by the committee into what he called the "unbelievable breakdown in security that allowed it to happen."

In testimony before the Senate Foreign Relations Committee in September, General Kelly said in answer to a question that the area of responsibility given the marines in the multinational force dictated their position and that the Marines Corps was satisfied with

Continued on Page A12, Column 3

Rescuers removing a wounded marine on a stretcher from the rubble of the bombed-out building that housed a U.S. Marine battalion in Beirut.

Associated Press

Beirut Bombing: How It Happened
Based on reports from Beirut and Washington.

To Beirut

Terminal

100 YARDS

The New York Times/Oct. 24, 1983

1. Truck passes Lebanese and Marine checkpoints on highway to airport . . .
2. . . . and turns left onto access road to parking lot in front of Marine headquarters.
3. Once in lot, driver guns engine and runs through barbed wire fence, swerves to avoid sandbag bunker and crashes through main gate in fence about 40 feet from building.
4. Driver swerves again to avoid sandbag blast wall. Behind it, at building entrance, is guard hut with sergeant-at-arms and sentry. Sergeant calls in report and sentry fires five shots before driver smashes through hut. Truck reaches central atrium and driver detonates bomb.

BUILDINGS BLASTED

Truck Loaded With TNT Wrecks Headquarters of a Marine Unit

By THOMAS L. FRIEDMAN
Special to The New York Times

BEIRUT, Lebanon, Oct. 23 — A suicide terrorist driving a truck loaded with TNT blew up an American Marine headquarters at the Beirut airport today, killing at least 161 marines and sailors and wounding 75.

In an almost simultaneous attack, another bomb-laden truck slammed into a French paratroop barracks two miles away.

According to Lebanese Civil Defense authorities, at least 27 French paratroopers were killed, 12 were wounded and 53 were reported missing and believed buried in rubble. Official Defense Ministry figures issued in Paris listed 12 French soldiers dead, 13 wounded and 46 missing.

It was the highest number of American military personnel killed in a single attack since the Vietnam War.

The identity of the attackers still had not been determined tonight.

Vehicle Smashes Barriers

According to a Pentagon spokesman, a Mercedes truck filled with some 2,500 pounds of TNT broke through a series of steel fences and sandbag barricades and detonated in the heart of the Marines' administrative headquarters building shortly after dawn. The explosion collapsed all four floors of the building, turning it into a burning mound of broken cement pillars and cinder blocks.

Although a marine sentry was able to fire about five shots at the suicide driver and another marine threw himself in front of the speeding, explosive-filled truck, neither could block its entry into the headquarters building, where it exploded in a fireball that left a crater 30 feet deep and 40 feet wide.

In a haunting scene late tonight, rescue workers using blow torches, pneumatic drills and cranes worked furiously under floodlights to pry out the dead and wounded still crushed beneath the smouldering debris. Marine spokesmen said there might have been as many as 300 men sleeping in the building — which doubled as a bunk house — at the time of the blast.

'Carnage' Like That in Vietnam

"I haven't seen carnage like that since Vietnam," the Marine spokesman, Maj. Robert Jordan, said shortly after emerging from the rescue operation with his forearms smeared with blood.

Today's blast brought to 184 the number of Americans killed in Lebanon since the bombing of the American Embassy here in April.

Rescue workers were hindered in their movements by unidentified snipers who intermittently fired shots into the Marine compound from the nearby southern suburbs of Beirut. The marines occasionally returned the fire.

Less that two minutes after the attack on the Marine compound, a truck laden with explosives slammed into a building used by the French as a headquarters for one of their 110-man companies in the southern Beirut suburb of

Continued on Page A6, Column 1

'DON'T LEAVE US,' TRAPPED MEN CRY

Survivors Recount the Horror of Scene at Marine Base

Special to The New York Times

BEIRUT, Lebanon, Oct. 23 — Gunnery Sgt. Herman Lange was one of the first marines to get down to the bombed Marine headquarters from a nearby barracks.

"Bodies were lying around all over," he said. "Other people were trapped under the concrete. I could hear them screaming. 'Get us out. Don't leave us.' I just started digging, picking men out and taking them away on a jeep. It was total devastation."

The blast at the Marines' headquarters building, which housed the Battalion Landing Team and was known by the marines as the BLT, was so massive it dug a crater in the heart of the building 30 feet deep and 40 feet across. In the crater, piles of reinforced concrete, marines still in their cots, files, air conditioners, clothes and crates all intermingled.

Playing Cards and Deodorant

Classified papers were blown all over the area and the marines who survived scrambled to pick them up. The pile of rubble was peppered with personal items — a can of deodorant, a jack of hearts from someone's deck of playing cards and a United States quarter, twisted out of shape by the blast. "It felt just like an earthquake," said Staff Sgt. Alfonso Hernandez.

"I was sleeping in my rack in a tent about 200 yards away," Sergeant Hernandez said. "We were all thrown out

Continued on Page A7, Column 1

Questions on Mission

By BERNARD GWERTZMAN
Special to The New York Times

WASHINGTON, Oct. 23 — The devastating attack on the American marines in Lebanon today stunned the Reagan Administration and put it under new pressure to come up with a clearer explanation of why the marines are there.

News Analysis

Tonight the White House, seeking to justify the presence of the marines in Lebanon, said they would remain there and not yield to "international terrorism." If they were withdrawn now, the White House said, "the civilized world" would suffer.

In the 13 months since the marines were sent to the Beirut area, the reasons for their presence there have shifted with the situation. At first they were dispatched to bolster the morale of the Lebanese Government and to be ready to help police areas that the United States had expected would be evacuated by the Israeli, Syrian and Palestinian forces.

But more recently, as the hopes for an early withdrawal of these forces faded, the marines, augmented by United States Navy ships, have become in effect a protector of the Lebanese Army, fighting off efforts by Syrian-backed Druse and Shiite factions to undermine the Lebanese Government. But even this role was ambiguous because the Administration would not sanction an all-out military role for the marines for fear of alienating Congress and friendly Arab nations.

Today President Reagan, clearly frustrated by the Marine casualties, vowed even before he had met with his National Security Council that the United States would not be driven out of Lebanon.

Yet after the morning meeting of the

Continued on Page A9, Column 1

French paratrooper holding trapped comrade's hand at site of second blast.

United Press International

Other News

Stirring Marathon Victory
Rod Dixon of New Zealand took the lead in the final mile to win the men's title. Grete Waitz won a fifth women's crown. SportsMonday, page C1.

Grenada Warns of Invasion
Grenada's radio issued a warning to the island's residents to expect an imminent invasion by the country's Caribbean neighbors. Page A4.

Mixed Signals for Bonn
The antimissile protests in West Germany conveyed signs of both disquiet and reassurance for Bonn and its allies. News analysis, page A3.

Augusta Suspect 'Troubled'
The suspect charged with taking hostages while President Reagan played golf is a 'troubled' man who may have been drinking. Page A14.

Food Tests Reviewed
A Louisiana laboratory's tests of chemicals for consumer use are being reviewed because a test on a coffee chemical was "sloppy." Page D12.

DeLorean Tape Shown
CBS News won a court battle and televised a videotape of the scene culminating in the arrest of John Z. DeLorean on drug charges. Page A16.

The New York Times

Late Edition

Weather: Mostly cloudy and cool, brisk northeasterly winds today; remaining cloudy and cool tonight and tomorrow. Temperatures: today 49-51 tonight 41-43; yesterday 46-53. Details, page C20.

VOL.CXXXIII . No. 45,843   Copyright © 1983 The New York Times   NEW YORK, WEDNESDAY, OCTOBER 26, 1983   50 cents beyond 75 miles from New York City, except on Long Island.   30 CENTS

1,900 U.S. TROOPS, WITH CARIBBEAN ALLIES, INVADE GRENADA AND FIGHT LEFTIST UNITS; MOSCOW PROTESTS; BRITISH ARE CRITICAL

Toll Climbs In Bombing In Lebanon

216 Americans Dead, 20 to 30 Missing

By THOMAS L. FRIEDMAN
Special to The New York Times

BEIRUT, Lebanon, Oct. 25 — Gen. Paul X. Kelley, the United States Marine commandant, arrived here from Washington today as the Marine contingent was placed on its highest state of alert.

Late in the day, it was announced that the number of American military personnel killed in Sunday's bombing of the Marine headquarters had risen to 216, with 20 to 30 bodies still believed buried in the rubble of the headquarters building at the Beirut airport.

• The alert was ordered after an early morning intelligence warning was passed to the marines by the Lebanese Army saying that three vehicles reportedly carrying high explosives were circling the area and might strike at the Marine compound.

[Vice President Bush left Washington for Beirut, where he will meet with President Amin Gemayel and visit with the Marine force, The Associated Press reported. Mr. Bush, whose trip was announced after his departure, is expected to return Wednesday night, a White House spokesman said.]

Removal of Barrier Reported

In another development, a marine officer familiar with the bombed compound said that two long, thick pipes that had been placed as barriers in front of the entryway of the headquarters to protect against car-bomb attacks had been removed several days before Sunday's attack.

This evening, a Marine spokesman, Maj. Robert Jordan, said he could not say for certain whether the pipes, which had apparently been installed months ago, had been in their position at the time of the attack.

General Kelley came to the Lebanese capital to review security measures at the Marine compound and to meet with the members of the American contingent in the multinational force here.

Replacements Arrive

Hours before General Kelley reached Beirut, 300 more marines arrived by plane from the United States to replace their fallen comrades.

General Kelley toured the ruins of the Battalion Landing Team headquarters, while marines and Lebanese civil defense workers continued to excavate bodies from the jagged wreckage of the

Continued on Page A6, Column 1

President Reagan, accompanied by Prime Minister Eugenia Charles of Dominica, holding a news conference on the Grenada invasion. Listening were Secretary of State George P. Shultz, Defense Secretary Caspar W. Weinberger and, behind them, David R. Gergen, the White House communications director.

United Press International

Key Events in Caribbean Invasion

Puerto Rico and Barbados: 1,200-member Marine unit reportedly assembles in Panama and in Puerto Rico, while 700 Army Rangers are said to leave from Barbados; 300 soldiers are provided by Organization of Eastern Caribbean States.

St. George's: Invaders reportedly seize most of southern half of capital, where Cubans had been living.

Medical School: Both campuses of school where Americans are enrolled are quickly secured.

Point Salines and Pearls Airport: 700 U.S. troops land at Point Salines, where Cubans were building an international airport; 600 Americans land at Pearls. Later 300 Caribbean soldiers are flown in, and 600 U.S. marines remain in helicopter carrier offshore.

The New York Times/Oct. 26, 1983

Agony of Lebanon Is Felt in Connecticut

By SUSAN CHIRA
Special to The New York Times

NAUGATUCK, Conn., Oct. 25 — Schoolchildren passed around Dwayne Wigglesworth's picture and talked about why people were killing one another in Lebanon. Older men talked about why the young always had to die, and young boys talked about whether they would have to fight, too.

Lance Corporal Wigglesworth, 19 years old, died Sunday in Beirut, a victim of the terrorist bombing against the Marines. Today, as word of his death spread, people here thought of how they could comfort members of his family, who live in this town of nearly 30,000. Neighbors and strangers called the Wigglesworth home, offering help or bringing food.

The fighting in Beirut came home to this town Monday morning, when three marines in dress blues knocked on the door of the Wigglesworths' home to tell them what they had been praying not to hear.

"The first reaction is anger, ha-

tred, all the frustration," said Henry Wigglesworth, Corporal Wigglesworth's father. "There are a lot of whys, a lot of questions, and we haven't had the answers yet to give anybody else."

The Wigglesworths have seven other sons and one daughter. Robyn, 21, is a marine stationed in Japan. Gary, 22, is in the Army, stationed at Fort Bragg, N.C.

Gary and Dwayne spent the last month before Corporal Wigglesworth was sent to Beirut "fishing and enjoying each other," their father said.

Today Robyn arrived home to be with his family, and Corporal Wigglesworth's death was the topic of

conversation at shoe stores and stationers, at schools and at City Hall.

"It's not only people outside that we don't know getting killed," said Paul DeFranzo, 18. "It's somebody from your own hometown. It makes you think even harder."

"I feel sorry for people who have to suffer because it's in the family," said Robin Henao, a 13-year-old seventh grader at the Hillside Middle School. Her teacher passed Corporal Wigglesworth's picture around her social studies class and read them news of Lebanon from the newspaper.

Five flags surrounded the war me-

Continued on Page A7, Column 1

An Invasion Prompted by Previous Debacles

By BERNARD GWERTZMAN
Special to The New York Times

WASHINGTON, Oct. 25 — Behind President Reagan's decision to invade Grenada today was his concern that the island not become either "another Iran," where Americans were held hostage for 444 days, or "another Beirut," where the United States was powerless to prevent the death of more than 200 marines, Administration officials said.

News Analysis

But in addition to these reasons, which Secretary of State George P. Shultz insisted were the paramount ones, there was additional motivation, officials said: to rid the Caribbean of a potential outpost for Cuba and the

Soviet Union and to stop what the Administration perceived as a drift toward more radicalism in the region.

Some officials said the White House could not afford "another Nicaragua," the Cuban ally in Central America, while others said a more real concern was that there not be "another Suriname," the former Dutch colony in northern South America that was taken over by leftists last year in a coup.

The move also demonstrated the determination of this Administration not to appear passive in the face of foreign crisis. A French diplomat, who derided the Grenada invasion, said the President looked as if he was "flailing around," striking at the Grenadians out of his frustration at not being able

to hit Damascus, Havana or Moscow. White House officials defended the President as being suitably cautious, but unwilling to run the risk of being compared to his predecessor, Jimmy Carter, whose handling of the hostage crisis in Iran may have caused him to lose the election to Mr. Reagan.

The invasion, however, has produced a new series of international problems for the Administration, already faced with a difficult crisis in Lebanon. Launching the action without advance consultation with Congress, and without the cooperation of its key North Atlantic Treaty Organization and Latin American allies, the Administration

Continued on Page A17, Column 2

Airports Seized, Drive on Capital Faces Stiff Fire

By MICHAEL T. KAUFMAN
Special to The New York Times

BRIDGETOWN, Barbados, Oct. 25 — An assault force spearheaded by United States troops invaded Grenada before dawn today and soon seized both of the island's airfields. But the advance of the invaders, who included contingents from seven Caribbean nations, was reportedly slowed in the afternoon by heavy fire in the capital.

According to military and intelligence sources in the Caribbean, the initial landings were made by helicopter. Fire from armed Cubans met those landing at a jet runway being completed by Cuban workers at Point Salines, four miles south of St. George's, the capital.

In the initial contact, 12 Cubans were killed and 24 captured, according to officials of the Barbados Government, one of the contributors of troops to the invading force.

Russians Reported Seized

The United States contingent consisted of marines and army rangers. At least one marine was reported here to have been killed; in Washington the Defense Department put the number of Marine dead at two.

Radio stations here reported that 30 Soviet advisers to the Grenadian Government had been seized. But officials here said they could not confirm that report.

By this afternoon, a source who had returned from Grenada reported that the invading force had established a perimeter that included the southern half of St. George's. The part of the city held by the multinational force included the deep-water harbor, the Prime Minister's residence and the Grenada Beach Hotel, the former Holi-

Continued on Page A17, Column 3

U.S. WAS WARNED BY MRS. THATCHER

She Urged Caution on Reagan — London Played No Role

By BARNABY J. FEDER
Special to The New York Times

LONDON, Oct. 25 — Prime Minister Margaret Thatcher said today that the British Government had urged President Reagan to reconsider his plans to launch an invasion of Grenada after learning of them Monday, and that no British ships or forces had taken part.

The announcement in the House of Commons that Grenada, a member of

The Soviet press called the invasion an "act of undisguised banditry." Cuba said its workers in Grenada had been ordered not to give up under any circumstances. Page A7.

the Commonwealth, had been invaded by an ally despite the Government's expressed misgivings led to harsh criticism of both the British Government and President Reagan by opposition parties and some of Mrs. Thatcher's own Conservatives.

France described the invasion as "a surprising action in relation to international law" and said it had not been informed of the action. [Page A17.]

Opposition Speaks of Deception

Sir Geoffrey Howe, the Foreign Secretary, underwent 45 minutes of tumultuous questioning when called upon to explain the events that had begun to unfold hours after he assured the House on Monday that there was no reason to anticipate any military intervention in Grenada.

Denis Healey, the Labor Party's spokesman on foreign affairs, said the United States and some Commonwealth nations in the Caribbean had deceived Britain about their plans.

"None of the objectives stated by President Reagan justifies the invasion of an independent state," Mr. Healey said.

The Government, however, refused to condemn the invasion. Mrs. Thatcher said, "We understand that what weighed heavily with the United

Continued on Page A17, Column 1

2 AMERICANS KILLED

Cubans Clash With Force — 30 Soviet Advisers Are Reported Safe

By HEDRICK SMITH
Special to The New York Times

WASHINGTON, Oct. 25 — President Reagan announced today that he had ordered a predawn invasion of Grenada by nearly 1,900 marines and Army airborne troops.

He said the invasion was intended to protect American citizens and to help restore democratic institutions on the Caribbean island.

The Defense Department said two Americans had been killed.

Four hours after the American landings began, the President said the

Reagan statement, page A16;
Shultz news conference, page A18.

operation was launched in response to an urgent request from some members of the Organization of Eastern Caribbean States, some of which provided 300 troops for the operation.

'No Choice But to Act'

The United States, President Reagan told a 9 A.M. news conference, "had no choice but to act strongly and decisively" to oppose "a brutal gang of leftist thugs" that had violently seized power on Oct. 12, later executed Prime Minister Maurice Bishop and other Cabinet ministers, recently imposed a "shoot on sight" curfew and shut down the international airports this weekend when some of the 1,000 Americans on the island wanted to leave.

The President said American forces had quickly "secured" the island's two airports. This afternoon, Secretary of State George P. Shultz said American troops had identified and were assuring the safety of 30 Soviet military advisers on the island and had also taken over part of the island's medical school, where more than 500 Americans were studying.

'Pockets of Resistance'

Mr. Shultz said American forces had encountered "pockets of resistance" around the capital city of St. George's and were also fighting some of the 600 armed Cuban construction workers building an airfield near Point Salines. But he gave no details. A Cuban broadcast, quoted by The Associated Press, said that "at nightfall the heroic resistance of our constructors and collaborators continued."

Tonight, at an urgent meeting of the United Nations Security Council called to discuss the situation in Grenada, the United States clashed sharply with Latin American countries critical of the invasion. [Page A18.]

Extremely tight secrecy surrounded the invasion and only at 9 P.M. did the Pentagon release its first combat communiqué, reporting that two American troops had been killed and 23 wounded

Associated Press
Gen. Hudson Austin, head of Grenada's military junta.

Continued on Page A16, Column 1

Days of Crisis for President: Golf, a Tragedy and Secrets

By FRANCIS X. CLINES
Special to The New York Times

WASHINGTON, Oct. 25 — At midday Saturday, as President Reagan was in the midst of a round of golf at the Augusta National Golf Course in Georgia, he had under active consideration a secret request from Caribbean nations to join in the invasion of Grenada.

The President, already a legend in the Administration for keeping his own counsel, had begun the most secretive and momentous week of his incumbency with a golf club in his hands.

One of his golfing partners, Secretary of State George P. Shultz, was receiving the latest details of Grenada invasion plans going on in Washington, and discussing them with the President on the golf course, according to White House officials.

On Sunday morning, the Grenada

issue was further laid out in Administration study papers as Mr. Reagan made a sudden return home and appeared standing in the rain outside the White House, grief-stricken and mourning the marines who had died in the shocking Beirut explosion a few hours earlier.

The national security meetings that followed were ostensibly devoted entirely to the Lebanon crisis, but today it became clear that they also advanced the Grenada invasion decision.

Continued on Page A22, Column 3

INSIDE

Civil Rights Dismissals

In an unexpected move, President Reagan removed three Democratic critics from the United States Commission on Civil Rights. Page A24.

Indian Pt. Change Urged

A panel told the Nuclear Regulatory Commission to change evacuation plans for the area around Indian Point nuclear plant. Page B2.

FOR HOME DELIVERY OF THE NEW YORK TIMES, call toll free 1-800-631-2500 In Boston, (617) 787-7919 In Washington (301) 587-3600.—ADVT.

The New York Times

VOL.CXXXIII...No. 45,951   Copyright © 1984 The New York Times   NEW YORK, SATURDAY, FEBRUARY 11, 1984   30 cents beyond 75 miles from New York City, except on Long Island   30 CENTS

Late Edition

Weather: Mostly cloudy, chance of morning showers today; partly cloudy tonight. Partly cloudy, mild tomorrow. Temperatures: today 51-53, tonight 41-43; yesterday 30-47. Details, page 54.

ANDROPOV IS DEAD IN MOSCOW AT 69; REAGAN ASKS 'PRODUCTIVE' CONTACTS AND NAMES BUSH TO ATTEND FUNERAL

LILCO WITHDRAWS FROM PARTNERSHIP IN UPSTATE PLANT

Misses $1.1 Million Payment for Building Nuclear Unit, Citing Financial Woes

By MATTHEW L. WALD

The Long Island Lighting Company defaulted yesterday on its partnership agreement with four other New York State utilities that are building the Nine Mile Point 2 nuclear power plant on the shore of Lake Ontario.

The company said that it had missed a $1.1 million payment due Thursday and that it would spend no more on the plant, which is still at least two years from operation, at an estimated cost of $4.2 billion for completion.

Lilco has invested about $500 million in the project since 1975, when it agreed to buy 18 percent of the reactor. This year its share would have been $180 million.

The utility is struggling to raise cash because of its troubles with the Shoreham reactor, which it is building alone on Long Island.

Mismanagement Charged

In another blow yesterday, the staff of the state's Public Service Commission recommended that Lilco, not its customers, should bear $1.5 billion of the reactor's cost of approximately $4 billion because of "serious mismanagement and inefficiency throughout the project." [Page 31.]

Governor Cuomo said he would meet with legislative leaders next week and "provide them with a comprehensive agenda for action including the problem of Shoreham and all other current energy concerns."

Lilco's four partners in the Nine Mile Point project had no comment yesterday on what they would do next to pick up the cost of the project and said they

Continued on Page 31, Column 3

400 Americans Are Evacuated From Lebanon

By THOMAS L. FRIEDMAN
Special to The New York Times

BEIRUT, Lebanon, Feb. 10 — With only a few hours' notice, more than 400 American citizens, protected by United States marines and Druse militiamen, were evacuated from Beirut today. Britain also evacuated hundreds of its citizens, and Italy prepared to do so.

The American Embassy had received many appeals from American citizens for transport out of Beirut, where they have been trapped by fighting. It announced this morning that "because of the unsettled conditions in Lebanon" it would evacuate any Americans or Lebanese in the process of taking up American citizenship.

On Thursday the embassy said it did not regard such a move as justified, and political sources close to the Americans said there was concern that an evacuation might upset negotiations aimed at keeping President Amin Gemayel in power.

Waiting for the Weather

Asked today why the embassy had waited to decide on an evacuation, its spokesman, John Stewart, said, "We were waiting to see if the weather was good."

In military action today, Israeli jets attacked targets in hills 12 miles east of Beirut in their first raids in Lebanon since Moslem militiamen took over West Beirut. The Israeli command said the raids, which came a day after rockets were fired into northern Israel from southern Lebanon, were against Palestinian guerrilla positions. [Page 5.]

[In Washington, a senior Reagan Administration official expressed optimism that the withdrawal of United States marines from the Beirut airport would begin "in a matter of days" and would be completed within a month. Page 5.]

According to the registration list, 410 Americans, Lebanese and diplomats from Egypt, Japan and South Korea were airlifted out of West Beirut

Continued on Page 5, Column 4

QUICK SIGNAL SENT

Shultz Emphasizes U.S. Is Ready for Effort to Improve Relations

By BERNARD GWERTZMAN
Special to The New York Times

WASHINGTON, Feb. 10 — President Reagan and Secretary of State George P. Shultz told Soviet leaders today that during this period of transition in Moscow the United States wanted to reaffirm its desire "for a constructive and realistic dialogue" with the Soviet Union.

Although some thought was given to having Mr. Reagan lead the American delegation to the funeral of Yuri V. Andropov, the White House said late today that Vice President Bush would head the delegation. [Page 7.]

In Santa Barbara, Calif., Larry Speakes, the White House spokesman, said that Mr. Reagan, in a message of condolences, called on the Kremlin to "join in peaceful purpose for all mankind."

Prompt Signal to Moscow

Mr. Shultz appeared before reporters in Washington to read an Administration statement that incorporated some of Mr. Reagan's message and some additional thoughts. The purpose of the publicity given the Administration's messages, State Department officials said, was to send a prompt signal to the Soviet leaders that Washington was more ready than ever for a significant improvement in relations, in keeping with the Administration's conciliatory policy of the last month.

Mr. Shultz was reported to have favored Mr. Reagan's going to the funeral, although other senior officials saw more merit at this time in Mr. Bush and Mr. Shultz heading the delegation, as they did at the funeral for Leonid I. Brezhnev in November 1982. In a telephone conversation with Mr. Reagan this morning, Mr. Shultz laid

Continued on Page 7, Column 1

Yuri Vladimirovich Andropov

Woodfin Camp / Lehtikuva Oy

BURIAL ON TUESDAY

Chernenko to Lead Rites — Role May Be a Hint on the Succession

By JOHN F. BURNS
Special to The New York Times

MOSCOW, Feb. 10 — The Soviet leadership announced today that Yuri V. Andropov died Thursday, less than 15 months after he succeeded Leonid I. Brezhnev as General Secretary of the Communist Party. He was 69 years old.

The two-paragraph announcement was read on radio and television at 2:30 P.M. (6:30 A.M. New York time) and was repeated throughout the day. It was followed by a series of bulletins on the causes of death and on arrangements for a funeral on Tuesday.

Konstantin U. Chernenko, 72 years old, a Brezhnev protégé who served as the second-ranking secretary, will lead the funeral commission. Foreign diplomats took this as an indication that he might succeed Mr. Andropov.

[Governments in Western Europe and Japan expressed regret and some indicated they would send high officials to the funeral. In Poland, the press mourned the Soviet leader, but people in the street reacted with sarcasm or indifference. Page 10.]

Absent for Six Months

The Soviet leadership said official mourning would last from Saturday until the burial in Red Square.

Mr. Andropov's death, from a chronic kidney ailment that had kept him from public functions for six months, left vacant several key positions. In addition to being party leader, he was chairman of the Presidium of the Supreme Soviet, the equivalent of

As Soviet leader, Yuri V. Andropov encountered major problems with the West and with a stagnating economy at home. An obituary, page 9.

head of state, and chairman of the Defense Council, with authority over the armed forces.

The official announcement said Mr. Andropov died at 4:50 P.M. on Thursday "after a long illness," identified by the medical bulletin as having involved nephritis, diabetes and hypertension "complicated by a chronic kidney deficiency."

The medical statement said he had been receiving treatment on an artificial kidney machine for 12 months, but had suffered a deterioration in his condition toward the end of January.

The pronouncements did not say where Mr. Andropov died. He had been reported hospitalized at a special clinic

Continued on Page 6, Column 1

Policy After Andropov

No Drastic Changes Expected in Moscow

By SERGE SCHMEMANN
Special to The New York Times

MOSCOW, Feb. 10 — Yuri V. Andropov's death put an end to the shortest period of rule in Soviet history, if Georgi M. Malenkov's week as titular Communist Party chief after Stalin's death can be overlooked.

But neither the worsening Soviet-American chill that marked Mr. Andropov's 15 months as leader nor the changes he set in motion through the Soviet Union's ponderous economic system and bureaucracy are considered likely to be altered anytime soon, no matter who succeeds him.

Ending the Stagnation

The chief reason, most diplomats agree, is that Mr. Andropov's economic experiments, his crackdown on corruption, and even his hard line in foreign relations found the support of a populace yearning for a tough "khozyain," or boss — and, more important, the support of powerful men and institutions.

Power brokers like Defense Minister Dmitri F. Ustinov, now arguably the most powerful man in the Politburo, or

Continued on Page 8, Column 2

Washington Foresees Continuing Conflicts

By LESLIE H. GELB
Special to The New York Times

WASHINGTON, Feb. 10 — The passing of a major political leader sometimes creates a sense of opportunity. But as seen by a range of Reagan Administration officials, Yuri V. Andropov's death offers not so much a chance for breakthroughs as a time for gestures that might lead to breakthroughs later on.

There is little evidence that anything fundamental has changed in either Moscow or Washington with Mr. Andropov's passing. Essentially, the same people have been running Soviet foreign policy for five or six years. Mr. Andropov was ill for almost one year of his 15-month tenure. His predecessor, Leonid I. Brezhnev, seemed inactive for his last three years. Soviet policy has been much the same throughout.

Profound Differences

Nor is there much evidence that President Reagan is prepared to propose new compromises that might help break the impasses over the Soviet intervention in Afghanistan or the Lebanon situation or the talks on nuclear arms. All that can be seen thus far is a

News Analysis

Continued on Page 8, Column 2

The Chief Mourner in Moscow

Konstantin Ustinovich Chernenko
Special to The New York Times

MOSCOW, Feb. 10 — The appointment of Konstantin U. Chernenko today to head Yuri V. Andropov's funeral commission marked at least a partial triumph for a veteran Communist who only 15 months earlier seemed to have reached the end of his political career.

Whether the appointment suggested that Mr. Chernenko had been tapped to succeed Mr. Andropov, or whether it was given him on the strength of his position as the second-ranking secretary, was likely to become clear only when the Central Committee named a new General Secretary.

But the fact that Mr. Chernenko would be on hand to supervise the burial of his former rival was in itself a feat of political survival not without an element of irony.

Mr. Chernenko, now 72 years old, had been the closest aide to Leonid I. Brezhnev and the clear choice of Mr. Brezhnev's entourage to succeed the late leader. But Mr. Andropov had outmaneuvered them all, and on Nov. 12, 1982, Tass, the official press agency, announced that Mr. Chernenko himself had nominated his rival to become the new Soviet chief.

This act of party loyalty apparently paid off. While many of Mr. Brezh-

Man in the News

nev's political allies found themselves retired or disgraced in the shuffles and crackdowns instigated by the new regime, Mr. Chernenko settled into a reasonably prestigious job. Although relieved of his post as chief of the Central Committee's General Department, with broad responsibility over the day-to-day work of the party and its personnel, he was handed the late Mikhail A. Suslov's stewardship over ideology and culture.

In that role, Mr. Chernenko made the keynote speech at a Central Committee meeting last spring and con-

Sketches of other leaders mentioned as possible successors, page 8.

Continued on Page 8, Column 1

Followed his patron, Leonid I. Brezhnev, up the party ladder.

Gamma-Liaison / Alain Mingam

Producer Prices Up 0.6% in Month, Led by Food

By JONATHAN FUERBRINGER
Special to The New York Times

WASHINGTON, Feb. 10 — Producer prices for finished goods, driven up by a sharp rise in food prices, climbed six-tenths of 1 percent in January, the Labor Department reported today. It was the largest monthly rise in more than a year.

The increase, which was as much as the Producer Price Index rose for all of 1983, surprised some economists but was not, several said, a cause for alarm. "This is not a fundamental turn," toward broadly higher inflation, said Otto Eckstein of Data Resources Inc.

"It just shows there is only so much luck you can have with fruit and vegetable prices and oil prices," he added, a reference to the slight increases in food prices and sharp declines in energy prices largely responsible for last year's almost stable index.

Over all, food prices rose 2.7 percent, the largest one-month jump since August 1980. In December, food prices rose seven-tenths of 1 percent. Pork, beef, veal and fish prices were up because of the cold weather, which killed

cattle or kept their weight down and disrupted the delivery of hogs. Poultry prices rose because of the loss of hundreds of thousands of chickens to avian flu, which also pushed up egg prices.

Because changes in producer prices of fresh food flow through quickly to retail prices, much of the January increase reported today may already be reflected in what consumers are paying at the store.

On the other hand, energy prices declined 1.2 percent in the January index, the sixth drop in the last seven months, and prices of other goods held rela-

Continued on Page 41, Column 5

FIND OUT ABOUT HOME OR OFFICE DELIVERY of The Times in New York, Boston, Philadelphia or Washington. Call toll-free, 1-800-631-2500—ADVT.

THE WAD FAMILY WISHES CHRISTANA A HAPPY 23rd BIRTHDAY—ADVT.

INSIDE

Diet May Cut Cancer Risk
The American Cancer Society issued new diet guidelines and urged Americans to avoid obesity to reduce the risk of cancer. Page 12.

British Skaters Take Lead
Jayne Torvill and Christopher Dean were given three perfect scores in ice dancing as skating began at the Olympic Winter Games. Page 21.

News Summary and Index, Page 29

Classified Ads ... 48-53   Auto Exchange ... 25

Britons boarding Royal Navy helicopters as foreign civilians, including Americans, began to leave Beirut.

United Press International

"All the News That's Fit to Print"

The New York Times

Late Edition
Weather: Morning fog and drizzle, afternoon rain, mild today, rain, fog tonight. Gradual clearing, mild tomorrow. Temperatures: today 49-51, tonight 41-43; yesterday 36-45. Details, page C10.

VOL.CXXXIII... No. 45,954   Copyright © 1984 The New York Times   NEW YORK, TUESDAY, FEBRUARY 14, 1984   30 cents beyond 75 miles from New York City, except on Long Island   30 CENTS

Elizabeth Hanford Dole

U.S. TELLS JORDAN OF ITS COMMITMENT DESPITE PULLBACK

Reagan Assures Hussein That American Support Against Syrians Will Continue

By STEVEN R. WEISMAN
Special to The New York Times

WASHINGTON, Feb. 13 — President Reagan assured King Hussein of Jordan today that his decision to pull back the marines from Beirut did not imply a weakening of his commitment to Jordan and Lebanon in their struggles against Syria.

Mr. Reagan's assurances came at a meeting with the King at the White House that marked the beginning of a round of discussions on the turbulent situation in the Middle East. The President is to follow up the session today with a meeting Tuesday with both King Hussein and President Hosni Mubarak of Egypt.

Mr. Mubarak and the King had dinner together Sunday night, but an American official said he did not regard their getting together as "historic" or "ice breaking." The two leaders had met twice before and the Administration has said their presence in town together is a coincidence.

'Terrorism Cannot Be Tolerated'

In his statement after the talk with King Hussein, Mr. Reagan criticized nations he said have supported terrorism in the Middle East. He did not single out any nations, but both he and the King have in the past charged that Syria had supported terrorist attacks against Jordan, the United States and others.

"We also agree that terrorism cannot be tolerated and that the leaders of all states must stand together against this new barbarism that threatens civilization," Mr. Reagan said. "States that condone terrorism undermine their own legitimacy."

The King, who is making an unofficial visit here after a medical checkup in Cleveland and a holiday in Colorado, thanked Mr. Reagan and said, "On all subjects, sir, that you were kind enough to address, I could not in all honesty say that I could have presented my views differently."

Support for U.N. Resolution

In a briefing after the meeting, an Administration official said the session was marked by expressions of friendship and like-mindedness, particularly on the need to oppose Syrian influence and to achieve progress in returning some autonomy to the Palestinians on the West Bank of the Jordan River.

Once more, the official said, Mr. Reagan told King Hussein that he supported United Nations Security Council Resolution 242, a position voiced earlier by Mr. Andropov in responding to Mr. Reagan's overture.

Continued on Page A6, Column 1

F.A.A. SET TO HIRE MORE INSPECTORS

Mrs. Dole Plans 30% Increase for Airline Safety Checks

By RICHARD WITKIN

Secretary of Transportation Elizabeth Hanford Dole, noting the recent temporary groundings of three small airlines for safety reasons, announced yesterday that the airline inspector force of the Federal Aviation Administration would be increased by more than 30 percent.

Mrs. Dole also said she had recommended to the White House that Adm. Donald D. Engen, retired, now on the National Transportation Safety Board, be nominated to head the aviation agency, which is part of her department.

The Reagan Administration has been criticized in Congress in recent months because of cutbacks made in the airline inspector force. The number dropped from 638 in 1981 to 534 last year, and another 7 percent cut had been set for the current fiscal year.

Under the turnaround announced by Mrs. Dole yesterday, 166 new inspectors would be added to the 508 now authorized. That would bring the total to 674, the number authorized in 1981.

Mrs. Dole, speaking at the National Press Club in Washington, did not say how the financing of the increased force would be arranged. Later an F.A.A. spokesman, Dennis Feldman, said: "We have to begin the process immediately of hiring the additional inspectors. And we'll have to absorb the increase within our present fiscal 1984

Continued on Page D27, Column 1

CHERNENKO IN TOP SOVIET POST; VOWS TO RETAIN ARMS BALANCE, WARNS AGAINST 'ADVENTURISTS'

Konstantin U. Chernenko, above at left, with Politburo members at the House of Unions in Moscow where Yuri V. Andropov lies in state. From the right are Dmitri F. Ustinov, Andrei A. Gromyko and Nikolai A. Tikhonov. Below: President Reagan signing book of condolences yesterday at the Soviet Embassy in Washington.

Associated Press, Tass

U.S. Says the Chernenko Speech Hints Door May Be Open to Talks

By BERNARD GWERTZMAN
Special to The New York Times

WASHINGTON, Feb. 13 — The United States said today that it welcomed some apparently conciliatory comments in the speech by the new Soviet leader, Konstantin U. Chernenko. American officials said the comments suggested that the door might be open to reviving a dialogue.

Senior Reagan Administration officials said Mr. Chernenko's speech, which he gave after being chosen as the new General Secretary of the Communist Party, broke no major new ground. But they said it appeared to respond indirectly to President Reagan's call for a new "constructive dialogue."

Late this afternoon, President Reagan arrived at the Soviet Embassy in Washington and signed the condolence book for Yuri V. Andropov that was opened to the public this morning. The White House said Mr. Reagan signed this message:

"Please accept my condolences on the death of Chairman Andropov and convey my sympathy to his family."

The White House said Mr. Reagan

had signed a similar book after the death of Leonid I. Brezhnev in 1982.

In responding to Mr. Chernenko's speech, State Department officials glossed over his tough-sounding words. Instead they focused on his comments about Soviet readiness to "cooperate with" countries that were prepared to help lessen tensions "through practical deeds."

From the context of his remarks, he could have been placing responsibility on the United States to come up with "practical deeds," a position voiced earlier by Mr. Andropov in responding to Mr. Reagan's overture.

But the State Department chose to put a more positive interpretation on Mr. Chernenko's remarks by making it appear that it was the Soviet Union that was ready to offer "practical deeds."

The senior Administration officials said they expected Mr. Chernenko to move cautiously in foreign affairs and rely, perhaps more than had any previ-

Continued on Page A13, Column 1

A Bolshevik Of Old Mold Rises to Top

By SERGE SCHMEMANN
Special to The New York Times

MOSCOW, Feb. 13 — In selecting Konstantin Ustinovich Chernenko to be the next leader of the Soviet Union, his comrades on the Politburo went for a Bolshevik from the old mold.

Mr. Chernenko is widely regarded here as an ideologue, low on formal education or managerial experience but high on old-fashioned propaganda and party loyalty.

If Yuri V. Andropov began his 15-month tenure saying that tired slogans would no longer suffice, Mr. Chernenko began his with a handful of slogans: "Our party's principled stand on these issues is clear, pure and noble," "The party, which is selflessly devoted to the masses, enjoys full trust of the masses," "The inexhaustible strength of Soviet Communists is in cohesion of their ranks."

The occasion, of course, was one that demanded some ceremonial platitudes. Mr. Andropov had not yet been buried and Mr. Chernenko had just been selected General Secretary of the Soviet Communist Party, and the theme of speeches on such occasions is invariably the unity, strength and inevitable triumph of the party.

But Mr. Chernenko's remarks fit neatly into the pattern of all his major pronouncements since he came to prominence as Leonid I. Brezhnev's closest ally on the Politburo.

It was a style probably derived from his years working in agitation and propaganda, or "agit-prop," in Siberia and Moldavia and on the party's Central Committee. But it also reflected a

Continued on Page A11, Column 3

NOTABLE COMEBACK

New Chief, 72, Succeeds the Rival Who Foiled Him in '82 Contest

By JOHN F. BURNS
Special to The New York Times

MOSCOW, Feb. 13 — Konstantin U. Chernenko was chosen by the Communist Party's Central Committee today to succeed Yuri V. Andropov as its General Secretary.

His assumption of the post automatically made Mr. Chernenko the Soviet Union's pre-eminent leader. At 72 years of age, he is the oldest of the men named to lead the party since the Bolshevik Revolution in 1917.

Mr. Chernenko immediately made a wide-ranging speech to the Central Committee in which he praised Mr. Andropov for the "tremendous prestige and respect" he had gained among the Soviet people and endorsed many of Mr. Andropov's domestic policies.

Excerpts from speech, page A11.

Selection Termed Unanimous

On relations with the United States, he said that while the Soviet Union remained committed to peaceful co-existence and elimination of the threat of nuclear war, it would insure that it had enough arms "to cool the hotheads of militant adventurists."

"We need no military superiority," he said. "We do not intend to dictate our will to others. But we will not permit the military equilibrium that has been achieved to be upset. And let nobody have even the slightest doubt about that: We will further see to it that our country's defense capacity be strengthened, that we should have enough means to cool the hot heads of militant adventurism."

An official announcement said that the 12 members of the ruling Politburo had unanimously recommended the appointment of Mr. Chernenko, and that the Central Committee, which has about 300 members, had also been unanimous in approving the nomination.

An Aide to Brezhnev

The appointment marked what appeared to be a remarkable political comeback for Mr. Chernenko, a Russian peasant's son from Siberia who left school at the age of 12 and worked his way through party ranks to the Kremlin as an aide and protégé of Leonid I. Brezhnev. He was the losing candidate 15 months ago when Mr. Andropov was named party leader in succession to Mr. Brezhnev and in the months

Continued on Page A11, Column 1

Salvador Is Faulted On Diversion of Aid In Auditors' Report

By RAYMOND BONNER

WASHINGTON, Feb. 13 — The Salvadoran Government lacks an effective mechanism for preventing the diversion of United States aid money, according to a confidential report prepared for the Agency for International Development.

One result, according to the report, is that a Salvadoran importer can "obtain foreign exchange for transfers to his offshore account." In addition, the report found that some Salvadoran businessmen were reporting "that either political influence or payoffs are necessary to obtain timely financing for imports."

The 100-page report was prepared by Arthur Young & Company, a private consulting company under contract to A.I.D., and completed in June 1983.

At a Congressional hearing late in January, Representative Michael D. Barnes, Democrat of Maryland and chairman of the House Foreign Affairs subcommittee on Latin American, referred to the report and said it showed "rampant corruption and mismanagement" in the use of United States aid to El Salvador.

He asked that the report be made public, but Administration officials re-

Continued on Page A9, Column 1

U.S. Captures Giant Slalom And Takes First Gold Medal

By JOHN TAGLIABUE
Special to The New York Times

SARAJEVO, Yugoslavia, Feb. 13 — The United States, which had won only one medal in the first four days of full-scale competition at the XIV Olympic Winter Games, picked up two more today when Debbie Armstrong won the gold and Christin Cooper the silver in the women's giant slalom.

The race marked the first time that Americans had ever taken the first two places in an Olympic skiing event. It also brought the first Olympic skiing gold medal to the United States since Barbara Ann Cochran won the women's slalom in 1972 at Sapporo, Japan.

Meanwhile, the United States' medal hopes brightened on another front. Scott Hamilton of Denver was in the lead after the first of three days of competition by male figure skaters.

In women's speed skating, Karin Enke of East Germany won her third

medal of the Games, and her second gold, by setting an Olympic record in the 1,000-meter race. The only other event in which medals were awarded today was the men's 15-kilometer cross-country ski race, won by Gunde Svan of Sweden.

The women's giant slalom, two

Continued on Page B8, Column 1

INSIDE

Iranian and Iraqi Shelling
Iran and Iraq attacked towns on each other's borders for a second day, and Iran said it had launched a major offensive into northeast Iraq. Page A6.

Alumni Donations Set Mark
Graduates of colleges in New York, New Jersey and Connecticut are sending donations in record amounts, college fund-raisers report. Page B2.

Debbie Armstrong celebrating her gold medal in the giant slalom — the first for the United States at Sarajevo.

Associated Press

"All the News That's Fit to Print"

The New York Times

Late Edition

Weather: Sunny and cool, brisk westerly winds today; cloudy, showers possible tonight. Sunny again tomorrow. Temperatures: today 63-67, tonight 45-50; yesterday 55-69. Details, page C22.

VOL.CXXXIII..No. 46,039

Copyright © 1984 The New York Times

NEW YORK, WEDNESDAY, MAY 9, 1984

50 cents beyond 75 miles from New York City, except on Long Island.

30 CENTS

OHIO AND INDIANA ARE WON BY HART, BUOYING HIS DRIVE

HE LOSES 2 STATES

Mondale Takes Maryland and North Carolina to Hold Delegate Lead

By HOWELL RAINES

Gary Hart won the Presidential primaries in Ohio and Indiana yesterday, denying Walter F. Mondale the victories he needed to bring the battle for the Democratic nomination to an early close.

By winning the primaries in North Carolina and Maryland, Mr. Mondale sustained his commanding lead in the competition for delegates. He has about two-thirds of the 1,967 needed for nomination.

But by narrowly achieving his first primary victories since the voting in Connecticut on March 27, Mr. Hart prevented the former Vice President from gaining the big prize of the day, Ohio. Democratic strategists and party leaders had agreed that if Mr. Mondale could add a victory there to his triumph in the Texas caucuses last Saturday, he could have sewn up the nomination, for practical purposes.

Showdown on June 5

Now, Mr. Hart said last night, the nomination battle will continue toward a showdown on the final day of the campaign season on June 5, when California, New Jersey and three other states hold primaries. Mr. Hart's strategy calls for weakening Mr. Mondale with a series of defeats in the late primaries and then overtaking him at the Democratic National Convention in July.

With his performance, Hart aides said the Colorado Senator "bought time" to execute his strategy. Mr. Hart sounded the same theme in an appearance before supporters in Washington. He said the Ohio results showed that "the Democrats of this nation are not prepared to have this contest and this debate end at this time."

Mr. Mondale conceded shortly before midnight, ending an evening in which Mr. Hart held a narrow but steady lead of one to two percentage points in Ohio and Indiana.

Mondale Blames Himself

Mr. Mondale blamed himself for failing to reach the voters, just as he did in his initial upset defeat this year in the New Hampshire primary.

"I think I did not make my case," Mr. Mondale said in Washington. "The contrasts were not drawn as they should have been." He added, however, that he remained "confident" of winning the nomination.

The Rev. Jesse Jackson placed third in Ohio, Indiana and North Carolina and, in late returns from Maryland,

Continued on Page B10, Column 1

United Press International

ATTACK REPORTED ON QADDAFI HOME

Libyan Leader Said to Survive an Assault by 20 Gunmen

By WERNER WISKARI

At least 20 gunmen yesterday reportedly attacked a barracks usually used as a residence by Libya's leader, Col. Muammar el-Qaddafi. After several hours of fighting, their attack was ended by Libyan troops, according to reports reaching the West from diplomats and an Italian journalist in Tripoli, the Libyan capital.

Information on the attack was sketchy and in some respects contradictory. But a diplomat said in Rome late in the day, according to The Associated Press, that Colonel Qaddafi had apparently survived another of the several attempts that have been made in recent years to overthrow him since he seized power in 1969 as the leader of a coup that ended the Libyan monarchy.

The journalist, representing the Italian news agency Ansa, said the episode began at 7 A.M. with 20 to 30 gunmen attacking the barracks on the southern outskirts of Tripoli with rocket-propelled grenades and automatic fire. He said it was not clear whether Colonel Qaddafi was inside at the time.

Nor was it established who the gunmen were and where they had come from, although people describing

Continued on Page A12, Column 1

PRIME LOAN RATE IS RAISED BY BANKS ½ POINT, TO 12½%

White House Says Monetary Rein of Federal Reserve Is Threat to the Recovery

By GARY KLOTT

The nation's leading banks raised their prime lending rate half a percentage point yesterday, to 12½ percent, the third such increase in two months.

The rise in the key interest rate to its highest level in 18 months brought sharp criticism by the White House of the Federal Reserve Board, which is the nation's central bank.

Larry Speakes, chief White House spokesman, said the Federal Reserve had been unduly restricting the supply of money to the national economy, thus driving up the cost of money — interest rates — and threatening to choke off the economic recovery. [Page D6.]

Economists said the rise in the prime rate, which is set by the banks, underscored the recent sharp run-up in interest rates caused by a surge in borrowing by both businesses and individuals as economic expansion continues at a stronger-than-expected pace.

Blow to Third-World Nations

Despite the comment by Mr. Speakes, the increase in the prime rate was not widely viewed among bankers as immediately threatening the general economic recovery. But it will complicate the problems of the many third-world nations whose vast debt payments are tied to the prime rate.

Further, the recent rise in mortgage and consumer loan rates has raised concerns that housing and auto sales — which are particularly sensitive to interest rate changes — will weaken.

Economists, who have been surprised by the enduring strength of the economy, said yesterday that additional rate increases were likely. "We have been anticipating further rate increases as long as the economy continues to be this strong," said Leif H.

Continued on Page D6, Column 3

Soldier in Quebec Opens Fire At Legislature, Killing Three

By DOUGLAS MARTIN
Special to The New York Times

QUEBEC, May 8 — A Canadian soldier who said his goal was to assassinate Quebec government officials burst into the Quebec National Assembly today, firing volleys of shots with a submachine gun. Three people were killed and 13 wounded.

"I came here to kill," the soldier shouted as he entered the Assembly building.

For a tense four and a half hours the soldier, later identified by military authorities as J. P. L. Denis Lortie, a 38-year-old corporal in the Royal 22d Regiment, held the Assembly's sergeant-at-arms hostage.

The police negotiated with Corporal Lortie by telephone as he and his hostage appeared to roam around the otherwise empty building.

Hostage Rescued Unharmed

Finally, at 2:25 P.M., the police, including a specially trained crisis team from Montreal, overwhelmed the soldier and rescued the hostage unharmed.

The soldier was dressed in military fatigues, a flak jacket and a beret. In addition to the submachine gun, he had two handguns and a hunting knife.

Little was known about the soldier. Military authorities said he was assigned to a base near Ottawa where he was a supply corporal, a job that might have given him access to weapons. The base, in effect, serves as a bunker for the Prime Minister and other Canadian leaders in the event of a nuclear war. Called Carp, it is some eight miles southwest of Ottawa.

Corporal Lortie's declared motivation

Continued on Page A6, Column 1

INSIDE

Democrats' Budget Loses

The Senate rejected, in a tie vote, a Democratic plan that would have cut projected deficits by $204 billion over the next three years. Page A28.

Trials Sought in Papal Case

A prosecutor recommended that three Bulgarians and four Turks be tried in connection with the attack on Pope John Paul II in 1981. Page A4.

About New York B3	Man in the News .A10
Around Nation A18	Movies C22
Books C23	Music C15
Bridge C15	Obituaries B4-9
Business Day ...D1-21	Op-Ed A27
Crossword C21	Real Estate D22
Dance C17,C21	Sports Pages ...B13-16
Day by Day B4	Theaters C22
Editorials A26	TV / Radio C24-25
Going Out Guide ..C24	U.N. Events A7
Living Section ..C14-15	Washington Talk .B12
	Weather C22
News Summary and Index, Page B1	
Classified Ads ..B16-25	Auto Exchange ..D25-27

MOSCOW WILL KEEP ITS TEAM FROM LOS ANGELES OLYMPICS; TASS CITES PERIL, U.S. DENIES IT

MAJOR EFFECT SEEN

If Soviet's Allies Follow, Quality Would Suffer More Than in 1980

By FRANK LITSKY

The absence of a Soviet team would drastically diminish the quality of competition at the 1984 Olympic Games in Los Angeles. If other Soviet bloc nations also stay away, many of the most successful and famous athletes in international sports will be absent — far more than when the United States withdrew from the 1980 Moscow Olympics.

The chairman of the Los Angeles Olympic Organizing Committee, Paul Ziffren, acknowledged today that the Olympic Committee faced a loss of income because of the Soviet withdrawal from the 1984 Games. But he said "adjustments" would be made in income and expenses to insure that the Games "are operated at a reasonable profit." [Page A17.]

The withdrawal of the Soviet Union from Los Angeles, if it is not reversed, would remove such gold-medal favorites as Sergei Bubka, the world's leading pole vaulter; Tamara Bykova, the world record-holder outdoors and indoors in the women's high jump; Vladimir Salnikov, winner of two swimming gold medals in 1980, and Anatoly Pisarenko, the world champion and world record-holder in super-heavyweight weight lifting.

Gymnastics Champions Affected

It would eliminate Dmitri Belozertchev and Natalia Yurchenko, the world overall gymnastics champions. It would leave at home the men's and women's basketball teams that ranked as favorites with the American teams and men's and women's volleyball teams that won gold medals in 1980.

A withdrawal by Eastern European countries allied to the Soviet Union would also eliminate East Germany, which has moved ahead of the Soviet Union in track and field and swimming. There will be 24 gold medals for

Continued on Page A17, Column 3

Reagan Speech Tonight

President Reagan scheduled a speech on his Central America policy for 8 o'clock tonight. It will be broadcast by the television networks.

United Press International

Mayor Tom Bradley of Los Angeles said he rejected reasons given for the Soviet decision.

SOVIET PUTS LIMITS ON SAKHAROV WIFE

Husband Starts Hunger Strike to Get Treatment for Her

Special to The New York Times

MOSCOW, May 8 — Yelena G. Bonner, the wife of Andrei D. Sakharov, is under investigation for "defaming the Soviet system" and has been barred from leaving the city of Gorky, a friend of the couple said today.

The friend said Dr. Sakharov, the dissident physicist who was banished to Gorky four years ago, has begun a hunger strike to demand medical treatment for his wife abroad.

The friend, Irina G. Kristi, a mathematician who managed to talk to Dr. Sakharov and his wife Sunday for three minutes in Gorky, said the couple told her Miss Bonner had been put under investigation and barred from leaving the city. She said Miss Bonner had also been threatened with charges of treason.

Dr. Sakharov, Mrs. Kristi said, began a hunger strike last Wednesday to seek help for his wife, who has had several heart attacks. Mrs. Kristi quoted Dr. Sakharov as saying of his wife that he would "fast to the very end if they do not let her go abroad for medical treatment."

Mrs. Kristi said that Dr. Sakharov and his wife were outside their building when she reached their home on Sunday, and that she managed to talk with them for three minutes before the police seized her.

Mrs. Kristi said Miss Bonner told her that an investigation had been opened

Continued on Page A7, Column 1

PROTESTS ARE ISSUE

Russians Charge 'Gross Flouting' of the Ideals of the Competition

By JOHN F. BURNS
Special to The New York Times

MOSCOW, May 8 — The Soviet Union announced today that it would not take part in the Olympic Games in Los Angeles this summer.

A statement issued by the Soviet National Olympic Committee said the participation of Soviet athletes was impossible because of "the gross flouting" of Olympic ideals by United States authorities. In particular, the statement, distributed by the press agency Tass, cited plans by groups to stage anti-Soviet demonstrations during the Games and the American refusal to ban such protests.

[The Reagan Administration said the Soviet decision was "a blatant political action for which there was no real justification." The Soviet charges were heatedly denied by White House and State Department officials, as well as by several members of Congress. Page A16.]

Boycott by U.S. Recalled

In 1980, the United States led nearly 60 other nations in boycotting the Moscow Olympic Games to protest the Soviet military intervention in Afghanistan. The Soviet statement today and others in recent months have carefully avoided any suggestion that revenge might be a factor in a decision not to go to the Games in Los Angeles. At the time of the Moscow Games, and repeatedly since, Soviet sports officials

The American boycott of the 1980 Olympics in Moscow appeared to be a factor behind the Soviet decision. News analysis, page A16.

cials have said they oppose sports boycotts in principle.

Apparently to maintain consistency with that position, they have taken to saying in recent months that although they would not boycott the Olympics in Los Angeles, they might not send a team, a distinction that they have not further explained. The announcement today did not use the word "boycott."

Other Nations May Follow

The Soviet announcement raised the strong possibility that several Eastern European nations, as well as Cuba, Vietnam and other countries allied with Moscow, would also stay away from the Los Angeles Games.

A common front on the issue was suggested when 12 Communist nations met in Moscow early last month to discuss the issue, and subsequent statements

Continued on Page A16, Column 1

Lila Wallace, Who Bestowed Reader's Digest Wealth, Dies

Lila Acheson Wallace, the co-founder and longtime co-chairman of Reader's Digest whose philanthropic donations totaled scores of millions of dollars, died of heart failure yesterday morning at her Mount Kisco, N.Y., home. She was 94 years old and had been in declining health for some time.

The shy, strong-willed daughter of a Presbyterian clergyman, Mrs. Wallace for years wielded extensive, though indirect, influence over the Reader's Digest publishing combine through her husband, DeWitt Wallace. Mr. Wallace, who founded the magazine with his wife in 1922, died in 1981 at the age of 91.

When Mrs. Wallace chose to exercise leadership at the Digest directly, she sometimes told associates simply, "Do your best."

Mrs. Wallace took enormous interest in, and pains over, her numerous philanthropies. They ranged from large gifts to The Juilliard School of Music and the New York Zoological Society, to restoring a mansion on the Hudson River, temples at Abu Simbel in Egypt and the painter Monet's house and grounds at Giverny, France, to providing daily fresh flowers in the Metropolitan Museum of Art's Great Hall.

Once, several years ago, while appreciatively sipping a martini from a 4,000-year-old gold Egyptian cup at her Mount Kisco home, Mrs. Wallace told

The New York Times, 1972

Lila Acheson Wallace

visitors: "If I displayed this cup, I might look at it once or twice a week. By using it, I get pleasure from it continually."

She also brought her energy and attention to detail to purchases of art, made in the magazine's name, that grew into a multimillion dollar collection. She once told one interviewer that she bought paintings not with regard to

Continued on Page B9, Column 1

POPE CELEBRATES MASS IN PAPUA NEW GUINEA: Pope John Paul II giving communion to a Catholic tribesman in Mount Hagen, Papua New Guinea. Mass was celebrated in pidgin English for 100,000 people. Page A2.

United Press International

The New York Times

VOL.CXXXIV.. No. 46,215   Copyright © 1984 The New York Times   NEW YORK, THURSDAY, NOVEMBER 1, 1984   80 cents beyond 75 miles from New York City, except on Long Island.   30 CENTS

GANDHI, SLAIN, IS SUCCEEDED BY SON; KILLING LAID TO 2 SIKH BODYGUARDS; ARMY ALERTED TO BAR SECT VIOLENCE

U.N. SAYS LEBANESE AND ISRAELIS PLAN TALKS ON PULLOUT

A Meeting of Military Teams Reported Set for Monday in South Lebanon Town

By JAMES FERON
Special to The New York Times

UNITED NATIONS, N.Y., Oct. 31 — The United Nations announced today that Israeli and Lebanese military teams would begin talks Monday in southern Lebanon on the subject of Israeli withdrawal from that region.

The conference, which is to take place at Naqura, headquarters of the United Nations Interim Force in Lebanon, also will deal with the security of Israel's northern border, which Israel has long demanded as a precondition for any withdrawal.

United Nations officials declined to discuss the agreement, indicating that to do so might jeopardize any prospect of success. Syria, which also occupies part of southern Lebanon, will not take part in the talks.

Apparently a Breakthrough

But a source familiar with the negotiations that prepared the way for the conference said that "the Israelis and the Lebanese want to get on with it and the Syrians don't want to get in the way." Diplomats here said Lebanon would almost certainly not have agreed to the negotiations without having consulted Syria.

The terse announcement appeared to represent a breakthrough in efforts by both Israel and Lebanon to end an occupation that has been costly to both. The Israelis invaded Lebanon in 1982 in an operation they said was intended to secure their northern border against attacks by Palestinians.

U.N. Role Not Specified

It was understood that the Israeli and Lebanese military teams probably would include senior staff officers. Israeli newspapers said today that the talks would be conducted directly by the two sides, but there was no confirmation of that here.

The United Nations role, similarly, was not spelled out. But the organization's involvement renewed speculation here that the role of the United Nations force in Lebanon might be expanded. Such a decision would require

Continued on Page A8, Column 1

Rebel Asserts C.I.A. Pledged Help in War Against Sandinistas

By JOEL BRINKLEY
Special to The New York Times

WASHINGTON, Oct. 31 — A senior director of the largest Nicaraguan rebel force says the Central Intelligence Agency recruited him to serve as a director two years ago and told him, "We are going to help you change the Government in Managua and do it within a year."

The officer, speaking in an interview, said the C.I.A. paid his family's expenses for more than a year and coached him and other rebel leaders on what to say in public so they would not anger members of Congress, who had to approve financing for the contras, as they are called.

In interviews at his home in Key Biscayne, Fla., the officer, Edgar Chamorro, one of seven directors of the Nicaraguan Democratic Force, gave a detailed description of the relationship between the group and the C.I.A.

He said he was telling the story now, contrary to orders he and other rebel officers received from the C.I.A., partly because he now believes that the United States is not likely to renew aid to the rebels. Aid was ended last spring.

Mr. Chamorro also said: "I resent some of the things the C.I.A. did."

Continued on Page A14, Column 1

The body of Indira Gandhi outside the All-India Institute of Medical Sciences before being taken to her residence. *Agence France-Presse*

Son in Charge In New Delhi

Rajiv Gandhi

By SANJOY HAZARIKA
Special to The New York Times

NEW DELHI, Oct. 31 — Rajiv Gandhi, who was chosen today to become India's new Prime Minister after the assassination of his mother, Indira, was propelled into public life after his younger, more politically ambitious brother, Sanjay, died in a stunt plane crash in 1980.

Man in the News

At the time, Sanjay was regarded as his mother's likely successor and, after Mrs. Gandhi, the most powerful politician in the country. Sanjay's death left a vacuum that Mrs. Gandhi and her followers urged Rajiv to fill.

Rajiv, who is now 40 years old, apparently reluctantly resigned his job with Indian Airlines and agreed to contest an electoral race to fill Sanjay's seat in Parliament the next year. He won the election by a large margin, promising to rid Indian politics of corruption and venality, a campaign that earned him the nickname "Mr. Clean."

Better Known as Indira's Son

Yet as a freshman Member of Parliament, Rajiv was still better known as Mrs. Gandhi's unassuming elder son. After his election he began helping his mother — screening appointments, advising her on reorganizing the affairs of her ruling but decaying Congress Party and receiving petitions. Recognizing him as a major influence on his mother, party leaders began to cultivate him.

Mrs. Gandhi, who increasingly turned to him for support and advice after Sanjay's death, is also known to

Continued on Page A24, Column 3

For India, Huge Void

Ability of Son Seen As Major Question

The writer of this dispatch, William K. Stevens, has been The Times's New Delhi correspondent since 1982.

Special to The New York Times

NEW DELHI, Oct. 31 — So thoroughly had Prime Minister Indira Gandhi dominated Indian politics over the last two decades that even some of her critics said she was what held the fractious country together.

News Analysis

Many called her Madam, Madamji, Mrs. G., Indiraji, Amma (Mother) or just "She." Not everyone thought of her in kind terms, but all knew who "She" was,

Facts and figures: a profile of India, in charts, page A22.

and her assassination leaves an incalculable void in the life of the country. Her sudden disappearance from the public scene represents a considerable challenge to the future of the Indian experiment in democracy.

Hours after her death, her 40-year-old son, Rajiv Gandhi, was sworn in as her successor. His abilities and performance are perhaps the biggest uncertainty for many people as the nation tries to adjust to the events of today.

Charan Singh, another former Prime Minister, who failed to hold an opposition Government together in 1979 and 1980, thereby paving the way for Mrs. Gandhi's return from three years out of power, expressed as much horror as anyone else when he heard the news of Mrs. Gandhi's assassination.

'Dynastic Rule' Feared

But when he heard about Rajiv Gandhi's rapid elevation, he said it confirmed his fear that "democracy is being gradually eroded in the country in order to establish a dynastic rule."

Whether that interpretation turns out to be correct, or whether Mr. Gandhi's swift installation as Prime Minister will exercise a stabilizing influence, is not clear.

What seems clearer is that Mr.

Continued on Page A19, Column 3

ATTACKS IN 8 CITIES

New Leader Tells Nation 'Maximum Restraint' Is Vital in Crisis

By WILLIAM K. STEVENS
Special to The New York Times

NEW DELHI, Thursday, Nov. 1 — Prime Minister Indira Gandhi was shot and killed at her home Wednesday by two gunmen identified by police officials as Sikh members of her personal bodyguard. Mrs. Gandhi's only surviving son, Rajiv, was sworn in Wednesday night as her successor.

Mrs. Gandhi was killed by at least eight bullets fired at close range from a submachine gun and a pistol by two men, according to police officials. One of the men was said to have been killed by other guards on the scene. The other was reported captured.

If Mrs. Gandhi was killed by Sikhs, it would be the second time since independence that an Indian leader had been the victim of a killing motivated by religious hatred. Mohandas K. Gandhi, who was not related to Mrs. Gandhi, was killed in 1947 by Hindu extremists opposed to partition.

The shooting occurred as Mrs. Gandhi, dressed in an orange-colored

The United States and the Soviet Union both assailed the assassination. Page A23.

Fierce condemnations also came from political and religious leaders in all parts of the world. Page A23.

sari, was walking from her house to her office in the same compound shortly before 9:30 A.M. (11 P.M. Tuesday, New York time). She was pronounced dead at a nearby hospital.

The assassination plunged this country, one-third the size of the United States and with more than 685 million people, into a major political crisis. As word of the assassination spread, Hindus began attacking Sikhs in the streets of the capital and in at least seven other cities. [Page A18.]

Apparently in anticipation of disorder, the army was put on alert. All military personnel on leave were called back to their posts. Approaches to New Delhi were sealed off, as were the approaches to the hospital and Mrs. Gandhi's residence.

Street violence was reported in at least six areas of New Delhi today.

Funeral Is Saturday

In his first radio broadcast to the nation as Prime Minister, Mr. Gandhi, 40 years old and previously the ranking general secretary of his mother's party, appealed for "maximum restraint" in view of the violence that was already beginning.

Mrs. Gandhi, a Hindu, had at age 66 led India for all but 3 of the last 18 years and was regarded as a major international figure. The Government announced that her funeral would be held Saturday and that she would then be cremated. Many world leaders are expected to attend the funeral.

Today, some mourners burst through barricades and surged to within 30

Continued on Page A18, Column 1

Rajiv Gandhi being sworn in as Prime Minister by President Zail Singh. *Associated Press*

Father and Daughter: A Remembrance

By A. M. ROSENTHAL

In India's great years of hope, when Jawaharlal Nehru was Prime Minister and the people called him their beloved jewel, the young woman was almost always with him, usually not at his side, but a few steps behind.

Indira, Nehru's only child, appeared with him at receptions and meetings in New Delhi, smiling, nodding, holding her hands together gently to her forehead in greeting, murmuring a word now and then.

Boosts Up the Ladder

In villages far from New Delhi she walked behind him down dusty roads. She sat motionless on platforms while he talked to city crowds of hundreds of thousands, millions sometimes, usually scolding them for their faults, a father quite loving but quick to anger.

She was close to him and he favored her. He gave her boosts up the political ladder within his Congress Party. Then, in 1964, Jawaharlal Nehru died, and two years later, Indira Gandhi was Prime Minister.

And now she is dead herself, one more victim of the religious hatreds of India against which her father used to harangue the crowds. Now she is dead

and her son Rajiv is Prime Minister. Rajiv, whom she had selected as her heir when her first choice, her younger son, Sanjay, died in a wild, senseless airplane stunt over New Delhi, almost within sight of his mother's offices.

Because of Indira Gandhi's open and obvious preparation to turn over rule to one of her sons, the theory of Indian dynasty has been growing and now will become written into history. Father to child to grandchild, just like the old Indian rajahs.

It is a neat theory, fitting comfortably into the stereotypes of India, but at best it is only half true — and it will take time to discover whether even that half holds.

For the fact is that there is no evidence that Jawaharlal Nehru ever really thought in dynasty terms, of turning over office to Indira.

There was a closeness between them, but also a certain aloofness. For years — the years he spent in fighting for Indian independence and the years in prison that were part of that struggle — he was remote, a father she knew mostly from his jail cell letters. Then her mother, the lonely, sad, often neglected Kamala, died and Indira went off to school abroad, far from home and father.

All this was in the 1920's and 30's, and

Continued on Page A19, Column 1

The Inquiry Report On the Vatican Plot

Mehmet Ali Agca, the man convicted of shooting Pope John Paul II, told Italian investigators that a second gunman had instructions to carry out the assassination if Mr. Agca was unable to get off at least five shots, according to a judicial report filed yesterday in Rome.

Key sections of the report, prepared by Judge Ilario Martella, begin on page D30.

Prime Minister Indira Gandhi with her son, Rajiv, who has succeeded her. *United Press International*

"All the News That's Fit to Print"

The New York Times

VOL.CXXXIV.. No. 46,221   Copyright © 1984 The New York Times   NEW YORK, WEDNESDAY, NOVEMBER 7, 1984   50 cents beyond 75 miles from New York City, except on Long Island.   30 CENTS

Late Edition

Weather: Mostly sunny and cool today, northwesterly winds; mostly clear tonight. Mostly sunny, mild tomorrow. Temperatures: today 50-53, tonight 33-37; yesterday 42-59. Details, page A24.

REAGAN WINS BY A LANDSLIDE, SWEEPING AT LEAST 48 STATES; G.O.P. GAINS STRENGTH IN HOUSE

Two Parties Still Split Control on Capitol Hill

House Power Battle

By STEVEN V. ROBERTS

Republicans cut into the Democratic majority in the House of Representatives last night, but their drive to shake the control of Democratic leaders seemed to fall short.

If last night's trends hold when the final votes are tallied, the House would continue to pose a major obstacle to President Reagan's legislative agenda, despite his overwhelming re-election victory.

Representative Thomas P. O'Neill Jr., the Speaker of the House, estimated that the Democrats would lose 10 to 12 seats from their majority of 90. In a television interview, he attributed the Democrats' strong showing to a widespread desire in the country check Mr. Reagan's more conservative proposals.

G.O.P. Needed 25 Seats

"I believe they wanted the Democrats in there as a safety net," he said. Speaking of President Reagan, Mr. O'Neill said, "He really hasn't had coat tails."

The Republicans needed a gain of about 25 seats to give them a chance to form the core of coalition with conservative Democrats that enacted many of Mr. Reagan's proposals during the first two years of his Presidency.

In many states, Democratic Representatives survived the Reagan landslide by distancing themselves from the national ticket and stressing their personal records of service to their constituents.

In North Carolina and Texas, the Republicans had a chance to make sweep-

Continued on Page A23, Column 1

Helms Senate Victor

By MARTIN TOLCHIN

Senate Republican candidates grasped President Reagan's coattails yesterday, but early returns indicated that they would be unable to solidify their control of the Senate.

Mr. Reagan, who spent the final week of his campaign appearing in behalf of Senate Republican candidates, seemed unable to translate his dramatic victory into significantly increasing the Republican margin in the Senate. But Democrats were similarly unable to make significant inroads into the Republican margin.

Should this pattern prevail, Mr. Reagan could expect to encounter the same resistance to some of his programs that he experienced in the last two years.

Helms Wins Bid

In the most acrimonious, expensive and closely watched Senate race, Senator Jesse Helms, Republican of North Carolina, leader of the New Right and a foe of abortion and supporter of organized school prayer, defeated Gov. James B. Hunt Jr., a moderate Democrat. The two had exchanged invectives right up to election day.

In Iowa, Senator Roger W. Jepsen, a Republican, was defeated by Representative Tom Harkin, a Democrat, in another campaign in which both candidates engaged in intensive negative campaigning.

Republicans appeared to have won an upset victory in Kentucky, where A. Mitchell McConnell, Jefferson County Judge, was narrowly leading Senator Walter D. Huddleston, a Democrat, although The Associated Press reported

Continued on Page A23, Column 3

President and Mrs. Reagan claiming victory last night in Los Angeles.

The New York Times/Paul Hosefros

MANDATE CLAIMED

Mondale Concedes Loss — Democrats Seek to Avert Realignment

By HOWELL RAINES

Ronald Wilson Reagan won a second term as President yesterday in an election that Republican leaders hailed as a sweeping personal triumph and a mandate for his policies.

Mr. Reagan secured clear landslide victories in both popular and electoral votes as he defeated Walter F. Mondale, the Democratic nominee, in at least 48 of the 50 states.

However, it remained unclear whether the powerful tide of support

Transcripts of speeches, page A21.

for Mr. Reagan ran deeply enough to carry enough Republican Congressional candidates into office to secure the "historic electoral realignment" that the President asked the voters to deliver.

With more than two-thirds of the popular vote counted, Mr. Reagan led Mr. Mondale by about 59 percent to 41 percent.

The President waited until after midnight, Eastern time, to claim the election that continued his tenure as the oldest man to occupy the White House.

Entering the ballroom of the Century Plaza Hotel in Los Angeles to the strains of "Hail to the Chief," Mr. Reagan received a tumultuous welcome from a crowd that chanted, "Four more years."

"I think that's just been arranged," said Mr. Reagan with a grin.

Policy Extension Planned

He said he would use his mandate to extend the economic and military policies of his first term. But, as if answering criticisms made by Mr. Mondale, he said he would also devote his second term to limiting nuclear weapons and to "lifting the weak and nurturing the less fortunate."

"You know, so many people act as if this election means the end of something," Mr. Reagan concluded in an indirect reference to the fact that this was the last election night of his career. "To each one of you I say, it's the beginning of everything," Mr. Reagan said. Then he stirred full-throated cheers by repeating an informal slogan of his campaign, "You ain't seen nothing yet."

Mondale Affirms Principles

Mr. Mondale, looking somber and drained, conceded shortly after 11:20 P.M., Eastern time. After complimenting the President on his victory, Mr. Mondale affirmed his commitment to the principles he had championed in a long, grinding campaign.

"Let us continue to seek an America that is just and fair," Mr. Mondale said. "Tonight especially I think of the

Continued on Page A20, Column 1

Economy the Key Issue

By HEDRICK SMITH

For all the careful orchestration of campaign rallies and political commercials, the televised debates, the partisan clashes over fine points of foreign and military policy, it was the economy that set the basic pattern for President Reagan's stunning re-election sweep yesterday and that fueled Republican gains in Congress.

News Analysis

In a very real sense the election returns followed the well-established script of the Reagan Presidency to make economic policy the central issue of American politics, according to a New York Times/CBS News Poll of 5,051 people as they left the voting booths. For Ronald Reagan vaulted into the White House in 1980 largely on the strength of his biting attacks on the economy under President Carter and his telling question, "Are you better off today than you were four years ago?" In the midterm Congressional elections two years ago, he suffered a stinging setback with the recession that eroded Republican ranks in the House of Representatives. Now this year, interviews showed, the President won a resounding vote of confidence for his handling of the economy and used it to power a coast-to-coast landslide for a second term in the White House.

His strategists were quick to contend that he had won a mandate for future policies. But the Times/CBS News poll showed that it was the electorate's feelings about the economy more than Mr. Reagan's appeals to traditional values or any specific vision for the future of what he likes to call his "second American revolution" that moved solid majorities in every region of the country into the President's column.

Broad Coalition for Reagan

Indeed, Walter F. Mondale gained more support than Mr. Reagan on his vision of the future, according to the poll. By nearly 2 to 1, however, the voters rejected Mr. Mondale's argument that a tax increase was necessary to reduce the Federal deficit, and Mr. Reagan won a big margin among those who opposed raising taxes.

Most significantly, the Election Day survey found that almost three-fifths of the voters felt the economy was better off today than four years ago, and that

Continued on Page A20, Column 2

PRESIDENT SWEEPS THE TRISTATE AREA

Connecticut Landslide Gives G.O.P. the Legislature

By FRANK LYNN

President Reagan swept New York, New Jersey and Connecticut yesterday. But except for Connecticut, he generally failed to translate his landslide margin into Republican victories in the House of Representatives and local offices.

In Connecticut, the Reagan tide enabled Republicans to gain control of both houses of the General Assembly for the first time in a decade, and to win the post held by Representative William R. Ratchford, a Democrat who was seeking his fourth term.

The President's victory over Walter F. Mondale, his Democratic opponent, in both New Jersey and Connecticut was approaching record proportions of at least 300,000 and 600,000 votes respectively.

He won New York State by at least 500,000 votes, triple his 1980 plurality in the state. He lost New York City by 300,000 votes but almost made up the entire deficit on Long Island, with victories of more than 100,000 votes each in Nassau and Suffolk Counties. The President lost only one upstate county, Albany, also a traditional Democratic stronghold.

In a hotly contested House campaign that was the most expensive in the country, Andrew J. Stein, the Democratic Manhattan Borough President,

Continued on Page B4, Column 1

State of Siege Is Imposed in Chile

By LYDIA CHAVEZ
Special to The New York Times

SANTIAGO, Chile, Nov. 6 — President Augusto Pinochet imposed a state of siege in Chile today for the first time in six years.

He acted after months of political unrest and a day after his Cabinet resigned to give him a freer hand to deal with the situation.

"It is precisely to save democracy and liberty that now more than ever it is necessary to be inflexible with respect to the institutional order that rules us," the President said at a ceremony at which he announced a new Cabinet.

Greater Powers for President

Minutes after the ceremony, a nightly curfew from midnight to 5 A.M. was imposed.

The President already had considerable powers to combat terrorism under the previous state of emergency. The press could be censored and political leaders exiled.

The main difference seems to be that under the state of siege the Government can hold terrorist suspects without charges for an indefinite period and trials can be delayed indefinately.

The new Cabinet brought only two minor changes. General Pinochet reappointed Interior Minister Sergio Onofre Jarpa, the chief minister, whose deci-

sion to step down Monday was followed immediately by the resignation of 15 other ministers.

Mr. Jarpa's resignation had been thought to be in protest against the Government's hard line against the opposition. But his decision to remain in the Cabinet indicated that he agrees with the Government's position.

The Government has taken an in-

Continued on Page A12, Column 1

Other News

Trade Talks With Russians

The United States and the Soviet Union plan talks in Moscow in January to explore ways to expand trade between the two nations. Page D1.

Catholics on Capitalism

A commission of conservative Roman Catholic business and professional leaders voiced strong support for American capitalism. Page A16.

Eleanor Mondale hugging her father as he appeared in St. Paul to make concession speech. Geraldine A. Ferraro was joined by her mother, Antonetta, and a daughter, Laura, in watching results at a Manhattan hotel.

The New York Times/Jim Wilson and Sara Krulwich

Bradley Wins Handily in Jersey Despite Strong Vote for Reagan

By JOSEPH F. SULLIVAN

Senator Bill Bradley, Democrat of New Jersey, easily won re-election to a second term yesterday.

With more than two-thirds of the votes counted, the 41-year-old Senator led Mary V. Mochary, a 42-year-old lawyer and former Mayor of Montclair, 63 to 37 percent.

Mr. Bradley gained his victory as hundreds of thousands of voters moved between the Democratic and Republican lines on the ballot to give President Reagan an overwhelming margin in the state as well.

Mr. Reagan held a a 64-to-36 percent lead over Walter F. Mondale with more than two-thirds of the votes counted. Mr. Reagan was leading in all 21 counties on his way to capturing the state's 16 electoral votes. The sweep would include Essex, Hudson and Mercer, three counties that he lost in 1980, when he won the state by 400,000 votes over President Jimmy Carter.

Mrs. Mochary telephoned Mr. Bradley at 8:45 P.M., 45 minutes after the polls closed, to congratulate him.

The Republican challenger was outspent by the incumbent, 3 to 1, and had to interrupt her campaign during the final three weeks to accompany her 44-year-old husband, Stephen, to the Stanford University Medical Center in California, where he is awaiting a heart transplant.

Mrs. Mochary said that she planned to leave for California this afternoon.

Mrs. Mochary, who talked to her supporters at the Somerset Hilton Hotel after telephoning Mr. Bradley, said she planned to run for office again, "and I'm not going to lower my sights."

Her comment prompted speculation she was thinking of running against New Jersey's other Democratic Sena-

Continued on Page B4, Column 5

Nicaragua Said to Get Soviet Attack Copters

By PHILIP TAUBMAN
Special to The New York Times

WASHINGTON, Wednesday, Nov. 7 — Nicaragua has received a number of Soviet-built attack helicopters in recent days, a senior Administration official said Tuesday night. He said the White House viewed their delivery as a "very serious development."

In addition, Administration officials said they were concerned about a Soviet freighter apparently headed for Nicaragua that intelligence reports indicated was carrying crates that could contain MIG fighter aircraft.

A spokesman for the Nicaraguan Embassy denied that helicopters had been delivered or that MIG's were on the way.

A senior Defense Department official said the Administration was considering a variety of responses to the delivery of the helicopters because they could have an important impact on the military balance in Central America.

Although they do not represent as serious an increase in Nicaraguan fire power as would the delivery of advanced fighter planes, he said, they presented a more serious "practical problem."

Specifically, he said, the helicopters, which Soviet forces have used extensively in Afghanistan to combat insur-

Continued on Page A12, Column 1

"All the News That's Fit to Print"

The New York Times

Late Edition
Weather: Sunny this morning, cloudiness increasing during the day. Snow or sleet tonight, becoming rain tomorrow. Temperatures: today 35-40, tonight 27-33; yesterday 34-42. Details, page D11.

VOL.CXXXIV .. No. 46,249   Copyright © 1984 The New York Times   NEW YORK, WEDNESDAY, DECEMBER 5, 1984   50 cents beyond 75 miles from New York City, except on Long Island   30 CENTS

REAGAN COMPLETES PROPOSALS ON CUTS IN MANY PROGRAMS

NO DECISION ON MILITARY

Projected Domestic Spending Would Be Cut $167 Billion in 3 Years Under Plan

By JONATHAN FUERBRINGER
Special to The New York Times

WASHINGTON, Dec. 4 — President Reagan today finished deciding how to cut domestic spending in his 1986 budget, White House officials said, leaving him to decide whether he also wants to slow his military buildup to reach his deficit-reducing goal.

The decision on military spending will not come until next week, after Defense Secretary Caspar W. Weinberger returns from Europe. Although the President has opposed slowing his military buildup, some of his top aides have said they expect him to accept some slowdown, partly because of pressure from Republican Congressional leaders to include the military in any package of spending cuts.

Officials said today that the President had not rejected a proposal from his top economic and budget advisers that would reduce his planned military buildup by $58 billion over three years and bring his total spending reductions close to the target of $237 billion over three years. If he does reject any military spending cuts, officials said, he could either look for deeper domestic spending cuts or change the targets.

Preliminary Budget Figures

The cuts in projected domestic spending to be proposed to Congress in January, according to officials, total about $32 billion in 1986, $60 billion in 1987 and $75 billion in 1988. The final figures are still being added up.

The President and his advisers have set an overall target of cutting projected programs by $42 billion in 1986, $85 billion in 1987 and $110 billion in 1988. With the savings in the military budget filling in the gap, these cuts, if approved by Congress, would reduce the Administration's projected deficit of $225 billion in 1988 to about $100 billion, the Administration said.

Among the major domestic decisions that have been approved by Mr. Reagan are these:

¶Eliminating for one year cost-of-living increases in all benefit and pension programs, except for Social Security, and freezing pay levels for civilian Government workers.

¶Freezing spending for much of Gov-

Continued on Page D23, Column 1

The New York Times/George Tames
TESTIFIES ON SOUTH AFRICA: Bishop Desmond M. Tutu, who appeared before House panel yesterday as protests against country's policies spread. Page A18.

Regan Declares New York Tax Could Be Cut

By DAVID E. ROSENBAUM
Special to The New York Times

WASHINGTON, Dec. 4 — Treasury Secretary Donald T. Regan said tonight that his proposal to revamp the Federal income tax system would provide greater tax revenues for New York State and that, therefore, the state could afford to reduce its own taxes.

In an interview, Mr. Regan granted that many New Yorkers would owe more Federal tax if Congress adopts his plan than they do now because the plan would abolish deductions for state and local taxes.

But if the state reduced its tax rates enough, the Secretary said, the combined taxes that New York residents pay to the Federal Government and the state together would not rise.

'They're a High-Tax State'

"New York has a problem," Mr. Regan said. "But I submit New York's problem has always been they're a high-tax state. If they're going to get more revenue, perhaps New York will want to cut its rates."

The Treasury tax plan was called "lethal" for New York and an invitation to regional conflict by Felix G. Rohatyn, chairman of the Municipal Assistance Corporation. [Page D23.]

The plan, presented last week, would reduce Federal tax rates — the per-

Continued on Page D23, Column 3

MADRID AND LISBON FACE NEW HURDLE TO MARKET ENTRY

Greece Threatens Veto Unless Members Pledge $5 Billion in Aid to Poor Farmers

By PAUL LEWIS
Special to The New York Times

DUBLIN, Dec. 4 — Greece today threatened to veto longstanding plans to admit Spain and Portugal as members of the European Economic Community unless the community agrees to pay poor southern European farmers up to $5 billion in special aid over the next five years.

As a result of this threat, issued by the Greek Prime Minister, Andreas Papandreou, a two-day meeting of Common Market heads of government ended in confusion and bitterness today, with other European leaders visibly angry at Greece's demands. Prime Minister Margaret Thatcher of Britain said at a news conference that Greece's request was "totally out of the question." Chancellor Helmut Kohl of West Germany and France's President, François Mitterrand, also rejected the Greek demand outright, according to their spokesmen. Other officials openly accused Greece of blackmailing the community.

'A New Shadow of Doubt'

Spain and Portugal can join the Common Market only if all the 10 members agree. And Prime Minister Garret FitzGerald of Ireland, who was chairman of the meeting here, said at a news conference that there was now "a new shadow of doubt" over plans to enlarge the Common Market.

The meeting's principal purpose had been to pave the way for the entry of Spain and Portugal into the Common Market at the start of 1986 by making final the membership terms the 10 present members will offer the new entrants.

Support for NATO Membership

All 10 have said they favor enlarging the Common Market to include Spain and Portugal for political reasons, despite the economic difficulties that would be caused, arguing that membership would strengthen these countries' still-fragile democratic systems. The Spanish Government also says it believes membership will help it win popular support for remaining in NATO in a referendum it is holding on a continued alliance membership early next year.

Earlier today, the Common Market nations appeared to have removed the last major economic obstacle to en-

Continued on Page A15, Column 1

GAS DEATHS IN INDIA EXCEED 1,000, WITH THOUSANDS HURT; GANDHI SEEKS COMPENSATION

Agence France-Presse
A woman, a victim of the toxic gas that spread through Bhopal, India, comforting a more seriously injured relative at a crowded hospital.

COMPANY IS PRESSED

Doctors Say 20,000 May Suffer Aftereffects — Acrid Odor Lingers

By Reuters

BHOPAL, India, Dec. 4 — At least 1,000 people were reported to have been killed by poison gas that leaked from an American-owned insecticide plant here Monday. Prime Minister Rajiv Gandhi broke off an election campaign tour to visit the city and said he would seek compensation.

A spokesman for the state government of Madhya Pradesh said the official death toll from the accident, one of the largest industrial accidents in history, had reached 546. But the United News of India said its reporters put the figure at 1,200.

Hundreds of Burials

The agency said that 345 victims had been buried at Bhopal's central Sirdaus Manzil graveyard and that 445 had been cremated in an area of the city called Chola Vishram Ghar.

[The Associated Press quoted two doctors as saying that at least 1,000 people had been killed. They were quoted as saying that they counted 500 corpses at the city's major hospitals and had reports of at least 500 more dead at hospitals on the outskirts of Bhopal. Doctors said as many as 200,000 people were affected, the AP reported, and one doctor estimated that 20,000 might suffer serious aftereffects. Some women may be sterile, he said, and some victims may be blinded.]

Staff at city hospitals said 4,000 people had been badly gassed and some died in neighboring towns after fleeing Bhopal, 300 miles south of New Delhi, when the gas cloud spread over the city.

Gandhi Breaks Off Campaign

Mr. Gandhi, who toured the area and visited victims in various hospitals, said emergency steps had been taken to stop the spread of toxic effects of the gas on animals and crops. He gave no details.

Mr. Gandhi told a news conference that the disaster was "a result of planning in an uncontrolled manner." He added, "We are concerned not only about this plant but about similar places as well."

He told reporters his Government

Continued on Page A12, Column 1

Jobs and Risks Are Linked At Sister Plant in the U.S.

By STUART DIAMOND
Special to The New York Times

INSTITUTE, W. Va., Dec. 4 — The sprawling Union Carbide chemical factory here, a sister plant to the one that leaked toxic gas in India this week, is an uneasy neighbor to the middle-class houses and college classrooms nestled among the hills and riverbanks around the mile-long tangle of steel machinery.

Balanced against thousands of jobs and millions of dollars in tax revenues are the occasional chemical releases, pitted car paint, evacuation notices and links to increased cancer.

It is a problem that has nagged at residents here for years but recently intensified when state officials fined Union Carbide for open-air burning of toxic wastes at another local plant and a state study said that thousands of tons of chemicals are being spewed into the air annually by local chemical companies.

Plant Tour Is Refused

Today, after initially indicating on Monday that they would probably show the plant to reporters, Union Carbide officials backed off and a plant official threatened to confiscate the camera of a photographer if he took pictures of the plant's exterior from the company driveway. A company spokesman said the refusal to permit examination of the equipment was a policy decision of top management.

In Danbury, Conn., Union Carbide executives said it might take two to three weeks to determine the cause of the poisonous gas leak at the plant in Bhopal, India, this week. Warren M. Anderson, Union Carbide's chairman, said he would go to Bhopal to determine the cause of the accident and decide what "appropriate relief measures" should be offered by the company. [Page A12.]

In Washington, officials of the Environmental Protection Agency said no regulations in this country control dangerous chemicals stored in underground tanks, such as the one that leaked in India. Several said a similar accident here was not unimaginable. [Page A13.]

The Union Carbide plant here is one of five major chemical factories in the

Continued on Page A12, Column 1

House Panel Decides Ferraro Violated Ethics Law

By JANE PERLEZ
Special to The New York Times

WASHINGTON, Dec. 4 — The House ethics committee found today that Representative Geraldine A. Ferraro violated the Ethics in Government Act of 1978 by failing to report details of her husband's finances.

But the panel ruled that the violations were not intentional, and it therefore did not recommend any sanctions against Mrs. Ferraro, the Queens congresswoman who was the Democratic candidate for Vice President.

Also today, Walter F. Mondale agreed to pay the Treasury $379,640 and a fine of $18,500 because of excess contributions for his Presidential campaign from political action committees organized by labor unions. [Page A21.]

Exemption Requirements Not Met

According to a Congressional aide familiar with the Ferraro inquiry, the 12-member House committee voted secretly, 10 to 2, to adopt the findings of its staff, with two Republicans advocating sterner action. Representative Hank Brown of Colorado, filed a written dissent, and Congressional aides said the other Republican "no" vote came from Representative James V. Hansen of Utah.

The committee said Mrs. Ferraro had benefited from her husband's financial interests and was thus wrong to claim an exemption that allows Government officials not to disclose a spouse's financial dealings on the

forms required by the ethics act.

To qualify for the exemption, Mrs. Ferraro needed to demonstrate that she had no knowledge of the finances of her husband, John A. Zacarro, a New York real estate businessman; that she had not benefited from them, and that she was entirely financially independent of him.

Mrs. Ferraro had benefited from her husband's financial activities, the report said. The "maintenance of the Forest Hills home, education of the children, and the purchase of vacation properties are three examples of expenses covered with John Zacarro's financial resources," it said.

"All facts point to error, oversight and misinterpretation as the reason for the incomplete disclosures," the report concluded.

The findings appeared to put to rest Congress's interest in Mrs. Ferraro's finances, which came under intense scrutiny and were a damaging issue in the national campaign.

But the Justice Department is still

Continued on Page A29, Column 1

William Curtsinger / © 1984 National Geographic Society
Bronze Age Shipwreck Is Found
Archeologists mapping wreck of a ship that sank off the southern coast of Turkey about 3,400 years ago. The earliest shipwreck ever to be excavated, it has yielded a treasure of Bronze Age artifacts, including the Canaanite amphora, at top right. The ship went down sometime in the 14th century B.C. Page A24.

U.S. Court Bars Excluding People As Jurors Solely Because of Race

By DAVID MARGOLICK

A divided Federal appeals court in Manhattan ruled yesterday that prosecutors could not systematically exclude people from juries solely because of their race.

The 2-to-1 decision, by the Court of Appeals for the Second Circuit, marks the first time that a Federal appellate court has invalidated such use of peremptory challenges, for which potential jurors can be rejected without cause. Such challenges have often been used to keep blacks and Hispanic people off juries.

The decision, the latest in a series of conflicting rulings on the subject, upheld a lower-court ruling issued last year in Brooklyn.

8 Were Excluded

In the case before the court, prosecutors from the Brooklyn District Attorney's office had in 1980 excluded seven blacks and one Hispanic person from the jury trying a black defendant for robbery. The defendant, Michael McCray, was subsequently convicted. An earlier trial of Mr. McCray, in which three of the jurors were black, resulted in a hung jury.

The systematic exclusion of jurors by race, the court held in an opinion by Judge Amalya L. Kearse, violates the right to a fair trial, guaranteed by the Sixth Amendment to the Constitution. While the state need not always assure juries that perfectly mirror the population, she wrote, it cannot "restrict unreasonably the possibility that the jury will comprise a fair cross section of the community."

Judge Kearse acknowledged that under longstanding practice, prosecutors have been permitted to use peremptory challenges whenever they wished. But under yesterday's ruling, she explained, where a defendant can show

a "substantial likelihood" that challenges are being used on racial grounds, the state violates the law unless it can prove otherwise.

"The responsibility of the state and its prosecutor is not to secure a conviction at all costs; it is to see that justice is done," she wrote. "The constitutional wisdom is that justice is best served by a jury that represents a cross section of the community, not one from which cognizable groups are systematically eliminated because of their group affiliation."

Judge Kearse termed "fallacious and pernicious" the notion that all persons of the same skin color "will ipso facto view matters in the same way."

Such attitudes, she wrote, "limit artificially the opportunity of blacks for

Continued on Page B4, Column 4

INSIDE

Grenada's New Leader
Herbert A. Blaize, sworn in as Grenada's Prime Minister, has a reputation for honesty and level-headedness. Man in the News, page A2.

U.S. Fight Against Terror
The United States has taken steps to defend against and possibly retaliate for terrorist violence. Last of four articles on counterterrorism, page A8.

Another Telephone Bill
Millions of telephone customers in New York State will begin to get a separate phone bill in January, for equipment rental. Page D1.

Developer of 'Pill' Dies
Dr. John Rock, a developer of the birth control pill, died at the age of 94. He also performed the first test tube fertilization. Page A29.

FOR A LIMITED TIME, HOME OR OFFICE delivery of The Times costs less than the newsstand price in most cities. Call toll-free, 1-800-631-2500 for details — ADVT.

RENT-A-PC   IBMPC/XT, APPLE IIc   leased delivery, free maint. 516-273-5595.—ADVT.

"All the News That's Fit to Print"

The New York Times

VOL.CXXXIV..No. 46,346   Copyright © 1985 The New York Times   NEW YORK, TUESDAY, MARCH 12, 1985   30 cents beyond 75 miles from New York City, except on Long Island   30 CENTS

Late Edition
Weather: Rain early today, tapering off to showers and ending in the afternoon; clearing tonight. Sunny tomorrow. Temperatures today 41-49, tonight 33-37; yesterday 39-62. Details on page B2.

CHERNENKO IS DEAD IN MOSCOW AT 73; GORBACHEV SUCCEEDS HIM AND URGES ARMS CONTROL AND ECONOMIC VIGOR

ISRAELI ARMY KILLS 24 IN RAID ON TOWN IN SOUTH LEBANON

Attack Across New Defense Line Follows Car-Bombing of a Military Convoy

By JOHN KIFNER
Special to The New York Times

ZRARIYAH, Lebanon, March 11 — Israeli troops stormed across their new defense line today and killed at least 24 people in a raid against this southern Lebanese village.

The raid, the fiercest of the current Israeli crackdown, came about 12 hours after a suicide car bomber crashed into an Israeli Army convoy, killing 12 Israeli soldiers.

The main street of this village was a scene of hysteria and chaos after the Israeli force withdrew just before dusk, with women shrieking and waving their hands in the air or sitting on the ground weeping.

The casualty figures were still in doubt tonight. An Israeli military announcement said 24 people it described as "terrorists" had been killed, but the Israeli radio later put the death toll at 30. The Lebanese police and local radio stations said 25 people had died.

Bodies in Burned-Out Cars

Western journalists saw six bodies in burned-out cars on the outskirts of the village and there were a number of others in the village itself.

The raid appeared to signal a determination by Israel that its "iron fist" policy would not be altered in the face of continued guerrilla resistance.

Today's raid, guerrillas and villagers said, actually began at about 11 P.M. Sunday when Israeli troops tried to infiltrate the village, which is a few miles north of their new second-stage defense line on the Litani River.

Members of the Amal Shiite militia, supported by a 30-man garrison that the Lebanese Army recently established here, fought back against the attack, militiamen and residents of the village said.

Israeli Force Put at 1,000

But at 6 A.M. today, after a heavy artillery barrage, the Israelis came from three directions in overwhelming force and pushed into the village of about 8,000 people, according to witnesses.

Militiamen and members of the local police force, who said they had been cuffed about by the Israelis, put the attacking force at as many as 1,000 soldiers and perhaps 200 to 300 vehicles.

Continued on Page A8, Column 4

Succession in Moscow

The announcement of the death of Konstantin U. Chernenko, above, the Soviet leader, was quickly followed by the naming of his successor, Mikhail S. Gorbachev. The move represents a shift to a new generation of Soviet leadership.

A Leader With Style — and Impatience

Special to The New York Times

MOSCOW, March 11 — Coming to power at the age of 54, Mikhail Sergeyevich Gorbachev, the peasant's son from southern Russia, is expected to bring a new style of leadership to the Kremlin. If the expectations prove correct, this leadership will be more open, perhaps, less obsessively suspicious, less burdened with memories of Stalin's terror and the war.

For the moment, Mr. Gorbachev seemed anxious to give fire to the program of economic change he inherited from his mentor, Yuri V. Andropov.

He revealed his impatience in a major speech last December when he said, "We will have to carry out profound transformations in the economy and in the entire system of social relations."

'Intensive Development'

There was an echo of that today when he said, "We are to achieve a decisive turn in transferring the national economy to the tracks of intensive development."

He added, "A good deal is to be done."

What remained to be seen, however, was how Mr. Gorbachev (pronounced gore-bah-CHAWFF) would translate his impatience into action by the enormous bureaucracy that manages the Soviet Union's ponderous, creaky, centralized economy.

For all the fervor, style and obvious achievement he has displayed in reaching the highest position in the Soviet power structure, Mr. Gorbachev and the generation he represents remain an untested and largely unknown political force.

These are people who were reared after the war and after the Stalinist terror, who grew up in a state more secure in its power and potential, men who got better educations than their predecessors and had more contact with the outside world.

Yet these are also men who have made their careers in a Communist Party that has changed from an idealistic elite into an entrenched, privileged and self-perpetuating bureaucracy intolerant of too much independence or nonconformism among its members.

Under Mr. Andropov, Mr. Gorbachev worked under a seasoned politician who knew the power structure intimately from within as consequence of his 15 years at the head of the K.G.B., the internal security and intelligence agency. And though he himself rose to the peak of Soviet power, Mr. Gorbachev's political biography did not conclusively prove his ability to wage the sort of brutal political struggle that is required to get change through the bureaucracy.

After a steady and apparently uneventful climb through the provincial party apparatus in the Stavropol region of southern Russia, north of the Caucasus, Mr. Gorbachev was brought to Moscow to take over as

Continued on Page A16, Column 1

Konstantin U. Chernenko was a dedicated Bolshevik but also a pragmatist. An obituary, page A14.

BUSH SENT TO RITES

Reagan Decides Against Trip, but Says He Is Ready for Meeting

By BERNARD WEINRAUB
Special to The New York Times

WASHINGTON, March 11 — President Reagan decided today against attending the funeral of Konstantin U. Chernenko, but he said he was "more than ready" to meet the new Soviet leadership.

White House officials said Vice President Bush, who is in Geneva after a visit to drought-stricken African nations, would lead the American delegation to Mr. Chernenko's funeral in Moscow on Wednesday.

Mr. Bush also represented the United States at the funerals of Leonid I. Brezhnev in 1982 and Yuri V. Andropov in 1984. He is to be joined by Secretary of State George P. Shultz and the United States Ambassador to Moscow, Arthur A. Hartman.

'Looking Forward' to Meeting

Mr. Reagan, in his first public comments after Mr. Chernenko's death, said he was "looking forward" to meeting the new Soviet leader, Mikhail S. Gorbachev. But the President voiced doubt that Soviet policies would change in any substantive way as a result of the selection of Mr. Gorbachev.

White House officials indicated that Mr. Reagan had seriously considered flying to Moscow for the funeral to underscore American resolve to improve relations. But after a morning meeting with leading aides, Mr. Reagan decided against the trip, largely because he felt little would be accomplished by a brief visit.

"As of 4 A.M. this morning I started

Continued on Page A17, Column 1

Arms Talks Still On

The United States and the Soviet Union agreed that a new round of arms talks would go ahead as scheduled on Tuesday. Page A20.

TRANSFER IS SWIFT

New Leader, 54, Loses No Time in Offering His Own Program

By SERGE SCHMEMANN

MOSCOW, March 11 — The Kremlin today announced the death of Konstantin U. Chernenko and, within hours, named Mikhail S. Gorbachev to succeed him as Soviet leader.

The announcement said Mr. Chernenko died Sunday evening after a grave illness at the age of 73. He had been in office 13 months, and had been ill much of the time, leaving a minor imprint on Soviet affairs.

The succession was the quickest in Soviet history, suggesting that it had been decided well in advance. Whereas the Central Committee had taken several days to name a successor to Leonid I. Brezhnev and Yuri V. Andropov, Mr. Gorbachev was confirmed in his new job 4 hours and 15 minutes after Mr. Chernenko's death was announced.

Youngest Leader Since Stalin

Mr. Gorbachev became, at 54, the youngest man to take charge of the Soviet Union since Stalin and the seventh to head the Soviet state.

"I am well aware of the great trust put in me and of the great responsibil-

Kremlin statement and speech by Gorbachev, pages A15-A16. Autopsy report, page A19.

ity connected with this," he said. "I promise you, comrades, to do my utmost to faithfully serve our party, our people and the great Leninist cause."

In his acceptance speech on being named General Secretary, he showed his impatience to start working.

"We are to achieve a decisive turn in transferring the national economy to the tracks of intensive development," he said. "We should, we are bound to attain within the briefest period the most advanced scientific and technical positions, the highest world level in the productivity of social labor."

Real Arms Cut Urged

In world affairs, he said he valued the "successes of détente, achieved in the 1970's." Referring to the Soviet-American arms talks starting Tuesday in Geneva, Mr. Gorbachev said the Soviet Union sought a "real and major reduction in arms stockpiles, not the development of ever-new weapon systems, be it in space or on earth."

The speech was one sign that the leadership intended to pursue business as usual despite Mr. Chernenko's

Continued on Page A15, Column 1

Young Team Takes Reins

Kremlin Starts Shift To a New Generation

By SETH MYDANS
Special to The New York Times

MOSCOW, March 11 — With the naming of Mikhail S. Gorbachev as its new leader, the Soviet Union has finally begun its long-awaited shift to a new generation of leadership.

News Analysis

The speed with which the announcement of his appointment was made and the fast pace of scheduled funeral rites suggested that plans for the succession had been firmly in place before the death of Konstantin U. Chernenko on Sunday.

The signposts of change contained in an address by the new leader, which was read immediately to the nation, showed that Mr. Gorbachev planned to take the Soviet Union forward toward changes in policy that have been on hold for the last year.

But Western and Soviet analysts here cautioned that although Mr. Gorbachev and his economic planners have been laying their plans for months, change in the Soviet Union comes slowly and with difficulty.

They said that although the new leader seemed to have stepped into his new role with vigor, it might take months or years for him to consolidate

Continued on Page A28, Column 1

Reagan's Doctors Find a Growth, But Stress His Health Is Excellent

By PHILIP M. BOFFEY
Special to The New York Times

WASHINGTON, March 11 — Doctors discovered a second small growth in President Reagan's intestinal tract in his annual physical examination Friday, but the growth was not a precursor of cancer, the White House announced today.

The doctors also detected signs of blood in the President's stool, Larry Speakes, the White House spokesman, told reporters at a briefing where the doctors were not present. He said they had not determined the cause but believed it to be from the polyp or a false reading caused by the President's diet.

Over all, the results of the physical, performed at the Naval Medical Center in Bethesda, Md., were excellent, according to Mr. Reagan's doctors.

Capt. Walter Karney, chief of internal medicine at the naval hospital, who led the examining doctors, was quoted by the White House as saying:

"President Reagan continues to enjoy good health. His overall physical and mental condition is excellent. I am especially impressed with the fact that his blood pressure is lower than a year ago — this is quite remarkable."

The President's blood pressure while lying down was measured at 130 over 74. His pulse while resting was reported as 57 beats a minute, which Mr. Speakes described as "probably lower than most of us."

Mr. Reagan, who is 74 years old, is the oldest person ever to be President. His health and ability to perform in office became an issue in last year's campaign after he appeared to stumble verbally in a debate with the Demo-

Continued on Page A28, Column 1

INSIDE

Jets Strike Cities in Gulf
Iranian planes attacked the outskirts of Baghdad and Iraqi planes hit Iranian cities as stepped-up fighting continued for an eighth day. Page A3.

Bid-Rigging Charged
Key contractors agreed to bar competition for concrete work on all major projects in New York City since 1978, a Federal lawsuit charged. Page B1.

Politburo members at the House of Unions in Moscow, where the body of Konstantin U. Chernenko lay in state. From the left were Vitaly I. Vorotnikov, Mikhail S. Gorbachev, the new Soviet leader, Prime Minister Nikolai A. Tikhonov, Foreign Minister Andrei A. Gromyko, Viktor V. Grishin and Grigory V. Romanov.

Tass via Associated Press

In U.S., Cautious Hopes for Better Relations

By HEDRICK SMITH
Special to The New York Times

WASHINGTON, March 11 — The shift to a new generation of Soviet leadership has raised cautious hopes in the Reagan Administration that in the long run it will bring new vigor and decisiveness in the Kremlin and could lead to improvements in Soviet-American relations.

News Analysis

But President Reagan and his top advisers expect no significant changes in Soviet foreign policy to emerge over the next several months from the new leadership of Mikhail S. Gorbachev, a 54-year-old party official with a reputation for interest in modest internal economic changes.

The Soviet decision to pursue arms talks in Geneva, with only a token ceremonial interruption, is seen by Government specialists as a deliberate Kremlin move to project both strength of leadership and continuity of policy despite the death of the third Soviet leader in 28 months.

"Preserving the image of continuity at this point is at least as important as the fact of continuity," a State Department official said. "They are embarrassed at the succession of infirm leaders they've had," another Government specialist said, "and they don't want

Chernenko's death to look as though it's hampering them."

The speed with which Mr. Gorbachev was named the General Secretary of the Communist Party was taken as evidence by officials here that the ruling Politburo made the key decision to select him as the new leader in late February, if not before.

Moreover, they see evidence that Mr. Gorbachev had been performing as the effective leader of both the party and the Soviet Defense Council in the final months of Konstantin U. Chernenko's life. Each of those developments adds

Continued on Page A17, Column 4

The New York Times

Late Edition

Weather: Variable sunshine and cloudiness today; cloudy tonight, chance of drizzle. Chance of light rain tomorrow. Temperatures: today 73-77, tonight 63-67; yesterday 63-79. Details, page D13.

VOL.CXXXIV. No. 46,457   Copyright © 1985 The New York Times   NEW YORK, MONDAY, JULY 1, 1985   50 cents beyond 75 miles from New York City, except on Long Island.   30 CENTS

39 AMERICAN HOSTAGES FREE AFTER 17 DAYS; GO FROM LEBANON TO SYRIA AND HEAD HOME

REAGAN HAILS MOVE

In White House Talk, He Also Warns Terrorists 'We'll Fight Back'

By BERNARD WEINRAUB
Special to The New York Times

WASHINGTON, June 30 — President Reagan welcomed the release of the American hostages today, but said the United States "will not rest until justice is done" in Beirut as well as El Salvador.

"Terrorists be on notice," Mr. Reagan said in a nationally televised speech from the Oval Office as the

Text of Reagan remarks, page A10.

freed Americans left Syria for West Germany. "We will fight back against you in Lebanon and elsewhere. We will fight back against your cowardly attacks on American citizens and property."

It was not clear from Mr. Reagan's strong words about hijackers and terrorists that he was hinting at the possibility that the United States would retaliate militarily for the Beirut hostage crisis.

But a ranking Administration official, who asked not to be identified, seemed to indicate that the United States had ruled out military retaliation against the Lebanese Shiites who seized Trans World Airlines Flight 847 on June 14, taking the passengers hostage and later killing one, a Navy diver named Robert Dean Stethem.

Knowledge of Terror Groups

Shortly after Mr. Reagan spoke, Secretary of State George P. Shultz appeared in the White House briefing room, where he emphasized what he said was the Government's determination to respond to terrorism.

Mr. Shultz added that terrorist groups "would perhaps be a little surprised to know how much we are getting to know about them."

"We want to find who in particular beat and shot Robert Stethem," Mr. Shultz said.

Although Mr. Reagan termed the release of the 39 hostages "a moment of joy," he added, "this is no moment for celebration."

7 Hostages Remain

"Let it be clearly understood," he said sternly, "that the seven Americans still held captive in Lebanon must be released, along with other innocent hostages from other countries; that the murderers of Robert Stethem and of our marines and civilians in El Salvador must be held accountable; that those responsible for terrorist acts

Continued on Page A10, Column 5

Associated Press

Hostages waving goodbye as they left school near Beirut airport for trip to Damascus. From left: Thomas Murry, Leo Byron, Jerome Barczak and Thomas Cullins. Hostage at center rear is unidentified.

In Beirut, Hooded Men Tell of Captives' Release

By JOHN KIFNER
Special to The New York Times

BEIRUT, Lebanon, June 30 — Two men who said they were the hijackers of the Trans World Airlines jet said today that they had committed the act to show the world "the ability of the oppressed to confront America."

Hoods over their heads and automatic pistols jammed in their pants, the men met reporters at the Beirut airport at almost the same moment that the 39 Americans were beginning their journey to Syria and freedom after 17 days in captivity.

"America is the great Satan," one of the men said in an angry tone as he read a 10-minute statement in Arabic. His head was covered by what appeared to be a pillowcase with eyeholes cut into it.

He said he and his comrade had hoped to die as martyrs in the hijacking, and he warned that they would strike again if the United States retaliated for the hostage-taking.

Speaking of the Syrian-brokered arrangement to free the Americans, he said: "We emphasize that in the event of any violation of commitments that had been agreed upon with a Syrian guarantee for the release of the prisoners in occupied Palestine" — a reference to Israel — "we address a strong warning to America, which knows we are capable of accomplishing."

"America's war machine is nothing but children's toys as far as we are concerned," the man said. "We also warn the United States anew against playing with fire, because we are determined to burn it with this fire."

The two men refused to answer reporters' questions and left after finishing the statement.

'The Great Satan'

The statement concluded with the phrase, "America is the great Satan," and it was signed, "The Oppressed on Earth." Both are phrases used by pro-Iranian Islamic fundamentalist groups.

Not far from the airport, in the suburban shantytown of Burj al Brajneh, the 39 Americans were piling into a caravan of 12 cars and one truck organized by the International Committee of the Red Cross.

As the caravan pulled away from the settlement amid the honking of horns and celebratory gunshots, militiamen of the mainstream Shiite movement Amal offered handshakes and pink and red roses.

"Go, go, goodbye," a bearded young militiaman shouted as the Americans waved.

The festive departure of the Americans, against the backdrop of the menacing words at the airport news conference, made for a strange moment, even by the standards that prevail in this shattered, anarchic city, where violence is so routine that residents do not flinch at the frequent bursts of automatic-weapons fire throughout the day and night.

The two young gunmen met with journalists at the airport transit lounge after striding from the red and white T.W.A. jet, which remained parked at

Continued on Page A7, Column 1

A KEY STATEMENT

U.S. Policy Affirmation Gained the Release, Officials Report

By BERNARD GWERTZMAN
Special to The New York Times

WASHINGTON, June 30 — A senior Reagan Administration official said today that the final obstacle to the release of the 39 American hostages was removed Saturday night when the Administration accepted a proposal by Syria to issue an old policy statement on Lebanon.

The statement said the United States "reaffirms its longstanding support for the preservation of Lebanon, its Government, its stability and security, and for the mitigation of the suffering of its people."

The statement fell far short of what the hostages' captors were demanding — a public pledge from the United States that it would not retaliate militarily after the hostages were released. But Syria, the American official said, had assured Washington that the issuing of the statement would induce the Shiite Lebanese Shiites to free the Americans.

The 39 Americans, who were aboard a Trans World Airlines jet when it was hijacked over Europe on June 14, were released today.

Praise for Syrian Leader

American officials praised President Hafez al-Assad of Syria for his part in ending the standoff over the hostages, and for what they said were his efforts in trying to find seven other Americans reported abducted or missing in Lebanon over the last 15 months.

The officials said that no deals had been struck with Syria, but they said they hoped the ending of the crisis might bring a period of better relations between the two Governments.

But they added that there continued to be sharp disagreements between Washington and Damascus over Middle East peace efforts, with the United States firmly supporting the recent peace initiative of King Hussein of Jordan and Yasir Arafat of the Palestine

Continued on Page A6, Column 3

'MOST HAPPY' GROUP

Spokesman Tells Parley on Stop in Damascus of Captives' Relief

By RICHARD BERNSTEIN

DAMASCUS, Syria, June 30 — Thirty-nine Americans were freed today by their Lebanese Shiite captors in Beirut, then were driven here in a convoy organized by the International Committee of the Red Cross. Within hours, the jubilant group was flying to West Germany, en route home after 17 days in captivity.

Their release, under an arrangement worked out with the help of the Syrian Government, ended a crisis that began June 14, when two Shiite gunmen com-

Statements in Damascus, page A7.

mandeered a Trans World Airlines jetliner over Europe. The assailants, who demanded the release of more than 700 mainly Shiite detainees held by Israel, beat and killed one American hostage early in the hijacking.

[The group landed at Frankfurt early Monday, where they were expected to undergo physical examinations, reunite with friends and relatives, and head home.

["You are back, and America did not compromise her principles to get you back," Vice President Bush said in greeting the hostages at Rhein-Main Air Base.]

Arrival in Damascus

The 39 Americans, waving and shouting happily to reporters, arrived in Damascus in 12 Red Cross cars and a truck that had left from the same schoolyard in southern Beirut where they had assembled the day before in hopes of leaving. Their departure was put off Saturday after their captors added a new demand, asking that the United States publicly guarantee that it would not retaliate militarily after the hostages were freed. The demand was apparently satisfied by a United States statement issued Saturday night.

The freed hostages, all men, appeared healthy and relaxed as they arrived here.

"We are most happy to be in Damascus with you people," their spokesman, 39-year-old Allyn B. Conwell of Houston, said at a brief news conference. He and his 38 colleagues sat at a long table, behind which hung a Syrian flag, a Sheraton hotel flag and a portrait of the Syrian President, Hafez al-Assad.

'I Don't Seek Retaliation'

Asked if he thought the United States should retaliate for the hijacking, Mr. Conwell said: "I don't really know who the people that took us are. Retaliation sounds an awful lot like revenge. I don't seek any retaliation or revenge."

"I think we all need to find a deeper understanding of the circumstances that led up to people taking a desperate act," he added. "And if we do that, that is without a doubt in my mind the surest way to finding a solution to the international terrorist dilemma."

Despite today's release, seven Americans who have disappeared in Lebanon over the last 15 months remain missing. Six are believed to be in the hands of Moslem militants. Late last

Continued on Page A6, Column 1

Space Arms Projects Ignite Debate On U.S.-Soviet Science Exchanges

By WILLIAM J. BROAD

Tensions are rising, because of the development of antimissile research programs, over the exchange of ideas and information taking place among scientists from the United States and the Soviet Union.

The exchanges revolve around nonmilitary matters and are limited to socalled pure, or theoretical, science, according to experts in the United States and Europe.

But a debate is intensifying over whether the meetings should be sharply curtailed. Many of these Russian and American scientists work in military laboratories and their meetings are occurring at a time when both nations are searching for powerful space weapons. These weapons have yet to be perfected and will almost certainly depend for their success on future developments in theoretical science.

Pressure to Curb Meetings

Members of opposing ideological camps are switching sides in this debate. Some Pentagon officials say Soviet scientists could gain not only ideas for exotic weaponry but state secrets as well and want the meetings promptly halted. They are allied in this desire with some liberals who want such "pure science" explorations stopped because they believe they will ultimately escalate the arms race.

On the other hand, different Government officials are allied with conservative weapons scientists, like Dr. Edward Teller, who argue that through discussion and shared research, nuclear weapons, as President Reagan proposed in his speech of March 1983, can be made "impotent and obsolete."

Continued on Page D10, Column 1

INSIDE

Wrapping It Up in Albany
The Legislature recessed after resolving the major remaining issue — extending rent controls for thousands of New York City tenants. Page B1.

Fire Burns 53 Coast Homes
Residents fled a San Diego neighborhood as 53 homes were destroyed by one of six brush fires within 150 miles of Los Angeles. Page A12.

Teacher Testing Backed
The National Education Association's leader urged the group to drop its often-criticized opposition to the testing of new teachers. Page A13.

Associated Press

Vice President Bush greeting Richard Young Moon, right, after hostages arrived at Rhein-Main Air Base in Frankfurt. At center is another hostage, the Rev. James W. McLoughlin.

AIDS Children Struggle With Tragic Legacy

By JANE GROSS

Dr. James Oleske pulled a plush rabbit from the pocket of his lab coat, but was unable to quiet his 4-year-old patient.

Instead, Dr. Oleske turned the restive boy from his back to his stomach and prescribed Valium as a sedative.

"See you, old buddy," Dr. Oleske said, leaving the hospital room with a salute and a strained smile. Then he approached a staff physician.

"Resuscitate," Dr. Oleske said, "but no respirator."

The child was dying of AIDS, the viral disease that destroys the immune system of both its adult and its child victims. Last fall the boy was walking and talking, holding his own, until

until the virus attacked his central nervous system.

Now, he lay at Children's Hospital in Newark, mute but for intermittent weeping, immobile but for spasmodic movements in his stiffened legs.

He is 1 of the about 600 children nationwide who health experts estimate have either AIDS, acquired immune deficiency syndrome, or preliminary symptoms of the disorder. More than 300 are in the New York area, most born to mothers who are intravenous drug users. Many of the mothers do not display symptoms but may themselves eventually sicken and die.

Since AIDS was identified in adults in 1981, the Federal Centers for Disease Control in Atlanta have reported 11,271 cases and 5,641 deaths, most of them male homosexuals and intravenous drug users.

According to the Federal definition of pediatric AIDS, which requires the presence of "an opportunistic, life-threatening infection" and the elimination of all other possible immunological disorders, 132 of these victims were children, 97 of whom have died.

Doctors, researchers and health-care professionals say that for every child with AIDS, there are three or four with a condition known as AIDS-related complex. The related condition

Continued on Page B10, Column 1

More News On Hostages

Israel: The Israeli Cabinet discussed the release but made no decision on when to free the 735 detainees it is holding. Page A7.

Families: Relatives of the 39 American hostages celebrated with champagne and smiles after learning the captives were free. Page A9.

7 Still Missing: Amid the joy over the freeing of the 39 was a call that seven Americans still held or missing in Lebanon not be forgotten. Page A9.

Managing the Crisis: The hostage crisis preoccupied the Administration to the exclusion of all else, and new details are emerging. Page A10.

Islamic Radicals: The fundamentalist Party of God, which is believed to be linked to the hijacking, is a growing force in the Middle East. Page A10.

Welcome in West Germany: The freed hostages were welcomed at Rhein-Main Air Base by relatives and Vice President Bush. Page A11.

Psychological Effects: Experts on the psychological effects of terrorism see deeper meanings in comments of the former hostages. Page A11.

"All the News
That's Fit to Print"

The New York Times

Late Edition
Weather: Chance of morning showers today, sunny and cool this afternoon; clear tonight. Mostly sunny tomorrow. Temperatures: today 63-67, tonight 45-49; yesterday 60-78. Details, page C31

VOL.CXXXV . No. 46,559   Copyright © 1985 The New York Times   NEW YORK, FRIDAY, OCTOBER 11, 1985   50 cents beyond 75 miles from New York City, except on Long Island.   30 CENTS

U.S. INTERCEPTS JET CARRYING HIJACKERS; FIGHTERS DIVERT IT TO NATO BASE IN ITALY; GUNMEN FACE TRIAL IN SLAYING OF HOSTAGE

OFFICIALS SAY C.I.A. DID NOT TELL F.B.I. OF SPY CASE MOVES

Court Papers Assert Suspect Told Colleagues He Might Give Secrets to Soviet

The following article is based on reporting by Stephen Engelberg and Joel Brinkley and was written by Mr. Brinkley.

Special to The New York Times

WASHINGTON, Oct. 10 — The Central Intelligence Agency failed to notify the Federal Bureau of Investigation after it learned more than a year ago that Edward L. Howard was considering becoming a Soviet spy, Government officials said today.

According to court records, Mr. Howard told two agency employees in September 1984 that he was thinking of disclosing classified information to the Soviet Union.

Law Calls For Reporting

The bureau has sole responsibility for domestic espionage investigations and, under Federal law, the intelligence agency and all other Government agencies are supposed to report suspected espionage to the F.B.I. It is illegal for the C.I.A. or any other Federal agency to carry out surveillance or other actions within the United States to stop potential spies.

Mr. Howard, 33 years old, a former intelligence agency officer who is now a fugitive, has been charged with espionage, accused of giving Soviet officials details of American intelligence operations in Moscow. Federal officials have called the disclosures serious and damaging.

Soviet Defector Was the Key

Federal officials said the C.I.A. told the F.B.I. nothing about Mr. Howard until after the bureau began an investigation this fall based on information from a Soviet defector, Vitaly Yurchenko, a once senior official of the K.G.B., the Soviet intelligence agency.

The bureau began surveillance of Mr. Howard last month, but he slipped out of his home at night and is believed to have fled the country.

Senator Patrick J. Leahy, the Vermont Democrat who is vice chairman of the Select Committee on Intelligence, said today: "If the C.I.A. did not give the F.B.I. adequate information

Continued on Page B8, Column 4

Planes from the carrier Saratoga near Albania intercepted jet south of Crete and escorted it to Sicily.

The New York Times Oct. 11, 1985

BUOYANT CAPITAL HAILS THE ACTION

Moynihan Sums Up the Mood: 'Thank God We Won One'

By BERNARD WEINRAUB

Special to The New York Times

WASHINGTON, Oct. 10 — Reagan Administration officials and legislators reacted exuberantly tonight to the news that American warplanes had seized the four hijackers who apparently killed an elderly American aboard an Italian cruise ship.

"Thank God we've won one," said Senator Daniel Patrick Moynihan, Democrat of New York.

The comment summed up the mood in this startled capital after years of witnessing the Carter and Reagan administrations struggling in vain to cope with Middle East terrorism and attacks against the United States.

Iran Crisis Recalled

Officials pointed out that it was nearly six years ago that Iranian revolutionaries seized the United States Embassy in Teheran and virtually made a hostage of the Carter Administration. Mr. Carter found himself unable to fulfill his threats against terrorists and, in the case of a military raid to rescue the Americans held hostage in Iran, failed in a humiliating manner.

Mr. Reagan took office after criticizing

Continued on Page A11, Column 4

Port in Israel Described as Target Of Terrorists Who Seized Vessel

By THOMAS L. FRIEDMAN

Special to The New York Times

JERUSALEM, Oct. 10 — The four Palestinians aboard the Achille Lauro intended to stay aboard as passengers until the cruise liner reached Ashdod, Israel, and then planned either to shoot up the harbor or take Israelis hostage, according to Israeli, Palestinian and other Arab informants. The Israelis were to be held to bargain for the release of 50 Palestinians held in Israeli jails.

The leader of the faction that ordered the operation, Mohammed Abbas, also known as Abul Abbas, is a close associate of Yasir Arafat, the chairman of the Palestine Liberation Organization, and was reportedly sent by Mr. Arafat to deal with the hijackers after their original plan to infiltrate Israel at Ashdod had gone awry.

Crew Discovered Arms Cache

According to the informants, the four members of the group aborted their plans and seized the ship when their weapons were discovered by the crew after the Achille Lauro had left Alexandria on Monday. The informants say the original plan and the hijacking were part of a bungled attempt to exact revenge for Israel's raid last week on the P.L.O. headquarters near Tunis.

When relations between the P.L.O. and Italy seemed jeopardized by the seizure of the ship and an American passenger was killed by the apparently panicked hijackers, Mr. Arafat and Abul Abbas ordered the hijackers to return to Port Said and surrender.

This picture was pieced together from information provided by Israeli Foreign Ministry and military officials, Arab analysts in Beirut and a statement issued today in Nicosia, Cyprus, by a spokesman of the Abul Abbas faction in the Palestine Liberation

Front, one of the guerrilla groups in the Palestine Liberation Organization.

A copy of the statement was delivered to Reuters in Nicosia and virtually all its main points have been confirmed by Israeli or Arab sources.

The statement, which apologized to the cruise passengers for the hijacking, was believed to be the first time that a Palestinian guerrilla group has expressed regret for an attack. It was apparently occasioned by widespread condemnation of the incident in Italy and in the Arab world.

Retaliation Was Aim

According to Arab and Palestinian sources in Beirut and Nicosia, the gunmen had planned the assault on Ashdod in retaliation for the Israeli attack on the P.L.O. headquarters in Tunisia, in which about 60 people were killed. The message to Israel was to have been: "If you can reach out 1,500 miles and strike at us, we can reach out 1,500 miles and strike back at you."

Israeli merchant marine and Government sources say Israel has been on the lookout for seaborne attempts at infiltration. The sources noted that Israeli naval vessels had been observed and photographed by unidentified men when they docked at Western European ports. Now that overland routes into Israel — from Lebanon, Jordan

Continued on Page A14, Column 1

PRAISE FOR PILOTS

Weinberger Will Not Say if Navy Planes Would Have Used Force

By BILL KELLER

Special to The New York Times

WASHINGTON, Friday, Oct. 11 — Secretary of Defense Caspar W. Weinberger praised Navy fighter pilots early this morning for "high military skill" in intercepting an Egyptian plane carrying four hijackers of an Italian cruise ship.

Mr. Weinberger, briefing reporters on the operation, refused to say whether the four F-14's from the aircraft carrier U.S.S. Saratoga had been prepared to use force if necessary to divert the Egyptian aircraft.

Mr. Weinberger also disclosed, in an apparent reference to American military special operations units reportedly deployed to the region, that before the hijackers of the Italian ship, the Achille Lauro, surrendered, the United States was "prepared to take action against the ship." He added, "We were prepared to do that, I think, effectively and successfully."

Details of Interception

Mr. Weinberger provided the first details of the interception.

He said the Saratoga was steaming west in the Eastern Mediterrean on a routine exercise near Albania when she received orders at about 9 P.M. local time Thursday to prepare for an interception.

At about 11 P.M., four swept-wing F-14 fighter planes took off, shortly before the Egyptian aircraft did so. Pentagon officials said two E-2C surveillance planes, smaller versions of the Awacs eavesdropping aircraft, had left the Cairo airport, and how they were certain they had the right plane. "I would say that we had very good intelligence," he said.

The fighters circled in the darkness near the island of Crete south of Greece and intercepted the Egyptian plane, a commercial Boeing 737 chartered by the Egyptian Government, at about 12:30 A.M., Mr. Weinberger said, and made radio contact.

"They were waiting in international

Continued on Page A10, Column 1

FLOWN FROM CAIRO

4 in Custody in Sicily — Washington Says It Wants Extradition

By BERNARD GWERTZMAN

Special to The New York Times

WASHINGTON, Friday, Oct. 11 — An Egyptian plane carrying the hijackers of an Italian cruise ship was intercepted by American Navy jets as it flew toward Tunisia Thursday night and was forced to land in Italy, the White House announced. A spokesman said the four terrorists had been taken into custody by Italian authorities.

In a late evening news conference, Larry Speakes, the White House spokesman, said President Reagan had ordered the dramatic military action after learning that Egypt had turned down repeated American pleas to prosecute the four gunmen and was flying them to freedom. The hijackers are believed to have killed an elderly American tourist aboard the cruise ship.

No Shots Fired

The United States intends to seek "the prompt extradition" of the hijackers from Italy, Mr. Speakes said. Later, Defense Secretary Caspar W. Weinberger said the United States hoped the Italians would waive their right to try the hijackers and would allow them to be prosecuted in the United States.

Mr. Speakes said that the Egyptian plane, a commercial 737 airliner with armed Egyptian security men aboard, was intercepted by the F-14's from the aircraft carrier Saratoga north of

News session excerpts, page A12.

Egypt in international waters. The F-14's "diverted" the plane to a joint Italian-NATO base at Sigonella in Sicily. Mr. Weinberger said four F-14's were involved.

The incident occurred without the American planes having to fire a shot, Mr. Speakes said.

Troops Surround Plane

He said the Egyptian aircraft had been headed for Tunisia but that the Tunisian Government had refused to grant it landing rights. For that, he said, the United States was grateful. Mr. Weinberger said the Egyptian plane had also been refused permission to land by authorities in Athens.

After the Egyptian plane landed, it was surrounded by American and Italian troops, Mr. Speakes said. Mr. Wein-

Continued on Page A10, Column 4

Orson Welles Is Dead at 70; Innovator of Film and Stage

Orson Welles, the Hollywood "boy wonder" who created the film classic "Citizen Kane," scared tens of thousands of Americans with a realistic radio report of a Martian invasion of New Jersey and changed the face of film and theater with his daring new ideas, died yesterday in Los Angeles, apparently of a heart attack. He was 70 years old and lived in Las Vegas, Nev.

An assistant coroner in Los Angeles, Donald Messerle, said Welles's death "appears to be natural in origin." He had been under treatment for diabetes as well as a heart ailment, his physician reported. Welles's body was found by his chauffeur.

An Unorthodox Style

Despite the feeling of many that his career — which evoked almost constant controversy over its 50 years — was one of largely unfulfilled promise, Welles eventually won the respect of his colleagues. He received the Lifetime Achievement Award of the American Film Institute in 1975, and last year the Directors Guild of America gave him its highest honor, the D. W. Griffith Award.

His unorthodox casting and staging for the theater gave new meaning to the classics and to contemporary works. As the "Wonder Boy" of Broadway in the 1930's, he set the stage on its ear with a "Julius Caesar" set in Fascist Italy, an all-black "Macbeth" and his presentation of Marc Blitzstein's "Cradle Will Rock." His Mercury Theater of the Air set new standards for radio drama, and in one perform-

SEE TODAY'S SPECIAL ARTS PROGRAM FEATURE FOR ART & DESIGN OPPORTUNITIES OPENING ON PAGE C20 IN THE WEEKEND SECTION-ADVT

United Press International
Orson Welles

ance panicked thousands across the nation.

In film, his innovations in deep-focus technology and his use of theater esthetics — long takes without close-ups, making the viewer's eye search the screen as if it were a stage — created a new vocabulary for the cinema.

By age 24, he was already being described by the press as a has-been — a cliche that would dog him all his life. But at that very moment Welles was creating "Citizen Kane," generally considered one of the best motion pictures ever made. This scenario was re-

Continued on Page B6, Column 1

INSIDE

40 Salvador Soldiers Killed
A leftist rebel unit killed at least 40 Salvadoran soldiers and wounded 68 in a raid on the main army training base near La Union. Page A3.

Yul Brynner Is Dead
The actor and director, the quintessential Siamese monarch in "The King and I," died in New York at the age of 65. Page B7.

Dodgers Go 2 Games Up
The Dodgers beat the Cardinals, 8-2, in Los Angeles and lead by 2-0, in the National League playoff, which shifts to St. Louis tomorrow. Page A29.

FOR THOSE FAVORING CREMATION WOODLAWN CEMETERY OFFERS A FREE PAMPHLET GIVING COMPLETE INFORMATION CALL 212-920-0600.-ADVT

"NEVER ON A SUNDAY" NOW YOU CAN SHOP AT EINSTEIN MOOMJY IN NEW YORK 7 DAYS A WEEK SEE AD IN SUNDAY'S PAPER-ADVT.

ALEX, HAPPY THIRTEEN, WE LOVE YOU A LOT MOM AND DAD-ADVT.

Hostage's Death: 'A Shot to Forehead'

By E. J. DIONNE Jr.

Special to The New York Times

PORT SAID, Egypt, Oct. 10 — Passengers from the hijacked Italian cruise liner were quoted today as describing how the terrorists had dragged an elderly American tourist in his wheelchair to the ship's side and shot him in cold blood.

The most vivid account, based on interviews with some of the more than 400 people held hostage aboard the Achille Lauro, came from the Italian Ambassador to Egypt, Giovanni Migliudo. The Ambassador told reporters that he had put together his account of the killing after six hours of interviews.

He said the killing of the tourist, Leon Klinghoffer, had taken place on Tuesday when the ship was near Tartus, Syria.

Answer 'Slow in Coming'

"The hijackers had asked to be put in contact with the Italian and U.S. Ambassadors in Damascus to demand the liberation of 50 Palestinians held in Israel," the Italian news agency, ANSA, quoted the Ambassador as saying. "But the answer was slow in coming and to exercise further pressure, the hijackers decided to kill a first hostage."

Mr. Migliudo said that all the American and British passengers on the ship were forced to lie on the deck.

"The hijackers pushed him in his chair and dragged him to the side of the ship — in cold blood — they fired a shot to the forehead. Then the body was dumped into the sea, together with the wheelchair," the Ambassador said.

The Ambassador's story was one of many that emerged today as the ship, the Achille Lauro, lay under a searing sun in the Suez Canal harbor here.

The Austrian Ambassador to Egypt,

Continued on Page A13, Column 1

Agence France-Presse
Marilyn Klinghoffer, whose husband, Leon, was slain, being escorted off ship in Port Said. A family friend, Neil Kantor of Metuchen, N.J., is at left.

The New York Times

Late Edition

Weather: Mostly sunny and cold today, westerly winds; clear and cold tonight. Partly sunny and milder tomorrow. Temperatures: today 30-35, tonight 20-25; yesterday 20-41. Details on page 46.

VOL.CXXXV.. No. 46,637   Copyright © 1985 The New York Times   NEW YORK, SATURDAY, DECEMBER 28, 1985   50 cents beyond 75 miles from New York City, except on Long Island   30 CENTS

AIRPORT TERRORISTS KILL 13 AND WOUND 113 AT ISRAELI COUNTERS IN ROME AND VIENNA

REAGAN TO TRADE TELEVISION TALKS WITH GORBACHEV

New Year's Day Greetings Are to Be Broadcast at Same Time in Both Nations

By GERALD M. BOYD
Special to The New York Times

LOS ANGELES, Dec. 27 — President Reagan and Mikhail S. Gorbachev have agreed to exchange videotaped New Year's Day greetings that are intended for broadcast in the United States and the Soviet Union, the White House announced today.

The announcement said the exchanges would give Mr. Reagan his first chance to talk to the Soviet people directly on television and would give the Soviet leader the same chance to speak to the American people.

The announcement came as Mr. Gorbachev, in Moscow, offered a cautiously upbeat assessment of relations between the Soviet Union and the United States, saying points of "potential convergence" had emerged in arms control talks. [Page 3.]

'Barbaric Methods' Assailed

Shortly before the announcement, Mr. Reagan, who flew here today to begin a weeklong vacation, issued his latest statement condemning the Soviet intervention in Afghanistan.

The statement, noting the sixth anniversary of the Soviet invasion, accused the Russians and their surrogates of resorting "to barbaric methods of waging war" to try to crush a liberation effort in Afghanistan. Mr. Reagan said the United States stood "squarely on the side of the people of Afghanistan."

The videotape exchange will achieve a longtime Administration goal of having Mr. Reagan talk on Soviet television.

Three to Five Minutes Long

Late today, the news divisions of the American networks indicated that they all planned to broadcast both addresses.

The speeches, both of which are to be broadcast on Wednesday, are to be three to five minutes long and will contain New Year's greetings, the officials said. One White House aide said Mr.

Continued on Page 3, Column 5

Further Growth In the Economy Forecast for '86

But Inflation and Jobless Rate Worry Analysts

By ROBERT D. HERSHEY Jr.
Special to The New York Times

WASHINGTON, Dec. 27 — The United States economy seems headed for a fourth consecutive year of expansion in 1986, but its course will be marred by gradually rising inflation and stubbornly high unemployment, according to a consensus of business and academic forecasters.

The possibility of a recession, which at various times in the last year has seemed just over the horizon, has receded and is no longer regarded as an apparent threat.

One important reason is the roaring bull market in stocks and bonds. By making investors richer, it has raised both confidence and the outlook for consumer spending, which accounts for two-thirds of the economy.

'Rather Sluggish Fashion'

"The prospects for the economy in 1986 are quite good," said A. Gilbert Heebner, chief economist for the Philadelphia National Bank, in a prediction that typifies current professional thinking. "It's going to seem like more of the same, with the economy growing but in a rather sluggish fashion."

The Reagan Administration, for its part, is believed to have tentatively adopted a 4 percent growth forecast for next year, somewhat higher than that of most private analysts.

To be sure, few economists or politicians are satisfied with the current rate of American growth, less than 2.5 percent for 1985 after 6.6 percent in 1984. This year's rate has been barely enough to keep unemployment from rising and it has left industry with large amounts of idle productive capacity.

Moreover, agriculture and parts of the oil, real estate and banking industries are in disarray despite an expansion that this month reached its third anniversary. Weak farm and crude oil prices, as well as a glut of unrented office space in some cities, could cause more problems for banks in 1986.

Yet most economists predict solid growth for 1986. They cite several factors for this tempered optimism. Both

Continued on Page 31, Column 4

VICTIMS: Bodies bearing tags affixed by police on the floor at Leonardo da Vinci Airport near Rome.

SUSPECT: A man suspected as a terrorist being taken into custody after the attack on the Rome airport.

4 ATTACKERS KILLED

Gunmen Fire Into Crowds and Throw Grenades Near Lines at El Al

By JOHN TAGLIABUE
Special to The New York Times

ROME, Dec. 27 — Terrorists hurled grenades and fired submachine guns at crowds of holiday travelers at airports in Rome and Vienna today in attacks on check-in counters of El Al Israel Airlines.

Authorities quoted by news services said the gunmen had killed at least 13 people, including 4 Americans, and wounded 113 in the two attacks. Four terrorists were killed, and three others were wounded and captured.

While El Al appeared to be a target in both attacks, the authorities said the terrorists in Rome had also thrown grenades and fired indiscriminately with Soviet-made assault rifles into crowds of New York-bound passengers checking in at Pan American World Airways and Trans World Airlines.

Terrorists Not Identified

The assailants, who were not immediately identified, left the two airline terminals strewn with bloodied and torn bodies, luggage, overturned furniture and broken glass.

Israeli Government officials asserted that the Palestine Liberation Organization might be responsible, but P.L.O. officials here and in Tunis denied any role in the apparently coordinated attacks.

Witnesses at the airport in Vienna said panic broke out as the explosions and firing began, with passengers and airport staff throwing themselves to the ground and crawling desperately for cover. [Page 4.]

Gunmen Jumped and Shrieked

Similar accounts were given in Rome, where survivors described chaos amid thundering explosions and raking bursts of gunfire unleashed by young masked men in blue jeans who jumped up and down and shrieked as their victims fell. Bystanders screamed and dived for cover.

"It was an inferno — they started throwing hand grenades and firing with submachine guns," said one witness who was wounded in Rome, Dora Silvestri. "We all threw ourselves to the ground. Blood spread over the floor. I

Washington said the attackers were "beyond the pale of civilization." Page 5. These comments were echoed worldwide. Page 6.

fell on the body of a girl, and a grenade splinter hit me in the face."

As the weary and shaken travelers caught in the airport attacks returned to New York, some of them told of their minutes of terror in a series of interviews. [Page 6.]

The authorities said seven terrorists were apparently involved — four in the attack in Rome, which began shortly after 9 A.M. (3 A.M. New York time), and three in the attack in Vienna, which started a few minutes later.

At Leonardo da Vinci Airport at Rome, three terrorists were slain and one was seized after being wounded in a gun battle with the police and plainclothes Israeli security men in the terminal. Security had been increased there after recent hijackings and official warnings that airports might be attacked during the Christmas holidays.

A total of 13 people were killed in the Rome attack, including three terrorists, and 70 wounded.

[A wounded American man died later at a Rome hospital, The Associated Press reported from Rome.]

At Schwechat Airport in Vienna, 3 were killed, including a gunman, and 47 wounded, one of them critically.

Two of the terrorists in Vienna were seized after a wild car chase and a run-

Continued on Page 4, Column 3

Road Repairs to Snarl Traffic On Both Sides of East River

By DEIRDRE CARMODY

A section of the Brooklyn-Queens Expressway near the Williamsburg Bridge will be closed in January for reconstruction, and the work is expected to cause heavy traffic on the Brooklyn and Manhattan ends of the bridge for more than a year.

The project, beginning in mid- to late January, is part of a five-year, $2.6 billion state program to rebuild many of the city's highways. The starting date depends on the availability of construction crews, according to the City Bureau of Traffic Operations.

70,000 Vehicles a Day

Westbound traffic on the expressway, which the Traffic Bureau says is used by about 70,000 vehicles a day, will be rerouted at the Wythe Avenue exit in Brooklyn onto Williamsburg Street West for two and a half blocks. Cars will be able to get back on the expressway at the Flushing Avenue entrance.

Williamsburg Street West has been widened by a lane and a shoulder has been added. The Flushing Avenue entrance has also been widened by a lane.

"It is not an easy detour, not one we look forward to," said Traffic Commissioner Samuel I. Schwartz.

The detour is not expected to be able to carry all the traffic, but according to Abel Silver, a spokesman for the City Transportation Department, some of the vehicles that normally take the Brooklyn and Manhattan Bridges into

Continued on Page 26, Column 1

The New York Times/Dec. 28, 1985

Williamsburg Bridge will carry more Manhattan-bound traffic.

Israel, Blaming P.L.O., Issues a Warning

By THOMAS L. FRIEDMAN
Special to The New York Times

JERUSALEM, Dec. 27 — Although the Palestine Liberation Organization denied involvement in the attacks in Rome and Vienna, Israeli officials blamed the guerrilla group today and made it clear that Israel would respond at the appropriate time and place.

"Israel is shocked and outraged by these two new acts of senseless terror against innocent civilians," a Foreign Ministry statement said.

"The terrorist attacks come against a background of declarations by the head of the P.L.O., and those Arab states that support this organization, that these terrorists will cease terror operations outside of Israel. Israel will continue its struggle against terrorism in every place and at any time it sees fit."

Syrian Missiles in Lebanon

Meanwhile, Israeli analysts said Israel's ability to retaliate for the attacks had been limited by Syria's decision to move mobile surface-to-air missiles into Lebanon.

In the past, Israel has often retaliated for terrorist attacks abroad by bombing Palestinian guerrilla bases in Lebanon, regarding these as convenient "return addresses."

To do so now, however, Israeli jets would have to penetrate the new curtain of surface-to-air missiles Syria has drawn across the Bekaa region in Lebanon, which could lead to an all-out war with Syria, the analysts said.

Since Israel already destroyed the main P.L.O. compound in Tunisia last October, that too is no longer an option for retaliation. The analysts said new P.L.O. offices in Baghdad would not be easy to reach and were widely dispersed. This would seem to leave as the only option for retaliation a more surgical strike against specific individuals, the analysts said.

A Political Statement

To appreciate the full Israeli quandary, officials said, it must be understood that the Syrian decision to deploy the SAM-6 and SAM-8 mobile batteries a few miles inside Lebanon, for the second time in a month, was as much a political statement as a strategic military maneuver.

It was apparently designed, Israeli

officials say, to send Israel and the United States clear signals about Damascus's intentions to change some of the rules in the Middle East.

To begin with, said Itamar Rabinovich, an authority on Syria at Tel Aviv University, the Syrians are apparently trying to establish a new relationship with Israel in Lebanon after the Israeli withdrawal.

While Israel wants to hold onto all of its old perquisites in Lebanon, particularly its freedom to fly reconnaissance missions over the Syrian-controlled Bekaa, the Syrians want to reverse once and for all this free Israeli access to their neighboring client state.

"By sending the missiles back, the

Continued on Page 5, Column 1

For Families of 2 Americans, Sudden Sorrow

By SARA RIMER

Natasha Simpson, the 11-year-old daughter of a foreign correspondent in Rome, was on her way to New York with her family for a three-week vacation with friends and relatives. John Buonocore 3d, a 20-year-old student, was on his way home to Wilmington, Del., after a semester in Rome, just in time for his father's 50th birthday.

Both died at Leonardo da Vinci Airport in Rome yesterday. They were among the 14 people killed there when terrorists hurled hand grenades and opened fire with submachine guns into crowds of holiday travelers. The Associated Press said two other Americans, Frederick Gage, of Madison,

Wis., and Don Maland, of New Port Richey, Fla., were also killed.

Natasha Simpson was killed apparently as her father, Victor L. Simpson, a New Yorker who is the news editor for The Associated Press in Rome, tried to shield her from the bullets. Mr. Simpson, 43, was wounded in the right wrist and hand.

'Put His Arm Around Her'

"I think he put his arm around her to try and push her down and that's how he injured his finger," said his wife, Daniela Petroff Simpson, who was reached by telephone at her parents' home in Rome.

Mrs. Simpson, 40, had been outside the terminal walking the family terrier

while her husband and two children — Natasha and 9-year-old Michael — checked in for their flight to Kennedy International Airport. Then she heard the exploding grenades.

"Suddenly there was a shattering noise as if something was collapsing," Mrs. Simpson, who is also a journalist, told The Associated Press in Rome. "And then there were machine-gun bursts. Two distinct machine-gun bursts. And then silence. I rushed into screams and cries and saw my husband dripping blood from his hand and my son on the floor shot in the stomach."

Mr. Simpson and his son were hospi-

Continued on Page 6, Column 3

INSIDE

3 on Miami Force Arrested
Three members of the Miami police force were charged with murder in the drownings of three men thought to have been dealing in drugs. Page 8.

West Side Rail Proposal
New York State and New York City are studying the possibility of a light rail line — perhaps a monorail — on Manhattan's West Side. Page 25.

"All the News That's Fit to Print"

The New York Times

Late Edition

Weather: Partly cloudy and cold today, chance of snow; chance of snow tonight. Partly cloudy, cold tomorrow. Temperatures: today 27-30, tonight 13-19; yesterday 14-23. Details, page C19.

VOL.CXXXV...No. 46,669   Copyright © 1986 The New York Times   NEW YORK, WEDNESDAY, JANUARY 29, 1986   50 cents beyond 75 miles from New York City, except on Long Island.   30 CENTS

THE SHUTTLE EXPLODES

6 IN CREW AND HIGH-SCHOOL TEACHER ARE KILLED 74 SECONDS AFTER LIFTOFF

11:39:13 A.M.

11:39:17 A.M.

ABC News; Agence France-Presse

Thousands Watch A Rain of Debris

By WILLIAM J. BROAD
Special to The New York Times

CAPE CANAVERAL, Fla., Jan. 28 — The space shuttle Challenger exploded in a ball of fire shortly after it left the launching pad today, and all seven astronauts on board were lost.

The worst accident in the history of the American space program, it was witnessed by thousands of spectators who watched in wonder, then horror, as the ship blew apart high in the air.

Flaming debris rained down on the Atlantic Ocean for an hour after the explosion, which occurred just after 11:39 A.M. It kept rescue teams from reaching the area where the craft would have fallen into the sea, about 18 miles offshore.

It seemed impossible that anyone could have lived through the terrific explosion 10 miles in the sky, and officials said this afternoon that there was no evidence to indicate that the five men and two women aboard had survived.

No Ideas Yet as to Cause

There were no clues to the cause of the accident. The space agency offered no immediate explanations, and said it was suspending all shuttle flights indefinitely while it conducted an inquiry. Officials discounted speculation that cold weather at Cape Canaveral or an accident several days ago that slightly damaged insulation on the external fuel tank might have been a factor.

Americans who had grown used to the idea of men and women soaring into space reacted with shock to the disaster, the first time United States astronauts had died in flight. President Reagan canceled the State of the Union Message that had been scheduled for tonight, expressing sympathy for the families of the crew but vowing that the nation's exploration of space would continue.

Killed in the explosion were the mission commander, Francis R. (Dick) Scobee; the pilot, Comdr. Michael J. Smith of the Navy; Dr. Judith A. Resnik; Dr. Ronald E. McNair; Lieut. Col. Ellison S. Onizuka of the Air Force; Gregory B. Jarvis, and Christa McAuliffe.

Mrs. McAuliffe, a high-school teacher from Concord, N.H., was to have been the first ordinary citizen in space.

After a Minute, Fire and Smoke

The Challenger lifted off flawlessly this morning, after three days of delays, for what was to have been the 25th mission of the reusable shuttle fleet that was intended to make space travel commonplace. The ship rose for about a minute on a column of smoke and fire from its five engines.

Suddenly, without warning, it erupted in a ball of flame.

The shuttle was about 10 miles above the earth, in the critical seconds when the two solid-fuel rocket boosters are firing as well as the shuttle's main engines. There was some discrepancy about the exact time of the blast: The National Aeronautics and Space Administration said they lost radio contact with the craft 74 seconds into the flight, plus or minus five seconds.

Two large white streamers raced away from the blast, followed by a rain of debris that etched white contrails in the cloudless sky and then slowly

Continued on Page A5, Column 4

Reagan Lauds 'Heroes'

President Reagan, shaken by the explosion of the space shuttle, postponed his State of the Union Message. "We mourn seven heroes," he said in a talk broadcast from the White House after the disaster. "There will be more shuttle flights and more shuttle crews and, yes, more volunteers, more civilians, more teachers in space."

He also sought to console the nation's pupils, many of whom saw telecasts of the loss of the teacher who was to have been sent into space. Article and transcript, page A9.

From the Beginning to the End

The last flight of the shuttle Challenger lasted about 74 seconds. Here is the transcript, as recorded by The New York Times, of its final moments, before and after liftoff.

PUBLIC AFFAIRS OFFICER: Coming up on the 90-second point in our countdown. Ninety seconds and counting. The 51-L Mission ready to go. . . .

T minus 10, 9, 8, 7, 6, we have main engine start, 4, 3, 2, 1. And liftoff. Liftoff of the 25th space shuttle mission and it has cleared the tower. . . .

MISSION CONTROL CENTER: Watch your roll, Challenger.

PUBLIC AFFAIRS OFFICER: Roll program confirmed. Challenger now heading down range. [Pause.] Engines beginning throttling down now at 94 percent. Normal throttle for most of flight 104 percent. Will throttle down to 65 percent shortly. Engines at 65 percent. Three engines running normally. Three good cells, three good ABU's. [Pause.] Velocity 2,257 feet per second, altitude 4.3 nautical miles, down range distance 3 nautical miles. [Pause.]

Engines throttling up, three engines now at 104 percent.

MISSION CONTROL: Challenger, go with throttle up.

FRANCIS R. SCOBEE, CHALLENGER COMMANDER: Roger, go with throttle up.

PUBLIC AFFAIRS OFFICER: One minute 15 seconds, velocity 2,900 feet per second, altitude 9 nautical miles, down range distance 7 nautical miles. [Long pause.]

Flight controllers here looking very carefully at the situation. [Pause.]

Obviously a major malfunction. We have no downlink [communications from Challenger]. [Long pause.]

We have a report from the flight dynamics officer that the vehicle has exploded.

How Could It Happen? *Fuel Tank Leak Feared*

By MALCOLM W. BROWNE

Debris from the explosion of the shuttle Challenger was scattered so widely over the Atlantic Ocean that investigators may never recover enough of it to pin down the cause of the disaster. But suspicions quickly focused on the craft's huge external fuel tank, a potential bomb that carried more than 385,000 gallons of liquid hydrogen and more than 140,000 gallons of liquid oxygen at liftoff.

The most logical explanation is that a large leak must have occurred either in the tank itself or in the pipeline and pumping system that carried liquid hydrogen to the orbiter's three main engines.

Barbara Schwartz, a spokesman for the Johnson Space Center, acknowledged that pure liquid or gaseous hydrogen cannot burn; only if the pure hydrogen carried in the rear section of the shuttle's tank were allowed to come into contact with air, or with the liquid oxygen in the tank's nose section, could it have burned or exploded.

Potential Dangers of Hydrogen Gas

But what might have started the leak, and what could have ignited the explosion that followed?

Parallel questions, never fully answered, were raised after the fire that destroyed the German airship Hindenburg as it was landing at Lakehurst, N.J., on May 6, 1937. The shuttle Challenger, like the Hindenburg, had been releasing hydrogen gas into the air shortly before the disaster, and some of the gas might have remained aboard the craft, mixed with air and ready to detonate if exposed to the smallest spark.

Neither NASA nor Martin Marietta Aerospace, the manufacturer of the external fuel tank, would comment yesterday on possible causes of the disaster.

But the geometry of the shuttle's external fuel tank, as described by official manuals from NASA and the Rockwell International Corporation, a major shuttle contractor, suggest one potential danger point in particular: the "intertank," or midsection of the structure, which separates the liquid oxygen tank from the liquid hydrogen tank. The bulk of the hydrogen fuel is closest to the liquid oxygen at this point, and a rupture or leak in the plumbing or walls of the intertank could have flooded the two fluids together to create a gigantic bomb.

Suggestions that the unseasonably cold weather at

Continued on Page A4, Column 1

After the Shock, a Need to Share Grief and Loss

By SARA RIMER

The nation came together yesterday in a moment of disaster and loss. Wherever Americans were when they heard the news — at work, at school or at home — they shared their grief over the death of the seven astronauts, among them one who had captured their imaginations, Christa McAuliffe, the teacher from Concord, N.H., who was to have been the first ordinary citizen to go into space.

Shortly before noon, when the first word of the explosion came, daily events seemed to stop as people awaited the details and asked the same questions: "What happened? Are there any survivors?"

In offices, restaurants and stores, people gathered in front of television sets, mesmerized by the terrible scene of the shuttle exploding, a scene that would be replayed throughout the day and night. Children who had learned

about Mrs. McAuliffe were watching in classrooms across the country.

It seemed to be one of those moments, enlarged and frozen, that people would remember and recount for the rest of their lives — what they were doing and where they were when they heard that the space shuttle Challenger had exploded. The need to reach out, to speak of disbelief and pain, was everywhere. Family members telephoned one another, friends telephoned friends.

"It was like the Kennedy thing," said John Hannan, who heard the news when his sister called him at his office, a personnel recruiting concern in Philadelphia. "Everyone was numb."

'I Felt Very Close to Her'

Florine Israel, a legal secretary at the New York Civil Liberties Union, echoed the sentiments of many who spoke of Mrs. McAuliffe not as an astronaut but as a friend. "I felt very close to her," she said. "She was ordinary people. She was a mother, a working woman. I felt like I was a part of it."

The image of the shuttle exploding flashed across 100 television sets in the electronics department of Macy's, in midtown Manhattan, where a crowd of workers from nearby offices and facto-

Continued on Page A3, Column 1

Francis R. Scobee
Commander

Michael J. Smith
Pilot

Judith A. Resnik
Electrical Engineer

Ellison S. Onizuka
Engineer

Ronald E. McNair
Physicist

Gregory B. Jarvis
Electrical Engineer

Christa McAuliffe
Teacher

317

"All the News
That's Fit to Print"

The New York Times

Late Edition

Weather: Mostly cloudy, windy today,
chance of snow; cloudy tonight. Partly
cloudy and continued cold tomorrow.
Temperatures: today 33-37, tonight 20-
25; yesterday 19-25. Details on page 48.

VOL.CXXXV...No. 46,679   Copyright © 1986 The New York Times   NEW YORK, SATURDAY, FEBRUARY 8, 1986   50 cents beyond 75 miles from New York City, except on Long Island.   **30 CENTS**

BOTH SIDES CLAIM THEY ARE LEADING IN PHILIPPINE VOTE

VIOLENCE REPORTED

Early Official Tally Gives Aquino Slight Edge — Marcos Confident

By SETH MYDANS
Special to The New York Times

MANILA, Saturday, Feb. 8 — Corazon C. Aquino claimed victory today in
the Presidential election while President Ferdinand E. Marcos said only, "I
probably have won."

The official Government vote count,
after coming to a near halt on the afternoon and night of Election Day Friday,
began moving slowly ahead and put
Mrs. Aquino in a slight lead in sketchy
early returns.

A respected poll-watching group that
is relied on here to offer an independent
assessment put Mrs. Aquino in the lead
by a larger margin with more than a
quarter of the vote recorded.

Aquino Statement

In a statement issued by her office,
Mrs. Aquino said: "The trend is clear
and irreversible. The people and I have
won and we know it. Nothing can take
our victory from us."

"Mrs. Aquino plans to call on Marcos
to arrange for an orderly transition of
power," an Aquino spokesman said today. He said the call would be made
"when the trend is irreversible, probably within the next 48 hours."

A spokesman for the President called
an urgent press conference at 3:30
A.M. to condemn Mrs. Aquino's statement and urged that no claims of victory be made until all returns are in.

'Systematic Harassment'

At least 30 people were reported
killed in Election Day violence amid
widespread reports of vote fraud and
intimidation at the polls.

Senator Richard Lugar, the co-chairman of an official delegation of American observers, accused the Government today of trying to "shape the return" by reporting votes from areas
where the President is strong while
holding back on the results from Manila, where Mrs. Aquino has her heaviest
support.

"The Manila vote has been held down
by systematic harassment," said the
Indiana Republican. "My own political
judgment is that the Government concluded the results from Manila would
not be good."

National Assembly's Role

Meanwhile, the speaker of the National Assembly, Nicanor Yniguez, appeared on Government television to remind voters that no matter what the
various counts showed, it is his Government body that will assess them and
declare the winner.

Mr. Yniguez, a close ally of Mr. Marcos, said the legislature would begin its

Continued on Page 6, Column 1

Gunmen Seize Votes At Polling Stations In Philippine Town

By FRANCIS X. CLINES
Special to The New York Times

MUNTINLUPA, the Philippines,
Feb. 7 — The voting ended at 3 P.M.,
and 30 minutes later, just as the ballot
boxes were unlocked for the counting,
the gunmen arrived at the Bayanan
elementary school.

They fired rifles into the air in the
courtyard and burst into classroom
after classroom, shouting and pointing
their weapons at voters and poll watchers, seizing ballot boxes to be carried
off or to be spilled and restuffed with
false ballots.

Screaming in fright, the people fell to
the floor and ducked under desks.
"Mother of God!" someone shouted as
the thugs darted past, wearing T-shirts
with the message, "Vote Intelligent-
ly."

The gunmen moved quickly, kicking
the long day's labor of marked ballots
aside like chaff and moving into the
room of Precinct 135 where they found
Pedro San Juan, the poll inspector,
defiantly hugging the voting box to his
chest.

The intruders struck him with a gun
butt. They cut his arm and finally tore
the box loose.

In an adjoining room, Christina

Continued on Page 6, Column 4

"GUIDE TO PROFESSIONAL SERVICES":
The not-banned section for legal services, health care
and nutrition, medical, dental and special advertising
starting Feb. 11 in Science Times. To advertise, call
Jamie Imbesi-lo at (212) 556-7542—ADVT

U.S. JUDGES HOLD NEW BUDGET LAW UNCONSTITUTIONAL

Supreme Court Is to Consider Ruling, Which Is Based on Separation of Powers

By ROBERT PEAR
Special to The New York Times

WASHINGTON, Feb. 7 — A panel of
three Federal judges ruled unanimously today that a key provision of a
new budget-balancing law was unconstitutional because it violated the principle requiring separation of powers
among the branches of Government.

The Court ruled that Congress could
delegate authority over the budget to
the President or people answerable to
him but could not shift it to the Comptroller General of the United States or
other people removable by Congress itself through legislation. The ruling now
goes to the Supreme Court for a final
determination of new law's constitutionality.

Significance in Many Areas

The decision by the Federal District
Court here has broad legal, political
and economic significance. The statute
in question was widely regarded as the
most important step taken by Congress
in many years to reduce the budget
deficit.

The provision the panel struck down
was intended to give teeth to the
budget-balancing law, and some legislative leaders said today that its loss
could undermine any effort to reach a
compromise on shrinking the deficit to
zero by 1991. [Page 9.]

More immediately, if upheld on appeal the decision would invalidate $11.7
billion of budget cuts for the current fiscal year that President Reagan ordered Saturday under the new law.

The judges stayed the effect of their
ruling to permit supporters of the law
to appeal. The law explicitly authorizes
a direct appeal to the Supreme Court.

Continued on Page 9, Column 3

A Victory for Reagan

The ruling striking down provisions of
the budget-balancing law is a significant but bittersweet victory for the
President. News analysis, page 9.

Kremlin Shifts On 'Star Wars,' Diplomats Say

By PHILIP TAUBMAN
Special to The New York Times

MOSCOW, Feb. 7 — The Soviet Union
will not insist that the United States
abandon development of a space-based
missile defense as a condition for an
agreement to reduce medium-range
nuclear weapons, Western diplomats
said today.

They said that after some weeks of
uncertainty about the Soviet position,
American officials were recently told
privately that Moscow would not link
an accord on medium-range nuclear
weapons to President Reagan's program to develop a space-based missile
shield. The program, the Strategic Defense Initiative, is popularly known as
the "Star Wars" plan.

Position Is 'Crystal Clear'

The diplomats said Mikhail S. Gorbachev, the Soviet leader, made a definitive statement about the issue in a
meeting Thursday in the Kremlin with
Senator Edward M. Kennedy, Democrat of Massachusetts.

"The Soviet position is now crystal
clear, and it increases the odds that an
interim agreement on medium-range
weapons can be reached before the
next summit meeting between Reagan
and Gorbachev," one diplomat said.

[A new Joint Chiefs of Staff assessment disputes President Reagan's
assertion that Moscow has violated a
commitment on deployment of missile launchers and intercontinental
bombers. Page 6.]

A Clear Separation

The diplomats said Moscow remained adamant in its insistence that
progress on limiting long-range nuclear weapons is impossible unless
Washington renounces development of
the space defense program.

Mr. Kennedy is to return to Washington on Saturday. American diplomats
said that he did not brief the United
States Embassy about his conversations with Soviet officials but that

Continued on Page 6, Column 5

DUVALIER FLEES HAITI TO END FAMILY'S 28 YEARS IN POWER; GENERAL LEADS NEW REGIME

President Jean-Claude Duvalier of Haiti, right, and his wife, Michèle, arriving at the airport in Port-au-Prince.
Associated Press

Jamaica Said to Play a Key Role In Persuading Duvalier to Leave

By BERNARD GWERTZMAN
Special to The New York Times

WASHINGTON, Feb. 7 — The Jamaican Government secretly played a
central role in persuading President
Jean-Claude Duvalier to flee Haiti,
United States and Jamaican officials
said today.

The officials said Jamaica had convinced Mr. Duvalier, who called himself President for Life, that he had to
leave for the sake of the people of Haiti
and the Caribbean.

Jamaica Tells the U.S.

Mr. Duvalier and his family and associates were flown to France from
Haiti early this morning aboard a
United States Air Force C-141. But the
primary impetus for his decision to
leave was attributed to senior State
Department officials to a member of
the Jamaican Government whom the
Duvalier family knew.

After the Jamaicans held discussions
with the Duvaliers and persuaded them
to leave, Jamaica told the United

States, and American officials added
pressure on Mr. Duvalier to leave, senior State Department officials said.

According to a Jamaican official,
who confirmed the initial account by
American officials, Prime Minister
Edward P. G. Seaga of Jamaica sent a
special representative to Haiti last
Sunday.

The representative was Dr. Neville
Gallimore, Minister of Social Security
in the Jamaican Government. He met
with Mr. Duvalier for three hours last
Sunday in Port-au-Prince and discussed the options "facing the regime,
and encouraged the President to leave
office for the good of his people and the
Caribbean in general," the Jamaican
official said.

2d Meeting Is Held

A second meeting was held for one
hour Monday, with Michèle Duvalier
joining her husband in the talks. In that
session, Dr. Gallimore requested a
decision by Tuesday on whether he
would leave.

On Tuesday, according to American
and Jamaican officials, Mr. Duvalier
told Dr. Gallimore that he would leave
Wednesday. But on Wednesday he had
no place to go to, and he began to
waver, American officials said.

The Governments of Greece, Spain
and Switzerland said Wednesday that
they had turned down requests for asylum from Mr. Duvalier. But a senior
American official said, "Those requests actually came from associates
of Michèle, we think, and not from
Duvalier himself."

The American Ambassador, Clayton
E. McManaway Jr., and his staff in
Haiti began telling all of President
Duvalier's associates that Washington
firmly believed that the only way he
could survive as President would be to

Continued on Page 5, Column 1

Immunity Granted General Dynamics As Navy Lifts Ban

By RICHARD HALLORAN
Special to The New York Times

WASHINGTON, Feb. 7 — The Navy
announced today that it had restored
the General Dynamics Corporation's
eligibility to bid for Government contracts because the company had made
progress in correcting its shortcomings.

In addition, the Navy granted the
leading military equipment contractor
immunity from further suspensions
that might be the consequence of new
indictments arising from three grand
jury investigations or 10 to 15 other investigations of the company that are
under way.

The Navy had banned the company
from receiving such orders Dec. 3, a
day after it and four former or current
executives were indicted on Federal
fraud charges.

Government regulations require that
a company be suspended from receiving all Government contracts if an indictment against it is handed up by a
grand jury.

Everett Pyatt, the Assistant Secretary of the Navy who negotiated the
agreement, told reporters late this afternoon that it would not make sense to
suspend General Dynamics, already
suspended twice in the last year, for
wrongdoing that it was correcting.

"We believe they are in a major
reformation in the way the company
operates," Mr. Pyatt said. Left unsaid

Continued on Page 35, Column 1

20 REPORTED DEAD

Cheers Turn to Violence —Ruler and Wife Fly to France in U.S. Jet

By JOSEPH B. TREASTER
Special to The New York Times

PORT-AU-PRINCE, Haiti, Feb. 7 —
President Jean-Claude Duvalier
boarded a United States Air Force jet
and fled to France before dawn today,
ending the 28-year grip of his family on
this impoverished Caribbean nation.

In a videotaped message broadcast
after he had been in the air several
hours, Mr. Duvalier said he had
stepped down after two months of
tumultuous anti-Government protests
to spare the nation of six million people
a "nightmare of revolt."

Moments later, Lieut. Gen. Henri
Namphy, the commander of the armed
forces, went on the air to announce that
the army had taken over. He said he
had acted with Haiti nearly paralyzed
and the "specter of civil war" rising.

Interim Council to Rule

He said the armed forces would govern the country with an interim six-
member ruling council that includes
two civilians.

Mr. Duvalier's flight came after
months of unrest over economic conditions and political repression in this
country, the poorest in the Western
hemisphere. It also came a week after
the White House issued an erroneous
announcement that Mr. Duvalier had
fled.

General Namphy, 53 years old, gave
assurances that the military did not
"entertain any political ambition," indicating that it expected to perform its
traditional mission of providing a
transition power until elections could
be held.

Cheers and Blaring Horns

Mr. Duvalier's departure, along with
his wife, Michèle, their children, his
mother and about 20 other relatives,
was greeted in the capital with a riot of
cheers and blaring horns. But the celebration soon turned violent.

A supervising doctor at the national
university hospital said 20 people had
been killed by early afternoon, half of
them members of Mr. Duvalier's special police force, known as the Tontons
Macoute. Seventy-five others were reported hurt.

At one point, mobs broke into the
stone mausoleum of François Duvalier, Jean-Claude's father and predecessor as President, next to the presi-

Continued on Page 4, Column 3

INSIDE

Conviction in Spy Case

A retired analyst for the Central Intelligence Agency was convicted by a
Federal jury of spying for the Chinese
for more than 30 years. Page 8.

Jobless Rate Drops to 6.6%

A sharp increase in job growth helped
push the nation's jobless rate in January down to 6.6 percent, the lowest
level in nearly six years. Page 50.

A Taste of Winter

Two storm systems with high winds
brought four to eight inches of snow —
the first real taste of winter — to New
York City and its suburbs. Page 30.

2 California Banks to Merge

Two San Francisco banks will merge
in a $1.06 billion transaction that will
create the nation's 10th largest banking company. Page 33.

*Haitians celebrating the departure of President Jean-Claude Duvalier as
they rode through Port-au-Prince. News of his leaving was heralded by the
ringing of a single church bell early yesterday morning. Page 4.*
Agence France-Presse

After 9 Babies Die in 14 Years, Mother Is Held

By AMY WALLACE
Special to The New York Times

SCHENECTADY, N.Y., Feb. 7 —
Year after year, one after the other, the
babies of Mary Beth Tinning died, nine
of them over the past 14 years. The
causes are listed variously as natural
or undetermined or sudden infant
death syndrome.

There were six autopsies, but never
any signs of abuse. There were whispers and suspicions. But somehow no
one — not the police, the coroner, doctors, social workers or neighbors, not
even Mrs. Tinning's husband — detected something evil in the strange
pattern of deaths.

"There were so many of us in on it, I
guess," said Dr. Robert L. Sullivan,
Schenectady County's Chief Medical
Examiner. "If anyone is negligent, I
suppose I am. I probably should have
said, 'There must be more to it than
this.' But we all think, and don't do."

It was not until Wednesday, when the
police charged Mrs. Tinning, who is 43
years old, with suffocating her
3-month-old daughter, Tami Lynne,
with a pillow last Dec. 20, that investigators said they believed that all nine
of her children, including one who was
being adopted, may have been murdered by their mother since 1972.

Dr. Sullivan, 57, who has been the
part-time medical examiner since 1968,

said there might have been incomplete
examinations of the deaths and lapses
of communication among doctors and
public officials.

The medical examiner, who is responsible for investigating all unexplained deaths, said he did not know
why four of the deaths were not reported to his office.

He also said he regretted that he and
other doctors who serve as his assistants had not been more diligent in noting the pattern of deaths.

Investigators began looking into the
case when an employee of St. Clare's
Hospital called the police after Tami
Lynne was brought to the hospital
dead. They said Mrs. Tinning had
made "statements and admissions" —
which they declined to make public —

Continued on Page 30, Column 5

Classified Ads   17-25   Auto Exchange   49

LOUIS EPSTEIN — HAPPY 25TH AND
forever! EB TSEB LOVE MOM & DAD.—ADVT

WAS THIS COPY OF THE TIMES delivered to you?
Home and office delivery is available in many U.S. cities.
Get details by calling toll-free 1-800-631-2500.—ADVT

318

"All the News
That's Fit to Print"

The New York Times

Late Edition

Weather: Mostly sunny and cold today; cloudy, chance of snow tonight. Continued cold, chance of snow tomorrow. Temperatures: today 28-32, tonight 20-23; yesterday 21-38. Details, page D11.

VOL.CXXXV .. No. 46,697   Copyright 1986 The New York Times   NEW YORK, WEDNESDAY, FEBRUARY 26, 1986   50 cents beyond 78 miles from New York City, except on Long Island   30 CENTS

MARCOS FLEES AND IS TAKEN TO GUAM; U.S. RECOGNIZES AQUINO AS PRESIDENT

ROCKET ENGINEERS TELL OF PRESSURE FOR A LAUNCHING

Testify NASA Forced Them to Reverse Decision-Making Role on Shuttle Safety

By PHILIP M. BOFFEY
Special to The New York Times

WASHINGTON, Feb. 25 — Rocket engineers testified today that pressure from the space agency to launch the space shuttle Challenger forced them to reverse their normal role — that instead of having to prove that the shuttle was ready to go, it was up to them to show that a launching would be unsafe.

The engineers from Morton Thiokol Inc., which manufactured the shuttle's booster rockets, described a series of tense meetings and telephone conferences on Jan. 27, the day before the launching that resulted in an explosion that killed seven astronauts. They said that in those discussions they felt pressure from NASA officials to allow the launching to proceed unless they could prove beyond doubt that disaster would result.

Key hearing testimony, page B6.

Meanwhile today, James M. Beggs resigned as Administrator of the National Aeronautics and Space Administration. He had been on leave while facing fraud charges resulting from his tenure as an executive of the General Dynamics Corporation. [Page B7.]

The Thiokol engineers' testimony came at a hearing of the Presidential commission that is investigating the Challenger accident. "I felt pressure," said one of them, Brian Russell. "I felt we were in the position of having to

Continued on Page B7, Column 1

The New York Times / Marilynn K. Yee
Allan J. McDonald, engineer for Morton Thiokol, as he testified.

High Court Backs Use of Zoning To Regulate Showing of Sex Films

By STUART TAYLOR Jr.
Special to The New York Times

WASHINGTON, Feb. 25 — The Supreme Court held today that local zoning officials have broad powers to restrict the location of movie theaters showing sexually explicit films.

Extending a 1976 decision that allowed Detroit to prevent "skid row" concentrations of adult theaters by dispersing them around the city, the Court ruled that a town may limit such theaters to a small area away from homes, schools, churches and parks.

The Justices announced several other decisions today, including their ruling that states cannot require utility companies to include in their billing envelopes the messages of groups with which they disagree. [Page A20.]

Limit on Protection Reaffirmed

In the sex movie case, the seven-Justice majority rejected arguments by a theater owner that the zoning ordinance in Renton, Wash., might effectively ban adult theaters altogether by restricting them to an industrial area where no "commercially viable" sites were available.

While the First Amendment guarantees sexually explicit entertainment facilities "a reasonable opportunity to open and operate," Associate Justice William H. Rehnquist wrote for himself and five others, it does not require zoning under which they "will be able to obtain sites at bargain prices."

On Monday, in striking down an Indianapolis law that outlawed pornographic materials that "subordinate women" as a form of sex discrimina-

Continued on Page A20, Column 1

THE FIRST OFFICIAL SPECTATOR'S GUIDE TO One Day of America by Brock Yates in The Sunday New York Times on April 2. Advertising details by calling 212-556-1164—ADVT

WAS THIS COPY OF THE TIMES delivered to you? Home and office delivery is available in many U.S. cities. Get details by calling toll free 1-800-631-2500—ADVT

Gorbachev Says U.S. Arms Note Is Not Adequate

Also Tells Party Change In Economy Is Urgent

By SERGE SCHMEMANN
Special to The New York Times

MOSCOW, Feb. 25 — Addressing a landmark meeting of the Soviet Communist Party, Mikhail S. Gorbachev today criticized President Reagan's recent response on arms reduction and said the timing of the next summit meeting could hinge on progress in arms control.

The Soviet leader's comments were included in a speech of five and a half hours on the state of the Soviet Union in

Excerpts from speech, page A11.

the opening session of the 27th congress of the ruling party.

Addressing 5,000 delegates and 152 foreign delegations, Mr. Gorbachev presented a sweeping overview of the problems facing the nation, most of which he blamed on stagnation under the 18-year rule of Leonid I. Brezhnev ending in 1982. Mr. Gorbachev said the key to the future was a qualitatively new approach to Soviet economic development.

Focus on Medium-Range Missiles

Two days ago, Mr. Reagan responded in a letter to a proposal made Jan. 15 by Mr. Gorbachev to eliminate nuclear arms by the year 2000 in a sequence of three stages. Mr. Reagan focused on the first of these stages, involving the elimination of medium-range nuclear missiles.

Mr. Gorbachev said in his speech that he presumed the timing of the response was intended to solicit his reaction at the congress.

He said that Mr. Reagan's proposal "seems to contain some reassuring opinions and theses," but that these "are swamped in various reservations, 'linkages' and 'conditions' ".

"To put it in a nutshell," Mr. Gorbachev said, "it is hard to detect in the letter we have just received any serious readiness of the United States Administration to get down to solving the cardinal problems involved in eliminating the nuclear threat."

'No Sense in Empty Talks'

On the question of a summit meeting, Mr. Gorbachev essentially made any further planning contingent on progress in arms control.

"There is no sense in holding empty talks," he said.

Mr. Gorbachev and Mr. Reagan had agreed last November in Geneva that the Soviet leader would visit the United States this year, but officials in Washington have been saying that Moscow has evaded setting a date.

Mr. Gorbachev made clear that this

Continued on Page A10, Column 3

Associated Press
A looter slashing a painting of Ferdinand E. Marcos at presidential palace, which was stormed last night.

Shultz Praises 'Peaceful Transition' in Philippines

By GERALD M. BOYD
Special to The New York Times

WASHINGTON, Wednesday, Feb. 26 — The Reagan Administration moved quickly Tuesday to recognize the new Government of Corazon C. Aquino.

At the same time, the Administration praised what it called the peaceful manner in which Ferdinand E. Marcos had relinquished his 20-year rule as President of the Philippines.

The Administration had issued a statement Monday urging Mr. Marcos to resign. Tuesday, Secretary of State George P. Shultz welcomed the new Government only hours after Mr. Marcos, his family and other associates fled the presidential palace in Manila aboard United States helicopters.

Administration's Involvement

Mr. Marcos's abrupt departure capped days of close involvement by the Administration in the Philippines situation. That involvement was deepened when Senator Paul Laxalt, after conferring with President Reagan, told Mr. Marcos "the time has come" for him to surrender power. Senator Laxalt, a Republican of Nevada and a close friend of Mr. Reagan, had served as his special emissary to Manila last October.

"With the peaceful transition to a new Government of the Philippines, the United States extends recognition to this new Government headed by President Aquino," Mr. Shultz said in a statement pledging United States cooperation.

U.S. Encourages Reconciliation

Larry Speakes, the White House spokesman, said the Administration welcomed Mrs. Aquino's call for "reconciliation and nonviolence" and looked forward to working with the new Government on changes in political, military and economic areas. He said Philip C. Habib, the special Reagan envoy, was en route to Manila to discuss how the United States could help.

A senior Administration official said Mr. Reagan would telephone both Mrs. Aquino and Mr. Marcos, possibly as early as today. He said Mr. Reagan wanted to wait before contacting the new President because things were "unsettled" in the Philippines.

Mr. Shultz said the shift in power should have no effect on relations be-

Continued on Page A14, Column 1

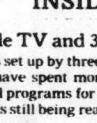

Reuters
Supporters of Corazon C. Aquino and Salvador H. Laurel rejoicing at palace.

From a Symbol to a Leader: The Rise of Corazon Aquino

Special to The New York Times

MANILA, Wednesday, Feb. 26 — Corazon C. Aquino began to exercise presidential power even before Ferdinand E. Marcos left the country today, telling some of the country's most powerful men what they would be doing in her Cabinet, and making a key decision about the nation's top financial institution.

She did so in the same quiet-spoken manner in which, as a self-described housewife, she had hovered in the background during the political career of her husband, Benigno S. Aquino Jr.

Her manner today, however, obscured a personal transformation that has been noted both by political analysts and by members of her own family, who say they have watched her grow in strength and confidence.

In the four months since she decided to run for office, Mrs. Aquino, a genuinely reluctant candidate, has moved from being a symbol around which the nation could unite to being a leader.

"It's astonishing," says a member of her husband's family. "She was just a housewife. Her strength has astonished all of us. The transformation is amazing. It has even affected her children, who have grown as well."

Mrs. Aquino's cool and even tone, her advisers say, overshadows the stubbornness and growing self-assurance that have put her in increasing command of their inner councils. The self-assurance, they say, has been reinforced by the broad popular support that has continued to grow for the woman who has styled herself "almost the complete opposite" of Mr. Marcos.

One Aquino adviser, Teodoro Locsin, said, "By the end of the election, she realized that now she was speaking for the entire nation."

Mrs. Aquino had also come to demonstrate a greater familiarity with the issues than she had in an interview published

Continued on Page A13, Column 1

20-YEAR ERA ENDS

'New Life' for Philippines Seen by Successor — Nation Celebrates

By SETH MYDANS
Special to The New York Times

MANILA, Wednesday, Feb. 26 — Ferdinand E. Marcos fled the Philippines Tuesday, ending 20 years as President. Corazon C. Aquino succeeded him, saying "a new life" had begun for her country.

Mr. Marcos, facing pressure from all sides to step down, left the presidential palace shortly after 9 P.M. (8 A.M. Eastern standard time) and traveled by helicopter to Clark Air Base.

There, accompanied by his wife, Imelda, and Gen. Fabian C. Ver, a close associate and former chief of the Philippines military forces, he boarded an American Air Force plane for Guam, a United States territory in the Pacific.

[A Defense Deapartment statement said 55 people were with Mr. Marcos's party aboard two aircraft, The Associated Press reported from Agana, Guam.]

Greeted by Acting Governor

Mr. Marcos arrived at Andersen Air Force Base in Guam this morning, where he was greeted by Acting Gov. Edward D. Reyes.

In Washington, officials said the 68-year-old leader, who reportedly suffers from a kidney ailment, would receive treatment at the Naval Medical Center on Guam. One official described his hospitalization as precautionary.

According to a Defense Department spokesman in Washington, Mr. Marcos was to leave Guam this evening (between 5 A.M. and 8 A.M. E.S.T.) for an unspecified air base near Honolulu.

The departure of Mr. Marcos from Manila ended a day in which he pleaded with Washington for help in clinging to office, then went through an inaugural ceremony that was held apparently after he had decided to leave.

Aquino Too Is Inaugurated

Mrs. Aquino was also inaugurated in the morning to head what was dubbed a provisional government, and although Mr. Marcos made no public resignation when he departed, the United States immediately recognized her administration.

The news of Mr. Marcos's departure set off celebrations in the capital as hundreds of thousands of Filipinos surged into the streets, honking horns, setting off firecrackers and burning tires.

As crowds converged on the presidential palace, fighting broke out between supporters and opponents of Mr. Marcos. Stones and knives were used in the clashes, and a number of injuries were reported. Eventually, a noisy crowd surged into the palace, tearing down portraits of Mr. Marcos and his wife and helping themselves to souvenirs.

Earlier, three civilians were reported killed in Manila during a pitched battle between loyalist and rebel troops for control of a television transmitting tower.

In Washington, the Reagan Administration hailed Mrs. Aquino for "her commitment to nonviolence" while praising Mr. Marcos for a decision "characterized by the dignity and strength that have marked his many years of leadership."

Request to Stay Rejected

The official said that even after Mr. Marcos arrived at Clark Air Base, he asked if he could remain in his home province in northern Luzon, but that the Aquino side refused.

Legal questions remained to be resolved about Mrs. Aquino's mandate following the Feb. 7 election in which Mr. Marcos was proclaimed the winner

Continued on Page A12, Column 3

For Marcos, a Restless Night of Calls to U.S.

By BERNARD GWERTZMAN
Special to The New York Times

WASHINGTON, Feb. 25 — It was about 3 A.M. today in Manila and President Ferdinand E. Marcos was telephoning to find out whether the message he had received from Washington calling for "a peaceful transition" to a new government actually meant he should quit.

Senator Paul Laxalt, who received the call in Washington — when it was then 2 P.M. Monday — said later that Mr. Marcos was "a desperate man, clutching at straws," even though he would be formally sworn in for another term as President in about nine hours.

Mr. Marcos told the Nevada Republican, whom he seemed to trust as a confidant of President Reagan, that he did not want to resign. Nor did he want to come to the United States, where he might be harassed by Congressional committees.

The telephone call touched off the events that led to Mr. Marcos's reluctant decision to give up his fight to remain as President only hours after his inaugural ceremony. But, according to senior Administration officials, Mr. Marcos has resisted accepting Mr. Reagan's offer of a safe haven in the United States.

Even after being taken to Clark Air Base by a United States Air Force helicopter, Mr. Marcos asked the United States Embassy to intercede with those close to Corazon C. Aquino and ask if he could be allowed to live in his home province of Ilocos Norte in northern Luzon.

According to a senior American official, the Aquino side refused on the grounds that passions were running too

Continued on Page A14, Column 4

INSIDE

Cable TV and 3 Boroughs
Groups set up by three borough presidents have spent more than $700,000 on local programs for cable television systems still being readied. Page B1.

Consumer Prices Up 0.3%
The Consumer Price Index increased last month by the smallest amount since September. Food and energy costs were restrained. Page D1.

The New York Times / Larry C. Morris
NETS' STAR BANNED: Micheal Ray Richardson, who was barred from playing in the N.B.A. after a positive cocaine test. Page B11.

CONCORDE/1ST CLASS DEEP DISCOUNT. NET FARE CORP (212) 844-1000—ADVT

MOOMBAY HITS METROPOLITAN AREA. HEAD FOR EINSTEIN MOOMBY—ADVT

"All the News That's Fit to Print"

The New York Times

Late Edition

Weather: Partly cloudy and cool today, southwesterly winds; fair tonight. Mostly sunny and milder tomorrow. Temperatures: today 53-57, tonight 40-43; yesterday 41-52. Details, page C18.

VOL.CXXXV. No. 46,724   Copyright © 1986 The New York Times   NEW YORK, TUESDAY, MARCH 25, 1986   30 cents beyond 78 miles from New York City, except on Long Island.   30 CENTS

U.S., CITING LIBYAN FIRE, REPORTS ATTACKING A MISSILE SITE AND SETTING 2 SHIPS ABLAZE

Aquino May Disband Legislature While a New Charter Is Drafted

By FRANCIS X. CLINES
Special to The New York Times

MANILA, March 24 — President Corazon C. Aquino is expected to abolish the National Assembly and begin exercising "nearly absolute power," the national television station reported tonight.

The plan was described as a temporary step to having voters approve a new constitution and legislature.

After considerable internal dispute, Mrs. Aquino's plan is likely to provide for the drafting of a proposed constitution by committee rather than by an elected convention and for national elections this fall, according to Government officials familiar with the plan.

The President's spokesman, Rene Saguisag, cautioned tonight against speculation about Mrs. Aquino's decision, which is scheduled to be announced Tuesday. The President, who has kept her own Cabinet guessing and, in fact, furiously debating the shape of a reformed government, could alter existing plans at the last minute, he said.

November Elections Possible

While Mr. Saguisag was cautionary, Vice President Salvador Laurel has indicated that elections may be proposed for November to renew both local executive offices and national legislative offices under a plan submitted to Mrs. Aquino by a committee of advisers.

Mr. Laurel indicated that her current thinking is to abolish the parliamentary-style National Assembly, formally known as the Batasang Pambansa, and seek a constitution providing for a system with an elected bicameral legislature.

Such a step presumably would obviate the question of whether the National Assembly should rescind its certification of Ferdinand E. Marcos as President and proclaim her instead. The assembly acted following the disputed Feb. 7 election amid a national outcry that Mr. Marcos's majority in the assembly was stealing the election from Mrs. Aquino.

Interim Council Proposed

Some advisers have recommended keeping the assembly at least temporarily as a token indication of her wish to share power and not be absolutist in this provisional stage. Others have said the National Assembly remains too much a symbol of the Marcos era since its majority had routinely backed his authoritarian rule.

One recommendation she was reported considering was to try and ease this "absolutist" charge by designating some of her Cabinet members and other appointees as a "legislative council" designed to provide an additional governmental presence. This would, however, be merely advisory.

One point of considerable debate has been whether to define Mrs. Aquino's interim rule as "revolutionary," as

Continued on Page A3, Column 1

World Bank Plans $1.5 Billion In New Aid to Latin Debtors

By CLYDE H. FARNSWORTH
Special to The New York Times

WASHINGTON, March 24 — The World Bank, beginning Tuesday, is expected to approve $1.5 billion in loans to Latin America as part of its effort to help resolve the debt crisis.

The loans, all expected to be approved before the end of April, represent the bank's largest commitment ever to Latin America in such a brief period. The aid includes $1 billion for Mexico, which has been crippled by the collapse of world oil prices.

The loan agenda, described by World Bank officials, is a sign that the bank is responding to a call for increased lending by Treasury Secretary James A. Baker 3d. "These loans are a product of what Baker advocated in Seoul," said a bank spokesman, Peter Riddleberger, referring to a speech Mr. Baker made in South Korea last October at the annual meeting of the World Bank and its sister institution, the International Monetary Fund.

The bank's board of directors, representing its 149 member governments, is scheduled Tuesday to approve $465 million in loans to Mexico, including $400 million for reconstruction needed as a result of an earthquake last Sept. 19 that severely damaged Mexico City.

Other large loans in the final stages of negotiation include $500 million to Mexico to assist in trade liberalization and $350 million to Argentina to speed agricultural reforms. Colombia and Ecuador are among the other countries expected to receive World Bank aid.

Focus Is on Economies

The external debt of Latin American countries is about $380 billion, two-thirds of which is owed to commercial banks, so the World Bank loans are just a small step in solving the crisis. They are not intended to repay other loans, but to make the economies of the borrowing nations grow faster.

The loan negotiations, which have been going on for more than a year in some cases, have been influenced by Secretary Baker's agenda and the nations' increasing willingness to do their part under the Baker proposal to deregulate and free up their economies.

Mr. Riddleberger said the loan agreements can proceed at this time because "this happens to be when the countries' internal policies now

Continued on Page D6, Column 5

Rocket Bombs Fired At the U.S. Embassy And Palace in Tokyo

By SUSAN CHIRA
Special to The New York Times

TOKYO, Tuesday, March 25 — Small homemade bombs were fired this afternoon at the United States Embassy and the Imperial Palace, the police said.

There were no injuries, and no damage was reported.

The bombs appeared to have been launched from parked cars outside the United States Embassy and the western gate of the Imperial Palace, known as the Hanzomon Gate, according to the Tokyo Metropolitan Police.

The bombs appeared to have been constructed from small aluminum cans that were filled with gasoline. The police found what appeared to be timing and launching devices inside the trunks of the cars.

The attacks occurred despite police measures to tighten security in preparation for the summit of industrialized nations to be held in Tokyo in May. The television news station NHK reported that Prime Minister Yasuhiro Nakasone called today for tighter security measures.

Police and United States Embassy officials said they did not know who had launched the bombs. But the police speculated that the attackers were left-

Continued on Page A3, Column 1

An A-7 warplane taking off from the U.S. carrier Saratoga yesterday in the Gulf of Sidra.

Reuters

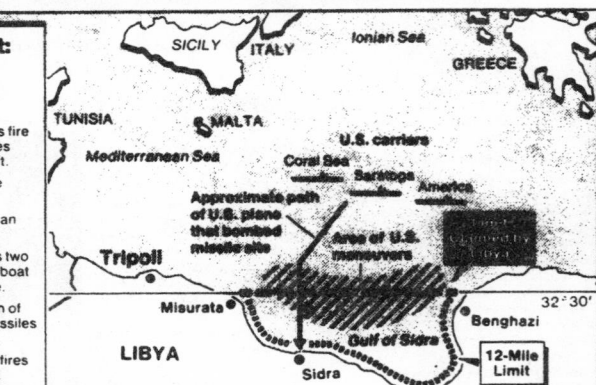

A Day of Combat: Washington's Account

All times are E.S.T.

7:52 A.M. Libyan forces fire two surface-to-air missiles from Sidra at U.S. aircraft.

12:45 P.M. Libyans fire three more missiles.

1:14 P.M. Another Libyan missile is fired.

2 P.M. U.S. aircraft fires two missiles at Libyan patrol boat near the 32-30 north line.

3 P.M. U.S. forces south of 32-30 line launch two missiles at Sidra.

4:20 P.M. U.S. aircraft fires at second Libyan vessel.

The New York Times/March 25, 1986

Haiti's Exiles, Returning Steadily, Carry Home Formulas for Change

By MARLISE SIMONS
Special to The New York Times

PORT-AU-PRINCE, Haiti, March 24 — Jean Dominique is in from New York and walked into what used to be Haiti's most outspoken radio station, now a place covered with dust, unraveled tapes and smashed cabinets. The transmitters were carted off five years ago by the political police.

Today, as Haiti is testing life without the Duvalier family, Mr. Dominique is back from exile, ready to start over, joining many Haitians eager to come home.

In recent days, the cautious trickle of exiles returning has become a steady flow, with men and women arriving from Africa, Europe, the United States. They are here, celebrating, asking questions, offering recipes for change. Undaunted by the shake-up in the ruling council last week, some have already declared themselves political candidates.

Old-timers, away for 20 years, do not recognize the capital, which has tripled in size to about a million people and, by most indicators, also in misery and in the number of millionaires. Returnees say they see more villas on the cool hillsides, but also a town center and slums that look sadder and filthier, and more people hawking minutiae such as five cigarettes or a handful of lemons.

There are no exact accounts of the hundreds of thousands who left in the past few decades, people who were expelled, threatened or just felt trapped by a corrupt and harsh system.

Writers, Politicians, Guerrillas

It was poverty that forced many people to flee on rickety boats to Florida. But Haiti also lost much of its skilled and professional class, the teachers, doctors and economists who were caught in the perennial purges and power shifts dictated by the palace, or the people who looked for some intellectual and creative space elsewhere. Their role, in many cases, has been taken over by foreigners, whose freedom and salaries come from churches and development agencies abroad.

Today, nearly 1.5 million Haitians live outside Haiti, at least half of them

Continued on Page A14, Column 4

LAWMAKERS BACK ACTIONS ON LIBYA

But Head of Committee Says Reagan Exceeded Powers

By ROBERT PEAR
Special to The New York Times

WASHINGTON, March 24 — Members of Congress today generally expressed support for the action taken by American warplanes against Libyan land and sea targets, but the chairman of the House Foreign Affairs Committee charged that President Reagan had not fully complied with the War Powers Resolution of 1973.

The chairman, Representative Dante B. Fascell, said the deployment of American naval forces off the coast of Libya "constituted from the outset a situation where imminent involvement in hostilities was a distinct possibility clearly indicated by the circumstances even prior to today's development."

'The Right Course,' O'Neill Says

While some lawmakers said they needed more information to say for sure whether military action was justified, leading Democrats and Republicans in the House said they agreed with Mr. Reagan's actions against Libya and its leader, Col. Muammar el-Qaddafi.

"The Administration's handling of this matter is on the right course. Its actions in protecting America's armed forces in international waters are justified," said Thomas P. O'Neill, Jr., the Speaker of the House. "Based upon the briefing given me at the White House," Mr. O'Neill continued, "the American

Continued on Page A11, Column 1

IN DISPUTED AREA

Libya Says It Downed 3 Jets, but Washington Reports No Losses

By BERNARD WEINRAUB
Special to The New York Times

WASHINGTON, March 24 — American and Libyan forces clashed today in and around the disputed waters off the Libyan coast.

The Reagan Administration announced that the encounter began in the Gulf of Sidra when Libyan ground batteries fired six missiles at American planes. It said United States Navy aircraft had retaliated by attacking

News session excerpts, page A10.

two Libyan patrol boats and a missile site on Libyan soil.

It said one Libyan vessel was set afire and was "dead in the water" and the other was "severely damaged."

Missile Site 'Out of Action'

The damage to the missile site, according to Defense Secretary Caspar W. Weinberger, was still being assessed, but he said the installation was "out of action." Mr. Weinberger said that Navy warplanes had used long-range air-to-surface missiles to strike the Libyan missile site and the two Libyan vessels. [Page A10.]

Earlier, the Libyan state television and the official Libyan press agency reported that three American jets had been shot down.

The White House spokesman, Larry Speakes, said, "We have no reports of any U.S. casualties, and no loss of U.S. aircraft or ships has been reported."

A 30-Ship Task Force

The incident occurred as a 30-ship Navy task force, led by three aircraft carriers, was conducting maneuvers in the Mediterranean off Libya. The maneuvers began over the weekend.

Asked directly today why the United States had chosen this particular time to enter waters claimed by Libya, White House officials would say only that the United States wished to assert its right to navigate in international waters.

"The President approved the rules of engagement on March 14 as part of a pattern of asserting U.S. rights to navigate in international waters," said one senior official. The official said the United States had gone into the Gulf of Sidra eight times since 1981.

"We just couldn't allow Qaddafi to assert a right of sovereignty over international waters," the official said, referring to the Libyan leader, Col. Muammar el-Qaddafi.

Libya claims the entire Gulf of Sidra as its territorial waters, extending as far as 100 miles from the gulf's southern shore. But the United States and

Continued on Page A16, Column 5

Hondurans Meeting Amid U.S. Reports Of Nicaraguan Raid

By STEPHEN KINZER
Special to The New York Times

MANAGUA, Nicaragua, March 24 — President José Azcona Hoyo of Honduras tonight called an urgent meeting of his National Security Council to discuss reports of a Nicaraguan military incursion into Honduran territory.

A Government spokesman, Lisandro Quesada, said the Government could not verify the reports, which had been circulated earlier in the day by Reagan Administration officials in Washington.

"At this time, we know nothing about these reports," Mr. Quesada told reporters in Tegucigalpa. "The situation is being investigated by the armed forces."

The Honduran Foreign Minister, Carlos López Contreras, said before the National Security Council meeting that he could give no details of the alleged incursion. "We know nothing official at this time," he said.

In Managua, Western diplomats said they knew nothing of the supposed raid.

Administration officials in Washington told reporters today that 1,500 Nicaraguan troops had crossed into Honduras in what was described as their boldest cross-border strike ever. The officials said the troops had penetrated 10 miles or more into Honduras.

The Senate is scheduled to vote this

Continued on Page A18 Column 1

INSIDE

Davis Bid for CBS Reported
Marvin Davis, the Denver millionaire, has apparently made an offer to buy CBS Inc., Wall Street sources disclosed last night. Page D1.

Genetic Test Draws Fine
A company accused of falsifying data has lost its permit to test a genetically engineered farm chemical and has been fined $20,000. Page A20.

Associated Press

OSCAR WINNERS: William Hurt, left, after being named best actor for "Kiss of the Spider Woman." With him were Anjelica Huston, best supporting actress for

"Prizzi's Honor;" Geraldine Page, best actress for "Trip to Bountiful," and Sydney Pollack, best director for "Out of Africa," also named best picture. Page C15.

"All the News That's Fit to Print"

The New York Times

Late Edition
Weather: Partly cloudy and cool today, chance of showers; rain likely tonight. Cloudy, with continued rain tomorrow. Temperatures: today 54-58, tonight 43-47; yesterday 41-67. Details, page C14.

VOL.CXXXV. No. 46,745   Copyright © 1986 The New York Times   NEW YORK, TUESDAY, APRIL 15, 1986   50 cents beyond 75 miles from New York City, except on Long Island.   **30 CENTS**

U.S. JETS HIT 'TERRORIST CENTERS' IN LIBYA; REAGAN WARNS OF NEW ATTACKS IF NEEDED; ONE PLANE MISSING IN RAIDS ON 5 TARGETS

FORECAST ON TRADE GAP: Prime Minister Yasuhiro Nakasone in Washington. He predicted a decline in Japanese trade surplus with U.S. by fall. Page D1.

The New York Times/Paul Hosefros

Crucial Portion Of Shuttle Joint Found in Ocean

By DAVID E. SANGER

Salvage crews off the Florida coast have recovered a burned-out section of the booster rocket joint whose rupture is thought to have led to the destruction of the space shuttle Challenger, the Navy said yesterday.

The discovery provides the first tangible evidence that a failure of the joint, whose questionable design had worried rocket engineers for nearly a year before the Jan. 28 explosion, caused the disaster, which took the lives of seven astronauts.

Key 4,000-Pound Segment

After discovery of the crew cabin, which was hauled ashore last month, the search for the booster joint was the top priority for the flotilla of surface ships and submarines still combing the ocean floor off Cape Canaveral.

The wreckage, a 4,000-pound section of the aft-center segment of the rocket, was recovered early Sunday morning by the salvage vessel Stena Workhorse and an unmanned submersible working in 560 feet of water. Along one edge, where a tang fits into a groove on an adjacent rocket segment, a 2-foot-wide hole is evident, burned through the hardened steel of the rocket casing.

"It looks like someone took a giant

Continued on Page C3, Column 3

PARIS BARRED JETS

Weinberger Says Rebuff Added 1,200 Miles to Flight From Britain

By NEIL A. LEWIS
Special to The New York Times

WASHINGTON, April 14 — President Reagan said today that the Western European allies had assisted the United States in its military attack against Libya, but according to other high officials the action was hampered by a lack of cooperation, notably from France.

According to Secretary of State George P. Shultz and Defense Secretary Caspar W. Weinberger, the degree of cooperation ranged from Britain's allowing American air bases there to be used to France's refusal to let the American planes fly through its airspace.

"With respect to our allies, we have a variety of opinions," Mr. Shultz said in the White House briefing room. Mr. Weinberger said Prime Minister Margaret Thatcher of Britain had allowed the use of her air bases.

Route Was 1,200 Miles Longer

But Mr. Weinberger said the pilots had to use a more dangerous route to avoid flying over countries that had barred the use of their airspace. He suggested that several countries had not cooperated, but in response to a question, he singled out France.

Mr. Weinberger, in showing the flight path on a map, said that the circuitous route was 2,800 nautical miles, 1,200 miles more than a direct route.

"Obviously, if we had permission to fly a direct route, we would not have subjected the pilots to such a long flight," he said.

'That Is a Fair Description'

In response to a question whether the United States sought and was refused permission to fly over France, he responded, "I think that is a fair description."

When asked whether countries other than France had refused permission to fly over their territory, Mr. Weinberger said, "No, that would have been the direct route," an allusion to French airspace.

Mr. Weinberger said that in addition to having to fly a longer route, pilots had to take evasive actions to avoid detection.

Mr. Reagan, in his speech, praised

Continued on Page A11, Column 1

United States conducted air strikes against five Libyan targets near Tripoli and Benghazi. The American jets were said to have taken off from a British base and from ships in the Mediterranean.

The New York Times April 15, 1986

In the Skies Over Libya's Capital, Planes Roar and Bombs Resound

By EDWARD SCHUMACHER
Special to The New York Times

TRIPOLI, Libya, Tuesday, April 15 — For nearly 10 minutes, the night sky was ablaze with explosions from missiles and tracers as the American planes soared out of the distance.

Hours later, doctors said 60 to 100 wounded civilians had come to a hospital. It was not known how many more might have been killed, and the doctors did not offer an estimate.

Bombs fell on an upper-middle-class neighborhood that included the French Embassy. When reporters toured the area after daybreak, it was littered with broken glass, collapsed walls and destroyed cars.

The reporters saw one body.

The target appeared to be a communications building with a large antenna on top and several antennas behind it. The building's function was not clear, and officials would not say.

The bombs fell short of the building, and although its windows were blown out, the antennas stood intact on the roof.

The attacks began shortly before 2 A.M. (7 P.M. Monday, New York

time), when the rumble of bombs could first be heard. For nearly 10 minutes afterward, the sky turned into a fireworks display of missiles and bombs. Missiles could be seen rising into the air, but no American planes appeared to be hit.

Volleys of Antiaircraft Fire

The air strikes were met by volleys of antiaircraft fire. Smoke could be seen rising in the capital.

The reaction here was slow. The city's lights were not blacked out until 20 minutes after the attack began.

Even during the bombing, there was a strange calm on the city streets. Cars moved beneath the street lights around the harbor.

The state-run Libyan radio asserted that bombs had fallen on the barracks where Col. Muammar el-Qaddafi, the Libyan leader, maintains his headquarters, and that some members of his family were wounded in the raids. The reports could not be confirmed.

Officials said a downed American

Continued on Page A12, Column 1

Plots on Global Scale Charged

By BERNARD GWERTZMAN
Special to The New York Times

WASHINGTON, April 14 — Secretary of State George P. Shultz said tonight that Libyan agents had been deployed around the world for attacks against United States embassies in as many as 30 countries.

At a news conference after the announcement of the American bombing attacks on Libya, Mr. Shultz said the raids had been necessary to deter Libya from future terrorist attacks and to retaliate for the bombing on April 5 of a West Berlin discotheque frequented by American soldiers.

He said that "we have reports and indications, quite substantial evidence, of Libyan efforts to attack — varying degrees of certainty on the evidence — up to 30 of our embassies."

Mr. Shultz said all United States embassies had been placed on special alert. Secretary of Defense Caspar W. Weinberger said United States military installations around the world were also on alert.

Administration officials said a plan

by the Joint Chiefs of Staff for surgical bombing strikes against Libya was approved by President Reagan eight days ago. [Page A11.]

Larry Speakes, the White House spokesman, said tonight that Libyans were known to have been conducting surveillance and planning attacks against American diplomatic and commercial installations in Africa, Europe, the Middle East and Latin America.

He said that 10 attacks were planned in Africa alone and that in one African country, which he did not name, three Libyan agents arrived last week with the objective of bombing the United States Embassy and chancery and kidnapping the American Ambassador.

'The Primary Objective'

Discussing the American action tonight, Mr. Shultz said, "It's not a question of settling scores; it's a question of acting against terrorism, of saying to terrorists that the acts they perpetrate will cost them.

"If you raise the costs, you do something that should eventually act as a deterrent," he said. "And that is the primary objective, to defend ourselves both in the immediate sense and prospectively."

In his broadcast address tonight, Mr. Reagan said that "our evidence is direct, it is precise, it is irrefutable" that

Continued on Page A11, Column 4

PENTAGON DETAILS 2-PRONGED ATTACK

British-Based Jets Hit Tripoli, Navy Planes to Benghazi

By MICHAEL R. GORDON
Special to The New York Times

WASHINGTON, April 14 — Officials said tonight that the United States attack on five Libyan targets was a complex operation that involved separate attacks by Air Force and Navy planes and the use of aircraft for refueling, intelligence and electronic jamming.

The operation involved two strikes on separate regions of Libya, the officials said.

In one attack, Pentagon officials said, 18 United States Air Force F-111 bombers left England and attacked three targets near Tripoli. The targets were the military side of the Tripoli airport; a port section called Sidi Bilal, where Libyan commandos are trained, and the military barracks called el-Azziziya.

Planes From Carriers

In a separate attack, 15 A-6 and A-7 aircraft from the Coral Sea and the America, the two United States Navy aircraft carriers in the central Mediterranean, attacked two Libyan bases near Benghazi, Defense Secretary Caspar W. Weinberger said. They included an air base called Benina and a barracks called Jamahiriya.

Mr. Weinberger said that all the F-111's were accounted for except for

Continued on Page A11, Column 1

STRIKES IN 2 AREAS

White House Lays 'Direct Responsibility' in Blast in Berlin to Qaddafi

By BERNARD WEINRAUB
Special to The New York Times

WASHINGTON, Tuesday, April 15 — The United States conducted a series of air strikes on Monday night against what the White House called "terrorist centers" and military bases in Libya.

President Reagan, in a nationally broadcast speech, said the American forces had "succeeded" in their mis-

Statements, pages A10 and A13.

sion of retaliating against Libya for what he termed the "reign of terror" waged by Col. Muammar el-Qaddafi, the Libyan leader, against the United States.

Defense Secretary Caspar W. Weinberger said later that one United States plane, an F-111 with a crew of two, "is not accounted for at this time." But he declined to say if the plane had been shot down.

Libya Says 3 Jets Downed

The Libyan radio, monitored in London, said that three United States aircraft had been shot down and that Libyans had killed their pilots and crew.

Mr. Reagan said: "Today we have done what we had to do. If necessary we shall do it again."

Congressional leaders generally expressed support for the attack on Libya, but a leading Democrat warned that the raid could lead to more violence. [Page A10.]

The French Foreign Ministry said the French Embassy in Tripoli was hit in the bombing raid, but a spokesman said no one was injured.

Foreign reporters in Tripoli, after a Government-conducted tour of a residential district today, said that the rear of the French Embassy was heavily damaged, with windows blown out, and that five or six houses in the district were also damaged. A Libyan Government spokesman said an unknown number of civilians had been killed.

5 Targets Near Cities

In his address on Monday night, Mr. Reagan said the American attack was a retaliation for what he asserted was the "direct" Libyan role in the bombing on April 5 of a West Berlin discotheque frequented by American servicemen. One American soldier and a Turkish woman died, and more than 200 people were wounded, including 50 other servicemen.

"We believe that this pre-emptive action against his terrorist installations will not only diminish Colonel Qaddafi's capacity to export terror, it will provide him with incentives and reasons to alter his criminal behavior," said a grim-faced Mr. Reagan.

An Administration official said five military targets near Libya's two major cities, Tripoli and Benghazi, were attacked.

Mr. Weinberger said American planes were forced to fly a long route to

Continued on Page A10, Column 3

The Recovered Piece Of the Booster Rocket

Burned-out section of the right booster rocket came from the aft-center segment. A two-foot-wide hole was found at the joint, whose failure is suspected of causing the Challenger disaster. The hole was at 300° (shown below) on the rocket near its aft attachment point to the external fuel tank.

Orbiter
149 feet
Section recovered
300°
0°
270°   90°
180°
Left booster rocket   External fuel tank   Right booster rocket

The New York Times/April 15, 1986

The New York Times/Paul Hosefros

President Reagan speaking to journalists last night after broadcast.

INSIDE

Soviet Missile Said to Fail
United States experts said the Soviet Union had tested its largest new land-based missile, but that the test had apparently failed. Page A8.

Mets Lose Home Opener
An error by the Met third baseman, Howard Johnson, triggered a four-run burst that enabled the Cardinals to win, 6-2, in 13 innings. Page A25.

Simone de Beauvoir Dies
Simone de Beauvoir, the author and intellectual whose work helped inspire the women's movement, died in Paris at the age of 78. Page B9.

Horowitz Returns to Russia
Vladimir Horowitz, who left the Soviet Union 61 years ago, vowing never to return, arrived in Moscow to perform two piano recitals. Page C13.

"All the News That's Fit to Print"

The New York Times

Late Edition

Weather: Mostly sunny, warm today; increasing cloudiness tonight. Mostly cloudy, chance of showers tomorrow. Temperatures: today 78-82, tonight 50-59; yesterday 52-71. Details, page A18.

VOL.CXXXV...No. 46,760   Copyright © 1986 The New York Times   NEW YORK, WEDNESDAY, APRIL 30, 1986   50 cents beyond 75 miles from New York City, except on Long Island.   30 CENTS

SOVIET, REPORTING ATOM PLANT 'DISASTER,' SEEKS HELP ABROAD TO FIGHT REACTOR FIRE

VIRTUAL CERTAINTY OF FAILURE SHOWN FOR SHUTTLE SEAL

New Tests Indicate That Cold and Design Flaws Doomed Challenger From Start

By DAVID E. SANGER
Special to The New York Times

WASHINGTON, April 29 — New and unpublished test results show that a failure of a safety seal on the space shuttle Challenger was virtually inevitable because of a combination of cold weather on the morning of the launching and serious design flaws.

The test results, conducted for the Presidential panel studying the accident and summarized for The New York Times, also determined that the joint would sometimes begin to fail at temperatures as high as 50 degrees Fahrenheit.

In the past, officials of the National Aeronautics and Space Administration have testified that they felt confident the shuttle could be launched at far lower temperatures without undue risk to the crew.

Failure Was Probable

The Challenger was launched Jan. 28 in 36-degree weather, but investigators estimate that the temperature of the joint that contained the failed seal was about 28 degrees, a temperature at which failure is more likely than not, the tests show.

The analysis of the accident, in which the seven crew members died, is expected to serve as the centerpiece of the Presidential commission's report, due in early June. On Monday panel members received a summary of the results, based on tests conducted in recent weeks primarily by NASA engineers and outside aerospace experts working for the commission's working group analyzing data and design.

'I Wouldn't Fly That Rocket'

"The bottom line is that temperature is the key variable, but temperature alone didn't cause it," Maj. Gen. Donald J. Kutyna, who led the working group, said in response to questions about the results. General Kutyna, a former fighter pilot, warned against a "quick fix" of the joint, saying that under the current design "even on a warm day I wouldn't fly that rocket."

The findings, when taken with testimony before the commission, strongly suggest that the middle-level NASA officials from the Marshall Space Flight Center who decided to go ahead with the launching, despite warnings about the low temperature from engineers working for the manufacturer of the booster rocket, acted with virtually no knowledge of the true performance limitations of the crucial joints and the synthetic rubber rings that were relied on to seal them.

Investigators say they are at a loss to

Continued on Page B7, Column 1

Agence France-Presse
AN IMPERIAL ANNIVERSARY: Emperor Hirohito reading a message at ceremony in Tokyo marking his 60th anniversary on the throne as well as his 85th birthday.

Indonesia Bars Two Journalists In Reagan Party

By GERALD M. BOYD
Special to The New York Times

DENPASAR, Bali, April 29 — President Reagan arrived today on this Indonesian island on the first major stop of his trip to the Far East, but the occasion was marred, White House officials said, when the Indonesian Government detained two Australian journalists in the President's party and barred them from the country.

In a separate incident, Indonesian authorities detained and expelled Barbara Crossette, a correspondent for The New York Times who was seeking to report on the Reagan visit. [Page A6.]

Moments before Mr. Reagan was greeted at the island's airport by President Suharto, the Indonesian leader, and colorfully clad Balinese dancers, Indonesian authorities removed the two Australians from the White House press plane.

Ordered to Leave Country

The journalists, from the Australian Broadcasting Corporation, were ordered to leave the country in a move that White House officials said highlighted sharp differences between the United States and Indonesia over press and political freedoms.

The two correspondents, Jim Middleton and Richard D. Palfreyman, are based in Washington and had been told that they would not be allowed to enter, despite the protests of American officials, following unfavorable reports in

Continued on Page A6, Column 1

ASSESSMENT OF U.S.

Intelligence Sources Say Accident Began Days Ago and Continues

By PHILIP M. BOFFEY
Special to The New York Times

WASHINGTON, April 29 — United States intelligence sources said today that the nuclear disaster in the Soviet Union started as long as four or five days ago and was continuing to spread radioactive material into the atmosphere.

Most experts agreed that the graphite core of the Chernobyl reactor, at Pripyat in the Ukraine, had caught fire and was burning fiercely.

Details of the accident remained scarce today, the day after the Russians announced that an accident had taken place at the reactor. Without such details, experts found it difficult to speculate about the short- and long-term dangers the disaster posed to health and the environment.

Soviet Technology Faulted

But they faulted Soviet technology, which uses graphite, a form of carbon, to moderate nuclear reactions. In the United States, water is used as a moderator.

They also said the stricken reactor was not encased in a protective concrete containment dome, as is customary in the United States. The external shell could cut down on the radioactive material spewed into the atmosphere.

The experts warned that such graphite fires can be very difficult to extinguish, and that an unextinguished fire continues to release more radioactivity over the Soviet Union and other countries downwind of the reactor.

"The graphite is burning and will continue to burn for a good number of days," said Kenneth L. Adelman, the United States arms control administrator. He told Congress that, because the reactor is on a river, "there is concern over water contamination."

Europeans Are Critical

European officials and nuclear experts criticized the Soviet Union for not disclosing the accident as soon as it occurred. Some United States intelligence officials say they believe it happened Friday or possibly even Thursday. Moscow did not reveal the accident until Monday.

The Associated Press quoted a ranking information official, who was not identified, as saying that today "smoke was still billowing from the site" at the reactor.

"The roof had been blown off and large portions of the walls had caved in, and it seemed at the time that the nuclear unit just above it might still be in some danger," The A.P. said, adding that it was understood — but not officially confirmed — that much of the American intelligence information had been gathered by a KH-11 spy satellite.

Zhores Medvedev, the exiled Russian

Continued on Page A11, Column 2

Reuters
Photograph published in the February issue of Soviet Life magazine shows cooling system of a reactor at the Chernobyl nuclear power plant near Kiev.

The Nuclear Disaster

What Happened

In an unusual public admission, the Soviet state radio said a "disaster" had occurred at a nuclear power plant in the Ukraine. West German and Swedish officials said Soviet officials had asked for help in controlling a burning nuclear reactor. The nuclear accident, described by Swedish experts as potentially the worst ever at a power plant, sent a radioactive cloud across parts of the Soviet Union, Eastern Europe and Scandinavia. Moscow provided few details, but intelligence sources believe that the accident occurred last Thursday or Friday and that radiation was continuing to spew yesterday. Western experts say they believe graphite used to moderate the nuclear reaction in the plant caught fire. They disagree on whether the fire was associated with a meltdown, in which nuclear fuel rods burn out of control.

The Health Damage

The Russians reported that four nearby localities had been evacuated, two people had died and others had been treated. Western experts say they fear that a great many more, perhaps thousands, who lived near the plant may become ill or die from radiation poisoning in coming years or suffer cancers and genetic mutations later. So far, radiation levels reaching Scandinavia are not considered dangerous.

Could It Happen Here?

American commercial reactors use water rather than graphite, a flammable material, to moderate nuclear reactions. They also, unlike the Soviet reactor in the accident, have steel and concrete containment structures designed to prevent the escape of radiation. But experts say they do not have enough information to tell whether the accident holds any lessons for nuclear power safety here.

Unanswered Questions

These are among the unanswered questions: When did the accident begin? What caused the accident? How much radiation of what types has been released? How many people have been killed, injured or exposed to dangerous radiation? Have soils, crops, water and livestock in the Ukraine been dangerously contaminated?

2 DEATHS ADMITTED

Moscow, in Terse Report, Asserts the 'Radiation Situation' Is Stable

By SERGE SCHMEMANN
Special to The New York Times

MOSCOW, April 29 — The Soviet Government was reported today to have asked West Germany and Sweden for assistance in handling a fire in a nuclear reactor core.

The reports, from officials in those countries, came amid indications that a reactor accident reported Monday in the Ukraine, 70 miles north of Kiev, was a major disaster, perhaps the worst in the history of nuclear power.

[The United States formally offered humanitarian and technical assistance to the Soviet Union to help it deal with the accident. Page 6.]

'Radiation Situation' Stable

The developments came as the Soviet Government issued its second official statement on the accident in the Chernobyl nuclear power station at Pripyat, saying that the "radiation situation has now been stabilized."

The four-paragraph statement disclosed for the first time that the accident at the four-reactor plant had occurred in the No. 4 reactor, which went into service in 1983, and that the three others were in operating order, but had been shut down. Each of the four reactors had an electrical generating capacity of 1,000 megawatts.

[At one point, according to Reuters, the Moscow radio referred to the accident as "a disaster," but later dropped the release word. United Press International quoted the radio as having said, "The disaster was the first one at a Soviet nuclear power plant in more than 30 years." There was a nuclear accident in the Urals in 1957 that the Soviet Government has never acknowledged.]

Four Localities Evacuated

The Soviet Government statement, which was read on the evening television news, said that two people had been killed in the accident and that the power-station settlement, an allusion to Pripyat, and three other nearby localities had been evacuated.

[Some Western officials questioned whether the death toll could be as low as two. In Washington, Kenneth L. Adelman, director of the Arms Control and Disarmament Agency, called the Soviet assertion "frankly preposterous."]

The reported Soviet request for assistance from West Germany and Sweden indicated to experts that the reactor's graphite core was burning uncontrollably, and therefore that the fuel rods in it might have melted down partly or completely. Some foreign scientists agreed that if this was the case, the accident was the worst nuclear-power disaster in history.

But the Soviet authorities provided

Continued on Page A10, Column 5

Casualties in Soviet Could Keep Rising, U.S. Experts Assert

By HAROLD M. SCHMECK Jr.

American experts said yesterday that deaths and injuries from the reactor accident in the Soviet Union may continue to mount for several weeks in the vicinity of the disaster if severe radiation has been released.

These experts on health and radiation said there appeared to be no danger for the Western Hemisphere and probably little in the Scandinavian countries, on the basis of what has been reported thus far.

When the Soviet Union announced that two people had been killed in the accident at the Chernobyl power plant in the Ukraine, there was no indication if the cause of death was radiation, fire or other nonnuclear effects.

There was an unconfirmed report from the area that many more may have died. If that report is confirmed, said Dr. Kenneth Mossman of Georgetown University Medical School, it would suggest extremely high levels of gamma radiation.

Two types of radiation exposure are likely to be involved in the damage at and near the reactor site.

The first and most immediately dangerous is external gamma radiation, which is similar to X-rays and equally penetrating. Gamma radiation can damage cells, genes and vital tissues,

Continued on Page A12, Column 1

The New York Times/Paul Hosefros
BODIES OF CHALLENGER'S CREW LEAVE FLORIDA: Coffin of Francis R. Scobee being carried from plane at Dover Air Force Base, Del. Remains of astronauts will be turned over to their families for burial. Page B7.

INSIDE

Dismissal in Secrets Case
Officials said a Pentagon aide was dismissed on the ground that he gave information about covert U.S. operations for a news article. Page A17.

Methodists' Nuclear Stand
The United Methodist Church's Council of Bishops voted to issue a pastoral letter declaring opposition to any use of nuclear weapons. Page A15.

Red Sox Pitcher Fans 20
Roger Clemens of Boston set a major league record by striking out 20 Seattle batters in the Red Sox 3-1 victory. He issued no walks. Page A27.

"All the News That's Fit to Print"

The New York Times

VOL.CXXXV . No. 46,826   Copyright © 1986 The New York Times   NEW YORK, SATURDAY, JULY 5, 1986   30 CENTS

Late Edition

Weather: Mostly sunny, humid today; hazy, warm and humid tonight. Mostly sunny, humid and very hot tomorrow. Temperatures: today 90-92, tonight 73-77; yesterday 55-77. Details, page 17.

30 cents beyond 75 miles from New York City, except on Long Island.

A VERY SPECIAL DAY

Millions Watch Festive Harbor Salute to Liberty

SAILING TALL: Ships proceeding through the harbor, part of a stately six-hour parade that delighted an audience of millions on land and on water.

The New York Times/Jim Wilson

FIREWORKS FILL SKY

21-Gun Salutes Thunder as Warships and Tall Ships Ply the Bay

By ROBERT D. McFADDEN

A procession of tall ships joined an armada of mighty warships in New York Harbor yesterday, and an enormous fireworks show turned the night sky to blazing color in a salute to the Fourth of July and the centennial of a rekindled Statue of Liberty.

As darkness fell on a day of stately nautical maneuvers, the biggest fireworks display in American history — a booming, 28-minute barrage of sky-rockets — burst like supernovas over the harbor and bathed millions of awed spectators and much of the metropolitan region in eerie light.

It was, to many, the highlight of a Fourth of July filled with delights, especially the spectacle of tall ships joining warships in the harbor, with President Reagan reviewing the fleet aboard the battleship Iowa and a parade of sail from Governors Island.

"We expected the best fireworks since Nero set Rome on fire, and we got them," Mayor Koch said after the fireworks.

40,000 Shells

From a necklace of 30 barges around the tip of Manhattan, stretching from the Brooklyn Bridge to the World Trade Center, more than 40,000 pyrotechnic shells shrieked skyward in a computer-controlled, nonstop cannonading, with smoke and blasts reminiscent of a battlefield.

Against the night sky, cascades of red, orange, yellow, blue, green and white exploded into gigantic flowerlike shapes of chrysanthemums, peonies, silvertails and morning glories. Others bloomed into palettes of swizzling color, forming dragonflies, swaying leaves, meteors.

The sound and light echoed and flashed off the towers of downtown Manhattan, washed over the floodlit Statue of Liberty, illuminated tens of thousands of boats dotting the harbor and overwhelmed the sparkling lights of the city in the distance.

Musical Score

The fireworks, choreographed by Grucci, Pyro Spectaculars and Zambelli Internationale, were accompanied by a musical score played on radio and television by the 140-member United States Marine Band aboard the aircraft carrier John F. Kennedy, anchored at midharbor. President Reagan and his wife, Nancy, had an admirable view from the deck of the carrier.

Millions of spectators, meanwhile, gasped, oooooed and aaaahed as they watched from the rim of the harbor and

Continued on Page 30, Column 1

STRIKE BY MINERS HITS SOUTH AFRICA

Workers at Diamond Company Seek Release of Unionists

By ALAN COWELL
Special to The New York Times

JOHANNESBURG, July 4 — Nearly 2,000 black mineworkers have gone on strike at four diamond mines to demand the release of detained labor leaders, their employer said today.

The stoppage at the De Beers mines, which started Thursday, is the first known protest in the economically crucial mining industry since the newest state of emergency was imposed June 12. South Africa's gold, diamond and other mines account for more than half the country's export earnings.

The police, meanwhile, said a bomb explosion, the 13th since the declaration of the emergency, wounded 20 people in a white suburb of Pretoria, the capital.

11 Blacks and 9 Whites Hurt

The Bureau for Information, the sole source of authorized news under the emergency decree, said the explosion was caused by a device left between two parked cars.

The bureau said 11 of the wounded were black — presumably blacks working for white employers in the area — and nine were white.

Three people have died and about 100, many of them white, have been wounded in bomb explosions since the emergency was declared. The overall death toll since June 12 is more than 100; most of the dead were blacks. Since September 1984, when the current period of protest and violence

Continued on Page 4, Column 4

INSIDE

Becker and Lendl in Final
Boris Becker, the champion last year, and Ivan Lendl, never the champion, advanced to tomorrow's singles final at Wimbledon. Page 19.

Neo-Nazi Dream Lives On
Members of a violent neo-Nazi group are dead or in prison, but their dream of a racist state in the Pacific Northwest refuses to die. Page 10.

Rudy Vallee Dies
Rudy Vallee, saxophonist, bandleader and singing idol of the 1930's and 40's, died at the age of 84 in his home in California. Page 8.

Family Sails Amid History For a Moment

By WILLIAM E. GEIST

Seven-year-old Josh Curtis wondered aloud yesterday what in the world the Statue of Liberty would say if she could speak. His question was lost in the roar of thousands of boat engines and the blare of their horns.

The boy had just entered New York Harbor, uttering a "Wow!" as the family motorboat emerged from a tributary. He beheld more boats than he had ever imagined existed — indeed, perhaps more than have ever been assembled — as they swirled about the statue's feet and swarms of

About New York

blimps, skywriters, helicopters and fighter planes buzzed around her head.

Josh's family had slept aboard their well-traveled, 26-foot boat at the New Elco Marina in Bayonne, N.J., for an early getaway. With American flags unfurled, they sailed across Newark Bay and down the Kill Van Kull, lined with salvage yards and oil tankers, a dreary approach that made the harbor view all the more dramatic.

His father, Skip Curtis, dressed in a red-white-and-blue "Liberty Park, New Jersey" T-shirt, enthusiastically loaded the family — Josh; his mother, Ellen, and Matthew, his 10-year-old brother — aboard, along with two coolers so full of beer, soda, cold cuts and nacho cheese chips that their sides were splitting. Also on board was a sack of fireworks and a radio playing rock-and-roll oldies.

Mr. Curtis, 42, said he wanted them to be "present and part of an unforgettable moment in American history." All they could do was hope this turned out better than Halley's comet, which he was also excited for them to see.

Mrs. Curtis went along reluctantly on the pilgrimage to the refurbished Statue of Liberty. Matthew had suggested to his father a little fluke fishing instead.

"They told us at school we had to contribute $5 to the statue," Matthew said, "or we were in trouble."

But now they were all excited — if occasionally afraid for their lives — as Mr. Curtis deftly wove them through this assemblage of virtually every type of vessel conceived by man to pay homage to the statue.

There were sloops, hydrofoils, junks, carriers, brigantines, the Queen Elizabeth 2, Jet-Skis, an oil barge with bleachers, schooners, water taxis, a submarine, a battleship and a thousand and one would-be Don Johnsons in sleek Cigarette boats.

The parade of breathtaking tall ships, the ostensible reason for the gathering of the masses, seemed but a sideshow at times.

The Curtis family, of North Bergen, N.J., beheld two seemingly crazed people out in a kayak in this hull-to-hull traffic. There was even a car, one of those small convertible automobiles that run on land or water, with waves breaking over the windshield wipers.

They next came upon what appeared

Continued on Page 27, Column 1

BURSTING IN AIR: Fireworks providing brief but brilliant rivalry for statue's torch.

The New York Times/Fred R. Conrad

New York Relaxes as It Savors a Celebration

By JOSEPH BERGER

People moved about more lazily. Faces were less taut and many wore radiant smiles. Even the sky was flawless — blue, then a starry black. .

In short, New Yorkers and out-of-town visitors yesterday were in a mood appropriate not only to the Fourth of July, but to a singular Fourth, one that celebrated their roots and their unabashed pride in their country.

"It's a custom-made day," said Gabriel De Los Rios, a 64-year-old Chilean-American pianist standing amid a light-hearted and relaxed throng on the Riverside Park promenade watching the tall ships glide up the Hudson.

"There's a brotherhood and everybody's friendly to everybody else," he added. "It happens on happy occasions."

"The last time I saw this was when the hostages came home from Iran and they had that rally," Police Officer Thomas Gulotta said as he took a lunch break on a shaded bench behind the promenade. "That's when everybody was pulling in the same direction. It's a pleasure. You don't mind working."

New Yorkers, who on most days seem to be heading in thousands of different directions, were indeed pulling in the same few directions yesterday and gently sharing an unspoken camaraderie.

Last night, as the fireworks began, the joyful screams of thousands matched the screams of thousands of rockets, and the whole of lower Manhattan seemed as if it had broken into a smile.

Couples embraced, children grasped their parents and those who could speak uttered superlatives and exclamations.

"Indescribable," said Jim Tully, a

Continued on Page 26, Column 2

For Ronald Reagan, The Ceremonies Stir Pride and Patriotism

By BERNARD WEINRAUB

President Reagan blended politics and patriotism yesterday in what aides described as one of the most exuberant days of his Presidency.

Celebrating Independence Day and the rededication of the Statue of Liberty, Mr. Reagan flew by helicopter in the morning to the battleship Iowa and steamed south on the sun-drenched Hudson River to pass an international flotilla of warships. Many of the vessels fired guns in salute as the Iowa, a recommissioned World War II vessel, cruised down the Hudson at 8 knots.

As Mr. Reagan sat in the viewing booth, moments after F-16 Thunderbirds flew over and left a red, white and blue trail in the cloudless sky, he said to Capt. Larry Seaquist, the ship's commanding officer: "Absolutely brilliant. No word to describe my pride."

Larry Speakes, the White House spokesman, said the President was "exuberant for sure" during his visit to New York, which ends this morning.

"There have been other days like these — inaugural days, the release of the Iranian hostages," Mr. Speakes said. "This ranks with them."

By nightfall Mr. Reagan and his

Continued on Page 31, Column 1

"All the News That's Fit to Print"

The New York Times

Late Edition

New York Today: Becoming cloudy, mild. High 66-72. Tonight, a few showers, mild. Low 53-58. Tomorrow, periods of rain. High 62-67. Yesterday: High 63, low 48. Details on page C18.

VOL.CXXXVI.. No. 46,926   Copyright © 1986 The New York Times   NEW YORK, MONDAY, OCTOBER 13, 1986   80 cents beyond 75 miles from New York City, except on Long Island.   30 CENTS

REAGAN-GORBACHEV TALKS END IN STALEMATE AS U.S. REJECTS DEMAND TO CURB 'STAR WARS'

A volunteer helping victims of the earthquake at a makeshift hospital set up on a San Salvador street.

Lack of Help Angers Poor In El Salvador

By JAMES LeMOYNE
Special to The New York Times

COMUNIDAD MODELO, El Salvador, Oct. 12 — The people of this miserable warren of mud shacks have been promised by the Government that it will help them rebuild from the earthquake that swept away their homes and buried their loved ones on Friday morning.

But tonight, as the rains of a violent thunderstorm added to their misery, they found it hard to believe that the promise would be kept any time soon.

"We have nobody, nobody," said Ana Lilia Vásquez Sibrian, 50 years old, as she watched friends dig out their crushed adobe home. "We are forgotten."

[The Salvadoran President, José Napoleón Duarte, said in a televised news conference late Sunday night that the death toll had risen to 890 and that some stricken areas had still not been reached to search for victims, the Associated Press reported. Mr. Duarte said 10,000 were injured and 150,000 left homeless.]

In his Sunday homily today, the Roman Catholic Archbishop of San Salvador, Arturo Rivera y Damas, harshly criticized the failure to provide greater relief services to the poor neighborhoods that appear to be those that sustained the most damage.

"What is most apparent, without of-

Continued on Page A11, Column 1

CLOSE AIDE TO BUSH LINKED TO FIGURE HELPING CONTRAS

National Security Adviser Had Served in C.I.A. With Man Directing Aid Flights

By PHILIP SHENON
Special to The New York Times

WASHINGTON, Oct. 12 — Vice President Bush acknowledged today that his national security adviser had ties to a Central Intelligence Agency veteran identified as a leader of a secret effort to supply Nicaraguan rebels.

But the Vice President continued to deny any involvement in overseeing the supply operations to the rebels, known as contras, who are fighting the Sandinista Government of Nicaragua.

Through a spokesman, the Vice President said he had met twice in his office with the former C.I.A. agent, known as Max or Felix Gomez and as Felix Rodriguez, but only to discuss El Salvador.

Worked for El Salvador

According to Mr. Bush's staff, Mr. Gomez had worked for the Salvadoran Air Force as a counterinsurgency specialist.

Mr. Bush's spokesman, Marlin Fitzwater, said in an interview that Mr. Gomez had been recommended for the job by Donald P. Gregg, a former intelligence agency official who is Mr. Bush's national security adviser.

Eugene Hasenfus, an American captured after his cargo plane was downed in Nicaragua last week, said Mr. Gomez was a C.I.A. employee and was running the supply operations to the rebels from a Salvadoran air base.

Denial by Agency

The Central Intelligence Agency has denied that Mr. Gomez works directly or indirectly for the agency.

Mr. Fitzwater said Mr. Bush had met twice with Mr. Gomez, most recently in May. On Saturday the Vice President called Mr. Gomez "a patriot."

Mr. Fitzwater said that the conversations in the Vice President's office in the Old Executive Office Building were brief, 10 to 15 minutes, and did not involve the Nicaraguan rebels.

The conversations, the spokesman said, "had been entirely related to El Salvador." He said Mr. Bush "has never had any conversation of any kind about the contras or contra aid or Nicaragua with Mr. Gomez."

The Vice President, Mr. Fitzwater said, did not know then or now that Mr. Gomez might be involved in aiding the rebels. Congress has barred direct American Government support of the guerrillas.

President Reagan and the C.I.A.

Continued on Page A7, Column 4

President Reagan listening yesterday as an interpreter translated the farewell remarks of Mikhail S. Gorbachev.   *The New York Times/Jose R. Lopez*

Sticking Points in Iceland

'Historic' Gains on Arms Cuts Were Near, But Talks Foundered on 'Star Wars' Issue

By LESLIE H. GELB
Special to The New York Times

REYKJAVIK, Iceland, Oct. 12 — President Reagan and his aides came here with the expectation that Moscow was prepared to reach tentative agreements on medium-range missiles and other arms issues without first solving the problem of space-based defenses.

News Analysis

And they had reason to believe this, based on the two leaders' pledge last November in Geneva to seek an "interim" accord on medium-range weapons, and based on more recent public statements by Soviet leaders.

But today in the dramatic finale to their two-day get-together, Mikhail S. Gorbachev told them they were wrong.

To the Soviet leader, every agreement to reduce arms depended on American willingness essentially to scrap Mr. Reagan's dream for space-based defenses against missile attacks.

And he had a basis for this belief as well. That same joint statement in Geneva pledged the two sides to "accelerate" efforts to "prevent an arms race in space."

While each side accused the other of responsibility for a failure to reach agreement, both sides were at the same time careful not to charge one another with bad faith.

Progress on Arms Reduction

Mr. Reagan and Secretary of State George P. Shultz spoke hopefully about the potential progress made here on reducing offensive arms and about trying to pick up the pieces in the continuing arms talks in Geneva.

But Mr. Shultz appeared grim in his news conference, a seriousness matched by Mr. Gorbachev in his news conference, although he too referred to "positive" elements.

From all indications, neither side

Continued on Page A9, Column 3

VIEW IN CONGRESS ON TALKS IS MIXED

Reagan Criticized and Praised for Stand on 'Star Wars'

By JOHN HERBERS
Special to The New York Times

WASHINGTON, Oct. 12 — Initial Congressional reaction tonight to the failure of President Reagan and Mikhail S. Gorbachev to reach agreement on nuclear arms control was mixed.

Some Democrats blamed the President for refusal to compromise on his missile defense program and some Republicans praised him for avoiding what they called a Soviet trap.

Senator Richard G. Lugar, Republican of Indiana and chairman of the Senate Foreign Relations committee, spoke out in Mr. Reagan's defense, saying the meeting was a "Soviet trap to put the United States in perpetual jeopardy of the remaining intercontinental ballistic missiles."

'Did Not Blink'

"The President did not blink," Mr. Lugar said, adding that he acted in an imaginative and proper way to "preserve the defense of our country."

Some leading Democrats, however, expressed disappointment that Mr. Reagan did not use his strategic defense initiative, popularly known as "Star Wars," as a bargaining chip.

"This is a sad day for mankind," said Senator Claiborne Pell of Rhode Island, ranking Democrat on the Foreign Relations Committee. "I deeply regret the failure to achieve an agreement

Continued on Page A8, Column 4

Reagan to Address Nation

President Reagan is to address the nation from the White House tonight at 8 P.M. All the television networks will carry the address live.

NO U.S. SUMMIT DATE

Effect on Ties Unclear — Understandings Cited on Certain Issues

By BERNARD GWERTZMAN
Special to The New York Times

REYKJAVIK, Iceland, Oct. 12 — President Reagan and Mikhail S. Gorbachev ended two days of talks here today with no agreement on arms control and no date for a full-fledged summit meeting in the United States.

While officials said that the two leaders had succeeded in developing tentative understandings on most arms con-

Remarks by Reagan and Gorbachev, page A10, and Shultz, page A9.

trol issues, a possible accord foundered over Soviet insistence that the United States scrap its space-based missile-defense plans.

Secretary of State George P. Shultz said at a news conference, "We are deeply disappointed by this outcome."

Future Outlook Is in Doubt

It was not immediately clear whether Soviet-American relations would worsen because of the failure to achieve an agreement, or whether the tentative understandings on medium-range and long-range forces and on nuclear testing could be revived even in the absence of an understanding on the missile-defense issue.

The two leaders, after 11 hours of talks and all-night discussions with their experts, displayed frustration and disappointment. Each held the other responsible for the lack of results.

Mr. Reagan, speaking to American forces at the Keflavik Air Base near here, before returning home, said, "We came to Iceland to advance the cause of peace and, though we put on the table the most far-reaching arms control proposal in history, the General Secretary rejected it."

Mr. Gorbachev, at a news conference, attributed the failure to American intransigence on the plan for a space-based missile defense, known officially as the Strategic Defense Initiative, and popularly as "Star Wars."

Gorbachev Sees Chance Missed

The Soviet leader said he had told the President at the end of their meeting: "We missed a historic chance. Never have our positions been so close."

When the Iceland meeting was first arranged, it was expected to set a date for a regular summit meeting in the United States in the coming months, as called for by the two leaders at their first meeting in Geneva last year.

But Secretary of State Shultz said at his news conference after an unscheduled final three-and-a-half-hour session that no date was set.

He said the United States would not pay the price for having Mr. Gorbachev go to the United States if it meant accepting constraints on the missile defense program.

He said that the tentative package of "extremely important potential agreements," extending into areas other than arms control, failed when Mr. Gorbachev insisted that the 1972 treaty limiting defensive missiles, known as the antiballistic missile treaty, be changed to prevent research, testing

Continued on Page A8, Column 1

BankAmerica Recalling Clausen, Gone 5 Years, as Chief Executive

By ANDREW POLLACK
Special to The New York Times

SAN FRANCISCO, Oct. 12 — The board of directors of the troubled BankAmerica Corporation, in a special meeting today, named A. W. Clausen, former president of the World Bank, to resume the helm of the banking company he once led.

Mr. Clausen, who is 63 years old, was chief executive officer of BankAmerica from 1970 until 1981, when he left to join the World Bank. He returns as chairman and chief executive officer of both the bank holding company and its subsidiary, the Bank of America.

He will face the task of restoring the giant California bank to health after a long period of huge losses from bad loans, management turmoil and high costs.

The action of the board follows the resignation Friday of Samuel H. Armacost, 47, as president and chief executive officer of the BankAmerica Corporation and chairman and chief executive of its bank. He had presided over the bank since 1981, as its fortunes steadily diminished.

The board today also announced that Leland S. Prussia, the chairman of the board of the BankAmerica Corporation, would take early retirement and that Thomas A. Cooper, the No. 2 man at the Bank of America behind Mr. Armacost, would be given additional responsibilities.

The choice of Mr. Clausen, which had been suspected since Friday, has already become controversial.

Mr. Clausen, who is also known as

Tom, led the bank during a decade of uninterrupted growth, as the bank rose to international prominence. Nevertheless, many analysts and bank officials say that the policies he put in place then were responsible for many of the problems that affected the bank after he left.

Still, the appointment is expected to end at least some uncertainty that had long permeated the bank because of rumors that Mr. Armacost was on the way out.

John R. Beckett, the chairman of the executive committee of the board of directors, said the board reached its decision reluctantly and took ac-

Continued on Page D3, Column 4

VISIT TO CHINA: Queen Elizabeth II being saluted by a youngster on her arrival in Peking for a six-day visit, the first to China by a British sovereign. At center is Lady Evans, wife of the British Ambassador to China. Page A5.   *Associated Press*

Apartment Builders Return to Prewar Design

By JOSEPH GIOVANNINI

A new generation of apartment buildings resembling the traditional prewar structures of New York is being built in Manhattan, challenging the tall, thin apartment towers standing in plazas that have been typical of the last 25 years.

Preservationists see the new buildings — which typically have storefronts on the street and whose upper stories step back in a "wedding cake" design — as compatible with older structures and with the social fabric of established neighborhoods.

After years of dismissing old neighborhoods, architects with a post-modernist interest in historical styles are now taking traditional buildings on old city blocks as architectural models.

Preservationists see the new generation of buildings as architecturally nice," said the director of the Manhattan office of the Department of City Planning, Con Howe.

The new generation of buildings is largely a result of zoning changes made by the department, which has encouraged the buildings where appropriate. A sweeping neighborhood-by-neighborhood zoning review, called the Quality Housing program, that is under way will make these buildings an alternative that will no longer require spe-

Continued on Page B4, Column 1

INSIDE

The Pill: A New Kind
A drug may soon be available in France that both blocks and terminates pregnancy, a World Health Organization official said. Page A15.

Brazilians Mourn Priestess
Mourning has continued for weeks in Salvador, Brazil, over the death of a 92-year-old cult priestess who was revered across the country. Page A4.

U.S. Plans to Aid Patients
In a reversal after efforts to cut regulation of nursing homes, the Reagan Administration plans new rules to protect patients' rights. Page A13.

WAS THIS COPY OF THE TIMES delivered to you? Home and office delivery is available in most U.S. cities. Get details by calling toll-free 1-800-631-2500. - ADVT.

METS LOSE TO ASTROS, 3-1: Alan Ashby, right, after hitting a two-run homer. Denis Menke, third base coach, is at left. League championship series is tied at two each. SportsMonday, page C1.   *The New York Times/Barton Silverman*

The New York Times

Late Edition

New York Today: Rain, heavy in afternoon. High 51-56. Tonight, rain changing to showers. Low 42-47. Tomorrow,
gradual clearing. High 48-53. Yesterday:
High 52, low 39. Details on page B9.

VOL.CXXXVI...No. 46,970   Copyright © 1986 The New York Times   NEW YORK, WEDNESDAY, NOVEMBER 26, 1986   50 cents beyond 75 miles from New York City,
except on Long Island   30 CENTS

IRAN PAYMENT FOUND DIVERTED TO CONTRAS; REAGAN SECURITY ADVISER AND AIDE ARE OUT

Friedman Is Guilty With 3 in Scandal

ALL PLAN TO APPEAL

Charges of Corruption in New York Case Carry Long Prison Terms

By RICHARD J. MEISLIN
Special to The New York Times

NEW HAVEN, Nov. 25 — A jury to-
day returned guilty verdicts against
Stanley M. Friedman, the Bronx Demo-
cratic leader and long one of New York
City's most powerful political figures,
on all charges against him in the first
Federal trial stemming from New
York City's corruption scandal.

Three other defendants were also
found guilty of charges including racketeering, conspiracy and mail fraud for
their participation in a "racketeering
enterprise" that transformed the city's
Parking Violations Bureau into a tool
for their corrupt personal profit.

The 12 jurors, their expressions
grim, delivered the verdict at 11:11
A.M. after deliberating for three days
on the eight weeks of testimony and argument in the case. The jury found Mr.
Friedman and each of his co-defend-
ants guilty of racketeering, conspiracy
and mail fraud charges carrying
lengthy prison sentences and heavy
financial penalties.

Sentencing Set for March 1

In addition to Mr. Friedman, those
found guilty were Lester N. Shafran,
the former director of the Parking
Violations Bureau; Michael J. Lazar, a
real-estate developer and former city
transportation administrator, and
Marvin B. Kaplan, the chairman of
Citisource Inc., a company chosen to
manufacture hand-held computers to
issue summonses for the parking bureau. Mr. Kaplan was also found guilty
of having perjured himself while testifying before the Securities and Exchange Commission last February.

Judge Whitman Knapp, who presided
over the trial, scheduled sentencing for
March 1 at 10 A.M. Lawyers for all four
defendants said they would file appeals
at that time.

The trial of the four defendants was
the first to stem from Federal investigations into corruption in the New
York City government, and the United
States Attorney in Manhattan, Rudolph

Continued on Page B3, Column 1

The New York Times/Jim Wilson
Stanley M. Friedman and his
daughter, Betty, leaving courthouse in New Haven yesterday
after guilty verdict. Rudolph W.
Giuliani, below, prosecuted case.

More Inquiries to Come

The verdicts in New Haven cleared
the way for other inquiries into New
York City corruption, perhaps lasting
for several years. Page B3.

Manila and Rebels Say Cease-Fire Could Be Signed in a Day or Two

By BARBARA CROSSETTE
Special to The New York Times

MANILA, Nov. 25 — The Government of President Corazon C. Aquino
said tonight that it might be within two
days of signing a cease-fire agreement
with Communist rebels.

Peace talks, broken off after the killing of a left-wing labor leader nearly
two weeks ago, resumed this afternoon,
less than 48 hours after the President
said the talks would be called off if no
accord was reached by Sunday.

Tonight, after eight hours of talks,
the leader of the Government team,
Agriculture Minister Ramon V. Mitra,
told reporters, "I like to think we have
just one more meeting, and then make
an announcement."

He implied that the final meeting
would take place Wednesday and that
an agreement would be announced
Thursday. "We are so close," he said.

'Technical Hitches' Cited

Declining to disclose the length of the
cease-fire agreed on, Mr. Mitra said it
was less than 100 days, the time sought
by the Communists, but more than 30
days, the Government's proposal.

At the outset of the talks aimed at establishing a cease-fire, both sides said
they hoped it would be a opportunity
for more comprehensive negotiations
to bring the insurgency to a formal end
and bring guerrillas back into society.

It was not made clear today whether
the Government had agreed to the
rebels' preconditions, which included
the scaling back of military deployment, the disbanding of certain paramilitary units and the restriction of the
police to civilian law-enforcement
duties.

The proposed truce, if begun early
next month as planned, would extend
through the Christmas season and pos-

Continued on Page A10, Column 1

INSIDE

Takeover Action Swings Up
A lull in merger activity abruptly
ended, with billion-dollar offers for
Chesebrough-Pond's, Borg-Warner
and Carter Hawley Hale. Page D1.

Bumpurs Case Revived
New York State's top court reinstated
charges against a policeman who
killed a knife-wielding, emotionally
disturbed woman in 1984. Page B1.

President Reagan deferring reporters' questions to Attorney
General Edwin Meese 3d at news
conference yesterday in Washington. With them were Donald
T. Regan, left, White House chief
of staff, and Larry Speakes, the
White House spokesman, next to
the President. Mr. Reagan had
just announced the resignation of
Vice Adm. John M. Poindexter,
far right, as national security adviser and the dismissal of Lieut.
Col. Oliver L. North, right, for his
role in the Iranian arms affair.

The New York Times/Paul Hosefros

The Iran Affair: A Presidency Damaged

Both Friends and Foes See Reagan as Isolated

By R. W. APPLE Jr.
Special to The New York Times

WASHINGTON, Nov. 25 — After six
years of seeming invulnerability,
President Reagan has been grievously
damaged by the crisis over secret
arms shipments to Iran.

With a unanimity rare in
Washington, leading Re-
publican and Democratic
politicians agreed today
that the disclosure of payments to the Nicaraguan rebels and the
departure of two White House aides
had probably hurt the Administration
more than it helped. Some think the
damage may be irreparable.

A week of almost unrelieved criticism of Mr. Reagan's secret decision to
send arms to Iran, and of startling public bickering among senior Administration officials, has created the image of
a President isolated, stuck with an unpopular policy and uncharacteristi-
cally defensive. The disclosures today
produced a sensation in Washington
unmatched, perhaps, since the days of
the Watergate crisis.

'Probably No Smoking Gun'

"There is probably no smoking gun
here," said a man who served in the
White House during the Watergate
years. "But there is a new mess in
Washington, if not a new Watergate.
There will be a whole string of fresh
disclosures in the months to come, and
that will throw the Administration off
stride.

"It will hurt the effort in Nicaragua,
it will hurt the campaign against terrorism and it will hurt Reagan — unless, of course, he gets lucky and something happens in Iran that shows he
was right after all."

In the weeks to come, Mr. Reagan
seems certain to find his credibility, his
competence and his control under
stern challenge.

On a personal level, Mr. Reagan remains the most popular President of
modern times, and he has shown enormous resilience in the past. But he approaches the last two years of his Administration — a time when the strongest Presidents have seen their power
slip slowly away — with the Senate and
the House of Representatives under
Democratic control, with severe budgetary problems demanding attention
and now with months or perhaps even

Continued on Page A12, Column 5

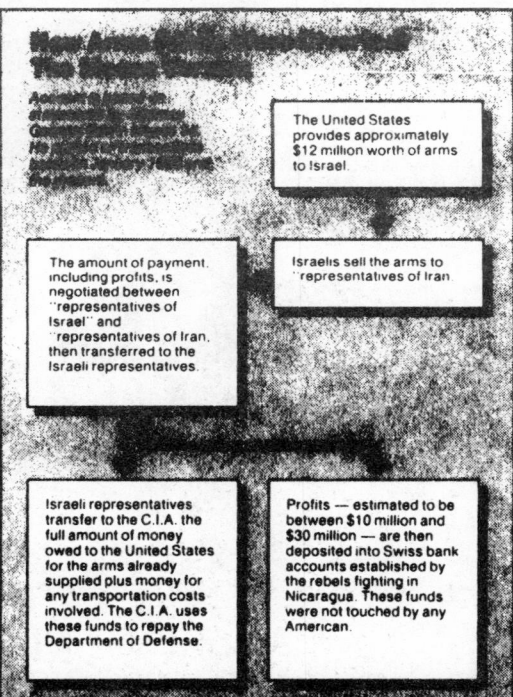

More on the Policy Crisis

Legal questions were raised by the
operation involving the Nicaraguan
rebels, including whether criminal
laws had been broken. Page A11.

The contra-aid mystery may be explained by the disclosure, Congressional investigators and Administration officials said. Page A13.

Israel said it sent arms to Iran at
the "request" of Washington and did
not know some payments were chan-
neled to the contras. Page A12.

A Saudi arms dealer played a central role in financing the Iranian purchase of arms, Israeli and American
sources said. Page A13.

Doubts were raised by intelligence
experts, officials and lawmakers con-

cerning the Administration's explanation of the arms shipments and assertions that only two American Government officials knew money was
going to the contras. Page A11.

A sister of an American hostage
held in Lebanon wrote to President
Reagan in support of his Iran initiative and expressed "a deep sense of
shame" that she had not spoken out
sooner. Page A16.

Alton G. Keel Jr., the acting national security adviser, is described
as an intelligent and hard-working
man who has seldom taken a visible
leadership role. Page A12.

Nancy Reagan dismissed the idea
that the President had been badly
damaged by the growing turmoil in
his Administration. Page A10.

HOME and OFFICE
DELIVERY of THE
NEW YORK TIMES
is available in most
major U.S. cities. For
details please call toll
free 1-800-631-2500
ADVT.

DISARRAY DEEPENS

Was Not 'Fully Informed' About Secret Moves, President Asserts

By BERNARD WEINRAUB
Special to The New York Times

WASHINGTON, Nov. 25 — President
Reagan said today that he had not been
in full control of his Administration's
Iran policy, and the White House said
that as a consequence up to $30 million
intended to pay for American arms had
been secretly diverted to rebel forces
in Nicaragua.

At the same time, the President announced that two men he held responsible — Vice Adm. John M. Poindexter,

*Statement by President Reagan
and Meese's comments, page A10.*

the national security adviser, and
Lieut. Col. Oliver L. North, a member
of the admiral's staff — had left their
posts.

With the Administration already in
turmoil over the earlier disclosure of
clandestine arms shipments to Iran,
and with speculation rampant about a
major overhaul of the White House
staff, the President's statement
seemed to deepen a sense of disarray.
By all accounts, Mr. Reagan now faces
the most serious crisis in his six-year
Presidency.

Shultz to Control Policy

The State Department, meanwhile,
said Secretary of State George P.
Shultz had been given control over future Iran policy, authority that apparently met his condition for remaining
in office. State Department officials, including Mr. Shultz, have said they were
left in the dark on much of the Iran
operation.

Mr. Reagan stunned legislators and
ranking Administration officials by announcing in a televised session with reporters that he had not been "fully informed" of some details of the Iran
operation and that Admiral Poindexter
and Colonel North were leaving after
"serious questions of propriety had
been raised."

Inquiry Still Under Way

Mr. Reagan said that, "although not
directly involved," Admiral Poindexter had "asked to be relieved of his assignment" and would return to Navy
duties. Colonel North, the President
said, "has been relieved of his duties on
the National Security Council staff."
Colonel North was widely reported to
be the central figure in the Iran arms
deal.

After Mr. Reagan's announcement,
Attorney General Edwin Meese 3d said
the Justice Department was still investigating how Nicaraguan rebel forces,
known as contras, received "somewhere between $10 and $30 million"

Continued on Page A11, Column 1

TOP LEGISLATORS PROMISE INQUIRY

Likely Violations of Law Cited — Contra Aid May Suffer

By STEVEN V. ROBERTS
Special to The New York Times

WASHINGTON, Nov. 25 — Congressional leaders expressed astonishment
today at the latest disclosures about
United States dealings with Iran and
vowed to investigate the Administration's actions.

The leaders asserted that several
laws had probably been violated when
funds paid by Iran for weapons were
transferred to the Nicaraguan rebels.

The leaders also said Congress would
probably approve legislation next year
cutting off aid to the Nicaraguan rebels
and would see to it that the head of the
National Security Council would have
to be confirmed by the Senate.

But the biggest question on Capitol
Hill today was whether President Reagan and his chief aides had known
about the operation.

Representative Jim Wright, the
Texas Democrat who will become
Speaker of the House in January,
voiced skepticism about White House
explanations that Vice Adm. John M.
Poindexter, the national security adviser, was the highest ranking official
to know about the operation.

It "defies logic," Mr. Wright told reporters, to believe that such a critical

Continued on Page A11, Column 1

"All the News That's Fit to Print"

The New York Times

VOL.CXXXVII ... No. 47,298   Copyright © 1987 The New York Times   NEW YORK, TUESDAY, OCTOBER 20, 1987   50 cents beyond 75 miles from New York City, except on Long Island.   30 CENTS

Late Edition

New York: Today, increasing clouds. High 62-67. Tonight, cloudy, breezy, showers likely. Low 51-57. Tomorrow, showers ending. High 58-65. Yesterday: High 68, low 48. Details on page B6.

STOCKS PLUNGE 508 POINTS, A DROP OF 22.6%; 604 MILLION VOLUME NEARLY DOUBLES RECORD

U.S. Ships Shell Iran Installation In Gulf Reprisal

Offshore Target Termed a Base for Gunboats

By STEVEN V. ROBERTS
Special to The New York Times

WASHINGTON, Oct. 19 — United States naval forces struck back at Iran today for attacks on American-registered vessels and other Persian Gulf shipping by shelling two connected offshore platforms that American officials said were a base for Iranian gunboats.

A few hours later, a naval commando detachment boarded a third platform five miles away and destroyed radar and communications equipment, Pentagon officials said.

No American casualties were reported in the actions, which occurred 120 miles east of Bahrain at about 2 P.M. (7 A.M., Eastern daylight time).

A 20-Minute Warning

American officials said the attacking force took pains to avoid killing Iranians, giving the crew on the first two platforms a 20-minute warning before four destroyers, stationed about three miles away, began the shelling.

At the United Nations, an Iranian delegate said "several innocent people" had been killed in the attack, but the assertion could not be confirmed.

With the bombardment, the Administration intended to send a message to Iran: The United States had shown restraint in the level of its attack this time, but might respond with greater force if Iran continued "unprovoked attacks" on gulf shipping. [Military analysis, page A10.]

'Prudent Yet Restrained'

President Reagan issued a statement describing the actions as a "prudent yet restrained response." Defense Secretary Caspar W. Weinberger warned that "stronger countermeasures" would be taken if Iranian attacks continued.

Administration officials acknowledged that today's action was unlikely to halt the cycle of violence that has ensnared American forces in the gulf since 11 Kuwaiti tankers were placed under their protection this summer. "Nobody thinks that this will end it," Vice President Bush said today.

But the actions were necessary, Mr. Bush added, because American credibility was at stake in the region after a

Continued on Page A10, Column 1

A Huge Blow to the Five-Year Bull Market

Dow's Record Fall
Yesterday's close was down 22.6 percent from Friday's close.

The Dow Jones industrial average, which has been marching up since August 1982, began a dramatic fall last week that continued through yesterday when it closed at 1,738.74. Shown: Weekly close of the Dow.

Source: Knight-Ridder Tradecenter

The New York Times/Oct. 20, 1987

Does 1987 Equal 1929?

By ERIC GELMAN

As stock prices soared this year, a chorus of pessimists warned that 1987 was looking more like 1929, when a stock market crash helped to usher in the Great Depression. Yesterday, after a plunge reminiscent of the worst days of 1929, one pressing question was whether the aftershocks would be as devastating to individuals and the nation.

News Analysis

The quick answer, many economists say, is no. The huge losses on Wall Street constitute a substantial blow to the economy at large. But there are many safeguards in place today — some instituted directly in response to the Depression — that would tend to prevent the cascading financial collapse that characterized the crash, impoverishing millions of Americans.

"A stock market crash doesn't ripple out into the economy with the same force" as it did in 1929, said Geoffrey H.

Moore, director of the Center for International Business Cycle Research at Columbia University.

To be sure, there are some unsettling similarities between the current era and the pre-Depression years. Like the Roaring Twenties, the 1980's have seen an astonishing boom on Wall Street. Now as then, individual and corporate debt are high, and some sectors of the economy are extremely weak. Trade relations are strained, with protectionist sentiment growing.

But today's economy is better equipped to handle financial shocks. "I don't see this decline in the stock market leading to a great breakdown in the economy," said Robert A. Kavesh, a professor of finance and economics at the New York University School of Business. "There are still many elements of strength in the economy —

Continued on Page D34, Column 5

Who Gets Hurt?

By ROBERT A. BENNETT

Unless the stock market bounces back quickly and substantially, most Americans are likely to be hurt by the dramatic decline in stock values — even those who own no stock at all.

Although it is a long jump from a record stock market plunge to a second Great Depression, it is much more likely that the plunging market may shake the economy and lead to a distinct downturn.

The biggest threat may be the spread of worry and fear. If investors feel poorer and employees begin to worry about the fortunes of their employers, consumers may draw back from spending of all kinds. They will postpone trading in the family car, do without a winter vacation and put off buying the home they wanted.

Reluctant to Build Plants

Similarly, businesses, stunned by the decline in their shares' value and facing the prospect of curtailed consumer spending, will shy away from building new plants or buying new equipment. Universities, churches, hospitals and other nonprofit institutions will likewise see their endowments shrink in value and are likely to brake their own spending.

And for all these diverse investors, the lower level of stock-market wealth will make it tougher to raise money by selling stock or borrowing against it.

"This affects even those who don't have direct investments in stocks," said Henry Kaufman, the chief economist of Salomon Brothers, a major

Continued on Page D34, Column 1

WORLDWIDE IMPACT

Frenzied Trading Raises Fears of Recession — Tape 2 Hours Late

By LAWRENCE J. De MARIA

Stock market prices plunged in a tumultuous wave of selling yesterday, giving Wall Street its worst day in history and raising fears of a recession.

The Dow Jones industrial average, considered a benchmark of the market's health, plummeted a record 508 points, to 1,738.74, based on preliminary calculations. That 22.6 percent decline was the worst since World War I and far greater than the 12.82 percent drop on Oct. 28, 1929, that along with the next day's 11.7 percent decline preceded the Great Depression.

Since hitting a record 2,722.42 on Aug. 25, the Dow has fallen almost 1,000 points, or 36 percent, putting the blue-chip indicator 157.5 points below the level at which it started the year. With Friday's plunge of 108.35 points, the Dow has fallen more than 26 percent in the last two sessions.

Unprecedented Trading

Yesterday's frenzied trading on the nation's stock exchanges lifted volume to unheard of levels. On the New York Stock Exchange, an estimated 604.3 million shares changed hands, almost double the previous record of 338.5 million shares set just last Friday.

With the tremendous volume, reports of brokers' trades on the New York Stock Exchange were delayed by more than two hours and at times. The New York Stock Exchange said that, as a result, it would not have definitive figures for the Dow's point decline and the exchange's volume until today.

Yesterday's big losers included International Business Machines, the bluest of the blue chips, which dropped $31, to $104. In August the stock was at $176. The other big losers among the blue chips were General Motors, which lost $13.875, to $52.125, and Exxon, which dropped $10.25, to $33.50.

More Than $1 Trillion Lost

According to Wilshire Associates, which tracks more than 5,000 stocks, the rout obliterated more than $500 billion in equity value from the nation's stock portfolios. That equity value now stands at $2.311 trillion. Since late summer, more than $1 trillion in stock values has been lost.

The losses were so great they sent shock waves to markets around the world, and many foreign exchanges posted record losses. In a sign of the continuing effect, the Tokyo Stock Exchange fell sharply today. The Nikkei Dow Jones average plummeted a record 3,395.95 yen, to 22,350.61, a drop of 13.2 percent, by late afternoon. Also, The Hong Kong exchange decided to close for the week.

In Washington yesterday, the White House spokesman, Marlin Fitzwater, issued a statement saying that President Reagan had "watched with concern" the stock market's collapse. But Mr. Reagan remained convinced that the economy was sound.

Economy Called Sound

Mr. Fitzwater said the President had directed Administration officials to contact leading financial experts. "Those consultations confirm our view that the underlying economy remains sound," he added.

Stock market analysts scrambled for explanations, which ranged from rising interest rates to the falling dollar to the possibility of war between the United States and Iran.

Indeed, the panic selling may have been bolstered by the news that the United States Navy destroyed an Iranian offshore oil platform in the central Persian Gulf yesterday, and Iran vowed retaliation.

But many experts seemed to think

Continued on Page D34, Column 1

INSIDE

Turnaround on Schools
A week after adopting a year-round term, the Los Angeles Board of Education reversed itself. A new vote was set for March 1. Page A17.

Senator Stennis to Retire
John C. Stennis, Democrat of Mississippi, will leave the Senate at the end of this term, when he will have served more than 41 years. Page A16.

Martin Back With Yankees
The Yankees promoted Lou Piniella to the post of general manager and brought Billy Martin back for his fifth stint as manager. Page B7.

Two connected Iranian offshore platforms on fire after being shelled by American destroyers. A U.S. warship can be seen in the background.
ABC News

Goetz Given 6-Month Term on Gun Charge

Bernhard H. Goetz, who ignited a nationwide debate about self-defense when he shot four teen-agers on a Manhattan subway train, was sentenced yesterday to six months in jail for carrying an unlicensed concealed pistol.

Mr. Goetz, who was acquitted of charges of attempted murder and assault at his trial last June, was also sentenced to five years' probation and ordered to undergo psychiatric counseling. He could have received as much as seven years' imprisonment.

The judge, Acting Justice Stephen G. Crane, stayed the sentence pending an

appeal by Mr. Goetz, who left the courtroom without making any comment to reporters.

Outside the courthouse, however, Mr. Goetz's lead lawyer, Barry I. Slotnick, said, "We think that he's being treated harsher as a result of the fact that he's Bernhard Goetz."

The case began Dec. 22, 1984, when Mr. Goetz shot the youths on a downtown IRT train with a .38-caliber revolver. From his surrender four months through his indictments, the long legal maneuvering and the trial, Mr. Goetz steadfastly insisted that he had shot the youths because they were about to rob him.

Article, page B1.

More About the Markets

Bonn and the United States agreed that the dollar should be stabilized near current levels. Disagreement on currency levels and interest rates had contributed to unrest in the markets. Page D1.

Small investors searched for news much of the day. Many held on to their stocks, as they tried to determine what really was happening in the stock market. Page D1.

Washington officials hesitated to offer investors immediate advice. The shouts of panic on Wall Street echoed only faintly in the corridors of the Reagan Administration. The White House maintained that the underlying economy remained sound. News analysis, page D32.

Investors bought U.S. securities in a search for a safe place to put their money. Some interest rates hovered just below 10 percent. Page D1.

Tokyo's stock market plummeted to record losses today and the Hong Kong market suspended trading for the week as Asian investors reacted in fright to the collapse on Wall Street. Page D1.

Business leaders were shaken by the collapse, which wiped out huge amounts of the market value of their companies. And they seemed to have been caught by surprise. But many leaders were confident the panic would pass. Page D32.

Overseas investors sold actively on Wall Street after years of having poured money into the bull market. Accounts of the volume of foreign selling varied widely. Page D32.

Wall Street firms are uncertain about the effect the historic drop could have on them, but some analysts fear that smaller and poorly capitalized firms may find rough going in the days ahead. Page D33.

Mutual funds sold stock shares in huge numbers, feeding the historic drop. Several mutual fund management companies said the number of phone calls from investors was about double the normal volume. Page D33.

New York City could be affected significantly because of its large number of securities industry employees. Some experts maintain that the city's economy has grown too reliant on Wall Street. Page D32.

Trading tested computers' ability to handle a volume of trading that had not been expected until the early 1990's. Page D34.

The dollar closed lower against leading currencies except the Canadian dollar. Analysts said trading was quiet as traders were preoccupied by the jarring news from the stock market. Gold was $486.50 an ounce, up $15.50 from Friday to reach its highest level in over four years. Page D26.

Democratic leaders called for talks with President Reagan on a deficit-reduction package that would include tax increases. Page D32.

In politics, two questions loomed: How badly were the Republicans' 1988 chances hurt? How were the Democrats' prospects helped? Political Memo. Page A30.

THE NEW YORK TIMES is available for home or office delivery in most major U.S. cities. Please call this toll-free number: 1-800-631-2500 ADVT.

Terrence J. McManus, a specialist with Spear, Leeds & Kellogg, on the floor of the New York Stock Exchange yesterday. Articles on Wall Street's day to remember and the sinking of investor hopes, page D1.
The New York Times/Marilynn K. Yee

The New York Times

Late Edition

New York: Today, partly sunny, breezy. High 45-50. Tonight, increasing clouds, colder. Low 26-36. Tomorrow, sunny periods, cold. High 35-40. Yesterday: High 70, low 48. Details on page C26.

VOL.CXXXVII.. No. 47,328   Copyright © 1987 The New York Times   NEW YORK, THURSDAY, NOVEMBER 19, 1987   50 cents beyond 75 miles from New York City, except on Long Island.   **30 CENTS**

IRAN-CONTRA REPORT SAYS PRESIDENT BEARS 'ULTIMATE RESPONSIBILITY' FOR WRONGDOING

Mortgage Rates And Housing Construction

New private housing started, in millions.* Mortgage rates, at key points, are in parentheses.†

(10.15%) (9.08%)
(9.70%)
(10.89%)
(11.26%)

M J J A S O N D J F M A M J J A S O
1986   1987
*Seasonally adjusted, annual rate
†30-year fixed rate mortgage, monthly average.
Source: Commerce Department; Federal Home Loan Mortgage Corp.

The New York Times/Nov. 19, 1987

Let Banks Enter Securities Field, Greenspan Says

By NATHANIEL C. NASH
Special to The New York Times

WASHINGTON, Nov. 18 — The Federal Reserve Board called today for repeal of legislation enacted during the Depression that places a barrier between the banking and securities industries.

Advocates of such change, including most banking regulators, say consumers would find a wider range of products at their banks and at lower cost.

Supporters of the barrier say enough competition already exists to provide consumers with a variety of investments at fair prices. There is not enough benefit, they argue, to allow the industries to combine.

Testifying before a House banking subcommittee, Alan Greenspan, chairman of the Federal Reserve Board, said the central bank wanted commercial banks to be able to engage in the broadest range of securities underwriting. As a safeguard, Mr. Greenspan recommended that securities operations be confined to a separate unit of a bank holding company.

The legislation under assault is the Glass-Steagall Act of 1933, one of the nation's landmark banking laws. It was intended to increase the stability of the banking industry by preventing it from speculating in stocks and other securities. Now a concerted effort to repeal some of its key provisions is being

Continued on Page D10, Column 4

32 Are Killed in Fire At London Subway; 80 Reported Injured

By HOWELL RAINES
Special to The New York Times

LONDON, Thursday, Nov. 19 — At least 32 people were killed and about 80 injured Wednesday night when a fire broke out in a subway station in central London.

Witnesses described a scene of panic and confusion in the King's Cross station as commuters were trapped in the ticketing areas and on platforms of the Piccadilly Line. They reported seeing people with their clothes and hair aflame, clawing desperately to make their way to the exits.

"People were running everywhere, panicking and treading on each other," said Paul Medland, a survivor.

Another commuter, Doug McAdam, told of arriving in the station in a train just as smoke billowed down toward the tracks. "It was like coming into a pub full of smoke," he said. "The escalator had been shut down and the station guards sent us toward the Victoria Line escalator, which was working. As we went up, the smoke was worse."

The blaze started at the foot of a wooden escalator at about 7:50 P.M., catching the last of Wednesday's evening rush hour crowd at the city's busiest underground station, where five subway lines converge.

Early reports were that the fire started in the equipment room under the escalator that links the Piccadilly Line platforms with the main ticketing concourse of the station. Officials did not rule out the possibility that an incendiary device was involved, but they

Continued on Page A2, Column 4

STARTS IN HOUSING FALL 8% IN MONTH TO HIT 4-YEAR LOW

Most of October Drop Tied to Rise in Rates That Ended When Stocks Plunged

By PETER T. KILBORN
Special to The New York Times

WASHINGTON, Nov. 18 — Home building plunged in October to its lowest level in more than four years, the Government reported today.

Economists attributed most of the decline to the rise in interest rates that ended with the plunge of the stock market. Since then, rates have receded, but they are expected to stay high enough in the next year or so to prevent any burst of new construction.

Construction of houses and apartments dropped in October to an annual rate of 1.51 million, 8.2 percent below the September rate, the sharpest one-month drop in three years.

Between Boom and Recession

Despite the severity of the drop, that annual rate is midway between boom levels and recession levels, and economists predicted it would remain there well into next year if mortgage rates continued in double digits, as they expect.

"We're busy as ever, just a little more nervous," said Richard A. Lewis, president of Lewis Homes in Upland, Calif., which builds 3,000 houses and apartments a year in one of the nation's strongest areas for new housing.

Economists predict little recovery from the October pace because they expect interest rates to remain above 10 percent; rates below that level lead to booms in construction. Rates for home mortgages, which were at a low of 9 percent on average last March, steadily rose to 10.5 percent in June, and then abated a bit in July.

At that point, investors and the Fed-

Continued on Page D11, Column 4

Biological Mother Is Granted Custody of Boy in Abuse Case

The New York Times/William E. Sauro
Nicole Bridget Smigiel, right, biological mother of Mitchell Steinberg, and her mother, Graceann, arriving at Family Court.

By KIRK JOHNSON

The biological mother of a 17-month-old boy raised by a Manhattan couple who have been charged in the death of another child won temporary custody of the boy yesterday.

The woman, Nicole Bridget Smigiel, argued in an emotional hearing that the boy, Mitchell, had never been legally adopted. Miss Smigiel, who is 18 and lives in Massapequa Park, L.I., is seeking permanent custody.

The couple who had been raising the boy, Joel B. Steinberg and Hedda Nussbaum, are charged with murdering the other child, Lisa, and with neglect in the care of Mitchell, who was taken from the Steinberg home in Greenwich Village by the police on Nov. 2.

Mitchell, who began living with Mr. Steinberg and Ms. Nussbaum immediately after birth, was found tied to a chair and drinking spoiled milk. He has been in city foster care since Nov. 2. Yesterday, attorneys for Mr. Steinberg

and Ms. Nussbaum strongly opposed Miss Smigiel's request for custody.

The court decision, at Family Court Building in lower Manhattan, was ordered held in abeyance by the judge, Jeffry H. Gallet, until 5 P.M. today to allow attorneys for Mr. Steinberg and Ms. Nussbaum to file appeals.

The attorneys for the city's Department of Social Services and the court-appointed lawyers speaking for Mitchell's interests supported the judge.

"I am not predeciding this case," Judge Gallet said in explaining the custody ruling, which will likely remain in effect pending a Family Court trial, to begin in January. "I just don't want this child bounced around," the judge said, referring to the foster-care program.

Under state law, blood relatives are given priority in temporary custody

Continued on Page B4, Column 4

The New York Times/Paul Hosefros
Senator Warren B. Rudman, Republican of New Hampshire, commenting yesterday on the majority report of the Congressional committees that investigated the Iran-contra affair. With him were, from the right, Representative Lee H. Hamilton, Democrat of Indiana, and Senators Daniel K. Inouye, Democrat of Hawaii; Paul S. Trible Jr., Republican of Virginia; Paul S. Sarbanes, Democrat of Maryland; George J. Mitchell, Democrat of Maine, and William S. Cohen, Republican of Maine.

U.S. Aides Say Panama General Proposed Sabotage in Nicaragua

By STEPHEN ENGELBERG
Special to The New York Times

WASHINGTON, Nov. 18 — Panama's military leader offered to undertake sabotage and possibly assassinations in Nicaragua for the Reagan Administration, Government officials said today, explaining a veiled allusion to the matter in the Iran-contra report.

The officials said Lieut. Col. Oliver L. North, then a White House aide, had accepted the sabotage offer on the instructions of Rear Adm. John M. Poindexter, then the President's national security adviser. But they said the plan put forward by the Panamanian, Gen. Manuel Antonio Noriega, never got off the ground.

They said computer messages reviewed by the Congressional committees but not disclosed in the report suggested that General Noriega was also offering to undertake assassinations, but that Admiral Poindexter told Colonel North not to become involved. American Government officials are prohibited by executive order from conducting or taking part in assassinations.

The Enterprise's Activities

The Congressional report provides the fullest account yet of the activities kept secret from Congress by the Administration. It says White House officials were planning many more operations when their secret network was exposed last year.

Although it does not describe in detail the other covert operations planned by "the Enterprise," the private companies run by Richard V. Secord, a retired Air Force major general, and Albert Hakim, an Iranian-born middleman, the report says they included gathering intelligence on terrorists, freeing hostages and underwriting secret propaganda efforts.

The report also details completed operations, including Colonel North's use of a Danish ship to ferry arms around the world and his payments to Drug Enforcement Administration agents hoping to free American hostages in Lebanon.

In discussing the activities attributed by officials to Panama, the Congressional report says only that "a third party" offered to carry out the operations, and it does not indicate that a foreign government was involved.

According to the report, Admiral

Continued on Page A11, Column 1

Worst Is Past For President

Damage to Reputation Was Done Long Ago

By JOEL BRINKLEY
Special to The New York Times

WASHINGTON, Nov. 18 — Even with its arresting descriptions of "pervasive dishonesty" and "disarray at the highest levels of Government," the Congressional report on the Iran-contra affair is not likely to do

News Analysis

significant new harm to the Reagan Presidency because the damage is already done.

The affair knocked President Reagan off his feet a year ago. As politicians of both parties say — and the failures, embarrassments and strident calls for stronger leadership of the last several months demonstrate — Mr. Reagan has never fully regained his stride.

'There Isn't Much New Here'

White House officials may be correct when they say, as one put it today, that "the public is tired" of the Iran-contra affair. In fact they were banking on that as they brushed off the report with a dismissive wave.

"There isn't much new here," said Marlin Fitzwater, the White House spokesman.

But while the White House may be correct that the report is not likely to set off new waves of criticism and angst, it is because the public view calcified many months ago that the affair had already diminished Mr. Reagan as a leader.

"The damage to Reagan's reputation came in the first two weeks," said an independent political consultant, Wil-

Continued on Page A11, Column 1

'CABAL OF ZEALOTS'

No Bush Role Is Found — Reagan Says It Is Time to Move On

By DAVID E. ROSENBAUM
Special to The New York Times

WASHINGTON, Nov. 18 — The Congressional committees on the Iran-contra affair blamed President Reagan in their final report today for failing to live up to his constitutional mandate to "take care that the laws be faithfully executed" and said he bore "the ultimate responsibility" for wrongdoing by his aides.

"Fundamental processes of governance were disregarded and the rule of law was subverted," the majority report of the committees asserted. "If the President did not know what his national security advisers were doing, he should have."

The White House reacted with a statement by Mr. Reagan's spokesman, Marlin Fitzwater, saying the President understood that mistakes had been made, accepted responsibility and believed that the time had come to move on to other, more pressing issues.

An Authoritative Narrative

The Congressional report provided the most accurate accounting to date on how nearly $48 million raised from the arms sales to Iran had been distributed and added some new details about other matters.

Although it included little important evidence that was not covered during the three months of public hearings last spring and summer, it marshaled the details of the complicated affair into an authoritative narrative that sought to underpin its severe judgments on the Reagan Administration.

The 11-month investigation, the most thorough and highly publicized Congressional inquiry since the Watergate scandal, grew out of the disclosures a year ago this month that the Reagan Administration had secretly sold arms to Iran and had run a clandestine operation to support the Nicaraguan rebels.

The focus now shifts to the special prosecutor, Lawrence E. Walsh, who is expected to seek indictments soon, perhaps in January.

Sweeping Criticism of Officials

"The Iran-contra affair was characterized by pervasive dishonesty and inordinate secrecy," the report said in a sweeping criticism of officials involved in the clandestine deals to ship arms to Iran and use the proceeds to finance the contras.

The report, which was accompanied

Continued on Page A10, Column 3

More on the Report

Key sections of the Congressional Iran-contra report and a transcript of the White House response are on pages A12-15. Also inside, a chronology, page A12; a cast of characters, page A13, and the special prosecutor's reaction, page A10.

INSIDE

Turmoil in Mexico
The peso fell by 59 percent against the dollar after the central bank stopped propping it up. And inflation reached 141 percent. Page D1.

Moscow Gives Arms Data
The Soviet Union gave the United States data on missiles as negotiators pressed to complete a missile treaty. Page A8.

New Post for Russian
Boris N. Yeltsin, removed as head of the Moscow Communist Party, was given a high post in the construction industry, Tass reported. Page A9.

Korean Fights His Past
For Roh Tae Woo, Government candidate for President of South Korea, unshackling himself from his military background is a key goal. Page A3.

Budget Plan Under Attack
Congressional negotiators criticized the emerging plan to reduce the budget deficit, raising doubts about its prospects for approval. Page A26.

CBS Returns to its Roots
CBS agreed to sell its records division to Sony for about $2 billion in cash, completing its sale of non-broadcast operations. Page D1.

B12   THE NEW YORK TIMES HEALTH THURSDAY, NOVEMBER 18, 1987

Parents of Premature Infants Thrust Into a Life-Saving Role

Personal Health Jane E. Brody

Encouraging News for the Absent Minded
Memory Can Be Improved, With Practice

New on Thursdays: The Health Page
A new life-saving role for parents of premature babies. And the Personal Health column reports on keeping the memory sharp. Page B12.

Also today: Parent & Child, a column starting this week in The Home Section, discusses neatness. Page C8.

Outlook for AIDS Victims
About 15 percent of the AIDS patients in New York City have survived at least five years, hinting at a less dire outlook for some victims. Page B1.

THE NEW YORK TIMES is available for home or office delivery...

"All the News That's Fit to Print"

The New York Times

Late Edition

New York: Today, partly sunny skies. High 48-58. Tonight, partly cloudy. Low 40-45. Tomorrow, variable clouds and sun, showers. High 50-55. Yesterday: High 48, low 32. Details, page C32.

VOL.CXXXVII...No. 47,348   Copyright © 1987 The New York Times   NEW YORK, WEDNESDAY, DECEMBER 9, 1987   50 cents beyond 75 miles from New York City, except on Long Island   30 CENTS

REAGAN AND GORBACHEV SIGN MISSILE TREATY AND VOW TO WORK FOR GREATER REDUCTIONS

A.B.A. Rates Kennedy

Judge Anthony M. Kennedy, the Supreme Court nominee, has received the American Bar Association's highest rating. Page A29.

Estimate of Risk Of Dioxin Is Cut In Cancer Study

By PHILIP SHABECOFF
Special to The New York Times

WASHINGTON, Dec. 8 — The Environmental Protection Agency, in a new draft study with the potential for far-reaching policy implications, has sharply reduced its estimate of the cancer-causing potential of dioxin, a widespread chemical pollutant.

Dioxin has been described as among the most potent toxic substances known to man. But in a new risk assessment, the E.P.A. concludes that dioxin's potency as a cancer-inducing substance is one-sixteenth that of the agency's original estimate two years ago.

Agency officials said, however, that even considering the revised risk levels, dioxin is still the most toxic of the cancer-linked substances regulated by the agency.

Under the new risk assumptions, dioxin is 10,000 times more likely to cause cancer than PCB's, or polychlorinated biphenyls, at the same level of exposure, one agency official said. But the new assessment lowers the risk of dioxin being in out or left field," the official said.

Since dioxin appears in such minute quantities, the effect of the reassessment might be that previously troubling levels will be considered far less dangerous or even safe. The new report appears to strike a compromise between those scientists who see the alarm over dioxin as exaggerated and

Continued on Page D27, Column 1

ECONOMY REPORTED HOLDING UP WELL SINCE STOCK SLIDE

A Recession Is Unlikely Soon, Analysts Say, Despite Slip in Consumer Spending

By ROBERT D. HERSHEY Jr.
Special to The New York Times

WASHINGTON, Dec. 8 — Defying widespread predictions, the economy has held up well since the stock market collapsed in mid-October and an imminent recession appears quite unlikely, private and Government analysts maintain.

Many forecasters who had initially slashed estimates for growth next year have been nudging them upward of late, prompted by successive sets of data indicating that the stock market tremors have yet to shake the economy's foundations.

These improved forecasts come despite consumer spending that slowed before the market plunge and seems to have lost further impetus since.

Spending Tied to Incomes

But while consumer spending has slowed, it has not dropped as sharply as many economists had feared. As best as economists can determine, people have apparently decided to base their spending on their incomes, not on their assets. And so their losses in the stock market have not dramatically affected their buying habits.

While the housing sector has been slumping, the decline in construction of new homes and sales of homes stems from the rising interest rates that preceded the stock market's collapse, and much of those increases have been reversed.

"I have zero evidence of an '88 early recession," said Joseph W. Duncan, chief economist for Dun & Bradstreet, who has just completed surveys of business expectations and production and investment plans. "Corporate America so far is saying, 'We're just going to move ahead because we have strong orders.' "

G.N.P. Loss 'Added Back'

An economist for a large New York bank said that, of a dozen economists with whom he lunched today, more than half had "added back" much or all of the loss of 1988 gross national product they had subtracted from their late-October G.N.P. estimates.

And in a survey last week, 51 economists polled by Blue Chip Economic Indicators, an Arizona-based newsletter,

Continued on Page D2, Column 5

HOW TO DESTROY THE 2,611 MISSILES

Treaty Details Ways but U.S. Withholds Data on Sites

By MICHAEL R. GORDON
Special to The New York Times

WASHINGTON, Dec. 8 — The text of the treaty signed today by President Reagan and Mikhail S. Gorbachev spells out how hundreds of American and Soviet inspectors will insure that 2,611 American and Soviet missiles are smashed, exploded, crushed, burned or launched to be destroyed.

But at American insistence, the text released today to the press and television does not include a 73-page annex that describes exactly where the weapons are kept.

American officials said that because of the danger from terrorists, the information was too sensitive to publish. Soviet officials, who have it, said that there was no reason why the information should be withheld and that it would be published in Moscow.

Rights of Inspectors

Under the treaty provisions, inspectors will have the right to visit installations on each side to confirm information provided by the other side. And when bases and support installations are eliminated, officials from each side will conduct special "close out" inspections. Inspectors will also observe the destruction of missiles.

Each side will have an annual quota of short-notice inspections for 13 years after the treaty goes into force.

Inspectors can make use of a camera that instantly produces two photographs, one for each side. The photos will be taken not by the inspectors but by escorts from the nation being inspected. But the escorts are to photograph what the inspectors want.

To carry out inspections in the Soviet Union, American officials will fly to Moscow or Irkutsk. Once there, they

Continued on Page A21, Column 1

A Tempered Optimism

At the End of an Unlikely Journey, Reagan And Gorbachev Are Mindful of Differences

By R. W. APPLE Jr.
Special to The New York Times

WASHINGTON, Dec. 8 — Even for this city, which long ago mislaid its sense of wonder, this was a thrilling day, bathed in a glow of satisfaction at what has been achieved and of optimism about what may lie just ahead.

News Analysis

Often Washington looks on the dark side, especially where the Soviet Union is concerned, but there were few in the capital who failed to feel a frisson of excitement as Mikhail S. Gorbachev stepped from his limousine and grasped Ronald Reagan's hand, few in the country who were immune to the drama of television pictures of the two leaders in profile with the red Soviet flag whipping in the wind behind them.

If, as Henry A. Kissinger once said, Americans oscillate between despair and euphoria in their attitudes toward the Soviet Union, today's emotions may be relatively short-lived. Certainly the hopes raised in June 1973, when Leonid I. Brezhnev was welcomed to the White House by Richard M. Nixon under steel-gray skies much like this morning's, proved ephemeral.

Both Mr. Reagan, with his call for "a heavy dose of realism," and Mr. Gorbachev, with his reminder of the "profound historical, ideological, socio-economic and cultural differences" that divide the superpowers, seemed to be warning of the limits of the process of accommodation they have begun.

But it is nonetheless remarkable that it has begun at all, and that these two men are those sponsoring it. For each, the moment at which they swapped pens after signing the treaty banning medium- and shorter-range nuclear arms represented the end of a long, im-

Continued on Page A20, Column 1

The Arms Treaty

The arms treaty and excerpts from the protocols to it are on pages A24-26. Additional coverage of yesterday's events, including remarks by President Reagan and Mikhail S. Gorbachev, appears on pages A20-23.

A MOOD OF WARMTH

As Summit Talks Begin, the Attention Shifts to Strategic Arms

By DAVID K. SHIPLER
Special to The New York Times

WASHINGTON, Dec. 8 — With fervent calls for a new era of peaceful understanding, President Reagan and Mikhail S. Gorbachev today signed the first treaty reducing the size of their nations' nuclear arsenals.

The President and the Soviet leader, beginning three days of talks aimed at even broader reductions, pledged to build on the accord by striving toward what Mr. Gorbachev called "the more important goal," reducing long-range nuclear weapons.

In their White House conversations, the leaders were said to have reviewed their previous proposals aimed at furthering those negotiations, and they established an arms-control working group of ranking officials to hold parallel sessions.

'Mine is Mikhail'

An immediate mood of warmth was established as the two leaders agreed this morning to call each other by their first names, a White House official said. He quoted the President as telling Mr. Gorbachev, "My first name is Ron."

Mr. Gorbachev answered, "Mine is Mikhail."

"When we're working in private session," Mr. Reagan reportedly said, "we can call each other that."

The new treaty, which provides for the dismantling of all Soviet and American medium- and shorter-range missiles, establishes the most extensive system of weapons inspection ever negotiated by the two countries, including placing technicians at sensitive sites on each other's territory.

The Mood for Talking

The signing, the fruition of years of negotiation, set the mood for two and a half hours of talks between the leaders. The talks were "very serious, substantive discussions," Secretary of State George P. Shultz said tonight before a formal dinner in the White House.

The visit to Washington by Mr. Gorbachev was the first by a Soviet leader since Leonid I. Brezhnev was here 14 years ago, and it took on immediate drama as Mr. Reagan, who entered office with deep suspicions of the Soviet Union, welcomed Mr. Gorbachev on the South Lawn of the White House.

"I have often felt that our people should have been better friends long ago," he told his guest as they stood

Continued on Page A20, Column 1

Air Crash Inquiry Is Said to Focus On Disgruntled Ex-Worker on Jet

By ROBERT REINHOLD
Special to The New York Times

TEMPLETON, Calif., Dec. 8 — The Federal Bureau of Investigation said today that criminal activity was strongly suspected in the crash of a jetliner that smashed into a cattle ranch here Monday after the pilot reported gunfire in the passenger cabin.

The crash killed all 43 people aboard the plane operated by Pacific Southwest Airlines, which last May was acquired by USAir.

Suspicion focused on a disgruntled former employee of USAir, dismissed last month on charges of stealing money from the company, who boarded the plane along with his former supervisor. The two men, together with all 36 other passengers and 5 crew members, died when the four-engine British Aerospace 146 Series 200 jet plunged into a green, oak-studded hillside near here in central California.

A Government official said he had been told that the employee, David A. Burke, had left a message on a friend's recording machine telling her that he was going to take care of the person who had dismissed him. But by the time she heard the message, the plane had crashed.

ABC News quoted unidentified officials as saying Mr. Burke left a suicide message indicating he intended to kill his former supervisor. The network said the authorities believed the former employee boarded the flight with a .44 magnum pistol.

Richard T. Bretzing, special agent in charge of the F.B.I.'s Los Angeles of-

Continued on Page D27, Column 3

The Emerging Candidate: Who Is Senator Simon?

By ROBIN TONER
Special to The New York Times

WASHINGTON, Dec. 8 — Senator Paul Simon of Illinois promises an administration of good deeds. He spins the vision of a nurturing Government.

If elected President, he says, he would give the unemployed an $8 billion-a-year job program. He would protect the elderly from the towering costs of nursing home care. The 11 books he has written bristle with Federal solutions to the nation's problems: a new program to rebuild the country's bridges and highways, a new Reconstruction Finance Corporation, a new drive to combat illiteracy.

"I want a Government that cares," he says. "I want a Government that helps people."

In a campaign dominated by

tests of character, Mr. Simon's test has arisen not in his personal life but around his public policy. The issue is the cost of his unquestioned good intentions, the practicality of a politician who often affects a disdain for politics, the credibility of a man whose slogan is, "Isn't it time to believe again?"

In the simplest terms, his rivals for the Democratic nomination now demand that he explain how he would pay for it all and balance the budget in three years, as he promises.

"Paul, you're not a pay-as-you-go Democrat, you're a promise-as-you-go Democrat," Representative Richard A. Gephardt declared last week in a nationally

Continued on Page A28, Column 1

Mr. Gorbachev applauding after he and Mr. Reagan signed copies of the treaty. At rear, staff members exchanged the copies so that each could be signed by the other leader.
The New York Times/Paul Hosefros

INSIDE

Sandinistas Down American
An American helicopter has been shot down over Nicaragua while "engaged in enemy activity," the Nicaraguan Defense Minister said. Page A3.

Reds Trade Dave Parker
The Cincinnati Reds traded Dave Parker, their aging but productive power hitter, to the Oakland Athletics for two young pitchers. Page A31.

Cardinal Krol to Retire
John Cardinal Krol, the Archbishop of Philadelphia, announced that he would retire on Feb. 11. Page A28.

The New York Times is available for home or office delivery in most major U.S. cities. Please call this toll-free number: 1-800. Out-of-town 1-800 APVT

$10 Million for Met Wing
Henry R. Kravis, a New York investor, has pledged $10 million to the Metropolitan Museum of Art to complete a new wing. Page C25.

Anti-Corruption Fund Asked
Top New York law-enforcement officials asked the Legislature for a $10 million fund to uncover corruption by officials and businesses. Page B1.

The New York Times

Late Edition

New York: Today, partly sunny and warmer. High 43-48. Tonight, clear and calm. Low 26-32. Tomorrow, sun then increasing clouds. High 45-50. Yesterday: High 43, low 29. Details, page C22.

VOL.CXXXVII.. No. 47,447   Copyright © 1988 The New York Times   NEW YORK, THURSDAY, MARCH 17, 1988   50 cents beyond 75 miles from New York City, except on Long Island.   30 CENTS

NORTH, POINDEXTER AND 2 OTHERS INDICTED ON IRAN-CONTRA FRAUD AND THEFT CHARGES

3 Killed by Grenades at I.R.A. Funeral

Mourners ducking for cover as grenades exploded at a burial service in Belfast, Northern Ireland.

Associated Press

U.S. TO SEND FORCE TO AID HONDURAS, CITING 'INCURSION'

White House Charges a Raid by the Nicaraguan Army — 3,200 Troops to Go

By STEVEN V. ROBERTS
Special to The New York Times

WASHINGTON, March 16 — President Reagan tonight ordered the deployment of four battalions of American troops, about 3,200 men, to Honduras as a sign of support for the Government there.

In announcing the move, Marlin Fitzwater, the President's spokesman, said Honduras had suffered a "significant cross-border incursion" by 1,500 to 2,000 Sandinista troops.

That contention is disputed by President Daniel Ortega of Nicaragua, who has invited international observers to view the border region. [Page A12.]

Troops Will Be Restricted

Mr. Fitzwater called the troop movement an "emergency deployment readiness exercise," and said the soldiers would not be sent "to any area of ongoing hostilities." The troops, from Fort Bragg, N.C., and Fort Ord, Calif., are to leave Thursday morning. They are to be confined to the area surrounding the Palmerola Air Base in Honduras, about 125 miles from the Nicaraguan border.

The spokesman said the troops represented "an important signal and a deterrence, just by being in the region." The President, he added, sees the American forces as "an important show of solidarity" with Honduras.

Mr. Fitzwater insisted that President José Azcona Hoyo of Honduras had requested the military assistance tonight after consultation with Everett Briggs, the American ambassador to Honduras. "We are responding to his request," the spokesman asserted.

Military officials said, however, that

Continued on Page A12, Column 1

Indicted

Lieut. Col. Oliver L. North

The New York Times/Paul A. Souders

Rear Adm. John M. Poindexter

The New York Times

The Prosecutor

Lawrence E. Walsh

Agence France-Presse

23 COUNTS DETAILED

Arms Middlemen Named — Walsh Acts After 14-Month Inquiry

By PHILIP SHENON
Special to The New York Times

WASHINGTON, March 16 — Lieut. Col. Oliver L. North, Rear Adm. John M. Poindexter and two other key participants in the Iran-contra affair were indicted today on charges of conspiracy to defraud the United States by illegally providing the Nicaraguan rebels with profits from the sale of American weapons to Iran.

The indictment was the most sweeping criminal action against former White House officials since the Watergate scandals, and presented to President Reagan the politically delicate issue of whether he should pardon his former aides before his term ends next January.

The long-awaited indictment, following a 14-month grand jury investigation, named Colonel North, who was a member of the National Security Council staff, and Admiral Poindexter, President Reagan's former national security adviser. It also named two middlemen in the arms transfer — Richard V. Secord, a retired Air Force major general, and Albert A. Hakim, an Iranian-American businessman.

'Exploiting for Own Purposes'

All four were accused in the 23-count indictment of stealing money belonging to the Government — proceeds from the arms sales to Iran in 1985 and 1986 — and transfering a portion of the money to rebel groups, known as the contras, battling the Sandinista Government of Nicaragua.

They also were accused of wire fraud — using telephones or other wire communications to further their scheme.

The four have repeatedly denied wrongdoing, arguing their actions in the Iran-contra affair were motivated strictly by patriotism.

Money Involved Not Specified

According to the indictment the defendants, as part of what prosecutors described as the central conspiracy, defrauded the Government by "deceitfully exploiting for their own purposes" the Iran-contra initiative, "rather than pursuing solely the specified governmental objectives of the initiative, including the release of Americans being held hostage in Lebanon." [Excerpts from indictment, page D26.]

Today's indictment did not specify how much money may have been stolen. It said the arms sales to Iran generated about $30 million, of which the United States Government was paid $12 million.

Each of the defendants faces a different set of charges, and they could all go to prison for decades under the indictment. Law-enforcement officials said it

Continued on Page D27, Column 1

Reagan Vetoes Bill That Would Widen Federal Rights Law

By JULIE JOHNSON
Special to The New York Times

WASHINGTON, March 16 — President Reagan disregarded warnings of a political backlash from Republican Congressional leaders today and vetoed a major civil rights bill.

The measure, which would expand the reach of Federal anti-discrimination laws that the Supreme Court had limited in 1984, was passed by both houses of Congress with more than enough votes to override a veto, and Senate leaders planned to call the bill up Thursday.

But Mr. Reagan offered an alternative that he said would "protect civil rights and at the same time preserve the independence of state and local governments, the freedom of religion and the right of America's citizens to order their lives and businesses without extensive Federal intrusion."

The President said Congress "has sent me a bill that would vastly and unjustifiably expand the power of the Federal Government over the decisions and actions of private organizations, such as churches and state and local governments," adding, "In the process, it would place at risk such cherished values as religious liberty."

The bill the President vetoed was intended to overturn the effects of a Supreme Court decision involving Grove City College in Pennsylvania. The

Continued on Page A14, Column 1

CONSUMER OUTLAYS SPURRING ECONOMY

Rebound From October Crash Surprises Many Analysts

By PETER T. KILBORN
Special to The New York Times

WASHINGTON, March 16 — The latest reports on jobs, consumer debt, production and the like are convincing many economists that the economy is a lot stronger these days than they were predicting just a few weeks ago. Today's announcement of an 8.9 percent jump in home construction last month is further evidence of the economy's surprising resilience.

The reason seems to be a consumer livelier than economists expected, particularly after the October rout of the stock market. Even without the rout, however, this was to have been a period when consumer spending, which had been pulling the economy through most of the last five years, would run out of steam.

The Earlier Assumption

The assumption had been that consumers would pass the baton to industry, which would sell more of its goods abroad, thanks to the cheaper dollar, and build more factories at home. During this first-quarter transition, the economy would slow down considerably and perhaps even slip into a recession.

But after pinching pennies for a month or two after the market's plunge, consumers are stepping up their spending again. They are still a lot more restrained than they were in recent years, but with industry pulling the weight expected of it, firmer consumer spending augurs a more robust economy than most forecasts showed. There is more talk now of inflation, the price the economy sometimes pays for strong growth, than of recession.

Right after the market collapsed, about half the members of the economics community revised their forecasts for the first quarter of this year from

Continued on Page D24, Column 1

INSIDE

College Credits for Police

Two or more years of college will be required for members of the New York City force seeking promotion to sergeant, lieutenant or captain, Commissioner Benjamin Ward said. Supervisors now holding such posts will keep them, however. Page B1.

Reagan Firm on Mideast

After meeting with Prime Minister Yitzhak Shamir of Israel, President Reagan pledged to pursue his Middle East negotiating plan. Page A3.

Rogue Software Is Loose

A program that can secretly spread from computer to computer and destroy data has been found in commercial software. Page D1.

Prado Gains Collection

The Prado Museum in Madrid has been chosen to house several hundred pieces of the Thyssen-Bornemisza art collection. Page C23.

Gunman Terrorizes Belfast Crowd Gathered at Rites for 3 Guerrillas

By FRANCIS X. CLINES
Special to The New York Times

BELFAST, Northern Ireland, March 16 — Three people were killed and dozens wounded today as an assailant threw grenades into a screaming crowd at a funeral and then fled across the graveyard from enraged mourners.

Panic broke out and grieving families dived for cover by the mud of the open grave as four grenades exploded amid thousands of mourners gathered for the burial of three Irish Republican Army guerrillas. The guerrillas, unarmed but on a bombing mission, were slain March 6 by British undercover agents in Gibraltar.

"Kill the bastard!" came cries from the crowd as dozens of mourners ignored the gunshots fired by the retreating assailant and chased him a quarter mile to an adjacent expressway.

Crowd Is Stunned

Families, clergy members, pallbearers and grave diggers watched stunned on the cemetery hill as the wounded mourners, who had been saying the rosary moments before, staggered bleeding among the headstones.

The collective screams of shock and panic soon changed to cheers when the crowd of more than 5,000 saw the blue-coated invader finally collared and pummelled after he coolly turned and threw the last of his grenades and fired bullets at furious pursuers.

"We beat him unmercifully," said George McMurray after racing down the hill toward the gunman, who was widely suspected of being on a terrorist mission for one of the paramilitary Protestant gangs. The gunman was rescued and arrested by officers of the Royal Ulster Constabulary.

Beyond the three dead men, four mourners were listed as seriously

The gunman firing at pursuers.

Agence France-Presse

wounded among the dozen who were hospitalized. More than 30 others were treated and released, according to the hospital.

The attack on the eve of St. Patrick's Day in Milltown Cemetery pushed this city toward a fresh cycle of the sectarian vendetta and street violence that has marked the last two decades of Northern Irish life. Cars were hijacked and set afire by youths as anger built at nightfall in the heavily policed ghettos

Continued on Page A6, Column 3

Noriega Foils Coup Attempt; Civilians Take to the Streets

By LARRY ROHTER
Special to The New York Times

PANAMA, March 16 — An attempt to overthrow Gen. Manuel Antonio Noriega failed here today, but it was followed by widespread civil disorders across Panama.

The uprising, which was marked by sharp exchanges of gunfire at military headquarters, was led by Col. Leónidas Macias, the chief of police, the Government said later.

General Noriega, the country's military leader, was apparently unhurt in the incident and later appeared on the doorstep of military headquarters to speak briefly to reporters.

No figure on the number of officers and men arrested in the coup attempt was given, and no mention was made of any casualties. But residents of the area around military headquarters said they had seen wounded soldiers being removed from the command building, which houses General Noriega's main office.

Senior United States officials in Washington said that the coup attempt demonstrated a deepening division within Panama's armed forces and police, but that they were uncertain whether it would weaken General Noriega's hold on power. [Page A6.]

The disturbances at military headquarters followed two days of demonstrations by doctors, teachers, dock workers and other Government employees protesting the Government's inability to pay them. The cash shortage stems from moves to block the Noriega Government from access to some $50 million in deposits in American banks.

A Display of Force

The United States has applied other economic sanctions as well in an effort to force the ouster of General Noriega, who is under indictment by two Federal grand juries in Florida on drug-trafficking and racketeering charges.

Rumors that the coup attempt had succeeded sent thousands of Panamanians into the streets of the capital this morning. They erected barricades, set cars, garbage dumpsters and tires on fire, brought traffic and commerce to a standstill and burned some buildings, including a military checkpoint.

But by midafternoon the military forces were back in action, firing shotguns and tear and pepper gas in a huge show of force as they sped down the palm-lined boulevards of the capital. Paramilitary squads in civilian clothes also took to the streets, firing shotguns and pistols at knots of confused civilians who had gathered on street corners to await the outcome of events.

"This morning, an attempt by some officers to seize and control the general headquarters of our institution was

Continued on Page A6, Column 4

Bush vs. Dole: Behind the Turnaround

This article was reported by Gerald M. Boyd, E. J. Dionne Jr. and Bernard Weinraub and was written by Mr. Dionne.

History is written by the victors, and that is true even of political campaigns not yet concluded. In retrospect, the winning side's decisions invariably appear brilliant, and losers almost always look foolish.

And so it is now with the battle between Vice President Bush and Senator Bob Dole for the Republican Presidential nomination. A Bush victory is now spoken of as the inevitable product of a long-term battle plan that worked out exactly as it was supposed to. All the organizing that Bush campaign did in 1986 and 1987, discounted at the time by some, is now seen as critical to his victory.

'Firewall' in the South

And after Mr. Bush's sweep of Southern primaries on March 8, nothing looks more brilliant than having set up the South as a "firewall" against possible early defeats.

Mr. Dole, once the hero of the political circuit and even at times described as the inevitable nominee, is

spoken of now in almost contemptuous terms, especially as he vows to continue his quest against impossible odds. His campaign, it is now clear, was marked by blunders, internal rivalries, and the unpredictable personality of a candidate who switched signals and traveling plans with abandon. Mr. Dole, the argument goes, failed to appoint a single, dominant campaign manager and allowed his organization to go on a 1987 spending binge that left the cupboard bare when it came time for television commercials on Super Tuesday.

George Bush's success in transforming himself from a loser to an almost certain winner in just 29 days is one of the remarkable political stories of recent American political history. It is also the lucky consequence of facing

off against a foe, Mr. Dole, who at crucial moments seemed to do everything wrong.

What follows is an account of the rise of Mr. Bush and the fall of Mr. Dole, based on interviews with top officials and former officials of both campaigns and other Republican political professionals.

Staff, Organization, Planning

Mr. Bush won in large part because he had a better staff, a keener sense of organization and a more prescient long-term plan.

But in politics, one brilliant last-minute decision can make up for months of bad ones and a key strategic miss can leave even the best organization in chaos.

Thus amid the praise that Mr. Bush's campaign manager, Lee Atwater, receives now, what is not mentioned is that Mr. Bush, according to several aides, was prepared to dismiss or demote him if Mr. Dole won the New Hampshire primary.

And Mr. Dole, in the meantime, had many opportunities in the last month to turn the race around.

In New Hampshire, many of his allies believe he could have won if he

Continued on Page B7, Column 1

DARLING GEORGE, MAY ALL YOUR BIRTHDAYS be green. Love, your Cheri.—ADVT.

0 354743 11

"All the News That's Fit to Print"

The New York Times

Late Edition

New York: Today, partly sunny, breezy. High 63-69 inland, 50-55 coast. Tonight, showers late. Low 44-51. Tomorrow, showers likely. High 60-65. Yesterday: High 76, low 46. Details on page B16.

VOL.CXXXVII... No. 47,455   Copyright © 1988 The New York Times   NEW YORK, FRIDAY, MARCH 25, 1988   50 cents beyond 75 miles from New York City, except on Long Island.   30 CENTS

An unidentified New York City restaurant inspector in F.B.I. custody yesterday after his arrest.
Associated Press

INSPECTORS SEIZED IN WIDE EXTORTION FROM RESTAURANTS

28 CHARGED IN NEW YORK

Health Code Threats Against 300 Establishments Cited — Visits Suspended

By SELWYN RAAB

Twenty-eight current and former New York City health inspectors and supervisors were charged yesterday with extorting hundreds of thousands of dollars from restaurants by threatening to close them or cite them for sanitation violations.

More than 300 restaurants were forced to make payoffs ranging from $50 to $1,400 in a systematic corruption scheme by Health Department employees that authorities said dated back at least to the early 1980's.

The head of the Federal Bureau of Investigation in the city, James M. Fox, said the payoffs had doubled the incomes of most of the inspectors and allowed several of them to lead "lavish life styles."

Cadillacs and Rolexes

"Some restaurant owners dreaded to see them coming, driving up in Cadillacs and wearing Rolex watches," Mr. Fox said in announcing the filing of the Federal charges. In a single day, a team of two inspectors obtained $3,000 of payoffs from six restaurants, Mr. Fox asserted.

Andrew J. Maloney, the United States Attorney in Brooklyn, said the evidence suggested that usually the inspectors, rather than overlook unsanitary conditions, had threatened to cite restaurants falsely for nonexistent violations unless payments were made. Mr. Maloney said restaurateurs "dreaded" financial losses if cited for health code irregularities in a weekly list that was issued by the Health Department and published in newspapers.

The department said routine inspections of restaurants would be suspended, except for emergencies, until at least next week.

The New York Times, The Daily News and New York Newsday said yesterday that they would not print the current list of health code violations. [Page B6.]

Law-enforcement officials declined

Continued on Page B6, Column 1

SANDINISTA-CONTRA CEASE-FIRE OPENS WAY TO A DURABLE PEACE, RIVAL NICARAGUAN FACTIONS SAY

Adolfo Calero, a contra leader, signing peace accord. Others included Defense Minister Humberto Ortega Saavedra, left, President Daniel Ortega Saavedra, third from left, and Miguel Cardinal Obando y Bravo.
The New York Times/Samuel L. Barreto

Reversal on 'Star Wars'

U.S. Adopts Moscow's View That the Issue Cannot Be Ignored in Strategic Arms Talks

By MICHAEL R. GORDON
Special to The New York Times

WASHINGTON, March 24 — The United States is taking a new approach to strategic arms talks that stems from a worry that a new treaty could otherwise be a disturbing source of misunderstanding.

News Analysis The new policy, disclosed by Secretary of State George P. Shultz on Wednesday night, is that the United States will try to negotiate a strategic arms pact and resolve the issue of space-based missile testing at the same time.

For years, the United States stressed the need to complete a strategic arms treaty even if the two sides couldn't resolve their differences over the development of the space-based missile defenses popularly known as "Star Wars." Moscow, in contrast, insisted the two issues had to be linked.

Under the latest American position, which has evolved over several years, the two sides finally agree on a basic negotiating approach, even though they remain far apart on what kind of testing and development of new anti-missile systems should be allowed.

'Predictability About Defenses'

Mr. Shultz, disclosing the new American position Wednesday after three days of meetings with Eduard A. Shevardnadze, the Soviet Foreign Minister, said: "I think that if we are going to have the kind of massive reductions in offensive arms that would be brought about by the strategic arms agreement, then we are as interested as they are in having predictability about defenses."

Asked if the two sides could conclude a strategic arms treaty while postponing a resolution of their differences over space defenses, Mr. Shultz said, "No, I don't think so." Last December, during the summit meeting in Washington, the American position was that the two sides had agreed to disagree over the issue while the negotiations on strategic arms moved ahead.

On Wednesday night, Mr. Shultz said that the two agreements in the two areas should be "completed more or less at the same time so the two things move in parallel."

The latest American approach

Continued on Page A11, Column 1

AT WHITE HOUSE, SOME 'DISCOMFORT'

Concern That the Rebels May Have Given Up Too Much

By JULIE JOHNSON
Special to The New York Times

WASHINGTON, March 24 — The Reagan Administration, caught by surprise by the terms of the cease-fire accord reached by the contras and Sandinistas, reacted ambivalently today.

Although Secretary of State George P. Shultz called the accord an important step forward, the White House pointedly declined to describe it as a positive development. In part this reflected concern in the Administration that the contras may have given up too much by agreeing to receive no more arms aid, thereby making moot the Administration's crusade for a renewal of such support for them.

U.S. Upset Over Terms

Lieut. Gen. Colin L. Powell, the President's national security adviser, told officials at a White House meeting today that he had been unaware that contras were about to sign such an accord.

"There is discomfort over what the contras are apparently agreeing to," said a senior Administration official who was at the meeting.

He noted that the contra leadership had also indicated feelings of being "sold out" in the United States and added, "That is why they are making these kinds of agreements."

The Administration is concerned about the accord's provision that all

Continued on Page A8, Column 5

TWO-MONTH TRUCE

Government to Release Prisoners in Steps — Exiles Can Return

By STEPHEN KINZER
Special to The New York Times

MANAGUA, Nicaragua, March 24 — Having recognized each other as authentic political forces for the first time, Government officials and contra leaders said today that the cease-fire agreement they signed Wednesday night held out the promise of a durable political settlement.

Under the agreement, the truce that was declared at the start of the talks on Monday will extend through May. During that time, contra leaders will meet with officials of the Sandinista Government here to discuss steps necessary to permanently end the six-year-old war.

The Government agreed that anti-Sandinista prisoners — those accused of contra activities and former members of the National Guard under the deposed Somoza family dictatorship — would be released in groups as the peace process advances, with the first 100 to be freed Sunday. The Sandinistas say there are 3,300 such prisoners.

Free Expression Guaranteed

The cases of former guardsmen are to be reviewed by the Inter-American Human Rights Court, which is part of the Organization of American States.

The Sandinistas also pledged to permit "unrestricted freedom of expression," and guaranteed that all exiles could return without fear of punishment for their "political-military activities." [Text of accord, page A8.]

In return, the contras agreed to recognize Sandinista rule and the legitimacy of President Daniel Ortega Saavedra. The contras embarked on a process aimed ultimately at disarming themselves and allowing them to return to a different and freer Nicaragua, although they will not be required to lay down their weapons until a final peace agreement is reached.

No Aid From the U.S.

The contras promised not to accept military aid from anyone, and to receive "humanitarian" aid — a term used in the agreement — only through "neutral organizations." This provision forbids them from receiving any form of direct aid from the United States.

If the plan succeeds, it would mark

Continued on Page A8, Column 1

Wedtech Figure Testifies He Hid Aid to D'Amato

By LYDIA CHAVEZ

A former Wedtech Corporation executive testified yesterday that he gave Senator Alfonse M. D'Amato more than $30,000 in illegal campaign contributions while the Senator was helping Wedtech win Government contracts.

But the witness, Mario Moreno, said that although he had hidden the contributions under different names, he did not feel he had bribed the Senator or been extorted by him. Mr. Moreno also testified that he saw nothing wrong in what Mr. D'Amato did for Wedtech.

Mr. D'Amato, a New York Republican, said through a spokesman that the allegations were "ridiculous."

Cooperating With Government

"We have absolutely no knowledge of any secret contributions," the spokesman, Edward Martin, said.

Mr. Moreno, Wedtech's former vice chairman, is cooperating with the Government in exchange for leniency. He testified yesterday under cross-examination by Maurice Nessen, the lawyer for the former Bronx Borough President, Stanley Simon.

Seven defendants, including Mr. Simon and Representative Mario Biaggi, Democrat of the Bronx, are on trial on charges of turning Wedtech, a Bronx military contractor, into a racketeering enterprise that used millions of dollars in bribes to get Government contracts set aside for minority-owned companies.

Mr. D'Amato intervened repeatedly with the Army, the Navy and the Small Business Administration in behalf of Wedtech in its efforts to win Government contracts, but there is no evidence that he received any personal

Continued on Page B4, Column 4

Democrats Close In On Bush Nationally, Latest Survey Shows

By E. J. DIONNE Jr.

After months of having their Presidential candidates regarded as inferior to Republican counterparts, the Democrats have emerged as highly competitive with the Republicans in the 1988 Presidential election, the latest New York Times/CBS News Poll shows.

The survey shows that about a fifth of the voters who said they had voted for President Reagan in 1984 now expect to vote for a Democrat. The Democrats also keep almost all their 1984 voters, and the result is that the two parties are just about even nationally.

Gov. Michael S. Dukakis of Massachusetts now leads the Democratic field, and the Rev. Jesse Jackson is his only close competitor. Mr. Jackson has improved his image among Democrats in general and whites in particular.

Bush Achieves Dominance

Vice President Bush, in the meantime, has translated his string of primary victories into overwhelming dominance in the Republican Party. Among likely Republican primary voters, he now leads Senator Bob Dole of Kansas by 63 percent to 20 percent.

The poll of 1,654 adults, 1,271 of whom said they were registered voters, found that when Mr. Bush and Mr. Dukakis were matched in a hypothetical election, the result was a virtual tie among the registered voters: Mr. Bush had 46 percent, Mr. Dukakis 45. The poll had a margin of sampling error of plus or minus 3 percentage points.

Mr. Bush enjoys a clear lead when he is matched against Mr. Jackson or Senator Albert Gore Jr. of Tennessee. But when the registered voters are asked — without any candidate's name being mentioned — which party's Presidential candidate they would

Continued on Page B8, Column 1

The New York Times/Jose R. Lopez

Iran-Contra Principals Plead Not Guilty

Rear Adm. John M. Poindexter, right, leaving court yesterday with his wife, Linda, and lawyer, Richard Beckler, after he was arraigned along with Lieut. Col. Oliver L. North and two arms dealers. Page A12.

U.S. Demand on Afghan Arms Aid Seen as Last Big Obstacle to Pact

By DAVID K. SHIPLER
Special to The New York Times

WASHINGTON, March 24 — The disagreement between the United States and the Soviet Union over the Reagan Administration's demand for a halt in Soviet weapon supplies to the Afghan Government has emerged as the only important obstacle to an accord on a Soviet troop withdrawal, American officials and Asian diplomats said today.

The other major problem was resolved because Pakistan has dropped its insistence that a transitional coalition government be established in Kabul before the withdrawal agreement is signed.

Instead, Pakistan is apparently ready to sign if the pro-Soviet Afghan Government commits itself to promoting the formation of an interim government, the officials said.

The American demand for a cutoff in Soviet military aid was recently added to conditions that Washington wants met before ending its military supplies to the Afghan guerrillas.

[In Geneva, officials said there was little chance the current talks on Afghanistan would produce a peace accord due to the aid dispute.]

In talks this week in Washington, the Soviet Foreign Minister, Eduard A. Shevardnadze, Secretary of State George P. Shultz proposed a moratorium in aid from both sides for three months longer than the time it takes the Soviet troops to leave, American officials said. Under the current plan for a nine-month withdrawal, the

Continued on Page A10, Column 1

Du Pont to Halt Chemicals That Peril Ozone

By PHILIP SHABECOFF
Special to The New York Times

WASHINGTON, March 24 — E.I. du Pont de Nemours & Company, the world's largest producer of chlorofluorocarbons, announced plans today to phase out all production of the chemicals that scientists say are contributing to the destruction of the earth's ozone shield.

While the company refused to set a target date for ending production of the chemicals, Joseph M. Steed, environmental manager of Du Pont's Freon products division, said that reducing output by at least 95 percent by the beginning of the next century is a "reasonable goal."

An International Agreement

Du Pont's action indicated a readiness to surpass the goals of an international agreement reached in Montreal last fall calling for an initial freeze on production levels and then a 50 percent reduction in their use by the end of the century.

The company's decision is bound to have wide influence because Du Pont

The company said it was taking the action, which would go well beyond its previous commitment only to reduce output of the chemicals, because of new scientific evidence that the threat to the atmospheric ozone layer was worse than had been thought.

accounts for about 25 percent of the world's production of chlorofluorocarbons, or CFC's. The chemicals, which are widely used in refrigerants, foam insulation and cleaning solvents, among other products, are believed to combine with and destroy ozone molecules in the upper atmosphere.

The ozone shield blocks harmful ultraviolet rays from the sun that can cause skin cancer in humans, damage plants and harm animals.

Du Pont urged today that more countries quickly ratify the Montreal protocol. It also called for immediate reassessment of the problem and consider-

Continued on Page A20, Column 1

INSIDE

New Life for Ancient Turtle
After hundreds of years perched above the Bronx River, an Indian petroglyph of a turtle is rediscovered. A drawing of it has been outlined to make it more visible. Page B1.

A New Terror in Punjab
Sikh militants are attacking entire Sikh families who will not cooperate with the separatist campaign. Page A10.

A Troubled Savings Industry
A third of the nation's savings and loan associations lost money last year, giving the industry a record $6.8 billion net loss. Page D1.

THE NEW YORK TIMES is available for home or office delivery in most major U.S. cities. Please call this toll-free number: 1-800-631-2500. ADVT.

FOR THOSE FAVORING CREMATION WOODLAWN Cemetery offers a free pamphlet giving complete information. Call 212-920-0500.—ADVT.

The New York Times

VOL.CXXXVII .. No. 47,469   Copyright © 1988 The New York Times   NEW YORK, FRIDAY, APRIL 8, 1988   50 cents beyond 75 miles from New York City, except on Long Island.   30 CENTS

Late Edition

New York: Today, rain and fog. High 44-48. Tonight, rain ending. Low 37-40. Tomorrow, clouds, fog, afternoon clearing. High 47-52. Yesterday: High 45, low 41. Details are on page A19.

The New York Times/David Jennings
Governor Cuomo yesterday.

MAJOR DEMOCRATS IN NEW YORK STATE BACKING DUKAKIS

AN INITIATIVE BY CUOMO

Urging Leaders to Choose, He Remains Neutral to Avoid Anger in Jackson Camp

By FRANK LYNN

Governor Cuomo yesterday urged top New York Democrats to choose a Presidential candidate to support, and, as he expected, most of them started lining up behind Gov. Michael S. Dukakis of Massachusetts.

The move, orchestrated through the Democratic state chairman, Laurence J. Kirwan, allowed the Governor to bow to the preference of most of the state's Democratic leaders. At the same time, it permitted him to maintain his own public neutrality and thus not offend New York supporters of the Rev. Jesse Jackson, with whom Mr. Cuomo will have to deal long after 255 delegates to the Democratic National Convention are picked in the state's Presidential primary April 19.

"The Dukakis campaign people have been complaining that they can't get anywhere in the state with the Governor hanging back," said a leading Democrat.

Dukakis a Clear Choice

He added, "They asked the Governor that if he did not endorse Dukakis, to at least release the Democratic leaders on the ground that Dukakis had played the Cuomo game, showing him respect and deference."

Mr. Cuomo gave no personal signal of his own preference, party officials said. But he was aware that Governor Dukakis was the clear favorite among county leaders, legislators and other public officials who make up the state's Democratic leadership, particularly after the sweeping Dukakis victory in the Wisconsin primary last Tuesday.

So he knew what to expect when Mr. Kirwan, saying that he was speaking for the Governor, urged the leaders yesterday to choose one of the party's three remaining active Presidential candidates: Mr. Dukakis, Mr. Jackson or Senator Albert Gore Jr. of Tennessee.

'I Want You to Pick'

Addressing about half of the 300-member Democratic State Committee at the New York Hilton in Manhattan yesterday afternoon, Mr. Kirwan said, "The Governor now feels that there are three candidates in this race, and 'I want you to pick one of the three.'"

The first party leader to take the advice was Joseph F. Crangle, the Erie

Continued on Page A18, Column 4

Hondurans Riot At U.S. Offices; Four Said to Die

By Reuters

TEGUCIGALPA, Honduras, Friday, April 8 — The United States Consulate was set afire Thursday night and at least four people were killed during a riot sparked by the expulsion of a suspected drug dealer to the United States, radio stations reported.

Witnesses said shots were fired from inside the consulate building and protesters responded with pistol fire. At least 4 students died and at least 2 were wounded as the crowd of 1,500 protesters scattered in panic, radio stations said. It was not clear who fired from inside the building.

The third floor of the consulate was reported burning fiercely and part of the outside of the main United States Embassy building across the street was also ablaze as firefighters arrived. Power was cut off, blacking out street lights and adding to the confusion as the shooting started, reports said.

20 Cars on Fire

The shots came after the protesters had set fire to part of the embassy, hurling rocks and flaming sticks, and had broken into the consulate building. At least 20 cars belonging to embassy personnel were burning in the street.

About 200 anti-riot officers and firefighters moved in to quell the violence, which was being called the worst anti-American riot ever in Honduras, traditionally a close American ally.

[The Associated Press quoted an embassy spokesman, Michael O'Brien, as saying that there was extensive damage to embassy buildings but that no American citizens had been injured. He said the Hondu-

Continued on Page A9, Column 1

Authorities Debate Increased Firepower For Narcotics Agents

By PETER KERR

A rise in the use of machine pistols by drug dealers in New York — and a decision to issue submachine guns this month to 300 Federal drug agents in the region — has officials arguing about the safest way to arm agents and the police in the densely populated city.

The growth of violent crack-dealing organizations in New York in the last two years has brought a new class of powerful handguns into general use in the underworld in the city, Federal officials said. The weapons hold 20 or more rounds and can be easily converted into machine guns that fire bursts of bullets with each pull of the trigger.

Crack organizations in Brooklyn and Queens are sending couriers, often by bus, to buy the guns in Texas, Georgia and Alabama, where firearms laws are more lax, according to the New York office of the Federal Bureau of Alcohol, Tobacco and Firearms.

Automatic weapons have been used by drug organizations in Florida and elsewhere in the country since the early 1980's. Drug dealers in New York have generally used cheaper less-powerful weapons, until recently.

The latest example of the danger posed by criminals armed with such weapons occurred Tuesday night, the police said, when four men sprayed a crowded Brooklyn intersection with

Continued on Page B5, Column 4

One Week of Killings

New York City police recorded 17 deaths by violence last week. Behind each police report is the story of a life. Page B1.

GORBACHEV AND AFGHAN LEADER SAY WAY SEEMS CLEAR TO START SOVIET TROOP PULLOUT BY MAY 15

Tass via Agence France-Presse
Najibullah, left, the Afghan leader, and Mikhail S. Gorbachev at meeting in Tashkent, U.S.S.R.

Tokyo's Surging Stock Prices Top Record Set Before October Crash

By SUSAN CHIRA
Special to The New York Times

TOKYO, Friday, April 8 — Prices on the Tokyo stock market continued today to rise above the peak reached before last fall's global market collapse. No other major stock market has returned to its pre-crash levels.

Yesterday, the Nikkei average of 225 stocks closed at 26,769.22 yen, well above the previous record of 26,646.43 yen reached on Oct. 14, five days before share prices around the world collapsed. That increase was 258.05 yen, or 97-hundredths of 1 percent. In trading today the Nikkei had risen another 141.68 yen, to 26,910.90, by the close of the morning session.

The surge in prices demonstrates the underlying strength in the Tokyo Stock Exchange, the world's largest in terms of money invested. While the Tokyo market has now exceeded pre-crash levels, the New York and London markets have posted comparatively modest advances and are well below their record levels.

[In a move to bolster investor confidence in the market, the New York Stock Exchange proposed a sharp increase in the level of capital required for specialist brokers to buy or sell stocks. Page D1.]

High corporate profits, low interest rates, continuing economic growth, and Government actions to prevent any drastic fall in stock prices have driven the Tokyo market's rebound, analysts here said.

Fears of Overheating

Some Japanese officials, notably Satoshi Sumita, governor of the Bank of Japan, have expressed fears that the Tokyo market could be overheating. Mr. Sumita told reporters yesterday that share prices were rising too fast in relation to the rate of economic growth.

Other analysts point out that any panic in other stock markets might spread to Tokyo, given the degree to

Continued on Page D6, Column 1

ACCORD INDICATED ON STABLE DOLLAR

Officials Expect Action When 7 Nations Meet Next Week

By PETER T. KILBORN
Special to The New York Times

WASHINGTON, April 7 — American and foreign officials indicated today that they expect the United States and six other leading industrial nations to agree next week to try to keep the dollar's value roughly at its current level for the foreseeable future.

The officials thus confirmed speculation in the financial markets that after a couple of weeks of currency turbulence the countries want a steady dollar and will do what they can to keep it steady. Some economists have suggested that the dollar, which closed today at 125.72 Japanese yen, should decline some more.

The officials also said the countries, known as the Group of Seven, could report some progress on a proposal by Treasury Secretary James A. Baker 3d to use prices of gold and other commodities in guiding their economic policies. But they said that while Mr. Baker favors the immediate adoption of such a price index in making Group of Seven policy, other nations could urge delay.

The anticipation by market traders of a renewed commitment to a stable

Continued on Page D2, Column 1

GENEVA PACT SEEN

Acceptance of U.S. Plan on Arms Aid Indicated in Joint Statement

By PHILIP TAUBMAN
Special to The New York Times

MOSCOW, April 7 — The Soviet Union and Afghanistan said today that they believed the last barriers to a negotiated settlement of the war in Afghanistan had been eliminated.

The two Governments indicated, but did not explicitly confirm, that they had accepted an American formula breaking the last remaining deadlock at the Geneva talks aimed at ending the eight-year-old war.

The compromise would permit Washington to continue providing military aid to the Afghan guerrillas during a withdrawal of Soviet forces at a level commensurate with the aid Moscow gives to the Afghan Government.

Signing Likely Next Week

Western diplomats here said the announcement appeared to clear the way for quick completion of the Geneva talks, with the signing of an agreement likely before the end of next week.

In Washington, Reagan Administration officials voiced cautious optimism that a settlement would soon be formally concluded and lead to a Soviet withdrawal. But they also said they were reserving final judgment until the United States received a formal response from the Soviet Union and reviewed the detailed Geneva accords. [Page A10.]

In a joint statement issued after a meeting today, Mikhail S. Gorbachev and the Afghan leader, Najibullah, said the Soviet Union would begin withdrawing its troops on May 15 if the Geneva accords were completed within the next few days. [Text of statement, page A10.]

Reagan Visit Seen as Factor

The departure date, originally set by Moscow for early February but postponed as the negotiations bogged down, suggested that Mr. Gorbachev wanted to start bringing Soviet soldiers home before President Reagan's visit to Moscow in late May.

Mr. Gorbachev and Mr. Najibullah met in the Soviet Central Asian city of Tashkent, 190 miles north of the Afghan border.

Mr. Gorbachev later told workers at two collective farms near Tashkent: "There is a certainty that an agreement will be signed on a political settlement. I think that Pakistan and Afghanistan will come to an agreement. And we with the Americans will agree to be guarantors, I think."

Resolution of the Afghan conflict, which Soviet forces entered in Decem-

Continued on Page A10, Column 3

Guard's Bullet Reportedly Struck Israeli Girl Killed on West Bank

By JOHN KIFNER
Special to The New York Times

ELON MOREH, Israeli-Occupied West Bank, April 7 — As angry, armed Jewish settlers turned the funeral here for a teen-age girl into a passionate rally, an army investigation was reported today to have found a bullet from an Israeli guard's rifle in the victim's body.

The report raised questions about the emotionally charged reports on Wednesday that the 15-year-old girl, Tirza Porat, had been stoned to death by Palestinian villagers. Army spokesmen said late tonight that it was not clear what had caused the girl's death and that an investigation was under way.

Israeli soldiers shot and killed a Palestinian youth outside the village of Beita today as they searched the hills surrounding the site where Wednesday's confrontation took place. The army said the unidentified youth was a suspect who was trying to flee. There was no independent confirmation of this report, and the death raised the number of Palestinians known to have been killed in four months of protest here to 123.

The army also blew up five houses in the sealed-off village, saying they were the homes of people known to have

taken part in the clash on Wednesday.

Palestinian accounts of the events in Beita were not immediately available because the village and the surrounding area were sealed off by the army. The military order to shut the Palestine Press Service, which maintained a

Continued on Page A3, Column 1

INSIDE

Eggs Linked to Illness

Clean, inspected Grade A eggs may be responsible for an increase in food poisoning in the Northeast, Federal researchers say. Page A16.

Speakes Roils the Capital

Larry Speakes, President Reagan's ex-spokesman, depicts him in a new book as inspiring but uninformed. Washington Talk, page A20.

[A comparative drawing showing the relative sizes of a pygmy tyrannosaur, center, a previously unknown species; a tyrannosaurus rex, a tiger and a polar bear.]

Robert T. Bakker

It Would Seem T. Rex Had a Pygmy Cousin

By MALCOLM W. BROWNE

Paleontologists reported yesterday that a peculiar dinosaur skull, unearthed 46 years ago but erroneously identified at the time, is actually that of a previously unknown genus, a pygmy tyrannosaur possibly related to modern birds.

The announcement yesterday at the Cleveland Museum of Natural History culminated a yearlong study of the skull by three scientists who recognized it as a fossil of extraordinary importance.

Many paleontologists believe that the dinosaurs never entirely died out but merely evolved into birds, and the iden-

tification of the new genus supports that theory. Differences of opinion persist, however, as to which dinosaurs might have been the ancestors of birds.

The skull was found in Montana in 1942 but had never stirred particular scientific interest because it was assumed to have come from a gorgosaur, a large flesh-eating dinosaur of the late Cretaceous period, of which many specimens have been collected and studied.

Over the years several scientists questioned this assumption, but it was

not until last year that Dr. Robert T. Bakker of the University of Colorado, on a visit to the museum, challenged the label on the skull and began an investigation.

He enlisted as collaborators Dr. Michael E. Williams of the Cleveland museum and Dr. Philip Currie of the Tyrrell Museum of Paleontology in Drumheller, Alberta, Canada. Dr. Currie is an expert in theropod, or "beast-footed," dinosaurs, a category to which the two-foot skull belonged.

"We found that this animal was much more like a tyrannosaur than a

Continued on Page A16, Column 1

THE NEW YORK TIMES is available for home or office delivery in most major U.S. cities. Please call this toll-free number: 1-800-631-2500. ADVT.

0 35475314

"All the News That's Fit to Print"

The New York Times

VOL.CXXXVII.... No. 47,556 Copyright © 1988 The New York Times   NEW YORK, MONDAY, JULY 4, 1988   50 cents beyond 75 miles from New York City, except on Long Island.   **30 CENTS**

New York: Today, mostly sunny and warm. High 81-87. Tonight, clear and mild. Low 59-66. Tomorrow, mostly sunny, very warm. High 84-90. Yesterday: High 88, low 61. Details, page 18.

U.S. DOWNS IRAN AIRLINER MISTAKEN FOR F-14; 290 REPORTED DEAD; A TRAGEDY, REAGAN SAYS

Two Churches in Paris Battle Across the Lefebvre Schism

Jean-Marie Cardinal Lustiger calling for Church unity at Notre Dame in Paris yesterday.

Agence France-Presse

By STEVEN GREENHOUSE
Special to The New York Times

PARIS, July 3 — It was a battle for the hearts, minds and souls of thousands of traditionalist followers of Marcel Lefebvre, the dissident Archbishop who was excommunicated Thursday.

It involved two churches less than a quarter mile apart. One was the rebel Left Bank church that Archbishop Lefebvre's ultraconservative followers took control of in 1977 in defiance of church superiors and the law, and the other was Notre Dame Cathedral, which was eager to win back the flocks that had strayed.

At St.-Nicolas-du-Chardonnet, the citadel of the Lefebvre movement in Paris, more than 2,000 worshipers flocked to morning Mass Sunday in defiance of Pope John Paul's threat that Catholics who continue to follow the rebel prelate might be excommunicated too.

Cardinal Gives Latin Mass

At the same time, Jean-Marie Cardinal Lustiger, the Archbishop of Paris, took a highly unusual step to woo back Lefebvre loyalists by holding the first traditional Latin Mass in Notre Dame in two decades. Five thousand worshipers, twice the usual number, crowded into Sunday's 10 A.M. Mass at the 12th-century landmark to hear the Cardinal implore traditionalists not to follow those who have broken with the Holy See.

As in most religious battles, the language was electric, and the stakes were high. Priests at St.-Nicolas sought to fight defections in the city where the Lefebvre movement is strongest, while Cardinal Lustiger struggled to bring unity back to Paris's Catholic Church. In ways it is a battle between those who want to bring the church into the 20th century and those who believe that the church is immutable and eternal and should not be tinkered with.

Archbishop Defied Pope

"A few of our people are anxious, but I can't say there is real fear about what the Vatican has done," said the Rev. François Pivert, a priest at St.-Nicolas. "We think the excommunications are null. Rome is excommunicating the real Catholics."

On Thursday, the Vatican said Archbishop Lefebvre was excommunicated because on that day he defied the orders of the Pope and consecrated four traditionalist bishops at his seminary

Continued on Page 28, Column 3

Because of holiday production requirements, The Times is printed today in two sections. SportsMonday begins on page 34, Business Day on page 29.

Israeli Decision On Emigré Curb Splits U.S. Aides

By MICHAEL R. GORDON
Special to The New York Times

WASHINGTON, July 3 — A debate has erupted in the State Department over whether the United States should counter a recent decision by the Israeli Cabinet that would require most Jews who leave the Soviet Union to settle in Israel.

Officials in the State Department's Office of Human Rights and Humanitarian Affairs say American refugee procedures should be changed so that Soviet Jews who travel to Israel would have the right to resettle in the United States quickly if they want to.

Broad Ramifications Seen

But this approach is opposed by the State Department officials in the Bureau of Near Eastern and South Asian Affairs, who say such a move would disrupt American-Israeli relations.

The issue, which has potential ramifications for refugees from other countries, has not yet been put to Secretary of State George P. Shultz for a decision.

At the heart of the dispute is a multifaceted legal, political and ethical debate about how best to aid Jewish emigration from the Soviet Union.

Under current arrangements, the overwhelming majority of Soviet Jews who are permitted to leave the Soviet Union do so by receiving Soviet exit permits and Israeli visas in Moscow. The Israeli visas are distributed by the Dutch Embassy in Moscow, which has represented Israel's interests there since the Soviet Union broke off rela-

Continued on Page 2, Column 3

Traffic Perils Economic Boom Of Suburbs Around New York

By RICHARD L. MADDEN

Jammed rush-hour traffic, once the bane of the big city, has become a pervasive part of daily life in the suburbs around New York City.

Fifty miles and more from Manhattan, highway traffic crawls bumper-to-bumper. Commuters, trying to avoid bottlenecks, leave home earlier, search out back roads, stay later at the office. Businesses that moved to the suburbs to escape the crowded city move again, even farther out.

What has happened, planners say, is that fundamental changes in where people work, where they live, and even

First of two articles.

how they live, have combined to overwhelm the metropolitan region's roads. The changes include these:

¶The spread of corporate headquarters and offices across Westchester County, Long Island, New Jersey and Connecticut has created hundreds of thousands of jobs in former bedroom communities. Since 1980 alone, the suburbs have created 763,000 jobs, for a total of 4.9 million, compared with New York City's 3.6 million, a gain of 306,000.

¶The dispersal of those jobs has created new commuting patterns between far-flung suburbs, leaving most people no choice but to drive; nearly all mass transit runs in and out of New York City, not across the region.

¶Soaring housing costs have pushed more and more people farther out to find affordable homes, leaving them long commutes over crowded country roads never designed for heavy traffic.

¶The increase in families with two income-earners has sent more husbands and wives out of the house in separate cars and, often, in opposite directions. One consequence: the number of cars in the suburbs has far outstripped population growth.

Choking Suburbs

The result, according to planners, transportation officials, business people and commuters, is worsening traffic that threatens to choke the suburbs on their own success in becoming places to live and work. And they see no immediate solutions.

"No one really has realized it until it's on us," said Dr. Robert W. Burchell, acting director of the Center for Urban

Continued on Page 26, Column 1

Downing of Flight 655: The U.S. Account

Events occurred Sunday. Information is based on a briefing by Adm. William J. Crowe Jr., chairman of the Joint Chiefs of Staff.

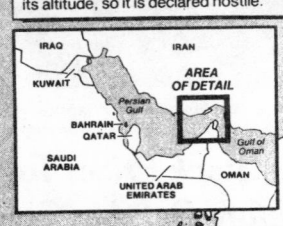

10:42 A.M. The Vincennes and the frigate Montgomery respond to the attack, sinking two Iranian boats and damaging a third.

10:47 A.M. An Iran Air jetliner, an Airbus A300, takes off from Bandar Abbas for Dubai.

10:47 A.M. The Vincennes detects a plane flying toward it. The plane is identified as an F-14 by electronic means.

10:49 A.M. The plane fails to respond to repeated radio warnings on civilian and military networks.

10:51 A.M. The plane continues toward the Vincennes and decreases its altitude, so it is declared hostile.

10:10 A.M. A helicopter from the U.S. cruiser Vincennes is fired on by a small Iranian boat.

10:54 A.M. With the plane nine miles away, the Vincennes fires two surface-to-air missiles. At least one missile hits the plane.

The U.S. later admits that the plane shot down was the Iranian passenger jetliner.

All times are local for the Persian Gulf. Eastern daylight time is eight hours earlier.

The New York Times/July 4, 1988

Failures Seen in Safeguards on Erroneous Attacks

By STEPHEN ENGELBERG
Special to The New York Times

WASHINGTON, July 3 — The downing of an Iranian jetliner is striking evidence of how split-second decisions in modern warfare may be based on incomplete electronic information.

Navy officers said today that based on the Government's account of the incident, it appeared that several precautions relied upon to prevent such an incident had inexplicably failed.

Iranian jetliners routinely monitor emergency frequencies used to send warnings and had always responded to such transmissions, these officers said, but the plane downed today did not answer three separate warnings on the civilian network. Four warnings were also sent on a military network, officials said.

Path Suited to Attack

Nor was radar able to identify the aircraft as a passenger plane. Civilian planes are supposed to be equipped with devices that emit signals identifying them on radar screens as civilian, but the Navy said no such signal had been received.

Finally, the Navy said the jetliner was following a path that was outside the normal civilian air corridors and would have been well suited to an attack on the American cruiser Vincennes in the Strait of Hormuz.

There are several unanswered questions about the incident, particularly how the jetliner and the control tower at Bandar Abbas in Iran failed to hear or heed the warnings said to have been sent by the Vincennes before it fired. It is not known whether the Reagan Administration will play tapes to establish that those warnings took place.

Navy officers asserted today that based on available information, the threat to the ship was sufficient to justify firing on the plane, and that, if anything, the captain of the Vincennes waited unusually long to fire his missiles. The Administration said the plane was nine miles away when the order was given, a distance well within the range of the air-to-surface missiles used by the Iranian military.

"If anything, the captain could be criticized for holding his fire as long as he did," said Joseph Metcalf 3d, the Navy's former deputy chief of naval operations for surface warfare. "From what they're saying, he waited a long

Continued on Page 6, Column 1

The cruiser Vincennes, which shot down an Iranian jetliner yesterday.

Reuters

Similarities With KAL Flight Are Rejected by U.S. Admiral

By STEVEN ERLANGER

The downing of an Iran Air passenger plane by American missiles yesterday prompted comparisons to the destruction of a South Korean airliner shot down by a Soviet fighter pilot nearly five years ago.

At a Washington news conference yesterday, the chairman of the Joint Chiefs of Staff, Adm. William J. Crowe Jr., rejected the comparison, citing "very fundamental differences" between the two events.

Unlike the Korean airliner, Admiral Crowe said, the Iran Air aircraft was flying in a war zone at low altitude during combat and had failed to change course or respond to three warnings on a civilian radio network and four warnings on a military network. Commercial pilots in the gulf have also been warned by the United States in recent months to identify themselves when challenged.

Admiral Crowe said there were reasons, including classified "electronic indications" he would not reveal, that led American crew members aboard the American cruiser Vincennes to be-

lieve that they were confronting an American-built F-14 of the Iranian Air Force.

But although the Navy said the Iranian plane was not emitting the signals that would have identified it as a commercial flight, the admiral did not explain in detail how a sophisticated American air defense system could confuse the radar signature of a small fighter jet and a wide-bodied passenger plane. This question of identification was raised both by the United States in the aftermath of the Korean airline disaster and by Iranian officials yesterday.

In the early hours of Sept. 1, 1983, Korean Air Lines Flight 007, flying 365 miles off its normal course from An-

Continued on Page 6, Column 1

SKIPPER DEFENDED

Admiral Plans a Review of Rules for Firing — Embassies Alerted

By RICHARD HALLORAN
Special to The New York Times

WASHINGTON, July 3 — A United States Navy warship in the Persian Gulf shot down an Iranian passenger plane today that the Navy said it mistook for a jet fighter, and Iran said 290 lives were lost.

The Chairman of the Joint Chiefs of Staff, Admiral William J. Crowe Jr., said the missile cruiser Vincennes, while seeking to protect itself from what was thought to be a hostile aircraft, shot down the airliner with a surface-to-air missile. The downing of the jetliner, Iran Air flight 655, took place over the Strait of Hormuz, at the southern end of the gulf. [Transcript of news conference, pages 4 and 5.]

President Reagan, in a statement issued from the Presidential retreat in Camp David, Md., and Admiral Crowe, in a briefing at the Pentagon, both said the United States regretted the loss of life on the plane but defended the judgment of the warship's captain, Will C. Rogers 3d, saying the commander's first responsibility was to protect his ship and crew.

KAL Comparison Rejected

Admiral Crowe rejected a comparison with the episode on Sept. 1, 1983, in which a Soviet fighter plane shot down a Korean Air Lines passenger jet over international waters in the Sea of Japan, killing all 269 on board. He said the main difference was that the Korean plane "was not in a war zone" and that "there was no combat in progress" when it was shot down. The admiral said such was the case in the attack today.

The admiral said the actions aboard the Vincennes would be reviewed by Rear Adm. William N. Fogarty of the Central Command, which has its headquarters in Tampa, Fla. The Central Command is responsible for United States military operations in the gulf region.

'Obligation' to Crew

Admiral Crowe also said the rules of engagement, which govern the circumstances under which a commander may fire his weapons, would be reviewed. But he emphasized that "the commanding officer had a very heavy obligation to protect his ship, his people."

At the State Department, officials said the downing should not force the United States to revise its policy of seeking to keep the Persian Gulf open

Continued on Page 4, Column 1

'Saddened' Reagan Decides to Remain At Maryland Retreat

By JULIE JOHNSON
Special to The New York Times

WASHINGTON, July 3 — After a series of telephone calls that began before dawn, President Reagan decided today to remain at his Camp David retreat rather than return to the White House to deal with the shooting down of an Iranian airliner by an American warship.

The President's decision, Administration officials said, indicated the degree to which aides sought to keep the events from being characterized as a crisis.

The White House issued a written statement from Mr. Reagan, who was notified of the military action shortly before 5 A.M. but did not learn with certainty for five more hours that it was a commercial jetliner that had been shot down. The statement said the President was "saddened" by the incident and offered his condolences to the passengers, crew and their families. [Text of statement, page 6.]

Telephone Conference Call

The capital, emptied of officials over the Fourth of July holiday, was slow to react to today's events. With the President in Maryland, Vice President Bush in Maine, Secretary of State George P. Shultz in Massachusetts and the national security adviser, Lieut. Gen. Colin L. Powell, in Tennessee, the consultations that led to the Administration's response were worked out by telephone conference call.

At the heart of the effort to keep the crisis level at a minimum, Administration officials said, was a sensitivity to

Continued on Page 6, Column 4

INSIDE

Inquiry Into Blimp Contract
The F.B.I. and the S.E.C. are investigating the competition between two military contractors for a $5 billion contract to build blimps. Page 10.

Rain at Wimbledon
The men's singles final between Boris Becker and Stefan Edberg was suspended by rain in the first set. It will resume today. Page 37.

Perestroika in China
China has largely undergone the type of economic restructuring sought by Moscow. But openness in public debate lags behind. Page 3.

Proudly Flies the Flag. . .
...and just about everywhere, too. Companies that make American flags say more and more people are showing their colors in a resurgence of patriotism. Page 7.

THE NEW YORK TIMES is available for home or office delivery in most major U.S. cities. Please call this toll-free number: 1-800-631-2500. ADVT.

The New York Times

Late Edition

New York: Today, sunny, windy, very cold. High 20-25. Tonight, clear, quite cold. Low 16-22. Tomorrow, partly sunny, windy, warmer. High 35-40. Yesterday: High 53, low 33. Details, page 49.

VOL.CXXXVIII.. No. 47,757   Copyright © 1989 The New York Times   NEW YORK, SATURDAY, JANUARY 21, 1989   50 cents beyond 75 miles from New York City, except on Long Island.   35 CENTS

BUSH TAKES OFFICE ASKING BIPARTISAN HELP IN FIGHTING SOCIAL ILLS DESPITE THE DEFICIT

F.B.I. INTENSIFYING COMMODITY INQUIRY ON CHICAGO TRADES

Suspects Said to Be Pressed to Name Others Involved in Fraudulent Dealings

By KURT EICHENWALD
Special to The New York Times

CHICAGO, Jan. 20 — Capitalizing on fears in the commodity markets after subpoenas were served on 50 to 100 floor traders, Federal investigators are pressing those implicated in possible fraud to name others, lawyers and other sources said today.

A number of commodity traders with the Chicago Mercantile Exchange and the Chicago Board of Trade, the nation's two largest commodity exchanges, have begun to cooperate with the Government, these sources said. Some traders have agreed to testify before the grand jury conducting the inquiry, they added.

The investigation involves potential fraud charges based on, among other things, agreements among traders in the futures pits to cheat customers by illegally manipulating trades, law enforcement sources said. They added that clients might have been defrauded of millions of dollars.

Key Element of Strategy

The growing concern that many people might go to prison, fueled by the extensive publicity the case is receiving, appears to have become a key element of a strategy to convince traders to cooperate with the Government and testify, the sources said.

"This thing is being done to create the maximum effect, to create this big aura of inevitability," said John Troelstrup, a commodity lawyer involved in the case. "It's trying to tell people, 'You had better cooperate now before it's too late.'" By cooperating with the Government in the early stages of investigations, defendants typically stand a better chance of receiving lenient treatment in the courts.

The Mercantile Exchange said it had begun an inquiry into trading activities on its floor. The Board of Trade, the world's largest futures market, has also begun an investigation, said some officials who asked not to be identified. A Board of Trade spokesman declined to comment. [Page 39.]

Case Remains Sketchy

Lawyers involved in the case said today that they were telling their clients not to cooperate, simply because the case is very sketchy.

But the Government's strategy of surprise has won some cooperation, people directly involved in the investigation said.

Some people who have cooperated with the investigators were stunned when agents of the Federal Bureau of Investigation beginning late Tuesday, armed with subpoenas and details of incriminating evidence against them.

Much of that evidence involved secret tape recordings, made on the trading floor, of conversations between the undercover agents and the people working at the exchanges.

In a scene more akin to a large drug

Continued on Page 39, Column 1

George Bush being sworn in yesterday by Chief Justice William H. Rehnquist as Barbara Bush held two Bibles, the Bush family Bible and the one used by George Washington 200 years ago. Mr. Bush's 87-year-old mother, Dorothy, standing with Marilyn Quayle and surrounded by other family members, watched along with Vice President Dan Quayle, Congressional leaders and others.
The New York Times/Angel Franco

No Reversal, But Changes

'New Breeze' Signals A Shift From Reagan

By R. W. APPLE Jr.
Special to The New York Times

WASHINGTON, Jan. 20 — President Bush swore his oath with the same 35 words that George Washington uttered two centuries ago, resting his left hand on the same Bible that George Washington used, and he spoke of the orderly transfer of power that the inaugural ceremony so compellingly symbolizes.

News Analysis

But the thoughts that George Bush laid before the nation today as he stood on "the front porch of democracy," as he called it, were all about change. There was, of course, no hint of repudiation of the works of Ronald Reagan, whom the new President served for eight years and whom he thanked for "the wonderful things" Mr. Reagan had done. There was, all the same, a clear call from Mr. Bush for subtle yet significant corrections in the nation's course.

"A new breeze is blowing," the President said again and again, and he called upon the winds of change to carry away greed, both public and private, and sterile bickering between the White House and Congress, and seeming indifference, both public and private, to the plight of the poor and the sick, and the painful cleavages that still remain from the Vietnam War.

Though he briefly re-identified himself with the foes of abortion, and though he warned that the national finances could not stand much new spending, his ___ was moderate, nonideological and ___ dest. Where Mr.

Continued on Page 7, Column 4

Transformation of Bush: His Own Man

By MAUREEN DOWD
Special to The New York Times

WASHINGTON, Jan. 20 — "I —" the new President blurted out, a beat ahead of the moment he was supposed to begin repeating the Presidential oath after Chief Justice William H. Rehnquist. George Bush smiled nervously and began again.

The slip could not have surprised anyone who had been watching Mr. Bush bounding about the White House and the country since his election.

"He's loaded for bear," said his old friend Senator Alan K. Simpson of Wyoming. "It's what he's planned on for a long, long time."

For Mr. Bush, as for most Americans, the idea of George Bush as President took some getting used to. The morning after his election, alone with friends and family, his eyes had a lost look, the vulnerability that can come with getting exactly what you have always wanted. At a private buffet in Houston after his first news conference as President-elect, an aide recalled that Mr. Bush seemed nervous and subdued, his voice uncommonly low.

From Faithful Follower to Confident Leader in About 2 Months

But by the next day, when he arrived in Florida for a vacation, where the new President would change into formal clothes tonight for the inaugural ball.

"He's loaded for bear," the tentativeness had evaporated in a spray of water sports, and he met the press on the beach with an easy and joyful air of confidence. He had shed the "deferential Episcopalian tilt," as one friend called the self-effacing manner he assumed as Ronald Reagan's Vice Preside___.

'The Man at the Desk'

After recalling all the Presidents he had known and worked for, after remembering all the contests he had endured and the jobs he had held to prepare himself, Mr. Bush was able to banish contemplation with the certainty that he was ready to be "the man at the desk."

"He was able to look at this whole thing and say, 'I can do this,'" said his friend and adviser Peter Teeley.

Or as his brother Jonathan put it in ebullient Bush fashion: "He's not cowed because he knows he has the combination of knowledge, experience and energy to form one great big assault on the management of the country."

Over the last 10 weeks, the 64-year-old Mr. Bush has made his passage from faithful and sometimes fumbling lieutenant to self-assured leader with an ease that has amazed all but those closest to him. Everyone has struggled for a metaphor to capture the striking change.

"It's as though a great shadow has lifted," said one of the men chosen for the Bush Cabinet. "It's like watching a balloon inflate," said another acquaintance.

But perhaps Jonathan Bush offered the best description of his older brother's giddy rush to self-expression: "It is as though you took a bottle of soda water and shook it up and down and then took the cork out, and boom goes

Continued on Page 9, Column 1

Ronald Reagan pausing to take a last look at his desk as he left the office of the President.
The New York Times/Jose R. Lopez

'WILL' OVER 'WALLET'

41st President Also Says of Drug Abuse, 'This Scourge Will Stop'

By BERNARD WEINRAUB
Special to The New York Times

WASHINGTON, Jan. 20 — George Herbert Walker Bush of Texas, promising new efforts to heal social wounds and to end two decades of divisiveness between the White House and Congress, was inaugurated today as the 41st President of the United States.

In an Inaugural Address delivered from the flag-draped West Front of the Capitol, Mr. Bush, his voice strong and his manner self-assured, emphasized the urgency of dealing with the Federal budget deficit.

That deficit, the new President said, means that the Government alone cannot solve all pressing social problems. But he asserted that the problems could nonetheless be solved. "We have more will than wallet; but will is what we need," he said.

'This Scourge Will Stop'

Indeed, Mr. Bush offered an unqualified promise to put an end to one of those ills, the epidemic of drug abuse. "Take my word," he said. "This scourge will stop."

The 20-minute speech, delivered before tens of thousands of people at the Capitol and on the grounds beyond, was also marked by a theme of harmony and conciliation, as when the 64-year-old Republican called on the Democrats who control Congress to join him in dealing with homelessness, poverty and "the rough crime of the streets."

"A new breeze is blowing," he said, "and the old bipartisanship must be made new again. To my friends, and yes, I do mean friends, in the loyal opposition, and yes, I mean loyal: I put out my hand."

Three Minutes Late

The inauguration took place on a clear, cold day, the azure sky flecked with white.

Barbara Bush, the nation's new First Lady, smiled faintly as Chief Justice William H. Rehnquist administered the Presidential oath at 12:03 P.M., three minutes after Ronald Reagan's term had officially come to an end under the provisions of the 20th Amendment to the Constitution. Mr. Bush had his left hand on two Bibles held by his wife. One was a family Bible; the other was used by George Washington at his swearing-in 200 years ago.

Immediately after Mr. Bush had taken the oath, the United States Army Band broke into "Hail to the Chief." A 21-gun salute followed, the sound of the cannons echoing across the Mall.

Shortly before Mr. Bush took the

Continued on Page 6, Column 1

Gorbachev Asks Stable Relations

Mikhail S. Gorbachev congratulated President Bush and expressed hope for stable relations.

Other countries also sent congratulations, while bidding farewell to Ronald Reagan.

Article, page 9.

INSIDE

Managua's Gesture to Bush
In a step to promote good relations with the new Bush Administration, Nicaragua lifted a freeze on visas for American diplomats. Page 5.

Zhukov on Stalin's War Role
Pravda published previously secret memoirs of Marshal Georgi K. Zhukov that shatter the Soviet image of Stalin as a war hero. Page 3.

Two Officers Wounded
Two New York City police officers were shot in Brooklyn when they tried to arrest a murder suspect. The man apparently escaped. Page 29.

Bea Lillie Dies at 94
The comedienne amused millions with her barbed wit and skillfully wielded cigarette holder. Page 34.

Tears, Handcuffs for Boy, 10, Facing Judge in Crack Sale

By MICHAEL WINERIP
Special to The New York Times

HAUPPAUGE, L.I., Jan. 20 — The 14-year-old boy drove the BMX bike, a Suffolk County police officer testified today. The 10-year-old sold crack from the back of the bike.

"I saw six such exchanges," the officer, John McGinley, testified in Family Court, describing how the boys, selling crack from a brown bag, rode up and down Straight Path in Wyandanch, a poor community plagued with drug dealing.

"God!" a relative of the 10-year-old said with a gasp.

In a highly unusual move this week, Suffolk County Judge Donald L.

Auperin opened Family Court hearings concerning the 10-year-old boy, who the police said was carrying three small plastic bags of crack and $226 when he and his friend were arrested last Sunday night. He requested that the boy not be identified because of his age.

At the end of today's hearing, the judge found a reasonable likelihood that a crime had been committed and ordered that the boy continue to be held in a juvenile jail until a fact-finding hearing, the Family Court equivalent of a trial, on Jan. 31. Brought to court in handcuffs and carrying a Marvel comic book, he was led away in handcuffs and tears.

Family Court in New York is almost always closed, but can be opened at a judge's discretion. Judge Auperin, who acted today despite objections from both the prosecutor and the boy's legal guardian — the Family Court equivalent of a defense lawyer — indicated that his concern with society's drug

Continued on Page 33, Column 1

Reagan Packs Up a Presidency and Its Memories

By MAUREEN DOWD
Special to The New York Times

WASHINGTON, Jan. 20 — Ronald Reagan was wistful. Nancy Reagan was worried.

Mrs. Reagan, teary all morning, kept searching through drawers in the family quarters, making sure she had packed up all her things. Finally, her press secretary, Elaine Crispin, told her to stop. "If you leave something behind," she said to Mrs. Reagan, "they'll send it to you. They have your address."

Before she left, she tucked a note for Mrs. Bush in an empty drawer in the bedroom, and left a small white orchid. Mrs. Reagan also put a humorous note

for Mr. Bush in his dressing room, where the new President would change into formal clothes tonight for the inaugural ball.

Mr. Reagan left a more serious handwritten note with his prayers and his affection for Mr. Bush in the top desk drawer in the Oval Office. He went to the office in the morning to take one last look around and seemed quite sad to see it emptied of his belongings, including his sunny sign — "It CAN be done."

"He wanted to freeze a few vignettes in his memory," said Marlin Fitzwater, Mr. Reagan's spokesman, who was staying on with Mr. Bush.

Standing behind his desk, his head lowered, Mr. Reagan put out both

hands to touch the desk as though to hold it in his memory. He received his last daily schedule from his personal secretary, Kathleen Osborne. He took a deep breath, lifted his head and walked out the door to the Rose Garden, stopping to look back.

Rex, the Reagans' energetic King Charles spaniel, dashed across the lawn and the President remarked, "There he goes — that's his last walk." This week the Presidential pet received a gift, a new doghouse built by Navy Seabees to resemble the White House and complete with a patch of carpet from Rex's favorite floor at Camp David.

Then Ronald Reagan carried on, in

Continued on Page 6, Column 1

"All the News
That's Fit to Print"

The New York Times

Late Edition

New York: Today, morning showers, thunderstorms, then clearing skies and windy. High 82. Tonight, clear. Tomorrow, chance of late showers. Yesterday: High 86, low 65. Details are on page 41.

VOL.CXXXVIII — No. 47,891   Copyright © 1989 The New York Times   NEW YORK, SUNDAY, JUNE 4, 1989 $1.50 beyond 75 miles from New York City, except on Long Island.   **$1.25**

TROOPS ATTACK AND CRUSH BEIJING PROTEST; THOUSANDS FIGHT BACK, SCORES ARE KILLED

Khomeini, Imam of Iran And Foe of U.S., Is Dead

By The Associated Press

NICOSIA, Cyprus, Sunday June 4. — Ayatollah Ruhollah Khomeini, Iran's spiritual and political leader, died today, 12 days after he underwent surgery for bleeding in his digestive system, the official Iranian news agency reported. He was believed to be 89 years old.

"The leader of the Islamic revolution and founder of the Islamic Republic, Imam Khomeini, passed away at a Teheran Hospital," the Islamic Republic News Agency reported in an urgent dispatch.

[Reuters reported that a statement from his son, Hojatlislam Ahmad Khomeini, his chief aide, accompanied the announcement.]

["The lofty spirit of the leader of Moslems and free men everywhere, His Excellency Imam Khomeini, has gone to Heaven and his heart, which was brimming with love for God and the oppressed of mankind, stopped beating," it said.]

The Ayatollah was referred to by Iranians as the imam, or spiritual leader. He led the 1979 revolution that toppled 2,500 years of monarchy and set up the Islamic Republic of Iran, turning the relatively Western-style country ruled by Shah Mohammed Riza Pahlevi into the most hard-line Islamic nation in the world.

He emerged as an implacable foe of the United States, which had supported the Shah, and it was under his direction that Iranian students overran the United States Embassy in Teheran and held many of the diplomats inside hostage for over a year, a development that was one of the chief causes of the electoral defeat of the Jimmy Carter Administration.

Reaction From Ex-Hostage

He was equally an enemy of the Soviet Union, referring to both the superpowers as "The Great Satans," and he led his country in an eight-year-war against neighboring Iraq.

A former American hostage in Iran said the Ayatollah's death ends a chapter for the former captives.

"I'm not the type to say I'm happy he's dead," said Barry Rosen, of Brooklyn, one of the 52 hostages held 444 days by radical Iranian students from 1979 to 1981. "But I do feel, to a certain degree, that that part of the

Associated Press, 1988
Ayatollah Ruhollah Khomeini

Continued on Page 39, Column 1

Soviet Emigré Mob Outgrows Brooklyn, and Fear Spreads

By RALPH BLUMENTHAL
with CELESTINE BOHLEN

A criminal underworld of Soviet émigrés, some of them skilled in white-collar crime and hardened by Soviet prison and labor camps, is reaching beyond its base in Brooklyn, using extortion and violence in its own neighborhoods and engaging in multimillion-dollar racketeering schemes on an international scale.

The network of Russian-speaking criminals is small and loosely grouped compared with the hierarchies of traditional American organized crime. But camouflaged within the country's growing Soviet immigrant communities, the network is fast outstripping the ability of local and Federal agencies to curb its illegal schemes, some of which are linked to Mafia crime families, officials of the Federal Bureau of Investigation and other agencies say.

Intelligence reports trace the network to black marketeers and other professional gangsters, many of whom plied their criminal trade in the Soviet Union before winning exit visas — or being planted — in the wave of Jewish emigration.

One mob boss who was said to have spent 10 years in Soviet prisons before turning up in Brooklyn was known to enforce his threats with an electric cattle prod he kept in his car. Investigators say he once extorted $15,000 from another immigrant by threatening to kill the man's daughter on her wedding day. Another crime kingpin, convicted of credit card fraud and now facing extradition from West Germany, is reputed to have amassed a fortune of more than $600 million from bootlegged gasoline in less than a decade after he arrived from Odessa.

Greater Numbers Coming

As Soviet emigration policies loosen up, greater numbers of Jews, Armenians and ethnic Germans have been given permission to leave. Since 1975, some 150,000 have come to the United States. About 50,000 have settled in the New York area; another 15,000 are expected to settle here this year.

Law-enforcement officials say that, while the network comprises no more than a few hundred active criminals out of all those who arrived, some of these are highly skilled mob enforcers, forgers and confidence men.

Their criminal activities range from old-fashioned jewelry swindles on 47th

Continued on Page 38, Column 1

Associated Press
A student placing debris in front of a moving armored personnel carrier early today in Tiananmen Square.

In the Streets, Anguish, Fury and Tears

By SHERYL WuDUNN
Special to The New York Times

BEIJING, Sunday, June 4 — As the crackle of automatic weapons filled the air today on the Avenue of Eternal Peace, tens of thousands of Beijing residents, even elderly men and women, rushed out to see what they could do to turn back the troops.

"The citizens have gone crazy," said a driver watching as a tank plowed its way down the main thoroughfare. "They throw themselves in front of the tank, and only when they see it won't stop, they scatter."

The driver himself was shaken by what he had seen: A tank had rammed into an army truck used as a barricade. As the truck turned over, it crushed a man to death. Elsewhere, he had seen three bloodied bodies lying in the street. Several soldiers still standing in their trucks were crying.

Students and workers threw beer bottles, gasoline bombs, lead pipes, whatever they could find, at the tanks and armed personnel trucks, which nevertheless continued rumbling down the avenue. One truck drove back and forth along the east side of the Changan Avenue, as the Avenue of Eternal Peace is known in Chinese, and did not stop when people stood in its path.

Amazement had already turned to fear and defiance earlier in the evening as citizens saw the military convoys entering the city. Some troops from other provinces practically paraded their AK-47 rifles as they stood in their trucks, stranded by the human blockades that had formed around the trucks.

By dark, tensions had soared throughout the city. Hundreds of people were impelled outdoors by their disbelief and anger, yet brought back to their homes by fear of the violence. The sound of tanks whizzing by and reports of open firing fanned their fears.

"You beasts! You beasts!" shouted the people at the troops.

'We Have to Obey Orders'

Around a convoy of about 45 military trucks in the eastern part of the city, people pushed and shoved their way to the troops, shouting and urging them to consider their role as fellow citizens. But the sympathy that had characterized the troops last week was gone; the soldiers seemed to have a certain resolve.

"Will you shoot at us if they order you to?" was a question asked by many of the people surrounding the truck. The soldiers gave weak assurances to the people that they would not fire, but they also admitted that

Continued on Page 20, Column 1

Reuters
A protester injured in a clash with troops yesterday at the Great Hall of the People in Beijing.

Gingrich, Pursuer of Democrats, Now Finds Himself the Pursued

By E. J. DIONNE Jr.

WASHINGTON, June 2 — Representative Newt Gingrich's role in bringing down House Speaker Jim Wright seems to have set him up for a Wright-style roasting that could determine his future as the leader of the young and aggressive backbenchers bidding for control of their party in the House.

Obviously a target for Democratic

The Polish Vote

The Solidarity labor union takes a step toward becoming a broad political movement today as Poles vote in the first openly contested elections in the Soviet bloc.

Some say that, four years hence, the opposition will be in control. Others predict a splintering of Solidarity's factions.

Article, page 18.

revenge, the 45-year-old Georgia Republican is also facing some criticism as a divisive figure within his own party.

One sign of Mr. Gingrich's political difficulties, party strategists say, is that his main competitor for leadership of the young conservatives, Representative Vin Weber of Minnesota, has already begun to distance himself from Mr. Gingrich, his longtime friend.

The strategists interpret recent comments by Mr. Weber as suggesting that while the party needs Mr. Gingrich's inspirational example right now, House members might want a cooler leader for the long haul.

Some Republicans scoff at Democratic suspicions that there is an organized "stink-tank" campaign under way, saying the majority party is merely suffering trouble that it brought on itself. [Page 34]

If Mr. Gingrich has his Republican

Continued on Page 34, Column 1

SQUARE IS CLEARED

General Strike Is Urged as Officials Announce End of 'Rebellion'

By NICHOLAS D. KRISTOF
Special to The New York Times

BEIJING, Sunday, June 4 — Tens of thousands of Chinese troops retook the center of the capital from pro-democracy protesters early this morning, killing scores of students and workers and wounding hundreds more as they fired submachine guns at crowds of people who tried to resist.

Troops marched along the main roads surrounding central Tiananmen Square, sometimes firing in the air and sometimes firing directly at crowds who refused to move.

Early this morning, the troops finally cleared the square after first sweeping the area around it. Several thousand students who had remained on the square throughout the shooting left peacefully, still waving the banners of their universities. Several armored personnel carriers ran over their tents and destroyed the encampment.

Casualty Reports Sketchy

Reports on the number of dead were sketchy. Three Beijing hospitals reported receiving at least 68 corpses of civilians and said many others had not been picked up from the scene. Four other hospitals said they had received bodies of civilians but declined to disclose how many. Students said, however, that at least 500 people may have been killed in the crackdown.

[A report on the state-run radio put the death toll in the thousands and denounced the Government for the violence, The Associated Press reported. But the station later changed announcers and broadcast another report supporting the governing Communist Party, the A.P. said.]

Most of the dead had been shot, but some had been run over by personnel carriers that forced their way through the protesters' barricades.

Official Version

The official news programs this morning reported that the People's Liberation Army had crushed a "counter-revolutionary rebellion." They said that more than 1,000 police officers and troops had been injured and some killed, and that civilians had been killed, but did not give details.

[President Bush called for an end to the violence. "I deeply deplore the decision to use force against peaceful demonstrators," he said. Page 20.]

Changan Avenue, or the Avenue of Eternal Peace, Beijing's main east-

Continued on Page 20, Column 4

Associated Press
Students in Beijing beating the driver of an armored personnel carrier after he rammed a crowd of protesters early today. The driver had been forced from the vehicle after demonstrators set fire to it.

INSIDE

TODAY'S SECTIONS

The New York Times/Dith Pran
$12.1 Million Desk
An 18th-century American desk, which sold at a price usually paid for famous paintings. Page 36.

"All the News That's Fit to Print"

The New York Times

Late Edition
New York: Today, increasing clouds, windy, cool. High 54. Tonight, clearing, breezy. Low near 40. Tomorrow, mostly sunny conditions. High 57. Yesterday: High 55, low 44. Details are on page 32.

VOL.CXXXIX .. No. 48,051   Copyright © 1989 The New York Times   NEW YORK, SATURDAY, NOVEMBER 11, 1989   50 cents beyond 75 miles from New York City, except on Long Island.   40 CENTS

JOYOUS EAST GERMANS POUR THROUGH WALL; PARTY PLEDGES FREEDOMS, AND CITY EXULTS

D'AMATO BACKED SUPPORTERS' BID FOR H.U.D. MONEY

Senator's '84 Letter Appears to Contradict Assertions He Never Urged Grants

By MICHAEL WINERIP

Senator Alfonse M. D'Amato urged the Federal Housing Secretary to approve a grant worth several million dollars for a Buffalo housing-renovation project run in part by two of the Senator's supporters, according to a newly obtained document.

In a March 15, 1984, letter written on Mr. D'Amato's Washington office stationery, the Senator asked Secretary Samuel Pierce of the Department of Housing and Urban Development to use "deliberate speed" in approving the moderate-rehabilitation grant for the 65-unit Buffalo project. Within two months the grant was approved.

The letter, marked as having been hand delivered, appears to contradict repeated assertions by the Senator that he never asked department officials to approve specific moderate-rehabilitation projects. A statement issued to The New York Times last month by the Senator's office said, "The Senator has made no contact with any officials of H.U.D. on behalf of any development or developer as it relates to mod rehab."

Links to Projects

In May 1984, when the department's Buffalo office informed local officials about the moderate-rehabilitation grants that had won approval that year, that letter was marked "cc: Sen. Alfonse M. D'Amato." He was the only elected official designated by the department to receive a copy of its letter about the Buffalo projects.

The Buffalo matter is the most recent in a series of disclosures that have linked the Senator with department projects that benefited his family members, friends and campaign contributors and that have stretched from his hometown, Island Park, L.I., throughout New York State and to Puerto Rico. Federal prosecutors and Congressional investigators are conducting inquiries into several of these programs although Mr. D'Amato has not been identified as a subject of any inquiry.

Allegations in '85

A spokeswoman for the Senator, Zenia Mucha, said last night that the Senator "can't be expected to remember every single letter over a nine-year period." She said that when Mr. D'Amato called on behalf of projects it was "based on merit and need, and no other factors were ever considered."

The moderate-rehabilitation program, which was intended to rebuild housing for low-income people, has been a central focus of inquiries by the department

Continued on Page 32, Column 1

East Germans pouring through a gate leading to the newly opened Berlin wall and, beyond it, West Berlin.
Agence France-Presse

An East German border guard handing a flower back to West Berliners who sat atop the Berlin wall. (Detail from a scene that appears on page 7.)
Reuters

Redefining Europe

As the Revelry Goes On, Politicians Ponder The Ramifications of Changes in Germany

By CRAIG R. WHITNEY
Special to The New York Times

WEST BERLIN, Nov. 10 — By the simple act of forcing their Communist rulers to open the Berlin wall and allow them to go wherever they wish, the people of East Germany have irrevocably changed the way Berlin, Germany and all of Europe have defined themselves for more than 40 years.

News Analysis

Thousands and thousands of East Berliners celebrated their triumph today by promenading up and down the elegant, tree-lined shopping boulevards of the western part of the city, which most of them had never before been allowed to see. They made the Kurfürstendamm into a street festival this evening as church bells pealed joyously into the night.

'A Different Relationship'

Willy Brandt, who was Mayor of West Berlin when the wall was built in 1961, said at a rally this evening, "The moving together of the German states is taking shape in reality in a different way than many of us expected." said. No one should act as if he knows in which concrete form the people in these two states will find a new relationship. But that they will find a relationship, that they will come together in freedom, that is the important point."

But the entire postwar European order has been based on the assumption that Germany, and Europe, would remain divided, and the countries of Eastern and Western Europe firmly anchored in their respective alliances.

In that assumption the United States, in the NATO alliance, guaranteed the security of Western Europe. And in that same assumption France, West Germany and the other major industrial countries of Western Europe began the economic and political unification of the European Community.

West German politicians, including Mr. Brandt and Chancellor Helmut

Kohl, who interrupted an official visit to Poland today to fly to Berlin, all insist that West Germany's commitment to West European integration and the alliance remains.

But politicians, diplomats and business leaders all over Europe are considering new implications for both institutions now that the end of German partition is at last imaginable.

"Europe, though Europeans did not always appreciate it, has been a haven of order these past 44 years," The Economist wrote today. "For East Europeans the price of that stability has been high: a lifetime wasted under a government you loathed. For West Europeans the stability has been marvelous. They could get rich, and start to build a new unity, within a clearly defined zone which ended at the river Elbe and the Bohemian forest."

Now, a NATO diplomat in Brussels said, "The end of the wall raises questions of what's going to happen in Europe. The whole concept of the European Community now may have to change."

So would the concept of the NATO alliance, this diplomat conceded: "Our role will be to design a new role for the alliance — maintaining a balance of stability with the East while all this change is going on.

"There's a reassessment of the War-

Continued on Page 9, Column 4

U.S. ENTHUSIASTIC, BUT HAS CONCERNS

New Order in Eastern Europe Astonishes Washington

By THOMAS L. FRIEDMAN
Special to The New York Times

WASHINGTON, Nov. 10 — Like the rest of the world, Washington is scrambling to keep pace with the changes unfolding by the hour in Eastern Europe. But in contrast with the pivotal role the United States played 40 years ago in shaping the postwar European order that now seems to be coming apart, Washington finds itself more of a bystander — astonished, enthusiastic and concerned.

Twice in the last 24 hours, Secretary of State James A. Baker 3d found himself being slipped notes from aides informing him of major changes in Eastern Europe that only a week earlier no one had imagined, let alone predicted. Officials said a policy review that Mr. Baker ordered three weeks ago on how the United States should relate to changes in East Germany will have to be tossed out and begun anew.

The political changes reverberating across Europe, and the diminished threat of military conflict, also promised to stir new debate in Washington about the need for maintaining a large, expensive American military presence in Western Europe. Moving quickly to deflate such speculation, Defense Sec-

Continued on Page 8, Column 1

BERLIN A FESTIVAL

Communist Leadership Announces a Program of Radical Change

By SERGE SCHMEMANN
Special to The New York Times

WEST BERLIN, Nov. 10 — As hundreds of thousands of East Berliners romped through the newly porous wall in an unending celebration, West German leaders today proclaimed this the moment Germans had yearned for through 40 years of division.

At the same time, change continued unabated in East Berlin, where the Communist Party's Central Committee concluded a three-day session with the announcement of a program of radical changes. They included "free, democratic and secret elections," a "socialist planned economy oriented to market conditions," separation of party and state, parliamentary supervision of state security, freedom of assembly and a new law on the press and broadcasting.

'In the Midst of an Awakening'

"The German Democratic Republic is in the midst of an awakening," the Central Committee declared in the prologue to the newly adopted program. "A revolutionary people's movement has brought into motion a process of great change. The renewal of society is on the agenda."

Though the West Berlin police could give no estimate of the numbers of East Berliners who crossed over in the last 24 hours, the authorities said that only 1,500 so far had announced their intention to stay.

Beyond Berlin, only one of many points along the border between the two Germanys where people could cross, 55,500 East Germans crossed over the border between the two Germanys since the wall was opened on Thursday, and 3,250 remained in West Germany, the West German Interior Ministry said.

Chancellor Helmut Kohl, who interrupted a state visit to Poland to come to West Berlin, told an emotional crowd of East and West Berliners gathered outside the West Berlin city hall: "I want to call out to all in the German Democratic Republic: We're on your side, we are and remain one nation. We belong together."

Speaking on the steps of the city hall, from which President John F. Kennedy had made his "Ich bin ein Berliner" speech shortly after the wall was raised, Mr. Kohl declared: "Long live a free German fatherland! Long live a united Europe!"

Kurfürstendamm Is Packed

All through the night and through the day, East Berliners continued to flood into West Berlin in vast numbers, filling the glittering Kurfürstendamm until traffic came to a halt, forming long lines to pick up the 100-mark "welcome money" — about $55 — that West Germany has traditionally given East Germans on their first time in the West, gaping at shop windows and drinking in the heady new feeling of freedom.

A festival air seized the entire city. West Berliners lined points to greet East Berliners with champagne, cheers and hugs. Many restaurants offered the visitors free food. A television

Continued on Page 6, Column 1

Bush Offers Housing Plan to Aid Poor, Homeless and New Buyers

By ANDREW ROSENTHAL
Special to The New York Times

DALLAS, Nov. 10 — President Bush today proposed a $7 billion, three-year package of housing programs and tax breaks to aid low-income families, first-time home buyers and the homeless "who live a nightmare in the midst of the American dream."

"This initiative will address the full range of housing concerns," Mr. Bush said in a speech to the National Association of Realtors here. He termed the program "a comprehensive agenda to help bring basic shelter and affordable housing within reach of millions of Americans."

The three-year program would provide mortgage assistance for low-income families and tax breaks for first-time home buyers, but it does not include money for building new public and low-income housing units, which some advocates for the homeless regard as essential. Instead, it seeks to generate additional housing units through a variety of means that Republicans have been urging.

For example, a major element of the proposal involves matching grants to local authorities and nonprofit organizations for the acquisition of property and the rehabilitation of housing units.

Democratic legislators, advocates of low-income housing and spokesmen for the housing industry praised it as signaling a new interest in housing problems after years of relative inattention

during the Reagan Administration. But several said the level of financing was insignificant compared to the needs of the homeless or people in substandard housing.

Jack F. Kemp, the Secretary of Housing and Urban Development, said the program was directed more toward stimulating the low-income housing industry than directly subsidizing individual purchases.

In announcing the plan, Mr. Bush

Continued on Page 13, Column 1

INSIDE

The Debate on Child Care

Deep divisions have emerged in Congress over how much money should be spent on child care and who should benefit. Page 12.

Over 30 and Unmarried

Researchers whose study saw poor marriage prospects for well-educated women over 30 omit those findings in a revised paper. Page 10.

Warnings From Koch

He didn't exactly criticize David N. Dinkins, but the Mayor made it clear that he and his successor differ on many important issues. Page 29.

Chairman to Leave Ford

Donald E. Petersen, who led the company from a financial crisis to record profits, plans to retire. Page 35.

Bulgarian Chief Quits After 35 Years of Rigid Rule

By CLYDE HABERMAN
Special to The New York Times

SOFIA, Bulgaria, Nov. 10 — Todor I. Zhivkov, Eastern Europe's longest-serving leader, resigned today as Bulgaria's President and Communist Party leader, after 35 years of guiding the country with old-line orthodoxy.

Mr. Zhivkov, 78 years old, was immediately replaced as the party's General Secretary by his longtime Foreign Minister, Petar T. Mladenov, who is viewed here as likely to take a somewhat more flexible approach toward economic and political restructuring. It will be up to the politically weak National Assembly to choose his successor as President.

Since Mr Zhivkov and other top officials recently began to talk about the need to separate state and party roles, it seemed possible that someone other than Mr. Mladenov could be selected. Mr. Zhivkov's resignation came as a surprise but not as a total shock to Western diplomats, who said that the Bulgarian leader had apparently fallen victim to the fast-paced changes elsewhere in Eastern Europe.

Bulgarian officials reportedly said in confidence that Mr. Zhivkov did not

want to stay too long and risk being forced from power in disgrace, as were Janos Kadar of Hungary or Erich Honecker of East Germany.

There were strong rumors of more shifts to come in top party echelons, but the state press agency and television network made no announcements. The prospects for genuine change here, several diplomats said, are likely to be determined by the extent of any future shake-up.

Doubts on Rapid Change

Mr. Mladenov, who is 53 and was Foreign Minister for 18 years, wasted no time as the new leader in warning that "there is no alternative to restructuring" Bulgaria's struggling economy and tightly controlled political apparatus. The present system has "handicapped progress in our society in all spheres," he told the party Central Committee, adding: "We have to turn Bulgaria into a modern, democratic and lawful country."

Despite his words, however, many

Continued on Page 9, Column 4

Todor I. Zhivkov
Agence France-Presse

"All the News That's Fit to Print"

The New York Times

Late Edition

New York: Today, mostly cloudy, afternoon showers, mild. High 52. Tonight, showers ending. Low 37. Tomorrow, partly cloudy, cooler. High 44. Yesterday: High 52, low 35. Details, page C22.

VOL.CXXXIX .. No. 48,105   Copyright © 1990 The New York Times   NEW YORK, THURSDAY, JANUARY 4, 1990   50 cents beyond 75 miles from New York City, except on Long Island.   40 CENTS

NORIEGA GIVES HIMSELF UP TO U.S. MILITARY; IS FLOWN TO FLORIDA TO FACE DRUG CHARGES

DINKINS WILL DELAY HIRING OF RECRUITS FOR POLICE FORCE

Says That 'Real World' Move Will Help New York City Face Its Budget Gap

By TODD S. PURDUM

In his first major act as Mayor of New York, David N. Dinkins said yesterday that he would indefinitely delay hiring 1,848 police officers who were to have gone on the payroll on Jan. 16 as recruits at the Police Academy. He said he might also have to delay another class that was scheduled to start in June.

Mr. Dinkins's decision means that the city's Police Department will almost certainly fall below its current strength of 25,971 officers during the year. It will also make it harder for the Mayor to keep his campaign promise to double the number of community patrol officers, who walk neighborhood beats, in his first term.

Mr. Dinkins said the move would save $4 million a month and help keep the city's budget balanced in the face of deep fiscal uncertainty.

'Represents a Hardship'

"I realize that this represents a hardship both for the recruits awaiting induction and for the people of the city, who expect and deserve the protection that these new officers would afford," Mr. Dinkins said yesterday. His announcement came unexpectedly in the middle of a news conference called to discuss Gov. Mario M. Cuomo's State of the State Message.

State officials have predicted a budget gap for the city of as much as $185 million in the rest of the fiscal year that ends June 30 and a gap of at least several hundred million dollars in the following year.

"As I have said consistently, I will be bound by the requirements of fiscal prudence in making the difficult decisions that affect our city and our people," said Mr. Dinkins, whose liberal policies created concern in some quarters during the mayoral campaign that he might overspend. He was also faulted by his opponents as indecisive or unwilling to make unpopular decisions.

Discussion With Brown

"I would wish that every announcement I would make would speak of enhancements," he said. "But that's just not the real world."

Mr. Dinkins had vowed repeatedly during the mayoral campaign and in his inaugural address on Monday to be "the toughest mayor on crime this city has ever seen."

The January class was to have had 1,476 recruits for the Police Department, 230 for the transit police and 142 for the housing police. The transit police has about 3,600 officers, while the housing police about 1,700. During his campaign, Mr. Dinkins had promised

Continued on Page B2, Column 1

The New York Times/Sara Krulwich
Gov. Mario M. Cuomo delivering his State of the State address.

Savings Agency Ordered to Sell Real Estate Fast

By NATHANIEL C. NASH
Special to The New York Times

WASHINGTON, Jan. 3 — The new agency created to manage the huge savings and loan bailout was instructed today to sell the real estate it inherited from hundreds of insolvent institutions as quickly as possible. The directive from the Bush Administration raised concerns among bankers that the properties could be "dumped" in an already weakened real estate market.

While the mandate to the newly formed Resolution Trust Corporation could mean that billions of dollars in homes, apartment buildings, shopping centers and raw land would be available to investors at bargain prices in 1990, bankers warned that an overzealous sales program could do more harm than good.

"Dumping is an acute political hot button, and if that is mishandled, then the political problems will end up right on George Bush's door," said Kenneth A. Guenther, executive vice president of the Independent Bankers Association.

Largest in Nation's History

On Tuesday, the savings agency listed more than 30,000 parcels of commercial and residential property as the first group it will put on the market, making the real estate sale the nation's largest ever. The vast majority of parcels, 26,813, are residential, of which 11,918 are single-family homes.

The nonresidential properties range from a golf course in South Padre Island, Tex., to a Dairy Queen in Woodland Park, Colo. Also on the list are nursing homes, theaters, marinas and churches.

The heaviest concentration of properties is in the troubled Southwest. Although the trust agency has not disclosed the total value of the real estate,

Continued on Page D5, Column 1

HEALTH INSURANCE FOR ALL CHILDREN IS URGED BY CUOMO

State of State Message Calls for Score of New Programs in an Election Year

By ELIZABETH KOLBERT
Special to The New York Times

ALBANY, Jan. 3 — Presenting an election-year array of new programs, Gov. Mario M. Cuomo today proposed a universal health insurance program for children and an overhaul of the method that the state uses to distribute education aid.

Starting with a detailed recitation of his accomplishments and ending with a score of proposals aimed at almost as many constituencies, the Governor, who delivered his eighth State of the State address, sounded very much like a man preparing for the 1990 gubernatorial campaign.

"Wherever the need was, we were there — rebuilding New York," Mr. Cuomo said, listing the achievements of state government during his time in office. [Excerpts from the address, page B4.]

At a time when the state is facing enormous budget problems, the Governor proposed several major spending initiatives. Besides the new health insurance program for children, they included substantial expansion of the state's drug-treatment program and a $1.9 billion environmental bond issue.

A 'More Beautiful' Future

"It's time now for another solid down-payment on a better and more beautiful future for the generations to follow us," Mr. Cuomo said.

For the first time, the Governor also called for legislation eliminating so-called building tenure for principals in New York City schools. This prevents the principals from being transferred between schools without hearings.

Some of Mr. Cuomo's proposals, like the environmental bond issue, would not require a significant state investment for several years. But the Governor left open the question of how he would finance other new programs, saying this would be dealt with in the

Continued on Page B4, Column 1

Agence France-Presse
After the surrender of Gen. Manuel Antonio Noriega, an American soldier and a Panamanian woman celebrated in Panama City.

As Word Spreads in Panama, Thousands Turn Out to Cheer

By LARRY ROHTER
Special to The New York Times

PANAMA, Jan. 3 — Jubilant street celebrations broke out tonight as the news spread in the capital that the country's deposed military ruler, Gen. Manuel Antonio Noriega, had voluntarily handed himself over to the United States authorities and would be tried in a United States court.

Thousands of Panamanians took to their cars, honking their horns and snarling traffic across the city. Thousands came out of their homes onto the lawns or verandas of their homes to bang pots and pans as soon as General Noriega's surrender to the United States was announced over national radio and television.

On street corners, youths waved Panamanian flags and sang and danced. Some lighted firecrackers and hoisted pineapple effigies of General Noriega pierced with knives.

"Our full liberation from the dictatorship of Noriega is now complete," Vice President Ricardo Arias Calderón told the nation in a televised address. "All Panamanians feel great jubilation because we know now that a new day has begun, a new day of democracy and being brothers again, so as to reconstruct our country."

On the streets, the sentiment was identical and even more fervently expressed. "Now we are finally free," read one banner waved by a middle-aged woman. "Justice has been served," said another.

"The dictator is gone, once and for all," shouted a young Panamanian

Continued on Page A12, Column 5

U.S. GOAL ACHIEVED

Bush Speaks of Vatican 'Assistance' in Ending Panama Standoff

By ANDREW ROSENTHAL
Special to The New York Times

WASHINGTON, Jan. 3 — President Bush announced tonight that Gen. Manuel Antonio Noriega had surrendered to the United States military authorities in Panama, giving the President the final victory he had been seeking in the invasion of Panama.

General Noriega, who had defied American efforts to drive him from power for more than four years, was removed under cover of night from the Vatican Embassy in Panama, where he had taken refuge 10 days ago. He was then flown by United States military helicopter to Howard Air Base in Panama City, where he was arrested by agents of the United States Drug Enforcement Administration.

The general is under indictment in two Federal courts in Florida on drug trafficking charges and Mr. Bush has made bringing him to trial in the United States a major justification for invading Panama on Dec. 20 and an important aspect of his Latin American policy in general.

Bush Thanks the Vatican

Mr. Bush appeared in the White House briefing room at about 9:40 P.M., less than an hour after General Noriega surrendered, to announce that the deposed Panamanian strongman was aboard an Air Force C-131 transport plane bound for Homestead Air Force Base in southern Florida.

Thanking the Vatican for its "evenhanded, statesmanlike assistance" in getting General Noriega into American hands, Mr. Bush told reporters at a hurriedly called White House briefing that the general would be arraigned in Federal District Court in Miami on the drug charges filed in Miami in 1988. He was also indicted in Tampa.

An Administration official who asked not to be identified said that the White House had been expecting a breakthrough in the negotiations for several days, but that General Noriega's final surrender came without warning.

General Sets 3 Conditions

The general had sought assurances earlier in the week that he would not face the death penalty if he surrendered and had been told that the charges against him did not carry the death penalty, the official said.

Tonight, General Noriega informed the United States through Vatican intermediaries that he was ready to surrender. The official said the general had set three conditions: he wanted the press to be kept away from the Vatican mission when he left, he wanted to be able to contact family and friends by telephone before being flown out of the country and he wanted to be able to wear his uniform when he surrendered.

The United States, acting through the Vatican diplomats, agreed to those conditions, the official said.

General Noriega left the mission at 8:48 P.M. and was aboard the C-131 transport plane by 9:08 P.M. His sur-

Continued on Page A12, Column 4

INSIDE

Federal AIDS Estimate Is Being Revised

Scientists say that while AIDS continues to rise sharply, there will be at least 10 percent fewer cases over the next three years than previously predicted. Experts are debating why the rate seems to be changing. Page D20.

Treatment for First Lady

Barbara Bush began the first of 10 daily radiation treatments to relieve the double vision, eye discomfort and tears caused by Graves' disease, a thyroid affliction. Page D20.

Oil Leak Threatens Birds

An Exxon pipeline has leaked more than 200,000 gallons of heating oil into the Arthur Kill between Staten Island and New Jersey, posing a threat to birds along the waterway. Page B1.

Tyrannosaurus Deflatus?

A leading paleontologist says a type of dinosaur as large and fierce as Tyrannosaurus rex flourished 30 million years earlier. Page A21.

Teen-Agers Who Won't Join When Drug Dealers Recruit

By DIRK JOHNSON
Special to The New York Times

CHICAGO, Jan. 3 — One recent Saturday afternoon on the South Side here, a 14-year-old boy received a telephone call from a gang leader. He was calling, he said, to recruit drug dealers. The boy, who did not know the gang leader, politely declined.

"Well then," the caller asked, "who's going to fight for you?"

Street gangs here, who thrive on the commerce of illegal drugs, have become far more aggressive and insistent in trying to broaden their operations, school and police officials say.

"The gangs used to be much more selective," said Mary Cannon, a counselor at Harper High School on the South

Side, where a 16-year-old gang member was recently stabbed to death in a classroom by rival gang members. "Now they want anybody and everybody. It's big dollars, big business."

Teen-agers everywhere contend with peer pressure to use drugs just to fit in. But in the inner city, where poverty and frustration can make a drug high seem all the more appealing, there is also the pressure of street gangs, and their threats can be more ominous than any anti-drug message.

Despite these daunting forces, many young people in inner-city neighborhoods manage to resist drugs. They choose to work behind the counters of fast-food restaurants at the minimum wage even though they have heard they could earn a lot more money by selling cocaine.

They endure taunts, insults, even beatings, because they will not sell or use drugs.

Lacrista Ewing, an energetic 18-year-old, was warned about her straitlaced ways by the girls of a street gang

Continued on Page A20, Column 4

Reuters
Contras Deny Part in Attack on Nuns in Nicaragua

Roman Catholic nuns sitting beside the coffin of Sister Maureen Courtney yesterday in Managua. A leader of the American-backed Nicaraguan rebels denied that the contras played any part in the attack that killed Sister Maureen, an American, and Sister Teresa Rosales, a Nicaraguan. Page A10.

Soviets Reinforcing Troops Along Iranian Border

By FRANCIS X. CLINES
Special to The New York Times

MOSCOW, Jan. 3 — The Soviet Government reinforced its troops along the Iranian border today in the face of continuing reports of destructive protests by Azerbaijani crowds demanding an open frontier.

Soviet officials said angry throngs of thousands of people had destroyed guard towers, crossing alarms and wire fencing along miles of the border, demanding that ancient cultural and political ties between Azerbaijanis or

both sides of the Soviet-Iranian border be restored.

Most of the Government reports of violence and protest, in which no deaths and only reports of gunfire have been reported, centered on the autonomous republic of Nakhichevan, an Azerbaijani region that shares with Iran 102 miles of a common border area that is closed to Western reporters.

According to accounts in Izvestia, a group identified as the Nakhichevan Popular Front began staging protest rallies at the Nakhichevan segment of the border a month ago, demanding union with neighboring "southern Azerbaijan," which is now a part of

The Soviet Union shares a vast frontier with Iran, and Izvestia, the Soviet Government newspaper, reported that "a complex situation has emerged" with crowd protests reported at times along much of that length.

Continued on Page A15, Column 3

"All the News That's Fit to Print"

The New York Times

Late Edition

New York: Today, light snow, becoming partly sunny. High 38. Tonight, clear, breezy late. Low 30. Tomorrow, partly cloudy, windy. High 49. Yesterday: High 48, low 32. Details, page C8.

VOL.CXXXIX...No. 48,144   Copyright © 1990 The New York Times   NEW YORK, MONDAY, FEBRUARY 12, 1990   50 cents beyond 75 miles from New York City, except on Long Island   40 CENTS

Mike Tyson applying a cold towel to his swollen eye during a news conference after the fight.

Boxing Officials Could Overturn Defeat of Tyson

By PHIL BERGER

James (Buster) Douglas knocked out Mike Tyson this weekend and won the world heavyweight championship in one of the greatest upsets in boxing history. But Douglas's victory in Tokyo may be undone by a rancorous dispute over a long count on Tyson's knockdown of Douglas in the eighth round.

Two of boxing's major governing bodies, the World Boxing Association and the World Boxing Council, suspended the result of the fight yesterday pending hearings into the controversy. The third major group that recognized Tyson as the champion, the International Boxing Federation, said it now considers Douglas to be the champion.

Tyson's corner had protested that Douglas received a long count and, according to the W.B.C., a formal protest was later lodged by Japanese boxing authorities.

The result of the bout, fought Sunday in Tokyo (Saturday night in the United States), could ultimately be determined by the political and legal wrangling of the governing bodies as well as the considerable influence of Tyson's promoter, Don King.

Tunney-Dempsey Recalled

But this much is clear: By dominating the fight and knocking out the undefeated and seemingly invincible Tyson in the 10th round, Douglas, a relative unknown, shocked the sports world. And he also apparently upset the carefully laid plans for Tyson's boxing future, including a projected $22 million payday for a title defense against Evander Holyfield in June.

The knockdown in dispute, recalling the famous long count in the 1927 Gene Tunney-Jack Dempsey title fight, occurred after Tyson, battered by Douglas for most of eight rounds, connected on a right uppercut to Douglas's jaw that sent the challenger backward to the canvas.

Referee Octavio Meyran Sánchez leaped to Douglas's side and, after a pause, began counting with his fingers

Continued on Page C4, Column 5

INSIDE

Not Quite Watchdogs Yet
Across Eastern Europe, the once mighty official press is in even bigger trouble than the Communist parties it has praised for so long. Some papers have fallen into oblivion. Others are hoping for independence. Page A12.

A Turn in the Drug War?
In what experts hope is a turning point, the crime rate in and around Washington, D.C., is growing more slowly, and the number of suspects testing positive for cocaine use has dropped in recent months. Page B9.

Crisis Among Counselors
As the problems they confront grow more serious than those of 20 or even 10 years ago, guidance counselors in New York schools remain heavily overloaded. Page B1.

Checking-Account Bonus
Some banks are giving customers insurance that automatically protects goods bought by check against damage or loss and extends manufacturers' warranties. Page D1.

REAL LOVE: BY THEODORE ISAAC RUBIN, M.D. is at your bookstore now! AD'VT.

U.S. INVITES IDEAS FROM THE SOVIETS ON STRATEGIC CUTS

AN ADMINISTRATION SHIFT

Moscow's Earlier Suggestions on Reducing Nuclear Arms Have Been Spurned

By MICHAEL R. GORDON
Special to The New York Times

WASHINGTON, Feb. 11 — In a shift of position, the Bush Administration has told Moscow that it is now prepared to receive Soviet proposals about reductions in long-range nuclear arms that go beyond the emerging strategic arms treaty, Administration officials disclosed today.

Until recently, the Bush Administration has rebuffed Moscow's suggestions that the two sides open discussions on a possible second arms treaty that would make deeper reductions in long-range nuclear weapons, like ocean-spanning ballistic missiles, cruise missiles and bombers, than does the arms treaty now under negotiation.

But Secretary of State James A. Baker 3d told Soviet leaders in Moscow last week that the Administration is now ready to entertain new Soviet ideas on what sort of subsequent reductions in long-range nuclear arms should be carried out after the current Strategic Arms Reduction Talks are concluded.

Thinking of 'Next Phase'

"Up to now we have not been willing to discuss the Soviet ideas on Start-2 on the ground that we still have work to do on Start-1," said a senior Administration official. "Now we are saying you can raise your ideas if you want to. We are getting to the point where we need to think a little bit about the next phase."

The question of whether to seek further reductions in long-range nuclear weapons after an agreement is reached has been a contentious one for the Bush Administration. Some Administration officials, like the White House national security adviser, Brent Scowcroft, have argued that reductions in nuclear weapons should not be pursued for their own sake, and the Administration has yet to formulate a basic position of what additional cuts in long-range nuclear arms, if any, might be sought.

The treaty currently under negotia-

Continued on Page A11, Column 1

The Price of Peace

Movements that fought in the trenches of the cold war are flushed out as peace breaks out in Central and Eastern Europe. Page A10.

MANDELA, FREED, URGES STEP-UP IN PRESSURE TO END WHITE RULE

Nelson Mandela leaving Victor Verster prison yesterday after spending 27 years in South African jails.

On Mandela's Walk, Hope and Violence

By JOHN F. BURNS
Special to The New York Times

PAARL, South Africa, Feb. 11 — When Nelson Mandela made his walk to freedom today, he did it with the same simplicity and command of occasion that made him a leader among millions of South African blacks when his imprisonment began more than 10,000 days ago.

At 4:14 P.M. on a sun-warmed day — 27 years, six months and one week after his arrest on Aug. 5, 1962 — Mr. Mandela stepped from the car that drove him to the last guard post at the Victor Verster prison.

From there, smiling gently, he passed under a raised barrier and flicked his right hand quickly out from his body in greeting. He then raised his right arm several times in the bolder, black nationalist salute, his left hand holding the hand of his wife, Winnie,

and walked to the point where the prison entrance road abuts the highway running through the undulating wine country of the Western Cape.

It was a walk of perhaps 70 yards, through a corridor of policemen, and as he made it, Mr. Mandela said not a word, at least none that could be heard by any in the crowd of 5,000 blacks and whites chanting his name. But to those who have come to know Mr. Mandela in the only way that was possible under the total ban that the South African Government threw around the black leader in prison — through his speeches and writings of a generation ago — there was no mistaking the symbolism involved in beginning his life outside jail on foot.

About the time in 1961 when President John F. Kennedy was spending his first summer in the White House, Mr. Mandela, then about the same age as

Mr. Kennedy, used a phrase that became the title of a book of Mr. Mandela's speeches and writings. The book has been passed hand to hand in dog-eared copies among South Africans, who were forbidden until today under censorship laws and statutes governing political prisoners to own any book by or about the black leader. There was, Mr. Mandela said, "no easy walk to freedom" for South African blacks after three centuries of white domination and repression.

Dignified and Resolute

The Nelson Mandela who made his own walk to freedom today, after more than 22 years in the fortress prison on Robben Island, in the gale-swept mouth of Cape Town harbor, and five more years in a series of other prisons, had hair that had turned to gray. He looked at least 30 pounds lighter than he had at his last public appearance, in June 1964 when, with the physique of the heavyweight boxer he had been in his youth, he stood in the dock at the Rivonia Trial in Johannesburg and acknowledged that he was guilty as charged of sabotage and attempting to overthrow the Government.

But in other respects, the 71-year-old

Continued on Page A14, Column 1

SPEECH IS RESOLUTE

He Asks Other Nations Not to Lift Sanctions Against Pretoria

By CHRISTOPHER S. WREN
Special to The New York Times

CAPE TOWN, Feb. 11 — After 27 and a half years in prison, Nelson Mandela finally won his freedom today and promptly urged his supporters at home and abroad to increase their pressure against the white minority Government that had just released him.

"We have waited too long for our freedom," Mr. Mandela told a cheering crowd from a balcony of Cape Town's old City Hall. "We can wait no longer."

"Now is the time to intensify the struggle on all fronts," he said. "To relax our efforts now would be a mistake which generations to come will not be able to forgive." [Transcript of the address, page A15.]

First Speech Since '64

Mr. Mandela's 20-minute speech, which he prepared before leaving prison today, constituted his first remarks in public since before he was sentenced in June 1964 to life imprisonment for conspiracy to overthrow the Government and engage in sabotage.

He asked the international community not to lift its sanctions against South Africa, despite the recent changes introduced by President F. W. de Klerk, which culminated in Mr. Mandela's release.

"To lift sanctions now would be to run the risk of aborting the process toward ending apartheid," he said.

An Eloquent Militancy

Mr. Mandela's voice sounded firm and his words as eloquently militant as when he defended violence as the ultimate recourse at his political trial in 1964. Though he looked all of his 71 years and was grayer than artists' renditions over the years had depicted, he walked out of Victor Verster prison erect and vigorous.

In Washington, President Bush rejoiced over the release of Mr. Mandela, spoke to him by telephone and invited the anti-apartheid leader to visit the White House. [Page A17.]

Mr. Mandela gave no evidence that his militant opposition to apartheid had been tempered by the more than 10,000 days he spent in confinement. But he also said nothing that would have surprised the Government he said it during his years of incarceration. Indeed, there appeared to be nothing in Mr. Mandela's initial remarks after his release to give the Government much consolation or encouragement.

Although he has been viewed as a potential leader for all South Africans, he stressed time and again that his loyalty lay with the African National Congress, for which he was working under-

Continued on Page A14, Column 1

A South African youth celebrating Nelson Mandela's release yesterday at an African National Congress rally in Soweto. Mr. Mandela urged supporters to increase their pressure against the white Government.

Bush Homeless Plan: 'Godsend' or False Hope?

By JASON DePARLE

On the night of Sept. 25, 1988, a previously obscure piece of Federal legislation was ushered onto political center stage before a television audience of millions.

During the season's first Presidential debate, a panelist asked George Bush what he would do for the homeless, "this voiceless segment of our society."

Mr. Bush answered without hesitation. "I want to see the McKinney Act fully funded," the Republican candidate said.

The McKinney Act?

The reference hardly resonated in the living rooms of America. Most viewers had never heard of the McKinney Act, and Mr. Bush's terse answer offered virtually no basis on which to judge it.

But Mr. Bush has kept his word. Last year, at his urging, Congress came close to fully financing most McKinney programs for the first time since the act was passed in 1987.

And the legislation remains a central provision of the Administration's plan for helping the home-

Federal Aid, New York Homeless
A special report.

less. As recently as last month, Mr. Bush pointed toward funds from the McKinney Act in telling a convention of home builders in Atlanta that "my Administration is going to do its part" in working to "solve the problems of the helpless and the homeless."

$67 Million for New York

The act itself is a quiver of 16 programs, each taking a different aim at homelessness. Some of the programs support shelters, with food or funds. Others provide services like job training, health care or treatment for alcohol or drug abuse.

The funds approved last year are likely to raise New York State's share to about $67 million, from $45 million. Because the money filters through a variety of governments and private organizations, it is im-

possible to determine how much of it is spent in New York City.

But despite the McKinney Act's broad aims and the recent increase in financing, many of those who provide shelter and services to the homeless say the McKinney Act falls short in at least these three respects:

¶It provides relatively little money.

¶It creates daunting bureaucratic obstacles.

¶It provides almost no funds for low-income housing, which advocates argue must be part of a solution to homelessness.

"It's much ado about nothing," said Douglas H. Lasdon of the Legal Assistance Center for the Homeless in Manhattan. "It gives people the impression that something's being done, but it's not."

Measured in paint or plaster, protein or pajamas, the law has made a difference in the lives of dozens of New York organizations. Some money from the act, named for Representative Stewart B. McKinney, a Connecticut Republican

Continued on Page B8, Column 1

Rural Doctor's Struggle to Care for the Poorest

By PETER APPLEBOME
Special to The New York Times

TCHULA, Miss. — There aren't many doctors like Ronald Myers, a jazz-playing, Baptist-preaching family practitioner whose dream has always been to practice medicine in the kind of place most other doctors wouldn't even stop for a tank of gas.

But there are plenty of places like Tchula, a forlorn patch of Mississippi Delta poverty where it is hard to find a street that's not rutted, a sign that's not crooked, a paint job that's not peeling or a life that's not perched on the brink of economic ruin.

Dr. Myers's story — how hard it has been for him to get here and how hard

it may be for him to stay — provides a dispiriting look at health care in rural America. The situation is worsening because the Government's program to provide doctors for the nation's neediest areas is being dismantled as health care needs continue to grow.

"Working in Tchula, Miss., is like working in a third world country," said Dr. Myers, who became Tchula's only doctor when he opened a clinic this month in an abandoned restaurant next to a grim liquor store. "The needs are that great. So how is it that here's a well-trained physician who wants to

come to an area that's desperately poor, and I can't get any assistance? I can't get a loan. I'll take a tongue depressor if someone will give me one. There's a problem somewhere."

In poor rural areas, particularly in the South, regular medical care is seldom more than a distant dream. In areas like Tchula and nearby Belzoni, where Dr. Myers previously worked, infant mortality rates are three times the national average, most women receive little if any prenatal care and people usually see a doctor only when they have no choice.

"The health problems in this area

THE NEW YORK TIMES IS AVAILABLE FOR home or office delivery in most major U.S. cities. Please call this toll free number 1-800-631-2580. ADVT.

Continued on Page B11, Column 1

The New York Times

VOL.CXXXIX . No. 48,316   Copyright © 1990 The New York Times   NEW YORK, FRIDAY, AUGUST 3, 1990   50 cents beyond 75 miles from New York City, except on Long Island   40 CENTS

Late Edition

New York: Today, sunny. High 89. Tonight, clear, not as cool. Low 70. Tomorrow, mostly sunny, very warm, more humid. High 91. Yesterday, high 89, low 65. Details are on page C22.

INVADING IRAQIS SEIZE KUWAIT AND ITS OIL; U.S. CONDEMNS ATTACK, URGES UNITED ACTION

INDICTMENT NAMES QUEENS LAWMAKER IN MISUSE OF FUNDS

Rep. Flake Faces 17 Federal Counts Involving Church and Housing Complex

By ARNOLD H. LUBASCH

Representative Floyd H. Flake, a powerful Queens minister who rode his popularity into Congress four years ago, has been indicted on charges of diverting tens of thousands of dollars in church funds to his own use.

The 17-count Federal indictment, which was unsealed yesterday, charges that Mr. Flake and his wife, Margarett, engaged in a two-pronged conspiracy involving his church and the housing complex for the elderly that it built in Jamaica under his stewardship. They are accused of fraudulently obtaining $66,700 from the church, embezzling $75,000 from the housing complex and evading income taxes on both amounts.

Pastor Since '76

The Representative, a Democrat whose Sixth Congressional District covers southern Queens, issued a detailed statement denying the charges. His lawyer said he still intended to run for re-election in November, and Mrs. Flake's lawyer added that the charges would fuel "a perception that minority politicians are being unfairly targeted for prosecution."

Since 1976, the 45-year-old Congressman has been pastor of the Allen A.M.E. Church in Jamaica, one of the largest and oldest black churches in New York City, with 6,000 members and a history reaching back into the 1830's. During his tenure, Mr. Flake has built up the church, and his own influence, with a network of social-services for the largely poor and largely black Jamaica neighborhood.

3d Congressman to Be Indicted

And yesterday, under the warm afternoon sun, there was a wary feeling of racism at work and an insistence that the charges against the pastor had to be false. [Page B4.]

Mr. Flake is the third New York City Congressman indicted in the last three years. The others, Mario Biaggi and Robert Garcia, both Bronx Democrats, were convicted in the Wedtech racketeering case. Mr. Garcia's conviction was overturned in June.

In announcing the unsealing of the indictment, the United States Attorney

Continued on Page B4, Column 5

The New York Times
Representative Floyd H. Flake

Covenant Report Is Said to Find Sex Misconduct

By M. A. FARBER

An investigation ordered by the Covenant House board of directors concludes that the Rev. Bruce Ritter, the charity's founder and longtime president, engaged in sexual misconduct with young men living at Covenant House shelters for runaway youths, according to people who have read the investigation's report.

They say the four-month investigation, headed by Robert J. McGuire, a former New York City Police Commissioner, finds that had Father Ritter not resigned last February, the board would have had to dismiss him.

A Secretive Personal Fund

The report, which is to be issued today, also says the Covenant House board, controlled by Father Ritter until this year, failed to exercise proper oversight. The report notes, for example, that the board did not know that Father Ritter was receiving a salary of $98,000, the bulk of which was going into a secretive personal fund.

The fund, called the Franciscan Charitable Trust, had accumulated close to $1 million. Plans now call for it to be liquidated, with the assets going to Covenant House, as Father Ritter says he intended all along.

Father Ritter, who has vehemently denied the allegations, calling them "garbage," has declined to be interviewed for months and is said to have refused to cooperate with Mr. McGuire's investigation. The 63-year-old

Continued on Page B4, Column 2

Soviet Smokers Vow Strikes As Cigarettes, Too, Disappear

By CELESTINE BOHLEN
Special to The New York Times

MOSCOW, Aug. 2 — It happens like clockwork, all over the city. A truck pulls up to a boarded-up kiosk, unloads its wares, the sale window opens and within minutes smokers appear out of nowhere to take places in line, hopeful that for this day, anyway, their addiction can be fed.

Along with other ills, the Soviet Union is now in the throes of a nicotine fit, brought on by a painful and puzzling withdrawal of cigarettes from a nation of heavy smokers.

In many parts of the country, the cigarette shortage — caused by a series of typical economic lapses — has galvanized the patient, line-suffering Soviet consumer into action.

In the city of Perm last week, a demonstration that began in front of an empty tobacco shop spilled into downtown streets, ending in a rally outside City Hall, where 2,000 people chanted and waved banners, badgering the Communist Party for cigarettes. "Hey, you up there, your people have nothing to smoke as well as nothing to eat," one banner read. "Party, have you got a smoke?" asked another.

Aircraft Workers Threaten Strike

In Kuibyshev, smokers at an aircraft plant threatened a strike over the cigarette shortage and protesters mounted a daily vigil at a local tobacco plant that had been shut for repairs.

Warning strikes have also been reported in Ulyanovsk and Ufa, while in Voronezh and Orel, angry smokers have smashed the windows of tobacco kiosks. This month, at the height of the harvest in the Krasnodar region, combine operators brought their machines to a stop with a nonnegotiable demand: "No tobacco, no work."

Such public vehemence has been absent during other shortages: when cheese, onions, lemons or sausages disappear from the stores, Soviet shoppers simply shift their queues from one

Continued on Page A4, Column 5

INSIDE

Why a Bishop Quit
The recent resignation of the Roman Catholic Archbishop of Atlanta came about after evidence of his "intimate relationship" with a woman, church officials said. Page A12.

A Troubled Savings Rescue
Almost a year after the Federal bailout of the savings and loan industry, economists see problems, including a danger to banks. Page D1.

Barry Case Goes to Jury
The drug case against Washington's Mayor is now in the hands of 12 of the city's residents. Page A12.

IRAQ'S ADVANTAGE LIMITS U.S. OPTIONS

Lack of Warning or Proximity Hinders American Action

By MICHAEL R. GORDON
Special to The New York Times

WASHINGTON, Aug. 2 — The Bush Administration faced the sobering reality today that despite a longstanding commitment to defend America's vital interests in the Persian Gulf, there was no easy military means to compel Iraq to withdraw its forces from Kuwait.

With the forces of pro-Western Arab powers like Saudi Arabia no match militarily for Iraq's powerful army, and with only a token American military presence in the area, the Administration's immediate responses included condemning the invasion, freezing Iraqi assets in the United States and calling for international sanctions.

Pentagon officials said that the United States had undertaken some military preparations as a result of the Iraqi attack. One aircraft carrier, the Independence, was under way at high speed from the Indian Ocean toward the Persian Gulf. It is expected to reach the area in several days.

A 2d Carrier Is Shifted

Another aircraft carrier, the Eisenhower, was being shifted to the Eastern Mediterranean Sea to put its attack planes within range of Iraq. The modest fleet of American ships in the Persian Gulf was expanded from six to eight. And some Air Force aerial refueling tankers were said to have been dispatched to the Indian Ocean region.

Defense Secretary Dick Cheney canceled plans to go with President Bush to Aspen, Colo., for Mr. Bush's speech on military issues and instead monitored the Gulf crisis from the Pentagon.

Continued on Page A8, Column 4

2 Teen-Agers Shot As Violence Persists On New York Streets

The tide of violence in New York City in the last two weeks — four children killed by stray gunfire, an advertising executive shot dead in the West Village, two cab drivers murdered, a young couple bludgeoned in Central Park — continued yesterday as officials struggled to respond to growing fears.

A 14-year-old Queens boy was shot and killed after he told another teenager to stop riding a friend's moped. In the Bronx, a 15-year-old girl standing with friends in a park was critically wounded when a youth fired a gunshot into her group. A homeless drifter was charged with Monday's fatal shooting of the ad executive at a phone booth.

And pressure grew on city officials to cope with the latest wave of violence. Mayor David N. Dinkins today will announce a crackdown on gun users. Police Commissioner Lee P. Brown, in an interview, contended that the police alone could not solve the problems of crime and violence.

Articles, pages B1 and B3.

Jim Perry/The New York Times
Iraqi invaders quickly moved into Kuwait City, taking control of Government buildings and the airport.

A New Gulf Alignment

Iraqis, Bargaining on Anti-U.S. Sentiment, May Profit by Intimidating the Monarchies

By YOUSSEF M. IBRAHIM
Special to The New York Times

News Analysis

PARIS, Aug. 2 — Iraq's invasion of Kuwait ushers in a new alignment in which Iraqis, Iranians and Palestinian hard-liners appear to share an interest in subduing the oil-rich monarchies of the region and challenging United States influence in the Arab world.

In ordering his forces to attack Kuwait, President Saddam Hussein of Iraq calculated that the odds were largely in his favor.

Arab diplomats and military experts said the only serious risk for Iraq was swift retaliation from the United States military forces. But that is a move that Washington may not be ready to take, given that the Iraqi armed forces are widely considered the most tested and best equipped in the Gulf region.

The Iraqis have much to gain from their invasion of Kuwait. A successful offensive could establish Baghdad as the dominant power in the Middle East, giving it a much greater say in decisions on oil production and prices.

Beyond that, the attack could become a rallying point for those in the Arab world who resent United States influence in world affairs and who feel that some Middle Eastern nations like Egypt have gone too far in accommodating Washington. Lastly, it could finally settle Iraq's longstanding border disputes with Kuwait.

The prospects for an effective counter to the attack appear slimmer in view of evidence that the Iraqis coordinated their move with Iran, which helped exert diplomatic pressure on Kuwait and the United Arab Emirates to raise prices last month at a meeting of the Organization of Petroleum Exporting Countries.

Iran officially condemned the Iraqi move late today, but the suspicion remained that it had at the very least not discouraged Baghdad's action.

Sense of Powerlessness

In the wake of the invasion, the Arab world is discovering how powerless it is in countering an Iraqi attempt to assert its dominance.

Saudi Arabia is Kuwait's closest ally in the region and the founder of the Gulf Cooperation Council, the alliance to which both Kuwait and the United Arab Emirates belong. But it has hardly lifted a finger to halt the Iraqi invasion, giving the impression that it is powerless and ever more dependent on American assistance. Although the Saudis have spent billions of dollars on

Continued on Page A10, Column 3

'NAKED AGGRESSION'

Bush Suggests Action by U.N. — Emir Flees to Saudi Arabia Exile

By R. W. APPLE Jr.
Special to The New York Times

WASHINGTON, Aug. 2 — Iraqi troops stormed into the desert sheikdom of Kuwait today, seizing control of its capital city and its rich oilfields, driving its ruler into exile and plunging the strategic Persian Gulf region into crisis and sending tremors of anxiety around the world.

President Bush condemned the invasion as "naked aggression" and sought to enlist world leaders in collective action against Iraq.

Faced with a dire threat from the truculent Iraqi leader, Saddam Hussein, to a region containing much of the world's oil reserves and with world financial markets in turmoil, Mr. Bush banned nearly all imports from Iraq and froze the nation's assets in the United States. At a news conference in Woody Creek, Colo., the President and Prime Minister Margaret Thatcher of Britain raised the possibility of economic or even military action by the United Nations.

Iraq Suspends Payments

In response, Iraq, which had been accusing Kuwait for weeks of stealing its oil and violating production limits set by the Organization of Petroleum Exporting Countries, suspended debt payments to the United States. Western experts asserted that Iraq had been motivated by a financial squeeze that only more oil dollars could ease and by ambitions for regional dominance.

Although oil prices rose sharply today, analysts noted that world inventories are unusually high, and they saw no immediate threat to supplies.

Witnesses in Kuwait said that hundreds of people were killed or wounded today as Iraqi ground forces, led by columns of tanks, surged into the desert emirate at the head of the gulf. Other troops came by air.

For Mr. Bush, the invasion posed manifold problems: the difficulty of direct military action despite the huge commitment of money and resources to the gulf in recent years; fear of another surge in oil prices, which could hurt economic growth and rekindle inflation; the potential disruption of the fragile budget negotiations between the White House and the Congress, in which a gasoline tax has been considered, and possible damage to the Re-

Continued on Page A8, Column 1

Reuters
Iraqi gunners yesterday on the coast near Kuwait City, where they fired on Kuwaiti naval vessels offshore.

The Iraqi Invasion: Global Reverberations

OIL PRICES Spot market prices surged, with the American benchmark crude rising to $23.11 a barrel, up $1.57. The invasion stirred fears of slower economic growth, higher inflation and OPEC domination of the world oil market. But price increases should be limited by a near-record stockpile worldwide. Page A9.

FINANCIAL MARKETS The dollar rose, gold prices jumped and most stock markets fell. Japan, dependent on imported oil, was hard hit. As of today's close in Tokyo, its stock market had fallen 4.3 percent since the invasion took place. Page D1.

THE SOVIET UNION Moscow announced a suspension in the delivery of arms and military hardware to

Iraq. The move interrupted Moscow's longtime role as Baghdad's chief arms supplier. Page A10.

UNITED NATIONS With Moscow and Washington in agreement, the Security Council voted 14 to 0 to condemn the invasion and demand an Iraqi withdrawal. Page A10.

DIPLOMACY Secretary of State James A. Baker 3d cut short a visit to Mongolia and plans to issue a joint statement with the Soviet Foreign Minister, Eduard A. Shevardnadze, condemning the invasion and called for an emergency Arab summit conference.

ISRAEL Israeli leaders condemned the invasion, but they also appeared

relieved by the move. For months, President Saddam Hussein has been sharply threatening Israel. Officials in Jerusalem were openly frustrated that the rest of the world did not seem adequately concerned. Page A10.

THE EUROPEAN ALLIES Western European countries unanimously condemned the invasion, with Britain and France joining the United States in freezing billions of dollars worth of Kuwaiti assets. Page A10.

338

"All the News That's Fit to Print"

The New York Times

Late Edition

New York: **Today,** sunny, becoming windy. High 73. **Tonight,** breezy, mild. Low 62. **Tomorrow,** quite windy, sunny, warmer. High 77. **Yesterday,** high 69, low 56. Details are on page C7.

VOL.CXL . . No. 48,377

Copyright © 1990 The New York Times

NEW YORK, WEDNESDAY, OCTOBER 3, 1990

50 cents beyond 75 miles from New York City, except on Long Island.

40 CENTS

TWO GERMANYS UNITE AFTER 45 YEARS WITH JUBILATION AND A VOW OF PEACE

DINKINS PROPOSES RECORD EXPANSION OF POLICE FORCES

Mayor Offers New Programs for Corrections and Youth to Help Combat Crime

By RALPH BLUMENTHAL

Seeking to take command of an issue that has shaken his leadership, Mayor David N. Dinkins announced a barrage of proposals yesterday to fight crime, including a record expansion of New York City's police forces and ambitious new corrections, youth and education programs. The total cost would be $1.8 billion over the next four years.

With New York City already in financial straits, the Mayor proposed paying for the initiatives through a rise in the real-property tax, a new city payroll tax to be shared by workers and employers and a 25-cent surcharge on state lottery tickets.

The taxes, which would rise from $138 million in what remains of the first fiscal year to $644 million in the fourth year, would require approval by the City Council and the State Legislature.

'Assault on All Fronts'

"We will not wage war by degree," Mr. Dinkins said, releasing a 535-page police manpower study and a 57-page mayoral report that began a day of briefings and culminated in a news conference timed for live television coverage on the evening news. "Our strategy calls for an assault on all fronts." [Excerpts, page B2.]

The anti-crime program was hailed by many community leaders, but reaction to the tax plan was mixed. The State Senate majority leader, Ralph J. Marino, voiced strong reservations about the potentially negative effect on commuters and businesses. Gov. Mario M. Cuomo said that if it were necessary for public safety, he "could" support the payroll tax, but that he had yet to review the plan in detail.

Assembly Speaker Mel Miller also urged caution. "We're going to have to go slowly in weighing the tax package," most of which, he noted, would not take effect until the fiscal year beginning next July. The City Council Speaker, Peter F. Vallone, voiced general support for the plan but seemed taken aback that it went so far beyond the Council's own proposal to hire more officers through a lottery surcharge.

Thomas Reppetto, president of the

Continued on Page B2, Column 1

In Appeal for Support for Budget, President Calls Plan Best for Now

By DAVID E. ROSENBAUM
Special to The New York Times

WASHINGTON, Oct. 2 — Faced with a revolt in his party's Congressional ranks and wariness around the country, President Bush appealed on television tonight for public support of the budget compromise he and Congressional leaders struck last weekend. He predicted "economic chaos if we fail to reduce the deficit."

In a show of bipartisanship that verged on coalition Government, the President was followed with a broadcast by Senator George J. Mitchell of Maine, the Democratic leader. He urged support for the President "because the nation is more important than partisan differences." [Transcripts of the Bush and Mitchell speeches appear on page D28.]

Tough Task for Bush

Mr. Mitchell was preaching to the converted for the most part. Despite considerable opposition among liberals, a majority of Congressional Democrats appear to support the agreement.

But Mr. Bush has the more difficult task of swaying enough dissident Republicans to win enactment of the plan.

The President said that neither he nor anyone else was completely satisfied with the compromise, but he said it was "the best agreement that can be legislated now."

In the strongest statement he has made about economic perils that might lie ahead, Mr. Bush emphasized: "If we fail to enact this agreement, our economy will falter, markets may tumble and recession will follow."

He called on the public to "tell your Congressmen and Senators you support this deficit-reduction agreement."

A Bipartisan Appeal

The President continued: "If they are Republicans, urge them to stand with the President. If they are Democrats, urge them to stand with their Congressional leaders."

"Those who dislike one part or another may pick our agreement apart," Mr. Bush said, "but if they do, believe me, the political reality is no one can put a better one back together again."

Senator Mitchell made almost identical points. He would have preferred "a budget that asks more from the wealthy and less from the elderly," he said. But as for the compromise, he

Continued on Page D27, Column 1

Pivotal Moment for Bush

By ANDREW ROSENTHAL
Special to The New York Times

WASHINGTON, Oct. 2 — With his speech tonight from the Oval Office, George Bush completed a fundamental transition: The President who succeeded for so long at giving Americans only good news is now telling them to prepare for economic pain at home and the possibility of war abroad.

News Analysis

With remarkable speed, Mr. Bush has moved from the most protracted honeymoon in recent White House history to twin crises that could determine the success of his Presidency.

The decision to confront the Republican rebellion on Capitol Hill over the budget agreement quickly and directly in a nationally televised speech represented a judgment that any delay could allow events to spin out of control. If the emerging prospects for passage of the budget package turn into defeat, Mr. Bush would immediately lose his calculated gamble that such an agreement would be good for the economy and thus bolster his re-election campaign in 1992.

For more than a year and a half, everything seemed to be going Mr. Bush's way, especially in Europe. Then on Aug. 8, six days after the Iraqi invasion of Kuwait, Mr. Bush went on national television to announce that he was sending troops to the Persian Gulf and to prepare the country for the possibility that American soldiers and civilians could die in a far-off war.

Tonight, less than two months later, Mr. Bush again spoke from the Oval

Continued on Page D27, Column 4

More on the Budget

A SECOND LOOK Some experts say the deficit will be cut less than predicted. Page D27.

TAX BREAKS Big companies may benefit from provisions aimed at small ones. Page D29.

PLANNING AHEAD How changes in deductions will affect some taxpayers. Page D29.

The German flag was unfurled in front of the Reichstag building in Berlin at midnight as the two Germanys were reunited.

Associated Press

Senate Confirms Souter, 90 to 9, As Supreme Court's 105th Justice

By RICHARD L. BERKE
Special to The New York Times

WASHINGTON, Oct. 2 — Ten weeks after President Bush nominated David H. Souter, a little-known New Hampshire judge, for the Supreme Court, the Senate voted overwhelmingly today to confirm him as the Court's 105th Justice.

The vote was 90 to 9, with only Democrats voting against confirmation. The balloting came after nearly four hours of speeches on the Senate floor in which supporters said they were confident Judge Souter would preserve fundamental constitutional values, while opponents said too much was not known about his positions on critical issues like abortion.

Case on Sensitive Issue

Chief Justice William H. Rehnquist will swear in Judge Souter at a relatively short ceremony at the Court on Tuesday morning, in time to sit for oral arguments later that day in the second week of the Court term.

On Wednesday, Judge Souter will be among the Justices hearing a major case on the lawfulness of corporate policies that exclude women from jobs that might endanger a developing fetus. Today the Court took up the major issue left unresolved from the era of official school segregation: what a school system that was segregated by law decades ago must do to free itself from Federal court supervision. [Education, page B8.]

With the Souter nomination behind him, Senator Joseph R. Biden Jr., the

Delaware Democrat who is chairman of the Judiciary Committee, was looking to future vacancies on the Court. He said he hoped that the Administration "will not learn the wrong lesson" from the strong bipartisan support the nominee received.

"Our overwhelming approval is not a sign that the Senate intends to be lax about exercising its advise-and-consent power, or intends to use that power only to screen out extremist nominees," Mr. Biden said. "Rather, it is a sign that we take this power seriously, and that we intend to exercise it responsibly. And in doing so, Judge Souter falls within the sphere of candidates acceptable to the Senate."

Mr. Biden emphasized, however, that he and several other Democrats who supported the nomination had serious misgivings because Judge Souter

Continued on Page A24, Column 1

A MILLION IN BERLIN

Flag at Reichstag Marks Start of a New Era at Center of Europe

By SERGE SCHMEMANN
Special to The New York Times

BERLIN, Wednesday, Oct. 3 — Forty-five years after it was carved up in defeat and disgrace, Germany was reunited today in a midnight celebration of pealing bells, national hymns and the jubilant blare of good old German oom-pah-pah.

At the stroke of midnight Tuesday, a copy of the American Liberty Bell, a gift from the United States at the height of the cold war, tolled from the Town Hall, and the black, red and gold banner of the Federal Republic of Germany rose slowly before the Reichstag, the scarred seat of past German Parliaments.

Then the President, Richard von Weizsäcker, drawing on the words of the West German Constitution, proclaimed from the steps of the Reichstag: "In free self-determination, we want to achieve the unity in freedom of Germany. We are aware of our responsibility for these tasks before God and the people. We want to serve peace in the world in a united Europe."

Singing of Anthem

With that, a throng estimated at one million joined in the West German national anthem, now the anthem for united Germany: "Unity and justice and freedom for the German fatherland . . ." The words are from the third stanza of the prewar anthem, whose opening verses, now banned, began, "Deutschland, Deutschland über Alles."

The moment marked the return of a nation severed along the front line between East and West to the center stage of Europe, this time as an economic powerhouse vowing never again to bring grief to a continent it had so terribly ravaged in the past century.

It is the smallest unified German state to rise in the 119 years since Otto von Bismarck first gathered the Germans under the Prussian crown.

Beer and Revelry

Hundreds of German flags waved and firecrackers snapped in the chilly autumn night. Beer and sparkling wine flowed freely and the strains of divergent bands mingled in a rowdy cacophony. Soon bottles began smashing on the pavement and celebration turned to intoxication, and by early morning the center of the new capital was deep in smashed bottles and weaving revelers.

A force of about 5,000 police officers had been massed in case radicals tried

Continued on Page A17, Column 1

Germany by the Numbers

In some respects, the united Germany is less than the sum of its parts. The statistical tale is told in charts and a map on page A16.

Bitter Dispute Is Threatening Program for Marrow Donors

By GINA KOLATA

A program that has the lofty goal of finding altruistic people to donate bone marrow to save the lives of dying patients has become enmeshed in a dispute that threatens its ability to function.

The conflict involves charges that a former subcontractor in the federally financed program provided misleading information to dying patients and volunteers who wanted to help them; withheld the names of thousands of potential marrow donors; and failed to account for families for large sums of money raised in their names.

The subcontractor, the Life-Savers Foundation of America, has denied the allegations and accused the National Marrow Donor Program of overcharging patients and being inefficient in matching patients and donors.

Registry of Potential Donors

The national program has amassed a file of 200,000 people who are willing to donate marrow if their tissue is compatible with that of a patient with leukemia or another disease. Without transplants, the patients will die, and the demand for donors far exceeds the supply.

But Federal officials, transplant surgeons and ethicists are worried that allegations of questionable conduct in the treatment of dying patients and their families could cause the network of

The national program has asserted in court and in a letter to Senator Al Gore, Democrat of Tennessee, that Life-Savers caused patients unnecessary anguish by raising false hopes that they would find a donor.

Officials of the national program, who say they have severed all ties with the subcontractor, say some families

Continued on Page A26, Column 1

Top Soviet General Tells U.S. Not to Attack in Gulf

Gen. Mikhail A. Moiseyev, left, chief of the Soviet General Staff, discussing options in the Persian Gulf crisis yesterday in New York City. With him was Gen. Colin L. Powell, the Chairman of the Joint Chiefs of Staff.

Jack Manning/The New York Times

By MICHAEL R. GORDON

The head of the Soviet military said yesterday that the economic sanctions against Iraq were working and that no force should be used in the Persian Gulf unless it was approved by the United Nations.

The remarks by the Soviet general, Mikhail A. Moiseyev, Chief of the Soviet General Staff, were the most explicit comments made so far by a Soviet official on the need for United Nations approval for the use of force by the United States and other nations that have opposed the Iraqi invasion of Kuwait.

The Soviet general's comments — in an unusual joint interview with Gen. Colin L. Powell, Chairman of the Joint Chiefs of Staff — signaled a basic disagreement with Washington about the circumstances under which military force could be used in the Persian Gulf.

"We cannot view the resolution of any crisis like this by means of using arms," said General Moiseyev, who is on a tour of the United States as a guest of General Powell. But General Powell pointedly said President Bush had not ruled out any options.

The two generals were interviewed by writers and editors of The New York Times.

Suggesting that military force was

not needed to force Iraqi troops out of Kuwait, General Moiseyev said the economic embargo was beginning to hurt Iraq.

"Saddam Hussein has really understood now finally how far he has gone," General Moiseyev said. "He is finding himself in economic and political isolation, and he can't survive very long that way."

General Moiseyev asserted that protests, uprisings and desertions in Iraqi were sapping the strength of the Iraqi military and impelling President Hussein to seek a diplomatic solution.

"You can't keep an army together

Continued on Page A12, Column 1

INSIDE

Air Crash Mystery in China
Did a cockpit struggle cause a hijacked Chinese plane to crash into a parked jet at Canton's airport, killing 127 people? Chinese officials would not confirm the report. Page A3.

South African Rift Persists
The leader of the Inkatha movement spurned a meeting with the African National Congress, dampening prospects for a reconciliation between the two warring groups. Page A3.

Melee in Pakistan
A mob stormed the courtroom where former Prime Minister Benazir Bhutto is to stand trial on corruption charges. Page A6.

Women in Locker Rooms
Three recent incidents in football have reopened the issue of access to locker rooms by women covering men's sports. Page D31.

"All the News That's Fit to Print"

The New York Times

Late Edition

New York: **Today,** partly cloudy, windy. High 49. **Tonight,** clear, cold winds. Low 32. **Tomorrow,** variable clouds. High 40. **Yesterday,** high 55, low 38. Details are on page D22.

VOL.CXL ... No. 48,483   Copyright © 1991 The New York Times   NEW YORK, THURSDAY, JANUARY 17, 1991   50 cents beyond 75 miles from New York City, except on Long Island.   **40 CENTS**

U.S. AND ALLIES OPEN AIR WAR ON IRAQ; BOMB BAGHDAD AND KUWAITI TARGETS; 'NO CHOICE' BUT FORCE, BUSH DECLARES

A TENSE WAIT ENDS

News of Attack Sweeps the Country, Stirring Profound Feelings

By JAMES BARRON

In one long moment yesterday, word that the United States had attacked Baghdad swept the country.

In split-level suburban homes on the East Coast where dinner was in the oven, in big-city restaurants in the Midwest where bars were jammed with the happy-hour crowd and in skyscraper offices on the West Coast where people were still at work, there was an odd mixture of apprehension, sadness and relief.

In malls, shoppers emptied out of stores and cried. In supermarkets, cashiers rushed to call relatives and share the news that after five months of waiting and wondering America was at war. In department stores, people crowded in front of television sets, with some saying they were stunned that President Bush had decided to act so soon after the United Nations deadline for Iraq to withdraw from Kuwait.

A Scene Out of World War II

Suddenly, in public places where cacophony is the norm, there was an unusual silence, eerie rather than giddy. Grand Central Terminal in Manhattan — where even whispers can take on an echoing, high-decibel intensity — was quiet. On trains to Connecticut, passengers gathered around people who had radios with headsets. "The people with the radios would listen to the news and then relay it to the other passengers," said Dan Brucker, a spokesman for the Metro-North Commuter Railroad, "kind of like World War II radio dispatchers delivering the news."

The word that waves of air strikes were striking Iraq silenced black-tie galas in Manhattan. And in a Houston hotel, the chatter around the bar stopped when the President began his speech from the Oval Office. Only the machine making frozen margaritas kept whirring.

Some people applauded Mr. Bush's decision to order the attack. "It was direct and to the point," Lester Alexander, a New Orleans real-estate investor, said of Mr. Bush's speech. "He did not try to sell me on his reasons, but he

Continued on Page A19, Column 4

OTHER NEWS

Gorbachev Is Moving To Muzzle the Press

Faced with mounting condemnation of the assault by Soviet forces on demonstrators in Lithuania, President Mikhail S. Gorbachev moved to undermine a law guaranteeing freedom of the press — a hallmark of the era of openness that he himself ushered in. Page A8.

In a show of defiance in the Lithuanian capital, hundreds of thousands of mourners streamed through the streets to bury the dead. Page A8.

Dinkins Offers Budget With Layoffs and Cuts

Mayor David N. Dinkins presented a preliminary New York City budget of $29.3 billion for the next fiscal year. The announcement was met with a mix of pain and uncertainty. The plan includes thousands of layoffs and service cuts. Page B1.

Daily News Threatens To Close or Sell

The management of The Daily News threatened to close or sell the paper unless it stems heavy losses. Both sides in the 12-week-old strike agreed the move was an ultimatum to the unions to make major concessions or lose their jobs for good. Page B1.

THE RAPE OF KUWAIT. READ IT AND FIND OUT why we're there. Now in paperback Knightsbridge $4.95 ADVT

THE NEW YORK TIMES is available for home of office delivery in most major U.S. cities. Please call this toll-free number 1-800- ADVT

Possible air strike targets
- ✈ Air bases
- 🏭 Oil refineries
- ⚙ Conventional weapons plants
- ⚗ Chemical, nuclear, biological warfare facilities

The New York Times

Raids, on a Huge Scale, Seek to Destroy Iraqi Missiles

By MICHAEL R. GORDON
Special to The New York Times

WASHINGTON, Thursday, Jan. 17 — The military campaign to evict Iraq from Kuwait began, as expected, with night air strikes on a huge scale at targets deep in Iraq and Kuwait.

According to early reports of the night operation from the Pentagon, no American aircraft were lost and grave damage appeared to have been done to Iraqi military forces. Cable News Network reported that another series of sorties began at midmorning Baghad time.

American officials said the first onslaught against Iraqi air defenses, communications and weapons sites included the firing of Tomahawk sea-launched cruise missiles, as well as F-117 Stealth fighter-bombers, F-15E fighter-bombers and a wide variety of other Air Force and Navy planes.

British and Saudis Join In

The American aircraft were accompanied by British and Saudi Tornado fighter-bombers, Saudi F-15's and Kuwaiti combat planes.

The aims of the nighttime attack were to damage the Iraqi military establishment by destroying command and control centers, including those in Baghdad, and to establish air superiority by knocking out Iraqi air defenses and airfields.

Pentagon officials said that all Navy planes in the night operation were reported to have returned safely. There

were no reported Air Force losses, though the return of some of the planes to an air base near Taif, Saudi Arabia, was being delayed by bad weather there. Britain reported that all of its planes had returned safely.

Pentagon officials said that its bomb-damage assessments were still being conducted, and they disputed reports that the attacks had decimated the Republican Guards, the elite of the Iraqi Army.

Satellite Reports Awaited

Pentagon officials said the attack on Iraq appeared to be very successful because the Iraqi Air Force had not challenged the attacking planes and because the United States has no confirmed reports of launchings of Iraqi Scuds, long-range surface-to-surface missiles that are considered a threat to the allies' bases and to Israel. But they added that they were still awaiting definitive satellite and other reconnaissance reports.

Gen. Colin L. Powell, the chairman of the Joint Chiefs of Staff, said at a Pentagon news conference that "there has been no air resistance" from the Iraqis. Pentagon officials said that they hoped to destroy the Iraqi planes in their hardened shelters.

The allied air forces also attacked Scud batteries and, as President Bush emphasized, American planes struck at Iraqi nuclear and chemical-weapons production sites. No ground forces were used in the operation, the Pentagon said.

In mounting the air attack, the United States is also trying to make good on assurances to the Israelis that Washington would blast the Scud missiles that threaten Israel to make it unnecessary for Israel to enter the war, the American officials said. Defense Secretary Dick Cheney said the Pentagon had no information to confirm that Iraqi Scud missiles had struck Saudi Arabia.

The timing of the attack was de-

Continued on Page A15, Column 1

No Ground Fighting Yet; Call to Arms by Hussein

By ANDREW ROSENTHAL
Special to The New York Times

WASHINGTON, Thursday, Jan. 17 — The United States and allied forces Wednesday night opened the long-threatened war to drive President Saddam Hussein's army from Kuwait, striking Baghdad and other targets in Iraq and Kuwait with waves of bombers and cruise missiles launched from naval vessels.

"The liberation of Kuwait has begun," President Bush said in a three-sentence statement confirming the start of the attack that was read by his spokesman, Marlin Fitzwater, shortly after the raids began.

Later, in a televised address to the nation from the Oval Office, a somber Mr. Bush said that after months of continuous diplomatic overtures had failed to produce movement by Iraq, the United States and its allies "have no choice but to force Saddam from Kuwait by force. We will not fail." [Transcript, page A6.]

No Planes Reported Missing

United States officials said shortly after midnight Wednesday that none of the planes that took part in the night-time raids were reported missing.

In Baghdad, Mr. Hussein said in a speech broadcast by the Iraqi radio that "the mother of all battles has

begun," according to news service reports. He called Mr. Bush a "hypocritical criminal" and vowed to crush "the satanic intentions of the White House." It was unclear when Mr. Hussein had read his remarks, whether they had been pre-recorded, or where he was at the time. [Page A18.]

Mr. Bush's goal "is not the conquest of Iraq, it is the liberation of Kuwait." But he also said, "We are determined to knock out Saddam Hussein's nuclear bomb potential. We will also destroy his chemical-weapons facilities."

3 Other Nations Take Part

Defense Secretary Dick Cheney and Gen. Colin L. Powell, Chairman of the Joint Chiefs of Staff, told reporters at the Pentagon Wednesday night that those targets had been among those assigned to the first wave of American F-117 Stealth fighter-bombers, F-15 fighter-bombers, British Tornado attack planes and Saudi and Kuwaiti F-15's that raided Iraqi military targets about 3 A.M. local time Thursday (7 P.M. Wednesday Eastern standard time).

Administration officials also said United States Navy ships in the waters off the Arabian Peninsula had fired ground-hugging cruise missiles at targets that had been programmed into their guidance systems for months. The officials said the ships fired a total of 50 Tomahawk missiles in an assault on Iraqi command and communications centers.

Seeking to Avoid Civilians

Mr. Cheney said the initial targets were spread throughout Iraq and Kuwait and were chosen to "do everything possible to avoid injury to civilians." Both officials declined to say if there had been any American or allied losses, or to describe in any detail how badly they thought they had damaged Baghdad or the other Iraqi targets.

"The response of the Iraqi forces at this point has been limited," Mr. Cheney said, leading analysts to conclude that the allies may have succeeded in their goal of largely incapacitating Iraq's Air Force at the outset.

But Mr. Cheney said that the war was just beginning and that "it is likely to run for a long period of time."

Reports of New Attack

Cable News Network reported that antiaircraft fire resumed in Baghdad about 9:30 A.M. Iraqi time and that its correspondents heard explosions that sounded like bombs in the far distance from their central Baghdad hotel.

The network also reported the first sighting of President Hussein since the start of the attacks, by a Western television technician at a Baghdad television center this afternoon.

Mr. Cheney said the United States could not confirm reports that Iraq had fired Soviet-made Scud missiles at allied positions after the attack began. Reuters reported from Bahrain that the civil defense authorities there had detected missile launches but that the weapons fell short of their targets.

Assuring Americans that ground forces were not yet engaged in the battle, the President added: "Five months ago, Saddam Hussein started this cruel war against Kuwait. Tonight, the battle has been joined."

He said initial reports indicated that "our operations are proceeding according to plan."

"Our objectives are clear," he said. "Saddam Hussein's forces will leave Kuwait, the legitimate Government of Kuwait will be restored to its rightful

Continued on Page A14, Column 1

ABC News
President Bush as he announced in a televised address last night that an air attack had been launched against Iraq.

Rumble in the Sky Ends a 5-Month Wait

By PHILIP SHENON
Special to The New York Times

IN SAUDI ARABIA, Thursday, Jan. 17 — "It's absolutely awesome, I mean the ground shook and you felt it," said Col. Ray Davies, describing the takeoff of the first planes to attack Iraq from a big Saudi air base where he is chief maintenance officer.

The 44-year-old colonel said the first group of jets left at 12:50 A.M., about an hour before the first word of attack was broadcast by television reporters in Baghdad.

"We've been waiting here for five months; now we finally got to do what

we were sent here to do," Colonel Davies told a group of American reporters who were brought to the base. "This is history in the making."

The F-15 fighter bombers, heavily loaded with bombs and supplemental underwing fuel tanks, thundered off in pairs into what had been a still desert night. The aircraft, which quickly became faint red dots, were also armed with cannon and air-to-air missiles to be used in their own defense.

The activity at the airfield, whose exact location cannot be identified under military reporting rules, was the first indication here that the assault

was under way. All commercial traffic at the airport had been suspended a short time earlier.

Just before 4 A.M. Saudi time, hundreds of journalists and other guests at the Dhahran International Hotel, including many Filipino and Pakistani workers, were herded into the bomb shelter in the hotel basement and instructed to put on gas masks. Sirens started to wail throughout the city.

Waiting for the Signal

As the guests, primarily journalists, waited for the signal "gas clear," a hotel employee serving as warden directed guests to spread out in the area, which serves as a kitchen. The air conditioning had been turned off to prevent the spread of chemical agents in case the hotel was hit by Iraqi missiles. The room was quiet except for the sound of a radio on which a news announcer was reporting that the attack had begun.

A British defense consultant who is working for the hotel, Philip Congdon,

Continued on Page A17, Column 6

MORE ON THE GULF

Bush Evokes Glory Of Past, Not Vietnam

To tell Americans that war with Iraq had started, President Bush harked back to one of the great days in American military history — D-Day, June 6, 1944. News analysis, page A16.

In Cairo, Jubilation Among Kuwaiti Exiles

Hundreds of Kuwaitis drove their cars through the Egyptian capital, honking and waving flags after hearing news of the American-led attack. "Thank God! Thank God!" was a cry heard over and over again. Page A18.

Israel on Alert

Israel declared a state of emergency minutes after word of the attack. There was no indication of an Iraqi attack on Israel. Page A18.

The War Begins

"The liberation of Kuwait has begun. In conjunction with the forces of our coalition partners, the United States has moved under the code name Operation Desert Storm to enforce the mandates of the United Nations Security Council.

"As of 7 o'clock P.M. Operation Desert Storm forces were engaging targets in Iraq and Kuwait."

STATEMENT, PRESIDENT BUSH, 7:06 P.M.

The New York Times

Late Edition

New York: Today, partly cloudy, not as cold. High 43. Tonight, some clouds. Low near 40. Tomorrow, some sun, windy, warmer. High 58. Yesterday, high 36, low 26. Details, page B14.

VOL. CXL .. No. 48,525   Copyright © 1991 The New York Times   NEW YORK, THURSDAY, FEBRUARY 28, 1991   50 cents beyond 75 miles from New York City, except on Long Island.   40 CENTS

BUSH HALTS OFFENSIVE COMBAT; KUWAIT FREED, IRAQIS CRUSHED

Under skies darkened by smoke from burning oil wells, Kuwaitis celebrated the recapture of Kuwait City from Iraq. The Kuwaiti flag, which had vanished from public display during Iraq's occupation, suddenly appeared everywhere. Page A6.

Associated Press

Gen. H. Norman Schwarzkopf as he discussed allied successes at a news briefing yesterday in Saudi Arabia.

Associated Press

MILITARY AIMS MET

Firing Ending After 100 Hours of Ground War, President Declares

By ANDREW ROSENTHAL
Special to The New York Times

WASHINGTON, Thursday, Feb. 28 — Declaring that "Kuwait is liberated" and Iraq's army defeated, President Bush ordered allied forces on Wednesday night to suspend offensive military operations against President Saddam Hussein's isolated and battered army.

Mr. Bush said the suspension, which began at midnight Eastern time, would continue as long as Iraq did not attack allied forces or launch missile attacks on any other country. In an address from the Oval Office that was televised around the world at 9 P.M. Eastern time, he called on Mr. Hussein to send his commanders to meet with allied officers in the war zone within 48 hours to settle the military terms of a permanent cease-fire.

For such a cease-fire to be approved, he said, Iraq must comply with all 12 United Nations resolutions concerning Kuwait, including measures calling for Iraq to void its annexation of the territory and agree in principle to pay reparations to Kuwait and other countries. Iraq must also free all prisoners of war and detained Kuwaiti citizens, and give the allies the location of all land and sea mines that Iraq had laid in the region, Mr. Bush said.

No Official Word From Iraq

Administration officials said they had received no authoritative response from the Iraqi Government. At the United Nations, Soviet diplomats said Iraq had submitted a letter signaling its willingness to comply with all 12 resolutions adopted by the Security Council. But the letter did not say whether Baghdad was willing to comply with the rest of Mr. Bush's demands, including the freeing of Kuwaiti civilians seized in recent days. [Text of the letter, page A10.]

Pentagon officials said this morning there were no reports of renewed Iraqi attacks on allied positions.

Speaking in a solemn voice, President Bush said: "This war is now behind us. Ahead of us is the difficult task of securing a potentially historic peace." [Transcript of his remarks, page A12.]

He seemed to invite the citizens of Iraq to overthrow the man who had defied the assembled military and political power of the international alliance. "Coalition forces fought this war only as a last resort," Mr. Bush said, "and look toward to the day when Iraq is led by people prepared to live in peace with their neighbors."

Unusually Low Casualties

Mr. Bush, who had staked his Presidency on being able to resolve a crisis that had shattered the post-cold war calm and led to the largest single American military offensive since World War II, declared an end to the war in his third nationally televised speech from the Oval Office since Iraq invaded Kuwait on Aug. 2.

To arrive at the point where he was able to declare victory last night, Mr. Bush had to command what military experts had said was one of the largest combat operations ever conducted with such low casualties, counter political opposition at home and navigate the shoals of diplomacy complicated by last-minute Soviet peace ventures that plainly irritated the President and his war council.

"At midnight tonight, Eastern standard time, exactly 100 hours since ground operations commenced and six weeks since the start of Operation Desert Storm, all United States and

Continued on Page A12, Column 1

Freed Kuwaitis Tell of Iraqi Abuse Including Some Cases of Torture

By CHRIS HEDGES
Special to The New York Times

KUWAIT CITY, Feb. 27 — On the third floor of a gutted mansion, a Kuwaiti Army major slowly pushed open a door with his foot to what was once a laundry room. It had been converted by the Iraqis, he said, into a torture chamber.

In one corner were metal box springs, raised off the floor by chairs. Next to the springs was a crude brown box with bare electrical wires protruding from black cords.

"They put the prisoners on the springs, poured water over them and then applied the current," said the Kuwaiti Army officer, Maj. Jamal al-Hassan, who was a leader in the underground during the occupation. "If they were not happy with the answers, they turned up the voltage."

Accounts of Torture

Kuwaitis who were picked up by the Iraqi secret police had their own stories to tell.

"They beat me, did not let me sleep and made me sit naked on a bottle of hot sauce," said 21-year-old Faisal al-Anizi. "This went on for three days in what used to be the reform school."

Others tell of being rubbed down with sandpaper, having their heads thrust into cold water and being hung by their hands from a hook.

When an American correspondent arrived in Kuwait City on Tuesday, ahead of entering allied troops, he found Kuwaitis who were eager to tell the world that Saddam Hussein brought more to Kuwait than Iraqi license plates and innumerable portraits of himself. He had also brought the techniques of control that have kept his authoritarian Government in power.

Members of the Kuwaiti underground, acting on information provided by people who said they were tortured by the Iraqi secret police, have identified places where Kuwaitis were questioned, beaten and tortured.

A visitor is overwhelmed by reports that hundreds, perhaps thousands of young men were taken by the Iraqis, many in the final hours before the Iraqi forces left the city on Monday. Their parents and friends fear that they may not reappear.

"A lot of people have disappeared in Iraq and never been seen since," said

Continued on Page A6, Column 4

IRAQ ELITE ROUTED, U.S. SOLDIERS SAY

Officers Brace for Prisoners as Hussein's Force Retreats

By PHILIP SHENON
Special to The New York Times

WITH U.S. VII CORPS, in Iraq, Feb. 27 — American troops described a ferocious armored battle between the United States and troops of Iraq's Republican Guards that resulted, they said in interviews tonight, in devastating losses for the Iraqis and a torrent of thousands of battle-weary Iraqi prisoners of war.

In battlefield interviews with troops from three of the four Army divisions involved in the assault on the guards, American soldiers said that the tank clash raged across dozens of miles of the southern Iraqi desert. Speaking before President Bush ordered military operations suspended, the soldiers said that the Iraqi guards were offering fierce resistance despite overwhelming odds.

Tanks Are Charred Bits of Steel

During a helicopter tour today close to the front lines, the devastation wrought by allied forces on the Iraqi military in recent days and weeks was made plain.

The burned-out shells of scores of Iraqi tanks, some smoldering, some still on fire, sat in what had been extensive dug-in fortifications of sand and dirt. All that remained of several Iraqi tanks and artillery installations were charred bits of steel spread across hundreds of square yards of scrub-covered desert floor.

From the air, large bands of captured Iraqi soldiers could be seen in the custody of American soldiers.

The Americans described prisoners captured today from other, regular Iraqi units as desperate for food, water and medical attention, after a month-long allied bombing campaign cut them off from supply lines.

Some of the Iraqis said they had not been fed for days. As many as one-third

Continued on Page A7, Column 1

Women Among War Dead

At least three women were reported to be among the 28 American soldiers who were killed in an Iraqi missile attack on Tuesday. Page A13.

Allies Destroy Iraqis' Main Force; Kuwait Is Retaken After 7 Months

By R. W. APPLE Jr.
Special to The New York Times

DHAHRAN, Saudi Arabia, Thursday, Feb. 28 — Hours before President Bush announced the conditional suspension of offensive military operations in the Persian Gulf, allied armored units, which had trapped Iraq's vaunted Republican Guard, cut it to pieces in a furious tank battle that began Wednesday and raged until early this morning, American officials said.

At midday Wednesday, United States Marines captured the Kuwait International Airport after a smaller but nonetheless intense two-day fight, and later, marines and Kuwaiti and other Arab troops rode in triumph down the broad boulevards of Kuwait City, past scenes of devastation and desolation. That essentially completed the expulsion of President Saddam Hussein's forces from Kuwait, which they had overrun in a surprise assault last Aug. 2.

Casualties among coalition forces were light and Iraqi losses heavy, the allied command said.

But the honking horns, waving flags and scenes of jubilation as the capital was retaken scarcely concealed the agony generated by tales of torture, kidnapping, rape and pillage over the final days of occupation. As many as 40,000 Kuwaitis were said to have been taken hostage by the Iraqis as they fled north on Tuesday.

Gen. H. Norman Schwarzkopf, commander of the American-led coalition that has trounced Iraq in a lightning-fast ground war reminiscent of the World War II blitzkrieg, said the Iraqi leader had been stripped of the offensive weapons that made his army one of the most fearsome in the Middle East.

'Not Enough Left'

"There's not enough left for him to be a regional threat," the general said in a detailed briefing on the campaign Wednesday night, adding pointedly, "unless someone chooses to rearm them in the future." [Excerpts, page A8.]

"We've accomplished our mission," General Schwarzkopf said, hours before Mr. Bush spoke, "and when the decision-makers come to the decision that there should be a cease-fire, nobody will be happier than me."

With his army shattered and reeling after 100 hours of ground combat, Mr.

Continued on Page A9, Column 1

Allied and Iraqi tanks fought in the desert west of Basra.

The New York Times

Ethics Unit Singles Out Cranston, Chides 4 Others in S.& L. Inquiry

By RICHARD L. BERKE
Special to The New York Times

WASHINGTON, Feb. 27 — Seeking to set standards for the way lawmakers raise money and do favors, the Senate Ethics Committee concluded today that Senator Alan Cranston engaged in "an impermissible pattern of conduct" that might warrant disciplinary action by the full Senate.

In written rebukes to four other Senators who were also investigated for their ties to Charles H. Keating Jr., a savings and loan executive and contributor to the Senators' campaigns or causes they supported, the committee asserted that their behavior reflected poor judgment at the very least.

The committee's finding on Mr. Cranston essentially clears the way for it to recommend that the full Senate reprimand him as the panel is expected to do. But the committee said the other lawmakers' actions were not significant enough to require such further action.

Aside from Mr. Cranston, a California Democrat, the findings against two other Democrats, Senators Dennis DeConcini of Arizona and Donald W. Riegle Jr. of Michigan, were the most stern. The committee said their conduct "gave the appearance of being improper and was certainly attended with insensitivity and poor judgment." The lightest rebukes went to Senators John Glenn, an Ohio Democrat, and John McCain, an Arizona Republican, who were found to have "exercised poor judgment." [Excerpts from the committee's statement, page B10.]

Today's announcement came after the committee voted unanimously on each Senator, ending a 14-month inves-

Continued on Page B10, Column 1

INSIDE

Condom Plan Approved

The New York City Board of Education narrowly approved a plan to make condoms available to the city's 250,000 high school students. Page B1.

New Rival to Phone Industry

Three cable television companies plan to build experimental networks that would allow people to use very small wireless telephones. Page D1.

Legions of bedraggled Iraqi warriors on buses, trucks and flatbed trailers voiced cheers of relief at the end of their fighting days. Page A10.

Pool photo via Associated Press

The New York Times

Late Edition

New York: Today, cloudy, cool, early sprinkles. High near 60. Tonight, partial clearing. Low 46. Tomorrow, cloudy, late clearing. High 56. Yesterday, high 61, low 50. Details, page 17.

VOL.CXLI .. No. 48,751   Copyright © 1991 The New York Times   NEW YORK, SATURDAY, OCTOBER 12, 1991   50 CENTS

SOVIET REPUBLICS AGREE TO CREATE AN ECONOMIC UNION

10 OF 12 PLEDGE SUPPORT

Yeltsin Leads Way in Pressing for an Accord — Gorbachev Calls Plan 'Last Hope'

By FRANCIS X. CLINES
Special to The New York Times

MOSCOW, Oct. 11 — Russia and a majority of the other republics announced their commitment today to soon forming a new economic community devoted to free-market resuscitation of the fallen Soviet nation.

President Boris N. Yeltsin of the Russian federation, the centerpiece republic in the complex plan, led the way in pressing nine other republics for a formal signing of the economic compact as early as next Tuesday.

The Soviet President, Mikhail S. Gorbachev, leading a meeting of 10 republic leaders at the Kremlin, warned that the economic plan represented the people's "last hope" for decisive action toward national reconstruction after the harrowing failed coup and collapse of the central Government in August.

Yeltsin's Return

"People's patience is at a breaking point," Mr. Gorbachev cautioned, according to the press agency Tass.

The news that Mr. Yeltsin was back from vacation and recommitting Russia to the economic plan immediately bolstered proponents of the free-market community.

In his absence for the last two weeks, critics of the plan came forward in his own cabinet to warn that Russia, the nation's dominant republic, would be slighted in creating such an economic monolith from the dregs of the Communist Soviet Union.

'Common Economic Space'

But Mr. Yeltsin reaffirmed his view that the plan for a "common economic space" of trade, currency, banking and customs procedures was the only hope for the crippled Soviet nation to turn itself toward reform and a chance of joining the global free market.

The most Mr. Yeltsin offered to critics, according to initial reports, was the possibility of a common banking system less central in nature. That was in concession to an apparent sensitive point among the now sovereign republics still fearful of echoes of the central monolith that marked Communism's handling of the economy.

The republics, meeting together as members of the new State Council 'emergency Government, also followed through on earlier agreements to reshape the K.G.B. state police into sepa-

Continued on Page 4, Column 6

Kiichi Miyazawa at a meeting of his party faction yesterday.

Miyazawa Gets Party Approval To Lead Japan

By DAVID E. SANGER
Special to The New York Times

TOKYO, Oct. 11 — Kiichi Miyazawa, a stalwart of Japan's governing party and one of the architects of the country's postwar economic ascent, was virtually assured election as the next Japanese prime minister tonight, ending a bruising weeklong scramble for the leadership.

Mr. Miyazawa, an urbane 72-year-old politician who has held virtually every key political post in Japan except prime minister, was endorsed this evening by the largest and wealthiest faction in the Liberal Democratic Party, controlled by former Prime Minister Noboru Takeshita.

At a news conference earlier in the day, Mr. Miyazawa said he expected no significant changes in Japan's relations with Washington, where he has been a well-known and influential player in Japanese-American relations for more than two decades.

'The Same Values'

"We have the same values," he said of Japan and the United States. "If we have something to complain about to each other, we should do so frankly."

It was the Takeshita faction that withdrew its support from Prime Minister Toshiki Kaifu a week ago, forcing him to abandon his hopes of seeking a second term. Political analysts said they expected Mr. Miyazawa, a far more senior member of the party and a leader of a major faction, to hold somewhat more independent sway over the conduct of the Government than did Mr. Kaifu, who was widely viewed as a weak leader entirely dependent on the good graces of Mr. Takeshita and his aging ally in the governing party, Shin Kanemaru.

For Mr. Miyazawa, known as one of the party's keenest minds and one of its most fluent English speakers, the endorsement today completes a stunning political turnaround. Less than three years ago, he was forced to step down

Continued on Page 5, Column 5

INSIDE

Bush Vetoes Benefits Bill

Citing a need for budget discipline, the President rejected legislation that would have given additional unemployment benefits to people out of work more than six months. Page 6.

One Step Closer

The President formed a Bush-Quayle '92 Primary Committee, a move that allows him to go ahead with already scheduled fund-raising events for his re-election campaign. Page 6.

Yes, He Is. No. Maybe.

Political contributors say Gov. Mario M. Cuomo told them he was considering running for President. But later he said he had no plans. Page 31.

Twins Win and Lead Playoff

A home run by Mike Pagliarulo in the 10th inning gave Minnesota a 3-2 victory over Toronto and a 2-1 lead in the American League playoff. Page 45.

News Summary

Obituaries

Weather

Haitians in New York Rally for Ousted Leader
Tens of thousands of Haitian demonstrators spilled across the Brooklyn Bridge into lower Manhattan yesterday in a spirited display of support for Haiti's ousted President, Jean-Bertrand Aristide. Page 31.

THOMAS ACCUSER TELLS HEARING OF OBSCENE TALK AND ADVANCES; JUDGE COMPLAINS OF 'LYNCHING'

Professor Anita F. Hill and Judge Clarence Thomas as they were sworn in yesterday before testifying.
Photographs by Jose R. Lopez/The New York Times

DRAMA IN SENATE

Court Nominee Rejects Charges Laid Out in Frank, Vivid Detail

By RICHARD L. BERKE
Special to The New York Times

WASHINGTON, Oct. 11 — Confronting a disputed nomination to the Supreme Court and a boiling political furor, the Senate Judiciary Committee heard gripping but contradictory testimony today from Judge Clarence Thomas and the woman accusing him of sexual harassment.

The proceedings in a jammed hearing room at the Russell Senate Office Building here amounted to a political drama centered on two extraordinarily composed figures, Judge Thomas and his accuser, Anita F. Hill, an Oklahoma law professor.

Judge Thomas and Professor Hill, who worked for him in two Federal agencies, both testified under oath and offered accounts of their social and professional relationships that differed so starkly that Senator Howell Heflin, an Alabama Democrat, said, "One of them is not telling the truth."

'I Had a Duty to Report'

Professor Hill complained of sexual approaches in vivid detail and said she had not volunteered to bring this issue to the Senate but was there because Senate aides asked her if she was aware of any harassment. "I felt I had a duty to report — I have no personal vendetta against Clarence Thomas," she said.

Judge Thomas angrily denied the charge and compared his ordeal to a "lynching." [Excerpts from the hearing appear on pages 10-15.]

Testifying first in a hearing that lasted 12 hours and 35 minutes, Judge Thomas sounded by turns defiant and sorrowful in insisting to committee members that he had never sexually harassed Professor Hill, depicting himself and his family as victims who had been betrayed by the professor and a Senate confirmation process that had run amok.

The Process on Trial

In his opening statement in the morning, and even more strongly when he returned to the Congress tonight to testify, Judge Thomas tried to rebut the charges against him by putting the process on trial — a political process that has been widely disdained as cutthroat and out of control.

He called it "a travesty" that such "sleaze," "dirt," "gossip" and "lies," which he said were improperly disclosed by the committee, should be "displayed in prime time to an entire nation." In answer to a question, he said that he did not watch Professor Hill's testimony.

Professor Hill said that she, too, had been tormented by the issue and the intense scrutiny. Facing sometimes sharp questions from Republicans and more gentle questioning from Democrats, Professor Hill testified for near-

Continued on Page 9, Column 1

On Thomas: More Questions, Not Fewer

A Political Process Becomes the Focus

By R. W. APPLE Jr.
Special to The New York Times

WASHINGTON, Oct. 11 — The choices presented to the United States Senate by today's lurid, gut-wrenching proceedings on Capitol Hill could hardly have been much starker.

News Analysis

By the time Anita F. Hill had finished her testimony, filled with vivid and often excruciating sexual detail that few had anticipated, but delivered with a prim earnestness that seemed to bespeak reserve and reluctance to discuss such subjects, the Senators who must vote on Tuesday were left with only two options: Either she was telling the truth or she is a sociopath; either these horrifying events took place or she, for some reason, invented them.

By the time Judge Clarence Thomas had made his response, the Senators had been rocked even further back on their heels by a blast that have had few precedents as a statement by a senior Federal official in an official forum. Dropping his usual accommodating manner, he let the fury pour out of him, calling the current inquiry "a national disgrace" and "a high-tech lynching for uppity blacks."

He stopped only a hair short of explicitly accusing the committee, composed entirely of white males, of racism.

He Said Them, Or He Didn't

What Judge Thomas asserted, and what Judge Thomas said in his implacably resolute testimony, made it crystal clear that this was no case of tragic misunderstandings nor of ambiguous conversations that could be interpreted as sexual harassment or not, depending on one's frame of reference or state of mind. Either he said these wretched things to her — things that one associates with the seamiest of criminal cases or the raunchiest of locker rooms, not with the Senate or Supreme Court — or he did not. Yes or no. Up or down.

If Judge Thomas did say them, few, if any, Senators would vote to confirm, whatever the pull of partisan solidarity. So a vote to confirm the judge, in the

rawest political terms, will mean the voter thinks Professor Hill fabricated (or was fed) these "ugly" incidents and phrases, to use her own word.

Such a vote will not be easy for the jury of 100 Senators, a group of professional politicians, a third of whom face re-election next year, who have already been burned by the wrath of women when they seemed willing to brush off Professor Hill's allegations earlier this week.

It will be harder because the judge's defenders struggled all day, with limited success, to suggest what kind of twisted motive she might have had for telling monstrous lies about him.

It will be hardest of all for the Democrats, and the arithmetic gives them the upper hand. If 51 of the 57 Democrats vote no on the nomination — vote, in effect, to back Professor Hill — then Judge Thomas will not make it to the Supreme Court, even if all 43 Republicans reject what she told them.

To bring about that result, only about five or six of the Democrats who had intended to support Judge Thomas before Professor Hill's allegations became public would have to change their minds. At least that many have indicated they had serious doubts by pressing to hold new hearings.

But what of Judge Thomas's testimony? Like Professor Hill a child of the civil rights movement, a success story that would have made the Rev. Dr. Martin Luther King Jr. beam with

Continued on Page 9, Column 1

In an Ugly Atmosphere, the Accusations Fly

By MAUREEN DOWD
Special to The New York Times

WASHINGTON, Oct. 11 — With a powerful invocation of racial imagery that he had not used in his public remarks before this day of testing, Clarence Thomas tried to put the Senate on trial tonight, accusing Congress of tactics that went "far beyond McCarthyism."

As his wife, Virginia, sat behind him with a trembling chin, wiping away tears, Judge Thomas delivered a forceful rebuttal to Anita F. Hill's accusations of sexual harassment with a stony face and a voice bristling with anger.

When his testimony, filled with racially charged images, collided with the counterpoint of the Oklahoma University law professor's cool, dispassionate testimony, nearly devoid of references to race, the hearing reached an emotional high point

Furious Denunciations

Confounding those who thought he would give up after the testimony by Professor Hill, testimony that many Senators found impressive and credible, President Bush's nominee put the process on trial and offered a furious denunciation of the Judiciary Committee's handling of the case.

"You are running the country," he told the senators, accusing them of going "far beyond McCarthyism." At

another point, he said that black men who did not "kowtow to an old order" would "be lynched, destroyed, caricatured by a committee of the U.S. Senate rather than hung from a tree."

In comparing his ordeal to a "high-tech lynching, for uppity blacks," Judge Thomas evoked one of the most powerful images of the civil rights movement, a movement with which he has long had an uneasy relationship.

It was during his tenure as chairman of the Equal Employment Opportunity Commission that he became an increasingly fervent spokesman against the approaches of the traditional civil rights groups. As his relations with those groups worsened, he complained in an interview with The Washington Post in 1984 that all the nation's traditional civil rights leaders do is, "bitch, bitch, bitch, moan and whine."

Offended by Justice Marshall

He said he was offended by Justice Thurgood Marshall who once complained that he did not want to celebrate the Constitution because it condoned slavery. But when he opened his testimony on Sept. 10, he was careful to give great credit to the civil rights movement for his own journey.

"So many others gave their lives, their talents. But for them, I would not be here today. Justice Marshall, whose seat I have been nominated to fill is one of those who had the courage and the intellect," he said.

Initially today, Mr. Thomas refused to rebut the individual charges, relying instead on monolithic outrage and a categorical denial. He said he had been "drawn and dragged" into a national forum to discuss allegations that "should have been discussed in a confidential way."

At first, Senator Howell Heflin

Continued on Page 9, Column 1

America Listens In On a Private Subject

In cities and towns across the country, Americans took time out from their workaday lives to tune into the riveting collision between Judge Clarence Thomas and Anita F. Hill.

The hearing capped a week in which Professor Hill's charges became the leading topic in offices and on university campuses, in restaurants and on street corners, with many women applauding public discussion of a frequently private subject and many men wondering about their own conduct.

Article, page 8.

"All the News
That's Fit to Print"

The New York Times

Late Edition
New York: **Today,** limited sun, perhaps a shower late. High 62. **Tonight,** cooler. Low 40. **Tomorrow,** cloudy, a light shower. High 41. **Yesterday,** high 59, low 45. Details are on page D10.

VOL.CXLI...No. 48,809   Copyright © 1991 The New York Times   NEW YORK, MONDAY, DECEMBER 9, 1991   50 CENTS

DECLARING DEATH OF SOVIET UNION, RUSSIA AND 2 REPUBLICS FORM NEW COMMONWEALTH

Frantic Moves Came to Light In Days Before Maxwell Died

As the Empire Was Crumbling
A special report.

Robert Maxwell

By STEVEN PROKESCH
Special to The New York Times

LONDON, Dec. 8 — At the time of his mysterious death on Nov. 5, Robert Maxwell almost certainly knew he was about to be caught.

He had drained hundreds of millions of dollars from his two flagship public companies and from employee pension funds in a frantic attempt to keep his heavily indebted publishing empire afloat.

The auditors of the Maxwell empire, Coopers & Lybrand Deloitte, were to conduct their next regular audit of the pension funds in a couple of months. And Coopers would have quickly discovered the transactions, said a person very familiar with the details of a special financial examination of the empire conducted for the banks after Mr. Maxwell's death. He agreed to discuss the report only if his identity was not disclosed.

'Basically Grabbing Cash'

The Coopers team also found evidence that some of the diverted money went to The Daily News in New York to cover its losses. That raises more doubts about the future of the newspaper, which Mr. Maxwell acquired in March.

The maneuvering by Mr. Maxwell to prop up the private companies that controlled his empire "was doomed to failure," the person familiar with the Coopers report said.

"It wasn't a sophisticated fraud like B.C.C.I.," he said, referring to the scandal surrounding the Bank of Credit and Commerce International. "The guy was basically grabbing cash, and Coopers found it out within days of going in." The Coopers team was led by Richard Stone, the partner in charge of the accounting firm's corporate finance division.

That discovery led the main holding companies of the Maxwell empire to file Thursday for the British equivalent of bankruptcy protection.

It is now apparent that the pressure on Mr. Maxwell to find money for the private companies was increasing sharply in the weeks before his death, according to the Coopers report, bankers, and directors and executives of the Maxwell empire.

"It would appear that there was a desperate need for cash from June

Continued on Page D3 Column 1

West Europeans Gather to Seek A Tighter Union

By ALAN RIDING
Special to The New York Times

MAASTRICHT, the Netherlands, Dec. 8 — In an atmosphere of great expectation tinged with no small apprehension, European Community leaders gathered here tonight for a crucial two-day summit meeting that should determine the region's place in the world well into the 21st century.

Their aim is to prepare the 12-nation community to compete with regional economic groups led by the United States and Japan and to exercise greater political influence in international affairs. To achieve this, they hope to speed up Europe's 34-year-old march toward political and economic integration.

They will therefore be taking up proposals to establish a single currency and a regional central bank, to move toward common foreign and security policies, to give more power to the European Parliament and to harmonize their approaches to social and environmental questions.

Nowhere Near Full Union

The measures fall far short of creating anything resembling a United States of Europe. While some politicians like to evoke the centuries-old dream of full union, it is at least decades away.

Yet if approved, the changes will significantly bolster the community's existing plan to form a single regional market of 340 million consumers on Jan. 1, 1993, eventually turning what is already the world's largest trading bloc into the world's dominant financial power.

Adoption of the Maastricht agenda is far from assured. Britain, long the

Continued on Page A10, Column 1

U.S. Seeks to Trim 'Friendly Fire' Toll

Alarmed by the number of American soldiers killed and wounded by "friendly fire" in the Persian Gulf war, the military has begun top-to-bottom changes to decrease the frequency of such incidents in future conflicts.

The changes in training, equipment and procedures will affect tens of thousands of soldiers, the Army said, and are the most significant shifts so far in American military practices resulting from lessons learned in the gulf war.

"We're committed to addressing this problem in an institutional and effective way," Gen. Gordon R. Sullivan, the Army Chief of Staff, said.

The changes are to be announced later this week, at which time senior Army generals are also expected to discuss new policies on notifying relatives of American soldiers who were accidentally killed by their own forces.

Article, page A12.

The New and the Old

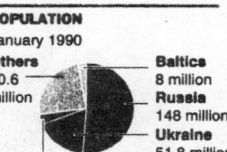

POPULATION
January 1990
Others 70.6 million
Baltics 8 million
Russia 148 million
Ukraine 51.8 million
Byelorussia 10.3 million

CONSUMER GOODS
Share of production 1988
Other 28.2%
Baltics 6.8%
Russia 47.0%
Ukraine 16.4%
Byelorussia 1.5%

AGRICULTURE
Share of total output, 1988
Other 21.4%
Baltics 4.4%
Russia 46.7%
Ukraine 22.1%
Byelorussia 5.4%

Source: The Statesman's Yearbook, 1991-92; U.S.S.R. Facts and Figures Annual, 1991

The New York Times

"We, the republic of Byelorussia, the Russian Federation and Ukraine . . . state that the U.S.S.R., as a subject of international law and geopolitical reality, is ceasing its existence."
— Brest declaration, Dec. 8, 1991

The Union Is Buried: What's Being Born?

By CELESTINE BOHLEN
Special to The New York Times

MOSCOW, Dec. 8 — Ever since the August coup d'état, the Soviet Union has been dying a lingering death, its final agony stretched over months of crisis and negotiations while it was kept alive largely by the frantic faith of one man, Mikhail S. Gorbachev, the Soviet President.

News Analysis

Today, the union died — if future historians will accept a death warrant signed by the patient itself as proof, which is how the leaders of Russia, Ukraine and Byelorussia intended their statement, signed in the Byelorus-

Gorbachev's Vain Pleas Make His Eclipse Clear

sian border town of Brest, to be read.

The Brest statement does not reckon with Mr. Gorbachev; it simply ignores him, which only made its appearance tonight on Soviet television all the more poignant as he once again pleaded, cajoled and banged his fists, making the case that without a union the country will fall apart.

But for some time now, Mr. Gorbachev's warnings have had a hollow ring, since for most people, the collapse he keeps warning about has already happened. This is a fact they can confirm with their daily lives, as they go to factories that have run out of materials, to office jobs where they have stopped getting salaries or to shops where there are no goods.

A Fresh Start?

By sweeping the old structures out of the way, President Boris N. Yeltsin of Russia, President Leonid M. Kravchuk of Ukraine and the Byelorussian leader, Stanislav Shushkevich, have cleared the way for something new — assuming, of course, that the military or other conservative forces mount no effort to restore the center.

What exactly the new shape of things will be was not totally clear from today's statement, nor could it be, given the absence of some major players, most notably representatives of Kazakhstan and the Central Asian republics.

But the absence of Mr. Gorbachev seemed to make no difference one way or the other. Once the Houdini of Soviet politics, the man who could turn setbacks to his advantage, the master of the surprise move, the Soviet President had become a Johnny-one-note whose insistence on renovating old structures — the word perestroika means reconstruction — in the end got in the way of more radical but in the view of others more constructive approaches.

By bypassing him publicly, the lead-

Continued on Page A9, Column 1

TAKE OVER A-ARMS

Newborn Bureaucracy Is Inheriting Functions of Old Authority

By SERGE SCHMEMANN
Special to The New York Times

MOSCOW, Dec. 8 — The leaders of Russia, Ukraine and Byelorussia declared today that the Soviet Union had ceased to exist and proclaimed a new "Commonwealth of Independent States" open to all members of the former union.

In a series of statements issued after a two-day meeting at a Byelorussian government retreat, the leaders of the three Slavic republics declared void all efforts to create a new union on the ruins of the old one. But they called for the creation of new "coordinating bodies" for defense, foreign affairs and the economy that would have their seat in Minsk, the capital of Byelorussia, and decided to maintain the ruble as the common currency.

They declared that the "norms" and activities of the former union ceased as of the moment of signing, and that the new commonwealth assumed all international obligations of the Soviet Union, as well as control over its nuclear arsenal.

Gorbachev's Move

"The U.S.S.R., as a subject of international law and geopolitical reality, is ceasing its existence," the leaders declared. [Text, page A8.]

The action essentially stripped President Mikhail S. Gorbachev of his office and authority, and the immediate question was whether the tough and tenacious Soviet leader would resist — and if he did, whether the military or other levers of power would support him.

The three cofounders of the new commonwealth — President Boris N. Yeltsin of Russia, President Leonid M. Kravchuk of Ukraine and Stanislav Shushkevich, Chairman of the Byelorussian Parliament — were scheduled to meet on Monday with Mr. Gorbachev and with Nursultan A. Nazarbayev, the President of Kazakhstan and the unofficial spokesman for the Muslim republics of Central Asia.

Portents of Disaster

Mr. Gorbachev had no immediate reaction. But in a taped interview with French television broadcast today, he argued fervently that the consequences of dismantling the union would make the war in Yugoslavia "a simple joke by comparison."

The Central Asian republics had all indicated an interest in retaining some form of union, and it was not immediately clear why Mr. Nazarbayev was excluded from the Byelorussian declaration, or how he would respond. Arriving in Moscow today, he declared that he was still in favor of preserving an association, and at least in maintaining joint control over the nuclear arsenal.

The predominantly Slavic republics declared that they drew their authority to dissolve the union from the fact that they were its original cofounders. They and the Trans-Caucasus republic, later

Continued on Page A8, Column 3

Short on funds, long on tolerance, Ira Levine and his team at Lafayette High School try to stay positive.

Jim Estrin for The New York Times

A Team Plays On in a Search for Normalcy

By HARVEY ARATON

Dexter Wooten's eyes grew wide and bright as he watched Antonio Carrasquillo score layup after layup against Midwood High School's undersized and helpless defenders under the basket.

"I could get me a lot of assists playing with Antonio," Wooten said as the game early last week, a smile breaking out from under the brim of his black-and-red Chicago Bulls cap.

That's what Ira Levine, the basketball coach at Lafayette High School, was thinking last June when Carrasquillo's improved class attendance enabled him to pass his academic subjects. Finally, as a senior, Carras-

Long Shots
A Bruising Season in Brooklyn

A periodic visit with the Lafayette High School basketball team.

quillo, an agile, 6-foot-9-inch basketball star-in-waiting, would make his debut in the New York City Public Schools Athletic League. He would arrive, unannounced, to make Levine's team a force in Brooklyn, a threat to the defending city champion and perennial divisional power, Lincoln.

But even the tallest and most gifted centers, as Patrick Ewing, the Knicks' $33 million man, knows, must be sur-

rounded by complementary players, and one by one Carrasquillo's began to disappear.

In many ways, the losses were just events in the life of public high school sports. They might have happened as easily at any other New York City school. They might have happened at a school in Chicago, Los Angeles or Detroit. The situation was trying, but not debilitating. Short on funds, long on tolerance, the high school coach and his team play on.

Lafayette's team turned into an urban soap opera early this fall when

Continued on Page C8, Column 3

INSIDE

Oiling the Machinery
The challenge for the President's new chief of staff will be to revitalize a domestic policy apparatus that rusted while John Sununu and Richard Darman held sway. Page A12.

Another View in Japan
Japan's Socialists said the nation had "turned its back on the historical truth" by refusing to "sincerely apologize" for wartime conduct. Page A7.

Who Knows Who Nanny Is?
Parents often know little about the people caring for their children, a fact highlighted by an au pair's arrest in a girl's arson death. Page B1.

Dallas Times Herald Shuts
The city's oldest daily newspaper ceases publication today, after selling its presses and subscription lists to its rival, The Morning News. Page D1.

The New York Times 1991

Focus of AIDS Debate Dies
Kimberly Bergalis, who stirred a national debate over AIDS testing of doctors and other health workers, died of AIDS at the age of 23. Page D9.

0 354713 50

"All the News That's Fit to Print"

The New York Times

Late Edition

New York: Today, clear, mild for the season. High 44. Tonight, cloudy late, breezy. Low 34. Tomorrow, cloudy, then colder, windy. High 45. Yesterday, high 40, low 28. Details, page D12.

VOL.CXLI...No. 48,826   Copyright © 1991 The New York Times   NEW YORK, THURSDAY, DECEMBER 26, 1991   50 CENTS

GORBACHEV, LAST SOVIET LEADER, RESIGNS; U.S. RECOGNIZES REPUBLICS' INDEPENDENCE

RETAILERS REPORT SALES FELL SHORT OF DIM FORECASTS

Last-Minute Buying Spree Fails to Carry Merchants Ahead of Last Year's Receipts

By EBEN SHAPIRO

Retailers would probably like to forget Christmas 1991. While most merchants had been prepared for a sluggish season, many said sales turned out to be even worse than expected. Even the last-minute shopping frenzy was not enough to give merchants anything to cheer about.

As recently as a month ago, many retailers had hoped to exceed last year's sales by 5 percent. But results through the close of business on Monday indicate that spending will be flat or up slightly in December. The major retail chains are scheduled to release their final monthly sales results next week.

"We are disappointed with the season," Stephen E. Watson, president of the Dayton Hudson Corporation in Minneapolis, said in a telephone interview on Tuesday.

'Too Little Too Late'

Business surged in the final days, and a number of retailers said that Monday was the busiest day of the year. But Mr. Watson said, "In our view, it's really been too little too late." Dayton Hudson, which relies on California for one-third of its business, was hit hard by the slowdown in that state's economy.

This is the third consecutive sluggish Christmas shopping season — the make or break season for retailers — and many analysts say this year's dismal results are likely to force thousands of companies into bankruptcy.

The economy received most of the

Continued on Page D8, Column 3

On Tom Harkin

Mixing pugilism and politics, the Iowa Senator is running for President with an appeal built on his combative personality.

Strategies: The Democrats and '92. Page D11.

Mikhail S. Gorbachev after announcing his resignation last night as President of the Soviet Union.

Associated Press

The Soviet State, Born of a Dream, Dies

By SERGE SCHMEMANN
Special to The New York Times

MOSCOW, Dec. 25 — The Soviet state, marked throughout its brief but tumultuous history by great achievement and terrible suffering, died today after a long and painful decline. It was 74 years old.

Conceived in utopian promise and born in the violent upheavals of the "Great October Revolution of 1917," the union heaved its last in the dreary darkness of late December 1991, stripped of ideology, dismembered, bankrupt and hungry — but awe-inspiring even in its fall.

The end of the Soviet Union came with the resignation of Mikhail S. Gorbachev to make way for a new "Commonwealth of Independent States." At 7:32 P.M., shortly after the conclusion of his televised address, the red flag with hammer-and-sickle was lowered over the Kremlin and the white-blue-red Russian flag rose in its stead.

No Ceremony, Only Chimes

There was no ceremony, only the tolling of chimes from the Spassky Gate, cheers from a handful of surprised foreigners and an angry tirade from a lone war veteran.

Reactions to the death varied widely, according to Pravda, the former mouthpiece of the empire: "Some joyfully exclaim, 'Finita la comedia!' Others, heaping ash on their heads, raise their hands to the sky in horror and ask, what will be?"

The reaction depended somewhat on whether one listened to the ominous gunfire from Georgia, or

End of an Empire

A special report.

watched spellbound the bitter if dignified surrender of power by the last leader of the Union of Soviet Socialist Republics, Mr. Gorbachev.

Most people vacillated. The taboos and chains were gone, but so was the food. The Soviet Union had given them pitifully little, but there was no guarantee that the strange-sounding "Commonwealth of Independent States" would do any better.

As for Mr. Gorbachev, public opinion polls indicated a virtually universal agreement that it was time for him to move on — not because he had failed, but because there was nothing more he could do.

It was perhaps a paradox that the ruler who presided over the collapse of the Soviet Union was the only one of its ill-starred leaders to leave office with a measure of dignity intact. It was possible that history would reach a different verdict, but among many thoughtful Russians, it was to his undying credit that he lifted the chains of totalitarian dictatorship. Whether he could also have saved the economy was another question.

"Gorbachev was unable to change the living standards of the people, but he changed the people," Komsomolskaya Pravda wrote in a sympathetic farewell that seemed to capture the dominant mood. He didn't know how to make sausage, but he did know how to give freedom. And if someone believes that the former is more impor-

Continued on Page A14, Column 1

Communist Flag Is Removed; Yeltsin Gets Nuclear Controls

By FRANCIS X. CLINES
Special to The New York Times

MOSCOW, Dec. 25 — Mikhail S. Gorbachev, the trailblazer of the Soviet Union's retreat from the cold war and the spark for the democratic reforms that ended 70 years of Communist tyranny, told a weary, anxious nation tonight that he was resigning as President and closing out the union.

"I hereby discontinue my activities at the post of President of the Union of Soviet Socialist Republics," declared the 60-year-old politician, the last leader of a totalitarian empire that was undone across the six years and nine months of his stewardship.

Mr. Gorbachev made no attempt in his brief, leanly worded television address to mask his bitter regret and concern at being forced from office by the creation of the new Commonwealth of Independent States, composed of 11 former republics of the collapsed Soviet empire under the informal lead of President Boris N. Yeltsin of Russia.

'A New World'

Within hours of Mr. Gorbachev's resignation, Western and other nations began recognition of Russia and the other former republics.

"We're now living in a new world," Mr. Gorbachev declared in recognizing the rich history of his tenure. "An end has been put to the cold war and to the arms race, as well as to the mad militarization of the country, which has crippled our economy, public attitudes and morals. The threat of nuclear war has been removed." [A transcript of Mr. Gorbachev's speech and excerpts from interviews with Mr. Gorbachev and Mr. Yeltsin are on pages A12 and A13.]

Mr. Gorbachev's moment of farewell was stark. Kremlin guards were preparing to lower the red union flag for the last time. In minutes, Mr. Gorbachev would sign over the nuclear missile launching codes for safeguarding to Mr. Yeltsin, his rival and successor as the dominant politician of this agonized land.

Yeltsin's Assurance on Weapons

Earlier today, Mr. Yeltsin told his Russian Parliament that "there will be only a single nuclear button, and other presidents will not possess it."

But he said that to "push it" requires the approval of himself and the leaders of Ukraine, Byelorussia and Kazakhstan, the four former republics that have strategic nuclear weapons on their soil.

"Of course, we think this button must never be used," Mr. Yeltsin said.

Out in the night beyond the walled fortress as Mr. Gorbachev spoke, a disjointed people, freed from their decades of dictated misery, faced a frightening new course of shedding collectivism for the promises of individual enterprise. It is a course that remains a mystery for most of the commonwealth's 280 million people.

"I am very much concerned as I am leaving this post," the union President told the people. "However, I also have feelings of hope and faith in you, your wisdom and force of spirit. We are the heirs of a great civilization and it now depends on all and everyone whether or not this civilization will make a comeback to a new and decent living."

Still Against Commonwealth

In departing, the Soviet leader took comfort in the world's supporting his singular achievements in nuclear disarmament. But even more, he firmly warned his people that they had not yet learned to use their newly won freedom and that it could be put at risk by the

Continued on Page A12, Column 1

BUSH LAUDS VISION OF SOVIET LEADER

In Farewell, President Cites Gorbachev's Historic Role

By MICHAEL WINES
Special to The New York Times

WASHINGTON, Dec. 25 — President Bush moved quickly tonight to recognize Russia and other former republics of the now-extinct Soviet Union.

After praising the former Soviet leader, Mikhail S. Gorbachev, Mr. Bush went out of his way to express support for President Boris N. Yeltsin of Russia, who has emerged as the first among equals in the new Commonwealth of Independent States and as the custodian of the old Soviet Union's nuclear arsenal.

In his brief televised speech, Mr. Bush said that the United States now recognized the independence of the 11 former Soviet republics that have banded together, as well as a 12th, Georgia, which has shunned the alliance. [Text of Mr. Bush's remarks, page A16.]

But he indicated that the equally important step of establishing diplomatic ties between Washington and all 12 parts of the old Soviet empire would be more complicated.

The President said he was satisfied with the assurances on nuclear controls that he has received from Mr. Yeltsin and from leaders of other former republics with nuclear arms on their soil. Mr. Bush said that the United States would move rapidly to establish diplomatic relations with Russia, Armenia, Ukraine, Byelorussia, Kazakhstan and Kirghizia.

Diplomatic relations with the re-

Continued on Page A16, Column 3

INSIDE

Health Care on Wheels

Home health care has emerged as a $15 billion industry with more than 12,500 companies and not-for-profit services, from simple nursing to mobile emergency rooms. Page D1.

11 Turks Die in Firebombing

Kurdish separatists threw firebombs at a department store in Istanbul, setting the seven-story building ablaze and killing 11. Page A5.

Television and radio news and listings appear today on pages D18-19.

Pineapple, After Long Affair, Jilts Hawaii for Asian Suitors

By ROBERT REINHOLD
Special to The New York Times

LANAI CITY, Hawaii — For the last 13 years Kathleen Ruaburo dressed for work in thick rubberized pants and goggles and spent her days, just as her immigrant Filipino father did, in the heat and the dust picking pineapples on the Dole plantation. Now she dons a crisp white jacket with gold buttons and sets tables for wealthy tourists at the new Manele Bay Hotel here.

Mrs. Ruaburo's transition tells the story of pineapples in Hawaii. The crop that symbolizes this state and for decades has been a mainstay of the islands' economy is almost gone. Hawaiian pineapples can no longer compete in the world market.

Over the next 18 months, crews will harvest the last planting on this island, once the largest pineapple plantation in the world. Then the fields will go to alfalfa and oats, and the pineapple crews will either have to accept jobs in two new luxury hotels or leave the island for work. It is a future that some welcome and some fear on this tidy island, where 2,144 residents still live an isolated plantation life that has scarcely changed since James Drummond Dole started growing pineapples

here 69 years ago.

A big worry is that the island's economy will be just as dependent as ever on one industry. When the hotels were first proposed, pineapple cultivation was expected to continue and tourism was intended as a way to diversify the types of jobs here. But gradually, Dole managers said, it became clear that pineapples were no longer profitable enough.

Seventy-two miles away in Honolulu the Dole Packaged Foods Company on Dec. 1 began laying off about 500 workers at the big cannery near downtown that has processed the Lanai fruits for more than half a century. Its largest competitor, Del Monte, quit canning almost a decade ago. Only one canner remains in Hawaii, the Maui Land and Pineapple Company, which produces private labels for supermarkets. The Dole brand will stay on the shelves, but the pineapples will come from its plantations in Asia, as some do now.

Some Hawaiian pineapples will be grown for local consumption and to provide fresh fruit to markets on the

Continued on Page A18, Column 2

Having a Home Is Not a Prerequisite for Having the Spirit of Christmas

Leroy Lewis built a Christmas tree at his sometime home under the Queensboro Bridge on First Avenue in Manhattan. Lenore Elners stopped yesterday to wish Mr. Lewis a merry Christmas.

Lee Romero/The New York Times

From L.I. to Angry Illinois: A 5-Day Trash Odyssey

By SARAH LYALL

TAYLORVILLE, Ill., Dec. 20 — The story of Ocke Ketelsen's garbage began Dec. 15, when he put it out on his curb in Westbury, L.I. It was nothing special, just things like an old milk carton and some scraps of aluminum foil, and Mr. Ketelsen didn't give it a second thought. "Garbage is garbage," he said.

Not really, not anymore.

Garbage has become a multimillion-dollar industry, a touchy environmental issue and a major headache for crowded states like New York and New Jersey. And the next day, while Mr.

Ketelsen stayed home, his trash began an odyssey that took it north, south, and finally 900 miles west to the flat, open community of Taylorville, where the major industries are farming, paper and New York State refuse.

The system that got Mr. Ketelsen's garbage here is as messy as trash itself. The Soviet Union now pays five times as much in waste-disposal taxes as he did 15 years ago. And as they deal with closing landfills, wildly varying environmental regulations, and a crazy-quilt pricing system that can draw garbage halfway across the country in search of a good deal, many municipalities are finding that garbage is their

biggest worry and their biggest expense.

"Garbage is the most serious problem that we face," said Ernest J. Strada, who, as Mayor of Westbury, is responsible for removing Mr. Ketelsen's trash. "The general public talks about it in a general sense — we make garbage and it goes away. But it doesn't."

In the uneven picture of garbage in America, few places are as complicated as Long Island. The Island has dozens of overlapping jurisdictions, no

Continued on Page B4, Column 1

The New York Times

Late Edition
New York: Today, becoming mostly sunny. High 57-62. Tonight, showers late. Low 47. Tomorrow, clouds breaking, breezy. High 72. Yesterday, high 62, low 42. Details are on page B16.

VOL.CXLI..No. 48,953   Copyright © 1992 The New York Times   NEW YORK, FRIDAY, MAY 1, 1992   50 CENTS

23 DEAD AFTER 2D DAY OF LOS ANGELES RIOTS; FIRES AND LOOTING PERSIST DESPITE CURFEW

SENATORS APPROVE A BILL TO CURTAIL CAMPAIGN SPENDING

Curbs on Unrestricted Money Pass in Vote With Margin Too Thin for Override

By ADAM CLYMER
Special to The New York Times

WASHINGTON, April 30 — On a near party-line vote, the Senate today passed a campaign finance bill that would set voluntary spending limits in Congressional races and sharply reduce the role of money raised outside of existing Federal rules on contributions.

The 58-to-42 vote sent the most sweeping campaign finance legislation in 18 years to the White House, where it faces a certain veto. President Bush has said he would reject any legislation providing public money for candidates and setting spending limits, a move that he says would favor incumbents.

Neither today's margin nor the 259-to-165 tally by which the House approved the Democratic bill on April 9 is close to the two-thirds' vote required to override a veto.

A Milestone Vote

Despite that hard reality and the bill's failure to say how the Government would pay for the benefits it offers, supporters called today's vote and the agreement between House and Senate Democrats a milestone on the way to changing the current system.

The spending limits were the subject of the most heated argument as the Senate ended a three-day debate today. Senator Bob Dole of Kansas, the Republican leader, said: "Often the only way a challenger can compete with the built-in advantages of incumbency is to spend money. The bottom line is that spending limits are designed to prevent change at a time when the American people are demanding change."

Senator George J. Mitchell of Maine, the majority leader, called such arguments "nonsense." He said incumbents almost always raised more than their challengers, often three or four times as much, and therefore limits would help even the odds in those contests.

That partisan division was reflected

Continued on Page A16, Column 3

Leadership And Its Limits

Political Needs Prevail In Check-Scandal Vote

By ADAM CLYMER

WASHINGTON, April 30 — The leaders wanted to resist. The followers didn't.

News Analysis
The leaders tried to look after the House as an institution. The ordinary members preferred to look after their own careers.

That is the quickest explanation of what happened when the House voted Wednesday night to comply with a subpoena from the Justice Department, asking for records of every check written on the now closed House bank between July 1988 and October 1991.

Indeed, dozens of members who voted to comply with the subpoena regarded it as an improper "fishing expedition" but one they could not effectively resist, and only 131 Democrats stood up and voted to challenge it in court. Perhaps 30 or 40 more had promised to do so if their votes mattered. They waited, saw it was hopeless and cast the vote that was easier to explain back home.

Spotlight on Foley

For months, some Democrats have faulted Speaker Thomas S. Foley for not anticipating the perils that the bank's tolerance of dubious checks posed for all of them. They also faulted him for being thoughtful and judicious but not political enough.

A Texan, John Bryant, took the floor four weeks ago to complain that the Speaker was not defending the House adequately. Mr. Foley is certainly not succeeding in defending the House against what he and most Democrats see as irresponsible intrusions by a zealous Justice Department. But on Tuesday night Mr. Bryant voted to surrender the records.

Yes, there are complaints about the leadership, but basically the followers have the leadership they want, leaders who plead with them but do not or cannot order them about. The demand that Mr. Foley become a stronger leader is not easily squared with the independent search for survival that marks the House today.

His circumstances were made al-

Continued on Page A24, Column 4

Flames engulfing a building in South-Central Los Angeles on Wednesday night as rioting spread.
Associated Press

Surprised, Police React Slowly as Violence Spreads

By ROBERT REINHOLD
Special to The New York Times

LOS ANGELES, April 30 — The Los Angeles Police, apparently caught off guard by the violent reaction to the acquittal of four white officers in the beating of a black motorist, were slow to react, even after the scope of the anarchy sweeping the city had become apparent.

As unruly demonstrators threatened to invade police headquarters downtown early Wednesday evening, Chief of Police Daryl F. Gates was attending an event in the affluent Brentwood area, about 11 miles away, to raise money to fight a proposal on the June ballot to limit the term of the police chief. Matthew Hunt, the deputy chief in charge of the affected area, was attending a community meeting about 6 miles from the police command center.

It was hours before the police entered many of the areas in South-Central Los Angeles where stores were being looted and motorists were being dragged from their cars and beaten.

Chief Resisted National Guard

As late as 11 P.M., with at least two dozen fires blazing out of control, Chief Gates resisted Mayor Tom Bradley's call for National Guard troops, telling Gov. Pete Wilson in a conference call with the Mayor that he was not sure the police needed help handling the situation, according to someone who is close to Mayor Bradley and who spoke on the condition of anonymity.

The Mayor prevailed with the Governor, and by this morning Mr. Gates agreed that the Guard was needed. But the first contingent, about 2,400 guardsmen, including about 100 military police, was not deployed on the streets until midafternoon today. The Governor traced the delay in part to a shortage of ammunition.

Fires Burned Unattended

Similarly, the Los Angeles Fire Department, had no special contingency plan apart from declaring a tactical alert, meaning engine companies moved in special teams. The department was forced to let many fires burn unattended, not because it lacked sufficient engines at first but because the police did not have enough officers to protect firefighters. There were barely enough officers on hand to prevent Parker Center, the police headquarters downtown, from being overrun.

The slow response was due in part to the fact that almost nobody, including the Mayor, anticipated such a sweeping acquittal of all four officers and

Continued on Page A22, Column 1

Suspected looters, handcuffed and forced to lie down, in police custody.
Reuters

Smell of Fear in Los Angeles

By JANE GROSS
Special to The New York Times

LOS ANGELES, April 30 — The City of Angels endured another siege of violence today with an acrid smell of smoke in its nostrils and a cold stone of fear heavy on its heart.

Hopes were dashed early that daylight would quiet the beating, looting and burning that followed Wednesday's verdict in the Rodney G. King case, and residents took to the streets warily, knowing that terrible things had happened here overnight, with more terrible things likely to come.

Throughout the sprawling metropolis, even in neighborhoods far from the epicenter of the violence, Angelenos sensed that the next car that passed might carry hooligans waving crowbars and axes, that the next

store to burn or be looted could be the one on their corner. This was not a disturbance with a clear perimeter, they came to understand, and while some street corners were safer than others, there was really no place to hide.

The roadways were emptier than usual, but chaotic as a bumper-car ride as nervous motorists navigated a shifting maze of barricades and craned their heads skyward to track the newest plume of smoke rising in the heavy haze. The drivers' eyes darted from side to side, taking the measure of the stranger in the car beside them, plotting new routes as they opened, and gazing in horror at the ravaged and smoldering stores that dotted the city.

Evacuation in Koreatown

In some neighborhoods more than others, one could almost smell the fear. Four miles north from the genesis of the violence, Koreatown, for instance, was an edgy place this morning, braced for trouble because of longstanding tensions between the black and Asian communities here.

By midafternoon, the bands of looters were moving in waves toward the small strip shopping centers near Olympic Boulevard and Vermont Street, the heart of the Koreatown, but hours earlier some Korean merchants decided they were taking no

Continued on Page A21, Column 3

900 REPORTED HURT

National Guard on Patrol — Violence Spreads to San Francisco

By SETH MYDANS
Special to The New York Times

LOS ANGELES, April 30 — Social order broke down today across a broad area of the nation's second-largest city as vandals and looters roamed the streets, carloads of young men attacked pedestrians and uncounted fires burned out of control.

Mayor Tom Bradley and the Police Chief, Daryl F. Gates, appealed for order and imposed a dusk-to-dawn curfew, saying they had been overwhelmed by the violence and rioting that broke out after Wednesday's acquittal of four white police officers on trial for beating a black motorist, Rodney G. King.

The authorities said at least 23 people had been killed, more than 900 injured and nearly 500 people arrested. Hundreds of buildings burned as the violence spread from South-Central Los Angeles into wealthier white areas, and entire inner-city blocks lay in ruins.

National Guard Arrives

As the night wore on, officials said, the violence and lawlessness increased even as National Guard troops summoned by Gov. Pete Wilson were put on the streets.

"The situation is getting worse, despite the dusk-to-dawn curfew," said Deputy Larry Mead of the Los Angeles County Sherrif's Department. "There's been an increase in looting and fires in the southern sections of the city of L.A. and L.A. County."

Near midnight there were signs that the number of new fires was decreasing, but the police were still trying to control roving bands of looters. A police spokesman, Lieut. John Dunkin, said officers had killed three people in separate incidents since nightfall.

In Washington, the Justice Department announced that it was reopening an investigation into the March 3, 1991, videotaped beating of Mr. King to prepare the ground for a possible civil rights case against the four officers who were acquitted.

Violence in Other Cities

But it was clear from the words of the rioters, as well as black elected officials and others, that their anger ran far deeper than reaction to the acquittal. There were demonstrations around the nation, gangs on the loose in Atlanta and San Francisco and fears that the violence, shown so vividly on television, might spread further. [Page A20.]

Just before 7 P.M., two white men on a motorcycle were attacked by a group of about 15 black men in Long Beach, south of Los Angeles. The two motorcyclists were beaten and shot, and one was killed, according to Comdr. Anthony Batts of the Long Beach Police Department.

The violence in Los Angeles spread today as smoke from burning buildings mingled with the city's smog. The first 1,200 of 4,000 National Guard members to be deployed took up positions this afternoon alongside hundreds of police and highway patrol officers in South-Central Los Angeles, the mostly black and Hispanic section where the violence began Wednesday afternoon. Governor Wilson this afternoon doubled the original summons of 2,000 troops as the violence spread through-

Continued on Page A20, Column 1

MORE ON THE RIOTS

'I Know It's Not Right'
In some areas, looters said they were expressing their bitterness at the status of blacks in America. Page A21.

Clinton and Bush Spar
Gov. Bill Clinton and aides to President Bush criticized each other's response to the events. Page A22.

Public Topic No. 1
On call-in programs, at rallies and on the job, Americans voiced apprehension about race relations. Page A23.

How Lawyers See the Case
Los Angeles lawyers who have followed the case dissected the tactics of prosecution and defense. Page A20.

Afghans' Battle Lines Are Drawn As One Rebel Denounces Another

By EDWARD A. GARGAN
Special to The New York Times

KABUL, Afghanistan, April 30 — Afghanistan's strongest guerrilla leader, Ahmad Shah Masood, took charge of the security of Kabul today after entering the capital overnight with a three-mile-long convoy of military vehicles and an estimated 10,000 troops.

Shortly after arriving, Mr. Masood denounced the lone guerrilla leader who has refused to take part in the coalition that proclaimed an Islamic republic in Afghanistan on Tuesday.

The holdout, Gulbuddin Hekmatyar, who heads the hard-line Islamic group Hezb-i-Islami, has marshaled his guerrillas just south of Kabul in Logar Province, from where he is continuing to mount attacks on the capital.

A barrage of rockets, presumably fired by Mr. Hekmatyar's forces, hit the airport this evening. Mr. Masood's forces did not counterattack, but the guerrilla leader's criticism of Mr. Hekmatyar left little doubt that a new round of fighting could be in store.

"Every group which is fighting the Government, which is acceptable to the majority of the people, is baghi," Mr. Masood said. The word refers to un-Islamic behavior akin to criminality.

As late as Wednesday the new Government, headed by Sibgatullah Mojadedi, was considering some way to placate Mr. Hekmatyar by giving him a role in the new administration. But today, with the continuing attacks, Mr. Hekmatyar was branded an enemy.

Full Attack Weighed

"He's out," said Assam Akram, a spokesman for Mr. Mojadedi, who is to hand over leadership of the ruling coalition in two months to the head of Mr. Masood's guerrilla group, Jamiat-i-Islami or Islamic Society. Mr. Akram accused Mr. Hekmatyar of sabotaging Kabul's electrical grid; the capital has been without power for two days.

Nurul Haq Ullumi, a general in the

Continued on Page A10, Column 4

INSIDE

Familiar End in Mideast Talks
Israelis and Arabs ended their fifth round of talks without signs of progress on major issues or a commitment on meeting again. Page A6.

Navy Report on Sex Assaults
The Navy said many women, not just a few, were abused at an aviators' convention and said many officers would not aid the inquiry. Page A14.

An Everglades Cleanup Idea
A system of trading pollution credits could help to rid the Everglades waters of phosphorous from fertilizers, economists believe. Law, page B18.

Exxon Official Still Missing
The disappearance of the president of Exxon International remained a mystery and officials refused to discuss the investigation. Page B1.

Nets Walk the Plank
New Jersey's season of near-mutiny ended in a 98-89 loss to the Cleveland Cavaliers in the fourth game of their N.B.A. playoff series. Page B9.

The New York Times

The New York Times

Late Edition

New York: Today, sun, then increasing clouds. High 44. Tonight, rain. Low 40. Tomorrow, morning rain, brighter by afternoon. High 46. Yesterday, high 43, low 27. Details are on page C20.

VOL.CXLII...No. 49,218   Copyright © 1993 The New York Times   NEW YORK, THURSDAY, JANUARY 21, 1993   50 CENTS

CLINTON TAKES OATH AS 42D PRESIDENT, URGING SACRIFICE TO 'RENEW AMERICA'

Bill Clinton being sworn in yesterday by Chief Justice William H. Rehnquist as the 42d President of the United States. With him outside the Capitol were his wife, Hillary, their daughter, Chelsea, and Vice President Al Gore, who had taken his oath of office moments earlier.

Jose R. Lopez/The New York Times

Amid Pageant of Diversity, Homage to Election Themes

By THOMAS L. FRIEDMAN
Special to The New York Times

WASHINGTON, Jan. 20 — William Jefferson Clinton became the 42d President of the United States today, and in an Inaugural Address striking in its appeal for sacrifice, he told Americans that if they assume greater responsibility for their country's future, "there is nothing wrong with America that cannot be cured by what is right with America."

The 46-year-old Governor of Arkansas, virtually unknown to most Americans 18 months ago and a long shot for the White House, took the oath of office under a stunningly blue sky from Chief Justice William H. Rehnquist. President George Herbert Walker Bush, who once seem ed sure to win a second term, watched stoically from his seat on the Capitol steps.

Under Mr. Clinton's left hand, his wife, Hillary, held a King James Bible given to Mr. Clinton by his grandmother. His 12-year-old daughter, Chelsea, stood at his right as he uttered the traditional oath at 11:58 A.M. Eastern time. He then spoke for 14 minutes to a sea of people, flowing down from the flag-draped Western facade of the Capitol to the Washington Monument.

'What America Does Best'

"We must do what America does best: offer more opportunity to all and demand more responsibility from all," Mr. Clinton declared in an echo of John F. Kennedy's Inaugural Address. "It is time to break the bad habit of expecting something for nothing, from our Government or from each other. Let us all take more responsibility, not only for ourselves and our families but for our communities and our country."

In a speech with the recurring theme of renewal, Mr. Clinton implored at one point: "To renew America we must be bold. We must do what no generation has had to do before." [Transcript, page A15.]

Washington never looked better, or felt better. Cheerful chaos reigned on the streets, in a subway system that is usually weirdly sedate and on the Mall, in front of the Capitol, where something like a quarter of a million people endured mobs and metal detectors and midwinter chill. Schools and Federal offices had a quadrennial holiday, so natives joined tourists beneath a Capitol that was dressed for the day in gowns of red, white and blue, and glittered in the January sun.

Walk Through the Crowd

In a day of ceremonies intended to be casual and intimate — with lots of Presidential bear hugs for friends and a conscious assertion of the passing of power to the post-World War II generation — the Clintons walked the last few blocks down Pennsylvania Avenue from the Capitol to the White House. Before the Clintons decided to get out of their new armor-plated Cadillac, the crowds along the route were chanting: "Walk! Walk!"

From the viewing stand in front of the White House's iron gates, the Clintons watched a politically inclusive parade, encompassing everyone from Arkansas bands to gay groups to Elvis impersonators — like the rest of the inaugural as meticulously scripted as any Hollywood production. Throughout, Mr. Clinton wore the amazed grin of a man whose lifelong dream had just come true.

The flag-waving crowds along the parade route were striking both for their enthusiasm and their racial diversity. The upbeat mood of the well-wishers seemed on track with that of recent national polls — one of guarded optimism about Mr. Clinton's prospects, coupled with a strong desire to give the new President a chance.

Short, Informal Speech

Mr. Clinton's Inaugural Address, far more compact than the lengthy oratory of his long 1988 Democratic National Convention speech, was informal and almost conversational.

It was typical of the New Age political style that helped him win the highest office in the land. While Mr. Clinton paid homage to many of the themes that won him the election — the need for renewal, health-care reform, economic revival and political reform — his address was not an agenda for action, but rather a call to service.

"You, my fellow Americans, have forced the spring," he said. "Now we must do the work the season demands."

The address was at times brutally frank in its assessment of the decline of the country under Mr. Bush and in its chastising of an aloof and self-absorbed

Continued on Page A14, Column 1

The Inauguration: Serious and Not So

DOWN TO BUSINESS As President Clinton's new team set about governing, the swirl of ceremony was almost an intrusion. Page A11.

CONFIRMING A CABINET The Senate confirmed new Secretaries of State, Defense and the Treasury, and agreed to move quickly on 11 other Cabinet posts. Page A12.

PRIVATE CITIZEN AGAIN Proclaiming his career "a hell of a ride," George Bush returned with little fanfare to Houston, where it began. Page A13.

STYLES AND PARTIES A new youthful feeling pervaded the fashions and forms of the Democrats' celebration. Page A16.

CLINTON SET TO END BAN ON GAY TROOPS

Military to Have Say on How Change Is Carried Out

By ERIC SCHMITT
Special to The New York Times

WASHINGTON, Jan. 20 — Refining a compromise on a volatile issue, President Clinton plans to issue an executive order that would lift the ban on homosexuals in the armed forces, but he will delay the directive for several months to give the Pentagon a chance to draft it, Clinton transition aides said today.

In the meantime, the military will be directed less formally to stop asking recruits about their sexual orientation and discharging people when they are found to be homosexuals. These are the two points that would be the main practical effect once an executive order is in effect.

Tug of War on Issue

Mr. Clinton is expected to announce his new policy in the next few days, officials said.

The two-step process buys the Clinton Administration time to consult with senior military leaders on details of the policy, while at the same time fulfilling a campaign pledge Mr. Clinton made to repeal the ban with an executive order.

Under intense pressure from the military to back off that commitment, Mr. Clinton's aides had been considering a plan to lift the ban without a Presidential order. Homosexual-rights advocates vigorously protested, contending

Continued on Page A17, Column 5

January High Noon: Hail Meets Farewell

Smiles and Grim Eyes as Winners Exult and the Losers Depart

By DAVID E. ROSENBAUM
Special to The New York Times

WASHINGTON, Jan. 20 — At 11:30 sharp this morning, the Marine Band played "Hail to the Chief" for George Bush for the last time.

He walked through the archway on the West Front of the Capitol and, unsmiling, walked down to his chair on the inauguration stage, hardly acknowledging the lawmakers, Supreme Court Justices and others already seated.

Moments later, Bill Clinton — William Jefferson Clinton, as the doorkeeper of the House of Representatives, James T. Molloy, announced him — walked through the same arch. With a wide grin, he waved and shook hands all the way to his seat. Hillary and Chelsea Clinton were already there. So were Al and Tipper Gore and their four children.

The contrast in the families' moods was palpable throughout the ceremony. From below, the Bushes seemed to be maintaining their composure, but close up, on television, their eyes, while dry, showed the strain. Mr. Bush's were drawn and gray. During the Rev. Billy Graham's invocation, Barbara Bush's eyes were shut unusually tight.

Most of the Clintons and Gores could hardly contain their excitement, and after Mr. Gore took the oath of office from Justice Byron R. White, the new Vice President and Mr. Clinton threw their arms around each other in the bear hug they favor at festive occasions.

Chelsea Clinton, on the other hand, seemed wiped out. She had gone to the entertainment gala on Tuesday night and did not get back to Blair House, where the family was staying, until nearly 1:30 A.M. — quite a night

for a 12-year-old. She appeared to fall asleep at this morning's service at the Metropolitan African Methodist Episcopal church, and she yawned several times during Mr. Graham's invocation. But later she seemed to get a second wind and listened wide-eyed to her father's address.

Hats Off to Clinton

The mid-January weather has often played havoc with inaugurations. Eight years ago, with the temperature in single digits, Ronald Reagan took the oath inside the Capitol and the parade was canceled.

But today, the temperature climbed into the 40's, the sky was clear and wind was still. Mr. Clinton and Mr. Gore even took off their overcoats when they took their oaths.

But it was nippy enough that many wore hats. Chief Justice William H. Rehnquist, a stickler for precedent and tradition, wore the same black, wool skull cap he wore four years ago at Mr. Bush's inauguration ceremony.

The cap, it seems, is part of the official garb for Chief Justices at outdoor, cold-weather events. Chief Justice Charles Evans Hughes wore it to three of Franklin D. Roosevelt's inaugurations. But it fell into disuse thereafter, until Justice Rehnquist,

Continued on Page A13, Column 2

A Change of Power, but Barely a Break in Stride

President Bush welcoming the new tenant to 1600 Pennsylvania Avenue yesterday before they left for the inauguration.

Agence France-Presse

In a Ritual of Continuity Bowing to History, Enter Clinton, With His Unwritten Chapter

By R. W. APPLE Jr.
Special to The New York Times

WASHINGTON, Jan. 20 — Today was the day of Bill Clinton's dreams, the day he and his party finished the arduous climb to a "joyful mountaintop of celebration," but like all Inauguration Days, it was more than that.

News Analysis It was a day when the nation committed itself once more, with the recital of a simple 18th-century oath, to what the new President felicitously termed "the mystery of American renewal." The solemn magic of the moment, in this most telling of national rituals, lies in what it symbolizes: the unquestioned acceptance by victor, vanquished and public alike of the continuity and legitimacy of governance.

The United States crowns no kings. But as he stood before the Capitol and spoke the words George Washington first uttered in lower Manhattan on April 30, 1789, Mr. Clinton embodied this nation's unity, in something of the way a monarch embodies Britain's at the hour of coronation in Westminster Abbey.

Jack Valenti, who worked in the White House three decades ago, calls the man in the Oval Office "the keeper of the national integrity and the steward of our civic virtue."

As such, Mr. Clinton starts with the good wishes of most Americans. But he is the leader of a Government as well

as an icon of nationhood, and in that capacity he begins with less than universal acceptance. He won the votes, after all, of only 43 percent of those who cast ballots last November, and since then, he has excited wariness as well as enthusiasm in the country.

Bitter Democratic Memories

Few will take exception to his message of hope and rebirth, but it is far less certain that he will carry the country with him in his appeal to "face hard truths and take strong steps" in a spirit of shared sacrifice. That will depend not only upon who is asked to give up what, and how fair the apportionment seems, but also upon Mr. Clinton's ability to stir a citizenry that has been more preoccupied with "me" than with "us" for much of the last two decades.

The Old Guard in his party remembers all too well the self-immolation of the last two Democratic Administrations, those headed by Lyndon B. Johnson and Jimmy Carter, and prays that

Continued on Page A12, Column 1

INSIDE

Serbs Accept Peace Pact
The Serbs' parliament in Bosnia voted reluctantly for a plan intended to keep the nation whole. Page A3.

U.S. Setback at U.N. Agency
Opposed by Washington, the head of the World Health Organization won a key vote to keep his post. Page A8.

Gaps in Shelter System
The slaying of a Bronx woman points to the lack of treatment for homeless people who are mentally ill. Page B1.

Jean Harris Granted Freedom
A parole board panel approved the release of Jean S. Harris, 13 years after she killed her lover. Page B7.

Audrey Hepburn Is Dead; Actress Epitomized Elegance
The Oscar-winning actress of "Roman Holiday" who went on to engrave such films as "Funny Face," "Breakfast at Tiffany's" and "Wait Until Dark" with her sylphlike elegance is dead at 63. Page D24.

354613

"All the News That's Fit to Print"

The New York Times

Late Edition
New York: **Today**, cold winds, mostly sunny. Clouds south of the city. High 33. **Tonight**, clear. Low 22. **Tomorrow**, mostly sunny, cold. High 35. **Yesterday**, high 27, low 21. Details, page 34.

VOL.CXLII .. No. 49,255   Copyright © 1993 The New York Times   NEW YORK, SATURDAY, FEBRUARY 27, 1993   50 CENTS

BLAST HITS TRADE CENTER, BOMB SUSPECTED; 5 KILLED, THOUSANDS FLEE SMOKE IN TOWERS

Associated Press; Carrie Boretz for The New York Times; Marilynn K. Yee/The New York Times

ELEVATORS, STAIRS

SHOPPING ARCADE

VISTA HOTEL

PERRY STREET

WEST STREET

LIBERTY STREET

LOADING DOCK AND GENERATOR

PATH TRACKS

PUBLIC PARKING

③

②

①

EMPLOYEE PARKING

EMPLOYEE PARKING

AIR-CONDITIONING, BACKUP GENERATOR

① The blast occurred in a parking garage on the second level of the multi-level basement of the north World Trade Center tower.

② It carved a 200- by 100-foot crater on the public parking level, blew through a ceiling and knocked a hole in a wall.

③ Cinder blocks and rubble from the collapsing wall fell to the tracks of the PATH station, and damaged lower levels.

This drawing is schematic and is based on information from reporters and officials at the scene.

Jean Rutter/The New York Times; illustration by David Montesino and Julie Shaver

Many Are Trapped for Hours In Darkness and Confusion

By ROBERT D. McFADDEN

An explosion apparently caused by a car bomb in an underground garage shook the World Trade Center in lower Manhattan with the force of a small earthquake shortly after noon yesterday, collapsing walls and floors, igniting fires and plunging the city's largest building complex into a maelstrom of smoke, darkness and fearful chaos.

The police said the blast killed at least five people and left more than 650 others injured, mostly with smoke inhalation or minor burns, but dozens with cuts, bruises, broken bones or serious burns. The police said 476 were treated at hospitals and the rest by rescue and medical crews at the scene.

The explosion also trapped hundreds of people in debris or in smoke-filled stairwells and elevators of the towers overhead and forced the evacuation of more than 50,000 workers from a trade center bereft of power for lights and elevators for seven hours.

No Bomb Fragments Found

The blast, which was felt throughout the Wall Street area and a mile away on Ellis and Liberty Islands in New York Harbor, also knocked out the police command and operations centers for the towers, which officials said rendered the office complex's evacuation plans useless. [Page 23.]

James Fox, an assistant director of the Federal Bureau of Investigation in charge of the agency's New York office, said that no bomb fragments were found but that a joint terrorist task force of Federal agents and city detectives had examined the wreckage and believed that a car bomb had caused the explosion.

There was no warning of an impending explosion, Police Commissioner Raymond W. Kelly said. Jack Killorin, a spokesman in Washington for the Treasury Department's Bureau of Alcohol, Tobacco and Firearms, said that after the blast, authorities received at least nine telephone calls claiming responsibility.

Mr. Killorin said the first call was made 15 minutes after the blast to a non-emergency number of a New York Police Department precinct by an individual who mentioned the conflict in Bosnia. He said other claims were made between an hour and several hours after the event by callers who cited that and a variety of other reasons for the attack. He declined to elaborate.

Some law-enforcement officials said an explosion of such size, without a claim of responsibility, might suggest that it went off accidentally.

Mr. Kelly was more oblique about the cause of the blast, saying only that a car bomb or other type of explosive device was not being ruled out.

Four hours after the explosion, a bomb threat forced the evacuation of the Empire State Building in midtown Manhattan, and there were numerous other bomb threats in the city, the police said. But it was unclear if any were related to the World Trade Center explosion or only the macabre work of pranksters.

As the day ended, a series of investigations began — into the cause of the explosion and its possible perpetrators, and into what went wrong in what many called a botched evacuation, with no alarms and no instructions for thousands caught in dark, smoky stairwells, in stark contrast to carefully laid plans.

Mayor David N. Dinkins, visiting in Osaka, Japan, was notified by City Hall and, in a telephone news conference, called the Fire Department response the largest for any non-natural disaster in the city's history. He said he had spoken with President Clinton and had thanked him for the cooperation of Federal investigators.

The effects of the blast radiated outward, disrupting most non-cable television transmissions throughout the metropolitan area, halting traffic in most of lower Manhattan and PATH train

Continued on Page 22, Column 1

Agence France-Presse
A man calling for help.

Manhattan Is Held in the Grip Of Traffic Snarls and Anxiety

By DEBORAH SONTAG

Traffic snarled to a standstill in lower Manhattan. Major arteries downtown closed, and a half-dozen subway lines were rerouted. Nervous relatives jammed the 911 emergency lines. And an anxiety that began in lower Manhattan at lunchtime yesterday grew infectious as the day grew long, generating a restless buzz throughout New York City.

As news spread that the explosion at the World Trade Center — which the F.B.I. said may have been caused by a car bomb — had been followed by a bomb scare at and evacuation of the Empire State Building, nerves began to fray. Drivers sitting bumper to bumper on Canal Street leaned on their horns, waiting over an hour to enter the Holland Tunnel. Subway riders jostled their way onto overcrowded trains, pondering their commuters' headaches as well as what seemed to be a different kind of urban terrorism.

An Eerie Quiet on Closed Streets

"It's frightening," said Charles Sampey, 34 years old, a building superintendent riding the IRT No. 3 downtown at 6 P.M. "You'd expect more to get robbed in New York than to get hit by a terrorist bomb."

After an underground explosion rocked the World Trade Center at noontime, the Franklin D. Roosevelt Drive, the West Side Highway, the Brooklyn Battery Tunnel and most side streets in lower Manhattan were closed to all but emergency vehicles. It grew eerily quiet — "like Sunday at dawn,"

said a Triborough Bridge and Tunnel Authority spokesman, Frank Pascual — but for the cry of sirens. With their antennae atop the Trade Center, all except one New York television station — WCBS, Channel 2 — went off the air.

As trading on five commodities exchanges was disrupted and thousands of employees were evacuated from the smoke-filled office complex, transportation officials immediately began making emergency plans for an imminent rush hour. They added buses, trains and ferries to New Jersey to

Continued on Page 22, Column 1

INSIDE

Economy Ended 1992 With Robust Growth

The gross domestic product grew at the robust rate of 4.8 percent in the final three months of 1992, the best quarterly performance in five years and a full percentage point higher than initial estimates. Page 35.

Judge Rebuffs Gay Group On St. Patrick's Parade

A Federal judge ruled that New York City cannot order the Ancient Order of Hibernians to include a gay contingent in the annual St. Patrick's Day Parade up Fifth Avenue. The city will not appeal. Page 21.

Bosnia Sees a Turning Point

After hearing of American plans to airdrop relief supplies, many Bosnians said they sensed a major change in their plight. Page 6.

PRESIDENT URGES MORE RUSSIAN AID

In a Speech on World Trade, He Seeks a 2-Way Street

By R. W. APPLE Jr.
Special to The New York Times

WASHINGTON, Feb. 26 — President Clinton declared today that having spent trillions of dollars to win the cold war, the United States must summon the will to spend much more than planned in Russia and the other former Soviet republics "to support democracy's success where Communism failed."

Documents sent to Capitol Hill with the President's economic message last week, but little noticed at the time, indicated the President will ask for $700 million in aid next year for the former Soviet republics, nearly doubling the $417 million allotted for this year. Mr. Clinton, who plans to meet with President Boris N. Yeltsin of Russia on April 4, said "the world will suffer" if Russia's tottering economic reforms collapse. [Excerpts, page 6.]

Wants America to Compete

In a speech at American University consciously evocative of one delivered there 30 years ago by John F. Kennedy, the President endorsed the broad thrust of former President George Bush's trade policies. But at the same time, he sent two signals of change with his call for greater support for Russia and a suggestion that he would demand progress on human rights as the price for continued growth in trade with China.

The speech was devoted to international economics and trade and was not

Continued on Page 6, Column 1

First, Darkness, Then Came the Smoke

By N. R. KLEINFIELD

It depended on where you were in the towers when it came. For some the warning was a trembling underfoot or just a blank computer screen and flickering lights. For others, it was a shocking noise. One woman was blown out of her high heels. Another, desk chair and all, sank into the floor. And then, instantly it seemed, came the billowing smoke and the chilling realization that you had to get out of there.

The Face of Death

There were those who panicked, those who coolly absorbed it, those who got sick to their stomach and those who saw the face of death. No one was sure what had happened; did a plane hit the building, was it an earthquake, had lightning struck? Many wondered why there seemed to be no evacuation plan and no guidance — not realizing that the blast had knocked out the center's operations center.

But thousands of people in the

For Workers in Offices, the First Imperative Was to Get Outside

World Trade Center yesterday afternoon knew they were in the grip of one of the most dreaded urban nightmares: they were in the city's tallest building and something was very wrong.

Joann Hilton was low. And, in this disaster, that was the worst place to be. A secretary working for the Port Authority of New York and New Jersey, she was at her desk in the command office on the B1 level of the building, musing about the weekend.

"All of a sudden, we heard this big boom," she said. "It sounded like an earthquake. And then the floor just collapsed and me and my chair sank into the floor. The ceiling started to come down, too, and I'm in my chair in the floor. Some of the lights went

out. And then it was all dark. Like a cave. Somebody pulled me out of that floor and we beat it out of there."

Denise Bosco was high. She was on the 82d floor, where she too works as a secretary for the Port Authority. "The whole building shook," she said. "The lights flashed on and off. The computers went down. Then, instantly, there was smoke. I was terrified. People panicked. They started pushing and shouting to get out. Some of them were throwing up. I said, 'Oh dear God, what is it? What is it? Is it my time? Is this the way?' "

Wrapped in a Bath Towel

Her coat was still in her office and she was wrapped in a white bath towel as she stood outside. She broke down into tears. "It was horrible," she said. "There was this awful feeling that we might not be able to get out. We were in the mighty, tall tower but we weren't getting out."

They didn't know whether to stay put or flee, but instinct said to run.

Continued on Page 22, Column 4

Reuters
The explosion that shook the World Trade Center yesterday left a crater 60 feet wide below the building.

THE NEW YORK TIMES is available for home or office delivery in most major US cities. Please call this toll-free number: 1-800-631-2500   ADVT

354613

The New York Times

Late Edition

New York: Today, partly sunny, warm winds. High 75, but cooler along south shores. Tonight, cloudy. Low 58. Tomorrow, showers. High 71. Yesterday, high 79, low 49. Details, page B16.

VOL.CXLII... No. 49,307   Copyright © 1993 The New York Times   NEW YORK, TUESDAY, APRIL 20, 1993   75 cents beyond 75 miles from New York City, except on Long Island   **50 CENTS**

SCORES DIE AS CULT COMPOUND IS SET AFIRE AFTER F.B.I. SENDS IN TANKS WITH TEAR GAS

The wood-frame compound of David Koresh and his cult followers turned into an inferno of death yesterday as a standoff of 51 days was ended.   *Agence France-Presse*

Apparent Mass Suicide Ends A 51-Day Standoff in Texas

By SAM HOWE VERHOVEK
Special to The New York Times

WACO, Tex., April 19 — Hours after Federal agents began battering holes in the walls of the Branch Davidian compound and spraying tear gas inside, David Koresh and more than 80 followers — including at least 17 children — apparently perished today when flames engulfed the sprawling wooden complex on the Texas prairie.

Officials of the Federal Bureau of Investigation said they believed that Mr. Koresh, a self-described messiah who prophesied to his followers that they would meet their end in an apocalyptic confrontation with the law, gave the order to burn the compound down in the 51st day of a standoff with Federal agents.

F.B.I. officials said smashing the walls and filling the building with tear gas was intended to increase pressure on the cult members, who had resisted all previous demands for surrender. But the officials insisted that the tear gas was not flammable and that the fire was set by cult members who poured fuel around the perimeter of the compound and lit matches.

'They All Willingly Followed'

"David Koresh, we believe, gave the order to commit suicide and they all willingly followed," said Bob A. Ricks, a senior F.B.I. agent who has been here for most of the standoff, which began seven weeks ago with a deadly shootout between cult members and agents from the Federal Bureau of Alcohol, Tobacco and Firearms who wanted to search the compound.

Mr. Ricks said only nine people were rescued from the compound today, including one woman who had sought to return to the burning building and tried to fight off a Federal agent who came to her aid. Ammunition in the cult's storehouse of weapons sporadically exploded during the afternoon, hindering rescue workers.

Mr. Ricks said that so far "several bodies" had been found in a bus buried on the compound, and only "two or three" other bodies. The authorities believed that some of these were cult members who had been killed in the original confrontation on Feb. 28, he said.

"We had hoped the women would grab their children and flee," Mr. Ricks said. "That did not occur and they bunkered down the children and allowed them to go up in flames with them." Mr. Ricks said that it was only speculation at this point but that the authorities had received reports, apparently from some of the survivors, that the children had been injected with some kind of poison to ease their pain.

F.B.I. officials said they believed that 95 people were inside the compound when the fire began, including 17 children under the age of 10, and that it only knew of the 9 survivors, 4 of whom were at hospitals this evening and 5 of

Continued on Page A20, Column 3

RENO SEES ERROR IN MOVE ON CULT

Fatigue of Agents and Failure of Talks Brought Assault

By STEPHEN LABATON
Special to The New York Times

WASHINGTON, April 19 — Attorney General Janet Reno conceded tonight that in hindsight the Government's plan to assault the heavily armed cult near Waco, Tex., had been a mistake.

"It was based on what we knew then," she said this evening on the "Larry King Live" program on CNN. "Based on what we know now, it was obviously wrong."

Earlier in the day, a shaken and somber Ms. Reno said she had worried over the weekend that the plan could bring mass suicide, but she decided that it was "highly unlikely" and approved the operation.

Taking responsibility for the assault, she acknowledged that it had in fact led to a mass suicide, as members of the Branch Davidian cult burned down their wooden compound.

She added that Federal agents had decided to move in this morning on the 51st day of the standoff because negotiations had proved fruitless, because the cult members were prepared to hold out for many months and because there was no backup team to replace weary agents. She also said that the authorities had received reports that children in the compound were being beaten.

Ms. Reno said that the gassing of the

Continued on Page A21, Column 1

Italians Support Political Reform By a Big Margin

By ALAN COWELL

ROME, April 19 — After months of scandal, recession and Government paralysis, Italians voted overwhelmingly for political change in a referendum on Sunday and today that repudiated the country's leadership of the last 48 years, but that left the future uncertain.

Final computer projections late tonight, 10 hours after polls closed, showed 82 percent of voters endorsing a proposal to scrap the current system of pure proportional representation for most of the Senate and replace it with the majority voting used in other parts of Europe and the United States.

The magnitude of the vote is expected to put heavy pressure on legislators to enact similar changes in the lower house, or Chamber of Deputies.

The ballot had assumed the proportions of a popular judgment on Italy's postwar political system, and the result was widely interpreted as a mandate for a new government to press through broader electoral reform.

That, in turn, would set a political calendar for new elections — and thus a fresh start — after a debilitating corruption scandal that has tainted much of the political and business elite and exposed ties between some government leaders and the Mafia.

While some of Italy's traditional parties, notably the Christian Democrats and the former Communists, would probably survive the process of re-

Continued on Page A8, Column 1

Vietnam Report on Prisoners A Fake, Reputed Author Says

By PHILIP SHENON
Special to The New York Times

HANOI, Vietnam, April 19 — A Vietnamese general denied today that he had written in 1972 that Hanoi held more than twice as many American prisoners as it ultimately released. Any such report attributed to Hanoi is a forgery, he declared.

And a special envoy, sent by President Clinton to tell the Vietnamese that relations could not improve until the matter was cleared up, said he saw no reason to disbelieve the Vietnamese denial.

Nearly two weeks ago, Russian archivists turned over to the United States a Russian translation of what was said to be a secret report to Hanoi's Politburo given by Gen. Tran Van Quang, described in the document as Deputy Chief of Staff of the Vietnamese armed forces at the time. The document said Hanoi held 1,205 American prisoners of war in September 1972.

591 Released in 1973

Because Vietnam released only 591 prisoners in 1973 and has maintained repeatedly that there were no other prisoners, the Russian translation raised the recurring question of whether Hanoi had kept some prisoners back, and if so, what happened to them. An alternative explanation offered by some experts was that Hanoi might have killed hundreds of prisoners.

Hanoi immediately denied the accuracy of the Russian document, saying it was a "fabrication."

In a meeting today, General Quang told President Clinton's special envoy, Gen. John W. Vessey Jr., that he did not write the 1972 report on which the

Russian translation was supposedly based. If the Vietnamese report exists, General Quang said, it is a forgery that may have been prepared by someone interested "in undermining advances in relations between Vietnam and the United States."

At a news conference today after meeting with General Vessey, General Quang said of the 1972 report: "I did not write it. I tell you, never in my life have I made such a report, because it was not in my area of responsibility."

He stressed that although he was

Continued on Page A6, Column 4

Law Firm for S. & L. Is Fined $51 Million

Jones, Day, Reavis & Pogue, one of the nation's biggest law firms, agreed to pay the Government $51 million to settle charges that it aided the financier Charles H. Keating Jr. in the fraud that brought on the costliest bankruptcy in the savings and loan debacle. The agreement came as a trial was about to begin.

The settlement, which is the largest against a law firm in the savings and loan rescue, also ends litigation against the Jones, Day partner in charge of work for Mr. Keating's Lincoln Savings and Loan Association, which collapsed in 1989 at a cost to taxpayers of $2.5 billion.

Business Day, page D1.

New Country Is Like Prison to Asenhat, 18

By DAVID GONZALEZ

Asenhat Gomez used to peer out the windows of her childhood home in the Dominican countryside and relish a landscape of willowy palm trees and verdant fields where her extended family would gather for daylong reunions.

In her new home in Brooklyn — a cramped apartment on Williamsburg's South Side — the windows frame a claustrophobic vista of brick walls, and the few relatives she has in this country are so preoccupied with making ends meet that family get-togethers seem as long gone as the father who died a dozen years ago.

It has been nearly a year since Asenhat was reunited with her mother, who six years before had left her children with their aunt and illegally entered the United States in search of the opportunities that had eluded the family in the Dominican Republic.

Longing for Home

But the immigrant journey of Asenhat Gomez is only beginning. For 18-year-old Asenhat, the joys of reunion are constantly tempered by the struggles of life in a hard new land. Hundreds of miles from all that was familiar, unable to shake her longing for home, she tentatively ventures into a future that beckons with equal measures of promise and fear.

In many ways, hers is the oldest of immigrant stories, played out time and again by wave after wave of newcomers to America's shores. But for today's immigrant children, in places like Williamsburg, that process of adjustment is made all the more difficult by the modern plagues of drugs, guns and recession.

Asenhat, a shy girl, has become even shyer since arriving last May, the strangeness and the frustrations coalescing in a sometimes overwhelming feeling that she is trapped.

'Sense of Confinement'

"Everybody talked about the sense of confinement," she said recently, recalling her first weeks in New York. "I expected that, but just not so much.

Monica Almeida/The New York Times

Children of the Shadows
The eighth of ten lives of the cities.

"Lying in bed I would think about what I left behind. There you got accustomed to visiting people, my friends from school, since we were infants. The whole place was different; you could go out to play. I miss my school."

Williamsburg — its bumpy narrow streets lined with age-worn two-family homes and apartment buildings closed in by the shadows of hulking waterfront factories and the Williamsburg Bridge — can seem forbidding to someone used to the easy freedom of the countryside. The family's two small bedrooms are shared by six people

who subsist on meager earnings.

Still, even as she bridles at her confinement, it has become her defense mechanism in a city whose ways and language are not her own. She seldom ventures beyond her neighborhood, partly from fear of getting lost on unexplored streets and subway lines and partly from fear of drug dealing and violent crime on nearby blocks.

"It makes you feel insecure," said Asenhat, a short girl whose floppy ponytail and baggy jeans give her the look of someone just entering her teen-age years. "You can be going down the street and not know what can happen."

She has few friends, feeling that she has little in common with American-born teen-agers, who she says are too "liberal" — so preoccupied with boyfriends, clothes and the latest fads that

Continued on Page B6, Column 1

John Kluge Gives Columbia $60 Million to Aid Minorities

By MARIA NEWMAN

John W. Kluge, the chairman of the Metromedia Company and a 1937 graduate of Columbia University, presented his alma mater last night with $60 million for minority scholarships. It is the largest gift the university has ever received.

In making his gift, Mr. Kluge recalled what a hardship it was for him to afford his tuition — only $500 a year at the time — when he was earning $7 a week working in the school dining hall. Fortunately for him, he said, Columbia helped by giving him a scholarship.

"Columbia made a difference really in my life and I really want to assure that it will continue to make a difference for others," Mr. Kluge said in an interview from his office in Manhattan. At 78, Mr. Kluge, who made his fortune building up a string of radio and television stations, is one of the wealthiest people in America.

By itself, the $60 million donation is believed to be the fifth largest to any university or college. When added to the $50 million Mr. Kluge already donated to Columbia in two previous gifts, it would be second only to the $125

million pledged to Louisiana State University in 1981 by Claude B. Pennington.

One of Mr. Kluge's two previous gifts, of $25 million, presented in 1987, was also for minority scholarships and the other, in 1990, went to aid young scholars and junior faculty members.

The new gift comes at a critical time as Columbia battles serious fiscal problems. With its $1 billion operating budget, the university has a $15 million deficit this year and is working to cut costs to balance its budget for next year.

Luring Minority Candidates

But officials of the university said it was unclear whether the gift, because it was specifically for scholarships for undergraduates, would have any impact on the deficit.

The gift would, they said, help the university attract minority candidates who might otherwise go to other universities better able to help them with steep college costs.

Fred Knubel, a spokesman for Columbia, said last night that the gift would provide at least 300 students a year with grants of $10,000. Mr. Knubel said that the money would be used in

Continued on Page B7, Column 1

INSIDE

Arrest in Capital Shootings

The police arrested a suspect in a series of shootings that had left three people dead and terrorized Washington since Feb. 23. Page A12.

Slain South African Buried

South Africa honored the burial of a slain black Communist into the biggest political rite since Nelson Mandela's release from prison. Page A8.

New Abortion-Rights Politics

Now that abortion-rights supporters finally have an ally in the White House, they face a new set of priorities and challenges. Page A18.

Rustling Scholarly Feathers

Flightless bird or feathered dinosaur, a turkey-sized fossil from Mongolia has scientists debating the history of flying. Science Times, page C1.

Today's TV Listings

Television and radio listings and advertising appear today on pages B16-17.

354613

Continued on Page B7, Column 1

"All the News That's Fit to Print"

The New York Times

Late Edition
New York: Today, partly sunny, windy, shower possible. High 84. Tonight, clearing, breezy. Low 57. Tomorrow, cool, windy. High 72. Yesterday, high 78, low 66. Details, page D17.

VOL.CXLII...No. 49,450   Copyright © 1993 The New York Times   NEW YORK, FRIDAY, SEPTEMBER 10, 1993   75 cents beyond the greater New York metropolitan area   50 CENTS

P.L.O. AND ISRAEL ACCEPT EACH OTHER AFTER 3 DECADES OF RELENTLESS STRIFE

Mr. Prime Minister . . .

The P.L.O. recognizes the right of the State of Israel to exist in peace and security . . . renounces the use of terrorism and other acts of violence. . . .

Sincerely,

YASIR ARAFAT
CHAIRMAN
THE PALESTINE LIBERATION ORGANIZATION

Mr. Chairman . . .

The Government of Israel has decided to recognize the P.L.O. as the representative of the Palestinian people. . . .

YITZHAK RABIN
PRIME MINISTER OF ISRAEL

VIOLENCE REJECTED

An Exchange of Letters Clears the Way for a Pact on Self-Rule

By CLYDE HABERMAN
Special to The New York Times

JERUSALEM, Sept. 9 — Enemies to the death for three decades, Israel and the Palestine Liberation Organization opened a new era in their blood-soaked history today by recognizing each other's legitimacy and the rights of both to represent their people's dreams.

Yasir Arafat, the P.L.O. chairman, said in a letter to Prime Minister Yitzhak Rabin that his group recognized Israel's right "to exist in peace and security," renounced "the use of terrorism and other acts of violence," and was ready to discipline any of its loyalists who break this pledge.

And in a separate letter to Norway's Foreign Minister, who had served for months as an intermediary in secret talks between the two sides, Mr. Arafat called on Palestinians in the Israeli-occupied West Bank and Gaza Strip to begin "the normalization of life." Israeli officials took that as an Arafat appeal to end the Palestinian uprising known in Arabic as the intifada, although that was not spelled out.

Rabin Stood Firm

The Israelis said Mr. Rabin was adamant that the intifada must be curtailed. It was a measure of Mr. Arafat's determination to reach an agreement that he yielded on this point even though most Palestinians in the territories consider the uprising an indispensable tool to resist the Israeli occupation.

For his part, Mr. Rabin wrote a terse letter to Mr. Arafat saying that in light of these Palestinian commitments, his Government has decided to recognize the P.L.O. as the representative of the Palestinian people and to commence negotiations within the Middle East peace process." Unlike Mr. Arafat, who closed his letter with the word "sincerely," Mr. Rabin dispensed with such pleasantries and simply put his name. [Texts of the three letters, page A12.]

Mr. Arafat signed his letter to Mr. Rabin behind closed doors late tonight in Tunis, where the P.L.O. is based. When Mr. Rabin follows suit in a signing ceremony in Jerusalem on Friday morning, it will clear the way for yet another agreement on a plan to transfer authority in the territories from Israeli to Palestinian hands, starting with a form of self-rule in Gaza and the West Bank city of Jericho.

Breathtaking Change

That accord, the product of months of secret negotiations conducted mainly in Norway, is to be signed at the White House on Monday by high-ranking officials on each side. No names have been announced, but the Israelis said they would probably be represented by Foreign Minister Shimon Peres, and the Palestinians are expected to send Mahmoud Abbas, the P.L.O. official who supervised the negotiations. Farouk Kaddoumi, the P.L.O. foreign minister, opposed the agreements.

Washington has been the locale of the most recent Middle East peace talks, and both sides seem to want United States involvement in the peace process.

No amount of protocol or formal language, however, could obscure the breathtaking change that has now swept across this land for which Jews and Arabs have fought and died across the last century.

For Israel, recognition of the P.L.O., formally endorsed by the Rabin Cabinet this evening, means that it is pre-

Continued on Page A12, Column 1

U.S. Troops Fire on Somalis; Death Toll May Reach 100

By MICHAEL R. GORDON
Special to The New York Times

WASHINGTON, Sept. 9 — In a battle that is expected to heighten the debate over the United States role in Somalia, American and Pakistani forces opened fire today on a crowd of Somali soldiers, women and children after United Nations peacekeeping troops came under attack.

Two American Cobra attack helicopters and Pakistani tanks and armored personnel carriers fired cannons and rockets at the Somalis in Mogadishu, the Somali capital. United Nations officials said as many as 100 Somalis may have been killed in the fighting, and that some appeared to be women and children.

A Pakistani soldier was also killed, bringing the toll of United Nations peacekeepers killed in Somalia to 48. Four peacekeepers were wounded today, including two Americans.

Justified by U.N. Aide

Maj. David Stockwell, the chief United Nations spokesman in Mogadishu, justified the shooting of women and children as a "last-ditch, last resort effort to protect the United Nations troops."

"We saw all the people swarming on the vehicles as combatants," he was quoted as saying in news agency reports. "We've seen this before. If they reach our soldiers they tear them limb from limb."

Among the unresolved questions left by the fight was whether some of the women hit were armed collaborators of Gen. Mohammed Farah Aidid, the fugitive leader of a powerful Somali faction, as U.N. officials suggested, or rather civilians caught in the crossfire.

United Nations and American officials gave this account of what appeared to be one of the deadliest battles

since American forces were deployed in Somalia in December.

The officials said the fighting began when a contingent of American combat engineers protected by Pakistani troops were ambushed while trying to clear a roadblock. The officials said the attack was carried out by a well-armed force of more than 100 militiamen commanded by General Aidid.,

The engineers and Pakistani troops withdrew, the officials said, while American attack helicopters and Pakistani tanks went to the scene.

During the three-hour battle, United Nations officials said, the Somali militiamen mingled with women and children, in what the officials called a common tactic intended to deter United Nations forces from firing back.

Small Arms and Rockets

During the intense fighting along 21 October Road in Mogadishu, the American helicopters, designed to kill troops and destroy vehicles in combat, responded with 20-millimeter cannon and rocket fire, blowing up a bulldozer that had been seized by the Somalis.

The United Nations said its troops came under fire from small arms, machine guns, rocket-propelled grenades and a 106-millimeter recoilless gun that destroyed one of the Pakistanis' M-48 tanks.

"I think this is part of a continuing military effort to attack the United Nations," Admiral Howe added in a telephone interview.

A United Nations spokesman said

Continued on Page A9, Column 1

The Brave New Middle East

By THOMAS L. FRIEDMAN
Special to The New York Times

WASHINGTON, Sept. 9 — The Middle East will never be the same.

The mutual recognition agreement between Israel and the Palestine Liberation Organization today fundamentally alters both the political and psychological maps of the region. It may not bring peace tomorrow or the day after, but it will reshape the Middle East more than any other single event since the establishment of Israel in 1948.

News Analysis

This agreement creates the potential for dramatically new alliances that could knit together both Israel and Arab countries; it unearths a mother lode of diplomatic opportunities for the United States, which will no longer have to choose between friendships with Israel or the Arab world; it will make it much easier for the pro-American Arab countries to be identified with Washington; it will deprive the Arab and Muslim fundamentalists of their most potent issue for mobilizing the Arab street — the war with Israel — and, most important, it will lay a real foundation for Arab-Israeli coexistence.

Some Prefer the Status Quo

But precisely because this event is so transforming it will not go down peacefully between the Nile and the Euphrates. Many Israelis and Palestinians were devoted to the status quo — Israelis who do not want to give up land because they believe it is their biblical patrimony, or because they do not trust P.L.O. promises, and Palestinians who will never resign themselves to the notion that the Jews have a legitimate claim to the land of Israel, or because do not trust Israeli promises.

All of them have quietly been counting on the notion that the day would never come when Israel made

New Vistas Revealed On Every Side of Fray

peace with the P.L.O. They will be as deeply threatened by it as the advocates of peace will be uplifted.

To appreciate just how unexpected, how mind-bending, this change is, consider the fact that several years ago Life magazine ran a demonstration of trick photography in which it seamlessly grafted the heads of different people onto the bodies of others. To prove how wild such photography could be, Life created a picture of President Ronald Reagan bringing Yitzhak Shamir, who was then the Israeli Prime Minister, and the P.L.O. leader, Yasir Arafat, into a handshake on the White House lawn. On Monday no trick photography will be needed. President Clinton is

expected to be the host to just such a handshake between senior Israeli and P.L.O. officials in his backyard.

It is the psychological impact of that ceremony — two neighbors who for years never recognized the other's legal title to Palestine/Israel finally acknowledging that they each have an equally valid claim — that will be the most enduring.

For the Israelis, that moment will not only signify the beginning of the healing of the Arab-Israeli conflict, but, in some ways, it could also signify the first signs of recovery of the Israeli people from the trauma of the Holocaust.

For years, said the Israeli political theorist Yaron Ezrahi, Israeli leaders from Golda Meir to Yitzhak Shamir drew from the Holocaust the pessimistic lesson that the only way Jews could survive in the post-Holocaust

Continued on Page A14, Column 1

A First Step Toward Peace

Accord clears the way for the granting of limited self-rule for Palestinians in the Gaza Strip and the West Bank town of Jericho.

Three pages on the Middle East accord: A12-14.

OTHER MAJOR NEWS

Proposed Settlement On Breast Implants

The Dow Corning Corporation announced a proposed $4.75 billion fund to compensate women with silicone breast implants. Lawyers on both sides of the bitter dispute said they expected it to be ratified. Women who have suffered any one of eight diseases would be eligible for compensation ranging from $200,000 to $2 million, while others, even those claiming no physical effects, could receive lesser amounts. Page A16.

Baseball's New Lineup

If the players' union goes along, major league baseball will have a new look next season: three divisions in each league, instead of the current two, and a new round of playoffs in October. Page B11.

Masson v. Malcolm, Again

A Federal district judge ordered a new trial in the libel case between Jeffrey Masson and the writer Janet Malcolm but severed The New Yorker from the case. Page A20.

Laura Pedrick for The New York Times

Wachtler Ordered to Prison

Sol Wachtler, above, New York State's former Chief Judge and one-time gubernatorial hopeful, was sentenced to 15 months in prison for threatening his ex-lover. Page B1.

Penalties Proposed For High Drug Prices

The Clinton Administration has told Congress that it wants the Government to review prices of new prescription drugs so that Medicare coverage can be denied for drugs whose prices are deemed excessive.

Such a penalty, proposed as part the new health care plan, would be a powerful means of restraining prescription drug prices, which have risen twice as quickly as other consumer prices. Page A17.

No Early Holtzman Report

The New York City Comptroller, Elizabeth Holtzman, said in a candidates' debate that she would not allow the early release of the findings of a city investigation into a campaign loan that she received last year. Page B5.

News Summary	A2
Business Day	D1-17
Editorial, Op-Ed	A26-27
International	A3-14
Metro	B1-6
National	A16-20, B6
SportsFriday	B11-17
Weekend	C1-28
Law	B9	Real Estate	B7
Media Business	D17	TV Listings	D19
Obituaries	B10	Weather	D17
Classified	A29	Auto Exchange	B17

P.L.O. Lining Up Palestinian Support for Accord

By YOUSSEF M. IBRAHIM
Special to The New York Times

TUNIS, Sept. 9 — In a mood of resignation and quiet satisfaction, top leaders of the Palestine Liberation Organization continued their final deliberations tonight on texts of agreements with Israel. And senior P.L.O. officials appeared to have made breakthroughs in taming opposition to the accords by Muslim militants and the organization's leftist flank.

A senior official asserted that the P.L.O. leadership in Tunis had succeeded in persuading Sheik Ahmad Yassin, the spiritual leader of the Palestinian Muslim militant Hamas movement in the Gaza Strip, who is held by the Israelis, to issue a statement calling on his followers not to use violence to

demonstrate their opposition to the deal.

Yasir Arafat, the P.L.O. leader, signed the letter recognizing Israel and renouncing violence in a simple ceremony in his office tonight in the presence of Norway's Foreign Minister, Johan Jurgen Holst, who had acted as broker in the secret negotiations that led to the agreement.

In Paris, Mahmoud Darwish, a Palestinian poet who resigned from the P.L.O.'s Executive Committee last week to underline his opposition to any deals with Israel, is also expected to issue a statement venting his misgivings against them, a P.L.O. official said.

Mr. Darwish, the P.L.O. official said, is expected to say that while he still opposes these accords, he now stands with the Palestinian leadership in its attempt to make them work and calls upon "all Palestinians" to do so.

Sheik Yassin has a great deal of influence among the rank and file of the Hamas movement, which has emerged as the most serious threat to the P.L.O.'s influence in Gaza and the West Bank.

It is too early to say whether his appeal will make a difference and it is not clear yet whether the P.L.O., with the cooperation of the Israeli authorities, has succeeded in proposing such a deal to him.

"We basically told him if you co-

Continued on Page A13, Column 1

The New York Times

"All the News That's Fit to Print"

Late Edition

New York: Today, patchy fog, then mostly sunny. High 86. Tonight, clear. Low 72. Tomorrow, sunshine mixed with clouds, humid. High 88. Yesterday, high 84, low 65. Details, page C16.

VOL.CXLII .. No. 49,454   Copyright © 1993 The New York Times   NEW YORK, TUESDAY, SEPTEMBER 14, 1993   75 cents beyond the greater New York metropolitan area.   50 CENTS

RABIN AND ARAFAT SEAL THEIR ACCORD AS CLINTON APPLAUDS 'BRAVE GAMBLE'

"The children of Abraham . . . have embarked together on a bold journey." — President Clinton.

Associated Press

Old Warriors Now Face Task Of Building Upon Foundation

By THOMAS L. FRIEDMAN
Special to The New York Times

WASHINGTON, Sept. 13 — In a triumph of hope over history, Yitzhak Rabin, the Prime Minister of Israel, and Yasir Arafat, the chairman of the P.L.O., shook hands today on the White House lawn, sealing the first agreement between Jews and Palestinians to end their conflict and share the holy land along the River Jordan that they both call home.

At 11:43 A.M. on the sun-splashed South Lawn of the White House, Foreign Minister Shimon Peres of Israel and Mahmoud Abbas, the foreign policy aide for the Palestine Liberation Organization, signed a Declaration of Principles on Palestinian self-government in Israeli-occupied Gaza and the West Bank. Three thousand witnesses watched in amazement, including former Presidents Jimmy Carter and George Bush.

Mr. Rabin, whose face is etched with the memories of every Arab-Israeli war, captured in his remarks the exhaustion of all parties with the centuries-old conflict. "We the soldiers who have returned from the battle stained with blood," he said, "we who have fought against you, the Palestinians, we say to you today in a loud and clear voice: 'Enough of blood and tears! Enough!'"

Mr. Arafat, relishing his moment of acceptance on the White House lawn, strove to give Mr. Rabin the appropriate response, declaring in Arabic: "Our two peoples are awaiting today this historic hope, and they want to give peace a real chance."

An Awkward Moment

And President Clinton, who gracefully shepherded Mr. Arafat and Mr. Rabin through their awkward moment of public reconciliation, hailed them both for their "brave gamble that the future can be better than the past." [Transcripts of the leaders' remarks are on page A12.]

The agreement, which will eventually allow Palestinians to run their own affairs as Israeli troops pull back within months from the Gaza Strip and Jericho in a first step, was reached during secret negotiations over the past few months between Israelis and

Palestinians, under the direction of Mr. Peres and Mr. Abbas, through the mediation of Norway.

The documents were signed on the same wooden table on which the Peace Treaty between Egypt and Israel was signed in 1979. That table stood today as a silent memorial to the assassinated Egyptian President, Anwar el-Sadat, whose path-breaking visit to Israel in 1977 and subsequent agreements at Camp David brought him denunciations as a traitor by Mr. Arafat.

But the audience in attendance, and perhaps the millions more watching back in the Middle East, seemed less interested in the formal signing than in the visual moment that would somehow make this tentative peace real: the handshake between the two old warriors who personified the conflict between their peoples.

A Nudge, a Hand, a Smile

Moments after the documents were signed, Mr. Clinton took Mr. Arafat in his left arm and Mr. Rabin in his right arm and gently coaxed them together, needing to give Mr. Rabin just a little extra nudge in the back. Mr. Arafat reached out his hand first, and then Mr. Rabin, after a split second of hesitation and with a wan smile on his face, received Mr. Arafat's hand. The audience let out a simultaneous sigh of relief and peal of joy, as a misty-eyed Mr. Clinton beamed away.

Two hands that had written the battle orders for so many young men, two fists that had been raised in anger at one another so many times in the past, locked together for a fleeting moment of reconciliation.

But much difficult work, many more compromises, will now have to be performed by these same two men to make it a lasting moment.

That reality was underscored by the fact that both Mr. Rabin and Mr. Arafat invoked their peoples' undying attachment to Jerusalem in their respective speeches.

[Later in Jerusalem, Israeli Radio reported that Mr. Rabin, accompanied by Foreign Minister Shimon Peres, was traveling to Morocco on Tuesday for a surprise meeting with King Hassan to discuss establishing diplomatic relations. The report said Tunisia was among several Muslim and Arab countries now ready to establish ties with Israel.]

In an opening speech that was both eloquent and moving, Mr. Clinton described the history of the effort to make peace in the Middle East and paid tribute to Mr. Rabin and Mr. Arafat. He also pledged United States support for their effort.

"The United States is committed to insuring that the people who are affected by this agreement will be made more secure by it and to leading the world in marshaling the resources necessary to implement the difficult details that will make real the principles

Continued on Page A13, Column 1

MORE ON THE ACCORD

Arafat's Strategy: '2 Olive Branches'

Transforming one's image from guerrilla leader to statesman is not easy, but Yasir Arafat was trying hard to make it happen. Efforts in the past have had mixed results for all the countries involved. "This time," he said just an hour after making peace with Israel, "I am coming with two olive branches." Page A15.

Arabs and Jews Reflect

As many speak out about the events of recent days, there are new hopes, on both sides, but fears from years past remain. Page A16.

Divisions in Syria

Thousands marched in Syria, waving black flags in protest against Mr. Arafat, but elsewhere in the nation the response was more stunned, disbelieving, silence. Page A17.

Security Surprises

Security for the dignitaries was about what you would expect in the capital, but despite the hardware and planning, there were surprises. Page A14.

A 45-Year Struggle

Over the years since the birth of Israel in 1948, the Palestinian movement has drawn support from Palestinians inside Israel, in Israeli-occupied territories and in neighboring Arab countries while pressing for nationhood or self-rule. Page A15.

The Next Challenge for the U.S.

By R. W. APPLE Jr.
Special to The New York Times

News Analysis

WASHINGTON, Sept. 13 — As he himself said, this was not Bill Clinton's day. It was not he who brought together the sober old soldier and the grinning guerrilla fighter in the leafy calm of the South Lawn of the White House, far from the battlefields of the Middle East, for a paean to peace.

However deft, however sagacious, he was but the master of ceremonies. He thanked those who had labored to bring about the latest in a series of once-inconceivable changes that have remade the world in five short years. He bestowed the congratulations of the world's only superpower. And he gave Yitzhak Rabin a timely little nudge when he seemed reluctant to grasp the outstretched hand of Yasir Arafat.

Now, though, President Clinton will have to assume the central role if the momentum toward a comprehensive peace settlement is not to be lost. That is likely to be a long, messy job of diplomatic donkey work in the dark corners of history — a much less gratifying chapter than today's carefully scripted pageant of good intentions.

Israel and Jordan are poised to move forward tomorrow. But the other Arab nations whose representatives watched today's ceremony from the front rows know that only the United States can provide the impetus needed for the next round of negotiations. Mr.

Peace Momentum Up to Washington

Arafat spoke for them, too, when he said his people "are relying on your role, Mr. President" to "usher in an age of peace."

So this President, who so longs to concentrate on problems at home, is thrust like so many of his predecessors into an international arena not of his choosing. Along with the rest of the world, the United States has a new ward, the inchoate entity called Palestine, and it has the main responsibility for fostering Israeli settlements with

its other neighbors while deepening the one with the Palestinians.

It will be up to Mr. Clinton, who does not much like doing so, to butt heads between the Israelis and the Syrians, and perhaps take considerable heat from American Jews in the process, which he did not have to endure this time.

Neither Mr. Clinton nor any other American President has ever wanted to do business with Mr. Arafat and the Palestine Liberation Organization. As Mr. Rabin, the Israeli Prime Minister, said in one of his many moments of eloquence this morning, "It's not so

Continued on Page A13, Column 6

President's Tie Tells It All: Trumpets for a Day of Glory

By MAUREEN DOWD
Special to The New York Times

WASHINGTON, Sept. 13 — The President who loves to stay up late told his aides that he went to bed at 10 P.M. on Sunday, so he could be rested for the historic day.

They did not believe him, of course.

"No way," said Dee Dee Myers, the White House press secretary. "He got the big hand and the little hand mixed up."

"It was Jerusalem time," suggested Mark Gearan, the White House communications director.

But what happened next is not in contention: The President said he woke up at 3 A.M. and could not go back to sleep. He was worrying about the speech he would make to mark what was sure to be one of the most remarkable events of his Presidency: the moment when the two men who had been bitter enemies for so long, the Israeli Prime Minister, Yitzhak Rabin, and the Chairman of the Palestine Liberation Organization, Yasir Arafat, would recognize each other's existence on the South Lawn of the White House.

With his wife and daughter still asleep, Mr. Clinton put on a blue jogging suit and went into the study in the White House residence. He picked up a Bible. He read the entire Book of Joshua, wanting to review the part about the trumpets in Jericho that toppled walls and making sure he put a reference in his speech contrasting

Continued on Page A14, Column 5

the victory of war and the victory of peace.

In another part of the White House, a team led by Jeremy Rosner, a National Security Council speechwriter, was scrambling to fulfill the President's last request: Mr. Clinton wanted a passage from the Koran to balance his Biblical allusions. The desperate White House staff members finally called Prince Bandar bin Sultan, the Saudi ambassador, who helped them pick out an appropriately soothing passage: "If the enemy inclines toward peace, do thou also incline toward peace."

Watching for the Dawn

At some point, Mr. Clinton moved from the study to the kitchen to read and drink coffee. He wanted to sit near the window, where he could keep track of when the dawn arrived and what the sky looked like.

The White House staff had worked over three days to compile a 26-page step-by-step log choreographing every movement that the leaders would make, as best as anyone that, with this most delicate of all diplomatic meetings, a million things could go wrong — a look, a word, a handshake, the weather.

At dawn, as he later told aides, who

Jim Estrin/The New York Times

Palestinian women dancing with joy in Jericho, on the West Bank.

Reuters

Israelis watching the signing on television on a Jerusalem street.

Palestinians: Glee And Flag-Waving

Special to The New York Times

JERICHO, Israeli-Occupied West Bank, Sept. 13 — Palestinians took to the streets of the West Bank and Gaza Strip today in rapturous and noisy celebrations of the Palestine Liberation Organization accord with Israel and what they said was the cornerstone of their future state.

In the sleepy city of Jericho, the seat of the future Palestinian self-governing authority, it looked as though every one of the 15,000 residents was in the streets.

Savoring a new reality few had dared to imagine just a few weeks ago, they danced all day and into the night. In the Gaza Strip they handed flowers to Israeli soldiers. In East Jerusalem they shouted "Shalom!" to Israeli well-wishers.

The accord also changed the face of the occupied territories and East Jerusalem, where Palestinian flags, which had technically been banned, flew with impunity.

Israelis: Searching For New Bearings

Special to The New York Times

BEIT ZAYIT, Israel, Sept. 13 — When Yitzhak Rabin shook hands with Yasir Arafat, six Israelis watching it on television together on the western outskirts of Jerusalem might as well have been struck by lightning. They could only sigh deeply in disbelief before their thoughts and emotions unscrambled themselves.

The dominant feeling, in the room and across the country, is that there is no alternative to having Israelis and Palestinians come to terms with each other, as they are now trying to do.

Like many Israelis, Eliezer Shemhav, a surgeon who had friends into watch the ceremony, wrestled with religious convictions that taught him that God intended all of the biblical Land of Israel to be in Jewish hands.

Articles, page A17.

INSIDE

Primary Candidates Work on Voter Turnout

Appearing at subway stops and centers for the elderly and monopolizing the talk shows, candidates in the Democratic primaries for New York City offices played to their surest supporters in the closing hours of the campaign. The races could hinge on voter turnout. Page B1.

POLLING PLACES will be open from 6 A.M. to 9 P.M. today in New York City, Westchester and Nassau, and from 6 A.M. to 8 P.M. in Connecticut.

Fall Air Fares Cut by 45%

The nation's airlines cut fares by up to 45 percent on domestic flights through Dec. 16, but tickets must be bought by Saturday. Page D1.

354613

The New York Times

VOL.CXLIII... No. 49,580
Copyright © 1994 The New York Times
NEW YORK, TUESDAY, JANUARY 18, 1994
75 cents beyond the greater New York metropolitan area
50 CENTS

SEVERE EARTHQUAKE HITS LOS ANGELES; AT LEAST 30 KILLED; FREEWAYS COLLAPSE

The body of a motorcycle police officer lying near the wreckage of his vehicle in the center of an overpass that collapsed onto Interstate 5. He drove off the edge and fell 25 feet.

An injured man being treated at an emergency unit set up outside Olive View Medical Center in Sylmar.

HUNDREDS INJURED

Predawn Tremor Levels Buildings and Ignites Dozens of Fires

By SETH MYDANS
Special to The New York Times

LOS ANGELES, Jan. 17 — A violent earthquake jolted millions of people out of bed before dawn today, crumpling freeway overpasses, leveling buildings and igniting scores of fires. Hundreds of people were injured and at least 30 were reported killed, including 15 at a three-level apartment complex that was reduced to two stories.

The quake, centered in the Northridge area in the San Fernando Valley, 20 miles northwest of downtown Los Angeles, measured 6.6 on the Richter scale of ground motion and was felt for hundreds of miles, knocking out power and water service for hundreds of thousands of residents.

In a region held together by its network of freeways, three overpasses collapsed, crippling major highways for weeks and possibly months. Roads cracked and buckled across the San Fernando Valley.

State of Emergency

People lingered on the streets throughout the day as the thuds of aftershocks sent dust rising above the mountains. Others formed long lines outside hardware stores and tried to buy batteries, water, propane or plywood to repair damaged homes. And when evening came, hundreds of people whose homes were destroyed or too dangerous to re-enter camped in city parks and on tennis courts in a nervously festive atmosphere, some of them with campfires and cases of beer.

A state of emergency was declared at the local, state and Federal levels in this latest disaster to strike the city. Aerial pictures of blocks of burning buildings evoked traumatic memories of the 1992 riots and last autumn's wildfires.

"I couldn't stop screaming as I ran out of the house," said Erik Wyler, 19, still shaking an hour after the quake. "I looked up and all I could see was darkness coming toward us, and it got real windy. I thought it was the sun exploding."

Hundreds of buildings were damaged, including Anaheim Stadium, which was expected to need $3.4 million in repairs. The quake, which struck at 4:31 A.M., was not the strongest to hit the region in recent years but was by far the most destructive because it struck in a heavily populated area.

Curfew Is Imposed

The Chief of Police, Willie L. Williams, addressed the city on television this evening, telling people to remain calm and to stay home from work on Tuesday if possible. He said that city offices would be open on Tuesday but that schools in the Los Angeles Unified School District would be closed.

He also announced a dusk-to-dawn curfew and issued a warning against any potential looters, with reference to the rampage that overtook the city during the 1992 riots.

"We're not going to tolerate what

Continued on Page A17, Column 1

Airborne in Bed: A Building Collapses, Leaving 15 Dead

By ELIZABETH KOLBERT
Special to The New York Times

LOS ANGELES, Jan. 17 — Erik Pearson heard a loud explosion and felt a jolt like a bomb. Still on their bed, he and his wife then fell 12 feet through the ceiling of the apartment below.

"We were airborne," said Mr. Pearson, a 27-year-old nursing student. "I heard the glass break from the glass sliding doors. Our apartment came down and pitched diagonally." The door was jammed shut, the couple said, but they climbed down to safety off their once third-floor, now second-floor, balcony.

But at least 15 other residents of the tan stucco apartment complex, the Northridge Meadows, did not. They died as building suffered some of the worst damage of the earthquake today and its residents bore the brunt of the casualties.

The building, half a block from California State University at Northridge, housed many college students. An identical building next to it, the Northridge, buckled but did not collapse.

The Meadows, a three-story, 164-unit apartment complex near the epicenter of the quake in the San Fernando Valley, looked like a cardboard box that someone had stepped on. In several sections of the building, the first floor no longer existed; it lay crushed beneath the two other floors. Windows had popped out of their frames, balconies dangled at odd angles and entire walls buckled.

Famous From Now On

Until 4:31 A.M. today this sleepy middle-class section of Los Angeles, about 20 miles northwest of downtown, was known only for its treelined branch of the California State University. From now, it will be known as the epicenter of a devastating 6.6 earthquake.

Simply put, city officials said the 15 deaths made this building the site of the largest number of earthquake fatalities in the city's history.

John William, 36, a survivor who lived on the first floor, managed to slither to safety by following a small path of light to a crack in the building's foundation.

"I pushed open the crack in the wall; my fiancée and I were pressed together, and we squeezed ourselves free," said Mr. William, who had cuts on both hands and arms. "I felt like we were going to lose circulation at any minute.

"I was hearing moans and whining and banging from people pinned in the other apartments. I'm not exaggerating: the second floor is now in the dirt. There is not two inches of room in my apartment."

Residents described a scene of panic in the hours before dawn as people tried to climb from their balconies or pick their way down dark staircases that had been torn apart by the quake.

Search for Bodies

This afternoon, many residents of the complex were still milling around in front of the ruined building, at 9565 Reseda Boulevard, as firefighters, sweaty and exhausted, continued to search the debris. Eight hours after the quake, firefighters held out little hope that anyone still trapped would be found alive, but they said they were inserting electronic listening devices into the rubble that could pick up sounds as soft as human breathing. Earlier, they brought in dogs trained to find survivors in building rubble.

There was no power in the area, most of the shops were closed and, in an incongruously festive gesture, people up and down the street had taken to eating half-melted ice cream cakes from a nearby Baskin-Robbins.

The force of the tremor ripped apart homes, businesses, roads and utilities, leaving thousands of people without water, power or shelter.

Reseda Boulevard, a main thoroughfare, resembled a war zone: broken water mains flooded streets; gas permeated the air, fuel for numerous fires that were controlled by the late afternoon. Traffic lights were knocked out, and accidents occurred throughout the area.

Many of the community's 20,000

Continued on Page A19, Column 1

OTHER MAJOR NEWS

U.S.-China Pact Averts Trade Fight

China and the United States reached an 11th-hour textile agreement, averting a major clash about the $7.3 billion in Chinese textiles sold annually in the American market.

The Clinton Administration had threatened to reduce Chinese textile imports by more than $1 billion unless a new agreement could be signed to end persistent instances of cheating by Chinese companies. Page D1.

Israelis Are Hopeful But Cautious on Syria

Israel said it saw a promise of peace, but expressed caution about remarks by Syria's President that he was ready for normal relations. "Normalization was also mentioned by the Syrians in the past," Prime Minister Yitzhak Rabin said. Page A8.

Facing Down Boos, Giuliani Praises King

After days of criticism over two confrontations between blacks and the police, Mayor Giuliani faced hecklers at a tribute to Martin Luther King Jr. He told his audience, "For you to succeed, I have to succeed." Page B1.

THE NEW YORK TIMES is available for home or office delivery in most major U.S. cities. Please call this toll free number 1-800-631-2500 ADVT

354613

Collapsed Freeways Cripple City Where People Live Behind Wheel

By BERNARD WEINRAUB
Special to The New York Times

LOS ANGELES, Jan. 17 — The earthquake that struck Los Angeles before dawn today crippled crucial freeways, raising the prospect that the American city most defined by its cars and interlocking highways would be gripped by traffic chaos for months.

The city's freeways and highways, mostly built since World War II, soar and wind like roller coasters, often resting atop columns as they crisscross one another. The buckling and collapse today of three heavily traveled elevated portions raised the prospect of at least partial paralysis for a city where the automobile is seen as intrinsic to the region's life.

As a result, city officials said, almost every facet of life for the nine million people in the Los Angeles area is likely to be disrupted for up to a year or more.

With nearly 3 million vehicles using 616.3 miles of freeway in Los Angeles during the evening rush hour, the city's residents are extraordinarily dependent on main highway arteries. The city has never confronted, until today, the possibility that many of these freeways would be partially unusable for long periods.

The city's new subway line, the Metro Red Line, which opened in January 1993, is expected to offer little help. It runs through just 4.4 miles of downtown Los Angeles, from Union Station to MacArthur Park.

'Not Going to Be Easy'

The area's Metrolink commuter trains will operate on Tuesday, though some stations and stretches of track that were damaged will be closed. The service will add passenger cars to trains on the line from Santa Clarita and Antelope Valley, the Associated Press reported. Freeways linking those areas to Los Angeles were severed by the quake.

"It's not going to be easy," a grim Mayor Richard J. Riordan said this afternoon as Gov. Pete Wilson stood beside him.

Patricia Reid, a spokesman at Cal

Continued on Page A18, Column 1

Lives and Nerves Shattered, but Not Civility

By JANE GROSS
Special to The New York Times

LOS ANGELES, Jan. 17 — Ventura Boulevard, the main highway through the devastated San Fernando Valley, was ghostly this morning, its shops a shambles, its sidewalks littered with broken glass, its traffic signals out and its automatic teller machines useless.

But the stillness was misleading.

Behind a shuttered Thrifty drugstore in the Studio City section, where the aisles were clogged with fallen ceiling tiles, a tangle of toys and broken cosmetic bottles, employees peddled batteries and flashlights to a stunned throng of men and women still shaking from the jolt of a lifetime, which occurred before dawn.

"I need a good flashlight! And eight D batteries! And a couple of Triple A's! And one of those heavy-duty things!" sputtered one man in line, as harried clerks dispensed these limited goods from a shopping cart and apologized that nothing else was for sale because the store was knee-deep in ruined merchandise.

Across the region — from the eastern edge of the San Fernando Valley, where buildings shuddered and fell, to the graffiti-scarred streets of downtown, to the manicured confines of Beverly Hills and Pasadena — residents were stunned and shaken, but largely composed.

Some homes were ruined. Most were without power. Some lacked telephone service. And all of their inhabitants were shaken to the core. But residents of the City of Angels, where disasters have lately been heaped one upon the other, kept their heads.

The closest thing to bedlam, as of nightfall, was the scene at Hughes Market, the only open grocery store for

Continued on Page A19, Column 6

THE RUSSIAN TEA ROOM HAS BEEN LIBERATED from the cable monopoly! Better building-wide service. Better prices. Call Liberty Cable 212/891-7777 – ADVT

HAIR PULLING? RESEARCH AND TREATMENT IN a university program. 960 5731 ADVT

The earthquake severed the freeway system in three places and killed 15 people in a building near its epicenter in the Northridge section.

"All the News That's Fit to Print"

The New York Times

Late Edition

New York: **Today,** showers then clouds. High 61. **Tonight,** clearing. Low 51. **Tomorrow,** sun, scattered showers, thunder. High 66. **Yesterday,** high 66, low 51. Details, page C14.

VOL.CXLIII...No. 49,686   Copyright © 1994 The New York Times   NEW YORK, THURSDAY, MAY 5, 1994   75 cents beyond the greater New York metropolitan area.   50 CENTS

Defense Dept. May Postpone Base Closings

Economic and Political Factors Are at Work

By ERIC SCHMITT
Special to The New York Times

WASHINGTON, May 4 — Fearful of damaging the economies of scores of communities nationwide, the Defense Department is preparing to seek authority to delay some decisions on base closings until after the 1996 elections, a senior Pentagon official said today.

Congress would have to approve such a plan. But Defense Secretary William J. Perry and Deputy Defense Secretary John M. Deutch favor dividing a final round of decisions scheduled for next year into two parts: choosing next year to close some bases and then waiting until 1997 or 1998 to decide the fate of many others, the official said.

By doing so, Mr. Perry and Mr. Deutch would place political and economic considerations above the strong objections of the Joint Chiefs of Staff, who are counting on saving billions of dollars by closing installations as quickly as possible to pay for future weapons, training and troop salaries.

Moreover, it would inject a political element into a process Congress invented four years ago specifically to be as free as possible from political influence. Critics say there is clearly a political incentive for President Clinton and some members of Congress to delay or diminish the economic pain of base closings until after the 1996 elections, or at least to limit closings in states like California, Texas and Florida, pivotal battlegrounds in 1996.

Three independent commissions, meeting in 1988, 1991 and 1993, have decided to close 70 major installations. It takes five to six years to shut a base. Lawmakers and Pentagon officials have predicted that the 1995 round of decisions, scheduled to be the last one, could close more installations than the previous three combined.

"As the defense budget goes down and we close bases, the issue now is the pace of closures and how communities can adjust," the senior

Continued on Page B14, Column 1

11 MORE OFFICERS TAKEN OFF DUTIES IN 30TH PRECINCT

NEW YORK INQUIRY GROWS

25 of 191 Assigned Have Now Been Removed and Bratton Expects More to Follow

By CLIFFORD KRAUSS

Eleven more police officers were taken off the job in the 30th Precinct in Harlem yesterday, as a corruption investigation into the precinct continued to grow. A Federal investigator said the 11 were suspected of either knowing of or participating in crimes like stealing, selling drugs and shaking down drug dealers.

The officers' guns and badges were confiscated and they were placed on desk duty with pay. Police Commissioner William J. Bratton would not detail the accusations against them, except to say they were "very significant and disturbing."

But a Federal investigator said the allegations were linked to the previous corruption uncovered in the precinct in northwest Harlem, in which 14 officers have been arrested on charges including narcotics conspiracy, robbery, assault and civil-rights violations. The investigator, who spoke on the condition that he not be named, said the 11 officers now under investigation knew of, witnessed or participated in those crimes.

Police officials said several of the 11 officers would probably be suspended in the next few weeks, while others would be arrested on criminal charges. The Federal investigator said the department decided to move against the officers first because the charges were imminent.

The reassignment of the 11 officers — known as "modified assignment" in department jargon — brings to 25 the number of officers taken out of the 191-member precinct. Commissioner Bratton has said that more officers would be arrested in the 30th Precinct, and last month he estimated that 25 percent of the precinct might be implicated.

Yesterday, the Commissioner repeated his assessment that corrup-

Continued on Page B4, Column 4

RABIN AND ARAFAT SIGN ACCORD ENDING ISRAEL'S 27-YEAR HOLD ON JERICHO AND THE GAZA STRIP

Agence France-Presse

Yasir Arafat caused an uproar in Cairo yesterday when he refused to sign part of the accord. Discussing the issue, which was resolved after 35 minutes of heated talks, were, from left, Foreign Minister Shimon Peres of Israel, Foreign Minister Andrei V. Kozyrev of Russia, Prime Minister Yitzhak Rabin of Israel, Foreign Minister Amr Moussa and President Hosni Mubarak of Egypt, and Mr. Arafat.

CEREMONY IN CAIRO

Pact Approved Despite Last-Minute Dispute Over Boundaries

By CHRIS HEDGES
Special to The New York Times

CAIRO, May 4 — Israel and the P.L.O. signed an agreement today that formally begins Israel's withdrawal from the Gaza Strip and the Jericho area of the West Bank — lands occupied for 27 years — and grants Palestinians a measure of self-government for the first time, though not sovereignty.

The accord, which follows up the agreement in principle signed in September in Washington, opens a new chapter in the Middle East. It provides for the possibility of Palestinian control of an area whose occupation by Israel has been a focus of Arab anger for decades, and holds the chance for reconciliation between Israeli and Palestinian.

But for any of that to happen, there will have to be further agreements between Israel and the Palestine Liberation Organization during the next five years. During that time the Palestinians will be tested to show that they can govern the limited areas now being given to them.

The World Bank and many countries, including the United States, are committed to helping the Palestinian authority, as it is called, to survive.

The ceremonies here were led by President Hosni Mubarak of Egypt, whose country has been the only Arab land to make peace with Israel, and were attended by many dignitaries. The agreement was signed by Prime Minister Yitzhak Rabin of Israel and Yasir Arafat, chairman of the P.L.O.

Until last summer's negotiations leading up to the White House signing in September, the Israelis and the P.L.O. had been bitter enemies; now they are united in defending their accord.

Mr. Arafat, whose name was once anathema to Israelis, described the accord as a "true beginning — to complete the march of peace, guarantee the legitimate rights of the Palestinian people, and realize justice and equality." [Excerpts from speeches and from the agreement are on pages A16 and A18.]

But the ceremony faltered in a last-minute dispute over the boundaries of Jericho, and the Palestinian leader signed only after 35 awkward minutes of on- and off-stage negotiations with Mr. Mubarak and Secretary of State Warren Christopher.

After the heated consultations, Mr. Arafat added a handwritten note that

Continued on Page A16, Column 1

Arafat Signs and the Gaza Strip Shrugs

By CLYDE HABERMAN
Special to The New York Times

SHATI, Gaza Strip, May 4 — The picture was fuzzy on the balky old television set, but it was clear enough for Salameh al-Arouqi. What he saw did not please him one bit.

There was Yasir Arafat, master of political pyrotechnics and chairman of the Palestine Liberation Organization, taking out his pen to sign the agreement that he had finally reached with Prime Minister Yitzhak Rabin of Israel.

"Don't sign, you donkey, stop!" Mr. Arouqi shouted at the screen, which he watched with several friends in the bare three-room house in this coastal refugee camp that his family of 11 fills to the brim.

When Mr. Arafat paid him no mind and put pen to paper, Mr. Arouqi, who supports a P.L.O. faction opposed to the chairman, pressed his lips togeth-

Some Palestinians Feel Only Abiding Distrust After a Long Wait

er and said quietly, "He's signing his own execution."

"For years we have been fighting and suffering, and this is the result — this silly document?" he said. "What is Gaza and Jericho?"

Not much, agreed the half-dozen friends who sat or knelt on cushions in the Arouqi home, watching the signing ceremony from Cairo.

Theirs was a widely shared view today across the Gaza Strip, where the dominant sound in ramshackle refugee camps and along garbage-lined city streets was that of one hand clapping even though this was one of those rare days that qualified imme-

diately as historic.

With the signing, Israeli control formally ended over little Jericho in the West Bank and over teeming Gaza, except for buffer zones around the 19 Jewish settlements in the strip. It meant that for the first time Israel had ceded authority in Palestinian areas that it captured in the 1967 Arab-Israeli war. It meant that Palestinian police officers could start pouring in and Israeli soldiers start heading home. It meant a chance, effectively the first, to show that Palestinians can rule themselves without terrifying their neighbors.

In short, it was a big deal.

Yet while so much seemed to change, nothing actually did, and most of the 800,000 or so Gazans went about their daily business, ignoring the Cairo events or shrugging them

Continued on Page A17, Column 1

Nations Help to Back Dollar As U.S. Acts to Show Resolve

By THOMAS L. FRIEDMAN
Special to The New York Times

WASHINGTON, May 4 — The United States teamed up with the central banks of 16 other nations today to buy dollars in a global campaign intended to show investors that the Clinton Administration is serious about maintaining the value of the ailing American currency.

It was the first such coordinated intervention since August 1992, and involved the Treasury Department and the Federal Reserve, joining with the central banks of Germany, France, Japan and 13 other countries. The move was planned in a series of secret phone calls overnight.

The dollar was sharply higher against the German mark and the Japanese yen in late trading in New York today, although it started to slip again near the end of the day. It ended at 1.6531 marks, up from 1.6370 on Tuesday, and at 101.88 yen, up from 101 on Tuesday.

Senior American Treasury officials said the main objective of Friday's effort and today's much larger intervention to support the dollar was to

counter what they saw as a widening perception in global currency markets that the Administration was ready to allow the dollar to drift lower, either as matter of deliberate policy or of benign neglect.

But the real question is whether this kind of market intervention alone can change the mood in trading.

Continued on Page D20, Column 1

INSIDE

Tokyo Official Speaks Out

A senior minister in Japan declared that the massacre of Chinese at Nanjing was a "fabrication." Page A9.

A Season for Goodbyes

In northern New England, the burying of those who died in winter is an unfailing sign of spring. Page A22.

News Summary   A2

Arts C14-22
Business Day D1-21
Editorial, Op-Ed A26-27
Home Section C1-13
International A3-19
Metro B1-9
National A20-24, B10-14
SportsThursday B16-23

Media Business .. D5 TV Listings .. C21
Obituaries .... B15 Weather C14

Classified .... B23 Auto Exchange .. D21

175 EAST 42nd STREET HAS BEEN LIBERATED from the cable monopoly! Better building-wide service. Better prices. Call Liberty Cable 212/891-7777 — Advt.

Federal Judge Says Ban on Suicide Aid Is Unconstitutional

By TIMOTHY EGAN
Special to The New York Times

SEATTLE, May 4 — Abortion and suicide, two ends of the spectrum of life, have been linked for the first time by a Federal judge, who ruled on Tuesday that the Constitution guarantees people not only the right to terminate pregnancies without Government interference, but also the right to end their own lives.

In striking down a 140-year-old Washington State ban on assisted suicide, Judge Barbara Rothstein of United States District Court in Seattle said the law violated the 14th Amendment clause against state infringement of individual liberty.

"The suffering of a terminally ill person cannot be deemed any less intimate or personal, or any less deserving of protection from unwarranted governmental interference than that of a pregnant woman," Judge Rothstein wrote in her ruling on Tuesday.

The decision, the first by a Federal court on assisted suicide, came one day after a Michigan jury acquitted Dr. Jack Kevorkian of charges that he had violated that state's law against helping people kill themselves.

After Judge Rothstein's ruling, a group in Seattle that has been helping terminally ill people end their lives

Continued on Page A24, Column 1

Agence France-Presse

In Jericho, Children Celebrate

The self-rule accord got a mixed reaction among Palestinians. While many went about their business with hardly a shrug, these children decorated a fence around the Israeli police station with flowers. Page A17.

Pact Breaks Grip of New York School Custodians

By CHARISSE JONES

Union negotiators for New York City's school custodians have agreed to concessions that would reduce the custodians' control over school buildings, a breakthrough that School Chancellor Ramon C. Cortines said would make schools cleaner for children and more accessible to community groups.

The tentative agreement between the union and the Board of Education, which is subject to the approval of union members and the Mayor's office, would effectively create a system of controls tying the promotion of the school system's 853 custodians to their job performance rather than

seniority, and holding them accountable to the principals at their schools.

No longer would some custodians be able to set their own cleaning standards, opting for example to mop the bathrooms or sweep the floors of a school once a week if they chose. Instead, their cleaning responsibilities would be established by the custodian, the principal and a plant manager. The principal would have the

primary responsibility to evaluate the custodians' performance every six months and decide whether or not those standards are being met.

"This tentative contract is not a small change from the previous one, as most labor settlements are," Chancellor Cortines said in a written statement. "It's revolutionary."

But while school officials applauded the tentative agreement, officials with the Mayor's office complained about how they learned of the agreement and what it included. They said they were informed of the preliminary settlement by press release and

Continued on Page B8, Column 3

Outcome of Voting In Zulu Heartland Remains in Doubt

By KENNETH B. NOBLE
Special to The New York Times

DURBAN, South Africa, May 4 — The outcome of elections in the volatile Zulu heartland of Natal remained uncertain today, with new vote totals showing a tight race between the African National Congress and its longtime adversary, the Inkatha Freedom Party.

Even though the polls closed five days ago, the battle for control of South Africa's most fiercely contested province intensified as officials of the Congress and Inkatha accused each other of widespread cheating. The latest tally showed the counting behind by 5 percentage points, with about half the vote still uncounted.

"We believe Inkatha had its own pirate polling stations, 54 of them," Ronnie Mamoepa, an African National Congress spokesman said. Other irregularities alleged by the African National Congress included tampering with the plastic seals used to close ballot boxes, chasing electoral monitors from polling stations and intimidating voters.

The Inkatha leader, Chief Mangosuthu G. Buthelezi, described the ac-

Continued on Page A13, Column 1

"All the News That's Fit to Print"

The New York Times

VOL.CXLIII... No. 49,693   Copyright © 1994 The New York Times   NEW YORK, WEDNESDAY, MAY 11, 1994   75 cents beyond the greater New York metropolitan area.   **50 CENTS**

Late Edition
New York: Today, sunny with a few high clouds. High 75. Tonight, breezy, mild. Low 60. Tomorrow, showers, windy, cooler. High 68. Yesterday, high 72, low 54. Details, page B14.

SOUTH AFRICANS HAIL PRESIDENT MANDELA; FIRST BLACK LEADER PLEDGES RACIAL UNITY

Giuliani's Budget Proposes Cuts For Spending and Work Force

By JAMES C. McKINLEY Jr.

Mayor Rudolph W. Giuliani proposed a $31.6 billion budget for New York City yesterday that would reduce spending slightly for the first time in 16 years and sharply cut the municipal work force in almost every major agency except the Police and Fire Departments.

Submitting his first executive budget to the City Council, Mr. Giuliani said the city "has been spending itself beyond its economy" for more than a decade, creating perennial gaps between what it spends and what its tax base can support. The Mayor said the city's overspending had drained the local economy, driving private industry from the city.

"The purpose of this budget is to redirect the economy of New York," Mr. Giuliani said. Saying the city was "hemorrhaging jobs" while the rest of the nation was recovering, Mr. Giuliani added, "We can't employ people through government alone."

In drafting his plan, Mr. Giuliani needed to close a $2.3 billion gap between projected spending and revenues for the fiscal year that begins on July 1. To do that, he has suggested about $1.2 billion in spending cuts from city agencies, mostly through cutting 15,000 workers, or 7 percent of the city-financed work force. Mr. Giuliani said those cuts could be made without serious damage to services if managers learned to run agencies more efficiently. Over all, spending would fall by $102 million.

He also proposed some modest tax cuts totaling about $35 million.

The extent of the service cuts is likely to figure in the debate over Mr. Giuliani's budget as it moves to the City Council, particularly since the budget makes no cuts in the Police or Fire Departments. Already some lawmakers are asking whether protecting those agencies is worth the pain for schools, youth programs and hospitals. [News analysis, page B5.]

Besides cutting jobs, the Mayor relied in his efforts to close the budget gap on some actions that will still require the cooperation of the State Legislature, the Federal Government

Closing the Gap

Principal measures the Mayor proposes in his budget for fiscal year 1995 and the PROJECTED SAVINGS (OR COST) in millions.

Cuts to spending in city agencies	**$1,269**
Increased state aid	275
Increased Federal aid	125
Union co-payments for retirees' benefits	200
Refinancing of city debt	225
Asset sales (WNYC-FM, U.N. Plaza Hotel)	110
Changes in payments on pension debt	51
Fiscal year 1994 surplus	98
Cuts in hotel tax and commercial rent tax	(35)
TOTAL SAVINGS	**$2,318**

Continued on Page B4, Column 4

Trail of Despair by a Father Leaves 4 Dead and Son Hurt

By CLIFFORD J. LEVY

After being dismissed last week from his $7.50-an-hour job at a paper factory in Brooklyn, Jose Luis Berroa grew despondent about how he would care for his 2-year-old son. He had lived on the grim streets of New York City with little Carlos before, his friends said, and he could not bear to return. So he decided to give Carlos back to the boy's mother, Awilda Enriquez.

But something snapped in Mr. Berroa when he arrived at the home of Ms. Enriquez's family in Newark, something that caused him to go on a rampage that left a trail of death yesterday, ending when he wounded the child and then killed himself after a confrontation with police officers on a stairwell in Washington Heights.

The night before in Newark, Mr. Berroa killed two of Ms. Enriquez's brothers, the police said, and shot to death a woman who had earned a reputation for kindness in the neighborhood by adopting 12 children. [Page B6.] He then fled with the boy in her car and sought refuge in Washington Heights with a woman who had helped him build a new life after he immigrated from Cuba a decade ago.

It was there that his life ended. The police said they caught up with him and, instead of surrendering, Mr. Berroa fired a bullet into his son's face before shooting himself.

He left only two small plastic bags that he lugged from place to place in recent months, his friends said. They contained Carlos's baby clothes and tiny sneakers, a broken toy motorcycle and a box that once held shells for a 9-millimeter gun, the weapon the police said Mr. Berroa had used on his victims and himself.

"He told us he was going crazy about maybe losing the baby," said Georgina Gonzalez, 26, the daughter of Emma Maria, 50, in whose Washington Heights building Mr. Berroa died. She recalled how her mother had persuaded Mr. Berroa to stay with her recently after he had spent much of the winter sleeping on park benches, huddling with the child against the cold.

The police said Mr. Berroa, 33, showed up unexpectedly about 6:30 P.M. on Monday at the home of Ms. Enriquez's family at 231 Sixth Ave-

Continued on Page B6, Column 4

INSIDE

Italian Government Formed
Italy's right-wing Prime Minister-designate formed a Government after weeks of wrangling, including five seats for neo-Fascists. Page A5.

Identifying a Real Lobbyist
The Government's new 30-page description of lobbying imposes micrometer precision on an activity that seemed kind of obvious. Page A16.

Collapse at Christie's
At an auction of Impressionist and modern art, only 38 of 76 works were sold; proceeds fell nearly $40 million below estimates. Page C18.

Nelson Mandela takes the oath of office as President from Chief Justice Michael Corbett in Pretoria.
Reuters

Dance for Joy! Come Dance a Toyi-Toyi!

By FRANCIS X. CLINES
Special to The New York Times

PRETORIA, South Africa, May 10 — Hours before Nelson Mandela took possession of the Government, and had his air force delight an outdoor throng with a fly-over wafting rainbow-hued vapors, Elsie Njokweni was dancing her shoes off in the most fitting of places.

She was a bobbing, crooning blur aboard one of the packed commuter trains from the Soweto ghetto, traditionally a sardine-can affair for the ostracized black underclass of apartheid, but today a vessel of historic exultation.

Numerous trains clacked and boomed along the rails with the special chanted resistance songs and the foot-stamping dances known as toyi-toyi that South African blacks turned into a swarming political art form in defeating racist oppression.

"I was arrested six years ago for behaving this way," Mrs. Njokweni said, sliding into a toyi-toyi with hip-swaying grace to join her neighbors from Soweto Extension No. 1, southwest of Johannesburg.

It was soon after dawn when they all crammed and capered onto one of the ceremonial excursion trains that carried scores of thousands of ordinary people to the grand Government Lawn to witness President Mandela's inaugural triumph.

Whatever the exuberance level of the formally choreographed proceedings, most of the watching world missed the full truth of South Africans' joy, not being aboard the toyi-toyi train nor trying to keep up with Mrs. Njokweni and three generations of her neighbors.

They were leaping, scuttling and back-sliding into a pounding version of "Hold On, Boys," a work-song for barracks laborers near the breaking point, a song intended to snatch courage from intimidation.

"Your gun, Mr. Policeman, only reminds me of our hero, Oliver Tambo," the Sowetans sang and danced, in praise of a founder of the African National Congress who died a year ago.

Their noise graced the passing countryside, stirring white suburbanites to wave V-signs and fists of triumph along the three-hour ride. More often, it was blacks looking out suddenly from their track-side shanties

Elsie Njokweni singing on her way to inauguration ceremonies.
Ozier Muhammad/The New York Times

Continued on Page A8, Column 1

President Is Said to Pick Babbitt For Court Despite Senate Concern

By GWEN IFILL
Special to The New York Times

WASHINGTON, May 10 — In spite of last-minute concerns expressed by members of the Senate over the weekend, President Clinton has settled on Interior Secretary Bruce Babbitt as his nominee to the Supreme Court, officials said today.

A senior White House official said there was a "95 percent chance" that Mr. Babbitt, a former Arizona Governor and Attorney General, would be Mr. Clinton's choice to replace Justice Harry A. Blackmun, who is retiring at the end of the current term. Other advisers said Mr. Clinton was satisfied that Mr. Babbitt could face down any objections.

The President has been leaning toward Mr. Babbitt for several days, but he only disclosed his list of finalists for the Court to senators last weekend in a series of telephone conversations.

Mr. Clinton held a final one-hour meeting with his Supreme Court search team today, and aides said afterward that he was still "going through the calculus" to weigh the selection. One aide acknowledged that Mr. Babbitt could be a "political lightning rod," but said that the White House had determined it could overcome opposition led by Senator Orrin G. Hatch of Utah, the senior Republican on the Senate Judiciary Committee.

In an interview, Senator Hatch described Mr. Babbitt "as a nominee who would be pushed by the far left" and as the kind of judge "who would legislate from the bench laws that the liberal community doesn't have a tinker's chance of getting through the people's elected representatives."

Mr. Hatch suggested that Democratic and Republican senators would join his campaign to block a Babbitt nomination, but two other Western Senators who have tangled with Mr. Babbitt over environmental issues, Harry Reid of Nevada and Ben Nighthorse Campbell of Colorado, said today that they would welcome his

Continued on Page A17, Column 1

NEWS SUMMARY   A2

DE KLERK PRAISED

An Inauguration Tumult for 'the Old Man' and His Diverse Guests

By BILL KELLER
Special to The New York Times

PRETORIA, South Africa, May 10 — With the commanding dignity that has carried him through more than half a century of defiance, captivity and conciliation, Nelson Rolihlahla Mandela became the first black President of South Africa today.

He stood before a crowd of world leaders who shunned this capital during its decades of infamy, and in a husky, resolute voice swore the oath to become the 10th leader of South Africa since its union in 1910, but the first elected with the participation of the black majority.

Then the 75-year-old leader opened his presidency with an intimate speech of shared patriotism, speaking of South Africans' common exhilaration in the seasons and the soil, their common pain for their country's humiliation before the world and their shared relief at being readmitted to the company of civilized nations.

"Never, never, and never again shall it be that this beautiful land will again experience the oppression of one by another and suffer the indignity of being the skunk of the world," he said. [Transcript, page A8.]

As a token of renewal, Mr. Mandela promised that an amnesty would soon be announced for "various categories" of prisoners.

He lavished praise on F. W. de Klerk, the President who collaborated with him in negotiating the end of white rule and who today took the oath as one of Mr. Mandela's two Vice Presidents in a unity Government.

In a post-inaugural visit to the 50,000 ordinary citizens celebrating on the lawn far below the Government buildings, Mr. Mandela held Mr. de Klerk's hand aloft and hailed his predecessor as "one of the greatest reformers, one of the greatest sons of our soil."

For the day, at least, blacks and whites were united by the mutual strain of taking in the recently unimaginable.

There was Fidel Castro on his first visit to the country that tried to pulverize his army in Angola, the only one among the scores of dignitaries singled out by the crowd for lusty shouts of "Viva!"

And Muslim and Hindu prayers broadcast into the air of what has been the most rigidly, officially Christian of capitals.

And the Navy band in dress whites entertaining the inaugural dignitaries with a Zulu migrant labor song.

And finally President Nelson Mandela, now Commander in Chief, reviewing the defense force that was built, in large part, to prevent some-

Continued on Page A8, Column 1

Fetal Harm Is Cited As Primary Hazard In Dioxin Exposure

By KEITH SCHNEIDER

In a report on dioxin, scientists at the Environmental Protection Agency have concluded that cancer is not the most serious health hazard at common exposure levels. Of greater concern, their report said, are subtle effects on fetal development and the immune system that may be the result of very low levels of exposure.

The scientists said that most people already have levels of dioxin in their bodies at or near the concentrations that cause such fetal and immune system problems in laboratory animals.

This new assessment of the risk of dioxin, one of a class of toxic chlorine-based compounds present everywhere in the environment, comes in a draft summary of a 2,000-page report scheduled to be made public this summer. The conclusion, that current levels of exposure may already pose human health problems, is based on new mathematical assumptions that have not been published in scientific journals.

And it has already caused a storm of dissent in Federal agencies, principally in the Food and Drug Administration and the Department of Agri-

Continued on Page A20, Column 1

A Rare Sight
A solar eclipse darkened skies yesterday at midday in a 150-mile-deep swath across the United States. Sunlight filtered through tree branches in Chicago, above, projected the rare annular eclipse. Page B7.

Associated Press
Agence France-Presse

The New York Times

Late Edition

New York: **Today**, clouds then sun, not as cool. High 65. **Tonight**, some clouds. Low 55. **Tomorrow**, partly sunny, pleasant. High 75. **Yesterday**, high 54, low 48. Details, page B10.

VOL.CXLIII.... No. 49,702   Copyright © 1994 The New York Times   **NEW YORK, FRIDAY, MAY 20, 1994**   75 cents beyond the greater New York metropolitan area.   **50 CENTS**

Jacqueline Kennedy Onassis Dies of Cancer at 64

Widow of President, Ailing, Spent Final Day at Her Home

By ROBERT D. McFADDEN

Jacqueline Kennedy Onassis, the widow of President John F. Kennedy and of the Greek shipping magnate Aristotle Onassis, died of a form of cancer of the lymphatic system yesterday at her apartment in New York City. She was 64 years old.

Mrs. Onassis, who had enjoyed robust good health nearly all her life, began being treated for non-Hodgkin's lymphoma in early January and had been undergoing chemotherapy and other treatments in recent months while continuing her work as a book editor and her social, family and other personal routines.

But the disease, which attacks lymph nodes, an important component of the body's immune system, grew progressively worse. Mrs. Onassis entered the New York Hospital-Cornell Medical Center for the last time on Monday but returned to her Fifth Avenue apartment on Wednesday after her doctors said there was no more they could do.

In recent years Mrs. Onassis had lived quietly but not in seclusion, working at Doubleday; joining efforts to preserve historic New York buildings; spending time with her son, daughter and grandchildren; jogging in Central Park; getting away to her estates in New Jersey, at Hyannis, Mass., and on Martha's Vineyard, and going about town with Maurice Tempelsman, a financier who had become her closest companion.

She almost never granted interviews on her past — the last was nearly 30 years ago — and for decades she had not spoken publicly about Mr. Kennedy, his Presidency or their marriage.

Although she was one of the world's most famous women — an object of fascination to generations of Americans and the subject of countless articles and books that re-explored the myths and realities of the Kennedy years, the terrible images of the President's 1963 assassination in Dal-

Jacqueline Kennedy Onassis

Susan Ragan/Associated Press, 1992

las, and her made-for-tabloids marriage to the wealthy Mr. Onassis — she was a quintessentially private person, poised and glamorous, but shy and aloof.

They were qualities that spoke of her upbringing in the wealthy and fiercely independent Bouvier and Auchincloss families, of mansion life in East Hampton and Newport, commodious apartments in New York and Paris, of Miss Porter's finishing school and Vassar College and circles that valued a woman's skill with a

verse-pen or a watercolor brush, at the reins of a chestnut mare or the center of a whirling charity cotillion.

She was only 23, working as an inquiring photographer for a Washington newspaper and taking in the capital nightlife of restaurants and parties, when she met John F. Kennedy, the young bachelor Congressman from Massachusetts, at a dinner party in 1952. She thought him quixot-

Continued on Page B8, Column 1

---

18 NAMED IN GRAFT TIED TO PROJECTS FOR SCHOOL BOARD

NEW YORK OFFICIALS HELD

Lease and Maintenance Unit, Shorn of Power to Build, Is Still Under Fire by U.S.

By SAM DILLON

Federal prosecutors charged yesterday that the division of the Board of Education that maintains schools and leases space remained rife with corruption, five years after it was stripped of the power to build new schools because of earlier scandals.

The prosecutors charged a senior lawyer for the Board of Education who resigned last week and 17 other people with paying or accepting bribes for awarding contracts, approving fake invoices and expediting board payments to contractors.

The sweeping charges against former board officials as well as lawyers and contractors underline how the Board of Education's management of its 1,100 buildings continues to be a target for bribery, fraud and racketeering, even though the State Legislature stripped the board of its power to build schools in 1989.

Before 1989, the racketeering detailed in the indictments focused largely on the construction of school buildings, particularly the badly botched construction of Fiorello H. La Guardia High School in the early 1980's. In 1989, after the La Guardia debacle and other troubles, the Legislature turned construction over to a new agency, the School Construction Authority, to stanch corruption in building schools. That agency was not involved in yesterday's allegations.

According to the indictments, since the change in 1989, corruption has largely focused on activities that have remained the responsibility of the board's Facilities Division, including leasing and renovating commercial buildings for use as schools, and removing asbestos and lead.

Because enrollments have surged amid the city's financial difficulties, the board has leased increasing numbers of buildings in recent years for use as schools and offices.

Responding to the indictments, the seven-member Board of Education voted in a closed session yesterday to suspend all new leasing, except the leasing of classroom space for the fall

Continued on Page B2, Column 4

Wide Immunity For Presidents Gains Support

Justice Dept. to Make Argument for Clinton

By NEIL A. LEWIS
Special to The New York Times

WASHINGTON, May 19 — The Justice Department is preparing to tell a Federal judge that the sexual harassment suit brought against President Clinton should be dismissed or delayed indefinitely because Presidents are entitled to broad immunity from lawsuits while in office, Administration officials said today.

The Justice Department argument is being readied to support a motion that Mr. Clinton's private lawyer, Robert S. Bennett, plans to file soon in Federal court in Little Rock. Mr. Bennett will ask that the suit brought by Paula Corbin Jones, a former Arkansas state employee, be dismissed or postponed until after the President leaves office. Mr. Bennett has indicated that he will argue that the President should be given immunity from all lawsuits because the need to defend himself would distract him from his official duties and throw the Government into disarray.

The Administration officials said that the Justice Department's Office of Legal Counsel is preparing a brief for the court that would back Mr. Bennett's claim of broad immunity for Presidents from civil lawsuits, even those resulting from actions before they take office.

Mr. Bennett's overall strategy is to crush Ms. Jones's suit at the earliest possible stage or to delay it until Mr. Clinton leaves office, according to a senior White House adviser who spoke on condition of anonymity.

The goal of Mr. Bennett and the President's other advisers is to avoid the spectacle of Mr. Clinton's testifying under oath about his behavior three years ago. Ms. Jones says in her legal complaint, which was filed on May 5, that she was invited to meet Mr. Clinton, then governor of Arkansas, in a Little Rock hotel room, where she alleges he made an explicit sexual overture.

White House officials acknowledged that Mr. Bennett's tactics are driven largely by political considerations, arising from the sexual nature of Ms. Jones's charges. "If this goes all the way to trial and the President wins, he will have really lost politically," said the senior White House adviser.

The official also said that any actions associated with the lawsuit, like

Continued on Page B20, Column 4

EXPERTS SAY U.S. FAILS TO ACCOUNT FOR ITS PLUTONIUM

DANGER OF THEFT IS CITED

Officials Say New Estimates Have Erased Large Gap in Bomb Fuel Inventory

By WILLIAM J. BROAD

Energy Secretary Hazel R. O'Leary's campaign to open the nation's atomic complex to public scrutiny has stumbled on the seeming inability of her department to assemble reliable figures on its production of plutonium, the main ingredient of nuclear warheads.

Experts say crude tallies and shifting numbers raise new doubts about the Government's attention to detail in guarding one of the deadliest substances on earth. In the past, private experts have charged that Federal plants were sloppy and prime targets for atomic theft and diversion.

The current trouble arose when private experts at the Natural Resources Defense Council, which specializes in nuclear issues, found a discrepancy between their calculations of plutonium production and what Mrs. O'Leary had announced last Dec. 7. The gap was 1.5 metric tons, enough to make 300 nuclear weapons.

Federal officials say the discrepancy and say they have raised their production estimate to erase virtually all of the calculated gap. But the private experts accuse the Government of a laxity that raises questions about the plutonium's whereabouts.

Inconsistent numbers might also have diplomatic repercussions, since the declassified figures on plutonium production that Mrs. O'Leary delivered to her counterpart in Russia have turned out to be wrong.

"The accounting is not what it should have been," Michael Gauldin, the Energy Department's chief spokesman, said in an interview. "We've been trying to reconstruct the stuff from the early days and having a hard time."

Dr. Thomas B. Cochran, a senior scientist at the Natural Resources Defense Council in Washington, said: "The Government has never been through this accounting exercise before. That's troubling. Banks do this kind of thing once a day."

If Russia reported such discrepancies, some experts say, the West would be shocked.

Dr. Everet H. Beckner, a senior Federal official involved in tracking the nuclear materials and their production history, said the problem was nothing more than harmless errors of accounting and production. But Dr. Beckner added that the Energy Department, which runs the nation's nuclear complex, was committed to clearing up all apparent discrepancies.

"There are technical differences that need to be resolved," Dr. Beckner said in an interview. "And we think it's important to resolve them."

In atomic bombs, plutonium is often the sole ingredient fueling the nuclear blast; in hydrogen bombs, it is used as an atomic trigger to ignite

Continued on Page A19, Column 1

INSIDE

Insurer to Offer Clinic Care

Anticipating sweeping health care changes, New Jersey's largest health insurer plans to establish a statewide system of private clinics. Page B1.

A Long Night for the Icemen

Stephane Matteau's goal at 6 minutes 13 seconds of double overtime gave the Rangers a 3-2 victory over the New Jersey Devils. Page B11.

Tennis Star Seeks Treatment

Jennifer Capriati, arrested Monday on a drug charge, has entered a Miami rehabilitation facility. Page B11.

Clinton Spells Out Reasons He Might Use Force in Haiti

By DOUGLAS JEHL
Special to The New York Times

WASHINGTON, May 19 — President Clinton today offered the clearest explanation yet of why his Administration is considering the use of military force in Haiti while resisting it elsewhere in the world.

"It's in our backyard," the President said at a White House news conference as he ticked off the first in a list of six reasons why he is weighing military action to oust Haiti's leaders if economic sanctions do not force them to step down.

He said Haiti's proximity to the United States and the danger that more of its citizens could seek refuge in southern Florida meant that his Administration had an obligation to promote an end to the military dictatorship there.

Mr. Clinton's comments, in response to a question at a joint appearance with India's Prime Minister, also represented a response to Republican critics who say it would be wrong to risk American lives to restore the exiled President, the Rev. Jean-Bertrand Aristide.

With a tighter United Nations embargo on Haiti to take effect at midnight on Saturday, aides to Mr. Clinton emphasized that no American military action there was imminent. After facing criticism on past occasions in which the Administration has appeared to back away from tough talk on Bosnia, the aides said no decision on whether to use military force in Haiti would be made until the sanctions have been given time to work.

But with opinion polls showing mounting public dissatisfaction with his conduct of foreign policy, the aides say that Mr. Clinton has grown concerned that he has failed to cast the challenges he faces in proper context and that, in particular, he has not adequately explained why his Administration is suddenly devoting so much attention to Haiti after 32 months of military tyranny there.

A senior White House official, who said Mr. Clinton had planned his an-

Continued on Page A2, Column 3

Looser Rules on Water

Eight years after it voted for drastic tightening of the purity standards for tap water, the Senate decided to loosen them again. But whether the changes would increase the tiny risks of drinking tap water was in dispute, as environmentalists argued that the strict standards were warranted.

Article, page A12.

Cause for Celebration, Twice

Barnard College graduates were showered with confetti and the fizz from a celebratory bottle yesterday as they joined their counterparts from Columbia University at commencement. The Barnard students, who celebrated at their own ceremony on Wednesday, received degrees yesterday. Page B6.

Angel Franco/The New York Times

Vietnamese Also Extending A Search for Their M.I.A.'s

By MALCOLM W. BROWNE
Special to The New York Times

Vietnam Revisited
A periodic report.

HANOI, Vietnam — "For 2,000 years, wars have seeded our land with the bones of the missing in action," the general told a visitor, "and the American war produced a particularly rich crop. We'll never find most of our own dead soldiers, but they remain in our hearts."

The speaker, Maj. Gen. Nguyen Trong Vinh, spent most of his 68 years fighting the French and the Americans, and he now publishes a monthly magazine for North Vietnamese and Vietcong veterans listing grave sites and missing soldiers and guerrillas.

Sometimes families who see the photographs, eyewitness reports and maps that the magazine publishes have been able to identify the resting places of missing husbands, fathers and sons.

The quest by the United States for

its war dead and missing in Vietnam seems to have brought increased efforts by Hanoi to account for Communist troops who remain missing.

Besides offering information that might help identify Communist dead, ordinary Vietnamese also sometimes respond to an American advertisement in the yellow pages of Hanoi's telephone book that asks for information that could lead to the recovery of American bones. The Veterans of Foreign Wars, which has given Hanoi a few tips on where to look for Vietcong remains, has thanked the Vietnamese who have helped in the search for American servicemen.

Most Vietnamese families gave up hope many years ago of learning the fates of their missing, most of whom were buried where they fell. During the war, this correspondent saw the unidentified corpses of hundreds of Communist soldiers shoveled into unmarked mass graves all over South

Continued on Page A8, Column 1

One of Africa's Last Dictators Bows to Democracy

By BILL KELLER
Special to The New York Times

JOHANNESBURG, May 19 — The last prominent ruler in the generation of African strongmen who displaced the European colonialists, Hastings Kamuzu Banda of Malawi, conceded today that voters had decisively ended his autocratic 30-year personality cult.

The self-proclaimed Life President, an eccentric leader in three-piece suit and homburg, accepted defeat in an extraordinary show of mutual graciousness. After a vote widely acclaimed as peaceful and fair, Dr. Banda, who is in his 90's, offered his

cooperation to the new Government and was offered in turn generous praise and a comfortable pension.

"I consider him to be a father of the nation," said Bakili Muluzi, the victor, in a telephone interview tonight from his home in Blantyre. "Therefore we definitely want to look after him as much as possible. We are not looking for vengeance or retribution at all."

The President-elect is a 51-year-old businessman whose style is more Chamber of Commerce than inquisi-

tional Star Chamber. He served in Dr. Banda's Cabinet and rose to the second-highest position in the governing party before resigning in 1982 because, he said tonight, he suspected Dr. Banda might have him killed.

Malawi is a land-locked sliver of mountain and lake whose 9.7 million people are among the poorest in the world.

Dr. Banda (he earned a medical degree from Meharry Medical College in Tennessee) outlasted all but one of the original African nationalists who took power from colonialists in the 1950's and 1960's and stamped

Continued on Page A10, Column 1

JEWISH WOMEN/GIRLS LIGHT SHABBAT candles today 18 min. before sunset. In NYC 7:52 P.M. Info 718-774-3060, outside NYC 1-800-SABBATH. In merit of Reizel Gutnick, OBM — ADVT.

"All the News That's Fit to Print"

The New York Times

Late Edition

New York: Today, hot and humid, a few thunderstorms. High 95. Tonight, partly cloudy. Low 71. Tomorrow, sunny, cooler. High 84. Yesterday, high 92, low 72. Details are on page 33.

VOL.CXLIII .. No. 49,732

Copyright © 1994 The New York Times

NEW YORK, SUNDAY, JUNE 19, 1994

$2.50 beyond the greater New York metropolitan area.

TWO DOLLARS

Simpson, Under Suicide Watch, Is Jailed on 2 Murder Charges

The police photo of O. J. Simpson being booked late Friday.

Former Football Star Is Described as Crying And Despondent

By SETH MYDANS
Special to The New York Times

LOS ANGELES, June 18 — O. J. Simpson, whose thrilling play on the football field seemed to symbolize freedom, today sat locked in a 9-foot-by-7-foot jail cell on a double-murder charge with only a toilet, a sink and a bunk for furnishings.

The authorities said they had taken sharp objects, shoelaces and his belt away from Mr. Simpson, who was described by his lawyer as being in tears today. Every few minutes, officials said, a deputy peered through a window into his cell to make sure he did not kill himself.

Mr. Simpson was admitted to Men's Central Jail at 10:20 on Friday night, said Sheriff's Deputy Angie McLaughlin, and was held without bail. His entry into jail ended an extraordinary day in which he was charged with murder in the slayings of his former wife and her friend, disappeared, and then led the police on a bizarre 90-minute tour of the freeways, broadcast live on television nationwide, before surrendering meekly at his house.

Al Cowlings, Mr. Simpson's driver in the chase, was freed early today on $250,000 bail after being arrested and booked for aiding and abetting a fugitive, the police said.

The police said Mr. Simpson could be arraigned as early as Monday, beginning what could be a long legal journey that will explore the brutal double killings of Nicole Brown Simpson, 35, and her friend Ronald Goldman, 25. On Friday, in a desperate open letter his lawyer described as a suicide note, Mr. Simpson denied involvement in the slayings.

Today, the lawyer, Robert Shapiro, talked to Mr. Simpson by telephone, and said his jailed client was deeply depressed and crying. "As bad as he has been in the past four days, it's the worst I've ever heard him," Mr. Shapiro told The Associated Press.

The police's handling of the case was being scrutinized today, with politicians and former police officials criticizing what they saw as lax treatment that allowed Mr. Simpson to escape and elude capture for nearly nine hours. [Page 21.]

There was a sense of awe in the city today at the bizarreness of the spectacle as Mr. Simpson, holding a gun to his head, led the police on a low-speed

Continued on Page 20, Column 1

Life, Meet TV

The broadcasts of the fugitive's stately procession along California highways seemed so real because the scene differed so much from television's professionally crafted reality.

The Week in Review, Section 4.

POLL FINDS A LACK OF FAITH IN POLICE

New Yorkers Concerned Over Protection and Integrity

By CLIFFORD KRAUSS

New Yorkers express anxiety about the Police Department's ability to protect them, and many say there is widespread corruption in the force, according to a New York Times/WCBS-TV News Poll.

The survey and follow-up interviews suggest a serious lack of confidence in the department because of a fear of crime and concern over revelations of corruption in several precincts.

Despite police reports of a slight though steady decrease in crime over the last four years, the poll found a general perception that crime has increased or remained at the same levels as last year. More than a third of those polled said that because of their fear of crime they had moved to new neighborhoods or were planning to. Many, especially in Hispanic and black neighborhoods, say they have taken measures like riding the subway less, staying home at night or avoiding places that they are afraid to go to.

The telephone poll of 1,189 adult residents conducted from June 12 to June 15 is just a snapshot, and the extent to which opinions might have changed recently is uncertain, because many questions were asked for the first time. But the findings suggest that the image of the department is badly bruised just when it is introducing new crime-fighting strategies that rely on community cooperation, like having beat officers seek intelligence on drug dealers and gun traffickers from residents.

The worries about crime and police performance span racial, economic and ethnic lines. But skepticism about the Police Department is expressed most strongly by minority-

Continued on Page 30, Column 1

TODAY'S SECTIONS

Africa is falling further behind the rest of the world in health, education and general living standards. In Nairobi, Kenya, a health clinic sits next to an open sewer in a suburban shantytown.

Liz Gilbert/Sygma, for The New York Times

'Lost Decade' Drains Africa's Vitality

By JOHN DARNTON
Special to The New York Times

OUAGADOUGOU, Burkina Faso — You don't have to be a detective to spot the decline in living standards in Africa. It hits you right away.

It can be seen in the shantytowns that surround every capital city, sprawls of humanity living in hovels with no windows, open sewers and garbage heaped in mounds chest-high.

It can be heard in the lessons sung out in ancient schoolrooms, where enrollments are dropping and yet class sizes swell to 120 pupils.

And it can be smelled in the fly-infested corridors of hospitals where diseases flourish, medication is scarce and people are increasingly turned away or left to suffer because they cannot afford treatment.

The countries south of the Sahara, the traditional division between black Africa and the Arab world, have turned in a decade and more of devastatingly bad economic performance. The economic failure is undercutting a drive for political liberalization, raising ethnic rivalries to a dangerous level and forcing countries to impose politically inflammatory austerity programs, often under the dictates of Western financial institutions.

But most of all it is spreading misery. In living standards, Africa is falling further behind the rest of

Survival Test

Can Africa Rebound?
First of three articles.

the world. It is now the only continent where most poor people are getting still poorer and where health and education are deteriorating.

As political changes similar to those that shook Eastern Europe and the Soviet Union four and five years ago now reverberate in Africa, Africans seem more concerned about the social and welfare problems caused by the economic decline. Their views emerged during scores of interviews in the course of a six-week trip through nine countries in East, West and Southern Africa.

The statistics roll by in a blur: More than four million children born this year will die before the age of five. Nearly one-third of children are severely malnourished. One in three goes without primary school education.

But it is the individuals who remain fixed in memo-

Continued on Page 10, Column 1

Two Koreas Plan Summit Talks on Nuclear Issue

By DAVID E. SANGER
Special to The New York Times

SEOUL, South Korea, June 18 — For the first time since the Korean peninsula was divided five decades ago, the Presidents of North and South Korea agreed today to hold a summit meeting, which is likely to focus on defusing tensions over the North's suspected effort to build a nuclear weapon.

The agreement was brokered by former President Jimmy Carter, who delivered the offer from North Korea's 82-year-old leader, Kim Il Sung, after returning to Seoul this morning from a three-day visit to Pyongyang.

South Korea's President, Kim Young Sam, immediately met Mr. Carter at Blue House, the presidential mansion in the mountains ringing Seoul, and told him that "the sooner the better," aides said.

But South Korean officials acknowledged that there was reason to question whether a summit meeting between the two countries, still technically at war, would ever take place. They noted that many agreements between North and South have been thrown onto the scrap heap.

The state-run Korean Broadcasting System suggested in a television analysis tonight that "this could be another attempt by the North to buy time and escape from a tense situation."

Mr. Carter also used his visit to deliver a stinging critique of the Clinton Administration's strategy of seeking United Nations sanctions against the North as part of an effort to force Mr. Kim to give up his nuclear weapons program.

At a news conference outside the American Ambassador's house here, Mr. Carter said he believed that economic sanctions were doomed to failure and would do nothing but further poison relations between the North and the rest of the world.

"The declaration of sanctions by the U.N. would be regarded as an insult by them, branding it as an outlaw country," he said. It would also constitute "a personal insult to their so-called Great Leader," Kim Il Sung, Mr. Carter said, "by branding him as a liar and a criminal.

"This is something in my opinion

Continued on Page 12, Column 3

ACCORD REACHED TO END WALKOUT AGAINST L.I.R.R.

PARTIAL SERVICE TODAY

Railroad Yields on Work Rules After Learning Congress Is Reluctant to Intervene

By MATTHEW L. WALD
Special to The New York Times

MELVILLE, L.I., June 18 — The Long Island Rail Road reached a contract agreement with its largest union late tonight, capitulating on work rule issues, after officials concluded that Congress would not step in soon to stop the strike.

The chairman of the Metropolitan Transportation Authority, Peter E. Stangl, appearing before reporters shortly before 11 P.M., said he had decided to settle the strike by giving up. "I made a decision that I'd pay the ransom before it got too bad out there," he said.

Mr. Stangl said he had been advised by Gov. Mario M. Cuomo and members of the state's Congressional delegation that Congress might not act soon. Senator Daniel Patrick Moynihan said the chance of Congressional action was "about 50-50."

Appearing after Mr. Stangl, Edward J. Yule Jr., the chairman of the United Transportation Union, said there was no ransom. "Ransom? I should have his money," Mr. Yule said of Mr. Stangl.

"That's called collective bargaining," he added. "We worked at this. I don't think we're winners."

Mr. Stangl said that between the pay package that had been agreed to and the failure to change the work rules, the accord would cost about $14 million more than the authority's last offer before the strike.

The deal ends a strike that began early Friday and promises limited service on Sunday and a normal Monday rush hour for 107,000 commuters.

The agreement was reached after a marathon day that began about 7:30 A.M., with the two sides meeting in separate rooms at the Huntington Hilton Hotel here, sending emissaries from room to room and conferring in hallways, elevators and the parking lot. The last contract expired nearly two and a half years ago.

But the deciding factor appears to have been Mr. Stangl's conclusion that he could not count on action by the Congress.

Presuming that the agreement is ratified by the union membership and the board of the M.T.A., it will be retroactive to Jan. 1, 1992, and will expire on New Year's Eve this year. Under the terms of the Railway Labor Act, the M.T.A. will send a notice to the union to begin renegotiation six months in advance of the expiration, which is less than two weeks from now. The schedule for the ratification vote was not certain tonight.

Governor Cuomo issued a statement saying, "We are grateful to the M.T.A. and the unions for saving the entire region from an enormous amount of inconvenience and damage. Reasonableness prevailed."

But the M.T.A.'s chief negotiator, Gary Dellaverson, said that the concession on work rules was "exceptionally damaging" to his agency's effort to win productivity improve-

Continued on Page 28, Column 3

A Bitter Harvest for Ukraine From an American Seed Deal

By RAYMOND BONNER
with JAMES BENNET
Special to The New York Times

KIEV, Ukraine — When an American company ventured into Ukraine last year with a deal to sell $70 million of corn seeds, herbicides and expensive farm equipment, it was hailed here and in Washington as a historic vote of confidence in this struggling nation and a model for cooperation between American businesses and former Communist countries.

Now, a year later, the deal looks like a model of a different sort, an embarrassing instance in which American companies took advantage of a country in turmoil to dispose of poor quality seeds it could not sell in the United States and reap large profits.

"It's a very black page," said David Sweere, chairman of the agriculture committee of the American Chamber of Commerce in Ukraine. "There was a time when the Ukrainian farmer held the American farmer in very high regard. Now, they have lost respect for us, because of deals like this. Yes, we in the West believe in commercial gain. But if that is your only goal, then this is what happens."

Some farms planted the seed and grew nothing. Most of the combines never moved from their sheds. And while the American seed company and brokers have been paid, Ukraine is struggling to repay the $70 million to Citibank, which financed the deal. If the country fails to repay the money, the United States Export-Import Bank, which guaranteed the loan, will have to repay it, a cost ultimately borne by American taxpayers.

The Ex-Im Bank, which promotes business abroad, is refusing to do business in Ukraine, partly because of the economic conditions here and delinquencies on the loan. This has dealt a blow to the Clinton Adminis-

Continued on Page 14, Column 1

Ireland Stuns a Struggling Italy

Ireland got its first soccer victory ever over Italy, 1-0, in the World Cup opening round. Ireland's Andy Townsend, on the ground, took down Roberto Baggio at the Meadowlands. SportsSunday, section 8.

David Cannon/Allsport

INSIDE

Fear of No Health Care Bill
As the fight to overhaul health care enters a crucial phase, a powerful pressure on Congress is a possibility that was unthinkable until recently: that there might not be a major health care bill this year. Page 18.

6 Slain in Northern Ireland
Gunmen killed six people watching Ireland's World Cup soccer victory over Italy in a Northern Ireland pub, the police said. The militant Protestant Ulster Volunteer Force claimed responsibility. Page 5.

354713

"All the News That's Fit to Print"

The New York Times

Late Edition

New York: Today, mostly cloudy, mild, a drizzle. High 68. Tonight, cloudy, cooler late. Low 47. Tomorrow, some sun. High 58. Yesterday, high 70, low 48. Details, page D26.

VOL.CXLIV . No. 49,875

Copyright © 1994 The New York Times

NEW YORK, WEDNESDAY, NOVEMBER 9, 1994

75 cents beyond the greater New York metropolitan area.

60 CENTS

G.O.P. WINS CONTROL OF SENATE AND MAKES BIG GAINS IN HOUSE; PATAKI DENIES CUOMO 4TH TERM

OTHER HIGHLIGHTS

VIRGINIA

In Brutal Battle, Robb Defeats North

Robb | North

In what may have been the bitterest fight of a bitter year, Senator Chuck Robb, a one-term Democrat, narrowly defeated Oliver North. Mr. North, the former national security aide to President Ronald Reagan, rallied an intensely loyal following among the religious right, opponents of gun control laws and bitter voters wanting to shake up Washington. But his involvement in the Iran-contra affair proved more damaging than the allegations of marital misconduct against Mr. Robb. Page B3.

GOVERNORSHIPS

Wilson and Weld Win; Bushes Split

Republicans swept all but one of the major governors' races. Gov. Pete Wilson, given up for politically dead two years ago as California staggered through a fierce recession, completed a stunning comeback by trouncing State Treasurer Kathleen Brown. Page B4.

In Massachusetts, Gov. William F. Weld easily turned back State Representative Mark Roosevelt, establishing himself as a possible player in the 1996 Republican Presidential sweepstakes. Page B3.

For two sons of President George Bush, it was a split decision, but not in the way experts had predicted. George W. Bush was elected in Texas, upsetting the incumbent, Ann Richards. But his younger brother, Jeb Bush, lost to Gov. Lawton Chiles

G.W. Bush | Wilson

in a close race in Florida.

MASSACHUSETTS

Kennedy Beats Back Romney

Kennedy

Senator Edward M. Kennedy proved that after more than three decades on Capitol Hill, he is not ripe for replacing. In the toughest race of his career, the 62-year-old Senator beat a political newcomer with a large personal fortune and another famous name, Mitt Romney.

Mr. Romney, the 47-year-old son of George W. Romney, the former Governor of Michigan, had tried to tap this year's anti-incumbent fervor, arguing that it was time for a change, but on the stump and in political debates, Senator Kennedy underscored his long experience, his command of the issues and his intimacy with the legislative process.

ILLINOIS

Chicago Earthquake: Rostenkowski Is Out

If any seat in the House seemed safe at the outset of the year, it was that of Dan Rostenkowski of Chicago, longtime chairman of the House Ways and Means Committee. But reeling under an indictment and an anti-Democratic wave in Illinois, the 66-year-old Mr. Rostenkowski lost to a 31-year-old political neophyte, Michael Patrick Flanagan. Page B2.

NEW YORK

Moynihan Wins A Fourth Term

Moynihan

In a year when liberal incumbents faced stiff challenges from the right, Senator Daniel Patrick Moynihan, a Democrat who is the chairman of the Senate Finance Committee, easily defeated the Republican candidate, Bernadette Castro. Page B12.

TENNESSEE

A Senate Sweep For the G.O.P.

Tennessee had two Democratic Senators. Now it will have two Republicans. Jim Sasser, a three-term Democratic incumbent who is chairman of the Senate Budget Committee and a close ally of President Clinton, lost to William Frist, a wealthy heart and lung surgeon who has never held public office.

And Fred Dalton Thompson, a lawyer for the Republicans on the Senate Watergate committee in 1973, defeated Representative Jim Cooper for the seat left vacant when Al Gore was elected Vice President. Page B3.

WASHINGTON, D.C.

The Redemption Of Marion Barry

Barry

Marion Barry came back from the ignominy of a drug conviction to return as Mayor of Washington, despite a strong challenge from Carol Schwartz. In 1990, after 11 years as Mayor, Mr. Barry was videotaped smoking crack in a hotel room. In this campaign, he stressed his strength of character in overcoming his weaknesses. Page B4.

PENNSYLVANIA

Upset Winner in '90 Is the Loser in '94

A pitched battle of ideological opposites ended with Representative Rick Santorum, a conservative Republican, narrowly defeating Senator Harris Wofford, a liberal Democrat. Mr. Santorum aggressively promoted less government, lower taxes, more military spending and his opposition to a ban on assault weapons. Mr. Wofford, whose own upset victory four years ago put health care at the top of the national agenda, made Social Security the pivotal issue in this election.

OHIO Metzenbaum's seat goes to the G.O.P.

NEW YORK Maloney defeats Millard on the Upper East Side.

TERM LIMITS Approved in Maine, Nebraska and Washington, D.C..

THE ELECTIONS: SECTION B

National coverage B1-5
State by state B6-8
The region B9-14

G. Paul Burnett/The New York Times

George E. Pataki celebrating at his Manhattan headquarters last night with his wife, Libby, after defeating Gov. Mario M. Cuomo. At right was Elizabeth McCaughey, who won election as Lieutenant Governor.

New York Voters End a Democratic Era

By KEVIN SACK

George Elmer Pataki, a lanky lawyer-legislator from the Hudson Valley who has promised to slash income taxes and restore the death penalty, was elected the 53d Governor of New York yesterday, ending 20 years of Democratic rule in Albany and toppling Mario M. Cuomo, a legendary figure in state and national politics.

In other New York races, H. Carl McCall became the first black New Yorker to win statewide elected office, defeating Herbert London in the race for state comptroller. Mr. McCall, a former State Senator, investment banker and president of the New York City Board of Education, was appointed Comptroller by the Legislature last year to fill a vacancy left by the midterm retirement of Edward V. Regan.

In the race for attorney general, the Republican, Dennis C. Vacco, a former United States Attorney from Buffalo, won a narrow victory over Karen S. Burstein, a former Family Court judge in Brooklyn.

Senator Daniel Patrick Moynihan, the New York Democrat, easily dispatched his Republican opponent, Bernadette Castro, to win a fourth term. But he lost the chairmanship of the Finance Committee to Senator

Rowland Wins Connecticut; Lautenberg Edges Haytaian

For the first time in a generation, Connecticut elected a Republican Governor yesterday, John G. Rowland.

His principal campaign promise was to repeal the 3-year-old state income tax, the legacy of Gov. Lowell P. Weicker Jr.

But because Mr. Rowland won only slightly more than a third of the vote in a five-way race, it will not be easy to deliver.

Mr. Rowland, 37, defeated William E. Curry, a Democrat, and Eunice S. Groark, the candidate of Mr. Weicker's A Connecticut Party, which stands to lose its major-party status.

With 98 percent of 820 precincts reporting, the vote was:

Rowland	36%
Curry	33%
Groark	19%
Scott	12%

| Zdonczyk | 1% |

In New Jersey, Senator Frank R. Lautenberg, a Democrat, won a third term, defeating Assembly Speaker Chuck Haytaian, a Trenton insider who had strong support from Gov. Christine Todd Whitman. Mr. Haytaian, tried to portray himself as an outsider during the campaign.

With 99 percent of 6,010 districts reporting, the vote was:

| Lautenberg | 50% |
| Haytaian | 47% |

Mr. Haytaian had been a legislative champion of Mrs. Whitman's plan to reduce state income taxes by 30 percent. But last night she said it had been "difficult to communicate Haytaian's ability to do in Washington what we were able to accomplish here."

Articles, pages B13 and B14.

CONGRESS AT A GLANCE As of 2:00 A.M. Eastern time.

	CURRENT BALANCE	AT STAKE	WINNERS	NEW BALANCE
SENATE				52 R / 47 D · 1 UNDECIDED
Democrat	56	22 (6 OPEN)	13	
Republican	44	13 (3 OPEN)	21	
HOUSE				188 D / 216 R · 36 UNDECIDED / 1 INDEPENDENT
Democrat	256	All 435 seats	182	
Republican	178		216	
Independent	1		1	

The New York Times

INSIDE

A Boost for Israel Talks
Israel agreed to pick up the pace of talks on Palestinian self-rule in an effort to blunt pressure from Islamic militants on Yasir Arafat. Page A10.

Black Ownership at Denny's
The Denny's chain, which has been accused of bias, said a black-owned company would run up to 47 outlets in the New York area. Page B15.

Bosnian Capital Bombarded
In its worst attack since February, Sarajevo was hit yesterday afternoon by artillery fire, probably from Bosnian Serb positions. Page A8.

BLOW FOR CLINTON

Democratic Mainstays Ousted in Big Upsets Around the Nation

By RICHARD L. BERKE

The Republican Party seized control of the Senate and moved within a few seats of capturing the House yesterday, winning eight Democratic seats in the Senate and at least 38 in the House. The gains were the Republicans' strongest in decades and put them in position to thwart President Clinton and his legislative proposals for the next two years.

The Republican tide also extended to the races for governor in several important states that will be critical to Mr. Clinton's hopes for re-election in 1996, including New York, Pennsylvania, Texas and California.

One after another, once unassailable Democrats like Gov. Mario M. Cuomo, Gov. Ann W. Richards of Texas, Representative Dan Rostenkowski of Chicago and Senators James Sasser of Tennessee and Harris Wofford of Pennsylvania fell to little-known Republican challengers.

But Republicans, who have held the Senate in only 6 of the last 40 years, were particularly overjoyed that they had picked up Democratic Senate seats in Pennsylvania, Michigan, Tennessee, Oklahoma, Minnesota, Michigan and Maine. Mr. Clinton had criss-crossed most of those states in a frenetic eight-day campaign swing, but it did no good. The Republicans ended the night with at least a 52-to-48 majority in the Senate.

"I've never known a better night in electoral politics for the Republican Party, and the best is yet to come," a beaming Bob Dole declared to an overflow crowd at the Republican National Committee headquarters in Washington. Mr. Dole, who will become the majority leader, studiously avoided saying whether he would focus on that job or on running for President in 1996, but the crowd was excited about the party's prospects, chanting, " '96! '96! '96!"

The Democrats were not completely shut out. Senator Charles S. Robb, a Democrat, defeated Oliver L. North in one of the most closely watched races in a particularly volatile election season, and Senator Edward M. Kennedy of Massachusetts hung on to his seat after the biggest scare of his political life.

In metropolitan area races, two

A HOMESPUN IMAGE

State Senator George E. Pataki, who will be New York's 55th Governor, is almost a millionaire, yet he comes off as homespun and unpretentious. Man in the News, page B1.

Bob Packwood of Oregon when the Senate went Republican.

Mr. Pataki, a 49-year-old State Senator, won by drawing a strong turnout in upstate New York counties where Republicans traditionally fare well, by taking narrow majorities in the suburbs surrounding New York City, by winning Staten Island and by faring well in Erie County.

B. Thomas Golisano, a millionaire businessman from Rochester who was the gubernatorial candidate of the Independence Fusion Party, proved less of a factor than some had anticipated in siphoning anti-Cuomo votes from Mr. Pataki.

With 97 percent of the precincts reporting, the results were:

Pataki	2,465,631 (49%)
Cuomo	2,223,567 (45%)
Golisano	196,327 (4%)

Mr. Pataki's election represents a political triumph for his patron, Senator Alfonse M. D'Amato, and a potentially devastating defeat for Mayor Rudolph W. Giuliani, who alienat-

Continued on Page B11, Column 1 · *Continued on Page B5, Column 1*

A Vote Against Clinton

By R. W. APPLE Jr.

It was an immoderate campaign, coarse in its tone and unedifying in its substance, and the nation's politics are likely to stay that way for the next two years and beyond.

News Analysis Dissatisfaction with President Clinton, with liberalism, with the Democratic Party and with Washington in general combined to create a surge by Republicans, especially conservative Republicans. If not quite a tidal wave, yesterday's results swept dozens of incumbents from office and set up two years of intense political confrontation between the White House and Congress.

Republicans will soon control the statehouses in seven of the eight largest states, giving them immensely useful building blocks for the next Presidential election. They will control the Senate for the first time since 1987, and perhaps Congress as a whole for the first time since the Eisenhower era.

Their leader in the House of Representatives, Representative Newt Gingrich, is at heart a revolutionary bent on fundamental change.

This was a realigning election that put the final nails in the coffin of the Solid South, the regional bastion upon which Democratic power was once built. Democratic seats in the House fell all across the region: three in Georgia, four in North Carolina, three in Tennessee.

If the victory of Senator Edward M. Kennedy of Massachusetts provided some balm, the defeats of major party luminaries — Representative Dan Rostenkowski of Illinois and Jack Brooks of Texas, Gov. Ann W. Richards of Texas and Gov. Mario M. Cuomo of New York — sent many Democrats into gloom bordering on despondency.

Stated most simply, the message from the electorate was disgust with big government and impatience with government activism, two of the things with which the Democrats are most closely identified.

The returns constituted a sharp rebuke to Mr. Clinton. Many of those

Continued on Page B5, Column 6

354613

"All the News That's Fit to Print"

The New York Times

Late Edition
New York: Today, cloudy, not as warm. Light rain, mainly east. High 54. Tonight, fog. Low 44. Tomorrow cloudy, cooler. High 48. Yesterday high 58, low 53. Details, page B8

VOL.CXLIV.. No. 49,943   Copyright © 1995 The New York Times   NEW YORK, TUESDAY, JANUARY 17, 1995   75 cents beyond the greater New York metropolitan area.   60 CENTS

AT LEAST 597 ARE KILLED IN JAPANESE QUAKE; KOBE DEVASTATED AS 2,000 BUILDINGS BUCKLE

Flu Casts Fevered Misery Across New York Region

By ELISABETH ROSENTHAL

Although her cubicle at the emergency room at St. Luke's-Roosevelt Hospital Center was uncomfortably warm, Martha Rivera of Manhattan wrapped herself in a sweater, scarf and thick winter coat, huddling fruitlessly against a chill that came from deep within.

"Oh, my God," she said. "I have never felt so terrible."

Her eyes were sunken, her nose red. "My joints hurt," she went on. "I have a splitting headache. Chills. A sore throat. A cough. My fever is 104. I feel like an old lady." (She is only 54.)

Two rooms down, Dan Auerbach, a 21-year-old violin student at Juilliard, slumped in his chair, coughing weakly; his shoes were untied, his hair on end. He had canceled all appointments for the day in deference to a cough, a high fever and a headache that would not go away.

The flu and cold season has singled out New York with particular fury this year. While much of the country has remained unusually healthy this winter, many New Yorkers have coughed, sneezed and wheezed their way into the new year.

Based on the surveillance system used by the Centers for Disease Control and Prevention and the World Health Organization, as of Jan. 6 more than 60 percent of the nation's flu cases were in New York, with Connecticut, Kentucky, Maryland and Virginia also reporting significant numbers of flu cases.

Most of the cases have been caused by the Shangdong strain of the influenza A virus. The strain is new to this country, so people have had no time to develop resistance to it, which may in part explain the large number of cases and their severity, experts say.

In addition to the flu, doctors say they have been deluged by patients with unusually severe coughs and intestinal problems.

"There seems to be a lot out there right now," said Steven J. Matthews, a spokesman for the New York City Department of Health. "Probably a lot of what people are suffering from is not really the flu. But you know what? If you got it, it don't make no difference."

Hospital emergency depart-

Continued on Page B2, Column 1

New York City's Undying Deficit: Slash It, and It Just Grows Back

By ALISON MITCHELL

Although he has already slashed $2 billion from city programs, Mayor Rudolph W. Giuliani still faces another budget gap in the next 18 months that will be as large, if not larger.

And those grim figures do not take into account the real possibility of large cuts in aid from Washington and from Albany, where Gov. George E. Pataki is looking for ways to solve the state's budget gaps and make good on his campaign promise of major cuts in taxes and spending.

"It's very, very bad," said City Comptroller Alan G. Hevesi. "The decisions are increasingly painful."

With business, sales and personal income tax collections all running lower than expected in December, the administration's first task is to close a gap now estimated at $600 million to $700 million in the $31.6 billion budget before the fiscal year ends in June.

At the same time, the Mayor must prepare a budget for next year to close a gap ranging from $2 billion, as his budget director predicts, to well above $2.5 billion, as several outside monitors expect.

To get through the year, administration officials are scrutinizing everything from a one-shot debt refinancing to cuts in contracts with nonprofit social-service providers. Next year, they are looking at vast reductions in welfare and Medicaid, as well as the elimination and con-

solidation of scores of city programs. The municipal unions, which all open new rounds of contract talks with the city this year, have been told that there will be no raises that are not paid for through increased productivity.

The recurrence of annual $2 billion deficits testifies to the depth of the city's fiscal problems. When he came into office a year ago, inheriting a $2.3 billion deficit, Mr. Giuliani, the first Republican Mayor in more than two decades, promised to end New York City's long tradition of expansive government. And he has worked single-mindedly to carry out that pledge, despite demonstrations by constituent groups, a court battle with the City Council and growing criticisms from parents troubled by reductions in school aid and closing youth programs.

He won City Council approval for a budget that reduced city spending for the first time in 16 years, and removed 15,000 workers from the

Continued on Page B3, Column 1

INSIDE

Budget Measure Unknowns

It is a good bet that an amendment calling for a balanced budget will pass the House of Representatives, but few can say what form the measure will take. Page A16.

Spotlight on Greenspan

Alan Greenspan, chairman of the Federal Reserve, is taking a more visible role in issues normally beyond his purview. Page D1.

Red Sprites and Blue Jets

Researchers have spotted bizarre lightning bolts, some red and others blue, that shoot upward from thunderheads. Science Times, page C1.

Bishop Is Found Dead

Bishop David E. Johnson, who was retiring as leader of the largest Episcopal diocese in the nation, apparently committed suicide. Page B7.

Part of the Hanshin Expressway, which runs from Kobe to Osaka, collapsed in Nishinomiya, near Kobe.
Associated Press

Russian Guns Pound Deeper in Chechen Capital

By ALESSANDRA STANLEY
Special to The New York Times

GROZNY, Russia, Jan. 16 — Russian bombers and helicopters swung low over the capital of the secessionist region of Chechnya today, and artillery pounded deeper south toward Chechen-held territory. The besieged Chechen rebels, who say they have forced the Russians to retreat from some buildings in the city, appeared tired and dangerously edgy.

As artillery and rocket fire continued to hit the capital, Grozny, the Russian Prime Minister, Viktor S. Chernomyrdin, appeared on television in Moscow. He called for immediate peace talks and a cease-fire in Chechnya, where the Russian military campaign to seize control from the secessionist government entered its sixth week today.

Mr. Chernomyrdin, who has proposed such talks before, said that any negotiations would mean the end to the attacks in and around Grozny.

"Our main goal today," he said, "is to stop the bloodshed." As before, however, he blamed "illegal armed bands" in Chechnya for the war.

The children of Grozny, the capital are becoming hardened to the violence around them.

Ramon Gabayev, 10, had no words to describe the rain of fire that has turned his neighborhood into a burned-out ruin, and little to say even about the sniper fire that wounded his mother in front of his eyes. He stood silent and embar-

Continued on Page A8, Column 3

MANY FIRES IGNITED

Heaviest Urban Losses From Quake Since Tokyo in 1923

By NICHOLAS D. KRISTOF
Special to The New York Times

TOKYO, Tuesday, Jan. 17 — A powerful earthquake shook major cities in western Japan today, killing at least 597 people, starting dozens of fires and trapping hundreds of residents in the wreckage of collapsed buildings.

The national police and other authorities said 2,198 people were injured and 531 missing, and the casualty figures were expected to rise as the authorities combed the rubble. In the initial confusion, the official toll of injured was given as 13,000 but that number was later retracted.

The earthquake occurred at 5:46 A.M. (3:46 P.M. on Monday, Eastern time), when most people were still in their beds.

Today's temblor, which measured 7.2 on the Richter scale, apparently was the biggest to hit urban areas of Japan since a catastrophic quake struck Tokyo in 1923. Building collapses and widespread fires killed an estimated 140,000 in that quake.

While this morning's quake was not nearly so lethal, it caused enormous amounts of structural damage in one of Japan's most important economic zones. But there was no damage reported in Tokyo, where the quake could scarcely be felt.

Kobe, a major port city of 1.4 million people 280 miles west of Tokyo, bore the brunt. A modern industrial hub that was rebuilt after World War II, Kobe was covered by black smoke caused by more than 70 fires. Fires were still raging out of control eight hours after the quake.

An elevated freeway toppled on its side like a long ribbon, smashing cars beside it. Rescuers frantically searched through 2,000 collapsed buildings in Kobe.

The Government held an emergency cabinet meeting and dispatched troops to search the rubble with specially trained dogs.

"Mother! Mother!" a man in his 20's called out, as a television crew filmed him wandering over the debris of what had been his house. He stared blankly at the shattered

Continued on Page A6, Column 1

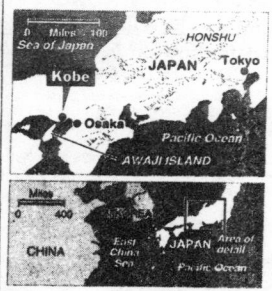
Center of quake was near Kobe.
The New York Times

Women's Five at Connecticut Make a Perfect Season Better

By MALCOLM MORAN
Special to The New York Times

STORRS, Conn., Jan. 16 — The players' joyful faces and the noise from all around transformed a basketball game into a milepost. And nobody wanted to leave.

The women from the University of Connecticut reached uncharted territory today by defeating the top-ranked Lady Vols of Tennessee. Their victory came before a roaring full house of 8,241 fans in Gampel Pavilion, before a national television audience and at the expense of the team whose three national championships make it the standard for challengers in women's college basketball.

The 77-66 victory was the 13th for the unbeaten and second-ranked Huskies this season, left them in position to become the top-ranked team in the nation for the first time, and preserved the only perfect record for men's and women's teams at the same major college.

This was the 25th time the top two women's teams had met in the 19 years that The Associated Press had conducted a women's poll. And it became the frantic start of a day that would turn the disease identified as Husky Mania into an epidemic.

The women received a standing ovation at the Hartford Civic Center tonight, where they held red roses

Continued on Page B11, Column 3

In the besieged Chechen capital, a handicapped woman and a dog competed for a piece of meat.
Reuters

The New York Times

Late Edition

New York: **Today,** sunny, mild, light winds. High 71. **Tonight,** increasing clouds. Low 50. **Tomorrow,** cloudy, cool, occasional rain. High 59. Yesterday, high 76, low 51. Details, page C13.

VOL.CXLIV...No. 50,037   Copyright © 1995 The New York Times   NEW YORK, THURSDAY, APRIL 20, 1995 $1 beyond the greater New York metropolitan area.   60 CENTS

AT LEAST 31 ARE DEAD, SCORES ARE MISSING AFTER CAR BOMB ATTACK IN OKLAHOMA CITY WRECKS 9-STORY FEDERAL OFFICE BUILDING

CLUES ARE LACKING

U.S. Officials Scurry for Answers — Reno to Ask Death Penalty

By DAVID JOHNSTON

WASHINGTON, April 19 — The Federal authorities opened an intensive hunt today for whoever bombed a Federal office building in Oklahoma City, and proceeded on the theory that the bombing was a terrorist attack against the Government, law-enforcement officials said.

President Clinton appeared this afternoon in the White House press room and somberly promised that the Government would hunt down the "evil cowards" responsible. "These people are killers," he said, "and must be treated like killers."

Attorney General Janet Reno, speaking to reporters at the White House in early evening, said that casualty figures from the scene were climbing and that of the 550 people who worked in the building, 300 were unaccounted for.

Ms. Reno said Federal prosecutors would seek the death penalty against the bombers. "The death penalty is available," she said, "and we will seek it."

But questions about the identity of the bombers swirled around the case. The only solid fact was the explosion itself.

Some law-enforcement officials said the bombing might be linked to the second anniversary today of the F.B.I.'s ill-fated assault on the Branch Davidian compound near Waco, Tex., an operation that ended in a fire that killed about 80 people, including many children. Among the offices housed by the Federal building in Oklahoma City was one quartering local agents of the Bureau of Alcohol, Tobacco and Firearms, the agency that Branch Davidians and their sympathizers blamed for the confrontation.

But other officials said that neither the Branch Davidians nor right-wing "militia" groups that have protested the Government's handling of the Davidians were believed to have the technical exper-

Continued on Page B8, Column 1

OTHER NEWS

Gas Fumes Create Panic in Yokohama

In a chilling reminder of the gas attack last month in Tokyo, caustic fumes spread through Yokohama's railroad station and through a train, sending about 300 people to hospitals. No one took responsibility for release of the gas. Page A10.

Court Upholds Anonymity

In a decision threatening state election laws, the Supreme Court ruled the Constitution guarantees the right to distribute anonymous campaign literature. Page A20. Add two more lines of type in all.

Lugar Declares Candidacy

Saying he has an unblemished character, Senator Richard Lugar of Indiana announced that he would seek the Republican nomination for President in 1996. Page A16.

Mayor Wants to End Relief

A day after touting the success of new rules for a welfare program, Mayor Giuliani said he really favors abolishing the program. Page B1.

David Longstreath/Associated Press

Charles H. Porter IV/Associated Press
Emergency workers remove a child injured in the explosion in downtown Oklahoma City, which occurred as employees began reporting for work yesterday. At least 31 were killed, including numerous children at a day-care center, and scores were injured or missing, some still buried in the rubble.

---

12 Victims Were Children in 2d-Floor Day-Care Center

By JOHN KIFNER

OKLAHOMA CITY, April 19 — A car bomb went off with a thunderous explosion here this morning, ripping through a Federal office building, collapsing walls and floors, and killing at least 31 people. Many others were buried in the wreckage, and the death toll seemed certain to rise.

At least 12 children whose parents had just dropped them off at a second-floor day-care center were among those immediately known dead in the deadliest bombing in the United States in 75 years.

As dusk fell, scores of the more than 500 people who normally work in the building were still missing. John Hansen, an Assistant Oklahoma City Fire Chief, said it appeared that dead and wounded victims were underneath the piles of concrete, plaster and glass. Late tonight, rain fell from the gray clouds that had threatened for much of the day, adding hardship to horror and raising the possibility the wreckage would shift, imperiling the trapped injured and their rescuers.

The National Guard has been called in, and late tonight limited martial law was declared to keep the streets clear.

Reflecting on the early report of the death toll, Fire Chief Gary Marrs said, "We're sure that it will go up, because we've seen fatalities in the building."

At the White House, President Clinton convened an inter-agency task force to coordinate Federal assistance and called on Americans to pray for the dead and stricken. He also dispatched a small army of Federal investigators to Oklahoma and pledged a relentless hunt for the killers.

Attorney General Janet Reno, noting that the dead children ranged from 1 to 7 years old, and that some had been burned beyond recognition in the day-care center just above the curb where the bomb detonated, said the crime was a capital one and that the Government would seek the death penalty if those responsible were caught. She also said that there were 550 people working in the building and that about 300 were still unaccounted for.

By late tonight, no one had claimed responsibility for the bombing, which occurred on the second anniversary of the Federal raid on

Associated Press
The Alfred P. Murrah building in Oklahoma City before its north side, facing left, was bombed.

the Branch Davidian compound near Waco, Tex., in which David Koresh and scores of his followers perished. There was no evidence that today's bombing, which was similar in intensity to the World Trade Center bombing in New York two years ago, but far more deadly, was linked to the Davidians.

Rescue teams, bringing in backhoes, bulldozers and other heavy equipment, dug in the rubble tonight in darkness, rain and a cutting wind, searching for victims in the flattened center of the nine-story Alfred P. Murrah Building.

Three survivors were pulled out of the wreckage by firefighters shortly after 9:30 P.M. There were cries from a woman in the basement, firefighters said, but they were having difficulty getting to her because there appeared to be bodies in the way. That vignette of horror was just one of hundreds played out all day long, from morning to dark.

Federal buildings in seven other cities were evacuated because of bomb threats, and security was tightened at Government buildings from coast to coast.

Shards of glass littered the street around the Federal building here, and much of the masonry was literally peeled away from the building, leaving a gaping nine-story hole. Federal Bureau of Investigation agents in bright yellow rain slickers,

Continued on Page B9, Column 1

In Shock, Loathing, Denial: 'This Doesn't Happen Here'

By RICK BRAGG

OKLAHOMA CITY, April 19 — Before the dust and the rage had a chance to settle, a chilly rain started to fall on the blasted-out wreck of what had once been an office building, and on the shoulders of the small army of police, firefighters and medical technicians that surrounded it.

They were not used to this, if anyone is. On any other day, they would have answered calls to kitchen fires, domestic disputes, or even a cat up a tree. Oklahoma City is still, in some ways, a small town, said the people who live here.

This morning, as the blast trembled the morning coffee in cups miles away, the outside world came crashing hard onto Oklahoma City.

"I just took part in a surgery where a little boy had part of his brain hanging out of his head," said Terry Jones, a medical technician, as he searched in his pocket for a cigarette. Behind him, firefighters picked carefully through the skeleton of the building, still searching for the living and the dead.

"You tell me," he said, "how can anyone have so little respect for human life."

The shock of what the rescuers found in the rubble had long since worn off, replaced with a loathing for the people who had planted the bomb that killed their friends, neighbors and children.

One by one they said the same thing: this does not happen here. It happens in countries so far away, so different, they might as well be on the dark side of the moon. It happens in New York. It happens in Europe.

It does not happen in a place where, debarking at the airport, passengers see a woman holding a sign that welcomes them to the Lieutenant Governor's annual turkey shoot.

It does not happen in a city that has a sign just outside the city limits, "Oklahoma City, Home of Vince Gill," the country singer.

"We're just a little old cowtown," said Bill Finn, a grime-covered firefighter who propped himself wearily up against a brick wall as the rain turned the dust to mud on his face. "You can't get no more Middle America than Oklahoma City. You

Continued on Page B11, Column 1

More on the Blast

THE RESCUE When rescuers found the hundreds of cut, burned and terrified victims, it became a matter of grasping for the living while trying to ignore the dead. Page B10.

AROUND THE NATION Shocked and fearful, government officials at Federal, state and some local levels shut down offices in at least eight cities, including New York. Page B10.

THE BOMB The powerful bomb was very likely made of ingredients that are widely available from gardening centers, chemical suppliers and gasoline stations. Page B8.

354613